THE

GOOD
PUB
GUIDE

2018

THE
FUZZY DUCK
ARMSCOTE

COTSWOLDS' COUNTRY PUB

LUXURY ROOMS

FINE BRITISH SEASONAL CUISINE

Ilmington Road | Armscote | CV37 8DD
twitter.com/fuzzyduckpub | facebook.com/fuzzyduckarmscote
01608 682 635 | **www.fuzzyduckarmscote.com**

The Good Pub Guide 2018

Edited by Fiona Stapley

Associate Editor: Patrick Stapley
Managing Editor: Fiona Wright
Editorial Assistant: Ruby Utting

Founded by Alisdair Aird in 1982

EBURY

Please send reports on pubs to:

The Good Pub Guide
FREEPOST RTXY–ZCBC–BBAZ, Stream Lane, Sedlescombe, Battle TN33 0PB

or **feedback@goodguides.com**

or visit our website: **www.thegoodpubguide.co.uk**

If you would like to advertise in the next edition of *The Good Pub Guide*,
please email **goodpubguide@tbs-ltd.co.uk**

10 9 8 7 6 5 4 3 2 1

Published in 2017 by Ebury Press, an imprint of Ebury Publishing

Ebury Press, an imprint of Ebury Publishing
20 Vauxhall Bridge Road,
London, SW1V 2SA

Text © Ebury Publishing 2017
Maps © PerroGraphics 2017
Fiona Stapley has asserted her right to be identified as the author of this Work
in accordance with the Copyright, Designs and Patents Act 1988

www.eburypublishing.co.uk

Penguin Random House is committed to a sustainable future for
our business, our readers and our planet. This book is made from
Forest Stewardship Council® certified paper.

To buy books by your favourite authors and register for offers,
visit www.penguin.co.uk

Typesetter: Integra
Designer: Jerry Goldie Graphic Design
Project manager and copy editor: Cath Phillips
Proofreader: Tamsin Shelton

Printed and bound by Clays Ltd, St Ives PLC

9781785036194

Contents

VOTED #1 CASK ALE OF 2016

Wainwright
THE GOLDEN BEER

Refreshingly rewarding crafted golden beer
4.1% ᴬᴸᶜ ᵛᴼᴸ

IF THERE WAS EVER A GOOD TIME TO STOCK WAINWRIGHT IT HAS TO BE NOW...

● OVER **13 MILLION** PINTS SOLD IN THE PAST YEAR

● ONE OF THE **FASTEST GROWING** BEERS IN THE MARKET

● VOTED **NUMBER ONE** CASK ALE OF 2016

● WINNER OF CAMPAIGN OF THE YEAR WITH **'FINDYOURMOUNTAIN'**

A SUPERB THIRST QUENCHING, REFRESHING BEER PACKED FULL OF FLAVOUR, LIGHTLY HOPPED WITH SUBTLE SWEET NOTES AND A DELICATE CITRUS AROMA.

STYLE: GOLDEN BEER / ABV: 4.1%
SEE: GOLDEN / SMELL: FRUIT, CITRUS
TASTE: REFRESHING, FRUITY, SWEET, CITRIC
BITTER: 2.5 / SWEET: 4.5

Wainwright
THE GOLDEN BEER

SEARCH 'WAINWRIGHTGOLDENBEER'
WWW.WAINWRIGHTGOLDENBEER.CO.UK f 🐦

*The MA Drinks List: Top 100 List

#FINDYOURMOUNTAIN

Introduction & The Good Pub Guide Awards 2018

Pubs make us happy – and they do so in a way that other businesses simply can't. As the wise Dr Johnson said: 'There is nothing which has yet been contrived by man, by which so much happiness is produced as by a good tavern or inn.' It's also heartening to learn that a recent Oxford University study fully endorses this! Apparently, people with a local pub near their home were 'significantly' happier, more satisfied with their life and had more friends (and also drank more moderately).

Step into a well run pub and you're greeted by gentle laughter and the murmur of voices, the sight of ale being pulled at the pump, the smell of good food, maybe a snoozing dog on the hearth by a roaring fire and, all importantly, a friendly smile. Good pubs are run by naturally hospitable people who provide an equally warm welcome to regulars and visitors – everyone should feel at home and valued.

A pub is where the various rites of passage are celebrated – not just births, deaths and marriages, but the first drink, the first job, perhaps even the first kiss. As the hub of a local community with customers from all walks of life, there's no need to make an appointment as there will always be someone there that you know, gossip to catch up on and news to share. We feel we belong, we matter and for a while the cares and clutter of daily life are left behind – and this makes us happy.

It's the air of mischievous energy and the inclusive sense of humour that, according to one of our top publicans, are key factors to enjoying both his own and other pubs. Plus the fact that he'll see someone walk through his door looking a bit weary or wilted and watch them leave later with spirits lifted and head held a little higher. And that makes him happy – he feels he's done a good job.

But enjoying a pub isn't simply because we're with friends or family in a convivial atmosphere; it's because pubs have changed so much over the last few years to suit our changing needs.

There are those, of course, who feel that some pubs have lost their true identity. That they are no longer the traditional boozers they used to be, with too much emphasis now placed on food and on modish dé that involves stubby candles in glass jars, rugs on bare boards a sea of Farrow & Ball paintwork. But pubs – and their landlords and landladies – are nothing if not adaptable. To run a successful pub you must pay attention to what your customers actually want from you and keep a keen eye on other nearby businesses.

In recent years, pubs, hotels, restaurants, coffee shops and cafés have seen a blurring of lines, with all of them now treading on one another's turf. Pubs started to take business from restaurants quite a while ago when customers wanted less formality and more flexibility in what and when they chose to eat. Keen young chefs took note of these changing demands and you'll now find some of the best food in Britain in a pub rather than a restaurant. A pub can offer a wide range of meals from breakfast (traditionally the staple of a café) to cake and morning coffee (move over, Starbucks) and on to imaginative, contemporary dishes fit for any special occasion. And as people's lifestyles change (and this seems especially apt for younger customers) they want to be able to eat at a time of their choosing – and of course with many pubs now open all day, this is easy to provide.

More and more people enjoy spending a few days away from home, and whereas hotels and guest houses were once the obvious option, pubs have jumped on the bandwagon by refurbishing rooms above the bar and renovating old outbuildings – all to a very high standard. Over a third of our Main Entries now hold a *Good Pub Guide* Stay Award. What appeals to our readers is the winning combination of a chatty bar with a cheerful mix of customers and a bedroom just upstairs.

Some pubs have little delis offering local and home-made produce and takeaway meal options. Others keep a room free for book clubs, knit-and-natter groups, live music or even small conferences. And, of course, many have set up outside catering services. You name it and pubs will have thought of it. It's this entrepreneurial spirit that will keep pubs alive and kicking for years to come, despite all the doom and gloom you read about in the press. Pubs hold all the trump cards and are the worthy winners in this free-for-all marketplace.

Drinks: the search for fair prices and top quality

Our national survey of beer prices shows a huge £1.09-a-pint difference in the cost of a pint of ale between Herefordshire and Yorkshire, the cheapest areas, and Surrey the most expensive. The average price for a pint of beer in Britain is now £3.60. How does your area rank? Here are the details, in average price order from cheapest upwards:

Bargain beer
Herefordshire, Yorkshire, Shropshire, Derbyshire, Cumbria, Worcestershire

TRUTH IN EVERY TASTE

Wherever you want your visit to the pub to take you, we've got the venue to fit your bill.

From rural landscapes with top quality dining and individual style, to live music venues with good old fashioned boozers in between, our range of pubs are just the ticket to your perfect outing.

Nestled amongst the Somerset countryside, paving the bustling streets of Bristol and Bath, glistening along the waterfront.

We have 29 pubs across Somerset, Wiltshire, Bristol, Bath and Cheltenham, and we'd love to see you for a drink!

www.butcombe.com/pubs

 /Butcombe    @ButcombeBrewery   butcombe

Fair-priced beer
Northumbria, Wales, Leicestershire, Northamptonshire, Staffordshire

Average-priced beer
Lancashire, Dorset, Devon, Somerset, Lincolnshire, Cornwall, Wiltshire, Gloucestershire, Suffolk, Cambridgeshire, Essex, Warwickshire, Bedfordshire, Nottinghamshire, Hampshire, Norfolk, Cheshire, Scotland

Expensive beer
Isle of Wight, Oxfordshire, Buckinghamshire, Kent, Berkshire, Scottish Islands, Hertfordshire, Sussex

Rip-off beer
London, Surrey

In 2005, Paul Halsey and James Minkin established the Purity Brewing Company on a working farm in lovely Warwickshire countryside. As the name suggests, it was important to them that the brewing process was eco-friendly and energy-efficient. The spent grain goes to the farm

cattle, yeast to the pigs, and their hops become fertiliser. The latest heat and steam exchange technology reduces energy consumption and, every day, thousands of gallons of water run through a series of reed beds behind the farm to purify the brewing waste before it flows back into the River Avon. As well as Purity Pure UBU (named after their old farm dog who was fondly known as Useless Bloody Urchin), their beers include Bunny Hop, Lawless Lager, Longhorn IPA, Mad Goose, Pure Gold and Saddle Black. Their ales can be found within a 120-mile radius of the brewery and are delivered to more than 500 outlets. Brewery tours are held on Saturdays at 10.30am and 2pm and include a brewing history talk and a pint in the visitor centre. For their award-winning beers, **Purity** is our **Brewery of the Year 2018**.

This year's Top Ten Beer Pubs are spread all over the country and include the **Bhurtpore** in Aston (Cheshire), **Beer Hall at Hawkshead Brewery** in Staveley (Cumbria), **Tom Cobley** in Spreyton (Devon), **Fat Cat** in Norwich (Norfolk), **Malt Shovel** in Northampton (Northamptonshire), **Fat Cat** in Ipswich (Suffolk), **Halfway House** in Pitney (Somerset), **Nags Head** in Malvern (Worcestershire), **Kelham Island Tavern** in Sheffield (Yorkshire) and **Guildford Arms** in Edinburgh (Scotland). Although all the pubs included here have a wonderful choice of quickly changing real ales, it's hard to beat Colin Keatley's

collection of 32 well kept beers, so the **Fat Cat** in Norwich is our **Beer Pub of the Year 2018**.

You typically save yourself 51p a pint if you drink at one of the own-brew pubs in this edition of *The Good Pub Guide*. Our Top Ten Own-Brew pubs are the **Brewery Tap** in Peterborough (Cambridgeshire), **Brown Horse** in Winster and **Watermill** at Ings (Cumbria), **Old Poets Corner** in Ashover (Derbyshire), **Church Inn** at Uppermill (Lancashire), **Grainstore** at Oakham (Leicestershire), **Dipton Mill Inn** at Diptonmill and **Ship** at Newton-by-the-Sea (Northumbria), **Gribble Inn** at Oving (Sussex) and **Weighbridge Brewhouse** in Swindon (Wiltshire). A long-standing favourite with many, the **Church Inn** at Uppermill is our **Own-Brew Pub of the Year 2018**.

Many of the pubs in these pages have extremely interesting and thoughtfully chosen wine lists and more than 375 of them hold one of our Wine Awards. Our Top Ten Wine Pubs are the **Old Bridge Hotel** in Huntingdon (Cambridgeshire), **Acorn** in Evershot (Dorset), **Inn at Whitewell** at Whitewell (Lancashire), **Kings Arms** in Wing and **Olive Branch** in Clipsham (Leicestershire), **Woods** in Dulverton (Somerset), **Duncombe Arms** in Ellastone (Staffordshire), **Crown** in Stoke-by-Nayland (Suffolk), **The Inn West End** at West End (Surrey) and **Griffin** in Felinfach (Wales). Mr Groves reckons he could put 1,000 different wines up on the bar and will open any of them (with a value of up to £100) for just a glass – **Woods** in Dulverton is our **Wine Pub of the Year 2018**.

Stocking quite extraordinary collections of malt whiskies, our Top Ten Whisky Pubs are the **Bhurtpore** in Aston and **Old Harkers Arms** in Chester (Cheshire), **Nobody Inn** at Doddiscombsleigh (Devon), **Acorn** in Evershot (Dorset), **Red Fox** at Thornton Hough (Lancashire), **Black Jug** in Horsham (Sussex), **Pack Horse** at Widdop (Yorkshire), **Bow Bar** in Edinburgh, **Bon Accord** in Glasgow and **Sligachan Hotel** on the Isle of Skye (Scotland). With over 400 whiskies, the friendly and cheerful **Bon Accord** in Glasgow is our **Whisky Pub of the Year 2018**.

Individual Inns is run by Ewan Harries (a former director at Bass) and Martin Clarkson (who has been running pubs for some years) and consists of six pubs in Cumbria, Lancashire and Yorkshire. A beautiful location is a requisite for each pub, alongside individual décor, imaginative food using local produce, a thoughtful choice of drinks and comfortable bedrooms. It's important too that the inns are very much part of the local community and host a wide range of events such as reading and creative writing groups, live music, quiz and games evenings, guided walks, drinks tastings and monthly cinema or dining nights. They are particularly welcoming to walkers (with their dogs), families and guests – which is just as well since the countryside around each pub is stunning. The pubs that make up Individual Inns are the Masons Arms at Cartmel Fell and Wheatsheaf at Brigsteer (Cumbria), Spread Eagle

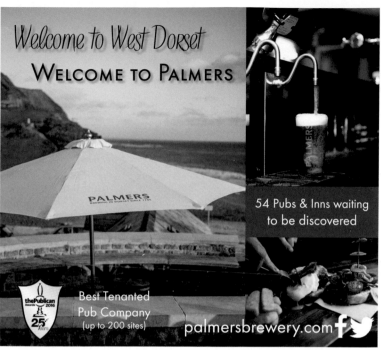

in Sawley (Lancashire) and Tempest Arms at Elslack, Wheatley Arms at Ilkley and Fountaine in Linton in Craven (all Yorkshire). **Individual Inns** is our **Pub Group of the Year 2018**.

The best pubs in town and country

Genuinely unspoilt and unchanging pubs run by dedicated landlords and landladies can be found all over Britain and our Top Ten are the **White Lion** in Barthomley (Cheshire), **Old Poets Corner** in Ashover and **Barley Mow** at Kirk Ireton (Derbyshire), **Digby Tap** in Sherborne and **Square & Compasses** at Worth Matravers (Dorset), **Harrow** at Steep (Hampshire), **Crown** at Churchill and **Halfway House** in Pitney (Somerset), **White Horse** near Petersfield (Hampshire) and **Birch Hall** at Beck Hole (Yorkshire). In the same family for 88 years and quite charming, the **Harrow** at Steep is **Unspoilt Pub of the Year**.

If you're out walking or away for the weekend, then a country pub with a roaring log fire is just what you're hoping to find. With this in mind our Top Ten Country Pubs are the **White Horse** in Hedgerley (Buckinghamshire), **Pheasant** in Burwardsley (Cheshire), **Rugglestone** in Widecombe (Devon), **Brace of Pheasants** at Plush (Dorset), **Royal Oak** in Fritham (Hampshire), **Royal Oak** in Ramsden (Oxfordshire), **Hatchet** at Lower Chute and **Malet Arms** in Newton Tony (Wiltshire), **Fleece** in Bretforton (Worcestershire) and **Harp** at Old Radnor (Wales).

In a peaceful spot, well placed for walks and with enjoyable food and comfortable bedrooms, the **Brace of Pheasants** at Plush is **Country Pub of the Year 2018**.

As a stranger in a town or city, a well run pub with a genuine welcome leaves you feeling much less alone. Our Top Ten Town Pubs are the **Punter** in Cambridge (Cambridgeshire), **Wykeham Arms** in Winchester (Hampshire), **Bank House** in King's Lynn (Norfolk), **Victoria** in Durham (Northumbria), **Kings Arms** in Woodstock (Oxfordshire), **Old Green Tree** in Bath (Somerset), **Eight Bells** in Saffron Walden (Suffolk), **Old Joint Stock** in Birmingham (Warwickshire), **Olde Mitre** (London) and **Kays Bar** in Edinburgh (Scotland). A winner in the past, the **Wykeham Arms** is an exceptional all-rounder and is our **Town Pub of the Year 2018**.

Nowadays, when so many people want a weekend or a few days away as a mini break, a pub with bedrooms is just the place to head for, with the bonus of a chatty bar in which to relax at the end of the day – in this edition, 293 pubs hold one of our Stay Awards. Our Top Ten Inns are the **Rock** at Haytor Vale (Devon), **Anchor** at Chideock (Dorset), **Kings Head** in Bledington (Gloucestershire), **Inn at Whitewell** at Whitewell (Lancashire), **Lord Crewe Arms** in Blanchland (Northumbria), **Old Swan & Minster Mill** in Minster Lovell (Oxfordshire), **Luttrell Arms** in Dunster (Somerset), **Cat** in West Hoathly (Sussex), **Blue Lion** at East Witton (Yorkshire) and **Red Lion**

Ridley Inns

Characterful, family-run pubs with great food

The Cock

Old Uckfield Road (A26), Near Ringmer, BN8 5RX

Food served 7 days a week lunchtime and evening
and all day Sunday.

Large Garden and Sun Terrace
Log Fire in Winter
Roasts served all day Sunday
Open all day on Bank Holidays
Vegetarian Menu always available (5 choices)
Real Ales incl. Harveys and other locally source
micro breweries
Home Cooked Food – something for every taste
diet and budget!

tel: 01273 812040
www.cockpub.co.uk

The Highlands Inn

Eastbourne Road, Ridgewood, Uckfield, TN22 5SP

Food served 7 days a week lunchtime and evening
and all day Sunday until 6.30pm

Sports Bar showing all BT and Sky Sports
fixtures with special Sports Bar menu
Formal Restaurant area with seating for 120
covers and separate Restaurant Bar Area
Real Ales incl. Harveys and other locally source
micro breweries
Extensive selection of wines by the glass
Large Sun Trap Garden with al fresco Dining

tel: 01825 762989
www.highlandsinn.co.uk

www.ridleyinns.co.uk

in East Chisenbury (Wiltshire). The lovely mid 13th-c abbot's guest house the **Lord Crewe Arms** in Blanchland, in the wilds of the North Pennine Moors, is our **Inn of the Year 2018**.

Looking for value and taste

Value Awards are given to pubs that have managed to keep at least some of their main course dishes at £11 or under – which is quite a struggle given the rising costs of raw materials. Our Top Ten Value pubs are the **Drake Manor** in Buckland Monachorum (Devon), **Yew Tree** in Lower Wield (Hampshire), **Red Lion** in Preston (Hertfordshire), **Church Inn** at Uppermill (Lancashire), **Dipton Mill Inn** in Diptonmill and **Olde Ship** at Seahouses (Northumbria), **Rose & Crown** in Oxford (Oxfordshire), **Old Castle** in Bridgnorth (Shropshire), **Blue Boar** in Aldbourne (Wiltshire) and **Crown & Trumpet** in Broadway (Worcestershire). The charming **Drake Manor** in Buckland Monachorum with its friendly, long-serving landlady is our **Value Pub of the Year 2018**.

Dining pubs at the top of their game provide some exceptional food, cooked by first class chefs using carefully sourced local and seasonal produce. This year's Top Ten Dining Pubs are the **Wellington Arms** in Baughurst (Hampshire), **Stagg** in Titley (Herefordshire), **Assheton Arms** at Downham (Lancashire), **Olive Branch** at Clipsham (Leicestershire), **Plough** in Kingham (Oxfordshire), **Horse Guards** at Tillington (Sussex), **Red Lion** at East Chisenbury (Wiltshire), **Shibden Mill** in Halifax (Yorkshire), **Burts Hotel** in Melrose (Scotland) and **Griffin** in Felinfach (Wales). The standards here are as high as you can get and the food (using some home-grown produce) is inspired – the **Stagg** at Titley is our **Dining Pub of the Year 2018**.

The best of the best

Every year we're lucky enough to find new entries that range from little country taverns to smart dining pubs, and this year our Top Ten New Pubs are the **Three Horseshoes** in Madingley (Cambridgeshire), **Nags Head** at Haughton Moss (Cheshire), **Ebrington Arms** in Ebrington and **Swan** in Southrop (Gloucestershire), **Watership Down** in Freefolk (Hampshire), **Crown** in Old Dalby (Leicestershire), **Smiths** in Bourne (Lincolnshire), **Woodstock Arms** in Woodstock (Oxfordshire), **Drawing Board** in Leamington Spa (Warwickshire) and **Timbrells Yard** in Bradford-on-Avon (Wiltshire). The golden-stone **Ebrington Arms** in Ebrington with its own-brewed ales, imaginative food and lovely bedrooms is our **New Pub of the Year 2018**.

Some of the best pubs in the country owe their appeal almost entirely to the caring, hard-working and welcoming personality of their landlady or landlord. Outstanding among those are **Philip and Lauren Davison** of the Fox in Peasemore (Berkshire), **Alex Clarke** who owns both the Black Bull in Balsham and the Red Lion in Hinxton (Cambridgeshire), M

Short of the Barley Mow in Kirk Ireton (Derbyshire), **Kathryn Horton** of the Ostrich in Newland (Gloucestershire), **Tim Gray** of the Yew Tree in Lower Wield (Hampshire), **Patrick Groves** of Woods in Dulverton (Somerset), **Gerry and Ann Price** of The Inn West End, West End (Surrey), **Rob and Liz Allcock** of the Longs Arms in South Wraxhall (Wiltshire), the **Mainey family** of the Crown in Roecliffe (Yorkshire) and the **Key family** of the Nags Head in Usk (Wales). For the warmth of the welcome and for the excellent landlord-cooked food, **Rob and Liz Allcock** of the Long Arms in South Wraxhall are **Licensees of the Year 2018**.

Our Top Ten pubs – vying for the Pub of the Year category – are really very special indeed and feature consistently in our readers' warmest reports. They are the **Cock** at Hemingford Grey (Cambridgeshire), **Pandora** at Mylor Bridge (Cornwall), **Kings Head** in Bledington (Gloucestershire), **Wykeham Arms** in Winchester (Hampshire), **Olive Branch** in Clipsham (Leicestershire), **Rose & Crown** in Snettisham (Norfolk), **Horse Guards** in Tillington (Sussex), **Bell** at Welford-on-Avon (Warwickshire), **Compasses** in Chicksgrove (Wiltshire) and **Blue Lion** at East Witton (Yorkshire). With its lively, friendly bar, excellent drinks selection, first class food and lovely bedrooms, the **Kings Head** in Bledington is our **Pub of the Year 2018**.

TOP TEN PUBS 2018

(in county order)

Cock in Hemingford Grey (Cambridgeshire)

Pandora in Mylor Bridge (Cornwall)

Kings Head in Bledington (Gloucestershire)

Wykeham Arms in Winchester (Hampshire)

Olive Branch in Clipsham (Leicestershire)

Rose & Crown in Snettisham (Norfolk)

Horse Guards in Tillington (Sussex)

Bell in Welford-on-Avon (Warwickshire)

Compasses in Chicksgrove (Wiltshire)

Blue Lion in East Witton (Yorkshire)

Discover an Individual Inn

Our eclectic traditional inns in stunning settings, all offer excellent food and service, a fine range of hand pulled beers and a great cellar of wine.

Each Individual Inn offers a welcoming environment, with delightful settings, cosy bars and eating areas with real Inn charm.

All the Inns have the advantage of comfortable accommodation with soft muted colours and beautifully appointed rooms, apartments and holiday cottages or our luxury bunkhouse.

MASONS ARMS

ROOMS FROM SUMMER 2017

THE WHEATSHEAF INN

LUMLEY FEE BUNKHOUSE

SPREAD EAGLE inn

The Tempest Arms

The Fountaine Inn

W THE WHEATLEY ARMS

Visit an Individual Inn, find out more information at...

individualinns.co.uk

Individual Inns - Publican Awards Best Accommodation Operator 2014
Wheatsheaf Inn - Cumbrian Life - Food and Drink Pub 2015
Masons Arms - North West Pub of the Year 2012
Tempest Arms - UK Pub of the Year 2011

Tell-tale signs

By **Christopher Winn**

What have the Romans ever done for us? Well, for a start, they've given us pub signs. As the Romans laid out their network of roads across Britannia, they built *tabernae*, or taverns, along the way where travellers could find food and lodging. *Tabernae* that sold wine would advertise the fact by hanging vine leaves from a pole outside – the first pub signs. In Britain, since vines were scarce, they would sometimes use evergreen bushes instead, giving us one of the earliest pub names, the Bush.

Over the following centuries, wine was largely replaced by ale and in 1393 King Richard II ordered that 'Whoever shall brew ale in the town for the intention of selling it, must hang out a sign, otherwise he shall forfeit his ale.' This was to make pubs easily identifiable to his 'ale tasters', who would travel the country inspecting ales for quality. One method they used, apparently, was to pour some ale on to a wooden bench and then sit on it – if they stuck to the bench then the beer was too sweet! I remember hearing that story over a pint of good ale at my local pub many years ago – I do hope it's true and not the sort of tale told at the sign of the Cock and the Bull...

Back to Richard II. Many landlords thought it prudent to show their allegiance to him by sporting his emblem, the White Hart – still one of the top ten most popular pub names to this day. Richard's all-powerful uncle John of Gaunt used a red lion as his heraldic symbol and this became a widely used pub sign too. The Red Lion moniker gained even greater popularity after the Union of the Crowns in 1603 when James VI of Scotland became also James I of England and decreed that the Red Lion of Scotland should be ubiquitously displayed, helping to make the Red Lion the most popular pub sign in Britain.

As the number of pubs grew so they began to use a wider variety of names and, since the majority of people couldn't read, pubs would use their signs to illustrate the story behind the name. The sign might be a model of a plough or a bell or a crown, but, more often, it would be a colourful picture.

Every picture tells a story

All pub signs tell a tale, some stranger than others. The Bucket of Blood at Phillack in Cornwall tells of a landlord who went to fetch water from the well and drew up a bucket full of blood instead – it turned out that the bloodied head of an unfortunate

exciseman had been thrown down the well. The Drunken Duck at Hawkshead in Cumbria relates to a landlady who found her ducks lying outside the back door, apparently dead. She started plucking them ready for the oven, when they woke up – it turned out they were not dead but dead drunk, having been sipping from a leaking beer barrel. In remorse, the landlady knitted them all waistcoats to keep them warm until the feathers grew back. The Rose Revived beside the Thames at Newbridge in Oxfordshire commemorates a visit by Oliver Cromwell. The rose he was wearing in his hat was wilting and so he placed it in a glass of ale and, hey presto, it revived!

Calling thirsty artists

Local artists were usually employed to paint pub signs, although some breweries maintained their own specialist artists. Alas, there is only one major brewery that still retains a full-time band of artists to hand-paint its pub signs, the Wadworth Brewery in Devizes, Wiltshire.

Bespoke hand-painted pub signs are becoming rare and sought after. One of the most talked about can be found in the We Three Loggerheads, near Mold in North Wales. A regular visitor in the 1780s was Richard Wilson, the first great British landscape painter and a founder of the Royal Academy. In return for a few free pints, Wilson agreed to paint the Loggerheads' pub sign, which then hung outside the pub for over 200 years. It was eventually taken down to preserve it from the weather and is now displayed inside. Experts disagree on its authenticity but the sign has become a pub legend and people still come from far and wide to see it.

Signs of the times

There are a number of different types of pub sign. The most common are signs mounted directly on to the outside wall of the pub or hanging ones that swing from a bracket projecting from the wall. Then there are freestanding signs, which stand away from the pub building, usually at the roadside as a means of drawing attention to a pub that's set back from the road.

The most unusual signs are gallows signs, which stretch across the road like an arch. As roads and vehicles have got wider and traffic busier, such signs have become increasingly rare and today there are only four left in Britain that I know of. Two belong to coaching inns: the George Hotel at Stamford, Lincolnshire, whose sign spans the main street into the town; and the sign for the Green Man & Black's Head Royal Hotel (now closed) at Ashbourne in Derbyshire. Then there is the Magpie at Stonham

Parva in Suffolk, which has a Grade II listed sign across the A140. Apparently, it also used to have a live magpie in a cage on the wall as a living pub sign. Finally, there's the wonderful Grade II listed sign for the Fox & Hounds at Barley, Hertfordshire, with a fox running across it pursued by five hounds and two mounted huntsmen.

My own favourite pub, the Withies in Compton near Guildford in Surrey, is a lovely 16th-century pub tucked away down a narrow country lane. It looks tiny, but is quite spacious inside and also cosy, with a huge inglenook. I've been going there since I was a child and it doesn't seem to have changed at all. The food is always excellent – especially the fresh crab sandwich for which the pub is famous. It's child-friendly too and the cottagey garden has plenty of tables. Compton is an exceptionally pretty village, famous for the Watts Gallery and Chapel and for Surrey's finest Norman church, celebrated for its unique double chancel.

Christopher Winn's first book was the bestselling *I Never Knew That About England,* followed by volumes on Ireland, Scotland, Wales, London and many more. His latest is *I Never Knew That About England's Country Churches* (Ebury Press, 2017).
Favourite pub Withies, Compton, Surrey.

Proper pub grub

By **Rick Stein**

Fish burger with red onion, lettuce, tomato and chipotle relish

The type of fish doesn't really matter – use whatever is cheap. It's well worth making the chipotle relish. It's very good with fried eggs too.

Serves 4

60g flour

1 egg

60g panko breadcrumbs

400g fish, cut into 1cm-thick slices

Salt

150ml vegetable oil, for frying

4 hamburger buns

60g little gem or iceberg lettuce, sliced

150g tomato, thinly sliced

60g red onion, thinly sliced

60g mayonnaise or Japanese Kewpie mayonnaise

60ml chipotle relish or a favourite brand of chilli tomato relish

1 fresh red chilli, thinly sliced

Put the flour, egg and breadcrumbs into three separate shallow dishes. Season the fish slices with salt and put them in the flour, then the egg, then the breadcrumbs. Shallow-fry the fish in oil over a medium heat until the breadcrumbs are light brown and crisp: about 1.5 minutes each side.

Cut the buns in half and assemble the burger. Start with the lettuce, then the tomato and onion, then the mayonnaise and the relish. Finally rest the fish on top, sprinkle with fresh chilli, top with the other half of the bun and serve straightaway.

My chipotle relish

200g onions, chopped

30g garlic, chopped

30ml vegetable oil

15g chipotle chilli

400g canned tomatoes

3 tbsp tomato purée

2 tsp salt

240ml malt vinegar

120g sugar

200ml water

Cook the onions and garlic in the oil for 10 minutes over a medium heat. Add all the other ingredients and cook very gently for 45 minutes until quite thick. Transfer to a sterilised jar unless using immediately.

Moules marinière

There was a time, long ago, when a bowl of moules marinière and a glass of muscadet, in Brittany, was to me simply the most exotic thing. You couldn't get mussels in Britain unless you picked them yourself off the rocks. Every time I cook this, I think of the past.

Serves 4

1.75kg mussels, cleaned
50g unsalted butter
1 medium onion, finely chopped
50ml dry white wine
1 tbsp coarsely chopped parsley

Put the mussels, butter, onion and white wine into a very large pan. Cover and cook over a high heat for 3-4 minutes, shaking the pan every now and then, until the mussels have opened. Discard any unopened ones. Spoon the mussels into bowls. Add the parsley to the remaining juices, then pour all but the last tablespoon or two, which might contain some grit, back over the mussels.

Rick Stein has always believed in showcasing local seafood and farm produce in his 12 restaurants in the south of England and in his pub, **The Cornish Arms**, in the village of St Merryn, Cornwall. The recipes above are taken from his book *Fish & Shellfish*. His most recent book is *Rick Stein's Long Weekends* (BBC Books), tying into the BBC2 television series of the same name.

Design for living
··
By **Kit Caless**

'All architecture is shelter.' - Philip Johnson

Che pub is the ultimate shelter. Once you're inside, it provides warmth, food and drink. The storm of everyday life is kept outside the pub doors and you can forget the changing weather of human existence for a few hours.

Most shelters are functional. The Anderson shelter, designed to protect people from bomb blasts during World War II, isn't considered the most beguiling of interior spaces. Perhaps a nice table feature doesn't matter when people are being wiped out by bombs, but the point still stands. The public house, however, is our most venerated shelter, and a cornucopia of design ideas and aesthetics that would turn Laurence Llewelyn-Bowen weak at the knees.

The problem with the pub is we barely see the design, caught as we are in the social melee of banter, camaraderie and drinking. We rarely look down, or up or even into the distance, focusing instead on our companions in front of us. It's only a weirdo who goes around the country taking pictures of pub carpets. But since I have literally done that (so you don't have to), I have decided there are four main areas of pub design. Variations exist on each theme, of course, but next time you're having a pint in your local, have a look around you and drink in the design. Maybe you'll see things you never knew were there.

1. Dry hops and brass, trinkets and paintings of *The Hunt*
This is classic country pub design. Large wooden tables with knots abound, the bar counter is made of dark wood that doesn't respond well to modern sanitiser spray and the hops flake off on to your shoulders like beery dandruff. There is home-made cider called something like 'Old Hazy' on tap. No one has heard of quinoa.

2. Dartboard, pictures of Tottenham Hotspur's 1981 FA Cup winning team, benches, red curtains bleached by the sun and ale coasters above the bar
Small town pubs that orbit London are not everyone's best bitter. They haven't changed for decades. However, on match days these pubs come alive with the possibility of happiness. The carpet may be old and faded, but the most interesting thing about the place is the array of photos behind the bar. Snapshots of regulars, old staff and pets tell stories of lost years in merriment, community and fellowship.

3. Renovated old cinema/bingo hall/corn exchange/church, ridiculous carpet, round tables, mismatched chairs

This is the pub where the carpet is king. Look down, you'll see. Patterns ranging from faux fleur-de-lys to constructivist, art deco, post-mortem, mathematical or downright lurid dominate this kind of pub.

4. School chairs, weak tables, craft beer, a huge mirror taken from a skip, menus written in Helvetica, wooden floors, candles that burn too quickly in jam jars

This pub has an island bar and serves Pilsner Urquell as the house lager. There are beards here you wouldn't believe, and tattoos you should never see. This is the pub you told your friends you would never drink in, but somehow, over time, you just kind of ended up here, didn't you?

Kit Caless is a writer and broadcaster. He is a regular contributor to *Vice* magazine and to publications as varied as *Architectural Digest*, the *Guardian* and *New Statesman*. He is co-founder and editor at Influx Press, a small independent publisher of fiction and creative non-fiction. He is also the author of *Spoon's Carpets: An Appreciation* (Square Peg, 2016).
Favourite pub Pembury Tavern, Amhurst Road, London E8.

Shake up your mocktail menu

By **Steve Carter**

Shake, stir and serve up more interest, variety and creativity from behind the bar, but make sure you do it for both your drinking and your non-drinking customers. A new generation of successful pub and bar owners are engaging and exciting their customers with a range of ingenious and imaginative drinks, and the best of the bunch aren't just relying on alcohol to do this. Never before has 'virgin' been so in vogue, as non-alcoholic cocktails – or mocktails – become mainstream and consumers increasingly look for a soft drink that makes them feel as special as if they were sipping a traditional Singapore Sling.

We've all become more health-conscious. There are now apps to measure sugar levels or to monitor your weekly intake of alcohol. With this, the UK's relationship with drinking and alcohol consumption is changing... but our relationship with the great British pub doesn't have to. One in five of us no longer drink alcohol, according to the Office for National Statistics, and that number rises when you consider younger adults or those living in London, where almost one in three are turning away from alcohol. Whether this represents a grand move to teetotalism, or just demonstrates the shift in choices that we make to reflect our busy lives, it would be a mistake to ignore the many potential customers out there that are looking for a soft drink to tempt them.

> We're increasingly seeing mixologists go back to basics to create their own breed of soft drink in the form of a signature mocktail

With an explosion of new and exciting soft drinks on the market, we're increasingly seeing mixologists go back to basics to create their own breed of soft drink in the form of a signature mocktail, or bar owners looking to premium soft drink brands for inspiration to create a fleet of mocktails for their menus. And these colourful creations are going down a storm, adding a point of difference to a standard soft drinks offering and quenching a non-drinker's thirst for something a little more memorable when enjoying an evening out.

Scan the soft drinks menu of an increasing number of pubs and bars across the country and you'll find their own take on non-alcoholic cocktails. These mocktails don't just mimic, they blend pure, premium-quality fruit juices, fragrant herbs and essences, colourful garnishes and equally colourful names.

They're matched to dishes on the menu, the changing seasons or a particular celebration. They're no longer just a cocktail with the alcohol removed, but a drink in their own right; they've become a considered choice and a special treat for all non-drinkers who don't resonate with a syrup-pumped carbonate just because they're having a night off the booze.

So, join the mocktail movement and squeeze more passion into your soft drinks. Here are my handy mocktail-making tips:

Make them interesting: Create enticing and eye-catching mocktails that will inspire, demonstrate creativity and make customers feel special.

Shaken and stirred: Go through the same theatrical ritual you would for a cocktail when making a mocktail. Shake, stir, strain and garnish before serving in the most gorgeous of glassware that's guaranteed to make a statement.

Mocktail not mimic: Don't just think of the non-alcoholic version of a cocktail when developing a mocktail, as these can often be unbalanced and lacking in flavour. Aim to create unique, standalone mocktails that can hold their own at the bar. Try to create a spectrum of flavour profiles from tart to sweet, and consider food matches and how each mocktail fits your customer's needs throughout the day.

Frobishers Spiced Apple Cooler

Frobishers Apple Juice
5 good slugs of Angostura Bitters
Soda water
Apple to garnish

Fill a collins or goblet glass with ice, then add the apple juice and bitters. Top up with soda water and garnish with a slice of apple.

Steve Carter began his career at Grand Met Brewing straight from university, and has worked within the drinks business ever since. He held senior positions at First Drinks and Taunton Cider before moving to premium fruit juice brand **Frobishers** in 2009, where he is sales and marketing director.
Favourite pub Beckford Arms, Fonthill Gifford, Wiltshire.

What is a Good Pub?

We hear about possible new entries in this *Guide* from our many thousands of correspondents who keep us in touch with pubs they visit – by post, by email at feedback@goodguides.com or via our website, www.thegoodpubguide.co.uk. These might be places they visit regularly (and it's their continued approval that reassures us about keeping a pub as a full entry for another year) or pubs they have discovered on their travels and that perhaps we know nothing about. And it's from these new discoveries that we make up a shortlist, to be considered for possible inclusion as new Main Entries.

What marks a pub out for special attention could be an out of the ordinary choice of drinks – a wide range of real ales (perhaps even brewed by the pub), several hundred whiskies, a remarkable wine list, interesting spirits from small distillers or proper farm ciders and perries. It could be delicious food (often outclassing many restaurants in the area) or even remarkable value meals. Maybe as a place to stay it's pretty special, with lovely bedrooms and obliging service. Or the building itself might be stunning (from golden-stone Georgian houses to part of centuries-old monasteries or extravagant Victorian gin-palaces) or in a stunning setting, amid beautiful countryside or situated by water.

Above all, what makes a good pub is its atmosphere. You should feel at home and genuinely welcomed by the landlord or landlady – it's their influence that can make or break a pub. It follows from this that a lot of ordinary local pubs, perfectly good in their own right, don't earn a place in the *Guide*. What makes them attractive to their regulars could make strangers feel a bit left out.

Another point is that there's not necessarily any link between charm and luxury. A basic unspoilt tavern may be worth travelling miles for, while a too smartly refurbished dining pub may not be worth crossing the street for.

The pubs featured as Main Entries do pay a fee, which helps to cover the *Guide*'s production costs. But no pub can gain an entry simply by paying this fee. Only pubs that have been inspected anonymously, and approved by us, are invited to join.

Using the *Guide*

The Counties

England has been split alphabetically into counties. Each chapter starts by picking out the pubs that are currently doing best in the area, or are specially attractive for one reason or another.

The county boundaries we use are those for the administrative counties (not the old traditional counties, which were changed back in 1976). We have left the new unitary authorities within the counties that they formed part of until their creation in the most recent local government reorganisation. Metropolitan areas have been included in the counties around them – for example, Merseyside in Lancashire. And occasionally we have grouped counties together – for example, Rutland with Leicestershire, and Durham with Northumberland to make Northumbria. If in doubt, check the Contents pages.

Scotland, Wales and London have each been covered in single chapters. Pubs are listed alphabetically (except in London, which is split into Central, East, North, South and West), under the name of the town or village where they are. If the village is so small that you might not find it on a road map, we've listed it under the name of the nearest sizeable village or town. The maps use the same town and village names, and additionally include a few big cities that don't have any listed pubs – for orientation.

We list pubs in their true county, not their postal county. Just once or twice, when the village itself is in one county but the pub is just over the border in the next-door county, we have used the village county, not the pub one.

Stars ★

Really outstanding pubs are awarded a star, and in one case two: these are the aristocrats among pubs. The stars do NOT signify extra luxury or specially good food – in fact, some of the pubs that appeal most distinctively and strongly are decidedly basic in terms of food and surroundings. The detailed description of each pub shows what its particular appeal is, and this is what the stars refer to.

Food Award 🄌

Pubs where food is really outstanding.

Stay Award ⇐

Pubs that are good as places to stay at (obviously, you can't expect the same level of luxury at £60 a head as you'd get for £100 a head). Pubs with bedrooms are marked on the maps as a square.

Wine Award ♀

Pubs with particularly enjoyable wines by the glass – often a good range.

Beer Award ◀

Pubs where the quality of the beer is quite exceptional, or pubs that keep a particularly interesting range of beers in good condition.

Value Award £

This distinguishes pubs that offer really good value food. In all the award-winning pubs, you will find an interesting choice at around £11.

Recommenders

At the end of each Main Entry we include the names of readers who have recently recommended that pub (unless they've asked us not to use their names).

Important note: the description of the pub and the comments on it are our own and not the recommenders'.

Also Worth a Visit

The Also Worth a Visit section at the end of each county chapter includes brief descriptions of pubs that have been recommended by readers in the year before the *Guide* goes to print and that we feel are worthy of inclusion – many of them, indeed, as good in their way as the featured pubs (these are picked out by a star). We have inspected and approved nearly half of these ourselves. All the others are recommended by our reader-reporters. The descriptions of these other pubs, written by us, usually reflect the experience of several different people.

The pubs in Also Worth a Visit may become featured entries in future editions. So do please help us know which are hot prospects for our inspection programme (and which are not!), by reporting on them. There are report forms at the back of the *Guide*, or you can email us at feedback@goodguides.com, or write to us at

The Good Pub Guide, FREEPOST RTXY–ZCBC–BBAZ,
Stream Lane, Sedlescombe, Battle TN33 0PB

Locating Pubs

To help readers who use digital mapping systems we include a postcode for every pub. Pubs outside London are given a British Grid four-figure map reference. Where a pub is exceptionally difficult to find, we include a six-figure reference in the directions. The Map number (Main Entries only) refers to the maps at the back of the *Guide*.

Motorway Pubs

If a pub is within four or five miles of a motorway junction we give special directions for finding it from the motorway. The Special Interest Lists at the end of the book include a list of these pubs, motorway by motorway.

Prices and Other Factual Details

The *Guide* went to press during the summer of 2017, after each pub was sent a checking sheet to get up-to-date food, drink and bedroom prices and other factual information. By the summer of 2018 prices are bound to have increased, but if you find a significantly different price please let us know.

Breweries or independent chains to which pubs are 'tied' are named at the beginning of the italic-print rubric after each Main Entry. That generally means the pub has to get most if not all its drinks from that brewery or chain. If the brewery is not an independent one but just part of a combine, we name the combine in brackets. When the pub is tied, we have spelled out whether the landlord is a tenant, has the pub on a lease, or is a manager. Tenants and leaseholders of breweries generally have considerably greater freedom to do things their own way, and in particular are allowed to buy drinks including a beer from sources other than their tied brewery.

Free houses are pubs not tied to a brewery. In theory they can shop around, but in practice many free houses have loans from the big brewers, on terms that bind them to sell those breweries' beers. So don't be too surprised to find that so-called free houses may be stocking a range of beers restricted to those from a single brewery.

Real ale is used by us to mean beer that has been maturing naturally in its cask. We do not count as real ale beer that has been pasteurised or filtered to remove its natural yeasts.

Other drinks. We've also looked out particularly for pubs doing enterprising non-alcoholic drinks (including good tea or coffee), interesting spirits (especially malt whiskies), country wines, freshly squeezed juices and good farm ciders.

Bar food usually refers to what is sold in the bar; we do not describe menus that are restricted to a separate restaurant. If we know that a pub serves sandwiches, we say so – if you don't see them mentioned, assume you can't get them. Food listed is an example of the sort of thing you'd find served in the bar on a normal day.

Children. If we don't mention children at all, assume that they are not welcome. All but one or two pubs allow children in their garden if they have one. 'Children welcome' means the pub has told us that it lets them in with no special restrictions. In other cases, we report exactly what arrangements pubs say they make for children. However, we have to note that in readers' experience some pubs make restrictions that they haven't told us about (children only if eating, for example). If you come across this, please let us know, so that we can clarify with the pub concerned for the next edition.

The absence of any reference to children in an Also Worth a Visit entry means we don't know either way. Children's Certificates exist, but in practice children are allowed into some part of most pubs in this *Guide* (there is no legal restriction on the movement of children over 14 in any pub). Children under 16 cannot have alcoholic drinks. Children aged 16 and 17 can drink beer, wine or cider with a meal if it is bought by an adult and they are accompanied by an adult.

Dogs. If Main Entry licensees have told us they allow dogs in their pub or bedrooms, we say so; absence of reference to dogs means dogs are not welcome. If you take a dog into a pub you should have it on a lead. We also mention in the text any pub dogs or cats (or indeed other animals) that we've come across ourselves, or heard about from readers.

Parking. If we know there is a problem with parking, we say so; otherwise assume there is a car park.

Credit cards. We say if a pub does not accept them; some that do may put a surcharge on credit card bills, to cover charges made by the card company. We also say if we know that a pub tries to retain customers' credit cards while they are eating. This is a reprehensible practice, and if a pub tries it on you, please tell them that all banks and card companies frown on it – and please let us know the pub's name, so that we can warn readers in future editions.

Telephone numbers are given for all pubs that are not ex-directory.

Opening hours are for summer; we say if we know of differences in winter, or on particular days of the week. In the country, many pubs may open rather later and close earlier than their details show (if you come across this, please let us know – with details). Pubs are allowed to stay open all day if licensed to do so. However, outside cities many pubs in England and Wales close during the afternoon. We'd be grateful to hear of any differences from the hours we quote.

Bedroom prices normally include full english breakfasts (if available), VAT and any automatic service charge. If we give just one price, it is the total price for two people sharing a double or twin-bedded room for one night. Prices before the '/' are for single occupancy, prices after it for double.

Meal times. Bar food is commonly served between the hours of 12-2 and 7-9, at least from Monday to Saturday. We spell out the times if they are significantly different. To be sure of a table it's best to book before you go. Sunday hours vary considerably from pub to pub, so it's advisable to check before you leave.

Disabled access. Deliberately, we do not ask pubs about this, as their answers would not give a reliable picture of how easy access is. Instead, we depend on readers' direct experience. If you are able to give us help about this, we would be particularly grateful for your reports.

Website, iPhone and iPad

You can read and search *The Good Pub Guide* via our website (www.thegoodpubguide.co.uk), which includes every pub in this *Guide*. You can also write reviews and let us know about undiscovered gems. The *Guide* is also available as an app for your iPhone or iPad and as an eBook for your Kindle.

Changes during the year – please tell us

Changes are inevitable during the course of the year. Landlords change, and so do their policies. We hope that you will find everything just as we say, but if not please let us know. You can email us at feedback@goodguides.com or use the Report Forms section at the end of the *Guide*.

Editors' acknowledgements

We could not produce the *Guide* without the huge help we have from the many thousands of readers who report to us on the pubs they visit, often in great detail. Particular thanks to these greatly valued correspondents: Chris and Angela Buckell, Tony and Wendy Hobden, Susan and John Douglas, Michael and Jenny Back, Gerry and Rosemary Dobson, Steve Whalley, Liz Bell, Michael Doswell, R K Phillips, Roger and Donna Huggins, Clive and Fran Dutson, David Lamb, Michael Butler, Tracey and Stephen Groves, Neil and Angela Huxter, Richard Tilbrook, Paul Humphreys, Ann and Colin Hunt, Ian Herdman, Peter Meister, Mrs Margo Finlay and Jörg Kasprowski, David Hunt, Gordon and Margaret Ormondroyd, Stuart Doughty, Tony and Jill Radnor, Brian Glozier, Simon and Mandy King, Simon Collett-Jones, Brian and Anna Marsden, Pete and Sarah, Dave Braisted, Richard Kennell, Dr J Barrie Jones, Phil and Jane Hodson, John Saville, Bob and Margaret Holder, John Beeken, Mr and Mrs P R Thomas, Edward Mirzoeff, Guy Vowles, Ian Phillips, Nigel Espley, Giles and Annie Francis, John and Sylvia Harrop, John Evans, Sara Fulton and Roger Baker, Hunter and Christine Wright, Ross Balaam, Mike and Mary Carter, R L Borthwick, S G N Bennett, Gerry and Julie Flanagan, Mr and Mrs Richard Osborne, David and Sally Frost, John and Eleanor Holdsworth, David Jackman, Martinthehills, M G Hart, Ann and Tony Bennett-Hughes, Taff Thomas, John Wooll, Ewan and Sue Hewitt, Suzy Miller, Sally and John Quinlan, Christian Mole, Robert W Buckle, Jamie and Sue May, Dr W I C Clark, Stephen Funnell, Sue Parry Davies, David Fowler, Barry Collett, John Evans, Dr and Mrs A K Clarke, John and Penny Wildon, Tony Scott, David Stewart, Derek and Sylvia Stephenson, Roy and Gill Payne, Comus and Sarah Elliott, Pat and Tony Martin, Mike and Eleanor Anderson, Theocsbrian, Conrad Freezer, J B and M E Benson, R T and J C Moggridge, Janet and Peter Race, Rod and Diana Pearce, the Dutchman, S Holder, Hugh Roberts, B and M Kendall, Minda and Stanley Alexander, Richard Cole, Marianne and Peter Stevens, Revd R P Tickle, Lewis Canning, Robert Kennedy, Alison Chalu, R C Hastings, Dave and Jan Pilgrim, Stephen Woad, Mike Kavaney, KC, David Edwards, Phil and Jane Villiers, William and Ann Reid, Tim and Moira Hurst, Darren and Jane Staniforth, Glenn and Julia Smithers, David and Judy Robison, Sally Melling, Martin Day, Tony Tollitt, Johnny Beerling, Tim Brogan, Katharine Cowherd, Dr A McCormick, Derek Stafford, Martin and Clare Warne, John and Enid Morris, Denis and Margaret Kilner, Stephen Green, Johnston and Maureen Anderson, Philip J Alderton, Graham and Carol Parker, Simon and Angela Thomas, Chris Parker, Kevin Chesson, M A Borthwick, Tony and Maggie Harwood, Sian Gillham, Pieter and Janet Vrancken, Anneliese Cameron, Ian and Rose Lock, Hilary Forrest, Nick and Meriel Cox, Fr Robert Marsh, Mrs Julie Thomas, Peter Raney, Gerald Warner, David Fellows, Dr A J and Mrs B A Tompsett, Nigel and Jean Eames, George Atkinson, Adam Bellinger, PL, Peter L Harrison, Christopher Mobbs, Geoffrey Kemp, David Thorpe, James Rickett, Peter and Pat Taylor, Peter and Anne Hollindale, James Castro-Edwards, Mr and Mrs D Hammond, Martin and Anne Muers, Mrs Zara Elliott, Ian Malone, Dr D J and Mrs S C Walker, Clifford Blakemore, David Cartwright, Richard Maccabee, Rob Unsworth, A W Johns, Dr J H Sewart, Morris family, Heather and Richard Jones, Philip Turton, Edward Barnaby, Nigel and Sue Foster, Robert Watt, V Brogden, Robert Lester, Colin McLachlan, Revd Michael Vockins, Alistair Forsyth, Richard Tingle, I D Barnett, Ron Corbett, Stuart Reeves, Michael Sargent, Andrew Bosi, Malcolm and Pauline Pellatt, David H Bennett, John and Jennifer Spinks, Bernard Stradling MBE, Mike and Margaret Banks, R and S Bentley, Phil and Helen Holt, Dr and Mrs RGJ Telfer, Robert Wivell, Peter Randell, Frank Price, M J Winterton, Trevor Burgess, John and Elspeth Howell, Brian and Jacky Wilson, Philip Crawford, David and Stella Martin, Dr and Mrs J D Abell, Dr and Mrs F McGinn, Guy and Caroline Howard, Lesley Broadbent, Peter Myers, Mrs P Sumner, Canon Michael Bourdeaux, Tim and Sue Halstead, Sally Anne and Peter Goodale, Mr and Mrs J Watkins, Dr Martin Owton, Mike and Anita Beach, Frank Blanchard, B and F A Hannam, Dave Snowden, the Griffiths family.

Thanks too to all those who helped us at The Book Service for their cheerful dedication: Maria Byrne, Carol Bryant, Peter Piechuta and Michele Csaforda. And particularly to John Holliday of Trade Wind Technology, who built and looks after our all-important database.

Fiona Stapley

ENGLAND

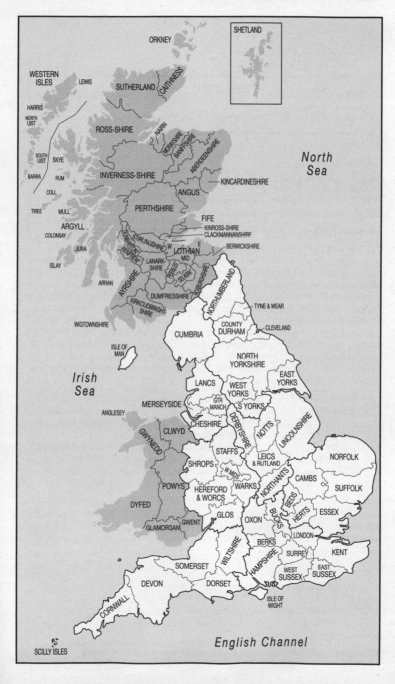

SHETLAND

ORKNEY

WESTERN
ISLES

LEWIS

HARRIS

NORTH
UIST

SUTHERLAND

CAITHNESS

SOUTH
UIST

SKYE

BARRA

RUM

COLL

ROSS-SHIRE

NAIRN

MORAYSHIRE

BANFFSHIRE

ABERDEENSHIRE

INVERNESS-SHIRE

TIREE

MULL

ARGYLL

ANGUS

KINCARDINESHIRE

COLONSAY

PERTHSHIRE

FIFE

JURA

KINROSS-SHIRE

CLACKMANNANSHIRE

ISLAY

STIRLINGSHIRE

W
DUNBARTON
RENFREW

LOTHIAN

MID

E

BERWICKSHIRE

ARRAN

LANARK-
SHIRE

PEEBLES

SELKIRK

AYRSHIRE

ROXBURGHSHIRE

DUMFRIESSHIRE

KIRKCUDBRIGHT-
SHIRE

NORTHUMBERLAND

TYNE & WEAR

WIGTOWNSHIRE

ISLE OF
MAN

CUMBRIA

COUNTY
DURHAM

CLEVELAND

NORTH
YORKSHIRE

*Irish
Sea*

LANCS

WEST
YORKS

EAST
YORKS

ANGLESEY

MERSEYSIDE

GTR
MANCH

S YORKS

CHESHIRE

DERBYSHIRE

NOTTS

LINCOLNSHIRE

GWYNEDD

CLWYD

STAFFS

LEICS
& RUTLAND

NORFOLK

SHROPS

W MIDS

POWYS

HEREFORD
& WORCS

WARKS

NORTHANTS

CAMBS

SUFFOLK

BEDS

DYFED

GLOS

OXON

BUCKS

HERTS

ESSEX

GWENT

GLAMORGAN

LONDON

BERKS

WILTSHIRE

HAMPSHIRE

SURREY

KENT

SOMERSET

DORSET

WEST
SUSSEX

EAST
SUSSEX

DEVON

ISLE OF
WIGHT

CORNWALL

SCILLY ISLES

*North
Sea*

English Channel

Bedfordshire

AMPTHILL
Prince of Wales
(01525) 840504 – www.princeofwales-ampthill.com

Bedford Street (B540 N from central crossroads); MK45 2NB

TL0338   Map 5

Civilised and with neat décor and up-to-date food; bedrooms

Although perhaps more of a bar-brasserie than a straightforward pub, there are plenty of chatty customers in this attractive red-brick place and they do keep Charles Wells Bombardier and Eagle on handpump, plenty of wines by the glass and good coffee; service is notably good. It's set on two levels with comfortable, stylish furnishings and modern prints on mainly cream walls (dark green and maroon accents at either end). The slightly sunken flagstoned area with wooden tables and chairs and a log fire in the exposed brick fireplace leads to a partly ply-panelled dining room with dark leather dining chairs around a mixed batch of sturdy tables; also, plenty of church candles and big burgundy leather armchairs and sofas at low tables on bare boards. Background music. The nicely planted, two-level lawn has picnic-sets, with more on a terrace by the car park.

🍴 Quite a choice of good food includes lunchtime sandwiches (not Sunday), tiger prawn skewers marinated in chilli, garlic and lime with avocado purée, chicken liver and brandy pâté with home-made piccalilli, chargrilled courgette and aubergine with marinated feta, olives and roasted red pepper sauce, salmon en croûte with white wine and dill, chicken breast filled with chorizo and a rich tomato sauce, pork belly with apple, sage and celeriac and cider jus, and puddings such as crème brûlée of the day and salted caramel tart with chocolate ice-cream; Thursday is steak night. *Benchmark main dish: pie of the day £11.95. Two-course evening meal £19.00.*

Wells & Youngs ~ Lease Richard and Neia Heathorn ~ Real ale ~ Open 11-11 (midnight Fri, Sat); 12-5 Sun ~ Bar food 12-2.30 (3 weekends), 6.30-9 (7-9.30 Fri, Sat); not Sun evening ~ Restaurant ~ Children welcome ~ Dogs allowed in bar and bedrooms ~ Wi-fi ~ Bedrooms: £55/£70 *Recommended by Richard Kennell, Susan and Jeremy Arthern, Maggie and Matthew Lyons, Susan and Tim Boyle*

BEDFORD
Park 🍷
(01234) 273929 – www.theparkbedford.co.uk

Corner of Kimbolton Road (B660) and Park Avenue, out past Bedford Hospital; MK40 2PA

TL0550   Map 5

Civilised and individual oasis – a great asset for the town

Customers drop in and out of this bustling and cheerful pub all day. There are all sorts of seating areas to choose from, each with appealing décor and thoughtful touches: a more or less conventional bar with heavy beams, panelled dado and leaded lights in big windows, a light and airy conservatory sitting room with easy chairs well spread on a carpet, and an extensive series of softly lit rambling dining areas, carpeted or flagstoned. Charles Wells Bombardier Burning Gold and Eagle and Courage Directors on handpump, inventive bar nibbles and an excellent choice of wines by the glass; background music. The sheltered brick-paved terrace has good timber furniture, some under canopies, and attractive shrubs.

🍽 Enjoyable food includes breakfasts (8.30-10.30am Thursday, Friday; 9-11am weekends), sandwiches, sharing boards, brie parcel with fruit chutney, chicken and tarragon terrine, a pasta and a risotto of the day, sausage and mash with onion gravy, steak and coriander burger with toppings and chips, trout fillet with roasted beetroot purée and blood orange, fennel and almond salad, pork belly and chorizo casserole, and puddings such as dark chocolate brownie with white chocolate ice-cream and rhubarb and ginger crumble with Grand Marnier crème anglaise; they also offer a two- and three-course weekday menu. *Benchmark main dish: steak in ale pie £12.00. Two-course evening meal £21.00.*

Little Gems Country Dining Pubs ~ Manager Steve Cook ~ Real ale ~ Open 8am-11.30pm; 9am-11.30pm Sat; 9am-11pm Sun ~ Bar food 12-3, 6-10; 12-10 Sat; 12-8 Sun ~ Restaurant ~ Children in one bar and restaurant ~ Dogs allowed in bar ~ Wi-fi *Recommended by Ruth May, Tony Smaithe, Charles Todd, Belinda Stamp*

FLITTON
White Hart ♀
TL0535 Map 5

(01525) 862022 – www.whitehartflitton.co.uk
Village signed off A507; MK45 5EJ

Simply furnished and friendly village pub with bar and dining area, real ales, interesting food and seats in the garden

There's little doubt that the main emphasis in this friendly village pub is on the extremely popular food, but they still keep B&T Golden Fox and Shefford Bitter on handpump and 20 wines – as well as champagne and prosecco – by the glass. The minimally decorated front bar has dark leather tub chairs around low tables, contemporary leather and chrome seats at pedestal tables, and Farrow & Ball painted walls; TV. Steps lead down to a good-sized, simply furnished back dining area with red plush seats and banquettes on dark wooden floorboards. The nice garden has neat shrub borders, and teak seats and tables on a terrace shaded by cedars and weeping willows. A 13th-c church is next door.

🍽 Their renowned steaks and daily fresh fish dishes dominate the menu and include crab, lime and chilli bruschetta with fennel, saffron and red pepper dressing, gilt-head bream with avocado, mango and chilli salsa, turbot with lemon and brown shrimp butter and aberdeen angus steaks with a choice of butters; they also serve sandwiches, home-made liver pâté with caramelised onion marmalade, sticky spicy pork ribs with chorizo, coleslaw chicken breast with creamed leeks, bacon, brie and pernod sauce, chargrilled lamb chops with feta and tomato salad, and puddings such as butterscotch pudding with butterscotch sauce and lemon, lime and ginger posset. *Benchmark main dish: grilled whole lemon sole £12.95. Two-course evening meal £20.00.*

Free house ~ Licensees Phil and Clare Hale ~ Real ale ~ Open 12-2.30, 6-midnight; 12-3, 6-1am Sat; 12-5 Sun; closed Sun evening, Mon ~ Bar food 12-2, 6.30-9 (9.30 Fri, Sat); 12-2.30 Sun ~ Restaurant ~ Children welcome ~ Dogs allowed in bar ~ Wi-fi *Recommended by Colin Humphreys, Diane Abbott, Andrea and Philip Crispin, Mark Morgan, Charles Todd*

IRELAND
TL1341 Map 5

GOOD PUB GUIDE

Black Horse ⭐ ♀ 🛏

(01462) 811398 – www.blackhorseireland.com

Off A600 Shefford–Bedford; SG17 5QL

Bedfordshire Dining Pub of the Year

Contemporary décor in old building, first class food, good wine list and lovely garden with attractive terraces; bedrooms

As well as a fine range of drinks, you can be sure of an excellent meal in this family-run 17th-c inn. The warm and relaxing bar has inglenook fireplaces, beams in low ceilings and timbering – plus Adnams Bitter, Fullers London Pride and Sharps Doom Bar on handpump, 28 wines by the glass, a dozen malt whiskies, Weston's cider and good coffee from the long green-slate bar counter; staff are courteous and helpful. There are leather armchairs and comfortable wall seats, a mix of elegant wooden and high-backed leather dining chairs around attractive tables on polished oak boards or sandstone flooring, original artwork and fresh flowers; background music. French windows open from the restaurant on to various terraces with individual furnishings and pretty flowering pots and beds. The chalet-style bedrooms (just across a courtyard in a separate building) are comfortable and well equipped; continental breakfasts are included and taken in your room. The Birch at Woburn is under the same ownership.

 From seasonal menus the impressive food includes lunchtime sandwiches, roast pigeon breast with carrot and walnut salad and blueberry jus, mussels in a sauce of the day, beetroot, pea and tomato pasta with basil mascarpone cream, a pie of the day, pork tenderloin with apple and mustard potato cake, creamed leeks and black pudding fritter, suprême of loch-reared trout on leek, tarragon and lemon risotto, honey-glazed duck breast with beetroot fondant, garlic shallots and blackberry and port jus, and puddings such as white chocolate and raspberry ripple tart with peach melba flavours and dark chocolate brownie with white chocolate fudge and cookies; they also offer a two- and three-course set menu (not Friday evening or weekends). *Benchmark main dish: lager-battered fish and triple-cooked chips £13.95. Two-course evening meal £23.00.*

Free house ~ Licensee Darren Campbell ~ Real ale ~ Open 12-3, 6-11; 12-11 Sat; 12-6 Sun ~ Bar food 12-2.30, 6.15-9.45; 12-5 Sun ~ Restaurant ~ Children welcome ~ Wi-fi ~ Bedrooms: /$89.95 *Recommended by Ruth May, Jack and Hilary Burton, Alison and Tony Livesley, Alison and Dan Richardson*

OAKLEY
TL0053 Map 5

GOOD PUB GUIDE

Bedford Arms ♀

(01234) 822280 – www.bedfordarmsoakley.co.uk

High Street; MK43 7RH

Updated 16th-c village inn with real ales, wines by the glass, fish and other popular food in two dining rooms, and seats in the garden

Each of the interconnected rooms here has different contemporary décor. The pubbiest part has straightforward wooden furniture on bare boards, flower prints on the walls, daily papers, a decorative woodburning stove with a flat-screen TV above it, and Wells Eagle and a couple of guests such as Black Sheep BAA BAA and St Austell Proper Job on handpump and up to 40 wines by the glass; darts and board games. The four cosy, individually decorated rooms leading off the main bar are the nicest places for a drink and chat. One has a large circular pine table (just right for a private party), another has farmhouse chairs and a cushioned pew beside a small fireplace, the third has ladder-back chairs and shiny tables on ancient floor tiles and the last is very much Victorian in style. The stone-floored dining rooms have tartan-covered seating or wicker chairs, while the light, airy conservatory overlooks the pretty garden where there are seats for warm-weather meals.

Daily fresh fish dishes play a big part here and might include swordfish loin with wasabi mayonnaise and pea and broad bean salad, moules marinière and grey mullet with pearl barley and celeriac risotto, black pudding and apple; they also serve lunchtime sandwiches, ham hock terrine with pineapple pickle, sharing boards, rhubarb and lentil curry with toasted coconut and greek yoghurt, cumberland sausages with caramelised onion gravy, corn-fed chicken with potato rösti, french-style peas and prosciutto crisps and puddings such as white chocolate cheesecake with red berry coulis and fruit crumble of the day. *Benchmark main dish: sea bass fillet with crushed new potatoes and spinach purée £14.00. Two-course evening meal £20.00.*

Wells & Youngs ~ Tenant Emma Avery ~ Real ale ~ Open 11-11; 12-8 Sun ~ Bar food 12-2.30, 6-9.30; 12-5 Sun; not Mon ~ Restaurant ~ Children welcome until 7pm ~ Dogs allowed in bar ~ Wi-fi *Recommended by Michael Butler, Michael Sargent, Holly and Tim Waite, Elise and Charles Mackinlay, Lucy and Giles Gibbon*

WOBURN
Birch ⭐🍴♀

SP9433   Map 4

(01525) 290295 – www.birchwoburn.com

3.5 miles from M1 junction 13; follow Woburn signs via A507 and A4012, right in village then A5130 (Newport Road); MK17 9HX

Well run dining establishment with focus on imaginative food, good wines and attentive service

This edge-of-town pub continues to get warm praise from our readers. The several individually and elegantly furnished linked rooms have contemporary décor and furnishings, and the upper dining area has high-backed leather or wooden dining chairs around tables on stripped and polished floorboards. The lower part occupies a light and airy conservatory with a pitched glazed roof, ceramic floor tiles, light coloured furnishings and original artwork and fresh flowers; background music. The bustling bar is similarly furnished and has a few high bar stools against the sleek, smart counter where they serve Adnams Bitter and Sharps Doom Bar on handpump, 15 good wines by the glass, a dozen malt whiskies and quite a few teas and coffees; background music. There are tables out on a sheltered deck, and in summer the front of the pub has masses of flowering hanging baskets and tubs. This is sister pub to the Black Horse at Ireland.

Enticing food includes scallop and prawn ravioli with chilli crayfish bisque, mixed game terrine with carrot and orange marmalade, beetroot and caramelised red onion tarte tatin with goats cheese, lamb rump with a mini shepherd's pie, honey-glazed baby rainbow carrots and jus, duck breast and confit duck bonbons with buttered savoy cabbage and apricot purée, venison steak with braised red cabbage and bacon and a redcurrant and pink peppercorn jus, and puddings such as honey and lavender crème brûlée with crystallised lavender and bitter lemon purée with star anise shortbread and a soufflé of the day. *Benchmark main dish: griddled sea bass fillet with a salsa of the day £15.95. Two-course evening meal £25.00.*

Free house ~ Licensee Mark Campbell ~ Real ale ~ Open 12-3, 6-11; 12-6 Sun ~ Bar food 12-2.30, 6.15-9.45; 12-5 Sun ~ Restaurant ~ Children welcome ~ Wi-fi *Recommended by Tim and Sarah Smythe-Brown, Lindy Andrews, Daniel King, Jeff Davies, Michael Sargent*

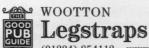

WOOTTON
Legstraps
TL0046 Map 4

(01234) 854112 – www.thelegstraps.co.uk

Keeley Lane; MK43 9HR

Bustling village pub with a nice range of food from open kitchen, local ales and wines by the glass

There's no doubt that the top quality food in this village pub is a highlight – but there are plenty of drinkers too and the kind, efficient staff welcome everyone. The low-ceilinged bar has an elegant feel with contemporary and comfortable upholstered chairs around all sizes of table, big flagstones, a woodburning stove in a brick fireplace with a leather sofa and box wall seats to either side, and leather-topped stools against the pale planked counter. They keep Fullers London Pride and Sharps Doom Bar on handpump, good wines by the glass and quite a few gins. The dining rooms have bold paintwork, similar furnishings to the bar, polished bare boards and flower prints on one end wall with butterflies wallpaper on another.

The thoughtful menu includes duck and spring onion croquettes with soy and honey dip, cornish mussels in garlic, cream and white wine, garlic and rosemary butternut squash with spinach and ricotta pithivier and parsley sauce, cider-braised pork belly with baked apple and apple and elderflower sauce, guinea fowl breast with poached thigh, pommes parisienne and red wine jus, and puddings such as spiced rum and vanilla crème brûlée and coffee ice-cream and strawberry iced parfait with rhubarb sorbet, caramelised rhubarb and apple crumble and a shot of pedro ximénez. *Benchmark main dish: beer-battered fish of the day £14.00. Two-course evening meal £20.00.*

Free house ~ Licensee Ian Craig ~ Real ale ~ Open 12-3, 5.30-11; 12-midnight Fri, Sat; 12-7 Sun; closed Mon ~ Bar food 12-2, 6-9 (9.30 Fri, Sat); 12-4 Sun ~ Restaurant ~ Children welcome ~ Dogs allowed in bar ~ Wi-fi *Recommended by S Holder, Ben and Diane Bowie, Tim and Sarah Smythe-Brown*

Also Worth a Visit in Bedfordshire

Besides the fully inspected pubs, you might like to try these pubs that have been recommended to us and described by readers. Do tell us what you think of them: feedback@goodguides.com

BEDFORD TL0550
d'Parys (01234) 340248
De Parys Avenue; MK40 2UA Dining pub in former red-brick Victorian hotel; contemporary revamp keeping original features such as parquet floors, stained glass, period fireplaces and sweeping staircase, open-plan drinking area with long wooden tables and benches, some leather button-back sofas, Charles Wells ales and plenty of wines by the glass, popular food including weekday set lunch and breakfasts (from 7am; 8am weekends), separate counter serving good coffee, ice-cream and traditional sweets, friendly helpful staff; children welcome, outside seating, 14 stylish bedrooms, open (and food) all day. *(Lindy Andrews)*

BEDFORD TL0549
Embankment (01234) 261332
The Embankment; MK40 3PD Revamped mock-Tudor hotel (Peach group) adjacent to the river; airy L-shaped front bar with mix of modern furniture on wood floor, pretty blue-tiled fireplace, Charles Wells ales and several wines by the glass, good choice of food from sandwiches and deli boards up including popular fixed-price menu, cheerful helpful service, restaurant; background music; children welcome, seats out on front terrace

We include some hotels with a good bar that offers facilities comparable to those of a pub.

looking across to Great Ouse, 20 bedrooms (best ones with river views), good breakfast, open (and food) all day. *(Daniel King)*

BEDFORD TL0450
Wellington Arms (01234) 308033
Wellington Street; MK40 2JX Friendly no-frills backstreet corner local, a dozen well kept ales including Adnams and B&T, real cider/perry and good range of continental beers, wooden tables and chairs on bare boards, lots of brewerania; no food or mobile phones, some live music; seats in backyard, open all day from midday. *(S Holder)*

BIDDENHAM TL0249
Three Tuns (01234) 354847
Off A428; MK40 4BD Refurbished part-thatched village dining pub with bar, lounge and restaurant extension, good varied menu from traditional favourites up, plenty of wines by the glass including champagne, well kept Greene King ales, efficient friendly service; spacious garden with picnic-sets, more contemporary furniture on terrace and decked area, open all day. *(Holly and Tim Waite)*

BLETSOE TL0157
★Falcon (01234) 781222
Rushden Road (A6 N of Bedford); MK44 1QN Refurbished 17th-c building with comfortable opened-up bar, low beams and joists, seating from cushioned wall/window seats to high-backed settles, woodburner in double-aspect fireplace, snug with sofas and old pews, panelled dining room, enjoyable food from pub standards up (plenty of gluten-free choices), Charles Wells ales and a guest, decent choice of wines by the glass and good coffee, efficient friendly service; unobtrusive background music, daily papers; decked and paved terrace in lovely big garden down to the Great Ouse, open (and food) all day. *(Lindy Andrews)*

BOLNHURST TL0858
★Plough (01234) 376274
Kimbolton Road; MK44 2EX Stylishly converted Tudor building with thriving atmosphere, charming professional staff and top notch food (must book Sat night), Adnams and a couple of interesting guests, good carefully annotated wine list (including organic vintages) with over a dozen by the glass, maybe home-made summer lemonade and tomato juice, airy dining extension, log fires; children welcome, dogs in bar, attractive tree-shaded garden with decking overlooking pond, remains of old moat, closed Sun evening, Mon and for two weeks after Christmas. *(Hugo Jeune, Michael Sargent, Peter Andrews)*

BROOM TL1743
Cock (01767) 314411
High Street; from A1 opposite Biggleswade turn-off, follow 'Old Warden 3, Aerodrome

2' signpost, first left signed Broom; SG18 9NA* Friendly and unspoilt 19th-c village-green pub, four changing ales tapped from casks by cellar steps off central corridor (no counter), Potton Press cider, enjoyable traditional home-made food such as steak and kidney pudding, good value two-course lunch deal, original latch doors linking one quietly cosy little room to the next (four in all), low ceilings, stripped panelling, farmhouse tables and chairs on old tiles, open fires, games room with bar skittles and darts; children and dogs welcome (resident jack russell), picnic-sets on terrace by back lawn, camping field, open all day, no food Sun evening. *(Lindy Andrews)*

CLOPHILL TL0838
Stone Jug (01525) 860526
N on A6 from A507 roundabout, after 200 metres, second turn on right into backstreet; MK45 4BY Secluded old stone-built local (originally three cottages), cosy and welcoming with traditional old-fashioned atmosphere, well kept B&T, Otter, St Austell and a couple of guests, popular good value pubby lunchtime food (not Sun, Mon), various rooms around L-shaped bar, darts in small games extension; background music; children and dogs welcome, roadside picnic-sets and pretty little back terrace, open all day Fri-Sun. *(Daniel King)*

GREAT BARFORD TL1351
Anchor (01234) 870364
High Street; off A421; MK44 3LF Open-plan pub by medieval arched bridge and church, good sensibly priced food from snacks up, Charles Wells ales and guests kept well, friendly staff, river views from main bar, back restaurant where children allowed; background music; picnic-sets in front looking across to Great Ouse, three bedrooms, open (and food) all day weekends. *(Charlie Timmins)*

HENLOW TL1738
Crown (01462) 812433
High Street; SG16 6BS Nicely updated beamed dining pub with good choice of popular food including children's menu, several wines by the glass, well kept Caledonian Flying Scotsman, Courage Directors and a guest, smiley helpful staff, woodburners (one in inglenook); quiet background music, free wi-fi, daily newspapers; terrace and small garden, five good bedrooms in converted stables, open (and food) all day. *(Daniel King)*

HENLOW TL1738
★Engineers Arms (01462) 812284
A6001 S of Biggleswade; High Street; SG16 6AA Traditional 19th-c village pub with up to a dozen changing ales plus good choice of ciders/perries, bottled belgian beers and wines by the glass, helpful knowledgeable staff, limited range of good

value snacks; comfortable carpeted front room with old local photographs, bric-a-brac collections and good open fire, smaller tiled inner area and another carpeted one; beer/cider/country wine festivals, monthly live music, disco and quiz nights, sports TVs, juke box and silent fruit machine; dogs allowed in bar, plenty of outside seating, open all day (till 1am Fri, Sat). *(Daniel King)*

HOUGHTON CONQUEST   TL0342
Chequers   (01525) 404853
B530 towards Ampthill; MK45 3JP
Roomy Little Gems pub being refurbished as we went to press (news please); decent choice of fairly priced food from pizzas and burgers up, three real ales and plenty of wines by the glass, friendly helpful service; children welcome, garden with play area, open all day, breakfast from 9am. *(Si Jamieson)*

HOUGHTON CONQUEST   TL0441
★ Knife & Cleaver   (01234) 930789
Between B530 (old A418) and A6, S of Bedford; MK45 3LA Refurbished and extended 17th-c village dining pub opposite church, good variety of well liked food from separate bar and restaurant menus, extensive choice of wines by the glass including champagne, Charles Wells ales and a guest, friendly staff; free wi-fi; children welcome, no dogs inside, nine chalet bedrooms arranged around courtyard and garden, good breakfast, free charging of electric cars for guests, quiz (Mon evening), open all day from 7am (8am weekends). *(Emma Scofield)*

HUSBORNE CRAWLEY   SP9635
White Horse   (01525) 280565
Mill Road, just off A507; MK43 0XE
Open-plan village pub arranged around central servery, a couple of real ales and good reasonably priced home-made food (vegetarians and special diets well catered for), friendly attentive staff, beams, wood and quarry-tiled floors, some stripped brickwork and woodburner; children welcome, tables outside, lovely hanging baskets, open (and food) all day, till 8pm (6pm) Sun. *(Harvey Brown, Mike Hickling)*

LITTLE GRANSDEN   TL2755
Chequers   (01767) 677348
Main Road; SG19 3DW Village local in same family for over 60 years and keeping its 1950s feel; simple bar with coal fire, darts and framed historical information about the pub, interesting range of own-brewed Son of Sid ales, step down to cosy snug with another fire and bench seats, comfortable back lounge with fish tank, no food apart from good fish and chips Fri evening (must book); open all day Fri, Sat. *(Si Jamieson)*

MAULDEN   TL0538
Dog & Badger   (01525) 860237
Clophill Road E of village, towards A6/A507 junction; MK45 2AD Attractive

neatly kept bow-windowed cottage, enjoyable food (booking advised weekends) including gluten-free choices, sharing boards, pizzas and grills, set lunch Mon-Sat and other deals, beams and exposed brickwork, high stools on bare boards by carved wooden counter serving Charles Wells and guests, mix of dining chairs around wooden tables, double-sided fireplace, steps down to two carpeted areas and restaurant; background music, sports TV; children welcome, tables and smokers' shelter in front, garden behind with sturdy play area, open all day Fri-Sun. *(Daniel King)*

MILTON BRYAN   SP9730
Red Lion   (01525) 210044
Toddington Road, off B528 S of Woburn; MK17 9HS Refurbished red-brick village dining pub under new ownership; Greene King ales and a guest, several wines by the glass, cocktails and good range of gins, well liked nicely presented food from bar snacks and sharing boards up, lunchtime/early evening set menu, good friendly service, central bar with dining areas either side, beams and open fire; quiz first Thurs of month; children and dogs welcome, big garden with pretty views, open all day Sat, till 7pm Sun, closed Mon. *(George Atkinson, Richard Kennell)*

NORTHILL   TL1446
★ Crown   (01767) 627337
Ickwell Road; off B658 W of Biggleswade; SG18 9AA Prettily situated village pub; cosy flagstoned bar with copper-topped counter, heavy low beams and bay window seats, woodburner here and in restaurant with modern furniture on light wood floor, steps up to another dining area with exposed brick and high ceiling, good brasserie-style food (not Sun evening) including lunchtime baguettes/panini, Greene King and guests, plenty of wines by the glass, good friendly service; soft background music; children welcome, no dogs inside, tables out at front and on sheltered side terrace, more in big back garden with play area, open all day Fri-Sun. *(Daniel King)*

ODELL   SP9657
Bell   (01234) 910850
Off A6 S of Rushden, via Sharnbrook; High Street; MK43 7AS Popular thatched village pub doing well under present welcoming licensees, several comfortable low-beamed rooms around central servery, log fire and inglenook woodburner, good reasonably priced home-made food (not Sun evening, booking advised) including Mon steak night, well kept Greene King, guest ales and good selection of wines/gins, friendly helpful young staff; children and dogs welcome, big garden backing on to river, handy for Harrold-Odell Country Park, open all day. *(Revd R P Tickle)*

OLD WARDEN   TL1343
Hare & Hounds (01767) 627225
*Village signposted off A600 S of Bedford
and B658 W of Biggleswade; SG18 9HQ*
Family-run dining pub with four cosy
refurbished rooms, tweed upholstered chairs
at light wood tables on stripped wood, tiled
or carpeted floors, log fire in one room,
inglenook woodburner in another, prints and
old photographs including aircraft in the
Shuttleworth Collection (just up the road),
popular food using local ingredients, good
value weekday set lunch, two Charles Wells
ales, a guest beer and several wines by the
glass, friendly attentive service; background
music; children welcome, garden stretching
up to pine woods behind, nice thatched village
and good local walks, closed Mon otherwise
open all day, no food Sun evening. *(John Saul)*

POTTON   TL2249
Old Coach House (01767) 260221
Village Square; SG19 2NP Comfortably
refurbished 18th-c coaching inn, well kept
ales such as Charles Wells and good range
of wines by the glass, cocktails, popular food
including burgers in bar or restaurant (pie
day Fri), afternoon teas with home-made
cakes, friendly helpful staff; background
music; children and dogs welcome, seats out
at front and in courtyard, 11 bedrooms, open
all day. *(Lindy Andrews)*

RAVENSDEN   TL0754
★ Horse & Jockey (01234) 772319
*Village signed off B660 N of Bedford;
pub at Church End, off village road;
MK44 2RR* Pleasantly modern pub
decorated in olive greys and deep reds,
leather easy chairs in bar with wall of
meticulously arranged old local photographs,
three real ales including Adnams and 20
wines by the glass, good food from shortish
but varied menu, friendly staff, bright dining
room with chunky tables and high-backed
seats; background music, board games, free
wi-fi; children and dogs (in bar) welcome,
modern tables and chairs under parasols on
sheltered deck, a few picnic-sets on grass,
handsome medieval church nearby, open all
day Sun till 8pm. *(Michael Sargent, Dennis and
Doreen Haward)*

RISELEY   TL0462
Fox & Hounds (01234) 709714
*Off A6 from Sharnbrook/Bletsoe
roundabout; High Street, just E of Gold
Street; MK44 1DT* Modernised village pub
dating from the 16th c; low beams, stripped
boards and imposing stone fireplace, Wells
Bombardier and Eagle, steaks cut to weight
and other food (including takeaway fish and

chips), separate dining room; children and
dogs (in bar) welcome, seats out in front and
in back garden with terrace, open (and food)
all day weekends. *(Michael Sargent)*

SALFORD   SP9339
Swan (01908) 281008
*Not far from M1 junction 13 – left off
A5140; MK17 8BD* Popular Edwardian
country dining pub (Peach group), well liked
food from sandwiches and deli boards to
dry-aged steaks, fixed-price menu weekdays
and Sat lunchtime, Sharps Doom Bar and
a guest, good range of wines, gins and
cocktails, friendly accommodating staff,
updated interior with drinking area to right
of central servery, sofas and leather chairs
on wood floor, restaurant to left with modern
country cottage feel and window view
into kitchen; background music; children
welcome, dogs in bar, seats out on decking,
open (and food) all day. *(S Holder)*

SHEFFORD   TL1439
Brewery Tap (01462) 628448
North Bridge Street; SG17 5DH
No-nonsense L-shaped bar notable for its
well kept/priced B&T ales brewed nearby
and guest beers; bare-boards and low ceiling,
beer bottle collection and other breweriana,
simple lunchtime food, friendly helpful staff;
darts and dominoes; children (in family area)
and dogs welcome, picnic-sets out behind,
open all day. *(Charlie Timmins)*

SHILLINGTON   TL1232
Musgrave Arms (01462) 711286
*Apsley End Road, towards Pegsdon
and Hexton; SG5 3LX* Friendly little low-
beamed 16th-c village local, well kept Greene
King ales and enjoyable home-made food
(not Mon) including good Sun roasts, log fire;
children and dogs welcome, big back garden
with play area, camping, open all day. *(Jake)*

SOULDROP   SP9861
Bedford Arms (01234) 781384
*Village signposted off A6 Rushden–
Bedford; High Street; MK44 1EY* Village
pub dating from the 17th c and doing well
under present management; cosy low-
beamed bar with snug and alcove, Black
Sheep, Greene King IPA and three guests,
several wines by the glass, tasty well priced
pubby food, cottagey dining area with more
low beams, broad floorboards and woodburner
in central fireplace, also roomy mansard-
ceilinged part with sofas by big inglenook;
open mike night first Sun of month, table
skittles, shove-ha'penny and darts; children
and dogs (in bar) welcome, garden tables,
open all day Fri-Sun, closed Mon.
(Lindy Andrews)

We checked prices with the pubs as we went to press in summer 2017.
They should hold until around spring 2018.

STEPPINGLEY   TL0135
French Horn (01525) 720122
Off A507 just N of Flitwick; Church End;
MK45 5AU Comfortable dining pub next
to church; linked rooms with stippled
beams, standing posts and wall timbers,
two inglenooks (one with woodburner),
eclectic mix of chesterfields, leather
armchairs, cushioned antique dining
chairs and other new and old furniture
on flagstones or bare boards, Greene King
IPA and a changing guest, good range of
wines by the glass and malt whiskies, well
liked freshly made food (all day weekends)
served by friendly staff, elegant dining
room; background music, TV, free wi-fi;
children and dogs (in bar) welcome, seats
outside overlooking small green, open all
day (till 1am Sat). *(Daniel King)*

STOTFOLD   TL2136
Fox & Duck (01462) 732434
Arlesey Road; SG5 4HE Welcoming
roadside pub-restaurant with light modern
interior, good food from varied menu
(panini up), Greene King IPA, a guest ale
and plenty of wines by the glass, friendly
accommodating staff, separate coffee lounge;
free wi-fi; children welcome, big enclosed
garden with play area, open all day.
(Rupert Hennen)

STUDHAM   TL0215
Red Lion (01582) 872530
Church Road; LU6 2QA Character
community pub with jovial hands-on landlord
and friendly staff; public bar and eating
areas filled with pictures and bits and
pieces collected over many years, house
plants, wood flooring, carpeting and old
red and black tiles, open fire, ales such as
Adnams, Fullers, Greene King and Timothy
Taylors, enjoyable pubby food (not Sun,
Mon or Tues evenings); background music;
children and dogs welcome, green picnic-
sets in front under pretty window boxes,
more on side grass, play house, open all day
Fri-Sun. *(Emma Scofield)*

SUTTON   TL2247
★John O'Gaunt (01767) 260377
Off B1040 Biggleswade–Potton;
SG19 2NE Friendly bustling village pub
just up from 14th-c packhorse bridge and
ford: beams and timbering, red-painted or
pretty papered walls, local artwork for sale,
flagstoned bar with leather seats and sofas
around ships' tables, open fire and hood
skittles, Adnams and Woodfordes ales, local
cider and 12 wines by the glass, good food
cooked by landlord-chef (Thurs fish and

chips), dining rooms with mix of furniture
on bare boards, woodburner; background
music, free wi-fi; children and dogs (in
bar) welcome, seats in sheltered garden,
pétanque, closed Sun evening, Mon (open
lunchtime on bank holidays, then closed
all Tues). *(Alison and Michael Harper)*

TILSWORTH   SP9824
Anchor (01525) 211404
Just off A5 NW of Dunstable; LU7 9PU
Comfortably modernised 19th-c red-brick
village pub; good food (all day Sun)
from MasterChef finalist, three real
ales including Greene King IPA, friendly
attentive service, dining conservatory;
children welcome, picnic-sets in large
garden, open all day weekends, closed
Mon, Tues. *(Lindy Andrews)*

TOTTERNHOE   SP9721
Cross Keys (01525) 220434
Off A505 W of A5; Castle Hill Road;
LU6 2DA Restored thatched and timbered
two-bar pub below remains of a motte and
bailey fort; low beams and cosy furnishings,
good reasonably priced food (all day Sat,
not Sun, Mon evenings) from sandwiches/
baguettes up, well kept ales such as Adnams
Broadside, Greene King IPA and Sharps
Doom Bar, dining room; quiz first Weds
of month, TV; children and dogs (in bar)
welcome, good views from attractive big
garden, plenty of walks nearby, open all day
Fri-Sun. *(Ross Balaam)*

TURVEY   SP9452
Three Cranes (01234) 881365
Off A428 W of Bedford; MK43 8EP
Renovated stone-built village pub on two
levels, good food (not Sun evening) from
sandwiches and sharing boards to daily
specials, up to five well kept ales, friendly
staff; children and dogs welcome, secluded
tree-shaded garden, five bedrooms, open all
day. *(Mrs Margo Finlay, Jörg Kasprowski)*

TURVEY   SP9352
★Three Fyshes (01234) 881463
A428 NW of Bedford; Bridge Street,
W end of village; MK43 8ER Well
maintained early 17th-c beamed village
pub; big inglenook with woodburner, mix of
easy and upright chairs around tables on
tiles or ancient flagstones, good well priced
home-made food including burger evening
Tues and steak night Thurs, cheery attentive
staff, Marstons Pedigree, Sharps Doom Bar
and a couple of guests, decent choice of
wines, carpeted side restaurant; background
music; children and dogs (in bar) welcome,
charming garden with decking overlooking

Post Office address codings confusingly give the impression that some pubs
are in Bedfordshire, when they're really in Buckinghamshire or Cambridgeshire
(which is where we list them).

bridge and mill on the Great Ouse (note the flood marks), car park further along the street, open all day. *(George Atkinson)*

WESTONING   SP0332

Chequers (01525) 712967

Park Road (A5120 N of M1 junction 12); MK45 5LA Nicely refurbished thatched village pub with enjoyable food including good value set lunch, steak night Weds, seafood evening Thurs, Adnams and Greene King ales, good choice of wines by the glass and various teas/coffees, helpful friendly service, low-beamed front bar, good-sized stables restaurant; free wi-fi; children and dogs (in bar) welcome, courtyard tables, open all day from 9am (10am weekends) for breakfast. *(Jake)*

WOBURN   SP9433

Bell (01525) 290280

Bedford Street; MK17 9QJ Traditional and comfortable with small beamed bar and longer bare-boards dining lounge up steps, pleasant décor and furnishings, enjoyable food including Mon steak night, Greene King and good selection of guest ales, real ciders and several gins, friendly helpful service; background music; children and dogs welcome, back terrace, hotel part across busy road, handy for Woburn Abbey/Safari Park, open (and food) all day. *(Daniel King)*

Berkshire

 BRAY

SU9079 Map 2

Crown 🎖 ⏣

(01628) 621936 – www.thecrownatbray.co.uk

1.75 miles from M4 junction 9; A308 towards Windsor, then left at Bray signpost on to B3028; High Street; SL6 2AH

Ancient low-beamed pub with 16th-c features in open-plan rooms, highly regarded food, real ales and seats in the large garden

Friendly and welcoming, the little bar area here has high stools around an equally high table, simple tables and chairs beside an open fire and regulars who drop in for a chat and a drink: Courage Best and Directors and a beer named for the pub on handpump and around 18 wines by the glass. The main emphasis is on dining (not surprising given that the owner is Heston Blumenthal). The snug rooms have panelling, heavy old beams – some so low you may have to mind your head – plenty of timbers at elbow height where walls have been knocked through, a second log fire and neatly upholstered dining chairs and cushioned settles; board games. The covered and heated courtyard has modern slatted chairs and tables and there are plenty of picnic-sets in the large, enclosed back garden.

🎖 As well as lunchtime sandwiches, the rewarding food includes lunchtime sandwiches, king prawn cocktail, confit potted rabbit with chargrilled bread, macaroni cheese with pickled mushrooms and charred spring onions, burger with pastrami, toppings and fries, stone bass fillet with spinach, tomato and shallots, confit duck leg with blackberry sauce and red cabbage, chargrilled sirloin steak with marrowbone sauce and fries, and puddings such as banana eton mess and chocolate parfait with honeycomb and chocolate oil. *Benchmark main dish: haddock and chips £17.95. Two-course evening meal £30.00.*

Heineken ~ Tenant David Hyde ~ Real ale ~ Open 11.30-11; 12-10 Sun ~ Bar food 12-2.15 (2.45 Sat), 6-9.15 (9.45 Fri, Sat); 12-5.45 Sun ~ Children welcome ~ Dogs allowed in bar ~ Wi-fi *Recommended by Dr and Mrs A K Clarke, Barry and Daphne Gregson, Susan Eccleston, John and Claire Masters*

CHIEVELEY

SU4574 Map 2

Crab & Boar 🎖 ⏣ 🛏

(01635) 247550 – www.crabandboar.com

North Heath, W of village; RG20 8UE

Stylish inn with a welcoming atmosphere, good drinks choice, imaginative food and charming staff; seats outside; well equipped bedrooms

The atmosphere here is gently civilised and friendly and the interconnected bars and dining rooms are smartly furnished. One end of the L-shaped bar is light and airy with tall green leather chairs lining a high shelf, a couple of unusual, equally high tables with garden planter bases, a contemporary chandelier and stools lining the shabby-chic counter where they keep Ringwood Razorback and West Berkshire Mr Chubbs on handpump and good wines by the glass. The other end is cosier, with leather armchairs and sofas facing one another across a low table in front of a woodburning stove in a large fireplace. The first room leading off here is really an extension of the bar, with beams and timbering, tartan-upholstered stall seating and leather banquettes, and framed race tickets on the walls. Dining rooms, linked by timbering and steps, are decorated with old fishing reels, a large boar's head, photos and prints, with an eclectic mix of attractive chairs and tables on bare floorboards or carpet; an end room is just right for a private party. The garden has elegant metal or teak tables and chairs on gravel and grass; there's also a fountain and an outside bar. The comfortable, well equipped bedrooms have fine country views and private courtyards, and five have their own hot tub as well.

Enterprising modern food includes cornish crab with sweet chilli, apple and cucumber, game terrine with pickled shallots and beetroot, tian of vegetables with hazelnuts, stone bass and octopus with butternut squash, cauliflower and spinach, loin of venison with venison pie, celeriac and cavolo nero, lamb and lamb kofta with a trio of artichoke (jerusalem, globe and japanese), giant prawns with greek salad and fries, and puddings such as blackberry soufflé with vanilla ice-cream and custard and date tart with rum and raisin ice-cream. *Benchmark main dish: sirloin steak with cherry tomato salsify with peppercorn or diane sauce £24.00. Two-course evening meal £26.00.*

Free house ~ Licensee Roger Swain ~ Real ale ~ Open 12-11 ~ Bar food 12-2, 6.30-9.30; 12-3, 6.30-8.30 Sun ~ Restaurant ~ Children welcome ~ Dogs allowed in bar and bedrooms ~ Wi-fi ~ Bedrooms: /£110 *Recommended by Sandra Morgan, R K Phillips, Brian and Susan Wylie, Alison and Dan Richardson*

CURRIDGE
Bunk ⚓

SU4871 Map 2

(01635) 200400 – www.thebunkinn.co.uk
Handy for M4 junction 13, off A34 S; RG18 9DS

A good mix of customers in bustling, extended pub with attractive bar and dining rooms, good modern food and seats outside; bedrooms

---

Handy for the M4 and Newbury Racecourse and with good woodland walks nearby, this extended pub is on the edge of the village. It's a friendly place with a sofa and chunky wooden armchairs facing one another before an open fire, leather-seated wall banquettes, farmhouse chairs and stools around pine tables on wide boards and more stools at the counter where they keep Upham ales. The dining room has painted, wooden and high-backed leather chairs around a mix of tables, rustic stable-door partitioning, a pale green dado with mirrors and artwork on brick walls above, fresh flowers and little plants in pots; there's also a spacious dining conservatory. Outside, terraces have tables and chairs and picnic-sets under parasols plus a heated hut. Bedrooms are well equipped and comfortable.

From a seasonal menu, the interesting food includes lunchtime sandwiches, goose terrine with cranberry and pickled shallots, moules marinière, cumberland sausage and mash with charred onions, roast cauliflower with cheese purée, pickled romanesco cauliflower and sage butter dressing, corn-fed chicken with crispy thigh, sweetcorn, king cabbage and delmonico potatoes, a pie of the day, duck breast with confit leg croquette, marmalade-glazed salsify, sprout tops and jus, and puddings such as warm chocolate and hazelnut brownie with vanilla ice-cream and blood orange parfait, doughnuts and blood orange carpaccio; they also offer a two- and three-course early bird menu (6-7pm Monday-Thursday). *Benchmark main dish: burger with toppings in a brioche bun with fries £15.00. Two-course evening meal £22.00.*

Upham ~ Manager George Sallitt ~ Real ale ~ Open 10am-11pm; 10am-10.30pm Sun ~ Bar food 12-2.30 (3 Sat, 4 Sun), 6-9.30 (6.30-9 Sun) ~ Restaurant ~ Children welcome ~ Dogs allowed in bar and bedrooms ~ Wi-fi ~ Live music monthly ~ Bedrooms: /£90
Recommended by William Pace, Caroline and Oliver Sterling, James and Becky Plath

HARE HATCH
SU8077   Map 2

Horse & Groom ♀ ☜

(0118) 940 3136 – www.brunningandprice.co.uk/horseandgroom
A4 Bath Road W of Maidenhead; RG10 9SB

Spreading pub with attractively furnished, timbered rooms, enjoyable food and seats outside

This 18th-c coaching inn was once one of the gates into Windsor Forest. There are plenty of signs of great age in the interconnected rooms – and much of interest too: beams and timbering, a pleasing variety of well spread individual tables and chairs on mahogany-stained boards, oriental rugs and some carpet to soften the acoustics, and open fires in attractive tiled fireplaces. Also, a profusion of mainly old or antique prints and mirrors, book-lined shelves, house plants and daily papers. Well trained, courteous staff serve a splendid range of drinks including a good changing range of 15 wines by the glass, Brakspears Bitter and Oxford Gold, Jennings Sneck Lifter and Wychwood Hobgoblin on handpump, two farm ciders, 50 gins and 40 malt whiskies. A sheltered back garden has picnic-sets and the front terrace has teak tables and chairs under parasols.

Good modern food includes sandwiches, salt and pepper squid with chilli and coriander dipping syrup, whole baked camembert with garlic and thyme and red onion marmalade, steak burger with toppings, coleslaw and chips, sweet potato, spinach and aubergine curry with coconut and coriander rice, spicy vietnamese king prawn and rice noodle salad with mint, coriander, chilli and lime dressing, rabbit, ham hock and barley casserole with tarragon dumplings, and puddings such as crème brûlée and white chocolate cheesecake. *Benchmark main dish: braised lamb shoulder with dauphinoise potatoes £17.95. Two-course evening meal £22.00.*

Brunning & Price ~ Manager John Nicholson ~ Real ale ~ Open 11.30-11 ~ Bar food 12-10 (9.30 Sun) ~ Children welcome ~ Dogs allowed in bar ~ Wi-fi *Recommended by Ian Herdman, Simon Rodway, DHV, George Sanderson, Max Simons, Sally and David Champion*

INKPEN
SU3764   Map 2

Crown & Garter ⭐️ ☞

(01488) 668325 – www.crownandgarter.co.uk
Inkpen Common: Inkpen signposted with Kintbury off A4; in Kintbury turn left into Inkpen Road, then keep on into Inkpen Common; RG17 9QR

Carefully run country pub with modern touches blending with original features, enjoyable food and seats outside; bedrooms

The friendly landlady here welcomes a wide mix of customers into her substantial and rather fine old brick inn. The spreading bar area has wooden stools against the counter where they serve West Berkshire Good Old Boy, Ramsbury Gold and a guest such as Flack Manor Flacks Double Drop on handpump and 13 wines by the glass, and leading off here is a snug area with a leather armchair and sofa by an open fire in a raised brick fireplace. Throughout, an assortment of upholstered dining chairs are grouped around simple tables on pale floorboards, with armchairs here and there, cushioned wall seating, mirrors and modern artwork on contemporary paintwork and wallpaper that depicts bookcases (in the smart restaurant) and old suitcases. The front terrace has seats and tables under parasols. The comfortable bedrooms are in a separate single-storey L-shaped building around an attractive garden. There's a separate bakery and coffee shop (which becomes a private dining space in the evening). Disabled access.

 Bolstered by daily specials and using seasonal, local produce, the highly rated food includes lunchtime sandwiches, crispy duck with hoisin sauce, shredded white cabbage and pickled carrots, baked camembert with honey and thyme, burger with toppings, pickles and chips, chicken, ham and cider pie, barley risotto with black truffle, celeriac and celery, lamb shank with lyonnaise potatoes, gurnard with chilli and lime, and puddings such as chocolate and hazelnut torte and rhubarb crumble with lemon and ginger sorbet. *Benchmark main dish: beer-battered fish and chips £14.50. Two-course evening meal £23.00.*

Free house ~ Licensee Romilla Arber ~ Real ale ~ Open 12-11; 12-10.30 Sun (12-6 Sun in winter) ~ Bar food 12-2 (3 Sun), 6.30-9 ~ Restaurant ~ Children welcome ~ Dogs allowed in bar ~ Wi-fi ~ Bedrooms: £105/£130 *Recommended by David and Judy Robison, Tom Stone, Mark Hamill, Angela and Steve Heard, Joe and Belinda Smart*

INKPEN

Swan

(01488) 668326 – www.theswaninn-organics.co.uk

SU3564 Map 2

Lower Inkpen; coming from A338 in Hungerford, take Park Street (first left after railway bridge); RG17 9DX

Country pub with rambling rooms, traditional décor, real ales and plenty of seats outside; comfortable bedrooms

Many customers come to this much extended pub after a walk. It's owned by local, organic beef farmers and you can buy their produce and ready-made meals and groceries in the interesting farm shop next door. The rambling beamed rooms have cosy corners, traditional pubby furniture, eclectic bric-a-brac and two log fires, and there's a flagstoned games area plus a cosy restaurant. Butts Jester and Traditional and a guest ale on handpump, several wines by the glass and home-made sloe gin; darts, shut the box and board games. The bedrooms are quiet and comfortable. There are picnic-sets on tiered front terraces overlooking a footpath.

Using their own produce, the popular food includes sandwiches, chicken liver pâté, a trio of smoked fish with horseradish cream, ricotta and spinach cannelloni, chilli con carne, beer-battered cod and chips, steak and kidney pudding, chicken breast stuffed with brie and basil wrapped in parma ham with dauphinoise potatoes, and puddings such as fruit crumble with custard and sticky toffee pudding. *Benchmark main dish: home-made sausages with mash and gravy £13.95. Two-course evening meal £20.00.*

Free house ~ Licensees Mary and Bernard Harris ~ Real ale ~ Open 12-2.30, 6.30-11; 12-11 Sat; 12-4 Sun; closed Mon, Tues, evening Sun ~ Bar food 12-2 (3 weekends), 7-9 ~ Restaurant ~ Children welcome ~ Wi-fi ~ Bedrooms: £80/£95 *Recommended by Charlie Parker, D J and P M Taylor, Jamie Green, Amy Ledbetter, Mike Swan*

> The details at the end of each featured entry start by saying whether the pub is a free house, or if it belongs to a brewery or pub group (which we name).

KINTBURY
Dundas Arms ♀ ⇖

SU3866 Map 2

(01488) 658263 – www.dundasarms.co.uk

Village signposted off A4 Newbury–Hungerford about a mile W of Halfway; Station Road – pub just over hump-back canal bridge, at start of village itself; RG17 9UT

Carefully updated inn with relaxed informal bar, good two-level restaurant and lovely waterside garden; comfortable bedrooms

Early in the 19th c this handsome pub was erected for the canal builders – it stands between the River Kennet and the Kennet & Avon Canal. As well as picnic-sets on decking, the large, pretty back garden (with water on each side) has plenty of well spaced tables on grass among shrubs and trees. The big windows of the smart two-level restaurant overlook this scene. At the other end is a smallish bar, taking its relaxed informal mood from the cheerful helpful staff. Here, there are sporting prints above a high oak dado, neat little cushioned arts-and-crafts chairs around a few stripped or polished tables on broad floorboards, and high chairs by the counter (decorated with highly polished old penny pieces), which serves Tutts Clump farm cider on handpump, as well as Battledown Sunbeam, Ramsbury Gold and West Berkshire Good Old Boy, and 14 wines by the glass; background music. Between the bar and restaurant is a cosy, tartan-carpeted sitting room with wing chairs and a splendid leather and mahogany settee, daily papers, a good winter log fire flanked by glass-fronted bookcases, and big silhouette portraits on topiary-print wallpaper. Pleasant nearby walks.

 Popular food includes thai monkfish with pickled chilli and ginger, rosemary and garlic baked camembert with onion marmalade and brioche (for two), wild mushroom and aged parmesan risotto with white truffle oil, chicken caesar salad, burger with toppings, battered pickle and chips, fillet of cod with crushed peas and parsley sauce, confit barbary duck leg with pak choi, field mushroom and red wine jus, and puddings such as sticky toffee pudding with honeycomb ice-cream and summer berry fool. *Benchmark main dish: burger with toppings and chips £14.00. Two-course evening meal £25.00.*

Free house ~ Licensee James Waterhouse ~ Real ale ~ Open 11-11 ~ Bar food 12-3, 6-9 (8 Sun) ~ Restaurant ~ Children welcome ~ Dogs allowed in bar and bedrooms ~ Wi-fi ~ Bedrooms: /£99 *Recommended by George Atkinson, Jack Trussler, Daniel King, Maggie and Matthew Lyons*

MAIDENS GREEN
Winning Post ⇖

SU9072 Map 2

(01344) 882242 – www.winningpostwinkfield.co.uk

Follow signs to Winkfield Plain W of Winkfield off A330, then first right; SL4 4SW

18th-c inn with beams and timbering in character rooms, good food and drinks choice, friendly feel and seats in garden; bedrooms

At weekends in particular there are lots of chatty locals with their families and dogs here, but as a visitor you'll get just as warm a welcome. It's a gently civilised place with beamed open-plan rooms connected by timbering (some with leather crash pads). The main bar area has leather and wood tub chairs around a table in one window, a long cushioned settle in another, and big flagstones and stools by the bar where efficient staff serve Upham Punter and Tipster on handpump and good wines by the glass. An end room, also with flagstones, has more tub chairs, wall seating and contemporary paintwork on planked walls; TV. The dining rooms are to the left of the bar: one long room has huge photos of horses taking up whole walls, there are tartan banquettes, cushioned dining chairs around wooden tables on bare boards, a woodburning stove, hanging lanterns and bowler-hat lights. A room to the back of the inn called the Winning Enclosure has horse-racing wall photos and a large raised fireplace. The partly covered terrace has good quality seats and tables and a rather smart conical smokers' hut. Quiet bedrooms, handy for Ascot and Henley, face the garden.

Quite a choice of good food includes breakfasts for non-residents (7.30-10am weekdays; 8-10am weekends), crab with celeriac, russet apple slaw, apple blossom and golden raisins, crispy duck salad with pomegranate, flatbread croutons and roast garlic dressing, halloumi with ras el hanout, quinoa and buckwheat stew, 6oz fillet of beef, braised ox cheek, spinach and mash, monkfish with samphire, black olives, pea purée and pesto, 18oz côte de boeuf with triple-cooked chips and béarnaise sauce (for two to share), and puddings such as hot chocolate and orange fondant with orange jelly and pineapple, coconut, lemon and lime frozen yoghurt with chia seeds; they also offer a two- and three-course set weekday lunch. *Benchmark main dish: chicken and wild mushroom risotto and truffle oil £15.50. Two-course evening meal £22.50.*

Upham ~ Manager Gregory Loison ~ Real ale ~ Open 11am-11.30pm (10.30pm Sun) ~ Bar food 12-9.30; 12-7.30 Sun ~ Restaurant ~ Children welcome ~ Dogs allowed in bar and bedrooms ~ Wi-fi ~ Bedrooms: /£120 *Recommended by Sarah Roberts, Millie and Peter Downing, Tom Stone, Angela and Steve Heard, Sylvia and Phillip Spencer, Monty Green*

NEWBURY

Newbury 🌟 ♀ ◖

SU4767 Map 2

(01635) 49000 ~ www.thenewburypub.co.uk
Bartholomew Street; RG14 5HB

Lively pub with thoughtful choice of drinks, good food and plenty of bar and dining space

With rewarding food and a cheerful atmosphere, this is a stylish town pub. The bar has an assortment of wooden dining chairs around sturdy farmhouse and other solid tables on bare boards, comfortable leather sofas, big paintings on pale painted walls and church candles. They keep a fantastic choice of drinks: a beer named for them (from Greene King), Ramsbury Gold and Same Again, Timothy Taylors Landlord and Upham Punter on handpump, a farm cider, 20 malt whiskies, around 23 wines by the glass, an extensive cocktail list and a fine range of coffees and teas (including tea grown in Cornwall). There is also an upstairs cocktail bar that leads out on to a roof terrace with an electric folding canopy roof. The light and airy dining rooms have wall benches and church chairs around more rustic tables on more bare boards, and local artwork. There are seats in the downstairs courtyard.

Making everything on site (bread, chutneys, ice-cream and so forth) the highly regarded food includes sandwiches, lots of lunchtime tapas-style nibbles, tempura king prawns on mussel and squid ink risotto with lemon jelly, chicken liver parfait with redcurrant gel, cajun or vegetarian burgers with toppings, lamb rump with basil mash and ratatouille, fresh tuna niçoise, corn-fed chicken with potato cake, onion purée and truffle jus, cod with black garlic mash, crispy kale, salsify and curried mussels, and puddings such as vanilla pannacotta with strawberry syrup and hot chocolate fondant with orange sorbet. *Benchmark main dish: duck breast with cherry purée and wild mushrooms £19.50. Two-course evening meal £25.00.*

Free house ~ Licensee Peter Lumber ~ Real ale ~ Open 11.30-midnight; 10-1am Sat ~ Bar food 12-3, 6-9 (10 Thurs); 12-3, 5.30-10 Fri; 12-10 Sat; 12-6 Sun ~ Restaurant ~ Children welcome ~ Dogs allowed in bar ~ Wi-fi *Recommended by Lionel Smith, Geoff and Ann Marston, Mary Joyce, Charles Welch, Diane Abbott*

PANGBOURNE

SU6376 Map 2

Elephant

(0118) 984 2244 – www.elephanthotel.co.uk

Church Road; RG8 7AR

Plenty of elephant detail in bar and dining rooms, fair choice of ales and food and seats in sizeable garden; bedrooms

Throughout the bars, dining room and seating areas there are indeed numerous elephants of all sizes – mainly indian in style and made of painted wood – on mantelpieces, on shelves, in a cabinet and a huge one on wheels in the reception hall; the gantry above the bar is inlaid with wooden panels painted with Babar escapades. The main bar has simple wooden furniture, some leather banquettes, bare boards, a log fire with a large mirror above it and West Berkshire Good Old Boy and Mr Chubbs and Sharps Doom Bar on handpump, 16 wines by the glass and two farm ciders; TV, background music and skittle alley. Two seating areas have comfortable sofas and armchairs and rugs on floorboards, while the dining room has plenty of tables and chairs on more rugs. In the big back garden are rattan-style sofas on flagstones, and picnic-sets on the lawn. Bedrooms are individually styled with bold colours and fine fabrics.

Quite a choice of food includes sandwiches, smoked salmon roulade with orange, fennel and celery slaw, potted duck liver parfait with red onion marmalade, spinach and goats cheese-filled portobello mushroom with roasted plum tomato sauce, pork belly and fillet stuffed with black pudding with butternut squash purée and honey and mustard sauce, venison steak with sweet potato and beetroot gratin and redcurrant jus, and puddings such as raspberry cheesecake and sticky toffee pudding. *Benchmark main dish: burger with toppings and chips £11.75. Two-course evening meal £20.00.*

Bluebelt Hospitality ~ Lease Dale Winrow ~ Real ale ~ Open 11-11 ~ Bar food 12-2.30, 6-9.30; 12-4, 5-9.30 Sat; 12-4, 5-8 Sun ~ Restaurant ~ Children welcome ~ Dogs allowed in bar and bedrooms ~ Wi-fi ~ Bedrooms: $90/$115 *Recommended by Sophie Ellison, Barbara Brown, Charles Welch, Michael Napier, Monty Green, David and Leone Lawson*

PEASEMORE

SU4577 Map 2

Fox

(01635) 248480 – www.foxatpeasemore.co.uk

4 miles from M4 junction 13, via Chieveley: keep on through Chieveley to Peasemore, turning left into Hillgreen Lane at small sign to Fox Inn; village also signposted from B4494 Newbury–Wantage; RG20 7JN

Friendly downland pub on top form under its expert licensees

Philip and Lauren Davison are first class licensees and continue to run their busy, cheerful pub in their inimitable, friendly and efficient style; it's so popular that you must book a table in advance. The long bare-boards bar has strategically placed high-backed settles (comfort guaranteed by plenty of colourful cushions), a warm woodburning stove in a stripped-brick chimney breast and, for real sybarites, two luxuriously carpeted end areas, one with velour tub armchairs. Friendly, efficient, black-clad staff serve West Berkshire Good Old Boy and a couple of changing guests on handpump, 15 wines by the glass and summer farm cider; background music. This is downland horse-training country, and picnic-table sets at the front look out to the rolling fields beyond the quiet country lane – on a clear day as far as the Hampshire border hills some 20 miles south; there are more picnic-sets on a smallish sheltered back terrace. Good walks.

🍴 Good quality food includes lunchtime open sandwiches and omelettes, crispy fried brie with berry fruit compote, a trio of fish with sweet chilli dip, portobello mushroom with stilton, pine nuts and wild mushrooms in a provençale tomato sauce, steak and kidney pie, local sausages with onion gravy, salmon and haddock fishcakes with tartare sauce, slow-cooked lamb shank in red wine and rosemary sauce, and puddings such as apple and berry crumble with custard and chocolate mousse with chocolate brownie and chocolate ice-cream. *Benchmark main dish: confit duck leg with merlot and cherry sauce and dauphinoise potatoes £13.50. Two-course evening meal £21.00.*

Free house ~ Licensees Philip and Lauren Davison ~ Real ale ~ Open 12-2.30, 6-11; 12-11 Sat; 12-6 Sun; closed Mon, Tues ~ Bar food 12-2, 6-9; 12-3, 5.30-9 Sat; 12-4 Sun ~ Restaurant ~ Children welcome ~ Dogs allowed in bar ~ Wi-fi *Recommended by Ian Herdman, Sarah Roberts, Mrs P Sumner, David and Judy Robison, Nigel and Sue Foster, Sally and David Champion*

 RUSCOMBE SU7976 Map 2

Royal Oak 🌟 🍺

(0118) 934 5190 – www.burattas.co.uk

Ruscombe Lane (B3024 just E of Twyford); RG10 9JN

Wide choice of popular food at welcoming pub with interesting furnishings and paintings and local beer and wine

The bars here (it's known locally as Buratta's) are open-plan and carpeted and cleverly laid out so that each area is fairly snug but maintains an overall feel of a lot of people enjoying themselves. A good variety of furniture runs from dark oak tables to big chunky pine ones with mixed seating to match; the two sofas facing each other are popular. Contrasting with the old exposed ceiling joists, mostly unframed modern paintings and prints decorate the walls, which are painted in cream, white and soft green. Binghams (the brewery is just across the road) Space Hoppy IPA and Twyford Tipple and Fullers London Pride on handpump, 16 wines by the glass (they stock wines from the village's Stanlake Park vineyard), a dozen malt whiskies and attentive service. Picnic-sets are ranged around a venerable central hawthorn in the garden behind (where there are ducks and chickens); summer barbecues. The pub is on the Henley Arts Trail. Do visit the friendly landlady's antiques and collectables shop, which is open during pub hours.

🌟 Well thought-of food includes sandwiches and panini, crispy crab, coriander and sweetcorn fritters with sweet chilli sauce, avocado, mozzarella and tomato salad with smoked garlic pesto, sharing platters, a pie of the week, mushroom and stilton risotto, chicken strips with mushrooms and shallots on brandy mustard sauce and rice, venison steak with redcurrant and rosemary sauce, saddle of rabbit in garlic cream sauce, and puddings such as Baileys cheesecake and chocolate brownie with chocolate sauce and vanilla ice-cream. *Benchmark main dish: monkfish wrapped in parma ham with peppercorn sauce £15.00. Two-course evening meal £22.00.*

Enterprise ~ Lease Jenny and Stefano Buratta ~ Real ale ~ Open 12-3, 6-11; 12-4 Sun; closed Sun and Mon evenings ~ Bar food 12-2.30, 6-9.30; 12-3 Sun ~ Restaurant ~ Children welcome ~ Dogs welcome ~ Wi-fi *Recommended by Paul Humphreys, Barry and Daphne Gregson, Andrew and Michele Revell*

 SHEFFORD WOODLANDS SU3673 Map 2

Pheasant 🌟

(01488) 648284 – www.thepheasant-inn.co.uk

Under 0.5 miles from M4 junction 14 – A338 towards Wantage, first left on B4000; RG17 7AA

Bustling bars, a separate dining room, highly thought-of food and beer and seats outside; bedrooms

Our readers enjoy their visits here – all mention the friendly service and good food. The various interconnecting bar rooms have been carefully refurbished with contemporary paintwork, lots of antiques and plenty of horse-related prints, photographs and paintings; there are elegant wooden dining chairs and settles around all sorts of tables, big mirrors here and there, leather banquettes and stools, and a warm fire in a little brick fireplace. One snug little room has newly upholstered armchairs and sofas. They keep a fantastic range of drinks that includes 36 gins, 15 vodkas, ten rums, 26 malt whiskies, cocktails and interesting liqueurs – plus a beer named for the pub (from Marstons), Marstons Pedigree, Ramsbury Gold and Ringwood Best on handpump and quite a few good wines by the glass. There's also a separate dining room; background music. Seats in the garden have attractive views. The 11 individually decorated and well equipped modern bedrooms are in a separate extension and breakfasts are good.

The interesting, popular food includes sandwiches, black pudding salad with pancetta, fried quail egg and honey and mustard dressing, scallops with saffron and leek purée, crispy leeks and grilled lemon vinaigrette, macaroni cheese with mushrooms and truffle shavings, ham and beef burger with toppings and skinny fries, cajun sea bass fillet with roast red pepper salsa, basil and polenta chips and sour cream, confit duck leg with red cabbage, bubble and squeak and orange and redcurrant sauce, and puddings such as clementine dumpling with passion-fruit sauce and citrus granita and chocolate mousse with hazelnut praline, honeycomb and white chocolate milkshake. *Benchmark main dish: beer-battered fish and chips £14.00. Two-course evening meal £20.00.*

Free house ~ Licensee Jack Greenall ~ Real ale ~ Open 11-11 (10.30 Sun) ~ Bar food 12-3, 6-9.30; 12-5, 6-9 Sun ~ Children welcome ~ Dogs allowed in bar and bedrooms ~ Wi-fi ~ Bedrooms: /£110 *Recommended by Michael Sargent, B and M Kendall, Guy Vowles, Simon Rodway, Nick Higgins, Patti and James Davidson, William and Sophia Renton*

SONNING
Bull 🛏️
SU7575 Map 2

(0118) 969 3901 – www.bullinnsonning.co.uk
Off B478, by church; village signed off A4 E of Reading; RG4 6UP

Pretty timbered inn in attractive spot, plenty of character in old-fashioned bars, friendly staff and good food; bedrooms

In early summer when the wisteria is flowering and the courtyard is full of pretty flowering tubs, this fine old black and white timbered inn looks its best. The two old-fashioned bar rooms have low ceilings and heavy beams, cosy alcoves, leather armchairs and sofas, cushioned antique settles and low wooden chairs on bare boards, and open fireplaces. Butcombe Rare Breed and Fullers HSB and London Pride and a seasonal guest on handpump served by helpful staff, 16 good wines by the glass, cocktails and a farm cider. The dining room has a mix of wooden chairs and tables, rugs on parquet flooring and shelves of books; TV. Bedrooms are comfortable and well equipped and get booked up well in advance. If you bear left through the ivy-clad churchyard opposite, then turn left along the bank of the river, you come to a very pretty lock. The Thames Valley Park is close by.

Imaginative food includes sandwiches (until 5pm), chilli and ginger squid with soy and lime dip, ham hock terrine with piccalilli, chicken caesar salad, butternut squash tarte tatin with goats cheese and hazelnut salad, pork and chorizo burger with toppings, minted mayonnaise and spiced potato wedges, calves liver with bacon and madeira cream sauce, hake fillet with crushed dill and crème fraîche potatoes and rainbow chard, and puddings such as white chocolate pannacotta with fruit compote and pear, plum and almond crumble with crème anglaise. *Benchmark main dish: steak in ale pie £14.50. Two-course evening meal £20.00.*

Fullers ~ Managers Sian and Jason Smith ~ Real ale ~ Open 10am-11pm; 12-10.30 Sun ~ Bar food 12-3, 6-9.30 winter weekdays; 12-9.30 Sat and summer weekdays; 12-8.30 Sun ~ Restaurant ~ Children welcome ~ Dogs allowed in bar ~ Wi-fi ~ Tribute acts monthly ~ Bedrooms: /£105 *Recommended by Allan Lloyd and family, Roy Hoing, Susan and John Douglas, Frank and Marcia Pelling, Penny and David Shepherd*

 SWALLOWFIELD   SU7364   Map 2

George & Dragon 🌟 ♀

(0118) 988 4432 – www.georgeanddragonswallowfield.co.uk
Church Road, towards Farley Hill; RG7 1TJ

Busy country pub with enjoyable bar food, real ales, friendly service and seats outside

At peak times this comfortable, easy-going pub is deservedly packed, so it's best to book a table in advance. The long-serving licensees are attentive and friendly and the various interconnected rooms have plenty of character: beams (some quite low) and standing timbers, a happy mix of nice old dining chairs and settles around individual wooden tables, rugs on flagstones, lit candles, a big log fire and country prints on red or bare brick walls; background music. Ringwood Best, Sharps Doom Bar and Upham Punter on handpump, quite a few wines by the glass and several gins and whiskies. There are picnic-sets on gravel or paving in the garden and the website has details of an enjoyable four-mile walk that starts and ends at the pub.

 Seasonal country cooking includes lunchtime ciabattas, devilled lambs kidneys, wild mushroom, tarragon and stilton filo parcels on creamy garlic spinach, thai-style crab cakes on rice noodle, peanut and chilli salad with spicy dipping sauce, venison sausages with a braised game faggot, roasted celeriac, braised red cabbage and red wine gravy, vegetarian burger with falafel cake, halloumi cheese, garlic and coriander yoghurt and chips, corn-fed chicken breast filled with mushroom duxelles, chestnut and tarragon, carrot and swede mash and red wine sauce, monkfish wrapped in prosciutto with cauliflower purée and roast sweet potato, and puddings such as lemon posset with marinated mixed berries and cappuccino crème brûlée. *Benchmark main dish: half shoulder of lamb with rosemary gravy £15.95. Two-course evening meal £21.00.*

Free house ~ Licensee Paul Dailey ~ Real ale ~ Open 12-11 (10 Sun) ~ Bar food 12-2.30, 7-9.30; 12-3, 7-9 Sun ~ Restaurant ~ Children welcome lunchtime only ~ Dogs allowed in bar ~ Wi-fi *Recommended by Tony and Jill Radnor, Mark Hamill, Rosie and John Moore, Colin and Daniel Gibbs*

 WHITE WALTHAM   SU8477   Map 2

Beehive 🌟 ◖

(01628) 822877 – www.thebeehivewhitewaltham.co.uk
Waltham Road (B3024 W of Maidenhead); SL6 3SH

Berkshire Dining Pub of the Year

Attractive village pub with welcoming staff and excellent food and drinks choice; seats in garden with table service

The atmosphere here is bustling and friendly – all helped along by the hospitable landlord and his friendly, impeccable staff. To the right of the entrance are several comfortably spacious areas with leather chairs around sturdy tables, while to the left is a neat bar brightened up by cheerful scatter cushions on built-in wall seats and captain's chairs. Rebellion IPA, Sharps Doom Bar, Timothy Taylors Landlord and a guest beer on handpump, 20 wines by the glass from a good list and farm cider; background music. An airy dining room has glass doors opening on to the front terrace where teak seats and picnic-sets take in the rather fine view. The bigger back garden has plenty of seats and tables and the village cricket field is opposite. Disabled access and facilities.

Cooked by the landlord, the food is exceptionally good: potted crab with fennel, blood orange and rosemary toast, lasagne of wild rabbit with wood blewit mushrooms and chervil, linguine of wild mushrooms, courgettes, cherry tomatoes and parmesan cream, chicken, ham and leek pie, monkfish with tarka dhal, cucumber, red onion and coriander salad, pot roast pheasant with creamed potatoes, onions, mushrooms and bacon, black angus rib-eye steak with peppercorn sauce and chips, and puddings such as chocolate fondant with toffee sauce and pistachio ice-cream and poached pear and almond tart with vanilla ice-cream. *Benchmark main dish: venison haunch with creamed spinach and sauce poivrade (a peppery game sauce) £24.00. Two-course evening meal £25.00.*

Enterprise ~ Lease Dominic Chapman ~ Real ale ~ Open 12-2.30, 5-11; 12-11 Sat; 12-6 Sun ~ Bar food 12-2.30, 6-9.30 (10 Fri, Sat); 12-4 Sun ~ Restaurant ~ Children welcome ~ Dogs allowed in bar ~ Wi-fi *Recommended by Dr Simon Innes, Charlie Parker, Simon Collett-Jones, Dr and Mrs A K Clarke, Gerald and Brenda Culliford, Alison and Tony Livesley, Mary and Douglas McDowell*

WOOLHAMPTON
SU5766 Map 2

Rowbarge ★ ♀ ◀

(0118) 971 2213 – www.brunningandprice.co.uk/rowbarge
Station Road; RG7 5SH

Canalside pub with plenty of interest in rambling rooms, six real ales, good bistro-style food and lots of outside seating

The position by the Kennet & Avon Canal certainly draws in the crowds in warm weather, and there are wooden chairs and tables on a decked terrace and picnic-sets among trees. Six rambling rooms with beams and timbering are connected by open doorways and knocked-through walls. The décor is gently themed to represent the nearby canal with hundreds of prints and photographs (some of rowing and boats) and oars on the walls, as well as old glass and stone bottles in nooks and crannies, big house plants and fresh flowers, plenty of candles and several open fires; the many large mirrors create an impression of even more space. Throughout there are antique dining chairs around various nice old tables, settles, built-in cushioned wall seating, armchairs, a group of high stools around a huge wooden barrel table, and rugs on polished boards, stone tiles or carpeting. Friendly, helpful staff serve Andwell Ruddy Darter, Fuzzy Duck Pheasant Plucker, Indigenous Frisky Mare, Stonehenge Spire Ale, Tring Side Pocket for a Toad and Triple fff Hunky Dory on handpump, 20 wines by the glass, 30 gins and 65 malt whiskies; background music and board games.

Good modern food includes sandwiches, smoked haddock kedgeree arancini with a quail egg, mango chutney and coriander, confit chicken and chorizo terrine wrapped in parma ham with tomato chutney, spiced pancakes with mushroom, paneer, cauliflower dhal, raita and coriander and tomato salad, sea bass fillets with mediterranean vegetables, tomato harissa sauce and couscous, duck breast croquettes with pomegranate jus and balsamic reduction, and puddings such as crème brûlée and hot waffle with butterscotch sauce and honeycomb ice-cream. *Benchmark main dish:*

chicken, ham hock and tarragon kiev with pea purée, baby carrots and fondant potato £13.95. Two-course evening meal £21.00.

Brunning & Price ~ Manager Stuart Groves ~ Real ale ~ Open 11-11 (10.30 Sun) ~ Bar food 12-10 (9.30 Sun) ~ Restaurant ~ Children welcome ~ Dogs allowed in bar ~ Wi-fi
Recommended by John Preddy, Ian Herdman, Andrew and Michele Revell, Brian and Susan Wylie

YATTENDON
Royal Oak 🏵️ ♟ 🛏️

SU5574   Map 2

(01635) 201325 – www.royaloakyattendon.co.uk

The Square; B4009 NE from Newbury; right at Hampstead Norreys, village signed on left; RG18 0UG

Civilised old inn with beamed and panelled rooms, imaginative food and seats in pretty garden; bedrooms

As the West Berkshire brewery is actually in the village, the Good Old Boy, Maggs Mild and Mr Chubbs on handpump are on tip top form; the 12 wines by the glass are well chosen. Many customers are here for the pleasing food, though you're more than welcome to drop in for just a drink. The charming bar rooms have beams and panelling, an appealing mix of wooden dining chairs around interesting tables, some half-panelled wall seating, rugs on quarry tiles or wooden floorboards, plenty of prints on brick, cream or red walls, lovely flower arrangements and four log fires. Under the trellising in the walled back garden are wicker armchairs and tables and there are picnic-sets under parasols at the front; boules. This is a comfortable place to stay and the light, attractive bedrooms overlook the garden or village square; breakfasts are good. The pub is only ten minutes from Newbury Racecourse and gets pretty busy on race days.

Top notch food includes sandwiches, rare vietnamese beef salad with toasted peanuts, coconut, chilli and lime, chalk-stream trout ceviche with a citrus and coriander dressing, butternut squash and spinach curry, beer-battered haddock and chips, crispy breaded chicken cordon bleu with ham and cheddar fries, garlic lamb rump with wild nettles, lovage and borlotti beans, and puddings such as warm chocolate fondant with salted caramel ice-cream and espresso crème brûlée; they also offer a two- and three-course weekday set lunch. *Benchmark main dish: braised shin of beef cottage pie £16.00. Two-course evening meal £25.00.*

Free house ~ Licensee Rob McGill ~ Real ale ~ Open 11-11 (midnight Sat); 12-11.30 Sun ~ Bar food 12-2.30 (3 weekends), 6.30-10 (9 Sun) ~ Children welcome ~ Dogs welcome ~ Wi-fi ~ Bedrooms: /£99 *Recommended by David and Stella Martin, Nick Sharpe, Andrew Lawson, Brian and Sally Wakeham, Mary Joyce*

Also Worth a Visit in Berkshire

Besides the fully inspected pubs, you might like to try these pubs that have been recommended to us and described by readers. Do tell us what you think of them: feedback@goodguides.com

ALDWORTH   SU5579

★**Bell** (01635) 578272
A329 Reading–Wallingford; left on to B4009 at Streatley; RG8 9SE Unspoilt and unchanging village pub in same family for over 250 years; simply furnished panelled rooms, beams in ochre ceiling, old photographs and ancient one-handed clock, woodburner, glass-panelled hatch serving well kept Arkells, West Berkshire and a monthly guest, Upton cider and nice house wines, good value rolls, ploughman's and winter soup, traditional pub games; no mobile phones or credit cards; well behaved children and dogs welcome, seats in quiet cottagey garden by cricket ground, animals in paddock behind pub, maybe Christmas

mummers and summer morris, closed Mon (open lunchtime bank holidays), can get busy weekends. *(Jamie Green)*

ALDWORTH   SU5579
Four Points (01635) 578367
B4009 towards Hampstead Norreys; RG8 9RL Attractive 17th-c thatched roadside pub with low beams, standing timbers and panelling, nice fire in bar with more formal seating area to the left and restaurant at back, enjoyable good value home-cooked food (all day weekends) from baguettes up, bargain OAP lunch deal Mon-Weds, local Two Cocks and Wadworths 6X, friendly helpful young staff; children and dogs (in bar) welcome, garden over road with play area. *(David and Leone Lawson)*

ARBORFIELD CROSS   SU7667
Bull (0118) 976 2244
On roundabout; RG2 9QD Light open-plan dining pub with most tables set for their popular food (need to book), extensive menu including one or two french dishes, well priced house wines, efficient friendly service; children welcome, picnic-sets in garden with play area, open all day Fri-Sun, closed Mon. *(John Pritchard)*

ASHMORE GREEN   SU4969
Sun in the Wood (01635) 42377
B4009 (Shaw Road) off A339, right to Kiln Road, left to Stoney Lane; RG18 9HF Updated and extended 19th-c dining pub; enjoyable food (not Sun evening) from stone-baked pizzas and pub favourites up, Thurs grill night, Wadworths ales and several wines by the glass, friendly helpful staff, spacious interior with light open feel, small side conservatory; background music, quiz nights; children and dogs (in bar) welcome, decked terrace and woodside garden, open all day weekends. *(Nick Higgins)*

ASTON   SU7884
★**Flower Pot** (01491) 574721
Off A4130 Henley–Maidenhead at top of Remenham Hill; RG9 3DG Roomy red-brick country pub with nice local feel, snug traditional bar and airy back dining area, lots of stuffed fish and other taxidermy, milk churn stools and roaring log fire, four well kept ales such as Brakspears and Ringwood, enjoyable food (not Sun evening) from baguettes to fish and game, quick friendly service; vocal parrot; very busy with walkers and families at weekends, dogs allowed in some parts, country views from big orchard garden, side field with poultry, Thames nearby, three bedrooms, open all day weekends. *(Edward Mirzoeff)*

BARKHAM   SU7866
Bull (0118) 976 2816
Barkham Road; RG41 4TL Traditional pub run by friendly thai family, opened-up carpeted interior with dining area to one end,

half a dozen ales such as Gales, Otter, St Austell and Sharps, popular food including good south-east asian choices; Mon quiz: children welcome, open all day (till 7pm Sun). *(John Pritchard)*

BEECH HILL   SU6964
Elm Tree (0118) 988 3505
3.3 miles from M4 junction 11: A33 towards Basingstoke, turning off into Beech Hill Road after about 2 miles; RG7 2AZ Five rooms, one with blazing fire, and nice rural views especially from more modern barn-style restaurant and conservatory, good food (not Sun evening) from lunchtime sandwiches and pub standards up, prompt friendly service, well kept ales such as Ringwood and Sharps, good choice of wines by the glass; children and dogs welcome, tables on heated front deck with palms, open all day. *(Robert Watt)*

BEENHAM   SU5868
Six Bells (0118) 971 3368
The Green; RG7 5NX Comfortable red-brick Victorian village pub with good food from landlord-chef including imaginative additions to standard pub menu, well kept West Berkshire Good Old Boy and a couple of guests, friendly staff, large bar area with armchairs and winter fires, dining conservatory; board games; children welcome at lunchtime, four bedrooms, closed Sun evening, Mon lunchtime. *(John Pritchard)*

CHARVIL   SU7776
Lands End (0118) 934 0700
Lands End Lane/Whistley Mill Lane near Old River ford; RG10 0UE Welcoming 1930s Tudor-style pub, reasonably priced traditional food from good baguettes to popular Sun roasts (best to book), well kept Brakspears and a dozen wines by the glass, efficient accommodating staff, open-plan bar with log fire, separate restaurant, various stuffed fish (good fishing nearby); children welcome, no dogs inside, sizeable garden with terrace picnic-sets, open all day Sun till 9pm. *(Charles Welch)*

CHEAPSIDE   SU9469
Thatched Tavern (01344) 620874
Off A332/A329, then off B383 at Village Hall sign; SL5 7QG Civilised dining pub with a good deal of character and plenty of room for just a drink; good up-to-date food (can be pricey) along with more traditional choices, plenty of wines by the glass including champagne from extensive list, Fullers London Pride, a beer named for the pub and a guest ale, big inglenook log fire, low beams and polished flagstones in cottagey core, three smart dining rooms off; children welcome, dogs in bar, tables on terrace and attractive sheltered back lawn, handy for Virginia Water, open (and food) all day, busy on Ascot race days. *(Nick Higgins)*

CHIEVELEY   SU4773

★**Olde Red Lion** (01635) 248379

*Handy for M4 junction 13 via A34
N-bound; Green Lane; RG20 8XB*
Welcoming village pub with three well
kept Arkells beers and good varied choice
of generously served food at reasonable
prices, friendly attentive service, low-
beamed carpeted bar with log fire, extended
back restaurant; background music, TV;
children and dogs welcome, wheelchair
accessible throughout, small garden, five
bedrooms in separate building, open all day
weekends. *(John and Enid Morris,
Mrs P Sumner)*

COOKHAM   SU8985

★**Bel & the Dragon** (01628) 521263

High Street (B4447); SL6 9SQ Smartly
updated 15th-c inn; heavy beams, log fires
and simple country furnishings in two-room
front bar and dining area, hand-painted
cartoons on pastel walls, more modern bistro-
style back restaurant, emphasis on good
food (separate bar and restaurant menus)
including weekend brunch, Rebellion IPA
and a local guest, plenty of wines by the
glass from extensive list, cocktails; children
welcome, dogs in bar, well tended garden
with tables on paved terrace, play area, five
bedrooms, Stanley Spencer Gallery almost
opposite, open all day, food all day Sun.
(Theocsbrian)

COOKHAM   SU8885

★**White Oak** (01628) 523043

The Pound (B4447); SL6 9QE
Modernised red-brick restauranty pub with
highly regarded interesting food including
good value set menus, large back area and
several other parts set for eating, front
bar with ales such as Greene King and
good choice of wines by the glass, friendly
efficient service; free wi-fi; children welcome,
sheltered back terrace with steps up to white
wirework tables on grass, closed Sun evening,
otherwise open all day. *(Simon Collett-Jones)*

COOKHAM DEAN   SU8785

★**Jolly Farmer** (01628) 482905

Church Road, off Hills Lane; SL6 9PD
18th-c pub owned by village consortium;
unspoilt linked rooms with open fires, five
well kept ales such as Rebellion and good
choice of wines by the glass, popular food
with some italian influences including
wood-fired pizzas, pleasant attentive service,
good-sized more modern eating area and
small dining room; occasional live music;
well behaved children and dogs welcome,
tables out in front and on side terrace,
garden with big play area, open all
day. *(Simon Rodway, Simon Collett-Jones)*

COOKHAM DEAN   SU8785

Uncle Toms Cabin (01628) 483339

*Off A308 Maidenhead–Marlow;
Hills Lane, towards Cookham Rise
and Cookham; SL6 9NT* Welcoming
small-roomed local with simple sensitively
modernised interior, four well kept
mainstream ales and plenty of wines by the
glass, good reasonably priced food cooked by
owner-chef, low beams (and doorways), wood
floors and grey-green panelling, gleaming
horsebrasses, open fire; children in eating
areas, dogs in bar, seats out at front and
in sheltered sloping back garden, peaceful
country setting, open all day Sat, closes at
9pm Sun and Mon. *(R K Phillips)*

CRAZIES HILL   SU7980

Horns (0118) 940 6041

*Warren Row Road off A4 towards
Cockpole Green, then follow Crazies Hill
signs; RG10 8LY* Revamped 16th-c beamed
village pub continuing well under present
welcoming licensees; good food cooked by
landlord-chef from lunchtime baguettes and
traditional favourites up, Brakspears ales in
top condition and nice choice of wines by
the glass, friendly helpful service, four rooms
including raftered barn restaurant; children
welcome, dogs in bar (resident black lab),
big garden with play area, summer
barbecues, open all day Fri and Sat, till 9pm
Sun, closed Mon (Tues after bank holiday).
(Paul Humphreys, Simon Collett-Jones)

DATCHET   SU9877

Royal Stag (01753) 584231

*Not far from M4 junction 5; The Green;
SL3 9JH* Ancient beamed pub next to
church overlooking green, well kept Fullers
London Pride and three Windsor & Eton
ales, enjoyable food including good Sun
roasts, friendly staff; Tues quiz; seats outside,
open (and food) all day. *(Daphne and Barry
Gregson)*

DONNINGTON   SU4770

Fox & Hounds (01635) 40540

Old Oxford Road; RG14 3AP Popular
family-owned pub (they also run a local
butchers and have a meat raffle every other
Sun); well kept Fullers, Sharps and West
Berkshire, decent wine range and good food
(not Sun evening) from pub favourites to
grills, friendly attentive young staff, back
dining room; children and dogs welcome,
tables out in front, handy for M4 (junction
13) and A34, closed Mon, otherwise open
all day. *(Ian Herdman)*

'Children welcome' means the pub says it lets children inside without any special
restriction; some may impose an evening time limit earlier than 9pm – please tell us
if you find this.

EAST GARSTON   SU3676
★**Queens Arms** (01488) 648757
*3.5 miles from M4 junction 14; A338
and village signposted Gt Shefford;
RG17 7ET* Friendly inn at the heart of
racehorse-training country; opened-up
bar with antique prints (many jockeys),
wheelbacks around well spaced tables on
bare boards, Ramsbury and Sharps Doom Bar,
plenty of wines by the glass and fair choice
of whiskies, lighter dining area with more
prints, good fairly traditional food (not Sun
evening); background music, TV for racing,
newspapers including *Racing Post*, free wi-fi;
children and dogs (in bar) welcome, seats
on sheltered terrace, spacious attractively
decorated bedrooms, fly fishing and shooting
can be arranged, good surrounding downland
walks, open all day. *(Mr and Mrs P R Thomas)*

EAST ILSLEY   SU4981
★**Crown & Horns** (01635) 281545
*Just off A34, about 5 miles N of M4
junction 13; Compton Road; RG20 7LH*
Civilised brick and tile pub in horse-training
country; rambling beamed rooms with
log fires, enjoyable home-made food from
sandwiches, pizzas and pub favourites up
including good Sun lunch, five real ales,
friendly efficient staff; background music;
children, dogs and muddy boots welcome,
tables in pretty courtyard, modern bedroom
extension, open all day and busy on Newbury
race days. *(Nick Higgins)*

FRILSHAM   SU5573
Pot Kiln (01635) 201366
*From Yattendon take turning S, opposite
church, follow first Frilsham signpost,
but just after crossing motorway go
straight on towards Bucklebury ignoring
Frilsham signposted right; pub on right
after about 0.5 miles; RG18 0XX*
Refurbished red-brick country dining pub,
small bare-boards bar with woodburner,
four West Berkshire ales including Brick
Kiln named for the pub, several wines by the
glass and maybe a couple of ciders, various
dining areas with wooden tables and chairs,
signature local game and other food from
ciabattas up; free wi-fi; children and dogs
welcome, unobstructed views from seats in
big suntrap garden with pizza oven, walks in
nearby woods, open all day Sat, till 5pm Sun,
closed Tues. *(Dr Simon Innes, Luke Morgan)*

HENLEY   SU7682
★**Little Angel** (01491) 411008
*Remenham Lane (A4130, just over
bridge E of Henley); RG9 2LS* Civilised
dining pub, more or less open-plan but with
distinct modernised seating areas, bare
boards throughout, little bar with leather
cube stools, tub and farmhouse chairs,
other parts with mix of dining tables and
chairs, artwork on Farrow & Ball paintwork,
contemporary food (all day weekends)

from sharing plates up, Brakspears ales
and several wines by the glass including
champagne, pleasant attentive service,
airy conservatory; background music; well
behaved children allowed, dogs in bar, tables
on sheltered floodlit back terrace overlooking
cricket pitch, open all day. *(Simon Rodway,
Roy Hoing, Gus Swan)*

HOLYPORT   SU8977
George (01628) 628317
*1.5 miles from M4 junction 8/9, via
A308(M)/A330; The Green; SL6 2JL*
Attractive 16th-c pub on picturesque village
green with duck pond, colourful history and
plenty of old-world charm, open-plan low-
beamed interior, cosy and dimly lit, with nice
fireplace, good food from pub favourites up,
well kept Fullers London Pride and a couple
of Rebellion ales, nice wines from sound
list, friendly helpful service; background
music, quiz first Mon of month; children and
dogs (in bar) welcome, picnic-sets on pretty
terrace, closed Sun evening, Mon.
(Jamie Green)

HUNGERFORD   SU3368
John O'Gaunt (01488) 683535
Bridge Street (A338); RG17 0EG
Welcoming 16th-c town pub with refurbished
bare-boards interior, enjoyable generously
served food from lunchtime sandwiches/
wraps (not Sun) to good Sun roasts, six
well kept mainly local ales including own
microbrews (tasting trays available), good
bottled range too and local cider, efficient
cheerful service from uniformed staff;
children and dogs welcome, small sheltered
garden, open all day, food all day Sun.
(Anthony Jones, David Shaw)

HUNGERFORD   SU3368
Three Swans (01488) 682721
High Street; RG17 0LZ Clean and
welcoming former coaching inn; cosy
panelled bar off to the right with three well
kept ales such as Fullers and Ramsbury,
large split-level restaurant on the left, good
reasonably priced food from sandwiches and
snacks up (nice fish and chips), efficient
friendly service; children and dogs (in
bar) welcome, some tables out at front,
25 bedrooms open all day from 9am for
breakfast; refurbishment planned, so may
be changes. *(Tony and Wendy Hobden,
Kristin Warry)*

HUNGERFORD NEWTOWN   SU3571
Tally Ho (01488) 682312
*A338 just S of M4 junction 14;
RG17 0PP* Traditional red-brick beamed
pub owned by the local community, friendly
and welcoming, with good food (not Sun
evening) from baguettes to specials and
popular Sun lunch, four well kept local ales
such as Ramsbury and West Berkshire, log
fire; occasional music and quiz nights, free
wi-fi; children welcome, a couple of picnic-

sets out in front, more tables on side terrace, three bedrooms, open all day. *(Dr and Mrs R E S Tanner)*

HURLEY   SU8281
Dew Drop (01628) 315662
Small yellow sign to pub off A4130 just W; SL6 6RB Old flint and brick pub tucked away in nice woodland setting, shortish choice of food including good lunchtime sandwiches, Brakspears and a guest ale, log fire; children and dogs welcome, pleasant views from back garden, good local walks, open all day Sat, till 6pm Sun, closed Mon. *(Paul Humphreys)*

HURST   SU7973
★Castle (0118) 934 0034
Church Hill; RG10 0SJ Popular old dining pub owned by church opposite; very good well presented food (not Sun evening, Mon) from fairly priced varied menu including daily specials, well kept ales such as Binghams and plenty of wines by the glass, efficient friendly staff, bar with restaurant on left, snug to the right, beams, wood floors and old brick nogging, some visible wattle and daub, roaring fire; children and dogs (in bar) welcome, garden picnic-sets, open all day weekends, closed Mon lunchtime.
(John Pritchard, Paul Humphreys, DHV)

HURST   SU8074
Green Man (0118) 934 2599
Off A321 just outside village; RG10 0BP Partly 17th-c pub with enjoyable food from sandwiches, sharing plates and pub favourites up, a couple of well kept Brakspears ales and a guest, several wines by the glass, friendly service, bar with dark beams and standing timbers, cosy alcoves, wall seats and built-in settles, hot little fire in one fireplace, old iron stove in another, dining area with modern sturdy wooden tables and high-backed chairs on solid oak floor; children and dogs welcome, sheltered terrace, picnic-sets under spreading oak trees in large garden with play area, open all day, food all day weekends. *(Paul Humphreys)*

LAMBOURN   SU3175
Hare (01488) 71386
aka Hare & Hounds; Lambourn Woodlands, well S of Lambourn itself (B4000/Hilldrop Lane); RG17 7SD Rambling 17th-c beamed restaurant-pub with well liked fairly priced food from lunchtime sandwiches/baguettes to good Sun roasts, several small linked rooms including a proper bar with ales such as Ramsbury and Sharps, friendly efficient service; background music, TV; children and dogs (in one part) welcome, garden behind, open all day (till 8pm Sun). *(Michael Sargent)*

LITTLEWICK GREEN   SU8379
Cricketers (01628) 822888
Not far from M4 junction 9; A404(M) then left on to A4 – village signed on left; Coronation Road; SL6 3RA Welcoming old-fashioned village pub in charming spot opposite cricket green (can get crowded); three well kept Badger ales and good choice of wines by the glass, enjoyable pub food (not Sun evening) from lunchtime sandwiches and baguettes to specials, traditional interior with three linked rooms, wood and quarry-tiled floors, huge clock above woodburner in brick fireplace; background music, TV, fortnightly quiz Tues; children and dogs (they have their own) welcome, pretty hanging baskets and a few tables out in front behind picket fence, open all day weekends (weekdays too if busy). *(Susan and John Douglas, D J and P M Taylor)*

MAIDENHEAD   SU8582
Pinkneys Arms (01628) 630268
Lee Lane, just off A308 N; SL6 6NU Refurbished dining pub with good food (not Mon) from pubby choices and pizzas up (some choices expensive), well kept ales (mainly Rebellion) and decent wines, friendly efficient service; outside gents', barn function room; children and dogs welcome, big garden, closed Mon lunchtime, otherwise open all day from midday. *(Paul Baxter)*

MARSH BENHAM   SU4267
Red House (01635) 582017
Off A4 W of Newbury; RG20 8LY Attractive thatched dining pub with good imaginative food from french chef-owner, also lunchtime sandwiches and pub favourites, steak night Tues and Fri, well kept West Berkshire and a guest such as Charles Wells, lots of wines by the glass, afternoon teas, roomy flagstoned/wood floor bar with woodburner, separate restaurant, good cheerful service; background music; children and dogs welcome, terrace and long lawns sloping to River Kennet water meadows, open (and food) all day. *(Ian Herdman)*

MIDGHAM   SU5566
Coach & Horses (0118) 971 3384
Bath Road (N side); RG7 5UX Comfortable main-road pub with good choice of food from baguettes up including lunchtime offers, cheerful efficient service, Fullers London Pride and West Berkshire Good Old Boy, flagstoned bar with sofa by brick fireplace, steps up to small half-panelled carpeted dining area with country-style furniture, second dining room; children welcome, garden behind, closed Sun evening, Mon. *(Jamie Green)*

If we know a pub has an outdoor play area for children, we mention it.

MORTIMER
SU6564

Horse & Groom (0118) 933 2813

The Street; RG7 3RD Double-fronted Victorian pub facing common, reliable well cooked food from pub favourites up including good daily specials (they list local suppliers), two or three real ales such as Timothy Taylors Landlord and decent wines by the glass, open fire; children and dogs welcome, picnic-sets on side lawn, parking opposite, open all day, no food Sun evening. *(Dr and Mrs R E S Tanner)*

NEWBURY
SU4767

Lock Stock & Barrel
(01635) 580550

Northbrook Street; RG14 1AA Modern pub approached down small alleyway and popular for its canalside (River Kennet) setting; low ceiling, light wood or slate flooring and painted panelling, lots of windows overlooking canal, varied choice of enjoyable sensibly priced food all day from sandwiches up, well kept Fullers/Gales beers, efficient friendly staff; occasional live music, free wi-fi; children welcome, outside seating including suntrap Astroturf roof terrace looking over a series of locks towards handsome church, moorings, open all day (till midnight Fri, Sat). *(Phil and Jane Villiers)*

OAKLEY GREEN
SU9276

★ Greene Oak (01753) 864294

Off A308 Windsor–Maidenhead at Twyford (B3024) signpost; Dedworth Road; SL4 5UW Several eating areas with variety of dining chairs, wall banquettes and tables from country kitchen-style to more formal, bare boards or flagstones, enjoyable modern cooking (not particularly cheap) from seasonal menu, dedicated drinkers' area to the right serving Greene King IPA and a couple of guests such as Rebellion and Windsor & Eton, plenty of wines by the glass, friendly helpful staff; background music, free wi-fi; children welcome (menu for them), dogs in bar, sizeable terrace behind with decked area, handy for Legoland and Ascot (racegoers' champagne dinner), open all day (till 7pm Sun). *(Simon Collett-Jones)*

OLD WINDSOR
SU9874

Oxford Blue (01753) 861954

Crimp Hill Road, off B3021 – itself off A308/A328; SL4 2QY Fully refurbished 19th-c restaurant-pub under new management; highly regarded upscale food (not cheap) from proprietor-chef, well kept local ales and good wines from extensive list, friendly professional service; well placed with open country views, terrace tables, open till 6pm Sun, closed Mon, Tues. *(Nick Higgins)*

PALEY STREET
SU8676

★ Royal Oak (01628) 620541

B3024 W; SL6 3JN Attractively modernised and extended 17th-c restaurant pub owned by Sir Michael Parkinson and son Nick; highly regarded british cooking (not cheap) and most here to eat, good service, dining room split by brick pillars and timbering with mix of well spaced wooden tables and leather chairs on bare boards or flagstones, smallish informal beamed bar with woodburner, leather sofas and cricketing prints, Fullers London Pride and wide choice of wines by the glass including champagne; background jazz; children welcome (no pushchairs in restaurant), seats outside among troughs of herbs, closed Sun. *(Daphne and Barry Gregson)*

READING
SU7173

★ Alehouse (0118) 950 8119

Broad Street; RG1 2BH Cheerful no-frills drinkers' pub with nine well kept quickly changing ales and three craft kegs, also lots of different bottled beers, farm ciders and perry; small bare-boards bar with raised seating area, hundreds of pump clips on walls and ceiling, corridor to several appealing panelled rooms, some little more than alcoves, no food; background music, TV; open all day. *(Susan Eccleston)*

READING
SU7272

Jolly Anglers (0118) 376 7823

Kennetside; RG1 3EA Simple two-room pub on River Kennet towpath, originally built for workers at the former Huntley & Palmers biscuit factory; four or more well kept changing ales and up to ten ciders/perries, good value home-made food including vegetarian/vegan choices, friendly landlord and staff, wood floors, original fireplaces, darts and other pub games, piano; open mike night Mon; resident dogs (others welcome), picnic-sets in back garden up steep steps, open (and food) all day. *(Jamie Green)*

READING
SU7174

Moderation (0118) 375 0767

Caversham Road; RG1 8BB Modernised airy Victorian pub with enjoyable reasonably priced food including good thai/indonesian choices, pleasant prompt service, three well kept changing ales, some eastern influences to the décor; background music, sports TV; seats out at front and in enclosed garden behind, open all day. *(Jamie Green)*

READING
SU7073

Nags Head 07765 880137

Russell Street; RG1 7XD Fairly basic mock-Tudor drinkers' pub just outside town

---

By law, pubs must show a price list of their drinks. Let us know if you're inconvenienced by any breach of this law.

centre attracting good mix of customers, a dozen well kept changing ales and 14 ciders, baguettes and pies (roasts on Sun), open fire, darts and cribbage; background and occasional live music, TV for major sporting events (busy on Reading FC match days); beer garden, open all day. *(John Pritchard, Jamie Green)*

READING   SU7173
★**Sweeney & Todd** (0118) 958 6466
Castle Street; RG1 7RD Pie shop with popular bar/restaurant behind (little changed in over 30 years); warren of private period-feel alcoves and other areas on various levels, enjoyable home-made food including their range of good value pies, cheery service, small bar with four well kept ales such as Adnams and Hook Norton, Weston's cider and decent wines; children welcome in restaurant area, closed Sun evening and bank holidays, otherwise open (and food) all day. *(John Pritchard, Chris and Pauline Sexton, Robin James)*

SHINFIELD   SU7368
Black Boy (0118) 988 3116
Shinfield Road (A327); RG2 9BP Recently refurbished Barons group pub; contemporary beamed interior with bow-windowed front bar and spreading back restaurant, painted half-panelling, some high tables and lots of booth seating, modern artwork and a couple of gas woodburners, three real ales including Greene King and good range of wines/gins, popular food from baguettes and sharing plates through burgers and pub favourites up, efficient helpful staff; background music; children welcome, back terrace with own bar and various covered seating areas, open all day. *(Darren and Jane Staniforth)*

SHINFIELD   SU7367
★**Magpie & Parrot** (0118) 988 4130
2.6 miles from M4 junction 11, via B3270; A327 just SE of Shinfield on Arborfield Road; RG2 9EA Unusual homely little roadside cottage with two cosy spic and span bars, warm fire and lots of bric-a-brac (miniature and historic bottles, stuffed birds, dozens of model cars, veteran AA badges and automotive instruments) Fullers London Pride and a local guest from small corner counter, weekday lunchtime snacks and evening fish and chips (Thurs, Fri), hospitable landlady; no credit cards or mobile phones; pub dogs (others welcome), seats on back terrace and marquee on immaculate lawn, open 12-7.30 (later some Thurs nights when live jazz), closed Sun evening. *(Daphne and Barry Gregson)*

SHURLOCK ROW   SU8374
★**Shurlock Inn** (0118) 934 9094
Just off B3018 SE of Twyford; The Street; RG10 0PS Cosy 17th-c village-owned pub with good food (all day

weekends) from pubby choices up, four ales including West Berkshire Mr Chubbs and one from Rebellion, nice wines with a dozen by the glass, log fire in double-sided fireplace dividing bar and larger dining room, new oak flooring, painted panelling and one or two old beams; background music, weekend papers, free wi-fi; children welcome, dogs in bar, black metal furniture on side and back terraces, lawned garden with picnic-sets under parasols and fenced play area, open all day Fri, Sat, till 9pm Sun. *(Tony and Jill Radnor)*

SULHAMSTEAD   SU6269
Spring (0118) 930 3440
Bath Road (A4); RG7 5HP Friendly old barn conversion with spacious bar and balustraded upstairs dining area under rafters, good variety of popular food from interesting sandwiches up, three real ales including Fullers and West Berkshire, nice range of wines by the glass, friendly efficient staff; children welcome, plenty of seats outside, open all day. *(Daphne Veale)*

SUNNINGHILL   SU9367
Carpenters Arms (01344) 622763
Upper Village Road; SL5 7AQ Restaurant village pub run by french team, good authentic french country cooking, not cheap but they do offer a reasonably priced set lunch (Mon-Sat), nice wines including house pichets, Sharps Doom Bar; no children in the evening, terrace tables, open all day and best to book. *(Alastair and Sheree Hepburn)*

SUNNINGHILL   SU9367
Dog & Partridge (01344) 623204
Upper Village Road; SL5 7AQ Bright contemporary décor and emphasis on good freshly made food (all day Sun) including set lunch menu, friendly helpful staff, Fullers, Sharps and a guest, good range of wines (a dozen by the glass); background music; children and dogs welcome, disabled facilities, part covered courtyard garden with pond and fountain, closed Mon, otherwise open all day. *(Nick Higgins)*

THEALE   SU6471
Bull (0118) 930 3478
High Street; RG7 5AH Modernised and extended old red-brick inn; large bar with tiled floor and dark half-panelling, carpeted dining area behind with banquettes, enjoyable good value food from pub favourites up delivered by dumb-waiter from upstairs kitchen, three or four well kept Wadworths ales, friendly staff; background and some live music, quiz nights; children and dogs (on leads) welcome, seats outside, open (and food) all day. *(Andrew Lawson)*

THEALE   SU6471
Fox & Hounds (0118) 930 2295
2 miles from M4 junction 12; follow A4 W, then first left signed for station,

over two roundabouts, then over narrow canal bridge to Sheffield Bottom; RG7 4BE Large neatly kept dining pub with well priced pubby food (not Sun evening) from baguettes to specials, five well kept Wadworths ales, Weston's cider, decent wines and coffee, L-shaped bar with dividers, traditional mix of furniture on carpet or bare boards including area with modern sofas and low tables, two open fires; pool and darts, Sun quiz; children and dogs welcome, outside seating at front and sides, lakeside bird reserve opposite, open all day Fri-Sun. *(John Pritchard)*

THREE MILE CROSS   SU7167
Swan (0118) 988 3674
A33 just S of M4 junction 11; Basingstoke Road; RG7 1AT Smallish traditional pub built in the 17th c and later a posting house; five well kept ales including Loddon and Timothy Taylors, enjoyable fairly standard home-made food at reasonable prices, friendly efficient staff, two beamed bars, inglenook with hanging black pots, old prints and some impressive stuffed fish; large well arranged outside seating area behind (also home to wolfhound Mr Niall, the London Irish RFC mascot), near Madejski Stadium and very busy on match days, closed Sun evening, otherwise open all day. *(John Pritchard)*

WALTHAM ST LAWRENCE SU8376
★ Bell (0118) 934 1788
B3024 E of Twyford; The Street; RG10 0JJ Welcoming 14th-c village local with well preserved timbered interior, good home-made food marked on blackboard from bar snacks including own pork pies up, friendly service, five well kept mainly local beers, up to eight real ciders and plenty of wines by the glass, also good choice of whiskies, two compact connecting rooms, another larger one off entrance hall, warming log fires, daily newspapers; children and dogs welcome, pretty back garden with extended terrace and shady trees, open all day weekends. *(Simon Collett-Jones)*

WARGRAVE   SU7878
Bull (0843) 289 1773
Off A321 Henley–Twyford; High Street; RG10 8DE Low-beamed 15th-c brick coaching inn run well by hospitable landlady; main bar with inglenook log fire, two dining areas (one up steps for families), enjoyable traditional home-made food from baguettes up, well kept Brakspears ales and a guest, friendly attentive staff; background music, free wi-fi; well behaved dogs welcome, walled garden behind, four bedrooms, open all day weekends. *(Simon Collett-Jones, DHV)*

WARGRAVE   SU7878
St George & Dragon (0118) 940 5021
High Street; RG10 8HY Spacious smartly updated dining pub in good Thames-side position with deck overlooking the water (they ask for a credit card if you eat outside), wide range of well presented food including fixed-price menu (weekdays till 6pm) and other deals, central fire giving cosy feel; children welcome, open (and food) all day, can get very busy and service may suffer. *(Susan and John Douglas)*

WEST ILSLEY   SU4782
Harrow (01635) 281260
Signed off A34 at E Ilsley slip road; RG20 7AR Appealing and welcoming family-run country pub in peaceful spot overlooking cricket pitch and pond; Victorian prints in deep-coloured knocked-through bar, some antique furnishings, log fire, good choice of enjoyable sensibly priced home-made food (not Sun or Mon evenings), well kept Greene King ales and nice selection of wines by the glass, afternoon teas; children in eating areas, dogs allowed in bar, big garden with picnic-sets, more seats on pleasant terrace, handy for Ridgeway walkers, may close early Sun evening if quiet. *(Jamie Green)*

WINDSOR   SU9676
Carpenters Arms (01753) 863739
Market Street; SL4 1PB Nicholsons pub rambling around central servery with good choice of well kept ales and several wines by the glass, reasonably priced pubby food from sandwiches up including range of pies, friendly helpful service, sturdy pub furnishings and Victorian-style décor with two pretty fireplaces, family areas up a few steps, also downstairs beside former tunnel entrance with suits of armour; background music; no dogs, tables out on cobbled pedestrian alley opposite castle, no nearby parking, handy for Legoland bus stop, open (and food) all day. *(Andrew Lawson)*

WINDSOR   SU9676
Two Brewers (01753) 855426
Park Street; SL4 1LB In shadow of Windsor Castle with three cosy unchanging rooms around central servery, well kept ales such as Fullers London Pride, St Austell Tribute and Sharps Doom Bar, good choice of wines by the glass and enjoyable freshly made food (not Fri-Sun evenings) from shortish mid-priced menu, friendly efficient service, thriving old-fashioned pub atmosphere, beams, bare boards and open fire, enamel signs, posters and old photographs; background music, daily

---

Post Office address codings confusingly give the impression that some pubs are in Berkshire, when they're really in Buckinghamshire, Oxfordshire or Hampshire (which is where we list them).

papers; no children inside, dogs welcome, tables and attractive hanging baskets out by pretty Georgian street next to Windsor Park's Long Walk, open all day. *(Simon Rodway)*

WINDSOR   SU9576
Vansittart Arms (01753) 865988
Vansittart Road; SL4 5DD Friendly three-room Victorian local with cosy corners and open fires, well kept Fullers/Gales beers, big helpings of enjoyable good value home-made food (all day weekends); background music, sports TV, pool, free wi-fi; children and dogs welcome, part-covered beer garden, open all day. *(Andrew Lawson)*

WINNERSH   SU7871
Wheelwrights Arms (0118) 934 4100
Off A329 Reading–Wokingham at Winnersh crossroads by Sainsbury's, B3030 signed Twyford; under A239(M) then right into Davis Way; RG10 0TR Popular refurbished beamed pub, enjoyable food from ciabattas and deli boards up at reasonable prices (smaller helpings available), friendly efficient service, well kept Wadworths ales and guests, big woodburner in brick fireplace, flagstone and wood floors, newer dining area; background music, daily newspapers; children, muddy boots and dogs

welcome, disabled access, picnic-sets out at front and in garden behind (some motorway noise), opposite Dinton Pastures, open all day, food all day Sat, till 4pm Sun. *(DHV)*

WRAYSBURY   TQ0174
George (01784) 482000
Windsor Road (B376); TW19 5DE Revamped beamed dining pub, good fairly priced food catering for special diets from sandwiches to specials, three real ales and nice range of wines by the glass, friendly helpful service; children and dogs welcome, rattan-style furniture out on decking, open all day. *(Nick Higgins)*

WRAYSBURY   TQ0074
Perseverance (01784) 482375
High Street; TW19 5DB Welcoming old community village pub; enjoyable good value home-made food from sandwiches up, three well kept ales including Otter and decent choice of wines by the glass, interesting selection of gins too, friendly helpful staff, beams and log fires (one in inglenook); Thurs quiz, live music Sun afternoon and first/third Tues of month, darts; children (till 9pm) and dogs welcome, nice back garden with pizza oven, open all day (till 9.30pm Sun), food all day Sat. *(Andrew and Michele Revell)*

Buckinghamshire

ADSTOCK   SP7330   Map 4

Old Thatched Inn 🌟 🍺

(01296) 712584 – www.theoldthatchedinn.co.uk

Main Street, off A413; MK18 2JN

Thatched dining pub with keen landlord, friendly staff, five real ales and good food

First class food in this pretty thatched dining pub continues to win warm praise from our readers. But there's a welcome for those who just want a drink and a chat with the enthusiastic landlord – they keep Brakspears Oxford Gold, Fullers London Pride, Sharps Doom Bar, Thwaites Wainwright and Vale Wychert on handpump, 14 wines by the glass, a dozen malt whiskies and four ciders. The small front bar area has low beams, sofas on flagstones, high bar chairs and an open fire. A dining area leads off with more beams and a mix of pale wooden dining chairs around miscellaneous tables on a stripped wooden floor; background music. There's also a modern conservatory restaurant at the back with well spaced tables on bare boards. The sheltered terrace has tables and chairs under a gazebo. This is an attractive village.

🌟 From a thoughtful menu, the highly thought-of food includes goats cheese and confit onion croquette with pineapple chilli relish, prawn and crayfish cocktail, linguine with feta, wild mushrooms and spinach, burger with toppings, sweetcorn slaw and chips, slow-cooked pork belly with spring onion and ginger pak choi, sautéed oriental vegetables and soy dressing, sea bass with crushed minted chilli peas and spicy tomato sauce, and puddings such as raspberry and rhubarb fool and banana bread with honeycomb butter, caramel sauce and vanilla ice-cream; they also offer a two- and three-course weekday set lunch. *Benchmark main dish: Aylesbury duck with dauphinoise potatoes, roasted pear and red wine and rosemary jus £17.50. Two-course evening meal £23.50.*

Free house ~ Licensee Andrew Judge ~ Real ale ~ Open 12-11 (midnight Sat, 10.30 Sun) ~ Bar food 12-2.30, 5-9; 12-8 Sun ~ Restaurant ~ Well behaved children welcome ~ Dogs allowed in bar ~ Wi-fi *Recommended by Tim and Sarah Smythe-Brown, Dave Braisted, Graham and Carol Parker, Richard Kennell, Jess and George Cowley*

AYLESBURY
SP8113 Map 4

Kings Head 🍺

(01296) 718812 – www.farmersbar.co.uk

Kings Head Passage (off Bourbon Street), also entrance off Temple Street; no nearby parking except for disabled; HP20 2RW

Fine old town centre pub with civilised atmosphere, good local ales (used in the food too) and friendly service

Only a part of this handsome 15th-c building (owned by the National Trust) is used as a pub and it's quite a surprise to come across it tucked away in a modern town centre. It contains the Farmers Bar, as well as the tourist information office and conference rooms. Three timeless rooms have been restored with careful and unpretentious simplicity: stripped boards, cream walls with minimal decoration, gentle lighting and a variety of seating which includes upholstered sofas and armchairs, cushioned high-backed settles and some simple modern pale dining tables and chairs dotted around. Most of the bar tables are of round glass, supported on low cask tops. The neat corner bar has Chiltern Ale, Beechwood Bitter and a seasonal guest beer on handpump, 11 wines by the glass, a farm cider and some interesting bottled beers. Service is friendly and there's no background music or machines. The atmospheric medieval cobbled courtyard has teak seats and tables, some beneath a pillared roof; summer barbecues and live events are held. Disabled access and facilities.

Popular food includes sandwiches, rarebit with cheese, bacon and ale, two-egg omelette, toad in the hole with cider gravy, ham and eggs, goats cheese tart with roasted peppers, creamy mushroom chicken breast, venison and blue cheese burger, superfood salad, a pie of the week, and puddings such as apple crumble and sticky toffee pudding. *Benchmark main dish: cheese and bacon burger with chips £11.95. Two-course evening meal £17.00.*

Chiltern ~ Manager George Jenkinson ~ Real ale ~ Open 11-11; 12-10.30 Sun ~ Bar food 11.30-3, 5-9 (not Mon or Tues evenings); 11.30-9 Fri, Sat; 12-6 Sun ~ Children welcome away from bar ~ Wi-fi *Recommended by Graham and Carol Parker, David and Charlotte Green, John Poulter, Robin and Anne Triggs*

BOVINGDON GREEN
SU8386 Map 2

Royal Oak 🏅 🍷

(01628) 488611 – www.royaloakmarlow.co.uk

0.75 miles N of Marlow, on back road to Frieth signposted off West Street (A4155) in centre; SL7 2JF

Civilised dining pub with nice little bar, a fine choice of wines by the glass, real ales and imaginative food

Even at their busiest, the staff in this particularly well run pub remain impressively efficient and courteous. The low-beamed cosy snug, closest to the car park, has three small tables and a woodburning stove in an exposed brick fireplace (with a big pile of logs beside it). They keep Rebellion IPA on handpump alongside a guest such as Purity Pure UBU, 24 wines by the glass (plus pudding wines), several gins and farm cider. Several other attractively decorated areas open off the central bar with half-panelled walls variously painted in pale blue, green or cream (though the dining room ones are red). Throughout, there's a mix of church chairs, stripped wooden tables and chunky wall seats, with rugs on the partly wooden, partly flagstoned floors, co-ordinated cushions and curtains, and a bright, airy feel. Thoughtful extra touches enhance the tone: a bowl of olives on the bar,

carefully laid-out newspapers and fresh flowers or candles on the tables.
Board games and background music. A sunny terrace with good solid tables
leads to an appealing garden with pétanque, ping pong, badminton and swing
ball; there's also a smaller side garden and a kitchen herb garden.

Using the best local, seasonal produce the enticing food includes gin-cured
gravadlax with smoked beetroot and horseradish, free-range chicken and leek
terrine with local sparkling wine jelly, goats cheese, walnut and fig tart with onion
jam, polenta chips and red pepper ketchup, local free-range pork sausages with gravy
and crispy onions, sea bass fillets with caramelised chicory, potato boudin and warm
hazelnut dressing, lamb rump with lamb faggot, confit potato, burnt onions and pea
purée, and puddings such as tiramisu with black cherry sorbet and shortbread crumble
and lady grey tea crème brûlée with ginger biscuits. *Benchmark main dish: bubble
and squeak with oak-smoked bacon, a poached egg and hollandaise £11.25. Two-course
evening meal £24.00.*

Salisbury Pubs ~ Manager James Molier ~ Real ale ~ Open 11-11; 12-11 Sun ~ Bar food
12-2.30, 6.30-9.30; 12-3, 6-10 Fri, Sat; 12-9 Sun ~ Restaurant ~ Children welcome ~ Dogs
welcome ~ Wi-fi *Recommended by Peter, Tracey and Stephen Groves, Ben and Diane Bowie,
Guy Henderson, Mary and Douglas McDowell*

BRILL   SP6514   Map 4

Pheasant

(01844) 239370 – www.thepheasant.co.uk
Windmill Street; off B4011 Bicester–Long Crendon; HP18 9TG

**Long-reaching views, a bustling bar with local ales, attentive staff
and tasty food; bedrooms**

If you stay here, the bedrooms are comfortable and two are in the former
bakehouse; good views and nearby walks too. The interior is more or
less open-plan, with a raftered bar area, leather tub seats in front of a
woodburner, and a good mix of customers – including chatty, friendly
regulars. Brains Rev James, Vale Brill Gold and a beer named for the
pub on handpump and a dozen wines by the glass served by charming,
attentive staff. Dining areas have high-backed leather or dark wooden
chairs, attractively framed prints and books on shelves; background music.
There are plenty of seats and tables on the decked area and in the garden,
with marvellous views over the windmill opposite (one of the oldest post
windmills still in working order) and into the distance across five counties.
Roald Dahl used to drink here, and some of the tales the locals told him were
worked into his short stories.

Good food includes lunchtime sandwiches, ravioli of dry-aged beef, tomato, shallot
and parsley sauce, salad of smoked and hot smoked salmon, crayfish tails and
bloody mary sauce, beetroot and burrata cheese with pesto, balsamic and pine nuts,
sausages and mash with onion rings and gravy, steak in ale pie, beef or cajun chicken
burger with toppings and french fries, curried tiger prawns with indian-style bread, and
puddings such as white chocolate and raspberry cheesecake and apple and blackberry
crumble; they also offer a limited weekday takeaway menu. *Benchmark main dish:
loin of local venison with black pudding £18.00. Two-course evening meal £22.00.*

Free house ~ Licensee Marilyn Glover ~ Real ale ~ Open 12-11 (midnight Fri, Sat); 12-10
Sun ~ Bar food 12-2.30, 6-9; 12-5 Sun ~ Children welcome ~ Dogs allowed in bar ~ Wi-fi ~
Bedrooms: £85/£110 *Recommended by David Jackman, John and Hilary Murphy, John Evans,
Alison and Graeme Spicer, Canon Michael Bourdeaux*

You can send reports directly to us at feedback@goodguides.com

BRILL

SP6513   Map 4

Pointer ⬤ ⚲

(01844) 238339 – www.thepointerbrill.co.uk

Church Street; HP18 9RT

• •

Buckinghamshire Dining Pub of the Year

Carefully restored pub in a pretty village with rewarding food, local ales and interesting furnishings

Tolkien is said to have based the village of Bree in *The Lord of the Rings* on this pretty village. The handsome pub is beside the village green and church, and is very stylishly furnished: low beams, windsor chairs, elegant armchairs and sofas with brocaded cushions, open fires or woodburners in brick fireplaces and animal-hide stools by the counter. A beer named for the pub (from the XT Brewing Company), Vale Gravitas and a guest from Rebellion on handpump, 11 wines by the glass, a dozen gins, 28 malt whiskies, and friendly, attentive staff. The airy and attractive restaurant has antique Ercol chairs around pale oak tables, cushioned window seats, rafters in a high vaulted ceiling and an open kitchen. French windows open on to the sizeable garden. Do visit their own butchers next door where they sell home-reared beef and free-range pork, free-range eggs, home-baked bread and home-made pies, sausage rolls and so forth (open 2.30-6.30pm Wednesday-Friday, 9am-2pm Saturday). Bedrooms should be open by the time this Guide is published.

 Using meat from their own farm and other seasonal, local produce, the creative food includes rare-breed beef tongue with crispy sweetbreads, celeriac slaw, apple and walnuts, chicken liver parfait with red onion marmalade and kumquat, wild mushroom risotto, pollack with lentils, curried mussels and caramelised cauliflower, pork belly with miso-glazed cheek, kohlrabi and caramelised pear purée, venison pie with cardamom gravy and beetroot ketchup, and puddings such as sticky date pudding with iced parfait and apple and butterscotch sauce and iced coconut with dark chocolate, matcha green tea and warm chocolate sauce. *Benchmark main dish: rare-breed rib-eye steak with dripping chips and béarnaise sauce £30.00. Two-course evening meal £32.00.*

Free house ~ Licensees David and Fiona Howden ~ Real ale ~ Open 12-11 (midnight Sat); 12-10 Sun; closed Mon and first week Jan ~ Bar food 12-2.30, 6.30-9; 12.30-5 Sun ~ Restaurant ~ Children welcome ~ Dogs allowed in bar ~ Wi-fi ~ Bedrooms: /£180 *Recommended by Brian Glozier, John Harris, Jim King, Camilla and Jose Ferrera, Peter and Alison Steadman*

BUTLERS CROSS

SP8407   Map 4

Russell Arms ⚲ 🍺

(01296) 624411 – www.therussellarms.co.uk

Off A4010 S of Aylesbury, at Nash Lee roundabout; or off A413 in Wendover, passing station; Chalkshire Road; HP17 0TS

Attractive old pub in quiet village with access to Chiltern hills; good food, local ales, friendly landlord and seats on sunny terrace

This is a brick and flint tiled former coaching inn that was also the servants' quarters for nearby Chequers, the prime minister's country retreat. The simply furnished bar has stools and chairs around polished tables on new pale floorboards, higher stools against the counter and well kept Brakspears Bitter, Chiltern Beechwood and Malt Starry Nights on handpump, 16 wines by the glass and artisan gins, all served by welcoming staff; background music and board games. The two dining areas have an open fire with logs piled high to either side of it and a woodburner in an inglenook, an eclectic collection of wheelback, mate's and elegant high-backed and cushioned chairs around scrubbed tables on bare boards, some panelling, tartan curtains and fresh flowers. One wall has a blown-up photo of Chequers with smaller photos of past prime ministers. French windows lead to a suntrap terrace with teak furniture, and there are steps up to the garden with picnic-sets. The pub is well placed for walks in the Chilterns.

From a seasonal menu, the attractively presented food includes goats cheese mousse with golden beetroot, pomegranate and yoghurt crisp, grilled sardines with smoked dill mayonnaise, a pie of the day, chicken suprême with jerusalem artichoke, wild mushrooms and baby leeks, pork belly with black pudding, croquette and turnip, lamb rump with pearl barley, haggis and swede, and puddings such as double chocolate brownie with caramelised white chocolate ice-cream and lemongrass and mango pannacotta with kaffir lime sorbet and spiced pineapple; they also offer a lunchtime house dish with a drink for £10. *Benchmark main dish: pollack with samphire and brown crab, caper and herb butter £16.50. Two-course evening meal £23.00.*

Free house ~ Licensee James Penlington ~ Real ale ~ Open 10am-11pm; 12-10.30 Sun; 12-6 Sun in winter; closed Mon ~ Bar food 12-2.30, 6.30-9; 12-4 Sun ~ Restaurant ~ Children welcome ~ Dogs allowed in bar ~ Wi-fi *Recommended by Julian Thorpe, Valerie Sayer, Lorna and Jack Mulgrave, Holly and Tim Waite*

COLESHILL   SU9594   Map 4
Harte & Magpies
(01494) 726754 – www.magpiespub.com

E of village on A355 Amersham–Beaconsfield, by junction with Magpie Lane; HP7 0LU

Friendly and busy roadside dining pub with enjoyable food, well kept local ales and seats in big garden

A wide mix of customers use this popular roadside pub – from families (there's a sturdy wooden play area for children) to walkers and their dogs (plenty of nearby walks) and those keen on live music (see the website for dates); a classic car club holds meetings here on the second Tuesday of the month from April to September. The open-plan interior has a rambling collection of miscellaneous pews, high-backed booths and distinctive tables and chairs making for plenty of snug corners. Also, a profusion of patriotic antique prints and candles in bottles, and maybe Scrumpy Jack the labrador. Chiltern Pale Ale and Rebellion Smuggler on handpump and nice wines by the glass served by friendly staff. A terrace has picnic-sets by a tree picturesquely draped with wisteria and a big sloping informal garden has more trees and more picnic-sets.

As well as breakfasts (10-5, not Sunday), the wide choice of food includes baguettes (12-5), shell-on garlic prawns, devilled kidneys on toast, pizzas, pasta with spicy tomato sauce, gammon with egg and pineapple, pie of the day, lamb shank in red wine and rosemary sauce, burger with toppings and chips, and puddings such as apple crumble and sticky toffee pudding with custard or cream. *Benchmark main dish: beer-battered cod and chips £13.00. Two-course evening meal £15.00.*

Free house ~ Licensee Stephen Lever ~ Real ale ~ Open 11-11; 11-9 Sun ~ Bar food 12-9.30 (8 Sun) ~ Children welcome except on live music evenings ~ Dogs welcome ~ Wi-fi ~ Live music and comedy evenings *Recommended by Charlie Parker, David Lamb, Edward Edmonton, Brian and Susan Wylie*

We say if we know a pub has background music.

EASINGTON

SP6810 Map 4

Mole & Chicken 🌟 ♟ ⇦

(01844) 208387 – www.themoleandchicken.co.uk

From B4011 in Long Crendon follow Chearsley, Waddesdon signpost into Carters Lane opposite indian restaurant, then turn left into Chilton Road; HP18 9EY

Fine country views, an inviting interior, real ales and very good food and drink; bedrooms

The five ensuite bedrooms in this civilised inn are simply but elegantly furnished and breakfasts are very good – our readers enjoy staying here. The opened-up interior is arranged so that the different parts seem quite snug and self-contained without being cut off from the relaxed and sociable atmosphere. The heavily beamed bar curves around the serving counter in a sort of S-shape, and there are cream-cushioned farmhouse chairs around oak and pine tables on flagstones or tiles, a couple of dark leather sofas, church candles and good winter log fires. Chiltern Pale Ale and a changing guest from Chiltern on handpump, several wines by the glass and quite a few malt whiskies; background music. In warm weather try to bag a table on the raised terrace and decked area behind the creeper-clad building – the views over Buckinghamshire and Oxfordshire are lovely.

 As well as breakfasts (also offered to non-residents 7.30-9.30am weekdays; 8-10am weekends), the first class food using the best british produce includes lunchtime sandwiches, house-cured salmon with honey and mustard sauce, thai-spiced crispy duck salad, smoked free-range ham and eggs, fresh tagliatelle with creamed wild mushrooms and pine nuts, hake with samphire, tomato, clams and mussels, corn-fed chicken breast with a haggis stovie, kale and veal jus, ox cheek with truffle and parmesan chips, onion purée and roast carrots, and puddings such as raspberry crème brûlée and warm chocolate fondant with honeycomb ice-cream; they also offer a two-course set menu (not Friday evening or weekends). *Benchmark main dish: lamb rump with crushed potatoes, carrots and artichoke crisps £19.50. Two-course evening meal £24.00.*

Free house ~ Licensee Steve Bush ~ Real ale ~ Open 7.30am (8am weekends)-11pm ~ Bar food 12-2.30, 6.30-9.30; 12-3.30, 6-9 Sun ~ Children welcome ~ Wi-fi ~ Bedrooms: £95/£125
Recommended by Jo Garnett, Tim and Sarah Smythe-Brown, Richard Kennell, Beth Aldridge, Patricia and Anton Larkham

FINGEST

SU7791 Map 2

Chequers

(01491) 638335 – www.chequersfingest.com

Off B482 Marlow–Stokenchurch; RG9 6QD

Friendly, spotlessly kept old pub with big garden, real ales and interesting food

A unique twin-roofed Norman church tower – probably the nave of the original church – is opposite this 15th-c, white-shuttered brick and flint pub. The unaffected public bar has real country charm, and other neatly kept old-fashioned rooms are warm, cosy and traditional, with large open fires, horsebrasses, pewter tankards and pub team photographs on the walls. Brakspears Bitter and Jennings Golden Host on handpump alongside quite a few wines by the glass, several malt whiskies and farm cider; board games and a house cat and dog. French doors from the smart back dining extension open to a terrace (plenty of picnic-sets), which leads to the big, beautifully tended garden with fine views over the Hambleden Valley. This is good walking country with quiet pastures sloping up to beechwoods, and you can walk from here to other pubs in this chapter.

🍴 Well thought-of food includes lunchtime sandwiches, omelette arnold bennett, spicy king prawns, roasted red pepper and feta linguine, pork and leek sausages with onion rings, burger with toppings and fries, cod fillet with creamed leeks and pancetta, and puddings. *Benchmark main dish: steaks with a choice of sauce £17.50. Two-course evening meal £22.00.*

Brakspears ~ Tenants Jaxon and Emma Keedwell ~ Real ale ~ Open 12-3, 5.30-11; 12-11 Sat; 12-10.30 Sun; closed Mon ~ Bar food 12-2 (3 Sat, 4 Sun), 7-9 (9.30 Fri, Sat) ~ Restaurant ~ Children welcome ~ Dogs allowed in bar ~ Wi-fi *Recommended by Edward and William Johnston, Isobel Mackinlay, Donald Allsopp, Lenny and Ruth Walters*

FORTY GREEN   SU9291   Map 2

Royal Standard of England 🍺

(01494) 673382 – www.rsoe.co.uk

3.5 miles from M40 junction 2, via A40 to Beaconsfield, then follow sign to Forty Green, off B474 0.75 miles N of New Beaconsfield; keep going through village; HP9 1XT

Full of history and character, with fascinating antiques in rambling rooms, and good choice of drinks and food

It's really worth looking at the leaflet documenting this extraordinary pub's ancient history – it's been trading for nearly 900 years. The rambling rooms have some fine old features to look out for: huge black ship's timbers, lovely worn floors, carved oak panelling, roaring winter fires with handsomely decorated iron firebacks and cluttered mantelpieces – there's also a massive settle apparently built to fit the curved transom of an Elizabethan ship. Nooks and crannies are filled with a collection of antiques, including rifles, powder-flasks and bugles, ancient pewter and pottery tankards, lots of tarnished brass and copper, needlework samplers and richly coloured stained glass. Chiltern Pale Ale, Hardys & Hansons Olde Trip, Navigation Britannia and Windsor & Eton Conqueror and Guardsman on handpump, a carefully annotated list of bottled beers and malt whiskies, farm ciders, perry, somerset brandy and around a dozen wines by the glass. You can sit outside in a neatly hedged front rose garden or under the shade of a tree; look out for the red gargoyle on the wall facing the car park. The inn is used regularly for filming television programmes such as *Midsomer Murders*.

🍴 Tasty food includes lunchtime sandwiches and baguettes, gin and beetroot-cured salmon with horseradish purée, baked camembert with garlic and rosemary, vegetarian quiche of the day, lambs liver and bacon with onion gravy, cod and chips, steak and kidney pudding, pork belly with bubble and squeak, red cabbage and apple sauce, and puddings such as apple crumble and custard and treacle tart with ginger cream; they also offer a two- and three-course set lunch. *Benchmark main dish: chicken, leek and mushroom pie £15.00. Two-course evening meal £21.00.*

Free house ~ Licensee Matthew O'Keeffe ~ Real ale ~ Open 11am-11.30pm; 12-10.30 Sun ~ Bar food 12-9.30 ~ Children welcome ~ Dogs welcome ~ Wi-fi *Recommended by James Allsopp, Julie Braeburn, Roy Hoing, Susan and John Douglas, Paul Humphreys, Martin and Sue Neville, Charlie May*

FULMER   SU9985   Map 2

Black Horse 🏨 ♀

(01753) 663183 – www.theblackhorsefulmer.co.uk

Village signposted off A40 in Gerrards Cross, W of junction with A413; Windmill Road; SL3 6HD

Appealingly reworked dining pub, friendly and relaxed, with up-to-date food, exemplary service and pleasant garden; bedrooms

In a charming conservation village and next to the church, this is an extended and thoughtfully run 17th-c pub that is usefully open all day. There's a proper bar in the middle and two cosy areas to the left with low black beams, rugs on bare boards, settles and other solid pub furniture and several open log fires. Greene King IPA and London Glory and Morlands Original on handpump, 21 wines by the glass and 22 malt whiskies; staff are friendly and efficient even when pushed. Background music, TV. The main area on the right is set for dining and leads to the good-sized suntrap back terrace where there's a summer barbecue bar. The two bedrooms are stylish and well equipped.

 Some sort of good quality food is served all day: molasses-cured salmon with celeriac rémoulade, baked camembert with pineapple chutney (to share), smoky barbecue ribs with coleslaw and skinny fries, wild mushroom risotto, pork faggots with creamy bacon mash and cider sauce, poached haddock fishcake with poached egg, crispy bacon and hollandaise, chicken korma, and puddings such as apple and rhubarb crumble and home-made sorbet and ice-cream. *Benchmark main dish: beer-battered haddock and chips £14.75. Two-course evening meal £25.00.*

Greene King ~ Lease Jane Gaunt ~ Real ale ~ Open 8.30am-11pm; 12-10.30 Sun ~ Bar food 8.30am-9.30pm (10pm Fri, Sat; 12 7 Sun) ~ Restaurant ~ Children welcome ~ Dogs allowed in bar ~ Wi-fi ~ Bedrooms: /£130 *Recommended by Julian Thorpe, Luke Morgan, Sally Wright*

GRANBOROUGH
Crown
SP7625 Map 4

(01296) 670216 – www.thecrowngranborough.co.uk
Winslow Road; MK18 3NJ

Perfect in good weather with several seating areas and an outside bar and kitchen, and cosy in winter with open fires and beams

There's plenty of space for both eating and drinking in this extended former coaching inn. The main bar is a long room with painted beams, high chairs at the counter and at elbow tables and a fire at one end; a second bar has leather tub chairs, more painted beams and a comfortable feel. Fullers London Pride, Sharps Doom Bar and Vale Wychert on handpump and several wines by the glass, served by friendly staff. The restaurant is a lovely room with high ceilings and oak beams, farmhouse and other chairs around solid tables on wooden boards and a woodburning stove in a sizeable fireplace; a smaller room is more intimate and similarly furnished. In warm weather you can sit on cushioned rattan-style sofas on the terrace, at wooden tables and chairs under parasols on gravel or at picnic-sets on grass (where there's also a climbing frame) – and they have an outside kitchen with a pizza oven and barbecue.

Using carefully sourced, seasonal produce, the food includes chicken liver parfait with onion chutney and poached pear, seared scallops with celeriac purée, black pudding and sauce vierge, sharing boards, butternut squash, spinach and pumpkin seed risotto with parmesan, venison, juniper and red wine pie, rabbit pasta with wild mushrooms, cream and brandy, molasses lamb loin, slow-cooked shoulder and chickpeas wrapped in filo with pistachios and yoghurt, and puddings such as golden syrup crème brûlée with orange shortbread and dark chocolate and salted caramel tart with honeycomb ice-cream. *Benchmark main dish: chicken breast and confit leg with mushroom cream sauce £15.00. Two-course evening meal £21.00.*

Free house ~ Licensee Andy Judge ~ Real ale ~ Open 12-11 (5-9 Mon); 12-8 Sun; closed
Mon lunchtime ~ Bar food 12-2.30, 5-9.30; 12-5 Sun; not Mon ~ Restaurant ~ Children
welcome ~ Dogs allowed in bar ~ Wi-fi *Recommended by John and Abigail Prescott,
Nicola and Nigel Matthews, Peter Pilbeam*

GREAT MISSENDEN
Nags Head

SP9000 Map 4

(01494) 862200 – www.nagsheadbucks.com

Old London Road, E – beyond Abbey; HP16 0DG

**Well run and pretty inn with beamed bars, an open fire, a good range
of drinks and modern cooking; bedrooms**

This is a quietly civilised dining pub – but it started life as three small
cottages built in the 15th c. There's a low-beamed area on the left, a loftier
part on the right, a mix of small pews, dining chairs and tables on carpet,
Quentin Blake prints on cream walls and a log fire in a handsome fireplace.
Rebellion IPA and a couple of guests such as Chiltern Beechwood Bitter
and Malt Missenden Pale on handpump from the unusual bar counter (the
windows behind face the road), 26 wines by the glass from an extensive list
and half a dozen vintage Armagnacs. There's an outside dining area beneath
a pergola and seats on the extensive back lawn. The beamed bedrooms are
well equipped and comfortable, and the breakfasts are very good. Roald Dahl
used this as his local and the Roald Dahl Museum & Story Centre is just a
short walk away.

Food is highly rated and includes breakfast for non-residents (8-10am), foie
gras terrine with smoked duck breast and fig roulade, white crab meat with
home-smoked salmon on blinis with chive cream, a vegetarian dish of the day, chicken
pie with rose wine gravy, wild boar with apple sausages with chive mash and red wine
gravy, medallion of sea trout with a green curry and chardonnay cream, lamb cannon
with parsnip croquette and marjoram jus, and puddings such as white chocolate and
raspberry jelly cheesecake with mixed berry and Chambord compote and lemon tart
with cassis sorbet. *Benchmark main dish: veal kidneys in a herb, cream and brandy
sauce £17.95. Two-course evening meal £24.00.*

Free house ~ Licensee Adam Michaels ~ Real ale ~ Open 11-11 (midnight Sat); 11-10.30
Sun ~ Bar food 12-2.30, 6.30-9.30; 12-7 Sun ~ Restaurant ~ Children welcome ~ Dogs
allowed in bar ~ Wi-fi ~ Bedrooms: £75/£95 *Recommended by Martin Day, Gerry and Rosemary
Dobson, Dan and Nicki Barton, Amanda Shipley*

HEDGERLEY
White Horse ★ ◀ £

SU9687 Map 2

(01753) 643225

*2.4 miles from M40 junction 2; at exit roundabout take Slough turn-off following
alongside M40; after 1.5 miles turn right at T junction into Village Lane; SL2 3UY*

**Convivial old place with lots of beers, home-made lunchtime food
and a cheery mix of customers**

This old-fashioned and charming country gem does get packed, particularly
at weekends. Most are here to enjoy the fine range of real ales, which
might include Rebellion IPA and up to seven daily changing guests, sourced
from all over the country and tapped straight from casks kept in a room
behind the tiny hatch counter. Their Easter, May, Spring and August bank
holiday beer festivals (they can get through about 130 beers during the May
event) are highlights of the local calendar. This marvellous range of drinks
extends to craft ales in cans or bottles, three farm ciders, 12 wines by the

glass, a dozen malt whiskies and winter mulled wine. The cottagey main bar has plenty of unspoilt character with beams, brasses and exposed brickwork, low wooden tables, standing timbers, jugs, ballcocks and other bric-a-brac, a log fire, and a good few leaflets and notices about village events. A little flagstoned public bar on the left has darts, shove-ha'penny and board games. A canopied extension leads out to the garden where there are tables, occasional barbecues and lots of hanging baskets; a few tables in front of the building overlook the quiet road. Good walks nearby and the pub is handy for the Church Wood RSPB reserve.

🍴 Lunchtime-only bar food includes good sandwiches, a salad bar with home-cooked quiches and cold meats, changing hot dishes such as soup, sausage or lamb casserole, and proper puddings such as plum sponge and bread and butter pudding. *Benchmark main dish: pie of the day £7.50.*

Free house ~ Licensees Doris Hobbs and Kevin Brooker ~ Real ale ~ Open 11-2.30, 5-11; 11-11 Sat; 12-10.30 Sun ~ Bar food 12-2 (2.30 weekends) ~ Children allowed in canopied extension area ~ Dogs allowed in bar ~ Wi-fi *Recommended by Dave Braisted, Roy Hoing, Len and Lilly Dowson, Val and Malcolm Travers, Tom and Lorna Harding, Susan and John Douglas*

LITTLE MARLOW
Queens Head 🌟

SU8787 Map 2

(01628) 482927 – www.marlowslittlesecret.co.uk
Village signposted off A4155 E of Marlow near Kings Head; bear right into Pound Lane cul-de-sac; SL7 3SR

Charmingly tucked-away country pub with good food and ales, friendly staff and appealing garden

This is a pretty tiled cottage – just before the church and opposite the manor house – with a friendly, unpretentious main bar. This has simple but comfortable furniture on polished boards and leads back to a sizeable squarish carpeted dining extension with good solid tables. Throughout are old local photographs on cream or maroon walls, panelled dados painted brown or sage, and lighted candles. On the right is a small, quite separate, low-ceilinged public bar with Fullers London Pride, Rebellion IPA and Sharps Doom Bar on handpump, several wines by the glass, quite a range of whiskies and good coffee; neatly dressed efficient staff and unobtrusive background music. On a summer's day, the front garden is a decided plus, though not large: sheltered and neatly planted, it has teak tables and quite closely arranged picnic-sets, and white-painted metal furniture in a little wickerwork bower.

🌟 Quickly changing food from seasonal menus includes lunchtime sandwiches, haddock and crab cake with lemongrass broth and lemon crème fraîche, rabbit and leek strudel with parma ham and mustard jus, artichoke, spinach and mushroom lasagne with red pepper sauce, calves liver with mash and onion and ginger jam, hake with sweetcorn hash, grilled aubergine and dill cream, venison suet pudding with truffle mash and port jus, and puddings such as sticky toffee pudding with banana ice-cream and Baileys crème brûlée. *Benchmark main dish: beer-battered haddock £11.95. Two-course evening meal £20.00.*

Punch ~ Lease Daniel O'Sullivan ~ Real ale ~ Open 11-11; 11-10 Sun ~ Bar food 12-2.30, 6.30-9.30; 12-4, 6.30-9.30 weekends ~ Restaurant ~ Children welcome ~ Wi-fi
Recommended by Peter Andrews, Bernard Stradling, Anne Taylor, Alexandra and Richard Clay

---

The star-on-a-plate award, 🌟, distinguishes pubs where the food is of exceptional quality. The knife-and-fork symbol just means the pub serves food.

LITTLE MISSENDEN

SU9298   Map 4

Crown ✦ £

(01494) 862571 – www.thecrownlittlemissenden.co.uk

*Crown Lane, SE end of village, which is signposted off A413 W of Amersham;
HP7 0RD*

**Long-serving licensees and pubby feel in little country cottage, with
several real ales and straightforward food; attractive garden**

For over 90 years, the same friendly family have been in charge here.
It's a traditional brick cottage with bustling bars that are more spacious
than they might first appear – and immaculately kept. There are old red
floor tiles on the left, oak parquet on the right, built-in wall seats, studded
red leatherette chairs and a few small tables and a winter fire. Oakham
JHB, Otter Bitter, St Austell Tribute and Timothy Taylors Boltmaker on
handpump or tapped from the cask, farm cider, summer Pimms and several
malt whiskies; darts and board games. The large attractive sheltered garden
behind has picnic-sets and other tables, and there are also seats out in
front. Bedrooms are in a converted barn (continental breakfasts in your
room only). Dogs may be allowed inside if well behaved. No children. The
interesting church in the pretty village is well worth a visit.

Honest lunchtime-only food (not Sunday) includes their famous bucks bite,
sandwiches, cornish pasty with baked beans, steak in ale or chicken and
mushroom pie, smoked haddock and spring onion fishcakes with a sweet chilli dip.
Benchmark main dish: sausage and mash with mushroom gravy £7.95.

Free house ~ Licensees Trevor and Carolyn How ~ Real ale ~ Open 11-2.30, 6-11; 12-3,
7-10.30 Sun ~ Bar food 12-2; not Sun ~ Wi-fi ~ Bedrooms: /£85 *Recommended by Roy Hoing,
William Slade, David Lamb, Edward May*

LONG CRENDON

SP6908   Map 4

Eight Bells ✦

(01844) 208244 – www.8bellspub.com

*High Street, off B4011 N of Thame; car park entrance off Chearsley Road, not 'Village
roads only'; HP18 9AL*

**Good beers and sensibly priced seasonal food in nicely traditional
village pub with charming garden**

This was originally called the Five Bells – until the church got eight bells
in 1771. The little bare-boards bar on the left has Banks's Sunbeam,
Ringwood Razorback, XT Four and a guest beer on handpump, 16 wines by
the glass, a range of gins and three farm ciders; service is cheerful. A bigger
low-ceilinged room on the right has a log fire, daily papers and a pleasantly
haphazard mix of tables and simple seats on ancient red and black tiles; one
snug little hidey-hole is devoted to the local morris men – frequent visitors.
Board games, TV and background music. The small back garden is a joy in
summer when there are well spaced picnic-sets among a colourful variety of
shrubs and flowers; aunt sally. The interesting old village is known to many
from TV's *Midsomer Murders*. Sister pub is the Black Boy in Oving.

Fair priced food includes sandwiches, garlic and chilli prawn cakes with avocado
dip, crispy fried lamb and mint croquettes with greek salad, spinach, feta and
sun-dried tomato strudel, pizzas (also to take away), honey-roast ham and free-range
eggs, beer-battered fish and chips, barbecue rack of ribs with coleslaw and skin-on
fries, confit duck leg with vegetable fricassée in tomato and herb sauce, and puddings
such as white chocolate and raspberry crème brûlée and rhubarb and ginger summer

pudding. *Benchmark main dish: steak burger with toppings and chips £13.25. Two-course evening meal £22.00.*

Free house ~ Licensee Paul Mitchell ~ Real ale ~ Open 12-11; 12-10 Sun ~ Bar food 12-9; 12-4 (pizzas till 8pm) Sun ~ Restaurant ~ Children welcome ~ Dogs welcome ~ Regular events; see website *Recommended by Ian Duncan, Peter Brix, Martin Jones, Elizabeth and Bill Humphries, Jill and Dick Archer*

OVING — Black Boy

SP7821   Map 4

(01296) 641258 – www.theblackboyoving.co.uk

Off A413 N of Aylesbury; HP22 4HN

Recently refurbished and reopened, partly 16th-c pub with friendly owners, popular food, local ales and lovely views from spacious garden

Seats and tables on spacious sloping lawns and the raised terrace behind this extended and recently refurbished 16th-c brick and timbered pub have expansive views of the Vale of Aylesbury; not surprisingly, it's best to arrive early on a sunny day. Inside, the dining rooms and bar are linked by brick arches and have beams, log fires (one in a huge inglenook), wooden chairs around tables of all sizes on bare boards or original black and red tiles, sofas and settles with scatter cushions, books on shelves and prints and photos on pale walls. Friendly staff serve Chiltern Beechwood Bitter, Leighton Buzzard Narrow Gauge and XT Four on handpump, nine wines by the glass, farm cider and a good range of spirits. Sister pub is the Eight Bells in Long Crendon.

A good choice of pleasing food includes toasted panini, beetroot and orange gravadlax with fennel salad, lamb samosa with minted yoghurt, pizzas (to eat here or take away), roasted aubergine stuffed with lightly spiced couscous topped with grilled halloumi and baba ganoush, thai green chicken curry, rack of ribs with skin-on chips, lamb rump with peas in a tomato and dill sauce, and puddings such as eton mess and peach tarte tatin with chantilly cream. *Benchmark main dish: burger with toppings, burger sauce and fries £13.25. Two-course evening meal £19.25.*

Free house ~ Licensee Paul Mitchell ~ Real ale ~ Open 12-11; 12-6 Sun ~ Bar food 12-9; 12-4 Sun ~ Children welcome ~ Dogs welcome ~ Wi-fi ~ Quiz last Tues of month
Recommended by Chloe and Tim Hodge, Martino and Fabio Lockley, Miles Green

STOKE MANDEVILLE — Bell 🍽 ♀

SP8310   Map 4

(01296) 612434 – www.bellstokemandeville.co.uk

Lower Road; HP22 5XA

Friendly landlord and staff, a fine choice of drinks, interesting food and seats outside

The atmosphere in the interconnected bar and dining areas here is relaxed, and you'll get a friendly welcome from the hands-on landlord. There are flagstones or polished pine floorboards, prints, drawings and maps of local interest plus hunting prints on the walls above a dark blue dado, and background music and board games. High stools line the counter where they keep Wells Bombardier and Youngs Bitter on handpump and 20 wines (including sweet wines) by the glass; there are some equally high stools and tables opposite. Throughout are high-backed cushioned wooden and farmhouse chairs, wall settles with scatter cushions, and rustic benches around a medley of tables, some painted beams and a woodburning stove; a snug alcove has just one table surrounded by cushioned wall seats. The little side terrace has picnic-sets and there are more on grass beside a weeping silver birch.

A good choice of tasty food includes smoked salmon mousse with dill cucumber, pigeon breast with black pudding, pear and watercress salad, sausages of the day with onion gravy, wild mushroom, pea and broad bean pasta with tomato sauce and herb crumb, indian-spiced mackerel with roast squash, couscous and cucumber raita, venison bourguignon with root vegetable hash, and puddings such as passion-fruit crème brûlée and chocolate marquise with champagne sorbet and orange syrup. *Benchmark main dish: pork belly, chorizo and butter bean cassoulet £14.95. Two-course evening meal £20.50.*

Distinct Pub Company ~ Lease James Penlington ~ Real ale ~ Open 10am-11pm; 12-10.30 Sun ~ Bar food 12-3, 6-9; 12-9 Fri-Sun ~ Restaurant ~ Children welcome ~ Dogs allowed in bar ~ Wi-fi *Recommended by Ruth May, David Longhurst, David Lamb, Nicola and Stuart Parsons, Kerry and Guy Trooper*

Also Worth a Visit in Buckinghamshire

Besides the fully inspected pubs, you might like to try these pubs that have been recommended to us and described by readers. Do tell us what you think of them: feedback@goodguides.com

AMERSHAM SU9597
Elephant & Castle (01494) 721049
High Street; HP7 0DT Refurbished twin-gabled low-beamed local, good value tasty food including sharing platters, stone-baked pizzas and burgers, Sun roasts, three well kept ales such as Sambrooks and Sharps from U-shaped counter, quick friendly service, woodburner in large brick fireplace, conservatory; garden behind, children and dogs welcome, open (and food) all day. *(David and Charlotte Green)*

AMERSHAM SU9597
Kings Arms (01494) 725722
High Street; HP7 0DJ Picture-postcard timbered inn (dates from the 1400s) in charming street, lots of heavy beams and snug alcoves, big inglenook, Brakspears, Rebellion and a guest, over a dozen wines by the glass and good range of enjoyable food from sandwiches up, afternoon teas, friendly helpful service, restaurant; children and dogs (in bar) welcome, 34 bedrooms, garden behind, open all day, food all day weekends. *(Guy Henderson)*

ASHERIDGE SP9404
Blue Ball (01494) 758305
Braziers End; HP5 2UX Small open-plan country pub with light airy décor, generous helpings of enjoyable good value food cooked to order including daily specials, well kept Courage Best, Fullers London Pride and Youngs Bitter, real cider, friendly landlady and staff; children (till 6pm) and dogs welcome, large well maintained back garden,

good Chilterns walking country, open all day, no food Sun or Mon evenings. *(Roy Hoing, Mrs P Sumner)*

ASTON ABBOTTS SP8519
Royal Oak (01296) 681262
Off A418 NE of Aylesbury; Wingrave Road; HP22 4LT Welcoming part-thatched beamed pub, generous helpings of enjoyable freshly made food, up to four real ales; sunny back garden, bedrooms, quite handy for Ascott House (NT). *(David Lamb)*

ASTON CLINTON SP8811
Bell (01296) 632777
London Road; HP22 5HP Comfortably refurbished old Mitchells & Butlers village inn-restaurant; good choice of enjoyable food from sandwiches and sharing boards up, Fullers London Pride, Sharps Doom Bar and a guest, plenty of wines by the glass including champagne, friendly efficient service; children welcome, tables out under trees, 11 bedrooms, car park over the road, open (and food) all day from 8am. *(John Poulter, David Lamb)*

AYLESBURY SP8114
Hop Pole (01296) 482129
Bicester Road; HP19 9AZ Friendly well looked-after end of terrace pub, own Aylesbury Brewhouse beers (brewed behind) along with Vale and several guests, also traditional cider and enjoyable fairly priced food including sharing platters and grills, back restaurant; seats out at front behind metal fence, open all day Fri-Sun, closed Mon lunchtime. *(Pesto)*

BEACHAMPTON
SP7736
Bell (01908) 418373
Main Street; MK19 6DX Big low-beamed pub with pleasant view down attractive streamside village street, updated interior with woodburner dividing bar from dining area, popular generously served food including weekday set lunch and Tues steak night, up to four changing ales (often local Silverstone), good friendly service; children welcome, large garden with paved terrace, open all day (till 8pm Sun). *(Graham and Carol Parker, Jess and George Cowley)*

BEACONSFIELD
SU9588
Hope & Champion (01494) 685530
M40, Beaconsfield Services; HP9 2SE UK's first pub (Wetherspoons) in a motorway service area; spacious spotlessly clean modern interior on two floors, five real ales including Sharps Doom Bar and enjoyable food from breakfast on, good fast service; TVs, free wi-fi; children welcome, no dogs inside, disabled access to ground floor only, seats out overlooking lake with fountain, open (and food) all day from 6am.
(Ross Balaam)

BEACONSFIELD
SU9490
Royal Saracens (01494) 674119
1 mile from M40 junction 2; London End (A40); HP9 2JH Former coaching inn with striking timbered façade and well updated open-plan interior; comfortable chairs around light wood tables, wood and tiled floors, massive beams and timbers in one corner, log fires, welcoming young staff, wide choice of enjoyable food from sandwiches and sharing plates up, Weds evening fixed-price menu for two (includes bottle of wine), well kept ales such as Fullers London Pride and Sharps Doom Bar, craft kegs and plenty of wines by the glass, large back restaurant; children welcome, attractive sheltered courtyard, open (and food) all day, busy at weekends when best to book.
(Jim King)

BLEDLOW RIDGE
SU7997
Boot (01494) 481499
Chinnor Road; HP14 4AW Welcoming village pub with fresh modern décor, good food from sandwiches, sharing plates and pub favourites up, well kept Rebellion ales and Sharps Doom Bar, several wines by the glass from extensive list, dining room with exposed rafters and large brick fireplace; background music; children and dogs welcome, terrace and in sizeable lawned garden, closed Mon, otherwise open all day (till 8pm Sun).
(David Lamb)

BOURNE END
SU8987
Bounty (01628) 520056
Cock Marsh, actually across the river along the Cookham towpath, but shortest walk – still about 0.25 miles – is from Bourne End, over the railway bridge; SL8 5RG Welcoming take-us-as-you-find-us pub tucked away in outstanding setting on bank of the Thames and accessible only by foot or boat; collection of flags on ceiling and jumble of other bits and pieces, well kept Rebellion ales from boat counter, basic standard food including children's meals, back dining area, darts and bar billiards; background music inside and out; dirty dogs and muddy walkers welcome, picnic-sets with parasols on front terrace, play area to right, open all day in summer (may be boat trips), just weekends in winter and closes early if quiet. *(Anne Taylor)*

BUCKINGHAM
SP6933
Villiers (01280) 822444
Castle Street; MK18 1BS Pub part of this large comfortable hotel with own courtyard entrance; big inglenook log fire, panelling and stripped masonry in flagstoned bar, beers from Hook Norton and Black Sheep, reliably good food from shortish menu, competent friendly staff, sofas and armchairs in more formal front lounges, restaurant with two large tropical fish tanks; children welcome till 9pm, no dogs, terrace tables, open all day.
(Edward Edmonton)

CHALFONT ST GILES
SU9895
Ivy House (01494) 872184
A413 S; HP8 4RS Old brick and flint coaching inn with tasty home-made food including good value set lunch, Fullers ales and a guest, friendly staff, U-shaped bar with wood or tiled floor, log fire, back beamed and flagstoned restaurant; background and some live music, quiz first Thurs of month, free wi-fi; children welcome, some seats out under covered front part by road, pleasant terrace and sloping garden, five comfortable bedrooms, good hearty breakfast, open all day (till 8pm Sun). *(Mr and Mrs J Watkins, Tracey and Stephen Groves)*

CHEARSLEY
SP7110
Bell (01844) 208077
The Green; HP18 0DJ Cosy traditional thatched and beamed pub on attractive village green, Fullers beers and good wines by the glass, enjoyable sensibly priced home-made food (not Sun or Mon evenings), efficient friendly service, inglenook with big woodburner; quiz (first Sun of month), bingo (first Tues); children in eating area, dogs welcome, plenty of tables in spacious back garden with heated terrace and play area. *(David Lamb)*

CHENIES
TQ0198
Bedford Arms (01923) 283301
2 miles from M25 junction 18; A404 towards Amersham, then village signposted on right; Chesham Road; WD3 6EQ Popular country-house hotel with bright modernised front bar, good food here or in more formal oak-panelled restaurant,

friendly efficient staff, Fullers London Pride, Tring Side Pocket for a Toad and a guest, decent choice of wines by the glass; tables on attractive front terrace and in lovely garden behind with mature oaks, 18 bedrooms, enjoyable walks, open all day. *(Brian Glozier, Graham and Pam Winton, Richard Kennell)*

CHENIES TQ0298
Red Lion (01923) 282722
2 miles from M25 junction 18; A404 towards Amersham, then village signposted on right; Chesham Road; WD3 6ED The long-serving landlord at this popular village pub has retired and renovations by new owners were underway as we went to press – news please.

CHESHAM SP9604
Black Horse (01494) 784656
Vale Road, N off A416 in Chesham; HP5 3NS Extended black-beamed country pub refurbished under newish owners; well liked pubby food (all day Sat, till 6pm Sun) from sandwiches up, Charles Wells ales with guests such as Haresfoot, good friendly service, inglenook log fire; fortnightly Sun quiz, some acoustic live music; children welcome, picnic-sets out in front and on back lawn, closed Mon, otherwise open all day. *(Edward Edmonton)*

CHESHAM SP9501
Queens Head (01494) 778690
Church Street; HP5 1JD Popular well run Fullers corner pub, two traditional beamed bars with scrubbed tables and log fires, their ales and a guest kept well, good thai food along with modest range of pub staples, restaurant, friendly staff and chatty locals; sports TV, free wi-fi; children welcome, tables in small courtyard used by smokers, next to little River Chess, open all day. *(Jim King)*

CLIFTON REYNES SP9051
Robin Hood (01234) 711574
Off back Road Emberton–Newton Blossomville; no-through road; MK46 5DR Stone-built 16th-c village pub with welcoming licensees and good friendly service, nice range of well liked food including wood-fired pizzas, three real ales such as St Austell, dark beams, woodburner in small lounge's inglenook, dining conservatory; bar billiards and darts; children and dogs (in bar) welcome, large recently revamped garden with terrace, summer barbecues and donkeys, riverside walks to Olney, closed Mon. *(Anne Taylor)*

COLNBROOK TQ0277
Ostrich (01753) 682628
1.25 miles from M4 junction 5 via A4/ B3378, then 'village only' road; High Street; SL3 0JZ Historic timbered inn (12th-c origins) with gruesome history – tales of over 60 murders; recently refurbished interior blending modern furnishings with oak beams and open fireplaces, three Shepherd Neame ales and good choice of wines, enjoyable sensibly priced food from sandwiches and pub favourites up, friendly service, restaurant; children welcome, 11 new bedrooms, teak furniture in courtyard, open (and food) all day including breakfast/ brunch for non-residents. *(David and Charlotte Green)*

CUBLINGTON SP8322
Unicorn (01296) 681261
High Street opposite church; LU7 0LQ Extended low-beamed 17th-c pub incorporating small village shop; popular sensibly priced food including set menu choices and Thurs steak night, Brakspears, Fullers, XT and a guest (May, Aug beer festivals), several wines by the glass, good friendly service, handsome fireplace at one end; Mon quiz and some live music; children welcome, dogs in bar, big enclosed garden behind, open all day (till 7pm Sun), breakfast served Sat from 9.30am. *(Graham and Carol Parker)*

CUDDINGTON SP7311
★ Crown (01844) 292222
Spurt Street; off A418 Thame–Aylesbury; HP18 0BB Thatched cottage with chatty mix of customers and nice atmosphere, comfortable pubby furnishings including cushioned settles in two low-beamed linked rooms, big inglenook log fire, well kept Fullers and guests, around 20 wines by the glass and good home-cooked food (not Sun evening) from shortish menu, competent friendly service, carpeted two-room back dining area with country kitchen chairs around mix of tables; children welcome; neat side terrace with modern garden furniture and planters, picnic-sets in front. *(Mike Kavaney, Mr and Mrs J Watkins, Graham and Carol Parker, David Lamb)*

DENHAM TQ0487
Green Man (01895) 832760
Village Road; next to the Swan; UB9 5BH Welcoming 18th-c red-brick pub in centre of this lovely village next to the Swan; refurbished beamed bar with flagstones and log fire, well kept Fullers, Rebellion, Sharps and a guest, good choice of popular food from baguettes up (surcharge if you pay by card), cheerful efficient service, conservatory dining extension; free wi-fi; children and dogs welcome, sunny back terrace and garden, open all day. *(Taff Thomas, David Lamb)*

DENHAM TQ0487
★ Swan (01895) 832085
Village signed from M25 junction 16; UB9 5BH Wisteria-clad Georgian dining pub (Little Gems group); stylishly furnished bars with nice mix of antique and old-fashioned chairs at solid tables, heavily draped curtains, log fires, Rebellion IPA and a guest, good sensibly priced wine list

and decent range of spirits, well liked food (all day Fri-Sun) including blackboard specials and Sat brunch, friendly efficient staff; background music, daily papers, free wi-fi; children and dogs (in bar) welcome, extensive floodlit back garden with sheltered terrace, open all day. *(David Jackman, Taff Thomas, Edward Mirzoeff, Nigel and Sue Foster)*

DINTON SP7610
Seven Stars (01296) 749000
Signed off A418 Aylesbury–Thame, near Gibraltar turn-off; Stars Lane; HP17 8UL Pretty 16th-c community-owned pub run by french landlady and popular locally; inglenook bar, beamed lounge and dining room, well kept Fullers, Rebellion and Vale, extensive wine list on two blackboards, good fairly priced food cooked to order from pub staples up including some french influences, friendly service; children welcome, no dogs inside, tables in sheltered garden with terrace, pleasant village, closed Sun evening. *(Mr and Mrs J Watkins, David Lamb, Graham and Carol Parker)*

DORNEY SU9279
Palmer Arms (01628) 666612
2.7 miles from M4 junction 7, via B3026; Village Road; SL4 6QW Modernised and extended dining pub in attractive conservation village, good popular food (best to book) from snacks and pub favourites to more restaurant dishes, friendly efficient service, Greene King ales, lots of wines by the glass (interesting list) and good coffee, open fires in civilised front bar and back dining room; background music, daily newspapers; children and dogs (in certain areas) welcome, disabled facilities, terrace overlooking mediterranean-feel garden, enclosed play area, nice riverside walks nearby, open (and food) all day. *(Anne Taylor)*

DORNEY SU9279
Pineapple (01628) 662353
Lake End Road; 2.4 miles from M4 junction 7; left on A4 then left on B3026; SL4 6QS Nicely old-fashioned pub handy for Dorney Court (where the first english pineapple was grown in 1661); shiny low Anaglypta ceilings, black-panelled dados, leather chairs around sturdy country tables (one very long, another in big bow window), woodburner and pretty little fireplace, china pineapples and other decorations on shelves in one of three cottagey carpeted linked rooms on left, well kept Black Sheep, Fullers London Pride and a beer named for the pub (actually Marstons EPA), over 1,000 varieties of sandwiches in five different fresh breads, roasts on Sun; background music, games machine; children and dogs welcome, rustic seats on roadside verandah, round picnic-sets in garden, fairy-lit decking under oak tree, some motorway noise, open (and food) all day. *(Edward Edmonton)*

EMBERTON SP8849
Bell & Bear (01234) 711565
Off A509 Olney–Newport Pagnell; High Street; MK46 5DH Old stone-built village pub with good interesting food cooked by landlord-chef including set lunch and tapas-style bar menu (Weds-Sat), four well kept changing ales, craft beers, real cider and good selection of other drinks, friendly efficient staff, bar with log fire and hood skittles, restaurant; well behaved children and dogs (in bar) welcome, garden tables, open all day Fri-Sun, closed Mon lunchtime, no food Sun evening, Mon, Tues lunchtime. *(David and Charlotte Green)*

FLACKWELL HEATH SU8889
Crooked Billet (01628) 521216
Off A404; Sheepridge Lane; SL7 3SG Steps up to cosily old-fashioned 16th-c pub, Brakspears and Youngs ales, reasonably priced traditional lunchtime food including sandwiches, charming landlord and friendly staff, eating area spread pleasantly through alcoves, low black beams and good open fire; lovely cottagey garden with nice views (beyond road), walks nearby. *(Andrew and Michele Revell)*

FRIETH SU7990
Prince Albert (01494) 881683
Off B482 SW of High Wycombe; RG9 6PY Friendly cottagey Chilterns local with low black beams and joists, high-backed settles, big black stove in inglenook and log fire in larger area on right, decent lunchtime food from sandwiches up (also Fri and Sat evenings – they ask you to book on Sat), well kept Brakspears ales; quiz every other Tues, folk night last Weds of month; children and dogs welcome, nicely planted informal side garden with views of woods and fields, good walks, open all day. *(Edward Edmonton)*

GAWCOTT SP6831
Crown (01280) 822322
Hillesden Road; MK18 4JF Welcoming black-beamed village pub with good value popular food including carvery (Weds and Sun), three well kept ales such as Sharps Doom Bar from herringbone brick counter, restaurant area; background music, Sky TV, pool; children welcome, long back garden with swings, open all day (no food Sun evening, Mon). *(Philip Kingsbury)*

GERRARDS CROSS TQ0089
★ Three Oaks (01753) 899016
Austenwood Lane, just NW of junction with Kingsway (B416); SL9 8NL Civilised dining pub facing Austenwood Common, efficient neatly dressed staff, two-room front bar with fireside bookshelves, tartan wing armchairs, sturdy wall settles and comfortable banquettes, well kept Fullers, Rebellion and several wines by the glass, dining part with three linked rooms,

popular highly regarded food including short set menu; soft background music, free wi-fi; children welcome, sturdy wooden tables on flagstoned side terrace, open all day. *(Simon Collett-Jones, David Lamb)*

GREAT BRICKHILL SP9029
Red Lion (01525) 261715
Ivy Lane; MK17 9AH Roadside village pub refurbished under newish licensees, enjoyable fairly traditional food (not Sun evening), a couple of Caledonian ales and a guest, good friendly service, log fire in small bar, woodburner in restaurant; background music, quiz nights; children and dogs welcome, lovely views over Buckinghamshire and beyond from enclosed back lawn, closed Mon, otherwise open all day. *(Jo and Belinda Smart)*

GREAT HAMPDEN SP8401
★ Hampden Arms (01494) 488255
W of Great Missenden, off A4128; HP16 9RQ Friendly village pub opposite cricket pitch, good mix of locals and visitors, comfortably furnished rooms (back one more rustic with big woodburner), well kept Rebellion IPA and a couple of guests, Addlestone's cider and several wines by the glass from small corner bar, enjoyable reasonably priced pubby food including one or two greek dishes, cheerful efficient service; children and dogs welcome, seats in tree-sheltered garden, good Hampden Common walks, open all day Sun. *(Ross Balaam, David Lamb)*

GREAT KINGSHILL SU8798
★ Red Lion (01494) 711262
A4128 N of High Wycombe; HP15 6EB Welcoming village pub across from cricket green; contemporary décor and relaxed informal atmosphere, well cooked brasserie-style food including fixed-price menu (Tues-Sat lunchtime, Tues-Thurs early evening), local beers such as Rebellion and good value wine list, 'lobby' and cosy little flagstoned bar with leather tub chairs by log fire, spacious candlelit dining room; well behaved children welcome, at few seats out at front and behind, closed Sun evening, Mon. *(Roy Hoing, David Lamb)*

GREAT MISSENDEN SP8901
★ Cross Keys (01494) 865373
High Street; HP16 0AU Friendly and relaxed village pub dating from the 16th c, unspoilt beamed bar divided by standing timbers, traditional furnishings including high-backed settle, log-effect gas fire in huge fireplace, well kept Fullers ales and often an unusual guest, enjoyable fairly priced food (not Sun evening) from sandwiches and pizzas up (special diets catered for), cheerful helpful staff, spacious beamed restaurant; free wi-fi; children and dogs welcome, picnic-sets on back terrace, open all day. *(Edward Edmonton)*

GROVE SP9122
★ Grove Lock (01525) 380940
Pub signed off B488, on left just S of A505 roundabout (S of Leighton Buzzard); LU7 0QU Overlooking Grand Union Canal and usefully open all day; open-plan with lofty high-raftered pitched roof in bar, squashy brown leather sofas on oak boards, eclectic mix of tables and chairs including butcher's block tables by bar, big open-standing log fire, steps down to original lock-keeper's cottage (now three-room restaurant area), enjoyable food from sandwiches to daily specials, Fullers ales and lots of wines by the glass; background music, free wi-fi; children welcome, seats on canopied deck and waterside lawn by Lock 28. *(David Lamb)*

HADDENHAM SP7408
Green Dragon (01844) 292826
Village signposted off A418 and A4129, E/NE of Thame; then follow Church End signs into Churchway; HP17 8AA Shuttered 18th-c village dining pub, open-plan modernised interior with two log fires, well kept ales such as Loddon and Loose Cannon, decent wines by the glass and good interesting food from chargrilled sandwiches up, friendly service; children, dogs and muddy boots welcome, sheltered terrace and appealing garden, open all day (till 9pm Sun). *(Douglas Harrison)*

HAMBLEDEN SU7886
★ Stag & Huntsman (01491) 571227
Off A4155 Henley–Marlow; RG9 6RP Friendly brick and flint pub in pretty Chilterns village; chatty locals in busy little bar, built-in cushioned wall seats and simple furniture on bare boards, Rebellion IPA, Sharps Doom Bar and a couple of guests, several wines by the glass, sizeable open-plan room with armchairs by woodburner, dining room with good mix of wooden tables and chairs, hunting prints and other pictures on floral wallpaper, popular food from breakfast on, good service; background music, free wi-fi, darts; children and dogs (in bar) welcome, country garden and nice walks nearby, comfortable bedrooms, open all day. *(Simon Collett-Jones, James Allsopp, Susan and John Douglas, Paul Humphreys)*

HUGHENDEN VALLEY SU8697
★ Harrow (01494) 564105
Warrendene Road, off A4128 N of High Wycombe; HP14 4LX Small cheerful brick and flint roadside cottage surrounded by Chilterns walks; traditionally furnished with tiled-floor bar on left, black beams and joists, woodburner in big fireplace, pewter mugs, country pictures and wall seats, similar but bigger right-hand bar with sizeable dining tables on brick floor, carpeted back dining room, good value tasty pub food (not Sun evening) from sandwiches up including

meal deal Mon–Weds, Courage Best, Fullers London Pride and Shepherd Neame Spitfire, friendly attentive staff; Tues quiz; children and dogs welcome, disabled access, plenty of picnic-sets in front with more on back lawn, play area, open all day. *(Simon Collett-Jones, David Lamb)*

HYDE HEATH   SU9300
Plough (01494) 774408
Off B485 Great Missenden–Chesham; HP6 5RW Small prettily placed pub with traditional bare-boards bar and carpeted dining extension, decent choice of fairly priced pubby food from sandwiches up, Fullers London Pride and a couple of guests, real fires and cosy friendly atmosphere; background music, TV; bikers welcome, picnic-sets on green opposite, open all day Fri–Sun. *(David Lamb)*

ICKFORD   SP6407
Rising Sun (01844) 339238
E of Thame; Worminghall Road; HP18 9JD Pretty thatched local with cosy low-beamed bar, friendly staff and regulars, Adnams, Black Sheep, Marstons and a weekly guest, enjoyable reasonably priced home-made food, log fire; Tues quiz; children, walkers and dogs welcome, pleasant garden with picnic-sets and play area, handy for Waterperry Gardens, open all day weekends. *(David Lamb)*

IVINGHOE ASTON   SP9518
Village Swan (01525) 220544
Aston; signed from B489 NE of Ivinghoe; LU7 9DP Village-owned pub managed by welcoming dutch couple; traditional beamed interior with open fire, enjoyable home-made food from varied menu including some dutch dishes, three real ales and nice wines by the glass; quiz first Mon of month, free wi-fi; children, walkers and dogs welcome, covered outside area and garden, handy for Ivinghoe Beacon and Icknield Way, open all day weekends, closed Mon and weekday lunchtimes. *(Guy Henderson)*

LACEY GREEN   SP8200
Black Horse (01844) 345195
Main Road; HP27 0QU Friendly mix of customers in this two-bar beamed country local; popular good value home-made food (not Sun evening, Mon) from baguettes up, breakfast from 9am Tues–Sat, four real ales including Brakspears and nice choice of wines by the glass, quotations written on walls, inglenook woodburner; darts, sports TV, free wi-fi; children and dogs welcome, picnic-sets in garden with play area and aunt sally, closed Mon lunchtime, open all day Thurs–Sun. *(Donald Allsopp)*

LACEY GREEN   SP8201
Pink & Lily (01494) 489857
A4010 High Wycombe–Princes Risborough, follow Loosley sign, then

Great Hampden, Great Missenden sign; HP27 0RJ Friendly updated 18th-c pub in pretty setting; enjoyable food from sandwiches and traditional choices up, four changing mainly local ales and several wines by the glass, pubby furniture and open fire in airy main bar, cosier side areas and conservatory-style extension with big arches, small tap room with built-in wall benches on red tiles, framed Rupert Brooke poem about the pub (he used to drink here) and broad inglenook, games room; occasional background music, free wi-fi; children, dogs and muddy walkers welcome, big garden with heated deck, futuristic glass pods, play area and barbecue, open all day. *(Tracey and Stephen Groves)*

LACEY GREEN   SP8100
Whip (01844) 344060
Pink Road; HP27 0PG Hilltop local under new licensees; mix of simple traditional furnishings in smallish front bar and larger downstairs dining area, popular generously served pubby food including range of home-made pies, six interesting well kept ales (May beer festival with live music), traditional ciders, friendly helpful staff; background music, sports TV, free wi-fi; children and dogs welcome, tables in mature sheltered garden looking up to windmill, open all day, no food Sun evening. *(Robert Watt)*

LEY HILL   SP9901
★Swan (01494) 783075
Village signposted off A416 in Chesham; HP5 1UT Friendly well looked-after pub – once three 16th-c cottages; character main bar (some steps) with original features including low beams, standing timbers, antique range and inglenook log fire, nice mix of furniture and collection of old local photographs, St Austell Tribute, Timothy Taylors Landlord and Tring Side Pocket for a Toad, several wines by the glass and tasty reasonably priced food, raftered dining section with french windows to terrace and lawn; children welcome till 9pm, pretty summer hanging baskets and tubs, common opposite with cricket pitch and a nine-hole golf course, closed Sun evening, Mon. *(Alistair Forsyth, Carol and Barry Craddock)*

LITTLE KINGSHILL   SU8999
Full Moon (01494) 862397
Hare Lane; HP16 0EE Picturesque brick and flint village pub with popular food from sandwiches up including Tues steak night and Wed burger night, well kept Adnams, Fullers London Pride, Youngs and a guest, nice wines, friendly helpful service from busy staff, traditional beamed and quarry-tiled bar with open fire, bigger dining room; Thurs quiz; children and dogs welcome, circular picnic-sets out at front, lawned garden with swings, good walks. *(David Lamb)*

LITTLE MISSENDEN   SU9298
Red Lion (01494) 862876
*Off A413 Amersham–Great Missenden;
HP7 0QZ* Unchanging pretty 17th-c cottage
with long-serving landlord; small black-
beamed bar, plain seats around elm pub
tables, piano squashed into big inglenook
beside black kitchen range packed with
copper pots, kettles and rack of old guns,
little country dining room with pheasant
décor, well kept Greene King IPA, Skinners
Betty Stogs and Tring Side Pocket for a
Toad, fair-priced wines, pubby food; live
music Sat; children welcome, dogs in bar,
picnic-sets out in front and on grass behind
wall, back garden with little bridge over
River Misbourne, two bedrooms, open all day
Fri-Sun. *(Roy Hoing)*

LITTLEWORTH COMMON   SP9386
Blackwood Arms (01753) 645672
*3 miles S of M40 junction 2; Common
Lane; SL1 8PP* Traditional little 19th-c
brick pub tucked away in lovely spot on
edge of beechwoods (features in the film *My
Week with Marilyn*), sturdy mix of furniture
on bare boards, roaring log fire, enjoyable
home-made (not Sun evening) from
open sandwiches up, well kept Brakspears
and guests, interesting selection of wines,
friendly accommodating staff; free wi-fi;
children and dogs welcome, hitching rail for
horses, nice garden and good local walks,
closed Mon, otherwise open all day (till
7.30pm Sun). *(Ross Balaam, Mark Wilson)*

LUDGERSHALL   SP6617
Bull & Butcher (01844) 238094
*Off A41 Aylesbury–Bicester; bear
left to The Green; HP18 9NZ* Nicely
old-fashioned country pub under newish
friendly management, bar with low beams
in ochre ceiling, pews and wheelback
chairs on dark tiles or flagstones, inglenook
woodburner, Greene King IPA and a guest,
enjoyable pubby food including themed
nights, back dining room; aunt sally
and dominoes teams, open mike night
fourth Thurs of month; children and dogs
welcome, picnic-sets on pleasant front
terrace, play area on green opposite,
circular walks from the door, open all
day weekends (till 8pm Sun), closed
lunchtimes Mon and Tues. *(David Lamb)*

MAIDS MORETON   SP7035
Wheatsheaf (01280) 822903
*Main Street, just off A413 Towcester–
Buckingham; MK18 1QR* Attractive
17th-c thatched local, well kept ales such as
Tring, Sharps and Skinners, good fairly pubby
food, friendly service, spotless low-beamed
bar with bare boards and tiled floors, two
inglenooks, conservatory restaurant; seats
on front terrace, hatch service for pleasant
enclosed back garden, closed Mon, otherwise
open all day. *(Jess and George Cowley)*

MARLOW   SU8586
Coach No phone
West Street; SL7 2LS Sister dining pub to
Tom Kerridge's Hand & Flowers restaurant;
very well liked food (tapas-style helpings, no
bookings) from open kitchen with rotisserie,
good helpful service, compact interior with
modern décor, bar area serving up to four
changing ales and nice wines by the glass
(maybe local fizz) from pewter-topped
counter; silent TVs; open all day from 8am for
breakfast. *(Tracey and Stephen Groves)*

MARLOW   SU8586
Two Brewers (01628) 484140
*St Peter Street, first right off Station
Road from double roundabout; SL7 1NQ*
18th-c red-brick beamed pub set just back
from the river; enjoyable fairly pubby food
from snacks up, good value lunchtime set
menu, friendly helpful service, well kept
Fullers London Pride and three Rebellion
ales, a dozen wines by the glass, various
dining areas including upstairs room and
cellar restaurant; free wi-fi; children and
dogs welcome, seats outside, open (and food)
all day, kitchen closes 5pm Sun. *(Simon
Collett-Jones)*

MEDMENHAM   SU8084
Dog & Badger (01491) 579944
A4155, opposite the church; SL7 2HE
Renovated low-beamed roadside bar-
restaurant with contemporary décor, good
if not cheap food from open kitchen, local
ales such as Rebellion, plenty of wines by
the glass and good selection of other drinks
including cocktails, friendly helpful staff;
live music Tues; children and dogs (in bar)
welcome, terrace tables, herb garden, six
stylish bedrooms in separate building, open
all day from 8am for breakfast. *(Anne Taylor)*

MILTON KEYNES   SP8737
Olde Swan (01908) 679489
*Newport Road, Woughton on the Green;
MK6 3BS* Spacious and picturesque timber-
framed Chef & Brewer overlooking village
green; refurbished beamed interior with good
log fires and nice nooks and corners, their
usual wide menu, Greene King ales and good
wine choice; children welcome, plenty of
seating in large garden, footpaths to nearby
lakes, open (and food) all day. *(Martin and
Alison Slainsby)*

MILTON KEYNES   SP8939
★Swan (01908) 665240
*Broughton Road, Milton Keynes village;
MK10 9AH* Good mix of customers at this
attractive thatched pub; interconnecting
rooms mixing original features with
contemporary furnishings, main beamed
and flagstoned bar with plush armchairs by
inglenook, high chairs and tables, cushioned
banquette and chunky tables, Wells
Bombardier, Youngs Bitter and guests,

30 wines by the glass, good popular food served by helpful young staff, spreading restaurant with open kitchen and doors to outside dining area overlooking garden; free wi-fi; well behaved children welcome, dogs in bar, open all day, food all day Fri-Sun. *(Valerie Sayer, Beth Aldridge, Ben and Diane Bowie, Michael Butler, Jess and George Cowley)*

NEWPORT PAGNELL SP8743
Cannon (01908) 211495
High Street; MK16 8AQ Friendly little bay-windowed drinkers' pub with interesting military theme, four well kept reasonably priced ales, carpeted half-panelled interior with gas woodburner in central fireplace, live music and comedy nights in room behind; TV, juke box; seats out in small backyard, open all day. *(Donald Allsopp)*

OLNEY SP8851
★ Swan (01234) 711111
High Street S; MK46 4AA Cosy little pub under same owners as the Rose & Crown at Yardley Hastings (see Northamptonshire); beamed and timbered linked rooms, popular good value food from sandwiches and british tapas to interesting blackboard choices, at least three well kept/priced changing ales and plenty of wines by the glass from good list, friendly attentive service, rather close-set pine tables, cheery log fires, small back bistro dining room (booking advised); courtyard tables, open all day (till 9pm Sun). *(Gerry and Rosemary Dobson, Michael Sargent)*

PENN SU9093
★ Old Queens Head (01494) 813371
Hammersley Lane/Church Road, off B474 between Penn and Tylers Green; HP10 8EY Stylishly updated old pub with open-plan rooms; well spaced tables, a modicum of old prints and comfortably varied seating on flagstones or broad dark boards, stairs up to attractive two-level raftered dining room, well liked food (special diets catered for) including Sat brunch from 9.30am, Greene King ales and lots of wines by the glass, a dozen gins, good friendly service, log fire in big fireplace; background music, daily papers, free wi-fi; children and dogs (in bar) welcome, sunny terrace overlooking church, picnic-sets on sheltered L-shaped lawn; beechwoods of Common or Penn Woods close by, open all day. *(Sandra and Nigel Brown, Tracey and Stephen Groves)*

PENN SU9093
★ Red Lion (01494) 813107
Elm Road, B474; HP10 8LF Bustling 16th-c pub opposite village duck pond (sister to the Royal Standard of England at Forty Green – see Main Entries); various bar rooms and mix of furniture including cushioned mate's chairs, settles and rustic tables with candlesticks, homely sofas and armchairs, rugs on ancient parquet or old quarry tiles,

fantastic collection of British Empire prints and paintings, windowsills and mantelpieces crammed with Staffordshire dogs, plates and old bottles, hop-strung beams, woodburner in big fireplace, Chiltern, Windsor & Eton and a guest, real cider, good choice of wines by the glass, well liked home-made pubby food; TV for major sporting events only, shove-ha'penny, board games; children and dogs welcome, seats on front terrace and small side garden, open all day; still for sale as we went to press so things may change. *(Roy Hoing)*

PENN STREET SU9295
★ Hit or Miss (01494) 713109
Off A404 SW of Amersham, keep on towards Winchmore Hill; HP7 0PX Welcoming traditional village pub; heavily beamed main bar with leather sofas and armchairs on parquet flooring, horsebrasses, open fire, two carpeted rooms with interesting cricket and chair-making memorabilia, more sofas, wheelback and other dining chairs around pine tables, good interesting food (highish prices) including daily specials, Badger ales; background music, free wi-fi; children and dogs (in certain areas) welcome, picnic-sets on terrace overlooking own cricket pitch, parking over the road, open all day. *(Roy Hoing)*

PENN STREET SU9295
Squirrel (01494) 711291
Off A404 SW of Amersham, opposite the Common; HP7 0PX Friendly sister pub to nearby Hit or Miss, open-plan bar with flagstones, log fire and mix of furniture including comfortable sofas, reasonably priced home-made pubby food from baguettes up (not Sun evening, Mon), good children's meals too, up to five well kept ales such as Rebellion, Tring, Vale and XT, Weston's cider, bric-a-brac and cricketing memorabilia (village cricket pitch is opposite), sweets in traditional glass jars; live acoustic music Fri, open mike last Sun of month, monthly quiz; dogs welcome, covered outside deck with sofas and logburner, play area in big back garden, lovely walks, closed Mon lunchtime, otherwise open all day. *(Tracey and Stephen Groves, David Lamb)*

PRESTWOOD SP8799
★ Polecat (01494) 862253
170 Wycombe Road (A4128 N of High Wycombe); HP16 0HJ Smallish civilised rooms opening off low-ceilinged bar, rugs and assorted tables and chairs on bare boards or red tiles, various stuffed animals (white polecats in one cabinet), good open fire, five real ales including Malt and Rebellion, 30 wines by the glass and quite a few gins, good tasty food; free wi-fi; children and dogs (in bar) welcome, attractive big garden with colourful hanging baskets and tubs, large play area, picnic-sets under parasols on neat

front grass beneath fairy-lit pear tree, open all day in summer, till 6pm Sun. *(William Slade, Tracey and Stephen Groves)*

PRINCES RISBOROUGH SP8104
Red Lion (01844) 344476
Whiteleaf, off A4010; OS Sheet 165 map reference 817043; HP27 0LL Comfortably worn-in 17th-c family-owned pub in charming village, Sharps Doom Bar and a couple of guests, decent pubby food at reasonable prices, flowers on tables, log fire; traditional games; children, walkers and dogs welcome (no muddy boots – covers provided), seats in garden behind, extensive views over to Oxfordshire, four bedrooms, open all day weekends, closed Mon. *(Jim King)*

QUAINTON SP7420
George & Dragon (01296) 655436
The Green; HP22 4AR Traditional flower-decked brick pub beside village green, half a dozen well kept changing ales, Weston's cider and good choice of reasonably priced food including blackboard specials and bargain OAP lunch Tues, friendly efficient staff, split-level bar, coffee shop, post office facility Weds; quiz nights and darts; children welcome, tables outside with good view of windmill, open all day Sat, closed Mon. *(David Lamb)*

SEER GREEN SU9691
★ Jolly Cricketers (01494) 676308
Chalfont Road, opposite the church; HP9 2YG Bustling brick Victorian pub with two parquet-floored bar rooms, woodburner in each, cushioned window seats, farmhouse and antique-style dining chairs around bare wood or painted tables, old cricketing photos, prints and bats, Rebellion, Vale and three guests, 16 good wines by the glass and 20 malt whiskies, good interesting food served by pleasant helpful staff, separate restaurant; background and some live music, quiz last Sun of month, TV, free wi-fi, board games; dogs and muddy boots in main bar, picnic-sets on back terrace, handsome wisteria at front (note the ironic pub sign), open all day (till midnight Fri, Sat), food all day Sun till 6pm. *(John Evans, Tracey and Stephen Groves, David Lamb)*

SKIRMETT SU7790
★ Frog (01491) 638996
From A4155 NE of Henley take Hambleden turn and keep on; or from B482 Stokenchurch–Marlow take Turville turn and keep on; RG9 6TG Pretty pub in Chilterns countryside; nice public bar with log fire, prints on walls, cushioned sofa and leather-seated stools on wood floor, high chairs by counter, Rebellion IPA, Gales Seafarer and a changing guest, 18 wines by the glass including champagne, 24 malt whiskies, two dining rooms in different styles – one light and airy with country kitchen furniture, the other more formal with dark

red walls, smarter furniture and candlelight, good interesting food cooked by chef-landlord from baguettes and deli boards up, friendly attentive staff; background music; children and dogs (in bar) welcome, side gate to lovely garden with unusual five-sided tables, attractive valley views and farmland walks, Chiltern Valley Winery & Brewery nearby, three comfortable bedrooms, closed Sun evening Oct-May. *(Andrew and Michele Revell)*

STOKE GOLDINGTON SP8348
★ Lamb (01908) 551233
High Street (B526 Newport Pagnell–Northampton); MK16 8NR Chatty village pub with friendly helpful licensees, up to five ales including Tring, real ciders and good range of wines, generous helpings of enjoyable home-made food (all day Sat, not Sun evening) from baguettes to good value Sun roasts, lounge with log fire and sheep decorations, two small pleasant dining rooms, darts and table skittles in public bar; may be soft background music, TV; children and dogs welcome, terrace and sheltered garden behind with play equipment, bedrooms in adjacent cottage, closed Mon lunchtime, otherwise open all day (till 7pm Sun). *(Lorna and Jack Mulgrave)*

STOKE MANDEVILLE SP8310
Woolpack (01296) 615970
Risborough Road (A4010 S of Aylesbury); HP22 5UP Thatched Mitchells & Butlers pub with boldly decorated contemporary interior, Brakspears Oxford Gold, Sharps Doom Bar and a guest, several wines by the glass, cocktails, good choice of food including fixed-price weekday menu (till 6pm), friendly service and relaxed atmosphere; free wi-fi; well behaved children allowed, seats in back garden and on the heated front terrace, open (and food) all day. *(Jim King)*

STONY STRATFORD SP7840
Crown (01908) 262888
Market Square; MK11 1BE Former coaching inn recently refurbished under new owner-chef, various areas arranged around central servery, bare boards, some stripped stonework and interesting modern artwork, back dining room with pitched ceiling, good food including tapas and range of burgers, special diets catered for, ales such as Adnams and Sharps Doom Bar, friendly staff; background and some live music; picnic-sets on brick terrace, closed Mon, otherwise open all day (till 7pm Sun). *(Edward Edmonton)*

THE LEE SP8904
★ Cock & Rabbit (01494) 837540
Back roads 2.5 miles N of Great Missenden, E of A413; HP16 9LZ Overlooking village green and run by same friendly italian family for over 25 years; much emphasis on their good italian cooking, also lunchtime baps and Weds evening

pasta deal, Greene King, Sharps and a beer named for the pub, plush-seated lounge, cosy dining room and larger restaurant; children welcome, dogs in bar, seats on verandah, terraces and lawn, good walks, open all day weekends. *(David and Charlotte Green)*

THE LEE · SP8904
★ Old Swan (01494) 837239
Swan Bottom, back road 0.75 miles N of The Lee; HP16 9NU Major structural work and extensions going on (maybe till early 2018) at this friendly tucked-away country pub; mainly 16th-c with attractively furnished linked rooms, heavy beams, flagstones and old quarry tiles, high-backed antique settles and window seats, log fire in inglenook cooking range, good food (not Sun evening, Mon) from sensibly short menu, Chiltern, Sharps and a guest such as Rebellion, several wines by the glass; free wi-fi; children and dogs (in bar) welcome, big, spreading back garden with picnic-sets and contemporary seating around rustic tables, play area, surrounding walks and cycling routes, open all day Fri, Sat, till 7pm Sun, closed Mon lunchtime. *(Richard Kennell, Emma Scofield, Mr and Mrs J Watkins, Peter Pilbeam)*

TURVILLE · SU7691
★ Bull & Butcher (01491) 638283
Valley road off A4155 Henley–Marlow at Mill End, past Hambleden and Skirmett; RG9 6QU Popular 16th-c black and white pub in pretty village (famous as film and TV setting); two traditional low-beamed rooms with inglenooks, wall settles in tiled-floor bar, deep well incorporated into glass-topped table, Brakspears ales kept well and decent wines by the glass, enjoyable good value locally sourced food cooked by chef-patron, friendly staff; background music (live last Fri of month); children and dogs welcome, seats by fruit trees in attractive garden, good walks (Chiltern Way runs through village), open all day weekends and can get very busy. *(Ross Balaam, Guy Vowles)*

WADDESDON · SP7316
Long Dog (01296) 651320
High Street; HP18 0JF Renovated village pub with good food from open-view kitchen including english tapas, friendly accommodating service, well kept ales and nice choice of wines by the glass, bar area with open fire; background music, live jazz every other Tues; children and dogs welcome, tables out front and back, very handy for Waddesdon Manor (NT), open all day, food all day weekends. *(R K Phillips)*

WEEDON · SP8118
★ Five Elms (01296) 641439
Stockaway; HP22 4NL Cottagey thatched pub with two welcoming little bars, low beams and log fires, ample helpings of good fairly priced food (notable steak and kidney pudding) cooked by landlord (best to book),

nice wines, interesting range of gins and a well kept ale such as XT Four, cheerful helpful service, old photographs and prints, separate compact dining room; games such as shove-ha'penny; children welcome (no under-9s in restaurant), dogs in bar, pretty hanging baskets and a few picnic-sets out in front, attractive village, closed Sun evening and lunchtimes Mon, Tues. *(Amaya Arias-Garcia)*

WENDOVER · SP8609
Village Gate (01296) 623884
Aylesbury Road (B4009); HP22 6BA Country dining pub under new management; interconnecting rooms including bar with woodburner in brick fireplace, Rebellion, Sharps, Tring and a guest, good choice of popular food (just pizzas Mon evening), friendly efficient young staff, other rooms laid for eating, one with high-raftered ceiling; children and dogs welcome, outside seating including deck, long-reaching country views, open all day, no food Sun evening. *(Emma Scofield)*

WEST WYCOMBE · SU8394
George & Dragon (01494) 535340
High Street; A40 W of High Wycombe; HP14 3AB Rambling hotel bar in preserved NT Tudor village; massive beams and sloping walls, big log fire, three well kept Rebellion ales along with St Austell Tribute, good range of wines and well liked food including fixed-price menus (can eat in bar or restaurant), prompt friendly service; children and dogs welcome, tables in nice garden, 11 bedrooms (magnificent oak staircase), handy for West Wycombe Park (NT) and the Hell-Fire Caves, open all day, meals 12-6 Sun. *(Jim King)*

WESTON TURVILLE · SP8510
Chequers (01296) 613298
Church Lane; HP22 5SJ Comfortably updated dining pub with low 16th-c beams, flagstones and large log fire, very good up-to-date food from chef-owner in bar or restaurant including set lunch, friendly helpful staff, well kept ales such as Rebellion and Sharps, wide choice of wines by the glass; children (no under-6s after 4pm) and dogs (away from dining areas) welcome, tucked away in attractive part of village, tables on large front terrace, open all day (Sun till 6pm), closed Mon. *(Roger and Penny Gudge, Penny Dathan, Jayne Muir, David Alexander, Michael Cookson, Ian Usher)*

WESTON UNDERWOOD · SP8650
Cowpers Oak (01234) 711382
Signed off A509 in Olney; High Street; MK46 5JS Wisteria-clad village pub with enjoyable home-cooked food (special diets catered for) from bar snacks up, well kept Hopping Mad, Woodfordes Wherry and a couple of guests, several wines by the glass, friendly helpful staff, beams, painted panelling and some stripped stone, nice

mix of old-fashioned furnishings including pews, two open fires, restaurant behind; background music, Mon quiz; children and dogs welcome, small suntrap front terrace, more tables on back decking and in big orchard garden, fenced play area, open all day weekends (till 9pm Sun).
(Guy Henderson)

WHELPLEY HILL   SP9501
White Hart (01442) 833367
Off B4505 Bovington–Chesham; HP5 3RL Cosy tile-hung village pub with good home-made food, well kept interesting beers and good selection of other drinks, friendly accommodating service, log fires; background music; children and dogs welcome, seats out at front and in big back garden, nice local walks, open all day, can get crowded at weekends. *(Roy Hoing)*

WINCHMORE HILL   SU9394
Plough (01494) 259757
The Hill; HP7 0PA Village pub-restaurant with good italian food from wood-fired pizzas up (landlord is from Campania), flagstones, low beams and open fires, linked dining area with polished wood floor, real ales and imported lagers, nice coffee, little shop selling italian wines and other produce; children welcome, tables on terrace and lawn, pleasant walks nearby, open all day from 9am for breakfast. *(John Evans)*

WINCHMORE HILL   SU9394
Potters Arms (01494) 726222
Fagnall Lane; HP7 0PH Welcoming 17th-c pub close to village green, ales such as Brakspears, Ringwood and Wychwood, enjoyable pubby food (not Sun evening)

from sandwiches and panini up, good helpful service, some black beams, leather sofa and armchairs by inglenook log fire; popular comedy night last Thurs of month; children welcome, tables in fenced front garden, four bedrooms, open all day Sat, till 7pm Sun.
(Roy Hoing)

WINSLOW   SP7627
Bell (01296) 714091
Market Square; MK18 3AB Fine old coaching inn, comfortable and atmospheric, with reasonably priced food in beamed bar and popular carvery restaurant, Greene King ales, friendly welcoming staff, snug with historical photos and log fire; courtyard tables, 39 bedrooms (some with four-posters), open all day. *(Dr W I C Clark)*

WOOBURN COMMON   SU9187
★**Chequers** (01628) 529575
From A4094 at Bourne End roundabout, follow for Wooburn, then straight over next roundabout into Kiln Lane; OS Sheet 175 map reference 910870; HP10 0JQ Bustling hotel with friendly low-beamed main bar, second bar to the left and smart restaurant – refurbishment/extension underway as we went to press, news please; good range of well liked food from sandwiches, wraps and some pubby choices up, Rebellion ales, Fullers London Pride and a dozen wines by the glass from good list, fair range of whiskies and brandies too; background music, TV, free wi-fi; children and dogs (in bar) welcome, spacious garden set away from the road, comfortable bedrooms, open (and food) all day. *(Tracey and Stephen Groves, Simon Collett-Jones, David Lamb, R K Phillips)*

Post Office address codings confusingly give the impression that some pubs are in Buckinghamshire, when they're really in Bedfordshire or Berkshire (which is where we list them).

Cambridgeshire

BALSHAM
TL5850 Map 5

THE GOOD PUB GUIDE

Black Bull  🍺 🛏

(01223) 893844 – www.blackbull-balsham.co.uk

Village signposted off A11 SW of Newmarket, and off A1307 in Linton; High Street; CB21 4DJ

Pretty thatched pub with bedroom extension – a good all-rounder – well thought-of food too

This is a handsome black and white timbered thatched inn that's particularly well run by the hands-on, convivial landlord – and our readers enjoy their visits very much. The beamed bar spreads around a central servery where they keep their own-label Red & Black Ale (from Nethergate) plus Adnams Ghost Ship, Crafty Beers Sauvignon Blonde and Woodfordes Wherry on handpump, 22 wines by the glass from a good list, 15 malt whiskies, draught lager and interesting juices. Dividers and standing timbers break up the space, which has an open fire (with leather sofas in front of it), floorboards and low black beams in the front part; furniture includes small leatherette-seated dining chairs. A restaurant extension (in a listed barn) has a high-raftered oak panelled roof and a network of standing posts and steel ties. The front terrace has teak tables and chairs by a long, pleasantly old-fashioned verandah and there are more seats in a small sheltered back garden. Smart, comfortable bedrooms are in a neat single-storey extension. This pub has the same good owners as the Red Lion at Hinxton.

 As well as pub classics plus sandwiches and baguettes, the interesting food includes pork rillette with saffron and thyme pickled onions, smoked haddock risotto with soft boiled egg and curry sauce, home-cooked ham and free-range eggs, crayfish linguine, chargrilled baby artichoke with pesto, harissa and pepper couscous, rabbit leg stuffed with tarragon and mushrooms with sherry reduction, lamb rump with confit garlic, feta gnocchi, pea foam and tomato jam, a fish dish of the day, and puddings such as egg custard tart with poached rhubarb and chocolate fondant with freeze-dried strawberry and cherry sorbet. *Benchmark main dish: steak in ale pie £14.00. Two-course evening meal £22.00.*

Free house ~ Licensee Alex Clarke ~ Real ale ~ Open 7.30am (8.30am weekends)-11pm (10.30pm Sun) ~ Bar food 12-2, 6.30-9; 12-2.30, 6.30-9.30 Fri, Sat; 12-3, 6.30-8.30 Sun ~ Restaurant ~ Well behaved children welcome ~ Dogs allowed in bar and bedrooms ~ Wi-fi ~ Bedrooms: £95/£125 *Recommended by Mrs Margo Finlay, Jörg Kasprowski, William Slade, Carol and Barry Craddock, Caroline Prescott, Guy Henderson, Gerry and Pam Pollard, Lee and Jill Stafford*

BRANDON CREEK
Ship ◖

TL6091 Map 5

(01353) 676228 – www.theshipbrandoncreek.co.uk

A10 Ely–Downham Market; PE38 0PP

Fine riverside spot near the A10 with plenty of outside seating, cosy snug and busy bar, four ales, good wines and well liked food

Seats on the terrace and in the garden make the most of the riverside position here and they have free moorings for visiting boats. It's a busy 17th-c pub, welcoming to both families and dogs, and the carefully modernised bar at the centre of the building has massive stone masonry in the sunken former forge area, a big log fire at one end and a stove at the other, interesting old fenland photographs and prints, and paintings by local artists for sale. Adnams Southwold, plus a couple of guests such as Cottage Try Me and Two Rivers Hares Hopping on handpump, a wide choice of wines and farm cider; board games and quiet background music. There's a cosy snug and a restaurant overlooking both the Great Ouse and the Little Ouse rivers.

🍴 The short choice of well liked food uses seasonal produce and includes sausages and mash with gravy, beer-battered haddock fillet, home-made pies such as chicken, bacon and sweetcorn; spinach, potato and stilton; pork, leek and cheddar; and smoked haddock and spring onion, and puddings such as bakewell tart and lemon meringue pie. *Benchmark main dish: steak and onion pie £11.00. Two-course evening meal £17.00.*

Free house ~ Licensee Mark Thomas ~ Real ale ~ Open 12-11; closed Mon ~ Bar food 12-3, 6-9; 12-9 Sat; 12-8 Sun ~ Restaurant ~ Children welcome ~ Dogs allowed in bar ~ Wi-fi ~ Live music or quiz first Fri evening of month *Recommended by Brian and Sally Wakeham, Nick Higgins, Susan and Callum Slade*

CAMBRIDGE
Punter

TL4459 Map 5

(01223) 3633221 – www.thepuntercambridge.com

Pound Hill, on corner of A1303 ring road; CB3 0AE

Good enterprising food in relaxed and interestingly furnished surroundings

There are plenty of nice nooks and crannies and the sound of chatty customers in this former coaching inn – it's an enjoyable place. The rambling and informal linked rooms have quite a bit of character with paintings, antique prints, old dark floorboards and a pleasing choice of seating such as pews, elderly dining chairs and Lloyd Loom easy chairs. One prized corner is down a few steps, behind a wooden railing. The scrubbed tables feature candles in bottles or assorted candlesticks, and staff are quick, friendly and efficient. Adnams Ghost Ship, Oakham Citra, Sharps Doom Bar and Turpins Cambridge Black on handpump and a dozen wines by the glass; board games and background jazz music. The flagstoned and mainly covered former coachyard has tables and picnic-table sets; beyond is a raftered barn bar, similar in style, with more pictures on papered walls, a large rug on dark flagstones and a big-screen TV. This is sister pub to the Punter in Oxford.

🍴 As well as their bargain £5 lunch, the appetising food includes ham hock terrine with brandy, caramelised apple and stem ginger, crab mayonnaise and avocado salad, sausages with olive oil mash and madeira sauce, vegetable and halloumi tagine with yoghurt and couscous, teriyaki salmon and soya udon noodles, chilli and ginger vinaigrette, confit duck leg with cherry sauce, chestnut purée and potato gratin, and puddings such as chocolate tart with strawberry ice-cream and sticky toffee pudding. *Benchmark main dish: hake with chorizo, black pudding, mushy pea croquette and mushroom sauce £13.50. Two-course evening meal £19.50.*

Punch ~ Lease Sarah Lee ~ Real ale ~ Open 12-midnight (11.30 Sun) ~ Bar food 12-3, 6-9 (10 Fri); 12-10 Sat; 12-9 Sun ~ Children welcome ~ Dogs welcome *Recommended by David Thorpe, Ivor Smith, Richard Tilbrook, Lyn and Freddie Roberts, Christopher Mannings, Donald Allsopp*

DUXFORD   TL4746 Map 5
John Barleycorn ♀ ⇖

(01223) 832699 – www.johnbarleycorn.co.uk
Handy for M11 junction 10; right at first roundabout, then left at main village junction into Moorfield Road; CB22 4PP

Traditional, pretty pub with friendly staff, an enjoyable atmosphere, good, interesting food and seats outside; bedrooms

As the Imperial War Museum Duxford is close by, this lovely early 17th-c inn with its low thatched roof and shuttered windows is the perfect place for lunch. It's got a lot of character and the standing timbers and brick pillars create alcoves and different drinking and dining areas: there are heavy beams and nice old floor tiles, a log fire, all manner of seating from rustic cushioned settles through white-painted and plain wooden dining chairs to some rather fine antique farmhouse chairs and quite a mix of wooden tables. Plenty to look at too – pub and air force memorabilia, china plates and old clocks, copper pans and plenty of pictures and paintings on blue or pale yellow walls. Greene King Abbot and IPA and guests such as Purity Pure UBU and Timothy Taylors Landlord on handpump and ten wines by the glass; background music. The front terrace has picnic-sets beside pretty hanging baskets and the back garden has more picnic-sets among flowering tubs and shrubs. This is a comfortable place to stay and the bedrooms are in a converted barn. The pub was used by the brave young airmen of Douglas Bader's Duxford Wing during World War II. Easy wheelchair access from the back car park.

Carefully presented, popular food includes sandwiches, moules marinière, chargrilled chicken and chorizo skewer with cherry tomato salad, sharing boards, wild mushroom risotto, cumberland pork sausages with creamy mash and veal jus, lamb and mint, wild boar or steak burgers with toppings, coleslaw and skin-on chips, salads such as hot-smoked salmon with a honey mustard dressing and a poached egg, venison haunch with horseradish mash and redcurrant jus, and puddings such as a cheesecake of the week and espresso crème brûlée. *Benchmark main dish: home-made pie of the day £11.95. Two-course evening meal £19.00.*

Greene King ~ Tenant Nicholas Kersey ~ Real ale ~ Open 11-11 ~ Bar food 12-3, 5-9.30; 12-3, 5-8.30 Sun ~ Children welcome ~ Dogs allowed in bar ~ Wi-fi ~ Bedrooms: /$85
Recommended by David Jackman, Simon and Mandy King, Minda and Stanley Alexander, Nicola and Holly Lyons, Monica and Steph Evans

ELTON   TL0894 Map 5
Crown ✪ ♀ ⇖

(01832) 280232 – www.crowninnelton.co.uk
Off B671 S of Wansford (A1/A47), and village signposted off A605 Peterborough–Oundle; Duck Street; PE8 6RQ

Pretty pub with interesting food, several real ales, well chosen wines and a friendly atmosphere; stylish bedrooms

To find this lovely golden-stone thatched pub, follow the brown sign towards Nassington (the pub is on the edge of this charming village). The softly lit, beamed bar has leather and antique dining chairs around a nice mix of chunky tables on bare boards, an open fire in a stone fireplace and good pictures and pubby ornaments on pastel walls. The beamed main dining area has fresh flowers and candles, and similar tables and chairs on stripped wooden flooring, and there's a dining extension too. High bar chairs against the counter are popular with locals, and they keep a house beer (from Kings Cliffe Brewery), Greene King IPA, Nobbys Best, Oakham JHB and Timothy Taylors Boltmaker on handpump, well chosen wines by the glass and farm cider; board games, background music and TV. There are tables outside on the front terrace, and Elton Mill and Lock are nearby. Bedrooms are smart, comfortable and well equipped and the breakfasts are especially good.

 The landlord cooks the appealing food: sandwiches, tempura squid with oriental dipping suace, sautéed mushrooms on chargrilled toast with truffle oil, omelettes, cider-glazed ham with free-range eggs, blue cheese and pine nut tart with basil oil salad, burger with toppings and french fries, beer-battered haddock and chips, 28-day dry-aged rib-eye steak with peppercorn or stilton sauce, and puddings such as banoffi cheesecake with caramelised banana and butterscotch sauce and dark chocolate brownie with white chocolate ice-cream and cherry compote. *Benchmark main dish: slow-roast lamb shoulder with redcurrant jus and dauphinoise potatoes £17.50. Two-course evening meal £21.00.*

Free house ~ Licensee Marcus Lamb ~ Real ale ~ Open 12-11; closed Mon lunchtime ~ Bar food 12-2 (4 bank holidays), 6.30-9 ~ Restaurant ~ Children welcome ~ Dogs allowed in bar ~ Wi-fi ~ Bedrooms: £80/£140 *Recommended by James Landor, Caroline and Steve Archer, Charlie Stevens, Elise and Charles Mackinlay, John Harris*

FEN DRAYTON
TL3468 Map 5

Three Tuns 🍺

(01954) 230242 – www.the3tuns.co.uk

Eastbound on A14, take first exit after Fenstanton, signed Fen Drayton and follow to pub; westbound on A14 exit at junction 27 and follow signs to village on Cambridge Road; High Street; CB24 4SJ

Lovely old pub with traditional furnishings in bar and dining room, real ales, tasty food and seats in garden

If you're looking for an enjoyable drink or meal in friendly surroundings – just head for this pretty thatched pub. The three rooms are more or less open-plan with a relaxed atmosphere, log fires in each, heavy-set moulded Tudor beams and timbers, a mix of burgundy cushioned stools, nice old dining chairs and settles in the bar, and wooden dining chairs and tables on red-patterned carpet in the dining room; framed prints of the pub too. Greene King IPA and Old Speckled Hen and a couple of guests such as Oakham JHB and Timothy Taylors Landlord on handpump and a dozen wines by the glass; they hold a beer festival over the August Bank Holiday weekend. A well tended back garden has seats and tables, a covered dining area and play equipment for children.

High quality traditional food includes lunchtime sandwiches, wraps and baguettes (not Sunday), deep-fried whitebait with tartare sauce, lamb samosas with minted yoghurt, a pie of the day, root vegetable tagine with couscous, home-baked honey roast ham with egg or pineapple, a curry of the day, chicken kiev, rib-eye steak with stilton or peppercorn sauce, and puddings such as sticky gingerbread pudding with ginger wine and brandy sauce and key lime pie; they have a two-for-one night on Wednesdays and a curry evening on the last Monday of the month. *Benchmark main dish: sizzling chicken fajitas £11.50. Two-course evening meal £15.00.*

Greene King ~ Tenants Mr and Mrs Baretto ~ Real ale ~ Open 12-3, 6-11; 12-12 Sat; 12-4 Sun ~ Bar food 12-2 (2.30 Sat), 6-9; 12-4 Sun ~ Restaurant ~ Children welcome ~ Dogs allowed in bar ~ Wi-fi ~ Live piano every other Fri *Recommended by Ivor Smith, Gordon and Margaret Ormondroyd, George Atkinson, Stephen Funnell*

GREAT WILBRAHAM
TL5558   Map 5

Carpenters Arms 🌟 �♍ ◪

(01223) 882093 – www.carpentersarmsgastropub.co.uk

Off A14 or A11 SW of Newmarket, following The Wilbrahams signposts; High Street; CB21 5JD

Inviting village pub with traditional bar, own-brew beers, highly regarded food in both the bar and the back restaurant; nice garden

Mr Hurley is informative and enthusiastic about his own-brewed beers – and about the particularly good food cooked by his wife. The low-ceilinged village bar on the right is properly pubby with bar billiards, a woodburning stove in a big inglenook, copper pots and iron tools, and cushioned pews and simple seats around solid pub tables on floor tiles. Their own brews (brewed at a local farm unit) are Crafty Beers Carpenters Cask, Sauvignon Blonde and Sixteen Strides on handpump and they keep a carefully chosen wine list (strong on the Roussillon region); background music, darts and board games. Service is spot-on: thoughtful, helpful and cheerful. On the left, a small cosy carpeted dining area has another big stone fireplace and overflowing bookshelves; this leads through to a sitting area with comfortable sofas and plenty of magazines. The light and airy extended main dining room has country kitchen chairs around chunky tables. A huge honeysuckle swathes the tree in the pretty back courtyard, and further on is an attractive homely garden, with fruit and vegetables, and circular picnic-sets shaded by tall trees.

 Everything is made in-house here by the landlady – and it's very good: rustic terrine with home-made chutney, scallops with puy lentils and provençale tomato sauce, a pie of the day and burger with toppings, both with triple-cooked chips, chicken forestière with creamy mash, baby carrots and green beans, confit duck leg with sautéed potatoes, slow-roast pork belly with cider sauce, sage and onion mash and braised red cabbage, and puddings such as chocolate mousse with chocolate hazelnut ice-cream and tarte tatin. *Benchmark main dish: tartiflette (potatoes, bacon and onion baked with reblochon cheese) £14.50. Two-course evening meal £19.95.*

Free house ~ Licensees Rick and Heather Hurley ~ Real ale ~ Open 11.30-3, 6.30-11; 11.30-3 Sun; closed Sun evening, Mon, Tues; 2 weeks June, 1 week Nov ~ Bar food 12-2, 7-9; 12-3 Sun ~ Restaurant ~ Children welcome ~ Wi-fi *Recommended by Mike and Mary Carter, Brian and Sally Wakeham, Ivor Smith, Chris Bell, Sally and Lance Oldham, Julie and Andrew Blanchett*

HEMINGFORD ABBOTS
TL2870   Map 5

Axe & Compass

(01480) 463605 – www.axeandcompass.co.uk

High Street; village signposted off A14 W of Cambridge; PE28 9AH

Thatched pub with several linked rooms, a good range of drinks and food served by friendly staff and seats outside

'Every village should have a pub as good as this,' says one reader, and we agree with him. It's very much at the heart of things, with a cheerful mix of customers and plenty of space in the interconnected rooms. The simple, beamed public bar has mate's chairs and stools around wooden tables on lovely ancient floor tiles, and an open two-way fireplace (not in use) into the snug next door where there's a woodburning stove. The main room has more beams and standing timbers, tweed tartan-patterned chairs and armchairs and cushioned wall seating around nice old tables on wood floors, local photographs, and stools against the counter where they serve Adnams Lighthouse, Sharps Doom Bar and Timothy Taylors Landlord on handpump, 12 wines by the glass and local cider. There's a second woodburner in a small brick fireplace; background music and board games. The long dining room has more photos on green walls and high-backed dark leather dining and other chairs around pale wooden tables. The garden, between the pretty thatched pub and the tall-spired church, has a fenced-off area with play equipment, contemporary seats and tables on the terrace and picnic-sets on grass; walks along the river. Disabled facilities.

¶¶ Rewarding, seasonal food at reasonable prices includes crispy duck with chilli and onion bhajis, cucumber salad and mint yoghurt, scallops with black pudding, pancetta, beetroot and cauliflower purée, sharing platters, root vegetable, pearl barley, parmesan and tomato casserole with mustard dumplings, corn-fed chicken suprême with dauphinoise potato purée, roast beetroot and mushroom and blue cheese sauce, sea bass fillet with champ mash and béarnaise sauce, and puddings such as lemon and lime mousse with citrus syrup, pistachios, meringue and brittle and chocolate orange torte with chocolate sauce and charred orange. *Benchmark main dish: burger with toppings, chips and coleslaw £10.00. Two-course evening meal £18.00.*

Enterprise ~ Lease Emma Tester ~ Real ale ~ Open 12-11 (10 Mon in winter) ~ Bar food 12-2.30, 6-9; 12-9 Sat; 12-4 Sun; maybe longer hours on summer weekends ~ Restaurant ~ Well behaved children welcome ~ Dogs allowed in bar ~ Wi-fi ~ Live music first Fri of month; quiz Tues *Recommended by D W Stokes, Sarah Nancollas, Mrs Margo Finlay, Jörg Kasprowski, Ted and Mary Bates, Miranda and Jeff Davidson*

HEMINGFORD GREY   TL2970   Map 5

Cock ★☆▣ ♀ ◖

(01480) 463609 – www.cambscuisine.com/the-cock-hemingford
Village signposted off A14 eastbound, and (via A1096 St Ives road) westbound; High Street; PE28 9BJ

Imaginative food in pretty pub with extensive wine list, four interesting beers, a bustling atmosphere and a smart restaurant

If you wish to enjoy the delicious food at this pretty little pub, you must eat in the restaurant as they've sensibly kept the public bar on the left for drinking only. This has an open woodburning stove on a raised hearth, bar stools, wall seats and a carver, and steps that lead down to more seating. Brewsters Hophead and Great Oakley Wagtail with guests such as Nene Valley DXB and Tydd Steam Piston Bob on handpump, 20 wines by the glass mainly from the Languedoc-Roussillon region, and Cromwell cider (made in the village). Other bar rooms have white-painted or dark beams and lots of contemporary pale yellow and cream paintwork, fresh flowers and church candles, artworks here and there, and a really attractive mix of old wooden dining chairs, settles and tables. In marked contrast, the stylishly rustic restaurant on the right – you must book to be sure of a table – is set for dining, with pale wooden floorboards and another woodburning stove. There are seats and tables among stone troughs and flowers on the terrace and in the neat garden, and pretty hanging baskets. This is in a delightful village on the River Ouse. Sister pubs are the Crown & Punchbowl at Horningsea and Tickell Arms in Whittlesford.

★ Creative, first class food includes sandwiches (not Sunday lunch), dorset snails with onion jam, lobster and crayfish bisque with tarragon cream, wild mushroom and goats cheese risotto, chicken suprême with potato and celeriac terrine, confit leeks and tarragon sauce, hake with green thai cauliflower, mango and sticky rice, braised beef with black olive and herb crust, beef dripping mash and caramelised onion, duck breast with pickled shallots, caramelised plum and walnut granola, and puddings such as rum-poached pineapple with coconut sorbet, pineapple crisp and coconut sponge and peanut butter crème brûlée with a banana cookie; Tuesday is steak night and they also offer a two- and three-course weekday set lunch. *Benchmark main dish: home-made sausages with mash and a choice of sauce £13.50. Two-course evening meal £24.00.*

Free house ~ Licensees Oliver Thain and Richard Bradley ~ Real ale ~ Open 11-3, 6-11; 11.30-11 Sat; 12-10.30 Sun ~ Bar food 12-2.30, 6.30 (6 Fri, Sat)-9; 12-8 Sun ~ Restaurant ~ No children after 6pm ~ Dogs allowed in bar ~ Wi-fi *Recommended by Mrs Margo Finlay, Jörg Kasprowski, Hilary De Lyon and Martin Webster, William Slade, Ivor Smith, Paul Farraday, Monty Green, Rosie and John Moore*

HINXTON

Red Lion 🌟 ⏟ 🍺 🛏

TL4945 Map 5

(01799) 530601 – www.redlionhinxton.co.uk

2 miles off M11 junction 9 northbound; take first exit off A11, A1301 N, then left turn into village – High Street; a little further from junction 10, via A505 E and A1301 S; CB10 1QY

16th-c pub with friendly staff, interesting bar food, real ales and a big landscaped garden; comfortable bedrooms

In warm weather, there's plenty of seating outside this pink-washed inn: teak tables and chairs on one terrace, huge parasols on a second terrace by the porch and picnic-sets on grass. There's also a dovecote and nice views of the village church. Inside, the low-beamed bar has a relaxed, friendly atmosphere, oak chairs and tables on bare boards, two leather chesterfield sofas, an open fire and an old wall clock. You'll find their own-label Red & Black Ale (from the local Nethergate Brewery) plus Adnams Ghost Ship, Woodfordes Wherry and a guest such as Crafty Beers Sauvignon Blonde on handpump, 22 wines by the glass, 15 malt whiskies and first class service. An informal dining area has high-backed settles, and the smart restaurant (with oak rafters and traditional dry peg construction) is decorated with various pictures and assorted clocks. Well equipped, pretty bedrooms are in a separate flint and brick building. The Imperial War Museum at Duxford is close by. They also own the Black Bull in Balsham just up the road.

First class food includes sandwiches, king scallops with sweet and sour peppers, mizuna leaves and aged balsamic, confit duck salad with pink grapefruit, crispy skin and bitter orange dressing, spinach and nutmeg gnocchi with jerusalem artichoke velouté and crispy kale, braised rabbit leg with bubble and squeak, button onions, crispy leeks and cider sauce, red mullet with crab croquette, saffron and fennel purée, queen scallops with lemon velouté, and puddings such as chocolate bouchon with espresso syrup, cacao nibs and honeycomb ice-cream and apple tarte tatin with caramel sauce and yoghurt sorbet. *Benchmark main dish: 12-hour slow-roast lamb with spring greens and bacon, madeira jus and thyme and garlic potatoes £17.00. Two-course evening meal £22.00.*

Free house ~ Licensee Alex Clarke ~ Real ale ~ Open 7.30am (8.30am weekends)-11pm (10.30pm Sun) ~ Bar food 12-2, 6.30-9; 12-2.30, 6.30-9.30 Fri, Sat; 12-3, 6-8 Sun ~ Restaurant ~ Well behaved children welcome ~ Dogs welcome ~ Wi-fi ~ Bedrooms: $99/$125 *Recommended by Paul Scofield, Julian Thorpe, Rona Mackinlay, Alison and Dan Richardson, Patti and James Davidson*

Virtually all pubs in this book sell wine by the glass. We mention wines if they are a cut above the average.

HORNINGSEA
TL4962 Map 5

Crown & Punchbowl ⭐ ♀ ⇦

(01223) 860643 – www.cambscuisine.com/the-crown-and-punchbowl

Just NE of Cambridge; CB25 9JG

Impressive food and thoughtful drinks choice in carefully refurbished old inn with seats outside; bedrooms

Ever since this carefully refurbished and extended 17th-c inn reopened, we've had nothing but warm praise from our readers. Original features and character have been maintained and the beamed bar has a woodburning stove in a brick fireplace, leather banquettes and rustic old chairs, stripped boards, terracotta walls and an attractively carved counter where they serve freshly carved ham and home-made pickles. Behind the bar they keep Brewsters Hophead, Milton Pegasus and a changing guest tapped from the cask and 20 wines by the glass (with a focus on the Languedoc-Roussillon region), home-made punches (alcoholic and non-alcoholic), lavender lemonade and local cider. The timbered dining room has leather cushioned chairs around wooden tables on pale boards, wall panelling and candlelight. Another conservatory-style room has large windows and ceramic light fittings (a nod to the village's history as a centre for Roman pottery). There are country seats out in front of the pub, while the five guest bedrooms upstairs are well equipped, light and comfortable. Sister pubs are the Cock at Hemingford Grey and Tickell Arms in Whittlesford.

 From a modern menu using local, seasonal ingredients, the appetising food includes sandwiches, rabbit, bacon and prune terrine with pickled vegetables, feta, broad bean and pea frittata with mint and lemon pesto, portobello mushroom with chargrilled vegetables, camembert and spiced tomato chutney, home-made sausages with mash and onion gravy, rack of lamb with a goats cheese and herb crust, baby aubergine, sunblush tomatoes and raspberry sauce, whole guinea fowl (for two) with parmentier potatoes, garlic butter, roasted vine tomatoes and rosemary gravy, and puddings such as sticky toffee pudding with salted caramel and raspberry pannacotta; they also offer a two- and three-course set menu (weekday lunchtimes and Sunday-Thursday evenings). *Benchmark main dish: fresh fish dish of the day £18.00. Two-course evening meal £23.00.*

Free house ~ Licensees Oliver Thain and Richard Bradley ~ Real ale ~ Open 12-3, 6 (5 Fri)-11; 12-11 Sat; 12-10.30 Sun ~ Bar food 12-2.30, 6.30-9; 12-2.30, 6-9.30 Fri, Sat; 12-3, 6.30-8.30 Sun ~ Restaurant ~ Children welcome ~ Dogs allowed in bar ~ Wi-fi ~ Bedrooms: /£120
Recommended by Belinda Stamp, Caroline Prescott, Lindy Andrews, Scott and Charlotte Havers, David Stewart, Penny and David Shepherd

HUNTINGDON
TL2471 Map 5

Old Bridge Hotel ⭐ ♀ ⇦

(01480) 424300 – www.huntsbridge.com

1 High Street; ring road just off B1044 entering from easternmost A14 slip road; PE29 3TQ

Proper bar in Georgian hotel with a splendid range of drinks, first class service and excellent food; individually styled bedrooms

Of course this is a lovely, civilised hotel and a special place to stay in luxurious bedrooms (some of which overlook the river) but there remains a wide mix of customers who very much enjoy the traditional pubby bar. This has a log fire, comfortable sofas and low wooden tables on polished floorboards, and Adnams Southwold and Nene Valley Blond Session Ale on handpump. They also have an exceptional wine list (up to 30 by the glass in the bar) and a wine shop where you can taste a selection of wines before you buy. Food is available in the big airy restaurant with floor-to-ceiling windows overlooking the garden, or in the bar/lounge. There are seats and tables on the terrace by the Great Ouse, and they have their own landing stage. This is sister pub to the Three Horseshoes at Madingley.

 Some sort of excellent food is available all day: hot and cold sandwiches, king prawns with samphire and garlic butter and avocado, pomegranate, chilli and leaf salad, venison terrine with pickled beetroot and onions, red onion tarte tatin with warm goats cheese, beef and crispy cheddar burger with skin-on chips, dressed crab on toast, pigeon breasts wrapped in pancetta with grilled cauliflower and roast squash, stuffed chicken with spinach risotto and crisp cavolo nero, slow-braised beef in puff pastry with horseradish mash, creamed cabbage and shallot sauce (for two), and puddings such as chocolate tart with rippled salted caramel ice-cream and pavlova with roasted pineapple and rum cream. *Benchmark main dish: slow-cooked pork belly with potato and gruyère bonbons and apple sauce £19.00. Two-course evening meal £27.00.*

Huntsbridge ~ Licensee John Hoskins ~ Real ale ~ Open 11-11 ~ Bar food 12.15-2.15, 6-9 (10 Sat); 12.15-3, 3.30-9 Sun ~ Restaurant ~ Children welcome ~ Dogs welcome ~ Wi-fi ~ Bedrooms: £99/£168 *Recommended by Michael Sargent, Mike and Mary Carter, Roy Shutz, Jennifer and Nicholas Thompson, Peter and Caroline Waites, Liz and Mike Newton*

KEYSTON
Pheasant ⏣ ⏥
TL0475 Map 5

(01832) 710241 – www.thepheasant-keyston.co.uk
Just off A14 SE of Thrapston; brown sign to pub down village loop road, off B663; PE28 0RE

Smart but friendly country dining pub with appealing décor and attractive garden

A charming thatched building serving exceptional food in civilised surroundings – it's not surprising our readers are so full of enthusiastic praise for this place. The main bar has pitched rafters high above, with lower dark beams in side areas, and the central serving area has padded stools beside the leather-quilted counter and dark flagstones, with hop bines above the handpumps for Adnams Southwold, Brewsters Hop A Doodle Doo and a guest beer, and a tempting array of 14 wines by the glass. Service by neat staff is attentive and courteous. Nearby are armchairs, a chesterfield, quite a throne of a seat carved in 17th-c style, other comfortable seats around low tables, and a log fire in a lofty fireplace. The rest of the pub is mostly red-carpeted with dining chairs around a variety of polished tables, large sporting prints, some hunting-scene wallpaper and lighted candles and tea-lights. The attractively planted and well kept garden behind has tables on lawn and terrace, and there are picnic-sets in front. This is a quiet farming hamlet.

 Cooked by the landlord, the impressive food includes sandwiches, pigeon breast with pearl barley, cauliflower purée and red wine sauce, monkfish satay with coconut basmati rice and sesame spinach, gnocchi with celeriac purée, beetroot, red onion, pumpkin seeds and parmesan, free-range pork sausages with confit swede, red onion and sage sauce, lamb with sweetbreads, potato fondant, braised red cabbage and salsa verde, skate wing with olive mash, braised fennel, mussels, dill and saffron butter, and puddings such as spotted dick with vanilla custard and local honey and orange sorbet; they also offer a two- and three-course set menu (not Saturday evening or Sunday lunch). *Benchmark main dish: chargrilled scotch beef fillet £18.00. Two-course evening meal £25.00.*

Free house ~ Licensee Simon Cadge ~ Real ale ~ Open 12-11; 12-5 Sun; closed Sun evening, Mon; 2-14 Jan ~ Bar food 12-2 (2.30 Fri, Sat), 6.30-9.30; 12-3.30 Sun ~ Restaurant ~ Children welcome ~ Dogs allowed in bar ~ Wi-fi *Recommended by Michael Sargent, Geoffrey Sutton, Katherine Matthews, Rupert and Sandy Newton, Max Simons*

MADINGLEY
Three Horseshoes 🌟 ♀

TL3960 Map 5

(01954) 210221 – www.threehorseshoesmadingley.co.uk

High Street; off A1303 W of Cambridge; CB23 8AB

• •

Cambridgeshire Dining Pub of the Year

Pretty thatched pub, newly refurbished, with excellent food and wines, charming staff and seats in the garden

We are as delighted as our readers that this attractive thatched pub is back again in the hands of John and Julia Hoskins, who had run it in the past for many years. It's been carefully refurbished to create a gently civilised but informally friendly atmosphere where both drinkers and diners feel welcome and the décor throughout is light and attractive. The bare-boards bar has high-backed cushioned settles and a mix of nice old dining chairs around wooden tables, prints on pale paintwork, a contemporary open fire and chairs against the counter where friendly, courteous staff serve Adnams Southwold and a changing ale from Nene Valley on handpump and 11 particularly good wines by the glass. The conservatory restaurant, overlooking the garden, has rattan-style chairs around white-clothed tables, flowers on windowsills and a woodburning stove in a brick fireplace. At the front of the building are solid benches and tables under parasols and the sunny back lawn has brightly painted picnic-sets and deckchairs. Sister establishment is the Old Bridge at Huntingdon.

 Using seasonal local produce, the imaginative food includes sharing plates with cured meats, vegetarian dips and oysters, fettucine with venison, chocolate, cinnamon and parmesan, cured sea trout with celeriac rémoulade and hazelnuts, lentil, ricotta and aubergine moussaka, stone bass fillet with clams, piquillo pepper, jerusalem artichoke and kale, pork belly with potato bake, caramelised onion, spinach and apple sauce, beef short-rib with parsnip purée and cavolo nero with sultanas, and puddings such as citrus salad with tangerine sorbet and goats cheese cheesecake and chocolate mousse with snow egg, passion fruit and almond; they also have an interesting cheeseboard (with cheeses from Somerset, Sussex and Spain). *Benchmark main dish: braised lamb shoulder with potato croquette, baby gem and baby carrots £16.00. Two-course evening meal £25.00.*

Free house ~ Licensee John Hoskins ~ Real ale ~ Open 11-11; closed Sun evening, Mon ~ Bar food 12-2.15, 6-9 (10 Sat) ~ Restaurant ~ Children welcome ~ Dogs allowed in bar ~ Wi-fi *Recommended by Muriel and Spencer Harrop, Alexandra and Richard Clay, Patricia and Anton Larkham, Mark and Mary Setting*

PETERBOROUGH
Brewery Tap ◗ £

TL1899 Map 5

(01733) 358500 – www.thebrewery-tap.com

Opposite Queensgate car park; PE1 2AA

Fantastic range of real ales including their own brews, popular thai food and a lively, friendly atmosphere

Of course the extraordinary building will grab your attention (it's a striking modern conversion of an old labour exchange), but so will the mix of their own-brewed Oakham Ales and thai food. The open-plan contemporary interior has an expanse of light wood and stone floors and blue-painted iron pillars holding up a steel-corded mezzanine level. It's stylishly lit by steel-meshed wall lights and a giant suspended steel ring with bulbs running around the rim. A band of chequered floor tiles traces the path of the long sculpted pale wood bar counter, which is boldly backed by an impressive display of bottles in a ceiling-high wall of wooden cubes. There's also a comfortable downstairs area, a big-screen TV for sporting events, background music and regular live bands and comedy nights. A two-storey glass wall divides the bar from the brewery, giving fascinating views of the two-barrel brew plan from which they produce their own Oakham Bishops Farewell, Citra, Inferno, JHB and seasonal ales; also, guest ales, quite a few whiskies and several wines by the glass. It gets very busy in the evening.

The incredibly popular thai food includes set menus and specials, as well as tom yum soup, chicken, beef, pork, prawn, duck and vegetable curries, stir-fried crispy chilli beef, talay pad cha (prawns, squid and mussels with crushed garlic, chilli and ginger), various noodle dishes, all sorts of salads and stir-fries and five kinds of rice. *Benchmark main dish: pad thai noodles £7.75. Two-course evening meal £18.00.*

Own brew ~ Licensee Jessica Loock ~ Real ale ~ Open 12-11 (1am Fri, 2am Sat); 12-10.30 Sun ~ Bar food 12-2.30, 5.30-10.30; 12-10.30 Fri, Sat; 12-3.30, 5.30-9.30 Sun ~ Restaurant ~ Children welcome during food service times only ~ Dogs allowed in bar ~ Wi-fi ~ Live band last Fri of month; DJs Sat evening *Recommended by Martin Jones, Neil Allen, Alison and Michael Harper, Lorna and Jack Mulgrave, Paddy and Sian O'Leary, Peter and Emma Kelly*

REACH
Dyke's End ◀
(01638) 743816 – www.dykesend.co.uk
From B1102 follow signpost to Swaffham Prior and Upware; village signposted; CB25 0JD

Candlelit rooms in former farmhouse with tasty food and own-brewed beer

If you're walking the nearby Devil's Dyke then this former farmhouse in its charming village-green setting is just the place for refreshment. It's a proudly traditional place with old-fashioned values such as no background music, games machines, food sachets or paper napkins, and the simply decorated ochre-walled bar has stripped heavy pine tables and pale kitchen chairs on dark boards. In a panelled section on the left are a few smarter dining tables with candles, and on the right there's a step down to a red-carpeted part with the small red-walled servery and sensibly placed darts at the back; board games. Adnams Southwold, Crafty Beers Sauvignon Blonde and Timothy Taylors Boltmaker on handpump, a decent wine list and Old Rosie cider. Picnic-sets are set under parasols on the front grass.

Honest food includes lunchtime sandwiches, mushroom pâté and roast figs with rosemary and thyme shortbread, caribbean-spiced beef dumplings with mango salsa, local sausages with onion gravy, aubergine and tomato lasagne, beer-battered haddock and chips, duck breast with apple sauce and potato and romaine salad, and puddings such as lemon crème brûlée and sticky toffee pudding with butterscotch sauce. *Benchmark main dish: steak frites £13.50. Two-course evening meal £25.00.*

Free house ~ Licensee George Gibson ~ Real ale ~ Open 12-2.30, 6-11; 12-11 Sat; 12-10.30 Sun; closed Mon ~ Bar food 12-1.45, 6.45-8.45; not Sun evening, Mon ~ Restaurant ~ Children allowed but must be well behaved ~ Dogs welcome ~ Wi-fi *Recommended by Ivor Smith, Peter Brix, Toby Jones, Mark Morgan, Mike Swan*

STILTON
Bell ♀ 🛏

TL1689 Map 5

(01733) 241066 – www.thebellstilton.co.uk

High Street; village signposted from A1 S of Peterborough; PE7 3RA

Fine coaching inn with character bars, popular food, thoughtful drinks choice and seats in a pretty courtyard; bedrooms

If the A1 is proving too much, this elegant and civilised hotel (a lovely example of a 17th-c coaching inn) is the perfect place for a break. Our favourite spot is the neatly kept right-hand bar which has a great deal of character: bow windows, sturdy upright wooden seats on flagstone floors, a big log fire in a handsome stone fireplace, partly stripped walls with large prints of sailing and winter coaching scenes, and a giant pair of blacksmith's bellows. This room has been opened up with the bistro to create a bar-cum-dining area with a bustling, chatty atmosphere. A beer named for the pub from Digfield, Grainstore Red Kite, Greene King IPA and Old Speckled Hen and Oakham Bishops Farewell on handpump, several malt whiskies and 14 wines by the glass; service is helpful and welcoming. Other rooms include a residents' bar and a restaurant; background music and TV. Through the fine coach arch is a very pretty sheltered courtyard with tables, and a well that dates from Roman times. The bedrooms mix old-world charm with modern facilities and three are on the ground floor.

Quite a choice of enjoyable food includes cornish crab on toast with bloody mary ketchup, buttermilk-fried chicken with thai sweet chilli mayonnaise, ham and free-range eggs, vegetable tart with charred leeks and parsnip, beer-battered haddock and chips, sea bass fillet with basil and potato purée, tapenade and pepperade, slow-cooked pork with charred greens and caramelised apples, and puddings such as iced banana and passion-fruit parfait with honey-roasted oats and treacle tart rice pudding with raisins. *Benchmark main dish: beef blade with parmesan and potato bake and mustard jus £16.50. Two-course evening meal £23.00.*

Free house ~ Licensee Liam McGivern ~ Real ale ~ Open 12-2.30, 6-11; 12-midnight Fri, Sat; 12-10.30 Sun ~ Bar food 12-2.15 (2.30 Sat), 6-9.30; 12-3, 6-9 Sun ~ Restaurant ~ Children welcome ~ Wi-fi ~ Bedrooms: £87.50/£112.50 *Recommended by B and M Kendall, David Stewart, Mr and Mrs P R Thomas, Richard Kennell, Andrew Lawson, John and Delia Franks*

SUTTON GAULT
Anchor 🍴 ♀ 🛏

TL4279 Map 5

(01353) 778537 – www.anchor-inn-restaurant.co.uk

Bury Lane off High Street (B1381); CB6 2BD

Charming candlelit inn with beamed rooms, excellent food, real ales and a thoughtful wine list; bedrooms

This is an enjoyable place to stay in comfortable, well equipped bedrooms that overlook the river, and the breakfasts are very good. It's a gently civilised inn and although space for drinks may be limited at weekends, at other times you can pop in for a pint of Milton Sparta and Nethergate Azzanewt on handpump or one of the dozen or so wines by the glass. The four heavily timbered rooms are stylishly simple, with two log fires, antique settles and wooden dining chairs around scrubbed pine tables, set with candles and nicely spaced on gently undulating floors. Service is helpful and friendly. There are seats outside and you can walk along the high embankment where bird-watching is good.

Impressive food includes ham hock terrine with pineapple and chilli chutney, king scallops with roasted cauliflower, almonds, butternut squash purée and curry oil, grilled goats cheese salad with orange segments, marinated artichoke and honey dressing, beef in ale pie with horseradish mash and gravy, cod with pea and leek risotto, pickled courgette and shrimp and caper butter, bacon-wrapped pork tenderloin and slow-cooked belly with apple and sage purée and cider jus, and puddings such as dark chocolate brownie with lemon curd and fig sorbet and elderflower pannacotta with pink champagne and raspberry sorbet; they also offer a two- and three-course set lunch. *Benchmark main dish: chicken with saffron risotto balls, carrot purée and spicy coconut and cream sauce £18.00. Two-course evening meal £23.00.*

Free house ~ Licensee Ina Nicolajsen ~ Real ale ~ Open 12-11 ~ Bar food 12-2, 7-9; 12-2.30, 6-9.30 Sat; 12-2.30, 6.30-8.30 Sun ~ Restaurant ~ Children welcome ~ Wi-fi ~ Bedrooms: £59.50/£79.50 *Recommended by Colin and Daniel Gibbs, Charlie Parker, Millie and Peter Downing, Martin and Clare Warne, Brian Glozier, Phil and Jane Villiers*

THORNEY
Dog in a Doublet

TL2799   Map 5

(01733) 202256 – www.doginad.co.uk
B1040 towards Thorney; PE6 0RW

Country inn with produce from own farm, tasty food and local ales, friendly service and seats outside; bedrooms

The River Nene and one of the biggest lock gates in Europe are just across the road from this friendly country dining pub. Much emphasis here is, of course, on the enjoyable food but the bar has sofas, comfortable seats and an open fire and Angles Ales Goat Tosser, Kings Cliffe 5C and RCH Old Slug Porter on handpump, several wines by the glass and farm cider. The restaurant leads off and has an open kitchen, solid wooden dining chairs around farmhouse tables, prints on red-painted walls and a monthly live pianist; background music. A deli counter offers their own produce and treats from further afield too. Outside, there are brightly painted picnic-sets under a gazebo. The four bedrooms have vaulted ceilings and their own balconies, and they have a campsite. The inn is handy for Hereward Way walks.

Their small farm provides free-range eggs, home-grown vegetables and home-reared pigs for the popular food, which includes smoked eel and smoked mackerel pâté with apple and horseradish, black pudding with a poached egg, smoked bacon and mustard cream, macaroni cheese with garlic mushrooms, a pie of the day, veal meatballs with tomatoes and capers on pasta, lamb burger with toppings and sweet potato fries, lamb shoulder in harissa with butternut and bourbon purée, parmentier potatoes and raita, and puddings such as eton mess and brownies with home-made irish cream. *Benchmark main dish: their own sausages £15.00. Two-course evening meal £20.00.*

Free house ~ Licensees John McGinn and Della Mills ~ Real ale ~ Open 12-2.30, 5-10.30; 12-11 Sat; 12-10.30 Sun; closed Mon and Tues lunchtimes ~ Bar food 12-2.30, 5-9; 12-9 Sat; 12-7 Sun ~ Children welcome ~ Dogs allowed in bar and bedrooms ~ Wi-fi ~ Bedrooms: £50/£70 *Recommended by Peter Brix, Edward Nile, Donald Allsopp*

UFFORD
White Hart

TF0904   Map 5

(01780) 740250 – www.whitehartufford.co.uk
Main Street; S on to Ufford Road off B1443 at Bainton, then right; PE9 3BH

Lots of interest in bustling pub, bar and dining rooms, good food and extensive garden; bedrooms

In warm weather the three acres of gardens at the back here are a huge bonus – they include a sunken dining area with plenty of chairs and tables, picnic-sets on grass, steps to various quiet corners and lovely flowers and shrubs. Inside, this former farm is now a comfortable, welcoming inn with plenty of drinking and dining space. The bar has an easy-going atmosphere, farm tools and chamber-pots, scatter cushions on leather benches, some nice old chairs and tables, a woodburning stove, exposed stone walls and stools against the counter where they serve Grainstore Red Kite, Oakham JHB and Timothy Taylors Landlord on handpump, 18 wines by the glass and 15 gins. There's also an elegant beamed restaurant and an airy Orangery. Four of the comfortable bedrooms are in the pub, two are in a converted cart shed and four more are in the Old Brewery.

Well thought-of food includes sandwiches, gin-cured salmon with fennel, cucumber and dill, potted ham hock with home-made piccalilli, honey and mustard glazed ham and eggs, chargrilled red pepper and halloumi burger with home-made coleslaw and sweet potato chips, beer-braised ox cheek with horseradish mash and roasted root vegetables, slow-roasted lamb shoulder with leek and potato dauphinoise, sea bass with braised fennel, samphire, caper butter and herb-crushed potatoes, and puddings such as chocolate brownie with chocolate sauce and white chocolate ice-cream and apple and blackberry crumble with calvados custard. *Benchmark main dish: pheasant with baby onions, smoked bacon and mushroom sauce and creamed potatoes £14.50. Two-course evening meal £25.00.*

Free house ~ Licensee Sue Olver ~ Real ale ~ Open 8am-11pm (midnight Sat); 8am-9pm Sun ~ Bar food 12-2.30, 6-9; 12-9 Sat; 12-7.30 Sun ~ Restaurant ~ Children welcome ~ Dogs allowed in bar and bedrooms ~ Wi-fi ~ Bedrooms: /£80 *Recommended by Jack and Hilary Burton, John Sargeant, Daniel King, David and Leone Lawson, Matt and Hayley Jacob*

WHITTLESFORD
TL4648   Map 5

Tickell Arms ⬤ ♟

(01223) 833025 – www.cambscuisine.com/the-tickell-whittlesford
2.4 miles from M11 junction 10: A505 towards Newmarket, then second turn left signposted Whittlesford; keep on into North Road; CB22 4NZ

Light and refreshing dining pub with good enterprising food and pretty garden

There are some fine architectural features here, so it's really worth wandering around the bars and dining rooms. The L-shaped bar has bentwood stools on floor tiles, ornate cast-iron pillars, a woodburning stove and – under bowler-hatted lampshades over the counter – Brewsters Hophead, Elgoods Cambridge Bitter and Milton Pegasus on handpump, 20 fairly priced wines by the glass including champagne, and farm cider. Also, there are three porcelain handpumps from the era of the legendarily autocratic regime of the Wagner-loving former owner Kim Tickell. Tables in the dining room vary from sturdy to massive, with leather-cushioned bentwood and other dining chairs and one dark pew, and fresh minimalist décor in palest buff. This opens into an even lighter limestone-floored conservatory area, partly divided by a very high-backed ribbed-leather banquette. Staff are neatly dressed and friendly. The side terrace has comfortable tables, and the secluded garden beyond has pergolas and a pond. This is sister pub to the Cock in Hemingford Grey and the Crown & Punchbowl at Horningsea.

Creative modern food using local, seasonal produce includes lunchtime sandwiches, pigeon breast with truffled pearl barley, apple purée, poached apples and crispy pork belly, seared squid with clam velouté, roasted shallots and tarragon, polenta with beetroot, balsamic caviar and puy lentils, sausage and mash with onion gravy, pork tenderloin with crispy ham hock, black pudding crumb, carrot purée and red wine gravy, sea trout with celery heart, crab bisque and tarragon oil, and puddings such as blueberry cheesecake with prosecco sorbet and sticky toffee pudding with toffee sauce and ice-cream; steak evening is Tuesday and they also offer a two- and three-course set menu (not Friday evening, Saturday or Sunday lunch). *Benchmark main dish: venison haunch with rosemary and potato croquettes, cauliflower purée and red wine sauce £19.00. Two-course evening meal £25.00.*

Free house ~ Licensees Oliver Thain, Richard Bradley, Max Freeman ~ Real ale ~ Open 12-3, 6-11; 12-11 Sat; 12-10.30 Sun ~ Bar food 12-2.30, 6.30-9; 12-2.30, 6-9.30 Fri, Sat; 12-3, 6-8 Sun ~ Restaurant ~ Children must be over 10 in pub and over 5 in evening restaurant ~ Dogs allowed in bar ~ Wi-fi *Recommended by Revd R P Tickle, Mrs Margo Finlay, Jörg Kasprowski, Sally Harrison, Gail and Frank Hackett, Katherine and Hugh Markham*

Also Worth a Visit in Cambridgeshire

Besides the fully inspected pubs, you might like to try these pubs that have been recommended to us and described by readers. Do tell us what you think of them: feedback@goodguides.com

ABBOTS RIPTON TL2377
Abbots Elm (01487) 773773
B1090; PE28 2PA Open-plan thatched dining pub reconstructed after major fire; well liked food from snacks and bar meals to interesting restaurant dishes using locally sourced and home-grown produce, extensive choice of wines by the glass including champagne, three well kept ales, good service; children and dogs welcome, four bedrooms, open all day Sat, till 4pm Sun, closed Mon. *(Christopher Mannings)*

AMPTHILL TL0337
Albion (01525) 634857
Dunstable Street; MK45 2JT Drinkers' pub with up to 12 well kept ales including local B&T and Everards, real ciders and a perry, friendly knowledgeable staff, no food apart from lunchtime rolls; monthly folk night and other live music; dogs welcome, paved beer garden, open all day. *(Caroline and Steve Archer)*

BARRINGTON TL3849
Royal Oak (01223) 870791
Turn off A10 about 3.7 miles SW of M11 junction 11, in Foxton; West Green; CB22 7RZ Rambling thatched Tudor pub with tables out overlooking classic village green, heavy low beams and timbers, mixed furnishings, Adnams and three guests, Aspall's and Thatcher's ciders, enjoyable food from pub favourites up, good wine list, friendly helpful service, airy dining conservatory; background music, free wi-fi; children and dogs welcome, classic car club meeting first Fri of month. *(Mike Swan)*

BOURN TL3256
★**Willow Tree** (01954) 719775
High Street, just off B1046 W of Cambridge; CB23 2SQ Light and airy dining pub with relaxed informal atmosphere despite the cut-glass chandeliers, sprinkling of Louis XVI furniture and profusion of silver-plated candlesticks; accomplished restaurant-style cooking (all day Sun till 8pm), Woodfordes and a local guest, several wines by the glass and inventive cocktails, friendly staff; live jazz Sun evening; children welcome, smart tables and chairs on back deck, grassed area beyond car park with fruit trees, huge weeping willow and tipi, open all day. *(Christopher Mannings)*

BOXWORTH TL3464
Golden Ball (01954) 267397
High Street; CB23 4LY Attractive partly thatched 16th-c village pub with pitched roof bar, restaurant and small conservatory, emphasis on good fairly priced food from baguettes through pubby choices and grills to blackboard specials, well kept Charles Wells ales, good wine and whisky choice; free wi-fi; children welcome, nice garden and heated terrace, pastures behind, 11 quiet bedrooms in adjacent block, open all day, food till 7pm Sun. *(John Harris)*

BRAMPTON TL2170
Black Bull (01480) 457201
Church Road; PE28 4PF 16th-c and later with updated low-ceilinged interior, stripped-wood floor and inglenook woodburner in split-level main bar, restaurant with light wood furniture on tiles, enjoyable well priced pubby food including good home-made pies, four real ales, friendly efficient staff; free wi-fi; children welcome, dogs in bar (treats for them), garden with play area, open (and food) all day, till 9pm (4pm) Sun. *(Mike Swan)*

BRINKLEY TL6254
Red Lion (01638) 508707
High Street; CB8 0RA Old country pub with beams and inglenook log fire, enjoyable food from fairly pubby menu, Sun brunch, Adnams and a couple of guests, friendly

service; free wi-fi; children and dogs (in bar) welcome, garden tables, closed Sun evening, Mon, Tues. *(Mark Morgan)*

BROUGHTON   TL2877
★ **Crown** (01487) 824428
Off A141 opposite RAF Wyton; Bridge Road; PE28 3AY Attractively tucked-away mansard-roofed dining pub opposite church; fresh airy décor with country pine tables and chairs on stone floors, some leather bucket seats and sofa, good well presented food (not Sun evening) from lunchtime sandwiches up, friendly service, real ales such as Mauldons, restaurant; background music; children and dogs welcome, disabled access and facilities, tables out on big stretch of grass behind, open all day Sun till 8pm, may close Mon and Tues evenings in winter. *(John Harris)*

BUCKDEN   TL1967
★ **George** (01480) 812300
High Street; PE19 5XA Handsome and stylish Georgian-faced hotel with bustling informal bar, fine fan beamwork, leather and chrome chairs, log fire, Adnams Southwold and a changing guest from chrome-topped counter, lots of wines including champagne by the glass, teas and coffees, popular brasserie with good modern food served by helpful enthusiastic young staff, also bar meals; background music; children and dogs welcome, tables under large parasols on pretty sheltered terrace with box hedging, 12 charming bedrooms named after famous Georges, smallish car park (free street parking), open all day. *(Michael Sargent)*

BUCKDEN   TL1967
Lion (01480) 810313
High Street; PE19 5XA Partly 15th-c coaching inn under newish ownership; dark beams and big inglenook log fire in airy bow-windowed bar, Adnams Southwold, several guest beers and a dozen wines by the glass, panelled back restaurant, enjoyable food from sandwiches up including set lunch Mon-Fri, friendly service; free wi-fi; children welcome, back courtyard, 14 bedrooms, open all day and handy for A1. *(David Stewart)*

CAMBRIDGE   TL4458
Anchor (01223) 353554
Silver Street; CB3 9EL Pub-restaurant in beautiful riverside position by punting station, popular with tourists and can get very busy; fine river views from upper dining room and suntrap terrace, five well kept beers and plenty of wines by the glass, good variety of food (fairly priced for the area), friendly service; live jazz Thurs; children and dogs welcome, open (and food) all day. *(Tony Scott)*

CAMBRIDGE   TL4658
★ **Cambridge Blue** (01223) 471680
85 Gwydir Street; CB1 2LG Friendly little backstreet local with a dozen or more interesting ales (some tapped from the cask – regular festivals), also six craft kegs, 200 bottled beers, six ciders and 70 whiskies, enjoyable well priced home-made food including seasonal specials, attractive conservatory and extended bar area with lots of breweriana and old advertising signs; free wi-fi; children and dogs welcome, seats in back garden bordering cemetery, open (and food) all day and can get very busy weekends. *(Mike Swan)*

CAMBRIDGE   TL4459
Castle (01223) 353194
Castle Street; CB3 0AJ Adnams range and interesting guest beers in big airy bare-boards bar, other pleasantly simple rooms including snug and quieter upstairs area, good value pub food from sandwiches and snacks to blackboard specials, efficient friendly young staff; background music, free wi-fi; children and dogs welcome, picnic-sets in good walled back courtyard, open all day. *(John Harris)*

CAMBRIDGE   TL4658
Clarendon Arms (01223) 778272
Clarendon Street; CB1 1JX Welcoming backstreet corner local; pubby furniture on flagstones or bare boards, lots of pictures including local scenes, step down to back bar, Greene King ales and enjoyable home-made food from snacks to Sun roasts, friendly helpful service; free wi-fi; children and dogs welcome, wheelchair access with help, seats in sunny back courtyard, open all day, no food Sun evening. *(Max Simons)*

CAMBRIDGE   TL4657
Devonshire Arms (01223) 316610
Devonshire Road; CB1 2BH Popular and welcoming Milton-tied pub with two cheerful chatty linked bars, their well kept ales and guests, real cider, also great choice of bottled beers, decent wines and a dozen malts, low-priced food (not Sun evening) from sandwiches and pizzas to steaks, creaky wood floors, mix of furniture including long narrow refectory tables, architectural prints and steam engine pictures, woodburner in back bar; wheelchair access, handy for the station, open all day. *(John Harris)*

CAMBRIDGE   TL4458
★ **Eagle** (01223) 505020
Benet Street; CB2 3QN Once the city's most important coaching inn; rambling rooms with two medieval mullioned windows and the remains of possibly medieval wall paintings, two fireplaces dating from around 1600, lovely worn wooden floors and plenty of pine panelling, dark red ceiling left unpainted since World War II to preserve signatures of british and american airmen made with Zippo lighters, candle smoke and lipstick, well kept Greene King ales including Eagle DNA (Crick and Watson announced the discovery of DNA's structure here in

1953) and two guests, decent choice of enjoyable food served efficiently considering the crowds; children welcome, disabled facilities, heavy wooden seats in attractive cobbled and galleried courtyard, open all day. *(John Wooll, Ivor Smith, Tony Scott)*

CAMBRIDGE TL4558
Elm Tree (01223) 502632
Orchard Street; CB1 1JT Traditional one-bar backstreet drinkers' pub with welcoming atmosphere, ten well kept ales including B&T and Charles Wells, good range of continental bottled beers plus local cider/perry usually poured from the barrel, friendly knowledgeable staff, no food, nice unspoilt interior with breweriana and other bits and pieces; some live music; wheelchair access, a few tables out at the side, open all day. *(Max Simons)*

CAMBRIDGE TL4559
Fort St George (01223) 354327
Midsummer Common; CB4 1HA Picturesque old pub (reached by foot only) in charming waterside position overlooking ducks, swans, punts and boathouses; extended around old-fashioned Tudor core, good value bar food including traditional Sun lunch, well kept Greene King ales and decent wines by the glass, oars on beams, historic boating photographs, open fire; free wi-fi ; children and dogs welcome, wheelchair access via side door, lots of tables outside, open (and food) all day. *(Ivor Smith)*

CAMBRIDGE TL4558
Free Press (01223) 368337
Prospect Row; CB1 1DU Unspoilt little backstreet pub with interesting décor including old newspaper pages and printing memorabilia (was printshop for a local paper); Greene King IPA, Abbot and Mild plus regularly changing guests, good range of wines by the glass, 25 malt whiskies and lots of gins and rums, tasty good value food, log fire; TV for major sports events, board games; children and dogs (in bar) welcome, wheelchair access, small sheltered paved garden behind, open all day. *(David Thorpe, John Wooll)*

CAMBRIDGE TL4557
Live & Let Live (01223) 460261
Mawson Road; CB1 2EA Popular backstreet pub with friendly relaxed atmosphere, five well kept ales including Oakham, proper cider and over 120 rums, snacky food, panelled interior with sturdy varnished tables on bare boards, some steam railway and brewery memorabilia,

old gas light fittings, cribbage and dominoes; dogs welcome, disabled access awkward but possible, closed Wed and Thurs lunchtimes. *(Sally Harrison)*

CAMBRIDGE TL4458
Mill (01223) 311829
Mill Lane; CB2 1RX Fairly compact old pub in picturesque spot overlooking mill pond (punt hire); seven mainly local ales and proper cider from plank-topped servery, reasonably priced food such as burgers, opened-up bar with bare boards, quarry tiles and some exposed brickwork, mix of old and new furniture including pews and banquettes, snug panelled back room; radiogram playing vinyl, Mon quiz, sports TV, free wi-fi; children welcome, open (and food) all day. *(Richard Tilbrook)*

CAMBRIDGE TL4458
Mitre (01223) 358403
Bridge Street, opposite St Johns College; CB2 1UF Popular Nicholsons pub close to the river and well placed for visiting the colleges; spacious rambling bar on several levels, good selection of well kept ales, farm cider and reasonably priced wines by the glass, their usual good value food including fixed-price menu, efficient friendly service; background music, free wi-fi; children welcome, disabled access, open (and food) all day. *(R T and J C Moggridge)*

CAMBRIDGE TL4559
Old Spring (01223) 357228
Ferry Path; car park on Chesterton Road; CB4 1HB Extended Victorian pub, roomy and airy, with enjoyable home-made food from traditional choices up, friendly efficient service, well kept Greene King IPA, Abbot and four guests, plenty of wines by the glass and good coffee, mix of seating including sofas on bare boards, log fires, conservatory; background music; well behaved children welcome, dogs outside only, disabled facilities, seats out in front and on large heated back terrace, open all day, food all day Sun. *(Ivor Smith)*

CAMBRIDGE TL4458
Pint Shop (01223) 352293
Peas Hill; CB2 3PN Revamped former university offices on two floors; front bar with restaurant behind, parquet floors, grey-painted walls, simple furnishings and pendant lighting, 16 craft/cask beers from smaller brewers listed on blackboard, good selection of wines and around 60 gins, unusual food from bar snacks up cooked on charcoal grill, set menu options Mon-Fri, further dining room upstairs;

Cribbage is a card game using a block of wood with holes for matchsticks or special pins to score with; regulars in cribbage pubs are usually happy to teach strangers how to play.

ground floor wheelchair access/loos, courtyard picnic-sets, handy for Cambridge Arts Theatre and Corn Exchange, open all day. *(Rupert and Sandy Newton)*

CASTOR   TL1298
★ **Prince of Wales Feathers**
(01733) 380222 *Peterborough Road, off A47; PE5 7AL* Friendly stone-built local with half a dozen well kept ales including Castor, craft beers and proper cider/perry, good value food cooked by landlady (not weekend evenings), open-plan interior with dining area to the left; Sat live music, Sun quiz, pool (free Thurs), TV; children and dogs welcome, disabled facilities, attractive front terrace, another at the back with large smokers' shelter, open all day, till late weekends. *(Sally Harrison)*

CATWORTH   TL0873
Racehorse (01832) 710123
B660, S of A14; PE28 0PF Welcoming 19th-c village pub with enjoyable food from sandwiches/panini and sharing boards up, three well kept changing ales and good choice of wines, whiskies and gins, cheerful helpful service, smallish bar connecting to more spacious dining areas, log fire, delicatessen/coffee shop; some live music, pool, TV; children and dogs welcome, café-style tables outside, five bedrooms in converted stables, closed Sun evening, otherwise open all day (till 10pm Mon-Thurs). *(Michael Sargent, Guy and Caroline Howard)*

CONINGTON   TL3266
White Swan (01954) 267251
Signed off A14 (was A604) Cambridge–Huntingdon; Elsworth Road; CB23 4LN Quietly placed 18th-c red-brick country pub; well kept Adnams and guests tapped from the cask, nine wines by the glass and good freshly made imaginative food (not Mon, Tues or Sun evening), friendly efficient service, traditional bar with tiled floor and log fire, restaurant extension, some old photographs and local artwork; children and dogs welcome, big front garden with play area, open all day. *(Christopher Mannings)*

DUXFORD   TL4745
Plough (01223) 833170
St Peters Street; CB22 4RP Popular early 18th-c thatched pub, clean bright and friendly, with enjoyable home-made food from shortish reasonably priced menu including OAP lunch Tues, Adnams, Everards and guests kept well, also a craft keg such as Oakham Green Devil IPA and four ciders, woodburner in brick fireplace; children

welcome, handy for IWM Duxford, open all day (no food Sun evening, Mon). *(John Harris)*

ELLINGTON   TL1671
Mermaid (01480) 891106
High Street; PE28 0AB Popular village dining pub dating in part from the 14th c; highly praised imaginative food (not Sun evening) from owner-chef including interesting tapas menu and plenty for vegetarians/vegans, a couple of Greene King ales and a guest from brick counter, several wines by the glass (good list), friendly obliging young staff, beams (some hiding coins left by US airmen), country furniture, woodburner, smallish dining rooms; background music (turned off on request); garden overlooking church, no proper car park, open all day weekends (till 8pm Sun), closed Mon. *(Michael Sargent, Roy Shutz, Mike and Mary Carter)*

ELSWORTH   TL3163
George & Dragon (01954) 267236
Off A14 NW of Cambridge, via Boxworth, or off A428; CB23 8JQ Neatly kept dining pub in same group as the Eaton Oak at St Neots and Rose at Stapleford; panelled and carpeted main bar opening on left to slightly elevated dining area with woodburner, garden room overlooking attractive terraces, more formal restaurant on right, wide choice of popular food including speciality fish/seafood, set menus and other deals, Greene King ales, a guest beer and decent range of wines, friendly service; steps down to lavatories, free wi-fi; children welcome, dogs in bar, open (and food) all day Sun. *(Michael and Jenny Back)*

ELSWORTH   TL3163
Poacher (01954) 267722
Brockley Road; CB23 4JS Restored 17th-c thatched and beamed corner local; well kept Woodfordes Wherry, St Austell Tribute and a couple of guests from tiny servery, good reasonably priced pubby food (not Sun evening), friendly service, painted pine furniture on bare boards or tiles, open fire; background and some live music, monthly quiz, TV; children and dogs welcome, a few picnic-sets out in front, more in revamped back garden, good walks, open all day weekends. *(Charlie Stevens)*

ELTON   TL0893
Black Horse (01832) 280591
Overend; B671 off A605 W of Peterborough and A1(M); PE8 6RU Honey-stone beamed dining pub with nicely updated and opened-up interior, good generously served food cooked by owner-chef, friendly accommodating service,

---

Half pints: by law, a pub should not charge more for half a pint than half the price of a full pint, unless it shows that half-pint price on its price list.

four real ales including Digfield, Greene King and a beer badged for the pub, decent wines; children welcome, dogs in bar (their westie is Molly), terrace and garden with views across to Elton Hall park and village church, open (and food) all day. *(John Preddy, Christopher Mobbs)*

ELY TL5479
Cutter (01353) 662713
Annesdale, off Station Road (or walk S along Riverside Walk from Maltings); CB7 4BN Beautifully placed riverside pub with bar, dining lounge and restaurant, enjoyable promptly served food from sandwiches, wraps and pizzas up, well kept Adnams, Sharps, Woodfordes and a guest from boat-shaped counter, nice wines by the glass and decent coffee, good views from window seats and terrace; children welcome, no dogs inside, moorings, open all day from 9am (food from midday). *(Ian and Amanda Seamark)*

ELY TL5480
Lamb (01353) 663574
Brook Street (Lynn Road); CB7 4EJ Good choice of food in popular hotel's panelled lounge bar or restaurant, friendly welcoming staff, Greene King ales and plenty of wines by the glass, decent coffee; children and dogs welcome, close to cathedral, 31 clean comfortable bedrooms, good breakfast (for non-residents), open (and food) all day. *(Ian and Amanda Seamark)*

ETTON TF1406
Golden Pheasant (01733) 252387
Just off B1443 N of Peterborough, signed from near N end of A15 bypass; PE6 7DA Former Georgian farmhouse (a pub since 1964); spacious bare-boards bar with open fire, five real ales such as Adnams, Greene King and Grainstore from central counter, decent choice of wines and spirits, good food (all day Sat, not Sun night) including competitively priced weekday set menu (lunchtime/early evening), prompt cheerful service, back panelled restaurant; some live music; children and dogs welcome, big tree-sheltered garden with play area, table tennis and table football in marquee, vintage car meetings, on Green Wheel cycle route, open all day Sat and Sun, closed Mon lunch. *(Liz and Mike Newton)*

FOWLMERE TL4245
★ Chequers (01763) 208558
High Street (B1368); SG8 7SR Popular 16th-c coaching inn with two comfortable downstairs rooms, long cushioned wall seats, dining chairs around dark tables, inglenook log fire, good traditional food served by friendly staff, Greene King, two guests and plenty of wines by the glass, attractive upstairs beamed and timbered dining room with interesting moulded plasterwork above one fireplace, spacious conservatory; children welcome, dogs in bar, terrace and garden with tables under parasols, four bedrooms, open all day weekends. *(Peter and Caroline Waites)*

GRANTCHESTER TL4355
★ Blue Ball (01223) 846004
Broadway; CB3 9NQ Character bare-boards free house rebuilt in 1900 on site of much older pub (cellars remain), sensitive renovation by present licensees (there's a list of publicans back to 1767), a couple of real ales such as Adnams and Woodfordes, Aspall's ciders and decent choice of wines by the glass, good log fire, cards and traditional games including shut the box and ring the bull, newspapers and lots of books; children and dogs welcome, tables on small terrace with lovely views to Grantchester Meadows, good heated smokers' shelter, new bedrooms, nice village, open all day (till 8pm Sun). *(Donald Allsopp)*

GRANTCHESTER TL4355
Red Lion (01223) 840121
High Street; CB3 9NF Comfortable and spacious thatched pub with attractively modernised open areas including pitched-roof dining room, beams, timbers and panelling, good variety of enjoyable food from baguettes up, children's menu, well kept Nene Valley, Greene King, Jo C's and Trumans, lots of wines by the glass and interesting gins such as Cambridge distilled nearby, friendly efficient service; background music; dogs and muddy boots welcome, sheltered terrace and good-sized lawn with play area, easy walk to river, open (and food) all day. *(Clive and Fran Dutson)*

GRANTCHESTER TL4455
Rupert Brooke (01223) 841875
Broadway; junction Coton Road with Cambridge–Trumpington Road; CB3 9NQ Smartly refurbished restauranty pub; contemporary wood-clad extension with huge windows, elegant dining chairs around polished tables on bare boards, back bar area with comfy sofas and two-level restaurant, brasserie-style food (not particularly cheap) from open kitchen, Woodfordes Wherry, a beer from Milton and several wines by the glass, courteous staff, upstairs club room and roof terrace; free wi-fi; children and dogs (in bar) welcome, open all day (till 7pm Sun). *(Paul Scofield, Sally Wright, Hilary and Neil Christopher, Mrs Margo Finlay, Jörg Kasprowski)*

GREAT ABINGTON TL5348
Three Tuns (01223) 891467
Off A1307 Cambridge–Haverhill, and A11; CB21 6AB Peacefully set 16th-c beamed village pub, low-backed settles on stripped-wood floors, open fires, good authentic thai food (traditional roast on Sun), three well kept changing ales, welcoming landlord and friendly efficient

staff; garden picnic-sets, nine well appointed bedrooms in modern block, open all day weekends. *(Mrs Margo Finlay, Jörg Kasprowski)*

GREAT CHISHILL — TL4239
★ **Pheasant** (01763) 838535
Follow Heydon signpost from B1039 in village; SG8 8SR Popular old split-level flagstoned pub with beams, timbers, open fires and some elaborately carved (though modern) seats and settles, good freshly made food (not Sun evening) using local produce, welcoming friendly staff, two or three ales including one for the pub from Nethergate and good choice of wines by the glass, small dining room (best to book); darts, cribbage, dominoes; no under-14s inside, dogs allowed, charming secluded back garden with small play area, open all day weekends.
(Charlie Stevens)

GREAT GRANSDEN — TL2655
Crown & Cushion (01767) 677214
Off B1046 Cambridge–St Neots; West Street; SG19 3AT Small thatched and beamed local in pretty village, two or three well kept ales such as Adnams and Oakham, authentic indonesian cooking from landlady (Fri evening, Sat, Sun), friendly staff, woodburner in big fireplace; live music; small garden, open all day weekends, closed Mon and lunchtimes Tues-Fri. *(John Harris)*

HADDENHAM — TL4675
Three Kings (01353) 749080
Station Road; CB6 3XD Popular 17th-c village pub, well kept Greene King IPA and guests, enjoyable home-made food from sandwiches and pub favourites up, good friendly service; children and dogs welcome, back courtyard, open all day, food all day weekends. *(Dipak Raxit)*

HARDWICK — TL3758
Blue Lion (01954) 210328
Signed off A428 (was A45) W of Cambridge; Main Street; CB23 7QU Attractive 18th-c split-level dining pub; good food using home-grown ingredients from landlord-chef in bar and extended dining area with conservatory, Greene King IPA and guests, friendly efficient young staff, beams and timbers, leather armchairs by copper-canopied inglenook; children welcome, pretty little front garden, more seats on decking and lawn with play area, handy for Wimpole Way walks, open all day (food all day weekends). *(Sally and Lance Oldham)*

HELPSTON — TF1205
Blue Bell (01733) 252394
Woodgate; off B1443; PE6 7ED Extended 17th-c stone pub refurbished under present owners, enjoyable food from snacks and sharing plates up, four well kept ales including Fullers London Pride and a house beer from local Star, good range of wines and gins, friendly staff; children and dogs welcome, four bedrooms, open all day weekends, no food Sun evening, John Clare's cottage next door (open Fri, Sat and Mon).
(John Harris)

HEYDON — TL4339
★ **King William IV** (01763) 838773
Off A505 W of M11 junction 10; SG8 8PW Rambling dimly lit rooms with fascinating rustic jumble (ploughshares, yokes, iron tools, cowbells and so forth) along with copperware and china in nooks and crannies, some tables suspended by chains from beams, central log fire, Fullers, Greene King and Timothy Taylors, good varied choice of well presented food including proper home-made pies, helpful staff; background music; children and dogs (in bar) welcome, teak furniture on heated terrace and in pretty garden, four bedrooms in separate building, open all day weekends. *(Patti and James Davidson)*

HISTON — TL4363
★ **Red Lion** (01223) 564437
High Street, off Station Road; 3.7 miles from M11 junction 1; CB24 9JD Impressive choice of draught and bottled beers along with traditional cider/perry (festivals Easter/early Sept); ceiling joists in L-shaped main bar packed with hundreds of beer mats and pump clips among hop bines and whisky-water jugs, fine collection of old brewery advertisements too, enjoyable traditional food (all day Sat, not Fri, Sun evenings), cheerful efficient service, log fires, comfortable brocaded wall seats, matching mate's chairs and pubby tables, extended bar on left (well behaved children allowed here) with darts, TV and huge collection of beer bottles; mobile phones discouraged, no dogs inside; disabled access/facilities, picnic-sets in neat garden, limited parking, four bedrooms, open all day. *(John Harris)*

KIMBOLTON — TL0967
New Sun (01480) 860052
High Street; PE28 0HA Up for sale as we went to press so could be changes; cosiest room is low-beamed front lounge with standing timbers, exposed brickwork, and comfortable seats by log fire, narrower locals' bar has Charles Wells ales, several wines by the glass and decent range of gins, well regarded food, traditionally furnished dining room and airy conservatory leading to terrace with smart furniture under giant umbrellas; background music, piano, board games and quiz machine; well behaved children welcome away from bar, dogs allowed in bar, note that some nearby parking has

---

We say if we know a pub allows dogs.

a 30-minute limit, open all day, no food Sun or Mon evenings. *(Carol and Barry Craddock, Edward Nile, Julian Richardson)*

LEIGHTON BROMSWOLD   TL1175
Green Man   (01480) 890238
Signed off A14 Huntingdon–Kettering; PE28 5AW Cosy traditional village pub with origins from the 13th c; four well kept changing ales and ample helpings of enjoyable good value food from ciabattas to specials, long-serving landlady and pleasant staff, heavy low beams, inglenook log fire, northants skittles; children welcome, picnic-sets outside, boules, closed Sun evening. *(Guy and Caroline Howard)*

LITTLE SHELFORD   TL4551
Navigator   (01223) 843901
2.5 miles from M11 junction 11: A10 towards Royston, then left at Hauxton, The Shelfords signpost; CB2 5ES Attractive little 16th-c village pub with bar and small restaurant, beams, painted panelling and some exposed brickwork, open fire, good authentic thai food (not Sun), mainstream ales and decent wines, friendly prompt service; children welcome, some picnic-sets outside, closed Sat lunchtime and Sun evening. *(Esther and John Sprinkle)*

NEWTON   TL4349
★Queens Head   (01223) 870436
2.5 miles from M11 junction 11; A10 towards Royston, then left on to B1368; CB22 7PG Lovely traditional unchanging pub run by same welcoming family for many years – lots of loyal customers; peaceful bow-windowed main bar with crooked beams in low ceiling, bare wooden benches and seats built into cream walls, curved high-backed settle, paintings and big log fire, Adnams ales tapped from the cask, farm cider and simple food such as soup and sandwiches, small carpeted saloon, traditional games including table skittles, shove-ha'penny and nine men's morris; no credit cards; children on best behaviour allowed in games room only, dogs welcome, seats out in front by vine trellis. *(Sarah Flynn, Ivor Smith)*

OFFORD D'ARCY   TL2166
Horseshoe   (01480) 810293
High Street; PE19 5RH Extended former 17th-c coaching house with two bars and restaurant, emphasis on good food including popular Sun carvery, friendly helpful service, up to five changing ales and well chosen wines, beams and inglenooks; children welcome, lawned garden with play area, open all day weekends. *(Charlie Stevens)*

ORWELL   TL3650
Chequers   (01223) 207840
Town Green Road; SG8 5QL Village dining pub with good food (not Tues or Sun evening) including popular themed nights, well kept ales and decent choice

of wines by the glass, pleasant helpful staff; children and dogs (in bar) welcome, disabled facilities, open all day Fri and Sat, till 8pm Sun, closed Mon. *(John Harris)*

PAMPISFORD   TL4948
★Chequers   (01223) 833220
2.6 miles from M11 junction 10: A505 E, then village and pub signed off; Town Lane; CB22 4ER Traditional neatly kept old pub with friendly licensees, low beams and comfortable old-fashioned furnishings, booth seating on pale ceramic tiles in cream-walled main area, low step down to bare-boards part with dark pink walls, Greene King IPA and a couple of guests, good fairly priced food including themed nights, Sun carvery and OAP lunch Weds, good friendly service; TV, free wi-fi; children and dogs welcome (their collie is Snoopy), picnic-sets in prettily planted small garden lit by black streetlamps, parking may be tricky, open all day (till 4pm Sun). *(Roy Hoing)*

PETERBOROUGH   TL1998
★Charters   (01733) 315700
Town Bridge, S side; PE1 1FP Interesting conversion of dutch grain barge moored on River Nene; sizeable timbered bar on lower deck with up to a dozen real ales including Oakham (regular beer festivals), restaurant above serving good value SE asian food, lots of wooden tables and pews; background music, live bands (Fri and Sat after 10.30pm, Sun from 3.30pm); children welcome till 9pm, dogs in bar, huge riverside garden (gets packed in fine weather), open all day (till 1am Fri, Sat). *(Christopher Mannings)*

PETERBOROUGH   TL1897
Coalheavers Arms   (01733) 565664
Park Street, Woodston; PE2 9BH Friendly old-fashioned little flagstoned local near football ground and busy on match days; half a dozen well kept ales including Milton, good range of bottled beers, traditional cider and several malt whiskies, basic snacks; Sun quiz, free wi-fi; dogs welcome, pleasant garden behind, open all day Fri-Sun, closed lunchtime Mon-Weds; for sale as we went to press, so may be changes. *(Mark Morgan)*

PETERBOROUGH   TL1898
Drapers Arms   (01733) 847570
Cowgate; PE1 1LZ Roomy open-plan Wetherspoons in converted 19th-c draper's, ten well kept ales and their usual good value food served all day, prompt friendly service; TV, free wi-fi; children welcome, open from 8am and can get very busy Fri, Sat evenings. *(Mark Morgan)*

ST IVES   TL3171
Oliver Cromwell   (01480) 465601
Wellington Street; PE27 5AZ Homely two-bar pub in little street just back from the river, enjoyable good value lunchtime food such as steak and kidney pudding, half

a dozen well kept changing ales (one always at a bargain price) and good choice of wines, friendly staff; live music Thurs, quiz first Tues of the month; small back terrace, open all day. *(Dave and Jan Pilgrim)*

ST NEOTS   TL1761
Eaton Oak (01480) 219555
Just off A1, Great North Road/ Crosshall Road; PE19 7DB Under same ownership as the George & Dragon at Elsworth and Rose at Stapleford; wide choice of popular food including grills, fresh fish and good value weekday set menu, Wells and Youngs ales plus a guest, good friendly service, plenty of nooks and crannies in older part, two front snugs, light airy dining area and conservatory; free wi-fi; children and dogs (in bar) welcome, disabled access and loo, tables out under parasols, hanging baskets and tubs of flowers, smokers' shelter, nine bedrooms, open all day (breakfast for non-residents). *(Michael and Jenny Back)*

STAPLEFORD   TL4651
Rose (01223) 843349
London Road; M11 junction 11; CB22 5DG Comfortable sister dining pub to the Eaton Oak at St Neots and George & Dragon at Elsworth, good choice of popular fairly pubby food including set menus and Mon, Tues early-bird deal, friendly uniformed staff, Courage Directors, Youngs Best and Wells Bombardier, small low-ceilinged lounge with inglenook woodburner, roomy split-level dining area; steps up to lavatories;

picnic-sets on back grass, open (and food) all day weekends. *(John Harris)*

THRIPLOW   TL4346
Green Man (01763) 208855
3 miles from M11 junction 10; A505 towards Royston, then first right; Lower Street; SG8 7RJ Welcoming little roadside pub owned by the village, good food from shortish daily changing menu along with blackboard tapas, four well kept ales and decent wines by the glass, efficient friendly service; free lift home for local evening diners (must book); children and dogs welcome, picnic-sets on small grassy triangle in front, two circular walks from the pub, closed Mon, otherwise open (and food) all day, till 7pm (6pm) Sun. *(Christopher Mannings)*

WHITTLESFORD   TL4648
Bees in the Wall (01223) 834289
North Road; handy for M11 junction 10 and IWM Duxford; CB22 4NZ Village-edge local with comfortably worn-in split-level timbered lounge, polished tables and country prints, small tiled public bar with old wall settles, darts, decent good value food from shortish menu, well kept Adnams Lighthouse and one or two guests, open fires; background and live music including folk club second Tues of month, small TV for major sporting events; children welcome, no dogs, picnic-sets in big paddock-style garden with terrace, bees still in the wall (here since the 1950s), closed all day Mon, lunchtimes Tues-Thurs (and Sat in winter), no food Sun evening or Tues. *(Peter and Emma Kelly)*

Post Office address codings confusingly give the impression that some pubs are in Cambridgeshire, when they're really in Bedfordshire, Lincolnshire, Norfolk or Northamptonshire (which is where we list them).

Cheshire

 ALDFORD SJ4259 Map 7

Grosvenor Arms ★ ♀ ◖

(01244) 620228 – www.brunningandprice.co.uk/grosvenorarms
B5130 Chester–Wrexham; CH3 6HJ

Spacious place with impressive range of drinks, wide-ranging imaginative menu, good service, suntrap terrace and garden

There's plenty of interest and individuality in the various chatty bars here. Spacious cream-painted areas are sectioned by big knocked-through arches with a variety of floor finishes (wood, quarry tiles, flagstones, black and white tiles), and the richly coloured turkish rugs look well against these natural materials. Good solid pieces of traditional furniture, plenty of pictures and attractive lighting keep it all intimate. A handsome room has tall bookshelves lining one wall; good selection of board games. Well trained, attentive staff serve Phoenix Brunning & Price Original, Weetwood Eastgate and Timothy Taylors Landlord with guests such as Big Hand Seren, Cheshire Brew Brothers Chester Gold, Phoenix Monkeytown Mild and Stonehouse Station Bitter from a fine-looking bar counter, and they offer 20 wines by the glass, more than 80 whiskies and 30 gins. Lovely on summer evenings, the airy terracotta-floored conservatory has lots of gigantic low-hanging flowering baskets and chunky pale wood garden furniture. It opens out to a large elegant suntrap terrace and a neat lawn with picnic-sets; the village green is opposite.

Interesting modern food includes sandwiches, haggis and black pudding hash cake with crisp pancetta, poached egg and grain mustard sauce, crab and cucumber salad with crab pannacotta and crab cake with lime and chilli marmalade, thai green sweet potato curry with pak choi, baby corn, cashew nuts and coconut rice, pork and leek sausages with onion gravy and mash, salmon fillet with orzo pasta salad, red pepper pesto and roasted courgettes, chicken breast with bacon, mushroom and barley risotto and red wine sauce, and puddings such as crème brûlée and Oreo and chocolate brownie cheesecake with white chocolate ice-cream. *Benchmark main dish: smoked salmon and haddock fishcakes £10.95. Two-course evening meal £22.00.*

Brunning & Price ~ Manager Justin Realff ~ Real ale ~ Open 11-11; 12-10.30 Sun ~ Bar food 12-9.30 (10 Fri, Sat); 12-9 Sun ~ Children welcome ~ Dogs allowed in bar ~ Wi-fi
Recommended by W K Wood, Aiden, Mike and Wena Stevenson, Michael and Sarah Lockley, John and Mary Warner, Peter and Emma Kelly

ALLOSTOCK
SJ7271 Map 7

Three Greyhounds Inn ⭑ 🏆

(01565) 723455 – www.thethreegreyhoundsinn.co.uk

4.7 miles from M6 junction 18: A54 E then fork left on B5803 into Holmes Chapel, left at roundabout on to A50 for 2 miles, then left on to B5082 towards Northwich; Holmes Chapel Road; WA16 9JY

Relaxing, civilised and welcoming, with enjoyable food and drink all day

A smashing choice of drinks here includes 14 interesting wines by the glass, 49 brandies and six local cider brandies, a farm cider and Three Greyhounds Bitter (named for the pub from Weetwood) plus quickly changing guests such as Caledonian Deuchars IPA, Storm Desert Storm, Tatton Ale and Titanic Anchor on handpump. The rooms are interconnected by open doorways, and décor throughout is restful: thick rugs on quarry tiles or bare boards, candles and soft lighting, dark grey walls (or interesting woven wooden ones made from old brandy barrels) hung with modern black-on-white prints. There's an appealing variety of wooden dining chairs, cushioned wall seats, little stools and plenty of plump purple scatter cushions around all sorts of tables – do note the one made from giant bellows; unobtrusive background music. Above the old farm barns is a restored private dining and party room called the Old Dog House. The big side lawn has picnic-table sets under parasols, with more tables on a decked side verandah with a Perspex roof. Shakerley Mere nature reserve is just across the road. The pub is owned by Tim Bird and Mary McLaughlin of Cheshire Cat Pubs & Bars.

 Carefully crafted food includes sandwiches, ham hock and candied apple terrine with spiced pear chutney, spicy crispy soft shell crab with coconut and chilli oil, cheese boards and sharing plates, feta, roasted sweet potato and red pepper tart, steak and marrow burger with treacle-cured bacon, coleslaw and chips, smoked haddock, salmon and spinach pie with parsley mash and cheese crumble, chicken, coconut and lemongrass curry with pineapple salsa, and puddings such as their own 'mess' with meringue, chantilly cream, caramelised apple and local cider brandy and milk chocolate and peanut butter brownie with vanilla ice-cream. *Benchmark main dish: chicken, ham, leek and tarragon pie £13.95. Two-course evening meal £19.00.*

Free house ~ Licensee James Griffiths ~ Real ale ~ Open 12-midnight; 12-11 Sun ~ Bar food 12-9.15 (9.45 Fri, Sat; 8.45 Sun) ~ Children welcome until 7pm ~ Dogs allowed in bar ~ Wi-fi ~ Live music every second Fri *Recommended by Brian and Sally Wakeham, John and Mary Warner, Caroline Prescott, Barry and Daphne Gregson, Jim King*

ASTBURY
SJ8461 Map 7

Egerton Arms £ 🛏

(01260) 273946 – www.egertonarms.co.uk

Village signposted off A34 S of Congleton; CW12 4RQ

Cheery pub with popular bar food, four real ales and large garden; nice bedrooms

You can be sure of a warm welcome from the hands-on licensees in this bustling 16th-c pub. The cream-painted rooms are decorated with newspaper cuttings relating to 'Grace' (the landlady's name), the odd piece of armour, shelves of books and quite a few mementoes of the Sandow Brothers (one of whom was the landlady's father) who performed as 'the World's Strongest Youths'. In summer, dried flowers replace the fire in the big fireplace; background music, games machine and TV. Robinsons Dizzy

Blonde, Double Hop, Unicorn and a guest beer on handpump, 13 wines by the glass, 15 malt whiskies and alcoholic winter warmers. There are picnic-sets on a terrace with more on grass, as well as a gazebo and a children's play area. This is a pretty spot with the church opposite and Little Moreton Hall (National Trust) nearby.

Food is reasonably priced and much liked: sandwiches and baps, crayfish cocktail, brie and pear salad, spinach and ricotta cannelloni, steak and kidney pudding, gammon and egg, lambs liver and onions in rich gravy, sweet and sour prawns with rice, and puddings such as chocolate fudge cake and lemon cheesecake; they also offer an OAP set lunch (not Sunday). *Benchmark main dish: beer-battered cod and chips £12.50. Two-course evening meal £17.00.*

Robinsons ~ Tenants Allen and Grace Smith ~ Real ale ~ Open 11.30-10.30 (11 Sat) ~ Bar food 11.30-2, 6-9; 12-7.30 Sun ~ Restaurant ~ Children welcome until 8pm ~ Wi-fi ~ Bedrooms: £60/£75 *Recommended by Anne Taylor, Paul Matthews, Mike and Wena Stevenson, Lionel Smith*

ASTON
Bhurtpore ★ ♀ ◖ £
SJ6146 Map 7

(01270) 780917 – www.bhurtpore.co.uk
Off A530 SW of Nantwich; in village follow Wrenbury signpost; CW5 8DQ

Warm-hearted pub with some unusual artefacts and an excellent range of drinks (especially real ales); big garden

They keep a fantastic choice of drinks here, with around 11 constantly changing real ales from all over the country. These might include Cheshire Brewhouse Sorachi Ace, Coastal Angelina, Hobsons Old Prickly, Idle Valley Unpretentious Declarant, Peakstones Rock Submission, Rat Rat Attack, Thornbridge McConnells Vanilla Stout and so forth. They also stock dozens of unusual bottled beers and fruit beers, a great many bottled ciders and perries and farm cider, over 100 different whiskies, 58 gins, 20 vodkas, 22 rums, carefully selected soft drinks and a dozen wines from a good list. The pub name commemorates the 1826 siege of Bhurtpore (a town in India) during which local landowner Sir Stapleton Cotton (later Viscount Combermere) was commander-in-chief. The connection with India also explains some of the quirky artefacts in the carpeted lounge bar – look out for the sunglasses-wearing turbanned figure behind the counter. There are also good local period photographs and some attractive furniture in the comfortable public bar; board games, pool, TV and games machine. Weekends tend to be pretty busy.

As well as their popular half a dozen curries, the tasty food includes breaded brie with cumberland dressing, onion bhajis with yoghurt and mint dip and mango chutney, chicken in creamy stilton and smoked bacon sauce, gammon with egg or pineapple, burger with coleslaw and chips, salmon fillet in white wine sauce, duck breast in plum sauce, quite a few daily specials, and puddings such as salted caramel cheesecake and raspberry crème brûlée. *Benchmark main dish: steak and kidney pie £11.00. Two-course evening meal £16.50.*

Free house ~ Licensee Simon George ~ Real ale ~ Open 12-11.30 (midnight Fri, Sat); 12-11 Sun ~ Bar food 12-2, 5.30-9.30 (8.30 Mon); 12-9.30 Fri, Sat; 12-9 Sun ~ Restaurant ~ Children welcome ~ Dogs allowed in bar ~ Wi-fi *Recommended by Andrew Vincent, Thomas Green, Nick Sharpe, Jo Garnett, Donald Allsopp, Buster and Helena Hastings*

The ◖ symbol shows pubs that keep their beer unusually well, have a particularly good range or brew their own.

BARTHOMLEY SJ7752 Map 7

White Lion £

(01270) 882242 – www.whitelionbarthomley.co.uk

M6 junction 16, B5078 N towards Alsager, then Barthomley signed on left; CW2 5PG

Timeless 17th-c thatched village tavern with classic period interior, up to half a dozen real ales and good value lunchtime food

This is a world away from the nearby M6. It's one of the most attractive buildings in a pretty village and is quite unspoilt and charming – and very much part of the local community. The bar has a blazing open fire, heavy oak beams dating from Stuart times, attractively moulded black panelling, prints of Cheshire on the walls, latticed windows and uneven wobbly old tables. Up some steps, a second room has another welcoming open fire, more oak panelling, a high-backed winged settle and a paraffin lamp hinged to the wall; shove-ha'penny. Local societies make good use of a third room. Jennings Cocker Hoop and Sneck Lifter, Marstons EPA and Pedigree, Sunbeam Best Bitter and Thwaites Wainwright on handpump served by genuinely friendly staff. The gents' are across an open courtyard. In summer, seats on cobbles outside offer nice village views. The early 15th-c red sandstone church of St Bertoline (where you can learn about the Barthomley massacre) is worth a visit.

 Good value, simple food is served only at lunchtime and includes sandwiches and baguettes, cottage pie, hotpots, sausage and mash with onion gravy, a changing pasta dish, and puddings such as fruit sponge and chocolate roll. *Benchmark main dish: steak and Guinness pie £7.95.*

Marstons ~ Tenant Peter Butler ~ Real ale ~ Open 12-11 (10.30 Sun) ~ Bar food 12-2 Mon, Tues; 12-3 Weds-Sun ~ Children welcome away from bar counter ~ Dogs allowed in bar ~ Wi-fi *Recommended by Charlie May, Mike Swan, Mike and Wena Stevenson, John Harris, Heather and Richard Jones*

BOSTOCK GREEN SJ6769 Map 7

Hayhurst Arms ♀ ◖

(01606) 541810 – www.brunningandprice.co.uk/hayhurstarms

London Road, Bostock Green; CW10 9JP

Interesting pub with a marvellous choice of drinks, a wide choice of rewarding food, friendly staff and seats outside

Right by the village green, this former stables and coach house is a social hub for locals but offers a warm welcome to visitors too. The long main bar is divided into different dining areas by elegant support pillars, and it's light and airy throughout: big windows, house plants, bookshelves, standard lamps, metal chandeliers and prints, old photographs and paintings arranged frame-to-frame above wooden dados. The varied dark wooden dining chairs are grouped around tables of all sizes on rugs, quarry tiles, wide floorboards and carpet, and three open fireplaces have big mirrors above them, with hefty leather armchairs to the sides. A couple of cosier rooms lead off; background music and board games. Phoenix Brunning & Price Original and Weetwood Eastgate Ale with guests such as Amber Ales Imperial IPA, Merlin Castle Black Stout and Wizard, Moorhouses Blond Witch and RedWillow Seamless on handpump, 25 wines by the glass, 70 malt whiskies and 25 gins; staff are efficient and courteous. The outside terrace has good quality tables and chairs under parasols, and the village green opposite has swings and a play tractor.

🍴 Good, interesting food includes sandwiches, spiced crab and salmon samosas with lime yoghurt and pineapple and mango salsa, air-dried beef with pickled radishes and english mustard mayonnaise, blue cheese, broccoli and leek quiche with crème fraîche new potato salad, steak in ale pudding, south indian-spiced sea bass fillets baked in a banana leaf with coconut sauce and lemongrass rice, chicken with chorizo, olives and pesto on pasta with tomato sauce, and puddings such as crème brûlée and bread and butter pudding with apricot sauce. *Benchmark main dish: braised lamb shoulder with dauphinoise potatoes £17.25. Two-course evening meal £25.00.*

Brunning & Price ~ Manager Christopher Beswick ~ Real ale ~ Open 11-11 (10.30 Sun) ~ Bar food 12-10 (9.30 Sun) ~ Children welcome ~ Dogs allowed in bar ~ Wi-fi
Recommended by Katherine Matthews, Barbara Brown, Dr Peter Crawshaw, Sabina and Gerald Grimshaw, Nik and Gloria Clarke

BUNBURY
Dysart Arms ♀ 🍺
SJ5658 Map 7

(01829) 260183 – www.brunningandprice.co.uk/dysart
Bowes Gate Road; village signposted off A51 NW of Nantwich; and from A49 S of Tarporley – coming in this way on northernmost village access road, bear left in village centre; CW6 9PH

Civilised chatty dining pub with thoughtfully laid-out rooms, enjoyable food and a lovely garden with pretty views

The meandering series of knocked-through rooms at this well run country pub give an intimate and homely but still very sociable atmosphere, and while cream walls keep it light and airy, deep venetian-red ceilings add cosiness. Each room (some with good winter fires) is nicely furnished with an appealing variety of well spaced sturdy wooden tables and chairs, a couple of tall filled bookcases and just the right amount of carefully chosen bric-a-brac, properly lit pictures and plants. Flooring ranges from red and black tiles to stripped boards and some carpet. Phoenix Brunning & Price Original and Weetwood Best Bitter with guests such as Pennine Real Blonde, Salopian Oracle, Storm Beauforts Ale and Titanic Plum Porter are served on handpump alongside a good selection of 17 wines by the glass, 30 gins and around 20 malts; background music and board games. There are sturdy wooden tables on the terrace and picnic-sets on the lawn in the neatly kept and slightly elevated garden, and the views of the splendid church at the end of this pretty village and the distant Peckforton Hills beyond are lovely.

🍴 Up-to-date food from an interesting menu includes sandwiches, potted brown shrimp and crayfish with pickled cucumber, curried mussels on bruschetta with coriander crème fraîche, sweet potato, cauliflower and chickpea tagine with tempura courgette and couscous, local sausages with mash and onion gravy, lemon and thyme chicken with chorizo croquette and tomato jus, and puddings such as apple, blackberry and hazelnut crumble and key lime pie. *Benchmark main dish: beef and stilton pie £14.95. Two-course evening meal £22.00.*

Brunning & Price ~ Manager Daniel Rose ~ Real ale ~ Open 11-11 (10.30 Sun) ~ Bar food 12-9.30 (9 Sun) ~ Children welcome ~ Dogs allowed in bar ~ Wi-fi *Recommended by Mary Joyce, Tony Smaithe, Mike and Wena Stevenson, Scott and Charlotte Havers, Sophia and Hamish Greenfield*

'Children welcome' means the pub says it lets children inside without any special restriction. If it allows them in, but to restricted areas such as an eating area or family room, we specify this. Some pubs may impose an evening time limit. We do not mention limits after 9pm as we assume children are home by then.

BURLEYDAM SJ6042 Map 7

Combermere Arms

(01948) 871223 – www.brunningandprice.co.uk/combermere

A525 Whitchurch–Audlem; SY13 4AT

Roomy and attractive beamed pub successfully mixing a good drinking side with imaginative all-day food

A fine range of drinks served by attentive, friendly staff are just two of the draws to this partly 16th-c pub. It's been cleverly extended without losing too much character and there are plenty of nooks and crannies in the rambling yet intimate-feeling rooms. Attractive and understated, they're filled with all sorts of antique cushioned dining chairs around dark wood tables, rugs on wood (some old, some new oak) and stone floors, prints hung frame-to-frame on cream walls, bookshelves and open fires. They serve Phoenix Brunning & Price Original and Weetwood Cheshire Cat Blonde Ale and guests such as Joules Slumbering Monk, Moorhouses White Witch, Salopian Oracle and Sharps Doom Bar on handpump, 100 malt whiskies, 20 wines by the glass from an extensive list and two farm ciders; board games and background music. Outside there are good solid wood tables and picnic-sets in a pretty, well tended garden.

Often inventive food includes sandwiches, potted crab and crayfish with samphire, caper and cucumber salad, chicken liver parfait with spiced pear and date chutney, basil gnocchi with warm gazpacho sauce, leeks and aubergine, steak burger with toppings, coleslaw and chips, sausages with onion gravy and mash, venison steak with rabbit and pigeon faggot, fondant potato and bramble gravy, sea bass fillet with brown shrimps, potato and caper cake and white wine sauce, and puddings such as lemon meringue roulade with raspberry sauce and dark chocolate and espresso tart with Baileys ice-cream. *Benchmark main dish: braised lamb shoulder with dauphinoise potatoes and rosemary gravy £17.25. Two-course evening meal £21.00.*

Brunning & Price ~ Manager Lisa Hares ~ Real ale ~ Open 12-11 (10.30 Sun) ~ Bar food 12-9.30 (10 Thurs-Sat); 12-9 Sun ~ Children welcome ~ Dogs allowed in bar ~ Wi-fi
Recommended by Ken Stein, Michael Butler, Dr Simon Innes, Jack Trussler, Chris Stevenson, Sally and David Champion

BURWARDSLEY SJ5256 Map 7

Pheasant ★

(01829) 770434 – www.thepheasantinn.co.uk

Higher Burwardsley; signposted from Tattenhall (which itself is signposted off A41 S of Chester) and from Harthill (reached by turning off A534 Nantwich–Holt at the Copper Mine); follow pub's signpost uphill from Post Office; OS Sheet 117 map reference 523566; CH3 9PF

Cheshire Dining Pub of the Year

Fantastic views and enjoyable food at this clever conversion of an old heavily beamed inn; good bedrooms

Plenty of walks surround this pretty 17th-c inn and the scenic Sandstone Trail along the Peckforton Hills is nearby. The attractive low-beamed interior is airy and modern-feeling in parts, and the various separate areas have nice old chairs spread spaciously on wooden floors and a log fire in a huge see-through fireplace. Local Weetwood Best, Cheshire Cat Blonde Ale and Eastgate and a guest such as Pheasant Gold (named for the pub, also from Weetwood) on handpump, 13 wines by the glass, ten malt whiskies and local farm cider served by friendly, helpful staff; quiet background music and daily newspapers. From picnic-sets on the terrace, you can enjoy one of the county's most magnificent views right across the Cheshire plains; on a clear day with the telescope you can see as far as the pier head and cathedrals in Liverpool. The comfortable, character bedrooms are in the main building or an ivy-clad stable wing and make a great base for exploring the area. Sister pubs are the Fishpool in Delamere and Bears Paw in Warmingham.

As well as sandwiches (until 6pm), the excellent food includes tiger prawn pil pil, guinea fowl breast with butternut squash gratin, apple purée and red wine sauce, sharing boards, crab, prawn and avocado salad with caviar, kiwi and pineapple, a pie of the day, broccoli, vintage cheddar and wild mushroom quiche with herb salad, sour cream dressing and black truffle, fillet of turbot with ox cheek fritters, pickled cucumber and chive oil, goosnargh duck breast with duck leg croquettes, pistachio and bacon crumb, roasted orange purée and truffle potato rösti, and puddings such as crème caramel with rosewater syrup and pearls, raspberry jam and honeycomb and dark chocolate fondant with orange and anise jelly and violet ice-cream. *Benchmark main dish: venison haunch with blackberry sauce, bacon crumb, polenta, parmesan and chive potatoes £16.25. Two-course evening meal £23.00.*

Free house ~ Licensee Andrew Nelson ~ Real ale ~ Open 11-11 (10.30 Sun) ~ Bar food 12-9.30 (10 Fri, Sat; 9 Sun) ~ Restaurant ~ Children welcome ~ Dogs welcome ~ Wi-fi ~ Bedrooms: £115/£125 *Recommended by Peter Harrison, Sylvia and Phillip Spencer, Matt and Hayley Jacob, Rosie and John Moore, Guy Henderson*

CHESTER
Albion ★ ◀ £

SJ4066 Map 7

(01244) 340345 – www.albioninnchester.co.uk
Albion Street; CH1 1RQ

Strongly traditional pub with comfortable Edwardian décor and captivating World War I memorabilia; pubby food and good drinks

This is a genuinely friendly, old-fashioned pub and the charming licensees have been amassing an absorbing collection of World War I memorabilia here for over 40 years; in fact, this is an officially listed site of four war memorials to soldiers from the Cheshire Regiment. The peaceful rooms are filled with big engravings of men leaving for war and similarly moving prints of wounded veterans, as well as flags, advertisements and so on. There are also leatherette and hoop-backed chairs around cast-iron-framed tables, lamps, an open fire in the Edwardian fireplace and dark floral William Morris wallpaper (designed on the first day of World War I). You might even be lucky enough to hear the vintage 1928 Steck pianola being played; there's an attractive side dining room too. The cats Charlie and Rosie appear after food service has finished. Big Rock Harvest Pale Ale and Moorhouses Pride of Pendle on handpump, new world wines, fresh orange juice, organic bottled cider and fruit juice, over 25 malt whiskies and a good selection of rums and gins. Bedrooms are small but comfortable and furnished in keeping with the pub's style (free parking for residents and a bottle of house wine if dining). An attractive way to reach the place is along the city wall, coming down at Newgate/Wolfsgate and walking along Park Street. No children. Please note: if the pub is quiet they may close early, so it's best to ring ahead and check.

The generously served 'trench rations' include club and doorstep sandwiches, corned beef hash with pickled red cabbage, fish pie with cheese topping, boiled gammon and pease pudding with parsley sauce, haggis and tatties, and lambs liver, bacon and onions with cider gravy. *Benchmark main dish: cottage pie £9.70. Two-course evening meal £15.00.*

Punch ~ Lease Mike and Christina Mercer ~ Real ale ~ Open 12-3, 5 (6 Sat)-11 (best to phone); 12-2.30 Sun; closed Sun evening ~ Bar food 12-2 (2.30 weekends), 5-8 (8.30 Sat) ~ Dogs allowed in bar ~ 1920s quartet; black tie Great War concerts ~ Bedrooms: £80/£90
Recommended by John Beeken, David and Leone Lawson, John and Delia Franks, David H Bennett, Steve Whalley

CHESTER
Architect ♀ ◖

SJ4066 Map 7

(01244) 353070 – www.brunningandprice.co.uk/architect
Nicholas Street (A5268); CH1 2NX

Lively pub by the racecourse with interesting furnishings and décor, attentive staff, a good choice of drinks and super food

On race days (there are views over Roodee Racecourse), this well run and friendly pub is even busier than normal and customers spill out on to the terrace. It's almost a place of two halves connected by a glass passage. The pubbiest part, with a more bustling feel, is the garden room where they serve Phoenix Brunning & Price Original and Weetwood Eastgate alongside guests such as Big Hand Savanna, Cheshire Brew Brothers Earls Eye Amber and Roodee Dark, Cheshire Brewhouse Cheshire Set and Lindow and Stonehouse Sunlander on handpump, 18 wines by the glass, 74 whiskies and farm cider. Throughout there are elegant antique dining chairs around a mix of nice old tables on rugs or bare floorboards, hundreds of interesting paintings and prints on green, cream or yellow walls, house plants and flowers on windowsills and mantelpieces, and lots of bookcases. Also, open fires, armchairs in front of a woodburning stove or tucked into cosy nooks, candelabra and big mirrors, and an easy-going atmosphere; background music and board games. Big windows and french doors look over a terrace, where there are plenty of good quality wooden seats and tables under parasols.

Pleasing contemporary food includes sandwiches, spiced crab samosas with fennel, cucumber and mint salad and lime yoghurt, deep-fried brie with candied pecans and pickled cramberries, sweet potato, pumpkin and chickpea tagine with lemon and coriander couscous, thai red fish curry with pak choi and coconut rice, steak in ale pudding with mustard mash, spiced duck with sweet potato fondant, parsnip purée and tamarind jus, and puddings such as crème brûlée and rhubarb and ginger trifle. *Benchmark main dish: wild boar burger topped with blue rarebit, cider and apple chutney and fries £13.75. Two-course evening meal £21.00.*

Brunning & Price ~ Manager Natalie Shaw ~ Real ale ~ Open 10.30am-11pm; 10.30-10.30 Sun ~ Bar food 12-10 (9.30 Sun) ~ Children welcome ~ Dogs allowed in bar ~ Wi-fi
Recommended by Sophie Ellison, Michael Butler, Peter Pilbeam, Isobel Mackinlay, Alfie Bayliss, Mungo Shipley

CHESTER
Mill ◖ £

SJ4166 Map 7

(01244) 350035 – www.millhotel.com
Milton Street; CH1 3NF

Big hotel with huge range of real ales, good value food and cheery service in sizeable bar; bedrooms

You would not expect this large modern hotel to stock up to a dozen real ales on handpump – in fact, they get through more than 2,000 guest beers a year. Weetwood Best and Mill Premium (brewed for them by Coach

House) are available all the time, with guests such as Castle Rock Harvest Pale, 8 Sail Victorian Porter, Oakham JHB, Phoenix Navvy, Rudgate Viking, Spitting Feathers Special Ale and Titanic Atlantic Red; also, a dozen wines by the glass, two farm ciders and 20 malt whiskies. You'll find a real mix of customers in the neatly kept bar which has some exposed brickwork and supporting pillars, slate-effect wallpaper, contemporary purple/grey upholstered seats around marble-topped tables on light wooden flooring, and helpful, friendly staff; a glass-walled dining extension has been added. One comfortable area is reminiscent of a bar on a cruise liner; quiet background music and unobtrusively placed big-screen sports TV. Converted from an old mill, the hotel straddles either side of the Shropshire Union Canal, with a glassed-in bridge connecting the two sections. The bedrooms are comfortable and rather smart.

There are several different menus, but the bar food includes sandwiches, chicken caesar salad, steak burger with coleslaw and home-made chips, vegetarian lasagne and steak and mushroom pie; more elaborate dishes include monkfish on a bed of samphire, milanese chicken with cucumber and yoghurt dip, and rib-eye steak with shallot and mushroom sauce, and puddings such as lemon curd cheesecake and sticky toffee pudding. *Benchmark main dish: beer-battered fish and chips £10.95. Two-course evening meal £20.00.*

Free house ~ Licensee Gordon Vickers ~ Real ale ~ Open 10am-midnight (11pm Sun) ~ Bar food 12-10 ~ Restaurant ~ Children welcome ~ Wi-fi ~ Live jazz Mon ~ Bedrooms: £74/£98 *Recommended by John Wooll, Peter Brix, John and Delia Franks, Lee and Jill Stafford, Mark and Sian Edwards*

CHESTER
SJ4166   Map 7

Old Harkers Arms ♀ ⌖

(01244) 344525 – www.brunningandprice.co.uk/harkers
Russell Street, down steps off City Road where it crosses canal; CH3 5AL

Well run canalside building with a lively atmosphere, fantastic range of drinks and extremely good food

There was indeed a Mr Harker who once ran a canalboat chandler's here right next to the Shropshire Union Canal – you can still watch the boats from the tall windows that run the length of the main bar. The striking industrial interior with its high ceilings is divided into user-friendly spaces by brick pillars. Walls are covered with old prints hung frame-to-frame, there's a wall of bookshelves above a leather banquette at one end, the mixed dark wood furniture is set out in intimate groups on stripped-wood floors and attractive lamps lend some cosiness; board games. Cheerful staff serve Phoenix Brunning & Price Original and Weetwood Cheshire Cat Blonde Ale with guests such as Abbeydale Moonshine, Big Hand Havok, Heavy Industry Freak Chick, Titanic Plum Porter and Woodfordes Norfolk Nog on handpump, 120 malt whiskies, 20 wines from a well described list, 30 gins and six farm ciders.

Brasserie-style food includes sandwiches, pulled pork croquettes with barbecue sauce and green chilli coleslaw, baked camembert with rosemary and garlic, sweet potato, cauliflower and chickpea tagine with lemon and coriander couscous, local sausages with mash and onion gravy, cumin and chilli chicken with tzatziki and sweet potato wedges, smoked haddock and salmon fishcakes with tomato and spring onion salad, slow-braised lamb shoulder with dauphinoise potatoes and gravy, and puddings such as crème brûlée and hot waffle with butterscotch sauce and honeycomb ice-cream. *Benchmark main dish: steak burger with toppings, coleslaw and chips £12.95. Two-course evening meal £19.50.*

Brunning & Price ~ Manager Paul Jeffery ~ Real ale ~ Open 10.30am-11pm; 12-10.30 Sun ~ Bar food 12-9.30 ~ Children welcome but no babies, toddlers or pushchairs ~ Dogs allowed in bar ~ Wi-fi *Recommended by Simon Collett-Jones, John Beeken, Jeremy Snaithe, David H Bennett, Andy and Louise Ramwell, Daniel King*

CHOLMONDELEY
SJ5550 Map 7
Cholmondeley Arms 🌟 ⌾ ♀ 🛏

(01829) 720300 – www.cholmondeleyarms.co.uk
Bickley Moss; A49 5.5 miles N of Whitchurch; SY14 8HN

Former schoolhouse with a decent range of real ales and wines, well presented food and sizeable garden; bedrooms

As well as an extraordinary number of gins – 370 as we went to press – they also keep Cholmondeley Best (from Weetwood) and three guests such as Big Shed Engineers Best, Coach House Gunpowder Strong Mild, Wincle Sir Philip and York Pure Gold on handpump and 15 wines by the glass in this interestingly converted schoolhouse. The bar rooms have lofty ceilings and tall Victorian windows plus huge old radiators and school paraphernalia (hockey sticks, tennis rackets, trunks and so forth). There's a lot of individuality such as armchairs by the fire with a massive stag's head above, big mirrors, all sorts of dining chairs and tables, warmly coloured rugs on bare boards, fresh flowers and church candles; background music. As well as plenty of seating on a sizeable lawn (which drifts off into open countryside), there's more in front overlooking the quiet road. The bedrooms are in the old headmaster's house opposite and named after real and fictional teachers; the pictures dotted about actually did belong to former headmasters. Cholmondeley Castle Gardens are nearby. The pub is owned by Tim Bird and Mary McLaughlin of Cheshire Cat Pubs & Bars.

As well as sandwiches, the reliably good food includes smoked salmon and crab cocktail with gin and tonic jelly, devilled lambs kidneys on toast, sharing plates, steak and kidney pie, smoked cheese, sage and onion sausages with bloody mary gravy, king prawn, scallop, lemongrass and chilli curry with sticky coconut rice, Guinness and treacle-braised short rib of beef with colcannon mash, wild garlic chicken with bacon and tarragon sauce, and puddings such as salted caramel brownie with vanilla ice-cream and mango, passion-fruit and coconut cheesecake with pineapple salsa and chilli and mint syrup. *Benchmark main dish: wagyu burger with treacle-cured bacon, onion rings and chips £14.95. Two-course evening meal £19.50.*

Free house ~ Licensee Timothy Moody ~ Real ale ~ Open 12-11 (11.30 Fri, Sat) ~ Bar food 12-9.30 (9.45 Fri, Sat) ~ No under-10s after 7pm ~ Dogs welcome ~ Wi-fi ~ Bedrooms: £85/£100 *Recommended by Peter Harrison, Roger and Anne Newbury, R T and J C Moggridge, Audrey and Paul Summers, Margo and Derek Stapley*

COTEBROOK
SJ5765 Map 7
Fox & Barrel 🌟 ♀

(01829) 760529 – www.foxandbarrel.co.uk
A49 NE of Tarporley, CW6 9DZ

Attractive building with stylishly airy décor, an enterprising menu and good wines

Despite the emphasis here on the first class food, drinkers feel quite at home on the high chairs against the bar counter or on the cushioned benches and settles. Friendly staff serve a beer named for the pub and Weetwood Eastgate plus a couple of guests such as Black Sheep Golden

Sheep and Wincle Waller on handpump; they also have 16 wines by the glass from a good list. A big log fire dominates the bar while a larger uncluttered beamed dining area has attractive rugs and an eclectic mix of period tables on polished floorboards, with extensive wall panelling hung with framed old prints. The front terrace has plenty of smart tables and chairs under parasols; at the back, there are picnic-sets on grass and some nice old fruit trees. There's a big new car park at the front.

Accomplished food includes sandwiches (until 6pm), pigeon and green peppercorn terrine and sticky shallots, flame-grilled and smoked mackerel with beetroot, orange and horseradish, chickpea dhal, tandoori tofu, roasted vegetables and naan, omelette arnold bennett, coq au vin, sea trout with giant couscous, spicy nuts and yoghurt, pork loin, marinated belly, plum and crispy potatoes, and puddings such as syrup sponge pudding with custard and white chocolate and passion-fruit mousse with pistachio sponge. *Benchmark main dish: beer-battered fish and chips £13.95. Two-course evening meal £19.00.*

Free house ~ Licensee Gary Kidd ~ Real ale ~ Open 12-11 (10.30 Sun) ~ Bar food 12-9.30 (9 Sun) ~ Children welcome ~ Dogs allowed in bar ~ Wi-fi *Recommended by Charles Fraser, Andrew Vincent, Colin and Daniel Gibbs, Robin and Anne Triggs, Mike Swan*

DELAMERE
Fishpool ♀ ◖
SJ5667   Map 7

(01606) 883277 – www.thefishpoolinn.co.uk
Junction A54/B5152 Chester Road/Fishpool Road, a mile W of A49; CW8 2HP

Something for everyone in extensive, interestingly laid-out pub, with a good range of food and drinks served all day

Plenty of snug, cosy areas lead off a big, cheerful open section in this cleverly and stylishly laid-out place, and the décor and furnishings are unusual and varied. A lofty central area, partly skylit – and full of contented diners – has a row of booths facing the long bar counter, and numerous other tables with banquettes or overstuffed small armchairs on pale floorboards laid with rugs; then comes a conservatory overlooking picnic-sets on a flagstone terrace, and a lawn beyond. Off on two sides are many rooms with much lower ceilings, some with heavy dark beams, some with bright polychrome tile or intricate parquet flooring: William Morris wallpaper here, dusky paintwork or neat bookshelves there, sofas, armchairs, a fire in an old-fashioned open range, lots of old prints and some intriguing objects including carved or painted animal skulls; background music. Weetwood Best, Cheshire Cat and Eastgate plus a guest named for the pub (from Cheshire Brew Brothers) on handpump, 13 wines by the glass, ten malt whiskies and farm cider; unobtrusive background music and upstairs lavatories. Sister pubs are the Pheasant in Burwardsley and the Bears Paw in Warmingham.

Pleasing food includes sandwiches, crispy ox cheeks and blue cheese fritters with truffled celeriac and port wine reduction and crayfish, crab and smoked halibut cocktail, crispy sweet chilli beef salad with shallots, carrots, celery and lime juice, steak burger with toppings and chips, prawn, haddock, salmon and hake pie, vegetarian thai green curry, lamb en croûte with parisienne potatoes, goats cheese, pine nuts and mint and honey-glazed vegetables, and puddings such as lemon and lime tart with berries and clotted cream and amaretto cheesecake with praline and vanilla chantilly. *Benchmark main dish: steak in ale pie £13.25. Two-course evening meal £21.00.*

Free house ~ Licensee Andrew Nelson ~ Real ale ~ Open 11-11 ~ Bar food 12-9.30 (10 Fri, Sat); 12-9 Sun ~ Restaurant ~ Children welcome ~ Dogs allowed in bar ~ Wi-fi
Recommended by Miles Green, Caroline Sullivan, Lindy Andrews, Patrick and Emma Stephenson

HAUGHTON MOSS

SJ5855 Map 7

Nags Head ♀

(01829) 260265 – www.nagsheadhaughton.co.uk

Off A49 S of Tarporley; CW6 9RN

Fine 17th-c pub with beams and timbering, character bar and dining rooms, good food and ales and pretty garden

Dating back in part to 1680, this handsome place is tucked away down country lanes. Great care has been taken to blend some stunning original features with up-to-date touches – and it works well. The bar, with leather saddle-style stools against the panelled counter and pale flagstones, has Merlin Gold, Thwaites 1629 (named for the pub), Weetwood Eastgate and a guest beer on handpump, 11 wines by the glass, 15 whiskies and several gins served by helpful staff. Several rooms lead off with lovely ancient beams and timbering, more built-in wall banquettes and tartan seats, open fires, wooden floors, and pictures and photos on painted or bare brick walls; background music and TV. The conservatory-style dining room has walls of windows, a high-pitched ceiling with rafters and joists, modern tartan, leather-seated or painted chairs around simple tables on parquet flooring, a long built-in wall banquette, and a woodburning stove. The neatly kept landscaped garden has seats and tables under parasols on the terrace and on lawns, and there's also croquet and bowls, a 'club house' and a tethering post for horses.

Using first class produce, the enjoyable food includes sandwiches, ham, chicken and black pudding terrine with a crispy egg and piccalilli, treacle-baked sticky pork ribs, cheese and onion pie with beetroot salad, lancashire hotpot with pickled red cabbage, devilled chicken breast with battered onion rings and dripping chips, fillet of bream with tempura queen scallops, chive mash and caper fish cream sauce, and puddings such as white chocolate cheesecake with caramelised pears and caramel ice-cream and lemon curd with berry compote and meringue. *Benchmark main dish: steak in ale pie £13.50. Two-course evening meal £18.00.*

Ribble Valley Inns ~ Manager James McAdam ~ Real ale ~ Open 12-11 (10.30 Sun) ~ Bar food 12-9 (9.30 Fri, Sat); 12-8 Sun ~ Restaurant ~ Children welcome ~ Dogs allowed in bar ~ Wi-fi *Recommended by Joe and Belinda Smart, Jane Rigby, Andrew Lawson, Louise and Oliver Redman, Maria and Henry Lazenby*

KETTLESHULME

SJ9879 Map 7

Swan

(01663) 732943

B5470 Macclesfield–Chapel-en-le-Frith, a mile W of Whaley Bridge; SK23 7QU

Charming 16th-c pub with enjoyable food, good beer and an attractive garden

After a walk in the relatively unfrequented north-west part of the Peak District National Park, our readers often head to this pretty white cottage for lunch. The interior is snug and cosy, with latticed windows, very low dark beams hung with big copper jugs and kettles, timbered walls, antique coaching and other prints and maps, ancient oak settles on a turkish carpet and log fires; the dining room has an open kitchen. Marstons Bitter on handpump with a couple of guest beers from breweries such as Abbeydale and Cheshire Brewhouse, 13 wines by the glass, a dozen gins and a dozen malt whiskies served by courteous, friendly staff. The front terrace has teak tables, while another two-level terrace has further tables and steamer benches under parasols.

The thoughtful menu features lots of fish dishes – such as a proper bouillabaisse, suprême of skrei cod with puy lentil and bacon casserole and crispy prosciutto, and wild turbot fillet with clam, streaky bacon and wild mushroom fricassée – as well as sandwiches, camembert fondue with warm bread and home-made chutney, spanish-style pork belly with chilli, honey and cannellini beans, cheese, potato and leek pie with white onion sauce, game pie with chips, saddle of rabbit with black pudding, pressed leg and parsnip and tarragon purée, and puddings such as brioche bread and butter pudding and Baileys cheesecake. *Benchmark main dish: beer-battered fish and chips £13.50. Two-course evening meal £25.00.*

Free house ~ Licensee Robert Cloughley ~ Real ale ~ Open 12-11 (midnight Sat); 4-8.30 Mon; 12-8 Sun; closed Mon lunchtime ~ Bar food 12-8.30; 12-4 Sun; no food Mon ~ Restaurant ~ Children welcome ~ Dogs allowed in bar ~ Wi-fi *Recommended by Alan Smith, Mary Joyce, Celia and Geoff Clay, Kerry and Guy Trooper, Thomas Green*

LOWER PEOVER $\qquad$ SJ7474 Map 7
Bells of Peover
(01565) 722269 – www.thebellsofpeover.com
Just off B5081; The Cobbles; handy for M6 junction 17; WA16 9PZ

Wisteria-covered pub in pretty setting with real ales and interesting food; lots of seating areas in the garden

Despite being off the beaten track in a quiet hamlet, plenty of customers find their way to this lovely old pub. The various rooms have beams, panelling and open fires that contrast cleverly with contemporary seating ranging from brown leather wall banquettes with scatter cushions to high-backed upholstered or leather dining chairs around an assortment of tables on bare boards; plenty of prints, paintings and mirrors on the walls. Robinsons Cumbria Way, Dizzy Blonde and Unicorn on handpump and several wines by the glass served by helpful, friendly staff; background music. Seats on the front terrace overlook the black and white 14th-c church, while at the side a decked area has rattan-style furniture under a pergola, and a spacious lawn with picnic-sets spreads down through trees all the way to a little stream.

 Good, enjoyable food includes lunchtime sandwiches and platters, pigeon breast with puy lentils, black pudding, hazelnuts and blackberry jus, chilli and garlic prawns with a herb crumb, halloumi thai green curry, a pie of the day, chicken breast with parmesan chive cream and braised lentils, hake loin with chorizo, chickpeas and coriander butter sauce, and puddings such as cheesecake of the day and chocolate brownie with ice-cream; Friday evening is steak night. *Benchmark main dish: confit pork belly with celeriac and potato dauphinoise, pork and apple fritters and madeira jus £16.25. Two-course evening meal £23.00.*

Robinsons ~ Manager Ben Antoniak ~ Real ale ~ Open 12-11 ~ Bar food 12-9 (9.30 Fri, Sat; 8 Sun) ~ Restaurant ~ Children welcome ~ Wi-fi *Recommended by Anne Taylor, Valerie Sayer, Hilary Forrest, Martin and Sue Neville, Nicola and Nigel Matthews, Rosie and Marcus Heatherley*

MACCLESFIELD $\qquad$ SJ9271 Map 7
Sutton Hall ◖
(01260) 253211 – www.brunningandprice.co.uk/suttonhall
Leaving Macclesfield southwards on A523, turn left into Byrons Lane signposted Langley, Wincle, then just before canal viaduct fork right into Bullocks Lane; OS Sheet 118 map reference 925715; SK11 0HE

Historic building set in attractive grounds, with a fine range of drinks and well trained, courteous staff

The hall at the heart of this former convent and manor house is especially noteworthy – in particular, the entrance space. It's nearly 500 years old and some of the remaining original features have been carefully restored to blend cleverly with up-to-date touches. There's a charming series of rooms (a bar, a library with books on shelves and a raised open fire and dining areas) divided by tall oak timbers: antique oak panelling, warmly coloured rugs on broad flagstones, bare boards and tiles, lots of pictures placed frame-to-frame and two more fires. Background music and board games. The atmosphere is nicely relaxed and a good range of drinks includes Phoenix Brunning & Price Original, Wincle Lord Lucan and Wibbly Wallaby and guests such as Bass, Castle Rock Harvest Pale and Timothy Taylors Landlord on handpump, 18 wines by the glass from an extensive list, 65 malt whiskies and 30 gins; service is attentive and friendly. The pretty gardens have spaciously laid-out tables (some on their own little terraces), sloping lawns and fine mature trees.

 Interesting, contemporary food includes sandwiches, tempura king prawns with pineapple, mint and chilli, maple-glazed pork belly with cauliflower purée, apple and caramelised baby onions, chicken caesar salad, steak burger with toppings, coleslaw and chips, cauliflower, chickpea and almond tagine with apricot and date couscous, fish pie with french-style peas, prosciutto-wrapped pork fillet with chorizo croquette, squash purée and red wine jus, and puddings such as glazed lemon tart with raspberry sorbet and white chocolate and passion-fruit cheesecake with passion-fruit coulis. *Benchmark main dish: braised shoulder of lamb with dauphinoise potatoes £16.95. Two-course evening meal £21.50.*

Brunning & Price ~ Manager Syd Foster ~ Real ale ~ Open 11-11 (10.30 Sun) ~ Bar food 12-10 (9.30 Sun) ~ Restaurant ~ Children welcome ~ Dogs allowed in bar ~ Wi-fi
Recommended by Jack and Hilary Burton, Brian and Sally Wakeham, Mike and Wena Stevenson, John Wooll, Dan and Nicki Barton, Katherine and Hugh Markham

MOBBERLEY
SJ7879 Map 7
Bulls Head ℗ ♀ ◖
(01565) 873395 – www.thebullsheadpub.co.uk
Mill Lane; WA16 7HX

Terrific all-rounder with interesting food and drink and plenty of pubby character

There's always something happening in this particularly well run, cheerful pub – live music, themed food nights, regular quizzes and so forth – so do check their website for dates. Our readers enjoy their visits here very much as there's always a good mix of customers and a fine range of drinks: a beer or two named for the pub (from Weetwood), Weetwood Cheshire Cat and guests from breweries such as Front Row, Merlin, Storm and Wincle on handpump (useful tasting notes too), 15 wines by the glass, around 80 whiskies and local gins. Several rooms are furnished quite traditionally but with just a touch of modernity, and there's an unpretentious mix of wooden tables, cushioned wall seats and chairs on fine old quarry tiles, black and pale grey walls contrasting well with warming red lampshades, and pink bare-brick walls and pale stripped-timber detailing; also, lots of mirrors, hops, candles, open fires, background music and board games. Dogs get a warm welcome (they're allowed in the snug) with friendly staff dispensing doggie biscuits from a huge jar, and they keep popular walk leaflets. There are seats outside in the big garden. The pub is owned by Tim Bird and Mary McLaughlin of Cheshire Cat Pubs & Bars.

Food is highly regarded and includes chicken livers with shallots in a creamy sherry sauce, ham hock and pistachio terrine with piccalilli, sharing plates, cheddar, smoked cheddar and onion potato cakes with plum and ale chutney, burger with toppings, coleslaw and chips, chicken breast with cherry tomato, soft cheese and herbs wrapped in ham with sauté potatoes, hake fillet with roasted sweet potato, courgette and spinach with mango and coriander cream sauce, and puddings such as toffee apple crumble with vanilla ice-cream and their own 'mess' with chocolate sponge, meringue, chantilly cream and cherries. *Benchmark main dish: home-made steak in ale pie with chips £13.95. Two-course evening meal £20.00.*

Free house ~ Licensee Barry Lawlor ~ Real ale ~ Open 12-10.30 (11.30 Sat) ~ Bar food 12-9.15 (9.45 Fri, Sat; 8.45 Sun) ~ Children welcome but no under-10s after 7pm ~ Dogs allowed in bar ~ Wi-fi ~ Live music twice a month *Recommended by Peter Brix, Lindy Andrews, Steve Whalley, Simon Day, Mike and Wena Stevenson, David and Charlotte Green, Martine and Lawrence Sanders*

MOBBERLEY
Church Inn ★ 🎯 ♀ 🍺

SJ7980 Map 7

(01565) 873178 – www.churchinnmobberley.co.uk
Brown sign to pub off B5085 on Wilmslow side of village; Church Lane; WA16 7RD

Nicely traditional, friendly country pub with bags of character; good food and drink

Head for the mainly medieval and Tudor St Wilfrid's Church to find this stylish and pretty brick pub just opposite. It's a friendly place with efficient young staff and the small, snug interconnected rooms have all manner of nice old tables and chairs on wide floorboards, low ceilings and plenty of candlelight. The décor in soothing greys and dark green, with some oak-leaf wallpaper, is perked up by a collection of stuffed grouse and their relatives, and a huge variety of pictures; background music and board games. Battlefield Saxon Gold, Mallorys Mobberley Best (George Mallory, lost near Everest's summit in 1924, is remembered in the church with a stained-glass window), Merlin Wizard and Tatton Church Ale-Alujah on handpump, and unusual and rewarding wines, with 16 by the glass; wine tastings can be booked in the upstairs private dining room. The sunny garden snakes down to an old bowling green with lovely pastoral views and a side courtyard has sturdy tables and benches. They give out a detailed leaflet describing a good four-mile circular walk from the pub, passing sister pub the Bulls Head en route. Dogs are welcomed in the bar with not just a tub of snacks on the counter, but maybe even the offer of a meaty 'beer'. The pub is owned by Tim Bird and Mary McLaughlin of Cheshire Cat Pubs & Bars.

🎯 Good, enjoyable food includes sandwiches, octopus carpaccio with lemon, aged balsamic and crispy rice, smoked haddock and cheddar fishcake with slow-cooked egg and braised baby gem, sharing plates, cottage pie with root vegetable gratin, black garlic gnocchi with roasted jerusalem artichoke, beer-battered fish and chips, corn-fed chicken breast with crispy wing, wild mushrooms, truffled mash and mushroom sauce, stone bass with sauerkraut, spiced sausage and onion sauce, and puddings such as chocolate ganache (layers of white chocolate and vanilla, milk chocolate and salted caramel and dark chocolate with pedro ximénez) and rhubarb and custard crumble tart. *Benchmark main dish: steak burger with toppings and chips £13.95. Two-course evening meal £25.00.*

Free house ~ Licensee Simon Umpleby ~ Real ale ~ Open 12-11 (10.30 Sun) ~ Bar food 12-9 (9.30 Fri, Sat) ~ Children welcome but no under-10s after 7pm ~ Dogs allowed in bar ~ Wi-fi *Recommended by Peter Andrews, Julie Braeburn, Ben and Diane Bowie, Dr and Mrs A K Clarke, John Watson, Jacqui and Alan Swan, Martine and Fabio Lockley*

We say if we know a pub has background music.

MOBBERLEY
SJ7879   Map 7

Roebuck ⍟ ♀ ⇔

(01565) 873939 – www.roebuckinnmobberley.co.uk

Mill Lane; downhill from sharp bend on B5085 at E edge of 30mph limit; WA16 7HX

Refurbished inn with a lot of individuality in bistro-style rooms, good range of drinks, enjoyable food and pretty multi-level garden; character bedrooms

Reopened just as we went to press in 2016, this has been completely renovated and restyled. It's very much an auberge in style with plenty of quirky touches: old shutters, reclaimed radiators, wood panelling and stripped brickwork, big gilt-edged mirrors, copper cooking pots and red and brick floor tiles. There's an open fire in the bar, chunky leather armchairs, lots of scatter cushions, an old trunk as a table, a two-way woodburner and an eclectic collection of art and photographs. Friendly staff serve Buck Bitter (named for the pub from Weetwood) and Deer Beer (from Dunham Massey) on handpump, a dozen wines and champagne by the glass, and a fine collection of liqueurs and aperitifs. The authentic-looking bistro has pots of herbs and candles in bottles on simple tables, café-style chairs and long leather wall banquettes; background music. To get to the garden you walk through the 'potting shed': upper and lower terraces, gazebos, herb beds and seats that range from rattan or elegant metal chairs to wooden benches and simple tables under parasols on decking or flagstones. The front of the building has a mediterranean feel with gnarly olive and standard box trees, flowering window boxes and a couple of benches. The rustic, shabby-chic bedrooms have much character and colour and dogs are allowed in one room; good breakfasts. They suggest both walking and jogging routes. The pub is owned by Tim Bird and Mary McLaughlin of Cheshire Cat Pubs & Bars.

 A thoughtful choice of interesting food includes sandwiches, crispy tiger prawns with lime, oregano, saffron and lemon mayonnaise, toulouse sausage cassoulet, sharing boards, parmesan risotto with aubergines, roasted tomatoes and pine nuts, thai chicken salad with sesame, chilli and coriander, monkfish with puy lentils, red wine and pancetta, venison bourguignon with dauphinoise potatoes, and puddings such as dark chocolate and date pudding with salted caramel sauce and vanilla ice-cream and banana sponge cake with banana jam, chocolate sauce and hazelnut ice-cream; they also offer Sunday brunch (10.30am-1pm). *Benchmark main dish: steak frites £15.95. Two-course evening meal £20.00.*

Free house ~ Licensee Charlie Mair ~ Real ale ~ Open 12-11 (10.30 Sun) ~ Bar food 12-2.30, 5-9, 12-9.30 Sat; 12-8 Sun ~ Children welcome but no under-10s after 7.30pm; not in bedrooms ~ Wi-fi ~ Bedrooms: £150/£135 *Recommended by Adam Bellinger, Sarah Roberts, Alice Wright, Frank and Marcia Pelling*

MOTTRAM ST ANDREW
SJ8878   Map 7

Bulls Head ♀ ◖

(01625) 828111 – www.brunningandprice.co.uk/bullshead

A538 Prestbury–Wilmslow; Wilmslow Road/Priest Lane; E side of village; SK10 4QH

Superb country dining pub with a thoughtful range of drinks and interesting food, plenty of character and well trained staff

Usefully open and serving food all day, this does have a bustling bar – though perhaps the main emphasis is on the dining areas at the far end. Four levels stack up alongside or above one another, each with a distinctive décor and style, from the informality of a sunken area with rugs on a tiled floor, through a comfortable library/dining room to another with an upstairs conservatory feel and the last, with higher windows and more of a special-occasion atmosphere. The rest of the pub has an appealing and abundant mix of old prints and pictures, comfortable seating in great variety, a coal fire in one room, a blazing woodburning stove in a two-way fireplace dividing two other rooms and an antique black kitchen range in yet another. Phoenix Brunning & Price Original and guests such as Happy Valley Lazy Daze, Pennine Amber Necker, Staffordshire Corkes IPA and Timothy Taylors Landlord on handpump, around 20 wines by the glass, 50 malt whiskies, 20 gins and several ciders, and an attractive separate tea-and-coffee station with pretty blue and white china cups, teapots and jugs. Also, background music, daily papers and board games. The lawn has plenty of picnic-sets beneath cocktail parasols.

 Highly thought-of modern food includes sandwiches, scallops with crispy ham fritters and pea purée, spiced lamb koftas with bombay potatoes and raita, wild mushroom, spinach and spring onion quiche, steak burger with toppings, coleslaw and chips, confit pork belly with black pudding hash cake and cider and pink peppercorn sauce, fish pie with french-style peas, crispy beef salad with sweet chilli dressing and spicy cashew nuts, and puddings such as glazed lemon tart with raspberry sorbet and bread and butter pudding with apricot sauce and clotted cream. *Benchmark main dish: braised lamb shoulder with dauphinoise potatoes and rosemary gravy £17.25. Two-course evening meal £20.00.*

Brunning & Price ~ Manager Andrew Coverley ~ Real ale ~ Open 11.30am-11pm (10.30 Sun) ~ Bar food 12-10 (9.30 Sun) ~ Children welcome ~ Dogs allowed in bar ~ Wi-fi
Recommended by Brian and Anna Marsden, W K Wood, Michael Butler, Peter Barrett, Mike and Wena Stevenson, Jacqui and Alan Swan, Chloe and Tim Hodge

NETHER ALDERLEY
SJ8576 Map 7
Wizard
(01625) 584000 – www.thewizardofedge.co.uk
B5087 Macclesfield Road, opposite Artists Lane; SK10 4UB

Bustling pub with interesting food, real ales, a friendly welcome and relaxed atmosphere

This enjoyable pub is on National Trust land and just a few minutes from lovely walks along Alderley Edge. The various rooms, connected by open doorways, are cleverly done up in a mix of modern rustic and traditional styles. There are beams and open fires, antique dining chairs (some prettily cushioned) and settles around all sorts of tables, rugs on pale floorboards, prints and paintings on contemporary paintwork and decorative items ranging from a grandfather clock to staffordshire dogs and modern lampshades. Hawkshead Cumbrian Five Hop, Ringwood Razorback and Storm PGA on handpump, 11 wines by the glass and farm cider; background music and board games. There are plenty of seats in the sizeable back garden. The pub is part of the Ainscoughs group.

 Popular food includes sandwiches, crispy squid with spicy mayonnaise, slow-roasted pork belly with black pudding, apple purée and smoked bacon crumb, beer-battered fish with triple-cooked chips, chickpea and sweetcorn burger with sweet potato fries, gammon and eggs, chicken thai green curry, sea bass with artichoke, asparagus, smoked bacon and red wine sauce, and puddings such as lemon cheesecake with lemon curd and toffee apple, pear and peach crumble with vanilla custard; they also offer a two- and three-course weekday early-bird menu. *Benchmark main dish: burger with toppings, onion rings and chips £13.50. Two-course evening meal £20.00.*

Free house ~ Licensee Stacey Goodwin ~ Real ale ~ Open 12-10 (11 Sat, 8 Sun) ~ Bar food 12-2.30, 6-9; 12-9 Sat; 12-7 Sun ~ Children welcome ~ Dogs welcome ~ Wi-fi
Recommended by Edward and William Johnston, Sandra King, Susan Eccleston

SANDBACH
Old Hall ♀ 🍺

SJ7560 Map 7

(01270) 758170 – www.brunningandprice.co.uk/oldhall

1.2 miles from M6 junction 17: A534 – ignore first turn into town and take the second – if you reach the roundabout double back; CW11 1AL

Glorious hall-house with impressive original features, plenty of drinking and dining space, six real ales and imaginative food

There are many lovely original architectural features here, particularly in the room to the left of the entrance hall, which is much as it has been for centuries with a Jacobean fireplace, oak panelling and priest's hole. This leads into the Oak Room, divided by standing timbers into two dining areas with heavy beams, oak flooring and reclaimed panelling. Other rooms in the original building have hefty beams and oak boards, three open fires and a woodburning stove; the cosy snugs are carpeted. The Garden Room is big and bright, with reclaimed quarry tiling and exposed A-frame oak timbering, and opens on to a suntrap back terrace with teak tables and chairs among flowering tubs. Throughout, the walls are covered with countless interesting prints, there's an appealing collection of antique dining chairs and tables of all sizes, and plenty of rugs, bookcases and plants. From the handsome bar counter, efficient and friendly staff serve Phoenix Brunning & Price Original, RedWillow Feckless and Three Tuns XXX with guests such as Abbeydale Moonshine, Beartown Ruby Bear and Titanic Iceberg on handpump, 16 good wines by the glass, 50 malt whiskies, 20 gins and farm cider; board games. There are picnic-sets in front of the building beside rose bushes and clipped box hedging.

 Popular brasserie dishes include sandwiches, potted smoked trout topped with shrimp butter, deep-fried brie with pickled cranberries and candied pecan salad, honey-roasted ham and eggs, malaysian fish stew with sticky coconut rice, chicken breast with smoked pancetta and butternut squash risotto, steak and kidney pudding, lamb hotpot with pickled red cabbage, and puddings such as hot waffle with boozy cherries and white chocolate chunk ice-cream and crème brûlée. *Benchmark main dish: braised lamb shoulder with dauphinoise potatoes and rosemary gravy £17.25. Two-course evening meal £20.00.*

Brunning & Price ~ Manager Chris Button ~ Real ale ~ Open 10.30-11; 9am-11pm Sat; 9am-10.30pm Sun ~ Bar food 12 (9 weekends)-10 (9.30 Sun) ~ Restaurant ~ Children welcome ~ Dogs allowed in bar ~ Wi-fi *Recommended by Tracey and Stephen Groves, Mike and Margaret Banks, Jeremy Snaithe, Alf Wright, M and A H, Mike and Wena Stevenson, Hugh Roberts, Paul Scofield*

SWETTENHAM
Swettenham Arms ⭐ ♀

SJ7967 Map 7

(01477) 571284 – www.swettenhamarms.co.uk

Off A54 Congleton–Holmes Chapel or A535 Chelford–Holmes Chapel; CW12 2LF

Big old country pub in a fine setting with shining brasses, five real ales and tempting food

After a walk in the pretty surrounding countryside or in the nearby Quinta Arboretum, head to this former nunnery for refreshment. It's been run by the same welcoming licensees for over 24 years and the three interlinked dark beamed areas are still nicely traditional with individual furnishings on bare floorboards or a sweep of fitted turkey carpet; also, a polished copper bar, three woodburning stoves, plenty of shiny brasses and a variety of old prints – military, hunting, old ships, reproduction Old Masters and so forth. Friendly efficient staff serve Black Sheep Best, Hydes Original Bitter, Tatton

Best, Thwaites Wainwright and Timothy Taylors Landlord on handpump, 12 wines by the glass, 20 malt whiskies and farm cider; background music. Outside behind, there are tables on a lawn that merges into a lovely sunflower and lavender meadow; croquet. They hold classic car evenings and vintage motorbike events, and can also hold civil ceremonies. Do visit the interesting village church which dates in part from the 13th c.

 Food is very good and includes sandwiches (until 5.30pm), duck confit and chicken terrine with a golden raisin and cognac purée, prawn cocktail, spinach, ricotta and caramelised red onion cannelloni, tempura langoustines with fennel and courgettes, beef stroganoff, gammon and duck egg with creamy cheese sauce, salmon with a fine herb crust, spring onion mash and white wine sauce with pancetta, and puddings such as chocolate and walnut brownie with vanilla ice-cream and vanilla cheesecake with blackcurrant compote. *Benchmark main dish: steak in ale pie £14.00. Two-course evening meal £20.00.*

Free house ~ Licensees Jim and Frances Cunningham ~ Real ale ~ No credit cards ~ Open 11.30am-11pm ~ Bar food 12-9 ~ Restaurant ~ Children welcome ~ Dogs allowed in bar ~ Wi-fi *Recommended by Mike and Margaret Banks, George Sanderson, Mike and Wena Stevenson, Charles Fraser, Margaret McDonald, Tom and Lorna Harding, Mark and Sian Edwards*

THELWALL
Little Manor ♀

SJ6587   Map 7

(01925) 212070 – www.brunningandprice.co.uk/littlemanor
Bell Lane; WA4 2SX

Restored manor house with plenty of room, lots of interest, well kept ales and tasty bistro-style food; seats outside

This is a big, handsome 17th-c house with six beamed rooms linked by open doorways and standing timbers. There are plenty of nooks and crannies and lots to look at, and flooring ranges from rugs on bare boards through carpeting to some fine old black and white tiles. There's an appealing variety of antique dining chairs around small or large, circular or square tables, as well as leather armchairs by open fires (note the lovely carved wooden one); background music. Lighting is from metal chandeliers, wall lights and standard lamps, and the décor includes hundreds of intriguing prints and photos, books on shelves and old glass and stone bottles on windowsills and mantelpieces; fresh flowers and house plants here and there too. Phoenix Brunning & Price Original and Coach House Cromwells Best Bitter with guests such as Dunscar Bridge Blonde, Mobberley HedgeHopper, Salopian Oracle, and Tatton Blonde on handpump, around 15 wines by the glass, 60 gins and 60 whiskies; the young staff are consistently helpful. In fine weather you can sit at the chunky teak chairs and tables on the terrace; some are under a heated shelter.

Quite a choice of good, seasonal food includes sandwiches, potted smoked trout topped with shrimp butter, capers, samphire and fennel, charcuterie sharing plate, mussels in smoked bacon, leeks and creamy cider, roasted sweet potato and goats cheese croquettes with red pepper salsa and onion crème fraîche, steak and kidney pudding, rump of lamb with mint gnocchi and salsa verde, beer-battered cod and chips, thai green chicken curry, and puddings such as glazed lemon tart with clotted cream ice-cream and apple and blackberry crumble. *Benchmark main dish: slow-braised lamb shoulder with dauphinoise potatoes and rosemary gravy £17.25. Two-course evening meal £23.00.*

Brunning & Price ~ Manager Jill Dowling ~ Real ale ~ Open 10.30am-11pm ~ Bar food 12-10 (9 Sun) ~ Children welcome ~ Dogs allowed in bar ~ Wi-fi *Recommended by Alistair Forsyth, Brian and Anna Marsden, Michael Butler, Mike and Wena Stevenson, Hilary Forrest, Alison and Michael Harper*

WARMINGHAM

SJ7161 Map 7

Bears Paw 🍺 🛏

(01270) 526317 – www.thebearspaw.co.uk

School Lane; CW11 3QN

Nicely maintained place with enjoyable food, half a dozen real ales and seats outside; bedrooms

Rooms work their way into one another in this extensive Victorian inn, each with plenty of individual character. We particularly like the two little sitting rooms with panelling, fashionable wallpaper, bookshelves and slouchy leather furniture with plumped-up cushions comfortably arranged by woodburning stoves in magnificent fireplaces; stripped wood flooring and a dado keep it all informal. An eclectic mix of old wooden tables and some nice old carved chairs are well spaced throughout the dining areas, with lofty windows providing a light and airy feel and lots of big pot plants adding freshness. There are stools at the long bar counter where cheerful, efficient staff serve Weetwood Best and Eastgate and a guest named for the pub (from Cheshire Brew Brothers) on handpump, 13 wines by the glass, 17 malt whiskies and local cider; background music. A small front garden by the car park has seats and tables. The well equipped bedrooms are comfortable and the breakfasts very good indeed. This is sister pub to the Pheasant in Burwardsley and the Fishpool at Delamere.

 As well as sandwiches (until 6pm), the reliably good food includes sticky eight-hour beef short-rib with horseradish rémoulade, chicken liver pâté with red onion jam, wild mushroom risotto with blue cheese, sharing boards, pork and apricot burger with tomato salsa and chips, thai green king prawn curry, lamb hotpot with pickled red cabbage, venison haunch with confit shin faggot and celeriac two-ways, and puddings such as sticky toffee and banana pudding with butterscotch sauce and banoffi ice-cream and plum and stem ginger tart with vanilla chantilly. *Benchmark main dish: steak in ale pie £14.50. Two-course evening meal £23.00.*

Free house ~ Licensee Andrew Nelson ~ Real ale ~ Open 11-11 (10.30 Sun) ~ Bar food 12-9.30 (10 Fri, Sat; 9 Sun) ~ Restaurant ~ Children welcome ~ Dogs welcome ~ Wi-fi ~ Bedrooms: £105/£115 *Recommended by Susan Allen, Susan Jackman, Rona Mackinlay, Katherine Matthews, Ivy and George Goodwill*

WHITELEY GREEN

SJ9278 Map 7

Windmill 🍷 🍺

(01625) 574222 – www.thewindmill.info

Brown sign to pub off A523 Macclesfield–Poynton, just N of Prestbury; Hole House Lane; SK10 5SJ

Extensive relaxed country dining bar with big sheltered garden and enjoyable food

You reach this pub up a long quiet lane in deepest leafy Cheshire countryside. Most of it is given over to dining tables, mainly in a pleasantly informal, painted base/stripped top style, on bare boards. The interior spreads around a big bar counter, its handpumps serving Storm Bosley Cloud and guests from breweries such as Merlin, Peak and Wincle; also, eight wines by the glass served by friendly and helpful staff. One area has several leather sofas and fabric-upholstered easy chairs; another by a log fire in a huge brick fireplace has more easy chairs and a suede sofa. Background music, daily papers and cribbage. The spreading lawns, surrounded by a belt of young trees, provide plenty of room for well spaced tables and picnic sets, and even a maze to baffle children. Middlewood Way (a sort of linear country park) and Macclesfield Canal (Bridge 25) are just a stroll away from the pub.

¶ The standard of food is high and dishes include sandwiches, salt beef hash cake with crispy poached egg and home-made brown sauce, crab salad with citrus mayonnaise, baby gem and avocado, tarte tatin of caramelised shallots and goats cheese, chicken in wild mushroom sauce with parmesan mash and truffle shavings, seafood tagliatelle with dill cream cheese, lamb loin stuffed with rosemary, apricots and garlic with bacon and butter bean broth, steaks with a choice of sauce, and puddings such as Baileys and dark chocolate cheesecake with chantilly cream and whisky and marmalade bread and butter pudding with apricot sauce. *Benchmark main dish: beer-battered fish and chips £10.00. Two-course evening meal £20.00.*

Mitchells & Butlers ~ Lease Peter and Jane Nixon ~ Real ale ~ Open 12-11 (10 Sun) ~ Bar food 12-2.30, 5-9 (9.30 Fri); 12-9.30 Sat; 12-7 Sun ~ Children welcome ~ Dogs allowed in bar ~ Wi-fi ~ Live acoustic music second Fri and live bands last Fri of month *Recommended by R W Batho, Harvey Brown, Belinda Stamp, Buster May, Barbara Brown, Daniel King*

Also Worth a Visit in Cheshire

Besides the fully inspected pubs, you might like to try these pubs that have been recommended to us and described by readers. Do tell us what you think of them: feedback@goodguides.com

ALLGREAVE   SU9767
Rose & Crown (01260) 227232
A54 Congleton–Buxton; SK11 0BJ
Welcoming 18th-c roadside pub in remote upland spot with good Dane Valley views and walks; refurbished beamed rooms, wood floors and log fires, good local food from bar and restaurant menus including daily specials, half a dozen well kept ales such as Jennings and Wincle from wood-clad servery; children and dogs welcome, lawned garden taking in the views, three bedrooms. *(Jack Trussler)*

ALPRAHAM   SJ5759
Travellers Rest (01829) 260523
A51 Nantwich–Chester; CW6 9JA
Timeless four-room country local in same family for three generations; friendly chatty atmosphere, well kept Tetleys and Weetwood, no food, leatherette, wicker and Formica, some flock wallpaper, fine old brewery mirrors, darts and dominoes; may be nesting swallows in outside gents'; dogs welcome, back bowling green, 'Hat Day' last Sun before Christmas when locals don unusual headgear, closed weekday lunchtimes (opens 6.30pm). *(Daphne and Barry Gregson)*

ASHLEY   SJ7784
Greyhound (0161) 871 7765
3 miles S of Altrincham; Cow Lane; WA15 0QR Refurbished and extended red-brick Lees pub, their well kept ales, decent wines and good choice of tasty reasonably priced food, friendly service, greyhound-theme décor and some old photos of nearby Tatton Hall (NT), wood floors, central woodburner; fortnightly quiz Tues, darts; children and dogs welcome, seats out on lawn and terrace, handy for the station, open (and food) all day. *(Gemma Clayton, Hilary Forrest)*

BARBRIDGE   SJ6156
Barbridge Inn (01270) 528327
Just off A51 N of Nantwich; CW5 0AY
Spacious open-plan family dining pub by lively marina at junction of Shropshire Union and Middlewich canals, enjoyable food from sandwiches and sharing boards to steaks served by friendly staff, three Weetwood ales and one or two guests, conservatory; background music; dogs allowed in a couple of areas, waterside garden with enclosed play area, moorings, open (and food) all day. *(Giles and Annie Francis, Roger and Anne Newbury)*

BARTON   SJ4454
★**Cock o' Barton** (01829) 782277
Barton Road (A534 E of Farndon); SY14 7HU Stylish contemporary décor in bright open skylit bar, good choice of well liked up-to-date food, cocktails and plenty of wines by the glass, ales such as Spitting Feathers and Stonehouse, Fri happy hour till 7pm, neat courteous staff, beamed restaurant areas; background music; children welcome (free main course for them on Sun), tables in sunken heated inner courtyard with canopies and modern

---

We include some hotels with a good bar that offers facilities comparable to those of a pub.

water feature, picnic-sets on back lawn, 14 bedrooms, open (and food) all day from 8am for breakfast. *(Tom and Lorna Harding)*

BIRKENHEAD   SJ3386
Refreshment Rooms
(0151) 644 5893 *Bedford Road E; CH42 1LS* Bow-fronted former 19th-c refreshment rooms for the Mersey ferry; three rooms with interesting collection of old photographs and other memorabilia, good selection of mainly local ales such as Liverpool Organic, Peerless and a house beer from Lees (HMS Conway), Rosie's welsh cider and a couple of interesting lagers, good competitively priced home-made food (using carefully sourced produce) including set deals, friendly prompt service; quiz Weds, live music last Fri of month, pool; children and dogs welcome, beer garden at back with play area, open (and food) all day. *(Paul Scofield)*

BOLLINGTON   SJ9377
Church House (01625) 574014
Church Street; SK10 5PY Welcoming village pub with good reasonably priced home-made food including OAP set lunch, efficient friendly service, three well kept ales including Adnams, nice open fire, separate dining room; children and clean dogs welcome, good place to start or end a walk, four comfortable well priced bedrooms, open all day weekends (food all day Sun).
(John and Mary Warner)

BOLLINGTON   SJ9477
Poachers (01625) 572086
Mill Lane; SK10 5BU Stone-built village local prettily set in good walking area, comfortable and welcoming, with enjoyable pubby food (all day Sun, not Mon) including bargain lunches, well kept Storm, Weetwood and three guests such as local Happy Valley, efficient friendly service, log fire and wood stove; charity quiz last Sun of month; children and dogs (towels and treats) welcome, sunny back garden, open all day weekends, closed Mon lunchtime. *(Maureen Wood)*

BOLLINGTON   SJ9377
Vale (01625) 575147
Adlington Road; SK10 5JT Friendly tap for Bollington brewery in three converted 19th-c cottages, their full range and a couple of guests (tasters offered), real ciders, enjoyable food (all day weekends) including range of locally made pies and daily specials, helpful efficient service, interesting photos, newspapers and books, roaring fire; picnic-sets out behind overlooking cricket pitch, near Middlewood Way and Macclesfield Canal, open all day Fri-Sun. *(John Wooll, Mike and Wena Stevenson)*

BOLLINGTON CROSS   SJ9177
Cock & Pheasant (01625) 573289
Bollington Road; SK10 5EJ Recently refurbished 18th-c red-brick Vintage Inn

at edge of village, their usual good value food including weekday set menus, real ales such as Sharps Doom Bar, craft beers and plenty of wines by the glass, pleasant helpful young staff, beams and open fire; Thurs quiz; children welcome, plenty of outside seating (some under cover), play area, good local walks, open all day. *(John Wooll)*

BRERETON GREEN   SJ7764
Bears Head (01477) 544732
Handy for M6 junction 17; set back off A50 S of Holmes Chapel; CW11 1RS Beautiful 17th-c black and white timbered Vintage Inn with civilised linked rooms, low beams, log fires and old-fashioned furniture on flagstones or bare boards, enjoyable well prepared food served by friendly staff, Sharps Doom Bar, Thwaites Wainwright and a guest; 25 bedrooms in modern Innkeepers Lodge, open (and food) all day. *(John Watson)*

BROOMEDGE   SJ7086
Jolly Thresher (01925) 752265
Higher Lane; WA13 0RN Spacious well appointed dining pub with enjoyable sensibly priced food including good value set lunch, well kept Hydes, lots of wines by the glass and good choice of other drinks, restaurant and dining conservatory (fish specials Fri); background music, free wi-fi; children and dogs welcome, tables on paved terrace and lawn, open (and food) all day. *(Hilary Forrest)*

BROXTON   SJ4858
Egerton Arms 01829 782241
A41/A534 S of Chester; CH3 9JW Large neatly kept mock-Tudor dining pub, well polished old furniture on wood or carpeted floors, dark panelling, lots of prints and books, open fires, wide choice of popular food from sandwiches and pub favourites up, four well kept changing beers and plenty of wines by the glass, efficient friendly staff; children and dogs welcome, wheelchair access, big garden with decking and play area, open all day. *(Scott and Charlotte Havers)*

BURTONWOOD   SJ5692
Fiddle i'th' Bag (01925) 225442
3 miles from M62 junction 9, signposted from A49 towards Newton-le-Willows; WA5 4BT Eccentric 19th-c country pub (not to everyone's tastc) crammed with bric-a-brac and memorabilia, three well kept changing ales and enjoyable uncomplicated home-made food (cash only), friendly staff; may be nostalgic background music; children welcome, open all day weekends. *(Jake)*

CHELFORD   SJ8175
★ Egerton Arms (01625) 861366
A537 Macclesfield–Knutsford; SK11 9BB Cheerful rambling old village pub, beams and nice mix of furniture including carved settles and a couple of wooden porter's chairs, grandfather clock, Copper Dragon

and up to six guests, several wines by the glass, well liked food including range of burgers and stone-baked pizzas, restaurant, steps down to little raftered games area with pool, darts and sports TV; background music (live last Fri of month including traditional jazz), quiz last Thurs; children and dogs welcome, picnic-sets on canopied deck and slate terrace, toddlers' play area, adjoining deli/coffee shop, open (and food) all day. *(John Wooll, John Watson)*

CHESTER   SJ4065

★**Bear & Billet**   (01244) 351002

Lower Bridge Street; CH1 1RU Handsome 17th-c timber and lattice-windowed Okells pub (an inn since the 18th c); their beers and three changing guests, belgian and american imports and nice range of wines by the glass, reasonably priced home-made pubby food including range of burgers, efficient friendly service, beamed bar with wood floor and panelling, open fire, scenes of old Chester in back dining part, further rooms above; quiz night and upstairs folk club (both Sun), sports TVs; children and dogs welcome, courtyard seating, open (and food) all day), kitchen closes 7pm Sun. *(John Beeken, David H Bennett, Dave Braisted)*

CHESTER   SJ4066

Boathouse   (01244) 328709

The Groves, off Grosvenor Park Road; on River Dee five-minute walk from centre; CH1 1SD Modernised pub on site of 17th-c boathouse with great River Dee views, well priced pubby food from sandwiches and sharing plates up, Lees ales and decent choice of wines by the glass, helpful staff; Weds quiz, free wi-fi; children welcome, dogs outside only, disabled access/facilities, tables and painted beach huts on paved terrace overlooking the water, little bridge to floating seating area, open (and food) all day. *(Chris Stevenson)*

CHESTER   SJ4065

★**Brewery Tap**   (01244) 340999

Lower Bridge Street; CH1 1RU Tap for Spitting Feathers brewery in interesting Jacobean building with 18th-c brick façade, steps up to lofty barrel-vaulted bar (former great hall) serving a couple of their well kept ales, five guest beers, a local cider and good choice of wines, hearty home-made food using local suppliers including produce from Spitting Feathers farm (rare-breed pork), pews and other rustic furniture on flagstones, tapestries on walls, large carved red-sandstone fireplace, also smaller plainer room; children and dogs welcome, no wheelchair access, open (and food) all day. *(Chris Stevenson)*

CHESTER   SJ4166

Cellar   (01244) 318950

City Road; CH1 3AE Laid-back Canal Quarter bar with well kept changing ales, craft beers and interesting selection of imports, decent wines and cocktails too, Mon happy hour 5-8pm, limited snacky food, basement bar for private functions; live music Fri and Sat from 10pm (can get packed), sports TV; closed Mon lunchtime, otherwise open all day till late. *(David H Bennett)*

CHESTER   SJ4066

Coach House   (01244) 351900

Northgate Street; CH1 2HQ Updated 19th-c coaching inn by town hall and cathedral; comfortable lounge with central bar, well kept Thwaites and guests, decent choice of wines and other drinks, enjoyable fairly priced home-made food including daily specials from semi-open kitchen, afternoon teas, prompt friendly service; children and dogs welcome, tables out in front, eight refurbished bedrooms, good breakfast, open (and food) all day, kitchen closes 7pm Sun. *(Michael Butler, David H Bennett)*

CHESTER   SJ4065

Cross Keys   (01244) 344460

Duke Street/Lower Bridge Street; CH1 1RU Small Victorian corner pub with ornate interior, dark panelling, etched mirrors and stained-glass windows, button-back leather wall benches and cast-iron tables on bare boards, open fire, well kept Joules ales and a guest, sensibly priced pubby food (not Mon, Tues), friendly service, upstairs function room; free wi-fi; no dogs inside, seats out in front, closed Mon and lunchtime Tues, otherwise open all day. *(Chris Stevenson)*

CHESTER   SJ4066

Olde Boot   (01244) 314540

Eastgate Row N; CH1 1LQ Lovely 17th-c Rows building; long narrow bar with heavy beams, dark woodwork, oak flooring and flagstones, old kitchen range in lounge beyond, settles and oak panelling in upper area, well kept/priced Sam Smiths beers, cheerful service and bustling atmosphere; no children. *(Michael Butler)*

CHESTER   SJ4066

Pied Bull   (01244) 325829

Upper Northgate Street; CH1 2HQ Old beamed and panelled coaching inn with roomy open-plan carpeted bar, good own-brewed ales (brewery tours) along with guests, enjoyable fairly priced traditional food from sandwiches and baked potatoes up, friendly staff and locals, imposing stone fireplace with tapestry above, divided inner dining area; background music, TV, machines; children welcome, tables under parasols on enclosed terrace, handsome Jacobean stairs to 13 bedrooms, open (and food) all day. *(David H Bennett)*

CHESTER   SJ4066

Telfords Warehouse   (01244) 390090

Tower Wharf, behind Northgate Street near railway; CH1 4EZ Large converted canal building with half a dozen well kept interesting ales and good variety of fairly priced food from sandwiches and snacks up, friendly efficient young staff, bare boards, exposed brickwork and high ceiling, big wall of windows overlooking the water, some old enamel signs and massive iron winding gear in bar, steps up to heavily beamed area with sofas, artwork and restaurant; late-night live music, bouncers on the door; tables out by canal, open all day (till late Weds-Sun). *(David H Bennett)*

CHURCH MINSHULL   SJ6660
Badger (01270) 522348
B5074 Winsford–Nantwich; handy for Shropshire Union Canal, Middlewich branch; CW5 6DY Updated 18th-c coaching inn in pretty village next to church, good food from sharing boards and pub favourites up, well kept ales such as Tatton, Titanic and Weetwood, Thatcher's cider, interesting range of wines and spirits, friendly helpful staff, bare-boards public bar, opened-up lounge/dining area leading to conservatory, woodburners; background music, free wi-fi; children and dogs (in bar) welcome, paved terrace with rattan-style furniture, five bedrooms, good breakfast, open (and food) all day. *(Paul Scofield)*

COMBERBACH   SJ6477
Spinner & Bergamot
(01606) 891307 *Warrington Road; CW9 6AY* Comfortable 18th-c beamed village pub named after two racehorses; good home-made food (smaller helpings available for some main courses), early-evening two-course deal Mon-Fri, well kept Robinsons ales and nice choice of wines, friendly attentive service, pitched-ceiling timber dining extension, two-room carpeted lounge and tiled-floor public bar where dogs allowed, log fires, some Manchester United memorabilia; unobtrusive background music, sports TV, Mon quiz; children welcome, small verandah, picnic-sets on sloping lawn, bowling green, open all day (food all day Sun). *(Mike and Wena Stevenson)*

CONGLETON   SJ8659
Horseshoe (01260) 272205
Fence Lane, Newbold Astbury, between A34 and A527 S; CW12 3NL Former 18th-c coaching inn set in peaceful countryside; three small carpeted rooms with decorative plates, copper and brass and other knick-knacks (some on delft shelves), mix of seating including plush banquettes and iron-base tables, log fire, well kept predominantly Robinsons ales, popular hearty home-made food at reasonable prices, daily specials, friendly staff and locals; children welcome, no dogs, rustic garden furniture, adventure play area with tractor, good walks. *(Mark and Sian Edwards)*

CONGLETON   SJ8762
Queens Head (01260) 272546
Park Lane (set down from flyover); CW12 3DE Friendly local by Macclesfield Canal, quaint dark interior with open fire, up to eight well kept ales, a real cider and good selection of malt whiskies, reasonably priced hearty pub food (all day Fri-Sun); table skittles, darts and pool (free Sun), sports TV; children and dogs welcome, steps up from towpath to nice garden with play area and boules, three bedrooms, handy for the station, open all day. *(Michael and Sarah Lockley)*

CONGLETON   SJ8662
Young Pretender (01260) 273277
Lawton Street; CW12 1RS Same ownership as the Treacle Tap in Macclesfield; one room (former shop) divided into smaller areas with local artwork on display, half a dozen well kept interesting ales and good selection of international draught/bottled beers, enjoyable food from snacks up including range of locally produced pies, friendly staff; various events such as live music, book club, Weds film night and Sun quiz; children (till 8pm) and dogs welcome, open (and food) all day. *(Tony Hobden)*

COTEBROOK   SJ5765
Alvanley Arms (01829) 760200
A49/B5152 N of Tarporley; CW6 9DS Welcoming refurbished roadside coaching inn, 17th-c behind its flower-decked Georgian façade, with beamed rooms and big open fire, Robinsons ales, several wines by the glass and good choice of other drinks, well liked reasonably priced food from wide-ranging menu, friendly efficient service; background music, free wi-fi; children welcome, disabled access, garden with deck and large pond, pleasant walks, seven comfortable bedrooms. *(Malcolm and Pauline Pellatt)*

CREWE   SJ7055
Borough Arms (01270) 748189
Earle Street; CW1 2BG Drinkers' pub with up to ten well kept changing ales (plans to reopen the on-site microbrewery), also good choice of continental beers and a couple of real ciders, friendly staff and regulars, two small rooms off central bar and downstairs lounge; occasional sports TV; picnic-sets on back terrace and lawn, open all day Fri-Sun, closed lunchtime other days. *(Jake)*

CREWE   SJ7055
Hops (01270) 211100
Prince Albert Street; CW1 2DF Friendly and relaxed belgian café-bar on two floors,

huge range of continental bottled beers (some also on draught), eight interesting ales including a house beer from Townhouse and good range of ciders, snacky lunchtime food (Weds-Sat), proper coffee; children and dogs welcome, disabled access/facilities, seats out at front, closed Mon lunchtime, otherwise open all day. *(Paul Scofield)*

DISLEY SJ9784
White Horse (01663) 762397
Buxton Old Road, car park down Ring O'Bells Lane by pub; SK12 2BB Proper straightforward pub popular with locals and well looked after by friendly hard-working licensees, four Robinsons ales and good value tasty food (all day weekends); free wi-fi; children welcome, no dogs inside, handy for Lyme Park (NT), open all day. *(John Wooll, Steve Whalley)*

DISLEY SJ9784
White Lion (01663) 762800
Buxton Road (A6); SK12 2HA Welcoming pub at east end of village, nine well kept changing ales and enjoyable food (not Mon) including good home-made pies, friendly efficient staff; dogs welcome in one part (food for them too), closed Mon lunchtime, otherwise open (and food) all day. *(Brian and Anna Marsden)*

EATON SJ8765
★**Plough** (01260) 280207
A536 Congleton–Macclesfield; CW12 2NH Cosy village pub with carefully converted traditional bar, beams, leaded windows and exposed brickwork, a couple of snug alcoves, cushioned wooden wall seats and comfortable armchairs on red-patterned carpet, woodburner in big stone fireplace, Storm, Charles Wells and a couple of guests, ten wines by the glass from decent list and 20 malt whiskies, well liked food including weekdays set menu, friendly efficient staff, heavily raftered barn restaurant (moved here from Wales); background music, board games and occasional TV, free wi-fi; children welcome, no dogs inside, big tree-filled garden with tables set for dining on covered/heated deck, fine views of Peak District fringes, appealingly designed bedrooms in converted stable block, open (and food) all day. *(Mark Morgan, Patricia Hawkins, William and Ann Reid)*

FADDILEY SJ5852
★**Thatch** (01270) 524223
A534 Wrexham–Nantwich; CW5 8JE Attractive thatched and timbered dining pub carefully extended from medieval core, low beams and open fires, raised room to right of bar, back barn-style dining room where children allowed, well kept ales such as Salopian and Timothy Taylors, good choice of popular food (booking advised weekends), friendly helpful service, relaxing atmosphere; soft background music, free wi-fi; charming

country garden with play area, open all day weekends, closed Mon, Tues. *(Chris Stevenson)*

FRODSHAM SJ5276
Travellers Rest (01928) 735125
B5152 Frodsham–Kingsley; WA6 6SL Popular family-run roadside dining pub with good food from sandwiches and pub favourites up, well kept Black Sheep and two guests, good selection of wines, attentive cheerful service; free wi-fi; children welcome, disabled access, superb views across Weaver Valley, open (and food) all day. *(Margaret McDonald)*

GAWSWORTH SJ8869
★**Harrington Arms** (01260) 223325
Off A536; Congleton Road/Church Lane; SK11 9RJ This unspoilt three-storey building is still part of a working farm; low 17th-c beams, tiled and flagstoned floors, snug corners and open fires, counter in narrow space on right serving Robinsons ales, a guest beer and good selection of wines and whiskies, several unpretentious rooms off with old settles and eclectic mix of tables and chairs, lots of pictures on red or pale painted walls, well liked hearty food from hot and cold sandwiches to daily specials, friendly relaxed atmosphere; background music (live folk Fri), free wi-fi; children and dogs (in bar) welcome, benches out on small front cobbled area, more seats in garden overlooking fields, lane leads to one of Cheshire's prettiest villages, open all day weekends. *(Michael Butler, Mike and Wena Stevenson)*

GOOSTREY SJ7770
Crown (01477) 532128
Off A50 and A535; CW4 8PE Extended and opened-up 18th-c red-brick village pub, beams and open fires, good choice of enjoyable food with some main courses available in smaller sizes, five well kept ales and plenty of wines by the glass, friendly efficient service; maybe Tues quiz; children welcome, close to Jodrell Bank, open (and food) all day. *(Paul Scofield)*

GRAPPENHALL SJ6386
★**Parr Arms** (01925) 212120
Near M6 junction 20 – A50 towards Warrington, left after 1.5 miles; Church Lane; WA4 3EP Renovated black-beamed pub in picture-postcard setting with picnic-sets out on cobbles by church, more tables on small canopied back terrace, good reasonably priced food from ciabattas and sharing plates to blackboard specials, friendly helpful service, well kept Robinsons from central bar, log fires; children and dogs welcome, open (and food) all day. *(John and Mary Warner)*

GREAT BUDWORTH SJ6677
★**George & Dragon** (01606) 892650
Signed off A559 NE of Northwich; High Street opposite church; CW9 6HF

Characterful building dating from 1722 (front part is 19th-c) in delightful village; Lees ales kept well and plenty of wines by the glass, welcoming friendly young staff, good choice of enjoyable reasonably priced home-made food from lunchtime sandwiches and baguettes to specials, good Sun lunch too, dark panelled bar with log fire, grandfather clock and leather button-back banquettes, back area more restauranty with wood floors and exposed brickwork, tables around central woodburner, some stuffed animals and hunting memorabilia; children and dogs (in bar) welcome, picnic-sets outside, open (and food) all day. *(Mike and Wena Stevenson)*

KERRIDGE
SJ9276
Lord Clyde (01625) 562123
Clarke Lane, off A523; SK10 5AH Converted from two mid 19th-c stone cottages, main emphasis on eating but can just pop in for a drink, good interesting food including tasting menus, also lunchtime sandwiches and ploughman's, well kept ales such as Greene King, Thwaites and Weetwood, friendly if not always speedy service; background music; no dogs inside, good local walks, open all day Fri-Sun, closed Mon lunchtime (no food Sat lunchtime, Sun evening, Mon). *(Brian and Anna Marsden)*

KNUTSFORD
SJ7578
Lord Eldon (01565) 652261
Tatton Street, off A50 at White Bear roundabout; WA16 6AD Traditional red-brick former coaching inn with four comfortable rooms, friendly staff and locals, beams, brasses, old pictures and large open fire, well kept Tetleys and a couple of guests, no food; music and quiz nights, darts; dogs welcome, back garden but no car park, handy for Tatton Park (NT), open all day. *(Margaret McDonald)*

KNUTSFORD
SJ7578
Rose & Crown (01565) 652366
King Street; WA16 6DT Beamed and panelled 17th-c inn with bar and Chophouse restaurant, well liked food from sandwiches (till 6pm), snacks and sharing plates up, a couple of changing ales, plenty of wines by the glass and some interesting gins, good friendly service; children and dogs (in bar) welcome, terrace tables, nine bedrooms, open (and food) all day. *(Scott and Charlotte Havers)*

LANGLEY
SJ9569
★ Hanging Gate (01260) 400756
Meg Lane, Higher Sutton; SK11 0NG Remote old place close to the moors with wonderful distant views to Liverpool Cathedral and even Snowdonia; cosy low-beamed rooms on different levels, log fires, very good well presented food from chef-patron including tasting menus, Hydes, a guest beer and nice selection of wines, friendly attentive service; background music, free wi-fi; children and dogs welcome, picnic-sets out on deck taking in the view, good circular walk, closed Sun evening, Mon, Tues lunchtime and Weds evening. *(Mike and Wena Stevenson)*

LANGLEY
SJ9471
★ Leather's Smithy (01260) 252313
Off A523 S of Macclesfield; OS Sheet 118 map reference 952715; SK11 0NE Isolated stone-built pub in fine walking country next to reservoir; well kept Theakstons and two or three guests, lots of whiskies, good food from sandwiches to blackboard specials, efficient friendly service, beams and log fire, flagstoned bar, carpeted dining areas, interesting local prints and photographs; unobtrusive background music; children welcome, no dogs inside but muddy boots allowed in bar, picnic-sets in garden behind and on grass opposite, lovely views, open all day weekends (till 8pm Sun). *(Mike and Wena Stevenson)*

LITTLE BOLLINGTON
SJ7387
Swan with Two Nicks
(0161) 928 2914 *2 miles from M56 junction 7 – A56 towards Lymm, then first right at Stamford Arms into Park Lane; use A556 to get back on to M56 westbound; WA14 4TJ* Extended red-brick village pub with good choice of enjoyable generously served food from sandwiches and baked potatoes up, well kept ales including Dunham Massey and a house beer from Coach House, decent wines and coffee, efficient service, beams, knick-knacks and log fire, back restaurant; children and (particularly) dogs welcome, tables outside, attractive hamlet by Dunham Massey (NT) deer park, walks by Bridgewater Canal, open (and food) all day. *(Dr D J and Mrs S C Walker, Tony Hobden, Mike and Wena Stevenson)*

LITTLE BUDWORTH
SJ5867
Cabbage Hall (01829) 760292
Forest Road (A49); CW6 9ES Restauranty pub (part of the Pesto chain) specialising in good tapas-style italian food (piattini), drinkers catered for in comfortable bar with real ales and decent wines by the glass, also italian-style afternoon teas, efficient friendly staff; children welcome, garden tables, open (and food) all day. *(Paul Scofield)*

LITTLE BUDWORTH
SJ5965
Egerton Arms (01829) 760424
Pinfold Lane; CW6 9BS Welcoming 18th-c

If you report on a pub that's not a featured entry, please tell us any lunchtimes or evenings when it doesn't serve bar food.

family-run country free house, enjoyable home-made food including wood-fired pizzas and range of burgers, six well kept local ales, good selection of bottled beers and interesting cocktails; weekend live music; children and dogs welcome, seats out in front and in garden behind overlooking cricket pitch, walks from the door, handy for Oulton Park racetrack, closed Mon (except bank holidays), otherwise open all day (from 3pm Tues, Weds in winter). *(Peter and Emma Kelly)*

LITTLE LEIGH   SJ6076
Holly Bush   (01606) 853196
A49 just S of A533; CW8 4QY Brick and timbered 17th-c thatched pub, good choice of enjoyable well priced food including several vegetarian options, charming helpful staff, Tetleys and a couple of mainstream guests, bar with open fire, restaurant extension; Sun quiz; children welcome, no dogs inside, wheelchair access, courtyard tables and garden with play area, 14 bedrooms in converted back barn, open all day weekends (food all day Sun). *(Mike and Wena Stevenson, Dr A McCormick)*

LOWER WHITLEY   SJ6178
Chetwode Arms   (01925) 640044
Just off A49, handy for M56 junction 10; Street Lane; WA4 4EN Rambling low-beamed dining pub dating from the 17th c, good food including range of exotic meats cooked on a hot stone, early-bird deal (before 7pm), welcoming efficient service, solid furnishings all clean and polished, small front bar with warm open fire, four real ales and good wines by the glass; well behaved children allowed but best to ask first, limited wheelchair access, tables outside along with tipi and own bowling green, open from 5pm (4-9pm Sun), may close Mon in winter. *(Margaret McDonald)*

LYMM   SJ7087
Barn Owl   (01925) 752020
Agden Wharf, Warrington Lane (just off B5159 E); WA13 0SW Popular comfortably extended pub in nice setting by Bridgewater Canal, Thwaites ales and three guests, decent wines by the glass, reasonable choice of good value pub food including OAP deals and Sun carvery, efficient service even when busy, friendly atmosphere; children and dogs welcome, disabled facilities, may be canal trips, moorings (space for one narrowboat), open (and food) all day. *(Mike and Wena Stevenson)*

LYMM   SJ6886
Church Green   (01925) 752068
Higher Lane; WA13 0AP Dining pub owned by celebrity chef Aiden Byrne, food can be very good (and pricey) in restaurant or smaller bar area, Caledonian and a guest beer, carefully chosen wines; background music; children welcome, disabled access/ facilities, pretty garden including heated

side deck, open (and food) all day, breakfast from 9am at weekends, kitchen shuts 7pm Sun. *(Sally and David Champion)*

MACCLESFIELD   SJ9173
Snow Goose   (01625) 619299
Sunderland Street; SK11 6HN Quirky laid-back bar with feel of an alpine ski lodge; well kept ales such as Storm and Wincle, several craft beers and good range of wines, unusual food from daily changing menu, bare-boards interior on three levels, woodburners, local artwork for sale, piano; background and live music, board games; children and dogs welcome, balcony overlooking back garden, open all day and can get very busy. *(Adam Bellinger)*

MACCLESFIELD   SJ9173
Treacle Tap   (01625) 615938
Sunderland Street; SK11 6JL Small one-room pub (former shop) with simply furnished bare-boards interior, three interesting mainly local ales and good selection of bottled beers (particularly belgian and german), other drinks too, short menu including meat/cheese platters and tasty locally made pies; regular events such as jam sessions, foreign language conversation evenings, a stitch'n'bitch night and Sun quiz; children welcome till 8pm, open (and food) all day. *(Tony Hobden)*

MOBBERLEY   SJ8179
Plough & Flail   (01565) 873537
Off B5085 Knutsford–Alderley Edge; at E end of village turn into Moss Lane, then left into Paddock Hill Lane (look out for small green signs to pub); WA16 7DB Extensive family dining pub tucked down narrow lanes; low-beamed bar with chunky cushioned chairs and stripped tables, flagstones and panelled dado, sofas in wood-floored side area, Lees ales, good choice of wines by the glass and enjoyable food including daily specials, comfortable airy dining room and conservatory; background music, free wi-fi; heated terraces with teak tables, picnic-sets on neat lawns, play area, open (and food) all day. *(Mike and Margaret Banks)*

MOULDSWORTH   SJ5170
Goshawk   (01928) 740900
Station Road (B5393); CH3 8AJ Comfortable Woodward & Falconer family dining pub (former station hotel); mix of furniture in extensive series of rooms including small 'library' area, masses of pictures, two-way log fire, good popular food from sandwiches to restauranty dishes, cheerful attentive uniformed staff, half a dozen well kept ales including couple of house beers from Hydes, nice wines by the glass; background and some live music; dogs allowed in bar, disabled facilities, good spot near Delamere Forest with big outdoor space

including play area and bowling green, open (and food) all day. *(Paul Scofield, Jake)*

NANTWICH   SJ6452
★ **Black Lion** (01270) 628711
Welsh Row; CW5 5ED Cosy old black and white pub with plenty of character, beams, timbered brickwork, bare boards and stone floors, open fire, good food (not Sun evening, Mon) from short but varied menu, four well kept Weetwood ales and a couple of guests, good service, upstairs rooms with old wooden tables and leather sofas on undulating floors; covered outside seating area, open all day weekends, closed Mon lunchtime. *(Brian and Anna Marsden)*

NANTWICH   SJ6552
Vine (01270) 619055
Hospital Street; CW5 5RP Black and white-fronted pub dating from the 17th c, modernised interior stretching far back with steps and quiet corners, woodburner, four well kept ales including Hydes, popular good value food from fairly pubby menu (till 6pm Sun), friendly staff and locals, raised seating areas; background music, sports TVs, darts; children and dogs welcome, small sunny outside seating area behind, open all day. *(Jacqui and Alan Swan)*

NESTON   SJ2976
Harp (0151) 336 6980
Quayside, SW of Little Neston; keep on along track at end of Marshlands Road; CH64 0TB Tucked-away little two-room country local; five well kept ales including Holts and Timothy Taylors, decent choice of bottled beers, wines by the glass and some good malt whiskies, enjoyable simple pub food (not Sun evening), log fire, pale quarry tiles and simple furnishings, interesting old photographs, hatch servery to lounge; children and dogs allowed, garden behind and picnic-sets up on front grassy bank facing Dee Marshes and Wales, glorious sunsets with wild calls of wading birds, good walks, open all day. *(Nik and Gloria Clarke)*

NORLEY   SJ5772
Tigers Head (01928) 788309
Pytchleys Hollow; WA6 8NT Friendly little village local near Delamere Forest, enjoyable good value home-made food including deals, well kept Marstons-related ales, tap room and lounge, upstairs skittle alley/function room; pool, darts, sports TV; children and dogs welcome, some seating out in front, more on paved terrace behind, bowling green, open all day Fri and Sat, till 9.30pm Sun, 8.30pm Mon, closed lunchtimes Mon-Thurs. *(Peter and Emma Kelly)*

PARKGATE   SJ2778
Boathouse (0151) 336 4187
Village signed off A540; CH64 6RN Popular 1920s black and white timbered pub (Woodward & Falconer) with attractive linked rooms, good choice of enjoyable food from snacks up, cheerful attentive staff, well kept Hydes and guests, several wines by the glass, big conservatory with great views to Wales over silted Dee estuary (RSPB reserve), may be egrets and kestrels; children and dogs (in bar) welcome, seats out on decking, open (and food) all day. *(Mike and Wena Stevenson)*

PARKGATE   SJ2778
Ship (0151) 336 3931
The Parade; CH64 6SA Far-reaching estuary views from hotel's bow-windowed bar, well kept Brimstage, Thwaites and three guests, several wines by the glass, over 50 whiskies and interesting range of gins, good reasonably priced home-cooked food including sandwiches (until 5pm), daily specials and popular Sun roasts, good friendly service, log fire; Weds quiz night; children welcome, no dogs inside, a few tables out at front and to the side, 25 bedrooms, open (and food) all day. *(John and Mary Warner)*

PEOVER HEATH   SJ7973
★ **Dog** (01625) 861421
Wellbank Lane; the pub is often listed under Over Peover instead; WA16 8UP Nicely renovated traditional country pub with intimate rooms, good variety of well liked generously served food (all day weekends), five ales including Weetwood, decent choice of wines by the glass and malt whiskies, friendly efficient staff; children welcome, dogs in tap room, picnic-sets out at front and in pretty back garden, can walk from here to the Jodrell Bank Discovery Centre and Arboretum, six bedrooms, open (and food) all day. *(Mike and Wena Stevenson)*

PLUMLEY   SJ7275
Golden Pheasant (01565) 722125
Plumley Moor Road (off A556 by the Smoker Inn); WA16 9RX Major recent refurbishment for this roomy country pub; enjoyable food from sandwiches up including good value weekday set lunch, well kept Lees ales and plenty of wines by the glass, friendly helpful staff; background music, Tues quiz, free wi-fi; children and dogs (in bar area) welcome, spacious garden with play area, nine bedrooms (two with four-posters), open (and food) all day. *(Mike and Wena Stevenson)*

POYNTON   SJ9283
Cask Tavern (01625) 875157
Park Lane; SK12 1RE Busy Bollington pub with five of their well kept ales and a guest, craft beers, real ciders and several wines by the glass including draught prosecco, friendly staff, some snacky food; dogs allowed, open all day Fri-Sun, from 4pm other days. *(Chris Stevenson)*

PRESTBURY   SJ9077
Admiral Rodney (01625) 828078
New Road; SK10 4HP Comfortable

and popular 17th-c beamed pub under newish management, well kept Robinsons ales and fairly simple reasonably priced lunchtime food from sandwiches, barm cakes and panini up, friendly attentive service, coal-effect gas fire; children welcome, rustic tables and benches outside, open all day. *(Margaret McDonald)*

PRESTBURY SJ8976

Legh Arms (01625) 829130

A538, village centre; SK10 4DG Beamed inn with divided-up bar and lounge areas, enjoyable food from sandwiches and traditional choices to daily specials, weekend set lunch, Robinsons ales and decent wines by the glass, soft furnishings, ladder-back chairs around solid dark tables, brocaded bucket seats, stylish french prints and italian engravings, two-way log fire and woodburner, cosy panelled back part with narrow offshoot; background music in one area, daily papers; children and dogs welcome, seats on heated terrace, eight bedrooms, good breakfast, open (and food) all day. *(Barbara Brown)*

RODE HEATH SJ8057

Broughton Arms (01270) 883203

Sandbach Road (A533); ST7 3RU Large Marstons pub by Trent & Mersey Canal, extensive range of good value food including several offers, efficient friendly service, spacious bright interior with conservatory; children and dogs welcome, picnic-sets on terrace and waterside lawn, moorings, open all day. *(Tony Hobden)*

STYAL SJ8383

Ship (01625) 444888

B5166 near Ringway Airport; SK9 4JE 17th-c beamed pub under same ownership as the Dog at Peover Heath; good variety of well liked food, ales such as Dunham Massey, Timothy Taylors and Weetwood, plenty of wines by the glass, friendly helpful service, lots of alcoves and snugs, some stripped brickwork and painted panelling, open fire; children welcome, seats out at front and on back terrace, attractive NT village with good walks on the doorstep, open (and food) all day. *(Jeremy King, Mike and Wena Stevenson, John Watson)*

SUTTON SJ9469

★**Ryles Arms** (01260) 252244

Hollin Lane, Higher Sutton; SK11 0NN Popular dining pub in fine countryside, very good food from extensive well priced menu, ales such as Black Sheep and Wincle,

decent wines and good choice of whiskies, pleasant décor, hill-view dining room with french windows to terrace; children welcome, good bedrooms in converted barn, open all day. *(Malcolm and Pauline Pellatt)*

SUTTON SJ9273

Sutton Gamekeeper (01260) 252000

Hollin Lane; SK11 0HL Attractively updated beamed village pub with good freshly made food from short but interestingly varied menu, Dunham Massey, Wincle and a guest, good friendly service, warm open fire; children welcome, well behaved dogs in bar, metal furniture in fenced garden behind, closed Mon (except bank holidays), otherwise open all day till 10pm, food all day weekends (till 7pm Sun). *(Chris Stevenson)*

TARPORLEY SJ5562

Swan (01829) 733838

High Street, off A49; CW6 0AG Elegant Georgian fronted inn (building actually dates from the 16th c) with rambling linked areas, beams and open fires, good food from sandwiches and snacks through pub favourites up, some main dishes available in smaller helpings, Weetwood ales and a couple of guests, lots of wines by the glass, efficient friendly staff; children and dogs (in bar) welcome, tables outside, 16 charming bedrooms, open (and food) all day. *(Malcolm and Pauline Pellatt)*

WESTON SJ7352

White Lion (01270) 587011

Not far from M6 junction 16, via A500; CW2 5NA Renovated 17th-c black and white inn; low-beamed lounge bar with slate floor, standing timbers and inglenook woodburner, popular food here or in restaurant, three well kept ales including Salopian, cocktail bar; background music; children in eating areas, dogs in bar, lovely garden with bowling green (not owned by the pub), 17 comfortable bedrooms, open all day. *(John and Mary Warner)*

WHITEGATE SJ6268

Plough (01606) 889455

Beauty Bank, Foxwist Green; OS Sheet 118 map reference 624684; off A556 just W of Northwich, or A54 W of Winsford; CW8 2BP Comfortable country pub with bar and extended dining area, wide choice of good home-made food (best to book) from panini and baked potatoes up, cheerful efficient service, four well kept Robinsons ales and plenty of wines by the glass; background music, free wi-fi; no under-14s inside, well behaved dogs allowed in tap

Post Office address codings give the impression that some pubs are in Cheshire, when they're really in Derbyshire (and therefore included in that chapter) or in Greater Manchester (see the Lancashire chapter).

room, disabled access, picnic-sets out at front
and in back garden, colourful window boxes
and hanging baskets, popular walks nearby,
open (and food) all day. *(Jack Trussler)*

WILDBOARCLOUGH   SJ9868
Crag (01260) 227239
*Village signed from A54; bear left at
fork, then left at T junction; SK11 0BD*
Old stone-built pub in charming little
sheltered valley below moors (good walk
up Shutlingsloe for great views), enjoyable
generously served home-made food
including Sun carvery, three well kept
local beers, genuinely friendly staff, plates
on delft shelving, various stuffed animals,
open fires; children, walkers and dogs
welcome, terrace with covered smokers'
shelter, open 12-6pm. *(Paul Scofield)*

WILMSLOW   SJ8481
Old Dancer (01625) 530775
Grove Street; SK9 1DR Mock Tudor-
fronted pub on pedestrianised street; bare-
boards interior with simple wooden furniture
and padded wall benches, some striking
murals, five well kept changing local ales,
craft beers and a proper cider, decent coffee
and good value food such as sandwiches,
sharing platters and pies, friendly staff,
second bar/function room upstairs (not
always open); regular events including live
music, film night (Weds) and quiz (Sun),
traditional games, free wi-fi; seats out in
front, open all day (till 1am Fri, Sat).
(M Hamilton)

WINCLE   SJ9665
★Ship (01260) 227217
*Village signposted off A54 Congleton–
Buxton; SK11 0QE* Friendly 16th-c
stone-built country pub; bare-boards
bar leading to carpeted dining room,
old stables area with flagstones, beams,
woodburner and open fire, good
generously served food (not Sun evening)
from varied well priced menu, three
Lees ales and several wines by the glass,
quick attentive service; children and dogs
welcome, tables in small side garden,
good Dane Valley walks, open all day.
(Guy Vowles, Malcolm and Pauline Pellatt)

WRENBURY   SJ5947
★Dusty Miller (01270) 780537
*Cholmondeley Road; village signed
from A530 Nantwich–Whitchurch;
CW5 8HG* Converted 19th-c corn
mill with fine canal views from gravel
terrace and series of tall glazed arches
in bar, spacious modern feel, comfortably
furnished with tapestried banquettes, oak
settles and wheelback chairs around rustic
tables, quarry-tiled area by bar with oak
settle and refectory table, old lift hoist up
under the rafters, Robinsons beers, farm
cider and good generously served food
(all day weekends), good friendly service;
background music, free wi-fi; children
and dogs welcome, disabled access/
loos, farm shop, closed Mon, otherwise
open all day. *(Giles and Annie Francis)*

Pubs close to motorway junctions are listed at the back of the book.

Cornwall

KEY   ★ Star Pub   🎯 Top Quality Food   🍺 Great Beer

🍷 Good Wines   £ Bargain Meals   🛏 Good Bedrooms   🍴 Serves Food

---

ANTONY   SX4054   Map 1

Carew Arms 🎯 🍷

(01752) 814440 – www.carewarms.com

Off A374; PL11 3AB

Renovated village pub with linked bar and dining rooms, imaginative food, well kept ales, good wines by the glass and downstairs farm shop

Below the church in a small village this neatly refurbished pub now also combines a general store and café. There are interconnected dining rooms with wide floorboards, painted farmhouse and other sturdy chairs around rustic wooden tables, wide stripped floorboards and immaculate pale paintwork; décor is minimal and includes a few pieces of artwork here and there and there's also an open fire. High chairs line the bar counter (tables here are reserved for those wanting just a drink and a chat) where they keep St Austell Tribute and Skinners Cornish Trawler on handpump and ten wines by the glass served by courteous staff. The old skittle alley downstairs has been transformed into a store-cum-farm-shop with a small café at one end and a woodburning stove. On Sunday evenings they hold film screenings, pub quizzes and so forth. Plans are afoot for a garden.

🎯 First class food using tip top local ingredients includes game terrine with fruit jelly, local mussel and sea green risotto, burger with pickles and chips, thyme-roasted beetroot and goats cheese 'in the hole', chicken with chorizo, borlotti beans and tomato, whole plaice with brown shrimp butter, rolled pork belly with puy lentils and apple, fish pie, and puddings such as chocolate and peanut slice with salted caramel, caramelised banana and honeycomb ice-cream and steamed rhubarb and orange pudding with vanilla anglaise. *Benchmark main dish: confit duck leg with braised carrots and clapshot £15.50. Two-course evening meal £18.00.*

Free house ~ Licensee Tremayne Carew Pole ~ Real ale ~ Open 12-11; 12-10 Sun; closed Mon ~ Bar food 12-2.30 (3 Sun), 6-9 ~ Restaurant ~ Children welcome ~ Dogs allowed in bar ~ Wi-fi ~ Quiz Sun evening *Recommended by Jane Rigby, Frances Parsons, Matt and Hayley Jacob, Peter L Harrison*

BOSCASTLE   SX0991   Map 1

Cobweb

(01840) 250278 – www.cobwebinn.com

B3263, just E of harbour; PL35 0HE

Plenty of interest in cheerful pub, several real ales and friendly staff

The name of this popular village pub comes from the pre-Food Safety Act practice of using spiders (and their cobwebs) to kill off the wine flies. Nowadays, as well as serving wines by the glass, they keep four real ales such as New Plassey Dragons Breath, St Austell Tribute, Tintagel Cornwalls Pride and a guest beer on handpump, a local cider and a dozen malt whiskies. The two interesting bars have quite a mix of seats (from settles and carved chairs to more pubby furniture), heavy beams hung with hundreds of bottles and jugs, lots of pictures of bygone years, and cosy log fires; the atmosphere is cheerful and bustling, especially at peak times. Games machine, darts and pool. The restaurant is upstairs. There are picnic-sets and benches outside (some under cover); dogs must be on a lead. A self-catering apartment is for rent.

Using local produce, the wide choice of food includes sandwiches and baguettes, chicken liver pâté, creamy crab, sea bream and kale risotto, stuffed peppers with herb couscous and tomato sauce, chicken caesar salad, pizzas (also available to take away), steak in ale pie, local sausages with mustard mash and onion gravy, a curry of the day, home-made chicken kiev with coleslaw, beef stroganoff, scallops with bacon, black pudding and colcannon, and puddings. *Benchmark main dish: Sunday carvery £8.95. Two-course evening meal £15.00.*

Free house ~ Licensee Adrian Bright ~ Real ale ~ Open 10.30am-11.30pm (midnight Sat); 11-11 Sun ~ Bar food 11.30-2.30, 5.15 (6 in winter)-9.30 ~ Restaurant ~ Children welcome ~ Dogs allowed in bar ~ Wi-fi *Recommended by Susan Jackman, John Sargeant, David Appleyard, Andrew Vincent, Alan and Alice Morgan*

CONSTANTINE
SW7328   Map 1

Trengilly Wartha ♀ ⇔

(01326) 340332 – www.trengilly.co.uk

Nancenoy; A3083 S of Helston, signposted Gweek near RNAS Culdrose, then fork right after Gweek; OS Sheet 204 map reference 731282; TR11 5RP

Well run inn surrounded by big gardens with a friendly welcome for all, an easy-going atmosphere and popular food and drink; bedrooms

Not far from the Helford River and tucked away on a peaceful hillside is this busy country inn with courteous licensees and charming staff. The long, low-beamed main bar has a sociable feel (especially in the evening when locals drop in), all sorts of tables, chairs and settles, a woodburning stove, lots of pump clips, and cricket team photos and bats on the walls. Cornish Chough Kynance Blonde, Penzance Potion No 9 and Skinners Cornish Knocker on handpump, lots of wines by the glass, 80 malt whiskies and 11 gins. Leading off the bar is the conservatory family room and there's also a cosy bistro. The six acres of gardens are well worth a wander and offer plenty of seats and picnic-sets under large parasols. The cottagey bedrooms are comfortable and breakfasts highly regarded.

Using local fish and other seasonal produce, the enjoyable food includes lunchtime sandwiches (the crab open sandwich is very popular in season), duck filo rolls with soy, honey and ginger dipping sauce, chicken liver pâté with home-made chutney, sun-dried tomato and wild garlic risotto, steak, mushroom and ale pie, fishcakes with tartare sauce, sausages with mustard mash and onion gravy, pork chop with a creamy pepper and red onion sauce, and puddings that include local ice-cream. *Benchmark main dish: creamy moules marinière £14.00. Two-course evening meal £25.00.*

Free house ~ Licensees Will and Lisa Lea ~ Real ale ~ Open 11-3.15, 6-11; 11-11 Sat; 12-11 Sun ~ Bar food 12-2.15, 6.30-9.30 ~ Restaurant ~ Children welcome away from bar area ~ Dogs allowed in bar and bedrooms ~ Wi-fi ~ Live music Weds and Sun evenings ~ Bedrooms: £75/£84 *Recommended by Colin McLachlan, Chris and Angela Buckell, Dave Braisted, Colin Humphreys, Mike and Sarah Abbot, Andrew and Ruth Simmonds, Victoria and James Sargeant*

DEVORAN
SW7938 Map 1

Old Quay

(01872) 863142 – www.theoldquayinn.co.uk

Devoran from new Carnon Cross roundabout A39 Truro–Falmouth, left on old road, right at mini roundabout; TR3 6NE

Light and airy bar rooms in friendly pub with four real ales, good wine and imaginative food and seats on pretty back terraces; bedrooms

This warmly friendly pub is next to the coast-to-coast Portreath to Devoran Mineral Tramway cycle path and just up from the quay, so you'll find quite a mix of chatty customers. The roomy bar has an interesting 'woodburner' set halfway up one wall, a cushioned window seat, wall settles and a few bar stools around just three tables on stripped boards, and bar chairs by the counter. Bass, Otter Bitter, Skinners Betty Stogs and Porthleven and Wells Bombardier on handpump and good wines by the glass. Off to the left is an airy room with pictures by local artists (for sale), built-in, cushioned wall seating, plush stools and a couple of big tables on the dark slate floor. To the other side of the bar is another light room with more settles and farmhouse chairs, attractive blue and white striped cushions and more sailing photographs; darts and board games. As well as benches outside at the front looking down through the trees to the water, there's a series of snug little back terraces with picnic-sets and chairs and tables. Nearby parking is limited unless you arrive early. There is wheelchair access through a side door.

Rewarding food includes lunchtime sandwiches, southern-fried chicken wings with barbecue sauce, slow-glazed pork belly with peanuts and crispy pork skin, wild mushroom and spinach risotto with local brie and white truffle oil, local mussels in thai green curry sauce, chicken and creamy basil pesto on pasta, fillet steak wrapped in bacon with potato rösti, shallots and beef jus, and puddings such as baked orange custard tart with vanilla ice-cream and chocolate fondant. *Benchmark main dish: burger with toppings, onion rings and triple-cooked chips £12.00. Two-course evening meal £22.00.*

Punch ~ Tenants John and Hannah Calland ~ Real ale ~ Open 11-11 ~ Bar food 12-3, 6-9 ~ Restaurant ~ Children welcome ~ Dogs allowed in bar ~ Wi-fi ~ Bedrooms: £63.50/£85
Recommended by Colin McLachlan, Chris and Angela Buckell, Julie Braeburn, Jean P & Myriam Alderson, Peter and Emma Kelly, Lee and Jill Stafford

GURNARDS HEAD
SW4337 Map 1

Gurnards Head Hotel

(01736) 796928 – www.gurnardshead.co.uk

B3306 Zennor–St Just; TR26 3DE

Interesting inn with lots of wines by the glass, good inventive food and fine surrounding walks; comfortable bedrooms

The open fires in the civilised but easy-going bars are a welcome refuge from the wild surroundings here – the Atlantic is just 500 metres away. There's bold, strong paintwork, books on shelves, work by local artists, fresh flowers, and all manner of wooden dining chairs and tables and sofas on stripped boards or rugs. St Austell Tribute, a beer named for the pub (from Cornish Chough) and guests such as Skinners Lushingtons and Penny Come Quick on handpump, 14 wines by the glass or carafe and a couple of ciders; background music, darts and board games. The large back garden has plenty of seats. Bedrooms are comfortable and have views of the rugged moors or the sea. This is under the same ownership as the Old Coastguard in Mousehole (also in Cornwall) and the Griffin at Felinfach (Wales).

Short, seasonal menu includes impressive modern food: beetroot with yoghurt za'atar, honey and smoked dates, thai mussels and octopus with coriander and chilli broth, sea trout with wild garlic, capers and hazelnuts, celeriac, blue cheese and hazelnut and spelt risotto, chicken breast with sage, bacon, cabbage and white onion and bread sauce, rump of beef with smoked mash and charred spring onions, ray wing with mussel, clam, pancetta and leek chowder, and puddings such as iced banana parfait with peanuts and caramel and rhubarb eton mess with rhubarb sorbet; they may offer a two- and three-course set lunch (not Sunday). *Benchmark main dish: crab, macaroni and parmesan gratin £16.00. Two-course evening meal £24.00.*

Free house ~ Licensees Charles and Edmund Inkin ~ Real ale ~ Open 11-11 ~ Bar food 12-2.30, 6-9.30 ~ Restaurant ~ Children welcome ~ Dogs allowed in bar and bedrooms ~ Wi-fi ~ Bedrooms: £100/£125 *Recommended by John Preddy, William Slade, Tony Smaithe, Andrew and Michele Revell, Patricia and Gordon Thompson, Angela and Steve Heard*

HALSETOWN TL5038 Map 1

Halsetown Inn

(01736) 795583 – www.halsetowninn.co.uk

B3311 SW of St Ives; TR26 3NA

Quite a mix of customers in bustling pub with local ales and wine suppliers, bold, often elaborate food and easy-going atmosphere

This quirky little stone-built pub is just a short drive from St Ives and is popular with locals, who sit at the high chairs by the bar with a pint, and those in for an interesting meal. It's run with environmental awareness (they use green energy and recycle as much as possible) and strong commitment to local producers (from farmers and fishermen to the local tea plantation). As well as the snug bar, there are simply furnished dining areas with an old range and a woodburning stove, an eclectic collection of wooden dining chairs and mismatched tables on quarry tiles, cushioned settles, candles and fresh flowers. Artwork and murals are bold and contemporary, with much created by local artists; we particularly liked the cardboard stag's head. Sharps Doom Bar and Skinners Betty Stogs on handpump, 12 wines by the glass, a dozen malt whiskies and cider; background jazz. The front terrace has a few picnic-sets.

Generous helpings of strongly flavoured, interesting food using local, seasonal produce includes lunchtime sandwiches, smoked trout with potato and parsley fritters and aioli, crispy spiced chicken wings with barbecue sauce, marinated cucumber, spring onion and coriander, cherry coke-glazed ham and eggs, mushroom and leek risotto cake with rosemary and parmesan cream, roasted cherry tomatoes and crispy onions, slow-roasted pork belly with black pudding and cheddar hash brown, onion rings and cider gravy, fillet of hake with laksa butter and asian salad, and puddings such as sticky ginger pudding with ginger toffee sauce and clotted cream and raspberry and prosecco posset with black pepper meringue and elderflower cream; they also offer a two- and three-course set menu (not Sunday). *Benchmark main dish: beef bourguignon £13.50. Two-course evening meal £20.00.*

Free house ~ Licensee Julia Knight ~ Real ale ~ Open 11 (midday in winter)-11; closed 5 Jan-5 Feb ~ Bar food 12-2, 6-9; 12-3 Sun ~ Restaurant ~ Children welcome ~ Dogs welcome ~ Wi-fi *Recommended by Matt and Hayley Jacob, Donald Allsopp, David Appleyard*

HELSTON SW6522 Map 1

Halzephron

(01326) 240406 – www.halzephron-inn.co.uk

Gunwalloe, village about 4 miles S but not marked on many road maps; look for brown sign on A3083 alongside perimeter fence of RNAS Culdrose; TR12 7QB

Bustling pub in lovely spot with tasty bar food, local beers and good nearby walks; bedrooms

This pub was built around 500 years ago and was well known as a smugglers' haunt. The bar and dining areas are neatly kept and have an informal, friendly atmosphere, some fishing memorabilia, comfortable seating, a warm winter fire in a woodburning stove and a good range of drinks: Sharps Doom Bar and guests such as Dynamite Valley Gold Rush and Skinners Porthleven on handpump, nine wines by the glass, 41 malt whiskies and summer farm cider. The dining gallery seats up to 30 people; board games. Picnic-sets outside look across National Trust fields and countryside. The pretty bedrooms have country views. Church Cove with its sandy beach is nearby, Gunwalloe fishing cove is just 300 metres from the pub and there are lovely coastal walks in both directions.

Fresh, seasonal food includes lunchtime sandwiches, mussels with white wine, shallots and cream, roasted brie and garlic with red onion marmalade, root vegetable and sweet potato stew with pearl barley and thyme, lambs liver and crispy bacon in onion sauce, local white crab meat in thermidor sauce topped with cheese, steak in ale pie, chicken strips with cashew nuts, mixed peppers and grain mustard sauce, and puddings. *Benchmark main dish: beer-battered cod fillet and chips £11.95. Two-course evening meal £20.00.*

Free house ~ Licensee Claire Murray ~ Real ale ~ Open 11-11; 12-10.30 Sun ~ Bar food 12-2.30 (3 Sun), 6-9 ~ Restaurant ~ Children welcome ~ Dogs allowed in bar and bedrooms ~ Wi-fi ~ Bedrooms: $55/$95 *Recommended by Barbara Brown, Ian Duncan, Jane and Kai Horsburgh, Sophia and Hamish Greenfield, Frank and Marcia Pelling*

LANLIVERY

Crown 🛏

SX0759 Map 1

(01208) 872707 – www.thecrowninncornwall.co.uk
Signposted off A390 Lostwithiel–St Austell (tricky to find from other directions); PL30 5BT

Chatty atmosphere in nice old pub, with traditional rooms and well liked food and drink; bedrooms

As one of Cornwall's oldest pubs, this pretty white-painted longhouse has a lot of character and history. The main bar has a good mix of both locals and visitors, a woodburning stove in a huge fireplace, traditional settles on big flagstones, church and other wooden chairs around all sorts of tables, old Cornwall photographs and beams in boarded ceilings. Sharps Doom Bar, Skinners Betty Stogs and a changing guest on handpump and several wines by the glass. A couple of other rooms have high-backed black leather dining chairs and built-in cushioned pews, there's another (smaller) woodburning stove and a simply furnished conservatory; darts. The porch has a huge well with a glass top and the quiet, pretty garden has picnic-sets. Bedrooms (in separate buildings) are clean and comfortable and overlook the rustic garden; breakfasts are good. The Eden Project is a ten-minute drive away.

Fair value simple food includes sandwiches, baked brie with red onion chutney, panko-breadcrumbed chicken strips with garlic mayonnaise and sweet chilli sauce, roasted mediterranean vegetable risotto, home-cooked ham and eggs, burger with toppings and chips, confit duck leg on rösti potato with spicy plum dressing, guinea fowl breast with beetroot reduction and a lemon, parsley and black onion seed dressing on crushed potatoes, and puddings such as toffee and hazelnut meringues and red berry and champagne jelly. *Benchmark main dish: lamb rump with garlic roasted new potatoes and red wine and mint jus £14.95. Two-course evening meal £18.00.*

Free house ~ Licensee Nigel Wakeham ~ Real ale ~ Open 11.30-11; 12-10.30 Sun ~ Bar food 12-2.30, 6-9 ~ Restaurant ~ Children welcome away from bar ~ Dogs allowed in bar and bedrooms ~ Wi-fi ~ Bedrooms: /£90 *Recommended by R T and J C Moggridge, Barry Collett, Bob and Margaret Holder, Tracey and Stephen Groves, Ian Herdman, Dr and Mrs F McGinn*

LONGROCK   SW5031   Map 1

Mexico Inn

(01736) 710625 – www.themexicoinn.co.uk
Riverside; old coast road Penzance–Marazion; TR20 8JB

Granite-stone pub with rustic charm, seasonal food cooked by both licensees and a friendly atmosphere

With two enthusiastic chefs at the helm, how could this cheerful, 200-year-old pub go wrong? Our readers have been quick to praise the easy-going atmosphere and enjoyable food and there's a warm welcome for all. It's the sort of place where everyone chats to everyone else, and customers include walkers with their dogs, windsurfers, locals in for a pint and a natter and families meeting up for the popular Sunday lunches. The open-plan rooms include one with leather tub chairs and a chesterfield sofa around a woodburning stove as well as dining rooms with wheelback and wooden chairs around nice antique tables on bare boards, bold aqua-green and orange paintwork, bookshelves, and stools against the counter where they serve Bath Gem, St Austell Proper Job and Trelawny on handpump, eight wines by the glass, several malt whiskies and farm cider; background music, darts and board games. At the front are a few picnic-sets while a small, enclosed back terrace catches the sun and has more picnic-sets.

A sensibly short menu lets the seasonal, local ingredients speak for themselves: crab soup, smoked haddock croquettes with soft boiled egg and curried mayonnaise, rigatoni pasta with peperonata, grilled sprouting broccoli and walnut pesto, burger with toppings and chips, sausages with mash, red cabbage and gravy, cassoulet (confit duck leg, sausage, smoked bacon, beans and cabbage), pork loin with crispy brawn, charcuterie sauce and champ potatoes, and puddings. *Benchmark main dish: beer-battered fish and chips £11.50. Two-course evening meal £19.00.*

Free house ~ Licensee Tom Symons ~ Real ale ~ Open 11.30-11.30 (midnight Sat); 12-10.30 Sun; closed winter Mon ~ Bar food 12.30-2.30, 6.30-9; 12.30-3 Sun ~ Restaurant ~ Children welcome ~ Dogs allowed in bar ~ Wi-fi ~ Live acoustic music last Sun of month
Recommended by Nicola and Stuart Parsons, Robin and Anne Triggs, Serena and Adam Furber, Heather and Richard Jones

LOSTWITHIEL   SX1059   Map 1

Globe ♀ ◖

(01208) 872501 – www.globeinn.com
North Street (close to medieval bridge); PL22 0EG

Traditional local with interesting food and drink, friendly staff and suntrap back courtyard

Luckily for the many loyal customers here, things are running as smoothly as ever. The unassuming and friendly bar, which is long and narrow, has a mix of pubby tables and seats, local photographs on pale blue plank panelling at one end and nice, mainly local prints (for sale) on walls above a coal-effect stove at the snug inner end; there's also a small front alcove. The ornately carved bar counter, with comfortable leatherette stools, dispenses Sharps Own, Skinners Betty Stogs and a guest such as Tintagel Pendragon on handpump, ten reasonably priced wines by the glass, 20 malt whiskies and two local ciders; background music, darts, board games and TV. The sheltered back courtyard is not large but has some attractive and unusual plants, and is a real suntrap (with an extendable awning and outside heaters). You can park in several of the nearby streets or the (free) town car park. The 13th-c church is worth a look and the ancient river bridge, a few metres away, is lovely.

Food remains good and includes lunchtime sandwiches and baguettes, moules marinière, chicken liver pâté, a pie of the week, chilli con carne, spaghetti carbonara, vegetarian roast with red onion, port and mushroom sauce, gammon with fresh pineapple and an egg, slow-roasted local lamb in its own gravy with creamy mash, a fresh fish dish of the day, and puddings such as ginger and black treacle sponge and sticky toffee pudding. *Benchmark main dish: jamaican-style lamb curry £10.95. Two-course evening meal £19.00.*

Free house ~ Licensee William Erwin ~ Real ale ~ Open 12-11 (midnight Fri, Sat) ~ Bar food 12-2, 6.30-9 ~ Restaurant ~ Children welcome but no pushchairs in restaurant ~ Dogs allowed in bar ~ Wi-fi ~ Live music Fri evening ~ Bedrooms: /£70 *Recommended by Dennis and Doreen Haward, Daphne and Robert Staples, Tracey and Stephen Groves, Gavin and Helle May, Buster May*

 MORWENSTOW
Bush 🛏
SS2015 Map 1

(01288) 331242 – www.thebushinnmorwenstow.com
Signed off A39 N of Kilkhampton; Crosstown; EX23 9SR

13th-c pub in fine spot, character bar, several dining rooms and outside dining huts and well liked food; bedrooms

Many of our readers come to this ancient little pub (it's one of the oldest in Britain) after a lovely coastal walk. The character bar has a warming woodburner in a large stone fireplace, traditional pubby furniture on big flagstones, horse tack and copper knick-knacks and welcoming staff. St Austell HSD and Tribute and a guest such as Sharps Atlantic on handpump, 13 wines by the glass, several whiskies and farm cider; background music, darts and board games. One beamed dining room has tall pale wooden dining chairs and tables on bare boards, small prints on cream-painted walls, fresh flowers and another woodburning stove; a second has big windows overlooking the picnic-sets and heated dining huts. The neat bedrooms have lovely sea views and breakfasts are served until 11am. Good surfing beaches nearby.

Pleasing food includes lunchtime baguettes, creamy garlic mushrooms, salt and pepper calamari with garlic mayonnaise, home-cooked honey-roast ham and free-range eggs, a pie of the day, beer-battered fish and chips, trio of sausages with creamy mash and onion gravy, vegetable and bean chilli, lamb shank with rosemary gravy, and puddings such as lemon crunch and fruit crumble. *Benchmark main dish: burger with toppings, coleslaw and chips £11.95. Two-course evening meal £20.00.*

Free house ~ Licensees Colin and Gill Fletcher ~ Real ale ~ Open 12-midnight (10.30 in winter); closed Mon in Jan ~ Bar food 12-9 (8 Sun) ~ Restaurant ~ Children welcome ~ Dogs allowed in bar ~ Wi-fi ~ Bedrooms: £65/£90 *Recommended by Sally Wright, Susan Busbridge, Sophie Ellison, Charles Todd, Julian Thorpe*

'Children welcome' means the pub says it lets children inside without any special restriction. If it allows them in, but to restricted areas such as an eating area or family room, we specify this. Some pubs may impose an evening time limit. We do not mention limits after 9pm as we assume children are home by then.

MOUSEHOLE
SW4726 Map 1

Old Coastguard ✪ ♀ ⇌

(01736) 731222 – www.oldcoastguardhotel.co.uk

The Parade (edge of village, Newlyn coast road); TR19 6PR

Lovely position for civilised inn with an easy-going atmosphere, good choice of wines and first rate food; bedrooms

The comfortable bedrooms here have a view of the sea across the rather special garden with its tropical palms and dracaena; a path leads down to rock pools and seats on the terrace look over to St Michael's Mount and the Lizard. The bar rooms have boldly coloured walls hung with paintings of sailing boats and local scenes, stripped floorboards and an atmosphere of informal but civilised comfort. The Upper Deck houses the bar and the restaurant, with a nice mix of antique dining chairs around oak and distressed pine tables, lamps on big barrel tables and chairs to either side of the log fire, topped by a vast bressumer beam. St Austell Tribute and a guest from Cornish Crown on handpump, 14 wines by the glass or carafe, a big choice of gins, vodkas and whiskies, a farm cider and a good choice of soft drinks. The Lower Deck has glass windows running the length of the building, several deep sofas and armchairs, and shelves of books and games; background music. This is sister pub to the Gurnards Head (also Cornwall) and the Griffin at Felinfach (Wales).

 Impressive food using local fish and beef includes breakfasts to non-residents (8-10am), mackerel with tempura sea vegetables, crab mayonnaise and blood orange, confit rabbit leg with waldorf salad, jerusalem artichoke and wild leek tart with duck egg, chanterelles, grapes and celery, gurnard with griddled pink fir potatoes, chicory and orange and saffron dressing, pancetta-rolled guinea fowl with celeriac and apple spelt risotto and truffle, and puddings such as rhubarb cheesecake with saffron ice-cream and lemon verbena posset with blackberry compote and meringue; they also offer a two- and three-course menu. *Benchmark main dish: fish stew with aioli £16.50. Two-course evening meal £25.00.*

Free house ~ Licensees Charles and Edmund Inkin ~ Real ale ~ Open 8am-midnight ~ Bar food 12.30-2.30, 6.30-9 (9.30 Fri, Sat); 12-2.15, 6.30-9 Sun ~ Restaurant ~ Children welcome ~ Dogs allowed in bar and bedrooms ~ Wi-fi ~ Bedrooms: £105/£140
Recommended by Peter Andrews, John Sargeant, R T and J C Moggridge, Rosie and Marcus Heatherley, Louise and Anton Parsons, Mark and Sian Edwards

MOUSEHOLE
SW4626 Map 1

Ship ⇌

(01736) 731234 – www.shipinnmousehole.co.uk

Harbourside; TR19 6QX

Busy little pub in pretty village with character bars, real ales and fair-priced food; bedrooms

Very popular with locals, this bustling place is right by the harbour in a lovely village. The opened-up main bar has black beams and panelling, built-in wooden wall benches and stools around low tables, sailors' fancy ropework, granite flagstones and a cosy open fire. St Austell Cornish Best, HSD and Tribute on handpump, several wines by the glass and perhaps background music. The bedrooms are above the pub or in the cottage next door and some overlook the water. It's best to park at the top of the village and walk down (traffic can be a bit of a nightmare in summer). The elaborate harbour lights at Christmas are well worth a visit.

🍴 Fair-priced food includes sandwiches (until 5pm), local crab and gruyère tart, pork rillettes with piccalilli, grilled whole mackerel with garlic and thyme vegetables, mushroom, red pepper and grilled halloumi stack with chilli jam and coleslaw, chicken with bacon and cheese in barbecue sauce, rump steak with trimmings and a choice of sauces, local dressed crab with nettle and ginger mayonnaise, and puddings. *Benchmark main dish: beer-battered fresh fish of the day and chips £13.00. Two-course evening meal £19.50.*

St Austell ~ Managers Barry Davy, Kate Murray ~ Real ale ~ Open 11-11 ~ Bar food 12-2.30, 6-8.30 ~ Restaurant ~ Children welcome ~ Dogs allowed in bar and bedrooms ~ Wi-fi ~ Bedrooms: /£120 *Recommended by Colin McLachlan, Alan Johnson, Andrew Stone, Julie Swift, Peter and Emma Kelly, Simon and Alex Knight*

MYLOR BRIDGE

Pandora ♀

SW8137 Map 1

(01326) 372678 – www.pandorainn.com

Restronguet Passage: from A39 in Penryn, take turning signposted Mylor Church, Mylor Bridge, Flushing and go straight through Mylor Bridge following Restronguet Passage signs; or from A39 further N, at or near Perranarworthal, take turning signposted Mylor, Restronguet, then follow Restronguet Weir signs, but turn left downhill at Restronguet Passage sign; TR11 5ST

Idyllically placed waterside inn with lots of atmosphere in beamed and flagstoned rooms, and all-day food

Even when this beautifully positioned medieval pub is at its busiest, staff manage to remain efficient and good-humoured. Seats at the front and on the long floating jetty are quickly snapped up, so do arrive early. Inside, there's a back cabin bar with pale farmhouse chairs, high-backed settles and a model galleon in a big glass cabinet. Several other rambling, interconnecting rooms have low beams, beautifully polished big flagstones, cosy alcoves, cushioned built-in wall seats and pubby tables and chairs, three large log fires in high hearths (to protect them against tidal floods) and maps, yacht pictures, oars and ships' wheels; church candles help with the lighting. St Austell HSD, Proper Job, Trelawny and Tribute on handpump, 17 wines by the glass and 18 malt whiskies. Upstairs, the attractive dining room has exposed oak vaulting, dark tables and chairs on pale oak flooring and large brass bells and lanterns. Because of the pub's popularity, parking is extremely difficult at peak times; wheelchair access.

🍴 Usefully, some sort of food is served all day: sandwiches (until 5pm), mussels in cider and cream, baked local camembert with spiced apple chutney, chargrilled cajun chicken salad, beer-battered fish of the day and chips, burger with toppings, coleslaw and chips, sausages with onion gravy and mash, bouillabaise, aubergine, chickpea and red pepper curry, and puddings such as strawberry pannacotta with toffee walnuts and banoffi pie with caramel sauce. *Benchmark main dish: fish pie £13.00. Two-course evening meal £20.00.*

St Austell ~ Tenant John Milan ~ Real ale ~ Open 10.30am-11pm ~ Bar food 10.30-9.30 ~ Restaurant ~ Children welcome away from bar area ~ Dogs allowed in bar ~ Wi-fi
Recommended by Chris and Angela Buckell, IAA, Maria Sansoni, Graeme and Sally Mendham, HMW, Amanda Shipley

---

Please keep sending us reports. We rely on readers for news of new discoveries, and particularly for news of changes – however slight – at the fully described pubs: feedback@goodguides.com, or (no stamp needed) The Good Pub Guide, FREEPOST RTXY–ZCBC–BBAZ, Stream Lane, Sedlescombe, Battle TN33 0PB.

PENZANCE
Turks Head

SW4730 Map 1

(01736) 363093 – www.turksheadpenzance.co.uk

At top of main street, by big domed building turn left down Chapel Street; TR18 4AF

Bustling atmosphere in well run pub with popular food and beer

As always, our readers enjoy their visits to this lively town pub with its cheerful mix of customers. The bar has old flat irons, jugs and so forth hanging from the beams, pottery above the wood-effect panelling, wall seats and tables and a couple of elbow-rests around central pillars; background music and board games. Sharps Doom Bar, Skinners Betty Stogs and a changing guest ale on handpump, ten wines by the glass, a dozen gins and 12 malt whiskies. The suntrap back garden has big urns of flowers, seats under a giant parasol and a barbecue. There's been a Turks Head here for over 700 years – though most of the original building was destroyed by a Spanish raiding party in the 16th c.

Well regarded food includes lunchtime sandwiches, potted rabbit topped with sage butter, crayfish cocktail, beer-battered local fish and skin-on chips, local sausages with onion and red wine jus, chicken burger with toppings and chips, lambs liver and bacon with mustard mash, 28-day-aged steaks with a choice of sauces, onion rings and chips, local seasonal game dishes, and puddings. *Benchmark main dish: seafood pie £13.95. Two-course evening meal £16.00.*

Punch ~ Lease Jonathan and Helen Gibbard ~ Real ale ~ Open 11.30-11.30 (midnight Sat); 12-11 Sun ~ Bar food 12-2.30, 6-10 ~ Restaurant ~ Children welcome ~ Dogs welcome ~ Wi-fi *Recommended by Alan Johnson, Thomas Green, Chris Stevenson, John and Mary Warner, Andrew Stone*

PERRANUTHNOE
Victoria 🌟

SW5329 Map 1

(01736) 710309 – www.victoriainn-penzance.co.uk

Signed off A394 Penzance–Helston; TR20 9NP

Cornwall Dining Pub of the Year

Carefully furnished inn with interesting food, a friendly welcome, local beers, and seats in pretty garden; bedrooms

With the South West Coast Path and the beaches of Mount's Bay so close, it makes sense to stay in the cosy bedrooms here and enjoy the surroundings. The imaginative food cooked by the chef-landlord is another draw but they do keep Sharps Doom Bar and guests such as Cornish Crown Mousehole and St Ives Boilers on handpump and over ten wines by the glass. The L-shaped bar has various cosy corners, exposed joists, a woodburning stove and an attractive array of dining chairs around wooden tables on oak flooring. The restaurant is separate; background music and board games. The pub spaniel is called Monty. The pretty tiered garden has seats and tables.

Well presented and particularly good food is cooked by the landlord and includes shredded ham hock with cauliflower purée, spiced pineapple salsa and duck egg, honey and truffle whipped goats cheese mousse with chicory, pear, walnuts and sherry vinegar, provençale fish and shellfish stew, roasted artichoke and pea tagliatelle with truffle oil, lemon zest, parmesan and crème fraîche, local plaice with leeks, cucumber, brown shrimps and dill and lemon butter sauce, garlic and thyme pork cutlet with apple butter, duck confit with white bean and thyme cassoulet, smoked bacon and savoy cabbage, and puddings such as chocolate slice with pistachios and passion fruit, and rhubarb and clotted cream rice pudding with saffron ice-cream; they also offer a good value three-course set menu (not Sunday). *Benchmark main dish: local pork belly with black pudding, root vegetable mash and rosemary jus £16.00. Two-course evening meal £25.00.*

Free house ~ Licensee Nik Boyle ~ Real ale ~ Open 12-11; 12-4.30 Sun; 12-3, 5.30-11 Tues-Sat in winter; closed Sun evening, winter Mon ~ Bar food 12-2, 6.15-9; 12-3 Sun ~ Restaurant ~ Children welcome but not in bedrooms ~ Dogs allowed in bar ~ Wi-fi ~ Bedrooms: /£95 *Recommended by Charlie Parker, Christopher Mannings, Nigel Reed, Tom and Ruth Rees, Sally Melling, Martine and Lawrence Sanders, Millie and Peter Downing*

POLGOOTH   SW9950   Map 1

Polgooth Inn ◖

(01726) 74089 – www.polgoothinn.co.uk
Well signed off A390 W of St Austell; Ricketts Lane; PL26 7DA

Welcoming pub in small village, plenty of space for eating and drinking, cornish ales, well liked food and seats on big front terrace

With the Lost Gardens of Heligan close by, it's a good idea to come to this spacious old pub for lunch. The spreading, linked rooms have dark beams and timbering, open fires and woodburning stoves, all sorts of seating ranging from high-backed settles to tartan upholstered dining chairs and banquettes and nice farmhouse seats around wooden tables on carpet, and old agricultural tools and photos on painted or exposed stone walls. St Austell Cornish Best, HSD, Proper Job and Tribute on handpump, good wines by the glass and a gin menu. A dining extension with country kitchen furniture has a modern woodburner against a black brick wall, contemporary lighting and french doors to the terrace. There are plenty of picnic-sets on grass (some under an awning), separate dining booths and a kitchen garden where they grow herbs and salads and keep chickens.

Quite a choice of food includes sandwiches and sharing platters, slow-braised pig cheeks with port and treacle reduction, scallops on chorizo and butter bean stew, burger with toppings in a tomato and rosemary bun, vegetable lasagne, lamb hotpot, monkfish and red mullet thai curry, chilli and barbecue pork ribs with celeriac coleslaw, chicken stir-fry with udon noodles, and puddings such as chocolate marquis and sticky toffee pudding with butterscotch sauce; they also offer breakfasts on Friday and Saturday (7.30-10.30am) and open daily for coffee (from 10am). *Benchmark main dish: beer-battered fish and chips £13.00. Two-course evening meal £18.00.*

St Austell ~ Tenants Alex and Tanya Williams ~ Real ale ~ Open 10am-11pm; 7.30am-midnight Fri, Sat; 11-11 Sun ~ Bar food 12 (7.30am Fri, Sat)-9.30 ~ Restaurant ~ Children welcome ~ Dogs allowed in bar ~ Quiz and tapas Tues evenings *Recommended by Chris and Dorothy Stock, Peter Pilbeam, Colin and Daniel Gibbs*

POLKERRIS   SX0952   Map 1

Rashleigh ◖

(01726) 813991 – www.therashleighinnpolkerris.co.uk
Signposted off A3082 Fowey–St Austell; PL24 2TL

Lovely beachside spot with sizeable sun terrace, five real ales and quite a choice of food

With a restored jetty and a fine beach a few steps away and the local section of the South West Coast Path being renowned for its striking scenery, there are plenty of customers here in fine weather. Another draw, of course, are the wonderful views from the front terrace towards the far side of St Austell and Mevagissey bays. The cosy bar has comfortably cushioned chairs around dark wooden tables at the front, and similar furnishings, local photographs and a winter log fire at the back. Adnams Broadside, Otter Bitter, Skinners Betty Stogs, Timothy Taylors Landlord and Boltmaker and Tintagel Harbour Special on handpump, several wines by the glass, two farm ciders and organic soft drinks; background music. All the tables in the restaurant have a sea view. Plenty of parking in either the pub's own car park or the large village one.

🍴 Carefully cooked food includes sandwiches and ciabattas, whole camembert with cranberry sauce, baked nachos with toppings, cornish pasties, local crab salad, steak in ale pie, local sausages with creamy mash and red onion gravy, chicken in a spicy tomato sauce on pasta, mixed bean chilli con carne, sea bass fillet with red onion and sunblush tomatoes, and puddings such as sticky toffee pudding and Baileys crème brûlée. *Benchmark main dish: local mussels in white wine and cream £11.95. Two-course evening meal £18.00.*

Free house ~ Licensees Jon and Samantha Spode ~ Real ale ~ Open 11-11 (10 winter Sun-Thurs) ~ Bar food 12-3, 6-9; snacks 3-5 ~ Restaurant ~ Children welcome ~ Dogs allowed in bar *Recommended by Sarah Roberts, Sally and David Champion, Geoff and Ann Marston, Patti and James Davidson*

POLPERRO   SX2050 Map 1

Blue Peter 🍺

(01503) 272743 – www.thebluepeterinn.yolasite.com
Quay Road; PL13 2QZ

Friendly pub overlooking harbour with fishing paraphernalia, real ales and carefully prepared food

Both locals and visitors enjoy the cosy low-beamed bar in this chatty little harbourside pub. It's a friendly place with an easy-going atmosphere, traditional furnishings that include a small winged settle and a polished pew, wooden flooring, fishing regalia, photographs and pictures by local artists, lots of candles and a solid wood bar counter. St Austell Tribute and guests such as Bays Gold, Cornish Crown SPA, Hanlons Yellowhammer and Sharps Own on handpump served by the friendly, long-serving licensees. One window seat looks down on the harbour, while another looks out past rocks to the sea; families must use the upstairs room. Background music and board games. There are a few seats outside on the terrace and more in an amphitheatre-style area upstairs. The pub gets crowded at peak times.

🍴 They specialise in fresh fish and as well as sandwiches (the crab is popular), the fair priced food includes crab soup, chicken liver pâté with red onion chutney, vegetable curry, home-cooked ham and free-range eggs, burgers with toppings and chips, a pie of the day, pork in cider casserole, tempura fish and chips, local steaks, and puddings such as toffee apple crumble and chocolate fudge cake. *Benchmark main dish: seafood platter £18.00. Two-course evening meal £17.50.*

Free house ~ Licensees Steve and Caroline Steadman ~ Real ale ~ Open 11-11 (11.30 Sat); 12-10.30 Sun ~ Bar food 12-2.30, 6-8.30; 12 3, 6-9 in high season ~ Restaurant ~ Children in upstairs family room only ~ Dogs allowed in bar ~ Wi-fi ~ Live music weekends and Thurs evening in high season *Recommended by Ian Herdman, Steve and Liz Tilley, Eddie Edwards, Tracey and Stephen Groves, Max Simons, Sally and David Champion*

Bedroom prices are for high summer. Even then you may get reductions for more than one night, or (outside tourist areas) weekends. Winter special rates are common, and many inns reduce bedroom prices if you have a full evening meal.

PORT ISAAC

SX0080 Map 1

Port Gaverne Inn 🛏

(01208) 880244 – www.portgavernehotel.co.uk

Port Gaverne signposted from Port Isaac and from B3314 E of Pendoggett; PL29 3SQ

Bustling small hotel with a proper bar and real ales, well liked food in several dining areas and seats in the garden; bedrooms

Our readers enjoy the bar here, which is full of locals and lively chat, and also the individually furnished and comfortable bedrooms, which are full of character – though the stairs up to most of them are fairly steep (staff will carry your luggage). In the bar are low beams, flagstones and carpeting, some exposed stone, a big log fire and St Austell Proper Job and Tribute, Skinners Betty Stogs and Timothy Taylors Landlord on handpump, 20 wines by the glass, 40 gins, 30 malt whiskies and farm cider. The lounge has some interesting old local photographs. You can eat in the bar or in the 'Captain's Cabin' – a little room where everything is shrunk to scale (old oak chest, model sailing ship, even the prints on the white stone walls). There are seats and tables under parasols at the front, with more in the terraced garden. This is a lovely spot just back from the sea and the inn is surrounded by splendid clifftop walks.

 Enjoyable food includes potato and truffle gnocchi with mushroom purée, creamed spinach and crispy leeks with parmesan, local sausages with creamed potatoes and ale, sage and onion gravy, local pollack, gurnard and squid curry with cucumber and yoghurt, whole poussin with glazed chicory, sauté potatoes and madeira jus, braised lamb shoulder with polenta, cavolo nero and pickled walnut pesto, and puddings such as local honey and whisky tart with elderflower ice-cream and passion-fruit pannacotta with pineapple, spiced ginger cake and coconut yoghurt sorbet. *Benchmark main dish: beer-battered haddock and chips £14.00. Two-course evening meal £22.00.*

Free house ~ Licensee Jackie Barnard ~ Real ale ~ Open 10am-midnight (11pm Sun) ~ Bar food 12-2.30, 5-9.30 ~ Restaurant ~ Children welcome ~ Dogs welcome ~ Wi-fi ~ Bedrooms: £95/£150 *Recommended by Colin McLachlan, Sandra Hollies, Ian Duncan, Charlie May, Celia and Rupert Lemming, Freddie and Sarah Banks*

PORTHLEVEN

SW6225 Map 1

Ship

(01326) 564204 – www.theshipinnporthleven.co.uk

Mount Pleasant Road (harbour) off B3304; TR13 9JS

Welcoming harbourside pub with fantastic views, pubby furnishings, real ales and tasty food and seats on terrace

Both the bustling bar and candlelit dining room in this friendly pub look over the sea and the harbour, which is interestingly floodlit at night; the seats and tables in the terraced garden also share these views. There are open fires in stone fireplaces, quite a mix of chairs and tables on flagstones or bare boards, beer mats and brasses on the ceiling and walls, and various lamps and pennants. Sharps Cornish Coaster and Doom Bar, Skinners Porthleven and a changing guest such as Cornish Crown Mousehole on handpump and six wines by the glass; background music. They also have a cosy, traditionally furnished and separate function room.

Well thought-of food includes lunchtime sandwiches, mussels in creamy leek and cider sauce, panko fish goujons with sweet chilli sauce, chicken, beef and vegetarian bean burgers with toppings, fries and coleslaw, gnocchi with blue cheese, spinach, chestnut mushrooms and toasted walnuts, crab salad with lemon mayonnaise, a changing pie, spare ribs and fries, and puddings such as treacle tart and apple crumble. *Benchmark main dish: beer-battered fish and chips £9.95. Two-course evening meal £16.00.*

Free house ~ Licensee Tom Harrison ~ Real ale ~ Open 11am-midnight ~ Bar food 12-2.30, 6-9 ~ Well behaved children welcome ~ Dogs welcome ~ Wi-fi ~ Occasional live music
Recommended by Alan Johnson, Ray White, Jack and Hilary Burton, Clifford Blakemore, Francis and Mandy Robertson, Melanie and David Lawson

 PORTHTOWAN   SW6948 Map 1
Blue
(01209) 890329 – www.blue-bar.co.uk
Beach Road, East Cliff; car park (fee in season) advised; TR4 8AW

Informal, busy bar by a stunning beach with modern food and wide choice of drinks

Cheerful, damp and sandy customers (often with their dogs) come straight off the fantastic adjacent beach to this bustling bar. They all pile in here throughout the day and the atmosphere is easy and informal; big picture windows look across the terrace to the huge expanse of sand and sea. The front bays have built-in pine seats, while the rest of the large room has wicker and white chairs around pale tables on grey-painted floorboards, cream or orange walls, several bar stools and plenty of standing space around the counter; ceiling fans, some big ferny plants and fairly quiet background music. St Austell Trelawny and Tribute, Sharps Doom Bar and a guest from Skinners on handpump, several wines by the glass, cocktails and shots, and all kinds of coffees, hot chocolates and teas.

Some kind of food is served all day including brunch (10-11.45am), nachos with toppings, antipasti platter, piri-piri chicken burger or bean burger, superfood salad, stone-baked pizzas, moules marinière, various curries, steaks, and puddings such as sticky toffee pudding with toffee sauce and belgian waffle with vanilla ice-cream and honey. *Benchmark main dish: steak burger with toppings, coleslaw and rustic chips £9.75. Two-course evening meal £16.00.*

Free house ~ Licensees Tara Roberts and Luke Morris ~ Real ale ~ Open 10am-11pm (midnight Fri, Sat); 10am-10.30pm Sun; closed Mon-Thurs evenings in winter ~ Bar food 10-9 ~ Children welcome ~ Dogs welcome ~ Wi-fi ~ Live music Sat evening
Recommended by Colin Humphreys, Claire Adams, Nigel Havers, Edward May, Karl and Frieda Bujeya, Martine and Fabio Lockley

 ROCK   SW9375 Map 1
Mariners ⭐ �
(01208) 863679 – www.themarinersrock.com
Rock Road; PL27 6LD

Modern pub with huge glass windows taking in the estuary views, highly popular food, three real ales and wines by the glass, friendly service and seats on front terrace

Of course, the food is the main draw here but they do keep Sharps Atlantic, Doom Bar, Wolf Rock and a guest beer on handpump and good wines by the glass. The lovely view over the Camel estuary is another reason for a visit – to make the most of this there's a front terrace with lots of seats and tables (people often sit on the wall too), a much coveted smaller terrace leading from the first-floor restaurant, and huge windows and folding glass doors. The bar is light and spacious with contemporary metal chairs and wall seats around pale wooden-topped tables on slate flooring; walls are partly bare stone and partly painted and hung with old black and white photos, modern prints and blackboards listing food and drink items. There's an open kitchen; background music and TV. The upstairs restaurant is similarly furnished and, if anything, the views are even better from here.

 Imaginative seasonal cooking includes lunchtime focaccia rolls, ham hock scrumpet with pease pudding and pickled walnuts, smoked and cured fish with pickles, lentil curry with eggs and an indian-style salad, breaded ling with apple and cider chutney and tarragon mayonnaise, lamb pie with mint sauce, slow-cooked shin of beef with horseradish mash, chargrilled chicken with satay dressing, peanut salad and coconut rice, and puddings such as chocolate tart with orange crème fraîche and steamed treacle and ginger sponge with custard. *Benchmark main dish: 8oz local rump steak with béarnaise sauce and chips £24.00. Two-course evening meal £23.00.*

Free house ~ Licensee Nathan Outlaw ~ Real ale ~ Open 11am-midnight ~ Bar food 11-3, 6-9 ~ Restaurant ~ Children welcome ~ Dogs welcome ~ Wi-fi ~ Live music every second Sun in summer *Recommended by Ben and Diane Bowie, Tim and Sarah Smythe-Brown, James Allsopp, Jill and Dick Archer, Alan and Linda Blackmore*

ST IVES

Queens 🖝

SW5441 Map 1

(01736) 796468 – www.queenshotelstives.com
High Street; TR26 1RR

Bustling inn just back from the harbour with a spacious bar, open fire, real ales and tasty food; bedrooms

This pub's location at the heart of this busy seaside town and just minutes from the harbour means plenty of cheerful customers ready to savour a pint or an enjoyable meal. The open-plan, spreading bar has a relaxed atmosphere, all sorts of wooden chairs around scrubbed tables on bare floorboards, tartan banquettes on either side of the Victorian fireplace, a wall of barometers above a leather chesterfield sofa and some brown leather armchairs; also, fresh flowers and candles on tables and on the mantelpiece above the open fire. Red-painted bar chairs line the white marble-topped counter where they serve St Austell HSD, Proper Job and Tribute and a guest such as Bath Gem on handpump, eight wines by the glass, a good choice of gins and rums and farm cider; background music, board games and TV for sports events. Bedrooms are attractive, airy and simply furnished, with cornish artwork on the walls and some period furniture. The window boxes and hanging baskets are quite a sight in summer.

Appealing food uses the best local, seasonal produce and includes lunchtime sandwiches, local mussels with white wine, garlic and cream, fresh local crab with lemon dressing, vegetable lasagne, burger with toppings, onion rings and chips, local sausages with mash and onion gravy, beer-battered fish and chips, honey-roasted ham with free-range eggs, and puddings such as chocolate brownie with rum and raisin ice-cream and apple crumble. *Benchmark main dish: beef stew with dumplings £10.00. Two-course evening meal £18.00.*

St Austell ~ Tenant Neythan Hayes ~ Real ale ~ Open 10.30am-11.30pm (midnight Sat) ~ Bar food 12-2.30, 6-9; 12-9 (6 winter) ~ Children welcome ~ Dogs allowed in bar ~ Wi-fi ~ Open mike Weds evening, live bands Sat evening ~ Bedrooms: £89/£109 *Recommended by Alan Johnson, Hilary and Neil Christopher, Pauline and Mark Evans, Rosie and John Moore*

Half pints: by law, a pub should not charge more for half a pint than half the price of a full pint, unless it shows that half-pint price on its price list.

ST MERRYN
Cornish Arms
SW8874 Map 1

(01841) 532700 – www.rickstein.com/eat-with-us/the-cornish-arms

Churchtown (B3276 towards Padstow); PL28 8ND

Bustling pub with lots of cheerful customers, bar and dining rooms, real ales, good pubby food, friendly service and seats outside

Certainly at peak times, this busy roadside pub appeals most to holidaymakers who find it usefully open all day. The main door leads into a sizeable informal area with a pool table and plenty of cushioned wall seating; to the left, a light, airy dining room overlooks the terrace. There's an upright modern woodburner, photographs of the sea and former games teams, and pale wooden dining chairs around tables on quarry tiles. This leads to two more linked rooms with ceiling joists; the first has pubby furniture on huge flagstones, while the end room has more cushioned wall seating, contemporary seats and tables and parquet flooring. There's also a dining room to the back. St Austell Proper Job, Trelawny and Tribute and a beer named for the pub – Chalkys Bite (from Sharps) – on handpump, 17 wines by the glass, a farm cider, friendly service, background music, board games and TV; they hold a beer and mussel festival every March. The window boxes are pretty and there are picnic-sets on a side terrace, with more on grass.

Well executed pubby favourites include sandwiches, chicken wings with tamarind and chilli sambal and mango, lime and coriander, devilled kidneys and mushrooms on sourdough toast, burger with toppings, chilli relish and chips, wild mushroom risotto, hake with soy butter sauce and champ mash, lancashire hotpot with pickled red cabbage, mussels and chips, and puddings such as cheesecake of the day with salted caramel sauce and rhubarb and apple crumble with vanilla ice-cream. *Benchmark main dish: beer-battered cod and chips £13.95. Two-course evening meal £20.00.*

St Austell ~ Tenant Siebe Richards ~ Real ale ~ Open 11.30-11 ~ Bar food 12-3, 5-9; 12-9 Sat; 12-8 Sun ~ Children welcome ~ Dogs welcome ~ Wi-fi *Recommended by Katherine Matthews, Peter and Emma Kelly, Alfie Bayliss, Adam Jones*

TREBURLEY
Springer Spaniel
SX3477 Map 1

(01579) 370424 – www.thespringerspaniel.co.uk

A388 Callington–Launceston; PL15 9NS

Cosy, friendly pub with highly popular, first class food, friendly staff and a genuine welcome for all

Although a proper pub with regular customers dropping in for a pint and a chat (often with a dog in tow who might get a biscuit), visitors in the 'know' are here for the impressive food. The friendly, easy-going little bar has beams, antlers and a few copper pans on an exposed stone wall above a woodburning stove, books on shelves, pictures of springer spaniels, a rather fine high-backed scttle and other country kitchen chairs and tables and old parquet flooring. A dining room has more bookcases, candles and similar tables and chairs, and stairs lead up to the main restaurant; a second woodburner is set into a slate wall with a stag's head above it. Dartmoor Jail Ale and St Austells Tribute on handpump and ten good wines by the glass (including sparkling); background music. Outside in the small enclosed, paved garden are picnic-sets.

Food includes pubby dishes plus creative modern choices: sandwiches, butternut squash and stilton ravioli with almond brown butter, honey and soy glazed pigeon with parsnip, venison and steak pasty, beer-battered fish and chips, beetroot risotto, burger with toppings, onion rings, slaw and triple-cooked chips, guinea fowl with heritage carrots and neeps and tatties, and puddings such as chocolate and hazelnut mousse and lemon parfait with fennel meringue and lime and cardamom gel. *Benchmark main dish: roast venison with chocolate and juniper £23.00. Two-course evening meal £30.00.*

Free house ~ Licensee Beth Martin ~ Real ale ~ Open 12-3, 5-11 ~ Bar food 12-3, 6-9; 12-6 Sun ~ Restaurant ~ Children welcome ~ Dogs allowed in bar *Recommended by Sarah Roberts, Tony Smaithe, Isobel Mackinlay, Edward May, Hazel Hyde*

TREVAUNANCE COVE
Driftwood Spars 🍺 🛏

SW7251 Map 1

(01872) 552428 – www.driftwoodspars.co.uk
Off B3285 in St Agnes; Quay Road; TR5 0RT

Friendly inn with plenty of history, own microbrewery, a wide range of other drinks and popular food; nearby beach; bedrooms

A fine range of drinks here includes seven real ales on handpump – their own Driftwood Alfies Revenge, Blackheads Mild, Lou's Brew and Spars with guests such as Penzance Potion No 9 and Tintagel Merlins Muddle (they hold two beer festivals a year), plus 25 malt whiskies, ten rums, seven gins and several wines by the glass; staff are knowledgeable and friendly. The three small bars are timbered with massive ships' spars (the masts of great sailing ships, many of which were wrecked along this coast), and furnishings include dark wooden farmhouse and tub chairs and settles around tables of different sizes, padded stools by the counter, old ship prints, lots of nautical and wreck memorabilia and woodburning stoves; table football and pool. It's said that an old smugglers' tunnel leads from behind the bar up through the cliff. The modern dining room overlooks the cove. Summer hanging baskets are pretty, there are seats in the garden and, being close to a dramatic cove and beach, the place is usefully open all day. Bedrooms are attractive and comfortable and have views of the coast.

🍴 A wide choice of food includes lunchtime sandwiches and platters, baked rosemary and garlic local brie with ale and red onion jam, mussels with fennel and shallots in beer and cream, burger with toppings, coleslaw and chips, sausages with onion gravy and mash, cauliflower and sweet potato curry, venison rump with garlic and thyme roast potatoes and blackberry jus, and puddings such as chocolate mousse with salted caramel and whisky ice-cream and sticky toffee pudding with butterscotch sauce. *Benchmark main dish: beer-battered fish and chips £12.95. Two-course evening meal £19.50.*

Own brew ~ Licensee Louise Treseder ~ Real ale ~ Open 11-11 (midnight Sat, 10 Sun) ~ Bar food 12-2.30, 6-9 ~ Restaurant ~ Well behaved children welcome away from main bar ~ Dogs welcome ~ Wi-fi ~ Live music some weekends (phone to check) ~ Bedrooms: /£92 *Recommended by Edward May, Simon Day, Charles Todd, Mr Yeldahn, Nicola and Holly Lyons, David Thorpe, Daniel King*

WADEBRIDGE
Ship 🍷

SW9972 Map 1

(01208) 813845 – www.shipinnwadebridge.co.uk
Gonvena Hill, towards Polzeath; PL27 6DF

One of the oldest pubs in town, with beams and open fires, carefully refurbished bars, real ales and good, seasonally changing food

There's a loyal local following and warmly friendly service in this old-fashioned pub, and our readers enjoy their visits. As well as plenty of nautical memorabilia on the rough whitewashed walls (the place was once owned by a shipbuilding family), seating in the bar area ranges from leather button-back wall banquettes to a collection of wooden dining chairs, stools and window seats topped with scatter cushions; also, flagstone or bare-boarded floors, books on shelves, church candles and open fires. High chairs line the counter where attentive staff serve Padstow Pride and Sharps Atlantic and Doom Bar on handpump and 12 wines by the glass (they hold a wine club on the first Tuesday of the month); background music. Of the two dining areas, one has high rafters and brass ship lights. The small, sunny decked terrace outside has seats and chairs.

A thoughtful menu includes smoked mackerel pâté with pickled cucumber, braised pig cheek with parsnip purée and parsnip crisps, a pie of the week, pumpkin, spinach and tallegio open ravioli with sage butter sauce, burgers with toppings, coleslaw and thin chips, gurnard fillets with bacon lardons and orange, calves liver with roasted shallots and onion sauce, guinea fowl breast with pancetta, fondant potato and whisky sauce, and puddings such as vanilla cheesecake with blackberries and mint and sticky toffee pudding with rum and raisin ice-cream; burger evening is Tuesday, veggie night is Wednesday and surf and turf on Thursday. *Benchmark main dish: lamb with dauphinoise potatoes and wild garlic sauce £15.50. Two-course evening meal £20.50.*

Punch ~ Tenants Rupert and Sarah Wilson ~ Real ale ~ Open 12-2.30, 5-11; 12-10 Sun ~ Bar food 12-2 (3 Sun), 5-9 (9.30 Fri, Sat); no food Sun evening except peak season ~ Children welcome ~ Dogs allowed in bar ~ Wi-fi ~ Wine club first Tues of month, folk club last Tues of month *Recommended by R T and J C Moggridge, Lindy Andrews, Jamie Green, Buster May, James and Sylvia Hewitt, Trish and Karl Soloman*

WAINHOUSE CORNER
Old Wainhouse
SX1895 Map 1

(01840) 230711 – www.oldwainhouseinn.co.uk
A39; EX23 0BA

Cheerful pub, open all day with friendly staff and a good mix of customers, plenty of seating spaces, real ales and tasty food; bedrooms

Happily, nothing has changed here under the newish owners and there's still a cheerful and easy-going atmosphere and plenty of chatty customers. The main bar has an attractive built-in settle, stripped rustic farmhouse chairs and dining chairs around a mix of tables on enormous old flagstones, a large woodburner with stone bottles on the mantelpiece above it, and beams hung with scythes, saws, a horse collar and other tack, spiles, copper pans and brass plates; do note the lovely photograph of a man driving a pig across a bridge. Off here is a simpler room with similar furniture, a pool table, darts and background music. The dining room to the left of the main door has elegant high-backed dining chairs around pale wooden tables, another woodburner and more horse tack. Sharps Atlantic, Cornish Coaster and Doom Bar on handpump and friendly service. Outside, a grass area to one side of the building has picnic-sets. The simply furnished but comfortable bedrooms are light and airy and look out towards the sea. The South West Coast Path is close by.

Well liked food includes chicken liver parfait with onion jam, thai scallop salad, red wine and blue cheese risotto with spiced walnuts, burger with relish and fries, beer-battered pollack and chips, tarragon-stuffed chicken breast wrapped in parma ham with jerusalem artichoke purée and red wine sauce, whole john dory with capers and parsley brown butter, and puddings such as sticky toffee pudding with butterscotch sauce and apple and cherry crumble with clotted cream. *Benchmark main dish: 21-day-aged sirloin steak and chips £18.95. Two-course evening meal £18.00.*

Enterprise ~ Lease Rob Tape ~ Real ale ~ Open 11am-midnight ~ Bar food 12-9 (9.30 Fri, Sat) ~ Restaurant ~ Children welcome ~ Dogs allowed in bar and bedrooms ~ Wi-fi ~ Live music first Sun of month ~ Bedrooms: £47.50/£95 *Recommended by Dr Simon Innes, George Sanderson, Maddie Purvis, Jim King, Justine and Neil Bonnett*

Also Worth a Visit in Cornwall

Besides the fully inspected pubs, you might like to try these pubs that have been recommended to us and described by readers. Do tell us what you think of them: feedback@goodguides.com

ALTARNUN   SX2280
Kings Head (01566) 86241
Five Lanes; PL15 7RX Old mansard-roofed beamed village pub, Greene King Abbot and guests such as local Penpont, Weston's cider, generous reasonably priced pubby food from sandwiches and baguettes up including popular Sun carvery, carpeted lounge set for dining with big log fire, slate floor restaurant and public bar with another fire, friendly staff and ghost of former landlady Peggy Bray; background music, TV, pool; children and dogs welcome, picnic-sets on front terrace and in small raised garden, refurbished bedrooms, open all day and handy for A30. *(Dr D J and Mrs S C Walker)*

ALTARNUN   SX2083
★ Rising Sun (01566) 86636
NW; village signed off A39 just W of A395 junction; PL15 7SN Tucked-away 16th-c pub with traditionally furnished L-shaped main bar, low beams, slate flagstones and coal fires, good choice of locally sourced food including excellent local seafood, specials board, Penpont, Skinners and guests, traditional cider, good friendly service; background music, pool, free wi-fi; well behaved children allowed in bar (not restaurant), dogs welcome outside of food times, seats on suntrap terrace and in garden, pétanque, camping field, nice village with beautiful church, open all day weekends. *(Chris Stevenson)*

BLISLAND   SX1073
★ Blisland Inn (01208) 850739
Village signposted off A30 and B3266 NE of Bodmin; PL30 4JF Traditional old-fashioned local with convivial landlord, six well kept west country ales (some tapped from the cask) including two badged for the pub from Sharps, also proper cider and fruit wines, generous helpings of tasty home-cooked food, beams and ceiling covered with pump clips and collection of mugs, toby jugs on beams, also a family room

with pool and table skittles; background and regular live music; dogs welcome, picnic-sets out on front grass overlooking village green, close to Camel Trail cycle path, open all day (till midnight Sat), no food Sun evening. *(Susan Jackman, Mr Yeldahn, Julian Richardson, Peter Brix, Ian Herdman)*

BODINNICK   SX1352
Old Ferry (01726) 870237
Across the water from Fowey; coming by road, to avoid the ferry queue, turn left as you go downhill – car park on left before pub; PL23 1LX 17th-c inn just up from the river with lovely views from terrace, dining room and some of its 12 comfortable bedrooms; traditional bar with nautical memorabilia, old photographs and woodburner, back room hewn into the rock, well kept Sharps ales and at least one guest, nice wines, good food from lunchtime sandwiches up including daily specials and children's menu, friendly french landlord and helpful staff; free wi-fi; good circular walks, lane by pub in front of ferry slipway is extremely steep and parking limited, open (and food) all day. *(Andrew Vincent)*

BOSCASTLE   SX0990
★ Napoleon (01840) 250204
High Street, top of village; PL35 0BD Welcoming 16th-c thick-walled cottage at the top of this steep quaint village (fine views halfway up); cosy rooms on different levels, slate floors, oak beams and log fires, interesting Napoleon prints and lots of knick-knacks, good food from daily changing menu in bar areas or small evening restaurant, well kept St Austell tapped from casks, decent wines and coffee, traditional games; background music (live Fri, singalong Tues), sports TV, free wi-fi; children and dogs welcome, small covered terrace and large sheltered garden, open all day. *(Max Simons)*

BOSCASTLE   SX0991
Wellington (01840) 250202
Harbour; PL35 0AQ Old hotel's long beamed and carpeted bar, good fairly priced food from varied menu, cornish ales kept

well, nice coffee and cream teas, roaring log fire, upstairs gallery area and separate evening restaurant with more upmarket menu; Weds folk night, quiz first Mon of month; children and dogs (in bar) welcome, big secluded garden, comfortable bedrooms and apartments in adjacent mill, open all day, food all day weekends. *(Julia Swift)*

BOTALLACK   SW3632

★**Queens Arms** (01736) 788318

B3306; TR19 7QG Honest welcoming old pub with good home-made food including local fish/seafood, meat sourced within 3 miles, well kept Sharps, Skinners and guests, good friendly service, log fires (one in unusual granite inglenook), dark wood furniture, tin mining and other old local photographs on stripped-stone walls, family extension; dogs welcome, tables out in front and pleasant back garden, wonderful clifftop walks nearby, lodge accommodation, open all day. *(Dr D J and Mrs S C Walker)*

BREAGE   SW6128

Queens Arms (01326) 564229

3 miles W of Helston just off A394; TR13 9PD Welcoming village corner pub with long part-carpeted bar, plush banquettes and woodburner at each end, up to eight well kept ales and good home-made pubby food (all day Sun) including daily specials, small restaurant with another woodburner, pool and darts in games part; background and live music, quiz nights, sports TV, free wi-fi; children and dogs welcome, seats outside under cover, barbecue and play areas, two bedrooms, caravan pitches, medieval wall paintings in church opposite, open all day. *(Mr and Mrs John Clifford)*

CADGWITH   SW7214

★**Cadgwith Cove Inn** (01326) 290513

Down very narrow lane off A3083 S of Helston; no nearby parking; TR12 7JX Friendly little pub in fishing cove with lovely walks in either direction; simply furnished front rooms with bench seating on parquet, log fire, local photos and nautical memorabilia, big back bar with huge fish mural, Otter, Sharps, Skinners and a guest from Atlantic, popular food including local fish/seafood (can be expensive); background music, folk night Tues, local singers (sea shanties) Fri, darts and board games; children and dogs welcome, front terrace overlooking old fishermen's sheds, comfortable bedrooms with sea views, coastal walks, open all day. *(David Eberlin, Piotr Chodzko-Zajko, R T and J C Moggridge, Adrian Johnson, Griffiths family)*

CALSTOCK   SX4368

Tamar (01822) 832487

The Quay; PL18 9QA Cheerful and relaxed 17th-c local opposite the Tamar with its imposing viaduct; dark stripped stone, flagstones, tiles and bare boards, pool room

with woodburner, more modern back dining room, good generous straightforward food and summer cream teas, well kept Sharps Doom Bar and other cornish ales, reasonable prices and friendly service; some live music; children (away from bar) and well behaved dogs welcome, nicely furnished terrace, heated smokers' shelter, hilly walk or ferry to Cotehele (NT). *(Tracey and Stephen Groves)*

CHAPEL AMBLE   SW9975

Maltsters Arms (01208) 812473

Off A39 NE of Wadebridge; PL27 6EU Country pub-restaurant with good food including Sun lunchtime carvery, friendly accommodating staff, Sharps ales and Weston's cider, log fire, beams, stripped stone and painted half-panelling, modern back extension; music and quiz nights; children and dogs (on slate-floored area) welcome, seats outside. *(James and Sylvia Hewitt)*

CHARLESTOWN   SX0351

Pier House (01726) 67955

Part of Pier House Hotel; PL25 3NJ Glass-fronted warehouse conversion alongside hotel, great spot looking over classic little harbour and its historic sailing ships; half a dozen ales including Bass, Sharps and Skinners, well liked reasonably priced food from sandwiches up, friendly efficient service; live music Sat, sports TVs, pool; children welcome, interesting film-set conservation village with shipwreck museum, good walks, parking away from pub. *(Dr A McCormick)*

CHARLESTOWN   SX0351

Rashleigh Arms (01726) 73635

Quay Road; PL25 3NX Modernised early 19th-c inn with public bar, lounge and dining area, five well kept St Austell ales, three guests and good wine choice, popular fairly priced food including burger menu and Sun carvery, quick friendly service; background music, fortnightly live bands Fri, trad jazz second Sun of month, free wi-fi; children welcome, dogs in bar, disabled facilities, front terrace and garden with picnic-sets, eight bedrooms (some with sea views), ten more in nearby Georgian house, Grade II listed car park (site of old coal storage yards), short walk to attractive harbour with tall ships, open (and food) all day. *(Ian McIntosh)*

COMFORD   SW7339

Fox & Hounds (01209) 820251

Comford; A393/B3298; TR16 6AX Attractive rambling low-beamed pub; stripped stone and painted panelling, high-backed settles and cottagey chairs on flagstones, some comfortable leather seating too, three woodburners, well liked freshly made food from interesting varied menu including daily specials, well kept St Austell ales, good friendly service; background music, newspapers, darts and board games; children and dogs (in bar) welcome, disabled facilities, nice floral displays in front, picnic-sets in back garden, open all day weekends, closed Mon. *(Trevor Burgess)*

COVERACK   SW7818
Paris (01326) 280258
The Cove; TR12 6SX Comfortable Edwardian seaside inn above harbour in beautiful fishing village; carpeted L-shaped bar with well kept St Austell ales and Healey's cider, large relaxed dining room with white tablecloths and spectacular bay views, wide choice of interesting if not always cheap food including good fresh fish, Sun lunchtime carvery, helpful cheery service, model of namesake ship (wrecked nearby in 1899); popular Weds quiz, pool, free wi-fi; children and dogs welcome, more sea views from garden and six bedrooms, limited parking. *(Geoff and Anne Marston)*

CRACKINGTON HAVEN   SX1496
Coombe Barton (01840) 230345
Off A39 Bude–Camelford; EX23 0JG Much extended old inn in beautiful setting overlooking splendid sandy bay (fine sunsets); good fairly priced food from shortish menu cooked by landlord-chef, three rotating cornish ales and decent wine choice, friendly helpful service; background and some live music, quiz and comedy nights, sports TV, darts and pool; children welcome, dogs in bar, picnic-sets on side terrace, lovely cliff walks, roomy bedrooms, open all day. *(Jim Slattery)*

CRAFTHOLE   SX3654
★Finnygook (01503) 230338
B3247, off A374 Torpoint road; PL11 3BQ 15th-c coaching inn with beams and joists in smart bar, long wall pews and carved cushioned dining chairs around wooden tables on bare boards, central log fire, high chairs and tables near counter serving St Austell Tribute and a couple of guests, decent choice of wines by the glass, ten malt whiskies and a real cider, dining room with fine views and unusual log-effect gas fire, dining library, enjoyable food from pub favourites up including daily specials, friendly helpful service; occasional live music Fri, quiz last Weds of month, free wi-fi; children and dogs welcome, good surrounding walks, bedrooms, open all day. *(Rosie and Marcus Heatherley)*

CROWS NEST   SX2669
Crows Nest (01579) 345930
Signed off B3264 N of Liskeard; OS Sheet 201 map reference 263692; PL14 5JQ New welcoming licensees for this characterful 17th-c pub; well kept St Austell ales, decent wines and good home-made food including daily specials, attractive furnishings under bowed beams, exposed stonework and big log fire, chatty locals; children and dogs welcome (they have three dogs), picnic-sets on terrace by

quiet lane, handy for Bodmin Moor walks, open all day weekends. *(Max Simons)*

CUBERT   SW7857
★Smugglers Den (01637) 830209
Off A3075 S of Newquay; TR8 5PY Big open-plan 16th-c thatched pub tucked away in small hamlet; good locally sourced food and up to four beers (May pie and ale festival), several wines by the glass, friendly staff, neat ranks of tables, dim lighting, stripped stone and heavy beam and plank ceilings, west country pictures and seafaring memorabilia, steps down to part with huge inglenook, another step to big side dining room, also a little snug area with woodburner and leather armchairs; background music; children and dogs welcome, occasional live music, small front courtyard and terrace (both decked) with nice country views, sloping lawn and play area, camping opposite, open all day. *(P and J Shapley)*

DULOE   SX2358
Plough (01503) 262556
B3254 N of Looe; PL14 4PN Popular restaurant pub with three country-chic linked dining rooms all with woodburners, dark polished slate floors, a mix of pews and other seats, good fairly priced locally sourced food (must book weekends) including some imaginative dishes, also lunchtime sandwiches and snacks, reasonably priced wines, well kept St Austell, Sharps and summer guests, friendly service; unobtrusive background music; children and dogs welcome, picnic-sets out by road. *(Tracey and Stephen Groves)*

EDMONTON   SW9672
★Quarryman (01208) 816444
Off A39 just W of Wadebridge bypass; PL27 7JA Welcoming busy family-run pub adjoining small separately owned holiday courtyard complex; gently refurbished three-room beamed bar with interesting decorations including old sporting memorabilia, fairly pubby food from shortish menu with good individual dishes such as sizzling steaks and portuguese fish stew, quick friendly service, well kept Exeter Avocet, Padstow May Day and Skinners Lushingtons, seven wines by the glass; well behaved children and dogs (on slate-floored area) allowed, disabled access (but upstairs lavatories – plans to move these downstairs), picnic-sets in front and courtyard behind, self-catering apartment, open all day. *(Chris Stevenson)*

EGLOSHAYLE   SX0071
Earl of St Vincent (01208) 814807
Off A389, just outside Wadebridge; PL27 6HT Pretty flower-decked beamed dining pub with over 200 working antique clocks (many chiming), also golfing memorabilia, art deco ornaments, old pictures and rich furnishings, enjoyable

home-made food from sandwiches to steaks, St Austell ales and Healey's cider; background music, outside loos; well behaved children allowed, no dogs inside, lovely garden. *(Andrew Vincent)*

FALMOUTH SW8132
5 Degrees West (01326) 311288
Grove Place, by harbourside car park; TR11 4AU Modern split-level open-plan bar with mixed furnishings including squashy sofas and low tables on stripped wood floors, log fire in driftwood-effect fireplace, local artwork, enjoyable food from snacks to grills, five real ales, three ciders and good choice of other drinks, back dining area; background music (live Thurs, Fri, Sun), quiz Mon, free wi-fi; children and dogs welcome, disabled facilities, seats out at front and on attractive sheltered back terrace, open (and food) all day. *(Chris Stevenson)*

FALMOUTH SW8032
Beerwolf (01326) 618474
Bells Court (opposite Marks & Spencer); TR11 3AZ Stairs up to intriguing old pub-cum-bookshop hidden down little alley in centre of town; a former working men's club with raftered ceilings and eclectic mix of furniture on bare boards, good range of well kept changing beers and ciders, decent coffee, no food but can bring your own, friendly laid-back atmosphere; games including table tennis and pinball, free wi-fi; children and dogs welcome, a few picnic-sets outside, open all day. *(Comus and Sarah Elliott, Guy Vowles)*

FALMOUTH SW8033
Boathouse (01326) 315425
Trevethan Hill/Webber Hill; TR11 2AG Two-level pub with buoyant local atmosphere, four well kept beers featuring some smaller cornish brewers such as Black Rock, Penpont and Rebel, good range of other drinks, enjoyable home-made food including fresh fish/seafood, friendly service; background and live music; children and dogs welcome, tables outside, upper deck with awning and fantastic harbour views, open all day. *(Chris Stevenson)*

FALMOUTH SW8132
★**Chain Locker** (01326) 311085
Custom House Quay; TR11 3HH This popular pub in fine spot by inner harbour was closed for extensive refurbishment as we went to press – news please.

FALMOUTH SW8033
★**Chintz Symposium** (01326) 617550
High Street/Brewery Yard; TR11 2BY Recently opened upstairs bar with Alice in Wonderland-inspired décor, welcoming and relaxed and run by two brothers; wood floors, rafters, comfortable plain furniture and hot little stove, plenty of quirky features including pitched ceiling decorated with

patchwork of wallpaper and prints, a gold room hidden behind a bookcase and loos with dinosaur and circus-tent themes; a couple of changing local ales, plenty of bottled beers, Healey's cider and 15 wines by the glass from carefully chosen list, also good range of spirits (some cornish ones), cheese and charcuterie boards, friendly service; live music and other events, board games; children and dogs (theirs is Pig) welcome, roof terrace, open all day weekends, from 5pm Mon, 2pm Tues-Fri; the Hand craft beer bar is below. *(IAA, HMW, Maria Sansoni)*

FALMOUTH SW8132
Front (01326) 212168
Custom House Quay; TR11 3JT Welcoming bare-boards drinkers' pub with good changing selection of well kept ales, some tapped from the cask, also foreign beers and ciders/perries, friendly knowledgeable staff, no food but can bring your own (fish and chip shop above), good mix of customers; seats outside, open all day. *(Max Simons)*

FALMOUTH SW8032
Seven Stars (01326) 312111
The Moor (centre); TR11 3QA Quirky 17th-c local, unchanging, unsmart and not to everyone's taste; friendly atmosphere with chatty regulars, up to six well kept ales tapped from the cask including Bass, Sharps and Skinners, quiet back snug; no food or mobile phones; dogs welcome, corridor hatch serving roadside courtyard, open all day. *(Chris Stevenson)*

FALMOUTH SW8032
Working Boat (01326) 314283
Greenbank Quay, off Stratton Place; TR11 2SP Part of the Greenbank Hotel by one of the upriver piers (town centre is a brisk ten minutes' walk); interior on varying levels with big windows overlooking the water, dark green walls and stripped plank wainscoting, some nautical touches and many interesting Falmouth pictures, black-tile or board floors, tables with lit candles in bottles, Skinners, St Austell and a couple of other real ales, decent wines by glass and good fairly priced food, friendly efficient service; background music, quiz nights; tables out overlooking the natural harbour, another good bar and restaurant in the hotel, open all day. *(Max Simons, Peter and Emma Kelly)*

FLUSHING SW8033
Royal Standard (01326) 374250
Off A393 at Penryn (or foot-ferry from Falmouth); St Peters Hill; TR11 5TP Compact pub set just back from the waterfront, bistro-bar feel with enjoyable fairly priced blackboard food including good spanish fish stew and Weds curry night, local ales and decent wines by the glass, friendly helpful staff; background and live music; children and dogs welcome, picnic-sets on

small front terrace, garden behind with harbour views, open all day. *(Laura Smyth)*

FLUSHING SW8033
Seven Stars (01326) 374373
Trefusis Road; TR11 5TY Old-style waterside pub with welcoming local atmosphere, good selection of well kept ales (third-pint tasters available), pubby food including Mon evening fish and chips, coal fire, separate dining room; darts and pool; children and dogs welcome, pavement picnic-sets, great views of Falmouth (foot-ferry across), open all day. *(Max Simons)*

FOWEY SX1251
Galleon (01726) 833014
Fore Street; from centre follow car-ferry signs; PL23 1AQ Superb spot by harbour and estuary, good beer range (local/national) and decent choice of wines, well liked food from extensive reasonably priced menu, friendly staff, slate-floor bar with modern décor, lots of solid pine and exposed stone, lofty river view dining area; live bands Fri night, jazz Sun lunchtime, projector TV, pool, free wi-fi; children welcome, disabled facilities, attractive waterside terrace and sheltered courtyard, seven bedrooms (two with estuary view), open all day. *(Ian Herdman)*

FOWEY SX1251
★ **King of Prussia** (01726) 833694
Town Quay; PL23 1AT Handsome quayside building with roomy upstairs bar, bay windows looking over harbour to Polruan, nice choice of enjoyable food from crab sandwiches and tapas boards up, St Austell ales and sensibly priced wines, friendly helpful staff, side restaurant; background music, pool, free wi-fi; children and dogs welcome, partly enclosed outside seating area, six pleasant bedrooms (all with views), open all day. *(Alan Johnson)*

FOWEY SX1251
Lugger (01726) 833435
Fore Street; PL23 1AH Centrally placed St Austell pub with up to three of their ales in top condition, spotless front bar with nautical memorabilia, small back dining area, good mix of locals and visitors (can get busy), generous helpings of enjoyable good value food including local fish, friendly helpful staff; children welcome, pavement tables, open all day. *(Alan and Linda Blackmore)*

FOWEY SX1251
★ **Ship** (01726) 832230
Trafalgar Square; PL23 1AZ Bustling old pub with open fire in bare-boards bar, maritime prints, nauticalia and other bits and pieces, St Austell ales and good wines by the glass, steps up to dining room with big stained-glass window, well liked interesting food along with pub favourites and sandwiches, friendly helpful service; background and live music; children and dogs welcome, bedrooms (some oak-panelled), open all day. *(Alan Johnson, Ian Herdman)*

GOLANT SX1254
Fishermans Arms (01726) 832453
Fore Street (B3269); PL23 1LN Partly flagstoned small waterside local with lovely views across River Fowey from front bar and terrace, good value generous pubby food and up to four well kept west country ales, friendly service, log fire, interesting old photographs; fortnightly quiz Tues; children and dogs welcome, pleasant garden, open all day in summer (all day Fri-Sun, closed Mon in winter). *(Max Simons)*

GORRAN CHURCHTOWN SW9942
Barley Sheaf (01726) 843330
Follow Gorran Haven signs from Mevagissey; PL26 6HN Built in 1837 by a local farmer and now owned and extensively refurbished by his great-(x3) grandson; enjoyable home-made food including popular Sun lunch, well kept Sharps Doom Bar and two cornish guests, local cider, friendly staff, upstairs overspill dining room; Tues quiz and some live music; children and dogs welcome, well tended sunny beer garden, open all day summer. *(Andrew Vincent)*

GRAMPOUND SW9348
Dolphin (01726) 882435
A390 St Austell–Truro; TR2 4RR Friendly St Austell pub with their well kept ales and decent choice of wines, good generous pub food (not Mon), two-level bar with black beams and some panelling, polished wood or carpeted floors, pubby furniture with a few high-backed settles, pictures of old Grampound, woodburner; Tues quiz, darts, pool, TV; children welcome, dogs in bar, wheelchair access from car park, beer garden, good smokery opposite, handy for Trewithen Gardens, open all day weekends, closed Mon lunchtime. *(Jill and Dick Archer)*

GWEEK SW7026
Black Swan (01326) 221502
Village signed from A394 at Edgcumbe; TR12 6TU Welcoming village pub with large open-plan bar, low beams and woodburner in big stone fireplace, well kept ales such as St Austell and Skinners, enjoyable reasonably priced food, roomy back restaurant; pool, TV; children (toys available) and dogs welcome, picnic-sets out at the side, short walk from seal sanctuary, four bedrooms, open all day. *(Max Simons)*

If we know a pub has an outdoor play area for children, we mention it.

GWITHIAN
SW5840
Red River (01736) 753223
Prosper Hill; TR27 5BW Stone-built
one-room village pub, several well
kept ales and eclectic range of popular
generously served food, welcoming
friendly staff; background and live music,
free wi-fi; children and dogs welcome,
picnic-sets in small garden across road,
near dunes, beach and coastal path,
open all day in summer, closed Mon
winter. *(Mr Yeldahn, Craig Burkinshaw)*

HELFORD
SW7526
Shipwrights Arms (01326) 231235
*Off B3293 SE of Helston, via Mawgan;
TR12 6JX* New tenants for this 17th-c
thatched pub by beautiful wooded creek (at
its best at high tide); nautical-themed bars
with old navigation lamps, ship models, boaty
wallpaper and appropriate artwork, even the
odd figurehead, painted high-backed dining
chairs, leather wall banquettes and scatter
cushions on window seats, woodburner,
St Austell Tribute and guests, several wines
by the glass and decent food; free wi-fi;
children and dogs welcome, seats on terraces
down to the water's edge making most of the
view, pontoon mooring and foot-ferry from
Helford Passage, good surrounding walks,
open (and food) all day. *(Colin McLachlan,
Helena and Trevor Fraser, Mrs L Gustine)*

HELFORD PASSAGE
SW7626
★Ferryboat (01326) 250625
Signed from B3291; TR11 5LB Busy
old pub in lovely position by sandy beach
(can book seats on terrace in advance);
bar with farmhouse and blue-painted
kitchen chairs, built-in cushioned wall
seats and stripped tables on grey slates,
woodburner, St Austell Proper Job, Tribute
and a guest, real cider and a dozen wines
by the glass, good food including local fish/
seafood, friendly service, arched doorway to
games room with pool and darts; some live
music, free wi-fi; children and dogs (in bar)
welcome, summer ferry from Helford village
across the water, can also hire small boats
and arrange fishing trips, walk down from
car park is quite steep, open (and food) all
day. *(Andrew Stone, Anne and Ben Smith)*

HELSTON
SW6527
★Blue Anchor (01326) 562821
Coinagehall Street; TR13 8EL Many (not
all) love this no-nonsense, highly individual,
15th-c thatched pub; quaint rooms off
corridor, flagstones, stripped stone, low
beams and well worn furniture, ancient
back brewhouse still producing distinctive
and very strong Spingo IPA, Middle and
seasonals such as Bragget with honey and
herbs, no food but can bring your own (good
pasty shop nearby), family room, traditional
games and skittle alley, friendly local
atmosphere; regular live music, Mon quiz;

back garden with own bar, four bedrooms
in house next door, generous breakfast,
open all day. *(Ray White, Peter Johnson)*

HESSENFORD
SX3057
Copley Arms (01503) 240209
A387 Looe–Torpoint; PL11 3HJ Friendly
17th-c village pub popular with passing
tourists; focus on enjoyable reasonably
priced food from sandwiches to grills in
linked carpeted areas, well kept St Austell
ales and nice choice of wines, variety of
teas and coffee, log fires, tables in cosy
booths, one part with sofas and easy chairs,
big family room; background and some live
music, Thurs quiz; dogs allowed in bar area,
a few roadside picnic-sets by small River
Seaton, fenced play area, five bedrooms,
open all day. *(Dennis and Doreen Haward)*

HOLYWELL
SW7658
St Pirans (01637) 830205
Holywell Road; TR8 5PP Great location
backing on to dunes and very popular
with holidaymakers; well kept ales such
as St Austell and Sharps, decent wines
and enjoyable food from sandwiches
and pub favourites up, cream teas,
friendly helpful staff; children and dogs
welcome, tables on large back terrace,
open all day, but closed out of season
and Mon in April. *(Jill and Dick Archer)*

HOLYWELL
SW7658
Treguth (01637) 830248
*Signed from Cubert, SW of Newquay;
TR8 5PP* Ancient whitewashed stone
and thatch pub near big beach, cosy
low-beamed carpeted bar with big stone
fireplace, larger dining room at back,
three real ales and popular food cooked
by landlord-chef, friendly service; regular
live music, Weds quiz, pool; children and
dogs welcome, handy for campsites and
popular with holidaymakers, open all day
weekends. *(Alan and Linda Blackmore)*

KINGSAND
SX4350
Devonport (01752) 822869
The Cleave; PL10 1NF Lovely bay views
from front bar of this popular pub, well
kept changing local ales and good food
including local fish/seafood, nice sandwiches
and afternoon teas too, friendly efficient
service even at busy times, light airy modern
décor, warming log fire; children and dogs
welcome, tables out by sea wall, closed Tues
during term time. *(Steve and Liz Tilley)*

LANIVET
SX0364
Lanivet Inn (01208) 831212
Truro Road; PL30 5ET Welcoming old
stone pub with long L-shaped bar, dining end
with woodburner and generous helpings of
popular good value food (best to book) from
sandwiches/wraps to daily specials, St Austell
ales and a guest, friendly efficient service;
background and live music, fortnightly quiz

Tues, pool, darts and TV; children and dogs (in bar) welcome, seats out at front and in fenced garden, handy for Saints Way trail, unusual pub sign recalling days when village supplied bamboo to London Zoo's pandas, open all day weekends. *(Chris Stevenson)*

LELANT   SW5436
Watermill (01736) 757912
Lelant Downs; A3074 S; TR27 6LQ
Mill-conversion family dining pub; working waterwheel behind with gearing in dark-beamed central bar opening into brighter airy front extension, upstairs evening (and Sun lunchtime) restaurant, Skinners Betty Stogs and a guest, enjoyable food served by friendly staff; live music Fri, quiz night Weds, free wi-fi; dogs welcome, good-sized pretty streamside garden, open all day. *(Alan Johnson)*

LIZARD   SW7012
Top House (01326) 290974
A3083; TR12 7NQ Neat clean pub with friendly staff and regulars, enjoyable local food from sandwiches and snacks up including fresh fish, children's meals and cream teas, well kept St Austell ales and guests, lots of good local sea pictures, fine shipwreck relics and serpentine craftwork (note the handpumps), warm log fire; folk music Mon; dogs welcome in bar, disabled access, sheltered terrace, eight bedrooms in adjoining building (three with sea views), good coastal walks, open all day in summer, all day weekends winter. *(Trish and Karl Soloman)*

LIZARD   SW7012
Witchball (01326) 290662
Lighthouse Road; TR12 7NJ Small friendly beamed pub popular with locals and visitors (booking recommended in summer), good food including fresh fish and seafood, Sun carvery, well kept ales such as Cornish Chough, St Austell and Skinners, cornish cider, cheerful helpful staff; Sat quiz; children and dogs welcome, front terrace, open all day summer, closed winter lunchtimes Mon-Wed. *(Clifford Blakemore)*

LOSTWITHIEL   SX1059
Earl of Chatham (01208) 872269
Grenville Road; PL22 0EP Traditional 16th-c split-level pub with beams, bare stone walls and open woodburner, generous helpings of enjoyable home-made food including popular Sun lunch (need to book), St Austell ales and nice choice of wines, friendly staff; children and dogs welcome, terrace picnic-sets, open all day. *(PL)*

LOSTWITHIEL   SX1059
Royal Oak (01208) 872552
Duke Street; PL22 0AG Welcoming old town pub doing well under present licensees; St Austell Tribute, Sharps Doom Bar and guests, traditional cider, several wines by the

glass and gin menu, good generously served pub food including Sun carvery, amiable helpful staff, bar, lounge and evening dining area, open fires; background and live music (Fri), free wi-fi; children welcome, dogs in bar (theirs is Radar), terrace picnic-sets under large willow, six comfortable clean bedrooms, open all day. *(Peter Foot)*

LUDGVAN   SW5033
White Hart (01736) 740175
Off A30 Penzance–Hayle at Crowlas; TR20 8EY Ancient stone-built village pub under new management, friendly and welcoming, with three west country beers tapped from the cask and enjoyable home-made food including blackboard specials, small unspoilt beamed rooms with wood and stone floors, nooks and crannies, woodburners; background music, quiz first Weds of month; children and dogs welcome, back garden with decked area, plans for glamping pods, interesting church next door, open all day, no food Sun evening in winter. *(Max Simons)*

MARAZION   SW5130
Godolphin Arms (01736) 888510
West End; TR17 0EN Revamped and extended former coaching inn with wonderful views across to St Michael's Mount; light contemporary décor and modern furnishings, well liked food from sandwiches and sharing plates up, St Austell and Skinners ales, lots of wines by the glass and good coffee, friendly staff; children welcome, beachside terrace and upper deck, ten stylish bedrooms (most with sea view, some with balconies), good breakfast, open all day from 8am. *(Phil and Jane Villiers)*

MARAZION   SW5130
Kings Arms (01736) 710291
The Square; TR17 0AP Old one-bar pub in small square, comfortable, cosy and welcoming with warm woodburner, good well presented food (best to book) including local fish from regularly changing menu, well kept St Austell ales, friendly helpful staff; children and dogs welcome, sunny picnic-sets out in front, open all day. *(Alan Johnson)*

MAWGAN   SW7025
Ship (01326) 221240
Churchfield, signed off Higher Lane; TR12 6AD Former 18th-c courthouse in nice setting near Helford river on the Lizard peninsula; high-ceiling bare-boards bar with woodburner in stone fireplace, end snug and raised eating area, emphasis on landlord's good food including local fish/seafood and seasonal game, takeaway fish and chips Tues, well kept ales and decent wine list, cheerful helpful young staff; well behaved children and dogs welcome, garden picnic-sets, closed lunchtimes and all day Sun, Mon. *(Alan and Linda Blackmore)*

MAWNAN SMITH SW7728
Red Lion (01326) 250026
W of Falmouth, off former B3291 Penryn–Gweek; The Square; TR11 5EP
Old thatched and beamed pub with cosy series of dimly lit rooms including raftered bar, enjoyable food from ciabattas and light lunches to daily specials, friendly helpful service, St Austell, John Smiths and Theakstons kept well, plenty of wines by the glass, woodburner in huge stone fireplace, country and marine pictures, stoneware bottles/flagons and some other bric-a-brac; background music, Tues quiz, daily papers; children (away from bar) and dogs welcome, disabled access, picnic-sets outside, handy for Glendurgan (NT) and Trebah Gardens, open all day. *(John and Mary Warner)*

MENHERION SX2862
Golden Lion (01209) 860332
Top of village by reservoir; TR16 6NW
Tucked-away little stone pub in nice spot by Stithians Reservoir; beamed bar and snug, woodburner, well kept St Austell ales and nice selection of wines by the glass, good generously served food from baguettes and pub favourites up, friendly staff, restaurant with lake view; folk night third Sat of month; children and dogs welcome, wheelchair access using ramps, disabled loo, attractive garden with heated shelter, good walks, camping, open (and food) all day weekends. *(Trevor Burgess)*

METHERELL SX4069
Carpenters Arms (01579) 351148
Follow Honicombe sign from St Anns Chapel just W of Gunnislake A390; Lower Metherell; PL17 8BJ Steps up to heavily black-beamed village local; huge polished flagstones and massive stone walls in cosy bar, carpeted lounge/dining area, three well kept ales such as St Austell, Sharps and Timothy Taylors Landlord, good reasonably priced food (not lunchtimes Mon-Thurs) cooked by landlord including themed nights, friendly staff and regulars; live music, free wi-fi; children and dogs welcome, front terrace, farmers' market and brunch first Sat of month, handy for Cotehele (NT), open all day Fri-Sun, from 2pm other days. *(Peter and Emma Kelly)*

METHERELL SX4069
Cross House (01579) 350482
Off A390 E of Callington; School Road – towards Metherell; PL17 8DN Substantial stone building (former farmhouse) with spreading carpeted bar, cushioned wall seats and stools around pub tables, some booth seating, hearty helpings of enjoyable reasonably priced home-made food, well kept Cotleigh, St Austell and guests, nice wines by the glass, good friendly service, open fire and woodburner, restaurant; monthly quiz, darts, free wi-fi; children and dogs (in bar)

welcome, disabled facilities, plenty of picnic-sets on good-sized lawn, play area, handy for Cotehele (NT), open all day. *(Max Simons)*

MEVAGISSEY SX0144
★ Fountain (01726) 842320
Cliff Street, down alley by Post Office; PL26 6QH Popular low-beamed fishermen's pub; slate floor, some stripped stone and a welcoming coal fire, old local pictures, piano, well kept St Austell ales and good reasonably priced food including local fish/seafood, friendly staff, back bar with glass-topped pit (the remains of an old fish-oil press), small upstairs evening restaurant; children and dogs welcome, pretty frontage with picnic-sets, three bedrooms, open all day in summer. *(Peter and Emma Kelly)*

MEVAGISSEY SX0144
Kings Arms (01726) 843904
Fore Street; PL26 6UW Small welcoming local tucked away behind the harbour; good varied choice of ales and other drinks from slabby-topped wooden counter, well liked freshly prepared food including home-smoked fish and own-baked bread; acoustic open mike night first Mon of month; opening times can vary. *(Claire Bethel)*

MEVAGISSEY SX0144
Ship (01726) 843324
Fore Street, near harbour; PL26 6UQ 16th-c pub with interesting alcove areas in big open-plan bar, low beams and flagstones, nautical décor, woodburner, fairly priced pubby food (small helpings available) including good fresh fish, well kept St Austell ales, cheery uniformed staff; background and some live music, Tues quiz, games machines, pool; children and dogs (in the bar) welcome, five bedrooms, open all day (food all day in summer). *(Chris Stevenson)*

MINIONS SX2671
Cheesewring (01579) 362321
Overlooking the Hurlers; PL14 5LE Homely village pub (claims to be the highest in Cornwall) useful for Bodmin Moor walks, good choice of reasonably priced home-made food, well kept ales including Sharps Doom Bar and St Austell, friendly staff, lots of brass and ornaments, woodburner; live music Sat; children and dogs welcome, bedrooms, open all day. *(Caroline Prescott)*

MITCHELL SW8554
★ Plume of Feathers
(01872) 510387/511125 *Off A30 Bodmin–Redruth, by A3076 junction; take southwards road then first right; TR8 5AX* 16th-c coaching inn with several linked bar and dining rooms, appealing contemporary décor with local artwork on pastel walls, stripped beams and standing timbers, painted dados and two open fires, generally well liked food from sandwiches and sharing plates up, Sharps, Skinners

and St Austell, several wines by the glass, impressive dining conservatory with centre olive tree; background music; children (away from bar) and dogs welcome, picnic-sets under parasols in well planted garden areas, comfortable stable-conversion bedrooms, open all day from 8am. *(R J Herd)*

MITHIAN   SW7450

★**Miners Arms** (01872) 552375
Off B3285 E of St Agnes; TR5 0QF Cosy old stone-built pub with traditional small rooms and passages, pubby furnishings and open fires, fine old wall painting of Elizabeth I in back bar, popular good value food, St Austell, Sharps and Skinners kept well, friendly helpful staff; background music, board games; children and dogs (in bar areas) welcome, seating in sheltered front cobbled forecourt, back terrace and garden, open all day. *(Chris Stevenson)*

NEWLYN   SW4629

★**Tolcarne** (01736) 363074
Tolcarne Place; TR18 5PR 17th-c quayside pub with very good food cooked by chef-landlord, much emphasis on local fish/seafood (menu changes daily) and booking advised, efficient service, St Austell Tribute, Skinners Betty Stogs and maybe a local microbrew; live jazz Sun lunchtime; children and dogs welcome, terrace (harbour wall cuts off view), good parking. *(Peter and Emma Kelly)*

NEWQUAY   SW8061

Fort (01637) 875700
Fore Street; TR7 1HA Massive pub in magnificent setting high above surfing beach and small harbour; decent food from sandwiches and baked potatoes up, full St Austell range, friendly staff coping well at busy times, open-plan areas divided by balustrades and surviving fragments of former harbourmaster's house, good solid furnishings from country kitchen to button-back settees, soft lighting, games part with two pool tables, excellent indoor children's play area; great views from long glass-walled side section and sizeable garden with multi-level terrace and further play areas, open (and food) all day. *(Alan Johnson)*

NEWQUAY   SW8061

Lewinnick Lodge (01637) 878117
Pentire headland, off Pentire Road; TR7 1QD Modern flint-walled bar-restaurant built into bluff above the sea – big picture windows for the terrific views; light airy bar with wicker seating, three or four well kept ales and several wines by the glass, spreading dining areas with contemporary furnishings on light oak flooring, popular bistro-style food from shortish menu, good service and pleasant relaxed atmosphere; children and dogs (in bar) welcome, modern seats and tables on terraces making most of the stunning

Atlantic views, ten bedrooms, open all day; same management as the Plume of Feathers in Mitchell. *(Mr and Mrs J Watkins)*

NORTH HILL   SX2776

Racehorse (01566) 786916
North Hill, off B3254 Launceston–Liskeard; PL15 7PG Comfortably reworked beamed dining inn (once the village school); bar, lounge and restaurant, good well presented food from short interesting menu, up to five well kept cornish ales and decent wines, friendly attentive service; free wi-fi; children welcome, country views from decking, three bedrooms, open all day. *(Hugo)*

PADSTOW   SW9175

★**Golden Lion** (01841) 532797
Lanadwell Street; PL28 8AN Old inn dating from the 14th c; cheerful black-beamed locals' bar and high-raftered back lounge with plush banquettes, Sharps Doom Bar, Skinners Betty Stogs and a guest, simple reasonably priced bar lunches including good crab sandwiches, evening steaks and fresh fish, friendly staff, coal fire and woodburner; pool in family area, background music, sports TV; dogs welcome, colourful floral displays at front, terrace tables, three good bedrooms, open all day (no food Sun evening). *(Alan and Alice Morgan)*

PADSTOW   SW9175

Harbour Inn (01841) 533148
Strand Street; PL28 8BU Attractive old-school pub just back from the harbour and a quieter alternative; long room with nautical bric-a-brac, front area with comfy sofas, woodburner, well kept St Austell ales and enjoyable generously served pub food including specials, good coffee, friendly helpful staff; children and dogs welcome, open all day.
(Max Simons, Alan and Alice Morgan)

PADSTOW   SW9175

London (01841) 532554
Lanadwell Street; PL28 8AN Intimate proper fishermen's local with lots of pictures and nautical memorabilia, mix of tables, chairs and built-in benches, friendly ex-merchant navy landlord, half a dozen well kept St Austell ales and decent choice of malt whiskies, good value bar food including fresh local fish, back dining area (arrive early for a table), two log fires; background and some live music; children and dogs welcome, four reasonably priced bedrooms named after boats, open all day. *(David Delaney)*

PADSTOW   SW9275

Old Custom House (01841) 532359
South Quay; PL28 8BL Large, bright and airy open-plan seaside bar, comfortable and well divided, with rustic décor and cosy corners, beams, exposed brickwork and bare boards, raised section, big family

area and conservatory, good food choice from baguettes up, four St Austell ales, efficient service (they swipe your card if running a tab), adjoining seafood restaurant; background and live music, TV; good spot by harbour with attractive sea-view bedrooms, open all day and can get very busy. *(Alan and Alice Morgan)*

PELYNT SX2054

★**Jubilee** (01503) 220312

B3359 NW of Looe; PL13 2JZ Popular early 17th-c beamed inn with wide range of good locally sourced home-made food (best to book in season), well kept St Austell ales and decent wines by the glass, friendly helpful young staff, spotless interior with interesting Queen Victoria mementoes (pub renamed in 1897 to celebrate her diamond jubilee), some handsome antique furnishings, log fire in big stone fireplace, separate bar with darts, pool and games machine; children and dogs welcome, disabled facilities, large terrace, 11 comfortable bedrooms, open all day (food all day weekends and all day in the summer). *(Andrew Vincent)*

PENDEEN SW3834

North (01736) 788417

B3306, opposite the school; TR19 7DN Friendly little creeper-clad village pub set back from the road, well kept St Austell ales and popular food including range of curries and good Sun roasts, single bar with interesting tin-mining memorabilia, upstairs restaurant looking over fields to the sea; children and dogs welcome, boules in big back garden, bedrooms and camping, good walks, open all day. *(Dr D J and Mrs S C Walker)*

PENDOGGETT SX0279

Cornish Arms (01208) 880335

B3314; PL30 3HH Old beamed coaching inn gently refurbished under friendly new owners; traditional oak settles on front bar's polished slate floor, well kept Sharps ales, a guest beer and several wines by the glass from good list, 27 gins, enjoyable food (all day weekends, not Mon lunchtime) including sandwiches and interesting burgers, friendly efficient service, comfortably spaced tables in dining room with wooden floor, proper back locals' bar with woodburner; children and dogs (in bars) welcome, disabled access, distant sea view from terrace, seven bedrooms, open all day. *(Andrew Vincent)*

PENELEWEY SW8140

Punch Bowl & Ladle

(01872) 862237 *B3289; TR3 6QY* Thatched dining pub with good home-made food from sandwiches up, helpful friendly

service, four St Austell ales, Healey's cider and good wine and whisky selection, black beams, some white-painted stone walls and oak panelling, rustic bric-a-brac and big sofas, steps down to lounge/dining area, restaurant; soft background music, free wi-fi; children (away from bar) and dogs welcome, wheelchair access (not from small side terrace), handy for Trelissick Garden (NT), open all day. *(Chris and Angela Buckell, Jean P & Myriam Alderson)*

PENZANCE SW4730

Admiral Benbow (01736) 363448

Chapel Street; TR18 4AF Wonderfully quirky pub, full of atmosphere and packed with interesting nautical paraphernalia; well kept cornish ales and enjoyable good value food including local fish, friendly helpful staff, cosy corners, log fire, downstairs restaurant in captain's cabin style, upper floor with pool table, pleasant view from back room; children and dogs welcome, open all day in summer; up for sale as we went to press, so may be changes. *(Andrew Vincent)*

PENZANCE SW4730

Crown (01736) 351070

Victoria Square, Bread Street; TR18 2EP Friendly little backstreet corner local with neat bar and snug dining room, own Cornish Crown beers, a guest ale and several wines by the glass, no food but can bring your own; Mon acoustic music night, board games; children and dogs welcome, seats outside, open all day. *(Chris Stevenson)*

PENZANCE SW4729

Dolphin (01736) 364106

Quay Street, opposite harbour after swing-bridge; TR18 4BD Old stone-built pub with enjoyable good value food including fresh fish, up to four well kept St Austell ales and good wines by the glass, roomy bar on different levels, nautical memorabilia and three resident ghosts; pool and darts; children and dogs welcome, pavement picnic-sets, three comfortable bedrooms with sea/harbour views, no car park (public one not far away), handy for Scillies ferry, open (and food) all day. *(Chris Stevenson)*

PERRANARWORTHAL SW7738

Norway (01872) 864241

A39 Truro–Penryn; TR3 7NU Large beamed pub with half a dozen linked areas, good choice of food including daily specials and carvery (Fri and Sat evenings, all day Sun, Tues lunchtime), St Austell ales and several wines by the glass, cream teas, good friendly service, open fires, panelling and mix of furniture on slate flagstones, restaurant; background music,

---

Virtually all pubs in this book sell wine by the glass. We mention wines if they are a cut above the average.

free wi-fi; children and dogs welcome, tables outside, four bedrooms, open (and food) all day. (Peter and Emma Kelly)

PERRANWELL STATION   SW7739
Royal Oak   (01872) 863175
Village signposted off A393 Redruth–Falmouth and A39 Falmouth–Truro; TR3 7PX Traditional old village pub, chatty and relaxed, with carpeted black-beamed bar, paintings by local artists, snug room behind with candlelit tables, big fireplace, St Austell Proper Job, Sharps Doom Bar, Skinners Lushingtons and a guest, proper cider and several wines by glass, hearty helpings of enjoyable home-cooked food including specials, good friendly service; free wi-fi; children and dogs (in bar) welcome, picnic-sets out at front, more seats in back garden, good surrounding walks, open all day weekends. (Chris and Angela Buckell)

PHILLEIGH   SW8739
★ Roseland   (01872) 580254
Between A3078 and B3289, NE of St Mawes just E of King Harry Ferry; TR2 5NB In small hamlet and handy for the King Harry Ferry and Trelissick Garden (NT); two cosy black-beamed bar rooms, one with flagstones, the other carpeted, wheelbacks and built-in red cushioned seats, old photographs, horsebrasses and some giant beetles and butterflies in glass cases, woodburner, tiny lower area liked by locals, side restaurant too, well kept Skinners Betty Stogs, Sharps Doom Bar and a guest, nice wines by the glass and enjoyable home-made food, friendly helpful service; folk night first Weds of month (not summer), free wi-fi; children and dogs (in bar) welcome, seats on pretty paved front terrace, may open all day weekends in high season. (R and S Bentley, Edward May, Phil and Jane Villiers, Mr and Mrs Richard Osborne)

POLPERRO   SX2051
Crumplehorn Mill   (01503) 272348
Top of village near main car park; PL13 2RJ Converted mill and farmhouse keeping beams, flagstones and some stripped stone, snug lower bar leading to long main room with cosy end eating area, well kept cornish ales, wide choice of popular food from snacks to blackboard specials (booking advised), friendly efficient service, log fire; children and dogs welcome, outside seating and working mill wheel, bedrooms and self-catering apartments, open all day. (Eddie Edwards)

POLPERRO   SX2050
Three Pilchards   (01503) 272233
Quay Road; PL13 2QZ Small low-beamed local behind fish quay, generous helpings of reasonably priced food from baguettes to good fresh fish, well kept St Austell Tribute, up to four guest beers and decent wines by the glass, efficient obliging service

even when busy, lots of black woodwork, dim lighting, simple furnishings, open fire in big stone fireplace; weekend live music; children and dogs welcome, picnic-sets on terrace up steep steps (lovely views), open all day. (Dennis and Doreen Haward)

POLRUAN   SX1250
★ Lugger   (01726) 870007
The Quay; back roads off A390 in Lostwithiel, or foot-ferry from Fowey; PL23 1PA Popular and friendly waterside pub; steps up to cosy beamed bar with open fire and woodburner, well kept St Austell ales, good freshly cooked food from bar snacks to daily specials including local fish/seafood, Sun carvery, restaurant on upper level; quiz and live music nights; children, dogs and boots welcome, not suitable for wheelchairs, good local walks, limited parking, open all day. (Jane and Kai Horsburgh)

PORT ISAAC   SW9980
★ Golden Lion   (01208) 880336
Fore Street; PL29 3RB Popular well positioned 18th-c pub retaining friendly local atmosphere in simply furnished old rooms; bar and snug with open fire, window seats and balcony tables looking down on rocky harbour and lifeboat slip far below, upstairs restaurant, enjoyable food including good local fish, well kept St Austell ales, amiable helpful staff; background music, darts; children and dogs welcome, dramatic cliff walks, open all day. (Andrew Vincent)

PORTHALLOW   SW7923
Five Pilchards   (01326) 280256
SE of Helston; B3293 to St Keverne, then village signed; TR12 6PP Sturdy old-fashioned stone-built local in secluded cove right by shingle beach; lots of salvaged nautical gear, interesting shipwreck memorabilia and model boats, woodburner, cornish ales and enjoyable reasonably priced food including local fish, friendly chatty staff, conservatory; children and dogs welcome, seats out in sheltered yard, sea-view bedrooms, closed in winter Mon lunchtime and all day Tues. (Peter and Emma Kelly)

PORTHLEVEN   SW6325
Atlantic   (01326) 562439
Peverell Terrace; TR13 9DZ Friendly buzzy pub in great setting above the harbour, good value tasty food including bargain OAP deal, ales such as Skinners and St Austell from boat-shaped counter, Weston's cider, big open-plan lounge with well spaced seating and cosier alcoves, good log fire in granite fireplace, dining room with trompe l'oeil murals; live music/entertainment Sat evening, Mon quiz, darts, free wi-fi; children and dogs welcome, lovely bay views from raised front terrace, open all day. (Adam Jones)

PORTHLEVEN   SW6225
Harbour Inn (01326) 573876
Commercial Road; TR13 9JB Large
neatly kept pub-hotel in outstanding
harbourside setting; expansive lounge and
bar with dining area off, big public bar,
well kept St Austell ales and good range
of pubby food, carvery Wed lunchtime
and Sun, well organised friendly service;
unobtrusive background music (live Sat),
Thurs quiz, free wi-fi; children and dogs
(in bar) welcome, picnic-sets on spacious
quayside terrace, 15 well equipped
bedrooms (some with harbour view), good
breakfast, open all day. *(Adam James)*

PORTLOE   SW9339
Ship (01872) 501356
At top of village; TR2 5RA Cheerful
traditional local in charming fishing village;
L-shaped bar with tankards hanging
from beams, nautical bric-a-brac, local
memorabilia and an amazing beer bottle
collection, straightforward dark pubby
chairs and tables on red carpet, open fire,
St Austell ales, cider/perry and six wines
by the glass, shortish choice of pubby food;
background music, sports TV, darts, free wi-fi;
children and dogs (in bar) welcome, sloping
streamside garden across road, comfortable
bedrooms, beach close by. *(Chris and Angela
Buckell, Keith Sturgess, Eddie Edwards)*

PORTSCATHO   SW8735
Plume of Feathers (01872) 580321
The Square; TR2 5HW Largely stripped-
stone coastal village pub with some
sea-related bric-a-brac and pictures in two
comfortable linked bars, also small side
bar and separate restaurant, St Austell ales
and enjoyable reasonably priced pubby
food, friendly staff; background music may
be intrusive, free wi-fi; children, dogs and
boots welcome, disabled access (steps to
restaurant and gents'), picnic-sets out under
awning, lovely coast walks, open all day in
summer (and other times if busy). *(Comus
and Sarah Elliott, Mr and Mrs J Watkins)*

ROSUDGEON   SW5529
Coach & Horses (01736) 763089
*Kenneggy Downs, A394 Penzance–
Helston; TR20 9AW* Low-ceilinged stone
pub under friendly new management,
comfortable contemporary refurbishment
with painted beams, light wood floors and
log fires in fine old fireplaces, some quirky
touches here and there, Keltek, Skinners
and a local guest, enjoyable home-made
food (not Sun evening); children (inside

play area for them) and dogs welcome,
open all day but may close Sun evening,
Mon out of season. *(Charlie May)*

ROSUDGEON   SW5529
Falmouth Packet (01736) 762240
A394; TR20 9QE Comfortably modernised
old pub with bare-stone walls, slate/
carpeted floors and open fire, good food
using local produce (booking advised),
own pickles, relishes etc for sale, well
kept Penzance ales and guests, family run
with good friendly service, conservatory;
children and dogs welcome, wheelchair
access, picnic-sets out at front and on
paved back terrace, self-catering cottage,
open all day (till 6.30pm Sun), closed
Mon in winter. *(Nick and Sylvia Pascoe)*

RUAN LANIHORNE   SW8942
★ Kings Head (01872) 501263
*Village signed off A3078 St Mawes Road;
TR2 5NX* Country pub in quiet hamlet
with interesting church nearby; relaxed
small bar with log fire, Skinners and a guest,
maybe farm cider, well liked food especially
local fish, dining area to the right divided in
two, lots of china cups hanging from ceiling
joists, cabinet filled with old bottles, hunting
prints and cartoons, separate restaurant to
the left; background music; well behaved
children allowed in dining areas, dogs
in bar only, terrace across road and nice
lower beer garden, walks along Fal estuary,
closed winter Sun evening and Mon; for
sale, so may be changes. *(Barry Collett)*

SENNEN COVE   SW3526
Old Success (01736) 871232
Cove Hill; Cove Road off A30; TR19 7DG
Glorious Whitesand Bay view from the
terraced garden or inside this seaside
hotel; beamed bar with lifeboat and other
nautical memorabilia, log fire, St Austell
ales from plank-fronted servery, enjoyable
food including fresh local fish and Sun
carvery, friendly helpful staff; background
and some live music; children and dogs
welcome, 12 comfortable bedrooms
(good breakfast), three self-catering
apartments, popular with surfers, open
all day. *(Roger and Donna Huggins)*

ST BREWARD   SX0977
Old Inn (01208) 850711
*Off B3266 S of Camelford; Churchtown;
PL30 4PP* Broad slate flagstones, low
oak beams, stripped stonework and two
massive granite fireplaces dating from the
11th c, Sharps Doom Bar and other well
kept ales, several wines by the glass and

A star symbol before the name of a pub shows exceptional character and appeal.
It doesn't mean extra comfort. Even quite a basic pub can win a star,
if it's individual enough.

enjoyable good value food including popular Sun carvery, roomy extended restaurant with tables out on deck; background music, darts, pool, free wi-fi; children and dogs welcome, moorland behind (cattle and sheep wander into the village), open all day in summer. (Alan McQuilan)

ST DOMINICK   SX4067
Who'd Have Thought It
(01579) 350214
Off A388 S of Callington; PL12 6TG Large comfortable country pub with popular reasonably priced home-made food (booking advised) including gluten-free and vegan choices, well kept St Austell ales, a guest beer and good value wine list, friendly competent service, superb Tamar views especially from conservatory, beams and open fire; live music and quiz nights; children and dogs (in bar) welcome, garden tables, handy for Cotehele (NT), open all day. (Ted George, John Evans)

ST EWE   SW9746
★ Crown (01726) 843322
Pub signed from Kestle and Polmassick; PL26 6EY Tucked-away 16th-c village pub with thoroughly traditional décor; low black-painted beams, big slate flagstones and carpet, two fireplaces decorated with shiny horse-brasses, china in glazed corner cupboards, wheelback chairs, pews and a splendid high-backed settle, four St Austell ales kept well and good value food from light lunchtime dishes up, also bargain OAP lunch Fri, friendly service, back overflow dining room up steps; children and dogs welcome, disabled access/facilities, very handy for Lost Gardens of Heligan. (IAA, HMW, Maria Sansoni)

ST ISSEY   SW9271
Ring o' Bells (01841) 540251
A389 Wadebridge–Padstow; Churchtown; PL27 7QA Traditional slate-clad 18th-c village pub with open fire at one end of beamed bar, pool the other, well kept Courage Best, Sharps Doom Bar and a guest, good choice of wines and whiskies, friendly service, enjoyable sensibly priced local food (own vegetables and pork) in long narrow side dining room; live music; children and dogs welcome, decked courtyard, pretty hanging baskets and tubs, three bedrooms, car park across road, open all day weekends and can get packed in summer. (Adam James)

ST IVES   SW5140
Lifeboat (01736) 794123
Wharf Road; TR26 1LF Thriving family-friendly quayside pub, decent choice of good value generously served food including fresh fish/seafood, well kept St Austell ales, spacious interior with harbour-view tables and cosier corners, nautical theme including lifeboat pictures, friendly helpful staff; background music, sports TV,

darts; no dogs, disabled access/facilities, open (and food) all day. (Barry Collett)

ST IVES   SW5441
Pedn Olva (01736) 796222
The Warren; TR26 2EA Hotel not pub, but has well kept reasonably priced St Austell ales in roomy bar, fine views of sea and Porthminster beach (especially from tables on roof terrace), all-day bar food and separate restaurant, good service; comfortable bedrooms. (Alan Johnson)

ST IVES   SW5140
★ Sloop (01736) 796584
The Wharf; TR26 1LP Popular low-beamed, panelled and flagstoned harbourside inn, bright St Ives School pictures and attractive portrait drawings in front bar, booth seating in back bar, good choice of food from sandwiches and baguettes to lots of fresh local fish, quick friendly service even though busy, well kept ales such as Greene King Old Speckled Hen and Sharps Doom Bar, good coffee, upstairs evening restaurant; background and live music, TV; children in eating area, beach view from roof terrace and seats out on cobbles, bedrooms, open all day (breakfast from 9am), handy for Tate gallery. (Alan Johnson, P and J Shapley)

ST IVES   SW5140
Union (01736) 796486
Fore Street; TR26 1AB Popular and friendly low-beamed local, roomy but cosy, with good value food from sandwiches to local fish, well kept Sharps Doom Bar and Weston's Old Rosie cider, decent wines and coffee, small hot fire, leather sofas on carpet, dark woodwork and masses of ship photographs; background music; dogs welcome. (Alan Johnson)

ST JUST IN PENWITH   SW3731
Kings Arms (01736) 788545
Market Square; TR19 7HF Friendly pub with three separate carpeted areas, granite walls, beamed and boarded ceilings, open fire, shortish menu of good home-made food (not Sun evening in winter), well kept St Austell ales and decent coffee; background music, Weds quiz, free wi-fi; children and dogs welcome, tables out in front, open all day. (Alan Johnson)

ST JUST IN PENWITH   SW3731
★ Star (01736) 788767
Fore Street; TR19 7LL Low-beamed two-room local with friendly landlord and relaxed informal atmosphere, five well kept St Austell ales, no food (bring your own lunchtime sandwiches or pasties), dimly lit main bar with old mining photographs on dark walls, ceiling covered in flags, coal fire; nostalgic juke box, live celtic music Mon, open mike Thurs, darts and euchre; tables in attractive backyard with smokers' shelter, open all day. (Alan Johnson)

ST KEW   SX0276

★**St Kew Inn** (01208) 841259
*Village signposted from A39 NE of
Wadebridge; PL30 3HB* Popular 15th-c
beamed pub next to village church;
unchanging slate-floored bar with fire in old
black range, two dining areas including neat
restaurant with stone walls, winged high-
backed settles and other traditional furniture
on tartan carpet, log fire in stone fireplace,
St Austell ales from cask and handpump,
gin menu, well liked food (not Sun evening
in winter) from lunchtime baguettes up,
friendly attentive service; live music every
other Fri; children away from bar and dogs
welcome, pretty flowering tubs and baskets
outside, picnic-sets in garden over road,
open all day in summer. *(Mrs Edna Jones)*

ST MAWES   SW8433

★**Rising Sun** (01326) 270233
The Square; TR2 5DJ Light and airy
pub across road from harbour wall; bar on
right with end woodburner and sea-view bow
window, rugs on stripped wood and a few
dining tables, sizeable carpeted left-hand
bar and conservatory, well prepared tasty
food from local fish to good steaks, cream
teas, well kept St Austell ales and nice
wines by the glass, friendly young staff,
buzzy atmosphere; background music, free
wi-fi; children and dogs welcome, awkward
wheelchair access, picnic-sets on sunny
front terrace, comfortable bedrooms,
open (and food) all day. *(Comus and
Sarah Elliott, Phil and Jane Villiers)*

ST MAWES   SW8533

St Mawes Hotel (01326) 270170
Marine Parade; TR2 5DN Refurbished
harbourside hotel's relaxed bar/restaurant,
woodburning stove, simple furnishings,
bare boards, enjoyable food from small
plates and pizzas up, a couple of real ales,
nice wines and good italian coffee, more
room upstairs with sofas, built-in wall
seats with big scatter cushions, quirky
décor and second woodburner, friendly
helpful young staff; children welcome, a
few tables out in front, good if not cheap
bedrooms (lovely sea views), open all day.
(Guy Vowles, Phil and Jane Villiers)

ST MAWES   SW8433

Victory (01326) 270324
Victory Hill; TR2 5DQ Popular pub tucked
up from the harbour; slate-floored locals' bar
on left, carpeted dining area to the right,
more formal upstairs restaurant with balcony,
well kept Otter, Sharps and Skinners, good
food including plenty of local fish, log fires,
friendly staff; background music; children

welcome, no wheelchair access, one or
two picnic-sets outside, two good value
bedrooms, open all day. *(Barry Collett)*

ST MAWGAN   SW8765

★**Falcon** (01637) 860225
*NE of Newquay, off B3276 or A3059;
TR8 4EP* A village inn since 1758; bar
with big fireplace, farmhouse chairs
and cushioned wheelbacks around an
assortment of tables on patterned carpet,
antique coaching prints and falcon pictures,
Dartmoor Legend, a couple of guests
and decent wines by the glass, enjoyable
reasonably priced food from sandwiches
up, friendly service, compact stone-floored
dining room; children (away from bar)
and dogs (in bar) welcome, picnic-sets
(some painted blue) in pretty garden with
wishing well, cobbled front courtyard,
comfortable bedrooms, open all day during
school holidays (all day weekends at other
times). *(Donald Allsopp, Ruth May, Anne Taylor)*

ST TUDY   SX0676

★**St Tudy Inn** (01208) 850656
Off A391 near Wadebridge; PL30 3NN
Landlady's good modern cooking is the
main draw here; bar with log fire in raised
hearth, cushioned window seats and mix
of tables and chairs on slate floors, Sharps
Doom Bar and a beer badged for the pub,
a couple of ciders and around 25 wines by
the glass, informal dining rooms with rugs
on bare boards, farmhouse and wheelback
chairs, fresh flowers, candlelight and another
log fire; background music, free wi-fi;
children and dogs (in bar) welcome, picnic-
sets under parasols at front, more seats
in garden, closed Sun evening, otherwise
open all day. *(R T and J C Moggridge, Caroline
Prescott, Lindy Andrews, Guy Henderson)*

TINTAGEL   SX0588

Olde Malthouse (01840) 770461
Fore Street; PL34 0DA Restored
14th-c beamed pub with inglenook bar
and restaurant, good generously served
home-made food (booking advised) from
ciabattas up, well kept local ales including
Tintagel, friendly helpful service; some
live music, free wi-fi; children and dogs
welcome, tables on roadside terrace,
bedrooms, good walks, open all day in
summer, closed Sun. *(Piotr Chodzko-Zajko)*

TOWAN CROSS   SW4078

Victory (01209) 890359
Off B3277; TR4 8BN Comfortable and
welcoming roadside local with four real
ales including Skinners and enjoyable
well priced food, good helpful service,
nice unfussy country décor and warm

All *Guide* inspections are anonymous. Anyone claiming to be a *Good Pub Guide*
inspector is a fraud. Please let us know.

relaxed atmosphere; pool and euchre; children and dogs welcome, beer garden, camping, handy for good uncrowded beaches, open all day. *(Caroline West)*

TREBARWITH   SX0586
Mill House (01840) 770200
Signed off B3263 and B3314 SE of Tintagel; PL34 0HD Former 18th-c corn mill wonderfully set in own steep woods above the sea; bar with white-painted beams, Delabole flagstones and mix of furniture including comfortable sofas, light and airy restaurant with pitched ceiling, enjoyable bar food and more upmarket evening menu, friendly staff, up to four local ales, decent wines by the glass and good coffee; background and live music, free wi-fi; children and dogs welcome, sunny terrace and streamside garden, eight bedrooms, open all day. *(Adam James)*

TREBARWITH   SX0585
Port William (01840) 770230
Trebarwith Strand; PL34 0HB Lovely seaside setting with glorious views and sunsets, waterside picnic-sets across road and on covered terrace, maritime memorabilia and log fires inside, enjoyable food from sandwiches and baked potatoes to daily specials (they may ask to swipe a card before you eat), St Austell ales; background music; children and dogs welcome, eight well equipped comfortable bedrooms, open all day. *(Adam James)*

TREEN   SW3923
★ Logan Rock (01736) 810495
Just off B3315 Penzance–Lands End; TR19 6LG Cosy traditional low-beamed bar with good log fire, well kept St Austell ales and tasty pub food from sandwiches and pasties to nice steaks, small back snug with collection of cricketing memorabilia (welcoming landlady eminent in county's cricket association), family room (no under-14s in bar); dogs welcome on leads, pretty split-level garden behind with covered area, good coast walks including to Logan Rock itself, handy for Minack Theatre, open all day in season and can get very busy. *(Ana Figueiredo)*

TREGADILLETT   SX2983
★ Eliot Arms (01566) 772051
Village signposted off A30 at junction with A395, W end of Launceston bypass; PL15 7EU Creeper-covered with series of small rooms, interesting collections including 72 antique clocks, 700 snuffs and hundreds of horsebrasses, also barometers, old prints and shelves of books/china, fine mix of furniture on Delabole slate from high-backed settles and chaises longues to more modern seats, open fires, well kept St Austell Tribute, Wadworths 6X and a guest, ample helpings of enjoyable pubby food, friendly staff and chatty locals; background

---

music, darts, games machine; children and dogs welcome, outside seating front and back, lovely hanging baskets and tubs, two bedrooms, open all day. *(Alan McQuilan)*

TREGONY   SW9244
Kings Arms (01872) 530202
Fore Street (B3287); TR2 5RW Light and airy 16th-c village coaching inn, long traditional main bar and two beamed and panelled front dining areas, St Austell ales, Healey's cider/perry and nice wines, enjoyable sensibly priced pub food using local produce, tea and coffee, prompt service and friendly chatty atmosphere, two fireplaces, one with huge cornish range, pubby furniture on carpet or flagstones, old team photographs, back games room; dogs very welcome and well behaved children, disabled access, tables in pleasant suntrap garden. *(A E Forbes)*

TREMATON   SX3960
Crooked Inn (01752) 848177
Off A38 just W of Saltash; PL12 4RZ Friendly family-run inn down long drive; open-plan bar with lower lounge leading to conservatory (lovely views), beams, straightforward furnishings and log fire, cornish ales and decent wines by the glass, good choice of popular freshly made food from sandwiches to daily specials, helpful service; children and dogs welcome, terrace overlooking garden and valley, play area, roaming ducks and other animals, 15 bedrooms, open all day. *(John Evans)*

TRURO   SW8244
★ Old Ale House (01872) 271122
Quay Street; TR1 2HD City-centre tap for Skinners brewery, five of their ales plus guests (some from casks behind bar), west country ciders and several wines by the glass including country ones, tasty food from snacks and sharing plates up, good cheerful service, dimly lit beamed bar with engaging mix of furnishings, sawdust on the floor, beer mats on walls and ceiling, some interesting 1920s bric-a-brac, life-size cutout of Betty Stogs, daily newspapers and free monkey nuts, upstairs room with table football; juke box, live music Mon and Sat evenings; children (away from bar) and dogs welcome, open all day. *(Alan Johnson)*

TRURO   SW8244
White Hart (01872) 277294
New Bridge Street (aka Crab & Ale House); TR1 2AA Compact old city-centre pub with nautical theme, friendly staff and locals, up to five well kept ales including Fullers London Pride, St Austell Tribute and Sharps Doom Bar, good reasonably priced traditional lunchtime food; background music, disco Fri and Sat, live music Sun afternoon, quiz Thurs; children and dogs welcome, open all day. *(Alan Johnson)*

TYWARDREATH SX0854
New Inn (01726) 813901
Off A3082; Fore Street; PL24 2QP
Welcoming 18th-c local in nice village
setting, St Austell ales and guests including
Bass tapped from the cask, good food (not
Tues) in back restaurant and conservatory,
friendly relaxed atmosphere; some live
music; children and dogs welcome,
large secluded garden behind with play
area, open all day. *(Charlie May)*

VERYAN SW9139
New Inn (01872) 501362
Village signed off A3078; TR2 5QA
Comfortable and homely one-bar beamed
local; good value food from sandwiches
up (can get busy in the evening so worth
booking), St Austell ales, Healey's cider and
decent wines by the glass, friendly attentive
service, inglenook woodburner, polished
brass and old pictures; background music,
quiz nights, darts, shove-ha'penny and ring
the bull; dogs and well behaved children
welcome, wheelchair access with help,
secluded beer garden behind, two bedrooms,
interesting partly thatched village not far
from nice beach, nearby parking unlikely
in summer. *(Peter J and Avril Hanson)*

WATERGATE BAY SW8464
Beach Hut (01637) 860877
B3276 coast road N of Newquay;
TR8 4AA Great views from bustling modern
beach bar with customers of all ages; planked
walls, cushioned wicker and cane armchairs
around scrubbed wooden tables, corner
snugs with banquettes and tile-topped
tables, weathered stripped-wood floor and
unusual sloping bleached-board ceiling, big
windows and doors opening to glass-fronted
deck with retractable roof looking across
sand to the sea, three real ales including
Skinners, decent wines by the glass and lots
of coffees and teas, enjoyable modern food
served by friendly young staff; background
music; dogs welcome in bar, easy wheelchair
access, open all day from 9am (10.30am-
5pm in winter). *(Peter and Emma Kelly)*

ZELAH SW8151
Hawkins Arms (01872) 540339
A30; TR4 9HU Homely 18th-c beamed
local, well kept St Austell, Skinners and
Otter, tasty well presented home-made
food from sandwiches to blackboard
specials, friendly staff, copper and brass
in bar and dining room, woodburner in
stone fireplace; occasional quiz nights;
children and dogs welcome, back and side
terraces, well equipped three-bedroom
static caravan for hire. *(Alfie Bayliss)*

ZENNOR SW4538
★Tinners Arms (01736) 796927
B3306 W of St Ives; TR26 3BY Friendly
welcome and good food from sandwiches
to fresh local fish, long unspoilt bar with
flagstones, granite, stripped pine and real
fires each end, back dining room, well
kept St Austell, Skinners and a house beer
(Zennor Mermaid) from Sharps, farm
cider, sensibly priced wines and decent
coffee, helpful staff coping well at busy
times, nice mix of locals and visitors;
Thurs folk night; children, muddy boots
and dogs welcome, tables in small suntrap
courtyard, lovely windswept setting near
coast path and church with 15th-c carved
mermaid bench, bedrooms in building
next door, open all day. *(Malcolm and
Pauline Pellatt, Phil and Jane Villiers)*

ISLES OF SCILLY

ST AGNES SV8808
★Turks Head (01720) 422434
The Quay; TR22 0PL One of the UK's
most beautifully placed pubs, idyllic sea
and island views from garden terrace, can
get packed on fine days; good food from
pasties to popular fresh seafood (best to
get there early), well kept ales such as
Skinners Betty Stogs, proper cider, friendly
licensees and good cheerful service;
children and dogs welcome, closed in winter,
otherwise open all day. *(Stephen Shepherd)*

ST MARTIN'S SV9116
Seven Stones (01720) 423777
Lower Town above Lawrence's Flats;
TR25 0QW Stunning location and sea and
islands views from this long single-storey
stone building (the island's only pub);
welcoming atmosphere and enjoyable food
from sandwiches to local fish, well kept
St Austell, Sharps and Skinners, five wines
by the glass; film and live music nights;
children and dogs allowed, lots of terrace
tables some on decking, lovely walks,
open all day in summer (Weds, Fri and
Sat evenings, all day Sun till early evening
in winter). *(Louise and Anton Parsons)*

ST MARY'S SV9010
Atlantic Inn (01720) 422323
*The Strand; next to but independent
from Atlantic Hotel; TR21 0HY* Spreading
and hospitable dark bar with well kept
St Austell ales, pubby food including
children's menu, sea-view restaurant, low
beams, hanging boat and other nauticalia,
mix of locals and tourists – busy evenings,
quieter on sunny lunchtimes; background
and live music, pool, darts, games machines,
free wi-fi; nice raised verandah with
wide views over harbour, good bedrooms
in adjacent hotel. *(Stephen Shepherd)*

ST MARY'S SV9010
Mermaid (01720) 422701
The Bank; TR21 0HY Splendid picture-
window views across town beach and
harbour from back restaurant extension,
unpretentious dimly lit bar with lots of

seafaring relics and ceiling flags, stone floor and rough timber, woodburner, steps down to second bar with tiled floor, boat counter and another woodburner, large helpings of enjoyable well priced food including children's choices, Sun carvery, well kept Ales of Scilly, Sharps and Skinners; background music, pool; dogs welcome in bar, open all day and packed Weds and Fri when the gigs race. *(Louise and Anton Parsons)*

ST MARY'S   SV9110
Old Town Inn (01720) 422301
Old Town; TR21 0NN Nice local feel in welcoming light bar and big back dining area, wood floors and panelling, good freshly made food (not Mon-Weds in winter) from daily changing menu, up to four well kept ales including Ales of Scilly and Sharps Doom Bar, great range of ciders; live music including monthly folk club, cinema in back function room, pool and darts; children and dogs welcome, wheelchair access, tables in garden behind, three courtyard bedrooms, handy for airport, open all day in season (from 5pm weekdays, all day weekends in winter). *(John and Mary Warner)*

TRESCO   SV8815
★New Inn (01720) 423006
New Grimsby; TR24 0QG Handy for ferries and close to the famous gardens; main bar with comfortable old sofas, banquettes, planked partition seating and farmhouse tables and chairs, a few standing timbers, boat pictures, collection of old telescopes and large model yacht, pavilion extension with cheerful yellow walls and plenty of seats on blue-painted floors, Ales of Scilly and Skinners, a dozen good wines by the glass, quite a choice of spirits and several coffees, enjoyable not especially cheap food including daily specials; background music, board games, darts and pool; children and dogs (in bar) welcome, seats on flower-filled sea-view terrace, 16 bedrooms and heated swimming pool, open all day in summer. *(Bernard Stradling, R J Herd)*

Ring the bull is an ancient pub game – you try to lob a ring on a piece of string over a hook (occasionally a bull's horn) on a wall or ceiling.

Cumbria

KEY	★ Star Pub	🔘 Top Quality Food	🍺 Great Beer
♀ Good Wines	£ Bargain Meals	🛏 Good Bedrooms	🍽 Serves Food

AMBLESIDE
NY3704 Map 9
Golden Rule 🍺

(015394) 32257 – www.goldenrule-ambleside.co.uk

Smithy Brow; follow Kirkstone Pass signpost from A591 on N side of town; LA22 9AS

Simple town tavern with a cosy, relaxed atmosphere and real ales

Unchanged over the years, this is an honest Lakeland local. The bar area
has built-in wall seats around cast-iron-framed tables (one with a local
map set into its top), horsebrasses on black beams, assorted pictures on the
walls, a welcoming winter fire and a relaxed atmosphere. Robinsons Cumbria
Way, Dizzy Blonde, Double Hop, Hartleys XB, Trooper and Wizard on
handpump and Weston's cider; they also offer various teas and good coffee
all day. A brass measuring rule hangs above the bar (hence the pub's name).
There's also a back room with TV (not much used), a room on the left with
darts and a games machine, and another room, down a couple of steps on the
right, with lots of seating. The backyard has benches and a covered heated
area, and the window boxes are especially colourful. There's no car park.

 The scotch eggs and pies (if they have them) run out fast, so don't assume you will
get something to eat.

Robinsons ~ Tenant John Lockley ~ Real ale ~ Open 11am-midnight ~ Children welcome
away from bar before 9pm ~ Dogs welcome ~ Wi-fi *Recommended by Carol and Barry
Craddock, Anne Taylor, Ruth May, Nick Sharpe, Mike Benton*

AMBLESIDE
NY3703 Map 9
Wateredge Inn ♀ 🛏

(015394) 32332 – www.wateredgehotel.co.uk

Borrans Road, off A591; LA22 0EP

**Family-run inn by lake with plenty of room both inside and out, six
ales on handpump and enjoyable all day-food; comfortable bedrooms**

The modernised bar here (originally two 17th-c cottages) has fine views
through big windows over the sizeable garden that runs down to Lake
Windermere. There's a wide mix of customers, a relaxed atmosphere, leather
tub chairs around wooden tables on flagstones and several different areas
leading off with similar furniture, exposed stone or wood-panelled walls and
interesting old photographs and paintings. A cosy and much favoured room
has beams and timbering, sofas, armchairs and an open fire. The real ales on
handpump served by friendly, cheerful staff include Jennings Cumberland
Ale and Sneck Lifter, Theakstons Best Bitter and Thwaites Nutty Black

and Wainwright, and they offer 17 wines by the glass and quite a choice of coffees. Background music and TV. In warm weather the picnic-sets close to the water get snapped up pretty quickly, and many of the stylish, comfortable bedrooms share these lake views; they have their own moorings.

¶¶ Food is good and served all day: sandwiches, chicken liver parfait, prawn cocktail, nachos with toppings (to share), vegetable curry, cumberland sausage with creamy mash and red wine, vegetable and onion gravy, beer-battered cod and chips, lamb hotpot, beef chilli with sour cream and rice, 16oz gammon steak with caramelised pineapple and a free-range egg, and puddings such as fruit crumble and a cheesecake of the day. *Benchmark main dish: flame-grilled burger with toppings, onion rings and fries £13.50. Two-course evening meal £20.00.*

Free house ~ Licensee Derek Cowap ~ Real ale ~ Open 11-11 ~ Bar food 12-9 ~ Children welcome ~ Dogs allowed in bar ~ Wi-fi ~ Live music Fri, Sat ~ Bedrooms: £60/£125
Recommended by Bernard Stradling, Denis and Margaret Kilner, Heather and Richard Jones, Max Simons

BASSENTHWAITE LAKE

NY1930 Map 9

Pheasant ★ 🎖 ♈ 🛏

(017687) 76234 ~ www.the-pheasant.co.uk
Follow Pheasant Inn sign at N end of dual carriageway stretch of A66 by Bassenthwaite Lake; CA13 9YE

Delightful, old-fashioned bar in smart hotel, with enjoyable bar food and a fine range of drinks; bedrooms

You'd never guess that a charming little bar of proper character (and used by chatty locals) was at the heart of this civilised and smart hotel. Nicely old-fashioned, it has mellow polished walls, cushioned oak settles, rush-seat chairs and library seats, and hunting prints and photographs. Coniston Bluebird Bitter, Cumbrian Legendary Loweswater Gold and Hawkshead Bitter on handpump, 16 good wines by the glass, 70 malt whiskies and ten gins and ten vodkas all served by friendly, knowledgeable staff. There's a front bistro, a formal back restaurant overlooking the garden and several comfortable lounges with log fires, beautiful flower arrangements, fine parquet flooring, antiques and plants. The garden has seats and tables and is surrounded by attractive woodland. Bedrooms are well equipped, comfortable and pretty, and two of them are pet friendly. There are plenty of walks in all directions.

🎖 Very good food can be eaten in the bar, bistro or lounges at lunchtime, and in the bistro and restaurant only in the evening: sandwiches (until 4.30pm), seafood plate with lemon aioli, ham hock tattie hash cake with poached egg and mushroom ketchup, chilli king prawns on spaghetti, gnocchi with sunblush tomatoes, spinach and crumbled feta, chicken curry with sticky rice, confit gressingham duck leg with colcannon potatoes and thyme and port jus, and puddings such as rhubarb crème brûlée with berry compote and baked chocolate and orange cheesecake; they also offer afternoon tea (3-5pm) and a two- and three-course set menu (12-2.30, 6-7pm). *Benchmark main dish: braised lamb shoulder with red wine jus £16.50. Two-course evening meal £23.00.*

Free house ~ Licensee Matthew Wylie ~ Real ale ~ Open 12-11 ~ Bar food 12-2.30, 6-9.30 ~ Restaurant ~ Children welcome but must be over 12 in bedrooms ~ Dogs allowed in bar and bedrooms ~ Wi-fi ~ Bedrooms: £105/£120 *Recommended by Pat and Stewart Gordon, Martin Day, Gordon and Margaret Ormondroyd, Edward Mirzoeff, Ian Herdman, Patricia and Gordon Thompson*

You can send reports directly to us at feedback@goodguides.com

BOWLAND BRIDGE
SD4189 Map 9

Hare & Hounds 🏵 � ☞

(015395) 68333 – www.hareandhoundsbowlandbridge.co.uk

Signed from A5074; LA11 6NN

17th-c inn in quiet spot with a friendly, cheerful landlady, real ales, popular food and fine views; good bedrooms

The comfortable bedrooms here make a good base for exploring the area – Lake Windermere is just three miles away and the valley views are lovely. The little bar has a log fire, daily papers to read and high chairs by the wooden counter where they serve Hare of the Dog (named for the pub by Tirril) and guests from breweries such as Coniston, Kirkby Lonsdale, Thwaites and Ulverston on handpump, a farm cider from half a mile away and a dozen wines by the glass. Leading off, other rooms are appealingly furnished with a mix of interesting dining chairs around all sorts of tables on black slate or old pine-boarded floors, numerous hunting prints on painted or stripped-stone walls, a candlelit moroccan-style lantern in a fireplace with neatly stacked logs to one side, and a relaxed atmosphere; background music and board games. The collie is called Murphy. If you'd like to sit outside, there are teak tables and chairs under parasols on the front terrace, with more seats in the spacious side garden.

Tempting food includes sandwiches (until 6pm), local game terrine with damson jam, hot smoked salmon and pink grapefruit tian, smoked chicken caesar salad, chickpea dhal with curried cauliflower purée, pea and mint beignet yoghurt dressing, beer-battered haddock and chips, beef in ale pie, slow-braised pork belly and pork fillet with fondant potato, apple purée, smoked pancetta and cider jus, stone bass, cod cheek and salmon with saffron potatoes and shellfish nage, and puddings such as blueberry and white chocolate cheesecake with berry compote and lemon and lime posset with chantilly cream and brown sugar meringue. *Benchmark main dish: duo of salt marsh lamb £19.00. Two-course evening meal £22.00.*

Free house ~ Licensee Kerry Parsons ~ Real ale ~ Open 12-11 (10.30 Sun) ~ Bar food 12-2, 6-9; all day weekends ~ Children welcome ~ Dogs allowed in bar and bedrooms ~ Wi-fi ~ Bedrooms: £95/£135 *Recommended by Lee and Liz Potter, Gerry and Pam Pollard, Robin and Anne Triggs, Gail and Frank Hackett*

BOWNESS-ON-WINDERMERE
SD4096 Map 9

Hole in t' Wall

(015394) 43488 – www.newhallinn.robinsonsbrewery.com

Fallbarrow Road, off St Martins Parade; LA23 3DH

Lively and unchanging town local with popular ales and friendly staff

Locals and visitors mingle happily here in the town's oldest pub (aka the New Hall Inn) and all are welcomed by the convivial licensees. There's a lot to look at in the character bar and the split-level rooms have beams, stripped stone and flagstones, lots of country knick-knacks and old pictures, and a splendid log fire beneath a vast slate mantelpiece; the upper room has some noteworthy plasterwork. Robinsons Dizzy Blonde, Hartleys XB and Unicorn plus a couple of guest beers on handpump, 23 malt whiskies, a dozen gins and 11 vodkas; juke box in the bottom bar. The small flagstoned front courtyard has sheltered picnic-sets and outdoor heaters.

Bar food includes pâté of the day, scampi and chips, a daily curry, fish pie, and puddings such as chocolate sponge and sticky toffee pudding. *Benchmark main dish: beef in ale pie £11.25. Two-course evening meal £19.00.*

Robinsons ~ Tenant Susan Burnet ~ Real ale ~ Open 11-11; 11am-11.30pm Fri, Sat; 12-11 Sun ~ Bar food 12-2.30, 6-8.30; 12-8 Fri, Sat; 12-5 Sun ~ Children welcome ~ Live music Fri and every other Sun Easter-Christmas *Recommended by Alf Wright, Sally Wright, Emma Scofield, Sandra Morgan*

BRIGSTEER
SD4889 Map 9

Wheatsheaf ♈

(015395) 68938 – www.thewheatsheafbrigsteer.co.uk

Off Brigsteer Brow; LA8 8AN

Bustling pub with interestingly furnished and decorated rooms, a good choice of food and drink, and seats outside; luxury bunkhouse bedrooms

Once again, we've had consistently warm praise for this friendly, well run pub. The various rooms have plenty of easy-going character throughout. The bar has a two-way log fire, carved wooden stools against the counter and Bowness Bay Swan Blonde, Hawkshead Bitter, Thwaites Wainwright and a changing guest beer on handpump, 16 wines by the glass and eight malt whiskies. There's an appealing variety of cushioned dining chairs, carved and boxed settles and window seats set around an array of tables on either flagstones or floorboards, walls with pale-painted woodwork or wallpaper hung with animal and bird sketches, cartoons or interesting clock faces, and lighting that is both old-fashioned and contemporary. Outside there are seats and tables along the front of the building and picnic-sets on raised terracing. Their luxury bunkhouse (half a mile up the road) has five ensuite rooms and fine country views; breakfasts are hearty.

Good, popular food includes sandwiches, local crab with baby gem, apple, crab ketchup, coriander, fennel seed crispbreads and chilli caramel, confit chicken with sage and onion terrine, truffle-marinated enoki mushrooms, celeriac remoulade and red wine reduction, sharing boards, pizzas and flatbreads with toppings, a pie of the day, red lentil, carrot and chickpea bake with cheese topping, beer-battered fresh haddock and chips, lamb shank with redcurrant and rosemary sauce, and puddings such as kendal mint cake liqueur chocolate mousse with mint chocolate chip ice-cream and lemon and basil posset with raspberry coulis. *Benchmark main dish: 12-hour brisket of beef £14.50. Two-course evening meal £20.00.*

Individual Inns ~ Managers Nicki Higgs and Tom Roberts ~ Real ale ~ Open 10am-11pm ~ Bar food 12-3, 5.30-9; snacks 3-5.30; 12-7.30 Sun ~ Restaurant ~ Children welcome ~ Dogs allowed in bar ~ Wi-fi ~ Bedrooms: /£70 *Recommended by Peter Andrews, Michael Doswell, David and Charlotte Green, Matt and Hayley Jacob, David Appleyard*

BROUGHTON MILLS
SD2190 Map 9

Blacksmiths Arms ⭐🍴

(01229) 716824 – www.theblacksmithsarms.com

Off A593 N of Broughton-in-Furness; LA20 6AX

Friendly little pub with rewarding food, local beers and open fires; fine nearby walks

Lovely countryside with peaceful walks and a delightful pub to head for makes a special day out for many of our readers. The four small rooms have a relaxed, friendly atmosphere and are simply but attractively decorated; three have original beams, slate floors and warm log fires. Three real ales such as Barngates Cracker, Chadwicks Kirkland Blonde and Cross Bay Nightfall Pale Bitter on handpump, nine wines by the glass and summer farm cider; darts, board games and dominoes. The hanging baskets and tubs of flowers in front of the building are very pretty in summer, and there are seats and tables under parasols on the front terrace.

 Very good food includes lunchtime sandwiches, potted smoked salmon with toasted sourdough, confit shredded duck leg with hoisin sauce, honey-roast ham with poached eggs, pea and parmesan risotto, cumberland sausage with spring onion mash, black pudding and red onion and balsamic gravy, salmon fillet on dill-crushed new potatoes with watercress mayonnaise and lemon syrup, slow-roasted pork belly with white bean mash, roasted root vegetables and mulled cider reduction, and puddings such as poached pear with chilli-spiced syrup and vanilla ice-cream and a cheesecake of the day; they also offer a two-course set lunch. *Benchmark main dish: slow-cooked lamb shoulder with dauphinoise potatoes £14.35. Two-course evening meal £19.50.*

Free house ~ Licensees Mike and Sophie Lane ~ Real ale ~ Open 12-11 (10.30 Sun); 12-2.30, 5-11 weekdays in winter; closed Mon lunchtime ~ Bar food 12-2, 6-9; not Mon ~ Restaurant ~ Children welcome ~ Dogs welcome *Recommended by Peter Meister, Lindy Andrews, Lee and Liz Potter, Tina and David Woods-Taylor, Elise and Charles Mackinlay, Nicola and Nigel Matthews*

CARLETON　　　　　　　　　　　　　　　NY5329　Map 9

Cross Keys ◖

(01768) 865588 – www.thecrosskeyspenrith.co.uk
A686, off A66 roundabout at Penrith; CA11 8TP

Friendly refurbished pub with several connected seating areas, real ales and popular food

The scenery and wildlife in this area are very special, so at lunchtime in particular there'll be plenty of outdoors lovers here. The beamed main bar has a friendly feel, pubby tables and chairs on light wooden floorboards, modern metal wall lights and pictures on bare stone walls, and Tirril 1823 and a guest such as Wells Bombardier on handpump. Steps lead down to a small area with high bar stools around a high drinking table and then upstairs to the restaurant: a light, airy room with big windows, large wrought-iron candelabras hanging from the vaulted ceiling, solid pale wooden tables and chairs, and doors leading to a verandah. At the far end of the main bar are yet another couple of small connected bar rooms with darts, games machine, pool, juke box and dominoes; TV and background music. There are views of the fells from the garden. This is under the same ownership as the Highland Drove in Great Salkeld.

Hearty pubby dishes plus interesting daily specials include prawn cocktail, chicken liver pâté, sharing platters, local cumberland sausage with mash and gravy, beer-battered fish and chips, lamb, pepper and mushroom kebab with greek salad, straw fries and garlic yoghurt dip, stilton, broccoli and cranberry en croûte with provençale sauce, chicken with bacon and cheddar croquette and rosemary sauce, and puddings such as chocolate brownie with chocolate sauce and crème brûlée. *Benchmark main dish: steak in ale pie £12.00. Two-course evening meal £18.00.*

Free house ~ Licensee Paul Newton ~ Real ale ~ Open 12-2.30, 5-1am; 12-2am Sat; 12-1am Sun ~ Bar food 12-2.30, 6-9 (8.30 Sun); 12-2.30, 5.30-9 Fri, Sat ~ Restaurant ~ Children welcome ~ Dogs allowed in bar ~ Wi fi *Recommended by Tracey and Stephen Groves, Peter Andrews, John Watson, Sarah Roberts, Frances Parsons*

CARTMEL FELL   SD4189 Map 9

Masons Arms 🌟 ⚏ ⬤

(015395) 68486 – www.masonsarmsstrawberrybank.co.uk

Strawberry Bank, a few miles S of Windermere between A592 and A5074; perhaps the simplest way to find the pub is to go uphill W from Bowland Bridge (which is signposted off A5074) towards Newby Bridge and keep right, then left at the staggered crossroads – it's then on your right, below Gummer's How; OS Sheet 97 map reference 413895; LA11 6NW

Wonderful views, beamed bar with plenty of character, interesting food and a good choice of ales and wines; self-catering cottages and apartments

The views over the Winster Valley to the woods below Whitbarrow Scar here are stunning and can be enjoyed from the rustic benches and tables on the heated covered terrace and from windows inside. The main bar has plenty of character, with low black beams in the bowed ceiling, and country chairs and plain wooden tables on polished flagstones. A small lounge has oak tables and settles to match its fine Jacobean panelling. There's also a plain little room beyond the serving counter with pictures and a fire in an open range, a family room with the atmosphere of an old parlour, and an upstairs dining room; background music and board games. Dent Aviator, Hawkshead Bitter and Thwaites Wainwright on handpump, quite a few foreign bottled beers, 12 wines by the glass, ten malt whiskies and farm cider; service is friendly and helpful. The self-catering cottages and apartments are stylish and comfortable and share the same fine outlook.

 Highly enjoyable food from a wide-ranging menu includes lunchtime hot and cold sandwiches (until 6pm weekends), baked camembert with pecan and maple syrup glaze, pork platter for sharing, green lentil chilli, a pie of the day, shredded duck burger with plum sauce, spring onion and cucumber, venison steak with honey and beetroot granola, dauphinoise potatoes and red wine jus, chicken topped with portobello mushrooms and cheddar with mango and brandy sauce, fishcakes with creamy dill sauce, and puddings such as damson gin crème brûlée and rice pudding with honey-roasted pear compote. *Benchmark main dish: spare ribs in sticky sauce with fries £13.95. Two-course evening meal £20.00.*

Individual Inns ~ Managers John and Diane Taylor ~ Real ale ~ Open 11.30-11; 12-10.30 Sun ~ Bar food 12-2.30, 6-9; 12-9 weekends ~ Restaurant ~ Children welcome ~ Dogs allowed in bedrooms ~ Wi-fi *Recommended by Christian Mole, Edward and William Johnston, Sandra King, Hugh Roberts, Charles and Maddie Bishop, Liz and Martin Eldon, Mr and Mrs Richard Osborne*

CLIFTON   NY5326 Map 9

George & Dragon 🌟 ⚏ 🛏

(01768) 865381 – www.georgeanddragonclifton.co.uk

A6; near M6 junction 40; CA10 2ER

Former coaching inn with attractive bars and sizeable restaurant, local ales, well chosen wines, well thought-of food and seats outside; smart bedrooms

Quite a few of our readers use the stylish, comfortable bedrooms here on a regular basis on journeys up to Scotland – the breakfasts are also very good. The relaxed reception room has bright rugs on flagstones, leather chairs around a low table in front of an open fire, and a table in a private nook to one side of the reception desk. Through wrought-iron gates is the main bar area with more cheerful rugs, assorted wooden farmhouse chairs and tables, grey panelling topped with yellow-painted walls, photographs of the Lowther Estate and of the family with hunting dogs, various sheep and fell pictures and some high bar stools by the bar counter. Eden Gold, Hawkshead Bitter and a changing guest beer on handpump, 20 wines by the glass from a well chosen list and interesting local liqueurs; background music and TV. The sizeable restaurant to the left of the entrance consists of four open-plan rooms: plenty of old pews and church chairs around tables set for dining, a woodburning stove and a contemporary open kitchen. Outside, tables and chairs are set in a decoratively paved front area and in a high-walled enclosed courtyard.

Using Lowther Estate produce, the interesting food includes lunchtime sandwiches, pressed ham terrine with pineapple, black pudding and crispy egg, torched mackerel with asparagus, cured egg yolk and charcoal mayonnaise, potato dumplings with glazed vegetables and sheeps curd, beef and bone marrow burger with toppings, mushroom and bacon jam and dripping chips, pollock with morels, asparagus, wild garlic hash and beurre blanc, glazed pig cheeks with local fennel salami and broad bean cassoulet, guinea fowl with sorrel pudding, black garlic and young vegetables, and puddings such as bitter chocolate tart with cocoa nib tuile, passion-fruit and vanilla and thyme brûleé with rhubarb and burnt white chocolate. *Benchmark main dish: chateaubriand with roast dripping potatoes and bordelaise sauce to share £55.00. Two-course evening meal £23.00.*

Free house ~ Licensee Charles Lowther ~ Real ale ~ Open 12-11 ~ Bar food 12-2.30, 6-9 ~ Restaurant ~ Children welcome ~ Dogs allowed in bar and bedrooms ~ Wi-fi ~ Bedrooms: £85/$100 *Recommended by Douglas Power, Geoffrey Sutton, Comus and Sarah Elliott, Rupert and Sandy Newton, Glen and Patricia Fuller*

CONISTON
Sun 🍺 ⌂

SD3098   Map 9

(015394) 41248 – www.thesunconiston.com
Signed left off A593 at the bridge; LA21 8HQ

Extended old pub in a fine spot with a lively bar, plenty of dining space, a fine choice of real ales, well liked food and seats outside; comfortable bedrooms

The cheerful bar with its range of up to eight real ales is a popular draw to this splendidly set 16th-c inn. On handpump these might include Barngates Cracker, Red Bull Terrier or Tag Lag, Coniston Bluebird Bitter and Cumbrian Legendary Loweswater Gold and frequent guests from other local brewers including Fell, Hardknott, Hawkshead and Ulverston; the friendly staff also keep ten wines by the glass, 20 malt whiskies, several gins and farm cider. There are beams and timbers, exposed stone walls, flagstones and a Victorian-style range – as well as cask seats, old settles and cast-iron-framed tables, quite a few Donald Campbell photographs (this was his HQ during his final attempt on the world water-speed record) and a good mix of customers (often with their dogs). Above the bar is another room with extra seating, more pictures, pool, darts and a TV for sport, and beyond that is a sizeable lounge. A big dining conservatory houses a new daytime café. Bedrooms are quiet and comfortable and their dramatic mountain views are shared by the seats and tables on the terrace and in the big tree-sheltered garden.

Tasty food includes lunchtime sandwiches, ham hock terrine with piccalilli, thai fishcakes with hot smoked salmon, prawns and dill mayonnaise, roast cauliflower risotto with goats cheese and curried onions, burger with toppings and chips, gammon steak and egg with pineapple ketchup, lamb rump with fondant potato, artichoke and gravy, 28-day-aged sirloin steak with onion rings and peppercorn sauce, and puddings such as apple and pear crumble with custard and chocolate brownie with raspberry ripple ice-cream. *Benchmark main dish: braised lamb casserole £13.50. Two-course evening meal £21.00.*

Free house ~ Licensee Alan Piper ~ Real ale ~ Open 11-11 ~ Bar food 12-3, 5.30-8.30 ~ Restaurant ~ Children welcome ~ Dogs allowed in bar and bedrooms ~ Wi-fi ~ Bedrooms: £65/£95 *Recommended by Paul Scofield, Maria and Henry Lazenby, Scott and Charlotte Havers, Andrew Vincent*

CROSTHWAITE
SD4491 Map 9

Punch Bowl

(015395) 68237 – www.the-punchbowl.co.uk

Village signed off A5074 SE of Windermere; LA8 8HR

Cumbria Dining Pub of the Year

Civilised dining pub with a proper bar and other elegant rooms, a fine wine list, impressive food and friendly staff; stylish bedrooms

Of course, many customers are here for the first class food or to stay in the lovely, well equipped bedrooms – but there is a proper public bar too, and plenty of chatty locals. This bar has rafters, a couple of eye-catching rugs on flagstones, bar stools by the slate-topped counter, Barngates Tag Lag and Bowness Bay Swan Blonde on handpump, 16 wines and two sparkling wines by the glass, 15 malt whiskies and local damson gin. To the right are two linked carpeted and beamed rooms with well spaced country pine furniture of varying sizes (including a big refectory table), and walls that are painted in restrained neutral tones with an attractive assortment of prints; winter log fire, woodburning stove, lots of fresh flowers and daily papers. On the left, the wooden-floored, light and airy restaurant area has comfortable high-backed leather dining chairs; background music. Tables and seats on a terrace are stepped into the hillside and overlook the pretty Lyth Valley.

Food is pretty special and includes lunchtime sandwiches, hand-dived scallops with carrot and chicken wings, black pudding with bubble and squeak and a crispy egg, turkey schnitzel with potato salad, smoked beetroot risotto with blue cheese and hazelnuts, guinea fowl breast with truffle, celeriac, potato layer and capers, local venison loin with smoked beetroot, chocolate, stuffed cabbage and fondant potato, and puddings such as lemon tart with damson sorbet and banana soufflé with toffee and lime sauce. *Benchmark main dish: cod loin with mussels, morteau sausage and boulangère potatoes £17.50. Two-course evening meal £25.00.*

Free house ~ Licensee Richard Rose ~ Real ale ~ Open 11-11 ~ Bar food 12-8.45 ~ Restaurant ~ Children welcome ~ Dogs allowed in bar ~ Wi-fi ~ Bedrooms: £95/£135 *Recommended by Lionel Smith, Daniel King, Anne Taylor, B R Merritt, Colin McLachlan, Hugh Roberts, Mr and Mrs Richard Osborne*

ELTERWATER
NY3204 Map 9

Britannia

(015394) 37210 – www.thebritanniainn.com

Off B5343; LA22 9HP

Much loved inn surrounded by wonderful walks and scenery, with up to seven real ales and well liked food; bedrooms

Being at the heart of the Lake District surrounded by spectacular scenery and with walks of every gradient right from the front door, this warmly friendly and unpretentious little pub is much loved by our readers. The small front bar has beams and a couple of window seats that look across to Elterwater through the trees, while the small back bar is traditionally furnished: thick slate walls, winter coal fires, oak benches, settles, windsor chairs and a big old rocking chair. A couple of beers are named for the pub – Britannia Special (from Coniston) and Britannia Gold (from Eden) – plus Coniston Bluebird Bitter, Cumberland Corby Ale and guests such as Dent Golden Fleece and Jennings Neddy Boggle and Sneck Lifter on handpump, and 12 malt whiskies. The lounge is comfortable, and there's also a hall and dining room. Plenty of seats outside, and visiting dancers (morris and step and garland) in summer. Bedrooms are warm and charming.

Some sort of enjoyable food is usefully served all day: sandwiches and rolls, grilled haggis with home-made plum jam, mackerel, salmon and trout fishcakes with garlic mayonnaise, cumberland sausage and mash with onion gravy, wild and button mushroom stroganoff, beer-battered fresh haddock and chips, steak and mushroom in ale pie, burger with toppings, red onion marmalade and chips, and puddings such as dark chocolate and mixed berry tart and a brûlée of the day. *Benchmark main dish: braised lamb shoulder in mint and spices with red wine gravy £15.95. Two-course evening meal £20.50.*

Free house ~ Licensee Andrew Parker ~ Real ale ~ Open 10.30am-11pm ~ Bar food 12-5, 6-9 ~ Restaurant ~ Children welcome ~ Dogs allowed in bar and bedrooms ~ Wi-fi ~ Bedrooms: £95/£105 *Recommended by Bernard Stradling, Tina and David Woods-Taylor, Peter Meister, Mr and Mrs Richard Osborne, Alan and Linda Blackmore, Heather and Richard Jones*

GREAT SALKELD
Highland Drove

NY5536 Map 10

(01768) 898349 – www.highlanddroveinnpenrith.co.uk
B6412, off A686 NE of Penrith; CA11 9NA

Bustling place with cheerful customers, good food and fair choice of drinks, and fine views from the upstairs verandah; bedrooms

Particularly well run by a friendly father and son team and with continuing warm praise from our readers, this remains an enjoyable all-rounder. The spotlessly kept, chatty main bar has sandstone flooring, stone walls, cushioned wheelback chairs around a mix of tables and an open fire in a raised stone fireplace. The downstairs eating area has more cushioned dining chairs around wooden tables on pale wooden floorboards, stone walls and ceiling joists, and a two-way fire in a raised stone fireplace that separates this room from the coffee lounge with its comfortable leather chairs and sofas. It's best to book to be sure of a table in the upstairs restaurant. A beer named for the pub from Eden, Theakstons Black Bull and Wells Bombardier on handpump, a dozen wines by the glass and 28 malt whiskies; background music, darts, pool and dominoes. The lovely views over the Eden Valley and the Pennines are best enjoyed from seats on the upstairs verandah; there are also seats on the back terrace. This is under the same ownership as the Cross Keys in Carleton.

Pleasing, popular food includes baguettes, oriental sticky pork ribs, blue cheese and caramelised apple pâté with walnut bread, sharing platters, spicy vegetable enchiladas with sour cream, steak burger with toppings, coleslaw and chips, gammon with fresh pineapple and two eggs, beer-battered haddock and chips, double barnsley lamb chop with parsley mash and mint and redcurrant sauce, and puddings. *Benchmark main dish: steak in ale pie £12.00. Two-course evening meal £18.00.*

Free house ~ Licensees Donald and Paul Newton ~ Real ale ~ Open 12-3, 6-1am; 12-1am Sat; 12-1am Sun; closed Mon lunchtime ~ Bar food 12-2, 6-9; 12-3, 6-8.30 Sun ~ Restaurant ~ Children welcome ~ Dogs allowed in bar ~ Wi-fi ~ Bedrooms: £60/£90

Recommended by Dave Arthur, Mr and Mrs Richard Osborne, Dave Sutton, Shona and Jimmy McDuff, Trish and Karl Soloman

HAWKSHEAD
NY3501   Map 9
Drunken Duck 🌟 ♀ 🍺 🛏
(015394) 36347 – www.drunkenduckinn.co.uk

Barngates; the pub is signposted from B5286 Hawkshead–Ambleside, opposite the Outgate Inn and from north first right after the wooded caravan site; LA22 0NG

Stylish little bar, several restaurant areas, own-brewed beers and bar meals as well as innovative restaurant choices; stunning views and lovely bedrooms

The delicious food and beautifully furnished bedrooms (some have their own balcony and overlook the garden and tarn) are what many customers are here to enjoy, of course – but there is a smart little bar that attracts walkers at lunchtime. And it's the own-brewed ales from their Barngates brewery that are the star attraction: Brathay Gold, Catnap, Cracker Ale, Goodhews Dry Stout, Pale, Red Bull Terrier and Tag Lag on handpump and a new own-brew weiss beer. They also offer 16 wines by the glass from a fine list, 25 malt whiskies and 17 gins. There's an easy-going atmosphere, leather bar stools by the slate-topped counter, leather club chairs, beams and oak floorboards, photographs, coaching prints and hunting pictures on the walls, and horsebrasses and some kentish hop bines as decoration. The three restaurant areas are elegant. Sit at the wooden tables and benches on grass opposite the building for spectacular views across the fells, and if you come in spring or summer the flowering bulbs are lovely.

 Inspired food includes lunchtime sandwiches, guinea fowl thigh with salt baked swede, bread sauce and chilli, kipper scotch egg with brown sauce, steak and stout pie, pork belly and fillet with kohlrabi and crackling, mushroom and chestnut suet pudding, stone bass with chicory jam, beetroot and verjus, and puddings such as melting chocolate tart with blood orange and rhubarb cobbler with popcorn ice-cream. *Benchmark main dish: hake with celeriac, hispi cabbage and monks beard (similar to samphire) £22.00. Two-course evening meal £30.00.*

Own brew ~ Licensee Steph Barton ~ Real ale ~ Open 11.30-11; 12-10.30 Sun ~ Bar food 12-4, 6.30-9 ~ Restaurant ~ Children welcome ~ Dogs allowed in bar ~ Wi-fi ~ Bedrooms: £78.75/£105 *Recommended by Bernard Stradling, Colin McLachlan, Malcolm and Pauline Pellatt, Peter Meister, Gordon and Margaret Ormondroyd, Sally Melling, Martin and Joanne Sharp*

INGS
SD4498   Map 9
Watermill 🍺 🛏
(01539) 821309 – www.watermillinn.co.uk

Just off A591 E of Windermere; LA8 9PY

Bustling, cleverly converted pub with fantastic range of real ales including own brews, and well liked food; bedrooms

The 11 changing beers on handpump here have a loyal following. Their own brews include Watermill A Bit'er Ruff, Blackbeard, Collie Wobbles, Dogth Vader, Isle of Dogs, Windermere Blonde, Ruff Justice and W'ruff Night, and there are guests such as Coniston Bluebird Bitter, Cumbrian Legendary Loweswater Gold and Theakstons Old Peculier. Also, scrumpy cider, a huge choice of foreign bottled beers and 40 malt whiskies. The chatty bar has beams, black leather, wheelback and kitchen or mate's dining chairs around solid tables on tartan carpet plus a woodburning stove in a stone fireplace.

Another room has lots of nice old posters on rough plastered walls, and the interconnected dining rooms, similarly furnished, have flagstones and exposed and painted stone walls; several open fires, darts and board games. There are seats in the gardens and lots to do nearby. Dogs may get free biscuits and water. Readers enjoy staying here.

 Generous helpings of all-day food using local produce includes lunchtime hot and cold sandwiches, crayfish cocktail, ham hock terrine with piccalilli, cumberland sausages with red onion marmalade, mustard chicken with chive mash and rosemary and black pepper sauce, vegetable curry, burger with toppings and chips, fish pie, game casserole, and puddings such as chocolate fudge cake and vanilla crème brûlée. *Benchmark main dish: beef in ale pie £11.95. Two-course evening meal £16.00.*

Own brew ~ Licensee Brian Coulthwaite ~ Real ale ~ Open 11am-11.30pm (10.30pm Sun) ~ Bar food 12-9 ~ Children welcome ~ Dogs allowed in bar and bedrooms ~ Wi-fi ~ Bedrooms: $49/$89 *Recommended by Denis and Margaret Kilner, Rona Mackinlay, Douglas Power, Robert Wivell, Tina and David Woods-Taylor, Gordon and Margaret Ormondroyd*

LANGDALE   NY2806 Map 9
Old Dungeon Ghyll 🍺 £
(015394) 37272 – www.odg.co.uk
B5343; LA22 9JY

Straightforward place in lovely position with real ales, traditional food and fine surrounding walks; bedrooms

Even on particularly sodden and chilly days there's always a boisterous atmosphere and plenty of fell walkers and climbers in the straightforward bar of this old inn. There's no need to remove boots or muddy trousers: you can sit on seats in old cattle stalls by the big warming fire and enjoy the fine choice of six real ales on handpump: Cumbrian Legendary Esthwaite Bitter, Hawkshead Bitter and Windermere Pale, Theakston Old Peculier and Yates Best Bitter and Solway Gold. Farm cider and several malt whiskies. It's a good place to stay, with warm bedrooms, a plush residents' lounge and highly rated breakfasts. It may get lively on a Saturday night (there's a popular National Trust campsite opposite).

 Tasty, honest food includes their own bread and cakes, lunchtime sandwiches, pâté of the day, prawn cocktail, beer-battered fish and chips, a pie of the day, spicy chilli con carne, vegetable goulash, gammon and free-range eggs, and puddings. *Benchmark main dish: cumberland sausage with onion gravy £10.95. Two-course evening meal £20.00.*

Free house ~ Licensee Neil Walmsley ~ Real ale ~ Open 11-11 (10.30 Sun) ~ Bar food 12-2, 6-9 ~ Restaurant ~ Children welcome ~ Dogs allowed in bar and bedrooms ~ Wi-fi ~ Bedrooms: $62.50/$125 *Recommended by Peter Meister, Julie Braeburn, Mr and Mrs D Hammond, Charles Todd*

LEVENS   SD4987 Map 9
Strickland Arms ♍ 🍺
(015395) 61010 – www.thestricklandarms.com
4 miles from M6 junction 36, via A590; just off A590, by Sizergh Castle gates; LA8 8DZ

Friendly, open-plan pub with popular food, local ales and a fine setting; seats outside

It's best to book a table in advance in this civilised place as it's close to the M6 and opposite the entrance to Sizergh Castle (owned by the National

Trust and open from April to October, Sunday to Thursday afternoons). The bar on the right has oriental rugs on flagstones, a log fire, Bowness Bay Raven Red and Swan Blonde, Hardknott Continuum and Lux Borealis and Lancaster Red on handpump, several malt whiskies and nine wines by the glass. On the left are polished boards and another log fire, and throughout there's a nice mix of sturdy country furniture, candles on tables, hunting scenes and other old prints on the walls, curtains in heavy fabric and some staffordshire china ornaments. Two of the dining rooms are upstairs; background music and board games. The flagstoned front terrace has plenty of seats; disabled access and facilities. The pub is part of the Ainscoughs group.

Using lamb from their own flock, the high quality food includes lunchtime sandwiches (until 5pm at weekends), salmon and cod fishcakes with lemon mayonnaise, home-made black pudding with mushrooms, bacon and cheese and topped with an egg, burger with toppings, pickles, relish and chips, pea and asparagus risotto, cumberland sausage with mash and onion cider gravy, beer-battered fish and chips, lancashire hotpot with pickled red cabbage, and puddings such as chocolate fudge brownie and vanilla pannacotta. *Benchmark main dish: pie of the day £12.50. Two-course evening meal £20.50.*

Free house ~ Licensee Michael Redmond ~ Real ale ~ Open 12-11 (10.30 Sun) ~ Bar food 12-9 ~ Children welcome ~ Dogs welcome ~ Wi-fi *Recommended by Rob Anderson, Mary Joyce, Andrew Vincent, Hugh Roberts, Donald Allsopp, Sally and David Champion*

LITTLE LANGDALE
Three Shires 🍺 ⛺

NY3103 Map 9

(015394) 37215 – www.threeshiresinn.co.uk
From A593 3 miles W of Ambleside take small road signposted 'The Langdales, Wrynose Pass'; then bear left at first fork; LA22 9NZ

Fine valley views from seats on the terrace, local ales, quite a choice of food and good service; comfortable bedrooms

Our readers enjoy this reliably well run and friendly inn very much. The comfortably extended back bar has green Lakeland stone and homely red patterned wallpaper, stripped timbers and a stripped beam-and-joist ceiling, antique oak carved settles, country kitchen chairs and stools on big dark slate flagstones and cumbrian photographs. The four real ales on handpump include Barngates Goodhews Dry Stout, Coniston Old Man Ale, Cumbrian Legendary Loweswater Gold and Hawkshead Bitter, and they also have over 50 malt whiskies and a decent wine list. The front restaurant has chunky leather dining chairs around solid tables on wood flooring, wine bottle prints on dark red walls and fresh flowers; a snug leads off here, and the residents' lounge has leather sofas and an open fire. Darts, TV and board games. The view from seats on the terrace down over the valley to the partly wooded hills below is stunning; there are more seats on a neat lawn behind the car park, backed by a small oak wood, and award-winning summer hanging baskets. The pretty bedrooms have fine views and they also offer two self-catering cottages. The three shires of the pub's name are the historical counties of Cumberland, Westmorland and Lancashire, which meet at the top of nearby Wrynose Pass.

Reliably good, enjoyable food includes lunchtime sandwiches, local smoked venison loin with chutney, Morecambe Bay potted shrimps, battered fresh haddock and chips, garlic and thyme-roasted mushroom risotto with truffle oil, beef in ale pie, chicken tikka masala, pork with black and white pudding, apple and cinnamon couscous and creamy mustard sauce, sea bass with wilted spinach, orange beurre blanc and burnt orange salad, and puddings such as caramel pannacotta with caramel sauce and fruit cake fritter with brandy custard. *Benchmark main dish: pheasant breast on leg meat pâté with herb mash and a honey and cream sauce £17.50. Two-course evening meal £22.00.*

Free house ~ Licensee Ian Stephenson ~ Real ale ~ Open 11-10.30 (11 Sat); 12-10.30 Sun; 11-3, 6-10 in winter; closed Jan ~ Bar food 12-2, 6-8.45; snacks in afternoon ~ Restaurant ~ Children welcome ~ Dogs allowed in bar ~ Wi-fi ~ Bedrooms: /£118 *Recommended by John Evans, Tracey and Stephen Groves, Christian Mole, Barry Collett, Tina and David Woods-Taylor, Mr and Mrs Richard Osborne*

LOWESWATER
NY1421 Map 9

Kirkstile Inn 🍺 ⇌

(01900) 85219 – www.kirkstile.com

From B5289 follow signs to Loweswater Lake; OS Sheet 89 map reference 140210; CA13 0RU

Fine location for this well run, popular inn with busy bar, own-brewed beers, good food and friendly welcome; bedrooms

It's only a short distance to the lakes of Loweswater and Crummock Water from this welcoming 16th-c inn and, with stunning surrounding walks, lunchtimes are particularly busy here. The main bar has a cosy atmosphere, thanks to the roaring log fire, plus low beams and carpeting, comfortably cushioned small settles and pews, partly stripped stone walls, board games and a slate shove-ha'penny board. As well as their own-brewed Cumbrian Legendary Esthwaite, Langdale and Loweswater Gold, they often keep a guest such as Watermill Collie Wobbles on handpump, plus nine wines by the glass and 20 malt whiskies. The stunning views of the peaks can be enjoyed from picnic-sets on the lawn, from the very attractive covered verandah in front of the building and from the bow windows in one of the rooms off the bar. Bedrooms are comfortable and breakfasts are especially good. Dogs are allowed only in the bar and not during evening food service.

Rewarding food includes lunchtime sandwiches, smoked haddock and leek risotto, smoked duck breast with feta, spring onion and watercress and hoisin dressing, wild mushroom risotto, local pork burger with toppings, ale onion rings and spicy tomato chutney, guinea fowl roulade with air-dried ham, chorizo bonbons, crispy sweet potato and rich jus, stone bass with ale battered anchovies and saffron cream, and puddings such as a fruit crumble of the day with custard and white chocolate and mango pannacotta with cassis sorbet. *Benchmark main dish: steak in ale pie £12.75. Two-course evening meal £21.00.*

Own brew ~ Licensee Roger Humphreys ~ Real ale ~ Open 11-11 ~ Bar food 12-2, 6-9; light meals and tea in afternoon ~ Restaurant ~ Children welcome ~ Dogs allowed in bar ~ Bedrooms: £63.50/£107 *Recommended by Tracey and Stephen Groves, Mike and Eleanor Anderson, Dr Peter Crawshaw, Peter Smith and Judith Brown*

LUPTON
SO5581 Map 7

Plough 🍽️⭐ ♀ ⇌

(015395) 67700 – www.theploughatlupton.co.uk

A65, near M6 junction 36; LA6 1PJ

Smart inn with open-plan smart rooms, a good choice of drinks, interesting food and seats outside; fine bedrooms

A stylish and historic 18th-c inn that's perfectly placed for exploring the Lake District. There are spreading open-plan bars with beams, a nice mix of antique dining chairs and tables, comfortable leather sofas and armchairs in front of a large woodburning stove and log fire, hunting prints and cartoons on grey-painted walls, rugs on wooden floors, fresh flowers and daily papers; background music and board games. High bar stools sit beside the granite-topped counter, where neatly dressed, friendly staff serve Fallen Dragonfly, Kirkby Lonsdale Monumental, Lancaster Blonde and Thwaites Wainwright on handpump, ten wines by the glass, ten gins and local vodka; board games. Outside, rustic wooden tables and chairs under parasols are set behind a white picket fence, with more in the back garden. Bedrooms are cosy, attractive and comfortable.

 Top quality, interesting food includes sandwiches (until 5pm), twice-baked local cheese and chive soufflé with sweet chilli jam, slow-cooked pork cheek with smoked brie and pearl barley risotto, poached salmon caesar salad, a pie of the day, nepalese curry of cauliflower, potato, chickpeas and spinach with mango chutney and flatbread, lamb rump with roasted baby onions and champ mash, butter-poached cod with white polenta, buttermilk crumb and scorched broccoli, chicken breast with butternut squash, swiss chard and parmesan gnocchi, chateaubriand (to share), and puddings such as dark chocolate mousse with peanut brittle, home-made fudge and caramel ice-cream and cherry liqueur pannacotta with cherry compote and almond crumble. *Benchmark main dish: Sunday roast lunch £13.95. Two-course evening meal £20.00.*

Free house ~ Licensee Paul Spencer ~ Real ale ~ Open 11-11; 12-11 Sun ~ Bar food 12-9 ~ Restaurant ~ Children welcome ~ Dogs allowed in bar and bedrooms ~ Wi-fi ~ Bedrooms: £85/£120 *Recommended by Michael Doswell, Alistair Forsyth, Lee and Liz Potter, Gordon and Margaret Ormondroyd, Amy and Luke Buchanan*

NEAR SAWREY
SD3795 Map 9

Tower Bank Arms 🍺 🛏

(015394) 36334 – www.towerbankarms.com
B5285 towards the Windermere ferry; LA22 0LF

Well run pub with several real ales, well regarded bar food and a friendly welcome; nice bedrooms

Many illustrations in the Beatrix Potter books can be traced back to their origins in this village, including the pub, which features in *The Tale of Jemima Puddle-Duck*. The low-beamed main bar has plenty of rustic charm with a rough slate floor, game and fowl pictures, a grandfather clock, a log fire and fresh flowers; there's also a separate restaurant. Barngates Cracker Ale and Tag Lag, Cumbrian Legendary Loweswater Gold and Hawkshead Bitter and Brodies Prime on handpump, nine wines by the glass, a dozen malt whiskies and four farm ciders; board games. There are pleasant views of the wooded Claife Heights from seats in the extended garden. The pretty bedrooms have a country outlook; good breakfasts.

Popular food includes lunchtime sandwiches, potted chicken liver and pistachio parfait with cumberland sauce, beer-battered chicken strips in sweet chilli and sesame seed sauce, spinach, mushroom and gnocchi in creamy tarragon sauce, cumberland sausage with caramelised red onion gravy and apple and sage mash, beer-battered haddock and chips, lamb shoulder in mint and red wine gravy on bubble and squeak, and puddings such as warm chocolate brownie with berries and banana ice-cream and raspberry eton mess. *Benchmark main dish: beef in ale stew £12.75. Two-course evening meal £18.50.*

Free house ~ Licensee Anthony Hutton ~ Real ale ~ Open 12-11 (10.30 Sun); closed Mon Nov-early Feb, 1 week early Dec, 1 week Jan ~ Bar food 12-2, 6-9 (8 Sun, winter Mon-Thurs and bank holidays) ~ Restaurant ~ Children welcome ~ Dogs allowed in bar and bedrooms ~ Wi-fi ~ Bedrooms: /£98 *Recommended by David Travis, Beth Aldridge, Charles Welch, Sandra Hollies, Sophia and Hamish Greenfield*

PENRITH

NY5130 Map 9

Dockray Hall ✪

(01768) 210676 – www.dockrayhall.com

Great Dockray/Cornmarket; CA11 7DE

Historic inn with interesting bar and dining areas, local ales and good wines, first class food and seats outside

Richard III once owned this historic 15th-c building – and it's been an inn since 1719. The renovations have been thoughtfully and carefully carried out to preserve the ancient character and there are plenty of bars and dining rooms to choose from. The main bar has a roaring log fire in an inglenook, built-in wall seats and settles with scatter cushions and all manner of wooden or leather chairs around dark tables on big flagstones and daily papers on a beer barrel; steps lead up to a panelled dining area with similar furnishings on checked carpeting, another open fire and a pretty bow window. Steps also lead down to another bar with solid furnishings on parquet flooring and plush little bar stools, and the Stables Bar has horse tack and other farming implements and traditional seats and tables on stripped wooden floorboards. Knowledgeable, friendly staff serve their own Cumbrian Legendary Loweswater Gold and Langdale and a couple of guest beers on handpump, nine good wines by the glass and ten malt whiskies. There's also a snug with comfortable upholstered winged and bucket seating. Outside in front, walled off from the road, are picnic-sets.

 Extremely good modern british food using local, seasonal produce includes sandwiches, twice-baked cheddar and spinach soufflé, chicken and black pudding terrine with home-made piccalilli, a pie of the day, wild mushroom and spinach pasta with wild garlic pesto, local venison burger with toppings, celeriac rémoulade and chips, local pork and ale sausages with bubble and squeak, crispy onions and gravy, haddock and salmon fish pie with parmesan mash, 28-day-aged sirloin steak with peppercorn sauce, and puddings such as orange parfait with chocolate and orange ganache with baked white chocolate and a crumble of the day with custard; they also offer brunch (10.30am-midday) and a two- and three-course set lunch. *Benchmark main dish: pie of the day £13.00. Two-course evening meal £25.00.*

Free house ~ Licensee Roger Humphreys ~ Real ale ~ Open 10.30am-11pm (midnight Sat); 12-10.30 Sun ~ Bar food 10.30-4, 6-9; 12-3, 6-8 Sun ~ Children welcome ~ Dogs allowed in bar ~ Wi-fi *Recommended by Alexandra and Richard Clay, Robert and Diana Myers, Neil Allen, Melanie and David Lawson*

RAVENSTONEDALE

NY7203 Map 10

Black Swan ✪ 🛏

(015396) 23204 – www.blackswanhotel.com

Just off A685 SW of Kirkby Stephen; CA17 4NG

Bustling hotel with thriving bar, several real ales, enjoyable food and good surrounding walks; comfortable bedrooms

There's plenty to do in this pretty village and surroundings, and the neatly kept Victorian hotel is at the heart of things. The popular U-shaped bar has hops on the gantry, quite a few original period features, stripped-stone walls, high wooden stools by the counter, a comfortable tweed banquette, various dining chairs and little stools around a mix of tables and fresh flowers; a cosy small lounge has armchairs and an open fire. You can eat in the bar or in two separate restaurants. Friendly, helpful staff serve Black Sheep Bitter, Timothy Taylors Boltmaker and a guest such as Coniston Bluebird Bitter on handpump, 11 wines by the glass, more than 30 malt whiskies, 25 gins and a good choice of fruit juices and pressés; background music, TV, darts, board games, newspapers and magazines. There are picnic-sets in the tree-sheltered streamside garden across the road and lots of good walks from the door; they have leaflets describing some routes. The bedrooms are individually decorated (some have disabled access, others are dog-friendly) and breakfasts are generous. They also run the village store, which has café seating outside.

Good, interesting food from a seasonal menu includes lunchtime sandwiches, scallops with a risotto of butternut squash, parma ham and sage, venison tartare with mustard, hazelnuts, nasturtium and bitter chocolate, celeriac rösti with a poached egg, stilton and walnuts and pickled apple dressing, beef bourguignon, chicken with black sesame, sweetcorn, miso and pulled chicken samosa, cod loin with pancetta, leeks and mussels, and puddings such as baked alaska with rhubarb and yoghurt and pistachio soufflé with pistachio ice-cream. *Benchmark main dish: lamb rump with yoghurt, pomegranate and chickpeas £18.50. Two-course evening meal £25.00.*

Free house ~ Licensee Louise Dinnes ~ Real ale ~ Open 8am-midnight (1am Fri, Sat) ~ Bar food 12-9 ~ Restaurant ~ Children welcome ~ Dogs allowed in bar and bedrooms ~ Wi-fi ~ Bedrooms: £80/£95 *Recommended by Sandra Hollies, John and Mary Warner, Beth Aldridge, Sophia and Hamish Greenfield*

RAVENSTONEDALE
NY7204 Map 10

Kings Head 🍺 🛏

(015396) 23050 ~ www.kings-head.com
Pub visible from A685 W of Kirkby Stephen; CA17 4NH

Riverside inn with beamed bar and adjacent dining room, attractive furnishings, three real ales and interesting food; comfortable bedrooms

A wide mix of customers gather in this easy-going place. It's been nicely opened up inside, and the beamed bar rooms have assorted rugs on lovely big flagstones, a wing chair by a log fire in a raised fireplace, an attractive array of fine wooden chairs and cushioned settles, a few prints on grey-painted walls and an old yoke above a double-sided woodburner and bread oven. Theakstons Best Bitter and a couple of guests such as Allendale Golden Plover and Jennings Sneck Lifter on handpump and eight wines by the glass, served by friendly staff; background music and a games room with darts and local photographs. The dining room is similarly furnished, but with some upholstered chairs on stone floors, tartan curtains, fresh flowers and a few prints. Bedrooms are comfortable and breakfasts hearty. There are picnic-sets by the river in a fenced-off area, and plenty of good surrounding walks.

Much liked food includes lunchtime sandwiches, chicken liver pâté with relish, scallops with crispy pancetta and cauliflower purée, ham hock with poached eggs, spinach and potato curry with minted yoghurt and naan, burger with toppings, coleslaw and chips, venison, juniper and rosemary pie, smoked haddock fishcake with dill and lemon mayonnaise and wilted spinach, lamb rump with garlic mash, salsa verde and pea and mint oil, and puddings such as lemon and ginger syllabub and chocolate and cherry brandy tart with champagne sorbet. *Benchmark main dish: beef and stilton pie £12.95. Two-course evening meal £22.00.*

Free house ~ Licensee Leigh O`Donoghue ~ Real ale ~ Open 12-11 (10.30 Sun) ~ Bar food 12-9 ~ Restaurant ~ Children welcome ~ Dogs allowed in bar ~ Wi-fi ~ Bedrooms: £80/£103 *Recommended by Graeme and Sally Mendham, Ben and Jenny Settle, Tom and Lorna Harding, John Evans*

It's very helpful if you let us know up-to-date food prices when you report on pubs.

STAVELEY   SD4798   Map 10

Beer Hall at Hawkshead Brewery ◀

(01539) 825260 – www.hawksheadbrewery.co.uk

Staveley Mill Yard, Back Lane; LA8 9LR

Hawkshead Brewery showcase plus a huge choice of bottled beers, brewery memorabilia and tasty food

From 14 handpumps, knowledgeable, friendly staff dispense the full range of Hawkshead Brewery ales. These might include Bitter, Brodies Prime, Cumbrian Five Hop, Dry Stone Stout, Lakeland Gold, Lakeland Lager, Red, Windermere Pale and seasonal beers; regular beer festivals. Also, 40 bottled beers, 25 gins and 50 whiskies with an emphasis on independent producers. It's a spacious and modern glass-fronted building and the main bar is on two levels with the lower level dominated by the stainless-steel fermenting vessels. There are high-backed chairs around light wooden tables, benches beside long tables and nice dark leather sofas around low tables (all on oak floorboards); a couple of walls are almost entirely covered with artistic photos of barley, hops and the brewing process. You can buy T-shirts, branded glasses and polypins and there are brewery tours. Parking can be tricky at peak times.

 As well as a dozen or so tapas-style dishes such as sticky barbecue ribs, breaded whitebait, beer-battered onion rings and gnocchi with tomato sauce and goats cheese, they offer a huge pork pie with wholegrain mustard, piccalilli and coleslaw, cheese, onion and potato or shepherd's pies, chicken curry, beer-battered fish and chips, and puddings such as chocolate brownie with vanilla ice-cream and a trio of puddings. *Benchmark main dish: yorkshire pudding filled with beef and horseradish sauce £6.50. Two-course evening meal £18.00.*

Own brew ~ Licensee Chris Ramwell ~ Real ale ~ Open 12-6 Mon-Thurs; 12-11 Fri, Sat; 12-8 Sun ~ Bar food 12-3 Mon-Thurs; 12-8.30 Fri, Sat; 12-6 Sun ~ Children welcome ~ Dogs allowed in bar ~ Wi-fi *Recommended by John Poulter, David Travis, Douglas Power, Nick Higgins, Penny and David Shepherd*

STAVELEY   SD4797   Map 9

Eagle & Child ◀ £ ⌂

(01539) 821320 – www.eaglechildinn.co.uk

Kendal Road; just off A591 Windermere–Kendal; LA8 9LP

Friendly inn with a good range of local beers and enjoyable food; bedrooms

There's always a cheerful crowd of customers here and the open fires are most welcome after a good walk. The bar has plenty of separate parts furnished with pews, banquettes, bow window seats and high-backed dining chairs around polished dark tables, and in the L-shaped flagstoned main area is a log fire beneath an impressive mantelbeam. Also, police truncheons and walking sticks, some nice photographs and interesting prints, a delft shelf of bric-a-brac, a few farm tools and another log fire. Five regularly changing ales come from breweries such as Barngates, Cumberland Legendary, Hawkshead, Jennings, Keswick, Kirkby Lonsdale and Ulverston on handpump, several wines by the glass, 30 malt whiskies, 20 gins and farm cider; background music, darts and board games. An upstairs barn-themed dining room has its own bar for functions. The bedrooms are comfortable and the breakfasts very generous. There are picnic-sets under cocktail parasols in a sheltered garden by the River Kent, with more on a good-sized back terrace and a second garden behind. This is a lovely spot with more walks that fan out from the recreation ground just across the road.

🍴 A good choice of enjoyable food includes sandwiches, pancake filled with prawns and smoked salmon in a creamy dill, lemon and mushroom sauce, a tapas platter, cajun chicken caesar salad, malaysian-style vegetable curry, beer-battered haddock and chips, chicken wrapped in smoked bacon with barbecue sauce and cheese topping, steak in ale pie, gammon with egg and fresh pineapple, and puddings such as hot chocolate fudge cake and vanilla cheesecake. *Benchmark main dish: moroccan lamb £11.95. Two-course evening meal £18.00.*

Free house ~ Licensees Richard and Denise Coleman ~ Real ale ~ Open 11.30-11; 12-10.30 Sun ~ Bar food 12-2.30, 6-9; 12-9 weekends ~ Restaurant ~ Children welcome ~ Dogs allowed in bar ~ Wi-fi ~ Bedrooms: £75/£85 *Recommended by Alf Wright, Julie Braeburn, Sandra King, Tina and David Woods-Taylor, Dave Braisted, Chris Stevenson, John and Mary Warner*

 STONETHWAITE   NY2513   Map 9

Langstrath 🍺 🛏

(017687) 77239 – www.thelangstrath.com
Off B5289 S of Derwentwater; CA12 5XG

Nice little place in a lovely spot, popular food with a modern twist, real ales and good wines, and seats outside; bedrooms

'A firm favourite' and 'a place I return to again and again' are just two enthusiastic comments from readers on this civilised and friendly small inn. The neat, simple bar – at its pubbiest at lunchtime – has a welcoming log fire in a big stone fireplace, rustic tables, plain chairs and cushioned wall seats, and walking cartoons and attractive Lakeland mountain photographs on its textured white walls. Jennings Cumberland Ale and Cocker Hoop, Keswick Thirst Gold and a guest from Keswick on handpump, 30 malt whiskies and several wines by the glass; background music and board games. The restaurant has fine views and there's a cosy residents' lounge too (in what was the original 16th-c cottage). The comfortable, warm bedrooms are just right as a base for a walking holiday and both the Cumbrian Way and the Coast to Coast path are close by. Outside, a big sycamore shelters several picnic-sets that look up to Eagle Crag.

🍴 Appetising food includes lunchtime sandwiches, a changing terrine, vegetable and feta lasagne, steak in ale pie, cumberland sausage with wholegrain mustard mash and onion gravy, chorizo and mushroom suet pudding with leeks in a white wine sauce, sea trout with spring onion and cheddar crushed potatoes and pesto dressing, and puddings such as sticky toffee pudding with butterscotch sauce and a crumble of the day. *Benchmark main dish: lamb shoulder with rosemary and red wine jus £18.90. Two-course evening meal £23.00.*

Free house ~ Licensees Guy and Jacqui Frazer-Hollins ~ Real ale ~ Open 12-10.30; closed Mon, all Dec, Jan ~ Bar food 12-4, 6-9 ~ Restaurant ~ Children welcome but not in bedrooms ~ Dogs allowed in bar ~ Wi-fi ~ Bedrooms: /£116 *Recommended by Martin Day, Tracey and Stephen Groves, Pat and Stewart Gordon, Helena and Trevor Fraser*

 TALKIN   NY5457   Map 10

Blacksmiths Arms 🍷 🛏

(016977) 3452 – www.blacksmithstalkin.co.uk
Village signposted from B6413 S of Brampton; CA8 1LE

Neatly kept and welcoming with tasty bar food, several real ales and fine nearby walks; bedrooms

A friendly family are in charge here – and in the 18th c, it really was the village blacksmiths. Several neatly kept, traditionally furnished bars include a warm lounge on the right with a log fire, upholstered banquettes and wheelback chairs around dark wooden tables on patterned red carpeting, with country prints and other pictures on the walls. The restaurant is to the left and there's also a long lounge opposite the bar, with a step up to another room at the back. Four real ales from breweries such as Black Sheep, Coniston, Cumbrian Legendary and Yates on handpump, 20 wines by the glass, 30 malt whiskies and local gin and vodka; background music, darts and board games. There are a couple of picnic-sets outside the front door with more in the back garden. The cottagey bedrooms are comfortable, and there are good walks in the attractive surrounding countryside.

Good pubby choices of well liked food includes sandwiches, thai-battered prawns with sweet chilli dip, chicken liver pâté with cumberland sauce, mushroom stroganoff, liver and bacon casserole, burger with toppings, onion rings and chips, chicken in creamy garlic, mushroom and bacon sauce, beef stroganoff, salmon fillet in white wine, parsley and cream sauce, and puddings. *Benchmark main dish: beer-battered haddock and chips £8.95. Two-course evening meal £14.00.*

Free house ~ Licensees Donald and Anne Jackson ~ Real ale ~ Open 12-midnight ~ Bar food 12-2 (2.30 Sun), 6-9 ~ Restaurant ~ Children welcome ~ Wi-fi ~ Bedrooms: £60/£80
Recommended by Alf Wright, Peter Pilbeam, Comus and Sarah Elliott, John and Sylvia Harrop, Daniel King

THRELKELD   NY3225 Map 9

Horse & Farrier £

(017687) 79688 – www.horseandfarrier.com
A66 Penrith–Keswick; CA12 4SQ

Well run and friendly 17th-c inn with good food and drinks and fine nearby walks; bedrooms

A t the foot of Blencathra, this popular place has walks from the back door and comfortable bedrooms with fine views. The linked mainly carpeted rooms (some have flagstones) have a mix of furniture from comfortably padded seats to pubby chairs and wall settles, candlelit tables, beams and open fires. Jennings Cumberland and guest ales are kept well on handpump served by efficient friendly staff. There's a partly stripped-stone restaurant; backround music, TV and board games. A few picnic-sets outside have fine views towards the Helvellyn range. They also have a self-catering cottage for rent. Disabled facilities.

A good varied choice of nicely presented food includes sandwiches, piri piri-marinated tiger prawn and chorizo skewers with a sweet chilli sauce, duck liver pâté with beetroot chutney, mushroom stroganoff, burger with toppings and chips, smoked haddock topped by an egg with chive mash and creamy white wine and parsley sauce, a curry of the day, pork belly with black and white pudding, grain mustard mash and apple, sage and spring onion sauce, and puddings such as ginger sponge pudding with orange and lemon sauce and chocolate fudge cake with fruit coulis. *Benchmark main dish: slow-cooked lamb shoulder with chive mash and redcurrant and mint sauce £15.95. Two-course evening meal £20.00.*

Jennings (Marstons) ~ Lease David Arkley ~ Real ale ~ Open 8am-midnight ~ Bar food 12-9 (10 Sat) ~ Restaurant ~ Children welcome ~ Dogs allowed in bar ~ Wi-fi ~ Bedrooms: £59.95/£91.90 *Recommended by Tina and David Woods-Taylor, Margaret and Peter Staples, Dr Peter Crawshaw, George Sanderson, Miles Green*

You can send reports directly to us at feedback@goodguides.com

TIRRIL   NY5026 Map 10

Queens Head

(01768) 863219 – www.queensheadinn.co.uk

B5320, not far from M6 junction 40; CA10 2JF

Dating from 1719 with two bars, real ales, speciality pies and seats outside; bedrooms

---

As this 18th-c inn is just a couple of miles from Ullswater, it does get pretty busy. The oldest parts of the main bar have original flagstones and floorboards, low beams and black panelling, and there are nice little tables and chairs on either side of the inglenook fireplace (always lit in winter). Another bar to the right of the entrance has pews and chairs around sizeable tables on a wooden floor, and candles in the fireplace, while the back locals' bar has heavy beams and a pool table; there are three dining rooms too. Robinsons Cumbria Way, Dizzy Blonde and Unicorn on handpump and several wines by the glass. Outside there are picnic-sets at the front, and modern chairs and tables under cover on the back terrace. The hard-working licensees also run the Pie Mill (you can eat their pies here) and the village shop. The pub is very close to several interesting places including Dalemain House and Garden at Dacre.

Food includes up to eight pies, plus sandwiches, creamy garlic mushrooms, vegetable lasagne, honey-roast ham and egg, a curry of the day, slow-roast lamb shoulder in redcurrant gravy, steaks with trimmings and chips, and puddings such as sticky toffee pudding and a fruit pie of the day. *Benchmark main dish: pie of the day £11.00. Two-course evening meal £17.00.*

Robinsons ~ Tenants Margaret and Jim Hodge ~ Real ale ~ Open 11-11 (11.30 Sat); 11am-11.30pm Sat; 12-10 Sun ~ Bar food 12-2.30, 5-8.30 ~ Restaurant ~ Children welcome ~ Dogs allowed in bar and bedrooms ~ Wi-fi ~ Bedrooms: £50/£80 *Recommended by Tina and David Woods-Taylor, Martin Day, Alastair and Sheree Hepburn, Ivor Smith, Neil and Angela Huxter, Shaun Mahoney*

ULVERSTON   SD3177 Map 7

Bay Horse 🍷 🛏

(01229) 583972 – www.thebayhorsehotel.co.uk

Canal Foot signposted off A590, then wend your way past the huge Glaxo factory; LA12 9EL

Civilised waterside hotel with lunchtime bar food, three real ales and a fine choice of wines; smart bedrooms

---

This is a fine place to stay and the bedrooms have french windows that open out to a panoramic view of the Leven estuary (the bird life is wonderful); breakfasts are excellent. The bar is at its most informal at lunchtime and has a relaxed atmosphere – despite its smart furnishings: cushioned teak dining chairs, paisley-patterned built-in wall banquettes, glossy hardwood traditional tables, a huge stone horse's head, black beams and props, and lots of horsebrasses. Magazines are dotted about, there's an open fire in the handsomely marbled, grey slate fireplace and decently reproduced background music; board games. Jennings Cocker Hoop and Cumberland on handpump, 14 wines by the glass (including champagne and prosecco) from a carefully chosen, interesting list and 15 malt whiskies. The conservatory restaurant has lovely views over Morecambe Bay and there are seats outside on the terrace.

In the evening, the emphasis is on the restaurant with one sitting (at 7.30pm) and light snacks only available in the bar. At lunchtime there might be sandwiches, duck liver pâté with quince and red chilli jelly, avocado and pink grapefruit salad with raspberry and passion-fruit dressing, beef, mushroom and Guinness casserole with white pudding mash, chicken marinated in coconut milk, lime and ginger with fresh pineapple and pancetta, lamb shank braised with orange, ginger and red wine, and puddings such as profiteroles filled with praline cream on a dark chocolate sauce and a trio of home-made sorbets. *Benchmark main dish: crab and salmon fishcake with a white wine and fresh herb cream sauce £19.00. Two-course evening meal £35.00.*

Free house ~ Licensee Robert Lyons ~ Real ale ~ Open 11-11; 12-10.30 Sun ~ Bar food 12-4 (3 in winter), 7.30-8.30 ~ Restaurant ~ Children welcome at lunchtime, must be over 9 in bedrooms ~ Dogs allowed in bar and bedrooms ~ Wi-fi ~ Bedrooms: £95/£120
Recommended by John Poulter, John and Sylvia Harrop, W K Wood, Tina and David Woods-Taylor, Denis and Margaret Kilner

WINSTER
SD4193 Map 9
Brown Horse 🍺 🛏

(015394) 43443 – www.thebrownhorseinn.co.uk

A5074 S of Windermere; LA23 3NR

Traditional coaching inn with character bar and dining room, own-brewed ales, good food and seats outside; bedrooms

The own-brew beers in this 19th-c coaching inn include Winster Valley Best Bitter, Chaser, Dark Horse, Hurdler, Lakes Blonde, and Old School – plus guests such as Banks's Sunbeam and Ringwood Boondoggle. Also, several wines by the glass, quite a few malt whiskies and an extraordinary list of 150 gins from all over the world with 13 different tonics to mix with them. The chatty beamed and flagstoned bar has church pews, a lovely tall settle and mate's chairs around a mix of tables, while the candlelit dining room has a medley of painted and antique chairs and tables, old skis, carpet beaters, hunting horns and antlers. The gents' is upstairs. There are seats outside among flowering tubs, with more on a raised terrace. The bedrooms are thoughtfully furnished and they also have three self-catering properties. This is a pretty valley with good walks.

🍴 Pleasing food includes sandwiches, game terrine with damson chutney, blue cheese pannacotta with caramelised walnut dressing, poached pear and figs, creamed wild mushroom and pine nut filo tart with smoked cheese and spinach, rump burger with toppings and sweet potato fries, toad in the hole with local sausages, mustard mash and caramelised onion gravy, fish pie with lemon samphire, lamb rump with slow-cooked shoulder pearl barley and vegetable broth and puddings such as praline cheesecake with passion-fruit sorbet and chocolate brownie with hot chocolate sauce and fudge ice-cream. *Benchmark main dish: curried cod with crispy squid, lentils and onions £18.50. Two-course evening meal £19.00.*

Free house ~ Licensees Karen and Steve Edmondson ~ Real ale ~ Open 11-11 ~ Bar food 12-2.30 (3 weekends), 6-9 ~ Restaurant ~ Children welcome ~ Dogs allowed in bar ~ Wi-fi ~ Bedrooms: /£115 *Recommended by Tim and Sarah Smythe-Brown, William Slade, Tina and David Woods-Taylor, Michael Butler, Gordon and Margaret Ormondroyd, Mr and Mrs Richard Osborne*

WITHERSLACK
SD4482 Map 10
Derby Arms 🍺

(015395) 52207 – www.thederbyarms.co.uk

Just off A590; LA11 6RH

Bustling country inn with half a dozen ales, good food and wine and a genuine welcome; bedrooms

As ever, the fine range of drinks here draws in many customers. On handpump they offer up to six real ales including Bowness Bay Swan Blonde, Cumbrian Legendary Esthwaite Bitter and Wychwood Hobgoblin Gold with three guests from breweries such as Hardknott, Hogshead and Thwaites; also, 11 wines by the glass and 22 malt whiskies. The main bar has sporting prints on pale grey walls, elegant old dining chairs and tables on large rugs over floorboards, and an open fire. A larger room to the right is similarly furnished (with the addition of some cushioned pews) and has local prints, another open fire, and alcoves in the back wall full of bristol blue glass, ornate plates and staffordshire dogs and figurines. Large windows lighten up the rooms, helped at night by candles in brass candlesticks; background music, TV and pool. There are two additional rooms – one with dark red walls, a red velvet sofa, sporting prints and a handsome mirror over the fireplace. Bedrooms are fairly priced and there's plenty to do nearby – Sizergh Castle (National Trust), Levens Hall and good walks around the Southern Lakes and Dales. This is part of the Ainscoughs group.

Food includes lunchtime sandwiches (until 5pm weekends), crispy whitebait with home-made tartare sauce, wild mushrooms on garlic and tomato bruschetta, cumberland sausage with mash and onion gravy, mixed bean and tomato cassoulet, beer-battered haddock and chips, chicken breast with bacon, spinach, potato rösti and cheese, and puddings such as lemon posset and white chocolate and raspberry crème brûlée; they also offer a two-course weekday lunch. *Benchmark main dish: steak in ale pie £13.50. Two-course evening meal £19.00.*

Free house ~ Licensee Barry Thomas ~ Real ale ~ Open 12-11 (midnight Sat) ~ Bar food 12-2, 6-9; 12-9 Sat; 12-8 Sun ~ Children welcome ~ Dogs allowed in bar and bedrooms ~ Wi-fi ~ Live music twice a month Fri or Sat ~ Bedrooms: /£75 *Recommended by John and Sylvia Harrop, Hugh Roberts, Sally Harrison, Len and Lilly Dowson*

YANWATH   NY5128 Map 9

Gate Inn ⭐ ♀

(01768) 862386 – www.yanwathgate.co.uk

2.25 miles from M6 junction 40; A66 towards Brough, then right on A6, right on B5320, then follow village signpost; CA10 2LF

Emphasis on imaginative food but with local beers and thoughtfully chosen wines, a cosy atmosphere and a warm welcome from helpful staff

Plenty of locals do drop in for a drink and a chat, but most customers are here for the excellent food. It remains a civilised and immaculately kept 17th-c pub and the cosy bar of charming antiquity has country pine and dark wood furniture, lots of brasses on beams, candles on all tables and an open fire in the attractive stone inglenook; background music and board games. Two real ales from Barngates and Yates on handpump, ten good wines by the glass, ten malt whiskies and Weston's Old Rosie cider; staff are courteous and helpful. The restaurant has been refurbished and has Farrow & Ball paintwork, oak floors and panelled walls, works by local artists, heavy beams and a woodburning stove. There are new seats and tables under parasols on the terrace and in the garden.

Delicious food using the best local, seasonal produce includes open sandwiches, wild nettle soup with poached oysters, swordfish ceviche with lemongrass, ginger and coriander, moroccan vegetarian tagine with spicy lemon harissa and coriander couscous, wild bass fillet with tiger prawn and chorizo risotto, roast poussin breast and confit leg with baby leeks, wild mushrooms and sauce au lait, rack of lamb with mustard mash and port gravy, and puddings such as orange and vanilla pannacotta with candied nuts and sticky date pudding with butterscotch sauce; they also offer a two- and three-course set lunch. *Benchmark main dish: beef shin in red wine with stockpot vegetables and braising juices £17.50. Two-course evening meal £25.00.*

Free house ~ Licensee Simon Prior ~ Real ale ~ Open 12-11; closed Mon ~ Bar food 12-2 (3.30 Sun), 6-8.45 ~ Restaurant ~ Well behaved children welcome ~ Dogs allowed in bar ~ Wi-fi *Recommended by Tina and David Woods-Taylor, Serena and Adam Furber, Freddie and Sarah Banks, Mark and Sian Edwards*

Also Worth a Visit in Cumbria

Besides the fully inspected pubs, you might like to try these pubs that have been recommended to us and described by readers. Do tell us what you think of them: feedback@goodguides.com

ALLITHWAITE　　　　　SD3876
Pheasant (015395) 32239
B5277; LA11 7RQ Welcoming family-run pub on village outskirts, enjoyable freshly cooked traditional food including blackboard specials and good Sun roasts, smaller appetites catered for, friendly helpful service, Thwaites Original and four other local beers, traditional bar with log fire, two dining areas off; Thurs quiz; children welcome (not in conservatory), dogs in bar, outside tables on deck with Humphrey Head and Morecambe Bay views, open (and food) all day. *(Peter Andrews)*

ALSTON　　　　　NY7146
Angel (01434) 381363
Front Street; CA9 3HU Simple 17th-c inn on steep cobbled street of this charming small Pennine market town, mainly local ales and generously served food including daily specials, reasonable prices, timbers, traditional furnishings and open fires, friendly local atmosphere; children and dogs welcome, tables in sheltered back garden, four bedrooms. *(Comus and Sarah Elliott)*

AMBLESIDE　　　　　NY4008
★**Kirkstone Pass Inn** (015394) 33888
A592 N of Troutbeck; LA22 9LQ Historic inn (Lakeland's highest pub) set in wonderful rugged scenery; flagstones, stripped stone and dark beams, lots of old photographs and bric-a-brac, open fires, enjoyable good value pubby food and changing cumbrian ales, hot drinks; soft background music, daily newspapers; well behaved children and dogs welcome, tables outside with stunning views to Windermere, bedrooms, bunkhouse and camping field, open all day in summer (till 6pm Sun), phone for winter hours. *(Geoff Owen)*

APPLEBY　　　　　NY6819
★**Royal Oak** (01768) 351463
B6542/Bongate; CA16 6UN Attractive and popular old beamed and timbered coaching inn on edge of town, popular generously served food including early-bird and OAP

deals, some themed nights, Black Sheep and one or two local guests, friendly efficient young staff, log fire in panelled bar, lounge with easy chairs and carved settle, traditional snug and restaurant; background music, TV; children and dogs welcome (menus for both), terrace tables, 11 bedrooms and self-catering cottage, good breakfast, open all day from 8am. *(John and Mary Warner)*

ASKHAM　　　　　NY5123
Punch Bowl (01931) 712443
4.5 miles from M6 junction 40; CA10 2PF Attractive 18th-c village pub on edge of green opposite Askham Hall; spacious beamed main bar, locals' bar, snug lounge and dining room, open fires, well kept Hawkshead and guests, decent choice of enjoyable food (all day weekends) from pub standards up, friendly staff; children and dogs welcome, picnic-sets out in front and on small raised terrace, six bedrooms, open all day. *(Martin Day)*

BAMPTON GRANGE　　　　　NY5218
★**Crown & Mitre** (01931) 713225
Opposite church; CA10 2QR Old inn set in attractive country hamlet (*Withnail and I* was filmed around here); opened-up bar with comfortable modern décor and nice log fire, separate dining room, popular good quality home-made evening food from pub favourites up, three well kept changing ales (two in winter) such as Eden, Hesket Newmarket and Keswick, friendly staff; children and dogs welcome, good walks from the door, eight bedrooms, shut lunchtimes (open from 5pm), winter hours may vary. *(Simon Day)*

BARBON　　　　　SD6282
Barbon Inn (015242) 76233
Off A683 Kirkby Lonsdale–Sedbergh; LA6 2LJ Charmingly set 17th-c fell-foot village inn, comfortable old world interior, log fires (one in an old range), some sofas, armchairs and antique carved settles, a couple of local ales and nice selection of wines, good food from bar meals up, restaurant, friendly staff and regulars; children and dogs welcome,

wheelchair access (ladies' loo is upstairs), sheltered pretty garden, good walks, ten bedrooms. *(John Poulter, John Evans)*

BASSENTHWAITE   NY2332
Sun (017687) 76439
Off A591 N of Keswick; CA12 4QP
White-rendered 17th-c village pub; rambling bar with low black beams and blazing winter fires in two stone fireplaces, built-in wall seats and heavy wooden tables, two Jennings ales and a guest, generous food served by friendly staff, cosy dining room; children and dogs welcome, terrace with views of the fells and Skiddaw, open all day Sun, from 4pm other days. *(Miles Green)*

BEETHAM   SD4979
Wheatsheaf (015395) 62123
Village (and inn) signed off A6 S of Milnthorpe; LA7 7AL Striking old building with fine black and white timbered cornerpiece, handily positioned on the old road to the Lake District; traditionally furnished rooms, opened-up lounge with exposed beams and joists, main bar (behind on the right) with open fire, two upstairs dining rooms and residents' lounge, a couple of real ales, several wines by the glass and decent range of malts, enjoyable food including bargain two-course weekday lunch, friendly service; children welcome, dogs in bar, plenty of surrounding walks, pretty 14th-c church opposite, five bedrooms, open (and food) all day. *(Glen and Patricia Fuller)*

BOOT   NY1701
Boot Inn (019467) 23711
Aka Burnmoor; signed just off the Wrynose/Hardknott Pass road; CA19 1TG Beamed country inn with Robinsons ales, decent wines and enjoyable home-made food, friendly helpful staff, blazing log fire in bar, conservatory; children and dogs welcome, garden with play area, lovely surroundings and walks, nine bedrooms, open (and food) all day. *(Neil Allen)*

BOOT   NY1701
★ Brook House (019467) 23288
From Ambleside, W of Hardknott Pass; CA19 1TG Lovely views and walks from this friendly family-run country inn, good sensibly priced food from sandwiches to specials, half a dozen well kept ales such as Barngates, Cumbrian Legendary, Hawkshead and Yates, Weston's cider/perry, decent wines and over 180 whiskies, relaxed comfortable raftered bar with log fire and stuffed animals, smaller plush snug, peaceful separate restaurant; children and dogs welcome, tables on flagstoned terrace, eight reasonably priced bedrooms, good breakfast (for nearby campers too), mountain weather

reports, excellent drying room, handy for Eskdale miniature railway terminus, open all day. *(Tina and David Woods-Taylor)*

BOOT   NY1901
Woolpack (019467) 23230
Bleabeck, midway between Boot and Hardknott Pass; CA19 1TH Last pub before the Hardknott Pass; warm welcoming atmosphere with main walkers' bar and more contemporary café-bar, also an evening restaurant (Fri, Sat), good home-made food including wood-fired pizzas, pies, steaks and daily specials, up to eight well kept ales, real cider and vast range of vodkas and gins; various events including Apr sausage and cider festival, March gin festival and June beer festival; pool room, some live music, big-screen sports TV; children and dogs welcome, mountain-view garden with play area, eight bedrooms, open (and food) all day. *(Tina and David Woods-Taylor)*

BOUTH   SD3285
★ White Hart (01229) 861229
Village signed off A590 near Haverthwaite; LA12 8JB Cheerful bustling old inn with popular generously served food, six well kept mainly local ales and 25 malt whiskies, friendly service, sloping ceilings and floors, old local photographs, farm tools and stuffed animals, collection of long-stemmed clay pipes, two woodburners; background music; children and dogs (in one part of bar) welcome, seats outside and fine surrounding walks, playground opposite, five comfortable bedrooms, adjoining self-catering cottage, open all day, food all day Sun. *(Lee and Liz Potter)*

BOWNESS-ON-
WINDERMERE   SD4096
Royal Oak (015394) 43970
Brantfell Road; LA23 3EG Family-run inn handy for the steamer pier; interconnecting bar, dining room and big games room, old photographs and bric-a-brac, open fire, well kept ales such as Coniston, Jennings, Sharps, Timothy Taylors and Tetleys, generous reasonably priced pub food from baguettes to specials, friendly efficient service; pool, darts and TV; children and dogs welcome, tables out in front, eight bedrooms, open (and food) all day. *(Neil Allen)*

BRAITHWAITE   NY2324
Middle Ruddings (017687) 78436
Middle Ruddings, road running parallel with A66; CA12 5RY Welcoming family-run country inn, good food in bar or carpeted dining conservatory with fine Skiddaw views (no mobile phones), friendly attentive service, three well kept changing local ales and good choice of bottled beers, several

---

We include some hotels with a good bar that offers facilities comparable to those of a pub.

ciders too and nice range of malt whiskies, afternoon teas; children and dogs welcome, garden with terrace picnic-sets, 14 bedrooms, good breakfast, open all day but no food weekday lunchtimes. *(Edward Mirzoeff)*

BRAITHWAITE   NY2323
Royal Oak (017687) 78533
B5292 at top of village; CA12 5SY Busy village pub with warm welcoming atmosphere; four well kept Jennings ales and hearty helpings of well priced traditional food (smaller servings available), prompt helpful service, beamed bar and restaurant; background music, TV, board games; children welcome, no dogs at mealtimes, ten bedrooms, open all day. *(Freddie and Sarah Banks)*

BROUGHTON-IN-FURNESS   SD2187
Manor Arms (01229) 716286
The Square; LA20 6HY End-of-terrace drinkers' pub on quiet sloping square, up to eight well priced changing ales and good choice of ciders, flagstones and nice bow-window seat in front bar, coal fire in big stone fireplace, old photographs and chiming clocks, limited food such as toasties; pool, free wi-fi; children and dogs allowed, bedrooms, open all day. *(Dr Peter Crawshaw)*

BUTTERMERE   NY1716
Bridge Hotel (017687) 70252
Just off B5289 SW of Keswick; CA13 9UZ Welcoming and popular with walkers, hotel-like in feel but with two traditional comfortable beamed bars (dogs allowed in one), four well kept cumbrian ales and good food, more upmarket menu in evening dining room; free wi-fi; children welcome, fell views from flagstoned terrace, 21 bedrooms and six self-catering apartments, open (and food) all day. *(Max Simons)*

CARLISLE   NY4056
Kings Head (01228) 533797
Fisher Street (pedestrianised); CA3 8RF 17th-c split-level pub, lots of beams (some painted), wood and stone floors, friendly bustling atmosphere, well kept Yates Bitter and guests, low-priced pubby lunchtime food from sandwiches and baked potatoes up, cheerful quick service, upstairs dining room; background and summer live music (in courtyard), TV; no children or dogs, historical plaque outside explaining why Carlisle is not in the Domesday Book, open all day. *(Pat and Graham Williamson, Comus and Sarah Elliott)*

CARTMEL   SD3778
Cavendish Arms (015395) 36240
Cavendish Street, off the Square; LA11 6QA Former coaching inn with simply furnished open-plan beamed bar, roaring log fire (even on cooler summer evenings), three or four ales featuring a house beer

from Cumberland, several wines by the glass and good range of gins, decent coffee, friendly staff, enjoyable fairly traditional food from lunchtime ciabattas up, restaurant; children welcome, dogs in bar, tables out in front and behind by stream (must pay in advance if you eat out here), nice village with notable priory church, racecourse and good walks, ten bedrooms – three more above their shop in the square, open (and food) all day. *(Lee and Liz Potter)*

CARTMEL   SD3778
Kings Arms (015395) 33246
The Square; LA11 6QB Bustling 18th-c pub close to the priory; cosy beamed rooms with flagstones and bare boards, log fires, nice mix of furniture including some comfortable sofas, Hawkshead ales and a guest, food from sandwiches to daily specials, friendly but not always speedy service; live weekend bands (pub open till 1am then), free wi-fi; children and dogs welcome, seats outside facing the lovely square, open (and food) all day. *(Gordon and Margaret Ormondroyd)*

CARTMEL   SD3778
★**Royal Oak** (015395) 36259
The Square; LA11 6QB Low-beamed flagstoned inn under same management as the Kings Arms next door; long rustic tables, settles, leather easy chairs and big log fire, cosy nooks, good value food including traditional choices, home-made pizzas, pasta and grills, well kept local ales such as Cumbrian Legendary, Hawkshead and Unsworth's Yard, good choice of wines, welcoming helpful staff; background and weekend live music, two sports TVs, free wi-fi; children and dogs welcome, some seats out in square, nice big riverside garden behind with heated terrace, four neat bedrooms, open (and food) all day. *(Simon Day)*

CASTERTON   SD6379
★**Pheasant** (015242) 71230
A683; LA6 2RX Welcoming 18th-c family-run inn with neatly furnished beamed rooms; highly regarded attractively presented food from imaginative menu, well kept ales including a house beer brewed by Tirril, nice wines and several malt whiskies, friendly helpful staff, arched and panelled restaurant; background music, free wi-fi; children and dogs welcome, a few roadside seats, more in pleasant garden with Vale of Lune views, near church with notable Pre-Raphaelite stained glass and paintings, ten bedrooms, closed Mon lunchtime, otherwise open all day. *(Michael Doswell)*

CASTLE CARROCK   NY5455
Duke of Cumberland (01228) 670341
Geltsdale Road; CA8 9LU Popular village-green pub under friendly family ownership; upholstered wall benches and mix of pubby furniture on slate floor,

coal fire, dining area with old farmhouse tables and chairs, a couple of well kept local ales, enjoyable nicely presented pub food at reasonable prices; children and dogs welcome, open all day weekends (shut Mon lunchtime). *(Mike Benton)*

CHAPEL STILE   NY3205
Wainwrights (015394) 38088
B5343; LA22 9JH Popular white-rendered former farmhouse, half a dozen ales including Jennings and plenty of wines by the glass, enjoyable well priced pubby food from good sandwiches up, friendly helpful service, roomy bar welcoming walkers and dogs, slate floor and good log fire, other spreading carpeted areas with beams, some half-panelling, cushioned settles and mix of dining chairs around wooden tables, old kitchen range; background music, TV and games machines, Tues quiz; children welcome, terrace picnic-sets, fine views, open (and food) all day. *(Simon Day)*

COCKERMOUTH   NY1230
Castle Bar (01900) 829904
Market Place; CA13 9NQ Busy 16th-c pub on three floors, beams, timbers and other original features mixing with modern furnishings, five well kept local beers such as Cumbrian Legendary and Jennings (cheaper 3-7pm Mon-Fri, all day Sun), Weston's cider, enjoyable home-made food including good value Sun roasts in upstairs dining room or in any of the three ground-floor areas, efficient service from friendly young staff; sports TV; children welcome, dogs downstairs, seats on sunny back tiered terrace, open all day. *(Mike and Eleanor Anderson)*

CONISTON   SD3097
Black Bull (015394) 41335/41668
Yewdale Road (A593); LA21 8DU Bustling 17th-c beamed inn brewing its own good Coniston beers; back area (liked by walkers and their dogs) with slate floor, more comfortable carpeted front part with log fire and Donald Campbell memorabilia, enjoyable food including daily specials, friendly helpful staff, lounge with Old Man of Coniston big toe (large piece of stone in the wall), restaurant; they may ask for a credit card if you run a tab; children welcome, plenty of seats in former coachyard, 15 bedrooms, open (and food) all day from 10am, parking not easy at peak times. *(John and Mary Warner)*

CROOK   SD4695
Sun (01539) 821351
B5284 Kendal–Bowness; LA8 8LA End-of-terrace roadside country pub under welcoming licensees; low-beamed bar with dining areas off, stone, wood and carpeted floors, log fires, a house beer from Theakstons and a couple of guests, enjoyable food from sandwiches up including weekday set lunch and themed evenings; children welcome (games for them), dogs

in certain areas, seats out at front by road, open (and food) all day. *(Mike Benton)*

DENT   SD7086
George & Dragon (015396) 25256
Main Street; LA10 5QL Two-bar corner pub in cobbled street, the Dent Brewery tap, with their full range kept well plus real cider and perry, old panelling, partitioned tables and open fires, enjoyable food from snacks up, friendly engaging young staff, steps down to restaurant, games room with pool and juke box; sports TV, free wi-fi; children, walkers and dogs welcome, ten bedrooms, lovely village, open all day. *(1suzinorman)*

DUFTON   NY6825
Stag (017683) 51608
Village signed from A66 at Appleby; CA16 6DB Traditional little 18th-c pub by pretty village's green; friendly licensees and regulars, good reasonably priced home-made food using local ingredients, interesting range of well kept regularly changing beers, two log fires, one in splendid early Victorian kitchen range in main bar, room off to the left, dining room; fortnightly quiz Thurs, darts; children, walkers and dogs welcome, tables out at front and in back garden with lovely hill views, handy for Pennine Way, self-catering cottage, open all day weekends, closed Mon and Tues lunchtimes. *(Alan and Eileen Ormrod)*

ENNERDALE BRIDGE   NY0716
Fox & Hounds (01946) 861373
High Street; CA23 3AR Popular community-owned village pub, clean beamed interior with woodburners, up to five well kept cumbrian ales including local Ennerdale, tasty reasonably priced home-made food (Thurs curries), friendly staff; children and dogs welcome, picnic-sets in streamside garden, three spacious bedrooms, handy for walkers on Coast to Coast path, open all day in summer. *(Max Simons)*

ENNERDALE BRIDGE   NY0615
Shepherds Arms (01946) 861249
Off A5086 E of Egremont; CA23 3AR Friendly well placed walkers' inn by car-free dale, bar with log fire and woodburner, up to five local beers and good generously served home-made food, can provide packed lunches, panelled dining room and conservatory; free wi-fi; children welcome, seats outside by beck, eight bedrooms, good breakfast. *(Martin Day)*

ESKDALE GREEN   NY1200
Bower House (01946) 723244
0.5 miles W of Eskdale Green; CA19 1TD Comfortably modernised 17th-c stone-built inn extended around beamed core, four regional ales including one named for the pub, enjoyable hearty food in bar and biggish restaurant, log fires, friendly atmosphere; Sun quiz, free wi-fi; children

and dogs welcome, sheltered garden with play area, charming spot by cricket field with great view of Muncaster Fell, good walks, bedrooms (some in converted barn), open all day, food all day weekends. *(Mike Benton)*

ESKDALE GREEN NY1400
King George IV (019467) 23470

E of village; CA19 1TS Whitewashed country pub with cheerful beamed and flagstoned bar, log fire in stone fireplace, interesting range of well kept ales and over 100 malt whiskies, sensibly priced plentiful pubby food from sandwiches up, friendly service, restaurant, games room with pool; free wi-fi; children, walkers and dogs welcome, disabled access/loos, nice views from outside tables (road nearby), lots of good walks, bedrooms and self-catering, open (and food) all day.
(Tina and David Woods-Taylor)

FAR SAWREY SD3795
Cuckoo Brow (015394) 43425

B5285 N of village; LA22 0LQ Renovated 300-year-old coaching house in lovely setting; opened-up bar with wood floors and central woodburner, steps down to former stables with tables in stalls, harnesses on rough white walls, even water troughs and mangers, well kept Coniston, Cumbrian Legendary, Loweswater and a couple of local guests, good hearty food served by friendly helpful staff; background music; children, walkers and dogs welcome, seats on nice front lawn, 14 bedrooms, open (and food) all day. *(John and Louise Gittins)*

FAUGH NY5054
String of Horses (01228) 670297

S of village, on left as you go downhill; CA8 9EG Welcoming 17th-c coaching inn with cosy communicating beamed rooms, log fires, oak panelling and some interesting carved furniture, tasty traditional food alongside latin american/mexican dishes, well kept local beers and nice house wines, restaurant; background music, sports TV, free wi-fi; children welcome, no dogs, a few picnic-sets out in front, 11 comfortable bedrooms, good breakfast, closed lunchtimes and all day Mon. *(Heather and Richard Jones)*

FOXFIELD SD2085
★ Prince of Wales (01229) 716238

Opposite station; LA20 6BX Cheery bareboards pub with half a dozen good changing ales including some bargains brewed here and at their associated Tigertops Brewery, bottled imports and real cider too, huge helpings of enjoyable home-made food (lots of unusual pasties), good friendly service and character landlord, hot coal

fire, pub games such as bar billiards, daily papers and beer-related reading matter; live music; children and dogs welcome, four reasonably priced bedrooms, open all day Fri-Sun, from 2.45pm Wed and Thurs, closed Mon, Tues. *(Mike Benton)*

GOSFORTH NY0703
Gosforth Hall (019467) 25322

Off A595 and unclassified road to Wasdale; CA20 1AZ Friendly well run Jacobean inn with interesting history; beamed and carpeted bar (popular with locals), fine plaster coat of arms above woodburner, lounge/reception area with huge fireplace, ales such as Hawkshead, Keswick and Yates, enjoyable home-made food including good range of pies, restaurant; nice big side garden, 22 bedrooms (some in new extension), open all day. *(Darren Ogden)*

GRASMERE NY3406
Travellers Rest (015394) 35604

A591 just N; LA22 9RR Welcoming 16th-c roadside coaching inn with attractive creeper-clad exterior; unmodernised linked rooms, settles, padded benches and other pubby furniture on flagstone or wood floors, local pictures and open fires, well kept Jennings ales and enjoyable reasonably priced food, good friendly service; background music; children and dogs welcome, seats outside with fell views, nine bedrooms, open (and food) all day.
(Gordon and Margaret Ormondroyd)

GREYSTOKE NY4430
Boot & Shoe (017684) 83343

By village green, off B5288; CA11 0TP Cosy two-bar 17th-c inn by green in pretty 'Tarzan' village; low ceilings, exposed brickwork and dark wood, good generously served traditional food including blackboard specials, well kept Black Sheep and local microbrews, bustling friendly atmosphere; live music, Thurs quiz; children (until 8pm) and dogs (in bar) welcome, seats out at front and in back garden, on national cycle route, 4 bedrooms, open all day. *(Max Simons)*

HARTSOP NY4011
Brotherswater Inn (01768) 482239

A592; CA11 0NZ Walkers' and campers' pub in magnificent setting at the bottom of Kirkstone Pass, ales such as Jennings and Thwaites, good choice of malt whiskies and generous helpings of enjoyable reasonably priced food, friendly staff; free wi-fi; dogs welcome, beautiful fells views from picture windows and terrace tables, six bedrooms, bunkhouse and campsite, open all day (from 8am for breakfast). *(Tracey and Stephen Groves)*

If you stay overnight in an inn or hotel, they are allowed to serve you an alcoholic drink at any hour of the day or night.

HAWKSHEAD · SD3598
Kings Arms · (015394) 36372
The Square; LA22 0NZ Old inn with low ceilings, traditional pubby furnishings and log fire, well stocked bar serving local ales such as Cumbrian Legendary and Hawkshead, good variety of enjoyable food from lunchtime sandwiches to daily specials, quick service, side dining area; background music, free wi-fi; children and dogs welcome, terrace overlooking central square of this lovely Elizabethan village, bedrooms, self-catering cottages nearby, free fishing permits for residents, open all day till midnight. *(Sally and David Champion)*

HAWKSHEAD · SD3598
Queens Head · (015394) 36271
Main Street; LA22 0NS Timbered pub in charming village; low-ceilinged bar with heavy bowed black beams, red plush wall seats and stools around hefty traditional tables, decorative plates on panelled walls, open fire, snug little room off and several eating areas, Robinsons ales, a guest beer and good range of wines and whiskies, enjoyable bar food plus more elaborate evening meals, friendly helpful staff; unobtrusive background music, TV, darts; children and dogs welcome, seats outside and pretty window boxes, 13 bedrooms, self-catering cottage, open all day. *(Jeff, Peter Meister)*

HAWKSHEAD · SD3598
Red Lion · (015394) 36213
Main Street; LA22 0NS Cheerful old inn with good selection of well kept local ales including Hawkshead, enjoyable traditional home-made food, original panelling and good log fire; quiz Sun evening; dogs very welcome (menu for them), eight bedrooms (some sloping floors), open all day. *(Max Simons)*

HAWKSHEAD · SD3598
Sun · (015394) 36236
Main Street; LA22 0NT Steps up to welcoming 17th-c beamed inn, Hawkshead, Jennings and a couple of guests, extensive range of gins, popular fairly priced food, sizeable restaurant; TV; children and dogs welcome, tables out in small front courtyard, eight bedrooms, open all day. *(Sue Parry Davies)*

HESKET NEWMARKET · NY3438
Old Crown · (016974) 78288
Village signed off B5299 in Caldbeck; CA7 8JG Straightforward cooperative-owned local in attractive village; small bar with bric-a-brac, mountaineering kit and pictures, woodburner, own good Hesket Newmarket beers (can book brewery tours), generous helpings of freshly made pub food (not Mon), reasonable prices and friendly service, dining room and garden room; folk night first Sun of month, juke box, pool and board games; children and dogs welcome, lovely walking country away from Lake District crowds (near Cumbria Way), open all day Fri-Sun, closed lunchtimes other days. *(Alastair and Sheree Hepburn)*

KENDAL · SD5192
Riflemans Arms · (01539) 241470
Greenside; LA9 4LD Old-fashioned local in village-green setting on edge of town, friendly regulars and staff, Greene King Abbot and guests, no food; Thurs folk night, Sun quiz, pool and darts (regular matches); children and dogs welcome, closed weekday lunchtimes, open all day weekends. *(Daniel King)*

KESWICK · NY2623
Dog & Gun · (017687) 73463
Lake Road; off top end of Market Square; CA12 5BT Smartly furnished beamed town pub; button-back leather banquettes, stools and small round tables on light wood flooring, collection of striking mountain photographs, reasonably priced hearty food including signature goulash (served in two sizes), friendly helpful staff, half a dozen or so well kept ales including Keswick and a house beer (Woof & Bang), log fire; poker night Weds; children till 9.30pm and dogs welcome, open (and food) all day, can get very busy in season. *(Tracey and Stephen Groves, Margaret and Peter Staples)*

KESWICK · NY2623
George · (017687) 72076
St Johns Street; CA12 5AZ Handsome 17th-c coaching inn with open-plan main bar and attractive traditional dark-panelled side room, old-fashioned settles and modern banquettes under black beams, log fires, four Jennings ales and a couple of guests kept well, ten wines by the glass, generous home-made food including signature cow pie and gluten-free dishes, friendly helpful service, restaurant; background music, daily papers; children welcome in eating areas, dogs in bar, 12 bedrooms, open all day. *(Daniel King)*

KESWICK · NY2624
Inn on the Square · (0800) 840 1247
Market Square; CA12 5JF Refurbished hotel with contemporary scandinavian-influenced décor, enjoyable food in front and back bars or steakhouse restaurant, good choice of wines and cocktails, well kept ales such as Keswick, efficient friendly service; children and dogs (in bar areas) welcome, 34 bedrooms, open all day. *(Comus and Sarah Elliott)*

KESWICK · NY2624
Pheasant · (017687) 72219
Crosthwaite Road (A66, a mile out); CA12 5PP Small 17th-c beamed roadside local, generous helpings of popular home-made food at reasonable prices, well kept Jennings and guests, good friendly service,

open fire, dining room; children (if eating) and dogs (in bar) welcome, a few picnic-sets out at front, beer garden up steps behind, bedrooms, near ancient church of St Kentigern, open all day. *(Richard Elliott)*

KESWICK
NY2623
Royal Oak (017687) 74584
Main Street; CA12 5HZ 18th-c coaching house with comfortable connecting rooms, wood flooring, grey-painted half-panelling and open fire, Thwaites ales, decent wines and good choice of sensibly priced food from sandwiches up, also weekday set menu till 5pm, pleasant service; children and dogs welcome, 19 bedrooms, open (and food) all day. *(Comus and Sarah Elliott)*

KESWICK
NY2421
Swinside Inn (017687) 78253
Newlands Valley, just SW; CA12 5UE Friendly pub in peaceful valley setting; carpeted low-beamed bar with upholstered settles and chairs around substantial tables, open fire, well kept Caledonian, Theakstons and a couple of guests, decent choice of reasonably priced pubby food, stripped-floor area beyond with woodburner, pool in back games part; background music and occasional live music, TV, free wi-fi; children and dogs welcome, tables in garden and on upper and lower terraces giving fine views across to the high crags and fells around Rosedale Pike, six bedrooms, big breakfast, open all day. *(Mr and Mrs Richard Osborne)*

KIRKBY LONSDALE
SD6178
Orange Tree (01524) 271716
Fairbank B6254; LA6 2BD Family-run inn acting as tap for Kirkby Lonsdale brewery, well kept guest beers too, a real cider and good choice of wines, carpeted beamed bar with central wooden servery, sporting cartoons and old range, enjoyable good value food in back dining room, friendly young staff; background music, pool and darts; children and dogs welcome, comfortable bedrooms (some in building next door), open all day. *(Steve Whalley)*

KIRKBY LONSDALE
SD6178
★Sun (015242) 71965
Market Street (B6254); LA6 2AU New licensees taking over this popular 17th-c inn as we went to press - news please; rambling beamed bar, flagstones and stripped oak boards, pews, armchairs and cosy window seats, woodburner, big landscapes and country pictures (Turner stayed here in 1818 when painting 'Ruskin's View'), back lounge and dining room with leather banquettes and another woodburner, Hawkshead, Thwaites and a guest beer; background music; children and dogs welcome, attractive comfortable bedrooms, Thurs market day, has opened all day from 9am (3pm Mon).
(Margaret McDonald, Jeremy Snow)

KIRKOSWALD
NY5641
Fetherston Arms (01768) 898284
The Square; CA10 1DQ Busy old stone inn with cosy bar and various dining areas, enjoyable food at reasonable prices including good home-made pies, interesting range of well kept changing beers, friendly helpful staff; bedrooms, nice Eden Valley village. *(Maria and Henry Lazonby)*

LANGDALE
NY2906
Sticklebarn (015394) 37356
By car park for Stickle Ghyll; LA22 9JU Glorious views from this roomy and busy Langdale Valley walkers'/climbers' bar owned and run by the NT; up to five well kept changing ales and a real cider, shortish choice of enjoyable home-made food (some meat from next-door farm), mountaineering photographs, two woodburners; background music (live Sat in season), films shown Tues in upstairs function room; children, dogs and boots welcome, big terrace with inner verandah, outside pizza oven and firepit, open (and food) all day, shuts winter at 6pm (9pm weekends). *(Peter Meister)*

LEVENS
SD4885
Hare & Hounds (015395) 60004
Off A590; LA8 8PN Welcoming old village pub handy for Sizergh Castle (NT), five well kept changing local ales and good home-made pub food including burgers and pizzas, partly panelled low-beamed lounge bar, front tap room with open fire and further seating down steps, also a barn dining room; Weds winter quiz; children, walkers and dogs welcome, disabled loo, good views from front terrace, four bedrooms, open (and food) all day. *(Mr and Mrs Richard Osborne)*

LORTON
NY1526
★Wheatsheaf (01900) 85199
B5289 Buttermere–Cockermouth; CA13 9UW Good local atmosphere in neatly furnished bar with two log fires and vibrant purple walls, Jennings ales and regularly changing guests, several good value wines, popular home-made food (all day Sun) from sandwiches up, smallish restaurant (best to book), affable hard-working landlord and friendly helpful staff; children and dogs welcome, tables out behind and campsite, open all day weekends, closed lunchtimes Tues, Weds (Mon-Thurs lunchtimes in winter). *(Pat and Stewart Gordon)*

LOW HESKET
NY4646
Rose & Crown (01697) 473346
A6 Carlisle–Penrith; CA4 0HG Welcoming 18th-c coaching inn with split-level interior; enjoyable home-made food including several vegetarian dishes and gluten-free choices, Jennings Bitter and guests, good service, pitched-roof dining room with railway memorabilia and central oak tree; background music, TV; children

welcome, closed Mon and lunchtimes apart from Sun. *(Chris Stevenson)*

LOWICK GREEN   SD3084
Farmers Arms (01229) 861853
Just off A5092 SE of village; LA12 8DT
Stable bar with heavy black beams, huge slate flagstones and log fire, cosy corners, some interesting furniture and pictures in plusher hotel lounge/dining area, tasty reasonably priced pubby food (all day weekends) from sandwiches and basket meals up, Thwaites Wainwright, Fullers London Pride and three guests, decent choice of wines by the glass, good friendly service; background music, TV, pool and darts, free wi-fi; children and dogs welcome, ten comfortable bedrooms, good breakfast, open all day. *(Scott and Charlotte Havers)*

MUNGRISDALE   NY3630
Mill Inn (017687) 79632
Off A66 Penrith–Keswick, 1 mile W of A5091 Ullswater turn-off; CA11 0XR
Part 17th-c pub in fine setting below fells with wonderful surrounding walks; neatly kept bar with old millstone built into counter, traditional dark wood furnishings, hunting pictures and woodburner in stone fireplace, Robinsons ales and good range of malt whiskies, traditional food from lunchtime sandwiches and baked potatoes up, friendly staff, separate dining room; darts, winter pool, dominoes; children and dogs welcome, wheelchair access, seats in garden by river, six bedrooms, open all day. *(Tina and David Woods-Taylor)*

NETHER WASDALE   NY1204
★Strands (01946) 726237
SW of Wast Water; CA20 1ET Lovely spot below the remote high fells around Wast Water, own-brew beers and popular good value food from changing menu, well cared-for high-beamed main bar with woodburner, smaller public bar with pool and table football, separate dining room, pleasant staff and relaxed friendly atmosphere; background music; children and dogs welcome, neat garden with terrace and belvedere, 14 bedrooms, good breakfast, open all day. *(Mike Benton)*

NEWBIGGIN   NY5649
Blue Bell (01768) 896615
B6413; CA8 9DH Tiny L-shaped one-room village pub, friendly and unpretentious, with a changing local ale and enjoyable pubby food cooked by landlady, fireplace on right with woodburner; darts and pool; children welcome, good Eden Valley walks, closed weekday lunchtimes. *(Daniel King)*

NEWBY BRIDGE   SD3686
★Swan (015395) 31681
Just off A590; LA12 8NB Substantial hotel (extended 17th-c coaching house) in fine setting by River Leven at southern tip of Windermere; good mix of customers in bustling bar, low ceilings, scrubbed tables on bare boards, cheerful upholstered dining chairs and window seats, pictures and railway posters on pink walls, log fire in little iron fireplace, Jennings, Cumbrian Legendary and a guest, plenty of wines by the glass and good popular food from varied menu (booking advised weekends), friendly smartly dressed staff, more space and another log fire towards the back, main hotel also has a sizeable restaurant; background music; children (till 7pm) and dogs (in bar) welcome, riverside terrace with iron-work chairs and tables, comfortable contemporary bedrooms, open (and food) all day. *(Caroline Sullivan, Margaret McDonald, Peter Barrett, Gordon and Margaret Ormondroyd, Mr and Mrs D Hammond)*

PENRUDDOCK   NY4227
Herdwick (01768) 483007
Off A66 Penrith–Keswick; CA11 0QU
18th-c inn at west edge of village; well kept Thwaites Wainwright and a Marstons-related guest from curved servery, decent wines and enjoyable generously served food, friendly efficient service, carpeted bar with good log fire, dining room with upper gallery, upstairs games room (pool and darts), also a little shop; free wi-fi; children and dogs welcome (they have three friendly dogs), seats out at back, five bedrooms, hearty breakfast, closed Mon and Tues lunchtimes (Mon-Fri lunchtimes in winter). *(Mike Benton)*

POOLEY BRIDGE   NY4724
Crown (017684) 25869
Centre of village; CA10 2NP Recent major refurbishment for this village pub, Thwaites ales and enjoyable reasonably priced food from sandwiches to grills; free wi-fi; children, walkers and dogs welcome, seats outside including roof terrace overlooking river, 17 bedrooms. *(Mike Benton)*

POOLEY BRIDGE   NY4724
Sun (017684) 86205
Centre of village (B5320); CA10 2NN
Friendly roadside local in row of whitewashed cottages, well kept Jennings and guests, decent choice of enjoyable fairly traditional food including hot and cold sandwiches, two bars with steps between (dogs allowed in lower one), restaurant; children welcome, picnic-sets in garden with play fort, nine reasonably priced comfortable bedrooms (three are dog-friendly). *(Mike Benton)*

RAVENSTONEDALE   NY7401
Fat Lamb (015396) 23242
Crossbank; A683 Sedbergh–Kirkby Stephen; CA17 4LL Isolated inn surrounded by great scenery and lovely walks; comfortable old-fashioned feel, pews in beamed bar with fire in traditional black range, interesting local photographs and bird plates, propeller from 1930s biplane over servery, good choice of enjoyable food

from sharing boards to daily specials, can eat in bar or separate dining room (less character), well kept Black Sheep, decent wines and around 60 malt whiskies, friendly helpful staff; background music; children and dogs welcome, disabled facilities, tables out by nature reserve pastures, 12 bedrooms, open all day. *(Graham and Carol Parker)*

ROSTHWAITE   NY2514
Scafell (017687) 77208
B5289 S of Keswick; CA12 5XB 19th-c hotel's big tile-floored back bar useful for walkers, weather forecast board and blazing log fire, up to five well kept local ales in season, 60 malt whiskies and enjoyable food from sandwiches up, afternoon teas, also cocktail bar/sun lounge and dining room, friendly helpful staff; background music, pool; children and dogs welcome, tables out overlooking beck, 23 smart contemporary bedrooms, open all day. *(Miles Green)*

RULEHOLME   NY5060
Golden Fleece (01228) 573686
Signed off A689; CA6 4NF Hospitable whitewashed inn with series of softly lit linked rooms, good interesting food, a couple of local ales and good range of wines by the glass, friendly attentive service; children welcome, seven comfortable well equipped bedrooms, hearty cumbrian breakfast, handy for Hadrian's Wall and Carlisle Airport, open all day weekends, closed weekday lunchtimes, all Mon. *(Daniel King)*

SANDFORD   NY7316
Sandford Arms (01768) 351121
Village and pub signposted just off A66 W of Brough; CA16 6NR Neatly modernised former 18th-c farmhouse in peaceful village, quite a choice of good food (all day weekends Apr-Oct) from chef-landlord, friendly helpful service, L-shaped part-carpeted main bar with stripped beams and stonework, well kept ales including a house beer from Tirril, comfortable raised and balustraded eating area, more formal dining room and second flagstoned bar, woodburner; background music; children and dogs welcome, seats in front garden and covered courtyard, four bedrooms, closed Tues and lunchtime Weds. *(Chris Stevenson)*

SANTON BRIDGE   NY1101
Bridge Inn (01946) 726221
Off A595 at Holmrook or Gosforth; CA19 1UX Old inn set in charming riverside spot with fell views, bustling beamed and timbered bar, some booths around stripped-pine tables, log fire, half a dozen well kept ales such as Jennings, enjoyable food (booking advised) including

blackboard specials and Sun carvery, friendly helpful staff, separate dining room and small reception hall with open fire and daily papers; background music, free wi-fi, World's Biggest Liar competition (Nov); children and dogs (in bar) welcome, seats outside by quiet road, plenty of walks, 16 bedrooms, open (and food) all day, breakfast for non-residents. *(Shona and Jimmy McDuff)*

SATTERTHWAITE   SD3392
Eagles Head (01229) 860237
S edge of village; LA12 8LN Nice little pub prettily placed on edge of beautiful Grizedale Forest (visitor centre nearby); low black beams and comfortable furnishings, various odds and ends including antlers, horsebrasses, decorative plates and earthenware, old tiled floor, woodburner, four ales such as Barngates, Coniston, Cumbrian Legendary and Hawkshead, popular pubby food from shortish menu including good home-made pies, friendly welcoming staff; occasional live music, local artwork for sale; children, dogs and muddy boots welcome, picnic-sets in attractive tree-shaded courtyard garden, open all day summer, closed Mon in winter, food all day weekends. *(Sally and David Champion)*

SCALES   NY3426
White Horse (017687) 79883
A66 W of Penrith; CA12 4SY Traditional Lakeland pub in lovely setting below Blencathra; log fire in flagstoned beamed bar, little snug and another room with black range, three real ales such as Cross Bay, Cumberland and Tirril, good pubby food (all day weekends); board games, free wi-fi; children and dogs welcome, picnic-sets out in front, bunkhouse, open all day. *(Max Simons)*

SEATHWAITE   SD2295
Newfield Inn (01229) 716208
Duddon Valley, near Ulpha (not Seathwaite in Borrowdale); LA20 6ED Friendly 16th-c whitewashed stone cottage under newish ownership, bar with unusual slate floor and interesting pictures, woodburner, four well kept changing local beers and good reasonably priced home-made food from sandwiches up; children and dogs welcome, tables in nice garden with hill views and play area, good walks, open (and food) all day. *(Dr Peter Crawshaw)*

SEDBERGH   SD6592
Red Lion (015396) 20433
Finkle Street (A683); LA10 5BZ Cheerful little beamed local opposite church, down to earth and comfortable, with good value generous home-made food including blackboard specials and nice fruit pies, well kept Jennings and other

---

If we know a pub has an outdoor play area for children, we mention it.

Marstons-related beers, good open fire; quiz and music nights, sports TV, free wi-fi; children and dogs welcome, gets very busy weekends, closed Mon. *(Derek Stafford)*

THRELKELD NY3225
Salutation (017687) 79614
Old Main Road, bypassed by A66 W of Penrith; CA12 4SQ Friendly modernised former 17th-c coaching inn; two or three changing ales and good range of ciders and wines by the glass, enjoyable sensibly priced pubby food (not Mon, Tues), low beams and open fire, raftered restaurant with high-backed leather chairs at light wood tables, games area with pool, darts and TV; background music, free wi-fi; dogs welcome, views from pleasant outside area, five bedrooms and self-catering cottage, sister pub to nearby Horse & Farrier (see Main Entries), open (and food) all day weekends. *(Dr Peter Crawshaw)*

TORVER SD2894
Church House (01539) 449159
A593/A5084 S of Coniston; LA21 8AZ Friendly 14th-c coach house with pubby bar, heavy beams (some painted), straightforward tables and chairs on slate floors, Lakeland bric-a-brac and big log fire in sizeable stone fireplace, enjoyable home-made food (all day weekends) from sandwiches and sharing plates up, four changing ales and seven wines by the glass from barrel-fronted counter, comfortable lounge, separate dining room; occasional live music; children and dogs (in bar) welcome, lawned garden, four bedrooms, standing for five caravans/motor homes, good nearby walks to Lake Coniston, open all day. *(Paul Scofield)*

TORVER SD2894
Wilson Arms (015394) 41237
A593; LA21 8BB Old family-run roadside inn with adjoining deli; beams, nice log fire and one or two modern touches, well kept cumbrian ales and good locally sourced food cooked to order in bar or dining room, friendly service; free wi-fi; children and dogs welcome, hill views (including Old Man of Coniston) from tables in large garden, area with pigs, goats and ducks, seven bedrooms and three holiday cottages, open (and food) all day. *(Paul Scofield)*

TROUTBECK NY4103
Mortal Man (015394) 33193
A592 N of Windermere; Upper Road; LA23 1PL Beamed and partly panelled bar with cosy room off, log fires, well kept local ales including a house beer from Hawkshead, several wines by the glass and well liked food in bar and picture-window restaurant; folk night Sun, open mike Tues, quiz Weds, storytelling Thurs, free wi-fi; children and dogs welcome, great views from sunny garden, lovely village and surrounding walks, bedrooms, open all day. *(Christian Mole)*

TROUTBECK NY4103
Queens Head (015394) 32404
A592 N of Windermere; Upper Road; LA23 1PW This 17th-c beamed coaching inn reopened recently after a devastating fire – reports please.

TROUTBECK NY3827
Troutbeck Inn (017684) 83635
A5091/A66; CA11 0SJ Former railway hotel with small bar, lounge and log-fire restaurant, a couple of Jennings ales and good food cooked by landlord-chef, efficient friendly service; children and dogs (in bar) welcome, seven bedrooms plus three self-catering cottages in converted stables, open all day in season. *(Max Simons)*

ULDALE NY2436
Snooty Fox (016973) 71479
Village signed off B5299 W of Caldbeck; CA7 1HA Comfortable and welcoming two-bar village inn; ample helpings of good-quality home-cooked food (not Weds) using local ingredients, up to four well kept changing ales including a summer brew named for the pub, decent selection of whiskies, friendly attentive staff, fox hunting memorabilia; winter pool, free wi-fi; children welcome in dining areas, dogs in snug, nice location with garden at back, three bedrooms, closed lunchtimes. *(Sandra Morgan)*

ULVERSTON SD2878
★**Farmers Arms** (01229) 584469
Market Place; LA12 7BA Attractively modernised convivial town pub; front bar with comfortable sofas, contemporary wicker chairs and original fireplace, quickly changing ales and a dozen wines by the glass, good varied choice of popular, fair-priced food from sandwiches and deli boards up, second bar leading to big raftered dining area (children here only); unobtrusive background music, Thurs quiz; seats on attractive heated front terrace, lots of colourful tubs and hanging baskets, Thurs market day (pub busy then), bedrooms and self-catering cottages, open all day from 9am. *(Alan and Linda Blackmore)*

UNDERBARROW SD4692
Punchbowl (01539) 568234
From centre of Kendal at town hall, turn left into Beast Banks signed for Underbarrow, then follow Underbarrow Road; LA8 8HQ Small friendly village local with open-plan beamed bar, mix of furniture including leather sofas on stone floor, woodburner, Hawkshead and a couple of local guests, good choice of enjoyable freshly prepared food, mezzanine restaurant; free wi-fi; children and dogs (in bar) welcome, picnic-sets and covered balcony outside, handy for walkers, open all day Fri-Sun and Weds, closed Tues. *(Daniel King)*

WARWICK-ON-EDEN   NY4656
Queens Arms (01228) 562283
*2 miles from M6, junction 43; signed off
A69 towards Hexham; CA4 8PA* Neatly
updated village inn with well kept ales
including Thwaites and several good value
wines by the glass, popular freshly made food
from open sandwiches up including set lunch,
prompt friendly service even when busy;
children and dogs welcome, nice garden with
terrace and play area, comfortable bedrooms,
open (and food) all day. *(Michael Doswell)*

WASDALE HEAD   NY1807
Wasdale Head Inn (019467) 26229
NE of Wast Water; CA20 1EX Mountain
hotel worth knowing for its stunning
fellside setting; roomy walkers' bar with
welcoming fire, several local ales and
good choice of wines, ample helpings of
enjoyable home-made food; residents' bar,
lounge and panelled restaurant; children
and dogs welcome, nine bedrooms, self-
catering apartments in converted barn and
camping, open all day. *(Chris Stevenson)*

WETHERAL   NY4654
Wheatsheaf (01228) 560686
Handy for M6 junctions 42/43; CA4 8HD
Popular 19th-c pub in pretty village,
three well kept changing ales and
enjoyable home-made food including daily
specials, good friendly service; Tues quiz,
sports TV; children and dogs welcome,
picnic-sets in small garden, open all day,
no food Mon, Tues. *(Charles Welch)*

WINDERMERE   SD4198
Crafty Baa (015394) 88002
*Victoria Street, beside the Queens;
LA23 1AB* Small atmospheric bar with
great selection of craft beers on tap and
in bottles (listed on blackboards), good
range of other drinks too including decent
coffee, enjoyable food from snacks to
more substantial cheese and charcuterie
combinations served on slates, friendly
knowledgeable staff, rustic décor with
bare boards, exposed stone walls and log
fire, some quirky touches, more room
upstairs; background music; dogs welcome
(theirs is Henry), a few seats out at front,
open (and food) all day. *(Mike Benton)*

WREAY   NY4349
Plough (016974) 75770
*Village signed from A6 N of Low Hesket;
CA4 0RL* Pretty village's welcoming
18th-c beamed pub, modernised split-level
interior with pine tables and chairs on
wood or flagstone floors, some exposed
stonework, woodburner, good choice of
enjoyable freshly prepared food (not Mon)
including specials, well kept Cumberland,
Hawkshead and a guest from brick-fronted
canopied bar, efficient friendly service;
live music (see website), quiz Mon
evening; children welcome, closed Mon
lunchtime and Tues. *(Sandra Hollies)*

Derbyshire

KEY ★ Star Pub  Top Quality Food 🍺 Great Beer

🍷 Good Wines £ Bargain Meals 🛏 Good Bedrooms ⅋ Serves Food

 ASHOVER   SK3462   Map 7

Old Poets Corner 🍺 £ 🛏
(01246) 590888 – www.oldpoets.co.uk

Butts Road (B6036, off A632 Matlock–Chesterfield); S45 0EW

**Cheerful owners keep interesting real ales (some own brew)
and ciders in characterful village; hearty food; bedrooms**

The enthusiastic and hard-working licensees here are the reason this unpretentious local does so well. And, of course, their own brews are quite a draw: Ashover Coffin Lane Stout, Light Rale, Littlemoor Citra, Poets Tipple, Red Lion and Zoo. Guests from breweries include Abbeydale, Blackjack, Blue Monkey, Gadds, Harviestoun, Kelham Island, Oakham, Roosters, Salopian, Sarah Hughes and Titanic, and they hold beer festivals in March and October. Also, a terrific choice of 12 farm ciders, a dozen fruit wines, 20 malt whiskies and belgian beers. The informal bar has an easy-going atmosphere and a mix of chairs and pews, while a small room opening off the bar has a stack of newspapers and vintage comics; background music. French doors lead to a tiny balcony with a couple of tables. They hold regular acoustic, folk and blues sessions (posters advertise forthcoming events) as well as quiz nights, poetry evenings and morris dancers. The bedrooms are attractive and there's a holiday cottage sleeping up to eight.

⅋ Food is honest and reasonably priced: sandwiches and baguettes, breaded brie wedges, crispy stuffed potato skins, beef cobbler, burger with toppings and chips, butternut squash wellington, a trio of sausages, and Sunday roasts; curry night is Sunday. *Benchmark main dish: steak in ale pie £11.25. Two-course evening meal £16.00.*

Own brew ~ Licensees Kim and Jackie Beresford ~ Real ale ~ Open 12-midnight ~ Bar food 12-2, 6-9; 12-9 Sat; 12-4, 6-9 Sun ~ Restaurant ~ Children welcome away from bar ~ Dogs allowed in bar and bedrooms ~ Wi-fi ~ Acoustic evenings Tues, Sun; quiz Weds ~ Bedrooms: £65/£75 *Recommended by Andrew Vincent, Miles Green, Malcolm Phillips, Charlie Stevens, Amanda Shipley, John Harris*

 BRADWELL   SK1782   Map 7

Samuel Fox  🍷 🛏
(01433) 621562 – www.samuelfox.co.uk

B6049; S33 9JT

**Friendly pub in the Hope Valley with real ales and fine food,
good service and neat bars; comfortable bedrooms**

If you want to make the most of the surrounding Peak District National Park, stay in the comfortable, quiet bedrooms here. Downstairs, the open-plan bar and interlinked dining rooms have a wide mix of customers and, although there's quite an emphasis on the interesting food, regulars do pop in for a pint of local ale and a chat. Red and dogtooth upholstered tub chairs are grouped around tables on striped carpet or wooden flooring, country scenes hang on papered walls above a grey dado, curtains are neatly swagged and there are several open brick fireplaces. Intrepid Blonde and Pennine Best Bitter on handpump, ten wines by the glass from a good list, and a farm cider served by helpful, courteous staff. The neat restaurant is similarly furnished but with red plush dining chairs. At the front of the building, white metal seating is arranged around small ornamental trees and there are some wooden seats too. No dogs inside. Wheelchair access.

Cooked by the chef-landlord, the modern british food is available as a two- or three-course fixed-price menu. Dishes include duck and pork terrine with pistachios and pickled beetroot, cured sea trout with fennel and orange, curried chickpeas with sweet potato, apple and cauliflower, beer-battered haddock and chips, slow-roasted pork belly with butternut squash, gnocchi, sage and cider sauce, braised beef cheek in ale with creamed potato and mushrooms, 28-day-aged steak with café de paris butter and chips, and puddings such as sticky toffee pudding with stout ice-cream and amaretto and blueberry trifle; they also offer a cheaper early-bird set menu (6-7pm). *Benchmark main dish: two-course set menu £27.00. Two-course evening meal £27.00.*

Free house ~ Licensee James Duckett ~ Real ale ~ Open 6-11 Weds-Sat; 1-10 Sun; closed Mon, Tues (except for residents); lunchtimes except Sun; first two weeks Jan ~ Bar food 6-9 Weds-Sat; 1-8 Sun ~ Restaurant ~ Children welcome ~ Wi-fi ~ Bedrooms: £100/£130 *Recommended by Miles Green, Colin and Daniel Gibbs, Geoff and Ann Marston, Alexandra and Richard Clay*

BRETTON
Barrel

SK2078 Map 7

(01433) 630856 – www.thebarrelinn.co.uk

Signposted from Foolow, which itself is signposted from A623 just E of junction with B6465 to Bakewell; can also be reached from either the B6049 at Great Hucklow, or the B6001 via Abney, from Leadmill just S of Hathersage; S32 5QD

Remote dining pub with traditional décor, popular food and friendly staff; bedrooms

Our readers enjoy their visits here and have praised the clean and comfortable bedrooms; good surrounding walks. Stubs of massive knocked-through stone walls divide the place into several spic and span areas. The cosy dark oak-beamed bar is charmingly traditional with gleaming copper and brass, a warming fire, patterned carpet, low doorways and stools lined up at the counter. Marstons Pedigree and EPA and Wychwood Hobgoblin on handpump, 28 malt whiskies, a farm cider and wines by the glass, all served by friendly, smartly dressed staff; maybe background radio. The outdoor seats on the front terrace by the road and in a courtyard garden are nicely sheltered from the inevitable breeze at this height, and on a clear day you can see five counties.

As well as seasonal game, the pubby food includes sandwiches, prawn cocktail, stilton mushrooms, toad in the hole with onion gravy, mediterranean vegetable pasta with fresh pesto, gammon and free-range eggs, lambs liver, onion and bacon with rich gravy, beef-battered fresh fish and chips, half a roast chicken with sage and onion stuffing, and puddings. *Benchmark main dish: steak in ale pie £12.60. Two-course evening meal £19.00.*

Free house ~ Licensee Philip Cone ~ Real ale ~ Open 11-3, 6-11; may open longer in summer; 11-11 Sat, Sun ~ Bar food 12-2, 6-9; 12-9 Sat, Sun ~ Well behaved children welcome ~ Wi-fi ~ Bedrooms: /£90 *Recommended by Simon Day, Ann and Tony Bennett-Hughes, Sue Parry Davies, Pieter and Janet Vrancken, Beverley and Andy Butcher, Andrew Wall, Anne Taylor*

CHELMORTON
SK1170 Map 7

Church Inn 🍺 £ 🛏

(01298) 85319 – www.thechurchinn.co.uk

Village signposted off A5270, between A6 and A515 SE of Buxton; keep on up through village towards church; SK17 9SL

Cosy, convivial, traditional inn beautifully set in High Peak walking country; good value food; bedrooms

Long-standing, experienced and convivial licensees run this warmly friendly old inn (the landlady was actually born in the village) and our readers continue to praise all aspects of the place. The chatty, low-ceilinged bar has an open fire and is traditionally furnished with built-in cushioned benches and simple chairs around polished cast-iron-framed tables (a couple still with their squeaky sewing treadles). Shelves of books, Tiffany-style lamps and house plants in the curtained windows, atmospheric Dales photographs and prints, and a coal-effect stove in the stripped-stone end wall all add a cosy feel. Abbeydale Moonshine, Kelham Island Pale Rider, Marstons Pedigree, Thwaites Original and a guest from Peak on handpump and nine wines by the glass; darts in a tile-floored games area on the left, TV and board games. The inn is opposite a mainly 18th-c church and is prettily tucked into woodland with fine views over the village and hills beyond from good teak tables on a two-level terrace. The cottagey bedrooms are comfortable and the breakfasts good.

Tasty, fairly priced food includes sandwiches, black pudding fritters with spicy chutney, prawn cocktail, vegetable rogan josh, lasagne, chicken wrapped in bacon with a creamy mushroom sauce, gammon with egg and pineapple, duck with orange and Grand Marnier sauce, pork medallions with wholegrain mustard sauce, beef in Guinness with stilton dumpling, and puddings. *Benchmark main dish: rabbit pie £13.95. Two-course evening meal £19.00.*

Free house ~ Licensees Julie and Justin Satur ~ Real ale ~ Open 12-11 ~ Bar food 12-8 ~ Children welcome ~ Dogs allowed in bar ~ Wi-fi ~ Quiz night Mon ~ Bedrooms: /£80 *Recommended by Kathleen I'Anson, Malcolm and Pauline Pellatt, Jane Rigby, Jane and Philip Saunders*

CHINLEY
SK0382 Map 7

Old Hall ★ 🍺 🛏

(01663) 750529 – www.old-hall-inn.co.uk

Village signposted off A6 (very sharp turn) E of New Mills; also off A624 N of Chapel-en-le-Frith; Whitehough Head Lane, off B6062; SK23 6EJ

Fine range of ales and ciders in splendid building with lots to look at and good country food; comfortable bedrooms

There's so much going for this wonderful old place, it's no wonder we get such enthusiastic reports from our readers. The warm bar – basically four small friendly rooms opened into a single area tucked behind a massive central chimney – contains open fires, broad flagstones, red patterned carpet, sturdy country tables and a couple of long pews and various other seats. Marstons Saddle Tank and guests from breweries such as Abbeydale, Howard Town, Marble, Kelham Island, Peak, RedWillow, Storm and Whim on handpump, as well as some interesting lagers on tap, 20 malt whiskies, eight cask ciders, a rare range of bottled ciders and around 50 bottled (mostly belgian) beers. They hold a beer festival with music in September. Also, around a dozen new world wines by the glass and friendly, helpful service. The dining room is surprisingly grand with a great stone chimney soaring into high eaves, refectory tables on a parquet floor, lovely old mullioned windows and a splendid minstrels' gallery. The pretty walled garden has picnic-sets under sycamore trees. Some of the attractive bedrooms look over the garden and there's also a self-catering cottage.

Rewarding food includes sandwiches, pressed ham hock with rhubarb chutney, corn beef fritters with a poached egg and home-made brown sauce, cheese, leek and apple pie, lamb and rosemary burger with toppings, coleslaw and triple-cooked chips, braised beef cheek with parsnip purée, spring onion hash cakes and red wine jus, guinea fowl confit with tarragon mash and madeira sauce, cod fillet with parmentier potatoes and black kale, and puddings such as stem ginger cheesecake with toffee apple gel and orange-infused poached pear with chocolate sauce and brandy-soaked raisins. *Benchmark main dish: steak in ale pudding £13.00. Two-course evening meal £20.00.*

Free house ~ Licensee Daniel Capper ~ Real ale ~ Open 12-midnight (11 Sun) ~ Bar food 12-2, 5-9 (9.30 Fri, Sat); 12-7.30 Sun ~ Restaurant ~ Children welcome ~ Dogs allowed in bar ~ Wi-fi ~ Bedrooms: £79/£95 *Recommended by Mary Joyce, Susan Jackman, Ross Balaam, Martine and Lawrence Sanders, Lindy Andrews*

FENNY BENTLEY
SK1750   Map 7
Coach & Horses
(01335) 350246 – www.coachandhorsesfennybentley.co.uk
A515 N of Ashbourne; DE6 1LB

Cosy inn with pretty country furnishings, roaring open fires and food all day

The traditional interior here has all the trappings you'd expect of a country pub, from roaring log fires, exposed brick hearths and flagstone floors to black beams hung with pewter mugs, and hand-made pine furniture that includes wall settles with floral-print cushions. There's also a conservatory dining room and a cosy front dining room. Marstons Pedigree and a changing guest such as Abbeydale Moonshine on handpump, a couple of farm ciders and seven wines by the glass; the landlord is knowledgeable about malt whiskies – he stocks around two dozen; quiet background music. A side garden by an elder tree (with views across fields) has seats and tables, and there are modern tables and chairs under cocktail parasols on a front roadside terrace. It's a short walk from the Tissington Trail, a popular cycling/walking path along a former railway line, which is best joined at the nearby picture-book village of Tissington. No dogs inside.

Popular food includes sandwiches, thai-style fishcakes with sweet chilli dip, pear, stilton and walnut salad, chicken stuffed with pork mince and cheddar, wrapped in bacon in a creamy leek sauce, spicy lentil and sweet potato cakes on caesar salad, rack of lamb and lamb belly with cranberry and rosemary sauce, sea bass fillets on ratatouille with balsamic sauce, and puddings. *Benchmark main dish: gammon and egg £10.95. Two-course evening meal £20.00.*

Free house ~ Licensees John and Matthew Dawson ~ Real ale ~ Open 11-11; 12-10.30 Sun ~ Bar food 12-9; 12-3, 6-9 Tues ~ Restaurant ~ Children welcome ~ Wi-fi *Recommended by Frances Parsons, Jim King, David and Leone Lawson, Frank and Marcia Pelling*

Pubs close to motorway junctions are listed at the back of the book.

GREAT LONGSTONE
Crispin

SK1971 Map 7

(01629) 640237 – www.thecrispingreatlongstone.co.uk

Main Street; village signed from A6020, N of Ashford in the Water; DE45 1TZ

Spotless traditional pub with emphasis on good, fairly priced pubby food; good drinks choice too

Good walks in the heart of the Peak District draw lovers of the outdoors here. In warm weather there are seats in the garden and picnic-sets out in front (one under a heated canopy) set well back above the quiet lane; the pub is usefully open all day. Décor throughout is traditional: brass or copper implements, decorative plates, a photo collage of regulars, horsebrasses on the beams in the red ceiling, cushioned built-in wall benches and upholstered chairs and stools around polished tables on red carpet, and a fire. A corner area is snugly partitioned off and there's a separate, more formal dining room on the right; darts, board games and maybe faint background music. Robinsons Dizzy Blonde, Double Hop, Magnum IPA, Unicorn and White Label Porter on handpump, Weston's Old Rosie cider and quite a choice of wines and whiskies.

The marvellous-value OAP lunch deal is still available alongside sandwiches, omelettes, chilli con carne, beer-battered fish and chips, burgers with toppings and chips, a pie of the day, show-cooked lamb shank, steaks with trimmings, and puddings. *Benchmark main dish: rack of lamb with leek and potato gratin £15.95. Two-course evening meal £22.00.*

Robinsons ~ Tenant Paul Rowlinson ~ Real ale ~ Open 12-3, 6-11; 12-midnight Sat; 12-11 Sun ~ Bar food 12-2.30, 6-9 ~ Restaurant ~ Children welcome ~ Dogs welcome ~ Wi-fi *Recommended by Malcolm and Pauline Pellatt, Jo Garnett, Daniel King, Heather and Richard Jones*

HASSOP
Old Eyre Arms

SK2272 Map 7

(01629) 640390 – www.eyrearms.com

B6001 N of Bakewell; DE45 1NS

Comfortable old farmhouse with long-serving owners, decent food and beer, and pretty views from the garden

At any time of year, this 17th-c former coaching inn is a fine sight – the hanging baskets make a lovely display in the summer and the creeper bursts into spectacular colour in the autumn; the delightful garden (with its gurgling fountain) looks straight out to fine Peak District countryside. The low-ceilinged beamed rooms are snug and cosy with log fires and traditional furnishings that include cushioned oak settles, comfortable plush chairs, a longcase clock, old pictures and lots of brass and copper. The tap room, snug and lounge are all traditionally furnished with cushioned oak benches, old pictures and an impressive collection of brass and copper; the tap room also has an impressive array of teapots. Darts and dominoes. Brunswick Usual, Peak Swift Nick and guests such as Bradfield Farmers Blonde and Kelham Island Easy Rider on handpump, ten wines by the glass, ten gins and 20 malt whiskies. Above the stone fireplace in the lounge is a painting of the Eyre coat of arms. Chatsworth House and Haddon Hall are both close by – as is the Monsal Trail cycling/walking path.

Good country cooking (using some home-grown produce) includes sandwiches and toasties, prawn cocktail, fishcakes with tartare sauce, bulgar wheat and walnut casserole, lasagne, steak and kidney pie, venison steak with cranberry, port and orange sauce, fresh fillet of lemon sole with parsley butter, chicken stuffed with leeks and stilton in a creamy sauce, and puddings. *Benchmark main dish: rabbit pie £17.95. Two-course evening meal £16.00.*

Free house ~ Licensees Nick and Lynne Smith ~ Real ale ~ Open 12-3, 6-11; 12-10.30 Sun; closed Mon evening ~ Bar food 12-2 (2.30 Sat), 6-9; 12-8 Sun ~ Children welcome ~ Dogs allowed in bar ~ Wi-fi *Recommended by Caroline Prescott, Emma Scofield, Donald Allsopp, John and Delia Franks, Alan and Linda Blackmore, Ann and Tony Bennett-Hughes*

HATHERSAGE
SK2380 Map 7
Plough 🏅 ♀ 🛏

(01433) 650319 – www.theploughinn-hathersage.co.uk
Leadmill; B6001 towards Bakewell; S32 1BA

Comfortable dining pub with well presented food, beer and wine and seats in a waterside garden; bedrooms

With well equipped bedrooms in a barn conversion (they make a good base for exploring the Peak District) and much enjoyed food, our readers make the most of their weekends here. The cosy, traditionally furnished rooms have rows of dark wooden chairs and tables (with cruets showing the emphasis on dining) and a long banquette running almost the length of one wall, and bright tartan and oriental patterned carpets; also, three woodburning stoves and decorative plates on terracotta walls. The neat dining room is slightly more formal. They have a good wine list (with 21 by the glass), 20 malt whiskies and Abbeydale Moonshine and Bradfield Yorkshire Farmer on handpump; quiet background music. The seats on the terrace have wonderful valley views and the nine-acre grounds are on the banks of the River Derwent – the pretty garden slopes down to the water.

Rewarding food includes sandwiches, an antipasti board, whitebait with pink peppercorn and lemon mayonnaise, crab two-ways (brown meat and rillettes) with a cucumber and melon sauce, home-made stone-baked pizzas with a wide choice of toppings, pasta with marinated cherry tomato, piquillo pepper and mozzarella sauce, sea trout with wild garlic gnocchi and braised baby gem, venison loin with dauphinoise potatoes and a port and redcurrant sauce, and puddings such as rhubarb flapjack crumble with stem ginger anglaise and white chocolate and strawberry cannelloni with pistachio nuts. *Benchmark main dish: rib-eye steak with trimmings and fries £23.00. Two-course evening meal £24.00.*

Free house ~ Licensees Bob, Cynthia and Elliott Emery ~ Real ale ~ Open 11-11; 12-10.30 Sun ~ Bar food 11.30-9.30; 12-8.30 Sun ~ Restaurant ~ Children welcome ~ Dogs welcome ~ Wi-fi ~ Bedrooms: £85/£110 *Recommended by Richard Cole, Tim and Sarah Smythe-Brown, Ben and Diane Bowie, Peter Wilson, Sue and Martin Neville, Patricia and Anton Larkham*

HAYFIELD
SK0387 Map 7
Royal 🛏

(01663) 742721 – www.theroyalathayfield.com
Market Street; SK22 2EP

Big, bustling inn with fine panelled rooms, friendly service and thoughtful choice of drinks and food; bedrooms

This is a traditional stone pub at the heart of an attractive village by the River Sett. The oak-panelled bar and lounge areas have open fires, a fine collection of seats from long settles with pretty scatter cushions through elegant upholstered dining chairs to tub chairs and chesterfields, around an assortment of solid tables on rugs and flagstones; house plants and daily papers. Happy Valley Sworn Secret, Marstons Pedigree, Salopian Shropshire

Gold, Thwaites Original and a guest from Howard Town on handpump, ten wines by the glass and two farm ciders; background music, TV and board games. The sunny front terrace is spacious and the bedrooms are well appointed and comfortable; breakfasts are good.

🍴 Quite a choice of well liked food includes sandwiches, ham hock terrine with pineapple and pickled vegetables, black pudding with a poached egg and mustard dressing, sharing platters, wild mushroom arancini with truffle oil and mushroom ketchup, a curry of the day, beer-battered fish and chips, pork belly with pork faggot, ham hock bubble and squeak and raspberry and elderflower dressing, and puddings such as lemon tart and a cheesecake of the day; they also offer a two- and three-course fixed lunch menu. *Benchmark main dish: pie of the day and chips £10.95. Two-course evening meal £14.50.*

Free house ~ Licensees Mark and Lisa Miller ~ Real ale ~ Open 11-11 (11.30 Sat); 11-10.30 Sun ~ Bar food 12-2.30, 5-8.30; 12-9 Sat; 12-7 Sun ~ Children welcome ~ Dogs allowed in bar and bedrooms ~ Wi-fi ~ Bedrooms: £65/£85 *Recommended by Ruth May, Hilary and Neil Christopher, Carol and Barry Craddoc,*

HURDLOW

SK1265 Map 7

Royal Oak 🍺

(01298) 83288 – www.peakpub.co.uk
Monyash–Longnor Road, just off A515 S of Buxton; SK17 9QJ

Bustling, carefully renovated pub in rural spot with beamed rooms, friendly staff and tasty, all-day food

A well earned pint and an honest meal is just what tired walkers and cyclists come for here. It's a hospitable pub and the two-roomed beamed bar has an open fire in a stone fireplace, lots of copper kettles, bed warming pans, horsebrasses and country pictures, cushioned wheelback chairs and wall settles around dark tables, and stools against the counter. Friendly staff serve Peak Bakewell Best Bitter, Sharps Doom Bar, Whim Hartington Bitter and Wincle Sir Philip on handpump, seven wines by the glass and two farm ciders; background music. The attractive dining room has country dining chairs, wheelback chairs, a cushioned pine settle in one corner on bare floorboards, pretty curtains and another open fire. For large groups, there's also a flagstoned cellar room with benches on either side of long tables. The terraced garden has plenty of seats and picnic-sets on grass. Both the self-catering barn with bunk bedrooms and the campsite are very popular.

🍴 Well presented food includes sandwiches, game terrine and tomato chutney, prawn cocktail, sharing platters, roast vegetable and stilton tart, local sausages on leek mash with black pudding fritter and gravy, blackened cajun salmon with lemon oil dressing, thai green chicken curry, lambs liver with smoked bacon, onions on leek mash and red wine gravy, rump steak and barbecue rib combo with coleslaw and chips, pork fillet with black pudding mash and Grand Marnier cream sauce, and puddings such as sticky toffee pudding with toffee sauce and apple and mixed berry crumble with custard. *Benchmark main dish: beef and stilton pie £11.50. Two-course evening meal £17.00.*

Free house ~ Licensee Paul White ~ Real ale ~ Open 10am-11pm; 8.30am-midnight Sat; 8.30am-11pm Sun ~ Bar food 10-9 ~ Children welcome ~ Dogs welcome ~ Wi-fi
Recommended by Daphne and Robert Staples, Emma Scofield, William and Sophia Renton, Buster May, Alf and Sally Garner

---

Post Office address codings confusingly give the impression that a few pubs are in Derbyshire, when they're really in Cheshire (which is where we list them).

KIRK IRETON   SK2650 Map 7

Barley Mow 🍺 🛏

(01335) 370306

Village signed off B5023 S of Wirksworth; DE6 3JP

Welcoming old inn that focuses on real ale and conversation; bedrooms

An inn since around 1800, this evokes how some grander rural pubs might have looked a century or so ago. It's a quite unchanging rural gem and has been run by the same long-serving, kindly landlady for over 40 years. The small main bar is relaxed and pubby with chatty locals, a roaring coal fire, antique settles on tiles or built into panelling, four slate-topped tables and shuttered mullioned windows. Another room has built-in cushioned pews on oak parquet and a small woodburning stove; a third has more pews, low beams and big landscape prints. In casks behind a modest wooden counter are five well kept ales including Whim Hartington IPA and four guests from breweries such as Abbeydale, Blue Monkey, Burton Bridge, Peak and Storm; french wines and farm cider too. There are two pub dogs. Outside you'll find a good-sized garden, a couple of benches at the front and a shop in what used to be the stable. This hilltop village is very pretty and within walking distance of Carsington Water. Bedrooms are comfortable, and readers enjoy the good breakfasts served in the stone-flagged kitchen. Dogs may be allowed in bedrooms if clean, but not at breakfast; the landlady tells us they have a newfoundland that is confined but does not like other dogs on her patch.

🍴 Very inexpensive filled rolls – lunchtime only – are the only food.

Free house ~ Licensee Mary Short ~ Real ale ~ No credit cards ~ Open 12-2, 7-11 (10.30 Sun) ~ Bar food lunchtime rolls only ~ Well behaved, supervised children lunchtime only ~ Dogs allowed in bar ~ Bedrooms: £45/£65 *Recommended by Ann and Colin Hunt, Luke Morgan, Maddie Purvis, John and Hilary Murphy*

LADYBOWER RESERVOIR   SK2084 Map 7

Yorkshire Bridge 🍺

(01433) 651361 – www.yorkshire-bridge.co.uk

A6013 N of Bamford; S33 0AZ

Just south of the dam, with several real ales, friendly staff, tasty food and fine views; bedrooms

This pleasantly genteel inn sits in dramatic country, beneath forested and moorland slopes just south of the Ladybower Reservoir dam; wonderful surrounding walks. The cosy bar has a woodburning stove, countless tankards hanging from beams, lots of china plates, photographs and paintings on red walls, horsebrasses and copper items, and red plush dining chairs around a mix of tables on red patterned carpeting. There's a lot of space in several other rooms – including a light and airy garden room with fine valley views – and an assortment of seating ranging from wicker and metal to bentwood-style chairs around all sorts of wooden tables, on carpeting or flagstones, plus many more decorative plates and photos. Friendly staff serve Acorn Barnsley Bitter, Bradfield Farmers Blonde, Howard Town Mill Town Mild, Peak Bakewell Best Bitter and a changing guest on handpump, and nine wines by the glass. Dogs are allowed in some bedrooms, but not in the bar at mealtimes.

🍴 Generous helpings of popular food include sandwiches, thai crab cake with asian salad and sweet chilli sauce, large yorkshire pudding filled with white onion sauce, brie, sun-dried tomato and red pepper quiche, chilli con carne, burgers with toppings and chips, gammon with egg or pineapple, lasagne, slow-cooked chicken in chasseur sauce, beer-battered fish of the day and chips, and puddings such as chocolate fudge cake and bakewell pudding. *Benchmark main dish: steak and kidney pie £10.75. Two-course evening meal £18.00.*

Free house ~ Licensee John Illingworth ~ Real ale ~ Open 11-11 (10.30 Sun) ~ Bar food 12-2.30, 5.30-8.30 (9 Fri); 12-9 Sat; 12-8.30 Sun ~ Children welcome ~ Dogs allowed in bar and bedrooms ~ Wi-fi ~ Bedrooms: £60/£96 *Recommended by Mark Hamill, Caroline Prescott, Nick Sharpe, David H Bennett, Jill and Dick Archer*

OLD BRAMPTON
SK3171 Map 7

Fox & Goose 🍷 🍺

(01246) 566335 – www.thefoxandgooseinn.com
Off A619 Chesterfield–Baslow at Wadshelf; S42 7JJ

Fine panoramic views for bustling pub with a restful bar, inventive food in light and airy restaurant, helpful staff and seats outside

This building was presented to the monks of Beauchief Abbey in a licence granted by Richard II in 1392. The name Fox & Goose was derived from the ancient Viking board game – fox and geese – which the monks used to play here. The character beamed bar has a woodburning stove in a big stone fireplace, mate's chairs and button-back wall seating surrounding a mix of wooden tables on large flagstones, Bradwell Farmers Blonde, Peak Bakewell Best Bitter and Chatsworth Gold and a couple of guest beers on handpump and a dozen wines by the glass served by friendly staff. A small snug leads off with heavy beams, button-back wall seats, beige carpeting and a small fireplace, and there's also a dining room with double-sided plush banquette seating. If eating, most customers head for the airy Orangery restaurant with its contemporary high-backed plush chairs around polished tables and lovely panoramic views through big picture windows. Outside, there are plenty of seats and tables under parasols on a terrace and decked area, and picnic-sets arranged on gravel.

🍴 Enjoyable food includes whitebait with squid ink aioli, twice-baked gruyère soufflé with fennel and pineapple salad, sausages of the day with rosemary mash and sweet red onion jus, roast mediterranean vegetables with gnocchi and pesto, beer-battered fish and chips, rabbit breast wrapped in pancetta with parmentier potatoes and raspberry purée, lamb rump with pea and mint risotto, wild garlic and jus, and puddings such as crème brûlée of the day and warm chocolate brownie with vanilla ice-cream. *Benchmark main dish: steak in ale pudding £12.95. Two-course evening meal £20.50.*

Free house ~ Licensee Craig Lynch ~ Real ale ~ Open 12-midnight (11 Sun); closed Mon-Thurs ~ Bar food 12-9 (9.30 Sat, 6 Sun) ~ Restaurant ~ Children welcome ~ Dogs allowed in bar ~ Wi-fi ~ Live music Sat evening *Recommended by Harvey Brown, Maddie Purvis, James Landor, John Harris, Millie and Peter Downing*

OVER HADDON
SK2066 Map 7

Lathkil 🍺

(01629) 812501 – www.lathkil.co.uk
Village and inn signposted from B5055 just SW of Bakewell; DE45 1JE

Long-serving owners of traditional pub with super views, a good range of beers and well liked food; bedrooms

The views from here are spectacular and can be enjoyed from seats in the walled garden and from windows in the bar. The inn is right at the heart of the Peak District National Park and popular with walkers and cyclists who use the warm, comfortable bedrooms as a base; breakfasts are hearty. The airy room on the right as you enter has a nice fire in an attractively carved fireplace, old-fashioned settles with upholstered cushions, chairs, black beams, a delft shelf of blue and white plates and some original prints and photographs. On the left, the sunny spacious dining area doubles as an evening restaurant and there's a woodburning stove. Adnams Mosaic, Blue Monkey BG Sips, Peak Summer Sovereign, Whim Hartington Bitter and a changing guest on handpump, a reasonable range of wines (including mulled wine) and a decent selection of malt whiskies; background music, darts, TV and board games. Dogs are welcome, but muddy boots must be left in the lobby.

Food is good and includes sandwiches, mini whole camembert with pear and kentish wine chutney, green-lipped mussels in garlic butter, spinach and ricotta cannelloni, steak and kidney pie, lasagne, salmon parcel with tomato and ginger jam, roast rack of lamb with marmalade and mustard crumb topping, venison and blackberry crumble, and puddings such as lemon meringue pie and cheesecake of the day. *Benchmark main dish: chicken in creamy stilton sauce with crispy prosciutto £12.95. Two-course evening meal £19.00.*

Free house ~ Licensee Alice Grigor-Taylor ~ Real ale ~ Open 11-11; 12-10.30 Sun ~ Bar food 12-2 (2.30 weekends), 6.30-8.30 ~ Restaurant ~ Children welcome but over-10s only in the bar ~ Dogs allowed in bar and bedrooms ~ Wi-fi ~ Bedrooms: £65/£80 *Recommended by Ann and Colin Hunt, Mike and Wena Stevenson, Geoff Rayner, Miranda and Jeff Davidson, Peter and Emma Kelly, Ann and Tony Bennett-Hughes*

STANTON IN PEAK
SK2364 Map 7
Flying Childers 🍺 £
(01629) 636333 – www.flyingchilders.com
Village signposted from B6056 S of Bakewell; Main Road; DE4 2LW

Top notch beer and inexpensive simple bar lunches in a warm-hearted, unspoilt pub – a delight

'What a splendid pub' says one of our readers – and, of course, many customers agree with him. The friendly landlord keeps Wells Bombardier and a couple of guests such as Stancill American Pale Ale and Storm Ale Force on handpump, and several wines by the glass. The best room in which to enjoy them is the snug little right-hand bar, virtually built for chat with its dark beam-and-plank ceiling, dark wall settles, single pew, plain tables, a hot coal and log fire, a few team photographs, dominoes and cribbage; background music. There's a bigger, equally unpretentious bar on the right. As well as seats out in front, there are picnic-sets in the well tended back garden. The surrounding walks are marvellous and both walkers and their dogs are warmly welcomed; they keep doggie treats behind the bar. In a beautiful steep stone village, this cottagey pub is named after an unbeatable racehorse of the early 18th c.

Cooked by the landlady, the simple lunchtime-only food includes filled rolls and toasties, home-made soups and weekend dishes such as local sausages, casseroles and home-made cake. *Benchmark main dish: casseroles £5.80.*

Free house ~ Licensees Stuart and Mandy Redfern ~ Real ale ~ No credit cards ~ Open 12-2 (3 weekends), 7-11; closed Mon and Tues lunchtimes ~ Bar food 12-2 ~ Children in lounge bar only ~ Dogs allowed in bar ~ Live acoustic music first Thurs of month *Recommended by Jeremy Snow, Max Simons, Geoff Rayner, Lorna and Jack Mulgrave, Mrs Julie Thomas, Barry and Daphne Gregson, Ann and Tony Bennett-Hughes*

WOOLLEY MOOR

SK3661 Map 7

White Horse

(01246) 590319 – www.thewhitehorsewoolleymoor.co.uk

Badger Lane, off B6014 Matlock–Clay Cross; DE55 6FG

Derbyshire Dining Pub of the Year

Attractive old dining pub with good food and drinks in pretty countryside; bedrooms

This lovely old inn was built on the original packhorse route from the toll bar cottage at Stretton to Woolley Moor toll bar; the views over the Amber Valley are splendid. It's neat and uncluttered – the bar, snug and dining room have wooden dining chairs and tables, stools and leather sofas on flagstoned or wooden floors, a woodburning stove (in the bar), an open fire (in the dining room), boldly patterned curtains and blinds and little to distract on the cream walls. Peak Bakewell Best Bitter and Chatsworth Gold and a changing guest on handpump and 13 wines by the glass. In the front garden you'll find picnic-sets under parasols on gravel, and boules. Contemporary bedroom suites (each with a private balcony) are well equipped and have floor-to-ceiling windows that give lovely views over the rolling countryside. Ogston Reservoir is just a couple of minutes' drive away.

From a seasonal menu using local produce, the enticing food includes filled ciabattas, smoked trout pâté, pork and fennel tortellini with crisp shallots and a red wine emulsion, beer-battered cod loin and chips, potato gnocchi with aubergine, vine tomatoes, olives and parsley, chicken breast with crushed potatoes and thyme cream, rump of local lamb with rosemary potatoes, spinach and red wine jus, and puddings such as banana parfait with blueberries and sesame brittle and chocolate brownie with salted caramel ice-cream. *Benchmark main dish: crispy pork belly with spring onion mash and smoked bacon sauce £14.95. Two-course evening meal £21.00.*

Free house ~ Licensees David and Melanie Boulby ~ Real ale ~ Open 12-11; 12-6 Sun; closed Mon lunchtime except bank holidays ~ Bar food 12-1.45, 6-8.45; 12-4 Sun ~ Restaurant ~ Children welcome ~ Wi-fi ~ Bedrooms: £139/£149 *Recommended by Helena and Trevor Fraser, Michael Butler, Alistair Forsyth, Dr Simon Innes, Jo Garnett, Malcolm Phillips, Chris Cook*

Also Worth a Visit in Derbyshire

Besides the fully inspected pubs, you might like to try these pubs that have been recommended to us and described by readers. Do tell us what you think of them: feedback@goodguides.com

ALDERWASLEY SK3153

Bear (01629) 822585

Left off A6 at Ambergate on to Holly Lane (turns into Jackass Lane) then right at end (staggered crossroads); DE56 2RD Unspoilt country inn with beamed cottagey rooms, one with large glass chandelier over assorted tables and chairs, another with tartan-covered wall banquettes and double-sided woodburner, other décor includes staffordshire china ornaments, old paintings/engravings and a grandfather clock, Timothy Taylors Landlord, Thornbridge Jaipur and guests, also own-brew Invader, several wines by the glass (decent list) and malt whiskies, enjoyable traditional food (all day Fri-Sun); children and dogs (in bar) welcome, seats in lovely garden with fine views, eight bedrooms and two self-catering cottages, open all day. *(Stephen Shepherd)*

ASHBOURNE SK1846

Smiths Tavern (01335) 300809

St John Street, bottom of marketplace; DE6 1GH Traditional little pub stretching back from heavily black-beamed bar through lounge to light and airy end room, up to seven well kept Marstons related ales plus a weekend guest (tasting glasses available), friendly knowledgeable staff, good pork pies; darts; children and dogs welcome, open all day. *(Jane and Philip Saunders)*

ASHFORD IN THE WATER SK1969
★**Ashford Arms** (01629) 812725
Off A6 NW of Bakewell; Church Street (B6465, off A6020); DE45 1QB
Attractive 18th-c inn set in pretty village; good quality reasonably priced food including Weds steak night (32oz rump if you're really hungry), well kept Black Sheep and two local guests, nice wines, restaurant and dining conservatory; free wi-fi; children and dogs welcome, plenty of tables outside, eight comfortable bedrooms, open all day Sun (food till 5pm). *(Daniel King)*

ASHFORD IN THE WATER SK1969
★**Bulls Head** (01629) 812931
Off A6 NW of Bakewell; Church Street (B6465, off A6020); DE45 1QB
Traditional 17th-c pub in attractive unspoilt village run by same family since 1953; cosy two-room beamed and carpeted bar with fires, one or two character gothic seats, spindleback and wheelback chairs around cast-iron-framed tables, local photographs and country prints on cream walls, four Robinsons ales and good choice of traditional food (not Tues evening), friendly efficient service; background music, daily papers; children welcome, overshoes for walkers, hardwood tables and benches in front and in good-sized garden behind with boules and Jenga, open all day weekends in summer. *(Ann and Colin Hunt, Brian and Anna Marsden)*

ASTON-UPON-TRENT SK4129
Malt (01332) 792256
M1 junction 24A on to A50, village signed left near Shardlow; The Green (one-way street); DE72 2AA
Comfortably modernised village pub with enjoyable good value food (not Sun evening, less choice Mon, Tues), well kept Bass, Marstons Pedigree, Sharps Doom Bar and three guests, friendly atmosphere; Tues quiz and some live music, TV; children and dogs welcome, back terrace, open all day. *(Alf and Sally Garner)*

BAKEWELL SK2168
Castle Inn (01629) 812103
Bridge Street; DE45 1DU Steps up to popular Georgian-fronted bay-windowed pub (actually dates from the 16th c) with well kept Greene King ales and a guest, decent competitively priced traditional food, three candlelit rooms with two open fires, flagstones, stripped stone and lots of pictures, good friendly service; background music; children and dogs welcome, tables out by road, attractive River Wye walks close by, four comfortable bedrooms,

good breakfast, open (and food) all day, gets busy Mon market day. *(John Wooll)*

BAMFORD SK2083
Anglers Rest (01433) 659317
A6013/Taggs Knoll; S33 0BQ Friendly community-owned pub with five good local beers and tasty home-made food including Tues pizzas, Weds pie night and Fri evening fish and chips, also has a café and post office; some live music, quiz Weds, free wi-fi; children, walkers and dogs welcome, open all day, no pub food Mon or lunchtimes Tues and Weds. *(Dr J Barrie Jones, David H Bennett)*

BASLOW SK2572
Devonshire Arms (01246) 582551
A619; DE45 1SR Modernised village inn with opened-up bar and dining areas; a couple of Peak ales and a guest, good wines by the glass and well liked imaginative food together with more traditional choices, friendly staff; rooms fan out from central bar with partitioning and swagged curtains creating cosy niches, notable circular dining room, range of seating including tub chairs, chesterfields and button-back leather wall banquettes, flagstones, tiles and carpeting, woodburner, coffee shop; background music, TV, free wi-fi; children and dogs welcome, 11 comfortable bedrooms, free parking but must enter your registration at the bar to avoid a fine, open all day (food all day weekends). *(Charlie Stevens)*

BASLOW SK2572
Wheatsheaf (01246) 582240
Nether End; DE45 1SR Cheerful Marstons inn (former coaching house) with comfortable carpeted interior, popular reasonably priced pub food including good children's menu, four well kept ales, prompt friendly service; free wi-fi; plenty of seats outside and play area, bedrooms, handy for Chatsworth House, open all day. *(Amanda Shipley)*

BEELEY SK2667
★**Devonshire Arms** (01629) 733259
B6012, off A6 Matlock–Bakewell; DE4 2NR Lovely 18th-c stone coaching inn in attractive Peak District village near Chatsworth House; original part with black beams, flagstones, stripped stone and cheerful log fires, contrasting ultra-modern bistro/conservatory, up to five well kept changing ales, several wines by the glass and nice range of malt whiskies, good imaginative food (not cheap) using local ingredients, helpful staff; background music; children welcome, dogs in bar and some of the 14 bedrooms, open all day. *(John and Penny Wildon)*

Real ale to us means beer that has matured naturally in its cask – not pressurised or filtered. We name all real ales stocked.

BIRCHOVER   SK2362
Red Lion (01629) 650363
Main Street; DE4 2BN Friendly early
18th-c stone-built pub with popular good
value italian-influenced food (landlord
is from Sardinia), also make their own
cheese and have a deli next door, Sun
carvery, Birchover ales (brewed here)
and four ciders, glass-covered well inside,
woodburners; acoustic music sessions and
quiz nights; children and dogs welcome, nice
rural views from outside seats, popular with
walkers, open all day weekends, closed all
Mon and Tues, Wed lunchtime. *(John Harris)*

BONSALL   SK2758
★**Barley Mow** (01629) 825685
*Off A5012 W of Cromford; The Dale;
DE4 2AY* Basic one-room stone-built local
with friendly buoyant atmosphere, beams,
pubby furnishings and woodburner, pictures
and plenty of bric-a-brac, well kept local
ales and real ciders, hearty helpings of good
value food from short daily changing menu
(be prepared to share a table); live music
Fri and Sat, outside loos; children and dogs
welcome, nice little front terrace, events
such as hen racing and world record-
breaking day, walks from the pub, camping,
open all day weekends, closed Mon and
lunchtimes Tues-Fri. *(John and Delia Franks)*

BONSALL   SK2758
Kings Head (01629) 822703
Yeoman Street; DE4 2AA Welcoming
17th-c stone-built village local with two
cosy beamed rooms, pubby furniture
including cushioned wall benches on carpet
or tiles, various knick-knacks and china,
woodburners, three Batemans ales and
enjoyable good value home-made food,
restaurant; karaoke last Sat of month, darts;
children and dogs welcome, seats out at front
and in back courtyard, handy for Limestone
Way and other walks, open all day weekends,
closed Mon lunchtime. *(Charlie Stevens)*

BRACKENFIELD   SK3658
Plough (01629) 534437
*A615 Matlock–Alfreton, about a mile
NW of Wessington; DE55 6DD* Much
modernised 16th-c former farmhouse in
lovely setting; three-level beamed bar with
cheerful log-effect gas fire, well kept ales and
plenty of wines by the glass, good popular
food including weekday lunchtime set deal
and blackboard specials, appealing lower-
level restaurant extension, friendly staff and
nice pub cat called Frank; children welcome,
large neatly kept gardens with terrace,
closed Mon, otherwise open all day (food till
5.30pm Sun). *(Patricia and Gordon Thompson)*

BRADWELL   SK1782
Samuel Fox (01433) 621562
B6049; S33 9JT This friendly stone pub
in the Peak District National Park was

up for sale as we went to press (has been
very food-oriented with landlord-chef in
charge of good kitchen); open-plan bar and
interlinked dining rooms with upholstered
tub chairs around tables on striped carpet
or wood flooring, country scenes on papered
walls above grey dado, several open brick
fireplaces; Bradfield Farmers Bitter and
Intrepid Explorer, real cider and ten wines
by the glass from good list, neat similarly
furnished restaurant; children welcome, no
dogs inside, wheelchair access, white metal
or wooden seating out in front, comfortable
bedrooms, only open Weds-Sat evenings
and Sun 1-5.30pm, closed all Jan. *(Miles
Green, Colin and Daniel Gibbs, Geoff and Ann
Marston, Alexandra and Richard Clay)*

BRASSINGTON   SK2354
★**Olde Gate** (01629) 540448
*Village signed off B5056 and B5035
NE of Ashbourne; DE4 4HJ* Wonderfully
unspoilt place – like stepping back in
time; mullioned windows, 17th-c kitchen
range with copper pots, old wall clock,
rush-seated chairs and antique settles,
beams hung with pewter mugs and shelves
lined with embossed Doulton stoneware
flagons, also a panelled Georgian room and,
to the left of a small hatch-served lobby, a
cosy beamed room with stripped settles,
scrubbed tables and open fire under huge
mantelbeam, Marstons, Thwaites and a
guest, decent fair value food; cribbage
and dominoes; well behaved children
welcome, dogs in bar, benches in small
front yard, garden with tables looking
out over pastures, open all day Fri-Sun,
closed Mon lunchtime. *(Kathleen I'Anson,
Julie and Andrew Blanchett, Patricia and
Gordon Thompson, Cliff and Monica Swan)*

BUXTON   SK0573
Old Sun (01298) 23452
High Street; SK17 6HA Revamped 17th-c
coaching inn with several cosy linked
areas, six well kept Marstons-related ales
and good choice of wines by the glass,
generous helpings of straightforward home-
made food (not Sun evening, Mon-Thurs
lunchtimes), low beams, panelling, bare
boards and flagstones, soft lighting, old local
photographs, open fire; background music,
Sun quiz; children till 7pm, no dogs inside,
roadside terrace, open all day. *(Barry Collett)*

BUXTON   SK0573
Tap House (01298) 214085
*Old Court House, George Street;
SK17 6AT* Buxton brewery tap with
their cask and craft range plus guests,
also good selection of bottled beers,
wines and spirits, tasty well priced food
including some cooked in smoker, various
interesting teas and coffees, friendly
knowledgeable staff; daily newspapers;
children welcome, a few seats outside, open
all day (till 1am Fri, Sat). *(Lindy Andrews)*

BUXWORTH
SK0282
Navigation (01663) 732072
*S of village towards Silkhill, off B6062;
SK23 7NE* Inn by restored Bugsworth
canal basin; half a dozen well kept ales
including Thwaites and Timothy Taylors,
good value pubby food from sandwiches
up, linked low-ceilinged rooms, canalia,
brassware and old photographs, open
fires, games room with pool and darts;
background and live music, free wi-fi;
children (away from main bar), walkers
and dogs welcome, disabled access,
tables on sunken flagstoned terrace,
six bedrooms, open (and food) all day.
(Tony Hobden, Brian and Anna Marsden)

CALVER
SK2374
Derwentwater Arms (01433) 639211
*In centre, bear left from Main Street into
Folds Head; Low Side; S32 3XQ* Elevated
stone-built village pub with big windows
looking down across car park to cricket pitch;
good fairly priced food (all day Sun) from
pizzas and pub favourites to daily specials,
three well kept ales including Bass and
Bradfield, friendly helpful service; children,
walkers and dogs (in bar) welcome, terraces
on slopes below (disabled access from
back car park), next-door holiday cottage,
open all day weekends. *(Jane Rigby)*

CASTLETON
SK1583
Olde Cheshire Cheese
(01433) 620330 *How Lane; S33 8WJ*
Cosy 17th-c inn with two linked beamed and
carpeted areas, six interesting ales such
as Acorn, Bradfield and Peak, good range
of popular reasonably priced wholesome
food and decent house wines, quick
friendly service, two gas woodburners,
lots of photographs, toby jugs, plates
and brassware, back dining room where
children welcome; background and some
live music, free wi-fi; dogs allowed in bar,
ten bedrooms, parking across road, open
(and food) all day. *(Eddie Edwards)*

CASTLETON
SK1582
★Olde Nags Head (01433) 620248
Cross Street (A6187); S33 8WH Small
solidly built hotel dating from the 17th c,
interesting antique oak furniture and coal
fire in civilised beamed and flagstoned bar,
adjoining snug with leather sofas, steps
down to restaurant, well kept Black Sheep,
Sharps Doom Bar and guests, nice coffee
and good locally sourced food, friendly
helpful staff; live music Sat; children and
dogs (in bar) welcome, nine comfortable
bedrooms, good breakfast, open all day.
(Martin Day, Stuart Paulley, David Hunt)

CHESTERFIELD
SK3871
Chesterfield Arms (01246) 236634
Newbold Road (B6051); S41 7PH
Popular and friendly 19th-c pub with 12 or
more real ales, craft beers, six ciders and
good choice of wines and whiskies, basic
snacks along with pie and curry nights,
open fire, oak panelling and stripped wood/
flagstoned floors, conservatory linking
barn room; Weds quiz, live music last
Thurs of month; dogs welcome, outside
tables on decking, open all day (from 4pm
Mon-Weds). *(Miranda and Jeff Davidson)*

CHESTERFIELD
SK3671
Manor (01246) 237555
*Old Road, Brampton; near the school;
S4 3QT* Converted manor house down
tree-lined drive, bar with tartan-upholstered
armchairs by open fire, high stools around
equally high tables, leather banquettes
down one side creating booths, wood and
flagstoned floors with chequered tiles by
servery, ales such as Brampton and Peak,
second room with tartan wall seating and
a wide mix of dining chairs, good range of
food from sandwiches and sharing plates
up including Sun carvery and themed
evenings, friendly staff; Tues quiz, Fri live
music, TV, fruit machine; children welcome,
tables under big parasols on front terrace,
second terrace by play area, open all day,
no food Sun evening. *(Charlie Stevens)*

CHESTERFIELD
SK3670
Rose & Crown (01246) 563750
Old Road; S40 2QT Popular Brampton
Brewery pub with their full range plus
Everards and two changing guests, Weston's
cider, enjoyable home-made food (not
weekend evenings) from baguettes up,
helpful staff and hands-on landlord, spacious
traditional refurbishment with leather
banquettes, panelling, wood or carpeted
floors, brewery memorabilia and cast-iron
Victorian fireplace, cosy snug area; Tues
quiz, trad jazz first Sun of month, free wi-fi;
tables outside, open all day. *(Daniel King)*

CHINLEY
SK0482
Paper Mill (01663) 750529
Whitehough Head Lane; SK23 6EJ Under
same management as next-door Old Hall (see
Main Entries); good selection of ales, craft
kegs and plenty of bottled belgian beers,
simple bar snacks including cheeseboards
and mini ploughman's, also a raclette
room (must book in advance – minimum
eight people), good choice of teas and
coffees, friendly helpful staff, flagstones,
woodburners and open fire, local artwork for
sale; TV for major sports; children, walkers

'Children welcome' means the pub says it lets children inside without any special
restriction; some may impose an evening time limit earlier than 9pm – please tell us
if you find this.

and dogs welcome, seats out at front and on split-level back terrace, plenty of good local walks, four bedrooms, open all day Sun, closed weekdays till 6pm, Fri till 5pm and Sat till 3pm. *(Frank and Marcia Pelling)*

CLIFTON
SK1645

Cock (01335) 342654

Cross Side, opposite church; DE6 2GJ Unpretentious two-bar beamed village local, comfortable and friendly, with enjoyable reasonably priced home-made pub food from baguettes up, well kept Marstons Pedigree, Timothy Taylors Landlord and a couple of guests, decent choice of wines by the glass, separate dining room; quiz first Tues of month, darts; children, walkers and dogs welcome, garden with play equipment, closed Mon lunchtime. *(Charlie Stevens)*

COMBS
SK0378

Beehive (01298) 812758

Village signposted off B5470 W of Chapel-en-le-Frith; SK23 9UT Roomy, neat and comfortable, with emphasis on good freshly made food (all day Sun) from baguettes to steaks and interesting specials, also very good value weekday set menu and Tues grill night, ales including Marstons Pedigree and a house beer from Wychwood, good choice of wines by the glass, log fire, heavy beams and copperware; background music, TV, Tues quiz; plenty of tables out in front, by lovely valley tucked away from main road, good walks, one-bed holiday cottage next door, open all day. *(G Whitehurst, Brian and Anna Marsden)*

CRICH
SK3454

Cliff (01773) 852444

Cromford Road, Town End; DE4 5DP Unpretentious little two-room roadside pub, well kept ales such as Blue Monkey, Buxton, Dancing Duck and Sharps, generous helpings of good value straightforward food (not weekend evenings or Mon), welcoming staff and friendly regulars, two woodburners; maybe Sun folk night, free wi-fi; children and dogs welcome, great views and walks, handy for National Tramway Museum, open all day weekends, closed weekday lunchtimes. *(Robert Turnham)*

CROWDECOTE
SK1065

Packhorse (01298) 83618

B5055 W of Bakewell; SK17 0DB Small three-room 16th-c pub in lovely setting, welcoming landlord and staff, good reasonably priced home-made food from weekday light bites and sandwiches up, four well kept changing ales, split-level interior with brick or carpeted floors, stripped-stone walls, open fire and two woodburners; Thurs quiz, pool and darts; children and dogs welcome, tables out behind, beautiful views and a popular walking route, closed Mon, Tues. *(Daniel King)*

DERBY
SK3538

Abbey Inn (01332) 558297

Darley Street; DE22 1DX Former abbey gatehouse opposite park (pleasant riverside walk from centre), massive 15th-c or older stonework remnants, brick floor, studded oak doors, coal fire in big inglenook, stone spiral staircase to upper bar (not always staffed) with oak rafters and tapestries, bargain Sam Smiths and reasonably priced bar food; the lavatories with their beams, stonework and tiles are worth a look too; children and dogs (downstairs) welcome, open all day. *(Richard Tingle)*

DERBY
SK3635

Alexandra (01332) 293993

Siddals Road; DE1 2QE Imposing Victorian pub, popular locally; two simple rooms with traditional furnishings on bare boards or carpet, railway prints/memorabilia, well kept Castle Rock and several quickly changing microbrewery guests, lots of continental bottled beers with more on tap, snack food such as pork pies and cobs; background music; children and dogs welcome, nicely planted backyard, 1960s locomotive cab in car park, four bedrooms, open all day. *(Jill and Dick Archer)*

DERBY
SK3535

Babington Arms (01332) 383647

Babington Lane; DE1 1TA Large open-plan Wetherspoons with 16 real ales and four proper ciders, good friendly service, usual well priced food, comfortable seating with steps up to relaxed back area; TVs, free wi-fi; children welcome, seats out at front by pavement, open all day from 8am for breakfast. *(Richard Tingle)*

DERBY
SK3536

Brewery Tap (01332) 366283

Derwent Street/Exeter Place; DE1 2ED 19th-c Derby Brewing Co pub (aka Royal Standard) with unusual bowed end; ten real ales including five of their own from curved brick counter, lots of bottled imports, knowledgeable staff, decent good value food all day (till 5pm Sun) from sandwiches and baked potatoes up, open-plan bare-boards interior with two high-ceilinged drinking areas, small upstairs room and roof terrace overlooking the Derwent; live music Tues; open all day (till 1am Fri, Sat). *(Daniel King)*

DERBY
SK3635

Brunswick (01332) 290677

Railway Terrace; close to Derby Midland Station; DE1 2RU One of Britain's oldest railwaymen's pubs, up to 16 ales including Everards and selection from own microbrewery, real ciders and good choice of bottled beers, cheap traditional lunchtime food from good sandwiches up, high-ceilinged panelled bar, snug with coal fire, chatty front parlour, interesting old train photographs and prints; live jazz upstairs first Thurs of month, darts, TV, games machine, free wi-fi; dogs welcome, walled beer garden behind, open all day. *(Dr J Barrie Jones)*

DERBY SK3435

Exeter Arms (01332) 605323

Exeter Place; DE1 2EU Victorian survivor amid 1930s apartment blocks and car parks; recently extended into next-door cottage, but keeping its traditional character including tiled-floor snug with curved wall benches and polished open range, friendly staff, well kept Dancing Duck, Marstons and two guests, good all-day food (till 6pm Sun) from snacks and pubby choices up; quiz Mon, summer live music Sat in small garden with outside bar (beer festivals), children and dogs welcome, open all day (till midnight Fri, Sat). *(Daniel King)*

DERBY SK3534

Falstaff (01332) 342902

Silver Hill Road, off Normanton Road; DE23 6UJ Big Victorian red-brick corner pub (aka the Folly) brewing its own good value ales, two friendly bars with interesting collection of memorabilia including brewerania, games room; children (till 6pm) and dogs welcome, outside seating area, open all day. *(Daniel King)*

DERBY SK3436

Five Lamps (01332) 348730

Duffield Road; DE1 3BH Corner pub with opened-up but well divided interior around central servery, wood-strip or carpeted floors, panelling, leather button-back bench seats and small balustrade raised section, a dozen well kept ales such as Everards, Oakham, Peak and Whim along with a house beer from Derby, real ciders, decent good value pubby food (not Sun evening); background music, TV; a few picnic-sets outside, open all day (till midnight Fri, Sat). *(Richard Tingle)*

DERBY SK3536

Olde Dolphin (01332) 267711

Queen Street; DE1 3DL Quaint 16th-c timber-framed pub just below cathedral; four small dark unpretentious rooms including appealing snug, big bowed black beams, shiny panelling, opaque leaded windows, lantern lights and coal fires, half a dozen predominantly mainstream ales, reasonably priced bar food and upstairs evening restaurant (Thurs-Sat); quiz and live music nights; children welcome at certain times (best to check), sizeable outside area for drinkers/smokers, open all day. *(Richard Tingle, Daniel King)*

DERBY SK3335

Rowditch (01332) 343123

Uttoxeter New Road (A516); DE22 3LL Popular character local with own microbrewery (well kept Marstons Pedigree

---

and guests too), friendly landlord, two bars and attractive little snug on right, coal fire; no children, dogs welcome at weekends, pleasant back garden, closed weekday lunchtimes. *(Daniel King)*

DERBY SK3536

Silk Mill (01332) 349160

Full Street; DE1 3AF Refurbished 1920s pub keeping traditional feel; central bar with lounge and skylit dining area off, plush banquettes, cushioned stools and cast-iron-framed tables on wood floors, open fires, one or two quirky touches such as fish wallpaper, a stuffed crocodile and antler chandelier, good choice of real ales and ciders, several wines by the glass, enjoyable food (all day weekdays, till 8pm Sun) from sandwiches and sharing boards up, friendly service; daily newspapers and free wi-fi; open all day. *(Richard Tingle)*

DUFFIELD SK3543

Pattern Makers Arms

(01332) 842844 *Crown Street, off King Street; DE56 4EY* Welcoming Edwardian backstreet local with well kept Bass (from the jug), Marstons, Timothy Taylors and guests, bargain lunchtime food, pubby furniture on wood or carpeted floors, upholstered banquettes, some stained-glass and etched windows; background music, TV, darts, pool and other games, Sun quiz; dogs welcome, beer garden behind, open all day Fri-Sun. *(Lindy Andrews)*

EARL STERNDALE SK0966

★ Quiet Woman (01298) 83211

Village signed off B5053 S of Buxton; SK17 0BU Old-fashioned unchanging country local in lovely Peak District countryside; simple beamed interior with plain furniture on quarry tiles, china ornaments and coal fire, well kept Marstons Bitter and guests, own-label bottled beers (available in gift packs), good pork pies, family room with pool, skittles and darts; no dogs inside, picnic-sets out in front along with budgies, hens, ducks and donkeys, you can buy free-range eggs, local poetry books and even hay, good hikes across nearby Dove Valley towards Longnor and Hollinsclough, small campsite next door with caravan for hire. *(Ann and Colin Hunt, M J Winterton)*

EDALE SK1285

Old Nags Head (01433) 670291

Off A625 E of Chapel-en-le-Frith; Grindsbrook Booth; S33 7ZD Relaxed well used traditional pub at start of Pennine Way, four well kept local ales, good value food from sandwiches up including carvery (Sat evening, Sun lunchtime), friendly service, log fire, flagstoned area for booted walkers, airy back family room; background music, TV, pool and darts; dogs welcome, front terrace and garden, two self-catering cottages, open (and food) all day in summer, closed Mon and Tues in winter, can get very busy weekends. *(David Eberlin)*

EDLASTON SK1842
Shire Horse (01335) 342714
Off A515 S of Ashbourne, just beside Wyaston; DE6 2DQ Timbered pub with good mix of drinkers and diners in large bar with open fire and separate restaurant/conservatory, friendly helpful staff, popular fairly priced food (not Sun evening) including specials board, well kept local ales, good house wines; children and dogs (in bar) welcome, tables out in front and in back garden with terrace, peaceful spot and nice views, open all day Sun. *(Greta and Gavin Craddock)*

ELMTON SK5073
★ Elm Tree (01909) 721261
Off B6417 S of Clowne; S80 4LS Popular competently run country pub with landlord-chef's good fairly traditional food including weekday set lunch, well kept Black Sheep and a guest, several ciders and wide range of wines, friendly obliging service even when busy, stripped stone and panelling, log fire, back barn restaurant (mainly for functions); children and dogs (in bar) welcome, garden tables, play area, closed Tues, otherwise open (and food) all day, till 8pm (6pm) Sun. *(Derek and Sylvia Stephenson)*

EYAM SK2276
Miners Arms (01433) 630853
Off A632 Chesterfield to Chapel-en-le-Frith; Water Lane; S32 5RG Three-roomed 17th-c beamed inn with enjoyable food (not Sun evening) from sandwiches up, Greene King and Theakstons ales, friendly efficient service; TV, background music, free wi-fi; children, walkers and dogs welcome, picnic-sets out at front and in back garden, nice walks nearby especially below Froggatt Edge, seven bedrooms, open all day. *(Dave Braisted)*

FOOLOW SK1976
★ Bulls Head (01433) 630873
Village signposted off A623 Baslow–Tideswell; S32 5QR Friendly pub by green in pretty upland village; simply furnished flagstoned bar with interesting collection of photographs including some saucy Edwardian ones, Black Sheep, Peak and two guests, over 30 malts, good food (all day Sun) with more elaborate choices Sat evening, OAP weekday lunch deal, step down to former stables with high ceiling joists, stripped stone and woodburner, sedate partly panelled dining room with plates on delft shelves; background music; children, walkers and dogs welcome, side picnic-sets with nice views, paths from here out over rolling pasture enclosed by dry-stone walls, three bedrooms, closed Mon. *(Jill and Dick Archer)*

FROGGATT EDGE SK2476
★ Chequers (01433) 630231
A625, off A623 N of Bakewell; S32 3ZJ Roadside dining pub surrounded by lovely countryside; opened-up bar and eating areas, cushioned settles, farmhouse and captain's chairs around mix of tables, antique prints, longcase clock and woodburner, well liked interesting food (all day weekends) along with more traditional choices, home-made chutneys and preserves for sale, Bradfield, Peak and a guest ale, several wines by the glass, friendly helpful staff; background music; children welcome, no dogs inside, garden with Froggatt Edge escarpment up through woods behind, six comfortable clean bedrooms, good breakfast, open all day. *(Mike and Wena Stevenson)*

FROGGATT EDGE SK2577
Grouse (01433) 630423
Longshaw, off B6054 NE of Froggatt; S11 7TZ Nicely old-fashioned beamed pub in same family since 1965; carpeted front bar with wall benches and other seating, log fire, back bar with coal-effect gas fire, small conservatory, enjoyable hearty home-made food (all day Sun, not Mon evening) from nice sandwiches to blackboard specials, four well kept Marstons-related beers and over 40 malt whiskies, friendly prompt service; children (in back room) and dogs welcome, terrace seating, lovely views and good moorland walks, open all day weekends. *(Charlie Stevens)*

GLOSSOP SK0394
Star (01457) 853072
Howard Street; SK13 7DD Unpretentious corner alehouse opposite station with four well kept changing ales and Weston's Old Rosie cider, no food, traditional layout including flagstoned tap room with hatch service, old local photographs; dogs welcome (resident alsatian is Heidi), open all day from 4pm (2pm Fri, noon Sat, Sun). *(Lindy Andrews)*

GRINDLEFORD SK2378
Sir William (01433) 630303
B6001, opposite war memorial; S32 2HS Popular refurbished pub-hotel under welcoming management; good food from sandwiches up, Greene King ales and guests, friendly helpful service, restaurant; Sun quiz, free wi-fi; children, walkers and dogs (in a couple of areas) welcome, splendid view especially from terrace, eight comfortable bedrooms. *(W K Wood)*

HARDWICK HALL SK4663
★ Hardwick Inn (01246) 850245
Quite handy for M1 junction 29; S44 5QJ Popular golden-stone pub dating from the 15th c at south park gate of Hardwick Hall (NT); several linked rooms including proper bar, open fires, fine range

of some 220 malt whiskies and plenty of wines by the glass, well kept Black Sheep, Peak, Theakstons and a house beer (Bess of Hardwick) from Brampton, generous helpings of good reasonably priced bar food plus carvery restaurant, long-serving licensees (in same family for three generations), efficient friendly staff; unobtrusive background music; children allowed away from bar areas, dogs in one part, tables out at front and in pleasant back garden, open (and food) all day. *(Derek and Sylvia Stephenson)*

HARTINGTON SK1260
Charles Cotton (01298) 84229
Market Place; SK17 0AL Popular stone-built hotel in attractive village centre; large comfortable bar-bistro with open fire, enjoyable food from lunchtime sandwiches up (more restauranty evening choice), ales including Jennings, Whim and a beer badged for the pub from Wincle, nice wines and italian coffee, friendly helpful service, restaurant and summer tea room; background and some live music; children, walkers and dogs (in bar) welcome, seats out at front and in small back garden, 17 bedrooms, open all day. *(Barry Collett)*

HARTINGTON SK1260
Devonshire Arms (01298) 84232
Market Place; SK17 0AL Traditional unpretentious two-bar pub in attractive village, welcoming and cheerful, with generous helpings of enjoyable home-made food (smaller servings available), ales such as Black Sheep and Jennings, log fires; maybe background music; children and dogs welcome, tables out in front facing duck pond, more in small garden, good walks, open (and food) all day weekends. *(Brian and Anna Marsden, Martyn Hooper)*

HARTSHORNE SK3220
Bulls Head (01283) 215299
Woodville Road; DE11 7ET Welcoming and popular red-brick local dating in part from 1600, big helpings of good value freshly cooked food including daily specials and meal deals, well kept Marstons Pedigree and a guest, several wines by the glass, cheery helpful staff; background music, free wi-fi; children welcome, clean comfortable bedrooms. *(Mike and Wena Stevenson)*

HATHERSAGE SK2381
★ Scotsmans Pack (01433) 650253
School Lane, off A6187; S32 1BZ Bustling inn equally popular with drinkers and diners; dark panelled rooms with lots of interesting knick-knacks, upholstered gingham stools and dining chairs, cushioned wall seats and assortment of tables, woodburner, five well kept Marstons-related ales and enjoyable food including daily specials, cream teas; background and some live music, quiz and bingo night Thurs, TV, darts; picnic-sets on terrace overlooking trout stream, plenty of surrounding walks, five bedrooms, open all day. *(Jane and Philip Saunders)*

HAYFIELD SK0388
Lantern Pike (01663) 747590
Glossop Road (A624 N) at Little Hayfield, just N of Hayfield; SK22 2NG This recently taken-over roadside pub still has its traditional red plush bar, warm fire and a few photos of the original *Coronation Street* cast (many were regulars along with series creator Tony Warren who based his characters on the locals), Abbeydale Moonshine, Timothy Taylors Landlord and a guest, decent pubby food; background music, live country bands Mon, TV and free wi-fi; children welcome, dogs may be allowed, tables on stone-walled terrace looking over towards Lantern Pike, plenty of surrounding walks on windswept moors, five bedrooms, closed Mon lunchtime, otherwise open all day. *(Gus Swan, Alf Wright, Julie and Andrew Blanchett, Donald Allsopp)*

HAYFIELD SK0387
Pack Horse (01663) 749126
Off A624 Glossop to Chapel-en-le-Frith; Market Street; SK22 2EP Modernised stone-built pub under newish welcoming licensees, good reasonably priced food from landlord-chef using local suppliers, four well kept ales and decent choice of wines, opened-up interior with some cosy areas, local artwork for sale, woodburners; background music; children, walkers and dogs welcome, a few seats out in front, open (and food) all day. *(Liz)*

HEAGE SK3750
Black Boy (01773) 856799
Old Road (B6013); DE56 2BN Modernised village pub-restaurant with popular good value food including fish specials in bar and upstairs dining room, well kept changing ales and real cider, friendly staff, open fire; live music and quiz nights; children welcome, no dogs, small outside seating area, open all day. *(Nick Sharpe)*

HOGNASTON SK2350
★ Red Lion (01335) 370396
Off B5035 Ashbourne–Wirksworth; DE6 1PR Traditional 17th-c village inn with open-plan beamed bar, three fires, attractive mix of old tables, curved settles and other seats on ancient flagstones, friendly service, good well presented home-made food from shortish menu in bar and conservatory, nice wines by the glass, Marstons Pedigree and guests; background music; children and dogs welcome, picnic-sets in field behind, boules, handy for Carsington Water, three good bedrooms, big breakfast. *(Jim King)*

HOLBROOK SK3645
★ Dead Poets (01332) 780301
Chapel Street; village signed off A6 S of Belper; DE56 0TQ Friendly

drinkers' local with up to nine real ales (some served from jugs), traditional ciders and good range of other drinks, helpful knowledgeable landlord, filled cobs and other good value lunchtime bar food, simple cottagey décor with beams, stripped-stone walls and broad flagstones, high-backed settles forming booths, big log fire, plenty of tucked-away corners, woodburner in snug, children allowed in back conservatory till 8pm; quiet background music, no credit cards; dogs welcome, seats out at back, open all day Fri-Sun. *(Charlie Stevens)*

HOPE   SK1783

★ **Cheshire Cheese** (01433) 620381
Off A6187, towards Edale; S33 6ZF
16th-c traditional stone inn with snug oak-beamed rooms on different levels, open fires, red carpets or stone floors, straightforward furnishings and gleaming brasses, up to five ales such as Abbeydale, Bradfield and Peak, a dozen malt whiskies and enjoyable food from sandwiches and pub favourites up, friendly service; Weds quiz, folk night first and third Thurs of month; children and dogs welcome, good local walks in the summits of Lose Hill and Win Hill or the cave district around Castleton, four bedrooms, limited parking, open all day weekends in summer, closed Mon. *(Jim King)*

HORSLEY WOODHOUSE   SK3944

Old Oak (01332) 881299
Main Street (A609 Belper–Ilkeston); DE7 6AW Busy roadside local linked to nearby Bottle Brook and Leadmill microbreweries, their ales and guests plus weekend back bar with another eight well priced beers tapped from the cask, farm ciders, basic snacks (can also bring your own food), beamed rooms with blazing coal fires; occasional live music; children and dogs welcome, hatch service to covered courtyard tables, nice views, closed weekday lunchtimes till 4pm, open all day weekends. *(Nick Sharpe)*

ILKESTON   SK4742

Dewdrop (0115) 932 9684
Station Street, Ilkeston junction, off A6096; DE7 5TE Large Victorian red-brick corner local in old industrial area, not strong on bar comfort but popular for its well kept beers (up to eight) such as Acorn, Blue Monkey, Bobs and Oakham, simple bar snacks, back lounge with fire and piano, connecting lobby to front public bar with pool, darts and TV, some Barnes Wallis memorabilia; children and dogs welcome, sheltered outside seating at back, walks by former Nottingham Canal, open all day weekends, closed weekday lunchtimes. *(Donald Allsopp)*

ILKESTON   SK4641

Spanish Bar (0115) 930 8666
South Street; DE7 5QJ Busy refurbished bar with half a dozen well kept/priced ales, traditional ciders and bottled belgian beers, friendly efficient staff, evening overspill room; Tues quiz, live music; dogs welcome, small back garden and skittle alley, open all day. *(Daniel King)*

INGLEBY   SK3427

John Thompson (01332) 862469
NW of Melbourne; turn off A514 at Swarkestone Bridge or in Stanton by Bridge; can also be reached from Ticknall (or from Repton on B5008); DE73 7HW Own-brews from the longest established microbrewery in the UK; comfortable neatly kept lounge with beams, old settles, button-back leather seats and sturdy oak tables, antique prints and paintings, log-effect gas fire, a couple of smaller cosier rooms off, simple good value lunchtime food including carvery, piano, TV and games in conservatory; background music, free wi-fi; children welcome till 9pm, dogs in bar and conservatory, seats on lawns or partly covered terrace, pretty surrounding countryside, self-catering chalets, open all day weekends, closed Mon. *(Peter Pilbeam, John Beeken, David Eberlin)*

KING'S NEWTON   SK3826

Hardinge Arms (01332) 863808
Not far from M1 junction 23A, via A453 to Isley, then off Melbourne/Wilson Road; Main Street; DE73 8BX New owners for this bright and spacious old pub; chunky low beams, brick, wood and flagstone floors, woodburner, enjoyable bar and evening restaurant food including Mon steak night, well kept local ales and good range of wines, quick friendly service; children in eating areas, bedrooms in converted stables, handy for Donington Park and East Midlands Airport, open all day, no food Sun evening. *(Peter Hawkins)*

LADYBOWER RESERVOIR SK1986

Ladybower Inn (01433) 651241
A57 Sheffield–Glossop, just E of junction with A6013; S33 0AX Batemans pub handy for the huge nearby reservoir; their ales and a couple of guests, enjoyable pubby food from sandwiches up, friendly service, various traditionally furnished carpeted areas, cast-iron fireplaces, Lancaster Bomber pictures recalling the Dambusters' practice runs on the reservoir; background music, darts, free wi-fi; children and dogs (in bar) welcome, picnic-sets out at front, annexe bedrooms, open (and food) all day. *(Martin Day, David H Bennett)*

All *Guide* inspections are anonymous. Anyone claiming to be a *Good Pub Guide* inspector is a fraud. Please let us know.

LITTLE LONGSTONE   SK1971
Packhorse (01629) 640471
*Off A6 NW of Bakewell via Monsal Dale;
DE45 1NN* Three comfortable linked
beamed rooms, pine tables on flagstones, well
kept Black Sheep, three Thornbridge ales
and a guest, popular generously served home-
made food from daily changing blackboard
including good Sun lunch, affordably
priced wine list, friendly accommodating
service, coal fires; Thurs quiz; children,
dogs and hikers welcome (on Monsal Trail),
terrace in steep little back garden, open
(and food) all day weekends. *(Dave and
Alison Baker, Ann and Tony Bennett-Hughes)*

LITTON   SK1675
Red Lion (01298) 871458
*Village signposted off A623, between
B6465 and B6049 junctions; also
signposted off B6049; SK17 8QU*
Welcoming traditional village pub, two linked
front rooms with low beams, panelling and
open fires, bigger stripped-stone back room,
three well kept ales and enjoyable home-
made food from sandwiches to daily specials;
dogs allowed, seats and tables in front with
more on village green, good walks in nearby
Dales, open (and food) all day. *(Alan Johnson,
Brian and Anna Marsden, Barry Collett, Mike and
Wena Stevenson, Ann and Tony Bennett-Hughes)*

LULLINGTON   SK2513
Colvile Arms (01827) 373212
*Off A444 S of Burton; Main Street;
DE12 8EG* New licensees for this popular
18th-c village pub; high-backed settles
in simple panelled bar, cosy comfortable
beamed lounge, well kept Bass, Marstons
Pedigree and two guests, over 30 gins, no food
except cobs, pleasant friendly atmosphere;
background music, free wi-fi; children (until
7.30pm) and dogs (in bar) welcome, picnic-
sets on small sheltered back lawn, closed
lunchtimes apart from Sun. *(Jim King)*

MAKENEY   SK3544
★ Holly Bush (01332) 841729
*From A6 heading N after Duffield, take
first right after crossing River Derwent,
then first left; DE56 0RX* Unspoilt 17th-c
two-bar village pub (former farmhouse);
beams and black panelling, tiled and
flagstone floors, three blazing fires, one
in old-fashioned range by snug's curved
high-backed settle, well kept changing ales
(some served from jugs), craft beers and
real cider, enjoyable lunchtime food from
rolls and pork pies up, lobby with hatch
service; beer festivals and occasional live
music; children, walkers and dogs welcome,

picnic-sets outside, open all day, no food
Mon, Tues. *(Julie and Andrew Blanchett)*

MARSTON MONTGOMERY SK1338
Crown (01889) 591430
*On corner of Thurvaston Road and
Barway; DE6 2FF* Refurbished red-brick
beamed village pub, clean and bright,
with friendly helpful staff, popular good
value food (till 7pm Sun), three real ales
including Marstons Pedigree and several
wines by the glass, restaurant; some
live music; children and dogs welcome,
disabled access, terrace tables, seven good
bedrooms, open all day. *(Buster May)*

MATLOCK   SK2960
Moca (01629) 258084
Dale Road; DE4 3LT Light café-style
bar with half a dozen or so well kept
local beers and snacky lunchtime food,
friendly knowledgeable staff, chunky pine
furniture on bare boards, black and white
photographs of musicians/bands; can
fill up as not large; dogs welcome, back
terrace, open all day. *(Jeremy King)*

MATLOCK   SK2960
Thorn Tree (01629) 580295
Jackson Road, Matlock Bank; DE4 3JQ
Superb valley views to Riber Castle from
this homely 19th-c stone-built local, Bass,
Greene King, Nottingham, Timothy Taylors
and guests, simple well cooked food (Tues-Fri
lunchtimes, Sun 5-6.30pm, Weds pie night),
friendly staff and regulars; free wi-fi; children
and dogs welcome, closed Mon lunchtime,
open all day Fri-Sun. *(Charlie Stevens)*

MAYFIELD   SK1444
★ Rose & Crown (01335) 342498
*Main Road (B5032 off A52 W of
Ashbourne); DE6 2JT* Welcoming dining
pub with good attractively presented
food cooked by owner-chef, reasonable
prices, well kept Marstons Pedigree and
nice range of good value wines, efficient
friendly service, woodburner in beamed
bar, restaurant; children welcome, no
dogs inside, terrace tables under parasols,
local walks, three bedrooms, closed Sun
evening, Mon, food served 12-1.30pm,
6.30-8.30pm. *(Brian and Anna Marsden)*

MILLERS DALE   SK1473
Anglers Rest (01298) 871323
*Just down Litton Lane; pub is PH on
OS Sheet 119 map reference 142734;
SK17 8SN* Creeper-clad pub in lovely
quiet riverside setting on the Monsal
Trail; two bars and dining room, log
fires, Adnams, Storm and a couple of

We mention bottled beers and spirits only if there is something unusual about them
– imported belgian real ales, say, or dozens of malt whiskies; so do please let us know
about them in your reports.

usually local guests, enjoyable simple food, cheery helpful service, reasonable prices; darts and pool; children welcome, muddy walkers and dogs in public bar, wonderful gorge views and river walks, self-catering apartment, open all day Sat, till 5pm Sun. *(Nick Sharpe)*

MILLTOWN   SK3561
Miners Arms (01246) 590218
Off B6036 SE of Ashover; Oakstedge Lane; S45 0HA Spotless stone dining pub with good freshly made food from well priced blackboard menu (booking advised), nice wines and one changing real ale, friendly staff, log fires; children welcome, no dogs inside, attractive country walks from the door, closed Mon-Weds (open Weds in Dec). *(Lorna and Jack Mulgrave)*

MONSAL HEAD   SK1871
★ Monsal Head Hotel (01629) 640250
B6465; DE45 1NL Outstanding hilltop location for this friendly inn; cosy stables bar with stripped timber horse-stalls, harness and brassware, farmhouse chairs and benches on flagstones, big open fire, good selection of mainly local ales including one badged for them from Pennine, german bottled beers and plenty of wines by the glass, enjoyable locally sourced food from lunchtime sandwiches up (they may ask to keep your credit card while you eat), elegant restaurant; children (over 3), muddy walkers and well behaved dogs welcome, big garden, stunning views of Monsal Dale with its huge viaduct, seven comfortable bedrooms, open (and food) all day. *(Ann and Colin Hunt)*

MONYASH   SK1566
★ Bulls Head (01629) 812372
B5055 W of Bakewell; DE45 1JH Rambling stone pub with high-ceilinged rooms, straightforward traditional furnishings including plush stools lined along bar, horse pictures and a shelf of china, log fire, four real ales such as Black Sheep and Peak, restaurant with high-backed dining chairs on heated stone floor, popular traditional food (all day weekends) from sandwiches and baked potatoes up, friendly service, small back room with darts, board games and pool; background music; children and dogs welcome, plenty of picnic-sets under parasols in big garden, gate leading to well equipped public play area, good surrounding walks, open all day in high summer, all day Fri-Sun other times. *(Ann and Colin Hunt)*

MOORWOOD MOOR   SK3656
White Hart (01629) 534888
Inns Lane; village signed from South Wingfield; DE55 7NU Cleanly updated country inn with good food including deals in bar and restaurant, helpful attentive staff, well kept Sharps Doom Bar, Timothy

Taylors Landlord and a couple of local guests; children welcome, ten modern bedrooms, open (and food) all day. *(Donald Allsopp)*

NEW MILLS   SJ9886
Fox (0161) 427 1634
Brook Bottom Road; SK22 3AY Tucked-away old-fashioned country local in good walking area at end of single-track road, Robinsons ales and good value pub food (no credit cards), log fire; darts and pool; children and dogs welcome, lots of tables outside, open all day Fri-Sun. *(Charlie Stevens)*

NEWTON SOLNEY   SK2825
Brickmakers Arms (01283) 702558
Main Street (B5008 NE of Burton); DE15 0SJ Friendly end-of-terrace beamed village pub owned by Burton Bridge Brewery and under newish licensees; four of their well kept ales and a couple of guests including Timothy Taylors Landlord, real ciders and plenty of bottled beers, no food (cheeseboard Sun lunchtime), two rooms off bar, one with original panelling and delft shelf displaying jugs and plates, pubby furniture, built-in wall seats and coal fires, area with books; Mon quiz, Tues bingo, Thurs poker, free wi-fi; tables on terrace, open all day weekends, closed lunchtimes during the week. *(Lindy Andrews)*

OCKBROOK   SK4236
Royal Oak (01332) 662378
Off B6096 just outside Spondon; Green Lane; DE72 3SE 18th-c village local run by same friendly family since 1953; good value honest food (not Sun evening) from good lunchtime cobs to steaks, well kept Bass and three interesting guest beers, tile-floored tap room, carpeted snug, inner bar with Victorian prints, larger and lighter side room, nice old settle in entrance corridor, open fires; darts and dominoes, some live music; children welcome, dogs in the evening, disabled access, sheltered cottage garden and cobbled front courtyard, separate play area, open all day weekends. *(Frances Parsons)*

OSMASTON   SK1943
Shoulder of Mutton (01335) 342371
Off A52 SE of Ashbourne; DE6 1LW Down-to-earth red-brick beamed pub with post office/shop, three well kept ales including Marstons Pedigree, enjoyable generous home-made food (all day weekends), good friendly service; fortnightly quiz Sun, free wi-fi; picnic-sets in attractive garden, farmland views, peaceful pretty village with thatched cottages, duck pond and good walks. *(Buster May)*

PARWICH   SK1854
Sycamore (01335) 390212
By church; DE6 1QL Friendly old country pub freshened-up under new management; flagstoned bar with mix of furniture including upholstered wall benches and

some painted tables, woodburner, three Robinsons ales and good reasonably priced home-made food, Tues steak night, a couple of back dining rooms, pub also houses the village shop; darts, free wi-fi; children and dogs welcome, picnic-sets in small front courtyard, more on side grass, good walks, open all day weekends. *(Jim King)*

PILSLEY SK2371

★ Devonshire Arms (01246) 583258

Village signposted off A619 W of Baslow, and pub just below B6048; High Street; DE45 1UL Civilised little country inn on the Chatsworth Estate; gentle contemporary slant with flagstoned bar and several fairly compact areas off (each with own character – some steps), log fires in stone fireplaces, comfortable seating and big modern paintings, three well kept Peak ales, a cider such as Lilley's Strawberry and several wines by the glass, food from lunchtime sandwiches up using Estate produce, friendly efficient staff; children and dogs welcome, a few picnic-sets out at front, Chatsworth farm shop at the top of lane, bedrooms, open all day. *(Ann and Colin Hunt, Stephen Woad)*

REPTON SK3027

Boot (01283) 346047

Boot Hill; DE65 6FT Restored 17th-c beamed inn (sister to the Dragon at Willington); own good microbrews (tasting notes provided) and very well liked interesting food (booking advised, particularly at weekends) including breakfast till 11am, friendly efficient young staff, modernised L-shaped interior; children and dogs (in bar area) welcome, split-level walled garden, nine bedrooms, open all day. *(Clive and Fran Dutson, Stephen Shepherd)*

REPTON SK3026

Bulls Head (01283) 704422

High Street; DE65 6GF Lively village pub with interesting décor in various interconnecting bars; beams and pillars, mix of wooden dining chairs, settles, built-in wall seats and squashy sofas on bare boards or flagstones, driftwood sculptures, animal hides and an arty bull's head, log fires, ales from Marstons, Purity and Shardlow, 15 wines by the glass and 20 malt whiskies, popular food including wood-fired pizzas, cheerful staff, upstairs restaurant; background music, free wi-fi; children and dogs (in bar) welcome, sizeable heated terrace with neatly set tables and chairs under big parasols, open (and food) all day. *(Stephen Shepherd)*

RIPLEY SK3950

Talbot Taphouse (01773) 742382

Butterley Hill; DE5 3LT New licensees for this traditional pub with full range of local Amber ales and changing guests, also traditional ciders, draught belgian and bottled beers, long narrow panelled room with comfy chairs, open fire in brick fireplace, bar billiards and table skittles, friendly atmosphere; open from 5pm weekdays, Fri 3pm, 2pm weekends. *(Buster May)*

ROWSLEY SK2565

★ Peacock (01629) 733518

Bakewell Road; DE4 2EB Civilised small 17th-c country hotel; comfortable seating in spacious modern lounge, inner bar with log fire, bare stone walls and some Robert 'Mouseman' Thompson furniture, good if not cheap food from lunchtime sandwiches to restaurant meals, Peak ales, nice wines and well served coffee, pleasant helpful staff; attractive riverside gardens, trout fishing, 15 good bedrooms. *(Lorna and Jack Musgrave)*

SHARDLOW SK4430

Malt Shovel (01332) 792066

3.5 miles from M1 junction 24, via A6 towards Derby; The Wharf; DE72 2HG Welcoming canalside pub in late 18th-c former maltings, interesting odd-angled layout with cosy corners and steps down to snug, Marstons Pedigree and a beer badged for the pub, very good value tasty home-made food from sandwiches and baked potatoes to specials, evening food Thurs only (thai/ english menu), quick friendly service, beams, panelling and central open fire; live music Sun, free wi-fi; children and dogs welcome, lots of terrace tables by Trent & Mersey Canal, pretty hanging baskets, open all day. *(Dr D J and Mrs S C Walker, John Beeken)*

SHARDLOW SK4429

Old Crown (01332) 792392

Off A50 just W of M1 junction 24; Cavendish Bridge, E of village; DE72 2HL Good value pub with half a dozen well kept Marstons-related ales and decent choice of malt whiskies, pubby food (all day Sat, not Sun evening, Mon) from sandwiches and baguettes up, beams with masses of jugs and mugs, walls covered with other bric-a-brac and breweriana, big inglenook; quiz Mon, fortnightly live music Tues; children and dogs welcome, garden with play area, open all day. *(Nick Sharpe)*

SHELDON SK1768

★ Cock & Pullet (01629) 814292

Village signed off A6 just W of Ashford; DE45 1QS Charming no-frills village pub with low beams, exposed stonework, flagstones and open fire, cheerful mismatch of furnishings, large collection of clocks and various representations of poultry (some stuffed), well kept Sharps Doom Bar, Timothy Taylors Landlord and a guest such as Peak, good simple food from shortish menu including popular Sun roasts (best to book), reasonable prices and friendly efficient service; quiet background music, pool and TV in plainer public bar; children and dogs welcome, seats and water feature on pleasant back terrace, pretty village just off Limestone Way and popular all year with walkers, clean bedrooms, open all day. *(John and Delia Franks)*

SHIRLEY   SK2141
Saracens Head (01335) 360330
Church Lane; DE6 3AS Modernised late 18th-c dining pub in attractive village; good range of well presented blackboard food from pubby choices to more expensive restaurant-style dishes, four Greene King ales, speciality coffees, simple country-style dining furniture and two pretty working art nouveau fireplaces; background music; children and dogs (in bar area) welcome, picnic-sets out in front and on back terrace, open all day Sun. *(Jim King)*

SOUTH WINGFIELD   SK3755
Old Yew Tree (01773) 833626
B5035 W of Alfreton; Manor Road; DE55 7NH Friendly 16th-c village pub with good reasonably priced home-made food (not Sun evening) including lunchtime/ early evening deal, Bass, a local guest (two at weekends) and a proper cider, log fire, beams and carved panelling, separate restaurant area; Sat night entertainment, TV, free wi-fi; children, walkers and dogs welcome, some rattan-style furniture out at the side, open all day Fri-Sun, closed Mon and Tues lunchtimes. *(Robert Turnham)*

STONEDGE   SK3367
Red Lion (01246) 566142
Darley Road (B5057); S45 0LW Revamped bar-bistro (former 17th-c coaching inn) on edge of the Peak District; good attractively presented food (pricey for the area) from sandwiches up using local ingredients including own vegetables, real ales such as Peak and good choice of wines, bare stone walls, flagstones and wood floors, some substantial timbers, lounge area with comfortable seating and open fire; picnic-sets out under parasols at back, 27 bedrooms in adjacent modern hotel, open all day. *(Buster May)*

SUDBURY   SK1632
Vernon Arms (01283) 585329
Off A50/A515; Main Road; DE6 5HS Rambling 17th-c brick pub with enjoyable reasonably priced food including good Sun roasts, four Marstons-related ales, friendly service, three main rooms with stairs to bar, log fires; background music, Sun quiz twice a month; children and dogs welcome, good big garden, handy for Sudbury Hall (NT), open all day. *(Charlie Stevens)*

SUTTON CUM
DUCKMANTON   SK4371
Arkwright Arms (01246) 232053
A632 Bolsover–Chesterfield; S44 5JG Friendly mock-Tudor pub with bar, pool room (dogs allowed here) and dining room, all with real fires, good choice of

well priced food (not Sun evening), up to 16 changing ales, ten real ciders and four perries (beer/cider festivals Easter/Aug bank holidays); TV, games machine; children welcome, seats at front and on side terrace, attractive hanging baskets, play equipment, open all day. *(Nick Sharpe)*

THORPE   SK1650
Old Dog (01335) 350990
Spend Lane/Wintercroft Lane; DE6 2AT Refurbished bistro-style village pub (former 18th-c coaching inn), lively and friendly, with popular food from sensibly short menu including good burgers, four well kept changing ales, good attentive service, candlelit tables on flagstones, woodburners; background music; children, walkers and dogs welcome, covered eating area outside, handy for Dovedale and Tissington Trail, open all day, food all weekends (till 7pm Sun). *(Lenny and Ruth Walters)*

TICKNALL   SK3523
★Wheel (01332) 864488
Main Street (A514); DE73 7JZ Stylish contemporary décor in bar and upstairs restaurant, enjoyable interesting home-made food (all day weekends) including daily specials, friendly efficient staff, well kept Marstons Pedigree and a guest; children welcome, no dogs inside, nice outside area with café tables on raised deck, near entrance to Calke Abbey (NT). *(R L Borthwick)*

TIDESWELL   SK1575
Horse & Jockey (01298) 872211
Queen Street; SK17 8JZ Friendly and relaxed family-run local; beams, flagstones, cushioned wall benches and coal fire in small public bar's traditional open range, bare boards, button-back banquettes and woodburner in lounge, well kept Tetleys and a couple of local guests, decent reasonably priced food (all day Sun), stripped-stone dining room; free wi-fi; children and dogs welcome, six comfortable bedrooms, good walks, open all day. *(Ann and Tony Bennett-Hughes)*

UPPER LANGWITH   SK5169
Devonshire (01623) 747777
Rectory Road; NG20 9RF Popular recently reopened/refurbished dining pub with several cosy areas, highly rated food from lunchtime sandwiches up including good fish dishes (best to book), well kept ales such as Hook Norton and Thwaites, decent wines, friendly attentive service; children welcome, easy disabled access, a few picnic-sets out at front, open all day (till 7pm Sun). *(Derek and Sylvia Stephenson)*

WARDLOW   SK1875
★Three Stags Heads (01298) 872268
Wardlow Mires; A623/B6465; SK17 8RW Basic unchanging pub (17th-c longhouse)

of great individuality; old country furniture on flagstones, heating from cast-iron kitchen ranges, old photographs, long-serving plain-talking landlord, locals in favourite corners, well kept Abbeydale ales including a strong house beer (Black Lurcher), lots of bottled beers, simple food on home-made plates (licensees are potters and have a small gallery), may be free roast chestnuts or cheese on the bar, folk music Sun afternoon; no credit cards or mobile phones; well behaved children and dogs welcome (resident lurchers), hill views from front terrace, good walking country, only open Fri evening and all day weekends. *(Ann and Tony Bennett-Hughes)*

WHITTINGTON MOOR   SK3873
Derby Tup   (01246) 269835
Sheffield Road; B6057 just S of A61 roundabout; S41 8LS Popular Castle Rock local with their ales along with Pigeon Fishers (landlord owns the brewery) and several guests, also craft beers, up to seven ciders and good range of other drinks, coal fire, simple furniture and lots of standing room, two side snugs; live music including jam session last Mon of month; dogs welcome, seats out on small back deck, open all day Fri-Sun (can get very busy weekend evenings and match days), closed Mon-Thurs lunchtimes. *(Beverley and Andy Butcher)*

WILLINGTON   SK2928
Dragon   (01283) 704795
The Green; DE65 6BP Renovated and extended pub backing on to Trent & Mersey Canal; enjoyable well cooked food (all day Fri-Sun) from sandwiches and sharing boards to pub favourites and grills, a couple of microbrews from sister pub the Boot at Repton and local guests; weekend live music, sports TV, free wi-fi; children and dogs (not in restaurant) welcome, picnic-sets out overlooking canal, moorings, open all day. *(Nick Sharpe)*

WINSTER   SK2460
★Bowling Green   (01629) 650219
East Bank, by Market House (NT); DE4 2DS Traditional old stone pub with good chatty atmosphere, character landlord and welcoming staff, enjoyable reasonably priced home-made food, at least three well kept changing local ales and good selection of whiskies, end log fire, dining area and family conservatory (dogs allowed here too); nice village with good surrounding walks, closed Mon, Tues and lunchtimes apart from Sun. *(Daniel King)*

WINSTER   SK2360
Miners Standard   (01629) 650279
Bank Top (B5056 above village); DE4 2DR Simply furnished 17th-c stone local, friendly and relaxed, with bar, snug and restaurant, well kept ales such as Greene King, Marstons and Wychwood, good value honest pub food (not Sun evening), big woodburner, lead mining photographs and minerals, lots of brass, a backwards clock and ancient well; background music; children (away from bar) and dogs welcome, fine view from garden, campsite next door, interesting stone-built village below, open all day. *(John Harris)*

If you report on a pub that's not a featured entry, please tell us any lunchtimes or evenings when it doesn't serve bar food.

Devon

BRAMPFORD SPEKE
SX9298 Map 1

Lazy Toad

(01392) 841591 – www.thelazytoadinn.co.uk

Off A377 N of Exeter; EX5 5DP

Well run dining pub in pretty village with popular food, real ales, friendly service and pretty garden

Although many customers are here to enjoy the very good food, this 18th-c inn is just as popular with those simply wanting a chat and a pint. The interconnected bar rooms have beams, standing timbers and slate floors, a comfortable sofa by an open log fire and cushioned wall settles and high-backed wooden dining chairs around a mix of tables; the cream-painted brick walls are hung with lots of pictures. Exeter 'fraidNot and St Austell Trelawny on handpump and several wines by the glass are served by attentive staff; the irish terrier is called Rufus. The courtyard (once used by the local farrier and wheelwright) has oak benches and tables, with more in the walled garden. It's worth wandering around this charming village of thatched cottages, and there are fine walks beside the River Exe and on the Exe Valley Way and Devonshire Heartland Way.

 High quality food includes sandwiches, grilled mackerel salad with pea and herb dressing, sautéed field mushrooms with toasted raisin bread, spinach, butternut squash and cheddar pie with herb cream, gammon and egg, steak in ale pie, corn-fed chicken with sweet potato mash and pancetta cream, duo of sea bass and salmon with bubble and squeak cake and pea purée, fillet of pork tenderloin with purple truffle potato mash and mustard cream, and puddings such as vanilla bean crème brûlée with berry compote and belgian chocolate amaretto tart with vanilla cream. *Benchmark main dish: fillet of local beef with sage fondant potatoes and peppercorn sauce £22.95. Two-course evening meal £21.00.*

Free house ~ Licensees Harriet and Mike Daly ~ Real ale ~ Open 12-3, 6-11; 12-4 Sun; closed Sun evening, Mon ~ Bar food 12-2, 6.30-9; 12-3 Sun ~ Children welcome but must be over 12 in bedrooms ~ Dogs allowed in bar ~ Wi-fi *Recommended by Comus and Sarah Elliott, Katherine and Hugh Markham, Rupert and Sandy Newton, Amy Ledbetter*

BRANSCOMBE
SY1888 Map 1

Fountain Head 🍺 £

(01297) 680359 – www.fountainheadinn.com

Upper village; W of Branscombe at Street; EX12 3BG

Friendly, old-fashioned pub with local beers and tasty, well priced food

A favourite with our readers, this 14th-c tavern is unchanging and nicely old-fashioned. The room on the left was once a smithy and has forge tools and horseshoes on high oak beams, cushioned pews and mate's chairs, and a log fire in the original raised hearth with its tall central chimney. There's Branscombe Vale Branoc, Golden Fiddle and Summa That on handpump (they hold a June beer festival), two local ciders and eight wines by the glass. On the right, an irregularly shaped snug room has another log fire, a white-painted plank ceiling with an unusual carved ceiling rose, brown-varnished panelling, a flagstone floor and local artwork for sale; darts and board games. You can sit outside on the front loggia and terrace listening to the little stream gurgling beneath the flagstoned path; barbecues and spit roasts are held on Sunday evening from 6pm (end July-early September). Good coastal walks from here.

Reasonably priced, well thought-of food includes lunchtime sandwiches, breaded butterfly prawns with garlic mayonnaise, chicken liver, wild mushroom and basil pâté with fig and peach chutney, vegetable lasagne, home-cooked honey-roast ham and eggs, a pie of the day, chicken filled with smoked bacon and cheese in a white wine sauce, lamb hotpot with boulangère potatoes, and puddings. *Benchmark main dish: beer-battered fresh cod and chips £11.50. Two-course evening meal £16.00.*

Free house ~ Licensees Jon Woodley and Teresa Hoare ~ Real ale ~ Open 11-3, 6-11; 12-10.30 Sun ~ Bar food 12-2, 6.30-9 ~ Restaurant ~ Children welcome away from main bar area ~ Dogs welcome *Recommended by Roger and Donna Huggins, Alfie Bayliss, Diane Abbott, Lucy and Giles Gibbon*

 BRANSCOMBE   SY2088 Map 1

Masons Arms ⇦

(01297) 680300 – www.masonsarms.co.uk

Main Street; signed off A3052 Sidmouth–Seaton, then bear left into village; EX12 3DJ

Rambling low-beamed rooms, woodburning stoves, a fair choice of real ales, popular food and seats on quiet terrace; spotless bedrooms

The heart of this 14th-c thatched inn remains the rambling main bar. This has comfortable seats and chairs on slate floors, ancient ships' beams, a log fire in a massive hearth, St Austell Proper Job and Tribute and guest beers such as Branscombe Vale Summa That and Otter Bitter on handpump and ten wines by the glass. A second bar also has a slate floor, a fireplace with a two-sided woodburning stove and stripped pine; the two dining rooms are smartly furnished. A quiet flower-filled front terrace, with thatched-roof tables, extends into a side garden. The neatly kept and comfortable bedrooms are above the inn or in converted cottages overlooking the gardens (dogs are allowed in these rooms). The sea is just a stroll away and the pretty village is worth exploring, so this popular place does get very busy at peak times.

Well liked food using local produce includes sandwiches, local mussels in garlic, white wine and cream, chicken liver pâté with red onion marmalade, roasted vegetables in thai-spiced coconut sauce, chargrilled chicken and quinoa salad with roasted chilli dressing, steak and kidney pie, burger with toppings, chips and sauce, rump steak with a choice of three sauces, and puddings. *Benchmark main dish: seafood platter £17.50. Two-course evening meal £21.00.*

St Austell ~ Managers Simon and Alison Ede ~ Real ale ~ Open 11-11; 12-10.30 Sun ~ Bar food 12-2.15, 6.30-9; some afternoon dishes and cream teas ~ Restaurant ~ Children welcome ~ Dogs allowed in bar and bedrooms ~ Wi-fi ~ Bedrooms: /£115 *Recommended by Colin McLachlan, Alastair and Sheree Hepburn, Ewan and Sue Hewitt, James and Sylvia Hewitt, John and Claire Masters*

BUCKLAND MONACHORUM

SX4968 Map 1

Drake Manor ⬤ £ ⇨

(01822) 853892 – www.drakemanorinn.co.uk

Off A386 via Crapstone, just S of Yelverton roundabout; PL20 7NA

Nice little village pub with snug rooms, popular food, quite a choice of drinks and pretty back garden; bedrooms

For 27 years the friendly landlady has run this charming little pub with great care and thought. The heavily beamed public bar on the left has a chatty, easy-going feel, brocade-cushioned wall seats, prints of the village from 1905 onwards, horse tack and a few ship badges and a woodburning stove in a very big stone fireplace; a small door leads to a low-beamed cubbyhole. The snug Drakes Bar has beams hung with tiny cups and big brass keys, a woodburning stove in another stone fireplace, horsebrasses and stirrups, and a mix of seats and tables (note the fine stripped-pine high-backed settle with hood). On the right is a small beamed dining room with settles and tables on flagstones. Darts and board games. Dartmoor Jail Ale, Sharps Doom Bar and St Austell Tribute on handpump, ten wines by the glass, a dozen malt whiskies and two farm ciders. There are picnic-sets in the prettily planted and sheltered back garden and the front floral displays are much admired; morris men perform regularly in summer. The bedrooms are comfortable and they also have an attractive self-catering apartment. Buckland Abbey (National Trust) is close by.

 Pleasing food uses home-reared pork, honey from their bees and includes lunchtime baguettes, potted rabbit with ale chutney, honey-roasted figs with candied walnuts and beetroot and blue cheese salad, ham and free-range eggs, cajun chicken with crème fraîche dressing, burgers with toppings and chips (they hold a burger evening on the first Tuesday of the month), butternut squash, spinach and ricotta cannelloni in goats cheese sauce, seafood pie, a trio of pork (tenderloin, cheek and belly) in apple and cider jus, and puddings such as raspberry and yoghurt pannacotta with raspberry sorbet and mixed berry granola and banana parfait with hazelnut praline, salted caramel sauce and millionaire shortbread ice-cream. *Benchmark main dish: beef in Guinness pie £10.50. Two-course evening meal £16.00.*

Punch ~ Lease Mandy Robinson ~ Real ale ~ Open 11.30-2.30, 6.30-11; 11.30-11.30 Fri, Sat; 12-11 Sun ~ Bar food 11.30-2, 6.30-9.30; 11.30-2.30, 6-9.30 Sat; 12-2.30, 6.30-9.30 Sun ~ Restaurant ~ Children welcome ~ Dogs allowed in bar ~ Wi-fi ~ Bedrooms: /£90
Recommended by Peter Andrews, Sandra and Nigel Brown, Jeremy Snaithe, Alison and Michael Harper, Donald Allsopp

CHAGFORD

SX7087 Map 1

Three Crowns ⇨

(01647) 433444 – www.threecrowns-chagford.co.uk

High Street; TQ13 8AJ

Stylishly refurbished bar and lounges in ancient inn, conservatory restaurant and good food and drinks; smart bedrooms

The ancient and modern features in this beautifully refurbished, part-thatched 13th-c former manor house blend together surprisingly well. There are massive beams and standing timbers, huge fireplaces with wood fires (lit all year), exposed stone walls, flagstones and mullioned windows, and a contemporary, glazed atrium dining room. The bar areas have leather armchairs and stools, built-in panelled wall seats and a few leather tub chairs. Dartmoor Jail Ale, St Austell Proper Job and Tribute on handpump, 20 wines by the glass and 21 gins served by friendly, hard-working staff.

Throughout the building are antique prints, photographs and polished copper kettles, pots and warming pans; background music and board games. The south-facing courtyard has sturdy tables and chairs among box topiary. Bedrooms are stylish and well appointed and blend character with modern design. Parking is limited to superior rooms only but there's also a nearby pay-and-display car park. Muddy boots and dogs are welcome.

🍴 Using local, seasonal produce, the reliably good food includes breakfasts, morning snacks and afternoon cream teas as well as sandwiches, local mussels in chorizo and tomato broth, smoked ham hock terrine with piccalilli, sharing platters, pea and mint tortellini with minted pea velouté, a trio of pork (belly, croquette and black pudding) with vanilla mash and salt-baked celeriac, sea bream fillet with truffle, mussel and white bean cassoulet, rare-breed rib-eye steak with confit shallots and thyme and red wine jus, and puddings such as apple and berry crumble with clotted cream and lemon cheesecake with lemon sorbet. *Benchmark main dish: luxury fish pie £16.00. Two-course evening meal £20.50.*

St Austell ~ Managers John Milan and Steve Bellman ~ Real ale ~ Open 10am-11pm; 10am-midnight Fri, Sat ~ Bar food 12-9 (9.30 Sat); 8-10am breakfast, 10am-midday snacks; 2.30-6pm sandwiches and cream teas ~ Restaurant ~ Children welcome ~ Dogs allowed in bar ~ Wi-fi ~ Bedrooms: £90/£110 *Recommended by Peter Andrews, George Sanderson, Dr A E and Mrs Forbes, Dr A McCormick, Professor James Burke, Amy and Luke Buchanan*

COCKWOOD
SX9780   Map 1
Anchor 🍺

(01626) 890203 – www.anchorinncockwood.com
Off, but visible from, A379 Exeter–Torbay, after Starcross; EX6 8RA

Busy dining pub specialising in seafood (other choices available), with up to six real ales

Of course, the position is quite a draw – the much prized tables on the sheltered front terrace look over the small harbour with its bobbing boats, swans and ducks; they also offer up to six real ales on handpump. An extension is made up of mainly reclaimed timber and decorated with over 300 ship emblems, brass and copper lamps and nautical knick-knacks, but there are also several small, low-ceilinged, rambling rooms with black panelling and good-sized tables in various nooks; the snug has a cheerful winter coal fire. Dartmoor Jail Ale, Otter Ale and St Austell Tribute with guests such as Beerd Monterey and South Hams Wild Blonde on handpump (beer festivals at Easter and Halloween), eight wines by the glass, 13 gins and 40 malt whiskies; background music, darts, cards and board games. Parking can be tricky at peak times.

🍴 As well as 19 ways of serving River Exe mussels, food includes sandwiches, smoked mackerel pâté with chutney, potted crab, vegetarian sausages and mash, steak in ale pie, chicken breast on mushroom and shallot sauce with peppers and leeks, scallops with lemon mayonnaise and dill pickles, surf and turf (fillet steak with king prawns and scallops), shared shellfish selection (for two people), and puddings such as sticky toffee pudding and passion-fruit bavarois. *Benchmark main dish: various ways with mussels £14.95. Two-course evening meal £22.00.*

Heavitree ~ Lease Malcolm and Katherine Protheroe, Scott Hellier ~ Real ale ~ Open 11-11; 11.30-10.30 Sun ~ Bar food 12-9 (9.30 Fri, Sat) ~ Restaurant ~ Children welcome if seated and away from bar ~ Dogs allowed in bar *Recommended by Toby Jones, Patricia Hawkins, Dr and Mrs A K Clarke, Graeme and Sally Mendham, Nick Higgins*

We say if we know a pub has background music.

COLEFORD

SS7701 Map 1

New Inn

(01363) 84242 – www.thenewinncoleford.co.uk

Just off A377 Crediton–Barnstaple; EX17 5BZ

Ancient thatched inn with welcoming licensees, good food and real ales; bedrooms

The small hamlet of thatched houses includes this 13th-c inn and as it's between Exmoor and Dartmoor there are always plenty of customers. The U-shaped building has the servery in the 'angle' with interestingly furnished areas leading off it: ancient and modern settles, cushioned stone wall seats, some character tables (a pheasant worked into the grain of one) and carved dressers and chests. Also, paraffin lamps, antique prints on the white walls, landscape-decorated plates on one beam and pewter tankards on another. Captain, the chatty parrot, may greet you with a 'hello' or even a 'goodbye'. Otter Ale and Sharps Doom Bar on handpump, local cider, 16 wines by the glass and a dozen malt whiskies; background music, darts and board games. There are chairs and tables on decking beneath a pruned willow tree by the babbling stream, and more in a covered dining area. Bedrooms are well equipped and comfortable and the breakfasts are very good indeed. At 600 years old, this warmly friendly place is one of the oldest 'new' inns in the country.

 Rewarding food includes lunchtime sandwiches and baguettes, venison and pork terrine with cranberry and orange compote, grilled goats cheese on poached pear with a honey, walnut oil and orange vinaigrette, aubergine and sweet potato moussaka with tomato and onion passata and crumbled feta cheese, sausages with yorkshire pudding and onion gravy, slow-cooked lamb shank with a red wine, pink peppercorn and mushroom sauce, chicken with crème fraîche, wholegrain mustard and tarragon sauce on charlotte potatoes, and puddings such as cappuccino brûlée and chocolate brownies. *Benchmark main dish: duck breast with raspberry sauce £15.50. Two-course evening meal £19.50.*

Free house ~ Licensees Carole and George Cowie ~ Real ale ~ Open 12-3, 6-11 (10.30 Sun) ~ Bar food 12-2, 6.30-9 ~ Restaurant ~ Children welcome ~ Dogs allowed in bar ~ Wi-fi ~ Monthly quiz Sun evening and summer hog roasts ~ Bedrooms: £70/£90 *Recommended by David Longhurst, Sally and David Champion, Jeremy Snaithe, Cliff and Monica Swan, Emma Scofield, Mike Benton*

DALWOOD

ST2400 Map 1

Tuckers Arms

(01404) 881342 – www.thetuckersarms.co.uk

Village signposted off A35 Axminster–Honiton; keep on past village; EX13 7EG

13th-c thatched inn with friendly, hard-working licensees, real ales and interesting bar food

The flagstoned bar in this thatched medieval longhouse is kept warm by a big inglenook log fireplace, and there are heavy beams, traditional furnishings including assorted dining chairs, window seats and wall settles, numerous horsebrasses and a friendly, bustling atmosphere. The back bar has an enormous collection of miniature bottles and there's also a more formal dining room; lots of copper implements and platters on display. Branscombe Vale Branoc, Exeter Avocet and Otter Bitter on handpump, several wines by the glass and up to 20 malt whiskies; background music and a double skittle alley. There are seats in the garden. The colourful summer window boxes, hanging baskets and tubs are really delightful and the pub is surrounded by narrow high-hedged lanes and hilly pasture countryside. Apart from the church, this is the oldest building in the parish.

Good, popular food includes lunchtime sandwiches, puff pastry pork belly with apricot, cider and raisin chutney and crackling, potted crab, an antipasti platter, pumpkin and sage ravioli, local moules marinière, steak in ale pie, smoked haddock florentine, lamb rump with redcurrant and rosemary gravy and bubble and squeak, and puddings such as butterscotch and ginger pudding with salted caramel ice-cream and lemon meringue slice. *Benchmark main dish: braised ox short rib in a creamy black pepper sauce £16.95. Two-course evening meal £21.00.*

Free house ~ Licensee Tracey McGowan ~ Real ale ~ Open 11.30-3, 6.30-11.30 ~ Bar food 12-2, 6.30-9 ~ Restaurant ~ Well behaved children in restaurant ~ Dogs allowed in bar ~ Wi-fi ~ Bedrooms: £45/£69.50 *Recommended by Tom Stone, Edward Nile, Julie Swift, Dr A McCormick, Ewan and Sue Hewitt, Andreas, Chris Stevenson, Jack Trussler*

DARTMOUTH
Royal Castle Hotel ♀ ⇌

SX8751 Map 1

(01803) 833033 – www.royalcastle.co.uk

The Quay; TQ6 9PS

350-year-old hotel by the harbour with a genuine mix of customers, real ales and good food; comfortable bedrooms

As this place was originally two Tudor merchant houses (although the façade is Regency), there's a great deal of character and many original features – some of the beams are said to have come from the wreckage of the Spanish Armada. The two ground-floor bars are quite different. The traditional Galleon bar (on the right) has a log fire in a Tudor fireplace, some fine antiques and maritime pieces, quite a bit of copper and brass and plenty of chatty locals. The Harbour Bar (to the left of the flagstoned entrance hall) is contemporary in style and rather smart, with a big-screen TV and live acoustic music on Thursday evenings. The more formal restaurant looks over the river; background music. Dartmoor Jail Ale, Otter Amber, Sharps Doom Bar and a weekly guest on handpump and 28 wines by the glass; service is helpful and friendly. This is a really enjoyable place to stay (breakfasts are excellent) and some of the stylish bedrooms overlook the water; dogs, welcome in all rooms, get treats and a toy. They also have their own secure parking.

Interesting food includes local mussels in cider and cream, goats cheese mousse with honey and thyme marinated beetroot, rocket and sun-dried tomato vinaigrette, sharing platters, ham and duck egg with piccalilli, cumberland sausage with onions and gravy, gnocchi with wild mushrooms, roasted butternut squash, courgette ribbons and lemon cream, a pie of the week, crab linguine with creamy shellfish bisque, lamb saddle and slow-cooked lamb croquette with roasted celeriac purée, and puddings such as chocolate brownie mousse with meringue and honeycomb and vanilla pannacotta with jellied berries. *Benchmark main dish: battered fresh fish and chips £14.95. Two-course evening meal £21.00.*

Free house ~ Licensees Nigel and Anne Way ~ Real ale ~ Open 8am-11pm (10.30pm Sun) ~ Bar food 8am-10pm ~ Restaurant ~ Children welcome ~ Dogs allowed in bar ~ Wi-fi ~ Live acoustic music Thurs evening, easy listening Sun afternoon ~ Bedrooms: £130/£180 *Recommended by Tony Scott, Scott and Charlotte Havers, Elisabeth and Bill Humphries, Charles Welch*

The details at the end of each featured entry start by saying whether the pub is a free house, or if it belongs to a brewery or pub group (which we name).

 DODDISCOMBSLEIGH   SX8586 Map 1

Nobody Inn ♀

(01647) 252394 – www.nobodyinn.co.uk

Off B3193; EX6 7PS

Busy old pub with plenty of character, a fine range of drinks, well liked bar food and friendly staff; bedrooms

Our readers continue to enjoy their visits here, with all of them praising the extraordinary choice of drinks: a beer named for the pub from Branscombe Vale and two changing guests such as Bath Gem and Yeovil Glory on handpump, 30 wines by the glass from a list of 200, 270 malt whiskies and three farm ciders. The beamed lounge bar of two character rooms contains handsomely carved antique settles, windsor and wheelback chairs, all sorts of wooden tables, guns and hunting prints in a snug area by one of the big inglenook fireplaces and fresh flowers; board games. The restaurant is more formal. In summer, try to bag one of the picnic-sets in the pretty garden with views of the surrounding wooded hill pastures. Do make the time to visit the local church, which has some of the best medieval stained glass in the west country.

Tasty food includes chicken and leek terrine with confit nut salad and truffle mayonnaise, battered salt and pepper squid with sweet chilli, barbecue poussin with charred vegetables, burger with toppings, coleslaw and french fries, pork belly with black pudding colcannon, pork jus and apple sauce, salmon en croûte with hollandaise, lamb rump with sauté potatoes and red wine jus, and puddings such as chocolate and salted caramel tart with praline and chocolate crumb and salted caramel ice-cream and coconut cake with mango sorbet and mango sauce. *Benchmark main dish: steak in ale pie £11.95. Two-course evening meal £22.00.*

Free house ~ Licensee Susan Burdge ~ Real ale ~ Open 11-11; 12-10.30 Sun ~ Bar food 12-2.30, 6-9 (9.30 Fri, Sat); 12-3, 6-9 Sun ~ Restaurant ~ Children welcome away from main bar; no under-5s in restaurant ~ Wi-fi ~ Bedrooms: £65/£99
Recommended by S G N Bennett, Piotr Chodzko-Zajko, Stephen Shepherd, Dr and Mrs J D Abell, Nicola and Holly Lyons, Beth Aldridge, Katherine and Hugh Markham

 EXETER   SX9192 Map 1

Fat Pig ◖

(01392) 437217 – www.fatpig-exeter.co.uk

John Street; EX1 1BL

Enthusiastically run pub with own-brew beers, home-distilled spirits, big-flavoured food and a buoyant atmosphere

You can be sure of a cheerful welcome and a lively, bustling atmosphere in this renovated Victorian pub. The big-windowed bar is simply furnished: elegant stools against a mahogany counter, more stools and long cushioned pews by sturdy pale wooden tables on bare boards, an open fire in a pretty fireplace, blackboards listing food choices and lots of mirrors. There's also a red-painted and red quarry-tiled conservatory with a happy jumble of hops and house plants, books and old stone bottles on shelves, more mirrors and long benches and settles with scatter cushions around rustic tables. They brew their own beers, which include Fat Pig Imperial Pirate Black IPA, Porco Rosso and Snout Stout, and have a guest or two on handpump, good wines by the glass, around 100 malt whiskies and their own Exeter Distillery gins (they have three), vodka and apple pie moonshine.

🍴 They source their rare-breed meat from nearby farms, shoot local game and make their own sausages, black pudding and dry-cured ham. The robust dishes include treacle-cured salmon and pickled cucumber, caramelised pork tongue with sauce gribiche, home-made sausages with mash and cider gravy, brined and smoked chicken with chimichurri sauce, goats cheese and leek pie, cinnamon and orange crispy smoked duck leg with sour chipotle cream, and puddings such as apple and rhubarb frangipane tart with ice-cream and hibiscus jelly with orange ice and fresh mint. *Benchmark main dish: english mustard and honey-smoked pork ribs and pickles with chips £15.00. Two-course evening meal £20.00.*

Free house ~ Licensee Paul Timewell ~ Real ale ~ Open 5pm-midnight; 12-midnight Sat; 12-6 Sun ~ Bar food 5-9; 5-10 Fri; 12-9 Sat; 12-4 Sun ~ Restaurant ~ Children allowed until 6pm ~ Dogs welcome ~ Wi-fi *Recommended by Geoffrey Sutton, Colin and Daniel Gibbs, Jamie and Sue May, Sophia and Hamish Greenfield, Adam Jones*

FROGMORE
SX7742 Map 1

Globe 🛏
(01548) 531351 – www.theglobeinn.co.uk
A379 E of Kingsbridge; TQ7 2NR

Extended and neatly refurbished inn with bar and several dining areas, real ales, popular food and seats outside; comfortable bedrooms

This is a lovely area to explore and the surrounding South Hams countryside is very pretty – so it makes sense to use the well equipped bedrooms here as a base; breakfasts are generous. The neatly kept bar has a double-sided woodburner with horsebrass-decorated stone pillars on either side, another fireplace filled with logs, cushioned settles, chunky farmhouse chairs and built-in wall seating around a mix of tables on wooden flooring, and a copper diving helmet. Attentive staff serve Otter Ale, Skinners Betty Stogs and South Hams Eddystone on handpump and several wines by the glass. The slate-floored games room has a pool table and darts. There's also a comfortable lounge with an open fire, cushioned dining chairs and tables on red carpeting, a big leather sofa, a model yacht and a large yacht painting – spot the clever mural of a log pile. Teak tables and chairs sit on the back terrace, with steps leading up to another level with picnic-sets; the summer window boxes are very pretty.

🍴 Well liked food includes lunchtime sandwiches and baguettes, smoked haddock and salmon fishcakes with horseradish mayonnaise, ham hock terrine with piccalilli, pizzas, steak in ale pie, beetroot and goats cheese salad with orange and candied hazelnuts, crab and prawn linguine, burger with toppings, red onion rings and chips, a curry of the day, pigeon on chorizo and pea risotto, pork tenderloin with confit garlic polenta and wild mushroom and red pepper purée, and puddings such as white chocolate cheesecake with stewed fruit compote and crème brûlée with Cointreau. *Benchmark main dish: seafood pancake £11.95. Two-course evening meal £17.00.*

Free house ~ Licensees John and Lynda Horsley ~ Real ale ~ Open 12-11 (10.30 Sun) except mid Sept-end June 12-2.30, 6-11 (10.30 Sun in winter); closed Mon lunchtime in winter ~ Bar food 12-2, 6-9 ~ Restaurant ~ Children welcome ~ Dogs allowed in bar and bedrooms ~ Wi-fi ~ Folk evenings first Tues, third Thurs and last Sun of month ~ Bedrooms: £70/£85 *Recommended by S G N Bennett, Rod and Chris Pring, Bob and Margaret Holder, B and F A Hannam, Paul Farraday, Jane Rigby*

We say if we know a pub allows dogs.

 GEORGEHAM   SS4639 Map 1

Rock ⭐ 🌟 ♀

(01271) 890322 – www.therockinn.biz

Rock Hill, above village; EX33 1JW

Beamed pub with good food, five real ales, plenty of room inside and out and a relaxed atmosphere

With enjoyable food and a genuine welcome, this 17th-c pub is popular with our readers. The big bustling bar is the heart of the place and is divided in two by a step. The pubby top part has half-planked walls, an open woodburning stove in a stone fireplace and captain's and farmhouse chairs around wooden tables on quarry tiles; the lower area has panelled wall seats, some built-in settles forming a cosy booth, old local photographs and ancient flat irons. Leading off here is a red-carpeted dining room with attractive black and white photographs of North Devon folk. Friendly young staff serve Bass, Exmoor Gold, Sharps Doom Bar and Timothy Taylors Landlord on handpump and more than a dozen wines by the glass; background music and board games. The light and airy back dining conservatory has high-backed wooden or modern dining chairs around tables under a vine, with a little terrace beyond. There are picnic-sets at the front beside pretty hanging baskets and tubs; wheelchair access.

 High quality food includes lunchtime sandwiches, shredded duck wraps with cucumber, spring onions and hoisin sauce, whole baked camembert with garlic and thyme, sharing platters, spanish-style chorizo and beef burger with manchego and serrano ham with aioli and chips, a pie of the week, thai green vegetable curry, beer-battered cod and chips, and puddings such as chocolate fondant and apple and rhubarb crumble with vanilla custard. *Benchmark main dish: spaghetti with king prawns, white wine, garlic, chilli and parsley £16.95. Two-course evening meal £20.00.*

Punch ~ Lease Daniel Craddock ~ Real ale ~ Open 11am-11.30pm (midnight Sat); 12-11.30 Sun ~ Bar food 12-2.30, 6-9; 12-8.30 Sun ~ Restaurant ~ Children welcome ~ Dogs allowed in bar ~ Wi-fi *Recommended by Stephen Shepherd, Margaret McDonald, Bob and Margaret Holder, Mike Benton, Andrew and Michele Revell*

HAYTOR VALE   SX7777 Map 1

Rock ★ 🌟 ♀ 🛏

(01364) 661305 – www.rock-inn.co.uk

Haytor signposted off B3387 just W of Bovey Tracey, on good moorland road to Widecombe; TQ13 9XP

● ●

Devon Dining Pub of the Year

Smart Dartmoor inn with lovely food, real ales and seats in pretty garden; comfortable bedrooms

This civilised place is on the edge of Dartmoor National Park and makes a marvellous base for walking: the smart, beamed bedrooms (with garden or moor views) are highly regarded by our readers and breakfasts are excellent. It's at its most informal at lunchtime. The two neatly kept, linked, partly panelled bar rooms have lots of dark wood and red plush, polished antique tables with candles and fresh flowers, old-fashioned prints and decorative plates, and warming winter log fires (the main fireplace has a fine Stuart fireback). Dartmoor IPA and Jail Ale on handpump, 15 wines (plus champagne and sparkling rosé) by the glass and 20 malt whiskies. There's also a light and spacious dining room in the lower part of the inn and a residents' lounge. The large, attractive garden opposite has some seating, with more on the little terrace adjacent to the pub. There is parking at the back of the building.

First class food includes lunchtime sandwiches, goats cheese mousse with balsamic and red wine poached fig, citrus-cured salmon with mixed beetroot, pork and apple burger with coleslaw, mustard mayonnaise and chips, roasted butternut squash, leek and sage risotto with crème fraîche and parmesan, chicken with tarragon mash and peppercorn sauce, stone bass with sweet potatoes, king prawns and chorizo butter, lamb rump with celeriac purée, fondant potato and red wine sauce, and puddings such as espresso crème brûlée and salted caramel tart with vanilla and ginger ice-cream. *Benchmark main dish: rib-eye steak with mushroom and truffle purée and peppercorn sauce £17.95. Two-course evening meal £21.00.*

Free house ~ Licensee Christopher Graves ~ Real ale ~ Open 11am-10.30pm (11pm Sat); 12-10.30 Sun ~ Bar food 12-2, 7-9 (8.30 Sun) ~ Restaurant ~ Children welcome away from main bar ~ Wi-fi ~ Bedrooms: $80/$100 *Recommended by Kim Skuse, Dr and Mrs F McGinn, Maggie and Matthew Lyons, Robin and Anne Triggs, James and Becky Plath*

HORNDON

SX5280 Map 1

Elephants Nest 🍺 £ 🛏

(01822) 810273 – www.elephantsnest.co.uk

If coming from Okehampton on A386, turn left at Mary Tavy Inn, then left after about 0.5 miles; pub signposted beside Mary Tavy Inn, then Horndon signposted; on OS Sheet it's named as the New Inn; PL19 9NQ

Isolated old inn with some interesting original features, real ales and changing food; good bedrooms

In warm weather, the spreading, pretty garden (with an area reserved for adults only) really comes into its own with picnic-sets under parasols and views across dry-stone walls to pastures and rougher moorland above. The main bar has lots of beer pump clips on the beams, high bar chairs by the bar counter, Dartmoor Jail Ale, Palmers IPA and a summer guest ale on handpump, a couple of farm ciders, several wines by the glass and 15 malt whiskies. Two other rooms have an assortment of wooden dining chairs around a mix of tables, and throughout there are bare stone walls, flagstones, horsebrasses and three woodburning stoves. Many people use the attractively furnished and deeply comfortable bedrooms here as a base while exploring the area – the breakfasts are especially good.

Tasty food includes lunchtime baguettes, pork terrine with pickled vegetables and apricot chutney, haddock mornay, new potato and onion tarte tatin with crispy capers and hazelnuts, beer-battered fresh haddock and chips, cumberland sausage with mash and onion gravy, loin of venison with celeriac and sour berry sauce, partridge breast with confit leg, smoked mash, roasted grapes and chestnut velouté, and puddings such as treacle tart with clotted cream and blackberry and apple crumble with custard. *Benchmark main dish: steak and kidney pudding £15.95. Two-course evening meal £21.00.*

Free house ~ Licensee Hugh Cook ~ Real ale ~ Open 12-3, 6.30-11 (10.30 Sun) ~ Bar food 12-2.30, 6.30-9 ~ Restaurant ~ Children welcome away from bar ~ Dogs welcome ~ Wi-fi ~ Bedrooms: /$120 *Recommended by Colin McLachlan, M G Hart, Stephen Shepherd, Alexandra and Richard Clay, Louise and Oliver Redman*

A star symbol after the name of a pub shows exceptional character and appeal. It doesn't mean extra comfort. And it's nothing to do with exceptional food quality, for which there's a separate star-on-a-plate symbol. Even quite a basic pub can win a star, if it's individual enough.

THE GOOD PUB GUIDE

IDDESLEIGH

SS5608 Map 1

Duke of York

(01837) 810253 – www.dukeofyorkdevon.co.uk

B3217 Exbourne–Dolton; EX19 8BG

Unfussy old place with simple furnishings, tasty food and a fair choice of drinks; charming bedrooms

This thatched pub is made up of four cottages, originally built for craftsmen rebuilding the church – it dates from the 15th c. The unspoilt bar has plenty of chatty locals and the homely character is helped along by rocking chairs, cushioned benches built into the wall's black-painted wooden dado, stripped tables and other simple country furnishings, banknotes pinned to beams, and a large open fireplace. Adnams Broadside, Bays Topsail and Otter Bitter tapped from the cask and a dozen wines by the glass. It can get pretty cramped at peak times. The dining room has a huge inglenook fireplace. Through a small coach arch is a little back garden with some picnic-sets. Three bedrooms are in the pub, with three more just a minute's walk away. Michael Morpurgo, author of *War Horse*, got the inspiration to write the novel after talking to World War I veteran Wilfred Ellis in front of the fire here almost 30 years ago.

A choice of food includes sandwiches, salt and pepper squid with chilli dip, creamy stilton mushrooms with crostini, five-bean mexican chilli, slow-roasted lamb shank with ale gravy, honey-roast ham and eggs, lambs liver and bacon with onion gravy, fish pie, beef in Guinness casserole, and puddings. *Benchmark main dish: steak and kidney pudding £13.95. Two-course evening meal £19.00.*

Free house ~ Licensee John Pittam ~ Real ale ~ Open 11-midnight ~ Bar food 12-3, 5.30-9; 12-9 Fri-Sun ~ Restaurant ~ Children welcome ~ Dogs allowed in bar and bedrooms ~ Wi-fi ~ Bedrooms: $55/$80 *Recommended by Alan and Alice Morgan, Simon and Alex Knight, Lindy Andrews, Frank and Marcia Pelling*

THE GOOD PUB GUIDE

KING'S NYMPTON

SS6819 Map 1

Grove ♀ ▥

(01769) 580406 – www.thegroveinn.co.uk

Off B3226 SW of South Molton; EX37 9ST

Thatched 17th-c pub in remote village with local beers, highly rated bar food and cheerful licensees

This is a lovely conservation village and the 17th-c thatched pub is very much part of it. The low-beamed bar has lots of bookmarks hanging from the ceiling, simple pubby furnishings on flagstones, bare stone walls and a winter log fire; darts and board games. A thoughtful and very good choice of drinks includes Country Life Shore Break, Exmoor Ale, Flying Monk Habit and Otter Ale on handpump (the particularly friendly landlord tries to source his ales as locally as possible and they hold a beer festival in July), 32 wines (and champagne) by the glass, 65 malt whiskies and six farm ciders. There's a self-catering cottage to rent, and the pub is surrounded by quiet rolling and wooded countryside.

Particularly good food includes sandwiches, duo of local trout with horseradish cream, breaded small-fry with garlic mayonnaise, all-day breakfast, hogs pudding with onion gravy, vegetable tagine with herbed couscous, rose veal burger with mature cheddar and chips, spit-roast chicken with red wine and rosemary sauce, individual beef fillet wellington, hake with salsa verde and rapeseed mash, and puddings such as burnt cream of local rhubarb and hot chocolate pudding with dairy vanilla ice.

Benchmark main dish: free-range chicken breast stuffed with local blue cheese and wild garlic £11.50. Two-course evening meal £16.00.

Free house ~ Licensees Robert and Deborah Smallbone ~ Real ale ~ Open 12-3, 6-11; 12-4, 7-10 Sun; closed Mon ~ Bar food 12-2, 6.30-9; 12-2.30 Sun ~ Restaurant ~ Well behaved children welcome ~ Dogs welcome ~ Wi-fi *Recommended by Guy Vowles, Barbara Brown, Alan and Alice Morgan, Penny and David Shepherd*

KINGSBRIDGE   SX7344   Map 1

Dodbrooke Inn ◧ £

(01548) 852068

Church Street, Dodbrooke (parking some way off); TQ7 1DB

Bustling local with friendly licensees, chatty locals and well thought-of food and drink

For 27 years this bustling, quaint local has been run by the same friendly licensees, who continue to welcome both regulars and visitors. It's a small terraced pub in a quiet residential area and the traditional bar has built-in cushioned stall seats and plush cushioned stools around pubby tables, some horse harness, local photographs and china jugs, a log fire and an easy-going atmosphere. Bass, Sharps Doom Bar, Youngs Bitter and a guest ale on handpump, local cider and eight wines by the glass. You can sit in the covered courtyard, which might be candlelit in warm weather.

Food continues to be fair value and includes sandwiches, deep-fried whitebait with tartare sauce, scallops and crispy bacon, ham and egg, beef stroganoff, beer-battered cod and french fries, sausage in a basket, minted lamb shank, and puddings. *Benchmark main dish: steaks with a choice of sauces £14.50. Two-course evening meal £16.00.*

Free house ~ Licensees Michael and Jill Dyson ~ Real ale ~ Open 12-2, 5-11; 12-2.30, 7-10.30 Sun; closed Mon-Weds lunchtimes ~ Bar food 12-1.30, 5.30-8.30 ~ Children welcome if over 5 ~ Wi-fi *Recommended by Brian and Sally Wakeham, Sandra and Nigel Brown, Peter Brix, Edward May*

LYDFORD   SX5285   Map 1

Dartmoor Inn ⦿ ♀ ⇌

(01822) 820221 – www.dartmoorinn.com

Downton, A386; EX20 4AY

Gently civilised inn with cheerful little bar, smartly informal dining rooms, excellent food and west country ales; pretty bedrooms

Situated on the edge of Dartmoor National Park, this attractive restaurant-with-rooms is at its most informal at lunchtime when customers (and their dogs) drop in after a walk. There's a cheerful small bar with a log fire, Otter Ale and St Austell Tribute on handpump and good wines by the glass. Several interconnected, civilised but relaxed dining rooms are individually furnished, with stylish contemporary décor, upholstered or painted wooden high-backed chairs around nice old tables on wooden floors, gilt-edged mirrors and open fires. Each of the three comfortable, well equipped and prettily decorated bedrooms has its own sitting area.

Much enjoyed food includes spiced crab soup, breaded goats cheese with apple and hazelnut salad, asparagus, saffron and leek risotto with a poached egg, hake fillet with indian spices, onion bhaji and wild garlic oil, lambs liver and kidneys with bacon and mash, slow-cooked duck confit with spiced red cabbage, steaks with herb butter, balsamic butter and chips, and puddings such as vanilla pannacotta and passion-fruit jelly and crème fraîche sorbet and chocolate fudge cake with chocolate sauce, honeycomb and brownie ice-cream. *Benchmark main dish: beer-battered fish and chips £13.95. Two-course evening meal £20.00.*

Free house ~ Licensee Philip Burgess ~ Real ale ~ Open 11.30-2.30, 6-11; 12-3 Sun; closed Sun and Mon evenings ~ Bar food 12-2.30, 6.30-9 ~ Restaurant ~ Children welcome ~ Dogs allowed in bar ~ Bedrooms: £85/£115 *Recommended by Beverley and Andy Butcher, Sally and Lance Oldham, Holly and Tim Waite*

MARLDON

Church House 🌟 ⚲

SX8663 Map 1

(01803) 558279 – www.churchhousemarldon.com
Off A380 NW of Paignton; TQ3 1SL

Pleasant inn with spreading bar rooms, particularly good food, fine choice of drinks, and seats on three terraces and in the garden

To find this attractive, bustling inn just head for the church. The pleasingly furnished, spreading bar with its woodburning stove has several different areas radiating off the big semicircular bar counter: unusual windows, some beams, dark pine and other nice old dining chairs around solid tables and yellow leather bar chairs. Leading off here is a cosy little candlelit room with four tables on bare boards, a painted dado and stone fireplace. There's a restaurant with a large stone fireplace and, at the other end of the building, a similarly interesting room, split into two, with a stone floor in one part and a wooden floor (and big woodburning stove) in the other. The old barn holds yet another restaurant with displays by local artists. Dartmoor Jail Ale, Teignworthy Gun Dog and Neap Tide and a guest beer on handpump, 16 wines by the glass, ten malt whiskies and local cider; background music and board games. There are picnic-sets on three carefully maintained grassy terraces behind the pub, and the village cricket field is opposite.

 Highly regarded food includes sandwiches, smoked salmon and spinach roulade with cucumber relish, tiger prawns with lime, ginger and coriander butter, spaghetti with tomato sauce, artichokes, pine nuts and parmesan, corn-fed chicken suprême with wild mushrooms and cheese with leek velouté, slow-cooked pork belly with sage and goats cheese pesto and pear and cider jus, monkfish with mussel, serrano ham and white bean stew with parsley pistou, and puddings such as coffee and walnut pudding with espresso sauce and lemon tart with mixed berry compote and ice-cream. *Benchmark main dish: slow-cooked lamb with redcurrant sauce £16.50. Two-course evening meal £24.00.*

Enterprise ~ Lease Julian Cook ~ Real ale ~ Open 11.30-2.30, 5.30-11; 12-3, 5.30-11 Sun ~ Bar food 12-2, 6.30-9.30 (9 Sun) ~ Restaurant ~ Children welcome ~ Dogs allowed in bar ~ Wi-fi *Recommended by Mike and Mary Carter, Jane and Kai Horsburgh, Jane and Philip Saunders, Louise and Oliver Redman, Ben and Jenny Settle*

MORETONHAMPSTEAD
Horse 🌟

SX7586 Map 1

(01647) 440242 – www.thehorsedartmoor.co.uk
George Street; TQ13 8NF

Attractive mediterranean-style courtyard behind simply furnished town pub, with a good choice of drinks and excellent food

'Visiting this smashing pub totally made our day' is just one enthusiastic report from our readers. It's an interesting place run by a genuinely friendly landlady and her chef husband. The bar has leather chesterfields and deep armchairs in front of a woodburning stove, all manner of wooden chairs, settles and tables on carpet or wooden floorboards, and rustic tools and horse tack alongside military and hunting prints on the walls; a dresser offers home-made cakes and local cider and juice for sale. There are stools by the green-planked counter where they serve Dartmoor Legend, Otter Amber and a guest beer on handpump, a dozen wines by the glass, ten malt whiskies, two farm ciders and quite a few coffees. A long light room leads off from here, and there's also a high-ceilinged barn-like back dining room; do look at forthcoming events as there's always something going on, from live bands to art shows. The sheltered inner courtyard, with metal tables and chairs, is popular in warm weather.

 Cooked by the landlord, the food is delicious: sandwiches and paninis, frittatas, tempura-battered haddock with home-made sauces and fries, tapas dishes such as cured yellowfin tuna carpaccio, crispy tiger prawns, lamb kofta, spanish hams and cheeses, mini vegetarian antipasti, and more substantial choices such as moules frites, crab linguine, harissa-marinated rump of lamb with fresh mint fregola and lemon and black olive caponata, sea bass fillets with ratatouille and fennel purée, and puddings. *Benchmark main dish: thin-crust pizzas £10.95. Two-course evening meal £20.00.*

Free house ~ Licensees Nigel Hoyle and Malene Graulund ~ Real ale ~ Open 12-3.30, 5-midnight; closed Mon lunchtime ~ Bar food 12.30-2.30, 6.30-9 ~ Restaurant ~ Children welcome ~ Dogs allowed in bar ~ Wi-fi ~ Live folk last Mon of month, rock/jam session third Thurs of month *Recommended by Anne and Ben Smith, Millie and Peter Downing, Graham and Carol Parker, Caroline and Peter Bryant, Margo and Derek Stapley*

POSTBRIDGE
Warren House
SX6780   Map 1

(01822) 880208 – www.warrenhouseinn.co.uk
B3212 0.75 miles NE of Postbridge; PL20 6TA

Isolated 18th-c pub, relaxing for a drink or meal after a Dartmoor hike

Deep in the heart of Dartmoor and built to serve the once busy tin mining community, this remote pub has a lot of local character. The cosy bar is straightforward, with simple furnishings such as easy chairs and settles beneath the beamed ochre ceiling, old pictures of the inn on partly panelled stone walls and dim lighting (powered by the pub's own generator); one of the open fires is said to have been kept alight since 1845. There's also a family room. Otter Ale plus guests such as Black Tor Pride of Dartmoor and Summerskills Start Point on handpump, local farm cider and malt whiskies. The picnic-sets on both sides of the road have moorland views.

Bar food includes baguettes, breaded king prawns with garlic dip, spinach and ricotta cannelloni, lamb shank with red wine and rosemary sauce, cajun chicken, smoked haddock and spring onion fishcakes with chips, gammon and pineapple, and puddings such as sticky toffee pudding and chocolate fudge cake. *Benchmark main dish: rabbit pie £13.50. Two-course evening meal £23.00.*

Free house ~ Licensee Peter Parsons ~ Real ale ~ Open 11-10; 12-10 Sun; 11-3 Mon, Tues in winter ~ Bar food 12-9 (8.30 Sun) ~ Restaurant ~ Children in family room only ~ Dogs allowed in bar *Recommended by Charlie May, Robert Watt, Scott and Charlotte Havers, Peter and Alison Steadman, Edward May*

Children – if the details at the end of a featured entry don't mention them, you should assume that the pub does not allow them inside.

RATTERY   SX7461   Map 1
Church House
(01364) 642220 – www.thechurchhouseinn.co.uk
Village signposted from A385 W of Totnes, and A38 S of Buckfastleigh; TQ10 9LD

Ancient place with friendly licensees, a good range of drinks, popular bar food and seats in the garden

Parts of this pub date from around 1030, making it one of Britain's oldest pubs. The rooms have plenty of character: massive oak beams and standing timbers in the open-plan bar, large fireplaces (one with a cosy nook partitioned around it), traditional pubby chairs and tables, some window seats and prints and horsebrasses on plain white walls. There's also a dining room, a lounge and a new separate restaurant with a new courtyard garden beside it equipped with smart seats and tables under big parasols. Dartmoor Jail Ale, Exeter Avocet and Otter Bitter on handpump, 19 malt whiskies and a dozen wines by the glass. There are picnic-sets at the front of the building with more on a large hedged-in lawn; the summer hanging baskets are pretty.

 From a seasonal menu, the good food includes lunchtime sandwiches, local pigeon breast with smoked pancetta and roast cauliflower, smoked haddock fishcakes with lemon mayonnaise, burger with toppings and chips, wild mushroom and truffle risotto, pork sausages with onion relish and gravy, salmon fillet with pepper and olive sauce vierge and fondant potato, chicken with mustard sauce and dauphinoise potatoes, and puddings. *Benchmark main dish: slow-roasted free-range pork belly with pancetta, lentils and cider sauce £15.00. Two-course evening meal £19.50.*

Free house ~ Licensees John and William Edwards ~ Real ale ~ Open 11.45-11 ~ Bar food 12-2.30, 6.30-9 ~ Restaurant ~ Children welcome ~ Dogs allowed in bar ~ Wi-fi
Recommended by Barry Collett, Hugh Roberts, Lynda and Trevor Smith, M J Daly, Charles and Maddie Bishop, Matt and Hayley Jacob

SALCOMBE   SX7439   Map 1
Victoria ♀
(01548) 842604 – www.victoriainn-salcombe.co.uk
Fore Street; TQ8 8BU

Friendly, bustling town-centre pub with plenty of character, west country ales, good food and back garden; bedrooms

An attractive 19th-c pub by the estuary, this is run with genuine care and thought by the hard-working, hands-on licensees. The beamed bar has an open fire in a big stone fireplace, huge flagstones and traditional furnishings that take in mate's chairs, built-in wall seats with scatter cushions and upholstered stools around sturdy tables. St Austell Proper Job, Tribute, a beer named for the pub and a regular guest on handpump, several wines plus champagne by the glass, a prosecco menu and around 22 gins; background music and board games. Several bright dining and drinking areas lead off with all manner of painted and wooden cushioned dining chairs around polished tables on stripped floorboards, lots of prints and mirrors above a blue dado, bookcase and china plate wallpaper and quite a collection of nautical items – lanterns, oars, glass balls, ropework and so forth. Upstairs has similar tables and chairs and button-back leather chesterfields and armchairs. The summer window boxes are very pretty and at the back is a large, sheltered, tiered garden with a play area for children and chickens and budgies. The quirky, comfortable bedrooms are in their Hobbit House and reached up a short flight of iron steps; no breakfasts but there are cafés and restaurants nearby.

🍴 Using local, seasonal produce (the beef comes from less than five miles away) and their own eggs, the enjoyable food includes sandwiches, local mackerel fillets with roasted cherry tomatoes and tapenade, whole baked camembert with garlic and herbs, butternut squash and chickpea burger with feta, spiced tomato and caramelised onion chutney, chicken thighs stuffed with chilli, herbs and gorgonzola, chive mash and chicken gravy, sea bass with crab cakes, roast fennel and salsa verde, and puddings such as passion-fruit posset with vanilla shortbread and chocolate and orange brownie with white chocolate sauce and clotted cream ice-cream. *Benchmark main dish: beer-battered fish and chips £13.00. Two-course evening meal £21.00.*

St Austell ~ Tenants Tim and Liz Hore ~ Real ale ~ Open 11-11 ~ Bar food 12-9 ~ Children welcome ~ Dogs allowed in bar ~ Wi-fi ~ Bedrooms: /£70 *Recommended by Elizabeth and Peter May, Edward and William Johnston, Rosie and John Moore, Alice Wright*

SANDFORD
Lamb 🍺 🛏️

SS8202 Map 1

(01363) 773676 – www.lambinnsandford.co.uk
The Square; EX17 4LW

16th-c inn with several real ales and decent wines by the glass, very good food and seats in garden; well equipped bedrooms

This is not a big place, but it is charming and well run and the linked beamed bar and dining area have an easy-going and friendly atmosphere. A good mix of both regulars and visitors gather in the bar which has red leather sofas beside a log fire, cushioned window seats, a settle and various dining chairs around a few tables on patterned carpet; towards the back is a handsome carved chest, a table of newspapers and magazines and a noticeboard of local news and adverts. Exeter Avocet, Otter Bitter, Powderkeg Speak Easy and Teignworthy Reel Ale on handpump, nine wines by the glass, cocktails, farm cider and 20 malt whiskies. The linked dining area has a woodburning stove, a cushioned wall pew, all manner of nice old wooden dining chairs and tables (each with a church candle) and similarly heavy beams; the large, cheerful animal paintings (which are also hung in the bedrooms) are by the landlord's wife. There's also a simpler public bar and a skittle alley; free film shows most weekends. The cobbled, three-level garden has fairy lights and simple seats and tables, and there are picnic-sets on grass beyond the hedge. Bedrooms are comfortable, modern and well equipped. Nearby parking is at a premium, but the village car park is just a few minutes' walk up the small lane to the right.

🍴 From a sensibly short menu, the highly thought-of food includes ciabatta sandwiches, duck liver parfait with red onion marmalade, barbecue mackerel with aubergine caviar, coriander and cumin, sausages and mash with onion gravy, a fish dish of the day, cannelloni of jerusalem artichoke, vitelotte potatoes, fine beans and almonds, cod with miso cauliflower, serrano ham, kohlrabi and shellfish bisque, and puddings such as sticky toffee pudding with clotted cream and apple, mixed berry and cinnamon crumble. *Benchmark main dish: duck breast with potato rösti and five-spice sauce £15.90. Two-course evening meal £21.50.*

Free house ~ Licensee Mark Hildyard ~ Real ale ~ Open 10am-11pm (midnight Sat) ~ Bar food 12-2.15, 6.30 (6 Fri, Sat)-9.15; 12-2.30, 6-8.30 Sun ~ Restaurant ~ Children welcome ~ Dogs welcome ~ Wi-fi ~ Folk night first Tues of month ~ Bedrooms: £69/£95 *Recommended by Douglas Power, Dr A McCormick, Richard and Penny Gibbs, Belinda Stamp, Edward May*

Real ale may be served from handpumps, electric pumps (not just the on-off switches used for keg beer) or – common in Scotland – tall taps called founts (pronounced 'fonts') where a separate pump pushes the beer up under air pressure.

SIDBURY SY1496 Map 1

Hare & Hounds ◀

(01404) 41760 – www.hareandhounds-devon.co.uk

3 miles N of Sidbury, at Putts Corner; A375 towards Honiton, crossroads with B3174; EX10 0QQ

Large, well run pub with log fires, beams and attractive layout, popular daily carvery and a big garden

The exceptionally highly thought-of carvery in this large roadside place is as popular as ever, so you'll need to book a table in advance at lunchtime. But plenty of customers do drop in for a pint and a chat and they keep Otter Ale and Bitter and St Austell Tribute tapped from the cask and eight wines by the glass. There are two log fires (and rather unusual wood-framed leather sofas complete with pouffes), heavy beams, fresh flowers and red plush cushioned dining chairs, window seats and leather sofas around plenty of tables on carpeting or bare boards. The newer dining extension, with a central open fire, leads on to a decked area; the seats here, and the picnic-sets in the big garden, have marvellous views down the Sid Valley to the sea at Sidmouth.

As well as the highly regarded carvery using the best local meat, they also offer a wide choice of dishes such as sandwiches, baguettes and panini, prawn cocktail with smoked salmon, deep-fried camembert with spiced peach chutney, vegetable burger with coleslaw and chips, smoked haddock fillet with three-cheese sauce, mexican chicken in a tortilla wrap with sour cream, beef casserole with dumplings, turkey curry, slow-cooked lamb shank with redcurrant and mint gravy, and puddings. *Benchmark main dish: daily carvery £10.75. Two-course evening meal £16.00.*

Heartstone Inns ~ Managers Graham Cole and Lindsey Chun ~ Real ale ~ Open 9am-11pm ~ Bar food 12-9 ~ Children welcome but no under-12s in bar ~ Dogs allowed in bar ~ Wi-fi *Recommended by William Slade, Julie Braeburn, Roy Hoing, Dylan, Jill and Dick Archer, Martine and Fabio Lockley*

SOUTH ZEAL SX6593 Map 1

Oxenham Arms 🛏

(01837) 840244 – www.theoxenhamarms.com

Off A30/A382; EX20 2JT

Wonderful 15th-c inn with lots of history, character bars, real ales, enjoyable food and big garden; bedrooms

If the weather is fine and you're stuck on the dreaded A30, stop at this ancient place to make the most of their four-acre garden. Reached up imposing curved stone steps it has plenty of seats and fine views – plus more tables under parasols out in front. First licensed in 1477, the building was constructed to combat the pagan power of the Neolithic standing stone that still forms part of the wall in the room behind the bar (there's actually 20 feet of stone below the floor). The heavily beamed and partly panelled front bar has elegant mullioned windows and Stuart fireplaces, all sorts of chairs and built-in wall seats with scatter cushions around low oak tables on bare floorboards, and bar stools against the counter where friendly staff serve Dartmoor Jail Ale and Merry Monk, a Red Rock beer named for the pub and Teignworthy Gun Dog on handpump; also, seven wines by the glass, 70 malt whiskies, 25 ports, local mead and three farm ciders. A small room has beams, wheelback chairs around polished tables, decorative plates and another open fire. Some of the bedrooms have four-poster beds. Charles Dickens, snowed up one winter, wrote a lot of *Pickwick Papers* here. It is possible to walk straight from the door on to the moor and they can provide details of walking tours.

🍴 Popular food using local produce includes lunchtime baguettes, a charcuterie board, ham hock terrine with pear and orange chutney, sweet potato and mushroom hash, sauté spinach and a poached egg with balsamic syrup, cider-braised pork belly with mustard mash, crackling and apple, fresh fish of the day with triple-cooked chips, lamb rump with rösti potato, ratatouille and crispy leeks, griddled chicken with fried potatoes, parma ham, spinach and cheese sauce, and puddings such as chocolate parfait and vanilla crème brûlée. *Benchmark main dish: steak in ale pie £11.95. Two-course evening meal £19.00.*

Free house ~ Licensees Simon and Lyn Powell ~ Real ale ~ Open 11-11 ~ Bar food 12-3, 6-9; light snacks all afternoon ~ Restaurant ~ Children welcome ~ Dogs allowed in bar ~ Wi-fi ~ Bedrooms: /£115 *Recommended by Comus and Sarah Elliott, Ron Corbett, Ian Herdman, Dr A McCormick, M J Daly, Serena and Adam Furber, Lenny and Ruth Walters*

SPARKWELL
Treby Arms 🍴⭐

SX5857 Map 1

(01752) 837363 – www.thetrebyarms.co.uk

Off A38 at Smithaleigh, W of Ivybridge, Sparkwell signed from village; PL7 5DD

Village pub offering excellent, imaginative food, real ales and good wines

Of course, most customers are here to enjoy the innovative food – but there is a little bar area used by locals which keeps the atmosphere nicely informal. This small room has stools against the counter, simple wooden dining chairs and tables, a built-in cushioned window seat and a woodburning stove in a stone fireplace with shelves of cookery books and guidebooks piled up on either side. Dartmoor Jail Ale, Sharps Two Tides and St Austell Proper Job and Tribute on handpump, several good wines by the glass from a list with helpful notes, 20 malt whiskies and local cider. Off to the right is the dining room with another woodburning stove, old glass and stone bottles on the mantelpiece and captain's and wheelback chairs around rustic tables; there's another carpeted dining room upstairs. The sunny front terrace has seats and tables.

⭐ Stylishly presented, the first class food includes calves sweetbreads with roasted salsify, black garlic and morel cream, brill with boudin blanc, celeriac and chicken juices, wild garlic and barley with roasted baby onion, confit egg yolk gel and moss, duck breast, heart and faggot with duck chips and foie gras gravy, lamb rump and shoulder with confit shallot, cockles and jus, braised oxtail with haricot blanc velouté, leek powder and puffed wild grains, and puddings such as lemon meringue pie with blood orange, tarragon and ale ice-cream and billionaire shortbread with milk ice-cream; they also offer a two- and three-course set weekday lunch. *Benchmark main dish: stone bass with sea vegetables, pickled kohlrabi and crab £27.00. Two-course evening meal £34.00.*

Free house ~ Licensee Clare Piotrowski ~ Real ale ~ Open 12-3, 6-11; 12-11 Fri, Sat; 12-10.30 Sun; closed Mon, Tues ~ Bar food 12-2, 6-9 ~ Restaurant ~ Children welcome ~ Dogs allowed in bar ~ Wi-fi *Recommended by Kate Moran, Sally and David Champion, Buster and Helena Hastings, Charles Todd*

Please keep sending us reports. We rely on readers for news of new discoveries, and particularly for news of changes – however slight – at the fully described pubs: feedback@goodguides.com, or (no stamp needed) The Good Pub Guide, FREEPOST RTXY–ZCBC–BBAZ, Stream Lane, Sedlescombe, Battle TN33 0PB.

SPREYTON
SX6996 Map 1
Tom Cobley
(01647) 231314 – www.tomcobleytavern.co.uk
Dragdown Hill; W out of village; EX17 5AL

Huge range of quickly changing real ales and ciders, and wide choice of food in friendly, busy village pub

With a warm, genuine welcome from the hospitable landlord and his cheerful staff and a fantastic range of up to 14 real ales well kept on handpump or tapped from the cask, this bustling village pub is a winner. The beers change all the time and might include Dartmoor Jail Ale, Holsworthy Original, Otter Ale, Plain India Plain Ale, St Austell Tribute, Tanners Box O'Frogs and Teignworthy Gun Dog; also, up to 14 farm ciders and perries. The comfortable bar has traditional pubby furnishings, an open fire and local photographs and country scenes on the walls. A large back dining room has beams and background music; darts. There are picnic-sets in the garden and more out in front by the quiet street. The bedrooms have been recently refurbished and all are now ensuite; several have Dartmoor views.

Good quality, traditional food includes sandwiches, prawn cocktail, duck spring rolls with hoisin sauce, home-made pasties, lunchtime omelettes, vegetable chilli, burger with toppings, onion rings, coleslaw and chips, full rack of barbecue ribs, steak and kidney pudding, lambs liver with bacon and onion gravy, smoked haddock and mozzarella fishcakes with chips, and puddings. *Benchmark main dish: home-made pies £9.95. Two-course evening meal £17.50.*

Free house ~ Licensees Roger and Carol Cudlip ~ Real ale ~ Open 12-3, 6-11 (midnight Fri, Sat); 12-4, 7-11 Sun; closed Mon lunchtime ~ Bar food 12-2, 7-9; set Sunday roast 1pm, 7-9 ~ Restaurant ~ Children welcome ~ Dogs allowed in bar ~ Bedrooms: £50/£100
Recommended by Comus and Sarah Elliott, Ian Herdman, Edward and William Johnston, David and Leone Lawson, Colin and Daniel Gibbs

STAVERTON
SX7964 Map 1
Sea Trout 🛏
(01803) 762274 – www.theseatroutinn.co.uk
Village signposted from A384 NW of Totnes; TQ9 6PA

Bustling old inn not far from the river with real ales, tasty food, helpful staff and back garden; bedrooms

Our readers continue to enjoy staying in the comfortable bedrooms here – some overlook the garden and some the country lane – and breakfasts are good. The neatly kept beamed lounge has fishing flies and stuffed fish on the walls, and traditional tables and chairs on the part-carpeted and part-wood floor. The simpler locals' bar has wooden wall and other seats, a stag's head, guns and horsebrasses, a huge stuffed pike, a woodburning stove and a cheerful mix of regulars and visitors. Palmers 200, Copper and Dorset Gold on handpump, 11 wines by the glass and several malt whiskies; background music and board games. There's also a smart, panelled restaurant and a conservatory. The attractive back garden has seats and tables. Fishing is available on the nearby River Dart (you can get daily permits).

Well liked food includes sandwiches, local white crab meat with lime mayonnaise, home-made onion bhajis, home-smoked duck breast with pickled pink ginger, wasabi and endive salad, sharing platters, mixed bean burger with red cabbage slaw and fries, apple and chilli roasted pork belly with sauté butter beans and honey star anise jus, lambs liver with crispy bacon and sweet onion jus, niçoise salad with fresh fish of the day, and puddings such as dark chocolate délice with peanut brittle and cherry purée and coconut pannacotta with pineapple and chilli salsa. *Benchmark main dish: beer-battered fish and chips £13.50. Two-course evening meal £20.50.*

Palmers ~ Tenants Nigel and Simon Hewhouse ~ Real ale ~ Open 11-11 (midnight Sat) ~ Bar food 12-2 (3 Sat), 6-9; 12-3, 6.30-9 Sun ~ Restaurant ~ Children welcome ~ Dogs allowed in bar and bedrooms ~ Wi-fi ~ Bedrooms: £80/£110 *Recommended by Mike and Margaret Banks, George Sanderson, Dr A McCormick, Sara Fulton, Roger Baker*

TIPTON ST JOHN   SY0991 Map 1
Golden Lion

(01404) 812881 – www.goldenliontipton.co.uk
Pub signed off B3176 Sidmouth–Ottery St Mary; EX10 0AA

Busy village pub with three real ales, well liked food and plenty of seats in the attractive garden

A good mix of villagers and diners from further afield mix quite happily in this bustling village pub. The main bar, split into two, has a comfortable, relaxed atmosphere, as does the back snug. Throughout are paintings by west country artists, art deco prints, Tiffany lamps and, hanging from the beams, hops, copper pots and kettles. A few tables are kept for those just wanting a pint and a chat. Otter Ale and Bitter and Sharps Doom Bar on handpump and 12 wines by the glass; background music. There are seats on the terracotta-walled terrace with outside heaters and grapevines and more seats on the grass edged by pretty flowering borders. Dog walkers and smokers may use a verandah.

Cooked by the chef-landlord, the good food includes lunchtime sandwiches, moules marinière, home-smoked duck salad with onion marmalade, home-cooked ham and egg, vegetable lasagne, steak and kidney pudding, rack of lamb dijonnaise, plaice with garlic butter, pheasant suprême with blueberries and rosemary, monkfish curry, and puddings such as tarte citron and crème brûlée. *Benchmark main dish: chunky fish soup £12.50. Two-course evening meal £19.50.*

Heavitree ~ Tenants François and Michelle Teissier ~ Real ale ~ Open 12-2.30, 6-10 (11 Fri, Sat); closed Sun evening ~ Bar food 12-2, 6-8.30 ~ Children welcome *Recommended by Diane Abbott, Charles Todd, Revd Michael Vockins, Susan and Callum Slade, Mark Hamill*

TOPSHAM   SX9687 Map 1
Globe 🛏

(01392) 873471 – www.theglobetopsham.co.uk
Fore Street; 2 miles from M5 junction 30; EX3 0HR

Thoughtfully refurbished inn with relaxed bar and dining areas, local ales, popular food and seats on big terrace; well equipped bedrooms

Original features in this handsome former coaching inn mix easily with contemporary touches and paintwork, and the atmosphere throughout is friendly and relaxed. The red-painted panelling in the bar is hung with old prints, there's an open fire in a small brick fireplace with logs piled to one side, armchairs in a corner and suede tub and pubby chairs around dark tables on bare floorboards. Another bar has pale painted panelling, a shelf of old glass bottles, a sizeable cushioned settle and more traditional chairs and tables on tartan carpet and a woodburning stove. The dining room is elegant with church candles in huge candlesticks, green paintwork above a grey dado and another open fire. St Austell Proper Job, Trelawny and Tribute on handpump and several wines by the glass served by helpful staff. Outside, the large terrace has plenty of good quality seats and tables under dark parasols. The individually decorated, modern bedrooms are well equipped and comfortable and breakfasts are good. The village is close to the Exe estuary and nature reserve.

As well as breakfasts for non-residents (7.30-11am, from 8am weekends), the pleasing food includes local mussels in white wine, garlic and cream, goats cheese mousse with apple and pickled walnuts, sharing boards, crispy polenta with roasted vegetables, parmesan and red pepper pesto, chicken caesar salad, pressed ham hock with pickled cabbage and free-range eggs, grilled fresh fish of the day with lemon and parsley butter, slow-cooked lamb shoulder with moroccan-style couscous and feta and pea salad, and puddings. *Benchmark main dish: pie of the day £13.95. Two-course evening meal £29.00.*

St Austell ~ Manager Jason Manton ~ Real ale ~ Open 10am-11pm (11.30pm Fri, Sat); 10am-10.30pm Sun ~ Bar food 12-9.30 (9 Sun) ~ Children welcome ~ Dogs allowed in bar and bedrooms ~ Wi-fi ~ Bedrooms: /£95 *Recommended by Adrian Johnson, Mike Swan, Shona and Jimmy McDuff*

TOTNES
Royal Seven Stars ⭐❘ 🛏

SX8060 Map 1

(01803) 862125 – www.royalsevenstars.co.uk
Fore Street, The Plains; TQ9 5DD

Handsome hotel just across the road from the River Dart, easy-going bar, several dining rooms and seats outside; bedrooms

The companionable bar in this well run and civilised old hotel is to the left of the interesting entrance hall (which has an imposing staircase, antlers and stag heads and big flagstones lined with leafy plant pots). This bar is friendly and easy-going with an open fire, button-back banquettes and cushioned wooden chairs around circular tables and stools against the bar where they keep New Lion Pandit IPA (the brewery is in the town), Dartmoor Jail Ale, Sharps Doom Bar and a guest ale on handpump and farm cider. Dining rooms have both antique and modern high-backed chairs, sofas, more banquettes, big gilt-edged mirrors, books on shelves, copper kettles, measuring jugs and warming pans, large paintings and stone jars. There are covered and heated seats and tables among box-planted troughs at the front of the building and the River Dart is just across the main road. The 21 bedrooms are lovely, individually styled and well equipped.

As well as breakfasts (8-11am), the food is particularly good and includes sandwiches, local white crab meat with lime mayonnaise, home-made onion bhajis, home-smoked duck breast with pickled pink ginger, wasabi and endive salad, sharing platters, mixed bean burger with red cabbage slaw and fries, apple and chilli roasted pork belly with sauté butter beans and honey star anise jus, lambs liver with crispy bacon and sweet onion jus, niçoise salad with fresh fish of the day, and puddings such as dark chocolate délice with peanut brittle and cherry purée and coconut pannacotta with pineapple and chilli salsa. *Benchmark main dish: local fish pie £13.95. Two-course evening meal £21.00.*

Free house ~ Licensees Anne and Nigel Way ~ Real ale ~ Open 8am-11pm (11.30pm Sat) ~ Bar food 11.30-9.30 ~ Children welcome ~ Dogs welcome ~ Wi-fi ~ Live music Fri evening ~ Bedrooms: /£150 *Recommended by Alan and Linda Blackmore, Maria and Henry Lazenby, George Sanderson*

If we don't specify bar meal times for a featured entry, these are normally 12-2 and 7-9; we do show times if they are markedly different.

UGBOROUGH
SX6755 Map 1

Anchor ♀ ⇦

(01752) 690388 – www.anchorinnugborough.co.uk

Off A3121; PL21 0NG

A wide mix of customers for 17th-c inn with beamed rooms, good food and drink and seats outside; bedrooms

Gently civilised and with pleasing, contemporary décor throughout, our readers enjoy their visits here very much. The beamed bar has an open fire, leather sofas and dining chairs around a mix of tables on wooden flooring, and stools against the planked bar counter where they keep Sharps Doom Bar and a guest such as Tavy Golden Ale on handpump and several wines by the glass; background music, TV and board games. The two-level beamed restaurant has elegant rattan dining chairs and wooden tables on flagstones in one part and more traditional dark wooden furniture in the lower area; there's a woodburning stove in a big fireplace and modern art on pale-painted walls. If you want to explore nearby Dartmoor National Park, you can stay in the comfortable, attractive and individually furnished bedrooms – six are in the main inn and four in courtyard cabins.

Interesting food includes breakfasts (8-10am), chargrilled local mackerel fillet with horseradish potato and beetroot, ham hock terrine with a fried quail egg and pineapple chutney, steak and green peppercorn pie, beetroot, chilli and baby spinach risotto with goats cheese, sea bass fillet with mussels, samphire and a white wine velouté, slow-braised pork belly with pulled pork fritter and pork sausage with apple purée and cider sauce, and puddings such as banana tarte tatin with belgian chocolate ice-cream and chocolate and Baileys fondant with salted caramel ice-cream and white chocolate sauce. *Benchmark main dish: bream fillet with king prawn in coconut sauce, panko king prawn and stir-fried vegetables £13.95. Two-course evening meal £20.00.*

Free house ~ Licensee Sarah Cuming ~ Real ale ~ Open 11-11 ~ Bar food 12-2.30, 6.30 (6 Fri, Sat)-9; 12-3, 6-8 Sun ~ Restaurant ~ Children welcome ~ Dogs allowed in bar ~ Wi-fi ~ Bedrooms: /£75 *Recommended by Charles Todd, Ben and Diane Bowie, Sandra King, Jeff Davies, Rosie and Marcus Heatherley*

WIDECOMBE
SX7276 Map 1

Rugglestone ◀

(01364) 621327 – www.rugglestoneinn.co.uk

Village at end of B3387; pub just S – turn left at church and NT church house, OS Sheet 191 map reference 720765; TQ13 7TF

Charming local with a couple of bars, cheerful customers, friendly staff, four real ales and traditional pub food

Just the place after a Dartmoor hike, this is a hidden gem of a pub. The unspoilt bar has just four tables, a few window and wall seats, a one-person pew built into the corner beside a nice old stone fireplace (with a woodburner) and a good mix of customers. The rudimentary bar counter dispenses Butcombe Bitter, Dartmoor Legend, Tavy Best and a beer named for the pub (from Teignworthy) tapped from the cask; local farm cider and a decent small wine list. The room on the right is slightly bigger and lighter in feel, with beams, another stone fireplace, stripped-pine tables and a built-in wall bench; there's also a small dining room. To reach the picnic-sets in the garden you have to cross a bridge over a little moorland stream. They have a holiday cottage to rent.

🍴 Tasty pubby food includes baguettes, deep-fried brie with redcurrant jelly, local potted crab, home-cooked ham and eggs, roasted vegetable or meaty lasagne, beer-battered fresh haddock and chips, spicy meatballs in tomato sauce with potato wedges, smoked trout salad with home-made coleslaw, and puddings. *Benchmark main dish: steak and stilton pie £10.50. Two-course evening meal £16.00.*

Free house ~ Licensees Richard and Vicki Palmer ~ Real ale ~ Open 11.30-3, 6-11.30; 11.30-3, 5-midnight Fri; 11.30am-midnight Sat; 12-11 Sun ~ Bar food 12-2, 6.30-9 ~ Restaurant ~ Children allowed away from bar area ~ Dogs welcome *Recommended by Elizabeth and Peter May, Peter Pilbeam, Anne and Ben Smith, Joe and Belinda Smart*

 WOODBURY SALTERTON SY0189 Map 1
Diggers Rest
(01395) 232375 – www.diggersrest.co.uk
3.5 miles from M5 junction 30: A3052 towards Sidmouth, village signposted on right about 0.5 miles after Clyst St Mary; also signposted from B3179 SE of Exeter; EX5 1PQ

Bustling village pub with real ales, well liked food and country views from the terraced garden

A former cider house, this place is 500 years old and very much the heart of the village. The main bar has antique furniture, local art on the walls and a cosy seating area by the open fire. The modern extension is light and airy and opens on to the garden. Otter Bitter and Ale and St Austell Tribute on handpump, 13 wines by the glass and Weston's cider; service is attentive and efficient. Background music, darts, TV and board games. The window boxes and flowering baskets are pretty in summer and there are fine walks around Woodbury Common and in the surrounding Otter Valley.

🍴 Rewarding food includes lunchtime sandwiches (available all afternoon on Saturday), duck liver and port pâté with ale chutney, king scallops with squash purée, pancetta and hazelnuts, wild mushroom and butternut squash risotto with truffle oil, local sausages with mash and onion gravy, honey-roast ham and eggs, pork three-ways (crispy belly, slow-cooked cheek, black pudding) with potato fritter and aubergine purée, plaice fillets with shrimps and cherry tomato, broad bean and chive cassoulet, and puddings such as sticky toffee pudding with butterscotch sauce and vanilla pannacotta. *Benchmark main dish: guinea fowl with beetroot, wild mushrooms and a mustard cream sauce £14.50. Two-course evening meal £19.50.*

Heartstone Inns ~ Licensee Laura Chappell ~ Real ale ~ Open 12-3, 5.30-11; 12-11 Sat; 12-10.30 Sun ~ Bar food 12-2, 6-9; 12-8 Sun ~ Restaurant ~ Children welcome ~ Dogs welcome ~ Wi-fi ~ Live music last Fri of month; quiz first Mon of month
Recommended by Mike and Margaret Banks, Roy Hoing, Neil Allen, Jacqui and Alan Swan

---

Also Worth a Visit in Devon

Besides the fully inspected pubs, you might like to try these pubs that have been recommended to us and described by readers. Do tell us what you think of them: feedback@goodguides.com

ABBOTSKERSWELL SX8568
Court Farm (01626) 361866
Wilton Way; look for the church tower; TQ12 5NY Attractive neatly extended 17th-c longhouse tucked away in picturesque hamlet; various rooms off long beamed and paved main bar, good mix of furnishings, woodburners, well priced popular food (worth booking) including weekday lunchtime bargains, friendly helpful service, Bass, Otter and other beers, farm cider and decent wines; background music, pool and darts; children welcome, picnic-sets in pretty lawned garden, open all day (food all day Thurs-Sun). *(Jack Trussler)*

APPLEDORE   SS4630
Beaver (01237) 474822
Irsha Street; EX39 1RY Relaxed, well
run harbourside pub with lovely estuary
view from popular raised dining area, well
priced food especially fresh local fish, prompt
friendly service, good choice of west country
ales, farm cider, decent house wines and
great range of whiskies; background and
some live music including jazz, quiz Weds,
pool in smaller games room, TV; children and
dogs (in bar) welcome, disabled access (but
no nearby parking), tables on small sheltered
water-view terrace. *(Barbara Brown)*

APPLEDORE   SS4630
Seagate (01237) 472589
The Quay; EX39 1QS Refurbished and
well run 17th-c quayside inn, good food from
lunchtime baguettes to fresh fish specials,
smaller appetites catered for, four real
ales, two ciders and ten wines by the glass,
friendly helpful service; children and dogs
welcome, terrace seating front and back, ten
updated bedrooms (some with estuary view),
open all day from 8am. *(Barbara Brown)*

ASHILL   ST0811
Ashill Inn (01884) 840506
*M5 junction 27, follow signs to Willand,
then left to Uffculme and Craddock on
B3440; Ashill signed to left; pub in
centre of village; EX15 3NL* Popular
19th-c village pub, cosy and friendly, with
well kept local ales and highly rated home-
cooked food including daily specials (booking
advised), reasonable prices, black beams,
woodburner in stone fireplace, modern
dining extension overlooking small garden;
some live music, darts and skittles, TV;
children welcome, closed Mon lunchtime,
no food Sun evening. *(Guy Vowles)*

ASHPRINGTON   SX8157
Durant Arms (01803) 732240
Off A381 S of Totnes; TQ9 7UP
Comfortably refurbished 18th-c village
inn with enjoyable home-cooked food
and three well kept ales, good friendly
service, slate-floored bar with stag's head
above woodburner, china on delft shelf,
other connecting rooms; vintage juke box;
children, walkers and dogs welcome, four
bedrooms (one in courtyard annexe),
closed Sun evening, Mon. *(Adam Jones)*

ASHPRINGTON   SX8056
Watermans Arms (01803) 732214
*Bow Bridge, on Tuckenhay Road;
TQ9 7EG* Whitewashed 17th-c creekside
inn; beamed and quarry-tiled main bar area,
built-in cushioned wall seats and wheelbacks
around stripped tables, log fire, dining room
with fishing-related décor, comfortable
lounge area down steps, four Palmers
ales and several wines by the glass, good
traditional food from lunchtime baguettes up,

friendly helpful service; background music;
children and dogs (in bar) welcome, seats
out by the water (maybe kingfishers) and in
garden, 15 bedrooms (some in purpose-built
annexe), car park over the road, open all day.
(Mike and Margaret Banks, I D Barnett)

AVONWICK   SX6958
★**Turtley Corn Mill** (01364) 646100
*0.5 miles off A38 roundabout at SW end
of South Brent bypass; TQ10 9ES*
Carefully converted watermill with series of
linked areas, mix of wooden dining chairs
and chunky tables, bookcases, fat church
candles and oriental rugs or dark flagstones,
woodburners, various prints and some framed
78rpm discs, big windows looking out over
grounds, Hanlons, Otter, St Austell and
Summerskills, nine wines by the glass and 30
malt whiskies, wide choice of brasserie-style
food, friendly service; free wi-fi; children and
dogs (in bar) welcome, extensive garden with
well spaced picnic-sets, giant chess set and
small lake, four bedrooms, open (and food)
all day from 8.30am for breakfast.
(John Evans, Lynda and Trevor Smith)

AXMOUTH   SY2591
★**Harbour Inn** (01297) 20371
B3172 Seaton–Axminster; EX12 4AF
Ancient thatched pub by estuary; heavily
beamed bar rooms with bare boards and
stripped stone walls, huge inglenook, lots of
model boats, old pictures, photographs and
accounts of shipwrecks, other partitioned
dining/seating areas including carpeted part
with armchairs by woodburner, Badger ales
and several wines by the glass, large helpings
of enjoyable good value food from sandwiches
and deli boards up, steak night Fri, friendly
service; background music; children and
dogs (in bar) welcome, modern furniture on
terrace, picnic-sets on grass, open (and food)
all day from 9am. *(Roger and Donna Huggins)*

AYLESBEARE   SY0490
Halfway (01395) 232273
*A3052 Exeter–Sidmouth, junction with
B3180; EX5 2JP* Modernised roadside
dining pub (same owners as the Bowd in
Sidmouth), well cooked food from fairly
priced pub favourites up including home-
made american-style burgers, good fresh fish/
seafood and two-course lunch/early evening
menu, Sun carvery, well kept Otter Bitter and
Greene King Abbot, efficient friendly service,
Dartmoor views from restaurant and raised
outside seating area; children welcome, open
(and food) all day. *(Roger and Donna Huggins)*

BAMPTON   SS9622
Quarrymans Rest (01398) 331480
Briton Street; EX16 9LN Village pub
with beamed and carpeted main bar, leather
sofas in front of inglenook woodburner,
dining chairs and some housekeepers'
chairs around wooden tables, enjoyable
home-made food and four well kept west

country ales, friendly service, steps up to comfortable stripped-stone dining room with high-backed leather chairs and heavy pine tables; pool and games machines; children and dogs welcome, picnic-sets in pretty back garden, more seats in front, four bedrooms, open all day. *(John and Sarah Perry)*

BAMPTON SS9522
Swan (01398) 332248
Station Road; EX16 9NG Popular, well run beamed village inn with spacious bare-boards bar, woodburners in two inglenooks, three changing local beers, decent wines and good home-made food (not Mon) from interesting varied menu, efficient friendly service; children and dogs welcome, well appointed bedrooms, big breakfast, closed Mon lunchtime otherwise open all day. *(Lenny and Ruth Walters)*

BANTHAM SX6643
★Sloop (01548) 560489
Off A379/B3197 NW of Kingsbridge; TQ7 3AJ Welcoming 14th-c split-level pub close to fine beach and walks, popular and relaxed, with good mix of customers in black-beamed stripped-stone bar, country tables and chairs on flagstones, blazing woodburner, well kept St Austell and a guest ale, enjoyable food from nice sandwiches to good fresh fish, friendly efficient service, restaurant; background music; children and dogs welcome, seats out at back, five bedrooms (a couple have sea views), open all day in summer. *(Lynda and Trevor Smith, Jane and Kai Horsburgh)*

BEER ST2289
Anchor (01297) 20386
Fore Street; EX12 3ET Sea-view inn with good choice of enjoyable food including local fish, Greene King, Otter and good value wines, refurbished open-plan interior with large eating area, friendly staff; background music, sports TV, free wi-fi; children well looked after, lots of tables in clifftop garden over road, six reasonably priced bedrooms, open (and food) all day. *(Donald Allsopp)*

BEESANDS SX8140
★Cricket (01548) 580215
About 3 miles S of A379, from Chillington; in village turn right along foreshore road; TQ7 2EN Popular pub-restaurant with pebbly Start Bay beach just over the sea wall; light airy new england-style décor with dark wood or leather chairs around chunky tables, stripped-wood flooring by the bar, carpet in the restaurant, some nautical bits and pieces including model boats, relaxed chatty atmosphere with a few tables kept for drinkers, Otter and St Austell ales, local cider and 14 wines by the glass, very good food with emphasis on fish/seafood; background music, TVs, free wi-fi; children and dogs (in bar) welcome, wheelchair

access/loo, picnic-sets by sea wall, seven attractive bedrooms (some overlooking sea), South West Coast Path runs through the village, open all day, food all day in high summer. *(Dave Braisted, Jane and Kai Horsburgh, Simon and Mandy King)*

BELSTONE SX61293
Tors (01837) 840689
A mile off A30; EX20 1QZ Popular small Victorian granite pub-hotel in peaceful Dartmoor-edge village, family-run and welcoming, with long carpeted bar divided by settles, well kept ales such as Dartmoor and Sharps, over 60 malt whiskies and good choice of wines, enjoyable food from baguettes to specials, cheerful prompt service, restaurant; children welcome and dogs (they have their own), disabled access, seats out on nearby grassy area overlooking valley, good walks, bedrooms, open all day in summer. *(Chris and Angela Buckell)*

BERE FERRERS SX4563
Old Plough (01822) 840358
Long dead-end road off B3257 S of Tavistock; PL20 7JL 16th-c pub in secluded River Tavy village; stripped stone and panelling, low beam-and-plank ceilings, slate flagstones and woodburner, enjoyable good value home-cooked food including decent vegetarian choice, well kept Hunters, Sharps Doom Bar and a couple of guests, real cider, warm local atmosphere, steps down to cosy restaurant; live music; children and dogs welcome, garden overlooking estuary, open all day Sun. *(Charles Welch)*

BICKLEIGH SS0307
Fishermans Cot (01884) 855237
A3072; EX16 8RW Much extended thatched riverside pub with wide choice of good local food and well kept Marstons ales, reasonable prices, friendly helpful service, lots of round tables on stone and carpet, pillars, plants and some panelled parts, fishing bric-a-brac, raised dining area, charming view over shallow rocky race below 1640 Exe bridge; background music; dogs welcome, terrace and waterside lawn, 19 good bedrooms, open all day and can get very busy, especially weekends. *(Jack Trussler)*

BISHOP'S TAWTON SS5629
★Chichester Arms (01271) 343945
Signed off A377 outside Barnstaple; East Street; EX32 0DQ Friendly 15th-c cob and thatch pub, good generous well priced food from sandwiches/baguettes to fresh local fish, quick obliging service even when crowded, St Austell Tribute, Charles Wells Bombardier and a guest, decent wines, heavy low beams, large stone fireplace, restaurant; free wi-fi; children and dogs welcome, awkward disabled access but staff very helpful, picnic-sets on front terrace and in back garden, open all day. *(Holly and Tim Waite)*

BOVEY TRACEY   SX8178
Cromwell Arms (01626) 833473
Fore Street; TQ13 9AE Welcoming 17th-c
beamed inn with popular good value food
and up to five St Austell ales, several areas
including separate restaurant; quiz Tues
and Sun evenings, games machines, free
wi-fi; children and dogs (in bar) welcome,
disabled access/facilities, small garden
with decking and pergola, 14 bedrooms,
open all day. *(Susan and Callum Slade)*

BRATTON CLOVELLY   SX4691
Clovelly (01837) 871447
*From S (A30), turn left at church,
pub is on the right; EX20 4JZ* Friendly
18th-c village pub with cosy bar and two
dining rooms, generous helpings of popular
reasonably priced traditional food, well
kept Dartmoor, St Austell and a guest,
cheerful staff, games room; may be live jazz
second Mon of month; children and dogs
welcome, 17th-c wall paintings in Norman
church, open all day weekends. *(M G Hart)*

BRAYFORD   SS7235
★**Poltimore Arms** (01598) 710381
*Yarde Down; 3 miles towards
Simonsbath; EX36 3HA* Ivy-clad 17th-c
beamed pub – so remote it generates
its own electricity, and water is from a
spring; good home-made food including
daily specials (best to book) and two
or three changing ales tapped from the
cask, friendly helpful staff, traditional
furnishings, woodburner in inglenook, two
attractive restaurant areas separated by
another woodburner, good country views;
free wi-fi; children and dogs (in bar)
welcome, picnic-sets in side garden, shop
and gallery, open all day. *(Barbara Brown)*

BRENDON   SS7547
★**Rockford Inn** (01598) 741214
*Rockford; Lynton–Simonsbath Road,
off B3223; EX35 6PT* Homely and
welcoming little 17th-c beamed inn
surrounded by fine walks and scenery (sister
to the Manor House at Ditcheat, Somerset);
neatly linked rooms with cushioned settles,
wall seats and other straightforward
furniture, country prints and horse tack,
open fires, good helpings of enjoyable well
priced pubby food (not Mon lunchtime),
a couple of well kept changing ales (often
Cotleigh) tapped from the cask, Adlestone's
and Thatcher's ciders, decent wines by the
glass, lots of pump clips and toby jugs behind
counter; background music, board games;
children and dogs (in bar) welcome, seats
across the road overlooking East Lyn river,
well appointed bedrooms, open all day.
(Theocsbrian, Bob and Margaret Holder)

BRENDON   SS7648
Staghunters (01598) 741222
Leedford Lane; EX35 6PS Idyllically set

family-run hotel with gardens by East Lyn
river, good choice of enjoyable reasonably
priced food, up to five well kept ales such as
Cotleigh, Exmoor and St Austell, real cider,
friendly efficient staff, bar with woodburner,
restaurant; can get very busy, though quiet
out of season; children, walkers and dogs
welcome, riverside tables, 12 good value
bedrooms, open all day weekends (and
weekdays if busy). *(Bob and Margaret Holder)*

BRIXHAM   SX9256
★**Maritime** (01803) 853535
*King Street (up steps from harbour –
nearby parking virtually non-existent);
TQ5 9TH* Single bar packed with bric-a-
brac; chamber-pots hanging from beams,
hundreds of key fobs, cigarette cards, pre-war
ensigns, toby jugs, mannequins, astronomical
charts, even a binnacle by the door, Hunters
Half Bore and Pheasant Plucker, over 80
malt whiskies, no food or credit cards,
long-serving landlady, lively terrier called
George and Mr Tibbs the parrot; background
music, small TV, darts and board games;
well behaved children and dogs allowed,
fine views over harbour, six bedrooms (not
ensuite), closed lunchtime. *(Tony Scott)*

BRIXHAM   SX9256
New Quay (01803) 883290
King Street; TQ5 9TW Refurbished early
18th-c pub tucked down side street; well kept
changing west country beers and ciders from
board-fronted servery, good range of wines
by the glass and gins, friendly helpful staff,
beam and plank ceiling, spindleback chairs
and mix of old tables on slate tiles, warming
woodburner, fairly traditional menu using
fresh local produce, upstairs restaurant with
another woodburner and old town views;
no children under 10, dogs welcome in bar,
closed Mon-Weds, open from 5.30pm Thurs-
Sat and 12-5.30pm Sun. *(David Delaney)*

BROADCLYST   SX9997
New Inn (01392) 461312
Wimple Road; EX5 3BX Friendly former
17th-c farmhouse with stripped brickwork,
boarded ceiling, low doorways and log fires,
well cooked reasonably priced pubby food,
Dartmoor, Hanlons, Otter and Sharps, good
attentive service, small restaurant; skittle
alley; children and dogs welcome, garden
with play area, open all day. *(Jack Trussler)*

BROADCLYST   SX9897
Red Lion (01392) 461271
B3121, by church; EX5 3EL Refurbished
16th-c pub under same owners as the
Hunters at Newton Tracey; heavy beams,
flagstones and log fires, St Austell and a
local guest, enjoyable well priced traditional
food (special diets catered for) in bar and
restaurant, good cheerful service; children
and dogs welcome, picnic-sets out in front
below wisteria, more in small enclosed
garden across quiet lane, nice village and

15th-c church, not far from Killerton (NT), open all day weekends. *(Donald Allsopp)*

BROADHEMBURY ST1004

Drewe Arms (01404) 841267

Off A373 Cullompton–Honiton; EX14 3NF Extended partly thatched family-run pub dating from the 15th c; carved beams and handsome stone-mullioned windows, woodburner and open fire, mix of furniture (some perhaps not matching age of building), modernised bar area, five well kept local ales and seven wines by the glass, enjoyable pubby food (all day weekends), friendly helpful service, skittle alley; children and dogs welcome, terrace seats, more up steps on tree-shaded lawn, nice setting near church in pretty village, open all day; up for sale as went to press, so could be changes. *(Roger and Donna Huggins)*

BUCKFAST SX7467

Abbey Inn (01364) 642343

Buckfast Road, off B3380; TQ11 0EA Lovely position perched on bank of River Dart; partly panelled bar with woodburner, three St Austell ales and Healey's cider, enjoyable reasonably priced pubby food from sandwiches and baguettes up, Sun carvery, big dining room with more panelling and river views; background music, free wi-fi; well behaved children and dogs (in bar) welcome, terrace and bedrooms overlooking the water, open all day. *(Charles Welch)*

BUCKLAND BREWER SS4220

★Coach & Horses (01237) 451395

Village signposted off A388 S of Monkleigh; OS Sheet 190 map reference 423206; EX39 5LU Friendly 13th-c thatched pub with heavily beamed bar (mind your head), comfortable seats, handsome antique settle and inglenook woodburner, smaller lounge with log fire in another inglenook, Exmoor Gold, Otter Ale and Sharps Doom Bar, local ciders and several wines by the glass, decent food including curries, small back games room (darts and pool) and skittle alley/function room; background music, games machine, occasional sports TV, free wi-fi; children and dogs (in bar) welcome, picnic-sets on front terrace and in side garden, holiday cottage next door. *(Bob and Margaret Holder)*

BURGH ISLAND SX6444

Pilchard (01548) 810514

300 metres across tidal sands from Bigbury-on-Sea; walk, or summer sea tractor if tide's in; TQ7 4BG Sadly, the splendid beamed and flagstoned upper bar with its lanterns and roaring log fire is reserved for guests at the associated flamboyantly art deco hotel, but the more utilitarian left-hand bar is still worth a visit for the unbeatable setting high above the sea swarming below this tidal island; Sharps, Thwaites and an ale named for the pub, lunchtime baguettes; children and dogs welcome, tables outside, some down by beach, open all day. *(George Sanderson)*

BUTTERLEIGH SS9708

Butterleigh Inn (01884) 855433

Off A396 in Bickleigh; EX15 1PN Traditional heavy-beamed country pub, friendly and relaxed with good mix of customers, enjoyable reasonably priced pubby food (not Mon) including Sun carvery, four well kept ales such as Cotleigh and Otter, real ciders and good choice of wines, unspoilt lived-in interior with two big fireplaces, back dining room; free wi-fi; children and dogs welcome, picnic-sets in large garden, four comfortable bedrooms, closed Sun evening, Mon lunchtime. *(Andrew and Michele Revell)*

CADELEIGH SS9107

★Cadeleigh Arms (01884) 855238

Village signed off A3072 W of junction with A396 Tiverton–Exeter at Bickleigh; EX16 8HP Attractive and friendly old pub owned by the local community; well kept Cotleigh, Dartmoor, St Austell and a guest, well liked, locally sourced food (not Sun evening) from favourites up, carpeted room on left with bay-window seat and ornamental stove, flagstoned room to the right with high-backed settles and log fire in big fireplace, valley views from airy dining room down a couple of steps; background music, games room (pool and darts) and skittle alley; children and dogs welcome, picnic-sets on gravel terrace with barbecue, more on gently sloping lawn, closed Mon lunchtime. *(Penny and David Shepherd)*

CALIFORNIA CROSS SX7053

California (01548) 821449

Brown sign to pub off A3121 S of A38 junction; PL21 0SG Neatly kept 18th-c or older beamed dining pub, red carpets, panelling and stripped stone, plates on delft shelving and other bits and pieces, log fire, good choice of enjoyable food from baguettes to steaks in bar and family area, popular Sun lunch (best to book), separate evening restaurant (Weds-Sun) and small snug, St Austell Tribute, Sharps Doom Bar and a local guest, traditional cider and decent wines by the glass, good friendly service; background music, free wi-fi; dogs welcome, attractive garden and back terrace, open all day. *(Adam Jones)*

CHAGFORD SX7087

Ring o' Bells (01647) 432466

Off A382; TQ13 8AH Welcoming old shuttered pub with good mix of locals and visitors, beamed and panelled bar, four well kept ales including Dartmoor and enjoyable home-made food at fair prices, friendly attentive service, woodburner in big fireplace; some live music, free wi-fi; well behaved children and dogs welcome (pub dog is Willow), sunny walled garden behind, nearby moorland walks, four comfortable spotless bedrooms, good breakfast, open all day. *(Dr A McCormick)*

CHALLACOMBE   SS6941
Black Venus (01598) 763251
B3358 Blackmoor Gate–Simonsbath; EX31 4TT Low-beamed 16th-c pub with two or three well kept changing ales, Thatcher's cider and decent wines by the glass, enjoyable fairly priced food from sandwiches to popular Sun lunch, friendly helpful staff, pews and comfortable chairs, woodburner and big fireplace, roomy attractive dining area, games room with pool and darts; free wi-fi; children and dogs welcome, garden play area, lovely countryside and good walks from the door, open all day in summer. *(Lynda and Trevor Smith)*

CHERITON BISHOP   SX7792
★ Old Thatch Inn (01647) 24204
Off A30; EX6 6JH Attractive thatched village pub with welcoming relaxed atmosphere, rambling beamed bar separated by big stone fireplace (woodburner), Otter, Dartmoor and a couple of guests, ciders such as Sandford's, good freshly prepared food (not Sun evening), efficient friendly service, restaurant; free wi-fi; children and dogs welcome, nice sheltered garden, two comfortable clean bedrooms; open all day. *(Charles Welch)*

CHERITON FITZPAINE   SS8706
Ring of Bells (01363) 860111
Off Barton Close, signed village centre; EX17 4JG Refurbished 14th-c thatched and beamed country pub; good food cooked by landlord-chef from blackboard menu, ales such as Branscombe Vale, Exe Valley and Teignworthy, local cider, friendly welcoming atmosphere, woodburners; children and dogs welcome (pub dog is Ruben), self-catering cottage, closed Sun evening, Mon. *(Mike and Lynne Steane)*

CHILLINGTON   SX7942
Bear & Blacksmiths (01548) 581171
A379 E of Kingsbridge; TQ7 2LD Old recently refurbished pub (former Open Arms) with clean modern interior, three well kept ales and good food from shortish menu, friendly staff; children welcome, tables on back terrace, closed Sun evening, Mon. *(Alistair Holdoway)*

CHITTLEHAMHOLT   SS6420
★ Exeter Inn (01769) 540281
Off A377 Barnstaple–Crediton, and B3226 SW of South Molton; EX37 9NS 16th-c thatched coaching inn with good food from sandwiches and traditional choices up, well kept ales such as Exmoor and Otter (some tapped from the cask), local ciders and good wine choice, friendly staff, barrel seats by open stove in huge

fireplace, beams dotted with hundreds of matchboxes, shelves of old bottles, traditional games, lounge with comfortable seating and woodburner, dining room and barn-style conservatory; background music; children and dogs welcome, gravel terrace, three bedrooms and four self-catering units. *(Lenny and Ruth Walters)*

CHRISTOW   SX8385
★ Teign House (01647) 252286
Teign Valley Road (B3193); EX6 7PL Former farmhouse in country setting, open fire in beamed bar, very good freshly made food from pub favourites up, also an asian menu, friendly helpful staff, up to five well kept local ales, own Brimblecombe's cider and nice wines, dining room; some live music; well behaved children and dogs welcome, garden and camping field, open all day weekends. *(George Sanderson)*

CHUDLEIGH   SX8679
Bishop Lacey (01626) 854585
Fore Street, just off A38; TQ13 0HY Partly 14th-c low-beamed church house, three well kept west country beers and enjoyable reasonably priced home-made food including Sunday lunch, cheerful obliging staff, two bars, log fire; children and dogs welcome, open all day. *(Jack Trussler)*

CHULMLEIGH   SS6814
Red Lion (01769) 580384
East Street; EX18 7DD Nicely updated 17th-c coaching inn, beams and open fires, enjoyable fairly priced food including burgers and pizzas, St Austell, Sharps and a guest, friendly helpful service; background music (live every other Sat), darts; children welcome, five bedrooms, open all day Fri-Sun, closed Mon lunchtime. *(Donald Allsopp)*

CLAYHIDON   ST1615
Half Moon (01823) 680291
On main road through village; EX15 3TJ Attractive old village pub with warm friendly atmosphere, wide choice of popular home-made food from sharing boards up, well kept Otter and a couple of guests, farm cider, good wine list, comfortable bar with inglenook log fire; some live music; children and dogs welcome, picnic-sets in tiered garden over road, lovely valley views, closed Sun evening, Mon. *(Guy Vowles, Mr and Mrs R G Spiller, Mrs Zara Elliott, David Thirkettle, Bob and Margaret Holder)*

CLOVELLY   SS3124
Red Lion (01237) 431237
The Quay; EX39 5TF Rambling 18th-c building in lovely position on curving quay below spectacular cliffs; beams, flagstones, log fire and interesting local photographs in character back bar (dogs allowed here), well kept Country Life and Sharps, bar food and upstairs restaurant, efficient service; great views, 11 attractive bedrooms (six more in

Sail Loft annexe), own car park for residents and diners, open all day. *(George Sanderson)*

CLYST HYDON   ST0201
★ **Five Bells** (01884) 277288
W of village, just off B3176 not far from M5 junction 28; EX15 2NT Thatched and beamed dining pub (former 16th-c farmhouse) with smartly updated interior; several different areas including raised dining part, assorted tables and chairs on wood or slate floors, woodburner in large stone fireplace, really good attractively presented food including set deal (12-1pm, 6-7pm), efficient friendly service, four well kept ales such as Butcombe and Otter, local cider and nice wines by the glass, games room with pool and sports TV; children welcome, dogs in bar, disabled access/loo, lovely cottagey garden with picnic-sets under parasols and country views, open all day Sun. *(Penny and David Sanderson)*

CLYST ST MARY   SX9791
Half Moon (01392) 873515
Under a mile from M5 junction 30 via A376; EX5 1BR Popular old beamed pub near disused 12th-c bridge over the River Clyst; good home-made food at reasonable prices including daily specials (best to book), many dishes available in smaller helpings, well kept ales such as Otter and decent choice of wines by the glass, friendly helpful staff, bar and separate lounge/dining area, stone floors, some red plush seating and log fire; quiz or bingo night Sun; children and dogs welcome, disabled access, open all day Fri-Sun. *(Roger and Donna Huggins)*

COCKWOOD   SX9780
★ **Ship** (01626) 890373
Off A379 N of Dawlish; EX6 8NU Comfortable traditional 17th-c pub set back from estuary and harbour – gets very busy in season; good food including some fish specials, five ales such as Hanlons, Otter and St Austell, friendly staff and locals, partitioned beamed bar with big log fire and ancient oven, decorative plates and seafaring memorabilia, small restaurant; background music; children and dogs welcome, nice steep-sided garden, open all day, food all day Sun. *(Matt Worthington)*

COMBE MARTIN   SS5846
Pack o' Cards (01271) 882300
High Street; EX34 0ET Unusual 'house of cards' building constructed in the late 17th c to celebrate a substantial gambling win – four floors, 13 rooms and 52 windows; snug bar area and various side rooms, three real ales such as Exmoor, St Austell and Wickwar, decent wines by the glass and good

range of well liked food including children's choices and all-day Sun carvery, cream teas, friendly helpful service even at busy times, restaurant; dogs welcome, pretty riverside garden with play area, six comfortable bedrooms, generous breakfast, open all day. *(R T and J C Moggridge, Roy and Gill Payne)*

COMBEINTEIGNHEAD   SX9071
Wild Goose (01626) 872241
Off unclassified coast road Newton Abbot–Shaldon, uphill in village; TQ12 4RA 17th-c pub under friendly family management; spacious back beamed lounge with agricultural bits and pieces on the walls, five west country ales and good freshly made food including daily specials, front bar with big fireplace, more beams, standing timbers and some flagstones, step down to area with another large fireplace, further cosy room with tub chairs; background and fortnightly live music, Sun quiz, TV projector for major sports; children and dogs welcome, nice country views from back garden, open all day weekends. *(David Leone Lawson)*

COUNTISBURY   SS7449
Blue Ball (01598) 741263
A39, E of Lynton; EX35 6NE Beautifully set heavy-beamed pub with friendly licensees, good range of generous local food in bar and restaurant, three or four ales including Exmoor and one badged for them, decent wines and proper ciders, log fires; background music, TV, free wi-fi; children, walkers and dogs welcome, views from terrace tables, good nearby cliff walks (pub provides handouts of four circular routes), comfortable bedrooms, open all day. *(Rosie and John Moore)*

CREDITON   SS8300
Crediton Inn (01363) 772882
Mill Street (follow Tiverton sign); EX17 1EZ Small friendly local (the 'Kirton') with long-serving landlady, well kept Hanlons Yellowhammer and up to nine quickly changing guests (Nov beer festival), cheap well prepared weekend food, home-made scotch eggs at other times, back games room/skittle alley; free wi-fi; open all day Mon-Sat. *(George Sanderson)*

CROYDE   SS4439
Manor House Inn (01271) 890241
St Marys Road, off B3231 NW of Braunton; EX33 1PG Friendly family pub with three well kept west country ales and good choice of enjoyable food from lunchtime sandwiches to blackboard specials, Sun carvery, cream teas, cheerful efficient service, spacious bar, restaurant and dining conservatory; background and

---

If you stay overnight in an inn or hotel, they are allowed to serve you an alcoholic drink at any hour of the day or night.

live music, sports TV, games end with pool and darts, skittle alley; free wi-fi; dogs welcome in bar, disabled facilities, attractive terraced garden with big play area, open all day. *(Neil and Brenda Skidmore)*

CROYDE
Thatch (01271) 890349   SS4439
B3231 NW of Braunton; Hobbs Hill; EX33 1LZ Lively thatched pub near great surfing beaches (can get packed in summer); rambling and roomy with beams and open fire, settles and other good seating, enjoyable pubby food from sandwiches and baked potatoes up, well kept changing local ales, morning coffee, teas, cheerful young staff, smart restaurant with dressers and lots of china; background and live music; children in eating areas, dogs in bar, flower-filled suntrap terraces and large gardens shared with neighbouring Billy Budds, good play area, simple clean bedrooms, self-catering cottage, open (and food) all day. *(Adrian Johnson, Neil and Brenda Skidmore)*

CULMSTOCK
Culm Valley (01884) 840354   ST1013
B3391, off A38 E of M5 junction 27; EX15 3JJ Friendly 18th-c pub with good choice of food from varied menu, four real ales including Otter, local cider and plenty of wines by the glass, country-style décor with hotchpotch of furniture, rugs on wood floors and some interesting bits and pieces, small front conservatory; free wi-fi; children and dogs (in bar) welcome, totem pole outside, tables on raised grassed area (former railway platform) overlooking old stone bridge over River Culm, open all day Fri-Sun. *(Adam Jones)*

DARTINGTON
★**Cott** (01803) 863777   SX7861
Pub signed off A385 W of Totnes, opposite A384 turn-off; TQ9 6HE Long 14th-c thatched pub with heavy beams, flagstones, nice mix of old furniture and two inglenooks (one with big woodburner), good home-made locally sourced food from traditional choices up in bar and restaurant, three well kept ales including local Hunters and Greene King, Ashridge's cider, nice wines by the glass, friendly efficient service; live music Sun; children and dogs welcome, wheelchair access (with help into restaurant), picnic-sets in garden and on pretty terrace, five comfortable bedrooms, open all day. *(Mike and Margaret Banks, John Evans)*

DARTMOUTH
★**Cherub** (01803) 832571   SX8751
Higher Street; walk along riverfront, right into Hauley Road and up steps at end; TQ6 9RB Ancient building (Dartmouth's oldest) with two heavily timbered upper floors jettying over the street, many original interior features, oak beams,

leaded lights and big stone fireplace, up to six well kept ales including a house beer from St Austell in bustling bar, low-ceilinged upstairs restaurant, enjoyable food from pub favourites to blackboard specials, efficient friendly service; background music; children welcome (no pushchairs), dogs in bar, open all day. *(Tony Scott)*

DARTMOUTH
Floating Bridge (01803) 832354   SX8751
Opposite Upper Ferry; Coombe Road (A379); TQ6 9PQ Busy pub in lovely quayside spot; bar with lots of stools by windows making most of waterside view, black and white photographs of local boating scenes, St Austell Tribute, Sharps Doom Bar and guests, several wines by the glass, enjoyable pubby food including daily specials, bare-boards dining room with leather-backed chairs around wooden tables; children and dogs (in bar) welcome, pretty window boxes, seats out by the river looking at busy ferry crossing, more on sizeable roof terrace, open (and food) all day. *(I D Barnett)*

DITTISHAM
★**Ferry Boat** (01803) 722368   SX8654
Manor Street; best to park in village car park and walk down (quite steep); TQ6 0EX Cheerful riverside pub with lively mix of customers; beamed bar with log fires and straightforward pubby furniture, lots of boating bits and pieces, tide times chalked on wall, flags on ceiling, picture-window view of the Dart, at least three real ales such as Otter and Sharps, a dozen wines by the glass and good range of tasty home-made food including pie of the day and various curries, efficient service; background and some live music, quiz night Thurs; children and dogs welcome, moorings for visiting boats on adjacent pontoon and bell to summon ferry, good walks, open (and food) all day. *(Dave Braisted, Lynda and Trevor Smith)*

DITTISHAM
Red Lion (01803) 722235   SX8654
The Level; TQ6 0ES Welcoming pub in lovely location looking down over attractive village and River Dart; enjoyable food including daily specials, Dartmoor, Palmers and a summer guest, carpeted bar and restaurant, open fires; also incorporates village store, tiny post office, library and craft shop; children and dogs welcome, eight bedrooms (some with river view), open from 8.30am, may shut Weds and weekend afternoons in winter. *(Charles Welch)*

DREWSTEIGNTON
Drewe Arms (01647) 281409   SX7390
Off A30 NW of Moretonhampstead; EX6 6QN Pretty thatched village pub under welcoming licensees; unspoilt room on left with basic wooden wall benches, stools and tables, original serving hatch, ales such as Dartmoor and Otter from tap room casks,

local cider, enjoyable sensibly priced pubby food including daily specials, two dining areas, one with Rayburn and history of Britain's longest serving landlady (Mabel Mudge), another with woodburner, darts and board games, some live music in back Long Room; free wi-fi; children and dogs welcome, seats under umbrellas on front terrace and in garden, pretty flowering tubs and baskets, two four-poster bedrooms, four bunk rooms, good local walks and handy for Castle Drogo (NT), open all day Sun (no evening food then). *(Barbara Brown)*

DUNSFORD   SX8189
Royal Oak (01647) 252256
Signed from Moretonhampstead; EX6 7DA Friendly comfortably worn-in village pub, generous helpings of traditional home-made food at reasonable prices, well kept ales such as Otter and Sharps, local cider, airy lounge with woodburner and view from sunny dining bay, simple dining room, steps down to pool room; background and some live music; children and dogs welcome, sheltered tiered garden with play area, various animals including donkeys, miniature ponies and alpacas, good value bedrooms in converted barn. *(Mr and Mrs P R Thomas)*

EAST ALLINGTON   SX7648
Fortescue Arms (01548) 521215
Village signed off A381 Totnes–Kingsbridge, S of A3122 junction; TQ9 7RA Pretty 19th-c wisteria-clad village pub; two-room bar with mix of tables and chairs on black slate floor, half-panelling and open fire, Dartmoor and St Austell ales, eight wines by the glass, spacious restaurant with high-backed dining chairs around pine tables and another fire in stone fireplace, enjoyable well priced traditional food cooked by landlord-chef, vegetarian menu too, warm friendly service; background and occasional live music, fortnightly Tues quiz, free wi-fi; children and dogs (in bar) welcome, wheelchair access, tables out at front with more on sheltered terrace, two bedrooms planned, closed Mon and lunchtime Tues. *(Simon and Mandy King)*

EAST BUDLEIGH   SY0684
Sir Walter Raleigh (01395) 442510
High Street; EX9 7ED Friendly little 16th-c low-beamed village local, well kept changing west country beers and good traditional food, restaurant down step; children and dogs on leads welcome, parking some way off, wonderful medieval bench carvings in nearby church, handy too for Bicton Park Botanical Gardens. *(Jack Trussler)*

EAST DOWN   SS5941
Pyne Arms (01271) 850055
Off A39 Barnstaple–Lynton near Arlington; EX31 4LX Welcoming old pub tucked away in small hamlet, cosy carpeted

bar with lots of alcoves, woodburner, good well presented food from traditional choices up, Exmoor, St Austell and a guest, good choice of wines, flagstoned area with sofas, conservatory; background music, free wi-fi; children and dogs welcome, small enclosed garden, good walks, handy for Arlington Court (NT), three comfortable bedrooms, open all day weekends, closed Mon lunchtime. *(Roy and Gill Payne)*

EAST PRAWLE   SX7836
Pigs Nose (01548) 511209
Prawle Green; TQ7 2BY Relaxed and quirky three-room 16th-c pub, lots of interesting bric-a-brac and pictures, mix of old furniture with jars of wild flowers and candles on tables, low beams, flagstones and open fire, local ales tapped from the cask, farm ciders and enjoyable simple pubby food, small family area with unusual toys, pool and darts; unobtrusive background music, hall for live bands (landlord was 1960s tour manager); friendly pub dogs (others welcome and menu for them), tables outside, pleasant spot on village green, closed Sun evening in winter. *(George Sanderson)*

EXETER   SX9390
Double Locks (01392) 256947
Canal Banks, Alphington, via Marsh Barton Industrial Estate; EX2 6LT Unsmart, individual and remotely located by ship canal; Wells & Youngs and guests, farm cider in summer, bar food (not Sun evening); background and some live music; children and dogs welcome, seats out on grass or decking with distant view to city and cathedral (nice towpath walk out), big play area, camping, open all day. *(Holly and Jim Waite)*

EXETER   SX9292
Georges Meeting House (01392) 454250 *South Street; EX1 1ED* Interesting Wetherspoons in grand former 18th-c chapel; bare-boards interior with three-sided gallery, stained glass and tall pulpit at one end, eight real ales from long counter, their usual good value food; children welcome, tables in attractive side garden under parasols, open all day from 8am. *(Roger and Donna Huggins)*

EXETER   SX9292
★Hour Glass (01392) 258722
Melbourne Street; off B3015 Topsham Road; EX2 4AU Old-fashioned bow-cornered pub tucked away in surviving Georgian part above the quay; good inventive food including vegetarian choices from shortish regularly changing menu, up to five well kept local ales (usually one from Otter) and extensive range of wines and spirits, friendly relaxed atmosphere, beams, bare boards and mix of furnishings, assorted pictures on dark red walls and various odds and ends including a stuffed

badger, open fire in small brick fireplace; background and live music; children (away from bar) and dogs welcome (resident cats), open all day weekends, closed Mon lunchtime. *(Roger and Donna Huggins)*

EXETER SX9193
★ Imperial (01392) 434050
New North Road (above St David's Station); EX4 4AH Impressive 19th-c mansion in own six-acre hillside park with sweeping drive; various different areas including two clubby little side bars, fine old ballroom with elaborate plasterwork and gilding and light airy former orangery with unusual mirrored end wall, interesting pictures, up to 14 real ales, standard good value Wetherspoons menu; popular with students and can get very busy; plenty of picnic-sets in grounds and elegant garden furniture in attractive cobbled courtyard, open all day. *(Roger and Donna Huggins)*

EXETER SX9192
Mill on the Exe (01392) 214464
Bonhay Road (A377); EX4 3AB Former paper mill in good spot by pedestrian bridge over weir; spacious opened-up interior on two floors (each with bar), bare boards, old bricks, beams and timbers, four well kept ales including St Austell, good house wines and popular food from snacks and sharing boards up, Sun carvery, large airy conservatory with feature raised fire; children and dogs welcome, river views from balcony tables, spiral stairs down to waterside garden (summer barbecues), 11 bedrooms in attached hotel side, open (and food) all day. *(Roger and Donna Huggins)*

EXETER SX9292
Old Fire House (01392) 277279
New North Road; EX4 4EP Relaxed city-centre pub in Georgian building behind high-arched wrought-iron gates; arranged over three floors with dimly lit beamed rooms and simple furniture, up to ten real ales, several ciders and good choice of bottled beers and wines, bargain food including late-night pizzas, friendly efficient staff; background music, live weekends, popular with young crowd (modest admission charge Fri, Sat night), Mon quiz; picnic-sets in front courtyard, open all day till late (3am Thurs-Sat). *(Roger and Donna Huggins)*

EXETER SX9292
Ship (01392) 272040
Martins Lane, near cathedral; EX1 1EY Historic heavy-beamed pub down alleyway, Greene King ales and guests, real cider, several wines by the glass and cocktails, decent reasonably priced food, steep narrow stairs up to comfortable quieter area with old easy chairs and sofas; background and live music, quiz nights, TV, machines; children and dogs welcome, open (and food) all day. *(IAA, HMW, Maria Sansoni)*

EXMINSTER SX9686
★ Turf Hotel (01392) 833128
From A379 S of village, follow the signs to the Swan's Nest, then continue to end of track, by gates; park and walk right along canal towpath – nearly a mile; EX6 8EE Remote but popular waterside pub reached by 20-minute towpath walk, cycle ride or 60-seater boat from Topsham quay (15-minute trip); several little rooms – end one with slate floor, pine walls, built-in seats and woodburner, simple room along corridor serves ales such as Exeter, Otter and Hanlons, local cider/juices and ten wines by the glass, interesting locally sourced food, friendly staff; background music, board games; children and dogs welcome, big garden with picnic-sets and summer barbecues, arrive early for a seat in fine weather, bedrooms and a yurt for hire, good breakfast, open all day in summer (best to check other times). *(Jack Trussler)*

EXMOUTH SY0080
Bicton Inn (01395) 272589
Bicton Street; EX8 2RU Traditional 19th-c backstreet corner local with friendly buoyant atmosphere, up to eight well kept ales and a proper cider, no food; regular live music including folk nights, pool, darts and other pub games; children and dogs welcome, open all day. *(Lucy and Giles Gibbon)*

EXMOUTH SX9980
Grapevine (01395) 222208
Victoria Road; EX8 1DL Popular red-brick corner pub (calls itself a pub-bistro), light and spacious with mix of wooden tables and seating, rugs on bare boards, modern local artwork, own Crossed Anchors beers plus changing west country guests, plenty of bottled imports and nice choice of wines by the glass, tasty well presented food including daily specials, friendly service and relaxed atmosphere; background music, live bands Fri and Sat, free wi-fi; children and dogs welcome, open all day. *(Jack Trussler)*

EXMOUTH SY9980
Grove (01395) 272101
Esplanade; EX8 1BJ Roomy high-gabled Victorian pub set back from beach, traditional furnishings, caricatures and local prints, enjoyable pubby food including local fish/seafood specials, friendly staff, Youngs ales and guests kept well, decent house wines, attractive fireplace at back, sea views from appealing upstairs dining room and balcony; background music, quiz Thurs; children welcome, picnic-sets in front garden, open all day (food all day weekends). *(PL)*

EXTON SX9886
Puffing Billy (01392) 877888
Station Road/Exton Lane; EX3 0PR Attractively opened-up dining pub with light

spacious interior, pitched ceiling bar area with flagstones and woodburner, restaurant part with wood-strip flooring and second woodburner in two-way fireplace, some painted tables and chairs and upholstered wall benches, good food from sharing plates and pub favourites up, beers such as Bath, Bays and Otter, good selection of wines and gins, friendly attentive service; background music, quiz last Sun of month; children welcome, tables out at front by road and on paved side terrace, on the Exe Estuary cycle trail, open all day, food all day weekends. *(Giles and Annie Francis)*

HARBERTON   SX7758

★**Church House** (01803) 863707

Off A381 S of Totnes; next to church; TQ9 7SF Ancient village inn (dates to the 13th c) with unusually long bar, blackened beams, medieval latticed glass and oak panelling, attractive 17th- and 18th-c pews and settles, woodburner in big inglenook, well kept ales including Salcombe and a house beer from Hunters, local cider and ten wines by the glass, good fairly priced food (not Sun evening), friendly efficient service, separate dining room; quiz and live music nights; children and dogs welcome (resident golden retriever), sunny walled back garden, comfortable bedrooms, open all day Sun, closed Mon and Tues lunchtimes. *(Rosie and John Moore)*

HATHERLEIGH   SS5404

Tally Ho (01837) 810306

Market Street (A386); EX20 3JN Friendly and relaxed old pub with own beers from back brewery plus a couple of guests such as Otter and St Austell, good food from ciabattas up, attractive heavy-beamed and timbered linked rooms, sturdy furnishings, big log fire and woodburner, restaurant, busy Tues market day (beer slightly cheaper then); background music, open mike night third Weds of month, darts; children and dogs welcome, tables in nice sheltered garden, three good value bedrooms, open all day. *(Matt and Hayley Jacob)*

HEMYOCK   ST1313

Catherine Wheel (01823) 680224

Cornhill; EX15 3RQ Popular and friendly village pub with bar, lounge and restaurant, Otter and Sharps Doom Bar, Thatcher's cider and plenty of wines by the glass, good interesting food (not Sun evening, Mon), fresh flowers on tables, leather sofas by woodburner, efficient service; Sun quiz, darts, pool and skittle alley, free wi-fi; children welcome, closed Mon lunchtime. *(Guy Vowles)*

HOLSWORTHY   SS3304

Rydon Inn (01409) 259444

Rydon (A3072 W); EX22 7HU Comfortably extended family-run dining pub, clean and tidy, with enjoyable food and well kept local ales, good friendly

---

service, raftered bar with thatched servery, woodburner in stone fireplace; background music; children and dogs welcome, disabled facilities, views over lake from conservatory and deck, well tended garden, open all day. *(George Sanderson)*

HONITON   ST1599

Heathfield (01404) 45321

Walnut Road; EX14 2UG Ancient thatched and beamed pub in contrasting residential area, well run and spacious, with a couple of Greene King ales and good value food from varied menu including the Heathfield Whopper (20oz rump steak), Sun lunchtime carvery, cheerful prompt service; skittle alley; children and dogs (in bar) welcome, seven bedrooms, open all day Fri-Sun. *(Bob and Margaret Holder)*

HONITON   SY1198

★**Holt** (01404) 47707

High Street, W end; EX14 1LA Charming little bustling pub run by two brothers, relaxed and informal, with just one room downstairs, chunky tables and chairs on slate flooring, shelves of books and coal-effect woodburner, full range of Otter beers (the family founded the brewery), bigger brighter upstairs dining room with similar furniture on pale floorboards, very good 'tapas' and other inventive food; cookery classes and quarterly music festivals; well behaved children welcome, dogs in bar, closed Sun, Mon. *(Revd R P Tickle)*

HOPE COVE   SX6740

Hope & Anchor (01548) 561294

Tucked away by car park; TQ7 3HQ Revamped seaside inn on two floors; open kitchen serving decent choice of popular food from sharing plates to local fish, St Austell ales and a west country guest, several wines by the glass, helpful amiable young staff, flagstones and bare boards, two woodburners, dining room views to Burgh Island; background music, free wi-fi; children and dogs welcome, sea-view tables out on decked balcony and terrace, 11 bedrooms, open (and food) all day from 8am for breakfast. *(Theocsbrian)*

HORNS CROSS   SS3823

★**Hoops** (01237) 451222

A39 Clovelly–Bideford, W of village; EX39 5DL Pretty thatched and beamed inn dating from the 13th c, friendly and relaxed, with traditionally furnished bar, log fires in sizeable fireplaces and some standing timbers and partitioning, more formal restaurant with attractive mix of tables and chairs, some panelling, exposed stone and another open fire, beers from Country Life, Forge and St Austell, over a dozen wines by the glass, enjoyable fairly straightforward food using local suppliers, welcoming helpful staff; may be background music; children and dogs allowed, picnic-sets under parasols in enclosed courtyard, more seats on terrace and in two acres of gardens, 13 well equipped bedrooms, open (and food) all day. *(Bob and Margaret Holder)*

HORSEBRIDGE   SX4074
★ **Royal** (01822) 870214
Off A384 Tavistock–Launceston; PL19 8PJ Dimly lit ancient local with dark half-panelling, log fires, slate floors, scrubbed tables and interesting bric-a-brac, good reasonably priced food, friendly landlord and staff, well kept Dartmoor, St Austell and Skinners direct from the cask, real cider; no children in the evening, dogs welcome, picnic-sets on front and side terraces and in big garden, quiet rustic spot by lovely old Tamar bridge popular with walkers and cyclists. *(Donald Allsopp)*

IDE   SX9090
Huntsman (01392) 272779
High Street; EX2 9RN Welcoming thatched and beamed country pub, tasty sensibly priced home-made food using local suppliers from sandwiches to good value Sun lunch and takeaway pizzas, three west country beers, friendly attentive service; regular events; children welcome, picnic-sets in pleasant garden. *(George Sanderson)*

IDE   SX8990
Poachers (01392) 273847
3 miles from M5 junction 31, via A30; High Street; EX2 9RW Cosy beamed pub in quaint village; Branscombe Vale Branoc and five changing west country guests from ornate curved wooden bar, enjoyable home-made food, mismatched old chairs and sofas, various pictures and odds and ends, big log fire, restaurant; free wi-fi; dogs welcome (they have a boxer), tables in pleasant garden with barbecue, three comfortable bedrooms, open (and food) all day (till late Fri, Sat). *(George Sanderson)*

IDEFORD   SX8977
★ **Royal Oak** (01626) 852274
2 miles off A380; TQ13 0AY Unpretentious little 16th-c thatched and flagstoned village local, friendly helpful service, a couple of changing local ales and generous helpings of tasty well priced pub food, navy theme including interesting Nelson and Churchill memorabilia, beams, panelling and big open fireplace; children and dogs welcome, tables out at front and by car park over road, closed Mon. *(Adam Jones)*

ILFRACOMBE   SS5247
George & Dragon (01271) 863851
Fore Street; EX34 9ED One of the oldest pubs here (14th c) and handy for the harbour, clean and comfortable with friendly local atmosphere, ales such as Exmoor, Sharps and Shepherd Neame, decent wines, traditional food including local fish, black beams, stripped stone and

open fireplaces, lots of ornaments, china etc; background and some live music, Tues quiz, no mobile phones; children and dogs welcome, open all day and can get very busy weekends. *(Serena and Adam Furber)*

ILFRACOMBE   SS5247
Ship & Pilot (01271) 863562
Broad Street, off harbour; EX34 9EE Bright yellow pub near harbour attracting friendly mix of regulars and visitors, six well kept changing ales (usually have Bass) and good range of proper ciders/perry, no food apart from rolls, traditional open-plan interior with lots of old photos; live music Sat evening, juke box, a couple of TVs for sport, darts; dogs welcome, tables outside, open all day. *(Lenny and Ruth Walters)*

ILSINGTON   SX7876
Carpenters Arms (01364) 661629
Old Town Hill; TQ13 9RG Unspoilt little 18th-c local next to the village church, beams and flagstones, country-style pine furniture, brasses, woodburners, enjoyable generously served home-made food (not Sun evening) and well kept changing ales, friendly atmosphere; darts; children, well behaved dogs and muddy boots welcome, tables out at front, good surrounding walks, no car park, open all day. *(George Sanderson)*

INSTOW   SS4730
Boat House (01271) 861292
Marine Parade; EX39 4JJ Well thought-of, modern high-ceilinged bar-restaurant with huge tidal beach just across lane and views to Appledore, wide choice of good food including plenty of fish/seafood, two well kept local ales and decent wines by the glass, friendly prompt service, lively family bustle; background music; roof terrace. *(Adam Jones)*

KENN   SX9285
Ley Arms (01392) 832341
Signed off A380 just S of Exeter; EX6 7UW Rambling old thatched dining pub in quiet spot near the church, good range of well presented popular food including blackboard specials, smaller appetites and special diets catered for, well kept west country ales and decent range of wines, cheerful helpful staff, beams, exposed stonework and polished granite flagstones, log fires, restaurant and garden room; children and dogs (theirs is Reggie) welcome, terrace tables under parasols, open all day, food all day weekends. *(Graham and Carol Parker)*

KENNFORD   SX9186
Seven Stars (01392) 834887
Centre of village; EX6 7TR Updated little village pub with three west country beers and good food including pies and takeaway pizzas, friendly atmosphere; Thurs quiz, open mike night first Fri of

month, pool, darts and sports TV; children and dogs welcome, closed Mon lunchtime, otherwise open all day. *(Charles Welch)*

KILMINGTON   SY2698
New Inn (01297) 33376
Signed off Gammons Hill; EX13 7SF
Traditional thatched local (originally three 14th-c cottages) under friendly licensees; good food especially Sun lunch and well kept Palmers ales; skittle alley and boules court, monthly quiz; children and dogs welcome, disabled access/loo, picnic-sets in large garden with tree-shaded areas, closed Mon lunchtime, no food Sun evening, Mon. *(Jack Trussler)*

KILMINGTON   SY2798
★ Old Inn (01297) 32096
A35; EX13 7RB Bustling 16th-c thatched and beamed pub, family-run and welcoming, with traditional food, well kept Branscombe Vale, Otter and a guest, decent choice of wines, attentive amiable service, small character front bar with traditional games (there's also a skittle alley), back lounge with leather armchairs by inglenook log fire, small restaurant; children welcome, wheelchair access, terrace and lawned area, closed Sun evening. *(Guy Vowles, Steve and Claire Harvey, Phil and Jane Villiers)*

KINGSBRIDGE   SX7343
Crabshell (01548) 852345
Embankment Road, edge of town; TQ7 1JZ Great waterside position, charming when tide is in, with lovely views from big windows and outside tables, emphasis on food including all day pizzas and good fish/seafood, half a dozen well kept ales including own microbrews, plenty of wines by the glass, friendly staff; children welcome, dogs ground floor only, open all day and can get very busy. *(Bob and Margaret Holder, Stuart Reeves)*

KINGSKERSWELL   SX8666
★ Bickley Mill (01803) 873201
Bickley Road, follow Maddacombe Road from village, under new ring road, W of Kingskerswell; TQ12 5LN Restored 13th-c mill tucked away in lovely countryside; rambling beamed rooms with open fires and rugs on wood floors, variety of seating from rustic chairs and settles to sofas piled with cushions, modern art and black and white photos on stone walls, good well presented food including pub favourites from sensibly priced menu, a couple of Bays ales and 14 wines by the glass, friendly helpful staff; monthly jazz Sun lunchtime, free wi-fi; children and dogs (in bar) welcome, seats on big terrace, also a subtropical hillside

garden, well appointed modern bedrooms, good breakfast, open all day. *(Kate Moran, Mike and Mary Carter, Kim Skuse)*

KINGSTON   SX6347
Dolphin (01548) 810314
Off B3392 S of Modbury (can also be reached from A379 W of Modbury); TQ7 4QE Peaceful and friendly 16th-c inn with knocked-through beamed rooms, traditional furniture on red carpeting, open fire, woodburner in inglenook fireplace, Otter, St Austell, Sharps and Timothy Taylors, a farm cider, straightforward food; children and dogs welcome, seats in garden, pretty tubs and summer window boxes, quiet village with several tracks leading down to the sea, three bedrooms in building across road, closed some Sun evenings in winter. *(Theocsbrian)*

KINGSWEAR   SX8851
★ Ship (01803) 752348
Higher Street; TQ6 0AG Attractive old beamed local by church, well kept Adnams, Exmoor, Otter and guests from horseshoe bar, Addlestone's cider and decent wines, popular food including local fish (good river views from restaurant up steps), nautical bric-a-brac and local photographs, two log fires; occasional live music, sports TV; children and dogs welcome, a couple of river-view tables outside, open all day in summer. *(Donald Allsopp)*

LAKE   SX5288
★ Bearslake (01837) 861334
A386 just S of Sourton; EX20 4HQ Rambling thatch and stone pub (former longhouse dating from the 13th c), leather sofas and high bar chairs on crazy-paved slate floor at one end, three more rooms with woodburners, toby jugs, farm tools and traps, stripped stone, well kept ales such as Dartmoor and Otter, good range of spirits, decent wines and enjoyable food, beamed restaurant; wi-fi through most of the building; children allowed, large sheltered streamside garden, Dartmoor walks, six comfortable bedrooms, good breakfast, closed Sun evening, otherwise open all day. *(George Sanderson)*

LANDSCOVE   SX7766
Live & Let Live (01803) 762663
SE end of village by Methodist chapel; TQ13 7LZ Friendly open-plan village local with decent freshly made food and well kept ales such as Teignworthy, impressive collection of miniatures, log fire; children and dogs welcome, tables on small front deck and in little orchard across lane, good walks, closed Sun evening, Mon. *(Adam Jones)*

Virtually all pubs in this book sell wine by the glass. We mention wines if they are a cut above the average.

LIFTON
SX3885
★Arundell Arms (01566) 784666
Fore Street; PL16 0AA Good imaginative food in substantial country-house fishing hotel including set lunch, warmly welcoming and individual, with professional service, good choice of wines by the glass, morning coffee and afternoon tea; also adjacent Courthouse bar, complete with original cells, serving good fairly priced pubby food (not Sun evening, Mon) including children's meals, well kept Dartmoor Jail and St Austell Tribute, darts and some live music; can arrange fishing tuition – also shooting, deer-stalking and riding; 25 bedrooms, useful A30 stop. *(Charlotte Gladstone-Millar)*

LITTLEHEMPSTON
SX8162
Pig & Whistle (01803) 863733
Newton Road (A381); TQ9 6LT Large welcoming former coaching inn, long bar with beams and stripped stone, ales such as Dartmoor and Teignworthy, enjoyable traditional food, extensive dining area; free wi-fi; children welcome, decked front terrace, two bedrooms, open all day. *(Mike and Margaret Banks)*

LOWER ASHTON
SX8484
Manor Inn (01647) 252304
Ashton signposted off B3193 N of Chudleigh; EX6 7QL Well run country pub under friendly hard-working licensees, good quality sensibly priced food including lunchtime set menu, well kept ales such as Dartmoor, Otter and St Austell, good choice of wines, Sun afternoon cream teas, open fires in both bars, back restaurant in converted smithy; dogs welcome, disabled access, garden picnic-sets with nice rural outlook, open all day Sun, closed Mon. *(Andrew and Michele Revell)*

LUPPITT
ST1606
★Luppitt Inn (01404) 891613
Back roads N of Honiton; EX14 4RT Unspoilt basic farmhouse pub tucked away in lovely countryside, an amazing survivor, with chatty long-serving landlady; tiny room with corner bar and a table, another not much bigger with fireplace, cheap Otter tapped from the cask, intriguing metal puzzles made by a neighbour, no food or music, lavatories across the yard; closed lunchtimes and all day Sun. *(Barbara Brown)*

LUSTLEIGH
SX7881
★Cleave (01647) 277223
Off A382 Bovey Tracey– Moretonhampstead; TQ13 9TJ Busy thatched pub in lovely Dartmoor National Park village; low-ceilinged beamed bar with granite walls and log fire, attractive antique high-backed settles and wheelbacks on red patterned carpet, Dartmoor, Otter and a guest, good variety of enjoyable home-cooked food, efficient friendly service, back room (formerly the old station waiting room) converted to light airy bistro with pale wooden furniture on wood-strip floor, doors to outside eating area; children and dogs (in bar) welcome, more seats in sheltered garden, good circular walks, shuts around 7.30pm Sun, otherwise open (and food) all day, but best to check there are no functions planned. *(Penny and David Shepherd)*

LUTON
SX9076
★Elizabethan (01626) 775425
Haldon Moor; TQ13 0BL Tucked-away, much-altered, low-beamed dining pub (once owned by Elizabeth I); wide choice of good well presented food including daily specials and popular Sun lunch, three well kept ales and several reasonably priced wines by the glass, friendly attentive service, thriving atmosphere; children welcome, pretty front garden, open all day Sun. *(Jack Trussler)*

LYDFORD
SX5184
Castle Inn (01822) 820241
Off A386 Okehampton–Tavistock; EX20 4BH Tudor inn owned by St Austell, traditional twin bars with big slate flagstones, bowed low beams and granite walls, high-backed settles and four inglenook log fires, notable stained-glass door, hearty helpings of popular well priced food, restaurant; free wi-fi; children and dogs welcome in certain areas, seats out at front and in sheltered back garden, lovely NT river gorge nearby, eight bedrooms, open all day. *(Barbara Brown)*

LYMPSTONE
SX9984
Redwing (01395) 222156
Church Road; EX8 5JT Modernised dining pub not far from the church, comfortable seating on oak or black slate floors, well kept local beers such as Hanlons, wide range of wines by the glass and good freshly made food from ciabattas and pub favourites up, friendly attentive service, converted loft restaurant; children and dogs (in bar) welcome, terrace tables, attractive unspoilt village. *(Giles and Annie Francis, Peter L Harrison)*

LYMPSTONE
SX9984
Swan (01395) 272644
The Strand, by station entrance; EX8 5ET Old beamed pub with enjoyable home-made food including local fish and bargain weekday set lunch, split-level dining area with big log fire, Hanlons Yellowhammer and four other west country ales, short but well chosen wine list; pool, free wi-fi; children welcome, picnic sets out at front, popular with cyclists (bike racks provided), shore walks, open all day. *(Adam Jones)*

LYNMOUTH
SS7249
Rising Sun (01598) 753223
Harbourside; EX35 6EG Nice old pub in wonderful position overlooking harbour; beamed and stripped-stone bar bustling

with locals and tourists, good fire, three Exmoor ales and a guest, popular food from comprehensive menu (emphasis on fish), upmarket hotel side with attractive restaurant; background music; well behaved children (till 7.30pm) and dogs welcome, gardens behind, bedrooms in cottagey old thatched building, parking can be a problem (expensive during the day, sparse at night), open all day. *(Richard and Penny Gibbs)*

LYNTON SS7248

Beggars Roost (01598) 753645

Manor Hotel; EX35 6LD Refurbished stone-built country pub with friendly relaxed atmosphere; good freshly made food and well kept ales including Exmoor and a house beer brewed by Marstons, helpful cheerful staff; children and dogs welcome, good bedrooms in hotel side, also camping next door, open all day. *(Paul Walker)*

LYNTON SS6548

Hunters (01598) 763230

Pub well signed off A39 W of Lynton; EX31 4PY Large Edwardian country inn set in four-acre grounds (roaming peacocks), superb Heddon Valley position by NT information centre down very steep hill, great walks including to the sea; two bars one with woodburner, up to six ales including Exmoor and Heddon Valley (brewed for them locally), good range of other drinks and enjoyable well priced food from fairly pubby menu, efficient friendly service, dining room overlooking back garden; quiz and music nights, pool, board games, free wi-fi; children and dogs welcome, ten bedrooms, open all day. *(Theocsbrian)*

MEAVY SX5467

★ **Royal Oak** (01822) 852944

Off B3212 E of Yelverton; PL20 6PJ Partly 15th-c pub taking its name from the 800-year-old oak on green opposite; heavy beamed L-shaped bar with church pews, red plush banquettes, old agricultural prints and church pictures, smaller locals' bar with flagstones and big open-hearth fireplace, separate dining room, good reasonably priced food served by friendly staff, four well kept ales including Dartmoor, farm ciders, a dozen wines by the glass and several malt whiskies; background music, board games; children and dogs (in bar) welcome, picnic-sets out in front and on the green, pretty Dartmoor-edge village, open all day. *(Lynda and Trevor Smith)*

MEETH SS5408

Bull & Dragon (01837) 811742

A386 Hatherleigh–Torrington; EX20 3EP Welcoming 15th-c beamed and thatched village pub with large open bar, inglenook woodburner, well kept ales such as Exmoor and Otter, good reasonably priced home-made food from shortish menu plus some blackboard specials (booking advised), friendly helpful

staff; children and dogs welcome, at end of Tarka Trail cycle route, closed Sun evening and Weds. *(Jamie and Sue May)*

MERTON SS5212

Malt Scoop (01805) 603924

New Street; EX20 3EA Thatched former farmhouse (a pub since the early 19th c), renovated interior with original slate floors and inglenook, enjoyable generously served bar food at fair prices using local produce (popular Sun lunch), St Austell ales, friendly service; free wi-fi; children and dogs welcome, two bedrooms, open all day Fri-Sun. *(Holly and Tim Waite)*

MOLLAND SS8028

London (01769) 550269

Village signed off B3227 E of South Molton; EX36 3NG Proper Exmoor inn at its busiest in the shooting season; two small linked rooms by old-fashioned central servery, local stag-hunting pictures, cushioned benches and plain chairs around rough stripped trestle tables, Exmoor Ale, attractive beamed room on left with famous stag story on the wall, panelled dining room on right with big curved settle by fireplace (good hunting and game bird prints), enjoyable home-made food using fresh local produce including seasonal game (not Sun evening, no credit cards), small hall with stuffed animals; fine Victorian lavatories; children and dogs welcome, picnic-sets in cottagey garden, untouched early 18th-c box pews in church next door, two bedrooms, closed Mon lunchtime. *(Lenny and Ruth Walters)*

MONKLEIGH SS4520

Bell (01805) 938285

A388; EX39 5JS Welcoming thatched and beamed 17th-c village pub with carpeted bar and small restaurant, well kept Dartmoor and a couple of guests, enjoyable reasonably priced food including daily specials, themed evenings and Sun carvery, friendly staff; background music, quiz nights, darts; children (till 9pm) and dogs (treats for good ones) welcome, wheelchair access, garden with raised deck, views and good walks, closed Mon. *(Jack Trussler)*

MORCHARD BISHOP SS7607

London Inn (01363) 877222

Signed off A377 Crediton–Barnstaple; EX17 6NW Prettily placed 16th-c village coaching inn run by mother and daughter team, thriving local atmosphere, good generous home-made food (best to book weekends), Fullers London Pride and a local guest, helpful friendly service, low-beamed open-plan carpeted bar with woodburner in large fireplace, small dining room; pool, darts and skittles; children and dogs welcome, closed Mon lunchtime. *(Barbara Brown)*

MORELEIGH   SX7652
New Inn (01548) 821326
*B3207, off A381 Kingsbridge–Totnes in
Stanborough; TQ9 7JH* Cosy old-fashioned
country local with friendly landlady (same
family has run it for several decades); large
helpings of enjoyable home-made food at
reasonable prices including popular steaks,
Timothy Taylors Landlord tapped from the
cask and a weekend guest, character old
furniture, nice pictures and good inglenook
log fire; only open from 6.30pm (12-2.30,
7-10.30 Sun). *(Paul and Karen Cornock)*

NEWTON ABBOT   SX8671
Olde Cider Bar (01626) 354221
East Street; TQ12 2LD Basic old-fashioned
cider house with plenty of atmosphere, around
30 interesting reasonably priced ciders (some
very strong), a couple of perries, more in
bottles, good country wines from the cask
too, baguettes, pasties etc, friendly staff,
stools made from cask staves, barrel seats
and wall benches, flagstones and bare boards;
regular live folk music, small back games
room with bar billiards; dogs welcome, terrace
tables, open all day. *(George Sanderson)*

NEWTON ABBOT   SX8468
Two Mile Oak (01803) 812411
*A381 2 miles S, at Denbury/Kingskerswell
crossroads; TQ12 6DF* Appealing two-bar
beamed coaching inn; black panelling,
traditional furnishings and candlelit alcoves,
inglenook and woodburners, well kept Bass,
Dartmoor and Otter tapped from the cask,
nine wines by the glass, enjoyable well priced
pubby food from sandwiches and baked
potatoes up (special diets catered for), decent
coffee, cheerful staff; background music;
children and dogs welcome, round picnic-sets
on terrace and lawn, open all day. *(S Holder)*

NEWTON FERRERS   SX5447
Dolphin (01752) 872007
*Riverside Road East: Newton Hill off
Church Park (B3186) then left; PL8 1AE*
Shuttered 18th-c pub in attractive setting;
L-shaped bar with a few low black beams,
pews and benches on slate floors and some
white plank panelling, open fire, up to
four well kept ales including St Austell,
decent wines by the glass, enjoyable
traditional food including good fish and
chips and daily specials, friendly staff;
children and dogs (in bar) welcome,
terraces over lane looking down on
River Yealm and yachts, open all day in
summer when can get packed, parking
limited. *(Penny and David Sanderson)*

NEWTON ST CYRES   SX8798
Beer Engine (01392) 851282
Off A377 towards Thorverton; EX5 5AX
Former railway hotel brewing its own beers
since the 1980s and continuing well under
friendly management; good home-made food

including specials and popular Sun lunch
(food all day Sun), log fire in bar; children
welcome, seats on decked verandah, steps
down to garden, open all day. *(Donald Allsopp)*

NEWTON TRACEY   SS5226
★Hunters (01271) 858339
B3232 Barnstaple–Torrington; EX31 3PL
Extended 15th-c pub with massive low beams
and two inglenooks, good reasonably priced
food from pub standards up including choices
for smaller appetites, well kept St Austell
Tribute and Sharps Doom Bar, decent wines,
efficient friendly service, skittle alley/
overflow dining area; soft background music;
children and dogs welcome, disabled access
using ramp, tables on small terrace behind,
open all day weekends. *(Jack Trussler)*

NOMANSLAND   SS8313
Mount Pleasant (01884) 860271
B3137 Tiverton–South Molton; EX16 8NN
Informal country local with good mix of
customers, huge fireplaces in long low-
beamed main bar, well kept ales such as
Cotleigh, Exmoor and Sharps, several wines
by the glass, Weston's cider, good range of
enjoyable freshly cooked food (special diets
catered for), friendly attentive service, happy
mismatch of simple well worn furniture
including comfy old sofa, candles on tables,
country pictures, daily papers, cosy dining
room (former smithy with original forge),
darts in public bar; background music;
well behaved children and dogs welcome,
picnic-sets and play area in back garden,
open (and food) all day. *(George Sanderson)*

NOSS MAYO   SX5447
★Ship (01752) 872387
*Off A379 via B3186, E of Plymouth;
PL8 1EW* Charming setting overlooking
inlet and visiting boats (can get crowded
in good weather); thick-walled bars with
bare boards and log fires, four well kept
local ales, good choice of wines and malt
whiskies, popular food from varied menu,
friendly efficient service, lots of local
pictures and charts, books, newspapers
and board games, restaurant upstairs;
children and dogs (downstairs) welcome,
plenty of seats on heated waterside terrace,
parking restricted at high tide, open (and
food) all day. *(Philip Crawford, Jan Gould,
Lynda and Trevor Smith, Tom and Ruth Rees)*

OAKFORD   SS9121
Red Lion (01398) 351592
Rookery Hill; EX16 9ES Friendly village
coaching inn dating from the 17th c (partly
rebuilt in Georgian times); well kept ales
such as Otter and reasonably priced pubby
food including Thurs OAP lunch deal and
Sun carvery till 3pm, woodburner in big
inglenook; children, walkers and dogs
welcome, four comfortable bedrooms,
open all day weekends (till 9pm Sun),
closed Mon lunchtime. *(Barbara Brown)*

OTTERTON
SY0885
Kings Arms (01395) 568416
Fore Street; EX9 7HB Big modernised village pub handy for families from extensive nearby caravan park; popular food from sandwiches and sharing plates through pub favourites to good fresh fish, Sun carvery, up to four well kept ales including Otter, decent wines, friendly helpful staff; quiz first Weds of the month, some live music, darts, free wi-fi; dogs very welcome (menu for them), attractive back garden with play area, also a covered terrace, 15 bedrooms (two with four-posters), open all day. *(Dr D J and Mrs S C Walker, Dr A J and Mrs B A Tompsett)*

OTTERY ST MARY
SY0995
Volunteer (01404) 814060
Broad Street; EX11 1BZ Welcoming early 19th-c pub, traditional front bar with darts and open fire, more contemporary restaurant behind, four gravity-fed beers including Otter, good reasonably priced home-made food (not Sun evening), friendly service; upstairs loos; open all day. *(Roger and Donna Huggins)*

PARKHAM
SS3821
★ Bell (01237) 451201
Rectory Lane; EX39 5PL Spotlessly kept thatched village pub with three communicating rooms (one on lower level), beams and standing timbers, pubby furniture on red patterned carpet, brass, copper and old photographs, grandfather clock, woodburner and small coal fire, model ships and lanterns hanging above bar serving Exmoor, Otter and Sharps, a dozen malt whiskies, popular food; darts, free wi-fi; well behaved children welcome, dogs in bar, picnic-sets on covered back terrace with fairy lights, open (and food) all day Sun. *(Charles Welch)*

PARRACOMBE
SS6644
★ Fox & Goose (01598) 763239
Off A39 Blackmoor Gate–Lynton; EX31 4PE Popular rambling Victorian pub, hunting and farming memorabilia and interesting old photographs, well kept Cotleigh and Exmoor, traditional cider and several wines by the glass, good variety of well cooked generously served food from blackboard menus, also takeaway pizzas, friendly staff, log fire, separate dining room; children and dogs welcome, small front verandah, riverside terrace and garden room, four bedrooms, open all day in summer. *(B R Merritt, Roy and Gill Payne)*

PETER TAVY
SX5177
★ Peter Tavy Inn (01822) 810348
Off A386 near Mary Tavy, N of Tavistock; PL19 9NN Old stone village inn tucked away at end of little lane, bustling low-beamed bar with high-backed settles on black flagstones, mullioned windows, good log fire in big stone fireplace, snug dining

area with carved wooden chairs, hops on beams and various pictures, up to five well kept west country ales, Winkleigh's cider and good wine/whisky choice, well liked food from varied menu including OAP lunch (not Sun) and early-evening deal, friendly attentive service, separate restaurant; children and dogs welcome, picnic-sets in pretty garden, peaceful moorland views, open all day weekends. *(Mrs Zara Elliott, Stephen Shepherd, Phil and Jane Villiers, Helen and Brian Edgeley)*

PLYMOUTH
SX4953
Bridge (01752) 403888
Shaw Way, Mount Batten; PL9 9XH Modern two-storey bar-restaurant with terrace and balcony overlooking busy Yacht Haven Marina, enjoyable food from sandwiches and pub favourites up, nice choice of wines by the glass, Sharps Doom Bar and St Austell Tribute, impressive fish tank upstairs; children welcome, well behaved dogs downstairs, open all day from 9am for breakfast. *(George Sanderson)*

PLYMOUTH
SX4854
Dolphin (01752) 660876
Barbican; PL1 2LS Unpretentious chatty local with good range of well kept cask-tapped ales including Bass and St Austell, open fire, Beryl Cook paintings (even one of the friendly landlord), no food but can bring your own; dogs welcome, open all day. *(John Poulter)*

PLYMOUTH
SX4854
Ship (01752) 667604
Quay Road, Barbican; PL1 2JZ Waterside corner pub with opened-up bare-boards interior, St Austell ales and quite a choice of enjoyable food, harbour views from upstairs restaurant, friendly attentive service; children and dogs (in bar) welcome, full wheelchair access, seats outside under umbrellas, open (and food) all day. *(Mike and Margaret Banks)*

PLYMOUTH
SX4753
Waterfront (01752) 226961
Grand Parade; PL1 3DQ Restored former 19th-c yacht club in great spot by Plymouth Sound, contemporary décor, varied choice of enjoyable food from sandwiches and sharing boards up, St Austell ales and guests, 20 wines by the glass, friendly helpful service; children and dogs welcome, decked terrace with superb views, open (and food) all day. *(Andrew and Michele Revell)*

PLYMTREE
ST0502
Blacksmiths Arms (01884) 277474
Near church; EX15 2JU Well run, friendly 19th-c beamed and carpeted village pub with good reasonably priced food cooked by landlord, three well kept changing local ales and decent choice of wines by the glass; pool room and skittle alley; children welcome, dogs on leads (their

leonberger is called Jagermeister), garden
with boules and play area, open all day
Sat, till 4pm Sun, closed Mon, lunchtimes
Tues-Fri. *(Matt and Hayley Jacob)*

PUSEHILL SS4228

Pig on the Hill (01237) 459222

Off B3226 near Westward Ho!; EX39 5AH
Extensively revamped restaurant pub
(originally a cowshed); good choice of highly
enjoyable, well presented food (must book
ahead), friendly helpful service, Country Life
and local guests, games room with skittle
alley; background music; children and dogs
(in bar) welcome, disabled facilities, good
views from terrace tables and picnic-sets on
grass, play area, boules, three self-catering
cabins, open all day. *(Martyn Stringer)*

RINGMORE SX6545

Journeys End (01548) 810205

*Signed off B3392 at Pickwick Inn,
St Anns Chapel, near Bigbury; best to
park opposite church; TQ7 4HL* Ancient
village inn (dates from the 13th c) with
friendly chatty licensees, character panelled
lounge and other linked rooms, Sharps Doom
Bar and local guests tapped from the cask,
farm cider, decent wines, well executed/
presented food from good shortish menu (not
Sun evening, best to book in summer), log
fires, family dining conservatory with board
games; children welcome throughout, garden
with picnic-sets on gravel, old-fashioned
streetlights and decked area, attractive
setting near thatched cottages and not
far from the sea, open all day weekends,
closed Mon. *(Philip Crawford, Theocsbrian)*

ROBOROUGH SS5717

New Inn (01805) 603247

Off B3217 N of Winkleigh; EX19 8SY
Tucked-away 16th-c thatched village
pub, cheerful and busy, with well kept
Teignworthy and a couple of guests, ten
proper ciders and several wines by the glass,
good variety of enjoyable locally sourced
food including takeaway pizzas, beamed bar
with woodburner, tiny back room leading
up to dining room, friendly helpful staff;
children and dogs welcome, seats on sunny
front terrace, open all day Fri-Sun, closed
lunchtimes Mon, Tues. *(Lucy and Giles Gibbon)*

ROCKBEARE SY0195

★ **Jack in the Green** (01404) 822240

*Signed from A30 bypass E of Exeter;
EX5 2EE* Neat welcoming dining pub (most
customers here to eat) run well by long-
serving owner; flagstoned lounge bar with
comfortable sofas, ales such as Butcombe,
Otter and Sharps, local cider, a dozen wines
by the glass (over 100 by the bottle), first
class food from interesting menu including
excellent puddings, carpeted dining rooms
with old hunting/shooting photographs and
high-backed leather chairs around dark
tables, big woodburner, also airy restaurant

and club-like ante-room with two-way stove,
good friendly service; background music;
well behaved children welcome, no dogs
inside, disabled facilities, plenty of seats in
courtyard, open all day Sun, closed 25 Dec-5
Jan, quite handy for M5. *(John Evans)*

SALCOMBE SX7439

Fortescue (01548) 842868

Union Street, end of Fore Street; TQ8 8BZ
Linked rooms with painted beams and
half-panelling, rugs and pine furniture on
quarry tiles, old local photographs and
some stuffed fish, woodburners, decent
pubby food and well kept ales such as Otter,
Salcombe and Sharps, public bar with
parquet floor, booth seating, games, TVs
and machines; children welcome, courtyard
picnic-sets, three new bedrooms, open (and
food) all day. *(Brian and Janet Braby)*

SAMPFORD COURTENAY SS6300

New Inn (01837) 82247

B3072 Crediton–Holsworthy; EX20 2TB
Attractive 16th-c thatched pub-restaurant
in picturesque village; good interesting food
from landlord-chef at reasonable prices
including set lunch, also tasting menus
and themed evenings, local ales tapped
from the cask, proper cider and good
range of gins, relaxed friendly atmosphere
with candlelit tables, beams and log fires;
quiz last Weds of month; children and dogs
(in bar) welcome, garden picnic-sets,
closed Mon. *(Barbara Brown)*

SANDY PARK SX7189

Sandy Park Inn (01647) 433267

*A382 Whiddon Down–
Moretonhampstead; TQ13 8JW* Little
thatched and beamed inn being
refurbished under new management
as we went to press – news please.

SHALDON SX9372

Clifford Arms (01626) 872311

Fore Street; TQ14 0DE Attractive 18th-c
open-plan pub on two levels, clean and
bright, with good range of home-made
blackboard food including Fri seafood, up
to four mainly local ales and eight wines
by the glass, low beams and stone walls,
wood or carpeted floors, log fire; live jazz
Mon and first Sun lunchtime of the month;
children over 5 welcome, front terrace and
decked area at back with palms, pleasant
seaside village. *(Serena and Adam Furber)*

SHALDON SX9472

London Inn (01626) 872453

Bank Street/The Green; TQ14 0DN
Popular bustling pub opposite bowling
green in pretty waterside village, ample
helpings of good reasonably priced food
using local suppliers, Otter and St Austell
ales, friendly efficient service; background
music, pool; children and dogs (in bar)
welcome, open all day. *(Holly and Tim Waite)*

SHALDON   SX9371
Ness House   (01626) 873480
Ness Drive; TQ14 0HP Georgian hotel on
Ness headland overlooking Teign estuary and
worth knowing for its position; comfortable
nautical-theme bar with mixed furniture
on bare boards, log fire, Badger ales and
decent wines by the glass, popular food in
beamed restaurant or small conservatory,
afternoon teas; free wi-fi; children welcome,
no dogs, disabled facilities, terrace with
lovely views, picnic-sets in back garden,
nine bedrooms, open all day. *(Adam Jones)*

SHEBBEAR   SS4309
Devils Stone Inn   (01409) 281210
*Off A3072 or A388 NE of Holsworthy;
EX21 5RU* Neatly kept 17th-c beamed
village pub reputed to be one of England's
most haunted; seats in front of open
woodburner, long L-shaped pew and second
smaller one, flagstone floors, St Austell
Tribute and a couple of local guests, decent
wines and enjoyable food in dining room
across corridor, plain back games room with
pool and darts; children and dogs welcome
(they have a rottweiler), picnic-sets on front
terrace and in garden behind, next to actual
Devil's Stone (turned by villagers on 5 Nov to
keep the devil at bay), eight bedrooms (steep
stairs to some), open all day Sun, closed
Weds lunchtime. *(Penny and David Shepherd)*

SHEEPWASH   SS4806
★ Half Moon   (01409) 231376
*Off A3072 Holsworthy–Hatherleigh at
Highampton; EX21 5NE* Ancient inn
loved by anglers for its 12 miles of River
Torridge fishing (salmon, sea and brown
trout), small tackle shop and rod room with
drying facilities; simply furnished main
bar, lots of beams, log fire in big fireplace,
well kept St Austell, Sharps and a local
guest, several wines by the glass, tasty
food, friendly service, separate extended
dining room; bar billiards; children and
dogs welcome, 13 bedrooms (four in
converted stables), generous breakfast,
tiny Dartmoor village off the beaten
track; open all day. *(George Sanderson)*

SIDFORD   SY1389
★ Blue Ball   (01395) 514062
A3052 just N of Sidmouth; EX10 9QL
Handsome thatched pub in same friendly
family for over 100 years; central bar with
three main areas each with log fire, pale
beams, nice mix of wooden dining chairs
around circular tables on patterned carpet,
prints, horsebrasses and plenty of bric-a-
brac, well kept Bass, Otter, St Austell and
Sharps, popular bar food, pleasant attentive
service, chatty public bar, board games,
darts and skittle alley; background music
and games machine; children and dogs
welcome, flower-filled garden, terrace and
smokers' gazebo, coastal walks close by,

bedrooms, open all day from 8am for good
breakfasts. *(Roger and Donna Huggins)*

SIDFORD   SY1390
Rising Sun   (01395) 516616
School Street; EX10 9PF Friendly
traditional local under new management;
well kept ales including Branscombe Vale
and Otter, well priced home-made pubby
food, mix of tables and chairs on wood floors,
old local photographs on white walls, open
fires, restaurant; children and dogs welcome,
steep garden behind, parking at nearby Spar
(free after 6pm). *(Roger and Donna Huggins)*

SIDMOUTH   ST1287
Anchor   (01395) 514129
Old Fore Street; EX10 8LP Welcoming
family-run pub popular for its fresh fish
and other good value food, well kept
Caledonian ales including one named
for them, decent choice of wines, good
friendly service, large carpeted L-shaped
room with nautical pictures and aquarium,
steps down to restaurant; darts; tables
out in front, more in back beer garden
with stage for live acts, open (and food)
all day. *(Roger and Donna Huggins)*

SIDMOUTH   SY1090
Bowd   (01395) 513328
Junction B3176/A3052; EX10 0ND
Large thatched and beamed dining pub with
enjoyable sensibly priced food (all day Sun)
including daily carvery, a couple of Otter
ales and Sharps Doom Bar, friendly helpful
staff, flagstone interior with standing
timbers and alcoves; children welcome,
plenty of seats in big garden, play area,
open all day. *(Roger and Donna Huggins)*

SIDMOUTH   SY1287
Dukes   (01395) 513320
Esplanade; EX10 8AR More brasserie
than pub, but long bar on left serves
Branscombe Vale and a couple of guests,
good food all day specialising in local fish
(best to book in the evening), friendly
efficient young staff, linked areas including
conservatory and flagstoned eating area
(once a chapel), smart contemporary
décor; big-screen TV, daily papers; children
welcome, disabled facilities, prom-view
terrace tables, bedrooms in adjoining
Elizabeth Hotel, open all day (may be
summer queues). *(Roger and Donna Huggins)*

SIDMOUTH   SY1287
★ Swan   (01395) 512849
York Street; EX10 8BY Cheerful old-
fashioned town-centre local, well kept Youngs
ales and enjoyable good value blackboard
food from sandwiches up, friendly helpful
staff, lounge bar with interesting pictures
and memorabilia, darts and woodburner
in bigger light and airy public bar with
boarded walls and ceilings, daily newspapers,
separate carpeted dining area; no under-14s,

dogs welcome (treats for them), flower-filled garden with smokers' area, open all day. *(Roger and Donna Huggins)*

SILVERTON   SS9503
Lamb (01392) 860272
Fore Street; EX5 4HZ Flagstoned local run well by friendly landlord, Exe Valley, Otter and a local guest tapped from stillage casks, inexpensive home-made pubby food including specials, separate eating area; quiz nights and other events, skittle alley, free wi-fi; children and dogs welcome, handy for Killerton (NT), open all day weekends. *(Adam Jones)*

SLAPTON   SX8245
★Tower (01548) 580216
Church Road off Prospect Hill; TQ7 2PN Close to some fine beaches and backed by Slapton Ley nature reserve, this old inn has a low-beamed bar with settles, armchairs and scrubbed oak tables on flagstones or bare boards, log fires, three or four well kept west country ales including one badged for them from St Austell, local cider and decent wines by the glass, good interesting food cooked by french chef from lunchtime sandwiches up, friendly accommodating service; free wi-fi; children and dogs (in bar) welcome, wheelchair access to dining area (but not to lavatories), picnic-sets in pretty back garden overlooked by ivy-covered ruins of 14th-c chantry, comfortable bedrooms reached by external stone staircase, good breakfast, lane up to the pub is very narrow and parking can be tricky particularly at peak times, closed Sun evening and Mon in winter (not during school holidays) and first two weeks of Jan. *(Nigel Smith and Karen Stafford-Smith, Simon and Mandy King, B and F A Hannam)*

SOURTON   SX5390
★Highwayman (01837) 861243
A386, S of junction with A30; EX20 4HN Unique place – a quirky fantasy of dimly lit stonework and flagstone-floored burrows and alcoves, all sorts of things to look at, one room a make-believe sailing galleon; a couple of local ales, proper cider and maybe organic wines, lunchtime sandwiches, home-made pasties and platters (evening food mainly for residents), friendly chatty service; nostalgic background music, open mike nights, poetry evenings; children allowed in certain areas, outside fairy-tale pumpkin house and an old-lady-who-lived-in-a-shoe, period bedrooms with four-posters and half-testers. *(Donald Allsopp)*

SOUTH BRENT   SX6960
Oak (01364) 72133
Station Road; TQ10 9BE Friendly village pub with well priced traditional and modern food, three well kept local ales and good choice of wines by the glass, welcoming helpful service, comfortable open-plan bar with some leather sofas, restaurant;

quiz and music nights including Weds folk session, meat raffle Fri evening; children and dogs welcome, small courtyard, five bedrooms, little nearby parking, open all day weekends, closed Mon and Tues lunchtimes. *(David and Teresa Frost)*

SOUTH POOL   SX7740
★Millbrook (01548) 531581
Off A379 E of Kingsbridge; TQ7 2RW New licensees for this small 17th-c whitewashed village pub; three simply decorated linked beamed rooms, bar with big open fire, dining part with woodburner, mix of country furniture including scrubbed tables, spindle and wheelback chairs, settles and wall benches, very good food from french chef (can be pricey), three well kept ales such as South Hams and decent choice of other drinks, friendly helpful service; children and dogs welcome, tables on narrow terrace by stream, cosy modern apartment upstairs, open all day. *(Richard Tilbrook, Roy Hoing, David Thornton)*

STICKLEPATH   SX6494
★Devonshire (01837) 840626
Off A30 at Whiddon Down or Okehampton; EX20 2NW Welcoming old-fashioned 16th-c thatched village local next to Finch Foundry museum (NT); low-beamed slate-floor bar with big log fire, longcase clock and easy-going old furnishings, key collection, sofa in small snug, well kept low-priced ales tapped from the cask, farm cider, good value sandwiches, soup and home-made pasties from the Aga, games room, lively folk night first Sun of month; £1 fine for using mobile phone; dogs welcome (pub has its own), wheelchair access from car park, good walks, bedrooms, open all day Fri, Sat, closed Sun evening. *(Chris and Angela Buckell)*

STOKE FLEMING   SX8648
Green Dragon (01803) 770238
Church Street; TQ6 0PX Popular and friendly village local with yachtsman landlord, well worn-in beamed and flagstoned interior, boat pictures and charts, snug with sofas, armchairs, grandfather clock and open fire, well kept ales such as Bass, Otter and Wadworths, Addlestone's and Aspall's ciders, good choice of wines by the glass and enjoyable local food including fresh fish and seasonal game, prompt service; children welcome, tables out on partly covered heated terrace, lovely garden with play area, handy for coast path. *(Richard Tilbrook)*

STOKE GABRIEL   SX8457
Church House (01803) 782384
Off A385 just W of junction with A3022; Church Walk; TQ9 6SD Popular early 14th-c pub; lounge bar with fine medieval beam-and-plank ceiling, black oak partition wall, window seats cut into thick butter-coloured walls, woodburner in huge fireplace, look out for the ancient

mummified cat, well kept Bass, Sharps Doom Bar and a guest, enjoyable good value food, also little locals' bar; background music, Sun quiz; well behaved children and dogs welcome, picnic-sets on small front terrace, old stocks (pub used to incorporate the village courthouse), limited parking, open all day. *(Caroline Prescott)*

STOKENHAM SX8042

Church House (01548) 580253

N of A379 towards Torcross; TQ7 2SZ
Extended old pub overlooking village green behind; three open-plan areas with low beams, mix of seating on flagstones and lots of knick-knacks, Otter ales and a guest, well liked food from good sandwiches up using local produce, dining conservatory; live music Tues; children and dogs (in bar) welcome, picnic-sets on lawn with play area, interesting church next door. *(Donald Allsopp)*

STOKENHAM SX8042

Tradesmans Arms (01548) 580996

Just off A379 Dartmouth–Kingsbridge; TQ7 2SZ Picturesque partly thatched 14th-c pub; traditional low-beamed cottagey interior with log fire, well kept west country beers and decent wine list (usually one from Devon), good locally sourced food from lunchtime sandwiches to blackboard specials (booking advised), restaurant; children and dogs welcome, seats over lane on raised area looking down on village green, nice bedrooms (they also have a self-catering apartment near the pub). *(Hazel Hyde)*

TEIGNMOUTH SX9372

Oldc Jolly Sailor (01626) 772864

Set back from Northumberland Place; TQ14 8DE Town's oldest pub (said to date from the 12th c), comfortable low-ceilinged interior with stripped-stone walls, various nooks and crannies, well kept Dartmoor Jail, Sharps Doom Bar and guests, tasty pub food (not Sun evening) including good sandwiches; live jazz Mon, sports TV, free wi-fi; children and dogs welcome, seats in front courtyard, more behind with estuary views, open all day. *(Brian Glozier)*

THORVERTON SS9202

Thorverton Arms (01392) 860205

Village signed off A396 Exeter–Tiverton; EX5 5NS Spacious former coaching inn with five adjoining areas with log-fire bar and restaurant, uncomplicated well cooked food at affordable prices (good fish and chips), Otter and a couple of other beers, friendly helpful staff; pool; children and dogs (in bar) welcome, wisteria-draped terrace and sunny garden, pleasant village, six comfortable bedrooms, good breakfast. *(Chris Hoyer Millar)*

TOPSHAM SX9688

★ Bridge Inn (01392) 873862

2.5 miles from M5 junction 30: Topsham signposted from exit roundabout; in Topsham follow signpost (A376) Exmouth, on the Elmgrove Road, into Bridge Hill; EX3 0QQ Very special old drinkers' pub (16th-c former maltings painted a distinctive pink), in landlady's family for five generations and with up to nine well kept ales tapped from the cask; quite unchanging and completely unspoilt with friendly staff and locals, character small rooms and snugs, traditional furniture including a nice high-backed settle, woodburner, the 'bar' is landlady's front parlour (as notice on the door politely reminds customers), simple food; live folk and blues, but no background music, mobile phones or credit cards; children and dogs welcome, picnic-sets overlooking weir. *(Holly and Tim Waite)*

TOPSHAM SX9688

Passage House (01392) 873653

Ferry Road, off main street; EX3 0JN Relaxed 18th-c pub with traditional black-beamed bar and slate-floored lower dining area, good food from sandwiches to local fish, well kept ales and decent wines, friendly service; quiz nights, free wi-fi; children and dogs welcome, peaceful terrace looking over moorings and river (lovely at sunset) to nature reserve beyond, open all day. *(Susan and Callum Slade)*

TORBRYAN SX8266

★ Old Church House (01803) 812372

Pub signed off A381; TQ12 5UR Character 13th-c former farmhouse with attractive bar (popular with locals), benches built into fine panelling, settle and other seats by big log fire, Hunters, Skinners, St Austell and a guest, several wines by the glass and around 35 malt whiskies, good variety of well liked food, cheerful helpful staff, discreetly lit lounges, one with a splendid deep Tudor inglenook; background and occasional live music; free wi-fi; children and dogs welcome, comfortable bedrooms (woodburner in one), good breakfast; closed Mon lunchtime, otherwise open all day. *(Matt and Hayley Jacob)*

TORCROSS SX8242

Start Bay (01548) 580553

A379 S of Dartmouth; TQ7 2TQ More fish and chip restaurant than pub but does sell Bass, Otter, local wine and cider; very much set out for eating and exceptionally busy at peak times with staff coping well, food is enjoyable and sensibly priced; wheelback chairs around dark tables, country pictures, some photographs of

---

storms buffeting the building, winter coal fire, small drinking area by counter, large family room; no dogs during food times, seats outside (highly prized) looking over pebble beach and wildlife lagoon, open all day. *(Penny and David Shepherd)*

TORQUAY SX9265

★**Cary Arms** (01803) 327110
Beach Road: off B3199 Babbacombe Road, via Babbacombe Downs Road; turn steeply down near Babbacombe Theatre; TQ1 3LX Charming higgledy-piggledy hotel reached down a tortuously steep lane; small, glass-enclosed entrance room with large ship lanterns and cleats, beamed grotto-effect bar overlooking the sea, rough pink granite walls, alcoves, hobbit-style leather chairs around carved wooden tables, slate or bare-board floors, woodburner, Bays, Hanlons and Otter, two local ciders and nine good wines by the glass, enjoyable if not particularly cheap food; free wi-fi; children and dogs (in bar) welcome, plenty of outside seating on various terraces, outside bar, barbecue and pizza oven, steps down to quay with six mooring spaces, boutique-style bedrooms, self-catering cottages (glorious views) and chic beach huts and shore suites, open all day. *(Roger and Donna Huggins, Dr and Mrs A K Clarke)*

TORQUAY SX9166

Crown & Sceptre (01803) 328290
Petitor Road, St Marychurch; TQ1 4QA Friendly two-bar local with eight well kept ales such as Butcombe, Dartmoor, Hanlons, Harveys and Otter, three proper ciders and basic good value lunchtime food (snacks any time), interesting naval memorabilia and chamber-pot collection; regular live music including jazz Tues, folk Fri; children and dogs welcome, sunny deck and garden, open all day Fri-Sun. *(Charles Welch)*

TORQUAY SX9163

Hole in the Wall (01803) 200755
Park Lane, opposite clock tower; TQ1 2AU Ancient two-bar local tucked away near harbour, enjoyable reasonably priced pubby food including good fresh fish, seven well kept ales such as Butcombe, Otter, St Austell and Sharps, real cider, good friendly service, smooth cobbled floors, low beams and alcoves, lots of nautical brassware, ship models and old local photographs, restaurant/function room; live music; children and dogs welcome, some seats in alley out at front, open all day and can get very busy at weekends. *(Tony Scott, Roger and Donna Huggins)*

TORRINGTON SS4919

Black Horse (01805) 622121
High Street; EX38 8HN Popular twin-gabled former coaching inn; beams hung with stirrups in smallish bar with solid furniture and woodburner, lounge with striking ancient oak partition wall, back restaurant, five well kept ales including Courage and St Austell, generous helpings of tasty home-made food served by friendly staff; background music, darts and shove-ha'penny; children and dogs welcome, disabled access, three bedrooms, open all day. *(Martyn Stringer)*

TOTNES SX8060

Albert (01803) 863214
Bridgetown; TQ9 5AD Unpretentious slate-hung pub near the river, small bar and two other rooms, low beams, flagstones, panelling, some old settles and lots of knick-knacks, friendly landlord brewing his own good Bridgetown ales, real cider and plenty of whiskies, honest reasonably priced pub food, friendly local atmosphere; quiz and music nights, darts, free wi-fi; dogs welcome, paved beer garden behind. *(Barbara Brown)*

TOTNES SX7960

Bay Horse (01803) 862088
Cistern Street; TQ9 5SP Welcoming traditional two-bar inn dating from the 15th c, four well kept local ales such as Dartmoor and New Lion, ciders such as Sandford Orchards, simple lunchtime food; background and regular live music including good Sun jazz; children and dogs welcome, nice garden behind, three bedrooms, good breakfast, open all day. *(Barbara Brown)*

TOTNES SX8059

★**Steam Packet** (01803) 863880
St Peters Quay, on W bank (ie not on Steam Packet Quay); TQ9 5EW Quayside inn with three distinct bar areas, light oak floor, some bare-stone and brick walls, dark half-panelling and delft shelving, squashy leather sofa in one part against wall of books, fireplace at either end, ales from Dartmoor, Salcombe and Sharps, proper cider and a dozen wines by the glass, popular fairly priced home-made food, friendly staff coping well at busy times, conservatory restaurant; background music, TV, free wi-fi; children and dogs welcome, seats on terrace overlooking River Dart, four bedrooms, open (and food) all day. *(Mike and Margaret Banks)*

TUCKENHAY SX8156

Maltsters Arms (01803) 732350
Ashprington Road, off A381 from Totnes; TQ9 7EQ Popular old pub (once owned by celebrity chef Keith Floyd) in lovely quiet spot by wooded Bow Creek, good food from bar snacks to fresh fish specials, well kept Bays and three west country guests, local ciders and great range of wines by the glass, friendly service, creek-view restaurant; background and some live music, free wi-fi; children and dogs welcome, waterside terrace with open-air bar, pontoon for visiting boats, six bedrooms (three with river views), open all day, food all day Fri-Sun during summer school holidays. *(Jack Trussler)*

UFFCULME ST0612
George (01884) 842556
Commercial Road; EX15 3EB Cleanly
modernised former 18th-c coaching inn, good
choice of well presented/priced food, three
well kept west country beers and decent
wines, friendly service, log fire; background
music, free wi-fi; children and dogs (in bar)
welcome, handy for M5 (junction 27), closed
Sun evening, Mon. *(Holly and Tim Waite)*

WEARE GIFFARD SS4722
Cyder Press (01237) 425517
Tavern Gardens; EX39 4QR Welcoming
village local with St Austell ales and
enjoyable fairly priced home-made food (not
Sun evening), black beams and timbers,
inglenook woodburner; Tues folk night,
morris dancing Mon; children (till 8.30pm)
and dogs welcome, seats outside, beautiful
countryside and handy for Tarka Trail, two
bedrooms, closed Mon and Tues lunchtimes,
otherwise open all day. *(Barbara Brown)*

WEMBURY SX5349
Odd Wheel (01752) 863052
Knighton Road; PL9 0JD Popular
modernised village pub with five well
kept west country ales and good fairly
traditional food from sandwiches/ciabattas
up, reasonable prices including good
value set lunch Mon-Fri, friendly helpful
service, back restaurant; pool, darts,
sports TV, free wi-fi; children and dogs
(in bar) welcome, seats out on decking,
fenced play area, open (and food) all day
weekends. *(Philip Crawford, Hugh Roberts)*

WEMBWORTHY SS6609
Lymington Arms (01837) 83572
Lama Cross; EX18 7SA Large early
19th-c beamed dining pub in pleasant
country setting, wide choice of enjoyable
food including some interesting specials,
character landlady and friendly staff,
well kept Sharps Doom Bar and a west
country guest, Winkleigh farm cider,
decent wines, comfortably plush seating
and red tablecloths in partly stripped-
stone bar, big back restaurant; children
welcome, picnic-sets outside, closed
Sun evening, Mon and Tues (and may
shut early if quiet). *(Jack Trussler)*

WESTON ST1400
★ Otter (01404) 42594
*Off A373, or A30 at W end of Honiton
bypass; EX14 3NZ* Big busy family pub
with heavy low beams, good choice of
enjoyable reasonably priced food (best to
book) including smaller appetites menu
and two-for-one deals, carvery Thurs and
Sun lunchtimes, cheerful helpful staff,
well kept Otter ales and a guest, carpeted
opened-up interior with good log fire;
background music, pool; dogs allowed in

one area, disabled access, picnic-sets on
big lawn leading to River Otter, open (and
food) all day. *(Bob and Margaret Holder)*

WHIMPLE SY0497
New Fountain (01404) 822350
*Off A30 Exeter–Honiton; Church Road;
EX5 2TA* Two-bar beamed village pub with
friendly local atmosphere, decent home-
made food (not Mon) using local ingredients,
well kept Teignworthy and a guest,
woodburner; children and well behaved
dogs welcome, some outside seating, local
heritage centre in car park (open Weds, Sat),
pub closes Mon lunchtime. *(Charles Welch)*

WIDECOMBE SX7176
Old Inn (01364) 621207
B3387 W of Bovey Tracey; TQ13 7TA
Busy dining pub (get there before about
12.30pm in summer to miss the coachloads),
spacious beamed interior including side
conservatory with large central woodburner,
enjoyable fairly standard food served by
friendly staff, well kept Badger, Dartmoor
and a guest; free wi-fi; children and dogs
welcome, nice garden with water features
and pleasant terrace, great walks from
this pretty moorland village, open (and
food) all day. *(Mike and Margaret Banks)*

WONSON SX6789
★ Northmore Arms (01647) 231428
*Between Throwleigh and Gidleigh;
EX20 2JA* Far from smart but a favourite
with those who take to its idiosyncratic
style (not all do); two simple old-fashioned
rooms, log fire and woodburner, low beams
and stripped stone, well kept ales such
as Dartmoor tapped from the cask, farm
cider and decent house wines, good honest
home-made food including popular Sun
lunch, darts and board games; free wi-fi;
children and dogs welcome, picnic-sets
outside, beautiful remote walking country,
closed Sun evening. *(Susan and Callum Slade)*

LUNDY SS1344
★ Marisco (01271) 870870
*Get there by ferry (Bideford and
Ilfracombe) or helicopter (Hartland
Point); EX39 2LY* One of England's
most isolated pubs – yet surprisingly busy
most nights, great setting, steep trudge up
from landing stage, galleried interior with
lifebelts and shipwreck salvage, open fire,
two St Austell ales named for the island
and its spring water on tap, Weston's cider
and reasonably priced house wines, good
basic food using Lundy produce, friendly
staff, books and games; no mobile phones;
children welcome, tables outside, souvenir
shop doubling as general store for the
island's few residents, open (and food) all
day from breakfast on. *(George Sanderson)*

Dorset

ASKERSWELL
SY5393 Map 2

Spyway £ 🛏

(01308) 485250 – www.spyway-inn.co.uk

Off A35 Bridport–Dorchester; DT2 9EP

Extremely popular family-run inn with a genuine welcome, unspoilt décor, real ales, well liked food and fine views; bedrooms

A favourite with our readers, this simple country local was once a smugglers' lookout. There's a charming landlord, cheerful customers and unspoilt little rooms cosily filled with cushioned wall and window seats and some tub chairs. Old photos of the pub and rustic scenes are displayed on the walls and jugs hang from the beams; the warm Rayburn is a bonus on chilly days. Otter Ale and Bitter on handpump, several wines by the glass and farm cider are served by friendly staff. The dining area has old oak beams and timber uprights, red-cushioned dining chairs around dark tables on patterned carpet, horse tack and horsebrasses on the walls, and a woodburning stove. Two smaller rooms lead off from here. There are marvellous views of the downs and coast from seats on the back terrace and in the garden, and a small children's play area. The comfortable bedrooms look over the grounds and breakfasts are excellent. The steep lane outside continues up Eggardon Hill, one of the highest points in the region.

🍴 Pleasing food includes sandwiches, duck spring rolls with barbecue sauce, pigeon and smoked bacon salad, butternut squash risotto with parmesan crisps, lambs liver, bacon and onions, battered haddock and chips, lamb shank with red wine gravy, chicken breast stuffed with haggis with whisky cream sauce, fish pie with smoked haddock, cod and salmon, slow-roasted pork belly with cider sauce, and puddings. *Benchmark main dish: steak and stilton pie £11.95. Two-course evening meal £16.00.*

Free house ~ Licensee Tim Wilkes ~ Real ale ~ Open 12-3, 6-11 ~ Bar food 12-3, 6-9 ~ Restaurant ~ Children welcome ~ Wi-fi ~ Bedrooms: £50/£80 *Recommended by Colin McLachlan, Peter J and Avril Hanson, P and J Shapley, Tracey and Stephen Groves, S G N Bennett, Pete and Sarah, John and Delia Franks, Rob Anderson*

BOURTON
ST7731 Map 2

White Lion

(01747) 840866 – www.whitelionbourton.co.uk

High Street, off old A303 E of Wincanton; SP8 5AT

Stone inn built in 1723, with beamed bar and dining room, pleasing food and ales and seats in the garden; bedrooms

After visiting nearby Stourhead (National Trust) make your way here for lunch. It's a handsome former coaching inn with convivial landlords, a traditionally furnished bar and a two-level dining room with nice old wooden chairs around a medley of tables. Throughout there are beams, bare boards, fine flagstones, stripped stone and half-panelling, bow window seats, church candles and a log fire in an inglenook fireplace. Otter Amber and a couple of guest beers such as Keystone Bedrock and King Alfred 871 on handpump and several wines by the glass; background music. The back terrace and raised lawn have picnic-sets. Bedrooms are comfortable and breakfasts good.

Well liked food includes sandwiches, potted hot smoked trout, filo prawns with sweet chilli dip, a curry of the day, burger with toppings, pickled cucumber and chips, wild mushroom tortellini with mushroom sauce and melted goats cheese, beer-battered cod and chips, local venison faggots with rosemary and redcurrant gravy, pork, mushroom and brandy stroganoff, and puddings. *Benchmark main dish: steak and kidney pie £13.50. Two-course evening meal £19.00.*

Free house ~ Licensee William Stuart ~ Real ale ~ Open 12-11 (10.30 Sun) ~ Bar food 12-2 (3 Sat), 6-9; 12-3, 7-9 Sun ~ Restaurant ~ Children welcome ~ Dogs welcome ~ Wi-fi ~ Live music Fri evening ~ Bedrooms: /£80 *Recommended by Miranda and Jeff Davidson, Edward Mirzoeff, David and Charlotte Green, M G Hart*

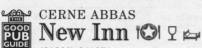

CERNE ABBAS   ST6601 Map 2
New Inn 🌟 ♀ ⇖

(01300) 341274 – www.thenewinncerneabbas.co.uk
Long Street; DT2 7JF

Carefully refurbished former coaching inn with character bar and two dining rooms, friendly licensees, local ales and inventive food; fine bedrooms

Our readers enjoy their visits to this lovely old inn very much – particularly if staying overnight. The bedrooms are smart and well equipped and located in either the charming 16th-c main building or the converted stable block. Not surprisingly, there's a lot of history here and many original features including mullioned windows, heavy oak beams and a pump and mounting block in the former coachyard. The bar has a solid oak counter, an attractive mix of old dining tables and chairs on slate or polished wooden floors, settles built into various nooks and crannies and a woodburner in the opened-up Yorkstone fireplace. Palmers Copper, Dorset Gold and IPA on handpump, ten wines by the glass, several malt whiskies and local cider. The dining room is furnished in a similar style; background music. There are seats on the terrace and picnic-sets beneath mature fruit trees or parasols in the back garden. You can walk from the charming stone-built village to the prehistoric Cerne Abbas Giant chalk carving and on to other villages.

Interesting, well presented food includes sandwiches, ham hock rillette with bubble and squeak and piccallili, cucumber and mint pannacotta with raita, dukkah and pakora, risotto verde with crispy egg, rabbit lasagne with home-made saffron pasta and aubergine, fish pie with pickled mussels, burger with toppings and fries, lamb rump with crispy kidney, spring roll, smoked kale and rocket pommes anna, chicken chasseur with dauphinoise potatoes, leeks and broth, and puddings such as treacle tart with marmalade ice-cream and rocky road brownie with nougat and hazelnuts. *Benchmark main dish: fresh fish dish of the day £18.50. Two-course evening meal £24.00.*

Palmers ~ Tenant Julian Dove ~ Real ale ~ Open 12-11 (10 Sun) ~ Bar food 12-2.30, 7-9; 12-3, 7-8.30 Sun ~ Restaurant ~ Children welcome ~ Dogs allowed in bar and bedrooms ~ Wi-fi ~ Occasional live music on Sun afternoons in courtyard ~ Bedrooms: £90/£105

Recommended by Alan Johnson, P and J Shapley, Clive and Fran Dutson, S G N Bennett, Mike Kavaney, Richard Cole, Matthew and Elisabeth Reeves, Frances and Hamish Porter

CHETNOLE ST6008 Map 2

Chetnole Inn 🛏

(01935) 872337 – www.thechetnoleinn.co.uk
Village signed off A37 S of Yeovil; DT9 6NU

Attractive country pub with beams and huge flagstones, real ales, popular food and seats in the back garden; bedrooms

With a friendly welcome, well kept ales and around ten wines by the glass, this is a nicely run beamed inn. The bar has a relaxed country kitchen feel with wheelback chairs and pine tables on huge flagstones and a woodburning stove. Butcombe Rare Breed, Ringwood Boondoggle and Thwaites Lancaster Bomber on handpump. Popular with locals, the snug has a leather sofa near another woodburner and stools against the counter; dogs are allowed in here. The airy dining room has more wheelback chairs around pale wooden tables on stripped floorboards and a small open fire. At the back, a delightful garden has picnic-sets and a view over fields. The comfortable bedrooms overlook the old church.

 Food is seasonal and includes duck cakes with hoisin and ginger with sweet chilli and mango relish, goats cheese pannacotta with onion and fig chutney, creamy smoked haddock and pea tagliatelle, a pie of the day, chicken breast with bacon, new potatoes and chicken broth, asparagus and goats cheese risotto, thyme and sage slow-roasted pork belly with root vegetable mash and tomato jus, and puddings such as vanilla crème brûlée and a tarte tatin of the day with chocolate soil and fruit gel. *Benchmark main dish: fillet steak cooked on a hot rock with herby butter and chips £23.00. Two-course evening meal £19.50.*

Free house ~ Licensees Simon and Maria Hudson ~ Real ale ~ Open 11-3, 6-11; 11-11 Sat; 12-4 Sun ~ Bar food 12-2, 6.30-9 ~ Restaurant ~ Children welcome ~ Dogs allowed in bar ~ Wi-fi ~ Bedrooms: /£105 *Recommended by Geoffrey Sutton, Peter Barrett, Clive and Fran Dutson, Alan and Linda Blackmore, Martin and Sue Neville, Holly and Tim Waite*

CHIDEOCK SY4191 Map 1

Anchor 🛏

(01297) 489215 – www.theanchorinnseatown.co.uk
Off A35 from Chideock; DT6 6JU

Stunning beach position for carefully renovated inn, lots of character, well kept ales and popular food and seats on front terrace; light, airy bedrooms

In warm weather if you wish to bag one of the seats and tables on the spacious front terrace here, you must arrive promptly as the location (just a few steps from the beach) is splendid. The inn also nearly straddles the South West Coast Path, so the surrounding walks are lovely. Inside, plenty of original character has been kept in the three smallish, light rooms: padded wall seating, nice old wooden chairs and stools around scrubbed tables on bare boards, a couple of woodburning stoves (one under a huge bressumer beam), tilley lamps, model ships and lots of historic photographs of the pub, the area and locals. From the wood-panelled bar they serve Palmers 200, Best, Copper and Dorset Gold on handpump, seven wines by the glass, 25 gins, over 35 rums and cocktails; background music. The attractive, airy bedrooms overlook the sea and are decorated with nautical touches using driftwood and ropework. You can park for free in front of the pub or across the road for £4 (refundable against a spend of £20 or more in the pub).

 Very good food includes filled rolls, hot smoked salmon mousse with shaved fennel, orange and marjoram, rare-breed pork and toasted almond terrine, peach and pepper pickle, char-roasted spiced cauliflower and spinach cheese, lamb burger with torched halloumi, mint harissa and chips, corn-fed chicken with rosemary mash and smoked portobello mushroom sauce, butter-roasted hake with wild garlic and pea purée risotto, and puddings such as coconut pannacotta with confit pineapple and lemon sorbet and rhubarb and custard tart with hibiscus syrup. *Benchmark main dish: vinegar and sea herb battered fish and chips £15.00. Two-course evening meal £20.50.*

Palmers ~ Tenant Paul Wiscombe ~ Real ale ~ Open 10am-11pm ~ Bar food 12-9 ~ Children welcome ~ Dogs allowed in bar ~ Wi-fi ~ Bedrooms: £155/£170 *Recommended by Richard and Penny Gibbs, Richard Tilbrook, A W Johns, Heather and Richard Jones, Nicola and Stuart Parsons, Kerry and Guy Trooper*

CHIDEOCK
George

SY4292 Map 1

(01297) 489419 – www.georgeinnchideock.co.uk
A35 Bridport–Lyme Regis; DT6 6JD

Comfortably traditional local with a thriving feel and well liked food and drink

If you're on the way to Cornwall and using the busy A35, then this thatched old inn is a good place for a break. The cosy, low-ceilinged, carpeted bar is nicely pubby, with Palmers 200, Copper, Dorset Gold, IPA and a guest beer on handpump, six wines by the glass and farm cider, warm log fires and brassware and pewter tankards hanging from dark beams. There are wooden pews and long built-in tongue-and-groove banquettes, cream walls hung with old tools and high shelves of bottles, plates and mugs; background music, TV, bar billiards, darts and board games. The garden room opens on to a pretty walled garden with a terrace and a much used wood-fired oven.

 As well as their wood-fired pizza evenings on Thursdays, food includes sandwiches, chorizo scotch egg with chipotle mayonnaise, macaroni cheese, cajun chicken burger topped with avocado and mozzarella, beetroot and halloumi caprese salad, grilled dover sole with parsley butter, rib-eye steak with beer-battered onion rings and chips, and puddings such as Baileys bread and butter pudding and sticky toffee pudding with caramel sauce. *Benchmark main dish: beer-battered fish and chips £11.95. Two-course evening meal £20.00.*

Palmers ~ Tenant Jamie Smith ~ Real ale ~ Open 12-3, 6-11 ~ Bar food 12-2.30, 6-9.30 ~ Restaurant ~ Children welcome except in snug bar ~ Dogs welcome ~ Wi-fi *Recommended by Andrew Stone, Edward May, Sabina and Gerald Grimshaw, Shona and Jimmy McDuff, Peter Brix*

CHURCH KNOWLE
New Inn ♀

SY9381 Map 2

(01929) 480357 – www.newinn-churchknowle.co.uk
Village signed off A351 N of Corfe Castle; BH20 5NQ

Cheerful pub with plenty of seating in various rooms, open fires, a thoughtful choice of drinks, good food and a friendly landlord

The linked character bar rooms in this partly thatched former farmhouse are full of interest: brass and copper measuring jugs, bed warmers, venerable board games and books, stone jars, china plates, a glass cabinet filled with household items from years ago, tilley lamps, a coastguard flag and an old diver's helmet. The main bar has an open fire in a stone fireplace, high-backed black leather dining chairs and cushioned wall settles around heavy rustic tables on red patterned carpet and quite a few stools against the counter. Butcombe Bitter, Ringwood Best and Sharps Doom Bar on handpump, six wines by the glass and farm cider; there's a wineshack from which you can choose your own wines, and also a wide choice of teas, coffees and local soft drinks. The similarly furnished dining room leads off here. There are picnic-sets on the lawn, and there's also a campsite. Corfe Castle ruins are nearby and there are fine walks too.

Popular seasonal food includes good fish dishes such as bouillabaisse, moules marinière, mixed seafood skewers, natural smoked haddock fillet with a poached egg and hollandaise sauce, and whole crab (24 hours notice), plus sandwiches, crispy duck salad with sesame, plum and honey dressing, steak in ale pie, chicken curry, lambs liver and bacon with red onion reduction, and puddings. *Benchmark main dish: roast of the day £11.95. Two-course evening meal £16.95.*

Punch ~ Tenants Maurice and Matthew Estop ~ Real ale ~ Open 10-3, 5-11; 12-3, 6-10 Sun ~ Bar food 12-2.15, 6-9; 12-3, 5-9.15 summer Sun ~ Restaurant ~ Children welcome ~ Wi-fi
Recommended by Dr J J H Gilkes, Alan and Angela Scouller, Jane and Kai Horsburgh, A W Johns, Mike Kavaney, Ian Wilson, Revd Carol Avery, Karl and Frieda Bujeya

CRANBORNE   SU0513   Map 2
Inn at Cranborne ⛹
(01725) 551249 – www.theinnatcranborne.co.uk
Wimborne Street (B3078 N of Wimborne); BH21 5PP

Neatly refurbished old inn with a friendly atmosphere, good choice of drinks, highly rated food and seats outside; comfortable bedrooms

The main bar area, divided into two by a partition, is a favourite place to sit: grey-planked and tartan-cushioned built-in wall seats and assorted chairs (farmhouse, wheelback, ladderback) on parquet flooring, flagstones or rugs, nightlights on each table and a woodburner in an inglenook fireplace. The rambling bars have heavy beams, open doorways, the odd standing timber and a chatty, relaxed atmosphere. Badger K&B Sussex Bitter and a guest from Badger on handpump and several wines by the glass served by friendly, helpful staff; background music, TV, darts and board games. The dining areas spread back from here, with similar furnishings and a little brick fireplace; there's also a second bar with white-painted or wooden furniture and another woodburning stove. Plenty of coaching prints on grey walls above a darker grey dado, and church candles. Outside, you'll find benches, seats and tables on neat gravel. The comfortable, well-equipped bedrooms are clean and bright and the breakfasts very good. Thomas Hardy visited the pub while writing *Tess of the D'Urbervilles*.

Using produce within a 30-mile radius, the interesting food includes hand-picked crab on toast with tarragon, confit duck terrine with madeira jelly, smoked haddock and salmon fishcake with a poached egg and chive butter sauce, burger with toppings and fries, chicken with trompette mushrooms, parisienne potatoes and sauce royale, braised shoulder of local lamb with creamy white bean sauce and rosemary jus, aged sirloin of beef with triple-cooked chips and peppercorn sauce, and puddings. *Benchmark main dish: beer-battered fish and chips £14.95. Two-course evening meal £22.00.*

Badger ~ Tenant Jane Gould ~ Real ale ~ Open 11-11 (11-10 Mon-Thurs in winter); 11-10 Sun ~ Bar food 12-2 (2.30 weekends), 6-9 (9.30 Fri, Sat) ~ Restaurant (evening only) ~ Children welcome ~ Dogs welcome ~ Wi-fi ~ Bedrooms: £85/£130 *Recommended by Ian Malone, Alison and Michael Harper, Sophie Ellison, Paddy and Sian O'Leary*

EVERSHOT

Acorn 🏅 ⚐ 🛏

(01935) 83228 – www.acorn-inn.co.uk

Off A37 S of Yeovil; DT2 0JW

ST5704   Map 2

Dorset Dining Pub of the Year

**400-year-old inn in a pretty village with character rooms, log fires
and knick-knacks and friendly licensees; bedrooms**

Immortalised as the Sow & Acorn in Thomas Hardy's *Tess of the
D'Urbervilles*, this friendly village inn is the heart of the community but
also offers a genuine welcome to visitors. The public bar has a log fire, lots of
beer mats on beams, big flagstones and high chairs against the counter where
they serve Dartmoor Legend, Dorset Jurassic and a guest beer on handpump,
39 wines by the glass and over 100 malt whiskies; dogs are looked after with
a bowl of water and biscuits behind the bar. A second bar has comfortable
beige leather wall banquettes and little stools around tables set with fresh
flowers, and a turkish rug on nice old quarry tiles. This leads to a bistro-
style dining room with ladderback chairs around oak tables; the slightly
more formal restaurant is similarly furnished. There's also a comfortable
lounge with armchairs, board games and shelves of books and a skittle
alley. Throughout are open fires, wood panelling, pretty knick-knacks, all
manner of copper and brass items, water jugs, wall prints and photographs;
background music, TV and darts. The walled garden has picnic-sets under
a fine beech tree. Each of the attractive bedrooms is individually decorated
and has a Thomas Hardy theme; breakfasts are first class and guests can use
the spa facilities at the nearby Summer Lodge hotel. Numerous nearby walks.

 Creative food using the best local produce includes sandwiches, smoked salmon
and mackerel terrine, open lasagne of confit rabbit with leeks, wild mushrooms
and rosemary jus, wholemeal spaghetti with puy lentil bolognese, rocket pesto and feta,
duck breast with sweet potato fondant, creamed confit leg and wild mushroom and port
jus, a trio of beef (fillet wrapped in smoked bacon, cottage pie and braised ox cheek)
with caramelised parsnip purée and red wine jus, and puddings such as pistachio cake
with lemon mousse, green tea mousse, green tea jelly and lemon coulis and sticky toffee
pudding with butterscotch sauce. *Benchmark main dish: beer-battered fish and chips
£14.00. Two-course evening meal £25.00.*

Free house ~ Licensee Natalie Read ~ Real ale ~ Open 11-11; 12-11 Sun ~ Bar food 12-2, 7-9
~ Restaurant ~ Children welcome ~ Dogs welcome ~ Wi-fi ~ Bedrooms: $89/$115
*Recommended by Tracey and Stephen Groves, Clive and Fran Dutson, Ian Malone, Nick Sharpe,
Charlie May*

FARNHAM

Museum 🏅 ⚐ 🛏

(01725) 516261 – www.museuminn.co.uk

Village signposted off A354 Blandford Forum–Salisbury; DT11 8DE

ST9515   Map 2

**Partly thatched smart inn with appealing rooms, brasserie-style food,
real ales and fine wines, and seats outside; comfortable bedrooms**

There's such a lot to see and do in the area surrounding this civilised
place that it makes sense to use the inn as a base. Four bedrooms are
in the main building, the remaining four in the converted stables; they also
have a large thatched self-catering cottage. There's a proper small bar with
beams, flagstones, a big inglenook fireplace and quite an assortment of dining
chairs around plain or painted wooden tables. Stools line the counter where

friendly staff serve Palmers Copper, Ringwood Best and Waylands Sixpenny 6D Best on handpump, ten wines by the glass, 20 malt whiskies, 30 gins and local spirits and ciders. Leading off here is a simply but attractively furnished dining room with cushioned window seats, a long dark leather button-back wall seat, similar chairs and tables on bare floorboards and quite a few photographs on patterned wallpaper. There's also a quiet lounge with armchairs around a low table in front of an open fire, books on shelves and board games. A terrace has cushioned seats and tables under parasols.

From a modern menu, the seasonal dishes include sandwiches, twice-baked local cheese soufflé, crab, dill and crème fraîche ravioli with tempura squid and sauce vierge, gnocchi with wild garlic, cauliflower purée and parmesan, pulled pork, chorizo and cider pie, haunch of venison with steamed venison pudding, sweet potato fondant and celeriac purée, tandoori-spiced hake fillet with cumin and chilli sticky rice and fennel bhaji, and puddings such as dark chocolate fondant with salted caramel ice-cream and coconut jelly with rum-soaked pineapple, meringue and mango purée. *Benchmark main dish: slow-roasted local pork belly with champ mash, roasted beetroot and jus £18.95. Two-course evening meal £20.00.*

Free house ~ Licensee Lee Hart ~ Real ale ~ Open 12-11 (10.30 Sun) ~ Bar food 12-2.30 (3 weekends), 6-9.30 ~ Restaurant open Fri and Sat evenings, Sun lunch ~ Children welcome ~ Dogs allowed in bar and bedrooms ~ Wi-fi ~ Bedrooms: /£110 *Recommended by Mungo Shipley, Dr Simon Innes, Peter Pilbeam, Joe and Belinda Smart*

KINGSTON
Scott Arms
SY9579 Map 2

(01929) 480270 – www.thescottarms.com
West Street (B3069); BH20 5LH

Wonderful views from a large garden, rambling character rooms, real ales and interesting food and an easy-going atmosphere; bedrooms

It's worth coming here for the views alone. From the big, attractive garden there's a magnificent outlook over Corfe Castle and the Purbeck Hills; there's also rustic-style seating and an outside summer kitchen with a jerk shack for caribbean-style food (the landlady is jamaican). Inside, the bar areas and more formal dining room are on several levels with stripped stone and brickwork, flagstones and bare boards, beams and high rafters, seats ranging from sofas and easy chairs through all manner of wooden chairs around tables of varying sizes, and open fires; stairs lead up from the bar to a small minstrels' gallery-like area with sofas facing one another across a table. Butcombe Bitter, Dorset Durdle Door and Jurassic and Otter Bitter on handpump, 11 wines by the glass and local cider; background music and board games. The four bedrooms are appealingly decorated, and the surrounding area has many good walks.

Well liked food includes sandwiches, prawn cocktail, country pâté with home-made pickles, local sausages with stockpot gravy and mash, moroccan vegetable stew, jerk chicken with sweet potatoes and coleslaw, beer-battered haddock and chips, pork tenderloin wrapped in serrano ham with cider cream sauce and dauphinoise potatoes, and puddings such as seasonal fruit crumble and warm chocolate brownie. *Benchmark main dish: clam chowder with mackerel, haddock and crab £16.00. Two-course evening meal £18.00.*

Greene King ~ Lease Ian, Simon and Cynthia Coppack ~ Real ale ~ Open 11-10 (11 Sat, 10.30 Sun) ~ Bar food 12-2.30, 6-8.30 ~ Children welcome ~ Dogs allowed in bar ~ Wi-fi ~ Bedrooms: £90/£105 *Recommended by Jenny and Brian Seller, Peter Meister, Peter Harrison, Tony Scott, Usha and Terry Patel*

MIDDLEMARSH

ST6607   Map 2

Hunters Moon 🛏

(01963) 210966 – www.hunters-moon.org.uk

A352 Sherborne–Dorchester; DT9 5QN

Plenty of bric-a-brac in several linked areas, reasonably priced food and quite a choice of drinks; comfortable bedrooms

Comfortable and neatly kept by the friendly hands-on licensees, this is a traditional 18th-c inn that our readers enjoy visiting on a regular basis. The beamed bar rooms are filled with a great variety of tables and chairs on red-patterned carpet, an array of ornaments from horsebrasses and horse tack to pretty little tea cups hanging from beams, and lighting in the form of converted oil lamps; the atmosphere is properly pubby. Booths are formed by some attractively cushioned settles, walls are of exposed brick, stone and some panelling and there are three log fires (one in a capacious inglenook); background music, children's books and toys and board games. Butcombe Bitter and changing guests from both Adnams and Theakstons on handpump, farm cider and 16 wines by the glass. A neat lawn has picnic-sets, including some circular ones.

 Popular food includes ciabatta sandwiches, honey and soy chicken skewers with garlic and herb dip, mussels in cider and bacon cream, local sausages with onion marmalade and gravy, mushroom, stilton and spinach wellington, a curry of the week, steak or lamb burgers with toppings, coleslaw and chips, chicken breast in a creamy garlic and white wine sauce, pork chops in cider and cream, and puddings such as dark chocolate marquise and poached pear with cinnamon eton mess. *Benchmark main dish: pie of the day £9.95. Two-course evening meal £19.00.*

Enterprise ~ Lease Dean and Emma Mortimer ~ Real ale ~ Open 10.30-2.30, 6 (5 Fri)-11; 10.30am-11pm Sat, Sun ~ Bar food 12-2, 6-9; all day weekends ~ Children welcome ~ Dogs welcome ~ Wi-fi ~ Bedrooms: £65/£75 *Recommended by Rob Anderson, Guy Vowles, Dr Simon Innes, Justine and Neil Bonnett*

NETTLECOMBE

SY5195   Map 2

Marquis of Lorne 🍺

(01308) 485236 – www.themarquisoflorne.co.uk

Off A3066 Bridport–Beaminster, via West Milton; DT6 3SY

Attractive country pub with enjoyable food and drink, friendly licensees and seats in big garden; bedrooms

Eggardon Hill, one of Dorset's most spectacular Iron Age hill forts with views over the coast and surrounding countryside, is within walking distance, so walkers often use this pub for lunch. The comfortable, bustling main bar has a log fire, mahogany panelling, old prints and photographs and neatly matching chairs and tables. Two dining areas lead off, the smaller of which has another log fire. The wooden-floored snug (liked by locals) has board games, table skittles and background music, and they keep Palmers Copper, Dorset Gold and IPA on handpump, with ten wines by the glass from a decent list. The big mature garden really comes into its own in warm weather with its pretty herbaceous borders, picnic-sets under apple trees and a rustic-style play area.

Good quality food includes sandwiches, chicken and duck liver pâté with spiced pears, tiger prawns in coriander and chilli tempura, home-baked mustard and brown sugar-baked ham with free-range eggs and piccalilli, aubergine filled with tomato, spinach and onion and glazed with goats cheese, venison and rosemary burger with toppings, house slaw and fries, lambs liver, bacon and mustard with battered onions and creamed mash, haddock and salmon fishcake on lemon cream topped with a poached egg and crispy spinach, and puddings. *Benchmark main dish: sea bass fillets with a creamy prawn velouté £16.00. Two-course evening meal £22.00.*

Palmers ~ Tenants Stephen and Tracey Brady ~ Real ale ~ Open 11.30-2.30, 6-10 ~ Bar food 12-2, 6-9 ~ Restaurant ~ Children welcome ~ Dogs allowed in bar ~ Wi-fi ~ Bedrooms: £85/£95 *Recommended by Belinda Stamp, Nick Sharpe, Jill and Hugh Bennett, Ian Wilson, Martine and Fabio Lockley*

PLUSH   ST7102 Map 2
Brace of Pheasants

(01300) 348357 – www.braceofpheasants.co.uk
Village signposted from B3143 N of Dorchester at Piddletrenthide; DT2 7RQ

16th-c thatched pub with friendly service, generously served food and pleasant garden; comfortable bedrooms

This is a lovely peaceful spot by Plush Brook and our readers enjoy staying in the attractively fitted out and comfortable bedrooms – each with a little outdoor terrace. The bustling, beamed bar has windsor chairs around good solid tables on patterned carpeting, a few standing timbers, a huge heavy-beamed inglenook at one end with cosy seating inside, and a good warming log fire at the other. Piddle Piddle, Ringwood Best and maybe a guest such as Flack Manor Double Drop are tapped from the cask and they offer a fine choice of wines with 18 by the glass and two proper farm ciders. A decent-sized garden includes a terrace and a lawn sloping up towards a rockery. The pub is well placed for walks – a pleasant bridleway behind the building leads to the left of the woods and over to Church Hill.

From a thoughtful menu, the enjoyable food includes a trio of smoked fish (gravadlax, smoked salmon and mackerel) with sweet beetroot relish, marinated thai beef spring rolls with crunchy coriander salad and sweet chilli sauce, warm marinated goats cheese salad with croutons, beetroot and walnuts, beer-battered fish of the day and chips, lambs liver and bacon with creamy mash and onion gravy, duck breast with caramelised orange and madeira sauce and potato rösti, and puddings such as flourless chocolate praline cake with chocolate sauce and warm malva pudding with a brandy glaze and stem ginger crème anglaise. *Benchmark main dish: duo of venison cutlets with root vegetable gratin and honey and lemon sauce £19.95. Two-course evening meal £23.00.*

Free house ~ Licensees Phil and Carol Bennett ~ Real ale ~ Open 12-3, 7-11 (10.30 Sun) ~ Bar food 12-2.30, 7-9 ~ Children welcome ~ Dogs allowed in bar ~ Wi-fi ~ Bedrooms: £109/£119 *Recommended by Mr and Mrs P R Thomas, Peter Harrison, Barry Collett, Ian Malone, Marianne and Peter Stevens, Richard Cole, Elisabeth and Bill Humphries, Scott and Charlotte Havers*

SHAFTESBURY   ST8622 Map 2
Grosvenor Arms 🛏

(01747) 850580 – www.thegrosvenorarms.co.uk
High Street; SP7 8JA

Relaxed hotel with a cheerful bar, several dining areas, enjoyable food and local ales, and seats in a courtyard; bedrooms

The civilised bar in this town-centre hotel is at the back of the building, with cheerful cushions on sofas and armchairs, cushioned settles, a woodburning stove, antlers on partly panelled walls, a coir and wood floor, and a few high chairs against the counter where they serve Otter Bitter and Palmers Dorset Gold on handpump and decent wines by the glass; service is friendly and helpful. A conservatory area (looking over a central courtyard with a fountain surrounded by metal and wood-slat chairs and tables) links this bar with several spreading dining rooms. There's a bistro-like area, a restaurant with brown leather dining chairs and tables on a wood floor, a small end room with bookcase wallpaper and another little dining room at the front. Bedrooms are comfortable and up to date.

Using seasonal produce from local farmers and growers, the popular food includes lunchtime sandwiches, duck, pork and pistachio terrine with pear salad, smoked pigs cheek with celeriac remoulade, spicy burger with paprika mayonnaise, toppings and chips, butternut and kale lasagne, chicken with coppa, honey-roast root vegetables and cider, wood-fired pizzas, hake and chorizo with roasted beetroot, spinach and capers, and puddings such as salted caramel and chocolate tart with honeycomb and cherry and rum bread and butter pudding with vanilla cream and butterscotch sauce. *Benchmark main dish: burger with toppings and chips £13.00. Two-course evening meal £21.50.*

Free house ~ Licensee Natalie Zvonek-Little ~ Real ale ~ Open 9am-11pm; 9am-10.30pm Sun ~ Bar food 9am-10pm ~ Restaurant ~ Children welcome ~ Dogs allowed in bar and bedrooms ~ Wi-fi ~ Bedrooms: /£90 *Recommended by Dan and Nicki Barton, Andy and Louise Ramwell, Sally and Lance Oldham*

SHERBORNE
Digby Tap ❦ £

ST6316   Map 2

(01935) 813148 – www.digbytap.co.uk
Cooks Lane; park in Digby Road and walk round corner; DT9 3NS

Regularly changing ales in simple alehouse, open all day with very inexpensive beer and food

There's always a wide mix of customers in this unpretentious, down-to-earth tavern – all keen to enjoy the fine ales and amazingly cheap food. The atmosphere, as ever, is lively, chatty and warmly welcoming and the straightforward flagstoned bar with its cosy corners is full of understated character. The small games room has a pool table and a quiz machine, and there's also a TV room; mobile phones are banned. The splendid selection of beers on handpump includes Black Sheep Bitter, Butcombe Heathcliff, Goffs Tournament and Otter Bitter. Also, several wines by the glass and a choice of malt whiskies. The glorious golden-stone Sherborne Abbey is just a stroll away.

Generous helpings of extraordinarily good value straightforward lunchtime food includes sandwiches and toasties, three-egg omelettes, sausages with free-range eggs, burgers and specials such as fish pie, sausage casserole and a mixed grill. *Benchmark main dish: ham, egg and chips £5.50.*

Free house ~ Licensees Oliver Wilson and Nick Whigham ~ Real ale ~ No credit cards ~ Open 11-11; 12-11 Sun ~ Bar food 12-2; not Sun ~ Children welcome until 6pm ~ Dogs allowed in bar ~ Wi-fi *Recommended by Tracey and Stephen Groves, Neil Allen, Patricia and Anton Larkham, Charlie Stevens, Lenny and Ruth Walters*

SHROTON
Cricketers

ST8512   Map 2

(01258) 860421 – www.thecricketersshroton.co.uk
Off A350 N of Blandford (village also called Iwerne Courtney); follow signs; DT11 8QD

Country pub with real ales, well liked food and pretty garden; nice views and walks nearby

This is a pleasant red-brick pub facing the village green. The bright, divided bar has a woodburning stove in a stone fireplace, cushioned high-backed windsor and ladderback chairs in one area and black leather ones in another, all sorts of tables, a settle with scatter cushions, and red and cream walls decorated with cricket bats and photos of cricket teams. There's also a cosy alcove and a spreading dining area towards the back. Butcombe Bitter, Otter Amber and Sharps Doom Bar on handpump (they may hold a beer festival on the early May Bank Holiday weekend) and several wines by the glass; background music. The back garden is secluded and pretty with seats on a terrace and lawn, and there are picnic-sets at the front. Walks up to the Iron Age ramparts on the summit reveal terrific views and the pub sits on the Wessex Ridgeway; walkers are requested to leave muddy boots outside and dogs are not allowed inside.

🍴 Good quality food includes lunchtime croque monsieur, twice-baked cheddar and stilton soufflé, japanese-style duck salad with sesame spinach, soy and lemon dressing and wasabi, leek and dolcelatte puff pastry slice with parmesan-fried courgettes and tomato relish, beer-battered cod and chips, lambs liver and bacon with mash and sage and onion gravy, roasted whole fish of the day, and puddings such as white chocolate and raspberry crème brûlée and sticky date, apricot and walnut pudding with clotted cream. *Benchmark main dish: pie of the day £11.00. Two-course evening meal £19.00.*

Heartstone Inns ~ Licensees Joe and Sally Grieves ~ Real ale ~ Open 12-3, 6-11; 12-10.30 Sun ~ Bar food 12-2.30, 6.30-9; no food Sun evening Sept-May ~ Children welcome ~ Wi-fi
Recommended by John Pritchard, Sophie Ellison, Nick Higgins, Julie Swift, Usha and Terry Patel

TRENT
Rose & Crown 🏵 🛏

ST5818 Map 2

(01935) 850776 – www.theroseandcrowntrent.co.uk
Opposite the church; DT9 4SL

Thatched pub with a friendly licensee, cosy rooms, open fires, a good choice of drinks and well thought-of food; bedrooms

'What a find' and 'a gem of a pub' are just two enthusiastic comments from readers on this well run, character place. The cosy little bar on the right has big, comfortable sofas and stools around a low table in front of an open fire, fresh flowers and candlelight. The bar opposite is furnished with nice old wooden tables and chairs on quarry tiles, and stools against the counter where they serve Wadworths 6X, Bishops Tipple, Horizon and IPA, and a guest beer such as St Austell Proper Job on handpump and 20 wines by the glass; board games. Two other interconnected rooms have similar wooden tables and chairs, settles and pews, a grandfather clock, pewter tankards and more fireplaces. Throughout are all sorts of pictures, including Stuart prints commemorating the fact that Charles II sought refuge in this village after the Battle of Worcester. The simply furnished back dining room leads to the garden with seats and tables and fine views (and sunsets); there are some picnic-sets at the front. The pretty bedrooms are in a converted byre just off the garden and breakfasts are first class. The church opposite is lovely.

🏵 Good, enjoyable food includes lunchtime sandwiches, ham hock terrine with a crispy free-range egg, pineapple and black pudding crumb, salt and pepper squid with cucumber, watercress, chilli and ginger dressing, grilled cauliflower with harissa dressing, rocket salad, black radish and dukkah crumbs, cumberland sausage with grain mustard mash and onion gravy, duck breast with puy lentils, red wine, bacon and pomegranate molasses, sea trout with scallop tortellini and watercress sauce, and puddings such as peanut butter and Baileys parfait with white chocolate and a strawberry doughnut and caramel and dark chocolate fondant with espresso ice-cream. *Benchmark main dish: best end of lamb with moroccan-spiced aubergines, freekeh, smoked almonds and pomegranate £19.50. Two-course evening meal £25.00.*

Wadworths ~ Tenant Nick Lamb ~ Real ale ~ Open 11-11 ~ Bar food 12-2.30, 6-9 ~ Children welcome ~ Dogs welcome ~ Wi-fi ~ Quiz last Sun of month ~ Bedrooms: £65/£85 *Recommended by Tracey and Stephen Groves, Liz and Martin Eldon, Guy Vowles, Michael Hill, Thomas Coke-Smyth, Cliff and Monica Swan*

 WEST BAY   SY4690   Map 1

West Bay ⭐ ⇌

(01308) 422157 – www.thewestbayhotel.co.uk
Station Road; DT6 4EW

Relaxed seaside inn with emphasis on seafood; bedrooms

You'll need to book a table in advance here – the position is special, looking out to sea and within strolling distance of the little harbour – and the fish and shellfish dishes are delicious. The fairly simple front part of the building, with bare boards, a coal-effect gas fire and a mix of sea and nostalgic prints, is separated by an island servery from the cosier carpeted dining area, which has more of a country kitchen feel; background music and board games. Palmers 200, Best, Copper, Dorset Gold and a seasonal guest are served on handpump alongside good house wines (including eight by the glass) and several malt whiskies. The pub's 100-year-old skittle alley does get used. There are tables in a small side garden and more in the large main garden, and bedrooms are quiet and comfortable. There are two unspoilt beaches on either side of the busy little harbour (much visited since the two *Broadchurch* TV series were filmed here).

🎯 The fresh fish and shellfish are the highlights and feature as daily specials, but they also offer sandwiches, whipped goats cheese, beetroot, charred fennel and pomegranate, beef carpaccio with parmesan, sage and hazelnut arancini with roast garlic and tomato sauce, home-cooked honey roast ham and eggs, beef stew with blue cheese dumplings, pressed pork belly with apple and cider cream reduction, calves liver and bacon with bubble and squeak and shallot and red wine jus, and puddings such as white chocolate and strawberry cheesecake and sticky toffee pudding. *Benchmark main dish: whole grilled fish of the day £17.00. Two-course evening meal £21.00.*

Palmers ~ Tenant Samuel Good ~ Real ale ~ Open 12-11 (midnight Sat, 10 Sun); 12-3, 6-11 Nov-Mar in winter ~ Bar food 12-2 (3 weekends), 6-9; 12-3, 6-8 Sun ~ Children welcome until 8pm ~ Dogs allowed in bar ~ Wi-fi ~ Bedrooms: £85/£115 *Recommended by A W Johns, Pete and Sarah, Julie and Andrew Blanchett, David Appleyard*

 WEST STOUR   ST7822   Map 2

Ship ⭐ ♀ 🍺 ⇌

(01747) 838640 – www.shipinn-dorset.com
A30 W of Shaftesbury; SP8 5RP

Civilised and pleasantly updated roadside dining inn offering a wide range of food and ales; bedrooms

The bedrooms here are attractive and comfortable with pastoral views, and breakfasts are hearty and particularly good. It's a smart and comfortable inn with a friendly landlord and highly enjoyable ales and food. The neatly kept rooms include a smallish but airy bar on the left with cream décor, a mix of chunky farmhouse furniture on dark boards and big sash windows that look beyond the road and car park to rolling pastures. The smaller flagstoned public bar has a good log fire and low ceilings. Fullers London

Pride, Plain Sheep Dip and Sharps Atlantic on handpump, 14 wines by the glass and four farm ciders. During their summer beer festival they showcase a dozen beers and ten ciders, all from the west country. On the right, two carpeted dining rooms with stripped pine dado, stone walls and shutters are similarly furnished in a pleasantly informal style, and have some interesting contemporary cow prints; TV, numerous board games and background music. The bedlington terriers are called Douglas and Toby. The garden behind the pub is lovely and there are rewarding surrounding walks.

 Highly enjoyable country cooking includes lunchtime sandwiches, lamb koftas with minted yoghurt and beetroot hummus, pâté of the day with gooseberry and coriander chutney, asparagus, sweet potato and feta filo pie with spinach puy lentils and red pepper and Pernod sauce, burger with toppings, beetroot slaw, onion rings and chips, caribbean-style goat curry, venison cottage pie, fillet of pork stuffed with black pudding with pear and calvados cream and smoked bacon bubble and squeak, and puddings such as mint choc chip cheesecake and bourbon and chocolate brownie with clotted cream ice-cream. *Benchmark main dish: cheese-topped posh fish pie £14.95. Two-course evening meal £22.00.*

Free house ~ Licensee Gavin Griggs ~ Real ale ~ Open 12-3, 6-11.30; 12-midnight Sat; 12-10.30 Sun ~ Bar food 12-2.30, 6-9; not Sun evening ~ Restaurant ~ Well behaved children in restaurant and lounge ~ Dogs allowed in bar ~ Wi-fi ~ Bedrooms: £60/£90 *Recommended by Anthony Wilkinson, Valerie Sayer, Tom and Ruth Rees, Allan Bentley, M G Hart, Robert Watt, Mike and Sarah Abbot, Martin and Joanne Sharp*

WEYMOUTH
Red Lion ◖ £

SY6878 Map 2

(01305) 786940 – www.theredlionweymouth.co.uk
Hope Square; DT4 8TR

Bustling place with sunny terrace, a smashing range of drinks, tasty food and lots to look at

The range of drinks here is splendid and served by friendly, efficient staff: Dorset Jurassic, Lifeboat Bitter (named for the pub, brewed by Otter with 10p per pint going towards the RNLI), Skinners Betty Stogs, St Austell Tribute and a changing guest on handpump, over 100 rums (they have a rum 'bible' to explain them) and 12 wines by the glass. Known as the lifeboatmen's pub, it features numerous pictures and artefacts relating to the lifeboat crews and their boats. The refurbished bare-boards interior, kept cosy with candles, has a cheerful, lively atmosphere, all manner of wooden chairs and tables, cushioned wall seats, some unusual maroon-cushioned high benches beside equally high tables, the odd armchair here and there, and plenty of bric-a-brac on stripped-brick walls. Some nice contemporary touches include the woven timber wall and loads of mirrors wittily overlapped; daily papers, board games and background music. There are plenty of seats outside that stay warmed by the sun well into the evening. The pub is owned by Tim Bird and Mary McLaughlin of Cheshire Cat Pubs & Bars.

Rewarding food includes lunchtime sandwiches, seafood chowder, moules marinière, sharing plates, a vegetarian pie topped with sweet potato mash, chicken or steak burgers with toppings, tomato and caramelised onion chutney and chips, smoked duck salad with blood orange, pickled walnuts, port and orange dressing and herb croutons, slow-braised pork belly with mustard mash and calvados sauce, smoked mackerel niçoise, and puddings such as chocolate brownie and date and sticky toffee pudding with rum and raisin ice-cream. *Benchmark main dish: steak in ale pie £12.50. Two-course evening meal £19.00.*

Free house ~ Licensee Brian McLaughlin ~ Real ale ~ Open 12-11 (10.30 Sun) ~ Bar food 12-9; may not serve food afternoons in winter ~ Children welcome until 7pm ~ Wi-fi ~ Live music outside Sun 2pm in summer *Recommended by John Harris, Alison and Michael Harper, JPC, Richard Cole, Jess and George Cowley, William and Sophia Renton, Glen and Patricia Fuller*

WIMBORNE MINSTER

SZ0199 Map 2

Green Man  £

(01202) 881021 – www.greenmanwimborne.com
Victoria Road, at junction with West Street (B3082/B3073); BH21 1EN

Cosy, warm-hearted town tavern with well liked food and Wadworths ales

New licensees have refurbished this cheerful town pub and reports from our readers are enthusiastic. Customers pop in and out all day and the small linked areas have some timbering, tartan banquettes, wheelback and farmhouse chairs around pubby tables on parquet flooring or carpet, some William Morris-style wallpaper, horsebrasses and a high shelf of stone bottles. The bar has a woodburning stove and high chairs line the counter where friendly staff keep Wadworths 6X, IPA and Swordfish and a guest beer on handpump and a farm cider. Darts, a silenced games machine and juke box; the Barn houses a pool table. In summer, the award-winning flowering tubs, hanging baskets and window boxes are quite amazing – there are more on the heated back terrace.

 Quality home-made food (lunchtime only) includes popular breakfasts, baguettes and sandwiches, baked potatoes, lasagne, ham and free-range eggs, burgers with toppings and chips, and beer-battered fish and chips. *Benchmark main dish: Sunday roast £7.95.*

Wadworths ~ Tenants Katherine Twinn and Scott Valenti ~ Real ale ~ Open 10-11; 11-11 Mon; 10-midnight Fri, Sat ~ Bar food 10-4; 10-midday Sun breakfast ~ Restaurant ~ Children welcome until 7pm ~ Dogs allowed in bar ~ Live music Fri, Sat evenings, occasional Sun 4-6pm *Recommended by Steve Whalley, Patricia Hawkins, Dr and Mrs A K Clarke, Andrew Wall, Lee and Jill Stafford*

WORTH MATRAVERS

SY9777 Map 2

Square & Compass ★

(01929) 439229 – www.squareandcompasspub.co.uk
At fork of both roads signposted to village from B3069; BH19 3LF

Unchanging country tavern with masses of character, in the same family for many years; lovely sea views and fine nearby walks

Little changes here, which is exactly how the customers of this much loved favourite want things to be. It's completely unspoilt and run by the charming Newman family who have owned the place for over a century. A couple of simple rooms have straightforward furniture on flagstones and wooden benches around the walls, a woodburning stove, a stuffed albino badger and a loyal crowd of chatty locals. Butcombe Heathcliff, Hattie Brown Crowblack, HBA and Moonlight and Thornbridge Jaipur tapped from the cask, and home-produced and ten other farm ciders are passed through the two serving hatches to customers in the drinking corridor; also, 20 malt whiskies. From the local stone benches out in front there's a fantastic view over the village rooftops down to the sea. There may be free-roaming chickens and other birds clucking around and the small (free) museum exhibits local fossils and artefacts, mostly collected by the current landlord and his father. Wonderful walks in the vicinity lead to some exciting switchback sections of the coast path above St Aldhelm's Head and Chapman's Pool – you'll need to park in the public car park (£2 honesty box) 100 metres along the Corfe Castle road.

🍴 Bar food consists of home-made pasties and pies.

Free house ~ Licensees Charlie Newman and Kevin Hunt ~ Real ale ~ No credit cards ~ Open 12-11; 12-3, 6-11 Mon-Thurs in winter ~ Bar food all day ~ Children welcome ~ Dogs welcome ~ Live music Sat evening and Sun lunchtime *Recommended by Alan Johnson, Steve Whalley, Peter Meister, Anne Evans, Tony Scott, Robert Watt, Bob and Melissa Wyatt, Greta and Gavin Craddock*

Also Worth a Visit in Dorset

Besides the fully inspected pubs, you might like to try these pubs that have been recommended to us and described by readers. Do tell us what you think of them: feedback@goodguides.com

BISHOP'S CAUNDLE   ST6913
White Hart (01963) 23301
A3030 SE of Sherborne; DT9 5ND
Smallish 17th-c roadside pub with modernised carpeted interior, dark beams, panelling, stripped stone and log fire, good well presented food from varied fair-priced menu including daily specials, Sharps Doom Bar and local guests, friendly service, restaurant; skittle alley; children and dogs welcome, country views from garden, closed Sun evening, Mon. *(Charlie Stevens)*

BLANDFORD FORUM   ST8806
Crown (01258) 456626
West Street; DT11 7AJ Civilised brick-built Georgian hotel on edge of town, spacious well patronised bar/dining area including snug with leather armchairs and roaring fire, full range of Badger ales from nearby brewery, numerous wines by the glass, cocktails, teas and coffee, enjoyable food from sandwiches and small plates up, separate restaurant; children welcome, dogs in bar, tables on big terrace with formal garden beyond, 27 recently refurbished bedrooms, open (and food) all day. *(Mr and Mrs Richard Osborne)*

BOURNEMOUTH   SZ1092
Cricketers Arms (01202) 551589
Windham Road; BH1 4RN Well preserved Victorian pub near station, separate public and lounge bars, tiled fireplaces and lots of dark wood, etched windows and stained glass, Fullers London Pride and two quickly changing guests, food weekend lunchtimes only from limited menu; folk night second and fourth Mon of the month, free wi-fi; children and dogs welcome, picnic-sets out in front, open all day. *(Dr and Mrs A K Clarke)*

BOURNEMOUTH   SZ0891
Goat & Tricycle (01202) 314220
West Hill Road; BH2 5PF Interesting Edwardian local (two former pubs knocked together) with rambling split-level interior; Wadworths ales and guests from pillared bar's impressive rank of ten handpumps, real cider, reasonably priced pubby food, friendly staff; background music, Sun quiz, free wi-fi; no under-18s, dogs welcome, good disabled access, part-covered yard, open (and food) all day. *(Dr and Mrs A K Clarke)*

BRIDPORT   SY4692
George (01308) 423187
South Street; DT6 3NQ Relaxed and welcoming old town pub; good food from open kitchen cooked by landlord-chef, well kept Palmers and decent wines by the glass, attentive friendly service; children and dogs (in bar) welcome, disabled facilities, open all day (from 10am for brunch on Sat market day). *(Ian Jenkins)*

BRIDPORT   SY4692
Ropemakers (01308) 421255
West Street; DT6 3QP Long rambling town-centre pub with lots of pictures and memorabilia, well kept Palmers ales and enjoyable home-made food from sandwiches up, good friendly service; regular weekend live music, Tues quiz, free wi-fi; children and dogs welcome, tables in back courtyard, open all day except Sun evening. *(Peter Brix)*

BRIDPORT   SY4692
★Stable (01308) 426876
At the back of the Bull Hotel; DT6 3LF Not a pub in any sense, but this lively cider/pizza bar is great fun and popular with customers of all ages; lofty barn-like room with rough planked walls and ceiling, big steel columns, two long rows of pale wooden tables flanked by wide benches, steps up to raised end area with cushioned red wall benches, over 80 ciders, St Austell Proper Job and six wines by the glass, good hand-made pizzas and other food such as pies, upstairs room (not always open); background music, free wi-fi; children

and dogs welcome, open (and food) all day weekends, from 5pm weekdays (all day during school holidays). *(Peter Brix)*

BRIDPORT   SY4692
Tiger (01308) 427543
Barrack Street, off South Street; DT6 3LY
Cheerful and attractive open-plan Victorian beamed pub with Sharps Doom Bar and five quickly changing guests, real ciders, no food except breakfast for residents; skittle alley, darts, sports TV, free wi-fi; dogs welcome, seats in heated courtyard, six bedrooms, open all day. *(Peter Brix)*

BUCKHORN WESTON   ST7524
★Stapleton Arms (01963) 370396
Church Hill; off A30 Shaftesbury–Sherborne via Kington Magna; SP8 5HS
Handsome Georgian inn with large civilised bar, sofas in front of fine stone fireplace, mix of other seating on flagstones or bare boards including farmhouse and chapel chairs around scrubbed tables, modern artwork on dark red walls, ales from Butcombe, Keystone and Plain, proper cider, 32 wines by the glass and 16 malt whiskies, good interesting food along with more traditional choices, separate elegantly furnished restaurant; some live music, free wi-fi; children and dogs (in bar) welcome, seats out at front and in charming back garden, good nearby walks, comfortable well equipped bedrooms, open all day weekends. *(Kate Moran)*

BURTON BRADSTOCK   SY4889
Anchor (01308) 897228
B3157 SE of Bridport; DT6 4QF Cheerful helpful staff in pricey but good seafood restaurant, other local food including nice steaks, village pub part too with blackboard choices from baguettes up, ales such as Dorset, St Austell and Sharps, decent wines by the glass and several malt whiskies; live music second Sun of month, games including table skittles; children and dogs (in bar) welcome, two bedrooms, open all day. *(Mr and Mrs N D Buckland)*

BURTON BRADSTOCK   SY4889
★Three Horseshoes (01308) 897259
Mill Street; DT6 4QZ Friendly thatched pub refurbished under present licensees; well kept Palmers ales, plenty of wines by the glass and good food cooked by dutch chef-landlord from bar snacks to specials, helpful accommodating service; children, dogs and muddy boots welcome, a few seats out in front, more in back garden with terrace, handy for nearby sandy beach, open all day in summer, all day weekends winter, no food Sun evening. *(A W Johns, Nick Buckland, Pete and Sarah)*

CHEDINGTON   ST4805
Winyards Gap (01935) 891244
A356 Dorchester–Crewkerne; DT8 3HY
Attractive dining pub surrounded by NT land

with spectacular view over Parrett Valley into Somerset; enjoyable food from sandwiches to daily specials, also Sun carvery and good value OAP weekday lunch, four well kept changing ales, local ciders, friendly helpful service, bar with woodburner, steps down to restaurant, skittle alley/dining room; children and dogs welcome, tables on front lawn under parasols, good walks, comfortable bedrooms, open all day weekends. *(David Appleyard)*

CHILD OKEFORD   ST8213
★Saxon (01258) 860310
Signed off A350 Blandford–Shaftesbury and A357 Blandford–Sherborne; Gold Hill; DT11 8HD Welcoming 17th-c village pub; snug bar with log fire and two dining rooms, Butcombe, Otter and guests, nice choice of wines and well liked reasonably priced home-made food including good Sun roast, efficient friendly service; children and dogs (in bar) welcome, attractive back garden, good walks on Neolithic Hambledon Hill, four comfortable bedrooms. *(Nick Higgins)*

CHRISTCHURCH   SZ1593
Rising Sun (01202) 486122
Purewell; BH23 1EJ Comfortably modernised old pub specialising in authentic thai food, Flack Manor and Sharps Doom Bar from L-shaped bar, good choice of wines by the glass, pleasant helpful young staff; terrace with palms and black rattan-style furniture under large umbrellas, open all day. *(Jake Stubbs)*

CORFE CASTLE   SY9681
Castle Inn (01929) 480208
East Street; BH20 5EE Welcoming little two-room pub mentioned in Hardy's *The Hand of Ethelberta*; popular generously served food including Fri fish night, good service, up to three real ales such as Dorset, Ringwood and Sharps, heavy black beams with fairy lights, exposed stone walls, flagstones and woodburner; background music; children welcome, no dogs inside, back terrace and big sunny garden with mature trees, steam train views, open all day. *(Sophie Ellison)*

CORFE CASTLE   SY9682
Greyhound (01929) 480205
A351; The Square; BH20 5EZ Bustling picturesque old pub in centre of this tourist village; three small low-ceilinged panelled rooms, steps and corridors, well kept ales such as Palmers, Ringwood and Sharps, local cider, good choice of interesting food from sandwiches and light dishes up, highish prices, traditional games including Purbeck longboard shove-ha'penny, family room; background and weekend live music; dogs welcome, garden with large decked area, great views of castle and countryside, pretty courtyard opening on to castle bridge, open all day. *(Tony Scott)*

DEWLISH SY7798
Oak (01258) 837352
Off A354 Dorchester–Blandford Forum; DT2 7ND Welcoming red-brick village pub, two or three well kept local ales and enjoyable good value food including specials and popular Sun lunch, friendly helpful service, woodburner and open fire in bar, small dining room; winter quiz; children welcome, good-sized garden behind, two bedrooms and self-catering cottage. *(Guy Vowles)*

DORCHESTER SY6990
Blue Raddle (01305) 267762
Church Street, near central short-stay car park; DT1 1JN Cheery pubby atmosphere in long carpeted and partly panelled bar, well kept ales such as Butcombe, Cerne Abbas, Fullers and St Austell, local ciders, good wines and coffee, enjoyable simple home-made lunchtime food (not Sun, Mon, Tues), evenings Thurs-Sat, coal-effect gas fires; background and live folk music (Weds fortnightly), darts and crib teams; no under-14s, dogs welcome, good disabled access apart from one step, closed Mon lunchtime. *(Barry Collett)*

EAST CHALDON SY7983
Sailors Return (01305) 854441
Village signposted from A352 Wareham–Dorchester; from village green, follow Dorchester, Weymouth signpost; note that the village is also known as Chaldon Herring; OS Sheet 194 map reference 790834; DT2 8DN Thatched village pub with five well kept ales such as Palmers, Otter and Ringwood, Thatcher's Gold cider and good food from short fairly pubby menu plus daily specials, Weds pie night, friendly attentive service, flagstone bar and various dining areas; Tues quiz in winter; children welcome, dogs in bar (not Fri evening), picnic-sets out at front and in side garden, useful for coast path, open all day weekends, closed Mon. *(S Holder)*

EAST MORDEN SY9194
★Cock & Bottle (01929) 459238
B3075 W of Poole; BH20 7DL Popular extended dining pub with wide choice of good if not especially cheap food (best to book), separate bar with open fire, well kept Badger ales and nice selection of wines by the glass, efficient cheerful service; children and dogs allowed in certain areas, outside seating and pleasant pastoral outlook, closed Sun evening. *(Mike Kavaney)*

EAST STOUR ST8123
Kings Arms (01747) 838325
A30, 2 miles E of village; The Common; SP8 5NB Extended dining pub with popular food from scottish landlord-chef including bargain lunch menu and all-day

Sun carvery (best to book), St Austell Tribute, Sharps Doom Bar and a guest, decent wines and good selection of malt whiskies, friendly efficient staff, open fire in bar, airy dining area with light wood furniture, scottish pictures and Burns quotes; gentle background music; children and dogs (in bar) welcome, good disabled access, picnic-sets in big garden, bluebell walks nearby, three bedrooms. *(Roy Hoing, R C Hastings)*

FIDDLEFORD ST8013
Fiddleford Inn (01258) 472886
A357 Sturminster Newton–Blandford Forum; DT10 2BX Beamed roadside pub with three linked areas; modern charcoal paintwork blending with traditional furnishings, old flagstones, carpets and some exposed stonework, two-way woodburner, well kept ales including one labelled for the pub, shortish choice of good traditional food, friendly young staff; children and dogs welcome, big fenced garden, four bedrooms, open (and food) all day, kitchen closes 6.30pm Sun. *(S J C Chappell)*

FONTMELL MAGNA ST8616
Fontmell (01747) 811441
A350 S of Shaftesbury; SP7 0PA Imposing dining pub with rooms, much emphasis on the enterprising modern cooking, but also some more straightforward cheaper dishes, good wine list, a house beer (Sibeth) from Keystone and two west country guests, small bar area with comfy sofas and easy chairs, restaurant overlooking fast-flowing stream that runs under the building; garden across road with two wood-fired pizza ovens, six comfortable well appointed bedrooms, open 9am-10pm (midnight Weds-Sat). *(Michael Doswell, Michael Hill)*

GILLINGHAM ST7926
Buffalo (01747) 823759
Off B3081 at Wyke 1 mile NW of Gillingham, pub 100 metres on left; SP8 4NJ Popular family-run Badger local, two linked bars and restaurant serving good well priced italian food (best to book), friendly attentive service; background and some live music; children welcome, back terrace by car park. *(Edward Mirzoeff)*

HINTON ST MARY ST7816
White Horse (01258) 472723
Just off B3092 a mile N of Sturminster; DT10 1NA Welcoming traditional little village pub dating from the early 17th c; good varied choice of food from changing menu cooked by south african landlord-chef (best to book), own-brew beers and decent house wines, unusual inglenook fireplace in cheerful bar, extended dining room; children, walkers and dogs welcome (pub dog is Pepper), picnic-sets in small well maintained garden, attractive setting, closed Sun evening, Mon. *(Frances and Hamish Porter)*

HURN
SZ1397
Avon Causeway (01202) 482714
*Village signed off A338, then follow
Avon, Sopley, Mutchams sign; BH23 6AS*
Comfortable and roomy hotel/dining pub
with enjoyable food from baguettes and pub
favourites up, well kept Wadworths ales,
helpful staff, interesting railway decorations
and pullman-coach restaurant (used for
functions) by former 1870s station platform;
children and dogs welcome, disabled
access, nice garden (some road noise) with
play area, 12 good value bedrooms, near
Bournemouth Airport (2 weeks' free parking
if you stay before or after you fly), open
all day, food all day Sun. *(Nick Higgins)*

IBBERTON
ST7807
Ibberton (01258) 817956
Village W of Blandford Forum; DT11 0EN
16th-c village pub (former Crown)
refurbished under welcoming new
owners; bar with flagstones and inglenook
woodburner, two dining areas (one carpeted,
the other where dogs allowed), three
local ales and Dorset Orchards' cider from
brick-faced servery, popular good value
food from traditional choices up, friendly
helpful staff; children welcome, picnic-
sets in front/side garden with stream,
beautiful spot under Bulbarrow Hill with
good walks, closed Mon, Tues and Sun
evening. *(Martin and Joanne Sharp)*

LANGTON MATRAVERS
SY9978
Kings Arms (01929) 422979
High Street; BH19 3HA Friendly old-
fashioned village local; ancient flagstoned
corridor to bar, simple rooms off, one with
a fine fireplace made from local marble,
well kept ales including Ringwood and
enjoyable good value pubby food, cheerful
helpful staff, splendid antique Purbeck
longboard shove-ha'penny; children and
dogs welcome, sunny picnic-sets outside,
good walks including to Dancing Ledge,
open all day. *(Usha and Terry Patel)*

LYME REGIS
SY3492
Cellar 59 (01297) 445086
Broad Street; DT7 3QF Recently opened
two-room bar down steps, flagstones and
stone walls, up to 14 real ales/craft kegs
chalked on blackboard including their
own Gyle 59 unfined beers, tasting trays
available, friendly knowledgeable staff,
tapas-style platters (vegetarians and vegans
catered for), shop above selling wide range
of bottled beers; outside seating area,
open all day. *(Roger and Donna Huggins)*

LYME REGIS
SY3391
Cobb Arms (01297) 443242
*Marine Parade, Monmouth Beach;
DT7 3JF* Spacious place with well kept
Palmers ales, decent wines and good choice
of reasonably priced freshly cooked food

(gluten-free options available), cream
teas, quick service, a couple of sofas, ship
pictures and marine fish tank, open fire; pool,
juke box, TVs; children and dogs welcome,
disabled access (one step up from road),
tables on small back terrace, well located
next to harbour, beach and coastal walk,
three bedrooms, open all day. *(Tony Scott)*

LYME REGIS
SY3391
Harbour Inn (01297) 442299
Marine Parade; DT7 3JF More
eating than pubby with thriving family
atmosphere, generally very well liked
food from lunchtime sandwiches to local
fish/seafood (not particularly cheap,
booking advised in season), Otter and
St Austell ales, good choice of wines by
the glass, tea and coffee, friendly if not
always speedy service, clean-cut modern
décor keeping some original flagstones
and stone walls (lively acoustic),
paintings for sale, sea views from front
windows; background and occasional live
music; dogs welcome, disabled access
from street, tables on verandah and
beachside terrace, open all day except
Sun evening in winter. *(Mike Kavaney)*

LYME REGIS
SY3492
Pilot Boat (01297) 443157
Bridge Street; DT7 3QA Popular bow-
fronted pub near waterfront; good fairly
priced food including blackboard specials,
Palmers ales and several wines by the glass,
helpful friendly service, back restaurant;
skittle alley; children and dogs welcome,
terrace tables, open (and food) all day; major
refurbishment (including bedrooms) planned
for autumn 2017 and pub may shut for
several months. *(Roger and Donna Huggins)*

LYME REGIS
SY3492
Volunteer (01297) 442214
*Top of Broad Street (A3052 towards
Exeter); DT7 3QE* Cosy old-fashioned
pub with long low-ceilinged bar, nice mix of
customers (can get crowded), a well kept
house beer from Branscombe Vale tapped
from the cask and west country guests,
enjoyable modestly priced food in dining
lounge (children allowed here), friendly
young staff, roaring fires; dogs welcome,
open all day. *(Alan and Linda Blackmoor)*

LYTCHETT MINSTER
SY9693
St Peters Finger (01202) 622275
Dorchester Road; BH16 6JE Sizeable
beamed roadhouse with popular food from
snacks and sharing boards up, smaller
helpings available for some dishes, Badger
ales and several wines by the glass, homely
mix of furnishings in different sections
giving cosy feel despite its size, end log
fire; free wi-fi; children and dogs welcome,
tables on big part-covered terrace, play
area, handy for nearby campsite, open
(and food) all day. *(Richard, S Holder)*

MANSTON
ST8116
Plough (01258) 472484
B3091 Shaftesbury–Sturminster Newton, just N; DT10 1HB Welcoming good-sized traditional country pub, four real ales including Palmers, Sharps and Timothy Taylors, Thatcher's cider and enjoyable fairly priced standard food, beams, richly decorated plasterwork, ceilings and bar front, red patterned carpets, dining conservatory; live music Fri; garden and adjacent caravan site, open (and food) all day. *(Charlie Stevens)*

MARNHULL
ST7818
Crown (01258) 820224
About 3 miles N of Sturminster Newton; Crown Road; DT10 1LN Part-thatched inn dating from the 16th c (the Pure Drop in Hardy's *Tess of the D'Urbervilles*); linked rooms with oak beams, huge flagstones or bare boards, log fire in big stone hearth in oldest part, more modern furnishings and carpet elsewhere, Badger ales, plenty of wines by the glass and enjoyable food including Sun carvery, good friendly service, restaurant; children welcome, peaceful enclosed garden, six bedrooms, open all day. *(Nick Higgins)*

MARTINSTOWN
SY6488
Brewers Arms (01305) 889361
Burnside (B3159); DT2 9LB Friendly family-run village pub (former 19th-c school) with attractively updated interior, good reasonably priced home-made food from lunchtime baguettes to specials, popular Tues curry night, well kept Palmers and Sharps, restaurant; Weds quiz and some live music; children and dogs welcome, picnic-sets out at front and in courtyard, historic sheepwash pool nearby (start of the annual duck race), good local walks, two bedrooms, closed Sun evening, Mon. *(Marianne and Peter Stevens)*

MELPLASH
SY4897
Half Moon (01308) 488321
A3066 Bridport–Beaminster; DT6 3UD 17th-c thatch and stone roadside pub comfortably revamped under newish owners; beams and log fire, well liked food from shortish varied menu cooked by landlord-chef, Palmers ales, hospitable attentive staff; free wi-fi; children and dogs welcome, a few picnic-sets out in front, more in back garden, good nearby walks, closed Sun evening, Mon. *(P and J Shapley)*

MILTON ABBAS
ST8001
Hambro Arms (01258) 880233
Signed off A354 SW of Blandford; DT11 0BP Pleasantly updated pub in beautiful late 18th-c landscaped thatched village; two beamed bars and restaurant, well kept Palmers, Otter and a couple of guests, good food from baguettes and sharing boards up, prompt friendly service; children welcome, dogs in bar, tables on front terrace, four bedrooms, open all day Fri-Sun, closed Mon and lunchtime Tues; changing hands as we went to press, so may be changes. *(Peter Brix)*

MOTCOMBE
ST8426
Coppleridge (01747) 851980
Signed from The Street, follow to Mere/Gillingham; SP7 9HW Welcoming country inn (former 18th-c farmhouse) with traditional bar and various dining rooms, good home-made food from ciabattas and pub favourites up including some imaginative choices, grill night Thurs, ales such as Butcombe and decent wines by the glass, friendly helpful staff; children welcome, dogs in bar and garden room, ten spacious courtyard bedrooms, barn function room (popular wedding venue), 15-acre grounds with play area and two tennis courts, lovely views over dorset countryside, open all day. *(Michael Doswell)*

NORDEN HEATH
SY94834
Halfway (01929) 480402
A351 Wareham–Corfe Castle; BH20 5DU Cosily laid-out partly thatched 16th-c pub; Badger beers, nice wines by the glass and enjoyable freshly cooked food including children's and vegetarian choices, good service, front rooms with flagstones, stripped stone and woodburners, snug little side area, pitched-ceiling back room; dogs welcome, picnic-sets on paved terrace and lawn, good nearby walks, open all day, food all day during school holidays. *(Alan and Angela Scouller)*

OSMINGTON MILLS
SY7381
Smugglers (01305) 833125
Off A353 NE of Weymouth; DT3 6HF Old partly thatched family-oriented inn, well extended, with cosy dimly lit timber-divided areas, woodburners, old local pictures, Badger ales, guests beers and several wines by the glass, food and service can be good; picnic sets on crazy paving by little stream, thatched summer bar, play area, lovely views from car park (parking charge refunded at bar), useful for coast path, four bedrooms, open (and food) all day. *(Barry Collett)*

PAMPHILL
ST9900
★Vine (01202) 882259
Off B3082 on NW edge of Wimborne: turn on to Cowgrove Hill at Cowgrove sign, then left up Vine Hill; BH21 4EE Simple old-fashioned place run by same family for three generations and part of Kingston Lacy Estate (NT); two tiny bars with coal-effect gas fire, handful of tables and seats on lino, local photographs and notices on painted panelling, narrow wooden stairs up to room with darts, a couple of real ales, local cider and foreign bottled beers, lunchtime bar snacks; quiet background music, no credit cards, outside lavatories; children (away from bar) and dogs welcome, verandah with grapevine, sheltered gravel

terrace and grassy area, Sept pumpkin and conker festival. *(Nick Higgins)*

PIDDLEHINTON SY7197

Thimble (01300) 348270

High Street (B3143); DT2 7TD Spacious thatched pub with log fires and deep glassed-over well in low-beamed core, enjoyable freshly made food from baguettes up including a gluten-free menu, good selection of well kept Palmers ales, friendly service; background and some live music, free wi-fi; children and dogs (in bar) welcome, disabled facilities, valley views from garden with stream, open all day Fri-Sun. *(David Appleyard)*

POOLE SZ0391

Bermuda Triangle (01202) 748087

Parr Street, Lower Parkstone (just off A35 at Ashley Cross); BH14 0JY Quirky 19th-c bare-boards local with four particularly well kept changing ales, two or three good continental lagers and many other beers from around the world, friendly staff, no food, dark panelling, snug old corners and lots of nautical and other bric-a-brac, additional side and back rooms; background music (can be loud); no children and a bit too steppy for disabled access, pavement picnic-sets, open all day Fri-Sun. *(Peter Brix)*

POOLE SZ0190

Poole Arms (01202) 673450

Town Quay; BH15 1HJ 17th-c waterfront pub looking over harbour to Brownsea Island, good fresh fish/seafood at fair prices, well kept ales such as Ringwood and St Austell, one comfortably old-fashioned room with boarded ceiling and nautical prints, good friendly service; outside gents'; no children, picnic-sets in front of the handsome green-tiled façade, almost next door to the Portsmouth Hoy, open all day. *(Gary)*

POOLE SZ0090

Portsmouth Hoy (01202) 673517

The Quay; BH15 1HJ Harbourside pub with views to Brownsea Island, old-world atmosphere with dark wood, beams and bare boards, good food including fresh fish, well kept Badger ales, friendly service; children and dogs welcome, outside tables shared with the Poole Arms, open all day. *(Peter Brix)*

POOLE SZ0090

Rope & Anchor (01202) 675677

Sarum Street; BH15 1JW Split-level Wadworths pub next to Poole Museum; good food including fresh fish, well kept beers and some nice wines by the glass, friendly accommodating staff; background music

---

(live Fri), daily papers, free wi-fi; children and dogs welcome, seats on back terrace, open (and food) all day. *(Will and George)*

PORTESHAM SY6085

Kings Arms (01305) 871342

Front Street; DT3 4ET Large modernised and extended pub in pretty village, ales such as Exmoor, Otter and St Austell, good seasonal food from light meals and sharing plates to specials and carve-your-own Sun roasts, attentive friendly service, coffee lounge with daily papers, open fires; regular live music, quiz last Thurs of month; children welcome, picnic-sets in sizeable garden with stream and summer pizza oven, three bedrooms, open all day, food all day too in summer. *(Marianne and Peter Stevens)*

PORTLAND SY6874

Boat that Rocks (01305) 823000

Portland Marina; DT5 1DX Modern bar/restaurant by the marina, popular range of food including burgers, pizzas and some mexican choices, good friendly service, four well kept ales such as Piddle and Shepherd Neame, upstairs cocktail bar; regular live music; children welcome, great boat views from balcony and terrace, open all day. *(Nick Higgins)*

PORTLAND SY6873

Cove House (01305) 820895

Follow Chiswell signposts – pub is at NW corner of Portland; DT5 1AW Low-beamed traditional 18th-c pub in superb position, effectively built into sea defences just above the end of Chesil Beach, great views from three-room bar's bay windows; Sharps Doom Bar and other well kept beers, enjoyable food including good crab sandwiches and blackboard fish specials, friendly service, steep steps down to gents'; background music, folk night Thurs; children and dogs welcome, tables out by seawall, open all day, no food Sun evening. *(Sophie Ellison)*

POWERSTOCK SY5196

Three Horseshoes (01308) 485328

Off A3066 Beaminster–Bridport via West Milton; DT6 3TF Tucked-away Edwardian pub under welcoming new owners; cheerful cosy bar with stripped panelling, windsor and mate's chairs around assorted tables on bare boards, Palmers ales and several wines by the glass, good freshly made food; children and dogs welcome, picnic-sets on back terrace with garden and country views, good surrounding walks, two comfortable bedrooms, closed Sun evening, Mon. *(Charlie Stevens)*

Half pints: by law, a pub should not charge more for half a pint than half the price of a full pint, unless it shows that half-pint price on its price list.

PUDDLETOWN
SY7594
Blue Vinny (01305) 848228
The Moor; DT2 8TE Large modernised village pub with beamed oak-floor bar and restaurant, good choice of highly regarded well presented food from lunchtime baguettes up (booking advised), well kept Sharps Doom Bar and a couple of guests, friendly helpful young staff; children welcome, dogs in one part, terrace overlooking garden with play area, open all day Fri-Sun, no food Sun evening.
(P and J Shapley, Marianne and Peter Stevens)

PUNCKNOWLE
SY5388
Crown (01308) 897711
Off B3157 Bridport–Abbotsbury; DT2 9BN 16th-c thatched inn under friendly new management (two brothers); enjoyable food from sandwiches and pub favourites up (smaller appetites catered for), Palmers ales and good choice of wines by the glass, beams and inglenook log fires, small shop selling local produce; board games; children and dogs (in bar) welcome, disabled facilities, valley views from peaceful pretty back garden, good walks, two bedrooms, open all day Sat, till 7pm Sun. *(Nicola and Stuart Parsons)*

SANDFORD ORCAS
ST6220
★ Mitre (01963) 220271
Off B3148 and B3145 N of Sherborne; DT9 4RU Thriving tucked-away country local with welcoming long-serving licensees, three well kept changing ales and proper ciders, wholesome home-made food (not Mon) from good soup and sandwiches up, flagstones, log fires and fresh flowers, small bar and larger pleasantly homely dining area; occasional open mike nights, games including shove-ha'penny and dominoes; children welcome and dogs (theirs are Finlay and Freya), pretty back garden with terrace, good local walks (on Macmillan Way and Monarch's Way), closed Mon lunchtime. *(David Appleyard)*

SHAPWICK
ST9301
Anchor (01258) 857269
Off A350 Blandford–Poole; West Street; DT11 9LB Welcoming red-brick Victorian pub owned by village consortium; popular freshly made food (booking advised) including blackboard specials, Sharps Doom Bar and a couple of guests, real cider, good service, scrubbed pine tables on wood floors, pastel walls and open fires; children and dogs welcome, tables out in front, more in attractive back garden with terrace, handy for Kingston Lacy (NT), closed Sun evening, Mon, otherwise open all day. *(Martin and Joanne Sharp)*

SPETISBURY
SY9102
Woodpecker (01258) 452658
A350 SE of Blandford; High Street;

DT11 9DJ Popular 1930s village pub with comfortable open-plan interior, enjoyable affordably priced home-made food (not Sun evening), four well kept changing ales, good range of ciders/perries and several wines by the glass, friendly helpful staff; background music, quiz first Tues of the month, bar billiards; children and dogs welcome, wheelchair access, tables in narrow roadside garden, open all day weekends, closed Mon. *(Charlie Stevens)*

STOBOROUGH
SY9286
Kings Arms (01929) 552705
B3075 S of Wareham; Corfe Road opposite petrol station; BH20 5AB Popular part-thatched 17th-c village pub, well kept Isle of Purbeck, Ringwood and up to three guests, good fairly priced food in bar and restaurant from snacks and pub favourites up including some interesting specials, cheerful efficient staff; children and dogs welcome, disabled access, flower-decked terrace and garden with play area, views over marshes to River Frome, open all day during summer school holidays (all day Fri-Sun at other times). *(Jenny and Brian Seller, Spencer Barratt)*

STOKE ABBOTT
ST4500
★ New Inn (01308) 868333
Off B3162 and B3163 2 miles W of Beaminster; DT8 3JW Welcoming 17th-c thatched pub with good home-cooked food including daily specials, well kept Palmers ales, woodburner in big inglenook, beams, brasses and copper, some handsome panelling, flagstoned dining room; children and dogs (in bar) welcome, wheelchair access, two attractive gardens, unspoilt quiet thatched village with good surrounding walks, street fair third Sat in July, closed Sun evening, all Mon and Tues lunchtime. *(Nick Higgins)*

STOURPAINE
ST8609
White Horse (01258) 453535
Shaston Road; A350 NW of Blandford; DT11 8TA Traditional country local extended from early 18th-c core (originally two cottages), popular food from landlord-chef including OAP deal, well kept Badger ales and sensible wine list, good friendly service, open-plan layout with scrubbed pine tables on bare boards, woodburners, games part with pool; post office and shop; well behaved children welcome, dogs in bar, seats out at front and on back deck, open (and food) all day. *(Peter Brix)*

STOURTON CAUNDLE
ST7115
Trooper (01963) 362405
Village signed off A30 E of Milborne Port; DT10 2JW Pretty little stone-built pub in lovely village setting (Enid Blyton's house opposite); friendly staff and atmosphere, well kept changing beers (their microbrewery is currently closed), real

ciders and good range of gins, food Weds and Fri (fish and chips) evenings only, tiny low-ceilinged bar, stripped-stone dining room, darts, dominoes and shove-ha'penny, skittle alley; background and some live music (folk and jazz), sports TV, outside gents'; children, walkers and dogs welcome, a few picnic-sets out in front, pleasant side garden with play area, camping, closed Mon and lunchtimes Tues-Thurs. *(Nicola and Stuart Parsons)*

STRATTON
SY6593
Saxon Arms (01305) 260020
Off A37 NW of Dorchester; The Square; DT2 9WG Traditional (though recently built) flint-and-thatch local, spacious open-plan interior with light oak tables and comfortable settles on flagstones or carpet, hop bines, log fire, well kept Butcombe, Timothy Taylors Landlord and two guests, good value wines, tasty generous food including deli boards and good choice of specials, large comfortable dining section on right; background music, traditional games; children and dogs welcome, terrace tables overlooking village green, open (and food) all day Fri-Sun. *(Marianne and Peter Stevens)*

STUDLAND
SZ0382
Bankes Arms (01929) 450225
Off B3351, Isle of Purbeck; Manor Road; BH19 3AU Creeper-clad stone pub in very popular spot above fine beach, outstanding country, sea and cliff views from huge garden over road with lots of seating; comfortably basic big bar with raised drinking area, beams, flagstones and good log fire, several real ales including own Isle of Purbeck (Aug beer festival), local cider, decent wines by the glass and generally well liked blackboard food from sandwiches up, darts and pool in side area; background music, machines, sports TV; over-8s and dogs welcome, just off coast path near Old Harry Rocks, can get very busy on summer weekends and parking complicated (NT car park), good-sized comfortable bedrooms, open (and food) all day. *(Jenny and Brian Seller, Brian Glozier, S Holder)*

STURMINSTER MARSHALL
SY9499
Golden Fox (01258) 857217
A350; BH21 4AQ Roadside country pub under newish management (was the Black Horse); popular good value food, a couple of real ales such as Sharps and Sixpenny, friendly helpful service, long comfortable beamed and panelled bar with log fire; games machines; children and dogs welcome, terrace seating, open all day Fri-Sun, closed Tues. *(David and Nicki Barton)*

STURMINSTER MARSHALL
SY9500
Red Lion (01258) 857319
Opposite church; off A350 Blandford–Poole; BH21 4BU Attractive village pub

opposite handsome church; bustling local atmosphere, wide variety of enjoyable food including good value set menu (Tues-Thurs, Sun evening), special diets catered for, Badger ales and nice wines, roomy U-shaped bar with log fire, good-sized dining room in former skittle alley; background music; children and dogs welcome, disabled access, back garden with wicker furniture and picnic-sets, open all day Sun, closed Mon. *(Nick Higgins)*

STURMINSTER NEWTON
ST7813
Bull (01258) 472435
A357, S of centre; DT10 2BS Cosy thatched and beamed 15th-c pub, Badger ales and enjoyable good value home-made food; children and dogs welcome, roadside picnic-sets, more in small back garden, closed Sun evening, Mon, otherwise open all day. *(Peter Brix)*

SWANAGE
SZ0278
Red Lion (01929) 423533
High Street; BH19 2LY Popular and unpretentious low-beamed local with great choice of ciders and up to six well kept ales such as Otter, Ringwood, Sharps and Timothy Taylors, good value food including curry night (Weds) and steak night (Fri), quick friendly service, brasses around log fire, restaurant; background and some live music, pool, darts and fruit machine; children welcome till 9pm, picnic-sets in garden with part-covered terrace, bedrooms in former back coach house, open all day. *(David Lamb)*

SYDLING ST NICHOLAS
SY6399
Greyhound (01300) 341303
Off A37 N of Dorchester; High Street; DT2 9PD Former coaching inn with beamed and flagstoned serving area, woodburner in brick fireplace, hops above counter, three well kept ales and a couple of ciders, carpeted bar with Portland stone fireplace, painted panelling and exposed stonework, popular food including good value set lunch, friendly welcoming staff, covered well in cosy dining room, flagstoned conservatory; children and dogs (in bar) welcome, picnic-sets in little front garden, six comfortable bedrooms, open all day Sun. *(Marianne and Peter Stevens)*

TARRANT MONKTON
ST9408
★ Langton Arms (01258) 830225
Village signposted from A354, then head for church; DT11 8RX Bustling thatched pub in picturesque spot next to 15th-c church; high-backed tartan dining chairs around wooden tables on carpeting, a cushioned window seat and a few high chairs against light oak counter, Flack Manor Double Drop and guests, real cider and decent choice of wines and whiskies, popular food using meat from own farm, two connecting beamed dining rooms with cushioned wooden chairs around

white-clothed tables, airy conservatory; background music, TV, board games; children and dogs (in bar) welcome, seats out at front and in back garden with play area, bedroom in brick buildings around courtyard and in neighbouring cottage, open all day, food all day weekends. *(Dr and Mrs A K Clarke, Mr and Mrs Richard Osborne)*

TOLPUDDLE   SY7994
Martyrs (01305) 848249
Former A35 W of Bere Regis; DT2 7ES
Village dining pub built in the 1920s, enjoyable home-made food including Mon curry, Fri fish and chips and Sun carvery, two or three Badger ales, friendly accommodating staff, opened-up bare-boards interior; background music; children welcome, good disabled access, small front terrace and garden behind, open (and food) all day. *(Alan and Linda Blackmoor)*

UPLODERS   SY5093
Crown (01308) 485356
Signed off A35 E of Bridport; DT6 4NU
Attractive stone-built village corner pub, log fires, dark low beams, flagstones and mix of old furniture including stripped pine, grandfather clock, good fairly traditional home-made food using local suppliers, three Palmers ales; background music; children and dogs (in bar) welcome, tables in pretty two-tier garden, closed Mon. *(Lenny and Ruth Walters)*

WAREHAM   SY9287
Kings Arms (01929) 552503
North Street (A351, N end of town); BH20 4AD Traditional thatched town local, five well kept changing ales, real cider and decent good value pubby food (till 6pm Sun), friendly staff, back serving counter and two bars off flagstoned central corridor, beams and inglenook log fire, carpeted dining room to the right, another at the back; some live music, free wi-fi; children and dogs welcome, steps up to garden behind with circular picnic-sets and smokers' shelter, open all day. *(Usha and Terry Patel)*

WAREHAM   SY9287
Old Granary (01929) 552010
The Quay; BH20 4LP Fine old brick building in good riverside position – can get very busy; emphasis on dining, but two small beamed rooms by main door for drinkers with well kept Badger ales and good wines by the glass, enjoyable fairly standard food at reasonable prices, friendly efficient young staff, airy dining room with leather high-backed chairs and pews around pale wood tables, brick walls and new oak standing timbers, two further rooms with big photographs of the pub, woodburners; quiet background music; children welcome, seats out overlooking the water and on covered roof terrace, boats for hire over bridge, limited nearby parking, open all day

from 9am (10am Sun), food served from midday on. *(Alan and Angela Scouller)*

WAREHAM   SY9287
Quay Inn (01929) 552735
The Quay; BH20 4LP Comfortable 18th-c inn in great spot by the water, enjoyable food including pubby favourites and cook-your-own meat on a hot stone, Tues steak night offer, well kept Isle of Purbeck, Ringwood and Timothy Taylors, friendly attentive service, two open fires (one gas); weekend live music; children and dogs welcome, terrace area and picnic-sets out on quay (boat trips), market day Sat, three bedrooms, nearby parking can be difficult, open all day. *(Robert Watt)*

WAREHAM FOREST   SY9089
★ **Silent Woman** (01929) 552909
Wareham–Bere Regis; Bere Road; BH20 7PA Long neatly kept dining pub divided by doorways and standing timbers, good choice of enjoyable food including daily specials, Badger ales kept well and plenty of wines by the glass, friendly helpful young staff, traditional furnishings, farm tools and stripped masonry; background music; no children inside, dogs welcome, wheelchair access, plenty of picnic-sets outside including a covered area, walks nearby, opening times vary during the year and it's a popular wedding venue, so best to check it's open. *(S Holder)*

WAYTOWN   SY4797
Hare & Hounds (01308) 488203
Between B3162 and A3066 N of Bridport; DT6 5LQ Attractive 18th-c country local up and down steps, friendly staff and regulars, well kept Palmers tapped from the cask, local cider, generous helpings of enjoyable good value food (not Sun evening) including popular Sun lunch, open fire, two small cottagey rooms and pretty dining room; children and dogs welcome, lovely Brit Valley views from sizeable well maintained garden, play area, occasional barbecues and live music. *(Nicola and Stuart Parsons)*

WEST BEXINGTON   SY5386
Manor Hotel (01308) 897660
Off B3157 SE of Bridport; Beach Road; DT2 9DF Relaxing quietly set hotel with long history and fine sea views; good choice of enjoyable food (highish prices) in beamed cellar bar, flagstoned restaurant or Victorian-style conservatory, well kept Otter, Thatcher's cider and several wines by the glass; children welcome, dogs on leads (not in restaurant), charming well kept garden, close to Chesil Beach, 13 bedrooms. *(Peter Brix)*

WEST KNIGHTON   SY7387
New Inn (01305) 852349
Off A352 E of Dorchester; DT2 8PE
Extended country pub with carpeted bar and restaurant, good home-made food using local

produce including daily specials and Sun carvery, a couple of real ales such as Palmers, friendly efficient staff; skittle alley, pool, free wi-fi; children welcome, dogs in bar, pleasant setting on edge of quiet village with farmland views, eight bedrooms, good breakfast, open all day Sun. (Mrs Sheila Davies)

WEST LULWORTH   SY8280
Castle Inn   (01929) 400311
B3070 SW of Wareham; BH20 5RN Pretty 16th-c thatched inn in lovely spot near Lulworth Cove, good walks and lots of summer visitors; beamed flagstoned bar with well kept changing local ales, over 40 ciders/perries and generous pubby food, maze of booth seating divided by ledges, cosy more modern-feeling lounge bar and restaurant; background music; children and dogs (particularly) welcome, front terrace, long attractive garden behind on several levels, 15 bedrooms, open (and food) all day. (Nick Higgins)

WEST LULWORTH   SY8280
Lulworth Cove   (01929) 400333
Main Road; BH20 5RQ Modernised inn with good range of enjoyable reasonably priced food from baguettes up, well kept Badger ales and several wines by the glass, friendly staff, seaside theme bar with bare boards and painted panelling; free wi-fi; children and dogs welcome, picnic-sets on sizeable terrace, short stroll down to cove, 12 bedrooms (some with sea-view balcony), open (and food) all day and can get very busy. (Jenny and Brian Seller)

WEYMOUTH   SY6778
Boot   07809 440772
High West Street; DT4 8JH Friendly unspoilt old local near the harbour; beams, bare boards, panelling, hooded stone-mullioned windows and coal fires, cosy gently sloping snug, ten well kept ales including Ringwood and other Marstons-related beers (tasting trays available), real cider and good selection of malt whiskies, no food apart from pork pies and pickled eggs (regulars bring own food on Sun to share); live music Tues, quiz Weds; free wi-fi; disabled access, pavement tables, open all day. (Sophie Ellison)

WEYMOUTH   SY6779
Handmade Pie & Ale House   (01305) 459342
Queen Street; DT4 7HZ Friendly and relaxed place opposite the station, wide range of good home-made pies plus other food, six well kept changing ales and plenty of ciders, more dining space in upstairs raftered room; children welcome, open (and food) all day. (Alan and Linda Blackmoor)

WEYMOUTH   SY6878
Nothe Tavern   (01305) 787300
Barrack Road; DT4 8TZ Comfortably refurbished 19th-c red-brick pub under friendly family management; enjoyable food from lunchtime sandwiches and bar snacks up including daily specials, also a vegan menu and weekend breakfasts, Brakspears, Ringwood and a dozen wines by the glass, restaurant with harbour and more distant sea views; children and dogs (in bar) welcome, more views from terrace, near Nothe Fort, open all day. (Tony Scott)

WIMBORNE MINSTER   SZ0199
Minster Arms   (01202) 840700
West Street; BH21 1JS Updated candlelit corner pub with log fires, leather sofas and an assortment of tables and chairs on wood floors, three real ales and extensive choice of wines by the glass, well liked food from varied menu, friendly service; live music Thurs; children and dogs welcome, courtyard area with heaters, comfortable modern bedrooms, open (and food) all day. (Adam Simmonds, Ian Malone)

WIMBORNE MINSTER   SU0100
★ Olive Branch   (01202) 884686
East Borough, just off Hanham Road (B3073, just E of its junction with B3078); BH21 1PF Handsome townhouse with spacious smartly revamped interior (some quirky touches), various opened-up dining areas, one with beams and view into kitchen, another more canteen-like with long tables and padded benches, popular food from range of small plates through burgers up, relaxed atmosphere and friendly young staff, Badger beers in comfortable panelled bar with woodburner, also a coffee bar and brick alcove with vaulted beer-bottle ceiling; rattan and other tables in mediterranean-style garden, open all day from 8am for breakfast. (Sophie Ellison)

WINTERBORNE STICKLAND   ST8304
Crown   (01258) 881042
North Street; DT11 0NJ Thatched village pub under welcoming new management; two rooms separated by servery, smaller one with inglenook woodburner, high-backed settle and dark tables and chairs on carpet, the other with low beams, more tables and chairs and darts, up to four real ales such as Ringwood, proper cider and good value traditional food; children and dogs welcome, pretty back terrace and steps up to lawned area with village view, open all day, till 7pm Sun. (Peter Brix)

Post Office address codings confusingly give the impression that some pubs are in Dorset, when they're really in Somerset (which is where we list them).

Essex

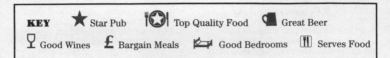

CHRISHALL   TL4439   Map 5

Red Cow 🍺

(01763) 838792 – www.theredcow.com

High Street; off B1039 Wendens Ambo–Great Chishill; SG8 8RN

Bustling, well run local with beamed rooms, four real ales, well liked food and seats in attractive garden

With candles in the windows at night, this thatched 16th-c pub looks very welcoming and cosy. The neat bar is bustling and atmospheric and both it and the dining room are heavily beamed and timbered, with a woodburning stove and an open fire, all sorts of wooden dining chairs around tables of every size on bare floorboards, and a comfortable sofa and armchairs. Friendly staff keep Adnams Southwold and Woodfordes Wherry plus two guest beers such as Timothy Taylors Landlord and Woodfordes Nelsons Revenge on handpump, eight wines by the glass, Aspall's cider and cocktails; they hold a music and beer festival in May. Terraces have picnic-sets and the garden is pretty. The pub is handy for the Icknield Way.

🍴 Food is good and includes paninis, goats cheese cheesecake with roasted beetroots and shallots, puff pastry filled with mussels in a garlic and herb cream sauce, spinach, herb and ricotta cannelloni, smoked haddock with spiced split lentils, spinach and herb casserole, steak burger with toppings, onion rings, coleslaw and chips, pheasant with roast vegetables and creamy mash, slow-cooked pork belly with cauliflower parcel and red wine sauce, and puddings such as rum pannacotta with mixed berries and a crumble of the day. *Benchmark main dish: pie of the day £12.75. Two-course evening meal £19.50.*

Free house ~ Licensees Toby and Alexis Didier Serre ~ Real ale ~ Open 12-3, 6 (5 Fri)-12; 12-midnight Sat; 12-10.30 Sun; closed Mon ~ Bar food 12-2, 6-9 (9.30 Fri); 12-9.30 Sat; 12-3.30 Sun ~ Restaurant ~ Children welcome ~ Dogs allowed in bar ~ Wi-fi ~ Live music monthly Fri *Recommended by Mrs Margo Finlay, Jörg Kasprowski, Greta and Gavin Craddock, Paul Farraday, Bob and Melissa Wyatt*

FEERING   TL8720   Map 5

Sun 🍺

(01376) 570442 – www.suninnfeering.co.uk

Just off A12 Kelvedon bypass; Feering Hill (B1024 just W of Feering proper); CO5 9NH

Striking 16th-c pub with six real ales, well liked food and pleasant garden

With enjoyable food and half a dozen ales, our readers are fond of this timbered and jettied pub. There's a good mix of customers in the busy slate-floored bar, an easy-going feel and two big woodburning stoves (one in the huge central inglenook fireplace, another by an antique winged settle on the left). Throughout, there are handsomely carved black beams and timbers galore, and attractive wild-flower murals in a frieze above the central timber divider. The beers on handpump include Shepherd Neame Bishops Finger, Hog Island, Spitfire and Whitstable Bay Pale, plus guest beers such as Navigation Britannia and St Austell Tribute, and they hold summer and winter beer festivals; also, 13 wines by the glass, eight malt whiskies and 15 gins served by cheerful staff. A brick-paved back courtyard has tables, heaters and a shelter, and in the garden beyond, tall trees shade green picnic-sets. The pub does have its own small car park through an archway in the middle of the adjoining terraced houses.

Food is well thought-of and includes sandwiches, mussel green thai curry, smoked chicken terrine with avocado purée and bacon crumb, wild boar and apple sausages with red onion mash and gravy, burgers with toppings and chips, chickpea, apricot and squash tagine with coriander yoghurt and spiced couscous, lamb kleftiko with roasted garlic quinoa, pomegranate and pink grapefruit salsa, cod loin with pea and crispy ham velouté and charred fennel, and puddings such as black forest truffle torte with cherry and kirsch ice-cream and lemongrass crème brûlée. *Benchmark main dish: beef, mushroom and stilton pie £12.50. Two-course evening meal £20.00.*

Shepherd Neame ~ Tenant Andy Howard ~ Real ale ~ Open 12-3, 5.30-11; 12-midnight Sat; 12-10.30 Sun ~ Bar food 12-2.30, 6-9; 12-3, 6-9.30 Fri, Sat; 12-8 Sun ~ Children welcome away from bar ~ Dogs welcome ~ Wi-fi *Recommended by Mrs Margo Finlay, Jörg Kasprowski, Ray White, David Fowler, Frank and Marcia Pelling*

FULLER STREET
Square & Compasses 🍽️ 🍺
TL7416 Map 5

(01245) 361477 – www.thesquareandcompasses.co.uk
Back road Great Leighs–Hatfield Peverel; CM3 2BB

Neatly kept country pub with two woodburning stoves, four ales and enjoyable food

There's a small extension at this 17th-c pub (originally two farm cottages) for walkers and dogs, as the place is in pretty countryside and handy for the Essex Way long-distance footpath. The L-shaped beamed bar has two woodburning stoves in inglenook fireplaces, and friendly staff serve Crouch Vale Essex Boys Best Bitter, Maldon Drop of Nelsons Blood and Mighty Oak Maldon Gold tapped from the cask, Bertie's dry cider and 18 wines by the glass; background jazz. The dining room features shelves of bottles and decanters against timbered walls, and an appealing variety of dining chairs around dark wooden tables set with linen napkins, on carpeting. Tables out in front on decking offer gentle country views.

From a seasonal menu, the rewarding food includes sandwiches, pheasant, partridge and pigeon bacon-wrapped terrine with beetroot relish, crab cake with lime, chilli and coriander with a spicy mayonnaise dip, fennel and carrot cheesecake with a crunchy parmesan base, local pork sausages with spring onion mash and onion gravy, home-cooked ham and free-range eggs, beer-battered fish of the day and chips, local lamb marinated in thyme and garlic on rosemary-roasted potatoes and red wine sauce, and puddings such as lemon tart with lemon crisps and syrup and spotted dick and custard. *Benchmark main dish: steak in ale pie £12.95. Two-course evening meal £21.00.*

Free house ~ Licensee Victor Roome ~ Real ale ~ Open 11.30-11; 12-midnight Sat; 12-11 Sun ~ Bar food 12-2 (2.30 Sat), 6.30-9.30; 12-5.45 Sun ~ Restaurant ~ Well behaved children welcome ~ Dogs allowed in bar *Recommended by Anne and Ben Smith, Alf Wright, Rob Anderson*

FYFIELD   TL5706 Map 5

Queens Head 🌟 ♀

(01277) 899231 – www.thequeensheadfyfield.co.uk

Corner of B184 and Queen Street; CM5 0RY

Essex Dining Pub of the Year

Friendly old pub with seats in riverside garden, a good choice of drinks and highly thought-of food

Once they've found this place, most customers return on a regular basis. On sunny days it's best to arrive early to bag a seat in the prettily planted back garden that runs down to the sleepy River Roding; the pub is usefully open all day at weekends. The compact, low-beamed, L-shaped bar has exposed timbers, pretty lamps on nice sturdy elm tables and comfortable seating from wall banquettes to attractive, unusual high-backed chairs, some in a snug little side booth. In summer, two facing fireplaces have church candles instead of a fire; background music. Adnams Broadside and Southwold and a guest such as Crouch Vale Brewers Gold on handpump and several good wines by the glass. The upstairs restaurant is more formal.

 Creative food includes king scallops with parsnip and vanilla purée, broad beans and crackling, pigs cheek ragoût on tagliatelle with parmesan, farfalle pasta with quail eggs, charred baby leeks, caper and shallot butter and crispy leeks, stone bass with confit chicken wings, wild mushrooms and artichoke purée, salmon fillet with salmon roe, truffle gnocchi, asparagus and wild garlic velouté, lamb rump with spring onion mash, radish, peas and salsa verde, and puddings such as hot chocolate tart with sugared pistachios, orange sorbet and raspberry caramel and blackberry soufflé with hazelnut crumble and pear ice-cream; they also offer a two- and three-course set menu. *Benchmark main dish: cod bourguignon £17.50. Two-course evening meal £21.00.*

Free house ~ Licensee Daniel Lamprecht ~ Real ale ~ Open 11-3.30, 6-11; 11-11 Sat; 12-10.30 Sun; closed Mon ~ Bar food 12-2.30 (4 Sat), 6.30-9.30; 12-6 Sun ~ Restaurant ~ Children welcome away from bar ~ Wi-fi *Recommended by Mark Hamill, Beth Aldridge, Mrs Margo Finlay, Jörg Kasprowski, Nicholas and Maddy Trainer, Rosie and John Moore*

GOLDHANGER   TL9008 Map 5

Chequers 🍺

(01621) 788203 – www.thechequersgoldhanger.co.uk

Church Street; off B1026 E of Heybridge; CM9 8AS

Cheerful and neatly kept pub with six real ales, traditional furnishings, friendly staff and tasty food

The half a dozen real ales and good food continue to draw happy customers here. There's a genuine welcome too, and the nice old corridor with its red and black floor tiles leads to six rambling rooms. These include a spacious lounge with dark beams, black panelling and a huge sash window overlooking the graveyard, a traditional dining room with bare boards and carpeting and a games room with bar billiards; woodburning stove, open fires, TV and background music. Adnams Ghost Ship, Crouch Vale Brewers Gold, St Austell Proper Job, Sharps Atlantic, Woodfordes Wherry and a guest such as Long Arm Shadow Wolf on handpump, and they hold spring and autumn beer festivals. Also, 16 wines by the glass, ten malt whiskies and several farm ciders. There are picnic-sets under umbrellas in the courtyard with its grapevine. Do look at the fine old church next door.

Popular food includes sandwiches, duck, orange and cognac pâté with cumberland sauce, garlic and rosemary-coated brie with balsamic onion chutney, macaroni cheese and spinach bake, lamb and mint pudding, cajun chicken with coleslaw and lattice fries, jamaican jerk sirloin steak with thai-battered prawns and chilli mayonnaise dip, sea bass with fennel and thyme, and puddings such as lemon meringue pie and chocolate pot. *Benchmark main dish: steak in stout pie £12.25. Two-course evening meal £19.00.*

Punch ~ Lease Philip Glover and Dominic Davies ~ Real ale ~ Open 11-11; 12-11 Sun ~ Bar food 12-3, 6.30-9; not Sun evening or Mon bank holiday evening ~ Restaurant ~ Children welcome except in tap room ~ Dogs allowed in bar ~ Wi-fi *Recommended by Ray White, George Atkinson, Chris MAC, John and Mary Warner, Rupert and Sandy Newton, Amy Ledbetter*

HATFIELD BROAD OAK
TL5416 Map 5
Dukes Head ♀
(01279) 718598 – www.thedukeshead.co.uk
B183 Hatfield Heath–Takeley; High Street; CM22 7HH

Relaxed, well run dining pub with enjoyable food in an attractive layout of nicely linked separate areas

Rambling around the central woodburner and side servery here are various cosy seating areas: good solid wooden dining chairs around a variety of chunky stripped tables with a comfortable group of armchairs and a sofa at one end, and a slightly more formal area at the back on the right. Cheerful prints on the wall and some magenta panels in the mostly cream décor make for a buoyant mood. Fullers London Pride, Greene King IPA, Sharps Doom Bar and Timothy Taylors Landlord on handpump and 30 wines by the glass from a good list, served by cheerful staff; background music and board games. In warm weather, head for the back garden with its sheltered terrace and chairs around teak tables under cocktail parasols; there are also picnic-sets at the front corner of the building which has some nice pargeting. Sam and Zac the pub dogs welcome other canines and there are always dog biscuits on offer.

 Reliably good food includes potted rabbit with fig jam, hot smoked salmon and crab fishcakes with crab bisque, macaroni cheese with wild mushrooms, crispy halloumi and fennel slaw, local sausages with shallot and thyme gravy and creamy mash, southern fried chicken with smoked bacon and sweetcorn fritter and double chicken sauce, smoked haddock fillet with bubble and squeak cake, a poached egg and hollandaise sauce, and puddings such as white and dark chocolate brownie with fudge sauce and apple, raisin and cinnamon crumble with custard. *Benchmark main dish: king prawn spaghetti £13.75. Two-course evening meal £20.00.*

Enterprise ~ Lease Liz Flodman ~ Real ale ~ Open 11.30-11 (4-11 Mon); 11.30-8 Sun; closed Mon lunchtime ~ Bar food 12-2.30, 6-9.30; 12-6 Sun ~ Restaurant ~ Children welcome ~ Dogs allowed in bar ~ Wi-fi *Recommended by Julie Braeburn, Jeremy Snaithe, Isobel Mackinlay, Shona and Jimmy McDuff, Paddy and Sian O'Leary*

HORNDON-ON-THE-HILL
TQ6783 Map 3
Bell ★☆◑ ♀ ◼ ⇔
(01375) 642463 – www.bell-inn.co.uk
M25 junction 30 into A13, then left after 7 miles on to B1007, village signposted from here; SS17 8LD

Lovely historic pub with fine food and a very good range of drinks; attractive bedrooms

This is a special place and has been run by the same friendly family for more than 75 years – our readers love it. The heavily beamed, panelled bar maintains a strongly pubby appearance with high-backed antique settles and benches, rugs on flagstones and highly polished oak floorboards, and an open log fire. Look out for the curious collection of ossified hot-cross buns hanging along a beam in the saloon bar – the first was put there in 1906 to mark the day (a Good Friday) that Jack Turnell became licensee. The timbered restaurant has numerous old copper pots and pans hanging from beams. An impressive range of drinks includes Crouch Vale Brewers Gold, Greene King IPA, Sharps Doom Bar and Shepherd Neame Hog Island and Spitfire Gold on handpump, and over 114 well chosen wines (16 by the glass). Two giant umbrellas cover the courtyard, which has very pretty hanging baskets in summer. Centuries ago, many important medieval dignitaries would have stayed here as it was the last inn before travellers heading south could ford the Thames at Highams Causeway. Today, it remains a lovely place to stay with individually styled, thoughtfully equipped bedrooms of all sizes.

 Impressive food includes sandwiches, warm pickled mackerel with crispy oyster mushrooms, shiitake mushroom broth and saffron-pickled lotus root, rabbit and tarragon ballotine wrapped in parma ham with sauté chorizo and rabbit mayonnaise, crispy caramelised onion and feta ravioli with aubergine and miso purée and red pepper jam, steak and kidney pudding, calves liver with maple syrup pancetta on wild garlic and shallots with jus, salmon fillet with rocket crust, potato gnocchi, sauté beetroot, beetroot mayonnaise and wild garlic oil, and puddings such as orange pannacotta with yoghurt sorbet, torched clementine, candied zest and orange crisp and raisin and croissant bread and butter pudding with custard. *Benchmark main dish: suckling pig with burnt apple purée and chicken velouté £19.95. Two-course evening meal £26.95.*

Free house ~ Licensee John Vereker ~ Real ale ~ Open 11-11; 12-10.30 Sun ~ Bar food 12-2, 6.30-9.45; 12-2.30, 7-9.45 Sun ~ Restaurant ~ Children welcome ~ Dogs allowed in bar and bedrooms ~ Wi-fi ~ Bedrooms: /£90 *Recommended by Mervyn and Susan English, Sarah Roberts, Valerie Sayer, Patricia and Gordon Thompson, Matt and Hayley Jacob, Charles Todd*

LITTLE WALDEN
TL5441   Map 5

Crown 🍺 £ 🛏

(01799) 522475 – www.thecrownlittlewalden.co.uk

B1052 N of Saffron Walden; CB10 1XA

Bustling old pub with a warming log fire, hearty food and bedrooms

The family involvement and commitment here contribute to making this 18th-c cottage just what a pub should be. It's very much the hub of the community and the low-ceilinged rooms have a cosy, chatty atmosphere and traditional furnishings, with book-room-red walls, floral curtains, bare boards, navy carpeting, cosy warm fires and an unusual walk-through fireplace. A higgledy-piggledy mix of chairs ranges from high-backed pews to little cushioned armchairs spaced around a good variety of closely arranged tables, mostly big, some stripped. The compact red-tiled room on the right has two small tables. Three changing beers, such as Adnams Broadside, Greene King Abbot and Woodfordes Wherry, and a guest ale are tapped straight from casks racked up behind the bar; TV, disabled access. Tables on the terrace have views over the tranquil surrounding countryside. Our readers love staying overnight here and the breakfasts are excellent.

🍴 Tasty, home-cooked food includes sandwiches and baguettes, creamy garlic mushrooms, devilled whitebait, four-cheese ravioli, honey roast ham and eggs, moussaka, pork fillets in cajun sauce, crispy battered fish and chips, caribbean-style king prawn curry, and puddings such as spicy apple crumble and chocolate sponge with chocolate sauce. *Benchmark main dish: pie of the day £10.95. Two-course evening meal £18.50.*

Free house ~ Licensee Colin Hayling ~ Real ale ~ Open 11.30-3, 6-11; 12-10.30 Sun ~ Bar food 12-2, 7-9; not Sun or Mon evenings ~ Restaurant ~ Children welcome ~ Dogs welcome ~ Wi-fi ~ Live jazz Weds ~ Bedrooms: /£80 *Recommended by Sara Fulton, Roger Baker, Guy Henderson, Colin and Daniel Gibbs, Elisabeth and Bill Humphries*

LITTLEY GREEN

TL6917 Map 5

Compasses ◀

(01245) 362308 – www.compasseslittleygreen.co.uk

Village signposted off B1417 Felsted road in Hartoft End (opposite former Ridleys Brewery), about a mile N of junction with B1008 (former A130); CM3 1BU

Charming brick tavern – a prime example of what is now an all too rare breed; bedrooms

In summer and at Christmas they hold beer festivals here featuring dozens of beers, alongside festivities that may include vintage ploughing in the field opposite. The companionable bar keeps a fine range of drinks all year: Bishop Nick Ridleys Rite (brewed in Felsted by the landlord's brother) as well as guests from Adnams, Crouch Vale, Green Jack, Mighty Oak, Red Fox, Skinners, Tyne Bank and two weekend guest ales, all tapped from casks in a back cellar. Also, constantly changing ciders from Biddenden, Carter's, Millwhites, Orchard Pig and so forth, and eight wines by the glass. The bar has very traditional brown-painted panelling and wall benches, plain chairs and tables on quarry tiles, with chat and laughter rather than piped music. There's a piano, darts and board games in one side room, and decorative mugs hanging from beams in another. There are picnic-sets out on the sheltered side grass and the garden behind, with a couple of long tables on the front cobbles by the quiet lane. Bedrooms are in a small newish block.

A big blackboard shows the day's range of huffers: big rolls with a hearty range of hot or cold fillings. They also serve ploughman's, baked potatoes and a few sensibly priced dishes such as chicken liver pâté, beer-battered fish and chips, a curry, gammon and egg, and rib-eye steak. *Benchmark main dish: beer-battered cod and chips £10.00. Two-course evening meal £16.00.*

Free house ~ Licensee Jocelyn Ridley ~ Real ale ~ Open 12-3, 5.30-11.30; 12-11.30 Thurs-Sun ~ Bar food 12-2.30 (4 Sat, 5 Sun), 7-9.30 ~ Children welcome ~ Dogs welcome ~ Wi-fi ~ Live folk music every third Mon of month ~ Bedrooms: /£70 *Recommended by Simon Day, Paul Scofield, Isobel Mackinlay, David Longhurst, Harvey Brown, Alf Wright, Donald Allsopp*

MARGARETTING TYE

TL6801 Map 5

White Hart ◀ £ ⇦

(01277) 840478 – www.thewhitehart.uk.com

From B1002 (just S of A12/A414 junction) follow Maldon Road for 1.3 miles, then turn right immediately after river bridge, into Swan Lane, keeping on for 0.7 miles; The Tye; CM4 9JX

Cheery pub with a fine choice of ales, good food, plenty of customers and a family garden; bedrooms

Always busy with both regulars and visitors, this is a particularly well run all-rounder. The open-plan but cottagey rooms have walls and wainscoting painted in chalky traditional colours that match well with the dark timbers, and a mix of old wooden chairs and tables; a stuffed deer head is mounted on the chimney breast above a woodburning stove. Tapped straight from the cask, the range of ales includes Adnams Broadside and Southwold, Mighty Oak IPA and Oscar Wilde and a couple of guests such as New River Twin Spring and Silks Whacker Payne; they hold beer festivals in July and November. Also, a german wheat beer, interesting bottled beers, quite a range of spirits and winter mulled wine. The neat carpeted back conservatory is similar in style to the other rooms, and the front lobby has a bookcase of charity paperbacks. Darts, board games and background music. There are plenty of picnic-sets out on grass and terracing around the pub, with a fenced duck pond and views across the fields; lovely sunsets.

Interesting food includes sandwiches, rabbit hotpot, king prawn cocktail, leek, pear and blue cheese pie, calves liver with smoked bacon and gravy, sea bream fillet with prawns, cauliflower and sauté kale, aberdeen angus burger with toppings, coleslaw, pickles and chips, chicken breast stuffed with spinach and ricotta, prosciutto and garlic risotto, veal chop with jerusalem artichokes, aparagus and ricotta, and puddings such as chocolate cream custard terrine with salted caramel ice-cream and apple tarte tatin with clotted cream. *Benchmark main dish: steak in ale pie £12.95. Two-course evening meal £18.00.*

Free house ~ Licensee Elizabeth Haines ~ Real ale ~ Open 11.30-3.30, 4-11.30; 11.30-11.30 Sat; 12-11 Sun; closed Mon evening in winter ~ Bar food 12-2.30, 6-9 ~ Restaurant ~ Well behaved children welcome ~ Dogs allowed in bar ~ Wi-fi ~ Bedrooms: /£80 *Recommended by Mervyn and Susan English, Mrs Margo Finlay, Jörg Kasprowski, Sylvia and Phillip Spencer, Louise and Oliver Redman*

MESSING
Old Crown 🏵

TL8919   Map 5

(01621) 815575 – www.oldcrownmessing.com
Signed off B1022 and B1023; Lodge Road; CO5 9TU

Bustling village pub with a friendly atmosphere, bar and dining rooms, highly regarded food and thoughtful choice of drinks; seats in garden

Very much the focal point of the village, this is an appealing late 17th-c village pub near a fine church. There's a convivial bar with an open fire, wheelback and farmhouse chairs around part-wood and part-painted tables on carpet, and stools against the pale-painted counter where friendly, cheerful staff serve Adnams Broadside and Southwold and Crouch Vale Brewers Gold on handpump and a dozen wines (including sparkling and champagne) by the glass. The two rooms of the restaurant have white-painted chairs around rustic tables on bare boards, another open fire and boating photos and paintings on canary yellow or modern papered walls. The back garden has picnic-sets under parasols and there are more in front. The deli – open 10.30am-9.30pm – is behind the pub and sells fresh local produce, ready-made meals, cakes, preserves and so forth.

Good, interesting food includes sandwiches, scallops with hazelnut and chive butter, pancetta and samphire, pigeon breast salad with caramelised apple, chorizo, celeriac purée and balsamic syrup, lamb moussaka with green salad, mushroom wellington with mushroom gravy, pancetta-wrapped pork fillet and slow-cooked belly with black pudding, apple croquette and cider and apple jus, game pie, sumatran fish curry, and puddings such as chocolate brownie with hot chocolate sauce and key lime pie. *Benchmark main dish: whole dover sole with lemon and caper butter £16.50. Two-course evening meal £24.00.*

Free house ~ Licensees Malcolm and Penny Campbell ~ Real ale ~ Open 12-11.30 (8.30 Sun) ~ Bar food 12-2.30, 6-9.30; 12-4 Sun ~ Restaurant ~ Children welcome ~ Dogs allowed in bar
Recommended by P Beardsell, Paddy and Sian O'Leary, Jacqui and Alan Swan, Max Simons

SAFFRON WALDEN
Eight Bells ♀

TL5338 Map 5

(01799) 522790 – www.8bells-pub.co.uk

Bridge Street; B184 towards Cambridge; CB10 1BU

Town pub with beautiful bar and dining rooms, helpful, courteous staff, enjoyable food and drink and seats in the garden

Carefully furnished to keep plenty of original features while adding some up-to-date touches, this is a handsomely timbered black-and-white Tudor inn with friendly staff and a relaxed and gently civilised atmosphere. The open-plan beamed bar area has leather armchairs, chesterfield sofas and old wooden settles on bare floorboards, a coal-effect gas fire in a brick fireplace and interesting old photographs. Woodfordes Wherry and a couple of guests such as Fullers London Pride and St Austell Tribute on handpump, ten wines by the glass and several malt whiskies. The back dining part is in a splendidly raftered and timbered barn with modern dark wood furniture and upholstered wall banquettes, a woodburning stove built into a log-effect end wall and display cabinets with old books, candlesticks and so forth; background music. There are seats and tables outside and a raised decked area. Audley End (English Heritage) is nearby, and there are some decent walks in the area too.

 Food is inventive and includes potato and herb gnocchi with parmesan cream, vegetable fricassée with crumbled gorgonzola and tarragon and walnut pesto, chicken breast with bread pudding, confit portobello mushroom, mushroom ketchup and chicken jus, and brioche and herb-crusted fillet of stone bass with grilled baby leeks, black venus rice and lemon velouté. They also do pub classics such as vegetable risotto with sheeps cheese, sausages of the week with caramelised red onion gravy, beer-battered fish of the day and chips, and puddings such as warm chocolate fondant with hazelnut praline and vanilla ice-cream and rhubarb and vanilla cheesecake with toasted oat granola. *Benchmark main dish: mustard and herb-crusted cannon of lamb with potato terrine, celeriac purée and lamb jus £19.50. Two-course evening meal £23.00.*

Cozy Pub Company ~ Lease Leanne Cutsforth ~ Real ale ~ Open 10am-11pm (midnight Sat); 10am-10.30pm Sun ~ Bar food 12-10; 12-6 Sun ~ Restaurant ~ Children welcome ~ Dogs allowed in bar ~ Wi-fi *Recommended by Max Simons, Andrew Stone, Sandra King, Nicholas and Maddy Trainer, Bridget and Peter Gregson*

SOUTH HANNINGFIELD
Old Windmill ⍟◑ ♀

TQ7497 Map 5

(01268) 712280 – www.brunningandprice.co.uk/oldwindmill

Off A130 S of Chelmsford; CM3 8HT

Extensive, invitingly converted pub with interesting food and a good range of drinks

The wide choice of drinks in this 18th-c pub attracts plenty of cheerful, chatty customers: Phoenix Brunning & Price Original and five guests such as Brentwood Boston Brown, Crouch Vale Brewers Gold, Slaters Premium and Ultra and Titanic Plum Porter on handpump, with a dozen wines by the glass, 70 malt whiskies and a good range of spirits. Cosy, rambling areas are created by a forest of stripped standing timbers and open doorways, and there's an agreeable mix of highly polished old tables and chairs spread throughout – as well as frame-to-frame pictures on cream walls, woodburning stoves and homely pot plants. Deep green or dark red dado and a few old rugs dotted on the glowing wood floors provide splashes of colour; other areas are more subdued with beige carpeting.

Background music. A back terrace has tables and chairs under parasols and there are picnic-sets on the lawn, and a few more seats out in front.

Modern brasserie food includes sandwiches, ham hock, rabbit, apricot and pistachio terrine with gooseberry chutney, sticky sesame pork belly with ginger and orange dressing, beetroot and quinoa salad with mint falafel, toasted seeds and pomegranate dressing, steak burger with toppings, coleslaw and chips, beef and Guinness sausages with mustard mash and shallot and stout sauce, tandoori hake with spinach and lentil dhal and creamy curried potatoes, and puddings such as honeycomb and chocolate brownie with chocolate sauce and apple and blackberry crumble with vanilla custard. *Benchmark main dish: chicken, ham hock and leek pie £13.95. Two-course evening meal £21.00.*

Brunning & Price ~ Manager Nick Clark ~ Real ale ~ Open 11.30-11; 12-10.30 Sun ~ Bar food 12-10 (9.30 Sun) ~ Restaurant ~ Children welcome ~ Dogs allowed in bar ~ Wi-fi *Recommended by Max Simons, Jeremy Snow, Celia and Geoff Clay, Millie and Peter Downing, John and Abigail Prescott, Neil Allen*

STOCK   TQ6999   Map 5

Hoop ◀

(01277) 841137 – www.thehoop.co.uk

B1007; from A12 Chelmsford bypass take Galleywood, Billericay turn-off; CM4 9BD

Cheerful weatherboarded pub with interesting beers, nice food and a large garden

A popular village local with a traditional bar and well kept ales, the atmosphere here is kept buoyant and chatty by the cheerful mix of customers. The open-plan bar has beams and standing timbers (hinting at the original layout when it was once three weavers' cottages), pubby tables and chairs and Adnams Bitter and guests such as Crouch Vale Amarillo, Mighty Oak Oscar Wilde and Youngs Special on handpump; they also hold a beer festival at the end of May featuring 100 real ales, 80 ciders, a hog roast and a barbecue. The dining room up in the timbered eaves is a fine space with an open fire in a big brick-walled fireplace, napery and elegant high-backed wooden chairs on bare boards. The large sheltered back garden, prettily bordered with flowers, has picnic-sets and a covered seating area. Parking is limited, so it's worth arriving early.

Food is popular and includes lunchtime sandwiches (until 5pm Sat), prawn and crab cocktail, salt beef terrine with mustard mayonnaise and pickles, a pie of the day, beer-battered cod and chips, burger with egg, toppings and skinny fries, treacle-cured ham with duck eggs, calves liver with bacon and onion rings, and puddings such as raspberry crème brûlée with raspberry sorbet and chocolate fondant with salted caramel ice-cream. *Benchmark main dish: toad in the hole £11.50. Two-course evening meal £20.00.*

Free house ~ Licensee Michelle Corrigan ~ Real ale ~ Open 11-11; 12-10.30 Sun ~ Bar food 12-2.30, 6-9; 12-9 Sat; 12-5 Sun ~ Restaurant ~ Children welcome on left-hand side of bar ~ Dogs allowed in bar ~ Wi-fi *Recommended by Sandra and Nigel Brown, Brian and Sally Wakeham, Patrick and Emma Stephenson, Patti and James Davidson, Lauren and Dan Frazer*

'Children welcome' means the pub says it lets children inside without any special restriction. If it allows them in, but to restricted areas such as an eating area or family room, we specify this. Places with separate restaurants often let children use them, and hotels usually let children into public areas such as lounges. Some pubs impose an evening time limit – let us know if you find one earlier than 9pm.

Also Worth a Visit in Essex

Besides the fully inspected pubs, you might like to try these pubs that have been recommended to us and described by readers. Do tell us what you think of them: feedback@goodguides.com

---

ARDLEIGH   TM0429

★**Wooden Fender** (01206) 230466

A137 towards Colchester; CO7 7PA
Pleasantly extended and furnished old pub with friendly attentive service, beams and log fires, good freshly made food from sharing plates through grills to daily specials, Greene King and guests, decent wines; children welcome in large dining room, dogs in bar, good-sized garden with play area, open all day Fri, Sat, till 9pm Sun. *(Jim King)*

ARKESDEN   TL4834

★**Axe & Compasses** (01799) 550272

Off B1038; CB11 4EX Comfortable part-thatched pub run by welcoming greek cypriot licensees; original part dating back to 1650 with low ceilings, original floor tiles and open fire in brick fireplace, upholstered chairs, cushioned wall seats and settles, Greene King IPA and Old Speckled Hen plus a guest, very good wine list (15 by the glass) and around two dozen malt whiskies, popular food including a few greek dishes in smartly converted stables with photographs of the pub and surrounding area; live music and quiz nights; children welcome, no dogs inside, pretty hanging baskets and benches out at front, more seats on side terrace, lovely village, shuts 8.30pm Sun (no food Sun evening in winter). *(Charlie Parker, Ruth May, Jim King)*

AYTHORPE RODING   TL5915

Axe & Compasses (01279) 876648

B184 S of Dunmow; CM6 1PP Attractive weatherboarded and part-thatched roadside pub, neatly kept and cosy, with beams, stripped brickwork and pale wood floors, modern furnishings, original part (on the left) has a two-way fireplace marking off a snug raftered dining area, popular food from light lunches up including deals, Adnams, Sharps and a guest, Weston's ciders and 13 wines by the glass; background and some live music, board games; small back garden with stylish modern furniture, views across fields to windmill, open all day from 9am for breakfast. *(Ray White)*

BELCHAMP ST PAUL   TL7942

Half Moon (01787) 277402

Cole Green; CO10 7DP Quaint 16th-c thatched and beamed pub overlooking village green, popular reasonably priced home-made food (not Sun evening, Mon), well kept Greene King IPA and guests, decent wines by the glass, friendly helpful staff, snug carpeted interior with woodburner, restaurant; Aug beer/music festival; children welcome, no dogs inside, tables out in front and in back garden, open all day weekends. *(Paul Farraday)*

BIRCHANGER   TL5122

★**Three Willows** (01279) 815913

Under a mile from M11 junction 8: A120 towards Bishop's Stortford, then almost immediately right to Birchanger Village; don't be waylaid earlier by the Birchanger Services signpost; CM23 5QR Welcoming dining pub feeling nicely tucked away; spacious carpeted bar with lots of cricketing memorabilia, well furnished smaller lounge, Greene King ales and good range of popular fairly traditional food including plenty of fresh fish, efficient friendly service; children welcome, dogs allowed in bar area, picnic-sets out in front and on lawn behind (some motorway and Stansted Airport noise), good play area, closed Sun evening. *(John Preddy)*

BISHOPS GREEN   TL6317

Spotted Dog (01245) 231598

High Easter Road; CM6 1NF Pretty 18th-c thatched pub-restaurant in quiet rural hamlet; good food cooked by landlord-chef including cheaper set menu choices (not Fri, Sat evenings or Sun lunchtime), friendly attentive staff, Greene King IPA and a guest beer, contemporary beamed interior with high-backed leather chairs at well spaced tables; background music; children welcome, rattan-style furniture out behind picket fence, closed Sun evening. *(Pauline Beardsell)*

BLACKMORE END   TL7430

Bull (01371) 851740

Off A131 via Bocking Church Street and Beazley End; towards Wethersfield; CM7 4DD Tucked-away village dining pub dating from the 15th c; cleanly restored opened-up interior with beams, stone or wood floors and back-to-back woodburners in central brick fireplace, generally well liked food from bar snacks and pub favourites up, Adnams Southwold, Sharps Doom Bar and a couple of guests, decent wines, friendly attentive service; live music first Fri of the month and other events; children welcome, no dogs inside, tables in side garden, closed Mon, otherwise open all day (till midnight Fri, Sat). *(Mrs Margo Finlay, Jörg Kasprowski)*

BOREHAM   TL7409

Lion (01245) 394900

Main Road; CM3 3JA Stylish bistro-bar with rooms, popular affordably priced food (order at bar) from snacks to daily specials, several wines by the glass, bottled beers and up to six well kept changing ales, efficient friendly staff, conservatory; monthly comedy club; children welcome, no dogs inside, 23 comfortable bedrooms, open all day. *(Donald Allsopp)*

BRAINTREE   TL7421
King William IV   (01376) 567755
London Road; CM77 7PU Small friendly drinkers' local with two simple bars, up to five real ales tapped from the cask including own Moody Goose brews, also proper ciders/perries, no food apart from snacks; folk night third Sun of month; picnic-sets in big garden, open all day Fri-Sun, from 3pm other days. *(Mark Crossley)*

BULMER TYE   TL8438
★ **Bulmer Fox**   (01787) 312277
A131 S of Sudbury; CO10 7EB Popular recently refurbished pub-bistro with good fairly priced food from varied menu, neatly laid tables with forms to write your order (can also order at the bar), Adnams and Greene King IPA, friendly well trained staff, bare boards with one or two 'rugs' painted on them, pastel colours and lively acoustics, quieter side room and intimate central snug, home-made chutneys, preserves etc for sale; children welcome, sheltered back terrace with arbour.
(Caroline and Peter Bryant)

BURNHAM-ON-CROUCH   TQ9495
★ **White Harte**   (01621) 782106
The Quay; CM0 8AS Cosy old-fashioned 17th-c hotel on water's edge overlooking yacht-filled River Crouch; partly carpeted bars with down-to-earth charm, assorted nautical bric-a-brac and hardware, other traditionally furnished high-ceilinged rooms with sea pictures on brown panelled or stripped brick walls, cushioned seats around oak tables, enormous winter log fire, good range of enjoyable well priced food including daily specials, beers from Adnams and Crouch Vale, friendly fast service; children and dogs welcome, outside seating jettied over the water, 19 bedrooms (eight with river view), good breakfast, open all day. *(Ian Phillips)*

BURTON END   TL5323
Ash   (01279) 814841
Just N of Stansted Airport; CM24 8UQ Thatched 17th-c country pub under new management; Green King IPA and Abbott plus a beer badged for the pub, decent range of wines by the glass and enjoyable generously served food from lunchtime sandwiches/baguettes and pubby choices up, friendly staff, black beams and timbers, quarry-tiled floors, woodburner, pitched-roof dining extension; sports TV, free wi-fi; children welcome, tables out on deck and grass, open (and food) all day.
(Mrs Margo Finlay, Jörg Kasprowski)

CASTLE HEDINGHAM   TL7835
Bell   (01787) 460350
St James Street B1058; CO9 3EJ Beamed and timbered three-bar pub dating from the 15th c, unpretentious, unspoilt and run by the same family since the late 1960s; Adnams, Mighty Oak and guests tapped from the cask (July and Nov beer festivals), popular pubby food along with turkish specials, good friendly service; background and live music including lunchtime jazz last Sun of month, quiz Sun evening; dogs welcome, children away from public bar, garden with hops and covered area, handy for Hedingham Castle, open all day Fri-Sun. *(Jeremy King)*

CHELMSFORD   TL7006
Orange Tree   (01245) 262664
Lower Anchor Street; CM2 0AS Bargain lunchtime bar food (also steak and curry night Thurs) in two-room brick local, eight well kept ales such as Dark Star, Harveys, Mighty Oak, Plain and Skinners (some tapped from the cask), efficient service; Tues charity quiz; dogs welcome in public bar, back terrace, handy for county cricket ground and can get very busy on match days, open all day. *(Tony Hobden)*

CHIGWELL ROW   TQ4693
Two Brewers   (020) 8501 1313
Lambourne Road; IG7 6ET Spacious Home Counties pub with relaxed atmosphere, all manner of tables and chairs and wall banquettes on flagstones or bare boards, heavy draped curtains, lots of pictures, photos and gilt-edged mirrors, two-way fireplace, good choice of real ales and wines by the glass, enjoyable food from varied menu, cheerful young staff; children and dogs welcome, nice three-mile circular walk from the pub, open (and food) all day. *(Neil Allen)*

CLAVERING   TL4832
★ **Cricketers**   (01799) 550442
B1038 Newport–Buntingford; CB11 4QT Busy dining pub with plenty of old-fashioned charm, inventive food and signed cookbooks by Jamie Oliver (his parents own it); main area with very low beams and big open fireplace, bays of deep purple button-backed banquettes and padded leather dining chairs on dark floorboards, split-level back part with carpeted dining areas and some big copper and brass pans on dark beams and timbers, three Adnams beers and 19 wines by the glass; background music, free wi-fi; children welcome, attractive front terrace with rattan-style chairs around teak tables, bedrooms, handy for Stansted Airport, open all day from 7am, food all day Sun. *(Ray White)*

COLCHESTER   TL9924
Fat Cat   (01206) 577990
Butt Road/Alexandra Road; CO3 3BZ Small corner pub sister to the Ipswich

and Norwich Fat Cats; eight well kept ales (including their own) and wide range of other beers all marked-up on blackboard, enjoyable inexpensive food (not Mon-Weds), friendly helpful staff; beer festivals, Sun quiz, sports TV; dogs welcome, open all day. *(Rob Anderson)*

COLNE ENGAINE   TL8530
Five Bells (01787) 224166
Signed off A1124 (was A604) in Earls Colne; Mill Lane; CO6 2HY Welcoming traditional village pub with list of landlords back to 1579; popular home-made food using local produce, six well kept changing ales including Adnams (Nov festival), friendly service, bare boards or carpeted floors, woodburners, old photographs, high-raftered dining area (former slaughterhouse), public bar with pool and sports TV; some live music, free wi-fi; children, walkers and dogs welcome, disabled facilities, attractive front terrace with gentle Colne Valley views, open (and food) all day.
(Mrs Margo Finlay, Jörg Kasprowski)

COPTHALL GREEN   TL4200
Good Intent (01992) 712066
Upshire Road, E of Waltham Abbey; EN9 3SZ Welcoming traditional family-run pub on edge of Epping Forest (just north of M25); enjoyable food including daily specials in bar or upstairs restaurant, well kept McMullens, friendly accommodating service; Weds live music, Thurs quiz; children and dogs welcome, some picnic-sets outside. *(Rupert and Sandy Newton)*

DANBURY   TL7805
Bakers Arms (01245) 227300
Maldon Road; CM3 4QH Pink-painted roadside pub with pleasant informal atmosphere, well kept ales such as Adnams and Sharps, enjoyable food (not Sun evening) including pizzas and four sizes of fish and chips, welcoming cheerful staff; children and dogs allowed (they have a mastiff and great dane), picnic-sets in back garden, open all day (till 8pm Sun).
(Tina and David Woods-Taylor)

DANBURY   TL7705
Griffin (01245) 699024
A414, top of Danbury Hill; CM3 4DH Renovated 16th-c pub with well divided interior, beams and some carved woodwork, mix of new and old furniture on wood, stone or carpeted floors, log fires, enjoyable food from pub standards, deli boards and pizzas up, changing real ales and nice choice of wines by the glass, friendly service; background and live music some Fri evenings; children

welcome, terrace seating, views, open all day (till 9pm Sun). *(Donald Allsopp)*

DEBDEN   TL5533
Plough (01799) 541899
High Street; CB11 3LE Welcoming village pub doing well under present licensees, good freshly made food from landlord-chef including daily specials, up to four well kept local ales and decent wines, cheerful helpful service, restaurant, log fire; children and dogs (in bar) welcome, fair-sized garden behind, open all day Fri-Sun, closed Mon and lunchtime Tues. *(Brian Farley)*

DEDHAM   TM0533
★Sun (01206) 323351
High Street (B2109); CO7 6DF Stylish Tudor coaching inn opposite church; popular food with some italian influences (should book at peak times), impressive wine selection with many by the glass/carafe, well kept Adnams, Crouch Vale and two guests, Aspall's cider, afternoon teas, pleasant young staff, historic panelled interior with high carved beams, handsome furnishings and splendid fireplaces, split-level dining room; background music, TV; children and dogs (in bar) welcome, picnic-sets on quiet back lawn with mature trees and view of church, characterful panelled bedrooms, good Flatford Mill walk, open all day. *(Hugh Roberts)*

DUNMOW   TL6222
★Angel & Harp (01371) 859259
Church Road, Church End; B1057 signposted to Finchingfield/The Bardfields, off B184 N of town; CM6 2AD Comfortable old place with linked rooms rambling around through standing timbers and doorways, mix of seating including armchairs, sofas and banquettes, stools line each side of the free-standing zinc 'counter' serving Adnams, Nethergate, a guest beer and 11 wines by the glass, good range of popular food (booking advised), friendly obliging service, substantial brick fireplace and some fine old floor tiles in low-ceilinged main area, steps up to interesting raftered room with one huge table, also attractive extension with glass wall overlooking flagstoned courtyard and grassed area beyond; background music, quiz last Weds of month, free wi-fi; children and dogs (in bar) welcome, open (and food) all day from 9am. *(Ian Herdman, David Jackman)*

DUTON HILL   TL6026
Three Horseshoes (01371) 870681
Off B184 Dunmow-Thaxted, 3 miles N of Dunmow; CM6 2DX Friendly traditional village local, well kept Mighty

---

A star symbol before the name of a pub shows exceptional character and appeal. It doesn't mean extra comfort. Even quite a basic pub can win a star, if it's individual enough.

Oak and a couple of guests (late May Bank Holiday beer festival), central fire in main bar, aged armchairs by another fireplace in homely left-hand parlour, lots of interesting memorabilia, small public bar with darts and pool, no food; dogs welcome, old enamel signs out at front, garden with pond and views, closed lunchtimes Mon-Thurs. *(Jim King)*

EARLS COLNE   TL8528
Lion (01787) 226823
High Street; CO6 2PA Restored village pub dating from the 15th c and under same ownership as the Five Bells at Colne Engaine; popular food from ciabattas and wood-fired pizzas up, well kept Adnams, Colchester and a guest, interesting wines (choose a bottle from their small shop to drink in or take away), friendly service; children and dogs welcome, courtyard tables, open (and food) all day from 9am (10.30am Sun) for breakfast. *(J B and M E Benson)*

EDNEY COMMON   TL6504
Green Man (01245) 248076
Highwood Road; CM1 3QE Comfortable country pub-restaurant, highly regarded, well presented food from interesting changing menu cooked by chef-owners, extensive wine list (several by the glass), a couple of real ales, friendly attentive staff, carpeted interior with black beams and timbers; children welcome, tables out at front and in garden, closed Sun evening, Mon. *(Matt and Hayley Jacob)*

EPPING FOREST   TL4501
Forest Gate (01992) 572312
Bell Common; CM16 4DZ Friendly open-plan pub dating from the 17th c and run by the same family for over 50 years; beams, flagstones and panelling, big woodburner, well kept Adnams and guests from brick-faced bar, inexpensive pubby food (they also have a smart upmarket restaurant next door); darts; dogs welcome, tables on front lawn popular with walkers, four bedrooms in separate building. *(Neil Allen)*

FINCHINGFIELD   TL6832
Fox (01371) 810151
The Green; CM7 4JX Pargeted 16th-c building with spacious beamed bar, exposed brickwork and central fireplace, patterned carpet, floor tiles by counter serving Adnams Southwold and guests, good choice of wines by the glass, popular freshly made food (not Sun evening) from sandwiches and pub favourites up, afternoon teas (must be pre-booked, not Sun); background and some live music; children and dogs welcome, picnic-sets in front overlooking village duck pond, open all day. *(Amy Ledbetter)*

FINGRINGHOE   TM0220
Whalebone (01206) 729307
Off A134 just S of Colchester centre, or B1025; CO5 7BG Old village pub geared for dining; airy country-chic rooms with cream-painted tables on oak floors, fresh flowers and log fire, good local food from interestingly varied menu, nice sandwiches too, four well kept beers including Adnams, friendly helpful staff, barn function room; background music; children and dogs welcome, charming back garden with peaceful valley view, front terrace, handy for Fingringhoe Wick nature reserve, open all day Sat, till 6pm Sun. *(Mrs Margo Finlay, Jörg Kasprowski)*

GESTINGTHORPE   TL8138
★ **Pheasant** (01787) 461196
Off B1058; CO9 3AU Civilised country pub with old-fashioned character in small opened-up beamed rooms, settles and mix of other furniture on bare boards, books and china platters on shelves, woodburners in nice brick fireplaces, Adnams Southwold, a house beer from Woodfordes and an occasional guest, nine wines by the glass, good food using local and some home-grown produce; children and dogs (in bar) welcome, seats outside under parasols with views over fields, five stylish bedrooms, closed Mon, lunchtimes Tues-Thurs and they also take days off Jan-May – so best to phone or check website. *(Neil Allen)*

GREAT CHESTERFORD   TL5142
Crown & Thistle (01799) 530278
1.5 miles from M11 junction 9A; pub signposted off B184, in High Street; CB10 1PL Substantial old building refurbished under present management; decorative plasterwork inside and out, particularly around the early 16th-c inglenook, low-ceilinged area by bar serving ales such as Oakham, Sharps and Woodfordes, enjoyable food from sandwiches and wraps through burgers and stone-baked pizzas up, long handsomely proportioned dining room; children, walkers and dogs (in bar) welcome, suntrap back courtyard, closed Sun evening. *(Jim King)*

GREAT EASTON   TL6126
Green Man (01371) 852285
Mill End Green; pub signed 2 miles N of Dunmow, off B184 towards Lindsell; CM6 2DN Popular well looked-after country dining pub down long winding lane; linked beamed rooms including bar with log fire, good food (best to book weekends) from pub favourites and tapas up, real ales, decent wines by the glass and cocktails, friendly helpful service; children welcome, dogs in bar, good-sized garden with terrace, open all day Sat, closed Sun evening, Mon. *(Mrs Margo Finlay, Jörg Kasprowski)*

GREAT HENNY   TL8738
Henny Swan (01787) 267953
Henny Street; CO10 7LS Welcoming dining pub in great location on River Stour; neatly kept bar, lounge and restaurant,

open fires, well kept Adnams, Woodfordes and a couple of guests, proper cider and plenty of wines by the glass, good food from separate bar and restaurant menus, friendly efficient service; background music; children in restaurant until 8pm, dogs in bar and lounge, disabled loos, terrace and waterside garden, may offer summer boat trips, open (and food) all day. *(Dr Peter Crawshaw)*

HARLOW   TL4411
Dusty Miller (01279) 424180
Junction Eastwick Road and Burnt Mill Lane; CM20 2QS Cream-painted brick and shuttered pub on rural outskirts, good food from varied menu including weekday lunch deal, McMullens ales, efficient friendly service, simple interior with traditional wooden tables and chairs on bare boards, open fires; children welcome, garden with play area, open all day Sat, closed Sun evening, Mon.
(Mrs Margo Finlay, Jörg Kasprowski)

HARWICH   TM2632
Alma (01255) 318681
Kings Head Street, CO12 3EE Popular old seafarers' local just back from the quayside; highly rated food (best to book) from sharing plates up including good fresh fish/seafood, well kept Adnams and good range of other beers, proper ciders and decent wines, friendly service; live music Fri, maybe a shanty group first Mon of month, quiz every other Tues; children and dogs welcome, cosy back courtyard, six bedrooms, open (and food) all day. *(Clem Luxford)*

HASTINGWOOD   TL4807
★ Rainbow & Dove (01279) 415419
0.5 miles from M11 junction 7; CM17 9JX Pleasantly traditional low-beamed country pub (originally a small farmhouse) with three cosy rooms, built-in cushioned wall seats and mate's chairs around pubby tables, some stripped stonework, woodburner in original fireplace, three well kept changing ales, good choice of wines by the glass and enjoyable fairly priced food from sandwiches up, breakfast from 9am Sat, friendly helpful staff, barn function room; background music; children and dogs welcome, tables out under parasols, smallholding with rare-breed pigs, goats and chickens (own sausages and eggs), closed Sun and Mon evenings. *(Caroline and Pater Bryant)*

HATFIELD HEATH   TL5115
Thatchers (01279) 730270
Stortford Road (A1005); CM22 7DU Thatched and weatherboarded 16th-c dining pub at end of large green, food generally good from varied menu, well kept Greene King IPA, St Austell Tribute and two guests from long counter, several wines by the glass, friendly attentive service, woodburners,

beams, some copper and brass and old local photographs; background music; children in back dining area, no dogs inside, tables out in front behind picket fence, open all day weekends (food till 7pm Sun). *(Patrick and Emma Stephenson)*

HENHAM   TL5428
Cock (01279) 850347
Church End; CM22 6AN Old timbered building striking good balance between community local and dining pub, enjoyable well priced home-made food from fairly pubby menu, Greene King IPA, a beer from Saffron (brewed in the village) and Sharps Doom Bar, decent wines, good open fires, restaurant with leather-backed chairs on wood floor, sports TV in snug; children welcome, dogs in bar, seats out at front and in tree-shaded garden behind, open all day Fri and Sat, till 7pm Sun. *(Rob Anderson)*

HERONGATE   TQ6491
★ Olde Dog (01277) 810337
Billericay Road, off A128 Brentwood–Grays at big sign for Boars Head; CM13 3SD Welcoming weatherboarded country pub dating from the 16th c; long attractive dark-beamed bar and separate dining areas, exposed brickwork, uneven wood floors and open fires, well kept ales tapped from the cask including a house beer from Crouch Vale, popular food from sandwiches up (all day Sat, till 6pm Sun), friendly staff; dogs welcome in one area, pleasant front terrace and big garden, open all day. *(Mrs Margo Finlay, Jörg Kasprowski, Paul Rampton, Julie Harding)*

HOWLETT END   TL5834
White Hart (01799) 599030
Thaxted Road (B184 SE of Saffron Walden); CB10 2UZ Comfortable well run pub-restaurant, two smartly set modern dining rooms either side of small bar, good food from sandwiches and pubby choices up, a real ale such as Nethergate and nice choice of wines, friendly helpful service; children welcome, terrace and big garden, closed Sun evening, Mon (open bank holiday lunchtime). *(Neil Allen)*

LANGHAM   TM0232
Shepherd (01206) 272711
Moor Road/High Street; CO4 5NR Roomy 1920s village pub on crossroads, L-shaped bar with areas off, wood floors and painted half-panelling, large OS map covering one wall, comfortable sofas, woodburner, two Adnams beers and a guest, plenty of wines by the glass and good selection of other drinks, enjoyable food (not Sun evening) from sharing plates up, efficient friendly service; quiz first Tues of month, occasional live music; children and dogs (in bar) welcome, side garden, open all day Fri, Sat, till 7pm Sun, closed Mon. *(Celia and Geoff Clay)*

LEIGH-ON-SEA   TQ8385
★**Crooked Billet** (01702) 480289
High Street; SS9 2EP Homely old pub
with waterfront views from big bay windows,
packed on busy summer days when service
can be frenetic but friendly, well kept
Adnams, Nicholsons, Sharps and changing
guests including seasonals, enjoyable
standard Nicholsons menu, log fires, beams,
panelled dado and bare boards, local fishing
pictures and bric-a-brac; background
music; children welcome, dogs outside only,
side garden and terrace, seawall seating
over road shared with Osborne's good
shellfish stall (plastic glasses for outside),
pay-and-display parking by flyover, open
(and food) all day. *(John and Enid Morris)*

LITTLE BRAXTED   TL8413
Green Man (01621) 891659
Kelvedon Road; signed off B1389;
OS Sheet 168 map reference 848133;
CM8 3LB Compact cream-painted village
pub opposite tiny green; modern décor
with old beams and log fires, enjoyable
reasonably priced traditional food from
sandwiches and baked potatoes up, OAP
set menu and other deals, Greene King ales
and a guest, Aspall's cider, friendly helpful
staff; children, walkers and dogs welcome,
picnic-sets out at front and in pleasant
sheltered garden, open all day Sat, till 7pm
Sun, closed Mon evening. *(Amy Ledbetter)*

LITTLE BROMLEY   TM1028
Haywain (01206) 390004
Bentley Road; CO11 2PL Popular 18th-c
pub freshened up under new owners;
carpeted/flagstoned interior with various
cosy areas leading off main bar, beams,
exposed brickwork, painted wainscoting and
open fires, well kept Adnams and a couple
of guests such as Sticklegs, enjoyable good
value food from snacks to grills, friendly
helpful service; children, walkers and dogs
welcome, small side garden, closed Mon
and Tues, otherwise open (and food) all
day from 9.30am for breakfast. *(Neil Allen)*

LITTLE TOTHAM   TL8811
Swan (01621) 331713
School Road; CM9 8LB Welcoming
little village local with eight well kept ales
tapped from the cask, farm ciders/perry
and straightforward good value lunchtime
food, low 17th-c beams, log fire, back dining
area, games bar with darts; live music
and quiz nights, beer festivals June and
Dec; children, dogs and walkers welcome,
disabled access, front lawned garden and
small terrace, open all day. *(Jim King)*

LITTLE WALTHAM   TL7013
★**White Hart** (01245) 360205
The Street; CM3 3NY Handsome village
pub with contemporary open-plan rooms;
wood, slate and tartan-carpeted floors,

seating from woven cane chairs through wall
banquettes and cushioned window seats to
upholstered armchairs, fireplaces (some
piled high with logs), metal deer heads,
antler chandeliers and candles in tall glass
lanterns, Adnams, Nethergate and guests,
Weston's cider and good wines by the glass,
popular reasonably priced food including
deals, efficient friendly service; free wi-fi;
children and dogs (in bar) welcome, garden
with cheerfully coloured metal chairs and
parasols along with rattan-style seating and
picnic-sets, open (and food) all day from 9am.
(Mrs Margo Finlay, Jörg Kasprowski)

LOUGHTON   TQ4296
Victoria (020) 8508 1779
Smarts Lane; IG10 4BP Chatty and
welcoming flower-decked Victorian local;
panelled bare-boards bar with small raised
end dining area, five real ales including
Sharps Doom Bar and Timothy Taylors
Landlord, decent range of whiskies and
good helpings of enjoyable home-made food;
children and dogs welcome, pleasant neatly
kept front garden, Epping Forest walks, open
all day weekends. *(Matt and Hayley Jacob)*

MATCHING GREEN   TL5310
Chequers (01279) 731276
Off Downhall Road; CM17 0PZ Red-brick
Victorian pub-restaurant in picturesque
village; not particularly cheap but very
enjoyable traditional and mediterranean-
style food from lunchtime ciabattas up,
also fixed-price weekday lunch, vegetarian
menu and children's choices, friendly
helpful staff dressed in black, nice wines
from comprehensive list, cocktails and
three well kept ales including Greene King
and Woodfordes; background music and
occasional cabaret/tribute nights; disabled
facilities, quiet spot overlooking large green,
good local walks, open all day Fri-Sun, closed
Mon except bank holidays. *(Donald Allsopp)*

MATCHING TYE   TL5111
Fox (01279) 731335
The Green; CM17 0QS Long 18th-c
village pub opposite tiny green, decent
range of popular well priced food, Greene
King IPA, Shepherd Neame Spitfire and
a guest, welcoming service, various areas
including beamed restaurant and raftered
barn room, comfortable dark wood
furniture, brasses, woodburners; regular
live music and quiz nights, TV; children
welcome, 11 bedrooms. *(Jim King)*

MILL GREEN   TL6401
★**Viper** (01277) 352010
*The Common; from Fryerning (which is
signposted off N-bound A12 Ingatestone
bypass) follow Writtle signposts;
CM4 0PT* Delightfully unpretentious
country local; cosy unchanging rooms with
spindleback and country kitchen chairs
around neat little tables, tapestried wall

seats and log fire, the fairly basic tap room is even more simple with parquet floor and coal fire, beyond is another room with sensibly placed darts; two beers named for the pub plus Animal Big Bang, Canterbury Brewers Nitro Engenius and Mighty Oak Oscar Wilde, Weston's cider/perry, straightforward lunchtime food; Easter and Aug beer festivals; children (at one end of bar) and dogs welcome, pretty cottagey garden (mass of summer colour) and lots of hanging baskets and window boxes, some seats on lawn, open all day weekends (busy with walkers and cyclists then). *(Maddie Purvis)*

MISTLEY   TM1131
★**Thorn** (01206) 392821

High Street (B1352 E of Manningtree); CO11 1HE Popular for American chef-landlady's good food (especially seafood), but there's also a friendly welcome if you just want a drink or coffee; high black beams give a clue to the building's age (Matthew Hopkins, the notorious 17th-c witchfinder general, based himself here), décor, though, is crisply up to date – bentwood chairs and mixed dining tables on terracotta tiles around central bar, cream walls above blue dado, colourful modern artwork, end brick fireplace with woodburner; newspapers and magazines, cookery classes; front pavement tables looking across to Robert Adam's fountain, interesting waterside village, 11 comfortable bedrooms, open all day. *(Ray White, Comus and Sarah Elliott)*

MOUNT BURES   TL9031
★**Thatchers Arms** (01787) 227460

Off B1508; CO8 5AT Well run modernised pub with good local food cooked to order, set lunch deal Tues-Fri, three or four well kept ales including Adnams and Crouch Vale, cheerful efficient staff; background music and occasional live music, film and quiz nights; children and dogs welcome, plenty of picnic-sets out behind, peaceful Stour Valley views, closed Sun evening, Mon, otherwise open all day. *(Celia and Geoff Clay)*

NEWPORT   TL5234
Coach & Horses (01799) 540292

Cambridge Road (B1383); CB11 3TR Welcoming beamed village pub with good freshly made food including specials (steak night is Friday), friendly prompt service, well kept Adnams, Timothy Taylors, Woodfordes and a guest; background music, free wi-fi; children welcome, garden with play boat, open all day Fri, Sat, till 6pm Sun. *(Paul Farraday)*

NORTH SHOEBURY   TQ9286
Angel (01702) 589600

Parsons Corner; SS3 8UD Conversion of timbered and partly thatched former post office/blacksmiths beside busy roundabout; Greene King, Woodfordes and a couple of guests, popular food including daily specials,

small quarry-tiled entrance bar flanked by tartan-carpeted dining rooms, step up to back bar with wood floor and some old local pictures, woodburner; background music, free wi-fi; children and dogs allowed in certain areas, disabled facilities, seats out at front, open all day weekends. *(Neil Allen)*

PAGLESHAM   TQ9492
Plough & Sail (01702) 258242

East End; SS4 2EQ Relaxed 17th-c weatherboarded dining pub in pretty country spot, popular fairly traditional food at affordable prices, friendly service, well kept changing ales, local cider and decent house wines, low black beams and big log fires, pine tables, lots of brasses and pictures, traditional games; background music; children welcome, front picnic-sets and pleasant side garden, open all day Sun. *(Patrick and Emma Stephenson)*

PAGLESHAM   TQ9293
Punchbowl (01702) 258376

Church End; SS4 2DP Weatherboarded 16th-c former sailmaker's loft under new management; low beams, pews, barrel chairs and lots of brass, local pictures, woodburners in two brick fireplaces, lower room laid for dining, Adnams Southwold, Sharps Doom Bar and three guests from brick and timber servery, popular fairly priced food including OAP menu (Tues, Thurs) and pie and mash night (Thurs), friendly attentive staff; background music, quiz last Weds of month; children welcome, no dogs inside, picnic-sets out by lane overlooking farmland, more seating to the side, open (and food) all day Sun. *(Patrick and Emma Stephenson)*

PELDON   TL9916
Plough (01206) 735808

Lower Road; CO5 7QR Welcoming little weatherboarded village pub (some recent refurbishment) with good choice of enjoyable food, Greene King London Glory, Sharps Doom Bar and decent wines by the glass, friendly efficient service, beams and woodburners, cosy restaurant; children and dogs welcome (their friendly victorian bulldog is Ponto), picnic-sets in back garden, open all day Sun, closed Mon lunchtime. *(Neil Allen)*

PELDON   TM0015
Rose (01206) 735248

B1025 Colchester–Mersea (do not turn left to Peldon village); CO5 7QJ Friendly new licensee for this popular old inn; dark bowed beams, standing timbers and little leaded-light windows, some antique mahogany and padded leather wall banquettes, arched brick fireplace, Adnams, Greene King and Woodfordes, several wines by glass and well liked food, cosy restaurant and smart airy garden room; children welcome away from bar, plenty of seats in spacious garden with pretty pond, comfortable country-style bedrooms, open all day. *(Paul Farraday)*

PENTLOW   TL8146
Pinkuah Arms (01787) 280857
Pinkuah Lane; CO10 7JW Contemporary furnishings in beamed country pub (aka Pinkers), well liked food from pub favourites to more restaurant dishes, good value lunchtime set menu and other deals, Adnams, Greene King, Timothy Taylors and Woodfordes kept well, friendly efficient service; quiz last Tues of month; children and dogs (in bar) welcome, garden and terrace with modern furniture, open all day, no food Sun evening, Mon. *(Jim King)*

PURLEIGH   TL8401
Bell (01621) 828348
Off B1010 E of Danbury, by church at top of hill; CM3 6QJ Cosy rambling beamed and timbered pub with fine views over the marshes and Blackwater estuary; bare boards, hops and brasses, inglenook log fire, well kept ales such as Adnams and Mighty Oak, plenty of wines by the glass (some local), good sensibly priced home-made food including specials, friendly staff; cinema and local art exhibitions in adjoining barn; children welcome, picnic-sets on side grass, good walks (on St Peter's Way), closed Sun evening, Mon (except bank holidays). *(Rupert and Sandy Newton)*

RIDGEWELL   TL7340
White Horse (01440) 785532
Mill Road (A1017 Haverhill–Halstead); CO9 4SG Comfortable beamed village pub with up to four well kept changing ales (some tapped from the cask), real ciders and decent wines by the glass, good generous food including lunchtime set menu (Tues-Sat), friendly service; background music, free wi-fi; well behaved children welcome, no dogs, tables out on terrace, modern bedroom block with good disabled access, closed Mon lunchtime and Tues afternoon, otherwise open all day. *(Matt and Hayley Jacob)*

SAFFRON WALDEN   TL5438
Cross Keys (01799) 522207
High Street; CB10 1AX Former medieval coaching inn with interesting jettied exterior, attractively updated inside with bar, restaurant and coffee shop, enjoyable well presented food from sharing plates to daily specials, good value set deal (Mon-Sat till 6pm), friendly service, ales such as Sharps Doom Bar, well chosen wines and extensive range of gins; children welcome, nine bedrooms, open (and food) all day. *(Dr Michael Smith, Michael Sargent)*

SAFFRON WALDEN   TL5438
Old English Gentleman
(01799) 523595 *Gold Street; CB10 1EJ* Busy 19th-c red-brick pub in centre of town; bare boards, panelling and log fires, plenty of inviting nooks and crannies, well kept Adnams Southwold, Woodfordes Wherry and a couple of guests, plenty of wines by the glass and good choice of enjoyable lunchtime only food from sandwiches and deli boards up, friendly staff; background music, TV; children welcome, part-covered heated terrace with modern furniture, open all day (till 1am Fri, Sat). *(Rob Anderson)*

SOUTHEND   TQ8885
Pipe of Port (01702) 614606
Tylers Avenue, off High Street; SS1 1JN Cellar bar (not strictly a pub) with plenty of atmosphere, sawdust and candlelight, well liked food including signature pies and good value set menu, excellent range of affordably priced wines and other drinks from craft beers to cocktails, friendly knowledgeable staff; wine tasting evenings; closed Sun and bank holidays. *(Dave Braisted)*

SOUTHMINSTER   TQ9699
Station Arms (01621) 772225
Station Road; CM0 7EW Popular weatherboarded local with unpretentious L-shaped bar, bare boards and panelling, well kept Adnams Southwold and several guests (beer festivals Jan, May), friendly chatty atmosphere; live blues and folk nights; back courtyard, open from midday (all day Sat from 2pm). *(Donald Allsopp)*

STAPLEFORD TAWNEY   TL5001
Mole Trap (01992) 522394
Tawney Common; signed off A113 N of M25 overpass – keep on; OS Sheet 167 map reference 500013; CM16 7PU Tucked-away, yet popular, little country pub with simple carpeted beamed bar (mind your head as you go in), brocaded wall seats and plain pub tables, steps down to similar area, log fires, well kept Fullers London Pride and guests, good value down-to-earth food (not Sun and Mon evenings); no credit cards, maybe quiet background radio; well behaved children welcome away from bar, small dogs allowed at quiet times, garden with rural views. *(Paul Farraday)*

STEEPLE BUMPSTEAD   TL6841
Fox & Hounds (01440) 731810
Chapel Street; CB9 7DQ Welcoming 15th-c beamed village pub with three eating areas, popular home-made food (booking advised) from varied menu including good value Mon evening two-course deal, well kept

Greene King IPA, three quickly changing guests and several wines by the glass, good friendly service, pine furniture, linen napkins and fresh flowers, log fire in bar; occasional live music; some seats out in front behind picket fence, more on little terrace behind, open all day Fri-Sun (no food Sun evening). *(Mrs Margo Finlay, Jörg Kasprowski)*

STOCK TQ6998
Bakers Arms (01277) 840423
Common Road, just off B1007 Chelmsford–Billericay; CM4 9NF
Popular open-plan beamed pub with good home-made food including some mediterranean influences, friendly attentive service, ales such as Adnams, Crouch Vale and Greene King, airy dining room with french windows to enclosed terrace, more seats out at front and in side garden; children welcome, open all day (food all day Fri-Sun). *(John and Enid Morris)*

STOW MARIES TQ8399
★Prince of Wales (01621) 828971
B1012 between South Woodham Ferrers and Cold Norton; CM3 6SA
Cheery atmosphere in this traditional weatherboarded pub, several little unspoilt low-ceilinged rooms, bare boards and log fires, conservatory dining area, half a dozen widely sourced ales, bottled/draught belgian beers including fruit ones and a couple of ciders, enjoyable food (all day Sun) with some interesting specials and home-smoked dishes; live jazz (third Fri of month); children in family room, terrace and garden tables, summer barbecues Sun, four good bedrooms in converted stable, open all day. *(Rupert and Sundy Newton)*

THEYDON BOIS TQ4598
Bull (01992) 812145
Station Approach; CM16 7HR
Cosy beamed pub dating from the 17th c, polished wood and carpeted floors, log fire, three well kept ales including Wells Bombardier, several wines by the glass and good home-made food from sandwiches to blackboard specials (booking advised, especially weekends), friendly staff; sports TV; children and dogs (in bar) welcome, paved beer garden, open all day, food all day Thurs-Sat, kitchen closed Sun evening. *(Roger and Pauline Pearce)*

UPSHIRE TL4100
Horseshoes (01992) 712745
Horseshoe Hill, E of Waltham Abbey; EN9 3SN Welcoming Victorian village pub with small bar area and dining room, good freshly made food from chef-landlord with some emphasis on fish, well kept McMullens beers, friendly helpful staff; children and dogs (in bar) welcome, garden overlooking Lea Valley, more tables out in front, good walks, open all day, no evening food Sun or Mon. *(Rob Anderson)*

WENDENS AMBO TL5136
★Bell (01799) 540382
B1039 W of village; CB11 4JY Cottagey local under new management; cheery bustle in low-ceilinged bars, brasses on ancient timbers, wheelback chairs at neat tables, winter log fire, Adnams, Oakham and Woodfordes and a couple of guests, real ciders and several wines by the glass, well liked food (not Sun evening), pizza van Thurs evening; background music, free wi-fi; children and dogs welcome, three-acre garden with seats under parasols on paved terrace, pond leading to River Uttle, woodland walk and timber play area, camping (glamping pods planned as we went to press), open all day. *(Caroline and Peter Bryant)*

WICKHAM ST PAUL TL8336
★Victory (01787) 269364
SW of Sudbury; The Green; CO9 2PT Old village dining pub by cricket green, attractive and spacious, with varied choice of tasty food including OAP weekday lunch and other deals, takeaway fish and chips Fri evening, friendly efficient service, Adnams and guests from brick-faced counter, beams and timbers, leather sofas and armchairs, inglenook woodburner; background music, pool and darts; children welcome, picnic-sets in neat front garden, open all day Fri-Sun, no food Sun evening. *(Paul Farraday)*

WIDDINGTON TL5331
★Fleur de Lys (01799) 543280
Signed off B1383 N of Stansted; CB11 3SG Welcoming unpretentious low-beamed and timbered village pub, enjoyable locally sourced food (not Sun evening, Mon, Tues) in bar and dining room from sandwiches to very good (if pricey) steaks, OAP set lunch Weds and Thurs, well kept Adnams, Woodfordes and a couple of guests chosen by regulars, decent wines, dim lighting, tiled and wood floors, inglenook log fire; pool and other games in back bar; children and dogs welcome, picnic-sets in pretty garden, open all day Fri-Sun, closed Mon and Tues lunchtimes. *(Matt and Hayley Jacob)*

WIVENHOE TM0321
Black Buoy (01206) 822425
Off A133; CO7 9BS Village pub owned by local consortium; open-plan partly timbered bare-boards bar, well kept ales such as Colchester, Mighty Oak and Red Fox, a craft keg, Aspall's cider and several wines by the glass, good sensibly priced home-made food (not Sun evening) from lunchtime sandwiches to daily specials, cheerful service, open fires, upper dining area glimpsing river over roofs; well behaved children and dogs allowed in certain areas, seats out on brick terrace, two smart bedrooms (up steep staircase), open all day. *(Patrick and Emma Stephenson)*

Gloucestershire

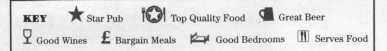

KEY ★ Star Pub | 🎯 Top Quality Food | 🍺 Great Beer
🍷 Good Wines | £ Bargain Meals | 🛏 Good Bedrooms | 🍴 Serves Food

---

BARNSLEY
SP0705 Map 4

Village Pub 🎯 🍷 🛏

(01285) 740421 – www.thevillagepub.co.uk

B4425 Cirencester–Burford; GL7 5EF

Bustling pub with first class food, a good choice of drinks and seats in the back courtyard; bedrooms

The excellent food remains the mainstay in this lovely country pub, but there's still a cheerful crowd of regulars who are as warmly welcomed for just a pint and a chat as those aiming for a full meal. The low-ceilinged bar rooms are smart and contemporary with pale paintwork, flagstones and oak floorboards, heavy swagged curtains, plush chairs, stools and window settles around polished candlelit tables, three open fireplaces and country magazines and newspapers. Corinium Gold, North Cotswold Best and a guest beer on handpump, an extensive wine list with a dozen by the glass and up to six farm ciders in summer. The sheltered back courtyard has solid wooden furniture under parasols, outdoor heaters and its own servery. Bedrooms are individually decorated and extremely comfortable and breakfasts are especially recommended.

🎯 First class food includes twice-baked cheddar cheese soufflé, shredded confit duck with an asian-style dressing, smoked haddock fishcakes with a poached egg and lemon butter sauce, polenta with mediterranean vegetable stew and mixed bean salad, cumberland sausage with creamy mash and gravy, half a roast cajun chicken with lime and yoghurt, black angus steaks with peppercorn or béarnaise sauce, and puddings such as walnut and chocolate brownie and spotted dick and custard. *Benchmark main dish: burger with bacon jam and chips £15.00. Two-course evening meal £21.00.*

Free house ~ Licensee Michael Mella ~ Real ale ~ Open 11-11 ~ Bar food 12-2.30, 6-9.30 (10 Fri); 12-3, 6-10 Sat; 12-9 Sun ~ Children welcome ~ Dogs allowed in bar ~ Wi-fi ~ Bedrooms: £119/£129 *Recommended by Mrs Zara Elliott, Michael Doswell, Anne Taylor, Susan Eccleston, Andrew Lawson, Caroline and Peter Bryant, Sabina and Gerald Grimshaw*

BLEDINGTON
SP2422 Map 4

Kings Head 🎯 🍷 🍺 🛏

(01608) 658365 – www.kingsheadinn.net

B4450 The Green; OX7 6XQ

•••
Gloucestershire Dining Pub of the Year
•••

16th-c inn with atmospheric furnishings, super wines by the glass, real ales and delicious food; smart bedrooms

Of course, much emphasis in this lovely, gently civilised former cider house is on the excellent food and smart bedrooms, but the main bar is lively, friendly and full of chatty locals. There are ancient beams and other atmospheric furnishings (high-backed wooden settles, gate-leg or pedestal tables), a warming log fire in a stone inglenook, ancient flagstones and sporting memorabilia of rugby, racing, cricket and hunting. To the left, a drinking area has built-in wall benches, stools and dining chairs around wooden tables, rugs on bare boards and a woodburning stove. Attentive, welcoming staff serve Hook Norton Best and guests from breweries such as Butcombe, Flying Monk, Hook Norton and Purity on handpump, a super wine list with ten by the glass, 20 malt whiskies and an extensive gin collection; background music, board games and cards. There are seats out in front and rattan-style armchairs around tables in the pretty back courtyard garden with a pagoda; maybe free-ranging bantams and ducks. This is an enjoyable place to stay (cosy rooms above the inn and more spacious ones in the courtyard) and the setting – opposite the green in a tranquil village – is most attractive. The same first class licensees also run the Swan at Swinbrook (in Oxfordshire).

 Free-range, organic and local produce is used on the imaginative seasonal menu: lunchtime open sandwiches, devilled lambs kidneys on toast, crab with green mango, asian slaw, coriander, roasted peanuts and nam jim dressing, chilli burger with bloody mary ketchup and skinny chips, asparagus risotto with mint and parmesan, grilled mackerel with pickled red cabbage and celeriac rémoulade, lamb chump with carrot purée, black pudding, squash and tarragon jus, and puddings such as bitter and white chocolate ganache with malt ice-cream and vanilla pannacotta with poached rhubarb. *Benchmark main dish: steak and mushroom in ale pie £14.50. Two-course evening meal £22.00.*

Free house ~ Licensees Nicola and Archie Orr-Ewing ~ Real ale ~ Open 11-11 ~ Bar food 12-2, 6.30-9; 12-2.30, 6-9.30 Fri, Sat; 12-3, 6.30-9 Sun ~ Restaurant ~ Children welcome ~ Dogs allowed in bar ~ Wi-fi ~ Bedrooms: $80/$100 *Recommended by P and J Shapley, Richard Tilbrook, Stephen Funnell, Keith Perry, Clive and Fran Dutson, Bob and Melissa Wyatt, Margo and Derek Stapley, Alun and Jennifer Evans*

BOURTON-ON-THE-HILL
Horse & Groom ♀ ⇔

SP1732   Map 4

(01386) 700413 – www.horseandgroom.info
A44 W of Moreton-in-Marsh; GL56 9AQ

Handsome old inn with a good range of drinks, enjoyable food, friendly staff and lovely views from seats outside; smart bedrooms

Of course, things will be very different here under the recently arrived new owners, but feedback from our readers has been warmly positive and the core values laid down by the Greenstock brothers, who ran this Georgian inn for some years, remain. The pubby bar is light, airy and simply furnished with a pleasing mix of farmhouse and other wooden chairs, settles, cushioned wall and window seats and tables on bare boards and a woodburning stove in a stone fireplace. They serve Banks's Amber, Marstons EPA and a guest such as Brakspears Oxford Gold on handpump, good wines by the glass, maybe a local farm cider and local gin. There are plenty of original features throughout; background music. Dining areas spread off from here – again, with a very attractive variety of dining chairs and rustic tables, rugs here and there, snug little corners, an open fire and pale-painted or exposed stone walls. The large back garden has lots of seats under parasols and fine countryside views. Bedrooms are individually styled and good breakfasts are well thought-of. It's best to arrive early to be sure of a space in the smallish car park. Batsford Arboretum is not far away.

Interesting food includes fish soup with rouille, baked cauliflower, butternut squash, chickpea and mascarpone parcel with curried tomato sauce, beef in ale pie, chicken breast with roasted sweet potato, piri-piri dressing and chive sour cream, rare-breed pork sausages with braised puy lentils, caramelised onions and green sauce, trout fillet with roasted jerusalem artichokes and chorizo crumbs, and puddings such as hazelnut and chocolate tart and rum baba with poached pear. *Benchmark main dish: longhorn rib-eye steak with tarragon and whole grain mustard butter £22.50. Two-course evening meal £25.00.*

Free house ~ Licensee Karl Soloman ~ Real ale ~ Open 11-11; 12-10 Sun ~ Bar food 12-2, 7-9 (9.30 Fri, Sat); 12-2.30 Sun ~ Restaurant ~ Children welcome ~ Dogs allowed in bar ~ Wi-fi ~ Bedrooms: /£120 *Recommended by Mrs J Ekins-Daukes, Richard Tilbrook, K H Frostick, Richard Cox, Bernard Stradling, R K Phillips, Mike and Mary Carter, Phil and Helen Holt, John and Penny Wildon*

BROCKHAMPTON SP0322 Map 4
Craven Arms ◖

(01242) 820410 – www.thecravenarms.co.uk
Village signposted off A436 Andoversford–Naunton – look out for inn sign at head of lane in village; can also be reached from A40 Andoversford–Cheltenham via Whittington and Syreford; GL54 5XQ

Friendly village pub with tasty bar food, real ales and seats in a big garden; bedrooms

This makes the perfect lunchtime base after an enjoyable walk across surrounding fields. The character bars have a chatty atmosphere, low beams, roughly coursed thick stone walls and some tiled flooring; although it's largely been opened out to give a sizeable eating area off the smaller bar servery, there's a feeling of several communicating rooms. The furniture is mainly pine, with comfortable leather sofas, wall settles and tub chairs; also, gin traps, various stuffed animal trophies and a woodburning stove. Served by attentive staff, drinks include Otter Bitter, Butcombe Legless Bob (20p per pint going to Diabetes UK) and Stroud Budding on handpump, eight wines by the glass and a farm cider; board games. The large garden has plenty of seats and the views are lovely. The two bedrooms are comfortable.

Good food includes their interesting barbecue-style 'hot rock' meat and fish choices with all sorts of sauces and dips, plus baguettes, smoked mackerel rillettes, baked blue brie with fig chutney, spiced squash, spinach, ricotta and pine nut tart, beef and mushroom in red wine pie, chicken in a basket with chipotle ketchup and fries, duck breast with fondant potato, pickled chard and white wine jus, monkfish and chorizo with samphire and beetroot, and puddings such as salted caramel cheesecake and white chocolate eton mess parfait. *Benchmark main dish: salmon fishcakes with sweet chilli mayonnaise £12.00. Two-course evening meal £19.00.*

Free house ~ Licensee Barbara Price ~ Real ale ~ Open 12-3, 6-11; 12-11 Sat; 12-5 Sun; closed Sun evening, Mon ~ Bar food 12-2 (2.30 Sat), 6.30-9; 12.30-3 Sun ~ Restaurant ~ Children welcome ~ Dogs allowed in bar ~ Wi-fi ~ Bedrooms: /£90 *Recommended by Richard Tilbrook, Katherine Matthews, Ian Duncan, Peter Young, Dr A J and Mrs B A Tompsett*

CHELTENHAM SO9624 Map 4
Royal Oak ♀ ◖

(01242) 522344 – www.royal-oak-prestbury.co.uk
Off B4348 just N; The Burgage, Prestbury; GL52 3DL

Cheerful pub with popular food, several real ales and wine by the glass, and seats in the sheltered garden

The warmly friendly landlord has been running this bustling pub with a great deal of care for more than 17 years; both regulars and visitors continue to enjoy their visits very much. The congenial low-beamed bar has fresh flowers and polished brasses, a comfortable mix of seating including chapel chairs on parquet flooring, some interesting pictures on the ochre walls and a woodburning stove in a stone fireplace. Efficient, helpful staff keep Dark Star American Pale Ale, Timothy Taylors Landlord and Wye Valley Butty Bach on handpump and seven wines by the glass; background music. Dining room tables are nicely spaced so that you don't feel crowded, and the skittle alley doubles as a function room; they hold a lot of fun events such as beer, sausage, cider and cheese festivals. There are seats and tables under canopies on the heated terrace and in a sheltered garden. Sister pub is the Gloucester Old Spot in Coombe Hill.

Food is good and includes lunchtime doorstep sandwiches, ham hock terrine with dijonnaise, queen scallop, king prawn and crab mornay with pickled samphire, steak burger with toppings and skin-on fries, wild and exotic mushroom and spinach lasagne, crispy pork belly, braised cheeks and chorizo with dauphinoise potatoes, duck breast and leg confit croquette with orange and star anise sauce, and puddings. *Benchmark main dish: beef bourguignon with mustard puff pastry £16.50. Two-course evening meal £23.00.*

Free house ~ Licensees Simon and Kate Daws ~ Real ale ~ Open 11-11; 12-10.30 Sun ~ Bar food 12-2, 6-9; 12-8 Sun · Restaurant ~ Children welcome in dining room and before 8pm in bar ~ Wi-fi *Recommended by Andy Dolan, Victor Sumner, Roger and Donna Huggins, Peter Young, Ian Herdman, Alf and Sally Garner, Charlie Stevens*

CHIPPING CAMPDEN
SP1539 Map 4
Eight Bells ¶ ⌖
(01386) 840371 – www.eightbellsinn.co.uk
Church Street (one-way – entrance off B4035); GL55 6JG

Lovely historic inn with massive timbers and beams, log fires, quite a choice of bar food, real ales and seats in a large terraced garden; bedrooms

There are log fires in up to three restored stone fireplaces, which makes the candlelit bars here especially cosy in winter. Also, heavy oak beams, massive timber supports, stripped-stone walls, cushioned pews, sofas and solid dark wood furniture on broad flagstones, and a cheerful, bustling atmosphere. A glass panel in the dining room floor reveals the passage from the church by which Roman Catholic priests escaped the Roundheads during the Civil War. Hook Norton Hooky, Goffs Jouster, Purity Pure UBU and Wye Valley HPA on handpump from the fine oak bar counter, seven wines by the glass and two farm ciders; background music and board games. There's a large terraced garden with plenty of seats, and striking views of the almshouses and church. If you stay in the attractive and comfortable bedrooms (breakfasts are highly regarded), you could then take the Cotswold Way, which leads to Bath.

As well as lunchtime sandwiches (not Sunday), the well liked food includes pork and chorizo meatballs on linguine with a tomato and basil sauce, salt and pepper-battered calamari with saffron aioli, mushroom stroganoff, chicken, asparagus and ham pie, greek-style lamb burger with tzatziki and garlic and rosemary fries, slow-pulled pork with sweet potato chips and coleslaw, red thai-style mussels in coconut cream, and puddings such as white chocolate cheesecake with raspberry coulis and mango pannacotta with red berry compote. *Benchmark main dish: beer-battered fish and chips £13.95. Two-course evening meal £20.00.*

Free house ~ Licensee Neil Hargreaves ~ Real ale ~ Open 12-11 (10.30 Sun) ~ Bar food 12-2, 6.30-9; 12-2.30, 6.30-9.30 Fri, Sat; 12-3, 6-9 Sun ~ Restaurant ~ Well behaved children welcome in dining room but not in bar after 7pm; must be over 6 in bedrooms ~ Dogs allowed in bar ~ Wi-fi ~ Bedrooms: £75/£99 *Recommended by Victoria and James Sargeant, Guy Vowles, Ivy and George Goodwill, Lorna and Jack Mulgrave*

CIRENCESTER
SP0202 Map 4

Fleece ⌂

(01285) 658507 ~ www.thefleececirencester.co.uk

Market Place; GL7 2NZ

Carefully renovated inn with various bars and lounges, enjoyable food and drink and seats on terrace; character bedrooms

Being at the centre of a bustling town, it's useful that this historic pub is open throughout the day – customers pop in and out all the time. The various bars, lounges and airy dining areas differ in style: wheelback and mate's chairs and high bar stools and tables around the counter, wicker tub and high-backed yellow or orange dining chairs around an assortment of wooden tables, shelves of glassware and pottery, and french windows that open on to the terrace where there are white metal tables and chairs under parasols. Throughout, there are bare floorboards, contemporary pale paintwork, plenty of prints and fresh flowers and good lighting; background music. Efficient, courteous staff serve Thwaites Original and Wainwright and guests from Cotswold Lion and Flying Monk on handpump, several wines by the glass and good coffees and teas. The comfortable, attractive and well equipped bedrooms (some with much character) make a good base for exploring the surrounding countryside; breakfasts are hearty.

Pleasing food includes sandwiches, smoked trout pâté, crispy duck pancakes with cucumber, spring onion and hoisin sauce, various platters, sweet potato, red pepper and coconut gnocchi, chicken or beef burger with toppings and fries, cumberland sausages with balsamic shallots and grain mustard jus, pepper-crusted salmon steak with whisky cream, 10oz rib-eye steak with trimmings and thick chips, and puddings such as chocolate brownie with peanut butter ice-cream and chocolate sauce and rhubarb three-ways (jelly, sorbet, poached) with meringue. *Benchmark main dish: chicken and chorizo pie £13.50. Two-course evening meal £19.00.*

Thwaites ~ Manager Phil Mehrtens ~ Real ale ~ Open 11-11 (10.30 Sun) ~ Bar food 7am-9.30pm ~ Restaurant ~ Children welcome ~ Dogs allowed in bar and bedrooms ~ Wi-fi ~ Bedrooms: £108/£116 *Recommended by Giles and Annie Francis, R T and J C Moggridge, Guy Vowles, Martin and Joanne Sharp, Patricia Healey, Lindy Andrews, Michael Sargent*

COOMBE HILL
SO8926 Map 4

Gloucester Old Spot ★ ◀

(01242) 680321 ~ www.thegloucesteroldspot.co.uk

Exit M5 junction 11 and use satnav GL51 9SY; access from junction 10 is restricted; GL51 9SY

Interestingly furnished country pub with much character, good ales and likeable food

Although this bustling and cheerful place is just outside Cheltenham, it has the feel of a proper country local. The quarry-tiled beamed bar has chapel chairs and other seats around assorted tables (including one in a bow-windowed alcove) and opens into a lighter, partly panelled area with cushioned settles and stripped kitchen tables. Purity Mad Goose, Timothy Taylors Boltmaker and Wye Valley Butty Bach on handpump, eight decent wines by the glass and farm cider and perry – all served by young, friendly staff. Decoration is in unobtrusive good taste, with winter log fires. A handsome separate dining room has similar country furniture, high stripped-brick walls, dark flagstones and candlelight. Outside, there are chunky benches and tables under parasols on a terrace, with some oak barrel tables on brickwork and pretty flowers in vintage buckets and baskets; heaters for cooler weather. It can get rather packed on race days. Sister pub is the Royal Oak in Prestbury, near Cheltenham.

Reliably good food includes sandwiches, twice-baked cheese soufflé with creamed leeks, pigeon breast with haggis beignet, poached egg and whisky and juniper dressing, shepherd's pie with Guinness and rosemary, pulled pork burger with toppings, red cabbage slaw and chips, lamb shoulder with merguez sausage, crushed swede and rosemary jus, pollack with a lemon and herb crust and white bean and smoked pork belly cassoulet, and puddings. *Benchmark main dish: rare-breed pork fillet with shoulder and black pudding terrine and madeira sauce £15.95. Two-course evening meal £22.00.*

Free house ~ Licensees Simon Daws and Hayley Flaxman ~ Real ale ~ Open 10.30am-10pm (11pm Fri, Sat) ~ Bar food 12-2, 6-9; 12-8 Sun ~ Restaurant ~ Children welcome until 8pm ~ Dogs allowed in bar ~ Wi-fi *Recommended by Mike and Mary Carter, Revd Michael Vockins, Simon Burne, Dave Braisted, Chloe and Tim Hodge*

COWLEY
Green Dragon 🏵 🛏

SO9714 Map 4

(01242) 870271 – www.green-dragon-inn.co.uk

Off A435 S of Cheltenham at Elkstone, Cockleford sign; OS Sheet 163 map reference 970142; GL53 9NW

17th-c inn with character bars, separate restaurant, popular food, real ales and seats on terraces; bedrooms

When it opened in 1643, this attractive stone-fronted pub was a cider house with its own orchard on the site of what's now the car park. Friendly staff still keep a good range of drinks – Hook Norton Old Hooky, Sharps Doom Bar and a guest such as Butcombe Bitter on handpump, ten wines by the glass, ten gins and ten malt whiskies. There's a good mix of both locals and visitors and the two beamed bars have plenty of character and a cosy, nicely old-fashioned feel; big flagstones, wooden floorboards, candlelit tables and winter log fires in two stone fireplaces. The furniture and the bar itself in the upper Mouse Bar were made by Robert Thompson – little mice run over the hand-carved tables, chairs and mantelpiece; there's also a small upstairs restaurant. Background music and a separate skittle alley. Bedrooms are comfortable and breakfasts generous. There are plenty of seats outside on terraces and this is good walking country. Wheelchair access and disabled loos.

High quality food includes sandwiches, avocado and prawns, chicken caesar salad, wild boar and chorizo pie with stilton cream sauce, roasted mediterranean vegetable risotto, cod steak with bacon lardons and wilted leeks, steak and kidney pudding, minted lamb steak with redcurrant gravy, pork escalope with apple and cider chutney, and puddings such as crème brûlée and banoffi pie. *Benchmark main dish: pulled ham hock with apple and mustard cream sauce £15.95. Two-course evening meal £23.00.*

Buccaneer Holdings ~ Managers Simon and Nicky Haly ~ Real ale ~ Open 11-11; 12-10.30 Sun ~ Bar food 12-2.30 (3 Sat), 6-10; 12-3.30, 6-9 Sun ~ Restaurant ~ Children welcome ~ Dogs allowed in bar ~ Wi-fi ~ Bedrooms: £70/£95 *Recommended by Mrs Zara Elliott, Chris and Angela Buckell, Simon Collett-Jones, Guy Vowles, Peter Young, Dr A J and Mrs B A Tompsett, Shona and Jimmy McDuff*

DIDMARTON
ST8187 Map 2

Kings Arms ♀ ⇐

(01454) 238245 – www.kingsarmsdidmarton.co.uk

A433 Tetbury road; GL9 1DT

Bustling pub with enjoyable food, a good choice of drinks, and pleasant back garden; bedrooms

With Westonbirt Arboretum nearby, this 17th-c former coaching inn is just the place for lunch. Several knocked-through beamed bar rooms work their way around a big central counter (where there are high chairs and stools against the counter), with grey-painted half-panelling, armchairs by a log fire in a stone fireplace, settles and window seats with scatter cushions, bare boards here and flagstones and rugs there, and a mix of farmhouse chairs and benches around wooden tables of all shapes and sizes. Church candles on shelves or in lanterns, antlers, prints and fresh flowers create interest; the jack russell is called Spoof. There's also a restaurant with another open fire. Bath Gem, Flying Monk Elmers and Wychwood Hobgoblin on handpump, and good wines by the glass; darts. There are plenty of seats and picnic-sets in the pleasant back garden. Bedrooms are individually furnished and comfortable and they also have self-catering cottages in a converted barn and stable block.

Using local game and seasonal produce, the well presented food includes lunchtime sandwiches, hot smoked salmon with beetroot and fennel salad and goats curd, chicken livers with spicy nut salad, wild mushroom arancini with parsley pesto, burger with toppings and skinny fries, duo of pork with spiced apple purée and cider jus, halibut with chorizo cassoulet, duck breast with jerusalem artichoke and spiced plums, and puddings such as tiramisu crème brûlée with tonka bean biscotti and salted caramel fondant with chocolate and pistachio parfait. *Benchmark main dish: burger with toppings and chips £14.25. Two-course evening meal £23.50.*

Free house ~ Licensee Mark Birchall ~ Real ale ~ Open 12-11 (10.30 Sun) ~ Bar food 12-2.30 (3 Sat), 6-9.30; 12-3, 6-8 Sun ~ Restaurant ~ Children welcome ~ Dogs allowed in bar and bedrooms ~ Wi-fi ~ Bedrooms: £60/£105 *Recommended by Harvey Brown, Geoffrey Sutton, Ruth May, Guy Vowles, Trish and Karl Soloman, Jill and Hugh Bennett*

DURSLEY
ST7598 Map 4

Old Spot ◀

(01453) 542870 – www.oldspotinn.co.uk

Hill Road; by bus station; GL11 4JQ

Unassuming and cheery town pub with a fine range of ales, regular beer festivals and good value lunchtime food

Cheerful, enthusiastic staff keep a fine range of drinks here. The seven real ales on handpump might include Uley Old Ric, with guests such as Bass, Harviestoun Schiehallion, Otter Bright, St Austell Trelawny, Tileys Pig Whisperer and Wye Valley HPA; they also hold two annual beer festivals and there are 30 malt whiskies, three farm ciders, half a dozen wines by the glass and artisan spirits. The front door opens into a deep-pink small room with stools on shiny quarry tiles beside a pine-boarded bar counter and old enamel beer signs on the walls and ceiling. A small room leads off on the left and the little wood-floored room to the right has a stone fireplace; there's plenty of porcine paraphernalia throughout. A step goes down to a cosy Victorian tiled snug and (to the right) a meeting room – which doubles as a family room. The heated and covered garden has benches and parasols. Wheelchair access but no disabled loos.

🍴 Decent lunchtime-only food includes sandwiches (the soup and sandwich deal is popular), chicken liver and sloe gin parfait with caramelised onion marmalade, prawn cocktail, lamb tagine with fruity couscous, vegetable and cream cheese tartlet, spicy chilli con carne, sea bass fillets with tomato ratatouille and watercress sauce, and puddings such as orange marmalade bread and butter pudding and chocolate and walnut tart with raspberry coulis. *Benchmark main dish: sausages with parsley mash and onion gravy £9.50.*

Free house ~ Licensee Ellie Sainty ~ Real ale ~ Open 12-11 ~ Bar food 12-3; 12-4 Sun ~ Children in family room ~ Dogs allowed in bar ~ Wi-fi *Recommended by Monty Green, Chris and Angela Buckell, Steve Crick, Angela and Steve Heard, Elisabeth and Bill Humphries, Maria and Henry Lazenby*

EASTINGTON
Old Badger 🍺

SO7705 Map 4

(01453) 822892 – www.oldbadgerinn.co.uk
Alkerton Road, a mile from M5 junction 13; GL10 3AT

Friendly, traditionally furnished pub with plenty to look at, five real ales, tasty food and seats in attractive garden

If you fancy a break from the M5, head for this busy, old-fashioned and friendly pub. The split-level connected rooms have an informal, easy-going feel and feature two open fires and traditional furnishings such as built-in planked and cushioned wall seats, settles and farmhouse chairs around all sorts of tables, quarry tiles and floorboards. There are stone bottles, bookshelves, breweriana on red or cream walls and even a stuffed badger. Bath Golden Hare, St Austell Trelawny, Tileys Pig Whisperer, Wickwar Falling Star and a quickly changing guest on handpump alongside ten wines by the glass, a dozen malt whiskies and farm cider; they hold beer and cider festivals with local musicians and brewery trips. The nicely landscaped garden has benches and picnic-sets on a terrace, a lawn and under a covered gazebo; the flowering tubs and window boxes are pretty. Wheelchair access to top bar/dining area only; disabled loos are shared with baby-changing facilities.

🍴 Decent pubby food includes a range of tapas, crayfish in lime and chilli mayonnaise, ham and egg, butternut squash with chilli, feta, pumpkin, butter beans and yoghurt dressing, tagliatelle with ragoût of lamb, lemon and herb crumb, burger with toppings, peppers and chips, slow-cooked beef with fried liver, puy lentils and smoked bacon, scallops with roasted cauliflower, pea purée, crispy bacon and garlic cream, and puddings such as caramelised orange pannacotta and dark chocolate fondant with caramel salted ice-cream. *Benchmark main dish: beer-battered fish and chips £12.00. Two-course evening meal £17.00.*

Free house ~ Manager Julie Gilborson ~ Real ale ~ Open 12-11 ~ Bar food 12-2.30, 6-9; 12-3 Sun ~ Children welcome away from bar area ~ Dogs welcome ~ Wi-fi ~ Live music monthly Sat *Recommended by David Houlihan, Mike and Mary Carter, Guy Vowles, Trish and Karl Soloman*

EBRINGTON
Ebrington Arms 🎯 ♀ 🍺 🛏

SP1839 Map 4

(01386) 593223 – www.theebringtonarms.co.uk
Off B4035 E of Chipping Campden or A429 N of Moreton-in-Marsh; GL55 6NH

Nice old pub in attractive village with own-brewed ales, thoughtful choice of food and seats in garden; bedrooms

We've been getting warm praise from our readers for the restoration work here and for the hard-working licensees who've created an easy-going atmosphere in the 17th-c character bar and dining room. There are beams, a log fire in a fine inglenook fireplace, a woodburning stove in a second fireplace (the ironwork is original) with armchairs beside it, an airy bow window seat, ladderback and farmhouse chairs and cushioned settles on old flagstones or bare boards, and fresh flowers and church candles. They keep three own-brewed Yubberton ales (Yubby Bitter, Yubby Goldie and the seasonal Yawnie Bitter) on handpump plus local guests such as North Cotswold Moreton Mild, Otter Bitter and Wye Valley Dorothy Goodbodys Wholesome Stout, good wines from a thoughtful list (with notes), nine gins, farm cider and winter mulled wine. Board games, bagatelle, shut the box and dominoes. An arched stone wall shelters seats and tables under parasols on the terrace and picnic-sets line the lawn. The well equipped, country-style bedrooms are very comfortable and breakfasts are good. The three venerable oak trees after which this old stone pub was once named still stand outside by the village green. Hidcote (National Trust) is nearby, as are Kiftsgate Court Gardens. This is sister pub to the Killingworth Castle in Wootton (see Oxfordshire).

The seasonal menu with interesting specials and pubby choices includes lunchtime sandwiches, rabbit leg ballotine with carrot jam, pistachio granola and pickled onions, salmon with cured beetroot, pickled fennel, orange and seaweed toast, vegetable pithivier with walnut and truffle dressing, burger with toppings and chips, duck breast and liver with celeriac, red wine-braised salsify and prune ketchup, seaweed-crusted cod brandade with mussel cream and sea vegetables, and puddings such as coconut pannacotta with rhubarb and lemonade parfait with citrus curd, puff pastry and meringue; they also offer a two-course set menu. *Benchmark main dish: pie of the day £14.00. Two-course evening meal £20.00.*

Free house ~ Licensees Claire and Jim Alexander ~ Real ale ~ Open 9am-11pm ~ Bar food 12-2.30, 6-9 (9.30 Fri, Sat); 12-3.30, 6-8.30 Sun; light snacks in the afternoon ~ Restaurant ~ Children welcome ~ Dogs allowed in bar ~ Wi-fi ~ Folk night first Mon of month ~ Bedrooms: £90/£99 *Recommended by Richard Tilbrook, Grace Ford, Mike and Sarah Abbot, Celia and Geoff Clay, Nicholas and Maddy Trainer, Frances Parsons*

FAIRFORD   SP1501 Map 4

Bull 🐂 🛏

(01285) 712535 – www.thebullhotelfairford.co.uk
Market Place; GL7 4AA

Lovely renovation of old coaching inn, character bars and dining rooms with interesting furnishings, good drinks and food; bedrooms

From the outside, this handsome stone former coaching inn looks just as it has done for hundreds of years. Inside, though, all has changed. The refurbishments have been done with great care and thought to keep the historic character and original features such as beams and timbering, while blending in new strong-coloured paintwork with old and new seating, using fine original fabrics and adding huge mirrors and reclaimed floorboards. The entrance leads directly into a left-hand sitting area with a vintage sofa and armchairs in front of a stone fireplace; opposite are two bar rooms with chapel chairs and settles around wooden tables, another open fire (with a gigantic bull's head above it) and steps that lead up to a light and airy room with purple and lime green velvet armchairs. Arkells 3B, Moonlight and Wiltshire Gold and a guest ale on handpump and 21 good wines by the glass (including sparkling ones). One dining room has nice old-fashioned chairs and window seats with scatter cushions, the other has walls made from reclaimed horseboxes and long banquettes. Lighting ranges from table lamps in lovely colours to antiqued iron pendants and chandeliers. The only downside is that there's no garden or courtyard and parking is on the street. As we went to press, the bedrooms were still being renovated. It is really worth visiting the church, which has Britain's only intact set of medieval stained-glass windows.

⬤ Rewarding food includes breakfasts (8-10am), antipasti plates such as chicken livers and chorizo with aged balsamic on crostini, hot seafood salad, and carpaccio of beef with fennel, rocket and pecorino – plus sandwiches, pizzas, open ravioli of crab, salt cod, chilli and coconut, rabbit, tarragon and chicken pie, beer-battered fish and skinny fries, calves liver and pancetta with cannellini beans and spinach, and puddings such as chocolate fondant with basil sorbet and raspberry panettone bread and butter pudding. *Benchmark main dish: escalope of veal saltimbocca with spinach, lemon and capers £17.00. Two-course evening meal £25.00.*

Arkells ~ Tenant Sebastian Snow ~ Real ale ~ Open 10am-11pm ~ Bar food 12-3, 6-9.30 (10 Fri, Sat); 12-3, 6-8.30 Sun ~ Restaurant ~ Children welcome ~ Dogs allowed in bar ~ Wi-fi ~ Bedrooms: £75/£120 *Recommended by Liz Bell, Jill and Dick Archer, Chris Stevenson, Caroline and Peter Bryant, Hilary Gardiner*

GLOUCESTER
Café René ◖

SO8318 Map 4

(01452) 309340 – www.caferene.co.uk

Southgate Street; best to park in Blackfriars car park (Ladybellegate Street) and walk through passageway – pub entrance is just across road; GL1 1TP

Interestingly placed bar with fair value food all day, and good choice of drinks

To get to this unusual 17th-c bar you walk down a flagstoned passageway beside the partly Norman church of St Mary de Crypt. There's some stripped brick and timbering plus an internal floodlit well with water trickling down into its depths, and a very subterranean feel – black beams, dim lighting and no windows. The long bar counter is made of dozens of big casks, and they keep three changing real ales tapped from the cask such as Arbor The Devil Made Me Brew It, Crafted Brewing The Revolution and Wickwar Falling Star, plus farm ciders and a good choice of wines by the glass (decoration consists mainly of great banks of empty wine bottles). Service remains friendly and efficient even when really pushed. One antique panelled high-backed settle joins the usual pub tables and wheelback chairs on carpet, and there's a sizeable dining area on the right. Well reproduced background music, a silenced games machine and big-screen TV (only for rugby). There's regular live music and they hold a popular rhythm and blues festival at the end of July. There are plenty of picnic-sets under parasols out by the churchyard.

🍴 Tasty all-day food includes sandwiches, prawn cocktail, garlic mushrooms in white wine and cream, trio of local sausages with wholegrain mustard mash and red onion gravy, sweet potato, goats cheese and spinach pie, gammon with egg and pineapple, beer-battered cod and chips, whole rack of baby back ribs in barbecue sauce, chargrilled steaks or mixed grill with a choice of sauces or butters, and puddings such as a cheesecake of the day and lemon tart. *Benchmark main dish: chargrilled burgers with toppings £9.95. Two-course evening meal £14.00.*

Free house ~ Licensee Paul Soden ~ Real ale ~ Open 11am-midnight (later Fri, Sat) ~ Bar food 12-10 ~ Restaurant ~ Wi-fi ~ Live music Weds and Fri evenings
Recommended by Julian Richardson, Daphne and Robert Staples, Maddie Purvis

GUITING POWER
Hollow Bottom
SP0924 Map 4

(01451) 850392 – www.hollowbottom.com

Village signposted off B4068 SW of Stow-on-the-Wold (still called A436 on many maps); GL54 5UX

Popular old pub with a good bustling atmosphere, real ales and enjoyable food; bedrooms

There's always a really good mix of customers (many from the racing fraternity) in this snug old stone cottage – all of whom are made to feel genuinely welcomed by the hard-working licensees and their helpful staff. The opened-up beamed bar has horse-racing pictures, wooden flooring, a woodburner in an unusual pillared stone fireplace, Greene King IPA and Old Speckled Hen and Ruddles County on handpump, several wines by the glass and 15 malt whiskies. The dining areas have exposed stone walls, fine old flagstones, built-in cushioned wall seats and painted farmhouse and wooden dining chairs around a medley of tables; background music and TV for racing. At the back, a decked area has all sorts of seats and tables, heaters, a firepit, a thatched outdoor bar and views towards sloping fields; good nearby walks. Bedrooms are comfortable (three are in the pub and two in an annexe; one is suitable for disabled guests).

Well liked food includes wraps, tiger prawns in garlic and chilli butter, duck liver pâté with redcurrant sauce, sharing boards, thin crispy pizzas, ham and free-range eggs, a vegetarian choice of the day, lightly battered chicken strips with slaw, rustic fries and sweet chilli sauce, local pheasant in port and redcurrant sauce with roasted root vegetables, calves liver with bacon, mash and gravy, steak and kidney pie, and puddings such as apple and blackberry crumble with custard and banoffi pie. *Benchmark main dish: chicken with white wine and thyme cream sauce, chickpea and chorizo mash and mangetout £16.00. Two-course evening meal £20.00.*

Free house ~ Licensees Hugh Kelly and Charles Pettigrew ~ Real ale ~ Open 9am-midnight ~ Bar food all day ~ Restaurant ~ Children welcome ~ Dogs allowed in bar ~ Wi-fi ~ Bedrooms: /£90 *Recommended by Michael Sargent, Nick Sharpe, Phoebe Peacock, Emma Scofield*

KILCOT
Kilcot Inn
SO6925 Map 4

(01989) 720707 – www.kilcotinn.com

2.3 miles from M50 junction 3; B4221 towards Newent; GL18 1NG

Attractively reworked small country inn, kind staff, enjoyable local food and drink; bedrooms

The M50 is just a couple of miles away, so this well run, friendly pub is a popular place for a break. The open-plan bar and dining areas have stripped beams, bare boards and dark flagstones, sunny bay-window seats, homely armchairs by one of the two warm woodburning stoves, tables with padded dining chairs and daily papers. Stools line the brick counter where the hard-working landlord and his courteous staff serve Marstons EPA and Wyc Valley Butty Bach on handpump, four draught ciders and perry (with more by the bottle), 20 malt whiskies, local wine and organic fruit juice; TV and maybe background music. The outside dining area has tables and chunky benches under thatched parasols next to a rose garden and there's also a children's play area; at the front are picnic-sets under cocktail-style parasols. Bedrooms are light, airy and comfortable and the breakfasts are praiseworthy. There's a smart shed for bicycle storage.

Well liked food uses produce grown within a 30-mile radius and includes lunchtime sandwiches, rabbit and wild boar terrine with pineapple pickle, scotch egg with prune and apple chutney, root vegetable and halloumi pie with olive oil mash, burger with toppings, garlic mayonnaise and skinny fries, cider-battered fish of the day with triple-cooked chips, hogget shoulder with creamed cauliflower and lyonnaise potatoes, chicken breast with pasta, mushrooms, cream and truffle oil, and puddings such as dark chocolate brownie and white chocolate and macadamia nut blondie with chocolate sauce and a seasonal crumble with custard. *Benchmark main dish: duck hash £12.50. Two-course evening meal £20.00.*

Free house ~ Licensee Mark Lawrence ~ Real ale ~ Open 11-11; 11-9 Sun; 11-3 Sun in winter ~ Bar food 12-2.30, 6-9; 12-3 Sun in winter ~ Restaurant ~ Children welcome ~ Dogs allowed in bar ~ Wi-fi ~ Bedrooms: £85/£95 *Recommended by Mike and Mary Carter, Nigel and Sue Foster, Richard Kennell, Dave Braisted, CSmith, Bridget and Peter Gregson*

LOWER SLAUGHTER
Slaughters Country Inn

SP1622 Map 4

(01451) 822143 – www.theslaughtersinn.co.uk
Village signposted off A429 Bourton-on-the-Water to Stow-on-the-Wold; GL54 2HS

Comfortable streamside inn with enticing food, real ales, attractive dining bar and fine grounds; smart bedrooms

Before this became a lovely hotel, it was a crammer for Eton College. A handsome stone building in an attractive village, it's set on the River Eye and the spacious grounds have tables and chairs under parasols on terraces and lawns that sweep down to the water. The spreading bar has a good mix of locals and visitors in several low-beamed linked rooms, plus well spaced tables on polished flagstones and a variety of seats from simple chairs to soft sofas. Log fires, medieval-motif curtains for mullioned windows, shelves of board games, a few carefully placed landscape pictures or stuffed fish on cream or puce walls create an air of understated refinement – and what really sets the style of the place is the thoroughly professional and efficient service. Brakspears Bitter and Wychwood Hobgoblin on handpump, and a dozen good wines by the glass. The smart evening restaurant looks over the lawn and the sheep pasture beyond. Bedrooms are comfortable and stylish and make a good base for exploring the area; some are in the main house, some across the courtyard.

Beautifully presented food includes lunchtime sandwiches, braised ham hock with cannellini bean stew and a poached egg, smoked mackerel croquette with pickled red cabbage and sour apple purée, charred seasonal vegetables with spiced aubergine and salsa verde, blade of beef with roasted onions, field mushroom, bacon and horseradish mash, cod fillet with parmesan gnocchi, cauliflower, pancetta and butter beans, cajun half chicken with aioli, corn on the cob and fries, and puddings such as dark chocolate crémeux with cherry sorbet and vanilla crème brûlée with prune compote. *Benchmark main dish: beer-battered fish and chips £14.50. Two-course evening meal £28.00.*

Free house ~ Licensee Stuart Hodges ~ Real ale ~ Open 12-midnight (11 Sun) ~ Bar food 12-3, 6.30-9; afternoon tea 3-5.30 ~ Restaurant ~ Children welcome ~ Dogs allowed in bar and bedrooms ~ Wi-fi ~ Bedrooms: /£190 *Recommended by Nigel and Sue Foster, George Atkinson, Bernard Stradling, Tracey and Stephen Groves, Martin and Sue Neville, Robin and Anne Triggs, Monica and Steph Evans*

The star-on-a-plate award, ⭐, distinguishes pubs where the food is of exceptional quality. The knife-and-fork symbol just means the pub serves food.

NAILSWORTH
Weighbridge

ST8699 Map 4

(01453) 832520 – www.weighbridgeinn.co.uk

B4014 towards Tetbury; GL6 9AL

Bustling pub with cosy old-fashioned bar rooms, a fine choice of drinks and food, friendly service and sheltered garden

This is a proper traditional pub with local ales and a warm welcome for regulars, families, walkers and their dogs. The relaxed bar has three cosily old-fashioned rooms with open fires, stripped-stone walls and antique settles, country chairs and window seats. The black-beamed ceiling of the lounge bar is thickly festooned with black ironware – sheep shears, gin traps, lamps and a large collection of keys, many from the old Longfords Mill opposite the pub. Upstairs is a raftered hayloft with an engaging mix of rustic tables. No noisy games machines or background music. Uley Old Spot, Wadworths 6X and a couple of guest beers such as Bath Gem and Great Western Maiden Voyage on handpump, 18 wines (and champagne and prosecco) by the glass, farm cider, 12 malt whiskies and 20 gins. A sheltered landscaped garden at the back has picnic-sets under umbrellas. Good disabled access and facilities.

Their famous two-in-one pies (also available for home baking) come in a divided bowl – one half contains the filling of your choice (perhaps steak, kidney and stout, salmon in cream sauce, or root vegetables with beans and pulses in tomato sauce) with a pastry topping, the other half with home-made cauliflower cheese (or broccoli mornay or root vegetables). Also, lunchtime baguettes, prawn cocktail, creamy mushrooms on toast, burger with toppings, coleslaw and fries, aubergine moussaka, slow-braised lamb shank with red wine and mint sauce, and puddings such as fruit crumble and black forest trifle. *Benchmark main dish: two-in-one pies £12.50. Two-course evening meal £18.00.*

Free house ~ Licensee Mary Parsons ~ Real ale ~ Open 12-10.30 (11 Fri, Sat); closes 10pm Mon-Thurs in winter ~ Bar food 12-9 ~ Restaurant ~ Children welcome in upstairs dining room ~ Dogs welcome *Recommended by Colin and Daniel Gibbs, Sandra Morgan, Tom and Ruth Rees, Jim and Sue James*

NETHER WESTCOTE
Feathered Nest ★

SP2220 Map 4

(01993) 833030 – www.thefeatherednestinn.co.uk

Off A424 Burford to Stow-on-the-Wold; OX7 6SD

Caring service, a happy atmosphere, attractive surroundings and exceptional food and drink; lovely bedrooms

This is a special place for a weekend stay with individually decorated, well equipped rooms and delicious breakfasts; our readers enjoy their visits very much. For many customers, of course, it's the beautifully presented food that remains the biggest draw – though it would be a shame to miss out on the companionable bar. This is cosy and friendly with Prescott Hill Climb and a guest beer on handpump and 22 wines by the glass from an impressive list; service is exemplary. Softly lit, the largely stripped-stone bar has real saddles as bar stools (some of the country's best racehorse trainers live locally), a carved settle among other carefully chosen seats, dark flagstones and low beams. This opens into an ochre-walled high-raftered room with deeply comfortable sofas by a vast log fire; background music and TV. A couple of attractively decorated dining rooms, both on two levels, have a pleasing mix of antique tables in varying sizes, and a lively, up-to-date atmosphere. A flagstoned terrace and heated shelter have teak tables and wicker armchairs, and a spreading lawn bounded by floodlit trees is set with groups of rustic seats, with the Evenlode Valley beyond.

Creative food using the best local, seasonal produce includes pollack with passion fruit, chilli, pawpaw and pisco, scotch egg with black pudding, piccalilli and apple, chicken with duck liver, morels, raviolo and wild garlic, stone bass with fennel, potato, taramasalata and lemon, turbot with mussels, monk's beard, sea kale and parsley root, and puddings such as crème caramel with salt-baked pineapple and coconut and sticky toffee pudding with lemon curd, pecans and clotted cream; they also offer a two- and three-course set lunch. *Benchmark main dish: brill with baby artichokes, Jersey Royals and a lemongrass and samphire foam £35.00. Two-course evening meal £55.00.*

Free house ~ Licensee Amanda Timmer ~ Real ale ~ Open 11-11 (7.30 Sun); closed Mon except bank holidays ~ Bar food 12-2.30, 6-9.30; 12-3.30 Sun ~ Restaurant ~ Children welcome ~ Dogs allowed in bar ~ Wi-fi ~ Bedrooms: £235/£285 *Recommended by Bernard Stradling, Caroline and Oliver Sterling, Daphne and Robert Staples, Clive and Fran Dutson, Victoria and James Sargeant, David and Leone Lawson*

NEWLAND
Ostrich ⊙ ♀ ◖

SO5509   Map 4

(01594) 833260 – www.theostrichinn.com

Off B4228 in Coleford; or can be reached from the A466 in Redbrook, by turn-off at the England–Wales border – keep bearing right; GL16 8NP

Super range of beers in welcoming country pub, with spacious bar, open fire and good interesting food

The charming, warmly friendly landlady and her helpful staff keep a fine choice of real ales on handpump here, such as Butcombe Gold, Cotswold Lion Shepherds Delight, Kingstone Abbey Ale, Otter Bright, RCH Pitchfork, Timothy Taylors Landlord and Wye Valley Butty Bach and HPA; also, several wines by the glass, a couple of farm ciders and a good range of soft drinks. The pub is mostly 16th-c and the low-ceilinged bar is spacious but cosily traditional, with a chatty, relaxed atmosphere, a roaring log fire, creaky floors, window shutters, candles in bottles on the tables, miners' lamps on uneven walls, and comfortable furnishings that include cushioned window seats, wall settles and rod-backed country kitchen chairs. Newspapers to read, perhaps quiet background jazz and board games. The walled garden has seats and tables, with more out in front, and the pub is popular with walkers and their dogs. The church opposite, known as the Cathedral of the Forest for its unusual size, is worth a visit.

Highly enjoyable food includes oak-roasted salmon tart with dill mustard cream, rabbit rillettes with rosemary jelly, wild mushroom (ceps, chanterelle, shiitake and oyster) risotto with crispy shallots and truffle oil, steak in ale pie, sausages with onion gravy and dauphinoise potatoes, pork ribs in a tangy sauce with garlic bread, rack of lamb with minted pea cream and crispy diced potatoes, fillet steak and pâté on a rosemary focaccia croûte with port and thyme jus, and puddings. *Benchmark main dish: salmon and spinach fishcakes with parsley sauce £13.50. Two-course evening meal £20.00.*

Free house ~ Licensee Kathryn Horton ~ Real ale ~ Open 12-3, 6.30-11.30; 12-3.30, 6-midnight Sat; 12-4, 6.30-11.30 Sun ~ Bar food 12-2.30, 6.30 (6 Sat)-9.30 ~ Restaurant ~ Children welcome ~ Dogs allowed in bar *Recommended by Amaya Arias-Garcia, Roger and Donna Huggins, Millie and Peter Downing, Julian Thorpe, Dr A J and Mrs B A Tompsett, Sean Cornforth, Chrissi Gower-Smith*

NORTH CERNEY

SP0208   Map 4

Bathurst Arms ♀ ⇔

(01285) 832150 – www.bathurstarms.co.uk

A435 Cirencester–Cheltenham; GL7 7BZ

Bustling inn with beamed bar, open fires, real ales and wines by the glass and tasty food; bedrooms

The heart of this handsome 17th-c inn remains the original beamed and panelled bar with its convivial atmosphere, flagstones, charming medley of old tables and chairs, old-fashioned window seats and a fireplace at each end – one is huge and houses an open woodburner. An oak-floored room off here has country tables and winged high-backed settles forming a few booths; background music and board games. The restaurant has another woodburning stove. Butcombe Bitter, North Cotswold Best and St Austell Tribute on handpump and ten good wines by the glass. The attractively landscaped garden has the River Chun running through it and plenty of seats; boules. The recently refurbished bedrooms are comfortable and well appointed and the hearty breakfasts are served in the bar. Cerney House Gardens are worth a visit and there are lots of surrounding walks in delightful countryside. Do visit the lovely church opposite.

Using locally sourced ingredients, the enjoyable food includes ciabattas, prawn and crayfish salad, chicken liver pâté with date chutney, wild mushroom and goats cheese risotto, home-baked ham and eggs, cumberland sausage and mash with onion gravy, burger with toppings and chips, lime sticky chicken, slow-roasted minted lamb shank on creamy mash with gravy, and puddings such as vanilla cheesecake and treacle sponge. *Benchmark main dish: pie of the day £11.95. Two-course evening meal £18.00.*

Free house ~ Licensees Rob and Mel Matthews ~ Real ale ~ Open 11-11; 12-10.30 (8 in winter) Sun ~ Bar food 12-2.30, 5.30-8.30; 12-8 (5 in winter) Sun ~ Restaurant ~ Children welcome ~ Dogs allowed in bar and bedrooms ~ Wi-fi ~ Bedrooms: £80 *Recommended by Dave Braisted, Giles and Annie Francis, James and Sylvia Hewitt, John and Claire Masters*

NORTHLEACH

SP1114   Map 4

Wheatsheaf ♀ ⇔

(01451) 860244 – www.cotswoldswheatsheaf.com

West End; the inn is on your left as you come in following the sign off A429, just SW of the junction with A40; GL54 3EZ

Attractive stone inn with contemporary food, real ales, candles, fresh flowers and a relaxed atmosphere; stylish bedrooms

After strolling around this lovely little town with its fine old market square, pop in here for a drink or a meal – they're open all day. The airy, big-windowed linked rooms have high ceilings, antique and contemporary artwork, church candles and fresh flowers, an appealing mix of dining chairs, big leather button-back settles and stools around wooden tables, flagstones in the central bar and wooden floors laid with turkish rugs in the dining rooms; also, three open fires. Black Sheep Best, Butcombe Bitter, Donnington On The Nose and Sharps Coastal on handpump, a dozen wines by the glass from a fantastic list of around 300 and local cider; background music, TV and board games. There are seats in the pretty back garden and they can arrange fishing on the River Coln. The comfortable bedrooms are individually styled and breakfasts are much enjoyed. Dogs are genuinely welcomed and they even keep a jar of pigs' ears behind the bar for them.

As well as serving breakfasts (8-10am), the high quality food includes pigeon and foie gras terrine with pickled pears, razor clams with monk's beard, chorizo and local cider, roasted romanesco with cauliflower purée, pine nuts and chilli, ray wing with brown butter and sea vegetables, calves liver with crispy bacon, sage and caramelised onion jus, steak frites with a choice of sauces, pot-roasted guinea fowl with bacon, chestnut mushrooms and savoy cabbage (for two people), and puddings such as blackberry crème brûlée and sticky date pudding with salted caramel sauce. *Benchmark main dish: chicken, mushroom and tarragon pie £15.00. Two-course evening meal £22.00.*

Free house ~ Licensees Sam and Georgina Pearman ~ Real ale ~ Open 8am-midnight ~ Bar food 12-2.30, 6-9 ~ Restaurant ~ Children welcome ~ Dogs welcome ~ Wi-fi ~ Bedrooms: /£155 *Recommended by Bernard Stradling, Giles and Annie Francis, Peter Young, Kevin, Cliff and Monica Swan, Simon Day*

 OAKRIDGE LYNCH   SO9103   Map 4
Butchers Arms
(01285) 760371 – www.butchersarmsoakridge.com
Off Eastcombe–Bisley Road E of Stroud; GL6 7NZ

Bustling country pub with nice old bars and dining room, real ales, food cooked by the landlady and seats in a big garden

Good walks and pretty countryside surround this attractive 18th-c pub. The beamed bar has a relaxed feel, an open fire in a big stone fireplace with large copper pans to each side, an attractive medley of chapel and other country chairs around tables of various sizes on wooden floorboards, and modern art on exposed stone walls. Stools line the central counter where they keep Wadworths 6X and IPA and a changing guest beer on handpump and several wines by the glass. The dining room is similarly furnished, with hunting prints and old photos on pale walls above a grey dado, a longcase clock and stone bottles on windowsills. The big garden with valley views is laid out with picnic-sets and other seats and tables. They also have a self-catering cottage next to the pub.

The landlady cooks the popular food: sandwiches, crab mornay, hot spicy chicken wings with blue cheese dip, home-cured ham and eggs, cottage pie, pizzas (also to take away), sausages and mustard mash with onion gravy, chicken kiev, red thai monkfish and prawn curry, irish steaks with a choice of three sauces, and puddings such as sticky toffee pudding with toffee sauce and lemon and vanilla set cream with berries. *Benchmark main dish: burger with toppings, coleslaw and fries £9.95. Two-course evening meal £19.00.*

Wadworths ~ Tenants Philip and Alison McLaughlin ~ Real ale ~ Open 12-3, 6-11; 12-11 Sat, Sun; may close earlier Sun in winter; closed Mon except bank holidays ~ Bar food 12-2, 6-9; not Sun evening, Mon ~ Restaurant ~ Children welcome ~ Dogs allowed in bar ~ Wi-fi
Recommended by Andrew Stone, Rob Anderson, Charles and Maddie Bishop, Chloe and Tim Hodge

 OLDBURY-ON-SEVERN   ST6092   Map 2
Anchor ♀ ◧ £
(01454) 413331 – www.anchorinnoldbury.co.uk
Village signposted from B4061; BS35 1QA

Friendly country pub with tasty bar food, a thoughtful range of drinks and a pretty garden with hanging baskets

In summer, the pretty garden here is a real bonus when the hanging baskets and window boxes look their best and seats are set underneath parasols or trees. Another big plus is the wide choice of drinks. Served by hard-working, attentive staff, there might be Bass, Butcombe Bitter and St Austell Trelawny on handpump, a dozen wines by the glass, three farm ciders and some 80 malt whiskies with helpful tasting notes. The neat lounge has black beams and stonework, cushioned window seats and a range of other wooden chairs, gate-leg tables, oil paintings of local scenes and a large log fire. The Village Bar has old and farming photographs on the walls, and there's a contemporary dining room towards the back of the building. You can walk from the pub to the River Severn and then along numerous footpaths and bridleways. Wheelchair access to the dining room and a disabled lavatory. Nearby St Arilda's church is interesting, set on an odd little knoll.

Likeable food includes sandwiches, scallops with pancetta, capers and thyme, wild boar terrine with apple and cider chutney, goats cheese and red onion marmalade filo parcel, goan fish curry, crispy pork belly and black pudding with mustard mash and creamed cabbage, duck breast with dauphinoise potatoes and port and cherry jus, and puddings such as rice pudding with rhubarb compote and chocolate brownie with salted caramel ice-cream and hot chocolate sauce; they also offer a two- and three-course set menu (not Fri evening, all day Sat or Sun lunch). *Benchmark main dish: steak and kidney pie with a stilton crust £11.95. Two-course evening meal £17.00.*

Free house ~ Licensees Michael Dowdeswell and Mark Sorrell ~ Real ale ~ Open 11.30-3, 6-10.30; 11.30-11 Fri, Sat; 12-10 Sun ~ Bar food 12-2 (2.30 Sat), 6-9; 12-3, 6-8 Sun ~ Restaurant ~ Children welcome ~ Dogs allowed in bar ~ Wi-fi ~ Bedrooms: £60/£85
Recommended by Chris and Angela Buckell, Amaya Arias-Garcia, Donald Allsopp, Margaret McDonald, Miranda and Jeff Davidson

SHEEPSCOMBE   SO8910   Map 4

Butchers Arms £

(01452) 812113 – www.butchers-arms.co.uk
Village signed off B4070 NE of Stroud; or A46 N of Painswick (but narrow lanes); GL6 7RH

Cheerful pub with open fire and woodburner, plenty to look at, several real ales and enjoyable food; fine views

Even on a cold, wet, midweek lunchtime, you'll find this place buzzing with happy customers. It's a proper country pub with a welcoming landlord, and the bar has farmhouse chairs and stools around scrubbed tables, two big bay windows with cushioned seats, low beams clad with horsebrasses, and flooring that's half parquet and half old quarry tiles. Also, delft shelves lined with china, brass and copper cups, lamps and blow torches (there's even a pitchfork) and walls decorated with hunting prints and photos of the village and surrounding area. Leading off here is a high-ceilinged room with exposed-stone walls hung with maps of local walks (there are many) and wheelback and mate's chairs around tables on bare boards. The more formal restaurant is carpeted and has an open log fire. Prescott Hill Climb and a couple of guests such as Exmoor Gold and Wye Valley HPA on handpump, ten wines by the glass and Weston's cider; daily papers, chess, cribbage and draughts. The view over the lovely steep beechwood valley is terrific, and the seats outside make the most of it. The area was apparently once a hunting ground for Henry VIII.

The comprehensive menu includes sandwiches, tempura-battered king prawns with sweet chilli dipping sauce, chicken liver pâté with plum and apple chutney, sharing platters, lasagne, local pork, apple and sage sausages with grain mustard mash and onion and thyme gravy, a pie of the week, vegetarian quiche of the day, salmon, cod and smoked haddock fishcakes with lemon mayonnaise, and puddings. *Benchmark main dish: burger with toppings, coleslaw and chips £11.50. Two-course evening meal £21.00.*

Free house ~ Licensees Mark and Sharon Tallents ~ Real ale ~ Open 11.30-3, 6.30-11; 11.30-11.30 Sat; 12-10.30 Sun ~ Bar food 12-2.30, 6.30-9.30; all day Sat; 12-8 (6 in winter) Sun ~ Restaurant ~ Children welcome ~ Dogs allowed in bar ~ Wi-fi *Recommended by Edward May, Stan Abrahams, Richard Tilbrook, Mike and Sarah Abbot, Amy and Luke Buchanan, Miles Hooper, Bridget and Peter Gregson, Revd Michael Vockins*

SOUTHROP
Swan 🏵 ♀
SP2003 Map 4

(01367) 850205 – www.thyme.co.uk

Off A361 Lechlade–Burford; GL7 3NU

Creeper-covered pub with a proper village bar, two dining rooms, imaginative food and a fine choice of drinks; seats in walled garden

In an attractive village-green setting, this handsome creeper-clad 17th-c pub is part of the Thyme company on the Southrop Manor Estate. There's a chatty, bustling bar with friendly locals (and maybe a dog or two), simple tables and chairs on flagstones, an open fire, stools against the counter, Hook Norton Hooky and Village Tipple (named for the pub from Sharps) on handpump, up to 15 wines by the glass from a well chosen list, and helpful staff. The two low-ceilinged dining rooms have tweed-upholstered chairs around a nice mix of tables, cushions on settles, rugs on flagstones, open fires and fresh flowers and candles. There are elegant metal chairs and tables on gravel in several sheltered walled garden areas and picnic-sets at the front; good surrounding walks.

 Creative food uses produce grown or raised on the Estate: citrus-cured salmon with dill, salmon roe and crème fraîche dressing, goats cheese and wild garlic mezzaluna, lemon, rosemary and capers, mussels in white wine, garlic and cream, burger with toppings, pickles and chips, hogget leg with lentils and salsa verde, guinea fowl breast with porcini, tarragon and crème fraîche, hake fillet with samphire and seaweed butter, and puddings such as dark chocolate mousse and buttermilk and honey pannacotta with rhubarb. *Benchmark main dish: aged rib-eye steak with grain mustard and tarragon butter and skinny fries £26.50. Two-course evening meal £23.00.*

Free house ~ Licensee Dominic Abbott ~ Real ale ~ Open 12-3.30, 6-10.30; 12-11.30 Sat; 12-5 Sun; closed Sun evenings ~ Bar food 12-2.30 (3.30 Sun), 6-9 (9.30 Fri); 12-3, 6-9.30 Sat ~ Restaurant ~ Children welcome ~ Dogs welcome ~ Wi-fi *Recommended by Jane and Philip Saunders, Louise and Oliver Redman, Graeme and Sally Mendham*

STOW-ON-THE-WOLD
Porch House 🏵 ♀ 🛏
SP1925 Map 4

(01451) 870048 – www.porch-house.co.uk

Digbeth Street; GL54 1BN

Fine old character inn with carefully refurbished bars and dining areas, and imaginative food; comfortable bedrooms

This is a beautifully restored pub dating from the 16th c and incorporating the original Saxon timber structure. There's plenty of space for both drinking and dining, with beams (some hop-draped), big flagstones or bare floorboards, exposed stone walls and open fireplaces. The bar areas have all sorts of cushioned wooden and upholstered chairs, little stools and settles with scatter cushions around myriad tables, church candles and lanterns, books on shelves, stone bottles on windowsills and a woodburning stove. The cosy snug is similarly furnished but also has sofas and armchairs. A beer named for the pub (from Brakspears) plus Brakspears Bitter and Oxford

Gold on handpump and good wines by the glass served by courteous, helpful staff. There's a dining room with upholstered, high-backed chairs (some with striking blue cushions), and also a conservatory. The atmosphere throughout is informal and gently civilised. A raised terrace has rattan chairs and cushioned wall benches around rustic tables intermingled with more contemporary seats. Bedrooms are individually designed and stylish and breakfasts particularly good. This is a lovely small town.

🏅 Robust, simple cooking using the best local produce includes lunchtime sandwiches, ham hock terrine with apple, sage and crispy quail egg, twice-baked cheddar soufflé with spinach and wholegrain mustard, burger with toppings and triple-cooked chips, rosemary and garlic chicken with mayonnaise and french fries, whole plaice with brown shrimps, lime butter and samphire, lamb rump with cream and garlic cannellini beans, red wine and anchovy crumb, and puddings. *Benchmark main dish: slow-cooked ox cheek with parsnip purée, spinach and gremolata £16.00. Two-course evening meal £20.00.*

Free house ~ Licensee Alex Davenport Jones ~ Real ale ~ Open 11-11; 11-10.30 Sun ~ Bar food 12-3 (4.30 Sat), 6.30-9.30; 12-4.30, 6.30-8.30 Sun ~ Restaurant ~ Children welcome ~ Dogs allowed in bar and bedrooms ~ Wi-fi ~ Bedrooms: /£99 *Recommended by Mike and Mary Carter, Maddie Purvis, NAJB, Patricia and Gordon Thompson, Joe and Belinda Smart*

TETBURY
ST8494 Map 4

Gumstool 🏅 ⓨ 🛏

(01666) 890391 – www.calcotmanor.co.uk

Part of Calcot Manor Hotel; A4135 W of town, just E of junction with A46; GL8 8YJ

Civilised bar with relaxed atmosphere, super choice of drinks and enjoyable food; bedrooms

As always, we receive enthusiastic, warm praise for this well run bar-brasserie – and you don't have to be staying in the very smart attached Calcot Manor Hotel to use it. The thoughtfully divided, stylish layout gives your table the feeling of having a snug area more or less to itself, without losing the friendly atmosphere of plenty going on around you. There are flagstones, elegant wooden dining chairs and tables, well chosen pictures and drawings and wooden 'stag's head and antlers' on mushroom-coloured walls, leather tub armchairs and stools and a neat row of copper cooking pans above the blazing log fire. From the long counter lined with modern chairs, they keep Hook Norton Hooky and Wadworths 6X on handpump, two dozen interesting wines by the glass and several malt whiskies; background music. The slightly sunken front courtyard has a few picnic-sets. Westonbirt Arboretum is not far away.

🏅 Food is excellent – they also have a fireside grill – and uses top quality local, seasonal produce: wild rabbit and ham hock terrine with spiced apple chutney, salt and pepper calamari with sweet chilly mayonnaise and lime, hake with chorizo, creamed spinach and crushed new potatoes, calves liver with pancetta, sage and capers, chicken with wild mushrooms and dauphinoise potatoes, pork belly with black pudding fritter, roast apple and wholegrain mustard mash, 28-day-aged sirloin steak with béarnaise or peppercorn sauce, and puddings such as vanilla pannacotta and chocolate fondant with mint chocolate ice-cream. *Benchmark main dish: beer-battered fish and chips £16.00. Two-course evening meal £23.00.*

Free house ~ Licensees Paul Sadler and Richard Ball ~ Real ale ~ Open 12-11 ~ Bar food 12-2 (2.30 Sat), 6-9.30; 12-4, 6-9 Sun ~ Children welcome ~ Wi-fi ~ Bedrooms: £184/£209 *Recommended by Andrew Vincent, Tom and Ruth Rees, Buster and Helena Hastings, Bernard Stradling, David Appleyard, IAA, HMW, Maria Sansoni*

TETBURY
Royal Oak 🏅 ♀ ◖ 🛏

ST8993 Map 4

(01666) 500021 – www.theroyaloaktetbury.co.uk

Cirencester Road; GL8 8EY

Golden-stone former coaching inn with a good mix of customers, character bar, upstairs dining room and seats outside; comfortable bedrooms

The boutique bedrooms in this fine 18th-c place are spotlessly kept and full of character; they're across a cobbled courtyard, and do need to be booked well in advance. Throughout, the renovations have been done with extreme care so that original features blend easily with up-to-date touches. The open-plan rambling bar (there are several snug areas too) has a roaring log fire at one end, green leather padded built-in wall seats, stools and a variety of chairs around dark tables on wide floorboards, a few elbow tables here and there, and a handsome carved counter. Courteous staff serve one of the '78s ales from Butcombe, Moor Nor'Hop, Stroud Tom Long and Wickwar Falling Star on handpump, ten wines by the glass, a farm cider, interesting spirits and a good choice of teas and coffee; the pretty piano does get used. Upstairs, a beamed and timbered dining room has dark polished furniture on more wide floorboards, creamy yellow paintwork, fresh flowers, candlelight and a fine raftered ceiling. Outside, there are seats and tables under parasols on terraces and a lawn; in summer, an Airstream trailer serves mexican street food, and boules. You can walk from the door into the woods; they're kind to dogs. Wheelchair access and disabled loos.

 Extremely good food includes lunchtime sandwiches, pigeon breast with beetroot purée, salsify and cashew crème, a charcuterie plate, beer-battered fish of the day with fries, beef, cajun chicken or vegetarian burgers with toppings and coleslaw, beer-braised oxtail with horseradish mash and salt-baked celeriac, pork fillet with red pepper hummus and pickled cauliflower, and puddings such as chocolate tart with thyme and lime parfait and cider-poached pear with coconut cream; they also have ice-creams with seven different toppings, and hold regular themed food events. *Benchmark main dish: chicken caesar salad £11.00. Two-course evening meal £20.50.*

Free house ~ Licensees Kate Lewis and Chris York ~ Real ale ~ Open 11-11 (11.30pm Fri, Sat); 12-11 Sun ~ Bar food 12-2.30, 6.30-9; 12-5 Sun ~ Restaurant ~ Children welcome until 8pm unless in restaurant ~ Dogs allowed in bar and bedrooms ~ Wi-fi ~ Live music Sun (best to phone) ~ Bedrooms: /£90 *Recommended by Chris and Angela Buckell, Ivy and George Goodwill, Andrew and Ruth Simmonds*

WESTON SUBEDGE
Seagrave Arms ♀ 🛏

SP1241 Map 4

(01386) 840192 – www.seagravearms.com

B4632; GL55 6QH

Golden-stone inn with friendly staff and enjoyable food; contemporary bedrooms

With a good value set lunch, this handsome old place is popular with walkers on the nearby Cotswold Way. It's got a lot of character – the cosy little bar has ancient flagstones, half-panelled walls, an open fire, padded window seats and a chatty, informal atmosphere. Hook Norton Hooky and Wychwood Jester Jack on handpump and 14 wines (plus prosecco and champagne) by the glass, served by helpful, friendly staff; background music, TV and board games. The two dining rooms have an appealing mix of wooden chairs and tables on floorboards. Outside, there are wicker chairs and tables on neat gravel at the front of the building and more seats in the back garden. Most of the well equipped, modern bedrooms are in the main house, with others in the converted stables; breakfasts are good and hearty.

🍴 Rewarding modern food includes lunchtime sandwiches, rabbit pie with morteau sausage, goose liver parfait with golden raisins, salt-baked celeriac with girolles and pesto, hake with jerusalem artichoke and cod brandade, pork belly and cheek with lovage potatoes and onions, beer-battered fish and chips, lamb belly with creamed polenta and kale, and puddings such as salt caramel tart with passion-fruit sorbet and and chocolate pave with praline ice-cream; they also offer a two- and three-course weekday set menu (12-2.30, 6-7). *Benchmark main dish: steak with king oyster mushrooms, charred onion and chips £20.00. Two-course evening meal £26.00.*

Free house ~ Licensee Fergus Gabb ~ Real ale ~ Open 12-11; 12-9 Sun ~ Bar food 12-2.30, 6-9.30; 12-9.30 Sat; 12-8 Sun ~ Restaurant ~ Children welcome ~ Dogs allowed in bar and bedrooms ~ Wi-fi ~ Bedrooms: /£80 *Recommended by Susan Jackman, Dave Braisted, Bernard Stradling, Margo and Derek Stapley*

WINCHCOMBE SP0228 Map 4
Lion 🌟 ♟ 🛏

(01242) 603300 – www.thelionwinchcombe.co.uk
North Street; GL54 5PS

Historic inn in fine town with drinking and dining spaces in character rooms, fresh flowers and candlelight and seats on pretty terraces; warm, TV-free bedrooms

They cleverly cater for all tastes here – morning coffee in comfortable chairs by the fire, a bar at the back for drinkers and chatters and a separate restaurant for those wanting more formal dining. It's a stylish 15th-c place with plenty of rustic-chic furnishings and an appealing and relaxed atmosphere. There are exposed golden-stone walls, portraits and gilt-edged mirrors on pale paintwork, flagstones, armchairs, scatter cushions on wall seats, stools and elegant wooden dining chairs around all shapes and sizes of table, jugs of fresh flowers and plenty of big stubby candles. Brakspears Oxford Gold, North Cotswold Windrush Ale, Prescott Chequered Flag and Wye Valley Butty Bach on handpump, good wines by the glass served by smiling, courteous staff; daily papers and background music. Wood and metal seats and tables sit on various terraced areas among shrubs and climbers and there are more seats on grass. Bedrooms are individually decorated in country-style; two have their own staircases and one is in a converted hayloft. Sudeley Castle is within walking distance and Cheltenham Racecourse is nearby.

🌟 Appetising food includes lunchtime sandwiches and pizzas, duck ballotine with carrot purée and crispy shallots, cured salmon with pickled kohlrabi, radish and orange salad, butternut squash and red onion tarte tatin, ricotta and red pepper piperade, smoked haddock with bubble and squeak cake, a poached egg and chive beurre blanc, sausages and mash with red onion gravy, pulled chicken and pancetta pasta with spinach and tarragon cream, and puddings such as peanut butter parfait with nut brittle, caramelised bananas and raisin purée and dark chocolate mousse with kirsch-soaked cherries, blackcurrant sorbet and baby meringues. *Benchmark main dish: slow-roast pork belly with pancetta £16.50. Two-course evening meal £24.00.*

Free house ~ Licensee Sue Chalmers ~ Real ale ~ Open 11-11 ~ Bar food 12-3, 6-9 (9.30 Fri, Sat); 12-4, 6-9 Sun ~ Restaurant ~ Children welcome ~ Dogs allowed in bar and bedrooms ~ Wi-fi ~ Bedrooms: /£150 *Recommended by Guy Vowles, Jo Rees, Richard Tilbrook, Mrs Julie Thomas, Mike and Mary Carter, Joe and Belinda Smart, Liz and Martin Eldon*

Also Worth a Visit in Gloucestershire

Besides the fully inspected pubs, you might like to try these pubs that have been recommended to us and described by readers. Do tell us what you think of them: feedback@goodguides.com

ALDSWORTH SP1510
Sherborne Arms (01451) 844346
B4425 Burford–Cirencester; GL54 3RB
Rural pub (former 17th-c stone farmhouse) set down from the road and run by same family since 1984; enjoyable good value home-made food including signature lamb and apricot casserole, often a weekday meal deal, two or three changing ales and proper cider, friendly service, beams, stripped stone and log fire, smallish bar and big dining area, conservatory, games/function room; background music, film night first Mon of month; children and dogs welcome, disabled access, pleasant front garden with smokers' shelter, closed Sun evening, Mon (except bank holidays). *(Margaret McDonald)*

AMBERLEY SO8401
Amberley Inn (01453) 872565
Steeply off A46 Stroud–Nailsworth – gentler approach from N Nailsworth; GL5 5AF Popular well located old stone inn with beautiful views and good local walks, two comfortable bars, snug and a more formal restaurant, well kept Stroud ales, nice wines and enjoyable locally sourced food from bar snacks up (special diets catered for), friendly helpful staff; may be a surcharge if paying by credit card; children and dogs (in bar) welcome, side terrace and back garden, 11 bedrooms. *(Joe and Belinda Smart)*

AMBERLEY SO8401
Black Horse (01453) 872556
Off A46 Stroud–Nailsworth to Amberley; left after Amberley Inn, left at war memorial; Littleworth; best to park by war memorial and walk down; GL5 5AL Two-bar pub with spectacular valley views from small conservatory and terraced garden; mix of pine furniture on wood and slate floors, exposed stone walls, modern artwork and two woodburners, up to five real ales such as Sharps, Stroud and Wickwar, Weston's cider and good range of gins, enjoyable reasonably priced fairly traditional food (not Sun evening) from sandwiches up, nice staff; outside gents'; children, walkers and dogs welcome, wheelchair access (highish step by gate), picnic-sets on front grass, more in split-level back garden, parking can be tricky, open all day. *(Chris and Angela Buckell)*

AMPNEY CRUCIS SP0701
Crown of Crucis (01285) 851806
A417 E of Cirencester; GL7 5RS
Modernised roadside inn with spacious split-level bar, beams and log fires, good choice of enjoyable food including competitively priced dish of the day (weekday lunchtimes), Sharps Doom Bar, a guest beer and decent choice of wines, friendly helpful service; children and dogs welcome, disabled facilities, tables out by Ampney Brook with wooden bridge over to cricket pitch, handy for Palladian Way walkers, quiet modern courtyard bedrooms, good breakfast, open (and food) all day. *(Guy Vowles)*

APPERLEY SO8627
Farmers Arms (01452) 780307
Lower Apperley (B4213); GL19 4DR
Extended country pub with beams, big open fire and split-level carpeted dining area, generous helpings of good well priced home-made food from traditional favourites up, Wadworths ales, friendly atmosphere; some live music including summer tribute band festival; children welcome, picnic-sets on terrace and in garden overlooking fields, closed Sun evening, Mon. *(Peter Young)*

ARLINGHAM SO7110
Red Lion (01452) 740700
High Street; GL2 7JH Old village corner pub owned by the local community, good generously served food from lunchtime sandwiches and pub favourites up, Uley Bitter and guests, friendly staff, updated interior with wood and carpeted floors, some beams and two woodburners; children and dogs welcome, picnic-sets out by the road, good circular walks (not far from the River Severn), closed Mon lunchtime, otherwise open all day (food all day Sat, till 6pm Sun, not Mon). *(Peter Young)*

ASHLEWORTH QUAY SO8125
Boat (01452) 700272
Ashleworth signposted off A417 N of Gloucester; quay signed from village; GL19 4HZ Tiny unpretentious old pub in lovely spot on the banks of the Severn; front parlour with mats on flagstones, built-in settle by scrubbed deal table, elderly chairs next to old-fashioned kitchen range, cribbage and dominoes, back quarry-tiled dining room with fireplace and a cosy snug, up to ten mostly local ales and good range of ciders, enjoyable food from baguettes to speciality burgers; live music and beer/cider festivals; children, dogs and muddy boots welcome, tricky for wheelchairs (friendly staff will help), sunny crazy-paved front courtyard, more seats to the side and on grass by river, moorings, near interesting 15th-c tithe barn (NT), open all day in summer

(all day Fri-Sun, closed Mon and lunchtime Weds in winter). *(Mike and Mary Carter)*

AYLBURTON SO6101

Cross (01594) 842823

High Street; GL15 6DE Popular family-run village pub, good choice of food from sandwiches and sharing plates through pub favourites to daily specials, changing ales such as Bath, Butcombe and Wye Valley, several wines by the glass and a dozen whiskies, welcoming helpful staff, open-plan split-level flagstoned bar, beams, modern furniture alongside high-backed settles, old local photographs, woodburners in large stone fireplaces, high-raftered dining room; free wi-fi; children and dogs welcome, wheelchair access from car park, pleasant garden with play area, open all day Fri-Sun. *(Louise and Oliver Redman)*

BIBURY SP1006

★**Catherine Wheel** (01285) 740250

Arlington; B4425 NE of Cirencester; GL7 5ND Bright cheerful old dining pub in beautiful Cotswold village; enjoyable freshly made food (best to book weekends) from sandwiches and pizzas up including good local trout, well kept Hook Norton, Sharps and a couple of guests, friendly efficient young staff, open-plan main bar and smaller back rooms, low beams, stripped stone and log fires, raftered dining room; children and dogs welcome, picnic-sets in front and in good-sized garden, handy for country and riverside walks, four bedrooms, open (and food) all day. *(R K Phillips, Peter Young)*

BISLEY SO9006

Bear (01452) 770265

Village signed off A419 E of Stroud; GL6 7BD Interesting 17th-c colonnaded inn (originally a courthouse); L-shaped bar with low ceiling, old oak settles, brass and copper implements around extremely wide stone fireplace, five well kept ales including Butcombe and Charles Wells, popular pubby food, friendly staff, separate stripped-stone family area; outside gents', ladies' upstairs; dogs welcome, small flagstoned courtyard, stone mounting blocks in garden across quiet road, one bedroom, open all day Sat and Sun. *(Ian Cooper)*

BLAISDON SO7016

Red Hart (01452) 830477

Village signposted off A4136 just SW of junction with A40 W of Gloucester; OS Sheet 162 map reference 703169; GL17 0AH Bustling village pub with plenty to look at in flagstoned main bar and attractive carpeted restaurant: woodworking and farming tools on magnolia walls and hanging from beams, old photographs of prize farm stock, a framed inventory of the pub in 1903 and lots of books, pot plants and some interesting prints, candles on traditional tables, cushioned wall and window seats,

Otter and three guests, real cider and ten wines by the glass, popular food from traditional choices up; background music, board games, free wi-fi; children welcome (family dining area), dogs in bar, wheelchair access, picnic-sets on terrace and in garden with play area, pretty summer window boxes, little church nearby also worth a visit. *(Mike and Mary Carter, Dr A J and Mrs B A Tompsett)*

BRIMPSFIELD SO9413

★**Golden Heart** (01242) 870261

Nettleton Bottom (not shown on road maps, so instead we list the pub under the name of the nearby village); on A417 N of the Brimpsfield turning northbound; GL4 8LA Traditional old roadside inn with low-ceilinged bar divided into five cosy areas, log fire in huge inglenook, exposed stone walls and wood panelling, well worn built-in settles and other old-fashioned furnishings, brass items, typewriters and banknotes, parlour on right with decorative fireplace leading into further room, well kept Brakspears with guests such as Jennings, Stroud and Wychwood, several wines by the glass, popular sensibly priced food from extensive blackboard menu including unusual choices like kangaroo and camel, several vegetarian/vegan options too, friendly staff; children and dogs welcome, seats and tables on suntrap terrace with pleasant valley views, nearby walks, open all day. *(Richard Tilbrook, Giles and Annie Francis, Guy Vowles)*

BROAD CAMPDEN SP1537

★**Bakers Arms** (01386) 840515

Village signed from B4081 in Chipping Campden; GL55 6UR 17th-c stone pub with tiny beamed character bar, stripped-stone walls and inglenook woodburner, half a dozen well kept ales such as North Cotswold, Stanway, Wickwar and Wye Valley, simply furnished beamed dining room serving popular pubby food (not Sun evening, Mon) plus blackboard specials; folk night last Weds of month, darts and board games; children (away from bar) and dogs (in bar) welcome, picnic-sets on terraces and in back garden, delightful Cotswold village and good nearby walks, open all day weekends, closed Mon lunchtime. *(Theocsbrian, Guy Vowles)*

BROADWELL SP2027

Fox (01451) 870909

Off A429, 2 miles N of Stow-on-the-Wold; GL56 0UF Golden-stone pub above broad village green; traditional furnishings and flagstones in log-fire bar, jugs hanging from beams, interesting bits and pieces on stripped-stone walls, well kept Donnington BB and SBA, lots of rums, winter mulled wine and enjoyable generously served food (not Sun evening) cooked by ex-military chef-landlord, efficient friendly staff, two carpeted dining areas; background music, darts and board games; children and dogs (in bar) welcome, picnic-sets on gravel in sizeable back garden, aunt sally, paddock with Herman the horse, camping. *(Dennis and Doreen Haward, Alun and Jennifer Evans, Keith Perry)*

BROCKWEIR   SO5301
Brockweir Inn (01291) 689548
Signed just off A466 Chepstow–Monmouth; NP16 7NG Welcoming country local near the River Wye; beams and stripped stonework, quarry tiles, sturdy settles and woodburner, nice snug with parquet floor and open fire, four well kept ales, three ciders and enjoyable food (not Sun evening) including OAP lunch deal (Tues, Thurs), small back dining area and room upstairs 'Devil's Pulpit' (games and books); live music first Tues of month; children and dogs welcome, little walled garden with clay oven, good walks, open all day weekends; for sale, so may be changes. *(Bill Farmer)*

BUSSAGE   SO8804
Ram (01453) 883163
At Eastcombe, take The Ridgeway and first right The Ridge; pub is 500 metres on left; GL6 8RB Tucked-away Cotswold stone local with roomy opened-up interior, enjoyable pub food (not Sun evening) from lunchtime sandwiches to daily specials, well kept ales such as Bath, Butcombe, Greene King and St Austell, varied choice of wines, friendly welcoming staff; background music, free wi-fi; children and dogs (in bar) welcome, a few picnic-sets outside, open all day Fri-Sun. *(Monica and Steph Evans)*

CAMP   SO9111
★ Fostons Ash (01452) 863262
B4070 Birdlip–Stroud, junction with Calf Way; GL6 7ES Open-plan dining pub (part of the small Cotswold Food Club group), light and airy, with good food from interesting light dishes and sharing plates up, three well kept ales such as Bath, Butcombe and Stroud, nice range of wines by the glass, welcoming helpful staff, one end with easy chairs and woodburner; background music, daily papers; children and dogs welcome, rustic tables in attractive garden with heated terrace and play area, good walks, open all day (food all day Sun). *(Guy Vowles)*

CHARLTON KINGS   SO9620
Royal (01242) 228937
Horsefair, opposite church; GL53 8JH Large 19th-c pub with clean modern décor, good food (all day weekends) in bar or dining conservatory, several well kept ales (tasting trays available) and decent wines, prompt friendly service; Sun quiz, some live music; children and dogs welcome, picnic-sets in garden overlooking church, open all day. *(Guy Vowles, Peter Young)*

CHEDWORTH   SP0608
Hare & Hounds (01285) 720288
Fosse Cross – A429 N of Cirencester, some way from village; GL54 4NN Rambling stone-built restauranty pub with good freshly made food including lunchtime set menu, well kept Arkells and nice wines, friendly efficient service, low beams and wood floors, soft lighting, cosy corners and little side rooms, two big log fires, small conservatory; children (away from bar) and dogs welcome, disabled access/facilities, ten courtyard bedrooms. *(Susan Eccleston)*

CHEDWORTH   SP0512
Seven Tuns (01285) 720630
Village signposted off A429 NE of Cirencester; then take second signposted right turn and bear left towards church; GL54 4AE Refurbished 17th-c village pub in remote valley close to famous Roman villa; well kept ales such as Hook Norton, Otter and local TAP, good interesting food from shortish menu plus daily specials, Tues steak night, Fri fish and chips, friendly helpful staff, linked characterful rooms with flagstone and wood floors, restored furniture along with newer comfortable seating, some curious artwork, embroideries and other bits and pieces, woodburners; upstairs skittle alley with darts and big-screen sports TV, open mike night last Tues of the month; children and dogs welcome, outside seating front and back, good walks, open all day weekends. *(Richard Tilbrook)*

CHELTENHAM   SO9622
Hewlett Arms (01242) 228600
Harp Hill, Battledown; GL52 6QG Compact split-level pebbledashed pub with good home-made food (not Sun evening) from lunchtime ciabattas to specials, well kept changing ales and decent range of wines by the glass, cheerful efficient service; background music; children and dogs welcome, picnic-sets under parasols in sunny front garden, open all day. *(Frank Hough)*

CHELTENHAM   SO9421
Jolly Brewmaster (01242) 772261
Painswick Road; GL50 2EZ Popular convivial local with open-plan linked areas around big semicircular counter, fine range of changing ales and ciders, friendly obliging young staff, newspapers, log fire; maybe quiz nights Mon, Weds; dogs welcome, coachyard tables, open from 2.30pm (midday Sat, Sun). *(Frank Hough)*

CHELTENHAM   SO9522
Old Restoration (01242) 522792
High Street; GL50 1DX Much altered 17th-c beamed pub, five well kept

---

It's very helpful if you let us know up-to-date food prices when you report on pubs.

changing ales (cheaper on Mon) and a couple of ciders, enjoyable, fair-priced food, friendly attentive staff, open fires; Mon quiz, sports TVs, darts; children (away from bar) and dogs welcome, open all day. *(Roger and Donna Huggins)*

CHELTENHAM SO9624
★**Plough** (01242) 222180
Mill Street, Prestbury; GL52 3BG
Convivial unspoilt thatched village local tucked away behind church; comfortable front lounge, service from corner corridor hatch in flagstoned back tap room, grandfather clock, old local photographs and big log fire, two or three well kept ales including Bath Gem and a house beer from Wickwar, proper ciders and good value home-made food (not Sun evening, Mon), friendly service; live folk music Thurs; lovely big flower-filled back garden with boules, open all day. *(Jeff Wright, Frank Hough)*

CHELTENHAM SO9321
Royal Union (01242) 519098
Hatherley Street; GL50 2TT Backstreet corner local with large bar and cosy snug up steps, around eight well kept local ales including Tivoli (brewed for the pub by TAP) plus craft kegs, reasonably priced wines and good range of whiskies/gins, enjoyable food (Weds-Sat evenings, Sun lunchtime), can also pre-book sharing dishes for up to ten people, informal restaurant in former skittle alley; Sun evening jazz/blues, Thurs quiz; well behaved children allowed (no under-5s), dogs on leads, courtyard behind, newly added bedrooms, open all day Sun, from 4pm other days. *(Guy Vowles)*

CHELTENHAM SO9522
Sandford Park (01242) 571022
High Street; GL50 1DZ Former nightclub converted to a popular pub, three bar areas and upstairs function room, up to nine real ales along with craft and continental beers, several ciders and good value home-cooked food from short menu (not Sun evening, Mon lunchtime), friendly staff; Sun quiz, bar billiards; large back garden, open all day. *(Guy Vowles, Theocsbrian, Giles and Annie Francis)*

CHIPPING CAMPDEN SP1539
Kings (01386) 840256
High Street; GL55 6AW Eclectic décor in 18th-c hotel's bar-brasserie and separate restaurant, good food from lunchtime sandwiches and pubby dishes to more upmarket choices, friendly helpful service, well kept Hook Norton Hooky and good choice of wines by the glass, afternoon teas, daily papers and nice log fire; secluded back garden with picnic-sets and terrace tables, 12 comfortable bedrooms, open all day. *(Liz and Martin Eldon)*

CHIPPING CAMPDEN SP1539
Noel Arms (01386) 840317
High Street; GL55 6AT Handsome 16th-c inn with beamed and stripped-stone bar, nice food from sandwiches to steaks, some good curries too from sri lankan chef (curry night last Thurs of month), well kept Hook Norton, local guests and good choice of wines by the glass, friendly efficient staff, coffee bar (from 9am), conservatory and separate restaurant; children and dogs welcome, sunny courtyard tables, 28 well appointed bedrooms, good breakfast, open all day. *(Margaret McDonald)*

CHIPPING SODBURY ST7381
Bell (01454) 325582
Badminton Road (A432); BS37 6LL Welcoming late 18th-c family-run inn, ales such as Butcombe Gold, Sharps Doom Bar and Wadworths 6X from ornate wooden counter, three ciders and decent choice of wines, wide choice of good pub food including set lunch deal Mon-Sat and other deals, friendly efficient young staff, dining rooms either side of bar area, some stripped stone and timbering, sofas and open fires; background music, TV; children welcome, four bedrooms, open all day Thurs-Sun. *(Dr and Mrs A K Clarke)*

CHIPPING SODBURY ST7282
Horseshoe 07780 505563
High Street; BS37 6AP Welcoming unpretentious little pub in former stationers' making most of the space; seven well kept ales and six ciders, low priced pubby lunchtime food (not Sun, Mon), curry night Weds, otherwise rolls on the bar, comfortable sofas and settles, another intimate room upstairs; occasional live music, sports TV; dogs welcome, small pretty garden behind, open all day (till midnight weekends). *(Roger and Donna Huggins)*

CIRENCESTER SP0103
Drillmans Arms (01285) 653892
Gloucester Road, Stratton; GL7 2JY Unpretentious two-room roadside local with welcoming long-serving landlady, well kept Sharps Doom Bar and three quickly changing guests, basic lunchtime food, low beams and woodburner; skittle alley, darts and pool; dogs welcome, tables out by small front car park, open all day Sat. *(Richard Tilbrook)*

CIRENCESTER SP0201
Marlborough Arms (01285) 651474
Sheep Street; GL7 1QW Busy bare-boards pub with eight well kept ales including Box Steam and North Cotswold, also proper ciders and continental draught/bottled beers, friendly landlord and good mix of customers, reasonably priced traditional lunchtime food (not Mon), brewery memorabilia, pump clips and shelves of bottles, open fire; live music and quiz nights, sports TV; enclosed back courtyard, closed Mon-Thurs

lunchtimes (open from 5pm), open all day Fri-Sun. *(Giles and Annie Francis)*

COATES SO9600
★ Tunnel House (01285) 770280

Follow Tarlton signs (right then left) from village, pub up rough track on right after railway bridge; OS Sheet 163 map reference 965005; GL7 6PW Lively bow-fronted stone house by entrance to derelict canal tunnel; rambling character rooms with beams, exposed stonework and flagstones, good mix of furnishings and plenty to look at including old enamel signs, railway lamps, racing tickets, stuffed animals, even an upside-down card table fixed to the ceiling (complete with cards and drinks), sofas by log fire, Box Steam, Sharps and Uley, a couple of Thatcher's ciders and several wines by the glass, popular food including daily specials and Sun carvery, good friendly service, more conventional dining extension and back conservatory; background music, free wi-fi; children and dogs welcome, disabled access/loos, impressive views from front terrace, big garden down to the canal, good nearby walks, open (and food) all day. *(Chris and Angela Buckell)*

COLESBOURNE SO9913
Colesbourne Inn (01242) 870376

A435 Cirencester–Cheltenham; GL53 9NP Civilised 19th-c grey-stone gabled coaching inn, decent choice of popular food from baguettes and deli boards up, smaller appetites and gluten-free diets catered for, friendly quick service, well kept Wadworths ales and lots of wines by the glass, linked partly panelled rooms, log fires, soft lighting, comfortable mix of settles, softly padded seats and leather sofas, candlelit back dining room; background music, TV above fireplace; dogs welcome, views from attractive back garden and terrace, nine bedrooms in converted stable block, good breakfast (for non-residents too), open (and food) all day. *(Dennis and Doreen Haward, Simon Collett-Jones, Peter Young)*

COMPTON ABDALE SP0717
★ Garniche at the Puesdown (01451)

860262 *A40 outside village; GL54 4DN* Spacious series of modernised linked bars and eating areas, mainly stripped-stone walls, rafter-effect or beamed ceilings, rugs on bare boards, chesterfield sofas and armchairs, high-backed dining chairs around mix of tables, log fire and two-way woodburner, a couple of Hook Norton ales and maybe a guest, good freshly made food from fairly pubby menu, morning coffee and afternoon tea, friendly helpful staff; background music, gift shop; children and dogs (in bar) welcome, tables in pretty back garden,

three comfortable ground-floor bedrooms, closed Sun evening, Mon, otherwise open (and food) all day. *(Peter Young)*

DOYNTON ST7174
Cross House (0117) 329 5830

High Street; signed off A420 Bristol–Chippenham E of Wick; BS30 5TF Welcoming 18th-c village pub with ales such as Bath Gem and Sharps Doom Bar, summer cocktails and well priced enjoyable food cooked by landlady, carpeted beamed bar, some stripped stone, simple pub furniture and woodburner, cottagey dining room; Tues quiz, board games; children welcome, dogs in bar (resident cats), picnic-sets out by the road, near fine walking country and Dyrham Park (NT), closed Mon, otherwise open all day. *(Dr and Mrs A K Clarke)*

DYMOCK SO6931
Beauchamp Arms (01531) 890266

B4215; GL18 2AQ Friendly parish-owned village pub with well kept ales such as Butcombe, local ciders and good value traditional food (not Sun evening, Mon) including fresh fish Weds, cheerful helpful staff, three smallish rooms, log fire; children and dogs welcome, pleasant little garden with pond, local walks among daffodils and bluebells, church with corner devoted to the Dymock Poets, closed Mon lunchtime. *(Alf and Sally Garner)*

EASTLEACH TURVILLE SP1905
Victoria (01367) 850277

Off A361 S of Burford; GL7 3NQ Traditional old stone pub under new management; open-plan low-ceilinged rooms around central servery, attractive seats built in by log fire, unusual Queen Victoria pictures, well kept Arkells and decent range of wines by the glass, enjoyable fairly priced food cooked by landlord from pubby choices up, friendly service; background and occasional live music; children and dogs welcome, small pleasant front garden with picnic-sets overlooking picturesque village (famous for its spring daffodils), more seats behind and aunt sally, good walks, open all day weekends, no food Sun evening. *(R K Phillips)*

ELKSTONE SO9610
★ Highwayman (01285) 821221

Beechpike; A417 6 miles N of Cirencester; GL53 9PL Interesting 16th-c building with rambling interior, low beams, stripped stone and log fires, cosy alcoves, antique settles among more modern furnishings, generous helpings of enjoyable food (gluten-free options) from lunchtime sandwiches up, Arkells beers

---

All *Guide* inspections are anonymous. Anyone claiming to be a *Good Pub Guide* inspector is a fraud. Please let us know.

and good house wines, friendly service; free wi-fi; children and dogs welcome, disabled access, outside play area, bedrooms, closed Sun evening, Mon. *(Peter Young)*

EWEN   SU0097

Wild Duck (01285) 770310

Off A429 S of Cirencester; GL7 6BY Character 16th-c village inn (former cottages and barns for Ewen Manor) now owned by the Lucky Onion group; old stone path to entrance with unusual duck clock up on right, dimly lit interior with appealing nooks and crannies, dark hop-strung beams, scrubbed pine tables on wood floors, crimson walls and antique furnishings, open fires including one in handsome Elizabethan fireplace, good if not particularly cheap food from interesting varied menu (service charge added), also set lunch offer Mon-Fri, ales such as Battledown, Butcombe, Otter, Sharps, Stroud and Timothy Taylors, good selection of wines by the glass from extensive list; children and dogs welcome, tables under parasols in heated courtyard and garden, Thames Path not far away, open all day; bedrooms and further works planned. *(Dave Snowden, Taff Thomas)*

FORD   SP0829

★ **Plough** (01386) 584215

B4077 Stow–Alderton; GL54 5RU 16th-c pub popular with the local horse-racing fraternity (it's opposite a famous stables); beamed and stripped-stone bar with racing prints and photos, old settles and benches around big tables on uneven flagstones, oak tables in a snug alcove, open fires and woodburners, Donnington BB and SBA, eight wines by the glass and a dozen malt whiskies, generous helpings of enjoyable reasonably priced food; background music, TV (for the races), free wi-fi, darts; children and dogs (in bar) welcome, picnic-sets and pretty hanging baskets in front, large garden behind with play fort, comfortable clean bedrooms (some with views of the gallops), Cotswold Farm Park nearby, open all day from 9am, food all day Fri-Sun, gets packed on race days. *(Sara Fulton, Roger Baker, Guy Vowles, K H Frostick, Richard Tilbrook, Tracey and Stephen Groves, Peter Young and others)*

FORTHAMPTON   SO8731

Lower Lode Inn (01684) 293224

At the end of Bishop's Walk by river; GL19 4RE Brick-built 15th-c coaching inn with River Severn moorings and plenty of waterside tables (prone to winter flooding); beams, flagstones and traditional seating, woodburners, enjoyable pubby food including Sun carvery, half a dozen well kept interesting beers, friendly helpful staff, restaurant, back pool room; children and dogs welcome, disabled facilities, four bedrooms and campsite, open all day. *(Ian Cooper)*

FRAMPTON COTTERELL   ST6681

Globe (01454) 778286

Church Road; BS36 2AB Popular white-painted pub next to church; large knocked-through bar-dining area with black beams and some stripped stone, usual furniture on parquet or carpet, woodburner in old fireplace, five well kept ales including Butcombe, Fullers and St Austell, Thatcher's ciders and well chosen wine list, enjoyable fairly priced pubby food from ciabattas up, Weds curry night, attentive friendly staff; background music, Tues quiz; children and dogs welcome, wheelchair access via side door, disabled/baby changing facilities, big grassy garden with play area and smokers' gazebo, on Frome Valley Walkway, open all day. *(Dr and Mrs A K Clarke)*

FRAMPTON MANSELL   SO9202

★ **Crown** (01285) 760601

Brown sign to pub off A491 Cirencester–Stroud; GL6 8JG Welcoming 17th-c country pub (former cider house) with pretty outlook; enjoyable food including daily specials, Butcombe, Sharps, Stroud, Uley and a guest, three ciders and good choice of wines, friendly helpful young staff, stripped stone and heavy beams, rugs on bare boards, two log fires and a woodburner, restaurant; various events including notable bonfire-night fireworks; children and dogs welcome, disabled access, picnic-sets in sunny front garden, 12 bedrooms in separate block, open all day from midday, food all day Sun. *(Giles and Annie Francis, Tom and Ruth Rees)*

FRAMPTON ON SEVERN   SO7407

Three Horseshoes (01452) 742100

The Green (B4071, handy for M5 junction 13, via A38); GL2 7DY Cheerfully unpretentious 18th-c pub by splendid green; welcoming staff and locals, well kept Sharps, Timothy Taylors and Uley from small counter, proper ciders/perry too, good value home-made food including speciality pies, lived-in interior with parquet flooring, cushioned wall seats and open fire in large brick fireplace, quieter back lounge/dining room; folk nights, darts; children, walkers and dogs welcome, wheelchair access, picnic-sets out in front, garden behind with two boules pitches, views over River Severn to Forest of Dean, parking can be tricky (narrow road), open all day weekends. *(Chris Stott)*

GLASSHOUSE   SO7121

★ **Glasshouse Inn** (01452) 830529

Off A40 just W of A4136; GL17 0NN Much extended beamed red-brick pub with series of small linked rooms, ochre walls and boarded ceilings, appealing old-fashioned and antique furnishings, hunting pictures and taxidermy, cavernous black hearth, well kept ales including cask-tapped Butcombe and Sharps, Weston's cider, good reasonably priced wines, some interesting malt whiskies and a couple of decent gins, enjoyable home-made food from sandwiches and basket meals up (no bookings except Sun lunch), good friendly service, big flagstoned conservatory; background music; no under-14s (in bars) or dogs, good disabled access, rustic furniture in neat garden with interesting topiary, flower-decked cider presses and lovely hanging baskets, nearby paths up wooded May Hill (NT), three self-catering lodges, closed Sun evening. *(Mike and Mary Carter, Christopher Mobbs)*

GLOUCESTER   SO8318
Fountain (01452) 522562
Westgate Street; GL1 2NW Tucked-away 17th-c pub off pedestrianised street, well kept ales such as Bristol Beer Factory, Butcombe, Dartmoor, St Austell and Thwaites, a couple of craft beers, Thatcher's and Weston's ciders and a modestly priced wine list, good value pubby food from well filled sandwiches and basket meals up, friendly chatty staff, opened-up carpeted bar with woodburner in handsome stone fireplace, some black beams and dark varnished dados, pubby furniture and built-in wall benches; background music; children welcome away from bar, disabled access/ loos, flower-filled courtyard with big gates to Berkeley Street, handy for cathedral, open all day (food all day Fri and Sat, till 5pm Sun). *(Chris and Angela Buckell, Alan Bird)*

GLOUCESTER   SO8218
Lord High Constable of England
(01452) 302890
Llanthony Warehouse, Llanthony Road; GL1 2EH Busy Wetherspoons on east side of the docks; spacious and comfortable with high raftered ceiling, good range of real ales and craft beers, their usual well priced food, efficient service; TVs, free wi-fi; children welcome, outside area overlooking canal, open all day from 8am. *(Theocsbrian, Mike and Mary Carter)*

GLOUCESTER   SO8318
New Inn (01452) 522177
Northgate Street; GL1 1SF Lovely beamed medieval building with galleried courtyard; Butcombe, Sharps and up to eight guests including smaller local breweries, decent wines, bargain daily lunchtime carvery and other good value food (all day Fri, Sat), friendly efficient service, restaurant and coffee shop; soft background music (live Fri, disco/karaoke Sat), sports TV, free wi-fi; children welcome, no dogs, wheelchair access to restaurant only,

33 affordably priced bedrooms, handy for cathedral, open all day. *(Richard Tilbrook)*

GREAT RISSINGTON   SP1917
★Lamb (01451) 820388
Turn off A40 W of Burford to the Barringtons; keep straight on past Great Barrington until Great Rissington is signed on left; GL54 2LP Cotswold-stone village inn dating from the 18th c, bar with pubby furnishings including padded wall benches and sewing-machine tables on strip-wood floor, woodburner, leather chairs against counter serving Brakspears, Wychwood Hobgoblin and a beer badged for the pub, decent wines by the glass and good choice of gins/malt whiskies, second woodburner in restaurant with collection of old agricultural tools, well liked interesting food along with sandwiches and a few pub standards, Weds steak day; background music, TV, free wi-fi; children and dogs (in bar) welcome, seats in sheltered hillside garden where Wellington bomber crashed in 1943 (see plaque and memorabilia), attractive circular walk, 13 bedrooms (four in converted outbuildings), open all day. *(Richard Tilbrook)*

GRETTON   SP0130
Royal Oak (01242) 604999
Off B4077 E of Tewkesbury; GL54 5EP Golden-stone pub under newish management; bar with painted kitchen chairs, leather tub chairs and pale wooden tables on bare boards or flagstones, open fires, airy dining room and conservatory, candelabras, antlers and big central woodburner, ales such as Goffs, Purity, Ringwood, St Austell and Wye Valley, plenty of wines by the glass, popular food from pub favourites to specials, good service; background music; children and dogs (in bar) welcome, wheelchair access but not to raised dining room, seats on back terrace with views over village to Dumbleton Hill and Malverns, play area and bookable tennis court, GWR steam trains run along bottom of garden in summer, open all day. *(Ian Herdman, Dr A J and Mrs B A Tompsett)*

GUITING POWER   SP0924
★Farmers Arms (01451) 850358
Fosseway (A429); GL54 5TZ Nicely old-fashioned with stripped stone, flagstones, lots of pictures and woodburner, well kept/ priced Donnington BB and SBA, wide blackboard choice of enjoyable honest food cooked by landlord including good rabbit pie and reasonably priced Sun roasts, welcoming prompt service, carpeted back dining part; games area with darts, dominoes,

---

Cribbage is a card game using a block of wood with holes for matchsticks or special pins to score with; regulars in cribbage pubs are usually happy to teach strangers how to play.

cribbage and pool, skittle alley; children welcome, garden with quoits, lovely village, good walks, bedrooms. *(Richard Tilbrook)*

HAM ST6898
Salutation (01453) 810284
On main road through village; GL13 9QH Welcoming unpretentious three-room country local; brasses on beams, horse and hunt pictures on Artex walls, high-backed settles, bench seats and other pubby furniture, six well kept local ales including home-brewed Tileys, nine real ciders/perries and good range of bottled beers, limited choice of simple low-priced lunchtime food such as ham, egg and chips (own pigs, hens and potatoes); folk night first Thurs of month and other live music, traditional games including shove-ha'penny, skittle alley, free wi-fi; wheelchair access, beer garden with views over deer park, handy for Berkeley Castle, open all day weekends, closed lunchtimes Mon-Thurs. *(Steve Crick)*

HAWKESBURY UPTON ST7786
★ Beaufort Arms (01454) 238217
High Street; GL9 1AU Unpretentious 17th-c pub in historic village; welcoming landlord and friendly chatty atmosphere, up to five well kept changing local ales and good range of ciders, popular no-nonsense food (all available to take away), extended uncluttered dining lounge on right, darts in more spartan stripped-brick bare-boards bar, interesting local and brewery memorabilia, lots of pictures (some for sale); skittle alley, free wi-fi; well behaved children allowed, dogs in bar, disabled access throughout and facilities, picnic-sets in smallish enclosed garden, on Cotswold Way and handy for Badminton Horse Trials, open all day. *(Lorna and Jack Mulgrave)*

HAWKESBURY UPTON ST7787
Fox (01454) 238558
High Street; GL9 1AU Welcoming 18th-c stone-built pub with four well kept changing ales, nice wines and good authentic italian cooking including two-course lunch deal, cheerful helpful service, restaurant; background music; children welcome, picnic-sets on front terrace, four bedrooms, closed Mon lunchtime, otherwise open all day (till 8.30pm Sun). *(Tom and Ruth Rees)*

HILLESLEY ST7689
Fleece (01453) 520003
Hawkesbury Road/Chapel Lane; GL12 7RD Comfortably updated old stone-roofed pub owned by the local community; well kept mainly local ales, good wines by the glass and decent range of gins, happy hour (4.30-6pm Mon-Fri), enjoyable good value pub food, friendly chatty staff and locals, bar with mix of pubby furniture, cushioned benches and wall seats, woodburner, steps down to dining room and snug; quiz first Sun of month, acoustic music second Sun,

darts, free wi-fi; children, walkers and dogs welcome (leave muddy boots in porch), wheelchair access to bar only, back garden with play area and smokers' shelter, small village in lovely countryside near Cotswold Way, closed till 4.30pm Mon, Tues, otherwise open all day. *(Chris and Angela Buckell)*

HINTON DYRHAM ST7376
★ Bull (0117) 937 2332
2.4 miles from M4 junction 18; A46 towards Bath, then first right (opposite the Crown); SN14 8HG 17th-c stone pub in nice setting; main bar with two huge fireplaces, low beams, oak settles and pews on ancient flagstones, stripped-stone back area and simply furnished carpeted restaurant, food from pub standards to specials, well kept Wadworths ales; background music; children and dogs welcome, difficult wheelchair access (steps at front, but staff willing to help), seats on front balcony and in sizeable sheltered upper garden with play equipment, handy for Dyrham Park (NT), open all day weekends (food till 6pm Sun), closed Mon. *(Mrs Zara Elliott, Dr and Mrs A K Clarke)*

KEMBLE ST9899
Thames Head (01285) 770259
A433 Cirencester–Tetbury; GL7 6NZ Roadside pub with opened-up modernised interior around central servery; faux black beams, stripped-stone walls and some rough-boarded dados/wall seats, fairly rustic furniture on tartan carpet, shelves of books, stoneware jugs and a bust of Old Father Thames, intriguing little front alcove, two open fires, popular reasonably priced food, well kept Arkells and good value wines, friendly chatty staff; background music, free wi-fi, skittle alley; children and dogs (in bar area) welcome, wheelchair access using ramp, disabled loo, tables outside, four barn-conversion bedrooms, good breakfast, walk (crossing railway line) to nearby Thames source, open (and food) all day. *(Peter Young)*

KILKENNY SP0118
Kilkeney Inn (01242) 820341
A436, 1 mile W of Andoversford; GL54 4LN Spaciously refurbished beamed pub (originally five stone cottages), stripped-stone and some plank-clad walls, wheelback, tub and leather dining chairs around tables on slate, wood or carpeted floors, open fire and woodburner, conservatory, Wells & Youngs ales, real cider and decent wines by the glass, well liked food from owner-chef including signature 'slow-cooked' dishes, good friendly service and buzzy atmosphere; background music; children welcome, wheelchair access from car park, lovely Cotswold views from tables out at front, more seating in back garden, one well appointed bedroom, closed Sun evening, Mon. *(Chris and Angela Buckell, Richard Tilbrook, Peter Young)*

KINETON
SP0926
Halfway House (01451) 850344
Signed from B4068 and B4077 W of Stow-on-the-Wold; GL54 5UG Welcoming 17th-c beamed village inn, good food from sandwiches and pub standards to more ambitious choices, well kept Donnington BB and SBA, Addlestone's cider and decent wines, separate dining area, log fire; pool and darts; children and dogs welcome, picnic-sets in sheltered back garden with pergola, good walks, bedrooms, open (and some food) all day. *(Richard Tilbrook)*

KNOCKDOWN
ST8388
Holford Arms (01454) 238669
A433; GL8 8QY Welcoming 16th-c beamed pub; bare-stone walls, flagstone or wood floors, leather sofas, armchairs and cushioned wall/window seats, candles on old dining tables, two woodburners (one in huge stone fireplace), six cask-tapped ales such as Cotswold Lion, Flying Monk and Stroud, own Sherston's cider and apple juice, good well balanced wine list, enjoyable food from sandwiches up including good value Sun lunch (own rare-breed pork), Mon steak night and Weds thai night, pleasant helpful service; background and live music (bluegrass Fri), skittle alley; children and dogs welcome, wheelchair access (no disabled loos), picnic sets in side and back gardens, outside summer bar, six bedrooms, camping, handy for Westonbirt Arboretum, Highgrove and Badminton Horse Trials, closed Mon and Tues lunchtimes, otherwise open all day. *(Chris and Angela Buckell, Michael Doswell)*

LECHLADE
SU2199
New Inn (01367) 252296
Market Square (A361); GL7 3AB Refurbished 17th-c brick coaching inn close to the church, roomy front bar with large log fire, Morland Original and a couple of guests, popular good value pubby food from sandwiches/panini up, back restaurant, friendly helpful staff; background music; children and dogs (in bar) welcome, big garden down to Thames, good walks, 30 bedrooms, open all day. *(Anita Kaila, Balinder Ladhar)*

LECHLADE
SU2199
Swan (01367) 253571
Burford Street; GL7 3AP Welcoming 16th-c inn with linked rooms around central servery; beam-and-plank ceilings, bare boards or carpeted floors, various odds and ends including old gramophones, musical instruments, farming memorabilia and enamel signs, even a couple of vintage petrol pumps, good log fires in two big stone fireplaces, restaurant part with modern pine furniture, Halfpenny and Old Forge beers (brewed at their sister pubs) and good choice of wines by the glass, sensibly

priced food (not Sun evening) including generous sandwiches and range of burgers; four bedrooms, handy for Thames Path walkers, open all day. *(Liz and Martin Eldon)*

LEIGHTERTON
ST8290
Royal Oak (01666) 890250
Village signposted off A46 S of Nailsworth; GL8 8UN Handsome early 18th-c mullioned-windowed village pub under new ownership; rambling beamed bar with two log fires, stripped stonework and pastel paintwork, mix of furniture including country pine, candles on tables, ales such as Flying Monk, Uley and Wye Valley, traditional cider and several wines by the glass, good food from interesting varied menu including some pub favourites, helpful friendly service; children and dogs welcome, disabled access, sheltered side courtyard with teak and metal furniture, surrounding walks (on Monarch's Way) and handy for Westonbirt Arboretum, closed Sun evening, Mon. *(Peter Brix, Alf Wright, Tom and Ruth Rees)*

LITTLE BARRINGTON
SP2012
Inn For All Seasons (01451) 844324
A40 3 miles W of Burford; OX18 4TN Handsome old coaching inn undergoing refurbishment as we went to press; attractive comfortable lounge bar with low beams, stripped stone, flagstones and log fire, a couple of ales such as Otter and St Austell, plenty of wines by the glass and nice range of malt whiskies, food can be very good too with emphasis on fish/seafood, restaurant and conservatory; background music, quiz night last Fri of every other month, cookery school; children and dogs (in bar) welcome, picnic-sets in garden with aunt sally, walks from the door, ten bedrooms, open all day weekends. *(R K Phillips, Peter Young)*

LITTLETON-UPON-SEVERN
ST5989
★White Hart (01454) 412275
3.5 miles from M48 junction 1; BS35 1NR Sympathetically refurbished 17th-c farmhouse with three main rooms; nice mix of country furnishings, log fires (loveseat in inglenook), flagstones at front, huge tiles at the back, well kept Youngs ales and guests, good range of ciders (including their own) and of other drinks, popular food cooked by landlord from bar snacks and traditional choices to more adventurous specials, good service; children and dogs welcome (theirs is Ralph), wheelchair access, tables on front lawn, more behind by orchard, vegetable patch and roaming poultry (eggs for sale), walks from the door, open all day, food all day Sun. *(Chris and Angela Buckell)*

LONGBOROUGH
SP1729
Coach & Horses (01451) 830325
Ganborough Road; GL56 0QU Traditional little 17th-c stone-built local, up to three well kept/priced Donnington ales, Weston's

cider and enjoyable reasonably priced pubby food including good ploughman's, friendly landlord and staff, leather armchairs on flagstones, inglenook woodburner, darts, dominoes and cribbage; background music, quiz last Sun of month; children and dogs welcome, tables out at front looking down on stone cross and pretty village, two simple clean bedrooms, handy for Sezincote house and gardens, open all day Fri-Sun. *(Mrs J Ekins-Daukes, Helene Grygar)*

LONGHOPE
SO6720
Farmers Boy (01452) 470105
Boxbush, Ross Road; A40 outside village; GL17 0LP Popular roadside country pub with a couple of Greene King ales and enjoyable range of food including signature pies, friendly service, heavy beams, log fire, restaurant and conservatory; background music and monthly tribute bands; children welcome, dogs in bar, picnic-sets in pleasant garden, eight courtyard bedrooms, open all day. *(Mike and Mary Carter)*

LOWER ODDINGTON
SP2326
★**Fox** (01451) 870555
Signed off A436; GL56 0UR Attractively presented 16th-c creeper-clad inn with emphasis on their excellent food including good value weekday set lunch, top notch service too from personable staff, Hook Norton and a couple of guests, Robinson's cider and well chosen wines, series of relaxed country-style flagstoned rooms with assorted chairs around pine tables, candles and fresh flowers, log fires including inglenook woodburner; background music; children and dogs (in bar) welcome, tables under parasols at front, enclosed cottagey back garden and heated terrace, pretty village, six comfortable bedrooms (three newly added in adjoining building). *(Alun and Jennifer Evans, Richard Tilbrook, Liz Bell, Martin Constable)*

LOWER SWELL
SP1725
Golden Ball (01451) 833886
B4068 W of Stow-on-the-Wold; GL54 1LF Welcoming 17th-c stone-built village local surrounded by good walks; well kept Donnington ales from the attractive nearby brewery and well prepared pubby food from landlord-chef, good attentive service, neatly kept beamed interior with some cosy nooks, woodburner; background music, sports TV, darts; children and dogs welcome, small garden and raised deck/balcony, aunt sally, one bedroom, open all day weekends, no food Sun evening. *(Michael and Jenny Back, Richard Tilbrook, Clive and Fran Dutson)*

MARSHFIELD
ST7773
★**Catherine Wheel** (01225) 892220
High Street; signed off A420 Bristol–Chippenham; SN14 8LR Attractive Georgian-fronted building in unspoilt village; high-ceilinged bare-stone front part with medley of settles, chairs and stripped tables, charming dining room with impressive open fireplace, cottagey beamed back area warmed by woodburners, three well kept ales such as Butcombe, Fullers and Wadsworths, interesting wines and other drinks, enjoyable sensibly priced food from pub favourites up; darts and dominoes, live music last Thurs of month, free wi-fi; well behaved children and dogs welcome, wheelchair access with help, flower-decked backyard, three bedrooms, open all day. *(Dr and Mrs A K Clarke)*

MAYSHILL
ST6882
New Inn (01454) 773161
Badminton Road (A432 Frampton Cotterell–Yate); BS36 2NT Popular largely 17th-c coaching inn with two comfortably carpeted bar rooms leading to restaurant, good choice of enjoyable generously served pub food at fair prices, friendly staff, three well kept changing ales, Weston's cider and decent wines by the glass, log fire; children and dogs welcome, garden with play area, open all day Fri-Sun, food all day weekends. *(Roger and Donna Huggins, Neil Hammacott)*

MEYSEY HAMPTON
SU1199
Masons Arms (01285) 850164
Just off A417 Cirencester–Lechlade; High Street; GL7 5JT Popular refurbished 17th-c village inn, good attractively presented food from sensibly short menu (all day Sun), well kept Arkells and several wines by the glass, welcoming helpful staff, longish open-plan beamed bar with big inglenook log fire at one end, tiled and boarded floors, scrubbed oak and pastel paintwork, restaurant; children and dogs (in bar) welcome, tables out on green, comfortable well appointed bedrooms, parking can be tricky, open all day weekends from midday (from 8.30am weekdays with a break 3-5pm). *(Sara Fulton, Roger Baker)*

MICKLETON
SP1543
★**Kings Arms** (01386) 438257
B4632 (ex A46); GL55 6RT 18th-c honey-stone pub with good imaginative food from lunchtime sandwiches to daily specials, real ales such as Greene King and Charles Wells, proper cider and several wines by the glass from interesting list, friendly helpful staff, atmospheric open-plan beamed lounge with nice mix of comfortable chairs, soft lighting and good log fire, lots of things to look at (some for sale), small locals' bar with darts, dominoes and cribbage; background music, free wi-fi; children and dogs welcome, circular picnic-sets under thatched parasols in courtyard, more tables in sizeable garden, attractive village, handy for Hidcote (NT) and Kiftsgate Court Gardens, open all day. *(Michael Doswell)*

MINCHINHAMPTON
SO8500
Old Lodge (01453) 832047
Nailsworth–Brimscombe – on common, fork left at pub's sign; OS Sheet 162 map reference 853008; GL6 9AQ Welcoming

dining pub (part of the Cotswold Food Club group) with civilised modern bistro feel, wood floors and stripped-stone walls, good food from pub favourites up, decent wines by the glass and well kept beers such as Otter and Stroud; children welcome, tables on neat lawn looking over NT common with grazing cows and horses, six bedrooms, open all day (food all day weekends). *(David Appleyard)*

MINCHINHAMPTON   SO8801
Ragged Cot (01453) 884643
Cirencester Road; NE of town; GL6 8PE
Attractively refurbished 17th-c Cotswold stone inn; front bar with open fire one end, woodburner the other, cushioned window seats and painted pine tables on wood-strip floor, connecting rooms including airy pitched-ceiling restaurant overlooking garden, emphasis on good (if not especially cheap) food from one or two pub favourites up, local ales including one badged for the pub, decent range of wines, good friendly service; outside café called 'the Shed', nine well appointed bedrooms. *(Jon Neighbour)*

MISERDEN   SO9308
Carpenters Arms (01285) 821283
Off B4070 NE of Stroud; GL6 7JA
Welcoming traditional country pub with opened-up low-beamed bar; stripped-stone walls, log fire and woodburner, some interesting old photographs, Wye Valley Butty Bach, HPA and a guest, several ciders and decent wines, ample helpings of enjoyable reasonably priced food using local/home-grown produce including good vegetarian choice, friendly staff; Weds folk night, quiz Thurs; children and dogs welcome, seats out in front and to the side, popular with walkers and handy for Miserden Park, open (and food) all day. *(Giles and Annie Francis)*

MORETON-IN-MARSH   SP2032
Black Bear (01608) 652992
High Street; GL56 0AX Unpretentious beamed and stripped-stone corner pub run by friendly welcoming family, no-frills locals' bar serving Donnington ales, generous helpings of tasty good value home-made food in airy dining room; sports TVs; children welcome. *(Richard Tilbrook)*

MORETON-IN-MARSH   SP2032
Inn on the Marsh (01608) 650709
Stow Road next to duck pond; GL56 0DW
Stone-built roadside pub with comfortable beamed bar, inglenook woodburner and some dutch influences to the décor, chef-landlady is dutch and cooks good value national dishes alongside pub favourites, well kept Marstons-related beers and guests, cheerful welcoming staff, modern conservatory restaurant;

background music from vintage vinyl or maybe landlord playing his guitar; children and dogs welcome, seats at front and in back garden, closed Mon lunchtime. *(Bill Farmer)*

MORETON-IN-MARSH   SP2032
Redesdale Arms (01608) 650308
High Street; GL56 0AW Relaxed 17th-c hotel (former coaching inn); alcoves and big stone fireplace in comfortable solidly furnished panelled bar on right, darts in flagstoned public bar, Wickwar ales, decent wines and coffee, enjoyable food from breakfast on served by courteous helpful staff, spacious child-friendly back brasserie and dining conservatory; background music, TVs, games machine; heated floodlit courtyard, 34 comfortable bedrooms (newer ones in mews), open all day from 8am. *(Dr and Mrs A K Clarke)*

MORETON-IN-MARSH   SP2032
White Hart Royal (01608) 650731
High Street; GL56 0BA Substantial 17th-c coaching inn with Charles II connection; cosy beamed quarry-tiled bar with fine inglenook and nice old furniture, adjacent smarter panelled room with Georgian feel, separate lounge and restaurant, Hook Norton and a guest ale, good choice of wines, well liked food from sandwiches and pub favourites up including children's choices, good friendly service; background music; courtyard tables, 28 bedrooms, good breakfast, open all day. *(Dr and Mrs A K Clarke)*

NAILSWORTH   ST8499
Britannia (01453) 832501
Cossack Square; GL6 0DG Large open-plan pub (part of the small Cotswold Food Club chain) in former manor house; popular bistro food (best to book evenings) including stone-baked pizzas, friendly helpful service, well kept Hook Norton, Wadworths and guests, good choice of wines by the glass, big log fire; children welcome, picnic-sets in front garden, open all day (food all day weekends). *(Julia Hanmer)*

NAUNTON   SP1123
★**Black Horse** (01451) 850565
Off B4068 W of Stow-on-the-Wold; GL54 3AD Welcoming locals' pub with well kept/priced Donnington BB and SBA, Weston's cider and popular home-made food from traditional favourites to daily specials such as seasonal game, bargain set menu Mon evening (must book), friendly efficient service, black beams, stripped stone, flagstones and log fire, dining room; background music, darts and dominoes; children and dogs welcome, small seating area outside, charming village

---

We checked prices with the pubs as we went to press in summer 2017.
They should hold until around spring 2018.

and fine Cotswold walks (walking groups asked to pre-order food), open all day Fri-Sun. *(Richard Tilbrook, Peter Young)*

NIBLEY   ST6982

Swan (01454) 312290

Badminton Road; BS37 5JF Part of small local pub group, friendly and relaxed, with good food from snacks to daily specials, Bath, Butcombe and Cotswold Spring, real cider and over a dozen wines by the glass, good service, modernised interior with fireside leather sofas one side, dining tables the other, separate restaurant; background music; children and dogs (in bar) welcome, garden picnic-sets, open all day. *(Ian Cooper)*

NORTH NIBLEY   ST7596

New Inn (01453) 543659

E of village itself; Waterley Bottom; GL11 6EF Former cider house in secluded rural setting popular with walkers; well kept Moles, Wickwar and a weekend guest from antique pumps, fine range of ciders and perries (more in bottles), enjoyable food cooked by landlord from lunchtime sandwiches and good ploughman's up, lounge bar with cushioned windsor chairs and high-backed settles, partly stripped-stone walls, simple cosy public bar with darts (no children here after 6pm), cider festivals and other events (maybe local mummers); no credit cards; dogs welcome, hitching rail and trough for horses, picnic-sets and swings on lawn, covered decked area with pool table, two bedrooms, open all day weekends, closed Mon lunchtime (evening too in winter). *(Susan Eccleston)*

OLD DOWN   ST6187

★**Fox** (01454) 412507

3.9 miles from M5 junction 15/16; A38 towards Gloucester, then Old Down signposted; turn left into Inner Down; BS32 4PR Tucked-away yet popular family-owned country pub; ales from Bath, Butcombe, Exmoor and Sharps, real cider and several wines by the glass, good reasonably priced traditional food (not Sun evening) from baguettes up, friendly helpful staff and warm local atmosphere, low beams, carpeted, wood or flagstone floors, magnolia walls with beige dados, log fire, plain modern wooden furniture, dark green faux leather wall seats in bar, snug family room; live music first Sat of month; dogs welcome, good disabled access (no loos), long verandah with grapevine, front and back gardens, play area, open all day Sun. *(Chris and Angela Buckell)*

OLD SODBURY   ST7581

Dog (01454) 312006

3 miles from M4 junction 18, via A46 and A432; The Hill (a busy road); BS37 6LZ Welcoming old pub under newish management; popular two-level carpeted bar, low beams, stripped stone and open fire, good fairly priced food from sandwiches

and baked potatoes to fresh fish and steaks, friendly young staff, Sharps Doom Bar and three Wickwar ales; children and dogs welcome, handy for Cotswold Way walkers, big garden with paved terrace, four annexe bedrooms, open all day. *(Tom and Ruth Rees, Stephen Woad, Giles and Annie Francis)*

PAINSWICK   SO8609

Falcon (01452) 814222

New Street; GL6 6UN Handsome stone-built inn dating from the 16th c; sympathetically updated open-plan layout with bar and two dining areas, good, popular food including daily specials, four well kept beers and good choice of wines by the glass, friendly young staff; occasional live music; children and dogs welcome, 12 comfortable bedrooms, opposite churchyard famous for its 99 yews. *(Peter Young)*

PARKEND   SO6107

Fountain (01594) 562189

Just off B4234; GL15 4JD Unpretentious 18th-c village inn by terminus of restored Dean Forest Railway; well kept Goffs, Sharps and Wye Valley, Weston's cider, wines in glass-sized bottles, enjoyable home-made traditional food including Sun carvery and OAP weekday lunch menu, welcoming helpful staff, assorted chairs and settles in two linked rooms, old tools, bric-a-brac, photographs and framed local history information, coal fire; quiz and live music nights; children, walkers and dogs welcome, wheelchair access, side garden, eight bedrooms and bunkhouse, open all day Sat. *(Monica and Steph Evans)*

PARKEND   SO6308

Rising Sun (01594) 562008

Off B4431; GL15 4HN Perched on wooded hillside and approached by roughish single-track drive – popular with walkers and cyclists; open-plan carpeted bar with modern pub furniture, Wickwar BOB and several guests, real ciders and well priced straightforward food from sandwiches and baked potatoes up, friendly service, lounge/games area with pool and machines; children and dogs welcome, wheelchair access with help, views from balcony and terrace tables under umbrellas, big woodside garden with play area and duck pond, self-catering accommodation, open (and food) all day. *(Louise and Oliver Redman)*

PAXFORD   SP1837

Churchill Arms (01386) 593159

B4479, SE of Chipping Campden; GL55 6XH 17th-c village dining pub under newish management; good well presented food from chef-owner including cheaper lunchtime set menu, a house beer (Winston) brewed by North Cotswold and two local guests, several wines by the glass from good list, friendly helpful service, attractively updated open-plan interior with flagstone and wood floors, some low painted beams and inglenook woodburner; children and dogs welcome, picnic-sets on small front terrace and gravelled back area, two bedrooms (may be adding a couple more), limited street parking, closed Sun evening and Mon, otherwise open all day. *(Jeff Wright)*

POULTON   SP1001
Falcon (01285) 850878
London Road; GL7 5HN Popular bistro-feel village dining pub with highly regarded food from chef-owner including good value set lunch, well kept Hook Norton Old Hooky, a local guest beer and nice wines by the glass, friendly attentive service, neat modern interior with some old black beams, relaxed easy-going atmosphere; background music; well behaved children welcome, closed Sun evening, Mon.
(Tom and Ruth Rees, Giles and Annie Francis)

QUENINGTON   SP1404
Keepers Arms (01285) 750349
Church Road; GL7 5BL Community local in pretty Cotswold village, cosy and comfortable, with stripped stone, low beams and log fires, friendly helpful landlord and staff, good fairly priced food in bar and restaurant from sandwiches to popular Sun lunch (no food Sun evening), well kept changing local beers and a traditional cider; dogs welcome, picnic-sets out in front, three bedrooms, closed Mon and Tues lunchtimes. *(Dennis and Doreen Haward, R K Phillips)*

SALFORD HILL   SP2629
Greedy Goose (01608) 646551
Junction A44/A436, near Chastleton; GL56 0SP Old roadside country dining pub with contemporary interior, enjoyable food from sandwiches and stone-baked pizzas up, three North Cotswold ales, friendly staff; children and dogs welcome, seats out at front and in back decked/gravelled area, camping, open all day. *(Ian Cooper)*

SAPPERTON   SO9403
★ Bell (01285) 760298
Village signposted from A419 Stroud–Cirencester; OS Sheet 163 map reference 948033; GL7 6LE Welcoming 250-year-old pub-restaurant with cosy connecting rooms around central bar, beams and exposed stonework, flagstone, wood and quarry-tiled floors, log fires, four well kept ales including a house beer from St Austell, plenty of wines by the glass and good choice of other drinks, well liked food (not Sun evening) from sandwiches, sharing boards and pub favourites to more ambitious choices, good friendly service; children and dogs welcome, seats out in front and in back courtyard

garden, tethering for horses, plenty of surrounding walks, open all day (till 9pm Sun). *(Alisongrindrod, Helene Grygar)*

SAPPERTON   SO9303
Daneway Inn (01285) 760297
Daneway; off A419 Stroud–Cirencester; GL7 6LN Quietly tucked-away 18th-c pub under new licensees; three sympathetically refurbished linked rooms with bare boards or carpet, woodburner in amazing floor-to-ceiling carved oak dutch fireplace, also an inglenook, up to four Wadworths ales including a summer elderflower beer (Rare Find, named for the Large Blue butterfly found here), traditional cider/perry and enjoyable uncomplicated food at fair prices, friendly staff, traditional games such as shove-ha'penny and ring the bull; folk night first/third Thurs of month, open mike second Sat, quiz third Tues; children and dogs welcome, tricky wheelchair access (there are disabled loos), terrace tables and lovely sloping lawn, good walks by disused canal with tunnel to Coates, surrounding nature reserves, campsite with shepherd's hut, open all day in summer (closed Sun and Mon evenings in winter). *(Nicholas and Maddy Trainer)*

SELSLEY   SO8303
Bell (01453) 753801
Bell Lane; GL5 5JY Attractively updated 16th-c village dining pub with rooms; good well presented food cooked by landlord-chef from pub favourites up, Stroud, Uley and a local guest, several wines by the glass including champagne and over 40 gins, friendly helpful service, three connecting rooms, open fire and woodburner, also garden room dining extension; children, walkers and dogs welcome (their dog is Bacchus), lovely valley views from terrace tables, near Selsley Common and Cotswold Way, two comfortable bedrooms, closed Sun evening (and 3-5pm Mon-Thurs in winter). *(Ruth Kelham, M Free)*

SHIPTON MOYNE   ST8989
Cat & Custard Pot (01666) 880249
Off B4040 Malmesbury–Bristol; The Street; GL8 8PN Popular early 18th-c pub (some recent expansion) in picturesque village; at least three real ales such as Flying Monk, Hook Norton and Wickwar, Weston's cider, some local gins and eight wines by the glass, enjoyable freshly made pubby food (not Sun evening), friendly service, deceptively spacious inside with several dining areas, beams and bric-a-brac, hunting prints, cosy back snug, woodburner; sports TV; children, walkers and dogs welcome, wheelchair access to bar only, shaded tables out on front lawn, handy for Beaufort Polo Club, Highgrove and Westonbirt Arboretum, five comfortable

---

Ring the bull is an ancient pub game — you try to lob a ring on a piece of string over a hook (occasionally a bull's horn) on a wall or ceiling.

bedrooms, open all day weekends. *(Michael and Jenny Back, Chris and Angela Buckell)*

SLAD   SO8707
Woolpack (01452) 813429
B4070 Stroud–Birdlip; GL6 7QA Popular early 19th-c hillside village pub with lovely valley views; four unspoilt little connecting rooms, interesting photographs including some of Laurie Lee who was a regular (his books for sale), log fire, good imaginative food (not Sun evening) along with pub favourites and Sun pizza night, well kept Uley ales and guests, local farm cider/perry and decent wines by the glass, friendly prompt service; some live music; children, walkers and dogs welcome, nice garden taking in the view, open all day. *(Jeff Wright)*

SLIMBRIDGE   SO7204
Tudor Arms (01453) 890306
Shepherds Patch; off A38 towards Slimbridge Wetlands Centre; GL2 7BP Much extended red-brick pub just back from canal swing bridge; welcoming and popular with six mainly local ales, eight ciders/perries and good wines by the glass, also some interesting whiskies and gins such as welsh Penderyn, enjoyable well priced food from baguettes to daily specials including weekday two-course lunch deal, prompt friendly service, linked areas with wood, flagstone or carpeted floors, some leather chairs and settles, comfortable dining room, conservatory; darts, pool and skittle alley; children and dogs (in back bar) welcome, disabled access/loos, tables on part-shaded terrace, boat trips, 12 annexe bedrooms, caravan site off car park, open (and food) all day from 7.30am for breakfast. *(Chris and Angela Buckell, Peter Young, B A Congreve)*

SNOWSHILL   SP0933
Snowshill Arms (01386) 852653
Opposite village green; WR12 7JU Unpretentious country pub in honeypot village – so no shortage of customers; well kept Donnington ales and reasonably priced straightforward (but tasty) food from sandwiches up, prompt friendly service, beams, log fire, stripped stone and neat array of tables, charming village views from bow windows, local photographs; skittle alley; children and dogs welcome, big back garden with stream and play area, handy for Snowshill Manor (NT), lavender farm and Cotswold Way walks. *(Eddie Edwards, Mr and Mrs Richard Osborne)*

SOMERFORD KEYNES   SU0195
Bakers Arms (01285) 861298
On main street through village; GL7 6DN Pretty little 17th-c stone-built pub with catslide roof; four well kept ales including Butcombe, Sharps and Stroud, Addlestone's cider, good house wines, generous helpings of tasty traditional food, friendly service, lots of pine tables in two linked areas,

fire in big stone fireplace; children and dogs welcome, nice garden with play area, lovely village, handy for Cotswold Water Park, open (and food) all day except Sun when shuts at 6pm. *(Martin Day)*

STANTON   SP0634
★ Mount (01386) 584316
Village signposted off B4632 SW of Broadway; keep on past village on no-through road uphill, bear left; WR12 7NE 17th-c pub with fine views over village towards the welsh mountains; flagstoned bars with heavy beams in low ceilings, inglenook log fire, well kept Donnington ales, good wines by the glass and popular food from baguettes to daily specials, prompt friendly service, picture-window restaurant taking in the view; darts and board games, free wi-fi; well behaved children and dogs welcome, seats on terrace and in quiet garden, good walks (Cotswold Way and Wyche Way nearby), closed Sun evening, Mon in winter. *(Phil and Jane Villiers, S Holder, Mrs Julie Thomas, Dr A J and Mrs B A Tompsett, Mr and Mrs Richard Osborne)*

STAUNTON   SO7829
Swan (01452) 840323
Ledbury Road (A417), on mini roundabout; GL19 3QA Revamped village pub owned by local farming family; enjoyable well priced food (including own lamb) from ciabattas and deli boards up, ales such as Butcombe and Wye Valley, Weston's cider, bar with sofas and woodburner, spacious restaurant and modern conservatory, attached barn for functions; live music last Sat of month, quiz nights, free wi-fi; children and dogs welcome, pretty garden, open all day Fri-Sun, closed Mon and Tues lunchtimes (no evening food on these days). *(Dan Gardiner)*

STAUNTON   SO5412
White Horse (01594) 834001
A4136; GL16 8PA Village pub on edge of Forest of Dean close to welsh border, welcoming and relaxed, with good freshly prepared food in bar or restaurant including popular Sun lunch, well kept local ales and ciders, friendly helpful service; small shop; children and dogs welcome, disabled access, picnic-sets in good-sized garden with glamping pods, open all day Sat, till 5pm Sun, closed Mon and lunchtime Tues. *(Margaret McDonald)*

STAVERTON   SO9024
House in the Tree (01242) 680241
Haydon (B4063 W of Cheltenham); GL51 0TQ Friendly old beamed and partly thatched pub, five real ales including Dartmoor, Otter and Sharps, traditional cider and decent wine list, well liked generously served food including daily specials, rambling linked areas, open fires; children and dogs welcome, plenty of tables in garden with

good play area and pets corner, handy for M5 (junction 10), open all day, food all day Sat, till 6pm Sun. *(David Shaw)*

STOW-ON-THE-WOLD   SP1925
★**Bell** (01451) 870916
Park Street; A436 E of centre; GL54 1AJ
Busy creeper-clad dining pub with comfortable homely décor, good well presented food from breakfasts and bar snacks up (best to book), friendly efficient service, lots of wines by the glass including champagne, a couple of Youngs ales and a guest, proper beamed and flagstoned bar with woodburner and piano; under-16s in dining part only, dogs welcome, picnic-sets outside, five bedrooms, eight more in nearby townhouse, open (and some food) all day. *(Bill Webster, Richard Tilbrook)*

STOW-ON-THE-WOLD   SP1925
Kings Arms (01451) 830364
The Square; GL54 1AF Revamped 16th-c coaching inn; black-beamed bar with wood floor, stripped stone and painted panelling, woodburner, Greene King ales (including one badged for the pub) and a guest, good up-to-date food here or in upstairs Chophouse restaurant with saggy oak floor, leopard-skin bar stools and ink-spot tables, prompt friendly service; children and dogs welcome, ten bedrooms including three courtyard 'cottages', open all day. *(I D Barnett, Guy Vowles)*

STOW-ON-THE-WOLD   SP1925
★**Talbot** (01451) 870934
The Square; GL54 1BQ Cheerfully bustling one-bar pub in good position on market square; light and airy modern décor with relaxed café-bar feel, well liked interesting food including good set lunch, four Wadworths ales and several wines by the glass, cocktails, afternoon teas and proper coffee, huge mirror over big log fire, upstairs function room (and lavatories); background and occasional live music, Tues quiz; no children inside, a few courtyard tables, open all day (till 6pm Sun). *(Richard Tilbrook)*

STROUD   SO8505
Ale House (01453) 755447
John Street; GL5 2HA Fine range of well kept beers and ciders/perries (third-of-a-pint tasting glasses available), enjoyable food including signature curries and good value Sun lunch, main high-ceilinged part with sofa by big open fire, other rooms off; well behaved dogs welcome (biscuits for them), small side courtyard, farmers' market Sat, open all day Fri-Sun. *(Alf and Sally Garner)*

SWINEFORD   ST6969
Swan (0117) 932 3101
A431, right on the Somerset border; BS30 6LN Popular 19th-c roadside pub, well kept Bath Ales and a guest, local ciders, decent wines and good range of whiskies and gins including Penderyn welsh whisky, enjoyable food from lunchtime sandwiches up, efficient friendly staff, updated interior with quarry tiles and light wood floors, pastel paintwork and bluey-green panelling, raised back dining area, open fire; daily newspapers; children and dogs welcome, wheelchair access to most parts, picnic-sets out at front and in large grassy garden with play area and chickens, open all day, food all day Fri-Sun. *(Michael Doswell, Chris and Angela Buckell, Ian and Rose Lock)*

TETBURY   ST8893
Close (01666) 502272
Long Street; GL8 8AQ Old stone hotel's contemporary bar, comfortable and stylish with blazing log fire, enjoyable food from sandwiches up, also brasserie and more formal dining room, coffee and afternoon teas, charming staff; children welcome, tables in lovely garden behind, open all day. *(Joe and Belinda Smart)*

TETBURY   ST8893
Priory (01666) 502251
London Road; GL8 8JJ Civilised restaurant-pub-hotel; central log fire in comfortable high-raftered stone-built former stables, popular food (booking advised) with emphasis on local produce, even a local slant to their good wood-fired pizzas, cheerful service, three well kept ales including Uley, proper ciders and several wines by the glass, comfortable coffee lounge; children very welcome, dogs in bar, wheelchair access (staff helpful), roadside terrace picnic-sets, 14 bedrooms, open all day. *(Frank Hough)*

TETBURY   ST8993
★**Snooty Fox** (01666) 502436
Market Place; GL8 8DD High-ceilinged stripped-stone hotel lounge, four well kept local ales, a real cider and good house wines, enjoyable all-day bar food from sandwiches up, leather sofas and elegant fireplace, nice side room and anteroom, restaurant; background music; children and dogs welcome, a few sheltered tables out in front, 12 bedrooms. *(Frank Hough)*

TEWKESBURY   SO8931
Gupshill Manor (01684) 292278
Gloucester Road (off A38 S edge of town); GL20 5SG Spacious old timbered building with series of lounge and dining areas, plenty of easy chairs and sofas, beams and open fires, good choice of enjoyable food including weekday set menu, friendly efficient staff, three well kept Greene King ales and a guest, decent wine list; background music, live jazz last Sun of month; children and dogs (in some parts) welcome, disabled access, tables out on partly covered terrace and grass, open (and food) all day from 9.30am (10am weekends) for breakfast. *(Peter Young)*

TEWKESBURY SO8932
Nottingham Arms (01684) 276346
High Street; GL20 5JU Popular old
black and white-fronted bare-boards local,
timbered bar with well kept St Austell,
Sharps and Wye Valley, Weston's cider,
enjoyable home-made food at reasonable
prices including good Sun lunch, well
priced wines too, friendly efficient
service, back dining room; music and
quiz nights; children and dogs welcome,
open all day. *(Dr J Barrie Jones)*

TEWKESBURY SO8932
Royal Hop Pole (01684) 274039
Church Street; GL20 5RT Wetherspoons
conversion of old inn (some parts dating
from the 15th c), their usual value-minded
all-day food and drink, good service; free
wi-fi; terrace seating and lovely garden
leading down to river, 28 bedrooms, open
from 7am. *(Theocsbrian)*

TEWKESBURY SO8932
Theoc House (01684) 296562
Barton Street; GL20 5PY Old pub now
more like a café/wine bar but with local
ales, good range of reasonably priced
food including tapas and vegetarian
choices, enthusiastic young staff,
spacious split-level interior, books and
board games; live jazz second and last
Weds of month, free wi-fi; children and
dogs welcome, open (and food) all day
from 8.30am breakfast. *(Guy Vowles)*

TODDINGTON SP0432
Pheasant (01242) 621271
*A46 Broadway–Winchcombe, junction
with A438 and B4077; GL54 5DT* Large
stone-built roadside pub with modern
open-plan interior, tartan carpets, blue
panelled dados and log fire, Donnington
ales and enjoyable good value food, friendly
attentive staff; children and dogs (in
bar area) welcome, handy for preserved
Gloucestershire Warwickshire Steam
Railway, open all day. *(Theocsbrian)*

TOLLDOWN ST7577
Crown (01225) 891166
*1 mile from M4 junction 18 – A46
towards Bath; SN14 8HZ* Cosy heavy-
beamed stone pub on crossroads; most
here for the good food (all day Sun) from
sandwiches and pub favourites to more
upmarket choices, efficient welcoming staff,
Wadworths ales, Thatcher's cider and plenty
of wines by the glass, warm log fires, candles
on pine tables, wood, coir and quarry-tiled
floors, animal prints on green rough plaster
walls, some bare stonework; children and
dogs (in bar) welcome, disabled access/
loos, sunny beer garden, nine bedrooms in
building behind, handy for Dyrham Park
(NT), open all day. *(Chris and Angela Buckell,
Dr and Mrs A K Clarke, Tom and Ruth Rees)*

ULEY ST7998
Old Crown (01453) 860502
The Green; GL11 5SN Unspoilt 17th-c
pub prettily set by village green just off
Cotswold Way; long narrow room with
settles and pews on bare boards, step up to
partitioned-off lounge, six well kept local
ales including Uley, decent wines by the glass
and small choice of well liked pubby food
from baguettes up, friendly service, open fire;
children and dogs welcome, a few picnic-sets
in front and attractive garden behind, four
bedrooms, open all day. *(David Appleyard)*

UPPER ODDINGTON SP2225
Horse & Groom (01451) 830584
*Village signposted from A436 E of
Stow-on-the-Wold; GL56 0XH* 16th-c
inn refurbished under new management;
beamed bar with pale polished flagstones,
stripped-stone walls and inglenook log
fire, three real ales including Brakspears
and Wye Valley, local cider and plenty of
wines by the glass, enjoyable food from pub
favourites up in bar, comfortable lounge or
restaurant; background music, free wi-fi;
children and dogs welcome, tables under
parasols on terrace and in garden, renovated
bedrooms in main house and 'cottage', open
all day. *(Bernard Stradling, David Travis)*

WESTONBIRT ST8690
★Hare & Hounds (01666) 881000
A433 SW of Tetbury; GL8 8QL
Substantial roadside hotel with separate
entrance to pub; good food from snacks
and sharing boards up, well kept regional
ales and ciders, lots of wines by the glass
and good whisky/gin selection, afternoon
teas, prompt polite service from uniformed
staff, flagstoned bar with another panelled
one to the left, series of interconnecting
rooms with polished wood floors, various
pictures including hares and hounds,
woodburner in two-way fireplace, more
formal restaurant; children welcome, muddy
boots and dogs in bar, disabled access/loos,
shaded wicker tables out on front paved
terrace, pleasant gardens, 42 bedrooms
(some in outbuildings), handy for the
Arboretum, open all day and gets very busy
(especially weekend lunchtimes). *(Chris
and Angela Buckell, IAA, HMW, Maria Sansoni)*

WILLERSEY SP1039
Bell (01386) 858405
*B4632 Cheltenham–Stratford, near
Broadway; WR12 7PJ* Imposing neatly
modernised 17th-c stone pub overlooking
village green and duck pond; popular
home-made food from sandwiches and
bar meals up, Purity UBU and Mad
Goose, good friendly service; children
welcome, dogs in bar, lots of tables in
big garden, good local walks (Cotswold
Way), five bedrooms in outbuildings,
open all day weekends. *(Dave Braisted)*

WINCHCOMBE   SP0228
★**White Hart** (01242) 602359
High Street (B4632); GL54 5LJ
Popular 16th-c inn with big windows
looking out over village street, mix of
chairs and small settles around pine
tables on bare boards, well kept ales such
as Goffs, Otter and Sharps, wine shop at
back (corkage added if you buy to drink
on premises), also good choice by the
glass, well cooked generous food including
specials, afternoon teas, good friendly
service, separate restaurant; children and
dogs (in bar and bedrooms) welcome,
open all day from 8am (9am weekends)
for breakfast. *(Lorna and Jack Mulgrave)*

WITHINGTON   SP0315
Mill Inn (01242) 890204
Off A436 or A40; GL54 4BE Idyllic
streamside setting for this mossy-roofed old
stone inn, plenty of character with nice nooks
and corners, beams, wood/flagstone floors,
two inglenook log fires and woodburner,
well kept/priced Sam Smiths tapped from
the cask and ample helpings of enjoyable
traditional food including basket meals,
four dining rooms, cheerful staff coping well
at busy times; children and dogs welcome,
picnic-sets in big garden, splendid walks,
open all day in summer (in winter open all
day Sat, closed Sun evening). *(Dennis and
Doreen Haward, Richard Tilbrook, Peter Young)*

WOODCHESTER   SO8403
Old Fleece (01453) 872582
*Rooksmoor; A46 a mile S of Stroud;
GL5 5NB* Old wisteria-clad roadside pub,
part of the small Cotswold Food Club chain;
decent choice of well presented popular
food from sharing plates up, well kept mostly
local beers and good wines by the glass,
friendly helpful service, bar, dining room
and snug, big mullioned windows, bare
boards, panelling and stripped stone, modern
paintings, large log fire; children welcome,
wheelchair access (except dining area –
you can eat in the bar), two front terraces,
open (and food) all day. *(Liz and
Martin Eldon)*

WOOLASTON COMMON   SO5900
Rising Sun (01594) 529282
*Village signed off A48 Lydney–Chepstow;
GL15 6NU* Traditional 17th-c stone
village pub on fringe of Forest of Dean,
friendly and welcoming, with enjoyable
reasonably priced home-made food including
signature pies, well kept Butcombe, Wye
Valley and a guest, good helpful service;
children and dogs welcome, seats out at
front and in large back garden, open all
day weekends in summer, closed Mon
and Tues lunchtimes. *(Dan Gardiner)*

Post Office address codings confusingly give the impression that some pubs are in
Gloucestershire, when they're really in Warwickshire (which is where we list them).

Hampshire

AMPORT
Hawk Inn 🛏

SU2944 Map 2

(01264) 710371 – www.hawkinnamport.co.uk

*Off A303 at Thruxton interchange; at Andover end of village just before Monxton;
SP11 8AE*

**Relaxed rambling pub with contemporary furnishings in front bar
and dining areas, helpful staff and well thought-of food; bedrooms**

The comfortable front bar in this rambling old place is open-plan and modern, with brown leather armchairs and plush grey sofas by a low table, a log fire in a brick fireplace and sisal matting on bare boards. To the left, a tucked-away snug room has horse-racing photographs, shelves of books and a TV. Two dining areas have smart window blinds, black leather cushioned wall seating and elegant wooden chairs (some carved) around pale tables, big oil paintings on pale walls above a grey dado, and a woodburning stove. Black-topped stools line the counter, where courteous staff serve Upham Punter and Tipster and a couple of guests such as Box Steam Piston Broke and Wadworths 6X on handpump and quite a few wines by the glass. The sunny sandstone front terrace has picnic-sets looking across the lane to more seating on grass that leads down to Pill Hill Brook. Bedrooms are up to date and comfortable. The famous Hawk Conservancy Trust is just down the road.

🍴 Food is good and starts with breakfasts (7.30-10.30am weekdays, 8.30-10.30am weekends), moving on to sandwiches, chicken and wild mushroom mousse with a chorizo crust, pickled wild mushrooms and mushroom salsa, sweet pepper and goats cheese quiche with pepper and leaf salad, sharing platters, local sausages of the day with bubble and squeak, a duck egg and red onion marmalade, slow-roast lamb breast with dauphinoise potatoes and redcurrant jus, hake fillet with tomato, prawn and spinach tagliatelle and basil beurre blanc, and puddings such as lemon and lime posset with clotted cream and dark chocolate brownie with chocolate sauce and raspberry sorbet. *Benchmark main dish: burger with toppings, home-made sauce, coleslaw and fries £14.50. Two-course evening meal £21.00.*

Free house ~ Licensee Becky Anderson ~ Real ale ~ Open 7.30am-11pm; 8.30am-11pm Sat; 8.30am-10.30pm Sun ~ Bar food 12-2.30, 6-9 (9.30 Fri, Sat) ~ Children welcome ~ Dogs allowed in bar ~ Wi-fi ~ Bedrooms: /£90 *Recommended by Emma Scofield, Simon Sharpe, Andrew Lawson, Liz and Martin Eldon*

If we know a featured-entry pub does sandwiches, we always say so – if they're not
mentioned, you'll have to assume you can't get one.

 BANK

SU2806   Map 2

Oak

(023) 8028 2350 – www.oakinnlyndhurst.co.uk

Signposted just off A35 SW of Lyndhurst; SO43 7FD

**New Forest pub with a good mix of customers, popular food
and interesting décor**

Even though this is in a peaceful New Forest spot, it gets pretty busy
at peak times. But the friendly staff offer a warm welcome to all and
remain efficient and helpful. The L-shaped bar has bay windows with built-in
red-cushioned seats, and two or three little pine-panelled booths with small
built-in tables and bench seats. The rest of the bare-boarded bar has low
beams and joists, candles in brass holders on a row of stripped old and
newer pale wood tables set against the wall and all manner of bric-a-brac:
fishing rods, spears, a boomerang, old ski poles, brass platters, heavy knives
and guns. There are cushioned milk churns along the bar counter and little
red lanterns among hop bines above the bar. Fullers London Pride, HSB and
Seafarers and a changing local guest on handpump and 14 wines by the glass;
background music. The pleasant side garden has picnic-sets and long tables
and benches by big yew trees.

 Much liked food includes sandwiches, black pudding rösti with bacon crisp and a
poached egg, crab salad with pickled apple and paprika mayonnaise, ricotta-filled
spinach gnocchi with tomato, artichoke, almonds and spinach, burger with toppings and
chips, a pie of the day, lamb, tomato and aubergine ragoût with sun-dried tomato and
cumin couscous and minted yoghurt, beer-marinated chicken with barley, peas, bacon
and gem lettuce, and puddings. *Benchmark main dish: beer-battered fish and chips
£14.50. Two-course evening meal £21.00.*

Fullers ~ Manager Carlos Dias ~ Real ale ~ Open 11.30-3, 5.30-11; 11.30-11 Sat; 12-10.30 Sun
~ Bar food 12-2.30, 6-9 (9.30 Fri); 12-5, 6-9.30 Sat; 12-5, 6-8 Sun ~ Children welcome until
6pm; must be over 10 after 6pm; no under-5s in restaurant in evening in school holidays ~
Dogs allowed in bar ~ Wi-fi *Recommended by M G Hart, Mr and Mrs D Hammond, Dave Braisted,
Alastair and Sheree Hepburn, Phil and Jane Villiers, Jane and Kai Horsburgh, Katharine Cowherd,
Darren and Jane Staniforth*

 BAUGHURST

SU5860   Map 2

Wellington Arms 🏅 ♀ 🛏

(0118) 982 0110 – www.thewellingtonarms.com

Baughurst Road, S of village; RG26 5LP

Hampshire Dining pub of the Year

**Small, pretty country pub-with-rooms, exceptional cooking
and a friendly welcome; character bedrooms**

Our readers love this delightful little country inn and it's beautifully kept
inside and out by the hands-on, hard-working owners and their courteous
staff. It is, of course, the marvellous food that most customers are here to
enjoy, but they do keep a couple of ales such as Longdog Bunny Chaser and
West Berkshire Good Old Boy on handpump, ten wines by the glass from a
smashing list, a farm cider and good aperitifs; background music. The dining
room is attractively decorated with an assortment of cushioned oak dining
chairs around a mix of polished tables on terracotta tiles, pretty blinds, brass
candlesticks, flowers and windowsills stacked with cookery books. The
garden has lovely herbaceous borders, teak tables and chairs under parasols
and some picnic-sets. The four bedrooms are charming and very well
equipped and breakfasts are first class.

Cooked by the landlord, the food (using their own vegetables, home-reared livestock, honey from their bees and other very carefully sourced produce) is delicious: pheasant, rabbit and pork terrine with spiced apple chutney, potato gnocchi with garlic, caramelised butternut squash, walnuts and sage, home-reared lamb with white wine and rosemary topped with flaky pastry, skate wing with brown butter, fried capers and anya potatoes, chargrilled local 28-day dry-aged 10oz rib-eye steak with red wine sauce, and puddings such as caramel custard with candied quince and raspberries and sherry trifle (jelly from their own elderflower cordial, raspberries, sponge, vanilla custard, whipped cream and almond praline); they also offer a simple two- and three-course set lunch. *Benchmark main dish: twice-baked cheddar soufflé on braised young leeks with cream and parmesan £9.85. Two-course evening meal £25.00.*

Free house ~ Licensees Simon Page and Jason King ~ Real ale ~ Open 9-3, 6-10.30 (11 Sat); 9-5 Sun ~ Bar food 12-1.30, 6-8.30 (9 Sat); 12-3 Sun ~ Children welcome ~ Dogs welcome ~ Wi-fi ~ Bedrooms: /£110 *Recommended by Kate Moran, Mark Morgan, Ben and Diane Bowie, Ron Corbett, Andrew and Ruth Simmonds, Nicholas and Maddy Trainer, John and Penny Wildon*

BEAULIEU

SU3902 Map 2

Montagu Arms

(01590) 614986 – www.montaguarmshotel.co.uk
Almost opposite Palace House; SO42 7ZL

Separate Monty's Bar, open all day for both drinks and food

Monty's Bar has its own entrance but is attached to the solidly built and civilised Montagu Arms hotel. Usefully open all day, this simply furnished bar has panelling, bare floorboards, bay windows and a mix of pale tables surrounded by tartan-cushioned dining chairs; winter log fire. There are still a couple of stools against the bar counter where they keep Ringwood Best and Fortyniner and a seasonal guest on handpump and several wines by the glass, served by cheerful, helpful bar staff. Across the entrance hall is a smarter panelled dining room. Do visit the hotel's tucked-away back garden which is quite charming in warm weather.

 Tasty food includes sandwiches, scallops with black pudding and broad bean purée, home-made local pork scotch egg with a soft-boiled free-range egg and spiced apple sauce, beer-battered haddock and chips, chicken caesar salad, burger with toppings and french fries, a pie and a risotto of the day, lamb rump with dauphinoise potatoes, crispy shoulder croquette and lamb jus, hake fillet with mussels, lemon fondant potato and wild mushrooms, and puddings. *Benchmark main dish: fish pie £12.95. Two-course evening meal £20.00.*

Free house ~ Licensee Sunil Kanjanghat ~ Real ale ~ Open 11-3, 6-11 (all day in school holidays); 11-3, 6-10.30 Sun ~ Bar food 12-2.30 (3 weekends), 6.30-9.30 ~ Restaurant ~ Children welcome ~ Dogs allowed in bar ~ Wi-fi ~ Bedrooms: /£149 *Recommended by Rob Anderson, Rona Mackinlay, Simon Day, Isobel Mackinlay, Usha and Terry Patel, Karl and Frieda Bujeya*

BRANSGORE

SZ1997 Map 2

Three Tuns 🌟 ◀

(01425) 672232 – www.threetunsinn.com
Village signposted off A35 and off B3347 N of Christchurch; Ringwood Road, opposite church; BH23 8JH

Pretty thatched pub with proper old-fashioned bar and good beers, a civilised main dining area and inventive food

Our readers enjoy their visits to this thatched 17th-c pub and return on a regular basis. It's run by helpful, friendly licensees who keep a good choice of ales that includes Otter Amber, Ringwood Best Bitter and Fortyniner and guests such as St Austell Proper Job and Thwaites Wainwright on handpump (they also hold a beer festival in September) plus a farm cider and a dozen wines by the glass. On the right is a separate traditional regulars' bar that seems almost taller than it is wide, with an impressive log-effect stove in a stripped-brick hearth, some shiny black panelling and individualistic pubby furnishings. The roomy low-ceilinged and carpeted main area has a fireside 'codgers' corner', as well as a good mix of comfortably cushioned low chairs around a variety of dining tables. The hanging baskets are lovely in summer and there are picnic-sets on an attractive, extensive, shrub-sheltered terrace with more tables on the grass looking over pony paddocks; pétanque. The Grade II listed barn is popular for parties – and they hold a civil ceremonies licence.

Creative food with some unusual touches includes sandwiches, snails in garlic pastry with crispy 'forest moss', wild mushrooms and watercress pesto, home-smoked salmon with shallot dressing, mussels with garlic, chilli, shallots and cider, local sausages and mash with crushed white beans and beef gravy, vegetarian moussaka, steak and heart pudding, venison bourguignon, prawn, mussels, cockles, clams, crab and lobster linguine with cream and aged parmesan, mini duck pie with pigeon and rabbit, chestnut purée, bacon and cassis jus, and puddings such as pumpkin pie with pumpkin ice-cream and deconstructed gin trifle. *Benchmark main dish: slow-roasted local pork with dauphinoise potatoes, dijonnaise sauce and compressed apple £14.95. Two-course evening meal £20.00.*

Enterprise ~ Lease Nigel Glenister ~ Real ale ~ Open 11-11; 11.30-10.30 Sun ~ Bar food 12-2.15, 6-9.15; 12-9.15 weekends and bank holidays ~ Restaurant ~ Children welcome ~ Dogs allowed in bar ~ Wi-fi *Recommended by Brian and Anna Marsden, Anne and Ben Smith, S Holder, Roy Shutz, Katharine Cowherd, Maria and Henry Lazenby, Jane and Philip Saunders, Phil and Jane Villiers*

CADNAM   SU2913 Map 2
White Hart ♀ ◖

(023) 8081 2277 – www.brunningandprice.co.uk/whitehartcadnam
Old Romsey Road, handy for M27 junction 1; SO40 2NP

New Forest pub with busy bar and dining rooms, a warm welcome, good choice of drinks and tasty food

The heart of things in this neatly extended, smart place is the bar with its long curved counter. Bustling with locals and visitors, this has an open fire, stools and tables on parquet flooring, Phoenix Brunning & Price Original, Flack Manor Double Drop, Hop Back Golden Best, Stonehenge Sign of Spring and Triple fff Moondance on handpump and good wines by the glass served by helpful, friendly staff. There's also a cosy area with a woodburning stove in a nice old brick fireplace, rugs and comfortable leather armchairs; background music and board games. Various dining rooms lead off with more rugs on carpet or tiles, all manner of cushioned dining chairs and wooden tables, frame-to-frame country pictures and photographs on pale walls above painted wooden dados, house plants on windowsills, mirrors and elegant metal chandeliers. The back terrace and garden have plenty of chairs and tables and there's a children's play area with a painted tractor.

A wide choice of well liked food includes sandwiches, prawn cocktail, mushrooms on toast with tarragon and garlic cream dressing, smoked haddock fishcake with a poached egg and chive and caper sauce, chicken, ham hock and leek pie, tandoori halloumi salad with pineapple, lime and mint, steak burger with toppings, coleslaw and chips, malaysian fish stew with sticky coconut rice, and puddings such as hot waffle with toffee apples and honeycomb ice-cream and lemon tart with lemon sorbet.

Benchmark main dish: braised lamb shoulder with dauphinoise potatoes and redcurrant jus £17.95. Two-course evening meal £21.00.

Brunning & Price ~ Manager Steve Butt ~ Real ale ~ Open 10.30am-11pm (10.30pm Sun) ~ Bar food 12-10; 12-10.30 Fri, Sat; 12-9.30 Sun ~ Restaurant ~ Children welcome ~ Dogs allowed in bar ~ Wi-fi *Recommended by Gerry and Rosemary Dobson, Tom Stone, Christopher Mannings, Victoria and James Sargeant, Rosie and John Moore*

 DROXFORD   SU6018   Map 2

Bakers Arms

(01489) 877533 ~ www.thebakersarmsdroxford.com
High Street; A32 5 miles N of Wickham; SO32 3PA

Welcoming, opened-up and friendly pub with good beers, interesting cooking and cosy corners

After enjoying one of the lovely walks along and around the nearby River Meon, head to this friendly place for a drink or a meal. There's an easy-going atmosphere and it's attractively laid out with the central bar as the main focus: Bowman Swift One and Wallops Wood (the brewery is only a mile away) and a guest such as Triple fff Altons Pride on handpump, local cider and 15 wines by the glass from a short, carefully chosen list. Well spaced tables on carpet or neat bare boards are spread around the airy L-shaped open-plan bar, with low leather chesterfields and an assortment of comfortably cushioned chairs at one end; a dark panelled dado, dark beams and joists and a modicum of country oddments emphasise the freshness of the crisp white paintwork; good log fire and board games. To one side, with a separate entrance, is the village post office. There are picnic-sets outside.

 Enjoyable food includes lunchtime baguettes (not Sunday), lots of tapas-type nibbles, whole baked camembert with chutney, local snails and ham hock in hot garlic butter with rarebit, prawn caesar salad, pie of the day, roast butternut squash and beetroot with cauliflower and kale, toasted seeds and wild garlic pesto, chicken breast with potato rösti and creamy wild mushroom sauce, local trout fillet with lemon and fennel risotto, local steak with beef dripping chips and a choice of sauce, and puddings such as crème brûlée and chocolate and fudge brownie with butterscotch ice-cream. *Benchmark main dish: crab thermidor with slaw, fries and lemon mayonnaise £17.50. Two-course evening meal £21.00.*

Free house ~ Licensees Adam and Anna Cordery ~ Real ale ~ Open 12-2, 6-11; 12-6 Sun ~ Bar food 12-2, 6-9; 12-2.30, 6-9.30 Fri, Sat; 12-4.30 Sun ~ Well behaved children welcome ~ Dogs allowed in bar ~ Wi-fi *Recommended by Kate Moran, Phil and Jane Villiers, Sophie Ellison, Ann and Colin Hunt, David Gunn, Martine and Fabio Lockley*

EAST STRATTON   SU5339   Map 2

Northbrook Arms

(01962) 774150 ~ www.thenorthbrookarms.com
Brown sign to pub off A33 4 miles S of A303 junction; SO21 3DU

Half a dozen beers and tasty food in pretty pub opposite the village green; bedrooms

Lord Northbrook owns this attractive brick-built pub and it's been part of his family estate for generations. The traditional tiled-floor bar on the right has beams and standing timbers, quite a mix of chairs and tables and up to five real ales on handpump, such as Andwell Resolute Bitter, Bowman Swift One, Butcombe Bitter, Sharps Cornish Coaster and Triple fff Altons Pride; quite a few wines by the glass too. The left-hand carpeted part is slightly more formal, ending in a dining room beyond a little central hall;

background music. The skittle alley is in the former stables. You can sit in the pretty country garden to the side or on the village green opposite. There are fine walks nearby.

🍴 Pleasing food includes sandwiches and hot ciabattas, home-made pork and black pudding scotch egg with crispy bacon, terrine of the day with piccalilli, sharing boards, honey and mustard-glazed ham with duck eggs, slow-cooked baby back ribs with sticky bourbon and cola glaze, slaw and sweet potato fries, beer-battered cod with tartare sauce, butternut squash, feta and spinach falafel burger with tzatziki and fries, lambs liver and bacon with red onion marmalade and port gravy, and puddings. *Benchmark main dish: pie of the day £13.95. Two-course evening meal £20.00.*

Free house ~ Licensee Ian Ashton ~ Real ale ~ Open 11-11 (10.30 Sun) ~ Bar food 12-3, 6-9; 12-9 Sat; 12-6 Sun ~ Restaurant ~ Children welcome ~ Dogs welcome ~ Wi-fi ~ Bedrooms: £80/£90 *Recommended by Simon and Alex Knight, Ted and Mary Bates, Sandra and Michael Smith, Tony and Jill Radnor*

FREEFOLK
SU4848 Map 2
Watership Down 🏅 ♥ 🍴 🛏
(01256) 892254 – www.watershipdowninn.com
Freefolk Priors, N of B3400 Whitchurch–Overton; brown sign to pub; RG28 7NJ

Cosy bar and open-plan dining rooms in refurbished country inn with five real ales, super food and pretty garden; bedrooms

This is an attractive 200-year-old brick-built inn at the foot of the North Wessex Downs with views over the River Test Valley. It's been carefully and thoughtfully refurbished, and the wood-floored bar has stools at the pale oak counter, high stools next to an elbow shelf and five real ales on handpump from within a 30-mile radius, such as Broken Bridge Henchman, Itchen Valley Pure Gold, Stonehenge Sign of Spring, Triple fff Moondance and West Berkshire Good Old Boy; there are several wines by the glass from a thoughtful list. Leading off here are two connected dining rooms with mate's chairs and cushioned settles (some draped with animal skins) around chunky tables on more bare boards or old brickwork, and a woodburning stove in a raised fireplace; throughout, plants line windowsills and modern art and photos are hung on pale paintwork above a grey-green dado. A conservatory with high-backed, cushioned wicker chairs around solid tables on floor tiles leads to a two-tiered terrace with seats and tables under big parasols; a large lawned area has plenty of picnic-sets. Three bedrooms (named after characters from the *Watership Down* novel) are airy and pretty and breakfasts are very good.

⭐ From a wide-ranging menu, the imaginative food includes ciabattas, scallops and sea bream fillet with vanilla parsnip purée and smoked pancetta, panko-coated goats cheese and thyme croquettes with candy beetroot purée, beer-battered halloumi with chargrilled aubergine, red onion and potatoes and tomato and chive sauce, greek-style chicken and pepper skewers with tzatziki, pork fillet with sweet potato purée and cider and sage sauce, 28-day-aged rare-breed steak with sauté wild mushrooms and potatoes and Jack Daniel's sauce, and puddings such as dark chocolate and salted caramel tart with vanilla bean ice-cream and cinnamon pain au raisin bread and butter pudding with Baileys anglaise; they also offer a two- and three-course set menu. *Benchmark main dish: steak burger with toppings, home-made tomato relish and chips £13.00. Two-course evening meal £22.00.*

Free house ~ Licensee Philip Denée ~ Real ale ~ Open 12-3, 6-11; 12-11.30 Fri-Sun ~ Bar food 12-2.30, 6.30-9; not Sun evening ~ Restaurant ~ Children welcome ~ Dogs allowed in bar ~ Wi-fi ~ Bedrooms: /£80 *Recommended by Martin and Sue Neville, Rupert and Sandy Newton, Andy and Louise Ramwell, Jess and George Cowley*

FRITHAM

Royal Oak ◖

SU2314 Map 2

(023) 8081 2606

Village signed from M27 junction 1; SO43 7HJ

Rural New Forest spot with traditional rooms, log fires, seven real ales and simple lunchtime food

'A gem' is how many of our readers describe this charming and quite unspoilt thatched pub. It's in a lovely spot right in the middle of the New Forest and part of a working farm, so there are ponies and pigs out on the green and plenty of livestock nearby. The three neatly kept, black-beamed rooms are straightforward but full of proper traditional character, with prints and pictures involving local characters on the white walls, restored panelling, antique wheelback, spindleback and other old chairs and stools with colourful seats around solid tables on oak floors, and two roaring log fires. The back bar has several books; darts and board games. Up to seven real ales are tapped from the cask including one named for the pub (from Bowman), Flack Manor Double Drop, Hop Back Summer Lightning, Ringwood Best and Fortyniner, Stonehenge Danish Dynamite and a guest ale from new local brewery Dancing Cows. Also, nine wines by the glass (mulled wine in winter), 14 country wines, local cider and a September beer festival; service remains friendly and efficient even when the pub is packed (which it often is). Summer barbecues may be held in the neatly kept big garden, which has a marquee for poor weather and a pétanque pitch. They have three shepherd's huts to rent for overnight stays.

 Good value, limited food – lunchtime only – consists of wholesome winter soup, a particularly good pork pie, quiche and sausages. *Benchmark main dish: home-cooked pork pie ploughman's £8.50.*

Free house ~ Licensees Neil and Pauline McCulloch ~ Real ale ~ Open 11-11; 12-10.30 Sun; 11-3, 5.30-11 weekdays in winter ~ Bar food 12-2.30 (3 weekends) ~ Children welcome ~ Dogs welcome *Recommended by Peter Meister, Ann and Colin Hunt, Philip Pascall, Patrick and Emma Stephenson, Buster and Helena Hastings*

HIGHCLERE

Yew Tree ♀ ⇌

SU4358 Map 2

(01635) 253360 – www.theyewtree.co.uk

Hollington Cross; RG20 9SE

Friendly country inn with character rooms, a good choice of drinks, enjoyable food and seats in garden; bedrooms

With Highclere Castle so close by, this bustling 17th-c place can get pretty packed at lunchtimes – particularly with *Downton Abbey* fans. The main door opens into a heavy-beamed character bar with leather tub chairs and a leather sofa in front of a two-way fireplace housing a chiminea stove, and stools and high chairs against the counter (church candles in chunky candlesticks to either side). Ringwood Best, West Berkshire Good Old Boy and a changing guest on handpump and good wines by the glass, served by friendly, helpful staff. Leading off to the left is a room with antlers and stuffed squirrels on the mantelpiece above an inglenook fireplace, books piled on shelves, a pale button-back leather window seat, a mix of wooden and painted dining chairs around nice old tables on red and black tiles or carpet and, at one end, a tartan and leather wall banquette; background music. Dining rooms to the left of the bar, divided by hefty timbers, have high-backed tartan seating creating booths and more wooden or painted chairs around a mix of tables on flagstones or sisal carpet. Doors go through to the garden where there's an outside bar and a variety of elegant metal and teak seats and tables either on gravel or raised decking. Well equipped and comfortable bedrooms (two on the ground floor) are named after trees; breakfasts are good.

🍴 The brasserie-style food includes crab and tarragon tortellini with fennel in bisque, pork terrine with rhubarb, garlic, spinach and spelt croquette with mushrooms and mustard leeks, half a roast chicken with cashews and bacon, beef and venison offal pie with cheese and potato topping, hake with mussels, crispy dumplings and white wine sauce, lamb rump with pressed shoulder, spiced aubergine and mint crème fraîche, and puddings such as vanilla cheesecake with berry compote and lemon tart with mango sorbet. *Benchmark main dish: beer-battered haddock and chips £13.95. Two-course evening meal £22.00.*

Free house ~ Licensee Tom Foster ~ Real ale ~ Open 8am-11pm (10pm Sun) ~ Bar food 12-2.30, 6-9 (8 Sun) ~ Children welcome ~ Dogs allowed in bar and bedrooms ~ Wi-fi ~ Bedrooms: /£120 *Recommended by Barbara Brown, Caroline Prescott, Emma Scofield, Andrew Wall, Susan and Tim Boyle*

HOOK
Hogget ◖
(01256) 763009 – www.thehogget.co.uk

SU7153 Map 2

1.1 miles from M3 junction 5; A287 N, at junction with A30 (car park just before traffic lights); RG27 9JJ

Well run and accommodating pub giving all-round good value

If you fancy a break from the nearby M3, then this cheerful, chatty pub is usefully open all day at weekends. The various rooms ramble around the central servery so there's plenty of space for all; the wallpaper, lighting and carpet pattern, plus high-backed stools and bar tables on the right at the back, give an easy-going and homely feel – as does the way the layout provides several smallish distinct areas. Ringwood Fortyniner, Thwaites Lancaster Bomber and a guest beer on handpump, 13 wines by the glass plus prosecco and plenty of neatly dressed staff; daily papers, background music and books (often cookbooks) on shelves. A sizeable terrace has sturdy tables and chairs, including some in a heated covered area.

🍴 Good food includes lunchtime sandwiches (not Sunday), sauté wild mushrooms on toast with a poached egg, moules marinière, halloumi, toad in the hole with onion gravy, crab and chorizo linguine, beer-battered fish and chips, slow-braised lamb shank in ale and rosemary with roast garlic mash and ale gravy, pork belly in cider with potato and celeriac dauphinoise and pan jus, and puddings such as rocky road chocolate brownie with vanilla ice-cream and sticky toffee pudding with salted caramel ice-cream. *Benchmark main dish: burger with toppings and chips £12.00. Two-course evening meal £20.00.*

Marstons ~ Lease Tom and Laura Faulkner ~ Real ale ~ Open 12-3, 6-11; 12-11 Sat; 12-6 Sun ~ Bar food 12-2.30, 6.30-9; 12-9 Sat; 12-6 Sun ~ Restaurant ~ Children welcome but not after 7pm Fri, Sat ~ Dogs allowed in bar ~ Wi-fi *Recommended by Mrs P Sumner, Mike Swan, Roger and Donna Huggins, Jo Garnett*

Please tell us if the décor, atmosphere, food or drink at a pub is different from our description. We rely on readers' reports to keep us up to date: feedback@goodguides.com, or (no stamp needed) The Good Pub Guide, FREEPOST RTXY–ZCBC–BBAZ, Stream Lane, Sedlescombe, Battle TN33 0PB.

HURSLEY
Kings Head ♀ ◀ ⇐
SU4225 Map 2

(01962) 775208 – www.kingsheadhursley.co.uk

A3090 Winchester–Romsey; SO21 2JW

Creeper-covered pub with an easy, friendly atmosphere, interestingly furnished rooms, well kept ales, good wines and enjoyable food; lovely bedrooms

There's an easy-going atmosphere in the character rooms here and a genuine welcome for all. The bar to the left has shutters by a cushioned window seat, high-backed plush green chairs and chunky leather stools around scrubbed tables on black floor slates, one high table with equally high chairs, and a raised fireplace with church candles on the mantelpiece above. Stools line the S-shaped, grey-painted counter where they serve Flack Manor Double Drop, Ringwood Best, Sharps Doom Bar and Upham Punter on handpump and 21 wines by the glass; background music, a piano, daily papers and board games. A character lower room has a fine end brick wall, a woodburning stove and wall banquettes with leather and tartan upholstery, and cushioned settles on floorboards. You can hire out the atmospheric downstairs skittle alley. The smart courtyard garden has wooden or metal seats and tables on brickwork or gravel, parasols and heaters. Bedrooms (named after previous owners of the Hursley Estate) are thoughtfully equipped and comfortable with original fireplaces and antiques. The ancient village church is opposite.

Appetising food includes sandwiches, home-made flatbread with various toppings, guinea fowl and chicken terrine with nut purée and pear chutney, mussels in cider, chicken, leek and bacon pie, goats cheese, shallot and thyme ravioli with basil pesto, sea bream with oak-smoked haddock kedgeree and mussel and shellfish sauce, duck breast with rosemary-roasted butternut squash, puy lentils, smoked bacon and black cherry sauce, and puddings such as lemon posset with lemon sorbet and pavlova with passion-fruit curd and berries. *Benchmark main dish: local rump steak with skinny chips and a choice of sauces £16.00. Two-course evening meal £24.00.*

Free house ~ Licensees Mark and Penny Thornhill ~ Real ale ~ Open 11-11 ~ Bar food 12-3, 6-9 (9.30 Fri); 12-9.30 Sat; 12-8 Sun ~ Restaurant ~ Children welcome ~ Dogs allowed in bar ~ Wi-fi ~ Bedrooms: $85/$115 *Recommended by Jack and Hilary Burton, Valerie Sayer, Tim King, Liz and Martin Eldon, Andrew Vincent*

HURSTBOURNE TARRANT
George & Dragon ◉ ♀ ⇐
SU3853 Map 2

(01264) 736277 – www.georgeanddragon.com

The Square (A343); SP11 0AA

Carefully renovated inn with plenty of original features, local ales, particularly good food and wine, and seats on a terrace; bedrooms

In a pretty village surrounding by walking country, this 15th-c former coaching inn has been carefully and thoughtfully renovated. At its heart is the beamed bar with a leather chesterfield and a couple of large upholstered pouffes on quarry tiles in front of a woodburning stove and stools against the counter where helpful, convivial staff keep Betteridges HBT (named for the pub – the brewery is just a few yards away) and Itchen Valley Hampshire Rose on handpump and 16 wines by the glass (also served by the carafe) from a carefully chosen list; it's all very relaxed and friendly. Carpeted dining areas have mate's chairs and wheelbacks, cushioned banquettes line cosy window alcoves and a second woodburner is fronted by button-back armchairs. There are seats and tables outside on a small secluded terrace, and eight comfortable, quiet and tastefully decorated bedrooms.

 Using the best local producers, the first class, seasonal food includes breakfasts (8-10am), crispy lamb belly with harissa, cauliflower and cumin, braised octopus with chorizo, potato and spring onion salad and aioli, a pie of the day, truffled potato, salsify and parmesan gratin with hazelnut purée, chicken breast with confit chicken rillettes, onions and kale, stone bass with mussel, saffron and tomato broth with polenta and samphire, lamb rump with roasted garlic gnocchi and mint salsa, and puddings such as toffee apple doughnuts with apple and cinnamon and dark chocolate and rosemary fondant with white chocolate and orange ice-cream. *Benchmark main dish: burger in a home-made brioche bun with toppings and fries £14.00. Two-course evening meal £21.50.*

Free house ~ Licensee Patrick Vaughan-Fowler ~ Real ale ~ Open 8am-11pm ~ Bar food 12-2.30, 6-9.30; 12-3, 6-8.30 Sun ~ Children welcome ~ Dogs welcome ~ Wi-fi ~ Bedrooms: /£75 *Recommended by Bridget and Peter Gregson, Professor James Burke, Simon Pyle, Val and Malcolm Travers*

LITTLETON
Running Horse 🛏
SU4532   Map 2

(01962) 880218 – www.runninghorseinn.co.uk
Main Road; village signed off B3049 NW of Winchester; SO22 6QS

Carefully renovated country pub with several dining areas, woodburning stove in the bar, enjoyable food and cabana in garden; pretty bedrooms

The spreading dining areas in this busy pub have a relaxed, friendly atmosphere and are attractively furnished with an appealing variety of chairs and tables on big flagstones or bare boards. Also, button-backed banquettes in a panelled alcove, an unusual wine-bottle ceiling light, old books on rustic bookshelves and big mirrors. A brick fireplace holds a woodburning stove, and leather-topped stools line the bar counter where they keep Upham Punter and Tipster and a changing guest on handpump, 14 wines by the glass and a farm cider. The front and back terraces have seats and tables and there are picnic-sets on the back grass by a spreading sycamore, and a popular cabana with cushioned seats. Bedrooms are well presented and breakfasts are good.

As well as tasty breakfasts (7.30-9.30am weekdays, 8-10.30am weekends), the reliably good food includes lunchtime sandwiches, chicken liver parfait with red onion marmalade, twice-baked cheddar soufflé with tomato and apple chutney, ham and eggs, vegetable cassoulet, rolled chicken breast with herb mousse and pan haggerty, pollack fillet with artichoke lyonnaise and artichoke emulsion, lamb two-ways (rump and confit shoulder cannelloni) with goats cheese, spinach and salsa verde, and puddings such as treacle tart with custard and vanilla rice pudding with ginger crumb and cranberry gel; they also offer a two-course set menu (not Friday evenings, not weekends). *Benchmark main dish: beer-battered fish and chips £13.00. Two-course evening meal £20.00.*

Upham ~ Licensee Anita Peel ~ Real ale ~ Open 11-11 (10.30 Sun) ~ Bar food 12-2.30, 6.30-9.30; 12-3.30, 6.30-9 Sun ~ Restaurant ~ Children welcome ~ Dogs allowed in bar ~ Wi-fi ~ Bedrooms: /£95 *Recommended by Terry and Eileen Stott, Ian Wilson, Mike Swan, Isobel Mackinlay, Amy and Luke Buchanan, James and Sylvia Hewitt*

Bedroom prices include full english breakfast, VAT and any inclusive service charge that we know of.

LONGSTOCK

Peat Spade ♀

SU3537 Map 2

(01264) 810612 – www.peatspadeinn.co.uk

Off A30 on W edge of Stockbridge; SO20 6DR

Former coaching inn with imaginative food, real ales and some sporting décor; stylish bedrooms

It's best to book a table in advance at this good-looking and well run pub – particularly in the evening when the highly regarded food is much in demand. The bars have lots of hunting and fishing pictures and prints and the odd stuffed fish on green walls and several old wine bottles dotted here and there. Both the bar and dining room have pretty windows, an interesting mix of dining chairs around miscellaneous tables on bare boards and candlelight. Upham Punter, Wadworths 6X and a guest ale on handpump, 12 wines by the glass, 19 gins and 28 malt whiskies; background music, TV and board games. Seating on the terrace or in the garden ranges from modern rattan-style through traditional wooden chairs and tables to a sunken area with wall seats around a firepit. Bedrooms are stylish and contemporary. The River Test, just 100 metres away, is world famous for its fly fishing.

Interesting food, attractively presented, includes sandwiches, pressed confit chicken and black pudding with spiced apple and carrot, crab cake and crayfish tails with avocado, sharing platters, butternut squash, artichoke and feta tart, dry-aged burger with wild mushrooms and truffle mayonnaise, lamb with grilled provençale vegetables, fondant potato and rosemary jus, butterflied chicken breast with bocconcini (small mozzarella balls), cherry tomato and basil salad, cod fillet with sauté potatoes, mushrooms, pancetta and rosemary sauce, and puddings. *Benchmark main dish: beer-battered hake fillet with pea purée and chips £13.00. Two-course evening meal £20.00.*

Upham ~ Licensees Richard and Liza McBain ~ Real ale ~ Open 10am-11pm (10.30pm Sun) ~ Bar food 12-2.30, 6.30-9; 12-3, 6.30-8.30 Sun ~ Restaurant ~ Children welcome ~ Dogs allowed in bar and bedrooms ~ Wi-fi ~ Bedrooms: /£89 *Recommended by Edward Mirzoeff, Guy Vowles, Jim King, John and Delia Franks, Martine and Lawrence Sanders*

LOWER FROYLE

Anchor ♀ ⇔

SU7643 Map 2

(01420) 23261 – www.anchorinnatlowerfroyle.co.uk

Village signposted N of A31 W of Bentley; GU34 4NA

Lots to look at in smart pub, real ales and good wines; bedrooms

This tucked-away country pub has log fires, candlelight, low beams and standing timbers, flagstones in the bar itself and stripped-wood floors elsewhere, sofas and armchairs dotted here and there, and a mix of attractive tables and dining chairs. Throughout are all sorts of interesting knick-knacks, books, copper items, horsebrasses and lots of pictures and prints on contemporary paintwork. High bar chairs line the counter where they keep Hogs Back TEA, Marstons EPA and Triple fff Altons Pride on handpump and nice wines by the glass. This is a comfortable place to stay overnight. Chawton Cottage (Jane Austen's house) is ten minutes away by car.

Up-to-date food includes lunchtime sandwiches, duck terrine with rhubarb chutney, soused mackerel with pomegranate and pear relish, beetroot quinoa with celeriac, parmesan and apple ginger, a pie of the day, burger with toppings, bacon jam, ruby slaw and triple-cooked chips, corn-fed chicken with baked sweet potato and broccoli jus, hake with onion buckwheat, braised chicory and beetroot kohlrabi, and puddings such as carrot and cinnamon sponge with coffee ice-cream and orange chocolate mousse cake with crème fraîche ice-cream. *Benchmark main dish: beer-battered haddock and chips £15.00. Two-course evening meal £22.50.*

Free house ~ Licensee Kiran Shukla ~ Real ale ~ Open 11-11 (10.30 Sun) ~ Bar food 12-2.30, 6.30-9 Mon-Thurs; 12-2.30, 6.30-9.30 Fri; 12-3, 6.30-9.30 Sat; 12-4, 6-8 Sun ~ Restaurant ~ Children welcome ~ Dogs allowed in bar and bedrooms ~ Wi-fi ~ Bedrooms: /£90
Recommended by Susan and Callum Slade, Elizabeth and Peter May, Usha and Terry Patel

LOWER WIELD
SU6339   Map 2

Yew Tree ⬤★ ♀ £

(01256) 389224 – www.the-yewtree.org.uk
Turn off A339 NW of Alton at 'Medstead, Bentworth 1' signpost, then follow village signposts; or off B3046 S of Basingstoke, signposted from Preston Candover; SO24 9RX

Bustling country pub with a delightful hard-working landlord, relaxed atmosphere and super choice of wines and food; sizeable garden

With a very special landlord at the helm, this tucked-away country pub continues to draw in warmly enthusiastic praise from our many readers – 'excellent in all respects' is just one comment. A small flagstoned bar area on the left has pictures above a stripped-brick dado, a ticking clock and a log fire. There's carpet around to the right of the serving counter (with a couple of stylish wrought-iron bar chairs), and miscellaneous chairs and mixed tables are spread throughout. Drinks include 13 wines by the glass from a well chosen list (with summer rosé and Louis Jadot burgundies), a beer named for the pub (from Triple fff) and Bowman Yumi on handpump, local Silverback gin and a locally made lager from Andwell. Outside, the front terrace has solid tables and chunky seats, a sizeable side garden has picnic-sets and there are pleasant views; the cricket field is across the quiet lane and there are walks nearby.

 Highly enjoyable food at reasonable prices includes sandwiches, goats cheese and horseradish mousse layered with sliced beetroot, smoked haddock, spring onion and mozzarella fishcake with citrus tartare, mediterranean vegetable crumble, cumberland sausages with parsley mash and onion gravy, goan chicken curry, local venison burger with toppings and chips, cod wrapped in parma ham with pea and mint risotto, and puddings such as chocolate, orange and raisin biscuit cake and peach schnapps-infused cherries in meringue with clotted cream. *Benchmark main dish: half lamb shoulder with dauphinoise potatoes and red wine jus £13.95. Two-course evening meal £19.00.*

Free house ~ Licensee Tim Gray ~ Real ale ~ Open 12-3, 6-11; 12-10.30 Sun; closed Mon, first two weeks Jan ~ Bar food 12-3, 6.30-9 ~ Children welcome ~ Dogs allowed in bar ~ Wi-fi *Recommended by Ann and Colin Hunt, Julian Thorpe, Geoffrey Sutton, Tony and Jill Radnor, B and M Kendall, Gill Waller*

LYMINGTON
SZ3295   Map 2

Angel & Blue Pig ⇌

(01590) 672050 – www.angel-lymington.com
High Street; SO41 9AP

Popular inn with plenty of space in several connected rooms, four real ales, enjoyable food and helpful staff; bedrooms

There's always a bustling, thriving feel to this town-centre pub and as it's open and serves food all day, customers pop in and out constantly. To the right of the door, a cosy front room has comfortable sofas and armchairs around a big chest, rugs on bare boards and an open fire; this leads into a pubby, flagstoned area with high tables and chairs and built-in leather wall seats. The two interconnected rooms to the left of the entrance – one carpeted, one with rugs on quarry tiles – have beams and timbers, upholstered dining chairs around a variety of tables, an old range in a brick fireplace, a large boar's head, lots of books on shelves and a bookshelf mural; throughout are numerous hunting prints and porcine paraphernalia. At the back, overlooking the terrace where there are seats and tables under blue parasols, is yet another area with some nice old leather armchairs beside a woodburning stove and the serving counter where they keep Blonde Angel (named for the pub from Ringwood), Ringwood Razorback and a couple of guests such as Dorset Ale Be Back and Itchen Valley Feline Good on handpump, 16 wines by the glass and a choice of coffees; service is friendly and attentive. The stylish modern bedrooms are comfortable and well equipped, and breakfasts are good.

Likeable brasserie-style food includes lunchtime sandwiches and baguettes, marinated duck skewers with spring onion, ginger and noodle salad and sticky soy dressing, cured salmon with pickled cucumber and fennel salad and horseradish cream, wild mushroom linguine with black truffle, mussels in cream, garlic and wine with skinny chips, maple-glazed pork chop with sage and onion mash and cider sauce, 28-day-aged charcoal-oven steaks with truffle butter and triple-cooked chips, and puddings such as coconut parfait with pineapple salsa, lime curd and coconut meringue and banoffi pie with toffee ice-cream. *Benchmark main dish: chicken with prosciutto, marinated mozzarella, herbed potatoes and chicken truffle sauce £12.95. Two-course evening meal £20.00.*

Free house ~ Licensee Matt England ~ Real ale ~ Open 9.30am-11pm (midnight Fri, Sat); 9.30am-10.30pm Sun ~ Bar food 12-10 (9 Sun) ~ Restaurant ~ Children welcome ~ Dogs allowed in bar ~ Wi-fi ~ Live music every second Fri ~ Bedrooms: £70/£90 *Recommended by Brian and Anna Marsden, Valerie Sayer, Harvey Brown, Ruth May, Greta and Gavin Craddock, Anne and Ben Smith, Phil and Jane Villiers*

LYMINGTON
Mayflower 🍴

SZ3394 Map 2

(01590) 672160 – www.themayflowerlymington.co.uk
Kings Saltern Road; SO41 3QD

Renovated inn by Lymington Marina with nautical décor, plenty of drinking and dining space, good food and drink and seats in garden; bedrooms

After a walk along the marina path, drop into this well run, popular pub for lunch. The high-ceilinged front rooms have patterned wallpaper or turquoise paintwork, built-in wall seats and leather-seated dining chairs around dark wooden tables, candles and fresh flowers, and logs piled neatly into the fireplace. Mayflower Bitter (named for the pub from Marstons) and changing guests such as Bath Gem and Otter Bitter on handpump and several wines by the glass served by cheerful, efficient young staff. At the back, two rooms have similar seats and tables, model yachts and big modern lanterns, yachting photographs on planked walls, books and a raised woodburning stove; background music and TV. You can walk from here out on to the covered terrace and then down steps to the lawn with its heavy rustic tables and benches. The refurbished, airy bedrooms have nautical touches and some overlook the coast.

As well as a two- and three-course menu, the pleasing food includes crispy ham hock terrine with a poached egg and lyonnaise salad, grilled sardines with salsa verde, a pie of the day, creamed leek, jerusalem artichoke and potato tart, cheese burger with toppings and skinny fries, crab and lobster linguine, slow-roast pork belly with champ and apple purée, beef bourguignon, and puddings such as toffee apple doughnut with salted caramel ice-cream and chocolate brownie with raspberry ripple ice-cream. *Benchmark main dish: seafood macaroni £16.95. Two-course evening meal £24.00.*

Free house ~ Licensee Gary Grant ~ Real ale ~ Open 11-11 (10 Sun) ~ Bar food 12-3, 6-9 (10 Fri); 12-10 Sat; 12-8 Sun ~ Restaurant ~ Children welcome ~ Dogs allowed in bar and bedrooms ~ Wi-fi ~ Bedrooms: /£90 *Recommended by Graham Smart, Edward Edmonton, Jeremy Snow, John Harris*

NORTH WARNBOROUGH
SU7352 Map 2
Mill House ♀ ◖

(01256) 702953 – www.brunningandprice.co.uk/millhouse
A mile from M3 junction 5: A287 towards Farnham, then right (brown sign to pub) on to B3349 Hook Road; RG29 1ET

Converted mill with an attractive layout, modern food, good choice of drinks and lovely waterside terraces

At the back is an extensive garden with lots of solid tables and chairs on terraces, even more picnic-sets on grass and appealing landscaping around the sizeable millpond; a couple of swings too. The sizeable raftered mill building has several linked areas on the main upper floor with heavy beams, plenty of well spaced tables in a variety of sizes and styles, rugs on polished boards or beige carpet, coal-effect gas fires in pretty fireplaces and a profusion of often interesting pictures. A section of floor is glazed to reveal the rushing water and mill wheel below, and a galleried section on the left looks down into a dining room, given a more formal feel by panelling. Well trained young staff serve Phoenix Brunning & Price Original, Andwell Spring Magic, Hogs Back TEA, Longdog Red Runner and Triple fff Hunky Dory on handpump, a fine range of 50 malt whiskies, 18 wines by the glass, around 30 gins and local farm cider; background music and board games.

Inventive, seasonal food includes sandwiches, black pudding with caramelised apple and red wine gravy, deep-fried brie with pickled cranberries, cheddar and potato pie with root vegetables and grain mustard gravy, steak and kidney pie, teriyaki sea bass with crispy wasabi rice balls, pickled ginger and chilli, soy and sesame dressing, lemon and thyme chicken with chorizo croquette and tomato jus, and puddings such as apple and berry crumble with custard and chocolate brownie with chocolate sauce. *Benchmark main dish: braised lamb shoulder with dauphinoise potatoes and red wine and rosemary jus £17.95. Two-course evening meal £20.00.*

Brunning & Price ~ Lease Katie-Jo Stoke Barnett ~ Real ale ~ Open 11-11 (10.30 Sun) ~ Bar food 12-10 (9.30 Sun) ~ Restaurant ~ Children welcome ~ Dogs allowed in bar ~ Wi-fi
Recommended by Edward Mirzoeff, Mrs P Sumner, Susan Eccleston, Heather and Richard Jones

OVERTON
SU5149 Map 2
White Hart

(01256) 771431 – www.whitehartoverton.co.uk
London Road; RG25 3NW

Smart town-edge inn with thoughtful renovations in bar and dining rooms, rewarding food and ales and suntrap garden; well equipped bedrooms

If you're a gin lover, do visit nearby Laverstoke Mill, home to the Bombay Sapphire distillery, and then come to this handsome 500-year-old inn for lunch. They've taken great care to keep the character of the place (beams, carvings, old fireplaces) during renovations, but have added contemporary, gently quirky touches too. The cosy bar has an open fire, cheerfully striped or leather armchairs, board games and daily papers and wooden stools against the carved counter where they keep Upham Punter and Tipster and a guest such as Upham First Drop on handpump, 12 wines by the glass and a cocktail list. An elegant two-level dining room, with a central woodburning stove, has green or bright pink seated chairs around wooden tables on a stripped-wood floor, and antlers and hand mirrors on the walls; another room has cushioned wall seating and similar tables and chairs. Folding doors open on to the suntrap garden (there's a heated awning for cooler days) with good quality chairs and tables under parasols. Bedrooms, in a converted stable block, are individually furnished and comfortable, and breakfasts are highly rated.

Interesting, up-to-date food includes lunchtime sandwiches and tacos, thai fishcake with asian slaw, pigeon and black pudding with cajun cauliflower, quinoa, blue cheese, pomegranate and cashew nut salad, burger with toppings and fries, sausage and mash with gravy, rainbow trout with pea and wild garlic purée with sausage vierge, lemongrass and tea-brined chicken breast with sweet potato, edamame beans and chickpeas, and puddings; they also offer breakfasts to non-residents (7.30-9.30am weekdays, 8-10am weekends). *Benchmark main dish: beer-battered fish and chips £12.50. Two-course evening meal £18.00.*

Upham ~ Manager Helen Zivanovic ~ Real ale ~ Open 10am-11pm (10.30pm Sun) ~ Bar food 12-3, 6-9.30; 12-3.30, 6-9 Sun ~ Restaurant ~ Children welcome ~ Dogs allowed in bar and bedrooms ~ Wi-fi ~ Live music first Fri of month ~ Bedrooms: /£110
Recommended by Lenny and Ruth Watson, Mark and Mary Setting, Freddie and Sarah Banks

PETERSFIELD
Old Drum 🏠 ♀ 🍴

SU7423 Map 2

(01730) 300544 – www.theolddrum.co.uk
Chapel Street; GU32 3DP

18th-c inn with friendly staff and atmosphere in bars and dining room, interesting ales and food, and seats in back garden; bedrooms

With the market and shops nearby, it's not surprising that this bustling, friendly pub has so much custom. The airy L-shaped bar has all manner of antique dining chairs and tables on bare boards, with a comfortable chesterfield and armchair by an open fire (there are three fires in all) and prettily upholstered stools against the counter. Bowman Wallops Wood, Dark Star Hophead and guests such as Flack Manor Double Drop, Listers Special Ale and Nelson Land of Hops & Glory on handpump, 16 wines by the glass, ten malt whiskies and farm cider and perry; background jazz and board games. A cosy beamed dining room leads off, with more interesting old cushioned chairs and tables on bare boards. Throughout there are prints, mirrors and the odd stag's head on pale paintwork or exposed bricks, modern lighting and fresh flowers. The back courtyard garden has chairs and tables and plants in raised flowerbeds. Bedrooms are stylish and comfortable and breakfasts well thought-of.

The up-to-date food is highly enjoyable: tapas choices, sandwiches, scallops with pancetta and lentil compote, coconut beer-battered tiger prawns with jalapeno shallot marmalade, root vegetable dauphinoise with field mushrooms, cheese and rooibos sauce, chilli and dill haddock with triple-cooked chips, lamb noisette with baby root vegetables and redcurrant jus, chargrilled chicken with roasted butternut squash, toasted pine nuts and garlic and sage sauce, and puddings such as banoffi tart with treacle and blueberries and honeycomb dust and chocolate ganache with salted caramel ice-cream. *Benchmark main dish: venison loin with rosemary fondant potatoes and redcurrant jus £19.00. Two-course evening meal £20.00.*

Free house ~ Licensee Maria Solovieth ~ Real ale ~ Open 9.30am-11pm (midnight Sat);
9.30am-8pm Sun ~ Bar food 12-3.30, 6-9.30; not Mon evening ~ Restaurant ~ Children
welcome until 8pm ~ Dogs allowed in bar ~ Wi-fi ~ Bedrooms: £90/£120 *Recommended by
R T and J C Moggridge, Ann and Colin Hunt, Len and Lilly Dowson, Jim and Sue James,
Patricia Healey*

PETERSFIELD
Trooper 🏅 🍺 🛏

SU7227 Map 2

(01730) 827293 – www.trooperinn.com

*From A32 (look for staggered crossroads) take turning to Froxfield and Steep;
pub 3 miles down on left in big dip; GU32 1BD*

**Courteous landlord, popular food, decent drinks, persian
knick-knacks and local artists' work; comfortable bedrooms**

After a visit to Ashford Hangers nature reserve, drop in here for lunch.
The bar has a log fire in a stone fireplace, all sorts of cushioned dining
chairs around dark wooden tables, old film star photos, paintings by local
artists (for sale), little persian knick-knacks, several ogival mirrors, lit
candles and fresh flowers. The charming landlord and his friendly staff keep
Bowman Swift One, Ringwood Best and Thwaites Wainwright on handpump,
good wines by the glass and several gins. There's also a sun room with
lovely downland views, carefully chosen background music, board games,
newspapers and magazines. The attractive raftered restaurant has french
windows to a paved terrace with views across the open countryside, and
there are lots of picnic-sets on an upper lawn. The horse rail in the car park
is reserved 'for horses, camels and local livestock'. Bedrooms are neatly kept
and the breakfasts very good.

🌟 Hearty food includes lunchtime ciabattas, potted shrimps, salmon and dill
fishcakes, angus burger with toppings, beer-battered onion rings and fries,
butternut squash, leek and butter bean stew, sausages (including vegetarian) with mash
and onion gravy, steak and kidney pudding, free-range chicken breast with tarragon and
creamy white wine sauce, pork medallions with mushroom, bacon and marsala sauce
and dauphinoise potatoes, and puddings such as chocolate brownie with warm chocolate
sauce and vanilla cheesecake with seasonal fruit compote; they also offer a two-course
set menu (not Friday evening or weekends) and Tuesday is steak night. *Benchmark
main dish: slow-roasted half shoulder of lamb with honey and mint gravy £19.50.
Two-course evening meal £21.00.*

Free house ~ Licensee Hassan Matini ~ Real ale ~ Open 12-3, 6-11; 12-4 Sun; closed
Sun evening, Mon lunchtime except bank holidays ~ Bar food 12-2, 6.30-9; 12-2.30 Sun ~
Restaurant ~ Children welcome ~ Dogs allowed in bar ~ Wi-fi ~ Bedrooms: £69/£99
*Recommended by Melanie and David Lawson, Trevor and Michele Street, Ivy and George Goodwill,
Alison and Tony Livesley*

PETERSFIELD
White Horse 🍺

SU7129 Map 2

(01420) 588387 – www.pubwithnoname.co.uk

*Up on an old downs road about halfway between Steep and East Tisted, near
Priors Dean – OS Sheet 186 or 197 map reference 715290; GU32 1DA*

**Much loved old place with a great deal of simple character,
friendly licensees and fantastic range of beers**

As ever, nothing really changes at this unspoilt old pub, which is just how
its loyal customers like it. The two parlour rooms remain charming and
idiosyncratic: open fires, oak settles and a mix of dark wooden dining chairs,

nice old tables (including some drop-leaf ones), various pictures, farm tools, rugs, a longcase clock, a couple of fireside rocking chairs and so forth. The beamed dining room is smarter with lots of pictures on the white or pink walls. A fantastic choice of up to ten real ales are kept on handpump – one or two are named for the pub plus Butcombe Bitter, Fullers London Pride, Ringwood Boondoggle and Fortyniner, St Austell Trelawny and quickly changing guests; lots of country wines, a dozen wines by the glass, 20 malt whiskies and two farm ciders. They hold a cider festival in September. There are some rustic seats outside and camping facilities.

As well as breakfasts (8.30am-midday), the popular food includes sandwiches, fishcakes with creamy mustard sauce, vegetable or beef nachos with chillies, cheese and sour cream, honey-glazed ham and free-range eggs, beetroot and feta risotto, smoked fish pie, sausages of the day with colcannon potatoes, onion marmalade and gravy, beer-battered haddock and chips, sirloin steak with sun-dried tomato and parmesan butter and chips, and puddings such as banana eton mess and fruit crumble with custard. *Benchmark main dish: steak in ale pie £14.00. Two-course evening meal £19.00.*

Gales (Fullers) ~ Managers Georgie and Paul Stuart ~ Real ale ~ Open 12-11 ~ Bar food 10-10; 12-2.30, 6-9 Mon ~ Restaurant ~ Children welcome ~ Dogs allowed in bar *Recommended by Tony and Jill Radnor, Ann and Colin Hunt, Lindy Andrews, Mark Hamill, Phil and Jane Villiers*

PORTSMOUTH

SZ6399 Map 2

Old Customs House ⬤ £

(023) 9283 2333 – www.theoldcustomshouse.com
Vernon Buildings, Gunwharf Quays; follow brown signs to Gunwharf Quays car park; PO1 3TY

Well converted historic building in a prime waterfront development with real ales and well liked food

Although part of an extensive modern waterside complex, this 18th-c former customs house is a lovely Grade I listed building and usefully open all day. The big-windowed high-ceilinged rooms have nautical prints and photographs on pastel walls, coal-effect gas fires, nice unobtrusive lighting and well padded chairs around sturdy tables of varying sizes on bare boards; the sunny entrance area has leather sofas. Broad stairs lead up to a carpeted restaurant with similar décor. Fullers ESB, HSB, London Pride and Seafarers and a couple of changing guests on handpump, a decent range of wines by the glass and good coffees and teas. Staff are efficient, the background music well reproduced and the games machines silenced. Picnic-sets out in front are just metres from the water; the bar has disabled access and facilities. The graceful Spinnaker Tower (170 metres high with staggering views from its observation decks) is just around the corner.

Food is well regarded and includes breakfasts (from 9am), lunchtime sandwiches, smoked salmon with caper butter and fresh horseradish, duck liver pâté with caramelised onion jam, sharing boards, beer-battered cod and chips, lentil, feta and squash salad, corn-fed chicken with sauté new potatoes and smoked bacon, burger with toppings and chips, pork belly in cider with black pudding mash, rump of lamb with fennel and quinoa salad, and puddings such as chocolate brownie with peanut brittle, salted caramel and vanilla ice-cream and passion-fruit crème brûlée. *Benchmark main dish: pie of the day £13.95. Two-course evening meal £19.00.*

Fullers ~ Manager Marc Duvauchelle ~ Real ale ~ Open 9.30am-11pm; 9.30am-midnight Fri, Sat ~ Bar food 9.30am-9pm ~ Children welcome ~ Dogs allowed in bar ~ Wi-fi *Recommended by Charlie May, John Harris, Neil Allen, Tony Scott, Tony and Wendy Hobden, Ann and Colin Hunt*

ROCKBOURNE
Rose & Thistle

SU1118   Map 2

(01725) 518236 – www.roseandthistle.co.uk

Signed off B3078 Fordingbridge–Cranborne; SP6 3NL

Homely cottage with hands-on landlord and friendly staff, informal bars, real ales and good food, and seats in garden

Originally, this cosy thatched pub was two 16th-c cottages and nice old features include beams, timbers and flagstones. The bar has homely dining chairs, stools and benches around a mix of old pubby tables, Butcombe Gold, Sharps Doom Bar and a changing local ale such as Flack Manor Double Drop on handpump, eight wines by the glass and Black Rat cider; board games. The restaurant has a log fire in each of its two rooms (one in a big brick inglenook), old engravings and cricket prints and an informal and relaxed atmosphere; background music. There are benches and tables under lovely hanging baskets at the front of the building, with picnic-sets under parasols on grass; good nearby walks. This is a pretty village on the edge of the New Forest.

Good, popular food includes lunchtime sandwiches, twice-baked parmesan soufflé, creamy garlic mushrooms, burger with toppings, gherkins and chips, butternut squash, shallot and feta open-top pie, chicken breast with parsnip purée and wild mushroom jus, confit rare-breed pork belly with truffle-infused mash, black pudding and red wine jus, venison steak with bubble and squeak and port and cherry jus, whole plaice with brown shrimp and dill butter, and puddings such as queen of puddings with ice-cream and vanilla pannacotta with honeycomb and blackcurrants. *Benchmark main dish: steak and kidney pudding £15.50. Two-course evening meal £21.00.*

Free house ~ Licensee Chris Chester-Sterne ~ Real ale ~ Open 11-3, 5-10.30; 11-10.30 Sat; 12-8 Sun ~ Bar food 12-2.15, 7-9.15; 12-2.15 Sun ~ Restaurant ~ Children welcome ~ Dogs allowed in bar ~ Wi-fi *Recommended by Christopher Mannings, Mike Swan, Ian Duncan, Robert and Diana Myers, Jill and Dick Archer*

ST MARY BOURNE
Bourne Valley ♀ ⇙

SU4250   Map 2

(01264) 738361 – www.bournevalleyinn.com

Upper Link (B3048); SP11 6BT

Bustling country inn with plenty of space, an easy-going atmosphere and enjoyable food and drink; good bedrooms

There's a good mix of customers here, particularly at weekends when dogs and children are very much part of the scene. It's an attractively updated old red-brick inn and the bar areas have sofas, all manner of wooden dining chairs and tables on coir or bare boards, empty wine bottles lining shelves and windowsills, and a warm log fire; at one end, a deli counter provides coffee and cake, afternoon tea and picnic hampers. Ringwood Best, Sharps Doom Bar, Upham First Drop and a guest beer on handpump and lots of wines by the glass served by helpful, friendly staff; background music and TV. A large barn extension, complete with rafters and beams, rustic partitioning and movable shelves made from crates, has big tables surrounded by leather, cushioned and upholstered chairs, more coir carpeting, a second open fire and doors that lead out to a terrace with picnic-sets and other seating. The comfortable, contemporary bedrooms are named after local lakes, brooks and rivers. Good nearby walks.

The modern food starts with breakfast (8.30-10.30am), plus duck terrine with rum and raisin chutney, cured local trout with avocado salsa and plantain crisps, ricotta and spinach tortellini with beurre noisette, parmesan and truffle, local venison sausages with celeriac purée, wild mushrooms and blackberry sauce, a pie of the day, lamb rump with creamed cabbage and bacon, caramelised figs and red wine jus, a fresh fish dish of the day, and puddings such as warm chocolate mousse with caramelised orange and sticky toffee pudding with toffee sauce; they also offer a two- and three-course set lunch. *Benchmark main dish: burger with toppings, onion rings and fries £12.95. Two-course evening meal £20.00.*

Free house ~ Licensee Ryan Stacey ~ Real ale ~ Open 11-11 ~ Bar food 12-2.30, 6-9; 12-3, 6-9.30 Fri, Sat; 12-3.30, 6-9 Sun ~ Children welcome ~ Dogs welcome ~ Wi-fi ~ Bedrooms: £75/£85 *Recommended by Jack and Hilary Burton, Charles Welch, Lauren and Dan Frazer, Deborah and Duncan Walliams, Sandra Hollies*

STEEP

SU7525   Map 2

Harrow 🍺 £

(01730) 262685 – www.harrow-inn.co.uk

Take Midhurst exit from Petersfield bypass, at exit roundabout take first left towards Midhurst, then first turning on left opposite garage, and left again at Sheet church; follow over dual-carriageway bridge to pub; GU32 2DA

Unchanging, simple place with long-serving landladies, beers tapped from the cask, unfussy food and cottage garden; no children inside

A favourite with so many of our readers, this charming small pub has been in the same family for 88 years and remains quite unspoilt and unchanging with no pandering to modern methods – no credit cards, no waitress service, no restaurant, no music and the rose-covered loos are outside. Everything revolves around village chat and the friendly locals are likely to involve you in light-hearted conversation. Adverts for logs sit next to calendars of local views (on sale in support of local charities) and news of various quirky competitions. The small public bar has hops and dried flowers (replaced every year) hanging from the beams, built-in wall benches on the tiled floor, stripped-pine wallboards, a good log fire in the big inglenook and wild flowers on scrubbed deal tables; dominoes. Bowman Swift One, Dark Star Hophead, Flack Manor Double Drop, Hop Back GFB, Langham Hip Hop and Ringwood Best are tapped straight from casks behind the counter, and they have local wine and apple juice; staff are polite and friendly, even when under pressure. The big garden has seats on paved areas surrounded by cottage garden flowers and fruit trees. The Petersfield bypass doesn't intrude much on this idyll, though you'll need to follow the directions above to find the pub. No children inside and dogs must be on leads. They sell honesty-box flowers outside for Macmillan nurses.

Honest food includes sandwiches, hot scotch egg, hearty soups, quiches, and puddings such as lemon crunch cheesecake and winter treacle tart. *Benchmark main dish: rare beef ploughman's £11.30. Two-course evening meal £16.00.*

Free house ~ Licensees Claire and Denise McCutcheon ~ Real ale ~ No credit cards ~ Open 12-2.30, 6-11; 11-3, 6-11 Sat; 12-3, 7-10.30 Sun; closed Sun evening in winter ~ Bar food 12-2, 7-9; not Sun evening ~ Dogs allowed in bar *Recommended by Tony and Jill Radnor, Ann and Colin Hunt, Lyn and Freddie Roberts, Andy and Rosemary Taylor, Serena and Adam Furber*

Bedroom prices are for high summer. Even then you may get reductions for more than one night, or (outside tourist areas) weekends. Winter special rates are common, and many inns reduce bedroom prices if you have a full evening meal.

TOTFORD

Woolpack ⭐ ♀ 🛏

SU5737 Map 2

(01962) 734184 – www.thewoolpackinn.co.uk

B3046 Basingstoke–Alresford; SO24 9TJ

Charming pub with carefully refurbished rooms, plenty of character, first class food and drink and seats outside; lovely bedrooms

Walkers with their dogs and cyclists come here while exploring the Candover Valley, so lunchtimes can get pretty busy. It's a handsome flint and brick pub and the bar has an easy-going atmosphere, leather button-back armchairs, little stools and wooden chairs around a mix of tables on wide floorboards, and high chairs against the counter where they offer Ramshead (a beer named for them from Marstons), Palmers Copper and a weekly changing guest such as Two Cocks 1643 Cavalier on handpump, 15 wines by the glass and a rather special bloody mary. Leading off here is a dining room with flagstones and carpet, a raised fireplace with guns, bellows and other country knick-knacks above it and chunky tables and chairs. Throughout the other rooms are rugs on flagstones, exposed brick and stonework, a few bits of timbering and beamery, church candles, lots of photos, some cosy booth seating and high-back upholstered dining chairs and leather wall seats around a medley of tables. The pool table converts into a dining table when they're really busy. Outside, on the terrace, on gravel and on grass are teak tables and chairs and picnic-sets under parasols, and distant views. The bedrooms, named after game birds, are very comfortable and well equipped.

 Good interesting food includes lunchtime sandwiches (not Sunday), crisp oxtail with pickled onions, watercress and roast shallots, smoked duck breast with fennel and blood orange salad, honey-roast ham and free-range eggs, baked parmesan gnocchi with jerusalem artichokes and leeks, pork faggots with mash and onion gravy, beef and sweet potato curry with spiced rice, peanuts and shallots, rose veal escalope with pepper tapenade and fondant potato, chargrilled local trout with smoked trout fishcake and herb hollandaise, and puddings such as apple and cinnamon crumble with custard and hot chocolate pudding with honeycomb ice-cream; they also offer breakfast (9-10.30am daily) and wood-fired pizzas (5.30-8.30pm summer Sundays). *Benchmark main dish: sea bass fillet with fennel purée, crushed new potatoes, charred radishes and herb oil £16.50. Two-course evening meal £21.00.*

Free house ~ Licensee Andrew Cooper ~ Real ale ~ Open 11-11 (midnight Sat); 12-10.30 Sun ~ Bar food 12-2.30 (3 Sat), 6.30-9; 12-3.30, 5.30-8.30 Sun ~ Restaurant ~ Children welcome ~ Dogs welcome ~ Wi-fi ~ Bedrooms: /£100 *Recommended by Julian Richardson, Hilary and Neil Christopher, Jacqui and Alan Swan, Tony and Jill Radnor*

WEST MEON

Thomas Lord ♀

SU6424 Map 2

(01730) 829244 – www.thethomaslord.co.uk

High Street; GU32 1LN

Cricketing knick-knacks in character bar rooms, a smarter dining room, helpful staff, local beers, well thought-of food and pretty garden

The relaxed, friendly bar in this bustling pub has plenty of cricketing memorabilia as the place is named after the founder of Lord's Cricket Ground: bats, gloves, balls, shoes, stumps, photographs and prints, and even stuffed squirrels playing the game in a display cabinet above the counter. Also, a leather chesterfield and armchairs beside a log fire, wooden chairs, animal-hide stools and corner settles on parquet flooring, and Upham Punter and Tipster and changing guests on handpump, a dozen wines by the glass and seasonal cocktails, served by chatty, helpful staff. A small room leads off the bar with similar furnishings, a brace of pheasant in the fireplace and antlers above; background music and board games. The dining room is slightly more formal, with long wide tartan benches beside long tables, green cushioned chairs and a big clock above another fireplace; another little room has a large button-back banquette, tables and a rustic mural. Plenty of candles throughout – in nice little teacups with saucers, in candlesticks, in silver glassware, in moroccan-style lanterns and in fireplaces. The sizeable garden has picnic-sets, herbaceous borders, an outdoor pizza oven, a barbecue area, a chicken run and a kitchen garden.

🍴 Good, modern food using their own eggs and home-grown produce includes sandwiches, chicken and smoked ham hock terrine with quince, gravadlax with swedish mustard, orange and roe, shallot tarte tartin with ceps and goats curd, dry-aged burger with barbecue sauce, truffle and parmesan fries, slow-cooked duck leg with pickled rhubarb and hasselback potatoes, local pigeon with french-style peas and dauphinoise potatoes, red mullet with jerusalem artichoke risotto, and puddings such as salted caramel and chocolate pot and rhubarb fool. *Benchmark main dish: beer-battered hake and chips £13.00. Two-course evening meal £20.50.*

Upham ~ Licensee Tabitha Money ~ Real ale ~ Open 12-11; 12-10.30 Sun ~ Bar food 12-2.30, 6-9.30 (10 Fri, Sat); 12-4, 6-9 Sun ~ Restaurant ~ Children welcome ~ Dogs allowed in bar ~ Wi-fi *Recommended by Anne and Ben Smith, James Landor, Peter Brix, Lindy Andrews, Holly and Tim Waite*

WINCHESTER
Wykeham Arms 🏮⭐ ♀

SU4829 Map 2

(01962) 853834 – www.wykehamarmswinchester.co.uk
Kingsgate Street (Kingsgate Arch and College Street are now closed to traffic; there is access via Canon Street); SO23 9PE

Tucked-away pub with lots to look at, several real ales, many wines by the glass and highly thought-of food; pretty bedrooms

To explore this fine old town and the surrounding countryside, many of our readers stay overnight in the lovely bedrooms here; some have four-posters and the two-level suite has its own sitting room. Downstairs, the series of bustling rooms have all sorts of interesting collections and three log fires – as well as 19th-c oak desks retired from Winchester College, kitchen chairs, deal tables with candles and big windows with swagged curtains. A snug room at the back, known as the Jameson Room (after the late landlord, Graeme Jameson), is decorated with a set of Ronald Searle 'Winespeak' prints. A second room is panelled. Fullers HSB, London Pride, Gales Seafarers, Southern Star and a guest such as Flowerpots Goodens Gold on handpump, 25 wines by the glass, 29 malt whiskies, a couple of farm ciders and quite a few ports and sherries; the tea list is pretty special. There are tables on a covered back terrace and in a small courtyard.

⭐ Excellent food includes lunchtime sandwiches, scallops with compressed apple, cauliflower purée and scallop ceviche, pigeon, pancetta and pomegranate salad with spinach and chilli-baked squash, olive oil gnocchi with mozzarella, peas, shallots and broccoli pesto, burger with toppings, house slaw and fries, corn-fed chicken breast with grapefruit, baby beetroot and chargrilled leeks, 35-day-aged chateaubriand with triple-cooked chips and béarnaise sauce (for two people), and puddings such as white chocolate and ginger pave with rhubarb sorbet and fig and almond crème brûlée. *Benchmark main dish: lamb rump with rosemary polenta, burnt aubergine purée and mint and anchovy dressing £20.50. Two-course evening meal £21.00.*

Fullers ~ Manager Jon Howard ~ Real ale ~ Open 11-11 (10.30 Sun) ~ Bar food 12-3, 6-9.30; 12-3.30, 6.30-9 Sun ~ Restaurant ~ Children over 8 allowed at lunchtime ~ Dogs allowed in bar and bedrooms ~ Wi-fi ~ Bedrooms: £99/£156 *Recommended by Neil and Angela Huxter, Ann and Colin Hunt, Dr and Mrs J D Abell, Phil and Jane Villiers, Jane and Kai Horsburgh, Tony Scott, Mark Morgan, Richard Tilbrook*

Also Worth a Visit in Hampshire

Besides the fully inspected pubs, you might like to try these pubs that have been recommended to us and described by readers. Do tell us what you think of them: feedback@goodguides.com

ALRESFORD   SU5832
Bell (01962) 732429
West Street; SO24 9AT Comfortable and welcoming Georgian coaching inn, good popular food including weekday fixed-price menu and plenty of daily specials, friendly helpful service, up to five well kept changing ales and extensive choice of wines by the glass, spic and span interior with bare boards, scrubbed tables and log fire, daily papers, separate smallish dining room, occasional live music (mainly jazz); children welcome, dogs in bar (resident spaniels Freddie and Teddy), attractive sunny back courtyard, six bedrooms, closed Sun evening, otherwise open all day (till 6pm Sun). *(David and Judy Robison, Ann and Colin Hunt, D J and P M Taylor, Tony and Jill Radnor)*

ALRESFORD   SU5832
Horse & Groom (01962) 734809
Broad Street; town signed off A31 bypass; SO24 9AQ Comfortable attractively updated Fullers pub with roomy well divided interior, pale beams (some supported by iron pillars), exposed brickwork and log fires, bow window seats and a few stepped levels, back restaurant area, well kept ales including a local guest such as Flowerpots, enjoyable food from fairly compact but varied menu, friendly young staff; background music, daily newspapers, free wi-fi; children and dogs welcome, small enclosed back terrace, open all day, food all day Sun till 7pm. *(Ann and Colin Hunt)*

ALRESFORD   SU5832
Swan (01962) 732302
West Street; SO24 9AD Long narrow bar in refurbished 18th-c hotel (former coaching inn), painted panelling and some rustic stall seating, well kept ales such as Itchen Valley, Sharps and Triple fff, decent wines, tea and coffee, popular reasonably priced food including Sun roasts, efficient friendly service, two dining rooms (one more formal); children welcome, café-style table on terrace, 22 bedrooms, open all day. *(Edward Edmonton)*

ALTON   SU7139
Ivy House (01420) 549011
Draymans Way; GU34 1SS Substantial centrally placed Wetherspoons linking a 17th-c building with a converted modern office block, Greene King, Sharps and several guests, good range of other drinks and extensive choice of inexpensive food from breakfast on, cheerful young staff coping well at busy times; TVs, free wi-fi; children welcome, plenty of outside seating, open all day from 8am (till 1am Fri, Sat). *(Minda and Stanley Alexander)*

AMPFIELD   SU4023
★White Horse (01794) 368356
A3090 Winchester–Romsey; SO51 9BQ Snug low-beamed front bar with candles and soft lighting, inglenook log fire and comfortable country furnishings, spreading beamed dining area behind, well kept Greene King, guest ales and several nice wines by the glass, good food including all-day snacks, efficient service, locals' bar with another inglenook; background music; children and dogs welcome, pergola-covered terrace and high-hedged garden with plenty of picnic-sets, cricket green beyond, good walks in Ampfield Woods and handy for Hillier Gardens, open all day. *(Simon Sharpe)*

ARFORD   SU8236
Crown (01428) 712150
Off B3002 W of Hindhead; GU35 8BT Low-beamed pub with log fires in several areas including local-feel bar and cosy upper dining room, well kept changing ales, decent wines by the glass and good food from pub favourites with a contemporary twist to blackboard specials, friendly staff; children welcome in eating areas, picnic-sets in peaceful dell by stream across road. *(John and Delia Franks)*

BARTON STACEY   SU4341
Swan (01962) 760470
Village signed off A303; SO21 3RL Refurbished beamed coaching inn with good affordably priced pubby food (not Sun

---

We say if we know a pub allows dogs.

evening, Mon) from lunchtime sandwiches and baked potatoes up, three real ales such as Alfreds Saxon Bronze and Sharps Doom Bar, friendly helpful young staff, bar with brick and timber walls, light wood flooring and inglenook log fire, back restaurant; board games, free wi-fi; children and dogs welcome, picnic-sets on front gravel and lawn, open all day Sat, till 6pm Sun, closed Mon lunchtime. *(Nigel James, Edward Mirzoeff)*

BASING   SU6653
Bartons Mill (Millstone)
(01256) 331153 *Bartons Lane, Old Basing; follow brown signs to Basing House; RG24 8AE* Busy converted watermill in tucked-away spot – lots of tables out by River Loddon looking across to viaduct through scrubland; Wadworths range kept well and a guest, proper cider and several wines by the glass, decent food (all day weekends) from baguettes and deli boards up, friendly staff, softly lit beamed and flagstoned interior; may be background music, Thurs quiz and other events, free wi-fi; children and dogs welcome, handy for Basing House ruins, open all day. *(Frances Parsons)*

BATTRAMSLEY   SZ3098
Hobler (01590) 623944
Southampton Road (A337 S of Brockenhurst); SO41 8PT Old roadside pub with several rooms, modern décor and furnishings alongside ancient heavy beams, wood and stone floors, log fire, tasty food from sandwiches and sharing plates up using fresh local ingredients, weekday set menu till 6pm, well kept Ringwood, Timothy Taylors and plenty of wines by the glass, friendly efficient service; children welcome, nice garden with some tables under cover, good New Forest walks, open (and food) all day. *(Phil and Jane Villiers)*

BEAUWORTH   SU5624
Milbury's (01962) 771248
Off A272 Winchester–Petersfield; SO24 0PB Traditional tile-hung country pub, beams, panelling and stripped stone, massive 17th-c treadmill for much older incredibly deep well, galleried area, three changing ales and straightforward reasonably priced food; skittle alley; children allowed in eating areas, dogs on leads (they have a cat called Bob), garden with fine downland views, good walks, regular classic car meetings including TVR, two bedrooms, closed Sun evening. *(Ann and Colin Hunt)*

BENTLEY   SU7844
Star (01420) 23184
Centre of village on old A31; GU10 5LW Small early 19th-c village pub under

welcoming new management; good reasonably priced food (smaller helpings available) cooked by landlady, Sharps Doom Bar, Triple fff Moondance and a guest, eight wines by the glass from decent list, open fire in brick fireplace, restaurant; quiz first Mon of the month, newspapers, free wi-fi; children and dogs welcome, garden with thatched gazebos, open all day, food all day Sun till 7pm. *(Charles Plumb)*

BENTWORTH   SU6740
Sun (01420) 562338
Well Lane, off Station Road; signed Shaldon/Alton; GU34 5JT Creeper-clad 16th-c country tavern under newish management; two little traditional rooms with scrubbed deal tables, high-backed settles, pews and wheelback chairs on bare boards, candles in bottles, various pictures and knick-knacks, three fireplaces, arch through to brick-floored room with another fire, half a dozen real ales and ample helpings of enjoyable pubby food from sandwiches and baked potatoes up; children and dogs welcome, seats out at front and in back garden, open all day Sun. *(Tony and Jill Radnor, Mrs Zara Elliott)*

BIGHTON   SU6134
English Partridge (01962) 732859
Bighton Dean Lane; village signed off B3046 N of Alresford; SO24 9RE Traditional country pub popular with locals and visitors alike; small simple room to left of the door with open fire, main bar with ancient parquet floor, hunting prints and game bird pictures, a stuffed pheasant in glass cabinet, woodburner in brick inglenook, ales from Otter and Triple fff, real cider and ten wines by the glass, honest country cooking (can eat in bar or dining room behind); background music, darts and board games, free wi-fi; children and dogs welcome, some benches out at front, large circular table to the side and more seats in sheltered back area, open all day Sun till 7pm, closed Mon and Tues (except summer school holidays). *(Helene Grygar, Ann and Colin Hunt, John Evans, Frances Parsons, Charles Todd)*

BISHOP'S WALTHAM   SU5517
Barleycorn (01489) 892712
Lower Basingwell Street; SO32 1AJ Relaxed 18th-c two-bar village local; popular generously served pub food at reasonable prices, good friendly service, well kept Greene King ales, a guest beer and decent wines, spic and span interior with beams and some low ceiling panelling, open fires; well behaved children and dogs welcome, large garden and back smokers' area, open all day. *(Ann and Colin Hunt)*

We include some hotels with a good bar that offers facilities comparable to those of a pub.

BISHOP'S WALTHAM   SU5517
★**Bunch of Grapes** (01489) 892935

St Peter's Street – near entrance to central car park; SO32 1AD Neat civilised little pub in quiet medieval street, smartly furnished keeping individuality and unspoilt feel (same family ownership for over a century), good chatty landlord and friendly regulars, a couple of ales such as Flack Manor and Flowerpots tapped from the cask, own wines from nearby vineyard, no food; charming walled garden behind, opening times may vary. *(Phil and Jane Villiers)*

BISHOP'S WALTHAM   SU5517
Crown (01489) 893350

The Square; SO32 1AF Spacious 16th-c beamed coaching inn attractively updated by Fullers; their ales including Gales and popular fairly priced food from sandwiches to daily specials, cheerful helpful staff, bar area on the left with bare boards, comfortable seating and log fire, split-level dining room to the right with three further fireplaces; background music, free wi-fi; children and dogs welcome, courtyard tables, opposite entrance to palace ruins, eight good bedrooms, open all day from 8.30am, food all day Fri-Sun. *(Ann and Colin Hunt)*

BOLDRE   SZ3198
★**Red Lion** (01590) 673177

Off A337 N of Lymington; SO41 8NE New Forest-edge dining pub with five black-beamed rooms and three log fires; pews, sturdy cushioned dining chairs and tapestried stools, rural landscapes on rough-cast walls, other rustic bits and pieces including copper and brass pans, a heavy horse harness and some ferocious-looking traps, old cooking range in cosy bar, well kept Ringwood and guests, good home-made food from varied menu, friendly service; dogs welcome, opposite village green with seats out among flowering tubs and hanging baskets, more tables in back garden, self-catering apartment, open all day Sun. *(Phil and Jane Villiers)*

BRAISHFIELD   SU3724
Wheatsheaf (01794) 368652

Village signposted off A3090 on NW edge of Romsey; SO51 0QE Friendly bay-windowed pub with four well kept beers and tasty home-cooked food, beams and cosy log fire; background music (live Thurs), sports TV, pool; children and dogs welcome, garden with play area and nice views, woodland walks nearby, close to Hillier Gardens, open all day. *(Phil and Jane Villiers)*

BRAMBRIDGE   SU4721
Dog & Crook (01962) 712129

Near M3 junction 12, via B3335; Church Lane; SO50 6HZ Bustling 18th-c pub with beamed bar and cosy dining room, enjoyable home-made food including good value set lunch and separate gluten-free menu, Wadworths 6X, a couple of local guests and several wines by the glass, friendly efficient service; background music, TV, fortnightly quiz Thurs; children and dogs welcome, disabled access/facilities, garden with covered deck, Itchen Way walks nearby, open all day Fri-Sun. *(Charles Todd)*

BRAMDEAN   SU6127
Fox (01962) 771363

A272 Winchester–Petersfield; SO24 0LP Popular and welcoming 17th-c part-weatherboarded roadside pub; open-plan bar with black beams and log fires, well kept Sharps Doom Bar and local guests, farmhouse ciders and several wines by the glass, good fairly traditional home-made food, cheerful helpful staff; children and dogs welcome, walled-in terraced area and spacious lawn under fruit trees, three shepherd's huts, good surrounding walks, open (and food) all day Fri-Sun. *(Ann and Colin Hunt, Helen and Brian Edgeley, Richard Tilbrook, John Evans)*

BREAMORE   SU1517
Bat & Ball (01725) 512252

Salisbury Road; SP6 2EA Dutch-gabled red-brick roadside pub with two linked bar areas and restaurant; well kept Ringwood ales and enjoyable reasonably priced food including fajitas and other mexican dishes, some south african influences too, friendly service; monthly quiz, live music; children and dogs welcome, pleasant side garden, Avon fishing and walks (lovely ones up by church and stately Breamore House), bedrooms in two apartments, open (and food) all day. *(Miranda and Jeff Davidson)*

BROCKENHURST   SU3000
Filly (01590) 623449

Lymington Road (A337 Brockenhurst–Lymington); SO42 7UF Old roadside pub with enjoyable well presented food (all day weekends) from lunchtime sandwiches to daily specials, friendly welcoming staff, a couple of changing local ales and decent selection of well priced wines, bare-boards bar with oak beams, carriage-lamp lighting and attractive fireplace, two dining rooms; children and dogs (in bar and garden room) welcome, sheltered tables outside and boules pitch, New Forest walks, five bedrooms, good breakfast, open all day. *(David and Sally Frost)*

BROCKENHURST   SU3002
Huntsman (01590) 622225

Lyndhurst Road (A337); SO42 7RH Large revamped roadside inn serving popular food from sandwiches and sharing plates up including wood-fired pizzas and chargrilled steaks, three or four real ales such as Ringwood, plenty of wines by the glass and cocktails, coffee bar; skittle alley; children and dogs (in bar) welcome, covered terrace and decent-sized garden,

13 well appointed bedrooms, open (and food) all day. *(Phil and Jane Villiers)*

BROOK SU2714
Bell (023) 8081 2214
B3079/B3078, handy for M27 junction 1; SO43 7HE Really a hotel with golf club, but has neatly kept flagstoned bar with lovely 18th-c inglenook fire, well kept ales such as Flack Manor, Ringwood and Wychwood, good cider and plenty of wines by the glass, nice food too from snacks to blackboard specials including good value lunchtime/early evening weekday set menu, afternoon teas (perhaps with a glass of house champagne), helpful friendly uniformed staff; children and dogs welcome, big garden, delightful village, 28 comfortable bedrooms, open all day. *(David and Sally Frost)*

BROOK SU2713
★ **Green Dragon** (023) 8081 3359
B3078 NW of Cadnam, just off M27 junction 1; SO43 7HE Thatched New Forest dining pub dating from the 15th c; popular food from pubby favourites to blackboard specials, well kept Wadworths ales and good range of wines by the glass, friendly helpful staff, linked areas with beams, log fires and traditional furnishings, lots of pictures and other bits and pieces including some old leather 'bends' showing brand marks of forest graziers; children and dogs (not in restaurant) welcome, disabled access from car park, attractive small terrace, garden with play area and paddocks beyond, picturesque village, open all day. *(David and Sally Frost, PL, Phil and Jane Villiers)*

BROUGHTON SU3032
Tally Ho (01794) 301280
High Street, opposite church; signed off A30 Stockbridge–Salisbury; SO20 8AA Welcoming village pub with light airy bar and separate eating area, well kept ales such as Ringwood, Sharps and Timothy Taylors, good food from pub favourites up (more elaborate evening choice), friendly service; children welcome, charming secluded back garden, good walks, open all day (food all day Fri-Sun). *(Nicholas and Maddy Trainer)*

BUCKLERS HARD SU4000
Master Builders House (01590)
616253 *M27 junction 2 follow signs to Beaulieu, turn left on to B3056, then left to Bucklers Hard; SO42 7XB* Sizeable red-brick hotel in lovely spot overlooking river; character main bar with heavy beams, log fire and simple furnishings, rugs on wooden floor, mullioned windows, interesting list of shipbuilders dating from 18th c, Ringwood Best and guests, stairs down to room with fireplace at each end, enjoyable bar and restaurant food from sandwiches and pizzas up, afternoon teas, prompt friendly service; children and dogs

welcome, picnic-sets on stepped terrace, small gate at bottom of garden for waterside walks, summer barbecues, 26 bedrooms, open (and food) all day. *(Tony Scott)*

BURGHCLERE SU4660
Carpenters Arms (01635) 278251
Harts Lane, off A34; RG20 9JY Friendly little village pub with enjoyable moderately priced home-made food (not Sun evening) from sandwiches up, bargain two-course OAP lunch Tues, Arkells and an occasional guest, good country views (Watership Down) from conservatory and terrace, log fire; background music; children, walkers and dogs welcome, tricky wheelchair access, handy for Sandham Memorial Chapel (NT) with its Stanley Spencer murals and Highclere Castle, six comfortable annexe bedrooms, open all day. *(Ian Herdman)*

BURLEY SU2103
Queens Head (01425) 403423
The Cross; back road Ringwood–Lymington; BH24 4AB Large brick and tile pub dating partly from the 17th c; several updated rambling rooms, open fire, enjoyable reasonably priced food (order at bar) including vegetarian/vegan choices, Greene King and local guests, helpful friendly staff; children and dogs (in one area) welcome, plenty of space outside including at front overlooking busy road, pub and New Forest village can get packed in summer, car parking fee refunded at bar, open all day. *(Tony Scott)*

BURLEY SU2202
White Buck (01425) 402264
Bisterne Close; 0.7 miles E, OS Sheet 195 map reference 223028; BH24 4AZ Well run 19th-c mock-Tudor hotel in lovely New Forest setting; Fullers ales in long bar with two-way log fire at either end, seats in big bow window, comfortable part-panelled shooting-theme snug and spacious well divided dining area on different levels, good choice of enjoyable attractively presented food (not overly expensive) and nice wines, helpful personable staff; background music, free wi-fi; children and dogs welcome, terraces and spacious lawn, excellent walks towards Burley itself and over Mill Lawn, good bedrooms, open all day. *(Lauren and Dan Frazer)*

BURSLEDON SU4909
Jolly Sailor (023) 8040 5557
Off A27 towards Bursledon Station, Lands End Road; handy for M27 junction 8; SO31 8DN Steps down to brick-built Badger dining pub worth knowing for its prime location overlooking yachting inlet; their ales (tasting trays available) and decent wine choice, enjoyable food from shortish menu (also daily specials), beams, bare boards and stone floors, some maritime bric-a-brac, log fires; dogs welcome, no wheelchair access and limited

nearby parking, nice outside seating area, pontoon for tidal mooring, open (and food) all day. *(Taff Thomas, Phil and Jane Villiers)*

CADNAM   SU3114
Compass (023) 8081 2237
Winsor Road, off Totton–Cadnam road at Bartley crossroads; OS Sheet 195 map reference 317143; SO40 2HE Tucked-away but popular 16th-c flower-decked pub, friendly and chatty, with well kept ales and reasonably priced gluten-free food, brasses on beams, pubby furniture on bare boards, woodburner in brick fireplace; dogs very welcome (food for them – their characterful jack russell is Boris), side garden with decorative arbour, charity shop, open all day, food all day weekends. *(Mark Hamill)*

CHALTON   SU7316
Red Lion (023) 9259 2246
Off A3 Petersfield–Horndean; PO8 0BG Largely extended timber and thatch dining pub, interesting old core around inglenook (dates to the 12th c and has been a pub since the 1400s); popular food (all day weekends) from sandwiches and pub favourites up, well kept Fullers/Gales beers, friendly helpful service; children and dogs welcome, disabled access and facilities, nice views from neat rows of picnic-sets on rectangular lawn by large car park, good walks, handy for Queen Elizabeth Country Park, open all day. *(Tony and Wendy Hobden, John and Enid Morris)*

CHERITON   SU5828
★ Flower Pots (01962) 771318
Off B3046 towards Beauworth and Winchester; OS Sheet 185 map reference 581282; SO24 0QQ Unspoilt 19th-c red-brick country local in same family since 1968; three or four good value cask-tapped ales from back brewery, enjoyable reasonably priced home-made food (not Sun evening or bank holiday evenings, and possible restrictions during busy times) including generous baps, range of casseroles and popular Weds curry night, cheerful welcoming staff, extended public bar with painted brick walls, tiled floor, open fire and glass-covered well, another straightforward but homely room with country pictures and small log fire; no credit cards or children; dogs welcome, seats on pretty front and back lawns (some under apple trees), vintage motorcycles Weds lunchtime, two bedrooms. *(Tony and Jill Radnor, Ann and Colin Hunt, David and Judy Robison)*

CHILBOLTON   SU3939
Abbots Mitre (01264) 860348
Off A3051 S of Andover; SO20 6BA Traditional 19th-c brick-built village pub refurbished under present owners; five well

kept local ales and decent wines by the glass, enjoyable food from sandwiches and pubby choices up including daily specials, friendly service; picnic-sets outside, River Test and other walks (circular one from the pub), open (and food) all day. *(Terry Gilmour)*

CHILWORTH   SU4118
Chilworth Arms (023) 8076 6247
Chilworth Road (A27 Southampton–Romsey); SO16 7JZ Modernised Mitchells & Butlers dining pub, good choice of popular food from sharing plates and home-made pizzas up, Sharps Doom Bar and a guest, lots of wines by the glass including champagne, cocktails, comfortable bar with log fires, conservatory-style restaurant; background music; children and dogs (in bar) welcome, disabled access/facilities, large neatly kept garden with terrace, open (and food) all day. *(Simon and Mandy King)*

COPYTHORNE   SU3115
Empress of Blandings
(023) 8081 2321 *Copythorne Crescent, just off A31; SO40 2PE* Country pub-restaurant with PG Wodehouse/pig theme (note spelling on Hall & Woodhouse sign), Badger ales and enjoyable moderately priced food from snacks and sharing boards up, good friendly service, roomy interior with some cosy corners; free wi-fi; children, welcome, dogs in one area, picnic-sets in front and back gardens, open (and food) all day. *(Phil and Jane Villiers)*

CRONDALL   SU7948
Plume of Feathers
(01252) 850245 *The Borough; GU10 5NT* Attractive 15th-c brick and timber village pub popular for its good range of generous home-made food from standards up, friendly helpful staff, well kept Greene King and some unusual guests, nice wines by the glass, beams and dark wood, red carpet, prints on cream walls, restaurant with log fire in big brick fireplace; soft background music, free wi-fi; children welcome, picnic-sets in back terrace garden (bookable barbecues), picturesque village, three bedrooms, open all day Sun. *(Sandra and Michael Smith)*

CROOKHAM   SU7952
Exchequer (01252) 615336 *Crondall Road; GU51 5SU* Welcoming smartly presented dining pub (part of the Red Mist group – Royal Exchange at Lindford, Wheatsheaf in Farnham (Surrey) etc); popular home-made food from sandwiches and sharing boards to blackboard specials in bar and restaurant, four well kept local ales and good choice of wines by the glass including champagne, interesting range of gins and cocktails, also cider and lager

from local Hogs Back, pleasant hard-working young staff, cosy woodburner, daily newspapers; children and dogs welcome, rattan-style furniture on split-level terrace, near Basingstoke Canal, open all day Fri-Sun, food all day Sun. *(Hugh Roberts, Roger)*

CURDRIDGE SU5314
Cricketers (01489) 784420
Curdridge Lane, off B3035 just under a mile NE of A334 junction; SO32 2BH Open-plan split-level Victorian village dining pub, popular food (all day weekends) from lunchtime sandwiches to specials, well kept Greene King and a guest, several wines by the glass, friendly staff; background music, free wi-fi; children and dogs welcome, picnic-sets on front lawn, pleasant walks, open all day except Mon in winter. *(Ann and Colin Hunt)*

DENMEAD SU6412
Fox & Hounds (023) 9226 5984
School Lane, Anthill Common; PO7 6NA Friendly village pub rescued from closure by the local community; modernised interior with comfortable log-fire bar and large back dining area, enjoyable own-grown and locally sourced food (order at the bar), four real ales, afternoon tea; children and dogs (theirs is Molly) welcome, paved terrace with pergola, open all day, no food Sun evening. *(Ann and Colin Hunt)*

DENMEAD SU6211
Horse & Jockey (023) 9263 2728
Hipley; W on Southwick Road, right into Forest Road; PO7 4QY Lots of tables laid for dining but still plenty of room for drinkers, three or four well kept ales such as Ringwood, popular generously served food including blackboard specials, good cheerful service, beams and knick-knacks, open fire in bar area, central woodburner in restaurant; occasional jazz nights; children welcome, terrace and streamside garden with play area, open all day. *(Ann and Colin Hunt)*

DROXFORD SU6118
Hurdles (01489) 877451
Brockbridge, just outside Soberton; from A32 just N of Droxford take B2150 towards Denmead; SO32 3QT Modernised dining pub (former 19th-c station hotel) with well liked interesting food from good lunchtime sandwiches to tasting menus; high ceilings and stripped-wood floors, leather chesterfield and armchairs by log fire in one room, dining areas with some eye-catching wallpaper and stripy chairs around shiny tables, well kept Bowman Swift One and Sharps Doom Bar, decent wines by the glass and good coffee, friendly service; background music; children and dogs (in bar) welcome, neat terraces (one covered and heated), flight of steps up to picnic-sets on sloping lawn by tall trees, open all day Sat, closed Sun evening, Mon. *(Jane and Kai Horsburgh)*

DUMMER SU5846
Queen (01256) 397367
Under a mile from M3 junction 7; take Dummer slip road; RG25 2AD Comfortable well divided beamed pub with lots of softly lit alcoves, Andwell, Otter and Sharps, decent choice of wines by the glass and popular food from lunchtime sandwiches and light dishes up, friendly service, big log fire, pictures of the Queen and some steeplechase prints; background music, free wi-fi; children welcome in restaurant, picnic-sets under parasols on terrace and in extended back garden, attractive village with ancient church. *(Lyn and Freddie Roberts)*

DUNBRIDGE SU3126
Mill Arms (01794) 340401
Barley Hill (B3084); SO51 0LF Much extended 18th-c coaching inn opposite station, welcoming informal atmosphere in spacious high-ceilinged rooms, scrubbed pine tables and farmhouse chairs on oak or flagstone floors, several sofas, two log fires, local ales such as Flack Manor and enjoyable food, dining conservatory; darts and two skittle alleys; children and dogs (in bar) welcome, big garden, plenty of walks in surrounding Test Valley, six comfortable bedrooms, open all day from 10am (till 5pm Sun). *(Charles Todd)*

DUNDRIDGE SU5718
★Hampshire Bowman (01489) 892940
Off B3035 towards Droxford, Swanmore, then right at Bishop's Waltham signpost; SO32 1GD Chatty mix of customers at this homely relaxed country pub, five well kept local ales tapped from the cask (beer festival last weekend in July), summer farm cider and good value food (all day Fri-Sun) from generous sandwiches and hearty pub dishes to specials using local produce, good cheerful service, stable bar and cosy unassuming original one; mobile phones discouraged; children and dogs (they have two) welcome, tables on heated terrace and peaceful lawn, play equipment, hitching post for horses, popular with walkers and cyclists, open all day. *(Val and Alan Green, Ann and Colin Hunt)*

DURLEY SU5116
Farmers Home (01489) 860457
B3354 and B2177; Heathen Street/ Curdridge Road; SO32 2BT Comfortable red-brick beamed country pub, spacious but cosy, with two-bay dining area and restaurant, enjoyable food including good steaks and popular Sun lunch, friendly service, room for drinkers too with decent wines by the glass and three well kept ales including Gales HSB and Ringwood, woodburner; children and dogs (in bar) welcome, big garden with pergola and play area, nice walks, open (and food) all day. *(Phil and Jane Villiers)*

DURLEY SU5217

★**Robin Hood** (01489) 860229

Durley Street, just off B2177 Bishop's Waltham–Winchester – brown signs to pub; SO32 2AA Quirky open-plan beamed pub with well prepared food from varied blackboard menu (order at bar), Greene King and a guest ale, nice wines, good informed service from accommodating staff, log fire and leather sofas in bare-boards bar, dining area with stone floors and mix of old pine tables and chairs, bookcase door to loos; background music; children and dogs welcome, disabled facilities, decked terrace with barbecue, garden with play area and country views, open all day Sun. *(Phil and Jane Villiers)*

EAST BOLDRE SU3700

Turf Cutters Arms (01590) 612331

Main Road; SO42 7WL Small dimly lit 18th-c New Forest local behind white picket fence; lots of beams and pictures, nicely worn-in furnishings on bare boards and flagstones, log fire, enjoyable home-made food from ciabattas up (worth booking evenings/weekends), well kept Ringwood ales and a guest, good friendly service and chatty relaxed atmosphere; children and dogs welcome, picnic-sets in large back garden, good heathland walks, bedrooms in nearby converted barn, open all day. *(Peter Meister, Dave T)*

EAST END SZ3696

★**East End Arms** (01590) 626223

Back road Lymington–Beaulieu, parallel to B3054; SO41 5SY Simple friendly pub (owned by former Dire Straits bass guitarist), determinedly unfussy bar with chatty locals and log fire, Ringwood Best or Fortyniner and several wines by the glass, enjoyable freshly made food (not Sun evening) served by cheerful helpful staff, attractive dining room; occasional live music, free wi-fi; children and dogs (in bar) welcome, picnic-sets in terraced garden, pretty cottagey bedrooms, open all day July-Sept (all day Fri-Sun other times). *(Phil and Jane Villiers)*

EAST MEON SU6822

Olde George (01730) 823481

Church Street; signed off A272 W of Petersfield, and off A32 in West Meon; GU32 1NH Atmospheric heavy-beamed village inn with well liked food from sandwiches and light lunches to more restauranty choices, Badger ales and decent selection of wines by the glass, cosy areas around central brick counter, inglenook log fires; children and dogs welcome, nice back terrace, five bedrooms, good breakfast, pretty

village with fine church and surrounding walks, open all day Sun. *(Frances Parsons)*

EAST WORLDHAM SU7438

Three Horseshoes (01420) 83211

Cakers Lane (B3004 Alton–Kingsley); GU34 3AE Welcoming early 19th-c brick and stone roadside pub with decent choice of enjoyable home-cooked food including daily specials, three Fullers ales and one or two guests, good wines by the glass, friendly helpful staff, wood floors and log fires; background and some live music including folk night first Tues of the month, quiz last Tues, free wi-fi; children and dogs welcome, pleasant secluded garden with lots of picnic-sets, five well appointed bedrooms, open all day Sat, till 5pm Sun, closed Mon lunchtime. *(Tony and Jill Radnor)*

EASTON SU5132

Chestnut Horse (01962) 779257

3.6 miles from M3 junction 9: A33 towards Kings Worthy, then B3047 towards Itchen Abbas; Easton then signposted on right – bear left in village; SO21 1EG 16th-c pub in pretty village of thatched cottages, open-plan interior but with a series of cosy separate areas, log fires, comfortable furnishings, black beams and joists hung with jugs, mugs and chamber-pots, three Badger ales, plenty of wines by the glass and good selection of whiskies and gins, food has been good (recent change of ownership); background music; children and dogs (in bar) welcome, seats and tables on smallish sheltered decked area, summer tubs and baskets, picnic-sets at the front; walks in Itchen Valley, open all day Fri-Sun, food all day Sun. *(Lindy Andrews)*

ECCHINSWELL SU4959

Royal Oak (01635) 297355

Ecchinswell Road; RG20 4UH Cosy and welcoming whitewashed village pub; bar with open fire, window seats and plush-topped stools around tables on wood floor, second room with another fire and airy dining room with country kitchen chairs and mix of tables on light boards, three well kept ales and enjoyable fair value food, good friendly service; children welcome, picnic-sets on front terrace behind picket fence, more in large back garden running down to stream. *(Dawn Saunders, Dr W I C Clark)*

ELLISFIELD SU6345

★**Fox** (01256) 381210

Green Lane; S of village off Northgate Lane; RG25 2QW Simple tucked-away country pub with friendly atmosphere; mixed collection of stripped tables, country chairs and cushioned wall benches on bare

---

If you stay overnight in an inn or hotel, they are allowed to serve you an alcoholic drink at any hour of the day or night.

boards and old floor tiles, some exposed masonry, open fires in plain brick fireplaces, Wadworth ales, enjoyable sensibly priced home-made food; outside gents'; children and dogs welcome, picnic-sets in nice garden, good walking country near snowdrop and bluebell woods, open all day. *(Simon Sharpe)*

EMERY DOWN   SU2808
★**New Forest** (023) 8028 4690
Village signed off A35 just W of Lyndhurst; SO43 7DY Well run 18th-c weatherboarded village pub in one of the best parts of the New Forest for walking; good sensibly priced home-made food including vegetarian choices, daily specials and popular Sun roasts (should book), friendly helpful uniformed staff, Ringwood and guests, real cider and several wines by the glass, coffee and tea; attractive softly lit separate areas on varying levels, each with own character, old pine and oak furniture, milk churn stools by bar, hunting prints and two log fires; background music; children and dogs welcome, covered terrace and nice little three-level garden, four good value simple bedrooms, open (and food) all day, can get very busy weekends. *(Sara Fulton, Roger Baker)*

EMSWORTH   SU7405
Blue Bell (01243) 373394
South Street; PO10 7EG Friendly and relaxed little 1940s red-brick pub close to the quay, old-fashioned lived-in interior with nautical and other memorabilia, good choice of popular reasonably priced home-made food including fresh fish (best to book weekends), bar nibbles Sun lunchtime, Sharps Doom Bar and a couple of well kept local guests from brick and timber servery; TV, daily newspapers; dogs welcome, seats on small front and side terraces, Sun market in adjacent car park, open all day. *(Ann and Colin Hunt, Michael Butler, Ken Board)*

EMSWORTH   SU7405
Coal Exchange (01243) 375866
Ships Quay, South Street; PO10 7EG Friendly little L-shaped Victorian local near harbour, well kept Fullers/Gales beers along with guests such as Butcombe, good value home-made lunchtime food (evenings Mon-Thurs including Weds pizza night), simple low-ceilinged bar with fire at each end; live music Sat and first/third Weds of the month, free wi-fi; children and dogs welcome, tables outside and smokers' shelter, handy for Wayfarer's Walk and Solent Way, open all day Fri-Sun. *(Ann and Colin Hunt)*

EVERSLEY   SU7762
Tally Ho (0118) 973 2134
Fleet Hill; RG27 0RR Home Counties group pub in extended old brick farmhouse, friendly chatty atmosphere, four real ales, lots of wines by the glass and enjoyable bistro-style food, beams and wood floors, built-in wall seats and cushioned dining chairs around wooden tables; children and dogs (in bar) welcome, tables on terrace and lawn, swings and play tractor, open (and food) all day. *(Edward Edmonton)*

EVERSLEY CROSS   SU7861
Chequers (0118) 402 7065
Chequers Lane; RG27 0NS Stylish Peach dining pub dating in part from the 14th c, good seasonal food from deli boards to daily specials, well kept Hogs Back and local guests, carefully chosen wines and gins, cocktails, friendly welcoming service, linked beamed rooms including restaurant; children welcome, tables out at front under parasols, open all day from 9.30am for breakfast. *(Patrick and Emma Stephenson)*

EVERTON   SZ2994
Crown (01590) 642655
Old Christchurch Road; pub signed just off A337 W of Lymington; SO41 0JJ Quietly set restaurant-pub on edge of New Forest, highly thought-of food cooked by landlord-chef including daily specials, friendly service, Greene King and Ringwood ales, decent wines, two attractive dining rooms off tiled-floor bar, log fires; children welcome, wheelchair access, picnic-sets on front terrace behind picket fence and in garden behind, closed Mon. *(Charles Todd)*

EXTON   SU6120
★**Shoe** (01489) 877526
Village signposted from A32 NE of Bishop's Waltham; SO32 3NT Popular brick-built country dining pub on South Downs Way; three linked rooms with log fires, good well presented food (best to book) from traditional favourites to more imaginative restaurant-style dishes including fresh fish and seasonal game, home-baked bread, well kept Wadworths ales and a guest, several wines by the glass including local sparkling, good service from friendly young staff; children and dogs welcome, disabled facilities, seats under parasols at front, more in garden across lane overlooking River Meon, open all day weekends. *(Ann and Colin Hunt, David and Judy Robison)*

FAREHAM   SU5806
Cams Mill (01329) 287506
Cams Hall Estate, off A27; PO16 8UP Large waterside Fullers pub (oak-framed re-creation of former tidal mill); roomy interior including high-raftered and galleried eating area, popular food, well kept ales and friendly young staff, Fareham Creek views from big windows and terrace; free wi-fi; children and dogs welcome, nice circular creekside walk, open (and food) all day. *(Ann and Colin Hunt)*

FAREHAM   SU5806
Cob & Pen (01329) 221624
Wallington Shore Road, not far from M27 junction 11; PO16 8SL Cheerful

old corner local near Wallington River; four well kept ales including Hop Back, St Austell and Sharps, enjoyable well priced home-made food from sandwiches up, log fire; some live music, TV, machines and darts; children and dogs welcome, large garden with play area and summer barbecues, open all day. *(Ann and Colin Hunt)*

FAREHAM SU5806
Golden Lion (01329) 234061
High Street; PO16 7AE Traditional 19th-c town local, well kept Fullers/Gales beers from dark wood servery, dining part to the right with decent reasonably priced pubby food from sandwiches and baked potatoes to regular themed food evenings, good friendly service; charity quiz Thurs, free wi-fi; children and dogs welcome, courtyard garden, open all day (till 6pm Sun). *(Ann and Colin Hunt)*

FARNBOROUGH SU8756
★ **Prince of Wales** (01252) 545578
Rectory Road, near station; GU14 8AL Ten well kept ales including five quickly changing guests at this welcoming Victorian local, three small linked areas with exposed brickwork, carpet or wood floors, open fire and some antiquey touches, generous lunchtime pubby food including Mon-Weds meal deal, good friendly service; quiz first Sun of month, some live music; well behaved children and dogs welcome, terrace and smokers' gazebo, open all day Fri-Sun. *(Roger and Donna Huggins)*

FAWLEY SU4603
Jolly Sailor (023) 8089 1305
Ashlett Creek, off B3053; SO45 1DT Cottagey waterside pub near small boatyard and sailing club, straightforward good value bar food, Ringwood Best and a guest, cheerful service, mixed pubby furnishings on bare boards, raised log fire, second bar with darts and pool; children and dogs welcome, tables outside looking past creek's yachts and boats to busy shipping channel, good shore walks, handy for Rothschild rhododendron gardens at Exbury, closed Tues otherwise open all day, no food Sun evening, Mon. *(Edward Edmonton)*

FROGHAM SU1712
Foresters Arms (01425) 652294
Abbotswell Road; SP6 2JA Refurbished New Forest pub (part of the Little Pub Group); enjoyable good value food from lunchtime baguettes and bagels up, well kept Wadworths ales and a guest, good friendly service, cosy rustic-chic interior with rugs on wood or flagstone floors, woodburners in brick fireplaces, pale green panelling, mix of old and new furniture including settles and pews, antlers and grandfather clock;

children, walkers and dogs (in bar) welcome, picnic-sets out at front under pergola and on lawn, maybe donkeys, open all day weekends. *(Phil and Jane Villiers, Neil Weddell)*

GOODWORTH CLATFORD SU3642
Royal Oak (01264) 324105
Longstock Road; SP11 7QY Comfortably modern L-shaped bar with ales such as Flack Manor and Ringwood, nice wines by the glass and good carefully sourced food from pub staples up, friendly efficient staff; Weds quiz night; children welcome, picnic-sets in pretty dell-like garden, attractive Test Valley village and good River Anton walks, closed Sun evening. *(Mike and Mary Carter)*

GOSPORT SZ6198
Fighting Cocks (023) 9252 9885
Clayhall Road, Alverstoke; PO12 2AJ Cosy and welcoming local in residential area, Wadworths ales and enjoyable good value pub food including Sat breakfast from 9.30am, friendly helpful service; children and dogs welcome (pub spaniels are Sophie and Henry), big garden with play equipment, open all day. *(Sandra and Michael Smith)*

GOSPORT SU6101
Jolly Roger (023) 9258 2584
Priory Road, Hardway; PO12 4LQ Popular extended waterfront pub with fine harbour views, traditional beamed bar with four well kept ales and decent house wines, good choice of home-made food from bar and restaurant menus, efficient friendly young staff, lots of bric-a-brac, log fire, attractive dining area with conservatory; children and dogs welcome, disabled access/facilities, seats outside, open all day. *(Ann and Colin Hunt)*

GOSPORT SZ6100
Queens 07974 031671
Queens Road; PO12 1LG Classic bare-boards corner local with five real ales such as Fallen Acorn, Ringwood and Youngs kept in top condition by long-serving landlady, popular Oct beer festival, three areas off bar, good log fire in interesting carved fireplace, sensibly placed darts, TV for major sports; no children or dogs, open all day Sat, closed lunchtimes Mon-Thurs. *(Ann and Colin Hunt)*

GRAYSHOTT SU8735
Fox & Pelican (01428) 604757
Headley Road; GU26 6LG Large village pub with enjoyable food (all day Fri and Sat, till 6pm Sun) from lunchtime sandwiches and light dishes up, Fullers/Gales beers and a guest, good friendly service, linked areas with comfortable seating on wood or carpeted floors, open fire in large fireplace, dining conservatory; quiz and tapas Thurs, darts, sports TV, games machines; children

and dogs welcome, wheelchair access, tables on paved terrace and lawn, fenced play area, open all day. *(John and Bernadette Elliott)*

GREYWELL   SU7151
Fox & Goose (01256) 702062
Near M3 junction 5; A287 towards Odiham, then first right to village; RG29 1BY Traditional two-bar village pub popular with locals and walkers, country kitchen furniture, open fire, enjoyable home-made pubby food from good lunchtime sandwiches up, Sun roast till 6pm, three well kept ales including Sharps Doom Bar; open mike night third Mon of month; children and dogs welcome, good-sized back garden and camping field, River Whitewater and Basingstoke Canal walks, open all day. *(D J and P M Taylor)*

GRIGGS GREEN   SU8231
Deers Hut (01428) 724406
Off A3 S of Hindhead; GU30 7PD Popular old country pub with horseshoe bar and several rustically furnished dining areas, good if slightly pricey food (service charge added) from baguettes and pub staples to daily specials, Sharps Doom Bar, Youngs Bitter and a couple of guests, good choice of other drinks, helpful young staff; children welcome, attractive woodland setting with picnic-sets on front terrace and green, handy for Shipwrights Way walkers, classic car event (Father's Day), open all day. *(Tony and Jill Radnor, Jonathan Powell)*

HAMBLE   SU4806
Bugle (023) 8045 3000
3 miles from M27 junction 8; SO31 4HA Bustling little 16th-c village pub just back from the River Hamble; beamed and timbered rooms with flagstones and polished boards, woodburner in fine brick fireplace, bar stools along herringbone-brick and timber counter, a beer named for the pub from Itchen Valley plus a couple of guests (often Flack Manor), popular food (all day Sun); background music, TV; children and dogs (in bar) welcome, picnic-sets on small raised front terrace with boat views, open all day. *(Alastair and Sheree Hepburn)*

HAMBLE   SU4806
King & Queen (023) 8045 4247
3 miles from M27 junction 8; High Street; SO31 4HA Popular with locals and visiting yachtsmen, this cheerful bustling pub has a simply furnished bar with log fire at one end, sofas and painted settles with scatter cushions, steps down to two small dining rooms, white-painted and plain wooden chairs, candelabra on straightforward tables, big yachting photographs and woodburner, three changing ales, good wines, cocktails and some 30 different rums, generous helpings of enjoyable food from sandwiches and pizzas up, friendly hard-working young staff; children and

dogs welcome, sunny front garden with planked tables and picnic-sets (some under parasols), open all day. *(Taff Thomas)*

HAMBLE   SU4806
Victory (023) 8045 3105
High Street; SO31 4HA Split-level 18th-c red-brick pub with four well kept ales and enjoyable reasonably priced bar food including popular Sun lunch, cheerful welcoming staff, nautical theme including Battle of Trafalgar mural (find the hidden faces), beams and half-panelling, wood, flagstone and carpeted floors; darts, sports TV; children and dogs welcome, terrace picnic-sets, open all day. *(Taff Thomas)*

HAMBLEDON   SU6716
★ Bat & Ball (023) 9263 2692
Broadhalfpenny Down; about 2 miles E towards Clanfield; PO8 0UB Extended dining pub opposite historic cricket pitch, log fires and comfortable modern furnishings in three linked rooms, lots of cricketing memorabilia (the game's rules are said to have been written here), Fullers ales and enjoyable food from well priced snacks up, panelled restaurant; free wi-fi; children and dogs welcome, tables on front terrace, garden behind with lovely downs views, good walks, open all day. *(Trevor and Michele Street)*

HAMBLEDON   SU6414
Vine (023) 9263 2419
West Street; PO7 4RW Popular 400-year-old village local, well kept Ringwood and other Marstons-related beers, decent choice of whiskies and gins, enjoyable sensibly priced home-made food (not Sun evening) from sandwiches up, Thurs steak night, friendly helpful staff, comfortable beamed interior with two-way log fire and illuminated well; some live music, darts, free wi-fi; children and dogs (in bar) welcome, nice garden with small covered deck, good walks, closed Mon, otherwise open all day. *(Ann and Colin Hunt)*

HAVANT   SU7106
Old House At Home (023) 9248
3464 *South Street; PO9 1DA* Black and white Tudor pub next to church; modernised two-bar interior with low beams and nice rambling alcovey feel, enjoyable sensibly priced food from sandwiches and bar snacks up, Fullers/Gales beers, friendly service; Tues quiz, juke box (some live music), TV, fruit machine, darts and board games; children (in smaller bar) and dogs welcome, pretty jettied frontage with hanging baskets, tables and smokers' shelter in back garden, open (and food) all day except Sun when kitchen closes at 5pm. *(Ann and Colin Hunt)*

HAVANT   SU7206
Wheelwrights Arms (023) 9247 6502
Emsworth Road; PO9 2SN Sizeable stylishly decorated Victorian pub, well kept beers and good range of enjoyable

food including OAP lunch deal Mon-Thurs, friendly service; children welcome, open all day Sun. *(Charles Todd)*

HAWKLEY   SU7429
Hawkley Inn (01730) 827205
Off B3006 near A3 junction; Pococks Lane; GU33 6NE Traditional tile-hung village pub with seven well kept mainly local ales from central bar, popular often interesting home-made food (not Sun evening), friendly staff, open fires (large moose head above one), rugs on flagstones, old pine tables and assorted chairs; children and dogs welcome, covered seating area at front, picnic-sets in big back garden, useful for walkers on Hangers Way, six comfortable bedrooms, open all day weekends. *(Tony and Jill Radnor)*

HAYLING ISLAND   SU7201
Maypole (023) 9246 3670
Havant Road; PO11 0PS Sizeable two-bar 1930s roadside local, well run and friendly, with good reasonably priced home-made pub food including Fri fish night, Fullers/Gales beers kept well, parquet floors and polished panelling, plenty of good seating, open fires; Thurs quiz, darts; children and dogs welcome, garden picnic-sets and play equipment, closed Sun evening. *(Frances Parsons)*

HECKFIELD   SU7260
New Inn (0118) 932 6374
B3349 Hook–Reading (former A32); RG27 0LE Rambling open-plan dining pub with good reasonably priced food (all day weekends) from sandwiches and baked potatoes up, well kept Badger ales and good choice of wines by the glass, efficient friendly service, attractive layout with some traditional furniture in original core, two log fires, restaurant; quiz and curry last Thurs; children welcome, good-sized heated terrace, 16 comfortable bedrooms in extension, open all day. *(Darren and Jane Staniforth)*

HERRIARD   SS6744
Fur & Feathers (01256) 384170
Pub signed just off A339 Basingstoke–Alton; RG25 2PN Light and airy Victorian country pub with popular freshly made food, four well kept ales including Sharps Doom Bar and good choice of wines, friendly staff, smallish bar with stools along counter, dining areas either side, pine furniture on stripped-wood flooring, painted half-panelling, old photographs and farm tools, two woodburners; background music; garden behind, open all day Fri and Sat, till 6pm Sun, closed Mon. *(John and Delia Franks)*

HORDLE   SZ2996
★ Mill at Gordleton (01590) 682219
Silver Street; SO41 6DJ Charming tucked-away country inn; small panelled bar to the right with leather armchairs and Victorian-style mahogany dining chairs

on parquet flooring, pretty corner china cupboard and feature stove, ales from Ringwood and Upham, 18 good wines by the glass and over 20 malt whiskies, also cosy lounge, spacious second bar and sizeable beamed restaurant extension, highly rated imaginative food (can be pricey), warm accommodating service; free wi-fi; children and dogs (in bar) welcome, lovely gardens with extensive series of interestingly planted areas and several pools, plenty of places to sit including main waterside terrace, good nearby walks, comfortable individually furnished bedrooms, open all day. *(Alison Chalu, I D Barnett, Darren and Jane Staniforth)*

HORSEBRIDGE   SU3430
John O'Gaunt (01794) 388644
Off A3057 Romsey–Andover, just SW of Kings Somborne; SO20 6PU New owners and refurbishment for this River Test village pub; L-shaped bar with mix of furniture including armchairs on bare boards, light wood dados, book wallpaper either side of woodburner, popular good value home-made food from baguettes up, Ringwood Razorback and three guests, a couple of Purbeck ciders and good selection of gins, friendly helpful service; children, walkers and dogs welcome, seats outside, open (and food) all day. *(Mrs Julie Thomas)*

HOUGHTON   SU3432
★ Boot (01794) 388310
Village signposted off A30 in Stockbridge; SO20 6LH Updated well maintained country pub with cheery log-fire bar and more formal dining room, well kept Flack Manor, Ringwood and a guest, Weston's cider, good bar and restaurant food (not Sun or Mon evening) from baguettes to blackboard specials, friendly helpful staff; children and dogs welcome, picnic-sets out in front and in spacious tranquil garden by lovely (unfenced) stretch of River Test, outside summer grill, opposite Test Way walking/cycling path, open all day Fri-Sun. *(John Allman, Helen and Brian Edgeley)*

KEYHAVEN   SZ3091
★ Gun (01590) 642391
Keyhaven Road; SO41 0TP Busy rambling 17th-c pub looking over boatyard and sea to Isle of Wight; low-beamed bar with nautical bric-a-brac and plenty of character (less in family rooms and conservatory), good fairly standard food including excellent crab sandwiches, well kept Ringwood, Sharps, Timothy Taylors and Charles Wells tapped from the cask, Weston's cider, lots of malt whiskies, prompt service from helpful young staff; bar billiards; tables out in front and in big back garden with swings and fish pond, you can stroll down to small harbour and walk to Hurst Castle, open all day Sat, closed Sun evening. *(Bob and Margaret Holder, David and Judy Robison, Brian Glozier, Alison Chalu, M J Daly)*

KINGSCLERE SU5258
Swan (01635) 299342
Swan Street; RG20 5PP Nicely updated 15th-c beamed village inn (Bel & The Dragon group), emphasis on dining with good bar and restaurant food including Josper grills, weekend brunch, three real ales, cocktails and good selection of wines by the glass including champagne, friendly helpful staff; children welcome, nine bedrooms, good surrounding walks, open all day. *(Nicholas and Maddy Trainer)*

LANGSTONE SU7104
★ Royal Oak (023) 9248 3125
Off A3023 just before Hayling Island bridge; Langstone High Street; PO9 1RY Charmingly placed waterside dining pub overlooking tidal inlet and ancient wadeway to Hayling Island – boats at high tide, wading birds when it goes out; four Greene King ales and good choice of wines by the glass, reasonably priced pubby food from sandwiches up, refurbished interior retaining spacious flagstoned bar and linked dining areas, log fire; children welcome in restaurant, dogs in bar, nice garden with pond, good coast paths nearby, open (and food) all day from 10am. *(Tony Scott, Suzy Miller)*

LINDFORD SU8036
Royal Exchange (01420) 488118
Liphook Road; GU35 0NX Revamped Red Mist pub with spacious bar and light modern dining room, enjoyable food from sandwiches and sharing boards to good specials, four real ales including a house beer from Andwell, craft beers, plenty of wines by the glass and interesting selection of gins, efficient friendly service; children and dogs welcome, seats outside, open all day Fri-Sun, food all day Sun. *(John Evans)*

LINWOOD SU1910
High Corner (01425) 473973
Signed from A338 via Moyles Court, and from A31; BH24 3QY Big rambling pub in splendid New Forest position at end of track; popular and welcoming with some character in original upper log-fire bar, big back extensions for the summer crowds, nicely partitioned restaurant, verandah lounge and other rooms, good helpings of enjoyable home-made food, well kept Wadworths ales and Weston's cider, friendly staff; children and dogs welcome, horses too (stables and paddock available), extensive wooded garden with play area, seven comfortable bedrooms, open all day in summer (all day weekends other times). *(Peter Meister, Phil and Jane Villiers)*

LISS SU7826
Jolly Drover (01730) 893137
London Road, Hill Brow; B2070 S of town, near B3006 junction; GU33 7QL Traditional pub with neatly carpeted low-beamed bar, leather tub chairs and a couple of chesterfield sofas in front of inglenook log fire, Bowman Wallops Wood, Sharps Doom Bar and Timothy Taylors Landlord, a dozen wines by the glass and good value honest food, chatty locals and long-serving landlord, two back dining sections; free wi-fi; children welcome, teak furniture on terrace, picnic-sets on lawn, bedrooms in two barn conversions, closed Sun evening. *(Colin and Daniel Gibbs, Mark Morgan, Andrew Vincent, Katherine Matthews)*

LITTLE LONDON SU6259
Plough (01256) 850628
Silchester Road, off A340 N of Basingstoke; RG26 5EP Tucked-away local, cosy and unspoilt, with log fires, low beams and mixed furnishings on brick or tiled floors (watch the step), well kept Palmers, Ringwood and interesting guests tapped from the cask, good value baguettes; bar billiards and darts; dogs welcome, attractive garden, handy for Pamber Forest and Calleva Roman remains. *(Frances Parsons)*

LONG SUTTON SU7447
Four Horseshoes (01256) 862488
Signed off B3349 S of Hook; RG29 1TA Welcoming unpretentious country pub with loyal band of regulars, open plan with black beams and two log fires, long-serving landlord cooking uncomplicated bargain food such as lancashire hotpot and fish and chips, friendly landlady serving three changing ales; monthly quiz and jazz nights; children and dogs welcome, disabled access, small glazed-in front verandah, picnic-sets and play area on grass over road, pétanque, bedrooms with country views, closed Mon and Tues lunchtimes. *(Tony and Jill Radnor)*

LONGPARISH SU4344
Cricketers (01264) 720335
B3048, off A303 just E of Andover; SP11 6PZ Cheerful village local with connecting rooms and cosy corners, beams, bare boards and flagstones, two woodburners (one two-way), assorted cricketing memorabilia, enjoyable freshly made food (not Sun evening) from good ciabattas to blackboard specials, well kept Wadworths ales; children and dogs welcome, back garden with terrace, closed Mon, otherwise open all day. *(Edward Mirzoeff)*

LYMINGTON SZ3293
Chequers (01590) 673415
Ridgeway Lane, Lower Woodside – dead end just S of A337 roundabout W of Lymington, by White Hart; SO41 8AH Old beamed pub with enjoyable food from traditional favourites up (smaller helpings available), Ringwood ales and good wines by the glass, bare boards and quarry tiles, mix of furniture including spindleback

chairs, wall pews and country pine tables, yacht-racing pictures, woodburner; well behaved children and dogs welcome, tables and summer marquee in neat walled back garden, good walks and handy for bird-watching on Pennington Marshes. *(Darren and Jane Staniforth, Phil and Jane Villiers)*

LYMINGTON SZ3295
Kings Head (01590) 672709
Quay Hill; SO41 3AR Friendly dimly lit old pub in steep cobbled lane of smart small shops; well kept Fullers London Pride, Ringwood, Timothy Taylors Landlord and a couple of guests, several wines by the glass, enjoyable uncomplicated home-made food from sandwiches up, pleasant helpful staff, nicely mixed old-fashioned furnishings in rambling beamed and bare-boarded rooms, log fire and woodburner; background music, daily papers; children and dogs welcome, nice little sunny courtyard behind, open all day and can get very busy. *(Darren and Jane Staniforth)*

LYNDHURST SU2908
Fox & Hounds (023) 8028 2098
High Street; SO43 7BG Big busy low-beamed pub, comfortable and much modernised/extended; good food including weekend brunch, Fullers/Gales beers and a guest, plenty of wines by the glass, cheerful helpful service, rambling interior with exposed brick and standing timbers, wood and stone floors, attached café/deli; regular live music, Mon quiz, free wi-fi; children and dogs welcome, disabled facilities, tables in courtyard with murals and enamel signs, covered seating in old barn, open all day (and food) Fri-Sun. *(Simon Sharpe)*

LYNDHURST SU2908
Waterloo Arms (023) 8028 2113
Pikes Hill, just off A337 N; SO43 7AS Thatched 17th-c New Forest pub with low beams, stripped-brick walls and log fire, two Ringwood beers and Sharps Doom Bar, pubby food including blackboard specials, friendly staff, comfortable bar and roomy back dining area; live music Sun; children and dogs welcome, terrace and nice big garden, open (and food) all day. *(Lindy Andrews)*

MAPLEDURWELL SU6851
★Gamekeepers (01256) 322038
Off A30, not far from M3 junction 6; RG25 2LU Dark-beamed dining pub with good upmarket food (not cheap and they add a service charge) from regularly changing blackboard menu, also some pubby choices and lunchtime baguettes, welcoming helpful landlord and friendly efficient staff, three well kept local ales including Andwell,

good coffee, a few sofas in flagstoned and panelled core, well spaced tables in large dining room; background music, TV; children welcome, terrace and garden, lovely thatched village with duck pond, good walks, open all day weekends. *(Guy Consterdine)*

MARCHWOOD SU3809
Pilgrim (023) 8086 7752
Hythe Road, off A326 at Twiggs Lane; SO40 4WU Popular and picturesque thatched pub (originally three 18th-c cottages), enjoyable sensibly priced food from lunchtime sandwiches up, well kept Fullers ales and decent wines, friendly helpful staff, open fires; children and dogs welcome, tree-lined garden with circular picnic-sets, 14 stylish bedrooms in building across car park, open all day. *(Phil and Jane Villiers)*

MATTINGLEY SU7357
Leather Bottle (0118) 932 6371
3 miles from M3 junction 5; in Hook, turn right-and-left on to B3349 Reading Road (former A32); RG27 8JU Old red-brick pub (Home Counties group) converted from three cottages; three local ales including Andwell, plenty of wines by the glass and popular varied choice of food, friendly efficient service, well spaced tables in linked areas, black beams, flagstones and bare boards, inglenook log fire, extension opening on to covered terrace; background music; children and dogs (in bar) welcome, disabled access/facilities, two garden areas, open (and food) all day including breakfast from 9am. *(Buster and Helena Hastings)*

MEONSTOKE SU6120
Bucks Head (01489) 877313
Village signed just off A32 N of Droxford; SO32 3NA Cleanly refurbished and opened up tile-hung pub in lovely village setting with ducks on pretty little River Meon; stone floors and log fires, popular traditional food from sandwiches up, three well kept ales including Greene King, good friendly service; children and dogs welcome, small walled gardens either side, one overlooking river, good walks, five bedrooms, open all day Sat, till 7pm Sun. *(Mark Hamill)*

MICHELDEVER SU5138
Half Moon & Spread Eagle (01962) 774339 *Brown sign to pub off A33 N of Winchester; SO21 3DG* Simply furnished 18th-c beamed village local; bare-boards bar with woodburner, horsebrasses and old banknotes pinned overhead, five real ales, ample helpings of enjoyable well priced food in carpeted dining side from baguettes up, steps up to games area with

---

Virtually all pubs in this book sell wine by the glass. We mention wines if they are a cut above the average.

pool and shelves of books; regular quiz nights; children and dogs welcome, sheltered back terrace and garden, pleasant walks nearby, open all day Sat, Sun till 6pm, closed Mon. *(Rupert and Sandy Newton)*

MILFORD-ON-SEA   SZ2891
Beach House (01590) 643044
Park Lane; SO41 0PT Civilised well placed Victorian hotel-dining pub owned by Hall & Woodhouse; restored oak-panelled interior, entrance hall bar with Badger First Gold, Tanglefoot and a guest, nice wines by the glass and enjoyable sensibly priced food from lunchtime sandwiches and sharing boards to specials, friendly attentive service, magnificent views from dining room and terrace; children welcome, dogs in bar, grounds down to the Solent looking out to the Needles, 15 bedrooms, open (and food) all day. *(David and Sally Frost, Alison Chalu)*

MINLEY MANOR   SU8357
Crown & Cushion (01252) 545253
A327, just N of M3 junction 4A; GU17 9UA Attractive and popular little pub dating from 1512, three well kept Shepherd Neame ales, a dozen wines by the glass and decent selection of gins, good fairly priced food from ciabattas and sharing plates up including signature barbecue ribs, prompt cheerful service, Sun carvery in big separate 'meade hall' with rafters, flagstones and huge log fire; children welcome, no dogs inside, terrace overlooking cricket pitch, open (and food) all day. *(KC)*

MINSTEAD   SU2810
★**Trusty Servant** (023) 8081 2137
Just off A31, not far from M27 junction 1; SO43 7FY Attractive 19th-c red-brick pub in pretty New Forest hamlet with wandering cattle and ponies and plenty of easy walks; two-room bare-boards bar and big dining room, open fires, well kept ales such as Flack Manor and several wines by the glass, good food from doorstep sandwiches and pub favourites to local game, friendly efficient service even when busy; children and dogs welcome, terrace and big sloping garden, interesting church where Sir Arthur Conan Doyle is buried, five recently added bedrooms, open (and food) all day. *(Tony Scott, Phil and Jane Villiers)*

NEW CHERITON   SU5827
★**Hinton Arms** (01962) 771252
A272 near B3046 junction; SO24 0NH Popular neatly kept country pub with cheerful accommodating landlord and friendly staff, three or four real ales including Bowman Wallops Wood and a house beer brewed by Hampshire, decent wines by the glass, large helpings of enjoyable food from sandwiches to daily specials, sporting pictures and memorabilia; TV lounge; well behaved children and dogs welcome, terrace and big garden, lots of colourful tubs and

hanging baskets, very handy for Hinton Ampner House (NT). *(Tony and Jill Radnor)*

NORTH WALTHAM   SU5645
★**Fox** (01256) 397288
3 miles from M3 junction 7: A30 southwards, then turn right at second North Waltham turn, just after Wheatsheaf; pub also signed from village centre; RG25 2BE Well run traditional flint pub with low-ceilinged bar, Andwell, Brakspears, West Berkshire and a guest, Aspall's cider (many more in bottles) and good range of wines and whiskies, padded country kitchen chairs on parquet floor, poultry prints above dark dado, big woodburner, good food from sandwiches/ baguettes to daily specials, larger separate dining room with high-backed leather chairs and blue tartan carpet; free wi-fi; children and dogs (in bar) welcome, picnic-sets under parasols in colourful garden with pergola walkway, pretty window boxes and hanging baskets, nice walks including one to Jane Austen's church at Steventon, open all day. *(Simon and Mandy King, Melanie and David Lawson, Miranda and Jeff Davidson, Joe and Belinda Smart, Mike and Sarah Abbot)*

OVINGTON   SU5631
Bush (01962) 732764
Off A31 W of Alresford; SO24 0RE 17th-c country pub in charming spot with streamside garden (lots of picnic-sets), low-ceilinged bar, high-backed settles, pews and lots of old pictures, log fire, well kept Wadworths ales and good choice of wines by the glass, popular food from ciabattas up, friendly service; free wi-fi; children and dogs welcome, good local walks, open (and food) all day Sun. *(Phil and Jane Villiers)*

PETERSFIELD   SU7423
George (01730) 233343
The Square; GU32 3HH Old building in square with café-style tables outside, clean contemporary interior, enjoyable food including well filled sandwiches, sharing plates and home-made burgers, three well kept ales, good choice of wines by the glass and decent coffee, friendly young staff; some weekend live music; children welcome, attractive courtyard garden with own bar, open all day from 9am for popular breakfast. *(Charles Todd)*

PETERSFIELD   SU7423
Square Brewery (01730) 264291
The Square; GU32 3HJ Friendly town-centre pub refurbished in modern-rustic style, three well kept Fullers ales and a guest, decent choice of wines and enjoyable sensibly priced food including good lunchtime sandwiches, wood floors, painted panelling and central woodburner; background music (live band Sat), monthly quiz first Thurs of month, free wi-fi; children and dogs welcome, seats out in front and

in covered courtyard behind, open all day, evening food Weds, Thurs and Sun (till 7pm) only. *(Ann and Colin Hunt)*

PHOENIX GREEN SU7555
Phoenix (01252) 842484
London Road, A30 W of Hartley Wintney; RG27 8RT 18th-c pub with lots of beams, timber dividers, rugs on bare boards and big end inglenook, good freshly made food from varied daily changing menu including speciality steaks, four well kept ales, a couple of good ciders and 16 wines by the glass, friendly prompt service, back dining room; children and dogs (in bar) welcome, pleasant outlook from sunny garden (hats provided). *(John and Delia Franks)*

PILLEY SZ3298
★ Fleur de Lys (01590) 672158
Off A337 Brockenhurst–Lymington; Pilley Street; SO41 5QG Ancient thatched and beamed village pub (11th-c origins); good popular restauranty food from shortish menu (booking advised), Courage Directors, Sharps Doom Bar and a guest, good wines, friendly helpful service, inglenook log fires; well behaved children and dogs welcome, pretty garden with old well, fine forest and heathland walks, open all day Sat, till 6pm Sun, closed Mon. *(Dr and Mrs F McGinn)*

PORTSMOUTH SZ6399
Bridge Tavern (023) 9275 2992
East Street, Camber Dock; PO1 2JJ Flagstones, bare boards and lots of dark wood, comfortable furnishings, maritime theme with good harbour views, Fullers ales, sensibly priced food including plenty of fish dishes; nice waterside terrace, open all day. *(Ann and Colin Hunt, Tony Scott, Jess and George Cowley)*

PORTSMOUTH SU6706
George (023) 9222 1079
Portsdown Hill Road, Widley; PO6 1BE Comfortable one-bar Georgian pub with friendly local feel (despite being surrounded by busy roads), seven well kept ales such as Adnams, Flowers, Greene King and Ringwood, popular pubby food including good ploughman's, helpful pleasant staff; live music Tues, quiz every other Sun; dogs welcome, picnic-sets on side terrace, views of Hayling Island, Portsmouth and Isle of Wight, hill walks across the road, open all day. *(Pat and Stewart Gordon)*

PORTSMOUTH SU6501
George (023) 9275 3885
Queen Street, near dockyard entrance; PO1 3HU Spotless old inn (Grade I listed) with two rooms (one set for dining), log fire, glass-covered well and maritime pictures, well kept Greene King Abbot, Sharps Atlantic and Doom Bar, well priced food (not Sun evening, Mon lunchtime) from sandwiches up, friendly staff; eight

bedrooms, handy for dockyard and HMS *Victory*, open all day. *(Ann and Colin Hunt)*

PORTSMOUTH SZ6399
Pembroke (023) 9282 3961
Pembroke Road; PO1 2NR Traditional well run corner local with good buoyant atmosphere, comfortable and unspoilt under long-serving licensees, Bass, Fullers London Pride and Greene King Abbot from L-shaped bar, simple cheap food including fresh rolls, coal-effect gas fire; darts and weekend live music; dogs welcome, open all day (break 4-7pm Sun). *(Ann and Colin Hunt)*

PORTSMOUTH SU6300
Ship Anson (023) 9282 4152
Victory Road, The Hard (opposite Esplanade Station, Portsea); PO1 3DT No-frills mock-Tudor pub close to dockyard entrance, spacious and comfortable, with well kept Greene King ales and a guest, generous pub food at bargain prices including coffee and cake, buoyant local atmosphere; fruit machines, sports TVs; children welcome, seats outside overlooking ferry port, very handy for HMS *Victory*, open all day. *(Jess and George Cowley, Ann and Colin Hunt)*

PORTSMOUTH SZ6299
Still & West (023) 9282 1567
Bath Square, Old Portsmouth; PO1 2JL Great location with superb views of narrow harbour mouth and across to Isle of Wight, especially from glazed-in panoramic upper family area and waterfront terrace; nautical bar with fireside sofas, Fullers ales and good choice of wines by the glass, enjoyable all-day food from sandwiches and sharing plates to good fish dishes; background music, free wi-fi; dogs welcome in bar, handy for Historic Dockyard, nearby pay-and-display parking, open from 10am (11.30am Sun). *(Ann and Colin Hunt)*

PORTSMOUTH SU6400
White Swan (023) 9289 1340
Guildhall Walk, next to Theatre Royal; PO1 2DD Popular mock-Tudor pub (Brewhouse & Kitchen) visibly brewing its own good beers, also decent choice of well priced food from wraps and sharing boards up, friendly helpful staff; children welcome, open (and food) all day. *(Phil and Jane Villiers, Ann and Colin Hunt)*

PRESTON CANDOVER SU6041
Purefoy Arms (01256) 389777
B3046 Basingstoke–Alresford; RG25 2EJ Relaxed red-brick dining pub under welcoming newish owners; good attractively presented food including daily specials, a couple of well kept local ales, good wines and some interesting cocktails, friendly helpful staff, log fires; background music, quiz nights; children and dogs welcome, sizeable sloping garden, more seats on a sheltered terrace, summer barbecues,

appealing village, open all day Sat, closed Sun evening, Mon. *(Charles Todd)*

RINGWOOD   SU1504
Railway (01425) 473701
Hightown Road; BH24 1NQ Traditional two-bar Victorian local with up to four well kept changing ales (usually one from nearby Ringwood), enjoyable home-made food including range of burgers, also vegan/vegetarian menu, friendly service; Thurs quiz, darts; children and dogs welcome, nice enclosed garden with play area, vegetable patch, ducks and chickens, open all day (Sun till 9pm). *(Charles Todd)*

ROMSEY   SU3523
Dukes Head (01794) 514450
A3057 out towards Stockbridge; SO51 0HB Attractive 16th-c roadside dining pub with warren of small comfortable linked rooms, beams and inglenook woodburner in main bar, enjoyable generously served food including affordable lunchtime specials, ales such as Flack Manor and Sharps, cheerful staff; music nights, free wi-fi; children welcome, sheltered back terrace and pleasant garden, pretty hanging baskets, handy for Hillier Gardens, open all day Sun (food till 7.30pm). *(Ann and Colin Hunt)*

ROMSEY   SU3521
Old House at Home (01794) 513175
Love Lane; SO51 8DE Attractive 17th-c thatched pub surrounded by new development; friendly and bustling, with comfortable low-beamed interior, wide choice of freshly made sensibly priced bar food including popular Sun lunch, well kept Fullers/Gales ales and guests, Aspall's cider, cheerful efficient service; regular folk sessions; children and dogs (in bar) welcome, split-level back terrace, open all day (no food Sun evening). *(Ann and Colin Hunt, R K Phillips, Tony and Wendy Hobden)*

ROMSEY   SU3520
Three Tuns (01794) 512639
Middlebridge Street (but car park signed straight off A27 bypass); SO51 8HL Good well presented food is the star at this old village pub but they do keep Flack Manor with guests such as Flowerpots and Upham plus a house beer from Andwell, local cider and 11 wines by the glass; bar with cushioned bow-window seat, dark wooden tables on flagstones, beer mats pinned to the walls and church candles in fireplace, dining areas either side, one with a huge stuffed fish over another fireplace, the other with prints on yellow walls above a black dado, a few rugs scattered around, heavy beams and antler chandeliers; background music, board games, free wi-fi; children

and dogs welcome (pub dogs are Alfie and Monty), back terrace with picnic-sets under parasols, more seats in front by the tiny street, open all day, no food Sun evening. *(R K Phillips, Phil and Jane Villiers)*

ROTHERWICK   SU7156
Coach & Horses (01256) 768976
Signed from B3349 N of Hook; also quite handy for M3 junction 5; RG27 9BG Friendly 17th-c pub with traditional beamed front rooms, well kept Badger ales and good reasonably priced pubby food using local suppliers, cheerful accommodating staff, log fire and woodburners, newer back dining area; open mike night first Weds of month, quiz fourth Tues; children, dogs and muddy boots welcome, tables out at front behind picket fence and on back terrace overlooking fields, pretty flower tubs and hanging baskets, good walks, open all day Sat, Sun till 6pm, closed Mon. *(Tony and Jill Radnor, Darren and Jane Staniforth)*

ROTHERWICK   SU7156
Falcon (01256) 765422
Off B3349 N of Hook, not far from M3 junction 5; RG27 9BL Well run open-plan country pub with good freshly made local food (highish prices), decent selection of wines and well kept ales such as Otter and Ringwood, friendly efficient service, rustic tables and comfy sofa in bare-boards bar, well laid flagstoned dining area, log fires; free wi-fi; children and dogs welcome, disabled access, tables out in front and in back garden, open all day, food all day Sun. *(Simon Sharpe)*

SHALDEN   SU7043
Golden Pot (01420) 80655
B3349 Odiham Road N of Alton; GU34 4DJ Airy light décor with timbered walls, bare boards and log fires, decent food from baguettes up including themed nights, friendly service, a couple of ales such as Sharps Doom Bar and Triple fff Altons Pride, local artwork for sale in smallish restaurant; background music, skittle alley; children and dogs welcome, benches out in covered area at front, garden with play area, open all day. *(Anne and Ben Smith)*

SHEDFIELD   SU5613
Samuels Rest (01329) 832213
Upper Church Road (signed off B2177); SO32 2JB Cosy and welcoming village local overlooking cricket pitch; well kept Wadworths ales and generous helpings of enjoyable sensibly priced home-made food, nice eating area away from bar, conservatory; some live music including folk night third Weds of month, pool and darts; children and dogs (in bar) welcome, aviary with

---

We say if we know a pub has background music.

parrots, good sized garden, lovely church nearby, closed Mon lunchtime, otherwise open all day. *(Ann and Colin Hunt)*

SHEDFIELD SU5513
Wheatsheaf (01329) 833024
A334 Wickham–Botley; SO32 2JG
Friendly no-fuss local with well kept/priced Flowerpots and guests tapped from the cask, proper cider, short sensible choice of enjoyable bargain lunches (evening food Tues and Weds), good service, woodburner and darts in public bar, smaller lounge; live music Sat; dogs welcome, garden, handy for Wickham Vineyard, open all day. *(Ann and Colin Hunt)*

SHERFIELD ENGLISH SU3022
Hatchet (01794) 322487
Romsey Road; SO51 6FP Beamed and panelled 18th-c pub with good choice of popular fairly priced food including two-for-one steak deal (Tues, Thurs evenings) and OAP lunch (Mon-Thurs), four well kept ales such as Dartmoor, St Austell, Sharps and Timothy Taylors, good wine choice, friendly hard-working staff, long bar with cosy area down steps, woodburner, more steps up to second bar with darts, TV and juke box; monthly quiz; children and dogs welcome, outside seating on two levels, play area, open all day weekends. *(Lyn and Freddie Roberts)*

SHIPTON BELLINGER SU2345
Boot (01980) 842279
High Street; SP9 7UF Village pub with vast range of enjoyable reasonably priced food including chinese, thai, italian and mexican alongside traditional english dishes, friendly staff; background music; children welcome, garden behind with decked area, open all day Sun. *(Lindy Andrews)*

SOBERTON SU6116
White Lion (01489) 877346
School Hill; signed off A32 S of Droxford; SO32 3PF Attractive 17th-c pub in nice spot opposite raised village green; enjoyable home-made food from baguettes up, a couple of Bowman ales, Sharps Doom Bar and good range of wines by the glass, friendly efficient service, low-ceilinged bar with built-in wall seats and open fire, restaurant; children welcome, sheltered garden and suntrap terrace, good walks nearby, stable-conversion bedrooms, open all day, food all day Sun. *(Jane and Kai Horsburgh)*

SOPLEY SZ1596
Woolpack (01425) 672252
B3347 N of Christchurch; BH23 7AX Pretty 17th-c thatched dining pub with rambling open-plan low-beamed bar, enjoyable traditional food plus daily specials and range of sandwiches and wraps, well kept Ringwood Razorback, Sharps Doom Bar and a guest, Thatcher's cider and good choice of wines by the glass, modern dining

conservatory overlooking weir; children and dogs (menu for them) welcome, terrace and charming garden with weeping willows, duck stream and footbridges, open (and food) all day. *(Edward Edmonton)*

SOUTHAMPTON SU4314
Butchers Hook (023) 8178 2280
Manor Farm Road; SO18 1NN
One-room micro-pub in former Bitterne Park butchers (some original features remain including tiling), interesting changing ales/craft kegs tapped from scaffold stillage (no bar), real cider and good range of bottled beers, friendly helpful service, no food (can bring your own); board games; well behaved dogs welcome, a few bench seats out in front, closed Mon, Tues and lunchtimes Weds-Fri, open all day Sat from 1pm, Sun from 2pm, gets packed at busy times. *(Dr Martin Owton)*

SOUTHAMPTON SU4111
Dancing Man (023) 8083 6666
Bugle Street/Town Quay; SO14 2AR
Ancient listed building with plenty of atmosphere and character, up to 12 interesting beers including eight from on-site brewery (tours available), shortish choice of enjoyable home-made food (all day Fri-Sun) from bar snacks and pies up, good friendly service, sweeping staircase to upper dining area with own bar and fine raftered ceiling; dogs welcome (menu for them), disabled access and lift, open all day. *(Phil and Jane Villiers)*

SOUTHAMPTON SU4111
★Duke of Wellington (023) 8033 9222
Bugle Street (or walk along city wall from Bar Gate); SO14 2AH Striking timber-framed building dating from the 14th c (cellars even older); heavy beams and fine log fire, up to nine well kept Wadworths ales (tasting trays available), plenty of wines by the glass and good fairly priced food (not Sun evening), friendly helpful service, background music (live jazz Fri), free wi-fi; children welcome, sunny streetside picnic-sets, handy for Tudor House & Garden, open all day. *(Phil and Jane Villiers)*

SOUTHAMPTON SU4213
Rockstone (023) 8063 7256
Onslow Road; SO14 0JL Popular relaxed place with well liked generous food from signature burgers to asian street food (booking advised), good variety of real ales, craft beers and ciders from well stocked bar, friendly hard-working staff; some live music; children welcome, seats out at front, open (and food) all day (till 1am Fri, Sat). *(Phil and Jane Villiers)*

SOUTHAMPTON SU4313
South Western Arms
(023) 8032 4542 *Adelaide Road, by St Denys station; SO17 2HW* Friendly

backstreet corner local with ten well kept changing ales, also good choice of bottled beers and whiskies, friendly staff and easy-going atmosphere, bare boards and brickwork, lots of woodwork, toby jugs, pump clips and stag's head on beams, old range and earthenware, darts, pool and table football in upper gallery allowing children; some live music, beer festivals; dogs welcome, picnic-sets in walled beer garden, open all day. *(Edward Edmonton)*

SOUTHAMPTON   SU4213
White Star   (023) 8082 1990
Oxford Street; SO14 3DJ Modernised opened-up bar with crescent-shaped banquettes, panelling and open fires, wood or stone floors, comfortable sofas and armchairs in secluded alcoves by south-facing windows, bistro-style dining area, good up-to-date food including brunch, nice wines by the glass and lots of cocktails, ales such as Itchen Valley, efficient attentive staff (may ask to keep a credit card while you eat), highish prices; background music (DJ Fri evening); sunny pavement tables on pedestrianised street, 13 boutique bedrooms, open all day from 7am (8.30am weekends). *(Edward Edmonton)*

SOUTHSEA   SZ6699
Artillery Arms   (023) 9273 3610
Hester Road; PO4 8HB Traditional two-bar Victorian backstreet local, seven well kept ales including Triple fff, no food apart from rolls on match days (near Fratton Park), friendly atmosphere; Mon quiz, sports TV, pool and darts; children and dogs welcome, garden with play equipment, open all day. *(Tony Scott)*

SOUTHSEA   SZ6498
Belle Isle   (023) 9282 0515
Osbourne Road; PO5 3LR Popular café-bar-restaurant in former shop, interesting continental-feel interior, three real ales, international bottled beers, cocktails and eclectic blackboard menu, decent coffee too; children welcome, a few seats out at front under awning, open all day. *(Ann and Colin Hunt)*

SOUTHSEA   SZ6698
Eastney Tavern   (023) 9282 6246
Cromwell Road; PO4 9PN Bow-fronted corner pub just off the seafront, spacious and comfortable, with various eating areas (plenty of room for drinkers too), popular good value food including Weds steak night and Thurs curry (reduced menu Mon), Sharps Doom Bar and a couple of local guests, decent choice of wines by the glass, good cheerful service; Tues quiz, live music last Fri of the month, sports TV; children and dogs welcome, seats in courtyard garden, nearby parking difficult, closed Mon lunchtime, otherwise open all day. *(Ann and Colin Hunt)*

SOUTHSEA   SZ6499
Eldon Arms   (023) 9229 7963
Eldon Street/Norfolk Street; PO5 4BS Tile-fronted Victorian backstreet pub under welcoming management, Fullers London Pride, St Austell Tribute and guests, simple well priced food, old pictures and advertisements, attractive mirrors, shelves of books and assorted bric-a-brac; some live music, bar billiards, darts and pool; children welcome, tables in back garden, open all day. *(Phil and Jane Villiers, Ann and Colin Hunt)*

SOUTHSEA   SZ6499
★ **Hole in the Wall**   (023) 9229 8085
Great Southsea Street; PO5 3BY Friendly unspoilt little local in old part of town, six interesting well kept/priced ales including Flowerpots Goodens Gold, four craft kegs and good range of bottled beers, real cider/perry, speciality local sausages, meat puddings and other simple good value food (evenings Tues-Sat, lunchtime Fri), nicely worn boards, dark pews and panelling, old photographs and prints, hundreds of pump clips on ceiling, little snug behind the bar and sweet shop; daily papers, quiz night Thurs, Oct beer festival; dogs welcome, small outside area at front with benches, side garden, open all day from 4pm (noon Fri, 2pm Sat and Sun). *(Phil and Jane Villiers)*

SOUTHSEA   SZ6499
King Street Tavern   (023) 9307 3568
King Street; PO5 4EH Newly refurbished corner pub with fine Victorian tiled façade set in attractive conservation area; four well kept Wadworths ales and a couple of guests, craft kegs and two proper ciders, short choice of good value home-made food such as burgers and smokehouse ribs, friendly atmosphere; live music including irish folk session second Thurs of the month, big-screen sports TV; children welcome, courtyard tables, open all day Fri and Sat, till 7pm Sun, closed lunchtimes Mon, Tues. *(Charles Todd)*

SOUTHSEA   SZ6598
Leopold   (023) 9282 9748
Albert Road; PO4 0JT Traditional green-tiled corner local with ten well kept ales (tasters offered), good choice of ciders and over 100 bottled beers including several from BrewDog, bright interior with hundreds of pump clips on the walls and pictures of old Portsmouth, no food; Mon quiz, unobtrusive TVs each end, darts; walled beer garden behind complete with own Tardis, open all day. *(Ann and Colin Hunt)*

SOUTHSEA   SZ6498
Meat & Barrel   (023) 9217 6291
Palmerston Road; PO5 3PT Sizeable bar-restaurant under same ownership as Southsea's Belle Isle, fine range of real ales and craft beers (tasters offered),

friendly knowledgeable staff, enjoyable food including range of burgers and various sausage and mash combinations; children welcome, open all day. *(Ann and Colin Hunt)*

SOUTHSEA   SZ6698
Sir Loin of Beef (023) 9282 0115
Highland Road, Eastney; PO4 9NH One-room corner pub with friendly staff and buoyant atmosphere, at least eight well kept frequently changing ales (tasters offered) including Gales and Titanic, real cider, no food, interesting submarine pictures and artefacts; bar billiards, juke box, some live music; open all day. *(John and Delia Franks)*

SOUTHSEA   SZ6499
Wine Vaults (023) 9286 4712
Albert Road, opposite King's Theatre; PO5 2SF Bustling Fullers pub with several chatty rooms on different floors, main panelled bar with long plain counter and pubby furniture on bare boards, seven well kept ales and decent choice of food including pizzas and range of burgers, good service, separate restaurant; background music, live jazz or folk Tues, sports TV, table football; children welcome, dogs in bar, smokers' roof terrace, open (and food) all day. *(Ann and Colin Hunt)*

SOUTHWICK   SU6208
Golden Lion (023) 9221 0437
High Street; just off B2177 on Portsdown Hill; PO17 6EB Welcoming two-bar 16th-c beamed pub (where Eisenhower and Montgomery came before D-Day); up to seven well kept local ales including two from Suthwyk using barley from surrounding fields, four ciders and a dozen wines by the glass, good locally sourced home-made food (not Sun or Mon evenings) from snacks up in bar and dining room, cosy lounge bar with sofas and log fire, live music including Tues jazz; good outside loos; children and dogs welcome, picnic-sets on grass at side, picturesque Estate village with scenic walks, next to Southwick Brewhouse shop/museum (over 250 bottled beers), open all day Sat, till 7pm Sun. *(Val and Alan Green, Ann and Colin Hunt, Suzy Miller)*

SPARSHOLT   SU4331
Plough (01962) 776353
Village signposted off B3049 (Winchester–Stockbridge), a little W of Winchester; SO21 2NW Neatly kept dining pub under new ownership; main bar with interesting mix of wooden tables and farmhouse or upholstered chairs, farm tools attached to the ceiling, Wadworths ales and good choice of wines by the glass, well regarded food from blackboard menu, dining tables on the left looking over fields to woodland; children and dogs welcome, disabled access/facilities, plenty of seats on terrace and lawn, play fort,

open all day from 9am. *(Dr and Mrs Paul Cartwright, David Jackman, Maren Webb, Phil and Jane Villiers, Neil and Angela Huxter)*

STOCKBRIDGE   SU3535
Greyhound (01264) 810833
High Street; SO20 6EY Substantial inn reworked as civilised pub-restaurant; log fires each end of bow-windowed bar (restaurant to the right), scrubbed old tables on woodstrip floor, dark low beams, highly regarded food from interesting varied menu (not cheap), three real ales including a house beer from Ringwood, good wine and whisky choice, friendly efficient staff (service charge added to bills); children and dogs allowed, tables in charming Test-side garden behind, ten bedrooms, good walks and fly fishing, open all day. *(Edward Mirzoeff)*

STOCKBRIDGE   SU3535
Three Cups (01264) 810527
High Street; SO20 6HB Lovely low-beamed building dating from 1500, spruced up and added to yet keeping country inn feel, some emphasis on dining with lots of smartly set tables, but also high-backed settles and some rustic bric-a-brac, four well kept interesting ales and nice wines by the glass, food and service can be good, back 'orangery' restaurant extension; children and dogs welcome, charming streamside garden with vine-covered terrace, eight bedrooms (back ones quieter), open all day. *(Miranda and Jeff Davidson)*

STOCKBRIDGE   SU3535
White Hart (01264) 810663
High Street; A272/A3057 roundabout; SO20 6HF Spacious village-edge pub with pleasantly busy divided beamed bar, attractive décor with antique prints, oak pews and other seats around pine tables, decent choice of enjoyable food from bar snacks to daily specials, well kept Fullers/Gales beers, good friendly service, comfortable restaurant with open fire (children allowed); dogs in bar, terrace tables and nice garden, 14 bedrooms, open all day. *(Edward Mirzoeff, Ann and Colin Hunt)*

SWANMORE   SU5716
Brickmakers (01489) 890954
Church Road; SO32 2PA Large restyled 1920s pub in centre of village, friendly and relaxed, with four well kept ales (Bowman Wallops Wood always on), decent wines and good food cooked by landlord-chef including popular Sun roasts and OAP weekday lunch deal, cheerful efficient service, leather sofas by log fire, dining area with local artwork; Tues quiz, some live music; children and dogs welcome (pub dog is Rosie), garden with raised deck, nearby walks, open (and food) all day, except Sun when kitchen closes at 5.30pm. *(Val and Alan Green, Ann and Colin Hunt)*

SWANMORE   SU5815
Rising Sun (01489) 896663
Droxford Road; signed off A32 N of Wickham and B2177 S of Bishop's Waltham, at Hillpound E of village centre; SO32 2PS Former brick coaching inn with low-beamed carpeted bar, comfortable seating by log fire, pleasant roomier dining area with brick barrel vaulting in one part, three local ales such as Flack Manor and Flowerpots, good range of wines by the glass and enjoyable reasonably priced pub food including daily specials, friendly speedy service; children and dogs (in bar) welcome, picnic-sets on side grass with play area, King's Way long-distance path nearby, closed Sun evening, Mon lunchtime. *(Shesh Bazzar)*

SWANWICK   SU5109
Elm Tree (01489) 579818
Swanwick Lane, off A3051 not far from M27 junction 9; SO31 7DX Welcoming two-bar pub with generous helpings of enjoyable good value food including Tues steak night, prompt friendly service, well kept Flowerpots, Sharps and a guest, dining extension; darts, free wi-fi; children and dogs welcome, tables in small garden, handy for Swanwick Lakes nature reserve, open all day. *(Ann and Colin Hunt)*

SWAY   SZ2898
Hare & Hounds (01590) 682404
Durns Town, just off B3055 SW of Brockenhurst; SO41 6AL Bright, airy and comfortable New Forest family dining pub with hearty helpings of home-cooked food including daily specials, well kept ales such as Itchen Valley, Ringwood, St Austell and Timothy Taylors, good friendly service, low beams and central log fire; background music, Sun quiz; dogs welcome, picnic-sets and play frame in neatly kept garden, open all day. *(Edward Edmonton)*

THRUXTON   SU2945
White Horse (01264) 772401
Mullens Pond, just off A303 eastbound; SP11 8EE Attractive old thatched pub (tucked below A303 embankment) with emphasis on enjoyable freshly made food, good friendly service, plenty of wines by the glass and well kept ales such as Greene King, spacious comfortably modernised interior with very low beams, woodburner and separate dining area; regular live music and other events; good-sized garden and terrace, summer barbecues, four bedrooms, open all day (Sun till 6pm). *(Mrs Zara Elliott)*

TICHBORNE   SU5730
★ Tichborne Arms (01962) 733760
Signed off B3047; SO24 0NA Welcoming old-fashioned thatched pub (rebuilt in the 1930s) in rolling countryside; half-panelled bare-boards bar with interesting pictures and other odds and ends, candlelit pine tables and raised woodburner, Palmers and guests tapped from cooled casks, local cider, good traditional home-made food (not Sun or Mon evenings, booking advised), locals' bar with piano, darts and open fire; children and dogs welcome (pub dogs are Honey and Rosie), sheltered terrace and large peaceful garden with water meadow views, close to Wayfarer's Walk and Itchen Way, open all day Sat, till 7.30pm Sun. *(Tony and Jill Radnor, David and Judy Robison)*

TIMSBURY   SU3325
Bear & Ragged Staff
(01794) 368602 *A3057 towards Stockbridge; pub marked on OS Sheet 185 map reference 334254; SO51 0LB* Roadside dining pub with good choice of popular food including blackboard specials, friendly service, lots of wines by the glass, three Fullers/Gales beers and a guest, good-sized beamed interior with log fire; children welcome in eating part, tables in extended garden with play area, handy for Mottisfont (NT), good walks, open all day. *(David Hartshorne, Phil and Jane Villiers)*

TITCHFIELD   SU5305
Queens Head (01329) 842154
High Street; off A27 near Fareham; PO14 4AQ Welcoming early 17th-c family-run pub with enjoyable home-made food and four well kept ales, cosy bar with old local pictures, window seats and warm winter fire in central brick fireplace, small dining room; Sun quiz, function room for nostalgic dinner-dance and theatre nights; children welcome, picnic-sets in prettily planted backyard, pleasant conservation village near nature reserve and walks to coast, open all day. *(Charles Todd)*

TITCHFIELD   SU5405
Wheatsheaf (01329) 842965
East Street; off A27 near Fareham; PO14 4AD Welcoming old pub with bow-windowed front bar and back restaurant extension, good food including small-plates menu, Tues steak night and popular Sun roasts, well kept ales such as Flowerpots and Palmers, log fires; background music, live acoustic session first Mon of month; terrace tables, open all day (food all day Fri and Sat, till 6.45 Sun). *(Ann and Colin Hunt)*

TWYFORD   SU4824
★ Bugle (01962) 714888
B3355/Park Lane; SO21 1QT Modern dining pub with good enterprising food (highish prices) from daily changing menu, also lunchtime sandwiches/snacks and Mon evening set deal, well kept ales such as Bowman, Flowerpots and Upham, nice wines by the glass, attentive friendly young staff; background music; seats on

attractive verandah, good walks nearby, three country-style bedrooms, open all day, no food Sun evening. *(Lindy Andrews)*

TWYFORD   SU4824
Phoenix (01962) 713322
High Street (B3335); SO21 1RF Cheerful open-plan local with raised dining area and big inglenook log fire, jovial long-serving landlord and friendly attentive staff, eight well kept ales including Greene King, good value wines and large helpings of enjoyable traditional food from reasonably priced menu; background music, sports TV, quiz nights, skittle alley; children welcome, side terraces, open all day in summer. *(Richard Heath, Mary Smith, Ann and Colin Hunt)*

UPHAM   SU5320
Brushmakers Arms (01489) 860231
Shoe Lane; village signed from Winchester–Bishop's Waltham downs road, and from B2177; SO32 1JJ Welcoming low-beamed village pub redecorated under present licensees; L-shaped bar divided by central woodburner, cushioned settles and chairs around mix of tables, various brushes (once made here) and related paraphernalia, little back snug, enjoyable locally sourced home-made food from daily changing menu, Bowman, Flack Manor, Flowerpots and a local guest, good choice of wines; quiz first Thurs of month, folk session third Sun (from 5pm); children and dogs welcome, big garden with picnic-sets on sheltered terrace and tree-shaded lawn, good nearby walks, open all day weekends, no food Sun evening in winter. *(Phil and Jane Villiers, Ann and Colin Hunt)*

UPPER CLATFORD   SU3543
Crook & Shears (01264) 361543
Off A343 S of Andover, via Foundry Road; SP11 7QL Cosy and welcoming 17th-c thatched pub, well kept Otter and Ringwood ales, Thatcher's cider and reasonably priced traditional food (not Sun evening) from good baguettes to enjoyable Sun roasts, also OAP weekday lunch deal and Tues steak night, friendly attentive service, open fires and woodburner, small dining room, back skittle alley with own bar; children and dogs welcome, pleasant secluded garden behind, closed Mon lunchtime. *(Frances Parsons)*

UPPER FARRINGDON   SU7135
Rose & Crown (01420) 588231
Off A32 S of Alton; Crows Lane – follow 'Church, Selborne, Liss' signpost; GU34 3ED Early 19th-c tile-hung village pub, L-shaped bar with bare boards and log fire, a couple of Triple fff ales along with Sharps Doom Bar and a guest, several gins including some local ones, good reasonably priced home-cooked food (not Sun evening), steak night Thurs, wood-fired pizzas Fri,

friendly helpful service, back dining room; children, walkers and dogs welcome, wide views from attractive garden, open all day weekends, closed Mon. *(Guy Vowles)*

UPTON   SU3555
Crown (01264) 736044
N of Hurstbourne Tarrant, off A343; SP11 0JS Old country pub refurbished under new licensees; good imaginative food (not Sun evening) from bar snacks up, two or three changing regional ales and well chosen wines by the glass including english sparkling, friendly helpful service, nice log fire, coffee lounge, restaurant and conservatory; children and dogs (in bar) welcome, small garden and terrace, closed Mon, otherwise open all day (from 9am Sun for breakfast). *(Mark Hamill)*

UPTON GREY   SU6948
Hoddington Arms (01256) 862371
Signed off B3349 S of Hook; Bidden Road; RG25 2RL Nicely updated 18th-c beamed pub; good food from varied menu (not Sun evening), Flowerpots, Ringwood and a local guest, ten wines by the glass, friendly staff; events including live music, movie nights and beer/cider festivals; children and dogs welcome, big enclosed garden with terrace, quiet pretty village with interesting Gertrude Jekyll garden, good walking/cycling, open all day Fri-Sun. *(Tony and Jill Radnor)*

VERNHAM DEAN   SU3456
George (01264) 737279
Centre of village; SP11 0JY Rambling open-plan 17th-c beamed and timbered pub with notable eyebrow windows, some exposed brick and flint, inglenook log fire, well kept Flack Manor, Greene King, Hop Back and a guest, popular home-made pubby food (not Sun evening), good friendly service; variety of events including Aug beer festival; children and dogs welcome, pretty garden behind, lovely thatched village and fine walks, open all day (Sun till 6pm). *(Patrick and Emma Stephenson)*

WALHAMPTON   SZ3396
Walhampton Arms (01590) 673113
B3054 NE of Lymington; aka Walhampton Inn; SO41 5RE Large comfortable Georgian-style family roadhouse handy for Isle of Wight ferry; popular well priced food including daily carvery in raftered former stables and two adjoining areas, pleasant lounge, Ringwood and Flack Manor ales and traditional cider, cheerful helpful staff; music quiz first Fri of month; attractive courtyard, good walks, open (and food) all day. *(Simon Sharpe)*

WALTHAM CHASE   SU5614
Black Dog (01329) 832316
Winchester Road; SO32 2LX Old brick-built pub with low-ceilinged carpeted front bar, three well kept Greene King ales and

a guest, over a dozen wines by the glass and good well priced food (all day Sun) from basket meals up, cheerful helpful service, log fires, back restaurant; some live music, sports TV; children and dogs welcome, tables under parasols in good-sized neatly kept garden with deck, play area and colourful hanging baskets, open all day weekends. *(Ann and Colin Hunt)*

WELL   SU7646

★ **Chequers** (01256) 862605

Off A287 via Crondall, or A31 via Froyle and Lower Froyle; RG29 1TL Appealing low-beamed country dining pub; very good restaurant-style food (some quite pricey) including fresh fish/seafood, also brasserie menu and lunchtime sandwiches, Badger ales kept well and good choice of wines, wood floors, panelling and log fires; free wi-fi; bench seating on vine-covered front terrace, spacious back garden overlooking fields, open (and food) all day. *(Peter and Adriana Gill)*

WEST TYTHERLEY   SU2730

Black Horse (01794) 340308

North Lane; SP5 1NF Compact unspoilt village local with welcoming chatty atmosphere, traditional beamed bar with a couple of long tables, woodburner in big fireplace, four mainly local ales and a real cider, nicely set dining area serving enjoyable reasonably priced food including good Sun roasts; quiz last Weds of month, skittle alley; children, walkers and dogs welcome, open all day Sun till 7pm, closed all Mon, lunchtime Tues. *(Charles Todd)*

WHERWELL   SU3839

Mayfly (01264) 860283

Testcombe (over by Fullerton, not in Wherwell itself); A3057 SE of Andover, between B3420 turn-off and Leckford where road crosses River Test; OS Sheet 185 map reference 382390; SO20 6AX Busy pub in lovely position overlooking fast-flowing River Test; spacious beamed and carpeted bar with fishing paraphernalia, rustic pub furnishings and woodburner, Fullers ales and extensive range of wines by the glass, generally well liked food (must book for a good table and they may add a surcharge if you pay by credit card), conservatory; background music; well behaved children and dogs welcome, plenty of riverside picnic-sets on decking and grass, open (and food) all day. *(Martin Day, Helen and Brian Edgeley)*

WHERWELL   SU3840

White Lion (01264) 860317

B3420; SP11 7JF Early 17th-c multi-level beamed village inn, popular and friendly, with good choice of enjoyable food including speciality pies, well kept Sharps, Timothy Taylors and a local guest, ciders such as Orchard Pig and several wines by the glass, cheery helpful staff, open fire, comfy

leather sofas and armchairs, dining rooms either side of bar; background music; well behaved children welcome, dogs on leads, teak furniture in sunny courtyard, Test Way walks, three bedrooms, open all day Fri and Sat, till 9pm Sun, closed Mon. *(Michael and Jenny Back, Martin Day, Edward Mirzoeff)*

WHITSBURY   SU1219

Cartwheel (01725) 518362

Off A338 or A354 SW of Salisbury; SP6 3PZ Welcoming tucked-away red-brick pub, ample helpings of good well presented home-made food (not Sun or Mon evenings), Ringwood ales (tasting trays available), pitched high rafters in one part, lower beams elsewhere, snug little side areas; may be background music; children and dogs welcome, garden with slide, open all day Fri-Sun, closed Mon evening in winter. *(Andrew and Ruth Simmonds)*

WICKHAM   SU5711

Greens (01329) 833197

The Square, at junction with A334; PO17 5JQ Civilised restauranty place with clean-cut modern décor, small bar with leather sofa and armchairs on light wood floor, extensive wine choice and a couple of real ales, obliging young staff, step down to split-level balustraded dining areas with good imaginative food including cheaper lunchtime/early evening set menus; background music; children welcome if eating, pleasant lawn overlooking water meadows, closed Sun evening, Mon. *(Lachlan Milligan)*

WINCHESTER   SU4829

Bishop on the Bridge

(01962) 855111 *High Street/Bridge Street; SO23 9JX* Neat efficiently run red-brick Fullers pub, their well kept beers (not cheap) and decent food from ciabattas up, leather sofas, old local prints; free wi-fi; children and dogs welcome, nice back terrace overlooking River Itchen, open all day. *(Val and Alan Green)*

WINCHESTER   SU4828

★ **Black Boy** (01962) 861754

B3403 off M3 junction 10 towards city, then left into Wharf Hill; no nearby daytime parking – 220 metres from car park on B3403; SO23 9NQ Wonderfully eccentric décor at this chatty old-fashioned pub, floor to-ceiling books, lots of big clocks, mobiles made of wine bottles or spectacles, variety of stuffed animals including a baboon, donkey and dachshund, two open fires, orange-painted room with big oriental rugs on red floorboards, barn room with open hayloft, five well kept local ales such as Alfreds, Flowerpots and Itchen Valley, real cider and decent straightforward home-made food (not Sun evening, Mon, Tues lunchtime) from sandwiches up, friendly service; table football and board games;

supervised children and dogs welcome, slate tables out in front and seats on attractive secluded terrace, ten bedrooms in adjoining building, open all day. *(Ann and Colin Hunt, Phil and Jane Villiers)*

WINCHESTER   SU4829
Eclipse (01962) 865676
The Square, between High Street and cathedral; SO23 9EX Picturesque unspoilt 16th-c local with massive beams and timbers in two small cheerful rooms, up to four well kept ales such as Sharps and Timothy Taylors, proper ciders and decent choice of wines by the glass, good value traditional lunchtime food including popular Sun roasts, oak settles and open fire; children in back area, seats outside, handy for the cathedral, open all day. *(Ann and Colin Hunt)*

WINCHESTER   SU4829
★**Old Vine** (01962) 854616
Great Minster Street; SO23 9HA Popular big-windowed town bar with four well kept ales including local Alfreds, plenty of wines by the glass and worn oak boards, larger dining side and modern conservatory (young children allowed here only), good variety of food from sandwiches and pub staples up, efficient friendly service even though busy; background music; dogs welcome in bar, wheelchair access to restaurant and bar using ramp (no access to lavatories), by cathedral with a few pavement seats, more tables in partly covered back terrace, charming bedrooms, open all day.
(Val and Alan Green, Richard Tilbrook)

WINCHESTER   SU4728
Queen (01962) 890542
Kingsgate Road; SO23 9PG Cottagey twin-gabled pub in attractive setting opposite College cricket ground; cosy interior with bare boards and log fire, up to ten well kept ales including own brews (tasting

trays available), enjoyable sensibly priced home-made food from sandwiches, bar snacks and sharing plates up, good friendly service, step to restaurant; children and dogs (in bar) welcome, paved front terrace and big garden behind, open all day (till late Fri, Sat). *(Tony and Jill Radnor)*

WINCHESTER   SU4729
St James (01962) 861288
Romsey Road; SO22 5BE Smallish corner pub (Little Pub Group) with attractively refurbished split-level interior; bare boards and flagstones, pews and wheelback chairs by scrubbed pine tables, some leather armchairs, painted panelling and a Victorian fireplace, plenty of pictures and other odds and ends, Wadworths ales, craft beers and good selection of wines by the glass, enjoyable food from sharing plates up including Mon burger night and Weds pie night, gluten-free diets also catered for, good friendly service; background and some live music, Tues quiz; children and dogs welcome (there's an amiable pub dog), pleasant little terrace behind, open all day. *(Phil and Jane Villiers)*

WINCHESTER   SU4829
Willow Tree (01962) 877255
Durngate Terrace; no adjacent weekday daytime parking, but Durngate car park is around corner in North Walls; a mile from M3 junction 9, by Easton Lane into city; SO23 8QX Popular 19th-c riverside pub, cosy pubby bar to the left with open fire, larger smarter restaurant to the right, well liked food from sandwiches and snacks up including good value weekday set lunch, up to four changing ales and several wines by the glass, friendly staff; Weds quiz, Thurs live music; children and dogs welcome, lovely waterside garden (summer wood-fired pizzas), Winnall Moors nature reserve over the road, closed Sun evening, Mon, otherwise open all day. *(Ann and Colin Hunt)*

Herefordshire

 CAREY   SO5631   Map 4

Cottage of Content 🍴⭐ 🛏

(01432) 840242 – www.cottageofcontent.co.uk

Village signposted from good back road betweeen Ross-on-Wye and Hereford E of A49, through Hoarwithy; HR2 6NG

Country furnishings in a friendly rustic cottage with interesting food, real ales and seats on terraces; bedrooms

You can make the most of the tranquil position of this nicely tucked-away medieval cottage by bagging one of the picnic-sets, either on the flower-filled front terrace or in the rural-feeling garden at the back. The place has much character and there's a friendly welcome, a multitude of beams and country furnishings such as stripped-pine kitchen chairs, long pews beside one big table and various old-fashioned tables on flagstones or bare boards. Hobsons Best and Wye Valley Butty Bach on handpump, a gin list and local cider and perry during the summer. The bedrooms are quiet and the breakfasts good.

🍴⭐ Rewarding food includes tapas on Friday evening (5.30-7pm), as well as venison terrine with fig jam, tian of smoked salmon, crab and mussels with celeriac rémoulade and mustard and dill sauce, mushroom, brie, hazelnut and cranberry wellington, honey-roast ham and free-range eggs, a pie of the day, duck breast with lime mash and black cherry jus, beef slow-cooked in ale and treacle with thyme-buttered cabbage, a fresh fish dish of the day, and puddings such as white chocolate and raspberry cheesecake and rice pudding brûlée with rhubarb and ginger. *Benchmark main dish: pork medallions, black pudding, chorizo, charred belly bacon, mustard mash and jus £15.25. Two-course evening meal £22.50.*

Free house ~ Licensees Richard and Helen Moore ~ Real ale ~ Open 12-2.30, 6.30 (6 Weds, 5.30 Fri)-10.30 (11 Fri); 12-2.30, 6-11 Sat; 12-2.30 Sun; closed Sun evening, Mon, winter Tues, one week Feb, one week Oct ~ Bar food 12-2, 6.30-9; 12-2 Sun ~ Restaurant ~ Children welcome ~ Dogs allowed in bar ~ Bedrooms: £65/£85 *Recommended by Philip J Alderton, Peter J and Avril Hanson, Mike and Mary Carter, Barry Collett, P and J Shapley*

 EARDISLEY   SO3149   Map 6

Tram £

(01544) 327251 – www.thetraminn.co.uk

Corner of A4111 and Woodseaves Road; HR3 6PG

Character pub with welcoming licensees, a lively mix of customers and good food and beer

The convivial licensees are sure to make you warmly welcomed at this handsome old place – and this, together with rewarding food and a cheerful atmosphere, continues to draw praise from our readers. The beamed bar on the left has local character, especially in the cosy back section behind sturdy standing timbers. Here, regulars congregate on the bare boards by the counter, which serves Hobsons Best, Wye Valley Butty Bach and a guest such as Ludlow Gold on handpump and three local organic ciders. Elsewhere there are antique red and ochre floor tiles, a handful of nicely worn tables and chairs, a pair of long cushioned pews enclosing one much longer table, a high-backed settle, old country pictures, interesting tram prints and a couple of pictorial Wye maps. There's a small dining room on the right, a games room (with pool and darts) in a converted brewhouse and a covered terrace; background music. The outside gents' is extremely stylish. The sizeable, neatly planted garden has picnic-sets on the lawn; pétanque. The famous black and white village is a big draw too.

Pleasing food using local produce includes sandwiches, chargrilled tiger prawns skewer in garlic butter, chicken, pork and apricot pâté with apple and mango chutney, brie, leek and pea tart with chilled minted pea purée, burger with toppings, coleslaw, onion rings and chips, beer-battered hake and chips, 28-day-aged sirloin steak, sea bass fillet, crayfish, tomato and spinach on tagliatelle in a parsley and lemon beurre blanc, and puddings such as chocolate and caramel torte with honeycomb ice-cream and lemon pavlova roulade with berry coulis. *Benchmark main dish: local beef in ale pie £9.75. Two course evening meal £20.00.*

Free house ~ Licensees Mark and Kerry Vernon ~ Real ale ~ Open 12-3, 6-11.30 (midnight Sat); 12-4, 7-10.30 Sun; closed Mon except bank holidays, Feb half-term ~ Bar food 12-3, 6-9; 12-3 Sun ~ Restaurant ~ Well behaved children welcome ~ Dogs allowed in bar ~ Wi-fi
Recommended by Mike and Mary Carter, P and J Shapley, John and Jennifer Spinks, David Edwards, Alan and Linda Blackmore, Jill and Hugh Bennett

KILPECK
Kilpeck Inn ♀

SO4430   Map 6

(01981) 570464 – www.kilpeckinn.com
Village and church signposted off A465 SW of Hereford; HR2 9DN

Imaginatively extended country inn in fascinating and peaceful village; bedrooms

With Offa's Dyke Path so close, there's plenty of good walking around this neat little country inn. The beamed bar with dark slate flagstones rambles happily around to provide several tempting corners, with an antique high-backed settle in one and high stools around a matching chest-high table in another. This opens into two cosily linked dining rooms on the left, with high panelled wainscoting. Three Tuns 1642 and Wye Valley Butty Bach on handpump, seven wines by the glass, a gin list (including local ones) and farm cider; background music. The neat back grass has picnic-sets. If you stay overnight, you can make the most of the interesting nearby castle ruins and the unique romanesque church. Green values matter a lot here: they have high-spec insulation, underfloor heating run by a wood pellet boiler, solar heating panels and a rainwater recycling system.

The landlord cooks the popular food using produce from close by: sandwiches, mussels in cider, sage and bacon, pigeon breast with puy lentils, bacon and red wine jus, wild garlic and chestnut mushroom risotto, burger with toppings, an egg and celeriac and apple coleslaw, duck breast with griottine cherries, herbed bulgar wheat and braised cabbage, pork loin steak with bacon and black pudding hash and a duck egg, and puddings such as limoncello semifreddo with orange shortbread and tonka bean rice pudding with apricot and fig compote. *Benchmark main dish: wild garlic-crusted lamb rack with aubergine dauphinoise and red wine jus £18.00. Two-course evening meal £24.00.*

Free house ~ Licensee Ross Williams ~ Real ale ~ Open 12-3, 5.30-11; 12-11 Sat; 12-4 Sun; closed Sun evening, Mon lunchtime ~ Bar food 12-2 (2.30 weekends), 6.30-9 ~ Restaurant ~ Children welcome ~ Dogs allowed in bar ~ Wi-fi ~ Bedrooms: /£90 *Recommended by Hugh Roberts, Melanie and David Lawson, WAH, P and J Shapley, Caroline and Steve Archer, Caroline and Peter Bryant*

LEDBURY
SO7137 Map 4

Feathers 🕮⭐ ⏻ 🛏
(01531) 635266 ~ www.feathers-ledbury.co.uk
High Street (A417); HR8 1DS

Handsome old hotel with chatty relaxed bar, more decorous lounge, good food and friendly staff; comfortable bedrooms

The elegant black and white external timbering here dates back to 1521 and although it is obviously a hotel rather than a pub, the convivial back bar-brasserie is always full of both drinkers and diners. Those wanting a pint and a chat congregate at one end: long beams covered in a mass of hop bines, prints and antique sale notices on stripped panelling, and stools lining the counter where they keep Fullers London Pride and a changing guest ale on handpump, a craft beer from Prescott, good wines by the glass from an extensive list and 40 malt whiskies. Staff are first class. In the main section, full of contented diners, there are cosy leather easy chairs and sofas by the fire, flowers and oil lamps on stripped kitchen and other tables, and comfortable bays of banquettes and other seats. The sedate lounge is just right for afternoon tea, with high-sided armchairs and sofas in front of a big log fire, and daily papers. In summer, the sheltered back terrace has seats and tables under parasols and abundant plant pots and hanging baskets. The bedrooms are individually furnished and stylish.

🕮 Food is attractively presented and particularly good: sandwiches, devilled chicken livers on a caramelised onion croûte, pigeon breast with chorizo, sweet pepper, smoked feta and balsamic syrup, beer-battered haddock and chips, oyster mushroom and rocket risotto, burger with toppings, spicy tomato salsa and fries, hake fillet with crab mash, samphire and sauce vierge, rack of lamb with parmentier potatoes, sweetbreads, baby onions and port jus, and puddings such as lime and coconut rice pudding with mango jelly and mango and chilli salsa and rocky road brownie tart with salted caramel mascarpone ice-cream. *Benchmark main dish: beer-battered fish and chips £12.50. Two-course evening meal £23.00.*

Free house ~ Licensee David Elliston ~ Real ale ~ Open 11-11 (10.30 Sun) ~ Bar food 12-2, 6.30-9.30 (10 Fri); 12-2.30, 6.30-10 Sat; 12-2.30, 6.30-9 Sun ~ Restaurant ~ Children welcome ~ Dogs allowed in bar and bedrooms ~ Wi-fi ~ Bedrooms: £99.50/£155 *Recommended by Comus and Sarah Elliott, Jeremy Snow, Jack and Hilary Burton, John and Claire Masters, Julia and Fiona Barnes*

LITTLE COWARNE
SO6050 Map 4

Three Horseshoes ⏻
(01885) 400276 ~ www.threehorseshoes.co.uk
Pub signposted off A465 SW of Bromyard; towards Ullingswick; HR7 4RQ

Long-serving licensees and friendly staff in bustling country pub with good food using home-grown produce; bedrooms

Mr and Mrs Whittall have been at the helm here for nearly 30 years, so you can be sure of a kind and genuine welcome. The L-shaped, quarry-tiled middle bar has upholstered settles, wooden chairs and tables, old local photographs above a woodburning stove, hop-draped beams and local guidebooks. Opening off one side is the garden room with wicker armchairs around tables, and views over the outdoor seating area and well kept garden; leading off the other side is the games room, with pool, darts, juke box, games machine and cribbage. Wye Valley Bitter and Butty Bach and a guest such as Greene King Old Speckled Hen on handpump, local Oliver's cider and perry, ten wines by the glass and home-made elderflower cordial. A popular Sunday lunchtime carvery is offered in the stripped-stone, raftered and spacious restaurant extension. There are well sited tables and chairs on the terrace and in the neat, prettily planted garden. The bedrooms are reached by outside stairs. Disabled access.

🍴 Using local and home-grown produce, the well thought-of food includes lunchtime sandwiches, smoked salmon and prawn fishcake with beetroot and horseradish relish, devilled lambs kidneys on toast, cheese, leek, celery, apple and walnut in filo pastry, chicken with cider and mushroom sauce, braised lamb shoulder with red wine gravy, whole plaice with lemon butter, pigeon with seville orange sauce, and puddings; they offer an OAP deal on Thursday lunchtime and fish and chips on Friday evening. *Benchmark main dish: steak in ale pie £13.50. Two-course evening meal £21.00.*

Free house ~ Licensees Norman and Janet Whittall ~ Real ale ~ Open 11-3, 6.30-11; 11-3, 6-11.30 Sat; 12-4 Sun; closed Sun evening, Tues ~ Bar food 12-2, 6.30-9.30; 12-2.30 Sun ~ Restaurant ~ Children welcome ~ Wi-fi ~ Bedrooms: £40/£70 *Recommended by Julian Richardson, John Sargeant, Revd Michael Vockins, Francis and Mandy Robertson*

MICHAELCHURCH ESCLEY SO3133 Map 6
Bridge Inn 🛏

(01981) 510646 – www.thebridgeinnmichaelchurch.co.uk
Off back road SE of Hay-on-Wye, along Escley Brook valley; HR2 0JW

Character riverside inn with warm, simply furnished bar and dining rooms, local drinks, hearty food and seats by the water; bedrooms

With interesting food and a peaceful location, this makes a splendid spot for lunch. The pub is tucked away in an attractive valley beside a river and there are stunning walks nearby. The simply furnished bar is homely and easy-going, with hops on dark beams, pine pews and dining chairs around rustic tables, a big woodburning stove and Wye Valley Butty Bach and HPA on handpump, good wines by the glass and local cider served by the friendly landlord. Background music. Two dining areas, with contemporary paintwork, have prints on the walls. The bedrooms in the 17th-c farmhouse (one minute's walk away) are warm and comfortable and there's a cosy sitting room too; they also have a yurt and a shepherd's hut for hire.

🍴 Creative food includes persian-style lamb with za'atar potatoes, steamed salmon with sushi ginger and lemon, burger with toppings, home-made onion rings and chips, chicken wrapped in serrano ham with creamy garlic sauce, steak frites, deep-fried hake with wakame and sesame tartare sauce, and puddings such as chocolate fudge brownie with chocolate sauce and 'banoffi lova' (a mix between banoffi pie and pavlova). *Benchmark main dish: beef in ale pie £13.75. Two-course evening meal £18.00.*

Free house ~ Licensee Glyn Bufton ~ Real ale ~ Open 12-3, 5.30-11; 6.30-11 Mon; 12-11 Sat; 12-10.30 Sun; closed Mon lunchtime ~ Bar food 12-2.30, 5.30 (6.30 Mon)-8.30; 12-3,

5.30-9.30 Sat; 12-3, 5.30-8.30 Sun ~ Restaurant ~ Children welcome ~ Dogs allowed in bar ~ Wi-fi ~ Live bands monthly (see website) ~ Bedrooms: /£100 *Recommended by Simon Daws, Paul Scofield, Geoffrey Sutton, Daniel King, Lauren and Dan Frazer*

ROSS-ON-WYE
SO5924 Map 6
Kings Head 🛏
(01989) 763174 – www.kingshead.co.uk
High Street (B4260); HR9 5HL

Welcoming bar in well run market-town hotel with real ales and tasty food; good bedrooms

The comfortable bedrooms have a lot of character with beams and wonky floors, as well as good bathrooms and excellent breakfasts. Parts of the friendly old hotel are said to date back to the 14th c, and the little beamed and panelled bar on the right has traditional pub furnishings, including comfortably padded bar seats and an antique cushioned box settle, stripped floorboards and a couple of black leather armchairs by a log-effect fire. Wye Valley Bitter and Butty Bach and a guest beer such as Purity Pure Ubu on handpump, three farm ciders and several wines by the glass at sensible prices. The beamed lounge bar on the left, also with bare boards, has some timbering, soft leather armchairs, padded bucket seats and shelves of books, and there's also a big carpeted dining room; background music. The sheltered back courtyard has contemporary tables and chairs.

Reliably good food includes sandwiches using home-baked bread, duck liver parfait with port jelly and fig and date chutney, goats cheese mousse with apple and lemon honey syrup, sharing boards, superfood vegetarian salad, pie of the day, chicken wrapped in parma ham with dauphinoise potatoes and mushroom and vegetable velouté, saddle of local venison with potato rösti and mixed berry and dark chocolate jus, hake fillet with lemon and caper sauce, and puddings such as bread and butter pudding and lemon posset; they also offer a two-course lunch menu. *Benchmark main dish: 28-day dry-aged rump steak with trimmings and triple-cooked chips £13.45. Two-course evening meal £20.00.*

Free house ~ Licensee James Vidler ~ Real ale ~ Open 11-11; 12-10.30 Sun ~ Bar food 12-2, 6-9 ~ Restaurant ~ Children welcome ~ Dogs allowed in bar and bedrooms ~ Wi-fi ~ Bedrooms: £60/£85 *Recommended by Dr J Barrie Jones, Helena and Trevor Fraser, Steve Whalley, Monty Green, Martine and Lawrence Sanders*

SYMONDS YAT
SO5616 Map 4
Saracens Head 🍺 🛏
(01600) 890435 – www.saracensheadinn.co.uk
Symonds Yat E; HR9 6JL

Lovely riverside spot with seats on waterside terraces, a fine range of drinks and interesting food; comfortable bedrooms

There's a buoyant atmosphere and plenty of chatty customers at this 17th-c inn, and its position by the River Wye, with plenty of seats on waterside terraces, means it's particularly busy in warm weather. The flagstoned bar has Sharps Doom Bar, Wye Valley Butty Bach and HPA and guests such as Bespoke Saved by the Bell, Kingstone Llandogo Trow and Wadworths 6X on handpump, 13 wines by the glass, 20 malt whiskies and several ciders. TV, background music. A cosy lounge and a modernised bare-boards dining room have fine old photos of the area and fresh flowers in jugs. Bedrooms in the main building have views over the water, while a boathouse annexe has two more contemporary rooms. There are walks in the nearby Forest of Dean.

One way to reach the inn is via the little hand ferry (pulled by one of the staff). Disabled access to the bar and terrace.

Food is good and includes sandwiches, twice-baked cheese soufflé, chicken liver parfait with red onion jam, pie of the day, spinach, ricotta and wild mushroom crêpe with mushroom velouté, local pork sausages with bubble and squeak cake and red onion gravy, slow-braised pork belly with ham and mustard croquette, pancetta and celeriac, gressingham duck breast, confit leg and vegetable spring roll with plum sauce, and puddings such as treacle tart with clotted cream ice-cream and chocolate fondant with coconut ice-cream. *Benchmark main dish: beer-battered haddock and chips £13.95. Two-course evening meal £23.00.*

Free house ~ Licensees P K and C J Rollinson ~ Real ale ~ Open 11-11; 11-10.30 Sun ~ Bar food 12-2.30, 6.30-9 ~ Restaurant ~ Children welcome but not in bedrooms ~ Dogs allowed in bar ~ Wi-fi ~ Bedrooms: £65/£90 *Recommended by Guy Vowles, Julian Richardson, Kate Moran, Mike and Mary Carter, Christine and Tony Garrett, Liz and Martin Eldon*

TILLINGTON
Bell 🍺

SO4645 Map 6

(01432) 760395 – www.thebelltillington.com
Off A4110 NW of Hereford; HR4 8LE

Relaxed and friendly pub with a snug character bar opening into civilised dining areas – good value

Even when this well run pub is at its busiest, you can still be sure of a genuine welcome from the hands-on landlord and his family. The snug parquet-floored bar on the left has assorted bucket armchairs around low, chunky, mahogany-coloured tables, brightly cushioned wall benches, team photographs and shelves of books; the black beams are strung with dried hops. There's Hobson Town Crier, Wye Valley Bitter and a guest such as Tiny Rebel Billabong on handpump, cider made on site, several wines by the glass and locally produced spirits from Chase, all served by notably cheerful staff; daily papers, background music and board games. The bar opens into a comfortable bare-boards dining lounge with stripy plush banquettes and a coal fire. Beyond that is a pitched-ceiling restaurant area with more banquettes and big country prints; through slatted blinds you can see a sunken terrace with contemporary tables, and a garden with teak tables, picnic-sets and a play area.

Highly rated food includes sandwiches, black pudding and apple hash topped with a fried egg, seafood chowder, a vegetarian quiche of the day, beef curry, seafood spaghetti, pork and cider burger with coleslaw and chips, beer-battered cod and chips, lamb rump with dauphinoise potatoes and lamb jus, monkfish and scallops on tomato and chorizo risotto, sirloin steak with a choice of four sauces, and puddings such as salted caramel and chocolate tart with butterscotch ice-cream and lemon and ginger cheesecake with lime syrup. *Benchmark main dish: steak in ale pie £13.95. Two-course evening meal £19.00.*

Free house ~ Licensee Glenn Williams ~ Real ale ~ Open 11-11 (midnight Sat); 12-10.30 Sun ~ Bar food 12-2.15, 6-9; all day Fri, Sat; 12-3 Sun ~ Restaurant ~ Children welcome ~ Dogs allowed in bar ~ Wi-fi *Recommended by Andy Dolan, John and Jennifer Spinks, Lindy Andrews, Nicholas and Maddy Trainer, Belinda Stamp*

People named as recommenders after the full entries have told us that the pub should be included. But they have not written the report – we have, after anonymous on-the-spot inspection.

TITLEY

Stagg ⊙ ⍭ ⇆

(01544) 230221 – www.thestagg.co.uk

B4355 N of Kington; HR5 3RL

Herefordshire Dining Pub of the Year

Terrific food in three dining rooms, real ales and a fine choice of other drinks, and seats in the two-acre garden; comfortable bedrooms

'Every aspect of our visit was memorable' and 'a wonderful inn' are just two enthusiastic comments from our readers. Commendable thought and effort go into maintaining the high standards here, and it shows. Of course, many customers are here for the exceptional food, but there's a pubby little bar at the heart of the place too. This convivial bar has plenty of chatty locals, a gently civilised feel and a really interesting choice of drinks served by courteous and genuinely welcoming staff. Wye Valley Butty Bach and HPA on handpump, 15 house wines by the glass (plus a carefully chosen bin list), cocktails, local cider and perry, a huge list of gins and several whiskies. Throughout, furnishings are simple: high-backed elegant wooden or leather dining chairs around a medley of tables on bare boards, candlelight and (in the bar) 200 jugs hanging from the ceiling. The two-acre garden has seats on a terrace and a croquet lawn. There are bedrooms above the pub and in a Georgian vicarage four minutes' walk away; super breakfasts. The inn is surrounded by good walking country and is handy for the Offa's Dyke Path.

Using their own eggs and home-grown vegetables and fruit (when available), the inspired food includes sandwiches on their own ciabatta bread, nibbles such as potted shrimps and barbecue pork bonbons, plus home-cured salmon, crab and avocado, lamb sweetbreads with onion, spinach and crisp potato, roasted and puréed cauliflower with spiced cauliflower couscous and parmentier potatoes, crispy duck leg with carrot and orange purée and fondant potato, snail fricassée with parsley, watercress, mushrooms and garlic croutons, chicken breast with puy lentils, bacon marmalade and little gem lettuce, cod fillet with leek, black olive tapenade and sauté new potatoes, and puddings such as three crème brûlées (vanilla, coffee, cardamom) and chocolate mousse with dark chocolate sorbet, white chocolate ice-cream and pear; on Friday there's usually a special fish choice such as turbot, squid, fennel and orange. *Benchmark main dish: fillet of local beef with salsa verde, mushrooms, red wine shallots and chips £24.90. Two-course evening meal £25.00.*

Free house ~ Licensees Steve and Nicola Reynolds ~ Real ale ~ Open 12-3, 6.30-11; 12-3.30, 6.30-10.30 Sun; closed Mon, Tues, one week Jan/Feb, one week June/July, two weeks Nov ~ Bar food 12-2, 6.30-9 (9.30 Sat); 12-3, 7-8.30 Sun ~ Restaurant ~ Children welcome ~ Dogs allowed in bar and bedrooms ~ Wi-fi ~ Bedrooms: £90/£110 *Recommended by Mike and Mary Carter, Simon and Alex Knight, Dave Sutton, P and J Shapley, Caroline and Oliver Sterling, Max and Steph Warren, Rosie and Marcus Heatherley*

UPPER COLWALL

Chase

(01684) 540276 – www.thechaseinnmalvern.co.uk

Chase Road, brown sign to pub off B4218 Malvern–Colwall, first left after hilltop on bend going W; WR13 6DJ

Gorgeous sunset views from nicely traditional tavern's garden, good drinks and traditional food

SO3359   Map 6

SO7643   Map 4

This is a cheerful country pub with a chatty and companionable atmosphere. There's a great variety of seats (from a wooden-legged tractor seat to a carved pew) and tables, an old black kitchen range and plenty of decorations – china mugs, blue-glass flasks, lots of small pictures. Four well kept ales are tapped from the cask, such as Bathams Best, Exmoor Gold, Ringwood Fortyniner and Woods Shropshire Lad, and friendly staff also serve eight wines by the glass, 18 gins, seven malt whiskies and a farm cider. Seats and tables on the steep series of small, pretty back terraces look across Herefordshire and even as far as the Black Mountains and the Brecon Beacons. Plenty of good surrounding walks.

Pubby food includes lunchtime sandwiches, deep-fried whitebait with tartare sauce, chicken liver pâté with pickles, burger with toppings, coleslaw and chips, seasonal vegetable risotto, beef in ale pie, free-range chicken with root vegetables and honey and mustard dressing, sea bass fillets with spinach and tarragon pearl barley and pea purée, breaded pork escalope with blue cheese sauce and fondant potatoes, and puddings; they offer takeaway fish and chips 6.30-9pm. *Benchmark main dish: beer-battered cod and chips £11.90. Two-course evening meal £18.00.*

Free house ~ Licensee Duncan Ironmonger ~ Real ale ~ Open 12-3, 5-11; 12-11 Sat; 12-10.30 Sun ~ Bar food 12-2 (2.30 weekends), 6.30-9 ~ Children welcome ~ Dogs allowed in bar ~ Wi-fi *Recommended by Charlie Parker, Colin and Daniel Gibbs, Emily and Toby Archer, Simon Day, Mike Benton*

WALFORD   SO5820   Map 4

Mill Race ⭐ ♀

(01989) 562891 – www.millrace.info

B4234 Ross-on-Wye to Lydney; HR9 5QS

Contemporary furnishings in uncluttered rooms, good quality food, real ales served by attentive staff, and terrace tables

The highly enjoyable food remains a big draw in this whitewashed pub, though the hospitable landlord gives a genuine welcome to drinkers too. It's all very civilised and stylish, with a row of strikingly high arched windows, comfortable leather armchairs and sofas on flagstones, and smaller chairs around broad pedestal tables. Photographs of the local countryside hang on the mainly cream or red walls and there's good unobtrusive lighting. One wall, stripped back to the stonework, contains a woodburning stove that's open to the comfortable, compact dining area on the other side; background music. From the granite-topped modern bar counter, friendly staff serve Wye Valley Bitter and HPA and a changing guest such as Hillside Legless Cow on handpump, farm cider and 22 fairly priced wines by the glass. There are seats on the terrace with views towards Goodrich Castle (English Heritage), and more seats and tables in the garden. There are some popular surrounding walks and the pub provides leaflets describing pleasant ones in the area.

Much of the produce comes from their nearby 1,000-acre farm and woodlands (cattle, rare-breed pigs, turkeys, geese, pheasant and ducks) and they list other local suppliers on their website. Dishes include lunchtime ciabattas, garlic mushrooms on toast with a poached egg and truffle oil, king prawn bloody mary cocktail with fennel, minted pea and goats cheese risotto, burger with toppings, red onion marmalade and sweet potato fries, chicken kiev with creamed mushrooms, pork belly with potato rösti and cider jus, mixed grilled fish with salsa verde and samphire, and puddings such as orange and cardamom crème brûlée and chocolate brownie with vanilla ice-cream. *Benchmark main dish: beer-battered fish and chips £13.00. Two-course evening meal £19.00.*

Free house ~ Licensee Luke Freeman ~ Real ale ~ Open 12-3, 5-10; 12-11 Sat; 12-9 Sun;
closed Mon ~ Bar food 12-2.30 (3 Sat), 6-9; 12-3 Sun ~ Restaurant ~ Children welcome ~
Dogs allowed in bar ~ Wi-fi *Recommended by Hilary De Lyon and Martin Webster, William Slade,
Claire Scott, Mike and Mary Carter, Lee and Jill Stafford, Andrew Wall*

 WOOLHOPE SO6135 Map 4
Butchers Arms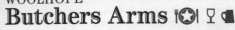
(01432) 860281 – www.butchersarmswoolhope.com
Off B4224 in Fownhope; HR1 4RF

**Pleasant country inn in peaceful setting, with an inviting garden,
interesting food and a fine choice of real ales**

Just outside the village and tucked away down a country lane, this is a
half-timbered inn with modern food and local ales. The bar has very low
beams, built-in cushioned wall seats, farmhouse chairs and stools around a
mix of old tables (some set for dining) on carpet, hunting and horse pictures
on cream walls and an open fire in a big fireplace; there's also a little beamed
dining room, similarly furnished. They serve their own-brewed Butchers
Arms Henry Hodges plus Wye Valley Butty Bach and Ledbury Gold on
handpump, six wines by the glass from a good list, 14 malt whiskies and a
couple of farm ciders. The parrot is called Max and they have a new fish tank.
There are picnic-sets in a pretty, streamside garden. To really appreciate the
surroundings, turn left as you come out of the pub and take the tiny left-hand
road at the end of the car park; this turns into a track and then a path, and
the view from the top of the hill is quite something.

Cooked by the landlord, the popular food includes twice-baked goats cheese
soufflé with apple and walnut salad, smoked salmon, avocado and crayfish with
lemon dressing, thai green vegetable curry, mackerel fillet with parmentier potatoes
and stewed rhubarb, meatballs in a tomato, basil and garlic sauce on tagliatelle, lamb
rump with dauphinoise potatoes and redcurrant and thyme sauce, pork belly with
smoked bacon, black pudding and apple sauce, and puddings such as cherry, chocolate
and brandy gateau and sticky toffee pudding with toffee sauce. *Benchmark main dish:
rabbit, apple and cider pie £12.95. Two-course evening meal £18.00.*

Free house ~ Licensee Philip Vincent ~ Real ale ~ Open 11-3, 6-11; 12-3.30 Sun; closed
Sun evening, Mon except bank holidays ~ Bar food 12-2.30, 6-9; 12-2.30 Sun ~ Restaurant
~ Children welcome ~ Dogs allowed in bar ~ Wi-fi *Recommended by Ben and Diane Bowie,
Harvey Brown, Ian Duncan, David and Charlotte Green*

 WOOLHOPE SO6135 Map 4
Crown
(01432) 860468 – www.crowninnwoolhope.co.uk
Village signposted off B4224 in Fownhope; HR1 4QP

Chatty village local with excellent ciders and perries, and popular food

Cider lovers head for this cheerful, busy pub as the landlord makes four
farm ciders (and keeps a couple of guest ciders) and serves around
two dozen bottled ciders and perrys from within a 15-mile radius; they also
hold a May Day Bank Holiday festival with live music, beer, cider and perry.
Also, Ledbury Bitter and Wye Valley Butty Bach and HPA on handpump and
several wines by the glass. The bar has painted farmhouse and other wooden
chairs, upholstered settles and rustic tables on wooden flooring, an open fire
and a woodburning stove, some standing timbers and stools against the bar
counter; background music, darts and board games. In summer, there's a bar
in the lovely big garden, which has a firepit and a particularly comfortable
smokers' shelter with cushions and darts; marvellous views. Disabled access.

🍴 Tasty seasonal food includes lunchtime baguettes, fire-roasted red pepper linguine with tempura courgettes, pigeon breast with black pudding, pickled shallots and a rich brown sauce, rabbit sausages with truffle and kibbled onion mash and onion gravy, a pie of the day, burger with toppings and chips, goat with goat croquette, tarka dhal, bhindi bhaji and bean salad, home-smoked trout niçoise salad, steaks with a choice of sauces and potatoes, and puddings such as tonka bean crème brûlée with hazelnut butter toffee and chocolate brownie with chocolate sauce. *Benchmark main dish: open venison pie with wild mushrooms and peppercorns £14.00. Two-course evening meal £20.00.*

Free house ~ Licensees Matt and Annalisa Slocombe ~ Real ale ~ Open 12-3, 6-11; 12-midnight Sat; 12-11 Sun ~ Bar food 12-2, 6-9 (9.30 Fri); 12-2.30, 6-9.30 Sat; 12-3.30, 6-9 Sun ~ Restaurant ~ Children welcome ~ Dogs allowed in bar ~ Wi-fi *Recommended by Martin Day, Guy Vowles, Katherine Matthews, Mike Swan, David and Stella Martin, Audrey and Paul Summers*

Also Worth a Visit in Herefordshire

Besides the fully inspected pubs, you might like to try these pubs that have been recommended to us and described by readers. Do tell us what you think of them: feedback@goodguides.com

ALMELEY   SO3351
Bells (01544) 327216
Off A480, A4111 or A4112 S of Kington; HR3 6LF Welcoming old country local with original jug-and-bottle entry lobby and carpeted beamed bar with woodburner, second bar has been converted to village shop/deli, a couple of well kept ales such as Three Tuns and Woods, traditional cider/perry and generous home-made food (not evenings) from sandwiches up; children and dogs welcome, garden with decked area and boules, on Wyche Way long-distance path, open all day. *(Guy Vowles)*

AYMESTREY   SO4265
★ Riverside Inn (01568) 708440
A4110, at N end of village, W of Leominster; HR6 9ST Black and white inn with terrace and tree-sheltered garden making most of lovely waterside spot by ancient stone bridge over the Lugg; cosy rambling beamed interior with some antique furniture alongside stripped country kitchen tables, warm fires, well kept Hobsons, Wye Valley and a guest, local ciders, very good imaginative food from chef-patron using local rare-breed meat and own fruit and vegetables (bar snacks only Sun evening), friendly helpful staff; quiet background music; children welcome, dogs in bar, lovely circular walks, six bedrooms (more planned), fly fishing for residents, good breakfast, closed Mon lunchtime, otherwise open all day. *(John and Jennifer Spinks)*

BISHOPS FROME   SO6648
Green Dragon (01885) 490607
Just off B4214 Bromyard–Ledbury; WR6 5BP Welcoming village pub with four linked rooms, unspoilt rustic feel, beams, flagstones and log fires (one in fine inglenook), half a dozen ales including Otter, Timothy Taylors and Wye Valley, real ciders and enjoyable traditional food (Tues-Sat evenings and Sun lunchtime); children and dogs welcome, tiered garden with smokers' shelter, on Herefordshire Trail, closed weekday lunchtimes, open all day Sat. *(Liz and Martin Eldon)*

BODENHAM   SO5454
Englands Gate (01568) 797286
On A417 at Bodenham turn-off, about 6 miles S of Leominster; HR1 3HU Attractive black and white 16th-c coaching inn, rambling interior with beams and joists in low ceilings around a vast central stone chimneypiece, sturdy timber props, exposed stonework and well worn flagstones (one or two steps), Hobsons, Wye Valley and a guest, traditional cider, fairly pubby food from lunchtime sandwiches up; background and occasional live music, July beer/cider/sausage festival; children welcome, dogs in bar, tables under parasols on terrace and in pleasant garden, modern bedrooms in converted coach house next door, open all day. *(Lauren and Dan Frazer)*

BOSBURY   SO6943
Bell (01531) 640285
B4220 N of Ledbury; HR8 1PX Timbered village pub opposite the church; log fires in both bars, Otter, Wye Valley and a guest, three ciders and good choice of wines by the glass, dining area serving popular sensibly priced traditional food (not Sun evening, Mon, Tues) including Sun carvery, friendly staff; pool and darts; children and dogs welcome, large garden with covered terrace

and play equipment, open all Sun, closed Mon and Tues lunchtimes. *(Ian Duncan)*

BRINGSTY COMMON   SO6954

★**Live & Let Live** (01886) 821462
Off A44 Knightwick–Bromyard 1.5 miles W of Whitbourne turn; take track southwards at Black Cat inn sign, bearing right at fork; WR6 5UW Bustling 17th-c timber and thatch cottage (former cider house) with cosy flagstoned bar, scrubbed or polished tables, cushioned chairs, long stripped pew and high-backed winged settle by log fire in cavernous stone fireplace, earthenware jugs hanging from low beams, old casks built into hop-strung bar counter, three well kept ales including Wye Valley Butty Bach, local ciders/apple juice and decent wines by the glass, good fairly traditional food served by friendly efficient staff, Thurs steak night, two dining rooms upstairs under steep rafters; children and dogs welcome, glass-topped well and big wooden hogshead as terrace tables, peaceful country views from picnic-sets and rustic benches in former orchard, handy for Brockhampton Estate (NT), closed Mon, otherwise open all day (best to check winter hours). *(Alan and Angela Scouller, Richard Stanfield)*

BROMYARD DOWNS   SO6755

★**Royal Oak** (01885) 482585
Just NE of Bromyard; pub signed off A44; HR7 4QP Beautifully placed low-beamed 18th-c pub with wide views; open-plan carpeted and flagstoned bar, log fire and woodburner, dining room with huge bay window, well kept Malvern Hills, Purity and Woods, real cider, enjoyable food (special diets catered for) including daily specials, friendly service; background music, pool and darts; children, walkers and dogs welcome, nice garden with front terrace and play area, closed Sun evening, Mon (open all day bank holiday weekends). *(Mike Swan)*

CANON PYON   SO4648

Nags Head (01432) 830725
A4110; HR4 8NY Welcoming 17th-c timbered roadside pub; beamed bar with log fire, flagstoned restaurant and overspill/function room, well kept Sharps Doom Bar and a guest, popular good value food (not Sun evening) cooked by landlady, pleasant attentive service; traditional pub games; children and dogs (in bar) welcome, extensive garden with play area, open all day Sun till 6pm, closed Mon, Tues. *(John and Claire Masters)*

CLIFFORD   SO2445

Castlefields (01497) 831554
B4350 N of Hay-on-Wye; HR3 5HB Rebuilt and enlarged family pub retaining some old features including a glass-covered well, generous helpings of popular good value food and a couple of changing ales, friendly

helpful staff, red-carpeted floors, woodburner in two-way stone fireplace, restaurant; pool, darts and various community-based events; lovely country views, camping, closed all day Mon, Tues afternoon, otherwise open all day. *(Ian Duncan)*

CLODOCK   SO3227

Cornewall Arms (01873) 860677
N of Walterstone; HR2 0PD Wonderfully old-fashioned survivor in remote hamlet by historic church facing the Black Mountains; friendly stable-door bar with open fire each end, a few mats and comfortable armchairs on stone floor, lots of ornaments and knick-knacks, photos of past village events, books for sale, games including darts and devil among the tailors, bottled Wye Valley and cider, no food or credit cards; dogs welcome, open all day weekends, closed weekday lunchtimes. *(Barry Collett)*

COLWALL   SO7440

★**Wellington** (01684) 540269
A449 Malvern–Ledbury; WR13 6HW Welcoming pub with highly thought-of food from bar snacks and standards to imaginative restaurant dishes (special diets catered for), well kept Goffs Tournament, a couple of guest ales and nice wines by the glass, friendly helpful landlord and staff, comfortably lived-in two-level beamed bar with red patterned carpet and quarry tiles, some built-in settles including unusual high-backed one framing a window, woodburner and open fire, spacious relaxed back dining area; occasional live music, daily newspapers; children and dogs welcome, picnic-sets on neat grass above car park, good local walks, closed evenings Sun and bank holiday Mon (shut all day Aug Bank Holiday Mon). *(Richard Kennell, Richard C Morgan)*

DORSTONE   SO3141

★**Pandy** (01981) 550273
Pub signed off B4348 E of Hay-on-Wye; HR3 6AN Ancient inn (12th-c origins) by village green, traditional rooms with low beams, stout timbers and worn flagstones, various alcoves and vast fireplace, several woodburners, four real ales including Three Tuns and Wye Valley, local cider and enjoyable reasonably priced food (not Sun evening) from changing blackboard menu, friendly attentive service; children and dogs (in bar) welcome, side garden with picnic sets and play area, four good bedrooms in purpose-built timber lodge (now run independently, but breakfast in the pub), closed Mon lunchtime, otherwise open all day (till 9.30pm Sun), in winter closed lunchtime Mon-Thurs. *(Mr Yeldahn)*

EWYAS HAROLD   SO3828

Temple Bar (01981) 240423
Village centre signed from B4347; HR2 0EU Popular creeper-clad Georgian inn run by welcoming family; good freshly

made food from bar meals to interesting evening restaurant dishes (weekly changing menu), Wye Valley Butty Bach and a couple of guests, local cider, modernised interior keeping original features such as oak beams, flagstones and log fire; children and dogs (in bar) welcome, disabled access, three comfortable bedrooms, hearty breakfast, open all day weekends, no evening food Sun, Mon or Tues. *(Peter and Jane Emmerson)*

FOWNHOPE   SO5734
Green Man (01432) 860243
B4224; HR1 4PE Striking 15th-c black and white dining inn; beams, standing timbers and big log fire in bare-boards bar, button-back wall benches, bentwood and windsor chairs at slabby-topped tables, restaurant with inglenook woodburner, separate function room, generally well liked food from interesting menu, three Wye Valley ales, good wines and coffee; background music; children welcome, no dogs, ramped wheelchair access from car park, attractive quiet garden, bedrooms and self-catering cottages, open (and some food) all day. *(David Fowler)*

FOWNHOPE   SO5734
New Inn (01432) 860350
B4224, centre of village; HR1 4PE Neat little local set back from the road; good pubby lunchtime food plus occasional pie/steak nights, well kept Hobsons, Wye Valley and a guest, efficient friendly service, small dining area; children, well behaved dogs and walkers welcome, tables outside, picturesque village with unusual church and nice views, open all day weekends. *(Jill and Hugh Bennett)*

GARWAY   SO4622
Garway Moon (01600) 750270
Centre of village, opposite the green; HR2 8RQ Attractive 18th-c pub in pretty location overlooking common; good freshly made food (not Mon) served by friendly staff, well kept ales such as Butcombe, Kingstone and Wye Valley, proper ciders, beams and exposed stonework, woodburner in inglenook, restaurant; children, dogs and muddy boots welcome, garden with terrace and play area, three bedrooms, open all day weekends, closed lunchtimes Mon and Tues. *(Mike Swan)*

GORSLEY   SO6726
Roadmaker (01989) 720352
0.5 miles from M50 junction 3; village signposted from exit – B4221; HR9 7SW Popular 19th-c village pub run by group of retired gurkhas; large carpeted lounge bar with central log fire, good nepalese food here and in evening restaurant, also Sun roasts and other english choices, well kept ales such as Brains and Butcombe, efficient courteous service; quiz first Sun of month; children welcome, no dogs, terrace with water feature, open all day. *(Alan and Linda Blackmore)*

HAMPTON BISHOP   SO5538
Bunch of Carrots (01432) 870237
B4224; HR1 4JR Spacious beamed country pub by River Wye, good daily carvery and choice of other pubby food (all day weekends), cheerful efficient service, well kept Wye Valley Butty Bach, Sharps Doom Bar and a couple of guests, local cider and several wines by the glass, traditional dimly lit bar area with wood and flagstone floors, woodburner, airy restaurant; children and dogs welcome, disabled access/loo, garden with play area, open all day. *(Jill and Hugh Bennett)*

HAREWOOD END   SO5227
Harewood End Inn (01989) 730637
A49 Hereford to Ross-on-Wye; HR2 8JT Roadside pub in two connecting buildings, compact bar and a couple of bare-boards dining rooms, high-backed chairs around scrubbed-top tables, interesting collection of enamel signs on panelled walls, open fire, good choice of enjoyable home-made food from lunchtime sandwiches up including 'build your own burger', three well kept ales and decent choice of wines, welcoming attentive staff; quiz last Sun of month, pool, darts and TV, free wi-fi; children and dogs welcome, nice garden and local walks, five bedrooms, closed Mon. *(Liz and Martin Eldon)*

HEREFORD   SO5139
Barrels (01432) 274968
St Owen Street; HR1 2JQ Friendly 18th-c coaching inn and former home to the Wye Valley brewery, up to seven of their well kept keenly priced ales from barrel-built counter (beer/music festival end Aug), Thatcher's cider, no food, cheerful efficient staff and good mix of customers (very busy weekends); live jazz first Mon of month, pool room, big-screen sports TV, juke box; dogs welcome, partly covered courtyard behind, open all day. *(Richard Scarle)*

HEREFORD   SO5039
★ Lichfield Vaults (01432) 266821
Church Street; HR1 2LR Popular place, a pub since the 18th c, in picturesque pedestrianised area near cathedral; dark panelling, some stripped brick and exposed joists, impressive plasterwork in big-windowed front room, traditionally furnished with dark pews, padded pub chairs and a couple of heavily padded benches, hot coal stove, charming greek landlord and friendly staff, five well kept ales such as Adnams, Caledonian and Sharps, enjoyable food from sandwiches up including greek dishes and good Sun roasts; faint background music, live blues/rock last Sun of month, TV projector for sports (particularly rugby), games machines, daily papers; children welcome, no dogs, picnic-sets in pleasant back courtyard, open all day. *(Andy Dolan, Richard Searle)*

HOARWITHY SO5429
New Harp (01432) 840900
*Off A49 Hereford to Ross-on-Wye;
HR2 6QH* Open-plan village dining pub
with cheerful bustling atmosphere; good
well presented local food from chef-landlord
including good value weekday two-course
lunch, friendly helpful service, ales such as
Wye Valley, Ledbury and Otter, Weston's cider
(maybe their own organic cider in summer),
pine tables on slate tiles, bay-window seats
and half-panelling, screened-off dining
area with light wood furniture, a couple
of woodburners; background and some
live music, sports TV; children, walkers
and dogs welcome, pretty tree-sheltered
garden with stream, picnic-sets and decked
area, little shop and Mon morning post
office, unusual italianate Victorian church
nearby, open all day. *(Barry Collett)*

KENTCHURCH SO4125
★ Bridge Inn (01981) 240408
B4347 Pontrilas–Grosmont; HR2 0BY
Ancient rustic pub bordering the River
Monnow (and Wales), welcoming staff and
warm local atmosphere, good reasonably
priced home-made food, well kept Otter
and a couple of guests, big log fire in bar,
pretty little back restaurant overlooking the
river (two miles of trout fishing); terrace
and waterside garden with pétanque,
handy for Herefordshire Trail, closed
Sun evening, Mon, Tues. *(Mike Swan)*

KINGSLAND SO4461
★ Corners (01568) 708385
*B4360 NW of Leominster, corner of
Lugg Green Road; HR6 9RY* Comfortably
updated, partly black and white 16th-c
village inn with snug nooks and corners;
log fires, low beams, dark red plasterwork
and some stripped woodwork, bow-window
seat and leather armchairs in softly lit
carpeted bar, well kept Hobsons, Wye
Valley and decent selection of wines, big
side dining room in converted hay loft
with rafters and huge window, enjoyable
reasonably priced food from pubby choices
up, cheerful attentive service; children
welcome, no garden, comfortable bedrooms
in modern block behind. *(Mike Swan)*

KINGTON SO3056
★ Olde Tavern (01544) 231945
*Victoria Road, just off A44 opposite
B4355 – follow sign to 'Town Centre,
Hospital, Cattle Market'; pub on right
opposite Elizabeth Road, no inn sign but
'Estd 1767' notice; HR5 3BX* Gloriously
old-fashioned with hatch-served side room
opening off small plain parlour and public
bar, plenty of dark brown woodwork, big
windows, settles and other antique furniture
on bare floors, gas fire, old local pictures,
china, pewter and curios, four well kept ales
including Hobsons and Ludlow, Weston's

cider, generous helpings of enjoyable home-
made food (Thurs-Sun), friendly atmosphere;
children and dogs welcome, little yard at
back, open all day weekends, closed Mon-
Thurs lunchtimes. *(Caroline and Peter Bryant)*

KINGTON SO2956
Oxford Arms (01544) 230322
Duke Street; HR5 3DR Traditional old-
fashioned beamed inn with woodburners in
main bar on left and dining area on right,
smaller lounge with sofas and armchairs,
Woods Shropshire Lad and a couple of guests,
enjoyable reasonably priced food including
Weds pie night and Thurs surf-and-turf, good
friendly service; some live music, summer
beer festivals, pool; children and dogs
welcome, terrace picnic-sets, bedrooms, open
all day Fri-Sun, closed Mon and lunchtimes
Tues-Thurs. *(Sylvia and Philip Spencer)*

KINGTON SO2956
Royal Oak (01544) 230484
Church Street; HR5 3BE Cheerful
and welcoming 17th-c pub with good thai
restaurant (carvery only on Sun), also well
kept ales such as Ringwood and Wye Valley
and a proper cider like Somersby's, two little
open fires, darts and sports TV in public
bar; children and dogs (in bar) welcome,
garden with terrace, handy for Offa's Dyke
walkers, three neat simple bedrooms, open
all day Fri-Sun, closed lunchtimes Mon
and Tues, no food Tues. *(Ian Duncan)*

KINGTON SO2956
Swan (01544) 230510
Church Street; HR5 3AZ Cleanly
modernised 17th-c dining pub by the square;
enjoyable freshly made food (not Sun
evening) from lunchtime sandwiches up, Sun
brunch, three local ales and good choice of
wines, friendly young staff, split-level interior
with three different eating areas, beams and
standing timbers, woodburner in central
stone fireplace; background music, free wi-fi;
children and dogs welcome. *(Guy Vowles)*

LEDBURY SO7137
★ Prince of Wales (01531) 632250
*Church Lane; narrow passage from
Town Hall; HR8 1DL* Friendly old
black and white local prettily tucked away
down narrow cobbled alley, seven well
kept ales, foreign draught/bottled beers
and Weston's cider, knowledgeable staff,
decent uncomplicated low-priced food
from sandwiches up, beams, nooks and
crannies and shelves of books, long back
room; background music, live blues Sun
afternoon, folk session Weds evening; dogs
welcome on leads, a couple of tables in
flower-filled backyard, open all day. *(Comus
and Sarah Elliott, Dr J Barrie Jones, David Dore)*

LEDBURY SO7137
Seven Stars (01531) 635800
Homend (High Street); HR8 1BN

16th-c beamed and timbered pub with good well presented food (all day weekends) using produce from own farm, three well kept ales including Shepherd Neame, friendly helpful staff, bar area with comfortable seating and cosy open fire, dining room behind; free wi-fi; children and dogs welcome, disabled access, walled back terrace, three bedrooms, open all day. *(Dr J Barrie Jones)*

LEDBURY
SO7137

Talbot (01531) 632963

New Street; HR8 2DX Comfortable 16th-c black and white fronted coaching inn; log-fire bar with Wadworths ales and guests, plenty of wines by the glass and good fairly traditional food from sharing boards and lunchtime sandwiches up, regular deals, friendly efficient service, oak-panelled dining room; courtyard tables, 13 bedrooms (six in converted stables), open all day. *(John and Claire Masters)*

LEINTWARDINE
SO4073

Lion (01547) 540203

High Street; SY7 0JZ Restored inn beautifully situated by packhorse bridge over River Teme; helpful efficient staff and friendly atmosphere, good well presented food from varied menu including some imaginative choices (can be pricey), Tues steak night, restaurant and two separate bars (both with woodburners), well kept beers such as Ludlow and Wye Valley; children welcome, safely fenced riverside garden with play area, eight attractive bedrooms, can arrange fishing trips, open all day (till 8pm Sun). *(Mike Swan)*

LEINTWARDINE
SO4073

★**Sun** (01547) 540705

Rosemary Lane, just off A4113; SY7 0LP Fascinating 19th-c time warp: benches and farmhouse tables by coal fire in wallpapered brick-floored front bar (dogs welcome here), three well kept ales including Hobsons tapped from the cask (Aug beer festival), another fire in snug carpeted parlour, pork pies and perhaps a lunchtime ploughman's (can bring food from adjacent fish and chip shop), friendly staff and cheery locals; open mike night last Fri of month; new pavilion-style building with bar and garden room, open all day. *(Lauren and Dan Frazer)*

LEOMINSTER
SO4959

★**Grape Vaults** (01568) 611404

Broad Street; HR6 8BS Compact two-room character pub, popular and friendly, with well kept ales such as Ludlow and local Swan, tasty good value traditional food (not Sun evening, no credit cards – ATM opposite), good cheerful service, two coal fires, beams and stripped woodwork, original dark high-backed settles and round copper-topped tables on bare boards, old local prints and posters, bottle collection, shelves of books in snug; tiny gents', live music Sun afternoon, occasional quiz nights, free wi-fi; dogs welcome, open all day. *(Guy Vowles, Roy and Gill Payne)*

LINTON
SO6525

Alma (01989) 720355

On main road through village; HR9 7RY Cheerful village local with up to five well kept ales, Weston's cider and several wines by the glass, enjoyable pub food (not Sun, Mon) including specials, friendly service, front bar with open fire, restaurant, pool in small back room; live music (mainly acoustic) including open mike first Thurs of month, also June festival, quiz last Sun of month; children and dogs welcome, good-sized garden behind with nice view, closed Mon lunchtime. *(Mike and Mary Carter)*

LUGWARDINE
SO5441

Crown & Anchor (01432) 850630

Just off A438 E of Hereford; Cotts Lane; HR1 4AB Cottagey timbered pub dating from the 18th c; ample helpings of enjoyable food from traditional favourites up, well kept Wye Valley and a guest beer, decent wines, good friendly service, various smallish opened-up rooms, inglenook log fire; children and dogs (in bar) welcome, seats in front and back gardens, open all day. *(Andy Dolan)*

MUCH DEWCHURCH
SO4831

Black Swan (01981) 540295

B4348 Ross-on-Wye to Hay-on-Wye; HR2 8DJ Roomy and attractive beamed local (partly 14th-c) with welcoming long-serving licensees; well kept Timothy Taylors Landlord and local guests, Weston's cider, decent wines and enjoyable straightforward home-made food using local produce, log fires in cosy well worn bar and lounge/eating area, pool room with darts, TV and juke box; Thurs folk night; children and dogs welcome, seats on front terrace, open all day Sun. *(Caroline and Steve Archer)*

MUCH MARCLE
SO6634

Royal Oak (01531) 660300

On A449 Ross-on-Wye to Ledbury; HR8 2ND Roadside country dining pub with lovely views; good reasonably priced food (all day Sun) using meat from local farms, lunchtime deals, grill night Mon, prompt friendly service, well kept Brakspears and Marstons Pedigree, Weston's cider and several wines by the glass, smallish bare-boards bar area, various dining sections including library room and large back function room; skittle alley; children and dogs welcome, garden and terrace seating, two bedrooms. *(Dr A J and Mrs B A Tompsett)*

ORLETON
SO4967

★**Boot** (01568) 780228

Off B4362 W of Woofferton; SY8 4HN Popular pub with beams, timbering, even some 16th-c wattle and daub, inglenook woodburner in charming cosy traditional bar, steps up to further bar area, spacious two-room dining part, good well presented food from shortish but varied menu, friendly quick service, Hobsons, Wye Valley and a local guest (July beer/music festival), real ciders; children and dogs welcome, seats in garden under huge ash tree, fenced-in play area, open all day weekends. *(Peter J and Avril Hanson)*

PEMBRIDGE   SO3958
New Inn (01544) 388427
Market Square (A44); HR6 9DZ Timeless ancient inn overlooking small black and white town's church, unpretentious three-room bar with antique settles, beams, worn flagstones and impressive inglenook log fire, well kept changing ales, farm cider and generous helpings of popular good value food, friendly service, quiet little family dining room; traditional games, downstairs lavatories; no dogs, simple bedrooms and two resident ghosts. *(Mike Swan)*

PETERSTOW   SO5524
Red Lion (01989)730546
A49 W of Ross; HR9 6LH Roadside country pub with good sensibly priced food cooked by landlord (smaller appetites catered for), good range of well kept ales and ciders, friendly staff, open-plan with large dining area and modern conservatory, log fires; children and dogs welcome, back play area, camping, open all day, except 3-6pm Sun. *(Ian Duncan)*

PRESTON   SO3841
Yew Tree (01981) 500359
Village W of Hereford; HR2 9JT Small tucked-away pub handy for River Wye, simple and welcoming, with two quickly changing ales tapped from the cask and real cider, good value home-made bar food including weekday early evening deal for two and Fri steak night; live music, free wi-fi; children and dogs welcome, bunkhouse, open (and food) all day. *(Liz and Martin Eldon)*

ROSS-ON-WYE   SO5924
Mail Rooms (01989) 760920
Gloucester Road; HR9 5BS Open-plan Wetherspoons conversion of former post office, up to five real ales including Greene King, Weston's cider and good choice of wines, enjoyable well priced food, friendly service; silent TV, free wi-fi; children welcome till 8pm, decked back terrace, open all day from 8am. *(Alan and Linda Blackmore)*

ROSS-ON-WYE   SO6024
White Lion (01989) 562785
Wilton Lane; HR9 6AQ Friendly riverside pub dating from 1650, well kept Wye Valley and a couple of guests, enjoyable traditional fare at reasonable prices, good service, big fireplace in carpeted bar, stone-walled gaol restaurant (building once a police station); free wi-fi; children

and dogs welcome, lots of tables in garden and on terrace overlooking the Wye and historic bridge, bedrooms and camping, open all day. *(Alan and Linda Blackmore)*

SELLACK   SO5526
Lough Pool (01989) 730888
Off A49; HR9 6LX Cottagey black and white country pub – some recent refurbishment but keeping character; bars with beams and standing timbers, rustic furniture on flagstones, open fire and woodburner, well kept Wye Valley ales and a guest, local farm ciders/perries and several wines by the glass, landlord-chef's good attractively presented food from interesting menu including daily specials, back restaurant, friendly attentive service; well behaved children and dogs (in bar) allowed, good surrounding walks, closed Sun evening, Mon. *(Martin Hartog)*

STAPLOW   SO6941
Oak (01531) 640954
Bromyard Road (B4214); HR8 1NP Popular roadside village pub with two snug bar areas, beams, flagstones and woodburners, four real ales and good choice of wines, open-kitchen restaurant serving good food from lunchtime sandwiches/ciabattas up, cheerful quick service; occasional live music; children and dogs welcome, garden picnic-sets, four comfortable bedrooms, open all day. *(John and Claire Masters)*

STAUNTON ON WYE   SO3844
Portway (01981) 500474
A438 Hereford–Hay, by Monnington turn; HR4 7NH Modernised 16th-c beamed inn with good food including Fri steak night and bargain OAP lunch Tues and Thurs, Ludlow Gold, Sharps Doom Bar and Wye Valley, log-fire bar, lounge and restaurant; background music, TV, pool; children welcome, picnic-sets in sizeable garden among fruit trees, nine bedrooms, open all day. *(Dave Braisted)*

STOCKTON CROSS   SO5161
★ Stockton Cross Inn (01568) 612509
Kimbolton; A4112, off A49 just N of Leominster; HR6 0HD Cosy half-timbered 16th-c drovers' inn; heavily beamed interior with huge log fire and woodburner, handsome antique settle, old leather chairs and brocaded stools, cast-iron-framed tables, well kept Wye Valley ales and guests, Robinson's cider, enjoyable food from pub favourites up, good friendly service; children and dogs welcome, pretty garden, handy for Berrington Hall (NT), open all day. *(R T and J C Moggridge)*

SUTTON ST NICHOLAS   SO5345
Golden Cross (01432) 880274
Corner of Ridgeway Road; HR1 3AZ Thriving modernised pub with enjoyable

good value food from ciabattas up, OAP lunch deal Mon-Fri, Wye Valley Butty Bach and two regularly changing guests from stone-fronted counter, good friendly service, clean décor, some breweriana, relaxed upstairs restaurant; live music Fri, pool and darts; children and dogs welcome, disabled facilities, no-smoking garden behind, pretty village and good surrounding walks, open all day Fri-Sun. *(Ian Duncan)*

SYMONDS YAT SO5515
Old Ferrie (01600) 890232
Ferrie Lane, Symonds Yat West; HR9 6BL Unpretentious lived-in old pub set in picturesque spot by River Wye (own hand-pulled ferry); decent choice of enjoyable food including lunchtime sharing boards, Wye Valley ales and local cider, friendly helpful staff, log fires; games room; children and dogs (in bar) welcome, waterside terrace, paddle boarding and good walks, bedrooms including two bunkhouses, open all day. *(Mike Swan)*

TRUMPET SO6639
Trumpet Inn (01531) 670277
Corner A413 and A438; HR8 2RA Modernised black and white timbered pub dating from the 15th c, well kept Wadworths ales and plenty of wines by the glass, good food (all day Sat, till 5pm Sun) from sandwiches to specials, Mon steak night, efficient service, carpeted interior with beams, stripped brickwork and log fires, restaurant; free wi-fi; children and dogs (in bar) welcome, tables in big garden behind, campsite with hard standings, open all day. *(Jill and Hugh Bennett)*

UPPER SAPEY SO6863
Baiting House (01886) 853201
B4203 Bromyard–Great Witley; WR6 6XT Recently refurbished 19th-c country inn; two bars with flagstone and wood-strip flooring, woodburners, very nice food from lunchtime sandwiches up (more adventurous evening menu), five well kept ales including Hobsons and Wye Valley, local ciders, several wines by the glass and good selection of gins, friendly attentive service, restaurant; separate room for darts and sports TV; children and dogs (in one bar and snug) welcome, disabled access, picnic-sets on brick terrace and raised lawn, six comfortable well appointed bedrooms, open all day, no food Sun evening, Mon. *(Anne Cheston)*

UPTON BISHOP SO6326
★ Moody Cow (01989) 780470
B4221 E of Ross-on-Wye; HR9 7TT Tucked-away dining pub with modern rustic décor; L-shaped bar with sandstone walls, slate floor and woodburner, biggish raftered restaurant and second more intimate eating area, highly regarded freshly made food (can be pricey, some dishes available in smaller helpings), well kept ales and decent wines

including some local ones, friendly efficient service; children, dogs and boots welcome, garden growing own fruit/vegetables, courtyard bedroom up spiral staircase, closed Sun evening, Mon and Tues. *(Ian Duncan)*

WALTERSTONE SO3424
★ Carpenters Arms (01873) 890353
Follow Walterstone signs off A465; HR2 0DX Charming unspoilt stone cottage with unchanging traditional rooms (known locally as the Gluepot – once you're in you don't want to leave); beams, broad polished flagstones, a roaring fire in gleaming black range warming ancient settles against stripped-stone walls, Wadworths 6X and a guest tapped from the cask, enjoyable straightforward food in snug main dining room with mahogany tables and oak corner cupboards, another little dining area with old oak tables and church pews on more flagstones; no credit cards, outside lavatories are cold but in character; children welcome, open all day Sat. *(R T and J C Moggridge, James Landor)*

WELLINGTON HEATH SO7140
Farmers Arms (01531) 634776
Off B4214 just N of Ledbury – pub signed right, from top of village; Horse Road; HR8 1LS Roomy open-plan beamed pub with enjoyable generously served food (booking advised) with daily specials and two-course lunch menu (Wed-Fri), various themed nights, Otter, Wye Valley Butty Bach and a guest, friendly staff; free wi-fi; children and dogs welcome, picnic-sets on paved terrace, good walking country, open all day weekends, closed Mon (except bank holidays 12-4pm) and Tues lunchtime. *(Ian Duncan)*

WEOBLEY SO4051
Salutation (01544) 318443
Off A4112 SW of Leominster; HR4 8SJ Old beamed and timbered inn at top of delightful village green, enjoyable food cooked by chef-landlord from bar snacks up including set lunch/early evening deal, well kept ales such as Otter, Thwaites and Wye Valley, Robinson's cider, pleasant helpful service, bar and various dining areas, inglenook log fires; quiz/curry night first Weds of month; children welcome, sheltered back terrace, three bedrooms, good breakfast, open all day. *(Liz and Martin Eldon)*

WESTON-UNDER-PENYARD SO6323
Weston Cross Inn (01989) 562759
A40 E of Ross; HR9 7NU Creeper-clad roadside pub with good choice of enjoyable well priced food in bar or restaurant, Bass, Otter and a guest, Stowford Press cider, friendly helpful staff; children, walkers and dogs welcome, good-sized garden with plenty of picnic-sets and play area, open all day Sat, limited menu Sun evening. *(Guy Vowles)*

WHITBOURNE
SO7156

Live & Let Live (01886) 822276

Off A44 Bromyard–Worcester at Wheatsheaf; WR6 5SP Welcoming pub on southern edge of the village; good freshly made food from blackboard menu including interesting specials, well kept ales such as Ludlow and Wye Valley, friendly helpful staff, beams and nice log fire, big-windowed restaurant; quiz second Sat of month, live music last Sun; children welcome, garden with country views, open all day weekends, closed Mon lunchtime. *(Jill and Hugh Bennett)*

WIGMORE
SO4168

Oak (01568) 770424

Ford Street; HR6 9UJ Restored 16th-c coaching inn mixing original features with contemporary décor, well liked interesting food (not Tues) from sensibly short menu including lunchtime sandwiches, Hobsons and guests such as Greene King, traditional cider, cheerful helpful service; children and dogs welcome, two spacious bedrooms, open all day Sat, till 5pm Sun, closed Mon and lunchtime Tues. *(Mike Swan)*

WINFORTON
SO2946

Sun (01544) 327677

A438; HR3 6EA Friendly unpretentious village pub offering enjoyable freshly cooked food all sourced locally, Wye Valley Butty Bach and real ciders, country-style beamed areas either side of central servery, stripped stone and woodburners; background music; children and dogs welcome, garden picnic-sets, closed Sun evening, Mon and Tues. *(Audrey and Paul Summers)*

YARPOLE
SO4664

Bell (01568) 780537

Just off B4361 N of Leominster; HR6 0BD Welcoming old black and white village pub; beamed and carpeted lounge with log fire, large high-raftered restaurant in former cider mill (the stone press remains), enjoyable well priced pubby food (not Sun evening), three ales such as Brains, Sharps and Wye Valley, friendly attentive staff; Sun quiz; children and dogs welcome, garden picnic-sets, handy for Croft Castle (NT), open all day weekends. *(John and Claire Masters)*

Post Office address codings confusingly give the impression that a few pubs are in Herefordshire when they're really in Gloucestershire or even Wales (which is where we list them).

Hertfordshire

KEY ★ Star Pub 🌟 Top Quality Food 🍺 Great Beer
🍷 Good Wines £ Bargain Meals 🛏 Good Bedrooms 🍴 Serves Food

ASHWELL
TL2739 Map 5
Three Tuns 🍷
(01462) 743343 – www.thethreetunsashwell.co.uk

Off A505 NE of Baldock; High Street; SG7 5NL

**Bustling inn with a fair choice of drinks, tasty food served
by helpful staff, and substantial garden; attractive bedrooms**

This is one of several pretty buildings in a charming village; it became
a pub in 1806. The airy bar has an open fire, a long settle and cushioned
wooden dining chairs around tables (each set with a flowering plant in a
small pot), bare floorboards, a few high chairs around equally high tables
and pictures on pale walls above a blue dado. The atmosphere is friendly
and relaxed. Greene King IPA and a guest such as Belhaven Wembley 67 on
handpump, a dozen wines by the glass and 15 gins; background music. The
long Victorian-style dining room has a woodburning stove, built-in wall seats
and more cushioned wooden dining chairs around a mix of tables, and rugs
on floorboards. There are seats on the terrace and in the large garden with
apple trees. Bedrooms are comfortable and attractive (one is dog-friendly)
and breakfasts are good.

🍴 Imaginative food includes sandwiches, hot smoked flaked salmon and smoked
salmon with horseradish cream, local pork sausage in yorkshire pudding with
parsnip purée, apple and cider compote and onion jus, blue cheese, mushroom and
spinach pasta, fresh tuna niçoise, gammon chop with a poached egg and mustard cream
sauce, thai coconut chicken with wilted asian greens, tempura-battered haddock and
chips, and puddings such as spiced carrot, pistachio and almond cake with rosewater
cream and tarte au citron. *Benchmark main dish: lamb tagine £14.50. Two-course
evening meal £21.00.*

Greene King ~ Lease Bev Robinson ~ Real ale ~ Open 12-11; 12-9 Sun ~ Bar food 12-2.30, 6-9;
12-4, 6-10 Sat; 12-5 Sun ~ Restaurant ~ Children welcome ~ Dogs allowed in bar ~ Wi-fi ~
Bedrooms: /£100 *Recommended by David Jackman, Diane Abbott, Colin and Daniel Gibbs,
Ivy and George Goodwill*

BARNET
TQ2599 Map 5
Duke of York 🍷
(020) 8449 0297 – www.brunningandprice.co.uk/dukeofyork

Barnet Road (A1000); EN5 4SG

**Imposing place with reasonably priced bistro-style food
and enjoyable garden**

This was an important coaching inn on the main London–York route, and it's a rather grand building. Open doorways and stairs cleverly divide up the spreading rooms, while big windows and mirrors keep everything light and airy. There's a friendly, easy-going atmosphere and an eclectic mix of furniture on tiled or wooden flooring, hundreds of prints and photos on cream walls, fireplaces and thoughtful touches such as table lamps, books, rugs, fresh flowers and pot plants. Stools line the impressive counter where friendly staff serve Phoenix Brunning & Price Original plus guests such as Redemption Rock the Kazbek, Sambrooks Scrumdown, Truman Gypsy Queen and Wychwood Hobgoblin Gold on handpump, 20 wines by the glass, 30 gins and a large choice of whiskies; background music. The garden is particularly attractive, with seats, tables and picnic-sets on a tree-surrounded terrace and lawn, and a tractor in the good play area.

Enterprising food includes sandwiches, scallops with carrot purée, crispy pancetta, chervil and lemon dressing, chicken liver parfait with fig chutney, mussels with white wine, garlic and cream, cauliflower, chickpea and almond tagine with apricot and date couscous, cumberland sausages with onion gravy and mash, king prawn, chorizo and squid salad with roasted mediterranean vegetables and gazpacho dressing, warm crispy beef salad with cashews and sweet chilli dressing, and puddings such as glazed lemon tart with raspberry sorbet and crème brûlée. *Benchmark main dish: braised lamb shoulder with dauphinoise potatoes and gravy £17.45. Two-course evening meal £22.00.*

Brunning & Price ~ Manager John Johnston ~ Real ale ~ Open 11-11 (10.30 Sun) ~ Bar food 12-10 (9 Sun) ~ Restaurant ~ Children welcome until 8pm ~ Dogs allowed in bar ~ Wi-fi *Recommended by Charles Gysin, Sally and David Champion, Melanie and David Lawson, Peter and Emma Kelly, Usha and Terry Patel, Greta and Gavin Craddock*

BERKHAMSTED   SP9807 Map 5
Highwayman ♀
(01442) 285480 – www.highwaymanberkhamsted.com
High Street; HP4 1AQ

Bustling town pub, attractively refurbished, with plenty of room for both drinking and dining

Food does play a major part here, but the relaxed bar is a social place with Sharps Atlantic and Doom Bar, Timothy Taylors Landlord and a guest beer on handpump and good wines by the glass. It's a busy place and usefully open all day, so customers are always popping in and out. There are upholstered and leather chairs around all sorts of tables, lots of church candles in stubby holders and big windows overlooking the street; young staff are cheerful and helpful. The dining room has dark green leather wall seating, cushioned dining chairs around tables with barley-twist legs on bare boards and a bookcase mural at one end. Up some stairs, a mezzanine with rustic wooden walls offers more seating. There are seats and tables outside on the back terraced garden.

Good, modern food includes potted crab with avocado, prawn butter and toasted sourdough, a charcuterie plate for two, goats cheese, pea and mint ravioli with wilted vegetables, chicken and green pawpaw salad with coriander, mint, cashews and thai dressing, bouillabaisse with garlic croutons, beef bourguignon, duck leg confit with black cherry sauce, pot-roasted vegetables and dauphinoise potatoes, 30-day dry-aged cornish steaks with a choice of sauce, and puddings such as summer berry pavlova and english gooseberry compote with almond, ginger and cinnamon crumble and vanilla ice-cream. *Benchmark main dish: pie of the week £12.50. Two-course evening meal £21.00.*

White Brasserie Company ~ Manager Mike White ~ Real ale ~ Open 11-11 (10.30 Sun) ~ Bar food 12-10 (10.30 Fri, Sat); 12-9 Sun ~ Restaurant ~ Children welcome ~ Dogs allowed in bar ~ Wi-fi ~ Live music monthly (see website) *Recommended by Lindy Andrews, Sandra Hollies, Liz and Martin Eldon, Julian Thorpe, Belinda Stamp*

COTTERED
Bull

TL3229   Map 5

(01763) 281243 – www.thebullcottered.co.uk
A507 W of Buntingford; SG9 9QP

Busy dining pub in nice village, recently refurbished rooms, an easy-going feel, several ales, interesting food and seats in sizeable garden

The large attractive garden behind this well run pub is popular, with seats and tables under fine old trees; more seats at the front enjoy the view of the charming thatched cottages opposite. The interconnected bar and dining rooms have bare boards, contemporary paintwork, a woodburning stove and a log-effect gas fire, upholstered or cushioned dining chairs around dark wooden tables, tartan armchairs and button-back banquettes; also, fresh flowers, candles in big white lanterns, country prints above wooden dados and stone bottles and carpentry planes. Greene King IPA and Abbot on handpump and nine decent wines served by helpful staff.

A good choice of freshly cooked food includes sandwiches and toasties, twice-baked parmesan cheese soufflé, scallops, black pudding and chive cream, burgers with toppings, coleslaw and chips, wild mushroom and cheese risotto, a pie of the day, calves liver with sage and bacon, trio of pork (belly, tenderloin, cumberland sausage) with savoy cabbage and bacon, salmon with caesar salad and fresh anchovies, and puddings. *Benchmark main dish: omelette arnold bennett £11.00. Two-course evening meal £21.00.*

Greene King ~ Tenant Darren Perkins ~ Real ale ~ Open 12-3, 6.15-11; 12-10.30 Sun ~ Bar food 12-2, 6.30-9.30; 12-3.30, 6-8.30 Sun ~ Restaurant ~ Children welcome but no highchairs or changing facilities ~ Wi-fi ~ Dinner dance monthly *Recommended by Mrs Margo Finlay, Jörg Kasprowski, Alan and Angela Scouller, John and Delia Franks, Michael Sargent, Nik and Gloria Clarke*

EPPING GREEN
Beehive

TL2906   Map 5

(01707) 875959 – www.beehiveeppinggreen.co.uk
Off B158 SW of Hertford, via Little Berkhamsted; back road towards Newgate Street and Cheshunt; SG13 8NB

Cheerful bustling country pub, popular for its food – especially fish

For lovers of fresh fish, this attractive weatherboarded country pub is the place to head for. It's traditionally furnished and the low-ceilinged, beamed bar has a friendly, informal atmosphere, ornamental brasses and a woodburning stove in a panelled corner. Helpful staff serve Greene King Abbot and IPA and a changing local guest on handpump alongside a good range of ten wines by the glass; background music. Between the low building and quiet country road is a neat lawn and decked area, with plenty of tables for enjoying the summer sunshine. There are good woodland walks nearby.

Delivered fresh from Billingsgate daily, the fish dishes include prawn and avocado salad, fresh calamari, moules marinière, smoked haddock with a poached egg, and sea bass fillets on basil pesto; non-fishy dishes include halloumi bruschetta with tomato and red onion salsa, spinach and ricotta cannelloni, steak and mushroom pie, lamb shoulder with thyme gravy, and puddings such as gingerbread cheesecake and gluten-free hot chocolate fudge cake. *Benchmark main dish: beer-battered cod and chips £13.25. Two-course evening meal £18.50.*

Free house ~ Licensee Martin Squirrell ~ Real ale ~ Open 12-3, 5.30-11; 12-10.30 Sun ~
Bar food 12-2.30, 6-9.30 (9 in winter); 12-4, 6-8.30 Sun ~ Children welcome ~ Wi-fi
Recommended by Julie Wilkinson, Alison and Michael Harper, Frank and Marcia Pelling,
Luke Morgan, Louise and Oliver Redman

FLAUNDEN
Bricklayers Arms ⭐ ♀

TL0101   Map 5

(01442) 833322 – www.bricklayersarms.com

4 miles from M25 junction 18; village signposted off A41 – from village centre follow
Boxmoor, Bovingdon road and turn right at Belsize, Watford signpost into Hogpits
Bottom; HP3 0PH

•••
Hertfordshire Dining Pub of the Year

Cosy country restaurant with fairly elaborate food;
very good wine list

This civilised 18th-c dining pub was once two cottages and there are signs of this inside. It's mainly open-plan with stubs of knocked-through oak-timbered walls indicating the original room layout, and the well refurbished low-beamed bar is snug and comfortable, with a roaring log fire in winter. Stools line the brick counter where they keep Paradigm Touch Point, Tring Side Pocket for a Toad and Vale VPA on handpump, an extensive wine list with 20 by the glass and a good choice of spirits; background music. In summer, the terrace and beautifully kept old-fashioned garden have seats and tables. Just up the Belsize road, a path on the left leads through delightful woods to a forested area around Hollow Hedge. The pub is just 15 minutes by car from the Warner Bros Studios where the Harry Potter films were made; you can tour the studios but must book in advance.

 Sophisticated food includes white crab meat with home-smoked salmon, chive cream and blinis, a charcuterie board for two, a risotto of the day, pigeon breast with thyme jus and tempura artichoke hearts, sausages of the day with red wine and onion jus and chive mash, sea bream fillet with saffron and vegetable broth, pork fillet with pig trotter stuffing and marsala jus, slow-cooked ox cheek with a honey glaze, parsnip crumb and marjoram jus, and puddings such as caramel cheesecake with apricot sorbet and apple and rhubarb tart with vanilla ice-cream. *Benchmark main dish: barbary duck breast and duck confit with fig jus £19.95. Two-course evening meal £25.00.*

Free house ~ Licensee Alvin Michaels ~ Real ale ~ Open 12-11.30 (midnight Sat);
12-9.30 Sun ~ Bar food 12-2.30, 6.15-9.30; 12-7 Sun and bank holidays ~ Restaurant ~
Children welcome ~ Dogs allowed in bar ~ Wi-fi *Recommended by David Longhurst,*
Renrag, Moira and John Wheeler, Daniel King, Karl and Frieda Bujeya

FRITHSDEN
Alford Arms ⭐ ♀

TL0109   Map 5

(01442) 864480 – www.alfordarmsfrithsden.co.uk

A4146 from Hemel Hempstead to Water End, then second left (after Red Lion) signed
Frithsden, then left at T junction, then right after 0.25 miles; HP1 3DD

Thriving dining pub with a chic interior, good food from imaginative
menu and a thoughtful wine list

The elegant, understated interior in this pretty Victorian pub has simple prints on pale cream walls, with blocks picked out in rich heritage colours, and an appealing mix of antique furniture from Georgian chairs to old commode stands on bare boards and patterned quarry tiles. A good mix of both drinkers and diners creates a cheerful atmosphere, and helpful staff serve Leighton Buzzard Borrowers Bitter, Tring Side Pocket for a Toad and a changing guest on handpump, 23 wines by the glass (including two sparkling ones), 18 gins and 22 whiskies and bourbons; background jazz and darts. There are plenty of tables outside, and the pub is surrounded by lovely National Trust woodland.

Good, contemporary food includes local goats cheese fondant with rhubarb chutney and home-made foccacia, grilled mackerel fillet with beetroot and horseradish salsa, moroccan-style sweet potato and chickpea stew with tahini yoghurt, rabbit leg bourguignon, local free-range sausages of the day, salmon fillet with baked beetroot and dill gnocchi, free-range confit pork belly with sweet potato mash, jerusalem artichoke and black garlic dressing, and puddings such as caramel popcorn pannacotta with salted popcorn and corn ice-cream and apple tarte tatin with muscovado ice-cream. *Benchmark main dish: bubble and squeak with oak-smoked bacon, free-range poached egg and hollandaise £11.75. Two-course evening meal £22.00.*

Salisbury Pubs ~ Lease Darren Johnston ~ Real ale ~ Open 11-11; 12-11 Sun ~ Bar food 12-2.30, 6.30-9.30; 12-3, 6-10 Fri, Sat; 12-9 Sun ~ Restaurant ~ Children welcome ~ Dogs allowed in bar ~ Wi-fi *Recommended by Alf Wright, Daniel King, Sandra Hollies, Ian Duncan, Patricia and Gordon Thompson, Professor James Burke, Margo and Derek Stapley, Tracey and Stephen Groves*

HERTFORD HEATH

College Arms

TL3510 Map 5

(01992) 558856 – www.thecollegearmshertfordheath.com
London Road; B1197; SG13 7PW

Light and airy rooms with contemporary furnishings, friendly service, good, interesting food and real ales; seats outside

This is a civilised, well run place with attention to detail and a good mix of locals and visitors – our readers enjoy their visits. The bar has long cushioned wall seats and pale leather dining chairs around tables on rugs or wooden floorboards, and a modern bar counter where attentive staff serve Goddards Fuggle-Dee-Dum and Wickwar Falling Star on handpump and 20 wines by the glass; background music. Another area has more long wall seats and an open fireplace piled with logs, and there's also a charming little room with brown leather armchairs, a couple of cushioned pews, a woodburning stove in an old brick fireplace, hunting-themed wallpaper and another rug on floorboards. The elegant, partly carpeted dining room contains a real mix of antique-style dining chairs and tables. On the back terrace are tables, seats and a long wooden bench among flowering pots.

The extremely good food is modern British with pub classics and includes sandwiches, bacon terrine with tomato jam and charred lettuce, smoked fishcake with a poached egg and béarnaise sauce, a pie of the day, roasted cauliflower, brie croquette, potato terrine and leeks, burger with toppings, burger sauce and fries, lamb saddle with wild garlic dumplings and green sauce, cod with prawn ravioli, sorrel and sea vegetables, ox cheek with watercress mash, onions and sour cream, and puddings. *Benchmark main dish: beer-battered fish and chips £13.00. Two-course evening meal £23.00.*

Punch ~ Lease Andy Lilley ~ Real ale ~ Open 12-11 (midnight Fri, Sat); 12-8 Sun ~ Bar food 12-3, 6-9; 12-7 Sun ~ Restaurant ~ Children welcome ~ Dogs allowed in bar ~ Wi-fi ~ Live music last Fri of month *Recommended by Sandra Morgan, Colin and Daniel Gibbs, Douglas Power, WAH, David Hunt*

POTTERS CROUCH
TL1105 Map 5

Holly Bush ◕ £

(01727) 851792 – www.thehollybushpub.co.uk

2.25 miles from M25 junction 21A: A405 towards St Albans, then first left, then after a mile turn left (ie away from Chiswell Green), then at T junction turn right into Blunts Lane; can also be reached fairly quickly, with a good map, from M1 exits 6 and 8; AL2 3NN

Neat pub with gleaming furniture, well kept Fullers beers, good value food and an attractive garden

The dreary M25 is just a couple of miles away, so this well tended cottage makes a welcome escape from the traffic jams. The long, stepped bar has particularly well kept Fullers ESB, London Pride, Seafarers and a Fullers seasonal beer on handpump and several wines by the glass. There are quite a few antique dressers (several filled with plates), a number of comfortably cushioned settles, a fox's mask, some antlers, a fine old clock with a lovely chime, daily papers and (on the right as you enter) a big fireplace. In the evening, neatly placed candles cast glimmering light over darkly varnished tables, all sporting fresh flowers. The fenced-off back garden has plenty of sturdy picnic-sets on a lawn surrounded by handsome trees.

Food is well liked and includes brussels pâté with apple and ale chutney, smoked salmon with lemon crème fraîche, sharing plates, steak and stilton pie, lamb koftas with feta salad, tzatziki and toasted flatbread, chilli beef con carne, chicken or spicy bean burgers with toppings and chips, teriyaki salmon with crispy kale and rice, and puddings such as golden syrup sponge with custard and chocolate fondant with ice-cream. *Benchmark main dish: steak in ale pie £12.50. Two-course evening meal £16.00.*

Fullers ~ Tenants Steven and Vanessa Williams ~ Real ale ~ Open 12-2.30, 6-11; 12-3, 7-10 Sun ~ Bar food 12-2 (2.30 Sun), 6-9; not Sun-Tues evenings ~ Children welcome
Recommended by Max and Steph Warren, Peter and Emma Kelly, Paul Farraday

PRESTON
TL1824 Map 5

Red Lion ◕ £

(01462) 459585 – www.theredlionpreston.co.uk
Village signposted off B656 S of Hitchin; The Green; SG4 7UD

Homely village local with changing beers, fair-priced food and neat colourful garden

There's a genuinely cheerful welcome for both locals and visitors in this village pub which has been owned by the community since 1982 – it was the first in the country to do this – and it's been a roaring success ever since. The main room on the left, with grey wainscoting, has sturdy, well varnished furniture including padded country kitchen chairs and cast-iron-framed tables on patterned carpet, a generous window seat, fox hunting prints and a log fire in a brick fireplace. The somewhat smaller room on the right has steeplechase prints, varnished plank panelling and brocaded bar stools on flagstones around the servery; background music, darts and dominoes. Fullers London Pride and Youngs Bitter on handpump with guests such as Oakham Akhenaten and Oldershaw Grantham Stout, four farm ciders, ten wines by the glass (including an english house wine), a perry and winter mulled wine. A few picnic-sets on grass at the front face lime trees on the peaceful village green opposite, while the pergola-covered back terrace and good-sized sheltered garden with its colourful herbaceous border have seats and picnic-sets (some shade is provided by a tall ash tree).

🍴 Reasonably priced food includes sandwiches, prawns with garlic and chilli, stilton-stuffed mushrooms, spinach and mushroom lasagne, chicken curry, chilli con carne, liver and bacon with onion gravy, fish dish of the day, venison bourguignon, and puddings such as crème brûlée and passion-fruit pavlova. *Benchmark main dish: fish pie £12.50. Two-course evening meal £16.00.*

Free house ~ Licensee Raymond Lambe ~ Real ale ~ Open 12-2.30, 5.30-11; 12-3.30, 5.30-midnight Sat; 12-3.30, 7-10.30 Sun ~ Bar food 12-2, 6.30-8.30; not Sun evening, Mon ~ Children welcome ~ Dogs welcome ~ Wi-fi *Recommended by Anne Taylor, Alan and Angela Scouller, Karum, William Pace, Charles Welch, Lindy Andrews*

REDBOURN
Cricketers 🍺

TL1011 Map 5

(01582) 620612 – www.thecricketersofredbourn.co.uk
3.2 miles from M1 junction 9; A5183 signed Redbourn/St Albans, at second roundabout follow B487 for Hemel Hempstead, first right into Chequer Lane, then third right into East Common; AL3 7ND

Good food and beer in attractively updated pub with a bar and two restaurants

Redbourn Common is opposite and many other walking and cycling opportunites surround this popular village pub. The relaxed front bar is decorated in country style: comfortable tub chairs, cushioned bench seating and high-backed bar stools on pale brown carpet, and a woodburning stove. Five quickly changing ales on handpump include St Austell Tribute and Tring Side Pocket for a Toad with guests such as Sharps Doom Bar, Shepherd Neame Spitfire and Tring Apache, 16 wines by the glass, farm cider, several malt whiskies and good coffee; background music. This bar leads back into an attractive, comfortably refurbished and unusually shaped modern restaurant; there's also an upstairs contemporary restaurant for private parties or functions. A side garden has plenty of seating and summer barbecues. They can help with information on the Redbourn Village Museum next door.

🍴 Likeable food includes sandwiches (not Sunday lunchtime), crispy fried squid with sweet chilli jam, ham hock terrine with pickles and piccalilli, gnocchi with asparagus, ricotta and wild mushrooms, beer-battered cod and chips, calves liver with bacon, bubble and squeak and onion gravy, chicken breast wrapped in pancetta and stuffed with blue cheese on chive mash with wild mushroom sauce, red mullet fillet with crab and creamy mussel sauce, and puddings such as vanilla pannacotta with strawberry and basil compote and chocolate torte with white chocolate mousse and cherry coulis. *Benchmark main dish: crayfish and chilli risotto £12.90. Two-course evening meal £20.00.*

Free house ~ Licensees Colin and Debbie Baxter ~ Real ale ~ Open 12-11; 12-11.30 Thurs; 12-midnight Fri, Sat; 12-10.30 Sun ~ Bar food 12-3, 6-9; 12-4 Sun ~ Restaurant ~ Children welcome ~ Dogs allowed in bar ~ Wi-fi *Recommended by Richard Kennell, Sarah Roberts, Carol and Barry Craddock, Lorna and Jack Mulgrave, Patrick and Emma Stephenson, John and Claire Masters*

SARRATT
Cricketers 🍷 🍺

TQ0499 Map 5

(01923) 270877 – www.brunningandprice.co.uk/cricketers
The Green; WD3 6AS

Plenty to look at in rambling rooms, up to six real ales, nice wines, enjoyable food and friendly staff; seats outside

It's really worth wandering around this cleverly refurbished pub before you decide where you want to sit as the interlinked rooms have numerous little snugs and alcoves – perfect for a quiet drink. There are all manner of antique dining chairs and tables on rugs or stripped floorboards, comfortable armchairs or tub seats, cushioned pews, wall seats and two open fires in raised fireplaces; decoration includes cricketing memorabilia, fresh flowers, large plants and church candles. Phoenix Brunning & Price Original plus guests such as 3 Brewers Dark Mild, Chiltern Earl Grey IPA, Otley American Brown and Timothy Taylors Dark Mild on handpump, good wines by the glass, 30 gins and 50 malt whiskies; background music and board games. Several sets of french windows open on to the back terrace where there are tables and chairs, with picnic-sets on grass next to a colourfully painted tractor; seats at the front overlook the village green and duck pond.

Interesting food includes sandwiches, smoked trout with lime crème fraîche, potted pork with juniper and thyme with caramelised apple and crackling, honey-roasted ham and eggs, butternut squash, spinach and blue cheese pie and port jus, sea bass fillets with potato cake and mussel and white wine sauce, cumberland sausages with mash and onion gravy, rump steak with garlic and horseradish butter and chips, and puddings such as hot waffle with caramelised banana, toffee sauce and honeycomb ice-cream and rhubarb cheesecake with lemon sorbet and ginger syrup. *Benchmark main dish: burger with toppings, coleslaw and chips £12.95. Two-course evening meal £22.00.*

Brunning & Price ~ Licensee David Stowell ~ Real ale ~ Open 10am-11pm (10.30pm Sun) ~ Bar food 12-10 (9.30 Sun) ~ Restaurant ~ Children welcome ~ Dogs allowed in bar ~ Wi-fi
Recommended by John Harris, Mrs Margo Finlay, Jörg Kasprowski, Geoff and Ann Marston, Martin Jones, Tracey and Stephen Groves

ST ALBANS
Prae Wood Arms ♀ ⬤
TL1308 Map 5

(01727) 229090 – www.brunningandprice.co.uk/praewoodarms
Garden House Lane; AL3 6JZ

Spreading manor house in extensive grounds, with interestingly furnished rooms with plenty to look at, a fine range of drinks and modern brasserie-style food

The lovely grounds surrounding this large and rather gracious pub include a partly covered big stone terrace with lots of good quality tables and chairs under green parasols, picnic-sets on grass and lawns that slope down to the River Ver at the bottom. Inside, the various interconnected bar and dining areas have five open fires (one with button-back leather armchairs to each side) and a lively, chatty atmosphere – though there are more intimate crannies too. Throughout, antique-style dining chairs and tables of every size and shape sit on bare boards, parquet and carpet, pale-painted walls are hung with portraits, prints and huge mirrors, elegant metal or glass chandeliers hang from high ceilings and the Brunning & Price trademark bookshelves, house plants and stone and glass bottles are much in evidence. Wooden stools line the counter where friendly, courteous young staff serve Phoenix Brunning & Price Original with guests such as 3 Brewers Dark Mild, London Fields Shoreditch Triangle IPA, Mad Squirrel Mister Squirrel, Redemption Hopspur and Tring Side Pocket for a Toad on handpump, 18 wines by the glass and 54 gins; background music and board games. The loos are upstairs.

Imaginative food includes sandwiches, almond-crusted squid with soy, lime and sesame seed dip, roast garlic mushrooms with crispy tarragon polenta and goats cheese, smoked mackerel, leek and sour cream quiche, steak in ale pie, pork belly with braised borlotti beans, chorizo, smoked paprika and rainbow chard, salmon fillet with salmon gravadlax, boiled egg, new potato salad and gribiche sauce, and puddings such as dark and white chocolate brownie with chocolate sauce and apple and blackberry crumble. *Benchmark main dish: burger with toppings, coleslaw and chips £12.95. Two-course evening meal £22.00.*

Brunning & Price ~ Manager Sal Morgan ~ Real ale ~ Open 11-11 (10.30 Sun) ~ Bar food 12-10.30 (9.30 Sun) ~ Children welcome ~ Dogs allowed in bar ~ Wi-fi *Recommended by Audrey and Paul Summers, Cliff and Monica Swan, Sandra Morgan, Nick Higgins*

 ST ALBANS   TL1407   Map 5
Verulam Arms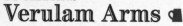
(01727) 836004 – www.the-foragers.com
Lower Dagnall Street; AL3 4QE

Quirky, enjoyable pub with foraged ingredients used in both the creative food and own-made drinks

Certainly different, this unusual pub is in a quieter part of town and, once found, our readers enjoy their visits here a lot. It's run by a team of hunters and gatherers who use wild game, fruit and fungi for their interesting food, and also brew their own ale with wild ingredients; they also make their own liqueurs and cocktails such as woodruff and apple vodka or a martini that uses sloe gin, vermouth and douglas fir syrup (a sort of christmas-tree-with-grapefruit taste). You can also buy tickets to join them on their foraging walks. Furnishings and décor throughout are simple: scrubbed tables surrounded by all manner of old dining chairs on floorboards, fireplaces with big gilt-edged mirrors above, a few prints on sage green paintwork, large blackboards with daily specials listed, frosted windows and candles. High chairs line the counter where they serve their own Foragers St Cloak Stout, Sling Shot and a quickly changing guest on handpump; also, beers from all over the world, tapped from the cask and in bottles, and cider. The gravelled garden has brightly painted picnic-sets and a heated awning where they grow hops and grapes.

Food is seasonal and creative and might include shredded slow-cooked muntjac and blue cheese risotto rice balls with wild berry syrup, sloe gin-cured sea trout with horseradish and lady's smock wasabi, pickled sea vegetables and wholemeal crisps, elderflower vegetable motley with elderflower cream with chestnuts and walnuts, water-mint butter and courgette fritters, hake with crushed new potatoes, chorizo and samphire, 24-hour birch-smoked lamb shank in hogweed seeds and paprika with hedge mustard mash, and puddings such as cheesecake using seasonal plants and sticky toffee pudding; they also offer a two- and three-course set menu (not Fri-Sun evenings or Sun lunch). *Benchmark main dish: pork belly with pickled crab apples, purée and mash with alexander seeds £14.50. Two-course evening meal £21.00.*

Free house ~ Licensee George Fredenham ~ Real ale ~ Open 12-11 (midnight Fri, Sat) ~ Bar food 12-3, 6.30-9 (10 Fri, Sat); 12-4 Sun ~ Restaurant ~ Well behaved children welcome ~ Dogs welcome ~ Wi-fi *Recommended by Kate Moran, Patricia Hawkins, Edward Nile, Paul Humphreys, James and Becky Plath, Andrea and Philip Crispin, Bridget and Peter Gregson, Peter and Emma Kelly*

 WATTON-AT-STONE   TL3019   Map 5
Bull
(01920) 831032 – www.thebullwatton.co.uk
High Street; SG14 3SB

Bustling old pub with beamed rooms, candlelight and fresh flowers, real ales and enjoyable food served by friendly staff

The huge inglenook fireplace in the middle of this charming 15th-c pub is a magnet for customers on chilly evenings. There's a relaxed atmosphere, friendly staff, fresh flowers, contemporary paintwork, a leather button-back chesterfield and armchairs, solid dark wooden dining chairs and plush-topped stools around tables on bare boards and a leather banquette beside a landscape-patterned wall. Adnams Ghost Ship and Sharps Atlantic and Doom Bar on handpump and good wines by the glass; background music. Near the entrance are some high bar chairs along counters by the windows; from here, it's a step up to a cosy room with just four tables, decorative logs in a fireplace, books on shelves, board games and an old typewriter. At the other end of the building is an elegantly furnished dining room (part-carpeted and part-slate floored). Outside, a covered terrace has seats and tables, there are picnic-sets on grass plus a small well equipped play area. This is a pretty village.

Food is enjoyable and includes sandwiches, baked camembert with red onion jam, potted crab and crayfish with tomato and basil butter, pea, tarragon and truffle risotto with a poached egg, barbecue pork spare ribs with coleslaw, beans and fries, lamb curry with onion bhaji, sag aloo and yoghurt, chicken, leek and mustard open pie, hake fillet with clam, mussel and crayfish chowder, and puddings such as sticky toffee pudding with toffee sauce and crème brûlée with apricot and almond compote. *Benchmark main dish: burger with toppings, coleslaw and fries £12.95. Two-course evening meal £22.00.*

Punch ~ Lease Alastair and Anna Bramley ~ Real ale ~ Open 9.30am-11pm; 12-6 Sun; closed Sun evening ~ Bar food 12-3, 6-10; 12-4, 6-10 Sat; 12-4 Sun ~ Restaurant ~ Children welcome ~ Dogs allowed in bar ~ Wi-fi *Recommended by Sally Wright, James Landor, Daphne and Robert Staples, Adam Jones, Amy Ledbetter, Nik and Gloria Clarke*

Also Worth a Visit in Hertfordshire

Besides the fully inspected pubs, you might like to try these pubs that have been recommended to us and described by readers. Do tell us what you think of them: feedback@goodguides.com

ALDBURY   SP9612
Greyhound (01442) 851228
Stocks Road; village signed from A4251 Tring–Berkhamsted, and from B4506; HP23 5RT Picturesque village pub with some signs of real age inside; inglenook in cosy traditional beamed bar, more contemporary area with leather chairs, airy oak-floored back barn restaurant with wicker chairs at big tables, Badger ales and a dozen wines by the glass, generally well liked food from lunchtime sandwiches, sharing plates and pubby choices up, set menu Mon-Thurs; children welcome, dogs in bar, front benches facing green with whipping post, stocks and duck pond, suntrap gravel courtyard, eight bedrooms (some in newer building behind), open all day, food all day weekends (till 7.30pm Sun). *(Julian Thorpe)*

ALDBURY   SP9612
★**Valiant Trooper** (01442) 851203
Trooper Road (towards Aldbury Common); off B4506 N of Berkhamsted; HP23 5RW Cheery traditional 17th-c village pub; appealing beamed bar with red and black floor tiles, built-in wall benches, a pew and small dining chairs around country tables, two further rooms (one with inglenook) and back barn restaurant, enjoyable generously served food (all day Sat, not Sun or Mon evenings), Chiltern, Tring and three guests, five ciders and plenty of wines by the glass, friendly helpful staff; background music, free wi-fi; children and dogs (in bar) welcome, enclosed garden with wooden adventure playground, well placed for Ashridge Estate beechwoods, open all day. *(Brian Glozier)*

ALDENHAM   TQ1498
Round Bush (01923) 855532
Roundbush Lane; WD25 8BG Cheery and bustling traditional village pub with plenty of atmosphere; two front rooms and back restaurant, popular generously served food at fair prices, well kept Charles Wells ales and a guest such as St Austell, friendly efficient staff; quiz first Weds of month, occasional live music, darts; children and dogs welcome, big enclosed garden with play area, good walks, open (and food) all day. *(Charles Welch)*

ALLENS GREEN TL4517
Queens Head (01279) 723393
Village signed from West Road, Sawbridgeworth; CM21 0LS Friendly semi-detached village drinkers' pub, four well kept beers (many more on the third weekend of the month) and good range of ciders/perries, straightforward reasonably priced food; live music and beer festivals; dogs welcome, large garden, open all day weekends, closed lunchtimes Mon and Tues. *(Kevin Bilton)*

ARDELEY TL3027
★Jolly Waggoner (01438) 861350
Off B1037 NE of Stevenage; SG2 7AH Traditional beamed pub with lots of nooks and corners, inglenook log fire, up to four well kept changing ales (usually one from Buntingford), plenty of wines by the glass including some organic ones, good reasonably priced home-made food with much sourced from farm opposite (rare-breed meat), friendly service, restaurant with linen tablecloths; children and dogs welcome, large garden, open all day, food all day Sat, till 7pm Sun. *(Jake)*

ASHWELL TL2639
Bushel & Strike (01462) 742394
Off A507 just E of A1(M) junction 10, N of Baldock, via Newnham; Mill Street opposite church, via Gardiners Lane (car park down Swan Lane); SG7 5LY Smartly modernised 19th-c village dining pub (originally a brewery), good attractively presented food (Sun till 6pm) from chef-landlord's interesting menus including set choices and occasional themed nights, Charles Wells ales and nice selection of wines by the glass, friendly service; wheelchair access, picnic-sets on lawn and small terrace with view of church, closed Mon, otherwise open all day (till 10pm Sun). *(Graham and Carol Parker)*

AYOT ST LAWRENCE TL1916
Brocket Arms (01438) 820250
Off B651 N of St Albans; AL6 9BT Attractive 14th-c country inn with low beams and inglenook log fires, good traditional food (special diets catered for) in bar and restaurant, friendly helpful staff, six real ales such as Greene King, Nethergate and Sharps, wide choice of wines by the glass; live music including jazz and open mike nights, quiz second Sun of the month; children welcome, dogs in bar, nice suntrap walled garden with play area, handy for George Bernard Shaw's house (Shaw's Corner – NT), six comfortable bedrooms, open all day, no food Sun evening. *(WAH)*

BALDOCK TL2433
Orange Tree (01462) 892341
Norton Road; SG7 5AW Unpretentious old two-bar pub with up to 13 well kept

ales including Buntingford and Greene King, four real ciders and large selection of whiskies, good value locally sourced home-made food (all day Sat, till 6pm Sun) including range of pies and blackboard specials, friendly young staff, games room with bar billiards; quiz Tues, folk club Weds; children welcome and dogs (theirs is Arthur), garden with play area and chickens, open all day Thurs-Sun. *(John Pritchard)*

BARKWAY TL3834
Tally Ho (01763) 848071
London Road (B1368); SG8 8EX Little village-edge pub with clean modern décor, mix of wooden furniture on light boarded floor, log fire in central brick fireplace, three changing ales and good range of other drinks, enjoyable home-made food (not Sun evening) from lunchtime sandwiches up, friendly efficient staff; quiz second Weds of month; children welcome, decked seating area at front, picnic-sets and weeping willow in garden beyond car park, open all day from 9am (till 7pm Sun). *(Ross Balaam)*

BENINGTON TL3023
Bell (01438) 869827
Town Lane; just past Post Office, towards Stevenage; SG2 7LA Traditional 16th-c pub in very pretty village, local beers such as Buntingford and enjoyable caribbean food (licensees are from Trinidad), low beams, sloping walls and big inglenook; occasional folk nights and other events; big garden with country views, handy for Benington Lordship Gardens, open all day Sun (food till 6pm), closed Mon and lunchtimes Tues and Weds. *(Melanie and David Lawson)*

BERKHAMSTED SP9907
Boat (01422) 877152
Gravel Path, by bridge; HP4 2EF Cheerfully refurbished open-plan Fullers dining pub in attractive canalside setting (can get packed in fine weather), their ales kept well and guests, cocktails and good choice of wines by the glass, popular food from lunchtime sandwiches and small plates to daily specials, mix of seating including padded stools and leather chesterfields on mainly parquet flooring, painted panelling and contemporary artwork, a couple of Victorian fireplaces; background music, live jazz Sun afternoon; children and dogs welcome, french windows to paved terrace overlooking towpath and canal, moorings, open (and food) all day. *(Taff Thomas, Richard Kennell)*

BERKHAMSTED SP9907
Old Mill (01442) 879590
London Road/Bank Mill Lane (A4251); HP4 2NB Sizeable Peach dining pub with attractive rambling layout, good choice of enjoyable food from deli boards up including weekday set menu (till 6pm), well kept Greene King IPA, Tring Side Pocket for

a Toad and a couple of guests, plenty of wines by the glass, interesting gins and cocktails, friendly service, two good fires; children and dogs (in bar) welcome, tables outside by mill race, some overlooking unspectacular stretch of Grand Union Canal, open (and food) all day. *(Ross Balaam)*

BERKHAMSTED   SP9907
Rising Sun (01442) 864913
George Street; HP4 2EG Victorian canalside pub known locally as the Riser; five well kept ales including one badged for them from Tring, up to 30 ciders/perries (four beer/cider festivals a year) and interesting range of spirits, two very small traditional rooms with a few basic chairs and tables, coal fire, snuff and cigars for sale, no food apart from substantial ploughman's, friendly service; background music, Thurs quiz; children and dogs welcome, chairs out by canal and well worn seating in covered side beer garden, colourful hanging baskets, open all day. *(Taff Thomas, Richard Kennell)*

BISHOP'S STORTFORD   TL5021
Nags Head (01279) 654553
Dunmow Road; CM23 5HP Well restored 1930s art deco pub (Grade II listed), McMullens ales from island servery and plenty of wines by the glass, wide choice of enjoyable reasonably priced food, good service; quiz last Weds of month, free wi-fi; children welcome, no dogs inside, garden with play area, open all day. *(Doug Jackson)*

BRAUGHING   TL3925
Axe & Compass (01920) 821610
Just off B1368; The Street; SG11 2QR Nice country pub in pretty village with ford; enjoyable freshly prepared food (all day Sat, till 6pm Sun) from varied menu, own-baked bread, well kept ales including Harveys and several wines by the glass, friendly uniformed staff, mix of furnishings on wood floors in two roomy bars, lots of old local photographs, log fires, restaurant with little shop selling home-made chutney and relish; well behaved children and dogs welcome, garden overlooking playing field, outside bar. *(Paul Faraday)*

BRAUGHING   TL3925
Brown Bear (01920) 822157
Just off B1368; The Street; SG11 2QF Steps up to traditional little low-beamed pub with inglenook log fire in bar, up to four well kept changing ales and enjoyable home-cooked pubby food (not Mon, Tues) from ciabattas to good fish and chips, friendly staff, dining room with another good fire; Thurs quiz, occasional live music, games including darts, dominoes and shove-ha'penny; tricky disabled access, picnic-sets in garden behind with pizza oven, barbecue and pétanque, attractive village, open 3-6pm Mon, 3-11pm Tues, closed Sun evening, otherwise open all day. *(Charles Welch)*

BRAUGHING   TL3925
Golden Fleece (01920) 823555
Green End (B1368); SG11 2PE 17th-c dining pub with good food (special diets catered for) from chef-landlord including some imaginative choices, popular tapas night last Weds of the month and curry evenings, Adnams Southwold and guests, plenty of wines by the glass, cheerful service, bare-boards bar and two dining rooms, beams and timbers, good log fire; summer beer festival; children welcome, circular picnic-sets out at front, back garden with metal furniture on split-level paved terrace, play area, open all day weekends (food till 6pm Sun). *(Peter and Emma Kelly)*

BRICKET WOOD   TL1302
Gate (01923) 678944
Station Road/Smug Oak Lane; AL2 3PW Popular family pub with good sensibly priced home-cooked food including british tapas, Charles Wells and guests, friendly service, bar with log fire and side dining area; quiz Mon, free wi-fi; dogs welcome, garden, open all day. *(Usha and Terry Patel)*

BUSHEY   TQ1394
Horse & Chains (020) 8421 9907
High Street; WD23 1BL Comfortably modernised dining pub with woodburner in big inglenook, good choice of wines by the glass, real ales and enjoyable bar food from sandwiches and sharing plates up, also separate restaurant menu, themed nights and Sun brunch, kitchen view from compact dining room, good friendly service; children welcome, open (and food) all day. *(Frank and Marcia Pelling)*

CHAPMORE END   TL3216
Woodman (01920) 463339
Off B158 Wadesmill–Bengeo; pub signed 300 metres W of A602 roundabout; OS Sheet 166 map reference 328164; SG12 0HF Early Victorian local in peaceful country hamlet; plain seats around stripped pub tables, floor tiles or broad bare boards, working period fireplaces, two well kept Greene King ales and guests poured from the cask, friendly staff, no food apart from summer Sun barbecues, conservatory; children and dogs welcome, picnic-sets out in front under a couple of walnut trees, bigger back garden with fenced play area and boules, closed Mon lunchtime, otherwise open all day. *(Max and Steph Warren)*

CHIPPERFIELD   TL0400
Cart & Horses (01923) 263763
Quickmoor Lane/Common Wood; WD4 9BA Smallish 18th-c wisteria-clad pub popular for its enjoyable generously served food including bargain specials, two or three well kept changing ales and good choice of wines by the glass, friendly staff; children and dogs welcome, picnic-sets in

big garden with marquee and play area, nice surrounding countryside and walks, open all day weekends, food all day Sun. *(Ian Duncan)*

CHORLEYWOOD   TQ0395
★ **Black Horse** (01923) 282252

Dog Kennel Lane, The Common; WD3 5EG Welcoming 18th-c country pub popular for its good value generous food (smaller helpings available) from sandwiches to daily specials, five well kept ales including Adnams, Wadworths, Wells and Youngs, decent wines, tea and coffee, good cheery service even when busy, low dark beams and two log fires in thoroughly traditional rambling bar; daily papers and free wi-fi, open mike night second Sun of month; children, walkers and dogs welcome, disabled access, picnic-sets overlooking common, parking can be difficult, open all day, food all day Sun till 7pm. *(Roy Hoing)*

CHORLEYWOOD   TQ0294
Land of Liberty, Peace & Plenty (01923) 282226

Long Lane, Heronsgate, just off M25 junction 17; WD3 5BS Traditional 19th-c drinkers' pub in leafy outskirts, half a dozen well kept interesting ales and good choice of ciders/perries, snacky food such as pasties, simple layout, darts, skittles and board games; background jazz, TV (on request), no mobile phones or children inside; dogs on leads welcome, garden with pavilion, open all day. *(Tim West)*

CHORLEYWOOD   TQ0295
Stag (01923) 282090

Long Lane, Heronsgate, just off M25 junction 17; WD3 5BT Open-plan Edwardian dining pub with good varied choice of food from sandwiches and tapas up, well kept McMullens ales and several wines by the glass, friendly attentive service, bar and eating areas extending into conservatory, woodburner in raised hearth; daily papers, free wi-fi; children and dogs welcome, tables on back lawn, open all day, food all day Weds-Sun. *(Jake, Brian Glozier, Richard Kennell)*

CHORLEYWOOD   TQ0396
White Horse (01923) 282227

A404, just off M25 junction 18; WD3 5SD Black-beamed roadside pub under good new management, food such as pizzas, tapas and panini, Greene King ales, helpful staff, big log fire; children and dogs (in bar) welcome, small back terrace, open all day. *(Mr and Mrs J Watkins)*

COLNEY HEATH   TL2007
Plough (01727) 823720

Sleapshyde; handy for A1(M) junction 3; A414 towards St Albans, double back at first roundabout then turn left; AL4 0SE Cosy 18th-c low-beamed thatched local with friendly chatty atmosphere, good value generous home-made food (not Sun-Tues evenings) from lunchtime baked potatoes up, well kept Greene King, St Austell and a guest, big log fire, small brighter back dining area; charity quiz first Tues of month, darts and dominoes, sports TV, free wi-fi; children welcome, no dogs during food times, front and back terraces, picnic-sets on lawn overlooking fields, open all day weekends. *(Doug Jackson)*

ESSENDON   TL2608
Candlestick (01707) 261322

West End Lane; AL9 6BA Peacefully located country pub under same ownership as the nearby Woodman at Wildhill; emphasis on dining but also three well kept beers and several wines by the glass, relaxed friendly atmosphere, good value freshly prepared bar and restaurant food, comfortable clean interior with faux black timbers, log fires; quiz nights; children and dogs welcome, plenty of seats outside, good walks, closed Mon and Tues, otherwise open all day (till 5pm Sun). *(Jestyn Phillips)*

FLAUNDEN   TL0100
Green Dragon (01442) 832269

Flaunden Hill; HP3 0PP Comfortable and chatty 17th-c beamed pub in same family for three generations; partly panelled extended lounge, back restaurant and traditional little tap bar, log fire, popular good value food (not Mon) with emphasis on thai dishes, Fullers, St Austell and Youngs, friendly helpful service; background music, darts and other pub games; children and dogs welcome, hitching rail for horses, well kept garden with smokers' shelter, pretty village, only a short diversion from Chess Valley Walk, closed Sun evening and Mon lunchtime. *(Jake)*

GILSTON   TL4313
Plume of Feathers (01279) 424154

Pye Corner; CM20 2RD Old beamed corner pub with decent choice of well priced food (all day Fri-Sun) including cook-your-own meat on a volcanic rock, Courage Best, Adnams Broadside and local guests, Weston's cider and maybe a mulled winter one, good choice of wines by the glass, pleasant staff, carpeted interior with brass-hooded log fire; background music, free wi-fi; children welcome, seats on terrace and fenced grassy area with play equipment. *(Jane and Philip Saunders)*

GOSMORE   TL1827
Bull (01462) 440035

High Street; SG4 7QG Popular 17th-c village pub, beams and open fires, good often imaginative food (not Mon) cooked by landlord-chef, Fullers, Sharps and a guest, friendly welcoming service, small back dining area; no under-14s in bar after 6pm or on Sun lunchtime, terrace tables, closed Sun evening, Mon lunchtime. *(Hugo Jeune)*

GREAT HORMEAD   TL4030
Three Tuns (01763) 289405
B1038/Horseshoe Hill; SG9 0NT
Old thatched and timbered country pub-
restaurant in lovely surroundings; enjoyable
home-made food including blackboard
specials, Buntingford Twitchell and a
couple of guests, good choice of wines by
the glass and local gin, small linked areas,
huge inglenook with another great hearth
behind, back conservatory extension;
free wi-fi; children, walkers and dogs
welcome, nice secure garden, open all day
Sun till 7pm, closed Mon. *(Ian Duncan)*

HALLS GREEN   TL2728
Rising Sun (01462) 790487
*NW of Stevenage; from A1(M) junction
9 follow Weston signs off B197, then
left in village, right by duck pond;
SG4 7DR* Welcoming 18th-c beamed
and carpeted country pub, good value
traditional home-made food (not Sun
evening) in bar or conservatory restaurant,
well kept McMullens ales, friendly
helpful service, woodburner and open
fire; children and dogs (in bar) welcome,
disabled access, big garden with terrace,
boules and plenty for kids including
swings and playhouse, closed Mon,
otherwise open all day. *(Jestyn Phillips)*

HARPENDEN   TL1312
★White Horse (01582) 469290
*Redbourn Lane, Hatching Green
(B487 just W of A1081 roundabout);
AL5 2JP* Smart up-to-date Peach group
dining pub; chatty split-level bar (one
side a former stables), prints on painted
panelling, stools by circular metal-based
tables, old parquet flooring, flagstones,
some timbers and inglenook log fire, ales
such as Haresfoot, Sharps and Tring,
several wines by the glass, airy dining room
with tartan-upholstered chairs, pews and
cushioned wall seats around pale wooden
tables on stripped boards, enjoyable food
including good value set menu; background
music, board games, free wi-fi; children
and dogs (in bar) welcome, contemporary
tables and chairs under parasols on large
sunny terrace, open (and food) all day
from 9.30am breakfast on. *(Sandra and
Nigel Brown, Edward May, Isobel Mackinlay)*

HATFIELD   TL2308
Eight Bells (01707) 272477
Park Street, Old Hatfield; AL9 5AX
Attractive old beamed pub (two buildings
knocked together) with Charles Dickens
association; small rooms on different levels,
wood floors and open fire, three well kept
ales including Sharps and Wells, good value
food; background music (live Tues, Sat),
games machine, free wi-fi; children and
dogs welcome, tables in backyard, open all
day Fri-Sun, closed Mon. *(Charles Welch)*

HATFIELD   TL2108
Harpsfield Hall (01707) 265840
*Parkhouse Court, off Comet Way
(A1001); AL10 9RQ* Newly built aviation-
theme Wetherspoons, large hangar-like
interior with interesting décor using some
old aircraft parts including a seating booth
made from a jet-engine housing, good range
of beers and other drinks from long servery
featuring time-zoned clocks in aeroplane
windows, their usual good value food, friendly
staff; TVs, free wi-fi; children welcome,
disabled access, tables on paved terrace,
open all day from 8am. *(Ross Balaam)*

HATFIELD   TL2308
Horse & Groom (01707) 264765
Park Street, Old Hatfield; AL9 5AT
Friendly old town local with up to half a
dozen well kept ales and good value pubby
lunchtime food (snacks at weekends), also
simple Tues and Sat suppers (free if you buy
a pint), dark beams and good winter fire,
old local photographs, darts and dominoes;
beer festivals, sports TV; dogs welcome, a
few tables out behind, handy for Hatfield
House, open all day. *(Isobel Mackinlay)*

HEMEL HEMPSTEAD   TL0411
Crown & Sceptre (01442) 234660
*Bridens Camp; leaving on A4146,
right at Flamstead/Markyate sign
opposite Red Lion; HP2 6EY* Traditional
rambling pub, welcoming and relaxed,
with well kept Greene King ales, up to six
guests and local cider, generous helpings
of good reasonably priced pubby food
including Tues pie night, cheerful efficient
staff, dining room with woodburner;
children allowed, dogs in outside bar/
games room, picnic-sets out at front and in
pleasant garden, good walks, open all day
weekends, no food Sun evening. *(Jake)*

HEMEL HEMPSTEAD   TL0604
Paper Mill (01442) 288800
Stationers Place, Apsley; HP3 9RH
Recently built canalside pub on site of
former paper mill; spacious open-plan
interior with upstairs restaurant, Fullers
ales and a couple of guests (usually local),
food from sandwiches and sharing plates up,
friendly staff, log fire; comedy, quiz and live
music nights, free wi-fi; children welcome,
tables out on balcony and by the water,
open (and food) all day. *(Paul Faraday)*

HERTFORD   TL3212
Old Barge (01992) 581871
The Folly; SG14 1QD Red-brick bay-
windowed pub by River Lee Navigation
canal; clean quaint interior arranged around
central bar, wood and flagstone floors, some
black beams and log fire, well kept Sharps
Doom Bar, Woodfordes Wherry and guests,
real ciders/perry, enjoyable reasonably priced
food (not Sun evening) from sandwiches

up, friendly staff; background music, Sun quiz, games machines; children welcome, a few tables out in front, more to the side, open all day. *(Quentin and Carol Williamson)*

HERTFORD HEATH TL3511
Goat (01992) 535788
Vicarage Causeway; SG13 7RT Popular 16th-c low-beamed pub facing village green, enjoyable fair-priced food including OAP set lunch Tues-Fri, Greene King IPA and a couple of guests, Aspall's cider, friendly helpful staff, restaurant; children and dogs (in lower bar) welcome, picnic-sets out at front, classic car meeting first Sun of month, open all day, no food Sun evening. *(J B and M E Benson)*

HIGH WYCH TL4614
Rising Sun (01279) 724099
Signed off A1184 Harlow–Sawbridgeworth; CM21 0HZ Opened-up 19th-c red-brick village local, up to five well kept ales including Courage, Mighty Oak and Oakham tapped from the cask, friendly staff and regulars, woodburner, no food; live music and monthly quiz nights, darts; walkers and dogs welcome, small side garden, closed Tues and Thurs lunchtime. *(Peter and Emma Kelly)*

HITCHIN TL1828
Half Moon (01462) 452448
Queen Street; SG4 9TZ Welcoming tucked-away local with up to ten well kept ales including Adnams and Youngs (beer festivals Apr and Oct), real cider/perry and plenty of wines by the glass too, good value food including tapas and burgers, some themed nights; open all day (till 1am Fri, Sat). *(Julian Thorpe)*

HITCHIN TL5122
Victoria (01462) 432682
Ickleford Road, at roundabout; SG5 1TJ Popular wedge-shaped Victorian corner local, Greene King ales and a couple of guests, enjoyable reasonably priced lunchtime food (also Mon and Fri evenings); events including live music, comedy and quiz nights, barn function room; children welcome, seats in sunny beer garden, open all day. *(Ivy and George Goodwill)*

HUNSDON TL4114
Fox & Hounds (01279) 843999
High Street; SG12 8NJ Village dining pub with good enterprising food from chef-landlord, not cheap but they do offer a weekday set menu, friendly efficient service, Adnams Southwold, a local guest beer and wide choice of wines by the glass, beams, panelling and fireside leather sofas, more formal restaurant with chandelier and period furniture, bookcase door to lavatories; children welcome, dogs in bar, heated covered terrace, closed Sun evening, Mon. *(Max and Steph Warren)*

LEY GREEN TL1624
Plough (01438) 871394
Plough Lane, Kings Walden; SG4 8LA Small brick-built rural local, plain and old-fashioned, with chatty regulars, two well kept Greene King ales and a guest, simple low-priced food (not Weds); folk session Tues (band second of month), free wi-fi; big informal garden with verandah, peaceful views, good walks nearby, closed lunchtimes Mon and Tues, otherwise open all day. *(Tim West)*

LITTLE HADHAM TL4322
Nags Head (01279) 771555
Hadham Ford, towards Much Hadham; SG11 2AX Popular and welcoming 16th-c country dining pub with small linked heavily black-beamed rooms, enjoyable food from snacks to daily specials including good Sun roasts, close-set tables in small bar with Greene King ales and decent wines, restaurant down a couple of steps; occasional quiz nights; children welcome in eating areas, no dogs inside, tables out at front and in pleasant garden behind, open all day Sun till around 9pm. *(Jake)*

LONG MARSTON SP8915
Queens Head (01296) 668368
Tring Road; HP23 4QL Welcoming beamed village local with well kept Fullers beers and enjoyable good value food from pub favourites up (not Sun evening), helpful friendly service, open fire; children welcome, seats on terrace, good walks nearby, two bedrooms in annexe, open all day. *(Usha and Terry Patel)*

MARSWORTH SP9114
Anglers Retreat (01442) 822250
Startops End; HP23 4LJ Homely unpretentious pub near Grand Union Canal; smallish L-shaped angler-theme bar with stuffed fish and live parrot, four well kept ales including Tring Side Pocket for a Toad, good value honest food from baguettes up, Mon pizza night, friendly staff; open mike Thurs and some live music Sun, outside gents'; children and dogs welcome, side garden with tables under parasols, old tractor and aviary, handy for Tring Reservoirs, bedrooms (some in separate building), open all day. *(Roy Hoing)*

MUCH HADHAM TL4219
★ Bull (01279) 842668
High Street; SG10 6BU Neatly kept old dining pub with good home-made food from sandwiches to daily specials, nice choice of wines by the glass including champagne, well kept Brakspears and guests, cheerful efficient service even at busy times, inglenook log fire in unspoilt bar with locals and their dogs, roomy civilised dining lounge and back dining room; children welcome, good-sized garden, Henry Moore

Foundation nearby, open all day weekends
(food till 6.30 Sun). *(Julian Thorpe)*

NUTHAMPSTEAD TL4134

★ **Woodman** (01763) 848328
Off B1368 S of Barkway; SG8 8NB
Tucked-away thatched and weatherboarded
village pub with comfortable unspoilt core,
17th-c low beams/timbers and nice inglenook
log fire, dining extension, enjoyable
home-made food (not Sun evening, Mon)
from traditional choices up, Buntingford,
Greene King and Woodfordes tapped from
the cask, friendly service, interesting
USAF memorabilia and outside memorial
(near World War II airfield); children in
family room with soft play area, dogs in bar,
benches out overlooking tranquil lane, two
comfortable bedrooms, open all day Tue-Sat,
Sun till 7pm, closed Mon. *(Charles Welch)*

POTTEN END TL0108

Martins Pond (01442) 864318
The Green; HP4 2QQ 1920s brick
dining pub facing village green and pond,
popular food especially Sun roasts (should
book), ales from local Red Squirrel and
a dozen wines by the glass, friendly staff,
conservatory; smallish paved garden,
circular walks from the door, open all
day (till 4pm Sun). *(Lewis Canning)*

RICKMANSWORTH TQ0594

Feathers (01923) 770081
Church Street; WD3 1DJ Quietly set off
the high street, beams, panelling and soft
lighting, well kept Fullers London Pride,
Tring and two guests, good wine list, varied
choice of freshly prepared seasonal food
from sandwiches up including lunchtime
deal and themed evenings, friendly young
staff coping well at busy times; children
allowed till 5pm, picnic-sets out behind,
open (and food) all day. *(Brian Glozier)*

RICKMANSWORTH TQ0592

Rose & Crown (01923) 773826
*Woodcock Hill/Harefield Road, off A404
E of Rickmansworth at Batchworth;
WD3 1PP* Wisteria-clad low-beamed
country pub under new owners; well kept
ales including Fullers London Pride,
enjoyable traditional home-cooked food
from sandwiches up, friendly young staff,
airy dining room and conservatory, open
fires; children and dogs welcome, large
peaceful garden with views and goats,
open all day. *(Brian Glozier, David Lamb)*

RIDGE TL2100

Old Guinea (01707) 660894
Crossoaks Lane; EN6 3LH Welcoming
modernised country pub with good pizzeria
alongside traditional bar, St Austell Tribute,
nice italian wines and proper italian coffee,
open fire; children welcome, dogs in bar,
large garden with far-reaching views, open
all day (food till 10pm). *(Paul Faraday)*

ROYSTON TL3540

Old Bull (01763) 242003
High Street; SG8 9AW Coaching inn
dating from the 16th c with bow-fronted
Georgian façade; roomy high-beamed bar,
exposed timbers and handsome fireplaces,
wood flooring, plenty of tables and some
easy chairs, papers and magazines, dining
area with wall-sized photographs of old
Royston, enjoyable pubby food including
good value Sun carvery, Greene King ales
and a guest, several wines by the glass,
helpful pleasant service; background music,
live folk second and last Fri of month;
children welcome, dogs in bar, suntrap
courtyard, 11 bedrooms, open all day from
8am (till 1am Fri, Sat). *(John Pritchard)*

RUSHDEN TL3031

Moon & Stars (01763) 288330
*Mill End; off A507 about a mile
W of Cottered; SG9 0TA* Cottagey
low-beamed pub in peaceful country
setting, good well priced home-made
food (not Mon) in bar or small dining
room, Adnams Southwold and a guest,
friendly service; children and dogs (in
bar) welcome, large back garden, closed
Sun evening, Mon. *(Isobel Mackinlay)*

SARRATT TQ0499

★ **Boot** (01923) 262247
The Green; WD3 6BL Early 18th-c dining
pub with good food (all day Sat, not Sun
evening) from lunchtime sandwiches and
sharing plates up, weekend breakfast
(9.30-11.30am), also tapas and pizzas Fri
and Sat evening, three well kept ales and
good choice of wines by the glass, friendly
young staff, rambling bar with unusual
inglenook, restaurant extension; children
and (in some parts) dogs welcome, good-
sized garden with polytunnel growing own
produce, pleasant spot facing green, handy
for Chess Valley walks, open all day.
(Ross Balaam, Chris and Pauline Sexton)

SARRATT TQ0498

Cock (01923) 282908
*Church End: a very pretty approach is
via North Hill, a lane N off A404, just
under a mile W of A405; WD3 6HH*
Comfortably traditional 17th-c pub; latched
back door opening directly into homely
tiled snug with cluster of bar stools, vaulted
ceiling and original bread oven, archway
through to partly oak-panelled lounge
with lovely inglenook log fire, red plush
chairs at oak tables, lots of interesting
artefacts and several namesake pictures
of cockerels, Badger ales and decent
choice of enjoyable food (not Sun evening)
including OAP deal, carpeted restaurant
in converted barn; background music
(live Sun afternoon), free wi-fi; children
and dogs (in bar) welcome, picnic-sets
in front looking over quiet lane towards

churchyard, more on sheltered lawn and terrace with open country views, play area, open all day. *(Roy Hoing)*

SAWBRIDGEWORTH   TL4814
Orange Tree (01279) 722485
West Road; CM21 0BP Dining pub on leafy outskirts, good freshly cooked food from interestingly varied menu including pub favourites and daily specials, set lunch deal and some themed nights, McMullens ales, friendly staff; children welcome, side garden, closed Mon. *(Max and Steph Warren)*

ST ALBANS   TL1406
Garibaldi (01727) 894745
Albert Street; left turn down Holywell Hill past White Hart – car park left at end; AL1 1RT Busy little Victorian backstreet local with well kept Fullers/Gales beers and a guest, good wines by the glass and reasonably priced tasty food including daily specials, friendly staff; live music, sports TV, free wi-fi; children and dogs welcome, picnic-sets on enclosed terrace, lots of window boxes and flowering tubs, open all day (from 2.30pm Mon), no food Sun evening, Mon. *(Professor James Burke)*

ST ALBANS   TL1507
Mermaid (01727) 568912
Hatfield Road; AL1 3RL Bay-windowed pub with several seating areas (including window seats) arranged around central servery, half a dozen well kept ales, a dozen ciders/perries and good selection of bottled beers, friendly knowledgeable staff, small menu serving Pieminister pies and selection of curries; background and live music, sports TV, darts; beer garden behind, open all day. *(Jake)*

ST ALBANS   TL1307
Rose & Crown (01727) 851903
St Michaels Street; AL3 4SG Proper old-fashioned pub dating from the 16th c, low beams, timbers and panelling, enjoyable fairly priced home-made food from speciality lunchtime sandwiches up, Adnams, Sharps, Thwaites and a guest, welcoming friendly service, big log fire, small snug; Tues quiz and some live music; children and dogs welcome, tables in pretty floral and ivy-hung beer garden, summer barbecues, handy for Verulamium Museum and Park, closed Mon lunchtime, otherwise open all day. *(Dr and Mrs J D Abell)*

ST ALBANS   TL1307
Six Bells (01727) 856945
St Michaels Street; AL3 4SH Rambling old pub with five well kept beers including Oakham, Timothy Taylors and Tring, reasonably priced home-made pubby food (not Sun evening) from good lunchtime sandwiches up, cheerful helpful staff, low beams and timbers, log fire, quieter panelled dining room; weekly live music, some quiz nights; children and dogs welcome, small back garden, handy for Verulamium Museum, open all day. *(Paul Humphreys, Jake)*

ST ALBANS   TL1406
White Hart Tap (01727) 860974
Keyfield, round corner from Garibaldi; AL1 1QJ Friendly 19th-c corner local with half a dozen well kept ales (beer festivals), decent choice of wines by the glass and reasonably priced home-made food (all day Sat, not Sun evening) including good fish and chips Fri; some live music, Weds quiz; tables outside, open all day. *(Professor James Burke)*

THERFIELD   TL3337
Fox & Duck (01763) 287246
Signed off A10 S of Royston; The Green; SG8 9PN Open-plan 19th-c bay-windowed pub in peaceful village setting with picnic-sets on small front green, good food (not Sun evening) from pub favourites up, Greene King and a couple of guests, friendly helpful staff, country chairs and sturdy stripped-top tables on stone flooring, smaller boarded area on left with darts, carpeted back restaurant; children welcome, garden behind with gate to park (play equipment), pleasant walks nearby, open all day weekends, closed Mon. *(Mrs Margo Finlay, Jörg Kasprowski)*

TRING   SP9313
Grand Junction Arms
(01442) 891400 *Bulbourne; B488 towards Dunstable, by bridge; HP23 5QE* Busy canalside pub on two levels; up to four well kept ales and 11 wines by the glass, good reasonably priced food cooked to order from pub favourites to more adventurous choices, friendly service, bar with simple furniture including stools and cushioned settles on bare boards or tiles, local artwork for sale, woodburner, raised dining section; Sun quiz and occasional live music; children welcome, waterside picnic-sets and big garden with fruit trees, beehives and wooden play house, open all day, no food Sun evening. *(Taff Thomas)*

TRING   SP9211
Kings Arms (01442) 823318
King Street; by junction with Queen Street (which is off B4635/Western Road – continuation of High Street); HP23 6BE Cheerful backstreet pub built in the 1830s; five well kept ales including

---

Post Office address codings confusingly give the impression that some pubs are in Hertfordshire, when they're really in Bedfordshire, Buckinghamshire or Cambridgeshire (which is where we list them).

Tring, real cider and decent choice of malt whiskies and gins, good value food (not Sun evening) from pub favourites up including daily specials, stools around cast-iron tables, cushioned pews, some pine panelling and two warm coal fires (unusually below windows), separate courtyard restaurant (Fri-Sun); darts, free wi-fi; children till 8.30pm, no dogs inside, open all day weekends from 10am for breakfast. *(Tracey and Stephen Groves)*

TRING   SP9211
Robin Hood (01442) 824912
Brook Street (B486); HP23 5ED Welcoming traditional local with four Fullers/Gales beers and a couple of guests kept well, good value pubby food (all day Sat), pop-up thai restaurant Sun evening, cosy atmosphere and genial service, several well cared-for smallish linked areas, main bar with banquettes and standard pub chairs on bare boards or carpet, conservatory with woodburner; background music, Wed quiz, free wi-fi; children welcome, dogs in bar (resident yorkshire terrier and westie), small back terrace, public car park nearby, open all day Fri-Sun. *(Julian Thorpe)*

WELL END   SU8987
Black Lion (01628) 520421
Marlow Road; SL8 5PL Simple comfortably furnished pub with well kept ales such as Aylesbury, Brakspears and Rebellion and good wines (landlord has separate wine business), enjoyable reasonably priced pubby food, friendly helpful staff, log fire; quiz Thurs, pool; children welcome, picnic-sets outside, open all day, no food Sun evening, Mon. *(Paul Baxter)*

WESTMILL   TL3626
Sword Inn Hand (01763) 271356
Village signed off A10 S of Buntingford; SG9 9LQ Beamed 14th-c colourwashed pub in pretty village next to church; good interesting food in bar and pitched-ceiling dining room from snacks to evening specials, welcoming attentive service, Greene King IPA and a guest from brick-faced counter, pine tables on bare boards or tiles, log fires; children and dogs (in one part of bar) welcome, attractive outside seating area, four comfortable bedrooms in outbuilding, open all day Fri, Sat, closed Sun evening. *(Mrs Margo Finlay, Jörg Kasprowski)*

WHEATHAMPSTEAD   TL1716
Cross Keys (01582) 832165
Off B651 at Gustard Wood 1.5 miles N; AL4 8LA Friendly 17th-c brick pub attractively placed in rolling wooded countryside; enjoyable reasonably priced pubby food (not Sun-Tues evenings) in bar and beamed restaurant including good Sun roasts, four well kept ales such as Adnams and Greene King, inglenook log fire; quiz second Mon of month; children, walkers

and dogs welcome, picnic-sets in large garden with play area, three bedrooms, open all day weekends. *(Paul Faraday)*

WILDHILL   TL2606
Woodman (01707) 642618
Off B158 Brookmans Park–Essendon; AL9 6EA Simple tucked-away country local with friendly staff and regulars, two well kept Greene King ales and four guests, open-plan bar with log fire, two smaller back rooms (one with TV), straightforward weekday bar lunches; darts, free wi-fi; children and dogs welcome, plenty of seating in big garden. *(Doug Jackson)*

WILLIAN   TL2230
★ Fox (01462) 480233
A1(M) junction 9; A6141 W towards Letchworth then first left; SG6 2AE Civilised contemporary dining pub; pale wood tables and chairs on stripped boards or big ceramic tiles, paintings by local artists, good inventive food along with more traditional choices including substantial sandwiches, Adnams, Fullers and three guests, good wine list (14 by the glass), attentive friendly young staff; background music, summer beer festival, TV; children and dogs (in bar) welcome, side terrace with smart tables under parasols, picnic-sets in good-sized back garden below handsome 14th-c church tower, open all day. *(John Gibbon, M G Hart)*

WILSTONE   SP9014
Half Moon (01442) 826410
Tring Road, off B489; HP23 4PD Traditional old village pub, clean and comfortable, with good value pubby food (not Sun or Mon evenings) from sandwiches/panini up, well kept ales including Malt, Tring and XT, friendly efficient staff, big log fire, low beams, old local pictures and lots of brasses; may be background radio, games including Scrabble, dominoes and darts, free wi-fi; children and dogs welcome, some seats out in front and in good-sized back garden, handy for Grand Union Canal walks, open all day. *(Paul Faraday)*

WINKWELL   TL0206
Three Horseshoes (01442) 862585
Just off A4251 Hemel–Berkhamsted; Pouchers End Lane, just over canal swing bridge; HP1 2RZ 16th-c pub worth knowing for its charming setting by unusual swing bridge over Grand Union Canal; low-beamed three-room core with inglenooks, traditional furniture including settles, a few sofas, three Charles Wells ales and good selection of wines by the glass, food from british tapas to burgers (they may ask to keep a credit card while you eat), bay-windowed extension overlooking canal; background music, comedy and quiz nights; children welcome, picnic-sets out by the water, open (and food) all day. *(Taff Thomas)*

Isle of Wight

 BEMBRIDGE   SZ6587 Map 2
Crab & Lobster
(01983) 872244 – www.crabandlobsterinn.co.uk

*Foreland Fields Road, off Howgate Road (which is off B3395 via Hillway Road);
PO35 5TR*

Clifftop views from terrace and delicious seafood; bedrooms

You wouldn't stumble across this busy pub unless you were in the know –
and it would be a great shame to miss it, given the wonderful view and
the excellent seafood. The interior is roomier than you might expect and
decorated in a parlour-like style, with lots of yachting memorabilia, old local
photographs and a blazing winter fire; darts, dominoes and cribbage. Helpful,
cheerful staff serve Goddards Fuggle-Dee-Dum, Sharps Doom Bar, Ringwood
Razorback and Wadworths 6X on handpump, ten wines by the glass, 16 malt
whiskies and good coffee. From picnic-sets on the terrace you look over the
Solent and the shore is just a stroll away. Two of the light and airy bedrooms
have sea views.

 The fresh fish and seafood are the highlight: crab ramekin, moules marinière,
red snapper fillet with cajun spices and lemon, and plaice fillet topped with
garlic king prawns, but there's also sandwiches and baguettes, wild mushroom
stroganoff, burger with toppings and triple-cooked chips, gammon and egg, a curry of
the day, trio of lamb cutlets with fondant potatoes and mint and port reduction, and
puddings such as chocolate brownie with vanilla ice-cream and fruit pavlova.
Benchmark main dish: seafood mixed grill £18.50. Two-course evening meal £20.00.

Character Inns ~ Lease Rob Benwell ~ Real ale ~ Open 11.30-10 (11 Fri, Sat) ~ Bar food
12-9 ~ Children welcome ~ Dogs allowed in bar ~ Bedrooms: /£100 *Recommended by Jack
and Hilary Burton, Daniel King, Holly and Tim Waite, William Pace, Thomas Green*

 FISHBOURNE   SZ5592 Map 2
Fishbourne Inn 🛏
(01983) 882823 – www.thefishbourne.co.uk

*From Portsmouth car ferry turn left into Fishbourne Lane (no through road);
PO33 4EU*

**Recently refurbished pub with a contemporary feel, real ales,
plenty of wines by the glass and all-day food; bedrooms**

Handy for the Wightlink ferry terminal, this attractive half-timbered
pub helpfully offers some sort of food all day. The open-plan bar has
tartan-upholstered built-in wall seats and wooden chairs on slate flooring,

a woodburning stove with a huge mirror above it and stools against the counter where friendly staff serve Goddards Wight Squirrel, Sharps Doom Bar and Ringwood Razorback on handpump and a dozen wines by the glass; leading off here is a comfortable, beamed lounge area with leather sofas, large pouffes, a couple of button-back armchairs and a flat-screen TV. There's also a bare-boards room with several clocks and a smart, airy dining room with high-backed black leather chairs around all sorts of tables, chandeliers and house plants. The outside seating areas have picnic-sets and contemporary tables and chairs. Bedrooms are comfortable and breakfasts are good. This is sister pub to the Boathouse in Seaview.

Quite a choice of popular food includes sandwiches and baguettes, seared scallops with cauliflower purée and black pudding, rosemary and garlic baked camembert with spiced tomato chutney (for two people), local sausages with mash and gravy, butternut squash and spinach risotto, a pie of the day, gluten-free battered fish of the day and chips, pork tenderloin with sticky red cabbage and red wine jus, lamb shank with rosemary-infused mash and silverskin onion gravy, and puddings such as spiced plum crumble and white chocolate and pistachio parfait with dark chocolate sauce. *Benchmark main dish: trio of fish £13.50. Two-course evening meal £22.00.*

Inns of Distinction ~ Lease Martin Bullock ~ Real ale ~ Open 9am-11pm (10.30pm Sun) ~ Bar food 9am-9.30pm ~ Restaurant ~ Children welcome ~ Dogs allowed in bar ~ Wi-fi ~ Live music summer Sun ~ Bedrooms: £85/£125 *Recommended by D J and P M Taylor, Max Simons, David Longhurst, John and Enid Morris, Isobel Mackinlay*

HULVERSTONE
Sun ☜
SZ3984 Map 2

(01983) 741124 ~ www.sunhulverstone.co.uk
B3399; PO30 4EH

Picture-postcard pub in fine setting with sea views, a bustling bar, real ales and tasty food; plenty of outside seats

A good mix of walkers and cyclists enjoy this pretty thatched pub – all hoping to bag a picnic-set in the secluded, split-level cottagey garden, which looks across to the sea. The low-ceilinged bar has a nice mix of character furniture (including a fine old settle) on flagstones and floorboards, brick and stone walls, and horsebrasses and ironwork around a woodburning stove; background music and darts. Courage Directors, Hancocks HB, Sharps Doom Bar and Wells Bombardier on handpump and ten wines by the glass. Large windows in the traditionally furnished and carpeted dining room take in the delightful view.

Popular food includes sandwiches and baguettes, moules marinière, ham hock terrine with piccalilli, wild mushroom and asparagus tagliatelle with truffle oil, steak in ale pie, a curry of the day, beer-battered cod and triple-cooked chips, chicken wrapped in bacon with barbecue sauce and mozzarella, crab thermidor with garlic butter, and puddings such as eton mess and crumble of the day. *Benchmark main dish: duck breast with black cherry glaze £14.95. Two-course evening meal £20.00.*

Character Inns ~ Lease Rob Benwell ~ Real ale ~ Open 12-11 ~ Bar food 12-9 ~ Restaurant ~ Children welcome ~ Dogs welcome *Recommended by Mrs Jillian Chave, Alfie Bayliss, Glen and Patricia Fuller, Alf and Sally Garner, Nicola and Holly Lyons*

Please tell us if the décor, atmosphere, food or drink at a pub is different from our description. We rely on readers' reports to keep us up to date: feedback@goodguides.com, or (no stamp needed) The Good Pub Guide, FREEPOST RTXY–ZCBC–BBAZ, Stream Lane, Sedlescombe, Battle TN33 0PB.

 NITON   SZ5075 Map 2

Buddle

(01983) 730243 – www.buddleinn.co.uk

St Catherines Road, Undercliff; off A3055 just S of village, towards St Catherines Point; PO38 2NE

Stone pub with sea views in clifftop garden, five real ales and tasty food

Surrounded by National Trust land and handy for the coast path, this 16th-c former smugglers' haunt keeps five real ales on handpump such as Courage Directors, Hancocks HB, Sharps Doom Bar, Wells Bombardier and a guest beer named for the pub (from Yates); also, 11 wines by the glass and a couple of farm ciders. The traditional bar rooms have plenty of character: heavy black beams, captain's chairs and wheelbacks or cushioned wall seats around solid wooden tables on big flagstones or carpet, and an open fire in a broad stone fireplace with a massive black oak mantelbeam; background music. Picnic-sets on both stone terraces and on the grass in the neatly kept garden look down to the sea.

🍴 Rewarding food includes sandwiches and baguettes, moules marinière, pâté of the day with chutney, vegetarian curry, chicken burger with coleslaw and triple-cooked chips, local sausages and mash with rich gravy, crab thermidor, gammon with pineapple and eggs, lamb steak and lyonnaise potatoes with cranberry and red wine jus, and puddings such as chocolate brownie and seasonal fruit crumble. *Benchmark main dish: pie of the day £11.95. Two-course evening meal £18.00.*

Character Inns ~ Lease Rob Benwell ~ Real ale ~ Open 11-11 ~ Bar food 12-9 ~ Restaurant ~ Children welcome ~ Dogs welcome ~ Wi-fi *Recommended by Edward May, William Wright, Heather and Richard Jones*

SEAVIEW   SZ5992 Map 2

Boathouse 🛏

(01983) 810616 – www.theboathouseiow.co.uk

On B3330 Ryde–Seaview; PO34 5AW

Contemporary décor in well run pub with real ales, quite a choice of food, a friendly welcome and seats outside; bedrooms

Some of the airy bedrooms in this extended blue-painted Victorian pub have a view of the sea – as do picnic-sets and other seats under parasols on the terrace. The appealing interior has a bar with built-in wall seats, armchairs and leather pouffes, a large model yacht on the mantelpiece above a woodburning stove with a huge neat stack of logs beside it, and Goddards Scrumdiggity, Ringwood Razorback and Sharps Doom Bar on handpump and 11 wines by the glass; background music. The dining rooms have elegant wooden and high-backed black leather dining chairs, portraits on pale blue walls and an ornate mirror over an open fire; one of these rooms has a dinghy (complete with oars) leaning against the wall. Throughout, the paintwork is light and fresh and there's a mix of polished bare boards, flagstones and carpet. The beach is just across the road. This is sister pub to the Fishbourne Inn at Fishbourne.

🍴 Well liked food includes sandwiches and baguettes, moules marinière, chicken liver parfait, steak in ale pie, pork and leek sausages with chive mash and onion gravy, vegetable tagliatelle with parmesan, cajun chicken with beer-battered onion rings and skin-on chips, slow-roasted pork belly with mustard mash, bacon and cider cream sauce, calves liver and bacon with balsamic red wine and onions, seafood platter, and puddings such as crème brûlée with berry compote and spiced rhubarb pudding with salted caramel ice-cream. *Benchmark main dish: bass fillet with herb-crushed potatoes and local asparagus £12.95. Two-course evening meal £20.00.*

Inns of Distinction ~ Lease Martin Bullock ~ Real ale ~ Open 9am-11pm (10.30pm Sun) ~ Bar food 12-9.30 ~ Restaurant ~ Children welcome ~ Dogs allowed in bar ~ Wi-fi ~ Live music on terrace summer Sun ~ Bedrooms: /£95 *Recommended by Peter Barrett, Jack and Hilary Burton, D J and P M Taylor, Stephen Funnell, Christopher May*

SHORWELL
SZ4582 Map 2

Crown ◀

(01983) 740293 – www.thecrowninnshorwell.co.uk
B3323 SW of Newport; PO30 3JZ

Popular pub with an appealing streamside garden and play area, pubby food and several real ales

Four opened-up rooms spread around a central bar with carpet, tiles or flagstones, and there's a warm welcome for all. Friendly staff serve Hancocks HB, Sharps Doom Bar and Wells Bombardier on handpump, 11 wines by the glass and a farm cider. The beamed, knocked-through lounge has blue and white china on an attractive carved dresser, country prints on stripped-stone walls and a winter log fire with a fancy tilework surround. Black pews form bays around tables in a stripped-stone room off to the left, with another log fire; background music. The peaceful, tree-sheltered garden has a little stream that broadens into a small trout-filled pool, plenty of closely spaced picnic-sets and white garden chairs and tables on grass, and a decent children's play area. This is an attractive rural setting.

Generous helpings of well liked food include parma ham salad with goats cheese and pear, a pâté of the day with chutney, burgers with toppings and triple-cooked chips, cauliflower and leek crumble, sausages and apple mash with gravy, tiger prawn and chorizo linguine with chilli and garlic, chicken breast stuffed with feta, spinach and sun-dried tomatoes wrapped in bacon on ratatouille, pork medallions with wild mushroom and marsala sauce, and puddings such as crème brûlée and clementine posset. *Benchmark main dish: steak in ale pie £12.45. Two-course evening meal £20.00.*

Character Inns ~ Lease Rob Benwell ~ Real ale ~ Open 11.30-10 ~ Bar food 12-9 ~ Children welcome ~ Dogs welcome ~ Wi-fi *Recommended by Tracey and Stephen Groves, Toby Jones, Thomas Green, Trish and Karl Soloman, Neil Allen*

Also Worth a Visit in Isle of Wight

Besides the fully inspected pubs, you might like to try these pubs that have been recommended to us and described by readers. Do tell us what you think of them: feedback@goodguides.com

ARRETON SZ5386
White Lion (01983) 528479
A3056 Newport–Sandown; PO30 3AA
White-painted former coaching inn, beamed bar with stripped-wood floor and comfortable seats by log fire, Sharps Doom Bar, Timothy Taylors Landlord and a guest, several wines by the glass, good choice of well liked fairly priced food, friendly helpful staff, restaurant; children and dogs welcome, pleasant terrace with view up to ancient church, nice walks, open (and food) all day. *(Neil Allen)*

BEMBRIDGE SZ6488
Pilot Boat (01983) 872077
Station Road/Kings Road; PO35 5NN
Recently redecorated harbourside pub shaped like a boat – even has portholes; good food from sandwiches to local seafood, well kept Goddards and guests, friendly staff, restaurant area with woodburner and local artwork for sale; sports TV, darts; children and dogs welcome, disabled access, tables out overlooking the water or in two pleasant courtyards behind, well placed

for coast walks, five bedrooms (overnight cycle storage), open all day. *(Ben Trueman)*

BEMBRIDGE SZ6487
Spinnaker (01983) 873572
Steyne Road; PO35 5UH Attractively refurbished Edwardian inn (sister to the island's Boathouse at Seaview and Fishbourne Inn in Fishbourne – see Main Entries); interesting mix of dining chairs and tables on wooden floors, some bold paintwork, photos and nautical memorabilia, sofas beside an open fire and a woodburner, ales such as Goddards Fuggle-Dee-Dum, several wines by the glass and good imaginative food using island produce, afternoon teas; seats outside, 14 comfortable bedrooms, open all day from 9am for breakfast. *(Ben Trueman)*

BONCHURCH SZ5778
★Bonchurch Inn (01983) 852611
Bonchurch Shute; from A3055 E of Ventnor turn down to Old Bonchurch; opposite Leconfield Hotel; PO38 1NU Quirky former stables with restaurant run by welcoming italian family (here since 1984); congenial bar with narrow-planked ship's decking and old-fashioned steamer-style seats, Courage ales tapped from the cask, decent wine list, bar food and good italian dishes, charming helpful service; background music, darts, shove-ha'penny and other games; children and dogs welcome, delightful continental-feel central courtyard (parking here can be tricky), holiday flat. *(Christopher May)*

BRADING SZ6086
Bugle (01983) 407359
High Street (A3055 Sandown–Ryde); PO36 0DQ Refurbished pub in same group as the Crown at Shorwell and Sun at Hulverstone (see Main Entries); three roomy beamed areas, painted or wooden chairs around tables of all sizes, tartan wall seating, button-back banquettes and a bright flowery sofa, wood or tiled floors, chunky candles and open fires, decent choice of good pubby food from baguettes to popular Sun carvery, three real ales; children and dogs welcome, attractive garden, open (and food) all day. *(Stan Jessop)*

CARISBROOKE SZ4687
★Blacksmiths Arms (01983) 529263
B3401 1.5 miles W; PO30 5SS Friendly family-run hillside pub; scrubbed tables in neat beamed and flagstoned front bars, superb Solent views from airy bare-boards family dining extension, ales such as Adnams, Island and Timothy Taylors, decent wines and cider, good food including fresh fish; children, dogs and walkers welcome (Tennyson Trail nearby), terrace tables and smallish back garden with same view, play area, open (and food) all day. *(William Pace)*

COWES SZ4995
Duke of York (01983) 295171
Mill Hill Road; PO31 7BT Welcoming inn with popular generously served pub food and well kept ales such as Goddards, Ringwood and Sharps, lots of nautical bits and pieces; free wi-fi; children and dogs welcome, well situated near high street and ferry, bedrooms, open all day. *(Neil Allen, Ben Trueman)*

COWES SZ5092
Folly (01983) 297171
Folly Lane signed off A3021 just S of Whippingham; PO32 6NB Glorious Medina estuary views from bar and waterside terrace of this cheery laid-back place; timbered ship-like interior with simple wood furnishings, wide range of sensibly priced food from breakfast on (may be queues at peak times but staff cope well), Greene King ales and a guest; background and live music, TV, fruit machine; children and dogs welcome, long-term parking, showers and weather forecasts for sailors, water taxi, open (and food) all day. *(Trish and Karl Soloman)*

COWES SZ4996
Union (01983) 293163
Watch House Lane, in pedestrian centre; PO31 7QH Old-town inn tucked back from the seafront; well kept Fullers beers and good value freshly made food, friendly staff, cosy areas around central bar, log fire, dining room and conservatory; some live music, Weds quiz, free wi-fi; children and dogs welcome, tables outside, short walk from ferry terminal and marina, six comfortable clean bedrooms, open all day. *(Trish and Karl Soloman)*

CULVER DOWN SZ6385
Culver Haven (01983) 406107
Seaward end, near Yarborough Monument; PO36 8QT Superb Channel views from this isolated clifftop pub, clean and modern, with popular fairly priced home-made food, well kept changing ales such as Goddards, Timothy Taylors and Wadworths, several wines by the glass and decent coffee, friendly service, big restaurant; children and dogs welcome, small terrace, good walks. *(Ben Trueman)*

FRESHWATER SZ3487
★Red Lion (01983) 754925
Church Place; from A3055 at E end of village by Freshwater Garage mini roundabout follow Yarmouth signpost, then take first real right turn signed to Parish Church; PO40 9BP Bay-windowed red-brick pub on quiet village street, popular with locals and visitors; well kept ales such as Goddards Fuggle-Dee-Dum, Sharps Doom Bar and West Berkshire Good Old Boy, 11 wines by the glass and enjoyable good value food from varied blackboard menu, friendly service,

open-plan bar with country-style furnishings on flagstones or bare boards, woodburner; children under 10 at landlord's discretion, dogs welcome, a couple of picnic-sets out at front with view of church, more tables in carefully tended back garden growing own herbs and vegetables, good walking on the nearby Freshwater Way. *(M G Hart, Chris)*

GODSHILL   SZ5281
★**Taverners** (01983) 840707
High Street (A3020); PO38 3HZ
Welcoming 17th-c pub with good food cooked by landlord-chef, emphasis on fresh locally sourced produce (some home-grown), booking advised weekends, well kept ales including Sharps and a house beer from Yates, plenty of wines by the glass and some interesting home-made liqueurs, good friendly service, spacious bar and two front dining areas, beams, bare boards and slate floors, woodburner; children and dogs welcome in certain parts, garden with terrace and play area, shop selling home-made and local produce, limited parking, handy for the Model Village, open all day, closed Sun evening (except bank and school summer holidays). *(D J and P M Taylor)*

GURNARD   SZ4796
Woodvale (01983) 292037
Princes Esplanade; PO31 8LE Large 1930s inn with splendid picture-window views of the Solent (great sunsets), good choice of food from sandwiches and baguettes to daily specials, Fullers London Pride, Ringwood Fortyniner and a couple of guests, plenty of wines by the glass, friendly staff; weekend live music, Mon quiz; children and dogs welcome, garden with terrace and summer barbecues, five bedrooms, open all day, food all day weekends. *(Stan Jessop)*

HAVENSTREET   SZ5590
White Hart (01983) 883485
Off A3054 Newport–Ryde; Main Road; PO33 4DP Welcoming old red-brick village pub with good choice of popular food (all day Sun, special diets catered for) from sandwiches up, Ringwood and Goddards ales, cosy log-fire bar and carpeted dining area; children and dogs welcome, tables in secluded garden behind, open all day. *(Christopher May)*

NEWCHURCH   SZ5685
★**Pointer** (01983) 865202
High Street; PO36 0NN Well run old two-room pub by Norman church, generous helpings of good fairly priced local food including blackboard specials (booking

advised in season), well kept Fullers ales and a guest, friendly service; children and dogs welcome, views from pleasant back garden, boules, open (and food) all day. *(S Holder)*

NEWPORT   SZ5089
Bargemans Rest (01983) 525828
Little London; PO30 5BS Quayside pub with spreading bare-boards interior packed with nautical memorabilia, good choice of generous reasonably priced pubby food including vegetarian and gluten-free options, Goddards, Ringwood and four guests; frequent live music, free wi-fi; children (away from bar) and dogs welcome, part-covered terrace overlooking River Medina, handy for Quay Arts Centre, open (and food) all day. *(Stan Jessop)*

NEWPORT   SZ4989
Newport Ale House 07791 514668
Holyrood Street; PO30 5AZ Steps up to intimate one-room pub with friendly chatty atmosphere, stools and leatherette bucket chairs on bare boards, half-panelling and some striking wallpaper, well kept changing ales tapped from the cask by knowledgeable landlord, pies, rolls and sandwiches; regular live music, darts; dogs welcome, open all day. *(Lisa Robertson)*

NINGWOOD   SZ3989
★**Horse & Groom** (01983) 760672
A3054 Newport–Yarmouth, a mile W of Shalfleet; PO30 4NW Roomy carefully extended pub liked by families; comfortable leather sofas grouped around low tables on flagstones, sturdy tables and chairs well spaced for relaxed dining, winter log fire, Ringwood Best, a couple of guest beers and a dozen wines by the glass, popular fair value food served by friendly staff (smaller appetites catered for); background music, games machine, board games, free wi-fi; dogs allowed in bar, garden with well equipped play area including bouncy castle and crazy golf, nearby walks, open all day from 9am for breakfast. *(Penny and Peter Keevil)*

NORTHWOOD   SZ4983
Travellers Joy (01983) 298024
Off B3325 S of Cowes; PO31 8LS Friendly pub with simple contemporary interior; up to eight well kept ales (tasters offered), enjoyable reasonably priced food from sandwiches and pubby choices to daily specials, long bar with log fire, dining conservatory, pool room; Sun quiz and some live music; children, walkers and dogs welcome, garden with pétanque and play area, open all day. *(Ben Trueman)*

'Children welcome' means the pub says it lets children inside without any special restriction. If it allows them in, but to restricted areas such as an eating area or family room, we specify this. Some pubs may impose an evening time limit. We do not mention limits after 9pm as we assume children are home by then.

RYDE SZ5992

S Fowler & Co (01983) 812112

Union Street; PO33 2LF Wetherspoons
in split-level former department store,
plenty of seating including upstairs
family area, a dozen real ales and good
choice of other drinks including decent
coffee, their usual food and affordable
prices, friendly staff; disabled access,
TVs for subtitled news, free wi-fi; open
all day from 7am. *(D J and P M Taylor)*

SEAVIEW SZ6291

Seaview Hotel (01983) 612711

*High Street; off B3330 Ryde–
Bembridge; PO34 5EX* Small gently
civilised but relaxed hotel, traditional
wood furnishings, seafaring paraphernalia
and log fire in pubby bare-boards bar,
comfortable more refined front bar (like
a naval wardroom), three well kept
ales including Goddards, eight wines
by the glass from good list and well
executed pub food, also more elaborate
restaurant menu specialising in fish/
seafood, pleasant helpful staff; background
music; children welcome, dogs in bar,
sea glimpses from tables on tiny front
terrace, 13 bedrooms (some with sea
views, seven in modern back annexe),
good breakfast, open all day. *(Ian Malone)*

SHALFLEET SZ4089

New Inn (01983) 531314

A3054 Newport–Yarmouth; PO30 4NS
New management for this pub-restaurant
near the quay (a former fishermen's
haunt); good food including local fish/
seafood, ales such as Island, St Austell
and Sharps, several wines by the glass,
rambling rooms with boarded ceilings,
pubby chairs and scrubbed pine tables
on stone or carpeted floors, log fires;
children and dogs (in bar) welcome,
seats on outside deck, open all day, food
all day weekends. *(David Longhurst, Ruth
May, Penny and Peter Keevil, Tracey and
Stephen Groves, John and Enid Morris)*

SHANKLIN SZ5881

★Fishermans Cottage (01983) 863882

Bottom of Shanklin Chine; PO37 6BN
Early 19th-c thatched cottage in terrific
setting tucked into the cliffs on Appley
beach, steep zigzag walk down beautiful
chine; two spotless little rooms with low
beams, flagstones and stripped-stone walls,
old local pictures, fireplace with two-tier
mantelpiece, Fullers London Pride and
a couple of Island beers, good value pub
food including plenty of fish, friendly staff;
background and some live music; children
and dogs welcome, sun-soaked terrace
overlooking sea, lovely walk to Luccombe,
open all day in summer, closed much of
winter (best to check times).
(Steve Whalley, Stephen Funnell)

SHANKLIN SZ5881

Steamer (01983) 862641

Esplanade; PO37 6BS Busy nautical-
theme beachfront bar, fun for holiday
families, with good choice of enjoyable
well priced food from snacks to daily
specials, ales such as Ringwood, Goddards
and Yates, hard-working staff, mix of
seating including cushioned pews and
leather sofas on quarry tiles; live music
most weekends; fine sea views from
part-covered two-tier terrace, eight
bedrooms, open all day. *(Steve Whalley)*

ST HELENS SZ6289

Vine (01983) 872337

Upper Green Road; PO33 1UJ Victorian
local overlooking cricket green; enjoyable
home-cooked food (all day Sat, Sun)
including stone-baked pizzas, ales
such as Island and Ringwood, cheerful
helpful staff; weekend live music, Weds
quiz, pool, free wi-fi; children and dogs
welcome, some seats out in front, play area
across road, open all day. *(A N Bance)*

VENTNOR SZ5677

Perks (01983) 857446

High Street; PO38 1LT Popular little
bar packed with interesting memorabilia
behind shop-window front, well kept ales
including Bass and good range of wines,
enjoyable well priced home-made food
from sandwiches and baked potatoes up,
bargain OAP two-course lunch, fast friendly
service; open all day. *(Christopher May)*

VENTNOR SZ5677

★Spyglass (01983) 855338

*Esplanade, SW end; road down is very
steep and twisty, and parking nearby
can be difficult – best to use pay-and-
display (free in winter) about 100
metres up the road; PO38 1JX* Perched
above the beach with a fascinating jumble
of seafaring memorabilia in snug quarry-
tiled interior, Ringwood ales and guests,
popular food including fish dishes (well
filled crab sandwiches), friendly helpful
service; background music, live daily in
summer; children welcome, dogs in bar,
sea-wall terrace with lovely views, coast
walk towards the Botanic Garden, heftier
hikes on to St Boniface Down and towards
the eerie shell of Appuldurcombe House,
four sea-view bedrooms, open all day.
(D J and P M Taylor)

WHITWELL SZ5277

White Horse (01983) 730375

High Street; PO38 2PY Popular extended
old pub (dates from 1454) with enjoyable
good value food from pub staples to daily
specials, well kept ales such as Goddards and
Yates, good friendly service, carpeted beamed
bar with exposed stonework, restaurant;
Mon quiz, darts and pool; children and dogs

welcome, picnic-sets among fruit trees in big garden with play area, open all day (food all day weekends). *(John and Sylvia Harrop)*

YARMOUTH   SZ3589

Bugle (01983) 760272

The Square; PO41 0NS Old coaching house in same group as the Crown at Shorwell, Sun in Hulverstone and Crab & Lobster in Bembridge (see Main Entries); long frontage and several linked rooms, chesterfields by open fire in low-ceilinged panelled lounge, farmhouse-style furniture in dining areas, books on shelves (and book wallpaper), restaurant with high-backed leather chairs around mix of tables on bare boards or carpet, generous helpings of enjoyable pub food including daily fresh fish, quick cheerful service, traditionally furnished bar with five real ales such as Courage and Sharps, conservatory; background music; children and dogs welcome, picnic-sets and lots of hanging baskets in large courtyard garden, seven bedrooms, handy for ferry, open (and food) all day. *(Neil Allen)*

YARMOUTH   SZ3589

Wheatsheaf (01983) 760456

Bridge Road, near ferry; PO41 0PH Opened-up and modernised Victorian pub with generous well priced food including good burgers, cheerful service, Goddards, Ringwood and a guest; pool; children and dogs welcome, outside seating, handy for the harbour, open (and food) all day. *(William Pace)*

A star symbol before the name of a pub shows exceptional character and appeal. It doesn't mean extra comfort. Even quite a basic pub can win a star, if it's individual enough.

Kent

BIDBOROUGH
Kentish Hare 🍷

TQ5643 Map 3

(01892) 525709 – www.thekentishhare.com

Bidborough Ridge; TN3 0XB

Plenty of drinking and dining space in well run pub with local ales, good wines, enjoyable food and attentive staff

With a thoughtful choice of drinks and particularly good food, this gently civilised but easy-going place is popular locally but highly thought-of by visitors too. The main bar has leather armchairs grouped around an open fire with antlers above it, some unusual stools made of corks, bookcase wallpaper and ales that include a beer named for them from Tonbridge plus Firebrick Coalface and Harveys Best on handpump, 30 wines by the glass, a locally brewed lager, a growing local gin collection and a local cider. A cosy middle room has a modern two-way woodburner at one end, leather sofas and armchairs, old photographs of the pub, local people and the area, lamps made from fire extinguishers and wallpaper depicting old leather suitcases. On the other side of the woodburner is a second bar, with attractive chunky wooden chairs and cushioned settles around various tables on wide dark floorboards – some in small booths. The airy back restaurant is similarly furnished with industrial-style lights hanging from painted joists, pots of fresh flowers and candles, exposed brick walls and an open kitchen; background music. A decked terrace with contemporary tables and chairs overlooks a lower terrace with picnic-sets.

 Good, modern food includes salmon ceviche with pink grapefruit and jalapeno, chicken liver parfait with apple jelly, aubergine and red pepper romesco with rigatoni, parmesan and pine nuts, pistachio crumb pork loin with pork belly, caramelised apple and braised baby gem, curried hake with onion bhaji, carrots, chicory and cucumber, lamb rump with braised shoulder, lamb bacon, peas and asparagus, local steaks with a choice of four sauces and triple-cooked chips, and puddings such as vanilla crème brûlée and sticky toffee pudding with caramel sauce; they also offer a two- and three-course set menu (not Saturday evening or Sunday). *Benchmark main dish: smoked haddock risotto £15.95. Two-course evening meal £21.00.*

Free house ~ Licensees Chris and James Tanner ~ Real ale ~ Open 11-3, 5-11; 11-11 Sat; 11-5 Sun; closed Sun evening, Mon ~ Bar food 12-2.30, 6-9.30; 12-4 Sun ~ Restaurant ~ Children welcome (under-5s eat free) ~ Dogs allowed in bar ~ Wi-fi *Recommended by Julian Richardson, Charlie Parker, Edward May, Charlie Stevens, Audrey and Paul Summers, Usha and Terry Patel*

BIDDENDEN

Three Chimneys ★ ⚲ 🛏

TQ8238 Map 3

(01580) 291472 – www.thethreechimneys.co.uk

Off A262 at pub sign, a mile W of village; TN27 8LW

Kent Dining Pub of the Year

Pubby beamed rooms of considerable individuality, log fires, imaginative food and big, pretty garden; comfortable bedrooms

Food at this appealing old cottage is excellent but this is not a straightforward dining pub – the public bar is quite down to earth, with darts, dominoes and cribbage and real ales tapped from the cask. Served by well trained staff, these include Adnams Southwold, Harveys Best and a guest such as Westerham Spirit of Kent, and they also stock 15 wines plus sparkling wine and champagne by the glass, local Biddenden cider and 13 malt whiskies. The small, low-beamed bar and dining rooms are civilised but informal with plenty of character. They're simply done out with plain wooden furniture and old settles on flagstones and coir matting, some harness and sporting prints on the stripped-brick walls and good log fires. A candlelit bare-boards restaurant has rustic décor and french windows that open into a conservatory looking over seats in the pretty garden, where raised beds contain herbs and other produce for the kitchen. At the front of the building is an extended and enclosed dining courtyard. Five lovely new bedrooms each have their own terrace, and breakfasts are very good. Sissinghurst gardens (National Trust) are nearby.

 Delicious seasonal food uses the best local produce and includes seared pigeon breast on parsnip purée with crispy pancetta and wild rocket, cheddar rarebit on toast with parma ham and sunblush tomato salad, pork and sage sausages with mash and port and red onion gravy, rack of lamb with butternut squash, dauphinoise potatoes and jus, smoked haddock fillet with creamed leeks, mixed mushrooms and chive velouté, duck breast with roasted carrot and swede, parmentier potatoes and jus, and puddings such as dark chocolate délice with pistachio ice-cream and apple and plum crumble. *Benchmark main dish: loin of local wild boar with caramelised apple and local cider jus £18.95. Two-course evening meal £22.50.*

Free house ~ Licensee Craig Smith ~ Real ale ~ Open 11.30-11; 12-10.30 Sun ~ Bar food 12-2.30 (3 Fri, Sat), 6.30-9.30; bar snacks 2-6.30; all day Sun ~ Restaurant ~ Children welcome ~ Dogs allowed in bar ~ Wi-fi ~ Bedrooms: £90/£135 *Recommended by Andrew Bosi, Miss A E Dare, Hunter and Christine Wright, Alexandra and Richard Clay, Serena and Richard Furber, Julia and Fiona Barnes*

CHIDDINGSTONE CAUSEWAY

Little Brown Jug

TQ5146 Map 3

(01892) 870318 – www.thelittlebrownjug.co.uk

B2027; TN11 8JJ

Bustling pub with interconnected bar and dining rooms, open fires, four real ales and enjoyable food; seats outside

There's plenty of space in this friendly spreading pub for both drinking and dining. The beamed front bar has rugs on bare boards or tiled floors, a roaring log fire, leather chesterfield sofas and chunky stools in one corner and high chairs against the carved counter where they keep Greene King Abbot, Kent Cobnut, Larkins Traditional and Old Dairy Copper Top on handpump and 22 wines by the glass; background music and board games. Throughout, various dining areas merge together with open doorways and timbering, all manner of cushioned wooden dining chairs, wall seats and settles with scatter cushions around polished dark wood or rustic tables, and more open fires. Also, hundreds of prints, framed old cigarette cards, maps and photos on painted walls, books on shelves, house plants, old stone bottles and candles on windowsills and big mirrors. A terrace has seats and tables, there are picnic-sets on grass and a children's play area; you can hire the 'dining huts' for £25, but you must book in advance.

From a wide menu, the highly thought-of food includes sandwiches, prawn cocktail, baked camembert with garlic and rosemary, a pie of the week, steak burger with toppings, skinny fries and aioli, pork and leek sausages with onion rings and onion gravy, vegetable nut roast with vegetarian gravy, lambs liver with black pudding bonbons, crispy bacon and lamb and mint jus, stout-glazed beef cheeks with celeriac purée, confit tomato and rich stout jus, and puddings such as chocolate brownie with chocolate sauce and orange cheesecake with orange emulsion and crispy honeycomb. *Benchmark main dish: beer-battered fish and chips £14.95. Two-course evening meal £20.00.*

Whiting & Hammond ~ Lease Duke Chidgey ~ Real ale ~ Open 10am-11pm; 9am-midnight Sat; 9am-11pm Sun ~ Bar food 12-9.30; 9am-9.30pm Fri, Sat; 9-9 Sun ~ Restaurant ~ Children welcome ~ Dogs allowed in bar ~ Wi-fi *Recommended by Christian Mole, Tony Scott*

CHIPSTEAD

George & Dragon ⊗ ♀

TQ5056 Map 3

(01732) 779019 – www.georgeanddragonchipstead.com
Near M25 junction 5; 39 High Street; TN13 2RW

Excellent food in popular village dining pub with three real ales, friendly, efficient service and seats in garden

Drinkers are quite at home here, of course, but it's the first class food that most customers want to enjoy. The opened-up bar has heavy black beams and standing timbers, grey-green panelling, framed articles about their suppliers on the walls, and an easy-going, friendly atmosphere; background music. In the centre, a comfortable sofa and table sit in front of a log fire, with a tiny alcove to one side housing a built-in wall seat and just one table and chair. Westerham George's Marvellous Medicine and Grasshopper and a weekly changing guest such as Whitstable East India Pale Ale on handpump and 21 wines by the glass served by courteous, helpful staff. Up a step to each side are two small dining areas with more panelling, an attractive assortment of nice old chairs around various tables on bare floorboards and two more (unused) fireplaces. Upstairs is a sizeable timbered dining room with similar furnishings and a cosy room that's just right for a private party. The back garden has benches, modern chrome and wicker chairs and tables under parasols, and raised beds for flowers, herbs and vegetables. Wheelchair access to the garden only.

Using carefully sourced local produce, the very good, up-to-date food includes sandwiches, pork, pistachio and onion seed terrine with baby crab apples and tomato chutney, seared king scallops with slow-roasted cherry tomatoes and tomato and chorizo salsa, black olive and sun-dried tomato risotto with goats cheese, duck breast with carrot and cumin purée and dauphinoise potatoes, lime pickle-marinated lamb rump with couscous and lime yoghurt, slow-cooked pork belly with savoy cabbage, pulled pork and apple sauce, and puddings such as raspberry and coconut tart with raspberry ripple ice-cream and chocolate and amaretti torte with coffee chantilly cream. *Benchmark main dish: venison with artichoke and truffle purée £15.95. Two-course evening meal £22.00.*

Free house ~ Licensee Ben James ~ Real ale ~ Open 12-11 (10.30 Sun) ~ Bar food 12-3 (4 Sat), 6-9.30; 12-4, 6-8.30 Sun ~ Restaurant ~ Children welcome ~ Dogs allowed in bar ~ Wi-fi *Recommended by Mrs Margo Finlay, Jörg Kasprowski, Simon and Mandy King, Gordon and Margaret Ormondroyd, Michael Breeze, Richard Cole*

GOUDHURST
Green Cross

TQ7037 Map 3

(01580) 211200 – www.greencrossinn.co.uk

East off A21 on to A262 (Station Road); TN17 1HA

Down-to-earth bar with real ales and more formal back restaurant

The marvellous fish and shellfish are still what most people covet here, but the properly pubby little two-roomed front bar is chatty and relaxed and they do keep Harveys Best and half a dozen wines by the glass. There are stripped floorboards, dark wooden furnishings, wine bottles on windowsills, hop-draped beams, brass jugs on a mantelshelf above the fire and a few plush bar stools by the counter; background music. Attractive in an old-fashioned sort of way, the back dining room has flowers on tables, dark beams in cream walls and country paintings for sale. You can sit out on a small terrace at the side of the pub.

Majoring on fish and shellfish, the menu includes baguettes, avocado and crab bake, tiger prawns in chilli and garlic, sausages with mash and onion gravy, moules frites, steak, mushroom and kidney pie, skate wing in brown butter, slow-roast pork belly with apple sauce, gravy and crackling, linguine with queen scallops, vermouth, tarragon and cream, sea bass fillets with spring onions, ginger, soy sauce and white wine, coquilles saint-jacques au gratin, seafood paella, and puddings. *Benchmark main dish: beer-battered fresh cod and chips £14.10. Two-course evening meal £22.00.*

Free house ~ Licensees Lou and Caroline Lizzi ~ Real ale ~ Open 12-3, 6-11; closed Sun evening ~ Bar food 12-2, 7-9 ~ Restaurant ~ Children welcome ~ Dogs allowed in bar ~ Wi-fi
Recommended by Allan Lloyd and family, Alan and Alice Morgan, Robin Waters, Harvey Brown, Emma Scofield, Sabina and Gerald Grimshaw

ICKHAM
Duke William

TR2258 Map 3

(01227) 721308 – www.thedukewilliamickham.com

Off A257 E of Canterbury; The Street; CT3 1QP

Friendly pub with character rooms, good food and ales and seats in pretty garden; bedrooms

The spreading bar in this gently civilised country pub has huge oak beams and stripped joists, seats that range from country kitchen to cushioned settles with animal skin throws, all manner of tables on stripped wooden floors and a log fire with a low barrel table in front of it. Seats line the bar where friendly staff serve Shepherd Neame Whitstable Bay Pale Ale, Timothy Taylors Landlord and a guest from a local brewery such as Ripple Steam on handpump, eight wines by the glass and a good choice of gins and whiskies. The low-ceilinged dining room is similarly furnished and a conservatory looks over the garden and fields beyond. Throughout, paintwork is contemporary, tables are set with fresh flowers and candles in stone bottles and there are interesting paintings, prints and china plates on the walls; background music and board games. Modern seats and tables are set under parasols on the partly covered terrace, with picnic-sets and a children's play area on grass. Bedrooms (named after the owner's culinary heroes) are attractively and simply furnished and breakfasts are generous. This is a nice village and Canterbury is just ten minutes away by car.

Pleasing food includes a weekend brunch (11am-3pm) and full afternoon tea (midday-4 weekdays) as well as sandwiches, potted shrimps on toasted sourdough, chicory salad with pear, candied walnuts and blue cheese, bubble and squeak with a fried egg, honey and mustard-glazed ham and eggs, free-range chicken breast with leeks and wild garlic mayonnaise, butterflied mackerel with baby gem and beetroot salad, lamb rump with minted vegetables, and puddings such as bakewell tart with clotted cream and rhubarb crumble. *Benchmark main dish: beer-battered cod and chips £14.75. Two-course evening meal £20.00.*

Free house ~ Licensee Mark Sargeant ~ Real ale ~ Open 12-11; 11am-midnight Sat; 11am-10.30pm Sun ~ Bar food 12-3, 6-9.30; 11-5 Sun ~ Restaurant ~ Live music twice a month ~ Dogs allowed in bar ~ Wi-fi ~ Bedrooms: /£120 *Recommended by Claire Adams, Nigel Havers, Colin Humphreys, Sarah Ridout, V Brogden, Peter and Emma Kelly, Deborah and Duncan Walliams, Heather and Richard Jones*

IVY HATCH
Plough ♀
TQ5854 Map 3

(01732) 810100 – www.theploughivyhatch.co.uk
High Cross Road; village signed off A227 N of Tonbridge; TN15 0NL

Country pub with highly thought-of food, real ales and seats in landscaped garden

Particularly popular at lunchtime (there are marvellous surrounding walks and the National Trust's Ightham Mote is very close), this tile-hung village pub has seats in the landscaped garden surrounded by cob trees; pétanque. The various rooms have pale wooden floors, leather chesterfields grouped around an open fire, quite a mix of cushioned dining chairs around assorted tables and high bar chairs by the wooden-topped bar counter. They serve Tonbridge Traditional and Westerham British Bulldog on handpump, 12 wines by the glass and farm cider. There's also an attractive conservatory; background music and board games.

 There are plenty of tasty options on the menu starting with breakfasts (9am-midday weekdays; 10am-midday weekends) plus sandwiches, venison carpaccio with shaved cheese and pomegranate molasses, smoked ham hock with pea, mint and cress salad, chicken caesar salad, wild boar and apple sausages with red onion marmalade and red wine jus, salmon fillet with warm sweet potato, spinach and herb salad, pork belly rib with sweet potato wedges, coleslaw and barbecue sauce, rare-breed steak with bone marrow butter and rustic chips, and puddings such as chocolate and hazelnut brownie with hazelnut praline ice-cream and lemon posset. *Benchmark main dish: duck breast with scotch broth and savoy cabbage £17.00. Two-course evening meal £21.00.*

Free house ~ Licensee Miles Medes ~ Real ale ~ Open 9am-11pm; 10am-11pm Sat; 10-6 Sun ~ Bar food 12-2.45, 6-9.30; 12-5.30 Sun ~ Restaurant ~ Children welcome ~ Dogs allowed in bar ~ Wi-fi *Recommended by Peter Brix, Lindy Andrews, Tina and David Woods-Taylor, Christian Mole, Peter and Alison Steadman, Louise and Anton Parsons*

LANGTON GREEN
Hare ♀ ◖
TQ5439 Map 3

(01892) 862419 – www.brunningandprice.co.uk/hare
A264 W of Tunbridge Wells; TN3 0JA

Interestingly decorated Edwardian pub with a fine choice of drinks and imaginative food

Despite the emphasis on the brasserie-style food, there are plenty of chatty regulars around the bar counter where they keep Greene King IPA and guests such as Brains Bread of Heaven, Felstar Hoppy Hen and Timothy Taylors Landlord on handpump, 30 wines by the glass, 75 malt whiskies, 25 gins and a farm cider. The high-ceilinged rooms are light and airy with rugs on bare boards, built-in wall seats, stools and old-style wooden tables and chairs, dark dados below pale-painted walls covered in old photographs and prints, romantic pastels and a huge collection of chamber-pots hanging from beams; background music and board games. French windows open on to a big terrace with pleasant views of the tree-ringed village green. Parking in front of the pub is limited but you can park in the lane to one side.

¶¶ Modern, bistro-style food includes sandwiches, crab rillettes on pickled cucumber carpaccio with caper and samphire salad, sticky sesame pork belly with ginger and orange dressing, ricotta and pine nut-stuffed aubergine with couscous, pomegranate and dates and harissa ketchup, chicken, ham and leek pie, steak burger with toppings, coleslaw and chips, sea trout with asparagus and seafood broth, crispy beef salad with cashew nuts, sweet chilli and wasabi dressing, and puddings such as chocolate and almond tart with chantilly cream and mixed berry crumble. *Benchmark main dish: braised lamb shoulder with dauphinoise potatoes and rosemary gravy £17.25. Two-course evening meal £22.00.*

Brunning & Price ~ Manager Rebecca Bowen ~ Real ale ~ Open 12-11 (midnight Sat); 12-10.30 Sun ~ Bar food 12-9; 12-10 Fri, Sat; 12-8 Sun ~ Restaurant ~ Children welcome ~ Dogs allowed in bar ~ Wi-fi *Recommended by Gerry and Rosemary Dobson, R and S Bentley, Mrs J Ekins-Daukes, Richard and Penny Gibbs, Monica and Steph Evans, Emily and Toby Archer*

MATFIELD   TQ6541   Map 3
Wheelwrights Arms 🔘 ⚲ 🍺

(01892) 722129 – www.thewheelwrightsarmsfreehouse.co.uk
The Green; TN12 7JX

Cosy, character village pub with friendly staff, good food, up to six real ales and decent wines; seats on a front terrace

As well as the fine range of real ales in this attractive weatherboarded pub, you can be sure of a particularly good meal too. It's run by enthusiastic and hard-working licensees and there are hop-strung beams, traditional dark pubby tables and chairs on bare floorboards, church candles and leather armchairs in front of a woodburning stove; background music. Larkins Traditional and guests such as Dark Star Crème Brûlée, Old Dairy Blue Top, Westerham Viceroy India Pale Ale and Whitstable Kentish Reserve on handpump, 14 good wines by the glass, 14 gins, 11 whiskies and cider brewed in the village; helpful, courteous service. The dining room leads off the bar with an inglenook fireplace, horse tack, old soda siphons and other knick-knacks dotted about; plenty of old photos of the pub and local area. Outside at the front, fruit and vegetables grow in troughs, the hanging baskets are colourful and there are comfortable seats and tables.

🔘 The landlord cooks the enticing food: scotch egg with piccalilli, seared pigeon with spiced parsnip purée, bacon crumbs and dandelion, scallops, cauliflower and pork belly with pig trotter and madeira sauce, beetroot, spinach and goats cheese pithivier with herb, apple and golden beetroot salad, pies with bone marrow pastry, cod fillet with cider beurre blanc, pancetta and parmentier potatoes, saddle of venison with brambles, mash and greens, and puddings such as chocolate fondant with honeycomb, burnt oranges and vanilla custard and almond milk pannacotta with greengage bakewell, meringue and greengage ice-cream. *Benchmark main dish: baked cod loin with braised beef rib, turnip and horseradish velouté, cabbage and jersey royals £17.00. Two-course evening meal £24.00.*

Free house ~ Licensees Rob and Gem Marshall ~ Real ale ~ Open 12-11 (4-11 Tues); 12-9 Sun; closed Mon except bank holidays, Tues lunchtime ~ Bar food 12-2.30, 6.30-8.45; 12-3.45 Sun; not Mon or Tues ~ Well behaved children welcome ~ Dogs welcome ~ Wi-fi *Recommended by Claire Adams, Peter Pilbeam, James Allsopp, Victoria and James Sargeant, Sylvia and Phillip Spencer, Dan and Nicki Barton, Martin and Sue Neville*

MEOPHAM

TQ6364 Map 3

Cricketers

(01474) 812163 – www.thecricketersinn.co.uk

Wrotham Road (A227); DA13 0QA

Busy village pub with friendly staff, plenty to look at, several real ales, good wines and well thought-of food

There's plenty of space for both drinking and dining here, though customers wanting just a pint and a chat tend to head for the front bar. This has cushioned wall settles, a medley of old-style wooden dining chairs and tables, a raised fireplace, newspapers to read and Caledonian Deuchars IPA, Fullers London Pride, Musket Flintlock, Tonbridge Golden Rule and a seasonal beer such as Bexley May Place on handpump and around a dozen wines by the glass; staff are hard-working and helpful. Glass partitioning separates an end room which has bookshelves either side of another fireplace, rugs on bare floorboards and big house plants. Down steps to one side of the bar is a sizeable dining room with another raised fireplace and similar chairs and tables on more rugs and boards. Throughout, there are frame-to-frame photos, prints and paintings, and church candles on each table; background music. Doors in the end family room open to sizeable outdoor seating areas (overlooking the windmill) with contemporary black rattan-style seats under parasols; there are a few seats out in front too. The village green is opposite.

Food is good and includes sandwiches, chicken liver parfait with shallot and brandy compote, mussels in garlic and cider, pork and leek sausages with red wine and onion gravy, wild mushroom risotto, cajun spatchcocked poussin with house slaw and cajun fries, slow-cooked lamb shoulder with dauphinoise potatoes and red wine jus, monkfish, sea bass and king prawn curry with lime-infused rice, and puddings such as sticky toffee pudding with toffee sauce and vanilla and orange cheesecake with chantilly cream. *Benchmark main dish: beer-battered cod and chips £14.95. Two-course evening meal £19.00.*

Whiting & Hammond ~ Manager Joel Dos Santos ~ Real ale ~ Open 9am-11pm (midnight Fri, Sat) ~ Bar food 12-9.30; breakfast 9-11am weekends ~ Restaurant ~ Children welcome ~ Dogs allowed in bar ~ Wi-fi *Recommended by Dave Braisted, B and M Kendall, Daniel King, Tina and David Woods-Taylor, Bridget and Peter Gregson*

PENSHURST

TQ5142 Map 3

Bottle House 🏅 ♀

(01892) 870306 – www.thebottlehouseinnpenshurst.co.uk

Coldharbour Lane; leaving Penshurst SW on B2188 turn right at Smarts Hill signpost, then bear right towards Chiddingstone and Cowden; keep straight on; TN11 8ET

Country pub with friendly service, a good choice of drinks, tasty food and sunny terrace; nearby walks

In a lovely rural setting and well placed for walking, this is a cottagey pub that's particularly popular at lunchtime. The bars have all sorts of joists and beams (a couple of particularly low ones are leather-padded) and the open-plan rooms are split into cosy areas by numerous standing timbers. Pine wall boards and bar stools are ranged along the timber-clad copper-topped counter where they keep Larkins Traditional and Westerham Spirit of Kent on handpump, 20 wines by the glass from a good list and local gin. There's also a hotchpotch of wooden tables (with fresh flowers and candles), fairly closely spaced chairs on dark boards or coir, a woodburning stove and photographs of the pub and local scenes; background music. Some walls are of stripped stone. The sunny, brick-paved terrace has teak chairs and tables under parasols, and olive trees in white pots. Parking is limited.

A good choice of enjoyable food includes sandwiches, pulled pork scotch egg with hot flaked smoked salmon, asparagus and chive hollandaise, devilled mackerel with samphire, potato and caper salad, wild mushroom and truffle stroganoff, calves liver and bacon with onion jus and creamy mash, chilli and lime-crusted hake with curried cream, duck breast with caramelised plum, garlic and chive mash and red wine jus, bourbon barbecue baby back ribs with coleslaw and skinny fries, and puddings such as chocolate brownie with toffee sauce and raspberry and mango mess. *Benchmark main dish: four-hour cooked pork belly with mustard mash, braised red cabbage and apple and cider jus £15.50. Two-course evening meal £20.00.*

Free house ~ Licensee Paul Hammond ~ Real ale ~ Open 11-11; 11-10.30 Sun ~ Bar food 12-10 (9 Sun) ~ Restaurant ~ Children welcome ~ Dogs allowed in bar ~ Wi-fi *Recommended by B and M Kendall, Christian Mole, Bob and Margaret Holder, Barry Collett, Andy and Rosemary Taylor*

PLUCKLEY   TQ9243 Map 3
Dering Arms 🌟 ⚹ 🛏
(01233) 840371 – www.deringarms.com
Pluckley station, which is signposted from B2077; or follow Station Road (left turn off Smarden Road in centre of Pluckley) for about 1.3 miles S, through Pluckley Thorne; TN27 0RR

Handsome building with stylish main bar, carefully chosen wines, three ales and good fresh fish dishes; comfortable bedrooms

Mr Buss, who has owned this fine place for over 30 years, continues to take a hands-on approach and offers a warm welcome to all. It has an imposing frontage, mullioned arched windows and dutch gables and was originally built as a hunting lodge on the Dering Estate. The high-ceilinged, stylishly plain main bar has a solid country feel with a variety of wooden furniture on flagstones, a roaring log fire in a big fireplace, country prints and some fishing rods. The smaller half-panelled back bar has similar dark wood furnishings, plus an extension with a woodburning stove, comfortable armchairs, sofas and a grand piano; board games. A beer named for the pub from Goachers on handpump, 11 good wines by the glass from a fine list, local cider, 30 malt whiskies and 20 cognacs. This is a comfortable place to stay overnight and the breakfasts are highly regarded. Classic car meetings (the landlord James has a couple of classic motors) are held here on the second Sunday of the month.

The excellent, varied fresh fish and shellfish dishes are the highlight (though non-fishy dishes are offered as well): provençale fish soup, oysters done five ways, confit duck with bubble and squeak potato cake and black cherry and ginger sauce, skate wing with caper butter, lamb rump with spring onion mash and minted stilton sauce, coq au vin, hake fillet with crayfish beurre noisette, and puddings such as sticky toffee pudding with walnut sauce and apple, sultana and calvados tart. *Benchmark main dish: sea bass with leeks, bacon and saffron sauce £14.95. Two-course evening meal £25.00.*

Free house ~ Licensee James Buss ~ Real ale ~ Open 11.30-3.30, 6-11; 12-4 Sun; closed Sun evening, Mon ~ Bar food 12-2.30 (3 Sat), 6.30-9; 12-3 Sun ~ Restaurant ~ Children welcome ~ Dogs allowed in bar ~ Bedrooms: £85/£95 *Recommended by Jeremy Snow, Sandra Morgan, Richard Kennell, Pieter and Janet Vrancken, Robert and Diana Myers, Elisabeth and Bill Humphries*

SEVENOAKS
Kings Head ♀

TQ5055   Map 3

(01732) 452081 – www.kingsheadbesselsgreen.co.uk
Bessels Green; A25 W, just off A21; TN13 2QA

Bustling pub with open-plan character rooms, quite a choice of ales, good food and seats in garden

Friendly staff serve up to eight well kept real ales on handpump here: these might include Phoenix Brunning & Price Original plus Long Man Long Blonde, Old Dairy Blue Top, Timothy Taylors Landlord, Tiny Rebel Cereal Killer and Westerham British Bulldog; also, a dozen wines by the glass, 50 malt whiskies, 30 gins and local cider. The little bar, liked by chatty locals, has black and white floor tiles and stools against the counter; leading off here is an attractive small room that has a two-way open fire and is dog-friendly. Spreading dining areas fan out from the bar with a wide mix of cushioned dining chairs, button-back wall seats and settles with scatter cushions around rustic or dark wooden tables on bare-board or tile floors. Also, open fires, frame-to-frame prints, old photos and maps on painted walls, house plants, church candles and old bottles on windowsills, and bookshelves; background music. Outside there are teak tables and chairs on a terrace, picnic-sets on grass and one or two circular 'dining huts' (bookable in advance for £25).

 Up-to-date, popular food includes sandwiches, breaded tiger prawns with creole mayonnaise and pawpaw salsa, smoked macaroni cheese croquettes with tomato compote, asian crispy beef salad, steak burger with toppings and skinny fries, chicken, bacon and leek pie, vegetable linguine, smoked haddock rarebit, harissa lamb with couscous sald and mint falafels, slow-braised venison hotpot with gruyère, and puddings such as dark chocolate délice and lemon meringue pie. *Benchmark main dish: slow-braised lamb shoulder with dauphinoise potatoes and red wine sauce £20.95. Two-course evening meal £22.00.*

Whiting & Hammond ~ Manager Jamie Owen ~ Real ale - Open 11-11 (midnight Sat); 11-10.30 Sun ~ Bar food 12-9.30 (9 Sun); breakfast 9-11.30am weekends ~ Children welcome ~ Dogs allowed in bar ~ Wi-fi *Recommended by B and M Kendall, Dave Braisted, Carol and Barry Craddock, William and Sophia Renton, Beverley and Andy Butcher*

SEVENOAKS
White Hart ♀

TQ5352   Map 3

(01732) 452022 – www.brunningandprice.co.uk/whitehart
Tonbridge Road (A225 S, past Knole); TN13 1SG

Well run coaching inn with lots to look at in character rooms, rewarding food and friendly, helpful staff

There's a lot to look at in the many atmospheric rooms (connected by open doorways and steps) of this carefully renovated old place: open fires and woodburners, antique-style chairs and tables, rugs and bare floorboards and hundreds of prints and old photographs of local scenes or schools on cream-painted walls. Fresh flowers, house plants and candles, too. Phoenix Brunning & Price Original and Old Dairy Blue Top plus guests from breweries such as Empire, Harveys, Timothy Taylors, Tonbridge and Westerham on handpump, 20 good wines by the glass, 50 malt whiskies and a farm cider; daily papers, board games and plenty of chatty, cheerful customers. At the front of the building are picnic-sets under parasols, with wooden benches and chairs around tables under more parasols on the back terrace.

🍴 Interesting food includes sandwiches, potted smoked trout with shrimp butter, samphire, capers and fennel, a charcuterie sharing plate, spicy vietnamese king prawn and rice noodle salad with lime and chilli dressing, basil gnocchi with warm gazpacho sauce, baby leeks and roast aubergine, pork and leek sausages with onion gravy, chicken, ham hock and leek pie with white wine sauce, braised lamb shoulder with dauphinoise potatoes and redcurrant and rosemary sauce, smoked haddock fishcake with tomato concasse and a poached egg, and puddings such as crème brûlée and spiced plum and almond bakewell with vanilla ice-cream. *Benchmark main dish: malaysian fish stew £15.95. Two-course evening meal £20.00.*

Brunning & Price ~ Manager Chris Little ~ Real ale ~ Open 11.30-11; 12-10.30 Sun ~ Bar food 12-10 (9 Sun) ~ Children welcome away from bar until 7pm ~ Dogs allowed in bar ~ Wi-fi *Recommended by Gordon and Margaret Ormondroyd, Jean P & Myriam Alderson, Alan Cowell, Martin Day, Adam Jones*

SHIPBOURNE

Chaser ♀

TQ5952   Map 3

(01732) 810360 – www.thechaser.co.uk
Stumble Hill (A227 N of Tonbridge); TN11 9PE

Busy country pub with rambling rooms and interesting décor, log fires, good choice of drinks, enjoyable food and seats outside

Always deservedly busy (particularly at weekends), this is a gently civilised but easy-going pub with helpful, courteous staff. The comfortably opened-up bar and dining areas have an eclectic mix of solid wood tables (each set with a church candle) surrounded by prettily cushioned dining chairs, stripped wooden floors and several roaring log fires. Frame-to-frame pictures, maps and old photos line the walls above pine wainscoting, house plants and antique glass bottles are placed on windowsills, and rows of books sit on shelves. Greene King Old Speckled Hen, Larkins Traditional, Musket Flintlock and Tonbridge Copper Nob and Union Pale on handpump, good wines by the glass, 20 malt whiskies and two farm ciders; background music. A striking, school chapel-like room at the back has wooden panelling and a high, timber-vaulted ceiling. French windows open on to an enclosed central courtyard with wicker-style tables and chairs on large flagstones and plants in wall pots; this has a retractable awning and a woodburning stove and creates extra family dining space. A side garden with hedges and shrubs has picnic-sets and is overlooked by the church. You can use the small back car park or park in the lane opposite by the green-cum-common; local walks.

🍴 Rewarding food includes sandwiches, cider pulled pork croquettes with mustard mayonnaise and apple chutney, garlic and rosemary-studded baked camembert with cranberry sauce, butternut squash, pea, sage and spinach risotto, beer-battered cod and chips, steak burger with toppings and skinny fries, whole plaice with lemon and caper butter and samphire, thai chicken curry, duck breast with pomegranate dressing and rocket and lentil salad, and puddings such as chocolate brownie with white chocolate sauce and lemon posset. *Benchmark main dish: herb and mustard-coated lamb shoulder with dauphinoise potatoes and redcurrant and rosemary gravy £20.95. Two-course evening meal £22.50.*

Whiting & Hammond ~ Manager Jan Webb ~ Real ale ~ Open 10am-11pm; 9am-11pm Thurs, Sat; 9am-10.30pm Sun ~ Bar food 12-9.30; 9am-9.30pm Thurs, Sat; 9-9 Sun ~ Children welcome ~ Dogs allowed in bar ~ Wi-fi *Recommended by Gordon and Margaret Ormondroyd, Penny and David Shepherd, Martin Day, Angela and Steve Heard, Paddy and Sian O'Leary*

There are report forms at the back of the book.

STALISFIELD GREEN

TQ9552 Map 3

Plough 🏮🌟

(01795) 890256 – www.theploughinnstalisfield.co.uk

Off A252 in Charing; ME13 0HY

Ancient country pub with rambling rooms, open fires, interesting local ales and smashing food

It's the imaginative food cooked by the landlord that is the mainstay here. But drinkers are just as welcome and the atmosphere is relaxed and cheerful. The hop-draped rooms ramble around, up and down, with open fires in brick fireplaces, interesting pictures, books on shelves, farmhouse and other nice old dining chairs around a mix of pine or dark wood tables on bare boards, and the odd milk churn dotted about; background music. Bexley Session Pale, Hopdaemon Incubus, Old Dairy Red Top and a guest beer on handpump, 14 wines by the glass, 11 malt whiskies, ten local ciders and a fair choice of gins, vodkas and bourbons. The pub appears to perch on its own amid downland farmland, and picnic-sets on a simple terrace overlook the village green below.

 The very highly regarded food is cooked by the landlord and includes lunchtime rolls, spiced crab cakes with brown crab mayonnaise and cucumber relish, pigeon breast with sweet potato purée, braised shallots and pickled cherries, cheese and wild garlic arancini with walnut and blue cheese sauce, burger with spiced tomato chutney, mustard mayonnaise and chips, scallops and crispy prawns with monks beard, lemon verbena and beurre blanc, duck breast with garlic duck hash, granola and clementine sauce, and puddings such as sticky toffee pudding with toffee sauce and burnt cream, lemon curd and meringue. *Benchmark main dish: pork belly with black pudding, serrano ham and carrot purée £15.95. Two-course evening meal £22.00.*

Free house ~ Licensees Richard and Marianne Baker ~ Real ale ~ Open 12-3, 6-11; 12-3, 5-11 Weds-Fri; 12-11 Sat; 12-6 Sun; closed Sun evening, Mon; first week Jan ~ Bar food 12-2 (3 Sat), 6-9; 12-3 Sun ~ Restaurant ~ Children welcome ~ Dogs allowed in bar
Recommended by Luke Morgan, Susan and Callum Slade, Pauline and Mark Evans, Barry and Daphne Gregson, Patricia and Gordon Thompson

STODMARSH

TR2160 Map 3

Red Lion

(01227) 721339 – www.theredlionstodmarsh.com

High Street; off A257 just E of Canterbury; CT3 4BA

Interesting country pub with lots to look at, good choice of drinks and well liked food; bedrooms

Nearby Stodmarsh National Nature Reserve is a popular spot, and visitors often drop into this friendly country pub for lunch. The bar rooms have country kitchen chairs and tables, books on shelves and windowsills, tankards hanging from beams, a big log fire and plenty of candles and fresh flowers. Greene King IPA and a guest such as Adnams Mosaic tapped from the cask, eight wines by the glass and a farm cider; background music. There are seats and tables in the back garden.

🍴 Good, popular food includes smoked ham hock terrine with pear chutney, goats cheese and thyme soufflé with parmesan cream, beer-battered cod and chips with tempura prawn, pea purée, caper mayonnaise and lemon ketchup, wild mushroom and spinach risotto, duck breast with carrot purée, pearl barley and honey and orange glaze, salmon with a pistachio crust and blood orange hollandaise, and puddings such as Valrhona chocolate tart with berry compote and banoffi cheesecake; they also offer a two- and three-course weekday set lunch. *Benchmark main dish: shin of beef with horseradish mash £14.95. Two-course evening meal £20.50.*

Free house ~ Licensee Jeremy Godden ~ Real ale ~ Open 11.30-11; 11.30am-midnight Fri, Sat; 12-10.30 Sun ~ Bar food 12-3, 6-9.30; 12-4.30, 6-9 Sun ~ Children welcome ~ Dogs allowed in bar ~ Wi-fi ~ Bedrooms: £90/£95 *Recommended by Anneke and Bert Bannink, Philip Meek and Jessica Sproxton Miller, Pieter and Janet Vrancken*

 STONE IN OXNEY   TQ9428 Map 3
Ferry
(01233) 758246 ~ www.oxneyferry.com
Appledore Road; N of Stone-cum-Ebony; TN30 7JY

Bustling small cottage with character rooms, candlelight, open fires, real ales and popular food

In warm weather the tables and benches on the front terrace and seats in the back garden at this former smugglers' haunt are much prized; a river runs along the bottom and the sunsets can be lovely. Inside, the main bar has hop-draped painted beams, a green dado and stools against the counter where they serve a beer named for the pub (from Goachers), Harveys Best, Sharps Doom Bar and a guest from Whitstable on handpump, eight wines by the glass and farm ciders. To the right is a cosy eating area with wheelback chairs and a banquette around a few long tables, a log fire in an inglenook with candles in wall sconces on either side. To the left of the main door is a dining area with big blackboards on red walls, a woodburning stove beneath a large bressumer beam and high-backed, light wooden dining chairs around assorted tables; up a couple of steps, a smarter dining area has modern chandeliers. Throughout, there are wooden floors, all sorts of pictures and framed maps, a stuffed fish, beer flagons, an old musket and various brasses. Background music, TV, games machine, darts and pool in the games room. Disabled access in the bar and on the terrace.

Good quality food includes prawn cocktail, rosemary-infused baby camembert with onion marmalade, chargrilled chicken salad with peanut butter and sweet chilli sauce, bacon, steak and free-range eggs with wholegrain mustard sauce, potato gnocchi with stilton and pear sauce, beer-battered cod with beef dripping chips, parmesan-coated guinea fowl with parmentier potatoes, duck breast with orange jus and roasted new potatoes, and puddings such as lemon and lime cheesecake and triple chocolate brownie with vanilla ice-cream. *Benchmark main dish: steak and chorizo burger with cheese and chutney in toasted tortilla with coleslaw £12.95. Two-course evening meal £20.00.*

Free house ~ Licensee Paul Withers Green ~ Real ale ~ Open 11-11; 12-10 Sun ~ Bar food 12-3, 6-9; 12-9 Sat; 12-8 Sun ~ Restaurant ~ Children welcome in restaurant and games room ~ Dogs allowed in bar ~ Wi-fi *Recommended by Bill Adie, Lindy Andrews, Julie Swift, V Brogden, Celia and Geoff Clay, Jane and Philip Saunders, Karl and Frieda Bujeya*

 TUNBRIDGE WELLS   TQ5839 Map 3
Sankeys ♀ ◀
(01892) 511422 ~ www.sankeys.co.uk
Mount Ephraim (A26 just N of junction with A267); TN4 8AA

Pubby bar, real ales, decent food and cheerful feel; downstairs brasserie (wonderful fish and shellfish) and seats on sunny back terrace

The street-level bar here has a cheerful atmosphere and well kept local ales. Also, comfortably worn leather sofas and pews around all sorts of tables on bare boards, a fine collection of rare enamel signs and antique brewery mirrors, and old prints, framed cigarette cards and lots of old wine bottles and soda siphons; a big flat-screen TV (for rugby only) and background music. There's a constantly changing range of real ales, craft beers, fruit beers, lagers and ciders, and they always feature Harveys Best, Larkins Traditional and Tonbridge Golden Rule on handpump; also, 16 wines by the glass and a wide choice of spirits. Downstairs is a sizeable new function room with french windows leading to an inviting suntrap deck.

Food in the upstairs bar includes shellfish bisque, duck spring roll with teriyaki dip, chicken caesar or thai beef salad, mexican-style vegetarian burger with nachos and toppings, a pie of the week, chilli con carne, smoked salmon and haddock fishcakes with horseradish and spinach sauce and sweet potato fries, moules done four ways, rib-eye steak with a choice of chips, and puddings. *Benchmark main dish: their own smokie £13.50. Two-course evening meal £20.50.*

Free house ~ Licensee Matthew Sankey ~ Real ale ~ Open 12pm-1am; 12-11 Sun ~ Bar food 12-3, 6-10; 12-10 Sat; 12-8 Sun ~ Restaurant ~ Children welcome ~ Dogs allowed in bar ~ Wi-fi *Recommended by Edward May, Harvey Brown, Alfie Bayliss, Monty Green, Buster and Helena Hastings, Bob and Melissa Wyatt*

ULCOMBE
TQ8550 Map 3

Pepper Box

(01622) 842558 – www.thepepperboxinn.co.uk

Fairbourne Heath; signposted from A20 in Harrietsham, or follow Ulcombe signpost from A20, then turn left at crossroads with sign to pub, then right at next minor crossroads; ME17 1LP

Friendly country pub with a fine log fire, well liked food, fair choice of drinks and seats in a pretty garden

Although this country pub is not easy to find, it's really worth the effort to get here. Well run by attentive and convivial licensees, it's a favourite with many customers. The homely bar has standing timbers and a few low beams (some hung with hops), copper kettles and pans on windowsills, and nice horsebrasses on the fireplace's bressumer beam; two leather sofas are set beside the splendid inglenook fireplace with its lovely log fire. A side area, furnished more functionally for eating, extends into the opened-up beamed dining room with a range in another inglenook and more horsebrasses. Shepherd Neame Master Brew and guests such as Shepherd Neame Spitfire and Whitstable Bay Pale Ale on handpump and 15 wines by the glass; background music. In summer, the hop-covered terrace and shrub-filled garden (looking out over a great plateau of rolling arable farmland) is just the place to relax after a walk along the nearby Greensand Way footpath. The village church is worth a look.

Attractively presented, seasonal food includes lunchtime sandwiches, ham hock and grain mustard terrine with piccalilli, home-made lamb samosas with chilli, coriander and mint yoghurt, aubergine and lentil moussaka, a pie of the day, local sausages with egg, tomatoes, mushrooms and chips, honey-marinated duck breast with garlic, soy and crispy noodles, fillet of bream with prawns and provençale sauce, and puddings such as white chocolate pannacotta with raspberry coulis and sticky toffee and walnut pudding with custard. *Benchmark main dish: steak and kidney pudding £13.00. Two-course evening meal £20.50.*

Shepherd Neame ~ Tenant Sarah Pemble ~ Real ale ~ Open 11-3, 6-11; 12-5 Sun ~ Bar food 12-2.15, 6.30-9.30; 12-3 Sun ~ Restaurant ~ Children over 7 only ~ Dogs allowed in bar ~ Wi-fi *Recommended by Christian Mole, Quentin and Carol Williamson, Michael Breeze, Nick Higgins, Justine and Neil Bonnett, Jill and Hugh Bennett*

WHITSTABLE   TR1066 Map 3

Pearsons Arms ♀

(01227) 773133 – www.pearsonsarmsbyrichardphillips.co.uk

Sea Wall off Oxford Street after road splits into one-way system; public parking on left as road divides; CT5 1BT

Seaside pub with an emphasis on imaginative food, several local ales and good mix of customers

Right on the beach with sea views, this weatherboarded pub is known for its good, interesting food. There are two front bars, divided by a central chimney: cushioned settles, captain's chairs and leather armchairs on a stripped-wood floor, driftwood walls and big flower arrangements on the bar counter. Adnams Ghost Ship, Gadds Dr Sunshine Special Friendly and Whitstable East India Pale Ale on handpump, 14 wines by the glass and an extensive choice of cocktails; background music. A cosy lower room has a bookcase mural and a couple of big chesterfields and dining chairs around plain tables on a stone floor. Up a couple of flights of stairs, the restaurant looks out over the water and features mushroom-coloured paintwork, contemporary wallpaper, more driftwood and church chairs and pine tables on nice wide floorboards.

Enjoyable food includes mussels in white wine, garlic and cream, local scallops with cauliflower purée, couscous and a pork and sage beignet, a changing vegetarian dish of the week, free-range chicken, mushroom and tarragon pie, smoked haddock with a poached egg, spinach and curry cream, best end of lamb, braised shoulder and croquette with rosemary-infused spinach and lamb jus, 40-day dry-aged steaks with a choice of three sauces and triple-cooked chips, and puddings such as lemon meringue pie with blackberry sorbet and white chocolate and rhubarb cheesecake. *Benchmark main dish: beer-battered fresh fish and triple-cooked chips £14.00. Two-course evening meal £21.00.*

Enterprise ~ Lease Jake Alder ~ Real ale ~ Open 12-midnight (11 Sun) ~ Bar food 12-2.30, 6.30-9.30 ~ Restaurant ~ Children welcome ~ Dogs allowed in bar ~ Wi-fi ~ Live music evenings Sun, Tues and last Fri of month *Recommended by Roy Hoing, Richard Kennell, Serena and Richard Furber, Max and Steph Warren, Richard Tilbrook, Lee and Jill Stafford*

WYE   TR0546 Map 3

Kings Head

(01233) 812418 – www.kingsheadwye.com

Church Street; TN25 5BN

Busy high-street pub with good food, ales and wines by the glass – and bright bedrooms

There's a good, bustling atmosphere here and quite a mix of customers. The bare-boards bar is divided by a two-way log fire, with a long brown button-back wall banquette in one part and armchairs beside the fire on the other side by a glass-topped trunk table. Other furnishings include comfortable chairs around all sorts of tables and pale-painted high chairs beside the counter where they keep Shepherd Neame Spitfire and Whitstable Bay Pale Ale on handpump and 13 good wines by the glass, plus an array of olives, cakes, home-made pork crackling and so forth; a dresser is lined with jams and flavoured olive oils for sale. The dining room has one long wall banquette and painted kitchen chairs around pine tables, with an open fire at one end. Throughout, there are rustic boarded walls, church candles, photographs of the local area, daily papers and background jazz. A small courtyard has a few tables and chairs, and bedrooms are airy and simply furnished.

🍴 As well as offering breakfasts (8-11am), the tasty, well liked food includes garlic and chilli prawns with guacamole, local cheese fondue with ham and crudités, a pie of the day, beetroot gratin with lentils, leeks and goats curd, burgers with toppings, green slaw, mustard mayonnaise and fries, smoked haddock with sauté potatoes and a poached duck egg, rump and slow-cooked lamb shoulder with roasting juices and greens, and puddings such as sticky date pudding with butterscotch sauce and crème fraîche sorbet and caramelised vanilla rice pudding. *Benchmark main dish: beer-battered fish and chips £14.00. Two-course evening meal £22.00.*

Shepherd Neame ~ Tenant Scott Richardson ~ Real ale ~ Open 8am-11pm (10pm Sun) ~ Bar food 12-3, 6-9; all day weekends (till 7pm Sun) ~ Restaurant ~ Children welcome ~ Dogs welcome ~ Wi-fi ~ Bedrooms: /£95 *Recommended by James Allsopp, Julie Braeburn, Tony Smaithe, Peter Pilbeam*

Also Worth a Visit in Kent

Besides the fully inspected pubs, you might like to try these pubs that have been recommended to us and described by readers. Do tell us what you think of them: feedback@goodguides.com

APPLEDORE   TQ9529
Black Lion (01233) 758206
The Street; TN26 2BU Bustling and enjoyable 1930s village pub with good generously served food (all day Fri-Sun), lamb from Romney Marsh and local fish, four or five well kept ales including Goachers, Biddenden cider, welcoming helpful staff, partitioned back eating area, log fire; background music, events such as bank holiday hog roasts; children welcome, tables out on green, attractive village and good Military Canal walks, open all day. *(Pete Clayton)*

BARHAM   TR2050
Duke of Cumberland
(01227) 831396 *The Street; CT4 6NY* Open-plan pub close to village green, enjoyable home cooking including good Sun roasts, well kept Harveys, Greene King, Timothy Taylors and a guest, friendly staff, plain tables and chairs on bare boards or flagstones, hops and log fire; quiz second Tues of month, board games and darts; children welcome, dogs in bar, garden with boules and play area, three bedrooms, handy for A2, open all day, food all day weekends. *(Daisy Kelly)*

BEARSTED   TQ8055
Oak on the Green (01622) 737976
The Street; ME14 4EJ Well run pub with bustling friendly atmosphere (sister to the Old Mill at Kennington); two hop-festooned bar areas with bare boards and half-panelling, wide choice of home-made food including some mexican dishes, four real ales such as 1648 and Harveys, restaurant (they also own the smaller fish restaurant next door); children and dogs (in bar) welcome, disabled access, seats out at front under big umbrellas, open (and food) all day. *(Justine and Neil Bonnett)*

BENENDEN   TQ8032
★**Bull** (01580) 240054
The Street; by village green; TN17 4DE Relaxed informal atmosphere in bare-boards or dark terracotta-tiled rooms, pleasing mix of furniture, church candles on tables, log fire in brick inglenook, ales such as Dark Star, Harveys, Larkins and Old Dairy from carved wooden counter, Biddenden cider, more formal dining room, tasty generously served food (not Sun evening) including speciality pies and popular Sun carvery, friendly helpful staff; background music (live Sun afternoon); children and dogs (in bar) welcome, picnic-sets out in front behind white picket fence, back garden, open all day. *(V Brogden)*

BETHERSDEN   TQ9240
George (01233) 820235
The Street; TN26 3AG Tile-hung village local with good buoyant atmosphere, well kept Brakspears, Harveys, Greene King Old Speckled Hen and a guest, generous sensibly priced food including good value carvery (Sun, Weds), large public bar with open fire, smaller lounge next to dining area; pool, free wi-fi; children and dogs welcome, open all day, no food Sun evening, Mon lunchtime. *(Buster May)*

BODSHAM   TR1045
Timber Batts (01233) 750083
Following 'Bodsham, Wye' sign off B2068 keep right at unsigned fork after about 1.5 miles; TN25 5JQ Quirky old rural pub under newish family ownership; traditional beamed bar with inglenook log fire, eclectic mix of furniture, taxidermy and other bits and pieces, three kentish ales and four ciders, some evening food (Thurs-Sat) including wood-fired pizzas Fri; board games; children and dogs welcome, lovely views over wide-spreading valley from garden with wandering chickens, camping, working forge

next door (landlord is a blacksmith), closed Mon-Weds, open from 4pm Thurs, all day Fri and Sat, till 7pm Sun. *(Lee and Jill Stafford)*

BOUGH BEECH   TQ4846
Wheatsheaf (01732) 700100
B2027, S of reservoir; TN8 7NU Attractive 14th-c pub with emphasis on food including children's meals, three Westerham ales along with Harveys and good choice of wines, friendly attentive service, beams and timbering, bare boards and log fires (one in a huge fireplace), high ceilinged dining room, more tables upstairs; dogs welcome, nice outside seating area and good walks including circular one around Bough Beech Reservoir, open all day (till 9pm Sun). *(Pete Clayton)*

BOXLEY   TQ7758
Kings Arms (01622) 755177
1.75 miles from M20 junction 7; opposite church; ME14 3DR Cosy dining pub in pretty village at foot of the downs, largely 16th/17th-c, with good choice of traditional seasonal food from lunchtime baguettes to weekly specials, four well kept ales including Fullers and Harveys, low black beams, red clusterfields by big brick fireplace; background music, monthly quiz; children and dogs welcome, picnic-sets and play area in appealing garden, good local walks, open (and food) all day. *(Martin Day)*

BRABOURNE   TR1041
★ Five Bells (01303) 813334
East Brabourne; TN25 5LP Popular 16th-c inn at foot of North Downs (same owners as the Globe in Rye, Sussex and Woolpack at Warehorne); opened-up interior with hop-strung beams, standing timbers and ancient brick walls, all manner of dining chairs and tables on stripped boards, wall seats here and there, two log fires, quirky decorations including candles in upturned bottles on the walls and a garland-draped mermaid figurehead, four well kept changing local ales, Biddenden cider and selection of kentish wines, well liked food from varied menu, friendly service, shop selling local produce, monthly arts and crafts market; some live music, unisex loos; children and dogs welcome, tables out at front under pergola, comfortable if eccentric bedrooms, open all day from 9am for breakfast. *(Richard and Penny Gibbs, Bob Hinchley, Peter Meister)*

BRASTED   TQ4654
Stanhope Arms (01959) 561970
Church Road; TN16 1HZ Welcoming old village pub next to the church; six real ales including Greene King and well liked pubby food (not Sun evening, Mon, limited choice Tues), good service, cosy traditional

bar with darts, bright cheerful restaurant with white tablecloths and napkins; children and dogs welcome (resident labradors), summer barbecues and bat and trap in back garden, closed Mon lunchtime, otherwise open all day. *(Alan Cowell, Martin Day)*

BRENCHLEY   TQ6841
★ Halfway House (01892) 722526
Horsmonden Road; TN12 7AX Beamed 18th-c inn with attractive mix of rustic and traditional furnishings on bare boards, old farm tools and other bric-a-brac, two log fires, cheerful staff and particularly friendly landlord, up to a dozen well kept changing ales tapped from the cask (two bank holiday beer festivals), enjoyable traditional home-made food including popular Sun roasts, two eating areas; quiz every other Weds; children and dogs welcome, picnic-sets and play area in big garden, summer barbecues, two bedrooms, open all day (no food Sun evening). *(Mick Sanderson)*

BROADSTAIRS   TR3967
Charles Dickens (01843) 600160
Victoria Parade; CT10 1QS Centrally placed with big busy bar, decent choice of beers and wines, popular food from snacks to good local fish/seafood, breakfast from 10am (9am weekends), friendly efficient service, upstairs restaurant with fine sea views; Sat live music, sports TV; children welcome, tables out overlooking Viking Bay, almost next door to Dickens House Museum, open all day. *(Tom and Ruth Rees, Tony Scott)*

BROADSTAIRS   TR3868
Four Candles 07947 062063
Sowell Street; CT10 2AT Quirky, much enjoyed one-room micropub in former shop, good selection of local beers chalked on blackboard including own brews, kentish wines, high tables and stools on sawdust floor, bucket lightshades and various odds and ends including pitchfork handles (the Two Ronnies famous sketch was inspired by a Broadstairs ironmonger), local cheese and pork pies, friendly chatty service; closed weekday lunchtimes, open all day Sat. *(Duncan)*

BROADSTAIRS   TR3967
Tartar Frigate (01843) 862013
Harbour Street, by quay; CT10 1EU Flint-faced harbourside pub dating from the 18th c, pleasantly old-fashioned bar with interesting local photographs and fishing memorabilia, hanging pots and brasses, log fire, well kept ales such as Gadds, lunchtime bar food (Mon-Sat) and good fish/seafood in popular upstairs restaurant with fine Viking Bay views, also good value four-course Sun lunch, friendly

---

If you report on a pub that's not a featured entry, please tell us any lunchtimes or evenings when it doesn't serve bar food.

hospitable staff; background and live music including Weds folk session; open all day, no food Sun evening. *(John Wooll)*

BROOKLAND TQ9724
Woolpack (01797) 344321
On A259 from Rye, about a mile before Brookland, take first right turn signposted Midley where main road bends sharp left, just after the expanse of Walland Marsh; OS Sheet 189 map reference 977244; TN29 9TJ Welcoming 15th-c cottage refurbished under present family management; lovely uneven brick floor in ancient entrance lobby, quarry-tiled main bar with low beams (maybe from local wrecks) and massive inglenook, dining room, good value generously served food from sandwiches and baked potatoes up (no bookings so best to arrive early), Shepherd Neame ales and several wines by the glass, pub cat; children welcome, picnic-sets in good-sized garden, local walks, open (and food) all day weekends. *(Conrad Freezer, B and M Kendall, Peter Meister)*

BURMARSH TR1032
Shepherd & Crook (01303) 872336
Shear Way, next to church; TN29 0JJ Traditional 16th-c marshside village local with smuggling history; well kept ales such as Hop Fuzz along with Weston's Rosie's Pig cider, good straightforward home-made food at reasonable prices including deals, friendly service, interesting photographs and blow lamp collection, open fire; bar games such as ring the bull; children and dogs welcome, seats on side terrace, closed Mon, otherwise open all day (Sun till 6pm). *(B and M Kendall)*

CANTERBURY TR1458
Dolphin (01227) 455963
St Radigunds Street; CT1 2AA Busy modernised dining pub with plenty of tables in light spacious bar, enjoyable fairly traditional home-made food from baguettes up, Sharps Doom Bar, Timothy Taylors Landlord and guests, nice wines including country ones, friendly staff, bric-a-brac on delft shelf, board games, flagstoned conservatory; free wi-fi; children welcome, dogs at management's discretion, disabled access, picnic-sets in good-sized back garden, summer barbecue van, open all day (food all day Sat). *(Martin and Sue Neville)*

CANTERBURY TR1457
Foundry (01227) 455899
White Horse Lane; CT1 2RU Pub in former 19th-c iron foundry, light and airy interior on two floors, six Canterbury Brewers beers from visible microbrewery plus local guests, craft lagers and kentish cider, pubby food (till 6pm Sun-Tues), helpful cheerful staff; disabled access, small courtyard area, open all day (till late Fri, Sat). *(Martin Gowing)*

CANTERBURY TR1457
Parrot (01227) 454170
Church Lane – the one off St Radigunds Street, 100 metres E of St Radigunds car park; CT1 2AG Ancient heavy-beamed pub with wood and flagstone floors, stripped masonry, dark panelling and three open fires, Shepherd Neame ales and well liked food including pre-theatre menu, extensive wine list, friendly service, upstairs vaulted restaurant; some live music in bar, free wi-fi; nicely laid out courtyard with central barbecue, open (and food) all day. *(Duncan)*

CANTERBURY TR1457
White Hart (01227) 765091
Worthgate Place, opposite tree-shaded square off Castle Street; CT1 2QX Friendly little pub serving Shepherd Neame ales and enjoyable well priced traditional food (all day weekends), opened up bare-boards interior with woodburner in side room; Tues quiz; children (till 9pm) and dogs welcome, large garden behind – one of very few in the city, open all day (till 9pm Sun). *(Duncan)*

CAPEL TQ6444
Dovecote (01892) 835966
Alders Road; SE of Tonbridge; TN12 6SU Cosy pub in nice country surroundings with open fire, beams and some stripped brickwork, up to six cask-tapped ales including Harveys, Weston's cider, enjoyable well priced food (not Sun evening, Mon) from pitched-ceiling dining end, friendly helpful staff; live acoustic music Mon, quiz every other Weds; well behaved children allowed, dogs in bar (not at food times), lots of picnic-sets in back garden with terrace and play area, bat and trap, open all day Sun, closed Mon lunchtime. *(Max and Steph Warren)*

CHARING TQ9551
Bowl (01233) 712256
Egg Hill Road; TN27 0HG Popular and friendly 16th-c pub high on the downs (near Pilgrims Way) run by father and daughter; beamed bare-boards bar with inglenook log fire, tusky boar's head behind dark-panelled counter, good selection of well kept kentish beers, carpeted dining area serving enjoyable fairly priced food (all day Sat, till 5pm Sun) from lunchtime sandwiches/baguettes up including range of burgers; July beer/cider/cocktail festival with live music; children and dogs welcome, chunky picnic-sets on front terrace, more tables in big lawned garden, good local walks, six bedrooms, open all day. *(Dan and Nicki Barton)*

CHARTHAM TR1054
Artichoke (01227) 738316
Rottington Street; CT4 7JQ Attractive timbered pub dating from the 15th c, enjoyable reasonably priced home-made food (till 5pm Sun) from sandwiches and baked

potatoes up (also a takeaway menu), well kept Shepherd Neame ales, good service, carpeted log-fire bar, dining area with light wood tables (one built around a glass-topped well); quiz last Thurs of the month, darts and bat and trap; children welcome, picnic-sets in back garden, open all day. *(Buster May)*

CHIDDINGSTONE HOATH TQ4943
★ **Rock** (01892) 870296
Hoath Corner on back road Chiddingstone–Cowden; OS Sheet 188 map reference 497431; TN8 7BS
Welcoming little tile-hung cottage with undulating brick floor, simple furnishings and woodburner in fine brick inglenook, well kept Larkins and good home-made food (not Sun evening) from varied menu, large stuffed bull's head for ring the bull, up a step to smaller room with long wooden settle by nice table; walkers and dogs welcome, picnic-sets out in front and on back lawn, open all day (Sun till 8pm). *(Tony Scott, Martin Day)*

CHILHAM TR0653
★ **White Horse** (01227) 730355
The Square; CT4 8BY 15th-c pub in picturesque village square; handsome ceiling beams and massive fireplace with lancastrian rose carved on mantel beam, chunky light oak furniture on pale wood flooring and more traditional pubby furniture on quarry tiles, four well kept ales including a house beer from Canterbury Ales, enjoyable, varied food (all day Sat, not Sun evening), amiable helpful service; live music and quiz nights, free wi-fi; children welcome, dogs in bar (friendly pub alsatian is Sean), handy for the castle, open all day. *(Celia and Geoff Clay)*

CHILLENDEN TR2653
★ **Griffins Head** (01304) 840325
SE end of village; 2 miles E of Aylesham; CT3 1PS Attractive 14th-c beamed and timbered pub surrounded by nice countryside, gently upscale local atmosphere in two bars and flagstoned back dining room, big log fire, full range of Shepherd Neame ales, good wine list and decent choice of popular home-made food, attentive friendly service; no under-8s, dogs welcome, summer weekend barbecues in pretty garden, vintage car meetings first Sun of the month, open all day (shuts 4pm Sun). *(Daisy Kelly)*

CHIPSTEAD TQ4956
★ **Bricklayers Arms** (01732) 743424
Chevening Road; TN13 2RZ Attractive flower-decked pub (originally three cottages) overlooking lake and green, relaxed chatty atmosphere, well kept Harveys from casks behind long counter, good choice of popular fairly priced food (not Sun evening) from baguettes up, cheerful helpful service,

heavily beamed flagstoned bar with open fire and fine racehorse painting, larger back restaurant; Tues quiz and monthly live music; children and dogs welcome, disabled access/loo, seats out in front, open all day. *(Martin Day, Tony Scott)*

CONYER QUAY TQ9664
Ship (01795) 520881
Conyer Road; ME9 9HR Renovated and extended 18th-c creekside pub owned by adjacent Swale Marina; bare boards and open fires, enjoyable home-cooked food (not Sun evening) including weekend breakfast from 10am, Adnams, Shepherd Neame and guests; live folk first and third Tues of month, jazz/blues dinner third Thurs; children and dogs welcome, useful for boaters, walkers (on Saxon Shore Way) and birders, seats out at front, open all day weekends (till 9.30pm Sun). *(Mick Sanderson)*

COWDEN TQ4640
Fountain (01342) 850528
Off A264 and B2026; High Street; TN8 7JG Good sensibly priced food from sandwiches up (not Sun evening) in attractive tile-hung beamed village pub, steep steps up to unpretentious dark-panelled bar, well kept Harveys and decent wines by the glass, friendly helpful staff, old photographs on cream walls, good log fire, mix of tables in adjoining room, woodburner in small back dining area with one big table; background music, Thurs quiz; children, walkers and dogs welcome, picnic-sets on small terrace and lawn, pretty village, open all day Sun. *(Barry Collett, Martin Day)*

COWDEN TQ4642
★ **Queens Arms** (01342) 850598
Cowden Pound; junction B2026 with Markbeech Road; TN8 5NP Friendly little Victorian time warp known as Elsie's after former long-serving landlady – present local owner has thankfully kept things much the same; two simple unpretentious rooms with open fires, a well kept/priced ale from Larkins, no food, darts, shove-ha'penny and other traditional games, piano; folk music (second and third Tues of month and some Sats), morris dancers and Christmas mummers; dogs welcome, open 5-10.30pm Mon, Tue, 5-7.30pm Weds, Thurs, 5-9pm Fri, 5-7.30pm Sat (longer if music), 12-3pm Sun. *(Tony Scott)*

CROCKHAM HILL TQ4450
Royal Oak (01732) 866335
Main Road; TN8 6RD Chatty old village pub owned by Westerham brewery, their ales kept well and good value fairly standard food (till 7pm Sun) from sandwiches and sharing plates up, friendly hard-working

---

Ring the bull is an ancient pub game – you try to lob a ring on a piece of string over a hook (occasionally a bull's horn) on a wall or ceiling.

staff, mix of furniture including comfy leather sofas on stripped-wood floor, painted panelling, original Tottering-by-Gently cartoons and old local photographs, log fire in right-hand bar; occasional live music, darts, free wi-fi; children, walkers and dogs welcome, small garden behind car park, handy for Chartwell (NT), open all day. *(Audrey and Paul Summers)*

DARGATE   TR0761
Dove (01227) 751360

Village signposted from A299; ME13 9HB Tucked-away 18th-c restauranty pub with rambling rooms, food can be very good and quite expensive, Shepherd Neame ales and guests, nice wines by the glass, efficient pleasant service, plenty of stripped-wood tables, woodburner in brick and stone fireplace; live music last Fri of month; children, walkers and dogs welcome, sheltered garden with bat and trap, summer classic car meetings, open all day Fri, Sat. *(Lee and Jill Stafford)*

DARTFORD   TQ5272
Horse & Groom (01322) 290056

Leyton Cross Road; DA2 7AP Refurbished pub next to Dartford Heath with large bar and restaurant extension, five mainly local ales, a dozen wines by the glass, and good food from regularly changing menu including some pub favourites, friendly if not always fast service; children welcome, open all day, food all day weekends. *(Dave and Jan Pilgrim)*

DARTFORD   TQ5473
Malt Shovel (01322) 224381

Darenth Road; DA1 1LP Cheerful 17th-c waney-boarded pub with two bars and conservatory, well kept Youngs, St Austell and a guest, several wines by the glass and good reasonably priced food (not Sun evening, Mon or Tues) from sandwiches and sharing plates up, friendly helpful staff; quiz Mon, folk night second Sun of the month, free wi-fi; children and dogs welcome, tables on paved part-covered terrace, closed Mon lunchtime, otherwise open all day. *(A N Bance, Quentin and Carol Williamson)*

DEAL   TR3751
Berry (01304) 362411

Canada Road; CT14 7EQ Small no-frills local opposite old Royal Marine barracks, welcoming enthusiastic landlord serving up to 11 well kept changing ales (tasting notes on slates, regular festivals), kentish farm cider and perry, no food, L-shaped carpeted bar with coal fire; Fri quiz, darts teams, pool and some live music; dogs welcome, small vine-covered back terrace, open all day (from 2pm Tues). *(Daisy Kelly)*

DEAL   TR3752
Bohemian (01304) 361939

Beach Street opposite pier; CT14 6HY Seafront bar with five real ales, around

70 bottled beers, 60 vodkas, 50 gins and 100 whiskies, popular traditional home-made food including Sun roasts, friendly staff, L-shaped room with mismatched furniture (some découpage tables), polished wood floor, lots of pictures, mirrors, signs and other odds and ends (customers encouraged to donate items), sofas and weekend papers, similar décor in upstairs cocktail bar with good sea views; background music; children and dogs welcome, sunny split-level deck behind and heated smokers' gazebo, open all day (from 10m weekends) and can get very busy, particularly at weekends. *(Daisy Kelly, Duncan)*

DEAL   TR3752
Just Reproach 07432 413226

King Street; CT14 6HX Popular and genuinely welcoming micropub in former corner shop; simple drinking room with sturdy tables on bare boards, stools and cushioned benches, friendly knowledgeable service from father and daughter team, three or four changing small brewery ales tapped from the cask, also real ciders and some organic wines, locally made cheese, friendly chatty atmosphere; no mobile phones (fine for using them); dogs welcome, closed Sun evening. *(Duncan)*

DEAL   TR3753
Prince Albert (01304) 375425

Middle Street; CT14 6LW Compact 19th-c corner pub in conservation area, bowed entrance doors, etched-glass windows and fairly ornate interior with assorted bric-a-brac, three changing local ales, popular food (served evenings Weds to Sat) and Sun carvery in back dining area, friendly staff; dogs welcome, small garden behind, bedrooms, closed lunchtimes except Sun. *(Daisy Kelly)*

DEAL   TR3752
Royal (01304) 375555

Beach Street; CT14 6JD Popular early 18th-c hotel right on the seafront; light and comfortable with plenty of casual drinkers in pubby bar, Shepherd Neame ales and good choice of enjoyable well priced food from sandwiches to fresh fish, friendly uniformed staff, restaurant; children and dogs (in bar) welcome, terrace overlooking the beach, 18 bedrooms (some with sea-view balconies), open (and food) all day from 8am for brunch. *(John Wooll, Duncan)*

DEAL   TR3753
Ship (01304) 372222

Middle Street; CT14 6JZ Traditional dimly lit two-room local in historic maritime quarter; five well kept/priced ales including Dark Star and Ramsgate served by friendly staff, no food, bare boards and lots of dark woodwork, stripped brick and local ship and wreck pictures, evening candles, cosy panelled back bar, open fire and woodburner; dogs welcome, small pretty walled garden, open all day. (Tony Scott)

DOVER
TR3241

Blakes (01304) 202194

Castle Street; CT16 1PJ Small flagstoned cellar bar down steep steps, brick and flint walls, dim lighting, woodburner, Adnams and six changing guests, farm ciders/perries, over 50 malt whiskies and several wines by the glass, well liked bar food from sandwiches up, panelled carpeted upstairs restaurant, friendly staff; well behaved children welcome, dogs in bar, side garden and suntrap back terrace, four bedrooms, open (and food) all day. (Mick Sanderson)

DUNGENESS
TR0916

Pilot (01797) 320314

Battery Road; TN29 9NJ Single-storey, mid 20th-c seaside café-bar by shingle beach; well kept Adnams, Courage, Harveys and a guest, decent choice of good value food from nice sandwiches to fish and chips, friendly efficient service (even when packed), open-plan interior divided into three areas, dark plank panelling (including the slightly curved ceiling), lighter front part overlooking beach, prints and local memorabilia, books for sale (proceeds to RNLI); background music, free wi-fi; children welcome, picnic-sets in side garden, open all day till 10pm (9pm Sun). (B and M Kendall)

DUNKS GREEN
TQ6152

★ Kentish Rifleman (01732) 810727

Dunks Green Road; TN11 9RU Relaxing Tudor country pub with bare-boards bar and two carpeted dining areas, various rifles and guns on low beams, cosy log fire, well kept ales such as Harveys, Tonbridge, Westerham and Whitstable, Biddenden cider, enjoyable reasonably priced food (service charge added) from light meals to popular Sun roasts, friendly efficient staff; children and dogs welcome, tables in pretty garden with well, good walks from the door, one bedroom, open all day Fri-Sun, no food Sun or Mon evenings. (B and M Kendall, Bob and Margaret Holder)

EAST PECKHAM
TQ6548

Man of Kent (01622) 871345

Tonbridge Road; TN12 5LA Traditional tile-hung pub dating from the 16th c, low black beams, mix of pubby furniture on carpet or slate tiles, fresh flowers, big two-way woodburner in central fireplace, ales such as Harveys, Sharps, Timothy Taylors and Tonbridge, enjoyable well priced home-made food (all day Sat, not Sun evening); children welcome, terrace seating by River Bourne, nearby walks, open all day. (Buster May)

EGERTON
TQ9047

Barrow House (01233) 756599

The Street; TN27 9DJ Stylishly refurbished 16th-c weatherboarded pub (was the George) under same ownership as the Milk House at Sissinghurst; back bar with high beams and light stone floor, inglenook log fire (plastered canopy has signatures of World War II airmen), main bar with more beams and standing timber partitions, attractive wooden counter serving well kept ales such as Dark Star and Harveys and good choice of wines, enjoyable food from snacks and sharing plates up, two-room bare-boards restaurant with painted tables and antler chandeliers, friendly staff; background and live music including folk/blues night last Tues of month; children, walkers and dogs welcome, disabled access via garden, three comfortable bedrooms, open all day from 9am. (Caroline Prescott)

FAVERSHAM
TR0161

Bear (01795) 532668

Market Place; ME13 7AG Traditional late Victorian Shepherd Neame pub (back part dates from the 16th c), their ales kept well and occasional guests, pubby lunchtime food (evenings Tues-Thurs) including popular Sunday roasts, friendly relaxed atmosphere, locals' front bar, snug and back dining lounge (all off side corridor); quiz last Mon of month, free wi-fi; a couple of pavement tables, open all day. (Pete Clayton)

FAVERSHAM
TR0161

Sun (01795) 535098

West Street; ME13 7JE Rambling 15th-c pub in pedestrianised street; unpretentious feel in small low-ceilinged partly panelled rooms, scrubbed tables and big inglenook, well kept Shepherd Neame ales and enjoyable bar food, smart restaurant attached; background and some live music, free wi-fi; wheelchair access possible (small step), pleasant back courtyard, eight bedrooms, open all day. (Pete Clayton)

FAVERSHAM
TR0161

Vaults (01795) 591817

Preston Street; ME13 8PA Centrally placed old pub (more spacious than it looks) with half a dozen well kept ales (at least one local) and a couple of real ciders, cheerful helpful staff, enjoyable good value food (all day Fri, Sat and till 4pm Sun) including nice steaks and carve-your-own Sun roasts; quiz and curry first Mon of the month, traditional games; children and dogs welcome, big back garden, open all day. (Ben Martin)

FINGLESHAM
TR3353

★ Crown (01304) 612555

Just off A258 Sandwich–Deal; The Street; CT14 0NA Neatly kept low-beamed country local dating from the 16th c, good value generous home-made food from usual pub dishes to interesting specials, afternoon cream tea (not Sun), friendly helpful service, four well kept local ales such as Ramsgate, Biddenden cider, softly lit split-level carpeted bar with stripped stone and inglenook log fire, two other attractive dining rooms; children and dogs welcome, lovely big garden with play area and bat and trap, campsite with five hook-ups, open all day Fri-Sun. *(Lee and Jill Stafford)*

FOLKESTONE TR2336
British Lion (01303) 251478
The Bayle, near churchyard; CT20 1SQ Popular 18th-c flower-decked pub tucked behind parish church, comfortable and cosy, with four well kept ales and a couple of real ciders, big helpings of good value traditional food, friendly helpful service; children welcome, tables out in small yard, open all day Sun. *(Dan and Nicki Barton)*

FORDCOMBE TQ5240
Chafford Arms (01892) 731731
B2188, off A264 W of Langton Green; TN3 0SA Picturesque 19th-c tile-hung pub, well kept Harveys and Larkins, good selection of wines and enjoyable food from sandwiches and baguettes to imaginative specials, helpful friendly staff, comfy leather armchairs in lounge bar, locals' bar (dogs allowed – their black lab is Charlie) and dining room, three woodburners; free wi-fi; children welcome (menu for them), picnic-sets on front terrace and in attractive sheltered back garden with Weald views, 1930s telephone box in car park, closed Sun evening, Mon, otherwise open (and food) all day. *(Nigel and Jean Eames)*

FORDWICH TR1759
George & Dragon (01227) 710661
Off A28 at Sturry; CT2 0BX Handsome old Home Counties group pub on the banks of the River Stour in Britain's smallest town; spreading character rooms with beams and timbers, rugs on polished boards or flagstones, assortment of nice old chairs and tables (one a giant bellows), armchairs either side of open fire, Phoenix Brunning & Price, Shepherd Neame and guests, good wines by the glass and well liked brasserie-style food, friendly helpful staff; children and dogs welcome, disabled access/facilities, picnic-sets and a play tractor in garden, open (and food) all day. *(Patric Curwen)*

FRITTENDEN TQ8141
Bell & Jorrocks (01580) 852415
Corner of Biddenden Road/The Street; TN17 2EJ Simple 18th-c tile-hung village local, well kept Harveys, Woodfordes Wherry and a couple of guests (Easter weekend beer festival), Weston's and Thatcher's ciders, good home-made food (not Sun evening, Mon, Tues), friendly welcoming atmosphere, beamed interior with propeller from german bomber above fireplace; regular live music and other events, sports TV, kentish darts; children and dogs welcome, closed Mon and Tues lunchtimes till 3pm, otherwise open all day. *(Duncan)*

GOODNESTONE TR2554
★Fitzwalter Arms (01304) 840303
The Street; NB this is in E Kent not the other Goodnestone; CT3 1PJ Old lattice-windowed beamed village pub, rustic bar with wood floor and open fire, Shepherd Neame ales and local wines, carpeted dining room with another fire, enjoyable reasonably priced home-made food (fish and chips Fridays, steaks Saturdays), friendly service; shove-ha'penny and bar billiards; well behaved children and dogs welcome, terrace with steps up to peaceful garden, lovely church next door and close to Goodnestone Park Gardens, three bedrooms, open all day, no food Sun evening. *(Audrey and Paul Summers)*

GOUDHURST TQ7237
Star & Eagle (01580) 211512
High Street; TN17 1AL Steps up to striking medieval building (now a small hotel) next to the church; settles and Jacobean-style seats in old-fashioned carpeted areas (some down steps), beams and log fires, good choice of enjoyable food including some spanish influences, well kept ales such as Brakspears and Harveys, afternoon teas, friendly service, restaurant; children welcome, no dogs inside, tables out at back with lovely views, attractive village, 11 character bedrooms, good breakfast, open all day. *(Allan Lloyd and family)*

GOUDHURST TQ7037
Vine (01580) 211105
High Street; TN17 1AG White-painted 17th-c tile-hung village pub (former coaching inn) under new management; four refurbished linked rooms (steps down to two on left), mix of old wooden tables and chairs on bare boards, some half-panelling and exposed timbers, various pictures, old photographs and a large boar's head, woodburner in brick fireplace, Harveys Best and three changing guests, several wines by the glass including english sparkling, decent choice of enjoyable mid-priced food from pub favourites to interesting daily specials, upstairs grill room (not Sun evening, Tues) and cocktail lounge; background music; children and dogs (in bar) welcome, picnic-sets out at front around olive tree, enclosed gravel terrace behind, closed Mon, otherwise open all day (till 9pm Sun). *(V Brogden)*

GRAVESEND TQ6474
Rum Puncheon (01474) 353434
West Street; DA11 0BL Handsome Georgian house by Tilbury ferry pier, eight real ales and plenty of foreign beers, low-priced food lunchtimes and Fri, Sat evenings, friendly staff, bare boards and chandeliers, historic river prints and photographs, log fire; background classical music or jazz; no under-14s in bar after 6pm, tables on raised river-view terrace with steps down

to paved garden, open all day (till 9pm Sun and Mon in winter). *(A N Bance)*

GROOMBRIDGE   TQ5337
★**Crown** (01892) 864742
B2110; TN3 9QH Charming tile-hung wealden inn with snug low-beamed bar, old tables on worn flagstones, panelling, bric-a-brac, fire in sizeable brick inglenook, well kept Harveys, Larkins and a guest, enjoyable pubby food (all day Sat, till 5pm Sun) from lunchtime sandwiches up including plenty of gluten-free options, good friendly service, refurbished two-room restaurant with smaller inglenook, background music, free wi-fi; children and dogs (in bar) welcome, tables on narrow brick terrace overlooking steep green, more seats in garden behind, four bedrooms, handy for Groombridge Place gardens, open all day Sat, till 9pm Sun.
(Hunter and Christine Wright, Martin Day)

HAWKHURST   TQ7531
★**Great House** (01580) 753119
Gills Green; pub signed off A229 N; TN18 5EJ Stylish white-weatherboarded restaurant pub (part of the Elite Pubs group); good variety of well liked if not always cheap food, ales such as Harveys, Old Dairy and Sharps from marble counter, polite efficient service, sofas, armchairs and bright scatter cushions in chatty bar, stools against counter used by locals, dark wood dining tables and smartly upholstered chairs on slate floor beside log fire, steps down to airy dining room with Aga (they cook on it) and doors out to terrace; background music, jazz afternoons and other events; children and dogs (in bar) welcome, open all day (food all day weekends). *(Pete Clayton)*

HAWKHURST   TQ7630
Queens (01580) 754233
Rye Road (A268 E); TN18 4EY Fine Georgian fronted inn (building actually dates from the 16th c) set back from the road; revamped main bar with heavy beams and bare boards, some barrel tables and high modern chairs, armchairs either side of inglenook woodburner, dining area and cosy snug, well liked food from bar meals up, ales such as Old Dairy, Rockin' Robin and Sharps, decent wines by the glass, good friendly service, separate restaurant to left of entrance with another inglenook; background music; children welcome, tables out in front, seven refurbished bedrooms, open all day. *(Edwina Watts)*

HERNE   TR1865
Butchers Arms (01227) 371000
Herne Street (A291); CT6 7HL The UK's first micropub (converted from a butchers in 2005), up to half a dozen well kept changing ales (mainly local) tapped from backroom casks, tasters offered by friendly former motorbike-racing landlord, good local cheeses, just a couple of benches and butcher's-block tables (seats about ten), lots of bric-a-brac; dogs welcome, disabled access, tables out under awning, open 12-1.30pm, 6-9pm, closed Sun evening, Mon. *(Duncan)*

HERNHILL   TR0660
Red Lion (01227) 751207
Off A299 via Dargate, or A2 via Boughton Street and Staple Street; ME13 9JR Pretty Tudor pub by church and attractive village green, some refurbishment under present management but keeping character; densely beamed with antique-style tables and chairs on flagstones or parquet, log fires, fairly traditional food from sharing boards up using local produce, well kept ales such as Sharps and Shepherd Neame, decent wines, friendly helpful staff, upstairs restaurant; background and some live music; children and dogs welcome, seats in front and in big garden, open all day. *(Martin and Sue Neville)*

HEVER   TQ4743
Greyhound (01732) 862221
Uckfield Lane; TN8 7LJ 19th-c country pub fully renovated after devastating fire; good popular food and three well kept ales including Harveys, friendly efficient service; handy for Hever Castle, five bedrooms. *(Justine Young)*

HEVER   TQ4744
Henry VIII (01732) 862457
By gates of Hever Castle; TN8 7NH Predominantly 17th-c with some fine oak panelling, wide floorboards and heavy beams, inglenook fireplace, Henry VIII touches to décor, emphasis on enjoyable fairly priced food from pubby choices up, well kept Shepherd Neame ales, friendly efficient staff, restaurant; no dogs even in garden; children welcome away from bar, outside covered area with a couple of leather sofas, steps down to deck and pondside lawn, open all day, food all day weekends (till 7pm Sun). *(Tony Scott, Martin Day, R and S Bentley)*

HODSOLL STREET   TQ6263
Green Man (01732) 823575
Signed off A227 S of Meopham; turn right in village; TN15 7LE Friendly family-run village pub with traditional furnishings in neat mainly carpeted rooms around central bar, painted half-panelling, old framed photographs and woodburner in standalone fireplace, Harveys, Sharps, Timothy Taylors and a guest, wide choice of enjoyable blackboard food from sandwiches/baguettes up including popular two-course

---

Pubs close to motorway junctions are listed at the back of the book.

weekday lunch deal; background music (live Sun), quiz Mon, free wi-fi; children and dogs welcome, picnic-sets in front overlooking small green, more tables and climbing frame on back lawn, open (and food) all day Fri-Sun. *(Michael Breeze)*

HOLLINGBOURNE TQ8455
Dirty Habit (01622) 880880
B2163, off A20; ME17 1UW Ancient dimly lit beamed pub in Elite Pubs group (Great House in Hawkhurst, Poacher & Partridge at Tudeley etc); ales including Harveys and Shepherd Neame, several wines by the glass and food (all day Sat, till 4pm Sun), armchairs and stools on slate floor in main bar area, panelled end room with mix of tables and chairs, low beamed dining room and a further raftered eating area with brick floor and woodburner; children welcome, good outside shelter with armchairs and sofas, on North Downs Way (leaflets for walkers) and handy for Leeds Castle, open all day. *(Daisy Kelly)*

HOLLINGBOURNE TQ8354
★Windmill (01622) 889000
M20 junction 8, A20 towards Lenham then left on to B2163 – Eyhorne Street; ME17 1TR Most people here for the impressive food but there is a small back bar serving Sharps Doom Bar, a guest beer and up to 15 wines by the glass; light and airy main room with white-painted beams, animal skins on bare boards and log fire in low inglenook, mix of furniture including armchairs, heavy settles with scatter cushions, red leather banquette and dark wood dining tables and chairs, two further dining rooms (steps up to one), candles and fresh flowers; background music (live Weds), free wi-fi; children and dogs (in bar) welcome, back terrace, summer barbecues, open all day. *(Miss A E Dare, Dave Braisted)*

IDE HILL TQ4851
Cock (01732) 750310
Off B2042 SW of Sevenoaks; TN14 6JN Pretty village-green local dating from the 15th c, chatty and friendly, with two refurbished bars (steps between), well kept Greene King ales and a beer badged for the pub, enjoyable good value traditional food including good steak and kidney pudding, decent affordably priced wine list, cosy in winter with inglenook log fire; children and dogs welcome, picnic-sets out at front, handy for Chartwell and Emmetts Garden (both NT), nice walks nearby, open all day.
(Paul Scott, Richard Mason, Ian Phillips)

IDEN GREEN TQ8031
★Woodcock (01580) 240009
Not the Iden Green near Goudhurst; village signed off A268 E of Hawkhurst and B2086 at W edge of Benenden; in village follow Standen Street sign, then fork left into Woodcock Lane;

TN17 4HT Part weatherboarded 17th-c country pub in quiet spot surrounded by good walks; low-ceilinged bar with a couple of big standing timbers, stripped-brick walls hung with horse tack, inglenook woodburner, Greene King ales and a guest, good choice of wines and enjoyable food including blackboard specials, small panelled dining room; free wi-fi; children and dogs (in bar) welcome, pretty cottage garden, open all day (till 7pm Sun), no food Sun evening, Mon. *(Mick Sanderson)*

IGHTHAM TQ5956
★George & Dragon (01732) 882440
The Street, A227; TN15 9HH Ancient half-timbered pub with bright spacious interior, enjoyable if not particularly cheap food from snacks to daily specials, well kept Shepherd Neame ales and decent wines, friendly attentive staff, sofas among other furnishings in long main bar, heavy-beamed end room, woodburner and open fires, restaurant; children and dogs welcome, back terrace, handy for Ightham Mote (NT), good walks, open all day from 10am for breakfast, no food Sun evening. *(Alan Cowell, Gordon and Margaret Ormondroyd, Quentin and Carol Williamson)*

IGHTHAM COMMON TQ5855
★Harrow (01732) 885912
Signposted off A25 just W of Ightham; pub sign may be hard to spot; TN15 9EB Smart and comfortable with emphasis on good food from daily changing menu, also some traditional choices and Sunday roasts, relaxed cheerful bar area to the right with candles and fresh flowers, dining chairs on herringbone wood floor, winter fire, charming little antiquated conservatory and more formal dining room, well kept Loddon and nice wines by the glass; background music; children welcome (not in dining room Sat evening), pretty little pergola-enclosed back terrace, handy for Ightham Mote (NT), closed Mon-Weds, Sun evening. *(Duncan)*

IGHTHAM COMMON TQ5955
Old House (01732) 886077
Redwell, S of village; OS Sheet 188 map reference 591559; TN15 9EE Basic two-room country local tucked down narrow lane, no sign, beams, bare bricks and huge inglenook, half a dozen interesting changing ales from tap room casks, no food; darts; dogs welcome, closed weekday lunchtimes, opens 7pm and may shut early if quiet. *(Martin Day)*

KENNINGTON TR0245
Old Mill (01223) 661000
Mill Lane; TN25 4DZ Updated and much extended dining pub dating from the early 19th c (same owners as the Oak on the Green at Bearsted); good choice of generously served food (some quite

expensive), real ales such as 1648 and good wine list, friendly service; children welcome, plenty of terrace and garden seating, open (and food) all day. *(Mick Sanderson)*

KINGSDOWN   TR3748
Kings Head (01304) 373915
Upper Street; CT14 8BJ Tucked-away split-level local with two cosy bars and L-shaped extension, black timbers, lots of old photographs on faded cream walls, woodburner, three real ales and popular reasonably priced food including blackboard specials, friendly landlord and staff; background music, a few vintage amusement machines and darts, occasional live music; dogs and children welcome, small side garden, skittle alley, open all day Sun, closed weekdays till 5pm. *(Andy and Rosemary Taylor)*

KINGSTON   TR2051
Black Robin (01227) 830230
Elham Valley Road, off A2 S of Canterbury at Barham signpost; CT4 6HS 18th-c pub named after a notorious highwayman who was hanged nearby; kentish ales and good helpings of enjoyable home-made food from shortish menu (can eat in bar or back restaurant extension), stone-baked pizzas to take away, friendly helpful staff; background and live music including some established folk artists, quiz second Tues of month, sports TV; children and dogs welcome, disabled access, seats out on decking, open all day (till 8pm Sun). *(Pete Clayton)*

LADDINGFORD   TQ6848
Chequers (01622) 871266
The Street; ME18 6BP Friendly old beamed and weatherboarded village pub with good sensibly priced food from sandwiches and sharing boards up, some themed nights (sausage night is Thurs), well kept Adnams Southwold and three guests; children and dogs welcome, big garden with play area, shetland ponies in paddock, Medway walks nearby, one bedroom, open all day weekends. *(Buster May)*

LEIGH   TQ5646
Plough (01732) 832149
Powder Mill Lane/Leigh Road, off B2027 NW of Tonbridge; TN11 9AJ Attractive opened-up Tudor country pub, lattice windows, hop-strung beams and parquet flooring, some cushioned pews and farmhouse chairs, massive grate in two-way inglenook, well kept Tonbridge Coppernob and up to three local guests, popular home-cooked food, friendly helpful staff, small flagstoned room behind servery with old mangle and darts; quiz third Thurs of month; children and dogs welcome, picnic-sets in garden with play area, old barn for weddings and other functions, open all day Sun till 9pm, closed Mon-Weds. *(Tony Scott)*

LINTON   TQ7550
Bull (01622) 743612
Linton Hill (A229 S of Maidstone); ME17 4AW Comfortably modernised 17th-c dining pub; good choice of food from sandwiches and light dishes to pub favourites and grills, popular Sun carvery, fine fireplace in nice old beamed bar, carpeted restaurant, well kept Shepherd Neame ales, friendly efficient service; children and dogs (in bar) welcome, side garden overlooking church, splendid far-reaching views from back decking, two gazebos, open all day. *(Lee and Jill Stafford)*

LITTLE CHART   TQ9446
Swan (01233) 840011
The Street; TN27 0QB Attractive 15th-c village pub with notable arched Dering windows, open fires and clean fresh décor in unspoilt front bar and good-sized dining area, flowers on tables, enjoyable home-made food (not Sun evening), well kept beers such as Old Dairy and decent wines by the glass, friendly service; Sun quiz; children and dogs (in bar) welcome, nice riverside garden, closed Mon, otherwise open all day. *(Miss A E Dare)*

LOWER HARDRES   TR1453
Granville (01227) 700402
Faussett Hill, Street End; B2068 S of Canterbury; CT4 7AL Spacious pub freshened up under present management; contemporary furnishings in several linked areas, one with unusual central fire under large conical hood, also a proper public bar with farmhouse chairs, settles and woodburner, enjoyable food (not Sun evening) from baguettes and pub favourites to more restauranty dishes (booking advised), good value set lunch, up to three Shepherd Neame ales including Master Brew, 13 wines by the glass; background music, maybe live jazz Tues, artwork for sale; children and dogs welcome, seats on small sunny terrace and in garden under large spreading tree, open all day. *(Alan Cowell)*

LUDDESDOWNE   TQ6667
★Cock (01474) 814208
Henley Street, N of village – OS Sheet 177 map reference 664672; off A227 in Meopham, or A228 in Cuxton; DA13 0XB Early 18th-c country pub under friendly long-serving no-nonsense landlord; at least seven well kept ales such as Adnams, Goachers, Musket and St Austell, also some good german beers, straightforward food including large filled rolls and basket meals, rugs on bare boards in bay-windowed lounge, beams and panelling, quarry-tiled locals' bar, woodburners, settles, cask tables and other pubby furnishings, aircraft pictures, masses of beer mats and bric-a-brac from stuffed animals to model cars, back dining conservatory; music quiz fourth Mon of

month, bar billiards and darts; no children inside or on part-covered heated back terrace, dogs welcome, big secure garden, good walks, open all day. *(Tony R)*

LYNSTED TQ9460
Black Lion (01795) 521229
The Street; ME9 ORJ Early 17th-c village pub under newish welcoming management; well kept Goachers and good freshly made pubby food (not Sun evening) including blackboard specials, settles and old tables on bare boards, log fires; some live music, pool; children and dogs welcome, well tended garden with play area, open all day. *(Duncan)*

MARDEN TQ7547
Stile Bridge (01622) 831236
Staplehurst Road (A229); TN12 9BH Friendly roadside pub with five well kept ales including Dark Star and Goachers, also lots of bottled beers, real ciders and extensive range of gins, good traditional food (not Sun evening); events including beer festivals, live music and comedy nights; dogs welcome in bar, back garden and terrace, open all day. *(Pete Clayton)*

MARKBEECH TQ4742
Kentish Horse (01342) 850493
Off B2026 Hartfield–Edenbridge; TN8 5NT Attractive village pub (originally three cottages) next to church, friendly and welcoming, with three well kept ales including Harveys and Larkins from brick counter, good value traditional food (not Sun or Mon evenings), friendly helpful staff, long carpeted bar with black beams and log fire, restaurant with woodburner in large brick fireplace, french windows to terrace; folk night second Sun of the month; children welcome, picnic-sets and fenced play area in big garden, nice views, open all day. *(Tony Scott)*

MARTIN TR3347
Lantern (01304) 852276
Off A258 Dover–Deal; The Street; CT15 5JL Pretty 17th-c brick pub (originally two farmworkers' cottages) in lovely setting; small recently refurbished bar with low beams, stripped brick and cosy corners, extensive range of craft beers and real ales from copper-topped counter, decent wines by the glass including prosecco on tap, cocktails, good food from traditional choices up, japanese evening every other Mon (must book), friendly helpful service, soft lighting, log fires, upstairs dining area being added as we went to press; background and some acoustic live music, events such as book club and wine tasting, shop selling home-made and local produce; children and dogs welcome, some tables out at front, more in good-sized back garden with big play house, open all day in summer, all day Fri-Sun winter. *(Daisy Kelly)*

MATFIELD TQ6642
Poet at Matfield (01892) 722416
Maidstone Road; TN12 7JH 17th-c beamed pub-restaurant named for Siegfried Sassoon who was born nearby; highly regarded modern cooking from south african chef-patron including good value weekday set menu, ales such as Harveys and Westerham, well chosen wines and some interesting gins, friendly efficient staff; closed Sun evening and Mon, otherwise open all day. *(Nick Taylor)*

MERSHAM TR0438
Farriers Arms (01233) 720444
The Forstal/Flood Street; TN25 6NU Large early 17th-c pub owned by the local community, beers from on-site microbrewery including seasonal ales, decent choice of wines and enjoyable home-made food from bar snacks to daily specials, Thurs steak night, friendly staff, opened-up interior with beams and log fires, restaurant; Sun quiz, live acoustic music first Tues of the month, May beer festival; children and dogs welcome, pretty streamside garden behind with pleasant country views, open all day (till 1am Fri, Sat). *(Justine and Neil Bonnett)*

NEWENDEN TQ8327
White Hart (01797) 252166
Rye Road (A268); TN18 5PN Popular 16th-c weatherboarded local; long low-beamed bar with big stone fireplace, dining areas off serving enjoyable reasonably priced pub food including good Sun roasts and themed evenings, well kept Harveys, Rother Valley and guests, friendly helpful young staff, back games area with pool; background music, quiz nights, sports TV; children and dogs welcome, boules in large garden, near river (boat trips to NT's Bodiam Castle), six bedrooms, open all day. *(V Brogden)*

NEWNHAM TQ9557
★George (01795) 890237
The Street; village signed from A2 W of Ospringe, outside Faversham; ME9 OLL Old pub with spreading open-plan rooms, beams, stripped brickwork and polished floorboards, candles and lamps on handsome tables, two inglenooks (one with woodburner), Shepherd Neame ales, real cider and ten wines by glass, well liked food; regular live music; children welcome, seats in spacious tree-sheltered garden, James Pimm (creator of Pimms) was born in the village, closed Sun evening (from 6.30pm). *(Mick Sanderson)*

NORTHBOURNE TR3352
Hare & Hounds (01304) 369188
Off A256 or A258 near Dover; The Street; CT14 OLG Welcoming 17th-c village pub with two or three well kept ales and good choice of wines from brick-faced servery, decent pubby food, bare-boards

and flagstoned bar separated by a couple of archways, nice log fire; children and dogs welcome, paved terrace and garden with play area, closed Mon lunchtime, otherwise open all day. *(Duncan)*

OARE TR0163

★**Shipwrights Arms** (01795) 590088
S shore of Oare Creek, E of village; signed from Oare Road/Ham Road junction in Faversham; ME13 7TU Remote marshland tavern with plenty of character; three dark simple little bars separated by standing timbers, wood partitions and narrow door arches, medley of seats from tapestry-cushioned stools to black panelled built-in settles forming booths, flags and boating pennants on ceiling, wind gauge above main door (takes reading from chimney), up to six kentish beers tapped from the cask (pewter tankards over counter), simple home-cooked lunchtime only; children (away from bar area) and dogs welcome, large garden with bat and trap, path along Oare Creek to Swale estuary, lots of surrounding bird life, closed Mon. *(Max and Steph Warren)*

OARE TR0063
Three Mariners (01795) 533633
Church Road; ME13 0QA Comfortable simply restored 18th-c pub with good food including fresh fish and evening set menu option, Shepherd Neame ales and plenty of wines by the glass, beams, bare boards and log fire; children and dogs (in bar) welcome, attractive garden overlooking Faversham Creek, good walks, open all day (till 9pm Sun). *(Lee and Jill Stafford)*

PAINTER'S FORSTAL TQ9958
Alma (01795) 533835
Signed off A2 at Ospringe; ME13 0DU Welcoming timbered and weatherboarded village local, homely and tidy, with well kept Shepherd Neame ales, decent wines and good value home cooking including notable steak and kidney pudding (no food Sun evening), helpful service; darts; children and dogs (in bar) welcome, picnic-sets in small enclosed garden, play area over the road, campsite nearby, closed Mon. *(Mick Sanderson)*

PENSHURST TQ5243
Leicester Arms (01892) 871617
High Street; TN11 8BT Refurbished inn close to Penshurst Place; beamed and timbered bars to right of entrance hall, middle one with armchairs in front of open woodburner, nice mix of cushioned dining chairs around dark tables and lovely wonky brick floor, steps up to airy dining room with half-panelling, contemporary paintwork and bookshelf wallpaper, rugs on wood floor, front bar with another woodburner, church candles and lots of suspended saddles, Harveys, Larkins and Tonbridge, several wines by the glass and quite a

choice of well liked food (not Sun evening), more formal restaurant; background music, board games, free wi-fi; children and dogs (in bar) welcome, comfortable bedrooms (some with four-posters), open all day. *(Nigel Havers, Lionel Smith)*

PENSHURST TQ5241
★**Spotted Dog** (01892) 870253
Smarts Hill, off B2188 S; TN11 8EP Quaint weatherboarded pub first licensed in 1520; heavy low beams and timbers, attractive moulded panelling, big inglenook fireplace, hops, horsebrasses and lots of country pictures, traditional furniture on bare boards or carpet, Harveys, Larkins, Tonbridge and Youngs, several wines by the glass, popular pubby food (not Sun evening); free wi-fi; children and dogs (in bar) welcome, terrace seating on several levels with good views over miles of countryside, open all day (till 10pm Sun). *(Mrs J Ekins-Daukes, Barry Collett)*

PETT BOTTOM TR1652
Duck (01227) 830354
Off B2068 S of Canterbury, via Lower Hardres; CT4 5PB Popular tile-hung pub in attractive downland spot; long bare-boards bar with scrubbed tables, pine-panelling and two log fires, very good freshly cooked food (not Sun evening, Mon, Tues, Weds evening) including weekday set lunch, friendly helpful service, two or three well kept beers such as Old Dairy and Timothy Taylors Landlord, Biddenden cider and good wine choice; children and dogs welcome, seats and old well out in front, garden behind where Ian Fleming used to make notes for his James Bond books (see blue plaque), camping close by, closed Mon and Tues, open all day Sun. *(Daisy Kelly)*

PETTERIDGE TQ6640
Hopbine (01892) 722561
Petteridge Lane; NE of village; TN12 7NE Unspoilt tiled and weatherboarded cottage in quiet hamlet, two small rooms with open fire between, traditional pubby furniture, hops and horsebrasses, well kept Tonbridge, Long Man and a guest, enjoyable good value home-made food including wood-fired pizzas, friendly staff, steps up to simple back part with brick fireplace; outside gents; terrace seating, open all day Fri-Sun, no food Mon. *(Buster May)*

PLUCKLEY TQ9144
Rose & Crown (01233) 840048
Mundy Bois – spelled Monday Boys on some maps – off Smarden Road SW of village centre; TN27 0ST Popular 17th-c tile-hung pub with good food (all day Sat and Sun) from french chef, three well kept beers such as Adnams, Harveys and Shepherd Neame, friendly attentive service, main bar with massive inglenook, small snug and restaurant; background music, beer festival

Aug; children and dogs (in bar) welcome, pretty garden and terrace with views, play area, open all day. *(Caroline Prescott)*

RAMSGATE TR3764
Artillery Arms (01843) 853202
West Cliff Road; CT11 9JS Old-fashioned little corner local on two levels, chatty and welcoming, with half a dozen well kept interesting beers and enjoyable food (all day weekends), artillery prints/memorabilia and fine listed windows depicting Napoleonic scenes; quiz Sun evening; dogs welcome, wheelchair access, open all day. *(Duncan)*

RAMSGATE TR3764
Conqueror 07890 203282
Grange Road/St Mildreds Road; CT11 9LR Cosy single-room micropub in former corner shop, welcoming enthusiastic landlord serving three changing ales straight from the cask, also local cider and apple juice, friendly chatty atmosphere, large windows and old photos of the cross-channel paddle steamer the pub is named after; dogs welcome, closed Sun evening, Mon. *(Pete Clayton)*

RAMSGATE TR3765
Great Tree (01843) 590708
Margate Road; CT11 7SP Quirky relaxed place with unusual café-bar décor, four real ales and 20 or so proper ciders, also interesting teas and good coffee, local artwork on show along with regular events such as jazz, folk, film and poetry evenings; children (away from bar) and dogs welcome, open Weds-Sun from 2pm, closed Mon lunchtime, Tues. *(Pete Clayton)*

ROCHESTER TQ7468
Coopers Arms (01634) 404298
St Margarets Street; ME1 1TL Ancient jettied building behind the cathedral, cosily unpretentious with two comfortable beamed bars, low-priced pub food and good range of well kept beers, list of landlords back to 1543 and ghostly tales of a walled-up monk (mannequin marks the spot); live music (Sun) and quiz nights; tables in attractive courtyard, open all day. *(Tony Scott)*

ROLVENDEN TQ8431
Bull (01580) 241212
Regent Street; TN17 4PB Welcoming tile-hung cottage with woodburner in fine brick inglenook, high-backed dining chairs around rustic tables on stripped boards, built-in panelled wall seats, well kept Harveys and Old Dairy, enjoyable food (not Sun evening in winter) from pub favourites and pizzas up, pale oak tables in dining room; background music; children and dogs (in bar) welcome, picnic-sets behind picket fence at front and side, more seats in sizeable back garden, open all day. *(Andy and Rosemary Taylor)*

ROLVENDEN LAYNE TQ8530
Ewe & Lamb (01580) 241837
Maytham Road; TN17 4NP Tile-hung village pub with beams, bare boards and log fires, well kept Adnams, Harveys and a guest, enjoyable home-made food from baguettes up including lots of gluten-free choices, daily specials and some themed nights, friendly efficient service, back restaurant; darts, free wi-fi; children and dogs welcome, seats out at front behind white picket fence, open all day. *(V Brogden)*

SANDWICH TR3358
★George & Dragon (01304) 613106
Fisher Street; CT13 9EJ Popular 15th-c backstreet dining pub run by two brothers (one cooks), very good often imaginative food from open kitchen (booking advised), four well kept ales including Otter, several bottled beers and nice choice of wines by the glass, good friendly service, open-plan beamed interior with three-way log fire, skylit dining extension opening on to paved terrace; children and dogs (in bar) welcome, open all day Sat, closed Sun evening. *(Alan Casey, Richard Tilbrook)*

SARRE TR2564
Crown (01843) 847808
Ramsgate Road (A253) off A28; CT7 0LF Historic 15th-c inn (Grade I listed) sandwiched between two main roads; front bar and other rambling rooms including restaurant, beams and log fires, well kept Shepherd Neame ales and decent fairly priced wines, own cherry brandy (pub known locally as the Cherry Brandy House), generous helpings of enjoyable locally sourced food from sandwiches up, good friendly service; children welcome, side garden (traffic noise), comfortable surprisingly quiet bedrooms, open all day. *(Allan Lloyd and family)*

SEASALTER TR0864
★Sportsman (01227) 273370
Faversham Road, off B2040; CT5 4BP Restauranty pub just inside seawall – rather unprepossessing from outside but surprisingly light and airy; imaginative contemporary cooking using plenty of seafood (not Sun evening, Mon, must book and not cheap), home-baked breads, good wine choice including english, a couple of well kept Shepherd Neame ales, knowledgeable landlord and friendly staff; two plain linked rooms and long conservatory, scrubbed pine tables, wheelback and basket-weave dining chairs on wood floor, local artwork; children welcome, plastic glasses for outside, wide views over marshland with grazing sheep and (from seawall) across to Sheppey, small caravan park one side, wood chalets the other, open all day Sun till 10pm. *(Andy and Rosemary Taylor)*

SEVENOAKS
TQ5555

★Bucks Head (01732) 761330
Godden Green, just E; TN15 0JJ
Welcoming and relaxed old flower-decked pub with neatly kept bar and restaurant area, good freshly cooked blackboard food from baguettes to Sun roasts, well kept Shepherd Neame and a guest, beams, panelling and splendid inglenooks; children and dogs welcome, front terrace overlooking informal green and duck pond, pretty back garden with mature trees, pergola and views over quiet country behind Knole (NT), popular with walkers. *(Pete Clayton)*

SEVENOAKS
TQ5355

Halfway House (01732) 463667
2.5 miles from M25 junction 5; TN13 2JD
Nicely updated old roadside pub with friendly staff and regulars, good competitively priced food from sensibly short menu, three changing ales, local wines and interesting flavoured vodkas, upper bar with record deck and LPs (can bring your own), some live music too; handy for the station, parking can be tricky, open all day (no food Mon). *(Daisy Kelly)*

SHOREHAM
TQ5161

Kings Arms (01959) 523100
Church Street; TN14 7SJ Part-weatherboarded 16th-c pub in quaint unspoilt village close to the River Darent, cosy and unpretentious, with good honest food and two or three well kept beers such as Sharps Doom Bar, friendly staff, log fire, plates and brasses, small restaurant area; children welcome, no dogs, picnic-sets outside, good walks, open all day in summer. *(Mrs Margo Finlay, Jörg Kasprowski)*

SHOREHAM
TQ5261

Olde George (01959) 522017
Church Street; TN14 7RY Traditional 16th-c pub opposite the church, low beams, uneven floors and a cosy fire, two or three well kept changing ales and enjoyable pubby food including bargain OAP lunch (Thurs), friendly attentive service, carpeted dining area to one side; children, walkers and dogs welcome, picnic-sets by road, open all day, no evening food Sun-Tues. *(B and M Kendall)*

SHOREHAM
TQ5161

Two Brewers (01959) 522800
High Street; TN14 7TD Busy family-run pub with two modernised beamed rooms, back part more restaurant, popular freshly made food from sharing plates to Sun roasts, three well kept changing kentish ales, friendly helpful staff, snug areas with comfortable seating, two woodburners; regular live music; handy for walkers, seats out in front behind picket fence, closed Sun evening, Mon and Tues. *(Victoria and James Sargeant)*

SISSINGHURST
TQ7937

★Milk House (01580) 720200
The Street; TN17 2JG Bustling village inn near Sissinghurst Castle Garden (NT); bar on right with grey-painted beams and handsome Tudor fireplace fronted by plush sofas, book wallpaper, candles in hurricane jars, milk churns on window sills and a wire cow, wicker-fronted counter serving Dark Star, Harveys and a local guest, real cider, 14 wines by the glass and good range of whiskies and gins, restaurant to the left with small room off (perfect for a private party), good popular food including pizzas from outside oven; background and winter live music (Weds from 6pm), board games, daily papers, free wi-fi; children and dogs (in bar) welcome, large side terrace with sturdy furniture under green parasols, garden picnic-sets and children's play hut by fenced-in pond, comfortable well equipped bedrooms, open all day from 9am. *(Ian Meeson, Mary Joyce, Sandra Hollies, David Jackman)*

SNARGATE
TQ9928

★Red Lion (01797) 344648
B2080 Appledore–Brenzett; TN29 9UQ
Unchanging 16th-c pub in same family for over 100 years; simple old-fashioned charm in three timeless little rooms with original cream wall panelling, heavy beams in sagging ceilings, dark pine Victorian farmhouse chairs on bare boards, an old piano and coal fire, local cider and four or five ales including Goachers tapped from casks behind unusual free-standing marble-topped counter, no food, traditional games like toad in the hole, nine men's morris and table skittles, friendly staff; children in family room, dogs in bar, outdoor lavatories, cottage garden, closed Mon evening. *(Lee and Jill Stafford)*

SPELDHURST
TQ5541

★George & Dragon (01892) 863125
Village signed from A264 W of Tunbridge Wells; TN3 0NN Handsome pub based around a 13th-c manorial hall (lovely original features); entrance hall with half-panelled room to the right, wheelback and other dining chairs, cushioned wall pew, small pictures and horsebrasses, doorway to another dining room with similar furnishings and second inglenook, bar to left of entrance has woodburner in small fireplace, high-winged cushioned settles and other wooden furniture on stripped-wood floor, interesting food from sandwiches up (not particularly cheap and they add a service charge), Harveys, Larkins and a guest, several wines by the glass, upstairs restaurant; background music, free wi-fi; children and dogs (in bar) welcome, teak furniture on front gravel terrace, covered back area and lower terrace with 200-year-old olive tree, open all day, no food Sun evening; up for sale as we went to press. *(Martin Day, Mary Joyce, Peter and Emma Kelly)*

ST MARGARET'S BAY   TR3744
★**Coastguard** (01304) 853051

Off A256 NE of Dover; keep on down through the village to the bottom of the bay, pub off on right by the beach; CT15 6DY At bottom of a steep winding road with lovely sea views (France visible on a clear day) from prettily planted balcony and beachside seating; newly refurbished bar with four changing ales, bottled continental beers, over 40 whiskies and a carefully chosen wine list (some from kent), straightforward pubby food including seafood specials, more fine views from restaurant with close-set tables on wood-strip floor; background music, free wi-fi (mobile phones pick up french signal); children and dogs allowed in certain areas, good walks, open all day. *(Tony Scott)*

ST MARY IN THE MARSH   TR0627
Star (01797) 362139

Opposite church; TN29 0BX Remote down-to-earth pub with Tudor origins; popular, straightforward food (not Sun, Mon or evenings Tues-Thurs), well kept ales including Youngs from brick-faced counter, friendly service, inglenook woodburner; bar billiards and darts, free wi-fi; children and dogs welcome, tables in nice garden, good value beamed bedrooms with Romney Marsh views, lovely setting opposite ancient church (Edith Nesbit, author of *The Railway Children*, buried here), popular with walkers and cyclists, open all day. *(Audrey and Paul Summers)*

STAPLEHURST   TQ7846
Lord Raglan (01622) 843747

About 1.5 miles from town centre towards Maidstone, turn right off A229 into Chart Hill Road opposite Chart Cars; OS Sheet 188 map reference 785472; TN12 0DE Country pub with cosy chatty area around narrow bar counter, hop-strung low beams, big log fire and woodburner, mix of comfortably worn dark wood furniture, good reasonably priced home-cooked food, Goachers, Harveys and a guest, farm cider and perry, good wine list; children and dogs welcome, reasonable wheelchair access, tables on terrace and in the side orchard, Aug onion festival, closed Sun. *(Mick Sanderson)*

STOWTING   TR1241
★**Tiger** (01303) 862130

3.7 miles from M20 junction 11; B2068 N, then left at Stowting signpost, straight across crossroads, then fork left after 0.25 miles and pub is on right; coming from N, follow 'Brabourne, Wye, Ashford' signpost to right at fork, then turn left towards Posting and Lyminge at T junction; TN25 6BA Peaceful 17th-c country pub near the Wye Downs and North Downs Way; traditionally furnished bare-boards rooms with woodburners, some faded rugs on stone floor towards the back, candles in bottles, books, paintings and brewery memorabilia, local ales including Shepherd Neame Master Brew and a house beer from Tonbridge, Biddenden cider and several wines by the glass, well liked food (not Sun evening) from snacks and pub favourites up; children and dogs (in bar) welcome, wheelchair access with help, seats on front terrace, closed Mon, Tues, otherwise open all day. *(Ian Herdman)*

SUNDRIDGE   TQ4855
White Horse (01959) 562837

Main Road; TN14 6EH Refurbished open-plan village pub on crossroads, decent range of well liked food (some choices available in smaller helpings at lunchtime), Adnams Southwold, St Austell Tribute and maybe a guest, several wines by the glass, good friendly service, log fires and low beams; children welcome, dogs in bar areas, picnic-sets under parasols on fenced lawn, open all day, no food Sun or Mon evenings. *(Gordon and Margaret Ormondroyd)*

SUTTON VALENCE   TQ8050
Plough (01622) 842555

Sutton Road (A274), Langley; ME17 3LX Recently refurbished roadside dining pub, main bar painted in shades of grey with mix of wooden and copper-topped tables, side bar with low tables with comfortable chairs, candlelit dining extension behind with view into kitchen, well kept Harveys, local Rockin' Robin and Sharps Doom Bar, several wines by the glass, enjoyable food from sandwiches and bar snacks to restaurant choices, friendly relaxed atmosphere; some live music; children and dogs welcome, tables and vintage plough out at front behind picket fence, open all day (Sun till 10pm). *(Peter Meister)*

TENTERDEN   TQ8833
White Lion (01580) 765077

High Street; TN30 6BD Comfortably updated beamed and timbered 16th-c inn behind Georgian façade, popular food including Josper grills and pizzas from open kitchen, mainly local ales such as Old Dairy and a beer badged for them, good choice of other drinks including cocktails, big log fire, friendly helpful staff; background music, free wi-fi; heated terrace overlooking street, nicely refurbished bedrooms, good breakfast, open (and food) all day. *(Celia and Geoff Clay)*

TOYS HILL   TQ4752
★**Fox & Hounds** (01732) 750328

Off A25 in Brasted, via Brasted Chart and The Chart; TN16 1QG Welcoming traditional country pub again under new management; bar area separated by two-way woodburner, plain tables and chairs on bare boards or stone floor, grey-painted half-panelling, modern carpeted dining extension with big windows overlooking tree-sheltered garden, well prepared/presented food (not Sun evening) from lunchtime ciabattas up, two Greene King ales and guest such as Westerham, nice wines by the glass, cheerful helpful staff; children and dogs (in bar) welcome, roadside verandah used by smokers, good local walks and views, handy for Chartwell and Emmetts Garden (both NT), open all day. *(Ian Phillips)*

TUDELEY TQ6145
Poacher & Partridge (01732)
358934 Hartlake Road; TN11 0PH
Renovated in smart country style by Elite Pubs (Great House in Hawkhurst, Dirty Habit at Hollingbourne etc); light interior with feature pizza oven, wide range of good food including daily specials, Tues steak night, ales such as Sharps Doom Bar and Timothy Taylors Landlord, good choice of wines by the glass, friendly attentive staff; live music including some afternoon jazz; children welcome, outside bar and grill, play area, nearby interesting church with Chagall stained glass (note roof paintings at pub's entrance), recommended local walks (leaflets provided), open (and food) all day. *(Buster May)*

TUNBRIDGE WELLS TQ5839
Black Pig (01892) 523030
Grove Hill Road; TN1 1RZ Up for sale as we went to press; long narrow bare-boards bar with leather sofas each side of woodburner, bookshelves, unusual cow wallpaper and a large antelope's head, overflow room up steps, Harveys Best and good wines by the glass, food from open kitchen has been interesting and popular, character dining room with contemporary wallpaper, panelling and oriental paintings, button-back wall banquettes and assortment of wooden tables and chairs; children and dogs (in bar) welcome, back gravel terrace, open all day (till 10pm Sun, Mon), food all day Sun. *(Yann, Katherine Matthews)*

TUNBRIDGE WELLS TQ5837
Bull (01892) 263489
Frant Road; TN2 5LH Friendly 19th-c pub towards the outskirts of town; two modernised linked areas with one or two quirky touches, chunky pine tables and kitchen chairs on stripped-wood floor, a couple of leather sofas by open fire, well kept Shepherd Neame ales, generous helpings of enjoyable home-cooked food from changing menu (not Sun evening, Mon); children (till 8.30pm) and dogs welcome, seats out on fenced roadside terrace, closed Mon lunchtime, otherwise open all day. *(Duncan)*

TUNBRIDGE WELLS TQ5838
Compasses (01892) 530744
Little Mount Sion; TN1 1YP Old pub tucked up from High Street and backing on to park; split-level beamed rooms around

central bar, bare boards or carpet, log fires (one in large brick fireplace), some stained and frosted glass, six well kept ales including Greene King and a beer badged for the pub, well priced food from snacks up; background music, free wi-fi, bar billiards; children and dogs welcome, teak and rattan-style furniture on good-sized front terrace, open (and food) all day. *(Pete Clayton)*

UNDERRIVER TQ5552
★White Rock (01732) 833112
SE of Sevenoaks, off B245; TN15 0SB
Attractive village pub with good food from pubby choices up (all day weekends, best to book), friendly helpful service, well kept Harveys, Tonbridge and a beer badged for the pub, decent wines, beams, bare boards and stripped brickwork in cosy original part with adjacent dining area, another bar in modern extension with woodburner; background and some live music, pool; children welcome, dogs may be allowed but ask first, small front garden, back terrace and large lawn with boules and bat and trap, pretty churchyard and walks nearby, open all day in summer, all day weekends winter. *(Martin Day, Gordon and Margaret Ormondroyd)*

UPNOR TQ7671
Ship (01634) 290553
Upnor Road, Lower Upnor; ME2 4UY
Smallish mock-Tudor pub overlooking the Medway and boats; good home-cooking including fish specials, ales such as Sharps, Shepherd Neame and Charles Wells, friendly staff, carpeted interior with marine knick-knacks; children welcome, picnic-sets out at front and in garden behind, open all day. *(Dave Braisted)*.

UPPER UPNOR TQ7570
Tudor Rose (01634) 714175
Off A228 N of Strood; High Street; ME2 4XG 16th-c pub down narrow cobbled street just back from the river next to Upnor Castle (best to use village car park at top); cosy beamed rooms with mix of old furniture and some nautical bits and pieces, Shepherd Neame ales and an occasional guest, popular pubby food (not Sun evening) from baguettes up, good friendly service; free wi-fi; children welcome, seats out at front made from an old boat, large enclosed garden behind with arbour, open all day. *(Mick Sanderson)*

WAREHORNE TQ9832
★Woolpack (01233) 732900
Off B2067 near Hamstreet; TN26 2LL
Part-weatherboarded 16th-c dining pub under same ownership as the Five Bells at Brabourne and the Globe in Rye (see Sussex); interesting interior with various connecting areas, beams, inglenook fire and woodburner, brick and quarry-tiled floors, walls (some boarded) hung with prints, old photographs, hops and ornate mirrors, lots of other bits and pieces including farming

implements, fishing rods, oars and a boar's head, candles on tables, four well kept regional ales direct from the cask, local cider and good wines by the glass, well liked food including daily specials (no bookings so best to arrive early), helpful service and friendly easy-going atmosphere; background jazz; children and dogs welcome, rows of outside seating overlooking quiet lane and 15th-c church, five comfortable quirky bedrooms, open all day. *(Peter Meister)*

WEALD   TQ5250

★**Windmill** (01732) 463330
Windmill Road; TN14 6PN Popular and friendly village pub with six well kept ales including Larkins, local ciders and good fair-priced food (not Sun evening, Mon) from interestingly varied menu, attentive helpful service, traditional hop-strung interior with etched windows and two fires, mix of seating including old pews and carved settles by candlelit tables, jugs and bottles on delft shelves, snug dining area; live music and quiz nights; children and dogs welcome, easy wheelchair access, nice quiet back garden, closed Mon lunchtime, otherwise open all day.
(Martin Day, Chris Billington, Jason Caulkin)

WEST PECKHAM   TQ6452
Swan on the Green (01622) 812271
*Off A26/B2016 W of Maidstone;
ME18 5JW* Attractively placed brick and weatherboarded pub facing village cricket green; own-brewed Swan beers in relaxed open-plan beamed bar, stripped brickwork, bare boards and mixed furnishings, two-way log fire, enjoyable freshly made food (not Sun evening) from varied menu, friendly efficient service; children and dogs welcome, next to interesting part-Saxon church, good walks including Greensand Way, open all day Sun till 9pm. *(Susan and Neil McLean)*

WESTBERE   TR1862
Old Yew Tree (01227) 710501
*Just off A18 Canterbury–Margate;
CT2 0HH* Heavily beamed 14th-c pub in pretty village, simply furnished bare-boards bar with inglenook log fire, good reasonably priced food from varied menu, Shepherd Neame Master Brew and a guest, friendly helpful staff; quiz first Weds of the month, open mike last Weds; picnic-sets in garden behind, open all day weekends, closed Mon. *(Dan and Nicki Barton)*

WESTERHAM   TQ4454
Grasshopper on the Green (01959) 562926 *The Green; TN16 1AS* Old black-beamed pub (small former coaching house) facing village green, three linked bar areas with log fire at back, well kept ales including Westerham, popular pubby food from sandwiches up, helpful pleasant service, restaurant upstairs; sports TV, free wi-fi; children and dogs welcome,

seating out at front and in back garden with play area, open all day. *(Martin Day)*

WESTGATE-ON-SEA   TR3270
Bake & Alehouse 07913 368787
Off St Mildreds Road down alley by cinema; CT8 8RE Friendly micropub in former bakery; simple little bare-boards room with a few tables (expect to share when busy), four well kept interesting ales tapped from the cask, real ciders – maybe a warm winter one (Monks Delight), kentish wines, local cheese, sausage rolls and pork pies, friendly chatty atmosphere; closed Sun evening, Mon. *(Duncan)*

WHITSTABLE   TR1066
Black Dog
High Street; CT5 1BB Quirky micropub (former deli) with five changing ales and several artisan ciders tapped from back room, friendly staff may offer tasters, snacky food, narrow dimly lit Victorian-feel bar with high tables and benches along two sides, intriguing mix of pictures and other bits and pieces on green walls, prominent chandelier suspended from red ceiling; eclectic background music and occasional folk sessions; open all day. *(Pete Clayton)*

WHITSTABLE   TR1066
Old Neptune (01227) 272262
Marine Terrace; CT5 1EJ Great view over Swale estuary from this popular unpretentious weatherboarded pub set right on the beach (rebuilt after being washed away in 1897 storm); Harveys, Shepherd Neame and a guest, reasonably priced lunchtime food from shortish menu including decent fish and chips, friendly young staff; weekend live music; children and dogs welcome, picnic-sets on the shingle (plastic glasses out here and occasional barbecues), fine sunsets, can get very busy in summer, open all day. *(B and M Kendall)*

WHITSTABLE   TR1066
Smack Inn (01227) 273056
*Middle Wall, next to Baptist church;
CT5 1BJ* Small Victorian backstreet local away from the tourist trail, three Shepherd Neame ales and shortish choice of enjoyable low-priced food including burgers and fish and chips, cheerful helpful staff, cosy interior arranged around central servery, panelling, stripped brickwork and log fire; regular live music, often in beach-theme back garden (barbecues); children and dogs welcome, open all day. *(Adam Bellinger)*

WICKHAMBREAUX   TR2258
Rose (01227) 721763
The Green; CT3 1RQ Attractive 16th-c and partly older pub in nice spot across green from church and watermill; enjoyable home-made food, Greene King IPA and three guests (May/Aug beer festivals), local ciders on rotation, friendly helpful staff, small

bare-boards bar with log fire in big fireplace, dining area beyond standing timbers with woodburner, hop-strung beams, panelling and stripped brick; quiz second Weds of the month; children and dogs welcome, enclosed side garden and small courtyard, open all day. *(Martin and Sue Neville)*

WILLESBOROUGH STREET · TR0341
Blacksmiths Arms (01233) 623975
The Street; TN24 0NA Well run, beamed village pub dating in part from the 17th c, Fullers London Pride and a couple of guests, good traditional home-cooked food (not Sun evening) from sandwiches and snacks up, daily blackboard specials, friendly service, open fires including inglenook; children and dogs welcome, picnic-sets in good-sized garden with play area, handy for M20 (junction 10), open all day. *(Andy and Rosemary Taylor)*

WINGHAM TR2457
★ Dog (01227) 720339
Canterbury Road (A257); CT3 1BB Pub/restaurant/hotel in recently refurbished Grade II* listed medieval building; comfortable contemporary styling blending with heavy beams, old brickwork, panelling and log fires, top notch imaginative food (not Sun evening) including good value weekday set lunch, ales such as Harveys, Old Dairy and Shepherd Neame, good range of wines and gins, helpful personable young staff, conservatory; eight well appointed stylish bedrooms, good breakfast, open all day (Sun till 9pm). *(Shaun Tilley)*

WROTHAM TQ6159
Bull (01732) 789800
1.7 miles from M20, junction 2 – Wrotham signed; TN15 7RF Restored 14th-c coaching inn with enjoyable if not always cheap food including smokehouse/barbecue menu, large beamed bar and separate restaurant, matching tables and chairs throughout, real ales such as Dark Star, craft beers and good wine list, friendly efficient service; Fri live music; children welcome, 11 comfortable bedrooms, open all day, food all day weekends. *(Gordon and Margaret Ormondroyd)*

WYE TR0546
New Flying Horse (01233) 812297
Upper Bridge Street; TN25 5AN 17th-c Shepherd Neame inn with beams and inglenook, enjoyable food including fixed-price menu in bar and restaurant, friendly accommodating staff; Sun quiz, occasional live music, free wi-fi; children welcome, good-sized pretty garden with play area and miniature thatched pub (a former Chelsea Flower Show exhibit), nine bedrooms (some in converted stables), open (and food) all day. *(Pete Clayton)*

WYE TR0446
Tickled Trout (01233) 812227
Signed off A28 NE of Ashford; TN25 5EB Popular summer family pub by River Stour; rustic-style carpeted bar with beams, stripped brickwork, stained-glass partitions and open fire, spacious conservatory/restaurant, good choice of food, ales such as Canterbury, Old Dairy and Sharps, kentish ciders and several wines by the glass, friendly helpful staff; live music Sun evening, quiz first Weds of month, free wi-fi; children and dogs welcome, tables on terrace and riverside lawn, open (and food) all day. *(Mick Sanderson)*

YALDING TQ6950
★ Walnut Tree (01622) 814266
B2010 SW of Maidstone; ME18 6JB Timbered village pub with split-level main bar, fine old settles, a long cushioned mahogany bench and mix of dining chairs on brick or carpeted floors, chunky wooden tables with church candles, interesting old photographs, big inglenook log fire, well kept Black Sheep, Harveys and Skinners, good bar food and more inventive restaurant menu, attractive raftered dining room with high-backed leather dining chairs on parquet flooring; background and occasional live music, TV; a few picnic-sets out by road, open all day, no food Sun evening. *(Daisy Kelly)*

A star symbol before the name of a pub shows exceptional character and appeal. It doesn't mean extra comfort. Even quite a basic pub can win a star, if it's individual enough.

Lancashire

with Greater Manchester, Merseyside and Wirral

KEY	★ Star Pub	 Top Quality Food	🍺 Great Beer
	♀ Good Wines	£ Bargain Meals	🛏 Good Bedrooms	🍴 Serves Food

BASHALL EAVES
SD6943 Map 7

Red Pump 🍴★ 🛏

(01254) 826227 – www.theredpumpinn.co.uk

NW of Clitheroe, off B6478 or B6243; BB7 3DA

Beautifully placed country inn with a cosy bar and first class food in contemporary, inviting dining rooms; bedrooms

---

You can stay in individually decorated and comfortable bedrooms here or in the new glamping yurts surrounded by lovely Forest of Bowland countryside; breakfasts are good and generous and residents can fish in the nearby river. The friendly licensees create a cheerful atmosphere and there are two inviting dining rooms and a cosy, traditional central bar: bookshelves, cushioned settles and wheelbacks on flagstones, and log fires. Three regional beers on handpump change weekly and might include a beer named for the pub, Bowland Hen Harrier and Lytham Blonde, plus eight wines by the glass and several malt whiskies; background music and board games. The views from seats on the terrace in front of the pub are splendid.

 Inventive food includes sandwiches, ham hock and white pudding terrine with mulled fruit chutney, salmon, prawn and avocado with roasted tomato dressing, pumpkin and pine nut risotto with sage pesto and parmesan, chicken in cider with smoked bacon and prune stuffing with champ mash, rare-breed burgers with toppings and chips, creamy fish pie, steak in ale pudding, lamb rump with tomatoes, garlic, olive and anchovy dressing, and puddings such as chocolate mousse and glazed lemon tart. *Benchmark main dish: rare-breed sirloin steak with a choice of butters and sauces £21.00. Two-course evening meal £25.00.*

Free house ~ Licensees Frances and Jonathan Gledhill ~ Real ale ~ Open 12-11 (5.30-11 Tues); closed Mon, Tues lunchtime; first two weeks Jan ~ Bar food 12-2, 6-9; 12-9 Sun ~ Restaurant ~ Children welcome ~ Dogs allowed in bar and bedrooms ~ Wi-fi ~ Bedrooms: £102/£120 *Recommended by Daniel King, Tim and Sarah Smythe-Brown, Caroline and Steve Archer, Lyn and Freddie Roberts, James and Sylvia Hewitt, Frances and Hamish Porter*

BAY HORSE
SD4952 Map 7

Bay Horse 🛏

(01524) 791204 – www.bayhorseinn.com

1.2 miles from M6 junction 33: A6 southwards, then off on left; LA2 0HR

18th-c former coaching inn with log fires, comfortable bar and restaurant, well regarded food, local ales and friendly staff; bedrooms

The series of small, rambling linked rooms at this family-owned 18th-c former coaching inn are friendly and gently civilised. The cosily pubby beamed bar has cushioned wall banquettes in bay windows, lamps on windowsills and a good log fire. Black Sheep, Moorhouses Pendle Witches Brew and Timothy Taylors Golden Best on handpump, 11 wines by the glass and a growing range of spirits served by friendly, efficient staff. The dining room has a woodburning stove and lovely views over the garden – where there are plenty of seats and tables. The bedrooms in the converted barn over the road are comfortable and just right if you want to explore the area or need to break a journey while on the nearby motorway.

The same rewarding food is served in both the bar and dining room and includes open sandwiches, black pudding scotch egg with english mustard mayonnaise, scorched gin-cured mackerel with celeriac, horseradish and orange, crispy egg with celeriac purée, kale, mushrooms and truffle, chicken breast with creamy leeks and bacon, hake with mussels and parsley and seaweed dressing, dry-aged local beef fillet with peppercorn sauce, and puddings such as crème brûlée with roast rhubarb and rosemary shortbread and chocolate torte with salted caramel and caramel ice-cream; they also offer a two- and three-course set menu (Wednesday-Friday). *Benchmark main dish: slow-cooked duck leg in port sauce £17.50. Two-course evening meal £25.00.*

Mitchells ~ Tenant Craig Wilkinson ~ Real ale ~ Open 12-3 (3.30 Sat), 6-11; 12-4.30, 6-9 Sun; closed Mon, Tues; one week Jan, second week Nov ~ Bar food 12-2 (2.30 Sat), 6-9; 12-3, 6-8 Sun ~ Restaurant ~ Children welcome ~ Dogs allowed in bar *Recommended by Claire Adams, Alf Wright, Bob and Melissa Wyatt, Graeme and Sally Mendham, Amy and Luke Buchanan, Nigel Havers*

BISPHAM GREEN
SD4813   Map 7

Eagle & Child ★ ♀ ◄

(01257) 462297 – www.eagleandchildbispham.co.uk
Maltkiln Lane (Parbold–Croston road, off B5246); L40 3SG

Civilised pub with antiques, enterprising food, an interesting range of beers and appealing rustic garden

As well as all the enjoyable pub attributes here, there's also a shop in a handsome side barn selling interesting wines and pottery, plus a proper butcher and a deli. The largely open-plan bar is carefully furnished with several handsomely carved antique oak settles (the finest made in part, it seems, from a 16th-c wedding bed-head), a mix of small old oak chairs, an attractive oak coffer, old hunting prints and engravings and hop-draped low beams. Also, red walls, coir matting, oriental rugs on ancient flagstones in front of a fine old stone fireplace and counter; the pub dogs are called Betty and Doris. Friendly young staff serve Bowland Hen Harrier, Hawkshead Windermere Pale, Moorhouses Pride of Pendle, Thwaites Original and Wainwright and Wychwood Hobgoblin on handpump, farm cider, ten wines by the glass, 15 gins and around 30 malt whiskies. A popular beer festival is usually held on the early May bank holiday weekend. The spacious garden has a well tended but unconventional bowling green; beyond is a wild area that's home to crested newts and moorhens. This is part of the Ainscoughs group.

Food is particularly good and includes sandwiches, crispy duck egg with home-cured spiced bacon, celeriac and dashi, chicken liver parfait with amontillado sherry jelly, sausages and black pudding with beer-battered onion rings and onion gravy, steak, ale and mushroom pie, chicken breast with truffle and olive mash, morels and jus, 28-day dry-aged steak with triple-cooked chips, portobello mushroom and a choice of sauces, and puddings such as treacle tart with raspberry ripple ice-cream and cappuccino crème brûlée. *Benchmark main dish: rack of lamb with dauphinoise potatoes and red wine jus £18.50. Two-course evening meal £25.00.*

Free house ~ Licensee Peter Robinson ~ Real ale ~ Open 12-11 (10.30 Sun) ~ Bar food 12-2, 5.30-8.30 (9 Fri); 12-9 Sat; 12-8 Sun ~ Children welcome ~ Dogs welcome ~ Wi-fi ~ Live music last Fri evening of month *Recommended by Martin Sargeant, W K Wood, Beth Aldridge, Julian Richardson, Alistair Forsyth, Patricia Healey, Steve Whalley*

 DOWNHAM   SD7844   Map 7

Assheton Arms

(01200) 441227 ~ www.seafoodpubcompany.com/the-assheton-arms
Off A59 NE of Clitheroe, via Chatburn; BB7 4BJ

Lancashire Dining Pub of the Year

Fine old inn with plenty of dining and drinking space, a friendly welcome, several real ales and creative food; bedrooms

The lovely, comfortable bedrooms (once a post office and two cottages) in this Grade II listed building make a fine base for exploring the area. A small front bar, with a hatch to the kitchen, has tweed-upholstered armchairs and stools on big flagstones around a single table, a woodburning stove surrounded by logs, and drawings of dogs and hunting prints on grey-green walls. Off to the right, a wood-panelled partition creates a cosy area where there are similarly cushioned pews and nice old chairs around various tables on a rug-covered wooden floor, and a couple of window chairs. The main bar, up a couple of steps, has old photographs of the pub and the village on pale walls and a marble bar counter where they serve Moorhouses Pride of Pendle, Thwaites Wainwright and Timothy Taylors Landlord on handpump, a dozen wines by the glass and farm cider. Staff are helpful and attentive. A two-level restaurant has carpet or wooden flooring, two fireplaces (one with a woodburning stove and the other with a lovely old kitchen range) and hunting prints. The setting at the top of a steep hill is very pretty, and picnic-sets and tables and chairs make the most of this. Do note the lovely church opposite. This is part of the Seafood Pub Company.

Exceptionally good food using the best seasonal produce includes sandwiches, queenie scallop and barbecue pork dumplings in mushroom and lemongrass broth, lettuce rolls with wok-fried chicken, cashews, ginger and green chilli, twice-baked cheese soufflé with spinach, cheese and chive sauce, lemon and oregano chicken breast with paprika potatoes, wood-roasted peppers and salsa verde, ravioli of the week, goan king prawn curry with coconut rice and flatbread, piggy grill (gammon rib-eye with a fried egg, pork fillet wrapped in streaky bacon with pineapple and grain mustard ketchup and glazed pork belly with black pudding fritter), and puddings such as passion-fruit and pineapple mess with Malibu cream, vanilla and mint and rocky road cheesecake with cherries, white chocolate, peanuts and popcorn. *Benchmark main dish: seafood skewer with cauliflower tabbouleh, spicy aubergines, yoghurt and chilli £19.50. Two-course evening meal £24.00.*

Free house ~ Licensee Jocelyn Neve ~ Real ale ~ Open 12-11 (midnight Sat, 10.30 Sun) ~ Bar food 12-9 (10 Fri, Sat, 8 Sun) ~ Restaurant ~ Children welcome ~ Dogs allowed in bar ~ Wi-fi *Recommended by W K Wood, Julie Swift, Caroline Sullivan, Millie and Peter Downing, Gary Baldwin, Martin and Joanne Sharp, Jim and Sue James, Emily and Toby Archer*

Bedroom prices are for high summer. Even then you may get reductions for more than one night, or (outside tourist areas) weekends. Winter special rates are common, and many inns reduce bedroom prices if you have a full evening meal.

FORMBY
SD3109 Map 7

Sparrowhawk ♀ ◀

(01704) 882350 – www.brunningandprice.co.uk/sparrowhawk

Southport Old Road; brown sign to pub just off A565 Formby bypass, S edge of Ainsdale; L37 0AB

Light and airy pub with interesting décor, good food and drinks choices and wooded grounds

Five acres of woods and parkland surround this well run country house and a flagstoned side terrace has sturdy tables, with picnic-table sets on lawns by a set of swings and an old Fergie tractor. The various open-plan rooms, spreading out from the central bar, have plenty of interest: attractive prints on pastel walls, church candles, flowers, snug leather fireside armchairs in library corners and seats and tables with rugs on dark boards by big bow windows. There's also a comfortably carpeted conservatory dining room; background music. A wide choice of drinks includes 21 wines by the glass, 89 malt whiskies, 49 gins and Phoenix Brunning & Price Original, Salopian Oracle, Titanic Plum Porter and guests such as Heavy Industry 77, Moorhouses Blond Witch and Peerless Triple Blond on handpump. A walk from the pub to coastal nature reserves might just yield red squirrels, still hanging on in this area.

Good, enjoyable food includes sandwiches, tempura king prawns with pineapple, mint and chilli salsa, chicken liver parfait with spiced pear and date chutney, smoked haddock fishcake with a poached egg and chive and caper sauce, sweet potato, aubergine and lentil moussaka, pork sausages with onion gravy, beef bourguignon, hake loin with tomato, butter bean and chorizo cassoulet, slow-roast pork belly with celeriac purée, black pudding croquette and quince jus, and puddings such as chocolate brownie with chocolate sauce and rhubarb and ginger trifle with pistachio granola. *Benchmark main dish: beer-battered cod and chips £13.45. Two-course evening meal £20.00.*

Brunning & Price ~ Manager Iain Hendry ~ Real ale ~ Open 12-11 (10.30 Sun) ~ Bar food 12-10 (9.30 Sun) ~ Children welcome ~ Dogs allowed in bar ~ Wi-fi *Recommended by Peter Pilbeam, Sandra Morgan, Colin Humphreys, Greta and Gavin Craddock, Margo and Derek Stapley*

GREAT MITTON
SD7138 Map 7

Aspinall Arms ♀ ◀

(01254) 826555 – www.brunningandprice.co.uk/aspinallarms

B6246 NW of Whalley; BB7 9PQ

Cleverly refurbished and extended riverside pub with cheerful helpful service and a fine choice of drinks and food

A good mix of customers (walkers, cyclists, anglers and locals) fills the various rambling rooms here and the atmosphere is friendly and relaxed. Set in the heart of the Ribble Valley, the pub sits on the banks of the river with picnic-sets on grass overlooking the water and seats and tables on a terrace. The bars have seating that ranges from attractively cushioned old-style dining chairs through brass-studded leather ones to big armchairs and sofas around an assortment of dark tables. Floors are flagstoned, carpeted or wooden and topped with rugs, while the pale-painted or bare stone walls are hung with an extensive collection of prints and local photographs. Dotted about are large mirrors, house plants, stone bottles and bookshelves and there are both open fires and a woodburning stove. From the central servery, knowledgeable staff serve Phoenix Brunning & Price Original and Moorhouses Aspinall Witch (named for the pub) with guests such as Goose Eye Chinook Blonde, Moorhouses Black Cat, Saltaire Blonde and Timothy

Taylors Golden Best on handpump, 15 wines by the glass, 50 gins, an amazing 150 malt whiskies and a farm cider; background music and board games.

 Up-to-date food choices include sandwiches, crispy duck and noodle salad with asian vegetables and mango and chilli dressing, scallops with black pudding, cauliflower purée and apple dressing, smoked haddock fishcake with a poached egg and chive and caper sauce, butternut squash and cauliflower dhal with spinach, onion bhaji and naan, pork and leek sausages with mash and onion gravy, lamb shoulder with dauphinoise potatoes and lamb jus, and puddings such as chocolate tart with boozy plums and bread and butter pudding with apricot sauce. *Benchmark main dish: burger with toppings, coleslaw and chips £12.95. Two-course evening meal £22.00.*

Brunning & Price ~ Manager Susanne Engelmann ~ Real ale ~ Open 10.30am-11pm (10.30pm Sun) ~ Bar food 12-10 (9.30 Sun) ~ Restaurant ~ Children welcome ~ Dogs allowed in bar ~ Wi-fi ~ Live music last Fri evening of month *Recommended by W K Wood, John and Sylvia Harrop, Peter Meister, Alf and Sally Garner, Francis and Mandy Robertson, James and Sylvia Hewitt*

GREAT MITTON   SD7139   Map 7
Three Fishes ♀ ◀

(01254) 826888 – www.thethreefishes.com
Mitton Road (B6246, off A59 NW of Whalley); BB7 9PQ

Stylish pub with tremendous attention to detail, excellent regional food given a modern touch and interesting drinks

In warm weather, the seats and tables on the terrace and in the garden here are quickly snapped up, as they have fine views over the Ribble Valley. Inside, it's imaginatively converted and cleverly laid out to include plenty of cosy corners. The areas closest to the bar are elegantly traditional with a couple of big stone fireplaces, rugs on polished floors and upholstered stools. Then there's a series of individually furnished and painted rooms with exposed stone walls, careful spotlighting, contemporary seats, tables and long button-back wall banquettes and wooden slatted blinds, ending with another impressive fireplace. Staff are young and friendly and there's a good chatty atmosphere: Bowland Pheasant Plucker, Moorhouses Premier Bitter, Reedley Hallows Pendleside and Thwaites 1814 on handpump, 11 wines by the glass, eight gins and 15 malt whiskies; background music.

 Very good, attractively presented food includes mussels with white wine, shallots and cream, venison bonbon scotch egg with pickled damson purée, roasted root vegetable, cheese and red wine shallot tart, lancashire hotpot, wild rabbit pie, maple-cured gammon with a poached egg and battered onion rings, seafood platter, and puddings such as sticky toffee pudding with ginger ice-cream and butterscotch sauce and spiced apple and brown sugar eton mess. *Benchmark main dish: fish pie £13.75. Two-course evening meal £19.00.*

Ribble Valley Inns ~ Manager Daniel McCarthy ~ Real ale ~ Open 12-11 (10.30 Sun) ~ Bar food 12-9 (9.30 Fri, Sat, 8 Sun) ~ Children welcome ~ Dogs allowed in bar ~ Wi-fi *Recommended by William and Sophia Renton, David Appleyard, Colin and Daniel Gibbs, Simon and Alex Knight*

LITTLE ECCLESTON   SD4240   Map 7
Cartford ⬤ ◀ ⇐

(01995) 670166 – www.thecartfordinn.co.uk
Cartford Lane, off A586 Garstang–Blackpool, by toll bridge; PR3 0YP

Attractively refurbished riverside coaching inn with a thoughtful choice of drinks and food; waterside bedrooms

The tidal River Wyre flows beneath a toll bridge within yards of this 17th-c coaching inn and the individually decorated bedrooms look over the water. The unusual four-level layout blends both traditional and contemporary elements with an appealing mix of striking colours, natural wood and polished floors, while the log fire and eclectic choice of furniture create a comfortable and relaxed feel in the bar lounge; background music. Giddy Kipper named for the pub (from Moorhouses) plus Hawkshead Lakeland Gold, Lancaster Black and Moorhouses Pride of Pendle on handpump, alongside speciality bottled beers, 18 wines by the glass, over 30 gins and a dozen malt whiskies. There's also another cosy lounge and a riverside restaurant. Tables in the front garden of this prettily placed inn look over the river, the Trough of Bowland and the peaks of the Lake District. The've just opened an on-site shop and delicatessen selling home-made food, artisan breads and cakes and top produce from around the region.

 Interesting food includes lunchtime sandwiches, smoked sea trout and scallops with sea rosemary, cauliflower purée and watercress coulis, marinated pork belly and watermelon with sweet pickled cucumber, mint, basil and goats curd, sharing platters, poussin with lemon and thyme stuffing, maple jersey potatoes, butternut squash and chorizo, miso-glazed cod and octopus with pak choi, aubergine and black garlic potato purée, oxtail, beef skirt and ale pudding with olive oil mash, and puddings such as dark chocolate mousse with espresso foam and cinnamon doughnut and vanilla custard tart with ginger and rhubarb. *Benchmark main dish: beer-braised jacob's ladder of beef with rosemary polenta £15.95. Two-course evening meal £24.00.*

Free house ~ Licensees Patrick and Julie Beaume ~ Real ale ~ Open 12-11; 5.30-11 Mon; 12-midnight Sat; 12-10 Sun; closed Mon lunchtime ~ Bar food 12-2, 5.30-9 (10 Fri, Sat); 12-8.30 Sun ~ Restaurant ~ Children must be over 10 after 8pm ~ Wi-fi ~ Bedrooms: £80/£130 *Recommended by Dave, Steve Whalley, W K Wood, Camilla and Jose Ferrera, Andy and Rosemary Taylor, Trish and Karl Soloman, John and Claire Masters*

MANCHESTER
Wharf ♀ ◖
SJ8297 Map 7

(0161) 220 2960 – www.brunningandprice.co.uk/thewharf
Blantyre Street/Slate Wharf; M15 4SW

Big wharf-like pub with large terrace overlooking the water and a fine range of drinks and food

Even when this huge place is packed, the hard-working staff remains unfailingly helpful and friendly. They serve a fine range of drinks: Phoenix Brunning & Price Original and Weetwood Cheshire Cat plus up to seven quickly changing guest ales on handpump, such as Front Row Land of Hops & Glory, Lancaster Red, Moorhouses White Witch, Staffordshire Rudyard Ruby Ale, Thirst Class Ale High Five, TicketyBrew Coffee Anise Porter and Wincle Sir Philip, as well as farm cider, 19 wines by the glass and over 50 malt whiskies. Despite being open-plan and on several levels, there are enough cosy nooks and alcoves to keep some sense of cosiness. Downstairs is more pubby and informal with groups of high tables and chairs, while the restaurant upstairs has table service. Throughout there's an appealing variety of pre-war-style dining chairs around quite a choice of dark wooden tables on rugs and shiny floorboards, hundreds of interesting prints and posters on bare-brick or painted walls, old stone bottles, church candles, house plants and fresh flowers on windowsills and tables, bookshelves and armchairs here and there, and large mirrors over open fires. The large front terrace has plenty of wood and chrome tables and chairs around a fountain, and picnic-sets overlooking the canal basin.

Bistro-style food includes sandwiches, sticky lime and ginger ribs with prawn crackers and sesame, scallops with crab fritters, pea purée and lemon dressing, saffron-braised fennel and quinoa salad with orange segments, pomegranate seeds and tahini dressing, steak in ale pudding, spicy vietnamese king prawn and rice noodle salad with toasted cashew nuts, lime and chilli dressing, chicken breast with fondant potato and soaked bacon with sherry sauce, and puddings such as clementine tart with blackcurrant sorbet and crème brûlée. *Benchmark main dish: beer-battered cod and chips £13.45. Two-course evening meal £21.00.*

Brunning & Price ~ Manager Siobhan Youngs ~ Real ale ~ Open 10.30am-11pm (midnight Fri, Sat, 10.30pm Sun) ~ Bar food 12-10 (9.30 Sun) ~ Restaurant ~ Children welcome ~ Dogs allowed in bar ~ Wi-fi ~ Live music Fri evening *Recommended by Rosie and John Moore, Susan and Callum Slade, Tony Hobden, Mike and Wena Stevenson, David and Charlotte Green, Shona and Jimmy McDuff*

MELLOR

SD6530 Map 7

Millstone 🍺 🛏
(01254) 813333 – www.millstonehotel.co.uk
The Mellor near Blackburn; Mellor Lane; BB2 7JR

Smart, popular dining pub with rewarding food, real ales and seats outside; bedrooms

This handsome and neatly kept 18th-c stone coaching inn was refurbished in 2017. The extensive panelling on both sides of the central bar has remained, and both here and in the dining rooms there are elegant wooden and painted, upholstered and up-to-date dining chairs around polished tables on carpet or parquet flooring and button-back wall seats. Also, several log fires, books on shelves, mirrors, flowers on tables and attractive prints on pale paintwork. Thwaites Original and Wainwrights and two weekly guest ales on handpump served by friendly staff and a dozen wines by the glass; background music. A side terrace has seats and tables under parasols. Bedrooms are well equipped and comfortable (some are in a separate block across the car park) and breakfasts are good.

A wide choice of good food includes sandwiches, smoked haddock kedgeree with slow-cooked duck egg yolk and pea purée, duck spring rolls with sticky plum sauce and oriental sesame seed salad, sharing boards, caramelised red onion and goats cheese tart with rosemary and polenta chips, beer-battered haddock and chips, confit lamb shank with chorizo and butter bean broth and garlic mash, tandoori chicken with bombay potatoes and raita, and puddings such as espresso crème brûlée and dark and white chocolate fondant with chocolate ice-cream. *Benchmark main dish: steak, kidney and ale pudding £14.95. Two-course evening meal £19.00.*

Thwaites ~ Manager Tim Parker ~ Real ale ~ Open 9am-midnight; 9am-10.30pm Sun ~ Bar food 12-9.30 (9 Sun) ~ Restaurant ~ Children welcome ~ Dogs allowed in bar ~ Wi-fi ~ Bedrooms: £70/£80 *Recommended by Brian and Anna Marsden, W K Wood, Edward Mirzoeff, Dr A McCormick*

NETHER BURROW

SD6175 Map 7

Highwayman ⅌
(01524) 273338 – www.highwaymaninn.co.uk
A683 S of Kirkby Lonsdale; LA6 2RJ

Substantial and skilfully refurbished old stone house with country interior serving carefully sourced food; lovely gardens

Even on a damp, cold winter's day you'll find plenty of cheerful customers in this substantial 17th-c stone pub in pretty Lune Valley countryside.

Although quite big, the stylishly simple flagstoned interior is nicely divided into intimate corners, with a couple of large log fires, wooden, leather-seated or tartan chairs around dark tables, and button-back or leather wall banquettes. There are some big photos on the walls and interesting modern lighting. Thwaites 1816, Original and Wainwright on handpump, 11 wines by the glass and 15 malt whiskies served by friendly, efficient staff; background music. French windows open out to a big terrace and lovely gardens with smart rattan-style furniture.

Championing local produce, the attractively presented food includes sandwiches, smoked salmon and prawn cocktail, pork belly and black pudding croquette with apple ketchup and pork quavers, sharing platters, black pea and chilli burger with toppings, piccalilli and skin-on fries, lancashire hotpot, fish dish of the day with seaweed butter, duck breast with braised onion tart, duck leg bonbon with green peppercorn sauce and dripping chips, and puddings such as dark chocolate slice with hot caramel sauce and crème brûlée with orange compote. *Benchmark main dish: cheese and onion pie £12.50. Two-course evening meal £17.50.*

Ribble Valley Inns ~ Manager Laura Bromwell ~ Real ale ~ Open 12-11; 12-10.30 Sun ~ Bar food 12-9; 12-9.30 Fri, Sat; 12-8 Sun ~ Restaurant ~ Children welcome ~ Dogs allowed in bar ~ Wi-fi *Recommended by John Poulter, Charlie May, Margaret McDonald, Sandra and Michael Smith, Audrey and Paul Summers*

PLEASINGTON
SD6528 Map 7
Clog & Billycock ♀
(01254) 201163 – www.theclogandbillycock.com
Village signposted off A677 Preston New Road on W edge of Blackburn; Billinge End Road; BB2 6QB

Carefully sourced local food in extremely appealing and well run stone-built village pub

This is a carefully modernised and attractive village pub run by friendly, hard-working licensees. It has the feel of an upmarket barn conversion and is light and airy with flagstoned floors, high ceilings with beams and joists and pale grey walls above a grey dado. Several rooms run together with leather seated or plush cushioned dining chairs and tartan wall banquettes around light wooden tables, big photographs, lamps in various niches and an open fire. Thwaites 1867, Copper Peel, Wainwright and a guest beer on handpump and good wines by the glass. The small garden has an awning-covered terrace with benches, seats and tables.

Local food producers are at the heart of the enjoyable food: sandwiches (until 6pm), free-range chicken caesar salad, plaice goujons with pickled cucumber and jalapeno dressing, burger with toppings, mustard mayonnaise and skin-on fries, mixed vegetable tempura with bulgar wheat salad and dips, lancashire hotpot with pickled red cabbage, whole plaice with morecambe bay shrimps and confit fennel and parsley, air-dried steaks with battered onion rings and dripping chips, and puddings such as treacle tart with raspberries and lemon sponge with vanilla ice-cream. *Benchmark main dish: pork belly, sausage, black pudding, crackling and gravy £14.00. Two-course evening meal £20.00.*

Ribble Valley Inns ~ Managers Andy Morris and Craig Bancroft ~ Real ale ~ Open 12-11 (10.30 Sun) ~ Bar food 12-9 (9.30 Fri, Sat, 8.30 Sun) ~ Children welcome ~ Dogs allowed in bar ~ Wi-fi *Recommended by W K Wood, Mark and Sian Edwards, Geoff and Ann Marston, Robert and Diana Myers*

> If we know a featured-entry pub does sandwiches, we always say so – if they're not mentioned, you'll have to assume you can't get one.

PRESTON
SD5634 Map 7

Haighton Manor ♀ ◖

(01772) 706350 – www.brunningandprice.co.uk/haightonmanor
Haighton Green Lane, Haighton; PR2 5SQ

Rather grand stone building surrounded by lawns and countryside, interesting furnishings in interconnected rooms, thoughtful drinks and food choice, and seats outside

This lovely 17th-c place, a former hospital, has been completely renovated and extended by Brunning & Price. The bustling bar has an open fire, a big farmhouse kitchen table with wooden chairs, elegant metal chandeliers and stools against the counter where plenty of cheerful staff serve Phoenix Brunning & Price Original plus guests such as Kelham Island Pale Rider, Lancaster Blonde, Moorhouses White Witch, Timothy Taylors Boltmaker and Tring Puma on handpump, 120 malt whiskies, 100 gins and six farm ciders; board games. Various open-plan rooms lead off here with rugs on wooden floors, wall-to-wall prints, photographs and mirrors on pale walls above painted dados, more open fires, antique-style cushioned dining chairs around dark tables, and house plants and candles. One cosy character room has armchairs and chesterfield sofas on flagstones and exposed stone walls, and there's a big, carpeted conservatory dining extension. Good quality chairs, benches and tables under parasols are set out on a terrace surrounded by lawns (on which there's a trademark tractor for children); pleasant country views.

 Good, modern food includes sandwiches, potted salmon and mackerel with pickled radish and cucumber salad, a charcuterie board, butternut squash, feta and spinach quiche, honey-roasted ham with eggs, steak and kidney pudding, sea bass with dhal, cauliflower beignets and mango dressing, duck breast with roasted plum and asian-spiced duck sauce, rump steak with tarragon and dijon butter, portobello mushrooms and chips, and puddings such as hot waffle with caramelised banana and toffee ice-cream and crème brûlée. *Benchmark main dish: braised lamb shoulder with dauphinoise potatoes and rosemary gravy £17.25. Two-course evening meal £22.00.*

Brunning & Price ~ Licensee Chris Humphries ~ Real ale ~ Open 11-11; 11-10.30 Sun ~ Bar food 12-10 (9.30 Sun) ~ Children welcome ~ Dogs allowed in bar ~ Wi-fi
Recommended by Nicola and Holly Lyons, Rosie and Marcus Heatherley, Amanda Shipley

SAWLEY
SD7746 Map 7

Spread Eagle ⇔

(01200) 441202 – www.spreadeaglesawley.co.uk
Village signed just off A59 NE of Clitheroe; BB7 4NH

Nicely refurbished pub with quite a choice of food, riverside restaurant and four real ales; bedrooms

There's so much to do and see around this attractive old coaching inn that it makes sense to stay a while in the individually furnished and comfortable bedrooms. The substantial ruins of a 12th-c cistercian abbey are close by and there are exhilarating walks in the Forest of Bowland. The bar rooms have a pleasing mix of nice old and quirky modern furniture – anything from an old settle and pine tables to up-to-date low chairs upholstered in animal print fabric – all set off well by the grey rustic stone floor. Low ceilings, cosy sectioning, a warming fire and cottage windows keep it all feeling intimate. The dining areas are more formal, with modern stripes and a bookshelf mural; background music. Bowland Sawley Duck, Dark Horse Hetton Pale Ale, Moorhouses White Witch and Thwaites Wainwright on handpump and several wines by the glass.

Rewarding food includes duck liver pâté with piccalilli, crab, avocado and plum tomato cocktail, sharing platters, indian-spiced lamb burger with onion bhaji, cucumber and mint yoghurt, spicy cauliflower and chickpea tagine with deep-fried falafel, slow-cooked beef daube on potato purée with bourguignon sauce, salmon with tartare velouté and baby spinach, duck with roasted beetroot and black cherry sauce, and puddings such as vanilla pannacotta with warm gingerbread, apple purée and spiced syrup and bread and butter ice-cream terrine with apricot sorbet and apricot sauce; they also have a £5 fish and chip deal on Wednesdays. *Benchmark main dish: battered haddock and chips £12.95. Two-course evening meal £19.50.*

Individual Inns ~ Managers Greg and Natalie Barns ~ Real ale ~ Open 11-11 (midnight Sat); 12-10.30 Sun ~ Bar food 12-2, 5.30-9; 12-2, 6-9.30 Sat; 12-7 Sun ~ Restaurant ~ Children welcome ~ Dogs allowed in bar and bedrooms ~ Wi-fi ~ Bedrooms: £92/£110
Recommended by Anne Taylor, Ruth May, Muriel and Spencer Harrop, Moira and John Wheeler, Adam Jones, Louise and Anton Parsons

THORNTON HOUGH  SJ2979 Map 7
Red Fox ♀ ◀
(0151) 353 2920 ~ www.brunningandprice.co.uk/redfox
Liverpool Road; CH64 7TL

Big spreading pub with a fine choice of beers, wines, gins and whiskies, courteous staff serving enjoyable food and large back garden

At the back of this substantial brick and sandstone pub you'll find terraces with good quality wooden chairs and tables under parasols, and steps down to picnic-sets around a fountain on a spreading lawn – the country views are pleasant. The spacious main bar is reached up stairs from the entrance: large central pillars divide the room into smaller areas with high stools and tables in the middle, dark wooden tables and chairs to each side and deep leather armchairs and fender seats by the large fireplace. This leads into a long, airy, carpeted dining room with two rows of painted iron supports, hefty leather and wood chairs around highly polished tables and a raised firepit; doors from here lead out to a terrace. Two additional dining rooms are similarly furnished, one with an elegant chandelier hanging from a fine moulded ceiling, the other with a huge metal elephant peeping through large house plants. Throughout there are photographs, prints and pictures covering the walls, big plants, stone bottles and shelves of books. Friendly, cheerful staff serve Phoenix Brunning & Price Original and Facers Sunlight Blonde with guests from breweries such as Brightside, Conwy, Liverpool Craft Beer Company, Merlins Micro Brewery and Peerless on handpump, 20 wines by the glass, 165 malt whiskies, 100 gins and eight farm ciders; background music and board games.

Brasserie-style food includes sandwiches, scallops with black pudding fritters, cauliflower purée and apple and sage dressing, chicken liver pâté with apple and rhubarb chutney, warm crispy beef salad with sweet chilli dressing and spicy peanuts, wild mushroom, butter bean and spinach pudding with thyme jus, steak burger with toppings, coleslaw and chips, duck breast with boulangère potatoes and blackberry and thyme jus, beer-battered cod and chips, chicken, ham hock and leek pie, and puddings such as clementine tart with raspberry sorbet and steamed apple and treacle sponge with custard. *Benchmark main dish: braised lamb shoulder with dauphinoise potatoes and gravy £17.25. Two-course evening meal £22.00.*

Brunning & Price ~ Manager David Green ~ Real ale ~ Open 10.30am-11pm (10.30pm Sun) ~ Bar food 12-10 (9.30 Sun) ~ Restaurant ~ Children welcome ~ Dogs allowed in bar ~ Wi-fi
Recommended by Lionel Smith, Jack and Hilary Burton, Edward May, Isobel Mackinlay, Matthew and Elisabeth Reeves, Christopher May

UPPERMILL
Church Inn 🍺 £

SD0006 Map 7

(01457) 820902 – www.churchinnsaddleworth.co.uk

From the main street (A607), look out for the sign for Saddleworth Church, and turn off up this steep narrow lane – keep on up; OL3 6LW

Community pub with big range of own-brew beers at unbeatable bargain prices and tasty food; children very welcome

The big range of own-brewed ales and incredible value food are what draw customers to this ancient pub – set all alone by an isolated church on a steep moorland slope. The big, unspoilt, L-shaped main bar has a cheerful, friendly atmosphere, high beams and some stripped stone, settles, pews, a good individual mix of chairs, lots of attractive prints, staffordshire and other china on a high delft shelf, jugs, brasses and so forth. They keep up to 11 of their own Saddleworth beers – though, if the water levels from the spring aren't high enough for brewing, they bring in guests such as Black Sheep and Copper Dragon. Some of their own seasonal ales are named after the licensee's children, only appearing around their birthdays; two home-brewed lagers on tap too. TV (for sporting events) and unobtrusive background music. A conservatory opens on to the terrace. The local bellringers arrive on Wednesdays to practise with a set of handbells kept here, and anyone can join the morris dancing on Thursdays. Children enjoy all the animals, including rabbits, chickens, dogs, ducks, geese, alpacas, horses, 14 peacocks in the next-door field and some cats that live in an adjacent barn; dogs are made to feel very welcome.

 Fair-priced, traditional food includes sandwiches, mushrooms in creamy garlic sauce, breaded prawns with barbecue sauce, full english breakfast, chilli con carne with rice, vegetable fajitas with sour cream, cheese and guacamole, deep-fried cod and chips, gammon with egg and pineapple, three-course roast lunch, and puddings such as apple crumble and hot chocolate fudge cake. *Benchmark main dish: steak and kidney pudding £9.95. Two-course evening meal £15.00.*

Own brew ~ Licensee Christine Taylor ~ Real ale ~ Open 12-midnight (1am Sat) ~ Bar food 12-3, 5-9; 12-9.30 Fri-Sun and bank holidays ~ Restaurant ~ Children welcome ~ Dogs allowed in bar ~ Wi-fi *Recommended by Colin and Daniel Gibbs, Kate Moran, Peter Barrett, Buster May, Steve Whalley, Jim and Sue James, Buster and Helena Hastings*

WHITEWELL
Inn at Whitewell ★ 🏵 🍷 🍺 🛏

SD6546 Map 7

(01200) 448222 – www.innatwhitewell.com

Most easily reached by B6246 from Whalley; road through Dunsop Bridge from B6478 is also good; BB7 3AT

Fine manor house with smartly pubby atmosphere, top quality food, exceptional wine list, real ales and professional, friendly service; luxury bedrooms

There are delightful views over the adjacent River Hodder and across towards the lovely high moors of the Forest of Bowland from the riverside bar and adjacent terrace at this elegant manor house hotel. The civilised bar rooms have handsome old wood furnishings, including antique settles, oak gate-leg tables and sonorous clocks, set off beautifully against powder blue walls neatly hung with big appealing prints. The pubby main bar has roaring log fires in attractive stone fireplaces and heavy curtains on sturdy wooden rails; one area has a selection of newspapers and magazines, local maps and guidebooks. There's a piano for anyone who wants to play, and board games. Early evening sees a cheerful bustle that later settles to a more tranquil and relaxing atmosphere. Drinks include a marvellous wine list of around 230 wines with 17 by the glass (reception has a good wine shop), 24 whiskies, eight gins, organic ginger beer, lemonade and fruit juices and Moorhouses Blond Witch, Timothy Taylors Landlord and Tirril Kirkstone Gold on handpump. The bedrooms are lovely (several have open fires), and there's also a self-catering holiday house. They own several miles of trout, salmon and sea trout fishing on the River Hodder; picnic hamper on request.

Food is delicious and uses the best local, seasonal produce: lunchtime sandwiches, home-made black pudding with mushrooms, bacon and new potatoes topped with a fried egg and mustard dressing, potted cornish crab with cucumber pickle and avocado purée, gnocchi with spinach, vine tomatoes and roast red onions, parmesan and a garlic croûte, corn-fed poussin in lemon and thyme with sage and onion croquette, bread sauce and roasting gravy, roast rack of lamb with rosemary and garlic tomatoes and lemon and mint jelly, sea bass with spinach and goats cheese couscous, crushed tomato on toast and harissa, and puddings such as chocolate and hazelnut brownie with chocolate sauce and sticky toffee pudding with butterscotch sauce. *Benchmark main dish: fish pie topped with cheese £11.50. Two-course evening meal £20.00.*

Free house ~ Licensee Charles Bowman ~ Real ale ~ Open 11am–midnight ~ Bar food 12–2, 7.30–9.30 ~ Restaurant ~ Children welcome ~ Dogs welcome ~ Wi-fi ~ Bedrooms: £97/£134
Recommended by John and Sylvia Harrop, W K Wood, Muriel and Spencer Harrop, John Poulter, Peter and Alison Steadman, Peter and Emma Kelly, Maria and Henry Lazenby, Professor James Burke

WORSLEY
Worsley Old Hall ♀ ◖
SD7401 Map 7

(0161) 703 8706 ~ www.brunningandprice.co.uk/worsleyoldhall
A mile from M60 junction 13: A575 Walkden Road, then after roundabout take first left into Worsley Park; M28 2QT

Very handsomely converted landmark building, now a welcoming pub scoring high on all counts

On a sunny day, the seats and tables on the big flagstoned terrace behind this impressive and rather grand timbered mansion are quickly snapped up; there's also a barbecue area, a neat lawn beyond the fountain with picnic-table sets and views over the golf course. The place has been carefully restored and has some lovely original architectural features: a gracefully arched inglenook and matching window alcove, handsome staircase, heavy beams and glowing mahogany panelling. The relaxed and chatty main area spreads generously around the feature central bar, where exceptionally well trained staff serve 17 good wines by the glass, over 100 malt whiskies and 38 gins. Also, Phoenix Brunning & Price Original and Brightside Brindley Blonde on handpump with guests such as Rudgate Jorvik, Saltaire Triple Chocoholic and Weetwood Old Dog and, from XT, Animal Brewing Co Moose. There's also the usual abundance of well chosen prints, fireside armchairs and a wide collection of cushioned dining chairs and wooden tables, and rugs on oak parquet; board games and background music. The Worsley Bridgewater Canal heritage area is a ten-minute walk away.

Usefully served all day from brunch onwards (9am–midday), the impressive food includes sandwiches, potted smoked mackerel topped with shrimp butter, capers, samphire and fennel, ham hock, pear and rhubarb salad, tarragon gnocchi with cep mushroom and madeira sauce, honey-roasted ham and eggs, warm crispy beef salad with sweet chilli dressing and cashew nuts, pork tenderloin, prosciutto, black pudding and braised pigs cheek with confit potato, apple purée and cider gravy, and puddings such as blackberry and apple crumble with vanilla custard and dark chocolate and hazelnut brownie with chocolate sauce. *Benchmark main dish: braised lamb shoulder with dauphinoise potatoes and gravy £17.25. Two-course evening meal £21.00.*

Brunning & Price ~ Manager David Green ~ Real ale ~ Open 9am-11pm (10.30pm Sun) ~ Bar food 12-10 (9.30 Sun) ~ Restaurant ~ Children welcome ~ Dogs allowed in bar ~ Wi-fi
Recommended by Michael Butler, W K Wood, Brian and Anna Marsden, Alun and Jennifer Evans, Amy Ledbetter

Also Worth a Visit in Lancashire

Besides the fully inspected pubs, you might like to try these pubs that have been recommended to us and described by readers. Do tell us what you think of them: feedback@goodguides.com

BARLEY   SD8240
★**Barley Mow** (01282) 690868
Barley Lane; BB12 9JX Bars and dining rooms resembling a hunting lodge; animal hide chairs and cushions, antlers and stuffed animals including a big boar's head, exposed-stone, cream-coloured or planked walls, woodburners (one in a raised two-sided fireplace), mix of furniture including long rustic wall seats on carpet, bare boards or flagstones, Moorhouses, Thwaites and Timothy Taylors, eight wines by the glass and well liked hearty food; background music, TV, board games, free wi-fi; children and dogs (in bar) welcome, comfortable bedrooms, open (and food) all day. *(Charlie Parker)*

BARLEY   SD8240
Pendle (01282) 614808
Barley Lane; BB12 9JX Friendly 1930s stone pub in shadow of Pendle Hill, three cosy rooms, two log fires and five well kept regional ales including Moorhouses, popular good value pubby food (all day weekends) using local produce including lamb from family farm, conservatory; fortnightly quiz, free wi-fi; picnic-sets on strip of lawn at front, small fenced play area across road by stream, lovely village and good walking country, bedrooms, open all day Fri-Sun. *(Emily and Toby Archer)*

BARNSTON   SJ2783
★**Fox & Hounds** (0151) 648 7685
3 miles from M53 junction 3: A552 towards Woodchurch, then left on A551; CH61 1BW Well run and welcoming early 20th-c pub; local Brimstage, Theakstons and guests, 60 malt whiskies, 20 gins and decent choice of wines by the glass, hearty helpings of good home-made food (all day Fri-Sun, not Mon evening), roomy carpeted bay-windowed lounge with built-in banquettes and plush-cushioned captain's chairs around solid tables, old local prints and collection of police and other headgear, charming quarry-tiled corner with antique range, copper kettles and earthenware, also small traditional locals' bar and snug where

children allowed; dogs welcome in bar areas, picnic-sets at back among tubs and hanging baskets, open all day. *(Paul Humphreys)*

BARTON   SD5137
Sparling (01772) 860830
A6 N of Broughton; PR3 5AA Contemporary dining pub with well liked food including set deals, roomy bar with comfortable sofas and other seats, plenty of tables in linked areas off, wood and flagstone floors, modern fireplaces, real ales such as Thwaites Wainwright and good choice of wines by the glass, friendly efficient young staff; free wi-fi; children welcome, handy for M6. *(Bob and Melissa Wyatt)*

BELMONT   SD6715
Black Dog (01204) 811218
Church Street (A675); BL7 8AB Nicely set Holts pub with enjoyable food, well kept beers and friendly staff, various modernised areas (some slightly raised), pubby furnishing including banquettes on light wood or carpeted floors, a couple of coal fires, picture-window dining extension; children and dogs welcome, seats outside with moorland views over village, attractive part-covered courtyard behind, good walks, three decent well priced bedrooms, open (and food) all day. *(Steve Whalley)*

BLACKBURN   SD6525
★**Oyster & Otter** (01254) 203200
1.8 miles from M65 junction 3: A674 towards Blackburn, turn right at Feniscowles mini roundabout, signposted to Darwen and Tockholes, into Livesey Branch Road; BB2 5DQ Distinctive clapboard and stone building in modern New England style; open-plan interior with cushioned dining booths by large windows on one side, other cosy seating areas divided by shoulder-high walls and big central hearth, end part with comfy sofas, very good food including signature fish/seafood from open kitchen, Thwaites Wainwright, a guest ale and a dozen wines by the glass, helpful young staff in aprons; background music (live first Fri of month),

free wi-fi; children welcome, seats on decking above road, open (and food) all day. *(Pat and Tony Martin, W K Wood, Douglas Power, John Watson)*

BOLTON SD7112
Brewery Tap (01204) 302837
Belmont Road; BL1 7AN Two-room corner tap for Bank Top, their full range kept well and a guest, knowledgeable friendly staff, no food; quiet background music, free wi-fi; children (until 7pm) and dogs welcome, disabled access, seats outside, open all day. *(David Appleyard)*

BRINDLE SD5924
★ Cavendish Arms (01254) 852912
3 miles from M6 junction 29, via A6 and B5256 (Sandy Lane); PR6 8NG Traditional village pub dating from the 15th c on corner adjacent to church; beams, cosy snugs with open fires, stained-glass windows (depicting the Battle of Brunanburh), carpets throughout, four Marstons-related ales and good inexpensive home-made food, friendly helpful service, back dining room; Tues quiz; children and dogs (in tap room) welcome, heated canopied terrace with water feature, more tables in side garden, good walks, open (and food) all day weekends, closed lunchtimes Mon and Tues (no food these days or lunchtimes Weds-Fri). *(Steve Whalley)*

BROUGHTON SD4838
Plough at Eaves (01772) 690233
A6 N through Broughton, first left into Station Lane under a mile after traffic lights, then left after 1.5 miles, Eaves Lane; PR4 0BJ Pleasantly unpretentious old country tavern with two beamed homely bars, well kept Thwaites ales and good choice of enjoyable reasonably priced food, friendly accommodating service, lattice windows and traditional furnishings, old guns over woodburner in one room, log fire in dining bar with conservatory; background music; children welcome, front terrace and spacious side/back garden, well equipped play area, open all day Fri-Sun. *(David Appleyard)*

BURY SD8008
Swan & Cemetery (0161) 764 1508
Manchester Road; BL9 9NS Renovated Thwaites pub with two bars and restaurant, their ales kept well and reasonably priced food from extensive menu including good choice of fish dishes, prompt service; Weds quiz; seats out on south-facing back deck, open all day. *(Gerry and Rosemary Dobson)*

BURY SD8313
Trackside (0161) 764 6461
East Lancashire Railway station, Bolton Street; BL9 0EY Welcoming busy station bar by East Lancashire steam railway; bright, airy and clean with ten real ales including a house beer from local Outstanding, also bottled imports, real ciders and great range of whiskies, enjoyable home-made food (Sat and Sun only); folk night last Thurs of month; children (till 7pm) and dogs welcome, platform tables under canopy, open all day. *(Patricia Healey)*

CARNFORTH SD5173
Longlands (01524) 781256
Tewitfield, about 2 miles N; A6070, off A6; LA6 1JH Popular family-run village inn with good food in bar and airy restaurant from pub favourites and pizzas up, four local beers, helpful friendly staff; children and dogs welcome (their black lab is Ronnie), bedrooms and self-catering cottages, Lancaster Canal and M6 nearby, open all day. *(John Evans)*

CHEADLE SJ8588
James Watts (0161) 428 3361
High Street (A560); SK8 1AX Newly refurbished mock-Tudor pub (former Star) owned by Hydes; fine range of cask and craft beers plus 100 more in bottles (all marked on little blackboard panels), good choice of wines and other drinks too, food from snacks to various sharing combinations served on slates, friendly helpful staff; live acoustic music Mon and Thurs, quiz Weds; back terrace, open all day (till midnight Fri, Sat). *(Mark and Sian Edwards)*

CHEADLE HULME SJ8785
Church Inn (0161) 485 1897
Ravenoak Road (A5149 SE); SK8 7EG Popular old family-run pub with decent food from varied menu including set deals, well kept Robinsons beers and nice selection of wines by the glass, gleaming brass on panelled walls, warming coal fire, pleasant staff and locals, back restaurant; live music most Sun evenings; children welcome, seats outside (some undercover), car park across road, open all day. *(Mike and Wena Stevenson)*

CHIPPING SD6141
★ Dog & Partridge (01995) 61201
Hesketh Lane; crossroads Chipping–Longridge with Inglewhite–Clitheroe; PR3 2TH Comfortable old-fashioned and much altered 16th-c dining pub in grand countryside, long-serving owners, enjoyable food (all day Sun), ales such as Thwaites and Tetleys, friendly service, beams, exposed stone walls and good log fire, small armchairs around close-set tables in main lounge, restaurant; free wi-fi; children welcome, no dogs inside, open all day Sun, closed Mon, Tues evening. *(Peter and Emma Kelly)*

If you know a pub is ever open all day, please tell us.

CLAUGHTON   SD5666
★ **Fenwick Arms** (01524) 221157

*A683 Kirkby Lonsdale–Lancaster;
LA2 9LA* Civilised 250-year-old black and
white pub in Lune Valley, mainly popular
for its particularly good fish and seafood;
smartly updated with white-painted beams
in wonky ceilings, open fires (one in a black
range) and painted panelling, upholstered
and antique-style dining chairs around all
shapes of table on carpet or bare boards,
window seats with scatter cushions, Thwaites
Wainwright, Timothy Taylor Landlord and
a guest, 14 wines by the glass and a good
choice of spirits, efficient friendly staff;
background music, free wi-fi; children
and dogs (in bar) welcome, picnic-sets on
front terrace, nine comfortable modern
bedrooms, open (and food) all day.
*(Maddie Purvis, John Sargeant, Steve Whalley,
Michael Butler, John and Sylvia Harrop)*

CLITHEROE   SD7441
Holmes Mill (01200) 401035

Greenacre Street; BB7 1EB Conversion
of town's last working cotton mill, cavernous
industrial interior keeping some of the old
machinery (giant flywheel in the engine
room), lovely flagged floor and plenty of
recycled fixtures and fittings, walls fitted
with leather benches and scrubbed plank
tables, sturdy canteen chairs and high-
backed stools elsewhere, vast U-shaped
counter serving 24 real ales including six
from Bowland (brewery visible behind
glass partitions), good selection of fast
food such as hot dogs, burgers and pies,
also has a café and other development
planned including boutique hotel; prominent
background and some live music; picnic-
sets outside along with covered seating in
shipping containers, open (and food) all
day, till 9pm (7pm) Sun. *(Steve Whalley)*

CLITHEROE   SD7441
New Inn (01200) 423312

Parson Lane; BB7 2JN Traditional
old-fashioned local with ten or more well
kept ales from central bar, knowledgeable
staff, cosy rooms with log fires; live music
including fortnightly irish sessions Sun
afternoon; dogs welcome, seats out at front
and back, open all day. *(John Poulter)*

COLNE   SD8940
Black Lane Ends (01282) 863070

Skipton Old Road, Foulridge; BB8 7EP
Country pub tucked away in quiet lane;
generous helpings of good sensibly priced
food, three well kept real ales including
Timothy Taylors Landlord and decent wine
choice, cheerful attentive staff, long bar with
spindleback chairs, padded wall benches
and scrubbed tables, large fireplace partially
separating small dining room with fire
blazing in cast-iron range; children welcome,
play area in back garden, nice views towards

Wycoller from terrace, handy for canal and
reservoir walks. *(Michael Breeze, Steve Whalley)*

DELPH   SD9809
Royal Oak (01457) 874460

*Off A6052 about 100 metres W of
White Lion, turn up steep Lodge Lane
and keep on up into Broad Lane;
OL3 5TX* Welcoming traditional 18th-c
pub opposite old moorland church in
steep narrow winding lane, great views
of surrounding valleys, real fires in three
small rooms, comfortable solid furniture,
four well kept ales including Millstone
and Moorhouses, no food; closed Mon
and lunchtimes apart from Sun when
open 12-6pm. *(Christopher May)*

DENSHAW   SD9710
Printers Arms (01457) 874248

Oldham Road; OL3 5SN Above Oldham
in shadow of Saddleworth Moor, modernised
interior with small log-fire bar and three
other rooms, popular good value food
including bargain set menu (till 6.30pm,
4pm Sat, not Sun), Black Sheep and Timothy
Taylors Golden Best, several wines by the
glass, friendly staff; children welcome,
lovely views from two-tier beer garden,
open (and food) all day. *(Stuart Paulley)*

DENSHAW   SD9711
Rams Head (01457) 874802

*2 miles from M62 junction 22; A672
towards Oldham, pub N of village;
OL3 5UN* Sweeping moorland views from
this roadside dining pub (don't be put off
by the rather austere exterior); generally
well liked food (all day weekends) including
seasonal game and seafood, ales such as
Marstons and Timothy Taylors kept well,
friendly service, four thick-walled little
rooms, beam-and-plank ceilings, panelling,
oak settles and built-in benches, log fires,
coffee shop and adjacent delicatessen
selling local produce; soft background music;
children welcome (not Sat evening), closed
Mon and Tues. *(Sandra and Michael Smith)*

DENTON   SJ9395
Lowes Arms (0161) 336 3064

Hyde Road (A57); M34 3FF Thriving
19th-c pub with own Westwood beers and
local guests such as Crossbay and Torrside,
jovial community-spirited landlord and
helpful friendly staff, reasonably priced
food including daily specials, bar with
pool and darts, restaurant; children and
dogs welcome, tables outside, smokers'
shelter, open all day. *(David Appleyard)*

DIGGLE   SE0007
Diggle (01457) 872741

*Village signed off A670 just N of
Dobcross; OL3 5JZ* Sturdy four-square
hillside pub in quiet spot just below the
moors overlooking end of Standedge Canal
tunnel; good value food (till 7pm Sun) from

snacks up, well kept ales such as Black Sheep, Millstone and Timothy Taylors, helpful staff; free wi-fi; children and dogs welcome, disabled access, picnic-sets out among trees, four bedrooms, closed Mon, otherwise open (and food) all day. *(Peter and Emma Kelly)*

DOLPHINHOLME — SD5153
Fleece (01524) 791233

A couple of miles from M6 junction 33; W of village; Chipping Lane/Anyon Road; LA2 9AQ Extensively renovated old stone inn (parts date from the 16th c), various rooms including black beamed bar with rugs on flagstones and log fire with unusual copper canopy, four well kept regularly changing ales and decent wines by the glass, popular sensibly priced food (good value set lunch), friendly efficient service, dining lounge with some modern booth seating and sofas in front of woodburner, little shop selling local produce; children and dogs welcome, modern rattan-style furniture on terrace, Trough of Bowland views, nine comfortable well appointed bedrooms, excellent breakfast, closed Mon, otherwise open all day. *(Richard Heath)*

DUNHAM TOWN — SJ7488
Axe & Cleaver (0161) 928 3391

School Lane; WA14 4SE Big 19th-c country house converted into spacious open-plan Chef & Brewer, good value popular food from light lunchtime choices and sharing plates up (best to book Sun lunch), three well kept ales, friendly service; children welcome, garden picnic-sets, handy for nearby Dunham Massey (NT), open (and food) all day. *(Jeremy King, Mike and Wena Stevenson)*

DUNHAM TOWN — SJ7288
Vine (0161) 928 3275

Barns Lane, Dunham Massey; WA14 5RU Tucked-away (but busy) old-fashioned little village local with friendly staff and regulars, well kept/priced Sam Smiths and several ciders, enjoyable generously served lunchtime food; children and dogs welcome, picnic-sets in good-sized garden, handy for Dunham Massey (NT), open all day. *(Hilary Forrest)*

EDENFIELD — SD7919
Coach (01706) 825000

Market Street; BL0 0HJ Updated and extended 19th-c dining pub under new management; good food from lunchtime sandwiches up, three real ales, over a dozen wines by the glass and good range of gins, friendly young staff; free wi-fi; children welcome, disabled access/facilities, a few tables on front pavement, open (and food) all day, except Mon when kitchen closed. *(Christopher May)*

FENCE — SD8237
Fence Gate (01282) 618101

2.6 miles from M65 junction 13; Wheatley Lane Road, just off A6068 W; BB12 9EE Imposing 18th-c dining pub with good choice of enjoyable food, five real ales and several wines by the glass, service friendly but not always speedy, refurbished panelled bar with pewter counter and woodburner in large stone fireplace, contemporary brasserie plus various function rooms, look out for their display of over 600 gins; background and regular live music; children welcome, rattan-style furniture out at front, open all day. *(Patricia Healey)*

FENCE — SD8237
★ **White Swan** (01282) 611773

Wheatley Lane; BB12 9QA Whitewashed village dining pub with comfortably renovated Victorian-style interior, highly regarded imaginative food (not cheap) from short daily changing menu, good friendly service, four well kept Timothy Taylors ales from curved polished wood servery, nice wines, own infused spirits and good coffee, old pictures of the pub, some antlers and stuffed animal heads, wall lights and chandeliers, fireplace at each end; children welcome, outside seating on two levels with chunky wooden tables, open all day, food till 6pm Sun, kitchen closed Mon. *(Steve Whalley)*

GARSTANG — SD4945
Th'Owd Tithebarn (01995) 604486

Off Church Street; PR3 1PA Creeper-clad tithe barn with big terrace overlooking Lancaster Canal marina and narrow boats; linked high-raftered rooms with red patterned carpet or flagstones, upholstered stools, armchairs and leather tub seats around assorted shiny tables, lots of cartwheels, rustic lamps, horse tack and a fine old kitchen range, four changing ales, fair value wines by the glass and well priced pubby food from hot and cold sandwiches to grills and specials; Tues quiz, TV, free wi-fi; children and dogs (in bar) welcome, open all day (food all day weekends). *(Geoff and Anne Marston)*

GISBURN — SD8248
White Bull (01200) 415805

Main Street (A59); BB7 4HE Spacious refurbished roadside pub; opened-up dining rooms on either side of entrance, more room further back to right of bar, taupe-painted walls and stone-effect wallpaper, nice mix of dark furniture on polished wood or flagstone floors, some beams and whitewashed standing timbers, good attractively presented food cooked by chef-owner from pub standards up, four well kept ales (including a Holts beer named for the pub) from semicircular counter with cherry wood top, friendly service; children and dogs (in one section) welcome, narrow access to large back car park, open all day. *(Steve Whalley)*

GOOSNARGH   SD5738
★ **Horns** (01772) 865230

On junction of Horns Lane and Inglewhite Road; pub signed off B5269, towards Chipping; PR3 2FJ Early 18th-c inn (same family ownership since 1952) with neatly kept carpeted rooms including a rare 'parlour' behind the servery; enjoyable home cooking from pub standards to local duck and game, own Goosnargh ales and an occasional microbrewery guest, plenty of wines by the glass and good choice of malts, courteous helpful service, log fires; background music, free wi-fi; children welcome, dogs in garden only, six bedrooms in converted stone barn (some with road noise), caravan park, not far from M6, open (and food) all day Sun, closed Mon lunchtime. *(Steve Whalley)*

GREAT ECCLESTON   SD4240
★ **Farmers Arms** (01995) 672018

Halsall Square (just off A586); PR3 0YE Popular attractively refurbished country pub not far from Fylde Coast and Blackpool; smart dining areas, on two floors, with painted panelled walls and eclectic collection of seating including cushioned settles on carpet or polished boards, woodburners in stone fireplaces, Thwaites Wainwright, Timothy Taylors Landlord and a guest, around 14 wines by the glass and highly regarded interesting food with emphasis on fish/seafood and grills, cheerful attentive service; free wi-fi; children and dogs (in bar) welcome, teak furniture on sheltered terrace, open (and food) all day. *(Gordon and Margaret Ormondroyd)*

GREAT HARWOOD   SD7332
Royal (01254) 876237

Station Road; BB6 7BA Popular Victorian local with half a dozen well kept changing ales and generous helpings of enjoyable pub food, friendly staff; some live music, pool and darts; children welcome, partly covered terrace, open all day. *(Martin and Joanne Sharp)*

GREENFIELD   SD9904
King William IV (01457) 873933

Chew Valley Road (A669); OL3 7DD Welcoming 19th-c village local with half a dozen well kept ales including local Greenfield and Millstone, enjoyable home-made food (not Mon, Tues or lunchtimes Weds, Thurs) helpful, friendly staff; sports TV, free wi-fi; children and dogs welcome, tables on walled front terrace, open all day. *(David Appleyard)*

GREENFIELD   SD9904
Railway Hotel (01457) 872307

Shaw Hall Bank Road, opposite station; OL3 7JZ Friendly four-room stone pub with half a dozen well kept mainly local ales, no food, old local photographs and open fire; live music Thurs, Fri and Sun, sports TV, upstairs games bar with darts and pool; children and dogs welcome, beer garden with good views, on the Transpennine Rail Ale Trail, open all day. *(Buster May)*

HEST BANK   SD4766
★ **Hest Bank Inn** (01524) 824339

Hest Bank Lane; off A6 just N of Lancaster; LA2 6DN Picturesque stone coaching house in nice setting close to Morecambe Bay, good choice of well liked food from snacks and pub favourites up, reasonable prices, well kept ales such as Black Sheep, Theakstons and Thwaites, decent wines, friendly helpful young staff, separate restaurant area; children welcome, plenty of tables out by Lancaster Canal, open all day. *(Roy and Gill Payne)*

HORNBY   SD5868
Castle (01524) 221204

Main Street; LA2 8JT Sizeable Georgian inn with interesting modernised interior, bar with leather sofas and open fires, bistro and restaurant, reasonably priced food from sandwiches, pub favourites and pizzas up, Black Sheep, Bowland and guests, good selection of other drinks; courtyard tables, six boutique bedrooms, open all day. *(Jim and Sue James)*

HURST GREEN   SD6837
★ **Shireburn Arms** (01254) 826678

Whalley Road (B6243 Clitheroe–Goosnargh); BB7 9QJ Welcoming 17th-c hotel with peaceful Ribble Valley views from big airy restaurant and neatly kept garden, food from sandwiches and traditional dishes to daily specials (all day weekends), leather armchairs, sofas and log fire in beamed and flagstoned lounge bar with linked dining area, two well kept ales such as Lancaster and Thwaites, several wines by the glass; occasional live music, daily papers; children and dogs welcome, pretty Tolkien walk from here, 22 comfortable bedrooms, open all day from 9am for coffee. *(Bob and Melissa Wyatt)*

HYDE   SJ9595
Sportsman (0161) 368 5000

Mottram Road; SK14 2NN Welcoming Victorian local with Rossendale ales and lots of changing guests (frequent beer festivals), bargain bar food and popular upstairs cuban restaurant, bare boards and open fires, pub games; children and dogs welcome, back terrace with heated smokers' shelter, open all day. *(David Appleyard)*

INGLETON SD6972

Masons Arms (01524) 242040

New Road (A65); LA6 3HL Welcoming roadside village inn fully refurbished by new owners; stools and upholstered chairs around mix of pubby tables on wood-strip flooring, tartan-carpeted dining end with woodburner, generous helpings of tasty straightforward food from lunchtime hot or cold sandwiches up (more evening choice), well kept ales such as Black Sheep, Dent, Kirkby Lonsdale and Sharps, decent wine list with half a dozen by the glass, good friendly service; children and dogs welcome, three bedrooms, open (and some food) all day. *(John and Sylvia Harrop)*

IRBY SJ2586

★**Irby Mill** (0151) 604 0194

Mill Lane, off Greasby Road; CH49 3NT Converted miller's sandstone cottage (original windmill demolished 1898), friendly and welcoming, with eight well kept ales including Caledonian Deuchars IPA, Greene King Abbot and Charles Wells Bombardier, good choice of wines by the glass and ample helpings of popular reasonably priced food from sandwiches up, efficient service, two low-beamed traditional flagstoned rooms and extended carpeted dining area, log fire, interesting old photographs and history; tables on terraces and revamped side area, good local walks, open (and food) all day, gets crowded evenings/weekends when parking limited. *(Paul Humphreys)*

LANCASTER SD4761

★**Borough** (01524) 64170

Dalton Square; LA1 1PP Popular city-centre pub, stylish and civilised, with chandeliers, dark leather sofas and armchairs, lamps on antique tables, high stools and elbow tables, eight ales including some from on-site microbrewery, lots of bottled beers, big dining room with central tables and booths along one side, enjoyable food with much emphasis on local suppliers, daily specials and meal deals, jams and local produce for sale; upstairs comedy night Sun; children and dogs welcome, lovely tree-sheltered garden, bedrooms, open (and food) all day from 8am. *(Buster May)*

LANCASTER SD4761

Sun (01524) 66006

Church Street; LA1 1ET Hotel's refurbished bar, ten well kept ales including five from Lancaster, plenty of continental beers and good choice of wines by the glass, popular food from doorstep sandwiches, deli boards and pub staples up, exposed stonework, panelling and several fireplaces, conservatory; background music, TV; children welcome away from servery, tables on walled and paved terrace, 16 comfortable bedrooms, open all day. *(Buster May)*

LANCASTER SD4761

Water Witch (01524) 63828

Parking in Aldcliffe Road behind Royal Lancaster Infirmary, off A6; LA1 1SU Attractive conversion of 18th-c canalside stables; flagstones, stripped stone, rafters and pitch-pine panelling, half a dozen well kept changing ales, fairly traditional food from sandwiches and deli boards up including weekday lunch deal, upstairs restaurant; Weds open mike night, Thurs quiz, free wi-fi; children in eating areas, picnic-sets out by water, moorings, open (and food) all day. *(Buster May)*

LANESHAW BRIDGE SD9141

Alma (01282) 857830

Emmott Lane, off A6068 E of Colne; BB8 7EG Attractively renovated 18th-c inn with popular food, several wines by the glass and three real ales including Moorhouses Pride of Pendle and Thwaites Wainwright, flagstoned bar, friendly helpful staff, part-panelled lounge with rugs on bare boards, open fires, large garden room extension; background music; well behaved children and dogs welcome, ten comfortable well appointed bedrooms, open (and food) all day, breakfast for non-residents. *(John and Eleanor Holdsworth)*

LITTLEBOROUGH SD9517

Moorcock (01706) 378156

Halifax Road (A58); OL15 0LD Long roadside inn high on the moors with far-reaching views; wide range of food (all day Thurs-Sun) from sandwiches and pub favourites up in flagstoned bar or restaurant, four well kept beers; sports TV; terrace tables taking in the view, seven comfortable reasonably priced bedrooms, open all day. *(Sandra and Michael Smith)*

LIVERPOOL SJ3489

Baltic Fleet (0151) 709 3116

Wapping, near Albert Dock; L1 8DQ Unusual bow-fronted pub with six interesting beers including Wapping (brewed in the cellar), real ciders and several wines by the glass, simple well cooked/priced lunchtime food such as traditional scouse, bare boards, big arched windows, simple mix of furnishings and some nautical paraphernalia, fires in parlour and snug; background music, TV; children welcome in eating areas, dogs in bar, back terrace, open all day. *(David Thorpe, David H Bennett)*

LIVERPOOL SJ3589

Belvedere (0151) 709 0303

Sugnall Street; L7 7EB Unspoilt 19th-c two-room pub with friendly chatty atmosphere, original features including etched glass and coal fires, four well kept changing ales such as Brimstage and

Liverpool Organic, good selection of bottled beers, real cider and fine choice of gins; dogs welcome, open all day. *(Helen McLagan)*

LIVERPOOL
SJ3589
Cracke (0151) 709 4171
Rice Street; L1 9BB Friendly unchanging local with five well kept ales including Phoenix and Thwaites, traditional cider, no food, small unspoilt bar with bare boards and bench seats, snug and bigger back room with unusual Beatles diorama, local artwork and some photos of John Lennon who used to drink here; juke box, sports TV; picnic-sets in sizeable tree-shaded back garden, open all day. *(David Appleyard)*

LIVERPOOL
SJ3590
Crown (0151) 707 6027
Lime Street; L1 1JQ Well preserved art nouveau showpiece; fine tiled fireplace and copper bar front, dark leather banquettes, panelling and splendid ornate ceiling, smaller back room with another good fireplace, impressive staircase sweeping up under cupola to handsome area with ornate windows, no real ales but bottled craft beers, good range of good value food; sports TV; very handy for the station, open all day from 8am for breakfast. *(Martin and Joanne Sharp)*

LIVERPOOL
SJ3490
Dead Crafty Beer 07977 228918
Dale Street opposite the old magistrates' court; L2 5TF New craft beer bar with 20 on tap and over 150 in bottles, tasters offered by friendly knowledgeable staff, compact fairly basic interior with bare boards and exposed brickwork, bar made from flight cases; unisex loos downstairs; open all day Fri-Sun, closed Mon and lunchtimes Tues-Thurs. *(Buster May)*

LIVERPOOL
SJ3589
Dispensary (0151) 709 2160
Renshaw Street; L1 2SP Small busy central pub worth knowing for its very well kept beers (up to ten), good choice of bottled imports too, no food, bare boards and polished panelling, wonderful etched windows, comfortable raised back bar with fireplace (not used), some Victorian medical artefacts; background music, silent TVs, notices on house rules; open all day (till midnight Fri, Sat). *(Buster May)*

LIVERPOOL
SJ3589
Fly in the Loaf (0151) 708 0817
Hardman Street; L1 9AS Former bakery with smart gleaming bar serving Okells, guest ales and several foreign beers, enjoyable simple home-made food at low prices, efficient, friendly service, long refurbished room with panelling and some raised sections; background music, sports TV, upstairs loos; open all day, till midnight Fri, Sat. *(David Appleyard)*

LIVERPOOL
SJ3490
Hole In Ye Wall (0151) 227 3809
Off Dale Street; L2 2AW Character 18th-c pub (the city's oldest) with thriving local atmosphere in high-beamed panelled bar, half a dozen changing ales fed by gravity from upstairs (no cellar as pub is on Quaker burial site), extensive gin range, baguettes, pies, burgers and so forth, friendly staff, plenty of woodwork, stained glass and old Liverpool photographs, coal-effect gas fire in unusual brass-canopied fireplace; live music evenings Mon, Fri and Sat, traditional sing-along Sun, sports TV, fruit machine; children allowed till 5pm, no dogs, open all day. *(Buster May)*

LIVERPOOL
SJ3490
Lion Tavern (0151) 236 1734
Moorfields, off Tithebarn Street; L2 2BP Beautifully preserved ornate Victorian corner pub, eight changing beers and extensive range of whiskies, good value simple lunchtime food including nice pork pies, friendly staff, sparkling etched glass and serving hatches in central bar, unusual wallpaper and matching curtains, big mirrors, panelling and tilework, two small back lounges one with fine glass dome, coal fire; juke box, sports TV, free wi-fi; open all day. *(Emily and Toby Archer)*

LIVERPOOL
SJ3590
Ma Egerton's Stage Door (0151) 345 3525 *Pudsey Street, opposite side entrance to Lime Street station; L1 1JA* Victorian pub behind the Empire Theatre and named after a former long-serving landlady/theatrical agent; refurbished but keeping old-fashioned character with green leather button-back banquettes (note the bell pushes), swagged curtains, wood floors, panelling and small period fireplace, lots of celebrity pictures and other memorabilia, a couple of changing ales and enjoyable food including sharing plates and pizzas, friendly staff; Mon quiz, Fri sing-along, bingo last Thurs of the month; open all day. *(Buster May)*

LIVERPOOL
SJ3589
Peter Kavanaghs (0151) 709 3443
Egerton Street, off Catherine Street; L8 7LY Character Victorian pub popular with locals and students; interesting décor in several small rooms, old-world murals, stained glass and all kinds of bric-a-brac (lots hanging from ceiling), piano, wooden settles and real fires, well kept Greene King Abbot and guests, friendly licensees; open all day (till 1am Fri, Sat). *(David H Bennett)*

LIVERPOOL
SJ3589
Philharmonic Dining Rooms
(0151) 707 2837 *36 Hope Street; corner of Hardman Street; L1 9BX* Beautifully preserved Victorian pub with wonderful period detail; centrepiece mosaic-faced

counter, heavily carved and polished mahogany partitions radiating out under intricate plasterwork ceiling, main hall with stained glass of Boer War heroes Baden-Powell and Lord Roberts, rich panelling, mosaic floor and copper panels of musicians above fireplace, other areas including two side rooms called Brahms and Liszt, the original Adamant gents' is also worth a look, ten real ales, several wines by the glass and decent choice of malt whiskies, fair-priced food; background music and machines; children welcome till 7pm, open (and food) all day. *(Susan and John Douglas, Mike and Wena Stevenson, David H Bennett)*

LIVERPOOL SJ3589

Roscoe Head (0151) 709 4365

Roscoe Street; L1 2SX Unassuming old local with cosy bar, snug and two other spotless unspoilt little rooms, friendly long-serving landlady, well kept Jennings, Tetleys and five guests, inexpensive home-made lunches (not weekends), interesting memorabilia; Tues quiz and traditional games such as crib; open all day. *(David Appleyard)*

LIVERPOOL SJ3490

Ship & Mitre (0151) 236 0859

Dale Street; L2 2JH Friendly local with fine art deco exterior and ship-like interior, up to a dozen unusual changing ales (many beer festivals), real ciders and over 70 bottled beers, decent choice of good value food (all day Fri-Sun) such as wraps, burgers and all-day breakfast, upstairs function room with original 1930s décor; well behaved children (till 7pm) and dogs welcome, open all day. *(David H Bennett)*

LIVERPOOL SJ3490

★ Thomas Rigbys (0151) 236 3269

Dale Street; L2 2EZ Spacious three-room Victorian pub; main bare-boards bar with iron pillars supporting sturdy beams, panelling and stained glass, Okells ales and guests from long counter, also good range of imported draught/bottled beers and several gins, back Nelson Room with impressive fireplace and an oak-panelled dining parlour where children allowed, enjoyable reasonably priced pubby food till early evening, attentive staff; sports TV; disabled access (although some steps and downstairs lavatories), seats in big courtyard, open all day. *(David H Bennett)*

LONGRIDGE SD6038

★ Derby Arms (01772) 782370

Chipping Road, Thornley; 1.5 miles N of Longridge on back road to Chipping; PR3 2NB Creeper-clad village pub with attractively refurbished bar and connecting dining rooms, wide floorboards or grey carpet, woodburner and open fire, assorted seating including high-backed chairs, settles with scatter cushions, wall banquettes and leather-topped stools,

Copper Dragon, Thwaites and Timothy Taylors from stylish oak-planked servery, nice selection of wines by the glass too, good food including chargrills and daily fish specials, cheerful helpful service; free wi-fi; children and dogs (in bar) welcome, good quality furniture on front terrace behind picket fence, comfortable airy bedrooms, open (and food) all day, breakfast for non-residents. *(Steve Whalley, David Fowler)*

LONGRIDGE SD6037

New Drop (01254) 878338

Higher Road, Longridge Fell, parallel to B6243 Longridge–Clitheroe; PR3 2YX Pleasant modernised dining pub in lovely moors-edge country overlooking Ribble Valley, good choice of reasonably priced food, decent wines and three well kept ales (usually Bowland Hen Harrier), friendly service; children welcome, open all day Sun, closed Mon. *(Sandra and Michael Smith)*

LYDGATE SD9704

★ White Hart (01457) 872566

Stockport Road; Lydgate not marked on some maps and not the one near Todmorden; take A669 Oldham–Saddleworth, right at brow of hill to A6050 after almost 2.5 miles; OL4 4JJ Smart up-to-date dining pub overlooking Pennine moors; mix of locals (in bar or simpler end rooms) and diners in elegant brasserie with smartly dressed staff, high quality food (not cheap), Lees, Timothy Taylors and a guest beer, 16 wines by the glass, old beams and exposed stonework contrasting with deep red or purple walls and modern artwork, open fires, newspapers; various events and a popular wedding/conference venue; children welcome, dogs in bar, picnic-sets on back lawn making most of position, 12 bedrooms, open all day. *(Bob and Melissa Wyatt)*

LYTHAM SD3627

★ Taps (01253) 736226

A584 S of Blackpool; Henry Street – in centre, one street in from West Beach; FY8 5LE Cheerful town pub just a couple of minutes from the beach; ten well kept ales including Greene King and a couple of proper ciders, simple good value lunchtime food (not Sun), friendly efficient staff, open-plan bar with wood or tiled floor, stripped brickwork and open fires, dining area leading through to sunny terrace; quiz Mon, TV for major sports, darts, fruit machine; children allowed till 7.30pm, parking nearby difficult (best to use West Beach car park on seafront, free Sun), open all day. *(Steve Whalley, Michael Butler)*

MANCHESTER SJ8498

Angel (0161) 833 4786

Angel Street, off Rochdale Road; M4 4BR Friendly place on edge of the Northern Quarter, good value home-made food, ten well kept ales including Saltaire, bottled beers and a couple of ciders/perries, piano in bare-boards bar, smaller upstairs restaurant with two log fires and local artwork; free wi-fi; children and dogs welcome, back beer garden, open all day. *(Patricia Healey)*

MANCHESTER SJ8398
Ape & Apple (0161) 839 9624
John Dalton Street; M2 6HQ Large open-plan pub with five well kept good value Holts beers plus guests, hearty traditional bar food including deals, comfortable seating, bare boards, carpet and tiles, lots of old prints and posters, upstairs restaurant/function room, friendly atmosphere; Weds comedy night, Tues quiz, juke box, games machines; children and dogs welcome, disabled access, heated central courtyard, open all day (till 9pm Sun). *(Jim and Sue James)*

MANCHESTER SJ8397
★ Britons Protection (0161) 236 5895
Great Bridgewater Street, corner of Lower Mosley Street; M1 5LE Lively unpretentious pub with rambling rooms and notable tiled murals of 1810 Peterloo Massacre (took place nearby); plush little front bar with tiled floor, glossy brown and russet wall tiles, solid woodwork and ornate red and gold ceiling, two cosy inner lounges, both served by hatch, with attractive brass wall lamps and solidly comfortable furnishings, coal-effect gas fire in simple art nouveau fireplace, five ales including Jennings, Robinsons and a Thwaites beer named for the pub from massive counter with heated footrail, also some 330 malt whiskies, straightforward lunchtime food Mon-Fri; occasional storytelling and live music; children till 5pm, tables in enclosed back garden, handy for Bridgewater Hall concerts, open all day (very busy lunchtime and weekends). *(Dr and Mrs A K Clarke)*

MANCHESTER SJ8498
Castle (0161) 237 0485
Oldham Street, about 200 metres from Piccadilly, on right; M4 1LE Restored 18th-c pub run well by former *Coronation Street* actor; simple traditional front bar, small snug, Robinsons ales and guests from fine bank of handpumps, Weston's Old Rosie cider; juke box, back room for regular live music and other events, overspill space upstairs; nice tilework outside, open all day till late. *(Patricia Healey)*

MANCHESTER SJ8497
Circus (0161) 236 5818
Portland Street; M1 4GX Traditional little two-room local with friendly staff serving well kept Robinsons and Tetleys from tiny corridor bar (or may be table service), leatherette wall benches and panelling, back room has football memorabilia and period fireplace; sports TV; open all day and can get crowded. *(Jim and Sue James)*

MANCHESTER SJ8398
City Arms (0161) 236 4610
Kennedy Street, off St Peters Square; M2 4BQ Friendly old-fashioned two-bar local sandwiched between two other pubs; eight well kept quickly changing ales, belgian bottled beers and decent range of whiskies and gins, simple weekday lunchtime food, bare boards, panelling and button-back banquettes, coal fires; background music, sports TV, darts and dominoes; wheelchair access but steps down to back lounge, open all day (till 8pm Sun). *(Jim and Sue James)*

MANCHESTER SJ8397
Dukes 92 (0161) 839 8642
Castle Street, below the bottom end of Deansgate; M3 4LZ Friendly informal atmosphere in refurbished former stables overlooking canal basin, modern furnishings on light tiled floor, exposed brickwork, stairs up to stylish gallery bar leading to roof terrace, a couple of local ales such as Seven Bro7hers, decent wines and wide range of spirits (happy-hour cocktails Mon-Thurs), good food choice from bar snacks and pizzas up; background music, DJs Fri and Sat, live music Sun; children welcome, no dogs inside, waterside tables on big terrace with outside bar/kitchen, open all day (till 1am Fri, Sat). *(Patricia Healey)*

MANCHESTER SJ8194
Font (0161) 871 2022
Manchester Road, Chorlton; M21 9PG Relaxed split-level bar with regularly changing beers including eight real ales and 16 craft kegs, also extensive bottled range and traditional ciders, fair-priced cocktails too, enjoyable food from sandwiches and wraps to burgers and burritos; weekend DJs, free wi-fi; children and dogs welcome, seats out at front behind railings, open (and food) all day (till 1am Fri, Sat). *(Christopher May)*

MANCHESTER SJ8397
Knott (0161) 839 9229
Deansgate; M3 4LY Modern glass-fronted café-bar under railway arch by Castlefield heritage site; seven well kept ales including Castle Rock and Marble, also lots of craft beers and continental imports, good value food; background music; upstairs balcony overlooking Rochdale Canal, open (and food) all day. *(Patricia Healey)*

MANCHESTER SJ8497
Lass o' Gowrie (0161) 273 5822
36 Charles Street; off Oxford Road; M1 7DB Traditional tile-fronted side-street local refurbished a few years ago but keeping Victorian character; big-windowed bar with cosy room off, wood floors and stripped brickwork, pendant lighting, various pictures including black and white photos of old Manchester, three well kept Greene King ales plus local guests, simple bargain food such

as home-made pies, friendly service; Thurs quiz, some live music; balcony overlooking River Medlock, open all day. *(Chris Parker)*

MANCHESTER   SJ8499
★**Marble Arch** (0161) 832 5914
Rochdale Road (A664), Ancoats; centre of Gould Street, just E of Victoria station; M4 4HY Cheery own-brew pub with fine listed Victorian interior; long narrow bar with high ceiling, extensive glazed brickwork, marble and tiling, sloping mosaic floor and frieze advertising various drinks, old stone bottles on shelves, their good Marble beers plus a couple of guests (brewery visible from windows in back dining room – tours by arrangement), well liked home-made food including separate cheese menu; background music; children welcome, small garden, open (and food) all day. *(Jim and Sue James)*

MANCHESTER   SJ8398
★**Mr Thomas's Chop House**
(0161) 832 2245 *Cross Street; M2 7AR*
Interesting late 19th-c pub with well preserved original features; generously served food including signature corned beef hash, ales such as Holts and Black Sheep and decent wines by the glass, front bar with panelling, old gas lamp fittings, framed cartoons, stools at wall and window shelves, back green-tiled eating areas have rows of tables on black and white Victorian tiles, archways and high ceilings; seats out at back, open (and food) all day. *(Christopher May)*

MANCHESTER   SJ8298
New Oxford (0161) 832 7082
Bexley Square, Salford; M3 6DB
Red-brick Victorian corner pub with up to 16 well kept changing ales (chalked on blackboard), plus extensive range of draught and bottled continental beers, real ciders too, light airy feel in small front bar and back room, coal fire, low-priced basic food till 6pm; open mike and quiz nights, juke box, free wi-fi; café-style seating out in square, open all day. *(Patricia Healey)*

MANCHESTER   SJ8398
★**Oast House** (0161) 829 3830
Crown Square, Springfields; M3 3AY
Quirky mock-up of a kentish oast house surrounded by modern high-rises; rustic lofty interior with bare boards, timbers and plenty of tables, good selection of draught and bottled beers, wines and cocktails, enjoyable fairly priced food from deli boards to barbecues and rotisserie grills, friendly helpful young staff, busy cheerful atmosphere; background and nightly live music; children welcome,

spacious outside seating area, open all day (till 2am Fri, Sat). *(Chris Parker)*

MANCHESTER   SJ8397
Paramount (0161) 233 1820
Oxford Street; M1 4BH Spacious busy Wetherspoons worth knowing for its interesting range of well priced beers, friendly service, usual food; TVs, free wi-fi; children welcome, disabled access, outside terrace, open all day from 7am. *(D W Stokes)*

MANCHESTER   SJ8397
★**Peveril of the Peak** (0161) 236 6364
Great Bridgewater Street; M1 5JQ Vivid art nouveau external tilework and three sturdily furnished old-fashioned bare-boards rooms, interesting pictures, lots of mahogany, mirrors and stained or frosted glass, log fire, four ales such as Brightside, Seven Bro7hers, Skinners and Timothy Taylors from central servery, cheap basic lunchtime food; background music, TV, table football and pool; children and dogs welcome, pavement tables, open all day. *(Jim and Sue James)*

MANCHESTER   SJ8498
Port Street Beer House (0161)
237 9949 *Port Street; M1 2EQ* Fantastic range of craft beers on draught and in bottles along with well kept changing ales, knowledgeable staff, no food, can get very busy but more room upstairs; events such as 'meet the brewer' and 'tap takeovers'; open all day weekends, from 2pm Fri, 4pm other days. *(Peter and Emma Kelly)*

MANCHESTER   SJ8397
Rain Bar (0161) 235 6500
Great Bridgewater Street; M1 5JG
Bare boards and lots of woodwork in former umbrella works, Lees ales and plenty of wines by the glass, good choice of enjoyable fair value food from sandwiches to grills, friendly relaxed atmosphere, nooks and corners, coal fire in small snug, large upstairs bar/function room; background music; good back terrace overlooking Rochdale Canal, handy for Bridgewater Hall, open (and food) all day, Sun till 8pm. *(Dr and Mrs A K Clarke)*

MANCHESTER   SJ8398
Sam's Chop House (0161) 834 3210
Back Pool Fold, Chapel Walks; M2 1HN
Downstairs dining pub (offshoot from Mr Thomas's Chop House) with original Victorian décor, generous helpings of plain english food including weekend brunch, formal waiters, well kept beers and good wine choice, a former haunt of LS Lowry (his statue sits contemplatively at the bar), back restaurant with black and white tiled floor; background music, sports TV; some pavement tables, open all day. *(Christopher May)*

Half pints: by law, a pub should not charge more for half a pint than half the price of a full pint, unless it shows that half-pint price on its price list.

MANCHESTER SJ8498
Smithfield (0161) 819 2767
Swan Street; M4 5JZ Simply presented pub on edge of the Northern Quarter owned by the Blackjack brewery, their ales and guests from six handpumps, also a dozen craft kegs, real cider and good selection of spirits, straightforward food such as sausages and pies, three main areas with vintage mismatched furniture on wood floors; occasional live music, traditional games including darts, shove-ha'penny and table skittles; dogs welcome, open all day weekends, from 2pm Fri, 4.30pm other days. *(Phil Hilton)*

MANCHESTER SJ8591
Woodstock (0161) 448 7951
Barlow Moor Road (A5145); M20 2DY Substantial red-brick Victorian house in leafy Didsbury, roomy interior arranged over two floors with plenty of period features, five real ales and good selection of other drinks, popular food from varied menu, friendly staff; background music, sports TV, free wi-fi; children welcome, tree-screened garden with fairy lights, tables under parasols, open all day (till 1am Fri, Sat). *(Chris Parker)*

MARPLE SJ9389
Hare & Hounds (0161) 427 0293
Dooley Lane (A627 W); SK6 7EJ Well run dining pub above River Goyt with modern layout and décor, tasty traditional food at reasonable prices from sandwiches up, Hydes ales and a guest, friendly service; background music; well behaved children welcome, outside seating, open (and food) all day. *(Simon and Alex Knight)*

MARPLE SJ9588
Ring o' Bells (0161) 427 2300
Church Lane; by Macclesfield Canal, bridge 2; SK6 7AY Popular old-fashioned local with assorted memorabilia in four linked rooms, well kept Robinsons ales and good reasonably priced food (all day weekends); quiz nights and some live music including brass bands in the waterside garden; children welcome, own narrowboat, one bedroom, open all day. *(Simon and Alex Knight)*

MARPLE BRIDGE SJ9889
Hare & Hounds (0161) 427 4042
Mill Brow; from end of Town Street in centre turn left up Hollins Lane and keep on uphill; SK6 5LW Comfortable, civilised and well run stone-built country pub in lovely spot; good modern cooking including a grazing menu and popular Sun lunch, well kept Robinsons ales and nice wines, quite small inside (can get crowded), log fires; children and dogs (in bar) welcome, garden behind, open all day weekends (food till 7pm Sun), closed lunchtimes Mon-Thurs. *(Buster May)*

MORECAMBE SD4264
Midland Grand Plaza (01524) 424000
Marine Road W; LA4 4BZ Classic art deco hotel in splendid seafront position; comfortable if unorthodox contemporary furnishings in spacious sea-view Rotunda Bar, rather pricey but enjoyable food from interesting lancashire tapas to restaurant meals (popular and very good afternoon tea), good service; children welcome, 44 bedrooms, open all day. *(Mark and Sian Edwards)*

NEWTON SD6950
★ Parkers Arms (01200) 446236
B6478 7 miles N of Clitheroe; BB7 3DY Arch-windowed pub on edge of village, friendly welcome and enjoyable locally sourced food from lunchtime sandwiches (home-baked bread) to imaginative specials, can eat in bar or restaurant, three real ales including Bowland, good range of wines and decent coffee, wood and flagstone floors, log fires; children and well behaved dogs welcome, disabled access, lovely views from picnic-sets on front lawn, one bedroom, closed Mon, Tues. *(Emily and Toby Archer)*

PARBOLD SD4911
Windmill (01257) 462935
Mill Lane; WN8 7NW Modernised and opened-up beamed pub next to village windmill and facing Leeds & Liverpool Canal; mix of furniture including settles and some interesting carved chairs, candles on tables, good coal fire, generally well liked food from pub favourites to more adventurous specials, six real ales (some from own microbrewery), several wines by the glass, friendly young staff; downstairs gents'; children and dogs welcome, seats out in front and behind, good local walks, open all day, food all day weekends. *(Mike and Wena Stevenson)*

PRESTON SD5329
Black Horse (01772) 204855
Friargate; PR1 2EJ Listed Victorian pub in pedestrianised street; splendid ornate curved and mosaic-tiled main bar serving eight well kept ales (Robinsons and guests), friendly helpful staff, panelling, stained glass and old local photographs, open fires, two quiet cosy snugs, mirrored back area and upstairs function room; no food or children; open all day from 10.30am (midday Sun). *(Bob and Melissa Wyatt)*

RABY SJ3179
★ Wheatsheaf (0151) 336 3416
Raby Mere Road, The Green; from A540 heading S from Heswall, turn left into Upper Raby Road, village about a mile further; CH63 4JH Up to nine well kept ales in pretty 17th-c black and white thatched pub, simply furnished rambling rooms with homely feel, cosy central bar and nice snug formed by antique settles around fine old fireplace, small coal fire in

more spacious room, well liked reasonably priced bar food including good range of sandwiches/toasties, à la carte menu in large former cowshed restaurant, good friendly service, conservatory; children welcome, dogs in bar, picnic-sets on terrace and in pleasant back garden, open all day and gets very busy at weekends, no food Sun or Mon evenings. *(Shaun Mahoney)*

RAMSBOTTOM SD8016
Eagle & Child (01706) 557181
Whalley Road (A56); BL0 0DL Friendly well run pub with good freshly made food (booking advised) using locally sourced produce including own vegetables, well kept Thwaites ales, real cider and decent choice of wines by the glass, good service; children welcome, interesting garden with valley views over rooftops to Holcombe Moor and Peel Tower, open all day Fri and Sat, till 7pm Sun. *(W K Wood, Robin Harris)*

RAMSBOTTOM SD8017
★ **Fishermans Retreat** (01706) 825314
Twine Valley Park/Fishery signed off A56 N of Bury at Shuttleworth; Bye Road; BL0 0HH Remote yet busy pub-restaurant with highly regarded food (can be pricey) using produce from surrounding Estate and trout lakes (they can arrange fishing), also have own land where they raise cattle; mountain lodge-feel bar with beams and bare stone walls, five well kept ales including Copper Dragon, Moorhouses, Timothy Taylors and Thwaites, over 300 malt whiskies and good wine list, small family dining room and restaurant/function room extension, helpful friendly staff; a few picnic-sets with lovely valley views, closed Mon, otherwise open (and food) all day. *(Martin and Joanne Sharp)*

RAMSBOTTOM SD7816
Major (01706) 826777
Bolton Street; BL0 9JA Welcoming end-of-terrace local with four well kept ales and inexpensive pub food (not Mon, Tues, lunchtimes Weds-Sat or after 6pm Sun), friendly obliging staff, old local pictures, two-way woodburner; Tues quiz, sports TV, pool and darts; children and dogs welcome, beer garden, closed lunchtimes Mon and Tues, otherwise open all day. *(Christopher May)*

RAWTENSTALL SD8213
Buffer Stops (0161) 764 7790
Bury Road; in East Lancashire Railway station; BB4 6EH Platform bar at Rawtenstall heritage station, five well kept changing ales such as Box Steam Piston Broke, real cider/perry and selection of bottled beers, snacky food and pies, popular with locals and railway enthusiasts, good friendly service; quiz night first and third Weds of month; children (in former waiting room) and

dogs welcome, platform tables, open all day (till 9pm Mon, Tues). *(Steve Whalley)*

RILEY GREEN SD6225
★ **Royal Oak** (01254) 201445
A675/A6061; PR5 0SL Cosy low-beamed four-room pub (former coaching inn) extended by present owners; popular freshly made food (all day Sat and Sun) served by friendly efficient staff, four Thwaites ales and maybe a guest from long back bar, ancient stripped stone, open fires and lots of nooks and crannies, impressive woodwork and some bric-a-brac, seats from high-backed settles to plush armchairs on carpet, comfortable dining rooms; children and dogs welcome, picnic-sets at front and in side beer garden, short walk from Leeds & Liverpool Canal, footpath to Hoghton Tower, open all day. *(Mark and Sian Edwards)*

ROCHDALE SD8913
Baum (01706) 352186
Toad Lane (off Hunters Lane) next to the Rochdale Pioneers (Co-op) Museum; OL12 0NU In surviving cobbled street and with plenty of old-fashioned charm, seven well kept changing ales and lots of bottled beers, good value food all day (Sun till 6pm) from sandwiches and tapas up including daily roast, cheerful welcoming young staff, bare boards, old advertising signs, conservatory; free wi-fi; children and dogs welcome, garden with pétanque, open all day (till midnight Fri, Sat). *(Frank Blanchard)*

ROMILEY SJ9390
Platform 1 (0161) 406 8686
Stockport Road next to station; SK6 4BN Updated red-brick Victorian pub, open and airy with tiled and woodstrip floors, some high tables and chairs, six mostly local ales including a well priced house beer, good value pubby food from sandwiches up, carpeted upstairs restaurant called Platform 2; occasional live music; children welcome, small decked seating area outside, open (and food) all day, kitchen closes 7pm Sun. *(Sandra and Michael Smith)*

SALESBURY SD6732
Bonny Inn (01254) 248467
B6245 Ribchester–Wilpshire; BB1 9HQ Cleanly refurbished and opened-up with light airy bar and split-level carpeted dining room, popular freshly made food including blackboard specials, four Thwaites ales and several wines by the glass, back conservatory with fine Ribble Valley views; children and dogs (in bar) welcome, sturdy picnic-sets out in front under awning, more seats and views on terrace behind, open all day, food all day Sun. *(Peter and Emma Kelly)*

SCARISBRICK SD4011
Heatons Bridge Inn (01704) 840549
Heatons Bridge Road; L40 8JG Pretty 19th-c pub by bridge over Leeds & Liverpool

Canal (popular with boaters), good value home-made food (not Sun evening, Mon, Tues), well kept Black Cat and two guests, friendly welcoming staff, four traditional cosy areas and dining room; free wi-fi; children and dogs welcome, pretty hanging baskets, garden with play area and World War II pillbox (pub hosts two vintage military vehicle events during the year), open all day. *(Buster May)*

SCOUTHEAD   SD9605
Three Crowns (0161) 624 1766

Huddersfield Road; OL4 4AT Refurbished stone dining pub with well liked food from snacks and pub favourites up including good value OAP set menu, cheerful efficient service, well kept ales such as Black Sheep and Timothy Taylors Landlord, decent choice of wines, local artwork and photographs; children welcome, open (and food) all day. *(Jake)*

SILVERDALE   SD4675
Royal (01524) 702608

Emesgate Lane; LA5 0RA Cleanly refurbished village-centre pub with smallish parquet-floored bar, three local ales from light wood counter, sofa and armchairs by woodburner in stone fireplace, good reasonably priced food including breakfast from 10am, friendly helpful service, small front conservatory and upstairs dining room; daily newspapers, sports TV; children welcome, no dogs inside, picnic-sets on terrace, two self-catering cottages, open all day, food all day weekends. *(David Coupe)*

STALYBRIDGE   SJ9598
Station Buffet (0161) 303 0007

The Station, Rassbottom Street; SK15 1RF Charming little Victorian buffet bar; period advertisements, old photographs of the station and other railway memorabilia on wood-panelled and red walls, fire below etched-glass mirror, Millstone, Timothy Taylors and six quickly rotating guests, two proper ciders, seven wines by glass and ten malt whiskies, straightforward low-priced food such as pie and peas (no credit cards), newish conservatory, plus extension into what was the ladies' waiting room and part of the stationmaster's quarters with original ornate ceilings; live folk Sat evening, free wi-fi; children and dogs welcome, open (and food) all day. *(Geoff and Anne Marston)*

STOCKPORT   SJ8990
★**Arden Arms** (0161) 480 2185

Millgate Street/Corporation Street, opposite pay car park; SK1 2LX Cheerful Victorian pub in handsome dark-brick building, several well preserved high-ceilinged rooms off island bar (one tiny old-fashioned snug accessed through servery), tiling, panelling and two coal fires, popular, sensibly priced food (not Sun-Weds evenings) from lunchtime sandwiches to interesting specials, half a dozen well kept Robinsons ales, friendly efficient service; background music, Mon jazz night, Tues quiz, free wi-fi; children and dogs welcome, tables in sheltered courtyard with smokers' shelter, open all day. *(Ruby King)*

STOCKPORT   SJ8989
Armoury (0161) 477 3711

Shaw Heath, by roundabout; SK3 8BD Friendly traditionally refurbished 19th-c local with three well kept Robinsons ales; darts, sports TV, free wi-fi; picnic-sets on back terrace, open all day and busy on Edgeley Park match days. *(Ruby King)*

STOCKPORT   SJ8990
Crown (0161) 480 5850

Heaton Lane, Heaton Norris; SK4 1AR Busy but welcoming partly open-plan Victorian pub popular for its well kept changing ales (up to 16), also bottled beers and real cider, three cosy lounge areas off bar, spotless stylish décor, bargain lunchtime food; frequent live music, darts; dogs welcome, tables in cobbled courtyard, huge viaduct soaring above, open all day. *(Tom Roberts)*

STOCKPORT   SJ8890
Magnet (0161) 429 6287

Wellington Road North; SK4 1HJ Busy pub with 14 cask ales including own Watts beers from on-site brewery, real cider, pizza van Fri evenings; pool and juke box; beer garden under renovation as we went to press, open all day Fri-Sun, from 4pm other days. *(Ruby King)*

STOCKPORT   SJ8990
Swan With Two Necks

(0161) 480 2341   *Princes Street; SK1 1RY* Traditional narrow pub with welcoming local atmosphere; front panelled bar, room behind with button-back wall benches, stone fireplace and skylight, drinking corridor, well kept Robinsons ales and decent lunchtime food (not Sun, Mon) from sandwiches up; small outside area, open all day Fri, Sat, other days till 7pm (6pm Sun). *(Jim and Sue James)*

STRINES   SJ9686
Sportsmans Arms (0161) 427 2888

B6101 Marple–New Mills; SK6 7GE Comfortable roadside local with panoramic

---

Post Office address codings confusingly give the impression that some pubs are in Lancashire when they're really in Cumbria or Yorkshire (which is where we list them).

Goyt Valley view from picture-window lounge bar, good changing ale range and enjoyable well priced honest food including specials, small separate bar, log fires; folk night first Weds of month, darts, sports TV; children and dogs welcome, tables out on narrow side decking with steps down to paved terrace and smokers' shelter, open all day weekends. *(Tony Hobden)*

TATHAM   SD6169
Tatham Bridge Inn (01524) 221326
B6480, off A683 Lancaster–Kirkby Lonsdale; LA2 8NL Popular 17th-c pub with cosy low-beamed bar, well kept ales such as Tetleys, good range of enjoyable fairly priced home-cooked food, friendly helpful staff, restaurant with woodburner; children and well behaved dogs welcome, large garden, camping, open all day except Weds and Thurs when closed 2-5pm. *(Emily and Toby Archer)*

TOCKHOLES   SD6623
Black Bull (01254) 581381
Between Tockholes and Blackburn; BB3 0LL Welcoming 19th-c country pub on crossroads high above Blackburn; home to the Three B's Brewery with their good beers including Black Bull Bitter from brick-fronted counter (tasting trays available), no food, opened-up neat interior with dark blue patterned carpet and leaf wallpaper, cushioned wall seats and high-backed chairs, woodburner, snug to left of entrance with another fire; background music; seats outside (some under cover – including summerhouse), good views, open all day weekends, otherwise from 4pm, closed Mon, Tues. *(Steve Whalley)*

TOCKHOLES   SD6621
Royal (01254) 705373
Signed off A6062 S of Blackburn, and off A675; Tockholes Road; BB3 0PA Friendly old pub with unpretentious little rooms and big open fires, four well kept ales such as local Three B's from tiny back servery, well priced pubby food including some blackboard specials (good steak night Weds); some live music, free wi-fi; children, walkers and dogs welcome, big garden with views from sheltered terrace, good walks including to Darwen Tower, closed Mon, otherwise open all day. *(Simon and Alex Knight)*

TUNSTALL   SD6073
Lunesdale Arms (01524) 274203
A683 S of Kirkby Lonsdale; LA6 2QN Welcoming relaxed atmosphere at this attractive 18th-c stone-built dining pub; opened-up bare-boards interior with good mix of stripped tables and chairs, woodburner in solid stone fireplace, snugger little flagstoned back part and games area with pool, Black Sheep and a couple of guests, enjoyable sensibly priced food from varied weekly changing menu, friendly staff; children and

dogs (in bar) welcome, pretty Lune Valley village, church has Brontë associations, closed Mon. *(Martin and Joanne Sharp)*

WADDINGTON   SD7243
Higher Buck (01200) 423226
The Square; BB7 3HZ Welcoming pub in picturesque village; smartly modernised open-plan interior with airy new england feel and nice mix of seating, good food including pub favourites (all day Sun till 8pm), well kept Thwaites from pine servery, good friendly service; background music; children welcome, tables out on front cobbles and in small back courtyard, seven attractively refurbished bedrooms, open all day. *(Peter and Emma Kelly)*

WADDINGTON   SD7243
★ Lower Buck (01200) 423342
Edisford Road; BB7 3HU Hospitable old stone village pub (newish owners) tucked away behind the church; four smartly presented little rooms, each with a warming coal fire, thriving front bar with scrubbed tables, large rug on bare boards and some stained glass panelling, five well kept real ales including Bowland, Moorhouses and Timothy Taylors, several wines by the glass and enjoyable reasonably priced food from sandwiches up; daily newspapers; children and dogs welcome, picnic-sets out on front cobbles and in the sunny back garden, good Ribble Valley walks nearby, open all day. *(Caroline Prescott, Isobel Mackinlay, Ruth May, Geoffrey Sutton, Freddie and Sarah Banks, Steve Whalley)*

WADDINGTON   SD7243
★ Waddington Arms (01200) 423262
Clitheroe Road (B6478 N of Clitheroe); BB7 3HP Character inn with four linked bars, left one snuggest with blazing woodburner in huge fireplace, other low-beamed rooms have fine oak settles, chunky stripped-pine tables and lots to look at including antique and modern prints and vintage motor-racing posters, tasty food, well kept Moorhouses and four guests, good choice of wines by the glass and a dozen malt whiskies; children and dogs welcome, wicker chairs on sunny front terrace looking over to village church, more seats on two-level back terrace and neat tree-sheltered lawn, comfortable bedrooms, good walks in nearby Forest of Bowland, open all day. *(Geoff and Anne Marston)*

WALLASEY   SJ3094
Queens Royal (0151) 691 0101
Marine Promenade opposite the lake; CH45 2JT Imposing double-fronted Victorian seafront hotel with airy modernised bar, mix of furniture including comfy leather sofas and high tables on wood floor, interesting old photographs of New Brighton, six regional ales and good range of ciders from marble-topped island servery, enjoyable

food including popular Sun roasts in bar or restaurant, afternoon teas, good friendly service; children welcome, front terrace with striking sea views, comfortable bedrooms, handy for Floral Pavilion theatre, open (and food) all day. *(Susan and John Douglas)*

WEST BRADFORD SD7444
Three Millstones (01200) 443339
Waddington Road; BB7 4SX Attractive old building, but more restaurant than pub, with all tables laid for owner-chef's highly praised good value food including set menu choices, four comfortable linked areas, beams, timbers and warming fires in two grand fireplaces, ales such as Bowland and Moorhouses, good choice of wines, friendly efficient service; five bedrooms in new block, closed Sun evening, Mon, Tues. *(John and Sylvia Harrop, John and Eleanor Holdsworth)*

WEST KIRBY SJ2186
White Lion (0151) 625 9037
Grange Road (A540); CH48 4EE Friendly proper pub in interesting 18th-c sandstone building, several small beamed areas on different levels, Black Sheep, Courage and a couple of quickly changing guests, good value simple bar lunches (not Sun), coal stove; no children, attractive secluded back garden up steep stone steps, fish pond, parking in residential side streets, open all day. *(David Appleyard)*

WHALLEY SD7336
★Swan (01254) 822195
King Street; BB7 9SN Modernised 17th-c former coaching inn with friendly staff and good mix of customers in big bar, a couple of Bowland ales plus Timothy Taylors Landlord, enjoyable food from fairly standard menu, further room with leather sofas and armchairs on bare boards; background music; children and dogs (in bar) welcome, picnic-sets on back terrace and on grass strips by car park, six bedrooms, open (and food) all day. *(Gordon and Margaret Ormondroyd)*

WHEATLEY LANE SD8338
★Sparrowhawk (01282) 603034
Wheatley Lane Road; towards E end of village road, which runs N of and parallel to A6068; one way to reach it is to follow Fence signpost, then turn off at Barrowford signpost; BB12 9QG Comfortably civilised 1930s feel in imposing black and white pub; oak panelling, parquet flooring and leather tub chairs, domed stained-glass skylight, six well kept ales including Reedley Hallows from cushioned leatherette counter, nice wines by the glass and good food from sandwiches and light lunches up, friendly young staff; background and live music, comedy nights; children and dogs (in bar) welcome, heavy wooden tables on spacious front terrace with good views to the moors beyond Nelson and Colne, open all day. *(Bev)*

WISWELL SD7437
★Freemasons Arms (01254) 822218
Village signposted off A671 and A59 NE of Whalley; pub on Vicarage Fold, a gravelled pedestrian passage between Pendleton Road and Old Back Lane in village centre (don't expect to park very close); BB7 9DF Civilised dining pub with three linked rooms; antique sporting prints on cream or pastel walls, rugs on polished flagstones, carved oak settles and variety of chairs around handsome stripped or salvaged tables, candles and log fires, Bank Top, Lancaster, Reedley Hallows and a guest, well chosen wines and highly praised imaginative food (all day Sun till 7pm), efficient friendly service from uniformed staff, more rooms upstairs; children and dogs (in bar) welcome, flagstoned front terrace with heaters and awning, open all day weekends, closed Mon and maybe first two weeks of Jan. *(John and Mary Warner, Alison and Michael Harper, Dr Peter Crawshaw)*

WOODFORD SJ8882
Davenport Arms (0161) 439 2435
A5102 Wilmslow–Poynton; SK7 1PS Popular red-brick country local (aka the Thief's Neck) run by same family since 1932; well kept Robinsons ales and enjoyable lunchtime food from snacks up (evening menu Fri and Sat), friendly service, refurbished snug rooms, log fires; sports TV; children and dogs welcome, tables on front terrace and in nice back garden with play area, open all day. *(Lee McLean)*

WRIGHTINGTON SD5011
Rigbye Arms (01257) 462354
3 miles from M6 junction 27; off A5209 via Robin Hood Lane and left into High Moor Lane; WN6 9QB 17th-c dining pub in attractive moorland setting, welcoming and relaxed, with wide choice of good sensibly priced food including game menu and Thurs steak night, hot and cold sandwiches too, well kept Timothy Taylors and two guests, decent wines, several carpeted rooms including cosy tap room, open fires, separate evening restaurant (Weds-Sat, booking required); free wi-fi; children welcome, garden and bowling green, regular car club meetings, open (and food) all day Sun. *(Patricia Healey)*

WRIGHTINGTON BAR SD5313
Corner House (01257) 451400
B5250, N of M6 junction 27; WN6 9SE Opened-up 19th-c corner pub-restaurant; good food (all day weekends) from traditional to more upscale choices, meal deals and daily specials, a local ale such as Southport and good quality wines, plenty of tables in different modernised areas; children welcome, no dogs, seats outside, open all day. *(Jim and Sue James)*

Leicestershire

and Rutland

BREEDON ON THE HILL
SK4022 Map 7

Three Horseshoes 🍴

(01332) 695129 – www.thehorseshoes.com

Main Street (A453); DE73 8AN

Comfortable pub with friendly licensees and staff and emphasis on popular food

---

Below the hillside church (which is interesting and can be seen for miles around) stands this carefully run and nicely restored 18th-c dining pub. The clean-cut central bar has a stylishly simple feel with heavy worn flagstones, green walls and ceilings, a log fire, pubby tables and a dark wood counter. Marstons Pedigree and maybe a guest beer on handpump and decent house wines served by friendly, helpful staff. Beyond the bar is a dining room with maroon walls, dark pews and tables, while a two-room dining area on the right has a comfortably civilised and chatty feel with big antique tables set quite closely together on coir matting, and colourful modern country prints and antique engravings on canary yellow walls. Even at lunchtime there are lit candles in elegant modern holders. The farm shop sells their own and other local produce: eggs, jams, meat, smoked foods and chocolates. Look out for the quaint conical village lock-up opposite.

🍴 Food is very good and includes sandwiches, fish and spinach pancake with cheese sauce, bacon, chicken and tomato salad, roast vegetable casserole, sausages with mash and onion gravy, lamb hotpot with garlic mash, duck breast with cabbage and bacon, blackened salmon with sweet potato and sour cream, cajun beef fillet with tzatziki, and puddings such as lemon cheesecake and sticky toffee pudding. *Benchmark main dish: beer-battered fish and chips £11.00. Two-course evening meal £19.00.*

Free house ~ Licensees Ian Davison, Jennie Ison, Stuart Marson ~ Real ale ~ Open 11.30-2, 5.30-10.30; 12-3.30 Sun; closed Sun evening, Mon ~ Bar food 12-2, 5.30-9; 12-3.30 Sun ~ Restaurant ~ Children welcome ~ Dogs allowed in bar ~ Wi-fi *Recommended by Jeremy Snow, Brian and Anna Marsden, Claire and Emma Braithwaite, Alison and Graeme Spicer, Clive and Fran Dutson*

'Children welcome' means the pub says it lets children inside without any special restriction. If it allows them in, but to restricted areas such as an eating area or family room, we specify this. Places with separate restaurants often let children use them, and hotels usually let children into public areas such as lounges. Some pubs impose an evening time limit – let us know if you find one earlier than 9pm.

CLIPSHAM

SK9716 Map 8

Olive Branch ★ 🍴⭐ ♀ 🍺 🛏

(01780) 410355 – www.theolivebranchpub.com

Take B668/Stretton exit off A1 N of Stamford; Clipsham signposted E from exit roundabout; LE15 7SH

Leicestershire Dining Pub of the Year

A special place for a drink, a meal or an overnight stay; bedrooms

A renovated Georgian house across the road from the main pub houses the individually decorated, restful bedrooms (our readers love staying here), and there's always warm praise for the delicious breakfasts. The various small and attractive bar rooms (once labourers' cottages) have a gently civilised, country feel, dark joists and beams, rustic furniture, an interesting mix of pictures (some by local artists), candles on tables and a cosy log fire in a stone inglenook fireplace; background music, bar billiards and board games. A carefully chosen range of drinks includes a beer named for the pub, Oldershaw Old Copper and a guest from Grainstore or Oakham on handpump, an enticing wine list (with at least 25 by the glass or carafe), a thoughtful choice of spirits and cocktails (they make their own using seasonal ingredients) and several british and continental bottled beers. Service is efficient and genuinely friendly. Outside, there are tables, chairs and big plant pots on a pretty little terrace, with seating on the neat lawn, sheltered in the crook of the two low buildings. The wine shop also sells their own jams and chutneys, you can order individual dishes to take away and they can even organise food for a dinner party at home.

 Cooked by the chef-patron, the exceptional food includes sandwiches, fillet of bream with chicory tart and orange salad, guinea fowl and cep terrine, wild mushroom and tarragon pasta, beer-battered haddock and chips, lamb chump with pearl barley tabbouleh and pomegranate, sea trout with cucumber, caper and white wine sauce, slow-cooked pork shoulder with sage and onion mash and piccolo parsnips, 28-day-aged rib-eye steak with pickled onion rings, pesto, tomato and lobster butter, and puddings such as banana pannacotta with caramel popcorn and cocoa sorbet and dark chocolate tart with raspberry sorbet; they also offer a two- and three-course set lunch. *Benchmark main dish: cod fillet with brown shrimp and samphire butter and spring onion potatoes £18.95. Two-course evening meal £26.00.*

Free house ~ Licensees Sean Hope and Ben Jones ~ Real ale ~ Open 12-11 (10.30 Sun) ~ Bar food 12-2 (2.30 Sat), 6.30-9.30; 12-3, 7-9 Sun ~ Restaurant ~ Children welcome ~ Dogs allowed in bar and bedrooms ~ Wi-fi ~ Bedrooms: £97.50/£115 *Recommended by Carol Borthwick, Paul Scofield, Simon Day, Barry Collett, Comus and Sarah Elliott, Ian Wilson, R L Borthwick*

GREETHAM

SK9314 Map 7

Wheatsheaf 🍴⭐ ♀

(01572) 812325 – www.wheatsheaf-greetham.co.uk

B668 Stretton–Cottesmore; LE15 7NP

Warmly friendly stone pub with interesting food, real ales, a dozen wines, and seats in front and back gardens

Even when really pushed (which they deservedly often are), the hard-working and welcoming licensees and their staff keep things running smoothly at this well run pub. The linked L-shaped rooms have a cheerful atmosphere, both a log fire and a blazing open stove, traditional settles and cushioned captain's chairs around tables of varying sizes, and Grainstore Ten

Fifty, Greene King IPA and Langton Inclined Plane on handpump, a dozen wines by the glass and home-made cordials; background music. A games room has TV, darts, pool and board games. The pub dogs are a dachshund and a labradoodle, and visiting dogs are welcome in the bar. There are chunky picnic-sets on the front lawn and more seats on a back terrace by a pretty stream with a duck house; pétanque. They sell their own pickles, chutneys and chocolates; ramp for wheelchairs.

From a weekly changing menu (the bread is home-baked daily), the tempting food cooked by the landlady includes lunchtime sandwiches, whole quail with potato pancake and truffle oil, whole baked mini camembert with apricot chutney, twice-baked cheese soufflé with leeks, beef in ale pie, black bream fillet with olive oil mash, chorizo, piquillo pepper and olive and caper dressing, duck breast with bacon, spring onion and cabbage potato cake and horseradish cream, roast rack of lamb with butternut squash dauphinoise and rosemary and anchovy sauce, and puddings such as buttermilk pannacotta with rhubarb and almond tart with poached plums. *Benchmark main dish: bavette steak with red onion and tarragon butter and chips £17.50. Two-course evening meal £20.50.*

Punch ~ Lease Scott and Carol Craddock ~ Real ale ~ Open 12-3, 6-11; 12-11 Fri, Sat; 12-10.30 Sun; closed Mon except bank holidays; two weeks Jan ~ Bar food 12-2 (2.15 Sat), 6.30-9; 12-2.45 Sun ~ Restaurant ~ Children welcome ~ Dogs allowed in bar ~ Wi-fi
Recommended by Michael and Jenny Back, Maddie Purvis, John and Mary Warner, Geoff and Ann Marston, Melanie and David Lawson

LYDDINGTON
SP8797 Map 4
Marquess of Exeter
(01572) 822477 – www.marquessexeter.co.uk
Main Street; LE15 9LT

Stone inn with contemporary décor, real ales and excellent food; bedrooms

Of course, the food is one of the main draws to this handsome, friendly inn, but the spacious open-plan areas have understated but stylish furnishings, and the fine flagstone or wooden floors, thick walls, beams and exposed stonework are left to speak for themselves. There's a mix of old tables and chairs, smart fabrics, leather sofas, pine chests and old barrels that might always have been here. In winter, it's all warmed by several open fires – one a quite striking piece in dark iron. A beer named for the pub, Marstons EPA and a changing guest on handpump and around a dozen wines by the glass. Outside, a terrace has seats and picnic-sets, with more in the tree-sheltered gardens that seem to merge with the countryside beyond. Bedrooms are comfortable and attractive. The pub is named after the Burghley family, which has long owned this charming village (Burghley House is about 15 miles away).

The landlord cooks the imaginative food: mussels in cream, garlic and white wine, a charcuterie plate with marinated shallots, mushroom, spinach and gorgonzola risotto, crab, chilli, tomato and garlic pasta, chicken caesar salad, lamb rump with dauphinoise potatoes and crispy seaweed, gurnard fillet with fondant potato, pickled cucumber and lemon dressing, flat-iron steak with café de paris butter, and puddings such as coconut and rum pannacotta with pineapple and lime salsa and clafoutis of quince with its own sorbet; they also offer a two- and three-course set lunch. *Benchmark main dish: rib of beef with pommes frites and béarnaise sauce (for two people) £48.50. Two-course evening meal £21.00.*

Marstons ~ Lease Brian Baker ~ Real ale ~ Open 11-11 (midnight Sat); 12-10.30 Sun ~ Bar food 12-2.30, 6.30-9.30; 12-3.30, 6.30-9 Sun; also, sandwiches and salads 12-6 ~

Restaurant ~ Children welcome ~ Dogs allowed in bar and bedrooms ~ Wi-fi ~ Bedrooms: £79.50/£99 *Recommended by Peter Andrews, Philippa & Felix, Heather and Richard Jones, Julie Braeburn, Beth Aldridge, Mark Morgan, Ted and Mary Bates*

OAKHAM
SK8509 Map 4

Grainstore £

(01572) 770065 – www.grainstorebrewery.com

Station Road, off A606; LE15 6RE

Super own-brewed beers in a former Victorian grain store, cheerful customers and pubby food

Since 1995, this converted railway grain warehouse has housed the excellent Grainstore brewery and the ten own-brews are the reason so many customers are here; staff will usually offer a sample or two to help you decide which to choose. They're served traditionally on handpump at the left end of the bar counter and through swan necks with sparklers on the right. Following the traditional tower system of production, the beer is brewed on the upper floors of the building directly above the down-to-earth bar; during working hours, you'll hear the busy noises of the brewery rumbling overhead. They offer beer takeaways and hold a beer festival (with over 80 real ales and live music) on the August Bank Holiday weekend; there's also a farm cider, several wines by the glass and 15 malt whiskies. Décor is plain and functional, with well worn wide floorboards, bare ceiling boards above massive joists supported by red metal pillars, a long brick-built bar counter with cast-iron stools, tall cask tables and simple elm chairs; games machine, darts, board games, giant Jenga and bottle-walking. In summer, the huge glass doors are pulled back, opening on to a terrace with picnic-sets. You can book a brewery tour (though not on Friday or Saturday evenings) – tickets are available online. Disabled access.

Well liked food includes sandwiches, baked whole camembert with spicy tomato salsa, chicken liver pâté with red onion chutney, sharing platters, sausages with mash and onion and ale gravy, wild mushroom tagliatelle, home-baked ham and eggs, cajun chicken with onion rings, rack of baby back ribs with barbecue sauce and coleslaw, and puddings such as american pancake stack with fruit compote and sticky toffee pudding with vanilla ice-cream; Tuesday is burger night and Wednesday is pie and a pint evening. *Benchmark main dish: burgers with toppings and skinny fries £9.95. Two-course evening meal £13.00.*

Own brew ~ Licensee Peter Atkinson ~ Real ale ~ Open 11-11 (midnight Fri); 9am-midnight Sat; 9am-11pm Sun ~ Bar food 12-3, 6-9; 9-9 Sat; 9-5 Sun ~ Children welcome ~ Dogs welcome ~ Wi-fi ~ Live music twice a month, comedy monthly *Recommended by Barry Collett, Beth Aldridge, Anne and Ben Smith, Guy Henderson, Matt and Hayley Jacob*

OAKHAM
SK8608 Map 4

Lord Nelson ★ ♀ ◖

(01572) 868340 – www.kneadpubs.co.uk

Market Place; LE15 6DT

Splendidly restored and full of interest, usefully open all day, real ales and ciders and enjoyable food

One of the main things here is the easy-going, good-natured atmosphere – it's very welcoming. The half a dozen rooms are spread over two floors and you can choose from cushioned church pews, leather elbow chairs, long oak settles, sofas, armchairs or, to watch the passing scene, a big bow-window seat; carpet, bare boards and ancient red and black tiles, plus paintwork in soft shades of ochre, canary yellow, sage or pink and William Morris wallpaper. There's plenty to look at too, from intriguing antique *Police News* and other prints – plenty of Nelson, of course – to the collections of mullers, copper kettles and other homely bric-a-brac in the heavy-beamed former kitchen with its Aga. Fullers London Pride and Oakham JHB with guest ales from breweries such as Hopshackle, Leeds Brewery and Tom Woods Beer on handpump; also a dozen gins with half a dozen tonics, three farm ciders and 17 wines by the glass. Background music and TV.

Likeable food includes plenty of nibbles such as honey and bacon doughballs, home-made scotch egg and yorkshire puddings with dipping gravy, plus pizzas with lots of toppings, lime and chilli beef salad with cucumber and mint dressing, smoked haddock with a poached egg and champ mash, chicken kiev with crushed smoked bacon potatoes and greens, moroccan-style chickpea and feta burger with harissa mayonnaise and pickles, slow-roast pork belly with chorizo potatoes, black pudding and wholegrain mustard sauce, and puddings such as vanilla crème brûlée and white wine poached pears and dark chocolate and salt caramel tart. *Benchmark main dish: indian-spiced burger with sag aloo and sweet onion bhaji £14.95. Two-course evening meal £20.00.*

Knead Pubs ~ Manager Lee Jones ~ Real ale ~ Open 10am-11pm; 12-11 Sun ~ Bar food 12-2.30, 6-9; 12-9 Sat; 12-8 Sun ~ Children welcome ~ Dogs allowed in bar ~ Wi-fi
Recommended by Nigel Havers, James Landor, Barry Collett, Trevor and Michele Street, Rosie and Marcus Heatherley, James and Becky Plath

OLD DALBY
Crown ♀ ◀
SK6723 Map 7

(01664) 820320 – www.thecrownolddalby.com
Debdale Hill; LE14 3LF

Interesting refurbishment for well run busy pub with local ales, a wide choice of good food and seats in sunny garden

Partly 17th-c, this bustling, extended, creeper-clad pub has been cleverly refurbished. The various cosy rooms in the original part of the building are decorated in a rustic style with plenty of reclaimed wood, nice old floorboards, flagstones and coir carpet, metal grillwork and interesting lamps and ceiling lights. There's an eclectic collection of old and new chairs, long cushioned wall seats and settles, tables of every shape and size, gilt-edged and advertising mirrors, lots of books on shelves, woodburning stoves and even a stuffed hare holding a shotgun. Charnwood Vixen and guests such as Belvoir Old Dalby or Goffs Tournament on handpump, 14 wines by the glass, cocktails and three ciders; background music, darts and board games. The partly covered garden room has fairy lights and simple furnishings and leads on to the south-facing garden with cast-iron tables and chairs under parasols on a terrace and on the lawn.

Good, popular food includes sandwiches (until 5pm), mussels in white wine and cream, pigeon with celeriac and vanilla purée and blackberry sauce, feta and vegetable hash with a fried duck egg and parmesan sauce, a pie of the week, barbecue half chicken with bourbon glaze, honey-roasted butternut squash and skin-on chips, scallops thermidor in the shell, lamb rump with sun-dried tomatoes, olives and honey balsamic sauce, and puddings such as baked rhubarb and orange cheesecake with rhubarb and custard ice-cream and dark chocolate croissant bread and butter pudding; Monday is pie or burger night and steak evening is Thursday. *Benchmark main dish: maple-glazed rack of ribs with kohlrabi slaw and cajun fries £16.95. Two-course evening meal £20.00.*

Little Britain Pub Company ~ Licensee Matthew Jenkinson ~ Real ale ~ Open 12-2.30, 5.30-11.30; 12-midnight Sat; 12-10 Sun; closed Mon lunchtime ~ Bar food 12-2.30, 5.30-9.30;

12-9.30 Sat; 12-6 Sun ~ Restaurant ~ Children welcome ~ Dogs allowed in bar ~ Wi-fi ~
Barbecues/live music monthly in summer, live music quarterly, quiz last Tues evening of
month *Recommended by Phil and Jane Hodson, Sabina and Gerald Grimshaw, Christopher May,
Emily and Toby Archer*

PEGGS GREEN
SK4117 Map 7

New Inn £

(01530) 222293 – www.thenewinnpeggsgreen.co.uk

*Signposted off A512 Ashby–Shepshed at roundabout, then turn immediately left down
Zion Hill towards Newbold; pub is 100 metres on the right, with car park on opposite
side of road; LE67 8JE*

**Intriguing bric-a-brac in unspoilt pub, friendly welcome, well liked
food at fair prices and real ales; cottagey garden**

Almost every inch of the walls and ceilings in the two cosy tiled front
rooms of this cheerful pub are covered with bric-a-brac – the genial
licensees have been collecting it since they first took over the place in 1978.
The little room on the left, a bit like an old-fashioned kitchen parlour (called
the Cabin), has china on the mantelpiece, lots of prints and photographs,
three old cast-iron tables, wooden stools and a small stripped kitchen table.
The room to the right has attractive stripped panelling and more appealing
bric-a-brac. The small back 'Best' room (good for private meetings) has a
stripped-wood floor and a touching display of vintage local photographs
including some colliery ones. Bass, Marstons Pedigree and a quickly
changing guest beer on handpump; background music and board games.
There are plenty of seats in front of the pub, with more in the peaceful back
garden. Do check the unusual opening and food service times carefully.

 There's a visiting fish and chip van on Monday evening and a pizza van on
Wednesday evening (you can eat both in the pub); Tuesday is pie night; chips
and toppings are on offer on Friday nights, and filled rolls on Friday and Saturday
lunchtimes; Sunday brunch (10-3) is for open toasties.

Enterprise ~ Lease Maria Christina Kell ~ Real ale ~ Open 12-2.30, 5.30-11; 12-3, 6.30-11 Sat;
10-3, 7-10.30 Sun; closed Mon-Thurs lunchtimes ~ Food 5-9 Mon; 6-8 Tues; 6-9 Weds; 6-10 Fri;
10-3 Sun; no food Sat, Sun or Thurs evenings ~ Well behaved children welcome ~
Dogs welcome ~ Wi-fi ~ Live folk club second Mon of month, quiz Thurs evening
*Recommended by Edward Nile, William Pace, Anne and Ben Smith, Brian and Sally Wakeham,
Shona and Jimmy McDuff*

SILEBY
SK6015 Map 7

White Swan

(01509) 814832 – www.whiteswansileby.co.uk

*Off A6 or A607 N of Leicester; in centre turn into King Street (opposite church), then
after mini roundabout turn right at Post Office signpost into Swan Street; LE12 7NW*

**Exemplary town local, a boon to its chatty regulars, with tasty
home cooking and a friendly welcome**

Mrs Miller has been running this honest local for over 30 years and it's
particularly popular with walkers from Cossington Meadows and
those moored at Sileby Marine. It has all the touches that mark the best
of between-the-wars estate pub design, such as an art deco-tiled lobby,
polychrome-tiled fireplaces, a shiny red Anaglypta ceiling and a comfortable
layout of linked but separate areas including a small restaurant (lined with
books). Packed with bric-a-brac from bizarre hats to decorative plates and
lots of prints, it quickly draws you in thanks to the genuinely bright and

cheerful welcome. Bass and maybe a guest beer on handpump and six wines by the glass. Mrs Miller also runs a highly successful outside catering business which includes meals you can buy from the pub to take home.

Good value food includes breaded mushrooms with garlic mayonnaise, prawn cocktail, puff pastry parcel filled with mushrooms, brie, cranberries and spinach with vegetable gravy, chicken parmesan topped with parma ham, salmon and prawn cake in a creamy cheese sauce, duck breast with port, redcurrant and black cherry sauce, rump steak with sausages and bacon, and puddings such as apple pie and chocolate brownie. *Benchmark main dish: beef cobbler £13.95. Two-course evening meal £17.50.*

Free house ~ Licensee Theresa Miller ~ Real ale ~ Open 6-10 Tues-Thurs; 12-2, 6-11 Fri, Sat; 12-3 Sun; closed Sun evening, all day Mon, lunchtimes Tues-Sat ~ Bar food 6-8.30 Tues-Sat; 12-1.30 Sun ~ Children welcome ~ Dogs allowed in bar ~ Wi-fi *Recommended by Harvey Brown, Emma Scofield, John Harris, Neil Allen, Jack Trussler, Simon and Alex Knight*

SUTTON CHENEY
SK4100   Map 4

Hercules Revived ⭐ ♀
(01455) 699336 – www.herculesrevived.co.uk
Off A447 3 miles S of Market Bosworth; CV13 0AG

Attractively furnished bar and upstairs dining rooms, highly thought-of food, real ales and helpful staff

The neat and careful refurbishment just a few years ago brought this 17th-c former coaching inn back to life. There's a genuine welcome for all customers – locals or visitors, drinkers or diners – and the atmosphere is easy-going and chatty. The long bar has brown leather wall seating with attractive scatter cushions, upholstered brown and white checked or plain wooden church chairs around various tables, rugs on wooden flooring, fresh flowers, prints and ornamental plates on creamy yellow walls and a big open fire; background music. There are high leather chairs against the rough hewn counter, where they serve Church End What the Foxs Hat and Sharps Doom Bar on handpump and ten wines by the glass. Upstairs, each of the interlinked, grey-carpeted dining rooms have their own colour scheme and tartan dining chairs around dark wooden tables; one wall is a giant map of the area. There are picnic-sets with parasols on the little back terrace, with views across a meadow to the church.

Rewarding food includes sandwiches and baguettes, trio of salmon (beetroot-marinated gravadlax, smoked salmon, poached salmon tian), chicken liver and smoked bacon pâté with red onion and cranberry chutney, tomato and thyme arancini with a poached egg and a warm salad of tomato, red onion and haricot beans, a curry of the day, duck breast with redcurrant jus and duck cottage pie, soda-battered fish and chips, chicken kiev with sweetcorn and potato rösti and garlic butter, and puddings such as dark chocolate tart and salted peanut caramel with white chocolate ice-cream and lemon pannacotta with lemon meringue and lemon curd ice-cream. *Benchmark main dish: slow-braised beef with smoked bacon, mushrooms, cheddar mash and suet cobbler £12.95. Two-course evening meal £15.00.*

Free house ~ Licensee Oliver Warner ~ Real ale ~ Open 12-3.30, 6-11; 12-11 Sat; 12-6 Sun ~ Bar food 12-2.30, 6-9; 12-4 Sun ~ Restaurant ~ Children welcome ~ Dogs allowed in bar *Recommended by Pauline and Mark Evans, Lindy Andrews, Alison and Michael Harper, Charles and Maddie Bishop*

The star-on-a-plate award, ⭐, distinguishes pubs where the food is of exceptional quality. The knife-and-fork symbol just means the pub serves food.

SWITHLAND

SK5512 Map 7

Griffin

(01509) 890535 – www.griffininnswithland.co.uk

Main Street; between A6 and B5330, between Loughborough and Leicester; LE12 8TJ

A good mix of cheerful customers and well liked food in a well run, busy pub

An appealing stone-built pub in a small tucked-away village, this is handy for walks, with Swithland Wood or Bradgate Park close by. The three beamed communicating rooms are cosy and traditional with some panelling, leather armchairs and sofas, cushioned wall seating, a woodburner, a nice mix of wooden tables and chairs and lots of bird prints. Stools line the counter where Adnams Southwold, Everards Original and Tiger and a couple of changing guests are well kept on handpump; also, a couple of farm ciders, several malt whiskies and wines by the glass from a good list; background music. The terrace, screened by plants, has wicker seats and there are more seats in the streamside garden overlooking open fields, as well as painted picnic-sets outside the Old Stables. They also have a café/deli selling local produce and artisan products. Good wheelchair access and disabled facilities.

Highly regarded food includes baguettes, moules marinière, ham hock and mustard terrine with piccalilli, roasted mediterranean vegetables in spicy tomato sauce topped with grilled goats cheese, lambs liver with onion gravy and crisp pancetta, steak, lamb, chicken or mixed bean burger with toppings, coleslaw and chips, a pie of the day, mint and mango slow-cooked lamb shank with mash, and puddings such as rhubarb and ginger fool and white chocolate and peanut butter cheesecake with raspberry jam; they also offer a two- and three-course lunch and early-bird set menu. *Benchmark main dish: beer-battered fresh haddock and chips £12.50. Two-course evening meal £20.00.*

Everards ~ Tenant John Cooledge ~ Real ale ~ Open 12-11 (10.30 Sun) ~ Bar food 12-2.30, 5.30-9; 12-9 Sat; 12-8 Sun ~ Restaurant ~ Children welcome ~ Dogs allowed in bar ~ Wi-fi
Recommended by Ian Herdman, Edward Nile, William Pace, David Longhurst, Susan Eccleston, Peter Pilbeam, Dr and Mrs A K Clarke, Justine and Neil Bonnett

WING

SK8902 Map 4

Kings Arms ★ ♀ ⌂

(01572) 737634 – www.thekingsarms-wing.co.uk

Village signposted off A6003 S of Oakham; Top Street; LE15 8SE

Nicely kept old pub with big log fires, super choice of wines by the glass and good modern cooking; bedrooms

Our readers enjoy their visits to this civilised former farmhouse very much, with particular praise for the first class food, attractive bars and comfortable bedrooms. The neatly kept and inviting long main bar has two large log fires (one in a copper-canopied central hearth), various nooks and crannies, nice old low beams and stripped stone, and flagstone or wood-strip floors. Friendly, helpful staff serve almost three dozen wines by the glass, as well as Black Sheep, Dark Star Partridge, Grainstore Cooking and a guest ale on handpump, 30 wines by the glass, ten gins, a dozen malt whiskies and 12 home-made hedgerow liqueurs; dominoes and cards. There are seats out in front, and more in the sunny yew-sheltered garden; the car park has plenty of space. If you stay here you can choose between the Old Bake House (the village's former bakery) or Orchard House (just up their private drive) – both have well equipped, pretty rooms, and breakfasts are particularly good. You'll find a medieval turf maze just up the road and it's only a couple of miles to one of England's two osprey hotspots.

Imaginative food uses produce from their own smokehouse, home-baked bread and home-made pickles, chutneys, preserves and so forth: sandwiches, black pudding fritters with relish, half rack of spicy pork ribs, open omelete of shallots, potatoes, herbs and cheese, pheasant curry, pulled pork or steak burgers with toppings, onion rings and fries, beer-battered fish of the day with dripping chips, fallow deer saddle and faggot with spiced red cabbage and butternut squash purée, smoked partridge caesar salad, and puddings such as chocolate mousse and vanilla crème brûlée with berry compote. *Benchmark main dish: 28-day-aged rump steak £19.50. Two-course evening meal £24.00.*

Free house ~ Licensee David Goss ~ Real ale ~ Open 12-3, 6.30 (5 Fri)-11; 12-11 Sat; 12-3 Sun; closed Sun evening, Mon lunchtime ~ Bar food 12-2, 6.30-8.30 (9 Fri, Sat) ~ Restaurant ~ Children welcome ~ Dogs allowed in bar and bedrooms ~ Wi-fi ~ Bedrooms: £75/£100
Recommended by Colin Chambers, Pat and Stewart Gordon, Susan Jackman, Mary Joyce, Peter Andrews, Martin and Clare Warne, S Holder, Kate Roberts, Martin and Sue Neville, Millie and Peter Downing

WYMONDHAM   SK8518   Map 7

Berkeley Arms ⭐

(01572) 787587 – www.theberkeleyarms.co.uk

Main Street; LE14 2AG

Well run village pub with interesting food, interlinked beamed rooms, a relaxed atmosphere and sunny terrace

Good walks surround this golden-stone inn, so lunchtimes can get pretty busy, but the hands-on, hardworking licensees keep things running smoothly and on top form. The atmosphere is easy-going and friendly, with knick-knacks, magazines, table lamps and cushions – and at one end (in front of a log fire), two wing chairs on patterned carpet beside a low coffee table. The red-tiled or wood-floored dining areas, dense with stripped beams and standing timbers, are furnished in a kitchen style with light wood tables and red-cushioned chunky chairs. Batemans XB, Castle Rock Harvest Pale, Woodfordes Wherry and a guest from Grainstore on handpump, 11 wines by the glass and local cider. Outside, on small terraces to either side of the front entrance, picnic-sets get the sun nearly all day long.

Food is extremely good and cooked by the landlord: rabbit and prune pâté with chutney, mussels with coconut milk, chilli, lemongrass and coriander, potato gnocchi with wild mushrooms, spinach, truffle oil and parmesan, local sausages with bubble and squeak and sage and red onion gravy, chicken breast with root vegetable gratin and wild mushrooms, honey-glazed duck breast with sweet potato, pak choi and orange and ginger glaze, lamb rump with spicy tomato and aubergine stew and herb couscous, and puddings such as passion-fruit cheesecake with passion-fruit sorbet and chocolate fondant with honeycomb and vanilla ice-cream. *Benchmark main dish: braised venison shoulder with caramelised walnuts and poached pear £18.50. Two-course evening meal £22.00.*

Free house ~ Licensee Louise Hitchen ~ Real ale ~ Open 12-3, 6-11; 12-5 Sun; closed Sun evening, Mon; first two weeks Jan, two weeks summer ~ Bar food 12-1.45, 6.30-9; 12-3 Sun ~ Restaurant ~ Children welcome ~ Dogs allowed in bar *Recommended by Max Simons, David Travis, Barry Collett, R L Borthwick, Rosie and John Moore, David Appleyard*

Real ale may be served from handpumps, electric pumps (not just the on-off switches used for keg beer) or – common in Scotland – tall taps called founts (pronounced 'fonts') where a separate pump pushes the beer up under air pressure.

Also Worth a Visit in Leicestershire

Besides the fully inspected pubs, you might like to try these pubs that have been recommended to us and described by readers. Do tell us what you think of them: feedback@goodguides.com

AB KETTLEBY   SK7519
Sugar Loaf (01664) 822473
Nottingham Road (A606 NW of Melton);
LE14 3JB Beamed roadside pub with
modern open-plan bar, wooden tables and
chairs on tartan carpet, old prints and
photographs on newly painted walls, wood-
strip end with coal-effect gas fire, airy dining
conservatory, enjoyable reasonably priced
pubby food from baguettes and light lunches
to daily specials, Sharps Doom Bar and
three guests, welcoming attentive service;
background and occasional live music,
TV, free wi-fi, darts; children welcome, no
dogs inside, seats on small side terrace and
grass, open (and food) all day. *(Johnston and
Maureen Anderson, John and Sylvia Harrop)*

ASHBY DE LA ZOUCH   SK3516
Tap at No 76 No phone
Market Street; LE65 1AP Recently opened
high-street micropub in former tea rooms,
fine range of ales and craft beers including
Tollgate (tasting trays available), proper
ciders and several wines by the glass, friendly
helpful staff, cosy interior with scatter-
cushion wall benches and high tables on
light wood floor, pendant lighting and good
woodburner, some old beams and a back
skylit area, snacky food such as pork pies;
open all day Thurs-Sun, closed Mon and
lunchtimes Tues, Weds. *(Hannah Barlow)*

BARROWDEN   SK9400
Exeter Arms (01572) 747365
*Main Street, just off A47 Uppingham–
Peterborough; LE15 8EQ* Former coaching
inn refurbished by current welcoming
family, open-plan bar with beams, stripped
stone and woodburner, Black Sheep,
Grainstore, Greene King and Sharps from
long central counter, enjoyable food from
pubby choices up including two-course
lunch deal Weds-Fri and steak night Weds,
friendly helpful service; quiz first Thurs of
the month, open mike third Thurs; children
and dogs welcome, picnic sets on narrow
front terrace with lovely views over village
green and Welland Valley, more tables and
boules in large garden behind, good local
walks, three bedrooms, closed Sun evening,
Mon and lunchtime Tues. *(Jim King)*

BELMESTHORPE   TF0410
Blue Bell (01780) 763859
*Village signposted off A16 just E of
Stamford; PE9 4JG* Cottagey 17th-c
stone pub in attractive remote hamlet;
good keenly priced home-made food
and decent range of well kept ales such

as Grainstore and Oakham, friendly
welcoming staff, comfortable dining areas
either side of central bar, beams and huge
inglenook; children and dogs welcome,
seats in garden, open all day weekends,
closed Mon lunchtime. *(Barry Collett)*

BRANSTON   SK8129
Wheel (01476) 870376
Main Street near the church; NG32 1RU
Beamed 18th-c stone-built village pub with
enjoyable food from sandwiches up including
set lunch/early evening deal, three well
kept changing ales such as Brewsters from
central servery (May beer festival), proper
cider and good choice of wines, friendly staff,
woodburner and open fires; background and
occasional live music, skittle alley; children
welcome, dogs in bar, attractive garden,
splendid countryside near Belvoir Castle,
open all day (till 8pm Sun). *(Mark Morgan)*

BRAUNSTON   SK8306
Blue Ball (01572) 722135
*Off A606 in Oakham; Cedar Street
opposite church; LE15 8QS* Pretty 17th-c
thatched and beamed dining pub, good
food (not Sun evening) including deals,
well kept Marstons-related ales and decent
wines (happy hour 5.30-6.30pm Fri), friendly
welcoming staff, log fires, leather furniture
and country pine in linked rooms, small
conservatory, artwork for sale; monthly jazz
Sun lunchtime; free wi-fi; children and dogs
(in bar) welcome, painted furniture outside
on decking, attractive village, open all day
Sat, till 8pm Sun, closed Mon. *(Patrick
and Barbara Knights, Barry Collett)*

BRAUNSTON   SK8306
Old Plough (01572) 722714
*Off A606 in Oakham; Church Street;
LE15 8QT* Comfortably opened-up
black-beamed village local continuing
well under new management; four well
kept changing ales, craft beers and good
range of gins, enjoyable food (not Sun
evening) from ciabattas to grills including
good value weekday lunch deal, friendly
efficient service, log fire, back dining
conservatory; free wi-fi; children, dogs
and muddy boots welcome, tables in
sheltered back garden with pétanque, five
bedrooms, open all day. *(Barry Collett)*

BRUNTINGTHORPE   SP6089
★**Joiners Arms** (0116) 247 8258
*Off A5199 S of Leicester: Church Walk/
Cross Street; LE17 5QH* More restaurant
than pub with most of the two beamed rooms
set for eating, drinkers have area by small

light oak bar with open fire; civilised relaxed atmosphere, candles on tables, elegant dining chairs and big flower arrangements, first class imaginative food served by efficient friendly staff, cheaper set menu option weekday lunchtimes/Tues evening, plenty of wines by the glass including champagne, one mainstream ale such as Greene King or Sharps; picnic-sets in front, closed Sun evening, Mon. *(Justine and Neil Bonnett)*

BUCKMINSTER SK8822

★**Tollemache Arms** (01476) 860477

B676 Colsterworth–Melton Mowbray; Main Street; NG33 5SA 19th-c country dining inn with good food from pub favourites up in bar or restaurant, OAP lunch Thurs and other deals; boarded floors in linked areas with mix of wooden furniture including some small hand-made pews, armchairs by open fire in bar, leather sofas in library room off restaurant, Grainstore, Oakham and a guest such as Wychwood, good choice of wines by the glass and several malt whiskies, friendly attentive service; background music, TV, free wi-fi; children and dogs (in bar) welcome, plenty of teak tables and chairs in sizeable garden, comfortable well equipped bedrooms, good breakfast, lovely village and handy for A1, open (and food) all day Sat, till 5pm Sun, closed Mon. *(Nick Judkins, Valerie Sayer, Toby Jones, Lauren and Dan Frazer, Deborah and Duncan Walliams)*

BURROUGH ON THE HILL SK7510

Grants (01664) 452141

Off B6047 S of Melton Mowbray; Main Street; LE14 2JQ Cosy old pub with own Parish ales (brewed next door) including the fearsomely strong Baz's Bonce Blower, well liked food served by helpful staff, open fires, restaurant and games room; occasional live music, sports TV, free wi-fi; children and dogs welcome, tables in garden, good walk to nearby Iron Age fort, open all day weekends, closed Mon. *(Jim King)*

BURTON OVERY SP6797

Bell (0116) 259 2365

Main Street; LE8 9DL Good interesting choice of well priced food (not Mon) from lunchtime sandwiches up in L-shaped open-plan bar and dining room (used mainly for larger parties), log fire, comfortable sofas, ales such as Langton and Timothy Taylors Landlord, pleasant unobtrusive service; children welcome, nice garden and lovely village, open all day weekends, closed lunchtimes Mon and Tues. *(R L Borthwick)*

CALDECOTT SP8693

Plough (01536) 770284

Main Street; LE16 8RS Welcoming pub in attractive ironstone village; carpeted bar with banquettes and small tables leading to spacious eating area, log fires, four well kept changing beers such as Grainstore and Langton, wide range of popular

inexpensive food including blackboard specials, prompt service; children and dogs welcome, good-sized garden at back, closed weekday lunchtimes. *(Ted and Mary Bates)*

COLEORTON SK4016

Angel (01530) 834742

The Moor; LE67 8GB Friendly and homely with good range of enjoyable reasonably priced food (all day Sun) including carvery, well kept beers such as Marstons Pedigree, hospitable attentive staff, beams and open fire; children welcome, tables outside, open all day Sun. *(Guy Henderson)*

COLEORTON SK4117

★**George** (01530) 834639

Loughborough Road (A512 E); LE67 8HF Traditional and homely with well divided beamed bar, scatter-cushioned pews and wall seats, church candles on tables, dark panelled dado with local photographs above, shelves of books, leather sofa and tartan-upholstered tub chairs by woodburner, Leatherbritches, Marstons and Tollgate, several wines by the glass and popular fair value food, friendly staff, bigger room on left with another woodburner and plenty to look at; background music, free wi-fi; well behaved children welcome, dogs in bar, spreading back garden with sturdy furniture and country views, open all day Fri, Sat, till 9pm Sun. *(Mark Morgan, Jeremy Snow, Lindy Andrews)*

CROXTON KERRIAL SK8329

Geese & Fountain (01476) 870350

A607 SW of Grantham; NG32 1QR Modernised 17th-c coaching inn with five real ales such as Brewsters, Grainstore and Oakham, several craft beers, organic wines and some interesting spirits, food from sandwiches and pizzas up, log fire in big open-plan beamed bar, dining room and garden room; occasional live music; children, walkers and dogs welcome, secure bike racks for cyclists, picnic-sets in inner courtyard and sloping garden with views, seven good bedrooms (separate block), open all day in summer, best to check winter hours. *(J P)*

DADLINGTON SP4097

Dog & Hedgehog (01455) 213151

The Green, opposite church; CV13 6JB Popular red-brick village dining pub with good choice of food including popular Sun lunch, friendly staff and hands-on character landlord, rebadged ales from brewers such as Quartz and Tunnel, nice wines, restaurant; children and dogs welcome, garden looking down to Ashby-de-la-Zouch Canal, closed Sun evening, otherwise open all day. *(Gareth Woods, Mike and Margaret Banks)*

DISEWORTH SK4524

Plough (01332) 810333

Near East Midlands Airport and M1 junction 23A; DE74 2QJ Extended

16th-c beamed pub, well kept Timothy
Taylor, Bass, Marstons and guests, low-
priced traditional food (not Sun evening),
friendly staff, bar and spacious well divided
restaurant, log fires; children and dogs
welcome, large paved terrace with steps
up to lawn, handy for Donington Park
race track, open all day. *(Mark Morgan)*

FOXTON
SP6989

★ **Foxton Locks** (0116) 279 1515
*Foxton Locks, off A6 3 miles NW of
Market Harborough (park by bridge
60/62 and walk); LE16 7RA* Busy
place in great canalside setting at foot
of spectacular flight of locks; large
comfortably reworked L-shaped bar,
popular pubby food including Sun carvery,
converted boathouse (not always open)
for snacks, friendly service, well kept
ales such as Greene King, Sharps and
Theakstons; some live music, free wi-fi;
children and dogs welcome, glassed-in
dining 'terrace' overlooking the water,
steps down to fenced waterside lawn,
good walks, open (and food) all day. *(Gerry and
Rosemary Dobson, Mike and Margaret Banks)*

GADDESBY
SK6813

Cheney Arms (01664) 840260
Rearsby Lane; LE7 4XE Friendly red-
brick country pub set back from the road;
bar with bare-boards and terracotta-tiled
floor, well kept Everards and a guest from
brick-faced servery, open fires including
inglenook in more formal dining room, big
helpings of reasonably priced food (not
Sun evening, Mon) from good lunchtime
baguettes up; sports TV, free wi-fi; children
welcome, disabled access, walled back
garden with smokers' shelter, lovely medieval
church nearby, four bedrooms, closed Mon
lunchtime. *(Millie and Peter Downing)*

GILMORTON
SP5787

Grey Goose (01455) 552555
Lutterworth Road; LE17 5PN Popular
bar-restaurant with good range of enjoyable
freshly made food including lunchtime/
early evening weekday set menu and
Sun carvery, ales such as Grainstore and
several wines by the glass, good friendly
staff coping well at busy times, light
contemporary décor, stylish wood and
metal bar stools mixing with comfortable
sofas and armchairs, woodburner in
stripped-brick fireplace; modern furniture
on terrace, closed Sun evening, otherwise
open all day. *(Mike and Margaret Banks)*

GLASTON
SK8900

Old Pheasant (01572) 822326
*A47 Leicester–Peterborough, E of
Uppingham; LE15 9BP* Attractive
much-extended stone inn; beamed bar
with inglenook and some comfortable
leather armchairs, well kept Grainstore
from central brick servery, good range of

generously served food including Weds grill
night, steps up to restaurant; bar billiards;
children welcome, picnic-sets on sheltered
terrace, good value bedrooms, open all day.
(Paul A Moore, Mike and Margaret Banks)

GREAT BOWDEN
SP7488

Red Lion (01858) 463571
*Off A6 N of Market Harborough; Main
Street; LE16 7HB* Attractively modernised
dining pub with good well presented food
using local produce (some from own garden),
carefully chosen wines and three real ales
including a house beer from Langton, friendly
attentive service; background music; children
welcome, no dogs during food times, tables
out on deck and lawn, open all day, no food
Sun evening, Mon. *(Mike and Margaret Banks)*

GREETHAM
SK9214

Plough (01572) 813613
B668 Stretton–Cottesmore; LE15 7NJ
Traditional village pub, comfortable and
welcoming, with good home-made food
including weekday deals, breakfast Sat
from 9.30am, can eat in cosy lounge or
fire-divided restaurant, Grainstore, Timothy
Taylors and guests, helpful friendly service;
children and dogs welcome, garden behind,
good local walks and not far from Rutland
Water, open all day Thurs, Sat and Sun,
closed Tues lunchtime. *(Susan Eccleston)*

GRIMSTON
SK6821

Black Horse (01664) 812358
*Off A6006 W of Melton Mowbray;
Main Street; LE14 3BZ* Steps up to
popular old village-green pub on two
levels, welcoming licensees and friendly
locals, well kept Adnams, Marstons and
a couple of guests, decent wines, fairly
priced traditional food from baguettes
to blackboard specials, open fire; darts;
children welcome, pétanque in back garden,
attractive village with stocks and 13th-c
church, closed Sun evening. *(Guy Henderson)*

GUMLEY
SP6890

Bell (0116) 279 0126
*NW of Market Harborough; Main Street;
LE16 7RU* Friendly beamed village local,
L-shaped bar with hunting prints and
two open fires, Timothy Taylors Landlord,
Woodfordes Wherry and guests, fair-priced
home-cooked food including blackboard
specials, weekday lunch deal and Weds
steak night; live music, sports TV; children
and dogs welcome, terrace garden with
pond, local walks and cycle routes, open
all day weekends. *(Ted and Mary Bates)*

HALLATON
SP7896

Bewicke Arms (01858) 555734
*On Eastgate, opposite village sign;
LE16 8UB* Attractive 18th-c thatched
dining pub; good interesting food from
sensibly short menu making use of local
ingredients, ales such as Grainstore

and Timothy Taylors, proper cider and well chosen wines, bar dining areas and restaurant, log fires and woodburners, memorabilia from ancient inter-village bottle-kicking match (still held on Easter Mon); children and dogs welcome, disabled facilities, big terrace overlooking paddock, play area, three bedrooms in converted stables, café and shop, closed Mon, otherwise open all day. *(Jim King)*

HARBY SK7531
Nags Head (01949) 869629
Main Street; LE14 4BN Popular old beamed pub with four comfortably refurbished linked rooms, good pubby food including burger menu and Tues evening deal, Jennings Cumberland, Thwaites Wainwright and a guest, friendly service, real fires; live music first Fri of month, sports TV, free wi-fi; picnic-sets in large garden, interesting Vale of Belvoir village, open all day Fri-Sun, closed Mon lunchtime. *(Phil and Jane Hodson)*

HINCKLEY SP4293
Railway (01455) 612399
Station Road; LE10 1AP Friendly chatty pub owned by Steamin' Billy, their ales and guests from seven pumps, also draught continentals and real cider, sensibly priced food including Weds pie and Thurs steak nights, friendly young staff, open fires; darts; dogs welcome, beer garden behind, handy for the station, open all day. *(Heather and Richard Jones)*

HOBY SK6717
Blue Bell (01664) 434247
Main Street; LE14 3DT Attractive well run thatched pub with good range of popular realistically priced food (smaller appetites catered for), friendly attentive uniformed staff, four well kept Everards ales and two guests, lots of wines by the glass, teas/coffees, open-plan and airy with beams, comfortable traditional furniture, old local photographs; background music, skittle alley and darts; children, walkers and dogs welcome, picnic-sets in valley-view garden with boules, open all day, food all day weekends. *(Mark Morgan)*

HOUGHTON ON THE HILL SK6703
Old Black Horse (0116) 241 3486
Main Street (just off A47 Leicester–Uppingham); LE7 9GD Welcoming village pub with enjoyable home-made food (not Sun evening, Mon) including Thurs pie night, well kept Everards, a guest beer and decent wines by the glass, opened up inside into distinct areas, mix of bare boards, tiles and carpet, some panelling; background and live music, regular quiz nights, sports TV, darts; children and dogs welcome, attractive big garden with boules, open all day Fri and Sun, closed Mon lunchtime. *(Mike and Margaret Banks)*

HUNGARTON SK6907
Black Boy (0116) 259 5410
Main Street; LE7 9JR Large partly divided restaurant bar with open fire, well priced food cooked to order by landlord-chef (weekend booking advised), various themed nights, changing ales such as Greene King, Fullers and Charles Wells, cheerful staff; background music; children welcome, picnic-sets on decking, closed Sun evening, Mon. *(Matt and Hayley Jacob)*

KIRBY MUXLOE SK5104
Royal Oak (0116) 239 3166
Main Street; LE9 2AN Modernish village pub with good food from sandwiches and pub favourites to more inventive dishes, lunchtime/early evening set deal and Mon pie and wine night, Everards ales including one badged for them and a guest, good wine choice, sizeable restaurant; Mon night quiz and Weds night bingo; children and dogs (in bar) welcome, disabled facilities, picnic-sets outside, 15th-c castle ruins nearby. *(Ted and Mary Bates)*

KNIPTON SK8231
Manners Arms (01476) 879222
Signed off A607 Grantham–Melton Mowbray; Croxton Road; NG32 1RH Handsome Georgian hunting lodge reworked as comfortable country inn; bare-boards bar with log fire, four well kept ales such as Batemans XXXB and Fullers London Pride, nice choice of wines by the glass, good reasonably priced food here or in sizeable restaurant with attractive conservatory, friendly helpful staff; background music; terrace with ornamental pool, lovely views over pretty village, ten comfortable individually furnished bedrooms, open all day. *(Susan Eccleston)*

KNOSSINGTON SK8008
Fox & Hounds (01664) 452129
Off A606 W of Oakham; Somerby Road; LE15 8LY Attractive 18th-c ivy-clad village dining pub, beamed bar with log fire and cosy eating areas, well liked food (best to book) from traditional choices to blackboard specials, Fullers London Pride, attentive friendly service; children (over 8) and dogs welcome, big back garden, closed Sun evening, Mon and lunchtimes Tues-Thurs. *(Jim King)*

LEICESTER SK5804
Ale Wagon (0116) 262 3330
Rutland Street/Charles Street; LE1 1RE Basic 1930s two-room corner local with nine well kept ales including own Hoskins Brothers beers, a traditional cider, no food apart from baps, coal fire, upstairs function room; background music; handy for Curve Theatre and station, open all day, closed Sun lunchtime. *(John Poulter)*

LEICESTER
SK5804

Criterion (0116) 262 5418
Millstone Lane; LE1 5JN 1960s building with dark wood and carpeted main room, up to a dozen well kept ales and extensive range of bottled beers, real ciders too, good value stone-baked pizzas plus some other snacky food, room on left with games and old-fashioned juke box; regular live music and quiz nights, annual comedy festival; picnic-sets outside, open all day; has recently changed hands but new owners intend to keep things much the same. *(Mark Morgan)*

LEICESTER
SK5804

Globe (0116) 253 9492
Silver Street; LE1 5EU Original character and lots of woodwork in partitioned areas off central bar, bare boards and some Victorian mosaic flooring, mirrors and working gas lamps, four Everards ales, three guests and a couple of real ciders, over a dozen wines by the glass, friendly staff, well priced food from bar snacks up including deals, function room upstairs; background music (not in snug); children and dogs welcome, metal café-style tables out in front, open all day. *(Mark Morgan)*

LEICESTER
SK5804

★ Rutland & Derby Arms
(0116) 262 3299 *Millstone Lane; nearby metered parking; LE1 5JN* Neatly kept modern town bar with open-plan interior; comfortable bar chairs by long counter, padded high seats including a banquette by chunky tall tables, some stripped brickwork and a few small prints of classic film posters, Everards and guests, 20 wines by the glass and good range of malt whiskies and other drinks, well liked food including pizzas and some german-influenced dishes; background and regular live music, Mon quiz, annual St Patrick's day Guinness and oyster festival, free wi-fi; children welcome, sunny courtyard with tables under parasols, more seats on upper terrace, closed Sun, otherwise open (and food) all day. *(Mark Morgan)*

LONG WHATTON
SK4823

Royal Oak (01509) 843694
The Green; LE12 5DB Compact smartly updated village dining pub, good well presented modern food along with pub favourites, set menu choices and Sun pie night, four well kept beers including Charnwood and St Austell, nice wines by the glass from extensive list, friendly efficient staff; comfortable spotless bedrooms in separate building, good breakfast, handy for East Midlands Airport, open all day. *(Michael Doswell)*

LYDDINGTON
SP8796

★ Old White Hart (01572) 821703
Village signed off A6003 N of Corby; LE15 9LR Popular and welcoming 17th-c inn across from small green; softly lit front bar with heavy beams in low ceiling, just a few tables, glass-shielded log fire, Greene King IPA and a guest, good food (not Sun evening in winter) including own sausages and cured meats (long-serving landlord is a butcher), half-price offer Mon-Thurs, efficient obliging service, attractive restaurant, further tiled-floor room with rugs, lots of fine hunting prints and woodburner; children welcome, seats by heaters in pretty walled garden, eight floodlit boules pitches, handy for Bede House (EH) and good nearby walks, ten bedrooms, open all day (may be a break Sun afternoon). *(Michael Sargent, Mike and Margaret Banks, Peter Andrews)*

MANTON
SK8704

Horse & Jockey (01572) 737335
St Marys Road; LE15 8SU Welcoming early 19th-c pub under same ownership as the Fox at Luffenham; updated low-beamed interior, modern furniture on wood or stone floors, woodburner, well kept ales such as Grainstore and Greene King plus a house beer (Fall at the First), decent fairly priced food from baguettes to blackboard specials, cheery service; background music; children and dogs welcome, colourful tubs and hanging baskets, terrace picnic-sets (they may ask for a card if you eat out here), nice location, on Rutland Water cycle route (racks provided), open all day in summer (all day Fri, Sat, till 7pm Sun in winter). *(P and D Carpenter, Mike and Margaret Banks, Barry Collett)*

MARKET OVERTON
SK8816

Black Bull (01572) 767677
Opposite the church; LE15 7PW Attractive low-beamed thatch and stone pub (dates from the 17th c) in pretty village well placed for Rutland Water, welcoming licensees and staff, good home-made food (booking advised) from pub staples up in long carpeted bar and two separate dining areas, well kept Black Sheep and a couple of guests, woodburner, banquettes and sofas; some background and live music, free wi-fi; children and dogs welcome, tables out in front by small carp pool, two bedrooms, open all day Sun till 6pm, closed Mon. *(M and GR, Barry Collett)*

MEDBOURNE
SP7992

★ Nevill Arms (01858) 565288
B664 Market Harborough–Uppingham; LE16 8EE Handsome stone-built Victorian inn facing stream and little footbridge; good bar and restaurant food served by friendly helpful staff, well kept ales such as Adnams, St Austell and Charles Wells, craft beers and good choice of wines by the glass including champagne, carpeted bar with beams and mullion windows, two woodburners (one in stone inglenook), modernised restaurant with banquettes and light wood furniture on white tiles;

children and dogs (in bar) welcome, streamside picnic-sets, back terrace and stable-conversion café (9am-5pm), ten bedrooms, open all day. *(Barry Collett)*

MELTON MOWBRAY   SK7519
Anne of Cleves   (01664) 481336
Burton Street, by St Mary's church; LE13 1AE Monks' chantry dating from the 14th c and gifted to Anne of Cleves by Henry VIII; heavy beams, flagstones and mullioned windows, tapestries on burnt orange walls, chunky tables, character chairs and settles, log fire, well kept Everards and guests, decent wines and generously served food, small end dining room; background music, free wi-fi; children and dogs welcome, tables in pretty little walled garden with flagstoned terrace. *(Susan Eccleston)*

MELTON MOWBRAY   SK7518
Boat   (01664) 500969
Burton Street; LE13 1AF Chatty and welcoming local with well kept Adnams, Bass, Wells Bombardier and a guest, over 40 malt whiskies, no food, bar with panelling and open fire in range, another fire (not often used) in snug; darts; dogs welcome, handy for the station, open all day Thurs-Sun (Fri from 2pm), closed lunchtimes Mon and Weds. *(Phil and Jane Hodson)*

MOUNTSORREL   SK5715
Swan   (0116) 230 2340
Loughborough Road, off A6; LE12 7AT Former coaching inn with split-level interior, log fires, old flagstones and stripped stone, good well priced often interesting food from baguettes up (best to book evenings), monthly themed nights such as Colombian and Thai, friendly efficient staff, Black Sheep and other well kept ales, good choice of wines, neat dining area and restaurant; dogs welcome in bar, pretty walled back garden down to canalised River Soar, open all day weekends. *(Justine and Neil Bonnett)*

MOWSLEY   SP6488
Staff of Life   (0116) 240 2359
Village signposted off A5199 S of Leicester; Main Street; LE17 6NT Gabled village pub with roomy fairly traditional bar, high-backed settles on flagstones, wicker chairs on shiny wood floor and stools around unusual circular counter, woodburner, Bass and Thwaites Wainwright, a dozen wines by the glass and decent whisky choice, interesting mid-priced food (not Sun evening), set evening deal (Tues, Weds); background music; well behaved children welcome (no under-12s Fri and Sat nights), no dogs, seats out in front and on nice leaf-shaded deck, open all day Sun, closed Mon and weekday lunchtimes. *(Heather and Richard Jones)*

NORTH LUFFENHAM   SK9303
Fox   (01780) 720991
Pinfold Lane; LE15 8LE Refurbished sister pub to the Horse & Jockey at Manton; flagstoned bar with woodburner, four well kept ales and several wines by the glass from light wood servery, lounge with comfortable seating on wood floor, exposed stone walls and another woodburner, good quality food in spacious modern dining room, friendly prompt service; darts and TV upstairs; children and dogs welcome, paved terrace with large planters and picnic-sets under parasols, pretty village, open all day weekends, closed Mon and Tues lunchtimes. *(Barry Collett)*

OADBY   SK6202
★Cow & Plough   (0116) 272 0852
Gartree Road (B667 N of centre); LE2 2FB Converted farm buildings with extraordinary collection of brewery memorabilia in two dark back rooms – enamel signs and mirrors advertising long-forgotten beers, an aged brass cash register, furnishings and fittings salvaged from pubs and even churches (there's some splendid stained glass behind the counter), own Steamin' Billy beers and several guests, two real ciders and a dozen malt whiskies, good generously served pubby food plus some interesting specials, long front extension and conservatory; background music, live jazz Weds lunchtime, TV, darts and board games, free wi-fi; children and dogs welcome, picnic-sets in the old yard, open all day, no food Sun evening. *(Barry Collett, O K Smyth)*

OAKHAM   SK8508
Wheatsheaf   (01572) 723458
Northgate; Church Street end; LE15 6QS Attractive and popular 17th-c local near church, well kept Everards and guests, good selection of wines by the glass and generous pubby food including specials, cheerful comfortable bar with open fires, quieter lounge, back conservatory; some live music; pretty suntrap courtyard, open all day Fri-Sun. *(Barry Collett)*

REDMILE   SK7935
★Windmill   (01949) 842281
Off A52 Grantham–Nottingham; Main Street; NG13 0GA Snug low-beamed bar with sofas, easy chairs and log fire in large raised hearth, comfortable roomier dining areas with woodburners, wide choice of good home-made food from sandwiches, burgers and stone-baked pizzas up, two-course deal Fri evening, steak night Sat, well kept ales such as Adnams, Marstons and Oldershaws, good wines by the glass; children welcome, no dogs inside, sizeable well furnished front courtyard, open all

---

If we know a pub has an outdoor play area for children, we mention it.

day Sat, till around 8pm Sun, closed Tues and Weds. *(Millie and Peter Downing)*

ROTHLEY   SK5812

Woodmans Stroke   (0116) 230 2785

Church Street; LE7 7PD Family-run 18th-c thatched pub with good value weekday lunchtime bar food from sandwiches up, well kept changing ales and nice wines by the glass, friendly service, beams and settles in front rooms, open fire, old local photographs plus rugby and cricket memorabilia; sports TV; pretty front hanging baskets, cast-iron tables in attractive garden with heaters, pétanque, open all day Sat. *(Mike and Margaret Banks, Barry Collett)*

RYHALL   TF0310

Wicked Witch   (01780) 763649

Bridge Street; PE9 4HH Village dining pub with highly regarded upmarket food cooked by chef-proprietor from weekly changing set menu, also occasional themed evenings, two dining areas and comfortable bar serving Banks's Mansfield and maybe a guest, nice wines, good friendly service; children welcome till 7pm, tables in back garden, closed Sun evening, Mon. *(Matt and Hayley Jacob)*

SADDINGTON   SP6591

Queens Head   (0116) 240 2536

S of Leicester between A5199 (ex A50) and A6; Main Street; LE8 0QH Welcoming village pub with well kept Everards, nice wines and good attractively presented food (all day Sat, till 6pm Sun) including Fri grill night, clean interior on different levels, country and reservoir views from dining conservatory and sloping terrace; free wi-fi; children welcome, garden play area, farm shop (9am-2pm), open all day Weds-Sun (closed 2.30-5.30pm Mon and Tues). *(Mike and Margaret Banks)*

SEATON   SP9098

George & Dragon   (01572) 747773

Main Street; LE15 9HU Stone-built pub dating from the 17th c; two cosy split-level bars (one a former bakery) and separate restaurant, three real ales including Bass and Grainstore, good traditional home-made food, attentive service and friendly local atmosphere; children and dogs welcome, outside tables, unspoilt hilltop village with good views of Harringworth Viaduct, bedrooms, open all day Sat, till 7pm Sun, closed Mon and lunchtime Tues. *(Barry Collett)*

SHAWELL   SP5480

White Swan   (01788) 860357

Main Street; village signed down declassified road (ex A427) off A5/A426 roundabout – turn right in village; not far from M6 junction 1; LE17 6AG Attractive little 17th-c beamed dining pub with clean contemporary interior, good interesting food from landlord-chef along with some pub staples, local Dow Bridge ales and guests, lots of wines by the glass (wine tasting evenings), champagne breakfast Sat; children welcome, closed Sun evening and Mon, otherwise open all day. *(Mark Morgan)*

SHEARSBY   SP6290

Chandlers Arms   (0116) 247 8384

Fenny Lane, off A50 Leicester–Northampton; LE17 6PL Comfortable old creeper-clad pub in attractive village, seven well kept ales including Dow Bridge (tasting trays, June beer festival), a summer cider and good value pubby food including range of 'sizzling' dishes; background music, monthly quiz, table skittles; children welcome, secluded raised garden overlooking green, open Sun till 7pm, closed Mon and lunchtime Tues-Thurs. *(Jim King)*

SILEBY   SK6015

Horse & Trumpet   (01509) 812549

Barrow Road, opposite church; LE12 7LP Beamed village pub with well kept Steamin' Billy beers and guests, real cider, fresh cobs; some live music including jazz second Mon of month, skittle alley, darts; well behaved dogs welcome, terrace picnic-sets, open all day. *(Guy Henderson)*

SOMERBY   SK7710

★Stilton Cheese   (01664) 454394

High Street; off A606 Oakham–Melton Mowbray, via Cold Overton, or Leesthorpe and Pickwell; LE14 2QB Friendly old ironstone pub with beamed bar/lounge, comfortable furnishings on red patterned carpets, country prints, plates and copper pots, stuffed badger and pike, Grainstore, Marstons and three guests, 30 malt whiskies, good reasonably priced pubby food along with daily specials, restaurant; children welcome, seats on terrace, peaceful setting on edge of pretty village. *(Mike and Margaret Banks, Phil and Jane Hodson)*

SOUTH LUFFENHAM   SK9401

★Coach House   (01780) 720166

Stamford Road (A6121); LE15 8NT Old roadside inn with stripped-stone and flagstoned bar, scatter cushions on small pews, log fire, three real ales including Adnams and Greene King, decent wines by the glass, good well priced food served by friendly staff, separate snug with neat built-in seating, smarter more modern dining room; children and dogs (in bar) welcome, small back deck, seven bedrooms, open all day Sat, till 5pm Sun, closed Mon lunchtime; for sale as we went to press. *(Justine and Neil Bonnett)*

SPROXTON   SK8524

Crown   (01476) 861608

Coston Road; LE14 4QB Friendly fairly compact 19th-c stone-built inn with spotless well laid-out interior, good reasonably priced food from bar snacks to restaurant dishes cooked by landlord-chef, three well kept changing ales, good wines and coffee, light airy bar with woodburner, lounge area and restaurant with glassed-off wine store; children and dogs (in bar) welcome, lovely sunny courtyard, pretty village and good local walks, three bedrooms, open all day weekends, closed lunchtimes Mon-Thurs. (*Susan Eccleston*)

STRETTON SK9415

★ **Jackson Stops** (01780) 410237
Rookery Lane; a mile or less off A1, at B668 (Oakham) exit; follow village sign, turning off Clipsham Road into Manor Road, pub on left; LE15 7RA Attractive thatched former farmhouse with plenty of character; meandering rooms filled with period features, black-beamed country bar with wall timbering, coal fires and elderly settle on worn tile and brick floor, a couple of Grainstore ales, eight wines by the glass and ten malt whiskies, smarter airy room on right with mix of ancient and modern tables on dark blue carpet, corner fire, two dining rooms, one with stripped-stone walls and old open cooking range, well liked food including deals, warm friendly service; rare nurdling bench (a game involving old pennies), background music; children and dogs (in bar) welcome, closed Sun evening, Mon. (*Gordon and Margaret Ormondroyd, Mike and Margaret Banks, Barry Collett*)

THORNTON SK4607

Reservoir (01530) 382433
Main Street; LE67 1AJ Busy pub with pleasant modern décor, decent home-made food from varied menu (not Sun evening) including good value set lunch, Weds burger night and Tues/Thurs pie and wine evenings, Steamin' Billy ales, friendly efficient service, restaurant; children welcome, muddy boots and dogs in bar, good circular walk around Thornton Reservoir, open all day Sat, closed Mon. (*Rosie and John Moore*)

THORPE LANGTON SP7492

★ **Bakers Arms** (01858) 545201
Off B6047 N of Market Harborough; LE16 7TS Civilised thatched restauranty pub with small bar; consistently good imaginative food (must book) from regularly changing menu including several seafood dishes, cottagey beamed linked areas and stylishly simple country décor, a well kept ale and good choice of wines by the glass, friendly licensees and efficient service, maybe a pianist; no under-12s or dogs, picnic-sets in back garden with country views, closed Sun evening, Mon and weekday lunchtimes. (*R L Borthwick*)

THRUSSINGTON SK6415

Star (01664) 424220
Village signposted off A46 N of Syston; The Green; LE7 4UH Neatly modernised 18th-c village inn; L-shaped bar with low stripped beams, broad floorboards and inglenook woodburner, unusual double-sided high-backed settle, Belvoir Star Bitter, a couple of guests and 14 wines by the glass, steps up to skylit dining room with banquettes and high-backed chairs, popular all-day food; background music, Sun quiz, TV, free wi-fi; children and dogs (in bar) welcome, side garden and flagstoned terrace, bedrooms, open all day from 8am for breakfast. (*Mark Morgan*)

TILTON ON THE HILL SK7405

Rose & Crown (0116) 259 7234
Main Street (B6047); LE7 9LF Friendly old beamed pub opposite village church, three knocked-together rooms, one with inglenook log fire, a couple of Greene King ales and generous helpings of inexpensive pub food; dogs welcome in bar, beer garden behind, closed Mon. (*Barry Collett*)

TUGBY SK7600

Fox & Hounds (0116) 259 8188
A47 6 miles W of Uppingham; LE7 9WB Attractively modernised village-green dining pub serving good well priced food (all day Sat, till 6pm Sun) from bar snacks to daily specials, efficient welcoming staff, ales such as Courage, Grainstore and Sharps, compact open-plan interior with stripped beams and quarry tiles, dining part with light-wood furniture and woodburner; background music, TV; fenced terrace by car park, open all day weekends. (*R L Borthwick, Barry Collett, Mike and Margaret Banks*)

UPPER HAMBLETON SK8907

Finchs Arms (01572) 756575
Off A606; Oakham Road; LE15 8TL 17th-c stone inn on Rutland Water peninsula; beamed and flagstoned bar with log fires and old settles, five real ales such as Castle Rock, Grainstore and St Austell, several wines by the glass including champagne, modern back restaurant opening on to spacious hillside terrace with lovely views over the water, well liked food from ciabattas and sharing boards up, also set menus and afternoon teas; children and dogs (in bar) welcome, good surrounding walks, ten bedrooms (four with reservoir views), open all day, food all day Sun. (*Guy Henderson*)

UPPINGHAM SP8699

Falcon (01572) 823535
High Street East; LE15 9PY Quietly refined old coaching inn, welcoming and relaxed, with oak-panelled bar, spacious nicely furnished lounge and restaurant, roaring fire and big windows overlooking market square, good food (not Sun evening) from bar snacks up, three Grainstore ales, efficient friendly service; children welcome, dogs in bar, back garden with terrace, bedrooms (some in converted stable block), open all day. (*Barry Collett*)

UPPINGHAM SP8699
Vaults (01572) 823259
Market Place next to church; LE15 9QH
Attractive old pub with compact modernised interior; enjoyable reasonably priced traditional food served by friendly staff, two Greene King ales, Marstons Pedigree, Theakstons Lightfoot and a house beer from Grainstore, several wines by the glass, two pleasant little upstairs dining rooms; background music, sports TVs; children and dogs welcome, some tables out overlooking picturesque square, four bedrooms (booking from nearby Falcon Hotel), open all day. *(Barry Collett)*

WALTHAM ON THE WOLDS SK8024
Royal Horseshoes (01664) 464346
Melton Road (A607); LE14 4AJ
Attractive sympathetically restored stone and thatch pub in centre of village; good varied choice of generous affordably priced blackboard food, well kept Castle Rock, Marstons, Sharps and three guests, interesting wine list and some 30 gins, two main rooms with beams and open fires; darts; children welcome, no dogs inside, courtyard tables, good value comfortable bedrooms in annexe, hearty breakfast, open all day weekends. *(Michael Doswell)*

WELHAM SP7692
Old Red Lion (01858) 565253
Off B664 Market Harborough–Uppingham; Main Street; LE16 7UJ
Popular comfortably updated corner dining pub (part of the King Henry's Tavern group); beamed rooms, some on different levels, including unusual barrel-vaulted back area, leather sofas by log fire, Fullers London Pride and Greene King IPA, nice selection of wines, decent coffee and extensive choice of enjoyable fairly pubby food including good steaks and Sun carvery, efficient friendly staff; children and walkers welcome (ramblers menu), no dogs, open (and food) all day. *(Guy and Caroline Howard, Mike and Margaret Banks)*

WHITWICK SK4316
Three Horseshoes (01530) 837311
Leicester Road; LE67 5GN Unpretentious and unchanging local with long quarry-tiled bar, old wooden benches and open fires, tiny snug to the right, well kept Bass and Marstons Pedigree, no food; piano, darts, dominoes and cards, outside loos; no proper pub sign so easy to miss, known locally as Polly's. *(Matt and Hayley Jacob)*

WOODHOUSE EAVES SK5214
★Curzon Arms (01509) 890377
Maplewell Road; LE12 8QZ Cheerful old beamed pub in pretty Charnwood Forest village (sister to the Crown at Old Dalby – see Main Entries); popular food (not Sun evening) from lunchtime sandwiches and pub favourites up, also Weds steak night and weekday lunchtime/early evening set menu, Sharps Doom Bar, Timothy Taylors Landlord and a couple of guests, several wines by the glass and range of cocktails, good friendly service, attractive up-to-date décor in linked areas; background music, Tues quiz, TV, free wi-fi; children and dogs welcome, ramp for wheelchairs, good-sized front lawn and terrace, open all day Fri-Sun. *(Ian Herdman, R L Borthwick)*

WOODHOUSE EAVES SK5313
Wheatsheaf (01509) 890320
Brand Hill; turn right into Main Street, off B591 S of Loughborough; LE12 8SS Brick and stone creeper-clad country pub with pretty window boxes and tubs; traditionally furnished beamed bar areas with open fires, some black and white motor-racing photographs, dining rooms with wheelback or high-back chairs around country pine tables, ales such as Adnams, Charnwood, Fullers and Timothy Taylors, several wines by the glass and generally well liked food, friendly service; children and dogs (in bar) welcome, seats outside in courtyard under parasols, open all day Sat, closed Sun evening. *(Ian Herdman, Phil and Jane Villiers)*

WYMESWOLD SK6023
Windmill (01509) 881313
Brook Street; LE12 6TT Bustling side-street village pub with enjoyable good value home-made food (not Sun evening) from lunchtime snacks up, three well kept rotating ales, good cheerful service even though busy; children welcome, dogs in bar, back garden with decked area, open all day Fri, Sat, till 9pm Sun. *(Mike and Margaret Banks)*

Post Office address codings confusingly give the impression that some pubs are in Leicestershire, when they're really in Cambridgeshire (which is where we list them).

Lincolnshire

KEY ★ Star Pub | 🎯 Top Quality Food | 🍺 Great Beer
🍷 Good Wines | £ Bargain Meals | 🛏 Good Bedrooms | 🍽 Serves Food

---

BARNOLDBY LE BECK
TA2303 Map 8

Ship 🎯 🍷

(01472) 822308 – www.the-shipinn.com

Village signposted off A18 Louth–Grimsby; DN37 0BG

Tranquil refined dining pub with plenty to look at

The Edwardian and Victorian collection of bric-a-brac here is really worth examining: stand-up telephones, violins, a horn gramophone, a bowler and top hats, old racquets, riding crops and hockey sticks. Heavy dark-ringed drapes swathe the windows and the furnishings fit in well, with pretty cushions on comfortable Lloyd Loom-style chairs, heavily stuffed gold plush Victorian-looking chairs on a new rust-coloured carpet and a warming winter coal fire. Axhome Cleethorpes Pale Ale, Batemans XB and Black Sheep on handpump, eight malt whiskies and good wines by the glass; background music. A fenced-off sunny area behind has hanging baskets and a few picnic-sets under parasols. This is a charming village.

🎯 Good, interesting food includes scallops with chorizo, sunblush tomatoes and aioli, chicken liver pâté with cumberland sauce, goats cheese and red onion filo tart with couscous, a pie of the day, duck breast with orange jelly and carrot purée, slow-cooked shin of beef with dauphinoise potatoes and red wine reduction, sea bass fillets on squid ink risotto with roasted vine tomatoes, and puddings such as chocolate brownie with Baileys mousse, honeycomb and chocolate sauce and whole baked apple with crumble and vanilla ice-cream. *Benchmark main dish: beer-battered fish and chips £10.95. Two-course evening meal £18.00.*

Free house ~ Licensee Michele Robinson ~ Real ale ~ Open 12-3, 6-11; 12-5 Sun; closed Sun evening ~ Bar food 12-2, 7-9; 12-5 Sun ~ Restaurant ~ Children welcome ~ Wi-fi
Recommended by Tim Rosamond, Tom Stone, Margaret McDonald, Daniel King, Lorna and Jack Mulgrave, Mike and Sarah Abbot

---

BASTON
TF1113 Map 8

White Horse 🎯 🍷 🍺

(01778) 560923 – www.thewhitehorsebaston.co.uk

Church Street; PE6 9PE

Refurbished village pub with four real ales, friendly staff and good, popular food

You'll find a wide mix of customers in this blue-painted, 18th-c village pub which has been interestingly renovated using reclaimed farm materials that include the bricks in the bay window, the boards in the ceiling, some of the beams and the huge piece of sycamore that acts as the counter in the snug bar. The main bar has built-in wall seats with scatter cushions, windsor and farmhouse chairs and stools around all sorts of tables on wooden flooring, a woodburning stove in a brick fireplace (with big logs piled into another) and horse-related items on pale paintwork; background music, TV, darts and board games. The dining area is similarly furnished. Stools line the blue-painted counter where they keep Adnams Southwold, Hopshackle Dead Legs, Oakham JHB and Stoney Ford Sheepmarket Supernova Straw on handpump, a dozen wines by the glass, several gins and ten malt whiskies; the resident springer spaniel is called Audrey. There are seats and tables set out on a side terrace.

Pleasing food includes pickled mackerel with celery, chervil and home-made sourdough, chicken terrine with rhubarb, tarragon and pistachio, burger with pink onions, cheese and chips, agnolotti pasta filled with pea, asparagus and ricotta, thyme-roasted chicken breast with braised pearl barley and glazed baby vegetables, fresh fish dish of the day, pork cutlet with rosemary and garlic dauphinoise and compressed apple, and puddings such as popcorn pannacotta with salted caramel fudge, popcorn and candied hazelnuts and banana tarte tatin with banana and spiced rum ice-cream, banana curd and banana crisps. *Benchmark main dish: roast lamb rump with caponata, white bean purée and salsa verde £17.95. Two-course evening meal £21.00.*

Free house ~ Licensees Ben and Germaine Larter ~ Real ale ~ Open 4-11 Mon, Tues; 12-11 Wed-Fri; 9.30am-midnight Sat; 9.30am-10.30pm Sun ~ Bar food 5.30-9 Tues; 12-2.30, 5.30-9 Wed-Fri; 9.30-9 Sat; 9.30-6 Sun ~ Restaurant ~ Children welcome until 9pm only ~ Dogs allowed in bar ~ Wi-fi ~ Quiz Sun evening fortnightly *Recommended by Patrick and Barbara Knights, Michael and Jenny Back, Lenny and Ruth Walters, Charles and Maddie Bishop, Martin and Joanne Sharp, Miranda and Jeff Davidson*

BOURNE
Smiths ◖

TF0920 Map 8

(01778) 426819   www.kneadpubs.co.uk

North Street; PE10 9AE

Former grocery store with intriguing bric-a-brac in many rooms, well kept ales, popular food and seats in garden

Interestingly converted from an old grocery store (with its lovely original frontage), this is a cleverly thought-out pub arranged over three floors. From the panelled front bar, there are a warren of interconnected rooms – a cook's pantry, one with hop-hung rafters, kitchenware on a big dresser and painted wooden settles, others with orange button-back banquettes set in semicircles and chunky leather dining chairs, benches and an eclectic mix of pubby chairs, and floors made up of nice old boards, flagstones and crazy-paved stone. The 'stables' is split into stalls with saddlery and horse tack, troughs and tin buckets, and even a horse cart. As well as woodburning stoves and open fires, the bare-brick walls are hung with vintage enamelled advertising signs and mirrors, and there are tilley lamps and a sizeable butterchurn, plus pots, pans and cauldrons and an old-fashioned butcher's bike. It's all great fun. Fullers London Pride, Oakham JHB and guests from Blue Monkey, Brewsters and Nene Valley on handpump, good wines by the glass and a gin menu; background music, TV and games machine. The partly covered, enclosed courtyard has metal seats and tables and the garden has picnic-sets on grass and a children's play area.

As well as good breakfasts, there are baguettes and open sandwiches, beer-battered king prawns with lemon mayonnaise, baked mini camembert with onion chutney, tasting boards, local sausages with mash and onion gravy, spicy lamb kebabs with feta, chickpea and black olive salad and minted yoghurt, roasted salmon caesar salad, pulled pork with garlic, herbs and french fries, chicken and chorizo cassoulet, and puddings such as warm chocolate cookie with white chocolate ice-cream, raspberry sauce and mini marshmallows and apple and toffee tart with honeycomb ice-cream. *Benchmark main dish: home-made stone-baked pizzas £8.95. Two-course evening meal £20.00.*

Knead Pubs ~ Manager Hayley Taylor ~ Real ale ~ Open 10am-11pm (midnight Fri); 8.30am-midnight Sat; 8.30am-11pm Sun ~ Children welcome ~ Dogs welcome
Recommended by Jim and Sue James, Trevor and Michele Street, Colin and Daniel Gibbs

 GREAT LIMBER   TA1308   Map 8

New Inn ⚝ 🍷 🛏

(01469) 569998 – www.thenewinngreatlimber.co.uk
High Street; DN37 8JL

Rather grand with an easy-going atmosphere, marvellous food, fine wines and large back garden; bedrooms

This is a quiet and comfortable place to stay and breakfasts are a highlight. It's handsome and civilised with quite a focus on the excellent food – though the proper working bar is popular with locals who drop in for a pint and a chat, quiz evenings or a game of darts. Here, there are windsor chairs, red button-back wall seats, some upholstered tub chairs and oak tables on pale floorboards, neatly stacked logs to either side of one fireplace and shelves of books by another, and chairs against the counter where efficient, friendly staff serve Batemans XXXB, Tom Woods Old Codger and a guest from Axeholme on handpump and a dozen wines by the glass. A snug little corner has a curved high-backed wall seat just right for a small group. The dining room is split into two, with cushioned wooden chairs in one part and comfortable red chairs and long wall seats with pretty scatter cushions in another. Throughout, the walls are hung with modern art, black and white photos and big mirrors; background music and TV. The landscaped back garden has both picnic-sets and tables and chairs.

 Food is impressive and uses produce from the Brocklesby Estate (of which this pub is part): lunchtime sandwiches, pressed pheasant and pancetta terrine with pickled vegetables, brown crab croquette with crab and lemon mayonnaise, lunchtime burgers with toppings and fries, beer-battered fresh fish and chips, corn-fed chicken with chorizo, sweetcorn and butter bean cassoulet and sweetcorn bhaji, hake with spiced tomato and prawn pasta, and puddings such as ginger crème brûlée with rhubarb and cinnamon crumble and warm coconut sponge with mango and raspberry. *Benchmark main dish: pigeon with maple shallots, girolles, fondant potato and thyme and madeira jus £16.95. Two-course evening meal £22.00.*

Free house ~ Licensee Chloe Kirby ~ Real ale ~ Open 12-11.30; 12-10.30 Sun ~ Bar food 12-2.30, 6.30-9; 12-2.30 Sun; not Sun evening, Mon lunchtime ~ Restaurant ~ Children welcome ~ Dogs allowed in bar and bedrooms ~ Wi-fi ~ Bedrooms: £88/£99 *Recommended by Miles Green, Andrew Vincent, Mark Morgan, Lucy and Giles Gibbon, Sally and Lance Oldham, Dr and Mrs A K Clarke*

 HEIGHINGTON   TF0369   Map 8

Butcher & Beast ◖

(01522) 790386 – www.butcherandbeast.co.uk
High Street; LN4 1JS

Traditional village pub with terrific choice of drinks, pubby food and a pretty garden by a stream

The thoughtful range of drinks kept by the hands-on and hard-working licensees here includes half a dozen ales such as Batemans XB, XXXB and Pilgrim Fathers IPA and guests such as Castle Rock Screech Owl, Everards Original and Oakham Citra on handpump, two farm ciders, eight wines by the glass, 30 gins and 20 malt whiskies. The simply decorated bar has button-back wall banquettes, pubby furnishings and stools along the counter, while the Snug has red-cushioned wall settles and high-backed wooden dining chairs. The beamed dining room – recently extended – is neatly set with an attractive medley of wooden or painted chairs around chunky tables on floorboards, and there's a woodburning stove; throughout, the cream or yellow walls are hung with old village photos and country pictures. The award-winning hanging baskets and tubs make quite a show in summer, and for warmer weather there are picnic-sets on a lawn that runs down to a stream.

Quite a choice of tasty food includes creamy garlic mushrooms with blue cheese, whitebait, tagine of pumpkin, red onion and cranberry with vegetable couscous, home-baked ham and egg, scampi with tartare sauce, burger with toppings, chicken with white wine, cream and apricot stilton cheese, moules frites, 10oz rib-eye steak with a choice of sauces, and puddings such as white and dark chocolate cheesecake and lemon sponge. *Benchmark main dish: steak in ale pie £12.95. Two-course evening meal £19.00.*

Batemans ~ Tenants Mal and Diane Gray ~ Real ale ~ Open 12-11 (10.30 Sun) ~ Bar food 12-2, 5-8; 12-2, 5-8.30 Fri, Sat; 12-2.30, 6-7.30 Sun ~ Restaurant ~ Children welcome away from bar ~ Dogs allowed in bar ~ Wi-fi *Recommended by Chris Johnson, William Pace, Sandra Morgan, Mark and Mary Setting, Caroline and Steve Archer, James and Sylvia Hewitt*

HOUGH-ON-THE-HILL
Brownlow Arms ⭐ ♀ 🛏
SK9246 Map 8

(01400) 250234 – www.thebrownlowarms.com

High Road; NG32 2AZ

Lincolnshire Dining Pub of the Year

Refined country house with beamed bar, real ales, imaginative food and graceful terrace; bedrooms

The bedrooms in this handsome 17th-c inn are well equipped and inviting and the breakfasts are very good. The comfortable beamed bar is warmly welcoming with plenty of panelling, some exposed brickwork, local prints and scenes, a large mirror, and a pile of logs beside a big fireplace. Seating includes elegant, stylishly mismatched upholstered armchairs, and the carefully arranged furnishings give the impression of several separate and cosy areas. Served by impeccably polite staff, the ales on handpump are Timothy Taylors Landlord and Woodfordes Wherry, there are ten wines by the glass and 15 malt whiskies; background music.

Delicious food using the best local produce includes fishcake with wholegrain mustard beurre blanc, parma ham and roast fig salad with raspberry coulis, a sharing charcuterie platter, chicken suprême with potato rösti, sauté leeks, crisp pancetta and chicken jus, twice-baked cheese soufflé with chestnut mushrooms and parmesan cream, pork tenderloin with calvados, sauté apples, black pudding and spinach, rack of lamb with dauphinoise potatoes, ratatouille and lamb jus, and puddings such as blackcurrant mousse with cassis compote, apple and blackcurrant sorbet and apple crisps and pistachio ice-cream 'baked alaska' with warm chocolate sauce. *Benchmark main dish: roast cod fillet wrapped in parma ham with braised little gem, puy lentil cassoulet and butternut purée £19.00. Two-course evening meal £27.00.*

Free house ~ Licensee Paul L Willoughby ~ Real ale ~ Open 12-2, 6-11; 12-4 Sun; closed Sun evening, Mon, Tues lunchtime ~ Bar food 12-2, 6.30-9; 12-4 Sun ~ Restaurant ~ Children welcome but must be over 8 in evening ~ Wi-fi ~ Bedrooms: £75/£120 *Recommended by Michael Doswell, John Preddy, Charles Fraser, George Sanderson, Ian Wilson, Mrs Julie Thomas, Jim King*

INGHAM
SK9483 Map 8

Inn on the Green 🌟

(01522) 730354 – www.innonthegreeningham.co.uk

The Green; LN1 2XT

Nicely modernised place serving thoughtfully prepared food and with a chatty atmosphere

If you want to enjoy the rewarding food here, it's very sensible to book a table in advance – but for a chat and a pint, simply head for the locals' bar. This is informal and pubby with a log fire, and caring staff who serve Sharps Doom Bar and guests such as Greene King Old Hoppy Hen, Pheasantry Pale Ale and Springhead Outlawed on handpump, 11 wines by the glass, 18 malt whiskies, 35 gins and home-made cordials; several tables may also be occupied by those enjoying the tasty food. The beamed and timbered dining room is spread over two floors, with lots of exposed brickwork, local prints and a warm winter fire. The lounge between these rooms has leather sofas and background music, and a bar counter where you can buy home-made jams, marmalade and chutney. There are attractive views across the village green. Dogs are allowed in the bar outside of food service times.

 Enjoyable food includes sandwiches, ham hock hash with a fried egg and home-made ketchup, beer-battered calamari with sweet chilli jam, vegetable curry with biryani rice, sausages with spring onion mash, southern fried chicken with coleslaw and fries, pork schnitzel with a fried egg, monkfish with curried crab and crayfish sauce, rabbit coq au vin, and puddings such as chocolate brownie with salted caramel parfait and Baileys crème brûlée; they also have an early-bird menu (12-1.45, 6-6.55pm) and a preserve and hamper list. *Benchmark main dish: pie of the day £10.85. Two-course evening meal £18.00.*

Free house ~ Licensees Andrew Cafferkey and Sarah Sharpe ~ Real ale ~ Open 11.30-3, 6-11 (midnight Sat); 12-10.30 Sun; closed Mon ~ Bar food 12-1.45 (2.45 Sun), 6-8.45; no food Sun evening, Mon, Tues ~ Restaurant ~ Children welcome ~ Dogs allowed in bar ~ Wi-fi *Recommended by Caroline Sullivan, Christopher Mannings, Peter Meister, Jeff Davies*

KIRKBY LA THORPE
TF0945 Map 8

Queens Head 🌟 £

(01529) 305743 – www.thequeensheadinn.com

Village and pub signposted off A17, just E of Sleaford, then turn right into Boston Road cul-de-sac; NG34 9NU

Reliable dining pub very popular for its good food and helpful, efficient service

Mr Clark has cooked the particularly good food in this gently traditional and neatly comfortable place for some 20 years now. There are open fires, elaborate flower arrangements and plenty of courteous dark-waistcoated staff, and the carpeted bar has stools along the counter, button-back banquettes, sofas and captain's chairs around shiny dark tables. The smart, beamed restaurant has high-backed, orange-upholstered dining chairs around linen-set tables on carpet, heavy curtains and a woodburning stove; there's also a popular dining conservatory. Nice decorative touches take in thoughtful lighting, big prints, china plates on delft shelves and handsome longcase clocks (it's quite something when they all chime at midday). Batemans XB and guests such as 8 Sail Windmill Bitter and Sharps Doom Bar on handpump; background music. Easy disabled access.

 As well as the lunchtime specials (at £9.95 – hence our Value Award), the tempting food includes sandwiches and baguettes, mussels with white wine, herbs and cream, goats cheese and spinach lasagne, omelettes with lots of fillings, dark sugar and mustard roast ham with free-range eggs, lambs liver with crispy bacon and caramelised onions, local sausages with mash and onion gravy, whole grilled lemon sole with brown shrimp and lemon butter, venison pie with red wine gravy, and puddings such as warm orange and marmalade tart with vanilla custard and new york raspberry and white chocolate cheesecake; they also offer early/late-bird specials (6-7pm, 7-9.30pm), steak evenings on Thursday and fish choices on Friday nights. *Benchmark main dish: steak and kidney pudding £14.95. Two-course evening meal £20.00.*

Free house ~ Licensee John Clark ~ Real ale ~ Open 12-3, 6-11; 12-10.30 Sun ~ Bar food 12-2.30, 6-9.30; 12-8.30 Sun ~ Restaurant ~ Children welcome until 7pm ~ Dogs allowed in bar ~ Wi-fi *Recommended by David Travis, Patricia Hawkins, Phoebe Peacock, Andrew Stone, Miranda and Jeff Davidson, Pauline and Mark Evans*

STAMFORD

TF0306 Map 8

George of Stamford 🌟 ⏰ 🛏

(01780) 750750 – www.georgehotelofstamford.com

High Street, St Martins (B1081 S of centre, not the quite different central pedestrianised High Street); PE9 2LB

Lovely coaching inn with traditional bar, several dining areas and lounges, excellent staff and top class food and drink; bedrooms

A favourite with our readers for many years, this handsome 16th-c place is very special and remains exceptionally well run with a gently civilised yet informal atmosphere. The various areas are furnished with all manner of seats from leather, cane and antique wicker to soft sofas and easy chairs, and there's a room to suit every occasion. The central lounge is particularly striking with sturdy timbers, broad flagstones, heavy beams and massive stonework. The properly pubby little York Bar at the front has Adnams Broadside, Oakham JHB and a guest from Stoney Ford on handpump alongside 20 wines from an exceptional list and 30 malt whiskies; service throughout is professional yet friendly. There's an amazing oak-panelled restaurant (jacket required) and a less formal Garden Room restaurant, which has well spaced furniture on herringbone glazed bricks around a central tropical planting. The seats in the charming cobbled courtyard are highly prized and the immaculately kept walled garden is beautifully planted; there are also sunken lawns and croquet. Also, individually and thoughtfully decorated bedrooms and splendid breakfasts.

 The simplest food option is the York Bar snack menu with sandwiches (their toasties are especially good), a proper ploughman's and a plate of smoked salmon with capers. First class food in the restaurants includes seared foie gras with caramelised orange and toasted brioche, sea bream with aubergine caviar and saffron aioli, potato gnocchi with roasted butternut squash, toasted pine nuts and deep-fried blue cheese, lobster and chilli spaghetti, asian-style chicken curry with deep-fried tempura and peanut satay, butter-poached halibut with fennel, radish and lime leaf essence, and puddings such as sherry trifle and a changing crème brûlée. *Benchmark main dish: sirloin of beef carved at the table with hot horseradish and yorkshire pudding £26.50. Two-course evening meal £50.00.*

Free house ~ Licensee Paul Reseigh ~ Real ale ~ Open 11-11 ~ Bar food 11-9.30; some sort of food available all day ~ Restaurant ~ Children must be over 8 in panelled dining room ~ Dogs allowed in bar and bedrooms ~ Wi-fi ~ Bedrooms: £125/£205 *Recommended by Caroline Sullivan, Hilary and Neil Christopher, William and Sophia Renton, James and Becky Plath, Michael Sargent, Sally Harrison*

 STAMFORD   TF0307 Map 8

Tobie Norris 🍺

(01780) 753800 – www.kneadpubs.co.uk
St Pauls Street; PE9 2BE

A warren of ancient rooms, a good period atmosphere, a fine choice of drinks, enjoyable food and seats outside

The charming series of little rooms here are full of character, and the best has been made of the building's great age: worn flagstones, meticulously stripped stonework, a huge hearth for one room's woodburning stove and steeply pitched rafters in one of the two upstairs room – it's been beautifully restored. There's a wide variety of furnishings from pews and wall settles to comfortable armchairs, and a handsomely panelled shrine to Nelson and the Battle of Trafalgar. Attentive, friendly staff serve Fullers London Pride, Oakham JHB and guests from breweries such as Adnams, Ossett and Thornbridge on handpump, farm cider and several wines by the glass. A snug end conservatory opens out to a narrow but sunny two-level courtyard with seats and tables.

🍴 Good, enjoyable food includes lots of nibbles such as baked mini garlic and rosemary camembert, yorkshire pudding with dipping gravy, pigs in blankets with mustard mayonnaise, plus sandwiches and pizza wraps, chickpea and beetroot bonbon with sweet herby tomato sauce and sweet potato fries, lamb kofta kebab with hummus, minted yoghurt and feta, olive and red onion salad, beer-battered fish and chips, beef and blue cheese pie, lime and chilli chicken salad with spicy chipotle sauce and raita, and puddings such as chocolate brownie and salted caramel ice-cream and banana sticky toffee pudding. *Benchmark main dish: home-made stone-baked pizzas £12.00. Two-course evening meal £20.00.*

Knead Pubs ~ Licensee James Keating ~ Real ale ~ Open 10am-11pm (midnight Fri, Sat); 12-11 Sun ~ Bar food 12-2.30, 6-9; 12-9.30 Fri, Sat; 12-8 Sun ~ Children welcome ~ Dogs welcome ~ Wi-fi *Recommended by Dr J Barrie Jones, Barry Collett, Mike and Sarah Abbot, Jane Rigby, Alice Wright, Ted and Mary Bates*

 WOOLSTHORPE   SK8334 Map 8

Chequers 🏅 ♀

(01476) 870701 – www.chequersinn.net
Woolsthorpe near Belvoir, signposted off A52 or A607 W of Grantham; NG32 1LU

Interesting food in comfortably relaxed inn with good drinks and appealing castle views from outside tables; bedrooms

Our readers enjoy their visits to this partly 17th-c inn very much, and if you want to explore the lovely Vale of Belvoir, it makes sense to stay in the comfortable bedrooms in the converted stables next door. The heavily beamed main bar has two big tables (one a massive oak construction), an inviting mix of seating including some handsome leather chairs and banquettes, and a huge boar's head above a good log fire in the big brick fireplace. Among cartoons on the wall are some of the illustrated claret bottle labels from the series commissioned from famous artists. There are more leather seats in a dining area on the left and a corridor leads off to the light and airy recently extended main restaurant and then to another bar; background music. Grainstore Rutland Bitter and guests on handpump such as Magpie Thieving Rogue, Sharps Doom Bar and York Yorkshire Terrier, around 30 wines by the glass, 50 malt whiskies, around 20 gins, a seasonal cocktail list and a farm cider. There are good quality teak tables, chairs and benches outside and, beyond these, some picnic-sets on the edge of the pub's cricket field, with views of Belvoir Castle.

Excellent food uses the best local, seasonal produce and includes sandwiches, home-smoked duck breast with chicory, pear, confit orange and walnut salad, scallops with mango, lime and chorizo confit, burger with toppings and chips, thai green vegetable curry with lime and coriander rice, free-range chicken breast with sweet potato rösti and chive velouté, spicy monkfish with saffron rice, butternut squash and apricots, and puddings such as dark chocolate brownie with white chocolate sorbet and confit and candied orange and sticky toffee pudding with butterscotch sauce. *Benchmark main dish: côte du boeuf with béarnaise and pepper sauce (for two) £48.00. Two-course evening meal £19.00.*

Free house ~ Licensee Justin Chad ~ Real ale ~ Open 12-11; 12-midnight Sat; 12-10.30 Sun ~ Bar food 12-2.30, 6-9.30; 12-4, 6-8.30 Sun ~ Restaurant ~ Children welcome ~ Dogs allowed in bar and bedrooms ~ Wi-fi ~ Bedrooms: £60/£80 *Recommended by Jo Garnett, Edward Nile, William Pace, Martin and Clare Warne, Dr and Mrs F McGinn, Malcolm Phillips, Jacqui and Alan Swan*

Also Worth a Visit in Lincolnshire

Besides the fully inspected pubs, you might like to try these pubs that have been recommended to us and described by readers. Do tell us what you think of them: feedback@goodguides.com

ALLINGTON
SK8540
★Welby Arms (01400) 281361
The Green; off A1 at N end of Grantham bypass; NG32 2EA Welcoming, well run and well liked inn with helpful friendly staff, large simply furnished bar divided by stone archway, beams and joists, log fires (one in attractive arched brick fireplace), comfortable plush wall banquettes and stools, up to six changing ales, over 20 wines by the glass and plenty of malt whiskies, good popular food including blackboard specials, reasonable prices, can eat in bar or back dining lounge; background music; children welcome, tables in walled courtyard with pretty flower baskets, picnic-sets on front lawn, comfortable bedrooms, open all day Sun. *(Gordon and Margaret Ormondroyd, Johnston and Maureen Anderson, Mike and Margaret Banks)*

ASLACKBY
TF0830
Robin Hood & Little John
(01778) 440681 *A15 Bourne–Sleaford; NG34 0HL* Old mansard-roofed roadside country pub; split-level bar with beams, flagstones and woodburners, fairly pubby food including vegetarian choices and daily specials (two-course deal Mon-Thurs), Greene King Abbot and guests, friendly staff, separate more modern oak-floored restaurant; children and dogs (in bar) welcome, tricky wheelchair access, three-level terrace, open (and food) all day weekends. *(Sally Harrison)*

BARHOLM
TF0810
Five Horseshoes (01778) 560238
W of Market Deeping; village signed from A15 Langtoft; PE9 4RA Welcoming old-fashioned village local, cosy and comfortable, with beams, rustic bric-a-brac and log fire, well kept Adnams, Oakham and four guests, good range of wines, Fri and Sat pizza van, occasional Sun barbecues; pool room with TV, some live music; children and dogs welcome, garden and shady arbour, play area, open all day weekends, closed weekday lunchtimes. *(James and Sylvia Hewitt)*

BASSINGHAM
SK9160
Five Bells (01522) 788269
High Street; LN5 9JZ Cheerful old red-brick pub with well liked food including good value lunchtime set menu (Mon-Thurs) and steak nights (Weds, Thurs), Greene King ales and good range of brandies, efficient friendly service, bare-boards interior with hop-draped beams, country furniture and cosy log fires, lots of brass and bric-a-brac, an old well in one part; children and dogs (particularly) welcome, a few tables out in front fenced from the road, open all day (food till 7pm Sun). *(Tony and Maggie Harwood)*

BELCHFORD   TF2975
★**Blue Bell** (01507) 533602
*Village signed off A153 Horncastle–
Louth; LN9 6LQ* 18th-c dining pub
with cosy comfortable bar, Batemans
XB, Worthington and guests, Thatcher's
cider, popular traditional and modern
food, efficient friendly service, restaurant;
children and dogs welcome, picnic-sets in
terraced back garden, good base for Wolds
walks and Viking Way (remove muddy
boots), open all day Sun. *(Daniel King)*

BICKER   TF2237
Red Lion (01775) 821200
A52 NE of Donnington; PE20 3EF
Nicely decorated 17th-c village pub,
enjoyable home-made food including set
lunch and popular Sun carvery, also a
'Lincolnshire tapas' menu, friendly helpful
service, Greene King IPA, Courage Directors
and a guest, bowed beams (some painted),
exposed brickwork and half panelling,
wood and flagstone floors, woodburners,
part-raftered restaurant; quiz first Weds of
month; children welcome, no dogs inside,
rattan-style furniture on brick terrace with
pergola, lawned garden, open all day Sun till
7pm, closed Mon, Tues. *(Mrs Julie Thomas)*

BILLINGBOROUGH   TF1134
★**Fortescue Arms** (01529) 240228
*B1177, off A52 Grantham–Boston;
NG34 0QB* Beamed village pub with
old stonework, exposed brick, panelling
and big see-through fireplace in carpeted
rooms, tables in bay windows overlooking
high street, well kept Greene King ales
and a guest, enjoyable home-made food
including some decent vegetarian options,
good friendly service even at busy times,
Victorian prints, brass and copper, a stuffed
badger and pheasant, dining rooms at each
end; Thurs quiz, free wi-fi; children and
dogs welcome, picnic-sets and rattan-style
furniture in sheltered courtyard with
flowering tubs, useful big car park, open
all day weekends. *(Mrs Julie Thomas)*

BOSTON   TF3244
Mill (01205) 352874
Spilsby Road (A16); PE21 9QN
Roadside pub run by friendly italian
landlord, reasonably priced food (not
Tues) including some italian choices and
blackboard specials, Batemans XB and a
guest; children welcome, tables out in front,
open all day. *(Lenny and Ruth Walters)*

BURTON COGGLES   SK9725
Cholmeley Arms (01476) 550225
Village Street; NG33 4JS Well kept ales
such as Fullers, Grainstore and Greene King
in small beamed pubby bar with warm fire,
generous helpings of good reasonably priced
home-made food (not Sun evening), friendly
accommodating staff, restaurant; farm

shop, four comfortable modern bedrooms
in separate building overlooking garden,
handy for A1, open all day weekends, closed
lunchtimes Mon, Tues. *(Michael Butler)*

CAYTHORPE   SK9348
Red Lion (01400) 272632
*Signed just off A607 N of Grantham;
High Street; NG32 3DN* Popular 17th-c
village pub, good fairly traditional home-
made food (not Sun evening) including
lunchtime/early evening deal (Weds-Fri) and
Tues fish and chips night, friendly helpful
staff, well kept Adnams and Everards, good
sensibly priced wines, bare-boards bar
with light wood counter, black beams and
roaring fire, modern restaurant; back terrace
by car park. *(Pauline and Mark Evans)*

CHAPEL ST LEONARDS   TF5672
Admiral Benbow (01754) 871847
The Promenade; PE24 5BQ Small
bare-boards beach bar serving three real
ales including Black Sheep and good choice
of foreign bottled beers, proper cider too,
sandwiches and snacks, cushioned bench
seats, stools and barrel tables, lots of bric-a-
brac and nautical memorabilia on planked
walls and ceiling; free wi-fi; children and
dogs welcome, picnic-sets out on mock-up
galleon, great sea views, open all day
summer (all Fri-Sun winter). *(Jane Rigby)*

CLAYPOLE   SK8449
Five Bells (01636) 626561
Main Street; NG23 5BJ Friendly brick-
built village pub, good-sized beamed bar with
smaller dining area beyond servery, well kept
Greene King IPA and mainly local guests, a
couple of ciders, good value home-made food
including range of burgers and daily specials;
pool and darts; children welcome, dogs in
bar, grassy back garden with play area, four
bedrooms, closed lunchtimes Mon and Tues,
otherwise open all day. *(Daniel King)*

CLEETHORPES   TA3009
No 2 Refreshment Room
07905 375587 *Station Approach beneath
the clock tower; DN35 8AX* Small
comfortable station bar with well kept
Hancocks HB, Rudgate Ruby Mild, Sharps
Doom Bar and guests, real cider too, friendly
staff, interesting old pictures of the station,
historical books on trains and the local area,
no food apart from free Sun evening buffet;
tables out under heaters, open all day from
7.30am (9am Sun). *(Lorna and Jack Mulgrave)*

CLEETHORPES   TA3008
Nottingham House (01472) 505150
Sea View Street; DN35 8EU Seafront
pub with lively main bar, lounge and snug,
seven well kept ales including Tetley Mild,
Timothy Taylors Landlord and Oakham Citra,
Weston's ciders, good reasonably priced food
(not Mon, Tues) from sandwiches and pub
favourites up in bar or upstairs restaurant,

helpful friendly staff; regular live music, annual winter beer festival; children and dogs (in bar) welcome, bedrooms, good breakfast, open all day. *(Chris Johnson)*

CLEETHORPES TA3108

★**Willys** (01472) 602145

Highcliff Road; south promenade; DN35 8RQ Popular mock-Tudor seafront pub with panoramic Humber views; open-plan interior with tiled floor and painted brick walls, own good ales from visible microbrewery, also changing guests and belgian beers, enjoyable home-made bar lunches at bargain prices, good mix of customers; children welcome, no dogs at food times, a few tables out on the prom, open all day (till 2am Fri, Sat). *(Chris Johnson)*

COLEBY SK9760

Bell (01522) 813778

Village signed off A607 S of Lincoln, turn right and right into Far Lane at church; LN5 0AH Restauranty pub with wide variety of very good food from owner-chef including early-bird menu (Weds-Fri), welcoming staff, well kept Timothy Taylors and several wines by the glass (not cheap), bar and three dining areas; children over 8 welcome, terrace tables, village on Viking Way with lovely fenland views, three bedrooms, open evenings Weds-Sat and lunchtime Sun. *(Daniel King)*

CONINGSBY TF2458

Leagate Inn (01526) 342370

Leagate Road (B1192 southwards, off A153 E); LN4 4RS Heavy-beamed 16th-c fenland pub run by same family for over 25 years; three cosy linked rooms, medley of furnishings including high-backed settles around the biggest of three log fires, ancient oak panelling, dim lighting, attractive dining room, even a priest hole; reasonably priced food from extensive menu, Adnams, Batemans and Charles Wells ales; free wi-fi; children welcome (they eat for free 6-7pm Mon-Fri), dogs in bar, pleasant garden with play area, site of old gallows at front, eight motel bedrooms, open all day Sun. *(Sally Harrison)*

DONINGTON ON BAIN TF2382

Black Horse (01507) 343640

Main Road; between A153 and A157, SW of Louth; LN11 9TJ Welcoming roadside village inn with two carpeted bars (back one with low beams) and restaurant, open fires and woodburner, good locally sourced food cooked by landlord-chef including daily specials, well kept John Smiths and guests, proper cider; games room with pool, darts and dominoes, free wi-fi; children and dogs (in bars) welcome, picnic-sets in back garden, eight motel-style bedrooms, on Viking Way and handy for Cadwell Park race circuit, closed Mon and Tues lunchtimes. *(Jane Rigby)*

DRY DODDINGTON SK8546

★**Wheatsheaf** (01400) 281458

Main Street; 1.5 miles off A1 N of Grantham; NG23 5HU Welcoming and well cared-for 16th-c village pub; front bar (basically two rooms) with woodburner, variety of built-in wall seats, settles and little wooden stools, windows looking out to green and lovely 14th-c church with its crooked tower, Greene King Abbot and IPA, several wines by the glass and good range of gins, well liked food from varied menu including lunchtime/early evening set menu and some themed nights, slight slope down to comfortable extended dining room (once a cow byre perhaps dating from the 13th c); background music, free wi-fi; children and dogs (in bar) welcome, side disabled access, neat tables under parasols on front terrace, closed Mon. *(John Saul)*

FOSDYKE TF3132

Ship (01205) 260764

Moulton Washway; A17; PE12 6LH Useful roadside pub with popular reasonably priced food from varied menu, Sun carvery, two Adnams beers and Batemans XB, friendly staff, simple pine and quarry tile décor, woodburner; quiz every other Mon; children and dogs welcome, garden tables, open all day. *(Daniel King)*

FULBECK SK9450

Hare & Hounds (01400) 272322

The Green (A607 Leadenham–Grantham); NG32 3JJ Converted 17th-c maltings overlooking attractive village green, modernised linked areas, easy chairs by bar's woodburner, highly regarded food from pub favourites up including 'hot rock' menu, friendly attentive service, four well kept ales and an affordable wine list, raftered upstairs function room; no dogs inside, terrace seating, eight good bedrooms in adjacent barn conversion, generous breakfast, open all day Sun till 8pm (food till 7pm). *(William and Ann Reid)*

GAINSBOROUGH SK8189

Eight Jolly Brewers (01427) 611022

Ship Court, Silver Street; DN21 2DW Small drinkers' pub in former warehouse, eight interesting real ales such as Dukeries, traditional cider and plenty of bottled beers, friendly staff and locals, beams and bare brick, more room upstairs; live music Thurs; seats outside, open all day. *(Lorna and Jack Mulgrave)*

GEDNEY DYKE TF4125

★**Chequers** (01406) 366700

Off A17 Holbeach–King's Lynn; PE12 0AJ Smartly presented dining pub serving first class food including some pub staples, beamed bar with high tables and chairs, exposed brickwork and open fire, Greene King Abbot and Woodfordes Wherry, plenty of wines by the glass from good list, wide range of spirits too, friendly professional service from aproned staff, linked carpeted dining rooms and conservatory with high-backed chairs around white-clothed tables; background music, free wi-fi; children and dogs (in bar) welcome, back terrace and fenced-off lawn, closed Sun evening, Mon, Tues and first week Jan. *(Charles Welch, Hilary and Neil Christopher, Carol and Barry Craddock)*

KIRKBY ON BAIN   TF2462
★ **Ebrington Arms**   (01526) 354560
Main Street; LN10 6YT Popular village pub with good value traditional food (not Mon, booking advised), half a dozen well kept ales such as Adnams, Timothy Taylors and Sharps, beer mats on low 16th-c beams, carpets and banquettes, open fire, restaurant behind; background music, darts; children and dogs welcome, wheelchair access, tables out in front by road, lawn to the side with play equipment, campsite next door, closed Mon lunchtime. *(Daniel King)*

LEADENHAM   SK9552
George   (01400) 272251
Off A17 Newark–Sleaford; High Street; LN5 0PN Solid old coaching inn with comfortable old-fashioned two-room bar, well kept ales, several wines by the glass and remarkable range of some 700 whiskies, good choice of enjoyable food from fairly pubby menu, Sun carvery, friendly helpful service, restaurant; events including folk sing-around first Thurs of the month; children and dogs welcome, outside seating, six annexe bedrooms, open all day. *(Tony and Maggie Harwood)*

LINCOLN   SK9871
Dog & Bone   (01522) 522403
John Street; LN2 5BH Comfortable and welcoming backstreet local with well kept Batemans, several guest beers and real cider, log fires, various things to look at including collection of valve radios, local artwork and exchange-library of recent fiction; background and live music, quiz nights, beer festivals; dogs welcome, picnic-sets on back terrace, open all day Fri-Sun, from 4.30pm other days. *(Lenny and Ruth Walters)*

LINCOLN   SK9771
Jolly Brewer   (01522) 528583
Broadgate; LN2 5AQ Popular no-frills pub with unusual art deco interior, half a dozen well kept ales such as Idle, Tom Woods and Welbeck Abbey, real cider and decent range of other drinks, friendly staff, no food; regular live music including Weds open mike night; back courtyard with covered area, open all day (till 8pm Sun). *(Tony and Maggie Harwood)*

LINCOLN   SK9771
Strugglers   (01522) 535023
Westgate; LN1 3BG Cosily worn-in beer lovers' haunt tucked beneath the castle

walls, built in 1841 and once run by the local hangman (note the pub sign); half a dozen or more well kept ales including Greene King and Timothy Taylors, bare boards throughout with lots of knick-knacks and pump clips, two open fires (one in back snug); some live acoustic music; no children inside, dogs welcome, steps down to sunny back courtyard with heated canopy, open all day (till 1am Fri, Sat). *(James and Sylvia Hewitt)*

LINCOLN   SK9771
Widow Cullens Well   (01522) 523020
Steep Hill; just below cathedral; LN2 1LU Ancient reworked building on two floors (upstairs open to the rafters), well kept/priced Sam Smiths beers and decent pubby food including children's choices, chatty mix of customers (busy evening and weekends), friendly service (they may add a surcharge if you pay by card), beams, stone walls and log fire, back extension with namesake well; dogs welcome, terrace seating, open all day. *(Jane Rigby)*

LINCOLN   SK9771
★ **Wig & Mitre**   (01522) 535190
Steep Hill; just below cathedral; LN2 1LU Civilised café-style dining pub with plenty of character and attractive period features over two floors; big-windowed downstairs bar, beams and exposed stone walls, pews and Gothic furniture on oak boards, comfortable sofas in carpeted back area, quieter upstairs dining room with views of castle walls and cathedral, antique prints and caricatures of lawyers/clerics, well liked food from breakfast on including good value set menus, extensive choice of wines by the glass from good list, Everards Tiger and guests such as Oakham, friendly service; children and dogs welcome, open 8.30am-midnight. *(Richard Tilbrook, Brian and Anna Marsden)*

LITTLE BYTHAM   TF0117
Willoughby Arms   (01780) 410276
Station Road, S of village; NG33 4RA Former 19th-c private railway station, six well kept ales including Abbeydale, Grainstore and Hopshackle, a proper cider and reasonably priced pubby food from baguettes to blackboard specials, friendly helpful staff, bare-boards bar and back dining extension; quiz second Tues of the month; children and dogs welcome, disabled access, picnic-sets in sizeable garden with splendid country views, seven bedrooms (four in mews building), open all day. *(Lorna and Jack Mulgrave)*

LONG BENNINGTON   SK8344
Reindeer   (01400) 281382
Just off A1 N of Grantham – S end of village, opposite school; NG23 5DJ 17th-c low-beamed pub refurbished under new management; fair value food from snacks and pub favourites up including Fri night pizzas, ales such as Fullers and

Timothy Taylors, log fire in stone fireplace; background music; picnic-sets under parasols on small front terrace, open all day Fri, Sat, closed Sun evening, Mon. *(Mike and Margaret Banks)*

LONG BENNINGTON SK8344
Royal Oak (01400) 281332
Main Road; just off A1 N of Grantham; NG23 5DJ Popular local with spacious open-plan bar serving Marstons ales, several wines by the glass and good sensibly priced home-made food including specials and popular Sun roasts, friendly helpful staff; children welcome, seats out in front and in big back garden with play area, path for customers to river, open all day. *(Sally Harrison)*

LOUTH TF3287
Wheatsheaf (01507) 606262
Westgate, near St James' church; LN11 9YD Welcoming traditional 17th-c low-beamed pub, half a dozen well kept ales including Bass, Greene King and Tom Woods, real cider, enjoyable pubby food served by friendly helpful staff, coal fires in all three bars, old photographs; children welcome, no dogs, tables outside, open all day and can get busy. *(Charles and Maddie Bishop)*

MARKET DEEPING TF1310
Bull (01778) 343320
Market Place; PE6 8EA Bustling local run by welcoming ex-footballer landlord; cosy low-ceilinged alcoves, little corridors and interesting heavy-beamed medieval Dugout Bar, well kept Everards Tiger and Original and a couple of guests including Adnams, enjoyable lunchtime food, restaurant, upstairs games room; quiz night first Mon of month, sports TV, darts, free wi-fi; children in eating areas, seats in coachyard, open all day. *(Daniel King)*

MARKET RASEN TF1089
Aston Arms (01673) 842313
Market Place; LN8 3HL Popular market-square pub serving generous helpings of inexpensive food, Theakstons, John Smiths and a guest, friendly staff, beamed bar, lounge and games area; children and well behaved dogs welcome, side terrace, open all day. *(Lorna and Jack Mulgrave)*

NORTON DISNEY SK8859
Green Man (01522) 789804
Main Street, off A46 Newark–Lincoln; LN6 9JU Old beamed village pub-restaurant; enjoyable popular food from chef-landlord (booking advised) including pub standards and daily specials, good Sun roasts, Black Sheep, Brains Rev James and a guest, friendly, helpful staff, opened-up

modernised interior; tables out in front and in spacious back garden, closed Sun evening, Mon lunchtime. *(Sally Harrison)*

PINCHBECK TF2326
Ship (01775) 711746
Northgate; PE11 3SE Popular thatched and beamed riverside pub refurbished under newish licensees; cosy split-level bar with warm woodburner, four real ales and enjoyable generously served food, friendly helpful staff, restaurant; traditional games such as shove-ha'penny; children and dogs welcome, tables out on decking, open all day Sat, closed Sun evening, Mon. *(James and Sylvia Hewitt)*

REVESBY TF2961
Red Lion (01507) 568665
A155 Mareham–Spilsby; PE22 7NU Former 19th-c red-brick coaching inn set back from the road, ample helpings of enjoyable home-made food from reasonably priced pubby menu, Sun carvery, can eat in comfortable lounge bar with open fire or separate dining room, well kept Batemans ales, friendly staff; games area with pool; children welcome, tables out at front and on large side lawn, four bedrooms, open all day. *(Brian Root)*

SCAMPTON SK9579
Dambusters (01522) 731333
High Street; LN1 2SD Welcoming pub with several beamed rooms around central bar, masses of interesting Dambusters and other RAF memorabilia, generous helpings of reasonably priced straightforward food (not Sun evening) from shortish menu, also home-made chutneys, pâté and biscuits for sale, six interesting ales including own microbrews (ceiling covered in beer mats), short list of well chosen wines, pews and chairs around tables on wood floor, log fire in big two-way brick fireplace, more formal seating at back; children and dogs welcome (their black labrador is Bomber), very near Red Arrows runway viewpoint, closed Mon, otherwise open all day (till 7.30pm Sun). *(Charles and Maddie Bishop)*

SKENDLEBY TF4369
Blacksmiths Arms (01754) 890662
Off A158 about 10 miles NW of Skegness; PE23 4QE Cottagey-fronted 17th-c pub with cosy old-fashioned two-room bar, low beams and log fire, view into the cellar from servery, well kept Batemans XB, a house beer from Horncastle and guest, good home-made food served by friendly staff, back dining extension with deep well; children and dogs welcome, unsuitable for wheelchairs, wolds views from back garden, closed Sun evening, Mon lunchtime. *(Jake)*

It's very helpful if you let us know up-to-date food prices when you report on pubs.

SKILLINGTON SK8925
Cross Swords (01476) 861132
The Square; NG33 5HB Unassuming
19th-c stone pub on crossroads in delightful
village, welcoming and homely, with very good
food (not Sun evening) cooked by landlord-
chef, up to three changing ales; background
music; no under-10s or dogs, three annexe
bedrooms, open all day Sun till 8pm,
closed Mon. *(Sally Anne and Peter Goodale)*

SOUTH FERRIBY SE9921
Hope & Anchor (01652) 635334
Sluice Road (A1077); DN18 6JQ
Refurbished nautical theme-pub; bar, snug
and back dining area with wide views
over confluence of Rivers Ancholme and
Humber (plenty for bird-watchers), popular
locally sourced food (all day Fri, Sat, not
Sun evening) from pub standards to more
restaurant choices including 40-day-aged
steaks (not cheap), Theakstons, Tom
Woods and a guest, several wines by the
glass including champagne, good friendly
service; children and dogs welcome, disabled
access/facilities, outside tables, closed Mon,
otherwise open all day. *(Daniel King)*

SOUTH ORMSBY TF3675
Massingberd Arms (01507) 480492
Off A16 S of Louth; LN11 8QS Unspoilt
little country pub with unusual arched
windows, well kept Thwaites and a
guest, short choice of good freshly made
food at reasonable prices (no credit
cards), restaurant; quiz Weds; children
welcome, no dogs inside, seats in pleasant
garden, good wolds walks, open all day
Sun, closed Mon. *(Sally Harrison)*

SOUTH RAUCEBY TF0245
Bustard (01529) 488250
Main Street; NG34 8QG Modernised
19th-c stone-built pub with good food from
shortish but varied menu (can be pricey,
early evening discount on some dishes),
well kept Batemans, Loxley and a house
beer Cheeky Bustard (actually Batemans
XB), plenty of wines by the glass, friendly
efficient staff, flagstoned bar with log fire,
steps up to bare-stone restaurant (former
stables); live jazz third and last Weds of
month; children welcome, no dogs inside,
attractive sheltered garden, open all day
Sat, closed Sun evening, Mon; pub for sale so
may be changes. *(Pauline and Mark Evans)*

SOUTH WITHAM SK9219
Angel (01572) 768302
Church Street; NG33 5PJ Welcoming old
stone pub next to the village church, good
value pubby food cooked by chef-owner

including Mon burger night, OAP lunch
(Tues, Thurs) and popular Sun carvery,
well kept Black Sheep, Wells Bombardier
and a guest; sports TV; dogs welcome,
handy for A1, open all day. *(Thomas Allen)*

SPALDING TF2422
Priors Oven 07972 192750
Sheep Market; PE11 1BH Friendly
micropub in ancient building (former
bakery), small octagonal room with
vaulted ceiling, island bar serving up to
six changing ales, local ciders and maybe
english wines, no food, spiral stairs up to
comfortable lounge with period fireplace;
open all day. *(Sally Harrison)*

STAMFORD TF0207
All Saints Brewery – Melbourn Brothers (01780) 7521865
All Saints Street; PE9 2PA Well reworked
old building (core is a medieval hall)
with warren of rooms on three floors;
upstairs bar serving bottled fruit beers
from adjacent early 19th-c brewery and
low-priced Sam Smiths on handpump,
food from pub favourites up including
set deals and good vegetarian options,
ground-floor dining area with log fire
and woodburner, top floor with leather
sofas and wing chairs; children and dogs
welcome, picnic-sets in cobbled courtyard,
brewery tours, open all day. *(Daniel King)*

STAMFORD TF0306
★ Bull & Swan (01780) 766412
High Street, St Martins; PE9 2LJ
Handsome former staging post with three
traditional linked rooms; low beams, rugs
on bare boards, portraits in gilt frames
on painted or stone walls, several open
fires and good mix of seating including
high-backed settles, leather banquettes
and bow-window seats, Adnams Southwold,
Sharps Doom Bar and guests such as
Grainstore and Nene Valley, 20 wines by
the glass and 30 malt whiskies, well liked
food from panini and sharing boards
up, helpful staff; background music,
free wi-fi; children and dogs welcome,
tables in back coachyard, character
bedrooms named after animals, open
all day. *(Lorna and Jack Mulgrave)*

STAMFORD TF0207
Crown (01780) 763136
All Saints Place; PE9 2AG Substantial
well modernised stone-built hotel with good
choice of popular food using local produce
(some from their own farm) including
weekday set lunch, friendly helpful staff,
well kept ales such as Fullers, Oakham
and Timothy Taylors, lots of wines by the

Post Office address codings confusingly give the impression that a few pubs are in
Lincolnshire, when they're really in Cambridgeshire (which is where we list them).

glass and cocktails, decent coffee and afternoon teas, spacious main bar with long leather-cushioned counter, substantial pillars, step up to more traditional flagstoned area with stripped stone and armchairs, restaurant; background music, free wi-fi; children and dogs welcome, seats in back courtyard, 28 comfortable bedrooms (some in separate townhouse), good breakfast, open (and food) all day. *(Barry Collett)*

STAMFORD   TF0207
Jolly Brewer (01780) 755141
Foundry Road; PE9 2PP Welcoming unpretentious 19th-c stone pub, six well kept ales including own Bakers Dozen, traditional cider and wide range of interesting whiskies (some from India and Japan), low-priced simple food (weekday lunchtimes and Fri evenings), open fire in brick fireplace; regular beer festivals and fortnightly Sun quiz, sports TV, pool, darts and other games; dogs welcome, picnic-sets out at front, open all day. *(Lorna and Jack Mulgrave)*

SURFLEET   TF2528
Mermaid (01775) 680275
B1356 (Gosberton Road), just off A16 N of Spalding; PE11 4AB Two high-ceilinged carpeted rooms, huge sash windows, banquettes, captain's chairs and spindlebacks, Adnams and a couple of guests, good choice of fairly standard food including a monthly themed night, restaurant; background music; pretty terraced garden with summer bar and seats under thatched parasols, children's play area walled from River Glen, moorings, four bedrooms, closed Sun evening, Mon. *(Jake)*

TATTERSHALL THORPE   TF2159
Blue Bell (01526) 342206
Thorpe Road; B1192 Coningsby–Woodhall Spa; LN4 4PE Ancient low-beamed pub (said to date from the 13th c) with friendly cosy atmosphere, RAF memorabilia including airmen's signatures on the ceiling (pub was used by the Dambusters), big open fire, three well kept ales such as local Horncastle and Tom Woods Bomber County, nice wines and enjoyable well priced pubby food, small dining room; some live music; garden tables, bedrooms, closed Sun evening, Mon. *(Sally Harrison)*

TETFORD   TF3374
White Hart (01507) 533255
East Road, off A158 E of Horncastle; LN9 6QQ Friendly bay-windowed village pub dating from the 16th c; Brains Rev James and a couple of guests, good value generous pubby food (not Mon), pleasant inglenook bar with curved-back settles and slabby elm tables on red tiles, other areas including pool room; regular live music; children and dogs welcome, sheltered back lawn with guinea pigs and rabbits, pretty countryside, bedrooms. *(Mike Swan)*

THEDDLETHORPE ALL SAINTS   TF4787
★ Kings Head (01507) 339798
Pub signposted off A1031 N of Maplethorpe; Mill Road; LN12 1PB Long 16th-c thatched pub under welcoming licensees; carpeted two-room front lounge with very low ceiling, brass platters on timbered walls, antique dining chairs and tables, easy chairs by log fire, central bar (more low beams) with well kept ales such as Batemans and a local cider, coal fire with side oven, shelves of books, stuffed owls and country pictures, long dining room, good local food from sandwiches and sharing plates to steaks and fresh Grimsby fish, popular Sun roasts; children and dogs welcome, one or two picnic-sets in front area, more on lawn, self-catering apartment, open all day weekends, closed Mon and lunchtime Tues (all day Tues winter); for sale, so may be changes. *(Lenny and Ruth Walters)*

THREEKINGHAM   TF0836
Three Kings (01529) 240249
Just off A52 12 miles E of Grantham; Saltersway; NG34 0AU Former coaching inn with big entrance hall, fire and pubby furniture in comfortable beamed lounge, also a panelled restaurant and bigger dining/function room, good choice of home-made food including Thurs steak night, Bass, Timothy Taylors Landlord and guests; Weds quiz; children and dogs (in bar) welcome, sunny paved terrace and small lawned area, various car club meetings, closed Mon. *(Sally Harrison)*

WAINFLEET   TF5058
★ Batemans Brewery (01754) 882009
Mill Lane, off A52 via B1195; PE24 4JE Circular bar in brewery's ivy-covered windmill tower, Batemans ales in top condition, czech and belgian beers on tap too, ground-floor dining area with cheap food including baguettes and a few pubby dishes, popular Sun carvery, old pub games (more outside), lots of brewery memorabilia and plenty for families to enjoy; no dogs inside, entertaining brewery tours and shop, tables on terrace and grass, bar open 11.30am-4pm, bistro 12-2pm, seasonal opening for brewery tours and shop. *(Pauline and Mark Evans)*

WASHINGBOROUGH   TF0170
Ferry Boat (01522) 790794
High Street; LN4 1AZ Friendly old village pub doing well under present management, enjoyable pubby food including good value two-course weekday lunch, three well kept ales, high-raftered central bar with low-beamed areas off including restaurant, bare-stone and stripped-brick walls, mix of furniture including leather sofas and tub chairs on wood floors, open fire; background and some live music, fortnightly quiz

Weds, games part with pool, darts and TV; children welcome, dogs in bar (maybe a treat), beer garden, good river walks nearby, open all day. *(Chris Johnson)*

WEST DEEPING   TF1009
Red Lion (01778) 347190
King Street; PE6 9HP Stone-built pub with long low-beamed bar, four well kept ales including Fullers London Pride and local Hopshackle, popular freshly made food from baguettes up including weekday evening deal, back dining extension; occasional live music, free wi-fi; children welcome, no dogs inside, tables in back garden with terrace and fenced play area, vintage car/motorcycle meetings, open till 4pm Sun, closed Mon. *(Jane Rigby)*

WILSFORD   TF0043
Plough (01400) 230304
Main Street; NG32 3NS Traditional old two-bar village pub next to church, beams and open fires, a couple of real ales, nice range of wines and good choice of well presented bar food (till 7.45pm Sun), pleasant friendly service, dining conservatory; pool and other games in adjoining room; children welcome, small

walled back garden, good local walks, open all day Fri and Sun. *(Pat and Stewart Gordon)*

WITHAM ON THE HILL   TF0516
Six Bells (01778) 590360
Village signed from A6121, SW of Bourne; PE10 0JH Well restored Edwardian stone inn with smart comfortable bar, enjoyable, popular food including wood-fired pizzas, well kept Bass and guests, good friendly service; children and dogs welcome, rattan-style furniture on front terrace, nice village, three well appointed bedrooms, good breakfast. *(Daniel King)*

WOODHALL SPA   TF1963
Village Limits (01526) 353312
Stixwould Road; LN10 6UJ Modernised country pub-restaurant on village outskirts; good locally sourced food cooked by landlord-chef from pub standards up, well kept ales including own badged beers from local Horncastle, friendly service, smallish beamed bar with banquettes, dining room with light wood furniture on wood-strip floor; children welcome, eight courtyard bedrooms, good views from garden, closed Mon lunchtime (and possibly Sun and Mon evenings in winter). *(Jane Rigby)*

Norfolk

 BAWBURGH   TG1508   Map 5

Kings Head 🎯 ♀ ☕ 🛏

(01603) 744977 – www.kingshead-bawburgh.co.uk

Harts Lane; A47 just W of Norwich then B1108; NR9 3LS

Busy, small-roomed pub with five real ales, good wines by the glass, interesting food and friendly service

From the moment you arrive at this gem of a 17th-c pub the friendly, helpful staff will make you feel welcome. The small rooms have plenty of low beams and standing timbers, leather sofas and an attractive assortment of old dining chairs and tables on wood-strip floors; also, a knocked-through open fire and a couple of woodburning stoves in the restaurant areas. Adnams Broadside, Lighthouse and Southwold, Woodfordes Wherry and a couple of changing guests on handpump, 11 wines by the glass and eight malt whiskies; background music. There are seats in the garden and the pub is opposite a little green. The six bedrooms are comfortable and pretty and in a separate building, and they now also offer two self-catering apartments.

🎯 Highly regarded and particularly good, the food includes sandwiches, gin and tonic-cured salmon with beetroot slaw, herb blini and dill oil, chicken livers with thyme polenta and wild mushroom duxelle, goats cheese wellington with butternut squash purée and roasted vegetables, smoked haddock and salmon fishcake with basil mayonnaise and pickled fennel, caramelised pork belly with chorizo and bean cassoulet and garlic aioli, honey-glazed duck breast with parmentier potatoes and parsnip and vanilla purée, and puddings such as fruit trifle and chocolate and espresso tart with milk sorbet and peanut praline. *Benchmark main dish: steak burger with toppings, red cabbage coleslaw and skin-on chips £12.00. Two-course evening meal £22.00.*

Free house ~ Licensee Anton Wimmer ~ Real ale ~ Open 11-11 (10.30 Sun) ~ Bar food 12-2, 5.30-9; 12-3, 5.30-8 Sun ~ Restaurant ~ Children welcome ~ Dogs allowed in bar ~ Wi-fi ~ Bedrooms: £90/£110 *Recommended by David Fowler, David Travis, Edward Nile, Charles Fraser, Glenn and Julia Smithers, Patti and James Davidson, Chloe and Michael Swettenham, Amanda Shipley*

 BURSTON   TM1383   Map 5

Crown ☕

(01379) 741257 – www.burstoncrown.com

Village signposted off A140 N of Scole; Mill Road; IP22 5TW

Friendly, relaxed village pub usefully open all day, with a warm welcome, real ales and well liked bar food

This is the sort of village pub where even visitors will feel immediately at home – you can be sure of a friendly welcome. Locals tend to gather in an area by the bar counter where they serve Adnams Broadside and Southwold and guests such as Bartrams Drink Responsibly Vote Responsibly and Shortts Farm Strummer on handpump or tapped from the cask, ten wines by the glass and seven malt whiskies. On a chilly day, the best place to sit in this heavily beamed, quarry-tiled bar room is on the comfortably cushioned sofas in front of a woodburning stove in a huge brick fireplace; there are also stools by a low chunky wooden table, and newspapers and magazines. The public bar on the left has a nice long table and panelled settle on an old brick floor in one alcove, a pool table, and more tables and chairs towards the back near a dartboard. Both rooms are hung with paintings by local artists; background music, board games, dominoes and cards. The simply furnished, beamed dining room has another big brick fireplace. Outside, there's a smokers' shelter, seats and tables on a terrace and in the secluded garden, and a play area for children.

Cooked by the landlord (and using their smokehouse for some dishes), the good food includes sandwiches, crispy chilli beef with oriental salad, chicken liver parfait with red onion marmalade, a pie of the week, courgette and feta cheese fritters with minted yoghurt dressing and sauté potatoes, chicken breast stuffed with black truffle mousse and tarragon jus, thai red monkfish curry, 10oz rib-eye steak with café de paris butter, and puddings such as coffee crème brûlée with almond praline and sticky toffee pudding with butterscotch sauce. *Benchmark main dish: beef, mustard and bacon pie £13.20. Two-course evening meal £20.00.*

Free house ~ Licensees Bev and Steve Kembery ~ Real ale ~ Open 12-11 (10.30 Sun) ~ Bar food 12-2, 6.30-9; 12-4 Sun; no food Sun evening, Mon ~ Restaurant ~ Children welcome ~ Dogs allowed in bar ~ Wi-fi ~ Live music Thurs 8.30pm, every second Sun from 5pm
Recommended by Caroline Sullivan, Patricia Hawkins, Ruth May, Melanie and David Lawson, Lucy and Giles Gibbon

CASTLE ACRE
Ostrich

TF8115 Map 8

(01760) 755398 – www.ostrichcastleacre.com
Stocks Green; PE32 2AE

Friendly old village pub with original features, fine old fireplaces, real ales and tasty food; bedrooms

Wandering around the various rooms in this mainly 18th-c pub you can still find features dating from a couple of hundred years earlier, such as the original masonry, beams and trusses. The L-shaped, low-ceilinged front bar (on two levels) has a woodburning stove in a huge old fireplace, lots of wheelback chairs and cushioned pews around pubby tables on a wood-strip floor and gold patterned wallpaper; there's a step up to an area in front of the bar counter where there are similar seats and tables and a log fire in a brick fireplace. Greene King Abbot, IPA, Old Speckled Hen and a beer named for the pub on handpump, around a dozen wines by the glass and several malt whiskies. There's a separate dining room with another brick fireplace. The sheltered garden has picnic-sets under parasols and the inn faces the tree-lined village green; nearby are the remains of a Norman castle and a Cluniac priory (English Heritage).

Tasty food includes sandwiches, chicken and apricot terrine with spiced pear chutney, peppered squid with chilli tartare sauce, vegetable burgers with toppings, chicken shawarma (spicy chicken with hummus, greek yoghurt and salad in self-rolled flatbreads), pizzas from their own oven (also to take away), seafood and antipasti platters, sirloin steak with peppercorn sauce and red onion marmalade, and puddings such as chocolate brownie with chocolate sauce and apple and blackberry frangipane. *Benchmark main dish: beer-battered fish and chips £13.95. Two-course evening meal £19.00.*

Greene King ~ Tenant Tiffany Turner ~ Real ale ~ Open 10am-11pm; 10am-midnight Sat ~ Bar food 12-3, 6-9; 12-3 Sun; no food Sun evening ~ Restaurant ~ Children welcome ~ Dogs allowed in bar ~ Wi-fi ~ Live music last Sun of month ~ Bedrooms: £75/£85
Recommended by David Jackman, Hilary De Lyon and Martin Webster, Andrea and Philip Crispin, Thomas Green, Mr and Mrs Richard Osborne, Paddy and Sian O'Leary

GREAT MASSINGHAM
Dabbling Duck 🏅◉❢

TF7922 Map 8

(01485) 520827 – www.thedabblingduck.co.uk
Off A148 King's Lynn–Fakenham; Abbey Road; PE32 2HN

Unassuming from the outside but with character bars, real ales and interesting food; comfortable bedrooms

Right by the village green with its big duck ponds, this is an easy-going place with three woodburning stoves for winter and plenty of outside furniture for summer. The relaxed bars have leather sofas and armchairs, a mix of antique wooden dining tables and chairs on flagstones or stripped-wooden floors, a very high-backed settle, 18th- and 19th-c quirky prints and cartoons, and plenty of beams and standing timbers. At the back of the pub is the Blenheim room, just right for a private group, and there's also a candlelit dining room. Adnams Broadside and Ghost Ship, Woodfordes Wherry and a guest ale on handpump and a dozen wines by the glass, served from a bar counter made of great slabs of polished tree trunk; background music, TV, darts and board games. Tables and chairs on the pub's front terrace take in the pleasant setting and there are more seats and a play area in the enclosed back garden. The nine bedrooms are named after famous local sportsmen and airmen from the World War II air base in Massingham. Wheelchair access.

 As well as breakfasts (8-10am), the good food from an often creative menu includes sandwiches, local pheasant with vanilla-pickled carrots and black garlic aioli, king scallops with white pudding, cauliflower and beetroot purée, compressed apple and black pudding crumb, vegetable rogan josh, four or five changing pizza choices, burgers with toppings, barbecue sauce and dripping fries, duck breast with pearl barley, cherry gel and jus, stone bass fillet with mussel popcorn and fennel pollen beurre blanc, and puddings such as white chocolate mousse with raspberry sorbet and baked coconut with chocolate snowball ice-cream and chocolate sauce. *Benchmark main dish: beer-battered fish and dripping chips £13.00. Two-course evening meal £21.00.*

Free house ~ Licensee Dominic Symington ~ Real ale ~ Open 12-11 (10.30 Sun) ~ Bar food 10-9 ~ Restaurant ~ Children welcome ~ Dogs allowed in bar and bedrooms ~ Wi-fi ~ Bedrooms: £75/£110 *Recommended by Millie and Peter Downing, Tracey and Stephen Groves, Patricia Hawkins, Peter and Alison Steadman, Elise and Charles Mackinlay*

HOLKHAM
Victoria ♀ ⇌

TF8943 Map 8

(01328) 711008 – www.victoriaatholkham.co.uk
A149 near Holkham Hall; NR23 1RG

Smart, handsome inn with pubby bar, plenty of character dining space, thoughtful choice of drinks, friendly staff and enjoyable food; bedrooms

You'll probably have to arrive very early or very late in order to bag an outside table here on sunny lunchtimes, as it's deservedly very popular – Holkham Beach with its vast stretches of sand backed by pine woods is just minutes away. There's plenty of seating on terraces plus an outside bar and seafood shack. Inside, the atmosphere is gently upmarket yet informal and friendly, with a proper bare-boards bar to the left that's popular with locals, and a spreading dining and sitting area with an appealing variety of antique-style dining chairs and tables on rugs and stripped floorboards, antlers and antique guns, and sofas by a big log fire. There's also a small drawing room to the right of the main entrance (for hotel guests only) with homely furniture, an open fire and an honesty bar. Adnams Broadside, Fullers London Pride and Woodfordes Nelsons Revenge and Wherry on handpump, 20 wines by the glass, good coffee and efficient, polite service. An airy conservatory dining room, decorated in pale beige, leads out to a back courtyard with green-painted furniture. Some of the stylish bedrooms have views of the sea and breakfasts are good and generous.

Served all day from 8am for breakfast and using Estate and other local produce, the enjoyable food includes sandwiches (until 6pm), orange and fennel-cured salmon with pickled cucumber, sauté duck livers with mustard cream and sourdough, vegetable crumble with warm potato salad, chicken breast with pea and mint fricassée, pavé of cod with rarebit crust, braised cabbage and red wine jus, venison suet pudding with haunch steak and juniper jus, and puddings such as honey and pear cheesecake and sticky toffee pudding and salted caramel ice-cream. *Benchmark main dish: beer-battered fish and chips £14.25. Two-course evening meal £21.00.*

Free house ~ Licensee Lord Coke ~ Real ale ~ Open 11-11; 12-10.30 Sun ~ Bar food 8-10am breakfast; 12-9 (half-hour break 6-6.30pm) ~ Restaurant ~ Children welcome ~ Dogs welcome ~ Wi-fi ~ Bedrooms: $135/$195 *Recommended by W K Wood, Jestyn Phillips, Julian Richardson, William and Sophia Renton, Peter and Emma Kelly, Tracey and Stephen Groves, Mr and Mrs Richard Osborne, Michael Sargent*

KING'S LYNN   TF6119   Map 8

Bank House 🏆 ♀ 🛏

(01553) 660492 – www.thebankhouse.co.uk
Kings Staithe Square via Boat Street and along the quay in one-way system; PE30 1RD

Georgian bar-brasserie with plenty of history and character, airy rooms, real ales and imaginative food from breakfast onwards; bedrooms

This particularly well run place is open all day, so you can drop in at any time to enjoy first class, up-to-date food and a genuine welcome. The various stylish rooms include the elegant bar (once the bank manager's office – the building was Barclays Bank's first opening in 1780) with sofas and armchairs, a log fire with fender seating, Adnams Broadside and Southwold and Woodfordes Wherry on handpump, 26 wines by the glass, 57 gins (including local ones; they also make their own tonic waters), 11 whiskies, interesting vodkas and cocktails; background music. The restaurant has antique chairs and tables on bare boards, an airy brasserie has sofas and armchairs around low tables and a big brick fireplace, and two other areas (one with fine panelling, the other with a half-size billiards table) have more open fires. The atmosphere throughout is gently civilised but easy-going and service is helpful and courteous. An outside area, flanked by magnificent wrought-iron gates, has fire pits for warmth on chillier evenings, and the riverside terrace (lovely sunsets) has an open-air bar. This is a splendid quayside spot and the Corn Exchange theatre and arts centre is just five minutes away. Sister pub is the Rose & Crown in Snettisham.

Impressive food using local, seasonal produce includes sandwiches, earl grey tea-cured sea trout with fennel and orange pickle, duck terrine with quince jelly, pumpkin, tomato and ginger bake with marmite dumplings, feta, edamame beans, green apple and toasted cashews with wild and brown rice, steak burger with toppings, barbecue sauce and french fries, spatchcock poussin with vegetable couscous and crispy parma ham, braised ox cheeks with dauphinoise potatoes, and puddings such as spotted dick with cinnamon custard and rum and raisin ice-cream and pistachio, pineapple and coconut trifle. *Benchmark main dish: grilled plaice with sauté potatoes, chargilled prawns and salsa verde £16.00. Two-course evening meal £22.00.*

Free house ~ Licensee Anthony Goodrich ~ Real ale ~ Open 11-11; 12-10.30 Sun ~ Bar food 12-9.30 (8.30 Sun) ~ Restaurant ~ Children welcome ~ Dogs allowed in bar ~ Wi-fi ~ Bedrooms: £85/£115 *Recommended by David Longhurst, Anne and Ben Smith, Colin Humphreys, John Wooll, Ian Duncan, Revd Michael Vockins, Ian Herdman*

LARLING
Angel 🍺 🛏

TL9889 Map 5

(01953) 717963 – www.angel-larling.co.uk
From A11 Thetford–Attleborough, take B1111 turn-off and follow pub signs; NR16 2QU

Good-natured, chatty atmosphere in busy pub with several real ales and tasty bar food; bedrooms

With the A11 nearby and good surrounding walks you can be sure of plenty of customers and a good bustling atmosphere here – especially at lunchtime. It's been run by the same friendly family since 1913 and they still have the original visitors' books from 1897 to 1909. The comfortable 1930s-style lounge on the right has squared panelling, cushioned wheelback chairs, a nice long cushioned panelled corner settle and some good solid tables for eating; also, a collection of whisky-water jugs on a delft shelf over the big brick fireplace, a woodburning stove, a couple of copper kettles and some hunting prints. Adnams Southwold and four guests from breweries such as Crouch Vale, Lacons, Oakham, Orkney and Swannay on handpump, 110 malt whiskies and ten wines by the glass; they hold an August beer festival with more than 100 real ales and ciders, live music and a barbecue. The quarry-tiled, black-beamed public bar has a good local feel, with darts, juke box, games machine, board games and background music. There's a neat grass area behind the car park with picnic-sets around a big fairy-lit apple tree and a fenced play area. The four-acre meadow is used as a caravan and camping site from March to October.

Popular food includes sandwiches, creamy mushroom pot, prawn cocktail, stilton and mushroom bake, various omelettes, sausage and egg, chicken with bacon, cheese and barbecue sauce, beer-battered fish of the day with chips, burgers with toppings and chips, smoked haddock provençale, mixed grill, and puddings such as chocolate fudge cake and local ice-creams and sorbets. *Benchmark main dish: steak and kidney pie £11.95. Two-course evening meal £18.00.*

Free house ~ Licensee Andrew Stammers ~ Real ale ~ Open 10am-11pm (11.30pm Sat) ~ Bar food 12-9.30 (10 Fri, Sat) ~ Restaurant ~ Children welcome ~ Wi-fi ~ Bedrooms: £60/£90 *Recommended by Patricia Hawkins, Hilary and Neil Christopher, Andrew Stone, Ruth May, Cliff and Monica Swan*

Please keep sending us reports. We rely on readers for news of new discoveries, and particularly for news of changes – however slight – at the fully described pubs: feedback@goodguides.com, or (no stamp needed) The Good Pub Guide, FREEPOST RTXY–ZCBC–BBAZ, Stream Lane, Sedlescombe, Battle TN33 0PB.

MORSTON

TG0043 Map 8

Anchor ⊙ 🍸

(01263) 741392 – www.morstonanchor.co.uk

A149 Salthouse–Stiffkey; The Street; NR25 7AA

Quite a choice of rooms filled with bric-a-brac and prints, real ales and enjoyable food

Our readers very much enjoy their visits to this whitewashed pub just up from the harbour in a small seaside village, and the hands-on licensees offer all their customers a genuine welcome. Three traditional rooms on the right have straightforward seats and tables on original wooden floors, coal fires, local 1950s beach photographs and lots of prints and bric-a-brac. Adnams Old Ale, local Winters Golden and Woodfordes Wherry on handpump, 20 wines by the glass and 13 gins; background music, darts and board games. The contemporary airy extension on the left, with comfortable benches and tables, leads into the more formal restaurant where work by local artists is displayed on the walls. You can sit outside at the front of the building. If parking is proving difficult at the pub, there's an overflow around the corner off-road and a National Trust car park five minutes' walk away. The surrounding area is wonderful for bird-watching and walking, and you can book seal-spotting trips here.

 Highly thought-of food using local produce includes sandwiches, twice-baked cheese soufflé with beetroot velouté and goats cheese, crispy squid with red pepper coulis, pesto, chorizo and olives, basil gnocchi with ratatouille and mozzarella, olive and sunblush tomato salad, beer-battered haddock and chips, chicken with wild mushrooms, parmentier potatoes, black pudding and red wine jus, burger with toppings, pickled slaw and skinny fries, and puddings such as crème brûlée and golden syrup pudding with custard. *Benchmark main dish: local mussels £16.00. Two-course evening meal £20.00.*

Free house ~ Licensees Harry Farrow and Rowan Glennie ~ Real ale ~ Open 9am-11pm (10.30pm Sun) ~ Bar food 12-3, 6-9 ~ Restaurant ~ Children welcome ~ Dogs allowed in bar ~ Wi-fi *Recommended by Roy Hoing, Victoria and James Sargeant, Phil and Jane Villiers, Monty Green, Caroline and Peter Bryant*

NORTH CREAKE

TF8538 Map 8

Jolly Farmers

(01328) 738185 – www.jollyfarmersnorfolk.co.uk

Burnham Road; NR21 9JW

Friendly village local with three cosy rooms, open fires and woodburners, well liked food and several real ales

Once you've found this well run old coaching inn, you'll become a regular visitor. Nothing is too much trouble for the kindly licensees and there arc three cosy and relaxed rooms, including the main bar with a large open fire in a brick fireplace, a mix of pine farmhouse and high-backed leather dining chairs around scrubbed pine tables on quarry tiles and pale yellow walls. Beside the wooden bar counter are some high bar chairs, and they keep Woodfordes Nelsons Revenge and Wherry tapped and Greene King Old Speckled Hen from the cask, 11 wines by the glass and a dozen malt whiskies; service is helpful and friendly. There's also a cabinet of model cars. A smaller bar has pews and a woodburning stove, while the red-walled dining room has similar furniture to the bar and another woodburner. The terrace outside has plenty of seats and tables.

Pleasing food includes sandwiches, pigeon and bacon salad with sweet dressing, crab savoury pot, home-roasted honeyed ham and eggs, macaroni with creamy stilton, walnut and tomato sauce, prawn and coconut curry, chicken caesar salad, mussels in wholegrain mustard, cream and local cider, lambs liver and bacon in red wine gravy, steak and stilton pie, and puddings such as dark chocolate, cherry and cherry wine tart and whisky and banana flummery. *Benchmark main dish: trio of lamb (breast, cutlets, minted lamb pattie) with minted yoghurt and minted glaze £16.00. Two-course evening meal £21.50.*

Free house ~ Licensees Adrian and Heather Sanders ~ Real ale ~ Open 12-2.30, 7-11; 12-7 Sun; closed Mon, Tues ~ Bar food 12-2, 7-9; 12-5.30 Sun ~ Children welcome ~ Dogs allowed in bar *Recommended by Barbara Brown, Derek and Sylvia Stephenson, Paul Faraday, Guy Henderson, Peter and Emma Kelly*

 NORWICH TG2109 Map 5
Fat Cat
(01603) 624364 – www.fatcatpub.co.uk
West End Street; NR2 4NA

A place of pilgrimage for beer lovers and open all day; lunchtime rolls and pies

Any beer lover is going to want to linger a while longer when visiting this lively pub. The knowledgeable landlord keeps an extraordinary range of up to 32 quickly changing ales and both he and his helpful staff can guide you through the choices. On handpump or tapped from the cask in a stillroom behind the bar – big windows reveal all – are their own beers (Fat Cat Bitter, Cat's Eyes, Marmalade Cat and Wild Cat), as well as guests such as Adnams Southwold, Crouch Vale Yakima Gold, Fullers ESB, Green Jack Mahseer IPA, Greene King Abbot, Oakham Green Devil IPA and Inferno, and Timothy Taylors Landlord – and many more choices from across the country. You'll also find imported draught beers and lagers, over 50 bottled beers from around the world and 20 ciders and perries. The no-nonsense furnishings include plain scrubbed pine tables and simple solid seats, lots of brewery memorabilia, bric-a-brac and stained glass. There are tables outside.

 Bar food consists of rolls and good pies at lunchtime (not Sunday).

Own brew ~ Licensee Colin Keatley ~ Real ale ~ No credit cards ~ Open 12-11 (midnight Thurs, Fri); 11-midnight Sat ~ Bar food filled rolls available until sold out; not Sun ~ Children allowed until 6pm ~ Dogs allowed in bar ~ Wi-fi *Recommended by Miles Green, Sophie Ellison, Edward May, Mike Swan, Mark Morgan, Dr J Barrie Jones*

OXBOROUGH TF7401 Map 5
Bedingfeld Arms 🍴☆ 🛏
(01366) 328300 – www.bedingfeldarms.co.uk
Near church; PE33 9PS

Attractively furnished Georgian inn with restful rooms, thoughtful choice of drinks, enjoyable food and good service; bedrooms

Both the village green and Oxburgh Hall (National Trust) are opposite this gently civilised 18th-c coaching inn. Our readers enjoy their visits here and the relaxed, wood-floored bar has green leather chesterfields, leather tub chairs and window seats around tables of varying heights, an open fire in a marble fireplace with a large gilt mirror above, fresh flowers and candles, and high chairs against the long bar counter. The airy dining room, with more fresh flowers and candles, is furnished with high-backed wooden and cushioned chairs around antique tables, wall seating with scatter cushions and bird prints on pale grey walls. Adnams Broadside, Woodfordes Wherry and a guest beer on handpump and ten wines by the glass, served by courteous, helpful staff; TV for major sporting events, background music. Local oak trees were used to construct the covered verandah extension which is furnished with leather armchairs and dining chairs, and the garden has seats and tables and a view of the church. Four of the lovely bedrooms are in the inn with another five in the coach-house annexe; breakfasts are highly recommended.

 As well as serving breakfasts (7.30-9.30am) and using rare-breed beef from their Estate farm, the highly rewarding food includes lunchtime sandwiches, duck terrine wrapped in parma ham, an antipasti plate, local honey and mustard roasted ham and eggs, coconut and vegetable thai curry, burgers with toppings, coleslaw, chilli chutney and chips, moules frites, lamb rump with dauphinoise potates, salsa verde and red wine, duck breast with crushed new potatoes, baby spinach and orange sauce, and puddings such as chocolate fondant with vanilla ice-cream and mango tart with mango sorbet and chantilly cream. *Benchmark main dish: langoustines with garlic butter and fries £19.95. Two-course evening meal £23.00.*

Free house ~ Licensees Stephen and Catherine Parker ~ Real ale ~ Open 11-11; 11-midnight Sat ~ Bar food 12-3, 6-9; 12-8 Sun ~ Restaurant ~ Well behaved children welcome ~ Dogs allowed in bar and bedrooms ~ Wi-fi ~ Bedrooms: £78.50/£88
Recommended by Maddie Purvis, Julie Braeburn, John Harris, Lyn and Freddie Roberts, Alexandra and Richard Clay, Max and Steph Warren

SALTHOUSE
Dun Cow 🍴 🍺

TG0743 Map 8

(01263) 740467 – www.salthouseduncow.com
A149 Blakeney–Sheringham (Purdy Street, junction with Bard Hill); NR25 7XA

Relaxed village pub, a good all-rounder and with enterprising food

Facing the bird-filled salt marshes, this cheerful pub has a flint-walled bar consisting of a pair of high-raftered rooms opened up into one area, with stone tiles around the counter where regulars congregate, and a carpeted seating area with a fireplace at each end. Also, scrubbed tables, one very high-backed settle, country kitchen chairs and elegant little red-padded dining chairs, with big sailing ship and other prints. Adnams Ghost Ship, Norfolk Brewhouse Moon Gazer Golden Ale, Woodfordes Wherry and a guest on handpump, 19 wines by the glass, 14 malt whiskies and a good relaxed atmosphere. Picnic-sets on the front grass look out towards the sea and there are more seats in a sheltered back courtyard and an orchard garden beyond. Bedrooms are self-catering.

 Tempting food includes sandwiches (until 5pm), herring roes on toast, crispy fried beef salad with asian-style dressing, pepper, chickpea and tomato stew with cumin, chilli and baked eggs, steak pie, a fish dish of the day, burger with toppings, relish and fries, tempura monkfish on chorizo and squid risotto, and puddings such as treacle tart and custard and crème brûlée. *Benchmark main dish: grilled local lobster with fries £18.00. Two-course evening meal £22.00.*

Punch ~ Lease Daniel Goff ~ Real ale ~ Open 11.30-11 ~ Bar food 12-9 ~ Children welcome ~ Dogs welcome ~ Wi-fi *Recommended by Camilla and Jose Ferrera, Alison and Graeme Spicer, Claire Adams, Alison and Dan Richardson, Lee and Jill Stafford*

We accept no free drinks or meals and inspections are anonymous.

SHOULDHAM
TF6708 Map

Kings Arms ◖

(01366) 347410 – www.kingsarmsshouldham.co.uk

The Green; PE33 0BY

Bustling local by the village green with local ales, interesting food and a buoyant atmosphere

Norfolk's first co-operative pub, this is attractively placed right on the village green; there are painted picnic-sets on grass in the garden. The bar rooms have beams, flagstones, exposed-stone or red-painted walls hung with prints, a homely mix of assorted dining chairs and tables, a leather button-back sofa and a woodburning stove in an inglenook fireplace. The three real ales tapped from the cask come from breweries such as Adnams, Beeston and Humpty Dumpty, there are ten wines by the glass, 14 malt whiskies, 17 gins and local cider; background music. There's also a café staffed by volunteers selling village-baked cakes and scones. They hold an annual beer, cider and music festival (check the website for dates) and on the first Sunday of the month there are classic car or motorcyle meetings.

 Using local produce and game from neighbouring estates, the good food includes lunchtime sandwiches, sweet, sticky marinated pork with sesame salad and miso dressing, grilled mackerel fillet with beetroot purée and pickled vegetables, ham and free-range eggs, vegetarian chilli with sour cream and cheese, burger with toppings, coleslaw, red pepper mayonnaise and chips, chicken breast stuffed with parmesan, basil and sun-dried tomatoes, wrapped in pancetta with rosemary and tomato sauce, sea bass fillet with salsa rossa and herbed potato cake, and puddings. *Benchmark main dish: pork belly with dauphinoise potatoes and cider jus £13.95. Two-course evening meal £20.00.*

Free house ~ Licensee Ian Skinner ~ Real ale ~ Open 12-3, 5-10.30; 12-11 Fri, Sat; 12-10.30 Sun; closed Mon lunchtime ~ Bar food 12-2 (2.30 Fri, Sat), 6-9; 12-4 Sun; not Sun evening or Mon ~ Restaurant ~ Children welcome ~ Dogs allowed in bar ~ Wi-fi ~ Live music throughout the year (see website) *Recommended by Sylvia and Phillip Spencer, Mike and Sarah Abbot, Daniel King*

SNETTISHAM
TF6834 Map 8

Rose & Crown ⭐ � ♟ ⊨

(01485) 541382 – www.roseandcrownsnettisham.co.uk

Village signposted from A149 King's Lynn–Hunstanton just N of Sandringham; coming in on the B1440 from the roundabout just N of village, take first left into Old Church Road; PE31 7LX

Particularly well run inn with log fires and interesting furnishings, imaginative food, a fine range of drinks and stylish seating on heated terrace; well equipped bedrooms

This remains a firm favourite with many of our readers – as it does with us too – and the professional, hands-on licensees and their neatly dressed, helpful staff continue to offer a warm welcome to all. The two main bars have distinct character and simple charm, with an open fire and woodburning stove, old quarry tiles or coir flooring, cushioned wall seating and wooden tables and chairs, candles on mantelpieces and daily papers. There are stools against the bar where locals enjoy Adnams Broadside and Southwold, Marstons Pedigree, Ringwood Boondoggle, Thwaites Lancaster Bomber, Woodfordes Wherry and Wychwood Hobgoblin on handpump; also, 16 wines by the glass, ten malt whiskies, artisan gins (including local ones), local cider and fresh fruit juices. A small wooden-floored back room has old sports equipment, the landlord's sporting trophies and photos of the pub's cricket team. The civilised little restaurant (decorated in soft greys) has cushions and picture mounts with splashes of bright green and flowers in old galvanised watering cans sitting on windowsills. At the back of the building, two rooms make up the bustling Garden Room, with sofas, wooden farmhouse and white-painted dining chairs around a mix of tables, church candles in large lanterns, attractive striped blinds and doors that lead to the pretty walled garden. Here there are plenty of contemporary seats and tables under cream parasols, outdoor heaters, colourful herbaceous borders and a wooden galleon-shaped climbing fort for children. Bedrooms are spacious and well appointed and breakfasts very good. Disabled lavatories and wheelchair ramp. This is sister pub to the Bank House in King's Lynn.

Good, imaginative food from thoughtful menus and using local, seasonal produce includes sandwiches, ham hock roulade with pickled wild mushrooms and celeriac rémoulade, beetroot-cured sea trout with pink radish, orange and avocado purée, wild garlic, courgette and toasted pine nut pasta, barbecue chicken and pulled pork burger with onion rings and fries, steak and mushroom in ale pudding, guinea fowl breast with confit leg, red wine risotto and grilled chicory, chargrilled mackerel with sicilian salad, and puddings such as lemon meringue pie and orange cheesecake with orange blossom, chocolate orange ganache and chocolate ice-cream. *Benchmark main dish: beer-battered haddock and chips with minted mushy peas £13.00. Two-course evening meal £20.00.*

Free house ~ Licensee Anthony Goodrich ~ Real ale ~ Open 11-11; 12-8.30 Sun ~ Bar food 12-9; 12-9.30 Fri, Sat; 12-8.30 Sun ~ Restaurant ~ Children welcome ~ Dogs welcome ~ Wi-fi ~ Bedrooms: £100/£120 *Recommended by Roger and Donna Huggins, Tony Scott, Roy Hoing, John Wooll, Katherine and Hugh Markham, Mark and Mary Setting, Muriel and Spencer Harrop*

THORNHAM
Lifeboat 🍺 🛏

TF7343   Map 8

(01485) 512236 – www.lifeboatinnthornham.com
A149 by Kings Head, then first left; PE36 6LT

Lots of character in traditional inn, plenty of space for eating and dining, real ales and super surrounding walks; bedrooms

The main bar in this character inn remains the same despite ownership changes, with beams, horse tack and farming implements, big lamps, brass and copper jugs and pans, cushioned window seats, chairs and settles around dark sturdy tables on quarry tiles and woodburning stoves – the antique penny-in-the-hole game is hidden under a bench cushion; a second bar, favoured by locals, is smaller with some fine carving around the counter. Adnams Southwold, Woodfordes Wherry and a couple of guest ales on handpump, good wines by the glass and nine gins; background music. The formal entrance hall now has sofas and fender seats by a big open fire, there's another room with more sofas and a cylindrical woodburner and also a simply furnished dining room. A quarry tiled conservatory (used for eating) has fairy lights and steps that lead up to the smartened-up back garden with grey-painted picnic-sets and a couple of cabanas; there are more picnic-sets at the front of the building. Bedrooms are warm and comfortable and you can walk from here to the salt marshes about a mile away.

Good, popular food includes sandwiches, chicory, pear and candied walnut salad with blue cheese dressing, smoked fish and shellfish platter, a pie of the day, beer-battered fish of the day and chips, crispy garlic and herb polenta with smoked bean chilli and coriander and spring onion salad, lambs liver with sweet potato mash, roasted shallots, pancetta and tomato and herb ragoût, hake with wild mushroom and leek fricassée and slow-roasted garlic potatoes, and puddings such as dark chocolate délice with hazelnut crumb and orange curd and honey and stem ginger brûlée. They also offer afternoon tea. *Benchmark main dish: moules marinière with frites £15.95. Two-course evening meal £21.00.*

Free house ~ Licensee James Green ~ Real ale ~ Open 11-11; 12-11 Sun ~ Bar food 12-9 ~ Restaurant ~ Children welcome ~ Dogs allowed in bar and bedrooms ~ Wi-fi ~ Bedrooms: £125/£140 *Recommended by Tracey and Stephen Groves, John Wooll, Patricia and Gordon Thompson, Monty Green*

THORNHAM

TF7343 Map 8

Orange Tree 🟊 ❎ ⏱ 🛏

(01485) 512213 – www.theorangetreethornham.co.uk

Church Street/A149; PE36 6LY

Norfolk Dining Pub of the Year

Nice combination of friendly bar and good contemporary dining, plus suntrap garden; bedrooms

There's always a cheerful mix of both locals and visitors in this well run, friendly pub and all get a genuine welcome from the courteous, hard-working staff. The most pubby part is the sizeable bar with white-painted beams, red leather chesterfields in front of a log fire, flowery upholstered or leather and wooden dining chairs and plush wall seats around a mix of tables on wood or quarry-tiled floors. There's Adnams Southwold and Woodfordes Nelsons Revenge and Wherry on handpump, over 30 wines by the glass, and 19 gins; background music, board games and flat-screen TV. A little dining room leads off here with silver décor, buddha heads and candles, and the two-part restaurant is simple and contemporary in style. In warm weather, the front garden is much in demand: lavender beds and climbing roses, lots of picnic-sets under parasols, outdoor heaters and a small smart corner pavilion. At the back of the building is a second outdoor area with children's play equipment. The bedrooms (our readers particularly recommend those in the Old Bakery) make a good base for this lovely stretch of the north Norfolk coast; breakfasts are good. They're kind to dogs and have a doggie menu plus snacks.

First class, creative food includes soft shell crab, pork rouille and king scallop with salt caramel and apple purée and apple pearls, crispy fried chicken with asian miso coleslaw, mango yoghurt, satay, nuts and seeds, goats cheese and fig crème brûlée with herb gnocchi, baby fennel, oyster mushroom, freekeh and tarragon oil, rare-breed burger with toppings, creamy thyme and mustard coleslaw and chips, seafood spaghetti, halibut with purple potato pie, smoked halibut, dashi and cockle chowder and sea purslane, and puddings such as Baileys profiteroles with chocolate sauce and banana split with chocolate ice-cream, chantilly cream, rum meringue and rum, raisin and chocolate sauce. *Benchmark main dish: free-range chicken and wild mushroom pie with smoked pancetta mash £16.75. Two-course evening meal £24.00.*

Punch ~ Tenant Mark Goode ~ Real ale ~ Open 12-11; 12-10.30 Sun ~ Bar food 12-9 ~ Restaurant ~ Children welcome ~ Dogs allowed in bar and bedrooms ~ Wi-fi ~ Bedrooms: £80/£89 *Recommended by Gordon and Margaret Ormondroyd, Chris Johnson, John Harris, Neil Allen, Tracey and Stephen Groves, John and Abigail Prescott, Patti and James Davidson*

Bedroom prices are for high summer. Even then you may get reductions for more than one night, or (outside tourist areas) weekends. Winter special rates are common, and many inns reduce bedroom prices if you have a full evening meal.

THORPE MARKET
TG2434 Map 8
Gunton Arms ♀
(01263) 832010 – www.theguntonarms.co.uk
Cromer Road; NR11 8TZ

Impressive place with an easy-going atmosphere, open fires and antiques, real ales, interesting food and friendly staff; bedrooms

Certainly not a straightforward pub, this individual place is a rather grand country house surrounded by a 1,000-acre deer park. The large entrance hall sets the scene; throughout, the atmosphere is easy-going and friendly, but definitely gently upmarket. The simply furnished bar has dark pubby chairs and tables on a wooden floor, a log fire, a long settle beside a pool table, and high stools against the mahogany counter where they serve Adnams Broadside and Southwold, Woodfordes Wherry and a guest beer on handpump, 13 wines by the glass, 16 malt whiskies and two ciders; staff are chatty and helpful. Heavy curtains line an open doorway into a dining room, where vast antlers hang above a big log fire (they often cook over this) and there are straightforward chairs around scrubbed tables on stone tiles. A lounge, with comfortable old leather armchairs and a sofa on a fine rug in front of yet another log fire, has genuine antiques and standard lamps. The restaurant is more formal with candles and napery, and there are also two homely sitting rooms for hotel residents. Many of the walls are painted dark red and hung with assorted artwork and big mirrors; background music, darts, TV and board games. The bedrooms have many original fittings, but no TV.

Using Estate produce, the food is rustic and hearty: sandwiches, smoked salmon with irish soda bread, deep-fried tiger prawns in matzo meal with garlic mayonnaise, crab pasta with chilli and coriander, chicken, bacon and leek pie, cod fillet with creamed leeks, bacon and peas, slow-roasted lamb shoulder with bubble and squeak, suckling pig with spinach and mustard, rib of beef to share with béarnaise sauce, and puddings such as chocolate and praline mousse and pistachio and griottine cherry cheesecake. *Benchmark main dish: venison sausages with mash and onion gravy £14.50. Two-course evening meal £24.00.*

Free house ~ Licensee Simone Baker ~ Real ale ~ Open 12-11; 12-10.30 Sun ~ Bar food 12-3, 6-10 (9 Sun) ~ Restaurant ~ Children welcome ~ Dogs allowed in bar and bedrooms ~ Wi-fi ~ Bedrooms: /£130 *Recommended by Tracey and Stephen Groves, David Jackman, Mark and Mary Setting, Alison and Graeme Spicer*

WIVETON
TG0442 Map 8
Wiveton Bell ⚫ ⊨
(01263) 740101 – www.wivetonbell.co.uk
Blakeney Road; NR25 7TL

Busy dining pub where drinkers are welcomed too, local beers, consistently enjoyable food and seats outside; bedrooms

Our readers very much enjoy staying here and the character bedrooms are comfortable and well equipped (three have their own small terrace); a continental breakfast hamper is delivered to your room each morning. The mainly open-plan rooms have some fine old beams, an attractive mix of dining chairs around wooden tables on a stripped-wood floor, a log fire and prints on yellow walls. The sizeable conservatory has smart beige dining chairs around wooden tables on coir flooring. Friendly, attentive staff serve only local ales – Norfolk Brewhouse Moon Gazer Amber Ale, Wolf Twenty 17, Woodfordes Wherry and Yetmans Red on handpump, and a dozen wines by the glass; complimentary sausage rolls and nibbles are on offer early on

Friday evening. Picnic-sets on the front grass look across to the church; at the back, stylish wicker tables and chairs on several decked areas are set among decorative box hedging. There's a self-catering cottage to rent.

 Excellent food uses produce grown or reared within ten miles of the pub and includes crispy pork fritters, pork terrine, apple mustard and puffed crackling, cured sea trout with cucumber, pear, sea trout tartar, horseradish buttermilk and dill, steak burger with toppings and burger sauce, truffle arancini with roast jerusalem artichoke and parmesan, cromer crab salad, gressingham duck breast with parsnip, rhubarb and dressed chicory, and puddings such as rum-soaked carrot cake with cream cheese frosting, orange and cinnamon and bittersweet chocolate parfait with peanut biscotti and marshmallow. *Benchmark main dish: free-range pork, confit belly and braised faggot £16.00. Two-course evening meal £22.00.*

Free house ~ Licensee Berni Morritt ~ Real ale ~ Open 12-11 (10.30 Sun) ~ Bar food 12-2, 6-9; 12-8.30 Sun ~ Children welcome ~ Dogs allowed in bar ~ Wi-fi ~ Bedrooms: /£130
Recommended by David Jackman, Barbara Brown, Peter and Emma Kelly, Dr Tony Whitehead, Roy Hoing, Revd Michael Vockins, Ian Herdman, Mr and Mrs Richard Osborne, Michael Sargent

WOLTERTON
Saracens Head 🍴 🛏

TG1732 Map 8

(01263) 768909 – www.saracenshead-norfolk.co.uk
Wolterton; Erpingham signed off A140 N of Aylsham, on through Calthorpe; NR11 7LZ

Remote inn with stylish bars and dining room and seats in courtyard; good bedrooms

While this civilised and friendly Georgian inn leans more towards dining, they do keep Woodfordes Wherry and a changing guest such as Panther Red Panther on handpump and several wines by the glass. The two-room bar is simple but stylish with high ceilings, light terracotta walls and tall windows with cream and gold curtains – all lending a feeling of space, though it's not large. There's a mix of seats from built-in wall settles to wicker fireside chairs, as well as log fires and flowers. The windows look on to a charming old-fashioned gravel stableyard with plenty of chairs, benches and tables. A pretty six-table parlour on the right has another big log fire. Bedrooms are comfortable and up to date.

 Food is imaginative and particularly good: ox tongue terrine with piccalilli, local crab and pink grapefruit salad with parmesan crisp, pea and mint ricotta cake with cherry tomato compote, grilled halibut and turbot on asparagus risotto with chive sauce, wild duck breast with braised red cabbage and apple, slow-roasted lamb shoulder with mash and green herb sauce, hake with parmesan and parsley crust and lemon sauce, sirloin steak with pink peppercorn sauce, and puddings; they also offer a two- and three-course set lunch (not Sun or Mon). *Benchmark main dish: duck breast with stir-fry of local shiitake mushrooms, peppers, ginger, chilli and soy £17.50. Two-course evening meal £22.00.*

Free house ~ Licensees Tim and Janie Elwes ~ Real ale ~ Open 11-3, 6-10.30; closed Sun evening in winter ~ Bar food 12-2, 6-8.30; 12.30-2.30, 6-8 Sun ~ Restaurant ~ Children welcome ~ Dogs allowed in bar and bedrooms ~ Wi-fi ~ Bedrooms: £75/£110 *Recommended by John Evans, David Jackman, Dr Tony Whitehead, John and Penny Wildon, Karl and Frieda Bujeya, Chloe and Tim Hodge*

'Children welcome' means the pub says it lets children inside without any special restriction. If it allows them in, but to restricted areas such as an eating area or family room, we specify this. Some pubs may impose an evening time limit. We do not mention limits after 9pm as we assume children are home by then.

WOODBASTWICK
Fur & Feather ◀

TG3214 Map 8

(01603) 720003 – www.thefurandfeather.co.uk

Off B1140 E of Norwich; NR13 6HQ

Full range of first class Woodfordes brewery ales, friendly service and popular bar food

This is a delightful pub in a lovely Estate village and as it's next door to Woodfordes brewery, the ales are perfectly kept. Tapped from the cask there's Bure Gold, Flagondry, Nelsons Revenge, Norfolk Nog, Reedlighter and Wherry. Efficient, helpful staff also serve a dozen wines by the glass and 12 malt whiskies. The style and atmosphere are not what you'd expect of a brewery tap – it's set out more like a comfortable and roomy dining pub with wooden chairs and tables on tiles or carpeting, plus sofas and armchairs; background music. There are seats and tables in the pleasant garden where they keep chickens. You can also visit the brewery shop.

Well regarded food includes ciabattas, twice-baked cheese and chive soufflé, pheasant and duck liver pâté with home-made piccalilli, beef or chicken burger with toppings, pickles, relish and sweet potato or chunky chips, sweet potato and butternut squash with pesto and parmesan, steak in ale pie, chicken stuffed with haggis in a creamy whisky sauce, pheasant two-ways with sauté cabbage, and puddings such as lemon posset with strawberry sorbet and double chocolate brownie with ice-cream. *Benchmark main dish: giant yorkshire pudding containing slow-braised steak in ale, mushrooms and onion gravy £11.95. Two-course evening meal £19.00.*

Woodfordes ~ Tenant Ian Cates ~ Real ale ~ Open 11-11 ~ Bar food 12-9 ~ Restaurant ~ Children welcome ~ Dogs allowed in bar ~ Wi-fi *Recommended by Christopher Maxse, Geoffrey Sutton, Roy Hoing, Beth Aldridge, Elise and Charles Mackinlay, Mark Morgan*

Also Worth a Visit in Norfolk

Besides the fully inspected pubs, you might like to try these pubs that have been recommended to us and described by readers. Do tell us what you think of them: feedback@goodguides.com

AYLMERTON TG1840
Roman Camp (01263) 838291
Holt Road (A148); NR11 8QD Large late 19th-c mock-Tudor roadside inn; comfortable panelled bar, cosy sitting room off with warm fire, and light airy dining room, decent choice of enjoyable sensibly priced food from sandwiches up, well kept Adnams, Greene King and a guest, friendly helpful service from uniformed staff; free wi-fi; children welcome, attractive sheltered garden behind with sunny terraces and pond, 15 bedrooms. *(Beth Aldridge)*

AYLSHAM TG1926
★**Black Boys** (01263) 732122
Market Place; off B1145; NR11 6EH Small friendly hotel with imposing Georgian façade and informal open-plan beamed bar,

popular generously served food from snacks up including good Sun roasts, various meal deals, Adnams, guest ales and decent wines, comfortable seating and plenty of tables on carpet or bare boards, helpful young uniformed staff coping well at busy times; children and dogs welcome, seats in front by marketplace, more behind, bedrooms, big cooked breakfast, open (and food) all day. *(Mrs Margo Finlay, Jörg Kasprowski)*

BANNINGHAM TG2129
★**Crown** (01263) 733534
Colby Road; opposite church by village green; NR11 7DY Welcoming 17th-c beamed pub in same family for over 25 years; good choice of popular food (they're helpful with gluten-free diets), well kept Greene King, local guest ales and decent wines, friendly efficient

We checked prices with the pubs as we went to press in summer 2017.
They should hold until around spring 2018.

service, log fires and woodburners; regular entertainment including comedy nights, TV, free wi-fi; children and dogs welcome, disabled access, open (and food) all day weekends. *(Peter and Emma Kelly)*

BARTON BENDISH TF7105
Berney Arms (01366) 347995
Off A1122 W of Swaffham; Church Road; PE33 9GF Attractive dining pub in quiet village; good freshly made food from pub favourites to more inventive dishes including good value set lunch, welcoming helpful staff, Adnams beers and several wines by the glass, afternoon teas, restaurant; children and dogs (in bar) welcome, nice garden with gazebos and unusual church-tower slide, good bedrooms in converted stables and forge (also two in main building), open all day from 8.30am for breakfast, food all day Sun. *(Sarah Flynn)*

BINHAM TF9839
Chequers (01328) 830297
B1388 SW of Blakeney; NR21 0AL Long low-beamed 17th-c local away from the bustle of the coastal pubs; comfortable bar with coal fires at each end, Adnams Southwold, Norfolk Brewhouse Moon Gazer Golden and guests, enjoyable pub food at reasonable prices, friendly staff; various games; children and dogs welcome, picnic-sets in front and on back grass, interesting village with huge priory church, open all day weekends. *(Roy Hoing)*

BLAKENEY TG0243
Kings Arms (01263) 740341
West Gate Street; NR25 7NQ A stroll from the harbour to this chatty 18th-c pub, three simple low-ceilinged connecting rooms and airy garden room, Adnams, Greene King, Morland and guests, generous wholesome food from breakfast on; children and dogs welcome, big garden, seven bedrooms, open (and food) all day from 9.30am (midday Sun). *(Mark Morgan)*

BLAKENEY TG0243
White Horse (01263) 740574
Off A149 W of Sheringham; High Street; NR25 7AL Friendly inn popular with locals and holidaymakers; long split-level carpeted bar with fine-art equestrian prints and paintings, high-backed brown leather dining and other chairs around light oak tables, Adnams ales and a dozen wines by the glass, well liked food including local fish/shellfish; wine tasting events; children and dogs welcome, wheelchair access to upper bar and dining conservatory only, seats in suntrap courtyard and pleasant paved garden, short stroll to harbour, bedrooms, open all day. *(Tony Scott)*

BLICKLING TG1728
Bucks Arms (01263) 732133
B1354 NW of Aylsham; NR11 6NF

Handsome Jacobean inn well placed by gates to Blickling Hall (NT); small proper bar, lounge set for eating with woodburner, smarter more formal dining room with another fire, Adnams and a guest, several wines by the glass and substantial helpings of enjoyable pub food, good friendly service; background music; children and dogs welcome, tables out on lawn, lovely walks nearby, three bedrooms, open all day (food all day Sun). *(John Wooll, Tom and Ruth Rees, Ian Herdman)*

BODHAM STREET TG1240
Red Hart (01263) 588270
The Street; NR25 6AD Old family-run village pub with well liked fairly traditional home-cooked food, ales including Woodfordes Wherry, efficient relaxed service; pool, sports TV, free wi-fi; children and dogs welcome (menus for both), open all day. *(Muriel and Spencer Harrop)*

BRAMERTON TG2905
Waters Edge (01508) 538005
Mill Hill, N of village, by river; NR14 7ED Clean modern pub-restaurant in great spot overlooking bend of River Yare; popular if not especially cheap food including daily specials (booking recommended in summer), ales such as Adnams and Woodfordes, plenty of wines by the glass including champagne, efficient friendly service; free wi-fi; children welcome, wheelchair access, picnic-sets on waterside deck, moorings, open all day in summer. *(Thomas Green)*

BRANCASTER TF7743
★ Ship (01485) 210333
London Street (A149); PE31 8AP Bustling roadside inn, part of the small Flying Kiwi chain; compact bar with built-in cushioned and planked wall seats, four well kept ales and nice wines by the glass from oak counter, several dining areas with woodburner in one and neatly log-piled fireplace in another, good modern food served by friendly helpful staff, contemporary paintwork throughout, pale settles and nice mix of other furniture on rugs and bare boards, bookcases, shipping memorabilia and lots of prints; background music, TV, daily papers; children and dogs welcome, gravelled seating area with circular picnic-sets out by car park, attractive well equipped bedrooms, open all day. *(Paulgermany, Tracey and Stephen Groves)*

BRANCASTER STAITHE TF7944
★ Jolly Sailors (01485) 210314
Main Road (A149); PE31 8BJ Unpretentious pub set in prime bird-watching territory on edge of NT dunes and salt flats; chatty mix of locals and visitors in simply furnished bars, wheelbacks, settles and cushioned benches around mix of tables on quarry tiles, photographs and local maps on the walls, woodburner,

their own Brancaster ales (brewery not on site) and guests, several wines by the glass, sizeable back dining room with popular food including pizzas (price reasonable for the area); children and dogs welcome, plenty of picnic-sets and play equipment in peaceful back garden, ice-cream hut in summer, vine-covered terrace, open all day (food all day in season). *(Derek and Sylvia Stephenson, Tracey and Stephen Groves, John Wooll)*

BRANCASTER STAITHE   TF8044

★**White Horse** (01485) 210262

A149 E of Hunstanton; PE31 8BY Popular restauranty place, but does have proper informal front bar serving own Brancaster ales and guests, lots of wines by the glass (including a local rosé) and good range of gins, log fire, pine furniture, historical photographs and bar billiards, middle part with comfortable sofas and newspapers, splendid views over tidal marshes from airy dining conservatory and new raised lounge, enjoyable bar and restaurant food including 'tapas' and plenty of fish, efficient attentive staff (may ask for a credit card if you run a tab); children welcome, dogs in bar, seats on sun deck taking in the view, more under cover on heated front terrace, nice bedrooms, coast path at bottom of garden, open (and food) all day. *(John Wooll, Tracey and Stephen Groves, Roy Hoing)*

BRISLEY   TF9521

Bell (01362) 668040

B1145; The Green; NR20 5DW Newly refurbished 17th-c pub in good spot on edge of sheep-grazed common (one of England's biggest); various areas ranging from cosy beamed snug with large open fire to airy garden room, well liked interesting food (not Sun evening) including set lunch, Adnams and local guests, nice wines and decent range of other drinks (norfolk whisky and gin), friendly efficient service; children and dogs welcome, terrace and good-sized garden (glamping planned), closed Mon, otherwise open all day. *(Lucy and Giles Gibbon)*

BROCKDISH   TM2179

Old Kings Head (01379) 668843

The Street; IP21 4JY Light and airy old pub at centre of village; several well kept changing ales including Adnams and Norfolk Brewhouse, decent wines by the glass and over 100 gins, enjoyable food with Italian slant including good pizzas, friendly helpful staff, L-shaped beamed bar with comfortable leather sofa, tub chairs, some scrubbed wooden tables and pews on bare boards, log fire, steps up to smaller seating area, café serving good coffee and cakes, local art for sale; live music nights; popular with Angles Way walkers, dogs welcome in the bar, a few tables out at the side, closed Mon, otherwise open (and food) all day, shuts 9pm Sun. *(Sheila Topham)*

BROOKE   TM2899

Kings Head (01508) 550335

Norwich Road (B1332); NR15 1AB Welcoming 17th-c village pub with enjoyable food from traditional choices up including regular themed evenings, four real ales and excellent choice of wines by the glass, maybe a Norfolk whisky, light and airy bare-boards bar with log fire, eating area up a step; occasional theatre nights and live music, free wi-fi; children welcome, tables in sheltered garden, open all day (from 9.30am weekends for breakfast). *(Mark Morgan)*

BROOME   TM3591

Artichoke (01986) 893325

Yarmouth Road; NR35 2NZ Unpretentious split-level roadside pub with up to ten well kept ales (some from tap room casks) including Adnams, belgian fruit beers and excellent selection of whiskies, good traditional home-made food in bar or dining room, friendly helpful staff, wood and flagstone floors, log fire in big fireplace; dogs welcome, garden picnic-sets, smokers' shelter, good walks nearby, closed Mon otherwise open all day. *(Claire Adams)*

BURNHAM MARKET   TF8342

Hoste (01328) 738777

The Green (B1155); PE31 8HD Stylish hotel's character front bar with informal chatty atmosphere, leather dining chairs, settles and armchairs (note the glass-topped suitcase table), wood-effect flooring, farming implements and cartoons on the walls, woodburner, Greene King and Woodfordes, 25 wines by the glass from extensive carefully chosen list and several malt whiskies, good if not cheap food including lunchtime sandwiches, courteous service, elegant dining areas, bustling conservatory and smart airy back restaurant, art gallery upstairs; children and dogs (in bar) welcome, attractive garden, luxurious bedrooms, open all day from 9am. *(Walter and Susan Rinaldi-Butcher)*

BURNHAM MARKET   TF8342

Nelson (01328) 738321

Creake Road; PE31 8EN Dining pub with nice food from sandwiches and pub favourites to more ambitious dishes in bar and restaurant, pleasant efficient staff, well kept Adnams Ghost Ship, Woodfordes Wherry and guests from pale wood servery, extensive wine list, L-shaped bar with leather sofas and armchairs, local artwork for sale; children and dogs welcome, terrace picnic-sets under parasols, four bedrooms (two in converted outbuilding), open all day. *(Tracey and Stephen Groves, Tony Scott)*

BURNHAM OVERY STAITHE   TF8444

★**Hero** (01328) 738334

Wells Road (A149); PE31 8JE Spacious recently refurbished roadside pub (sister to the Anchor at Morston – see Main Entries); nice variety of well liked often inventive food from sandwiches and snacks up (booking advised), three real ales such as Adnams and Grain, decent wines and good range of gins, friendly young staff, large bar and separate pitched-ceiling restaurant, woodburners; children and dogs welcome, terrace seating front and back, bedrooms, open all day from 9am. *(David Stewart)*

CHEDGRAVE   TM3699
White Horse (01508) 520250
Norwich Road; NR14 6ND Welcoming pub with Timothy Taylors Landlord and four other well kept ales, decent wines by the glass and good choice of popular sensibly priced food (all day Sun) including healthy options menu (pre-order) and themed nights, friendly attentive staff, log fire and sofas in bar, restaurant; live music, monthly quiz, beer festivals, pool and darts; children and dogs welcome, garden picnic-sets, open all day. *(Camilla and Jose Ferrara)*

CLEY-NEXT-THE-SEA   TG0443
★ George (01263) 740652
Off A149 W of Sheringham; High Street; NR25 7RN Large red-brick village inn overlooking the salt marshes; small carpeted front bar with long settle and sturdy dark wooden chairs, photographs of Norfolk wherries and other local scenes, Greene King, Woodfordes, Yetmans and a guest, 13 wines by the glass and well liked locally sourced food (good fish and chips), candlelit dining rooms, good cheerful service; newspapers and free wi fi; children and dogs (in bar) welcome, tables in little garden across lane, comfortable bedrooms, open all day, food all day summer. *(Lionel Smith, Dr Simon Innes, Carol and Barry Craddock, Peter and Anne Hollindale, Denis and Margaret Kilner)*

COCKLEY CLEY   TF7904
Twenty Churchwardens (01760)
721439 *Off A1065 S of Swaffham; PE37 8AN* Informal pub in converted school next to church, three linked beamed rooms, good open fire, decent well-priced food including nice home-made pies, well kept Adnams Southwold; newspapers, second-hand books for sale, no credit cards; children and dogs (particularly) welcome, tiny unspoilt village. *(Mark and Sarah Abbot)*

COLKIRK   TF9226
Crown (01328) 853028
Village signposted off B1146 S of Fakenham, and off A1065; Crown Road; NR21 7AA Friendly red-brick local under new management; bar and left-hand dining room, log fires, Greene King IPA and Abbot plus a guest like Timothy Taylors Landlord, generous helpings of good value pubby food (not Sun evening, Mon, Tues); quiz nights, pool; children and dogs (in bar)

welcome, suntrap terrace and pleasant garden, open all day. *(Edward Barnaby)*

COLTISHALL   TG2719
Kings Head (01603) 737426
Wroxham Road (B1354); NR12 7EA Dining pub close to River Bure and moorings, imaginative food from owner-chef (especially fish/seafood), also bar snacks, lunchtime set menu and children's choices, well kept Adnams and good wines by the glass, open fire, fishing nets and stuffed fish including a monster pike; background music; seats outside (noisy road), four bedrooms, open (and food) all day Sun. *(Claire Adams)*

CONGHAM   TF7123
Anvil (01485) 600625
St Andrews Lane; PE32 1DU Tucked-away modern country pub with welcoming licensees, wide choice of generously served home-made food (smaller helpings available) including good value Sun carvery, quick friendly service, three or more well kept ales (at least one local); live music and quiz nights; children welcome, picnic-sets in small walled front garden, campsite, open all day weekends, closed Mon Oct-Apr. *(Alison and Graeme Spicer)*

CROMER   TG2242
Red Lion (01263) 514964
Off A149; Tucker Street/Brook Street; NR27 9HD Substantial refurbished Victorian hotel with elevated sea views, original features including panelling and open fires, five well kept ales such as Woodfordes in bare-boards flint-walled bar, good food from sandwiches and platters up including daily specials, efficient friendly service, restaurant and conservatory; background music; children and dogs welcome, disabled facilities, tables in back courtyard, 14 bedrooms, open all day. *(Anne Evans)*

DEREHAM   TF9813
George (01362) 696801
Swaffham Road; NR19 2AZ Welcoming 18th-c inn-restaurant with enjoyable generously served food at fair prices, Fri steak night and some themed evenings, Adnams and Woodfordes ales, friendly helpful staff, panelled interior with decent sized bar, dining room and conservatory; children and dogs welcome, heated terrace, six bedrooms (two in annexe), open all day. *(Tony and Wendy Hobden)*

DERSINGHAM   TF6930
Feathers (01485) 540768
B1440 towards Sandringham; Manor Road; PE31 6LN Refurbished Jacobean carrstone inn once part of the Sandringham Estate; two adjoining bars (main one with big open fire), well kept Adnams, Woodfordes and a guest, enjoyable good value food including OAP lunch deal Mon-Fri, welcoming helpful

service, back dining room, function room in converted stables; background music; children and dogs welcome, large garden with play area, six bedrooms, open all day, food all day weekends. *(John Wooll, Tracey and Stephen Groves)*

EAST RUDHAM   TF8228

★**Crown** (01485) 528530

A148 W of Fakenham; The Green; PE31 8RD Civilised open-plan beamed pub with log fire at each end of main bar, brown leather dining chairs around mixed tables on rugs and stripped boards, bookshelves and a grandfather clock, pubbier part with built-in cushioned seats and high chairs against slate-topped counter, well kept Adnams, Black Sheep, Woodfordes and a guest, 20 wines by the glass and enjoyable up-to-date food at fair prices, friendly service, also snug lower area with comfortable seating and upstairs pitched-roof dining room; TV, free wi-fi; children and dogs welcome, picnic-sets under parasols on front gravelled terrace, bedrooms, open all day, food all day Sun. *(Tom Stone, Margaret McDonald, Tony Scott, Freddie and Sarah Banks, Monica and Steph Evans)*

EAST WINCH   TF6916

Carpenters Arms (01553) 841228

A47 Lynn Road; PE32 1NP Useful roadside pub with good value home-made food including daily specials in bar or separate restaurant, several beers and ciders; quiz night third Thurs of month, free wi-fi; children welcome, no dogs inside, open (and food) all day. *(Claire Adams)*

EDGEFIELD   TG0934

★**Pigs** (01263) 587634

Norwich Road; B1149 S of Holt; NR24 2RL Friendly bustling pub with carpeted bar, Adnams, Greene King, Woodfordes and a house beer from Wolf tapped from casks, arches through to simply furnished area with mixed chairs and pews on broad pine boards, airy dining extension in similar style split into stalls by standing timbers and low brick walls, nice variety of well priced food (all day Sun) including Norfolk tapas, good service, games room with bar billiards, also children's playroom; background music; dogs allowed in bar, good wheelchair access, rustic furniture on big covered front terrace, adventure playground, boules, ten bedrooms (seven with spa facilities including sauna and outside bath), open all day from 8am (breakfast for non-residents). *(Tracey and Stephen Groves, Alan McQuilan)*

ELSING   TG0516

Mermaid (01362) 637640

Church Road; NR20 3EA Welcoming 17th-c pub in quiet little village, L-shaped carpeted bar with woodburner, well kept Adnams, Woodfordes and guests tapped from the cask, enjoyable home-made food

including range of pies and suet puddings (signature steak and kidney roly-poly), indian and thai curries also available, friendly helpful service; pool and other games such as dominoes and shut the box, free wi-fi; children and dogs welcome, handy for walkers on Wensum Way, nice garden, 14th-c church opposite with interesting brasses, closed Mon lunchtime. *(Andrew Bebbington)*

GAYTON   TF7219

Crown (01553) 636252

Lynn Road (B1145/B1153); opposite church; PE32 1PA Low-beamed village pub with plenty of character, three main areas and a charming snug, reasonable value food including buffet lunch (Mon-Sat) and carvery (Tues-Fri evenings, all day Sun), well kept Greene King ales, sofas and good log fire, games room; children welcome in restaurant, dogs in bar, disabled access, attractive sheltered garden, four bedrooms, open (and food) all day. *(Mark Morgan)*

GREAT BIRCHAM   TF7632

Kings Head (01485) 578265

B1155, S end of village (called and signed Bircham locally); PE31 6RJ Handsome Edwardian hotel with cheerful little bar, comfortable sofas, tub chairs and log fire, four local ales such as Norfolk Moongazer and Woodfordes, good range of wines, whiskies and over 80 gins, lounge areas and airy modern restaurant with enjoyable varied choice of food, friendly helpful staff; background music, free wi-fi; children and dogs welcome, tables out at front and in back garden with nice country views, 12 comfortable bedrooms, open all day, food all day summer school holidays. *(Donald Allsopp, Julie Swift)*

GREAT CRESSINGHAM   TF8401

★**Windmill** (01760) 756232

Village signed off A1065 S of Swaffham; Water End; IP25 6NN Shuttered red-brick pub with interesting pictures and bric-a-brac in warren of rambling linked rooms, plenty of cosy corners, wide range of bar food from baguettes to chargrills, half a dozen ales including Adnams, Greene King, a house beer (Windy Miller) brewed by Purity and two guests, good choice of wines by the glass, 60 malt whiskies and decent coffee, friendly efficient staff, games room with pool and other pub games; background music, big sports TV in side snug; children and dogs welcome, large garden with picnic-sets and good play area, caravan parking, bedrooms, open all day. *(Paul Rampton, Julie Harding)*

GREAT HOCKHAM   TL9592

Eagle (01953) 498893

Harling Road; IP24 1NP Friendly 19th-c red-brick corner local, half a dozen well kept ales including Adnams, Greene King and Woodfordes, pubby food all day Fri, Sat and till 6pm Sun, just lunchtime snacks other days; fortnightly quiz Weds, pool, darts, free wi-fi; children and dogs welcome, open all day weekends. *(Alison and Graeme Spicer)*

HARPLEY   TF7825
Rose & Crown (01485) 521807
Off A148 Fakenham–King's Lynn; Nethergate Street; PE31 6TW Friendly old village pub competently run by welcoming licensees, good generously served home-made food including popular Sun roasts, well kept Woodfordes Wherry and guests, Aspall's cider, modernised interior with open fires; children and dogs welcome, garden picnic-sets, closed Sun evening, Mon and lunchtime Tues. *(John Wooll)*

HEYDON   TG1127
★ **Earle Arms** (01263) 587376
Off B1149; NR11 6AD Popular old dutch-gabled pub overlooking green and church in delightfully unspoilt Estate village; well kept Adnams, Woodfordes and a guest, food from varied if not extensive menu using local fish and meat (gluten-free choices marked), decent wine list, racing prints, some stuffed animals and good log fire in old-fashioned candlelit bar, more formal dining room; free wi-fi; children and dogs welcome, picnic-sets in small cottagey back garden, open all day Sun (no evening food then), closed Mon. *(Thomas Green)*

HICKLING   TG4123
Greyhound (01692) 598306
The Green; NR12 0YA Small popular village pub with welcoming open fire, good choice of enjoyable pubby food in bar and neat restaurant, well kept local ales and ciders, friendly long-serving landlord; well behaved children and dogs welcome, seats out at front and in pretty back garden with terrace, handy for nature reserve. *(Roy Hoing)*

HILBOROUGH   TF8200
Swan (01760) 756380
Brandon Road (A1065); IP26 5BW Welcoming early 18th-c pub with good quality home-made food including interesting blackboard specials, Sun carvery, up to four well kept beers and good value wine list, pleasant helpful staff, small back restaurant; free wi-fi; children and dogs (in bar) welcome, picnic-sets on sheltered lawn, eight bedrooms, open all day, food all day Fri-Sun. *(Guy Smith)*

HINGHAM   TG0202
White Hart (01953) 850214
Market Place, just off B1108 W of Norwich; NR9 4AF Georgian-fronted coaching inn with character rooms arranged over two floors; beams and standing timbers,

stripped floorboards with oriental rugs, mix of furniture including comfortable sofas in quiet corners, lots of prints and photographs, woodburners, galleried long room up steps from main bar with egyptian frieze, upstairs dining/function room, good choice of enjoyable food including british tapas, four real ales, lots of wines by the glass and cocktails; background music, bar billiards; children welcome, dogs downstairs, modern benches and seats in gravelled courtyard, pretty village with huge 14th-c church, five newly refurbished bedrooms, open all day, food all day Sat and Sun. *(Peter and Emma Kelly, Mark Morgan)*

HOLME-NEXT-THE-SEA   TF7043
White Horse (01485) 525512
Kirkgate Street; PE36 6LH Attractive old-fashioned place, cosy and rambling, with warm log fires, ample choice of enjoyable fair-priced food including local fish, friendly efficient service, Adnams, Greene King and decent wines, side extension; children and dogs welcome, small back garden, more seats out in front and on lawn opposite, play area, open all day. *(Katherine and Hugh Markham)*

HOLT   TG0738
Feathers (01263) 712318
Market Place; NR25 6BW Relaxed hotel with popular locals' bar comfortably extended around original panelled area, open fire, antiques in attractive entrance/reception area, good choice of enjoyable fairly priced food including blackboard specials, friendly accommodating service, Greene King ales and decent wines, good coffee, restaurant and dining conservatory; background music; children welcome, no dogs, 13 comfortable bedrooms, open all day. *(John Evans)*

HONINGHAM   TG1011
Buck (01603) 880393
Just off A47 W of Norwich; The Street; NR9 5BL Picturesque 16th-c pub with smartly renovated interior, beamed and timbered bar with flagstones and inglenook woodburner, Lacons beers and plenty of wines by the glass including champagne, very good imaginative food from unusual snacks up, friendly attentive service, comfortable restaurant with upholstered chairs and banquettes; seats on sheltered lawn, eight clean modern bedrooms in converted outbuildings, open all day, food all day Sun till 7pm. *(Chris and Diana Aylott)*

HORSEY   TG4622
★ **Nelson Head** (01493) 393378
Off B1159; The Street; NR29 4AD Unspoilt nicely tucked-away red-brick country pub, impressive range of beers (some direct from the cask) as well as ciders, good

---

If you report on a pub that's not a featured entry, please tell us any lunchtimes or evenings when it doesn't serve bar food.

sensibly priced bar food (not Sun evening in winter) from sandwiches and snacks to daily specials, friendly chatty staff, good log fire and lots of interesting bric-a-brac including various guns, small side dining room; quiet background music; children welcome, well behaved dogs in bar, outside seating including some in field opposite, good coast walks (seals), open all day. *(Beth Aldridge)*

HORSTEAD   TG2619
Recruiting Sergeant (01603) 737077
B1150 just S of Coltishall; NR12 7EE
Light, airy and spacious roadside pub, enjoyable generously served food from fresh wraps and jacket potatoes up including good fish choice (booking recommended), efficient friendly service, up to half a dozen changing ales such as Adnams, Greene King, Timothy Taylors and Woodfordes, plenty of wines by the glass, big open fire; children welcome, terrace and garden tables, variety of local walks, bedrooms, open all day. *(Lucy and Giles Gibbon)*

INGHAM   TG3926
★**Swan** (01692) 581099
Off A149 SE of North Walsham; signed from Stalham; NR12 9AB Smart 14th-c thatched dining pub nicely placed for the Broads and coast; rustic main area divided by massive chimneybreast with woodburner on each side, low beams and hefty standing timbers, bare boards or parquet, some old farm tools, quieter small brick-floored part with leather sofas, very good well presented restaurant-style food including set menus, seasonal ingredients from own farm, well kept Woodfordes, local cider and good selection of wines, friendly service; children welcome, picnic-sets on sunny back terrace, more at side, four comfortable bedrooms in converted stables, good breakfast. *(Camilla and Jose Ferrara)*

ITTERINGHAM   TG1430
★**Walpole Arms** (01263) 587258
Village signposted off B1354 NW of Aylsham; NR11 7AR Beamed 18th-c pub close to Blickling Hall (NT); good modern cooking using fresh local ingredients (some from own farm) along with more traditional choices, efficient friendly service, well kept Adnams, Woodfordes and nice wines by the glass, sizeable open-plan bar with woodburner, stripped-brick walls and dark wood dining tables on red carpet, light airy restaurant opening on to vine-covered terrace; jazz nights and Weds quiz; children welcome, dogs in bar, two-acre landscaped garden, open all day Sat, closed Sun evening. *(Alan and Angela Scouller)*

KENNINGHALL   TM0485
Red Lion (01953) 887849
B1113 S of Norwich; East Church Street; NR16 2EP 16th-c pub with stripped beams, bare boards and old floor tiles,

decent home-made food from baguettes and baked potatoes up, Sun brunch, well kept Greene King IPA, Woodfordes Wherry and guests, friendly helpful staff, bar with woodburner, cosy panelled snug and back restaurant; regular live music and quiz nights, free wi-fi; children (not in bar) and dogs welcome, tables out by back bowling green, bedrooms in former stable block, open all day Fri-Sun. *(Mike and Sarah Abbot)*

KING'S LYNN   TF6120
Crown & Mitre (01553) 774669
Ferry Street; PE30 1LJ Old-fashioned unchanging pub in great riverside spot, lots of interesting naval and nautical memorabilia, up to six well kept ales (the long-serving landlord still hopes to brew his own), good value straightforward home-made food, river-view back conservatory; no credit cards; well behaved children and dogs allowed, quayside tables. *(John Wooll)*

KING'S LYNN   TF6119
Marriotts Warehouse (01553) 818500 *South Quay; PE30 5DT*
Bar-restaurant-café in converted 16th-c brick and stone warehouse; well priced food from lunchtime sandwiches and light dishes up (greater evening choice), good range of wines, beers such as Sharps Doom Bar and Woodfordes Wherry, cocktails, small upstairs bar with river views; children welcome, quayside tables, open all day from 10am. *(Max and Steph Warren)*

LESSINGHAM   TG3928
Star (01692) 580510
School Road; NR12 0DN Popular little village pub with low ceilings and inglenook woodburner, local ales and ample helpings of enjoyable unpretentious food, warm friendly service, side restaurant; children and dogs welcome, good-sized garden, two bedrooms in back block, closed Mon, no food Sun evening. *(Roy Hoing)*

LETHERINGSETT   TG0638
Kings Head (01263) 712691
A148 (Holt Road) W of Holt; NR25 7AR Country house-style dining inn now under same ownership as the Jolly Sailors in Brancaster; rugs on quarry tiles, hunting/ coaching prints and open fires, own Brancaster beer along with Norfolk Moongazer and Woodfordes, food from sandwiches and pubby dishes up can be good, part skylit bare-boards dining room with built-in wall seating, farm tools on cream-painted flint and cob walls, back area under partly pitched ceiling with painted rafters; background music, sports TV, free wi-fi; children and dogs welcome, picnic-sets out at front and in big garden with play area, four bedrooms, open (and food) all day. *(Gordon and Margaret Ormondroyd, David Jackman, Charles Gysin, Denis and Margaret Kilner)*

LYNG   TG0617
Fox (01603) 872316
The Street; NR9 5AL Old beamed village
pub with several refurbished linked areas
and separate restaurant, ample helpings
of good inexpensive home-made food (not
Mon), Tues steak night and midweek two-
course lunch deal, ales such as Adnams and
Woodfordes, friendly staff; pool and giant
chessboard in one part; children and dogs
(in front bar) welcome, enclosed garden
with view of church, open all day in summer
apart from Mon lunchtime. *(Claire Adams)*

MARSHAM   TG1924
Plough (01263) 735000
Old Norwich Road; NR10 5PS Welcoming
18th-c inn with split-level open-plan
bar, enjoyable food using local produce
(special diets catered for) including good
value set lunch, Adnams Southwold and
a couple of local guests, friendly helpful
staff; free wi-fi; children welcome, dogs
in garden only, comfortable bedrooms,
open all day. *(Mark Morgan)*

MUNDFORD   TL8093
Crown (01842) 878233
*Off A1065 Thetford–Swaffham; Crown
Road; IP26 5HQ* Unassuming 17th-c
pub with heavy beams, huge fireplace and
interesting local memorabilia, Courage
Directors and one or two guests, over 50
malt whiskies, enjoyable generously served
food at sensible prices, friendly staff, spiral
iron stairs to two restaurant areas (larger
one has separate entrance accessible to
wheelchairs), locals' bar with sports TV;
children and dogs welcome, back terrace and
garden with wishing well, Harley-Davidson
meeting first Sun of month, bedrooms (some
in adjoining building), also self-catering
accommodation, open all day. *(Claire Adams)*

NEW BUCKENHAM   TM0890
Inn on the Green (01953) 860172
Chapel Street; NR16 2BB Modern
renovation of late Victorian red-brick
pub by little green close to the Kings
Head; good freshly prepared food from
pub favourites to more restaurranty dishes
including blackboard specials, Adnams
and Woodfordes, good selection of wines,
pleasant efficient staff; quiz second Thurs of
month; children (away from bar) and dogs
(in bar) welcome, terrace tables, handy for
Banham Zoo, closed Mon. *(Monty Green)*

NEW BUCKENHAM   TM0890
Kings Head (01953) 861247
Market Place; NR16 2AN Family-run
17th-c pub by small green opposite medieval
market cross, ales such as Adnams Southwold
and generous helpings of reasonably priced

pubby food, helpful service, modern open-
plan bar with beams and inglenook, big back
dining area; pool, free wi-fi; five bedrooms,
open all day. *(Monty Green)*

NORTH TUDDENHAM   TG0413
Lodge (01362) 638466
Off A47; NR20 3DJ Modernised dining
pub with good sensibly priced food from
traditional choices up including burger menu
and daily specials, local beers (just one in
winter) such as Woodfordes Reedlighter,
friendly attentive service; monthly quiz;
children and dogs (in bar) welcome,
tables outside (some on deck), closed Sun
evening and Mon, otherwise open (and
food) all day. *(Tony and Wendy Hobden)*

NORTHREPPS   TG2439
Foundry Arms (01263) 579256
Church Street; NR27 0AA Welcoming
village pub with good reasonably priced
traditional food (not Sun evening) from
generous sandwiches up, well kept
Woodfordes Wherry and a couple of guests,
decent choice of wines, good friendly
service, woodburner, smallish comfortable
restaurant; pool and darts in separate area;
children and dogs welcome, picnic-sets in
back garden, open all day. *(Lana Wood,
Peter and Anne Hollindale)*

NORWICH   TG2309
Adam & Eve (01603) 667423
*Bishopgate; follow Palace Street from
Tombland, N of cathedral; NR3 1RZ*
Ancient pub dating from at least 1240 when
used by workmen building the cathedral,
has a Saxon well beneath the lower bar
floor and striking dutch gables (added in
14th and 15th c); old-fashioned small bars
with tiled or parquet floors, cushioned
benches built into partly panelled walls and
some antique high-backed settles, three
ales including Adnams and Theakstons Old
Peculier, Aspall's cider and around 40 malt
whiskies, traditional pubby food (not Sun
evening), friendly service; background music;
children allowed in snug till 7pm, no dogs
inside, picnic-sets out among pretty tubs
and hanging baskets, open all day, closed
25, 26 Dec, 1 Jan. *(Peter and Emma Kelly)*

NORWICH   TG2408
Coach & Horses (01603) 477077
Thorpe Road; NR1 1BA Light and
airy tap for Chalk Hill brewery (tours
available), friendly staff, standard food
from baguettes and panini up, lunch deals
and Sat brunch, L-shaped bare-boards
bar with open fire, pleasant back dining
area; sports TVs, gets very busy on home
match days; disabled access possible
(not to lavatories), front terrace, open
all day. *(Alison and Graeme Spicer)*

NORWICH   TG2210

Duke of Wellington (01603) 441182

Waterloo Road; NR3 1EG Rambling corner local with huge range of well kept quickly changing ales including Fullers, Oakham and Wolf, many served from tap-room casks, foreign bottled beers too, no food apart from sausage rolls and pies (can bring your own) and weekend summer barbecue, real fire; live music and quiz nights, traditional games, free wi-fi; well behaved dogs welcome, nice back terrace (Aug beer festival), open all day. *(Lucy and Giles Gibbon)*

NORWICH   TG2308

Edith Cavell (01603) 765813

Tombland/Princes Street; NR3 1HF Corner pub-restaurant named after the gallant World War I Norfolk nurse; popular fairly priced food from sandwiches to good steaks cooked on hot rocks, three real ales including a house beer from Wolf, friendly helpful service, smallish bar, upstairs restaurant (and loos); diagonally across from Erpingham Gate into cathedral green, open all day (till 1am Fri, Sat). *(John Wooll)*

NORWICH   TG2408

Fat Cat & Canary (01603) 436925

Thorpe Road; NR1 1TR Newest of this Norwich brewer's three pubs, their well kept beers and several guests, real ciders and good range of other drinks, some snacky food, traditional interior with black and white floor tiles, friendly atmosphere; quiz and music nights; sheltered seating area outside, open all day. *(Muriel and Spencer Harrop)*

NORWICH   TG2310

Fat Cat Tap (01603) 413153

Lawson Road; NR3 4LF 1970s shed-like building home to the Fat Cat brewery and sister pub to the Fat Cat (see Main Entries) and Fat Cat & Canary; their beers and up to 12 guests along with draught continentals, lots of bottled beers and eight or more local ciders/perries, no food apart from rolls, pork pies and cheeseboards; regular live music; children (till 6pm) and dogs welcome, seats out front and back, open all day. *(Mark Morgan)*

NORWICH   TG2309

★ Kings Head (01603) 620468

Magdalen Street; NR3 1JE Traditional Victorian local with good friendly atmosphere in two simply furnished bare-boards bars (front one is tiny), a dozen very well kept changing regional ales, good choice of imported beers and a local cider, no food except pork pies; bar billiards in

back bar, free wi-fi; dogs welcome, open all day. *(Tracey and Stephen Groves)*

NORWICH   TG2208

Plough (01603) 661384

St Benedicts Street; NR2 4AR Little city-centre pub owned by Grain, their ales and guests kept well, good wines and cocktails, food limited to sausage pie, cheeseboards and summer barbecues, simply updated split-level interior with bare boards and open fire; background music; good spacious beer garden behind, open all day. *(Mark Morgan)*

NORWICH   TG2308

Ribs of Beef (01603) 619517

Wensum Street, S side of Fye Bridge; NR3 1HY Welcoming and comfortable riverside pub, nine real ales including Oakham, four traditional ciders and good wine choice, deep leather sofas and small tables upstairs, attractive smaller downstairs room with river view, generous well priced lunchtime food (till 5pm weekends), quick cheerful service; Sun live music; children welcome, seats out on narrow waterside terrace, open all day. *(John Wooll)*

NORWICH   TG2308

St Andrews Brew House (01603)

305995 *St Andrews Street; NR2 4TP* Interesting place visibly brewing its own good beers (also plenty of guest ales, craft kegs and bottled beers), utilitarian bare-boards interior with exposed ducting, rough masonry walls and eclectic mix of seating including some button-back booths, popular sensibly priced food from british tapas and sharing boards up, busy efficient staff, upstairs function room; background music, sports TV, Tues quiz and occasional comedy nights; children welcome, pavement tables, open all day, breakfast from 8am Mon-Fri. *(Tracey and Stephen Groves)*

NORWICH   TG2309

Wig & Pen (01603) 625891

St Martins Palace Plain; NR3 1RN Popular 17th-c beamed pub opposite cathedral close; good value food from sandwiches up, prompt friendly service, six ales including Adnams, Humpty Dumpty and Woodfordes, well priced wines; background music, sports TVs, spring beer festival; metal café-style furniture out at front, open all day (till 6.30pm Sun). *(Mark Morgan)*

OLD HUNSTANTON   TF6842

Lodge (01485) 532896

Old Hunstanton Road (A149); PE36 6HX Old red-brick roadside pub with clean contemporary décor, popular food in bar or

---

Anyone claiming to arrange, or prevent, inclusion of a pub in the *Guide* is a fraud. Pubs are included only if recommended by readers and if our own anonymous inspection confirms that they are suitable.

restaurant from pizzas and pub favourites up, well kept local beers such as Woodfordes Wherry and good choice of wines by the glass, friendly helpful staff, plenty of seating on wood floors including booths and sofas by woodburner; sports TV, occasional live music; children and dogs (in bar) welcome, tables on covered terrace and small lawn, 16 good bedrooms, open all day. *(Jim Taylor)*

OVERSTRAND   TG2440
Sea Marge (01263) 579579
High Street; NR27 0AB Substantial half-timbered sea-view hotel (former Edwardian country house) with separate entrance to spacious bar, enjoyable food from ciabattas to local seafood including weekday deal till 6pm on some main courses, real ales and decent wines by the glass, panelled restaurant with more upmarket menu; children welcome, dogs in some areas, five-acre grounds with terraced lawns down to clifftop and steep steps to coast path and beach, 26 comfortable bedrooms, open (and bar food) all day. *(David Jackman)*

OVERSTRAND   TG2440
White Horse (01263) 579237
High Street; NR27 0AB Comfortably modernised red-brick pub with good choice of well liked food in bar, dining room or barn restaurant (also used for functions), up to five well kept regional ales, friendly attentive staff, pool room; background music, silent sports TV; children and dogs welcome, picnic-sets in front, more in garden behind with play equipment (may be bouncy castle), short walk to beach, eight bedrooms, open all day from 8am. *(David Jackman)*

RINGSTEAD   TF7040
★Gin Trap (01485) 525264
Village signed off A149 near Hunstanton; OS Sheet 132 map reference 707403; PE36 5JU Attractive 17th-c coaching inn doing well under present management; original beamed bar with woodburner, farmhouse and mate's chairs around solid pine tables on bare boards, yellow tartan window seats, pub photos on walls, horse tack and coach lamps, Adnams, Woodfordes and a guest, several wines by the glass and around 30 gins, decent choice of popular food served by friendly staff; step up to quarry-tiled room with conservatory beyond, character back snug with red painted walls and nice old floor tiles; children and dogs (in bar) welcome, picnic-sets and play area in back garden, more seats out in front, handy for Peddars Way, comfortable well equipped bedrooms, open all day in summer (can get very busy), closed winter afternoons.
(Tracey and Stephen Groves, Philip and Susan Philcox, Cynthia Armitage, O.Thompson, Lisa Walker, Katherine and Hugh Markham)

ROYDON   TF7022
Three Horseshoes (01485) 600666
The one near King's Lynn; Lynn Road; PE32 1AQ Refurbished brick and stone village pub under same ownership as nearby Congham Hall Hotel; pleasant pastel décor with simple wood furniture, stone-floor bar and split-level part-carpeted restaurant, woodburner in each, decent uncomplicated food (all day Sun) from reasonably priced blackboard menu, weekday OAP lunch deal, three real ales including Greene King IPA, friendly helpful staff; children and dogs (in bar) welcome, tables outside, closed Mon, Tues, otherwise open all day. *(Max and Steph Warren)*

SCULTHORPE   TF8930
★Sculthorpe Mill (01328) 856161
Inn signed off A148 W of Fakenham, opposite village; NR21 9QG Welcoming dining pub in rebuilt 18th-c mill, appealing riverside setting with seats out under weeping willows and in attractive garden behind; light, airy and relaxed with leather sofas and sturdy tables in bar/dining area, good reasonably priced food from sandwiches to daily specials, attentive service, Greene King ales and good house wines, upstairs restaurant; background music, free wi-fi; six comfortable bedrooms, open all day in summer (all day weekends in winter). *(Camilla and Jose Ferrara)*

SEDGEFORD   TF7036
King William IV (01485) 571765
B1454, off A149 Kings Lynn–Hunstanton; PE36 5LU Homely inn handy for beaches and bird-watching; bar and dining areas decorated with paintings of north Norfolk coast and migrating birds, high-backed dark leather dining chairs around pine tables on slate tiles, log fires, Adnams, Greene King and Woodfordes, ten wines by the glass, straightforward food; magazines and daily papers; children welcome (no under-4s in main restaurant after 6.30pm), dogs allowed in bar and a couple of the bedrooms, seats on terrace and under parasols on grass, also an attractive covered dining area surrounded by flowering tubs, closed Mon lunchtime, otherwise open all day. *(Roy Hoing, Tracey and Stephen Groves)*

SHERINGHAM   TG1543
Lobster (01263) 822716
High Street; NR26 8JP Almost on seafront and popular with locals and tourists, friendly panelled bar with log fire and seafaring décor, wide range of ales including Adnams, Greene King and Woodfordes, two or three ciders and decent wines by the glass, generous reasonably priced bar food from good sandwiches up, restaurant with seasonal seafood including lobster and crab; some live music; children and dogs welcome, two courtyards, open all day. *(Dr J Barrie Jones)*

SMALLBURGH   TG3324
Crown (01692) 536314
A149 Yarmouth Road; NR12 9AD
Character thatched and beamed village inn
dating from the 15th c; well kept Adnams,
Fullers, Timothy Taylors, Woodfordes
and a guest, enjoyable home-made food
including blackboard specials and regular
african themed nights (friendly landlady
is from the Ivory Coast), can eat in log-fire
bar or small dining room; monthly quiz,
occasional live music, darts; children and
dogs welcome, picnic-sets in pretty back
garden, Aug anglo-african festival, two
bedrooms, open all day. *(Monty Green)*

SOUTH LOPHAM   TM0481
White Horse (01379) 688579
*A1066 Diss–Thetford; The Street;
IP22 2LH* Popular beamed village pub
with well kept Adnams, Woodfordes and an
occasional guest, enjoyable home-made food
including vegetarian options and blackboard
specials, log fires; live music, karaoke and
quiz nights, TV; children welcome, big garden
with play area, handy for Bressingham
Gardens, open all day. *(Beth Aldridge)*

SOUTH WALSHAM   TG3613
Ship (01603) 270049
The Street (B1140); NR13 6DQ
Modernised village pub under newish
management; enjoyable home-made food
(all day Sun till 7.30pm) from sandwiches/
wraps and traditional choices up, efficient
friendly service, well kept ales such as
Green Jack, stripped bricks and beams,
restaurant; children welcome, tables on
front elevated terrace and on tiered back
one, open all day. *(Revd Carol Avery)*

SOUTHREPPS   TG2536
★Vernon Arms (01263) 833355
Church Street; NR11 8NP Popular
old-fashioned brick and cobble village pub,
welcoming and relaxed, with good home-
made food (booking advised), takeaway
fish and chips (Tues-Fri evenings), friendly
helpful staff, well kept Adnams, Greene
King, Woodfordes and a guest, good choice
of wines and malt whiskies, big log fire;
darts and pool, occasional live music;
tables outside, children, dogs and muddy
walkers welcome, open all day, no evening
food Sun or Mon. *(Dr Tony Whitehead)*

SPORLE   TF8411
Peddars Inn (01760) 788101
The Street; PE32 2DR Welcoming
beamed pub with inglenook bar, dining
room and little conservatory, good sensibly
priced food from traditional favourites to
specials, themed nights, well kept Adnams
and a couple of local guests, Aspall's cider,
friendly service; occasional live music
and charity quiz nights; children and dogs
welcome, a few seats outside on grass,
well placed for Peddars Way walkers, open
all day Sat, closed Sun evening, Mon and
lunchtime Tues. *(Philip and Susan Philcox)*

STANHOE   TF8037
★Duck (01485) 518330
*B1155 Docking–Burnham Market;
PE31 8QD* Smart pub with emphasis on
good imaginative food; little entrance bar
with cushioned Edwardian-style chairs
around wooden tables on dark slate floor,
stools against fine slab-topped counter
serving Adnams Ghost Ship, Elgoods
Cambridge and a dozen wines by the glass,
woodburner in small area off, two dining
rooms with scatter-cushion wall seats,
scrubbed tables and local seascapes; free
wi-fi; children and dogs (in bar) welcome,
good disabled access/loo, tables out on
front gravel and under fruit tree in small
garden, there's also a garden room with
fairy lights and candles, comfortable well
appointed bedrooms, good breakfast,
open all day, food all day Sun. *(Tracey and
Stephen Groves, Ian Duncan, Sarah Flynn)*

STOW BARDOLPH   TF6205
Hare Arms (01366) 382229
*Just off A10 N of Downham Market;
PE34 3HT* Cheerful bustling village pub
under long-serving licensees; bar with
traditional pub furnishings and interesting
bric-a-brac, log fire, Greene King ales
and a couple of well kept guests, nine
wines by glass and several malt whiskies,
good value generous food (all day Sun),
two refurbished dining rooms and family
conservatory, pub cats; children welcome
in some parts, no dogs inside, plenty of
seats in front and back gardens, maybe
wandering peacocks, Church Farm Rare
Breeds Centre nearby, open (and food) all
day weekends. *(Tracey and Stephen Groves)*

SURLINGHAM   TG3107
Ferry House (01508) 538659
Ferry Road: far end by river; NR14 7AR
Welcoming unpretentious pub by River Yare;
well kept regional ales and generous helpings
of good inexpensive home-made food from
baguettes up, helpful accommodating service,
central woodburner in brick fireplace; some
live music; children and dogs welcome,
very busy with boats and visitors in summer
– free mooring, picnic-sets on waterside
lawn, handy for RSPB reserve, open (and
food) all day. *(Denis and Margaret Kilner)*

THOMPSON   TL9296
Chequers (01953) 483360
*Griston Road, off A1075 S of Watton;
IP24 1PX* Picturesque 16th-c thatched
dining pub tucked away in attractive setting;
enjoyable food including bargain weekday
lunch offer and regular themed nights,
ales such as Greene King and Woodfordes,
friendly atmosphere, series of quaint rooms
with low beams, inglenooks and some

stripped brickwork; children and dogs (in bar) welcome, seats out in front and in back garden with swing, bedroom block, open (and food) all day Sun. *(Mark Morgan)*

THORNHAM   TF7343
Chequers (01485) 512229
High Street (A149); PE36 6LY 16th-c roadside inn refurbished in contemporary style (same owners as the nearby Lifeboat – see Main Entries); two front bar rooms with pale-painted beams, wooden chairs or cube seats around mix of wooden tables on carpet or painted floorboards, some local photographs, open fire, a few stools at counter serving two local ales and decent wines by the glass, well liked food from 'tapas' and pizzas up, cosy room off with sofas, armchairs and woodburner, modern back dining room; children welcome, painted picnic-sets out at front, more seating in back courtyard garden with a couple of cabanas, 11 comfortable modern bedrooms, open all day. *(Tracey and Stephen Groves)*

WALSINGHAM   TF9336
Black Lion (01328) 820235
Friday Market Place; NR22 6DB Attractively renovated beamed village inn (dates from the 15th c); nice mix of old furniture on flagstones or quarry tiles, candlelit tables, shelves of books, farming tools and other bits and pieces including a tandem on one wall, woodburners and open fire, tractor-seat stools by blue counter serving Adnams, Woodfordes and a guest, a dozen wines by the glass and good traditional home-made food, friendly service; background and some live music; children and dogs welcome, a few tables out at front, more on little terrace with old well, six comfortable bedrooms, open all day. *(Denis and Margaret Kilner)*

WALSINGHAM   TF9336
Bull (01328) 820333
Common Place/Shire Hall Plain; NR22 6BP Quirky pub in pilgrimage village; lived-in bar with shelves of curious knick-knacks, pictures of archbishops and clerical visiting cards, a half-size statue of Charlie Chaplin, even a mirror ball in one part, three well kept changing ales and tasty reasonably priced food (not weekend evenings), welcoming friendly service, roaring fire, typewriter in snug, old-fashioned cash register in the gents'; TV, free wi-fi; children welcome, courtyard and attractive flowery terrace by village square, dovecote stuffed with plastic lobsters and crabs, outside games room, nice snowdrop walk in nearby abbey garden, bedrooms, open all day. *(Dr J Barrie Jones)*

WARHAM   TF9441
Three Horseshoes (01328) 710547
Warham All Saints; village signed from A149 Wells-next-the-Sea to Blakeney, and from B1105 S of Wells; NR23 1NL New owners and renovation for this popular old-fashioned pub; should reopen in autumn 2017 – news please.

WEASENHAM ST PETER   TF8522
Fox & Hounds (01328) 838868
A1065 Fakenham–Swaffham; The Green; PE32 2TD Traditional 18th-c beamed local with bar and two dining areas (one with inglenook woodburner), spotless and well run by friendly family, three changing ales, good reasonably priced home-made food (not Sun evening), pubby furniture and carpets throughout, brasses and lots of military prints; children welcome, big well maintained garden and terrace, closed Mon. *(Thomas Green)*

WELLS-NEXT-THE-SEA   TF9143
Albatros 07979 087228
The Quay; NR23 1AT Bar on 1899 quayside clipper, charts and other nautical memorabilia, Woodfordes ales served from the cask, dutch food including speciality pancakes, seats on deck with good views of harbour and tidal marshes; regular live music; children and dogs welcome, not good for disabled, cabin accommodation with shared showers, open all day. *(John Poulter)*

WELLS-NEXT-THE-SEA   TF9143
Bowling Green (01328) 710100
Church Street; NR23 1JB Welcoming 17th-c pub in quiet spot on outskirts, Greene King, Woodfordes and a guest, generous helpings of reasonably priced traditional food, bargain OAP lunch Tues, L-shaped bar with corner settles, flagstone and brick floor, two woodburners, raised dining end; children and dogs welcome, sunny back terrace, two bedrooms in converted barn, also self-catering accommodation. *(Mike and Sarah Abbot)*

WELLS-NEXT-THE-SEA   TF9143
Crown (01328) 710209
The Buttlands; NR23 1EX Smart old coaching inn (part of Flying Kiwi group) overlooking tree-lined green; rambling bar on several levels with beams and standing timbers, grey-painted planked wall seats and brown leather dining chairs on stripped floorboards, ales such as Adnams and Woodfordes, several wines by the glass, good modern food including daily specials, friendly accommodating staff, airy dining room and elegant more formal restaurant; background

---

If you stay overnight in an inn or hotel, they are allowed to serve you an alcoholic drink at any hour of the day or night.

music; children and dogs (in bar) welcome, 12 bedrooms, open all day from 8am for breakfast, can get very busy. *(Derek and Sylvia Stephenson, Comus and Sarah Elliott)*

WELLS-NEXT-THE-SEA   TF9143
Edinburgh (01328) 710120
Station Road/Church Street; NR23 1AE Traditional 19th-c pub near main shopping area, good home-made food and three well kept ales including Woodfordes, open fire, sizeable restaurant, also 'lifeboat' dining room decorated in RNLI colours; background music, free wi-fi; children and dogs welcome, disabled access, courtyard with heated smokers' shelter, three bedrooms, open all day. *(Dr J Barrie Jones)*

WELLS-NEXT-THE-SEA   TF9143
★Globe (01328) 710206
The Buttlands; NR23 1EU Handsome Georgian inn a short walk from the quay; plenty of space and nice atmosphere in opened-up contemporary rooms, tables on oak boards, big bow windows, well kept Adnams beers, thoughtful wine choice and enjoyable food including Weds steak night, good service; background and some live music; children and dogs welcome, attractive courtyard with pale flagstones, more seats at front overlooking green, seven bedrooms and nearby holiday house, open all day. *(Phil and Jane Villiers)*

WEST ACRE   TF7815
Stag (01760) 755395
Low Road; PE32 1TR Small family-run local with three or more well kept changing ales in appealing unpretentious bar, good value home-made food including set Sun lunch, efficient friendly service, neat dining room; quiz third Sun of month; attractive spot in quiet village, closed Mon. *(John Wooll)*

WEYBOURNE   TG1143
Ship (01263) 588721
A149 W of Sheringham; The Street; NR25 7SZ Popular traditional 19th-c village pub; well kept Woodfordes Wherry and two local guests, good wine choice, big bar with pubby furniture and woodburner, two dining rooms, good reasonably priced home-made food (should book weekends) from lunchtime sandwiches through pub favourites to local fish/seafood, efficient friendly young staff; background music, monthly quiz, free wi-fi; well behaved children welcome, dogs in bar, seats out at front and in nice side garden handy for Muckleburgh military vehicle museum, open all day in season, no food Sun evening. *(M and GR, Mr and Mrs Richard Osborne)*

WYMONDHAM   TG1001
★Green Dragon (01953) 607907
Church Street; NR18 0PH Picturesque heavily timbered medieval pub with plenty of character; small beamed bar and snug, bigger dining area, interesting pictures, log fire under Tudor mantelpiece, three well kept changing ales and over 50 whiskies, winter mulled wine, big helpings of popular good value food including daily specials (best to book), friendly helpful staff, upstairs function room (quiz Thurs, open mike night third Sun of month, ukulele group third Tues); children and dogs welcome, garden behind with raised deck, near glorious 12th-c abbey church, open all day (food all day Fri-Sun). *(Alan McQuilan)*

Post Office address codings confusingly give the impression that a few pubs are in Norfolk, when they're really in Cambridgeshire or Suffolk (which is where we list them).

Northamptonshire

ASHBY ST LEDGERS
SP5768 Map 4

Olde Coach House 🛏

(01788) 890349 – www.oldecoachhouse.co.uk

*Main Street; 4 miles from M1 junction 18; A5 S to Kilsby, then A361 S towards
Daventry; village also signed off A5 N of Weedon; CV23 8UN*

**Much character in ex-farmhouse with real ales, good wines,
well liked food and plenty of outside seating; bedrooms**

This is a lovely place to stay: 11 of the well equipped, contemporary
bedrooms are located in the converted stables, and breakfasts are good.
The opened-up bar on the right, full of original charm, has stools against the
counter where friendly staff serve Wells Bombardier, Youngs Bitter and a
guest beer on handpump and 16 wines by the glass. Several informal dining
areas take in paintwork ranging from white and light beige to purple, and
flooring that includes stripped wooden boards, original red and white tiles
and beige carpeting. All manner of pale wooden tables are surrounded by
assorted church chairs, high-backed leather dining chairs and armchairs,
with comfortable squashy leather sofas and pouffes in front of a log fire.
There are hunting pictures, large mirrors, an original old stove and fresh
flowers; background music and TV. The back garden has picnic-sets among
shrubs and trees, modern tables and chairs out in front under pretty hanging
baskets, and a dining courtyard. The church is of interest and the nearby
manor house was once owned by one of the gunpowder plotters.

🍴 A wide choice of rewarding food includes sandwiches, crispy calamari with garlic
aioli, ham and cheese croquettes with tomato salsa, stone-fired pizzas, rare-breed
sausages with creamy mash, blackened chicken and quinoa salad, lamb or sweet potato
burgers with toppings, dips and chips, venison and wild mushroom pie, plaice fillets
with minted pea fricassée and salsa verde, steaks from grass-fed beef with a choice of
sauce, and puddings such as dark chocolate pots with boozy cherries and raspberry
crème brûlée; they also offer a two- and three-course set menu (weekday lunchtimes
and 6-7pm Mon-Thurs). *Benchmark main dish: steak in ale pie £12.95. Two-course
evening meal £20.00.*

Quicksilver Management ~ Lease Mark Butler ~ Real ale ~ Open 12-11 (10 Sun) ~ Bar food
12-2, 6-9.30; 12-8 Sun ~ Restaurant ~ Children welcome ~ Dogs allowed in bar ~ Wi-fi ~
Bedrooms: /£95 *Recommended by George Atkinson, Mike and Mary Carter, Robert Wivell,
Greta and Gavin Craddock, Charles Fraser*

Virtually all pubs in this book sell wine by the glass. We mention wines
if they are a cut above the average.

FARTHINGHOE

Fox 🛏

SP5339 Map 4

(01295) 713965 – www.foxatfarthinghoe.co.uk

Just off A422 Brackley–Banbury; Baker Street; NN13 5PH

Bustling stone inn with a neat bar and dining rooms, tasty food, helpful service and seats in the garden; bedrooms

To be sure of enjoying the rewarding food in this stylish golden-stone pub, it's best to book a table in advance. The dark beamed bar has stools and a log fire in a stripped-stone fireplace, and the dining areas have seats ranging from leather tub chairs to banquettes, cushioned wall seats with scatter cushions and quite a range of wooden dining chairs – all arranged around rustic wooden tables; mirrors and country prints on pastel walls. Courage Directors, Wells Bombardier and Youngs Bitter on handpump, nine wines by the glass and a good choice of gins; background music. The terrace and lawn have picnic-sets under a giant parasol. Bedrooms in an adjoining barn conversion are quiet and comfortable; one is suitable for disabled customers.

Popular food includes tian of crab and avocado with mango salsa and lime mayonnaise, chicken liver parfait with truffle and onion jam, wild mushroom and spinach risotto with parmesan, beer-battered fish and chips, burger with toppings, coleslaw and onion rings, sea bass with lemon and chive beurre blanc and rösti potatoes, calves liver and bacon with horseradish mash and onion gravy, lamb rump with minted pea purée, dauphinoise potatoes and redcurrant jus, summer vegetable strudel with new potatoes, and puddings such as chocolate and pistachio nut marquise with toffee popcorn and glazed lemon tart with crushed raspberries. *Benchmark main dish: risotto of the day £11.50. Two-course evening meal £19.00.*

Charles Wells ~ Lease Neil Bellingham ~ Real ale ~ Open 12-11; 12-10.30 Sun ~ Bar food 12-2.30, 6-9.30; 12-4, 6-8 Sun ~ Restaurant ~ Children welcome ~ Dogs allowed in bar ~ Wi-fi ~ Bedrooms: £75/£85 *Recommended by Jo Garnett, Daniel King, Julia and Fiona Barnes, Edward Nile, Frances and Hamish Porter*

FARTHINGSTONE

Kings Arms ◖ £

SP6155 Map 4

(01327) 361604

Off A5 SE of Daventry; village signed from Litchborough; NN12 8EZ

Individual place with cosy traditional interior, carefully prepared food and lovely garden

You can expect plenty of chatty customers and a genuine welcome from the hard-working landlord in this cheerful little 18th-c pub. It's nicely traditional and the cosy flagstoned bar has a huge log fire, comfortable homely sofas and armchairs near the entrance, whisky-water jugs hanging from oak beams, and lots of pictures and decorative plates on the walls. A games room at the far end has darts, dominoes, cribbage, table skittles and board games. The ever-changing beers are kept in top condition and might include Butcombe Bitter, Elgood Cambridge Bitter, St Austell Tribute, Towcester Mill Mill Race, Tyne Bank EPA and Woodfordes Wherry on handpump; also Weston's Old Rosie cider and a short but decent wine list. Look out for the interesting, newspaper-influenced décor in the outside gents'. The handsome gargoyled stone exterior is nicely weathered and very pretty in summer when the hanging baskets are at their best; there are seats on a tranquil terrace among plant-filled, painted tractor tyres and recycled art, and they've recorded over 200 species of moth and 20 different butterflies. This is a picturesque village and good walks nearby include the Knightley Way. It's worth ringing ahead to check the opening and food times.

Tasty food – served weekend lunchtimes only – includes sandwiches, popular cheese, meat and fish platters with home-made chutney, cassoulets, casseroles, and puddings such as gingerbread pudding and meringues. *Benchmark main dish: yorkshire pudding filled with beef casserole £8.50.*

Free house ~ Licensees Paul and Denise Egerton ~ Real ale ~ Open 7-11 Mon-Thurs; 6.30-11.30 Fri; 12-11 Sat; 12-5, 9-11 Sun; 12-4.30, 6-11 Sat in winter; closed all Mon, weekday lunchtimes ~ Bar food 12-2.30 weekends; maybe evening snacks ~ Children welcome ~ Dogs allowed in bar ~ Wi-fi ~ Live music occasional Sat *Recommended by George Atkinson, Ian Duncan, Katherine Matthews, Victoria and James Sargeant, Justine and Neil Bonnett*

FOTHERINGHAY
Falcon ⊙ ♀

TL0593 Map 5

(01832) 226254 – www.thefalcon-inn.co.uk
Village signposted off A605 on Peterborough side of Oundle; PE8 5HZ

Northamptonshire Dining Pub of the Year

Upmarket dining pub with a good range of drinks and modern british food, and attractive garden

You'll get a genuine welcome in this stylish pub whether you're dropping in for a pint and a chat or are here to enjoy the particularly appealing food. The atmosphere is gently civilised and there are winter log fires in stone fireplaces, fresh flowers, cushioned slatback armchairs, bucket chairs and comfortably cushioned window seats and bare floorboards. The Orangery restaurant opens on to a charming lavender-surrounded terrace with lovely views of the huge church behind and of the attractively planted garden; plenty of seats under parasols. The thriving little locals' tap bar has a fine choice of drinks including Fullers London Pride, Greene King IPA and a guest from local breweries such as Digfield, Kings Cliffe, Nobbys and Oakham on handpump, 16 good wines by the glass and several malt whiskies; darts team and board games. This is a lovely village (Richard III was born here) with plenty of moorings on the River Nene; the ruins of Fotheringhay Castle, where Mary, Queen of Scots was executed, is nearby.

As well as summer Sunday barbecues and pizzas from their wood-fired oven, the highly enjoyable food includes prawn cocktail, confit duck with sweet pickled raisin and potato stack, potato gnocchi with spring onions, peas, mint and spinach, sausages and mash with onion gravy, free-range chicken breast with rösti potato, bacon and bean roll and thyme gravy, sea bream fillets with ratatouille, pak choi and sauté potatoes, barnsley lamb chop with chorizo and potato gratin and rosemary jus, and puddings such as banana tarte tatin with caramel ice-cream and turkish delight pannacotta with poached rhubarb; they also offer a two- and three-course set menu (not Saturday evening or Sunday). *Benchmark main dish: pie of the day £12.50. Two-course evening meal £22.00.*

Free house ~ Licensee Sally Facer ~ Real ale ~ Open 12-11; 12-5 Sun (12-10 June-Sept) ~ Bar food 12-2, 6-9; 12-3 Sun (12-3, 5.30-8 June-Sept) ~ Restaurant ~ Children welcome ~ Dogs allowed in bar ~ Wi-fi *Recommended by Michael Sargent, Mike and Margaret Banks, Charles Fraser*

We mention bottled beers and spirits only if there is something unusual about them – imported belgian real ales, say, or dozens of malt whiskies; so do please let us know about them in your reports.

GREAT BRINGTON
SP6664 Map 4

Althorp Coaching Inn

(01604) 770651 – www.althorp-coaching-inn.co.uk

Off A428 NW of Northampton, near Althorp Hall; until recently known as the Fox & Hounds; NN7 4JA

Friendly golden-stone thatched pub with some fine architectural features, tasty popular food, well kept real ales and sheltered garden

With half a dozen real ales kept well on handpump, this 16th-c former coaching inn always has plenty of happy customers. Changing regularly, these might include Greene King Abbot and IPA, Hook Norton Hooky, Phipps India Pale Ale, St Austell Tribute and Sharps Doom Bar; also, eight wines by the glass, a dozen malt whiskies and farm cider. The ancient bar has all the traditional features you'd wish for, from a dog or two sprawled by the huge log fire, to old beams, sagging joists and an appealing mix of country chairs and tables (set with fresh flowers) on broad flagstones and bare boards. There are snug alcoves, nooks and crannies with some stripped-pine shutters and panelling, two fine log fires and an eclectic medley of bric-a-brac ranging from farming implements to an old clocking-in machine and country pictures. There's a function room in a converted stable block next to the lovely cobbled and paved courtyard (also accessible by the old coaching entrance) with sheltered tables and colourful tubs of flowers; there is more seating available in the charming garden.

A wide choice of pleasing food includes lunchtime sandwiches and baguettes (not Sunday), moules marinière, thai-spiced fishcakes with sweet chilli sauce, three-bean vegetarian chilli, a pie of the day, corn-fed chicken with wild mushroom and dijon mustard sauce, hake fillet on mediterranean vegetables with a tomato, basil and oregano sauce, slow-braised lamb shank with red wine root vegetables and garlic mash, and puddings such as Baileys profiteroles with chocolate sauce and lemon tart with raspberry coulis. *Benchmark main dish: slow-cooked pork belly with black pudding mash, cider gravy and chunky apple sauce £13.95. Two-course evening meal £18.00.*

Free house ~ Licensee Michael Krempels ~ Real ale ~ Open 11-11 (midnight Sat); 12-11 Sun ~ Bar food 12-3, 6-9 ~ Restaurant ~ Children welcome ~ Dogs allowed in bar ~ Wi-fi ~ Quiz Mon evening, live music Tues evening *Recommended by Luke Morgan, John and Sarah Webb, David Appleyard, Alice Wright*

NORTHAMPTON
SP7559 Map 4

Malt Shovel £

(01604) 234212 – www.maltshoveltavern.com

Bridge Street (approach road from M1 junction 15); no parking in nearby street, best to park in Morrisons central car park, far end – passage past Europcar straight to back entrance; NN1 1QF

Friendly, well run real ale pub with bargain lunches and more than a dozen varied beers

Up to 13 real ales are served by knowledgeable, enthusiastic staff in this genuinely cheerful, lively tavern. From a battery of handpumps lined up on the long counter there might be Dow Bridge Acris, Fullers London Pride, Hook Norton Old Hooky, Lancaster Blonde, Nethergate Priory Mild, Oakham Bishops Farewell and JHB, Phipps NBC India Pale Ale, Rat White Rat, Twisted Barrel Gods Twisted Sister and Yeovil Spring Forward. They also stock belgian draught and bottled beers, 50 malt whiskies, 17 rums, 17 vodkas, 17 gins and Cheddar Valley farm cider; regular beer festivals. It's also home to quite an extensive collection of carefully chosen brewing memorabilia – look out for the rare Northampton Brewery Company star, displayed outside the pub, and some high-mounted ancient beer engines; darts, daily papers and background music. The secluded backyard has tables and chairs and a smokers' shelter; disabled facilities.

🍴 Lunchtime-only food includes baguettes and wraps, broccoli, mushroom and stilton pasta bake, burger and chips, shepherd's pie, gammon and egg, and lambs liver and bacon casserole. *Benchmark main dish: a changing curry £7.00.*

Free house ~ Licensee Scott Whyment ~ Real ale ~ Open 11.30-11 ~ Bar food 12-2; 12-4 Sun ~ Well behaved children welcome in bar ~ Dogs allowed in bar ~ Wi-fi ~ Blues Weds evening
Recommended by Dr J Barrie Jones, George Atkinson, Caroline Sullivan, Tony Hobden, Sabina and Gerald Grimshaw, Bob and Melissa Wyatt

OUNDLE
Ship 🍺 £
TL0388 Map 5

(01832) 273918 – www.theshipinn-oundle.co.uk
West Street; PE8 4EF

Bustling down-to-earth pub with interesting beers and good value pubby food; bedrooms

The buoyantly cheerful atmosphere in this traditional town local owes a lot to the genuinely welcoming brothers in charge. Off to the left of the central corridor, the heavily beamed lounge consists of cosy areas with a mix of leather and other seats, sturdy tables and a warming log fire in a stone inglenook. A charming little panelled snug at one end has button-back leather seats. The wood-floored public bar has poker evenings on Wednesdays, while the terrace bar has pool, darts, TV, board games and background music. Friendly staff serve Brewsters Hophead, Nene Valley NVB Bitter, Sharps Doom Bar and Timothy Taylors Boltmaker on handpump, eight wines by the glass and eight malt whiskies. The wooden tables and chairs on the series of small sunny, covered terraces are lit at night.

🍴 Food is fairly priced and includes rolls and baguettes, a changing pâté, whitebait with tartare sauce, ham and eggs, a pie of the day, sausages and mash with onion gravy, chilli with sour cream and rice, and a choice of steaks; they offer smaller helpings of some dishes at reduced rates for OAPs. *Benchmark main dish: burger with toppings, coleslaw and fries £7.95. Two-course evening meal £13.50.*

Free house ~ Licensees Andrew and Robert Langridge ~ Real ale ~ Open 11am-11.30pm; 12-11 Sun ~ Bar food 12-3, 6-9; 12-6 Sun ~ Children welcome ~ Dogs welcome ~ Wi-fi ~ Bedrooms: £39/£69 *Recommended by Amy and Luke Buchanan, Heather and Richard Jones, Julie Swift, Mike Benton*

SPRATTON
Kings Head 🍽️
SP7170 Map 4

(01604) 847351 – www.kingsheadspratton.co.uk
Brixworth Road, off A5199 N of Northampton; NN6 8HH

Part brasserie and part bar with contemporary furnishings, an easy-going atmosphere, real ales and particularly good food; seats outside

The different parts of this enterprising place blend together really well – it actually describes itself as 'three in one': bar, restaurant and coffee shop. There are pale flagstones and ancient stripped stonework mixing well with handsome new wood flooring and up-to-date décor, plus leather chesterfields, an antique settle, café chairs around stripped brasserie-style tables and a woodburning stove in a brick fireplace. Friendly staff serve Shepherd Neame Spitfire and a changing guest from Grainstore on handpump, eight wines by the glass and artisan spirits; background music. The coffee shop at the back has a glass wall overlooking a courtyard with modern metal and wood tables and chairs.

Food is good and includes goats cheese mousse macaron with textures of beetroot, crispy black pudding with confit cherry tomatoes, caramelised onion purée and soft quail egg, feta and spinach filo parcels with warm spicy aubergine salad, crispy polenta and carrot, cumin and coriander purée, breast of chicken wrapped in pancetta with local asparagus spears, wilted spinach, tarragon gnocchi and beurre blanc, lamb rump with crispy lamb shoulder, cabbage and red wine jus, lemon sole with ratatouille, tomato consommé, chorizo and parmentier potatoes, and puddings such as fennel pannacotta with blood orange sorbet, fennel and orange flapjack and yuzu gel and chocolate truffle with passion-fruit jelly, toasted marshmallow and passion-fruit sorbet. *Benchmark main dish: tandoori cod and curried peas £17.95. Two-course evening meal £23.00.*

Free house ~ Licensee Joanna Elmore ~ Real ale ~ Open 12-11; 12-11.30 Fri, Sat; 12-10.30 Sun ~ Bar food 12-2.30, 6-9; 12-4 Sun; coffee shop 8.30-5 (closed Sun) ~ Restaurant ~ Children welcome ~ Dogs allowed in bar ~ Wi-fi *Recommended by Mike and Margaret Banks, Gerry and Rosemary Dobson, Edward May*

Also Worth a Visit in Northamptonshire

Besides the fully inspected pubs, you might like to try these pubs that have been recommended to us and described by readers. Do tell us what you think of them: feedback@goodguides.com

ABTHORPE   SP6446
★ **New Inn** (01327) 857306
Signed from A43 at first roundabout S of A5; Silver Street; NN12 8QR Traditional partly thatched country local run by cheery farming family, fairly basic rambling bar with dining area down a couple of steps, four well kept Hook Norton beers and Weston's cider, good pubby food (not Sun evening) using own meat and home-grown herbs, blackboard specials, beams, stripped stone and inglenook woodburner, darts and table skittles; quiz last Sun of month, occasional live music, free wi-fi; children, dogs and muddy boots welcome, garden tables, bedrooms in converted barn (short walk across fields), open all day Sun, closed Mon lunchtime. *(Jim Taylor)*

ARTHINGWORTH   SP7581
Bulls Head (01858) 525637
Kelmarsh Road, just above A14 by A508 junction; pub signed from A14; LE16 8JZ Steps up to much extended black-beamed pub with various seating areas in L-shaped bar, pubby furniture and upholstered banquettes on patterned carpet, woodburner, enjoyable good value food including Weds steak deal, well kept Adnams and a couple of guests (May beer festival), efficient cheery service, restaurant; background music, TV, darts and skittles, free wi-fi; disabled access (from back) and facilities, terrace picnic-sets, eight bedrooms in separate block, handy for Kelmarsh Hall, open all day weekends (food till 7.30pm Sun). *(Max and Steph Warren)*

ASHTON   TL0588
Chequered Skipper (01832) 273494
The Ashton NE of Oundle, signed from A427/A605 roundabout; PE8 5LD Handsomely rebuilt thatched pub on chestnut-tree green of elegant Estate village; well kept changing local ales and good home-made food from snacks and stone-baked pizzas up (gluten-free diets catered for), helpful friendly young staff, spacious open-plan layout with dining areas either side; free wi-fi; children welcome, well behaved dogs in bar, good 4-mile circular walk, open all day weekends. *(Michael and Jenny Back, Peter Andrews)*

AYNHO   SP5133
Cartwright (01869) 811885
Croughton Road (B4100); handy for M40 junction 10; OX17 3BE Welcoming 16th-c coaching inn with linked areas, contemporary furniture on wood or tiled floors, some exposed stone walls, leather sofas by big log fire in small bar, ales such as Adnams and Butcombe, nice wines and good coffee, popular well presented food including set deals, friendly helpful uniformed staff; background music, TV, daily papers and free wi-fi; children welcome, a few seats in pretty corner of part-cobbled coachyard, 21 bedrooms,

good breakfast, pleasant village with apricot trees growing against old cottage walls, open all day. *(George Atkinson)*

AYNHO
SP4932

★Great Western Arms (01869)
338288 *On B4031 1.5 miles E of Deddington, 0.75 miles W of Aynho, adjacent to Oxford Canal and Old Aynho station; OX17 3BP* Attractive old pub with series of linked cosy rooms; fine solid country tables on broad flagstones, golden stripped-stone walls, warm cream and deep red plasterwork, fresh flowers and candles, log fires, well kept Hook Norton and guests, good wines by the glass and enjoyable fairly pubby food served by friendly attentive young staff, elegant dining area on right, extensive GWR collection including lots of steam locomotive photographs, daily papers and magazines; background music, skittle alley, pool; children and dogs welcome, white cast-iron furniture in back former stable courtyard, moorings on Oxford Canal and nearby marina, bedrooms, open all day, food all day Sun. *(Michael Sargent)*

BARNWELL
TL0584

Montagu Arms (01832) 273726
Off A605 S of Oundle, then fork right at Thurning/Hemington sign; PE8 5PH Attractive old stone-built pub with well kept Adnams, Digfield (brewed in village) and guests, real ciders, good helpings of enjoyable home-cooked food (not Sun evening, Mon), cheerful staff, log fire, low beams, flagstones or tile and brick floors, back dining room and conservatory; children and dogs welcome, big garden with play area, pleasant streamside village, nice walks, open all day weekends, closed Mon lunchtime. *(Steve Alderton)*

BRAUNSTON
SP5465

Admiral Nelson (01788) 891900
Dark Lane, Little Braunston, overlooking Lock 3 just N of Grand Union Canal tunnel; NN11 7HJ 18th-c ex-farmhouse in peaceful setting by canal and hump bridge; good freshly made food (not Sun evening) from sandwiches/baguettes and traditional favourites up, well kept ales including one brewed for them by local MerriMen, efficient service, L-shaped bar with log fire and two seating areas to the right (sofas at low tables), a couple of steps down to cosy dining alcove, brick-partitioned restaurant extension to the left with sturdy tables and high-backed leather chairs; some live music including Aug festival, hood skittles and darts, free wi-fi; well behaved children and dogs welcome, wheelchair access, lots of waterside picnic-sets, closed Mon lunchtime in winter, otherwise open all day. *(Clive and Fran Dutson, Simon and Mandy King, Gerry and Rosemary Dobson)*

BRAYBROOKE
SP7684

Swan (01858) 462754
Griffin Road; LE16 8LH Nicely kept thatched pub with Everards ales and good choice of other drinks, popular sensibly priced food (not Sun evening) from sandwiches and pub favourites up, friendly attentive staff, fireside sofas, soft lighting, beams and some exposed brickwork, restaurant; quiet background music, quiz second Tues of month; children and dogs welcome, disabled facilities, pretty hedged garden with covered terrace, open all day Sat, closed Mon. *(Mike and Margaret Banks)*

BRIXWORTH
SP7470

Coach & Horses (01604) 880329
Harborough Road, just off A508 N of Northampton; NN6 9BX Welcoming early 18th-c stone-built beamed pub, popular good value food from fairly straightforward menu plus more adventurous specials including seasonal game, lunchtime and early evening set deals, well kept Marstons-related ales, prompt friendly service, log-fire bar with small dining area off, back lounge; tables on gravelled terrace behind, bedrooms in converted outbuildings, charming village with famous Saxon church, open (and food) all day Sun; still for sale so could be changes. *(Mike and Margaret Banks, Gerry and Rosemary Dobson)*

CHACOMBE
SP4943

George & Dragon (01295) 711500
Handy for M40 junction 11, via A361; Silver Street; OX17 2JR Welcoming 17th-c pub under new management; beams, flagstones, panelling and bare stone walls, two inglenook woodburners and deep glass-covered well, good popular food (not Sun evening) in three dining areas including various deals, Everards ales and a guest from brass-topped counter, several wines by the glass; background and maybe some live music, charity quiz first Sun of month; children and dogs (in bar) welcome, picnic-sets on suntrap terrace, pretty village with interesting church, open all day. *(George Atkinson)*

CHAPEL BRAMPTON
SP7366

★Brampton Halt (01604) 842676
Pitsford Road, off A5199 N of Northampton; NN6 8BA Popular well laid out McManus pub on Northampton & Lamport Railway (which is open some weekends) in much-extended former stationmaster's house; railway memorabilia and train theme throughout, wide choice of enjoyable good value food from sandwiches to blackboard specials, meal deal Mon-Thurs, well kept Fullers London Pride, Sharps Doom Bar and four guests (beer

---

If we know a pub has an outdoor play area for children, we mention it.

festivals), several wines by the glass, cheery attentive service even when very busy, large restaurant; background music, TV in bar; children welcome, no dogs inside, lots of tables in big garden with awnings and heaters, summer barbecues and marquee, pretty views over small lake, Nene Way walks, open (and food) all day. *(Gerry and Rosemary Dobson, George Atkinson, Adrian Johnson, Mike and Margaret Banks)*

CLIPSTON   SP7181
Bulls Head (01858) 525268
B4036 S of Market Harborough; LE16 9RT Welcoming village pub with popular good value food (not Mon) served in bar and restaurant, Everards ales and up to five guests, log fire and heavy beams (coins inserted by World War II airmen); background music, Tues quiz, TV; children and dogs welcome, terrace tables, three comfortable bedrooms, open all day weekends, closed Mon lunchtime. *(Tony Hooper)*

COLLINGTREE   SP7555
Wooden Walls of Old England
(01604) 760641 *1.2 miles from M1 junction 15; High Street; NN4 0NE* Cosy thatch and stone village pub dating from the 15th c and named as a tribute to the navy; four well kept Marstons-related ales and good choice of wines by the glass, generous helpings of home-made food (smaller appetites also catered for), weekday early-bird deal (5-6.30pm), friendly staff, beams and stone fire; sports TV, table skittles, free wi-fi; big back garden with terrace, open all day Fri-Sun, closed Mon and till 4pm Tues-Thurs, no food Sun evening. *(Frances and Hamish Porter)*

COLLYWESTON   SK9902
★ **Collyweston Slater** (01780) 444288
The Drove (A43); PE9 3PQ Roomy 17th-c main road inn with good popular pub food, well kept Everards ales and decent selection of wines, friendly service, contemporary interior with brown leather sofas and easy chairs, smart modern two-part dining room plus some more informal areas, one with raised woodburner in dividing wall, beams, stripped stone and mix of dark flagstones, bare boards and carpeting; background music, TV, darts; children welcome, dogs in bar areas, teak furniture on flagstoned terrace, boules, three bedrooms, open all day, no food Sun evening, Mon. *(Colin McLachlan)*

COSGROVE   SP7942
Barley Mow (01908) 562957
The Stocks; MK19 7JD Friendly old village pub close to Grand Union Canal, well kept Everards ales and a guest, decent range of wines and enjoyable reasonably priced home-made food, beamed interior with various connecting areas, dark furniture on carpet or light stone floors, some half-panelling,

two-way woodburner in stone fireplace; occasional live music, TV, free wi-fi; children and dogs welcome, tables on terrace and lawn down to the canal, open all day, food all day weekends. *(Amy and Luke Buchanan)*

CRICK   SP5872
★ **Red Lion** (01788) 822342
1 mile from M1 junction 18; in centre of village off A428; NN6 7TX Nicely worn-in stone and thatch coaching inn run by same family since 1979; traditional low-ceilinged bar with lots of old horsebrasses (some rare) and tiny log stove in big inglenook, straightforward low-priced lunchtime food, more elaborate evening menu (not Sun) including popular steaks, plenty for vegetarians too, Adnams Southwold, Wells Bombardier and a guest, good friendly service; Sun quiz, free wi-fi; children (under-12s lunchtime only) and dogs welcome, picnic-sets on terrace and in Perspex-covered coachyard with pretty hanging baskets. *(Stuart Doughty)*

DUDDINGTON   SK9800
Royal Oak (01780) 444267
High Street, just off A43; PE9 3QE Stone-built inn on edge of pretty village; modern bar area with leather sofas and chairs on flagstones, panelling and log fire, three Grainstore ales from brick servery, restaurant with stone walls, wood floor and light oak furniture, enjoyable food from pub favourites up including weekday set lunch; background music; children welcome, disabled facilities, tables on small grassy area at front, six bedrooms, open (and food) all day Fri-Sun. *(Tony Hooper)*

EAST HADDON   SP6668
★ **Red Lion** (01604) 770223
High Street; village signposted off A428 (turn right in village) and off A50 N of Northampton; NN6 8BU Substantial and elegant golden-stone thatched hotel with sizeable dining room, log-fire lounge and bar, emphasis on their well presented imaginative food and most tables set for dining, but they do keep Charles Wells ales and offer over a dozen wines by the glass, efficient friendly service; background music, cookery school; children welcome, attractive grounds including walled side garden, seven comfortable bedrooms and two-bed cottage, good breakfast, closed Sun evening. *(Gerry and Rosemary Dobson, Michael Butler)*

EASTON ON THE HILL   TF0104
Blue Bell (01780) 763003
High Street; PE9 3LR Welcoming stone-built village pub with strong italian leaning to menu and staff, decent food (not Sun evening, Mon), three changing ales inlcuding Grainstore and plenty of wines by the glass, restaurant; pool and TV in games area, May beer festival;

children welcome, picnic-sets in good-sized sheltered garden behind, open all day Sun, closed Mon lunchtime. *(Steve Alderton)*

EASTON ON THE HILL   TF0104
★**Exeter Arms** (01780) 756321
Stamford Road (A43); PE9 3NS Carefully renovated 18th-c pub with friendly easy-going atmosphere; country-feel bar with cushioned captain's chairs, wall/window seats and copper pans above woodburner, tractor seats by counter serving several wines by the glass and ales such as Shepherd Neame and local Stoney Ford, good food (not Sun evening) from varied menu, restaurant and airy orangery opening on to sunken terrace; free wi-fi; children and dogs (in bar) welcome, picnic-sets on lawn, light, comfortable bedrooms, open all day, reduced menu choice Sun evening. *(William Pace, R L Borthwick, Pieter and Janet Vrancken)*

ECTON   SP8263
Worlds End (01604) 414521
A4500 Northampton–Wellingborough; NN6 0QN Extended 17th-c roadside inn (sister to the Olde Coach House at Ashby St Ledgers – see Main Entries); contemporary décor in L-shaped bar and dining room down steps, well liked food from sandwiches, sharing boards, pizzas and pubby choices up, Hook Norton, Sharps and often a guest (weekday happy hour 5-7pm), good selection of wines by the glass, friendly service; background music (live last Fri of the month); children welcome, no dogs inside, garden with decked terrace, 22 bedrooms in separate block, open all day (till 9pm Sun). *(Mike and Margaret Banks, George Atkinson, Gerry and Rosemary Dobson)*

EYDON   SP5450
★**Royal Oak** (01327) 263167
Lime Avenue; village signed off A361 Daventry–Banbury, and from B4525; NN11 3PG Interestingly laid-out 300-year-old ironstone dining pub, some lovely period features including fine flagstone floors and leaded windows, cosy snug on right with cushioned benches built into alcoves, seats in bow window, inglenook log fire, long corridor-like central bar linking three other small characterful rooms, very good well presented food (not Mon, Tues or evening Sun) from owner-chef, friendly attentive staff; children and dogs welcome, terrace seating (some under cover), open all day Thurs-Sun. *(Buster and Helena Hastings)*

FLORE   SP6460
White Hart (01327) 341748
A45 W of M1 junction 16; NN7 4LW Welcoming pub with good range of enjoyable affordably priced food from lunchtime baguettes up, three real ales including Sharps Doom Bar, modernised interior (some contemporary touches) with several linked areas around central bar including

restaurant; TV, free wi-fi; tables on back deck by car park, open (and food) all day, till 9pm (6pm) Sun. *(Richard Kennell)*

GRAFTON REGIS   SP7546
★**White Hart** (01908) 542123
A508 S of Northampton; NN12 7SR Thatched roadside dining pub with several linked rooms, good pubby food (not Sun evening) including range of home-made soups and popular Sun roasts (best to book), Greene King Abbot and IPA, Aspall's cider and nice wines by the glass, friendly helpful staff coping well when busy, restaurant with open fire; background music; children and dogs welcome (they have a couple of boxers and a parrot), terrace tables and gazebo in good-sized garden, closed Mon. *(Jim Taylor)*

GREAT BILLING   SP8162
Elwes Arms (01604) 407521
High Street; NN3 9DT Thatched 16th-c village pub with two bars (steps between), wide choice of good value tasty food (all day weekends) including weekday lunch deal, Black Sheep, Wadworths 6X and Shepherd Neame Spitfire, friendly service, pleasant dining room (children allowed); background music, quiz Thurs and Sun, sports TV, darts, free wi-fi; no dogs, garden tables and nice covered decked terrace, play area, open all day Sat, closed Sun evening. *(Tony Hooper)*

GREAT OXENDON   SP7383
George (01858) 452286
A508 S of Market Harborough; LE16 8NA Recently reopened after major refurbishment – same owners as the Joiners Arms at Bruntingthorpe (see Also Worth a Visit in Leicestershire); small front bar with Greene King Old Speckled Hen and a craft beer, all other areas for dining/pre-dining with bistro-style décor, good well presented food from shortish but varied menu including a few blackboard specials, higher than average prices, efficient well trained staff; children welcome, no dogs inside, terrace overlooking garden, eight bedrooms (four in annexe), open (and food) all day. *(Gerry and Rosemary Dobson)*

HACKLETON   SP8054
White Hart (01604) 870271
B526 SE of Northampton; NN7 2AD Comfortably traditional 18th-c country pub; wide choice of enjoyable food from sandwiches and baked potatoes up, curry night Tues, friendly helpful staff, Fullers London Pride, Greene King IPA and a guest, decent choice of wines and other drinks, flagstone bar with log fire, dining area up steps, beams, stripped stone and brickwork, illuminated well; background music, TV, pool and hood skittles; supervised children and dogs welcome, disabled access, picnic-sets in sunny garden, open all day, no food Sun evening. *(John and Claire Masters)*

HARRINGTON

SP7780

Tollemache Arms (01536) 711770

High Street; off A508 S of Market Harborough; NN6 9NU Pretty thatched and beamed Tudor pub revamped under present licensees (also have the Red Lion at East Haddon), good food including sharing boards, pizzas and burgers, three well kept ales from Wells and Youngs, good choice of wines by the glass, cocktails and a local artisan gin, friendly attentive staff; children and dogs (in bar) welcome, back garden with country views and play area, lovely quiet ironstone village, handy for Carpetbagger Aviation Museum, open all day weekends (till 8pm Sun). *(Gerry and Rosemary Dobson, Mike and Margaret Banks, Sophie Marple)*

HARRINGWORTH

SP9197

White Swan (01572) 747035

Seaton Road; village SE of Uppingham, signed from A6003, A47 and A43; NN17 3AF Handsome 16th-c coaching inn refurbished under welcoming new management; large stone fireplace dividing flagstoned bar and dining area with high-backed leather chairs, woodstrip floor and painted beams, three changing ales, Weston's cider and enjoyable fairly traditional food including Fri fish and chips; free wi-fi; children and dogs (in bar) welcome, tables on paved terrace with pretty hanging baskets, not far from magnificent 82-arch viaduct spanning the Welland, five bedrooms, open all day weekends, closed Mon, Tues. *(David Appleyard)*

HIGHAM FERRERS

SP9668

Griffin (01933) 312612

High Street; NN10 8BW Welcoming 17th-c pub-restaurant (bigger than it looks) with enjoyable food including fresh fish and popular Sun carvery (till 3.30pm), five well kept rotating ales and good selection of wines and malt whiskies, comfortable front bar with log fire, large back restaurant and dining conservatory, friendly service; free wi-fi; tables on heated terrace, open all day Fri-Sun. *(Dr W I C Clark, Stuart Doughty)*

HINTON-IN-THE-HEDGES

SP5536

Crewe Arms (01280) 705801

Off A43 W of Brackley; NN13 5NF Updated 17th-c stone-built village pub, well kept ales including Hook Norton, enjoyable home-made food (not Sun evening) from bar snacks to specials, good friendly service, log fire; background music, free wi-fi; children and dogs welcome, picnic-sets in garden, two comfortable bothy bedrooms, open all day. *(Jim Taylor)*

KETTERING

SP8778

Alexandra Arms (01536) 522730

Victoria Street; NN16 0BU Backstreet real ale pub with up to 14 changing quickly, hundreds each year, knowledgeable landlord, basic opened-up bar with pump clips covering walls and ceiling, back games room with darts, hood skittles and TV, some snacky food; quiz night Weds; dogs welcome, a couple of picnic-sets out in front, small beer garden with benches behind, open all day (from 2pm Mon-Thurs). *(David Appleyard)*

KILSBY

SP5671

★George (01788) 822229

2.5 miles from M1 junction 18: A428 towards Daventry, left on to A5 – pub off on right at roundabout; CV23 8YE Welcoming pub handy for the motorway; proper old-fashioned public bar, wood-panelled lounge with plush banquettes and coal-effect gas stove opening into smarter comfortably furnished area, well kept Adnams, Fullers, Timothy Taylors and a guest, fine range of malt whiskies, enjoyable good value home-made food including daily specials and themed evenings; Sun quiz, free-play pool tables, darts, TV; children welcome if eating, dogs in bar, garden picnic-sets, six bedrooms, open Sun till 6pm. *(Tony Hooper)*

KISLINGBURY

SP6959

Cromwell Cottage (01604) 830288

High Street; NN7 4AG Sizeable dining pub tucked away near River Nene; comfortable modernised bar/lounge with some beams and open fire, civil war themed pictures, maps and a large mural on one wall, smart dining room, popular food (booking advised) from snacks to specials including weekend brunch from 9am, well kept changing ales and nice wines, friendly neat staff; no dogs, plenty of seats on paved terrace, open (and food) all day. *(Mike and Margaret Banks, George Atkinson)*

KISLINGBURY

SP6959

Sun (01604) 833571

Off A45 W of Northampton; Mill Road; NN7 4BB Welcoming thatch and ironstone village pub popular with locals and visitors alike; ales such as Greene King, Hoggleys, St Austell and Sharps (June beer festival), enjoyable fairly traditional food including Tues pizza night, L-shaped bar/lounge and small separate dining area; occasional live music, sports TV, free wi-fi; children and dogs welcome, disabled access, a few picnic-sets out in front, open all day weekends, no food Sun evening, Mon or lunchtime Tues. *(Frances and Hamish Porter)*

LITCHBOROUGH

SP6353

Old Red Lion (01327) 830064

Banbury Road, just off former B4525 Banbury–Northampton; opposite church; NN12 8JF Attractive beamed pub owned by local farming family and doubling as village shop; four rooms including cosy flagstoned bar with woodburner in big inglenook, three real ales such as Great Oakley and MerriMen, shortish choice of enjoyable food (not Sun evening, Mon) from snacks up, friendly relaxed atmosphere, barn-conversion restaurant at back; table skittles, darts; children welcome, popular with walkers, terrace seating, open all day Sun till 8pm, closed Mon lunchtime. *(Dan Clayton)*

LITTLE BRINGTON SP6663

★**Saracens Head** (01604) 770640
4.5 miles from M1 junction 16, first right off A45 to Daventry; also signed off A428; Main Street; NN7 4HS Friendly old village pub with enjoyable fairly priced food (not Sun evening, Mon) from lunchtime sandwiches up, well kept Greene King IPA, Timothy Taylors Landlord and a guest, several wines by the glass, roomy U-shaped beamed lounge with woodburner, flagstones, bare boards and tiled floors, chesterfields and lots of old prints, book-lined dining room (proper napkins); gentle background music; plenty of tables out on gravel/paved area with country views, walks nearby and handy for Althorp House and Holdenby House. *(Mike and Margaret Banks)*

LITTLE HARROWDEN SP8671

Lamb (01933) 673300
Orlingbury Road/Kings Lane off A509 or A43 S of Kettering; NN9 5BH Popular pub in delightful village; split-level carpeted lounge bar with log fire and brasses on 17th-c beams, dining area, good promptly served food including Thurs steak night, Wells Eagle and a couple of guests, short sensibly priced wine list; games bar with darts, hood skittles and machines; background music, Fri quiz, free wi-fi; children welcome, small raised terrace and garden, open all day weekends. *(Buster and Helena Hastings)*

LODDINGTON SP8178

Hare (01536) 710337
Main Street; NN14 1LA Welcoming 17th-c stone-built dining pub with modernised interior, good home-made food including some reduced lunchtime/early evening choices, five well kept ales such as Greene King, Sharps Doom Bar and Wells Bombardier; background music, TV, Sun quiz; children and dogs welcome, picnic-sets on front lawn, open (and food) all day weekends. *(Mike and Margaret Banks)*

LOWICK SP9780

Snooty Fox (01832) 733434
Off A6116 Corby–Raunds; NN14 3BH Solidly built 17th-c village pub with spacious lounge bar, woodburner in sizeable fireplace, stripped stone and handsomely moulded dark oak beams, leather sofas, bucket chairs and stools on big terracotta tiles, formidable carved counter serving two changing ales, a real cider and lots of wines by the glass, more formal dining rooms with chunky tables on pale wood floor, food can be good and some choices expensive, italian night last Thurs of month; background music, free wi-fi; children and dogs (in bar) welcome, picnic-sets under parasols on front grass, play area, open all

day weekends, closed Mon. *(Michael Sargent, Mike and Margaret Banks, Peter Andrews)*

MOULTON SP7866

Telegraph (01604) 648228
West Street; NN3 7SB Spacious old stone-built village pub, popular and welcoming, with good promptly served food (not Sun evening) from sandwiches and pizzas up, well kept Fullers, Sharps and a couple of guests, maybe an interesting craft keg, log fire in bar, back restaurant extension; children welcome, open (and food) all day Fri and Sat. *(Michael Nicholas)*

NETHER HEYFORD SP6658

Olde Sun (01327) 340164
1.75 miles from M1 junction 16; village signposted left off A45 westbound; Middle Street; NN7 3LL Popular quirky place with small atmospheric linked rooms, bric-a-brac packed into nooks and crannies and hanging from the ceilings including brassware, 1930s cigarette cards, railway memorabilia, advertising signs and World War II posters, nice old cash till on one of the two counters serving Banks's, Greene King, Wychwood and a guest, well priced food including Sun carvery, beams and low ceilings, partly glazed dividing panels, steps between some areas, rugs on parquet, red tiles or flagstones, big inglenook log fire, games room with hood skittles and darts; background music; children and dogs welcome, lots of old farm equipment outside, open all day, no food Sun evening. *(George Atkinson, John Evans)*

NORTHAMPTON SP7560

Albion Brewery Bar (01604) 946606
Kingswell Street; NN1 1PR Tap for the revived 19th-c Albion Brewery (visible through glass partition, tours available); half a dozen Phipps/Hoggleys ales in top condition plus a guest and local cider, also their own Kingswell gin, bar snacks available Tues-Sat, friendly staff, pitched-ceiling bar with big windows and reclaimed fittings (many from closed Phipps pubs), traditional games including Northamptonshire skittles and bar billiards; live music (upstairs concert venue planned for autumn 2017); children and dogs welcome, disabled access/loo, open all day Fri, Sat, closed Sun evening and Mon. *(Richard Kennell, Stuart Doughty)*

NORTHAMPTON SP7261

Hopping Hare (01604) 580090
Harlestone Road (A428), New Duston; NN5 6PF Spacious Edwardian pub-restaurant-hotel on edge of housing estate; contemporary, stylish and comfortable, with good nicely presented food from lunchtime sandwiches and pub favourites to sharing boards and up-to-date restaurant dishes, well kept Adnams, Black Sheep and a guest, good choice of wines by the glass including champagne, prompt

friendly service; background music, daily newspapers, free wi-fi; tables out on deck, 18 comfortable modern bedrooms, good breakfast, open all day, food all day weekends (and weekdays during school summer holidays). *(Gerry and Rosemary Dobson, George Atkinson, Lesley and Brian Lynn)*

NORTHAMPTON   SP7560

Lamplighter (01604) 631125
Overstone Road; NN1 3JS Popular Victorian corner pub in the Mounts area, friendly and welcoming, with wide choice of draught and bottled beers, good value generously served food including range of burgers, good vegetarian options and popular Sun roasts; regular live music (open mike Mon), quiz Weds; children welcome if eating, picnic-sets in heated courtyard, open (and food) all day. *(David Appleyard)*

NORTHAMPTON   SP7661

Olde England 07742 069768
Kettering Road, near the racecourse; NN1 4BP Quirky conversion of Victorian corner shop over three floors (steepish stairs to upper level and down to cellar bar), ground-floor room with assorted tables and chairs on bare boards, 20 well kept changing ales and similar number of ciders served from hatch on stairs, lots of pictures with medieval or Arthurian themes, plus the odd banner, flag and suit of armour, cheap food with more extensive choice at weekends when pub is at its busiest, friendly staff and broad mix of customers; folk sessions and poetry readings, quiz nights, cards and board games; children and dogs welcome, closed Mon-Fri lunchtimes, otherwise open all day. *(Jim Taylor)*

NORTHAMPTON   SP7560

Wig & Pen (01604) 622178
St Giles Street; NN1 1JA Long L-shaped beamed room with bar running most of its length, up to a dozen well kept ales (tasters offered) including Adnams, Fullers and Greene King, traditional ciders and good choice of bottled beers, whiskies and gins, generous servings of nicely presented food (not weekend evenings) from sandwiches, tapas and deli boards up, brunch from 10am, friendly young staff; Tues jazz and other live music, sports TVs; split-level walled garden, handy for Guildhall and Derngate Theatre, open all day (till 1.30am Fri, Sat) and busy on Saints rugby days.
(George Atkinson, Dr J Barrie Jones)

OLD   SP7873

White Horse (01604) 781297
Walgrave Road, N of Northampton between A43 and A508; NN6 9QX Popular and welcoming village pub with good sensibly priced food from shortish menu supplemented by some interesting daily specials, three well kept ales, craft beers, proper ciders and decent wines by the glass, friendly efficient staff, additional dining area upstairs; quiz night first Thurs of month, live music last Fri, free wi-fi; well behaved children and dogs welcome, garden and deck overlooking 13th-c church, outside pizza oven, open all day Fri and Sat, till 7pm Sun, closed Mon. *(Gerry and Rosemary Dobson, Mike and Margaret Banks)*

OUNDLE   TL0388

Talbot (01832) 273621
New Street; PE8 4EA Hotel in handsome former merchant's house; various rooms including comfortably modernised bar, a couple of real ales such as Digfield and Mad Hatter, enjoyable food from sandwiches and sharing plates up, good helpful service, restaurant; children welcome, seats in courtyard and garden, 40 bedrooms, open (and food) all day. *(Amy and Luke Buchanan)*

PITSFORD   SP7567

Griffin (01604) 880346
Off A508 N of Northampton; High Street; NN6 9AD Friendly pub in pretty village near Pitsford Water/Brixworth Country Park; cosy beamed bar, back lounge with steps up to small eating area and pleasant restaurant extension, some interesting bits and pieces dotted about, Potbelly, St Austell and a guest, well liked reasonably priced home-made food from bar snacks up (evening restuarant menu), meal deal Tues-Sat (12-6pm); Sun quiz and occasional live music; children welcome, dogs in front bar, a few picnic-sets outside, open all Fri-Sun, closed Mon. *(Justine and Neil Bonnett)*

RAVENSTHORPE   SP6670

Chequers (01604) 770379
Chequers Lane; NN6 8ER Cosy old creeper-clad brick pub with L-shaped bar and restaurant, well kept ales including Oakham, Sharps and Thwaites, good choice of enjoyable food from light snacks to steaks and daily specials, banquettes, cushioned pews and sturdy tables, coal-effect fire; children and dogs welcome, partly covered side terrace, play area and separate building for Northamptonshire skittles, handy for Ravensthorpe Reservoir and Coton Manor Garden, open all day weekends. *(Steve Alderton)*

RUSHDEN   SP9566

Station Bar (01933) 318988
Station Approach; NN10 0AW Not a pub but part of station HQ of Rushden Historical Transport Society (non-members can sign in for £1); bar in former ladies' waiting room with gas lighting, enamel signs and railway memorabilia, seven ales including Dark Star and Phipps, tea and coffee, filled rolls and perhaps some hot food, friendly staff; also museum and summer train rides, table skittles in a Royal Mail carriage; outside benches, open all day weekends, closed weekday lunchtimes. *(Tony Hooper)*

RUSHTON   SP8483

Thornhill Arms (01536) 710251

Station Road; NN14 1RL Busy family-run dining pub opposite lovely village's cricket green, enjoyable food including keenly priced set menu (weekday evenings, Sat lunchtime) and carvery (Sun, Mon evening), gluten-free menu too, up to four well kept ales such as Black Sheep and Sharps, smart high-beamed back restaurant and several other neatly laid-out dining areas, open fire; children welcome, garden with decked area, open (and food) all day Sun. *(John and Claire Masters)*

SLIPTON   SP9579

★ Samuel Pepys (01832) 731739

Off A6116 at first roundabout N of A14 junction, towards Twywell and Slipton; NN14 3AR Old stone pub under friendly new management; long modernised bar with heavy low beams, wood flooring, log fire and great central pillar, up to seven well kept ales such as Digfield, Nene Valley and Sharps, traditional cider and 16 wines by the glass, good food from pub favourites up (more restaurant evening choices), two dining areas, one extending into roomy conservatory with country views; background music, free wi-fi; children and dogs (in bar) welcome, wheelchair access, sheltered garden with gazebo and heated terrace, open all day Fri-Sun, closed Mon, no food Sun evening. *(Mike and Margaret Banks, Clive and Fran Dutson)*

STANWICK   SP9871

Duke of Wellington (01933) 622452

Church Street; NN9 6PS Refurbished 19th-c stone pub next to the church, fresh contemporary décor in split level interior, good well presented food (not Sun evening) from lunchtime sandwiches and pub favourites up, real ales such as Greene King Abbot and IPA, friendly staff; background music, open mike night first Fri of month, quiz Weds; children welcome, picnic-sets out at front under parasols, more behind, closed Mon, otherwise open all day (till 10pm Tues-Thurs, 9pm Sun). *(Steve Sanford)*

STAVERTON   SP5461

Countryman (01327) 311815

Daventry Road (A425); NN11 6JH Beamed and carpeted dining pub with popular food from smallish menu including some interesting vegetarian options, Phipps IPA, Wells Bombardier and a guest, bar divided by brick pillars, restaurant; background music; children and dogs (in bar) welcome, disabled access, some tables out at front and in small garden behind, open (and food) all day Sun. *(Jim Taylor)*

STOKE BRUERNE   SP7449

Boat (01604) 862428

3.5 miles from M1 junction 15 – A508 towards Stony Stratford, then signed on right; Bridge Road; NN12 7SB Old-world flagstoned bar in picturesque canalside spot by lock, half a dozen Marstons-related ales and maybe a local guest, Thatcher's cider, enjoyable fairly standard food (not Sun evening) from baguettes up including deals, friendly service, more modern central-pillared back bar and bistro, comfortable upstairs bookable restaurant with separate menu; background music; children and dogs welcome, disabled facilities, tables out by towpath opposite canal museum, shop for boaters and trips on own narrowboat, open all day and can get very busy in summer, especially weekends when parking nearby difficult. *(Mike and Margaret Banks)*

STOKE DOYLE   TL0286

★ Shuckburgh Arms (01832) 272339

Village signed (down Stoke Hill) from SW edge of Oundle; PE8 5TG Relaxed 17th-c pub in quiet hamlet; four traditional rooms with some modern touches, low black beams in bowed ceilings, pictures on pastel walls, lots of pale tables on wood or carpeted floors, stylish art deco seats and elegant dining chairs, inglenook woodburner, ales such as Nene Valley and Black Sheep from granite-top bar, well selected wines and popular food including Thurs steak night, helpful attentive staff; soft background music; children welcome, garden with decked area and play frame, bedrooms in separate modern block, closed Sun evening, Mon. *(Peter Andrews)*

SUDBOROUGH   SP9682

Vane Arms (01832) 730033

Off A6116; Main Street; NN14 3BX Old thatched pub in pretty village, low beams, stripped stonework and inglenook fires, well kept Everards Tiger and guests, enjoyable freshly cooked food, friendly staff, restaurant; book club third Weds of month, free wi-fi; children and well behaved dogs (in bar) welcome, disabled loo, terrace tables, three bedrooms in nearby building, closed Sun evening. *(Justine and Neil Bonnett)*

SULGRAVE   SP5545

★ Star (01295) 760389

Manor Road; E of Banbury, signed off B4525; OX17 2SA Handsome creeper-clad inn under new management; woodburner in fine inglenook, working shutters, old doors and flagstones, moss or plum-coloured walls, mix of antique, vintage and retro furniture, polished copper and brass, Hook Norton ales, several wines by the glass and

---

We say if we know a pub has background music.

enjoyable fairly standard food including Weds evening meal deal, friendly efficient service, dining room with working range, snug in former farmhouse kitchen; children and dogs welcome, back garden with vine-covered trellis, aunt sally, short walk to Sulgrave Manor (George Washington's ancestral home), four bedrooms, closed Sun evening, Mon. *(George Atkinson)*

THORNBY
SP6675

★ **Red Lion** (01604) 740238

Welford Road; A5199 Northampton–Leicester; NN6 8SJ Popular old village pub with interesting choice of up to five well kept/priced changing ales, good home-cooked food (not Sun evening, Mon) from standards up including popular steak and stilton pie, smaller helpings available for some lunchtime dishes, prompt friendly service, recently redecorated interior with beams and log fire, lots of old local photos, back dining area; children and dogs welcome, garden picnic-sets, accommodation in converted barn, open all day Fri-Sun when can get very busy (booking advised Sat night), closed Mon lunchtime. *(Mike and Margaret Banks, Gerry and Rosemary Dobson)*

THORPE MANDEVILLE
SP5344

★ **Three Conies** (01295) 711025

Off B4525 E of Banbury; OX17 2EX Attractive and welcoming 17th-c ironstone pub, well kept Hook Norton ales and good choice of enjoyable locally sourced food (not Sun evening, Mon), beamed bar with some stripped stone, mix of old tables and comfortable seating on bare boards, log fires, large dining room; background music (live Fri), TV, wood skittles; children and dogs welcome, disabled facilities, tables out in front, more behind on decking and lawn, closed Mon lunchtime, otherwise open all day. *(Gerry and Rosemary Dobson)*

TOWCESTER
SP7047

Folly (01327) 354031

A5 S, opposite racecourse; NN12 6LB Early 18th-c thatched and beamed dining pub with good food (booking advised) from pub favourites to more expensive restaurant-style dishes, gluten-free menu too, good selection of wines and well kept beers, friendly efficient staff, small bar with steps up to dining area; children welcome till 8pm, picnic-sets outside, open all day Sun till 9pm, closed Mon. *(Mike Kavaney, Gerry and Rosemary Dobson)*

TOWCESTER
SP6948

Towcester Mill (01327) 437060

Chantry Lane; NN12 6YY Old mill tucked away behind market square surrounded by redevelopment; nice little bare-boards bar acting as tap for on-site brewery (tours Mon and Tues evenings – book ahead), seven ales including a couple of guests, also good range of ciders and country wines, friendly

knowledgeable staff, fish and chips Thurs evening (pies at other times); shop selling their beers, June and Sept beer/music festivals; walkers and dogs welcome, garden behind with seats by millrace and pond, open all day summer (winter from 5pm Mon-Thurs, 3pm Fri, all day Sat, till 8pm Sun), closes 8pm Mon. *(Ian Herdman, Andy Brown)*

TURWESTON
SP6037

Stratton Arms (01280) 704956

E of crossroads in village; pub itself just inside Buckinghamshire; NN13 5JX Friendly chatty local in picturesque village, five well kept ales including Otter and good choice of other drinks, enjoyable reasonably priced traditional food (Weds-Sun lunchtimes, Fri and Sat evenings), low ceilings and two log fires, small restaurant; background music, sports TV; children and dogs welcome, large pleasant garden by Great Ouse with barbecue and play area, camping, open all day Weds, Fri and Sat, till 8pm other days, closed Tues. *(David Appleyard)*

TWYWELL
SP9578

Old Friar (01832) 732625

Lower Street, off A14 W of Thrapston; NN14 3AH Welcoming pub with enjoyable food including set lunch menu and carvery (Thurs-Sat evenings, all day Sun), Greene King and a couple of guests, modernised split-level interior with beams and some exposed stonework; children and dogs welcome, garden with good play area, open (and food) all day weekends. *(Mike and Margaret Banks)*

UPPER BODDINGTON
SP4853

Plough (01327) 260364

Warwick Road; NN11 6DH Renovated 18th-c thatched village inn keeping much of its original character, small beamed and flagstoned bar, lobby with old local photos, Greene King IPA, Shepherd Neame Spitfire and a guest, good value fairly traditional food (Thurs curry night), in restaurant, snug or intimate 'Doll's Parlour' named after former veteran landlady, friendly efficient service, woodburners; quiz first Sun of month, occasional live music and beer festivals, free wi-fi; children and dogs welcome, five bedrooms (some sharing bathroom), usually closed weekday lunchtimes, open all day weekends, no food Sun evening, Mon. *(Clive and Fran Dutson)*

WADENHOE
TL0183

★ **Kings Head** (01832) 720024

Church Street; village signposted (in small print) off A605 S of Oundle; PE8 5ST Beautifully placed 17th-c country pub with picnic-sets on sun terrace and among trees on grassy stretch by River Nene (moorings); uncluttered partly stripped-stone bar with woodburner in fine inglenook, pale pine furniture and a couple of cushioned wall seats, simple bare-boards public bar and attractive little beamed dining room with more pine furniture, good well presented food (booking advised), three changing ales and several wines by the glass, friendly efficient service; games room with darts, dominoes and table skittles; children and dogs (in bar) welcome, good nearby walks, closed Sun evening, Mon. *(Tony Hooper)*

WALGRAVE   SP8072
Royal Oak (01604) 781248
Zion Hill, off A43 Northampton–Kettering; NN6 9PN Welcoming old stone-built village local, generous helpings of good fairly priced food (best to book) including very popular two-for-one Tues evening deal on main courses, well kept Adnams, Greene King and three guests, decent wines, friendly prompt service, long three-part carpeted beamed bar, small lounge, restaurant extension behind; quiz nights, sports TV in back bar; children welcome, no dogs inside, small garden with play area, open all day Sun. *(Gerry and Rosemary Dobson, Mike and Margaret Banks)*

WEEDON   SP6458
★Narrow Boat (01327) 340333
3.9 miles from M1 junction 16: A45 towards Daventry, left on to A5, pub then on left after canal, at Stowe Hill – junction Watling Street/Heyford Lane; NN7 4RZ Big draw here is its Grand Union Canal position – plenty of seats on covered deck and in garden sloping down to the water, outside summer bar and children's play trail; rambling interior with comfortable dark banquettes and padded chairs around neat tables, woodburner, a couple of Charles Wells ales and several wines by the glass, wide choice of generously served food (all day weekends), carpeted conservatory with heavy curtains for cooler nights; background music; children and dogs (in bar) welcome, disabled facilities, well equipped comfortable bedrooms in separate block, open all day. *(Mike and Margaret Banks)*

WELFORD   SP6480
Wharf Inn (01858) 575075
Pub just over Leicestershire border; NN6 6JQ Spacious castellated Georgian folly in delightful setting by two Grand Union Canal marinas; six well kept ales such as Grainstore, Marstons and Oakham in unpretentious bar, popular reasonably priced food (all day Sun) including good steak and kidney pudding and some interesting specials, efficient enthusiastic service,

pleasant dining section; children and dogs welcome, wheelchair access using portable ramps (disabled loo), big waterside garden and good local walks, open all day. *(Simon and Mandy King, Gerry and Rosemary Dobson, R T and J C Moggridge, Stuart Doughty)*

WELTON   SP5866
White Horse (01327) 702820
Off A361/B4036 N of Daventry; behind church, High Street; NN11 2JP Beamed 17th-c village pub on different levels, well kept Adnams, Purity, Oakham and a guest, local cider and nice house wines, reasonably priced food (not Sun evening, Mon, Tues) including good value steak deal Weds-Sat, woodburners, separate games bar with darts and skittles, small dining room; fortnightly Sun quiz; children and dogs welcome in one part, attractive garden and terrace, open all day Fri-Sun, closed Mon and Tues lunchtimes. *(Hilary Colpus)*

WHITTLEBURY   SP6943
Fox & Hounds (01327) 858048
High Street; NN12 8XJ Double-fronted 19th-c village bar-restaurant, smartly refurbished modern interior with wood flooring and comfy stylish seating, four well kept ales including local Gun Dog and one badged for the pub, nice selection of wines and good well presented food from thick-cut sandwiches and sharing boards up (separate bar and restaurant menus), friendly helpful service; children and dogs welcome, picnic-sets on suntrap gravelled terrace, handy for Silverstone, open all day weekends. *(George Atkinson, Brian Glozier)*

YARDLEY HASTINGS   SP8656
★Rose & Crown (01604) 696276
Just off A428 Bedford–Northampton; NN7 1EX Spacious and popular 18th-c dining pub in pretty village; flagstones, beams, stripped stonework and quiet corners, step up to big comfortable dining room, flowers on tables, good well presented food from interesting changing menu along with bar snacks and pubby choices, efficient friendly young staff, six well kept ales including a house beer from local Hart Family, four ciders and decent range of wines; background and occasional live music, daily newspapers; children welcome till 9pm, dogs in bar, tables under parasols in split-level garden, boules, open all day (from 5pm Mon). *(Mike and Margaret Banks, S Holder, Stuart Doughty)*

A star symbol before the name of a pub shows exceptional character and appeal. It doesn't mean extra comfort. Even quite a basic pub can win a star, if it's individual enough.

Northumbria

(County Durham, Northumberland and Tyneside)

KEY	★ Star Pub	🍽 Top Quality Food	🍺 Great Beer
	🍷 Good Wines	£ Bargain Meals	🛏 Good Bedrooms	𝗜𝗜 Serves Food

BLANCHLAND
Lord Crewe Arms ★ 🍽 🍷 🍺 🛏

NY9650 Map 10

(01434) 675469 – www.lordcrewearmsblanchland.co.uk

B6306 S of Hexham; DH8 9SP

Wonderful historic building, with unique Crypt bar, cosy dining rooms and spacious character restaurant; comfortable, well equipped bedrooms

This is a special place. It was built as a guest house in 1235 for the neighbouring Premonstratensian monastery and the architecture is remarkable. The unique Crypt bar is a medieval vaulted room sculpted by thick stone walls, lit by candlelight and with family crests on the ceiling. There are high wooden stools by wall shelves and against the armour-plated counter, cushioned settles and plush stools around a few little tables, with Hadrian Border Tyneside Blonde, Wylam Red Kite and Lord Crewe Brew (named for the pub from Wylam) on handpump, 14 wines by the glass, ten malt whiskies and a farm cider; background music and board games. One character sitting area has a leather sofa and two big tartan armchairs on flagstones in front of a large open fire, while the grand yet informal restaurant features a fine old wooden floor, cushioned wall seating and leather-cushioned dining chairs around oak-topped tables, fresh flowers, antlers on the walls and a big central candelabra. The bedrooms are lovely. Derwent Reservoir is nearby.

🍽 Food is exceptionally good and includes grilled sardines with spiced tomatoes, marinated steak with kentish cobnuts and chargrilled cabbage, scrambled duck eggs with home-cured smoked salmon, vegetarian sausage and black pudding plate with seasonal vegetables, sweet-cured bacon chop with fried sweetcorn and roasted chorizo, gurnard fillets with creamed potatoes and brown shrimps, lamb grill with a loin chop, kidney and rump with samphire and girolles, and puddings such as chocolate mousse with roasted apricots and crème catalan; they also offer afternoon tea. *Benchmark main dish: west country veal with artichokes £14.95. Two-course evening meal £23.00.*

Free house ~ Licensee Tommy Mark ~ Real ale ~ Open 11-11; 12-10.30 Sun ~ Bar food 12-2.30, 6-9; 12-3, 6-9.30 Sat; 12-3.30, 6.30-8.30 Sun ~ Restaurant ~ Children welcome ~ Dogs allowed in bar and bedrooms ~ Wi-fi ~ Bedrooms: £90/£99 *Recommended by David and Betty Gittins, Comus and Sarah Elliott, Elise and Charles Mackinlay, Mark and Mary Setting, Barry Collett, Stuart Doughty*

The details at the end of each featured entry start by saying whether the pub is a free house, or if it belongs to a brewery or pub group (which we name).

CARTERWAY HEADS
NZ0452 Map 10

Manor House Inn ■ ⌂

(01207) 255268 – www.themanorhouseinn.com

A68 just N of B6278, near Derwent Reservoir; DH8 9LX

Handy after a walk, with a traditional bar, comfortable lounge, bar food and five real ales; bedrooms

Not surprisingly, this friendly country inn is popular for miles around – with both regulars and visitors. Homely and old-fashioned, the locals' bar has an original boarded ceiling, pine tables, chairs and stools, old oak pews and a mahogany counter. The carpeted lounge bar (warmed by a woodburning stove) and restaurant are comfortably pubby with wheelback chairs, stripped-stone walls and picture windows that make the most of the fine setting. Greene King Old Speckled Hen and a couple of guests such as Adnams Lighthouse and Allendale Wagtail Best Bitter on handpump, alongside ten wines by the glass, 20 malt whiskies and Weston's Old Rosie cider; darts, board games and background music. Derwent Valley and Reservoir are close by and there are stunning views over the water and beyond from picnic sets on the terrace. The comfortable bedrooms share the same lovely outlook.

 Highly regarded food using local, seasonal produce and game from the moors includes tempura king prawns with sweet chilli dipping sauce, chicken liver pâté with red onion chutney, mushroom and potato rösti tart with courgette provençale and a herb cream, a trio of sausages with red onion marmalade, pigeon breasts with black pudding and apple salad with sweet plum reduction, tuna niçoise, slow-cooked pork belly with carrot and swede mash, crackling and redcurrant jus, venison with mash and whisky, wild mushroom and cream sauce, and puddings such as chocolate and Guinness meringue pie and a changing pannacotta. *Benchmark main dish: lamb rump with fondant potatoes and madeira and port jus £15.00. Two-course evening meal £22.00.*

Enterprise ~ Licensee Chris Baxter ~ Real ale ~ Open 12-11 (10.30 Sun) ~ Bar food 12-9; 12-8 (6pm winter) Sun ~ Restaurant ~ Children welcome ~ Dogs allowed in bar and bedrooms ~ Wi-fi ~ Bedrooms: £75/£85 *Recommended by Lesley and Peter Barrett, Robert Wivell, Deborah and Duncan Walliams, Claire Adams, Charlie Stevens*

CORBRIDGE
NY9964 Map 10

Angel ✱ ■ ⌂

(01434) 632119 – www.theangelofcorbridge.com

Main Street; NE45 5LA

Enterprising food and fine range of drinks in modernised coaching inn; comfortable bedrooms

This imposing coaching inn is nicely set at the end of a broad street, facing a handsome bridge over the River Tyne. The best sense of the building's age comes from the separate lounge where there are button-back armchairs, a sofa, oak panelling and a big stone fireplace; look out for the fine 17th-c arched doorway in the left-hand porch. The sizeable bar is modern in style, light and airy, with pale wooden tables and chairs and a few prints on pastel walls. Cumberland Corby Ale, Hadrian Border Tyneside Blonde, Mordue Workie Ticket, Jarrow Rivet Catcher, Wylam 005 Dr Rudi and a beer named for the pub (from Wylam) on handpump, a dozen wines by the glass, 30 malt whiskies and Weston's cider; daily papers and background music. There's also a carpeted lounge bar with a mix of up-to-date seats and more homely armchairs. You can sit out in front under parasols and outdoor heaters. Bedrooms are warm and comfortable and breakfasts are hearty; you can borrow bikes and boots.

As well as breakfasts (7.30-9.30am Monday-Friday; 7.30-10am Saturday; 8-10am Sunday), the highly rated, interesting food includes sandwiches (until 6pm), pressed ham hock with cranberries and wholegrain mustard, pease pudding and cumberland sauce, potted mackerel rillettes with brown shrimp cocktail, cumin and honey-roasted sweet potato and butternut squash with cheese and herb crumb, pork, black pudding and apple sausages with sage and onion gravy, sea trout fillet with sea greens and pepper and red onion salsa, lamb rump with aubergine, pan haggerty potatoes and rosemary gravy, chicken breast with wild mushroom, bacon and leek cream sauce and dauphinoise potatoes, and puddings such as warm chocolate brownie with salted caramel ice-cream and treacle tart with clotted cream. *Benchmark main dish: lambs liver with smoked bacon and rich jus £12.95. Two-course evening meal £20.00.*

Free house ~ Licensee Kevin Laing ~ Real ale ~ Open 11-11 (midnight Sat); 12-10.30 Sun ~ Bar food 12-9 (9.30 Fri, Sat; 8 Sun) ~ Restaurant ~ Children welcome ~ Wi-fi ~ Bedrooms: /£95 *Recommended by Comus and Sarah Elliott, Robert Wivell, Moira and John Wheeler, Andrea and Philip Crispin, Stuart Doughty*

COTHERSTONE
NZ0119 Map 10
Fox & Hounds 🛏
(01833) 650241 – www.cotherstonefox.co.uk
B6277; DL12 9PF

Bustling inn with cheerful beamed bar, good food and quite a few wines by the glass; bedrooms

The bright, clean and comfortable bedrooms in this Georgian country inn make a good base for exploring the fine surrounding walks. There's a cheerful, simply furnished beamed bar with a partly wooden floor (elsewhere it's carpeted), a good winter log fire, thickly cushioned wall seats and local photographs and country pictures in various alcoves and recesses. You'll find Black Sheep and a couple of guest beers from breweries such as Pennine and York on handpump, alongside eight wines by the glass, around 15 malt whiskies from smaller distilleries and several gins. There are seats outside on a terrace and quoits.

As well as some interesting specials using produce from the landlady's father's garden and daily fresh fish, the popular food includes cheese and hazelnut pâté with caramelised onion relish, smoked salmon, melon and prawn platter, vegetable bake, beer-battered fresh haddock and chips, steak and black pudding in ale pie, lambs liver with mustard mash and crispy bacon and rich gravy, gammon with tomato and cheese melt and chips, and puddings. *Benchmark main dish: cheese-filled chicken in creamy leek sauce £11.80. Two-course evening meal £16.00.*

Free house ~ Licensee Nichola Swinburn ~ Real ale ~ Open 12-3, 6-11.30 (11 Sun); closed Mon-Weds lunchtimes Nov-Easter ~ Bar food 12-2 (1.30 winter), 6-8.30 ~ Restaurant ~ Children welcome ~ Dogs allowed in bar and bedrooms ~ Wi-fi ~ Bedrooms: £47.50/£80 *Recommended by Miles Green, Julian Richardson, David Milton, S G N Bennett, Julie and Andrew Blanchett, Buster and Helena Hastings*

CRASTER
NU2519 Map 10
Jolly Fisherman
(01665) 576461 – www.thejollyfishermancraster.co.uk
Off B1339, NE of Alnwick; NE66 3TR

Stunning views, very good food and plenty of seasonal visitors

You can always be sure of a genuine welcome here, and the bustling bar, full of locals and ramblers, has a warming winter fire that's just right after a coastal walk; the route from here along the cliff to Dunstanburgh Castle (English Heritage) is popular. Also, leather button-back wall banquettes and upholstered and wooden dining chairs around hefty tables on bare boards, a few stools scattered here and there, and photographs and paintings in gilt-edged frames; background music. Black Sheep, Mordue Workie Ticket, Timothy Taylors Landlord and a changing guest on handpump served by friendly staff. From big windows in the upstairs dining room you look down on the charming harbour and out to sea. Seats and tables in the garden have the same outlook – and get snapped up pretty quickly. They have a couple of fishermen's cottages and an apartment available for rent as well as a café and gift shop opposite the pub.

Enjoyable food includes sandwiches, scottish moules marinière, a fish board, venison pudding with caramelised onion mash, red cabbage and game jus, sea bream with braised chicory, celeriac velouté and parmentier potatoes, calves liver with smoked bacon crisps, black pudding croutons and dauphinoise potatoes, a proper bouillabaisse, braised oxtail with parsnip purée, venison cottage pie and creamed vegetables, and puddings such as lemon posset and double chocolate cheesecake. *Benchmark main dish: crab sandwich £7.95. Two-course evening meal £20.00.*

Punch ~ Lease David Whitehead ~ Real ale ~ Open 11-11; 12-10.30 Sun ~ Bar food 11-3, 5.30-8.30; 12-4, 5-8.30 Sun (not Sun or Mon evenings in winter) ~ Restaurant ~ Children welcome ~ Dogs allowed in bar ~ Wi-fi *Recommended by Comus and Sarah Elliott, John and Sylvia Harrop, Pat and Stewart Gordon, Roger and Donna Huggins, Martinthehills, Barry Collett*

DIPTONMILL
Dipton Mill Inn ♥ ◖ £

NY9261 Map 10

(01434) 606577 – www.diptonmill.co.uk
S of Hexham; off B6306 at Slaley; NE46 1YA

Own-brew beers from on-site microbrewery, bargain bar food and waterside terrace

Home-brewed ales and amazing value food remain the mainstays of this tucked-away country local. The neatly kept snug bar has genuine character, dark ply panelling, low ceilings, red furnishings, a dark red carpet and two welcoming open fires. All six beers of the family-owned Hexhamshire Brewery are well kept on handpump: Blackhall English Stout, Devils Elbow, Devils Water, Old Humbug, Shire Bitter and Whapweasel. Also, 14 wines by the glass, 21 malt whiskies, Weston's Old Rosie cider and a guest cider. The garden is peaceful and pretty with attractive planting and seats on grass by a restored mill stream. Hexham Racecourse is not far away and there are woodland walks nearby.

The incredibly cheap, tasty food includes sandwiches, chicken liver pâté, smoked salmon and prawns, cheese and onion flan, lambs liver with sausages, chicken breast in sherry sauce, mince and dumplings, haddock baked in tomato and basil, and puddings such as syrup sponge with custard and creamy lemon tart. *Benchmark main dish: steak pie £7.50. Two-course evening meal £13.00.*

Own brew ~ Licensee Mark Brooker ~ Real ale ~ No credit cards ~ Open 12-2.30, 6-10.30 (11 Sat); 12-3 Sun; closed Sun evening ~ Bar food 12-2, 6.30-8.30; 12-2 Sun ~ Children welcome ~ Wi-fi *Recommended by Comus and Sarah Elliott, Stephen Woad, Celia and Rupert Lemming, Colin and Daniel Gibbs, Martinthehills*

The ◖ symbol shows pubs that keep their beer unusually well, have a particularly good range or brew their own.

DURHAM
NZ2742   Map 10
Victoria ◀

(0191) 386 5269 – www.victoriainn-durhamcity.co.uk

Hallgarth Street (A177, near Dunelm House); DH1 3AS

Unchanging and neatly kept Victorian pub with royal memorabilia, cheerful locals and well kept regional ales; bedrooms

Attractive bedrooms, hearty breakfasts and free off-street parking make this little gem perfect for exploring the city's castle and cathedral. Run by long-serving owners, the inn remains charmingly unspoilt and immaculately kept with original Victorian décor. Three small rooms lead off a central bar and have mahogany, etched and cut glass and mirrors, colourful William Morris wallpaper over a high panelled dado, some maroon plush seats in little booths, leatherette wall seats and long narrow drinkers' tables. Also, coal fires in handsome iron and tile fireplaces, photographs and articles showing a real pride in the pub, lots of period prints and engravings of Queen Victoria, and staffordshire figurines of her and the Prince Consort. Anarchy Blonde Star, Big Lamp Bitter, Durham White Gold, Hadrian Border Farne Island Pale Ale, Titanic Plum Porter and Wylam Gold Tankard on handpump, over 35 irish whiskeys, 60 scottish malts and cheap house wines; dominoes. Credit cards are accepted only for accommodation. No food.

Free house ~ Licensee Michael Webster ~ Real ale ~ No credit cards ~ Open 12-11; 12-10.30 Sun ~ Children welcome ~ Dogs welcome ~ Bedrooms: £65/£85
Recommended by Colin and Daniel Gibbs, Andrew Stone, Martinthehills, Edward May

ELLINGHAM
NU1625   Map 10
Pack Horse 🛏

(01665) 589292 – www.packhorseinn-ellingham.co.uk

Signed off A1 N of Alnwick; NE67 5HA

Stone-built inn with attractive rooms, good food, friendly staff and pretty garden; bedrooms

This charming small pub is a firm favourite with many of our readers. The flagstoned bar has masses of jugs hanging from beams, a long settle and upholstered stools around pubby tables, a log fire and tall stools against the counter where friendly staff serve Black Sheep and Timothy Taylors Landlord with a guest from the local Rigg & Furrow brewery on handpump; background music. The snug has a woodburning stove in a big stone fireplace with a stag's head above and captain's chairs and other seats on bare floorboards. The restaurant is divided into two with high-backed black leather chairs around pale tables on tartan carpet. As well as picnic-sets in the enclosed garden, there's an area where they grow their own vegetables. The pretty bedrooms make an excellent base for exploring the dramatic coastline and nearby castles.

 Interesting food includes scallops with warm tomato gazpacho and grilled chorizo, ham hock terrine with parma ham, egg and apple sauce, mediterranean vegetable ragoût with cream and grilled parmesan breadcrumbs, sea bass with vegetable stir-fry, tempura prawn and sweet chilli sauce, chicken milanese with fries, beef bourguignon, pork belly and black pudding fritter with scallops and port sauce, roasted lamb with thyme and garlic, and puddings such as chocolate brownie sundae and pannacotta with strawberry ice-cream. *Benchmark main dish: pie of the day £13.95. Two-course evening meal £20.00.*

Free house ~ Licensee Oliver Simpson ~ Real ale ~ Open 12-2, 6-11; 12-3, 7-10 Sun ~
Bar food 12-2, 6-9; 12-2 Sun ~ Restaurant ~ Children welcome ~ Dogs allowed in bar and
bedrooms ~ Wi-fi ~ Bedrooms: /£85 *Recommended by Claire Adams, Nigel Havers, David Travis,
Michael Doswell, Andrew Lawson, Patrick and Emma Stephenson*

GILSLAND   NY6366 Map 10

Samson ◨

(016977) 47880 – www.thesamson.co.uk

B6318, E end of village; CA8 7DR

**Friendly village pub in wonderful countryside, with cheerful
atmosphere in cosy bar, local ales and enjoyable food; bedrooms**

Three local farmers run this charming little pub which is just 30 metres
from Hadrian's Wall Path National Trail and on Hadrian's Cycleway.
The cosy bar has a chatty, easy-going atmosphere, red patterned carpeting,
swagged curtains, woodburning stoves, cushioned settles, traditional chairs
and stools around sewing machine-treadle and other pubby tables, and plush
stools at the carved wooden counter. Allendale Pennine Pale, Silverstone
Pitstop Bitter and a guest from Muckles on handpump and several wines
by the glass served by friendly staff; throughout the year they hold quiz
nights, themed evenings and live music events. In the dining room are beige
tartan-upholstered chairs around white-clothed tables on wide floorboards
and prints on red or yellow walls. There are picnic-sets on the back lawn.
Bedrooms are warm and attractive and make a good base for exploring the
area. They also run Willowford Farm B&B just outside the village.

Rewarding food uses their own lamb and other local, seasonal produce, and
includes smoked salmon fishcakes with horseradish dip, pork belly with black
pudding, crispy crackling and apple sauce, beetroot and shallot tarte tatin with blue
cheese dressing and sweet potato fries, sausages with caramelised onion gravy and
mash, rare-breed beef burger with toppings and chips, chicken in lemon, vermouth and
tarragon sauce, breaded cod with dauphinoise potatoes and tartare sauce, and puddings
such as a pastry tart filled with rum and spice-infused dates, ginger and raisins with
ice-cream and chocolate torte topped with chocolate mousse. *Benchmark main dish:
lamb tagine £12.50. Two-course evening meal £19.50.*

Free house ~ Licensees Liam McNulty and Lauren Harrison ~ Real ale ~ Open 12-10.30 ~
Bar food 12-2.30, 6-8.30 ~ Children welcome ~ Dogs allowed in bar ~ Wi-fi ~ Acoustic night
second Sun of month ~ Bedrooms: £60/£80 *Recommended by Comus and Sarah Elliott,
Alan McQuilan, Carol and Barry Craddock, Caroline Prescott*

HEDLEY ON THE HILL   NZ0759 Map 10

Feathers ⦿ ♚ ▽ ◨

(01661) 843607 – www.thefeathers.net

*Village signposted from New Ridley, which is signposted from B6309 N of Consett;
OS Sheet 88 map reference 078592; NE43 7SW*

• •

Northumbria Dining Pub of the Year

**Imaginative food, interesting beers from small breweries
and friendly welcome in quaint tavern**

Playing an important role in village life, but with a warm welcome for
visitors as well as locals, this is a special place, lucky to have friendly,
hands-on licensees who care about their customers and their inn – and
it shows. The two neat, homely bars are properly pubby, with open
fires, tankard-hung beams, stripped stonework, solid furniture including

settles, and old black and white photographs of local places and farm and country workers. Quickly changing beers include Allendale Golden Plover, Cullercoats Lovely Nelly, Hexhamshire Devils Elbow and Mordue Workie Ticket on handpump, as well as eight farm ciders, 30 wines by the glass, 30 malt whiskies and home-produced cordials; they regularly hold wine and beer evenings, festivals and other events (see their website). The picnic-sets in front are a nice place to sit and watch the world drift by.

 The excellent food uses only produce 'grown, reared, foraged and caught in the North East' and they create everything in-house – even fermenting beer for their vinegar. Dishes include home-produced charcuterie with celeriac coleslaw and gherkins, salt cod fishcakes with aioli, baked local goose egg with fermented wild garlic, pink fir apples and cheese straws, rare-breed pork sausages with creamy mash and real ale gravy, halibut fillet with mussels in cider velouté, lamb, mint and potato pie, beef fillet wellington with field mushroom and chicken liver parfait and madeira gravy, and puddings such as rhubarb and almond tart with clotted cream and dark chocolate brownie with vanilla ice-cream. *Benchmark main dish: pot-roast roe deer with red cabbage and ale gravy £14.00. Two-course evening meal £21.00.*

Free house ~ Licensees Rhian Cradock and Helen Greer ~ Real ale ~ Open 6-11 Mon-Weds; 12-11 Thurs-Sat; 12-10.30 Sun; closed Mon-Weds lunchtimes ~ Bar food 6-8.30 Weds; 12-2, 6-8.30 Thurs, Fri; 12-2.30, 6-9 Sat; 12-4.30 Sun ~ Children welcome ~ Wi-fi
Recommended by Comus and Sarah Elliott, Dr Simon Innes, Claire Adams, Lucy and Giles Gibbon, John and Abigail Prescott

NEWTON
NZ0364 Map 10
Duke of Wellington 🍽️⭐ ♀ 🍺 🛏️
(01661) 844446 – www.thedukeofwellingtoninn.co.uk
Off A69 E of Corbridge; NE43 7UL

Big stone pub with modern and traditional furnishings, well kept ales, good wines by the glass and highly thought-of food; bedrooms

In fine weather, the seats on the back terrace have lovely views across the Tyne Valley; on chillier days, it's warm and cosy inside. The bustling bar has leather chesterfields, built-in cushioned wall seats, farmhouse chairs and tables on honey-coloured flagstones, a woodburning stove with a shelf of books to one side, and rustic stools against the counter. Here they keep Greene King Old Speckled Hen and Hadrian Border Tyneside Blonde with guests from local breweries such as Anarchy, Mordue and Wylam on handpump, a dozen wines by the glass and 12 malt whiskies; TV, darts, dominoes and daily papers. The L-shaped restaurant has elegant tartan and wood dining chairs around pale tables on bare boards, modern art on exposed stone walls, and french windows that lead out to the terrace. Paintwork throughout is contemporary. They hold event evenings (gin tastings, open mike nights and so forth) – see their website for details. Bedrooms are comfortable and well equipped and our readers use them regularly.

The impressive food, served all day, includes breakfasts for non-residents (8-10am), goats cheese pannacotta with beetroot gel and goats milk foam, gin-cured salmon with herb yoghurt, ruby grapefruit, dehydrated fennel and a quail egg, charred cauliflower, pea croquette and corn purée with roasted corn, tempura courgette flower, leeks, parsley sauce and a crispy egg, spiced lamb kofta with raita and pitta bread, turbot with a crispy oyster, fennel and dill purée, a spring onion potato cake, sea vegetables and crab bisque steaks with a choice of sauce and triple-cooked chips, and puddings such as coconut milk rice pudding with roasted pineapple, rum compressed pineapple and Malibu ice-cream and dark chocolate fondant with raspberry compote. *Benchmark main dish: steak in ale pie £12.95. Two-course evening meal £19.00.*

Free house ~ Licensee Rob Harris ~ Real ale ~ Open 11-11 ~ Bar food 12-9; 12-5 Sun ~ Restaurant ~ Children welcome ~ Dogs allowed in bar ~ Wi-fi ~ Bedrooms: £95/£120
Recommended by Comus and Sarah Elliott, Pat and Stewart Gordon, Katherine Matthews, Lionel Smith, Andy and Louise Ramwell

 NEWTON-BY-THE-SEA   NU2424 Map 10

Ship ◄

(01665) 576262 – www.shipinnnewton.co.uk
Low Newton-by-the-Sea, signed off B1339 N of Alnwick; NE66 3EL

In a charming square with good simple food and own-brew beers; best to check winter opening times

This row of converted fishermen's cottages, now a cosy pub, is in a lovely spot and brews its own beers to boot. On handpump there are usually four on at any one time from a choice of 26 – maybe Ship Inn Dolly Daydream, Indian Summer, Squid Ink and a guest beer; also 14 malt whiskies and half a dozen wines by the glass. The plainly furnished but cosy bare-boards bar on the right has nautical charts on dark pink walls, while another simple room on the left has beams, hop bines, some bright modern pictures on stripped-stone walls and a woodburning stove in a stone fireplace; darts, dominoes. It can get extremely busy at peak times, so it's best to book in advance   and there might be a queue for the bar. Tables outside look across the sloping village green and down to the sea and you can walk along the massive stretch of empty, beautiful beach with views all the way to Dunstanburgh Castle (English Heritage). There's no nearby parking from May to September, but there's a car park up the hill.

Good, honest food includes sandwiches and ciabattas, kipper pâté with oatcakes, local salami with piccalilli, home-made pesto with roasted cherry tomatoes and cheese on pasta, local hand-picked crab salad, slow-cooked pork belly with cider gravy and apple sauce, rib-eye steak with onion marmalade, and puddings such as apple and berry crumble and chocolate pecan pie. *Benchmark main dish: crab sandwich £6.95. Two-course evening meal £20.00.*

Own brew ~ Licensee Christine Forsyth ~ Real ale ~ Open 11-11; 12-10 Sun (11-5 Mon-Weds; 12-5 Sun in winter) ~ Bar food 12-2.30, 7-8; not Sun-Tues evenings ~ Well behaved children welcome ~ Dogs welcome ~ Wi-fi ~ Live music – check website *Recommended by Comus and Sarah Elliott, Noel and Judy Garner, James and Becky Plath, Serena and Richard Furber, Freddie and Sarah Banks, Martinthehills*

 NORTH SHIELDS   NZ3668 Map 10

Staith House ⬤ ♀

(0191) 270 8441 – www.thestaithhouse.co.uk
Fish Quay/Union Road; NE30 1JA

Smashing food and real ales in refurbished dining pub with friendly staff and seats outside

It's best to arrive early – or book a table in advance – if you're hoping to enjoy the first class food. The attractive interior blends stripped wood, brickwork and stone with upholstered armchairs and dining chairs, captain's chairs and tartan wall seating, a medley of wooden tables and slate flooring and bare boards; to one end are some high bar chairs around equally high tables. Above the white woodburning stove are candles on a big mantlebeam and a large, rustic mirror, while the walls have ships' lamps and vintage photographs of the Tyne. Caledonian Golden XPA, Robinsons Dizzy Blonde and Theakstons Lightfoot Bitter on handpump and ten wines by the glass are served by enthusiastic welcoming staff. Picnic-sets and solid benches and tables are arranged on side terraces and the hanging baskets look pretty against the blue-painted pub walls.

 Using the best local produce and cooked by the landlord (a former *MasterChef* finalist), the creative food includes confit duck leg and duck liver mousse with toasted nuts and seeds, grilled mackerel fillet with tomato essence, cucumber and watermelon, pollack fillets with brown shrimp tartare sauce, samphire and chips, roast leg of local lamb with fresh mint sauce, loin of fallow deer with slow-roasted beetroot, cheese and wild mushrooms, smoked eel with parsley mash, crispy onions and cabbage, and puddings such as treacle tart with coconut, rum and lime sorbet and caramel chocolate mousse with griottine cherries. *Benchmark main dish: corn-fed chicken breast with garlic purée, madeira and lemon £16.50. Two-course evening meal £22.00.*

Free house ~ Licensee John Calton ~ Real ale ~ Open 11-11; 12-11 Sun ~ Bar food 12-3, 6-9; 12-3.30, 6-9.30 Sat; 12-4.30 Sun ~ Children welcome until 7.30pm ~ Dogs allowed in bar ~ Wi-fi ~ Live music Sun 3pm *Recommended by Peter Pilbeam, Alf and Sally Garner, Patricia Hawkins, John Stephenson, Glen and Patricia Fuller, John and Claire Masters*

ROMALDKIRK NY9922 Map 10
Rose & Crown ★
(01833) 650213 – www.rose-and-crown.co.uk
Just off B6277; DL12 9EB

18th-c coaching inn with accomplished cooking, attentive service and a fine choice of drinks; bedrooms

This is a lovely Teesdale village and this handsome old inn faces the green where you can still see the original stocks and water pump. The beamed bar area has lots of brass and copper, old-fashioned seats facing a warming log fire, a Jacobean oak settle, a grandfather clock, and old farm tools and black and white pictures of Romaldkirk on the walls. Black Sheep and Thwaites Wainwright with maybe a seasonal guest such as Village Brewer White Boar on handpump, seven wines by the glass, 22 malt whiskies and several gins. The hall has wine maps and other interesting prints, a cosy little snug has sofas and armchairs by a woodburning stove and there's an oak-panelled restaurant. Picnic-sets line the front terrace. The comfortable bedrooms (in the main building, the courtyard or Monk's Cottage) make a civilised base for the area, and breakfasts are highly thought-of. The village church is interesting and the exceptional Bowes Museum and High Force waterfall are nearby; the owners provide an in-house guide for days out in the area, and a *Walking in Teesdale* book.

 Inventive food includes lunchtime sandwiches, pigeon breast with beetroot, pearl barley, cobnuts, smoked bacon and sorrel, red cabbage-cured salmon with beetroot rémoulade, orange and herring roe, broccoli risotto with blue cheese emulsion, crispy cauliflower leaves, braised leeks and parmesan, chicken caesar salad, burger with toppings, fried onions and triple-cooked chips, sea trout with saffron potatoes, samphire, brown shrimps and scallop roe, and puddings such as dark chocolate and hazelnut brownie with white chocolate sauce and coffee ice-cream and vanilla pannacotta with rhubarb textures and passion fruit. *Benchmark main dish: Pork, sage and apple pie with mustard mash, parsnips and creamed cabbage £14.50. Two-course evening meal £21.00.*

Free house ~ Licensee Cheryl Robinson ~ Real ale ~ Open 11am-11.30pm; closed first week Jan ~ Bar food 12-2.30, 6-9 ~ Restaurant ~ Children welcome but under-8s must leave by 8pm ~ Dogs allowed in bar and bedrooms ~ Wi-fi ~ Bedrooms: £130/£140 *Recommended by Mark Hamill, Julie Swift, Gail and Frank Hackett, Camilla and Jose Ferrera, Muriel and Spencer Harrop, Ruby and Simon Swettenham*

SEAHOUSES
NU2232 Map 10
Olde Ship ★ ◖ £ ⇌
(01665) 720200 – www.seahouses.co.uk

Just off B1340, towards harbour; NE68 7RD

Lots of atmosphere and maritime memorabilia in busy little inn, with views across harbour to Farne Islands; bedrooms

The same friendly family have been running this harbourside stone inn since it was first licensed in 1812 to serve visiting herring fishermen. The old-fashioned bar has a cheerful, bustling atmosphere, a rich assemblage of nautical bits and pieces and even the floor is made of scrubbed ships' decking: lots of shiny brass fittings, ships' instruments and equipment, a knotted anchor made by local fishermen and sea pictures and model ships (including fine ones of the North Sunderland lifeboat and the Seahouses' Grace Darling lifeboat). There's also a model of the *Forfarshire*, the paddle steamer that local heroine Grace Darling went to rescue in 1838 (you can read more of the story in the pub), and even the ship's nameboard. An anemometer takes wind-speed readings from the top of the chimney. It's all gently lit by stained-glass sea-picture windows, lantern lights and a winter open fire. Simple furnishings include built-in leatherette pews around one end, stools and cast-iron tables. Black Sheep, Greene King Old Speckled Hen, Hadrian Border Farne Island Pale Ale and Theakstons Best Bitter on handpump (summer guests too), eight wines by the glass from a good wine list and 35 malt whiskies; background music and TV. The battlemented side terrace (you'll also find fishing memorabilia out here) and one window in the sun lounge look across the harbour to the Farne Islands (as do some bedrooms); if you find yourself here as dusk falls, the light of the Longstones lighthouse shining across the fading evening sky is a charming sight. The pub is not really suitable for children – though there is a little family room, and children are welcome on the terrace (as are walkers). You can book boat trips to the Farne Islands at the harbour, and there are bracing coastal walks, notably to Bamburgh, Grace Darling's birthplace.

 The sensibly short menu includes a wide choice of hot and cold sandwiches and paninis, pork terrine with apricot and gherkins, moules marinière, chilli bean stew, trio of mixed grilled fish (salmon, plaice and sea bass) with dill mayonnaise, minted lamb casserole, fresh crab salad, barbecue pork ribs with chips, gammon with egg and pineapple, rib-eye steak with peppercorn sauce, and puddings such as chocolate fudge gateau and banana and butterscotch pudding. *Benchmark main dish: beer-battered fish and chips £9.25. Two-course evening meal £18.00.*

Free house ~ Licensees Judith Glen and David Swan ~ Real ale ~ Open 11-11; 12-11 Sun ~ Bar food 12-2.30, 7-8.30 ~ Restaurant ~ Children allowed in lounge and dining room if eating, but must be over 10 in bedrooms ~ Wi-fi ~ Bedrooms: £48/£96 *Recommended by Comus and Sarah Elliott, Noel and Judy Garner, Peter Smith and Judith Brown, Martinthehills, John and Sylvia Harrop, Pieter and Janet Vrancken*

STANNERSBURN
NY7286 Map 10
Pheasant £ ⇌
(01434) 240382 – www.thepheasantinn.com

Kielder Water road signposted off B6320 in Bellingham; NE48 1DD

Friendly village inn with quite a mix of customers, homely bar food and streamside garden; bedrooms

With Kielder Water nearby, this family-run inn is particularly popular at lunchtime. The low-beamed lounge has ranks of old local photographs on stripped stone and panelling, brightly polished surfaces, shiny brasses, dark wooden pubby tables and chairs and upholstered stools ranged along the counter; there are several open fires. The separate public bar is simpler and opens into another snug seating area with beams and panelling. The friendly licensees and courteous staff serve Timothy Taylors Landlord and a couple of guests such as Mordue Northumbrian Blonde and Wylam 007 Vic Secret on handpump, wines by the glass, 38 malt whiskies and a couple of farm ciders. There are picnic-sets in the streamside garden, plus a pony paddock. Staying overnight in the comfortable bedrooms gives you time to explore the beautiful surrounding countryside, and they have now got a self-catering cottage as well.

🍴 Well thought-of food using local produce includes twice-baked cheese soufflé, chicken liver parfait with apple and ginger chutney, a daily vegetarian dish, chicken breast filled with cream cheese and sun-dried tomatoes and wrapped in parma ham, moroccan-style baked cod with roasted vegetable couscous, game and mushroom pie, salmon, lemon sole, monkfish or sea bass grilled with herb butter or served with a light cream sauce, and puddings such as lemon and lime cheesecake and seasonal fruit crumble; they'll also do you a packed lunch. *Benchmark main dish: slow-cooked lamb with rosemary and redcurrant sauce £14.50. Two-course evening meal £20.00.*

Free house ~ Licensees Walter and Robin Kershaw ~ Real ale ~ Open 12-3, 6-11; closed Mon, Tues Nov-Mar ~ Bar food 12-2.30, 6-8.30 ~ Restaurant ~ Children welcome ~ Dogs allowed in bedrooms ~ Wi-fi ~ Bedrooms: £80/£110 *Recommended by John Poulter, Comus and Sarah Elliott, Peter Smith and Judith Brown, Simon and Alex Knight, Dr Peter Crawshaw, Jill and Hugh Bennett*

 WARK

NY8676 Map 10

Battlesteads 🍺 🛏

(01434) 230209 – www.battlesteads.com

B6320 N of Hexham; NE48 3LS

Eco pub with good local ales, fair value interesting food and a relaxed atmosphere; comfortable bedrooms

Close to Wark Forest, this pretty pub is in a village on a scenic road by the North Tyne River. The nicely restored, low-beamed, carpeted bar has a woodburning stove with a traditional oak surround, comfortable seats including some deep leather sofas and easy chairs, and old *Punch* country life cartoons on the terracotta walls above a dark dado. As well as 13 wines by the glass, 20 malt whiskies, 35 gins and a farm cider, they keep four good changing local ales such as Durham Magus, Fyne Jarl, Hadrian Border Secret Kingdom and High House Farm Nels Best on handpump at the heavily carved dark oak bar counter; service is excellent. Background music and TV. There's also a restaurant, a spacious conservatory and tables on the terrace. Some of the ground-floor bedrooms have disabled access, and they're licensed to hold civil marriages. The owners are extremely conscientious about the environment and gently weave their beliefs into every aspect of the business – they grow their own produce, have a charging point in the car park for electric cars and use a biomass boiler.

🍴 Produce is carefully sourced and some is home-grown: sandwiches, game terrine with mustard butter and onion bread, seared scallops with kimchi (korean spicy fermented vegetables), chicken fajitas with sour cream, salsa, guacamole and cheese, beer-battered hake and chips, roasted pepper, goats cheese and pine nut ravioli, braised beef cheek with buttery mash, moroccan-style lamb with couscous and harissa, venison bourguignon, and puddings such as orange and chocolate cheesecake and banana parfait with toffee sauce. *Benchmark main dish: cajun chicken with cream, prawns, bacon and sauté potatoes £13.95. Two-course evening meal £22.00.*

Free house ~ Licensees Richard and Dee Slade ~ Real ale ~ Open 11-11 ~ Bar food 12-3, 6.30-9 ~ Restaurant ~ Children welcome ~ Dogs allowed in bar and bedrooms ~ Wi-fi ~ Bedrooms: £70/£120 *Recommended by Comus and Sarah Elliott, Mark Hamill, R L Borthwick, Peter Smith and Judith Brown, Caroline and Steve Archer, Charlie Stevens, Martinthehills*

WINSTON
NZ1416 Map 10

Bridgewater Arms ⭐🍴 ♀

(01325) 730302 – www.thebridgewaterarms.com
B6274, just off A67 Darlington–Barnard Castle; DL2 3RN

Former schoolhouse with quite a choice of appealing food, three real ales and seats outside

Before or after visiting this carefully converted Victorian schoolhouse, do stroll down to the fine old bridge across the River Tees – it's really worth a look. The high-ceilinged bar has an informal, friendly atmosphere, an open log fire, cushioned settles and chairs, a wall lined with bookcases and high chairs against the counter where they keep Brakspears Bitter, Rudgate Jorvik Blonde and a guest beer on handpump, a dozen wines by the glass and 12 malt whiskies. The two rooms of the restaurant have high-backed black leather dining chairs around clothed tables on stripped wooden flooring or tartan carpet, wine bottles lining a delft shelf and various prints and pictures on pale yellow walls. There are some picnic-sets at the front.

Fish and shellfish play a big part in the food here: mussels with shallots, garlic, tarragon and cream, langoustines in garlic butter, monkfish and bacon on curried prawn risotto, and sole fillets and crab with spinach, wild garlic and parsley butter sauce. They also offer cheddar and spinach soufflé, confit duck leg with wild garlic mash and red wine sauce, venison loin with wild mushrooms and pancetta, and puddings such as chocolate pudding with chocolate sauce and Armagnac-soaked prune frangipane tart with salted caramel ice-cream. *Benchmark main dish: sea bass and scallops with stir-fried vegetables and sweet chilli sauce £24.00. Two-course evening meal £30.00.*

Free house ~ Licensee Paul Grundy ~ Real ale ~ Open 12-3, 6-11; closed Sun, Mon ~ Bar food 12-2, 6-9 ~ Restaurant ~ Well behaved children welcome ~ Wi-fi *Recommended by Isobel Mackinlay, Edward May, Edward and William Johnston, Dave Sutton, Max and Steph Warren, Belinda Stamp*

Also Worth a Visit in Northumbria

Besides the fully inspected pubs, you might like to try these pubs that have been recommended to us and described by readers. Do tell us what you think of them: feedback@goodguides.com

ACOMB NY9366
Miners Arms (01434) 603909
Main Street; NE46 4PW Friendly little 18th-c village pub with good value traditional food (not Sun evening, Mon) including weekday set menu and popular Sun roasts, Wylam, Yates and guests, comfortable settles in carpeted bar, huge fire in stone fireplace, back dining area; acoustic night first Mon of month, quiz last Thurs; children and dogs welcome, a couple of tables out in front, more in back courtyard, open all day weekends, closed weekday lunchtimes. *(Charles Fraser)*

ALLENDALE NY8355
Golden Lion (01434) 683225
Market Place; NE47 9BD Friendly 18th-c two-room pub with enjoyable good value traditional food, well kept Wylam, Timothy Taylors and guests alongside beers from new on-site brewery, games area with pool and darts, upstairs weekend restaurant; regular live music; children and dogs welcome, Allendale Fair first weekend June, New Year's Eve flaming barrel procession, open all day (till late Fri, Sat). *(Comus and Sarah Elliott)*

We say if we know a pub allows dogs.

ALNMOUTH NU2410
★**Red Lion** (01665) 830584
Northumberland Street; NE66 2RJ
Friendly former coaching inn with peaceful
sheltered garden and raised deck giving
wide views over the Aln estuary; pleasant
relaxed bar with heavy black beams, classic
leather wall banquettes and window seats,
old local photographs on dark mahogany
brown panelling, cheerful fires, well
kept ales such as Black Sheep, Roosters,
Tempest and Tyne Bank (Oct beer festival),
half a dozen wines by the glass, popular
often interesting food from good paninis
up, stripped-brick restaurant with flagstones
and woodburner; background and monthly
live music, Tues quiz, free wi-fi; children
and dogs (in bar) welcome, comfortable
well equipped bedrooms, open all day
from 9.30am. *(Comus and Sarah Elliott,
Noel and Judy Garner)*

ALNMOUTH NU2410
Sun (01665) 830983
Northumberland Street; NE66 2RA
Comfortable banquettes in long low-beamed
bar with open fire one end, woodburner
the other, carpet or bare boards, sturdy
candlelit pine tables and plenty to look
at including driftwood decorations, small
contemporary dining area, decent well
priced traditional food from sandwiches
and hot baguettes up, ales such as Adnams
and Black Sheep, friendly staff and chatty
locals; background music; children welcome,
attractive seaside village, four bedrooms,
open all day. *(Michael Doswell)*

ALNWICK NU1813
John Bull (01665) 602055
Howick Street; NE66 1UY Popular
chatty drinkers' pub – essentially the front
room of an early 19th-c terraced house;
good selection of well kept changing ales,
real cider, extensive choice of bottled
belgian beers and well over 100 malt
whiskies; fortnightly live music Mon,
darts and dominoes, annual beer festival;
small beer garden, closed weekday
lunchtimes. *(Justine and Neil Bonnett)*

ALNWICK NU1813
Plough (01665) 602395
Bondgate Without; NE66 1PN Smart
contemporary pub-boutique hotel in
Victorian stone building (under same
management as the Jolly Fisherman
at Craster – see Main Entries); well
kept Timothy Taylors Landlord and a
guest, several wines by the glass and
extensive range of gins, good food (not
Sun evening) in bar, bistro or upstairs
restaurant, friendly helpful staff; children
and dogs welcome, pleasant streetside
raised terrace, seven bedrooms, open
all day. *(Andy and Louise Ramwell)*

ALNWICK NU1813
Tanners Arms (01665) 602553
Hotspur Place; NE66 1QF Welcoming
little drinkers' pub with three well kept local
ales and a decent glass of wine, flagstones
and stripped stone, warm woodburner,
plush stools and wall benches, small tree
in the centre of the room; juke box and
some live acoustic music, TV; dogs welcome,
open all day weekends, closed weekday
lunchtimes. *(Andy and Louise Ramwell)*

ANICK NY9565
★**Rat** (01434) 602814
*Village signposted NE of A69/A695
Hexham junction; NE46 4LN* Popular
country pub with cosy traditional bar; coal
fire in kitchen range, cottagey knick-
knacks such as floral chamber-pots hanging
from beams, china and glassware on a
delft shelf, well kept Allendale, Blythe,
Hexhamshire, Tyne Bank, Timothy Taylors
and Wylam, farm cider, a dozen wines by
the glass (including champagne) and a
local gin, good well presented interesting
food (not Sun evening), efficient service,
conservatory; background music, free
wi-fi; children welcome, charming garden
with dovecote, statues and lovely North
Tyne Valley views, limited parking (you
can park around the village green),
open all day. *(Comus and Sarah Elliott,
Noel and Judy Garner, Michael Doswell)*

AYCLIFFE NZ2822
★**County** (01325) 312273
*The Green, Aycliffe; just off A1(M)
junction 59, off A167 at West Terrace
and then right to village green; DL5 6LX*
Smart inn with open-plan rooms in red,
green and cream, seating from cushioned
dining chairs to tartan banquettes, stripy
carpets, painted ceiling joists and log
fires, highly regarded imaginative food in
minimalist wood-floored restaurant, Thwaites
Lancaster Bomber, two guests ales, a craft
beer and 11 wines by the glass, friendly
service; free wi-fi; children welcome, no
dogs inside, metal tables and chairs out
at front, seven attractive bedrooms, open
all day, food all day Sun till 7pm, useful A1
stop. *(Edward Nile, Tom Stone, Donald Allsopp)*

BAMBURGH NU1834
★**Castle** (01668) 214616
Front Street; NE69 7BW Clean and
comfortably old-fashioned pub with generous
helpings of reasonably priced food including
good crab sandwiches, a couple of well kept
ales such as Alnwick and decent house
wines, expanded dining area to cope with
summer visitors, local artwork for sale,
open fires (one in old range); free wi-fi;
children welcome, no dogs inside, circular
picnic-sets in nice beer garden, open (and
food) all day. *(Comus and Sarah Elliott)*

BAMBURGH NU1834
Lord Crewe Arms (01668) 214243
Front Street; NE69 7BL Small early
17th-c hotel prettily set in charming coastal
village dominated by Norman castle; bar and
restaurant (Wynding Inn) with painted joists
and panelling, bare stone walls and light
wood floor, warm woodburner, beers from
Northumberland and Charles Wells, good
varied menu; sheltered garden with castle
view, short walk from splendid sandy beach,
ten comfortable bedrooms. *(Comus and Sarah
Elliott, William and Ann Reid, Barry Collett)*

BARDON MILL NY7566
Twice Brewed (01434) 344534
*Military Road (B6318 NE of Hexham);
NE47 7AN* Large busy inn well placed for
fell-walkers and major Hadrian's Wall sites;
up to half a dozen ales including some from
newly opened microbrewery, craft beers
and good value home-cooked food (shortish
menu), winter steak nights Tues and Thurs,
cheerful helpful service, freshened-up
interior with warm woodburners, artwork
for sale; children and dogs welcome,
disabled access, picnic-sets in back garden,
18 bedrooms, open (and food) all day.
(John Poulter, John and Sylvia Harrop)

BARNARD CASTLE NZ0516
Old Well (01833) 690130
The Bank; DL12 8PH Welcoming 17th-c
coaching inn with two bars, restaurant and
conservatory, enjoyable reasonably priced
food (not Sun evening) including some
good indian dishes, five well kept regional
ales and decent wines by the glass, friendly
helpful staff; Thurs open mike night and
other live music, Tues quiz; children and dogs
welcome, secluded terrace over town walls,
ten bedrooms, useful for Bowes Museum,
open all day. *(Tony and Maggie Harwood)*

BARRASFORD NY9173
★Barrasford Arms (01434) 681237
*Village signposted off A6079 N of
Hexham; NE48 4AA* Bustling sandstone
inn with owner-chef's highly praised
interesting food (not Sun evening) including
good value set lunch, welcoming local
atmosphere and friendly helpful staff,
traditional log-fire bar with old photographs
and bric-a-brac, up to three real ales such
as Sharps and Wylam, two dining rooms, one
with wheelback chairs around neat tables
and stone chimneybreast hung with guns
and copper pans, the other with comfortably
upholstered dining chairs; background music,
TV, darts; children welcome, plenty of nearby
walks, handy for Hadrian's Wall, 11 bedrooms
and well equipped bunkhouse, open all day
weekends, closed Mon. *(Charles Fraser)*

BEADNELL NU2229
Beadnell Towers (01665) 721211
The Wynding, off B1340; NE67 5AY
Large pub-hotel with good food in log-fire
bar or restaurant including local fish/seafood
(can get busy with summer tourists and
booking advised), well kept ales such as
Black Sheep, Hadrian Border and Jarrow,
decent wines from shortish list, pleasant
helpful staff; some live music; children
welcome, seats outside, ten bedrooms
(a bit of a climb to some), open all day
weekends. *(Comus and Sarah Elliott)*

BEAMISH NZ2154
Beamish Hall (01207) 233733
NE of Stanley, off A6076; DH9 0YB
Converted stone-built stables in courtyard
at back of hotel, popular and family-friendly
(can get crowded), with five or six beers
from own microbrewery (tours available),
decent wines and enjoyable food including
some interesting choices, uniformed staff;
regular events such as live music, barbecues
and a summer festival; plenty of seats
outside, big play area, open (and food)
all day. *(Peter Smith and Judith Brown)*

BEAMISH NZ2055
Black Horse (01207) 232569
*Red Row (off Beamishburn Road NW,
near A6076); OS Sheet 88 map reference
205541; DH9 0RW* Late 17th-c country
dining pub with contemporary/rustic interior,
heritage colours blending with beams,
flagstones and some exposed stonework,
enjoyable fairly traditional food (not Sun
evening) from hot or cold sandwiches up,
half a dozen well kept changing beers
and decent wines by the glass, friendly
attentive staff, cosy fire-warmed front
room extending to light spacious dining
area with central bar, another dining
room upstairs, airy conservatory; children
welcome, dogs in bar, restful views from big
paved terrace, more tables on grass, open
all day. *(Peter Smith and Judith Brown)*

BERWICK-UPON-TWEED NT9952
Barrels (01289) 308013
Bridge Street; TD15 1ES Small friendly
pub with interesting collection of pop
memorabilia and other bric-a-brac, some
eccentric furniture including barber's
chair in bare-boards bar, red banquettes
in back room, Anarchy Blonde Star and
four guests kept well, also foreign bottled
beers, snacky food; regular live acoustic
music (often in basement bar) and good
quality background music; children and
dogs welcome, open all day. *(Tony Scott)*

CATTON NY8257
★Crown (01434) 618351
*B6295, off A686 S of Haydon Bridge;
NE47 9QS* Welcoming 18th-c village pub
in good walking country; inner bar with
stripped-stone and bare boards, dark tables,
mate's chairs and a traditional settle,
good log fire, well kept Allendale beers
and enjoyable home-cooked blackboard

food, efficient staff, extension with folding glass doors opening on to small garden, lovely Allen Valley views; folk night Thurs, quiz every other Tues, bar billiards; children and dogs welcome, open (and food) all day weekends, closed till 5pm weekdays. *(Comus and Sarah Elliott)*

CHATTON NU0528
Percy Arms (01668) 215244
B6348 E of Wooler; NE66 5PS
Sympathetically refurbished stone-built country inn (same owners as the Northumberland Arms at Felton); good well presented food in flagstoned log-fire bar or light panelled dining room (booking advised), six well kept ales including Allendale and a house beer from local Hetton Law, good whisky and gin choice, efficient friendly staff, open fire and woodburner; May beer festival, darts; children and dogs (in bar) welcome, picnic-sets on small front lawn, five well appointed bedrooms, good breakfast, quiet village with sweeping views of the Cheviot Hills, open (and food) all day. *(Simon and Alex Knight)*

CORBRIDGE NY9864
★**Black Bull** (01434) 632261
Middle Street; NE45 5AT Rambling 18th-c beamed pub with four linked rooms, mix of traditional pub furniture including leather banquettes, wood, flagstone or carpeted floors, log fires (one in open hearth with gleaming copper canopy), ceramic collection in front room and information about Hadrian's Wall, enjoyable reasonably priced pubby food, three Greene King ales, a guest beer and good choice of wines by the glass, efficient cheery service; children welcome, no dogs, seats out on two-level terrace, open all day. *(Comus and Sarah Elliott)*

CORBRIDGE NY9868
★**Errington Arms** (01434) 672250
About 3 miles N of town; B6318, on A68 roundabout; NE45 5QB Busy 18th-c stone-built pub by Hadrian's Wall attracting good mix of diners and walkers; beamed bars with pine panelling, stone and burgundy walls, farmhouse and other chairs around pine tables on strip-wood flooring, log fire and woodburner, good choice of popular fresh food from interesting sandwiches up, several wines by the glass and well kept ales such as Jennings and Wylam, friendly helpful staff; background music; children welcome, a few picnic-sets out in front, closed Sun evening, Mon. *(Comus and Sarah Elliott, Pat and Stewart Gordon, Martin Day)*

CORNHILL-ON-TWEED NT8539
Collingwood Arms (01890) 882424
Main Street; TD12 4UH Restored and comfortably updated Georgian stone hotel; nice little bar with decent wines, around 25 malt whiskies and a well kept local ale

such as Alnwick, good reasonably priced food in adjoining dining room or more pricey restaurant, friendly helpful staff, open fires; free wi-fi; children and dogs (in bar) welcome, tables out in lovely grounds, local fishing and shooting, 15 well appointed bedrooms (named after ships from the Battle of Trafalgar), good breakfast, open all day. *(Pat and Stewart Gordon)*

CROOKHAM NT9138
Blue Bell (01890) 820252
Pallinsburn; A697 Wooler–Cornhill; TD12 4SH Welcoming 18th-c roadside country pub with enjoyable freshly prepared food and well kept ales such as Fyne and Greene King, friendly attentive service; dogs welcome in bar, comfortable clean bedrooms, good breakfast, open (and food) all day weekends. *(Bob and Melissa Wyatt)*

DARLINGTON NZ2814
Number Twenty 2 (01325) 354590
Coniscliffe Road; DL3 7RG Popular long Victorian pub with high ceiling, wood and carpeted floors, exposed brickwork and striking red and gold wallpaper, up to 13 quickly changing ales (tasters offered) including own Village Brewer range, draught continentals and decent wine selection, snacky food till 7pm in back part, good friendly service; closed Sun, otherwise open all day. *(Colin Chambers)*

DINNINGTON NZ2073
White Swan (01661) 872869
Prestwick Road; NE13 7AG Large open-plan pub-restaurant popular for its wide range of good value food including gluten-free menu, reasonably priced wines and a well kept changing ale, efficient friendly service even at busy times; background music; family area (children's menu till 5.30pm), no dogs inside, disabled facilities, orangery and attractive garden with pond, handy for Newcastle Airport, open all day Sun till 6pm. *(Gerry and Rosemary Dobson)*

DUNSTAN NU2419
Cottage (01665) 576658
Off B1339 Alnmouth–Embleton; NE66 3SZ Comfortable single-storey beamed inn, enjoyable reasonably priced food (smaller helpings available) from fairly standard menu, three well kept ales, restaurant and conservatory; live music, quiz nights, free wi-fi; children and dogs welcome, attractive garden with terrace and play area, ten bedrooms, open all day. *(John and Sylvia Harrop)*

DURHAM NZ2742
Dun Cow (0191) 386 9219
Old Elvet; DH1 3HN Unchanging backstreet pub in pretty 16th-c black and white timbered cottage; tiny chatty front bar with wall benches, corridor to long narrow back lounge with banquettes, well kept

ales such as Black Sheep and Camerons, good value simple food, friendly staff; background and occasional live music, Mon quiz, free wi-fi; children and dogs welcome, open all day. *(Freddie and Sarah Banks)*

DURHAM
Head of Steam (0191) 383 2173
Reform Place, North Road; DH1 4RZ Hidden-away pub close to the river, modern open-plan interior on two floors, good range of well kept changing ales, real ciders and plenty of bottled continental beers, competitively priced food till early evening (4pm Sun) including burgers and pizzas; background music (live upstairs); dogs welcome, outside tables, open all day. *(Dr J Barrie Jones, Peter Smith and Judith Brown)*

DURHAM   NZ2742
Market Tavern (0191) 386 2069
Market Place; DH1 3NJ Narrow Taylor Walker pub in the heart of old Durham; traditionally refurbished interior including some cosy leather seating booths, six well kept changing ales and a proper cider, enjoyable pubby food, efficient service, popular with students (university-run folk night Weds); looks out on marketplace at front and to indoor market behind, open (and food) all day. *(Richard Tilbrook, Dr J Barrie Jones, Paul Humphreys)*

DURHAM   NZ2642
Old Elm Tree (0191) 386 4621
Crossgate; DH1 4PS Comfortable friendly old pub on steep hill across from castle, two-room main bar and small lounge, four well kept ales including Caledonian Deuchars IPA and Wychwood Hobgoblin (occasional beer festivals), reasonably priced home-made food, open fires, folk and quiz nights; dogs welcome, small back terrace, open all day. *(Peter Smith and Judith Brown)*

DURHAM   NZ2742
Shakespeare (0191) 340 9438
Saddler Street; DH1 3NU Friendly 19th-c brick pub (bigger inside than it looks) retaining some of its original character; compact front bar incorporating the former snug, larger back lounge, well kept Caledonian Deuchars IPA, Fullers London Pride and two guests, pubby lunchtime food; Weds folk night; children (till 5pm) and dogs welcome, convenient for castle, cathedral and river, can get crowded (particularly weekends), open all day. *(Paul Humphreys)*

DURHAM   NZ2742
Swan & Three Cygnets
(0191) 384 0242 *Elvet Bridge; DH1 3AG* Victorian pub in good bridge-end spot high above river, city views from big windows

and terrace, bargain lunchtime food and Sam Smiths ales, helpful friendly young staff, popular with locals and students; open all day. *(Freddie and Sarah Banks)*

EACHWICK   NZ1069
Plough (01661) 853555
Stamfordham Road (extension of B6324), S of village; NE18 0BG Large remote stone inn recently reopened after extensive refurbishment; open-plan split-level lounge with comfortable furniture including sofas, tub and winged-back chairs on wood or carpeted floors, good choice of enjoyable generously served food from snacks to specials, Caledonian Deuchars IPA and a couple of guests kept well, fairly priced wines, efficient service, separate restaurant (Fri and Sat evenings, Sun lunchtime); outside seating, three bedrooms, open all day Fri and Sat, till 6.30pm Sun, closed Mon. *(Comus and Sarah Elliott, Michael Doswell)*

EARSDON   NZ3273
★ Beehive (0191) 252 9352
Hartley Lane; NE25 0SZ Popular well run 18th-c country pub with cosy linked rooms, low painted beams, soft lighting, woodburners and one or two quirky touches, three well kept hatch-served ales (tasting trays available), good fairly priced home-made food (best to book weekends) from sandwiches, light dishes and sharing boards up, friendly service; background and some live music, TVs; children welcome, dogs in certain areas, picnic-sets out overlooking fields, summer bar and separate family garden with play area, open (and food) all day, kitchen shuts 6pm Sun. *(Michael Doswell, Martinthehills)*

EDMUNDBYERS   NZ0150
Punch Bowl (01207) 255545
B6278; DH8 9NL Small village's community local; well kept ales and good choice of reasonably priced food including daily specials, friendly service; TV, free wi-fi; children and dogs (in bar) welcome, fishing on nearby Derwent Reservoir (permits available from the pub), six updated bedrooms, good breakfast, open (and food) all day. *(John Poulter, Robert Wivell)*

EGGLESCLIFFE   NZ4213
Pot & Glass (01642) 651009
Church Road; TS16 9DQ Friendly little 17th-c village pub with up to seven well kept ales including Black Sheep and Caledonian Deuchars IPA, good value home-made food (some themed nights); monthly folk club; children welcome, picnic-sets on back terrace with play area, lovely setting behind church, open all day weekends, closed Mon lunchtime. *(Pete Jennings)*

Pubs close to motorway junctions are listed at the back of the book.

EGLINGHAM   NU1019

★**Tankerville Arms** (01665) 578444
B6346 Alnwick–Wooler; NE66 2TX
Traditional 19th-c stone pub with contemporary
touches and cosy friendly atmosphere; beams,
bare boards and some stripped stone,
banquettes and warm fires, well kept Hadrian
Border and a guest, good wines, enjoyable
nicely presented food from shortish menu,
raftered split-level restaurant; free wi-fi;
children, walkers and dogs welcome, lovely
country views from back garden, attractive
village, three bedrooms, closed lunchtimes
Mon, Tues, otherwise open (and food) all day.
(Comus and Sarah Elliott, Michael Doswell)

ELLINGTON   NZ2791
Plough (01670) 861761
Front Street/Ashington Street; NE61 5JB
Comfortably refurbished pub in former pit
village, enjoyable reasonably priced food
from traditional choices up including some
appealing vegetarian options, ales such as
Black Sheep and Greene King, friendly young
staff, spacious panelled restaurant, back
bar; TV, fruit machine; children welcome,
bedrooms, open all day. *(Michael Doswell)*

EMBLETON   NU2322
Dunstanburgh Castle Hotel
(01665) 576111 *B1339; NE66 3UN*
Comfortable hotel in attractive spot near
magnificent coastline, good choice of
enjoyable bar and restaurant food using
local meat and fish, good for vegetarians
too, efficient friendly service, local ales
and decent wines (five by the glass),
two lounges for coffee with open fires;
children welcome, seats in nice garden,
bedrooms and self-catering cottages,
open all day. *(John and Sylvia Harrop)*

EMBLETON   NU2322
Greys (01665) 576983
*Stanley Terrace off W T Stead Road, turn
at the Blue Bell; NE66 3UY* Welcoming
pub with carpeted bar and cottagey back
dining room, well priced home-made food
(wider evening choice) including good crab
sandwiches and local fish, interesting range
of well kept regional beers such as Hadrian
Border and Wylam; juke box, sports TV;
children and dogs welcome, small walled
back garden, raised decking with village
views, open all day. *(Charles Fraser)*

ESH   NZ1944
Cross Keys (0191) 373 1279
Front Street; DH7 9QR Friendly 18th-c
village local; hearty helpings of good well
priced food (not Sun evening) including
blackboard specials, half a dozen ales
such as Big Lamp and Black Sheep,
afternoon teas; children welcome, colourful
hanging baskets at front, good country
views from behind, closed Mon, otherwise
open all day. *(Bob and Melissa Wyatt)*

FELTON   NU1800
Northumberland Arms (01670)
787370 *West Thirston; B6345, off A1
N of Morpeth; NE65 9EE* Stylish 19th-c
inn across road from River Coquet (same
owners as the Percy Arms at Chatton);
beams, stripped stone/brickwork and
woodburner in roomy open-plan lounge
bar, flagstones and nice mix of furnishings
including big sofas, restaurant with mix
of light wood tables on bare boards, good
sensibly priced food from bar snacks and
standard dishes up (best to book), bread
from their own bakery, three or four well
kept mainly local beers and nice wines by the
glass from short well chosen list; Thurs quiz,
monthly folk night (fourth Tues); children
welcome, dogs in bar, six good bedrooms,
open (and food) all day. *(Pete Jennings)*

FROSTERLEY   NZ0236
★**Black Bull** (01388) 527784
Just off A689 W of centre; DL13 2SL
Unique in having its own peal of bells
(licensee is a campanologist); great
atmosphere in three interesting traditional
beamed and flagstoned rooms with coal
fires (one in old range), landlord's own
good photographs and three grandfather
clocks, four well kept local ales, farm cider
and perry, carefully chosen wines and
malt whiskies, good food using local and
organic ingredients (best to book evenings),
popular Sun lunch; some acoustic live
music; well behaved children and dogs
welcome, attractive no-smoking terrace
with wood-fired bread oven and old railway
furnishings (opposite steam line station),
closed Sun evening to Weds, otherwise
open all day. *(Max and Steph Warren)*

GATESHEAD   NZ2563
Central (0191) 478 2543
Half Moon Lane; NE8 2AN Unusual
19th-c wedge-shaped pub (Grade II listed)
restored by the Head of Steam group; well
preserved features including notable buffet
bar, great choice of changing local ales, real
ciders and lots of bottled beers, low-priced
food such as burgers from short menu,
upstairs function rooms and roof terrace;
some live music; dogs welcome, open all day
(till 1am Fri, Sat). *(Simon and Alex Knight)*

GREAT WHITTINGTON   NZ0070
Queens Head (01434) 672516
*Village signed off A68 and B6018
N of Corbridge; NE19 2HP* Handsome
golden stone village pub; dark leather chairs
around sturdy tables, some stripped-stone
walls and soft lighting, nice hunting mural
above old fireplace in long narrow bar, ales
such as Firebrick and High House Farm,
friendly helpful service, popular chinese
restaurant at back; background music,
quiz nights, pool; children and dogs (in
bar) welcome, picnic-sets under parasols

on little front lawn, closed lunchtimes (all day Mon Oct-Apr). *(Martinthehills)*

GRETA BRIDGE   NZ0813
★**Morritt** (01833) 627232
Hotel signposted off A66 W of Scotch Corner; DL12 9SE Striking 17th-c country house hotel popular for weddings and the like; properly pubby bar with big windsor armchairs and sturdy oak settles around traditional cast-iron-framed tables, open fires and remarkable 1946 mural of Dickensian characters by JTY Gilroy (known for Guinness advertisements), big windows looking on to extensive lawn, Thwaites Major Morritt (named for them) and Timothy Taylors Landlord, 19 wines by the glass from extensive list, bar and restauarant food, afternoon teas, friendly staff; background music; children and dogs (in bar and bedrooms) welcome, attractively laid-out split-level garden with teak tables and play area, open all day. *(Barry Collett, WAH)*

HALTWHISTLE   NY7166
Milecastle Inn (01434) 321372
Military Road; B6318 NE – OS Sheet 86 map reference 715660; NE49 9NN Sturdy stone-built pub on remote moorland road running alongside Hadrian's Wall; small rooms off beamed bar, brasses, horsey and local landscape prints, two log fires, ales such as Big Lamp and a few wines by the glass, traditional food, small comfortable restaurant; children welcome, no dogs inside, tables and benches in big sheltered garden with dovecote and stunning views, self-catering cottage next door. *(Comus and Sarah Elliott, Hilary and Neil Christopher, Max Simons, Peter Hacker, Peter Lowe)*

HART   NZ4634
White Hart (01429) 265468
Just off A179 W of Hartlepool; Front Street; TS27 3AW End of terrace pub with old ship's figurehead outside, fires in both bars (one in old range), wide choice of fairly traditional food (not Sun evening) cooked by friendly landlady, ales such as Camerons Strongarm; live music; children welcome, no dogs inside, open all day. *(Charles Fraser)*

HAYDON BRIDGE   NY8364
★**General Havelock** (01434) 684376
Off A69 Corbridge–Haltwhistle; B6319 (Ratcliffe Road); NE47 6ER Old darkly painted pub, a short stroll upstream from Haydon Bridge itself; L-shaped bar with open fire and some Philip Larkin memorabilia, well kept Great North Eastern Rivet Catcher and a guest, decent choice of wines by the glass and highly rated generously served food (not Sun evening, Mon) cooked by owner-chef, elegant stripped-stone barn dining room and terrace with fine South Tyne river views; children and dogs (in bar) welcome, closed Mon lunchtime. *(Comus and Sarah Elliott, Louella Miles, Michael Doswell)*

HEXHAM   NY9464
Heart of Northumberland
(01434) 608013 *Market Street; NE46 3NS* Renovated old local with five real ales such as Allendale, Timothy Taylors and Wylam, craft beers and proper ciders, plenty of wines by the glass too and well cooked reasonably priced food from pub favourites up, good cheerful service, painted panelling and exposed stonework, traditional furniture on bare boards, woodburner in big fireplace; live music Tues; children and dogs welcome, open (and food) all day including brunch from 11am. *(Comus and Sarah Elliott)*

HIGH HESLEDEN   NZ4538
Ship (01429) 836453
Off A19 via B1281; TS27 4QD Popular Victorian inn with half a dozen well kept changing ales and good food cooked by landlady including some interesting specials, sailing ship models including big one hanging with lanterns from boarded ceiling, log fire; sea views over farmland from garden, six bedrooms in new block, closed Mon lunchtime. *(Des Mannion)*

HOLWICK   NY9126
Strathmore Arms (01833) 640362
Back road up Teesdale from Middleton; DL12 0NJ Attractive and welcoming old stone-built country pub in beautiful scenery just off Pennine Way; four well kept ales including a house beer (Strathmore Gold) brewed by Mithril and several real ciders, good low-priced traditional food, beams, flagstones and open fire; live music Fri, quiz first Weds of month, pool, free wi-fi; well behaved dogs welcome, popular with walkers, four bedrooms, closed Tues, otherwise open all day. *(Michael Doswell)*

HOLY ISLAND   NU1241
Crown & Anchor (01289) 389215
Causeway passable only at low tide, check times (01289) 330733; TD15 2RX Comfortably unpretentious pub-restaurant by the priory; a couple of well kept Hadrian Border ales and enjoyable traditional home-made food including specials (maybe local oysters), cosy little bar with open fire, more roomy modern back dining room; children and dogs (in bar) welcome, garden with lovely views (they may ask for a credit card if you eat out here), four bedrooms, open all day. *(Trevor)*

HOLY ISLAND   NU1241
Ship (01289) 389311 *Marygate; TD15 2SJ* Nicely set pub and busy in season; beamed bar with wood floors, stone walls and maritime memorabilia, big stove, steps down to carpeted lounge/dining area, popular pubby menu including fish/seafood, Holy Island Blessed Bitter badged for them plus one or two guests, 30 malt whiskies;

background music; children welcome and usually dogs (but do ask first), sheltered sunny garden, four bedrooms, may close at quiet times. *(Andy and Louise Ramwell)*

HORSLEY   NZ0965
Lion & Lamb (01661) 852952
B6528, just off A69 Newcastle–Hexham; NE15 0NS 18th-c former coaching inn; main bar with scrubbed tables, stripped stone, flagstones and panelling, up to four changing ales and a real cider, good food from sandwiches, tapas and hearty traditional choices up, maybe summer seafood and winter game, efficient service, bare-boards restaurant; children and dogs (not evenings) welcome, Tyne views from attractive sunny garden with roomy terrace, play area, open all day. *(Comus and Sarah Elliott, Michael Doswell)*

HURWORTH-ON-TEES   NZ2814
★ Bay Horse (01325) 720663
Church Row; DL2 2AQ Popular dining pub (best to book, particularly weekends) with very good imaginative food, quite pricey but they do offer a fixed-price alternative (lunchtimes Mon-Sat, evenings Mon-Thurs), also vegetarian menu and children's meals, three well kept changing ales, extensive wine list, efficient friendly young staff, sizeable bar with good open fire, restaurant, and another dining room upstairs; seats on back terrace and in well tended walled garden, charming village by River Tees, open all day. *(Richard Cole)*

HURWORTH-ON-TEES   NZ3110
Otter & Fish (01325) 720019
Off A167 S of Darlington; Strait Lane; DL2 2AH Pleasant village setting across road from the Tees; up-to-date open-plan layout with flagstones and stripped wood, open fires and church candles, nice mix of dining furniture, comfortable armchairs and sofas by bar, popular well presented local food including set deals and decent vegetarian and children's choices (best to book especially weekends), friendly helpful staff, ales such as Black Sheep and several wines by the glass; closed Sun evening. *(Mike Swan)*

KNARSDALE   NY6754
Kirkstyle (01434) 381559
Signed off A689; CA8 7PB Welcoming 18th-c country pub in lovely spot looking over South Tyne Valley to hills beyond; enjoyable reasonably priced food (not Mon) including range of sausages and some interesting specials, well kept Yates and a summer guest, dining room; games area with darts and pool; children and dogs welcome, handy for Pennine Way, South Tyne Trail and South Tynedale Railway (Lintley terminus), closed Sun evening, Tues and may shut from 9pm if quiet. *(Comus and Sarah Elliott)*

LANGDON BECK   NY8531
Langdon Beck Hotel
(01833) 622267 B6277 Middleton–Alston; DL12 0XP Isolated unpretentious inn with two cosy bars and spacious lounge, well placed for walks including Pennine Way; good choice of enjoyable generous food using local Teesdale beef and lamb, Black Sheep and Ringwood, friendly helpful staff, interesting rock collection in 'geology room'; children and dogs welcome, events including Easter 'egg jarping' and late May beer festival; wonderful fell views from garden, seven bedrooms (some sharing bathrooms), open all day, closed Mon in winter. *(Pete Jennings)*

LANGLEY ON TYNE   NY8160
Carts Bog Inn (01434) 684338
A686 S, junction B6305; NE47 5NW Isolated 18th-c moorside pub with heavy beams and stripped-stone walls, old photographs, spindleback chairs around mix of tables on red carpet, nice open fire, enjoyable generously served food from sandwiches up including signature Bog Pie (steak and mushroom suet pudding) and popular Sun lunch (best to book), two or three well kept local ales, friendly efficient young staff, games room with pool and darts; children and dogs welcome, picnic-sets in big garden with views, quoits, open all day weekends, closed Mon, Tues. *(John Poulter, Martinthehills)*

LESBURY   NU2311
★ Coach (01665) 830865
B1339; NE66 3PP Picturesque stone pub at heart of pretty village; low-beamed rooms with pubby furniture on tartan carpet, dark leather stools by counter serving well kept Timothy Taylors Landlord and a guest, snug off to left with sofas and armchairs, small dining room and restaurant both with woodburners, popular good value home-made food including daily specials, friendly staff; background music; children and dogs (not in restaurant) welcome, picnic-sets on front terrace and in back garden, lovely flowering tubs and baskets, handy for Alnwick Castle, open (and food) all day in summer, closed afternoons in winter and no Sun evening food. *(Dr Nick Wright)*

LONG NEWTON   NZ3716
Vane (01642) 580401
Darlington Road; TS21 1DB Revamped 19th-c pub gaining reputation for landlord-chef's good food from pub favourites to imaginative restaurant dishes, lunchtime/early-evening set menu, Black Sheep and a couple of guests, warm friendly service, pale green walls contrasting solid dark dining tables and chairs, upholstered banquettes, cosy bar with log fire; background music; children and dogs (in bar) welcome, picnic-sets in garden with far-reaching

views across fields, three bedrooms, open all day Sun, closed Mon lunchtime, no food Sun evening, Mon. *(Michael Doswell)*

LONGFRAMLINGTON NU1301
Granby (01665) 570228
Front Street; NE65 8DP Welcoming old coaching inn run by same family for three generations; highly regarded food cooked by chef-proprietor from well executed pub favourites to creative restaurant dishes, also good value set lunch and afternoon teas, a real ale such as Sharps Doom Bar kept well and several malt whiskies, comfortable traditional beamed interior with bar, lounge and small restaurant; children welcome, no dogs, five bedrooms, open (and food) all day. *(Michael Doswell)*

LONGFRAMLINGTON NU1301
Village Inn (01665) 570268
Just off A697; Front Street; NE65 8AD Friendly 18th-c stone inn arranged into three distinct areas; tasty freshly prepared pub food including good Sun carvery, own-brewed VIP beers along with local guests; some live music, Mon quiz, pool room; comfortable bedrooms and self-catering cabins (just outside the village), open all day. *(Simon and Alex Knight)*

LONGHORSLEY NZ1494
Shoulder of Mutton (01670) 788236
East Road; A697 N of Morpeth; NE65 8SY Comfortable bar and restaurant with welcoming staff, good choice of enjoyable reasonably priced food from lunchtime baguettes up, weekday deals and popular Sun carvery till 6pm (must book), Courage Directors, Caledonian Deuchars IPA and a guest, good selection of other drinks; background music, TV, fruit machine; children and dogs (in bar) welcome, picnic-sets in back garden, two bedrooms, open all day, food all day Thurs-Sun. *(Guy and Caroline Howard)*

MAIDEN LAW NZ1749
Three Horseshoes (01207) 520900
A6067 N of Lanchester; DH7 0QT Spacious whitewashed roadside dining pub, family-run, with enjoyable good value food from varied menu including several vegetarian options, also bargain weekday two-course lunch deal and afternoon teas, neatly kept open-plan interior with central beamed and quarry-tiled bar, mix of high-backed cane chairs, leatherette sofas and tub chairs, two-way woodburner, conservatory; children welcome, disabled parking and wheelchair access, garden with play area, open all day Sat, till 5pm Sun, closed Mon. *(Michael Doswell)*

MICKLETON NY9724
★**Crown** (01833) 640381
B6277; DL12 0JZ Bustling pub under friendly hands-on licensees, simply furnished

bars and dining areas, cushioned settles, upholstered leather and wooden dining chairs around all sorts of tables on polished boards, country prints and photographs, woodburner flanked by two leather armchairs, Jennings, Banks's and local guests, several wines by the glass and good quality food; children and dogs welcome, rustic picnic-sets in garden with fine rural views, two self-catering properties and campsite, open (and food) all day, till 9pm (6pm) Sun. *(Lesley and Peter Barrett, Michael Doswell, Alison and Dan Richardson, Patti and James Davidson)*

MIDDLETON NZ0685
Ox (01670) 772634
Village signed off B6343, W of Hartburn; NE61 4QZ Warmly welcoming Georgian country pub in small tucked-away village, a couple of local ales such as Acton and Wylam, tasty straightforward home-made food (not Sun evening); children and dogs welcome, seats outside, handy for Wallington (NT), open all day weekends, closed weekday lunchtimes. *(Charles Fraser)*

MILFIELD NT9333
Red Lion (01668) 216224
Main Road (A697 Wooler–Cornhill); NE71 6JD Comfortable 18th-c coaching inn with good fairly priced food from chef-owner including weekday set lunch, well kept ales such as Black Sheep and Thwaites, a dozen wines by the glass and decent coffee, friendly efficient service; Weds quiz; children welcome, pretty garden by car park at back, six bedrooms, good breakfast, open all day. *(Michael Doswell)*

MORPETH NZ1986
Tap & Spile (01670) 513894
Manchester Street; NE61 1BH Cosy and easy-going two-room pub with up to eight well kept ales such as Everards, Greene King and Timothy Taylors, Weston's cider, short choice of good value lunchtime food, friendly staff, traditional pub furniture and interesting old photographs, quieter back lounge (children allowed here) with coal-effect gas fire, board and other games; background and live music including good folk session Sun afternoon, sports TV; dogs welcome in front bar, open all day Fri-Sun. *(Pete Jennings)*

NETHERTON NT9807
Star (01669) 630238
Off B6341 at Thropton, or A697 via Whittingham; NE65 7HD Simple unchanging village local run by charming long-serving landlady (licence has been in her family since 1917), large high-ceilinged room with wall benches and many original features, friendly regulars, range of bottled beers, no food, music, children or dogs; quiz first Weds of the month; open evenings only from 7.30pm, closed Mon and Thurs. *(Justine and Neil Bonnett)*

NEWBROUGH NY8768
Red Lion 01434 674226
Stanegate Road; NE47 5AR Former
coaching inn with light airy feel and buoyant
atmosphere; log fire, flagstones and half-
panelling, old local photographs and some
large paintings, good sensibly priced food
(not Sun evening, Mon) in bar and two
dining areas from well filled baguettes up
(more elaborate evening menu), a couple
of well kept local ales, friendly efficient
service, games room with pool and darts,
little shop selling local crafts and artwork;
children and dogs (not at food times)
welcome, garden behind with decking,
good local walks and on NCN cycle route
72, six bedrooms, open all day. *(Gray)*

NEWBURN NZ1665
Keelman (0191) 267 1689
*Grange Road: follow Riverside Country
Park brown signs off A6085; NE15 8ND*
Former 19th-c pumping station with eight
well kept Big Lamp beers (brewed on
site), relaxed atmosphere and good mix
of customers in airy high-ceilinged bar
with lofty arched windows, well spaced
tables and chairs, more seating in upper
gallery, fair value traditional food, modern
dining conservatory; background music,
free wi-fi; children welcome, spacious
terraces among flower tubs and shrub beds,
good play area, comfortable bedrooms
in two separate buildings, open (and
food) all day. *(Bob and Melissa Wyatt)*

NEWCASTLE UPON TYNE NZ2464
★ Bacchus (0191) 261 1008
*High Bridge E, between Pilgrim Street
and Grey Street; NE1 6BX* Smart,
spacious and comfortable Fitzgerald pub
with ocean liner look; two-level interior
with lots of varnished wood, pillars, ship
and shipbuilding photographs, good value
lunchtime food (not Sun) from sandwiches
and panini to pubby mains and some unusual
specials, nine very well kept changing
ales (beer festivals), plenty of bottled
imports, farm cider and splendid range
of whiskies, decent coffee too, friendly
helpful staff; background music; disabled
facilities, handy for Theatre Royal, open
all day and can get very busy. *(Jeremy
King, Peter Smith and Judith Brown)*

NEWCASTLE UPON TYNE NZ2464
Bodega (0191) 221 1552
Westgate Road; NE1 4AG Majestic
Edwardian drinking hall next to Tyne
Theatre; eight real ales including Big
Lamp, Fyne and Oakham, good range
of bottled beers, friendly service, snug
front cubicles, spacious back area with
two magnificent stained-glass cupolas;
background music, Thurs quiz, big-screen
TVs (very busy on match days), darts,
free wi-fi; open all day. *(Pete Jennings)*

NEWCASTLE UPON TYNE NZ2563
★ Bridge Hotel (0191) 232 6400
*Castle Square, next to high-level bridge;
NE1 1RQ* Big, well divided, high-ceilinged
bar around servery with replica slatted
snob screens, well kept Anarchy Blonde
Star, Sharps Doom Bar and eight quickly
changing guests, real cider, friendly helpful
staff, bargain lunchtime food, magnificent
fireplace, great river and bridge views from
raised back area, live music upstairs including
long-standing Mon folk club; background
music, sports TV, games machines; flagstoned
back terrace overlooking part of old town
wall, open all day. *(Roger and Donna Huggins)*

NEWCASTLE UPON TYNE NZ2563
Bridge Tavern (0191) 261 9966
Under the Tyne Bridge; NE1 3UF
Bustling place under same ownership as the
Town Wall; airy interior with brick walls and
lots of wood, industrial-style ceiling, view
into back microbrewery (joint venture with
Wylam), a dozen or so beers including local
guests (tasting trays available), generous
helpings of well liked often unusual food
(all day, till 7pm Fri-Sun) from snacks and
sharing boards up, friendly helpful staff;
background music; well behaved children
and dogs allowed before 7pm, upstairs bar
and good roof terrace, open all day (till
1am Fri, Sat). *(Comus and Sarah Elliott,
Peter Smith and Judith Brown, David Thorpe)*

NEWCASTLE UPON TYNE NZ2563
Broad Chare (0191) 211 2144
*Broad Chare, just off quayside opposite
law courts; NE1 3DQ* Traditional feel
although only recently converted to a pub,
popular british-leaning food from bar snacks
such as crispy pigs ears and Lindisfarne
oysters to hearty main courses, four real
ales including a house beer from Wylam
(Writer's Block), good choice of bottled
beers, wines and whiskies, bare-boards bar
and snug, old local photographs, upstairs
dining room; background music; children
welcome till 7pm (later upstairs), no dogs,
next door to the Live Theatre, open all day
(no food Sun evening). *(Pete Jennings)*

NEWCASTLE UPON TYNE NZ2464
Centurion (0191) 261 6611
Central Station, Neville Street; NE1 5HL
Glorious high-ceilinged Victorian décor with
tilework and columns in former first class
waiting room, well restored with comfortable
leather seats giving club-like feel, half a dozen
ales including Black Sheep and Caledonian,
good value food till early evening; background
music, big-screen sports TV; useful café-deli
next door, open all day. *(Paul Humphreys,
Comus and Sarah Elliott,)*

NEWCASTLE UPON TYNE NZ2464
City Tavern (0191) 232 1308
Northumberland Road; NE1 8JF

Revamped half-timbered city-centre pub on different levels, ten real ales including a couple badged for them, decent wine list and some 60 gins, good food from reasonably priced varied menu (plenty for vegetarians), friendly staff; children and dogs (theirs are Alfie, Hector and Dillon) welcome, open (and food) all day, kitchen closes 7pm Sun. *(Comus and Sarah Elliott, Gray)*

NEWCASTLE UPON TYNE NZ2664
Cluny (0191) 230 4474
Lime Street; NE1 2PQ Bar-café-music venue in interesting 19th-c mill/warehouse (part of the Head of Steam group); low-priced home-made food including various burgers and hot dogs, Sun brunch, up to eight well kept ales, good selection of other beers, ciders and some exotic rums, good friendly service, sofas in comfortable raised area with daily papers and art magazines, back gallery featuring local artists; background music and regular live bands (also in Cluny 2 next door); children (till 7pm) and dogs allowed, picnic-sets out on green, striking setting below Metro bridge, parking nearby can be difficult, open (and food) all day. *(Paul Humphreys)*

NEWCASTLE UPON TYNE NZ2365
Cosy Dove (0191) 260 2895
Hunters Road, Spital Tongues; NE2 4NA Newly refurbished pub on city fringe (former Spital House); opened-up interior blending contemporary and traditional features, exposed stonework and quirky colour scheme, leather sofas and rugs on wood floor, bookcases and open fire, good fairly priced food from open kitchen including range of burgers and some clay oven dishes, well kept Batemans, Deuchars, Theakstons and a beer labelled for the pub, good range of wines and gins, friendly welcoming staff; background music, quiz nights and sports TV; revamped exterior with tables behind planters, open all day, no food Sun evening. *(Michael Doswell)*

NEWCASTLE UPON TYNE NZ2563
★ Crown Posada (0191) 232 1269
The Side; off Dean Street, between and below the two high central bridges (A6125 and A6127); NE1 3JE City's oldest pub, just a few minutes' stroll from the castle; long narrow room with elaborate coffered ceiling, stained-glass counter screens and fine mirrors with tulip lamps on curly brass mounts (matching the great ceiling candelabra), long green built-in leather wall seat flanked by narrow tables, old photos of Newcastle and plenty of caricatures, Allendale, Hadrian Border, Highland, Titanic and Wylam, may do sandwiches, heating from fat low-level pipes, music from vintage record player; no credit cards; well behaved children in front snug till 6pm, open all day (midnight Fri, Sat) and can get packed at peak times. *(Paul Humphreys, Roger and Donna Huggins, Gray)*

NEWCASTLE UPON TYNE NZ2664
Cumberland Arms (0191) 265 1725
James Place Street; NE6 1LD Unspoilt traditional 19th-c pub with half a dozen well kept mainly local ales along with good range of craft beers and ciders, two annual beer festivals, limited choice of good value snacky food, friendly obliging staff, bare boards and open fires; events most nights including regular folk sessions, film and quiz evenings; dogs welcome, tables out overlooking Ouseburn Valley, four bedrooms, open all day weekends, from 5pm Mon-Weds, 3pm Thurs, Fri. *(Denis and Margaret Kilner)*

NEWCASTLE UPON TYNE NZ2664
Free Trade (0191) 265 5764
St Lawrence Road, off Walker Road (A186); NE6 1AP Splendidly basic and unpretentious with outstanding views up river from big windows, terrace tables and seats on grass; up to seven real ales, traditional ciders and plenty of bottled beers and whiskies, good sandwiches/pasties and regular pizza nights, warm friendly atmosphere, original Formica tables and coal fire, free juke box, steps down to back room and loos; open all day. *(Pete Jennings)*

NEWCASTLE UPON TYNE NZ2266
Old George (0191) 260 3035
Cloth Market, down alley past Pumphreys; NE1 1EZ Attractive refurbished 16th-c pub (former coaching inn) in cobbled yard, beams and panelling, comfortable armchairs by open fire, well kept/priced ales including Bass, plenty of wines by the glass and cocktails, good value food served by friendly staff; background music at one end, DJ Fri and Sat, open mike Thurs and Sun, sports TV, free wi-fi; children welcome, open all day (till 2am Fri, Sat). *(Pete Jennings)*

NEWCASTLE UPON TYNE NZ2463
Split Chimp
Arch 7, Westgate Road; NE1 1SA Two-floor micropub built into a railway arch; ground-floor bar with cask tables, stools, pews and leather sofas, six well kept ales, five craft beers (more in bottles), real cider and some wines by the glass, snacky food, upstairs skittle alley; live music; open all day Fri and Sat, till 8pm Sun, from 3pm other days. *(Roger and Donna Huggins)*

NEWCASTLE UPON TYNE NZ2463
Town Wall (0191) 232 3000
Pink Lane; across from Central Station; NE1 5HX Newish pub in handsome listed building (sister pub is Bridge Tavern); spacious bare-boards interior with dark walls, button-back banquettes and mix of well spaced tables and chairs, pictures in heavy gilt frames, up to a dozen ales (one badged for them), good choice of bottled

beers and several wines by the glass, well priced food including sharing boards, burgers and pub favourites, basement overspill/function room; background music, free wi-fi; well behaved children and dogs welcome, open all day (till 1am Fri, Sat), food till 7pm Fri-Sun. *(Comus and Sarah Elliott)*

NEWTON-BY-THE-SEA   NU2325
★**Joiners Arms** (01665) 576112
High Newton-by-the-Sea, by turning to Linkhouse; NE66 3EA Updated open-plan village pub-restaurant; flagstoned bar with big front windows and open fire, wood-clad dining area behind, well presented food from interesting sandwiches and sharing plates up, four local ales including Anarchy, carefully chosen wines; background music; children and dogs welcome, picnic-sets out at front and back, good coastal walks, five stylish bedrooms, open all day. *(Comus and Sarah Elliott)*

NEWTON-ON-THE-MOOR   NU1705
Cook & Barker Arms
(01665) 575234 *Village signed from A1 Alnwick–Felton; NE65 9JY* Traditional stone-built country inn; rustic beamed bar with partly panelled walls, upholstered wall benches by scrubbed pine tables, bottles and bric-a-brac on delft shelf, fire in old range one end, woodburner the other, Black Sheep, two guests and seven wines by the glass from extensive list, popular food including early-bird deal Weds and Thurs, friendly helpful staff, separate restaurant with exposed stonework and raftered ceiling; background music; children welcome, dogs in snug and lounge, small outside seating area, 16 bedrooms, Boxing Day hunt starts here, open (and food) all day. *(John and Penny Wildon, John and Sylvia Harrop, Peter Smith and Judith Brown, Johnston and Maureen Anderson)*

PONTELAND   NZ1771
Badger (01661) 867931
Street Houses; A696 SE, by garden centre; NE20 9BT Early 18th-c pub (Vintage Inn) with warren of rooms and alcoves, good log fire, well kept beers such as Bass, Black Sheep and Timothy Taylors, decent range of wines by the glass and enjoyable food, helpful friendly service; background music; children welcome, handy for Newcastle Airport, open (and food) all day. *(Comus and Sarah Elliott, Jeremy King)*

PONTELAND   NZ1773
Blackbird (01661) 822684
North Road opposite church; NE20 9UH Imposing ancient stone pub with opened-up interior, mix of furniture including several high tables and button-back banquettes, wood, slate and tartan-carpeted floors, striking old map of Northumberland and etching of Battle of Otterburn either side of fireplace, larger Tudor stone fireplace in unusual Tunnel Room, good popular food

from bar snacks to restauranty dishes, six well kept ales including one badged for them and over 50 gins, friendly service; background music, sports TV, free wi-fi; children and dogs welcome, picnic-sets out at front, more tables on back lawn, open all day, food till 5pm Sun. *(Michael Doswell, Gerry and Rosemary Dobson)*

RENNINGTON   NU2118
★**Horseshoes** (01665) 577665
B1340; NE66 3RS Comfortable and welcoming family-run pub with nice local feel (may be horses in car park), a couple of well kept ales including Hadrian Border Farne Island, decent wines by the glass and ample helpings of enjoyable locally sourced food, friendly efficient service, simple neat bar with flagstones and woodburner, carpeted restaurant; darts, free wi-fi; children welcome, picnic-sets out on small front lawn, attractive quiet village near coast, Aug scarecrow competition, closed Mon. *(Guy and Caroline Howard)*

ROCHESTER   NY8497
Redesdale Arms (01830) 520668
A68 3 miles W of Otterburn; NE19 1TA Isolated old roadside inn (aka the First & Last) surrounded by unspoilt countryside, warm and cosy, with enjoyable food such as lamb prepared three ways cooked by landlord, Allendale ales, friendly attentive staff; ten bedrooms, open (and food) all day. *(Simon and Alex Knight)*

SEATON SLUICE   NZ3477
Kings Arms (0191) 237 0275
West Terrace; NE26 4RD Friendly busy old pub in pleasant seaside location perched above tidal Seaton Sluice Harbour; good range of beers and enjoyable pubby food (not Sun evening) including gluten-free choices and blackboard specials, beamed and carpeted bar with old photographs and a woodburner at each end, restaurant; children welcome, a few picnic-sets on sunny front grass, more seats in enclosed beer garden behind, open all day. *(Arthur Shackleton)*

SEDGEFIELD   NZ3528
Dun Cow (01740) 620894
Front Street; TS21 3AT Popular 18th-c village inn with low-beamed bar, back tap room and restaurant, extensive choice of enjoyable reasonably priced food including good Sun roast, cheerful efficient staff, four well kept ales such as Black Sheep and Theakstons; children welcome, six comfortable bedrooms, open (and food) all day weekends. *(D M and B K Moores)*

SHINCLIFFE   NZ2940
Seven Stars (0191) 384 8454
High Street N (A177 S of Durham); DH1 2NU Comfortable and welcoming 18th-c village inn, varied choice of good generous food (not Mon) from pub

favourites up, weekday set menu and other deals, three well kept ales such as Durham and Thwaites, coal-effect gas fire in lounge bar, panelled dining room; children welcome in eating areas, dogs in bar, some picnic-sets outside, eight bedrooms, closed Mon lunchtime, otherwise open all day. *(Max and Steph Warren)*

SLALEY NY9757

Rose & Crown (01434) 673996

Church Close; NE47 0AA Welcoming 17th-c pub owned by the village, enjoyable good value food from sandwiches up (not Sun evening, may be reduced choice Mon), local ales such as Allendale, beams and log fires; Sun quiz; children and dogs welcome, garden with long country views, two bedrooms, open all day in summer. *(Charles Fraser)*

SLALEY NY9658

Travellers Rest (01434) 673231

B6306 S of Hexham (and N of village); NE46 1TT Attractive stone-built country pub, spaciously opened up, with farmhouse-style décor, beams, flagstones and polished wood floors, huge fireplace, comfortable high-backed settles forming discrete areas, friendly staff, enjoyable food (not Sun evening, Mon) in bar or quieter dining room, real ales such as Black Sheep and Caledonian; children and dogs welcome, tables outside and well equipped adventure play area, three good value bedrooms, open all day. *(Gray)*

SOUTH SHIELDS NZ3567

Alum Ale House (0191) 427 7245

Ferry Street (B1344); NE33 1JR Welcoming 18th-c bow-windowed pub adjacent to North Shields ferry, open-plan bare-boards bar with fire in old range, a dozen well kept Marstons-related ales; music and quiz nights; seats on front deck overlooking the river, handy for marketplace, open all day. *(Pete Jennings)*

SOUTH SHIELDS NZ3566

Steamboat (0191) 454 0134

Mill Dam/Coronation Street; NE33 1EQ Friendly 19th-c corner pub with nine well kept changing ales, lots of nautical bric-a-brac, bar ceiling covered in flags, raised seating area and separate lounge; near river and marketplace, open all day. *(John Poulter)*

STANNINGTON NZ2179

★ Ridley Arms (01670) 789216

Village signed off A1 S of Morpeth; NE61 6EL Extended Fitzgerald pub handy for A1; several separate areas, each with different mood and style, proper front bar with open fire and cushioned settles, stools

along counter serving up to nine local ales including Alnwick and Hadrian Border, a dozen wines by the glass and good coffee, decent choice of enjoyable reasonably priced food, pleasant helpful staff, several dining areas with comfortable upholstered bucket chairs around dark tables on bare boards or carpet, cartoons and portraits on cream, panelled or stripped-stone walls; background music, Tues quiz, free wi-fi; children welcome, good disabled access, picnic-sets in front and on back terrace, open (and food) all day. *(Comus and Sarah Elliott, Martinthehills)*

SUNDERLAND NZ4057

Ivy House (0191) 567 3399

Worcester Terrace; SR2 7AW Friendly Victorian corner pub off the beaten track, five well kept changing ales such as Dark Star and Maxim, interesting bottled beers and good range of spirits, popular reasonably priced food from open kitchen including burgers and pizzas; background and live music, Weds quiz, sports TV; open (and food) all day. *(Andy and Louise Ramwell)*

TYNEMOUTH NZ3669

Hugos at the Coast (0191) 257 8956

Front Street; NE30 4DZ Welcoming Sir John Fitzgerald pub with open-plan split-level interior, four changing ales and good choice of wines, freshly prepared bar food from sandwiches up, reasonable prices and cheerful service; Weds quiz, sports TV, darts; some pavement seating, open all day, food till 6pm (4pm Sun). *(Peter and Eleanor Kenyon)*

TYNEMOUTH NZ3668

Turks Head (0191) 257 6547

Front Street; NE30 4DZ Friendly John Barras pub with good selection of real ales and craft beers, pie and mash menu, steps between two comfortable small bars, ancient stuffed border collie called Willie and accompanying sad story (the pub is known locally as the Stuffed Dog); background music, sports TVs, darts; open all day. *(Roger and Donna Huggins)*

WARDEN NY9166

Boatside (01434) 602233

Village signed N of A69; NE46 4SQ Old stone-built pub refurbished after flooding, modern décor but still cosy, enjoyable fairly priced food from varied menu, a couple of local ales and decent selection of new world wines, good friendly service; sports TV; children welcome, small neat enclosed garden, attractive spot by Tyne bridge, bedrooms in adjoining cottages (some self-catering), open (and food) all day. *(Comus and Sarah Elliott)*

All *Guide* inspections are anonymous. Anyone claiming to be a *Good Pub Guide* inspector is a fraud. Please let us know.

WARENFORD   NU1429
White Swan (01668) 213453
Off A1 S of Belford; NE70 7HY Friendly
simply decorated bar with a couple of
changing ales such as Alnwick and Greene
King, steps down to cosy restaurant
with William Morris wallpaper, good
carefully presented imaginative food
(reduced lunchtime choice), cheerful
efficient service, warm fires; children
and dogs (in bar) welcome, open all day
Sun. *(Michael Doswell, William and Ann Reid)*

WARKWORTH   NU2406
Hermitage (01665) 711258
Castle Street; NE65 0UL Rambling
former coaching inn with good choice of
popular home-made food including Sun
carvery, Jennings, Marstons and guests,
decent range of wines, friendly staff,
quaint décor with fire in old range, small
upstairs restaurant; background and some
live music; children and dogs welcome,
attractive setting with benches and hanging
baskets out in front, bedrooms, open (and
food) all day. *(Pat and Stewart Gordon)*

WELDON BRIDGE   NZ1398
★ **Anglers Arms** (01665) 570271
*B6344, just off A697; village signposted
with Rothbury off A1 N of Morpeth;
NE65 8AX* Traditional coaching inn nicely
located by bridge over River Coquet; two-part
bar with cream walls or oak panelling,
shiny black beams hung with copper pans,
profusion of fishing memorabilia, taxidermy
and a grandfather clock, some unexpectedly
low tables with matching chairs, sofa by
coal fire, three changing ales, around
40 malt whiskies and decent wines, well
liked generous food, friendly helpful staff;
background music; children and dogs (in
bar) welcome, attractive garden and good
play area with assault course, fishing rights,
comfortable bedrooms, open (and food) all
day. *(Comus and Sarah Elliott, Martinthehills)*

WEST BOLDON   NZ3460
Red Lion (0191) 536 4197
Redcar Terrace; NE36 0PZ
Bow-windowed, flower-decked pub with
various cosy linked areas; beamed bar
with open fire, three real ales including
Black Sheep and Mordue from ornate wood
counter, separate snug and conservatory
dining room, good choice of popular well
priced food, friendly service and relaxed
atmosphere; seats out on back decking,
open all day. *(Roger and Donna Huggins)*

WEST WOODBURN   NY8986
Bay Horse (01434) 270218
A68; NE48 2RX Modernised 18th-c
roadside inn with horse-themed décor,
Belhaven and other Greene King ales,
decent wines and good range of reasonably
priced food including Sun carvery, friendly

service, can eat in carpeted log-fire bar or
separate restaurant; background music;
children and dogs welcome, riverside garden,
seven bedrooms. *(Freddie and Sarah Banks)*

WHITFIELD   NY7857
Elks Head (01434) 345282
*Off A686 SW of Haydon Bridge;
NE47 8HD* Extended old stone pub
attractively set in steep wooded valley, light
and spacious, with bar and two dining areas,
good value tasty food, Fullers London Pride
and a couple of local guests, several wines by
the glass, friendly helpful service; children
and dogs (in bar) welcome, picnic-sets in
small pretty front garden by little river,
scenic area with good walks, ten bedrooms
(some in adjacent cottage), open all day
in summer. *(Comus and Sarah Elliott)*

WHITLEY BAY   NZ3742
Left Luggage Room
Metro Station, Northam Road; NE26 3NR
Quirky micropub in former station room,
high vaulted ceiling and brick walls left
in original rough condition adding to the
character, mismatched wooden furniture on
boarded floor, artwork for sale, old suitcases
and trunks stacked below bar counter,
changing craft beers, ales, ciders and good
range of other drinks including several
whiskies and gins (all listed on blackboards),
no food apart from bar snacks, friendly
knowledgeable staff and vibrant chatty
atmosphere; live music some evenings; dogs
welcome, open all day. *(Martinthehills)*

WHORLTON   NZ1014
Fernavilles Rest (01833) 627341
High Stakes, N of village green; DL12 8XD
Refurbished old stone pub on pretty
village's green; log-fire bar and well
divided half-panelled restaurant, popular
reasonably priced food, a house beer
from local Mithril and two guests kept
well, friendly smartly dressed young staff;
children, walkers and dogs welcome (their
black lab is Ralph), three good value
comfortable bedrooms, near historic narrow
suspension bridge over the Tees and handy
for Bowes Museum, closed lunchtimes
(opens around 5pm). *(Michael Doswell)*

WYLAM   NZ1164
★ **Boathouse** (01661) 853431
*Station Road, handy for Newcastle–
Carlisle railway; across Tyne from village
(and George Stephenson's Birthplace
– NT); NE41 8HR* Convivial two-room pub
with a dozen real ales, traditional ciders and
good choice of malt whiskies, thai menu and
some snacky food, friendly knowledgeable
staff, light interior with one or two low
beams and woodburner; fortnightly buskers
night (Tues), juke box, sports TV; children
and dogs welcome, seats outside, close to
station and river, open all day (evenings can
be very busy). *(Comus and Sarah Elliott)*

Nottinghamshire

CAYTHORPE   SK6845 Map 7

Black Horse 🍺 £

(0115) 966 3520 – www.caythorpebrewery.co.uk

Turn off A6097 0.25 miles SE of roundabout junction with A612, NE of Nottingham;
into Gunthorpe Road, then right into Caythorpe Road and keep on; NG14 7ED

Quaintly old-fashioned little pub brewing its own beer, with simple
interior and enjoyable homely food; no children, no credit cards

The good value food and own-brewed ales continue to draw customers
into this old country local. It's been run by three generations of the
same friendly family and little has changed during that time. The homely,
uncluttered, carpeted bar has just five tables, along with brocaded wall
banquettes and settles, decorative plates on a delft shelf, a few horsebrasses
attached to the ceiling joists, and a coal fire. Cheerful regulars might occupy
the few bar stools to enjoy Caythorpe Bitter, Dover Beck and a seasonal ale
brewed in outbuildings here and served alongside a couple of guests such as
Bass on handpump; seven wines by the glass and half a dozen whiskies too.
Off the front corridor is an inner room, partly panelled with a wall bench
running all the way round three unusual, long, copper-topped tables; there
are several old local photographs, darts and board games. Down on the left,
an end room has just one huge round table. There are seats outside. The pub
is close to the River Trent where there are waterside walks.

🍴 Good value home-cooked food (you'll need to book a table in advance) includes
sandwiches, prawn cocktail, mushrooms on toast, three-egg omelettes, lamb chops
with creamed potatoes, gammon and eggs, fish in parsley sauce, and puddings such
as sticky toffee pudding and treacle sponge with custard. *Benchmark main dish:*
beer-battered fish and chips £12.00. Two-course evening meal £17.00.

Own brew ~ Licensee Sharron Andrews ~ Real ale ~ No credit cards ~ Open 12-3, 5.30-11;
12-5, 8-11 Sun; closed Mon except bank holidays ~ Bar food 12-2, 6-8.30; not Sat evening;
all day Sun ~ Dogs allowed in bar ~ Wi-fi *Recommended by Sally and David Champion,*
Anne and Ben Smith, Maddie Purvis

CLAYWORTH   SK7288 Map 7

Blacksmiths

(01777) 818171 – www.blacksmithsclayworth.com

Town Street; DN22 9AD

Bustling dining pub with stylish décor and good, enjoyable food

This interestingly refurbished pub has dining areas with a stylish, contemporary feel that includes some bold paintwork, cushioned walls seats and high-backed chairs around a mix of tables; dramatic flower arrangements and candles in large glass jars add to the overall comfortable feel. The bar has leather chesterfields and armchairs together with upholstered cube seats by a woodburning stove, and bar stools by the counter where you can while away an hour over a pint of Timothy Taylors Landlord and a guest beer on handpump or one of the several wines by the glass. Stairs lead up to a private dining area with a balcony overlooking the countryside. The sunny walled garden contains plenty of tables and chairs and a quirky water feature. The Chesterfield Canal, which circles the village, is popular with bird-watchers, walkers and cyclists. The local church is decorated with lovely murals by the renowned Scottish artist Phoebe Anna Traquair.

 Rewarding food includes sandwiches, chicken liver parfait with red onion marmalade, ham hock and pea tortellini with smoked bacon foam and fresh pea velouté, asparagus and pea risotto with parmesan and lemon, butter-poached cod with sea vegetables, white wine sauce and dill oil, lamb neck with crispy lamb breast, french-style peas and confit potatoes, 10oz rib-eye steak with tomato compote and onion rings, and puddings such as salted caramel eclair with crème anglaise and banana sticky toffee pudding with butterscotch sauce. *Benchmark main dish: burger with toppings and triple-cooked chips £12.95. Two-course evening meal £22.00.*

Free house ~ Licensees William and Vicki Foers ~ Real ale ~ Open 12-3, 5.30-11; 12-8 Sun; closed Mon except bank holidays when they close on Tues instead ~ Bar food 12-2.30, 6-9 (9.30 Fri, Sat); 12-4.30 Sun ~ Children welcome ~ Wi-fi ~ Bedrooms: £108/£120
Recommended by Stephen Woad, Peter and Emma Kelly, Brian and Sally Wakeham, Paul Sherfield, Dr and Mrs A K Clarke

COLSTON BASSETT
Martins Arms ★ ♀ ◀

SK6933 Map 7

(01949) 81361 – www.themartinsarms.co.uk
Village signposted off A46 E of Nottingham; School Lane, near market cross in village centre; NG12 3FD

Nottinghamshire Dining Pub of the Year

Smart dining pub with impressive food, good range of drinks including seven real ales and attractive grounds

The fine choice of drinks in this Elizabethan farmhouse includes a beer named for the pub, Bass, Black Sheep, Elgoods Black Dog Mild, Marstons Pedigree, Ringwood Boondoggle and Timothy Taylors Landlord on handpump, 28 wines by the glass or carafe (including prosecco, champagne and sweet wines) and a fair choice of whiskies and Armagnacs; staff are neatly uniformed. There's a civilised and comfortably relaxed atmosphere, warm log fires in Jacobean fireplaces, fresh flowers and candlelight, and the smart décor includes period fabrics and colours, antique furniture and hunting prints; dominoes and cards. The main dining room is painted in a warm red with gold silk curtains. The lawned garden (with summer croquet and barbecues) backs on to National Trust parkland. Do visit the church opposite and Colston Bassett Dairy (just outside the village) which produces and sells its own stilton cheese.

 Creative food includes pear and cheese salad with truffle honey, walnuts and gingerbread croutons, venison carpaccio with beef tongue, celeriac and black truffle and piccalilli pickled egg, sea bass with caramelised cauliflower purée, capers, raisins and vanilla cockles, cep risotto with brie and beer pickled onions, lamb rump with kofta, miso, yoghurt, aubergine and polenta, pork fillet and faggot with rösti potato, cabbage and scrumpy cream, and puddings such as crispy rice pudding with kaffir lime sorbet, brioche and pineapple purée and white chocolate and milk chocolate mousse with whipped coffee custard, hazelnuts and blood orange. *Benchmark main dish: short ribs cooked in malt and black treacle £22.00. Two-course evening meal £24.00.*

Free house ~ Licensees Lynne Strafford Bryan and Salvatore Inguanta ~ Real ale ~ Open 12-3 (4 Sat), 6-11; 12-4, 7-10.30 Sun ~ Bar food 12-2, 6-9; 12-2.30 Sun ~ Restaurant ~ Children welcome ~ Wi-fi *Recommended by Ian Duncan, Barbara Brown, Elizabeth and Peter May, Sandra King, Jacqui and Alan Swan, Adam Jones*

NEWARK
Prince Rupert ◧

SK7953 Map 7

(01636) 918121 – www.theprincerupert.co.uk
Stodman Street, off Castle Gate; NG24 1AW

Thoughtfully restored historic pub with fine original features, interestingly furnished small bars, local ales and tasty food

Close to the market square in the town centre, this is a timber-framed 15th-c pub that has been carefully renovated recently. It's a lively place with regular events and plenty of chatty locals – though visitors are always warmly welcomed by the friendly, helpful staff. The cosy rooms have a lot of character with some very fine high-backed settles, cushioned wall seats, pubby chairs around polished antique tables, advertising mirrors and old enamelled wall signs, hops, open fires and floors of terracotta tiles, bare floorboards and some carpet. A light and airy conservatory has tricycles hanging from the ceiling, and doors that lead out to the terraced garden. Ales served on handpump from the ornately carved counter include Brains Rev James, Oakham JHB and guests from breweries such as Blue Monkey, Ilkley, St Austell and Stoney Ford Brew and they also offer 22 wines by the glass; background music and TV.

As well as sandwiches, ciabattas and pizza wraps, the pleasing food includes tempura prawns with tartare sauce, mini baked rosemary and garlic camembert, spinach and ricotta cannelloni, beer-battered haddock and chips, chicken caesar salad, pizzas with lots of toppings, sea bass, squid and mussel stew, spicy lamb burger with cajun-style sweet potato fries and mint yoghurt, and puddings such as chocolate orange brownie with vanilla ice-cream and sticky toffee pudding with butterscotch sauce. *Benchmark main dish: steak, ale and blue cheese pie £14.95. Two-course evening meal £20.00.*

Knead Pubs ~ Managers Sam Johnson and Nikki Booth ~ Real ale ~ Open 11-11 (1am Sat) ~ Bar food 12-2.30, 6-9; 12-9 Sat; 12-8 Sun ~ Children welcome ~ Dogs welcome ~ Wi-fi *Recommended by David Hunt, Tony and Maggie Harwood, Professor James Burke*

Also Worth a Visit in Nottinghamshire

Besides the fully inspected pubs, you might like to try these pubs that have been recommended to us and described by readers. Do tell us what you think of them: feedback@goodguides.com

AWSWORTH SK4844
Gate (0115) 932 9821
Main Street, via A6096 off A610 Nuttall–Eastwood bypass; NG16 2RN
Friendly Victorian free house with seven well kept ales including Burton Bridge, bar with woodburner, coal fire in lounge, some snacky food; occasional live music and comedy nights, skittle alley; dogs welcome, disabled facilities, back courtyard and roof terrace, near site of once-famous railway viaduct, open all day. *(Toby Jones)*

BAGTHORPE SK4751

Dixies Arms (01773) 810505

A608 towards Eastwood off M1 junction 27, right on B600 via Sandhill Road, left into School Road; Lower Bagthorpe; NG16 5HF Friendly unspoilt 18th-c brick local with DH Lawrence connections; beams and tiled floors, well kept Greene King Abbot, Theakstons Best and a guest, no food, entrance bar with tiny snug, good fire in small part-panelled parlour's fine fireplace, longer narrow room with toby jugs, darts and dominoes; live music Sat, quiz Sun, beer/folk festival June, free wi-fi; children and dogs (on leads) welcome, picnic-sets out at front, big garden and play area behind, open all day. *(Maggie Dyson)*

BEESTON SK5236

Crown (0115) 925 4738

Church Street; NG9 1FY Everards pub with 14 well kept ales, real ciders/perry and good choice of other drinks, friendly knowledgeable staff, no hot food but fresh cobs and snacks; front snug and bar with quarry-tiled floor, carpeted parlour with padded wall seats, Victorian décor and new polished bar in lounge, beams, panelling and bric-a-brac including an old red telephone box; weekend live music, regular quiz nights and beer festivals; dogs welcome, terrace tables (some under cover), open all day. *(Johnston and Maureen Anderson, David Hunt)*

BEESTON SK5336

Star (0115) 854 5320

Middle Street; NG9 1FX Refurbished three-room inn with fine range of well kept changing ales and extensive choice of whiskies, friendly knowledgeable staff, enjoyable keenly priced pub food along with freshly baked pizzas; live music and quiz nights, separate games room with pool, darts and sports TV; children and dogs welcome, permanent marquee leading through to heated terrace and large grassy garden with play equipment, eight good value bedrooms, open all day. *(Johnston and Maureen Anderson, David Hunt)*

BEESTON SK5336

★Victoria (0115) 925 4049

Dovecote Lane, backing on to the station; NG9 1JG Genuine down-to-earth all-rounder (former red-brick station hotel) attracting good mix of customers; up to 16 real ales (regular beer festivals), two farm ciders, 120 malt whiskies and 30 wines by the glass, good sensibly priced food (order at bar) from varied blackboard menu including plenty for vegetarians, efficient service, three fairly simple unfussy rooms with original long narrow layout (last one for diners only), solid furnishings, bare boards and stripped woodwork, stained-glass windows, some brewerania, open fires; live music and other events including July VicFest, newspapers and board games; children welcome till 8pm, dogs in bar, seats out on covered heated area overlooking platform (trains pass just a few feet away), limited parking, open (and food) all day. *(Clive and Fran Dutson, Dr Martin Owton, Johnston and Maureen Anderson, David Hunt)*

BINGHAM SK7039

Horse & Plough (01949) 839313

Off A52; Long Acre; NG13 8AF Castle Rock pub in 1818 Methodist chapel, low beams, flagstones and stripped brickwork, comfortable open-plan seating including pews, prints and old brewery memorabilia, good selection of beers including their own (tasters offered), real cider and decent wine choice, enjoyable reasonably priced bar food and popular upstairs grill room with open kitchen, good friendly service; background music; children and dogs welcome, disabled facilities, open all day. *(Howard Nicholls)*

BLYTH SK6287

White Swan (01909) 591222

High Street; S81 8EQ Old whitewashed pub opposite the village green, beams, flagstones and exposed brickwork, mix of dining chairs and padded banquettes around assorted tables on flagstones or carpet, Black Sheep, Sharps Doom Bar and Timothy Taylors Landlord, enjoyable pubby food including Sun carvery, friendly service; Sun quiz, TV; children welcome, no dogs inside, tables out in front and in small back garden, open all day. *(Martin Day, Malcolm Phillips, John Saville)*

BRAMCOTE SK5037

White Lion (0115) 925 7841

Just off A52 W of Nottingham; Town Street; NG9 3HH Small friendly 18th-c village pub, three well kept Greene King ales and a couple of guests from bar serving two split-level adjoining rooms, good choice of low-priced pubby food (not Sun or Mon evenings) including Thurs grill night, good value wines too; events such as quiz and poker evenings, live music last Sat of month, darts; children and dogs welcome, tables in garden behind, open all day. *(Richard Tilbrook)*

BUNNY SK5829

Rancliffe Arms (0115) 984 4727

Loughborough Road (A60 S of Nottingham); NG11 6QT Substantial old former coaching inn with linked dining areas, emphasis on good food including popular carvery (Mon evening, Weds, Sat and Sun)

Post Office address codings confusingly give the impression that a few pubs are in Nottinghamshire, when they're really in Derbyshire (which is where we list them).

with excellent range of fresh vegetables, friendly welcoming staff, chunky country chairs around mixed tables on flagstones or carpet, well kept changing range of Marstons-related beers in comfortable log-fire lounge bar with leather sofas and armchairs; background music; children welcome, seating on decking outside, open all day Fri-Sun. *(Gerry and Rosemary Dobson, Johnston and Maureen Anderson)*

CAR COLSTON   SK7242
Royal Oak (01949) 20247
The Green, off Tenman Lane (off A46 not far from A6097 junction); NG13 8JE
Good well priced traditional food (not Sun evening) in biggish 19th-c pub opposite one of England's largest village greens, four well kept Marstons-related ales and decent choice of wines by the glass, woodburner in lounge bar with tables set for eating, public bar with unusual barrel-vaulted brick ceiling; skittle alley; children and dogs welcome, picnic-sets on spacious back lawn, heated smokers' den, camping, open all day Fri-Sun. *(Comus and Sarah Elliott)*

CAUNTON   SK7459
★Caunton Beck (01636) 636793
Newark Road; NG23 6AE Reconstructed low-beamed dining pub made to look old using original timbers and reclaimed oak; scrubbed pine tables and country kitchen chairs, open fire, Black Sheep, Oakham JHB and a beer from sister pub's microbrewery (see Bottle & Glass at Harby), over two dozen wines by the glass, well presented popular food from breakfast on, cheerful obliging staff and relaxed atmosphere; daily newspapers, free wi-fi; children and dogs (in bar) welcome, seats on flowery terrace, handy for A1, open (and food) all day from 8.30am. *(Malcolm Phillips)*

CAYTHORPE   SK6846
Old Volunteer (0115) 966 5822
Caythorpe Road; NG14 7EB Refurbished village dining pub with good food, decent wines and four well kept ales including Timothy Taylors and Theakstons, friendly helpful service, upstairs dining room with view over fields; children and dogs (in bar) welcome, seats out at front and on back deck, open (and food) all day, may close early if quiet. *(Dawn Rooney, Philip Turton)*

CUCKNEY   SK5671
Greendale Oak (01623) 844441
A616, E of A60; NG20 9NQ Refurbished country pub with good sensibly priced all-day food (till 7pm Sun) from sandwiches, sharing boards and pizzas up, eight real ales including Everards, good friendly service, restaurant; children welcome, no dogs inside, sturdy bench seating on front terrace, garden behind, handy for Clumber Park (NT), open all day (till 1am Fri, Sat). *(Derek and Sylvia Stephenson)*

EDWINSTOWE   SK6266
Forest Lodge (01623) 824443
Church Street; NG21 9QA Friendly 18th-c inn with enjoyable home-made food in pubby bar or restaurant, good service, five well kept ales including Wells Bombardier and a house beer from Welbeck Abbey, beams and log fire; Thurs quiz; children welcome, 13 bedrooms, handy for Sherwood Forest. *(Sam Tindall)*

EPPERSTONE   SK6548
Cross Keys (0115) 966 9430
Main Street; NG14 6AD Refurbished dining pub with chef-proprietor's good well presented/priced food from regularly changing menu, three real ales including Nottingham and nice wines by the glass, friendly efficient service, woodburner separating lounge bar and restaurant; quiz Sun; children welcome, muddy walkers and dogs in boot room, a few picnic-sets out at front, more in back garden with raised deck, pretty village and surrounding countryside, open (and food) all day, kitchen closes 6pm Sun. *(Gerry and Rosemary Dobson)*

FARNDON   SK7652
Boathouse (01636) 676578
Off A46 SW of Newark; keep on towards river – pub off Wyke Lane, just past the Riverside pub; NG24 3SX Big-windowed contemporary bar-restaurant overlooking the Trent, emphasis on food but they do serve a couple of changing ales, good choice of wines and some interesting cocktails, main area indeed reminiscent of a boathouse with high ceiling trusses supporting bare ducting, simple modern tables and upholstered chairs, shallow step up to second similarly furnished dining area, good variety of food including early-bird deal; background and Sun live music, July garden party with live bands, free wi-fi; children welcome, wicker chairs around teak tables on heated terrace, own moorings, open all day, food all day Sun. *(Professor James Burke)*

FISKERTON   SK7351
Bromley Arms (01636) 830789
Main Street; NG25 0UL Popular Trentside pub with modernised opened-up interior, fairly compact bar area with upholstered stools and leather armchairs/sofas, two-way fireplace, three well kept Greene King ales plus a beer badged for the pub, decent range of wines by the glass, river-view dining part with upholstered chairs on patterned carpet (some matching wallpaper), substantial helpings of enjoyable fairly priced food (discount 4-6pm Mon-Fri), friendly helpful service; background music, live acoustic session Thurs; children welcome, rattan-style furniture on narrow walled terrace, picnic-sets by edge of wharf giving boat views, open (and food) all day and can get very busy in summer. *(Clive and Fran Dutson, Gerry and Rosemary Dobson)*

GRANBY   SK7436
★**Marquis of Granby** (01949) 859517
Off A52 E of Nottingham; Dragon Street;
NG13 9PN Friendly 18th-c pub in attractive
Vale of Belvoir village, tap for Brewsters with
their well kept ales and interesting guests
from chunky yew counter, no food, two small
comfortable rooms with broad flagstones,
some low beams and striking wallpaper, open
fire; children and dogs welcome, open all day
weekends, from 4pm Mon-Fri. *(Peter Brix)*

HARBY   SK8870
Bottle & Glass (01522) 703438
High Street; village signed off A57 W
of Lincoln; NG23 7EB 19th-c dining
pub with pair of bay-windowed front bars,
enjoyable food including set-menu choices
and blackboard specials, well kept Black
Sheep and a couple of beers from on-site
microbrewery, good choice of wines, friendly
service, recently refurbished restaurant
extension, open fire and woodburners; shop
selling general provisions and gifts; children
welcome, dogs in bar, modern wrought-iron
furniture on back terrace, picnic-sets on
grass beyond and out at front, open (and
food – except Sun evening) all day, breakfast
from 10am (9am weekends). *(Liz Steward)*

HOCKERTON   SK7156
Spread Eagle (01636) 813322
Caunton Road; A617 Newark–Mansfield;
NG25 0PL Village corner pub reopened
after recent refurbishment; compact interior
with linked beamed rooms, a couple of
woodburners, smallish bar area serving
Black Sheep, a guest beer and decent
choice of wines, generous helpings of good
freshly made food from baguettes to daily
specials, friendly accommodating staff;
children welcome, dogs in one area, outside
seating (beer garden and separate deck),
closed Mon, otherwise open (and food) all
day, till 8pm (7pm) Sun. *(Sean O'Keefe)*

KIMBERLEY   SK4944
★**Nelson & Railway** (0115) 938 2177
Station Road; handy for M1 junction
26 via A610; NG16 2NR Welcoming
Victorian beamed pub in same family for
over 40 years, popular and comfortable,
with decent attractively priced home-made
food from snacks to blackboard specials,
well kept Greene King ales and guests,
mix of Edwardian-looking furniture,
brewery prints (was tap for defunct Hardys
& Hansons Brewery) and railway signs,
dining extension; juke box, games machine,
darts, free wi-fi; children and dogs allowed,

disabled access, nice front and back
gardens, 11 good value bedrooms, proper
breakfast, open all day, food all day Sat, till
6pm Sun. *(Stephen Woad, Stuart Doughty)*

KIMBERLEY   SK5044
Stag (0115) 938 3151
Nottingham Road; NG16 2NB Friendly
18th-c traditional local spotlessly kept
by good long-serving landlady; two cosy
rooms, small central counter and corridor,
low beams, dark panelling and settles, old
Shipstones Brewery photographs, table
skittles and working vintage slot machines,
well kept Adnams, Timothy Taylors Landlord
and three guests (summer beer festival), no
food; children and dogs welcome, attractive
back garden with play area, opens 5pm
(1.30pm Sat, midday Sun). *(Jake)*

LAXTON   SK7266
★**Dovecote** (01777) 871586
Off A6075 E of Ollerton; NG22 0NU
Red-brick pub handy for A1; cosy country
atmosphere in three traditionally furnished
dining areas, nice range of well liked
home-made food including good value set
lunch, well kept Castle Rock and guests,
proper cider and several wines by the
glass, efficient caring staff; background
music, free wi-fi; children welcome,
no dogs inside, small front terrace and
sloping garden with views towards church,
interesting village still using the medieval
'strip farming' system, two bedrooms,
open all day Sat, Sun till 9pm (food till
6.30pm). *(Derek and Sylvia Stephenson)*

LOWDHAM   SK6646
Worlds End (0115) 966 3857
Plough Lane; NG14 7AT Small 18th-c
village pub with long carpeted bar/dining
room, enjoyable traditional home-made food
(all day Fri, Sat, not Sun evening), friendly
service, three changing ales from brick-faced
counter, beams and open fire; background
music, free wi-fi; children and dogs welcome,
some covered seats out at front among
colourful tubs and baskets, picnic-sets on
lawned area, open all day. *(Howard Nicholls)*

MANSFIELD   SK5363
Railway Inn (01623) 623086
Station Street; best approached by
viaduct from near Market Place;
NG18 1EF Friendly traditional local with
four changing ales, real cider and good
bargain home-made food (till 5pm Sun),
two little front rooms leading to main
bar, another cosy room at back, laminate
flooring throughout; some live music;

Please tell us if the décor, atmosphere, food or drink at a pub is different
from our description. We rely on readers' reports to keep us up to date:
feedback@goodguides.com, or (no stamp needed) The Good Pub Guide,
FREEPOST RTXY–ZCBC–BBAZ, Stream Lane, Sedlescombe, Battle TN33 0PB.

children and dogs welcome, small courtyard and beer garden, handy for Robin Hood Line station, open all day. *(David Hunt)*

MAPLEBECK SK7160
Beehive

Signed down pretty country lanes from A616 Newark–Ollerton and from A617 Newark–Mansfield; NG22 0BS Unpretentious little beamed country tavern in nice spot, welcoming chatty landlady, tiny front bar with slightly bigger side room, traditional furnishings and antiques, open fire, a couple of well kept ales, no food; children and dogs welcome, tables on small terrace with flower tubs and grassy bank running down to stream, play area, may be closed weekday lunchtimes, busy weekends and bank holidays. *(Sam Tindall)*

MORTON SK7251
Full Moon (01636) 830251

Pub and village signed off Bleasby–Fiskerton back road, SE of Southwell; NG25 0UT Attractive old brick pub tucked away in remote hamlet close to River Trent; modernised pale-beamed bar with two roaring fires, comfortable armchairs, eclectic mix of tables and other simple furnishings, Timothy Taylors Landlord and guests, nine wines by the glass, enjoyable sensibly priced food (not Sun evening) from ciabattas up including good value lunchtime/early evening set menu, separate carpeted restaurant; background music, board games, free wi-fi; children and dogs (in bar) welcome, picnic-sets out at front, more on peaceful back terrace and sizeable lawn with sturdy play equipment, open all day weekends. *(Derek and Sylvia Stephenson)*

NEWARK SK8054
Castle Barge (01636) 677320

Town Wharf next to Trent Bridge; NG24 1EU Old grain barge moored near the castle; top deck has enclosed dining area, below is cosy bar, lots of changing local beers (cheaper Thurs and Sun evenings) and proper cider, cocktail happy hour 5-8pm, good value straightforward food including pizzas, friendly service; Weds quiz, free wi-fi; children (not in bar) and dogs welcome, picnic-sets out on wharf, open all day. *(David Hunt, Tony and Maggie Harwood)*

NEWARK SK7953
Just Beer 07983 993747

Swan & Salmon Yard, off Castle Gate (B6166); NG24 1BG Welcoming one-room micropub tucked down alley, four or five interesting quickly changing beers from brick bar, real cider/perry, limited range of other drinks, bright airy minimalist décor with some brewery memorabilia, half a dozen tables on stone floor, eclectic mix of customers; darts, dominoes and board games; dogs welcome, open all day (from 1pm weekdays). *(David Hunt, Nikki Squires)*

NORMANTON ON THE WOLDS SK6232
Plough (0115) 937 2401

Off A606 5 miles S of Nottingham; NG12 5NN Ivy-clad pub on edge of village, warm and welcoming, with good food from extensive menu including nice steaks, popular Sun lunch (booking advised) and evening deals, Black Sheep, Timothy Taylors and a couple of guests, friendly uniformed staff, fires in bar and extended restaurant; soft background music; children welcome, big garden with play area and summer barbecues, open all day, no food Sun evening. *(Peter Brix)*

NOTTINGHAM SK5739
★ Bell (0115) 947 5241

Angel Row; off Market Square; NG1 6HL Deceptively large pub with late Georgian frontage concealing two much older timber-framed buildings; front Tudor Bar with glass panels protecting patches of 300-year-old wallpaper, larger low-beamed Elizabethan Bar with half-panelled walls and maple parquet flooring, and upstairs Belfry with more heavy panelling and 15th-c crown post; up to a dozen real ales including Greene King and Nottingham from remarkable deep sandstone cellar (can arrange tours), ten wines by the glass, reasonably priced straightforward bar food; background and regular live music including trad jazz, TV, silent fruit machine; children welcome in some parts, pavement tables, open all day (till 1am Sat). *(Jacqui and Alan Swan)*

NOTTINGHAM SK5843
Bread & Bitter (0115) 960 7541

Woodthorpe Drive; NG3 5JL In former suburban bakery still showing ovens, three bright and airy bare-boarded rooms with defunct brewery memorabilia, around a dozen well kept ales including Castle Rock, good range of bottled beers, traditional cider and decent choice of wines, reasonably priced pub food from cobs to specials, friendly welcoming staff; quiz/curry night Mon, live music every other Tues; well behaved children and dogs welcome, open (and food) all day, kitchen closes 7pm Sun. *(Toby Jones)*

NOTTINGHAM SK5739
Canalhouse (0115) 955 5060

Canal Street; NG1 7EH Converted wharf building with bridge over indoors canal spur (complete with narrowboat), lots of bare brick and varnished wood, huge joists on steel beams, long bar serving Castle Rock and three guests, well over 100 bottled beers and good choice of wines, sensibly priced food from snacks up including range of burgers; background music; masses of tables out on attractive waterside terrace, open all day (till 1am Fri, Sat), food till 7pm Sun. *(Jess and George Cowley)*

NOTTINGHAM SK5739
Cock & Hoop (0115) 948 4414
*High Pavement opposite Galleries of
Justice; NG1 1HF* Cosy panelled front
bar with fireside armchairs and flagstoned
cellar bar attached to the Lace Market
Hotel; characterful décor, enjoyable fairly
priced food from sandwiches to good
Sun roasts, Castle Rock and several local
guests; children and dogs welcome, covered
outside seating area, 42 bedrooms (ones
by the street can be noisy at weekends),
open (and food) all day. *(Howard Nicholls)*

NOTTINGHAM SK5739
★ Cross Keys (0115) 941 7898
Byard Lane; NG1 2GJ Restored Victorian
city-centre pub on two levels, lower carpeted
part with leather banquettes, panelling and
chandeliers, upper area with old wooden
tables and chairs and some bucket seats
on bare boards, interesting pictures/prints
and more pendant lighting, well kept
Navigation beers and a couple of guests,
good reasonably priced food from breakfast
on, friendly service, upstairs function/dining
room; sports TV; seats outside, open all day
from 9am. *(Howard Nicholls)*

NOTTINGHAM SK5739
Fellows Morton & Clayton
(0115) 950 6795 *Canal Street (part of
inner ring road); NG1 7EH* Flower-
decked former canal warehouse, up to
nine well kept real ales such as Black Sheep,
Fullers, Nottingham, Sharps and Timothy
Taylors, very good value pubby food (not
evenings Sun-Weds), softly lit downstairs
bar with alcove seating, wood floors and
lots of exposed brickwork, two raised areas,
upstairs restaurant/function room; monthly
quiz first Thurs, several sports TVs, free wi-fi;
tables outside, open all day, till midnight
Fri, Sat. *(Dave Braisted, Dr J Barrie Jones)*

NOTTINGHAM SK5642
Gladstone (0115) 912 9994
Loscoe Road, Carrington; NG5 2AW
Welcoming mid-terrace backstreet local, half
a dozen well kept ales such as Castle Rock,
Fullers, Oakham and Timothy Taylors, good
range of malt whiskies, comfortable lounge
with collection of books, basic bar with
old sports memorabilia and darts, upstairs
folk club Weds, quiz Thurs; background
music, sports TV, free wi-fi; tables in back
garden among colourful tubs and hanging
baskets, open all day weekends, closed
weekday lunchtimes. *(David Hunt)*

NOTTINGHAM SK5640
Hand & Heart (0115) 958 2456
Derby Road; NG1 5BA Unexceptional
exterior but unusual inside with bar and
dining areas cut deep into back sandstone;
a house beer from Dancing Duck, Maypole
and guests, two real ciders and good wine

and whisky choice, enjoyable fairly priced
traditional food from sandwiches and snacks
up, set lunch deal Mon-Sat, friendly helpful
service, glassed-in upstairs room overlooking
street; background and interesting live
music Thurs; children welcome till 7pm
if eating, dogs in bar, open all day (till
midnight Fri, Sat). *(Jess and George Cowley)*

NOTTINGHAM SK5739
★ Kean's Head (0115) 947 4052
St Mary's Gate; NG1 1QA Cheery pub
in attractive Lace Market area; fairly
functional single room with simple wooden
café furnishings on bare boards, some
exposed brickwork and red tiling, low sofa
by big windows overlooking the street,
stools by wood counter, small fireplace,
Castle Rock and three guests, draught
belgian beers and interesting bottled
range, 20 wines by the glass, around 60
malt whiskies and similar number of gins,
teas/coffees, popular fairly traditional
food (not Sun evening), friendly service;
background music, daily papers and free
wi-fi; children welcome till 7pm, church
next door worth a look, open all day.
(Peter Smith and Judith Brown)

NOTTINGHAM SK5539
King William IV (0115) 958 9864
*Manvers Street/Eyre Street, Sneinton;
NG2 4PB* Victorian corner local (the King
Billy) with plenty of character, well kept
Oakham, Black Iris and five guests from
circular bar, also craft beers and real cider,
good fresh cobs and sausage rolls, friendly
staff; irish folk session Thurs, monthly quiz,
silent sports TV, pool upstairs, free wi-fi;
dogs welcome, seats on roof terrace, handy
for cricket, football and rugby grounds, open
all day (from 2pm Mon). *(Howard Nicholls)*

NOTTINGHAM SK5740
★ Lincolnshire Poacher
(0115) 941 1584 *Mansfield Road; up
hill from Victoria Centre; NG1 3FR*
Impressive range of drinks at this popular
down-to-earth pub (attracts younger
evening crowd), 13 well kept ales including
Castle Rock, lots of continental draught/
bottled beers, half a dozen ciders and
over 70 malt whiskies, shortish choice of
reasonably priced uncomplicated food;
big simple traditional front bar with wall
settles, wooden tables and breweriana,
plain but lively room on left and corridor to
chatty panelled back snug with newspapers
and board games, conservatory overlooking
tables on large heated back area; live
music Weds and Sun, free wi-fi; children
(till 8pm) and dogs welcome, open all day
(till midnight Thurs-Sat). *(David Hunt)*

NOTTINGHAM SK5541
★ Lion (0115) 970 3506
*Lower Mosley Street, New Basford;
NG7 7FQ* Around ten real ales (tasters

available) including Bass and Castle Rock from one of the city's deepest cellars (glass viewing panel – can be visited at quiet times), also plenty of craft beers and proper ciders, good well priced burger/ hot dog menu (all day weekends); big open-plan room with feel of separate areas, bare bricks and polished dark oak boards, old brewery pictures and posters, open fires; regular live music including popular Sun lunchtime jazz, Weds quiz; children welcome till 6pm, no dogs, disabled facilities, garden with terrace and smokers' shelter, open all day. *(Sam Tindall)*

NOTTINGHAM   SK5739

Malt Cross (0115) 941 1048

St James's Street; NG1 6FG Former Victorian music hall with vaulted glass roof and gallery looking down on bar area, bare boards and ornate iron pillars, comfortable sofas, good selection of drinks including some interesting real ales, decent well priced food from shortish menu, teas, coffees and daily newspapers; Mon quiz, regular music nights; cellars converted into art gallery/workshop areas, ancient caves (tours available); open all day (till 9pm Sun). *(Howard Nicholls)*

NOTTINGHAM   SK5739

Newshouse (0115) 952 3061

Canal Street; NG1 7HB Friendly two-room 1950s Castle Rock pub with blue tiled exterior, their ales and half a dozen changing guests, belgian and czech imports, decent fresh lunchtime food, mix of bare boards and carpet, local newspaper/radio memorabilia, beer bottles on shelves, darts, table skittles and bar billiards; background music, big-screen sports TV; a few tables out in front, walking distance from both football grounds, open all day and popular on match days. *(Peter Brix, Howard Nicholls)*

NOTTINGHAM   SK6141

Old Volunteer (0115) 987 2299

Burton Road, Carlton; NG4 3DQ Imposing 19th-c community pub acting as tap for Flipside, their well kept ales and several guests, good range of whiskies, friendly helpful staff, some food; live music and beer festivals; dogs welcome, picnic-sets on side terrace, open all day. *(Toby Jones)*

NOTTINGHAM   SK5739

★Olde Trip to Jerusalem

(0115) 947 3171 *Brewhouse Yard; from inner ring road follow 'The North, A6005 Long Eaton' signpost until in Castle Boulevard, then right into Castle Road; pub is on the left; NG1 6AD*
Unusual rambling pub seemingly clinging

to sandstone rock face, largely 17th-c and a former brewhouse supplying the hilltop castle; downstairs bar carved into the stone with dark panelling and simple built-in seats, tables on flagstones, some rocky alcoves, Greene King IPA and H&H Olde Trip plus guests (tasting trays available), good value food all day, efficient staff dealing well with busy mix of customers; popular little tourist shop with panelled walls soaring into dark cavernous heights; children welcome, seats and ring the bull in snug courtyard, open all day (till midnight Fri, Sat). *(Peter Smith and Judith Brown, Richard Tilbrook, Jess and George Cowley)*

NOTTINGHAM   SK5640

Organ Grinder (0115) 970 0630

Alfreton Road; NG7 3JE Tap for Blue Monkey with up to nine well kept ales including guests, a couple of ciders and a perry, good local pork pies, open-plan interior with bare boards and woodburner; sports TV; well behaved dogs welcome, seats out behind, open all day. *(Howard Nicholls)*

NOTTINGHAM   SK5739

Pitcher & Piano (0115) 958 6081

High Pavement; NG1 1HN Remarkable lofty-roofed conversion of 19th-c church, enjoyable all-day food and good range of drinks including cocktails; some live music; outside bar and terrace, open all day (till late Thurs-Sat). *(Jess and George Cowley)*

NOTTINGHAM   SK5540

Plough (0115) 970 2615

St Peters Street, Radford; NG7 3EN Friendly 1930s local with its own good value Nottingham ales brewed behind, also guest beers and traditional cider, weekday sandwiches, two bars (one carpeted, the other with terrazzo flooring), banquettes, old tables and chairs, bottles on delft shelving, coal fires; Thurs quiz, TV, traditional games including outside skittle alley; dogs welcome (may get a treat), beer garden with covered smokers' area, open all day. *(Peter Brix)*

NOTTINGHAM   SK5344

Roebuck (0115) 979 3400

St James's Street (pedestrianised) off Old Market Square; NG1 6FH Light airy Wetherspoons conversion of interesting 18th-c building, high ceilings and some original features, extensive choice of well kept ales (tasting paddles available), ciders/ perry and good wine choice, their usual reasonably priced food from toasties up, friendly staff, upper galleried area and enclosed roof terrace; muted TV; disabled facilities; children welcome, open all day from 8am. *(David Hunt, Toby Jones)*

Ring the bull is an ancient pub game – you try to lob a ring on a piece of string over a hook (occasionally a bull's horn) on a wall or ceiling.

NOTTINGHAM   SK5739
Salutation (0115) 947 6580
*Hounds Gate/Maid Marian Way;
NG1 7AA* Low beams, flagstones, ochre
walls and cosy corners including two small
quiet rooms in ancient lower back part,
plusher modern front lounge, up to eight
real ales and good choice of draught/
bottled ciders, quickly served food till
8pm (6pm Sun, no food Mon), helpful
friendly staff (ask them to show you the
haunted caves below the pub); background
music, live bands upstairs; open all day
(till 3am Fri, Sat). *(Howard Nicholls)*

NOTTINGHAM   SK5640
Trent Bridge (0115) 977 8940
Radcliffe Road; NG2 6AA Good
Wetherspoons in sizeable Victorian pub next
to the cricket ground (very busy on match
days), comfortably refurbished linked rooms
with panelling and cricketing memorabilia,
several well kept ales and decent good value
food; sports TVs, free wi-fi; children welcome,
open all day from 8am. *(Maggie Dyson)*

NOTTINGHAM   SK5838
Trent Navigation (0115) 986 5658
Meadow Lane; NG2 3HS Welcoming
tile-fronted Victorian pub close to canal
and home to the Navigation Brewery,
their beers and guests from half a dozen
pumps along with ciders/perries, popular
food including deals; regular live music
and well attended Sun quiz, sports TVs
(pub is next to Notts County FC); children
welcome, brewery shop at back, open all
day, food all day Thurs-Sun. *(Peter Brix)*

NOTTINGHAM   SK5739
★Vat & Fiddle (0115) 985 0611
*Queens Bridge Road; alongside Sheriffs
Way (near multi-storey car park);
NG2 1NB* Open-plan 1930s brick pub – tap
for next door Castle Rock Brewery; varnished
pine tables, bentwood chairs and stools on
parquet or terrazzo flooring, some brewery
memorabilia and interesting photographs
of demolished local pubs, up to 13 real ales,
bottled continentals, traditional ciders and
over 30 malt whiskies, decent food (not Sun
evening) including range of burgers and
Thurs curry night, modern dining extension,
visitors' centre with own bar; some live
music, free wi-fi; children and dogs welcome,
picnic-sets out at front by road, open all day
(till midnight Fri-Sat). *(Maggie Dyson)*

RADCLIFFE ON TRENT   SK6439
Horse Chestnut (0115) 933 1994
Main Road; NG12 2BE Smart pub with
plenty of Victorian/Edwardian features,
well kept Oakham, Fullers, St Austell and
four guests, decent wines by the glass and
sensibly priced home-made food (not Sun
evening) including some italian choices
(good pizzas), friendly service, two-level

main bar, parquet and mosaic floor,
panelling, big mirrors and impressive lamps,
handsome leather wall benches and period
fireplaces; some live music; children and
dogs welcome, disabled access, terrace
seating, open all day. *(Jacqui and Alan Swan)*

RAMPTON   SK7978
Eyre Arms (01777) 248771
Main Street; DN22 0HR Shuttered
red-brick village pub with enjoyable good
value food from chef-owner including
extensive specials menu and weekday
lunchtime bargains, well kept local ales,
friendly helpful service, refurbished dining
area overlooking pleasant garden, locals
bar with pool; open all day. *(Sam Tindall)*

RUDDINGTON   SK5733
Three Crowns (0115) 846 9613
Easthorpe Street; NG11 6LB Open-
plan pub known locally as the Top House,
well kept Fullers, Blue Monkey and
three guests (beer festivals), very good
indian food in back Three Spices evening
restaurant; open all day weekends, closed
lunchtimes Mon and Tues. *(Liz Steward)*

SCAFTWORTH   SK6692
King William (01302) 710292
A631 Bawtry–Everton; DN10 6BL
Popular red-brick country pub with friendly
relaxed atmosphere, good well presented
home-made food (not Mon, best to book
Sun lunch), Theakstons Best, a couple of
regional guests and good choice of wines
by the glass, bar, snug and two dining
rooms with old high-backed settles, plain
tables and chairs and log fires; background
music; children and dogs welcome, big back
garden with swings, open all day Fri-Sun,
from 4.30pm other days. *(Toby Jones)*

SELSTON   SK4553
★Horse & Jockey (01773) 781012
*Handy for M1 junctions 27/28; Church
Lane; NG16 6FB* Interesting pub on
different levels dating from the 17th c, low
heavy beams, dark flagstones, individual
furnishings and good log fire in cast-iron
range, friendly staff, Greene King Abbot
and Timothy Taylors Landlord poured from
the jug and up to four guests, real cider,
no food, games area with darts and pool;
folk night Weds, quiz Sun; dogs welcome,
terrace and smokers' shelter, pleasant
rolling countryside. *(Sean O'Keefe)*

SOUTHWELL   SK7054
★Final Whistle (01636) 814953
Station Road; NG25 0ET Popular
railway-themed pub commemorating the
long defunct Southwell line; ten well kept
ales including Bass, Everards and two
house beers from Ashover (beer festivals),
real ciders/perries, foreign bottled beers
and good range of wines, cheeseboard and
other snacky food, traditional opened-up

bar with tiled or wood floor, settles and armchairs in quieter carpeted room, corridor drinking area, two open fires, panelling, lots of railway memorabilia and other odds and ends; quiz Tues and Sun, occasional live music; children and dogs welcome, back garden with wonderful mock-up of 1920s platform complete with track and buffers, on Robin Hood Way and Southwell Trail, open all day. *(Professor James Burke)*

SOUTHWELL   SK7053
Hearty Goodfellow (01636) 919176
Church Street (A612); NG25 0HQ
Welcoming open-plan mock-Tudor pub, Everards Tiger and Sunchaser, guest beers, traditional ciders and good range of house wines, popular fairly straightforward food (not Sun evening) at reasonable prices, also takeaway fish and chips and pop-up fish/seafood restaurant in converted outbuilding, cheerful young staff, lots of polished wood, beams and two brick fireplaces; background and some live music, sports TVs; children and dogs welcome, covered terrace and nice big tree-shaded garden beyond car park, play area, handy for Southwell Workhouse (NT) and Minster, open all day Fri-Sun. *(Michael Butler)*

TUXFORD   SK7471
Fountain (01777) 872854
Lincoln Road on edge of village near East Coast railway line; NG22 0JQ
Comfortably updated family dining pub with welcoming atmosphere, enjoyable affordably priced food (not Sun evening) from pub favourites and grills to daily specials, local ales and ciders such as Welbeck Abbey and Scrumpy Wasp, friendly service; free wi-fi; picnic-sets out in fenced area, open all day Fri-Sun, closed lunchtimes Mon, Tues. *(Derek and Sylvia Stephenson)*

UPTON   SK7354
★Cross Keys (01636) 813269
Main Street (A612); NG23 5SY 17th-c pub in fine spot with rambling heavy-beamed bar, log fire in brick fireplace, own Mallard ales (brewed in Maythorne) and good home-made food (not Sun evening) from lunchtime sandwiches to specials, friendly staff, back extension; seats on decked terrace, British Horological Institute opposite, open all day Fri-Sun, closed lunchtimes Mon and Tues. *(Jake)*

WEST BRIDGFORD   SK5838
Larwood & Voce (0115) 981 9960
Fox Road; NG2 6AJ Well run open-plan dining pub (part of the small Moleface group); good locally sourced home-made food in bar and restaurant area including some imaginative choices, plenty of wines by the glass, cocktail menu and three well kept ales, attentive cheerful

staff; sports TV; children welcome away from bar, seats out on raised deck with heaters, on edge of the cricket ground and handy for Nottingham Forest FC, open all day, from 10am weekends for breakfast. *(Peter Smith and Judith Brown, Vanessa and Jerry Hockin, David Hunt)*

WEST BRIDGFORD   SK5938
Poppy & Pint (0115) 981 9995
Pierrepont Road; NG2 5DX Converted former British Legion Club backing on to bowling green and tennis courts; large bar with raised section and family area, around a dozen real ales including Castle Rock and a couple of ciders, decent food from breakfast on, friendly atmosphere; monthly folk night and other events; dogs welcome in bar, open all day from 9.30am (10am Sun). *(David Hunt)*

WEST BRIDGFORD   SK5837
★Stratford Haven (0115) 982 5981
Stratford Road, Trent Bridge; NG2 6BA Good Castle Rock pub; bare-boards front bar leading to linked areas including airy skylit back part with relaxed local atmosphere, up to 14 well kept ales, interesting bottled beers, proper ciders and good wine and whisky choice, wide range of reasonably priced home-made food including themed nights, fast friendly service; some live music (nothing loud), regular beer events, daily papers; children (during the day) and dogs welcome, tables outside, handy for cricket ground and Nottingham Forest FC (busy on match days), open (and food) all day. *(Howard Nicholls)*

WEST STOCKWITH   SK7994
White Hart (01427) 892672
Main Street; DN10 4EY Small refurbished country pub at junction of Chesterfield Canal and River Trent, own good Idle beers from next-door brewery plus guests, enjoyable well priced traditional food (not Sun evening) including blackboard specials and regular evening deals, friendly atmosphere; live music Fri, pool and sports TV; children and dogs welcome, garden overlooking the water, open all day. *(Sean O'Keefe)*

WYSALL   SK6027
Plough (01509) 880339
Keyworth Road; off A60 at Costock, or A6006 at Wymeswold; NG12 5QQ Attractive 17th-c beamed village local; popular good value lunchtime food from shortish menu, cheerful staff, Bass, Greene King Abbot, Timothy Taylors Landlord and three guests, rooms either side of bar with nice mix of furnishings, soft lighting, big log fire; Tues quiz, pool; dogs welcome (after 2.30pm), french doors to pretty terrace with flower tubs and baskets, open all day. *(Peter Brix)*

Oxfordshire

KEY   ⭐ Star Pub   🍴 Top Quality Food   🍺 Great Beer

🍷 Good Wines   £ Bargain Meals   🛏 Good Bedrooms   🍴 Serves Food

---

ASTHALL   SP2811   Map 4

Maytime 🍴 🛏

(01993) 822068 – www.themaytime.com

Off A40 at W end of Witney bypass, then first left; OX18 4HW

17th-c former coaching inn with individually furnished bar and dining rooms, good food and seats outside; smart bedrooms

Our readers enjoy this lively, very popular Cotswold-stone inn a great deal. The careful refurbishment offers much character: the lofty bar has exposed roof trusses, flagstones, leather sofas, cushioned wall seats and stools against the counter where friendly staff serve two quickly changing ales such as Pig & Porter Ashburnham Pale Ale and Saltaire Elderflower Blonde on handpump, at least 15 good wines by the glass and a fine collection of 85 gins; background music and board games. Several white-painted beamed rooms lead off on several levels with cushioned window seats, a mix of tartan upholstered and traditional wooden chairs around tables of varying size on black slates or bare boards, and pictures on painted or stone walls; one room has a glass ceiling. The pub springer is called Alfie. Seats and tables sit under parasols on the back terrace with more seats in the extended garden overlooking the River Windrush. This is a lovely place to stay, with stylish and well equipped bedrooms and highly thought-of breakfasts; there are good walks from the door.

🍴 The impressive food uses local, seasonal produce in generous helpings: lunchtime sandwiches, moules marinière, ham hock and chicken terrine with tonka bean mayonnaise, sharing boards, spinach, sweet potato and feta tart, beer-battered haddock and chips, chicken thighs with tarragon mousse, wild mushrooms and cep sauce, a risotto of the day, braised pork cheeks with sultana ragoût, leeks and caraway jus, and puddings such as lemon meringue pie with poached oranges and basil sorbet and chocolate brownie with banana ice-cream and toffee sauce. *Benchmark main dish: wild boar burger with toppings and chips £13.00. Two-course evening meal £22.00.*

Free house ~ Licensee Dominic Wood ~ Real ale ~ Open 11-11 ~ Bar food 12-2.30 (3 Sun), 6-9.30 ~ Restaurant ~ Children welcome but not in bedrooms ~ Dogs allowed in bar ~ Wi-fi ~ Live music every other Sun 3-5pm ~ Bedrooms: $85/$95 *Recommended by M G Hart, Sophia and Hamish Greenfield, Tracey and Stephen Groves*

BANBURY

SP4540 Map 4

Olde Reindeer ◀ £

(01295) 270972 – www.yeoldereindeer.co.uk

Parsons Street, off Market Place; OX16 5NA

Fine town pub with a friendly welcome, real ales and simple food

Despite being deservedly busy – which this splendid old inn often is – staff remain friendly and attentive. There's plenty of history here and the front bar has a good, bustling atmosphere, heavy 16th-c beams, very broad polished oak floorboards, a magnificent carved overmantel for one of the two roaring log fires and traditional solid furnishings; some interesting breweriana too. It's worth looking at the handsomely proportioned Globe Room used by Oliver Cromwell as his base during the Civil War. Quite a sight, it still has some very fine 17th-c carved dark oak panelling. Hook Norton Hooky, Old Hooky, Hooky Mild and a couple of seasonal guest beers on handpump, 12 wines by the glass, fruit wines and several malt whiskies. The little back courtyard has tables and benches under parasols, aunt sally and pretty flowering baskets.

 Fair value, honest food includes sandwiches, breaded camembert wedges with cranberry dip, chicken liver pâté with red onion dip, butterflied chicken schnitzel salad topped with honey mustard and cashews, root vegetable, apricot and nut bake topped with goats cheese and a poached egg, lamb chump on mustard mash with feta, mint, capers and pomegranate, rump steak with pepper sauce and skinny fries, and puddings such as plum and apple crumble with custard and chocolate fondant torte with clotted cream. *Benchmark main dish: venison burger with toppings and chips £13.00. Two-course evening meal £16.00.*

Hook Norton ~ Tenant Jeremy Money ~ Real ale ~ Open 11-11 (midnight Fri, Sat); 12-10.30 Sun ~ Bar food 12-3, 6-9; 12-3 Sun ~ Restaurant ~ Children welcome ~ Dogs allowed in bar ~ Live music Sat 9pm, quiz Thurs 8pm *Recommended by George Atkinson, Edward Edmonton, Rosie and John Moore, Ian Herdman, Cliff and Monica Swan, Maria and Henry Lazenby*

BESSELS LEIGH

SP4501 Map 4

Greyhound ♀ ◀

(01865) 862110 – www.brunningandprice.co.uk/greyhound

A420 Faringdon–Botley; OX13 5PX

Cotswold-stone inn with rambling rooms, up to half a dozen real ales, lots of wines by the glass and enjoyable food

'A winning formula' is how one enthusiastic reader describes this handsome old pub. It's particularly well run, with a welcome for both drinkers and diners, and the knocked-through rooms have plenty of character and interest: all manner of old photographs and pictures cover the half-panelled walls, individually chosen cushioned dining chairs, leather-topped stools and dark wooden tables are grouped on carpeting or rug-covered floorboards, and there are books on shelves, glass and stone bottles on windowsills, big gilt mirrors, three fireplaces (one housing a woodburning stove) and sizeable pot plants. Wooden bar stools line the counter where they serve Phoenix Brunning & Price Original and Timothy Taylors Landlord with guests such as Otley O2 Croeso, Three Castles Old Dragon and West Berkshire Maggs Magnificent Mild on handpump, 17 wines by the glass, 44 gins, 102 malt whiskies and a farm cider. By the back dining extension is a white picket fence-enclosed garden with picnic-sets under green parasols; the summer window boxes and hanging baskets are particularly delightful.

🍴 Interesting food includes sandwiches, rabbit, ham hock and tarragon croquettes with piccalilli, scallops with black pudding, butternut squash purée and apple dressing, thai red sweet potato and aubergine curry with coconut rice and tempura pak choi, teriyaki-marinated sea trout with stir-fry vegetables, wasabi noodles and toasted sesame seeds, steak in ale pie, chicken breast with fondant potato and smoked bacon, onion and sherry sauce, braised lamb shoulder with dauphinoise potatoes and rosemary gravy, and puddings such as hot waffle with caramelised banana, toffee sauce and vanilla ice-cream and chocolate brownie with dark chocolate sauce. *Benchmark main dish: beer-battered cod and chips £13.45. Two-course evening meal £22.00.*

Brunning & Price ~ Manager Damien Mann ~ Real ale ~ Open 11.30-11; 11.30-10.30 Sun ~ Bar food 12-10 (9.30 Sun) ~ Well behaved children welcome ~ Dogs allowed in bar ~ Wi-fi
Recommended by Taff Thomas, Neil and Angela Huxter, Richard Tilbrook, Nigel and Sue Foster, Emily and Toby Archer, Charles Fraser

 BRIGHTWELL BALDWIN   SU6594   Map 4
Nelson 🌟 ♀
(01491) 612497 ~ www.thenelsonbrightwell.co.uk
Off B480 Chalgrove–Watlington, or B4009 Benson–Watlington; OX49 5NP

Attractive inn with several character bars, real ales, good wines by the glass and enjoyable well regarded food; bedrooms

Opposite the church in a quiet village, this is a 300-year-old inn with 18th-c gable ends and an attractive arched verandah. The bar has candles and fresh flowers, wine bottles on windowsills, horsebrasses on standing timbers, lots of paintings on white or red walls, wheelback and other dining chairs around assorted dark tables and a big brick inglenook fireplace. One cosy room has cushions on comfortable sofas, little lamps on dark furniture, ornate mirrors and portraits in gilt frames; background music. Rebellion Angel, IPA and Zebedee on handpump, 20 wines (including champagne) by the glass, a dozen malt whiskies and winter mulled wine. There are seats and tables on the back terrace and in the willow-draped garden.

🌟 Pleasing food includes duck liver parfait with chilli jam, local pigeon breast with smoked bacon, black pudding and red wine sauce, leeks, parmesan and kale risotto, burger with toppings, coleslaw and fries, rabbit casserole, smoked haddock on colcannon topped with a poached egg and wholegrain mustard sauce, half a roast duck with dauphinoise potatoes and orange sauce, rack of lamb with rosemary and red wine sauce, and puddings such as banana crêpe with warm toffee sauce and ice-cream and tipsy bread and butter pudding. *Benchmark main dish: whole lemon sole with skinny fries £18.95. Two-course evening meal £24.00.*

Free house ~ Licensees Roger and Carole Shippey ~ Real ale ~ Open 12-3, 6-11; 12-5 Sun ~ Bar food 12-2.15, 6-10; 12-4 Sun ~ Restaurant ~ Children welcome ~ Dogs allowed in bar ~ Wi-fi ~ Bedrooms: £75/£100 *Recommended by Roy Hoing, Caroline and Peter Bryant, Valerie Sayer, Trish and Karl Soloman*

 **BURFORD**   SP2512   Map 4
Highway ♀ 🛏
(01993) 823661 ~ www.thehighwayinn.co.uk
Village signposted off A40 W of Oxford; High Street (A361); OX18 4RG

Comfortable old inn with a good choice of wines, well liked bar food and seats outside; comfortable bedrooms

Set in the centre of a bustling village and helpfully open all day, this pub has customers dropping in and out all the time. There are all sorts of interesting touches in the bars, but the main feature is the pair of big windows overlooking the bustle of the pretty High Street; each consists of several dozen panes of old float glass and has a long cushioned window seat. Do notice the stag candlesticks for the rather close-set tables on well worn floorboards, the neat modern dark leather chairs, the nice old station clock above the big log fire in a pleasingly simple stone fireplace and the careful balance of ancient stripped stone with black and pale blue filigree wallpaper. A small corner counter has Hook Norton Hooky and a guest such as Two Cocks 1643 Roundhead on handpump, 20 wines (including champagne) by the glass and 13 malt whiskies; they hold a beer festival and barbecue in the second week of June. Background music, TV and board games. On the right, a second bar room, with another big window seat, is carpeted but otherwise similar in style; there's also a downstairs cellar bar that's open for tapas at the weekend. A few picnic-sets stand above the pavement at the front and the high-walled courtyard garden has painted chairs and picnic-sets under parasols. The bedrooms are individually decorated in a country house style and breakfasts are good.

High quality food includes lunchtime sandwiches, ham hock terrine with piccalilli, mushroom fricassée on brioche toast with honey mustard drizzle, moroccan-spiced nut roast with apricot and date quinoa and mint yoghurt, steak in ale pie, seafood basket (calamari, prawns, whitebait and scampi) with spiced aioli and sweet chilli dips, burgers using wagyu beef, chicken, pork and a vegetarian choice all with toppings, coleslaw and skinny fries, sea bass fillet with lemon thyme butter and roasted vegetables, confit duck leg with dauphinoise potatoes and orange and veal jus, and puddings. *Benchmark main dish: rack of lamb with garlic mash, mint sauce and redcurrant and port jus £18.00. Two-course evening meal £22.00.*

Free house ~ Licensees Dan, Jane and Michelle Arnell ~ Real ale ~ Open 12-11.30 (midnight weekends); closed first two weeks Jan ~ Bar food 12-3, 6-9 ~ Restaurant ~ Children welcome ~ Dogs allowed in bar and bedrooms ~ Wi-fi ~ Bedrooms: £90/£130
Recommended by Roy Hoing, Audrey and Paul Summers, Margo and Derek Stapley, Caroline Prescott

BURFORD
Lamb 🎯 ♈ 🍺 🛏

SP2412   Map 4

(01993) 823155 ~ www.cotswold-inns-hotels.co.uk/lamb
Village signposted off A40 W of Oxford; Sheep Street (B4425, off A361); OX18 4LR

Lovely old inn with a bustling bar, real ales and an extensive wine list, interesting bar and restaurant food, and pretty gardens; bedrooms

Even when busy, service at this 500-year-old inn is attentive and helpful and the atmosphere is one of old-fashioned dignity and character. The cosy bar has armchairs on rugs and flagstones in front of log fires, china plates on shelves, Hook Norton Hooky and Wickwar Cotswold Way on handpump, an extensive wine list with 17 by the glass and 26 malt whiskies. The roomy beamed main lounge is charmingly traditional with distinguished old chairs, oak tables, seats built into stone-mullioned windows, polished floorboards, fresh flowers and antiques and other fine decorations. A pretty terrace with teak furniture leads down to neatly kept lawns surrounded by flowers, shrubs and small trees. The garden, enclosed by the warm stone of the surrounding buildings, is a real suntrap. They're kind to dogs and even have a special menu for them.

Accomplished food includes sandwiches, scallops with vegetable couscous, eggs benedict, deli boards, sausage and mash with red onion gravy, wild mushroom linguine with parmesan, chicken caesar salad, fishcakes with sweet chilli sauce and skinny chips, burger with toppings and chips, game pie, 31-day-aged steaks with a choice of sauces, and puddings such as lemon posset with berry coulis and chocolate tart with passion-fruit ice-cream; they also offer afternoon tea (3-6pm). *Benchmark main dish: braised lamb shank £15.95. Two-course evening meal £25.00.*

Cotswold Inns & Hotels ~ Manager Bill Ramsay ~ Real ale ~ Open 11-11 ~ Bar food 12-9.30 ~ Restaurant ~ Children welcome ~ Dogs allowed in bar and bedrooms ~ Wi-fi ~ Bedrooms: £175/£185 *Recommended by Richard Tilbrook, George Atkinson, R K Phillips, M G Hart, Val and Malcolm Travers*

CHURCHILL
Chequers 🎖️ 🍺

SP2824   Map 4

(01608) 659393 – www.thechequerschurchill.com
Church Road; B4450 Chipping Norton to Stow-on-the-Wold (and village signed off A361 Chipping Norton–Burford); OX7 6NJ

Simple furnishings in spacious bars and dining rooms, friendly relaxed atmosphere, up to six ales and popular food

Particularly well run and always busy, this is a golden-stone pub in a picture-postcard village. The relaxed and friendly bar has an armchair and other comfortable chairs around an old trunk in front of the inglenook fireplace, some exposed stone walls, cushioned wall seats, and a mix of wooden and antique leather chairs around nice old tables on bare floorboards. Rugs are dotted about and stools line the counter which is presided over by a big stag's head: Black Sheep, Butcombe Bitter, Hook Norton Hooky, Sharps Atlantic, Timothy Taylors Landlord and Wye Valley HPA on handpump, 13 wines by the glass (and several champagnes), 11 malt whiskies, mocktails and a farm cider; darts and background music. At the back is a large extension with soaring rafters, big lantern lights, long button-back leather banquettes and other seating, while upstairs is another similarly and simply furnished dining area and a room just right for a private party. The landscaped and flagstoned back terrace has lots of good quality wooden chairs and tables and climbing plants. The church opposite is impressive and worth a visit. Wheelchair access.

Consistently good modern british food includes sandwiches, devilled kidneys on toast, twice-baked cheese soufflé, swiss chard and ricotta malfatti (dumplings) with roasted squash and sage butter, rabbit with rocket, dandelion and aioli (for two people), chicken kiev with wild garlic and pickled walnuts, poached smoked haddock with spinach, a poached egg and hollandaise sauce, pot-roast duck leg with bacon, peas and baby gem, steak frites, and puddings such as strawberry knickerbocker glory and hot chocolate, salted caramel and peanut butter pudding. *Benchmark main dish: liver and bacon £16.00. Two-course evening meal £22.00.*

Free house ~ Licensee Peter Creed ~ Real ale ~ Open 11-11 ~ Bar food 12-3, 6-9.30 (10 Fri, Sat); 12-4, 6-9 Sun ~ Restaurant ~ Children welcome ~ Dogs welcome ~ Wi-fi *Recommended by Roger White, Helena and Trevor Fraser, Liz Bell, Brian Glozier, Guy Vowles, Frances and Hamish Porter, P and J Shapley*

EAST HENDRED
Eyston Arms 🎖️

SU4588   Map 2

(01235) 833320 – www.eystonarms.co.uk
Village signposted off A417 E of Wantage; High Street; OX12 8JY

Attractive bar areas with low beams, flagstones, log fires and candles, imaginative food and helpful service

Many customers are here to enjoy the particularly good food in this welcoming pub, but plenty of locals pop in for a drink and a chat, which keeps the atmosphere bustling and easy-going. There are seats at the bar and they keep a few tables free for drinkers keen to try the Hook Norton Hooky, Sharps Doom Bar and Wadworths 6X on handpump, ten wines by the glass, 14 gins and ten malt whiskies. Several separate-seeming candlelit areas have contemporary paintwork and modern country-style furnishings, low ceilings and beams, stripped timbers and the odd standing upright, nice tables and chairs on flagstones, some cushioned wall seats and an inglenook fireplace; background music and TV. Picnic-sets outside overlook the pretty lane and there are seats in the back courtyard garden.

 First class creative food includes sandwiches, carpaccio of beef with rocket, lemon oil and parmesan, kiln-potted salmon with shrimp butter and pickled celeriac, burger with toppings and string chips, superfood vegetarian salad, king prawn and smoked salmon spaghetti with chilli oil, guinea fowl breast with white wine and butter, gnocchi, pancetta, cream and tarragon and parmesan breadcrumbs, penang duck curry with carrot, orange, chilli and coriander salad, a fresh fish dish of the day with herb mash and béarnaise sauce, and puddings such as dark chocolate mousse with espresso cream and nutty granola and sticky toffee pudding with cream. *Benchmark main dish: pil pil king prawns £18.95. Two-course evening meal £25.00.*

Free house ~ Licensees George Dailey and Daisy Barton ~ Real ale ~ Open 11-11; 11-9 Sun ~ Bar food 12-2, 6-9; 12-3.30, 6-8 Sun; light menu 2-6 Sat ~ Restaurant ~ Well behaved children allowed lunchtimes ~ Dogs allowed in bar ~ Wi-fi *Recommended by Sally Wright, John Sargeant, R K Phillips, Sandra and Michael Smith, Paul Farraday*

FILKINS
Five Alls 🏵 🍽
SP2304 Map 4

(01367) 860875 – www.thefiveallsfilkins.co.uk
Signed off A361 Lechlade–Burford; GL7 3JQ

Thoughtfully refurbished inn with creative food, quite a range of drinks, a friendly welcome and seats outside; bedrooms

Bedrooms in this country stone inn are comfortable and attractively refurbished and make a good base for exploring the area. Popular locally, the beamed bar has a cosy area with three leather chesterfields grouped around a table by an open fire, an informal dining space with farmhouse chairs and cushioned pews around tables on bare boards and a nice little window seat for two. Stools line the bar where friendly staff serve a beer named for the pub (from Brakspears) plus Brakspears Oxford Gold, Otter Amber and Wychwood Hobgoblin on handpump, 16 wines by the glass and six malt whiskies. Décor in the dining room includes some unusual postage-stamp wallpaper, an attractive mix of chairs and tables on rugs, floorboards and flagstones, plus chandeliers, church candles, fresh flowers and modern artwork on pale painted walls; background music and TV. The back terrace has chunky tables and chairs under parasols and there are a few picnic-sets at the front. Sister pub is the Plough at Kelmscott.

 Imaginative food cooked by the landlord includes sandwiches, avocado with crab, grapefruit, gem lettuce and pumpkin seed salad, chicken liver and foie gras parfait with plum and apple chutney, local sausages and mash, seafood linguine, pork with caramelised apples and white bean and sage cassoulet, chicken milanese with griddled vegetables and salsa verde, roast lamb chump with imam bayildi (stuffed aubergine), couscous and garlic cream, and puddings such as raspberry bread and butter pudding with crème anglaise and Grand Marnier chocolate mousse. *Benchmark main dish: beer-battered fish and chips £14.50. Two-course evening meal £20.00.*

Free house ~ Licensee Sebastian Snow ~ Real ale ~ Open 12-11; 12-9 Sun ~ Bar food 12-2.30, 6-9.30; 12-3, 6-10 Fri, Sat; 12-3 Sun ~ Restaurant ~ Children welcome ~ Dogs allowed in bar ~ Wi-fi ~ Bedrooms: £95/£120 *Recommended by Charles Fraser, Carol and Barry Craddock, Bernard Stradling, Keith Perry, Nicholas and Maddy Trainer, P and J Shapley*

HEADINGTON

SP5407 Map 4

Black Boy

(01865) 741137 – www.theblackboy.uk.com

Old High Street/St Andrews Road; off A420 at traffic lights opposite B4495; OX3 9HT

Enterprising dining pub with good, enjoyable food and useful summer garden

Highly enjoyable food and the helpful, friendly staff are what our readers praise most here. It's a stylish place with black leather seats on dark parquet, large mirrors, silvery patterned wallpaper, nightlights in fat opaque cylinders and glittering bottles behind the long bar counter. The feel is light and airy, particularly at the two tables in the big bay window; just to the side are lower, softer seats beside an open fire. Crisp white tablecloths and bold black and white wallpaper lend the area on the left a touch of formality. Everards Midland Red, Burton Bridge Stairway to Heaven and a changing guest on handpump, 20 wines by the glass, ten malt whiskies and several coffees and teas. Behind the building is an appealing terrace with picnic-sets under alternating black and white parasols on smart pale stone chippings, and a central seat encircling an ash tree. As we went to press they were about to open five ensuite bedrooms.

 Appetising food includes lunchtime ciabattas (not Sunday), beetroot and vodka-infused gravadlax with pickled cucumber, shallots and lemon, black pudding with a poached egg and pancetta, wild mushroom and spinach lasagne with beurre blanc and herb salad, burger with toppings, gherkins and fries, swordfish with mango and chilli salsa, thai green chicken curry, confit duck leg with pickled red cabbage, butter beans, tomato concasse and sauce vierge, and puddings such as plum clafoutis with port and plum compote and iced white chocolate and raspberry mousse with raspberry coulis and raspberry sorbet. *Benchmark main dish: slow-roast pork belly, garlic and thyme mash and cider jus £14.95. Two-course evening meal £24.00.*

Greene King ~ Lease Abi Rose and Chris Bentham ~ Real ale ~ Open 12-11; 12-10.30 Sun ~ Bar food 12-2.45, 6-9.15 ~ Restaurant ~ Children welcome ~ Wi-fi ~ Bedrooms: £100/£140
Recommended by Neil Allen, John Poulter, Susan Eccleston, Ruby and Simon Swettenham, Bridget and Peter Gregson, Frank and Marcia Pelling

KELMSCOTT

SU2499 Map 4

Plough 🏮 🛏

(01367) 253543 – www.theploughinnkelmscott.com

NW of Faringdon, off B4449 between A417 and A4095; GL7 3HG

Lovely spot for tranquil pub with character bar and dining rooms, attractive furnishings and friendly owners; bedrooms

There's a warm welcome for all (including dogs in the bar) at this attractive country pub in its quiet hamlet setting. The small, traditional, beamed front bar has ancient flagstones and stripped-stone walls, along with a good log fire and the relaxed, chatty feel of a real village pub. A beer named for the pub (from Hook Norton) plus Butcombe Bitter, Hook Norton Hooky and Sharps Doom Bar on handpump, good wines by the glass and maybe farm cider. The dining room has elegant wooden or painted dining chairs around all sorts of tables, striped and cushioned wall seats, cartoons on exposed stone walls, rugs on the floor and plants on windowsills. The garden has seats and tables (some under cover). Bedrooms are comfortable and breakfasts are good. The Oxfordshire Cycleway runs close by and the inn is handy for Kelmscott Manor (open Wednesdays and Saturdays April-October). This is sister pub to the Five Alls at Filkins.

Using the best local produce and cooked by the landlord, the interesting food includes sandwiches, sauté duck livers and wild mushrooms on toast with shallot and sherry sauce, smoked local trout with fennel, cucumber, watercress, blood orange and pomegranate, monkfish, scampi and chips in a basket, mushroom and spinach lasagne, chicken kiev with thyme and duck fat roast potatoes, rocket and smoked tomato ketchup, grilled fillet of sea bream with herb-crushed potatoes and green olive dressing, slow-cooked lamb shoulder with crispy haggis, braised pearl barley and swede purée, and puddings such as blood orange and vodka trifle and dark chocolate and black cherry mousse cake with pistachio ice-cream; they also offer a two- and three-course set weekday menu (12-2.30, 6-7). *Benchmark main dish: pie of the day £17.50. Two-course evening meal £24.00.*

Free house ~ Licensee Sebastian Snow ~ Real ale ~ Open 12-11; 12-8 Mon ~ Bar food 12-2.30, 6-9.30 (not Mon evening); 12-3, 6-10 Sat; 12-7 Sun ~ Restaurant ~ Children welcome ~ Dogs allowed in bar ~ Wi-fi ~ Bedrooms: £70/£90 *Recommended by R K Phillips, Liz Bell, Bernard Stradling, Sally and John Quinlan*

KINGHAM   SP2624 Map 4
Plough 🏆 ⌂

(01608) 658327 – www.thekinghamplough.co.uk

Village signposted off B4450 E of Bledington; or turn S off A436 at staggered crossroads a mile SW of A44 junction – or take signed Daylesford turn off A436 and keep on; The Green; OX7 6YD

Oxfordshire Dining Pub of the Year

Friendly dining pub combining an informal pub atmosphere with creative food; bedrooms

The food here is exceptional – but this Cotswold-stone inn is also a proper pub with all that goes with that. The little bar, looking over the village green, has a simple feel, cheerful staff and keeps an interesting choice of drinks. There are some nice old high-backed settles and brightly cushioned chapel chairs on broad dark boards, candles on stripped tables and cheerful farmyard animal and country prints; at one end is a big log fire, at the other a woodburning stove. A snug one-table area is opposite the servery where they keep Hook Norton Hooky and a guest such as Goffs Lancer on handpump, 11 wines by the glass including three sparkling ones, 14 malt whiskies and local cider. The fairly spacious and raftered two-part dining room is up a few steps. The bedrooms are comfortable and pretty and the breakfasts very good.

Delicious, modern british food cooked by the landlady celebrates local produce and includes sandwiches, duck liver parfait with carrot marmalade and dandelion and carrot salad, asparagus and king oyster mushrooms with a soft-boiled quail egg, tarragon butter and chargrilled potato bread, vegetable tart with flowering herbs, burger with toppings and skinny chips, pigeon with onions, steamed herb dumplings, lemon and parsley salad, lemon sole with pickled cockles and asparagus, and puddings such as earl grey tea jelly with clotted cream ice-cream and lemon curd and warm sticky gingerbread with pear ice-cream. *Benchmark main dish: beef or lamb wellington £24.00. Two-course evening meal £35.00.*

Free house ~ Licensees Emily Watkins and Miles Lampson ~ Real ale ~ Open 12-11 ~ Bar food 12-2.30, 6.30-9 (lighter meals all day); 11.30-3 Sun (lighter meals 6-8) ~ Children welcome ~ Dogs allowed in bar and bedrooms ~ Wi-fi ~ Bedrooms: £110/£145 *Recommended by David Jackman, Neil and Angela Huxter, Terry Davis, Professor James Burke, John and Claire Masters*

Pubs close to motorway junctions are listed at the back of the book.

KIRTLINGTON

SP4919 Map 4

Oxford Arms ✪| ♀

(01869) 350208 – www.oxford-arms.co.uk

Troy Lane, junction with A4095 W of Bicester; OX5 3HA

Civilised and friendly stripped-stone pub with enjoyable food using local produce and good wine choice

This inviting stone-built pub by the post office in a lovely village is run with thought and care by the hands-on licensees. The long line of linked rooms is divided by a central stone hearth with a great round stove, and by the servery itself – where you'll find Black Sheep and Hook Norton Hooky on handpump, an interesting range of 13 wines by the glass, nine malt whiskies, farm cider and organic soft drinks. Past the bar area with its cushioned wall pews, creaky beamed ceiling and age-darkened floor tiles, dining tables on parquet have neat high-backed chairs; beyond that, leather sofas cluster round a log fire at the end. Also, church candles, fresh flowers and plenty of stripped stone. A sheltered back terrace has teak tables under giant parasols with heaters, as well as white metal furniture and picnic-sets on neat gravel. The geranium-filled window boxes are pretty. Dogs must be kept on a lead.

 The interesting daily specials are the highlight here: hot smoked salmon and leek tart, pasta with pea, asparagus and parmesan, local lamb shepherd's pie with greens, gurnard fillet with tiger prawns in bouillabaisse, and warm pigeon salad with black pudding, bacon and blueberries. Other choices include potted shrimps on toast, salmon and prawn fishcakes with sweet chilli sauce, 28-day-aged rib-eye steak with mustard and horseradish butter and triple-cooked chips, and puddings such as spiced rum and chocolate mousse with berries and olive oil cake with pistachio ice-cream. *Benchmark main dish: venison burger with toppings and triple-cooked chips £15.00. Two-course evening meal £23.00.*

Punch ~ Lease Bryn Jones ~ Real ale ~ Open 12-3, 6-11; 12-4 Sun; closed Sun evening, bank holiday Mon evening ~ Bar food 12-2.30, 6.30-8.30 ~ Restaurant ~ Well behaved children welcome ~ Dogs welcome *Recommended by Dr Peter Crawshaw, Mr and Mrs J Watkins, Brian and Sally Wakeham, Dave Braisted, Anya Van Gulck, Louise and Oliver Redman, Camilla and Jose Ferrera*

LONGWORTH

SU3899 Map 4

Blue Boar ♀

(01865) 820494 – www.blueboarlongworth.co.uk

Tucks Lane; OX13 5ET

Smashing old pub with good wines and beer, and well thought-of food

A bustling, easy-going atmosphere in this handsome country pub is helped along by a good mix of regulars and visitors. It's warmly traditional inside and the three low-beamed, characterful small rooms have brasses, hops and assorted knick-knacks (skis, an old clocking-in machine) on the walls and ceilings, scrubbed wooden tables and benches, faded rugs and floor tiles, fresh flowers on the bar, a coal fire and two blazing log fires (the one by the bar is noteworthy). The main eating area is the red-painted room at the end and there's a quieter restaurant extension too. Brakspears Bitter and Otter Ale on handpump, 20 malt whiskies, 15 gins and a dozen wines by the glass. There are tables outside in front and on the back terrace, and a circular two-mile walk starts at the front door.

Pleasing food includes sandwiches, skewered prawns with aioli, a sharing antipasti board, wild mushroom spinach and pine nut linguine, malaysian chicken curry, salad of merguez sausages, roasted piquillo peppers, olives and tzatziki, cider-battered fish and chips, pizzas, venison loin fillet with haggis, sweet potato mash and cranberry and port jus, cod loin fillet with asparagus and lemon beurre blanc, duck breast with sauté potatoes and griottine cherry jus, and puddings such as sticky toffee pudding with butterscotch sauce and warm treacle tart with vanilla ice-cream. *Benchmark main dish: burger with toppings and chips £11.95. Two-course evening meal £20.00.*

Free house ~ Licensee Paul Dailey ~ Real ale ~ Open 12-11 (midnight Sat) ~ Bar food 12-2.30, 6.30-9.30 (10 Fri, Sat); 12-3, 6.30-9 Sun; light snacks during afternoon ~ Restaurant ~ Children welcome ~ Dogs allowed in bar ~ Wi-fi *Recommended by John Pritchard, Neil and Angela Huxter, R K Phillips, Keith Perry, Julie Swift, Jill and Hugh Bennett*

MILTON UNDER WYCHWOOD   SP2618 Map 4
Hare ♀
(01993) 835763 – www.themiltonhare.co.uk
High Street; OX7 6LA

Renovated stone inn with linked bar and dining rooms, attractive contemporary furnishings, real ales, good food and seats in the garden

All manner of hare paraphernalia can be found throughout this bustling village pub – photos, paintings, statues, a large glass case with stuffed boxing hares, motifs on scatter cushions and so forth. There's a bar and a couple of little drinking areas warmed by a woodburning stove, and various dining areas leading off: wooden floors, dark grey-painted or exposed stone walls, painted beams, big gilt-edged mirrors and seating that includes stools, wooden or leather dining chairs, long button-back wall seats and cushioned settles around tables of every size – each set with a little glass oil lamp. Splashes of bright colour here and there brighten things considerably. Stools line the counter, where friendly, well trained staff serve Otter Bitter and guests such as Butcombe Rare Breed and Church Farm Browns Porter on handpump and good wines by the glass; on Fridays at 5pm it's champagne happy hour. The garden has tables, benches and chairs on a terrace and on a lawn.

Fish and seafood fresh from Cornwall is the speciality here, but they also offer lunchtime sandwiches, pressed rabbit terrine with courgette piccalilli, lamb kofta kebabs with warm pitta bread, mint crème fraîche and shredded lettuce, roasted beetroot, feta, spinach and sweet potato pie with red chard, pea shoot and pesto salad, burger with toppings, carrot and dry-roasted peanut slaw and fries, chicken breast stuffed with whipped goats cheese, sunblush tomatoes and basil and wrapped in parma ham, crispy pork belly with cheese and pancetta dauphinoise potatoes and tarragon sauce, and puddings such as rhubarb and apple crumble with vanilla bean ice-cream and espresso and honeycomb cheesecake sundae. *Benchmark main dish: fresh fish dish of the day £17.00. Two-course evening meal £23.00.*

Free house ~ Licensees Sue and Rachel Hawkins ~ Real ale ~ Open 12-3, 5.30-11; 11-11 Sat, Sun ~ Bar food 12-2.30, 6-9 (9.30 Sat); 12-8 Sun ~ Restaurant ~ Children welcome but not in the bar at weekends ~ Dogs allowed in bar ~ Wi-fi *Recommended by Liz Bell, Barry Collett, Tim and Sarah Smythe-Brown, Liz and Martin Eldon, Len and Lilly Dowson*

MINSTER LOVELL   SP3211 Map 4
Old Swan & Minster Mill ▣ ♀ ⇦

(01993) 774441 – www.oldswanandminstermill.com
Just N of B4047 Witney–Burford; OX29 0RN

Ancient inn with old-fashioned bar, real ales, a fine wine list, excellent food and acres of gardens and grounds; exceptional bedrooms

Of course, much emphasis is placed on the hotel and restaurant side of this rather lovely 15th-c building, but it would be a great pity to miss the unchanging and tranquil little bar. Here, you'll find stools at the wooden counter, Brakspears Oxford Gold, North Cotswold Windrush Ale and Wychwood Hobgoblin on handpump, good wines by the glass from a fine list, 30 malt whiskies and quite a choice of teas and coffees. Leading off are several attractive low-beamed rooms with big log fires in huge fireplaces, comfortable armchairs, sofas, dining chairs and antique tables, rugs on bare boards or ancient flagstones, antiques, prints, lots of horsebrasses, bed-warming pans, swords, hunting horns and even a suit of armour; also, fresh flowers, background music and board games. Seats are dotted around the 65 acres of grounds (the white metal ones beside the water are much sought after) and they have fishing rights to a mile of the River Windrush, as well as tennis courts, boules and croquet. The bedrooms have plenty of character; some are positively luxurious.

Especially good food from a seasonal menu includes sandwiches, smoked pigeon breast with black pudding and apple and parsnip purée, tian of hot smoked salmon with charred cucumber, radish and dandelion leaf, pumpkin and sage ravioli with baby spinach and pumpkin seed pesto, rare-breed burger with air-dried ham and triple-cooked chips, chicken with puy lentils, chervil root and parmesan potato purée, asian-spiced brill fillet with spiced cauliflower, baby spinach and creamed cockle tartlet, and puddings such as lemon posset with madeira cake and blood orange and vanilla pannacotta with poached pineapple, pink grapefruit and passion-fruit sorbet. *Benchmark main dish: beer-battered fresh fish and chips £15.00. Two-course evening meal £23.00.*

Free house ~ Licensee Oscar Garcia ~ Real ale ~ Open 10am-midnight ~ Bar food 12.30-9 (10 for snacks) ~ Restaurant ~ Children welcome ~ Dogs allowed in bar and bedrooms ~ Wi-fi ~ Live music last Sun of month ~ Bedrooms: £165/£175 *Recommended by Richard Kennell, Guy Vowles, Gail and Frank Hackett, Patti and James Davidson*

OXFORD   SP5106   Map 4

Bear ◖

(01865) 728164 – www.bearoxford.co.uk
Alfred Street/Wheatsheaf Alley; OX1 4EH

**Delightful pub with friendly staff, two cosy rooms, six real ales
and well liked bar food**

This easy-going and charming small tavern dates from 1242, making it the oldest drinking house in the city. The two small rooms are beamed, partly panelled and have a chatty, bustling atmosphere (in term time it's often packed with students), winter coal fires, thousands of vintage ties on the walls and up to six real ales from handpumps on the fine pewter bar counter: Fullers ESB, HSB, London Pride and Olivers Island and a guest such as Shotover Prospect. Staff are friendly and helpful; board games. There are seats under parasols in the large terraced back garden where summer barbecues are held.

Bar food includes sandwiches, cheddar rarebit with tomato chutney, home-made scotch egg with ale chutney and piccalilli, sausages and mash with red wine gravy, moroccan vegetable hotpot, burgers with toppings and chips, chicken, ham and leek pie, seared salmon with spinach and tartare sauce, and puddings such as chocolate brownie and vintage ale sticky toffee pudding. *Benchmark main dish: beer-battered fish and chips £12.75. Two-course evening meal £18.00.*

Fullers ~ Manager James Vernede ~ Real ale ~ Open 11-11 (midnight Fri, Sat); 11.30-10.30 Sun ~ Bar food 12-4, 5-9; 12-9 Fri-Sun ~ Children welcome but no pushchairs inside ~ Dogs welcome ~ Wi-fi *Recommended by MarkandDi, Daniel England, Richard Tilbrook, Charles Fraser, Paddy and Sian O'Leary*

OXFORD

SP4907 Map 4

Perch ♀

(01865) 728891 – www.the-perch.co.uk

Binsey Lane, on right after river bridge leaving city on A420; OX2 0NG

A fine mix of customers for beautifully set inn with riverside gardens, local ales, popular food and friendly service

Even the most seasoned of pub-goers could not fail to be charmed by this thatched 17th-c limestone pub. It's a special place, especially in warm weather, with a lovely garden running down to the Thames Path where there are moorings. A partly covered terrace has seats and tables, there are picnic-sets on the lawn, a summer bar and an attractively furnished marquee. But on cooler days customers have just as much to look forward to in the heavily beamed bar with its red leather chesterfields in front of a woodburning stove, a very high-backed settle, little stools around tables and fine old flagstones. Hook Norton Hooky and guests such as Prescott Hill Climb and XT Eight on handpump and plenty of wines by the glass; background music and board games. Leading off here are the dining areas with bare floorboards, scatter cushions on built-in wall seats, wheelbacks and other chairs around light tables, a second woodburner with logs piled to the ceiling next to it and a fine brass chandelier. Service is helpful and friendly; they hold an annual beer and cider festival, outdoor film evenings in summer and a folk festival. It's said that this might be one of the first places that Lewis Carroll gave public readings of *Alice in Wonderland*.

From a thoughtful menu using local produce, the good food includes wild rabbit and ham hock terrine with grape chutney, potted smoked salmon with watercress mousse and cucumber pickle, a fish or vegetarian platter, butternut squash, roast pepper and butter bean salad with a soft-boiled duck egg, local sausages with blue cheese mash and caramelised onion gravy, beer-battered fish with triple-cooked chips, braised lamb shoulder with black pudding and rosemary pie, and puddings such as spiced plum, blackberry and almond crumble and sticky toffee pudding. *Benchmark main dish: braised ox cheeks with champ mash £16.95. Two-course evening meal £23.00.*

Free house ~ Licensee Jon Ellse ~ Real ale ~ Open 10.30am-11.30pm; 10am-11pm Sun; closes 10.30pm in winter ~ Bar food 12-10 (9 in winter) ~ Restaurant ~ Children welcome ~ Dogs welcome *Recommended by Neil and Angela Huxter, Laura Moore, Beth Aldridge, Melanie and David Lawson*

OXFORD

SP5005 Map 4

Punter

(01865) 248832 – www.thepunteroxford.com

South Street, Osney (off A420 Botley Road via Bridge Street); OX2 0BE

Easy-going atmosphere in bustling pub overlooking the water with plenty of character and enjoyable food

'On a sunny day overlooking the Thames with a plate of good food – this was perfect,' says one reader summing up his visit here. Run by an enthusiastic landlord and his friendly staff, the place has a boathouse feel; the lower area has attractive rugs on flagstones and an open fire, while the upper room has more rugs on bare boards and a single big table surrounded by oil paintings – just right for a private group. Throughout are all manner of nice old dining chairs around an interesting mix of tables, art for sale on whitewashed walls and a rather fine stained-glass window. Greene King

Morlands Original and Old Golden Hen and a guest such as Mad Squirrel Mister Squirrel on handpump from the tiled counter and several wines by the glass; board games.

🍴 Highly popular food includes their £5 lunch special, as well as free-range scotch egg with apple and plum chutney, crab mayonnaise with mango and avocado salsa, halloumi with tenderstem broccoli and giant couscous with chestnut mushrooms, baby spinach and chestnut vinaigrette, moules frites, lamb meatballs with pearl barley and vegetable stew with crème fraîche, smoked haddock fillet with vegetable risotto and a poached egg, venison haunch steak with red miso butter and giant couscous and green bean salad, and puddings. *Benchmark main dish: burger with toppings, mustard mayo and frites £12.50. Two-course evening meal £20.00.*

Greene King ~ Lease Tom Rainey ~ Real ale ~ Open 12-midnight; 12-11.30 Sun ~ Bar food 12-3, 6-10; 12-10 Sat; 12-9 Sun ~ Children welcome ~ Dogs welcome ~ Wi-fi *Recommended by Richard Tilbrook, Harvey Brown, Phoebe Peacock, John Harris*

OXFORD
SP5107   Map 4

Rose & Crown ◧
(01865) 510551 – www.roseandcrownoxford.com
North Parade Avenue; very narrow, so best to park in a nearby street; OX2 6LX

Lively friendly local with a fine choice of drinks and proper home cooking

As always, this is a particularly well run pub with long-serving licensees who give the place plenty of individuality. The front door opens into a passage with a small counter and shelves of reference books for crossword buffs. This leads to two rooms: a cosy one at the front overlooking the street, and a panelled back room housing the main bar and traditional pub furnishings. A good mix of customers of all ages enjoy well kept Adnams Southwold, Hook Norton Old Hooky, Purple Moose Glaslyn Ale and Shotover Scholar on handpump, around 30 malt whiskies and 20 wines by the glass (including champagne and sparkling wine). The pleasant walled and heated back courtyard can be covered with a huge awning; at the far end there is a 12-seater dining/meeting room. The loos are rustic.

🍴 Honest food at fair prices includes sandwiches and baguettes, potted shrimps and potted crab, dips with hot pitta bread, a choice of omelettes, a pint of sausages, breaded cod or chicken with a honey glaze all with chips, english breakfast, salad niçoise, gammon with egg and pineapple, locally sourced sirloin steak with garlic butter or peppercorn sauce, and puddings such as apple pie or a hot pudding. *Benchmark main dish: pie and mash £11.00. Two-course evening meal £15.00.*

Free house ~ Licensees Andrew and Debbie Hall ~ Real ale ~ Open 11-11; 11-2.30, 4.30-11 Aug-early Sept ~ Bar food 12-2.15 (3 Sun), 6-9 ~ Wi-fi ~ Live jazz Sun evening *Recommended by Andy Dolan, John Harris, Barbara Brown, Nick Higgins, Gus Swan*

RAMSDEN
SP3515   Map 4

Royal Oak ♀ ◧
(01993) 868213 – www.royaloakramsden.com
Village signposted off B4022 Witney–Charlbury; OX7 3AU

Busy pub with long-serving licensees, large helpings of varied food, carefully chosen wines and seats outside; bedrooms

To really appreciate the surrounding countryside and fine walks, it makes sense to stay in the comfortable bedrooms in the converted coach house and stable block. The inn has been run by Mr Oldham for over 30 years and the unpretentious bar rooms (refurbished after a fire) are relaxed and friendly with old settles and tables and old-fashioned pub fittings; open fires. Gales HSB, Loose Cannon Abingdon Bridge, Wye Valley Bitter and changing guests from Cotswold Lion and Ramsbury on handpump, 40 wines by the glass from a carefully chosen list and three farm ciders. Folding doors from the dining room give easy access to the back terrace, and there are some tables and chairs out in front. The village church is opposite.

Popular food includes sandwiches, chicken liver parfait with red onion chutney, avocado and prawn gratin, a jamaican curry, a pie of the week, a vegetarian dish of the day, creamed haddock smokies cooked in whisky and cream with a cheese topping, steak burger with toppings and fries, jerk chicken with rice, scallops with smoked bacon and piquant citrus dressing, duck confit with dauphinoise potatoes and citrus and berry sauce, and puddings. *Benchmark main dish: steak and kidney pudding £14.50. Two-course evening meal £20.00.*

Free house ~ Licensee Jon Oldham ~ Real ale ~ Open 11.30-3.30, 6.30-11; 11.30-11 Sat; 12-10 Sun ~ Bar food 12-2, 7-9.30; 12-9.30 Sat; 12-8 Sun ~ Restaurant ~ Children welcome ~ Dogs allowed in bar ~ Wi-fi ~ Bedrooms: £55/£85 *Recommended by Tim King, Charles Welch, Keith Perry, Steve Whalley, Pieter and Janet Vrancken, Harvey Brown*

SHILTON
Rose & Crown ⭐

SP2608 Map 4

(01993) 842280 – www.shiltonroseandcrown.com
Just off B4020 SE of Burford; OX18 4AB

Simple and appealing small pub with particularly good food, real ales and fine wines

This is a pretty little 17th-c gem and very much the focus point of this lovely village – our readers consistently enjoy their visits. The friendly and chatty small front bar has an unassuming but civilised feel, low beams and timbers, exposed stone walls, a log fire in a big fireplace and half a dozen or so farmhouse chairs and tables on the red-tiled floor. There are usually a few locals at the planked counter where they serve Butcombe Rare Breed, Hook Norton Old Hooky and Youngs Bitter on handpump, along with ten wines by the glass, seven malt whiskies and farm cider. A second room, similar but bigger, is used mainly for eating, and has another fireplace. An attractive side garden has picnic-sets.

Enjoyable food cooked by the chef-owner includes ciabattas, goats cheese and beetroot salad with walnut oil dressing, soused mackerel fillets, aubergine parmigiana with mozzarella, lambs liver and bacon, pheasant with cabbage, bacon and mash, smoked haddock, salmon and prawn fish pie, flat-iron steak with garlic butter and chips, and puddings such as bread and butter pudding and vanilla pannacotta with butterscotch sauce, praline and pistachios. *Benchmark main dish: steak and mushroom in ale pie £13.50. Two-course evening meal £19.00.*

Free house ~ Licensee Martin Coldicott ~ Real ale ~ Open 11.30-3, 6-10.30; 11.30-10.30 Sat; 12-10 Sun ~ Bar food 12-2 (2.45 weekends and bank holidays), 7-9 ~ Children welcome at lunchtime and until 7pm ~ Dogs allowed in bar ~ Wi-fi *Recommended by R K Phillips, John Evans*

'Children welcome' means the pub says it lets children inside without any special restriction. If it allows them in, but to restricted areas such as an eating area or family room, we specify this. Some pubs may impose an evening time limit. We do not mention limits after 9pm as we assume children are home by then.

SHIPLAKE

SU7779   Map 2

Baskerville 🏵 ♈ ▪ 🛏

(0118) 940 3332 – www.thebaskerville.com

Station Road, Lower Shiplake (off A4155 just S of Henley); RG9 3NY

Emphasis on imaginative food but a proper public bar too, interesting sporting memorabilia and a pretty garden; bedrooms

This is a first-class pub run with care and thought by a hands-on family – there's always a good mix of customers and a genuine welcome for all. The bar has a few beams, red leather tub chairs, pale wood dining chairs and tables on oak floors or patterned carpet, plush red banquettes by the windows and a couple of log fires in brick fireplaces. Flowers and large house plants are dotted about, and the red walls are hung with a fair amount of sporting memorabilia and pictures (especially old rowing photos – Henley is very near) as well as signed rugby shirts and photos, and maps of the Thames. Bar chairs line the light, modern counter where they keep Loddon Hoppit, Rebellion IPA, Sharps Doom Bar and Timothy Taylors Landlord on handpump, 15 wines by the glass from a thoughtfully chosen list, 40 malt whiskies and farm cider, all served by neat staff; they support WaterAid by charging 75p for a jug of iced water and at the time of writing have raised £8,000. Background music and TV. There's a separate restaurant and a small room for private parties. The pretty garden has a covered barbecue area, teak furniture under huge parasols and some rather fun topiary statues cut from box hedging. The bedrooms are well equipped and comfortable and the breakfasts excellent.

 Extremely good food from a well judged menu includes open sandwiches, soft-boiled duck egg with porcini purée, pancetta, pine nuts and balsamic croûte, king scallops with black pudding, pea purée, pancetta crisp and truffle oil, chicken, ham and leek pie, asparagus and pea risotto with spinach and mint, lamb rack with cashew nut crust, white bean cassoulet and wild garlic purée, skate with chilli and lime tagliatelle, samphire and clams, 28-day dry-aged, grass-fed local sirloin steak with slow-roasted tomatoes, sauté mushrooms and chips, and puddings such as a trio of chocolate mousse with caramelised banana and peanut brittle and vanilla cheesecake with blueberry compote and salted caramel. *Benchmark main dish: burger with toppings and french fries £14.50. Two-course evening meal £24.00.*

Free house ~ Licensee Allan Hannah ~ Real ale ~ Open 11-11; 12-10.30 Sun ~ Bar food 12-9 (12-3, 6-9 Jan-Mar, Oct, Nov); 12-3.30 Sun ~ Restaurant ~ Children welcome but not in restaurant after 7pm Fri, Sat ~ Dogs allowed in bar and bedrooms ~ Wi-fi ~ Bedrooms: £100/£110 *Recommended by Richard Kennell, Allan Lloyd and family, Holly and Tim Waite, Alison and Dan Richardson*

SPARSHOLT

SU3487   Map 2

Star 🏵 ♈ 🛏

(01235) 751873 – www.thestarsparsholt.co.uk

Watery Lane; OX12 9PL

Excellent food, real ales and good wines by the glass, helpful friendly staff and seats in the garden; comfortable bedrooms

With delicious food served by efficient, charming staff and an easy-going and informal atmosphere, this appealing 16th-c pub is a winner. The simply furnished bar is also used by those just wanting a pint and a chat; they keep Purity Gold and Sharps Doom Bar on handpump and several wines by the glass. Background music and board games. The dining rooms have pale farmhouse chairs around chunky tables on floorboards or big flagstones, hops on beams, an open fire and old stone bottles and plants dotted about.

The two pub dogs are called Minnie and Ella. There are seats in the back garden and eight attractive, contemporary bedrooms in a smartly converted barn. You can enjoy walks along the Ridgeway and a carpet of spring snowdrops in the churchyard.

 Using some home-grown produce and other top quality local, seasonal ingredients, the first-class, imaginative food includes mackerel with lime, pomegranate, tomato and quinoa salsa, guacamole and jalapeno sorbet, chicken and chorizo croquette with red pepper and caraway jam, braeburn apple and parsley, burger with toppings and skin-on fries, puy lentil saag aloo with saffron-braised onion, spring vegetables, coconut and coriander sauce, smoked ham hock, onion and cheese pie with black truffle mash, lamb shoulder and crispy sweetbreads with spring onion champ, redcurrant jam and mint sauce, fresh fish of the day with ras el hanout couscous, courgette, pepper and basil beurre blanc, and puddings such as sticky toffee soufflé with salted caramel parfait and butterscotch and dark chocolate delice with pistachios and black cherry sorbet; they also offer a two- and three-course set lunch (not Sunday). *Benchmark main dish: sea trout with wild garlic, asparagus, truffle and hazelnut hollandaise £19.50. Two-course evening meal £25.00.*

Free house ~ Licensee Caron Williams ~ Real ale ~ Open 12-11 (midnight Sat); 12-11 Sun ~ Bar food 12-2.30, 6.30-9 (9.30 Fri, Sat); 12-8 Sun ~ Restaurant ~ Children welcome ~ Dogs welcome ~ Wi-fi ~ Bedrooms: £85/£105 *Recommended by Diane Abbott, Ben and Diane Bowie, Liz Bell, R K Phillips, Neil and Angela Huxter*

STANFORD IN THE VALE
SU3393 Map 4
Horse & Jockey ♀ £
(01367) 710302 – www.horseandjockey.org

A417 Faringdon–Wantage; Faringdon Road; SN7 8NN

Bustling, traditional village local with real character, highly thought-of and good value food and well chosen wines; bedrooms

As this is racehorse-training country, the walls in this charming pub are hung with big Alfred Munnings racecourse prints, card collections of Grand National winners and other horse and jockey pictures. The convivial, hands-on licensees are warmly friendly to all. The place is split into two sections: a contemporary dining area and an older part with flagstones, wood flooring, low beams and raftered ceilings. There are old high-backed settles and leather armchairs, a woodburning stove in a big fireplace and an easy-going atmosphere. A beer named for the pub (from Greene King), Belhaven Grand Slam and Greene King Windmill Pale on handpump, carefully chosen wines by the glass, 16 gins and a dozen malt whiskies; background music and board games. As well as tables under a heated courtyard canopy, there's a separate enclosed informal garden. The bedrooms, housed in another building, are quiet and comfortable.

Reasonably priced, well liked food using some home-grown produce includes sandwiches, salt, pepper and chilli tempura prawns, chicken liver pâté with fruit chutney, meat or cheese sharing boards, chicken caesar salad, wild mushroom stroganoff, local pork and leek sausages, stone-baked pizzas (available to take away too), breadcrumbed chicken with smoked paprika fries, coleslaw and spiced beans, and puddings such as a dozen home-made ice-creams and triple chocolate brownie. *Benchmark main dish: steak burger with toppings, smoked chilli relish and skinny fries £10.50. Two-course evening meal £16.00.*

Greene King ~ Lease Charles and Anna Gaunt ~ Real ale ~ Open 11-3, 5-midnight; 11am-12.30am Sat; 11-11 Sun ~ Bar food 12-2.30, 6.30-9 (9.30 Fri, Sat); 12-2.30 Sun ~ Restaurant ~ Children welcome but not in bedrooms ~ Dogs allowed in bar ~ Wi-fi ~ Bedrooms: £65/£80 *Recommended by Peter Barrett, James Landor, R K Phillips, Shona and Jimmy McDuff, Luke Morgan*

STONESFIELD
SP3917   Map 4

White Horse

(01993) 891063 – www.whitehorsestonesfield.com

Village signposted off B4437 Charlbury–Woodstock; Stonesfield Riding; OX29 8EA

Carefully kept little pub with a relaxed atmosphere and enjoyable food and beer

A t weekend lunchtimes, this attractively upgraded small country pub does get pretty busy as it's on the Oxfordshire Way long-distance footpath. There's a friendly, uncluttered feel – just a few pieces of contemporary artwork on green and cream paintwork – and the cosy bar has a woodburning stove, country-style chairs and plush or leather stools around solid tables on bare boards, XT One, Thirteen and Fifteen on handpump and six wines by the glass; background music. The dining room has similar but more elegant furnishings. Doors open on to a neat walled garden with picnic-sets and interesting plants in pots and there are more seats in the courtyard. It's handy for the Roman villa at nearby North Leigh (English Heritage), but do note the pub's restricted opening hours.

Some home-grown produce and their own free-range eggs are used in the tasty food: filled rolls, goats cheese and beetroot salad, creamy garlic mushrooms, linguine with peppers and spicy tomato sauce, scampi and frites, burger with toppings and chips, calves liver and bacon, sea bass thai-style, grilled chicken breast and sirloin steak with a choice of sauces, and puddings such as rhubarb crumble and sticky toffee pudding; they hold barbecues on Wednesday evenings in summer. *Benchmark main dish: pie of the day £12.95. Two-course evening meal £20.00.*

Free house ~ Licensees Clare Villiers and Marina Barnes ~ Real ale ~ Open 5-11; 12-2, 5-11 Fri; 12-2, 6-11 Sat; 12-3 Sun; closed Sun evening, Mon, lunchtimes Tues-Thurs ~ Bar food 6-9; 12-2, 6-9 Fri, Sat; 12-3 Sun ~ Restaurant ~ Children welcome ~ Dogs allowed in bar ~ Wi-fi *Recommended by Edward May, Isobel Mackinlay, Emma Scofield, Amanda Shipley*

SWERFORD
SP3830   Map 4

Masons Arms

(01608) 683212 – www.masons-arms.com

A361 Banbury–Chipping Norton; OX7 4AP

Well liked food and fair choice of drinks in bustling dining pub with relaxed atmosphere and country views

O ur readers enjoy the neat back garden here in warm weather – there are picnic-sets on grass and pretty views over the Oxfordshire countryside. The friendly bar is welcoming at any time of year, with a big brown leather sofa facing a couple of armchairs in front of a log fire in a stone fireplace, rugs on pale wooden floors, Brakspears Bitter and Jennings Cumberland on handpump and 13 wines by the glass. The light and airy dining extension has pastel-painted dining chairs around nice old tables on beige carpet, and steps lead down to a cream-painted room with chunky tables and contemporary pictures. Around the other side of the bar is another spacious dining room with great views by day, candles at night and a civilised feel; background music.

Good, enjoyable food includes sandwiches, crayfish cocktail, baked brie parcels with cranberry and red onion chutney, honey-roast ham and eggs, roasted pepper, leek and mushroom lasagne, chicken with black pudding and pancetta with red wine, baby onion and mushroom sauce, duo of local lamb (cutlet and crispy belly) with rosemary roast potatoes and redcurrant, red wine and mint jus, duck breast with sweet potato bubble and squeak and brambleberry jus, and puddings such as apricot, mango, mandarin and passion-fruit mess and dark chocolate parfait with kirsch, black cherry compote and morello cherry ice-cream. *Benchmark main dish: rib-eye steak with stuffed mushrooms and beer-battered onion rings £18.95. Two-course evening meal £23.00.*

Free house ~ Licensee Louise Davies ~ Real ale ~ Open 11-3, 6-11; 11-6 Sun ~ Bar food 12-2.15, 6-9 (9.30 Sat); 11-6 Sun ~ Restaurant ~ Children welcome ~ Dogs allowed in bar ~ Wi-fi *Recommended by Maddie Purvis, Daphne and Robert Staples, Peter Meister, Chris and Pauline Sexton, Monty Green, Patricia Healey*

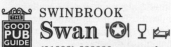

SWINBROOK
Swan 🌟 ⌾ 🍷 🛏

SP2812   Map 4

(01993) 823339 – www.theswanswinbrook.co.uk
Back road a mile N of A40, 2 miles E of Burford; OX18 4DY

Smart old pub with handsome oak garden rooms, antiques-filled bars, local beers and contemporary food; bedrooms

As this civilised place is owned by the Devonshire Estate, there are plenty of interesting Mitford family photographs blown up on the walls. The little bar has simple antique furnishings, settles and benches, an open fire and (in an alcove) a stuffed swan; locals drop in here for a pint and a chat. A small dining room leads off from the bar to the right of the entrance, and there are also two garden rooms with high-backed beige and green dining chairs around pale wood tables and views across the garden and orchard. Hook Norton Hooky and a couple of changing guests from breweries such as Flying Monk and Otter on handpump, nine wines by the glass, farm ciders and local draught lager; background music, board games and TV. The outdoor seats and circular picnic-sets make the best of this 400-year-old stone pub's position by a bridge over the River Windrush. The elegant bedrooms are in a smartly converted stone barn beside the pub, with five by the water. The Kings Head in Bledington (Gloucestershire) is run by the same first class licensees.

Accomplished cooking includes lunchtime sandwiches, rabbit hash with chicory and orange dressing and a fried duck egg, twice-baked blue cheese soufflé with grape, hazelnut and celery salad, buffalo mozzarella, sunblush tomato and basil risotto cakes with green olive tapenade, crispy fishcake with a free-range poached egg and hollandaise, confit pork belly with black pudding, red cabbage apple sauce and cider jus, sea bream with confit fennel, saffron parmentier potatoes and mussel velouté, and puddings such as chocolate tarte with lime butterscotch sauce and hazelnut ice-cream and apple crumble with cinnamon ice-cream. *Benchmark main dish: burger with toppings, sun-dried tomato mayonnaise and skinny chips £12.50. Two-course evening meal £25.00.*

Free house ~ Licensees Archie and Nicola Orr-Ewing ~ Real ale ~ Open 11-11 ~ Bar food 12-2, 7-9 ~ Restaurant ~ Children welcome ~ Dogs allowed in bar ~ Wi-fi ~ Bedrooms: £100/£125 *Recommended by Richard Tilbrook, Julia and Fiona Barnes, Chloe and Tim Hodge*

TADPOLE BRIDGE
Trout 🌟 ⌾ 🍷 🛏

SP3200   Map 4

(01367) 870382 – www.trout-inn.co.uk
Back road Bampton–Buckland, 4 miles NE of Faringdon; SN7 8RF

Busy country inn with waterside garden and moorings, civilised bar and dining rooms and a fine choice of drinks and food; bedrooms

'A perfect pub in a perfect location,' says one reader when describing this 17th-c inn on the banks of the Thames; there are moorings for six boats.

The smartly refurbished bar has a large stuffed trout, exposed stone walls, beams and standing timbers, a woodburning stove with logs neatly piled to one side, leather armchairs and stools, scatter cushions on window seats, and wooden floors and flagstones. Upholstered stools line the blue-painted counter where courteous, friendly staff serve a beer named for the pub (from Ramsbury), Banks's Bitter, Ringwood Boondoggle and White Horse Black Beauty on handpump, ten wines by the glass from a wide-ranging, carefully chosen list, 21 malt whiskies and two farm ciders. Dining rooms have green-and-brown-checked chairs around a mix of nice wooden tables, fresh flowers and candlelight; the pale wood or blue-painted tongue-and-groove walls are hung with trout and stag prints, oars and mirrors. The pretty garden has good quality chairs and tables under parasols, and the six bedrooms (three open on to a small courtyard) are attractive and comfortable.

Good, enterprising food includes confit duck ballotine with blood orange and smoked potato salad, crispy ham hock with black pudding and celeriac, local sausages of the day with shallot and red wine sauce, spring onion risotto with red peppers, goats cheese and pine nuts, chicken, leek and mushroom pie, gurnard with cannellini beans, leeks and white wine jus, glazed ox cheek with horseradish mash and pickled shallots, and puddings such as raspberry cheesecake and white chocolate sorbet and almond cake with quince sorbet. *Benchmark main dish: beer-battered haddock and chips £14.50. Two-course evening meal £24.00.*

Free house ~ Licensee Ricardo Canestra ~ Real ale ~ Open 12-11 ~ Bar food 12-2.30, 6.30-9 (8.30 Sun); ~ Restaurant ~ Children welcome ~ Dogs allowed in bar and bedrooms ~ Wi-fi ~ Bedrooms: /£130 *Recommended by John Poulter, Roy Davies, Neil and Angela Huxter, Richard Tilbrook, Mrs Zara Elliott, Chloe and Michael Swettenham, Ben and Jenny Settle*

WOLVERCOTE
Jacobs Inn ⍟◔ ♀
SP4809   Map 4

(01865) 514333 ~ www.jacobs-inn.com
Godstow Road; OX2 8PG

Enjoyable pub with enthusiastic staff, simple furnishings, inventive cooking and seats in the garden

On the edge of Port Meadow, this is a cheerfully run pub with interesting, hearty food, a bustling yet easy-going atmosphere and slightly quirky décor. The simply furnished bar has leather armchairs and chesterfields, some plain tables and benches, wide floorboards, a small open fire and high chairs at the counter where they keep Brakspears Bitter, Jennings Cumberland, and Wychwood Hobgoblin and Pinhead on handpump, 13 wines by the glass, a good choice of spirits and lots of teas and coffees; background music. You can eat at plain wooden tables in a grey panelled area with an open fire or in the smarter knocked-through dining room. This has standing timbers in the middle, a fire at each end and shiny, dark wooden chairs and tables on floorboards; there are standard lamps, stags' heads, a reel-to-reel tape recorder, quite a few mirrors and various deli items for sale. Several seating areas outside have good quality tables and chairs under parasols, picnic-sets on decking, and deckchairs and more picnic-sets on grass. Pigs and chickens roam in a large grassy enclosure. This is sister pub to the Woodstock Arms in Woodstock – a new Main Entry in this chapter.

Robust, inventive food using home-reared pigs, free-range eggs and other local produce includes potted kiln-roast salmon with pickled cucumber, pigeon breast and green bean salad with quince and sherry dressing, crab salad with spiced lemon and garlic aioli, asparagus and wild mushroom spaghetti with watercress and smoked garlic pesto, wild boar burger with celeriac and horseradish slaw and chips, rolled lamb belly with purple sprouting broccoli, mint purée and goats cheese curd, and puddings such as passion-fruit parfait with mango sorbet and chocolate pot with caramel shortbread. *Benchmark main dish: home-made pies £13.00. Two-course evening meal £22.00.*

Marstons ~ Lease Damion Farah and Johnny Pugsley ~ Real ale ~ Open 9am-11pm ~ Bar food 9am-10pm (9.30pm Sun) ~ Restaurant ~ Children welcome ~ Dogs allowed in bar ~ Wi-fi *Recommended by John Evans, William Slade, Thomas Green, Michael and Margaret Cross, Rosie and John Moore*

 WOODSTOCK   SP4416 Map 4

Kings Arms £ 🛏

(01993) 813636 – www.kingshotelwoodstock.co.uk
Market Street/Park Lane (A44); OX20 1SU

Bustling town-centre hotel with well liked food, a wide choice of drinks and an enjoyable atmosphere; comfortable bedrooms

Of all the pubs in this smart and attractive old town, it's this stylish place right in the heart of things that our readers enjoy the most. The unfussy bar has a cheerful mix of locals and visitors, an appealing variety of old and new furnishings including brown leather seats on the stripped-wood floor, smart blinds and black and white photographs; at the front is an old wooden settle and a modern woodburning stove. The neat restaurant has high-backed black leather dining chairs around a mix of tables on black and white floor tiles, and piles of neatly stacked logs on either side of another woodburning stove; background music. Fullers London Pride, Olivers Island and Spring Sprinter on handpump, 11 wines (plus champagne) by the glass and 35 malt whiskies. There are seats and tables on the street outside.

Good, enjoyable food includes duck scotch egg with anchovies and duck egg mayonnaise, pork terrine with beetroot and red onion jam, spiced chickpea and sweet potato burger with melted cheese, pickled carrots and chips, ham, free-range eggs, brown caper butter and sweet potato chips, free-range chicken breast with shallot and mushroom stuffing with stout gravy, jerusalem artichokes and celeriac dauphinoise, slow-cooked pork belly with creamy cabbage and bacon and sage-crushed pink fir potatoes, and puddings such as roast fig and honey possett and pear cheesecake. *Benchmark main dish: cod with lemon butter sauce and prawn croquettes £16.75. Two-course evening meal £23.00.*

Fullers ~ Manager Sebastian Speke ~ Real ale ~ Open 7am-11pm ~ Bar food 12-2.30, 6-9.30; 12-4, 6-9 Sun ~ Restaurant ~ Children welcome ~ Dogs allowed in bar ~ Wi-fi ~ Bedrooms: /£99 *Recommended by Phil and Helen Holt, Bob and Melissa Wyatt, Karl and Frieda Bujeya, Richard Tilbrook*

WOODSTOCK   SP4416 Map 4

Woodstock Arms 🌟 ♀ 🛏

(01993) 811251 – www.woodstockarms.com
Market Street; OX20 1SX

Cheerful town pub with enjoyable food and drink, back courtyard and knowledgeable staff; bedrooms

A refurbishment plus enthusiastic praise from our readers means this old place was going to be a winner from the outset. Set in the estate town to stunning Blenheim Palace, it's a pretty stone inn with three comfortable, contemporary and compact bedrooms upstairs and plenty of welcoming space for drinking and dining downstairs. The bar has a few leather wingbacked chairs, wooden tables and chairs on patterned floor tiles or large rugs, hops on beams, bare stone walls, a log fire beneath a large copper hood and high chairs by the green-painted counter. Greene King IPA and Old

Speckled Hen and a guest such as Shotover Prospect on handpump and good wines by the glass, served by cheerful staff. The hop-strung, dark beamed dining room has chunky tables and dark wooden chairs on parquet flooring, scatter cushions or animal hides on wall seating and a woodburning stove. It's all very easy-going and friendly. The back courtyard has rustic benches and chairs and tables on flagstones, and there are a few seats out in front, too. This is sister pub to the Jacobs Inn at Wolvercote.

Using carefully sourced produce, the rewarding british food includes sandwiches (until 4pm), crab fritter with pea shoots and cocktail sauce, confit chicken, chestnut and mushroom terrine with red onion marmalade, roasted butternut squash gnocchi with wild mushroom, smoked cheese and crème fraîche salad, wild boar burger with celeriac and horseradish slaw and chips, chicken and ham pie, pork cutlet with black pudding and apple sauce, lobster and crayfish spaghetti with clams, bacon and shellfish sauce, and puddings such as chocolate sundae with vanilla and honeycomb and apple tarte tatin with spiced ginger ice-cream. *Benchmark main dish: rare-breed sirloin steak with a choice of sauces £18.00. Two-course evening meal £24.00.*

Greene King ~ Lease Damion Farah and Johnny Pugsley ~ Real ale ~ Open 8am-11pm ~ Bar food 8am-10pm ~ Restaurant ~ Children welcome ~ Dogs allowed in bar ~ Wi-fi ~ Bedrooms: /£100 *Recommended by Louise and Anton Parsons, Katherine and Hugh Markham, Paul Dunleavy, Robin and Anne Triggs*

WOOTTON
Killingworth Castle 🛏

SP4320 Map 4

(01993) 811401 – www.thekillingworthcastle.com
Glympton Road; B4027 N of Woodstock; OX20 1EJ

Handsome, welcoming 17th-c stone inn with simply furnished bar and dining rooms, open fires, own-brews and good wines, highly regarded food and pretty back garden; lovely bedrooms

A striking three-storey coaching inn dating from 1640, this has been renovated by the same people who own the Ebrington Arms at Ebrington (see Gloucestershire). The bare-boards bar has a woodburning stove at one end, benches and wall seats around wooden tables and plush-topped stools at the counter where friendly staff serve their own-brewed Yubberton Goldie, Yubby and Yawnie ales on handpump, plus a couple of guests such as Fullers London Pride and Loose Cannon Abingdon Bridge, local cider, a thoughtful wine list and a good range of gin and whisky. The simply furnished and candlelit dining rooms have built-in wall seats plus chapel and other chairs around rustic tables on more floorboards and there's an open log fire. As well as seats out in front of the inn, there's a back garden with picnic-sets under parasols. Boutique-style bedrooms, some on the ground floor, some on the first, are well equipped and extremely appealing.

Reliably good, seasonal food includes sandwiches, duck liver parfait with vanilla and pear chutney, cider-steamed mussels with pancetta, garlic and cream, burger with toppings, confit onions and fries, calves liver with mash, shallots and smoked bacon, barbary duck breast with truffle mash, wild mushrooms and golden beetroot, sea bream with fish velouté and samphire, and puddings such as chocolate ganache with honeycomb and pistachios and apple tarte tatin with apple and cinnamon ice-cream; they also offer a daily one-course choice at lunchtime for £8.50 and a two-course menu (12-2.30pm Monday-Friday and 6-6.30pm Monday-Thursday). *Benchmark main dish: home-brewed beer-battered fish and chips £13.50. Two-course evening meal £20.00.*

Free house ~ Licensees Claire and Jim Alexander ~ Real ale ~ Open 9am-11pm ~ Bar food 12-2.30, 6-9 (9.30 Fri, Sat); 12-3.30, 6-8.30 Sun ~ Restaurant ~ Children welcome ~ Dogs allowed in bar ~ Wi-fi ~ Bedrooms: £90/£99 *Recommended by Paul Scofield, Scott and Charlotte Havers, Christine and Tony Garrett*

Also Worth a Visit in Oxfordshire

Besides the fully inspected pubs, you might like to try these pubs that have been recommended to us and described by readers. Do tell us what you think of them: feedback@goodguides.com

ABINGDON   SU4997
Brewery Tap (01235) 521655
Ock Street; OX14 5BZ Former tap for defunct Morland Brewery but still serving Original along with changing guests (autumn beer festival), proper ciders and good choice of wines, enjoyable well priced food (not Sun evening) from bar snacks to popular Sun roasts, stone floors and panelled walls, two log fires; background and weekend live music, darts, free wi-fi; children and dogs welcome, enclosed courtyard where aunt sally is played, three bedrooms, open all day (till 1am Fri, Sat). *(John Harris)*

ADDERBURY   SP4735
★ **Red Lion** (01295) 810269
The Green; off A4260 S of Banbury; OX17 3NG Attractive 17th-c stone coaching inn with good choice of enjoyable well priced food (all day weekends) including deals, helpful friendly staff, Greene King ales, good wine range and coffee, linked bar rooms with high stripped beams, panelling and stonework, big inglenook log fire, old books and Victorian/Edwardian pictures, more modern restaurant extension; background music, games area; children (in eating areas) and dogs welcome, picnic-sets out on roadside terrace, 13 character bedrooms, good breakfast, open all day in summer. *(Terry Davis)*

ALVESCOT   SP2704
Plough (01993) 842281
B4020 Carterton–Clanfield, SW of Witney; OX18 2PU Stone-built village pub freshened up and improved under present management, Wadworths ales and enjoyable food from sandwiches and pub standards up, good friendly service; children welcome, dogs in bar, back terrace and garden with play area, open (and food) all day. *(Ben and Jenny Settle)*

ARDINGTON   SU4388
Boars Head (01235) 835466
Sgned off A417 Didcot–Wantage; OX12 8QA Modernised 17th-c timber-framed pub with good value popular food from daily changing menu (more evening choice), friendly attentive staff, well kept ales including Loose Cannon, Fullers London Pride and one badged for them, low beams and log fires; background music (maybe live piano); children and dogs (in one area) welcome, terrace seating, peaceful attractive village. *(Keith Perry)*

ARDLEY   SP5427
Fox & Hounds (01869) 346883
B430 (old A43), just SW of M40 junction 10; OX27 7PE Roadside pub dating from the early 19th c with later additions; long opened-up low-beamed dining lounge with big fireplace at each end, enjoyable home-made food from lunchtime snacks to daily specials, two changing ales and good wine choice, helpful friendly staff, another open fire in cosy carpeted bar; sports TV; children welcome, no dogs inside, attractive beer garden, bedrooms, open all day Sat. *(Dave Braisted)*

ASCOTT UNDER WYCHWOOD   SP2918
Swan (01993) 832332
Shipton Road; OX7 6AY Renovated 16th-c coaching inn now under same ownership as the Bull at Charlbury; stylishly revamped interior with blue panelling, wood floors, limed beams and shuttered windows, easy chairs by inglenook, Hook Norton ales and a beer named for the pub, well chosen wines and good range of spirits, enjoyable food from pub standards up including some vegetarian options, restaurant with seagrass flooring, striking wallpaper and woodburner; children and dogs welcome, back courtyard garden, handy for Oxfordshire Way and Wychwood Way, eight individually styled bedrooms (two in outbuilding), open (and food) all day. *(Liz Bell)*

ASHBURY   SU2685
Rose & Crown (01793) 710222
B4507/B4000; High Street; SN6 8NA Friendly 16th-c coaching inn with roomy open-plan beamed bar, three well kept Arkells beers and decent range of wines by the glass, good food from 'grazing platters' and pub favourites up, polished woodwork, traditional pictures, chesterfields and pews, a raised section with oak tables and chairs, separate restaurant and games room (table tennis, pool and darts); background and occasional live music, quiz nights, sports TV; children and dogs welcome, disabled facilities, tables out at front and

---

Anyone claiming to arrange, or prevent, inclusion of a pub in the *Guide* is a fraud. Pubs are included only if recommended by readers and if our own anonymous inspection confirms that they are suitable.

in garden behind, lovely view down pretty village street of thatched cottages, handy for Ridgeway walks, eight bedrooms, open all day summer. *(Paul Farraday)*

ASTON TIRROLD — SU5586
Sweet Olive (01235) 851272
Aka Chequers; Fullers Road; village signed off A417 Streatley–Wantage; OX11 9EN Newish owners for this rustic dining pub; main room with wall settles, mate's chairs and sturdy tables on quarry tiles or slate floor, small brick fireplace, well liked food from pub favourites to more pricey restaurant dishes, Sharps Doom Bar and West Berkshire Mr Chubbs, nice wines by the glass, friendly service; background music; children and dogs (in bar area) welcome, tables in small cottagey garden, closed Sun evening. *(Charles Fraser)*

BANBURY — SP4540
Three Pigeons (01295) 275220
Southam Road; OX16 2ED Nicely renovated 17th-c coaching inn handy for town centre; several small rooms surrounding central bar, beams, flagstones, bare boards and gas woodburners (no logs because of part-thatched roof), good friendly atmosphere, shortish choice of well prepared food (all day weekends) from sandwiches to restaurant dishes, also set menu, three changing ales, decent selection of wines by the glass and around 30 malt whiskies, decent coffee too; children welcome, tables under parasols on paved terrace, three well equipped up-to-date bedrooms, useful but limited parking, open all day. *(Patricia Healey)*

BEGBROKE — SP4713
Royal Sun (01865) 374718
A44 Oxford–Woodstock; OX5 1RZ Welcoming old stone-built pub with modernised bare-boards interior, wide choice of enjoyable good value food from snacks to Sun carvery, well kept Hook Norton and a guest, good friendly service; may be background music, big-screen sports TV, free wi-fi; children welcome, no dogs inside, tables on terrace and in small garden, open all day. *(Emily and Toby Archer)*

BLEWBURY — SU5385
Red Lion (01235) 850403
Nottingham Fee – narrow turning N from A417; OX11 9PQ Attractive red-brick downland village pub; highly regarded food from interesting varied menu including set lunch, well kept Brakspears and good choice of wines, efficient friendly service, beams, tiled floor and big log fire, separate dining area; free wi-fi; children and dogs (in bar) welcome, peaceful enclosed back garden, three bedrooms, closed Sun evening, Tues. *(Sandra and Michael Smith)*

BLOXHAM — SP4235
★Joiners Arms (01295) 720223
Old Bridge Road, off A361; OX15 4LY Golden-stone pub dating from the 16th c opposite small green, rambling rooms with wood floors, exposed stonework and open fires, old well in raftered room off bar, Marstons, Ringwood and guests, enjoyable fairly traditional food including deals (popular Tues steak night); quiz every other Weds; children and dogs welcome, seats out under parasols on various levels – most popular down steps by stream, open all day from 10am for breakfast. *(John and Claire Masters)*

BRIGHTWELL — SU5890
Red Lion (01491) 837373
Signed off A4130 2 miles W of Wallingford; OX10 0RT Busy community-oriented village pub; four or five well kept ales such as Loddon and West Berkshire, wines from nearby vineyard, enjoyable good value home-made food including popular pies, friendly efficient staff, two-part bar with snug seating by log fire, dining extension to the right; live music Sun, quiz last Mon of the month, free wi-fi; children and dogs welcome, seats in front and back gardens, open all day weekends. *(John Pritchard)*

BRITWELL SALOME — SU6793
Red Lion (01491) 613140
B4009 Watlington–Benson; OX49 5LG Brick and flint pub with freshly modernised bar and dining room in pastel greys, assorted tables and chairs on wood or carpeted floors, open fires, ales such as West Berkshire and XT, real cider and good choice of wines by the glass, well liked food from varied menu including good seafood and charcuterie plates, friendly efficient service; children welcome, seats in courtyard garden, closed Sun evening. *(Chloe and Tim Hodge)*

BROUGHTON — SP4238
★Saye & Sele Arms (01295) 263348
B4035 SW of Banbury; OX15 5ED Attractive old stone house, part of the Broughton Estate (castle just five minutes away); sizeable bar with polished flagstones, cushioned window seats and dark wooden furnishings, a few brasses, three real ales including Sharps Doom Bar and nine wines by the glass, good food cooked by landlord, friendly service, two carpeted dining rooms with exposed stone walls, open fires, over 240 ornate water jugs hanging from beams; monthly quiz; children welcome, no dogs inside, picnic-sets and hanging baskets on terrace, neat lawn with tables under parasols, pergola and smokers' shelter, aunt sally, closed Sun evening. *(P and J Shapley)*

BUCKLAND — SU3497
★Lamb (01367) 870484
Off A420 NE of Faringdon; SN7 8QN

Carefully run 18th-c stone-built dining pub in lovely Estate village, highly praised interesting food cooked by chef-owner, can eat in low-beamed bar with log fire or restaurant, a couple of changing local ales and good choice of wines by the glass, also local gin and vodka, friendly helpful staff; well behaved children and dogs welcome (resident cocker is Oats), seats in courtyard and pleasant tree-shaded garden, good walks (close to Thames Path), three comfortable well equipped bedrooms, closed Sun evening, Mon. *(Isobel Mackinlay, Nick Sharpe, Keith Perry)*

BURFORD SP2512
Angel (01993) 822714
Witney Street; OX18 4SN Long heavy-beamed dining pub in interesting 16th-c building, warmly welcoming with roaring log fire, good popular food from sandwiches and pub favourites up, Hook Norton ales and well chosen wines; Aug beer festival, TV; children and dogs welcome, big secluded garden, three comfortable bedrooms, open (and food) all day. *(Camilla and Jose Ferrera)*

BURFORD SP2512
Mermaid (01993) 822193
High Street; OX18 4QF Handsome beamed dining pub with flagstones, stripped stone and nice log fire, decent food (all day weekends) at sensible prices including gluten-free menu, efficient friendly service, well kept Greene King ales and a guest, bay window seating at front, further airy back dining room and upstairs restaurant, afternoon cream teas; background music (live Fri); children and dogs welcome, tables out at front and in courtyard behind, open all day. *(Robert Lester)*

CAULCOTT SP5024
★ **Horse & Groom** (01869) 343257
Lower Heyford Road (B4030); OX25 4ND Pretty 16th-c roadside thatched cottage; L-shaped red-carpeted room with log fire in big inglenook (brassware under its long bressumer), plush-cushioned settles, chairs and stools around a few dark tables at low-ceilinged bar end, Black Sheep and a couple of guests (July beer festival), decent house wines, popular food (not Sun evening, booking essential) cooked by french owner-chef, also O'Hagans sausage menu, dining room at far end with jugs hanging on black joists, decorative plates, watercolours and original drawings, small side sun lounge; shove-ha'penny and board games; well behaved over-5s welcome, awkward for disabled customers (some steps and no car park), picnic-sets in nice little front garden, closed Mon. *(George Atkinson)*

CHADLINGTON SP3222
Tite (01608) 676910
Off A361 S of Chipping Norton; Mill End; OX7 3NY Friendly 17th-c country pub;

bar with eating areas either side, beams and stripped stone, pubby furniture including spindleback chairs and settles, flagstones and bare boards, woodburner in large fireplace, well kept Sharps Doom Bar and a couple of guests, Weston's cider and a dozen wines by the glass, enjoyable fairly traditional home-cooked food (not Sun evening), good service; occasional live music, winter quiz nights; well behaved children and dogs welcome, lovely shrub-filled garden with split-level terrace, good walks nearby, open all day. *(Bernard Stradling, Keith Perry)*

CHALGROVE SU6397
Red Lion (01865) 890625
High Street (B480 Watlington–Stadhampton); OX44 7SS Attractive beamed village pub owned by local church trust since 1637; good variety of freshly made food (not Sun evening) from sandwiches to blackboard specials, popular pudding evening second Tues of the month, well kept Butcombe, Fullers London Pride, Rebellion Mild and two guests, friendly helpful staff, quarry-tiled bar with big open fire, separate carpeted restaurant; children and dogs welcome, nice gardens (front one borders stream), public car park across the road, open all day Sun (and Sat if busy). *(David Lamb)*

CHARLBURY SP3519
Bull (01608) 810689
Sheep Street; OX7 3RR Stylishly refurbished 16th-c beamed dining pub (sister pub to Swan at Ascott under Wychwood); shabby-chic décor with exposed stone and grey-painted walls, colourful modern artwork, scrubbed tables and rugs on wood floors, linen cushioned window seats and comfy chairs by inglenook log fire, three real ales including one named for them from unusual drawer-fronted servery, plenty of wines by the glass and enjoyable food from snacks and pub favourites up, friendly helpful staff; children and dogs welcome, attractive sunny back terrace with vine-covered pergola, eight good bedrooms (four in converted barn), open (and food) all day from 8am. *(Liz Bell)*

CHARLTON-ON-OTMOOR SP5615
Crown (01865) 331850
Signed off B4027 in Islip; High Street, opposite church; OX5 2UQ Refurbished 17th-c village local with welcoming relaxed atmosphere in bar and separate restaurant, well kept Brakspears and a guest, decent wines and popular interesting food from landlord-chef (not weekday lunchtimes); children and dogs welcome, closed Mon. *(Caroline and Peter Bryant)*

CHARNEY BASSETT SU3794
Chequers (01235) 868642
Chapel Lane off Main Street; OX12 0EX Welcoming 18th-c village-green pub with spacious modernised interior, Marstons-

related ales and enjoyable fairly priced food from lunchtime sandwiches/baguettes to steaks (booking advised), log fire; free wi-fi; children and dogs (in bar) welcome, picnic-sets in small garden, three bedrooms. *(Val and Malcolm Travers)*

CHAZEY HEATH   SU6979
Packhorse (0118) 972 2140
Off A4074 Reading–Wallingford by B4526; RG4 7UG Attractive 17th-c beamed village dining pub (part of Home Counties group); good choice of well liked food from sandwiches and light dishes up, Loddon, West Berkshire and three guests, plenty of wines by the glass and some interesting gins, friendly staff, polished tables on wood and rug floors, built-in leatherette banquettes, shelves of books and lots of framed pictures, big log fire in raised hearth; background music; children and dogs (in main bar) welcome, disabled facilities, parasol-shaded tables in back garden, handy for Mapledurham house and watermill, open (and food) all day.
(John Cadge, Darren and Jane Staniforth)

CHECKENDON   SU6684
★**Black Horse** (01491) 680418
Village signed off A4074 Reading–Wallingford; RG8 0TE This charmingly old-fashioned country tavern, tucked into woodland away from main village, has been run by the same family since the 1900s; relaxing and unchanging series of rooms, back one with West Berkshire and Rebellion tapped from the cask, one with bar counter has some tent pegs above the fireplace (they used to be made here), homely side lounge with some splendidly unfashionable 1950s-style armchairs and another room beyond that, only baguettes and pickled eggs; no credit cards; children allowed but must be well behaved, dogs outside only, seats on verandah and in garden, popular with walkers and cyclists, closed Sun evening in winter and may shut early if quiet. *(Len and Lily Dowson)*

CHIPPING NORTON   SP3127
Blue Boar (01608) 643108
High Street/Goddards Lane; OX7 5NP Spacious recently refurbished former coaching inn (first licensed in 1683); four well kept Youngs ales and popular well priced food, friendly helpful staff, woodburner in big stone fireplace, raftered back restaurant and airy flagstoned garden room; background and weekend live music, Weds quiz, darts, sports TV, free wi-fi; children and dogs welcome, open (and food) all day. *(Robin and Anna Triggs)*

CHIPPING NORTON   SP3127
Chequers (01608) 644717
Goddards Lane; OX7 5NP Bustling traditional town pub with three softly lit beamed rooms, no frills but comfortable and with lots of character, flagstones, low

ochre ceilings and log fire, up to eight mainly Fullers ales, 15 wines by the glass and enjoyable food (not Sun evening) from shortish menu, friendly staff, airy conservatory restaurant behind; TV, free wi-fi; children and dogs (in bar) welcome, theatre next door, open all day. *(John Harris)*

CHISLEHAMPTON   SU5998
Coach & Horses (01865) 890255
B480 Oxford–Watlington, opposite B4015 to Abingdon; OX44 7UX Extended 16th-c coaching inn with two homely and civilised beamed bars, big log fire, sizeable restaurant with polished oak tables and wall banquettes, good choice of popular reasonably priced food (not Sun evening), friendly obliging service, three well kept ales usually including Hook Norton; background music; neat terraced gardens overlooking fields by River Thame, some tables out in front, nine bedrooms in courtyard block, closed 3.30-7pm Sun, otherwise open all day. *(Andy Dolan, Roy Hoing)*

CHRISTMAS COMMON   SU7193
Fox & Hounds (01491) 612599
Off B480/B481; OX49 5HL Old Chilterns pub in lovely countryside, spacious front barn restaurant serving enjoyable home-made food from open kitchen, Brakspears and a guest, decent wines and some gins flavoured with herbs from the garden, two compact beamed bar rooms simply but comfortably furnished, bow windows, red and black floor tiles and big inglenook, snug little back room too; board games; children, walkers and dogs (in bar) welcome, rustic benches and tables outside, open all day. *(Paul Farraday)*

CHURCH ENSTONE   SP3725
★**Crown** (01608) 677262
Mill Lane; from A44 take B4030 turn-off at Enstone; OX7 4NN Popular 17th-c beamed country pub, pleasant bar with straightforward furniture, old local photographs on stone walls and log fire in large fireplace, well kept Hook Norton and guests, good fairly priced food cooked by landlord from pub favourites up, friendly service, carpeted dining room with red walls, slate-floored conservatory; children welcome, dogs in bar, white metal furniture on front terrace overlooking lane, picnic-sets in sheltered back garden, closed Sun evening. *(Andy Dolan, Hunter and Christine Wright, Barry Collett)*

CHURCH HANBOROUGH   SP4212
Hand & Shears (01993) 881392
Opposite church; signed off A4095 at Long Hanborough, or off A40 at Eynsham roundabout; OX29 8AB Cotswold-stone village pub with opened-up interior on different levels, L-shaped bare-boards bar with exposed stonework, some rustic half-panelling and a couple of cushioned window seats, sofa by log fire, Charles Wells ales from stone-faced

counter, steps down to spacious part-raftered dining area divided by balustrades, fairly short choice of enjoyable home-made food including bargain set lunch (Tues-Fri), attentive friendly service; children welcome. *(Keith Perry)*

CLANFIELD · SP2802
Clanfield Tavern (01367) 810117
Bampton Road (A4095 S of Witney); OX18 2RG Pleasantly extended 17th-c stone pub (former coaching inn) adjacent to the Plough; opened-up beamed interior keeping feel of separate areas, mostly carpeted with mix of pubby furniture including some old settles (built-in one by log fire), smallish bar with comfortable seating in snug flagstoned area with woodburner, Marstons-related ales and enjoyable sensibly priced food (not Sun evening) including daily specials, more contemporary dining conservatory; background music, quiz last Weds of month, free wi-fi; children welcome, dogs in bar, picnic-sets on small flower-bordered lawn looking across to village green, open all day. *(R K Phillips)*

CLANFIELD · SP2802
Plough (01367) 810222
Bourton Road; OX18 2RB Substantial old stone inn with lovely Elizabethan façade, civilised atmosphere and plenty of character, log fires in comfortable beamed lounge bar, various dining areas, good food, particularly fish and seasonal game, well kept Hook Norton Hooky and a guest, over two dozen wines by the glass and more than 180 gins (can organise tasting sessions), attentive service; children and dogs welcome, pretty gardens with teak tables on sunny front terrace, 12 bedrooms, open all day. *(R K Phillips)*

CLIFTON · SP4931
Duke of Clifton (01869) 226334
B4031 Deddington–Aynho; OX15 0PE Recently reopened thatch and stone pub (was the Duke of Cumberland's Head); attractively refurbished low-beamed interior with flagstones and log fire in vast fireplace, enjoyable food (not Mon) including good value set lunch and daily specials, well kept Hook Norton and guests, friendly helpful service; children and dogs welcome, nice back garden, ten-minute walk from canal, five comfortable bedrooms and on-site camping, closed Mon lunchtime, otherwise open all day. *(Monty Green)*

COLESHILL · SU2393
Radnor Arms (01793) 861575
B4019; village signposted from Faringdon and Highworth; SN6 7PR Pub and village owned by NT; small quarry-tiled bar with cushioned settle, upholstered

carver chairs and woodburner, more seating in back alcove, steps down to main dining area, once a blacksmiths' forge with lofty beamed ceiling, log fire and some old tools on the walls, Old Forge ales brewed on site (tasters offered), proper ciders and enjoyable well priced home-made food including specials, friendly staff; children, walkers and dogs welcome, picnic-sets on narrow side terrace, garden beyond car park with some unusual tree-trunk furniture, play area, open all day. *(Keith Perry)*

CRAWLEY · SP3412
★Lamb (01993) 708792
Steep Hill; just NW of Witney; OX29 9TW Relaxed 18th-c stone-built dining pub with highly regarded food from owner-chef, not especially cheap but they do offer a good value set lunch, friendly attentive staff, beamed bar with polished boards and lovely inglenook log fire, Brakspears and Wychwood ales, various dining areas with cushioned settles, high-backed chairs and built-in wall seats, exposed stone walls throughout, prints, paintings, antlers and church candles; dogs welcome in bar, views from tables on back terrace and lawn, summer barbecues and wood-fired pizzas, pretty village, good walks (on Palladian Way), open all day Sat, closed Sun evening, Mon and Tues. *(Carol and Barry Craddock, Guy Vowles, Bernard Stradling)*

CROWELL · SU7499
Shepherds Crook (01844) 355266
B4009, 2 miles from M40 junction 6; OX39 4RR Welcoming and popular old village pub, good varied choice of freshly prepared food (not Sun evening) including daily specials, up to half a dozen ales such as Adnams, Rebellion, St Austell and Timothy Taylors, extensive wine list (ten by the glass), 30 or so whiskies, beamed bar with stripped brick and flagstones, woodburner, high-raftered dining area; some live music; children and dogs welcome, tables out on front terrace and small green, nice walks, open all day. *(Taff Thomas)*

CUDDESDON · SP5902
Bat & Ball (01865) 874379
S of Wheatley; High Street; OX44 9HJ Old coaching inn with low beams (mostly painted), flagstones and wood floors, exposed stone/brickwork and lots of cricketing memorabilia, three well kept Marstons-related ales from brick-faced counter, decent wines and cocktails, enjoyable pubby food from ciabatta and panini up, helpful friendly young staff, tables laid for dining throughout (feels more pubby at the front); background music; children and dogs (in bar area) welcome, sunny back terrace, seven bedrooms (some quite small), open all day. *(Richard Kennell)*

You can send reports directly to us at feedback@goodguides.com

CUMNOR SP4503
Bear & Ragged Staff (01865)
862329 *Signed from A420; Appleton Road; OX2 9QH* Extensive restaurant-pub dating from 16th c, contemporary décor in linked rooms with wood floors and painted beams, good food from sandwiches and sharing plates (create your own) through pub favourites up, Thurs steak night, flagstoned bar with log fire, well kept Greene King ales and good wine choice, airy garden room; background music, TV, free wi-fi; children welcome, decked terrace and fenced play area, nine bedrooms, open (and food) all day weekends. *(Sandra and Michael Smith)*

CURBRIDGE SP3208
Lord Kitchener (01993) 772613
Lew Road (A4095 towards Bampton); OX29 7PD Cosy modernised roadside pub, wide range of food including gluten-free choices and popular pies, Greene King Old Speckled Hen and a beer badged for the pub, several wines by the glass; live music Fri; children welcome, closed Sun evening, Mon. *(Helene Grygar)*

CUXHAM SU6695
Half Moon (01491) 612165
4 miles from M40 junction 6; S on B4009, then right on B480 at Watlington; OX49 5NF 16th-c thatched and beamed pub in sleepy village surrounded by fine countryside; sensibly priced italian-leaning food including popular pizzas, Rebellion IPA and Smuggler and several wines by the glass, proper italian coffee, friendly accommodating staff; free wi-fi; children and dogs welcome, nice garden behind, open (and food) all day. *(Chloe and Tim Hodge)*

DENCHWORTH SU3891
Fox (01235) 868258
Off A338 or A417 N of Wantage; Hyde Road; OX12 0DX Comfortable 17th-c thatched and beamed pub in pretty village, good sensibly priced food from extensive menu including Sun carvery (best to book) and OAP lunchtime deal Mon-Thurs, friendly efficient staff, well kept Greene King ales and good choice of reasonably priced wines, plush seats in low-ceilinged connecting areas, two log fires, old prints and paintings, airy dining extension; children and dogs (on lead) welcome, tables under umbrellas in pleasant sheltered garden with heated terrace, play area and aunt sally. *(John Harris)*

DORCHESTER-ON-THAMES SU5794
Fleur de Lys (01865) 340502
Just off A4074 Maidenhead–Oxford; High Street; OX10 7HH Traditional 16th-c coaching inn opposite abbey; knocked-through split-level bar/dining area with open fire and woodburner, plain wooden tables and some interesting old photographs of the pub, good imaginative evening set menu, more straightforward lunchtime food, a couple of changing ales, friendly efficient service; children (away from bar) and dogs welcome, picnic-sets on front terrace, more in back garden with play area and aunt sally, five bedrooms, closed Sun evening, Mon lunchtime. *(John Pritchard, Bridget Barker, Sally and John Quinlan)*

DUCKLINGTON SP3507
Bell (01993) 700341
Off A415, a mile SE of Witney; Standlake Road; OX29 7UP Pretty thatched and beamed village local, good value home-made food including stone-baked pizzas and Sun carvery, bargain OAP lunch Mon-Sat, Greene King ales, friendly service, big stripped-stone and flagstoned bar with scrubbed tables, log fires and glass-covered well, old local photographs and farm tools, hatch-served public bar, roomy back restaurant with bells hanging from beams; background music, sports TV, pool, free wi-fi; children welcome, seats outside and play area, aunt sally, five bedrooms, open all day (till 9.30pm Sun), no food Sun evening. *(Ben and Jenny Settle)*

EATON SP4403
Eight Bells (01865) 862261
Signed off B4017 SW of Oxford; OX13 5PR Popular unpretentious old pub with relaxed local atmosphere, two small low-beamed bars with open fires and a dining area, five well kept ales including Loose Cannon, traditional low-priced food (not Sun evening) served by friendly helpful staff; children and dogs welcome, pleasant garden with aunt sally, nice walks, open all day weekends, closed Mon. *(Emily and Toby Archer)*

EPWELL SP3540
★**Chandlers Arms** (01295) 780153
Sibford Road, off B4035; OX15 6LH Warmly welcoming little 16th-c stone pub with good freshly made food (booking advised) from sandwiches and bar meals up, well kept Fullers London Pride and Hook Norton, proper coffee, bar with country-style furniture, two dining areas, good attentive service; free wi-fi; children welcome, no dogs, pleasant garden with aunt sally and summer entertainment, attractive out-of-the-way village near Macmillan Way long-distance path, open all day. *(Bernard Stradling, Guy Vowles)*

EWELME SU6491
Shepherds Hut (01491) 836636
Off B4009 about 6 miles SW of M40 junction 6; High Street; OX10 6HQ Extended bay-windowed village pub with beams, bare boards and woodburner, good home-made food (not Sun evening) from ciabattas up, Greene King ales and a guest, friendly helpful staff, back dining area; children, walkers and dogs

welcome, terrace picnic-sets with steps up to lawn and play area, open all day. *(Anthony Waters, David Lamb)*

EXLADE STREET   SU6582

★**Highwayman** (01491) 682020

Just off A4074 Reading–Wallingford; RG8 0UA Whitewashed brick building with two beamed bar rooms, mainly 17th-c (parts older), with interesting rambling layout and mix of furniture, inglenook woodburner, good freshly cooked food from landlord-chef including lunchtime set menu, three well kept beers and plenty of wines by the glass, friendly efficient service, airy conservatory dining room; soft background music; children and dogs welcome, terrace and garden with fine views, closed Sun evening, Mon. *(Bill Gulliver and Harry Thomson, John Pritchard, Tracey G)*

FERNHAM   SU2991

★**Woodman** (01367) 820643

A420 SW of Oxford, then left into B4508 after about 11 miles; village another 6 miles on; SN7 7NX 17th-c country dining pub under new licensees; heavily beamed character main rooms, candlelit tables and a big open fire, also some newer areas, up to four changing ales, several gins/malt whiskies and decent choice of wines by the glass, good food from pub standards up including Tues steak night (free minibus for eight or more local diners), friendly helpful service; background and some live music; children and dogs welcome, disabled access/facilities, seats on small front lawn and heated back terrace, good walks below the downs, open all day weekends, closed Mon. *(R K Phillips, Keith Perry)*

FINSTOCK   SP3616

★**Plough** (01993) 868333

Just off B4022 N of Witney; High Street; OX7 3BY Thatched low-beamed village pub with long rambling bar, leather sofas by massive stone inglenook, pictures of local scenes and some historical documents connected with the pub, spacious dining room with candles on stripped-pine tables, popular home-made pubby food (best to book), two or three well kept ales including Adnams Broadside, traditional cider, several wines by the glass and decent choice of whiskies, friendly landlord and staff; soft background music, bar billiards; children and dogs (in bar) welcome, seats in neatly kept garden with aunt sally, woodland walks and along River Evenlode, open all day Sat, closed Sun evening, Mon lunchtime. *(Caroline and Peter Bryant)*

FRINGFORD   SP6028

Butchers Arms (01869) 277363

Off A421 N of Bicester; Main Street; OX27 8EB Welcoming partly thatched creeper-clad local in Flora Thompson's 'Candleford' village; traditional food including good Sun roasts (three sittings, must book), well kept Black Sheep, Hook Norton and Sharps (June beer festival), charming efficient service, unpretentious interior with L-shaped bar and back dining room, good log fire; children and dogs welcome, picnic-sets out at front beside cricket green, open all day. *(Dave Snowden)*

FYFIELD   SU4298

★**White Hart** (01865) 390585

Main Road; off A420 8 miles SW of Oxford; OX13 5LW Grand medieval hall with soaring eaves, huge stone-flanked window embrasures and minstrels' gallery, contrasting cosy low-beamed side bar with woodburner in large inglenook, fresh flowers and evening candles, civilised friendly atmosphere and full of history; good imaginative modern food (not Sun evening, best to book) cooked by licensee-chef using home-grown produce, Loose Cannon and a couple of guests, around 12 wines by the glass and several malt whiskies, cocktails too (Fri happy hour from 5.30pm); background music; well behaved children welcome, elegant furniture under umbrellas on spacious heated terrace, lovely gardens, good Thames-side walks, open all day weekends, closed Mon. *(Paul Farraday)*

GALLOWSTREE COMMON   SU6980

Reformation (0118) 972 3126

Horsepond Road; RG4 9BP Friendly and welcoming black-beamed village local, enjoyable varied choice of home-made food, Brakspears and a couple of Marstons-related guests, plenty of wines by the glass, open fires, conservatory; some live music, other events such as tractor runs and log-splitting competitions; children and dogs welcome, garden with 'shipwreck' play area, closed Sun evening, Mon. *(Patricia Healey)*

GODSTOW   SP4809

★**Trout** (01865) 510930

Off A40/A44 roundabout via Wolvercote; OX2 8PN Pretty 17th-c Mitchells & Butlers dining pub in lovely riverside location (gets packed in fine weather); good choice of food from varied menu including set weekday deal till 6pm (booking essential at busy times), four beamed linked rooms with contemporary furnishings, flagstones and bare boards, log fires in three huge hearths, Brakspears, Sharps and a guest, several wines by the glass; background music; children and dogs (in bar) welcome, plenty of terrace seats under big parasols, footbridge to island (may be closed), abbey ruins opposite, car park fee refunded at bar, open (and food) all day. *(Robert Wivell)*

GORING   SU5980

★**Catherine Wheel** (01491) 872379

Station Road; RG8 9HB Friendly 18th-c village pub with two cosily traditional bar areas, especially the more individual lower room with its dark beams and inglenook log fire, popular home-made food (not Sun evening) from seasonal menu, well kept Brakspears and other Marstons-related ales, Aspall's cider and a dozen wines by the glass, back restaurant, notable doors to lavatories; background and some live music, monthly quiz, TV, free wi-fi; children and dogs welcome, sunny garden with gravel terrace and summer pizza oven, handy for Thames Path, open all day. *(M A Borthwick)*

GORING   SU5980
John Barleycorn (01491) 872509
Manor Road; RG8 9DP Friendly low-beamed cottagey local with cosy unpretentious lounge bar and adjoining dining room, Brakspears, Ringwood and a guest, seven wines by the glass and popular good value pubby food (not Sun evening) from lunchtime sandwiches up, efficient cheerful service, public bar with log fire and bar billiards; children welcome, enclosed beer garden, short walk to the Thames, three bedrooms, open all day. *(Taff Thomas)*

GORING   SU5980
★ **Miller of Mansfield** (01491) 872829
High Street; RG8 9AW Handsome inn with excellent food cooked by chef-patron; simple unfussy décor in beamed bars, armchairs around open fires or in bay windows, plain wooden tables on bare boards, exposed stone and brick walls, a few prints and gilt-edged mirrors, Hook Norton, Sharps and West Berkshire, 16 wines by the glass from well chosen list, courteous staff, dining rooms with antique-style or contemporary chairs on more boards; background music, free wi-fi; children and dogs (in bar) welcome, solid furniture in multi-level terraced garden, 13 individually decorated bedrooms, woodland walks nearby, open all day. *(Sally Wright, Sarah Roberts)*

GREAT TEW   SP3929
★ **Falkland Arms** (01608) 683653
The Green; off B4022 about 5 miles E of Chipping Norton; OX7 4DB Part-thatched 16th-c golden-stone pub in lovely village; unspoilt partly panelled bar with high-backed settles, stools and plain tables on flagstones or bare boards, lots of mugs and jugs hanging from beam-and-plank ceiling, interesting breweriana and dim converted oil lamps, shutters for mullioned lattice windows, log fire in fine inglenook, Wadworths and guests, Weston's cider, country wines and some 30 malt whiskies, snuff for sale, locally sourced freshly made food, friendly service, separate dining room; folk night Sun; children and dogs welcome, tables out at front and under parasols in back garden, six bedrooms and cottage, open all day from 8am (breakfast for non-residents). *(Keith Perry, Guy Vowles, Peter Meister)*

HAILEY   SP3414
Bird in Hand (01993) 868321
Whiteoak Green; B4022 Witney–Charlbury; OX29 9XP Attractive 17th-c extended stone inn, enjoyable food including some welsh influences from owner-chef (best to book summer weekends), good value set menu Mon-Thurs, helpful friendly service, well kept ales such as Brains and Hook Norton, several wines by the glass, beams, timbers and stripped stone, comfortable armchairs on polished boards, large log fire, cosy corners in carpeted restaurant, witty references to Wales and rugby dotted about, lovely Cotswold views; parasol-shaded terrace tables, 16 bedrooms in modern block around grass quadrangle, open all day from 8am. *(John and Penny Wildon)*

HAILEY   SU6485
★ **King William IV** (01491) 681845
The Hailey near Ipsden, off A4074 or A4130 SE of Wallingford; OX10 6AD Popular fine old pub in lovely countryside, beamed bar with good sturdy furniture on tiles in front of big log fire, three other cosy seating areas opening off, enjoyable freshly made food (not Sun evening) from baguettes to specials, Brakspears and guests tapped from the cask, helpful friendly staff; children and dogs welcome, terrace and large garden enjoying peaceful far-reaching views, good walking (Chiltern Way and Ridgeway), leave muddy boots in porch, open all day weekends in summer (closed Sun evening winter). *(Bob and Margaret Holder, Colin McLachlan)*

HAILEY   SP3512
★ **Lamb & Flag** (01993) 702849
B4022 a mile N of Witney; Middletown; OX29 9UB Rambling 17th-c stone-built village pub with plenty of character, beams, some ancient flagstones and inglenook woodburner, freshly made food at affordable prices including good Sun lunch, friendly attentive staff, well kept Thwaites Lancaster Bomber and guests, good choice of wines by the glass; children welcome, lovely garden, open all day weekends, closed Mon and lunchtimes Tues-Thurs. *(Keith and Caroline Bowerman)*

HAMPTON POYLE   SP5015
Bell (01865) 376242
From A34 S, take Kidlington turn and village signed from roundabout; from A34 N, take Kidlington turn, then A4260 to roundabout, third turning signed for Superstore (Bicester Road); village signed from roundabout; OX5 2QD Front bar with three snug rooms, lots of big black and white photo prints, sturdy simple furnishings, scatter cushions and window seats, a stove flanked by bookshelves one end, large fireplace the other, open kitchen with feature pizza oven in biggish inner room, spreading restaurant with plenty of tables on

pale limestone floor, inventive well liked food including cheaper weekday set menu, good choice of wines by the glass, ales such as Hook Norton and Wye Valley, friendly service and cheerful buzzy atmosphere; background music; children and dogs (in bar) welcome, modern seats on sunny front terrace by quiet village lane, nine good bedrooms, open all day. *(Val and Malcolm Travers)*

HANWELL   SP4343

Moon & Sixpence (01295) 730544

Main Street; OX17 1HW Refurbished stone-built pub in attractive village setting, good food cooked by owner-chef from pub favourites up including set menu choices, comfortable bar and dining areas with view into kitchen, well kept Charles Wells ales and several wines by the glass from carefully chosen list; children welcome, disabled access, seats on back terrace, open till 6pm Sun. *(Patricia Healey)*

HEADINGTON   SP5406

Butchers Arms (01865) 742470

Wilberforce Street; OX3 7AN Welcoming backstreet local attracting good mix of customers, bare-boards interior with roaring fire, well kept Fullers beers and good value tasty food including ciabattas, pub favourites and stone-baked pizzas; Sun quiz, live jazz first Mon of month, darts, free wi-fi; children and dogs welcome, disabled access, heated terrace with smokers' shelter, open all day Fri-Sun. *(Robin and Anna Triggs)*

HEADINGTON   SP5407

White Hart (01865) 761737

St Andrews Road, Old Town; OX3 9DL Traditional split-level 18th-c stone pub facing the church; well kept Everards and changing guests, real cider, reasonably priced wines and reliable pubby food including range of pies, friendly staff; children welcome, delightful sunny back garden, open (and food) all day, kitchen closes 5pm Sun. *(Alex Mentzer)*

HENLEY   SU7682

Anchor (01491) 574753

Friday Street; RG9 1AH Beamed pub just back from the river; opened-up gently updated interior with wood and stone floors and grey/green panelling, some high tables and chairs in two small front rooms, step up to back dining area, popular food from panini and sharing plates up, well kept Brakspears and a guest such as Jennings, several wines by the glass; background music, TV; children welcome, nice enclosed terrace behind with rattan-style furniture, open all day. *(Mungo Shipley)*

HENLEY   SU7682

Angel on the Bridge (01491)

410678 *Thames-side, by the bridge; RG9 1BH* 17th-c and worth knowing for its prime Thames-side position (packed during the regatta); small front bar with

log fire, downstairs back bar and adjacent restaurant, beams, uneven floors and dim lighting, Brakspears ales and maybe a guest such as Ringwood, good choice of wines by the glass, enjoyable food from sandwiches and pubby choices up, cheerful efficient service; tables under parasols on popular waterside deck (plastic glasses here), moorings for two boats, open all day at least in summer. *(Richard Kennell)*

HENLEY   SU7582

★Three Tuns (01491) 410138

Market Place; RG9 2AA Small heavy-beamed front bar with fire, all tables set for eating (stools by counter for drinkers), well kept Brakspears and guests such as Ringwood, good well presented home-made food (not Sun evening), also good value weekday set lunch (not during regatta week), nice wines, friendly attentive service, lighter panelled back dining area with painted timbers and wood floor; live music Sun; children and dogs (in bar) welcome, tables in attractive little back courtyard, closed Mon, otherwise open all day. *(Paul Humphreys)*

HIGHMOOR   SU6984

★Rising Sun (01491) 640856

Witheridge Hill, signposted off B481; OS Sheet 175 map reference 697841; RG9 5PF Welcoming 17th-c pub in small Chilterns village, cosy beamed bar with red and black quarry-tiled floor, comfortable sofa by inglenook woodburner, Brakspears Bitter and a couple of Marstons-related guests, a dozen wines by the glass, three linked eating areas with rugs and pubby furniture on bare boards, pictures on dark red walls, log fire, well thought-of food (not Sun evening) from baguettes up; background music, free wi-fi; children and dogs (in bar) welcome, picnic-sets and white metal tables and chairs in pleasant back garden, good surrounding walks, open all day Sat, till 9pm Sun. *(John Pritchard, Jeremy Snaithe, Sandra King, M A Borthwick)*

HOOK NORTON   SP3534

★Gate Hangs High (01608) 737387

N towards Sibford, at Banbury–Rollright crossroads; OX15 5DF Tucked-away old stone pub with cosy low-ceilinged bar, traditional furniture on bare boards, attractive inglenook, good reasonably priced home-made food from bar snacks to daily specials, well kept Hook Norton ales and a guest, decent wines, friendly helpful service, side dining extension; background music; children and dogs (in bar) welcome, pretty courtyard and country garden, four bedrooms, camping, quite near Rollright Stones (EH), open all day. *(Peter Meister)*

HOOK NORTON   SP3533

Sun (01608) 737570

High Street; OX15 5NH Refurbished pub in centre of village; beamed and flagstoned bar with big fireplace, two dining areas, good range of enjoyable food from sandwiches and platters up, well kept Hook Norton and several wines by the glass, friendly helpful staff; children and dogs welcome, tables out in front and on back terrace, six comfortable bedrooms (ones above bar can be noisy), hearty breakfast, open all day (till 6pm Sun). *(Helene Grygar)*

HORNTON
SP3945

Dun Cow (01295) 670524

West End; OX15 6DA Traditional 17th-c thatch and ironstone village pub, friendly and relaxed, with sensibly short seasonal choice of good fresh food from lunchtime sandwiches up using local suppliers (must book by Fri for Sun lunch), Hook Norton and Purity, a dozen wines by the glass; charity quiz first Weds of the month; children and dogs welcome, appealing small garden behind, open all day weekends, closed lunchtimes Mon-Thurs, no food Sun evening, Mon or Tues. *(Mungo Shipley)*

KIDMORE END
SU6979

New Inn (0118) 972 3115

Chalkhouse Green Road; signed from B481 in Sonning Common; RG4 9AU Extended black and white pub by village church; beams and big log fire, enjoyable freshly made food, well kept Brakspears ales and decent wines by the glass, pleasant restaurant; children welcome, tables in large sheltered garden with pond, six bedrooms, open all day Thurs-Sat, till 5pm Sun. *(John Harris)*

KINGHAM
SP2523

★**Wild Rabbit** (01608) 658389

Church Street; OX7 6YA Former 18th-c farmhouse with plenty of rustic chic, antique country furniture, limestone floors, exposed stone walls, beams and huge fireplaces, contemporary artwork and fresh flowers, Hook Norton Hooky and a couple of guests, several wines by the glass including champagne, excellent food (they have a Michelin star) from lighter bar meals up, spacious restaurant with kitchen view, pleasant helpful young staff; children welcome, dogs in bar, paved front terrace with topiary rabbits, 12 sumptuously appointed individual bedrooms, open all day. *(Bernard Stradling)*

LAUNTON
SP6022

Bull (01869) 248158

Just E of Bicester; Bicester Road; OX26 5DQ Cleanly modernised, part-thatched 17th-c village pub, enjoyable good value food including OAP lunch deal (Mon-Fri) and Tues steak night, Greene King IPA and a couple of guests, friendly staff; background music, Sun quiz; children and dogs welcome, wheelchair access from car park, garden with terrace, open all day, no evening food Sun or Mon. *(Monty Green)*

LEWKNOR
SU7197

★**Olde Leathern Bottel** (01844) 351482 *Under a mile from M40 junction 6; off B4009 towards Watlington; OX49 5TW* Popular old village pub with two heavy-beamed bars, understated décor and rustic furnishings, woodburners (one in brick inglenook), well kept Brakspears, Marstons Pedigree and a guest, several wines by the glass and tasty pub food including specials, good friendly service, family room separated by standing timbers; dogs welcome, nice garden with lots of picnic-sets under parasols, play area, boules and aunt sally, handy for walks on Chiltern escarpment. *(R K Phillips, David Reed)*

LONG HANBOROUGH
SP4214

★**George & Dragon** (01993) 881362 *A4095 Bladon–Witney; Main Road; OX29 8JX* Substantial pub with original two-room bar (17th-c or older), low beams, stripped stone and two woodburners, Charles Wells ales and decent range of wines, roomy thatched restaurant extension with comfortably padded dining chairs around sturdy tables, wide choice of good food from lunchtime sandwiches and baked potatoes up, Thurs pie night, prompt friendly service; background music, Weds 'quiz and fizz' night; children and dogs (in bar) welcome, large back garden with picnic-sets among shrubs, tables beneath canopy on separate sheltered terrace, summer barbecues, open (and food) all day. *(Chloe and Tim Hodge)*

LONG WITTENHAM
SU5493

Plough (01865) 407738

High Street; OX14 4QH Welcoming 17th-c two-bar local with low beams, inglenook fires and lots of brass, two or three well kept ales including Butcombe, good reasonably priced home-cooked food (not Sun evening) from sandwiches and traditional choices to interesting specials, efficient service, dining room, games in public bar; children and dogs welcome, two bedrooms, Thames moorings at bottom of long garden, play area, open all day. *(David Lamb)*

LONGCOT
SU2790

King & Queen (01793) 784348

Shrivenham Road, off B4508; SN7 7TL Cosy beamed pub with good food cooked by landlord-chef, up to four well kept ales such as Loose Cannon and Ramsbury, two proper ciders and several wines by the glass from good value list, friendly attentive service, snug seating areas including sofa by two-way woodburner, restaurant and garden room; bar billiards, sports TV, free wi-fi; children and dogs (they have a couple) welcome, tables on paved terrace, seven bedrooms, open all day Sun, closed Mon lunchtime. *(George Paton, Brian Glozier)*

MAIDENSGROVE   SU7288
Five Horseshoes (01491) 641282
Off B480 and B481, W of village;
RG9 6EX Character 16th-c dining pub set
high in the Chilterns; rambling bar with low
ceiling and log fire, well liked food (not Sun
evening) from changing menu including
home-cured sea trout and seasonal game,
set lunch Tues-Fri, friendly service, well
kept Brakspears and good choice of wines
by the glass, airy conservatory restaurant;
regular jazz evenings; children and dogs
(in bar) welcome, plenty of tables in
suntrap garden with rolling countryside
views, good walks, open all day Sat, closed
Mon and evening Tues. *(Mungo Shipley)*

MARSH BALDON   SU5699
Seven Stars (01865) 343337
The Baldons signed off A4074 N of
Dorchester; OX44 9LP Competently run,
community-owned beamed pub on edge of
village green; good food including plenty
of gluten-free and vegetarian choices, well
kept Fullers London Pride and three mainly
local guests, helpful staff coping well at
busy times, modernised bar areas, seats
by corner fire, raftered barn restaurant;
monthly quiz and occasional live music;
children, dogs and muddy boots welcome,
seats outside overlooking fields and horses,
open all day (till midnight Fri, Sat), closes
7pm Sun in winter. *(Neil and Angela Huxter)*

MURCOTT   SP5815
★ Nut Tree (01865) 331253
Off B4027 NE of Oxford, via Islip and
Charlton-on-Otmoor; OX5 2RE Despite
its Michelin star, this 15th-c beamed and
thatched place manages to keep a relaxed
pubby atmosphere; first-rate imaginative
cooking (not cheap) using own produce
including home-reared pigs, good attentive
(but not intrusive) service from friendly staff,
Vale, two guest beers and carefully chosen
wines, well spaced tables with crisp white
cloths, leather chesterfields in bar area;
background music; children and dogs (in bar)
welcome, terrace and pretty garden, unusual
gargoyles on front wall (modelled loosely on
local characters), closed Sun evening, Mon
(including bank holidays). *(Michael Lamb)*

NEWBRIDGE   SP4001
Maybush (01865) 300101
A415 7 miles S of Witney; OX29 7QD
Revamped 18th-c 'eco' dining pub in lovely
Thames-side setting by ancient bridge; clean
modern interior with light stone floors,
some stripped beams and woodburners in
two-way fireplaces, good well presented
food, a couple of real ales such as Sharps
Doom Bar, craft beers from Cotswold and
decent wines by the glass, friendly attentive
staff; children and dogs (in bar) welcome,
waterside terrace and garden, on the
Thames Path, moorings and shepherd's

hut accommodation, closed Sun evening,
otherwise open all day. *(Lindy Wildsmith)*

NORTH MORETON   SU5689
Bear at Home (01235) 811311
Off A4130 Didcot–Wallingford; High
Street; OX11 9AT Village pub dating
from the 16th c run by friendly father and
daughter team; traditional bar, cosy fireside
areas and dining part with stripped-pine
furniture, lots of beams, carpeted floors,
pictures on rough walls, enjoyable sensibly
priced home-made food including daily
specials, Timothy Taylors, a house beer
from West Berkshire and a couple of local
guests, Weston's cider and a dozen wines by
the glass; regular quiz nights; children and
dogs welcome, nice back garden overlooking
cricket pitch (July beer and cricket festival),
pretty village, open all day Sat, closed Sun
evening. *(Bill Gulliver and Harry Thomson)*

NORTHMOOR   SP4202
Red Lion (01865) 300301
B4449 SE of Stanton Harcourt;
OX29 5SX Renovated 15th-c village
pub owned by the local community; good
range of well presented freshly made food
using local and home-grown produce,
up to four real ales and plenty of wines
by the glass, friendly young staff, cosy
atmosphere with heavy beams and bare
stone walls, scrubbed tables, open fire
one end, woodburner the other; maybe
summer movie nights and car boot sales,
free wi-fi; children, walkers and dogs
welcome, garden tables, open all day Sat,
closed Sun evening, Mon. *(Paul Farraday)*

OXFORD   SP5106
Anchor (01865) 510282
Hayfield Road; OX2 6TT 1930s red-brick
dining pub, wood-floored bar with padded
wall benches and stools around light
wood tables, log fire in small carved stone
fireplace, a couple of well kept Wadworths
ales (not cheap) and a guest from oak-
panelled servery, good range of wines, bistro-
feel dining room with black and white tiles
and another fireplace (woodburner), nice
food including daily specials and some good
vegetarian options, efficient service; children
welcome, café-style tables and chairs
on paved terrace, open all day, weekend
brunch from 10am. *(Clive and Fran Dutson)*

OXFORD   SP5106
Chequers (01865) 727463
Off High Street; OX1 4DH Narrow
16th-c courtyard pub tucked away down
small alleyway, several areas on three
floors with interesting architectural
features, beams, panelling and stained
glass, eight or so well kept ales and
enjoyable good value Nicholsons menu,
afternoon tea, friendly service; background
music; walled garden, open (and food)
all day. *(Tony and Wendy Hobden)*

OXFORD   SP5106
Eagle & Child (01865) 302925
St Giles; OX1 3LU Long narrow Nicholsons
pub dating from the 16th c, two charmingly
old-fashioned panelled front rooms with
Tolkien and C S Lewis connections (the
Inklings writers' group used to meet here
and referred to it as the Bird & Baby),
Brakspears, Hook Norton and guests, bustling
atmosphere, stripped-brick dining extension
and conservatory; children allowed in back
till 8pm, open all day. *(David Thornton, Tony
Scott, Philip J Alderton, Richard Tilbrook)*

OXFORD   SP5203
Isis Farmhouse (01865) 243854
*Off Donnington Bridge Road; no car
access; OX4 4EL* Early 19th-c former
farmhouse in charming waterside spot
(accessible only to walkers/cyclists), relaxed
lived-in interior with two woodburners,
short choice of enjoyable home-made
food (sensible prices, no credit cards),
Appleford and a guest ale, nice wines and
interesting soft drinks, afternoon teas with
wonderful home-baked cakes; some live
music; children and dogs welcome, terrace
and garden picnic-sets, canoe hire, short
walk to Iffley Lock and nearby lavishly
decorated early Norman church, open all
day Thurs-Sat in summer (Fri-Sun in winter)
and all bank holidays including Christmas,
may close in bad weather. *(John Harris)*

OXFORD   SP5106
Kings Arms (01865) 242369
Holywell Street/Parks Road; OX1 3SP
Relaxed corner pub dating from the early
17th c opposite the New Bodleian Library;
popular with locals and students (Wadham
College owns it), various cosy rooms up and
down steps, lots of panelling and pictures,
open fires, well kept Youngs ales and
guests, several wines by the glass, pubby
food from baked potatoes and sandwiches
up; free wi-fi; children and dogs welcome,
a few pavement tables, open (and food)
all day. *(Andy Dolan, Terry Davis)*

OXFORD   SP5106
Lamb & Flag (01865) 515787
St Giles/Banbury Road; OX1 3JS
Old college-owned pub with Thomas Hardy's
Jude the Obscure connection; modern airy
front room with light wood panelling and
big windows over street, more atmosphere
in back rooms with stripped stonework and
low-boarded ceilings, a beer by Palmers
for the pub (Lamb & Flag Gold), Skinners
Betty Stogs and guests, real cider/perry,
some lunchtime food including sandwiches
and home-made pies; no credit cards;
open all day. *(Andy Dolan, John Harris)*

OXFORD   SP5006
Old Bookbinders (01865) 553549
Victor Street; OX2 6BT Dark and mellow

family-run local tucked away in the Jericho
area; friendly and unpretentious, with old
fittings and lots of interesting bric-a-brac,
Greene King ales and three guests, decent
choice of whiskies and other spirits,
enjoyable french-leaning food including
speciality crêpes and lunchtime/early-
evening set menu; shove-ha'penny and
board games, quiz Tues, open mike night
Sun; children, dogs and students welcome,
some entertaining features such as multiple
door handles to the gents', closed Mon,
otherwise open all day. *(Andy Dolan)*

OXFORD   SP5105
Royal Blenheim (01865) 242355
Ebbes Street; OX1 1PT Popular 19th-c
corner pub opened by Queen Victoria during
her Golden Jubilee – now tap for the White
Horse Brewery; their range and many
interesting guests, good value straightforward
food (all day till 5pm weekends) including
some decent vegetarian options, Sun
breakfast, friendly chatty staff, single airy
room with original tiled floor and raised
perimeter booth seating; Mon open mike
night, Weds quiz, big-screen sports TV; open
all day (till midnight Fri, Sat). *(John Harris)*

OXFORD   SP5107
Royal Oak (01865) 310187
*Woodstock Road, opposite Radcliffe
Infirmary; OX2 6HT* Characterful old
pub with maze of little rooms meandering
around central bar, low beams, bare boards
and one or two contemporary touches, four
well kept ales along with interesting foreign
beers and good choice of other drinks, fairly
traditional food including decent Sun roast,
open fire; background music; children and
dogs welcome, pavement tables, smallish
garden and raised terrace with picnic-sets,
open all day. *(Richard Tilbrook)*

OXFORD   SP5106
Turf Tavern (01865) 243235
*Bath Place; via St Helens Passage,
between Holywell Street and New College
Lane; OX1 3SU* Interesting characterful
pub hidden away behind high walls; small
dark-beamed bars with lots of snug areas, up
to a dozen constantly changing ales including
Greene King, Weston's cider and maybe
winter mulled wine, popular reasonably
priced food from sandwiches up, pleasant
helpful service; newspapers and free wi-fi;
children and dogs welcome, three walled-in
courtyards (one with own bar), open (and
food) all day. *(Andy Dolan, Tony Scott)*

OXFORD   SP5208
Victoria Arms (01865) 241382
*Signed from Mill Lane, Marston;
OX3 0QA* Old beamed and carpeted pub
in lovely spot looking over River Cherwell
and meadows beyond; tasty food including
good value weekday set lunch, Wadworths
ales, a guest beer and lots of wines by the

glass, friendly accommodating service; children and dogs welcome, picnic-sets on terrace and grass down to the water, popular punting stop, open (and food) all day weekends. *(Richard Tilbrook)*

OXFORD   SP5106
White Horse (01865) 204801

Broad Street; OX1 3BB Bustling place squeezed between parts of Blackwell's bookshop; small narrow bar with snug raised back alcove, low beams and timbers, beautiful view of the Clarendon Building and Sheldonian, Brakspears, Marstons, Sharps, Shotover and White Horse, enjoyable home-made food, friendly staff; open all day (till 10pm Sun) and popular with students; used in filming the *Inspector Morse* TV series and more recently *Lewis*. *(Barry Collett)*

PISHILL   SU7190
★**Crown** (01491) 638364

B480 Nettlebed–Watlington; RG9 6HH 15th-c inn at heart of the Chilterns; beamed bars with old local photographs, prints and maps, some panelling and nice mix of wooden tables and chairs, well kept Brakspears and Rebellion ales, seven wines by the glass and a dozen malt whiskies, tasty generously served food, good service, knocked-through back area with standing timbers and three log fires (not always lit); priest hole is said to be one of the largest in the country; well behaved children welcome, dogs in bar, seats in pretty garden with thatched barn for functions, lots of nearby walks, self-catering cottage, closed Sun evening. *(David and Judy Robison)*

ROKE   SU6293
Home Sweet Home (01491) 838249

Off B4009 Benson–Watlington; OX10 6JD Wadworths country pub with two smallish bars, heavy stripped beams, big log fire and traditional furniture, carpeted room on right leading to restaurant area, good food including weekday set menu, friendly staff; background music, Rokefest music/beer festival late May Bank Holiday; children and dogs welcome, attractive low-walled front garden, open all day Sat, till 5.30pm Sun (food till 3.30pm), closed Mon. *(David Lamb)*

ROTHERFIELD GREYS   SU7282
★**Maltsters Arms** (01491) 628400

Can be reached off A4155 in Henley, via Greys Road passing Southfields long-stay car park; or follow Greys Court signpost off B481 N of Sonning Common; RG9 4QD Chilterns country pub with black-beamed front bar, comfortable wall banquettes and woodburner, Brakspears and other Marstons-related beers, Aspall's cider and eight wines by the glass, linked lounge and restaurant, good sensibly priced food from fairly pubby menu plus several blackboard specials, friendly staff; background music; children and dogs (in

bar) welcome, terrace tables under big heated canopy, picnic-sets on grass looking over paddocks and rolling countryside, good walks nearby and handy for Greys Court (NT), open all day Sun. *(Ross Balaam, Penny and Peter Keevil, R K Phillips, David Lamb)*

ROTHERFIELD PEPPARD   SU7081
Unicorn (01491) 628674

Colmore Lane; RG9 5LX Attractive country pub with bustling log-fire bar, Brakspears ales and good wines by the glass, dining room with high-backed chairs around mix of tables on stripped boards, well liked interesting food including lunchtime sandwiches and daily specials, friendly service; children and dogs welcome (pub dogs are Alfie and Betsy), seats out in front and in pretty back garden, accommodation planned, open all day weekends, closed Mon lunchtime. *(Paul Farraday)*

SHENINGTON   SP3742
Bell (01295) 670274

Off A422 NW of Banbury; OX15 6NQ Unpretentious 17th-c two-room pub with popular home-made food (vegetarians recommended to pre-book), well kept Hook Norton Hooky, a guest beer and good range of wines by the glass, friendly service, heavy beams, some flagstones, stripped stone and pine panelling, two woodburners; children welcome in eating areas, dogs in bar, picnic-sets out at front, charming quiet village with good surrounding walks, closed Sun evening, Mon and lunchtime Tues. *(Patricia Healey)*

SHIPTON-UNDER-WYCHWOOD   SP2717
★**Lamb** (01993) 830465

High Street; off A361 to Burford; OX7 6DQ Handsome stone inn under new management; beamed bar with oak-panelled settle, farmhouse chairs and polished tables on wood-block flooring, stripped-stone walls, log fire, Greene King IPA and a couple of guests, good wines (plenty by the glass) and several malt whiskies, well liked food including children's menu and Weds pie night, friendly service, restaurant area; free wi-fi; dogs allowed in bar, wheelchair access, garden with modern furniture on terrace, five bedrooms, open all day, food all day weekends. *(Charles Fraser)*

SHIPTON-UNDER-WYCHWOOD   SP2717
Wychwood Inn (01993) 831185

High Street; OX7 6BA Refurbished former coaching inn run by mother and son team; contemporary décor in recently extended open-plan bar/dining area, more period character in flagstoned public bar with black beams and inglenook, Greene King IPA and three guests, plenty of wines by the glass and enjoyable food from wraps to grills, friendly young staff, private dining room in glassed-in coach entrance; TV for major sporting events;

children and dogs welcome, picnic-sets on small terrace, five bedrooms, open all day. *(Bernard Stradling, Charles Fraser)*

SIBFORD GOWER SP3537
Wykham Arms (01295) 788808
Signed off B4035 Banbury to Shipston-on-Stour; Temple Mill Road; OX15 5RX
Cottagey 17th-c thatched and flagstoned dining pub, good food (not Sun evening) from light dishes up, friendly attentive staff, two well kept changing ales and over 20 wines by the glass, comfortable open-plan interior with low beams and stripped stone, glass-covered well, inglenook; children and dogs welcome, country views from big garden, lovely manor house opposite and good walks nearby, open all day Sun, closed Mon. *(Sandra and Michael Smith)*

SOULDERN SP5231
Fox (01869) 345284
Off B4100; Fox Lane; OX27 7JW
Early 19th-c pub set in delightful village; open-plan beamed interior with woodburner in two-way fireplace, well kept Hook Norton and guests such as Otter and Black Sheep, several wines by the glass and good fairly priced food from shortish menu, friendly attentive service; regular quiz nights; terrace and walled garden, aunt sally, four bedrooms, open all day Sat, till 5pm Sun. *(John and Claire Masters)*

SOUTH NEWINGTON SP4033
Duck on the Pond (01295) 721166
A361; OX15 4JE Spotless roadside dining pub with small flagstoned bar and linked carpeted eating areas up a step, very well liked food (till 7pm Sun) from lunchtime baguettes up including some good vegetarian choices and popular Sun lunch, Hook Norton Hooky and a couple of guests, cheerful pleasant staff, lots of duck-related items, woodburner; children welcome, no dogs inside, spacious grounds with tables on deck and lawn, pond with waterfowl and little River Swere winding down beyond, open all day weekends. *(George Atkinson)*

STANTON ST JOHN SP5709
Talk House (01865) 351654
Middle Road/Wheatley Road (B4027 just outside village); OX33 1EX Attractive part-thatched dining pub; older part on left with steeply pitched rafters soaring above stripped-stone walls, mix of old dining chairs and big stripped tables, large rugs on flagstones; rest of building converted more recently but in similar style with massive beams, flagstones or stoneware tiles, and log fires below low mantelbeams, good if not cheap food from sandwiches up, three Fullers ales and several wines by the glass; children welcome, inner courtyard with teak tables and chairs, a few picnic-sets on side grass, four bedrooms, open all day except Sun evening. *(Emily and Toby Archer)*

STEEPLE ASTON SP4725
★**Red Lion** (01869) 340225
Off A4260 12 miles N of Oxford; OX25 4RY Cheerful village pub with neatly kept beamed and partly panelled bar, antique settle and other good furnishings, well kept Hook Norton ales and decent wines by the glass, enjoyable food from shortish menu including pizzas, obliging young staff, back timber-framed dining extension; Mon quiz; well behaved children welcome till 7pm, dogs in bar, suntrap front garden with lovely flowers and shrubs, parking can be be awkward, open all day Sat, till 5pm Sun. *(David Lamb)*

STEVENTON SU4691
North Star
Stocks Lane, The Causeway, central westward turn off B4017; OX13 6SG
Very traditional little village pub through yew tree gateway; tiled entrance corridor, main area with ancient high-backed settles forming booth in front of brick fireplace, three well kept ales from side tap room, hatch service to another room with plain seating, a couple of tables and coal fire, simple lunchtime food, friendly staff; children and dogs welcome, tables on front grass, aunt sally, open all day weekends, closed weekday lunchtimes. *(John Harris)*

STOKE LYNE SP5628
Peyton Arms 07546 066160
From minor road off B4110 N of Bicester fork left into village; OX27 8SD
Beautifully situated and largely unspoilt one-room stone alehouse, character landlord (Mick the Hat) and loyal regulars, very well kept Hook Norton ales from casks behind small corner bar, no food apart from filled rolls, inglenook fire, tiled floor and lots of memorabilia, games area with darts and pool; no children or dogs; pleasant garden with aunt sally, open all day weekends till 7pm, closed weekday lunchtimes apart from Tues, and may shut early if quiet. *(Ben and Jenny Settle)*

STOKE ROW SU6884
Cherry Tree (01491) 680430
Off B481 at Highmoor; RG9 5QA
Sympathetically modernised 18th-c pub-restaurant (originally three cottages), enjoyable often interesting food from sharing plates to daily specials, Weds steak night, Fri fish and chips, Brakspears ales and good range of wines by the glass, helpful friendly staff, small linked rooms mainly set for dining, heavy low beams, stripped boards and flagstones; background music, Sun quiz, TV in bar; well behaved children and dogs welcome, lots of tables in attractive garden, nearby walks, four good bedrooms in converted barn, open all day (food all day Sun). *(Katharine Cowherd, Bob and Margaret Holder)*

STOKE ROW   SU6884
★**Crooked Billet** (01491) 681048
*Nottwood Lane, off B491 N of Reading –
OS Sheet 175 map reference 684844;
RG9 5PU* Nice place, but more restaurant
than pub; charming rustic layout with
heavy beams, flagstones, antique pubby
furnishings and fine inglenook log fire,
crimson Victorian-style dining room, very
good interesting food cooked by owner-chef
using local and home-grown ingredients,
cheaper set lunches Mon-Fri, helpful
friendly staff, Brakspears Oxford Gold
tapped from the cask (no counter), good
wines, relaxed homely atmosphere; weekly
live music often including established
artists; children very welcome, big garden
by Chilterns beechwoods, open all day,
food all day weekends. *(Colin McLachlan)*

SUNNINGWELL   SP4900
Flowing Well (01865) 735846
Just N of Abingdon; OX13 6RB
Refurbished timbered pub in former 19th-c
rectory; good food including british tapas,
range of burgers and gluton free menu, a
couple of Greene King ales and a guest,
good choice of wines; free wi-fi; children
welcome, dogs in bar, large heated raised
terrace, more seats in garden with small well,
open (and food) all day. *(Paul Farraday)*

SWINFORD   SP4308
Talbot (01865) 881348
B4044 just S of Eynsham; OX29 4BT
Roomy and comfortable 17th-c beamed
pub, well kept Arkells tapped from
cooled casks and good choice of wines,
enjoyable reasonably priced pubby food
from sandwiches and basket meals up
including deals, Sun carvery, friendly staff,
long attractive flagstoned bar with some
stripped stone, cheerful log-effect gas
fire; charity quiz second Mon of month;
children and dogs welcome, garden with
decked area overlooking Wharf Stream,
nice walk along lovely stretch of the
Thames towpath, moorings quite nearby,
11 bedrooms, open all day. *(Brian Glozier)*

THAME   SP7105
Cross Keys (01844) 218202
Park Street/East Street; OX9 3HP
Friendly one-bar 19th-c corner local,
eight well kept ales including own Thame
beers (not always available) and half a
dozen ciders, no food apart from scotch
eggs and occasional cheese and wine
nights but can bring your own; Weds quiz
and regular comedy nights; courtyard
garden, open all day Sun. *(Monty Green)*

THAME   SP7006
★**Thatch** (01844) 214340
Lower High Street; OX9 2AA Characterful
timbered and thatched 16th-c dining pub
(Peach group); good interesting food from
deli boards to daily specials, well kept
ales, nice wines and some interesting gins,
friendly service, cosy bar and appealing
collection of little higgledy-piggledy rooms,
heavy beams, old quarry tiles, flagstones and
double-sided inglenook, smart contemporary
furnishings and bold paintwork; children
welcome, prettily planted terraced garden
with tables under parasols, open (and food)
all day. *(Len and Lily Dowson)*

TOOT BALDON   SP5600
★**Mole** (01865) 340001
*Between A4074 and B480 SE of Oxford;
OX44 9NG* Light open-plan restauranty
pub with good if not cheap food (booking
advisable) including light lunch and weekly
changing set menus, friendly attentive
service, nice wines by the glass and a couple
of well kept ales such as Hook Norton Hooky,
leather sofas by bar, neat country furniture or
more formal leather dining chairs in linked
eating areas including conservatory, stripped
18th-c beams and big open fire; background
music; children welcome, no dogs inside,
lovely gardens, open all day. *(M A Borthwick)*

UFFINGTON   SU3089
Fox & Hounds (01367) 820680)
High Street; SN7 7RP Traditional beamed
village local with three changing ales and
enjoyable fairly priced home-made food
including daily specials, friendly attentive
staff, garden room extension with view
of White Horse Hill; live music and quiz
nights, sports TV, free wi-fi; children and
dogs welcome, picnic-sets outside, handy
for Tom Brown's School Museum, four
ground-floor bedrooms, open all day, no
food Sun evening. *(Patricia Healey)*

WALLINGFORD   SU6089
Partridge (01491) 839305
St Marys Street; OX10 0ET More
restaurant than pub, contemporary and
airy, with comfortably modern furnishings
including leather sofas and armchairs on
bare boards, open fires, good well presented
food (not especially cheap) from lunchtime
sandwiches to popular Sun roasts, well
chosen wines, West Berkshire bottled beers
and some upmarket gins, neat helpful staff;
children welcome, pleasant back terrace,
four bedrooms (three sharing bathroom),
closed Sun evening, Mon. *(Colin McLachlan)*

WANTAGE   SU3987
★**Royal Oak** (01235) 763129
Newbury Street; OX12 8DF Popular
two-bar corner local with well kept
West Berkshire ales (one named for the
friendly knowledgeable landlord) along
with Wadworths 6X and plenty of guests,
excellent range of ciders and perries too,
lots of decorative pump clips, old ship
photographs; several group meetings such as
choral society, book club, cribbage and darts;
closed weekday lunchtimes. *(Dave Evans)*

WARBOROUGH
SU6093

Six Bells
(01865) 858265

The Green S; just E of A329, 4 miles N of Wallingford; OX10 7DN Thatched 16th-c pub opposite village cricket green, well kept Brakspears and enjoyable fairly pubby food (not Sun or Mon evenings) from sandwiches and sharing boards up, friendly attentive staff, low beams and attractive country furnishings in small linked areas off bar, bare boards, stripped stone and big log fire; tables out in front and in pleasant orchard garden behind where aunt sally is played, open all day weekends. *(Paul Humphreys, Roy Hoing, Keith Perry, Colin McLachlan, Barry Collett)*

WARDINGTON
SP4946

Hare & Hounds
(01295) 750645

A361 Banbury–Daventry; OX17 1SH Comfortable and welcoming traditional village local, well kept Hook Norton ales and enjoyable home-made food including bargain OAP lunch, low-ceilinged bar leading to dining area, woodburner; quiz nights, darts and dominoes; children and dogs welcome, garden with play area and aunt sally, open all day Fri, Sat, till 8pm Sun. *(Charles Fraser)*

WATLINGTON
SU6994

Fat Fox
(01491) 613040

Shireburn Street; OX49 5BU Centrally placed 17th-c inn with beamed inglenook bar and separate restaurant, good food from changing menu using local produce, four real ales including Brakspears and good choice of wines by the glass, friendly helpful staff; free wi-fi; children and dogs (in bar) welcome, Ridgeway walks, nine bedrooms (seven in converted back barn), good breakfast, handy for M40 (junction 3). *(Taff Thomas)*

WEST HANNEY
SU4092

Plough
(01235) 868 987

Just off A338 N of Wantage; Church Street; OX12 0LN Refurbished 16th-c thatched and beamed village pub owned by the local community; light modern décor, four well kept ales including Greene King IPA, generous helpings of popular home-made food (not Sun evening, Tues), friendly service; free wi-fi; children and dogs on leads welcome, nice walled garden behind, aunt sally, good walks from the door, open all day weekends, closed Mon. *(Monty Green)*

WHITCHURCH
SU6377

Ferry Boat
(0118) 984 2161

High Street, near toll bridge; RG8 7DB Welcoming comfortably updated 18th-c pub with airy log-fire bar and restaurant, good variety of home-made food including stone-baked pizzas, real ales such as Black Sheep and Timothy Taylors, several wines by the glass; background music, free wi-fi; children welcome away from bar, well behaved dogs in bar only, café-style seating in courtyard garden, closed Sun evening, Mon. *(Charles Fraser)*

WHITCHURCH
SU6377

Greyhound
(0118) 343 3016

High Street, just over toll bridge from Pangbourne; RG8 7EL Attractive former ferryman's cottage under new management; small knocked-together low-beamed rooms, three changing ales and good value pubby food, friendly efficient staff; monthly live music; children and dogs welcome, small sheltered back garden, attractive village on Thames Path, open all day Sat, till 6pm Sun, closed Mon and lunchtime Tues. *(John Harris)*

WITNEY
SP3509

Angel
(01993) 703238

Market Square; OX28 6AL Unpretentious 17th-c town local with wide choice of enjoyable well priced food from good sandwiches up, Marstons-related ales including a house beer from Wychwood and an occasional guest, efficient friendly service even when packed, beams and open fire; background music (live Fri), sports TVs; lovely hanging baskets, back terrace with smokers' shelter, parking nearby can be difficult, open (and food) all day. *(Sandra and Michael Smith)*

WITNEY
SP3509

★ Fleece
(01993) 892270

Church Green; OX28 4AZ Smart civilised town pub (part of the Peach group), popular for its wide choice of good often imaginative food from sandwiches and deli boards up, fixed-price menu too (Mon-Fri 12-6pm), Greene King and a couple of guests, decent coffee, leather armchairs on wood floors, restaurant; background and occasional live music, daily papers; children welcome, café-style tables out at front overlooking green, ten comfortable affordable bedrooms, good breakfast, open (and food) all day from 9am. *(R K Phillips)*

WITNEY
SP3509

Hollybush
(01993) 708073

Corn Street; OX28 6BT Popular modernised 18th-c pub under same ownership as the Horseshoes across the road; front bar with woodburner in big fireplace, settles and window seats, various dining areas off, good food from sandwiches

---

Post Office address codings confusingly give the impression that some pubs are in Oxfordshire, when they're really in Berkshire, Buckinghamshire, Gloucestershire or Warwickshire (which is where we list them).

and deli boards up, weekday lunchtime set menu and other offers, three well kept ales including a house beer from Greene King and nice selection of wines, efficient friendly staff; background music, free wi-fi; children and dogs welcome, open (and food) all day. *(John and Claire Masters)*

WITNEY
SP3510

Horseshoes (01993) 703086
Corn Street, junction with Holloway Road; OX28 6BS Attractive 16th-c stone pub with good freshly made food (all day weekends) from pubby choices up, also gluten-free choices, deli counter and weekday set lunch deal, three changing ales and decent wines by the glass, heavy beams, stripped-stone walls, oak floors and log fires, separate back dining room; children and dogs welcome, a few seats out at front, tables on sunny paved terrace behind, open all day. *(Steve Whalley)*

WOLVERCOTE
SP4909

Plough (01865) 556969
First Turn/Wolvercote Green; OX2 8AH Comfortably worn-in pubby linked areas, armchairs and Victorian-style carpeted bays in main lounge, well kept Greene King and guests, traditional cider and decent wines by the glass, friendly helpful staff and bustling atmosphere, enjoyable good value usual food in flagstoned stables dining room and library (children allowed here), OAP lunchtime menu, traditional snug, woodburner;

dogs welcome in bar, picnic-sets on part-decked terrace looking over rough meadow to canal and woods, open all day Fri-Sun. *(Tony and Jill Radnor)*

WOODSTOCK
SP4417

Black Prince (01993) 811530
Manor Road (A44 N); OX20 1XJ Old pub with one modernised low-ceilinged bar, timbers, stripped stone and log fire, suit of armour, good value home-made food (not Sun evening) from sandwiches to specials, well kept St Austell and guests such as Downlands, Elgoods and Loddon, friendly service; some live music, outside lavatories; children, walkers and dogs welcome, tables in pretty garden by small River Glyme, aunt sally, nearby right of way into Blenheim parkland, open all day. *(John Harris, Camilla and Jose Ferrara)*

WOOLSTONE
SU2987

White Horse (01367) 820726
Off B4507; SN7 7QL New management for this appealing partly thatched black and white pub; prominent gables and latticed windows, spacious beamed bar with stone flooring and two open fires, Arkells ales and enjoyable food from regularly changing menus, wood-fired pizzas Thurs and Sun evenings in summer, restaurant; well behaved children and dogs allowed, plenty of seats in front and back gardens, secluded interesting village handy for White Horse and Ridgeway (good circular walk), six bedrooms, open all day. *(Patricia Healey)*

Shropshire

KEY ★ Star Pub 🎙️ Top Quality Food 🍺 Great Beer
🍷 Good Wines £ Bargain Meals 🛏️ Good Bedrooms 🍽️ Serves Food

BASCHURCH   SJ4221   Map 7
New Inn
(01939) 260335 – www.newinnbaschurch.com
Church Road; SY4 2EF

**A good mix of customers for bustling village pub with several beers
and highly popular food; seats outside**

The food in this handsome whitewashed pub is particularly good, but this
is no straightforward dining pub – five real ales on handpump are served
by friendly, cheerful staff and the interlinked, attractively refurbished rooms
have an easy-going atmosphere. At one end, the bar has a woodburning
stove, leather sofas and armchairs, pale wooden chairs and stools around
contemporary tables on quarry tiles and bare boards, and lots of wall prints.
Hobsons Best Bitter, Salopian Shropshire Gold and Stonehouse Station Bitter
on handpump and 13 wines by the glass. The two heavily beamed dining
rooms have logs piled into brick fireplaces, high-backed leather-seated chairs
around more light tables and candles in glass jars and lanterns; the table
flowers are pretty. There are seats outside on decking.

🍽️ Enjoyable food using local produce includes goats cheese and maple mousse with
saffron pickled pear and candied walnuts, confit duck leg hash with a fried duck
egg and home-made brown sauce, steak in ale pie, beer-battered haddock and chips,
steak burger with toppings and parmesan and truffle fries, spiced paneer and vegetable
patty with saag aloo and golden raisin and coconut curry sauce, hot smoked salmon or
smoked chicken caesar salad, braised lamb shoulder with garlic and thyme fondant
potato and french-style peas, and puddings such as green apple mousse with cinnamon
shortbread and sticky toffee pudding with toffee sauce. *Benchmark main dish: sea
bass with truffle and celeriac purée, sea vegetables and sorrel oil £15.50. Two-course
evening meal £21.00.*

Free house ~ Licensees Graham and Clare Jenkins ~ Real ale ~ Open 12-3, 6-11; 12-11 Sat;
12-8 Sun; closed Mon ~ Bar food 12-2, 6-9; 12-6 Sun ~ Restaurant ~ Children welcome ~
Dogs allowed in bar ~ Wi-fi *Recommended by Jacqui and Alan Swan, Caroline and Peter Bryant,
Nick Higgins*

BRIDGNORTH   SO7192   Map 4
Old Castle 🍺 £
(01746) 711420 – www.oldcastlebridgnorth.co.uk
West Castle Street; WV16 4AB

**Cheerful town pub, relaxed and friendly, with generous helpings of
good value pubby food, well kept ales and sizeable suntrap terrace**

First licensed in 1740, this is a bustling place that was once two cottages. The low-beamed, open-plan bar is properly pubby with some genuine character: you'll find tiles and bare boards, cushioned wall banquettes and settles around cast-iron-framed tables, and bar stools arranged along the counter where the friendly landlord and his staff serve Hobsons Town Crier, Sharps Doom Bar and Wye Valley Butty Bach and HPA on handpump. A back conservatory extension has darts, pool and a games machine; background music and big-screen TV for sports events. A big plus here is the sunny back terrace with picnic-sets, lovely hanging baskets, big pots of flowers, shrub borders and decking at the far end that gives an elevated view over the west side of town; children's playthings. Do walk up the street to see the ruined castle – its 20-metre Norman tower tilts at such an extraordinary angle that it makes the leaning tower of Pisa look like a model of rectitude.

Good pubby food at fair prices includes sandwiches and baguettes (not after 3pm), devilled whitebait, chicken dippers with barbecue sauce, burgers with toppings, onion rings and chips, sweet potato, red pepper and spinach lasagne, chilli con carne, minted lamb shank with mash and gravy, gammon and egg, mixed grill, and puddings. *Benchmark main dish: steak in ale pie £9.50. Two-course evening meal £15.00.*

Punch ~ Tenant Bryn Charles Masterman ~ Real ale ~ Open 11.30-11; 11.30-10.30 Sun ~ Bar food 12-3, 6.30-8.30 ~ Children welcome ~ Dogs welcome ~ Wi-fi *Recommended by Geoff and Ann Marston, Andrew and Michele Revell, Julian Richardson, Rona Mackinlay*

CARDINGTON
Royal Oak

SO5095   Map 4

(01694) 771266 – www.at-the-oak.com
Village signposted off B4371 Church Stretton–Much Wenlock, pub behind church; also reached via narrow lanes from A49; SY6 7JZ

Heaps of character in well run and friendly rural pub with seasonal bar food and real ales

Not much has changed over the centuries at this enjoyable place, which is said to be the oldest continually licensed pub in Shropshire – it's been enjoyed by our readers for many years. The rambling low-beamed traditional bar has a roaring winter log fire, a cauldron, black kettle and pewter jugs in a vast inglenook fireplace, aged standing timbers from a knocked-through wall, and red and green tapestry seats solidly capped in elm; board games and dominoes. Ludlow Best and Sharps Doom Bar with guests such as Hobsons Town Crier and Stonehouse Cambrian Gold on handpump, eight wines by the glass, ten gins, several malt whiskies and farm cider. A comfortable dining area has exposed old beams and studwork. This is glorious country for walks, such as the one to the summit of Caer Caradoc, a couple of miles to the west (ask for directions at the pub), and the front courtyard makes the most of its beautiful position.

Well liked food using local produce includes baguettes, chicken liver pâté, spicy crab cakes with sweet chilli dip, apricot and goats cheese nut roast with tomato and basil sauce, pork loin and black pudding tower with leek and bacon sauce, fish pie, duck breast with plum, shallot and red wine sauce, steak and kidney pudding, gammon and egg, steaks with a choice of sauce, and puddings. *Benchmark main dish: rump of lamb with redcurrant, red wine and rosemary sauce £13.95. Two-course evening meal £17.50.*

Free house ~ Licensees Steve and Eira Oldham ~ Real ale ~ Open 12-2.30, 6-11; 12-11 Sat, Sun; 12-4 Sun in winter; closed Mon except bank holiday lunchtime ~ Bar food 12-2.30, 6-9 ~ Restaurant ~ Children welcome ~ Dogs allowed in bar ~ Wi-fi *Recommended by Charles Todd, Michael Butler, Paddy and Sian O'Leary, Barbara Brown*

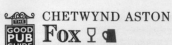

CHETWYND ASTON

SJ7517 Map 7

Fox ♀ ◖

(01952) 815940 – www.brunningandprice.co.uk/fox

Village signposted off A41 and A518 just S of Newport; TF10 9LQ

Civilised dining pub with generous helpings of well liked food and a fine array of drinks served by ever attentive staff

The large garden behind this handsome Edwardian pub is quite lovely, with a sunny terrace, picnic-sets tucked into the shade of mature trees and extensive views across quiet country fields; there's a Brunning & Price trademark play tractor for children. The interior, despite being large and spreading, has cosy corners too – all filled with a cheerful crowd of customers. The linked rooms (one with a broad arched ceiling) has plenty of tables in varying shapes and sizes, some quite elegant, and a loosely matching diversity of comfortable chairs on parquet, polished boards or attractive floor tiles. Masses of prints and photographs line the walls, there are three open fires and big windows and careful lighting contribute to the relaxed atmosphere; board games. Bar stools line the long bar counter where courteous, efficient staff keep some 23 wines by the glass, 50 rums, 80 gins, 100 malt whiskies, two farm ciders and Phoenix Brunning & Price Original, Three Tuns XXX, Woods Shropshire Lad and three quickly changing guests such as Heavy Industry 77, Phoenix Wobbly Bob and Tatton Blonde on handpump. Good disabled access.

 Imaginative food includes sandwiches, crispy chicken wings with korean kimchi salad and chilli dressing, smoked mackerel rillettes with pickled apple and cucumber, puy lentil, carrot and wild mushroom wellington with seasonal vegetables and red wine gravy, tempura king prawns with watermelon, pak choi, pickled ginger and mango, chilli and lime dressing, steak in ale pudding, pork and leek sausages with mash and onion gravy, tandoori hake fillet with red lentil and spinach dhal and cauliflower bhaji, and puddings such as crème brûlée and lemon and lime tart with strawberry sorbet. *Benchmark main dish: beer-battered fish and chips £13.45. Two-course evening meal £21.00.*

Brunning & Price ~ Manager Samantha Forrest ~ Real ale ~ Open 11-11; 11-10.30 Sun ~ Bar food 12-10 (9.30 Sun) ~ Children welcome ~ Dogs allowed in bar ~ Wi-fi
Recommended by Phoebe Peacock, John Evans, Tony Smaithe

CLUN

SO3080 Map 6

White Horse ◖ £

(01588) 418139 – www.whi-clun.co.uk

The Square; SY7 8JA

Bustling local with own-brewed and guest ales and good value traditional food; bedrooms

Attentive staff keep the own-brewed Clun beers here very well – they include Citadel, Loophole and Pale, with guests such as Hobsons Best and Wye Valley Butty Bach on handpump. Also, five wines by the glass, half a dozen malt whiskies and two farm ciders. There's always a friendly mix of both regulars and visitors. The low-beamed front bar is snug and friendly and warmed in winter by a cosy inglenook woodburning stove; from here, a door leads into a separate little dining room with a rare plank and munton screen. In the games room at the back you'll find a TV, games machine, darts, pool, juke box and board games; there is a small garden. The bedrooms are quiet and comfortable.

🍴 Fair priced food includes sandwiches and baguettes, wild boar pâté, scampi salad, mushroom stroganoff, chicken korma, beef bourguignon, local sausages with mash and gravy, red bean and coconut pottage, burger with toppings, onion rings and chips, lamb cutlets with new potatoes, 28-day hung steaks with onion rings and a choice of sauces, and puddings such as syrup sponge and rice pudding. *Benchmark main dish: steak and kidney pudding £11.95. Two-course evening meal £16.00.*

Own brew ~ Licensee Jack Limond ~ Real ale ~ Open 11am-midnight ~ Bar food 12-3, 6-9 ~ Restaurant ~ Children welcome ~ Dogs allowed in bar and bedrooms ~ Wi-fi ~ Live music every second Fri and second Weds ~ Bedrooms: £45/£70 *Recommended by Andy Dolan, Lance and Sarah Milligan, John Watson, John and Sharon Hancock*

COALPORT
Woodbridge 🍷 🍽
SJ7002 Map 4

(01952) 882054 – www.brunningandprice.co.uk/woodbridge
Village signposted off A442 1.5 miles S of A4169 Telford roundabout; down in valley, turn left across narrow bridge into Coalport Road, pub immediately left; TF8 7JF

Superb Ironbridge Gorge site for extensive, handsomely reworked pub, an all-round success

N amed after the wooden bridge that once connected the pub to the village, this 18th-c place is on the banks of the River Severn, with tables and chairs on a big deck looking over the water. Inside, the spreading series of linked rooms are comfortable and civilised with log fires and Coalport-style stoves, rugs on broad boards as well as tiles or carpet, black beams in the central part and plenty of polished tables and cosy armchair corners. A mass of mainly 18th- and 19th-c prints, often of local scenes, line the walls and are well worth a look; background music and board games. Phoenix Brunning & Price Original and guests such as Gorgeous Beer Company Blonde, Hobsons Twisted Spire, Salopian Lemon Dream, Three Tuns XXX and Weetwood Old Dog Bitter on handpump, 14 wines by the glass, 50 malt whiskies and 20 gins; service is quick and friendly.

🍴 Brasserie-style food includes sandwiches, deep-fried brie with pickled cranberries and apple salad, five-spiced duck leg with spring onion, cucumber, hoisin sauce and pancakes, butternut squash tortellini with warm gazpacho dressing, game pudding with braised red cabbage, prosciutto-wrapped pork fillet with chorizo croquette, squash purée and red wine gravy, smoked haddock fishcake with a poached egg and white wine, dill and caper sauce, chicken breast with smoked bacon and baby onion sherry sauce and fondant potato, and puddings such as raspberry and almond tart with custard and crème brûlée. *Benchmark main dish: beer-battered fish and chips £13.45. Two-course evening meal £23.00.*

Brunning & Price ~ Manager Vrata Krist ~ Real ale ~ Open 11.30-11; 11.30am-midnight Fri, Sat; 11.30-10.30 Sun ~ Bar food 12-10; 12-9.30 Sun ~ Restaurant ~ Children welcome ~ Dogs allowed in bar ~ Wi-fi *Recommended by Lynda and Trevor Smith, Dave Braisted, Max Simons, David Seward, Richard and Tessa Ibbot*

HODNET
Bear 🍽 🛏
SJ6128 Map 6

(01630) 685214 – www.bearathodnet.co.uk
Drayton Road (A53); TF9 3NH

Black and white timbered former coaching inn with beamed rooms, four real ales, enjoyable food and seats outside; bedrooms

T he rambling, open-plan main room in this nice old pub has heavy 16th-c beams and timbers creating separate areas, wooden tables and chairs on rugs or flagstones, and a woodburning stove in a large stone fireplace (there are three other woodburners as well); you can look into the former bear pit through a glass top in the floor. The smaller, beamed and quarry-tiled bar has Black Sheep, Salopian Shropshire Gold, Timothy Taylors Landlord and Weetwood Best Bitter on handpump, 13 wines by the glass, 20 malt whiskies and around 30 gins served by friendly staff; the pub jack russell is called Jack and the cocker spaniel is Betsy. The garden has picnic-sets and a play area, and the refurbished bedrooms are well equipped and comfortable. Hodnet Hall Gardens are opposite and the inn is handy for Hawkstone Park; good walks in lovely surrounding countryside.

Enjoyable food includes crispy whitebait with marie rose sauce, pear, blue cheese, walnut and chicory salad, moroccan-style vegetable tagine with spiced tomato sauce, slow-cooked asian-style pork belly with wasabi mayonnaise and asian slaw, lamb and mint burger with coleslaw, tzatziki and triple-cooked chips, hoisin duck leg with frites, salmon with dijon mustard cream sauce, and puddings such as cherry bakewell tart and ginger and black pepper pudding with butterscotch sauce. *Benchmark main dish: fresh fish dish of the day £12.95. Two-course evening meal £20.00.*

Free house ~ Licensees Gregory and Pia Williams ~ Real ale ~ Open 5-11; 12-11 Fri, Sat; 12-10 Sun; 12-7 Sun in winter; closed Mon-Thurs lunchtimes ~ Bar food 5-9.30; 12-9.30 Fri-Sun ~ Restaurant ~ Children welcome ~ Dogs allowed in bar ~ Wi-fi ~ Bedrooms: £65/£120 *Recommended by Roger and Anne Newbury, Maddie Purvis, Neil and Brenda Skidmore, Paul Scofield*

IRONBRIDGE
Golden Ball 🏠

SJ6703 Map 4

(01952) 432179 – www.goldenballironbridge.co.uk
Brown sign to pub off Madeley Road (B4373) above village centre – pub behind Horse & Jockey, car park beyond on left; TF8 7BA

Low-beamed, partly Elizabethan pub with popular food and drink; bedrooms

If you stay overnight here, the bedrooms are comfortable and breakfasts are good. The bar has worn floorboards, red-cushioned pews, one or two black beams and a woodburning stove. Gorgeous Beer Company Blonde and Golden Bitter, Purity Pure UBU and Wye Valley HPA on handpump, quite a few belgian bottled ales, nine wines by the glass and several gins and whiskies; background music and TV. A pretty fairy-lit pergola path leads to the door and on the sheltered side courtyard there are tables under parasols. This friendly inn is tucked away in a little hamlet of other ancient buildings; you can walk down to the River Severn, and beyond – but it's rather steep getting back up again.

Tasty food includes chicken liver pâté, tropical king prawn skewers with sweet chilli jam, wild mushroom, spinach and ricotta filo parcel with tomato and basil sauce, beer-battered cod and chips, honey-roasted duck breast with berry sauce, salmon fillet with herb crumb topping and a white wine and dill sauce, chicken thighs in chasseur sauce, and puddings such as chocolate fudge cake and rhubarb and ginger tart. *Benchmark main dish: chicken breast wrapped in bacon with grain mustard sauce £10.95. Two-course evening meal £18.00.*

Enterprise ~ Lease Jessica Janke ~ Real ale ~ Open 12-11.30; 12-10.30 Sun ~ Bar food 12-9; 12-7 Sun ~ Restaurant ~ Children welcome ~ Dogs allowed in bar and bedrooms ~ Wi-fi ~ Live band Fri monthly, open mike second Sun of month ~ Bedrooms: £60/£65 *Recommended by Mark Morgan, George Sanderson, Dr Simon Innes, Ben and Jenny Settle, Alexander and Trish Gendall*

LUDLOW
Charlton Arms ♨ ⇔

SO5174 Map 6

(01584) 872813 – www.thecharltonarms.co.uk

Ludford Bridge, B4361 Overton Road; SY8 1PJ

Fine position for bustling pub near town centre, plenty of space for both drinking and dining and extensive terraces looking over the river; bedrooms

If you stay in the well equipped and cosy bedrooms here, you'll have a marvellous view over the River Teme; the two balconies with seats and tables share the same outlook which leads down to the massive medieval bridge. The character bar has proper pubby tables and chairs on tiled and bricked floors, gluggle jugs along the gantry, a double-sided woodburner, and stools against the hop-hung counter where friendly staff serve Hobsons Best Bitter and Twisted Spire, Ludlow Gold and Stairway and Wye Valley Butty Bach on handpump, 15 wines by the glass and a farm cider. The two rooms of the lounge (sharing a two-way woodburning stove) are comfortable and chatty with tub chairs, armchairs and high-backed black leather seats on pale wooden floors. The dining room looks over the fine bridge; background music and board games.

Popular food includes sandwiches, potted shrimps, cheese soufflé with chive sauce, cauliflower steak with olive and artichoke salad and polenta chips, corn-fed chicken with turnip fricassée and boulangère potatoes, burger with toppings, barbecue sauce and chips, dressed crab salad with lemon mayonnaise and skinny fries, fish and shellfish pie, and puddings such as lemon tart and strawberry ice-cream and vanilla crème brûlée. *Benchmark main dish: beer-battered fish and chips £12.95. Two-course evening meal £21.00.*

Free house ~ Licensee Cedric Bosi ~ Real ale ~ Open 11-11 (midnight Fri, Sat); 12-10.30 Sun ~ Bar food 12-3, 6-9 (8.30 Sun) ~ Restaurant ~ Children welcome ~ Dogs allowed in bar ~ Wi-fi ~ Bedrooms: £95/£100 *Recommended by John Jenkins, Ian Herdman, Michael Butler, JPC, Graeme and Sally Mendham*

LUDLOW
Church Inn ♨

SO5174 Map 4

(01584) 874034 – www.thechurchinn.com

Church Street, behind Butter Cross; SY8 1AW

Splendid range of real ales in character town-centre pub

This old beamed town-centre pub is just up the road from the castle. It's been refurbished recently and the ground floor is divided into three appealingly decorated areas, with hops hanging from heavy beams and comfortable banquettes in cosy alcoves; the pulpit and pews come from a local church. A long central area has a fine stone fireplace, a chess table and board games, while, upstairs, the civilised lounge bar has vaulted ceilings and gives good views of St Laurence's church and the surrounding countryside. A fine range of ales served by friendly staff includes Hobsons Best Bitter, Ludlow Boiling Well, Gold and Stairway and Tiny Rebel Cwtch on handpump, 14 wines by the glass, 25 gins and a farm cider.

Reasonably priced food includes breaded whitebait with aioli, chorizo scotch egg with fruit chutney, chilli and cheese hot dog with sour cream and skinny fries, spring onion bubble and squeak with a poached egg and white wine sauce, lamb moussaka with garlic bread, beef in ale pie, monkfish cheek scampi with tartare sauce, southern fried chicken with coleslaw and fries, and puddings such as chocolate fondant with choocolate mint ice-cream and lemon tart with raspberry sorbet. *Benchmark main dish: chicken and ham hock pie £11.95. Two-course evening meal £18.00.*

Free house ~ Licensee Matt Tommey ~ Real ale ~ Open 11-11; 11am-midnight Fri, Sat; 12-10.30 Sun ~ Bar food 12-3, 6-9 (8.30 Sun) ~ Restaurant ~ Children welcome ~ Dogs allowed in bar ~ Wi-fi *Recommended by Roy and Gill Payne, Shona and Jimmy McDuff, Christopher May*

MAESBURY MARSH   SJ3125 Map 6
Navigation
(01691) 672958 – www.thenavigation.co.uk
Follow Maesbury Road off A483 S of Oswestry; by canal bridge; SY10 8JB

Versatile and friendly canalside pub with cosy bar and local seasonal produce in a choice of dining areas

All are warmly welcomed – and that includes dogs and children – at this 18th-c wharf building beside the Montgomery Canal. It's a cheerfully run traditional pub and the quarry-tiled bar on the left has squishy brown leather sofas by an old-fashioned black range blazing in a big red-brick fireplace, little upholstered cask seats around three small tables, and dozens of wrist- and pocket-watches hanging from the beams. A couple of steps lead up to a carpeted area beyond a balustrade, with armchairs and sofas around low tables, and a piano; off to the left is a dining area with paintings by local artists. The main beamed dining room, with some stripped stone, is beyond another small bar (they serve cocktails here) with a coal-effect gas fire – and an amazing row of cushioned carved choir stalls complete with misericord seats. Stonehouse Station Bitter and a guest such as Woods Shropshire Lad on handpump, 11 wines by the glass, nine malt whiskies (one from Wales) and a farm cider (in summer); quiet background music and board games. There are picnic-sets beside the water and the windows in the dining room share the same view. The hands-on licensees also run a book exchange, a shop where you can buy fresh local produce (including fish and shellfish) and offer a two-pint takeaway service.

Using free-range meat and local produce, the tasty food includes lunchtime sandwiches (Wednesday-Saturday), duck liver pâté with orange marmalade, potted white crab and prawns, roasted peppers stuffed with feta, garlic and tomato couscous with tzatziki, burger with toppings, sauce and chips, a trio of free-range pork sausages with mash and gravy, chicken caesar salad, a seasonal risotto, salmon fillet with crushed new potatoes, sauté leeks and herb yoghurt, and puddings such as white chocolate and orange cheesecake and caramelised baked apple with ice-cream; they also offer a two- and three-course set menu. *Benchmark main dish: free-range chicken wrapped in bacon with sauté leeks and mushrooms and white wine sauce £14.00. Two-course evening meal £20.00.*

Free house ~ Licensees Brent Ellis and Mark Baggett ~ Real ale ~ Open 12-2, 6-11; 12-6 Sun; closed Sun evening, all day Mon, lunchtime Tue; first two weeks Jan ~ Bar food 12-2, 6-8.30; 12-2 Sun ~ Restaurant ~ Children welcome ~ Dogs allowed in bar ~ Wi-fi ~ Folk music last Weds of month *Recommended by Isobel Mackinlay, Jeremy Snow, Sally Harrison, Jeff Davies*

NEENTON   SO6387 Map 4
Pheasant
(01746) 787955 – www.pheasantatneenton.co.uk
B4364 Bridgnorth–Ludlow; WV16 6RJ

Renovated village pub owned by locals, traditionally furnished bar and dining room, local ales and tasty food; seats in orchard garden

The local community own this refurbished village pub in the pretty Shropshire hills. The cosy front bar has leather sofas and armchairs by a woodburning stove, rugs on tiles and stools by the counter where they serve Hobsons Town Crier and Twisted Spire, Wye Valley HPA and a guest from Hop & Stagger on handpump, 14 wines by the glass, quite a few gins and farm cider; background music, darts and board games. Staff are friendly and helpful. The airy dining room is in an oak-framed extension at the back with a homely medley of cushioned chairs and wooden tables on bare boards. The three bedrooms are comfortable and breakfasts are good. There are picnic-sets on the lawn and under trees in the orchard, and a children's play area.

A thoughtful choice of food includes sandwiches, black pudding scotch egg with tomato pickle and bacon crisp, omelette arnold bennett, caramelised red onion and goats cheese tart with basil pesto, chicken breast with wild mushroom and herb risotto and baby leeks, burger with skin-on chips, fillets of black bream with pancetta and mustard and tarragon sauce, duck breast with crushed potatoes and bitter orange jus, pork chop with champ potatoes, black pudding and mustard jus, and puddings such as banoffi pie with salted caramel ice-cream and buttermilk pannacotta with poached rhubarb and thyme biscuit crumble. *Benchmark main dish: home-made pies £14.95. Two-course evening meal £19.00.*

Free house ~ Licensees Mark Harris and Sarah Cowley ~ Real ale ~ Open 12-3, 6-11; 12-11 Sat; 12-10 Sun ~ Bar food 12-2.30, 6-9; 12-3, 6-9.30 Sat; 12-4.30 Sun ~ Restaurant ~ Children welcome ~ Dogs allowed in bar and bedrooms ~ Wi-fi ~ Bedrooms. /£75
Recommended by Amy and Luke Buchanan, Emily and Toby Archer, George Sanderson

NORTON
Hundred House ♀ ⇋
SJ7200 Map 4

(01952) 730353 – www.hundredhouse.co.uk
A442 Telford–Bridgnorth; TF11 9EE

Family-run inn with rambling rooms, open fires, quite a choice of drinks and good food; large, comfortable bedrooms

The lovely garden behind this carefully kept, family-run inn has old-fashioned roses, herbaceous plants and a big working herb garden (with around 50 varieties); they've also got a rescue donkey too. The rambling bar rooms have log fires in handsome fireplaces (one has a great Jacobean arch with fine old black cooking pots) and a variety of interesting chairs and settles with long colourful patchwork leather cushions around sewing machine tables. Hops and huge bunches of dried flowers and herbs hang from beams, and bunches of fresh flowers brighten the tables and counter in the neatly kept bar. Steps lead up past a little balustrade to a partly panelled eating area, where the stripped brickwork looks older than it does elsewhere. Three Tuns Rantipole plus changing guests such as Heritage Victoria Pale Ale, Marstons Pedigree and Sadlers Boris Citrov on handpump, 12 wines by the glass, a dozen malt whiskies and a farm cider; background music. The bedrooms have antique four-posters or half-testers, Victorian-style baths and rain showers, and their trademark velvet-cushioned swing.

Enjoyable food includes chicken liver pâté with onion chutney, black pudding, apple and chorizo stack with smoked cheese sauce, roast butternut squash, thyme and ricotta tart with courgettes and sun-dried tomatoes, herb-crusted hake fillet with creamy fish sauce, chicken breast stuffed with emmental cheese and ham with leek and parsnip potato cake and mushroom sauce, venison pudding with juniper sauce, smoked duck breast and duck croquette with potato purée and blueberry port sauce, and puddings such as raspberry crème brûlée and pears poached in red wine, cinnamon and star anise with vanilla ice-cream. *Benchmark main dish: local sirloin steak £19.95. Two-course evening meal £23.00.*

Free house ~ Licensees Henry, Stuart and David Phillips ~ Real ale ~ Open 11-11 ~
Bar food 12-2.30, 6-9; 12-9 Sun ~ Restaurant ~ Children welcome ~ Dogs allowed in bar
and bedrooms ~ Wi-fi ~ Bedrooms: £75/£85 *Recommended by R T and J C Moggridge,
Peter and Emma Kelly, Chloe and Tim Hodge*

SHIPLEY   SO8095   Map 4

Inn at Shipley ♀ ◗

(01902) 701639 – www.brunningandprice.co.uk/innatshipley
Bridgnorth Road; A454 W of Wolverhampton; WV6 7EQ

Light and airy country pub – a good all-rounder

Several woodburning stoves and log fires surround the central bar in this
handsome 18th-c building – one in a big inglenook in a cosy, traditionally
tiled black-beamed end room and another by a welcoming set of wing and
other leather armchairs. All sorts of dining chairs are grouped around a
variety of well buffed tables in the rambling rooms, rugs are set on polished
boards, attractive pictures are hung frame-to-frame and big windows let in
plenty of daylight; church candles, careful spotlighting and chandeliers add
atmosphere. The various areas are interconnected but manage to also feel
distinct and individual; upstairs is a separate private dining room. Phoenix
Brunning & Price Original, Salopian Oracle and Three Tuns XXX and three
quickly changing guest ales on handpump, 17 wines by the glass, 80 malt
whiskies, 70 gins and two farm ciders; good neatly dressed staff, background
music and board games. There are plenty of sturdy tables outside, some on
a sizeable terrace with a side awning, others by weeping willows on the main
lawn behind the car park, more on smaller lawns around the building.

Contemporary food includes sandwiches, beetroot pannacotta with crumbled
goats cheese and basil dressing, seared scallops with celeriac purée and pig cheek
fritters, king prawn and clam spaghetti with white wine, cream, chilli and garlic sauce,
chicken, ham hock and leek pie, courgette, red pepper and manchego cheese fritters
with roasted mediterranean vegetables and romesco sauce, duck breast with confit duck
leg croquette, braised chicory and cherry sauce, sea bass fillets with mussels, clams and
samphire in white wine sauce and saffron potatoes, and puddings such as hot waffle
with glazed bananas and banoffi ice-cream and bread and butter pudding with apricot
sauce and clotted cream. *Benchmark main dish: slow-braised lamb shoulder with
dauphinoise potatoes, carrot purée and rosemary gravy £17.25. Two-course evening
meal £21.50.*

Brunning & Price ~ Manager Oliver Parrish ~ Real ale ~ Open 10.30am-11pm (10.30pm
Sun) ~ Bar food 12-10 (9.30 Sun) ~ Restaurant ~ Children welcome ~ Dogs allowed in
bar ~ Wi-fi *Recommended by Lynda and Trevor Smith, Edward Nile, Sandra and Michael Smith,
Patricia Healey*

SHREWSBURY   SJ4812   Map 6

Armoury ♀ ◗

(01743) 340525 – www.brunningandprice.co.uk/armoury
Victoria Quay, Victoria Avenue; SY1 1HH

**Vibrant atmosphere in interestingly converted riverside warehouse
with tempting all-day food**

The good food, fantastic range of drinks and buzzy atmosphere all come in
for high praise at this large, airy 18th-c former warehouse. The spacious
open-plan interior has long runs of big arched windows with views across
the broad River Severn – but, despite its size, it also has a personal feel,
helped by the eclectic décor, furniture layout and cheerful bustle. A mix of

wood tables and chairs are grouped on stripped-wood floors, the huge brick walls display floor-to-ceiling books or masses of old prints mounted edge-to-edge, and there's a grand stone fireplace at one end. Colonial-style fans whirr away on the ceilings, which are supported by green-painted columns, and small wall-mounted glass cabinets display smokers' pipes. Phoenix Brunning & Price Original, Longden The Golden Arrow, Salopian Oracle, Woods Shropshire Lad and a couple of guest beers on handpump, 17 wines by the glass, 100 malt whiskies, 30 gins, lots of rums and vodkas, a variety of brandies and a farm cider. The hanging baskets are quite a sight in summer. The pub doesn't have its own car park, but there are plenty of parking places nearby.

Highly regarded food includes sandwiches, potted smoked trout with shrimp butter, samphire and fennel, braised pig cheek with apple and cider purée and crackling, wild mushroom ravioli with sautéed mushrooms and leeks and sherry reduction, local pork sausages with mash and onion gravy, steak in ale pudding, lamb rump with lyonnaise potatoes, roasted plums, carrot purée and redcurrant minted jus, malaysian fish stew, coq au vin, and puddings such as jam roly-poly with custard and lemon meringue cheesecake with raspberry ripple ice-cream. *Benchmark main dish: beer-battered fish and chips £13.45. Two-course evening meal £21.00.*

Brunning & Price ~ Manager Emily Periam ~ Real ale ~ Open 10.30am-11pm (midnight Fri, Sat; 10.30pm Sun) ~ Bar food 12-10 (9.30 Sun) ~ Children welcome but not after 7.30pm Fri, Sat ~ Dogs allowed in bar ~ Wi-fi *Recommended by Steve Whalley, Claire Adams, Sandra Hollies, Michael Butler, Usha and Terry Patel, Gill and Hugh Bennett*

SHREWSBURY
Lion & Pheasant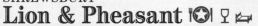

SJ4912   Map 6

(01743) 770345 – www.lionandpheasant.co.uk
Follow City Centre signposts across the English Bridge; SY1 1XJ

Shropshire Dining Pub of the Year

Civilised bar and upstairs restaurant in comfortable, neatly updated and well placed inn; bedrooms

Original features in this thoughtfully run 16th-c inn blend seamlessly with more contemporary touches, making the décor throughout extremely appealing. The big-windowed bar consists of three linked levels, the lowest of which has armchairs on dark flagstones by a big inglenook; elsewhere, there's a cushioned settee or two, but most of the seats are at sturdy stripped tables on dark floorboards. A few modern paintings, plentiful flowers and church candles brighten up the restrained cream and grey décor, as do the friendly staff and background music. Hobsons Best Bitter, Salopian Oracle and Three Tuns XXX on handpump and 14 wines by the glass. Off quite a warren of corridors, the restaurant is in the older back part of the building with beams and timbering (you can eat from the restaurant menu in the bar too). Outside, there are seats and tables under parasols with olive trees and flowering pots dotted about. This is a lovely place to stay in comfortable rooms – some of which provide glimpses of the River Severn below the nearby English Bridge – and breakfasts are good.

Imaginative food includes lunchtime sandwiches, rabbit gala pie with pickled vegetables, mustard mayonnaise and tarragon and apricot jam, charred mackerel with goats milk yoghurt, fennel, pomegranate and rye crumble, omelette arnold bennett, smoked artichokes, baby leeks and king oyster mushrooms with grilled halloumi and chestnut, truffle and leek sauce, pork fillet with beer-glazed pig cheeks, potato mousse, turnip, spinach, figs and crackling and a bacon and shallot crumb, butter-poached turbot with tortellini, spring vegetables, crayfish cream sauce and lemon thyme oil, and puddings such as chocolate délice with salted caramel chocolate, caramelised pecan and condensed milk ice-cream and lemon tart with pink peppercorn and dill iced parfait, italian meringue and blood orange; they also offer a two- and three-course set menu and afternoon tea (until 4.30pm). *Benchmark main dish: rib-eye steak with a choice of sauces* £24.00. Two-course evening meal £24.00.

Free house ~ Licensee Jim Littler ~ Real ale ~ Open 10am-11pm ~ Bar food 12-2.30, 6-9.30 ~ Restaurant ~ Children welcome ~ Wi-fi ~ Bedrooms: £99/£119
Recommended by Peter Harrison, Isobel Mackinlay, Edward May, Julia and Fiona Barnes

---

Also Worth a Visit in Shropshire

Besides the fully inspected pubs, you might like to try these pubs that have been recommended to us and described by readers. Do tell us what you think of them: feedback@goodguides.com

ADMASTON   SJ6313
Pheasant (01952) 251989
Shawbirch Road; TF5 0AD Red-brick Victorian pub with locally sourced food (all day Sat, till 7pm Sun), three or four well kept ales including Salopian and Woods; Thurs quiz; children welcome, garden with picnic-sets and play area, open all day. *(Nick Higgins)*

BISHOP'S CASTLE   SO3288
★**Castle Hotel** (01588) 638403
Market Square, just off B4385; SY9 5BN Substantial coaching inn at top of lovely market town, clubby little beamed and panelled bar with log fire, larger rooms off with big Victorian engravings and another fire, well kept Hobsons, Six Bells and Three Tuns, local cider, ten wines by the glass (maybe one from nearby vineyard) and some 30 malt whiskies, popular food served by friendly staff, handsome panelled dining room; background music, darts and board games; children and dogs welcome, pretty hanging baskets at front, garden behind with terrace seating, pergolas and climbing plants, surrounding walks, 12 spacious bedrooms, good breakfast, useful big car park, open all day. *(Mr and Mrs D J Nash)*

BISHOP'S CASTLE   SO3288
★**Six Bells** (01588) 630144
Church Street; SY9 5AA Friendly 17th-c pub with character landlord and own-brew beers (microbrewery tours available); smallish no-frills bar with mix of well worn furniture, old local photographs and prints, bigger room with stripped-stone walls, benches around plain tables on bare boards and inglenook woodburner, country wines and summer cider, July beer festival, sandwiches only lunchtimes Mon-Sat, good value home-made food Thurs-Sat evenings including themed nights, Sun roast; no credit cards; well behaved children and dogs welcome, café in brewery, open all day. *(Patricia Healey)*

BISHOP'S CASTLE   SO3288
★**Three Tuns** (01588) 638797
Salop Street; SY9 5BW Extended old pub adjacent to unique four-storey Victorian brewhouse (a brewery is said to have existed here since 1642); busy chatty atmosphere in public, lounge and snug bars, Three Tuns beers (including 1642) from old-fashioned handpumps (cheaper 5-7pm Fri), several wines by the glass, tasty good value food (not Sun evening) from sandwiches up, friendly young staff, modernised dining room done out in smart oak and glass; lots going on including film club, music nights, July beer festival and maybe morris men or brass band in the courtyard garden; children and dogs welcome, open all day. *(Mike and Eleanor Anderson, Michael Butler)*

BOULDON   SO5485
Tally Ho (01584) 841811
W end of village, set back from road; SY7 9DP Welcoming tucked-away pub owned by group of villagers; good local beers such as Hobsons and Ludlow, enjoyable fairly priced food from sandwiches and light meals up, service with a smile, rugs on quarry tiles, woodburner in big stone fireplace, various pictures and other memorabilia; some traditional games; children and dogs welcome, country views from nice garden with sturdy furniture, open all day weekends, closed Mon lunchtime. *(Michael Butler)*

BRIDGES   SO3996
★**Bridges** (01588) 650260
Pub signed from Pulverbatch–Wentnor road, W of Ratlinghope; SY5 0ST Old renovated beamed country pub owned by Three Tuns with their full range in excellent condition, bare-boards bar to right, large dining room to left, woodburner, enjoyable fairly traditional home-made food including daily specials, helpful friendly staff; occasional live music; children and well behaved dogs welcome, tables out by little River Onny (some on raised deck), bedrooms, also camping and youth hostel

nearby, great walking country, open (and food) all day. *(Peter and Emma Kelly)*

BRIDGNORTH SO6890

★**Down** (01746) 789539

The Down; B4364 Ludlow Road 3 miles S; WV16 6UA Good value roadside dining pub overlooking rolling countryside, enjoyable food (all day weekends) including popular daily carvery, efficient friendly service, a house beer (Down & Out) from Three Tuns and a couple of local guests; background music; children welcome, nine comfortable bedrooms, open all day. *(Christopher May)*

BRIDGNORTH SO7193

Kings Head (01746) 762141

Whitburn Street; WV16 4QN 17th-c timbered coaching inn with high-raftered back stable bar, popular food from well balanced menu including some good vegetarian options, friendly helpful staff, Hobsons and Wye Valley plus a couple of guests, winter mulled wine, log fires, beams and flagstones, pretty leaded windows; children and dogs welcome, courtyard tables, open all day. *(Christopher May)*

BRIDGNORTH SO7192

★**Railwaymans Arms** (01746) 760920

Severn Valley Railway station, Hollybush Road (off A458 towards Stourbridge); WV16 5DT Bathams, Hobsons and plenty of other well kept ales in chatty old-fashioned converted waiting room at Severn Valley steam railway terminus, bustling on summer days; old station signs and train nameplates, superb mirror over fireplace; snacky food such as pork pies; children and dogs welcome, wheelchair access with help, tables out on platform – the train to Kidderminster (station bar there too) has an all-day bar and bookable Sun lunches, open all day. *(Christopher May)*

BRIDGNORTH SO7192

White Lion (01746) 763962

West Castle Street; WV16 4AB Fairly compact 18th-c two-bar pub with seven well kept ales including own Hop & Stagger brews, Thatcher's cider, reasonably priced bar food such as home-made scotch eggs and butcher-made pies, friendly helpful staff, comfortable carpeted lounge with open fire; regular events including folk club (first Tues of month), storytelling (second Tues) and charity quiz (last Tues); children and dogs welcome, lawned garden with terrace, four good value clean bedrooms (no breakfast), open all day. *(Dave Braisted)*

BRIDGNORTH SO7093

Woodberry (01746) 762950

Victoria Road/Sydney Cottage Drive; WV16 4LF Welcoming dining inn with good choice of enjoyable locally sourced food, ales such as Battlefield

and Hobsons, friendly efficient service; background music, free wi-fi; children welcome, large garden with benches, comfortable bedrooms, good breakfast, open (and food) all day. *(Nick Higgins)*

BROMFIELD SO4877

★**Clive** (01584) 856565

A49, 2 miles NW of Ludlow; SY8 2JR Sophisticated minimalist bar-restaurant taking its name from Clive of India who once lived here; emphasis mainly on the imaginative well presented food (all day weekends) but also Hobsons and Ludlow ales, several wines by the glass and a bar menu, welcoming well trained staff, dining room with light wood tables, door to sparsely furnished bar with metal chairs, glass-topped tables and sleek counter, step down to room with soaring beams and rafters, exposed stonework and woodburner in huge fireplace; background music, free wi-fi; children welcome, tables under parasols on secluded terrace, garden with children's play area, fish pond, 15 stylish bedrooms, good breakfast, open all day. *(Chloe and Tim Hodge)*

BUCKNELL SO3574

★**Baron** (01547) 530549

Chapel Lawn Road; just off B4367 Knighton Road; SY7 0AH Modernised family-owned country inn, friendly and efficiently run, with enjoyable good value home-made food from panini and pizzas up, well kept Ludlow and Wye Valley, log fire in carpeted front bar, back pitched-roof dining room with small gallery, old cider press and grindstone, conservatory; free wi-fi; children welcome, peaceful setting with lovely views from big garden, five bedrooms plus three new garden rooms, open all day Sat, till 6pm Sun, closed lunchtimes Mon-Thurs. *(Brian and Jacky Wilson)*

BURLTON SJ4526

Burlton Inn (01939) 270284

A528 Shrewsbury–Ellesmere, near B4397 junction; SY4 5TB Welcoming attractively updated 18th-c inn under newish management; enjoyable pubby food and well kept Robinsons ales (maybe a guest), friendly helpful staff, beams, timbers and log fires, comfortable snug, restaurant with garden room; children and dogs (in bar) welcome, disabled access/facilities, teak furniture on pleasant terrace, six comfortable well equipped bedrooms, open all day Sun (food till 7pm). *(Phil and Margaret Walker)*

BURWARTON SO6185

★**Boyne Arms** (01746) 787214

B4364 Bridgnorth–Ludlow; WV16 6QH Handsome Georgian coaching inn with welcoming cheerful staff, enjoyable generous food (not Sun evening, Mon) including good value deals and Fri steak night, up to three real ales such as Enville and Timothy Taylors, Robinson's and Thatcher's cider, decent coffee, separate restaurant and public bar (dogs allowed here), function room with pool and other games; children welcome, good timber adventure playground in pretty garden, hitching rail for horses, open all day weekends, closed Mon lunchtime. *(Christopher May)*

CHURCH STRETTON   SO4593
Bucks Head (01694) 722898
High Street; SY6 6BX Old town pub with several good-sized modernised areas including restaurant, up to four well kept Marstons ales and guests, decent good value pubby food plus vegetarian options, friendly attentive staff, black beams and timbers, mixed dark wood tables and chairs; newspapers, sports TV, free wi-fi; garden with picnic-sets, four bedrooms, open all day (till 1am Fri, Sat). *(Nick Higgins)*

CHURCH STRETTON   SO4593
Housmans (01694) 724441
High Street; SY6 6BX Buzzing and welcoming restaurant-bar with good wine and cocktail lists plus a couple of well kept ales from Three Tuns, nice range of food including tapas-style sharing plates and specials, local art on walls; occasional live jazz and other acoustic music; children welcome, open all day weekends. *(Jake)*

CLAVERLEY   SO8095
Woodman (01746) 710553
B4176/Danford Lane; WV5 7DG Rural 19th-c red-brick dining pub; contemporary beamed interior arranged around central bar, good popular food (must book) making use of local produce including some from farm opposite, well kept Black Sheep and Enville, lots of wines by the glass and interesting range of gins, efficient service; terrace and garden tables, closed Sun evening, Mon. *(Patricia Healey)*

CLUN   SO3080
Sun (01588) 640559
High Street; SY7 8JB Beamed and timbered 15th-c pub in peaceful village surrounded by lovely rolling countryside; traditional flagstoned public bar with woodburner in inglenook, larger carpeted lounge, four well kept Three Tuns ales and enjoyable home-made food (not Sun evening) from lunchtime sandwiches up, friendly helpful staff; children (in snug), walkers and dogs (in bar) welcome, paved back terrace, four bedrooms (some in converted outbuildings), open all day Fri-Sun, closed lunchtimes Mon-Thurs. *(Nick Higgins)*

CLUNTON   SO3381
Crown (01588) 660265
B4368; SY7 0HU Welcoming old country local with three well kept ales including Hobsons and Stonehouse, enjoyable generously served food cooked by landlord (Thurs-Sat evenings), also popular Weds fish

and chips and good value Sun lunch, log fire in cosy flagstoned bar, dining room, games room with TV; folk night last Mon of month; small garden, open all day Fri-Sun, closed lunchtimes other days. *(Chloe and Tim Hodge)*

COALPORT   SJ6902
Shakespeare (01952) 580675
High Street; TF8 7HT Welcoming early 19th-c inn by pretty Severn gorge; timbering, bare stone walls and tiled floors, well kept Everards, Hobsons, Ludlow and a guest, good value generously served food from sandwiches through pub standards to international dishes; children welcome, picnic-sets in tiered garden with play area, handy for Coalport China Museum, four bedrooms, open all day weekends, closed weekdays till 5pm. *(Sam Cole)*

CORFTON   SO4985
Sun (01584) 861239
B4368 Much Wenlock–Craven Arms; SY7 9DF Lived-in unchanging three-room country local with own good Corvedale ales (including an unfined beer), friendly long-serving landlord often busy in the back brewery, decent pubby food from baguettes to steaks, lots of breweriana, basic quarry-tiled public bar with darts, pool and juke box, quieter carpeted lounge, dining room with covered well; children and dogs (in bar) welcome, good wheelchair access throughout and disabled loos, tables on terrace and in large garden with good play area. *(Robert W Buckle)*

ELLERDINE HEATH   SJ6122
Royal Oak (01939) 250300
Hazles Road; TF6 6RL Friendly little country pub known locally as the Tiddly (Wink), half a dozen well kept ales and good value straightforward food (not Mon, Tues), open fires; folk night third Tues of the month, pool; children and dogs welcome, good sized garden, open all day. *(Patricia Healey)*

ELLESMERE   SJ3034
Red Lion (01691) 622632
Church Street; SY12 0HD Popular and welcoming 16th-c coaching inn next to church; ample helpings of good value tasty food from sandwiches up, OAP deal Mon-Sat, Thwaites ales, friendly helpful service; children welcome, comfortable bedrooms (courtyard ones suitable for disabled), good breakfast, open (and food) all day. *(John Wooll)*

GRINDLEY BROOK   SJ5242
Horse & Jockey (01948) 662723
A41; SY13 4QJ Extended 19th-c roadside pub with enjoyable good value food from varied menu, friendly helpful service, eight well kept ales including a house beer from Woods named after resident chocolate labrador Blaze, teas and coffees, well divided open-plan interior with mix of furniture on

wood or carpeted floors, woodburners and some interesting bits and pieces; sports TV, pool; children, dogs and muddy boots welcome, play area on side lawn, handy for Sandstone Trail and Llangollen Canal, open (and food) all day. *(Mike and Wena Stevenson)*

HIGHLEY   SO7483
Ship (01746) 861219
Severnside; WV16 6NU Refurbished 18th-c inn set in lovely riverside location, good pubby food including popular Sun carvery, five real ales such as Banks's, Hobsons and Thwaites; children welcome, disabled access and facilities, tables on raised front deck, handy for Severn Way walks (and Severn Valley Railway), fishing rights, bedrooms and nearby camping, open all day. *(Stephen Shepherd)*

HINDFORD   SJ3333
Jack Mytton (01691) 679861
Village and pub signed from A495; SY11 4NL Refurbished canalside pub with opened-up interior, log-fire bar, lounge, raftered dining room and conservatory, four local ales including a house beer (Growling Bear) from Joules, over 40 gins and some interesting whiskies, well executed pub food including burgers and grills, friendly service; background music, free wi-fi; children and dogs welcome, wheelchair access via side door, disabled loo, picnic-sets in waterside garden, good-sized courtyard with carved bear (pub is named after an eccentric local squire who rode a bear), outside bar (Mar-Oct), moorings and good canalside walks, open all day summer (all day Fri-Sun, closed lunchtimes Mon-Thurs in winter). *(Mike and Wena Stevenson)*

HOPE   SJ3401
Stables (01743) 891344
Just off A488 3 miles S of Minsterley; SY5 0EP Hidden-away little 17th-c beamed country pub (former drovers' inn) under new ownership, friendly and welcoming, with good home-made food and a couple of well kept ales such as Three Tuns XXX, log fires; dogs welcome, fine views from garden, two bedrooms and a shepherd's hut, open all day weekends, closed weekday lunchtimes. *(Christopher May)*

HOPTON WAFERS   SO6376
Crown (01299) 270372
A4117; DY14 0NB Attractive 16th-c creeper-clad inn, comfortably lived-in with beams and inglenook, good food (all day Sun) in three separate dining areas, weekday set deal lunchtime/early evening, ales such as Ludlow and Wye Valley, good choice of wines and decent coffee, cheerful helpful staff, relaxed atmosphere; free wi-fi;

children and dogs welcome, inviting garden with terraces, duck pond and stream, 18 bedrooms (eight in new adjoining building), open all day. *(Sam Cole)*

KNOCKIN   SJ3322
Bradford Arms (01691) 682358
B4396 NW of Shrewsbury; SY10 8HJ Sizeable neatly kept village local with notable three-faced roof clock, popular good value pubby food (best to book) and well kept Marstons-related beers, friendly welcoming staff, games rooms; TV, free wi-fi; children and dogs welcome, garden behind by car park, open (and food) all day. *(Nick Higgins)*

LEEBOTWOOD   SO4798
★ Pound (01694) 751477
A49 Church Stretton–Shrewsbury; SY6 6ND Thatched cruck-framed building dating from 1458 – thought to be oldest in the village; stylishly modern bar rooms with minimalist fixtures and wooden furnishings, enjoyable interesting food cooked by chef-owner from light meals up, also pub favourites, a couple of real ales from Ludlow and nice wines by the glass, friendly efficient service; background music; seats on flagstoned terrace, disabled parking (level access to bar), closed Sun evening, Mon and Tues. *(Chloe and Tim Hodge)*

LEIGHTON   SJ6105
Kynnersley Arms (01952) 510233
B4380; SY5 6RN Victorian building built on remains of ancient corn mill; coal fire and woodburner in main opened-up area, armchairs and sofas in back part with stairs to lower level containing mill machinery (there's also a 17th-c blast furnace), five well kept mainly local ales including Salopian Shropshire Gold, Three Tuns XXX and a guest, traditional food along with pizzas and pasta dishes, Sun carvery, friendly helpful staff; background and occasional live music, regular quiz, sports TV, pool, free wi-fi; children and dogs welcome, good walks nearby, open all day. *(Nick Higgins)*

LEINTWARDINE   SO4175
★ Jolly Frog (01547) 540298
A4113 Ludlow–Knighton, E edge of village; The Toddings; SY7 0LX Cheerful well run place (more bar-bistro than pub) in glorious countryside; front bar with just a few tables on light oak boards, check tablecloths and red leatherette dining chairs, woodburner at each end and frenchified décor (kepis and other hats hanging from stripped beams, Paris street signs and a Metro map), similarly furnished dining room up a few steps, ales such as Otter and Three Tuns, nice wines by the glass and good food from wood-fired pizzas to fresh fish/seafood,

---

Post Office address codings confusingly give the impression that some pubs are in Shropshire, when they're really in Cheshire (which is where we list them).

friendly professional staff; background music, free wi-fi; children welcome, inner courtyard with tables under sail canopy, more seating on upper deck with wide pastoral views, closed Mon. *(Michael Butler, Frank Price)*

LITTLE STRETTON   SO4491

★**Green Dragon** (01694) 722925
Village well signed off A49 S of Church Stretton; Ludlow Road; SY6 6RE Popular village pub at the foot of Long Mynd; wide choice of good reasonably priced food from sandwiches and sharing boards up in bar or adjacent dining area (well behaved children allowed here), well kept Bass, Hobsons, Ludlow, Salopian, Wye Valley and a guest, proper cider, friendly efficient staff, cosy beamed interior with warm woodburner, area for muddy paws and boots; tables outside and play area, handy for Carding Mill Valley (NT), open (and food) all day. *(John Watson, Brian Glozier)*

LITTLE STRETTON   SO4492

★**Ragleth** (01694) 722711
Village well signed off A49 S of Church Stretton; Ludlow Road; SY6 6RB Characterful opened-up 17th-c dining pub; light and airy bay-windowed front bar with eclectic mix of old tables and chairs, some exposed brick and timber work, huge inglenook in heavily beamed brick and tile-floored public bar, four mainly local beers such as Hobsons, good food including plenty of fish dishes, cheerful attentive owners and staff; background music, TV, darts and board games; children welcome, dogs in bar, lovely garden with tulip tree-shaded lawn and good play area, thatched and timbered church and fine hill walks nearby, open all day Sat (summer) and Sun.
(Mr and Mrs D J Nash, Bernard Stradling)

LITTLE WENLOCK   SJ6507

Huntsman (01952) 503300
Wellington Road; TF6 5BH Welcoming modernised village pub, enjoyable food (till 7pm Sun) from lunchtime ciabattas and pub standards up, four well kept/priced changing ales and good selection of wines, black beamed bar with stone floor and central log fire, carpeted restaurant with high-backed upholstered chairs at light wood tables and woodburner in big fireplace; occasional live music; children and dogs (in bar) welcome, terrace seating, bedrooms, handy for Wrekin walks, open (and food) all day. *(Mr and Mrs D J Nash)*

LUDLOW   SO5174

Blue Boar (01584) 878989
Mill Street; SY8 1BB Recently renovated former coaching inn with lots of linked areas, well kept ales such as Black Sheep, Hobsons and Three Tuns, good choice of wines by the glass and enjoyable well priced home-made food (not Sun evening), friendly staff; upstairs live music, book club first

Thurs of month, quiz third Thurs; children and dogs welcome, back suntrap courtyard, bedrooms, open all day. *(Roy and Gill Payne)*

LUDLOW   SO5174

Queens (01584) 879177
Lower Galdeford; SY8 1RU Welcoming and popular 19th-c family-run pub, good reasonably priced food with emphasis on fresh local produce (booking advised, particularly Sun lunchtime), four well kept ales including Hobsons, Ludlow and Wye Valley, helpful friendly service, long narrow oak-floor bar, steps down to vaulted-ceiling dining area; some live music; children welcome (not in bar after 6pm), dogs allowed in one area, modern seating on enclosed deck, courtyard accommodation, open all day. *(Roy and Gill Payne)*

MAESBURY   SJ3026

Original Ball (01691) 654880
Maesbury Road; SY10 8HB Old brick-built pub with hefty beams and woodburner in central fireplace, Marstons Pedigree, Stonehouse Station Bitter and a guest, decent wines and enjoyable reasonably priced pub food (not Mon) including weekday deals and Sun carvery, friendly helpful staff; some live music, TV, pool; children and dogs welcome, open all day weekends, from 4pm other days. *(Ben and Jenny Settle)*

MARKET DRAYTON   SJ6734

Red Lion (01630) 652602
Great Hales Street; TF9 1JP Extended 17th-c coaching inn acting as tap for Joules Brewery; back entrance to attractive modern bar with light wood floor and substantial oak timbers, traditional dark-beamed part to the right, updated but keeping original features, with pubby furniture on flagstones, brewery mirrors and signs, woodburner, more breweriana in dining/function room to left featuring 'Mousey' Thompson carved oak panelling and fireplace; Joules Blonde, Green Monkey, Pale Ale, Slumbering Monk and a seasonal beer (tasting trays available), good selection of wines, fairly standard home-made food (all day Fri-Sun) including Sun carvery till 4pm; some live music; picnic-sets outside, brewery tours 7pm Mon-Thurs, open all day. *(Jacqui and Alan Swan)*

MARTON   SJ2802

★**Sun** (01938) 561211
B4386 NE of Chirbury; SY21 8JP Welcoming family-run dining pub, clean and neatly kept, with high standard of cooking including seasonal game and good fresh fish, light and airy black-beamed bar with comfortable sofa and traditional furnishings, woodburner in big stone fireplace, Hobsons Best and several wines by the glass, chunky pale tables and ladder-back chairs in restaurant; children welcome, dogs in bar (but do ask first),

front terrace, closed Sun evening, Mon and lunchtimes Tues and Wed. *(Nick Higgins)*

MUCH WENLOCK   SO6299
Gaskell Arms (01952) 727212
High Street (A458); TF13 6AQ 17th-c coaching inn with comfortable old-fashioned lounge divided by two-way woodburner, brassware and prints, three well kept ales such as Swan, Three Tuns and Wye Valley, enjoyable straightforward food served by friendly attentive staff, civilised beamed restaurant and separate locals' bar; background music, free wi-fi; well behaved children allowed, no dogs, disabled facilities, spacious walled garden behind with terrace, 14 bedrooms, open all day. *(Christopher May)*

MUCH WENLOCK   SO6299
★George & Dragon (01952) 727312
High Street (A458); TF13 6AA Busy town pub filled with fascinating collection of pub paraphernalia – old brewery and cigarette advertisements, bottle labels, beer trays and George and the Dragon pictures, also 200 jugs hanging from beams; main quarry-tiled room with antique settles and open fires in two attractive Victorian fireplaces, timbered back dining room, Greene King, Hobsons, St Austell and guest, big helpings of well priced food (not Weds or Sun evenings), good friendly service; background and some live music: children and dogs (in bar) welcome, pay-and-display car park behind, open all day. *(Mike and Wena Stevenson)*

MUNSLOW   SO5287
★Crown (01584) 841205
B4368 Much Wenlock–Craven Arms; SY7 9ET Former courthouse with imposing exterior and pretty back façade showing Tudor origins; lots of nooks and crannies, split-level lounge bar with old-fashioned mix of furnishings on broad flagstones, bread oven by log fire, another fire in traditional snug, eating area with more beams, flagstones and stripped stone, also upstairs restaurant (weekends only), good food from sandwiches and sharing boards through pub standards to restaurant dishes, popular Sun lunch, steak nights Tues and Weds, ales such as Otter, Three Tuns and Wye Valley, local bottled cider and nice wines, helpful efficient staff, friendly bustling atmosphere; background music; children welcome, level wheelchair access to bar only where dogs allowed, bedrooms, closed Sun evening, Mon. *(Robert W Buckle)*

NESSCLIFFE   SJ3819
Old Three Pigeons (01743) 741279
Off A5 Shrewsbury–Oswestry (now bypassed); SY4 1DB 16th-c pub with

two bar areas and restaurant, fairly priced food including fresh fish and plenty of daily specials, Thurs spanish evening and Tues burger night, well kept local ales (maybe one from on-site microbrewery), nice wines by the glass, black beams, wood floors and warm log fires; children and dogs (in bar) welcome, picnic-sets in garden with fountain and covered area, self-catering accommodation, opposite Kynaston's Cave, good cliff walks, open all day. *(Sam Cole)*

NEWPORT   SJ7419
New Inn (01952) 812295
Stafford Road; TF10 7LX Refurbished and extended Joules pub on crossroads, five of their ales and over 50 gins, good uncomplicated home-made food (not Sun evening) served by friendly staff, opened-up interior with some cosy corners, log fire and woodburner; live music Sun, beer and gin festivals; children and dogs welcome, picnic-sets under parasols on terrace and lawn, open all day. *(Mick Allen)*

PICKLESCOTT   SO4399
Bottle & Glass (01694) 751252
Off A49 N of Church Stretton; SY6 6NR Remote 17th-c country pub with plenty of character in quarry-tiled bar and lounge/dining areas, low black beams, oak panelling and log fires, assortment of old tables and chairs, good traditional home-made food (not Sun evening) from baps up, will cater for special diets, well kept ales such as Hobsons and Three Tuns, friendly helpful service; TV; children welcome, dogs in bar, seats out on raised front area, good walks, three bedrooms, open till 7pm Sun, closed Mon lunchtime (and evening winter). *(Revd Carol Avery)*

SHAWBURY   SJ5621
Fox & Hounds (01939) 250600
Wytheford Road; SY4 4JG Light and spacious 1960s pub, various opened-up areas including book-lined dining room with woodburner, rugs and assorted dark furniture on wood floors, cream-painted dados and lots of pictures, good fairly priced food from light lunches and sharing boards to daily specials, four or five well kept ales such as Greene King and Rowton, good choice of wines, efficient helpful service; free wi-fi; children welcome, picnic-sets on terrace and lawn, open (and food) all day. *(Nick Higgins)*

SHIFNAL   SJ74508
White Hart (01952) 461161
High Street; TF11 8BH Nine well kept interesting ales in chatty 17th-c timbered pub, quaint and old-fashioned with separate bar and lounge, good home-made

---

We include some hotels with a good bar that offers facilities comparable to those of a pub.

lunchtime food (not Sun), several wines by the glass, friendly welcoming staff; no credit cards; children and dogs (in bar) welcome, couple of steep steps at front door, back terrace and beer garden, open all day. *(Peter and Emma Kelly)*

SHREWSBURY SJ4912
Admiral Benbow (01743) 244423
Swan Hill; SY1 1NF Great choice of regional ales, also ciders and bottled belgian beers, friendly staff; free wi-fi; no children, beer garden behind, closed lunchtimes except Sat. *(Mick Allen)*

SHREWSBURY SJ4812
Boat House Inn (01743) 231658
New Street/Quarry Park; leaving centre via Welsh Bridge/A488 turn into Port Hill Road; SY3 8JQ Well positioned by footbridge to Severn park with river views from long bar and terrace tables; pastel blue panelling, painted tables and chairs on bare boards, some beams and timbering, log fire, well kept regional ales and enjoyable food from sandwiches to grills; background music, TV; children welcome, no dogs inside, summer bar on decked riverside terrace, open all day. *(Mick Allen)*

SHREWSBURY SJ4812
Bricklayers Arms (01743) 366032
Copthorne Road/Hafren Road; SY3 8NL Spotless 1930s suburban pub (walkable from the town centre) owned by Joules, their beers in top condition and generous helping of popular traditional food including good Sun lunch, cheerful efficient service, bare boards, panelling and open fire, screens and gleaming stained glass, one wall with examples of different bricklaying patterns; children and dogs welcome, picnic-sets out in front, open (and food) all day Thurs-Sun, from 4pm other days. *(Robert W Buckle, Mick Allen)*

SHREWSBURY SO4912
Coach & Horses (01743) 365661
Swan Hill/Cross Hill; SY1 1NF Relaxed beamed corner local off the beaten track; chatty panelled bar, cosy little side room and back dining lounge, well kept Salopian, Stonehouse and guests, real cider, happy hour (5-7pm Mon-Fri, 7-10pm Sun), enjoyable freshly made food including popular Sun carvery; background music; children allowed in dining room, dogs in bar, open all day. *(Michael Butler, Robert W Buckle)*

SHREWSBURY SJ4913
Dolphin (01743) 247005
A49 0.5 mile N of station; SY1 2EZ Traditionally refurbished little 19th-c pub with friendly welcoming staff and good mix

of regulars and visitors, well kept Joules and three guests, short choice of good bar snacks/simple meals, reasonable prices, original features including gas lighting, log fires; music and charity quiz nights, darts, free wi-fi; dogs welcome; seats on sunny back deck, open (and food) all day. *(Mick Allen)*

SHREWSBURY SJ4912
Loggerheads (01743) 360275
Church Street; SY1 1UG Chatty old-fashioned local with panelled back room, flagstones, scrubbed-top tables, high-backed settles and coal fire, three other rooms with lots of prints, bare boards and more flagstones, quaint linking corridor and hatch service for the half dozen well kept Marstons-related ales, no food, friendly service; weekly live folk music; dogs welcome (in some areas), open all day. *(Nick Higgins)*

SHREWSBURY SJ4912
Nags Head (01743) 362455
Wyle Cop; SY1 1XB Attractive old two-room pub, small, unpretentious and welcoming, with good range of well kept ales such as Hobsons and Wye Valley, no food; TV, juke box; dogs welcome, remains of ancient timbered building (used as a smokers' shelter) and garden behind, open all day (till 1am Fri). *(Nick Higgins)*

SHREWSBURY SJ4812
Shrewsbury Hotel (01743) 236203
Mardol/Mardol Quay; SY1 1PU Refurbished partly open-plan Wetherspoons (former coaching inn) opposite the river, seven well kept/priced ales and their usual good value food, helpful friendly service; TVs for subtitled news, free wi-fi; children welcome, tables out in front, 22 bedrooms (residents' car park), open all day from 7am. *(Ian Phillips)*

SHREWSBURY SJ4912
★Three Fishes (01743) 344793
Fish Street; SY1 1UR Timbered and heavily beamed 16th-c pub in quiet cobbled street, small tables on flagstones around three sides of central bar, old pictures, half a dozen well kept beers from mainstream and smaller brewers, good value wines and enjoyable fairly priced food (not Sun) from baguettes to blackboard specials, good friendly service even when busy; free wi-fi; dogs welcome, open all day Fri-Sun. *(Mick Allen)*

STIPERSTONES SJ3600
★Stiperstones Inn (01743) 791327
Village signed off A488 S of Minsterley; SY5 0LZ Cosy traditional pub useful for a post-walk drink – some stunning hikes on Long Mynd or up dramatic quartzite ridge

---

We say if we know a pub has background music.

of the Stiperstones; small carpeted lounge with comfortable leatherette wall banquettes and lots of brassware on ply-panelled walls, plainer public bar with darts, TV and fruit machine, a couple of real ales such as Six Bells and Stonehouse, good value bar food usefully served all day, also afternoon teas with freshly baked cakes and home-made jams, friendly helpful service; background music; children and dogs (in bar and garden) welcome, two comfortable bedrooms, open all day. *(Ben and Jenny Settle)*

STOTTESDON SO6782
Fighting Cocks (01746) 718270
High Street; DY14 8TZ Welcoming old half-timbered community pub in unspoilt countryside; carpeted split-level interior with low ceilings and log fire, good home-made food using local produce, well kept Enville, Hobsons and a couple of guests, real ciders; regular live music; children and dogs welcome (their collie is Buddy), nice views from garden and good walks, small shop behind, open all day weekends, closed Mon. *(Don Beattie)*

UPTON MAGNA SJ5512
Haughmond (01743) 709918
Pelham Road; SY4 4TZ Welcoming refurbished village pub; log-fire bar with painted beams, oak-strip flooring and carpet, a house beer (Antler) brewed by Marstons and two local guests from brick servery, good food in brasserie including tasting menu, village shop/café; children and dogs (in bar) welcome, great view to the Wrekin from attractive back garden, handy for Haughmond Hill walks and Attingham Park (NT), five bedrooms named after deer, open all day weekends, closed Mon lunchtime. *(R T and J C Moggridge)*

WALL UNDER HEYWOOD SO5092
Plough (01694) 771833
B4371; SY6 7DS Welcoming country pub with good generously served food including Sun carvery, five well kept ales such as Thwaites, Ludlow and Wye Valley, log fire and various odds and ends in small front bar, snug with darts, comfortable 'piano' lounge and dining conservatory; live music including Sun lunchtime jazz; children and dogs welcome, tables in back garden, good local walks, open all day. *(Patricia Healey)*

WELLINGTON SJ6511
Cock (01952) 244954
Holyhead Road (B5061 – former A5); TF1 2DL Welcoming 18th-c coaching inn with well kept Hobsons and five quickly changing guests usually from small breweries, handpulled cider and extensive range of bottled beers; friendly helpful staff, some food such as pies, big fireplace; free wi-fi; dogs welcome, beer garden with covered area, bedrooms, closed lunchtime Mon-Weds, otherwise open all day. *(Sam Cole)*

WELLINGTON SJ6410
Old Orleton (01952) 255011
Holyhead Road (B5061, off M54 junction 7); TF1 2HA Modernised 17th-c red-brick coaching inn with restaurant and bar, enjoyable varied choice of well presented food including vegetarian options and shorter good value Mon evening menu, a couple of Hobsons beers and Weston's cider, welcoming helpful staff; nice view of the Wrekin, ten well appointed comfortable bedrooms, good breakfast. *(Sam Cole)*

WELLINGTON SJ6411
Pheasant (01952) 260683
Market Street; TF1 1DT Town-centre pub under new management, one long room with seven well kept ales including Everards Tiger and up to three from own Rowton brewery, two real ciders and enjoyable good value lunchtime food served till 4pm (not Sun at the moment), friendly helpful staff; children and dogs welcome, disabled access and facilities, beer garden behind, open all day. *(Sam Cole, Christopher May)*

WELSHAMPTON SJ4335
Sun (01948) 710847
A495 Ellesmere–Whitchurch; SY12 0PH Extended roadside village pub with good choice of enjoyable reasonably priced food, Stonehouse Station Bitter and three guests, friendly helpful service; live music and quiz nights; children and dogs welcome, tables in fenced back garden, 15-minute walk to Llangollen/Shropshire Union Canal, three bedrooms, open (and food) all day. *(Peter and Emma Kelly)*

WHITCHURCH SJ5441
Black Bear (01948) 663800
High Street/Bargates; SY13 1AZ Black and white building opposite church (a pub since 1667), half a dozen well kept interesting beers including Stonehouse, enjoyable home-made food from open sandwiches up, characterful interior and good atmosphere; regular live music; children and dogs (in bar) welcome, beer garden behind, open all day weekends. *(Nick Higgins)*

WHITCHURCH SJ5441
Old Town Hall Vaults (01948) 662251
St Marys Street; SY13 1QU Red-brick 19th-c Joules local (birthplace of composer Sir Edward German), four of their ales and a guest, good value straightforward food from snacks up, main room divided into distinct areas with bar in one corner, oak panelling, stained glass, mirrors and signs, sturdy furniture including bench seating and cast-iron-framed tables, log fires, further room with glazed ceiling; outside listed gents'; dogs welcome, partly covered yard with barrel tables, open (and food) all day. *(Giles and Annie Francis)*

WHITCHURCH   SJ5345
Willey Moor Lock (01948) 663274
Tarporley Road; signed off A49 just
under 2 miles N; SY13 4HF Large
opened-up pub in picturesque spot by
Llangollen Canal; two log fires, low beams
and countless teapots and toby jugs,
cheerful chatty atmosphere, half a dozen
changing local ales and around 30 malt
whiskies, good value quickly served pub
food from sandwiches up; background
music, games machine, no credit cards
(debit cards accepted); children away
from bar, well behaved dogs in some areas,
terrace tables, secure garden with big
play area. *(Mike and Wena Stevenson)*

WISTANSTOW   SO4385
Plough (01588) 673251
Off A49 and A489 N of Craven
Arms; SY7 8DG Welcoming village
pub adjoining the Woods brewery, their
beers in peak condition and enjoyable
home-made food including daily specials
(all day Sat, till 7.30pm Sun), friendly
efficient service, smallish bar, airy
high-ceilinged modern restaurant and
games part with darts, dominoes and
pool; background music, sports TV,
free wi-fi; children and dogs (in bar)
welcome, some tables outside, open all
day Fri-Sun, closed Tues. *(Sam Cole)*

Somerset

KEY ★ Star Pub 🍽️ Top Quality Food 🍺 Great Beer
🍷 Good Wines £ Bargain Meals 🛏️ Good Bedrooms 🍴 Serves Food

 ASHCOTT   ST4337 Map 1
Ring o' Bells 🍺
(01458) 210232 – www.ringobells.com
High Street; pub well signed off A39 W of Street; TA7 9PZ

**Friendly village pub with homely décor in several bars,
separate restaurant, tasty bar food and changing local ales**

The long-serving family who run this traditional 18th-c pub welcome both
loyal regulars and visitors; as the RSPB Ham Wall reserve is nearby,
the place gets pretty busy, especially at lunchtime. The three main bars,
on different levels, are all comfortable, with maroon plush-topped stools,
cushioned mate's chairs and dark wooden pubby tables on patterned carpet,
horsebrasses along the bressumer beam above a big stone fireplace and a
growing collection of hand bells; background music. Changing local ales
include Black Bear Bitter and Black Tor Raven on handpump, eight wines
by the glass and local farm cider. There's also a separate restaurant, a skittle
alley/function room, and plenty of picnic-sets arranged both out on the
terrace and in the garden.

🍴 Pleasing food using local suppliers includes sandwiches, brie fritters with
cranberry sauce, grilled sardines, celery, almond and cashew nut roast with
cheese sauce, chicken with bacon, mozzarella and barbecue sauce, gammon with
egg or pineapple, pork escalope with apricot and brandy sauce, whole sole grilled
with lemon and parsley butter, lambs kidneys in sherry with bacon and mushrooms,
and puddings such as chocolate, orange and Cointreau pot and raspberry, white
chocolate and amaretto cheesecake. *Benchmark main dish: home-made pies £11.50.
Two-course evening meal £17.50.*

Free house ~ Licensees John and Elaine Foreman and John Sharman ~ Real ale ~
Open 12-3, 7-11; 12-3, 7-10.30 Sun ~ Bar food 12-2, 7-10 ~ Restaurant ~ Children welcome ~
Dogs allowed in bar ~ Wi-fi ~ Folk music first Sat and third Weds of month
Recommended by Edward May, Mr and Mrs J Watkins, Frank Willy, Dr A J and Mrs B A Tompsett

 BABCARY   ST5628 Map 2
Red Lion 🍷 🛏️
(01458) 223230 – www.redlionbabcary.co.uk
*Off A37 S of Shepton Mallett; 2 miles or so N of roundabout where A37 meets
A303 and A372; TA11 7ED*

**Thatched pub with comfortable rambling rooms, interesting food
and local beers and seats outside; bedrooms**

Once they've discovered this well run thatched inn, customers tend to come back on a regular basis. Several distinct areas work their way around the bar counter. To the left is a longish room with dark red walls, a squashy leather sofa and two winged armchairs around a low table by a woodburning stove – plus a few well spaced tables and captain's chairs. There are elegant rustic wall lights, clay pipes in a display cabinet, daily papers and magazines and board games. A more dimly lit public bar with lovely dark flagstones has a high-backed old settle and other more straightforward chairs; table skittles, board games and background music. In the good-sized dining room a large stone lion's head sits on a plinth above a large open fire, and tables and chairs are set on polished boards. Exmoor Gold, Otter Amber and Teignworthy Reel Ale on handpump, 18 wines by the glass, farm cider and cocktails. The Den, set in a pretty courtyard, has light modern furnishings and doubles as a party, wedding and conference venue. The long informal garden has a play area and plenty of seats. Bedrooms are comfortable and well equipped and the pub is handy for the Fleet Air Museum at Yeovilton, the Haynes Motor Museum in Sparkford and for shopping at Clarks Village in Street. Wheelchair access.

Well thought-of food includes sandwiches, venison tortellini with blue cheese cream, smoked eel with celeriac rémoulade, apple purée and crispy bacon, pumpkin, chickpea and cashew nut curry, coq au vin, a pie of the day, gurnard with saffron potatoes, braised fennel salad and crab bisque, braised pig cheeks with buttered mash and liquor, 28-day dry-aged sirloin steak with a choice of sauces, and puddings such as caramelised pineapple with passion-fruit sorbet, toasted coconut and pineapple and chilli salsa and sticky toffee pudding with stem ginger ice-cream. *Benchmark main dish: steak burger with toppings and frites £12.95. Two-course evening meal £23.00.*

Free house ~ Licensee Charles Garrard ~ Real ale ~ Open 11-3, 6-11; 11am-midnight Sat, Sun ~ Bar food 12-2.30 (3 weekends), 6.30-9.30 ~ Restaurant ~ Children welcome ~ Dogs allowed in bar ~ Wi-fi ~ Bedrooms: £90/£110 *Recommended by Daphne and Robert Staples, Bob and Margaret Holder, Ewan and Sue Hewitt, Ian and Rose Lock*

BATH
Old Green Tree ◖

ST7564 Map 2

(01225) 448259
Green Street; BA1 2JZ

Tiny, unspoilt local with up to six real ales and lots of cheerful customers

As ever, this firm favourite with our readers continues happily unchanged. It's a charming little 18th-c tavern with oak panelling and low ceilings of wood and plaster, and just three small rooms. These include a comfortable lounge on the left as you go in – its walls decorated with wartime aircraft pictures (in winter) and local artists' work (in spring and summer) – and a back bar. The big skylight lightens things attractively. Half a dozen beers on handpump might include Green Tree Bitter (named for the pub by Blindmans Brewery) and Butcombe Bitter with guests such as Blindmans Maverick Amber, Elland 1872 Ruby Mild (in May only) and Exmoor Gold; also, seven wines by the glass from a nice little list with helpful tasting notes, 36 malt whiskies and a farm cider. The gents' is basic and reached down steep steps. No children and no dogs.

Lunchtime-only food includes sandwiches, soup, pâté, sausages with ale and onion gravy, vegetable curry, burger with toppings and chips, and lambs liver with bacon and roast garlic mash. *Benchmark main dish: sausage and mash with a choice of three gravies £8.50.*

Free house ~ Licensee Tim Bethune ~ Real ale ~ No credit cards ~ Open 11-11; 12-4.30
Sun; 12-6.30 Sun in winter ~ Bar food 12-2.30 (3 Sat); not evenings or Sun *Recommended by
Taff Thomas, Dr J Barrie Jones, Ben and Diane Bowie, Melanie and David Lawson, Richard Mason,
Roger and Donna Huggins, Dr and Mrs A K Clarke, Stuart Doughty*

BATH ST7565 Map 2
Star ⌷
(01225) 425072 – www.abbeyales.co.uk
Vineyards; The Paragon (A4), junction with Guinea Lane; BA1 5NA

**Quietly chatty and unchanging old town local, the brewery tap
for Abbey Ales**

You get a strong sense of the past in this bustling old tavern, which attracts
a good mix of loyal regulars and visitors. The four small linked rooms have
many original features such as traditional wall benches (one is known as Death
Row), panelling, dim lighting and open fires. Abbey Bellringer plus guests such
as Banfield Tunnel Vision, Bass, Coach House Cheshire Gold, Lancaster Blonde
and St Austell Proper Job tapped from the cask, several wines by the glass,
30 malt whiskies and Cheddar Valley cider; darts, shove-ha'penny, cribbage and
board games – and complimentary snuff. The place gets particularly busy at
weekends and is just five minutes' walk from the city centre.

Food consists of filled rolls.

Punch ~ Lease Paul Waters and Alan Morgan ~ Real ale ~ Open 12-2.30, 5.30-midnight;
noon-1am Fri, Sat; 12-midnight Sun ~ Children welcome ~ Dogs welcome ~ Wi-fi ~ Singing
session Sun evening, irish folk Fri evening, quiz first Sun of month *Recommended by Taff
Thomas, Andrew and Michele Revell, Jack and Hilary Burton, Dr J Barrie Jones, Stuart Doughty*

BISHOPSWOOD ST2512 Map 1
Candlelight ✪⌷ ⌷
(01460) 234476 – www.candlelight-inn.co.uk
Off A303/B3170 S of Taunton; TA20 3RS

**Neat dining pub with a good choice of drinks, enjoyable food
and seats in the garden; handy for A303**

There were a few changes when new licensees took over at the end of
2016, but the neatly kept open-plan rooms (separated into different areas
by standing stone pillars and open doorways) remain more or less the same.
The beamed bar has high chairs by the counter where they serve Exeter
Avocet, Exmoor Gold and Otter Bitter tapped from the cask, good wines by
the glass and maybe a farm cider. Also, captain's chairs, pews and cushioned
window seats around a mix of wooden tables on sanded floorboards, books
on shelves, an open fire and a woodburning stove; background music.
Outside, there are picnic-sets on decking and a neatly landscaped garden.

 Particularly good food includes ham hock terrine with piccalilli, scallops with
black pudding, pea purée and pancetta, wild mushroom and truffle tortellini with
caramelised shallot purée and parmesan, beer-battered fish and chips, duck breast with
crushed sweet potato, sesame pak choi and teriyaki sauce, marinated lamb rump with
warm niçoise salad, hake with bombay potatoes and pickled fennel, and puddings such
as caramelised chocolate brownie sundae with salted caramel ice-cream and sticky
toffee pudding with butterscotch sauce; they also offer a two- and three-course weekday
lunch. *Benchmark main dish: burger with toppings, aioli, chutney and chips £13.00.
Two-course evening meal £20.00.*

Free house ~ Licensee Mike Rose ~ Real ale ~ Open 12-2.30, 6-11; 12-11 Sat, Sun ~ Bar food 12-2, 7-9; 12-2.30, 7-9.30 Fri, Sat; 12-4, 7-9 Sun ~ Children welcome ~ Dogs allowed in bar ~ Wi-fi *Recommended by Hugh Roberts, Roy Hoing, Bob and Margaret Holder, John Watson, Margo and Derek Stapley, Julia and Fiona Barnes*

BRISTOL   ST5873   Map 2

Highbury Vaults 🍺 £

(0117) 973 3203 – www.highburyvaults.co.uk

St Michael's Hill, Cotham; BS2 8DE

Cheerful town pub with up to eight real ales, good reasonably priced food and friendly atmosphere

A lock-up for condemned men in its early Georgian days, this unpretentious pub is an altogether jollier place now, with a bustling atmosphere and plenty of chatty customers. The fine range of quickly changing ales on handpump includes Youngs Bitter and London Gold plus guests such as Bath Gem, Purity Pure UBU, St Austell Tribute and Teignworthy Mad Hatters; also, six wines by the glass and eight malt whiskies. They offer hot sausage rolls from the oven on Thursday and Friday evenings at 10pm. The little front bar, with a corridor beside it, leads through to a series of small rooms: wooden floors, green and cream paintwork and old-fashioned furniture and prints (including plenty of royal family period engravings and lithographs in the front room). A model railway runs on a shelf the full length of the pub, with tunnels through the walls; bar billiards, TV and board games. The attractive back terrace has tables built into a partly covered flowery arbour; disabled access to main bar (but not the loos).

 Good value food includes filled rolls, baked potatoes, burgers with coleslaw, tortilla chips with salsa, beef in ale pie, lasagne, daily specials, and puddings such as sticky toffee pudding and chocolate puddle pudding with custard. *Benchmark main dish: fish pie £9.50. Two-course evening meal £15.00.*

Youngs ~ Manager Bradd Francis ~ Real ale ~ Open 12-midnight (11 Sun) ~ Bar food 12-2 (2.30 Sat), 5.30-8.30; 12-5 Sun ~ Children welcome ~ Wi-fi *Recommended by Carol and Barry Craddock, Lindy Andrews, John and Mary Warner, Peter Myers*

CHARLTON HORETHORNE   ST6623   Map 2

Kings Arms 🎖 ⇔

(01963) 220281 – www.thekingsarms.co.uk

B3145 Wincanton–Sherborne; DT9 4NL

Bustling inn with relaxed bars and more formal restaurant, good ales and wines and enjoyable food; bedrooms

A lthough many customers are here to enjoy the interesting food, the hands-on landlord offers just as warm a welcome to those popping in for a pint and a chat. It's a smart place and the main bar has an appealing assortment of local art (all for sale) on dark mulberry or cream walls, nice old carved wooden dining chairs and pine pews around a mix of tables, a slate floor and a woodburning stove. Leading off is a cosy room with sofas and newspapers on low tables. Butcombe Bitter and a couple of guests such as Butcombe Heathcliff and Dorset Tom Browns on handpump are served from the rather fine granite bar counter; they also keep 14 wines by the glass, nine malt whiskies and local farm cider. To the left of the main door is an informal dining room with Jacobean-style chairs and tables on a pale wooden floor and more local artwork. The back restaurant (past the open kitchen which is fun to peek into) has decorative wood and glass mirrors, wicker or black leather high-backed dining chairs around chunky, polished, pale wooden tables on coir carpeting, and handsome striped curtains. The attractive courtyard at the back of the inn has chrome and wicker chairs around teak tables under green parasols; a smokers' shelter overlooks a croquet lawn. Bedrooms are comfortable, well equipped and contemporary.

 Impressive food includes sandwiches, home-cured hot smoked salmon with pickled cucumber and mooli with horseradish crème fraîche, potted pork belly with tomato chutney, wild mushroom and mascarpone risotto, rump burger with toppings, red onion marmalade and chips, steak in ale pie, chicken breast with moroccan-style couscous, charred aubergine and saffron yoghurt, hake with nettle pesto and tomato salad, confit duck leg with chestnut and oyster mushroom fricassée with broad bean, pancetta and dauphinoise potatoes and red wine jus, and puddings such as lemon posset with raspberry sorbet and salted caramel tart with banana ice-cream. *Benchmark main dish: lamb rump with champ mash, honeyed parsnips and rosemary jus £19.50. Two-course evening meal £23.00.*

Free house ~ Licensee Tony Lethbridge ~ Real ale ~ Open 8am-11pm; 8am-10pm Sun ~ Bar food 12-2, 7-9.30 (10 Fri, Sat); 12-2, 7-9 Sun ~ Restaurant ~ Children welcome ~ Dogs allowed in bar ~ Wi-fi ~ Bedrooms: /£145 *Recommended by Edward Mirzoeff, Maddie Purvis, Claire Adams, Trish and Karl Soloman, Simon and Alex Knight*

CHURCHILL
ST4459 Map 1

Crown ◗ £
(01934) 852995

The Batch; in village, turn off A368 into Skinners Lane at Nelson Arms; BS25 5PP

Unchanging small cottage with friendly customers and staff, super range of real ales and homely lunchtime food

With its fine selection of real ales, chatty, friendly customers and completely untouched interior, this little tavern is much loved by a great many of our readers – though it's not the place for those keen on more modern comforts. Tapped from the cask, the seven beers include Bath Gem, Butcombe Bitter, Exmoor Gold, Palmers IPA, RCH IPA, St Austell Tribute and a quickly changing guest; several wines by the glass and five local ciders too. The small and rather local-feeling stone-floored and cross-beamed room on the right has a big log fire in a large stone fireplace and steps that lead up to another seating area. The left-hand room – with a slate floor, window seats and a log burner – leads through to the Snug. There's no noise from music or games (except perhaps dominoes). The outside lavatories are basic. There are garden tables at the front, more seats on the back lawn and hill views; the Mendip morris men visit in summer and some of the best walking on the Mendips is nearby. There isn't a pub sign outside, but no one seems to have a problem finding the place.

Traditional, lunchtime-only food includes sandwiches (the rare roast beef is popular), beef casserole, cauliflower cheese, lasagne, and puddings. *Benchmark main dish: chilli beef £6.40.*

Free house ~ Licensee Brian Clements ~ Real ale ~ No credit cards ~ Open 11-11; 12-10.30 Sun ~ Bar food 12-2.30 ~ Well behaved children allowed ~ Dogs allowed in bar ~ Wi-fi *Recommended by Taff Thomas, Hugh Roberts, Millie and Peter Downing, Tracey and Stephen Groves, Peter Myers, Dr and Mrs A K Clarke*

Bedroom prices are for high summer. Even then you may get reductions for more than one night, or (outside tourist areas) weekends. Winter special rates are common, and many inns reduce bedroom prices if you have a full evening meal.

CLAPTON-IN-GORDANO

ST4773 Map 1

Black Horse 🍺 £

(01275) 842105 – www.thekicker.co.uk

4 miles from M5 junction 19; A369 towards Portishead, then B3124 towards Clevedon; in North Weston opposite school, turn left signposted Clapton, then in village take second right, may be signed 'Clevedon, Clapton Wick'; BS20 7RH

Unpretentious old pub with lots of cheerful customers, friendly service, real ales, cider and simple lunchtime food; pretty garden

Local farmers and walkers with their dogs love this old-fashioned 14th-c tavern but there's always a genuine welcome for visitors too. The partly flagstoned, partly red-tiled main room has winged settles and built-in wall benches around narrow, dark wooden tables, window seats, a big log fire with stirrups and bits on the mantelbeam, and amusing cartoons and photographs of the pub. A window in an inner snug retains metal bars from the days when this room was the petty sessions gaol; also, high-backed settles – one with a marvellous carved and canopied creature, another with an art nouveau copper insert reading 'East, West, Hame's Best' – lots of mugs hanging from black beams and numerous small prints and photographs. A simply furnished room is the only place that families are allowed; background music. Bath Gem, Butcombe Bitter, Courage Best, Exmoor Gold and St Austell Tribute on handpump or tapped from the cask, six wines by the glass and three farm ciders. There are rustic tables and benches in the garden, with more to one side of the car park – the summer flowers are quite a sight. Paths from the pub lead up Naish Hill or to Cadbury Camp (National Trust) and there's access to local cycle routes. Although there is wheelchair access there are no disabled loos.

 Honest lunchtime-only food includes baguettes and baps with lots of hot and cold fillings and daily specials such as soup, sausage and mediterranean vegetable casserole, mushroom stroganoff, shepherd's pie, chilli con carne, beef in red wine and pork and cider casserole. *Benchmark main dish: corned beef hash with a fried egg £9.25.*

Enterprise ~ Lease Nicholas Evans ~ Real ale ~ Open 11-11; 12-9.30 Sun ~ Bar food 12-2.30; not evenings or Sun ~ Children in family room only ~ Dogs welcome ~ Wi-fi
Recommended by Taff Thomas, R T and J C Moggridge, Chris and Angela Buckell, Roy Hoing

COMBE HAY

ST7359 Map 2

Wheatsheaf 🎯 ⏣ 🛏

(01225) 833504 – www.wheatsheafcombehay.co.uk

Village signposted off A367 or B3110 S of Bath; BA2 7EG

Smart country dining pub with first class food and drink; attractive bedrooms

There's a civilised but informally friendly atmosphere here and a good mix of customers. Walkers with their dogs and those just wanting a drink and a chat can sit in a central area by a big fireplace where there are sofas on dark flagstones, and daily papers and current issues of *The Field* and *Country Life* on a low table. Friendly staff serve Butcombe Bitter and Gold and Otter Bright on handpump, 16 wines by the glass from a very good list, 18 malt whiskies and a farm cider. Other areas have stylish high-backed grey wicker dining chairs around chunky modern dining tables, on parquet or coir matting. It's fresh and bright, with block-mounted photo-prints, contemporary artwork and mirrors with colourful ceramic mosaic frames (many for sale) on white-painted stonework or robin's-egg-blue plaster walls. The sills of the many shuttered windows house anything from old soda siphons to a stuffed kingfisher and a Great Lakes model tugboat. Glinting glass wall chandeliers and nightlights in entertaining holders supplement the ceiling spotlights; background music. The two-level front garden has picnic-sets and a fine view over the church and valley; good surrounding walks. Bedrooms are quiet, spacious and comfortable.

Food is excellent: sandwiches, potted shrimp, prawn and crayfish, ham hock and smoked chicken terrine with piccalilli, beer-battered fish and skinny chips, wild mushroom and blue cheese tagliatelle, braised beef short rib with watercress mash and bourguignon, duck breast with duck and orange rösti and cherry jus, wild sea bass with herb mash and scallop velouté, braised lamb shoulder shepherd's pie, and puddings such as dark chocolate pannacotta with passion-fruit curd and treacle tart with crème fraîche sorbet. *Benchmark main dish: fresh fish dish of the day £19.00. Two-course evening meal £29.00.*

Free house ~ Licensee Ian Barton ~ Real ale ~ Open 10.30-3, 6-11; 10.30-3 Sun; closed Sun evening, Mon except bank holidays ~ Bar food 12-2.30, 6.30-9 ~ Restaurant ~ Children welcome ~ Dogs welcome ~ Wi-fi ~ Bedrooms: /£120 *Recommended by Richard Mason, George Sanderson, Julian Thorpe, Dr and Mrs A K Clarke*

CORTON DENHAM
Queens Arms 🎯 ♈ 🍺 🛏

ST6322   Map 2

(01963) 220317 – www.thequeensarms.com
Village signposted off B3145 N of Sherborne; DT9 4LR

Handsome 18th-c inn with super choice of drinks, interesting food and a sunny garden; comfortable, stylish bedrooms

Cadbury Castle hill fort is not far away and there are fine surrounding walks, so at lunchtime in particular this Georgian stone inn gets pretty busy. There's a gently civilised atmosphere and the bustling, high-beamed bar has rugs on flagstones and two big armchairs in front of an open fire, some old pews, barrel seats and a sofa, church candles and big bowls of flowers. There's also a couple of separate restaurants, one of which has cushioned wall seats and chunky leather chairs around dark wooden tables, mirrors down one side and a drop-down cinema screen (screenings are held twice a month). A beer named for the pub (from Gyle 59) plus Gyle 59 Toujours and guests from breweries such as Cheddar, Church End, Exmoor, Otter and Plain on handpump, 22 wines (including champagne) by the glass from a carefully chosen list, 57 malt whiskies, 26 gins, unusual bottled beers from Belgium, Germany and the US, and four local apple juices. A south-facing back terrace has teak tables and chairs under parasols (or heaters, if the weather is cool) and colourful flower tubs. The comfortable bedrooms have lovely country views and breakfasts are particularly good.

As well as offering breakfasts to non-residents (8-9.30am) and using their own farm produce and other home-grown and local ingredients, the inviting food includes sandwiches, piri-piri chicken terrine with sour cream, wild garlic, pine nuts and smoked pepper, asparagus salad with a poached duck egg and chervil mustard dressing, rare-breed beef burger with toppings, pickles and chips, smoked pork loin and eggs, lamb three-ways (prime, poached, spicy sausage) with scorched spring greens, crispy onions and sun-dried tomato jus, brill fillet with crushed jersey potatoes, fennel and smoked mussel cream, and puddings such as dark chocolate torte, passion-fruit curd and raspberry crumb and treacle and almond tart with grapefruit sauce and clotted cream; they also offer afternoon tea (3-5.30pm). *Benchmark main dish: guinea fowl with pancetta, shiitake mushrooms and cabbage £17.95. Two-course evening meal £25.00.*

Free house ~ Licensees Jeanette and Gordon Reid ~ Real ale ~ Open 8am-11pm; 8am-11.30pm Sat; 8am-10.30pm Sun ~ Bar food 12-3, 6-9 ~ Restaurant ~ Children welcome ~ Dogs allowed in bar and bedrooms ~ Wi-fi ~ Bedrooms: £95/£125 *Recommended by Carol and Barry Craddock, Stuart Reeves, Miles Green, Marianne and Peter Stevens, Ian Herdman, Julian Thorpe*

CROSCOMBE
George 🍺 🛏

ST5844   Map 2

(01749) 342306 – www.thegeorgeinn.co.uk
Long Street (A371 Wells–Shepton Mallet); BA5 3QH

Warmly welcoming, family-run coaching inn with charming canadian landlord, enjoyable food, good local beers and attractive garden; bedrooms

This is both very well run and genuinely welcoming and our readers continue to enjoy their visits very much. The main bar has a good mix of customers, stripped stone, dark wooden tables and chairs and more comfortable seats, a settle by one of the log fires in the inglenook fireplaces, and the family's grandfather clock; a snug area has a woodburning stove. As well as four farm ciders, they keep George & Dragon and King George the Thirst (both from Blindmans) and three guests such as Bath Gem, Cotleigh Barn Owl and Hop Back Crop Circle on handpump or tapped from the cask, ten wines by the glass and home-made elderflower cordial. The attractive dining room has more stripped stone, local artwork and family photographs on burgundy walls and high-backed cushioned dining chairs around a mix of tables. The back bar has canadian timber and a pew reclaimed from the local church, and there's a family room with games and books for children. Darts, a skittle alley, board games, shove-ha'penny and a canadian wooden table game called crokinole. The pub dog Tessa has been joined by Pixy the labrador/spaniel cross. The attractive, sizeable garden has seats on a heated and covered terrace, flower borders, a grassed area, a wood-fired pizza oven (used on Fridays) and chickens; children's swings. Bedrooms are clean and comfortable and breakfasts are good.

Tasty, popular food includes lunchtime sandwiches and baguettes, hot smoked salmon pâté, garlic mushrooms gratin, cashew nut terrine with red wine jus, ham and egg, lasagne, slow-cooked pork belly with apple purée and cider jus, hake fillet with mussels and basil pesto linguine, lamb cutlet, braised shoulder and lamb and apricot ballotine with crispy kale and medlar jus, and puddings such as apple crumble with custard and raspberry crème brûlée. *Benchmark main dish: pie of the day £11.95. Two-course evening meal £20.00.*

Free house ~ Licensees Peter and Veryan Graham ~ Real ale ~ Open 7.30-3, 6-11; 7.30-3, 5-midnight Fri; 8am-midnight Sat; 8am-11pm Sun ~ Bar food 7.30-2.30, 6-9; 8am-9pm Sat; 8-8 Sun ~ Restaurant ~ Children welcome ~ Dogs allowed in bar ~ Wi-fi ~ Bedrooms: £60/£80 *Recommended by Ray White, Taff Thomas, Dr J Barrie Jones, Tim and Moira Hurst, Freddie and Sarah Banks*

DULVERTON
Woods ★ 🍽⭐ ♀

SS9127   Map 1

(01398) 324007 – www.woodsdulverton.co.uk
Bank Square; TA22 9BU

Smartly informal place with exceptional wines, real ales, first rate food and a good mix of customers

This is a very special place that our readers enthuse about year after year – on all aspects. There are satisfied diners to the right and happy lunchtime drinkers nursing their pints to the left. The pub is on the edge of Exmoor, so there are plenty of good sporting prints on salmon pink walls, antlers and other hunting trophies, stuffed birds and a couple of salmon rods. By the bar counter are bare boards, daily papers, tables partly separated by stable-style timbering and masonry dividers, and (on the right) a carpeted area with a woodburning stove in a big fireplace; maybe unobjectionable background music. The marvellous drinks choice includes Dartmoor Jail Ale, Hop Back Crop Circle and St Austell Cornish Best tapped from the cask, farm cider, many sherries and some unusual spirits – but it's the stunning wine list that draws the most attention. Mr Groves reckons he could put 1,000 different wines up on the bar and will open any of them (with a value of up to £100) for just a glass. He is there every night and will happily chat to tables of restaurant customers about any wines they might be interested in. Large windows look on to the quiet town centre (there's also a couple of metal tables on the pavement) and in the small suntrap back courtyard there are a few picnic-sets.

 Using produce from their own farm, the food is delicious: sandwiches, pigeon breast with pak choi and beetroot purée, smoked salmon with citrus mayonnaise, quail egg, pickled cucumber and avruga caviar, wild mushroom linguine with white wine cream sauce and truffle oil, braised leg and crispy pork belly with apple jam and cider sauce, confit shoulder, chop and miniature pie of lamb with onion purée, wild garlic and lamb sauce, fillet of sea bass with rösti potato, wild mushrooms and pancetta and shallot sauce, and puddings such as salt peanut parfait with caramel and white chocolate mousse with caramelised banana and pomegranate crème brûlée with lemon sorbet. *Benchmark main dish: seared steak and bacon salad £11.50. Two-course evening meal £20.00.*

Free house ~ Licensee Patrick Groves ~ Real ale ~ Open 12-3, 6-11; 12-3, 7-11 Sun ~ Bar food 12-2, 6-9.30; 12-2, 7-9 Sun ~ Restaurant ~ Children welcome ~ Dogs welcome ~ Wi-fi
Recommended by Richard and Penny Gibbs, Ian and Rose Lock, Lynda and Trevor Smith, Hugh Roberts, Charles and Maddie Bishop, Graham Smart

DUNSTER
Luttrell Arms 🏅 � 🛏

SS9943 Map 1

(01643) 821555 – www.luttrellarms.co.uk
High Street; A396; TA24 6SG

Character bars and dining areas in lovely hotel, a thoughtful choice of drinks, enjoyable food and seats in courtyard and garden; luxurious bedrooms

Full of history, this civilised and imposing old place is based around a great hall built for the Abbot of Cleeve some 500 years ago and it has some fine medieval features. The Old Kitchen Bar retains the workings of the former kitchen with meat hooks on the beamed ceiling and a huge log fire and bread oven. The main bar – popular locally – has swords and guns on the wall above a massive fireplace, cushions on antique chairs, horsebrasses, copper kettles, plates and warming pans, animal furs dotted here and there, a stag's head and an antler chandelier, and various country knick-knacks. Exmoor Ale, Otter Amber and a guest from Cotleigh on handpump, 25 good wines by the glass, a dozen malt whiskies and three farm ciders; staff are courteous and helpful. There's also the Boot Bar with a lovely panelled wall seat and rugs on quarry tiles, a small snug and a deeply comfortable sitting room with one beautiful panelled wall, a woodburning stove and plenty of armchairs, sofas and window seats; board games. The delightful garden is designed on several levels with seats on lawns or terraces and haunting castle views; a little galleried courtyard has metalwork chairs and tables. Some of the bedrooms are opulently furnished with four-posters, antiques and carved fireplaces; breakfasts are first class.

 Imaginative food includes sandwiches, hand-picked crab and prawn salad with candied lemon and lime dressing, pressed rabbit terrine with pickled pear purée, butternut squash, quinoa and buckwheat risotto with courgette, red pepper and parmesan cream, cumberland sausages with horseradish mash and red onion gravy, oak-smoked salmon linguine with pine nuts, capers and dill, chicken kiev with sweet potato pie, chestnuts, caramelised shallots and baby turnips, 10oz sirloin steak with truffle mash and peppercorn sauce, and puddings such as rice pudding crème brûlée and a seasonal crumble with clotted cream; they also offer afternoon tea (3-5.30pm). *Benchmark main dish: beer-battered fish and chips £12.00. Two-course evening meal £22.00.*

Free house ~ Licensee Tim Waldren ~ Real ale ~ Open 10am-11pm; 12-11 Sun ~ Bar food 7.30am-9.30pm ~ Restaurant ~ Children welcome ~ Dogs allowed in bar and bedrooms ~ Wi-fi ~ Bedrooms: £100/£140 *Recommended by Martin Jones, Isobel Mackinlay, Peter Myers, Rosie and John Moore, Elizabeth and Peter May, Gerry and Rosemary Dobson*

EXFORD   SS8538 Map 1
Crown 🛏
(01643) 831554 – www.crownhotelexmoor.co.uk
The Green (B3224); TA24 7PP

17th-c coaching inn in pretty moorland village, character bar with real ales and enjoyable food, and big back garden; comfortable bedrooms

The bedrooms here are warm and comfortable and make a good base for exploring Exmoor. The two-room bar is easy-going and has a log fire in a big stone fireplace, plenty of stuffed animal heads and hunting prints on grey walls, some hunting-themed plates and old photographs of the area, cushioned benches and other traditional pubby tables and chairs on bare boards. There are stools against the counter where they serve Exmoor Ale and Gold and St Austell Tribute on handpump, 16 wines by the glass, ten malt whiskies, eight gins and farm cider; TV and board games. The dining room is rather smart. At the front of the building are some tables and chairs, with more on a back terrace; there's also a stream threading its way past gently sloping lawns in the three-acre garden. They're very dog-friendly, have stabling for horses and can arrange riding, fishing, shooting, hunting, wildlife-watching, cycling and trekking.

Well liked food includes sandwiches, chicken liver and foie gras pâté with fig relish, pigeon breast wrapped in parma ham with smoked bacon and lentils, mint and pea risotto with parmesan, wild boar and apple sausages with wholegrain mustard mash and caramelised onion sauce, a curry of the day, hake fillet on chorizo amd mediterranean vegetable stew, chicken breast with dauphinoise potatoes and pancetta and shiitake mushroom sauce, and puddings such as sticky toffee pudding with honeycomb ice-cream and butterscotch sauce and caramelised almond tart with mixed berry compote. *Benchmark main dish: beef in ale pie £13.50. Two-course evening meal £20.00.*

Free house ~ Licensee Sara Whittaker ~ Real ale ~ Open 12-11 ~ Bar food 12-2.30, 6-9.30 ~ Restaurant ~ Children welcome ~ Dogs allowed in bar and bedrooms ~ Wi-fi ~ Bedrooms: £75/£135 *Recommended by Geoff and Ann Marston, William Slade, Sandra and Michael Smith, Sophie Ellison*

We say if we know a pub allows dogs.

FROME
ST7747 Map 2
Archangel
(01373) 456111 – www.archangelfrome.com

King Street; BA11 1BH

Ancient place with contemporary design, several eating and drinking areas, a bustling atmosphere, rewarding food and drink and courtyard seats; bedrooms

Although this inn first opened its doors in 1311 and is full of history – it's quite a surprise inside. They've kept the ancient beams and walls and added contemporary artwork and touches of glass, steel, slate and leather throughout. The bar is bustling and convivial with a good mix and age range of customers sitting on wall banquettes or at high tables and chairs dotted around the room; the brick walls are painted white and there's a strip of blue neon lighting at ground level. They have a beer named for them (from Milk Street), Ringwood Boondoggle or Fortyniner and a guest from a brewery such as Blindmans or Box Steam on handpump, good wines by the glass and a large cocktail list. Stairs lead up to the restaurant with its rather dramatic glass-enclosed mezzanine cube, there are mustard yellow and pale green leather chairs around a mix of tables on big floorboards, high rafters lined with electric candles and a large carved angel on a plinth; background music. A long slate-floored passageway links this main part to a two-roomed snug area that has spacious leather sofas and armchairs and an open fire, and a small rather cosy dining room. The central courtyard has colourful tables and chairs and a mediterranean feel.

 Good quality food includes lunchtime sandwiches, moules frites, home-smoked chicken terrine with cauliflower purée and jerusalem artichoke crisps, king prawn, chorizo and chilli linguine, beef, bacon and mushroom pie, beetroot and blue cheese soufflé with celeriac rémoulade and pickled walnut dressing, cajun chicken breast with mushroom, bacon and fine bean fricassée, smoked haddock with dauphinoise potatoes and smoked haddock chowder, and puddings such as chocolate marquise with orange sorbet and treacle tart with salted praline and clotted cream; they also offer afternoon tea (2.30-5pm). *Benchmark main dish: slow-cooked sirloin of beef £19.95. Two-course evening meal £20.00.*

Free house ~ Licensee Ross Nicol ~ Real ale ~ Open 11-11 ~ Bar food 12-2.30, 6-9.30 ~ Restaurant ~ Children welcome ~ Dogs allowed in bar and bedrooms ~ Wi-fi ~ Live music last two Sun of month ~ Bedrooms: $70/$80 *Recommended by Geoff and Ann Marston, Lance and Sarah Milligan, Edward Mirzoeff, Andrew Lawson*

HINTON ST GEORGE
ST4212 Map 1
Lord Poulett Arms 🏆 ♀ 🛏
(01460) 73149 – www.lordpoulettarms.com

Off A30 W of Crewkerne and off Merriott road (declassified – former A356, off B3165) N of Crewkerne; TA17 8SE

Somerset Dining Pub of the Year

Thatched 17th-c stone inn with top class food, good choice of drinks and pretty garden; attractive bedrooms

As a highly enjoyable and civilised break from the dreaded A30, this old inn is hard to beat. The several attractive and cosy linked bar areas have hop-draped beams, walls made of honey-coloured stone or painted in bold Farrow & Ball colours and rugs on bare boards or flagstones; also, open fires (one in an inglenook, another in a raised fireplace that separates two rooms), antique brass candelabra, fresh flowers and candles, and some lovely old farmhouse, windsor and ladderback chairs around fine oak or elm tables. Butcombe Bitter, Otter Ale and St Austell Trelawny on handpump, 13 wines by the glass, home-made cordial, some interesting spirits and local bottled cider and perry; background music, chess and backgammon. The pub cat is called Honey. Outside, beneath a wisteria-clad pergola, are white metalwork tables and chairs in a mediterranean-style, lavender-edged gravelled area, and picnic-sets in a wild-flower meadow; boules. Bedrooms are pretty and the breakfasts splendid. This is a peaceful and attractive village and there are enjoyable surrounding walks.

Enticing food includes sandwiches, cockle and tomato risotto with malt vinegar and samphire salad, roast local venison with creamed celeriac, pak choi and szechuan pepper, chargrilled cauliflower steak with saag aloo, mint yoghurt and pickled cucumber, pheasant schnitzel with a fried egg and caesar salad, cod braised in truffle emulsion with leeks, chestnut gnocchi and mushrooms, confit duck leg with sweet and sour parsnips, duck fat crouton and thyme jus, and puddings such as apricot bavarois with earl grey-soaked apricots and mango sorbet and rocky road with chantilly cream and blueberry sorbet; they also offer a two- and three-course set menu. *Benchmark main dish: cider-battered fish and chips £14.75. Two-course evening meal £21.00.*

Free house ~ Licensees Steve Hill and Michelle Paynton ~ Real ale ~ Open 12-11 ~ Bar food 12-2.30, 6.30-9.15; 12-3.30, 7-9.15 Sun ~ Children welcome ~ Dogs allowed in bar ~ Wi-fi ~ Bedrooms: £65/£95 *Recommended by Ian Malone, Tim and Sarah Smythe-Brown, Charles Todd, Sylvia and Phillip Spencer, Patricia and Anton Larkham*

HOLCOMBE   ST6649   Map 2

Holcombe Inn 🍽 🛏

(01761) 232478 – www.holcombeinn.co.uk

Off A367; Stratton Road; BA3 5EB

Charming inn with far-reaching views, cosy bars, a wide choice of drinks and good food; lovely bedrooms

As there are plenty of places to visit nearby and good surrounding walks, the well equipped bedrooms here make an excellent base for exploring the area; some have views over peaceful farmland to Downside Abbey's school. Downstairs, the cosy room to the right of the main entrance has sofas around a central table and an open woodburning stove. To the left is the bar: fine old flagstones, window seats and chunky captain's chairs around pine-topped tables, and a carved wooden counter where they serve Bath Gem, Butcombe Bitter and Otter Ale on handpump, 21 wines and champagne by the glass, 25 malt whiskies, cocktails and a thoughtful choice of local drinks (cider, vodka, sloe gin, various juices); board games and background music. A two-way woodburning stove also warms the dining room, which is partly carpeted and partly flagstoned, and has partitioning creating snug seating areas, and a mix of high-backed patterned or leather and brass-studded dining chairs around all sorts of tables; daily newspapers. A little sitting area leads off here and serves specialist teas and coffees. There are picnic-sets arranged on a terrace and side lawn, and the sunsets can be stunning. Dogs are welcome everywhere (except the restaurant) and in two of the lodges by prior arrangement.

The standard of food is high and dishes include lunchtime sandwiches, grilled quail with onion purée, diced celeriac, caramelised apple and meat juices, salt pork and pistachio terrine with spiced oranges, baked buckwheat pancakes filled with mushrooms and spinach in a béchamel sauce, honey-roast ham and eggs, crayfish, lime, chilli and ginger linguine, venison steak with fondant potato, wild mushrooms and red wine sauce, lamb rump with deep-fried lambs tongue, ratatouille and dauphinoise potatoes, confit duck leg with mash, sweet pickled red cabbage and madeira cream sauce, and puddings such as coffee crème caramel with praline and bakewell tart with vanilla ice-cream. *Benchmark main dish: pie of the day £13.95. Two-course evening meal £20.00.*

Free house ~ Licensee Julie Berry ~ Real ale ~ Open 8am-11pm ~ Bar food 12-2.30, 6-9; 12-9 Sat, Sun ~ Restaurant ~ Children welcome ~ Dogs allowed in bar and bedrooms ~ Wi-fi ~ Bedrooms: £75/£120 *Recommended by Cynthia Awad, Isobel Mackinlay, Taff Thomas, Toni, Lyn and Geoff Hallchurch, Christopher May, Ben and Jenny Settle*

 HUISH EPISCOPI   ST4326   Map 1

Rose & Crown  £

(01458) 250494

Off A372 E of Langport; TA10 9QT

17th-c pub with local cider and real ales, simple food and a friendly welcome from long-serving licensees

There's a real sense of family history in this unspoilt thatched inn. Known locally as 'Eli's' after the licensees' grandfather, it's now been run by the same family for more than 147 years. There's no bar as such, just a central flagstoned still room where drinks are served: Teignworthy Reel Ale and a couple of guests such as Glastonbury Mystery Tor and Hop Back Summer Lightning, local farm cider and Somerset cider brandy. The casual little front parlours, with their unusual pointed-arch windows, have family photographs, books, cribbage, dominoes, shove-ha'penny and bagatelle and attract a good mix of both locals and visitors. A much more orthodox big back extension has pool, a games machine and a juke box. There are plenty of seats and tables in the extensive outdoor area and two lawns – one is enclosed and has a children's play area; pub customers can camp (by arrangement) on the adjoining paddock. There's also a separate skittle alley, a large car park, morris men (in summer) and fine nearby river walks; they hold a Friday evening organic produce co-op in one of their rooms (4.30-7pm). The site of the Battle of Langport (1645) is not far away.

 Fair-priced, home-made food includes sandwiches, good soups, cottage pie, a vegetarian tart, pork, apple and cider cobbler, chicken in tarragon sauce, and puddings such as sticky toffee pudding and apple crumble. *Benchmark main dish: steak in ale pie £8.75. Two-course evening meal £13.00.*

Free house ~ Licensees Maureen Pittard, Stephen Pittard and Patricia O'Malley ~ Real ale ~ No credit cards ~ Open 11.30-2.30, 5.15-11; 11.30-11.30 Fri, Sat; 12-10.30 Sun ~ Bar food 12-2, 5.30-7.30; not Sun evening ~ Children welcome ~ Dogs welcome ~ Wi-fi ~ Open mike last Thurs of month, folk sing-around third Sat of month (except June-Aug) *Recommended by David Longhurst, Lindy Andrews, Edward May, Isobel Mackinlay*

MELLS   ST7249   Map 2

Talbot 🏵 🍴 ♈ 🛏

(01373) 812254 – www.talbotinn.com

W of Frome, off A362 or A361; BA11 3PN

Carefully refurbished and interesting old coaching inn, real ales and good wines, inventive food and seats in courtyard; lovely bedrooms

Until the dissolution of the monasteries in the early 16th c, this village was owned by Glastonbury Abbey. The handsome old inn has a nicely informal, candlelit bar with various wooden tables and chairs on big quarry tiles, a woodburning stove in a stone fireplace, and stools (particularly popular with locals) against the counter where friendly, helpful staff serve a beer named for the pub (from Keystone), Butcombe Bitter and a couple of guests such as Butcombe Rare Breed on handpump, several good wines by the glass and a farm cider. Two interconnected dining rooms have brass-studded leather chairs around wooden tables, a log fire with candles in fine clay cups on the mantelpiece above and lots of coaching prints on the walls; quiet background music and board games. There's a mediterranean feeling to the courtyard with its pale green metalwork chairs and tables. Off here, in separate buildings, are the enjoyable, rustic-feeling sitting room with sofas, chairs and tables, smart magazines, a huge mural and enormous glass bottles (free films or popular TV programmes are shown here on Sunday evenings), and the grill room, where food is cooked simply on a big open fire overlooked by 18th-c portraits. The bedrooms are smart and stylish and breakfasts are excellent. Do visit the lovely church where the poet Siegfried Sassoon is buried; the walled gardens opposite the inn are very pretty. This is sister pub to the Beckford Arms at Fonthill Gifford (Wiltshire).

Food is creative and seasonal: sandwiches, squid with a spicy marinated salad and grilled lemon, steak tartare with dijon mustard, egg yolk, shallots and capers, burger with toppings, pickle, coleslaw and chips, maple-roasted squash with salt-baked celeriac, buckwheat and pumpkin granola and crispy nettles, cod with brown crab butter, jerusalem artichokes, seaweed, flaked almonds and sea herbs, lamb with mash, cabbage, charred shallots and roasting juices, 42-day dry-aged rump steak with smoked beetroot, bone marrow and horseradish butter and chips, and puddings such as dark chocolate mousse with hazelnut praline and peanut ice-cream and rhubarb posset with ginger shortbread and rhubarb sorbet. *Benchmark main dish: fish stew £18.00. Two-course evening meal £22.00.*

Free house ~ Licensee Matt Greenlees ~ Real ale ~ Open 8am-11pm ~ Bar food 12-3, 6-9.30 ~ Restaurant ~ Children welcome ~ Dogs welcome ~ Wi-fi ~ Bedrooms: /£100
Recommended by S G N Bennett, Edward Mirzoeff, Chris and Angela Buckell, Richard Mason, Taff Thomas, Matthew and Elisabeth Reeves

MILVERTON
Globe 🔴

ST1225   Map 1

(01823) 400534 – www.theglobemilverton.co.uk
Fore Street; TA4 1JX

Bustling and friendly inn with a welcome for all, good ales, quite a choice of tasty food and seats outside; bedrooms

It's the good food that most customers come for, but regulars do pop in for a pint and a chat and staff are helpful and cheerful to all. This is a handsome former coaching inn and the opened-up rooms have solid rustic tables surrounded by an attractive mix of wooden or high-backed black leather chairs, artwork on pale-painted walls above a red dado, and a big gilt-edged mirror above a woodburning stove in an ornate fireplace; background music and board games. Bar chairs line the counter where they keep Exeter Avocet, Otter Bitter and St Austell Trelawny on handpump, ten wines by the glass and local farm cider. The sheltered outside terrace has raffia-style chairs and tables and cushioned wall seating under parasols. The two bedrooms are comfortable and breakfasts are continental.

Particularly good food using seasonal produce includes sandwiches, crispy spiced squid with orange, fennel and wholegrain mustard salad, chicken liver pâté with red onion jam, gnocchi with tomato sauce, roasted vegetables, mozzarella and pesto, burger with toppings and chips, lambs liver and smoked bacon with gravy, smoked haddock with pancetta, leeks, sauté potatoes and a poached egg, free-range chicken breast with smoked bacon and pea risotto, and puddings such as chocolate brownie with chocolate sauce and vanilla ice-cream and vanilla crème brûlée with caramelised banana. *Benchmark main dish: slow-roast pork belly with honey and roasted shallots £14.95. Two-course evening meal £21.00.*

Free house ~ Licensees Mark and Adele Tarry ~ Real ale ~ Open 12-3, 6-11 (11.30 Sat); 12-3 Sun; closed Sunday evening, Mon lunchtime ~ Bar food 12-2, 6.30-9 ~ Restaurant ~ Children welcome ~ Dogs allowed in bar ~ Wi-fi ~ Bedrooms: £65/£70 *Recommended by Lyn and Geoff Hallchurch, Valerie Sayer, Colin and Daniel Gibbs, Bob and Margaret Holder*

MONKTON COMBE
ST7761 Map 2
Wheelwrights Arms 🛏
(01225) 722287 – www.wheelwrightsarms.co.uk
Just off A36 S of Bath; Church Cottages; BA2 7HB

18th-c stone pub with cheerful staff, helpful landlord and staff, good food and seats outside; comfortable bedrooms

This is an enjoyable place to stay – the bedrooms, in a restored annexe, are quiet, well equipped and comfortable. The bar-dining room has an open fire in a raised fireplace at one end, cushioned and wood-planked built-in wall seats, rush-seated or cushioned high-backed dining chairs around tables (each set with a small lamp), parquet flooring or carpet, and old photographs and oil paintings (the one above the fireplace of a dog is particularly nice). The middle room has some pretty frieze work, a high shelf of wooden wader birds and stools against the green-painted counter where they keep Butcombe Bitter and Otter Bitter on handpump, 13 wines by the glass, several gins and farm cider; background jazz and board games. A small end room is just right for a group. The gravelled terraces have wood and metal tables and chairs and picnic-sets. The peaceful village is surrounded by picturesque hills and valleys.

Highly regarded food – using home-baked bread and home made yoghurt – includes sandwiches, crab, crayfish and chilli linguine, ham hock terrine with capers, venison burger with red cabbage slaw and chips, cheese and truffle macaroni with fennel salad, beer-battered fish with triple-cooked chips, confit duck leg with red wine risotto, lamb ragoût with mint and pomegranate gremolata and pasta, and puddings such as chocolate mousse with griottine cherries and stout sticky toffee pudding with salted caramel sauce; they offer a two-course weekday lunch and a pizza oven was being installed as we went to press. *Benchmark main dish: sea bream with clams, samphire and chargrilled cauliflower £17.50. Two-course evening meal £23.00.*

Free house ~ Licensee David Munn ~ Real ale ~ Open 8am-11pm ~ Bar food 12-2, 6-9.30 ~ Children welcome ~ Wi-fi ~ Bedrooms: £85/£155 *Recommended by Richard Mason, John and Abigail Prescott, Holly and Tim Waite, Rosie and John Moore*

ODCOMBE
ST5015 Map 2
Masons Arms 🍺 🛏
(01935) 862591 – www.masonsarmsodcombe.co.uk
Off A3088 or A30 just W of Yeovil; Lower Odcombe; BA22 8TX

Own-brew beers and tasty food in pretty thatched cottage; bedrooms

The own-brews served by friendly staff here continue to draw in customers. The simple little bar has joists and a couple of standing timbers, a mix of cushioned dining chairs around all sorts of tables on cream and blue patterned carpet, and a couple of tub chairs and a table in the former inglenook fireplace. Up a step is a similar area, while more steps lead down to a dining room with a squashy brown sofa and a couple of cushioned dining chairs in front of a woodburning stove; the sandstone walls are hung with black and white local photographs and country prints. Their own ales are Odcombe No.1, Roly Poly and seasonal beers on handpump, they make their own sloe and elderflower cordials, have 11 wines by the glass and serve farm cider. There's a thatched smokers' shelter and picnic-sets in the garden, plus a vegetable patch and chicken coop and a campsite. Bedrooms are well equipped and comfortable and the breakfasts are good and hearty.

Enjoyable food uses home-grown and other local produce: lunchtime sandwiches and ciabattas, deep-fried brie with cranberry sauce, crab cakes with sweet chilli sauce, eggs benedict, a full breakfast, butternut squash, goats cheese and spinach lasagne, liver and bacon with bubble and squeak, onion rings and gravy, corn-fed chicken with parmentier potatoes, chorizo, shallots and red wine jus, baby barbecue back ribs with crispy onions and rustic chips, szechuan prawn stir-fry, and puddings such as chocolate and cherry mousse and vanilla pannacotta with rhubarb compote. *Benchmark main dish: burger with toppings, sauce, sweet potato slaw and chips £12.75. Two-course evening meal £19.00.*

Own brew ~ Licensees Drew Read and Paula Tennyson ~ Real ale ~ Open 8am-3pm, 6-midnight ~ Bar food 12-2, 6.30-9.30 ~ Children welcome ~ Dogs welcome ~ Wi-fi ~ Bedrooms: £60/£90 *Recommended by Edward Lubbock, JPC, Paddy and Sian O'Leary, Richard and Tessa Ibbot*

PITNEY
Halfway House 🍺 £

ST4527 Map 1

(01458) 252513 – www.thehalfwayhouse.co.uk
Just off B3153 W of Somerton; TA10 9AB

Bustling, friendly local with nine real ales, local ciders and good simple food

There's a cheerful mix of customers in this unpretentious village local – most are here to sample the fine range of up to ten regularly changing beers. The atmosphere is chatty and easy-going and the three old-fashioned rooms have communal tables, roaring log fires and a homely feel underlined by a profusion of books, maps and newspapers. Tapped from the cask, the ales might include Bad Seed Columbus Pale Ale, Butcombe Haka, Cheddar Potholer, Dark Star American Pale Ale, Hop Back Summer Lightning, Otter Bright, Teignworthy Neap Tide and Reel Ale and Yeovil Stout Hearted; also, four farm ciders, a dozen malt whiskies and several wines by the glass; board games. There are tables outside.

Fairly priced, simple food includes lunchtime sandwiches, ham and eggs, faggots with mash and onion gravy, a pie of the day, venison burger with red onion jam and chips, a casserole of the day and chilli beef. *Benchmark main dish: beer-battered fish and chips £10.00. Two-course evening meal £16.00.*

Free house ~ Licensee Mark Phillips ~ Real ale ~ Open 11.30-3, 4-11; 11.30-11.30 Sat; 12-11 Sun ~ Bar food 12-2.30, 7-9.30; 1-5 Sun ~ Children welcome ~ Dogs welcome ~ Wi-fi *Recommended by Richard and Penny Gibbs, S G N Bennett, Bob and Margaret Holder, Edward May*

We mention bottled beers and spirits only if there is something unusual about them – imported belgian real ales, say, or dozens of malt whiskies; so do please let us know about them in your reports.

PRIDDY
ST5250   Map 2

Queen Victoria £

(01749) 676385 – www.thequeenvicpriddy.co.uk

Village signed off B3135; Pelting Drove; BA5 3BA

**Stone-built country pub with a friendly atmosphere, real ales
and honest food; seats outside**

Things have been brightened up here with some fresh paintwork
and new lighting, and it remains extremely popular with locals and
visiting cyclists and walkers (often with their dogs). The various rooms
and alcoves have a lot of character and plenty of original features, and
there's both an open fire in a big grate (with a huge cauldron to one side)
and a woodburning stove in a back bar. There are flagstoned or slate
floors, bare stone walls (the smarter dining room is half panelled and half
painted), horse tack, farm tools and photos of Queen Victoria. Furniture is
traditional: cushioned wall settles, farmhouse and other solid chairs around
all manner of wooden tables, a nice old pew beside a screen settle making
a cosy alcove, and high chairs next to the bar counter where they serve
Butcombe Bitter and Rare Breed and a guest such as Bristol Beer Factory
No 7 on handpump, two farm ciders, nine malt whiskies, nine gins and nine
wines by the glass. There are seats in the front courtyard and more across
the lane where there's also a children's playground, the smokers' shelter is
a converted dray waggon. Wheelchair access.

 Food is fair value and traditional: baguettes, chicken liver and bacon pâté, smoked
salmon and prawn cocktail, roasted beetroot, horseradish and toasted cheese tart,
ham and eggs, chilli beef, chicken curry, fish pie, gammon with egg or pineapple, rump
steak with onion rings and chips, and puddings such as chocolate fudge cake and lemon
meringue cake. *Benchmark main dish: beef in ale pie £9.95. Two-course evening
meal £14.00.*

Butcombe ~ Tenant Mark Walton ~ Real ale ~ Open 12-11; 12-10.30 Sun ~ Bar food 12-9
(12-3, 5-9 Nov-May); 12-9 Sat; 12-8 Sun ~ Children welcome ~ Dogs welcome ~ Wi-fi ~
Occasional live music Sun afternoon *Recommended by Dave Sutton, Sophie Ellison,
Chris and Angela Buckell, M G Hart, Peter Myers, Ivy and George Goodwill*

SOMERTON
ST4828   Map 2

White Hart 🏠 ★ ♀ 🛏

(01458) 272273 – www.whitehartsomerton.com

Market Place; TA11 7LX

**Attractive old place with several bars, open fires, spacious dining
room and enjoyable food; bedrooms**

'This is a real find,' says one of our readers with enthusiasm. There's
a thoughtful choice of drinks, good popular food and a really buzzy
atmosphere. The main bar has long wall seats with attractive scatter
cushions, stools around small tables, big wall mirrors and Bath Gem,
Cheddar Potholer, Otter Ale and a local guest on handpump, 22 wines by
the glass and local cider; staff are helpful and friendly. A doorway leads
to a cosy room with a leather sofa, armchairs, a chest table and an open
fire, and another snug bar is similarly furnished, while a simpler room has
straightforward wooden dining chairs and tables, a little brick fireplace
and some stained glass. Throughout, there are rugs on parquet flooring
(some plain bare boards too), church candles, contemporary paintwork and
interesting lighting – look out for the antler chandelier with its pretty hanging
lampshades; background music and board games. Outside, the flower-filled

terrace has tables and chairs under parasols with more on grass. Some of the airy, well equipped and comfortable bedrooms overlook the square and church. This is a lovely village.

 As well as breakfasts (9-11am) and lunchtime sandwiches, the highly regarded food includes wood-fired pizzas, smoked lamb scrumpets with rémoulade, radish, chicory and chives, spiced chicken terrine with spring onion, raita and naan crispbread, half a grilled chicken with lemon and thyme, romesco sauce, crispy polenta and slow-cooked courgettes, grilled mackerel fillets with roasted beetroot and quinoa, ewes cheese, pickled fennel and shaved asparagus, dry-aged flat-iron steak with garlic and parsley butter, chips and a choice of sauces, and puddings such as elderflower pannacotta with berries and salted caramel and chocolate tart with honeycomb. *Benchmark main dish: chimichurri burger with toppings, paprika mayonnaise and crispy onions £13.00. Two-course evening meal £22.00.*

Free house ~ Licensee Abbie Windust ~ Real ale ~ Open 9am-11pm ~ Bar food 9am-9.45pm ~ Restaurant ~ Children welcome ~ Dogs allowed in bar and bedrooms ~ Wi-fi ~ Bedrooms: /£85 *Recommended by Peter and Emma Kelly, Richard Tilbrook, Charles Todd, Mark Hamill, Miranda and Jeff Davidson*

STANTON WICK
ST6162 Map 2
Carpenters Arms 🌟 ⏷ 🛏
(01761) 490202 – www.the-carpenters-arms.co.uk
Village signposted off A368, just W of junction with A37 S of Bristol; BS39 4BX

Bustling, friendly dining pub on country lane with pleasing food, helpful staff and fine choice of drinks; nice bedrooms

Once a row of miners' cottages, this is now a neatly kept pub well run by a friendly licensee and his attentive staff. Coopers Parlour on the right has a couple of beams, seats around heavy tables on a tartan carpet and attractive curtains; in the angle between here and the bar area is a wide woodburning stove in an opened-through fireplace. The bar has wall settles with cushions, stripped-stone walls and a big log fire in an inglenook. There's also a snug inner room (brightened by mirrors in arched recesses) and a restaurant with leather sofas, easy chairs and a lounge area at one end. Butcombe Bitter and Sharps Cornish Coaster and Doom Bar on handpump, ten wines by the glass (and some interesting bin ends) and several malt whiskies; TV in the snug. There are picnic-sets on the front terrace along with pretty flower beds, hanging baskets and tubs. Bedrooms are quiet and comfortable. The hanging baskets are very pretty and the surrounding countryside is peaceful with good walks.

 Enjoyable food includes sandwiches, confit duck with orange, walnuts and maple syrup, pheasant pâté with tomato and caramelised onion chutney, sharing boards, thai chicken curry, roasted red pepper, sun-dried tomatoes and courgette linguine with parmesan, six-hour braised beef with mash and red wine, thyme and baby onion sauce, hake fillet with smoked salmon, prawns and peas in herb cream sauce on pasta, lamb rump with smoked garlic mash, butternut squash purée and red wine and rosemary sauce, and puddings such as white chocolate and raspberry cheesecake and bakewell tart with clotted cream. *Benchmark main dish: local rib-eye steak with a choice of three sauces £18.95. Two-course evening meal £22.90.*

Buccaneer Holdings ~ Manager Simon Pledge ~ Real ale ~ Open 11-11; 12-10.30 Sun ~ Bar food 12-2.30, 6-9.30 (10 Fri, Sat); 12-9 Sun ~ Restaurant ~ Children welcome ~ Dogs allowed in bar ~ Wi-fi ~ Bedrooms: £80/£120 *Recommended by Mr and Mrs P R Thomas, Phil and Helen Holt, Mr and Mrs J Watkins, Dr and Mrs A K Clarke, Trish and Karl Soloman, Taff Thomas*

WATERROW

ST0525 Map 1

Rock

(01984) 623293 – www.rockinnwaterrow.co.uk

B3227 Wiveliscombe–Bampton; TA4 2AX

Handsome inn with local ales, interesting food and a nice mix of customers; comfortable bedrooms

The relaxed and informal bar area in this striking timbered inn on the edge of Exmoor National Park has wheelback chairs and cushioned window seats around scrubbed kitchen tables on tartan carpet, sympathetic lighting and a woodburning stove in a stone fireplace. High black leather bar chairs line the copper-topped bar counter where they serve Otter Bitter and St Austell Tribute on handpump, ten wines by the glass, a dozen malt whiskies and farm cider; background music, darts and board games. The elegant restaurant is up some steps from the bar with pale grey-painted panelled walls, a large stag's head and high-backed wooden chairs around chunky kitchen tables on pale floorboards; there's also a snug with sofas and leather armchairs. In front of the building are seats under umbrellas. The cottagey bedrooms are pretty, with good breakfasts. Parking outside is limited but there is more on the far side of the main road over the bridge.

 Using local produce and cooked by the landlord, the carefully crafted food includes sandwiches, white crab layered with avocado and smoked salmon, pigeon breast with black pudding on truffle oil-dressed salad, sweet potato-flavoured gnocchi with spinach, red onion, pine nuts and grilled artichoke, honey-roast venison haunch with girolle mushrooms, horseradish mash and port and pepper sauce, honey-roasted free-range duck breast with parsnip purée, merlot and orange-scented sauce and truffle dauphinoise potatoes, 29-day-hung aberdeen angus steak with café de paris butter, and puddings. *Benchmark main dish: short rib of aberdeen angus beef £17.00. Two-course evening meal £25.00.*

Free house ~ Licensees Daren and Ruth Barclay ~ Real ale ~ Open 12-3, 6-11; closed Sun evening, all day Mon, Tues lunchtime -- Bar food 12-2, 6.30-9 ~ Restaurant ~ Children welcome ~ Dogs welcome ~ Wi-fi ~ Bedrooms: £75/£85 *Recommended by Mrs K M King, Mike and Mary Carter, Pat Mitchell, Gary Wilkinson*

WEDMORE

ST4348 Map 1

Swan

(01934) 710337 – www.theswanwedmore.com

Cheddar Road, opposite Church Street; BS28 4EQ

Lively place with a friendly, informal atmosphere, lots of customers, efficient service and tasty food; bedrooms

With a cheerful, bustling atmosphere throughout, this handsome place is open and offers some kind of food and drink all day. Mirrors dotted about give the open-plan layout a feeling of even more space. The main bar has all sorts of wooden tables and chairs on floorboards, a wall seat with attractive scatter cushions, a woodburning stove, suede stools against the panelled counter and a rustic central table with daily papers; background music. Cheddar Potholer, Otter Bitter and Bright and a guest beer on handpump, 20 wines by the glass and two farm ciders are served by quick, friendly staff. At one end of the room, a step leads down to an area with rugs on huge flagstones, a leather chesterfield, armchairs and brass-studded leather chairs, then down another step to more sofas and armchairs. The airy dining room has attractive high-backed chairs, tables set with candles in glass jars and another woodburner. There are plenty of seats and tables on the terrace and lawn, and the metal furniture among flowering tubs at the front of the building gives a continental feel.

 Imaginative food includes sandwiches, game terrine with chutney, smoked pigs cheek with celeriac rémoulade and caper dressing, sharing boards, parsnip and polenta gnocchi with mushroom ragoût, olives and truffle oil pesto, chicken and ham hock pie, hake fillet with chorizo, butter beans and dill, oak-smoked lamb rump with celeriac and potato gratin, slow-cooked beef with roasted squash and mash, dry-aged steaks with roast garlic and parsley butter, and puddings such as rhubarb trifle with vanilla custard and salted caramel and chocolate tart. *Benchmark main dish: chimichurri beef burger with toppings and chips £13.00. Two-course evening meal £21.00.*

Free house ~ Licensee Natalie Zvonek-Little ~ Real ale ~ Open 9am-11pm (10.30 Sun) ~ Bar food 9am-10pm; snacks in afternoon ~ Restaurant ~ Children welcome ~ Dogs allowed in bar and bedrooms ~ Wi-fi ~ Bedrooms: /£75 *Recommended by John and Mary Warner, Taff Thomas, R T and J C Moggridge, Bob and Melissa Wyatt*

WRAXALL
ST4971   Map 2

Battleaxes 🛏

(01275) 857473 – www.flatcappers.co.uk
Bristol Road B3130, E of Nailsea; BS48 1LQ

Bustling pub with relaxed dining and drinking areas, helpful staff and good food; big bedrooms with contemporary bathrooms

It's all very easy-going here and the spacious interior is split into separate areas: polished floorboards or flagstones, portraits and pictures on walls above painted and panelled dados, mirrors on boldly patterned wallpaper, fresh flowers and house plants, books on windowsills and church candles. The bar has leather-topped stools against the counter where they keep a beer named for the pub (from Vale) and a couple of guests such as Electric Bear Werrrd! and Prescott Chequered Flag on handpump and several wines by the glass; background music. Throughout there are long pews with scatter cushions, church chairs and a medley of other wooden dining chairs around chunky tables and groups of leather armchairs. There are picnic-sets outside and some of the spacious bedrooms have country views. Tyntesfield (National Trust) is nearby. Wheelchair access using ramps.

Popular food includes breakfasts (8-11am), plus sharing boards, burger with toppings, coleslaw and chips, sausages of the week, mushroom and mozzarella wellington with sultanas and soy jus, calves liver and bacon with lyonnaise sauce, chicken suprême with rainbow chard and smoked paprika sauce, smoked haddock and cockle chowder, lamb rump with fondant potato, mushroom purée and red wine jus, and puddings such as a crumble of the day and chocolate and hazelnut brownie. *Benchmark main dish: beer-battered fish and chips £11.95. Two-course evening meal £20.50.*

Flatcappers ~ Manager Jacques Fourie ~ Real ale ~ Open 8am-11pm ~ Bar food 8am-10pm (9pm Sun) ~ Children welcome ~ Dogs allowed in bar ~ Wi-fi ~ Bedrooms: /£100 *Recommended by Dr Simon Innes, Gus Swan, R T and J C Moggridge, Dr and Mrs A K Clarke*

WRINGTON
ST4762   Map 2

Plough

(01934) 862871 – www.theploughatwrington.co.uk
2.5 miles off A370 Bristol–Weston, from bottom of Rhodiate Hill; BS40 5QA

Welcoming pub with bustling bar and two dining rooms, good food, well kept beer and seats outside

Facing a small green and smart period houses, this is a well run and neatly kept village pub. The bar is chatty and convivial with locals perched on stools against the counter where they keep Butcombe Bitter (the brewery is in the village), St Austell Tribute, Youngs Special and a guest such as Bath Golden Hare on handpump and 18 wines by the glass, served by friendly and efficient staff. The two dining rooms (the one at the back has plenty of big windows overlooking the gazebo and garden) have open doorways, and throughout you'll find (three) winter fires, slate or wooden floors, beams and standing timbers, plenty of pictures on the planked, red or yellow walls and all manner of high-backed leather or wooden dining or farmhouse chairs around tables of many sizes. Also, fresh flowers, table skittles and a chest containing games. There are picnic-sets at the front and on the back grass; boules. They hold a farmers' market on the second Friday of the month. This is sister pub to the Rattlebone at Sherston (Wiltshire). Disabled access.

Reliably good food includes sandwiches and ciabattas, chargrilled octopus with asian salad, honey and hoisin dressing and crispy seaweed, smoked chicken and chorizo terrine with apple, apricot and almond salad and curried mayonnaise, sharing boards, herb gnocchi with wild garlic and tomato ragoût and lime, chilli and poppy seeds, rosemary and apricot pork sausages with onion marmalade gravy, fillet of sea trout with herbs, salad and butter sauce, thai green curry, nine-hour braised lamb shank with bean sprout, mango and basil salad, and puddings such as warm carrot cake with spiced raisin purée and candied walnuts and iced dark chocolate and peanut parfait with salted caramel chocolate crumb; Wednesday is steak night. *Benchmark main dish: slow-roast pork belly with celeriac purée, apple, black pudding crisp and jus £13.95. Two-course evening meal £20.50.*

Youngs ~ Tenant Jason Read ~ Real ale ~ Open 12-3, 5-11 Mon, Tues; 12-11 Weds, Thurs, Sun; 12-midnight Fri, Sat ~ Bar food 12-2.30, 6-9.30; 12-9.30 Fri, Sat; 12-4, 7-9 Sun ~ Restaurant ~ Children welcome ~ Dogs welcome ~ Wi-fi *Recommended by Michael Doswell, Bob and Margaret Holder, Chris and Angela Buckell, Tracey and Stephen Groves, Peter Myers, Dr and Mrs A K Clarke*

Also Worth a Visit in Somerset

Besides the fully inspected pubs, you might like to try these pubs that have been recommended to us and described by readers. Do tell us what you think of them: feedback@goodguides.com

AXBRIDGE   ST4354
Lamb (01934) 732253
The Square; off A371 Cheddar–Winscombe; BS26 2AP Big rambling carpeted pub with heavy 15th-c beams and timbers, stone and roughcast walls, old settles and large stone fireplaces, unusual bar front with bottles set in plaster, Butcombe and a guest, well chosen wines and good coffee, enjoyable food (all day weekends) from sandwiches and baked potatoes up, two-course lunch Thurs and other deals; board games, table skittles and alley, sports TV; children and dogs allowed, seats out at front and in small sheltered back garden, farmers' market in square first Sat of month, medieval King John's Hunting Lodge (NT) opposite, open all day. *(Peter Myers)*

BACKWELL   ST4969
George (01275) 462770
Farleigh Road; A370 W of Bristol; BS48 3PG Modernised and extended main road dining pub (former coaching inn), well liked food in bar and restaurant from sandwiches and sharing boards up, well kept Bath, Butcombe, St Austell and a guest, good choice of wines; background music in some areas; children and dogs welcome, gravel terrace and lawn behind, seven bedrooms, open (and food) all day. *(Darrell Barton)*

BARRINGTON   ST3918
Barrington Boar (01460) 259281
Opposite church; TA19 0JB Old stone-built dining pub in pretty village, good variety of well liked food (not Sun evening,

Mon) from lunchtime sandwiches and light meals up, friendly helpful service, Exmoor, St Austell and a beer badged for them, Thatcher's cider, updated interior with solid modern furnishings, wood and stone floors, woodburners (boar's head above one); children and dogs welcome, picnic-sets in front and in pleasant beer garden behind, four bedrooms, handy for Barrington Court (NT), open all day weekends (till 9pm Sun), closed Mon lunchtime. *(Alan and Angela Scouller)*

BATCOMBE ST6839

★ **Three Horseshoes** (01749) 850359
Village signposted off A359 Bruton–Frome; BA4 6HE Handsome honey-stone inn with long narrow main room, beams, local pictures, built-in cushioned window seats and nice mix of tables, woodburner one end, open fire the other, Butcombe, Wild Beer and guests, local ciders, around a dozen wines by the glass and several malt whiskies, very good food (best to book, especially weekends), helpful friendly service, attractive stripped-stone dining room; open mike night last Thurs of month; children and dogs welcome, three simple but pretty bedrooms, lovely church next door, open all day weekends. *(Pete and Sarah)*

BATH ST7464

Bath Brew House (01225) 805609
James Street West; BA1 2BX Interesting spaciously converted pub visibly brewing its own James Street beers (brewery tours available), also guest ales and craft kegs, food from open kitchen including spit-roasts, various events such as comedy nights in upstairs room with own bar and sports TV; well behaved children and dogs allowed in some areas, sizeable split-level beer garden with covered eating area, summer barbecues, open (and food) all day. *(Dr and Mrs A K Clarke)*

BATH ST7565

Bell (01225) 460426
Walcot Street; BA1 5BW Long narrow split-level pub owned by the local community; nine real ales, traditional ciders and some basic good value food, lots of pump clips and gig notices, a couple of fires (one gas), bar billiards and table football; packed and lively in the evening with regular live music and DJ sets, board games, free wi-fi; canopied garden, even has its own laundrette, open all day. *(Dr and Mrs A K Clarke)*

BATH ST7564

Boater (01225) 464211
Argyle Street, by Pulteney Bridge; BA2 4BQ Refurbished Fullers pub in good spot near the river, fairly traditional bare-boards bar with at least five well kept ales, fine range of draught/bottled craft beers and good choice of wines by the glass, popular fairly priced food from lunchtime sandwiches and pub favourites up, quick friendly service, upstairs restaurant with view of Pulteney weir, cosy cellar bar; children and dogs welcome, sizeable back terrace on two levels, open all day (till 1am Fri, Sat). *(Dr and Mrs A K Clarke)*

BATH ST7465

Chequers (01225) 360017
Rivers Street; BA1 2QA Busy 19th-c city-centre pub with good interesting food (can be pricey) along with more standard choices, Bath Gem, Butcombe Bitter and several wines by the glass, friendly service, parquet-floored bar with wedgwood-blue paintwork and some fine plasterwork, cushioned wall pews, chapel, farmhouse and kitchen chairs around mix of flower-topped tables, coal-effect gas fire, attractive little candlelit restaurant upstairs with view into kitchen; children and dogs (in bar) welcome, pavement picnic-sets under awning, open all day. *(Luke Morgan, Richard Mason, Dr and Mrs A K Clarke)*

BATH ST7564

★ **Coeur de Lion** (01225) 463568
Northumberland Place, off High Street; BA1 5AR Tiny stained-glass-fronted single-room pub, simple, cosy and friendly, with candles and log-effect gas fire, well kept Abbey ales and guests, good well priced traditional food from snacks and baguettes up (vegetarian options), Christmas mulled wine, more room and loos upstairs; may be background music; tables out in charming flower-filled flagstoned pedestrian alley, open all day, food till 6pm. *(Stuart Doughty, Dr and Mrs A K Clarke)*

BATH ST7564

★ **Crystal Palace** (01225) 482666
Abbey Green; BA1 1NW Spacious two-room Fullers pub, rugs on wood floors and comfortable mix of seating, panelled walls and groups of pictures, popular sensibly priced food from lunchtime sandwiches up, Somerset cheese and port menu, speedy friendly service, four well kept ales from plank-faced bar, log fire, garden room opening on to nice sheltered courtyard; background music, sports TV, free wi-fi; children and dogs welcome, handy for Roman Baths and main shopping areas, open (and food) all day. *(Dr and Mrs A K Clarke, Michael Sargent)*

BATH ST7464

Garricks Head (01225) 318368
St Johns Place/Westgate, beside Theatre Royal; BA1 1ET Civilised and relaxed dining pub with good food including pre-theatre menu; bar with tall windows, wheelback and other chairs around wooden tables on bare boards, candles and a couple of sizeable brass chandeliers, gas-effect coal fire with fine silver meat domes on wall above, four interesting regional ales, real

ciders and decent wines by the glass, proper cocktails, separate smartly set dining room; may be soft background jazz; children and dogs (in bar) welcome, pavement tables, open all day. *(Dr and Mrs A K Clarke)*

BATH ST7564
Graze (01225) 429392
Behind Bath Spa station; BA1 1SX
Spacious Bath Ales bar-restaurant (part of the city's Vaults development) arranged over upper floor and served by lift; modern steel and glass construction with leather chairs and benches on wood-strip flooring, slatted ceiling with exposed ducting and pendant lighting, good selection of beers (some from on-site microbrewery, can be pricey), extensive range of wines and spirits, enjoyable food cooked in open kitchen from light dishes and sharing boards to Josper grills, happy helpful staff; prominent background music; children welcome, disabled facilities, two sizeable terraces overlooking Bath one side, the station the other, life-size models of cows, pigs and chickens, open all day. *(Dr and Mrs A K Clarke, Chris and Angela Buckell)*

BATH ST7464
Griffin (01225) 420919
Monmouth Street; BA1 2AP Cleanly refurbished little corner pub with fine range of well kept ales, craft beers and ciders, enjoyable freshly made food from shortish menu including good Sun roasts, friendly staff; comfortable bedrooms, open (and food) all day, kitchen closes 3pm Sun. *(Kate Ritcher)*

BATH ST7465
Hall & Woodhouse (01225) 469259
Old King Street; BA1 2JW Conversion of stone-fronted warehouse/auction rooms; big open-plan interior on two floors, steel girders and glass, palms and chandeliers, mix of modern and traditional furniture including old-fashioned iron-framed tables with large candles and some simple bench seating, parquet and slate floors, Badger ales from full-length servery on the right, sweeping stairs up to another bar and eating area (disabled access via lift), roof terrace, decent choice of food from pub favourites to specials, helpful chatty staff; gets very busy with after-work drinkers when standing room only, open (and food) all day from 9am for breakfast. *(Dr and Mrs A K Clarke)*

BATH ST7467
★Hare & Hounds (01225) 482682
Lansdown Road, Lansdown Hill; BA1 5TJ Wonderful far-reaching views over villages and fields from inside and out; long single bar with easy-going feel, chapel chairs and cushioned wall settles around pale wood-topped tables on bare boards, minimal decoration on pale walls above blue-grey dado, Butcombe Bitter, Theakstons Vanilla Stout and a Caledonian

beer badged for the pub from attractively carved counter, several wines by the glass, good food from breakfasts on, log fire with bronze hare and hound above, small slate-floored conservatory; background music, free wi-fi; children and dogs welcome, decked terrace, more seats and tables down steps, open all day from 8.30am. *(Michael Doswell, Dr and Mrs A K Clarke, Sally and David Champion, Richard Mason)*

BATH ST7465
★Hop Pole (01225) 446327
Albion Buildings, Upper Bristol Road; BA1 3AR Bustling family-friendly Bath Ales pub, their beers and guests kept well, decent wines by the glass and good choice of whiskies and other spirits, nice food (all day Fri-Sun) from sandwiches and traditional favourites up in bar and former skittle alley restaurant, friendly helpful staff, settles and other pub furniture on bare boards in four linked areas, lots of dark woodwork, ochre walls, some bric-a-brac; background music, Mon quiz, discreet sports TV; wheelchair access to main bar area only, pleasant two-level back courtyard with boules, fairy-lit vine arbour and heated summerhouses, opposite Victoria Park (great kids' play area), open all day. *(Chris and Angela Buckell, Taff Thomas, Dr and Mrs A K Clarke)*

BATH ST7565
King William (01225) 428096
Thomas Street/A4 London Road; BA1 5NN Cosy corner dining pub with well cooked food from short daily changing menu, four local ales and good choice of wines by the glass, chunky old tables on bare boards, steep stairs up to restaurant (a little more formal); background music; children and dogs welcome, open all day weekends. *(Dr and Mrs A K Clarke, Stuart Doughty)*

BATH ST7465
★Marlborough (01225) 423731
35 Marlborough Buildings/Weston Road; BA1 2LY Busy pub centrally placed and usefully open all day from 8am (9am weekends); U-shaped bare-boards bar with candles in sizeable jars on windowsills and above the fireplace, seating ranging from thick button-back wall seats to chapel, kitchen and high-backed dining chairs, flowers on tables, Butcombe, guest beers and several wines by the glass, well liked food from breakfasts up, cheerful staff; background music, free wi-fi; children and dogs welcome, suntrap courtyard garden. *(Peter Barrett, Dr and Mrs A K Clarke, James Allsopp)*

BATH ST7565
Pig & Fiddle (01225) 460868
Saracen Street; BA1 5BR Lively place (particularly weekends) with five well kept ales and fairly simple affordably priced food including range of burgers, friendly staff,

bare-boards interior with two big open fires and collection of sporting memorabilia, steps up to bustling servery and little dining area, games part; live music and DJ nights, several TVs for sport; picnic-sets on big heated terrace, open all day, food till early evening. *(Dr and Mrs A K Clarke)*

BATH ST7565
Pulteney Arms (01225) 463923

Daniel Street/Sutton Street; BA2 6ND Cosy, cheerful and largely unspoilt 18th-c pub, Box Steam Piston Broke, Fullers London Pride, Timothy Taylors Landlord and guests, Thatcher's cider, enjoyable freshly made food at sensible prices, traditional furniture on wooden floors, old gas lamps, woodburner and lots of Bath RFC memorabilia; background music, sports TV, darts, Mon quiz; children and dogs welcome, pavement tables and small back terrace, handy for Sydney Gardens and charming Holburne Museum, open all day Fri-Sun, no food Sun evening. *(Taff Thomas, Dr and Mrs A K Clarke)*

BATH ST7464
Raven (01225) 425045

Queen Street; BA1 1HE Small buoyant 18th-c city-centre free house serving two well kept ales for the pub from Blindmans and four guests, craft beers and a changing cider, decent wines by the glass too, limited choice of food (good Pieminister pies), quick friendly service, bare boards, some stripped stone and an open fire, newspapers, quieter upstairs bar; storytelling evenings and monthly open mike night; no under-14s or dogs; open all day. *(Dr and Mrs A K Clarke)*

BATH ST7466
Richmond Arms (01225) 316725

Richmond Place, off Lansdown Road; BA1 5PZ Cosy bow-windowed pub in Georgian terrace quietly located off the tourist track; well liked sensibly priced home-made food (not Sun evening, Mon) including daily specials, Butcombe, Sharps Doom Bar and a guest, ciders from Symonds and Thatcher's, lots of wines by the glass, friendly service, mix of tables and chairs on bare boards, local artwork for sale; monthly quiz; children and dogs welcome, enclosed pretty front garden, may be summer barbecues, open all day. *(Dr and Mrs A K Clarke)*

BATH ST7364
Royal Oak (01225) 481409

Lower Bristol Road; near Oldfield Park station; BA2 3BW Friendly roadside pub with well kept Butts, Downton and up to five guests, good range of ciders/perries and bottled beers, no food, two bare-boards bar areas with open fires; regular live music, Tues quiz; dogs welcome (they have two huskies), side beer garden, open all day (from 2pm Mon-Thurs). *(Dr and Mrs A K Clarke)*

BATH ST7464
Salamander (01225) 428889

John Street; BA1 2JL Busy city local tied to Bath Ales, their full range and a guest kept well, good choice of wines by the glass, bare boards, black woodwork and ochre walls, popular food from sandwiches up (more choice evenings/weekends), friendly helpful young staff, upstairs restaurant with open kitchen; background music, daily papers; children till 8pm, no dogs, open all day (till 1am Fri, Sat), gets packed on Bath RFC days. *(Taff Thomas, Dr and Mrs A K Clarke, Richard Mason, Philip J Alderton, Mike Gleave)*

BATH ST7564
Volunteer Riflemans Arms

(01225) 425210 *New Bond Street Place; BA1 1BH* Friendly little city-centre pub with leather sofas and a few close-set tables, wartime/military posters, open fire, well kept ales including a house beer from Moles, a couple of draught ciders and good value tasty lunchtime food, small upstairs dining room and roof terrace; background music; pavement tables, open all day. *(Dr and Mrs A K Clarke)*

BATH ST7564
White Hart (01225) 338053

Widcombe Hill; BA2 6AA Bistro-style pub with scrubbed pine tables on bare boards, candles and fresh flowers, good imaginative if not cheap food, well kept Butcombe from traditional panelled counter, proper cider and plenty of wines by the glass, quick friendly service; background music; children and dogs welcome, pretty back garden, bedrooms (some sharing bathroom), open all day (Sun till 5pm). *(Dr and Mrs A K Clarke)*

BATHFORD ST7866
Crown (01225) 852426

Bathford Hill, towards Bradford-on-Avon, by Batheaston roundabout and bridge; BA1 7SL Welcoming bistro pub with good blackboard food including weekday set deals, ales such as Bath and Timothy Taylors Landlord, nice wines, charming french landlady; children and dogs welcome, tables out in front and in back garden with pétanque, open all day. *(Dr and Mrs A K Clarke)*

BICKNOLLER ST1139
Bicknoller Inn (01984) 656234

Church Lane; TA4 4EW Welcoming old thatched pub nestling below the Quantocks, traditional flagstoned front bar, side room and large back restaurant with open kitchen, popular food from pub favourites up, Sun carvery (booking advised), friendly helpful service, four well kept Palmers ales and a couple of real ciders, skittle alley, free wi-fi; children and dogs (in bar) welcome, courtyard and nice back garden, boules, attractive village, open all day weekends. *(Peter Rogan)*

BISHOPS LYDEARD   ST1629
Lethbridge Arms (01823) 433467
Off A358 Taunton–Watchet; Gore Square;
TA4 3BW Welcoming 16th-c beamed
coaching inn with good well presented/priced
traditional food from sandwiches and baked
potatoes up, Sun carvery, well kept Quantock
Wills Neck and Sharps Doom Bar, Thatcher's
and Weston's ciders, efficient smiling
service; pool and darts, free wi-fi; children
and dogs welcome, bedrooms, open all day
weekends. *(Diana Hill and Brian Sturgess)*

BLAGDON   ST5058
New Inn (01761) 462475
Signed off A368; Park Lane/Church
Street; BS40 7SB Village pub with lovely
view over Blagdon Lake from garden
picnic-sets; well kept Wadworths and
guests, decent wines and good choice of
enjoyable reasonably priced food from
baguettes to grills (maybe fresh local
trout), bustling bars with two inglenook log
fires, heavy beams hung with horsebrasses
and tankards, comfortable antique settles
and mate's chairs among more modern
furnishings, old prints and photographs,
plainer side bar; no under-10s, dogs
welcome, wheelchair access best from
front. *(M G Hart, Tim and Moira Hurst)*

BLEADON   ST3457
★Queens Arms (01934) 812080
Just off A370 S of Weston; Celtic Way;
BS24 0NF Popular 16th-c beamed village
pub; informal chatty atmosphere in carefully
divided areas, generous reasonably priced
food (not Sun evening) from lunchtime
baguettes to steaks, friendly service,
Butcombe and other well kept ales tapped
from the cask, local cider and decent
wines by the glass, stripped-stone back bar
with woodburner, sturdy tables, winged
settles and old hunting prints, flagstoned
restaurant; occasional live music, quiz first
Mon of the month; children (away from
bar) and dogs welcome, partial wheelchair
access, picnic-sets on pretty heated terrace,
open all day. *(Bob and Melissa Wyatt)*

BRADFORD-ON-TONE   ST1722
White Horse (01823) 461239
Fairly near M5 junction 26, off A38
towards Taunton; TA4 1HF Popular
17th-c stone-built village pub across from
the church, enjoyable good value food from
fairly pubby menu including blackboard
specials and weekday light lunch deal,
friendly helpful staff, well kept ales such as
Hanlons, Otter and St Austell, bare-boards
bar with leather sofas and armchair by
woodburner, linked dining areas; background
music, skittle alley; children and dogs
welcome, picnic-sets in pleasant lawned
garden (look out for Percy the peacock),
unusual glass pub sign, closed Sun evening,
Mon lunchtime. *(Bob and Margaret Holder)*

BRISTOL   ST5773
Alma (0117) 973 5171
Alma Vale Road, Clifton; BS8 2HY
Two-bar pub with west country beers,
Aspall's and Thatcher's ciders and several
wines by the glass, good range of whiskies
too, very well liked imaginative food along
with more standard choices including good
Sun roasts, friendly hard-working staff,
dark panelled traditionally furnished front
bar with wood flooring, more contemporary
back room with bright modern wallpaper
and local artwork on display, thriving
upstairs theatre (10% food discount for
ticket holders); background music, jazz
pianist Sun; easy wheelchair access, small
paved terrace behind (not late evening),
open all day. *(Chris and Angela Buckell)*

BRISTOL   ST5873
Bank (0117) 930 4691
John Street; BS1 2HR Small proper
single-bar pub, centrally placed (but
off the beaten track) and popular with
office workers; four changing local ales
(may include a porter), real ciders
and enjoyable well priced food till 4pm
including sandwiches, burgers and one or
two unusual choices, comfortable bench
seats, newspapers, books on shelf above
fireplace; background and regular live
music, Tues quiz, free wi-fi; children and
dogs welcome, wheelchair access, tables
under umbrellas in paved courtyard, open
all day (till 1am Thurs-Sat). *(Taff Thomas)*

BRISTOL   ST5972
Barley Mow (0117) 930 4709
Barton Road; The Dings; BS2 0LF Late
19th-c Bristol Beer Factory pub in old
industrial area close to floating harbour; up
to eight well kept changing ales, excellent
selection of craft kegs and bottled beers,
proper cider and decent choice of wines by
the glass, enjoyable good value food (not
Sun evening) from short menu catering
for vegetarians, cheerful chatty staff, wood
floors, off-white walls and blue half-panelling,
cushioned wall seats and pubby furniture,
various odds and ends dotted about, open
fire in brick fireplace; Mon quiz, free wi-fi;
disabled access, open all day (till 10pm Sun).
(Matthew and Elizabeth Reeves)

BRISTOL   ST5872
Beer Emporium (0117) 379 0333
King Street, opposite the Old Vic;
BS1 4EF Cellar bar-restaurant with two
vaulted rooms; long stone-faced counter
under stained-glass skylight, 24 regularly
changing ales/craft beers (tasters offered)
plus over 150 in bottles from around the
world, good selection of malt whiskies and
other spirits, interesting wine list, coffees
and teas, italian food including range of
pizzas and good weekday lunchtime deal,
cheerful chatty staff; some live music;

wheelchair access via lift, disabled loos, open (and food) all day (till 2am Mon-Sat), can get crowded. *(Edward May)*

BRISTOL   ST5872
BrewDog (0117) 927 9258
Baldwin Street, opposite church;
BS1 1QW Corner bar serving own BrewDog beers and guests from other craft breweries (draught and bottled), tasters offered by knowledgeable young staff, limited but interesting selection of bar snacks, starkly modern feel with exposed brick, stainless-steel furniture and granite surfaces; can get noisily busy; wheelchair access, open all day till midnight (Thurs-Sat till 1am). *(Edward May)*

BRISTOL   ST5874
Chums 07757 681261
Chandos Road; BS6 6PF Micropub in former corner shop, mismatched furniture on boarded floor, painted half-panelling and lots of modern artwork for sale, six real ales (listed on blackboard) from pine-planked servery, real ciders and range of bottled belgian beers, snacky food; mobile phones discouraged; wheelchair access using ramp (staff will help), open all day weekends, from 4pm other days. *(Chris and Angela Buckell)*

BRISTOL   ST5872
Commercial Rooms (0117) 927 9681
Corn Street; BS1 1HT Spacious colonnaded Wetherspoons (former early 19th-c merchants' club) in good location; main part with lofty stained-glass domed ceiling, large oval portraits of Bristol notables and gas lighting, comfortable quieter back room with ornate balcony, note the unusual wind gauge above horseshoe servery; good changing choice of real ales, local ciders and nice chatty bustle (busiest weekend evenings), their usual food and low prices; ladies' with chesterfields and open fire; children welcome, no dogs, side wheelchair access and disabled facilities, open all day from 8am and till late Fri-Sun. *(Chris and Angela Buckell, Dr and Mrs A K Clarke)*

BRISTOL   ST5872
Cornubia (0117) 925 4415
Temple Street, opposite fire station;
BS1 6EN Tucked-away 18th-c real ale pub with fine selection including a good locally brewed house beer, also interesting bottled beers, farm ciders and perry, snacky food such as pasties and pork pies, friendly helpful service, walls and ceilings covered in pump clips, union jacks and other patriotic memorabilia, open fire and an aquarium for turtles; Thurs blues night, quiz first Tues of month; dogs welcome, not suitable for wheelchairs, picnic-sets in secluded front beer garden (summer barbecues), boules pitch, closed Sun evening, otherwise open all day. *(Taff Thomas, Dr and Mrs A K Clarke)*

BRISTOL   ST5773
Eldon House (0117) 922 1271
Lower Clifton Hill, Clifton; BS8 1BT
Extended terrace-end Clifton pub; bare boards and mix of wooden tables and chairs, circular stone-walled dining area with glazed roof, snug with original stained glass and half-door servery, well kept Bath Ales, a couple of guests and several wines by the glass, popular good value food (not Sun evening) including blackboard specials, friendly staff; background and regular live music, Mon quiz and other events, free wi-fi; children (till 8pm) and dogs (in bar) welcome, open all day Fri-Sun, closed lunchtimes Mon-Weds. *(Julian Richardson)*

BRISTOL   ST5876
Gloucester Old Spot (0117) 924
7693 *Kellaway Avenue; BS6 7YQ*
Popular refurbished community pub with opened-up interior; well kept ales such as Butcombe, Exmoor and Timothy Taylors from dark wood horseshoe servery, decent wines and good range of spirits, enjoyable reasonably priced food (not Sun evening) from sandwiches and sharing boards up, friendly prompt service, back bar and large parquet-floored dining lounge opening on to verandah and AstroTurf beer garden; Tues quiz, free wi-fi; children and dogs welcome, wheelchair access using portable ramp (staff will help), play area with wendy house, open all day from 9am for breakfast. *(Chris and Angela Buckell)*

BRISTOL   ST5872
Golden Guinea (0117) 987 2034
Guinea Street; BS1 6SX Steps up to cosy backstreet pub, well kept changing ales such as Black Flag and Tiny Rebel, real ciders and simple bargain home-made food, friendly staff, pews, wing armchairs and farmhouse tables on bare boards, some flock wallpaper and contemporary street art; occasional live music, comedy and quiz nights, sports TV; seats out in front and behind, closed lunchtimes Mon and Tues, otherwise open all day. *(Edward May)*

BRISTOL   ST5772
Grain Barge (0117) 929 9347
Hotwell Road; BS8 4RU Converted 100-ft barge owned by Bristol Beer Factory, their ales kept well and fair priced food including good sandwiches, burgers and Sun roasts, steak night Thurs, great harbour views from seats out on top deck, tables and sofas in wood floor bar below, also a 'hold bar' for functions and Fri live music; open all day. *(Taff Thomas)*

BRISTOL   ST5873
Green Man (0117) 925 8062
Alfred Place, Kingsdown; BS2 8HD
Cosy local with country pub feel, bare boards and dark woodwork, well kept Dawkins

and guests, real cider, several wines by the glass and around 60 gins, extensive burger menu and popular Sun roasts, friendly knowledgeable staff; background and regular live music, Weds quiz, free wi-fi; children and dogs (on leads) welcome, wheelchair access possible with help, open all day Fri and Sat, till 9pm Sun, from 4pm other days. *(Dan Beswick)*

BRISTOL ST5772
★ Hope & Anchor (0117) 929 2987
Jacobs Wells Road, Clifton; BS8 1DR
Welcoming 18th-c pub opposite 11th-c Jacobs Well; half a dozen changing ales from central bar, nice wines and good choice of malt whiskies, tables of various sizes (some shaped to fit corners) on bare boards, darker back area, enjoyable food including home-made pizzas, friendly staff; background and occasional live music, Sun quiz; children welcome, disabled access, attractive tiered back garden, parking nearby can be tricky, open (and food) all day. *(Taff Thomas)*

BRISTOL ST5873
Horts City Tavern (0117) 025 2520
Broad Street; BS1 2EJ Open-plan 18th-c Youngs pub, their well kept ales along with Bath Gem, good fairly priced food including burgers and sharing boards, big windows overlooking street, 26-seat cinema at back (free entry if you have a meal, free children's film Sun); background music, Thurs quiz, sports TV; tables in cobbled courtyard, open all day. *(Edward May)*

BRISTOL ST5977
Inn on the Green (0117) 952 1391
Filton Road (A38), Horfield; BS7 0PA
Busy open-plan pub with up to 12 changing ales and half a dozen ciders/perries, good selection of whiskies and gins too, enjoyable generously served food, helpful friendly staff, wood or slate floors, lots of mirrors and old prints, modern pub furniture along with sofas and armchairs, more screened seating areas in former skittle alley dining area; monthly folk night upstairs, bar billiards, darts; children and dogs welcome, disabled access/facilities, beer garden with sheltered pool table and summer table tennis, open (and food) all day. *(Chris and Angela Buckell)*

BRISTOL ST5774
Jersey Lily (0117) 973 8590
Whiteladies Road; BS8 2SB Compact corner pub with matt-black frontage, bare boards, magnolia/light grey walls and woodwork, some high tables and chairs, raised area with red leather wall seating, well kept Wickwar ales and guests, interesting wines (shortish list) and good range of gins, enjoyable reasonably priced food from pubby staples to more exotic specials, friendly helpful staff; some live music, sports TV, free wi-fi; wheelchair access to bar area only, pavement seats and awning,

decked side area through arch, open all day. *(Chris and Angela Buckell, Edward May)*

BRISTOL ST5874
Kensington Arms (0117) 944 6444
Stanley Road; BS6 6NP Dining pub (aka the Kenny) in centre of Redland under good new management; highly regarded food at fair prices from chef-patron including interesting snacks, well executed pub favourites and daily specials, Sat brunch from 10am, well kept Butcombe, Greene King and guests, Thatcher's cider and plenty of wines by the glass from comprehensive list, friendly attentive staff; background music, monthly comedy and quiz nights upstairs; children and dogs welcome, disabled facilities (no wheelchair access to dining room, but can eat in bar), heated front terrace, open all day, food till 7pm Sun. *(Charles Todd)*

BRISTOL ST5972
Kings Head (0117) 929 2338
Victoria Street; BS1 6DE Welcoming and relaxed little 17th-c pub; traditional bar with big front window and splendid mirrored bar-back, corridor to cosy panelled snug with serving hatch, toby jugs on joists, old-fashioned local prints and photographs, five well kept ales including Castle Rock, Harveys and Sharps, range of pies; a few pavement tables, open all day. *(Dr and Mrs A K Clarke)*

BRISTOL ST5972
Knights Templar (0117) 930 8710
The Square; BS1 6DG Glass and stainless-steel Wetherspoons very handy for Temple Meads station; spacious carpeted room with raised area, their usual good value food served from breakfast till late, well kept beers and good range of other drinks, helpful staff; lots of TVs; children welcome, disabled access/loos, plenty of outside seating, open all day. *(Taff Thomas, Chris and Angela Buckell)*

BRISTOL ST5276
Lamplighters (0117) 279 3754
End of Station Road, Shirehampton; BS11 9XA Popular 18th-c riverside pub; well kept Bath Ales and a guest, Thatcher's ciders, teas and coffees, competitively priced traditional food (not Sun evening) including children's choices, OAP meal deals and themed nights, modern bar furniture on carpet or bare boards, some faux leather sofas and armchairs, pastel walls with darker greeny-blue dados, bold patterned wallpaper here and there, mezzanine dining area and cellar bar (not always open); occasional live music; disabled access/facilities, picnic-sets on paved front terrace, limited parking nearby (beware of the high spring tides), riverside walks, open all day. *(Charles Todd)*

BRISTOL ST5976
Lazy Dog (0117) 924 4809
Ashley Down Road; BS7 9JR Popular local with two bar areas (one upstairs), ales

such as Bath, Bristol Beer Factory, Purity and Wye Valley, local ciders, some interesting wines and good range of spirits, well liked food from fairly extensive blackboard menu including some unusual dishes, helpful chatty staff, charcoal grey interior with wood panelled alcoves, white marble-effect bar counter, leather wall benches, sofas and armchairs on light wood floors, family room with metal furniture (children till 7pm); vintage juke box, fortnightly quiz (Tues), film night (Weds); dogs welcome, disabled access/loos, seats out at front and in partly decked back garden, open all day. *(Chris and Angela Buckell)*

BRISTOL ST5673
Mall (0117) 974 5318
The Mall, Clifton; BS8 4JG Recently smartened-up corner pub with good selection of draught and bottled beers, lots of wines by the glass and interesting range of other drinks including cocktails, popular modern pub food, helpful friendly staff, mix of old and new furniture on wood floors, tall windows, some panelling and ornate ceilings, downstairs bar; free wi-fi; children (till 9pm) and dogs welcome, tiered garden behind (summer barbecues), open (and food) all day. *(Peter Myers)*

BRISTOL ST5772
Nova Scotia (0117) 929 7994
Baltic Wharf, Cumberland Basin; BS1 6XJ Old local on south side of floating harbour with views to Clifton and Avon Gorge; Courage Best and guests, local scrumpy and generous helpings of enjoyable pub food, four linked areas, snob screen, mahogany and mirrors, nautical charts as wallpaper, welcoming relaxed atmosphere and friendly regulars; wheelchair access with help through snug's door, plenty of tables out by water, bedrooms sharing bathroom. *(Chris and Angela Buckell, Dr and Mrs A K Clarke)*

BRISTOL ST5872
Old Duke (0117) 927 7137
King Street; BS1 4ER Corner pub in interesting cobbled area between docks and Bristol Old Vic; named after Duke Ellington and festooned with jazz posters and one or two musical instruments, good bands nightly and Sun lunchtime, four real ales including Otter and Sharps, simple food, usual pub furnishings; open all day (till 1am Fri, Sat), gets packed evenings. *(Taff Thomas, Peter Myers, Dr and Mrs A K Clarke)*

BRISTOL ST5872
Old Fish Market (0117) 921 1515
Baldwin Street; BS1 1QZ Imposing brick-built former fish market, relaxed friendly atmosphere, well kept Fullers/Gales beers and fine range of whiskies and gins from handsome wooden counter, enjoyable food from pizzas up including various chowders;

background music, Sun live jazz from 7pm, sports TVs, free wi-fi; open all day (food all day weekends). *(Dr and Mrs A K Clarke)*

BRISTOL ST5672
Portcullis (0117) 973 0270
Wellington Terrace; BS8 4LE Compact pub in Regency terrace close to Clifton Suspension Bridge, five well kept ales including two from Dawkins, traditional cider and good range of wines and spirits, low-priced pubby food (not Weds), friendly service, flame-effect gas fire, dark wood and usual pubby furniture, upstairs room leading to beer garden; occasional acoustic live music, board games, free wi-fi; dogs welcome, tricky wheelchair access, open all day Fri-Sun, closed lunchtimes Mon-Thurs (also Fri in winter). *(Taff Thomas, Peter Myers)*

BRISTOL ST5772
Pump House (0117) 927 2229
Merchants Road; BS8 4PZ Spacious well converted dockside building (former 19th-c pumping station); charcoal-grey brickwork, tiled floors and high ceilings, good food in bar and smart candlelit mezzanine restaurant, ales such as Bath, Butcombe and St Austell, decent wines from comprehensive list and over 400 gins, good selection of rums and whiskies too, friendly staff and cheerful atmosphere; waterside tables, open all day. *(Chris and Angela Buckell)*

BRISTOL ST5872
River Station (0117) 914 4434
The Grove; opposite Hole in the Wall pub; BS1 4RB Modern harbourside bar-restaurant converted some years ago from a former police building, now owned by Youngs and given a major refit; light and airy split-level bar/dining area with tiled and polished wood floors, mix of seating including sofas and squashy banquettes, good views from french windows opening on to waterside terrace, Youngs ales, Orchard Pig cider and several international bottled beers, good selection of wines, spirits and cocktails too, spacious upstairs restaurant with high curved ceiling and lots of glass, further terraces overlooking the water, well liked food from interesting varied menu including weekend brunch, helpful staff; background music; limited wheelchair access, open (and food) all day. *(Chris and Angela Buckell)*

BRISTOL ST5872
Royal Naval Volunteer
(0117) 316 9237 *King Street; BS1 4EF* Modernised 17th-c pub in cobbled street, wide range of draught and bottled british beers, ciders/perries and a dozen wines by the glass, friendly knowledgeable staff, good interesting food in back restaurant; weekend live music, sports TV; dogs welcome, terrace seating. *(Taff Thomas, Dr and Mrs A K Clarke, Edward May)*

BRISTOL ST5972
Seven Stars (0117) 927 2845
Thomas Lane; BS1 6JG Unpretentious
one-room real ale pub near harbour (and
associated with Thomas Clarkson and slave
trade abolition), popular with students
and local office workers, up to eight well
kept changing ales (20 from a featured
county on first Mon-Thurs of the month),
some interesting malts and bourbons, dark
wood and bare boards, old local prints
and photographs, no food – can bring
in takeaways; weekend folk music, juke
box, pool, games machine; dogs welcome,
disabled access (but narrow alley with
uneven cobbles and cast-iron kerbs),
open all day. *(Chris and Angela Buckell)*

BRISTOL ST5872
Small Bar No phone
King Street; BS1 4DZ Bustling real ale/
craft beer pub with over 30 choices including
own Left Handed Giant, all served in smaller
glasses (up to two-thirds of a pint), good
range of bottled beers too, good food such as
burgers and hotdogs along with vegetarian/
vegan choices, bare boards and flagstones,
roughly exposed brickwork here and there
and wood plank walls, some barrel tables
and a couple of old fireplaces, upstairs
area with armchairs, sofas and shelves
of books; background music; open all day
(till 1am Fri, Sat). *(Julian Richardson)*

BRISTOL ST5871
Steam Crane (0117) 923 1656
North Street; BS3 1HT Fine selection of
ales/craft beers and well liked food including
good burgers and Sun roasts, friendly staff,
large bare boards room with patterned
wallpaper above cerise dado, mismatching
furniture including leather sofas, chandeliers
and maybe local artwork for sale; background
music, regular live bands, swing nights and
DJs, sports TV; children and dogs welcome,
seats on back terrace, open all day (till 1am
Fri, Sat). *(Taff Thomas)*

BRISTOL ST5872
Three Tuns (0117) 907 0689
St Georges Road; BS1 5UR Popular
city-centre pub; seven real ales including
local Arbor, craft kegs and interesting
selection of bottled beers, several ciders
too, monthly changing menu, pine tables
on bare boards, a couple of small leather
sofas in alcoves, open fire; regular events
including Weds quiz, art exhibitions, live
music, film screenings and magic nights
second and last Tues of the month; covered
and heated back terrace down steps, near
cathedral, open all day. *(Edward May)*

BRISTOL ST5773
Victoria (0117) 974 5675
Southleigh Road, Clifton; BS8 2BH
Popular little two-room pub that can get
crowded, half a dozen or more changing
small brewery ales including a couple from
Dawkins, interesting bottled belgian beers,
local cider and good selection of gins, basic
snacks such as pies and sausage rolls, big
mirrors and open fire; Tues quiz, free wi-fi;
dogs welcome, disabled access (a few low
kerbs/steps), open all day weekends, from
4pm Mon-Fri. *(Chris and Angela Buckell)*

BRISTOL ST5973
Volunteer (0117) 955 8498
New Street, near Cabot Circus; BS2 9DX
Tucked-away local with friendly relaxed
atmosphere, good choice of changing
ales/craft beers, a couple of ciders and
decent wines by the glass, well liked
reasonably priced home-made food
including range of burgers and popular
Sun roasts; live music and beer festivals;
children and dogs welcome, walled garden
behind, open all day. *(Taff Thomas)*

BRISTOL ST5976
Wellington (0117) 951 3022
Gloucester Road, Horfield (A38); BS7 8UR
Updated and opened-up 1920s red-brick pub
on edge of Horfield Common; well kept Bath
Ales and St Austell, craft beers, local cider
and good choice of other drinks including
nice range of gins, enjoyable reasonably
priced food till 10pm, pleasant efficient
service, separate dining area opening on to
sunny paved terrace and grassy beer garden;
children welcome, wheelchair access from
back door (or front using ramp), disabled
loos, popular boutique bedrooms (best
to book early), open all day (from 9am
weekends for breakfast). *(Chris and Angela
Buckell, Dr and Mrs A K Clarke)*

BRISTOL ST5672
White Lion (0117) 403 0210
*Avon Gorge Hotel, Princes Buildings,
Clifton; BS8 4LD* Recently refurbished
hotel worth knowing for its terrace bar
overlooking the Avon Gorge and Clifton
Suspension Bridge; dark grey walls and
modern industrial lighting, rustic bench
tables and chairs on polished wood or
tiled floors, beers such as BrewDog and
Butcombe, good wine list, food served
all day till late, full height windows
opening on to the huge terrace with large
parasol-shaded tables and fantastic views;
background music (turned down on request),
silent TV for sport; disabled access/loos,
bedrooms. *(Chris and Angela Buckell)*

BRISTOL ST5872
Wild Beer (0117) 239 5693
*Gaol Ferry Steps, Wapping Wharf,
behind the M Shed Museum; BS1 5WE*
Busy bar/eatery in new development
overlooking the old docks; over 20 craft
beers (including Wild Beer) listed on
blackboards and served in third, half and
two-thirds of a pint glasses (tasters offered),

interesting wines and good selection of whiskies/gins, unusual but enjoyable food including selection of panko, tempura and taco dishes plus sharing boards and interesting snacks, good fish and chips with seaweed salted chips, cheerful helpful staff, flagstones, pale green walls and floor-to-ceiling windows, exposed ducting and a large mural on one wall, a couple of steps up to dining area with open kitchen; background music; children welcome, disabled access/facilities, split-level terrace with deckchairs and picnic-sets, nearby parking difficult, open all day. (Chris and Angela Buckell)

BURROW BRIDGE   ST3530
King Alfred (01823) 698379
Main Road, by the bridge; TA7 ORB Old-fashioned local under newish ownership, relaxed friendly atmosphere in flagstoned bar, well kept ales such as Butcombe and Otter, local ciders and decent wines by the glass, landlord-chef's good food (not Sun evening) from pub standards up, comfortable dining room upstairs with view over River Parrett and Somerset Levels, roof terrace; live music and quiz/curry nights; dogs welcome, open all day (till 9pm Sun). *(Susan Crabbe, Bob and Margaret Holder, Tessa Barton)*

BUTLEIGH   ST5133
Rose & Portcullis (01458) 850287
Sub Road/Barton Road; BA6 8TQ Welcoming stone-built country pub with enjoyable good value home-made food (not Sun evening), five well kept ales and good range of local ciders, helpful friendly staff, bar and airy dining extension; sports TV, free wi-fi; children and dogs welcome, tables outside. *(Stuart Reeves)*

CASTLE CARY   ST6432
George (01963) 350761
Just off A371 Shepton Mallet–Wincanton; Market Place; BA7 7AH Old-fashioned thatched country-town hotel (former 15th-c coaching inn), popular front bar with big inglenook, bistro-bar and restaurant (evenings only), well liked food from sandwiches up including good steaks, three changing real ales and decent wines by the glass, friendly staff; free wi-fi; children welcome, 17 bedrooms (some in courtyard), open all day. *(Richard Tilbrook)*

CHARLTON MUSGROVE   ST7229
Smithy (01963) 824899
B3081, 5 miles SE of Bruton; about a mile off A303; BA9 8HG Recently restored 18th-c pub (had been closed for six years) under friendly licensees; bar with stripped stone, heavy beams and inglenook woodburner, mismatch of furniture (some tables made from old cheeseboards), rugs on flagstone/concrete floor, Greene King ales and guests from plank-fronted servery, well liked uncomplicated food, intimate dining area overlooking garden,

restaurant in former skittle alley; background and monthly live music, quiz nights, TV for major sports; children and dogs welcome, bedrooms planned, open (and food) all day. *(Holly and Tim Waite)*

CHEDDAR   ST4653
White Hart (01934) 741261
The Bays; BS27 3QN Welcoming village local with well kept beers, traditional cider and enjoyable fairly priced home-made food from good ploughman's to Sun carvery, log fire; live music and quiz nights, free wi-fi; children welcome, picnic-sets out in front and in back garden with play area, open (and food) all day. *(Taff Thomas, Tony Scott)*

CHEW MAGNA   ST5763
Pelican (01275) 331777
South Parade; BS40 8SL Welcoming village pub with modern opened-up interior, mix of furniture on wood floors including leather sofas, some old pew chairs and high-backed settles, candles on chunky tables, log fires in stone fireplaces, well kept changing ales such as Butcombe, Otter and St Austell, local cider, plenty of wines by the glass and some interesting malt whiskies, good fairly priced food including weekday set lunch and daily specials, efficient service; children and dogs welcome, wheelchair access from back courtyard, grassy beer garden, open all day (Sun till 6pm). *(Chris and Angela Buckell, Dr and Mrs A K Clarke)*

CHEW MAGNA   ST5861
★**Pony & Trap** (01275) 332627
Knowle Hill, New Town; from B3130 in village, follow Bishop Sutton, Bath signpost; BS40 8TQ Michelin-starred dining pub in nice rural spot near Chew Valley Lake; first rate food from snacks and some lunchtime pubby choices through to beautifully presented restaurant dishes (must book), professional friendly service, Butcombe ales and a guest, front bar with cushioned wall seats and built-in benches on parquet, old range in snug area on left, dark plank panelling and housekeeper's chair in corner, lovely pasture views from two-level back dining area with white tables on slate flagstones; children welcome, dogs in bar, more furniture on back terrace, picnic-sets on grass with chickens in runs below, front smokers' shelter, good walks. *(Mr and Mrs A H Young, Ian and Rose Lock, Steve and Liz Tilley, Dr and Mrs A K Clarke)*

CHEWTON MENDIP   ST5953
Waldegrave Arms (01761) 241384
High Street (A39); BA3 4LL Friendly village pub run by the same family for over 30 years, traditional food from sandwiches up, well kept local ales such as Butcombe, Cottage and Cheddar; quiz nights and darts leagues; dogs welcome in bar, colourful

window boxes and hanging baskets, flower-filled garden behind, open (and food) all day Sun. *(R T and J C Moggridge)*

CHISELBOROUGH ST4614
★**Cat Head** (01935) 881231
Cat Street; leave A303 on A356 towards Crewkerne; take the third left (at 1.4 miles) signed Chiselborough, then left after 0.2 miles; TA14 6TT Character 15th-c hamstone pub refurbished quite recently under good licensees; bar and two dining areas, flagstones, mullioned windows and two permanently lit woodburners (one in fine inglenook), well executed fairly traditional food cooked by landlady, a couple of ales such as Sharps and Butcombe, friendly service; classical background music; children and dogs (in bar) welcome, picnic-sets in lovely back garden, closed Sun evening, Mon. *(Ewan and Sue Hewitt)*

COMBE FLOREY ST1531
★**Farmers Arms** (01823) 432267
Off A358 Taunton–Williton, just N of main village turn-off; TA4 3HZ This popular 15th-c thatched and beamed pub is expected to reopen early 2018 following severe fire damage – news please. *(Ian Jenkins, Richard and Penny Gibbs, Bob and Margaret Holder)*

COMPTON DANDO ST6464
Compton Inn (01761) 490321
Court Hill; BS39 4JZ Welcoming stone-built village pub in lovely setting; enjoyable home-made food (not Sun evening), well kept Butcombe, Sharps and a guest, wood-floored bar with dining area at each end (one down a couple of steps), two-way woodburner in stone fireplace; charity quiz first Mon of month, TV; children, walkers and dogs welcome, picnic-sets out in front, garden behind with boules, open all day. *(Mark Hamill)*

COMPTON MARTIN ST5457
Ring o' Bells (01761) 221284
A368 Bath–Weston; BS40 6JE Old village pub with traditional beamed front bar, log fire in big inglenook, pubby seats on flagstones, steps leading up to spacious back area with oak boards, stripped-stone walls and various odds and ends including gold discs and signed celebrity photos, Butcombe and a guest ale, good wine and whisky choice, enjoyable food (not Sun evening) from sandwiches up; background and live music (artists such as Coldplay, Duran Duran and Kylie Minogue have played here), monthly quiz, board games, free wi-fi; children allowed till 8.30pm, dogs in bar, big garden backing on to Mendip Hills, play area, good surrounding walks, two spacious bedrooms, open all day Fri-Sun. *(Gus Swan, Neil Allen, Dr and Mrs A K Clarke)*

CONGRESBURY ST4363
Old Inn (01934) 832270
Pauls Causeway, down Broad Street opposite The Cross; BS49 5DH Popular 16th-c low-beamed local, deep-set windows, flagstones and huge fireplaces, one with stove opening to both bar and dining area, mix of old furniture including pews and upholstered benches, leather ceiling straps, good choice of enjoyable reasonably priced pubby food (not Sun evening), well kept Youngs and a couple of guests such as St Austell and Butcombe tapped from casks, Thatcher's cider and decent wines; children and dogs welcome, tables in back garden with pétanque, open all day (till midnight Fri, Sat). *(Bob and Margaret Holder)*

CONGRESBURY ST4363
★**Plough** (01934) 877402
High Street (B3133); BS49 5JA Popular old-fashioned character local – a pub since the 1800s; half a dozen well kept changing west country ales such as Butcombe, St Austell and Twisted Oak, ciders from Moles and Thatcher's, quick smiling service, generous helpings of well cooked food (not Sun evening) including daily specials, several small interconnecting rooms off flagstoned main bar, mix of old and new furniture, built-in pine wall benches, old prints, photos, farm tools and some morris dancing memorabilia, log fires; Sun quiz; no children inside, dogs welcome, wheelchair access from car park, garden with rustic furniture and boules. *(Bob and Margaret Holder, Taff Thomas)*

CORFE ST2319
White Hart (01823) 421388
B3170 S of Taunton; TA3 7BU Friendly traditional 17th-c village pub with enjoyable sensibly priced pubby food (not Tues) including some vegetarian options, curry night last Thurs of the month (booking advised), well kept ales such as Butcombe and Exmoor, beams, woodburner and open fire; bar billiards, skittle alley; dogs welcome, open all day Sat, closed Tues lunchtime. *(Sophie Ellison)*

CRANMORE ST6643
Strode Arms (01749) 880450
West Cranmore; signed with pub off A361 Frome–Shepton Mallet; BA4 4QJ Pretty stone dining pub (former 15th-c farmhouse) overlooking village duck pond, rambling beamed rooms with log fires in handsome fireplaces, carpeted or flagstone floors, country furnishings,

---

If you report on a pub that's not a featured entry, please tell us any lunchtimes or evenings when it doesn't serve bar food.

enjoyable generously served food (not Sun evening) from snacks up, Wadworths ales and decent wines by the glass, good friendly service; children, walkers and dogs welcome, seats on front terrace, handy for East Somerset Steam Railway, open all day weekends. *(Pete and Sarah)*

CROSS ST4254
New Inn (01934) 732455
A38 Bristol–Bridgwater, junction A371; BS26 2EE Steps up to friendly roadside pub with five well kept ales such as Bath and Bristol, good choice of enjoyable fairly traditional food from baguettes and baked potatoes up; annual beer festival; children and dogs welcome, nice hillside garden with play area, open (and food) all day. *(Tessa Barton)*

CROWCOMBE ST1336
Carew Arms (01984) 618631
Just off A358 Taunton–Minehead; TA4 4AD Interesting 17th-c beamed country inn attracting good mix of customers; hunting trophies, huge flagstones and good inglenook log fire in small lived-in front bar, up to five well kept ales including Exmoor and St Austell, real cider, enjoyable reasonably priced home-made food (not Sun evening in winter) with daily specials and decent choice for vegetarians, friendly service, dining room allowing children; outside skittle alley; dogs, walkers and cyclists welcome, tables in good-sized garden, six bedrooms, open all day in summer (all day Fri-Sun winter). *(Ian and Rose Lock, S G N Bennett)*

CURRY RIVEL ST3925
Firehouse (01458) 887447
Church Street; TA10 0HE Stylishly renovated village pub with light beams, exposed stonework and log fires, cosy bar with tractor-seat stools at counter serving four real ales (always Butcombe), decent wines and cocktails, well liked fairly pubby food plus pizzas from feature oven, lunchtime/early evening deal (Mon-Fri), friendly helpful young staff, various dining areas including upstairs raftered area and cellar bar with fine 14th-c vaulted ceiling; live music and quiz nights; children welcome, circular picnic-sets on paved terrace, open all day. *(Stuart Reeves)*

DINNINGTON ST4013
Dinnington Docks (01460) 52397
NE of village; Fosse Way; TA17 8SX Good cheery atmosphere in large old-fashioned rural local, unspoilt and unfussy, with good choice of inexpensive genuine home cooking from blackboard menu, well kept Butcombe and guests, farm ciders, friendly attentive staff, memorabilia to bolster myth that there was once a railway line and dock here, log fire, family room; skittle alley in adjoining

building; children and dogs welcome, large garden behind, good walks, open all day Fri-Sun. *(Ivy and George Goodwill)*

DITCHEAT ST6236
★Manor House (01749) 860276
Signed off A37 and A371 S of Shepton Mallet; BA4 6RB Pretty 17th-c red-brick village inn (sister to the Rockford Inn at Brendon, Devon); buzzy atmosphere and popular with jockeys from nearby stables, enjoyable home-made food from ciabattas and pub favourites to more sophisticated choices, well kept Butcombe and guests, friendly helpful staff, unusual arched doorways linking big flagstoned bar to comfortable lounge and restaurant, open fires; skittle alley; children welcome, tables on back grass, handy for Bath & West Showground, five bedrooms, good breakfast, open all day. *(Mr and Mrs P R Thomas, Hugh Roberts)*

DOWLISH WAKE ST3712
New Inn (01460) 52413
Off A3037 S of Ilminster, via Kingstone; TA19 0NZ Comfortable and welcoming dark-beamed village pub, good home-made food including blackboard specials, well kept Butcombe and Otter, local cider, friendly helpful staff, woodburners in stone inglenooks, pleasant dining room; quiz first Sun of the month; dogs welcome, attractive garden and village, Perry's cider mill and shop nearby, four bedrooms in separate annexe. *(Ewan and Sue Hewitt)*

DULVERTON SS9127
Bridge Inn (01398) 324130
Bridge Street; TA22 9HJ Welcoming unpretentious little pub next to River Barle; reasonably priced food using local suppliers, up to four well kept ales including Exmoor, some unusual imported beers, Addlestone's cider and 20 gins, comfortable sofas, woodburner; occasional live music and events, fortnightly quiz, free wi-fi; children and dogs welcome, two terraces, open all day summer. *(Vera Smith)*

DUNDRY ST5666
Carpenters (0117) 964 6423
Wells Road; BS41 8NE Welcoming village pub with well kept ales such as Bath and Butcombe, Thatcher's cider and enjoyable fairly priced traditional food including specials and Tues steak night, helpful friendly staff; free wi-fi; children and dogs welcome, disabled access, picnic-sets on lawn, open all day Fri-Sat, till 6pm Sun. *(Charles Todd)*

DUNSTER SS9843
★Stags Head (01643) 821229
West Street (A396); TA24 6SN Friendly accommodating staff in unassuming 16th-c roadside inn, popular good value food including daily specials, Exmoor and a guest ale, beams, timbers and inglenook log fire,

steps up to small back dining room; dogs welcome in bar area, comfortable simple bedrooms, good breakfast, open all day in summer, no food Weds. *(R L Borthwick)*

EAST HARPTREE ST5453
Castle of Comfort (01761) 221321
B3134, SW on Old Bristol Road; BS40 6DD Former coaching inn set high in the Mendips (last stop before the gallows for some past visitors); hefty timbers and exposed stonework, cushioned settles and other pubby furniture on carpet, log fires, Butcombe, Sharps and a guest, ample helpings of reasonably priced traditional food including good steaks, friendly staff; children (away from bar) and dogs welcome, wheelchair access, big garden with raised deck and play area, fine walks nearby. *(Bob and Melissa Wyatt)*

EAST LAMBROOK ST4218
Rose & Crown (01460) 240433
Silver Street; TA13 5HF Old-fashioned stone-built dining pub spreading extensively from compact 17th-c core with inglenook log fire, friendly helpful staff and relaxed atmosphere, good choice of well liked freshly made food using local suppliers, steak night Weds, curry Thurs, fish and chips Fri, Palmers ales, Thatcher's cider and several wines by the glass, decent whisky selection too, restaurant extension with old glass-covered well, skittle alley; quiz third Thurs of month; children and dogs (in bar) welcome, disabled access from the side, picnic-sets on neat lawn, opposite East Lambrook Manor Garden, closed Sun evening, Mon. *(Ewan and Sue Hewitt, M J Winterton)*

EAST WOODLANDS ST7944
★ Horse & Groom (01373) 462802
Off A361/B3092 junction; BA11 5LY Small pretty pub (aka the Jockey) tucked away down country lanes, friendly and relaxed, with good choice of enjoyable well priced food including some real bargains, quickly changing ales and real ciders, pews and settles in flagstoned bar, woodburner in comfortable lounge, big dining conservatory; traditional games; children welcome in eating areas, dogs in bar, disabled access, nice front garden with more seats behind, handy for Longleat. *(Darrell Barton)*

EVERCREECH ST6336
Natterjack (01749) 860253
A371 Shepton Mallet–Castle Cary; BA4 6NA Welcoming former Victorian station hotel (line closed 1966), good choice of popular generously served food at reasonable prices, cheerful service (may be slow at busy times), Butcombe and a couple of guests, real cider and nice range of wines, long bar with eating areas off; dogs welcome, lots of tables under parasols in big neatly kept garden, five bedrooms in restored cider house, open all day. *(Mr and Mrs P R Thomas)*

EXFORD SS8538
★ Exmoor White Horse
(01643) 831229 *B3224; TA24 7PY* Popular and welcoming old three-storey creeper-clad inn, more or less open-plan bar with good log fire, high-backed antique settle among more conventional seats, scrubbed deal tables, hunting prints and local photographs, Exmoor ales, Thatcher's cider and over 150 malt whiskies, good locally sourced bar and restaurant food including Sun carvery; children and dogs welcome, tables outside by river, pretty village, Land Rover Exmoor safaris, 28 comfortable bedrooms, open (and food) all day. *(Richard and Penny Gibbs, Lynda and Trevor Smith)*

FAULKLAND ST7555
★ Tuckers Grave (01373) 834230
A366 E of village; BA3 5XF Tiny place named after Edward Tucker who hanged himself nearby in 1747 and was buried at the pub crossroads; unspoilt and unchanging, with chatty locals and warm friendly atmosphere, flagstoned entrance opening into simple room with casks of Butcombe and Thatcher's Cheddar Valley cider in alcove on left, perhaps lunchtime sandwiches, two high-backed settles facing each other across a single table on right, side room with shove-ha'penny, open fires, skittle alley; children welcome in one area, lots of tables and chairs on attractive back lawn, good views, closed Mon lunchtime (except bank holidays). *(Taff Thomas, Dr and Mrs A K Clarke)*

FRESHFORD ST7960
Inn at Freshford (01225) 722250
Off A36 or B3108; BA2 7WG Roomy 16th-c flower-decked village pub in lovely spot near River Frome; new management and good recent refurbishment, well kept Box Steam and guests, a couple of local ciders and shortish but well chosen wine list, some interesting whiskies and gins too, popular home-made food from well balanced menu (all day Sat, not Sun evening, Mon) including sandwiches (12-6pm), friendly helpful young staff; background music; children and dogs welcome, wheelchair access, nice hillside garden overlooking valley with outside bar and barbecue, good waterside walks, closed Mon, otherwise open all day (till 7pm Sun). *(Chris and Angela Buckell, Dr and Mrs A K Clarke)*

FROME ST7748
Griffin (01373) 467766
Milk Street; BA11 3DB Unpretentious bare-boards bar with etched glass and open fires, long counter serving good Milk Street beers brewed here by friendly landlord, hot food Weds (usually a themed night) and Sun, easy-going mixed crowd; regular live music and quiz nights; small garden, open all day weekends, otherwise from 5pm (Fri 4pm). *(Charles Todd)*

FROME   ST7747
Three Swans   (01373) 452009
King Street; BA11 1BH Appealing and
quirky 17th-c beamed pub; well kept Abbey
Bellringer, Butcombe and a local guest, nice
wines by the glass, snacky food such as home-
made pork pies and scotch eggs, also popular
Sun roasts (must book), good friendly service,
upstairs function room; events such as quiz,
poetry, open mike and board game evenings;
children (till 7pm) and dogs welcome, part-
covered beer garden, open all day Fri-Sun,
closed other days till 5pm. *(Christopher Moss)*

GLASTONBURY   ST4938
George & Pilgrim   (01458) 831146
High Street; BA6 9DP Comfortable 15th-c
inn with magnificent carved stone façade and
some interesting features, carpeted bar with
handsome stone fireplace, moulded beams,
oak panelling and traceried stained-glass
bay window, Otter, St Austell and guests,
traditional cider, pubby food including
children's choices, OAP lunch Mon-Thurs
and other deals, restaurant; 14 bedrooms,
open all day. *(Richard Tilbrook)*

GLASTONBURY   ST5039
Who'd A Thought It   (01458) 834460
Northload Street; BA6 9JJ Interesting pub
filled with oddments and memorabilia – red
phone box (complete with mannequin),
bicycle chained to the ceiling, lots of
enamel signs and old photographs, coal
fire in old range, beams, flagstones,
stripped brick and pine panelling, well
kept Palmers ales and decent wines by
the glass, good freshly cooked food; free
wi-fi; children and dogs welcome, terrace
picnic-sets, five comfortable bedrooms,
open (and food) all day. *(Emma Scofield)*

HALLATROW   ST6357
★ Old Station   (01761) 452228
A39 S of Bristol; BS39 6EN Former
1920s station hotel with extraordinary
collection of bric-a-brac including railway
memorabilia, musical instruments, china
cows, postboxes, even half an old Citroën,
wide mix of furnishings too, Brains Rev
James, Butcombe Bitter and a guest, several
wines by the glass and good choice of highly
regarded food cooked by landlord-chef,
Pullman carriage restaurant, cheerful helpful
service; children and dogs (in bar) welcome,
café-style furniture on decking, picnic-sets
on grass, also crazy golf, football pitch and
polytunnel growing own vegetables, five
bedrooms in converted outbuilding (no
breakfast), open all day Fri-Sun. *(Ian and
Rose Lock, Dr and Mrs A K Clarke, M G Hart)*

HARDWAY   ST7234
★ Bull   (01749) 812200
*Off B3081 Bruton–Wincanton at brown
sign for Stourhead and King Alfred's
Tower; Hardway; BA10 0LN* Charming

17th-c country dining pub under friendly
long-serving landlord, good popular food
in comfortable bar and character dining
rooms, well kept Butcombe and a couple of
guests, farm cider and reasonably priced
wines by the glass, good informal service,
beams and log fire; unobtrusive background
music; children and dogs welcome, tables in
lovely garden behind (summer barbecues),
more seats in pretty rose garden over road,
closed Sun evening. *(Stuart Reeves)*

HASELBURY PLUCKNETT   ST4711
White Horse   (01460) 78873
North Street; TA18 7RJ Popular open-plan
village dining pub, good enterprising food
cooked by chef-landlord from bar snacks up
including set menu choices, west country ales
tapped from the cask, local ciders and ten
wines by the glass, friendly helpful service,
candlelit tables on flagstones or bare boards,
leather sofa by inglenook log fire; children
and dogs welcome, pretty back terrace with
roses and old well, closed Sun evening, Mon
and Tues. *(Gareth and Dorothy Thomas)*

HILLFARRANCE   ST1624
Anchor   (01823) 461334
*Oake; pub signed off Bradford-on-Tone
to Oake road; TA4 1AW* Comfortable
village pub with dining area off attractive
two-part bar, good choice of enjoyable
fairly priced food including Sun carvery,
nice friendly atmosphere, three local ales;
children welcome, garden with play area,
bedrooms and holiday apartments, closes
10pm Mon-Thurs, 11pm Fri, Sat, open all day
Sun till 9.30pm. *(Bob and Margaret Holder)*

HINTON BLEWETT   ST5956
★ Ring o' Bells   (01761) 452239
Signed off A37 in Clutton; BS39 5AN
Charming and welcoming low-beamed
stone-built country local opposite village
green, old-fashioned bar with solid furniture
including pews, log fire, enjoyable good
value food cooked by landlady catering
for gluten-free diets, obliging service,
Butcombe, Fullers and guests, good wines
by the glass, dining room; children, walkers
and dogs welcome, nice view from tables in
sheltered front yard, open all day weekends,
no food Sun evening. *(Taff Thomas)*

HOLCOMBE   ST6648
Duke of Cumberland   (01761)
233731 *Edford Hill; BA3 5HQ*
Modernised riverside pub with enjoyable
fairly priced food including home-made
pizzas, Blindmans, Butcombe, Wadsworth
and a guest, ciders such as Long Ashton
and Thatcher's, friendly helpful staff,
flagstoned bar with easy chairs by log fire,
table skittles and other traditional games,
also a skittle alley in the dining area;
background and some live music, sports TV;
children and dogs welcome, small waterside
garden, open all day. *(Taff Thomas)*

HOLFORD ST1541
Plough (01278) 741652
A39; TA5 1RY Welcoming beamed village
local, well kept ales such as Exmoor and
Otter, decent wines and hearty helpings of
enjoyable pubby food, friendly helpful staff,
log fire; dogs welcome, attractive garden,
wonderful Quantocks walks. *(Vera Smith)*

HORSINGTON ST7023
Half Moon (01963) 370140
*Signed off A357 S of Wincanton;
BA8 0EF* Beamed pub dating from the
17th c, light and airy knocked-through bars,
stripped stone and oak floors, inglenook
log fires, decent sensibly priced pubby
food, up to five well kept ales, decent wines
and a dozen gins, evening restaurant;
skittle alley, free wi-fi; children and dogs
welcome, disabled access, attractive
sloping front garden and big back one, good
walks nearby, ten bedrooms in separate
buildings behind, closed Sun evening, best
to check winter hours. *(Stuart Reeves)*

HORTON ST3214
★ Five Dials (01460) 55359
Hanning Road; off A303; TA19 9QH
Cleanly updated village pub run by friendly
helpful couple, popular reasonably priced
home-made food including good steaks and
fish, Otter, Sharps Doom Bar and a guest,
local ciders and good choice of wines by the
glass, restaurant; children and dogs welcome,
six comfortable bedrooms, open all day
Fri-Sun, closed Mon. *(Julian Richardson)*

KELSTON ST7067
Old Crown (01225) 423032
Bitton Road; A431 W of Bath; BA1 9AQ
Nicely updated 17th-c creeper-clad inn
with four small rooms, beams and polished
flagstones, carved settles and cask tables,
logs burning in ancient open range, also
woodburner and coal-effect gas fire, well
kept Bass, Butcombe and guest, real cider,
enjoyable food from shortish menu including
range of burgers and daily specials in bar or
restaurant, sandwiches available till 6pm;
children and dogs welcome, wheelchair
access with help, picnic-sets under apple
trees in sheltered sunny back garden with
covered deck, outside bar and barbecue,
open all day, food all day weekends (till
7pm Sun). *(Taff Thomas, Dr and Mrs A K Clarke)*

KEYNSHAM ST6669
★ Lock-Keeper (0117) 986 2383
*Keynsham Road (A4175 NE of town);
BS31 2DD* Welcoming riverside pub with
relaxed worn-in feel and plenty of character;
simple left-hand bar with big painted settle,
cushioned wall benches, trophy cabinet
and old local photographs, two more little
rooms with assorted cushioned dining chairs,
more photographs and rustic prints, Wells
and Youngs ales plus guests, Thatcher's

ciders and good range of wines, whiskies
and gins, popular well priced bar food from
ciabattas up served by cheerful helpful
young staff, light modern conservatory
(quite different in style); background music and
weekend live music; children welcome,
dogs in bar, disabled access/facilities,
teak furniture and giant parasols on big
heated deck overlooking water, steps down
to picnic-sets on grass, outside bar and
barbecue, pétanque, open all day and can
get very busy. *(Taff Thomas, Chris and Angela
Buckell, Tony Hobden, Dr and Mrs A K Clarke)*

KINGSDON ST5126
Kingsdon Inn (01935) 840543
*At Podimore roundabout on A303,
follow sign to Langport (A372) then
right on B3151; TA11 7LG* Pretty little
thatched cottage; main quarry-tiled bar
with woodburner, built-in cushioned wall
seats and country chairs around scrubbed
kitchen tables, Butcombe Bitter and
St Austell Tribute, local cider and 14 wines
by the glass, steps up to carpeted dining
area with a few low sagging beams and half-
panelled walls, similar furnishings including
one table set into former inglenook, fair
choice of popular food, second dining
area and separate attractive restaurant;
background classical music, TV, free wi-fi;
children and dogs (in bar) welcome, picnic-
sets on grass, herb garden, handy for the
Fleet Air Arm Museum, bedrooms.
*(P and J Shapley, Mrs Zara Elliott, Ian Herdman,
Andrew Vincent, Ewan and Sue Hewitt)*

KINGSTON ST MARY ST2229
Swan (01823) 451383
*Lodes Lane, in centre of village;
TA2 8HW* Cosy 17th-c roadside village pub,
neat and tidy, with long knocked-through
panelled bar, modern furniture on carpets,
black-painted beams and rough plastered
walls with signed cricket bats (landlord
is keen cricketer), big stone fireplaces,
popular home-made pubby food (not Sun
evening), well kept Dartmoor, Exmoor
and Sharps, Thatcher's Cheddar Valley
cider, cheerful helpful staff; background
music; children welcome, no dogs inside,
front wheelchair access, garden with play
area, skittle alley, handy for Hestercombe
Gardens. *(Chris and Angela Buckell, Bob and
Margaret Holder, Mrs Zara Elliott, Martin Day)*

KNAPP ST3025
Rising Sun (01823) 491027
*Village W of North Curry (pub signed
from here); TA3 6BG* Tucked-away
15th-c longhouse surrounded by lovely
countryside; handsome beams, flagstones
and two inglenooks with woodburners,
Exmoor and Sharps Doom Bar, proper cider,
good pubby food including popular Sun
roasts, friendly helpful staff; children and
dogs welcome, sunny little front terrace,
open all day Sat, closed Sun evening

(except first Sun of month when there's a quiz), Mon. *(Charles and Maddie Bishop)*

KNOLE   ST4825
Lime Kiln (01458) 241242
A372 E of Langport; TA10 9JH Creeper-clad beamed 17th-c country pub set back from the road, good range of decent locally sourced food, some main courses available in smaller helpings, Mon steak night, well kept Butcombe ales, Thatcher's Cheddar Valley cider, flagstoned bar and large carpeted dining room, inglenook log fire; children welcome, pleasant garden with southerly views, open (and food) all day weekends. *(Helen and Brian Edgeley)*

LANGFORD BUDVILLE   ST1122
★Martlet (01823) 400262
Off B3187 NW of Wellington; TA21 0QZ Cosy and comfortable 17th-c village pub with friendly landlady and staff, good generously served food (becomes more restauranty in the evening with fewer drinkers), popular OAP lunch deal Weds-Fri, well kept/priced local ales including Exmoor and Otter, beams and flagstones, central woodburner and inglenook, steps up to dining room, conservatory; children welcome, terrace picnic-sets, closed Sun evening, Mon and lunchtime Tues. *(Emma Scofield)*

LANGPORT   ST4625
★Devonshire Arms (01458) 241271
B3165 Somerton–Martock, off A372 E of Langport; TA10 9LP Handsome gabled inn (former hunting lodge) on village green; simple flagstoned back bar with high-backed chairs around dark tables, up to three west country ales tapped from the cask, several wines by the glass and local cider brandy, stylish main room with comfortable leather sofas and glass-topped log table by fire, scatter cushions on long wall bench, church candles, elegant dining room with wicker chairs and pale wood tables on broad boards, good interesting food from lunchtime sandwiches up (local suppliers listed), charming efficient service, maybe evening pianist; wheelchair access from car park, teak furniture out at front, pretty box-enclosed courtyard behind with water-ball feature, more seats on raised terraces, nine comfortable bedrooms, good breakfast. *(Richard and Penny Gibbs)*

LANSDOWN   ST7268
Blathwayt Arms (01225) 421995
Next to Lansdown Golf Club and Bath Racecourse; BA1 9BT Hilltop stone pub with well prepared food (not Sun evening) from ciabattas up including daily specials, Box Steam, Otter and St Austell, from dark wood bar, also Weston's cider, decent wines and good range of gins, pleasant prompt service, mix of carpeted, wood and stone flooring, pubby furniture, some raised areas in bar and conservatory, local photos and a map of the Battle of Lansdown (Civil War); background music; children welcome, wheelchair access to most areas, disabled loo, racecourse view from garden, play area open all day. *(Chris and Angela Buckell)*

LITTON   ST5954
Litton (01761) 241554
B3114, NW of Chewton Mendip; BA3 4PW Partly 15th-c pub reopened after major refurbishment (former Kings Arms); airy interior with wood and flagstone floors, main bar with long polished elm servery and mix of furniture including spindleback and bentwood chairs around scrubbed tables, some high cask tables, leather chesterfields and fur-draped settles, good varied choice of food from snacks and bar meals to interesting restaurant dishes, friendly helpful staff, local beers and ciders and plenty of wines by the glass, separate whisky bar with copper-topped counter, woodburners; children and dogs welcome, disabled access/loos, courtyard seating with steps up to lawned area, also terrace overlooking River Chew, good reservoir walks nearby, 12 comfortable individually styled bedrooms, open all day. *(Pete and Sarah)*

LONG ASHTON   ST5370
Bird in Hand (01275) 395222
Weston Road; BS41 9LA Painted stone dining pub (sister to the Pump House in Bristol), good modern food from seasonal menu including popular Sun roasts, well kept Bath Gem, St Austell Tribute and two guests, Ashton Press cider, nice wines and some interesting gins, friendly young staff, spindleback chairs and blue-painted pine tables on wood floors, collection of old enamel signs, open fire and woodburner; children and dogs welcome, side terrace, parking can be tricky, open all day. *(Holly and Tim Waite)*

LONG ASHTON   ST5370
Miners Rest (01275) 393449
Providence Lane; BS41 9DJ Welcoming three-room country pub, comfortable and unpretentious, with well kept Butcombe and an occasional guest tapped from the cask, five good traditional ciders, generous helpings of simple inexpensive lunchtime food, cheerful prompt service, local mining memorabilia, log fire, darts; no credit cards; well behaved children and dogs welcome, wheelchair access possible with some heroics, vine-covered verandah and suntrap terrace, open all day. *(Edward May)*

LOWER GODNEY   ST4742
★Sheppey Inn (01458) 831594
Tilleys Drove; BA5 1RZ Although rather unprepossessing from the outside, this quirky fun place is full of character and surprisingly popular for its remote location; eclectic mix of furniture on bare boards including plastic chairs by chunky wooden tables, cushioned

wall benches and some 1950s retro, various stuffed animals, old photographs, modern artwork and assorted kitsch, at least six ciders tapped from the barrel along with local ales and craft beers, imaginative choice of well liked food, some cooked in charcoal oven, friendly staff, black beams and log fire, long dining area with high pitched ceiling; background and regular live music; children and dogs welcome, seats on deck overlooking small River Sheppey, open all day weekends. *(Stuart Reeves, Hugh Roberts)*

LUXBOROUGH SS9837
Royal Oak (01984) 641498
Kingsbridge; S of Dunster on minor roads into Brendon Hills; TA23 0SH Welcoming atmospheric old inn set deep in Exmoor National Park; compact beamed bar with ancient flagstones, several fine settles, scrubbed kitchen tables and huge brick inglenook, back bar with cobbled floor, some quarry tiles and stone fireplace, cosy side room set for eating plus two further dining rooms, Exmoor and a couple of guests, good food from pub favourites up including seasonal game; pool, shove-ha'penny and board games in back room, also a radiogram with stack of old LPs; children and dogs welcome, seats in lovely sunny back courtyard, eight bedrooms, good walks nearby including Coleridge Way, closed Mon, otherwise open all day, no food Sun evening. *(Richard and Penny Gibbs, Lynda and Trevor Smith)*

LYDFORD ON FOSSE ST5630
Cross Keys (01963) 240473
Just off A37; TA11 7HA Beamed and flagstone pub with good traditional home-made food including generous ploughman's and award-winning pies, cheerful service, half a dozen well kept ales tapped from the cask such as Downton, proper ciders and nice wines by the glass, connecting rooms (main dining area at front), chunky rustic furniture and log fires in substantial old fireplaces; live music and other events in function room; children and dogs welcome, disabled access/loos, seats on covered terrace and in sunny garden, six comfortable well equipped bedrooms, camping field, popular with Fosse Way walkers, open all day. *(Richard Tilbrook, Dave Grindley, Chris and Angela Buckell)*

MIDFORD ST7660
★ Hope & Anchor (01225) 832296
Bath Road (B3110); BA2 7DD 17th-c pub near Colliers Way and close to walks on the disused Somerset & Dorset railway; neatly kept open-plan interior with civilised bar, heavy-beamed flagstoned restaurant with mix of dark wooden furniture and woodburner, modern back conservatory liked by families, enjoyable good value food cooked by landlord including daily specials, Otter Amber, Sharps Doom Bar and a guest, traditional cider and 11 wines

by the glass, courteous staff; dogs welcome in bar, seats on two-tier back terrace, open all day weekends. *(Harvey Brown, Julian Richardson, Tim King, Dr and Mrs A K Clarke)*

MINEHEAD SS9746
Old Ship Aground (01643) 703516
Quay West; TA24 5UL Friendly Edwardian harbourside pub owned by local farming family; Marstons-related ales and a guest such as Cotleigh, Thatcher's cider, enjoyable food using own meat and other local produce, Sun carvery, cheerful helpful service even when busy, faux black beams, pubby furniture and window-seat views; background music (live Fri), free wi-fi; children and dogs welcome, wheelchair access via side door, disabled loo, outside tables overlooking harbour, 12 bedrooms, open all day. *(Revd R P Tickle, Simon Boughey)*

MONKSILVER ST0737
Notley Arms (01984) 656095
B3188; TA4 4JB Bustling pub in lovely village on edge of Exmoor National Park; open-plan bar rooms with log fires and woodburners, cushioned window seats and settles, appealing collection of old dining chairs around mixed wooden tables on slate tiles or flagstones, paintings on cream or panelled walls, fresh flowers and church candles, tractor-seat stools by counter serving Exmoor, St Austell and a guest, proper cider, 30 wines by the glass and 20 malt whiskies, very good often interesting food; background music; children and dogs welcome, neat garden with plenty of picnic-sets, heated pavilion and a clear-running stream at the bottom, attractive comfortable bedrooms in former coach house, open all day from 8am. *(Mike and Mary Carter, Richard and Penny Gibbs, Lynda and Trevor Smith, Bob and Margaret Holder, Mrs Zara Elliott)*

MONTACUTE ST4917
Kings Arms (01935) 822255
Bishopston; TA15 6UU Extended 17th-c stone inn next to church; stripped-stone bar with comfortable seating and log fire, contemporary restaurant, three real ales including Greene King, nice house wines and good food from bar snacks to restaurant dishes, friendly courteous staff; background music, quiz second Sun of the month; children welcome, pleasant garden behind, 15 bedrooms (most ensuite), handy for Montacute House (NT). *(Alan and Angela Scouller)*

NAILSEA ST4469
Blue Flame (01275) 856910
Netherton Wood Lane, West End; BS48 4DE Small friendly 19th-c farmers' local with two unchanging lived-in rooms, coal fire, well kept ales from casks behind bar, traditional ciders and some snacky food such as fresh rolls and pork pies, pub games; outside lavatories including

roofless gents', limited parking (may be filled with Land Rovers and tractors); children's room, sizeable informal garden, open all day weekends, closed lunchtimes Mon, Tues. *(Taff Thomas, Peter Myers)*

NEWTON ST LOE   ST7065
Globe (01225) 872891
A4/A36 roundabout; BA2 9BB Popular 17th-c Vintage Inn, large and rambling, with dark wood partitions, pillars and timbers giving secluded feel, log fire, their usual food including set deals, well kept Butcombe, St Austell and a guest, prompt friendly service from uniformed staff; children welcome, nice back terrace, open (and food) all day. *(Dr and Mrs A K Clarke)*

NORTH CURRY   ST3125
Bird in Hand (01823) 490248
Queens Square; off A378 (or A358) E of Taunton; TA3 6LT Friendly village pub with cosy main bar, old pews, settles, benches and yew tables on flagstones, some original beams and timbers, good inglenook log fire, well kept ales and decent wines by the glass, enjoyable good value food in separate dining part; background music; children, dogs and muddy boots welcome, closed Sun evening. *(Bob and Melissa Wyatt)*

NORTON ST PHILIP   ST7755
★**George** (01373) 834224
A366; BA2 7LH Wonderful building full of history and interest – an inn for over 700 years; heavy beams, timbering, stonework and panelling, vast open fires, distinctive furnishings, plenty of 18th-c pictures, fine pewter and heraldic shields, Wadworths ales and enjoyable food from varied menu, good friendly service; children and particularly dogs welcome, appealing galleried courtyard, atmospheric bedrooms (some reached by Norman turret), worth strolling over meadow to attractive churchyard, open all day. *(Dr and Mrs A K Clarke, R K Phillips, Taff Thomas)*

NUNNEY   ST7345
George (01373) 836458
Church Street; signed off A361 Shepton Mallet–Frome; BA11 4LW Smart 17th-c coaching inn set in quaint village with ruined castle; comfortably modern open-plan lounge with beams, stripped stone and woodburner in big fireplace, good well presented food from sharing plates, burgers and pizzas up, Wadworths ales and a guest, nice wines by the glass and good coffee, friendly helpful staff, separate restaurant; background music; children and dogs (in bar) welcome, attractive split-level walled garden, rare 'gallows' inn-sign spanning the road, nine bedrooms, open all day. *(Revd Michael Vockins, Tony Scott)*

OAKHILL   ST6347
Oakhill Inn (01749) 840442
A367 Shepton Mallet–Radstock; BA3 5HU

Dining pub with sofas and easy chairs among candlelit tables around bar, friendly welcoming atmosphere, enjoyable food including pizzas and chargrills, a beer brewed for them plus three local ales, craft kegs, real cider and plenty of wines by the glass from good list, dining extension in former skittle alley, rugs on bare boards, wall of clocks, log fires; background music; children and dogs welcome, nice views from garden, five bedrooms, open all day weekends, food all day Sun. *(Taff Thomas)*

OVER STRATTON   ST4315
Royal Oak (01460) 240906
Off A303 via Ilminster turn at South Petherton roundabout; TA13 5LQ Popular thatched family dining pub, enjoyable reasonably priced food including bargain two-course lunch (Tues-Sat), well kept Badger ales, linked rooms with attractive rustic décor, oak beams, flagstones and thick stone walls, scrubbed kitchen tables, pews and settles, log fires; tables outside, secure play area, closed Mon. *(Ewan and Sue Hewitt)*

PITMINSTER   ST2219
Queens Arms (01823) 421529
Off B3170 S of Taunton (or reached direct); near church; TA3 7AZ Popular village pub-restaurant with good competitively priced food from varied set menus (best to book), well kept west country ales, Thatcher's ciders and decent wines, friendly helpful staff; downstairs skittle alley, picnic-sets out at back, closed Sun evening, Mon. *(Bob and Margaret Holder)*

PORLOCK   SS8846
★**Ship** (01643) 862507
High Street; TA24 8QD Picturesque old thatched pub with beams, flagstones and big inglenook log fires, popular reasonably priced food from sandwiches up, well kept ales such as Exmoor, Otter and St Austell, friendly service, back dining room, small locals' front bar with games; children welcome, attractive split-level sunny garden with decking and play area, nearby nature trail to Dunkery Beacon, five bedrooms, open all day; known as the Top Ship to distinguish it from the Ship at Porlock Weir. *(Darrell Barton)*

PORLOCK WEIR   SS8846
★**Ship** (01643) 863288
Porlock Hill (A39); TA24 8PB Unpretentious thatched pub in wonderful spot by peaceful harbour – can get packed; long and narrow with dark low beams, flagstones and stripped stone, simple pub furniture, woodburner, west country ales including Exmoor and Otter, real ciders and a perry, good whisky and soft drinks choice, enjoyable pubby food served promptly by friendly staff, games rooms across small backyard, tea room; background music and big-screen TV; children and dogs welcome,

sturdy picnic-sets in front and at side, good coast walks, three decent bedrooms, limited free parking but pay-and-display opposite; calls itself the Bottom Ship to avoid confusion with the Ship at Porlock. *(Darrell Barton)*

PORTISHEAD   ST4576
★**Windmill** (01275) 818483
M5 junction 19; A369 into town, then follow Sea Front sign and into Nore Road; BS20 6JZ Busy dining pub perched on steep hillside with panoramic Severn estuary views; curving glass frontage rising two storeys (adjacent windmill remains untouched), contemporary furnishings, four Fullers ales and a couple of guests, plenty of wines by the glass, decent range of enjoyable food from sandwiches and baked potatoes to daily specials, early-bird deal (3-7pm Mon-Fri, 3-5pm Sat), efficient friendly staff; children welcome, dogs allowed in bar, disabled access including chairlift, metal furniture on tiered lantern-lit terraces and decking, open (and food) all day. *(Chris and Angela Buckell)*

PRIDDY   ST5450
★**Hunters Lodge** (01749) 672275
From Wells on A39 pass hill with TV mast on left, then next left; BA5 3AR Welcoming and unchanging farmers', walkers' and potholers' pub above Ice Age cavern, in same family for generations, well kept local beers tapped from casks behind bar, Thatcher's and Wilkin's ciders, simple cheap food, log fires in huge fireplaces, low beams, flagstones and panelling, old lead mining photographs, Tues folk night; no mobiles or credit cards; children and dogs in family room, wheelchair access, garden picnic-sets. *(Taff Thomas)*

PRISTON   ST6960
Ring o' Bells (01761) 471467
Village SW of Bath; BA2 9EE Unpretentious old stone pub with large knocked-through bar, good reasonably priced traditional food cooked by licensees using nearby farm produce, real ales from small local brewers including a house beer from Blindmans, quick friendly service, flagstones, beams and good open fire; skittle alley; children, dogs and boots welcome, benches out at front overlooking little village green (maypole here on May Day), good walks, two bedrooms, closed Mon and lunchtimes Tue-Thurs, no food Sun evening. *(Taff Thomas)*

RICKFORD   ST4859
Plume of Feathers (01761) 462682
Very sharp turn off A368; BS40 7AH Cottagey 17th-c local with enjoyable reasonably priced home-made food in bar and dining room, friendly service, well kept Butcombe and guests, local cider and good choice of wines, black beams and half-panelling, mix of furniture including cast-iron tables and settles, log fires; table skittles,

darts and pool; well behaved children and dogs welcome, rustic tables on narrow front terrace, pretty streamside hamlet, bedrooms, open all day. *(Dr and Mrs A K Clarke)*

RIMPTON   ST6021
White Post Inn (01935) 851525
Rimpton Hill, B3148; BA22 8AR Small modern dining pub straddling Dorset border (boundary actually runs through the bar); highly rated imaginative food from chef-owner including reworked pub favourites and tasting menus, local ales and ciders, a dozen wines by the glass and interesting list of spirits including a milk vodka, friendly helpful staff, cosy carpeted bar area with leather sofas and woodburner, fine country views from restaurant and back terrace; children welcome, three bedrooms, closed Sun evening, Mon. *(Charles and Maddie Bishop)*

RODNEY STOKE   ST4850
Rodney Stoke Inn (01749) 870209
A371 Wells-Weston; BS27 3XB Comfortable dining pub with modern décor, extensive choice of good generously served food, well kept local ales and good range of wines by the glass, friendly accommodating service, airy high-beamed restaurant extension; children welcome, roadside terrace and back garden with play area, camping, open (and food) all day Sun. *(Tim and Moira Hurst)*

SALTFORD   ST6867
Bird in Hand (01225) 873335
High Street; BS31 3EJ Comfortable and friendly, with busy front bar, four well kept ales including Butcombe and Sharps, good choice of popular fairly priced food (all day weekends) from well filled rolls up, prompt cheerful service, pubby furniture including settles, carpets throughout, back conservatory dining area; Mon quiz, free wi-fi; wheelchair access at front (not from car park), picnic-sets down towards river, pétanque, handy for Bristol & Bath Railway Path. *(Dr and Mrs A K Clarke)*

SALTFORD   ST6968
Jolly Sailor (01225) 873002
Off A4 Bath-Keynsham; Mead Lane; BS31 3ER Worth knowing for its great River Avon setting by lock and weir; good range of food from bar snacks to authentic indian curries, three Wadworths ales, flagstones, low beams and two log fires, conservatory dining room overlooking the water; background and some live music; children and dogs (in bar) welcome, disabled access/facilities, paved lockside terrace, open (and food) all day. *(Dr and Mrs A K Clarke)*

SHEPTON MONTAGUE   ST6731
★**Montague Inn** (01749) 813213
Village signed off A359 Bruton-Castle Cary; BA9 8JW Simply but tastefully

furnished dining pub with welcoming licensees, popular for civilised meal or just a drink, stripped-wood tables and kitchen chairs, inglenook log fire, nicely presented often interesting food including range of burgers from shortish menu plus a few specials, well kept ales such as Bath, Cottage and Wadworths tapped from the cask, ciders such as Orchard Pig, good wine and whisky choice, friendly well informed young staff, bright spacious restaurant extension behind; children and dogs (in bar) welcome, disabled access, garden and big terrace with teak furniture, maybe summer Sun jazz, peaceful farmland views, closed Sun evening. *(Edward Mirzoeff)*

SIMONSBATH   SS7739
★ **Exmoor Forest Inn** (01643) 831341

B3223/B3358; TA24 7SH Welcoming 19th-c inn beautifully placed in remote countryside; split-level bar with circular tables by counter, larger area with cushioned settles, upholstered stools and mate's chairs around mix of tables, hunting trophies, antlers and horse tack, woodburner, good reasonably priced traditional food alongside more imaginative choices including local game, well kept ales such as Clearwater, Exmoor and Otter, Weston's cider, good range of wines and malt whiskies, airy dining room, residents' lounge; children and dogs welcome, seats in front garden, fine walks along River Barle, own trout and salmon fishing, ten comfortable bedrooms and self-catering cottage, open all day in high season. *(Paul Baxter, Bob and Margaret Holder)*

SOUTH CHERITON   ST6924
White Horse (01963) 370394

A357 Wincanton–Blandford; BA8 0BL Renovated 17th-c roadside country pub under friendly family management, well kept ales, craft beers and decent range of wines by the glass, good home-made food (not Sun evening) in bar or restaurant (separate menus), cheerful service; some live music, skittle alley; children and dogs welcome, picnic-sets in small back garden, open all day weekends. *(Stuart Reeves)*

SOUTH STOKE   ST7461
Pack Horse (01225) 832060

Off B3110, S edge of Bath; BA2 7DU Historic village pub (former medieval priory) saved from developers by the local community and being restored as we went to press – news please.

SPAXTON   ST2336
Lamb (01278) 671350

Barford Road, Four Forks; TA5 1AD Welcoming simply furnished little pub at foot of the Quantocks; open-plan beamed

bar with woodburner, well kept beers and enjoyable good value food (not Sun evening) cooked by landlady including notable local steaks, booking advised; quiz last Sun of month; tables on lawn behind, closed all day Mon and lunchtimes apart from Sun. *(Ivy and George Goodwill)*

STANTON DREW   ST5963
Druids Arms (01275) 332230

Off B3130; BS39 4EJ Refurbished pub in stone-circle village (there are some standing stones in the garden); linked flagstoned rooms with low black beams, bare stone walls and green dados, cushioned window seats and pubby furniture, candles here and there, open fires, tractor-seat stools by pale wood bar serving Butcombe and Sharps Doom Bar, Thatcher's cider and modest wine list, enjoyable often creative food from bar snacks up, Tues OAP lunch deal; occasional live music, darts, free wi-fi; children welcome, front wheelchair access using portable ramp, picnic-sets out by lane and in garden backing on to 14th-c church, open all day. *(Mark Hamill)*

STAPLE FITZPAINE   ST2618
Greyhound (01823) 480227

Off A358 or B3170 S of Taunton; TA3 5SP Rambling country pub with decent choice of popular home-made food (not Mon), smaller helpings available on some main courses, well kept Badger ales and good wines by the glass, welcoming helpful staff, flagstones and inglenooks, nice mix of settles and chairs, old pictures, farm tools and so forth; children and dogs welcome, four comfortable well equipped bedrooms, good breakfast, closed Mon lunchtime, otherwise open all day. *(Sara Fulton, Roger Baker, Bob and Margaret Holder, Guy Vowles)*

STOKE ST GREGORY   ST3527
Rose & Crown (01823) 490296

Woodhill; follow North Curry signpost off A378 by junction with A358 – keep on to Stoke, bearing right in centre, passing church and follow lane for 0.5 miles; TA3 6EW Popular dining pub with good food (best to book) and two or three local ales, friendly helpful staff, more or less open-plan, with stools by curved brick and wood counter, long high-raftered flagstoned dining room and two further beamed eating areas, one with glass-covered well; background music; children welcome, seats on sheltered front terrace, one bedroom, closed Sun evening. *(Bob and Margaret Holder)*

STOKE SUB HAMDON   ST4717
Prince of Wales (01935) 822848

Ham Hill; TA14 6RW Traditional stone pub on top of Ham Hill with superb views,

---

If you know a pub is ever open all day, please tell us.

changing real ales tapped from the cask and good food from sandwiches and west country deli boards up, friendly staff; children, dogs and muddy boots welcome, open all day from 8.30am for breakfast. *(Richard Mason)*

TARR SS8632

★ Tarr Farm (01643) 851507

Tarr Steps – narrow road off B3223 N of Dulverton; deep ford if you approach from the W (inn is on E bank); TA22 9PY Fine Exmoor position for this 16th-c inn above River Barle's medieval clapper bridge; compact unpretentious bar rooms with good views, leather chairs around slabby rustic tables, some stall and wall seating, game bird pictures on wood-clad walls, three woodburners, well kept Exmoor ales and several wines by the glass, good food using local produce, residents' end with smart evening restaurant, friendly helpful service, log fire in pleasant lounge with dark leather armchairs and sofas; children and dogs welcome, slate-topped stone tables outside making most of setting, extensive grounds, good bedrooms (no under-10s), open all day but may be closed early Feb. *(Bob and Margaret Holder)*

TAUNTON ST2525

Hankridge Arms (01823) 444405

Hankridge Way, Deane Gate (near Sainsbury's); just off M5 junction 25 – A358 towards city, then right at roundabout, right at next roundabout; TA1 2LR Interesting nicely restored Badger dining pub based on 16th-c former farmhouse – quite a contrast to the modern shopping complex surrounding it; different-sized linked areas, beams, timbers and big log fire, popular food from lunchtime sandwiches through pubby choices up, well kept (if pricey) ales and decent wines by the glass, friendly efficient young staff; background music; dogs welcome, plenty of tables in pleasant outside area, open (and food) all day weekends. *(R T and J C Moggridge)*

TAUNTON ST2225

Plough (01823) 324404

Station Road; TA1 1PB Popular little pub with three or four local ales including Otter and Bath tapped from cooled casks, up to ten racked ciders with more on draught and seven wines by the glass, simple food including range of pies, bare boards, panelling, candles on tables, cosy nooks and open fire, hidden door to lavatories; background music (live weekends); dogs welcome, handy for station, open (and food) all day (till 3am Fri, Sat). *(Darrell Barton)*

TAUNTON ST2223

Vivary Arms (01823) 272563

Wilton Street; across Vivary Park from centre; TA1 3JR Popular low-beamed 18th-c local (Taunton's oldest), good value fresh food from light lunches up in snug plush lounge and small dining room, takeaway fish and chips, friendly helpful young staff, well kept ales including Butcombe, decent wines, interesting collection of drink-related items; pool and darts; lovely hanging baskets and flowers, beer garden behind. *(Bob and Margaret Holder)*

TINTINHULL ST5019

★ Crown & Victoria (01935) 823341

Farm Street, village signed off A303; BA22 8PZ Handsome golden-stone inn, carpeted throughout, with high bar chairs at light oak counter serving four well kept ales including Butcombe and Sharps, farmhouse furniture and big woodburner, good popular food using free range/organic ingredients, efficient friendly service, dining room with more pine tables and chairs, former skittle alley also used for eating, end conservatory; well behaved children welcome, disabled facilities, big garden with play area, five bedrooms, handy for Tintinhull Garden (NT), closed Sun evening. *(Ewan and Sue Hewitt)*

TRULL ST2122

Winchester Arms (01823) 284723

Church Road; TA3 7LG Cosy streamside village pub with good value generous food including blackboard specials and popular Sun lunch, curry night first Weds of the month, west country ales and ciders, friendly helpful service, small dining room; Sun quiz, skittle alley, free wi-fi; dogs welcome, garden with decked area and summer barbecues, six bedrooms. *(Charles Todd)*

TUNLEY ST6959

King William (01761) 470408

B3115 SW of Bath; BA2 0EB Updated 17th-c coaching inn with good fairly priced pub food from baguettes to daily specials (smaller helpings available and plenty of gluten-free choices), well kept ales such as Butcombe and decent wines, friendly efficient staff, bar popular with locals, other room set for dining; courtyard tables, three comfortable bedrooms, open all day Sat, till 6pm Sun, closed Mon. *(Ian and Rose Lock)*

UPTON ST0129

Lowtrow Cross Inn (01398) 371220

A3190 E of Upton; TA4 2DB Welcoming old pub under new management; character low-beamed bar with open fire and woodburner, bare boards and flagstones, two country-kitchen dining areas, one with enormous inglenook, three real ales such as Exmoor Gold and Wychwood Hobgoblin, Thatcher's cider, popular reasonably priced home-made food (not Tues) including good steaks, fish and chips deal Weds, Thurs; children and dogs welcome, lovely surroundings, two bedrooms, camping next door, closed Sun evening, Mon. *(Sophie Ellison)*

VOBSTER ST7049

★**Vobster Inn** (01373) 812920

Lower Vobster; BA3 5RJ Spacious old stone-built dining pub with popular reasonably priced home-made food (special diets catered for) including evening set menu, Butcombe, Ashton Press cider and nice wines by the glass, three comfortable open-plan areas with antique furniture, plenty of room for just a drink; children and dogs (in bar) welcome, seats on lawn, boules, four bedrooms (also nearby yurts), closed Sun evening, Mon and lunchtime Tues. *(Taff Thomas)*

WASHFORD ST0440

White Horse (01984) 640415

Abbey Road/Torre Rocks; TA23 0JZ Welcoming and popular old local, good selection of well kept ales and enjoyable reasonably priced pubby food including specials and deals, can eat in bar or separate restaurant, log fires; pool; children welcome in restaurant; large smokers' pavilion over road next to trout stream, field with interesting collection of fowl and goats, handy for visits to Exmoor National Park, bedrooms, good traditional breakfast, open all day. *(Richard and Penny Gibbs)*

WATCHET ST0743

Pebbles (01984) 634737

Market Street; TA23 0AN Popular, welcoming and relaxed little bar in former shop near Market House Museum and harbour; extensive range of regional ciders (tasters offered), also cask-tapped ales such as Exmoor, Moles and Otter and good choice of whiskies, cider brandies and other drinks, friendly helpful staff, no food but can bring your own (plates and cutlery supplied, fish and chip shop next door); regular live music (some impromptu) including folk and jazz, sea shanty and poetry evenings, free wi-fi; dogs on leads welcome, open all day. *(Richard and Penny Gibbs)*

WATCHET ST0643

Star (01984) 631367

Mill Lane (B3191); TA23 0BZ Late 18th-c beamed pub at end of lane just off Watchet harbour; main flagstoned bar with other low-ceilinged side rooms, some exposed stonework and rough wood partitioning, mix of traditional furniture including oak settles, window seats, woodburner in ornate fireplace, good selection of pubby food mostly sourced locally including fresh fish, four well kept west country ales such as Butcombe and Stonehenge, Sheppy's cider and a few malt whiskies, cheerful helpful staff; background music; children and dogs (on leads) welcome, wheelchair access, picnic-sets out in front and in sloping beer garden behind, handy for marina and West Somerset Railway. *(Patricia and Anton Larkham)*

WEDMORE ST4347

New Inn (01934) 712099

Combe Batch; BS28 4DU Welcoming unpretentious village pub popular with locals and visitors alike, well kept Butcombe and guests, real cider and big helpings of enjoyable sensibly priced home-made food from baguettes up, comfortable dining area; skittle alley, darts, sports TV and lots of events including penny chuffing, conker competitions and the Turnip Prize (for worst piece of local artwork); children and dogs welcome, open all day weekends, closed lunchtimes Mon and Tues. *(Gordon Harold)*

WELLOW ST7358

Fox & Badger (01225) 832293

Signed off A367 SW of Bath; BA2 8QG Popular opened-up village pub under same owners as the White Hart at Widcombe Hill (Bath); flagstones one end, bare boards the other, woodburner in massive hearth, some snug corners, Butcombe, Otter and a guest, real ciders and good range of much liked food (booking advised weekends), friendly service; children and dogs welcome, picnic-sets in covered courtyard, open all day Fri, Sat, closed Sun evening. *(Alistair Holdoway, Taff Thomas, S G N Bennett)*

WELLS ST5445

★**City Arms** (01749) 677768

High Street; BA5 2AG Bustling town-centre pub (former 16th-c jail) with four well kept ales, three ciders and reasonably priced food from varied menu (all day Sat) including themed nights, friendly service, modernised main bar and restaurant areas; background music, free wi-fi; children and dogs welcome, cobbled courtyard and first-floor terrace, three bedrooms, open all day. *(Dr J Barrie Jones)*

WELLS ST5445

Crown (01749) 673457

Market Place; BA5 2RF Former 15th-c coaching inn overlooked by cathedral, various bustling areas with light wooden flooring, plenty of matching chairs and cushioned wall benches, Butcombe, Palmers, St Austell and Sharps, popular reasonably priced food in bar and bistro including good value set menu (must book weekends), friendly efficient service; background music, TV; children welcome till 8pm, dogs in bar, small heated back courtyard, 15 bedrooms, open all day. *(Steve and Liz Tilley, Richard Tilbrook, Ian Phillips)*

WELLS ST5546

★**Fountain** (01749) 672317

St Thomas Street; BA5 2UU Relaxed restauranty place with big comfortable bar, interesting décor and large open fire, quite a choice of popular food here or in upstairs dining room (booking advised weekends), Mon steak night, ales such as

Bath, Box Steam and Butcombe, several wines by the glass, courteous helpful staff; unobtrusive background music; children and dogs (in one area) welcome, pretty in summer with window boxes and shutters, handy for cathedral and moated Bishop's Palace, closed Sun evening, Mon lunchtime. *(Stephen Funnell, R K Phillips)*

WEST HUNTSPILL ST3145
Crossways (01278) 783756
A38, between M5 junctions 22 and 23; TA9 3RA Rambling 17th-c tile-hung pub with split-level carpeted areas, beams and log fires, six well kept mostly local ales (tasting trays available, Aug beer festival), good choice of enjoyable generously served food at reasonable prices (booking recommended), cheerful efficient staff; skittle alley, pool, TV, free wi-fi; children and dogs welcome, disabled facilities, garden with play area and heated smokers' shelter, seven bedrooms, open all day. *(Holly and Tim Waite)*

WEST MONKTON ST2628
★ Monkton (01823) 412414
Blundells Lane; signed from A3259, TA2 8NP Popular and welcoming village dining pub with good choice of freshly made food including some south african influences (best to book weekends), bare-boards bar with central woodburner and snug off, separate restaurant with strip-wood floor, well kept Exmoor, Otter and Sharps, Orchard Pig and Thatcher's ciders, nine wines by the glass, good friendly service; children and dogs welcome, wheelchair access from the front, lots of tables in big garden bounded by stream, play area. *(Bob and Margaret Holder)*

WEST PENNARD ST5438
Red Lion (01458) 832941
A361 E of Glastonbury; Newtown; BA6 8NH Traditional 16th-c stone-built village inn under newish management; bar and dining areas off small flagstoned black-beamed core, enjoyable home-made food from pub favourites up, ales such as Butcombe and Otter, inglenook woodburner and open fires; background and some live music including folk club, free wi-fi; children and dogs welcome, tables on big forecourt, skittle alley, good nearby walks, seven bedrooms in converted side barn. *(Darrell Barton)*

WIDCOMBE ST2216
Holman Clavel (01823) 421070
Culmhead, on ridge road W of B3170, follow sign for Blagdon; 2 miles S of Corfe; TA3 7EA Country local dating from the 14th c and revitalised under present owners; friendly and relaxed with good food from short but varied menu (vegetarian and gluten-free diets catered for), Butcombe Bitter and Gold, guest beers and good local cider including Tricky, flagstoned bar with woodburner in big fireplace, room off has

a long dining table (seats 24); some live music; children, dogs and muddy boots welcome, handy for Blackdown Hills, open all day Fri-Sun, closed Tues. *(Guy Vowles)*

WINCANTON ST7028
Nog Inn (01963) 32998
South Street; BA9 9DL Welcoming old split-level pub with Otter, Sharps and a couple of guests, real cider and continental beers, good reasonably priced traditional food including Sun carvery (not summer) and blackboard specials, bare boards, carpet and flagstones, pump clips on bar ceiling, log fires; background and some live music, charity quiz (second Thurs of month), darts; well behaved children and dogs welcome, pleasant back garden with heated smokers' shelter, open (and food) all day. *(Charles Todd)*

WINFORD ST5262
Crown (01275) 472388
Crown Hill, off Regil Road; BS40 8AY Popular old pub set in deep countryside, linked beamed rooms with mix of pubby furniture including settles on flagstones or quarry tiles, old pictures and photographs on rough walls, copper and brass, leather sofas in front of big open fire, enjoyable generous home-made food (all day Sun) at very reasonable prices, Thurs evening deal, Butcombe, Wadworths and a guest, good choice of wines by the glass, friendly landlord and staff; table skittles and skittle alley, folk night first Sun of month; children and dogs welcome, wheelchair access with help, tables out in front and in back garden, closed Mon-Weds lunchtime, otherwise open all day. *(Patricia and Anton Larkham)*

WINSFORD SS9034
★ Royal Oak (01643) 851455
Off A396 about 10 miles S of Dunster; TA24 7JE Prettily placed thatched and beamed Exmoor inn, enjoyable well priced home-made food (greater evening choice), Exmoor ales and west country ciders, friendly helpful staff, carpeted bar with woodburner in big stone fireplace, large bay window seat looking across to village green and foot and packhorse bridges over River Winn, restaurant and other lounge areas; children and dogs (in bar) welcome, disabled facilities, eight good bedrooms some with four-posters. *(Bob and Margaret Holder)*

WITHAM FRIARY ST7440
★ Seymour Arms (01749) 850742
Signed from B3092 S of Frome; BA11 5HF Well worn-in unchanging flagstoned country tavern, in same friendly family since 1952; two simple rooms off 19th-c hatch-service lobby, panelled benches and open fires, well kept Cheddar Potholer and an occasional guest, Rich's local cider tapped from back room, low prices, no food but can bring your own; bar billiards, darts and table

skittles; children and dogs welcome, garden by main rail line, cricket pitch over the road, open all day. *(Taff Thomas)*

WITHYPOOL   SS8435
Royal Oak (01643) 831506
Village signed off B3233; TA24 7QP
Prettily placed country inn – where R D
Blackmore stayed while writing *Lorna
Doone*; lounge with raised working fireplace,
comfortably cushioned wall seats and slat-
backed chairs, sporting trophies, paintings
and copper/brass ornaments, enjoyable food
here and in restaurant, well kept Exmoor
and a guest, real cider, character locals' bar;
walkers and dogs welcome (leave muddy
boots in porch), children in eating areas,
wooden benches on terrace, attractive
riverside village with lovely walks, grand
views from Winsford Hill just up the road,
eight bedrooms (twisting staircase to top
floor); for sale as we went to press, so may be
changes. *(Lynda and Trevor Smith, Peter Myers)*

WOOKEY   ST5245
★**Burcott** (01749) 673874
B3139 W of Wells; BA5 1NJ Beamed
roadside pub with two simply furnished
old-fashioned front bar rooms, flagstones,
some exposed stonework and half-
panelling, lantern wall lights, old prints,
woodburner, a couple of ales such as Hop
Back Summer Lightning and a real cider,
enjoyable food from snacks up in bar and
restaurant (children allowed here), good
service, small games room with built-in
wall seats; soft background music; no dogs,
wheelchair access, front window boxes
and tubs, picnic-sets in sizeable garden
with Mendip Hills views, four self-catering
units in converted stables, closed Sun
evening, Mon. *(Holly and Tim Waite)*

WOOKEY HOLE   ST5347
Wookey Hole Inn (01749) 676677
High Street; BA5 1BP Open-plan
family dining pub usefully placed opposite
the caves, welcoming and relaxed, with

unusual contemporary décor, wood or
tiled floors, tables with paper cloths
for drawing on (crayons provided), two
woodburners, good food from pub favourites
to daily specials, three changing local
ales, several belgian beers, ciders and
perry, efficient friendly staff; background
music; dogs allowed, pleasant garden with
various sculptures, five individually styled
bedrooms, open all day apart from Sun
evening. *(Matthew and Elizabeth Reeves)*

WRAXALL   ST4971
★**Old Barn** (01275) 819011
*Just off Bristol Road (B3130) in
grounds of Wraxall House; BS48 1LQ*
Idiosyncratic gabled barn conversion,
scrubbed tables, school benches and soft
sofas under oak rafters, stripped boards and
flagstones, various pictures and odds and
ends, welcoming atmosphere and friendly
service, five well kept ales including
Butcombe, Fullers and Palmers tapped
from the cask, farm ciders, good wines
by the glass, simple sandwiches, unusual
board games; occasional background
music and sports TV; dogs welcome,
nice garden with terrace barbecue
(bring your own meat) and smokers'
shelter, open all day. *(Taff Thomas)*

YARLINGTON   ST6529
Stags Head (01963) 440393
Pound Lane; BA9 8DG Old low-ceilinged
and flagstoned country pub tucked away
in rustic hamlet; well kept Bass, Greene
King and Otter from small central bar,
woodburner, chapel chairs and mixed pine
tables on left, carpeted dining area on right
with big log fire, modern landscape prints
and feature cider-press table, second dining
room with doors on to terrace, traditional
food including monthly themed nights, good
friendly service; background music; well
behaved children welcome, dogs in bar,
sheltered back garden with small stream,
maybe summer morris men, three bedrooms,
closed Sun evening. *(Bob and Melissa Wyatt)*

Staffordshire

BREWOOD
Oakley 🍷 🍺

SJ8708   Map 4

(01902) 859800 – www.brunningandprice.co.uk/oakley

Kiddemore Green Road; ST19 9BQ

Lots to look at in substantial, cleverly extended pub with interesting food and drink and seats outside

The open-plan rooms in this sizeable place have been furnished with thought and care, and the many windows and pastel paintwork keep it all very light and airy. Partitioning and metal standing posts split larger areas into cosier drinking and dining spaces. Throughout there are big house plants in pots with smaller ones on windowsills, mirrors above open fires (some in pretty Victorian fireplaces), books on shelves, elegant metal chandeliers, standard lamps, stubby candles and fresh flowers. Seating ranges from groups of leather armchairs to all manner of cushioned wooden dining chairs around character tables, the walls (some half-panelled) are hung with hundreds of prints, and flooring consists of rugs on big boards and, in the restaurant, carpet. From the long counter, friendly, helpful staff serve Phoenix Brunning & Price Original, Salopian Oracle and Purity Pure UBU with guests such as Hobsons Town Crier, Rudgate Viking, Woods Shropshire Lad and Wye Valley Butty Bach on handpump, 16 wines by the glass, 100 whiskies, 120 gins and 80 rums; background music and board games. The spreading back terrace has lots of seats and benches among flowering tubs and raised flower beds and overlooks a lake. There's a rack outside for cyclists. Disabled parking and loos.

Good, up-to-date food includes sandwiches, korean-style chicken wings with kimchi salad, lamb koftas with tzatziki, feta cheese, butternut squash and pearl barley cakes with pea purée and citrus salad, chicken, ham and leek pie, crispy beef salad with cashew nuts and sweet chilli dressing, bouillabaisse with saffron aioli, pork tenderloin with colcannon potatoes, red apple purée and cider reduction, and puddings such as plums with marmalade cream and crushed meringue and hot waffle with toffee apples and honeycomb ice-cream. *Benchmark main dish: braised shoulder of lamb with dauphinoise potatoes and rosemary gravy £17.00. Two-course evening meal £21.00.*

Brunning & Price ~ Manager John Duncan ~ Real ale ~ Open 11-11 (10.30 Sun) ~ Bar food 12-10 (9.30 Sun) ~ Restaurant ~ Children welcome ~ Dogs allowed in bar ~ Wi-fi
Recommended by Hilary and Neil Christopher, James Landor, Kate Moran, Tony Selinger, Andrew and Ruth Simmonds, Edward May

CAULDON   SK0749   Map 7

Yew Tree ★★ £

(01538) 309876 – www.yewtreeinncauldon.co.uk

Village signposted from A523 and A52 about 8 miles W of Ashbourne; ST10 3EJ

A unique collection of curios in friendly pub with good value snacks and bargain beer; very eccentric

This extraordinary roadside local is a treasure trove of fascinating curiosities and antiques, the most impressive pieces being the working polyphons and symphonions – 19th-c developments of the musical box, some taller than a person, each with quite a repertoire of tunes and elaborate sound effects. There are also two pairs of Queen Victoria's stockings, an amazing collection of ceramics and pottery including a Grecian urn dating back almost 3,000 years, penny-farthing and boneshaker bicycles and the infamous Acme Dog Carrier. Seats include 18th-c settles, plenty of little wooden tables and a four-person oak church choir seat with carved heads that came from St Mary's church in Stafford. Look out for the array of musical instruments ranging from a one-string violin (phonofiddle) through pianos and sousaphones to the aptly named serpent. Drinks are very reasonably priced, so it's no wonder the place is popular with locals. Burton Bridge Bitter, Rudgate Ruby Mild and a guest or two on handpump, ten interesting malt whiskies, eight wines by the glass and farm cider; they hold a music and beer festival in July and a vintage vehicle rally in September. Darts, table skittles and board games. There are seats outside the front door and in the cobbled stable yard, and they have a basic campsite for pub customers and a small caravan for hire. The pub is almost hidden by a towering yew tree.

🍴 The modest menu includes sandwiches, locally made pies, vegetable or beef chilli, beef stew with mash, and puddings. *Benchmark main dish: steak in ale pie £8.00. Two-course evening meal £11.00.*

Free house ~ Licensee Dan Buckland ~ Real ale ~ Open 12-3, 6-11; 12-midnight Sat; 12-11 Sun ~ Bar food 12-9; 12-3 Mon, Thurs; evening food available if pre-booked ~ Children welcome away from bar area ~ Dogs welcome ~ Wi-fi ~ Regular open mike and quiz evenings – see website *Recommended by Helen McLagan, Alf Wright, Len and Lilly Dowson, Dan and Nicki Barton*

 CHEADLE   SK0342   Map 7

Queens at Freehay

(01538) 722383 – www.queensatfreehay.co.uk

A mile SE of Cheadle; take Rakeway Road off A522 (via Park Avenue or Mills Road), then after a mile turn into Counslow Road; ST10 1RF

Gently civilised dining pub with three real ales and attractive garden

The neat rooms in this welcoming 18th-c pub have some cottagey touches that blend in well with the modern refurbishments. The comfortable lounge bar has pale wood tables on stripped wood floors, small country pictures and curtains with matching cushions. It opens via an arch into a simple light and airy dining area with elegant chairs and tables on tartan carpeting. Helpful staff serve Lancaster Bomber, Marstons Pedigree and Ringwood Mauler on handpump and eight wines by the glass; some seating is set aside for those who want just a drink and a chat. In warm weather, the attractive and immaculately kept little back garden is a fine place to sit, with picnic-sets among mature shrubs and flowering tubs.

Good, enjoyable food includes panko-breaded chicken goujons with sweet chilli sauce, tiger prawns with garlic, lemon and parsley butter, sausage, egg and chips, pasta with sunblush tomatoes and garlic, basil and cheese sauce, moroccan-style harissa chicken with apricot sauce, slow-roasted lamb shank with garlic mash, fresh mint and madeira gravy, 34-day-aged rib-eye steak with crispy fried onions and a choice of sauces, and puddings such as raspberry amaretti sundae and sticky toffee pudding; burger evening is Tuesday and grill nights are Monday and Wednesday. *Benchmark main dish: beef in red wine pie £13.95. Two-course evening meal £20.50.*

Free house ~ Licensee Adrian Rock ~ Real ale ~ Open 12-2.30, 6-11; 12-3, 6.30-10.30 Sun ~ Bar food 12-2, 6-9.30; 12-2.30, 6.30-9.30 Sun ~ Restaurant ~ Children welcome ~ Wi-fi
Recommended by Dr Simon Innes, Victor Sumner, Frank and Marcia Pelling, George Sanderson

ELLASTONE
SK1143 Map 7

Duncombe Arms ⭐ ♀

(01335) 324275 – www.duncombearms.co.uk

Main Road; DE6 2GZ

• •

Staffordshire Dining Pub of the Year

Nooks and crannies, a thoughtful choice of drinks, friendly staff and lovely food; seats and tables in large garden

This stylishly refurbished village pub creates an easy-going, friendly atmosphere that attracts a wide range of customers, and there's somewhere interesting to sit whatever the occasion. As well as beams, the rooms have bare brick, exposed stone and painted walls, open fires and woodburners, horse prints and photos, big bold paintings of pigs, sheep, cows and chickens, large clocks and fresh flowers, church candles on mantelpieces, in big glass jars and on tables – and flooring that ranges from carpet to flagstones, bare floorboards and brick. Furnishings are just as eclectic: long leather button-back and cushioned wall seats, armchairs, all manner of wooden or upholstered dining chairs and tables made from mahogany, pine and even driftwood. They serve a beer named for the pub plus Marstons Pedigree and Ringwood Razorback on handpump, 50 wines by the glass from a fine list, 20 gins and over 20 malt whiskies; background music. An appealing terrace has wooden or rush seats around tables under parasols, braziers for cooler evenings and a view down over the garden to Worthy Island Wood.

Imaginative food includes sandwiches, salmon rillettes with horseradish mayonnaise, chicken liver parfait with burnt orange and madeira jelly, vegetable risotto with buffalo mozzarella and truffle pesto, beef and onion pie, rump of hogget with aubergine, beans, confit tomato, ewes curd and black olives, lemon sole meunière with cockles, monk's beard, lemon and sea lettuce sauce, chicken with roasted barley, girolles, charred onion and parsley, and puddings such as dark chocolate délice with chocolate foam, caramelised peanut and chocolate sorbet and buttermilk pannacotta with almond granola, apple compote and honey madeline; they also offer a two- and three-course weekday set lunch. *Benchmark main dish: braised beef cheek with watercress pesto and burnt onions £18.00. Two-course evening meal £25.00.*

Free house ~ Licensees Johnny and Laura Greenall ~ Real ale ~ Open 12-10 (11 Sat); closed 1 week Jan ~ Bar food 12-2.30, 6-9; 12-5 Sun ~ Restaurant ~ Children welcome ~ Dogs allowed in bar ~ Wi-fi *Recommended by Brian and Anna Marsden, Millie and Peter Downing, Elise and Charles Mackinlay, Brian and Sally Wakeham*

If we know a featured-entry pub does sandwiches, we always say so – if they're not mentioned, you'll have to assume you can't get one.

LONGDON GREEN   SK0813   Map 7

Red Lion ♀ ⊜

(01543) 490410 – www.brunningandprice.co.uk/redlion

Hay Lane; WS15 4QF

Large, well run pub with interesting furnishings, a fine range of drinks, enjoyable food and spreading garden

Although the interior of this handsome pub has been extended and thoughtfully opened up, the bustling bar remains the heart of the place, with spreading rooms and nooks and crannies leading off. One dining room has skylights, rugs on nice old bricks, house plants lining the windowsill, an elegant metal chandelier and a miscellany of cushioned dining chairs around dark wooden tables. Similar furnishings fill the other rooms, and the walls are covered with old photos, pictures and prints relating to the local area and big gilt-edged mirrors; background music and board games. Open fires include a raised central fire pit. You'll find Phoenix Brunning & Price Original, Blythe Bagots Bitter and Timothy Taylors Boltmaker with guests from breweries such as Purity, Salopian, Weetwood and Wye Valley on handpump, 20 wines by the glass, 50 malt whiskies, 30 gins and two farm ciders. Staff are friendly, courteous and helpful. The large garden has seats and tables on a suntrap terrace, picnic-sets on grass, a gazebo and swings and a play tractor for children; you can also watch cricket matches being played on the village green opposite.

Rewarding food includes sandwiches, potted smoked mackerel and spiced brown shrimps with apple and grain mustard salad, korean-style chicken wings with kimchi salad, feta, pea and mint quiche with herbed crème fraîche potato salad, honey-roast ham and free-range eggs, manchego-glazed hake with patatas bravas, wilted spinach and chorizo salsa, duck breast with bubble and squeak cake, rainbow carrots and port jus, tempura king prawns with watermelon, pak choi, pickled ginger and chilli and lime dressing, and puddings such as spiced cheesecake with berry compote and hazelnut praline and strawberry jam tart with vanilla cream. *Benchmark main dish: beer-battered cod and chips £13.45. Two-course evening meal £21.00.*

Brunning & Price ~ Manager Paul Drain ~ Real ale ~ Open 9.30am-11pm (10.30pm Sun) ~ Bar food 12-10 (9.30 Sun) ~ Restaurant ~ Children welcome ~ Dogs allowed in bar ~ Wi-fi
Recommended by Belinda May, Peter Brix, Susan Jackman, Luke Morgan, Christine and Tony Garrett, Usha and Terry Patel

SALT   SJ9527   Map 7

Holly Bush £

(01889) 508234 – www.hollybushinn.co.uk

Village signposted off A51 S of Stone (and A518 NE of Stafford); ST18 0BX

Delightful medieval pub with all-day food

You can be sure of a genuine welcome in this charming thatched pub with its cheerful mix of customers. From the standing-only serving section, several cosy areas spread out with high-backed cushioned pews, old tables and more conventional seats. The oldest part has a heavy-beamed and planked ceiling (some of the beams are attractively carved), a woodburning stove and a salt cupboard built into a big inglenook, with other nice old-fashioned touches including copper utensils, horsebrasses and an ancient pair of riding boots on the mantelpiece. A modern back extension, with beams, stripped brickwork and a small coal fire, blends in well. Adnams Southwold, Marstons Pedigree and a beer named for the pub (from Marstons) on handpump, alongside ten wines by the glass. They operate a secure locker system for credit cards, which they'll ask to keep if you run a tab. The hanging baskets and tubs are lovely and the back garden is beautifully looked after and filled with flowers, with rustic picnic-sets set out on a big lawn. This is a pretty village.

▐▌ Using local produce, the fair-priced food includes half a rack of barbecue pork ribs, baked camembert topped with apricot preserve, steak and kidney pudding, burger with toppings, coleslaw, onion rings and chips, chicken stuffed with spiced pork and wrapped in smoked bacon with Guinness gravy, a fresh fish and vegetarian dish of the day, venison casserole, 28-day-aged steak with a choice of sauces, and puddings. *Benchmark main dish: greek lamb in herbs and red wine £11.95. Two-course evening meal £19.00.*

Admiral Taverns ~ Licensees Geoffrey and Joseph Holland ~ Real ale ~ Open 12-11 (10.30 Sun) ~ Bar food 12-9.30 (9 Sun) ~ Children welcome ~ Wi-fi *Recommended by Stephen Shepherd, Ian and Rose Lock, Dr D J and Mrs S C Walker, Alistair Forsyth, Belinda Stamp*

SWYNNERTON
Fitzherbert Arms ♀ ◖

SJ8535   Map 7

(01782) 796782 – www.fitzherbertarms.co.uk
Off A51 Stone–Nantwich; ST15 0RA

Thoughtfully renovated pub with character rooms, interesting décor, local ales and rewarding food; seats outside with country views

On Lord Stafford's Estate and at the centre of the village, this is a charming pub that's been carefully refurbished. Through an impressive glass door, the bar sits to the right with a raised fireplace styled like a furnace along with blacksmiths' tools and relics. Down a step to the left is the older part of the pub, with button-back leather armchairs beside a two-way fireplace, rugs on flagstones, hops and some fine old brickwork. Fitzherbert Best (from Weetwood) and Swynnerton Stout (from Titanic) on handpump with a couple of guests from breweries within a 35-mile radius; also, 15 good wines by the glass, a fantastic and carefully chosen array of 30 ports with helpful notes (they hold port tasting evenings – phone for details) and a farm cider from the Apple County Cider Company. Staff are helpful and friendly. The beamed dining room is similarly furnished – a nice mix of old dining chairs and tables – plus window seats with scatter cushions, gilt-edged mirrors, black and white photographs and chandeliers; background music and board games. Do look out for the glass-topped giant bellows and anvil tables, door handles made of historic smithy irons, and candles in old port bottles. Outside, a covered oak-timbered terrace has contemporary seats around rustic tables, heaters, fairy-lit shrubs in pots and country views; there are more seats in a small hedged garden. The pub is on a circular walk (details on their website – time it right to arrive back for lunch); dogs are greeted with a biscuit and a water bowl. The pub is owned by Tim Bird and Mary McLaughlin of Cheshire Cat Pubs & Bars.

▐▌ Interesting food includes prawn and crab tart with red pepper chilli jam, chicken liver and port pâté with red onion marmalade, staffordshire oatcakes filled with mushrooms, walnuts and goats cheese, pork and caramelised onion sausages with red cabbage and onion gravy, smoked fish pie, chicken breast with sweet potato fondant and tarragon sauce, beer-battered haddock and chips, lamb rump with asparagus and a tomato and anchovy dressing, and puddings such as banoffi mess with toffee sauce and mango and passion-fruit posset with coconut shortbread. *Benchmark main dish: steak in stout pie £13.95. Two-course evening meal £19.00.*

Free house ~ Licensee Leanne Wallis ~ Real ale ~ Open 12-11 (10.30 Sun) ~ Bar food 12-9; 12-9.30 Fri, Sat; 12-8.45 Sun ~ Children welcome but no under-10s after 7pm ~ Dogs allowed in bar ~ Wi-fi *Recommended by Margaret McDonald, Patricia Hawkins, Diane Abbott, Martin and Joanne Sharp, Jane Rigby, Joe and Belinda Smart*

WRINEHILL
SJ7547   Map 7
Hand & Trumpet ♀ ◗
(01270) 820048 – www.brunningandprice.co.uk/hand
A531 Newcastle–Nantwich; CW3 9BJ

All-day food in big attractive dining pub with a good choice of ales and wines by the glass, served by courteous staff

The linked, open-plan areas here work their way around the long, solidly built counter, with a mix of dining chairs and sturdy tables on polished tiles or stripped oak boards with rugs. There are nicely lit prints and mirrors on cream walls between a mainly dark dado, plenty of house plants, open fires and deep red ceilings. Original bow windows and a large skylight keep the place light and airy, and french windows open on to a spacious balustraded deck with teak tables and chairs, and a view down to ducks swimming on a big pond in the sizeable garden. Friendly attentive staff serve Phoenix Brunning & Price Original, Salopian Oracle, Stonehouse Station Bitter and guests such as Acorn Zeus IPA, Joules Slumbering Monk, and Titanic White Star on handpump, as well as 16 wines by the glass, 20 rums, 40 gins, 20 bourbons and about 70 whiskies; board games. Good disabled access and facilities.

Food is appealing and includes sandwiches, scallops with crispy ham fritters and pea purée, chicken liver pâté with carrot and apricot chutney, goats cheese and mushroom burger with roasted red peppers and sweet potato fries, satay chicken salad with chinese leaves, noodles, pineapple, spring onion and roasted peanuts, pork and leek sausages with mash and onion gravy, sea bass with roasted fennel, saffron potatoes and tomato and chilli broth, tikka-spiced lamb kebab with mint yoghurt and puy lentil salad, and puddings such as crème brûlée and chocolate brownie with chocolate sauce and vanilla ice-cream. *Benchmark main dish: braised lamb shoulder with gravy £17.25. Two-course evening meal £20.00.*

Brunning & Price ~ Manager Ryan Platt ~ Real ale ~ Open 12-11 (10.30 Sun) ~ Bar food 12-10 (9.30 Sun) ~ Children welcome ~ Dogs allowed in bar ~ Wi-fi *Recommended by Laura Reid, Chris Stevenson, Sabina and Gerald Grimshaw, Caroline and Peter Bryant*

Also Worth a Visit in Staffordshire

Besides the fully inspected pubs, you might like to try these pubs that have been recommended to us and described by readers. Do tell us what you think of them: feedback@goodguides.com

ABBOTS BROMLEY   SK0824
Coach & Horses (01283) 840256
High Street; WS15 3BN Modernised 18th-c village pub with good choice of well liked home-made food (not Sun evening) from baguettes and pizzas up, also good value weekday deals, beamed bar with stone floor and button-back banquettes, dark wood pubby furniture in carpeted restaurant, log fire, three well kept ales and several wines by the glass; children and dogs (in bar) welcome, pleasant garden with circular

picnic-sets, open all day Fri-Sun, closed Mon lunchtime. *(Martin and Joanne Sharp)*

ALSAGERS BANK   SJ8048
Gresley Arms (01782) 722469
High Street; ST7 8BQ At the top of Alsagers Bank with wonderful far-reaching views from the back, welcoming and popular, with eight or more interesting ales from smaller breweries and several real ciders, good value pubby food with deals including bargain Thurs steak night (must book) and eat-for-£1 Mon if you buy

a drink (no food Mon-Weds lunchtimes or Sun evening), traditional slate-floor bar with beams and open fire, comfortable lounge, picture-window dining room taking in the view, and a lower family room; Mon quiz; walkers and dogs welcome, garden picnic-sets, Apedale Heritage Centre nearby, open all day Thurs-Sun, otherwise from 3pm. *(Brian and Anna Marsden)*

ALSTONEFIELD   SK1355
★**George** (01335) 310205
Village signed from A515 Ashbourne–Buxton; DE6 2FX Simply furnished family-run pub in pretty village overlooking small green; chatty bar with low beams and quarry tiles, old Peak District photographs and pictures, log fire, Marstons-related ales and a dozen wines by the glass from copper-topped counter, really good imaginative food (can be pricey) using some home-grown produce, friendly efficient service, small snug and neat dining room with woodburner, simple farmhouse furniture, candlelight; free wi-fi, children and dogs (in bar) welcome, picnic-sets out at front, more seats in big sheltered stableyard behind, open all day Fri and Sat, till 9.30pm Sun. *(Derek and Sylvia Stephenson, Belinda May, Edward Nile, Clive and Fran Dutson)*

ARMITAGE   SK0716
Plum Pudding (01543) 490330
Rugeley Road (A513); WS15 4AZ Canalside pub and italian restaurant, good food in bar and dining room including selection of small plates (piattini) and daily specials, well kept Bass, Greene King Old Speckled Hen and a guest, friendly helpful staff; children welcome, no dogs inside, tables on waterside terrace and narrow canal bank, moorings, open (and food) all day. *(Robert W Buckle)*

BIDDULPH   SJ8959
Talbot (01782) 512608
Grange Road (N, right off A527); ST8 7RY Vintage Inn family dining pub in 19th-c stone building, enjoyable freshly made food including weekday set menus, well kept Bass and a couple of guests, raised two-way log fire in restaurant part, some secluded areas; background music; handy for Biddulph Grange (NT), open (and food) all day. *(Suzy Miller)*

BLACKBROOK   SJ7638
Swan with Two Necks (01782) 680343 *Nantwich Road (A51); ST5 5EH* Country pub-restaurant with smart modern décor in open-plan split-level dining areas, good well presented food (booking advised) from sharing boards up, Timothy Taylors Landlord, three guest ales and plenty of wines by the glass including champagne, efficient friendly service; background music; children welcome,

comfortable tables out on decking, open (and food) all day. *(Len and Lilly Dowson)*

BLITHBURY   SK0819
Bull & Spectacles (01889) 504201
Uttoxeter Road (B5014 S of Abbots Bromley); WS15 3HY Friendly 17th-c pub with good choice of generously served food including bargain lunchtime Hot Table (half a dozen or so main dishes with help-yourself vegetables, and some puddings), also good value steak night (Mon, Thurs), a couple of changing ales, good service; children and dogs welcome, next door to reindeer farm, open all day Sun till 7.30pm. *(Sandra Hollies)*

BURSLEM   SJ8649
Leopard (01782) 819644
Market Place; ST6 3AA Traditional Victorian city-centre pub with three rooms including a snug, good choice of enjoyable home-made food (Tues-Sun lunchtimes), Bass and up to five changing guests, well priced wines, friendly helpful service; regular live music, ghost tours in derelict hotel part; open all day. *(Susan Jackman)*

BURTON UPON TRENT   SK2523
★**Burton Bridge Inn** (01283) 536596
Bridge Street (A50); DE14 1SY Friendly down-to-earth local with good Burton Bridge ales from brewery across old-fashioned brick yard; simple little front area leading into adjacent bar with pews, plain walls hung with notices, awards and brewery memorabilia, 16 malt whiskies and lots of country wines, small beamed and oak-panelled lounge with simple furniture and flame-effect fire, upstairs dining room and skittle alley, short choice of low-priced lunchtime food Thurs-Sat, steak night first Tues of month, fish night third Tues; no credit cards; children and dogs (in bar) welcome, open all day Fri, Sat, closed Mon lunchtime. *(Colin Gooch)*

BURTON UPON TRENT   SK2423
★**Coopers Tavern** (01283) 532551
Cross Street; DE14 1EG Traditionally refurbished 19th-c backstreet local tied to Joules – was tap for the Bass brewery and still has some glorious ephemera including mirrors and glazed adverts; homely and warm with coal fire, straightforward front parlour, back bar doubling as tap room with up to half a dozen guest beers (including Bass) and good selection of ciders/perries, cheese boards and pies only but can bring your own food (or take beer to next-door curry house); regular live music; children (till 8pm) and dogs welcome, small back garden, open all day Thurs-Sun, from 4pm other days. *(Jake)*

BURTON UPON TRENT   SK2423
Old Cottage Tavern (01283) 511615
Rangemoor Street/Byrkley Street; DE14 2EG Friendly unpretentious corner local acting as tap for Burton Old Cottage, their ales in top condition and three guests,

bars front and back and a snug, upstairs games room with skittle alley; folk nights, free wi-fi; bedrooms, open all day. *(Jake)*

CANNOCK WOOD   SK0412
Park Gate   (01543) 682223
Park Gate Road, S side of Cannock Chase; WS15 4RN Large red-brick dining pub with good food including various deals and children's menu (Sun booking essential), ales such as Sharps and Thwaites, rustic-feel bar with woodburner, other comfortably modernised areas and conservatory; background and occasional live music; children and dogs (in bar) welcome, nice secluded back garden with plenty of picnic-sets and play area, by Castle Ring Iron Age hill fort, good Cannock Chase walks, open all day. *(Sandra Hollies)*

CHEDDLETON   SJ9752
Black Lion   (01538) 360620
Leek Road, by the church; ST13 7HP Popular 19th-c village local, well kept Bass, Welbeck Abbey and two guests, freshly made traditional lunchtime food (just snacks such as local pork pies in the evening), woodburner; some live music, pool and darts; dogs welcome, seats out in front and in fenced back garden, open all day. *(Frank and Marcia Pelling)*

CHEDDLETON   SJ9751
Boat   (01538) 360521
Basford Bridge Lane, off A520; ST13 7EQ Cheerful unpretentious canalside local handy for Churnet Valley steam railway, flint mill and country park; long bar with low plank ceiling, well kept Marstons-related ales and enjoyable honest food from sandwiches to steaks, dining room behind; children welcome, dogs in bar, seats out overlooking Caldon Canal, open all day. *(Chris and Dorothy Stock, Tony Hobden)*

CODSALL   SJ8603
Codsall Station   (01902) 847061
Chapel Lane/Station Road; WV8 1BY Converted vintage waiting room and ticket office of working station, comfortable and welcoming, with well kept Holdens ales and a couple of guests, good value pubby food including blackboard specials (just sandwiches Sun), lots of railway memorabilia, open fire, conservatory; terrace seating, open all day. *(Stephen Shepherd, Mark Writtle)*

CONSALL   SK0049
Black Lion   (01782) 550294
Consall Forge, OS Sheet 118 map reference 000491; best approach from Nature Park, off A522, using car park 0.5 miles past Nature Centre; ST9 0AJ Traditional take-us-as-you-find-us place tucked away in rustic canalside spot by restored steam railway station; generous helpings of enjoyable pub food, five well kept ales including Peakstones Rock and several ciders, flagstones and good coal fire; background music; children and dogs welcome, seats out overlooking canal, area for campers and shop for boaters, good walks, open (and food) all day, can get very busy weekend lunchtimes. *(Tony Hobden)*

COPMERE END   SJ8029
Star   (01785) 850279
W of Eccleshall; ST21 6EW Friendly two-room 19th-c country local with well kept Bass, Titanic Anchor, Wells Bombardier and a couple of guests, good choice of reasonably priced food from sandwiches up (not Sun evening), open fire and woodburner, piano; children and dogs welcome, tables and play area in back garden overlooking mere, good walks, open all day weekends, closed Mon. *(Jeff Sampson)*

DENSTONE   SK0940
Tavern   (01889) 590847
College Road; ST14 5HR Welcoming 17th-c stone-built pub with good food (not Mon) including freshly made pizzas (Fri-Sat evenings) and Sun carvery, well kept Marstons ales and good range of wines by the glass, pleasant service, comfortable lounge with antiques, dining conservatory; darts, some live music, free wi-fi; children and dogs welcome, picnic-sets out at front among tubs and hanging baskets, village farm shop and lovely church, open all day Fri-Sun, closed Mon lunchtime. *(Sandra Hollies)*

DUSTON   SP7262
Hopping Hare   (01604) 580090
Hopping Hill Gardens; NN5 6PF Imposing red-brick former manor surrounded by housing; largish bar adjacent to entrance, log fires and lots of different dining areas, well kept Adnams, Black Sheep and a guest, good range of wines by the glass and highly rated attractively presented food, friendly efficient service; children welcome, seats out on decking, 21 bedrooms, open (and food) all day. *(Gerry and Rosemary Dobson)*

ECCLESHALL   SJ8329
Old Smithy   (01785) 850564
Castle Street; ST21 6DF Pub-restaurant with comfortable clean modern décor, good freshly made food at fair prices including decent vegetarian options and some themed nights, four mainstream ales and good choice of other drinks, friendly efficient staff; children welcome, open all day. *(Jake)*

ECCLESHALL   SJ8329
Royal Oak   (01785) 859065
High Street; ST21 6BW Restored beamed and colonnaded coaching inn run by father and son team, well kept Joules ales and enjoyable locally sourced food including Mon and Tues bargains, friendly chatty staff; children and dogs (in bar) welcome, beer garden, open all day, food all day Sun. *(Jake)*

FLASH   SK0267

Travellers Rest/Knights Table

(01298) 236695 *A53 Buxton–Leek;*
SK17 0SN Isolated main-road pub and
one of the highest in Britain, clean and
friendly, with good reasonably priced
traditional food (not Sun evening), four
well kept ales and good selection of wines,
beams, bare stone walls and open fires,
medieval knights theme; free wi-fi; children
very welcome, great Peak District views
from back terrace, classic car meeting last
Thurs of month, bedrooms, closed Mon and
Tues, otherwise open all day. *(John Wooll)*

FRADLEY   SK1414

White Swan (01283) 790330

Fradley Junction; DE13 7DN Terrace-
row pub (aka the Mucky Duck) in good
canalside location at Trent & Mersey and
Coventry junction; Everards ales and three
guests, enjoyable reasonably priced food
including pizzas, cheery traditional public
bar with woodburner and open fire, quieter
lounge and lower vaulted dining room
(former stable); Thurs folk night, open mike
Sun; children and dogs welcome, waterside
tables, classic car/motorbike meetings,
open all day. *(Len and Lilly Dowson)*

GNOSALL   SJ8220

Boat (01785) 822208

Gnosall Heath, by Shropshire Union
Canal Bridge 34; ST20 0DA Popular
little canalside pub run by friendly family,
comfortable first-floor bar with curved
window seat overlooking narrowboats,
decent choice of reasonably priced
pub food (not Sun or Mon evenings),
Marstons-related ales, open fire; darts and
dominoes; children and dogs welcome,
tables out by canal, moorings and nice
walks, open all day weekends, closed Mon
lunchtime. *(Frank and Marcia Pelling)*

HANLEY   SJ8847

Coachmakers Arms (01782) 262158

Lichfield Street; ST1 3EA Chatty
traditional 19th-c town local with four
small rooms and drinking corridor, five
well kept ales including Bass, darts, cards
and dominoes, original seating and local
tilework, open fires; children and dogs
welcome, open all day Thurs-Sun, from 4pm
other days. *(Christine and Tony Garrett)*

HARTSHILL   SJ8645

Jolly Potters 07875 586902

Hartshill Road (A52); ST4 7NH
Welcoming traditional drinkers' pub (some
recent refurbishment) with five rooms off
central corridor, well kept Bass, Black Sheep

and up to three guests, good selection of
gins, no food apart from summer pizzas and
occasional barbecues/hog roasts); pool and
darts; children and dogs welcome, garden
with stage for live music, open from 3pm
Fri-Sun (4pm other days). *(Jeff Sampson)*

HAUGHTON   SJ8620

Bell (01785) 780301

A518 Stafford–Newport; ST18 9EX
Refurbished 19th-c village pub with good value
popular food (not Sun or Mon evenings, best
to book), lunchtime deal Mon-Sat and monthly
steak night, five well kept ales including
Marstons and Timothy Taylors, friendly
attentive service; children welcome, no dogs
inside, picnic-sets in back garden, open all
day Fri-Sun. *(Caroline and Peter Bryant)*

HIGH OFFLEY   SJ7725

Anchor (01785) 284569

Off A519 Eccleshall–Newport; towards
High Lea, by Shropshire Union Canal
Bridge 42; Peggs Lane; ST20 0NG Built
around 1830 to serve the Shropshire Union
Canal and little changed in the century
or more this family has run it; two small
simple front rooms, one with a couple of
fine high-backed settles on quarry tiles,
Wadworths 6X and Weston's cider, sandwiches
on request, owners' sitting room behind bar,
occasional weekend sing-alongs; outbuilding
with semi-open lavatories (swallows may
fly through); no children inside, lovely
garden with hanging baskets and notable
topiary anchor, small shop, moorings (near
Bridge 42), caravans/camping, closed
Mon-Thurs in winter. *(Helen McLagan)*

HIMLEY   SO8990

★ Crooked House (01384) 238583

Signed down long lane from B4176
Gornalwood–Himley, OS Sheet 139 map
reference 896908; DY3 4DA Extraordinary
sight, building thrown wildly out of kilter
by mining subsidence, one side 4-ft lower
than the other and slopes so weird that
things appear to roll up them; public bar
(dogs allowed here) with grandfather
clock and hatch serving Banks's and other
Marstons-related ales, lounge bar, good
food from snacks and pub standards to
more unusual choices, some local antiques
in level extension, conservatory; children
welcome in eating areas, big outside
terrace, closed Mon, otherwise open all
day (till 6pm Sun). *(Susan Jackman)*

HULME END   SK1059

Manifold Inn (01298) 84537

B5054 Warslow–Hartington; SK17 0EX
Fairly isolated stone coaching inn near River
Manifold; enjoyable traditional home-made

Virtually all pubs in this book sell wine by the glass. We mention wines
if they are a cut above the average.

food at reasonable prices including Mon steak night, four well kept ales such as Cottage, Leatherbritches, Marstons and Thwaites, pleasant friendly staff, log fire in traditional carpeted bar, adjacent restaurant and conservatory; background music, TV; children and dogs (in some parts) welcome, disabled facilities, tables outside, ten bedrooms (eight in converted barns), self-catering cottage, good walks including Manifold Trail, open (and food) all day. *(Derek and Sylvia Stephenson)*

KNIGHTON   SJ7240

White Lion (01630) 647300

B5415 Woore–Market Drayton; TF9 4HJ Welcoming roadside country pub continuing well under present management, good food from interestingly varied menu, well kept local ales (including one badged for them) and extensive range of gins, friendly attentive service, beams and open fires, dining conservatory; some live music, darts; children and dogs welcome (pub dog is Ted), tables outside, closed lunchtimes Mon and Tues. *(Simon H)*

LEEK   SJ9956

Earl Grey (01538) 372570

Ashbourne Road; ST13 5AT Traditional little red-brick corner pub attracting good mix of customers; freshly refurbished split-level interior, a house ale brewed by Whim plus several other interesting changing beers (tasters offered), real ciders and decent range of whiskies and gins, friendly knowledgeable staff, no food; juke box, some live music and quiz nights; dogs welcome (they have one), open all day Fri-Sun, from 5pm Mon, 3pm other days. *(Tony Hobden)*

LEEK   SJ9856

★**Wilkes Head** 07976 592787

St Edward Street; ST13 5DS Friendly lived-in three-room local dating from the early 18th c (still has back coaching stables), owned by Whim with their ales and interesting guests, real ciders and good choice of whiskies and gins, no food apart from rolls, lots of pump clips, pub games; juke box in back room and regular live music events including festivals organised by musician landlord; children allowed in one room (not really a family pub), dogs on leads welcome but do ask first, fair disabled access, garden with stage, open all day except Mon lunchtime. *(Jeff Sampson)*

LICHFIELD   SK1109

Beerbohm (01543) 898252

Tamworth Street; WS13 6JP Popular fairly new bar (former café) under enthusiastic friendly owners; four real ales including

Salopian and a beer badged for them, plenty of international beers (draught and bottled) and good choice of other drinks, helpful knowledgeable staff, cosy bar with rug on wood floor, some comfortable seating including armchairs and banquette by iron-framed tables, similar décor in upstairs lounge with prints, old beer advertising signs and large mirrors on plum or grey painted walls, no food but can bring your own (plates and cutlery supplied), tea and coffee; background music, free wi-fi; well behaved dogs welcome, closed Sun and Mon, otherwise open all day. *(Suzy Miller)*

LICHFIELD   SK0705

Boat (01543) 361692

From A5 at Muckley Corner, take A461 signed Walsall; pub is on right just before M6 Toll; WS14 0BU Under new management but emphasis continues on the food side and initial reports good; views into kitchen from skylit entrance part with leather tub chairs and sofas around coffee tables and potted palms, split-level bar/dining areas with sturdy modern pine furniture on carpet or lino, views of canal, three changing ales and several wines by the glass; background music; children welcome, wheelchair access, garden with seats on raised deck, closed Mon, otherwise open all day till 10pm. *(Frank and Marcia Pelling)*

LICHFIELD   SK1109

Duke of York (01543) 300386

Greenhill/Church Street; WS13 6DY Old beamed pub with split-level front bar, cosy carpeted lounge and converted back stables, inglenook woodburners, well kept Joules ales and guests, simple lunchtime food (not Sun) served by pleasant staff; some live music, Apr beer festival; no children but dogs allowed, terrace picnic-sets behind and own bowling green, open all day. *(Sandra Hollies)*

LICHFIELD   SK1308

Horse & Jockey (01543) 262924

Tamworth Road (A51 Lichfield–Tamworth); WS14 9JE Cosy old-fashioned pub with wide range of popular freshly prepared food including good home-made pies and fish specials (booking advised), ales such as Castle Rock, Marstons and Sharps, good friendly service, open fire; darts; children welcome if eating, no dogs, open (and food) all day. *(Jeff Sampson)*

LITTLE BRIDGEFORD   SJ8727

Mill (01785) 282710

Worston Lane; near M6 junction 14; turn right off A5013 at Little Bridgeford; ST18 9QA Dining pub in attractive 1814

If you stay overnight in an inn or hotel, they are allowed to serve you an alcoholic drink at any hour of the day or night.

watermill, enjoyable sensibly priced food including children's menu and Sun carvery, Greene King ales, good friendly service; Thurs quiz; nice grounds with adventure playground and nature trail (lakes, islands etc); open (and food) all day. *(Sandra Hollies)*

LONGDON
SK0814
Swan with Two Necks (01543)
491570 *Off A51 Lichfield–Rugeley; Brook Lane; WS15 4PN* Welcoming village pub with long low-beamed quarry-tiled bar, two-way woodburner and some leather wall benches, separate wood-floored lounge/restaurant with a couple of open fires, good range of enjoyable food catering for special diets, Marston Pedigree, Sharps Doom Bar and two guests, friendly helpful service; live music and quiz nights, TV; children (away from bar) and dogs (in bar) welcome, garden with play area, open all day, food all day Sat, not Sun evening. *(Mr and Mrs John Clifford)*

LONGNOR
SK0965
Old Cheshire Cheese
(01298) 83218 *High Street; SK17 0NS* Relaxed 17th-c village pub, three well kept Robinsons ales and enjoyable good value food including blackboard specials and Weds steak night, open fire, bric-a-brac and pictures in traditional main bar, two dining rooms, pool and TV in separate rooms; free wi-fi; children, walkers and dogs welcome, tables out in front and on back grass, four bedrooms in converted stables over road, open (and food) all day, kitchen closes 6pm Sun. *(Jake)*

MARCHINGTON
SK1330
Dog & Partridge (01283) 820394
Church Lane; ST14 8LJ Flower-decked 18th-c village pub with various beamed and tile-floored rooms, Bass and three changing guests (beer festivals), good food (not Sun evening) including themed nights and bargain two-course lunch deal, good value wines, attentive friendly staff, real fires and some interesting bits and pieces; background music, live music Sun from 5.30pm, free wi-fi; children and dogs (in bar) welcome, tables under parasols in paved back terrace by car park, open all day weekends. *(Jeff Sampson)*

MEERBROOK
SJ9960
Lazy Trout (01538) 300385
Centre of village; ST13 8SN Popular country dining pub with good sensibly priced home-made food including daily specials, friendly helpful staff, small bar area serving five well kept ales such as Greene King, Marstons and Wincle from curved stone counter, log fire in comfortable dining lounge on the right, another dining room to the left with quarry tiles, pine furniture and old cooking range; juke box; children welcome, dogs and muddy boots in some parts, seats out at front by quiet lane and in appealing

garden behind with splendid views to the Roaches and Hen Cloud, good walks, open (and food) all day. *(Dr D J and Mrs S C Walker, Malcolm and Pauline Pellatt)*

NEWBOROUGH
SK1325
Red Lion (01283) 576182
Duffield Lane; DE13 8SH Old pub facing church in quiet village, comfortable bar with open fire, Marstons-related ales including Pedigree and good choice of other drinks, enjoyable fair-priced food from snacks and sharing plates up, smallish dining room, friendly accommodating staff; children welcome, seats out at front, open all day, food till 6pm Sun. *(Martin and Joanne Sharp)*

PENKRIDGE
SJ9214
Littleton Arms (01785) 716300
St Michaels Square/A449 – M6 detour between junctions 12 and 13; ST19 5AL Cheerfully busy dining pub-hotel (former coaching inn) with contemporary open-plan interior, good variety of enjoyable well presented food from sandwiches and sharing boards to popular Sun lunch, five well kept changing ales and appealing choice of wines/gins from island servery, afternoon teas, friendly accommodating staff; background music; children and dogs (in bar area) welcome, terrace seating under parasols, ten bedrooms, open all day (till midnight Fri, Sat), brunch from 10am. *(Richard Moore, Tony Hobden)*

SEIGHFORD
SJ8725
Hollybush (01785) 281644
3 miles from M6 junction 14 via A5013/B5405; ST18 9PQ Modernised and extended beamed pub owned by the village, good value locally sourced pubby food (not Sun evening, Mon lunchtime) from sandwiches and light choices up, ales including Titanic and Everards; Sun quiz, portable skittle alley; children and dogs welcome, beer garden, open all day Fri-Sun. *(Susan Jackman)*

SHEEN
SK1160
Staffordshire Knot (01298) 84329
Off B5054 at Hulme End; SK17 0ET Welcoming traditional 17th-c stone-built village pub, nice mix of old furniture on flagstones or red and black tiles, stag's head and hunting prints, two log fires in hefty stone fireplaces, good interesting food cooked by landlady (booking advised), well kept local Whim Hartington and reasonably priced wines, friendly helpful staff; closed Mon. *(Jake)*

SHENSTONE
SK1004
Plough (01543) 481800
Pinfold Hill, off A5127; WS14 0JN Revamped village dining pub with clean modern interior, enjoyable food (not Sun evening) from sandwiches, sharing boards and pizzas up, ales such as Greene King

and Holdens and good range of wines by the glass, friendly service; children welcome, dogs in bar, tables out on front terrace, open all day. *(Christine and Tony Garrett)*

STAFFORD SJ9322
Spittal Brook 01785 245268
Lichfield Road, just off A34; ST17 4LP Friendly local on outskirts of town, front bar and larger back dining area, five well kept ales including Sharps Doom Bar, enjoyable reasonably priced pubby food (not Sun evening), good log fire; Tues folk night, Weds quiz, TV, darts; children and dogs welcome, garden fenced off from main railway line, five bedrooms, open all day Fri-Sun. *(Tony Hobden)*

STAFFORD SJ9323
Swan (01785) 258142
Greengate Street; ST16 2JA Modernised 18th-c two-bar coaching inn, well kept Marstons-related ales and guests, good sensibly priced bar and brasserie food including themed evenings and lunchtime set menu, coffee shop, friendly helpful staff; tables and occasional live music in courtyard, 31 bedrooms, open (and food) all day. *(Jeff Sampson)*

STANLEY SJ9352
Travellers Rest (01782) 502580
Off A53 NE of Stoke; ST9 9LX Comfortable old stone village pub with large restaurant/bar area, beams and some exposed stonework, pubby tables and chairs on patterned carpet, button-back banquettes, brassware and knick-knacks, well kept Bass, Marstons Pedigree and guests from central servery, wide choice of reasonably priced popular food (booking advised) including set menu and other deals, friendly helpful service; children allowed away from bar, tables out in front under parasols, self-catering cottage, open all day, food all day weekends. *(Tony Hobden)*

STOKE-ON-TRENT SJ8649
Bulls Head (01782) 834153
St Johns Square, Burslem; ST6 3AJ Old-fashioned two-room tap for Titanic with up to ten real ales (including guests) from horseshoe bar, also good selection of belgian beers, ciders and wines, well cared-for interior with varnished tables on wood or carpeted floors, coal fire; bar billiards, table skittles and good juke box; drinking area outside (may be barbecue if Port Vale are at home), open all day Fri-Sun, closed till 3pm other days. *(Jake)*

STOKE-ON-TRENT SJ8745
Glebe (01782) 860670
35 Glebe Street, by the Civic Centre; ST4 1HG Well restored 19th-c Joules corner pub, their ales, real cider and good reasonably priced wines from central

mahogany counter, William Morris leaded windows, bare boards and panelling, some civic portraits and big fireplace with coat of arms above, wholesome bar food (not Sun, Mon evening) from good doorstep sandwiches up, friendly staff; quite handy for station, open all day. *(Dr J Barrie Jones)*

STOKE-ON-TRENT SJ8647
Holy Inadequate 07771 358238
Etruria Old Road; ST1 5PE Drinkers' pub with well kept Joules Pale Ale and several guest ales, craft kegs, german lagers and lots of bottled beers, snacky food such as pies and scotch eggs, friendly staff; open all day Fri-Sun, from 4pm other days. *(Tony Hobden, Jake)*

STONE SJ9034
Royal Exchange (01785) 812685
Corner Radford Street (A520) and Northesk Street; ST15 8DA Refurbished end-of-terrace pub with up to a dozen well kept ales including Everards and Titanic along with some craft beers, snacky lunchtime food, friendly helpful staff, three seating areas (steps) and two fires; dogs welcome, open all day. *(Tony Hobden)*

STONE SJ8933
Wayfarer (01785) 811023
The Fillybrooks (A34 just N); ST15 0NB Sizeable 1930s pub beside dual-carriageway, contemporary décor and same owners as the Swan with Two Necks at Blackbrook; good food from varied menu including sharing plates and stone-baked pizzas, beers such as Sharps and Timothy Taylors, lots of wines by the glass including champagne, friendly attentive staff; free wi-fi; children welcome, no dogs inside, terrace seating, rear deck with tables under umbrellas, open (and food) all day. *(Frank and Marcia Pelling)*

STOWE SK0027
Cock (01889) 270237
Off A518 Stafford–Uttoxeter; ST18 0LF Popular bistro-style conversion of old beamed village pub (calls itself Bistro le Coq), well executed french food (not Mon) from sensibly short set menus, good affordably priced wines, small bar area serving real ale, friendly efficient service; well behaved children welcome, closed Sun evening, Mon. *(Martin and Joanne Sharp)*

TAMWORTH SK2004
Market Vaults (01827) 66552
Market Street, next to Town Hall; B79 7LU Popular and friendly traditional little pub with front bar and raised back lounge, dark oak, brass and original fireplaces, well kept Joules Pale Ale and seven guests, up to 16 real ciders and bargain lunchtime food (not Mon); regular live music, TV, free wi-fi; nice garden behind, open all day. *(Colin Gooch)*

TRYSULL   SO8594
Bell (01902) 892871
Bell Road; WV5 7JB Extended 18th-c
red-brick village pub next to church; cosy
bar, inglenook lounge and large high-
ceilinged back dining area, well kept
Bathams and guests, reasonably priced
wines and enjoyable food; children and
dogs (in bar) welcome, paved front terrace,
open all day Fri-Sun. *(Sandra Hollies)*

WETTON   SK1055
Olde Royal Oak (01335) 310287
*Village signed off Hulme End–
Alstonefield road, between B5054 and
A515; DE6 2AF* Old stone pub in lovely
NT countryside – a popular stop for walkers;
traditional bar with white ceiling boards
above black beams, small dining chairs
around rustic tables and log fire in stone
fireplace, carpeted sun lounge, four well
kept changing ales and a good selection of
malt whiskies, fairly priced home-made food
from sandwiches up; background and live
music, darts, dominoes and shove-ha'penny,
monthly quiz; children and dogs welcome,
picnic-sets in shaded garden, open (and
food) all day. *(Len and Lilly Dowson)*

WHEATON ASTON   SJ8512
Hartley Arms (01785) 840232
*Long Street (canalside, Tavern Bridge);
ST19 9NF* Popular roomy pub in pleasant
spot just above Shropshire Union Canal
(Bridge 19), good affordably priced food
from landlord-chef including OAP lunch
deal, Sun carvery and Mon curry night,
well kept Banks's and Marstons-related
guests, efficient friendly service; children
welcome, no dogs, picnic-sets outside,
open all day. *(Caroline and Peter Bryant)*

Post Office address codings confusingly give the impression that some pubs
are in Staffordshire, when they're really in Cheshire or Derbyshire
(which is where we list them).

Suffolk

KEY	★ Star Pub	🔘 Top Quality Food	🍺 Great Beer
♉ Good Wines	£ Bargain Meals	🛏 Good Bedrooms	🍴 Serves Food

ALDEBURGH
TM4656 Map 5

Cross Keys

(01728) 452637

Crabbe Street; IP15 5BN

16th-c pub with seats outside near the beach, chatty atmosphere, friendly licensee and local beers; bedrooms

Given its position on the seafront, this popular old pub gets busy at weekends and in high season – the seats on the sheltered back terrace offer views across the promenade and shingle to the water. It's a traditional place and the low-ceilinged interconnecting bars come with a cheerful, bustling atmosphere and a welcome from the obliging landlord, as well as antique and other pubby furniture, miscellaneous paintings on the walls and log fires in two inglenook fireplaces. Adnams Southwold, Broadside and Ghost Ship on handpump, decent wines by the glass and several malt whiskies; background music and games machine. The bedrooms are attractively furnished.

 Food is well liked and includes sandwiches, smoked mackerel pâté, goats cheese tart, ham and eggs, steak and kidney pie, fresh fish dishes such as mussels, whole plaice, skate wing with brown butter and crab, and puddings such as fruit crumble and sticky toffee pudding. *Benchmark main dish: beer-battered cod and chips £10.95. Two-course evening meal £17.00.*

Adnams ~ Tenants Mike and Janet Clement ~ Real ale ~ Open 11am-midnight; 12-midnight Sun ~ Bar food 12-2.30, 6.30-8.30; 12-3 Sun ~ Children welcome away from bar ~ Dogs welcome ~ Wi-fi ~ Bedrooms: £75/£95 *Recommended by Alan Cowell, Ian Herdman, Comus and Sarah Elliott, Brian and Susan Wylie, Sandra Morgan*

BRANDESTON
TM2460 Map 5

Queen 🔘 🛏

(01728) 685307 – www.thequeenatbrandeston.co.uk

The Street/Low Lane; IP13 7AD

Welcoming country pub with first class food, local ales, simple furnishings and seats in the garden; shepherd's huts

The particularly good food cooked by the chef-patron of this attractive brick-built place is one of the main reasons so many customers find their way here – but it's also still a proper pub with locals dropping in for a pint and a chat. The open-plan rooms are simply decorated with settles, built-in wall seats, grey-painted and cushioned dining chairs around rustic tables on stripped floorboards, an open fire, a woodburning stove and a few wall prints. Adnams Ghost Ship and Southwold and a changing guest on handpump, several wines by the glass and home-made fruit cordials; background music. Outside, teak tables and chairs sit among planter boxes on gravel. The three refurbished shepherd's huts are comfortable, warm and great fun as accommodation.

Using home-grown produce, the interesting modern food includes breakfasts (8-11am Thurs-Sun), sandwiches, quail with roast and pickled heritage carrots and a quail egg, brown crab with hispi cabbage and apple, lemon sole with mussels, violette potatoes and samphire, braised rare-breed beef with wild garlic, russian kale and cauliflower, fallow deer haunch with celeriac, cavolo nero and hazelnuts, pollock with peas, baby gem lettuce and warm tartare sauce, and puddings such as hot marmalade pudding with orange curd and bitter orange sorbet and chocolate brownie with vanilla ice-cream. *Benchmark main dish: herdwick lamb with cauliflower, set yoghurt and preserved lemon £16.00. Two-course evening meal £21.00.*

Free house ~ Licensee Alexander Aitchison ~ Open 12-11 Tues, Weds; 8am-11pm Thurs-Sat; 8am-10pm Sun ~ Bar food 12-2.30, 6-9 Thurs-Sat; 12-6 Sun ~ Children welcome ~ Dogs welcome ~ Wi-fi ~ Bedrooms: /£95 *Recommended by Jim King, Matt and Hayley Jacob, David Appleyard*

BROMESWELL
Unruly Pig ⊛ ⍩

TM3050   Map 5

(01394) 460310 – www.theunrulypig.co.uk
Orford Road, Bromeswell Heath; IP12 2PU

Refurbished dining pub with local ales, creative food, an informal feel, helpful, attentive staff and seats outside

The first class food in this neat, partly 16th-c pub is the reason most people visit, but they do keep three real ales and the atmosphere is relaxed and friendly. The bar has button-back leather wall seats, black leather dining chairs, simple tables, rugs on floorboards, a small woodburning stove and contemporary seats against the counter where charming, courteous staff serve Adnams Southwold and Woodfordes Wherry on handpump, 60 good wines by the glass, home-made cordials and interesting non-alcoholic drivers' drinks. The various linked dining rooms have beams and standing timbers, modern art and photos of well known pop stars on painted panelling, more up-to-date leather chairs and banquettes and rugs on bare boards; background music. There are seats and tables under cream parasols on the front terrace and they have bicycle racks. The pub is just a few minutes' drive from Sutton Hoo (National Trust).

Excellent british dishes with italian influences use the best local, seasonal produce: lunchtime sandwiches (not Sunday), chicken liver and foie gras parfait with clementines and endive, smoked mackerel and oyster velouté with celery and apple, halloumi and aubergine burger with fries and onion rings, ragoût of braised rabbit with guinea fowl, pancetta and spaghetti, cod loin with brown crab, prawns, cockles, chilli and almonds, braised ox cheek with bucatini pasta, wild garlic and lemon, poussin with leeks, chanterelle mushrooms and sauté potatoes, steaks with roasted bone marrow and dripping chips, and puddings such as rhubarb sorbet with poached rhubarb and almond and amaretto cake with blood oranges; they also offer a two- and three-course set menu. *Benchmark main dish: burger with toppings and chips £13.95. Two-course evening meal £18.00.*

Punch ~ Lease Brendan Padfield ~ Real ale ~ Open 12-3, 6-11; 12-11 Sat; 12-10.30 Sun ~ Bar food 12-2.30, 6-9; 12-3, 5-9.30 Sat; 12-8 Sun ~ Restaurant ~ Children welcome ~ Dogs welcome ~ Wi-fi *Recommended by Freddie and Sarah Banks, Clare and Andrew Reid, Camilla and Jose Ferrera*

CHELMONDISTON

TM2037 Map 5

Butt & Oyster

(01473) 780764 – www.debeninns.co.uk/buttandoyster

Pin Mill – signposted from B1456 SE of Ipswich; continue to bottom of road; IP9 1JW

Chatty old riverside pub with pleasant views, good food and drink and seats on the terrace

Happily, little changes here and this remains a simple old bargeman's pub in a fine spot by the River Orwell – seats on the terrace make the most of its setting. The half-panelled little smoke room is pleasantly worn and unfussy with high-backed and other old-fashioned settles on a tiled floor. There's also a two-level dining room with country kitchen furniture on bare boards, and pictures and boat-related artefacts on the walls above the dado. Adnams Mosaic and Southwold and a couple of guests tapped from the cask by friendly, efficient staff, several wines by the glass and local cider; board games. The annual Thames Barge Race (end June/early July) is fun. The car park can fill up pretty quickly.

The menu is strong on fish dishes such as scallops with crispy bacon and honey and mustard dressing, fritto misto (fish goujons, whitebait, crispy squid and tempura prawns with tomato and red onion salad with sweet chilli sauce) and seafood grill (sea bass, mackerel, garlic prawns and scallops) with olive, tomato and halloumi couscous with harissa yoghurt; non-fishy choices include superfood salad with chicken, vegetarian stir-fry, pork and apple burger with toppings and chips, lamb chops with dauphinoise potatoes and minted gravy, 10oz rib-eye steak with beer-battered onion rings and chips, and puddings. *Benchmark main dish: beer-battered fish and chips £12.95. Two-course evening meal £18.00.*

Adnams ~ Lease Steve Lomas ~ Real ale ~ Open 9am-11pm ~ Bar food 9am-9.30pm ~ Restaurant ~ Children welcome ~ Dogs allowed in bar ~ Wi-fi *Recommended by Mike and Mary Carter, Richard and Penny Gibbs, Dan and Nicki Barton, Patricia and Anton Larkham*

DUNWICH

TM4770 Map 5

Ship 🍺 ⇌

(01728) 648219 – www.shipatdunwich.co.uk

St James Street; IP17 3DT

Friendly, well run and pleasantly traditional pub in a coastal village, tasty bar food and local ales; bedrooms

The landlord and his friendly staff are warmly welcoming and the pub is cosy with a cheerful atmosphere; it's very different to when it was once the haunt of smugglers and seafarers. The traditionally furnished main bar has benches, pews, captain's chairs and wooden tables on a tiled floor, a woodburning stove (left open in cold weather) and lots of sea prints. Adnams Southwold and guests from breweries such as Grainstore, Green Jack, Humpty Dumpty and Woodfordes are served from antique handpumps at the handsomely panelled bar counter, as well as several wines by the glass; board games. A simple conservatory looks on to a back terrace, and the large garden is very pleasant, with well spaced picnic-sets, two large anchors and an enormous fig tree. The comfortable bedrooms make an excellent base for exploring the area and breakfasts are hearty. The RSPB reserve at Minsmere and nearby Dunwich Museum are worth visiting and there are enjoyable walks in Dunwich Forest.

Pleasing food includes pork and black pudding scotch egg with piccalilli, deep-fried brie with chilli jam, free-range ham with free-range eggs, roasted beetroot and red onion tart with honey-glazed goats cheese, steak burger with toppings, coleslaw and chips, chicken and ham pie, slow-braised ox cheeks with chive mash and an ox tongue fritter, beer-battered fish and chips, tiger prawns and clams with tomatoes, chilli and ginger on linguine, and puddings such as lemon posset with rhubarb compote and stem ginger mascarpone and sticky toffee pudding with cream. *Benchmark main dish: fish pie £13.95. Two-course evening meal £21.50.*

Free house ~ Licensee Gareth Clarke ~ Real ale ~ No credit cards ~ Open 8am-11pm ~ Bar food 12-3, 6-9; 12-9 weekends ~ Restaurant evening only ~ Children welcome ~ Dogs allowed in bar and bedrooms ~ Bedrooms: £90/£120 *Recommended by Donald Allsopp, Millie and Peter Downing, Ian Herdman, Comus and Sarah Elliott, S Holder, Julie Swift, Robin and Anne Triggs*

 EASTBRIDGE   TM4566   Map 5

Eels Foot 🛏

(01728) 830154 – www.theeelsfootinn.co.uk
Off B1122 N of Leiston; IP16 4SN

Country local with hospitable atmosphere, fair value food and Thursday evening folk sessions; bedrooms

There's an abundance of birds close to this simple, friendly inn bordering the freshwater marshes, and RSPB Minsmere is nearby; a footpath leads directly to the sea. At lunchtime in particular there are plenty of walkers as well as bird-watchers – they don't take bookings, so it's best to arrive promptly. The upper and lower parts of the bar have light modern furnishings on stripped-wood floors, a warming fire, Adnams Broadside, Ghost Ship, Mosaic, Southwold and a guest ale on handpump, 11 wines by the glass, several malt whiskies and a farm cider; darts in a side area, board games, cribbage and a neat back dining room. The terrace has seats and tables and the lovely big back garden has benches around more tables. The comfortable, attractive and quiet bedrooms are in a separate building (one room has wheelchair access); breakfasts are tasty. They are a certified Caravan Club site and can provide electric hook-ups.

🍽 Quite a choice of honest food includes pigeon breast salad with balsamic dressing, king prawns in garlic butter, lasagne, stuffed butternut squash, crab salad, a pie of the day, monkfish skewers with saffron sauce, winter casseroles, and puddings such as boozy bread and butter pudding and sticky toffee pudding; their wood-fired pizza oven is used at weekends. *Benchmark main dish: beer-battered fish and chips £10.95. Two-course evening meal £18.00.*

Adnams ~ Tenant Julian Wallis ~ Real ale ~ Open 12-3, 6-11; 12-11 Fri; 11.30-11 Sat; 11.30-11.30 Sun ~ Bar food 12-2.30, 6-9; 12-9 Fri-Sun ~ Children welcome ~ Dogs welcome ~ Wi-fi ~ Live folk music Thurs and last Sun of month ~ Bedrooms: £85/£115 *Recommended by Mary Joyce, Max Simons, Roy Hoing, Holly and Tim Waite, Alison and Dan Richardson*

 HASKETON   TM2450   Map 5

Turks Head 🍽⭐ 🍷

(01394) 610343 – www.theturksheadhasketon.co.uk
Top Road; follow village signs taking B1079 from second Woodbridge roundabout; IP13 6JG

Neatly renovated pub with airy bar, snug and dining room, local ales, imaginative food, attentive service and seats outside

A lot of hard work went into the recent refurbishment of this country dining pub and the fresh modern décor is light and appealing. The bar has white-painted beams, traditional chairs, stools and cushioned wall seats around tables on big flagstones, a woodburning stove in a large fireplace, books on shelves and high chairs against the pale oak counter where courteous staff serve Adnams Ghost Ship, Greene King Old Speckled Hen and Woodfordes Wherry with a guest such as Cliff Quay Roaring Forties on handpump and 16 wines by the glass. There's a similarly furnished snug with a small woodburner (dogs are allowed in here) and a spreading, high-raftered, airy dining room with doors out to the terrace, cushioned chairs and cream upholstered banquettes around dark tables on floorboards, and animal sketches and butterfly prints on RAF-blue paintwork; background music and board games. There are plenty of chairs and tables under large parasols on the terrace and picnic-sets on a lawn; boules.

 Excellent, attractively presented modern food includes interesting lunchtime sandwiches, spicy pork vindaloo with a shot of buttermilk tequila, squid ink tapioca wafers with scallops and seaweed, porcini mushroom risotto with chervil root salad, chicken with grilled avocado, crispy egg and pancetta salad, lemon sole with sorrel butter, capers and red chicory, pork chop with black pudding croquette, pak choi and cider and raisin jus, sea trout with keralan coconut stew, prawns and steamed south indian pancake, and puddings such as ginger pannacotta with honey and lemon syrup and banoffi pie with caramelised banana; they also offer a two- and three-course weekday lunch. *Benchmark main dish: beer-battered fish and chips £14.00. Two-course evening meal £21.00.*

Free house ~ Licensee Jemima Withey ~ Real ale ~ Open 10am-11pm; 10am-midnight Fri, Sat; 11-8 Sun ~ Bar food 12-3, 6-9; 12-6 Sun ~ Restaurant ~ Children welcome ~ Dogs allowed in bar ~ Wi-fi *Recommended by Gail and Frank Hackett, Mary Joyce, Patti and James Davidson*

IPSWICH
Fat Cat ◖

TM1844 Map 5

(01473) 726524 – www.fatcatipswich.co.uk
Spring Road, opposite junction with Nelson Road (best bet for parking is up there); IP4 5NL

Wonderful choice of changing real ales in a well run town pub; garden

Not surprisingly, there's always a cheerful crowd here, all keen to try the fantastic range of up to 18 real ales from around the country on handpump or tapped from the cask. There might be Adnams Southwold, Crouch Vale Brewers Gold and Yakima Gold plus Dark Star Hophead, Earl Soham Victoria, Exmoor Gold, Fat Cat Honey Ale, Hop Back Summer Lightning, Mighty Oak Maldon Gold, Navigation Eclipse, Pheasantry Mikado Mild, St Austell Tribute, Skinners Porthleven, Titanic Plum Porter and Woodfordes Wherry. They also stock quite a few belgian bottled beers, farm cider and seven wines by the glass. The bars have a mix of café chairs and stools, unpadded wall benches and cushioned seats around cast-iron and wooden pub tables, bare floorboards and lots of enamel brewery signs and posters; board games and shove-ha'penny. There's also a spacious back conservatory and several picnic-sets on the terrace and lawn. Very little nearby parking. Well behaved dogs are welcome but must be kept on a lead.

They keep a supply of rolls, spicy scotch eggs and sausage rolls made in their small kitchen and are happy for you to bring in takeaway food (not Friday or Saturday).

Free house ~ Licensees John and Ann Keatley ~ Real ale ~ No credit cards ~ Open 12-11; 12-midnight Fri; 11.30am-midnight Sat; 12-11 Sun ~ Bar food all day while it lasts ~ Dogs welcome ~ Wi-fi *Recommended by James Landor, Daphne and Robert Staples, Mike Swan, Richard and Penny Gibbs, Edward May*

PETTISTREE
Greyhound

TM2954 Map 5

(01728) 746451 – www.greyhoundinnpettistree.co.uk

The Street; brown sign to pub off B1438 S of Wickham Market, 0.5 miles N of A12; IP13 0HP

Neatly kept village pub with enjoyable food and drink; seats outside

With interesting food and a genuine welcome, our readers enjoy their visits here. It's basically just two smallish rooms with open fires, some rather low beams, chunky farmhouse chairs and cushioned settles around dark wooden tables on bare floorboards and candlelight. Earl Soham Victoria Bitter and guests such as Adnams Ghost Ship and Lacons Encore on handpump, several wines by the glass and quite a few malt whiskies; it's best to book in advance to be sure of a table. The well kept side garden has picnic-sets under parasols, with more beside the gravelled front car park. The village church is next door.

Cooked by the landlady using local produce, the rewarding food includes shredded confit duck with orange and sugar snap salad, crispy skin and honey mustard dressing, gin-cured scottish salmon with tonic jelly, cucumber pickle, dill cream and potato scone, courgette, carrot and butternut squash vegetable spaghetti with spinach pesto, goats cheese and soda bread croutons, pork fillet wellington stuffed with black pudding with cider gravy and apple sauce, hanger steak marinated in rosemary and garlic with cracked pepper butter and chips, and puddings such as chocolate brownie with hazelnut praline and cacao nib ice-cream and meringue with lemon curd cream and roasted rhubarb. *Benchmark main dish: hake fillet with beetroot mash and red pepper romesco sauce £14.00. Two-course evening meal £20.50.*

Free house ~ Licensees Stewart and Louise McKenzie ~ Real ale ~ Open 12-3, 6-11; 12-4 Sun; closed Sun evening, Mon, two weeks Jan ~ Bar food 12-2.30, 6-9; 12-3 Sun ~ Restaurant ~ Children welcome ~ Dogs allowed in bar ~ Wi-fi *Recommended by Michael Williamson, George Sanderson, JER, Dr A E and Mrs Forbes, Sally and Lance Oldham, Jeff Davies, Sarah and David Gibbs*

REDE
Plough

TL8055 Map 5

(01284) 789208

Village signposted off A143 Bury St Edmunds–Haverhill; IP29 4BE

Well liked and promptly served food in a 16th-c pub, with several wines by the glass and friendly service

The cheerful landlord keeps his quaint, partly thatched and cream-washed pub spic and span, and it's in a nice quiet spot at the end of the village green. Traditional and with low beams, the pretty bar has wheelback chairs and plush red wall banquettes around dark pubby tables, and a solid-fuel stove in a brick fireplace. Changing ales include Harveys Best, Ringwood Best Bitter and Timothy Taylors Boltmaker on handpump and they keep several wines by the glass; background music. There are picnic-sets in the sheltered cottagey garden and at the front.

Chalked on boards, the lengthy choice of food includes game terrine, salt and pepper squid with chilli sauce, ham and eggs, calves liver and bacon, oxtail casserole, chicken with pears and roquefort cheese, rabbit stew, a fresh fish dish of the day, and puddings such as apple lattice tart and bread and butter pudding. *Benchmark main dish: slow-cooked rioja lamb £13.95. Two-course evening meal £19.00.*

Admiral Taverns ~ Tenant Brian Desborough ~ Real ale ~ Open 11-3, 6.30-11.30; 12-3,
7-11 Sun ~ Bar food 12-2, 6.30-9; 12-2 Sun ~ Restaurant ~ Children welcome until 8pm ~
Wi-fi *Recommended by Katherine and Hugh Markham, Lucy and Giles Gibbon,
Christopher Mannings, Mark and Sian Edwards*

SIBTON
White Horse

TM3570 Map 5

(01728) 660337 – www.sibtonwhitehorseinn.co.uk

Halesworth Road/Hubbard's Hill, N of Peasenhall; IP17 2JJ

● ●

Suffolk Dining Pub of the Year

**Particularly well run inn with nicely old-fashioned bar, good mix
of customers, real ales and imaginative food; bedrooms**

Even when really busy – which it deservedly usually is – the hands-on
licensees and their friendly staff are able to keep things running
smoothly with a smile. The appealing bar has a roaring log fire in a large
inglenook fireplace, horsebrasses and tack on the walls, vintage settles and
pews, Adnams Southwold, Wolf Golden Jackal and Woodfordes Wherry on
handpump, eight wines by the glass and 15 malt whiskies served from an old
oak-panelled counter. A beer festival is held in August and a viewing panel
reveals the working cellar and its ancient floor. Steps lead up past an old
partly knocked-through timbered wall into a carpeted gallery, and there's
also a smart dining room and a secluded (and popular) dining terrace. The
big garden has plenty of seats. The bedrooms, housed in a separate building
next door, are warm, contemporary and well equipped.

They grow their own produce, use free-range meat and poultry and other
seasonal, local ingredients for the first class food and have a new smoking shed:
sandwiches, goats cheese pannacotta with beetroot, walnut and apple with a balsamic
reduction, cod fishcake with celeriac, pickled cucumber and truffle mayonnaise, leek,
apple and parsnip charlotte with garlic potato purée, apple fondant and mustard
cream, chicken with smoked cheddar dauphinoise, bacon crisp and walnut pesto, local
venison haunch steak with herb dumplings and port jus, 28-day-hung sirloin steak with
horseradish mash, wild mushrooms and bourguignon sauce, and puddings such as
orange and passion-fruit tart, mascarpone, mango and basil and sticky toffee pudding
with earl grey prunes, toffee sauce and praline ice-cream. *Benchmark main dish:
pork belly with sage mash, sultana chutney and cider jus £14.75. Two-course evening
meal £19.25.*

Free house ~ Licensees Neil and Gill Mason ~ Real ale ~ Open 12-3, 6.30 (6 Sat)-11; 12-4,
7-10.30 Sun; closed Mon lunchtime ~ Bar food 12-2, 6.30-9; 12-2.30, 7-8.30 Sun ~ Restaurant
~ Well behaved children welcome but must be over 6 in evening; not in bedrooms ~ Dogs
allowed in bar ~ Wi-fi ~ Bedrooms: £90/£100 *Recommended by Thomas Green, Simon Rodway,
R L Borthwick, Elise and Charles Mackinlay, Holly and Tim Waite, Buster and Helena Hastings*

SNAPE
Plough & Sail

TM3957 Map 5

(01728) 688413 – www.theploughandsailsnape.co.uk

The Maltings, Snape Bridge (B1069 S); IP17 1SR

**Nicely placed dining pub extended airily around an older bar, real ales
and well liked food using local seasonal produce; seats outside**

Twin brothers run this 16th-c former smugglers' haunt – Alex is front of
house and Oliver is head chef. It's a friendly place and mostly open-plan
with a clever blend of the traditional and modern: wicker and café-style

furnishings are set around an older heart which has an open fire, high bar chairs by the serving counter and rustic pine dining chairs and tables on terracotta tiling. Another cosy little room has comfortable sofas and low coffee tables by a woodburning stove. Most diners head for the simply furnished bar hall and spacious airy dining room with rattan or pale wooden chairs around tables on light, woodstrip flooring and high ceilings with A-frame beams; motifs illustrating the history of the Maltings decorate the walls. Another restaurant upstairs has similar furnishings; background music. Adnams Broadside and Southwold and Greene King Abbot and IPA on handpump and several wines by the glass. The flower-filled terrace has plenty of chairs and tables and there are some picnic-sets arranged at the front. The shops and other buildings in the attractive complex are interesting to wander through.

Good, modern food includes sandwiches, duck liver parfait with fruit chutney, spiced king prawn and vegetable bhaji with mango and chilli compote, butternut squash, feta and spinach open lasagne with butternut velouté and sage crisps, chicken kiev with wild garlic pistou, pancetta and parmentier potatoes, bass with thai-style egg noodles and vegetable broth, duo of pork with shallot puree, dauphinoise potatoes, creamed cabbage, apple compote and jus, and puddings such as plum frangipane tartlet with vanilla poached plum and stem ginger ice-cream and caramelised white chocolate tart with raspberries, chocolate soil and raspberry sorbet. *Benchmark main dish: beer-battered fish and chips £12.50. Two-course evening meal £20.50.*

Suffolk Dining ~ Lease Alex Burnside ~ Real ale ~ Open 11-11; 12-10.30 Sun ~ Bar food 12-2.30 (3 Sun), 6-9; they serve food earlier and later during concert season ~ Restaurant ~ Children welcome ~ Dogs allowed in bar ~ Wi-fi *Recommended by Phil and Jane Villiers, Simon Rodway, Tracey and Stephen Groves, Graham Smart, Jamie Green*

STOKE-BY-NAYLAND TL9836 Map 5
Crown ★ 🌟 ♀ 🛏
(01206) 262001 – www.crowninn.net
Park Street (B1068); CO6 4SE

Smart dining pub with attractive modern furnishings, imaginative food, real ales and a great wine choice; good bedrooms

'First class' is how many readers describe this particularly well run and civilised inn. The extensive open-plan dining bar is carefully laid out to give several distinct-feeling areas: a sofa and easy chairs on flagstones near the serving counter, a couple of armchairs under heavy beams by the big woodburning stove, one sizeable table tucked nicely into a three-sided built-in seat and a lower side room with more beams and cheerful floral wallpaper. Tables are mostly stripped veterans, with high-backed dining chairs, but there are more modern chunky pine tables at the back; also, contemporary artwork (mostly for sale) and daily papers. Served by friendly staff, there's Adnams Ghost Ship, Crouch Vale Brewers Gold, Woodfordes Wherry and a changing guest on handpump and Aspall's cider. Wine is a key feature, with 30 by the glass and hundreds more from the glass-walled 'cellar shop' in one corner – you can buy wine there to take away too. The sheltered flagstoned back terrace has comfortable teak furniture, heaters, big terracotta-coloured parasols and a peaceful view over rolling, lightly wooded countryside. Bedrooms are well equipped and comfortable. Good disabled access. This pretty village is worth exploring and there are plenty of well marked surrounding footpaths.

Enticing food includes rabbit terrine with pear chutney, crab and spiced pepper tortelloni with roast pepper dressing and crispy sea vegetables, chargrilled vegetable lasagne with cheese and hazelnut crumb, warm salad of liver and bacon with garlic croutons and raspberry and green peppercorn vinaigrette, braised guinea fowl legs with wild mushrooms, red wine sauce, tempura asparagus and champ mash, cod fillet with chorizo and crayfish butter and roasted garlic mash, rib-eye steak for two on the bone with lemon, garlic and thyme butter, peppercorn sauce and herb-crusted tomatoes, and puddings such as dark chocolate tart with blood orange ice-cream and blood orange marmalade and irish cream cheesecake with coffee granita, meringue and coffee syrup. *Benchmark main dish: beer-battered haddock and chips £14.75. Two-course evening meal £25.00.*

Free house ~ Licensee Richard Sunderland ~ Real ale ~ Open 11-11; 12-10.30 Sun ~ Bar food 12-2.30, 6-9.30 (10 Fri, Sat); all day Sun ~ Children welcome ~ Dogs allowed in bar ~ Wi-fi ~ Bedrooms: £100/£145 *Recommended by Mrs Margo Finlay, Jörg Kasprowski, MDN, Alan Cowell, Andrea and Philip Crispin, Caroline and Steve Archer, Ted and Mary Bates*

STRATFORD ST MARY
Swan 🏵 ♀ ◗

TM0434 Map 5

(01206) 321244 – www.stratfordswan.com

Lower Street; CO7 6JR

Excellent food and drink in 16th-c coaching inn; riverside seats

In warm weather there's plenty of room outside this lovely timbered inn, with teak tables and chairs under parasols on a terrace, more seats on a big lawn and across the road, and some tables under willow trees by the River Stour (where there's a landing stage). The two beamed bars have a log fire in a Tudor brick fireplace and a coal fire in the other, and an eclectic range of old furniture on parquet or brick floors; board games. Adnams Ghost Ship and a guest such as Loch Lomond 60/- on handpump, nine craft ales, 130 bottled beers from around the world, 14 wines by the glass, 53 malt whiskies, 11 vodkas, 19 gins, a farm cider and several interesting bottled ciders. The compact and timbered back restaurant is rather elegant.

Creative food (dishes are paired with an ale and a wine) includes pig head croquette with parsley, caper and raisin salad, marinated herring with roast beetroot and horseradish cream, artichoke and chestnut gnocchi gratin with pickled shiitake mushrooms, whole boned stuffed roast pigeon with mash and kale, butter-poached lemon sole with rainbow chard and roasted anya potatoes, rib-eye steak with sliced potato cake and garlic butter or red wine jus, and puddings such as bitter chocolate and salted caramel tart with crème fraîche and carrot and hazelnut cake with coconut cream and vanilla ice-cream. *Benchmark main dish: sea bass with mediterranean vegetables and almond rice £15.75. Two-course evening meal £21.00.*

Free house ~ Licensee Jane Dorber ~ Real ale ~ Open 11-11 (10.30 Sun); closed Mon, Tues ~ Bar food 12-3, 6-9; 12-4 Sun ~ Restaurant ~ Children welcome ~ Dogs allowed in bar ~ Wi-fi *Recommended by Maddie Purvis, Jack and Hilary Burton, Adam Jones, Andy and Rosemary Taylor, Paul Farraday*

WALBERSWICK
Anchor 🏵 ♀ 🛏

TM4974 Map 5

(01502) 722112 – www.anchoratwalberswick.com

The Street (B1387); village signed off A12; IP18 6UA

Friendly, bustling pub with good food and thoughtful choice of drinks; bedrooms and chalets

There's often something happening at this well run and much enjoyed pub – breakfasts (8.30-10am), steak and curry evenings, summer Sunday barbecues (until October half term), a cask ale and oyster festival and their Beer Academy courses. The simply furnished front bar, divided into snug halves by a two-way open fire, has big windows, heavy stripped tables on original oak flooring, sturdy built-in green leather wall seats and nicely framed black and white photographs of fishermen that are displayed on colour-washed panelling; daily papers and board games. Helpful, friendly staff serve Adnams Broadside, Ghost Ship and Southwold on handpump, 50 bottled beers and around 20 wines by the glass; they hold a beer festival in August. The extensive dining area stretches back from a small more modern-feeling lounge. There are plenty of seats in the attractive garden, and an outdoor bar and wood-fired pizza oven serving the flagstoned terraces. The six spacious chalet-style rooms in the garden have views of either the water or beach huts and sand dunes, while from the bedrooms in the main house you can hear the sea just a few hundred metres away; dogs are allowed in some rooms. As well as the coast path, there's a pleasant walk to Southwold.

 Using local producers and seasonal ingredients, the imaginative food includes pork, rabbit and pistachio with chutney, fish soup with rouille and croutons, smoked haddock and salmon fishcake with creamed leeks, rare-breed burger with jalapeno tartare sauce and chips, polenta with goats cheese, mushrooms and roasted vegetables, pork belly with mustard mash, choucroute (like sauerkraut), bacon and lentils, scallops with parsnip purée, pancetta and fennel salad, and puddings such as lime cheesecake with passion-fruit curd and tonka bean and buttermilk pannacotta with poached rhubarb; they also hold regular Friday curry evenings. *Benchmark main dish: crab linguine £14.75. Two-course evening meal £20.00.*

Boudica Inns ~ Lease Mark and Sophie Dorber ~ Real ale ~ Open 11-11 ~ Bar food 12-3, 6-9 ~ Restaurant ~ Children welcome ~ Dogs allowed in bar and bedrooms ~ Wi-fi ~ Bedrooms: £120/£145 *Recommended by Sheila Topham, Thomas Green, Simon Rodway, Tracey and Stephen Groves, Nicola and Holly Lyons, Louise and Anton Parsons*

WALDRINGFIELD
Maybush

TM2844 Map 5

(01473) 736215 – www.debeninns.co.uk/maybush
Off A12 S of Martlesham; The Quay, Cliff Road; IP12 4QL

Busy pub with tables outside by the riverbank; nautical décor and a fair choice of drinks and good value food

Since it's in such a lovely spot by the River Deben, it makes sense for this family-friendly pub to be open – and serve food – all day. Lots of picnic-sets on a terrace make the most of the view, but they do get snapped up pretty quickly in fine weather. River cruises are available nearby (though you have to pre-book). Some of the window tables inside also look over the water and the spacious knocked-through bar is divided into separate areas by fireplaces or steps. There's a nautical theme, with an elaborate ship's model in a glass case and a few more in a light, high-ceilinged extension, as well as lots of old lanterns, pistols and aerial photographs; background music and board games. Adnams Southwold and Ghost Ship and a guest beer on handpump and a fair choice of wines by the glass; board games. There is a large pay and display car park (charges are refunded to pub customers).

Well regarded food includes sandwiches, tandoori chicken skewer with raita, prawn and crayfish cocktail, wild mushroom linguine, gammon and free-range eggs, burgers with toppings, coleslaw and chips, raita and balsamic-braised lamb shank with sweet potato mash and braised red cabbage, chicken topped with barbecue sauce, crispy bacon and smoked cheese, king prawn and chorizo linguine in creamy tomato sauce, 28-day-aged aberdeen angus steaks with beer-battered onion rings and chips, and puddings such as pear and spiced ginger crumble with custard and banoffi pie. *Benchmark main dish: beer-battered cod and chips £11.95. Two-course evening meal £19.00.*

Adnams ~ Lease Steve and Louise Lomas ~ Real ale ~ Open 9am-11pm ~ Bar food 9am-9pm ~ Restaurant ~ Children welcome ~ Dogs allowed in bar ~ Wi-fi *Recommended by Bob and Margaret Holder, Mark Morgan, Tim King, Lenny and Ruth Walters, Mark and Sian Edwards, Nik and Gloria Clarke*

WESTLETON
Crown 🌟 🍷 🛏

TM4469 Map 5

(01728) 648777 – www.westletoncrown.co.uk

B1125 Blythburgh–Leiston; IP17 3AD

Bustling old inn with a cosy chatty bar, carefully chosen drinks and interesting food; bedrooms

Our readers enjoy staying in the comfortable and spotlessly kept bedrooms here (some are in the main inn, others are in converted stables and cottages – ask for the larger ones); breakfasts are excellent. This is a stylish old coaching inn and its heart remains the attractive little bar with its lovely log fire and plenty of original features. Locals drop in here for a pint and a chat, which keeps the atmosphere informal and relaxed, and they serve Adnams Southwold and three guest beers such as Grain Redwood, Wolf Golden Jackal and Woodfordes Wherry on handpump, 16 wines by the glass from a thoughtful list and 13 malt whiskies; background music and board games. There's also a parlour, a dining room and a conservatory, with all manner of wooden dining chairs and tables and historic photographs on some fine old bare-brick walls. The charming terraced garden is set out with plenty of seats and tables.

 From a varied menu using local, seasonal produce, the food includes ham hock and pigeon terrine with apple and pear chutney, gin, orange and fennel-cured salmon with celeriac slaw, flatcap mushroom and blue cheese tarte tatin with honey-roasted parsnips, sauté potatoes and blue cheese cream sauce, fillet of sea bass with herb-crushed new potatoes, spinach, leeks and cockle and prawn chowder, slow-cooked lamb shank with tomato and red pepper cassoulet, crispy black cabbage and toulouse sausage, and puddings such as cherry bakewell tart with cherry and almond ice cream and cherry jam and dark chocolate fondant with pistachio cream, raspberries and popcorn; they also offer cream teas (3-6pm). *Benchmark main dish: honey-roasted pork tenderloin and braised cheek with carrot purée and cider jus £17.50. Two-course evening meal £24.00.*

Free house ~ Licensee Gareth Clarke ~ Real ale ~ Open 7am-11pm ~ Bar food 12-2.30, 6.30-9.30 ~ Restaurant ~ Children welcome ~ Dogs allowed in bar and bedrooms ~ Wi-fi ~ Bedrooms: £95/£100 *Recommended by Andrew Vincent, Ian Herdman, Roy Hoing, Tracey and Stephen Groves, Peter and Alison Steadman, Mark and Mary Setting*

WHEPSTEAD
White Horse

TL8258 Map 5

(01284) 735760 – www.whitehorsewhepstead.co.uk

Off B1066 S of Bury; Rede Road; IP29 4SS

Charming partly 17th-c country pub with attractively furnished rooms and well liked food and drink

The hands-on licensees and their friendly staff work hard to make sure their customers – both locals and visitors – enjoy their visits. The dark-beamed bar has a woodburning stove in a low fireplace, stools around pubby tables on floor tiles, and Woodfordes Wherry and a guest from St Peters on handpump served from the copper-topped counter. Linked rooms have country kitchen tables and chairs, some rather fine old farmhouse chairs and traditional wall seats with pretty scatter cushions on antique floor tiles or carpet; the walls are hung with artworks. Skye is the friendly pub dog. The Tuck Shop sells sweeties, chocolate and ice-cream. A sheltered back terrace has seats and tables under parasols and there are picnic-sets on grass and a children's play area with swings and a climbing frame. Plenty of surrounding walks.

Pleasing food includes smoked mackerel and horseradish pâté, grilled vanilla-infused goats cheese with cranberry and walnut salad, sweet potato, cauliflower and chickpea curry with cucumber yoghurt, peppered duck breast with black cherry purée and sauté potatoes, free-range chicken breast with roasted balsamic tomatoes, feta crumb and butter sauce, moroccan-spiced lamb with red pepper couscous and tomato and coriander tagine, and puddings such as Baileys bread and butter pudding with vanilla custard and potted lemon curd cheesecake with raspberry coulis; they also offer a two- and three-course weekday set menu. *Benchmark main dish: beer-braised beef with red onion jam and chips £14.95. Two-course evening meal £19.00.*

Free house ~ Licensees Hana and Lee Saunders ~ Real ale ~ Open 11.30-3, 6-11; 11.30-4 Sun; closed Sun evening, Mon except bank holidays ~ Bar food 12-2, 6-9 ~ Restaurant ~ Children welcome ~ Dogs welcome ~ Wi-fi *Recommended by Brian and Sally Wakeham, Tim King, Alf and Sally Garner, Charlie Stevens, Conrad Freezer*

Also Worth a Visit in Suffolk

Besides the fully inspected pubs, you might like to try these pubs that have been recommended to us and described by readers. Do tell us what you think of them: feedback@goodguides.com

ALDEBURGH TM4656
White Hart (01728) 453205
High Street; IP15 5AJ Friendly one-room local in former high-ceilinged reading room, panelling, stained-glass windows and open fire, Adnams ales and guests, decent wines by the glass, summer pizzas in back courtyard; no children inside, dogs welcome, open all day. *(Graham Smart)*

ALDRINGHAM TM4461
Parrot & Punchbowl (01728) 830221 *B1122/B1353 S of Leiston; IP16 4PY* Welcoming 17th-c beamed country pub, good fairly priced traditional food catering for special diets, well kept Adnams Southwold and a couple of guests, two-level restaurant; children and dogs (in bar) welcome, nice sheltered garden, also family garden with adventure play area, open all day Fri-Sat. *(Andy and Rosemary Taylor)*

BADINGHAM TM3068
White Horse (01728) 638280
A1120 S of village; IP13 8JR Welcoming 15th-c low-beamed pub (former coaching inn), generous helpings of good reasonably priced food including themed nights and OAP lunch Mon-Thurs, Earl Soham and three guests, Aspall's and Weston's ciders, inglenook log fire and a couple

of woodburners; occasional live music, monthly charity quiz, May cider festival; children, dogs and muddy boots welcome, neat bowling green and nice rambling garden, two bedrooms accessed by spiral staircase, open all day. *(Dr Peter Crawshaw)*

BARHAM TM1251
Sorrel Horse (01473) 830327
Old Norwich Road; IP6 0PG Friendly open-plan beamed and timbered country inn with good log fire in central chimneybreast, well kept ales including Greene King, popular home-made pubby food (all day weekends); free wi-fi; children and dogs welcome, disabled facilities, picnic-sets on side grass with big play area, bedrooms in converted barn, open all day Weds-Sun. *(Floras23)*

BILDESTON TL9949
★**Crown** (01449) 740510
B1115 SW of Stowmarket; IP7 7EB Picturesque 15th-c timbered country inn; smart beamed main bar with leather armchairs and inglenook log fire, contemporary artwork in back area, ales such as Adnams and Greene King along with good choice of wines, gins and cocktails, highly praised imaginative food from snacks and reworked pub favourites up including set lunch (Mon-Thurs) and tasting menus, afternoon teas maybe

with a glass of champagne, more formal dining room; children welcome, disabled access and parking, tables laid for eating in appealing central courtyard, more in large beautifully kept garden with decking, 13 bedrooms. *(Christopher Mannings)*

BILDESTON   TL9949
Kings Head (01449) 741434
High Street; IP7 7ED Small 16th-c beamed village pub with own good beers (brewery behind – can view by appointment) plus local guests, enjoyable well priced home-made food (Fri lunchtime, Sat, Sun lunchtime only), pleasant chatty staff, wood floor bar with inglenook woodburner; games and live music evenings including Weds open mike, quiz last Thurs of month, May beer festival; children and dogs welcome, back garden with terrace and play equipment, open all day weekends, closed Mon, Tues and lunchtimes Weds-Fri. *(Sandra Morgan)*

BLAXHALL   TM3656
Ship (01728) 688316
Off B1069 S of Snape; can be reached from A12 via Little Glemham; IP12 2DY Charming country setting for this popular and friendly low-beamed 18th-c pub; good reasonably priced traditional food in bar and restaurant, well kept Adnams Southwold, Woodfordes Wherry and guests; various folk music events including sing-around session Mon afternoon and June festival, free wi-fi; children in eating areas, dogs in bar, eight chalet bedrooms, good breakfast, open all day weekends. *(Alexander and Trish Gendall)*

BOXFORD   TL9640
Fleece (01787) 211183
Broad Street (A1071 Sudbury–Ipswich); CO10 5DX Old coaching inn (partly 15th-c) with plenty of character; beautiful Corder Room with attractive period furniture, dark panelled wainscoting, William Morris wallpaper and sweeping red curtains, beamed bar on left has woodburner in terracotta-tiled front part, bare-boards back area with old stripped tables and a big fireplace, own Little Earth ales and guests (beer festivals), real cider and good varied choice of enjoyable food (not Sun evening), friendly service, upstairs function room; live music Weds including folk, Sun quiz; children and dogs (in bar) welcome, courtyard seating (barbecues), open all day. *(Ian Duncan, Charles Fraser, Giles and Annie Francis)*

BRAMFIELD   TM3973
Queens Head (01986) 784214
The Street; A144 S of Halesworth; IP19 9HT Smartly refurbished village pub next to interesting church; various rooms with heavy beams, timbering and tiled floors, woodburner in impressive brick fireplace in high-raftered dining room, Adnams and guests such as Lacons, good food from fairly pubby menu including plenty of gluten-free

choices, friendly service; children welcome, tiered garden, open (and food) all day, Sun till 6pm (4pm). *(Mary Joyce)*

BRENT ELEIGH   TL9348
★Cock (01787) 247371
A1141 SE of Lavenham; CO10 9PB Timeless and friendly thatched country pub, Adnams, Greene King Abbot and a guest, organic farm cider, enjoyable traditional food cooked by landlady, cosy ochre-walled snug and second small room, antique floor tiles, lovely coal fire, old photographs of village (church well worth a look); darts, shove-ha'penny and toad in the hole; well behaved children and dogs welcome, picnic-sets up on side grass with summer hatch service, one bedroom, open (and food) all day Fri-Sun. *(Val and Malcolm Travers)*

BROCKLEY GREEN   TL7247
Plough (01440) 786789
Hundon Road; CO10 8DT Neatly kept knocked-through bar, beams, timbers and stripped brick, scrubbed tables and open fire, generally well liked food from lunchtime sandwiches and deli boards up, Tues steak night, three changing ales, good choice of wines by the glass and several malt whiskies, restaurant; quiz first Thurs of month; children and dogs welcome, attractive grounds with peaceful country views, comfortable bedrooms, open all day. *(Sandra Morgan)*

BUNGAY   TM3389
Castle (01986) 892283
Earsham Street; NR35 1AF Pleasantly informal 16th-c dining inn with good interesting food from chef-owner including themed nights; opened-up beamed interior with restaurant part at front, two open fires, Cliff Quay Sea Dog, Earl Soham Victoria and a couple of craft beers, Aspall's cider, nice choice of wines by the glass and several gins, afternoon teas, friendly efficient staff, french windows to pretty courtyard garden shaded by an indian bean tree; children welcome, dogs in bar area, four comfortable bedrooms, closed Sun evening, Mon (also Tues evening in winter), otherwise open all day. *(Deborah and Duncan Walliams)*

BURY ST EDMUNDS   TL8463
Dove (01284) 702787
Hospital Road; IP33 3JU Friendly 19th-c alehouse with rustic bare-boards bar and separate parlour, half a dozen well kept mainly local beers such as Mauldons and some real ciders; quiz third Sun of the month, regular folk and acoustic sessions; some seats out at front, closed weekday lunchtimes. *(Jamie Green)*

BURY ST EDMUNDS   TL8564
★Nutshell (01284) 764867
The Traverse, central pedestrian link off Abbeygate Street; IP33 1BJ Very small

simple local with timeless interior (can be a crush at busy times), lots of interest such as a mummified cat (found walled up here) hanging from dark brown ceiling along with companion rat, bits of a skeleton, vintage bank notes, cigarette packets, military and other badges, a wooden propeller and a great metal halberd, short wooden benches along shopfront windows and a cut-down sewing-machine table, Greene King ales, no food; background music, steep narrow stairs up to lavatories; children (till 7pm) and dogs welcome, open all day. *(Jamie Green)*

BURY ST EDMUNDS   TL8564
Old Cannon (01284) 768769
Cannon Street, just off A134/A1101 roundabout at N end of town; IP33 1JR Up for sale as we went to press; early Victorian town house with own brewery in bar (two huge gleaming stainless-steel vessels and views up to balustraded malt floor above the counter), Old Cannon Best, Gunner's Daughter and seasonal ales, also Adnams Southwold, guest ales and good choice of wines by the glass, tasty food (not Sun evening) from pub favourites up including specials, assortment of old and new furniture on well worn bare boards; background music, free wi-fi; children over 10 allowed, comfortable bedrooms in old brewhouse across courtyard, open all day. *(Martin Day, Katherine Matthews, Jack Trussler, Nicola and Nigel Matthews, Andy and Louise Ramwell)*

BURY ST EDMUNDS   TL8564
One Bull (01284) 848220
Angel Hill; IP33 1UZ Smartly updated pub with own Brewshed beers and local guests, extensive choice of wines by the glass and good food from sandwiches and sharing boards up (all day Sat), friendly helpful staff; free wi-fi; children till 6pm in bar (8pm restaurant), closed Sun evening, otherwise open all day. *(Jeremy King)*

BURY ST EDMUNDS   TL8563
★Rose & Crown (01284) 755934
Whiting Street; IP33 1NP Cheerful black-beamed corner local with long-serving affable licensees, bargain simple lunchtime home cooking (not Sun), particularly well kept Greene King ales (including XX Mild) and guests, pleasant lounge with lots of piggy pictures and bric-a-brac, good games-oriented public bar, rare separate off-sales counter; background radio, no credit cards or under-14s; pretty back courtyard, open all day weekdays. *(Jamie Green)*

BUXHALL   TM9957
★Crown (01449) 736521
Off B1115 W of Stowmarket; Mill Road; IP14 3DW A pub of two halves; steps down to cosy low-beamed bar on left with woodburner in brick inglenook, timbered dining area beyond, well kept

Adnams Broadside, Earl Soham Victoria and nice choice of wines by the glass; light airy dining room to the right with its own bar and another woodburner, very good if not particularly cheap food from interesting menu, friendly service; children and dogs welcome, plenty of tables on terrace with views over open country (ignore the pylons), herb garden, closed Sun evening, Mon. *(Jeremy King)*

CAMPSEA ASHE   TM3356
Dog & Duck (01728) 746211
Station Road; IP13 0PT Refurbished roadside pub under new management, good varied choice of popular food including set lunch menu, Adnams, a guest beer and several wines by the glass from copper-topped counter, friendly welcoming staff, bar with woodburner, restaurant; children and dogs welcome, wheelchair access, nice garden with gazebo, open all day, food till 6pm Sun. *(Andrew and Clare Reid)*

CAVENDISH   TL8046
Bull (01787) 280245
A1092 Long Melford–Clare; CO10 8AX Traditional old pub with heavy beams, timbers and open fires, Greene King IPA and a couple of guests, real cider and enjoyable reasonably priced pub food including sandwiches and highly rated Sun roasts (till 4.30pm), good friendly service; charity quiz first Sun of month; children in eating areas, dogs in bar (but best to ask first), paved back terrace with steps up to car park (useful in this picturesque honeypot village), closed Sun evening, Mon and Tues. *(Mrs Margo Finlay, Jörg Kasprowski)*

CAVENDISH   TL8046
★George (01787) 280248
A1092; The Green; CO10 8BA Restaurant 16th-c inn with contemporary feel in two bow-windowed front areas, beams and timbers, big woodburner in stripped-brick fireplace, well liked food (not Sun evening) from short but varied menu, also set deal, two Nethergate ales and plenty of wines by the glass, Aspall's cider, back servery and further eating area, charming helpful staff, daily newspapers; children and well behaved dogs welcome, stylish furniture on sheltered back terrace, tree-shaded garden with lovely village church behind, five bedrooms up rather steep staircase, good breakfast, open all day. *(Ray White)*

CHELSWORTH   TL9848
Peacock (01449) 743952
B1115 Sudbury–Needham Market; IP7 7HU Prettily set village dining pub with lots of Tudor brickwork and exposed beams, separate pubby bar with grandfather clock and inglenook woodburner, local ales and decent home-cooked food from lunchtime sandwiches/baguettes up, friendly

service; children and dogs welcome, five bedrooms, attractive small garden, closed Sun evening. *(Val and Malcolm Travers)*

CHILLESFORD   TM3852
★ **Froize** (01394) 450282
B1084 E of Woodbridge; IP12 3PU
More restaurant than pub and only open during mealtimes, reliably good if not cheap buffet-style food from owner-chef using carefully sourced local produce including seasonal game, nice wines by the glass and well kept Adnams, warmly welcoming service, little deli next to bar; occasional live folk music; seats on terrace, no dogs inside, closed evenings Sun-Thurs, all day Mon. *(Richard and Tessa Ibbot)*

CREETING ST MARY   TM1155
Highwayman (01449) 760369
A140, just N of junction with A14; IP6 8PD Attractively modernised 17th-c pub with two bars and pleasant galleried barn extension, welcoming landlord and friendly relaxed atmosphere, popular freshly cooked food from landlady-chef, well kept Greene King IPA and guests, decent wines; unobtrusive background music; children welcome, no dogs inside, tables on gravel terrace and back lawn with pretty pond, closed Sun evening, Mon. *(Graham Smart)*

CRETINGHAM   TM2260
Bell (01728) 685419
The Street; IP13 7BJ Attractive and welcoming old beamed and timbered pub, good traditional home-made food from sandwiches up, well kept ales such as Adnams and Earl Soham, nice wines by the glass, bare-boards bar, dining tables in tiled second room with woodburner in big fireplace; regular live music; children and dogs (in snug) welcome, garden picnic-sets. *(Sandra Morgan)*

EARL SOHAM   TM2263
Victoria (01728) 685758
A1120 Yoxford–Stowmarket; IP13 7RL
Simple two-bar pub popular with locals, well kept Earl Soham beers (used to be brewed here) and reasonably priced home-cooked food, friendly service, kitchen chairs, pews and scrubbed country tables on bare boards or tiled floors, panelling and open fire; outside gents'; children and dogs welcome, seats out in front and on raised back lawn, handy for working windmill at Saxtead (EH), open all day Fri-Sun (May to Sept). *(Neil)*

EDWARDSTONE   TL9542
★ **White Horse** (01787) 211211
Mill Green, just E; village signed off A1071 in Boxford; CO10 5PX
Unpretentious pub with own good Mill Green beers and guests (beer/cider/music festivals), various sized bars with lots of beer mats, rustic prints and photos on the walls, second-hand tables and chairs including an

old steamer bench and panelled settle on bare boards, woodburner and open fire, well liked food (booking advised); live music, bar billiards, darts, ring the bull and other games, free wi-fi; children and dogs welcome, end terrace with sturdy teak furniture, attractive smokers' shelter, makeshift picnic-sets on grass, two scandinavian-style self-catering chalets plus campsite with shower block, open all day. *(Jeremy King)*

EYE   TM1473
Queens Head (01379) 870153
Cross Street; IP23 7AB Popular three-room beamed pub; Adnams and local guests such as Bullards tapped from the cask (July beer festival), 11 wines by the glass and good fairly priced food (not Sun evening) cooked by landlord including fish specials, friendly accommodating staff, interesting local artwork, woodburner; background music, monthly quiz and karaoke, free wi-fi; children and dogs (theirs is Franco) welcome, garden with play area, open all day (Sun till 9pm). *(Rob Wynne-Jones)*

FELIXSTOWE   TM3134
Fludyers Arms (01394) 691929
Undercliff Road E; IP11 7LU Restored and extended Edwardian pub-hotel on seafront, opened-up bare-boards bar and several dining areas including panelled restaurant, Adnams, Woodfordes and guests, popular food from bar snacks up including set menu, good friendly service; events such as live jazz; children welcome, sea views from heated front terrace, 12 bedrooms and mews apartment, open (and food) all day. *(J B and M E Benson)*

FELIXSTOWE FERRY   TM3237
Ferry Boat (01394) 284203
Off Ferry Road, on the green; IP11 9RZ
Much-modernised 17th-c pub tucked between golf links and dunes near harbour, martello tower and summer rowing-boat ferry; good fair value food including range of fish dishes, friendly efficient staff, well kept Adnams Southwold, Woodfordes Wherry and a guest, decent coffee, warm log fire; background music; children and dogs welcome, tables out in front, on green opposite and in fenced garden, good coast walks, open all day weekends and busy in summer. *(Mary Joyce)*

FRAMLINGHAM   TM2862
Station Hotel (01728) 723455
Station Road (B1116 S); IP13 9EE
Simple high-ceilinged big-windowed bar with scrubbed tables on bare boards, half-panelling and woodburner, well kept Earl Soham ales and good choice of house wines, popular freshly cooked food from interesting menu, also wood-fired pizzas Thurs-Sat evenings, friendly relaxed atmosphere, back snug with tiled floor; free wi-fi; children and dogs welcome, picnic-sets in pleasant garden. *(Christopher Mannings)*

FRESSINGFIELD   TM2677
★Fox & Goose (01379) 586247
Church Street; B1116 N of Framlingham;
IP21 5PB Relaxed dining pub in beautifully
timbered 16th-c building next to church,
highly regarded food from bar meals to
tasting menus served in cosy informal
heavy-beamed rooms and upstairs restaurant,
friendly efficient service, good wines by
the glass, Adnams and a guest tapped from
the cask in side bar; faint background
music; children welcome, downstairs
disabled facilities, tables out by duck pond,
closed Mon. *(John and Jennifer Spinks)*

FRISTON   TM4160
Old Chequers (01728) 688039
Just off A1094 Aldeburgh–Snape;
IP17 1NP Refurbished under friendly
newish licensees; brightened-up L-shaped
bar with wood flooring and woodburner,
enjoyable home-made food and well kept ales
such as Adnams, Greene and Woodfordes
from brick-faced servery; well behaved
children and dogs welcome, sunny back
terrace, nice circular walks to Aldeburgh
and Snape, closed Mon, otherwise open all
day (not Tues lunchtime, and till 8pm Sun
in winter). *(Tracey and Stephen Groves)*

GREAT BRICETT   TM0450
Red Lion (01473) 657863
B1078, E of Bildeston; IP7 7DD New
owners have refurbished this extended old
beamed pub, blue walls and white tables
and chairs, still serving the very good
vegetarian and vegan food at competitive
prices (nothing for meat eaters), children's
menu and takeaways too, real ales such as
Greene King; dogs welcome in bar, garden
with deck and play equipment, closed Sun
evening, Mon. *(Sandra Morgan)*

GREAT GLEMHAM   TM3461
Crown (01728) 663693
Between A12 Wickham Market–
Saxmundham and B1119
Saxmundham–Framlingham; IP17 2DA
Traditionally restored early 19th-c red-brick
village pub; two big fireplaces and some nice
old suffolk furniture on wood and quarry-tiled
floors, mostly local beers from old brass
handpumps, good interesting food (not Sun
evening, Tues) along with pub favourites,
back coffee lounge with freshly baked
cakes, friendly helpful staff; some acoustic
music and themed events, monthly quiz,
darts, table skittles, free wi-fi; well behaved
children and dogs welcome, disabled
facilities, cast-iron furniture on back lawn,
closed Tues lunchtime. *(Sandy Maclean)*

GREAT WRATTING   TL6848
Red Lion (01440) 783237
School Road; CB9 7HA Popular village
pub with a couple of ancient whale bones
flanking the entrance; log fire in bar

and plenty of copper and brass, well
kept Adnams and generous helpings
of enjoyable pubby food, friendly staff,
restaurant, children and dogs welcome,
big back garden with play equipment,
open all day Sat. *(Matt and Hayley Jacob)*

GRUNDISBURGH   TM2250
Dog (01473) 735267
The Green; off A12 via B1079 from
Woodbridge bypass; IP13 6TA Friendly
pink-washed pub with villagey public bar,
log fire, settles and dark wooden carvers
around pubby tables on tiles, Adnams, Earl
Soham, Woodfordes and a guest, half a
dozen wines by the glass, good value food
including daily specials, themed nights
and set lunch (Tues-Sat), carpeted lounge
linking to bare-boards dining room; free
wi-fi; children and dogs welcome, picnic-
sets out in front by flowering tubs, more
seats in wicker-fenced mediterranean-
feel back garden, play area, open all day,
closed Mon. *(Michael and Sarah Lockley)*

HADLEIGH   TM0242
Kings Head (01473) 828855
High Street; IP7 5EF Modernised
Georgian-fronted pub (building is actually
much older) with popular food from daily
changing menu including good wood-fired
pizzas, well kept Adnams and guests,
Aspall's cider, friendly helpful staff; Apr
beer festival; children and dogs (in some
areas) welcome, open all day from 9.30am
(midday Sun). *(Rupert and Sandy Newton)*

HADLEIGH   TM0242
Ram (01473) 822880
Market Place; IP7 5DL Smartly updated
bar-restaurant (sister to the Swan at Long
Melford) facing Georgian corn exchange;
good well presented food (not particularly
cheap) including vegetarian/vegan choices,
brunch from 10am, plenty of wines by
the glass from extensive list, interesting
gins, cocktails and a beer from Greene
King, efficient service; children welcome,
small courtyard garden behind, open
all day (Sun till 7pm). *(Jamie Green)*

HARTEST   TL8352
Crown (01284) 830250
B1066 S of Bury St Edmunds; IP29 4DH
Old pub by church behind pretty village
green; good food (all day Sun) from
sandwiches and sharing boards up, popular
Weds pie and pint night, own Brewshed
beers plus a couple from Greene King, plenty
of wines by the glass, friendly attentive
uniformed staff, well modernised split-level
beamed interior (note the coins left by
departing World War I soldiers), good log
fire in big fireplace; free wi-fi; children (not
in bar after 8pm) and well behaved dogs
welcome, tables on big back lawn and in
sheltered side courtyard, good play area,
open all day. *(Marianne and Peter Stevens)*

HAUGHLEY   TM0262
Kings Arms   (01449) 614462
Off A45/B1113 N of Stowmarket; Old Street; IP14 3NT 16th-c extended village pub under welcoming new licensees (some refurbishment), enjoyable reasonably priced food cooked by landlord-chef from pub favourites up, set menu choices Weds-Sat, Greene King ales (Abbot ale was named here by a landlord in 1950), also a guest beer and decent choice of wines, friendly service, spacious timbered interior with plenty of room for diners, woodburner in big brick fireplace; children and dogs (in bar) welcome, tables in back garden, open all day Weds-Sat, closed Sun evening, Mon and lunchtime Tues. *(Jeremy King)*

HAWKEDON   TL7953
Queens Head   (01284) 789218
Off A143 at Wickham Street, NE of Haverhill; and off B1066; IP29 4NN Flint Tudor pub in pretty setting looking down broad peaceful green to interesting largely Norman village church; quarry-tiled bar with dark beams and ochre walls, plenty of pews and chapel chairs around scrubbed tables, elderly armchairs by antique woodburner in huge fireplace, cheerful helpful staff, Adnams, Woodfordes and guests, proper cider/perry and nice choice of wines, good food (not Mon, Tues) using home-reared meat, dining area stretching back with country prints and a couple of tusky boars' heads; some live music and occasional games nights; picnic-sets out in front, more on back terrace overlooking rolling country, little shop (Fri and Sat mornings) selling their own bacon, pies, casseroles etc, open all day Fri-Sun, closed lunchtimes Mon-Thurs. *(Val and Malcolm Travers)*

IPSWICH   TM1644
Dove Street   (01473) 211270
St Helens Street; IP4 2LA Over 20 well kept quickly changing ales including their own brews (regular beer festivals), farm ciders, bottled beers and good selection of whiskies, low priced simple pub food including substantial pork pies, bare-boards bar, carpeted snug and back conservatory; free wi-fi; children (till 7pm) and dogs welcome, seats on heated covered terrace, two bedrooms across the road along with the brewery shop, open (and food) all day. *(Jamie Green)*

IPSWICH   TM1645
Greyhound   (01473) 252862
Henley Road/Anglesea Road; IP1 3SE Popular 19th-c pub close to Christchurch Park; cosy front bar, corridor to larger lounge/dining area, five well kept Adnams ales and a couple of guests, good home cooking including bargain weekday lunch and daily specials, quick friendly service; Sun quiz, sports TV, free wi-fi; children welcome, picnic-sets under parasols on back terrace, open all day Fri-Sun. *(Jamie Green, Graham Smart)*

IPSWICH   TM1747
Railway Inn   (01473) 252337
Westerfield Road, close to the station; IP6 9AA Roadside pub popular locally for its reasonably priced food (all day weekends) including set menus (Mon-Sat) and daily specials, three well kept ales from Adnams and several wines by the glass; children and dogs (in bar area) welcome, four bedrooms, outside tables and colourful hanging baskets, open all day Fri-Sun. *(Graham Smart)*

IPSWICH   TM1744
Woolpack   (01473) 215862
Tuddenham Road; IP4 2SH Welcoming traditional red-brick pub dating from the 1600s, Adnams and four other well kept beers, several wines by the glass and proper coffee, popular fairly priced home-cooked food including blackboard specials, two bars, snug and back dining area, corner with piano and board games; live music including jazz last Weds of the month, quiz second Sun; dogs welcome, seats on heated front terrace, opposite Christchurch Park, open all day from 10am for breakfast. *(Jamie Green)*

KESGRAVE   TM2346
Kesgrave Hall   (01473) 333741
Hall Road; IP5 2PU Country hotel with comfortably contemporary bare-boards bar, Adnams and a couple of guests from granite-topped servery, several wines by the glass and cocktails, popular often imaginative food in open-kitchen brasserie (no booking so best to arrive early), friendly efficient staff; children and dogs welcome, attractive heated terrace with huge retractable awning, 23 stylish bedrooms, open (and food) all day. *(Mike and Mary Carter)*

LAVENHAM   TL9149
Swan   (01787) 247477
High Street; CO10 9QA Smart hotel incorporating handsome medieval buildings; appealing network of beamed and timbered alcoves and more open areas, tiled-floor inner bar with log fire and memorabilia from its days as a local for US 48th Bomber Group, well kept Adnams and a guest, lots of wines by the glass from extensive list and good range of other drinks including cocktails, well thought-of interesting food, can eat in bar, informal brasserie or lavishly timbered restaurant, afternoon teas, efficient friendly young staff; children and dogs welcome, sheltered courtyard garden, 45 bedrooms, open all day. *(Marianne and Peter Stevens)*

LAXFIELD   TM2972
★ Kings Head   (01986) 798395
Gorams Mill Lane, behind church; IP13 8DW Unspoilt thatched pub with no bar counter – Adnams ales and a guest

poured in tap room; interesting little chequer-tiled front room dominated by three-sided booth of high-backed settles by range fire, two other rooms with pews, old seats and scrubbed deal tables, well liked food including good home-made pies; occasional live music; children and dogs welcome, neatly kept garden with arbour and small pavilion for cooler evenings, boules, three bedrooms, open all day, no food Sun evening and kitchen may close early other days if quiet. (Alexander and Trish Gendall)

LAXFIELD TM2972
Royal Oak (01986) 798666
High Street; IP13 8DH Extended Tudor pub next to 14th-c church; beams, old quarry tiles and inglenook, half a dozen well kept ales including Adnams and Woodfordes, good value food (not Sun evening) served by friendly staff; quiz and music nights, free wi-fi; children and dogs welcome, tables out in front, open all day. (Christopher Mannings)

LONG MELFORD TL8646
★ Black Lion (01787) 312356
Church Walk; CO10 9DN Civilised hotel in handsome street opposite the village green; back bar liked by locals with comfortable sofas, leather wing chairs and open fire, Adnams Southwold and 18 carefully chosen wines by the glass, dining rooms with attractive antique or high-backed leather chairs around candlelit tables, oil paintings and another open fire, well regarded food from lunchtime sandwiches and set choices up, afternoon teas, efficient friendly service; background music, free wi-fi; children and dogs (in bar) welcome, seats in charming Victorian walled garden, well equipped individually decorated bedrooms, good breakfast, open all day from 7.30am (8.30am weekends); up for sale as we went to press. (Alison and Michael Harper, John Harris, Lenny and Ruth Walters, Freddie and Sarah Banks)

LONG MELFORD TL8645
Crown (01787) 377666
Hall Street; CO10 9JL Partly 17th-c inn with four well kept ales such as Adnams and St Austell, central servery with unusual bar chairs, log fire, some stripped brickwork and tartan carpet, oak-floored restaurant with high-backed chairs and vibrant red walls, good locally sourced food (all day Sun) from bar snacks up, friendly helpful service; free wi-fi; tables under parasols on attractive split-level terrace, 12 well equipped bedrooms, open all day. (Martin Day)

LONG MELFORD TL8645
Swan (01787) 464545
Hall Street; CO10 9JQ Well run beamed dining pub (same group as Ram at Hadleigh); enjoyable imaginative food (best to book) including vegetarian choices, brunch from 10am, well selected wines, interesting gins,

cocktails and a couple of real ales, obliging service, split-level interior with pastel décor and some unusual wallpaper, high-backed dining chairs and mix of tables on wood or carpeted floors, log fire, newly opened deli; unobtrusive background music; children welcome, tables out on terrace and lawn, seven good bedrooms (four in next-door building), open all day. (Hayley Ransome)

MELTON TM2850
Olde Coach & Horses (01394) 384851 *Melton Road; IP12 1PD*
Attractively modernised beamed former staging inn, good choice of enjoyable fairly priced food from sandwiches, snacks and sharing plates up (special diets catered for), lunchtime meal deal Mon-Sat, Adnams, Woodfordes Wherry and decent wines by the glass, good friendly service; free wi-fi; children welcome, dogs in wood-floored area, tables out under parasols among colourful hanging baskets and planters, open (and food) all day. (Christopher Mannings)

MIDDLETON TM4267
★ Bell (01728) 648286
Off A12 in Yoxford via B1122 towards Leiston; also signposted off B1125 Leiston–Westleton; The Street; IP17 3NN New people had just taken over this partly thatched old place as we went to press – reports please; traditional bar with log fire in big hearth, low plank-panelled ceiling, old local photographs, bar stools and pews, Adnams ales tapped from the cask, several wines by the glass and enjoyable fairly priced food, informal two-room carpeted lounge/ dining area on the right with padded mate's and library chairs around dark tables under low black beams, woodburner; children and dogs welcome, picnic-sets out in front, handy for RSPB Minsmere and coast walks, open all day Sat, till around 9pm Sun, closed Mon. (Anne Taylor, Andrew Vincent, Peter Pilbeam, Val and Malcolm Travers)

MONKS ELEIGH TL9647
Swan (01449) 763163
A1141 NW of Hadleigh; IP7 7AU Refurbished thatched and beamed pub overlooking small village green (same owners as Anchor at Nayland and Angel at Stoke-by-Nayland), good interesting food (not Sun evening) using locally sourced ingredients, some cooked/smoked over charcoal, Adnams Southwold and a guest, plenty of wines by the glass including champagne, friendly accommodating staff; children welcome, dogs in bar, open all day Fri and Sat, till 9pm Sun, closed Mon. (MDN, Lesley Bernard Rose)

MOULTON TL6964
Packhorse (01638) 751818
Bridge Street; CB8 8SP Stylish place with very good food from bar snacks to inventive restaurant choices (not cheap and must book), well kept Adnams,

Woodfordes and a guest, good wines by the glass, pleasant attentive service; children and dogs welcome, adjacent to delightful 15th-c bridge across the Kennett and handy for Newmarket races, eight good bedrooms, open all day. *(M and GR)*

NAYLAND   TL9734
★**Anchor** (01206) 262313
Court Street; just off A134 – turn-off S of signposted B1087 main village turn; CO6 4JL Friendly pub by River Stour under same ownership as the Angel at Stoke-by-Nayland and Swan at Monks Eleigh; bare-boards bar with assorted wooden dining chairs and tables, big gilt mirror on silvery wallpaper one end, another mirror above pretty fireplace the other, five changing ales and several wines by the glass, popular food including some home-smoked dishes and flame grills, two other rooms behind and steep stairs up to cosy restaurant; children welcome, dogs in bar, terrace tables overlooking river, open all day, food till 6pm Sun. *(Lesley Bernard Rose)*

NEWBOURNE   TM2743
Fox (01473) 736307
Off A12 at roundabout 1.7 miles N of A14 junction; The Street; IP12 4NY Pink-washed 16th-c pub decked in summer flowers; low-beamed bar with slabby elm and other dark tables on quarry-tiled floor, stuffed fox in inglenook, comfortable carpeted dining room with various mirrors, Adnams Southwold, guest ales and decent wines by the glass, good choice of popular food including deals; background music, free wi-fi; children and dogs (in bar) welcome, wheelchair access, attractive grounds with rose garden and pond, open (and food) all day from 9am breakfast on. *(Michael and Sarah Lockley, Mary Joyce)*

ORFORD   TM4249
★**Jolly Sailor** (01394) 450243
Quay Street; IP12 2NU Welcoming old pub under mother and daughter team; several snug rooms with exposed brickwork, boating pictures and other nautical memorabilia, four well kept Adnams beers and popular sensibly priced food from good lunchtime sandwiches up, efficient cheerful service, unusual spiral staircase in corner of flagstoned main bar by brick inglenook, horsebrasses and local photographs, two cushioned pews and long antique stripped-deal table; maybe local sea shanty group, free wi-fi; children and dogs welcome, tables on back terrace and lawn with views over marshes, popular with walkers and bird-watchers, bedrooms, open all day weekends. *(Phil and Jane Villiers, Bob and Margaret Holder, JER, David Fowler)*

ORFORD   TM4249
★**Kings Head** (01394) 450271
Front Street; IP12 2LW Friendly village inn surrounded by fine walks and lovely

coastline; partly 700 years old and plenty of authentic atmosphere, snug main bar with heavy low beams straightforward furniture on red carpeting, Adnams ales and several wines by the glass, enjoyable home-made food (not Sun evening) from generously filled sandwiches to daily specials, dining room with nice old stripped-brick walls and rugs on ancient boards, woodburners; children and dogs welcome, four bedrooms open all day Fri-Sun. *(Derek and Sylvia Stephenson, Barry Collett)*

POLSTEAD   TL9938
Cock (01206) 263150
Signed off B1068 and A1071 E of Sudbury, then pub signed; Polstead Green; CO6 5AL 16th-c beamed and timbered village local; bar with woodburner, Greene King IPA and two guests, good choice of wines and enjoyable reasonably priced home-made food from lunchtime sandwiches up, light and airy barn restaurant; background music; children and dogs welcome, disabled facilities, picnic-sets overlooking small green, closed Sun evening, Mon. *(Graham Smart)*

RAMSHOLT   TM3041
Ramsholt Arms (01394) 411209
Signed off B1083; Dock Road; IP12 3AB Lovely isolated spot overlooking River Deben; modernised open-plan bar with log fire, enjoyable good value food from lunchtime sandwiches up, Adnams, a couple of guest beers and decent choice of wines by the glass; children and dogs welcome, plenty of tables outside taking in the view, handy for bird walks and Sutton Hoo (NT), best to check opening times. *(Comus and Sarah Elliott)*

REYDON   TM4977
★**Randolph** (01502) 723603
Wangford Road (B1126 just NW of Southwold); IP18 6PZ Stylish inn with quite an emphasis on dining and bedroom side; bar with high-backed leather dining chairs around chunky wooden tables on parquet floor, a couple of comfortable armchairs and sofa, prints of the pub from 1910 and photographs of Southwold beach, Adnams beers, more high-backed chairs in carpeted restaurant with pretty Victorian fireplace, popular food from short but varied menu including lunchtime sandwiches and snack baskets, pleasant staff; background music, TV; children welcome, dogs in small back bar, wheelchair access, picnic-sets on decked area and grass, ten bedrooms and self-catering bungalow, good breakfast, open all day. *(Jamie Green)*

ROUGHAM   TL9063
★**Ravenwood Hall** (01359) 270345
Off A14 E of Bury St Edmunds; IP30 9JA Country-house hotel with two compact bar rooms, tall ceilings, patterned wallpaper

and big heavily draped windows overlooking sweeping lawn with stately cedar, back area set for eating with upholstered settles and dining chairs, sporting prints and log fire, very good well presented food (own smoked meats and fish), well kept Adnams, good choice of wines and malt whiskies, pleasant attentive staff, comfortable lounge area with horse pictures, a few moulded beams and early Tudor wall decoration above big inglenook, separate more formal restaurant; background music; children and dogs welcome, teak furniture in garden, swimming pool and croquet, big enclosures for geese, pygmy goats and shetland ponies, 14 bedrooms, open 9am-midnight. *(Comus and Sarah Elliott)*

SAXTEAD GREEN   TM2564
Old Mill House   (01728) 685064
B1119; The Green; IP13 9QE Roomy dining pub across green from windmill; beamed carpeted bar and neat country-look flagstoned restaurant extension, good choice of fresh food (all day Sun) including daily carvery, well kept Greene King ales and decent wines; discreet background music; children very welcome, attractive garden with terrace and good play area, open all day Sun. *(Rupert and Sandy Newton)*

SHOTTISHAM   TM3244
Sorrel Horse   (01394) 411617
Hollesley Road; IP12 3HD Charming 15th-c thatched community-owned local; well kept Adnams, Earl Soham, Woodfordes and guests tapped from casks, decent choice of home-made traditional food including deals, attentive friendly young staff, good log fire in tiled-floor bar with games area (bar billiards), woodburner in attractive dining room; fortnightly Weds quiz, free wi-fi; children and dogs welcome, tables out on sloping front lawn and in small garden behind, open all day weekends. *(Annette Wilkins)*

SNAPE   TM3958
★ Crown   (01728) 688324
Bridge Road (B1069); IP17 1SL Small well laid-out 15th-c beamed pub with brick floors, inglenook log fire and fine double suffolk settle, well kept Adnams ales, good fresh food using local ingredients including own meat (reared behind the pub), reasonable prices, efficient friendly young staff; folk night last Thurs of month, darts, free wi-fi; children and dogs welcome, garden, two bedrooms. *(Simon Rodway, Comus and Sarah Elliott)*

SNAPE   TM4058
Golden Key   (01728) 688510
Priory Lane; IP17 1SA Welcoming traditionally furnished village pub; low-beamed lounge with old-fashioned settle and straightforward tables and chairs on chequerboard tiled floor, log fire, small snug

and two cosy dining rooms, well kept Adnams ales, local cider and several wines by the glass, reasonably priced pubby food, cheerful helpful service; children and dogs welcome, two terraces with pretty hanging baskets and seats under large parasols, handy for the Maltings, three comfortable bedrooms, open all day weekends. *(Sara Fulton, Roger Baker, Derek and Sylvia Stephenson, Phil and Jane Villiers, Simon Rodway, Comus and Sarah Elliott)*

SOUTH ELMHAM   TM3385
St Peters Brewery   (01986) 782288
St Peter South Elmham; off B1062 SW of Bungay; NR35 1NQ Beautifully but simply furnished manor dating from the 13th c (much extended in 1539) with own St Peters ales and bottled beers, bar and dining hall with dramatic high ceiling, elaborate woodwork and flagstoned floor, antique tapestries, woodburner in fine fireplace, two further rooms reached up steepish stairs, short choice of food including sandwiches, afternoon teas; children and dogs (in bar) welcome, outside tables overlooking original moat, open all day Fri and Sat, till 6pm Sun, Weds and Thurs, closed Mon, Tues (although may open in high summer), they do host weddings and other events, so best to check. *(Rob Wynne-Jones)*

SOUTHWOLD   TM5076
★ Crown   (01502) 722275
High Street; IP18 6DP Changes afoot as we went to press for this comfortable civilised hotel; informal chatty back bar liked by locals, bare boards, oak panelling and antique tables and chairs, well kept Adnams ales, many wines by the glass from splendid list, several malt whiskies and other interesting spirits, beamed front brasserie bar with settles and carved fireplace, impressive food from regularly changing menu, good friendly service; children and dogs (in bar) welcome, sheltered corner terrace, 14 comfortable well equipped bedrooms, good breakfast, open all day. *(Tracey and Stephen Groves, W K Wood, Phil and Jane Villiers, Brian and Sally Wakeham, John and Abigail Prescott, Tom and Lorna Harding and others)*

SOUTHWOLD   TM4975
★ Harbour Inn   (01502) 722381
Blackshore, by the boats; from A1095, turn right at the Kings Head, and keep on past the golf course and water tower; IP18 6TA Former fisherman's pub in great waterside spot; back bar with dark panelling, built-in wall seats and scrubbed tables, low ceiling draped with ensigns, signal flags, pennants and a line strung with ancient dried fish, lots of nautical bric-a-brac, old stove, Adnams ales and 16 wines by the glass, lower front bar and large elevated dining room with panoramic views of the harbour, lighthouse, brewery and churches beyond the marshes, popular food including good fresh

fish; folk singers Thurs and Sun evenings; children and dogs welcome in certain areas, picnic-sets on terrace overlooking boats on Blyth estuary, more seats behind, can walk from here to Walberswick and return by the one-man ferry, open (and food) all day; changes planned as we went to press – news please. *(Sheila Topham, Bob and Margaret Holder, Simon Rodway, Rupert and Sandy Newton, Michael and Sarah Lockley)*

SOUTHWOLD   TM5076
★ **Lord Nelson** (01502) 722079
East Street, off High Street (A1095); IP18 6EJ Busy local near seafront with partly panelled traditional bar and two small side rooms, coal fire, light wood furniture on tiles, lamps in nice nooks and corners, interesting Nelson memorabilia including attractive nautical prints and fine model of HMS *Victory*, five well kept Adnams ales, several wines by the glass and decent pubby food, good friendly service; board games, free wi-fi; children (away from the bar) and dogs welcome, disabled access not perfect but possible, seats out in front with sidelong view of the sea, sheltered and heated back garden with Adnams brewery in sight, open all day. *(Sheila Topham, Simon Rodway, John Wooll)*

SOUTHWOLD   TM5076
Red Lion (01502) 722385
South Green; IP18 6ET Under new management and some redecoration; front bar with big windows looking over green towards the sea, sturdy wall benches and bar stools on wood floor, well kept Adnams including seasonals, back room with mate's chairs, pews and polished dark tables, lots of framed black and white photographs, popular food served by friendly staff, three linked dining rooms; background music (live Sun afternoon); tables out in front and in small sheltered back courtyard, next to the Adnams retail shop. *(Val and Malcolm Travers, John Wooll)*

SOUTHWOLD   TM5076
Sole Bay (01502) 723736
East Green; IP18 6JN Busy pub near Adnams Brewery, their full range kept well and good wine choice, cheerful efficient staff, enjoyable reasonably priced simple food including good fish and chips, airy interior with well spaced tables, conservatory; sports TV; children and dogs welcome, disabled facilities, picnic-sets outside, moments from sea and lighthouse, open (and food) all day. *(Comus and Sarah Elliott)*

SOUTHWOLD   TM5076
Swan (01502) 722186
Market Place; IP18 6EG This smart Adnams-owned hotel with its popular back bar will reopen in autumn 2017 after major refurbishment – reports please.

STANSFIELD   TL7851
Compasses (01284) 789263
High Street; CO10 8LN Simple little country pub with good often interesting food cooked by character landlord (some ingredients from next-door farm), own-brewed beers and local guests, beams, bare boards and large woodburner; occasional live music, Fri quiz night, children, walkers and dogs welcome, outside tables with lovely rural views, open all day weekends, closed Mon-Weds. *(Sandra Morgan)*

STOKE ASH   TM1170
White Horse (01379) 678222
A140/Workhouse Road; IP23 7ET Sizeable 17th-c roadside coaching inn, beams and inglenook fireplaces, generous helpings of good reasonably priced pub food all day from 8am, well kept Adnams, Greene King and Woodfordes, local Calvors lager and Aspall's cider, efficient service from friendly staff; free wi-fi; children welcome, bedrooms in modern annexe, open (and food) all day. *(Sandy Maclean)*

STOKE-BY-NAYLAND   TL9836
★ **Angel** (01206) 263245
B1068 Sudbury–East Bergholt; CO6 4SA Elegant and comfortable 17th-c inn (same owners as the Swan at Monks Eleigh and Anchor at Nayland); lounge with handsome beams, timbers and stripped brickwork, leather chesterfields and wing armchairs around low tables, more formal room featuring deep glass-covered well, chatty bar with straightforward furniture on red tiles, well kept Adnams and Woodfordes, several wines by the glass and good range of gins, very well liked food including lunchtime set menu, efficient friendly service; children and dogs (in some parts) welcome, seats on sheltered terrace, six individually styled bedrooms, good breakfast, open all day from 10am. *(MDN, Dr Michael Smith, Lesley Bernard Rose)*

STOWUPLAND   TM0759
Crown (01449) 490490
Church Road (A1120 just E of Stowmarket); IP14 4BQ Extended thatched pub set back from the road behind white picket fence, refurbished interior blending traditional and contemporary features, well liked sensibly priced food from pub favourites up including good stone-baked pizzas (visible oven), real ales and a dozen wines by the glass, friendly efficient service, bar with log fire, restaurant; children and dogs welcome, good-sized garden, open all day, no food Mon, just pizzas Sun evening. *(Mrs Margo Finlay, Jörg Kasprowski)*

STUTTON   TM1434
Gardeners Arms (01473) 328868
Manningtree Road, Upper Street (B1080); IP9 2TG Cottagey roadside

pub on edge of small village, well kept Adnams Southwold and guests, good value home-made food including daily specials, friendly helpful service, cosy L-shaped bar with log fire, side dining room and larger area stretching to the back, lots of bric-a-brac, film posters and musical instruments; children and dogs welcome, two-tier back garden with pond, open all day Sun, closed Mon. *(Richard and Tessa Ibbot)*

SUDBURY   TL8741
Brewery Tap (01787) 370876

East Street; CO10 2TP Corner tap for Mauldons brewery, their range and guests kept well, good choice of malt whiskies, bare boards and scrubbed tables, some food (can bring your own); darts, cribbage and bar billiards, live music, comedy night first Weds of month, quiz third Weds; dogs welcome, open all day. *(Andy and Rosemary Taylor)*

SWEFFLING   TM3464
White Horse (01728) 664178

B1119 Framlingham–Saxmundham; IP17 2BB Traditional little two room country pub, friendly and laid back, with woodburner in one room, range in the other, up to three well kept changing east anglian beers served from tap room door, real cider and some interesting local wines and spirits, simple food such as ploughman's and locally made winter pies; some live acoustic music, bar billiards, darts and other traditional games; children and dogs welcome, self-catering cottage and campsite with yurts, closed lunchtimes apart from Sun, and evenings Tues-Thurs. *(Deborah and Duncan Walliams)*

SWILLAND   TM1852
Moon & Mushroom (01473) 785320

Off B1078; IP6 9LR Popular 16th-c country local serving east anglian beers from racked casks behind long counter, old tables and chairs on quarry tiles, log fire, enjoyable good value home-made food such as local game; quiz first Weds of month; children and dogs welcome, heated terrace with grapevines and roses, closed Sun evening, Mon. *(Graham Smart)*

THORNDON   TM1469
Black Horse (01379) 678523

Off A140 or B1077, S of Eye; The Street; IP23 7JR Friendly 17th-c village pub with decent food including lunchtime carvery, also curry and fish and chip takeaways, three well kept local ales such as Adnams and Woodfordes, beams, lots of timbering, stripped brick and big fireplaces; well behaved children and dogs (in bar) welcome,

tables on lawn, country views behind, open all day Sun till 9pm. *(Jamie Green)*

THORNHAM MAGNA   TM1070
Four Horseshoes (01379) 678777

Off A140 S of Diss; Wickham Road; IP23 8HD Extensive thatched dining pub dating from the 12th c, well divided dimly lit carpeted bar, Greene King ales and good choice of wines and whiskies, enjoyable reasonably priced food with main courses available in two sizes, popular Sun carvery, friendly helpful staff, very low heavy black beams, country pictures and brass, big log fireplaces, illuminated interior well; background music; children and dogs (in bar) welcome, disabled access, handy for Thornham Walks and interesting thatched church, picnic-sets on big sheltered lawn, seven comfortable bedrooms, open all day. *(Sally)*

THORPENESS   TM4759
★ Dolphin (01728) 454994

Just off B1353; Old Homes Road; village signposted from Aldeburgh; IP16 4FE Neatly kept extended dining pub in interesting seaside village (all built in the early 1900s); main bar with scandinavian feel, pale wooden tables and assortment of old chairs on broad modern quarry tiles, log fire, Adnams, Woodfordes and a guest, several wines by the glass (good value list), more traditional public bar with pubby furniture on stripped-wood floor, built-in cushioned wall seats and old local photographs, airy dining room with country kitchen-style furniture, good food from shortish but interesting menu, friendly service; background music, TV, free wi-fi; children and dogs welcome, spacious garden, three refurbished bedrooms, open all day weekends, closed Mon in winter. *(Tracey and Stephen Groves, Simon Rodway)*

THURSTON   TL9165
Fox & Hounds (01359) 232228

Barton Road; IP31 3QT Rather imposing former 19th-c station inn, well kept Adnams Broadside, Greene King IPA and four guests, pubby furnishings in carpeted lounge (back part set for dining), ceiling fans and lots of pump clips, big helpings of reasonably priced pubby food (not Sun evening or Mon lunchtime) with regular themed nights, friendly service, bare-boards public bar with pool, darts and machines; background and some live music, quiz and bingo nights; children and dogs welcome, picnic-sets on grassed area by car park and on small covered side terrace, pretty village, self-catering apartment, open all day. *(Mary Joyce)*

A star symbol before the name of a pub shows exceptional character and appeal. It doesn't mean extra comfort. Even quite a basic pub can win a star, if it's individual enough.

TUDDENHAM TM1948
Fountain (01473) 785377
The Street; village signed off B1077 N of Ipswich; IP6 9BT Popular dining pub in nice village; several linked café-style rooms with heavy beams and timbering, stripped floors, wooden dining chairs around light tables, open fire, lots of prints (some by cartoonist Giles who spent time here after World War II), wide choice of well cooked food (all day Sun till 7pm) including set menus and blackboard specials, Adnams Southwold and good selection of wines by the glass, decent coffee; background music; no under-10s in bar after 6.30pm, wicker and metal chairs on covered heated terrace, rows of picnic-style tables under parasols on sizeable lawn. *(Christopher Mannings)*

UFFORD TM2952
★ **Crown** (01394) 461030
High Street; IP13 6EL Quite a mix of customers for this well liked family-run pub-restaurant, good food cooked by landlady's brother from interestingly varied menu, redecorated bar and dining areas with cushioned wooden dining chairs and leather banquettes around medley of dark tables, shelves of books, modern ceiling lights, open fires in brick fireplaces, stools against counter serving Adnams Southwold, Earl Soham Victoria Bitter and a dozen good wines by the glass, friendly service; children and dogs (in bar) welcome, seats out at front, picnic-sets under parasols in back garden, open all day weekends (till 9pm Sun), closed Tues. *(Jack Trussler, Liz and Martin Eldon, Sandra King, Deborah and Duncan Walliams, Christopher Mannings)*

UFFORD TM2952
White Lion (01394) 460770
Lower Street (off B1438, towards Eyke); IP13 6DW 16th-c village pub near quiet stretch of River Deben; home to the Uffa Brewery with their beers and guests tapped from the cask, enjoyable generous home-made food (own pigs, free-range hens and bees), raised woodburner in large central fireplace, captain's chairs and spindlebacks around simple tables, shop/deli; regular events including quiz nights, Aug beer festival and vintage car rallies; nice views from outside tables, summer barbecues, closed Sun evening, Mon lunchtime. *(Michael and Sarah Lockley)*

WALBERSWICK TM4974
★ **Bell** (01502) 723109
Just off B1387; IP18 6TN Changes planned for this 600-year-old inn but has had plenty of original character in its various rooms; charming rambling bar with antique carved settles, cushioned pews and window seats, scrubbed tables and two huge fireplaces (one with elderly woodburner), fine old flooring encompasses sagging ancient bricks, broad boards, flagstones and red and black tiles, Adnams ales, 16 good wines by the glass and several malt whiskies, enjoyable food from sandwiches up, barn café, friendly staff and nice relaxed atmosphere; background music, darts; dogs welcome in bar, children away from it, smart oak furniture in sheltered back garden, pétanque, summer rowing-boat ferry to Southwold nearby, bedrooms (some with sea or harbour views), open all day. *(George Sanderson, Julian Richardson, R L Borthwick, Comus and Sarah Elliott, S Holder)*

WANGFORD TM4679
Angel (01502) 578636
Signed just off A12 by B1126 junction; High Street; NR34 8RL Handsome old coaching inn with airy beamed and carpeted bar, enjoyable good value food from sandwiches up, pleasant efficient service, Adnams, Brakspears, Greene King and a guest, decent wines, family dining room; dogs welcome, seven comfortable bedrooms (the church clock sounds on the quarter), good breakfast, open all day Sun. *(Matt and Hayley Jacob)*

WENHASTON TM4274
Star (01502) 478240
Hall Road; IP19 9HF Friendly well run 19th-c country pub, Adnams Southwold and guests, good wine choice and wide range of enjoyable inexpensive home-made food; children, dogs and muddy boots welcome, sizeable lawn with boules, nice views, open all day Sun. *(Rob Wynne-Jones)*

WESTLETON TM4469
White Horse (01728) 648222
Darsham Road, off B1125 Blythburgh–Leiston; IP17 3AH Friendly and relaxed traditional pub with well liked home-cooked food from blackboard menu including specials, four well kept Adnams ales, high-ceilinged bar with central fire, steps down to stone-floored back dining room; quiz nights, darts, free wi-fi; children and dogs welcome, picnic-sets in cottagey garden with climbing frame, more out by village duck pond, four bedrooms, good breakfast, open all day Fri-Sun. *(Ian Herdman)*

WINGFIELD TM2276
De La Pole Arms (01379) 384983
Off B1118 N of Stradbroke; Church Road; IP21 5RA Timbered 16th-c pub revamped under new welcoming licensees;

Post Office address codings confusingly give the impression that some pubs are in Suffolk, when they're really in Cambridgeshire, Essex or Norfolk (which is where we list them).

enjoyable food from sandwiches to daily specials, Sun carvery, well kept Adnams and St Peters, decent wines by the glass, good friendly service, beams, flagstones and quarry tiles, bar with log fire in big fireplace, raftered restaurant, deli/café; children and dogs (in bar) welcome, disabled access, parasol-shaded tables on sunny terrace, closed Mon, otherwise open all day from 10am (till 7pm Sun). *(Mary Joyce)*

WOODBRIDGE   TM2648
Cherry Tree (01394) 384627
Opposite Notcutts Nursery, off A12; Cumberland Street; IP12 4AG Opened-up 17th-c pub (bigger than it looks) with well kept Adnams and guests, good wines by the glass and ample helpings of reasonably priced tasty food including specials, friendly service, beams and two log fires, mix of pine furniture, old local photographs; Thurs quiz and regular beer festivals; children and dogs (in bar) welcome, garden with play area, three bedrooms in converted barn, good breakfast (for non-residents too), open all day. *(Rupert and Sandy Newton)*

WOODBRIDGE   TM2748
Crown (01394) 384242
Thoroughfare/Quay Street; IP12 1AD Stylish 17th-c dining inn, well kept ales such as Adnams from glass-roofed bar (boat suspended above counter), lots of wines by the glass and cocktails, good imaginative food from light meals up including set menu, afternoon teas, pleasant young staff, various

eating areas with contemporary furnishings; live jazz last Thurs of month; children and dogs (in bar) welcome, courtyard tables, ten well appointed bedrooms, open all day. *(Comus and Sarah Elliott)*

WOODBRIDGE   TM2749
Olde Bell & Steelyard (01394)
382933 *New Street, off Market Square; IP12 1DZ* Ancient and unpretentious timber-framed pub with two smallish beamed bars and compact dining room, brassware and old china, log fire, Greene King ales and guests from canopied servery, traditional ciders, standard home-made food from huffers up; traditional games including bar billiards, sports TV, free wi-fi; children and dogs welcome, disabled access, back terrace, steelyard still overhanging street, open all day weekends. *(Christopher Mannings)*

WOOLPIT   TL9762
Swan (01359) 240482
The Street; IP30 9QN Welcoming old coaching house pleasantly situated in village square, heavy beams and painted panelling, mixed tables and chairs on carpet, roaring log fire at one end, good inventive food from daily changing blackboard menu, prompt friendly service, well kept Adnams from slate-top counter and lots of wines by the glass; maybe background music, quiz last Sun of the month; walled garden behind, four bedrooms in converted stables, closed Sun, Mon. *(Jeremy King)*

Surrey

KEY ★ Star Pub 🔟 Top Quality Food 🍺 Great Beer
♇ Good Wines £ Bargain Meals 🛏 Good Bedrooms 🍴 Serves Food

BUCKLAND
TQ2250 Map 3

Pheasant ♇ 🍺

(01737) 221355 – www.brunningandprice.co.uk/pheasant
Reigate Road (A25 W of Reigate); RH3 7BG

**Busy roadside pub with a thoughtful range of drinks and food served
by friendly staff, character rooms and seats on terrace and lawn**

Always full of cheerful customers, this carefully extended and attractive weatherboarded pub has various interconnected areas that are split up by timbering and painted standing pillars. A couple of dining rooms at one end, separated by a two-sided open fire, have captain's chairs and cushioned dining chairs around a mix of tables on bare boards or rugs – and throughout there are wall-to-wall prints and pictures, gilt-edged mirrors, house plants, old stone bottles and elegant metal chandeliers. The busy bar has a long high table with equally high chairs, another two-way fireplace with button-back leather armchairs and sofas in front of it and stools against the counter where they keep Brunning & Price Phoenix Original plus guests such as Adnams Prop Hop, Dark Star Hophead, Hogs Back TEA, Tillingbourne The Source Spring Ale and Twickenham Redhead on handpump, 24 wines by the glass, 60 whiskies and 73 gins; background music and board games. One of the two other dining rooms has a big open fire pit in the middle. Out on the terrace is another open fire pit surrounded by built-in seats plus solid tables and chairs, while the lawn has plenty of picnic-sets and a children's play tractor.

🍴 Brasserie-style food includes sandwiches, curried crab croquettes with lime, coriander and mango salad, pigeon with puy lentils, black pudding beignets and golden beetroot, sweet potato, aubergine and almond with lemon couscous, pork sausages with mash and onion gravy, devilled sea bass with cucumber, mint and tomato salad and saffron mayonnaise, confit duck leg with flageolet bean stew and roasted thyme celeriac, szechuan-style belly pork with pak choi, watermelon and toasted cashew nut salad, and puddings such as lemon meringue roulade with raspberry sorbet and crème brûlée. *Benchmark main dish: steak and stilton pie £13.95. Two-course evening meal £21.00.*

Brunning & Price ~ Manager Bethany Wells ~ Real ale ~ Open 10am-11pm; 9am-11pm Sat; 9am-10.30pm Sun ~ Bar food 12-10; 9am-10pm Sat; 9am-9.30pm Sun ~ Restaurant ~ Children welcome ~ Dogs allowed in bar ~ Wi-fi
Recommended by Sarah and David Gibbs, John Branston, Donald Allsopp, Ann and Chris Heaps, M G Hart, Chantelle and Tony Redman

We accept no free drinks or meals and inspections are anonymous.

CHIDDINGFOLD

SU9635 Map 3

Swan 🌟 ⇔

(01428) 684688 – www.theswaninnchiddingfold.com

Petworth Road (A283 S); GU8 4TY

Open-plan light and airy rooms in well run inn, with local ales, modern food and seats in terraced garden; bedrooms

The bedrooms in this stylishly updated tile-hung inn are well equipped and comfortable and make a good base for exploring the area – there's plenty to do and see nearby. The bar has an open fire in an inglenook fireplace with leather armchairs in front and antlers above, wooden tables and chairs and cushioned wall seats on pale floorboards and leather-topped stools against the counter where they keep Upham Punter, Sprinter and Tipster on handpump, 19 wines by the glass and a good choice of spirits. Staff are helpful and friendly. The dining room leads off here with modern chairs and chunky tables set with fresh flowers on more bare boards. Outside, a three-tiered terraced garden has plenty of seats and tables.

 Rewarding food includes lunchtime sandwiches, crayfish and avocado salad with lemon and lime dressing, seared foie gras with gingerbread toast and rhubarb compote, burger with toppings and shoestring fries, root vegetable terrine with artichoke purée, goats cheese and pumpkin seed bonbon truffle, whole plaice, clams and capers with lemon beurre noisette sauce and sauté new potatoes, pheasant breast and crispy leg with a fennel fritter, puy lentil and vegetable casserole and celeriac gratin, venison haunch with romanesco and broccoli fricassée, cider fondant potatoes and mulled jus, and puddings such as banana bread and butter pudding with poppy seed ice-cream and dark chocolate, marzipan and caramel délice with toffee popcorn and lemon sorbet. *Benchmark main dish: lamb rump with lamb shoulder pastilla, spiced aubergine, sweet potato and harissa £15.95. Two-course evening meal £22.00.*

Upham ~ Managers Zach and Sinead Leach ~ Real ale ~ Open 7am-11pm; 9am-11pm Sat; 9am-10.30pm Sun ~ Bar food 12-3, 6.30-9.30 (9 Sun); snacks 3-6.30 ~ Children welcome ~ Dogs allowed in bar ~ Wi-fi ~ Bedrooms: /£85 *Recommended by Helena and Trevor Fraser, Tim and Sarah Smythe-Brown, Sally and David Champion, Bryce, Bridget and Peter Gregson, Miss A E Dare, Alison and Dan Richardson*

CHILWORTH

TQ0347 Map 2

Percy Arms 🌟 ♔

(01483) 561765 – www.thepercyarms.net

Dorking Road; GU4 8NP

Popular pub with stylish décor, attentive staff serving highly regarded food and lots of outside seating

Extended and attractively decorated, this is a particularly well run, bustling pub with courteous, efficient staff. From the entrance hall with its cubed tartan stools, rustic planked chairs and a button-back leather armchair, you turn right for the two bar rooms. The smaller one has logs piled neatly above a woodburning stove, a long slate-topped table lined with an equally long pew and cushioned bench and an L-shaped settle with scatter cushions next to another table; TV. The flagstoned main room is similarly furnished with tartan-cushioned chairs against the counter where they keep a beer named for the pub (from Greene King), Greene King Abbot, IPA and a guest beer on handpump and 16 wines by the glass. Dining rooms to the left of the entrance have upholstered tub and high-backed chairs on bare boards or rugs and a self-service carvery. There are further dining rooms, down steps from the bar, with alcoves, built-in cushioned wall seats, high-backed spindle and other chairs on wooden floors, antler chandeliers and doors out to a decked terrace. Paintwork is contemporary, pictures have large rustic frames and here and there are antlers and animal skins. The two-part garden is connected by a bridge over a small stream and has children's play equipment and picnic-sets.

Interesting food includes south african specialities such as boerewors (traditional farmers' sausage) with chakalaka (a spicy tomato and bean relish), bobotie (spicy beef with a fluffy egg topping) and a Durban-style curry. Also, bourbon-glazed pork belly with chive and sour cream dip, gnocchi with tomato, basil and mozzarella, thai sticky beef salad with noodles, beer-battered cod and chips, burgers with unusual toppings and sweet potato fries, ostrich medallions with berry jus and fondant potato, 35-day dry-aged steaks with a choice of sauces, and puddings such as sticky toffee pudding with toffee sauce and banoffi sundae; they also offer a two-course weekday set lunch. *Benchmark main dish: south african sharing board £21.95. Two-course evening meal £22.00.*

Greene King ~ Lease Janine Hunter ~ Real ale ~ Open 7am-10pm; 8am-11pm Sat; 8am-10pm Sun ~ Bar food 12-3, 6-10; 12-10 Sat; 12-9 Sun ~ Children welcome ~ Dogs allowed in bar ~ Wi-fi *Recommended by Julie Braeburn, Charles Todd, Sandra and Nigel Brown, Ian Phillips, Rosie and Marcus Heatherley, Elise and Charles Mackinlay*

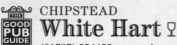

CHIPSTEAD
White Hart ⧉

TQ2757   Map 3

(01737) 554455 – www.brunningandprice.co.uk/whitehartchipstead
Hazelwood Lane; CR5 3QW

Airy open-plan rooms, a thoughtful choice of drinks, interesting food and friendly staff

There's plenty to look at in this well run, busy pub that is opposite rugby playing fields with far distant views. The raftered dining room to the right has elegant metal chandeliers, rough-plastered walls, an open fire in a brick fireplace and a couple of carved metal standing uprights. Helpful staff serve Phoenix Brunning & Price Original and Sambrooks Wandle with guests such as Adnams Broadside, Hammerpot Madgwick Gold and Sharps Doom Bar on handpump, 20 wines by the glass, more than 35 gins and up to 60 malt whiskies; background music and board games. The long room to the left is light and airy, with wall panelling at one end, a woodburning stove and numerous windows overlooking the seats on the terrace. Throughout, there's a fine mix of antique dining chairs and settles around all sorts of tables, rugs on bare boards, hundreds of interesting cartoons, country pictures, cricketing prints and rugby team photographs, large ornate mirrors and, on the windowsills and mantelpieces, collections of old glass and stone bottles, clocks, books and plants.

Highly regarded food includes sandwiches, scallops with warm pea, lettuce and bacon salad, chicken liver pâté with fig and plum chutney, aubergine and tomato tart with greek-style salad, feta pannacotta and tapenade, steak in ale pie, spicy vietnamese king prawn and noodle salad with toasted peanuts and chilli and lime dressing, chicken breast with heritage carrots, warm potato terrine, broad beans, crisp sage and thyme jus, and puddings such as bread and butter pudding with apricot sauce and hot belgian waffle with honeycomb ice-cream and butterscotch sauce. *Benchmark main dish: braised lamb shoulder with dauphinoise potatoes and gravy £17.45. Two-course evening meal £22.00.*

Brunning & Price ~ Manager Ollie Simmonds ~ Real ale ~ Open 11.30-11; 12-10.30 Sun ~ Bar food 12-10 (9.30 Sun) ~ Restaurant ~ Children welcome ~ Dogs allowed in bar ~ Wi-fi *Recommended by Paul A Moore, John Branston, M G Hart, Robert and Diana Ringstone, Sally and Colin Allen*

CHOBHAM

White Hart ♀ ◀

SU9761 Map 2

(01276) 857580 – www.brunningandprice.co.uk/whitehartchobham
High Street; GU24 8AA

Brick-built village inn with cheerful customers and a thoughtful choice of food and drink

The opened-up bar remains the heart of this handsome old place and has white-painted beams, standing pillars, rugs on parquet or wide boards, an assortment of dark wooden dining chairs and tables, and armchairs beside two fireplaces. High chairs line the counter where cheerful, well trained staff serve Phoenix Brunning & Price Original, Park Spankers IPA, Surrey Hills Shere Drop, Thurstons Horsell Gold and Tillingbourne Falls Gold on handpump, 24 wines by the glass, 40 gins and 43 malt whiskies. An L-shaped dining room has a leather wall banquette and leather and brass-studded dining chairs around a mix of tables and lots of old photos and prints on exposed-brick or painted walls. There's also a comfortable dining room with similar furniture, carpeting and a big elegant metal chandelier. The little side garden has seats under parasols.

As well as weekend breakfasts (9-11am), the interesting food includes sandwiches, duck rillettes with pickled root vegetables, potted crab and crayfish with samphire, caper and cucumber salad, honey-roasted ham and eggs, sweet potato, aubergine and spinach malaysian curry, monkfish risotto with smoked sausage, king prawns and mascarpone, slow-cooked ox cheek bourguignon with horseradish mash, chicken saltimbocca with crisp pancetta on pasta, and puddings such as peanut butter parfait with chocolate ganache and salted caramel and portuguese cinnamon custard tart with warm chocolate sauce. *Benchmark main dish: braised lamb shoulder with dauphinoise potatoes and rosemary gravy £17.95. Two-course evening meal £21.00.*

Brunning & Price ~ Manager Rebecca Bowen ~ Real ale ~ Open 11-11; 12-10.30 Sun ~ Bar food 12-10 (9.30 Sun) ~ Restaurant ~ Children welcome away from the bar; not suitable for babies/toddlers in evening ~ Dogs allowed in bar ~ Wi-fi *Recommended by Dr Simon Innes, Simon Collett-Jones, Jo Garnett, Liz and Martin Eldon*

ELSTEAD
Mill at Elstead

SU9044 Map 2

(01252) 703333 – www.millelstead.co.uk
Farnham Road (B3001 just W of village, which lies between Farnham and Milford); GU8 6LE

Fascinating building with sizeable attractive waterside garden, Fullers beers and well liked food

This is a special place for a drink in warm weather: there are picnic-sets dotted about by the River Wey and a lovely millpond with swans and weeping willows. It's a sensitively converted, largely 18th-c watermill and a series of rambling linked bar areas on the spacious ground floor have big windows that make the most of the view; there's an upstairs restaurant too. You'll find brown leather armchairs and antique engravings by a longcase clock, neat modern tables and dining chairs on bare boards, big country tables on broad ceramic tiles, iron pillars, stripped masonry and a log fire in a huge inglenook. Fullers ESB, London Pride, Spring Sprinter and Sticky Wicket on handpump, 15 wines by the glass and several malt whiskies and gins; background music, board games and TV.

Quite a choice of food includes grilled sardines with pesto, meze platter, rigatoni pasta with tomato, spinach, rosemary and chilli breadcrumbs, chicken caesar salad, moroccan-style lamb tagine, pork chop with fennel coleslaw, roast sweet potato and apple ketchup, beer-battered cod and chips, cumberland sausages with mash and onion gravy, sirloin steak with chips and a choice of sauce, and puddings such as apple and blackberry crumble and bread and butter pudding with custard; steak night is Friday. *Benchmark main dish: tea- and hop-smoked haddock with a poached egg and hollandaise £15.00. Two-course evening meal £21.00.*

Fullers ~ Manager Paul Stephens ~ Real ale ~ Open 11-11; 12-10.30 Sun ~ Bar food 12-9; 12-7 Sun ~ Restaurant ~ Children welcome ~ Dogs welcome ~ Wi-fi ~ Quiz night Weds *Recommended by Geoff and Ann Marston, Edward and William Johnston, Heather and Richard Jones*

ENGLEFIELD GREEN
Bailiwick ♀ ◖

SU9869 Map 2

(01784) 477877 – www.brunningandprice.co.uk/bailiwick
Wick Road; TW20 0HN

Fine position by parkland for busy pub, with lots of interest in various bars and dining rooms, well liked food and drink and super staff

Smaller than many of the other Brunning & Price pubs, this busy place has an open-plan bar area at the front (where dogs are allowed) with cushioned dining chairs around wooden tables on rugs and bare boards, and a pretty Victorian fireplace with a large mirror above. Stools line the counter where knowledgable, warmly friendly staff serve Phoenix Brunning & Price Original, Rebellion IPA, Windsor & Eton Parklife and a guest beer on handpump, 21 good wines by the glass and farm cider. Steps lead down to a dining area and on again to a bigger room with caramel-coloured leather dining chairs, banquettes and tables of every size. Throughout there are elegant metal chandeliers, prints and black and white photographs, lots of house plants and windowsills full of old stone and glass bottles. Seats and tables on the small front terrace overlook ancient woodland, and a circular walk leads from the pub and follows the south-east corner of Windsor Great Park – you can also see the polo lawns, Virginia Water lake and the vast expanses of landscaped parkland. There's no car park but there are 20 free spaces in the long lay-by on Wick Road; if these are full there's a large pay-on-entry car park alongside.

As well as weekend brunch (9-11am), the good, popular food includes sandwiches, scallops with pea purée and crisp parma ham, rabbit, ham hock and tarragon croquettes with piccalilli, wild mushroom, spinach and gruyère quiche with potato salad, steak burger with toppings, coleslaw and chips, confit pork belly with caramelised apple purée, charred asparagus, almonds and marjoram jus, malaysian fish stew with pak choi, lamb rump with potato rösti, salsa verde and red wine jus, and puddings such as dark chocolate torte with raspberry sorbet and crème brûlée. *Benchmark main dish: braised lamb shoulder with dauphinoise potatoes and rosemary gravy £17.95. Two-course evening meal £22.00.*

Brunning & Price ~ Manager Paolo Corgiolu ~ Real ale ~ Open 11-11; 12-10.30 Sun ~ Bar food 12-9.30 (9 Sun) ~ Children welcome but only in downstairs dining room after 6pm; no prams ~ Dogs allowed in bar ~ Wi-fi *Recommended by Sophie Ellison, Donald Allsopp, Miles Green, Alexander and Trish Gendall*

ESHER
Marneys

TQ1566 Map 3

(020) 8398 4444 – www.marneys.co.uk

Alma Road (one-way), Weston Green; heading N on A309 from A307 roundabout; after 0.5 miles turn left into Lime Tree Avenue (signposted to All Saints Parish Church), then left at T junction into Chestnut Avenue; KT10 8JN

Country-feeling pub with good value food and attractive garden

Cottagey and rather charming, this friendly little pub feels surprisingly rural – given the area. The chatty low-beamed bar has a good mix of customers, Fullers London Pride, Sharps Doom Bar and Youngs Bitter on handpump, 16 wines by the glass, ten malt whiskies and perhaps horse-racing on the unobtrusive corner TV. To the left, past a little cast-iron woodburning stove, the dining area has big pine tables, pews, pale country kitchen chairs and cottagey blue-curtained windows; background music. There are seats and wooden tables on the front terrace, which has views over the wooded common, village church and duck pond, and more seats on the decked area in the pleasantly planted sheltered garden. The pub is handy for visiting Hampton Court Palace.

At fair prices for the area, the well liked food includes sandwiches, baked camembert with chutney, king scallops and chorizo with cauliflower purée and balsamic reduction, steak in ale pie, thai-style salmon fishcakes with sweet chilli sauce, lamb burger with goats cheese, caramelised onions and fries, pear, roquefort and walnut salad, sausages with mustard mash and onion gravy, and puddings such as hot chocolate brownie and sticky toffee pudding. *Benchmark main dish: crab salad £13.50. Two-course evening meal £20.00.*

Free house ~ Licensee Thomas Duxberry ~ Real ale ~ Open 11-11; 12-10.30 Sun ~ Bar food 12-2.30, 6-9; 12-3.30 Sun; not Fri-Sun evenings ~ Restaurant ~ Children welcome away from bar ~ Dogs allowed in bar ~ Wi-fi *Recommended by Belinda May, Tom and Ruth Rees, Julie Braeburn, Dan and Nicki Barton*

MICKLEHAM
Running Horses

TQ1753 Map 3

(01372) 372279 – www.therunninghorses.co.uk

Old London Road (B2209); RH5 6DU

Country pub with plenty of customers in bar and dining rooms, enjoyable food and drink and seats on big front terrace; bedrooms

The stylish and spacious bar here has cushioned wall settles and other dining chairs around straightforward tables on parquet flooring, racing cartoons and Hogarth prints on the walls, lots of race tickets hanging from a beam and a log fire in an inglenook fireplace; some wood-panelled booths have red leather banquettes. Stools line the counter where friendly, helpful staff serve Brakspears Bitter and Oxford Gold, Fullers London Pride and a monthly guest beer on handpump and around 20 wines by the glass; background music. The panelled restaurant is furnished with an attractive mix of upholstered and wooden dining chairs around a medley of tables on tartan carpet. On a warm day, the front terrace is a fine place to sit among the pretty flowering tubs and hanging baskets, and there's a peaceful view of the old church with its strange stubby steeple. Parking is in a narrow lane (you can also park on the main road).

Food is good and includes lunchtime sandwiches, black pudding and pancetta croquettes with truffle mayonnaise, twice-baked cheddar soufflé with grain mustard and spinach, salmon and herb fishcake with pea purée, a poached egg and hollandaise, caramelised white onion tarte tatin with roasted chicory, stilton, pear and walnut salad, duck breast with parsnip, blackberries and port, sea bass with sauce vierge, olive-crushed potatoes and grilled fennel, beef wellington with dauphinoise potatoes and madeira sauce, and puddings such as treacle tart with clotted cream and hot chocolate mousse with salted caramel ice-cream. *Benchmark main dish: calves liver and bacon £14.00. Two-course evening meal £20.50.*

Brakspears ~ Manager Iain Huddy ~ Real ale ~ Open 12-11 ~ Bar food 12-3, 6-9 (10 Fri, Sat); 12-6 Sun ~ Restaurant ~ Children welcome ~ Dogs allowed in bar ~ Wi-fi ~ Bedrooms: /£125 *Recommended by Ian Phillips, Ron Corbett, David and Sally Frost, Professor James Burke, Jennifer and Nicholas Thompson*

 MILFORD   SU9542   Map 2

Refectory ♀ ◖

(01483) 413820 – www.brunningandprice.co.uk/refectory
Portsmouth Road; GU8 5HJ

Beamed and timbered rooms of much character, six real ales and other thoughtful drinks and well liked food

This is a lovely golden stone and timbered building – it's hard to think that it grew from what was a lowly cattle barn. The L-shaped, mainly open-plan rooms are spacious and interesting with exposed stone walls, stalling and standing timbers creating separate seating areas, strikingly heavy beams and a couple of big log fires in fine stone fireplaces. A two-tiered and balconied part at one end has a wall covered with huge brass platters; elsewhere there are nice old photographs and a variety of paintings. Dining chairs and dark wooden tables are grouped on wooden, quarry-tiled or carpeted floors, and there are bookshelves, big pot plants, stone bottles on windowsills and fresh flowers. High wooden bar stools line the long counter where they serve Phoenix Brunning & Price Original, Hogs Back TEA, Dark Star Hophead and three guests such as Adnams Broadside, Crafty Brewing Dunsfold Best and Little Beer Corporation Little & Often on handpump, a dozen wines by the glass, 50 gins, around 80 malt whiskies and two farm ciders. The back courtyard – adjacent to the characterful pigeonry – has teak tables and chairs. Wheelchair facilities and disabled parking.

A fine choice of modern food includes sandwiches, prawn and crayfish cocktail, chicken liver pâté with apple and cider chutney, five-bean and sweet potato chilli with coriander rice, guacamole, taco crisps and lime crème fraîche, beer-battered cod and chips, warm crispy beef salad with sweet chilli dressing and cashew nuts, chicken, ham hock and leek pie, braised lamb shoulder with minted potatoes and rosemary gravy, sea bass and king prawn laksa with coconut noodles and pak choi, and puddings such as crème brûlée and eton mess. *Benchmark main dish: steak burger with toppings, coleslaw and chips £12.95. Two-course evening meal £21.00.*

Brunning & Price ~ Manager Nicholas King ~ Real ale ~ Open 10.30am-11pm; 12-10.30 Sun ~ Bar food 12-10 (9.30 Sun) ~ Restaurant ~ Children welcome ~ Dogs allowed in bar ~ Wi-fi *Recommended by Miss A E Dare, Brian and Susan Wylie, Jeff Davies, Edward May*

 NORWOOD HILL   TQ2342   Map 3

Fox Revived ♀ ◖

(01293) 229270 – www.brunningandprice.co.uk/foxrevived
Leigh–Charlwood back road; RH6 0ET

Extended, well run pub with attractive, interesting bar and dining areas, excellent staff, interesting food and a fine range of drinks; seats outside

There's a five-mile walk right from the door of this recently refurbished pub, and the seats and tables on the stone terrace in the garden look over the hills beyond. Inside, life centres around the bustling bar where they keep Phoenix Brunning & Price Original and Surrey Hills Shere Drop with guests such as Adnams Freewheel, Dark Star Festival and Long Man Long Blonde on handpump, 18 wines by the glass, 17 rums, 40 gins and 20 whiskies all served by courteous, helpful staff; background music and board games. There are button-back armchairs and stools by open fires and the various dining areas and nooks are divided up by balustrading and standing timbers. Walls are hung with photos, prints and gilt-edged mirrors, big house plants are scattered here and there or arranged on windowsills, elegant metal chandeliers hang from ceilings and antique-style and high-backed leather dining chairs are grouped around tables of varying sizes on rugs, bare boards and carpet; one area has scatter cushions on a long L-shaped settle and lots of books on shelves.

Good, brasserie-style food includes sandwiches, scallops with crispy ham fritters and pea purée, korean chicken wings with kimchi salad, mussels with smoked bacon, leeks, cider and cream, blue cheese and potato pie with wholegrain mustard sauce, pork and leek sausages with mash and onion gravy, sicilian fish stew, sticky pork belly with watermelon, pineapple and pickled ginger salad with chilli dressing, rump steak with dijon and tarragon butter, portobello mushrooms and chips, and puddings such as crème brûlée and sticky toffee pudding with toffee sauce. *Benchmark main dish: steak burger with toppings, coleslaw and chips £12.95. Two-course evening meal £21.00.*

Brunning & Price ~ Manager Ryan Martinez ~ Real ale ~ Open 10.30am-11pm (10.30pm Sun) ~ Bar food 12-10 (9.30 Sun) ~ Restaurant ~ Children welcome ~ Dogs allowed in bar ~ Wi-fi *Recommended by Gail and Frank Hackett, Lucy and Giles Gibbon, Belinda Stamp, Andy and Louise Ramwell*

RIPLEY

Anchor ⊛ 🍷

TQ0556 Map 2

(01483) 211866 – www.ripleyanchor.co.uk
High Street; GU23 6AE

Stylish dining pub with first class food, real ales, friendly service and sunny courtyard

Best known for its creative food, this is a 16th-c, brick-built former almshouse. The several low-ceilinged rooms are interlinked and have heavy beams, slate floors and open fires and are decorated in a stylish, simple way that's immediately inviting. There are church chairs around polished tables in the bar, dark wooden chairs and cushioned wall seats in the dining areas, contemporary paintwork or exposed brick walls and elegant flower arrangements. Despite the emphasis on eating, there's an easy-going atmosphere and those just wanting a drink and a chat are more than welcome. Timothy Taylors Landlord and a couple of guests such as Courage Best and Wimbledon Common Pale Ale on handpump and ten good wines by the glass; background music. Outside, a sunny, decked back courtyard has cushioned wicker chairs and sofas.

As well as sandwiches, the imaginative food includes leek ballotine, pickled shiitake, a soft poached egg and mushroom milk sauce, pressed pig head with black pudding and gribiche sauce, roast leek tart with garlic purée, cep ketchup and mushroom shortbread, burger with toppings, red onion marmalade and skinny chips, guinea fowl breast with swede purée and mustard sauce, gurnard with dill, carrot and coconut sauce, and puddings such as caramelised mango, pine nut meringue and lemon and rhubarb ballotine with whisky gel and rice pudding ice-cream; they also offer a two- and three-course set menu (12-2.30pm, 6-7pm). *Benchmark main dish: rib-eye steak with sauerkraut and wild mushrooms £26.00. Two-course evening meal £25.00.*

~ Licensee Michael Wall-Palmer ~ Real ale ~ Open 12-11 (9 Sun); closed Mon ~ Bar food 12-2.30, 6-9.30; 12-9.30 Fri, Sat; 12-8 Sun ~ Restaurant ~ Children welcome until 7.30pm ~ Wi-fi *Recommended by Geoffrey Kemp, Robin Waters, Mary and Douglas McDowell, Andrew Wall*

SHAMLEY GREEN
Red Lion
TQ0343 Map 3

(01483) 892202 – www.redlionshamleygreen.com
The Green; GU5 0UB

Pleasant dining pub with popular food and attractive gardens

L ooking over the village green and cricket pitch, this is a friendly pub with a wide mix of chatty customers. The two interconnected bars are fairly traditional with a mix of new and old wooden tables, chairs and cushioned settles on bare boards and red carpet, stripped standing timbers, fresh white walls, deep red ceilings and open fires. Arundel Sussex Gold, Sharps Doom Bar and Youngs Bitter on handpump, 11 wines by the glass and several gins and malt whiskies; background music. There are plenty of hand-made rustic tables and benches outside, both at the front and at the back – which is more secluded and has seats on a heated, covered terrace and grassed dining areas.

🍴 Tasty food includes sandwiches, warm bacon and scallop salad, crispy duck with oranges and hoisin sauce, greek-style spinach and feta pie, sausages and mash with onion gravy, lambs liver and bacon with red wine gravy, beer-battered haddock and chips, lamb shank in red wine sauce with shallots and redcurrant jelly, beef curry, chicken breast stuffed with feta, sun-dried tomatoes, lemon and rosemary with fries, and puddings. *Benchmark main dish: veal schnitzel with a fried egg and fries £15.95. Two-course evening meal £20.00.*

Punch ~ Lease Debbie Ersser ~ Real ale ~ Open 11.30-11; 12-10 Sun (12-8 in winter) ~ Bar food 12-2.30 (3 Sat), 6.30-9.30; 12-3, 6.30-8.30 Sun; no food Sun evening in winter ~ Restaurant ~ Children welcome ~ Dogs allowed in bar ~ Wi-fi *Recommended by Graeme Bennet, Gerry and Pam Pollard, Margaret McDonald*

SUNBURY
Flower Pot 🛏
TQ1068 Map 3

(01932) 780741 – www.theflowerpotsunbury.co.uk
1.6 miles from M3 junction 1; follow Lower Sunbury sign from exit roundabout, then at Thames Street turn right; the pub is on next corner, with Green Street; TW16 6AA

Former coaching inn with appealing, contemporary bar and dining room, real ales and all-day food; bedrooms

A former coaching inn in a villagey area with waterside walks, this handsome place has elegant wrought-iron balconies and pretty summer hanging baskets. The airy bar has leather tub chairs around copper-topped tables, high chairs upholstered in brown and beige tartan around equally high tables in pale wood, attractive flagstones, contemporary paintwork and stools against the counter; there's also a couple of comfortably plush burgundy armchairs. The bar leads into a dining area with pale blue-painted and dark wooden cushioned dining chairs around an assortment of partly painted tables on bare boards, artwork on papered walls and a large gilt-edged mirror over an open fireplace; candles in glass jars, fresh flowers, background music and newspapers. Brakspears Bitter, Marstons 61 Deep and

Wychwood Hobgoblin on handpump and 15 wines by the glass. A side terrace has wood and metal tables and chairs. Bedrooms are smart and comfortable.

🍴 As well as breakfasts for non-residents, the popular food includes chicken liver pâté with chutney, tiger prawn skewers with coriander, lime and chilli yoghurt, sharing boards, roast chicken and crispy chorizo salad with parmesan and aioli, linguine with asparagus, spinach, roasted red peppers and creamy tomato and mascarpone sauce, battered hake and chips, burger with toppings, coleslaw and chips, stone-baked pizzas, a pie of the day, and puddings such as seasonal crumble and chocolate brownie with chocolate sauce and vanilla ice-cream. *Benchmark main dish: corn-fed chicken with dauphinoise potatoes and pink peppercorn sauce £12.95. Two-course evening meal £20.00.*

Authentic Inns ~ Tenant Simon Bailey ~ Real ale ~ Open 7am-11pm; 8am-11pm Sat, Sun ~ Bar food 7am-3pm, 6-9pm (10pm Fri, Sat); 8am-9pm Sun ~ Restaurant ~ Children welcome ~ Dogs allowed in bar ~ Wi-fi ~ Live music last Fri of month ~ Bedrooms: /£99
Recommended by Edward Edmonton, Pauline and Mark Evans, Diana and Bertie Farr

WALTON ON THE HILL
Blue Ball

TQ2255 Map 3

(01737) 819003 – www.theblueball.co.uk
Not far from M25 junction 8; Deans Lane, off B2220 by pond; KT20 7UE

Popular pub with spreading drinking and dining areas, helpful staff, well liked food and drink and lots of outside seating

Always busy with a wide mix of customers, this sizeable pub is well run by friendly, efficient staff. The entrance bar has a chatty atmosphere, colourful leather-topped stools at the counter plus rugs on bare boards, house plants on windowsills, all manner of old pictures and photographs on the walls, antique-style cushioned, farmhouse and high-backed kitchen chairs around tables of every size, and a large wine cage. A beer named for the pub (from Caledonian), Caledonian Deuchars IPA, St Austell Tribute and a changing guest ale on handpump and good wines by the glass. Leading back from here, several dining rooms have multicoloured button-back leather banquettes, similar chairs and tables on more rugs and wooden floors, bookshelves, gilt-edged mirrors, and a big central conical open fire; background music. The outside terrace has lots of seats and tables as well as a fire pit under a gazebo, and you can hire cabanas for a private group (you will need to book in advance, especially in warm weather when they're extremely popular).

🍴 Well thought-of food includes sandwiches (until 6pm), salt and pepper squid with paprika aioli, chicken liver parfait with red onion marmalade, honey-glazed ham and free-range eggs, goats cheese burger with sweet potato fries, pork and leek sausages with mash and onion gravy, veal and pork meatballs on tagliatelle with herbed tomato sauce, bacon-wrapped cod loin with truffle cream and mash, onglet steak with rosemary butter and fries, and puddings such as blueberry cream and cider jelly trifle and sticky toffee pudding with toffee sauce. *Benchmark main dish: burger with toppings, coleslaw and skinny fries £11.95. Two-course evening meal £20.50.*

Whiting & Hammond ~ Manager Jo Thiede ~ Real ale ~ Open 10am-11pm; 9am-11pm Sat; 9am-10.30pm Sun ~ Bar food 12-9.30; 9am-9.30pm Sat; 9-9 Sun ~ Restaurant ~ Children welcome ~ Dogs allowed in bar ~ Wi-fi *Recommended by Caroline Sullivan, Valerie Sayer, Charlie Parker, Maggie and Matthew Lyons, Charles Fraser*

Real ale may be served from handpumps, electric pumps (not just the on-off switches used for keg beer) or – common in Scotland – tall taps called founts (pronounced 'fonts') where a separate pump pushes the beer up under air pressure.

WEST END
SU9461   Map 2

The Inn West End 🔯 ⚑

(01276) 858652 – www.the-inn.co.uk

Just under 2.5 miles from M3 junction 3; A322 S, on right; GU24 9PW

Surrey Dining Pub of the Year

Plenty of dining and drinking space in carefully refurbished rooms, excellent wines and inventive food; bedrooms

The enthusiastic, hard-working and hands-on licensees here tell us their little wine shop is to be converted into two more very well equipped and comfortable bedrooms; some of these rooms allow dogs and one has disabled facilites. Breakfasts are first class. It's an airy place with a relaxed, friendly atmosphere, and the bar has white-painted beams, slatted and cushioned wooden benches and elegant chairs around a mix of tables on bare floorboards, pretty curtains, a large central barrel and chairs against the counter where they keep Fullers London Pride, Otter Bitter and Thurstons Horsell Gold on handpump. Wine plays a big role, with 20 by the glass from a fantastic list of around 500 (Iberia is the speciality); they also have several sherries, sweet wines and port, 34 malt whiskies, 17 gins and six vodkas. Do ask about the unusual clock. There's an extended restaurant and a lounge area with books on shelves, daily papers and an open fire; Sunny and Teddy are the pub dogs. The pretty garden and terrace have plenty of seats for warm weather. Children are only allowed if dining with adults.

As well as breakfasts (7-10.30am weekdays, 8.30-11am weekends) and championing local game and other first class produce from the area, the impressive food includes sandwiches, seared king scallops with cauliflower purée and chorizo, goats cheese bonbons with pickled beetroot, pear and walnuts, wild mushroom tagliatelle with leeks and parmesan cream, hake fillet with pancetta and garlic crust, creamed leeks and parmentier potatoes, slow-braised ox cheek with bone marrow crumb and red wine jus, haunch of red deer with carrot purée, roasted root vegetables and redcurrant jus, and puddings such as Baileys and chocolate cheesecake with honeycomb and apple and blackberry crumble with crème anglaise; they also offer a two-course set menu (not Friday evening or weekends). *Benchmark main dish: venison loin with mash and broccoli £20.00. Two-course evening meal £26.00.*

Free house ~ Licensees Gerry and Ann Price ~ Real ale ~ Open 7am-11pm; 7am-midnight Fri; 8.30am-midnight Sat; 8.30am-10.30pm Sun ~ Bar food 12-2.30, 6-9.30; 12-3, 6-9 Sun ~ Restaurant ~ Dogs allowed in bedrooms ~ Wi-fi ~ Bedrooms: /£90 *Recommended by Guy Vowles, Edward Mirzoeff, Susan and John Douglas, Peter and Alison Steadman, Guy Consterdine, Alison and Dan Richardson*

Also Worth a Visit in Surrey

Besides the fully inspected pubs, you might like to try these pubs that have been recommended to us and described by readers. Do tell us what you think of them: feedback@goodguides.com

ALBURY   TQ0447
Drummond Arms (01483) 202039
Off A248 SE of Guildford; The Street; GU5 9AG Modernised 19th-c pub in pretty village; four ales such as Adnams, Courage and Hogs Back, good choice of wines and enjoyable food from sandwiches and sharing plates up, opened-up bar with leather chesterfields, log fire and newspapers, parquet-floored dining room, conservatory; children welcome, good-sized pretty back garden by little River Tillingbourne, summer barbecues and hog roasts, pleasant walks nearby, nine bedrooms, open all day, food all day weekends. *(Jim and Sue James)*

ALFOLD
TQ0435
Alfold Barn (01403) 752288
Horsham Road, A281; GU6 8JE
Beautifully preserved 16th-c building with
bar and restaurant, very good locally sourced
home-made food from daily changing menu
with some emphasis on fish and shellfish
including lobster (Sun booking esential),
friendly attentive service, up to three well
kept ales from nearby breweries, beams
and rafters, mixed furniture on flagstones
or carpet, warming log fires; children
welcome, garden with play area and
animals including Rosie the goat, closed
Sun evening, Mon. *(Gerry and Pam Pollard)*

ALFOLD
TQ0334
Three Compasses (01483) 275729
Dunsfold Road; GU6 8HY Revamped
400-year-old pub under new management;
well kept Otter and a couple of guests, good
fairly priced food (not Sun evening, Mon) in
bar and restaurant areas, big log fire; regular
quiz and live music nights; children and dogs
welcome, good-sized garden, on back lane to
former Dunsfold Aerodrome (now Dunsfold
Park with little museum), Wey & Arun Canal
nearby, open all day. *(Gerry and Pam Pollard)*

ASH VALE
SU8952
Swan (01252) 325212
*Hutton Road, off Ash Vale Road
(B3411) via Heathvale Bridge Road;
GU12 5HA* Three-room Chef & Brewer on
Basingstoke Canal, wide choice of popular
well priced food including evening set
menu (Mon-Thurs), up to five real ales and
extensive wine list, friendly service, mix of
furniture on wood or carpeted floors, beams
and timbers, large log fires; background
music; children and dogs (in designated
area) welcome, garden with seating alongside
fenced canal, open (and food) all day. *(KC)*

BATTS CORNER
SU8140
Blue Bell (01252) 792801
Batts Corner; GU10 4EX Busy tucked-way
country pub with linked stone-floor rooms,
light fresh décor and mix of furniture
including sofas by big log fire, well kept
ales such as Frensham, Langham and
Triple fff, good home-made food from
sandwiches to popular Sun lunch (must
book), helpful friendly staff; children
and dogs on leads welcome, attractive
spacious garden with rolling views, summer
barbecues and good play area, handy for
Alice Holt Forest, open all day Sat, till 8pm
Sun. *(Tony and Jill Radnor, Patric Curwen)*

BLETCHINGLEY
TQ3250
Bletchingley Arms (01883) 743711
High Street (A25); RH1 4PE Spacious
modernised Barons group pub with plenty
of opened-up areas (some steps) including
beamed part with flagstones and woodburner,
good choice of well prepared sensibly
priced food from snacks up, three real
ales, plenty of wines by the glass and good
range of gins, friendly staff; background
music, newspapers, sports TV; children
and dogs (in bar) welcome, outside seating
areas with own bar, beach huts and good
play area, open all day. *(Ian Phillips)*

BLETCHINGLEY
TQ3250
Red Lion (01883) 743342
Castle Street (A25), Redhill side; RH1 4NU
Modernised and well looked-after beamed
village dining pub, decent range of good
home-made food such as steak and kidney
pudding and beef stroganoff, well kept Greene
King ales and a dozen wines by the glass,
friendly staff; frequent music nights;
children welcome, heated part-covered
terrace, secret garden, open (and food)
all day. *(Liz and Martin Eldon)*

BLINDLEY HEATH
TQ3645
Red Barn (01342) 830820
*Tandridge Lane, just off B2029, which
is off A22; RH7 6LL* Splendid farmhouse/
barn conversion; contemporary furnishings
alongside 17th-c beams and timbers, central
glass-sided woodburner with soaring flue,
large model plane suspended from rafters,
one wall with shelves of books, another
hung with antlers, clever partitioning
creating cosier areas too; red cooking range
and big wooden tables in farmhouse-style
room, adjacent bar with sofas by large
fireplace, one or two real ales and good
wine list, food and service can be good;
background and some live music; children
and dogs (in bar) welcome, solid granite
tables on lawn, open all day. *(Tony Scott)*

BRAMLEY
TQ0044
★ Jolly Farmer (01483) 893355
High Street; GU5 0HB Family-run village
pub with traditional beamed interior packed
with collections of plates and old bottles,
enamel signs, sewing machines, antique
tools and so forth, timbered semi-partitions
and open fire, Bowman, Youngs and up
to six guests, a couple of real ciders and
over a dozen wines by the glass, fairly
pubby food including good Sun carvery;
background music, board games, free
wi-fi; children and dogs (in bar) welcome,
tables out by car park, walks up St Martha's
Hill and handy for Winkworth Arboretum
(NT), bedrooms, open all day. *(Mrs Zara
Elliott, Peter Hailey, Sarah and John Webb)*

BROCKHAM
TQ1949
Inn on the Green (01737) 845101
Brockham Green; RH3 7JS Restaurant
pub facing village green (part of the small
Grumpy Mole group), good food from
traditional choices up including cook-your-
own steaks on a hot stone, helpful friendly
service, well kept Fullers London Pride
and Surrey Hills Shere Drop, several wines
by the glass, afternoon teas, conservatory;

children welcome, picnic-sets out at front, garden behind, open all day, food all day weekends. *(Milena Duncan, Malcolm Phillips)*

BROCKHAM
TQ1949
Royal Oak (01737) 843241
Brockham Green; RH3 7JS Nice spot on charming village green below North Downs; bare-boards bar and light airy dining area, well kept Fullers, Sharps, Shepherds Neame and Youngs, freshly cooked pub food at reasonable prices, newspapers and log fires; quiz last Tues of the month, jazz first Weds; children and dogs allowed, tables out in front looking across to fine church, more seats in back garden, handy for Greensand Way, open all day. *(Ian Phillips)*

BROOK
SU9238
Dog & Pheasant (01428) 682763
Haslemere Road (A286); GU8 5UJ Popular friendly pub looking across busy road to cricket green, long beamed bar divided up by standing timbers, cushioned wall settles, open fire in brick fireplace, four well kept ales such as Ringwood and Sharps from linenfold counter, dining area on right, further room to left with big inglenook, generally well liked food including Weds grill night; children and dogs welcome, picnic-sets on back decking and grass, play equipment, open all day, food till 4pm Sun. *(Pauline and Mark Evans)*

BURROWHILL
SU9763
Four Horseshoes (01276) 856257
B383 N of Chobham; GU24 8QP Busy pub attractively set by village green, updated interior with beams and log fires, up to four well kept ales including Fullers London Pride and a Caledonian house beer (Shoes), popular food from sandwiches and sharing boards up, cheerful helpful staff, dining extension; children, dogs and muddy boots welcome, tables out at front (some under ancient yew), also back terrace and garden with picnic-sets and deck chairs, open all day (Sun till 7pm). *(Mr and Mrs Johnson-Poensgen, Ian Phillips)*

CARSHALTON
TQ2764
Hope (020) 8240 1255
West Street; SM5 2PR Chatty community-owned local; Downton, Windsor & Eton and five guests, also craft beers, real cider/perry and over 50 bottled beers, generous low-priced pubby food (limited evening choice), 1950s-feel U-shaped bar with open fire, lots of pump clips, larger back room with bar billiards; live acoustic music second Weds of month, regular beer and cider festivals, board games; dogs welcome, garden, open all day. *(Geordie Simms)*

CATERHAM
TQ3254
Harrow (01883) 343260
Stanstead Road, Whitehill; CR3 6AJ Simple 16th-c beamed pub high up in open country by North Downs Way; L-shaped bare-boards bar and carpeted back dining area, several real ales (sometimes tapped from the cask) such as Ringwood and Fullers, well-liked food including daily specials (no food Sun evening), friendly service and good local atmosphere; beer festivals; children and dogs welcome, garden picnic-sets, popular with walkers and cyclists, open all day. *(Graham Smart)*

CHARLESHILL
SU8844
Donkey (01252) 702124
B3001 Milford–Farnham near Tilford; coming from Elstead, turn left as soon as you see pub sign; GU10 2AU Old-fashioned beamed dining pub with enjoyable home-made food including set menus and other deals, up to three well kept changing ales and good choice of wines by the glass, prompt friendly service, conservatory restaurant; children and dogs welcome, attractive garden with paddock for much-loved donkeys Pip and Dusty, good walks, open all day weekends. *(Maria and Bertie Farr)*

CHARLWOOD
TQ2441
Half Moon (01293) 863414
The Street; RH6 0DS Old pub next to churchyard, good-sized L-shaped bar with front part open to original upstairs windows, well kept Sharps Doom Bar, St Austell Tribute and a guest, enjoyable sensibly priced traditional food from sandwiches up, friendly service, back dining room; children and dogs (in bar) welcome, picnic-sets in nice courtyard area, attractive village handy for Gatwick Airport, open all day, food all day weekends. *(Tony Scott)*

CHERTSEY
TQ0466
Olde Swan (01932) 562129
Windsor Street; KT16 8AY Former coaching house run by McLean Inns, generous helpings of popular reasonably priced food including pizzas, burgers and good Sun lunch, Sharps Doom Bar, Thwaites Wainwright and a couple of guests from well stocked bar, good friendly service, opened-up split-level interior with rugs on bare boards, candles on tables, comfortable seating and lots of pictures, mirrors and other bits and pieces; weekend live music; children and dogs welcome, nice outside area, seven bedrooms, open all day, food till 6pm Sun. *(Hunter and Christine Wright)*

CHIDDINGFOLD
SU9635
★Crown (01428) 682255
The Green (A283); GU8 4TX Lovely 700-year-old timbered building with strong sense of history; bar and linked dining rooms with massive beams (some over 2-ft thick), oak panelling, moulded plasterwork and fine stained-glass windows, magnificently carved fireplace, mate's and other pubby chairs, cushioned wall seats and some nice antique

tables, lots of portraits, simple split-level back public bar with open fire, up to five changing ales and several wines by the glass, enjoyable often interesting food (all day Fri-Sun); quiz first Thurs of the month; children welcome (there's a playroom), dogs in some areas, seats out looking across village green to interesting church, more tables in sheltered central courtyard, character creaky bedrooms, open all day Fri-Sun. *(Chris and Pauline Sexton, Alastair and Sheree Hepburn)*

CHIPSTEAD   TQ2555
Well House   (01737) 830640
Chipstead signed with Mugswell off A217, N of M25 junction 8; CR5 3SQ
Originally three 16th-c cottages (converted from tea rooms to pub in 1955); log fires in all three rooms, low beams and rustic décor, bric-a-brac and pewter tankards hanging from ceiling, well kept Fullers, Surrey Hills and local guests, Millwhite's cider, food from ciabattas up, friendly staff, small conservatory, resident ghost is Harry the Monk; Tues quiz, free wi-fi; children and dogs allowed (they have cats), large pleasing hillside garden with ancient well (reputed to be mentioned in the Domesday Book), delightful country setting, open all day. *(Graham Smart)*

CHOBHAM   SU9761
Sun   (01276) 859190
High Street, off A319; GU24 8AF
Pub-brasserie (part of Raymond Blanc's White Brasserie group) with spacious but cosy beamed and timbered interior; four real ales, lots of wines by the glass and some interesting gins, good food (separate bar and restaurant menus) including set deal till 6.30pm, friendly helpful service; children and dogs (in bar) welcome, disabled access, nice back garden, open (and food) all day. *(Dr Martin Owton)*

CHURT   SU8538
Crossways   (01428) 714323
Corner of A287 and Hale House Lane; GU10 2JE Friendly down-to-earth local attracting good mix of customers; quarry-tiled public bar and carpeted saloon with panelling and plush banquettes, good beer range (some served direct from the cellar) and four real ciders, enjoyable well priced pub lunches (not Sun) including home-made pies, evening food Weds only, cheerful staff; no credit cards or children under 10, darts, TV, beer/cider festivals; dogs welcome, picnic-sets in lawned garden, open all day Fri, Sat. *(Tony and Jill Radnor)*

CLAYGATE   TQ1563
★ Foley   (01372) 462021
Hare Lane; KT10 0LZ Beautifully restored 19th-c Youngs pub; pubby part at front with wooden tables and chairs on bare boards, leather armchairs and sofas by Victorian fireplace, lots of interconnected sitting and dining areas leading off, their well kept ales and a guest, 30 wines by the glass, interesting spirits and good range of coffees and teas, well thought-of food from open kitchen, some prices on the high side; background music, sports TV, daily papers and free wi-fi; children and dogs (in bar) welcome, seats on two-level terrace, good modern bedrooms, open (and food) all day including breakfast from 7.30am (8.30am Sun). *(David and Sally Frost)*

CLAYGATE   TQ1563
Hare & Hounds   (01372) 465149
The Green; KT10 0JL Renovated 19th-c flower-decked village pub, good sensibly priced french food along with some pub favourites in bar or smaller restaurant, nice wines and well kept changing ales including local Brightwater, friendly caring service; Sun quiz, regular live music, free wi-fi; children and dogs welcome, disabled access/loo, tables on attractive front terrace and in small back garden with play area, open (and food) all day, coffee and cakes from 10am. *(Sean, Geoffrey Kemp, Robin Waters)*

COBHAM   TQ1058
Cricketers   (01932) 862105
Downside Common; 3.75 miles from M25 junction 10; take A3 S, first left signed Effingham/Hatchford; at Black Swan pub (Ockham Lane) turn left for Downside, under motorway then right into Chilbrook Lane; at junction straight over down lane; KT11 3NX
Old pub recently refurbished by White Brasserie group; open-plan modernised areas with crooked standing timbers and low oak beams (some painted), wood and flagstoned floors, log fires, Sharps Doom Bar, Timothy Taylors Landlord and a guest, lots of wines by the glass and good choice of popular food from bar meals up prepared in open kitchen, friendly efficient service; background music, Mon quiz; children and dogs (not in restaurant) welcome, lovely views across village green from terrace, open (and food) all day. *(Jim and Sue James)*

COBHAM   TQ1159
Running Mare   (01932) 862007
Tilt Road; KT11 3EZ Attractive old flower-decked pub overlooking green (can get very busy); well kept Fullers, Hogs Back and Youngs, good food including popular Sun lunch, efficient friendly service, two timbered bars and restaurant; regular live music; children very welcome, a few tables out at front and on rose-covered back terrace, open all day. *(Robin Waters)*

COLDHARBOUR   TQ1544
Plough   (01306) 711793
Village signposted in the network of small roads around Leith Hill; RH5 6HD Former 17th-c beamed coaching house refurbished and opened up under present welcoming licensees – also incorporates

the village shop; own-brew Leith Hill beers and guests, proper cider and a dozen wines by the glass, good popular food in bar or restaurant; background music, TV, free wi-fi, events in barn room such as live music, food fairs, bridge nights and french lessons; children, walkers and dogs welcome, seats out at front and on back terrace overlooking fields, comfortable bedrooms, open all day. *(Ian and Rose Lock)*

COMPTON SU9646
★**Withies** (01483) 421158
Withies Lane; pub signed from B3000; GU3 1JA Civilised gently old-fashioned 16th-c pub with atmospheric low-beamed bar, some 17th-c carved panels between windows, splendid art nouveau settle among old sewing-machine tables, log fire in massive inglenook, well kept Adnams, Greene King, Hogs Back and Sharps, very well liked food (restaurant choices can be pricey and they add a service charge), efficient bow-tied staff; children welcome, no dogs inside, seats on terrace, under apple trees and creeper-hung arbour, flower-edged neat front lawn, on edge of Loseley Park, near Watts Gallery and Chapel, closed Sun evening. *(Ron Corbett, Helen and Brian Edgeley, Susan and John Douglas, Dr W I C Clark, Miss A E Dare)*

CRANLEIGH TQ0739
Park Hatch (01483) 274374
Bookhurst Road, Parkmead Estate – towards Shere; GU6 7DN Refurbished 17th-c brick and tile dining pub, low beams, flagstones and big inglenook with woodburner, enjoyable food cooked by owner-chef including set lunch menu, five well kept changing ales, good friendly service, new oak-framed dining extension; children and dogs (in some parts) welcome, garden picnic-sets, open all day (till 1am Fri, Sat), food all day Sat, till 6pm Sun. *(Mike Benton)*

CRANLEIGH TQ0539
★**Richard Onslow** (01483) 274922
High Street; GU6 8AU Busy Peach group pub with cheerful small bar, leather tub chairs and built-in sofa, slate-floored drinking area, Firebird, Greene King, Hook Norton and Surrey Hills, a proper cider and ten wines by the glass, good interesting food in two dining rooms with open fires and sizeable restaurant with pale tables on wood floor, modern flowery wallpaper and big windows overlooking the street; background music, board games, free wi-fi; children and dogs (in bar) welcome, seats out at front and in terraced back garden, ten smart well equipped bedrooms, open (and food) all day from 7am (7.30am weekends) for breakfast. *(Mike Benton, Jim and Sue James)*

DORKING TQ1649
Cricketers (01306) 889938
South Street; RH4 2JU Chatty and relaxed little Fullers local, up to five well kept ales and simple weekday lunchtime food, friendly service, some cricketing memorabilia on stripped-brick walls; events including beer festivals, Scalextric championship and onion-growing competition, darts, sports TV, free wi-fi; nice split-level suntrap back terrace, open all day. *(Professor James Burke)*

DORKING TQ1649
Old House at Home (01306) 889664
West Street; RH4 1BY Bustling old Youngs pub with opened-up beamed interior, good food from bar snacks up (not Sun evening, Mon), friendly staff; Fri live music; dogs welcome, back terrace with heated beach huts, closed Mon lunchtime, otherwise open all day (till 8pm Sun). *(Professor James Burke)*

DORMANSLAND TQ4042
Old House at Home (01342) 836828
West Street; RH7 6QP Friendly 19th-c village pub refurbished under new management; beamed bar with traditional furniture on parquet floor, two-way woodburner, Shepherd Neame ales and several wines by the glass from unusual barrel-fronted counter, good well priced traditional food (not Sun evening, Mon), restaurant with wood and stone floor, darts and TV in snug; some live music, free wi-fi; children and dogs (in bar) welcome, tables out in front, closed Mon lunchtime, otherwise open all day. *(Graham Smart)*

DORMANSLAND TQ4042
Plough (01342) 832933
Plough Road, off B2028 NE; RH7 6PS Friendly traditional old pub in quiet village; well kept Fullers, Harveys and Sharps, Weston's cider and decent wines, good choice of enjoyable lunchtime bar food including specials, thai restaurant (Mon-Sat), log fires and original features; children welcome, disabled facilities, good-sized garden, open all day. *(Tony Scott, Martin Day)*

DUNSFOLD TQ0036
Sun (01483) 200242
Off B2130 S of Godalming; GU8 4LE Old double-fronted pub with four rooms (brighter at the front), beams and some exposed brickwork, scrubbed pine furniture and two massive log fires, ales such as Adnams, Harveys and Sharps, decent wines and enjoyable reasonably priced home-made food including popular Sun lunch (best to book) and curry evenings, good friendly service; open mike nights, darts; children and dogs welcome, seats on terrace and common opposite, good walks. *(Jennifer and Nicholas Thompson)*

EASHING SU9543
★**Stag on the River** (01483) 421568
Lower Eashing, just off A3 southbound; GU7 2QG Civilised, gently upmarket riverside inn with Georgian façade masking much older interior; attractively opened-up

rooms including charming old-fashioned locals' bar with armchairs on red and black quarry tiles, cosy log-fire snug beyond, Hogs Back TEA, one or two Marstons-related ales and a beer badged for the pub, Hazy Hog cider, plenty of emphasis on food with several linked dining areas including river room up a couple of steps, attentive courteous staff; children welcome, dogs in bar, extensive terrace with wicker or wooden furniture under parasols (some by weir), picnic-sets on grass, seven bedrooms, open all day. *(Gerry and Pam Pollard)*

EAST CLANDON   TQ0551
★ **Queens Head** (01483) 222332
Just off A246 Guildford–Leatherhead; The Street; GU4 7RY Busy attractively refurbished dining pub in same small group as Duke of Cambridge at Tilford, Stag at Eashing and Wheatsheaf in Farnham; well liked food (best to book) from light dishes to good daily specials, set lunch deal (Mon-Thurs), a beer badged for them and a couple of guests from fine elm-topped counter, also Hazy Hog cider and nice wines by the glass, good friendly service, comfortable linked rooms, log fire in big inglenook; daily newspapers and free wi-fi, silent TV in bar; children welcome, tables out in front and on side terrace, handy for Hatchlands (NT), open (and food) all day Fri and Sat, shuts 9pm Sun. *(John Allman, John Evans)*

EFFINGHAM   TQ1153
Plough (01372) 458121
Orestan Lane; KT24 5SW Youngs pub with well kept ales, plenty of wines by the glass and decent home-made food including children's menu, friendly efficient staff, open interior around central bar, grey-painted beams, delft shelving and half panelling, wood floors, two coal-effect gas fires; plenty of tables on forecourt and in pretty garden with fruit trees, disabled access and parking, handy for Polesden Lacey (NT), closed Sun evening. *(Glen Locke)*

ELSTEAD   SU9043
Woolpack (01252) 703106
B3001 Milford–Farnham; GU8 6HD Comfortably modernised tile-hung dining pub run by italian family, enjoyable home-cooked food including stone-baked pizzas and weekly themed nights, cask-tapped ales and decent wines by the glass, friendly efficient service, long main bar, restaurant, open fires; children welcome, garden with picnic-sets, open all day Sun. *(Mary and Douglas McDowell)*

EPSOM   TQ2158
Rubbing House (01372) 745050
Langley Vale Road (on Epsom Downs Racecourse); KT18 5LJ Restaurant pub popular for its fantastic racecourse views – can get very busy but staff cope well; attractive modern décor, sensibly

priced promptly served food including children's menu, tables perhaps a little close together, well kept ales such as Sharps and plenty of wines by the glass from good list, upper balcony for Derby days; background music; seats out by the course, open (and food) all day. *(Geordie Simms)*

ESHER   TQ1364
Wheatsheaf (01372) 464014
The Green; KT10 8AG Refurbished early 19th-c dining pub with neat opened-up bar area, light wood flooring, blue-painted panelling and mix of furniture including sofas and easy chairs, lots of colourful artwork and a couple of Victorian fireplaces, four well kept beers and plenty of wines by the glass, good food from upscale bar snacks, sharing plates and traditional favourites to more enterprising restauranty dishes, friendly staff, high-ceilinged back dining extension with small outside eating area; background music, sports TV, daily newspapers and free wi-fi; well behaved children till 7.30pm, dogs in bar, teak tables under parasols on front paved terrace looking across to green, open (and food) all day. *(Rob Unsworth, Hunter and Christine Wright)*

FARNHAM   SU8545
Spotted Cow (01252) 726541
Bourne Grove, Lower Bourne (towards Tilford); GU10 3QT Welcoming red-brick dining pub run by two brothers and tucked away on edge of town in nice wooded setting (good walks nearby), highly regarded fairly priced food from pub favourites and sharing boards up (booking advised), two changing local ales and decent range of wines including house carafes, friendly helpful staff; children and dogs welcome, big garden, open all day weekends, food all day Sun till 7pm. *(Patric Curwen, Mr and Mrs J Watkins)*

FARNHAM   SU8346
Wheatsheaf (01252) 717135
West Street; GU9 7DR Stylishly updated old pub in same group as the Queens Head at East Clandon, Stag at Eashing and Duke of Cambridge at Tilford; enjoyable food (all day Fri-Sun) from open kitchen including weekday set menu, gluten-free diets catered for, well kept local ales such as Hogs Back, craft beers and good choice of wines and whiskies, friendly helpful staff; free wi-fi; children welcome, seats in back courtyard, open all day, no nearby parking. *(Graham Smart)*

FICKLESHOLE   TQ3960
White Bear (01959) 573166
Featherbed Lane/Fairchildes Lane; off A2022 just S of A212 roundabout; CR6 9PH Long 16th-c country dining pub with lots of small rooms, beams, flagstones and open fires, tasty food (orders taken at the bar), Brakspears, Pilgrim and a couple of guests; children and well behaved dogs

welcome, picnic-sets and stone bear on front terrace, sizeable back garden with pond and summer weekend 'burger shack', closed Tues evening, otherwise open all day, food till 7pm Sun. *(Eric Shanes)*

FRIDAY STREET   TQ1245
Stephan Langton (01306) 730775
Off B2126; RH5 6JR Refurbished 1930s pub prettily placed in tucked-away hamlet; imaginative food from sandwiches up, well kept local Tillingbourne beers and guests, nice wines and fine gin selection, friendly staff; children and dogs welcome, wooded setting with pond, good nearby walks, closed Mon (except bank holidays), otherwise open all day (till 7pm Sun). *(Martin Day)*

GODALMING   SU9643
Star (01483) 417717
Church Street; GU7 1EL Friendly 17th-c local in cobbled pedestrian street, cosy low-beamed and panelled L-shaped bar, up to eight well kept changing ales (four tapped from the cask) including Greene King, five proper ciders/perries and simple bar food (not weekend evenings), more modern back room; Mon folk night, Sun quiz; no dogs, heated back terrace, open all day. *(Robert Kennedy)*

GOMSHALL   TQ0847
Gomshall Mill (01483) 203060
Station Road; GU5 9LB Attractive timber-framed and weatherboarded medieval mill with interesting multi-level interior, part of the Home Counties pub group and quite restauranty; good sensibly priced food from extensive menu including sandwiches and children's meals, four well kept local ales and several wines by the glass, nice cafetière coffee, friendly helpful staff; terrace with view of River Tillingbourne running under the pub, open all day. *(Richard Kennell, Calum Stewart, Dr Nick Fletcher, Ian Wilson)*

GRAYSWOOD   SU9134
Wheatsheaf (01428) 644440
Grayswood Road (A286 NE of Haslemere); GU27 2DE Welcoming family-run dining pub with light airy décor, enjoyable freshly made food in bar and restaurant, good range of well kept beers, friendly helpful staff; quiz first Tues of the month, free wi-fi; children and dogs welcome, front verandah, side terrace, six bedrooms in extension, good breakfast. *(Gerry and Pam Pollard)*

GUILDFORD   SU9949
Weyside (01483) 568024
Shalford Road, Millbrook; across car park from Yvonne Arnaud Theatre, beyond boatyard; GU1 3XJ Big riverside pub (former Boatman) refurbished by Youngs, their ales and enjoyable food from sharing dishes and pub favourites up, friendly service, large split-level bar

dropping down to back dining conservatory, also barn-room restaurant; children and dogs welcome, terrace overlooking River Wey, open all day. *(Pauline and Mark Evans)*

GUILDFORD   SU9949
White House (01483) 302006
High Street; GU2 4AJ Refurbished Fullers pub in pretty waterside setting, their ales and good range of wines, enjoyable food from small plates up, sizeable bar with conservatory, upstairs rooms and roof terrace; children welcome, a few picnic-sets out by River Wey, open (and food) all day. *(Pauline and Mark Evans)*

HEADLEY   TQ2054
★**Cock** (01372) 377258
Church Lane; KT18 6LE Relaxed opened-up pub in same group as the Stag on the River at Eashing, Queens Head at East Clandon and Duke of Cambridge at Tilford; light airy modern refurbishment (parts date from the 18th c) with open fires and comfortable seating, good food (all day Fri-Sun) from lunchtime sandwiches and sharing plates up, steak and grill night Mon, a house beer (Red Mist) and a couple of guests, interesting wines including champagne by the glass, friendly attentive service; children welcome, dogs in one area, disabled access using lift from upper car park, terrace tables under parasols, attractive setting and good woodland walks, open all day. *(John Evans, Glen Locke)*

HOLMBURY ST MARY   TQ1144
Kings Head (01306) 730282
Pitland Street; RH5 6NP Welcoming old pub tucked away in hillside village, decent food (not Sun evening) cooked by landlord-chef, well kept Dark Star Hophead, Otter and a guest, bare boards, exposed brickwork and two log fires; background music, darts, outside gents'; children and dogs welcome, pretty spot with a few seats out at front, more in big sloping back garden, good walks, open all day weekends (till 9pm Sun), closed Mon. *(Ian Phillips)*

HORSELL   SU9959
★**Red Lion** (01483) 768497
High Street; GU21 4SS Large popular pub with airy split-level bar, comfortable sofas and easy chairs, clusters of pictures on cream-painted walls, Fullers London Pride, St Austell Tribute and a guest from long wooden servery, a dozen wines by the glass, back dining room with exposed brick walls, old pews and blackboards listing the good bistro-style food; free wi-fi; children allowed till 7pm, ivy-clad passage to garden and tree-sheltered terrace, good walks, open (and food) all day. *(Colette Grace)*

HORSELL COMMON   TQ0160
Sands at Bleak House
(01483) 756988 *Chertsey Road, The Anthonys; A320 Woking–Ottershaw; GU21 5NL* Smart contemporary

pub-restaurant on edge of Horsell Common; grey sandstone floor (and bar front), brown leather sofas and cushioned stools, two dining rooms with dark wood furniture, woodburners, good well presented food (can be pricey) including set menu, Andwell, Hogs Back and Sharps, friendly attentive uniformed staff; background music, TV, free wi-fi; children welcome, courtyard with picnic-sets and smokers' shelter, good shortish walk to sandpits that inspired H G Wells's *The War of the Worlds*, seven bedrooms, open all day, till 6pm Sun. *(Graham Smart)*

LALEHAM   TQ0568
★ **Three Horseshoes** (01784) 455014
Shepperton Road (B376); TW18 1SE
Bustling dining pub near pleasant stretch of the Thames; bar with white walls and contrasting deep blue woodwork, easy-going mix of tables and chairs on bare boards, log fire fronted by armchairs and squashy sofa, well kept Fullers/Gales beers and plenty of wines by the glass, highly regarded food including blackboard specials (booking advised), efficient friendly staff, dining areas with assorted tables and chairs, pictures and mirrors on grey walls; soft background music, free wi-fi; children welcome till 8pm, attractive flagstoned terrace, picnic-sets on grass, open (and food) all day. *(Geoffrey Kemp, Hunter and Christine Wright)*

LEIGH   TQ2147
★ **Seven Stars** (01306) 611254
Dawes Green, south of A25 Dorking–Reigate; RH2 8NP Attractive tile-hung country dining pub, comfortable beamed and flagstoned bar with traditional furnishings and inglenook, Fullers, Harveys, Sharps and Youngs from glowing copper counter, several wines by the glass and enjoyable sensibly priced food, plainer public bar and sympathetic restaurant extension where children allowed; dogs welcome in bar areas, plenty of outside seating, open all day, food all day Sat and till 6pm Sun. *(Caroline West)*

LIMPSFIELD CHART   TQ4251
Carpenters Arms (01883) 722209
Tally Road; RH8 0TG Friendly open-plan pub owned by Westerham, their full range kept well (tasting trays available), popular nicely prepared food (not Sun evening) from light lunches up, friendly helpful staff, garden room; free wi-fi; dogs welcome, tables on terrace and lawn, delightful setting by village common, lovely walks and handy for Chartwell (NT), open all day weekends. *(Ian Phillips)*

MICKLEHAM   TQ1753
King William IV (01372) 372590
Just off A24 Leatherhead–Dorking; Byttom Hill; RH5 6EL Steps up to small nicely placed country pub, well kept Hogs Back TEA, Surrey Hills Shere Drop and

a guest, enjoyable food from lunchtime sandwiches to blackboard specials, friendly attentive service, pleasant outlook from cosy plank-panelled front bar, carpeted dining area with grandfather clock and log fire; background music, live summer jazz outside (Sun 4-7pm); children and dogs welcome, plenty of tables in pretty terraced garden (some in open-sided timber shelters), lovely valley views, open (and food) all day. *(Professor James Burke)*

MOGADOR   TQ2453
Sportsman (01737) 246655
From M25 up A217 past second roundabout, then Mogador signed; KT20 7ES Modernised and extended low-ceilinged pub on edge of Walton Heath (originally 16th-c royal hunting lodge); well kept ales including Sharps and Youngs, good food from interesting varied menu, restaurant with raised section; quiz and curry Mon, free wi-fi; children welcome (no pushchairs), dogs in bar, seats out on common, front verandah and back lawn, popular with walkers and riders, open all day. *(Tony Scott)*

OCKLEY   TQ1337
Punchbowl (01306) 627249
Oakwood Hill, signed off A29 S; RH5 5PU Attractive 16th-c tile-hung country pub with slabby Horsham stone roof – recent change of ownership and some refurbishment; good value food (not Sun evening) including range of burgers and Weds steak night, three changing ales, central bar with flagstones and low beams, inglenook log fire decorated with horsebrasses, carpeted restaurant on the left, another bar to the right; children (until 9pm) and dogs welcome, picnic-sets in pretty garden, quiet spot with good walks including Sussex Border Path, open all day. *(Nick Higgins)*

OUTWOOD   TQ3246
★ **Bell** (01342) 842989
Outwood Common, just E of village; off A23 S of Redhill; RH1 5PN Attractive 17th-c extended dining pub; smartly rustic beamed bar with oak and elm furniture (some Jacobean in style), soft lighting, low beams and vast stone inglenook, Fullers London Pride, ESB and a guest, 20 wines by the glass and wide range of spirits, popular food from pub standards up (best to book, especially evenings when drinking-only space limited); background music, free wi-fi; children and dogs (in bar) welcome, well maintained garden looking out past pine trees to rolling fields, open all day, food all day weekends. *(Tony Scott)*

OUTWOOD   TQ3146
Dog & Duck (01342) 844552
Prince of Wales Road; turn off A23 at station sign in Salfords, S of Redhill – OS Sheet 187 map reference 312460; RH1 5QU Relaxed beamed country pub

with enjoyable fairly priced home-made food
in bar or large two-part restaurant, four well
kept Badger ales and good range of wines,
friendly helpful service; children and dogs
(in bar) welcome, sizeable garden with
raised decking, fenced duck pond and play
area (also circuit for motorised kids' jeeps),
open all day (till 9pm Sun). *(Tony Scott)*

OXTED   TQ4048
Grumpy Mole (01883) 722207
*Caterfield Lane, Staffhurst Wood, S of
town; RH8 0RR* Recently refurbished
country pub (formerly the Royal Oak),
welcoming and popular, with ales such as
Greene King, Godstone and Westerham, lots
of wines by the glass and good food from
sandwiches and pub staples up including
cook your own steak on a hot stone,
afternoon teas, friendly obliging service,
well divided bar and dining areas, open
fire; children and dogs welcome, rattan-
style furniture on paved terrace, picnic-sets
on lawn, lovely views across fields, open
all day. *(Simon Rodway, Martin Day)*

PUTTENHAM   SU9347
Good Intent (01483) 810387
*Signed off B3000 just S of A31
junction; The Street/Seale Lane;
GU3 1AR* Convivial beamed village local,
Otter, Sharps, Timothy Taylors and three
guests, reasonably priced traditional
food (not Sun evening) from sandwiches
up, Tues burger night, big log fire in cosy
front bar with alcove seating, some old
farming tools and photographs of the
pub, parquet-floored dining area; darts,
free wi-fi; well behaved children and dogs
welcome, small sunny garden, good walks,
open all day weekends. *(Mrs J Ekins-Daukes)*

PYRFORD LOCK   TQ0559
Anchor (01932) 342507
*3 miles from M25 junction 10 – S on A3,
then take Wisley slip road and go on past
RHS Wisley garden; GU23 6QW* Light
and airy waterside dining pub (can get very
busy and may be queues), enjoyable good
value food from sandwiches up, Badger ales
and several wines by the glass, simple tables
on bare boards, quieter more comfortable
panelled back area, narrowboat memorabilia,
pleasant oak-framed conservatory with
raised woodburner, daily papers; children
welcome, dogs in some areas, splendid
terrace by bridge and locks on River Wey
Navigation (moorings), large car park across
road, handy for RHS Wisley, open (and food)
all day. *(Ian Phillips, Tony Hobdon)*

REDHILL   TQ2750
Garland (01737) 764612
Brighton Road; RH1 6PP Friendly 19th-c
Harveys corner local with their full range
kept well including seasonals, enjoyable well
priced traditional food cooked by landlord
(lunchtimes, Fri evening, Sun till 4pm);

live music Sat, bar billiards, darts, free wi-fi;
children (till 7.30pm) and well behaved
dogs welcome, picnic-sets in back garden,
open all day. *(Tony Hobden, Tony Scott)*

REDHILL   TQ2749
Plough (01737) 766686
Church Road, St Johns; RH1 6QE Early
17th-c beamed pub with warm friendly
atmosphere, lots of bits and pieces to look
at including copper and brass hanging from
the ceiling, Fullers, Youngs and a couple of
guests, enjoyable sensibly priced blackboard
food (not Sun evening), open fire; Weds
quiz; no under-10s inside, dogs welcome,
back garden and terrace (barbecues and
spit roasts), open all day. *(Tony Scott)*

REIGATE HEATH   TQ2349
Skimmington Castle (01737) 243100
*Off A25 Reigate–Dorking via Flanchford
Road and Bonnys Road; RH2 8RL*
Nicely located small country pub with
emphasis on enjoyable home-made food
from good baguettes up (can get very busy
and best to book), well kept Harveys,
St Austell and a couple of guests, friendly
efficient service, snug beamed and panelled
rooms, log fires; children, dogs and muddy
boots welcome, seats out on three sides
(some heaters), open all day, food till
7.30pm Sun. *(Tony Scott, Ian Phillips)*

RIPLEY   TQ0456
Seven Stars (01483) 225128
Newark Lane (B367); GU23 6DL Neat
1930s pub with snug areas, enjoyable food
from extensive menu, Greene King, Fullers,
Sharps and Shepherd Neame, good wines and
coffee, red patterned carpet, gleaming brasses
and open fire; quiet background music;
picnic-sets and heated wooden booths in well
tended garden, river and canalside walks,
closed Sun evening. *(Maria and Bertie Farr)*

SEND   TQ0156
New Inn (01483) 762736
Send Road, Cartbridge; GU23 7EN
Well placed old pub by River Wey Navigation,
long bar and dining room, Adnams, Fullers,
Greene King, Sharps and a guest, good choice
of generously served food (all day weekends)
from ciabattas to blackboard specials,
friendly helpful service, beams and log-effect
gas fires; children and dogs welcome, large
waterside garden with moorings, open all
day and can get very busy in the summer.
(John Pritchard, Roger and Pauline Pearce)

SHACKLEFORD   SU9345
Cyder House (01483) 810360
Peper Harow Lane; GU8 6AN Recently
refurbished 1920s village pub in pleasant
leafy setting, Badger ales, proper ciders/
perry and nice selection of wines by the
glass, good home-made food from lunchtime
sandwiches and baked potatoes up, airy
linked areas around central servery, wood

floors, log fire; Mon quiz night (limited menu then), free wi-fi; children and dogs welcome, back terrace with steps up to play area, good walks, closed Tues, otherwise open all day, food all day weekends (till 7pm Sun). *(Margaret Hawkes)*

SHALFORD   TQ0047
Queen Victoria (01483) 566959
Station Row; GU4 8BY Tile-hung, bay-windowed local with compact modernised interior around central bar, enjoyable reasonably priced food (not Sun evening) from lunchtime sandwiches up, a beer badged for the pub along with Otter and a weekend guest, woodburner; some live music, quiz first and third Thurs of month, TV; children welcome, seats out at front and on back terrace, open all day. *(Tony and Wendy Hobden)*

SHALFORD   TQ0047
Seahorse (01483) 514351
A281 S of Guildford; The Street; GU4 8BU Gently upmarket Mitchells & Butlers dining pub with wide range of food including popular set menu (weekdays till 6pm), friendly young staff, Adnams and Sharps Doom Bar, good choice of wines and other drinks, contemporary furniture and artwork, two-way log fire, smart dining room, comfortable part near entrance with sofas and huge window; children welcome, picnic-sets in big lawned garden, covered terrace, handy for Shalford Mill (NT), open (and food) all day. *(Bridget and Gerry Gregson)*

SHAMLEY GREEN   TQ0343
Bricklayers Arms (01483) 898377
Guildford Road, S of the green; GU5 0UA Red-brick village pub with five well kept ales such as Exmoor, Fullers and Surrey Hills, enjoyable pubby food (not Sun evening) including themed evenings, U-shaped layout (a couple of steps) with bare boards, carpets and flagstones, exposed brick and stripped wood, old local photographs, sofas by woodburner, games area with pool, darts and machines; quiz and poker nights, TV; children and dogs welcome, a couple of picnic-sets out in front, more seats behind, open all day. *(Pauline and Mark Evans)*

SHEPPERTON   TQ0866
Red Lion (01932) 244526
Russell Road; TW17 9HX In nice position across from the Thames; bistro-style renovation (oldest part a pub since the 18th c), good well presented food (all day weekends) from varied regularly changing menu, Fri evening takeaway fish and chips, Sat brunch and popular Sun lunch, Fullers, Theakstons and a guest, good range of other drinks, friendly helpful staff; children and dogs welcome, modern furniture on picket-fenced front terrace, more seats over road on riverside deck, open (and food) all day. *(Gerry and Rosemary Dobson, Robin Waters)*

SHERE   TQ0747
White Horse (01483) 202518
Shere Lane; signed off A25 3 miles E of Guildford; GU5 9HS Splendid Chef & Brewer with several rooms off small bar, uneven floors, massive beams and timbers, Tudor stonework, oak wall seats and two log fires (one in huge inglenook), interesting range of enjoyable food, Greene King IPA and a couple of guests, Weston's cider and plenty of wines by the glass, good, friendly service; children and dogs (in bar) welcome, seats out at front and in big garden behind, beautiful film-set village, open (and food) all day. *(Tony Scott, John Evans, Ian Phillips)*

SHERE   TQ0747
William Bray (01483) 202044
Shere Lane; GU5 9HS Dining pub with good well presented locally sourced food, four real ales such as Brakspears, Ringwood and Surrey Hills and decent range of wines, friendly helpful staff, roomy contemporary bar with stone floor and woodburner, more formal airy restaurant with comfortable leather chairs; background music; children and dogs welcome, split-level front terrace and pretty landscaped side garden, useful car park, open (and some food) all day. *(Mary and Douglas McDowell)*

SHOTTERMILL   SU8832
Mill (01428) 643183
Liphook Road (B2131, off A287 W of Haslemere); GU27 3QE Refurbished and extended 17th-c pub with low beamed bar and more spacious modern restaurant, popular food (all day Thurs-Sun) from sandwiches, sharing plates and pizzas up, Wadworths ales and large choice of wines by the glass, friendly service; free wi-fi; children and dogs welcome, terrace and garden behind, open all day. *(Martin and Alison Stainsby)*

STAINES   TQ0371
Bells (01784) 454240
Church Street; TW18 4ZB Comfortable and sociable Youngs pub in old part of town, their well kept ales and a guest, decent choice of wines and good promptly served fresh food (not Sun evening), central fireplace; sports TV; dogs allowed in bar, tables in nice back garden with heated terrace, limited roadside parking, open all day. *(Mike Benton)*

STOKE D'ABERNON   TQ1259
★**Old Plough** (01932) 862244
Station Road, off A245; KT11 3BN Popular nicely updated 300-year-old pub in same group as the Onslow Arms at West Clandon, Red Lion at Horsell and Three Horseshoes in Laleham; good freshly made food including daily specials, Fullers/Gales beers and a couple of guests, plenty of wines by the glass, competent friendly

staff, restaurant with various knick-knacks; newspapers and free wi-fi; children (not in bar after 7pm) and dogs welcome, seats out under pergola and in attractive garden, open (and food) all day. *(Charles North, Ron Corbett)*

SUTTON ABINGER
TQ1045
Volunteer (01306) 730985
Water Lane; just off B2126 via Raikes Lane, 1.5 miles S of Abinger Hammer; RH5 6PR Picturesque family-run pub in delightful setting above clear stream, low-ceilinged linked rooms, log fires, Badger ales and several wines by the glass, fairly priced traditional food from lunchtime sandwiches and baked potatoes up, good friendly service, restaurant; children and dogs welcome, terrace and suntrap lawns stepped up behind, nice local walks, open (and food) all day Sat, closed Sun evening. *(Geordie Simms)*

SUTTON GREEN
TQ0054
Olive Tree (01483) 729999
Sutton Green Road; GU4 7QD Large rambling country dining pub; bar area with comfortable seating by open fire, ales including Sharps Doom Bar and Timothy Taylors Landlord, good range of wines by the glass and well liked food from open sandwiches to daily specials, restaurant specialises in fish/seafood, friendly helpful service; children and dogs (in bar) welcome, seats out in front and on back terrace, open all day, food all day Sat, till 5pm Sun. *(Nigel and Sue Foster)*

TADWORTH
TQ2355
★ Dukes Head (01737) 812173
Dorking Road (B2032 opposite common and woods); KT20 5SL Roomy and comfortably modernised 19th-c pub, popular for its good varied choice of food (booking advised), five well kept ales including Fullers, Youngs and a house beer (KT20) from Morlands, Aspall's cider, good choice of wines by the glass, helpful friendly staff, three dining areas and two big inglenook log fires; background music, Weds quiz; children welcome (no highchairs), dogs in some areas, lots of hanging baskets and plenty of tables in well tended terraced garden, open (and food) all day, till 8pm (6.30pm) Sun. *(John Branston)*

THAMES DITTON
TQ1667
Red Lion (020) 8398 8662
High Street; KT7 0SF Extended pub with some quirky features; enjoyable home-made food from regularly changing menu, decent wines and coffee, ales such as Surrey Hills and Twickenham from servery clad in reclaimed doors, colander lampshades overhead, mismatched furniture on bare boards, open fires, back conservatory; vinyl night second Weds of the month; children and dogs welcome, seats on split-level enclosed terrace with Lego wall, open (and food) all day. *(Tom and Ruth Rees)*

TILFORD
SU8742
Duke of Cambridge (01252) 792236
Tilford Road; GU10 2DD Refurbished dining pub in same small local group as the Queens Head at East Clandon, Stag at Eashing and Wheatsheaf at Farnham; nice food from varied menu including gluten-free and children's choices, good selection of wines and gins (some local), ales such as Hogs Back and Surrey Hills, helpful service; May charity music festival; children and dogs welcome, terrace and garden with outside bar/grill, good play area, open all day. *(Gerry and Pam Pollard)*

VIRGINIA WATER
SU9968
Rose & Olive Branch (01344) 843713 *Callow Hill; GU25 4LH* Small unpretentious red-brick pub with good choice of food including speciality pies and several vegetarian and gluten-free options, two Greene King ales and a guest, decent wines, friendly busy staff; background music; children and dogs welcome, tables on front terrace and in garden behind, good walks, open (and food) all day weekends. *(Graham Smart)*

WALLISWOOD
TQ1138
Scarlett Arms (01306) 627243
Signed from Ewhurst–Rowhook back road, or off A29 S of Ockley; RH5 5RD Cottagey 16th-c village pub with low beams and flagstones, simple furniture and two log fires (one in big inglenook), well kept Badger ales and enjoyable good value food (not Sun evening) including malaysian menu, friendly prompt service, various smaller rooms off main bar; background music, darts; children and dogs welcome, tables out at front and in garden under parasols, good walks, open all day Fri, Sat, till 9.30pm Sun, closed Mon lunchtime. *(Gerry and Rosemary Dobson)*

WALTON-ON-THAMES
TQ0966
Anglers (01932) 223996
Riverside, off Manor Road; KT12 2PF Roomy dining pub on Thames towpath, enjoyable food from varied menu (not overlong and can be pricey), real ales including a house beer from Caledonian, craft beers and lots of wines by the glass, friendly efficient service, wooden tables and chairs on bare boards, log fire, more seating in upstairs river-view room with own copper-topped bar; background music; children welcome, solid wooden tables and benches out by the water, open (and food) all day. *(Minda and Stanley Alexander)*

WARLINGHAM
TQ3955
Botley Hill Farmhouse (01959) 577154 *S on Limpsfield Road (B269); CR6 9QH* Refurbished 16th-c country pub set high on the North Downs; low-ceilinged linked rooms up and down steps, fresh flowers and candles, popular food from

sandwiches and pub standards up (till 7pm Sun, booking advised), well kept local ales such as Pilgrim and Westerham tapped from the cask (tasters offered), a dozen wines by the glass, good friendly service, big log fireplace in one room, tea shop selling local produce; children and dogs welcome, disabled access, terrace and garden with fine views, good local walks, open all day, weekend breakfast from 9am. *(Richard Cole)*

WEST CLANDON TQ0451

★**Bulls Head** (01483) 222444

A247 SE of Woking; GU4 7ST Comfortably old-fashioned village pub based around 1540s timbered hall-house, enjoyable good value pubby food (not Sun evening) including proper home-made pies, friendly helpful staff, ales from Sharps, Surrey Hills and Youngs, good coffee, small lantern-lit beamed front bar with open fire and some stripped brick, old local prints and bric-a-brac, simple raised back inglenook dining area, games room with darts and pool; children and dogs welcome, disabled access from car park, play area in neat little garden, nice walks. *(Jim and Sue James)*

WEST CLANDON TQ0452

★**Onslow Arms** (01483) 222447

A247 SE of Woking; GU4 7TE Busy modernised pub with heavily beamed rambling rooms leading away from central bar; wooden dining chairs and tables on wide floorboards, painted panelling, all sorts of copper implements, hunting horns and pictures, leather chesterfields in front of open fire, ales including Sharps, Surrey Hills and a house beer brewed by Caledonian, good popular food from lunchtime sandwiches and traditional choices up; live music first Weds of month, TV, daily papers and free wi-fi; children (till early evening) and dogs welcome, pretty courtyard garden with tables under parasols, open (and food) all day.

(Mrs J Ekins-Daukes, Miss A E Dare, Robin Waters)

WEST HORSLEY TQ0853

Barley Mow (01483) 282693

Off A246 Leatherhead–Guildford at Bell & Colvill garage roundabout; The Street; KT24 6HR Welcoming tree-shaded traditional pub, low beams, mix of flagstones, bare boards and carpet, two log fires, well kept ales such as Fullers, Greene King and Surrey Hills, decent wines, good thai food along with more conventional lunchtime menu, barn function room; background music; children and dogs welcome, picnic-sets in good-sized garden, open all day, no food Sun. *(Pauline and Mark Higgins)*

WEST HORSLEY TQ0752

King William IV (01483) 282318

The Street; KT24 6BG Comfortable and welcoming early 19th-c village pub; low entrance door to front and side bars, beams, flagstones and log fire, back conservatory

restaurant, good variety of decent food (not Sun evening) including gluten-free menu, four real ales such as Charles Wells and Surrey Hills, decent choice of wines by the glass and good coffee; background and occasional live music, quiz nights, free wi-fi; children and dogs welcome, disabled access, small sunny garden with deck and play area, open all day. *(Maria and Bertie Farr)*

WEYBRIDGE TQ0765

★**Old Crown** (01932) 842844

Thames Street; KT13 8LP Comfortably old-fashioned three-bar pub dating from the 16th c, good value traditional food (not Sun-Tues evenings) from popular sandwiches to fresh fish, Courage, Youngs and a guest kept well, good choice of wines by the glass, friendly efficient service, family lounge and conservatory, coal-effect gas fire; may be sports TV in back bar with Lions RFC photographs, silent fruit machine; secluded terrace and smokers' shelter, steps down to suntrap garden overlooking Wey/Thames confluence, mooring for small boats, open all day. *(Professor James Burke)*

WEYBRIDGE TQ0664

Queens Head (01932) 839820

Bridge Road; KT13 8XS 18th-c pub owned by Raymond Blanc's White Brasserie Company, emphasis on dining with good food from open kitchen including well priced lunchtime/early-evening set menu (not Sun), also a proper bar serving real ales and plenty of wines by the glass, friendly staff; soft background music, newspapers; children welcome, tables out on small front terrace, open (and food) all day. *(Geoffrey Kemp)*

WINDLESHAM SU9464

Brickmakers (01276) 472267

Chertsey Road (B386, W of B383 roundabout); GU20 6HT Airy red-brick country dining pub, updated linked areas in pastel shades or vibrant reds, light wood furniture on flagstone and wood floors, two-way woodburner, good freshly prepared food (all day Fri-Sun when best to book) using local suppliers, Courage Best, Fullers London Pride and Sharps Doom Bar, good choice of wines by the glass and decent coffee, efficient friendly service, conservatory; well behaved children allowed, appealing garden with pergola, open all day from 9am for breakfast. *(Colette Grace, Ian Phillips)*

WITLEY SU9439

White Hart (01428) 683695

Petworth Road; GU8 5PH Picture-book beamed Tudor pub, well kept St Austell Tribute, Youngs Bitter and a guest, craft beers, plenty of wines by the glass and extensive range of whiskies, popular food (not Sun evening) including signature home-smoked/chargrilled meats, friendly helpful staff, bar, restaurant and cosy panelled snug with inglenook (where George Eliot used to drink); children and dogs welcome, tables on cobbled terrace and in garden, nice walks nearby, open all day (till 6pm Sun). *(Graham Smart)*

WOKING TQ0058
Herbert Wells (01483) 722818
Chertsey Road; GU21 5AJ Corner Wetherspoons named after H G Wells, busy with shoppers yet with lots of cosy areas and side snugs, fine selection of beers and ciders and their usual competitively priced all-day food, friendly helpful staff, old local pictures; free wi-fi and daily papers; children welcome, a few pavement tables, open from 8am. *(Tony Hobden)*

WONERSH TQ0145
Grantley Arms (01483) 893351
The Street; GU5 0PE Popular recently refurbished 16th-c village pub; opened-up beamed and timbered bar with mix of new and old furniture on light wood floor, a couple of steps up to long pitched-roof dining area, four real ales and interesting wine list, good well presented food from lunchtime sandwiches up including themed evenings, cosy space in former bakery for private dining, friendly helpful staff; occasional live music and quiz nights, free wi-fi; children (until 7.30pm) and dogs (in bar) welcome, ramp for wheelchairs, attractive paved terrace, open (and food) all day. *(Geordie Simms)*

WOOD STREET SU9550
Royal Oak (01483) 235137
Oak Hill; GU3 3DA 1920s village local with half a dozen well kept ales including Black Sheep and Thwaites, good value traditional home-cooked food (not Sun evening, Mon), pizzas Thurs and Fri, friendly staff; music and quiz nights, Aug beer festival, free wi-fi; children and dogs welcome, good-sized garden, open all day Fri and Sat, till 8pm Sun, closed Mon lunchtime. *(Liz and Martin Eldon)*

WORPLESDON SU9854
Jolly Farmer (01483) 234658
Burdenshott Road, off A320 Guildford–Woking, not in village; GU3 3RN Old Fullers pub in pleasant country setting; their well kept ales in beamed and flagstoned bar with small log fire, fairly traditional food from lunchtime sandwiches up, bare-boards dining extension under pitched roof; background music, free wi-fi; children and dogs welcome, garden with parasol-shaded tables and pergola, open all day. *(Mike Benton)*

WRECCLESHAM SU8344
Bat & Ball (01252) 792108
Bat & Ball Lane, South Farnham; approach from Sandrock Hill and Upper Bourne Lane, then narrow steep lane to pub; GU10 4SA Fairly traditional pub tucked away in hidden valley; decent range of enjoyable food (all day weekends) from pubby choices up, special diets catered for, six well kept local ales and plenty of wines by the glass, friendly helpful staff; regular live music including open mike last Thurs of month and June beer/music festival, Tues charity quiz, free wi-fi; children and dogs welcome, disabled facilities, attractive terrace with vine arbour, more tables in garden with substantial play fort, open all day. *(Jennifer and Nicholas Thompson)*

WRECCLESHAM SU8244
Royal Oak (01252) 728319
The Street; GU10 4QS 17th-c black-beamed village local with enjoyable good value home-made food (all day Sun) including themed evenings, three Greene King ales, friendly helpful staff, log fire; Sun quiz, sports TV, darts; children and dogs welcome, big garden with play area, open all day. *(Tony and Jill Radnor)*

Post Office address codings confusingly give the impression that some pubs are in Surrey when they're really in Hampshire or London (which is where we list them). And there's further confusion from the way the Post Office still refers to Middlesex – which disappeared in local government reorganisation nearly 50 years ago.

Sussex

 **ALFRISTON**   TQ5203   Map 3

George ♀

(01323) 870319 – www.thegeorge-alfriston.com
High Street; BN26 5SY

Venerable 14th-c timbered inn with comfortable, heavily beamed bars, good wines and several real ales; bedrooms

Walkers are fond of this fine old place because two long-distance paths (the South Downs Way and Vanguard Way) cross here, and the quietly beautiful Cuckmere Haven is nearby. There's plenty of character throughout and the long bar, dominated by a huge stone inglenook fireplace with a winter log fire (or summer flower arrangement), has massive hop-hung low beams, settles and chairs around sturdy stripped tables, soft lighting and lots of copper and brass. Greene King Abbot and Old Speckled Hen, Dark Star Hophead and a guest beer on handpump, 15 wines by the glass (including champagne and a pudding wine) and 18 gins served by friendly staff; background music. The lounge has comfortable sofas, standing timbers and rugs on the wooden floor, and the restaurant is cosy and candlelit. There are seats in the spacious flint-walled garden, and the beamed bedrooms are comfortable; there's no car park but you can park a couple of minutes away. This is a lovely village to wander around.

🍴 Pleasing, all-day food includes lunchtime sandwiches and toasties, scallops with black pudding and pea purée, pork and mushroom terrine with chutney, sharing boards, sweet potato, chickpea and spinach curry, chicken with gnocchi in a wild mushroom and chestnut sauce, burger with toppings, red onion marmalade and chips, king prawn and chorizo linguine with chilli and tomatoes, venison casserole with dumplings, and puddings such as banoffi pie and spiced apple and almond cake with crème fraîche. *Benchmark main dish: slow-cooked pork belly with apple and cider sauce £16.50. Two-course evening meal £23.00.*

Greene King ~ Lease Roland and Cate Couch ~ Real ale ~ Open 11-11; 12-11 Sat, Sun ~ Bar food 12-9 ~ Restaurant ~ Children welcome ~ Dogs welcome ~ Wi-fi ~ Bedrooms: £75/£100 *Recommended by Tony and Jill Radnor, John Beeken, Chantelle and Tony Redman, Kerry and Guy Trooper*

 CHARLTON   SU8812   Map 2

Fox Goes Free ♀

(01243) 811461 – www.thefoxgoesfree.com
Village signposted off A286 Chichester–Midhurst in Singleton, also from Chichester–Petworth via East Dean; PO18 0HU

Comfortable old pub with beamed bars, popular food and drink and big garden; bedrooms

With Goodwood close by, this well run pub gets particularly busy on race days – when it's best to book a table in advance. The bar, the first of several cosy separate rooms, has old irish settles, tables and chapel chairs and an open fire. Standing timbers divide up a larger beamed bar, which has a huge brick fireplace and old local photographs on the walls. A dining area overlooks the garden. The family extension is a clever conversion from horse boxes and the stables where the 1926 Goodwood winner was once housed; darts, board games, TV and background music. A beer named for the pub (from Arundel) and Flack Manor Flack Catcher on handpump, 15 wines by the glass and Addlestone's cider. The attractive back garden has picnic-sets under apple trees and the South Downs as a backdrop, and there are rustic benches and tables on the gravelled front terrace too. The bedrooms have been redecorated. You can walk up to Levin Down nature reserve, or stroll around the Iron Age hill fort on the Trundle with far-reaching views to the Isle of Wight; the Weald & Downland Living Museum and West Dean Gardens are nearby too.

Good, enjoyable food includes home-made flatbread with toppings, duck rillettes with apricot and cherry tomato compote, citrus-poached salmon with avocado, red onion and courgettes with pesto dressing, pulled honey and mustard ham with bubble and squeak and free-range eggs, crispy cajun-spiced halloumi cheese with couscous and sweet potato fritters, a fish dish of the day, lamb steak with chive mash and tarragon and redcurrant jus, steaks with chips and a choice of sauce, and puddings such as mint chocolate torte with orange mascarpone and berry compote and sticky toffee pudding with toffee sauce. *Benchmark main dish: fish pie £14.50. Two-course evening meal £22.00.*

Free house ~ Licensee David Coxon ~ Real ale ~ Open 11am-11.30pm; 12-11 Sun ~ Bar food 12-2.30, 6.15-9.30; 12-10 Sat; 12-9 Sun ~ Restaurant ~ Children welcome ~ Dogs allowed in bar ~ Wi-fi ~ Bedrooms: £73/£98 *Recommended by Katharine Cowherd, Caroline Sullivan, Roy Hoing, Christian Mole, Suzy Miller, Susie and Spencer Gray*

CHILGROVE   SU8214   Map 2

White Horse ⭐ ♈ 🛏

(01243) 519444 – www.thewhitehorse.co.uk
B2141 Petersfield–Chichester; PO18 9HX

Handsome coaching inn with a thoughtful choice of drinks, first class food and plenty of outside seating; bedrooms

There are plenty of original features in this 18th-c whitewashed inn and a gently civilised atmosphere. The bar area has leather armchairs in front of a woodburning stove and daily papers on the light oak counter where friendly staff serve a beer named for the pub (from Ringwood), Langham Hip Hop and a guest from Ballards on handpump and 18 good wines by the glass. Just off here, a room with leather button-back wall seats and mate's and other dark wooden dining chairs has all sorts of country knick-knacks: stuffed animals, china plates, riding boots, flower paintings, dog drawings, stone bottles and books on shelves. The dining room to the other side of the bar has a huge painting of a galloping white horse, a long suede wall banquette, high-backed settles creating stalls, elegant chairs, lots of mirrors and big metal chandeliers. Throughout, there are fat candles in lanterns, flagstones and coir carpet, beams and timbering, and animal skin throws; background music and board games. A two-level terrace has dark grey rattan-style seats around glass-topped tables under parasols among pretty flowering tubs; an area up steps has rustic benches and tables and there are picnic-sets on grass at the front. Each of the comfortable, contemporary and light bedrooms has a little private courtyard (two have a hot tub). There are enjoyable surrounding walks.

Highly thought-of food using local, seasonal produce includes chicken and tarragon ballotine with apricot, broad beans, spring onion and pistachio, chilli salt squid with aioli, a pie and a risotto of the day, herb and parmesan gnocchi with wild mushrooms, crispy egg and creamy white wine sauce, sea bream niçoise with sauce vierge, lamb rump with confit cherry tomatoes and rosemary jus, and puddings such as rum baba with vanilla roasted pineapple and coconut sorbet and blueberry and lime baked cheesecake with crème fraîche sorbet. *Benchmark main dish: burger with toppings, red cabbage slaw and fries £14.95. Two-course evening meal £24.00.*

Free house ~ Licensee Niki Burr ~ Real ale ~ Open 11-11 ~ Bar food 12-3, 6-9; 12-9.30 Sat; 12-9 Sun ~ Restaurant ~ Children welcome ~ Dogs allowed in bar and bedrooms ~ Wi-fi ~ Bedrooms: /£99 *Recommended by Mungo Shipley, Nick Sharpe, Malcolm and Sue Scott, Mark Hamill, Hunter and Christine Wright, Katherine Matthews, Celia and Geoff Clay*

COPTHORNE
TQ3240 Map 3
Old House ♀ ⭑

(01342) 718529 – www.theoldhouseinn.co.uk
B2037 NE of village; RH10 3JB

Charming old pub with plenty of character, real ales, enjoyable food and attentive staff; attractive bedrooms

On the way to or from Gatwick Airport, this timbered higgledy-piggledy building is just the place for a break. There are several interconnected rooms with nooks and crannies and the immediately warming little bar has an easy-going feel, a brown leather chesterfield sofa, armchairs and carved wooden chairs around all sorts of tables, a big sisal mat on flagstones, a decorative fireplace and nightlights. Ringwood Best Bitter, Sharps Doom Bar and a guest beer on handpump, several good wines by the glass and a couple of huge glass flagons holding Sipsmith vodka and gin; staff are friendly and helpful. Off to the left is a charming small room with a woodburning stove in an inglenook fireplace and two leather armchairs in front, white-painted beams in a low ceiling (this is the oldest part, dating from the 16th c), cushioned settles and pre-war-style cushioned dining chairs around varying tables. A teeny back room, like something you'd find on an old galleon, has button-back wall seating up to the roof, a few chairs and heavy ropework. The dining rooms are beamed (some painted) and timbered with parquet, quarry tiles or sisal flooring, high-backed leather and other dining chairs, more wall seating and fresh flowers and candles; background music and board games. The terraced garden has heavy rustic tables and benches and a converted barn houses the smartly comfortable bedrooms.

Rewarding food includes sausage and black pudding scotch egg with brown sauce, fried whitebait with aioli, burger with toppings and skin-on fries, a pie of the day, corn-fed chicken with asparagus and sauce vierge, 32-day dry-aged 10oz rib-eye steak with a choice of sauce, salmon, lime and paprika fishcake with chilli tomato salsa, slow-roast pork belly with black pudding mash, caramelised apple and cider sauce, and puddings such as raspberry pannacotta with raspberry sorbet and molten chocolate fondant with mint choc chip ice-cream. *Benchmark main dish: pie of the day £13.95. Two-course evening meal £22.00.*

Free house ~ Licensee Stephen Godsave ~ Real ale ~ Open 12-11 (8 Sun) ~ Bar food 12-3, 6-9 (9.30 Fri, Sat); 12-4, 6-8 Sun ~ Restaurant ~ Children welcome ~ Dogs allowed in bar and bedrooms ~ Wi-fi ~ Bedrooms: /£90 *Recommended by Michael Rugman, Sophie Ellison, Mrs Zara Elliott, Andrew and Michele Revell*

DANEHILL
TQ4128 Map 3

Coach & Horses ⭐ ♈

(01825) 740369 – www.coachandhorses.co

Off A275, via School Lane towards Chelwood Common; RH17 7JF

Well run dining pub with bustling bars, welcoming staff, very good food and ales and sizeable garden

This is an enjoyable pub with highly regarded food and a fine big garden. The little bar to the right has half-panelled walls, simple furniture on polished floorboards, a woodburner in a brick fireplace and a big hatch to the bar counter: Harveys Best and Larkins Traditional Ale on handpump, local Black Pig farmhouse cider and a dozen wines by the glass including prosecco and Bluebell sparkling wine from Sussex. A couple of steps lead down to a half-panelled area with a mix of dining chairs around characterful wooden tables (set with flowers and candles) on a fine brick floor, and changing artwork on the walls. Down another step is a dining area with stone walls, beams, flagstones and a woodburning stove; background music. The adults-only terrace beneath an enormous maple tree is quite a draw in warm weather and the large garden has picnic-sets, a children's play area and views of the South Downs.

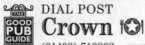 First class food includes lunchtime sandwiches, treacle-cured salmon with rhubarb relish, soft-boiled duck egg with bombay potatoes, sour mango and lime coriander toastie, red onion tarte tatin with butternut squash and pickled enoki mushrooms, moroccan-spiced lamb with almond couscous and roasted sweet potatoes, guinea fowl with burnt onion hash, caramelised celeriac and sage velouté, stone bass with salsify, parsnip purée and thyme vinaigrette, and puddings such as pistachio rice pudding with caramelised white chocolate and rhubarb frangipane tart with custard. *Benchmark main dish: crisp pork belly with roasted apple and mustard cream £15.00. Two-course evening meal £22.00.*

Free house ~ Licensee Ian Philpots ~ Real ale ~ Open 12-3, 5.30-11; 12-11 Sat; 12-10.30 Sun ~ Bar food 12-2 , 6.30-9; 12-2.30, 6.30-9.30 Sat; 12-3 Sun ~ Restaurant ~ Children welcome ~ Dogs allowed in bar ~ Wi-fi *Recommended by Mr and Mrs R A Bradbrook, John Preddy, Chris Bell, Tracey and Stephen Groves, Robert and Diana Ringstone*

DIAL POST
TQ1519 Map 3

Crown ⭐

(01403) 710902 – www.crown-inn-dialpost.co.uk

Worthing Road (off A24 S of Horsham); RH13 8NH

Tile-hung village pub with interesting food and a good mix of drinkers and diners; bedrooms

With a bustling atmosphere and a good mix of drinkers and diners, this remains a popular pub with our readers. The beamed bar has a couple of standing timbers, brown squashy sofas, pine tables and chairs on the stone floor and a small woodburning stove in a brick fireplace. Downlands Bramber, Hammerpot Shooting Star and Long Man Best Bitter on handpump are served from the attractive herringbone brick counter, alongside eight wines by the glass plus prosecco, champagne and a local cider. To the right of the bar, the restaurant (with more beams) has an ornamental woodburner in a brick fireplace, a few photographs, chunky pine tables and chairs, a couple of cushioned pews and a shelf of books; steps lead down to an additional dining room; background music and board games. The pub dog is called Chops. The straightforwardly furnished dining conservatory, facing the village green, is light and airy, and there are picnic-sets in the back garden.

 Good quality food includes sandwiches and wraps, hand-potted crab with lemon crème fraîche, duck and chicken liver pâté with sweetcorn relish, beetroot, black bean and chickpea falafel with tzatziki and sweet potato fries, steak in ale pie, persian-style chicken with aubergine and saffron rice and pomegranate and walnut sauce, rainbow trout with wild garlic butter and sauté potatoes, liver and bacon with onion gravy, and puddings such as dark chocolate and marshmallow mousse and treacle and raspberry tart with home-made ice-cream. *Benchmark main dish: steak burger with interesting toppings and chips £11.50. Two-course evening meal £20.00.*

Free house ~ Licensees James and Penny Middleton-Burn ~ Real ale ~ Open 12-3, 6-11; 12-4 Sun ~ Bar food 12-2, 6-9; 12-3 Sun ~ Restaurant ~ Children welcome ~ Dogs welcome ~ Wi-fi ~ Bedrooms: £51/£69 *Recommended by R and M Thomas, Elisabeth and Bill Humphries, Barbara and Phil Bowie*

DITCHLING
Bull 🏅 🍷 🍴 🛏

TQ3215 Map 3

(01273) 843147 – www.thebullditchling.com
High Street (B2112); BN6 8TA

500-year-old local in centre of village with three bars and dining rooms, a good choice of ales and popular food; bedrooms

At weekends in particular this former coaching inn is busy with walkers and cyclists (the South Downs Way is close by), but there are plenty of efficient staff to keep things running smoothly. The beamed main bar is a cosy haven in winter with a log fire in a sizeable inglenook fireplace, benches, scrubbed wooden tables and leather chesterfields on bare boards and modern artwork and historic photos of the village on the walls. Bedlam Benchmark and Golden Ale, Timothy Taylors Landlord and guests such as Burning Sky Aurora and Gipsy Hill Beatnik on handpump, 22 wines by the glass and a large choice of spirits; daily papers and background music. A couple of other rooms lead off to the left from the main entrance. You can sit in the garden under apple trees or on a terrace; the kitchen garden provides fruit, vegetables and herbs for the pub's excellent menu. Bedrooms are well equipped and comfortable.

 Highly enjoyable food includes lunchtime sandwiches, crispy poached egg with pancetta, pickled mushrooms and candied walnuts, monkfish with spiced lentil dhal, yoghurt and coriander, wild garlic gnocchi with garlic purée, feta, wild mushrooms and pine nuts, burger with toppings, smoked onion mayonnaise, coleslaw and chips, whole plaice with cockle emulsion, peas and leeks, chicken and chorizo pie, pepper-crusted pork fillet with black pudding bonbons, apple and butternut squash, and puddings such as chocolate brownie with chocolate ice-cream and carrot cake with mascarpone ice-cream and candied carrots. *Benchmark main dish: beer-battered cod and chips £13.50. Two-course evening meal £23.00.*

Free house ~ Licensee Dominic Worrall ~ Real ale ~ Open 11-11 (10.30 Sun) ~ Bar food 12-2.30, 6-9.30; 12-9.30 Sat; 12-9 Sun ~ Restaurant ~ Children welcome ~ Dogs allowed in bar ~ Wi-fi ~ Bedrooms: /£100 *Recommended by B and M Kendall, Tracey and Stephen Groves, Tony Scott, Chloe and Michael Swettenham*

DUNCTON
Cricketers

SU9517 Map 3

(01798) 342473 – www.thecricketersduncton.co.uk
Set back from A285; GU28 0LB

Charming old coaching inn with friendly licensees, real ales, popular food and suntrap back garden

For horse-racing and motor sport at Goodwood, this 16th-c pub is perfectly placed. The traditional bar has a display of cricketing memorabilia, a few standing timbers, simple seating and an open woodburning stove in an inglenook fireplace. Steps lead down to a dining room with farmhouse chairs around wooden tables. Crafty Brewing Loxhill Biscuit, Dark Star Partridge Best Bitter and Triple fff Moondance on handpump, nine wines by the glass and three farm ciders; board games. There are picnic-sets out in front beneath the flowering window boxes and more on decked areas and under parasols on grass in the picturesque back garden. The pub got its present name from the 19th-c owner John Wisden, the cricketer who published the famous *Wisden Cricketers' Almanack*.

Good quality food includes lunchtime sandwiches, chicken liver parfait, moules marinière, butternut squash risotto, chicken caesar salad, a trio of sausages with mash and onion gravy, catalan-style fish stew, chicken breast stuffed with goats cheese and red pepper with parmentier potatoes, teriyaki rib-eye steak with oriental noodle salad, and puddings. *Benchmark main dish: steak and mushroom in ale pie £11.95. Two-course evening meal £20.50.*

Free house ~ Licensee Martin Boult ~ Real ale ~ Open 11-11; 12-10.30 Sun ~ Bar food 12-2.30, 6-9; 12-9 weekends; cream teas 2.30-6pm ~ Children welcome ~ Dogs welcome ~ Wi-fi
Recommended by Peter Barrett, Ruth May, Simon Sharpe, Chris and Sophie Baxter

EARTHAM
SU9309 Map 2

George ♀ 🍺
(01243) 814340 – www.thegeorgeeartham.com
Signed off A285 Chichester–Petworth, from Fontwell off A27, from Slindon off A29; PO18 0LT

170-year-old pub in tucked-away village with country furnishings and contemporary touches, local ales and enjoyable food

Our readers consistently enjoy their visits here – either in winter when there are three open fires, or in warmer weather when the large garden has picnic-sets on grass and seats and tables under a gazebo. The light, airy bar is prettily decorated with scatter cushions on a long wall pew and painted dining chairs around wood-topped tables (each set with fresh flowers and candles) on parquet flooring, and there are sofas, armchairs, a dresser with country knick-knacks, paintings on cream-painted walls above a grey-planked dado and stone bottles and books. The pretty beamed restaurant has high-backed grey tartan chairs and pale settles on pale floorboards; background music and board games. A beer named for the pub (from Otter) and guests such as Arundel Springtide, Dark Star Crème Brûlée and Langham Halfway to Heaven on handpump, 13 wines by the glass, 25 gins, 20 malt whiskies and farm cider. There are some lovely walks and cycle routes in the surrounding South Downs. Easy disabled access.

Interesting food using local produce includes sandwiches, smoked salmon, prawn and crab platter with a gin bloody mary sauce, broccoli and blue cheese quiche, beer-battered fish and chips, timbale of lamb shoulder with celeriac purée and redcurrant reduction, cod with a herb crust, saffron mash and mussel velouté, confit duck leg with spiced Grand Marnier jus and spring green medley, and puddings such as chocolate and ale cake with salted caramel sauce and hazelnut ice-cream and fruit crumble of the day. *Benchmark main dish: pie of the day £13.25. Two-course evening meal £19.00.*

Free house ~ Licensees James and Anita Thompson ~ Real ale ~ Open 11.30-11; 12-6 Sun; closed Mon ~ Bar food 12-3, 6-9 (9.30 Fri, Sat); 12-4 Sun ~ Restaurant ~ Children welcome ~ Dogs allowed in bar *Recommended by Nick Sharpe, Alf Wright, Tracey and Stephen Groves, Lionel Smith, Adam and Natalie Davis*

EAST DEAN

TV5597 Map 3

Tiger ♀ ⇐

(01323) 423209 – www.beachyhead.org.uk

Off A259 Eastbourne–Seaford; BN20 0DA

Pretty old pub with bar and dining room, an informal and friendly atmosphere and own-brewed beers; bedrooms

The cottage-lined green beside this busy pub is delightful; in good weather, customers sit on the grass here or at picnic-sets on the flower-filled terrace. If you'd like a table, you do need to arrive early as they only take table reservations from October to March. The focal point of the little beamed main bar is the open woodburning stove in a brick inglenook surrounded by polished horsebrasses, and there are just a few rustic tables with benches, simple wooden chairs, a window seat and a long cushioned wall bench. The walls are hung with fish prints and a stuffed tiger's head, and a couple of hunting horns hang above the long bar counter. As well as their own-brewed Beachy Head Legless Rambler and Parsons Porter, they keep Gun Project Babylon Pale Ale, Harveys Best, Long Man Long Blonde and St Austell Tribute on handpump, nine wines by the glass and local gin and cider. Down a step on the right is a small room with an exceptionally fine high-backed curved settle, a couple of other elderly settles and nice old chairs and wooden tables on coir carpeting; on the walls are an ancient map of Eastbourne and Beachy Head and photographs of the pub. The dining room to the left of the main bar has a cream woodburner and hunting prints. Bedrooms are comfortable and breakfasts good. The walks to the coast and along the clifftops of the Seven Sisters and up to Belle Tout Lighthouse and Beachy Head are splendid.

 Bar food includes duck and orange pâté, deep-fried whitebait with aioli, vegetable moussaka, gammon and eggs, chicken curry, lamb cobbler, moules marinière, steak in ale pie, and puddings such as chocolate brownie and banoffi pie. *Benchmark main dish: burger with toppings, onion rings and chips £11.95. Two-course evening meal £18.00.*

Free house ~ Licensee Rebecca Vasey ~ Real ale ~ Open 11-11; 11am-midnight Sat; 11-10.30 Sun ~ Bar food 12-3 (4 weekends), 6-9 ~ Restaurant ~ Children welcome ~ Dogs allowed in bar ~ Wi-fi ~ Bedrooms: /£140 *Recommended by David and Judy Robison, Martin Day, Trevor and Michele Street, Maggie and Matthew Lyons*

ERIDGE GREEN

TQ5535 Map 3

Nevill Crest & Gun ♀ ◀

(01892) 864209 – www.brunningandprice.co.uk/nevillcrestandgun

A26 Tunbridge Wells–Crowborough; TN3 9JR

Handsome old building with lots of character, plenty to look at, six real ales and enjoyable modern food

There's over 500 years of history here and the Neville Crest refers to the Earls of Abergavenny on whose estate the pub was built. It's been cleverly opened up and extended with standing timbers and doorways keeping some sense of separate rooms. Throughout, there are heavy beams (some carved), panelling, rugs on wooden floors and woodburning stoves and open fires in three fireplaces (the linenfold carved bressumer above one is worth seeking out). Also, all manner of individual dining chairs around dark wood or copper-topped tables, lots of pictures, maps and photographs relating to the local area, and windowsills crammed with toby jugs, stone and glass bottles and plants. Phoenix Brunning & Price Original plus Black

Cat Original, Kent Session Pale, Long Man Best Bitter, Old Dairy Spring Top, Three Legs Red and 360 Degree Single Hop on handpump, 15 wines by the glass and lots of gins and malt whiskies; board games and background music. There are a few picnic-sets in front of the building and teak furniture on the back terrace, next to the newer dining extension with its large windows, light oak rafters, beams and coir flooring.

Brasserie-style food includes sandwiches, deep-fried squid with avocado, sweetcorn, coriander, lime and sweet chilli sauce, baked whole garlic and rosemary camembert (for two) with plum and ginger chutney, honey-roast ham and free-range eggs, grilled red mullet on pea and tomato risotto with parmesan crisps, sticky harissa lamb with couscous and feta, pomegranate and mint falafels, steak in ale pie, warm crispy beef salad with sweet chilli dressing, watermelon, pak choi, mouli, carrots and cashew nuts, and puddings such as vanilla pannacotta with rhubarb coulis and millionaire cheesecake with salted caramel sauce. *Benchmark main dish: steak burger with toppings, coleslaw and chips £12.95. Two-course evening meal £20.00.*

Brunning & Price ~ Manager Edward Hoskins ~ Real ale ~ Open 11.30-11; 12-10 Sun ~ Bar food 12-10 (9 Sun) ~ Children welcome ~ Dogs allowed in bar ~ Wi-fi *Recommended by Hilary and Neil Christopher, Isobel May, Paddy and Sian O'Leary, Nicola and Stuart Parsons*

EWHURST GREEN
TQ7924 Map 3

White Dog ★☆

(01580) 830264 – www.thewhitedogewhurst.co.uk

Turn off A21 to Bodiam at S end of Hurst Green, cross B2244, pass Bodiam Castle, cross river then bear left uphill at Ewhurst Green sign; TN32 5TD

Welcoming village pub run by father and daughter team with a nice little bar, several real ales and popular food; bedrooms

There can be few pubs with a view as stunning as the one over Bodiam Castle (National Trust) from the seats and tables in the back garden here. Inside, the bar has a roaring log fire in an inglenook fireplace, beams, wood panelling and a mix of chairs and tables on old brick or flagstoned floors. Four real ales from breweries such as Ewhurst Ales, Harveys, Rother Valley and Tonbridge on handpump and 20 wines by the glass. A dining room has sturdy wooden tables and chairs on more flagstones, while the games room (which opens on to the front terrace) has darts and pool; background music. The bedrooms are light and airy and one has a view over the castle.

 Good, seasonal food includes thai-style fishcakes with spicy cucumber relish, home-made scotch egg with piccalilli, tortellini filled with wild mushrooms and topped with cheese, home-cooked ham and eggs, pot-roasted rabbit in mustard cream sauce with mash, a local fish dish of the day, honey-glazed confit duck leg with herby puy lentils and braised peas, roast rack of local lamb on grain mustard mash with port wine jus, and puddings such as chocolate fondant and apple and blackberry crumble; wood-fired pizzas on Thursday evenings. *Benchmark main dish: burger with toppings, spicy tomato salsa and chips £11.95. Two-course evening meal £20.00.*

Free house ~ Licensees Harriet Bull and Dale Skinner ~ Real ale ~ Open 12-11 (11.30 Sat) ~ Bar food 12-2, 6.30-9 ~ Restaurant ~ Children welcome ~ Dogs allowed in bar and bedrooms ~ Wi-fi ~ Live music in bar Sun afternoons ~ Bedrooms: /£95
Recommended by Rob Newland, David Jackman, Mr. Frederick Peach, Mandy and Gary Redstone

---

'Children welcome' means the pub says it lets children inside without any special restriction. If it allows them in, but to restricted areas such as an eating area or family room, we specify this. Some pubs may impose an evening time limit. We do not mention limits after 9pm as we assume children are home by then.

 FIRLE   TQ4607 Map 3

Ram

(01273) 858222 – www.raminn.co.uk

Village signed off A27 Lewes–Polegate; BN8 6NS

Bustling country pub with three open fires, character rooms, good food and drink and seats in garden; bedrooms

Tucked beneath the South Downs in a small village, this 500-year-old pub is popular with walkers at lunchtime. The main bar has a log fire, captain's and mate's chairs and a couple of gingham armchairs around dark pubby tables on bare boards or quarry tiles, gilt-edged paintings on dark brown walls, Harveys Best and guest beers such as Beachy Head South Downs Ale and Goldmark Liquid Gold on handpump, 21 wines by the glass and eight malt whiskies; service is welcoming and helpful. A cosy bar leads off here with another log fire, olive-green built-in planked and cushioned wall seats and more dark chairs and tables on parquet flooring. Throughout, there are various ceramic ram's heads or skulls, black and white photos of the local area, candles in hurricane jars and daily papers; darts and toad in the hole. The back dining room is up some steps and overlooks the flint-walled garden where there are tables and chairs on a terrace and picnic-sets on grass; more picnic-sets under parasols are available at the front. Bedrooms are comfortable and breakfasts good.

 Using produce from the Firle Estate, the food includes lunchtime ciabattas, venison kofta with sweet chilli relish, local goats cheese with caramelised onion and apple croquette, sharing boards, burger with toppings, coleslaw and skinny fries, tomato, bocconcini cheese and parmesan salad with roast garlic aioli and grilled artichoke hearts, lamb steak with charred aubergine, pickled courgette, beetroot and salsa verde, stone bass with beetroot and truffle purée and crab, shrimp and caper butter, and puddings such as dark chocolate torte with berry compote and raspberry custard pot. *Benchmark main dish: hake with samphire, clams and basil and garlic courgettes £16.00. Two-course evening meal £21.00.*

Free house ~ Licensee Hayley Bayes ~ Real ale ~ Open 9am-11pm ~ Bar food 9am-9.30pm ~ Children welcome away from bar ~ Dogs welcome ~ Wi-fi ~ Live folk music first Mon of month *Recommended by Michael Rugman, Douglas Power, PL, Matthew and Elisabeth Reeves, Tony Scott, Harvey Brown*

 FLETCHING   TQ4223 Map 3

Griffin 🍴 ◉ ♀ 🛏

(01825) 722890 – www.thegriffininn.co.uk

Village signposted off A272 W of Uckfield; TN22 3SS

Busy, gently upmarket inn with a fine wine list, real ales, bistro-style bar food and a big garden; pretty bedrooms

'An exceptional pub' and 'worth all its accolades' are just two enthusiastic comments from readers. It's a civilised place and very much the focal point of this handsome village; the beamed and quaintly panelled bar rooms have blazing log fires, old photographs and hunting prints, straightforward close-set furniture including some captain's chairs, and china on a delft shelf. A small bare-boarded serving area is off to one side and there's a cosy separate bar with sofas and a TV. The place gets pretty packed at weekends. Harveys Best and guests such as Beachy Head LightHouse Ale, Burning Sky Plateau and Gun Project Babylon Pale Ale and Scaramanga on handpump, plus 20 wines by the glass from a good list (including champagne, prosecco and sweet wine); they hold a monthly wine club with supper (on a Thursday evening). At the garden entrance there's an outside bar and wood oven, tables and chairs under parasols and a stunning view over Sheffield Park; there are more seats on a sandstone terrace. The bright and pretty bedrooms are comfortable and breakfasts are good. There are ramps for wheelchairs.

Excellent food includes scallops with celeriac purée, bacon crumb and veal jus, sausage meat and black pudding scotch egg with curried mayonnaise and mint salad, wild mushroom pasta with truffle cream, pine nuts and parmesan, lamb and mint burger with toppings, chilli and garlic aioli and chips, king prawn and monkfish curry, rare-breed pork chops with parsley mash and calvados jus, crab linguine with fennel, chilli and white wine, and puddings such as dark chocolate fondant with clotted cream ice-cream and honeycomb crumbs and treacle and apple tart with rum and raisin ice-cream. *Benchmark main dish: beer-battered cod with pea purée and chips £14.50. Two-course evening meal £23.00.*

Free house ~ Licensees James Pullan and Samantha Barlow ~ Real ale ~ Open 11am-midnight; 11am-1am Sat, Sun ~ Bar food 12-3, 7-9.30; 12-9.30 weekends ~ Restaurant ~ Children welcome ~ Dogs allowed in bar and bedrooms ~ Wi-fi ~ Live music Fri evening, Sun lunch ~ Bedrooms: £70/£100 *Recommended by Carol and Barry Craddock, Daniel King, Richard Kennell, Ian Herdman, Robin Waters, Amanda Shipley*

FRIDAY STREET   TV6203 Map 3

Farm at Friday Street ♀ ◖

(01323) 766049 – www.farmfridaystreet.com

B2104, Langney; BN23 8AP

Handsome 17th-c house with lots to look at, efficient staff serving popular food and drink and seats outside

The old farmhouse core here (houses have replaced the fields that used to surround it) has many newer extensions, but it's been done well and there are plenty of both drinking and dining areas. The open-plan rooms are split by brick pillars into cosier areas with sofas, stools and all manner of wooden dining chairs and tables on bare boards, creamy coloured flagstones, coir or carpet. Throughout, there are open fires, big house plants, stubby church candles, frame-to-frame prints and pictures and farming implements; the atmosphere is easy-going and friendly. Bath Gem, Long Man Best Bitter, Musket Trigger, St Austell Cornish Best and Wadworths IPA on handpump and 14 wines by the glass. The dining room is on two levels with timbered walls, glass partitions, a raised conical roof and an open kitchen. The front lawn has plenty of picnic-sets.

Appetising modern food includes sandwiches, pork spring roll with noodles and sweet and sour sauce, box-baked garlic and rosemary camembert with cranberry compote, three-cheese macaroni with garlic ciabatta, toad in the hole with onion gravy, burger with toppings, barbecue sauce and skinny fries, sea bass with bacon-wrapped asparagus and white wine and crayfish sauce, sirloin steak with garlic butter or peppercorn sauce, and puddings such as sticky toffee pudding with butterscotch sauce and salted caramel ice-cream and pistachio parfait with white chocolate cookie. *Benchmark main dish: half shoulder of lamb with dauphinoise potatoes and rosemary and redcurrant jus £20.95. Two-course evening meal £22.00.*

Whiting & Hammond ~ Manager Paul Worman ~ Real ale ~ Open 9am-11pm (10.30pm Sun) ~ Bar food 12-9.30 (9 Sun) ~ Restaurant ~ Children welcome ~ Dogs allowed in bar ~ Wi-fi *Recommended by Anne and Ben Smith, Peter and Elizabeth May, Greta and Gavin Craddock, John Harris, Chloe and Tim Hodge*

It's very helpful if you let us know up-to-date food prices when you report on pubs.

HASTINGS
Crown ♀ ◀

TQ8109 Map 3

(01424) 465100 – www.thecrownhastings.co.uk

All Saints Street, Old Town; TN34 3BN

Informal and friendly corner pub with interesting food, local ales and simple furnishings – a good find

Enjoyable and gently quirky, this is a deservedly busy Old Town pub that our readers are very pleased to have found. The simply furnished bar has bare boards, plain chairs around tables inlaid with games and set with posies of flowers, a log fire and plenty of windows to keep everything light (despite the dark paintwork). A snug has leather armchairs in front of another open fire, a couple of tables, and books and house plants on a windowsill and mantelpiece; board games. Stools line the counter where they keep four changing ales such as Bedlam India Pale Ale, Burning Sky Plateau, Franklins Mama Knows Best and Three Legs Dark on handpump, 14 good wines by the glass, 15 gins, 15 whiskies and local cider; service is friendly and helpful. There's a dining area at one end of the bar with scatter cushions on wall seats, mismatched chairs and some large tables. Local art (for sale) hangs on the walls and one window is hung with bright neckties and lined with shelves of local pottery, greetings cards and hand-made purses; daily papers and background music. Dogs and children receive a genuinely warm welcome. There are a few picnic-sets outside at the front.

🍴 Popular, enterprising food includes good weekend brunches (11am-2pm), beer-battered fish finger sandwich with root vegetable slaw, pigeon, mushroom and bacon ragoût on toast, squash, pumpkin and mushroom pie with mushroom cream, fillet of bream with breaded smoked roe, smoked salmon and root vegetable rösti with creamed wild garlic and caper butter, kiev, breast and terrine of chicken with tarragon sauce, and puddings such as pear and oatcake sponge with salted caramel filling and custard and eccles cake with brown sugar and crème fraîche ice-cream. *Benchmark main dish: haddock and pea fishcake with a poached egg, kohlrabi and cucumber salad and tartare sauce £10.00. Two-course evening meal £20.00.*

Free house ~ Licensees Tess Eaton and Andrew Swan ~ Real ale ~ Open 11-11 (10.30 Sun) ~ Bar food 12 (11 weekends)-5, 6-9.30 ~ Children welcome ~ Dogs welcome ~ Wi-fi
Recommended by Alice Wright, Jenny Shepherd, Peter Meister, Julie and Andrew Blanchett, Angela and Steve Heard

HORSHAM
Black Jug ♀ ◀

TQ1730 Map 3

(01403) 253526 – www.brunningandprice.co.uk/blackjug

North Street; RH12 1RJ

Busy town pub with wide choice of drinks, attentive staff and rewarding food

Especially in the early evening, this well run pub is deservedly packed – though staff remain efficient and friendly. The single, large, early 20th-c room has a long central bar, a nice collection of sizeable dark wood tables and comfortable chairs on a stripped-wood floor, bookcases and interesting old prints and photographs above a dark wood-panelled dado on cream walls; background music and board games. A spacious, bright conservatory has similar furniture and lots of hanging baskets. Harveys Best and Marstons Pedigree New World with guests such as Long Man Best Bitter, Moorhouses White Witch, Robinsons Wizard and St Austell Proper Job on handpump, 16 wines by the glass, 170 malt whiskies, 50 gins, 30 rums, 30 bourbons and farm cider. The pretty, flower-filled back terrace has plenty of garden furniture; parking is in the council car park next door, as the small one by the pub is for staff and deliveries only.

Good, modern food includes sandwiches, deep-fried brie with pickled cranberries and candied pecan salad, pigeon breast with celeriac purée and blackberry jus, wild mushroom tortellini with poached pear, pickled walnuts and gorgonzola cream, miso-baked salmon with chinese salad and teriyaki noodles, harissa chicken breast salad with giant couscous and pomegranate and saffron yoghurt, lamb shoulder with dauphinoise potatoes and carrot purée, and puddings such as crème brûlée and hot waffle with caramelised banana, toffee sauce and vanilla ice-cream. *Benchmark main dish: steak burger with toppings, coleslaw and chips £12.95. Two-course evening meal £21.00.*

Brunning & Price ~ Tenant Alastair Craig ~ Real ale ~ Open 11.30am-11pm; 12-10.30 Sun ~ Bar food 12-10 (9.30 Sun) ~ Children welcome till 5pm ~ Dogs allowed in bar ~ Wi-fi
Recommended by Simon Day, Millie and Peter Downing, Tony Scott, Gail and Arthur Roberts, Sarah and David Gibbs

HORSTED KEYNES
TQ3828   Map 3
Crown 🏆 ☆ ♀

(01825) 791609 – www.thecrownhorstedkeynes.co.uk
The Green; RH17 7AW

Super food in beamed 16th-c inn, character bar with real ales, fine wines and seats outside; bedrooms

The accomplished cooking by the chef-patron here is first class, but this is no straightforward dining pub as there's a proper bar too. This has heavy beams, big flagstones, a huge inglenook fireplace, simple furniture and chairs against the counter where they keep Bedlam Phoenix, Dark Star Hophead and Harveys Best on handpump and 20 wines by the glass, and helpful, friendly staff. There's also a two-way fireplace with a leather sofa on one side and spreading dining areas on the other, with all manner of high-backed wooden and leather dining chairs around rustic-style tables on red patterned carpet, more beams and timbering and bare brick walls. Seats in the terraced back garden overlook the village green and cricket pitch and there are also picnic-sets at the front. The four comfortable bedrooms are decorated in a pretty country style.

Highly enjoyable modern food includes ham hock terrine with piccalilli, gin-cured salmon with caramelised lemon gel and crispy capers, shallot tatin with jerusalem artichokes, parmesan and truffle oil, smoked haddock risotto with a poached egg and parmesan crisp, chicken with haggis, dauphinoise potatoes and whisky sauce, venison haunch with pearl barley and carrots, and puddings such as chocolate and rosemary ganache with rhubarb and pistachios and blackcurrant parfait with apple and granola; last Friday of the month is steak night, and they also offer a two- and three-course set menu (5.30-6.45pm). *Benchmark main dish: burger with toppings, coleslaw and fries £12.50. Two-course evening meal £20.50.*

Free house ~ Licensee Simon Dennis ~ Real ale ~ Open 12-3, 5-11; 12-9 Sun ~ Bar food 12-2.30, 6-9; 12-4 Sun ~ Restaurant ~ Children welcome ~ Dogs allowed in bar ~ Wi-fi ~ Bedrooms: £70/£90 *Recommended by Sally and David Champion, Penny and David Shepherd, Sophia and Hamish Greenfield, Geoff and Ann Marston, Patricia and Anton Larkham, Lucy and Giles Gibbon*

We checked prices with the pubs as we went to press in summer 2017. They should hold until around spring 2018.

LICKFOLD
Lickfold Inn ⭐ ♟

SU9226 Map 2

(01789) 532535 – www.thelickfoldinn.co.uk

NE of Midhurst, between A286 and A283; GU28 9EY

Tudor inn with impressive food in bars and upstairs restaurant, friendly staff, a thoughtful choice of drinks and attractive garden

The exceptionally good food in this tucked-away country pub is obviously the highlight – but locals do drop in for a chat and a drink in the bar, which has a great deal of easy-going character. The two bar rooms have heavy Tudor beams, a fine herringbone brick floor, comfortable sofas to each side of a woodburning stove, chapel chairs, armchairs, Georgian settles and nice old tables (some with fine inlaid panels); it's fun watching the kitchen hard at work behind a big glass window. Goldmark American Hop Idol, Langham Best Bitter and a couple of guest beers on handpump, a dozen wines by the glass and several gins. Upstairs, the restaurant has more heavy beams, pale grey upholstered dining chairs around dark polished wood tables on bare boards, a few standing timbers and another woodburning stove. Outside, a terrace has plenty of seats and tables and there's also a garden across the drive on several levels with more seats.

 Innovative food using the best local, seasonal ingredients includes enterprising bar nibbles such as barbecue salmon with dill and seaweed, wild rabbit, tarragon and apricot terrine and scotch egg plus ricotta tortellini with lemon, broad beans, local asparagus and a coddled egg, local venison with baked celeriac and hay, pork with crisp salsify and wild mushrooms, lamb rump with garlic purée, truffle and asparagus, guinea fowl with barbecued asparagus and walnuts, and puddings such as bitter chocolate, orange and passion fruit and buttermilk pannacotta with rhubarb and sorrel; they also offer a two- and three-course set lunch. *Benchmark main dish: halibut with cauliflower purée, pickled sloes and sea beets £28.00. Two-course evening meal £30.00.*

Free house ~ Licensee Tom Sellers ~ Real ale ~ Open 11.30-10; 11.30-11 Sat; 11.30-8 Sun; closed Mon, winter Tues, first two weeks Jan ~ Bar food 12-9 ~ Restaurant ~ Children welcome ~ Dogs allowed in bar ~ Wi-fi ~ Live music first Sun evening of month
Recommended by Jack Trussler, Andrew and Michele Revell, Brian and Sally Wakeham, Diana and Bertie Farr, Celia and Rupert Lemming

LOWER BEEDING
Crabtree ⭐ ♟

TQ2225 Map 3

(01403) 892666 – www.crabtreesussex.co.uk

Brighton Road; RH13 6PT

Airy bar and cosy dining rooms in bustling pub with excellent food, helpful service and pretty garden

Although this family-run roadside pub has a Victorian façade, it's much older inside with Tudor beams and a huge inglenook (dated 1537). The front bar is light, airy and simply furnished: a green leather chesterfield, plush stools around just three tables on parquet flooring, a warming woodburning stove, fresh flowers and nightlights and maybe background jazz. Badger Leaping Legend and Tanglefoot and King & Barnes Sussex on handpump and good wines (some organic) by the glass served by knowledgeable staff. A garden room leads off with wicker chairs, leather wall banquettes and a dresser full of home-made jellies and chutney. Several dining rooms towards the back are interlinked and cosy with beams and brick floors, high-backed dining chairs around wooden-topped painted tables and country paintings (which are for sale); a small room to the right of the entrance is similarly furnished. The lovely landscaped garden has picnic-sets and a wendy house and views of the countryside. The pub is handy for Nymans (National Trust).

◉ Imaginative modern food includes citrus-cured salmon with charred chicory, pickled cucumber and lemon curd, potted pork with sticky apple and crackling salad, parsley and garlic risotto with beetroot and hazelnuts, burger with toppings, chips and cornichon salad, smoked haddock and salmon fishcakes with celeriac rémoulade and caper salad, venison haunch with junipers, braised red cabbage and port jus, slow-cooked pork belly with pomme purée, pear and caramelised shallots, and puddings such as rhubarb and custard pannacotta with meringue and raspberries and treacle tart with clotted cream and salt caramel; they also offer a two- and three-course weekday set lunch. *Benchmark main dish: dry-aged wagyu rump steak £26.00. Two-course evening meal £24.00.*

Badger ~ Tenant Simon Hope ~ Real ale ~ Open 11-11 (midnight Sat); 11-9 Sun ~ Bar food 12-3, 6.30-9.30; 12-5 ~ Restaurant ~ Children welcome ~ Dogs allowed in bar ~ Wi-fi
Recommended by Edward Edmonton, Susan and Callum Slade, David and Leone Lawson, David and Charlotte Green

LURGASHALL SU9327 Map 2

Noahs Ark 🏠

(01428) 707346 – www.noahsarkinn.co.uk
Off A283 N of Petworth; GU28 9ET

Busy old pub in nice spot with neatly kept rooms, real ales and pleasing food using local produce

There's always a good mix of customers in this 16th-c place – both locals and visitors – and the atmosphere is chatty and relaxed. The simple, traditional bar has stools by the counter where they serve Greene King IPA and Abbot and a guest such as St Austell Liquid Sunshine on handpump, 20 wines by the glass and a fine bloody mary. There are also beams, a mix of wooden chairs and tables, parquet flooring and an inglenook fireplace. Open to the top of the rafters, the dining room is spacious and airy with church candles and fresh flowers on light wood tables, and a couple of comfortable sofas facing each other in front of an open woodburning stove; background music and board games. The border terrier is called Gillie and visiting dogs may get a dog biscuit. There are tables in a large side garden and the village green and cricket pitch are opposite.

¶¶ Well liked food includes potted hot smoked salmon with wild garlic salad, confit duck croquettes with plum jelly dipping sauce, caramelised chicory, feta and thyme tarte tatin with watercress and toasted pecan salad, beer-battered haddock and chips, lamb rump with pomme purée, salsa verde and jus, shellfish and fish stew with gruyère croutes and garlic mayonnaise, rib-eye steak with chips, portobello mushrooms and peppercorn sauce, and puddings such as treacle tart with clotted cream and triple chocolate brownie with salted caramel sauce. *Benchmark main dish: burger with toppings and chips £14.00. Two-course evening meal £21.00.*

Greene King ~ Lease Henry Coghlan and Amy Whitmore ~ Real ale ~ Open 11-11; 11am-midnight Sat; 12-8 Sun ~ Bar food 12-2.30, 7-9.30; 12-3 Sun ~ Restaurant ~ Children welcome ~ Dogs allowed in bar ~ Wi-fi *Recommended by Alastair and Sheree Hepburn, Edward May, Miss A E Dare, Jennifer and Nicholas Thompson, Liz and Mike Newton*

Bedroom prices are for high summer. Even then you may get reductions for more than one night, or (outside tourist areas) weekends. Winter special rates are common, and many inns reduce bedroom prices if you have a full evening meal.

MARK CROSS
Mark Cross Inn ♀

TQ5831 Map 3

(01892) 852423 – www.themarkcross.co.uk

A267 N of Mayfield; TN6 3NP

Sizeable pub with interconnected rooms, real ales and popular food, and good views from seats in the garden

This is a big spreading pub on several linked levels but it's kept cosy with church candles and open fires, shelves lined with books and stone bottles, gilt-edged mirrors, big clocks, large house plants and fresh flowers. There's all manner of seating from farmhouse, mate's and cushioned dining chairs to settles and stools grouped around dark shiny tables on rugs and bare boards, and the walls are lined almost frame-to-frame with photographs, prints, paintings and old newspaper cuttings. Helpful staff serve Caledonian Deuchars IPA, Fullers London Pride, Long Man Best Bitter and Shepherd Neame Spitfire on handpump and good wines by the glass; daily papers and background music. In warm weather, the benches and tables on the terrace and the picnic-sets on grass get snapped up quickly by customers keen to enjoy the far-reaching views; there's also a children's play fort.

Usefully served all day, the generous helpings of food include sandwiches, chicken liver parfait with red onion jam, prawn cocktail, beer-battered cod and chips, wild mushroom risotto, rabbit hash with spicy tomato sauce, steak burger with toppings, aioli and skinny fries, confit duck leg cassoulet with garlic sausage and cannellini beans, sea bass with lime and lemon butter sauce, and puddings such as chocolate brownie with chocolate sauce and honeycomb ice-cream and banana pannacotta with caramelised bananas. *Benchmark main dish: lamb shoulder with dauphinoise potatoes and red wine sauce £20.95. Two-course evening meal £21.00.*

Whiting & Hammond ~ Manager Simon Wilson ~ Real ale ~ Open 9am-11pm (midnight Fri, Sat); 9am-10.30pm Sun ~ Bar food 12-9.30 (9 Sun) ~ Restaurant ~ Children welcome ~ Dogs allowed in bar ~ Wi-fi *Recommended by Charles Welch, Caroline Sullivan, Edward Nile, Jo Garnett, Rob Anderson*

OVING
Gribble Inn ◀

SU9005 Map 2

(01243) 786893 – www.gribbleinn.co.uk

Between A27 and A259 E of Chichester; PO20 2BP

Own-brewed beers in bustling village pub with well liked bar food and pretty garden

Our readers enjoy their visits to this 16th-c thatched pub – not least because of the own-brewed beers. On handpump, these might include Fuzzy Duck, Gribble Ale, Pig's Ear, Plucking Pheasant, Quad Hopper, Reg's Tipple and three seasonal ales, such as Sussex Quad Hopper or strong Wobbler Ale; they also stock 30 gins, 30 vodkas and unusual rums. The chatty bar features a lot of heavy beams and timbering while the other various linked rooms have a cottagey feel and sofas around two roaring log fires; board games. The barn houses a venue for parties. There are seats outside in a covered area and more chairs and tables in the pretty garden with its apple and pear trees.

Tasty food from a seasonal menu includes game terrine with pickled vegetables, twice-baked goats cheese soufflé with gooseberry jelly, pork sausages with creamy mash and onion gravy, wild mushroom and potato cannelloni, steak burger with toppings, red onion and ale confit and chips, braised rabbit leg in white wine and cream with roasted loin and braised fennel, monkfish wrapped in pancetta with tagliatelle and pesto, venison and game pudding, and puddings such as fruit crumble and sticky toffee pudding with toffee sauce. *Benchmark main dish: slow-roasted pork belly in cider with cabbage and bacon £14.95. Two-course evening meal £20.00.*

Badger ~ Licensees Simon Wood and Nicola Tester ~ Real ale ~ Open 11-11; 12-10 Sun ~ Bar food 12-9; 12-4 Sun ~ Restaurant ~ Children welcome away from bar ~ Dogs allowed in bar ~ Wi-fi *Recommended by Dave Snowden, John Beeken, Ian and Barbara Rankin, Christian Mole, Suzy Miller, Tony Selinger, Phil and Jane Villiers, Philippa Ward, Sally and John Quinlan*

PETWORTH   SU9721   Map 2

Angel 🌟 ♈ 🛏

(01798) 342153 – www.angelinnpetworth.co.uk

Angel Street; GU28 0BG

Medieval building with 18th-c façade, chatty atmosphere in beamed bars, friendly service and good, interesting food; bedrooms

In a market town famed for its antique shops, this smart pub has the feel of a country inn and a good mix of customers. The interconnected rooms have kept many of their original features. The front bar has beams, a log fire in an inglenook fireplace and an appealing variety of old wooden and cushioned dining chairs and tables on wide floorboards. It leads through to the main room with high chairs by the counter where they keep a beer named for the pub (from Langham), Arundel Castle and Langham Hip Hop on handpump, 24 wines by the glass from an extensive list and ten gins; board games. Staff are courteous and helpful. There are also high-backed brown leather and antique chairs and tables on pale wooden flooring, the odd milk churn and french windows to a three-level terrace garden. The cosy and popular back bar is similarly furnished, with a second log fire. Bedrooms are comfortable and the breakfasts good.

Rewarding food includes lunchtime sandwiches, beetroot and gin-cured salmon with shaved fennel, radishes and lemon dressing, breaded camembert with piccalilli, herb risotto with asparagus, broad beans and parmesan, chicken, bacon and avocado salad with garlic mayonnaise and croutons, organic beef burger with toppings, smoky sauce and french fries, pulled pork hash with spring onion, capers, gherkins, sauté potatoes and a fried egg, confit duck leg with pak choi, chilli and szechuan pepper jus, and puddings such as chocolate brownie with chocolate sauce and sesame brittle and orange posset with poached rhubarb and grenadine. *Benchmark main dish: fishcake with a poached egg and wholegrain mustard and vermouth velouté £14.50. Two-course evening meal £21.00.*

Free house ~ Licensee Will Morley ~ Real ale ~ Open 10.30am-11pm; 11.30-10.30 Sun ~ Bar food 12-2.30, 6.30-9.30; 12-2.30, 6-9 Sun ~ Children welcome ~ Dogs welcome ~ Wi-fi ~ Bedrooms: £110/£150 *Recommended by Tracey and Stephen Groves, Sally and John Quinlan, John Evans, Belinda and Neil Garth*

PETWORTH   SU9921   Map 2

Welldiggers Arms 🛏

(01798) 344288 – www.thewelldiggersarms.co.uk

Low Heath; A283 E; GU28 0HG

Civilised inn with character bar and airy dining room, four real ales and good wines, helpful service and seats on terrace; bedrooms

On our chilly winter visit it was the character bar in this civilised place that we enjoyed the most. Central to this was a warming woodburner with long wooden slab tables to either side (each set with candles in brass sticks and a plant), wall banquettes and settles with scatter cushions, wheelback chairs, white-painted beams and stools against the counter where cheerful, attentive staff serve Teds Tickle (named for them by Hepworth), Langham Halfway to Heaven and Ringwood Boondoggle on handpump and good wines by the glass. An end room is just right for a small group with a wooden settle and chunky chairs around a single table, and horse and hunting pictures. The big, airy dining room at the back has spreading country views from large picture windows, wall settles and more wheelbacks and country kitchen chairs with pretty cushions around tables of all sizes on flagstones, and a busy open kitchen. Through french windows is the terrace, largely enclosed by a marquee and with teak tables and chairs. The cottagey-style bedrooms (either in the pub or in a separate annexe and all with views) are comfortable, and dogs are allowed in all of them.

Good, interesting food using local, seasonal produce includes duck hash with an egg and crispy bacon crumb, warm cheese scone with whipped goats cheese and beetroot jam, roast cauliflower with cheese croquette, curry spices and seared baby gem, sausage and mash with onion gravy, cod with white beans, chorizo and jerusalem artichokes, 30-day-hung rib-eye steak with roasted shallots, a choice of sauce and chips, and puddings such as double chocolate and hazelnut brownie and treacle tart with clotted cream; they also offer a two- and three-course set lunch. *Benchmark main dish: sticky slow-braised beef with pickled girolles and garlic crumb £16.95. Two-course evening meal £22.50.*

Free house ~ Licensee Niki Burr ~ Real ale ~ Open 11-11; 12-3 Sun; closed Sun evening, Mon ~ Bar food 12-3, 6-9; 12-3 Sun ~ Restaurant ~ Children welcome ~ Dogs allowed in bar and bedrooms ~ Wi-fi ~ Live jazz Sun lunchtime ~ Bedrooms: /£90 *Recommended by Richard Tilbrook, Sandra and Miles Spencer, Belinda and Neil Garth*

RINGMER
TQ4313   Map 3

Cock ⚓ £

(01273) 812040 – www.cockpub.co.uk
Uckfield Road – blocked-off section of road off A26 N of village turn-off; BN8 5RX

Country pub with a wide choice of popular bar food, real ales in character bar, and plenty of seats in the garden

Tucked well away from the main road, this is a 16th-c former coaching inn with convivial licensees. The unspoilt bar has traditional pubby furniture on flagstones, heavy beams, a log fire in an inglenook fireplace, Harveys Best and a couple of guests such as Beachy Head Legless Rambler and Dark Star Hophead on handpump, nine wines by the glass and a dozen malt whiskies. There are also three dining areas; background music. Outside, on the terrace and in the garden, are lots of picnic-sets with views across open fields to the South Downs. The owners' dogs are called Bailey and Tally, and visiting canines are offered a bowl of water and a chew. This is sister pub to the Highlands at Uckfield.

The well liked, wide range of food includes sandwiches, salt and pepper squid, deep-fried camembert with cranberry sauce, home-cooked ham and free-range eggs, mushroom and red pepper stroganoff, chicken curry, local venison burger with spicy relish and chips, liver and bacon with onion gravy, slow-braised lamb shank with red wine and rosemary gravy, salmon fillet with cream and watercress sauce, and puddings such as banoffi pie and fruit crumble. *Benchmark main dish: steak in ale pie £11.95. Two-course evening meal £19.00.*

Free house ~ Licensees Ian, Val, Nick and Matt Ridley ~ Real ale ~ Open 11-3, 6-11.30; 11-10 Sun ~ Bar food 12-2.15 (2.30 Sat), 6-9.30; 12-8.30 Sun ~ Restaurant ~ Well behaved children welcome but no toddlers ~ Dogs allowed in bar ~ Wi-fi *Recommended by John Beeken, William Pace, James and Sylvia Hewitt, Martine and Fabio Lockley*

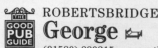

ROBERTSBRIDGE

TQ7323 Map 3

George 🛏

(01580) 880315 – www.thegeorgerobertsbridge.co.uk

High Street; TN32 5AW

Former coaching inn with good food and ales and seats in courtyard garden; bedrooms

With a friendly welcome and a good mix of customers, this is a handsome old village inn with hands-on licensees. The bar area to the right has a log fire in a brick inglenook with a leather sofa and a couple of armchairs in front – just the place for a quiet pint and a chat – plus high bar stools by the counter where they serve Harveys Best and guests such as Battle Abbey Pale and Whitstable Pearl of Kent on handpump, good wines by the glass and a farm cider. The dining area is opposite with elegant high-backed beige tartan or leather chairs around a mix of tables (each with fresh flowers and a tea-light) on stripped floorboards and more tea-lights in a small fireplace; background music. The back terrace has plenty of seats and tables. Bedrooms are comfortable and the breakfasts well thought-of.

Pleasing food includes sandwiches, pork and chorizo terrine with chutney, twice-baked goats cheese soufflé, sharing boards, cajun chicken with yoghurt dip, beef, chicken or five-bean and sweet potato burger with toppings and chips, slow-roast pork belly with pear compote and cider gravy, local rib-eye steak with peppercorn sauce and chips, lamb rump with red onion and rosemary and blackberry jus, and puddings such as crème brûlée of the day and lemon cheesecake. *Benchmark main dish: tempura-battered local cod and chips £12.50. Two-course evening meal £19.00.*

Free house ~ Licensees John and Jane Turner ~ Real ale ~ Open 12-11; 12-9 Sun; closed Mon ~ Bar food 12-2.30, 6.30-9; 12-7 Sun ~ Children welcome but must be accompanied by an adult at all times ~ Dogs allowed in bar ~ Wi-fi
Recommended by Valerie Sayer, Robert Mitchell, Peter Meister, Heather and Richard Jones

RYE

TQ9220 Map 3

Ypres Castle 🍺

(01797) 223248 – www.yprescastleinn.co.uk

Gun Garden; steps up from A259, or down past Ypres Tower; TN31 7HH

Traditional pub with several real ales, quite a choice of bar food and seats in garden

In warm weather, the tables in the sheltered garden here with views down over the River Rother get quickly snapped up – so it's best to arrive early. It's an unpretentious and traditional place and the main bar has wall banquettes with pale blue cushions, an open fire in a stone fireplace with a mirror above and easy chairs in front, assorted chairs and tables (each set with a modern oil lamp) and local artwork. Stools line the blue-panelled counter where they keep Harveys Best and guests from breweries such as Long Man, Old Dairy, Weltons and Westerham on handpump, eight wines by the glass and farm cider; background music and board games. The back dining room has paintings and pictures of Rye and similar furnishings to the bar; there's another dining room at the front. The pub is perched beside a stepped path just beneath the medieval Ypres Tower.

Popular food includes baguettes, crayfish and avocado salad, chicken liver pâté with cider apple chutney, tofu linguine with chilli and tomato sauce, smoked haddock, salmon and pea fishcakes with tomato salad, honey-roast ham and duck egg, chicken breast burger topped with pesto and mozzarella, and puddings such as chocolate fudge cake and apple crumble with custard. *Benchmark main dish: beer-battered fish and chips £11.80. Two-course evening meal £18.00.*

Free house ~ Licensee Garry Dowling ~ Real ale ~ Open 12-11 (10.30 Sun) ~ Bar food 12-3, 6-9; 12-3 Sun ~ Children welcome ~ Dogs welcome ~ Wi-fi ~ Live music Fri evening, Sun 4pm *Recommended by Stephen Shepherd, Jo Garnett, Tony Scott, Alexandra and Richard Clay*

SALEHURST
TQ7424   Map 3

Salehurst Halt ◗ £

(01580) 880620 – www.salehursthalt.co.uk
Village signposted from Robertsbridge bypass on A21 Tunbridge Wells–Battle; Church Lane; TN32 5PH

Bustling country local in quiet hamlet with easy-going atmosphere, real ales, well liked bar food and seats in pretty back garden

As ever, this particularly well run, chatty local gets warmly enthusiastic reports from our readers. To the right of the door is a small bareboards area with a couple of tables, a settle, a TV and a woodburning stove. Furniture includes a nice long scrubbed pine table, a couple of sofas and a mix of more ordinary pubby tables and wheelback and mate's chairs on the wood-strip floor; occasional background music, board games and books on shelves. Harveys Best and guests such as Dark Star American Pale Ale and Franklins English Garden on handpump, farm cider, several malt whiskies and eight wines by the glass. The cottagey and charming back garden has Rother Valley views and there's a terrace with metal chairs and tiled tables.

As well as the popular summer Wednesday evening pizzas from the wood-fired oven, the tasty food includes sandwiches, home-cured bresaola with citrus salad, smoked mackerel pâté, bacon, spinach and ricotta-stuffed field mushrooms, egg and cheddar pie, spicy italian sausages in tomato sauce with creamed parmesan polenta, steak and kidney open pie, pork chop and black pudding with cider sauce, sweet and sour prawn curry, moroccan-style lamb, and puddings such as rhubarb bakewell sponge and salted caramel torte. *Benchmark main dish: warm smoked trout niçoise £11.00. Two-course evening meal £19.00.*

Free house ~ Licensee Andrew Augarde ~ Real ale ~ Open 12-11.30 (10.30 Sun); closed Mon except bank holidays ~ Bar food 12-2.30, 6.30-8.30; 12-2.30 Sun ~ Children welcome ~ Dogs welcome ~ Wi-fi *Recommended by B and M Kendall, Nick Sharpe, Robert Mitchell, Nigel and Jean Eames*

SOUTH HARTING
SU7819   Map 2

White Hart ♀ ⇔

(01730) 825124 – www.the-whitehart.co.uk
B2146 SE of Petersfield; GU31 5QB

Enjoyable old village pub with a good mix of locals and visitors, interesting food, real ales, and seats in garden; bedrooms

Even when this sympathetically renovated and charming 16th-c village inn is at its busiest, you'll still get a genuine welcome from the friendly, efficient staff. The bars and dining area have beams and standing timbers, a couple of woodburning stoves and an open fire, bare boards and flagstones, and an attractive mix of cushioned wooden dining chairs, cushioned window seats and settles, leather armchairs and all sorts of rustic tables; there's a mural of a white hart, country prints, antlers, candles and fresh flowers. Upham Punter and Tipster and a guest beer such as Castle Rock Preservation

Fine Ale on handpump, 17 wines by the glass (from Berry Brothers of London), a dozen malt whiskies and farm cider. The terrace and garden have seats and picnic-sets under parasols, and there's a fine magnolia. If you stay in the comfortable, character bedrooms you can make the most of the lovely surrounding countryside – Uppark (National Trust) is close by.

Using local, seasonal produce, the rewarding food includes breakfasts for non-residents (7.30-10am weekdays, 8-10am weekends) plus baguettes, smoked salmon terrine with keta caviar, barbecue pork belly with sweet potato purée, burnt corn and coleslaw, sharing boards, chickpea and potato cakes with almond and coconut curry and cucumber and onion salad, burger with toppings and fries, plaice with mussels, cockles, clams and sea vegetables, pork chop with confit belly, charred leeks, fondant potato and apple, lamb tagine with couscous and tapenade, and puddings such as orange cheesecake with poached rhubarb and raspberry gel and treacle tart with brown bread ice-cream. *Benchmark main dish: ham hock with duck egg and chips £13.00. Two-course evening meal £20.00.*

Upham ~ Manager Dana Tase ~ Real ale ~ Open 7.30am-11pm; 8am-11pm Sat, Sun ~ Bar food 12-3, 6-9 (9.30 Fri); 12-9.30 Sat; 12-7 Sun (tapas only 3-6 weekends) ~ Restaurant ~ Children welcome ~ Dogs allowed in bar and bedrooms ~ Wi-fi ~ Live music – see website; quiz first Sun of month 5.30pm ~ Bedrooms: £114/£134 *Recommended by Douglas Power, Anne and Ben Smith, Daphne and Robert Staples, John Evans*

TICEHURST
Bell 🛏

TQ6830   Map 3

(01580) 200234 – www.thebellinticehurst.com
High Street; TN5 7AS

Carefully restored inn with heavily beamed rooms, real ales and good wines by the glass, popular food and friendly service; bedrooms

There's always something going on in this character pub – a craft fair, live music and comedy evenings, a film night or maybe a talk or debate. Everyone congregates in the heavily beamed bar with its inglenook fireplace, tables surrounded by cushioned wooden dining chairs on bare boards, quirky decorations such as a squirrel in a rocking chair, and stools by the counter where cheerful staff serve Harveys Best, Long Man Long Blonde and Old Dairy Copper Top on handpump, seven wines by the glass, local gin and a dozen malt whiskies. The dining room continues from the bar and is similarly furnished, with the addition of cushioned wall settles and an eclectic choice of paintings on the red walls; background music. A snug has comfortable sofas grouped around a low table in front of another open fire, interesting wallpaper, a large globe, an ancient typewriter and various books and pieces of china. What was the carriage room holds a long sunken table with benches on either side (perfect for an informal party) and there's an upstairs function room too. At the back is a courtyard garden with seats and tables and built-in cushioned seating up steps on a raised area. The bedrooms in the coaching inn are comfortable and very individually decorated and there are also separate lodges (each with their own little garden built around a fire pit).

Food is well liked and includes sandwiches, ham croquettes with spicy mayonnaise, smoked prawns with aioli, wild mushroom macaroni with cheese, a changing risotto, corn-fed chicken with smoked paprika, baby leeks, curried raisins and black sesame, beer-battered cod and chips, pork belly with celeriac purée and wild mushrooms, a fresh fish dish of the day, 28-day-hung sirloin steak with chimichurri sauce and chips, and puddings such as chocolate fondant with pistachio ice-cream and crème brûlée. *Benchmark main dish: steak burger with toppings and chips £14.00. Two-course evening meal £22.00.*

Free house ~ Licensee Howard Canning ~ Real ale ~ Open 7am-midnight ~ Bar food 12-3, 6-9.30; 12-4, 6-9 Sun ~ Restaurant ~ Children welcome ~ Dogs allowed in bar and bedrooms ~ Wi-fi ~ Bedrooms: /£90 *Recommended by Carol and Barry Craddock, John and Penny Wildon, Barbara and Phil Bowie, Belinda Stamp*

TILLINGTON SU9621 Map 2
Horse Guards

(01798) 342332 – www.thehorseguardsinn.co.uk

Off A272 Midhurst–Petworth; GU28 9AF

● ●

Sussex Dining Pub of the Year

300-year-old inn with beams, panelling and open fires in rambling rooms, inventive food and charming garden; cottagey bedrooms

'This pub makes me so happy' is a lovely comment from one of our readers. And so many others agree. It's a gently civilised and particularly well run 18th-c inn, and the neatly kept, beamed front bar has good country furniture on bare boards, a chesterfield in one corner and a fine view beyond the village to the Rother Valley from a seat in the big panelled bow window. High bar chairs line the counter where they keep Arundel Castle, Harveys Best and Skinners Betty Stogs on handpump, 18 wines by the glass, home-made liqueurs and local farm juices. Other rambling beamed rooms have similar furniture on brick floors, rugs and original panelling and there are fresh flowers throughout; background music and board games. When the weather is fine, the leafy, lush and sheltered garden has picnic-sets, day beds, deck chairs and even a hammock, and there's also a charming terrace. The cosy country bedrooms are comfortable and breakfasts are good. Constable and Turner both painted the medieval church with its unusual 'Scots crown' spire; Petworth mansion and park (National Trust) is nearby.

Exceptional food includes sandwiches, salt fish fritters with aioli, local game terrine with rowan jelly, purple sprouting broccoli with cheese, cornmeal porridge, red pepper salsa and parmesan, bouillabaisse with rouille, goan pork curry with sticky coconut rice, slaw and onion raita, organic local rose veal fillet with wild mushrooms, spinach, potato and cauliflower cheese gratin and truffle oil, 35-day-hung organic steak with smoked garlic butter or peppercorn sauce, and puddings such as lemon polenta cake with home-made seville orange marmalade and crème fraîche and iced crumble parfait with oat and pecan crumb and poached rhubarb. *Benchmark main dish: venison haunch with root vegetable gratin, beetroots and red wine gravy £17.50. Two-course evening meal £22.00.*

Enterprise ~ Lease Sam Beard ~ Real ale ~ Open 12-midnight ~ Bar food 12-2.30, 6.30-9 (9.30 Fri); 12-3, 6-9.30 Sat; 12-3.30, 6.30-9 Sun ~ Children welcome ~ Dogs welcome ~ Wi-fi ~ Bedrooms: £90/£110 *Recommended by Miss A E Dare, Richard Tilbrook, John Evans*

UCKFIELD TQ4720 Map 3
Highlands

(01825) 762989 – www.highlandsinn.co.uk

Eastbourne Road/Lewes Road; TN22 5SP

Busy, well run pub with plenty of space, real ales and well thought-of food; seats outside

This is a big bustling place, so perhaps head for our favourite spot around the bar counter. Here, customers chat over a pint or a glass of wine or browse the newspapers, and there are high tartan benches, high leather chairs around equally high tables, and armchairs. Harveys Best and two quickly changing local guests on handpump, 11 wines by the glass, a dozen malt whiskies and a cocktail menu; service from friendly, helpful young staff is good. The large, spreading restaurant on the right is split into two by a dividing wall with bookcase wallpaper, and has painted rafters in high ceilings, big glass lamps and walls decorated with local photographs and animal pictures. Also, all manner of cushioned dining and painted farmhouse chairs, long chesterfield sofas, upholstered banquettes and scatter cushions on settles around wooden tables on the part carpeted, part wooden and part ceramic flooring; background music. There's also an end bar with more long chesterfields, a pool area, TV, games machine and an open fire. Outside is a decked smokers' shelter, a children's play area and a refurbished front terrace. This is sister pub to the Cock at Ringmer.

Quite an extensive choice of food includes sandwiches, tiger prawns with sweet chilli and garlic butter, baked camembert with chutney, pork and herb sausages with mash and onion gravy, a pie of the day, sweet potato, spinach, cauliflower and chickpea curry, gammon with egg and pineapple, chicken breast topped with bacon, smoked cheddar and barbecue cream sauce, sea bass fillet with spinach, mushroom and white wine sauce, steaks with a choice of sauce and chips, and puddings such as treacle and ginger tart with custard and banoffi pie with caramel ice-cream. *Benchmark main dish: burgers with toppings, coleslaw and fries £11.50. Two-course evening meal £20.00.*

Ridley Inns ~ Managers Ian, Val, Nick and Matt Ridley ~ Real ale ~ Open 11-11; 11am-midnight Fri, Sat; 11-10.30 Sun ~ Bar food 12-2.30, 6-9.30; 12-9.30 Sat; 12-6 Sun ~ Restaurant ~ Children welcome ~ Dogs allowed in bar ~ Wi-fi *Recommended by Tony and Wendy Hobden, Andrea and Philip Crispin, Charlie Stevens*

WARNINGLID
Half Moon ♀

TQ2425 Map 3

(01444) 461227 – www.thehalfmoonwarninglid.co.uk
B2115 off A23 S of Handcross or off B2110 Handcross–Lower Beeding; RH17 5TR

Simply furnished pub with real ales, rewarding food, lots of wines by the glass and seats in sizeable garden; bedrooms

If it's just a drink and a chat you want, head for the lively locals' bar where there's a proper pubby atmosphere, straightforward wooden furniture on bare boards and a small Victorian fireplace; a room just off here has oak beams and flagstones. A couple of steps lead down to the dining areas, which have a mix of wooden chairs, cushioned wall settles and nice old tables on floorboards, plank panelling and bare brick, and old village photographs; there's also another open fire and a glass-covered well. Adnams Ghost Ship, Harveys Best and Youngs Bitter on handpump, around 18 wines by the glass, several malt whiskies and a farm cider. The sizeable sheltered garden has picnic-sets on a lawn and a spectacular avenue of trees with uplighters that glow at night-time. Bedrooms are contemporary and comfortable and breakfasts highly rated.

As well as bar choices, there are modern dishes such as home-smoked pigeon breast with morello cherries, gingerbread and pistachio crumb, halibut and cod fishcake with fennel and beetroot salad and caper dressing, mozzarella, cherry tomato and herb risotto with vegetarian parmesan, duck breast and confit leg with bubble and squeak and red wine jus, sea bass fillet with sauté sweet potato, red peppers, chorizo, tiger prawns and coriander dressing, and puddings such as passion-fruit and coconut crème brûlée with mango and pineapple salsa and coconut and lime ganache and dark chocolate and Grand Marnier marquise with white chocolate crumb and stem ginger ice-cream. *Benchmark main dish: calves liver and bacon with button onion gravy £16.00. Two-course evening meal £22.00.*

Free house ~ Licensee James Amico ~ Real ale ~ Open 11.30-3, 5.30-11; 12-9 Sun ~
Bar food 12-2, 6-9.30; 12-3 Sun ~ Restaurant ~ Children welcome ~ Dogs allowed in bar ~
Wi-fi ~ Bedrooms: /£95 *Recommended by John Harris, Belinda May, Sophie Ellison,
Andrew Stone, Belinda Stamp, Margo and Derek Stapley*

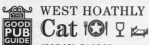

WEST HOATHLY   TQ3632   Map 3

Cat 🏅 ♉ 🛏

(01342) 810369 – www.catinn.co.uk

Village signposted from A22 and B2028 S of East Grinstead; North Lane; RH19 4PP

**16th-c inn with old-fashioned bar, airy dining rooms, local real ales,
tempting food and seats outside; lovely bedrooms**

The friendly hands-on landlord in this particularly well run old place keeps
things as tip top as ever. There's always a good mix of both drinkers
and diners and the lovely old bar has beams, pubby tables and chairs on an
old wooden floor, and a fine log fire in an inglenook fireplace. Harveys Best
and Old Ale and guests such as Larkins Traditional and Long Man Number
Eight on handpump, as well as two local farm ciders, local apple juice
and over 20 wines by the glass or carafe (plus four locally made sparkling
wines) from a carefully chosen list; look out for the glass cover over the
75-ft deep well. The light, airy dining rooms have a nice mix of wooden
dining chairs and tables on pale wood-strip flooring, and throughout there
are hops, china platters, brass and copper ornaments and a gently upmarket
atmosphere. The contemporary-style garden room has glass doors that open
on to a terrace with teak furniture. The cocker spaniel is called Harvey. The
comfortable and well equipped bedrooms were refurbished in 2017 and
breakfasts remain very good. Steam train enthusiasts can visit the Bluebell
Railway, and the Priest House in the village is a fascinating museum in a
cottage endowed with an extraordinary array of ancient anti-witch symbols.
Parking is limited but there is a public car park 300 metres away.

Appetising food includes sandwiches, black pudding scotch egg with smoked
bacon mayonnaise, salt and pepper squid with crayfish, chorizo, apple and sweet
chilli, chicken caesar salad, goats cheese hash brown with a poached egg, spinach
and tomatoes, guinea fowl and ham hock crumble with roasted red peppers and wild
mushrooms, cod fillet with milk-poached salsify, popcorn mussels and beurre blanc,
pork belly with pancetta, cranberries and mustard velouté, and puddings such as
blackberry and raspberry sherry trifle and chocolate brownie with honeycomb ice-
cream. *Benchmark main dish: steak and mushroom in ale pie £14.50. Two-course
evening meal £22.00.*

Free house ~ Licensee Andrew Russell ~ Real ale ~ Open 12-11; 12-10 Sun ~ Bar food 12-2,
6-9; 12-2.30, 6-9.30 Fri, Sat; 12-2.30, 6-8.30 Sun ~ Children over 7 welcome ~ Dogs allowed
in bar and bedrooms ~ Wi-fi ~ Bedrooms: £95/£125 *Recommended by Tina Wright, Tony Scott,
Peter Meister, Robin Waters, Robert and Diana Ringstone*

WITHYHAM   TQ4935   Map 3

Dorset Arms ♉ 🛏

(01892) 770278 – www.dorset-arms.co.uk

B2110; TN7 4BD

**Friendly, bustling inn with beamed rooms, real ales and good wines,
interesting food and seats in garden; bedrooms**

Once discovered, customers tend to come back to this 18th-c inn on a
regular basis – and although there's a strong emphasis on the particularly
good food, it's a proper pub with a working bar. To the left, the friendly and

informal beamed bar has fender seats around an open fire, scatter cushions on a built-in wall seat, a couple of armchairs, a few simple seats and tables, and darts. Harveys Best and a couple of guests such as Long Man Copper Hop and Shepherd Neame Spitfire on handpump and good wines by the glass, served by friendly, courteous staff. The dining room has a cottagey feel with pretty curtains, bookshelves to each side of a small fireplace, horse pictures and paintings, rosettes and pieces of china, a long red leather wall seat and wheelback and farmhouse chairs around dark wooden tables. A small room leads off with high-backed red leather chairs around more dark tables, a big ornate gilt-edged mirror, antlers and a chandelier; a lower room with contemporary seats and tables has a retractable roof. Outside there are seats on the front terrace and picnic-sets on grass, and steep steps lead up to a lawned garden with more picnic-sets. The six bedrooms are attractively decorated and comfortable.

🍴 Pleasing food includes devilled lambs kidneys on toast, prawn cocktail, macaroni cheese, endive, green bean and roquefort salad, steak and kidney pudding, grilled flat-iron chicken with rocket salad and frites, burger with toppings and chips, sea bass on saffron and chorizo risotto, and puddings such as chocolate and hazelnut brownie with hot fudge sauce and vanilla ice-cream and rice pudding with blackberry compote. *Benchmark main dish: whole lemon sole with brown shrimp butter and samphire £18.00. Two-course evening meal £22.00.*

Free house ~ Real ale ~ Open 12-11 (10.30 Sun) ~ Bar food 12-2.30, 6-9; 12-9 Sat; 12-8 Sun ~ Restaurant ~ Children welcome ~ Dogs allowed in bar and bedrooms ~ Wi-fi ~ Bedrooms: /£105 *Recommended by Nigel and Jean Eames, Gerry and Rosemary Dobson, R and S Bentley, Hunter and Christine Wright*

Also Worth a Visit in Sussex

Besides the fully inspected pubs, you might like to try these pubs that have been recommended to us and described by readers. Do tell us what you think of them: feedback@goodguides.com

ALBOURNE   TQ2514
Ginger Fox (01273) 857888
Take B2117 W from A23; pub at junction with A281; BN6 9EA Thatched country dining pub with simple rustic interior, emphasis on restaurant side (there is a small bar area serving local ales such as Harveys), highly regarded modern cooking, not cheap but they also do a good value two-course weekday lunch and popular Sun roasts (booking recommended), lots of wines by the glass from good list, friendly professional service; children welcome, attractive garden with downs views, play area, open all day. *(Edward Edmonton)*

ALCISTON   TQ5005
Rose Cottage (01323) 870377
Village signposted off A27 Polegate–Lewes; BN26 6UW Part tile-hung pub (two cottages); simple furnishings in bar and dining rooms, beams, log fires and some country bric-a-brac, good popular food from pub favourites up, Burning Sky, Harveys and a guest, several wines by the glass, friendly helpful service; children and dogs welcome, tables in front garden,

you can walk straight to the South Downs from here, three self-catering apartments, closed Sun evening. *(Michael Rugman)*

ALFOLD BARS   TQ0333
Sir Roger Tichborne (01403) 751873 *B2133 N of Loxwood; RH14 0QS* Renovated and extended beamed country pub keeping original nooks and crannies, five well kept ales including local Firebird and Youngs, popular well presented food (not Sun evening) from varied reasonably priced menu, friendly prompt service, flagstones and log fires, restaurant; children welcome, dogs in bar, back terrace and sloping lawn with lovely rural views, good walks, open all day. *(Tony and Wendy Hobden)*

ALFRISTON   TQ5203
Olde Smugglers (01323) 870241
Waterloo Square; BN26 5UE Black-beamed 14th-c village inn, wood and brick floors, panelling and various nooks and crannies, sofas by big inglenook, Harveys and a couple of guests, Weston's Old Rosie cider and half a dozen wines by the glass, reasonably priced traditional food (all day summer, all day Fri-Sun

winter) from sandwiches to daily specials, conservatory; background music, quiz first Thurs of month; children and dogs welcome, tables on back suntrap terrace and lawn, four bedrooms (two sharing bathroom), open all day. *(John Beeken, Tony Scott)*

ALFRISTON   TQ5203
★**Star** (01323) 870495

High Street; BN26 5TA Handsome 13th-c timbered inn decorated with fine medieval carvings, the striking red lion on the corner (known as Old Bill) was probably the figurehead from a wrecked dutch ship; heavy dark beams in character front bar, cushioned settles, stools and captain's chairs around pubby tables on bare boards, log fire in Tudor fireplace, tankards hanging over counter serving Harveys, Long Man and ten wines by the glass, steps down to big two-level bar (one level has lovely herringbone brick floor), rustic tables, chapel chairs, open fire and woodburner, further room with book wallpaper, plush burgundy armchairs/sofas and another woodburner, good locally sourced food served by friendly young staff, live music Fri, TV, comfortable contemporary bedrooms, open all day, food all day Fri-Sun. *(David and Judy Robison, John and Mary Warner, Gerald and Brenda Culliford, Robin Waters, Tracey and Stephen Groves)*

AMBERLEY   TQ0211
Bridge (01798) 831619

Houghton Bridge, off B2139; BN18 9LR Welcoming open-plan dining pub, comfortable and relaxed, with good mix of locals and visitors, pleasant bar and two-room dining area, candles on tables, log fire, wide range of popular reasonably priced food from good sandwiches up, well kept ales including Harveys and two guests, cheerful efficient young staff; children and dogs welcome (Bridget is the pub dog), seats out in front, more tables in enclosed side garden, handy for station, open all day. *(Tony Scott, Rod and Diana Pearce, Suzy Miller)*

AMBERLEY   TQ0313
Sportsmans (01798) 831787

Crossgates; Rackham Road, off B2139; BN18 9NR Popular 17th-c tile-hung pub refurbished under new licensees; well kept local Greyhound ales and fairly priced home-cooked food from good sandwiches up, friendly staff, three bar rooms including brick-floored one, great views over Amberley Wildbrooks nature reserve from back conservatory and decked terrace; children and dogs welcome, seats in pretty little front garden, good walks, five bedrooms (three taking in the view), open all day Fri-Sun. *(Alastair and Sheree Hepburn, Johnny Beerling)*

ANGMERING   TQ0604
Lamb (01903) 774300

The Square; BN16 4EQ Airy updated village coaching inn, popular food (not

Sun evening) from varied menu including good value two-course lunch, ales such as Fullers and Harveys from light wood servery, good choice of wines by the glass, helpful friendly service, painted half-panelling and wood-strip floors, inglenook log fire in bar, woodburner on raised plinth in restaurant; children and dogs welcome, modernised bedrooms, open all day. *(Julian Thorpe)*

ANGMERING   TQ0704
Spotted Cow (01903) 783919

High Street; BN16 4AW Up to six well kept ales including Harveys, Sharps and Timothy Taylors, decent wines by the glass and good choice of popular food from traditional choices up, efficient friendly service, smallish bar to the left, long dining extension with large conservatory on right, two fires; occasional live music, regular quiz nights, free wi-fi; children and dogs (in bar) welcome, disabled access (outside gents'), hedged garden with pretty flower borders and hanging baskets, also lower garden with country views, boules and play area, nice walk to Highdown Hill Iron Age fort, open all day Fri-Sun. *(Tony and Wendy Hobden)*

ARDINGLY   TQ3430
★**Gardeners Arms** (01444) 892328

B2028 2 miles N; RH17 6TJ Well liked food (all day Sun) from sandwiches and pub favourites up in old linked rooms, Badger ales, pleasant efficient service, standing timbers and inglenooks, scrubbed pine furniture on flagstones and broad boards, old local photographs, mural in back part, lighted candles and nice relaxed atmosphere; children and dogs welcome, disabled facilities, café-style furniture on pretty terrace and in side garden, opposite South of England showground and also handy for Borde Hill Garden and Wakehurst (NT), open all day. *(Martin Day)*

ARLINGTON   TQ5507
Old Oak (01323) 482072

Caneheath; off A22 or A27 NW of Polegate; BN26 6SJ 17th-c former almshouse with open-plan L-shaped bar, beams, log fires and comfortable seating, well kept Harveys and Long Man, enjoyable traditional food (all day weekends) from sandwiches to specials, afternoon teas; background music, toad in the hole played here; children and dogs welcome, circular picnic-sets out in front and in garden with play area, walks in nearby Abbots Wood, open all day (food all day weekends). *(Celia and Geoff Clay)*

ARLINGTON   TQ5407
Yew Tree (01323) 870590

Off A22 near Hailsham, or A27 W of Polegate; BN26 6RX Neatly cared-for Victorian village pub under long-serving family; generous helpings of good home-made food (booking advised), well kept Harveys and Long Man, decent wines, prompt friendly service, log fires, hop-covered beams and old local photographs, darts in thriving bare-boards bar, bigger plush dining lounge and comfortable conservatory; children welcome, play area in nice big garden, paddock with farm animals, good local walks. *(John Beeken, Tony Scott, Fr Robert Marsh)*

ARUNDEL   TQ0106
Kings Arms (01903) 885569
Tarrant Street/Kings Arms Hill; BN18 9DN Welcoming two-bar 17th-c local with five well kept ales including Fullers London Pride, no food but can bring your own (they provide plates and cutlery, decent takeaways nearby), good fire in lounge, candles and flowers on tables, more lively public bar with juke box and darts, third small room up a step; children and dogs welcome, tables out at the side and in small sunny back garden, open all day. *(Alfie Bayliss)*

ARUNDEL   TQ0107
Red Lion (01903) 882214
High Street; BN18 9AG Centrally placed red-brick pub with good value food including moules frites menu and Sat breakfast (10am-midday), four well kept ales such as Arundel, Dark Star, Fullers and Sharps, Thatcher's cider, bare-boards front bar with leather sofas either side of welcoming fire (huge red lion above), back restaurant; regular live music (Thurs-Sat), sports TV, free wi-fi; children and dogs welcome (pub dog is Roxy), garden behind with sandpit, open (and food) all day. *(Tony and Wendy Hobden, Jestyn Phillips, Tony Scott)*

ARUNDEL   TQ0107
Swan (01903) 882314
High Street; BN18 9AG Georgian inn's comfortably relaxed L-shaped bar, well kept Fullers/Gales beers and occasional guests, popular fairly priced food including deals and weekend breakfasts, friendly efficient young staff, wood flooring, sporting memorabilia and old photographs, open fire, connecting restaurant; 14 bedrooms, no car park (pay-and-display opposite), open all day. *(Dr and Mrs J D Abell, Jestyn Phillips, Tony and Wendy Hobden, Tony Scott)*

ASHURST   TQ1816
★ Fountain (01403) 710219
B2135 S of Partridge Green; BN44 3AP Attractive 16th-c pub with plenty of character; rustic tap room on right with log fire in brick inglenook, country dining chairs around polished tables on flagstones, opened-up snug with heavy beams and another inglenook, Harveys Best, guest beers and several wines by the glass, well liked home-cooked food from varied menu (weekend breakfasts 8.30-11.30am), skittle alley/function room; children (not in front bar) and dogs welcome, seats on

front brick terrace, pretty garden with raised herb beds, orchard and duck pond, summer barbecues, open (and food) all day. *(Alastair and Sheree Hepburn, Tony Scott)*

BALLS CROSS   SU9826
★ Stag (01403) 820241
Village signed off A283 at N edge of Petworth; GU28 9JP Cheery unspoilt 17th-c country pub; cosy flagstoned bar with log fire in huge inglenook, a few seats and bar stools, Badger beers, Weston's Old Rosie cider and several wines by the glass, second tiny room and appealing old-fashioned bare-boards cottagey restaurant, fishing rods, horse tack, country knick-knacks and old photographs, enjoyable pubby food (not Mon or Sun evenings), good service; bar skittles, darts and board games in separate room, outside loos; well behaved children allowed away from main bar, dogs welcome, seats out in front and in pretty back garden, open all day weekends. *(Julian Thorpe, Heather and Richard Jones, Susan Eccleston, Tony and Wendy Hobden)*

BARCOMBE   TQ4416
Anchor (01273) 400414
Barcombe Mills; BN8 5BS Late 18th-c pub with lots of tables out by winding River Ouse (boat hire), well kept ales including Harveys and good reasonably priced pubby food, two beamed bars, restaurant and small front conservatory; children and dogs welcome, self-catering chalet, open all day and can get crowded summer weekends. *(Sally Taylor)*

BARCOMBE CROSS   TQ4212
Royal Oak (01273) 400418
Off A275 N of Lewes; BN8 5BA Welcoming family-run village pub with good mix of locals and visitors, well kept Harveys ales and reasonably priced wines, generously served food from bar snacks up including Sat curry night (kitchen closes Sun evening-Weds, pizza van Mon evening), long bar with restaurant attached, beams, bare boards and open fire, local art for sale; Sun quiz, skittle alley; children and dogs welcome, a few tables out in front and in small tree-shaded garden, open all day. *(David and Leone Lawson)*

BARNS GREEN   TQ1227
Queens Head (01403) 730436
Chapel Road; RH13 0PS Welcoming traditional tile-hung pub, good generous home-made food from short menu (all day Sat, till 7pm Sun) including daily specials and curry night third Weds of the month, five well kept ales such as Fullers, St Austell and Sharps, good range of wines by the glass, acoustic music first Weds of the month, quiz second Tues, classic car event Aug; children and dogs welcome, tables out at front and in back garden with play area, open all day. *(Chloe and Tim Hodge)*

BERWICK
TQ5105
★ Cricketers Arms (01323) 870469
Lower Road, S of A27; BN26 6SP
Charming brick and flint local with three small unpretentious bars, huge supporting beam in each low ceiling, simple country furnishings on quarry tiles, cricketing pictures and bats, two log fires, friendly staff, four Harveys ales tapped from the cask, country wines and good coffee, well cooked uncomplicated food at reasonable prices, old Sussex coin game toad in the hole; children in family room only, dogs welcome, delightful cottagey front garden with picnic-sets among small brick paths, more seats behind, Bloomsbury Group wall paintings in nearby church and handy for Charleston, good South Downs walks, open (and food) all day Sat, shuts 8pm Sun. *(John Beeken, Tony Scott)*

BILLINGSHURST
TQ0830
Blue Ship (01403) 822709
The Haven; hamlet signposted off A29 just N of junction with A264, then follow signpost left towards Garlands and Okehurst; RH14 9BS Unspoilt pub in quiet country spot, beamed front bar with wall benches and scrubbed tables on brick floor, inglenook woodburner, cask-tapped Badger ales served from hatch, good home-made food from pub favourites up, two small carpeted back rooms; darts, bar billiards, shove-ha'penny, cribbage and dominoes; children and dogs welcome, tables out at front and in side garden with play area, camping, closed Sun evening, Mon. *(Sarah and David Gibbs)*

BILLINGSHURST
TQ0725
Limeburners (01403) 782311
Lordings Road, Newbridge (B2133/ A272 W); RH14 9JA Friendly characterful local in converted row of cottages, three Fullers ales and enjoyable pubby food from snacks up, part-carpeted bar with horsebrasses on dark beams and inglenook at each end; background and live music, quiz nights, bar billiards, TV; children and dogs welcome, picnic-sets in pleasant front garden with play area, campsite behind. *(Tony and Wendy Hobden)*

BILLINGSHURST
TQ0825
Olde Six Bells (01403) 782124
High Street (A29); RH14 9QS Picturesque partly 14th-c timbered pub, updated interior with large bar and split-level restaurant, flagstone and wood floors, inglenook log fire, four well kept Badger ales and enjoyable reasonably priced pubby food (not Sun evening) from baguettes and baked potatoes up; games room, free wi-fi; children and dogs

welcome, roadside garden and terrace, open all day. *(Tony and Wendy Hobden)*

BINSTED
SU9806
Black Horse (01243) 553325
Binsted Lane; about 2 miles W of Arundel, turn S off A27 towards Binsted; BN18 0LP Modernised 17th-c dining pub with good varied choice of food from sandwiches up, ales such as Harveys and local Listers, wood-floored bar and separate dining room; regular live music; children and dogs welcome, plenty of outside seating on terrace with covered well, lawn and in open-fronted cart lodge, valley views over golf course, closed Sun evening, Mon. *(Tony and Wendy Hobden)*

BLACKBOYS
TQ5220
★ Blackboys Inn (01825) 890283
B2192, S edge of village; TN22 5LG Old weatherboarded inn set back from the road; main bar to the right with beams, timbers, dark wooden furniture and log fire, locals' bar to left with lots of bric-a-brac, Harveys ales including seasonals, several wines by the glass and wide choice of enjoyable food (all day Sat, till 8pm Sun), panelled dining areas; background and some live music including open mike nights; children and dogs (in bar) welcome, sizeable garden with seats under trees, on terrace and under cover by duck pond, good walks (Vanguard Way passes the pub, Wealdway close by), open all day. *(Amanda Shipley)*

BODIAM
TQ7825
Castle Inn (01580) 830330
Village signed from B2244; opposite Bodiam Castle; TN32 5UB Bustling country pub very handy for Bodiam Castle (NT); Shepherd Neame ales and a couple of guests, good choice of wines, popular reasonably priced food from sandwiches up, friendly helpful service, plain tables and chairs in snug bar with log fire, back restaurant; occasional live music; picnic-sets on big sheltered terrace, open all day, food all day weekends. *(Stephen Shepherd, Conrad Freezer)*

BOGNOR REGIS
SZ9201
Royal Oak (01243) 821002
A259 Chichester Road, North Bersted; PO21 5JF Old-fashioned two-bar beamed local (aka the Pink Pub), well kept ales such as Wadworths and Shepherd Neame, shortish choice of popular reasonably priced food till 6.30pm (2.30pm Sun), friendly service; occasional live music, Thurs quiz, bar billiards, darts, sports TV, free wi-fi; children and dogs welcome, open all day. *(Angela and Steve Heard)*

Half pints: by law, a pub should not charge more for half a pint than half the price of a full pint, unless it shows that half-pint price on its price list.

BOLNEY   TQ2623
Bolney Stage (01444) 881200
*London Road, off old A23 just N of
A272; RH17 5RL* Sizeable 16th-c black
and white dining pub (part of the Home
Counties group) with good varied choice of
popular food, four changing ales (blackboard
descriptions) and good selection of wines
by the glass, friendly prompt service, low
beams and polished flagstones, nice mix of
old furniture, woodburner and big two-way
log fire; children and dogs (in main bar)
welcome, disabled facilities, tables on terrace
and lawn, play area, handy for Sheffield Park
(NT), Bluebell Railway and a useful M23/A23
resting place, open (and food) all day.
(Alastair and Sheree Hepburn, Tony Scott)

BOLNEY   TQ2622
Eight Bells (01444) 881396
The Street; RH17 5QW Popular village
pub with wide choice of good sensibly
priced food from baguettes up, breakfasts
(7.30-11.30am), set menu choices and OAP
meals (weekdays till 6pm), efficient friendly
young staff, well kept Harveys and a couple of
guests, decent choice of wines, brick-floored
bar with eight handbells suspended above
servery, second flagstone bar set for eating,
open fires, timbered dining extension;
bar billiards, pool and darts; children
welcome, disabled facilities, tables out on
deck under huge canopy, outside bar and
play area, various events including annual
pram race (Easter Mon), three bedrooms
in separate beamed cottage. *(Tony Scott)*

BOSHAM   SU8003
★ **Anchor Bleu** (01243) 573956
High Street; PO18 8LS Waterside inn
overlooking Chichester Harbour; two
simple bars with low ochre ceilings, worn
flagstones and exposed timbered brickwork,
lots of nautical bric-a-brac, robust furniture
(some tables close together), up to six
real ales and popular sensibly priced bar
food, efficient friendly staff (they may ask
for a credit card if you run a tab), upstairs
dining room; children and dogs welcome,
seats on front terrace and raised back one
(access through massive wheel-operated
bulkhead door), lovely views over sheltered
inlet, can park by water but note tide
times, church up lane figures in Bayeux
Tapestry, village and shore worth exploring,
open all day in summer and can get very
crowded. *(Roy Hoing, Miss A E Dare)*

BOSHAM   SU8105
White Swan (01243) 696465
*A259 roundabout; Station Road;
PO18 8NG* Spic and span 18th-c dining pub
with enjoyable sensibly priced food (not Sun
evening) including daily specials, four well
kept ales such as Dark Star and Hop Back,
friendly helpful service, good-sized flagstoned
bar, restaurant beyond with old bread oven,

darts in snug; fortnightly quiz Weds, sports
TV; children and dogs welcome in certain
areas, open all day. *(Ann and Colin Hunt)*

BREDE   TQ8218
Red Lion (01424) 882188
A28 opposite church; TN31 6EJ Popular
family-run beamed village pub; plain
tables and chairs on bare boards, candles
and inglenook log fire, good competitively
priced home-made food (should book)
including local fish and Sun carvery, own-
baked bread, well kept Harveys, Sharps,
Youngs and guests, good value wines from
short list, friendly efficient service, back
dining area decorated with sheet music
and instruments (occasional live music);
children and dogs welcome, garden
behind with roaming chickens (may have
eggs for sale), narrow entrance to car
park, open all day Fri-Sun. *(V Brogden)*

BRIGHTON   TQ3104
★ **Basketmakers Arms** (01273)
689006 *Gloucester Road – the E end,
near Cheltenham Place; off Marlborough
Place (A23) via Gloucester Street;
BN1 4AD* Cheerful bustling backstreet
local with eight pumps serving Fullers/
Gales beers and guests, decent wines by
the glass, over 100 malt whiskies and good
choice of other spirits, well liked/priced
bar food, two small low-ceilinged rooms,
lots of interesting old tins, enamel signs,
photographs and posters; background music;
children welcome till 8pm, dogs on leads,
a few pavement tables, open all day (till
midnight Fri, Sat). *(Phil and Jane Villiers)*

BRIGHTON   TQ3004
Brighton Beer Dispensary
(01273) 205797 *Dean Street; BN1 3EG*
Popular little terraced pub jointly owned
by Brighton Bier and Late Knights Brewery,
their ales along with many guests, craft beers
and an extensive bottled range, four hand-
pulled ciders too, well informed friendly
staff, bar snacks and burgers plus Sun roasts,
small back conservatory; quiz nights; open
all day and can get packed. *(Julian Thorpe)*

BRIGHTON   TQ3203
Bristol Bar (01273) 605687
Paston Place; BN2 1HA Kemptown
pub overlooking the sea; well kept
Harveys and plenty of wines by the
glass, enjoyable fairly priced bistro-style
food from open kitchen, friendly staff;
children till 5pm and dogs welcome
(resident labrador is Drogo), wheelchair
access, open all day. *(Fr Robert Marsh)*

BRIGHTON   TQ3005
Chimney House (01273) 556708
Upper Hamilton Road; BN1 5DF
Red-brick corner pub in residential area,
bare-boards interior arranged around central
bar, one or two quirky touches such as antler

chandeliers, good innovative food from open kitchen using local ingredients (some foraged), three real ales including Harveys, home-made jams, chutney and bread for sale; folk night Sun; children and dogs welcome, closed Mon, otherwise open all day, no food Sun evening. *(Edward Edmonton)*

BRIGHTON TQ3104
Colonnade (01273) 328728
New Road, off North Street; by Theatre Royal; BN1 1UF Small richly restored theatre bar with ornate frontage – note Willie the 19th-c automaton in small bay window; shining brass and mahogany, plush banquettes, velvet swags and gleaming mirrors, interesting pre-war playbills and signed theatrical photographs, three well kept ales including Fullers London Pride, good range of wines and interesting gins; downstairs lavatories; pavement seats overlooking Pavilion gardens, open all day. *(A N Bance)*

BRIGHTON TQ3004
Craft Beer Company (01273)
723736 *Upper North Street; BN1 3FG* Busy corner pub with fine selection of interesting draught and bottled beers, friendly knowledgeable staff, pubby food from snacks up, simple L-shaped bar with raised back section; closed weekday lunchtimes, open all day weekends. *(Tony Scott)*

BRIGHTON TQ3004
★ Evening Star (01273) 328931
Surrey Street; BN1 3PB Chatty drinkers' pub with good mix of customers, simple pale wood furniture on bare boards, up to four well kept Dark Star ales (originally brewed here) and lots of changing guests including continentals (in bottles too), traditional ciders/perries and country wines, lunchtime baguettes, friendly staff coping well at busy times; background and some live music, free wi-fi; pavement tables, open all day. *(Edward Edmonton)*

BRIGHTON TQ3203
Ginger Dog (01273) 620990
College Place, Kemptown; BN2 1HN Restauranty Kemptown pub in same small group as the Ginger Pig (Hove) and Ginger Fox (Albourne); well regarded modern food from changing menu (not especially cheap), good wines, cocktails and three local beers, well informed friendly service, fairly traditional bare-boards interior; children and dogs welcome, open all day. *(Charles North)*

BRIGHTON TQ2804
★ Ginger Pig (01273) 736123
Hove Street; BN3 2TR Bustling place just minutes from the beach; informal bare-boards bar area with plush stools and simple wooden dining chairs around mixed tables, armchairs and sofas here and there, Harveys Best and a guest, nice wines by the glass

and interesting local spirits and soft drinks, raised restaurant part with long button-back wall seating and more wooden tables and chairs, contemporary cow paintings, enterprising modern food (highish prices) served by friendly attentive staff; background jazz; children welcome, 11 stylish ensuite bedrooms, open all day. *(Julian Thorpe)*

BRIGHTON TQ3103
Hand in Hand (01273) 699595
Upper St James Street, Kemptown; BN2 1JN Brighton's smallest pub, but the canary yellow exterior makes it hard to miss; own-brewed ales along with five well kept changing guests, plenty of bottled beers and a real cider, dimly lit bar with a few tables and benches, tie collection and lots of newspaper cuttings on the walls, photographs including Victorian nudes on the ceiling, food limited to local sausage rolls, welcoming cheerful service and colourful mix of customers; interesting background music (live jazz Sun), veteran fruit machine; dogs welcome, open all day and can get crowded. *(Liz and Mike Newton)*

BRIGHTON TQ3105
★ Jolly Poacher (01273) 683967
Ditchling Road; BN1 4SG Emphasis on owner-chef's imaginative food prepared in open kitchen including two-course set menu (not Sat), plenty of rustic character in U-shaped bar/dining room, high-backed cushioned wooden chairs around mix of tables on wide boards, modern artwork on pale walls above grey-green dado, contemporary lighting suspended from high ceiling, a couple of fireplaces, Harveys Best, 11 good wines by the glass and cocktails (two-for-one 4-7pm); background music, free wi-fi; children and dogs welcome, metal furniture on narrow side terrace, closed Mon, otherwise open all day. *(Julian Thorpe)*

BRIGHTON TQ3004
Lion & Lobster (01273) 327299
Sillwood Street; BN1 2PS Backstreet pub spread over three floors (three bars and restaurant), softly lit interior with quirky portraits on red walls, well kept ales such as Dark Star and Harveys, extensive choice of enterprising well presented food (booking advised) including daily specials and late-night menu, friendly efficient young staff; regular jazz evenings, Mon quiz, sports TV; large terrace on two levels (can get very busy in summer), open (and food) all day, till 2am Fri and Sat. *(Tony Scott, John Beeken)*

BRIGHTON TQ3309
Stanmer House (01273) 680400
Stanmer Park; BN1 9QA Whiting & Hammond pub-restaurant in 18th-c parkland mansion; three impressive front rooms with button-back leather chesterfields on bare boards or marble, ornate fireplaces, gilt-edged mirrors and chandeliers, stone

lions/metal sculptures in wall recesses, old local photographs and shelves of books, well kept Park Life (brewed for them by Turners) and guests, 16 wines by the glass, enjoyable interesting food and popular afternoon teas, dining rooms (to left) with Victorian and Edwardian-style chairs around heavy dark tables, big portraits, church candles and opulent flower arrangements; children and dogs (in some parts) welcome, rustic furniture on terrace and around garden's pond, contemporary seats on front flagstones, open (and some food) all day from 10am. *(Mungo Shipley, John Harris, Guy Vowles)*

BROWNBREAD STREET   TQ6714
Ash Tree   (01424) 892104
Off A271 (was B2204) W of Battle; first northward road W of Ashburnham Place, then first fork left, then bear right into Brownbread Street; TN33 9NX
Tranquil 17th-c country local tucked away in isolated hamlet, enjoyable affordably priced home-made food including specials, good choice of wines and well kept ales such as Harveys Best, cheerful service, cosy beamed bars with nice old settles and chairs, stripped brickwork, interesting dining areas with timbered dividers, good inglenook log fire; children (in eating area) and dogs welcome, pretty garden, closed Sun and Mon evenings, otherwise open all day. *(William and Sophia Renton)*

BURPHAM   TQ0308
★George   (01903) 883131
Off A27 near Warningcamp; BN18 9RR
Busy 17th-c community-owned pub with attractively updated beamed interior; ales such as Arundel, Hammerpot and Harveys, wide range of wines including local fizz, interesting gins and vodkas (some made nearby), cocktails and decent coffee, good freshly made food from ciabattas to daily specials, nice selection of Sussex cheeses, efficient courteous service; free wi-fi; children and dogs welcome, picnic-sets out in front, hilltop village with splendid views down to Arundel Castle and river, open all day weekends, closed Mon evening, till 6pm Sun in winter. *(John Preddy, Robin Waters)*

BURWASH   TQ6724
Rose & Crown   (01435) 882600
Inn sign on A265; TN19 7ER Welcoming old tile-hung local tucked down lane (parking can be tricky) in pretty village, well kept Harveys, decent wines and enjoyable food (not Sun and Mon evenings) served by friendly staff, very low ceilings with banknotes stuck to beams near servery, pubby furniture on patterned carpet, inglenook log fire, restaurant to the left with another inglenook, glass-covered well just inside front door; children and dogs welcome, small side garden and pleasant back terrace, four bedrooms, handy for Batemans (NT), open all day. *(Richard Kennell)*

BURY   TQ0013
Squire & Horse   (01798) 831343
Bury Common; A29 Fontwell–Pulborough; RH20 1NS 16th-c roadside dining pub with very good attractively presented food from australian chef, well kept Harveys, a guest ale and good choice of wines, several partly divided beamed areas, plush wall seats, hunting prints and ornaments, log fire; children welcome, no dogs inside, pleasant garden and pretty terrace (some road noise), open all day Sun. *(Robert Mitchell)*

BYWORTH   SU9821
★Black Horse   (01798) 342424
Off A283; GU28 0HL Popular chatty country pub with smart simply furnished bar, pews and scrubbed tables on bare boards, pictures and old photographs, open fires, four ales such as Flowerpots and Fullers, Weston's Old Rosie cider, enjoyable food (not Sun evening) from light lunchtime dishes up, children's menu, back restaurant with nooks and crannies and old range, spiral staircase to heavily beamed function/dining room, games area with pool and darts; occasional live music and other events; dogs allowed in bar, attractive garden with tables on steep grassy terraces, lovely downs views, converted stable-block bedroom, open all day. *(Kerry and Guy Trooper)*

CHICHESTER   SU8605
Chichester Inn   (01243) 783185
West Street; PO19 1RP Georgian pub (quieter than the city-centre ones) with half a dozen local ales such as Dark Star, Langham and Harveys, good value pubby food from snacks up, friendly service, smallish front lounge with plain wooden tables and chairs, sofas by open fire, larger back public bar; live music and other events such as comedy nights, sports TV, pool; courtyard garden with smokers' shelter, four bedrooms, open all day. *(Julian Thorpe)*

CHICHESTER   SU8504
Crate & Apple   (01243) 539336
Westgate; PO19 3EU Country-style pub with interesting food from lunchtime sandwiches up, local ales, good range of wines by the glass and several gins, friendly attentive service, modern/rustic décor with simple tables and chairs on wood or stone floors, painted dados, leather sofas by woodburner; regular events including live music and quiz nights; children welcome, sunny front terrace with umbrellas, more seats behind, closed Sun evening, otherwise open (and food) all day. *(Miss A E Dare, Charlotte Bull, Craig Adfield)*

CHICHESTER   SU8604
Eastgate   (01243) 774877
The Hornet (A286); PO19 7JG Welcoming town pub with light airy interior extending

back, three Fullers ales and a guest, well cooked affordably priced traditional food, cheerful prompt service, woodburner; background with weekend live music, darts, pool and cribbage; children and dogs welcome, small heated back terrace, open all day. *(Phil and Jane Villiers)*

CHICHESTER SU8605
Park Tavern (01243) 785057
Priory Road; PO19 1NS Friendly buoyant pub in pleasant spot opposite Priory Park, good choice of Fullers/Gales beers and enjoyable reasonably priced pub food (not Sun evening), smallish front bar, extensive back eating area; quiz Tues, live music Sun; dogs welcome (they have two), open all day. *(Phil and Jane Villiers, Tony and Wendy Hobden)*

CHIDDINGLY TQ5414
★**Six Bells** (01825) 872227
Village signed off A22 Uckfield–Hailsham; BN8 6HE Lively unpretentious village local run well by hard-working hands-on landlord; small linked bars with interesting bric-a-brac, local pictures and posters, old furniture, cushioned window seats and log fires, family extension giving much-needed extra space, well kept Courage, Harveys and a guest, decent wines by the glass and a proper cider, bargain food; regular live music including blues/folk night every other Tues, free wi-fi; dogs welcome in bar, seats at the back by big raised goldfish pond, boules, monthly vintage and kit-car meetings, church opposite with interesting Jefferay Monument, open all day. *(Amanda Shipley)*

CHIDHAM SU7804
★**Old House at Home** (01243) 572477
Off A259 at Barleycorn pub in Nutbourne; Cot Lane; PO18 8SU Neat 18th-c red-brick pub in remote unspoilt farm hamlet; good choice of popular food from open sandwiches to fish specials, lunchtime set menu, several wines by the glass and at least four real ales including a house beer from Langham, friendly service, low beams and timbering, log fire; children allowed in eating areas, tables on front terrace and in attractive back garden, Chichester Harbour walks nearby, open all day. *(Tony and Jill Radnor, David and Judy Robison, J A Snell)*

CHILGROVE SU8116
★**Royal Oak** (01243) 535257
Off B2141 Petersfield–Chichester, signed Hooksway; PO18 9JZ Unchanging country pub close to South Downs Way; two simple cosy bars with huge log fires, country kitchen furniture and cottagey knick-knacks, Bowman, Exmoor and Fullers, good honest food, homely dining room with woodburner, plainer family room; background music (live last Fri of month), cribbage, dominoes and shut the box, free wi-fi; dogs welcome in bar (pub staffies are Twiglet and Amber

– the parrot is Gilbert), pretty garden with picnic-sets under parasols, closed Sun evening, Mon. *(Tony and Jill Radnor)*

CLAPHAM TQ1105
Coach & Horses (01903) 694721
Arundel Road (A27 Worthing–Arundel); BN13 3UA Friendly 18th-c former coaching inn beside dual carriageway; well liked food from sandwiches to blackboard specials including Mon deal, four well kept changing ales, local gins and vodka, rugs on wood floor, open fire in brick fireplace, flagstoned dining area to left of bar; background music, quiz second and last Weds of month, TV; children and dogs welcome, some tables out at front under parasols, more seating and play area behind, open all day, food all day Sat, till 7pm Sun. *(Tony and Wendy Hobden)*

COCKING CAUSEWAY SU8819
Greyhound (01730) 814425
A286 Cocking–Midhurst; GU29 9QH Pretty 18th-c tile-hung pub set back from the road, five well kept changing ales and enjoyable good value home-made food (all day weekends – should book), friendly welcoming staff, open-plan but cosy beamed and panelled bar with alcoves, log fire, pine furniture in big back dining conservatory; monthly quiz; children and dogs welcome, grassed area at front with picnic-sets and huge eucalyptus, sizeable garden and play area behind, open all day. *(John Beeken, Tony and Wendy Hobden)*

COLEMANS HATCH TQ4533
★**Hatch** (01342) 822363
Signed off B2026, or off B2110 opposite church; TN7 4EJ Quaint and appealing little weatherboarded Ashdown Forest pub dating from 1430, big log fire in quickly filling beamed bar, small back dining room with another fire, popular freshly made food (not Sun evening) from varied menu, well kept Harveys, Larkins and one or two guests, friendly staff and good mix of customers including families and dogs; picnic-sets on front terrace and in beautifully kept big garden, not much parking so get there early. *(Tony Scott)*

COMPTON SU7714
Coach & Horses (02392) 631228
B2146 S of Petersfield; PO18 9HA 17th-c two-bar local in charming downland village not far from Uppark (NT); beams, panelling, shuttered windows and log fires, up to four changing ales including a house beer from Ballards, good food cooked by landlord-chef; bar billiards; dogs welcome, tables out by village square, lovely surrounding walks, closed Mon. *(Andrea and Philip Crispin)*

COOLHAM TQ1423
★**George & Dragon** (01403) 741320
Dragons Green, Dragons Lane; pub signed off A272; RH13 8GE Tile-hung

cottage surrounded by fine countryside; cosy bar with massive unusually low beams (date cut into one is either 1577 or 1677), heavily timbered walls, traditional furniture and log fire in big inglenook, Dark Star Hophead, Harveys Best, Skinners Betty Stogs and a guest, decent wines by the glass and enjoyable food (not Sun, Mon or Tues evenings), dining room with pale farmhouse chairs around rustic tables on wood floor; children and dogs (in bar) welcome, pretty garden, two attractive double bedrooms in converted outbuilding, open all day Fri-Sun. *(Mungo Shipley, Nick Sharpe, Tony and Wendy Hobden)*

COOTHAM TQ0714
Crown (01903) 742625
Pulborough Road (A283); RH20 4JN
Extended roadside village pub with L-shaped bar on two levels, Harveys and a couple of guests, wide choice of popular food from bar snacks up (smaller helpings available), also set menus, friendly service, two open fires, large back dining area and games room (darts and pool); children and dogs welcome, big garden with play area and goats, handy for Parham House, open (and food) all day Sun. *(Tony and Wendy Hobden)*

COUSLEY WOOD TQ6533
★**Old Vine** (01892) 782271
B2100 Wadhurst–Lamberhurst; TN5 6ER
Popular 16th-c weatherboarded pub with linked rooms, heavy beams and open timbering, attractive old pine tables surrounded by farmhouse chairs, several settles, wood or brick flooring (restaurant area is carpeted), good inglenook log fire, well kept ales and several wines by the glass from green-painted servery, enjoyable good value home-made food; background and occasional live music; children and dogs welcome, picnic-sets on front terrace, three bedrooms, open all day Fri, Sat, closed Sun evening, Mon lunchtime; for sale as we went to press. *(Caroline Prescott)*

COWFOLD TQ2122
Hare & Hounds (01403) 865354
Henfield Road (A281 S); RH13 8DR
Small friendly village pub under new management, well kept Harveys, Shepherd Neame and a house beer Cowfold Village Ale brewed by Caledonian, decent fair-priced traditional food, flagstoned bar with log fire, little room off to the right, carpeted dining room to the left; quiz nights; children and dogs welcome, a couple of picnic-sets out in front, more seating on back terrace, open all day weekends. *(Tony and Wendy Hobden)*

CRAWLEY TQ2636
Brewery Shades (01293) 514105
High Street; RH10 1BA Popular old tile-hung pub in town centre, ten well kept beers including Greene King, several ciders and enjoyable pubby food (surcharge if you pay

by credit card), friendly helpful staff; sports TVs; seats outside in pedestrianised area, open all day (till 1am Fri, Sat). *(Tony Scott)*

CUCKFIELD TQ3025
Rose & Crown (01444) 414217
London Road; RH17 5BS 17th-c former coaching inn run by father and son team, good if not cheap food from regularly changing menus (not Sun evening), well kept Harveys and a guest, local Hepworth lagers and good choice of wines; children and dogs welcome, tables out in front and in nice garden behind, closed Mon, otherwise open all day (Sun till 9pm). *(Kerry and Guy Trooper)*

DALLINGTON TQ6619
★**Swan** (01424) 838242
Woods Corner, B2096 E; TN21 9LB
Old tile-hung roadside local with cheerful chatty atmosphere, well kept Harveys and a guest, decent wines by the glass and good blackboard food including popular two-course Mon evening deal, efficient friendly service, bare-boards bar divided by standing timbers, old enamel signs (on walls and floor), mixed furniture including cushioned settle and high-backed pew, candles in bottles, swan ornaments, big woodburner, simple back restaurant with far-reaching views to the coast; occasional background music, board games; children and dogs welcome, steps down to loos and garden, may close early if quiet. *(Peter Meister)*

DELL QUAY SU8302
Crown & Anchor (01243) 781712
Off A286 S of Chichester – look out for small sign; PO20 7EE 19th/20th-c beamed pub in splendid spot overlooking Chichester Harbour – best at high tide and quiet times (can get packed on sunny days and parking difficult); comfortable bow-windowed lounge and panelled public bar (dogs welcome), two log fires, well kept Youngs and a couple of guests, lots of wines by the glass including champagne, enjoyable freshly made food from pub favourites to specials, friendly staff; children and dogs welcome, views from large terrace, nice walks, open (and food) all day. *(Ian Phillips, J A Snell, Suzy Miller)*

DONNINGTON SU8501
Blacksmiths (01243) 785578
B2201 S of Chichester; PO20 7PR Neatly kept little roadside pub; bar with pale wooden wall seats, plush-topped stools and metal-legged tables on wide floorboards, open fire, a rail hung with old hammers and other tools, high wicker chairs against counter serving a couple of changing ales from Arundel or Langham, ten wines by the glass, popular food from sandwiches up, dining room with another open fire, grey leather or wooden chairs around simple wooden tables, watercolours on the walls, second dining room with alcove

perfect for a little group; live music Sun evening in summer, free wi-fi; children and dogs (in bar) welcome, teak tables under parasols on terrace enclosed by glass panels, fire pit and country views, attractive comfortable bedrooms, open all day (till 6pm Sun). *(Alan and Alice Morgan, Simon and Alex Knight, Tony Smaithe)*

EAST ASHLING   SU8207
Horse & Groom (01243) 575339
B2178; PO18 9AX Busy country pub run by long-serving landlord, five well kept ales including Dark Star, Hop Back and Youngs, decent choice of wines by the glass and well priced tasty food from sandwiches and baguettes up, unchanging front drinkers' bar with old pale flagstones and inglenook range, scrubbed trestle tables in carpeted area, airy extension with solid country kitchen furniture; children and dogs allowed in some parts, garden picnic-sets under umbrellas, 11 neat bedrooms (some in barn conversion), open all day (closes 6pm Sun evening). *(Pieter and Janet Vrancken, Ann and Colin Hunt)*

EAST CHILTINGTON   TQ3715
★ Jolly Sportsman (01273) 890400
2 miles N of B2116; Chapel Lane – follow sign to 13th-c church; BN7 3BA Impressive and inventive modern food cooked by landlord in this civilised place; small character log-fire bar for drinkers, Dark Star and Harveys tapped from the cask, excellent range of malt whiskies, cognacs and armagnacs and very good wine list, smart but cosy restaurant with contemporary light wood furniture and modern landscapes, garden room; free wi-fi; children and dogs (in bar) welcome, rustic tables under trees in front garden, more seats on big back lawn with views towards the South Downs, closed Sun evening, Mon. *(Mrs Julie Thomas, Ollie, Sally Taylor, Tracey and Stephen Groves)*

EAST DEAN   SU9012
Star & Garter (01243) 811318
Village signed with Charlton off A286 in Singleton; also signed off A285; PO18 0JG Brick and flint dining pub in peaceful village setting; pleasant bar and restaurant with exposed brickwork, panelling and oak floors, furnishings from sturdy stripped tables and country kitchen chairs through chunky modern to antique carved settles, Arundel ales tapped from the cask and several wines by the glass, good food including local fish/seafood (booking recommended), friendly service; background music, free wi-fi; children and dogs (in bar) welcome, teak furniture on heated terrace, smokers' shelter, steps down to walled lawn with picnic-sets, near South Downs Way, bedrooms, open (and food) all day weekends. *(Andrew and Michele Revell)*

EAST HOATHLY   TQ5216
Kings Head (01825) 840238
High Street/Mill Lane; BN8 6DR Creeper-clad 17th-c pub on crossroads (was the village school), own 1648 ales (brewed next door) plus Harveys Best, long open-plan room with wood floor, brick walls and log fire, pubby furniture including upholstered settles, reasonably priced traditional food, function room; TV, free wi-fi; children and dogs welcome, steps up to walled back garden, open all day. *(Jasper)*

EAST LAVANT   SU8608
★ Royal Oak (01243) 527434
Pook Lane, off A286; PO18 0AX Pretty dining pub with low beams, crooked timbers and exposed brickwork in open-plan rooms, log fires and church candles, drinking part at front with wall seats and sofas, one or two changing ales tapped from the cask, many wines by the glass and some 20 malt whiskies, dining area with leather chairs and scrubbed pine tables, popular imaginative food including specials, good friendly service; background music, free wi-fi; children and dogs (in bar) welcome, flagstoned front terrace with far-reaching views to the downs, more seats to the side and back, stylish bedrooms and self-catering cottages, car park across the road, handy for Goodwood, open all day. *(Miss A E Dare, Tracey and Stephen Groves, Graham Forbes)*

EASTBOURNE   TV6098
Bibendum (01323) 735363
Grange Road/South Street opposite Town Hall; BN21 4EU Roomy 19th-c corner pub with wine bar feel, well kept ales such as Harveys and Long Man, several wines by the glass and interesting selection of gins, enjoyable varied choice of food from snacks and different types of ploughman's up, friendly helpful staff, restaurant; quiz first Sun and third Tues of month; seats out in front under awning, open (and food) all day. *(Liz and Mike Newton)*

EASTBOURNE   TV5999
Lamb (01323) 720545
High Street; BN21 1HH Ancient inn arranged around central servery, lounge bar with sturdy beams and substantial stone fireplace, latticed bow windows and antique furnishings, steps down to half-panelled bare-boards dining area with mix of old tables and chairs and another big fireplace, well kept Harveys ales, good choice of wines and enjoyable home-made food at fair prices, friendly efficient service, internal glass-covered well and historic cellars; upstairs folk club first and third Weds of the month, TV and darts in public

bar; children and dogs welcome, by 12th-c church away from seafront, five bedrooms, open all day. *(Tony Scott)*

EASTBOURNE TV6199
Marine (01323) 720464
Seaside Road (A259); BN22 7NE Comfortable spacious pub under welcoming long-serving licensees, near the seafront and well known for its extravagant Christmas decorations; panelled bar, lounge with sofas and tub chairs, log fire, three well kept ales, good choice of wines and around 45 whiskies/brandies, generous helpings of good freshly made food including up to a dozen daily specials, back conservatory; children welcome, terrace and covered smokers' area, open (and food) all day Sun. *(Alan Johnson, Fr Robert Marsh)*

EASTBOURNE TV6097
Pilot (01323) 723440
Holywell Road, Meads; just off front below approach from Beachy Head; BN20 7RW Busy renovated corner inn with good fairly priced home-cooked food from lunchtime sandwiches up, well kept ales such as Harveys and Sharps, good selection of wines by the glass, friendly staff; free wi-fi; children welcome, dogs in bar, seats out in front and in nice split-level beer garden behind, walks up to Beachy Head, three bedrooms, open (and food) all day. *(Liz and Mike Newton)*

EASTERGATE SU9405
Wilkes Head (01243) 543380
Just off A29 Fontwell–Bognor; Church Lane; PO20 3UT Small friendly red-brick local with two traditional bars and back dining extension, beams, flagstones and inglenook log fire, enjoyable reasonably priced blackboard food from sandwiches up, Adnams Southwold, several guest ales and proper cider; acoustic music night second Sun of the month, beer festivals, darts; children welcome, tables in big garden with play area, open all day weekends. *(Tony and Wendy Hobden)*

ELSTED SU8320
Elsted Inn (01730) 813662
Elsted Marsh; GU29 0JT Attractive and welcoming Victorian country pub under new licensees; good interesting food from shortish regularly changing menu using local produce, three or four well kept ales and plenty of wines by the glass, friendly accommodating service, two log fires, nice country furniture on bare boards, old Goodwood racing photos (horses and cars), dining area at back; folk night first Sun of the month, classic car meeting second Weds; children and dogs (in bar) welcome, revamped downs-view garden with large part-covered terrace, four comfortable bedrooms, open all day, restaurant closed Sun evening, Mon (but some snacky food available). *(James Stock)*

ELSTED SU8119
★Three Horseshoes (01730) 825746
Village signed from B2141 Chichester–Petersfield; from A272 about 2 miles W of Midhurst, turn left heading W; GU29 0JY Good mix of customers and a congenial bustle at this pretty white-painted old pub; beamed rooms, log fires and candlelight, ancient flooring, antique furnishings and interesting prints/photographs, up to five real ales tapped from the cask such as Bowman, Flowerpots, Langham and Youngs, summer cider, highly rated food from extensive blackboard menu, good service; children allowed, dogs in bar, two delightful connecting gardens with plenty of seats, lovely roses and fine South Downs views, good surrounding walks. *(Miss A E Dare, Tony and Jill Radnor, John Beeken, S G N Bennett)*

ERIDGE STATION TQ5434
★Huntsman (01892) 864258
Signed off A26 S of Eridge Green; TN3 9LE Brick and tile country local under new ownership; two cosy opened-up rooms with painted half-panelling and lots of old photographs and prints, mix of furniture on bare boards including scrubbed pine, one table with 'Eridgeopoly' board game, sofa in front of log fire, three well kept Badger ales and several wines by the glass, good home-made food (not Sun evening) from baguettes up, friendly helpful service, downstairs function/overflow room; children and dogs welcome, tables on fenced front terrace, picnic-sets in garden set down behind, next to Eridge station with lots of cars parked on the road (pub has its own parking), closed Mon, otherwise open all day. *(Alf Wright)*

FALMER TQ3508
Swan (01273) 681842
Middle Street (just off A27 bypass); BN1 9PD Long thin building with seating areas either side of small central bar, Palmers and local guests, straightforward sensibly priced lunchtime food (evenings Thurs and Fri), barn function room; some live music, sports TV, free wi-fi; dogs welcome, seats on little terrace, near Sussex University (student discounts), closed Mon evening, otherwise open all day, busy on Albion match days. *(Robert Kennedy)*

FERNHURST SU9028
Red Lion (01428) 643112
The Green, off A286 via Church Lane; GU27 3HY Friendly 16th-c wisteria-clad pub tucked quietly away on edge of green and cricket pitch; heavy beams and timbers, attractive furnishings, inglenook woodburner, good food (not Sun evening) from sandwiches and snacks up, well kept Fullers/Gales beers and a guest, decent wines, restaurant; children and dogs welcome, seats out in front and in back garden with well, walks from the door, open all day. *(Andy and Sallie James)*

FERRING TQ0903
Henty Arms (01903) 241254
Ferring Lane; BN12 6QY Popular
19th-c local with five well kept changing
ales and a real cider, generous helpings
of well priced food (can get busy so best
to book), breakfast 9am-midday Tues-Sat,
friendly staff, opened-up lounge/dining area,
log fire, separate bar with TV and games
including bar billiards; children and dogs
welcome, garden tables, play area, open
(and food) all day. *(Tony and Wendy Hobden)*

FINDON TQ1208
Gun (01903) 873206
High Street; BN14 0TA Welcoming low-
beamed pub with opened-up bar area and
restaurant, very good food (not Sun evening)
including burger night (Mon), french
night (Tues) and popular Sun lunch, four
well kept Marstons-related beers, friendly
chatty staff, log fire; free wi-fi; children and
dogs (in bar) welcome, sheltered garden,
pretty village below Cissbury Ring (NT),
open all day. *(Sally and John Quinlan)*

FISHBOURNE SU8304
Bulls Head (01243) 839895
*Fishbourne Road (A259 Chichester–
Emsworth); PO19 3JP* Former 17th-c
farmhouse with traditional interior, copper
pans on black beams, some stripped brick
and panelling, paintings of local scenes, good
log fire, well kept Fullers/Gales beers and
enterprising reasonably priced home-made
food, friendly efficient service, intimate
dining room; background music and daily
newspapers; children welcome, dogs in bar,
tables on small covered deck, four bedrooms
in former skittle alley, handy for Fishbourne
Roman villa, open all day weekends.
(John Beeken, Christian Mole, Miss A E Dare)

FITTLEWORTH TQ0118
Swan (01798) 865154
*Lower Street (B2138, off A283 W of
Pulborough); RH20 1EN* Pretty tile-hung
dining inn under new management; beamed
main bar with mix of furniture including
windsor chairs, high-backed stools and
button-backed banquettes on wood flooring,
wall of pictures and old pub sign one end,
big inglenook log fire the other, ales such
as Harveys, Hogs Back and Langham,
several wines by the glass and traditional
cider, good food from pubby choices up
in bar and separate panelled restaurant,
efficient friendly staff; background and
occasional live music, monthly quiz, free
wi-fi; children and dogs (in bar) welcome,
big back lawn with plenty of tables, good
walks nearby, 17 comfortable well priced
bedrooms, open all day from 8.30am for
breakfast. *(Alastair and Sheree Hepburn)*

FRANT TQ5835
Abergavenny Arms (01892) 750233
A267 S of Tunbridge Wells; TN3 9DB
Attractively refurbished beamed dining
pub, good freshly cooked food (noteworthy
steaks) from varied menu including themed
evenings, six well kept local ales such as
Harveys, Larkins, Long Man and Tonbridge
(maybe bank holiday beer festivals), good
choice of wines by the glass and several
interesting gins, friendly efficient staff,
leather sofas by big woodburner in brick
inglenook, three separate dining areas;
background music, daily papers; children
welcome, terrace seating on different
levels, front part looking over road to
Eridge Park (good walks), open (and food)
all day. *(Martin Day, Gavin Markwick)*

FULKING TQ2411
Shepherd & Dog (01273) 857382
*Off A281 N of Brighton, via Poynings;
BN5 9LU* 17th-c bay-windowed pub in
beautiful spot below the South Downs;
low beams, panelling and inglenook, fine
range of real ales and craft beers including
Downlands (brewed a couple of miles
away), also bottled beers, ciders and plenty
of wines by the glass, enjoyable food from
tapas-style plates up, friendly young staff;
beer, cider and 'gin and jazz' festivals, free
wi-fi; children and dogs welcome, terrace
and pretty streamside garden with own
bar, straightforward climb to Devil's Dyke,
open all day. *(Tony and Wendy Hobden)*

FUNTINGTON SU7908
★ Fox & Hounds (01243) 575246
Common Road (B2146); PO18 9LL
Bustling old bay-windowed pub with updated
beamed rooms in grey/green shades,
welcoming log fires, good food from open
sandwiches and snacks to daily specials
and popular Sun carvery (booking advised
weekends), well kept Timothy Taylors and
guests, lots of wines by the glass and good
coffee, friendly service, comfortable spacious
dining extension; free wi-fi; children and
dogs (in bar) welcome, tables out in front
and in walled back garden, village shop,
open (and food) all day, from 9am weekends
for breakfast. *(Susan and Callum Slade)*

GUN HILL TQ5614
Gun (01825) 872361
*Off A22 NW of Hailsham, or off A267;
TN21 0JU* Big 15th-c country dining pub
with bistro-style food; large central bar

Anyone claiming to arrange, or prevent, inclusion of a pub in the *Guide* is a fraud.
Pubs are included only if recommended by readers and if our own anonymous
inspection confirms that they are suitable.

with nice old brick floor, stools against counter, Aga in corner, small grey-panelled room off with rugs on bare boards, animal skins on cushioned wall benches and mix of scrubbed and dark tables, logs piled into tall fireplace, well kept ales such as Harveys and Timothy Taylors, decent wines by the glass, close-set tables in two-room cottagey restaurant, beams and open fires, old bottles and glasses along gantry, gun prints and country pictures; background music; children welcome, picnic-sets in garden and on lantern-lit front terrace, Wealdway walks, open (and food) all day. *(M and GR)*

HALNAKER SU9008

★**Anglesey Arms** (01243) 773474

A285 Chichester–Petworth; PO18 0NQ Georgian pub belonging to the Goodwood Estate; bare boards, settles and log fire, four well kept ales such as Harveys and Youngs, decent wines, good varied if not particularly cheap food including local organic produce and Selsey fish, friendly accommodating service, simple L-shaped dining room (children allowed) with woodburners, stripped pine and some flagstones; traditional games, occasional live music; dogs welcome in bar, tables in big tree-lined garden, good nearby walks, open all day Fri-Sat. *(Julie and Andrew Blanchett)*

HAMMERPOT TQ0605

★**Woodman Arms** (01903) 871240

On N (eastbound) side of A27; BN16 4EU Refurbished pretty thatched pub with beams, timbers and inglenook woodburner, good choice of well liked food (smaller helpings available) including popular Sun lunch and Tues curries, three or four Fullers/Gales beers and decent wines by the glass, attentive friendly staff, comfortable bar with snug to the left, restaurant to the right; occasional live music, free wi-fi; children welcome if eating (not in bar), no dogs inside, tables in nice garden, open till 5pm Sun. *(Tony and Wendy Hobden, Ann and Colin Hunt)*

HANDCROSS TQ2629

Red Lion (01444) 400292

High Street; RH17 6BP Extensive stylishly reworked dining pub; beamed bar with wood and polished stone floor, armchairs and long thickly cushioned banquette facing circular copper-topped tables, Harveys and Sharps, plenty of wines by the glass and good range of other drinks including cocktails, side area with some ancient recycled timbers and stripped tables on nice oak boards, another part with lower white-painted plank ceiling, rather more contemporary furnishings and big two-way fireplace, good choice of popular well presented food from sandwiches, sharing plates and pizzas up, weekday set lunch, friendly service; background music; children and dogs (in bar) welcome, handy for Nymans (NT), open all day. *(IAA, HMW, Maria Sansoni)*

HANDCROSS TQ2529

Royal Oak (01444) 401406

Horsham Road (B2110), W of A23; RH17 6DJ Traditional comfortably refurbished tile-hung village pub under friendly new canadian landlady, well kept Fullers, Harveys and a guest, Weston's Old Rosie cider, decent wines and nice coffee, good food cooked to order including canadian recipes such as barbecue ribs, happy hour 3-5pm weekdays; fortnightly quiz Tues, free wi-fi; children and dogs welcome, seats out at front and on small terrace overlooking fields and woods, handy for Nymans (NT), open all day. *(Peter Meister, Ian Phillips, Tony Scott)*

HANDCROSS TQ2328

Wheatsheaf (01444) 400472

B2110 W; RH13 6NZ Welcoming country pub with Badger ales and good range of generous home-made food using local produce, efficient staff (they may ask to swipe a card if running a tab), two simply furnished bars with lots of taxidermy, horse tack and farm tools, log fires, caged parrot called Smirnoff; children welcome, garden with covered terrace and play area, near Nymans (NT), open all day (till 7pm Sun). *(Tony Scott)*

HARTFIELD TQ4634

Gallipot (01892) 770008

B2110 towards Forest Row; TN7 4AJ Traditional stone and weatherboarded country pub, long narrow beamed interior with central bar and fire at one end, good home-made food from baguettes to daily specials (not many tables so best to book), three well kept local beers including Harveys and Larkins, friendly helpful staff; some live music; children and dogs welcome, pleasant sloping garden behind with good views, handy for Pooh Bear country, open all day. *(Mrs J Ekins-Daukes)*

HASTINGS TQ8109

Dolphin (01424) 431197

Rock-a-Nore, off A259 at seafront; TN34 3DW Friendly tile-hung pub facing the fishermen's huts, smallish carpeted interior with masses of fishing/maritime paraphernalia, enjoyable food including fresh fish, well kept Dark Star, Harveys, Youngs and guests plus craft beers; background and regular live music, quiz Thurs; children (till 7pm) and dogs welcome, raised front terrace, open all day, food till 6pm (9pm Mon). *(Tony and Wendy Hobden)*

HASTINGS TQ8209

First In Last Out (01424) 425079

High Street, Old Town; TN34 3EY Congenial and chatty pub serving its own FILO beers (brewed close by) and a guest ale, good fairly priced food from varied menu including evening tapas (Mon) and indian thali (Thurs), friendly helpful staff, open-plan carpeted bar with 1970s Artex walls, dark wood booths and feature central raised log fire, lighter back dining room; regular live music, quiz first Sun of month; open all day, no food Sun or lunchtime Mon. *(Tony and Wendy Hobden)*

HEATHFIELD — TQ5920

★**Star** (01435) 863570

Church Street, Old Heathfield, off A265/B2096 E; TN21 9AH Nice old country pub next to church, ancient heavy beams, built-in wall settles, window seats, panelling and inglenook log fire, doorway to similarly decorated room set up more for eating, upstairs dining room with striking barrel-vaulted ceiling, Harveys Best and guests, 11 wines by the glass and well liked food; background music, free wi-fi; children and dogs welcome, seats in pretty garden with views of rolling pasture dotted with sheep and lined with oak trees, open all day. *(Claire Adams, James Landor, Gerald and Brenda Culliford)*

HENLEY — SU8925

★**Duke of Cumberland Arms** (01428) 652280

Off A286 S of Fernhurst; GU27 3HQ Pretty country cottage with two small low-ceilinged rooms; big scrubbed oak tables on brick or flagstoned floors, rustic decorations and open fire, Harveys and a couple of guests tapped from the cask, several wines by the glass and well liked food (not Sun or Mon evenings), more modern dining extension with sofas in front of woodburner; background music, board games, free wi-fi; well behaved children and dogs (in bar) welcome, seats and picnic-sets on decking and in big tiered garden with trout ponds, beautiful views, open all day. *(Miss A E Dare, John and Bernadette Elliott, John Evans, S G N Bennett, John Davis, Christopher and Elise Way)*

HERMITAGE — SU7505

★**Sussex Brewery** (01243) 371533

A259 just W of Emsworth; PO10 8AU Bustling little 18th c pub on the West Sussex/ Hampshire border; small bare-boards bar with good fire in brick inglenook, simple furniture, flagstoned snug, well kept Youngs ales and guests, ten wines by the glass and popular hearty food including speciality sausages (even vegetarian ones), small upstairs restaurant; children and dogs welcome, picnic-sets in back courtyard, open all day. *(Elisabeth and Bill Humphries)*

HIGH HURSTWOOD — TQ4925

★**Hurstwood** (01825) 732257

Hurstwood Road, off A272; TN22 4AH Although the main draw to this small country pub is their excellent inventive food (must book), they still attract some loyal local drinkers; open-plan U-shaped interior with beams and bare boards, high spindleback chairs against counter serving Harveys and Sharps, good wines by the glass and cocktails, friendly attentive young staff, area by tiled Victorian fireplace with sofas and armchairs, dining tables set with red gingham napkins, little plants and church candles, hunting prints and other artwork above painted dado, various lamps/lanterns and a piano (which does get played); children and dogs (in bar area) welcome, french windows on to deck with lawn beyond, open all day (till 5.30pm Sun). *(Nick Sharpe, Marianne and Peter Stevens, Miles Green, Charles Welch, David Jackman)*

HOOE — TQ6910

Red Lion (01424) 892371

Denbigh Road; off B2095; TN33 9EW Attractive old local behind screen of pollarded lime trees – originally a farmhouse but a pub since the 17th c; plenty of original features including hop-strung beams, flagstones and two big inglenooks, generous helpings of popular home-cooked food (worth booking), well kept Harveys, a guest and plenty of continental beers, good friendly service, main bar and back snug, overflow function room and further eating space upstairs; children and dogs welcome, wheelchair access, seats out at front and in garden behind, open all day. *(Nigel and Jean Eames, Simon and Mandy King)*

HOUGHTON — TQ0111

★**George & Dragon** (01798) 831559

B2139 W of Storrington; BN18 9LW 13th-c beams and timbers in attractive spic and span bar rambling up and down steps, note the elephant photograph above the fireplace, good Arun Valley views from back extension, enjoyable reasonably priced food, Marstons-related ales and decent wines by the glass, good friendly service; background music; children and dogs welcome, tables on decked terrace taking in the views (they may ask for a credit card if you eat out here), charming sloping garden, good walks, open all day Fri and Sat, till 9pm Sun. *(Alastair and Sheree Hepburn, Tony Scott, Tony and Wendy Hobden)*

HURSTPIERPOINT — TQ2816

New Inn (01273) 834608

High Street; BN6 9RQ Popular 16th-c beamed village pub, Harveys and a couple of guests, good wines by the glass and enjoyable food (not Sun evening) from pub favourites up, seafood specials (Fri, Sat) and themed evenings, friendly staff, linked areas including oak-panelled back bar with log fire and more formal restaurant with large skylight; quiz first Tues of the month, sports TV; children and dogs welcome, good sized enclosed garden with terrace and play area, open all day. *(Angela and Steve Heard)*

ICKLESHAM — TQ8716

★**Queens Head** (01424) 814552

Off A259 Rye–Hastings; TN36 4BL Friendly well run country pub, extremely popular locally (and at weekends with cyclists and walkers), open-plan areas around big counter, high timbered walls and vaulted roof, bottles on shelves and plenty of farming implements and animal traps, pubby furniture on brown patterned carpet, other areas with inglenooks and a back room with old bicycle memorabilia, up to eight well kept ales including Greene King and Harveys, local cider, several wines by the glass and good choice of reasonably priced home-made food; background jazz and blues (live 4-6pm Sun), occasional pub quiz; well behaved children till 8.30pm, dogs welcome, picnic-sets, boules and play area in peaceful garden with fine Brede Valley views, you can walk to Winchelsea from here, open all day (food all day weekends). *(V Brogden, Peter Meister, Tony Scott)*

ICKLESHAM   TQ8716
★ **Robin Hood**   (01424) 814277
Main Road; TN36 4BD Friendly family-run beamed pub with buoyant local atmosphere, good value unpretentious home-made food (all day Sun) including blackboard specials, well kept Greene King IPA and up to six guests, three proper ciders, hops overhead and lots of copper bric-a-brac, log fire, games area with pool, back dining conservatory; free wi-fi; children and dogs (in bar) welcome, play area and boules in big garden, lovely Brede Valley views, open all day Fri-Sun. *(Amanda Shipley)*

ISFIELD   TQ4417
Laughing Fish   (01825) 750349
Station Road; TN22 5XB Opened-up bustling Victorian local with affable landlord and cheerful efficient staff, enjoyable good value home-cooked food (not Sun evening) including specials board and some good vegetarian options, well kept Greene King ales with three local guests (always one from Isfield), open fire; bar billiards and other traditional games, various events including entertaining beer race Easter Mon; children and dogs welcome, disabled access, small pleasantly shaded walled garden with enclosed play area, field for camping, right by Lavender Line railway (pub was station hotel), post office facilities Thurs morning, open all day. *(John Beeken, Ann and Colin Hunt, Tony and Wendy Hobden)*

JEVINGTON   TQ5601
Eight Bells   (01323) 484442
Jevington Road, N of East Dean; BN26 5QB Friendly village pub in good walking country; simple furnishings, heavy beams, panelling, parquet floor and inglenook, popular home-made food from sandwiches and good ploughman's up, well kept ales including Harveys; background music (live Mon), Tues quiz; children and

dogs welcome, front terrace and secluded downs-view garden, adjacent cricket field, open all day. *(Gene and Kitty Rankin, Martin Day)*

KINGSTON   TQ3908
Juggs   (01273) 472523
Village signed off A27 by roundabout W of Lewes; BN7 3NT Tile-hung village pub with heavy 15th-c beams and very low front door, lots of neatly stripped masonry, sturdy wooden furniture on bare boards and stone slabs, log fires, smaller eating areas including a family room, food from sandwiches and pub standards up, Harveys and Shepherd Neame, good wines and coffee; background music, fortnightly quiz; dogs welcome, disabled access/facilities, lots of outside tables including covered area with heaters, tubs and hanging baskets, play area, nice South Downs walks, open all day. *(John Beeken, Ian Phillips, PL)*

LEWES   TQ4110
Black Horse   (01273) 473653
Western Road; BN7 1RS Bow-windowed pub with knocked-through bar keeping traditional feel, two log fires, wood floor, panelling and lots of old pictures, half a dozen ales mainly from smaller local brewers and some interesting gins, enjoyable home-made food including tapas, friendly service; quiz nights, sports TV, bar billiards and toad in the hole; children welcome, beer garden, open (and food) all day. *(Tony Scott)*

LEWES   TQ4210
Gardeners Arms   (01273) 474808
Cliffe High Street; BN7 2AN Unpretentious little bare-boards local opposite Harveys brewery shop, lots of beer mats on gantry, homely stools, built-in wall seats and plain scrubbed tables around three narrow sides of bar, dog water bowl by blocked-up fireplace, Harveys and five interesting changing guests, farm ciders, some lunchtime food including sandwiches, pasties and pies, bar nibbles on Sun, photos of Lewes bonfire night; background music, TV, darts; no children, dogs welcome; open all day. *(Julian Thorpe)*

LEWES   TQ4210
★ **John Harvey**   (01273) 479880
Bear Yard, just off Cliffe High Street; BN7 2AN Bustling tap for nearby Harveys brewery, four of their beers including seasonals kept in top condition (some poured from the cask), small choice of enjoyable well priced traditional food (not Sun evening), friendly efficient young staff, beamed and flagstoned bar with woodburner, huge vat halved to make two

---

If you report on a pub that's not a featured entry, please tell us any lunchtimes or evenings when it doesn't serve bar food.

snug seating areas, lighter room on left and upstairs restaurant/function room; live music first Sun of the month; a few tables outside, open all day. *(Tony Scott, Fr Robert Marsh, Ann and Colin Hunt)*

LEWES TQ4110

★**Lewes Arms** (01273) 473152

Castle Ditch Lane/Mount Place – tucked behind castle ruins; BN7 1YH Cheerful unpretentious little local with five well kept Fullers ales and two guests, 30 malt whiskies and plenty of wines by the glass, generous helpings of enjoyable reasonably priced bar food including good Sun roasts; tiny front bar on right with stools along curved counter and bench window seats, two other simple rooms hung with photographs and information about the famous Lewes bonfire night, beer mats pinned over doorways, poetry and folk evenings and more obscure events like pea throwing and dwyle flunking; background music; children (away from front bar) and dogs welcome, picnic-sets on attractive split-level back terrace, open all day (till midnight Fri, Sat). *(Ann and Colin Hunt, Tony Scott)*

LEWES TQ4110

★**Pelham Arms** (01273) 476149

At top of High Street; BN7 1XL Popular 17th-c beamed pub with character rambling interior, good well presented food (not Mon, booking advised) including some interesting vegetarian choices and meat/fish from on-site smokehouse, friendly efficient service, own Abyss beers and guests; children and dogs (in bar) welcome, small courtyard garden, closed Mon lunchtime, otherwise open all day. *(Ann and Colin Hunt)*

LEWES TQ4110

Rights of Man (01273) 486894

High Street; BN7 1YE Central Harveys pub close to the law courts, five of their ales kept well and enjoyable food (Sun till 6pm) including tapas, Victorian-style décor with a series of booths, another bar at the back and roof terrace; background music, free wi-fi; open all day. *(Julian Thorpe)*

LEWES TQ4210

★**Snowdrop** (01273) 471018

South Street; BN7 2BU Welcoming pub tucked below the chalk cliffs; narrowboat theme with brightly painted servery and colourful jugs, kettles, lanterns etc hanging from curved planked ceiling, wide mix of simple furniture on parquet flooring, old sewing machines and huge stone jars, slightly bohemian atmosphere; well kept range of ales such as Burning Sky and Dark Star, a couple of ciders and hearty helpings of enjoyable reasonably priced food (till 6pm Sun) including some good vegetarian options, nice coffee, cheerful efficient staff (may ask for a card if running a tab), more tables in upstairs room (spiral stairs) with bar billiards and darts; background and

frequent live music; dogs very welcome (menu for them), outside seating on both sides with pretty hanging baskets, open (and food) all day. *(Ann and Colin Hunt)*

LINDFIELD TQ3425

Bent Arms (01444) 483146

High Street; RH16 2HP Surprisingly spacious 16th-c village coaching inn with low black beams, timbers and some stained glass, most tables set for their popular affordably priced food including lunchtime sandwiches and ploughman's using own bread, good value evening set menu, three well kept Badger ales, friendly service; children welcome, sizeable back garden with covered area, nine bedrooms and cottage. *(Mrs P R Sykes, Tony Scott)*

LITLINGTON TQ5201

Plough & Harrow (01323) 870632

Between A27 Lewes–Polegate and A259 E of Seaford; BN26 5RE Neatly extended 17th-c flint village pub; large beamed and wood-floored bar with smaller rooms off, candles on tables, brewery mirrors and old farming implements on the walls, snug with inglenook, half a dozen well kept ales including at least three from Long Man, decent wines by the glass and good choice of generously served food from lunchtime pub staples to more enterprising dishes using local produce, friendly attentive service; monthly live music and Aug beer festival, pub quiz every second Weds; children and dogs welcome, attractive back garden, good walks (pub is on South Downs Way), open all day, food all day weekends. *(PL, John Beeken)*

LITTLEHAMPTON TQ0202

★**Arun View** (01903) 722335

Wharf Road; W towards Chichester; BN17 5DD Refurbished pub in lovely harbour spot with busy waterway directly below windows; popular good value food (all day Sun) from sandwiches/ciabattas to good fresh fish, well kept Arundel, Fullers and Ringwood, several wines by the glass, cheerful helpful staff, flagstoned and panelled back bar with banquettes and dark wood tables, large dining conservatory; background and regular live music and events, TVs, pool; children and dogs welcome, disabled facilities, flower-filled terrace, interesting waterside walkway to coast, four bedrooms, open all day. *(Tony and Wendy Hobden, Peter Meister)*

LITTLEHAMPTON TQ0202

Steam Packet (01903) 715994

River Road; BN17 5BZ Renovated 19th-c corner pub just across from the Arun View; open-plan interior providing several separate seating areas, well kept Courage Directors and guests such as Downlands, Greyhound and Langham, enjoyable food from snacks to daily specials; quiz Thurs, regular live jazz; seats out in small area facing river, raised back garden, closed Mon, otherwise open all day, no food Sun evening. *(Tony and Wendy Hobden, Tony Scott)*

LITTLEWORTH   TQ1921
Windmill (01403) 710308
Pub signed off B2135; village signed off A272 southbound, W of Cowfold; RH13 8EJ Refurbished brick and tile inn dating from the 17th c, two flagstoned bars, one with inglenook log fire, the other with woodburner, beams and lots of old farming tools etc on walls and ceiling, enjoyable home-made food (all day weekends) from sandwiches and pub standards up, well kept Harveys and a couple of guests, restaurant; bar billiards, darts, TV, free wi-fi; children and dogs welcome, picnic-sets in peaceful garden overlooking fields, bedrooms, open all day. *(Edward Edmonton)*

LODSWORTH   SU9321
Halfway Bridge Inn (01798) 861281
Just before village, on A272 Midhurst–Petworth; GU28 9BP Restauranty 17th-c coaching inn with character rooms, good oak chairs and individual mix of tables, log fires (one in polished kitchen range), interconnecting restaurant areas with beams and wooden floors, good if not especially cheap food from interesting menu along with pub favourites and set lunch, ales such as Arundel and Langham, wide range of wines by the glass, pleasant helpful staff; background music, newspapers and free wi-fi; children and dogs (in bar) welcome, small back terrace, seven bedrooms in former stable yard, open all day (food all day weekends). *(Patric Curwen)*

LODSWORTH   SU9223
Hollist Arms (01798) 861310
Off A272 Midhurst–Petworth; GU28 9BZ In lovely spot by village green; small snug room on right with open fire, public bar on left serving local Langham, two guest beers and a dozen wines by the glass, enjoyable fairly traditional food (not Sun evening) including some european influences, L-shaped dining room with wood-strip floor, inglenook and comfortable seating area, interesting prints and paintings (some by the chef); free wi-fi; children and dogs welcome, steps up to cottagey back garden, picnic-sets on terrace or you can sit under a huge horse chestnut on the green, good walks nearby, open all day. *(Julie and Andrew Blanchett)*

LYMINSTER   TQ0204
Six Bells (01903) 713639
Lyminster Road (A284), Wick; BN17 7PS Unassuming 18th-c flint pub with opened-up bar and separate dining room, well kept Fullers London Pride, Sharps Doom Bar and good house wines, generous helpings of enjoyable food cooked by landlord (best to book weekends), friendly efficient staff, low black beams, wood floor and

big inglenook with horsebrasses, pubby furnishings; background music, free wi-fi; children and dogs (in one area) welcome, terrace and garden seating. *(John Beeken)*

MAREHILL   TQ0618
White Horse (01798) 872189
Mare Hill Road (A283 E of Pulborough); RH20 2DY White-painted roadside country pub with several linked areas, enjoyable food including daily specials, well kept Fullers/Gales beers and several wines by the glass, friendly staff, two open fires, nice views from restaurant; some live music; children and dogs welcome, attractive garden behind, handy for RSPB Pulborough Brooks reserve, open all day. *(Richard Tilbrook)*

MAYFIELD   TQ5826
Middle House (01435) 872146
High Street; TN20 6AB Handsome 16th-c timbered inn, L-shaped beamed bar with massive fireplace, several well kept ales including Harveys, local cider and decent wines, quiet lounge area with leather chesterfields around log fire in ornate carved fireplace, good choice of enjoyable food, friendly staff coping well at busy times, attractive panelled restaurant; background music; children welcome, terraced back garden with lovely views, five bedrooms, open all day. *(Tony Scott)*

MAYFIELD   TQ5927
★ Rose & Crown (01435) 872200
Fletching Street; TN20 6TE Pretty 16th-c weatherboarded pub set down lane from village centre; two cosy front character rooms with coins stuck to low ceiling boards, bench seats built into partly panelled walls and simple furniture on floorboards, inglenook log fire, tankards above bar serving Harveys and a guest, several wines by the glass, decent all-day food including tapas night last Thurs of the month, further small room behind servery and larger carpeted one down steps; regular live music, Tues quiz, free wi-fi; children (till 8.30pm) and dogs welcome, raised front terrace, decked back garden, open all day (till midnight Fri, Sat). *(Susan and Callum Slade)*

MID LAVANT   SU8508
Earl of March (01243) 533993
A286 Lavant Road; PO18 0BQ Updated and extended with emphasis on eating, but with seats for drinkers in flagstone log-fire bar, well kept Harveys, Timothy Taylors and a guest, nice wines by the glass including champagne and english fizz, good if pricey food with much sourced locally, plush dining area and conservatory with seafood bar, pleasant staff; free wi-fi; children and dogs welcome, delightful spot with view up to Goodwood from neatly kept garden, local walks, open all day.
(Miss A E Dare, Mrs J Ekins-Daukes, John Evans, Hunter and Christine Wright)

MILLAND SU8328
Rising Sun (01428) 741347
Iping Road junction with main road through village; GU30 7NA Busy 20th-c red-brick Fullers pub, three of their ales and varied choice of fresh well presented food including specials and weekday lunchtime/ early-evening offers, friendly helpful staff, three linked rooms including cheery log-fire bar and bare-boards restaurant; live music Fri, free wi-fi; children and dogs welcome, extensive lawns attractively divided by tall yew hedge, canopied heated terrace and smokers' gazebo, good walking area, open all day (Fri-Sun). *(John Evans)*

MILTON STREET TQ5304
Sussex Ox (01323) 870840
Off A27 just under a mile E of Alfriston roundabout; BN26 5RL Extended country pub (originally a 1900s slaughterhouse) with magnificent downs views; bar area with a couple of high tables and chairs on bare boards, old local photographs, three real ales including Harveys and good choice of wines by the glass, lower brick-floored room with farmhouse furniture and woodburner, similarly furnished dining room (children allowed here), further front eating area with high-backed rush-seated chairs, generally well liked food from traditional choices up, friendly service; dogs welcome in bar, teak seating on raised back deck taking in the view, picnic-sets in garden below and more under parasols at front, open all day weekends. *(Tony Scott)*

NETHERFIELD TQ7118
Netherfield Arms (01424) 838282
Just off B2096 Heathfield–Battle; TN33 9QD Welcoming low-ceilinged 18th-c country dining pub, wide choice of enjoyable food including good specials and vegetarian dishes, friendly attentive service, decent wines and a well kept ale such as Long Man, inglenook log fire, cosy restaurant; picnic-sets in lovely back garden, far-reaching views from front, closed Sun evening, Mon. *(Edward Edmonton)*

NETHERFIELD TQ7118
White Hart (01424) 838382
Darwell Hill, B2096; TN33 9QH Smartened-up country pub with busy little front bar, cushions on built-in wall seats, log fire at one end, hops and country prints, stools by counter serving well kept Harveys and Shepherd Neame, lounge area with sofas and scatter cushions, huge stag's head and bookshelves, generous helpings of enjoyable food including OAP weekday lunch menu, friendly helpful service, dining room has rush-seated chairs around dark tables on coir, some half-panelling and woodburner; children and dogs welcome, white metal tables and chairs out on gravel with far-reaching views, closed Sun evening, Mon. *(Edward Edmonton)*

NEWHAVEN TQ4500
Hope (01273) 515389
Follow West Beach signs from A259 westbound; BN9 9DN Big-windowed pub overlooking busy harbour entrance; long bar with raised area, open fires and comfy sofas, upstairs dining conservatory and breezy balcony tables with even better view towards Seaford Head, well kept ales such as Dark Star and Harveys, good choice of generous well priced food (till 7pm Sun), friendly staff; regular live music; tables on grassed waterside area, open all day. *(Liz and Mike Newton)*

NUTBOURNE TQ0718
Rising Sun (01798) 812191
Off A283 E of Pulborough; The Street; RH20 2HE Unspoilt creeper-clad village pub dating partly from the 16th c (same owner for 36 years); front bar with beams, exposed brickwork and woodburner, scrubbed tables on bare boards, some 1920s fashion and dance posters, Fullers London Pride, local Greyhound and a couple of guests, good well presented food (not Sun evening) from pub favourites up, friendly service, second bar leading through to quarry-tiled restaurant, cosy back family room; background and live music; dogs welcome, small pond and smokers' shelter, archway through to lawned area. *(Tony Scott)*

NUTHURST TQ1926
Black Horse (01403) 891272
Off A281 SE of Horsham; RH13 6LH Welcoming 17th-c country pub with plenty of character in its several small rooms, low black beams, flagstones/bare boards and inglenook log fire, enjoyable good value food served by friendly attentive staff, four real ales including Fullers London Pride; popular charity quiz Weds; children and dogs welcome, pretty streamside back garden, more seats on front terrace, open all day weekends. *(Andrea and Philip Crispin)*

OFFHAM TQ3912
Blacksmiths Arms (01273) 472971
A275 N of Lewes; BN7 3QD Popular open-plan dining pub with good food from pub favourites up (not Sun evening, Mon, Tues), well kept ales such as Goldstone and Harveys, efficient friendly service, clean updated interior with a couple of woodburners, one in huge end inglenook; children and dogs (in bar) welcome, french windows to terrace, four bedrooms (steep stairs) open all day Weds-Sat. *(Amanda Shipley)*

PARTRIDGE GREEN TQ1819
★ Green Man (01403) 710250
Off A24 just under a mile S of A272 junction – take B2135 at West Grinstead signpost; pub at Jolesfield, N of Partridge Green; RH13 8JT Relaxed gently upmarket dining pub with popular enterprising food,

well chosen wines by the glass including champagne, Hurst, Longman, Palmers and a guest, good friendly service; unassuming front area by counter with bentwood bar seats, stools and library chairs around one or two low tables, old curved high-back settle, main eating area widening into back part with pretty enamelled stove and pitched ceiling on left, more self-contained room on right with stag's head, minimal decoration but plenty of atmosphere; cast-iron seats and picnic-sets under parasols in neat back garden, closed Sun evening, Mon. *(Andrew and Michele Revell)*

PARTRIDGE GREEN   TQ1819
Partridge (01403) 710391
Church Road/High Street; RH13 8JS
Spacious 19th-c village pub (former station hotel) now tap for Dark Star, their full range and maybe a guest, real cider, enjoyable sensibly priced home-made food (not Sun evening) including blackboard specials and deals, friendly relaxed atmosphere; darts and pool, free wi-fi; children and dogs welcome, garden with large terrace and play equipment, open all day. *(Julian Thorpe)*

PATCHING   TQ0705
Fox (01903) 871299
Arundel Road; signed off A27 eastbound just W of Worthing; BN13 3UJ Neatly kept pub with high standards of generous home-made food including popular Sun roasts (best to book), quick friendly service even at busy times, two or three well kept local ales, large dining area off roomy panelled bar, dark pubby furniture on patterned carpet, hunting pictures; quiet background music; children and dogs welcome, disabled access, colourful hanging baskets and good-sized tree-shaded garden with well laid-out seating, heaters and play area, open all day Sun till 9pm. *(Tony and Wendy Hobden)*

PEASMARSH   TQ8822
Horse & Cart (01797) 230034
School Lane; TN31 6UW Recently refurbished village pub, light beams and wood floors, red leather sofa and armchair by open fire, back restaurant separated by woodburner (gas) in two-way brick fireplace, good mix of seating from pews to banquettes, a beer badged for the pub from Romney Marsh along with local Three Legs, extensive wine list (several by the glass and carafes of house wine), very good food from pub stables up (can be pricey), also takeaway pizzas and weekend breakfast from 8am, friendly helpful service; games including shove-ha'penny; children and dogs welcome, a couple of tables out at front with more on back terrace and lawn, pétanque, four bedrooms, closed Sun evening and Mon, otherwise open all day. *(Caroline Prescott, James Castro-Edwards, Sue Kinder)*

PETT   TQ8713
Royal Oak (01424) 812515
Pett Road; TN35 4HG Friendly brick and weatherboarded village pub, roomy main bar with big open fire, well kept Harveys and a couple of changing guests, popular home-made food (not Sun evening) including several fish dishes, two dining areas, efficient helpful service; monthly live music (often irish) and quiz nights, traditional games; dogs welcome, small garden behind, open all day. *(Peter Meister)*

PETT   TQ8613
Two Sawyers (01424) 812255
Pett Road, off A259; TN35 4HB Meandering low-beamed rooms including bare-boards bar with stripped tables, tiny snug and restaurant down sloping passageway, open fires, well kept Harveys, Ringwood and guests, local cider/perry and wide range of wines, popular good value home-made food, friendly helpful service; background and some live music; children (in restaurant) and dogs (in bar) welcome, suntrap front courtyard, back garden with shady trees and well spaced tables, three (soon to be four) bedrooms, open all day. *(Jasper)*

PETWORTH   SU9719
Badgers (01798) 342651
Station Road (A285 1.5 miles S); GU28 0JF Restaurant dining pub with good up-to-date food including tapas, seasonal game and seafood, frequent Sun hog/lamb roasts, can eat in bar areas or restaurant, friendly accommodating staff, a couple of changing ales such as Sharps and Youngs, good choice of wines, cosy fireside area with sofas; free wi-fi; over-5s allowed in bar's eating area, stylish tables and seats on terrace by water lily pool, summer barbecues, three well appointed bedrooms, good breakfast. *(Kerry and Guy Trooper)*

PETWORTH   SU9721
Star (01798) 342569
Market Square; GU28 0AH Airy opened-up old pub with well kept Fullers/ Gales beers and decent wines, good choice of enjoyable food (not Sun evening), friendly helpful service, log fire; free wi-fi; children welcome, a few seats on terrace looking on to market square, open all day. *(Kerry and Guy Trooper)*

PLUMPTON   TQ3613
Half Moon (01273) 890253
Ditchling Road (B2116); BN7 3AF Enlarged beamed and timbered roadside dining pub with good locally sourced food from pub favourites up, local ales and plenty of wines by the glass, log fire with

---

We say if we know a pub has background music.

unusual flint chimneybreast; background
music; children and dogs (in bar) welcome,
tables in wisteria-clad front courtyard and
on back terrace, big downs-view garden
with picnic area, good walks, open all
day (till 6pm Sun). *(Julian Thorpe)*

RINGMER TQ4512
Green Man (01273) 812422
Lewes Road; BN8 5NA Welcoming
1930s roadside pub with busy mix of locals
and visitors, six real ales from brick-
faced counter including Greene King,
wide range of generous good value food,
efficient friendly service, long bar with
log fire, large restaurant, conservatory;
children and dogs welcome, terrace tables,
more on lawn under trees, play area, open
(and food) all day. *(John Beeken)*

RODMELL TQ4105
Abergavenny Arms (01273) 472416
Back road Lewes–Newhaven; BN7 3EZ
Welcoming beamed and raftered ex-barn,
large open-plan bar with wood and tiled
floors, several recesses and log fire in big
fireplace, good selection of enjoyable bar
food (not Sun evening), well kept Harveys
and one or more local guests, upstairs
eating area, games room; occasional live
music, free wi-fi; children welcome, large
two-level back terrace, handy for Virginia
Woolf's Monk's House (NT) and South
Downs Way, open all day. *(John Beeken)*

ROWHOOK TQ1234
★Chequers (01403) 790480
Off A29 NW of Horsham; RH12 3PY
Attractive 15th-c country pub, beamed
and flagstoned front bar with portraits and
inglenook log fire, step up to low-ceilinged
lounge, well kept Harveys and guests,
decent wines by the glass and good food
from chef-landlord using local ingredients
including home-grown vegetables, efficient
service from friendly chatty young staff,
separate restaurant; background music;
children and dogs welcome, tables on front
terraces and in pretty garden behind, good
play area, closed Sun evening. *(John Preddy,
Ian and Rose Lock, Hunter and Christine
Wright, Sally and John Quinlan)*

RUSPER TQ1836
★Royal Oak (01293) 871393
*Friday Street, towards Warnham – back
road N of Horsham, E of A24 (OS Sheet
187 map reference 185369); RH12 4QA*
Old-fashioned and well worn-in tile-hung
pub in very rural spot on Sussex Border Path;
small carpeted top bar with leather sofas
and armchairs, log fire, steps down to long
beamed main bar with plush wall seats, pine
tables and chairs and homely knick-knacks,
half a dozen well kept ales including Surrey
Hills Ranmore, real ciders and perries, short
choice of enjoyable low-priced lunchtime
food, (evenings and Sun lunch by pre-

arrangement), plain games room with darts;
no children inside, a few picnic-sets on grass
by road and in streamside garden beyond
car park, roaming chickens (eggs for sale),
bedrooms, closes at 9pm (4pm Sun).
(Alastair and Sheree Hepburn, Tony Scott)

RUSPER TQ2037
Star (01293) 871264
Off A264 S of Crawley; RH12 4RA
Several linked rooms in cosy 15th-c
beamed coaching inn, with well kept
Fullers London Pride, Greene King
Abbot and Ringwood Razorback, decent
food from sandwiches and light meals
up including some greek dishes, wood
floors, old tools on walls, fine brick
inglenook; children and dogs welcome,
small back terrace. *(Edward Edmonton)*

RYE TQ9220
★George (01797) 222114
High Street; TN31 7JT Sizeable hotel
with popular beamed bar, mix of furniture
including settles on bare boards, log fire, ales
such as Dark Star, Franklins, Harveys and Old
Dairy, continental beers on tap too, friendly
service from neat young staff, interesting
bistro-style food and good selection of wines,
big spreading restaurant to right of main
door; may be background jazz; children and
dogs welcome, attractive bedrooms, open all
day. *(Nigel and Jean Eames, Caroline Prescott)*

RYE TQ9220
★Globe (01797) 225220
Military Road; TN31 7NX Small
weatherboarded pub under same owners as
the Five Bells at Brabourne and Woolpack
at Warehorne (both in Kent); revamped
interior full of quirky touches such as
corrugated iron-clad walls, hanging lobster-
pot lights and eclectic range of furniture
from school chairs to a table made from
part of an old fishing boat, even hay bale
seats in one part, scatter cushions, fresh
flowers, candles and paraffin lamps, two log
fires, good locally sourced food from open
kitchen with wood-fired oven, interesting
local ales and ciders (no bar counter), also
some wines from nearby Chapel Down,
shelves of home-made preserves for sale,
quick cheerful service; unisex loos; children
and dogs welcome, seats on side decking,
Sat market, open all day. *(Alice Wright)*

RYE TQ9220
★Mermaid (01797) 223065
Mermaid Street; TN31 7EY Fine old
timbered inn on famous cobbled street
(cellars date from 12th c, although pub was
rebuilt in 1420); civilised antiques-filled
bar, Victorian gothick carved chairs, older
but plainer oak seats and huge working
inglenook with massive bressumer, Fullers,
Greene King and Harveys, good selection of
wines and malt whiskies, bar food (not Sat
evening) or more elaborate and expensive

restaurant choices, efficient friendly service, reputedly haunted by five ghosts; background music; children welcome, seats on small back terrace, bedrooms (most with four-posters), open all day. *(Stephen Shepherd)*

RYE　　　　　　　　　　　　TQ9120

Ship　(01797) 222233

The Strand, at the foot of Mermaid Street; TN31 7DB 16th-c inn with unusual blend of quirkiness and comfort; ground floor opened up from the sunny big-windowed front part to snugger back section with log fire below a stuffed boar's head, mix of flooring including composition, stripped boards and flagstones, a bit of carpet in the armchair corner, beams and timbers, mixed bag of rather second-hand-feeling furnishings – a cosy group of overstuffed leather armchairs and sofa, random stripped or Formica-topped tables and various café chairs – that suit it nicely, as do the utilitarian bulkhead wall lamps; Long Man, Old Dairy and Rother Valley, several wines by the glass and range of cocktails, generally well liked food from short menu; Sun quiz, board games, free wi-fi; children and dogs (in bar) welcome, simply furnished but comfortable bedrooms, also single-storey cottage and house for rent, picnic-sets out by quiet lane, open all day from 8am for breakfast. *(Stephen Shepherd, Peter Meister, Paul Rampton, Julie Harding, Mike and Eleanor Anderson)*

RYE　　　　　　　　　　　　TQ9120

★Standard　(01797) 225231

The Mint, High Street; TN31 7EN Ancient pub sympathetically opened up and renovated; moulded beams, exposed brickwork and panelling, brown leather and farmhouse chairs at rustic tables on quarry tiles, candles and log fires (stag's head above one), four well kept ales including nearby Three Legs, good fairly priced food using local ingredients (fish from the harbour), nice wines and decent coffee, friendly accommodating staff; outside gents'; well behaved children and dogs welcome, picnic sets on small back terrace, five well appointed character bedrooms, open all day. *(Caroline Prescott, Peter Meister, Mike and Eleanor Anderson)*

RYE HARBOUR　　　　　　　TQ9419

Inkerman Arms　(01797) 222464

Rye Harbour Road; TN31 7TQ Welcoming 19th-c end-of-terrace pub near nature reserve, enjoyable food including good fish and chips, well kept ales such as Old Dairy and Longman; children and dogs welcome, picnic sets in sheltered back terrace with pond, open all day Fri-Sun. *(William and Sophia Renton)*

RYE HARBOUR　　　　　　　TQ9419

William the Conqueror

(01797) 223315 *Opposite lifeboat station, bottom of Harbour Road; TN31 7TU* Welcoming recently refurbished harbourside

pub, well kept Shepherd Neame ales and good choice of wines by the glass, popular reasonably priced food including local fish and some mediterranean dishes, friendly helpful staff; background and occasional live music; children and dogs welcome, picnic-sets out in front, open all day (till 10pm Mon-Thurs, 6pm Sun). *(John Hills)*

SEDLESCOMBE　　　　　　　TQ7817

Queens Head　(01424) 870228

The Green; TN33 0QA Attractive tile-hung village-green pub (watch out for the wandering geese); beamed main bar on right with mixed tables and wheelback chairs on wood floor, church candles and fresh flowers, a huge cartwheel and some farming odds and ends, Harveys and Sharps Doom Bar from plank-fronted servery, side room laid for dining with brick fireplace, sofas in back lounge, another dining room to left of entrance with sisal flooring and huge working inglenook, good popular food from shortish menu (best to book); quiet background music; children and dogs welcome, garden picnic-sets, open all day, food all day Sat. *(Caroline Prescott, Will Wright)*

SHORTBRIDGE　　　　　　　TQ4521

★Peacock　(01825) 762463

Piltdown; OS Sheet 198 map reference 450215; TN22 3XA Civilised and welcoming old country dining pub with two fine yew trees flanking entrance, dark beams, timbers and big inglenook, some nice old furniture on parquet floors, good food from ciabattas up (all day weekends, till 6pm winter Sun), two or three well kept ales and decent wines by the glass, friendly attentive staff, restaurant; children welcome, back garden and terrace. *(Tony Scott)*

SIDLESHAM　　　　　　　　SZ8697

★Crab & Lobster　(01243) 641233

Mill Lane; off B2145 S of Chichester; PO20 7NB Restaurant-with-rooms rather than pub but walkers and bird-watchers welcome in small flagstoned bar for light meals, Harveys, Sharps and lots of wines by the glass including champagne, stylish upmarket restaurant with good imaginative (and pricey) food including excellent local fish, competent friendly young staff; background music; children welcome, tables on back terrace overlooking marshes, smart bedrooms, self-catering cottage, open all day (food all day weekends). *(Tracey and Stephen Groves, Richard Tilbrook)*

SINGLETON　　　　　　　　SU8713

Partridge　(01243) 811251

Just off A286 Midhurst–Chichester; PO18 0EY Pretty 16th-c pub in attractive village setting; all sorts of light and dark wood tables and dining chairs on polished wooden floors, flagstones or carpet, some country knick-knacks, open fires and woodburner, well kept Fullers London Pride, Harveys Best and a summer guest, several wines by the glass, tasty food, friendly service; background music, daily papers and board games; children and dogs welcome, plenty of seats under parasols on terrace and in walled garden, handy for Weald & Downland Living Museum. *(John Evans)*

SLINDON   SU9708
Spur (01243) 814216
Slindon Common; A29 towards Bognor; BN18 0NE Roomy 17th-c pub with good choice of popular food from bar snacks and pub favourites up (regular themed nights), Courage Directors and Sharps Doom Bar, friendly staff, pine tables and two big log fires, large panelled restaurant, games room with darts and pool, also a skittle alley; quiz fourth Weds of the month, some live music; children welcome, dogs in bar, pretty garden (some traffic noise), good local walks, open all day Sun. *(Tony and Wendy Hobden)*

SMALL DOLE   TQ2112
Fox (01273) 491196
Honfield Road; BN5 0XE Busy roadside village pub with good choice well liked/priced home-made food including popular weekday set menu, quick friendly service even at busy times, well kept Harveys and one or two guests, large dining area off roomy panelled bar, dark pubby furniture on patterned carpet, hunting pictures; quiet background music; children and dogs welcome, disabled access, colourful hanging baskets and good-sized tree-shaded garden with play area, open all day weekends (food all day Sun till 8pm). *(Tony and Wendy Hobden)*

SOMPTING   TQ1605
Marquis of Granby (01903) 231102
West Street; BN15 0AP Big 1930s pub with large sofas and raised dining area in updated part-flagstoned lounge, Fullers and Sharps ales kept well, good reasonably priced food (not Sun evening) from baguettes, burgers and pizzas up including daily specials and popular Sun roasts, friendly welcoming staff, pool, darts, fruit machine and TV in sports bar; live music and other events; children and dogs welcome, garden with picnic-sets, play area and marquee, open all day (till 6pm Sun). *(Nigel and Jean Eames)*

SOUTHWATER   TQ1528
Bax Castle (01403) 730369
Two Mile Ash, a mile or so NW; RH13 0LA Early 19th-c country pub with well liked/priced home-made food (all day Sat) including wood-fired pizzas and Sun carvery, three Marstons-related ales, friendly staff, sofas next to big log fire, barn restaurant; background music; children and dogs welcome, pleasant garden with play area, near Downs Link path on former railway track, open all day (till 7pm Sun). *(Tony and Wendy Hobden)*

STAPLEFIELD   TQ2728
Jolly Tanners (01444) 400335
Handcross Road, just off A23; RH17 6EF Split-level local by cricket green, welcoming landlord and pub dogs, two good log fires, padded settles and lots of china, brasses and old photographs, Fullers, Harveys and four guests (beer festivals), real cider, enjoyable pubby food including range of 'sizzling' dishes, friendly chatty atmosphere; background and some live music; children and dogs welcome, attractive suntrap garden, quite handy for Nymans (NT), open all day Fri-Sun. *(Tony Scott, Tony and Wendy Hobden)*

STAPLEFIELD   TQ2728
Victory (01444) 400463
Warninglid Road; RH17 6EU Pretty little shuttered dining pub overlooking cricket green (and London to Brighton veteran car run, first Sun in Nov), friendly welcoming staff, good choice of popular home-made food (all day Sat, till 5pm Sun) with smaller helpings for children, well kept Harveys Best and a guest, local cider and decent wines from zinc topped counter, beams and woodburner; dogs welcome in bar, nice tree-shaded garden with play area, closed Mon, otherwise open all day. *(Tony Scott, Ian Phillips)*

STEDHAM   SU8522
Hamilton Arms (01730) 812555
School Lane (off A272); GU29 0NZ Village local run by friendly thai family, standard pub food as well as popular thai bar snacks and restaurant dishes (you can buy ingredients in their little shop), good value Sun buffet, reasonably priced wines and four or more well kept ales, games room; background music; pretty hanging baskets on front terrace overlooking small green, nearby walks, open all day Thurs-Sun, closed Mon. *(Julian Thorpe)*

STOPHAM   TQ0318
★White Hart (01798) 874903
Off A283 E of village, W of Pulborough; RH20 1DS Fine old beamed pub by medieval River Arun bridge, well kept Harveys and Sharps, good food from ciabattas, sharing plates and stone-baked pizzas up, friendly efficient service; regular summer Sun afternoon music; children and dogs (in bar) welcome, waterside tables, open all day, food all day Sat. *(Alastair and Sheree Hepburn)*

STOUGHTON   SU8011
Hare & Hounds (02392) 631433
Signed off B2146 Petersfield–Emsworth; PO18 9JQ Airy pine-clad country dining pub with good reasonably priced fresh food from sandwiches to Sun roasts, up to six well kept ales and Weston's cider, cheerful service, flagstones and big open fires, locals' bar with darts; quiz nights; children (in eating areas)

and dogs welcome, tables on pretty front terrace and grass behind, lovely setting near Saxon church, good walks, open all day. *(Ann and Colin Hunt)*

SUTTON SU9715
★**White Horse** (01798) 869221
The Street; RH20 1PS Cleanly modernised country inn close to Bignor Roman Villa; bar with open brick fireplace at each end, tea-lights on mantelpieces and cushioned high bar chairs, up to three well kept ales and good wines by the glass, two-room barrel-vaulted dining area with minimalist décor and another little fire, good value well thought-of food from sandwiches up, friendly helpful young staff; children welcome, dogs in bar (there are two resident labradors), steps up to lawn with plenty of picnic-sets (more seats at front), good surrounding walks, bedrooms, closed Mon and Sun evenings. *(Tony and Wendy Hobden)*

THAKEHAM TQ1017
White Lion (01798) 813141
Off B2139 N of Storrington; The Street; RH20 3EP Steps up to 16th-c pub in pretty village (level access from back car park); heavy beams, panelling, bare boards and traditional furnishings, four changing ales and decent wines by the glass, well liked food (not Sun evening) including good selection of blackboard specials, efficient service, pleasant dining room with inglenook; children and dogs welcome, sunny terrace and small enclosed lawn, open all day. *(Alastair and Sheree Hepburn, David Jackman)*

TICEHURST TQ6831
★**Bull** (01580) 200586
Three Leg Cross; off B2099 towards Wadhurst; TN5 7HH Attractive 14th-c country pub popular with good mix of customers, big log fires in two heavy-beamed old-fashioned bars, well kept Harveys and a couple of guests, contemporary furnishings in light airy dining extension serving good food (not Sun evening), friendly service; children and dogs welcome, charming front garden (busy in summer), bigger back one with play area, good PYO fruit farm nearby, four bedrooms, open all day. *(Peter Meister)*

TURNERS HILL TQ3435
★**Red Lion** (01342) 715416
Lion Lane, just off B2028; RH10 4NU Old-fashioned, unpretentious and welcoming country local; snug parquet-floored bar with plush wall benches and small open fire, steps up to carpeted dining area with inglenook log fire, cushioned pews and settles, old photos and brewery memorabilia, well kept Harveys ales and good home-made food (lunchtime only – must book Sun); occasional live music and fortnightly quiz night; children

(away from bar) and dogs welcome, picnic-sets on side grass overlooking village, open all day weekends. *(Mrs P R Sykes)*

UDIMORE TQ8818
Plough (01797) 223381
Cock Marling (B2089 W of Rye); TN31 6AL Popular refurbished and extended 17th-c roadside pub; good freshly made food including tapas, bargain main course deal Weds evening, well kept Harveys, Long Man and Three Legs, good choice of wines by the glass, friendly welcoming staff, L-shaped main bar with wood floor, separate back dining room, two woodburners; Fri happy hour (5.30-7pm) followed by live music; children and dogs welcome, tables on good-sized sunny back terrace, Brede Valley views, self-catering apartment, closed Sun evening. *(Peter Meister, Mike and Eleanor Anderson, Will Wright)*

UPPER DICKER TQ5409
Plough (01323) 844859
Coldharbour Road; BN27 3QJ Extended 17th-c pub with small central beamed bar, seats by inglenook, two dining areas off to the left and step up to larger dining bar on right with raised section, well kept Harveys and Shepherd Neame, enjoyable food from pubby choices up; background and occasional live music, free wi-fi; children and dogs welcome, good-sized garden with play area, open all day. *(Chloe and Tim Hodge)*

WALBERTON SU9705
Holly Tree (01243) 553110
The Street; BN18 0PH Grey-painted 19th-c village pub (newish licensees) with fun quirky décor, enjoyable food from sandwiches up including breakfast (10-11.30am), themed food nights and various deals, friendly well trained young staff, happy hour 4-6pm; quiz nights; children and dogs welcome, café-style furniture and planters on front terrace, open (and food) all day. *(Paul Humphreys, Suzy Miller)*

WALDERTON SU7910
Barley Mow (02392) 631321
Stoughton Road, just off B2146 Chichester–Petersfield; PO18 9ED Popular country pub (newish licensees) with good food including Sun carvery, ales such as Adnams, Ringwood and Sharps, friendly service, two log fires in U-shaped bar with roomy dining areas; skittle alley; children welcome, big streamside back garden, good walks (Kingley Vale nearby) and handy for Stansted Park, open all day weekends, food till 4pm Sun. *(Ann and Colin Hunt)*

WALDRON TQ5419
★**Star** (01435) 812495
Blackboys–Horam side road; TN21 0RA Pretty pub in quiet village across from the church; beamed main bar with settle next to good log fire in brick inglenook,

wheelbacks around pubby tables on old quarry tiles, several built-in cushioned wall and window seats, old local pictures and photographs, high stools by central counter serving a couple of well kept Harveys ales and a guest, maybe own apple juice, good food (not Sun evening) including bar snacks, pubby dishes and specials, dining areas with painted chairs around pine-topped tables on parquet or bare boards, bookshelf wallpaper, chatty local atmosphere and friendly staff; quiz Mon evening; picnic-sets in pleasant back garden, wassailing on Twelfth Night, small café and shop next door. *(PL)*

WARBLETON   TQ6018
★Black Duck (01435) 830636
S of B2096 SE of Heathfield; TN21 9BD Friendly licensees at this small renovated pub tucked down from church; L-shaped main room with pale oak flooring, cushioned leather sofas in front of roaring inglenook, beams and walls hung with horsebrasses, tankards, musical instruments, farm tools, even an old typewriter, high-backed dining chairs around mix of tables, good pubby food including daily specials, bar area up a step with stools along counter, Harveys and a guest, nice wines by the glass, cabinet of books and board games; background and occasional live music; picnic-sets in back garden with sweeping valley views, more on front grass, open all day Fri-Sat. *(Andrea and Philip Crispin)*

WARNHAM   TQ1533
Sussex Oak (01403) 265028
Just off A24 Horsham–Dorking; Church Street; RH12 3QW Cheerfully busy country pub with heavy beams and timbers, mix of flagstones, tiles, wood and carpeting, big inglenook log fire, well kept Fullers, Harveys, Timothy Taylors and guests from carved servery, real cider and plenty of wines by the glass, enjoyable fairly traditional food (all day weekends), high-raftered restaurant; background music, Thurs quiz, darts, free wi-fi; children and dogs welcome, disabled facilities/parking, picnic-sets in large garden, good local walks, open all day. *(Christopher Maxse, Tony Scott, Tony and Wendy Hobden)*

WARTLING   TQ6509
★Lamb (01323) 832116
Village signed with Herstmonceux Castle off A271 Herstmonceux–Battle; BN27 1RY Popular family-owned country pub; small entrance bar with open fireplace, Harveys Best and a couple of local guests, several wines by the glass from good list, two-level beamed and timbered dining room to the left with inglenook woodburner,

bigger back bar and restaurant, well liked food including blackboard specials, friendly service; children and dogs welcome, steps up to garden with chunky seats, five bedrooms, closed Sun evening, otherwise open all day. *(V Brogden, Edward Edmonton)*

WEST ASHLING   SU8007
Richmond Arms (01243) 572046
Just off B2146; Mill Road; PO18 8EA Village dining pub in quiet pretty setting near big millpond with ducks and geese, good interesting food (quite pricey, best to book) from bar snacks up, also wood-fired pizzas cooked in a vintage van (Fri, Sat evenings), well kept Harveys ales and plenty of wines by the glass, competent friendly staff; children welcome, two nice bedrooms, closed Sun evening, Mon and Tues. *(Tracey and Stephen Groves, John Evans)*

WEST WITTERING   SZ8099
Lamb (01243) 511105
Chichester Road; B2179/A286 towards Birdham; PO20 8QA Modernised 18th-c tile-hung country pub, three Badger ales and enjoyable home-cooked food including popular Sun roasts, friendly capable staff, bar with painted beams and timbers, assorted furniture on wood floor including kitchen chairs and scrubbed pine tables, woodburner in brick fireplace, two bare-boards dining rooms off with some interesting artwork; background music; children and dogs welcome, tables out in front and in small sheltered back garden, closed Sun evening, otherwise open all day. *(Elisabeth and Bill Humphries)*

WESTFIELD   TQ8115
New Inn (01424) 752800
Main Road; TN35 4QE Popular village pub with light open-plan interior, pubby furniture including wheelback and captains' chairs on pale wood floors, sparsely decorated white walls, conservatory, four or five mainly local ales including Harveys, enjoyable reasonably priced home-made food from weekly changing menu, cheerful helpful staff; children and dogs welcome, disabled access, seats out on gravel terrace, open all day (till 8pm Sun). *(Caroline Prescott, Emma Scofield)*

WILMINGTON   TQ5404
★Giants Rest (01323) 870207
Just off A27; BN26 5SQ Popular early 20th-c country pub with long wood-floored bar, adjacent open areas with simple furniture, rural pictures and pot plants, log fire, two or three well kept Long Man ales and South Downs cider (made in the village), good enterprising food cooked by

---

A star symbol before the name of a pub shows exceptional character and appeal. It doesn't mean extra comfort. Even quite a basic pub can win a star, if it's individual enough.

french chef-landlord including specials and gluten-free options, friendly helpful staff; background music from vinyl collection, puzzles and games, children and dogs welcome, picnic-sets on front grass, surrounded by South Downs walks and village famous for chalk-carved Long Man, closed Sun evening, Mon. *(John Beeken)*

WINEHAM TQ2320
★ **Royal Oak** (01444) 881252
Village signposted from A272 and B2116; BN5 9AY Splendidly old-fashioned local with log fire in big inglenook, Harveys Best and guests tapped from stillroom casks, enjoyable home-cooked food (not Sun evening), jugs and ancient corkscrews on very low beams, collection of cigarette boxes and old bottles, various stuffed animals including a stoat and crocodile, more bric-a-brac and old local photographs in back parlour with views of quiet countryside; occasional folk music and morris men; children away from bar and dogs welcome, picnic-sets out at front, closed evenings 25 and 26 Dec, 1 Jan. *(Tony Scott)*

WISBOROUGH GREEN TQ0626
Bat & Ball (01403) 700199
Newpound Lane; RH14 0EH Refurbished 18th-c red-brick Badger dining pub set in six-acre site, their ales and 20 wines by the glass including champagne from counter faced in wine box ends, shortish choice of enjoyable if slightly pricey food, connecting beamed rooms with cosy corners and plenty of rustic charm including high-raftered restaurant with wine glass chandeliers; children and dogs (in bar) welcome, pretty garden with pond at front, camping facilities, handy for Fishers Farm Park, open all day (till 8pm Sun). *(Sally and John Quinlan)*

WISBOROUGH GREEN TQ0526
Cricketers Arms (01403) 700369
Loxwood Road, just off A272 Billingshurst–Petworth; RH14 0DG Attractive old pub on edge of village green, four or five well kept ales such as Dark Star, Fullers, Harveys and St Austell, good choice of food including specials, cheerful staff, open-plan with two big woodburners and pleasing mix of country furniture on parquet flooring, stripped-brick dining area on left; maybe weekend live music; children welcome, tables out in front, open all day. *(Alastair and Sheree Hepburn, Tony Scott)*

WISBOROUGH GREEN TQ0525
Three Crowns (01403) 700239
Billingshurst Road (A272); RH14 0DX Well looked-after beamed pub with rather quirky interior, enjoyable freshly made food (all day Sun) from sharing boards and pub favourites up, prompt friendly service, well kept Harveys, Shepherd Neame and four guests, extensive choice of wines by the glass including champagne and good range of gins, afternoon teas; live music; children welcome, sizeable tree-shaded back garden, open all day. *(Edward Edmonton)*

WIVELSFIELD GREEN TQ3519
Cock (01444) 471668
North Common Road; RH17 7RH Pleasant red-brick village pub with good choice of enjoyable reasonably priced food including themed nights, Harveys and guests, helpful friendly staff, two bars and restaurant, log fire; quiz nights, darts, bar billiards, pool and sports TV; children, walkers and dogs welcome, seats out in front and in garden behind, open all day, food all day weekends. *(Patric Curwen)*

WOODMANCOTE SU7707
Woodmancote (01243) 371019
The one near Emsworth; Woodmancote Lane; PO10 8RD Village pub with unusual contemporary décor – plenty of quirky touches; good popular food (best to book) from sandwiches and sharing boards up, weekly themed nights, three real ales including one badged for them and St Austell Tribute, several wines by the glass, restaurant; regular quiz nights; children and dogs (in bar) welcome, seats out under cover, open (and food) all day. *(Susan and Callum Slade)*

WORTHING TQ1402
Egremont (01903) 600064
Brighton Road; BN11 3ED Refurbished 19th-c pub near seafront, up to six real ales including Harveys and a couple from Goldmark badged for them, good range of interesting gins, enjoyable reasonably priced pubby food from ciabattas and sharing plates up, friendly helpful staff, split-level mainly bare-boards interior arranged around central bar, one part laid for dining, mix of furniture including button-back banquettes, stools, sofas and some high tables, original Kemptown Brewery stained glass, old enamel signs and other interesting bits and pieces; quiz and live music nights, TV for major sports; children and dogs welcome, pavement picnic-sets, open all day (till 1am Fri, Sat). *(Tony and Wendy Hobden)*

WORTHING TQ1502
Selden Arms (01903) 234854
Lyndhurst Road, between Waitrose and hospital; BN11 2DB Friendly unchanging 19th-c backstreet local opposite gasworks, welcoming long-serving licensees, six well kept ales (Jan beer festival), craft kegs and continental draught/bottled beers, bargain lunchtime food (not Sun) including doorstep sandwiches and various pies, curry night Fri and Sat, comfortably worn interior with photographs of old Worthing pubs, pump clips on ceiling, log fire; occasional live music, quiz last Weds of month, darts; dogs welcome (resident cat), open all day. *(Tony and Wendy Hobden, Alastair and Sheree Hepburn)*

Warwickshire

with Birmingham and West Midlands

KEY ⭐ Star Pub   🌟 Top Quality Food   🍺 Great Beer

🍷 Good Wines   £ Bargain Meals   🛏 Good Bedrooms   🍴 Serves Food

---

ALDERMINSTER   SP2348   Map 4
Bell 🌟 🍷 🛏

(01789) 450414 – www.thebellald.co.uk

A3400 Oxford–Stratford; CV37 8NY

**18th-c inn with sympathetically modernised character bars,
a two-storey restaurant, excellent modern cooking and thoughtful
choice of drinks; bedrooms**

Gently civilised and friendly – and part of the Alscot Estate – this
Georgian coaching inn has a good mix of customers and an easy-going
atmosphere. The open-plan rooms cleverly manage to create a contemporary
feel that fits in well with the many original features: beams, standing timbers,
flagstoned or wooden floors and open fires. The bustling bar serves Alscot
Ale (named for the pub from North Cotswold), North Cotswold Jumping
Jack and Purity Pure UBU on handpump, a dozen wines by the glass and
cocktails. The bar is comfortably furnished with a mix of traditional wooden
chairs and tables, upholstered sofas, armchairs in front of open fires, high
bar chairs by the blue-painted counter and daily papers; background music.
The two-storey restaurant is stylish and modern. The bottom floor, with
stunning chandeliers and circular wall mirrors, is decorated in soft pastels
and silvers and has folding doors leading directly to the terrace, while the top
floor has attractive chairs around polished copper tables on dark floorboards,
seats on a balcony and panoramic views across the Stour Valley; there's
also a private dining room with its own decked area and lawn. An appealing
courtyard and gardens have seats and tables looking over water meadows
and the lovely valley. The well equipped and comfortable bedrooms are
individually decorated and boutique in style.

🌟 As well as interesting snacks (12-6; not Sunday) such as crispy pork belly with
teriyaki dip, three different sliders on a mini brioche and tempura king prawns
in lime mayonnaise, the tempting food includes lunchtime sandwiches, crayfish and
lobster cakes with guacamole and smoked chilli mayonnaise, grazing boards, falafel,
chicken or steak burgers with toppings and chips, stone bass fillet with parmentier
potatoes, sorrel sauce and cherry tomato dressing, a duo of organic chicken with carrot
and lemongrass purée and fondant potatoes, and puddings such as chocolate brownie
with berries, dulce de leche and vanilla ice-cream and rhubarb eton mess; they also
offer a two- and three-course menu (not Friday evening or weekends). *Benchmark
main dish: duo of lamb with aubergine purée, minted potatoes and red wine jus
£20.95. Two-course evening meal £23.00.*

Free house ~ Licensee Emma Holman-West ~ Real ale ~ Open 9am-11pm ~ Bar food 12-2.30,
6.30-9 (9.30 Fri, Sat); 12-3, 6.30-8.30 Sun ~ Restaurant ~ Children welcome ~ Dogs allowed
in bar ~ Wi-fi ~ Bedrooms: £70/£100 *Recommended by P and J Shapley, Dr and Mrs A K Clarke,
John Harris, William and Sophia Renton*

ARMSCOTE   SP2444 Map 4

Fuzzy Duck

(01608) 682635 – www.fuzzyduckarmscote.com

Off A3400 Stratford–Shipston; CV37 8DD

**Interestingly refurbished former coaching inn with real ales,
a good wine list, inventive food and seats outside; bedrooms**

With Stratford-upon-Avon nearby and plenty of walks in the rolling
surrounding countryside, the deeply comfortable, well equipped and
pretty bedrooms here (each named after a species of duck) make a perfect
base for exploring. The bustling bar has an open fire, high chunky leather
chairs around equally high metal tables on flagstones, with more leather
chairs against the counter where friendly staff serve Purity Mad Goose
and a weekly guest such as North Cotswold Shagweaver on handpump, a
dozen wines by the glass, 12 malt whiskies and a farm cider; a wall of glass-
faced boxes holds bottles of spirits belonging to regular customers. Three
interconnected dining rooms have a mix of dark wooden tables surrounded
by leather and other elegant chairs on pale floorboards, a sofa here and
there and a two-way woodburning stove in an open fireplace. Throughout,
cartoons and arty photographs hang on pale or dark grey walls and flowers
are arranged in big vases; background music and board games. At the
back, another dining room (also used for private parties) leads to a decked
terrace furnished with basket-weave armchairs, cushioned sofas and
small modern metal chairs and tables under large parasols; there's also
a small lawn with fruit trees.

 Imaginative food using the best local, seasonal produce and their own bread and
ice-creams includes lunchtime sandwiches, chorizo scotch duck egg with tomato
and red pepper chutney, grilled mackerel fillet with pickled cucumber, horseradish
and apple, asparagus, spinach and parmesan risotto with almonds and rocket, chicken,
leek and pancetta pie with thyme cream sauce and champ mash, sea bass fillet with
baby pak choi and sweetcorn, wild rice and sesame and soy dressing, sirloin steak with
confit garlic butter and skin-on chips, and puddings such as lemon curd and meringue
tart and raspberry sorbet and dark chocolate brownie with caramelised banana
compote and honeycomb ice-cream. *Benchmark main dish: lamb breast and rump
with dauphinoise potatoes, pea purée and red wine jus £19.50. Two-course evening
meal £24.00.*

Free house ~ Licensee Annabelle Lyall ~ Real ale ~ Open 10am-11pm; 11-5 Sun;
closed Sun evening, Mon ~ Bar food 12-2.30, 6.30-9; 12-3 Sun ~ Restaurant ~ Children
welcome ~ Dogs welcome ~ Wi-fi ~ Bedrooms: /£140 *Recommended by Miles Green,
Charles Welch, Patricia Hawkins, Michael Doswell, Dr and Mrs A K Clarke, Ian Herdman*

BARSTON   SP1978 Map 4

Malt Shovel

(01675) 443223 – www.themaltshovelatbarston.com

*3 miles from M42 junction 5; A4141 towards Knowle, then first left into Jacobean
Lane/Barston Lane; B92 0JP*

**Well run country dining pub full of happy customers, with an
attractive layout, good service and seats in sheltered garden**

The food here is first class and service is exemplary – but you'll feel just as welcome if it's only a drink and chat that you've come for. The light and airy bar rambles extensively around the zinc-topped central counter, with big terracotta floor tiles neatly offset by dark grouting, and cream, tan and blue paintwork. Black Sheep, Salopian Treasure Trove and Sharps Doom Bar on handpump, 22 wines by the glass and 17 malt whiskies. Furnishings are comfortable, with informal dining chairs and scatter-cushioned pews around stripped-top tables of varying types and sizes, there are cheerful fruit and vegetable paintings on the walls, and french café-style shutters. The barn restaurant to the side is partially panelled with distressed dark grey paintwork that's topped with rows of pewter plates. The sheltered back garden has a weeping willow and picnic-sets, and the terrace and verandah have cushioned teak seats and tables.

Highly regarded food includes sandwiches, lamb kidneys with bacon, field mushrooms and jus, chicken and chorizo patties with sun-dried tomato and chilli hummus, superfood salad, shallot and artichoke tarte tatin with fig syrup, chicory and watercress pesto, moroccan-spiced rack of lamb with couscous and mint yoghurt, tandoori chicken with sweet potato and almond purée and onion and ginger pickle, and puddings such as brioche bread and butter pudding with orange and cocoa and white chocolate cream and eton mess with Pimms-soaked strawberries. *Benchmark main dish: salmon fishcakes with tarragon hollandaise and free-range eggs £14.95. Two-course evening meal £23.50.*

Free house ~ Licensee Helen Somerfield ~ Real ale ~ Open 12-midnight; 12-7 Sun; closed Sun evening ~ Bar food 12-2.30, 6-9.30; 12-4 Sun ~ Restaurant ~ Children welcome away from restaurant ~ Dogs allowed in bar *Recommended by Peter J and Avril Hanson, Dave Braisted, Susan and John Douglas, Ian Herdman, Alison and Graeme Spicer*

BIRMINGHAM
Old Joint Stock ◧ £

SP0686 Map 4

(0121) 200 1892 – www.oldjointstocktheatre.co.uk
Temple Row West; B2 5NY

Big bustling Fullers pie-and-ale pub with impressive Victorian façade and interior, and a small back terrace; own theatre

Most nights there's something on in the smart, purpose-built, first-floor theatre here – and you can book a two-course pre-theatre meal in advance. Downstairs, the pub is impressively flamboyant: chandeliers hang from the soaring pink and gilt ceiling, gently illuminated busts line the top of the ornately plastered walls and there's a splendid cupola above the centre of the room. Photographs of the historic building's past line the walls; there's also a big dining balcony reached up a grand sweeping staircase. The place is packed to the gunnels at peak times, but efficient and helpful staff manage to remain friendly and serve Fullers ESB, London Pride, Olivers Island and a guest such as Hook Norton Lion on handpump, and 14 wines by the glass; background music. The small back terrace has cast-iron tables and chairs and wall-mounted heaters.

As well as breakfasts (8-11am weekdays, 9-11am Saturday, 10am-midday Sunday), the popular food includes sandwiches, sharing plates, tea and hop-smoked haddock, salmon and leek or homity pies, ham and eggs with pineapple salsa, chargrilled vegetable and pine nut salad with spelt (you could add a leg of lamb), beer-battered fish and chips, and puddings such as bakewell tart and vanilla crème anglaise and banoffi cheesecake with salted caramel sauce. *Benchmark main dish: steak in ale pie £12.95. Two-course evening meal £18.00.*

Fullers ~ Manager Paul Bancroft ~ Real ale ~ Open 8am-11pm; 9am-11pm Sat; 10-5 Sun; closed Sun evening ~ Bar food 8am-10pm; 9am-4 Sun; not Sun evening ~ Restaurant ~ Children allowed until 6pm ~ Wi-fi ~ Regular live entertainment in theatre *Recommended by Mrs Julie Thomas, John Evans, Barry Collett, Alan Johnson, Susan and John Douglas, Colin Gooch*

BIRMINGHAM   SP0585 Map 4

Physician

(0121) 272 5900 ~ www.brunningandprice.co.uk/physician
Harborne Road, Edgbaston; B15 3DH

Large, extended pub with plenty of drinking and dining space, fantastic range of drinks including eight ales, interesting food and friendly atmosphere; seats outside

This substantial building once housed the Sampson Gangee Library for the History of Medicine. Brunning & Price have used the grand 19th-c rooms with their high ceilings and big sash windows to great effect; after a complete renovation, the pub opened at the end of 2016. The interlinked areas of all shape and size have leather armchairs in front of open fires, a medley of cushioned wooden dining chairs and mate's chairs around polished solid tables on bare boards, rugs or carpet, lots of old prints on pale-painted walls, large gilt-edged mirrors and big house plants, stone bottles and books on shelves and lighting that ranges from table lamps to elegant metal chandeliers. Friendly, well trained staff serve Phoenix Brunning & Price Original and Timothy Taylors Boltmaker and guests such as Backyard The Hoard, Purity Mad Goose, Sadlers Sweet Leaf, Silhill Blonde Star, Titanic Plum Porter and Wye Valley HPA on handpump, up to 25 wines by the glass, 50 gins, 50 rums, 90 malt whiskies and farm cider; background music and board games. Terraces have good quality wooden seats and tables under green parasols among flowering tubs and flower beds.

Quite a choice of good modern food includes sandwiches, korean chicken wings with kimchi salad, smoked mackerel rillettes with pickled cucumber, apple and crispy capers, sweet potato, cauliflower and chickpea tagine with tempura courgette and couscous, malaysian chicken curry, steak and kidney pudding, daube of pork with apples, cider, bacon sauce and colcannon mash, sea bass with potato terrine, beetroot purée and fennel salad, and puddings such as dark chocolate tart with raspberry sorbet and crème brûlée. *Benchmark main dish: braised lamb shoulder with dauphinoise potatoes and rosemary gravy £17.25. Two-course evening meal £22.00.*

Brunning & Price ~ Manager Lisa Rogers ~ Real ale ~ Open 10am-11pm (10.30pm Sun) ~ Bar food 12-10 (9 Sun) ~ Children welcome ~ Dogs allowed in bar ~ Wi-fi *Recommended by Chris and Sophie Baxter, Mandy and Gary Redstone, Audrey and Paul Summers*

GAYDON   SP3654 Map 4

Malt Shovel

(01926) 641221 ~ www.maltshovelgaydon.co.uk
Under a mile from M40 junction 12; B4451 into village, then over roundabout and across B4100; Church Road; CV35 0ET

Bustling pub in a quiet village with a nice mix of pubby bar and smarter restaurant

If you want a break from the M40, head for this cheerful village pub where the tasty food cooked by the landlord continues to draw in customers from far and wide. Varnished mahogany floorboards through to bright carpeting link the entrance with the bar counter to the right and a woodburning stove on the left. The central area has a high-pitched ceiling, milk churns and earthenware containers in a loft above the bar and three steps that lead up to a space with comfortable sofas overlooked by a big stained-glass window; reproductions of classic posters line the walls. Exmoor Gold, Sharps Doom Bar and Youngs Special on handpump, with 11 wines by the glass and three farm ciders. A busy dining area has fresh flowers on a mix of kitchen, pub and dining tables; background music, darts. The pub's jack russell is called Mollie.

 Popular food includes sandwiches, baguettes and paninis, Brixworth pâté with plum and apple chutney, smoked haddock welsh rarebit, goats cheese and pesto cannelloni with basil and tomatoes, three-egg omelettes with three fillings, gammon with egg, steak and kidney pudding, beer-battered haddock and chips, beef and horseradish casserole with dijon mustard mash, and puddings such as lemon cheesecake and chocolate, cherry and brandy fudge slice. *Benchmark main dish: pie of the day £10.95. Two-course evening meal £17.00.*

Enterprise ~ Lease Richard and Debi Morisot ~ Real ale ~ Open 11-3, 5-11; 11-11 Fri, Sat; 12-10.30 Sun ~ Bar food 12-2, 6.30-9 ~ Restaurant ~ Children welcome ~ Dogs allowed in bar ~ Wi-fi *Recommended by M and A H, Tony Smaithe, John Watson, Frances and Hamish Porter, Frank and Marcia Pelling*

HAMPTON-IN-ARDEN   SP2080   Map 4
White Lion ◀
(01675) 442833 – www.thewhitelioninn.com
High Street; handy for M42 Junction 6; B92 0AA

Popular village local with a good choice of ales; bedrooms

Occupying a former farmhouse in an attractive village, this bustling pub is well known locally for its fine range of real ales. On handpump there might be Castle Rock Harvest Pale, Hobsons Best, Holdens Golden Glow, M&B Brew XI, St Austell Proper Job and Sharps Doom Bar. The carpeted bar is nice and relaxed, with a mix of furniture tidily laid out, neatly curtained small windows, low-beamed ceilings and some local memorabilia on the cream-painted walls; background music, TV and board games. The modern dining areas are fresh and airy with light wood and cane chairs on stripped floorboards. The bedrooms are quiet and comfortable. The church opposite is mentioned in the Domesday Book.

 Well liked food includes sandwiches and croques, haddock fishcake with spinach, a poached egg and wine sauce, ham hock terrine with apricot chutney, sharing boards, creamy mushroom risotto, local sausages and mash with onion gravy, steak burger with toppings, coleslaw and chips, seafood linguine with chilli, moules à la crème with frites, beef bourguignon, and puddings such as chocolate brownie with vanilla ice-cream and sticky toffee pudding with custard; they also offer a two- and three-course set lunch. *Benchmark main dish: pie of the day £10.95. Two-course evening meal £16.00.*

Free house ~ Licensee Chris Roach ~ Real ale ~ Open 12-11; 12-midnight Sat; 12-10.30 Sun ~ Bar food 12-2.30, 6-9.30; 12-4 Sun ~ Restaurant ~ Children welcome ~ Dogs welcome ~ Wi-fi ~ Bedrooms: £90/£100 *Recommended by R T and J C Moggridge, Ian and Rose Lock, Andrew Wall, Dr and Mrs A K Clarke, Gerry and Pam Pollard*

HUNNINGHAM   SP3768   Map 4
Red Lion
(01926) 632715 – www.redlionhunningham.co.uk
Village signposted off B4453 Leamington–Rugby just E of Weston, and off B4455 Fosse Way 2.5 miles SW of A423 junction; CV33 9DY

Civilised and friendly place, with a good range of drinks and well liked food

In warm weather, the picnic-sets in the garden here are much prized as they look across to the arched 14th-c bridge over the River Leam; there's a basket of rugs for customers to take outside and more picnic-sets are set out at the front. Friendly and easy-going, the light, open-plan interior has been cleverly divided up and appealingly furnished. There are pews with scatter cushions, an assortment of antique dining chairs and stools around nice polished tables on bare boards (with a few big rugs here and there) and contemporary paintwork. A cosy room has tub armchairs around an open coal fire. They keep a beer named for the pub, Purity Bunny Hop and Warwickshire Beer Company Duck Soup on handpump, 16 wines by the glass and 40 malt whiskies; background music.

Good food includes sandwiches (until 5pm), garlic prawn skewers with mango and chilli salsa, chicken liver parfait with red onion chutney, sharing boards, roast butternut squash with red beans, quinoa and cheesy tomato sauce with a crisp tortilla, beer-battered fish and chips, Josper oven barbecue beef short rib with red coleslaw and chips, pork loin with beetroot purée, mash and crispy apple, and puddings such as sticky toffee pudding with toffee sauce and banana ice-cream and crumble of the day with raspberry ripple ice-cream. *Benchmark main dish: burger with toppings and chips £13.50. Two-course evening meal £22.00.*

Free house ~ Licensee Richard Merand ~ Real ale ~ Open 11-11 (10.30 Sun) ~ Bar food 12-9 ~ Restaurant ~ Children welcome ~ Dogs allowed in bar ~ Wi-fi *Recommended by George Atkinson, Jeremy Snaithe, Sandra King, Dr and Mrs A K Clarke, Belinda and Neil Garth*

ILMINGTON
SP2143   Map 4

Howard Arms ♀

(01608) 682226 – www.howardarms.com

Village signed with Wimpstone off A3400 S of Stratford; CV36 4LT

Lovely mellow-toned interior, lots to look at and enjoyable food and drink; bedrooms

The various beamed and flagstoned rooms in this golden-stone inn have a nice mix of furniture ranging from pews and rustic stools to leather dining chairs around all sorts of tables, rugs on bare boards, shelves of books, candles and a log fire in a big inglenook. Purity Pure UBU, Stratford Upon Avon Mosaic, Timothy Taylors Landlord and Wye Valley HPA on handpump, 15 wines by the glass and a fair choice of whiskies and brandies; background music, TV. The big back garden has seats under parasols and a colourful herbaceous border. Bedrooms are well equipped and comfortable and the breakfasts highly regarded. Good nearby hill walks.

Well liked food includes lunchtime sandwiches (not Sunday), spiced lamb kofta kebabs with red pepper salsa and tzatziki, scotch duck egg with piccalilli, wild mushroom and tomato macaroni, burger with toppings and chips, cod fillet with samphire, golden beetroot and chive velouté, steak in ale pie, lamb chump with peas and lettuce, cherry tomato compote and jus, duck breast with puy lentils, local asparagus, blackberries and jus, and puddings such as apple and rhubarb crumble with custard and white and dark chocolate brownie with vanilla ice-cream. *Benchmark main dish: calves liver with mash and smoked bacon gravy £14.00. Two-course evening meal £21.00.*

Free house ~ Licensee Robert Jeal ~ Real ale ~ Open 10am-11pm; 12-10.30 Sun ~ Bar food 12-2.30 (3 Sat), 6-9.30; 12-8 Sun ~ Restaurant ~ Children welcome ~ Dogs allowed in bar ~ Wi-fi ~ Bedrooms: $88/$110 *Recommended by Geoff and Ann Marston, Alan and Alice Morgan, Chantelle and Tony Redman*

LEAMINGTON SPA
Drawing Board ♀ ▪

SP3265   Map 4

(01926) 330636 – www.thedrawingboard.pub

Newbold Street; CV32 4HN

Town-centre pub with interesting, quirky décor, a thoughtful choice of food and drinks; good fun

This place is fun and overseen by a first class landlord. It's handy for the centre of town and local theatres and has a bustling, cheerful atmosphere and some intriguing design features. Over two floors there are rugs on bare boards, flagstones, leather sofas and chesterfields, mismatched dining chairs and rustic tables interspersed with contemporary furniture, large house plants, antlers, several woodburning stoves – and even a bike. But it's the framed vintage comic books on the grey walls and shelves of old-fashioned boys' and girls' annuals that are really worth looking at – along with some pop art and neon lighting. Church Farm Pale Ale, Dark Star American Pale Ale, Purity Bunny Hop and Tiny Rebel Juicy on handpump, several craft ales, 18 wines by the glass, 63 malt whiskies, 26 gins, 26 bourbons and 24 rums, all served by friendly, young staff; background music, TV, a retro arcade games machine and board games.

Good, interesting food includes filled brioche buns, tapas (falafel with mint yoghurt, honey panko prawns and portuguese beef trinchado), tempura soft shell crab with thai dressing, salt beef brisket croquette with egg, pickles and onions, lentil, goats cheese and sun-dried tomato pie with parsley pesto, corn-fed chicken with sweet potato purée, daikon, tamarind and pak choi, rare-breed burger with toppings, onion dipping stew and french fries, slow-cooked beef with wild garlic, potato purée, chargrilled cabbage and bacon with red wine jus, and puddings such as turkish meringue with orange curd and orange jelly and bitter chocolate tart with cherries. *Benchmark main dish: tempura sea bass with thai-spiced butternut squash, peas and mint £13.95. Two-course evening meal £23.00.*

Free house ~ Licensee Sam Cornwall Jones ~ Real ale ~ Open 11-11; 12-10.30 Sun ~ Bar food 12-3, 5.30-9.30; 12-9.30 Sat; 12-6 Sun ~ Children welcome ~ Dogs welcome ~ Wi-fi
Recommended by Chris and Sophie Baxter, Charlie and Mark Todd, Bridget and Peter Gregson

LONG COMPTON
Red Lion ◉

SP2832   Map 4

(01608) 684221 – www.redlion-longcompton.co.uk

A3400 S of Shipston-on-Stour; CV36 5JS

Traditional character and contemporary touches in comfortably furnished coaching inn; bedrooms

This lovely old coaching inn is a special place to stay with pretty bedrooms and particularly good breakfasts. The roomy, charmingly furnished lounge bar has some exposed stone and beams and nice rambling corners with cushioned settles among pleasantly assorted and comfortable seats and leather armchairs; there are tables on flagstones and carpets, animal prints on warm paintwork and both an open fire and a woodburning stove. Hook Norton Hooky and Wickwar Cotswold Way with a guest such as Robinsons Dizzy Blonde on handpump and a dozen wines by the glass; the chocolate labrador is called Cocoa. The simple public bar has darts, pool, a juke box and a TV; background music. There are tables out in the big back garden, as well as a play area for children.

Rewarding food includes sandwiches, crispy duck samosas with sweet chilli dip, goats cheese salad with beetroot, rocket and walnuts, savoury herb pancakes with spinach, red peppers, brie, cream and parmesan, herb-crumbed chicken schnitzel with cranberry sauce, pancetta-wrapped guinea fowl with wild mushrooms and madeira and thyme jus, seared salmon with samphire and crayfish tails and lime butter sauce, slow-braised lamb shank with roasted vegetables and rosemary jus, and puddings such as chocolate nut torte with salted caramel ice-cream and chocolate sauce and vanilla pannacotta with wild berry compote; they also offer a two- and three-course weekday menu (until 7pm). *Benchmark main dish: steak in ale pie £14.50. Two-course evening meal £22.00.*

Cropthorne Inns ~ Manager Lisa Phipps ~ Real ale ~ Open 10am-11pm ~ Bar food 12-2.30, 6-9.30; 12-9.30 Fri, Sat; 12-9 Sun ~ Children welcome ~ Dogs welcome ~ Wi-fi ~ Regular charity quiz nights ~ Bedrooms: £60/£95 *Recommended by Alun and Jennifer Evans, J A Snell, Michael Doswell, Tracey and Stephen Groves, Mitchell Cregor*

LOWER BRAILES
SP3139 Map 4
George 🍴 £
(01608) 685788 – www.georgeinnbrailes.com
B4035 Shipston–Banbury; OX15 5HN

Fine old stone inn with welcoming landlord and customers and well liked food; bedrooms

Set in a lovely village, this handsome 14th-c inn has a friendly, bustling back bar that's beamed and panelled and has plenty of cheerful, chatty locals. There's also a spacious front bar with dark oak chairs and tables on flagstones and an inglenook fireplace, and a separate restaurant. Hook Norton Hooky, Old Hooky, Hooky Mild and a guest on handpump, nine wines by the glass and farm cider; background music, TV, games machine, darts, pool, juke box and board games. There's aunt sally and picnic-sets (some blue-painted) in the sizeable and sheltered back garden and on the terrace; also a few tables and chairs out in the front. The comfortable bedrooms are fair value. Good nearby walks. The inn was built in the 14th c to house the stonemasons constructing the interesting church.

🍴 As well as some dishes that qualify for our Value Award, the tasty food includes garlic and sweet chilli king prawns, eggs benedict, sharing boards, spinach and ricotta tortellini with creamy pesto sauce, ham and egg, beer-battered haddock and chips, beef curry or pork casserole, salmon suprême with piquant tomato and spinach sauce, and puddings. *Benchmark main dish: pie of the day £10.00. Two-course evening meal £16.00.*

Free house ~ Licensee Baggy Saunders ~ Real ale ~ Open 12-11; 5-11 Mon; 12-midnight Fri, Sat; 12-11 Sun; closed Mon lunchtime ~ Bar food 12-2.30, 6-8.45; 12-3 Sun ~ Restaurant ~ Children welcome but not in bar after 8pm Fri, Sat ~ Dogs allowed in bar and bedrooms ~ Wi-fi ~ Bedrooms: £50/£70 *Recommended by R T and J C Moggridge, Richard Tilbrook, Clive and Fran Dutson, Sally Harrison*

PRESTON BAGOT
SP1765 Map 4
Crabmill 🍴 ♟ ♥
(01926) 843342 – www.thecrabmill.co.uk
A4189 Henley-in-Arden to Warwick; B95 5EE

Comfortable décor, open fires and particularly good food and drink in converted mill

Once our readers have discovered this rambling former cider mill, they're always keen to return. There's a gently civilised atmosphere and it's attractively decorated throughout, with contemporary furnishings and warm colour combinations. A smart two-level lounge has comfortable sofas and chairs, low tables, big table lamps and a couple of rugs on bare boards. The elegant, low-beamed dining area is roomy with caramel leather banquettes and chairs at pine tables, while the beamed and flagstoned bar area has stripped-pine country tables and chairs and snug corners; open fires. From the gleaming metal bar counter they serve Purity Pure Gold and Sharps Atlantic and Doom Bar on handpump and nine wines by the glass; background music. The large, attractive, decked garden has plenty of tables, some of which are under cover.

 Highly enjoyable food includes lunchtime sandwiches, baguettes and wraps, braised venison faggot with crispy shallots and beer jus, hot smoked salmon, crayfish and chive fishcake with tartare sauce, rigatoni pasta with wild mushrooms, local cheese, parsley and garlic crumb, maple-smoked bacon loin with a poached egg, chips and home-made tomato ketchup, duck breast with redcurrant compote, celeriac purée and jus, hake with brown shrimps, samphire and béarnaise sauce, beef bourguignon with dauphinoise potatoes, and puddings such as salted caramel and dark chocolate brownie with praline ice-cream and plum bakewell tart with stem ginger ice-cream. *Benchmark main dish: sea bass, sweet potato and spinach curry £17.95. Two-course evening meal £22.00.*

Free house ~ Licensee Dillyn Saunders ~ Real ale ~ Open 11-11; 12-7 Sun ~ Bar food 12-2.30, 6-9.30; 12-4.30 Sun ~ Restaurant ~ Children welcome ~ Dogs allowed in bar ~ Wi-fi
Recommended by Clive and Fran Dutson, Jenni Owen, Laura Reid, Lance and Sarah Milligan, Dr and Mrs A K Clarke, Sandra Hollies

SHIPSTON-ON-STOUR

SP2540 Map 4

Black Horse 🍺

(01608) 238489 – www.blackhorseshipston.com
Station Road (off A3400); CV36 4BT

16th-c pub with simple country furnishings, well kept ales, an extensive choice of thai food and seats outside

This chocolate-box pretty stone tavern is the oldest – and only thatched – building in the village and has been a pub since 1540; in summer, the flowering baskets and tubs are lovely. Low-beamed, character bars lead off a central entrance passage with some fine old flagstones and floor tiles and two open fires (one an inglenook). There are also wheelbacks, stools, rustic seats and tables and built-in wall benches, half-panelled or exposed stone walls, and plenty of copper kettles, pans and bedwarmers, horse tack and toby jugs. Friendly staff serve Prescott Hill Climb, Ringwood Old Thumper and Wye Valley Butty Bach on handpump, several wines by the glass, a dozen gins and ten malt whiskies; background music, TV, darts and board games. The little dining room has pale wooden tables and chairs on bare boards. There are a couple of benches on the front cobbles, contemporary seats and tables on a partly covered, raised decked area at the back and picnic-sets on grass.

The popular food is thai: tom yum soups, steamed dumplings, chicken satay, spicy salads such as seafood, lots of curries, chicken, duck and pork in tamarind, sweet soy and plum sauces, stir-fries and a big choice of dishes with noodles and rice. *Benchmark main dish: chicken or prawn thai curries £7.99. Two-course evening meal £16.50.*

Free house ~ Licensee Gabe Saunders ~ Real ale ~ Open 12-3, 6-11; 6-11 Mon; 12-11 Fri-Sun; closed Mon lunchtime ~ Bar food 12-2.30, 6-10; not Mon ~ Restaurant ~ Children welcome ~ Dogs allowed in bar ~ Wi-fi *Recommended by Jo Garnett, Charles Welch, Buster May, Trevor and Michele Street*

SHIPSTON-ON-STOUR

SP2540 Map 4

Horseshoe 🍺 £

(01608) 662190 – www.horseshoeshipston.com

Church Street; CV36 4AP

**Cheerful local with welcoming regulars, traditional furnishings,
real ales and honest food and seats outside**

It's the friendly, chatty, easy-going atmosphere that our readers particularly like in this pretty 17th-c timbered coaching inn. The two rooms that form the open, carpeted bar have straightforward red-upholstered cushioned wall seats and wheelback chairs around scrubbed wooden tables, country prints on lemon-yellow walls, copper pans hanging on the bressummer beam over the open fire (with books and stone jars on shelves to one side) and stools against the counter; juke box. Exmoor Fox, Timothy Taylors Boltmaker and Wye Valley HPA on handpump and several wines by the glass, and service is cheerful and courteous. The end dining room is similarly furnished. The back terrace has contemporary seats and tables on decking; aunt sally.

 Well liked food includes hot and cold sandwiches and baguettes, pâté of the day, king prawn cocktail, cauliflower cheese with new potato salad, a curry and casserole of the day, steak and kidney pudding, all-day breakfast (from 10.15am), chicken breast with stilton sauce, burger with toppings and chips, gammon with free-range eggs and pineapple, beer-battered haddock and chips, and puddings. *Benchmark main dish: south african bobotie £10.50. Two-course evening meal £16.00.*

Enterprise ~ Manager Baggy Saunders ~ Real ale ~ Open 10am-11pm ~ Bar food 12-2.30, 6-9; not Sun evening ~ Children welcome ~ Dogs welcome ~ Wi-fi ~ Folk second Tues of month, quiz third Tues of month *Recommended by Julian Thorpe, Douglas Power, Des Mannion, Mark Hamill, Jim King*

WARMINGTON

SP4147 Map 4

Falcon 🍷 🍺

(01295) 692120 – www.brunningandprice.co.uk/falcon

B4100 towards Shotteswell; OX17 1JJ

**Carefully extended roadside pub with spreading bar and dining
rooms, a fine choice of drinks and food, and seats outside**

This 18th-c pub (now beautifully restored) was originally built to take advantage of what was a busy turnpike road. It's a handsome golden-stone inn and the interconnected bar and dining areas have much character and plenty to look at. There are beams, mirrors over several open fires, rugs on pale floorboards, elegant metal chandeliers, prints and photos covering pale-painted walls, bookshelves, house plants and stone bottles. Cushioned Edwardian-style chairs and leather armchairs are grouped around a wide mix of tables and the main dining room has a central fire pit. Friendly young staff serve Phoenix Brunning & Price Original and guests such as Church End Grave Diggers Ale, Gun Dog Chilly Dog, Hook Norton Hooky, Silverstone Chequered Flag and Timothy Taylors Landlord on handpump, 15 wines by the glass, 100 gins and numerous malt whiskies; background music. The garden has good quality seats and tables under a gazebo.

 Brasserie-style food includes sandwiches, tempura squid with spiced chickpeas and red pepper aioli, basil pannacotta with black olive tapenade, smoked haddock fishcake with a poached egg and white wine and caper sauce, steak and mushroom in ale pie, thai vegetable curry with coconut rice, pork sausages with mash and onion gravy, warm crispy beef salad with sweet chilli dressing and cashews, chicken suprême on wild mushroom risotto with roasted cherry tomatoes and basil oil, and puddings such as lemon tart with blackcurrant sorbet and triple chocolate brownie with chocolate sauce and vanilla ice-cream. *Benchmark main dish: burger with toppings, coleslaw and chips £12.95. Two-course evening meal £21.00.*

Brunning & Price ~ Manager Peter Palfi ~ Real ale ~ Open 11-11 (10.30 Sun) ~ Bar food 12-10 (9.30 Sun) ~ Restaurant ~ Children welcome ~ Dogs allowed in bar ~ Wi-fi
Recommended by Peter and Emma Kelly, Melanie and David Lawson, Jason Caulkin, Terry Davis, Peter and Caroline Waites

WELFORD-ON-AVON
SP1452   Map 4
Bell 🏅🍴 🍷 🍺

(01789) 750353 – www.thebellwelford.co.uk
Off B439 W of Stratford; High Street; CV37 8EB

● ●
Warwickshire Dining Pub of the Year

Enjoyably civilised pub with appealing ancient interior, good carefully sourced food, a great range of drinks and a pretty garden with table service

'The best pub for miles around' and 'the happy, helpful staff always make you feel welcome' are just two comments from our readers about this particularly well run pub. The attractive and atmospheric interior – with plenty of signs of the building's venerable age – is divided into five comfortable areas, each with its own character, from the cosy terracotta-painted bar to a light and airy gallery room with antique wood panelling, solid oak floor and contemporary Lloyd Loom chairs. Flagstone floors, stripped or well polished antique or period-style furniture and three good fires (one in an inglenook) add warmth and cosiness. You'll find Hobsons Best, Purity Bunny Hop, Pure Gold and Pure UBU and a guest beer on handpump and 18 wines (including prosecco and champagne) by the glass; background music. In summer, the virginia creeper-covered exterior is festooned with colourful hanging baskets. The lovely garden has solid teak furniture, a vine-covered terrace, water features and gentle lighting.

Using the best seasonal produce from local producers, the especially good food includes sandwiches, deep-fried brie with apricot and ginger compote, breaded chicken goujons with spiced crème fraîche, lunchtime brunch, peppered sirloin steak strip salad with blue cheese dressing, tagliatelle with mushrooms in creamy madeira sauce, creamy smoked haddock and prawn lasagne, steak, tomato and cider pie, faggots with sage and onion gravy, gammon with free-range eggs or fresh pineapple, thai green monkfish curry, mixed grill, and puddings such as white chocolate and strawberry mousse and salted caramel and Rolo cheesecake. *Benchmark main dish: breaded garlic chicken breast stuffed with smoked cheddar on sweet potato mash £15.95. Two-course evening meal £24.00.*

Free house ~ Licensees Colin and Teresa Ombler ~ Real ale ~ Open 11.30-3, 6-11.30; 11.30-11.30 Sat; 11.45-10.30 Sun ~ Bar food 11.45-2.30, 6.30-9.30 (10 Fri); 11.45-10 Sat; 12-9.30 Sun ~ Children welcome ~ Wi-fi *Recommended by Jeff Humphries, Doreen Allen, Dave Braisted, Phil and Jane Villiers, Mr and Mrs C Skellon, Mrs Sheila Lupton, Jamie Thompson, Steve Whalley, Douglas Powell, Alan Organ, Phil and Helen Holt, Clive and Fran Dutson, Peter Northover and Sheila Ward*

Real ale may be served from handpumps, electric pumps (not just the on-off switches used for keg beer) or – common in Scotland – tall taps called founts (pronounced 'fonts') where a separate pump pushes the beer up under air pressure.

Also Worth a Visit in Warwickshire

Besides the fully inspected pubs, you might like to try these pubs that have been recommended to us and described by readers. Do tell us what you think of them: feedback@goodguides.com

ALCESTER SP0957
Holly Bush (01789) 507370
Henley Street (continuation of High Street towards B4089; not much nearby parking); B49 5QX Welcoming 17th-c Everards pub with six smallish rooms; their beers and one or two guests kept well, three real ciders and decent choice of wines by the glass, enjoyable good value traditional food from sandwiches up, simple furniture including pews and wall benches, bare boards, flagstones and carpet, some dark panelling, two woodburners and an open fire; quiz Thurs, monthly folk night, TV, free wi-fi; children and dogs welcome, seats in pretty back garden, summer barbecues, open all day. *(Andrew Jones)*

ALCESTER SP0857
Turks Head (01789) 765948
High Street, across from church; B49 5AD Updated old town pub with good friendly atmosphere, small front room and another off corridor, well kept Wye Valley and three guests, several bottled beers and decent choice of wines and whiskies, enjoyable food (not Sun evening) from sharing plates and pizzas up including good fish and chips, Sat brunch; free wi-fi; children welcome, tables in walled garden behind, open all day. *(Mr and Mrs D M Fishleigh, Dave Braisted)*

ALDRIDGE SK0900
Old Irish Harp (01922) 455968
Chester Road, Little Aston (A452 over Staffordshire border); WS9 0LP Popular (particularly with families) modernised beamed pub, good choice of enjoyable well priced food including speciality rotisserie chicken, meal deal Mon-Fri, Banks's Bitter, Jennings Cumberland and Marstons Pedigree, decent wines, extensive dining area; free wi-fi; children welcome, plenty of tables outside with parasols and heaters, open all day. *(Clifford Blakemore)*

ALDRIDGE SK0500
Turtles Head (01922) 325635
Croft Parade; off High Street; WS9 8LY Friendly micropub in row of 1960s shops; simple drinking area with leather sofa and some tub chairs on light wood floor, four well kept/priced ales, proper ciders and decent choice of other drinks, snacky food such as rolls and pork pies, very popular with locals; closed Mon lunchtime, otherwise open all day (till 9pm Sun). *(Suzy Miller)*

ALLESLEY SP3082
White Lion (024) 763 32841
Hawkes Mill Lane; on junction with Wall Hill Road; CV5 9FQ Cottage-fronted Vintage Inn with softly lit separate areas, good range of enjoyable reasonably priced food including fixed-price menus, three well kept ales and decent wines, beams and open fires; background music, upstairs lavatories; children and dogs welcome, tables in small front garden, open all day. *(David Hunt)*

ALVESTON SP2356
Ferry (01789) 269883
Ferry Lane; end of village, off B4086 Stratford–Wellesbourne; CV37 7QX Comfortable beamed dining pub with enjoyable food and well kept ales such as Black Sheep and Wye Valley, friendly staff; quiz first Tues of month, occasional live music; children and dogs welcome, nice spot with seats out at front (some on raised deck), open all day Sat, closed Sun evening, Mon. *(Dave Warren)*

ARDENS GRAFTON SP1153
Golden Cross (01789) 772420
Off A46 or B439 W of Stratford, corner of Wixford Road/Grafton Lane; B50 4LG 18th-c stone pub under new management (some refurbishment); beamed bar with dark flagstones, mix of furniture including chapel chairs and pews around kitchen tables, woodburner in big old fireplace, Wells Bombardier and a couple of guests, eight wines by the glass, tasty uncomplicated home-made food including deals, friendly helpful service, attractive lounge with unusual coffered ceiling, big mullioned bay window and log fire; background music, free wi-fi; children and dogs (in bar) welcome, wheelchair access, picnic-sets in good-sized back garden, more sturdy rustic furniture on terrace, nice views, open (and food) all day. *(Chris and Sophie Baxter)*

BARSTON SP2078
★Bulls Head (01675) 442830
From M42 junction 5, A4141 towards Warwick, first left, then signed down Barston Lane; B92 0JU Unassuming and unspoilt partly Tudor village pub, four well kept ales including Adnams Southwold and Purity Mad Goose, popular traditional home-made food from sandwiches to specials (not Sun evening), cheerful helpful staff, log fires, comfortable lounge with pictures and plates, oak-beamed bar and separate dining room; children and dogs allowed, good-sized

secluded garden alongside pub and barn, open all day Fri-Sun. *(Malcolm Phillips, Clive and Fran Dutson)*

BILSTON SO9496

Trumpet (01902) 493723

High Street; WV14 0EP Holdens pub with their ales and guests kept well, main draw is the good nightly (and Sun lunchtime) jazz, lots of musical memorabilia and photographs, friendly atmosphere. *(Andy Knight)*

BINLEY WOODS SP3977

Roseycombe (024) 7654 1022

Rugby Road; CV3 2AY Warm and friendly 1930s pub with wide choice of bargain home-made food (not Mon evening, Sun), Bass, Fullers London Pride and Greene King IPA; Weds quiz night, some live music; children welcome, big garden. *(Alan Johnson)*

BIRMINGHAM SP0788

★ **Bartons Arms** (0121) 333 5988

High Street, Aston (A34); B6 4UP Magnificent listed Edwardian landmark standing alone in a rather daunting area; impressive richly decorated linked rooms from the palatial to the snug, original tilework murals, stained glass and mahogany, decorative fireplaces, sweeping stairs to handsome upstairs rooms, well kept Oakham ales from ornate island bar with snob screens, interesting imported bottled beers and frequent mini beer festivals, well priced thai food, good service from friendly young staff; open all day. *(David Edwards)*

BIRMINGHAM SP0686

Brasshouse (0121) 633 3383

Broad Street; B1 2HP Spacious bank conversion with enjoyable good value food from sandwiches, burgers and pizzas up, various deals, well kept ales including Marstons and Timothy Taylors and good range of other drinks, efficient friendly service; children welcome in dining area till 6pm, canalside seats, handy for National Sea Life Centre, International Convention Centre and Symphony Hall, open all day from 8am. *(Richard Tingle)*

BIRMINGHAM SP0688

Lord Clifden (0121) 523 7515

Great Hampton Street (Jewellery Quarter); B18 6AA Fairly traditional pub with some contemporary touches, leather banquettes and padded stools around dimpled copper-top tables, interesting collection of street art including Banksy's, bustling atmosphere, wide choice of good value generous food from sandwiches to daily specials, Wye Valley and guests plus draught continentals, prompt friendly service; darts in front bare-boards section, sports TVs (outside too), Thurs quiz night and weekend DJs; plenty of seats in

enclosed part-covered beer garden with table tennis and table football, open all day (till late Fri, Sat). *(Dave Braisted)*

BIRMINGHAM SP0786

Old Contemptibles (0121) 200 3310

Edmund Street; B3 2HB Spacious Edwardian corner pub (Nicholsons) with lofty ceiling and lots of woodwork, good choice of real ales and enjoyable well priced food including range of sausages, friendly efficient young staff; upstairs lavatories; no children, handy central location and popular at lunchtime with office workers, open all day (till 6pm Sun). *(Alan Johnson)*

BIRMINGHAM SP0784

Old Moseley Arms (0121) 440 1954

Tindal Street; B12 9QU Tucked-away red-brick Victorian pub, five well kept ales such as Church End, Enville, Holdens and Wye Valley (regular favourites), nice selection of gins and good value authentic indian food (evenings and all day Sun); live music, sports TVs, darts; outside seating area, handy for Edgbaston cricket ground, open all day. *(Dave Braisted)*

BIRMINGHAM SP0384

Plough (0121) 427 3678

High Street, Harborne; B17 9NT Popular place with spacious modern interior (one or two steps), enjoyable range of food including stone-baked pizzas and chargrilled burgers, regular offers, well kept Purity, Wye Valley and guests, plenty of wines by the glass and some 50 whiskies, good coffee too, friendly staff; background music, TVs and various events such as wine/gin tasting evenings; well behaved children welcome, paved garden with covered area, open all day from 8am (9am weekends) for breakfast. *(Simon Matthews)*

BIRMINGHAM SP0686

Post Office Vaults (0121) 643 7354

New Street/Pinfold Street; B2 4BA Two entrances to this simple downstairs bar with 13 interesting ciders/perries, eight real ales including Hobsons and Salopian and over 300 international bottled beers, friendly knowledgeable staff, no food but can bring your own (plates and cutlery provided); handy for New Street station, open all day. *(Simon Matthews)*

BIRMINGHAM SP0686

Purecraft Bar & Kitchen

(0121) 237 5666 *Waterloo Street; B2 5TJ* Industrial chic-style bar with excellent range of cask and craft beers including several from Purity, interesting bottled range too along with Dunkerton's cider and a dozen wines by the glass, open kitchen serving good food (not Sun evening) from sandwiches and deli boards up (dishes matched with beer), friendly helpful service; children welcome, open all day. *(David Thorpe, Simon Matthews)*

BIRMINGHAM   SP0687
Rose Villa (0121) 236 7910
*By clocktower in Jewellery Quarter
(Warstone Lane/Vyse Street); B18 6JW*
Listed 1920s brick building standing
in splendid isolation; front saloon with
impressive stained glass leading through
to small but magnificent bar, floor-to-
ceiling green tiles and massive tiled arch
over fireplace, original parquet flooring,
quirky touches here and there such
as antler chandeliers and a red phone
box, four or five well kept ales including
Sharps Doom Bar, cocktails, reasonably
priced food from american diner menu;
live music and DJs Fri, Sat till late – can
get very busy; open all day, from 11am
weekends for brunch. *(Dave Braisted)*

BIRMINGHAM   SP0686
★Wellington (0121) 200 3115
Bennetts Hill; B2 5SN Traditionally
renovated high-ceilinged pub with 16 well
kept interesting ales (listed on TV screens)
including three from Black Country, also
real ciders, bottled beers and good range
of gins/whiskies, experienced landlord and
friendly staff, no food but plates and cutlery
if you bring your own, more room and roof
terrace upstairs; regular beer festivals and
quiz nights, darts; open all day and can get
very busy. *(Helen McLagan, Alan Johnson)*

BRIERLEY HILL   SO9286
★Vine (01384) 78293
*B4172 between A461 and (nearer)
A4100; immediately after the turn
into Delph Road; DY5 2TN* Popular
black country pub (aka the Bull & Bladder)
offering a true taste of the West Midlands;
down-to-earth welcome and friendly chatty
locals in meandering series of rooms, each
different in character, traditional front bar
with wall benches, comfortable extended
snug with solidly built red plush seats,
tartan-decorated back bar, well kept/priced
Bathams from brewery next door, a couple
of simple very cheap lunchtime dishes
plus cobs and snacks all day; TV, games
machine, darts and dominoes; children
and dogs welcome, tables in backyard,
open all day. *(Mandy and Gary Redstone)*

BROOM   SP0853
★Broom Tavern (01789) 778199
High Street; off B439 in Bidford; B50 4HL
Spacious 16th-c brick and timber village pub,
relaxed and welcoming, with good interesting
food from chef owners including excellent
Sun roasts, four well kept ales such as North
Cotswold, Purity, Sharps and Wye Valley, well

balanced wine list with several by the glass,
good attentive (but not intrusive) service,
main room divided into two parts, one
with cottage-style tables and chairs, the
other with oak furniture, black beams and
log fire, also a snug perfect for a group of
diners; Mon quiz; children welcome, dogs
in lower bar area, tables out on grass either
side, handy for Ragley Hall, open all day
weekends, no food Sun evening. *(Theocsbrian,
David and Catharine Boston)*

CHERINGTON   SP2836
Cherington Arms (01608) 685183
Off A3400; CV36 5HS Recently
refurbished 17th-c stone-built village
pub, popular food (not Mon) from french
landlord-chef including open sandwiches,
pub favourites and blackboard specials,
Tues evening fish and chips, Sun carvery,
well kept Hook Norton and a couple
of guests, welcoming efficient service,
beamed bar with log fire, separate dining
room; some live music; children and dogs
welcome, tables on terrace and in big
garden bordering River Stour, good nearby
walks, open all day Fri and Sat, till 6pm
Sun, closed Mon lunchtime. *(Cameron
Townsend, Clive and Fran Dutson)*

CLAVERDON   SP2064
★Red Lion (01926) 842291
*Station Road; B4095 towards Warwick;
CV35 8PE* Upmarket beamed Tudor dining
pub with highly regarded food including some
middle eastern influences, well kept Hook
Norton Lion and several wines by the glass,
friendly landlord and staff, log fires in linked
rooms, back area with country views over
sheltered heated deck and gardens; children
welcome, no dogs inside, open all day Sat,
closed Sun evening. *(Roger Braithwaite, Clive
and Fran Dutson, David and Catharine Boston)*

COVENTRY   SP3279
Old Windmill (024) 7625 1717
Spon Street; CV1 3BA Friendly 15th-c
pub with lots of tiny rooms (known locally
as Ma Brown's), exposed beams in uneven
ceilings, inglenook woodburner, seven well
kept ales including Sharps, Theakstons
and Timothy Taylors, good local pork pies;
live music, juke box, sports TV and games
machines, darts; closed Mon lunchtime,
otherwise open all day (till 1am Fri, Sat),
busy at weekends. *(Dave Braisted)*

COVENTRY   SP3379
Town Wall (024) 7622 0963
*Bond Street, among car parks behind
Belgrade Theatre; CV1 4AH* Busy
Victorian city-centre local with half a dozen

We mention bottled beers and spirits only if there is something unusual about them
– imported belgian real ales, say, or dozens of malt whiskies; so do please let us know
about them in your reports.

well kept ales including Adnams and Bass, Weston's cider, enjoyable good value pub food (not Sun evening, Mon) from lunchtime sandwiches up, unspoilt basic front bar and tiny snug, engraved windows, bigger back lounge with actor/playwright photographs and pictures of old Coventry, open fires; big-screen sports TV, juke box; no children, open all day. *(Alan Johnson, Dave Braisted)*

EARLSWOOD   SP1274
Blue Bell Cider House
(01564) 702328 *Warings Green Road, not far from M42 junction 4; B94 6BP* Welcoming 19th-c red-brick pub by Stratford Canal, roomy lounge, cosy bar and conservatory, good value generous food including OAP weekday lunch and popular Sun carvery, own-brew organic beers plus guests, traditional ciders, friendly helpful staff; Weds quiz; children and dogs welcome, plenty of outside seating, moorings, open all day. *(Dave Braisted)*

EASENHALL   SP4679
Golden Lion (01788) 833577
Main Street; CV23 0JA Bar in 16th-c part of busy comfortable hotel; white-painted beams, half-panelling and log fire, some original wattle and daub and fine 17th-c carved bench depicting the 12 apostles, a couple of real ales (usually one from Charles Wells) and good food including cook your own meat/fish on hot rocks, prompt friendly service, more formal restaurant; background music; children and small dogs welcome, disabled access/loos, tables on side terrace and spacious lawn, 17 well equipped bedrooms (some with four-posters), attractive village, open (and food) all day. *(Helen McLagan, Gerry and Rosemary Dobson)*

EDGE HILL   SP3747
★Castle (01295) 670255
Off A422; OX15 6DJ Crenellated octagonal tower built in 1742 as gothic folly (marks where Charles I raised his standard at the Battle of Edgehill); major renovation creating bar and four dining areas, plenty of original features including arched windows and doorways, beams and stone fireplaces, fantastic views (some floor-to-ceiling windows), good food (not Sun evening), also deli bar for sandwiches, coffee and afternoon teas, well kept Hook Norton ales, friendly enthusiastic young staff; downstairs lavatories; children welcome, seats in lovely big garden with more outstanding views, beautiful Compton Wynyates nearby, four refurbished bedrooms, parking can be tricky at busy times, open all day Sat, till 7pm Sun. *(Andy Dolan, Susan and John Douglas)*

ETTINGTON   SP2748
★Chequers (01789) 740387
Banbury Road (A422); CV37 7SR Good enterprising food is the main draw here,

but they do keep three real ales including a beer badged for them from Marstons and a decent range of wines by the glass; bar and restaurant areas with variety of comfortable and rather elegant dining chairs on dark wood flooring, big mirrors, a piano and richly figured velvet curtains and wall hangings, good service and relaxed friendly atmosphere; background music, free wi-fi; well behaved children welcome, dogs in bar, sheltered back garden with picnic-sets on lawn and stylish furniture on terrace, open all day Sat, till 6pm Sun, closed Mon. *(R T and J C Moggridge, Mike and Mary Carter, Mrs Zara Elliott, Michael Doswell)*

FARNBOROUGH   SP4349
Kitchen (01295) 690615
Off A423 N of Banbury; OX17 1DZ Refurbished golden-stone dining pub in NT village; bar with painted beams, wood floor and cushioned window seats, red woodburner in big fireplace, saddle- and tractor-seat stools at blue-panelled counter serving Purity ales and good wines by the glass, enjoyable food from interesting if not especially cheap menu, two room dining area; jazzy background music, free wi-fi; children and dogs welcome, neat sloping garden with blue picnic-sets and pizza oven, local walks, open all day weekends, closed Tues, Weds and lunchtime Thurs. *(Audrey and Paul Summers)*

FENNY COMPTON   SP4152
Merrie Lion (01295) 771134
Brook Street; CV47 2YH Spotless early 18th-c beamed village pub; three well kept beers including one badged for them, decent range of wines and good freshly made food from pubby choices up, friendly welcoming atmosphere; quiz nights and other events; dogs welcome, tables outside, handy for Burton Dassett Hills Country Park, open all day weekends. *(Andy Knight)*

FILLONGLEY   SP2787
Cottage (01676) 540599
Black Hall Lane; CV7 8EG Popular country dining pub on village outskirts, good value fairly traditional food including OAP lunch, early-evening deal and Tues curry night, beers such as Bass, St Austell and Timothy Taylors, friendly service; back terrace and lawn overlooking fields, closes Sun evening 6pm. *(Dave Warren)*

FIVE WAYS   SP2270
★Case is Altered (01926) 484206
Follow Rowington signs at junction roundabout off A4177/A4141 N of Warwick, then right into Case Lane; CV35 7JD Convivial unspoilt old cottage licensed for over three centuries; Old Pie Factory, Wye Valley and three guests served by friendly long-serving landlady, no food, simple small main bar with fine old poster of Lucas, Blackwell & Arkwright Brewery (now flats), clock with hours spelling out

Thornleys Ale (another defunct brewery), and just a few sturdy old-fashioned tables and a couple of stout leather-covered settles facing each other over spotless tiles, modest little back room with old bar billiards table (takes sixpences); no children, dogs or mobile phones; full disabled access, stone table on small brick courtyard. *(Peter and Caroline Waites)*

FLECKNOE   SP5163
Old Olive Bush (01788) 891134
Off A425 W of Daventry; CV23 8AT
Unspoilt little Edwardian pub in quiet photogenic village, friendly chatty atmosphere, enjoyable traditional food cooked by landlady (Weds-Sat evenings, Sun lunchtime), well kept changing ales and decent wines, open fire in bar with stripped-wood floor, steps up to games room (table skittles), small dining room with etched-glass windows and another fire; Thurs quiz; children welcome, pretty garden, closed weekday lunchtimes and all day Mon. *(Chantelle and Tony Redman)*

FRANKTON   SP4270
Friendly (01926) 632430
Just over a mile S of B4453 Leamington Spa–Rugby; Main Street; CV23 9NY Popular 16th-c village pub living up to its name, four well kept ales including Greene King IPA, good reasonably priced traditional home-made food (not Sun evening, Mon), two low-ceilinged rooms, open fire; dogs welcome, open all day weekends, closed Mon lunchtime. *(Darren and Jane Staniforth)*

HALESOWEN   SO9683
Waggon & Horses (0121) 550 4989
Stourbridge Road; B63 3TU Popular refurbished and extended 19th-c red-brick corner pub; Black Country ales along with plenty of interesting guests (tasting trays available) and four real ciders, friendly knowledgeable staff, limited food such as cobs and pork pies, open fire; dogs welcome, open all day. *(Nigel Espley, Tea Belly)*

HAMPTON LUCY   SP2557
Boars Head (01789) 840533
Church Street, E of Stratford; CV35 8BE
Welcoming unpretentious village pub with nicely decorated interior, beams and log fires, good range of changing local ales and enjoyable modestly priced pubby food from sandwiches up (all day Sat, not Sun evening), deli counter selling sauces, spices, olives etc; children welcome, seats in enclosed back courtyard, near lovely church, and handy for Charlecote Park (NT) and M40, open all day. *(Susan and John Douglas)*

HARBOROUGH MAGNA   SP4779
Old Lion (01788) 833238
3 miles from M6 junction 1; B4112 Pailton Road; CV23 0HQ Welcoming

village pub with stylish modern décor, emphasis on good well presented home-cooked food from pub favourites and stone-baked pizzas to steaks and daily specials, friendly attentive staff, Greene King ales including one badged for them and maybe a guest, nice choice of wines; children and dogs (in bar) welcome, terrace seating, open (and food) all day Sat, till 6pm Sun. *(Chris and Sophie Baxter)*

HARTSHILL   SP3394
Anchor (024) 7639 3444
Mancetter Road (B4111); CV10 0RT
Welcoming cleanly presented canalside pub run by father and son, three Everards ales and good choice of enjoyable home-made food including Sun carvery; sports TV, free wi-fi; children and dogs welcome, garden with bouncy castle, goats and chickens, open all day (till 8pm Sun). *(Ben Caunter)*

HATTON   SP2367
★Falcon (01926) 484281
Birmingham Road, Haseley (A4177, not far from M40 junction 15); CV35 7HA
Smartly updated dining pub with relaxing rooms around island bar, lots of stripped brickwork and low beams, tiled and oak-planked floors, good moderately priced food from sandwiches, sharing boards and pub favourites up, lunchtime/early-evening deal Mon-Fri, friendly service, nice choice of wines by the glass and well kept Marstons-related ales, barn-style back restaurant; children welcome, disabled facilities, garden (dogs allowed here) with heated covered terrace, eight bedrooms in converted barn, open (and food) all day. *(John Preddy, Ian Herdman)*

HENLEY-IN-ARDEN   SP1566
Bluebell (01564) 793049
High Street (A3400, off M40 junction 16); B95 5AT Impressive timber-framed dining pub with fine coach entrance, good imaginative food served by cheerful staff, rambling old beamed and flagstoned interior with contemporary furnishings creating stylish but relaxed atmosphere, big fireplace, well kept ales such as Church End and Purity, 20 wines by the glass, coffee and afternoon teas, daily papers; occasional art exhibitions and live music, free wi-fi; children welcome if eating, dogs allowed, tables on back decking, open till 7.30pm Sun, closed Mon, otherwise open all day. *(Simon Matthews)*

KENILWORTH   SP2872
Clarendon Arms (01926) 852017
Castle Hill; CV8 1NB Busy pub opposite castle and under same ownership as next-door Harringtons restaurant; several rooms off long bare-boards bustling bar, ales such as Hook Norton, Purity and Slaughterhouse, tasty reasonably priced pub food, cheerful staff, largish peaceful upstairs dining room; children and dogs (in bar) welcome, metal tables on small raised terrace, daytime car

park fee deducted from food bill, open (and food) all day weekends. *(Ian Herdman)*

KENILWORTH   SP2872
Old Bakery (01926) 864111
High Street, off A452; CV8 1LZ Friendly small hotel with cosy two-room bar popular with older customers, four well kept ales including Wye Valley HPA and good choice of wines by the glass; no music, TVs or machines; 14 comfortable bedrooms, good english breakfast, open evenings only from 5.30pm (5pm Fri-Sun) and can get very busy, food served Mon. *(Dave Warren)*

KENILWORTH   SP2871
Queen & Castle (01926) 852661
Castle Green; CV8 1ND Modernised beamed Mitchells & Butlers dining pub opposite castle, good range of enjoyable food, three real ales and plenty of wines by the glass; children welcome, open all day. *(Ian Herdman)*

KENILWORTH   SP2872
★Virgins & Castle (01926) 853737
High Street; CV8 1LY Small snugs by entrance corridor and maze of intimate rooms off inner servery, flagstones, heavy beams and lots of woodwork, coal fire, four well kept Everards ales and a couple of guests, good food at reasonable prices including some filipino dishes and weekday set lunch, friendly service, games bar upstairs; children in eating areas, disabled facilities, tables in sheltered garden, parking can be a problem, open all day. *(Dave Warren)*

LADBROKE   SP4158
★Bell (01926) 811224
Signed off A423 S of Southam; CV47 2BY Refurbished beamed country pub set back from the road, smallish bar with tub chairs by log fire, snug off with library wallpaper and another fire in little brick fireplace, three well kept ales including Ringwood and plenty of wines by the glass, very good well presented food from pub favourites and grills up, also gluten-free choices and weekday set menu, airy candlelit restaurant with light oak flooring, friendly efficient young staff; background music, free wi-fi; children and dogs (in bar) welcome, a few picnic-sets out in front and on side grass, pleasant surroundings, closed Sun evening, Mon. *(Clive and Fran Dutson, Mike Fountain, Nigel and Sue Foster, Michael Doswell)*

LAPWORTH   SP1871
★Boot (01564) 782464
Old Warwick Road; B4439 Hockley Heath–Warwick – 2.8 miles from M40 junction 1, but from southbound carriageway only, and return only to northbound; B94 6JU Popular upmarket dining pub near Stratford Canal, good range of food from interesting menu including weekday fixed-price offer, efficient cheerful

young staff, upscale wines, well kept Purity Pure UBU and Sharps Doom Bar, stripped beams and dark panelling, big antique hunting prints, cushioned pews and bucket chairs on ancient quarry tiles and bare boards, warm fire, charming low-raftered upstairs dining room; background music; children and dogs welcome, tables on side terrace (some under extendable canopy), more seating on grass beyond with tipi, nice walks, open all day. *(Ian Herdman)*

LAPWORTH   SP1970
Navigation (01564) 783337
Old Warwick Road (B4439 SE); B94 6NA Modernised beamed pub by the Grand Union Canal; slate-floor bar with woodburner, bare-boards snug and restaurant, well kept ales such as Byatts, Purity, Timothy Taylors and Wadworths, unusually Guinness also on handpump, decent wines and enjoyable reasonably priced food (all day Fri-Sun) from sandwiches and other bar choices up, breakfast from 10am weekends, good Sun roasts, friendly efficient staff; children welcome, dogs in bar, covered terrace and waterside garden, handy for Packwood House and Baddesley Clinton (both NT), open all day. *(Chris Francis, Clive and Fran Dutson)*

LEAMINGTON SPA   SP3165
Cricketers Arms (01926) 881293
Archery Road; CV31 3PT Friendly town local opposite bowling greens; fairly priced food (all day Sat) using meat from good local butcher, popular Sun roasts (till 6pm), also nice home-made sausage rolls and scotch eggs, well kept Slaughterhouse and a couple of guests such as Timothy Taylors from central tap, Weston's cider, some panelling and cricketing memorabilia, comfortable banquettes, open fires; fortnightly quiz Mon, poker night Weds, sports TV, darts, free wi-fi; children and dogs welcome, heated back terrace, open all day. *(Peter and Caroline Waites)*

LEAMINGTON SPA   SP3166
★Star & Garter (01926) 359960
Warwick Street; CV32 5LL Bustling open-plan town-centre pub (part of the Peach group); bare-boards bar with cushioned wall seats upholstered in quirky eastern european fabric, blue leather banquettes, red leather armchairs and small wooden stools around mixed tables, Greene King ales (including one named for the pub) and St Austell Tribute, plenty of wines by the glass and good selection of gins/whiskies, wide choice of enjoyable food including weekend brunch from 9am, dining area with back-to-back banquettes down one side and open kitchen, steps up to second bar area with blue tub seats, bright scatter cushions and some bold paintwork, friendly helpful staff; background music, free wi-fi; children and dogs (in bar) welcome, open all day. *(Miles Green, Donald Allsopp)*

LEEK WOOTTON   SP2868
Anchor (01926) 853355
Warwick Road; CV35 7QX Neat and
well run dining lounge popular for its good
fresh food including range of burgers and
daily specials, well kept ales such as Bass,
Hook Norton and Purity, good selection of
affordably priced wines and soft drinks,
attentive friendly service, lots of close-set
pine tables, smaller overflow dining area;
background music, sports TV, free wi-fi;
children welcome, no dogs inside, long
garden behind with play area, open (and
food) all day weekends. *(Andy Knight)*

LIGHTHORNE   SP3455
Antelope (01926) 651188
*Old School Lane, Bishops Hill; a mile SW
of B4100 N of Banbury; CV35 0AU*
Attractive early 18th-c stone-built pub
in pretty village setting, two neatly kept
comfortable bars and separate dining area,
beams, flagstones and big open fire, well
kept Greene King IPA, Sharps Doom Bar
and a couple of guests, enjoyable food (all
day Sun) from good sandwiches up, friendly
efficient service; children and dogs welcome,
picnic-sets out by well and on small grassy
area, open all day Fri-Sun. *(Simon Matthews)*

LITTLE COMPTON   SP2530
★Red Lion (01608) 674397
*Off A44 Moreton-in-Marsh to Chipping
Norton; GL56 0RT* Low-beamed 16th-c
Cotswold-stone inn under new management;
well liked food (not Sun evening) cooked by
landlord-chef from fairly traditional menu,
Donnington ales and good choice of wines
by the glass, friendly helpful service, snug
alcoves, inglenook woodburner; darts and
pool in public bar; well behaved children
and dogs welcome, white-painted metal
furniture in pretty garden, two comfortable
bedrooms, open all day (but may shut in
the afternoon if quiet). *(Martin Constable,
R K Phillips, D L Frostick, Bernard Stradling)*

LONG ITCHINGTON   SP4165
Duck on the Pond (01926) 815876
*Just off A423 Coventry–Southam; The
Green; CV47 9QJ* Fully refurbished
village pub with stylish modern interior,
good well presented food (not Sun
evening) including set lunchtime/early-
evening menu, Charles Wells ales and
over a dozen wines by the glass, efficient
cheerful service; children welcome, rattan-
style furniture in fenced front garden,
open all day. *(John and Mary Ling)*

LONG ITCHINGTON   SP4164
Two Boats (01926) 812640
*A423 N of Southam, by Grand Union
Canal; CV47 9QZ* Traditional brick-
built pub with lovely canal views from
waterfront terrace and alcove window
seats in long picture-filled main room,
enjoyable generously served food from
good value pubby menu, Wells, Youngs
and guests, friendly helpful staff; TV
and darts in side bar; children and dogs
welcome, moorings, open all day, no food
Sun evening. *(Mr and Mrs D Hammond)*

LONGFORD   SP3684
Greyhound (024) 7636 3046
*Sutton Stop, off Black Horse Road/
Grange Road; junction of Coventry and
North Oxford canals; CV6 6DF* Cosy
19th-c canalside pub with plenty of
character, half a dozen well kept ales and
good range of enjoyable food including
lunchtime sandwiches and home-made
pies, friendly helpful staff, coal-fired stove,
unusual tiny snug; children and dogs
(in bar) welcome, tables on attractive
waterside terrace, nice spot (if you ignore
the pylons), open all day. *(Alex Ivinson)*

LYE   SO9284
★Windsor Castle (01384) 897809
*Stourbridge Road (corner A458/A4036;
car park in Pedmore Road just above
traffic lights – don't be tempted to use
the next-door restaurant's parking!);
DY9 7DG* Interesting well kept beers from
impressive row of handpumps including
own Sadlers ales (brewery tours available);
central flagstoned part with bar stools by
counter and window shelf overlooking road,
several snugger rooms off, some brewing
memorabilia, enjoyable home-cooked food
(not Sun evening), friendly service; free
wi-fi; children and dogs (in bar) welcome,
disabled facilities, terrace and verandah
seating, four bedrooms, handy for Lye
station, open all day (from 9am Sat for
breakfast). *(Gerry and Ram Pollard)*

NAPTON   SP4560
Folly (01926) 815185
*Off A425 towards Priors Hardwick;
Folly Lane, by locks; CV47 8NZ*
Beamed red-brick pub in lovely spot on
Oxford Canal by Napton Locks and Folly
Bridge (113): three bars on different
levels, mix of furnishings and two big
fireplaces (one with woodburner), lots of
interesting bric-a-brac, pictures and old
framed photographs, good straightforward
home-made food (not Sun evening),
well kept ales including Hook Norton;
sports TV, free-wi-fi; children and dogs
welcome, open all day. *(Dave Warren)*

NETHER WHITACRE   SP2292
Gate (01675) 481292
Gate Lane; B46 2DS Welcoming
traditional community pub, seven well
kept Marstons-related ales and good
honest local food, log-fire bar, lounge and
dining conservatory, games room with
pool; children and dogs (in bar) welcome,
garden picnic-sets and play area, open
all day, no food Mon. *(Sarah Watkinson)*

NETHERTON   SO9488
★**Old Swan** (01384) 253075
Halesowen Road (A459 just S of centre);
DY2 9PY Victorian tavern full of traditional
character, known locally as Ma Pardoe's
after former long-serving landlady; charming
unspoilt front bar with big swan centrepiece
in patterned enamel ceiling, engraved
mirrors, traditional furnishings and old-
fashioned cylinder stove, other rooms
including cosy back snug and more modern
lounge, own well priced ales and enjoyable
good value bar food (best to book/check
times), upstairs restaurant (evenings only
and Sun lunch); no under-16s, dogs allowed
in bar, open all day. *(Nigel Espley)*

NEWBOLD ON STOUR   SP2446
White Hart (01789) 450205
A3400 S of Stratford; CV37 8TS
Welcoming dining pub with proper pubby
atmosphere and run by same family for many
years, enjoyable varied choice of home-made
food (not always Sun evening), Adnams and
Hook Norton, decent wines, long airy beamed
bar with good log fire in large stone fireplace,
flagstones and big bay windows, back bar and
separate dining room; pool, darts and ring the
bull; children and dogs welcome, picnic-sets
out at front and on back lawned area, open
all day weekends. *(Mandy and Gary Redstone)*

OFFCHURCH   SP3665
★**Stag** (01926) 425801
*N of Welsh Road, off A425 at Radford
Semele; CV33 9AQ* Popular 16th-c
thatched and beamed village pub; oak-floored
bar with log fires, ales such as Hook Norton,
Purity and St Austell, a dozen wines by the
glass and good interesting food served by
friendly efficient young staff, more formal
cosy restaurant areas with bold wallpaper,
striking fabrics, animal heads and big
mirrors; children and dogs (in bar) welcome,
nice garden with rattan-style furniture on
terrace, open all day. *(Clive and Fran Dutson)*

OLD HILL   SO9686
Waterfall (0121) 559 9198
Waterfall Lane; B64 6RG Friendly
unpretentious two-room local, well kept
Bathams, Holdens and several guests,
good straightforward low-priced home-
made food, tankards and jugs hanging
from boarded ceiling; dogs welcome, seats
on small raised front area and in back
garden, open all day. *(Simon Matthews)*

OXHILL   SP3149
★**Peacock** (01295) 688060
Off A422 Stratford–Banbury; CV35 0QU
Popular stone-built country pub with good
varied menu including blackboard specials
and gluten-free choices, friendly attentive
young staff, a house beer from Wychwood
and guests, good selection of wines by the
glass, cosy beamed bar with big solid tables

and woodburner, half-panelled bare-boards
dining room; unobtrusive background
music; children and dogs (in bar) welcome,
nice back garden, pretty village, open
all day Sun. *(Chris and Sophie Baxter)*

PRIORS MARSTON   SP4857
Holly Bush (01327) 260934
*Off A361 S of Daventry; Holly Bush
Lane; CV47 7RW* 16th-c pub under recent
new management; beams, flagstones and
lots of stripped stone in rambling linked
rooms, log fire and woodburners, good
home-made food, ales such as Black Sheep
and Hook Norton; darts, free wi-fi; terrace
and sheltered garden. *(Andy Knight)*

RATLEY   SP3847
Rose & Crown (01295) 678148
Off A422 NW of Banbury; OX15 6DS
Ancient golden-stone village pub, charming
and cosy, with five well kept changing ales
(St Austell Tribute and Wells Bombardier
feature regularly), blackboard list of
wines, enjoyable good value food (not Sun
evening, Mon) including daily specials,
friendly officient staff, carpeted black-
beamed bar with woodburner each end,
traditional furniture and window seats, cosy
snug; background music, darts; children,
walkers and dogs welcome, tables on sunny
split-level terrace, aunt sally, near lovely
church in sleepy village, handy for Upton
House (NT), open all day Fri-Sun, closed
Mon lunchtime. *(Clive and Fran Dutson)*

ROWINGTON   SP1969
Tom o' the Wood (01564) 782252
*Off B4439 N of Rowington, following
Lowsonford sign; Finwood Road;
CV35 7DH* Spaciously modernised and
extended canalside pub, good home-
cooked food (not Sun evening) from
sharing baskets and stone-baked pizzas
up, pie night Thurs, well kept Greene
King IPA and a guest, Weston's Rosie's
Pig cider, friendly staff and pub labrador
Boris, conservatory; live music Fri, free
wi-fi; children and dogs welcome, tables
on terrace and side lawn, open all day
(may close early Sun). *(Alex Ivinson)*

RUGBY   SP5075
Merchants (01788) 571119
Little Church Street; CV21 3AN Open-
plan pub tucked away near main shopping
area, cheerfully busy, with nine quickly
changing ales (some unusual for the
area), real ciders and huge selection of
belgian and other bottled imports, regular
beer/cider/gin festivals, shortish choice
of low-priced lunchtime food including
speciality fish and chips, quite dark inside
with beams, bare boards and mat-covered
flagstones, lots of interesting breweriana;
background music (live Tues), quiz last
Mon of month, sports TVs; open all day,
till 1am Fri, Sat. *(Dave Warren)*

RUGBY SP5075

Seven Stars (01788) 535478

Albert Square; CV21 2SH Traditionally refurbished 19th-c red-brick local with great choice of ales including Everards, Gun Dog and Oakham, friendly landlord and staff, main bar, lounge, snug and conservatory; occasional charity events with live music; some outside seating, open all day. *(Dave Warren)*

RUSHALL SK03001

Manor Arms (01922) 642333

Park Road, off A461; WS4 1LG Interesting low-beamed 18th-c pub (on much older foundations) by Rushall Canal, three rooms in contrasting styles, one with big inglenook, well kept Banks's ales from pumps fixed to the wall (there's no counter), simple snacky food, friendly staff; children and dogs welcome, waterside garden with moorings, next to Park Lime Pits nature reserve, open all day. *(Peter and Caroline Waites)*

SEDGLEY SO9293

★ Beacon (01902) 883380

Bilston Street; A463, off A4123 Wolverhampton–Dudley; DY3 1JE Plain old brick pub with own good Sarah Hughes ales from traditional Victorian tower brewery behind; cheery locals in simple quarry-tiled drinking corridor, little snug on left with wall settles, imposing green-tiled marble fireplace and glazed serving hatch, old-fashioned furnishings such as velvet and net curtains, mahogany tables on patterned carpet, small landscape prints, sparse tap room on right with blackened range, dark-panelled lounge with sturdy red leather wall settles and big dramatic sea prints, plant-filled conservatory (no seats), little food apart from cobs; no credit cards; children allowed in some parts including garden with play area, dogs not allowed. *(Chantelle and Tony Redman)*

SHIPSTON-ON-STOUR SP2540

George (01608) 661453

High Street; CV36 4AJ Popular hotel with splendid Georgian façade; spacious opened-up interior with several updated linked areas, enjoyable food from reasonably compact menu including lunchtime sandwiches, Brakspears and Marstons-related guests, over a dozen wines by the glass and good range of other drinks including cocktails (two-for-one Thurs evening), efficient helpful service; children and dogs (in bar area) welcome, teak tables and chairs in courtyard behind, 15 well appointed bedrooms, open all day from 8am for breakfast. *(Guy Vowles)*

SHUSTOKE SP2290

★ Griffin (01675) 481205

Church End, a mile E of village; 5 miles from M6 junction 4; A446 towards Tamworth, then right on to B4114 straight through Coleshill; B46 2LB Unpretentious country local with a dozen well kept changing ales including own Griffin (brewed in next-door barn), farm cider and country wines, standard lunchtime bar food (not Sun); cheery low-beamed L-shaped bar with log fires in two stone fireplaces (one a big inglenook), fairly simple décor including cushioned café seats, elm-topped sewing trestles and a nice old-fashioned settle, beer mats on ceiling, conservatory (children allowed here); games machine; dogs welcome, old-fashioned seats on back grass with distant views of Birmingham, large terrace, play area and summer marquee (live music), camping field, open all day Sun. *(Audrey and Paul Summers)*

SHUSTOKE SP2290

Plough (01675) 481557

B4114 Nuneaton–Coleshill; B46 2AN Old-fashioned feel with rooms arranged around central bar, well kept Bass and four guests, good choice of fairly straightforward food served by friendly helpful staff, separate dining room, black beams, open fire and gleaming brass; regular quiz nights (usually Mon), pool and darts, fruit machine, free wi-fi; children and dogs welcome, seats out at back along with caged rabbits and exotic birds, open all day Fri-Sun. *(Simon Matthews)*

STOCKTON SP4365

Boat (01926) 812657

A426 Southam–Rugby; CV23 8HQ Fairly traditionally updated canalside pub, open-plan split-level interior (raised part mainly for dining) with dark wood furniture on wood or pale stone floor, woodburner in brick fireplace, brewery mirrors and advertising signs, bottles on delft shelf, a house beer from Nethergate and three guests, popular reasonably priced pubby food (not Sun evening), friendly staff, little deli; children and dogs (in bar) welcome, picnic-sets out by the water (moorings), garden behind with play area, open all day. *(George Atkinson)*

STOCKTON SP4363

Crown (01926) 812255

High Street; CV47 8JZ Friendly village pub with well kept St Austell and local guests, popular straightforward food, restaurant in ancient barn, log fires; children and dogs welcome, garden with play area, open all day. *(Alex Ivinson)*

STOURBRIDGE SO9084

Duke William (01384) 440202

Coventry Street; DY8 1EP Friendly and popular Edwardian corner pub in semi-pedestrianised area, own Craddocks beers from on-site microbrewery (tours available) plus guests and draught/bottled imports, good pie, mash and peas menu, traditional old black country feel with long corridor, open fire in bar and cosy snug; plenty of events including music, quiz and film nights (some in upstairs function room); no children, beer garden, open all day. *(Gerry and Pam Pollard)*

STOURBRIDGE   SO8983
Plough & Harrow   (01384) 397218
Worcester Street; DY8 1AX Friendly little bay-windowed end-of-terrace local (sister to the nearby Duke William), well kept Craddocks ales and guests, snacky food (nothing hot), cosy horseshoe bar with log fires and piano; dogs welcome, no children inside, partly covered beer garden with woodburner, close to Mary Stevens Park, open all day. *(Gerry and Pam Pollard)*

STRATFORD-UPON-AVON   SP1955
Old Thatch   (01789) 295216
Rother Street/Greenhill Street; CV37 6LE Cosy and welcoming 15th-c thatched pub on corner of market square, well kept Fullers ales, nice wines and popular fairly priced food including Sun carvery, rustic décor, beams, slate or wood floors, sofas and log fire, back dining area; children and dogs welcome, covered tables outside, open all day. *(Alan Johnson)*

STRATFORD-UPON-AVON   SP2055
One Elm   (01789) 404919
Guild Street; CV37 6QZ Peach group pub with fresh modern décor on two floors, well liked food from sandwiches and sharing boards up, good value weekday set menu till 6pm, Purity, Sharps and one or two guests, plenty of wines by the glass and interesting range of gins, cocktails, friendly efficient service; children and dogs welcome, seats out at front and in attractive courtyard behind, open all day. *(Dr and Mrs J D Abell)*

STRATFORD-UPON-AVON   SP1955
White Swan   (01789) 297022
Rother Street; CV37 6NH Extensively renovated historic hotel (dates from 1450) with warren of connecting heavily beamed areas around central bar (one or two steps), good mix of seating including leather armchairs/sofas and antique settles, Shakespearean themed pictures and prints, oak-panelled dining room with two fine carved fireplaces and 16th-c wall painting of Tobias and the Angel, five Fullers/Gales beers, several wines by the glass and good choice of food to suit all tastes and occasions, quick friendly service; background music, daily newspapers, free wi-fi; children welcome, seats out at front overlooking market square and to the side, character bedrooms, open (and food) all day. *(Susan and John Douglas)*

STRATFORD-UPON-AVON   SP1954
Windmill   (01789) 297687
Church Street; CV37 6HB Ancient pub (with town's oldest licence) beyond the striking Guild Chapel, very low beams, panelling, mainly stone floors, big

fireplace (gas fire), Greene King, Purity UBU and guests, enjoyable good value food including range of burgers, friendly efficient staff; background music, sports TV, games machines, free wi-fi; courtyard tables, open all day. *(Andy Knight)*

STRETTON-ON-FOSSE   SP2238
★Plough   (01608) 661053
Just off A429; GL56 9QX Popular little 17th-c village local with welcoming landlady; central servery separating small bar and snug dining area, four changing mainly local ales, good home-cooked food (not Sun evening) including blackboard specials, low oak beams, stripped brick/stone walls and some flagstones, inglenook log fire; dominoes and cribbage, free wi-fi; children welcome, no dogs, a few tables outside, closed Mon lunchtime. *(K H Frostick)*

SUTTON COLDFIELD   SP1195
Brewhouse & Kitchen
(0121) 796 6838 *Birmingham Road; B72 1QD* Revamped mock-Tudor pub with own microbrewery (tours available), eight real ales (mainly theirs) plus good range of craft kegs and bottled beers, around a dozen wines by the glass and enjoyable reasonably priced food from snacks, burgers and ribs up (menu matches beers with food), friendly helpful staff, spacious modern interior with plenty of different seating areas including a boothed dining part; children welcome, open (and food) all day. *(Dave Braisted)*

TANWORTH-IN-ARDEN   SP1071
Warwickshire Lad   (01564) 742346
Broad Lane/Wood End Lane, Wood End; B94 5DP Beamed country pub with broad choice of enjoyable food cooked by landlord-chef, well kept St Austell, Wye Valley and a couple of guests, friendly service; open mike night last Sun of month; children and dogs welcome, popular with walkers (bridleway opposite), seats outside, open (and food) all day and fairly convenient for M42 (junction 3). *(Nick Hales, Elaine Powis)*

TEMPLE GRAFTON   SP1355
Blue Boar   (01789) 750010
1 mile E, towards Binton; off A422 W of Stratford; B49 6NR Welcoming stone-built dining inn with good food from sandwiches and tapas-style snacks up, well kept Banks's, Wychwood and a couple of guests, afternoon teas, beams, stripped stonework and log fires, glass-covered well with goldfish, smarter dining room up a couple of steps; occasional live music, sports TV, free wi-fi; children and dogs welcome, picnic-sets outside, bedrooms. *(Sharon and John Hancock)*

TIDDINGTON   SP2255
Crown   (01789) 297010
Main Street; CV37 7AZ Refurbished family-friendly pub with good well priced home-made food (smaller helpings

available), four well kept ales including Sharps Doom Bar, friendly staff; darts, pool and TV in side bar; dogs welcome, garden with play area, open all day Fri-Sun, no food Sun evening. *(Alan Johnson)*

TIPTON   SO9492
Pie Factory (0121) 557 1402
Hurst Lane, Dudley Road towards Wednesbury; A457/A4037; DY4 9AB Eccentric décor and quirky food – mixed grill served on a shovel, and you're awarded a certificate if you finish their massive Desperate Dan Cow Pie (comes with pastry horns) – other pies and good value food including Sun carvery, well kept Lump Hammer house ales brewed by Enville plus a guest; background music (live weekends), TV; children welcome, bedrooms, open (and food) all day. *(Alex Ivinson)*

UFTON   SP3762
White Hart (01926) 612976
Just off A425 Southam–Leamington; CV33 9PJ Friendly old pub in elevated roadside position next to church; modernised beamed bar with log fire, high-backed leather chairs and some booth seating, stripped-stone walls, a few stages here and there, well kept ales such as Greene King, St Austell and Slaughterhouse, several wines by the glass and enjoyable good value food, efficient service; children welcome, picnic-sets in hilltop garden with panoramic views, closed Sun evening, Mon. *(Clive and Fran Dutson)*

UPPER BRAILES   SP3039
Gate (01608) 685212
B4035 Shipston-on-Stour to Banbury; OX15 5AX Traditional low-beamed village local, well kept Hook Norton and a guest, Weston's cider and enjoyable reasonably priced food including good fish and chips, efficient friendly service, coal fire; quiz third Sun of month, occasional live music, TV, darts; children welcome, play area and aunt sally in extensive back garden, pretty hillside spot with lovely walks, two comfortable bedrooms, good breakfast, closed weekday lunchtimes, no food Sun evening, Mon. *(Peter and Caroline Waites)*

UPPER GORNAL   SO9292
★Britannia (01902) 883253
Kent Street (A459); DY3 1UX Popular old-fashioned 19th-c local with friendly chatty atmosphere (known locally as Sally's after former landlady), particularly well kept/priced Bathams, coal fires in front bar and time-trapped little back room with its wonderful wall-mounted handpumps, some bar snacks including good local pork pies; sports TV; dogs welcome, nice flower-filled backyard, open all day. *(Dave Braisted, Kevin)*

WALSALL   SP0198
Black Country Arms (01922)
640588 *High Street; WS1 1QW* Imposing pub on three levels (dates from the 17th c), pillared frontage with big Georgian-style windows, high-ceilinged bar with large portraits above traditional wooden servery, great choice of well kept ales including Black Country, craft beers and real ciders, enjoyable home-made pubby food at bargain prices, good friendly service; background and live music, quiz nights, sports TV; no dogs, small side terrace, open all day (till midnight Fri, Sat), kitchen shuts 4pm Sun and Mon. *(Dave Braisted, Liz and Brian Barnard)*

WARWICK   SP2864
★Rose & Crown (01926) 411117
Market Place; CV34 4SH Friendly bustling Peach group inn with uncluttered modern décor, good choice of interesting sensibly priced food including fixed-price menu, well kept ales such as Purity, good wines, cocktails and coffee, cheerful efficient service; background music, newspapers; children and dogs (in front bar) welcome, tables out under parasols, 13 comfortable bedrooms, open (and food) all day from 8am for breakfast. *(Alan Johnson, Lesley and Brian Lynn, Ian Herdman)*

WARWICK   SP2967
★Saxon Mill (01926) 492255
Guys Cliffe, A429 just N; CV34 5YN Rambling Mitchells & Butlers dining pub in charmingly set converted mill; beams and blazing log fire, contemporary tables and chairs on polished boards and flagstones, cosy corners with leather armchairs and big rugs, mill race and turning wheel behind glass, enjoyable food in bar and (best to book) upstairs family restaurant including weekend brunch from 9am, local beers and several wines by the glass, friendly helpful service; background music; ground-floor wheelchair access and loo, tables out on terraces by broad willow-flanked river, more over bridge, delightful views across to Guys Cliffe House ruins, open (and food) all day. *(Simon and Mandy King)*

WEST BROMWICH   SO9992
Sow & Pigs (0121) 553 1191
Hill Top, towards Wednesbury; B70 0PS Refurbished by Two Crafty Brewers in contemporary style but keeping original features, their well kept beers and up to three guests, good value food (not Sun evening-Weds) including burgers, pizzas and a nice steak and ale pie; live music; children welcome, open all day. *(Dave Cooper, Dave Braisted)*

Pubs close to motorway junctions are listed at the back of the book.

WHICHFORD SP3134
Norman Knight (01608) 684621
*Ascott Road, opposite village green;
CV36 5PE* Sympathetically extended
beamed and flagstoned pub, own Stratford
Upon Avon beers with guests such as Hook
Norton, enjoyable home-made food using
local produce including organic meat
from the family farm, prompt friendly
service; quiz last Mon of month, occasional
live music; children and dogs welcome,
picnic-sets on front lawn facing lovely
village green, aunt sally, three glamping
pods and self-catering apartment, good
walks, open all day Fri, Sat, till 6pm Sun,
closed Mon lunchtime. *(Guy Vowles)*

WILLEY SP4984
Sarah Mansfield (01455) 553133
*Just off A5, N of A427 junction; Main
Street; CV23 0SH* Comfortable 17th-c
beamed village pub with good choice of
enjoyable well priced food, friendly attentive
staff, four real ales including Brains and
Greene King from stone-faced servery, open
fire, pool and darts, free wi-fi, children
welcome, a few tables outside, closed Mon
lunchtime. *(Mike and Margaret Banks)*

WILLEY SP4885
Wood Farm (01788) 833469
Coalpit Lane; CV23 0SL Modern visitor
centre attached to (and with view into)
Wood Farm Brewery, up to eight of their
ales and occasional guests, ample helpings
of enjoyable reasonably priced food from
sandwiches and baked potatoes up, cheerful
helpful service, upstairs galleried function/
overflow room; children welcome, no dogs,
substantial terrace with country views,
camping, brewery tours (must pre-book,
not Sun), open all day (till 6pm Sun).
(George Atkinson, Alan Johnson)

WILLOUGHBY SP5267
Rose (01788) 891180
*Just off A45 E of Dunchurch; Main
Street; CV23 8BH* Neatly decorated old
thatched dining pub; low beam and plank
ceiling, wood or tiled floors, some panelling

and inglenook woodburner, good range of
popular food cooked by italian chef-landlord
including weekday set italian menu, well
kept Hook Norton and Sharps Doom Bar,
reasonably priced house wines, friendly
attentive young staff; children and dogs
welcome, disabled facilities, seating in side
garden with gate to park and play area,
closed Sun evening, Mon. *(Andy Knight)*

WIXFORD SP0854
Fish (01789) 778593
B4085 Alcester–Bidford; B49 6DA
Old pub by pretty brick bridge over River
Arrow; enjoyable reasonably priced food
including bargain weekday set menu
and Thurs steak night, three real ales,
contemporary bare-boards interior with
plenty of quirky touches, log fire; children
and dogs welcome, big riverside garden,
open (and food) all day. *(Simon Matthews)*

WOLVERHAMPTON SO9298
★Great Western (01902) 351090
*Corn Hill/Sun Street, behind railway
station; WV10 0DG* Cheerful pub hidden
away in cobbled lane down from mainline
station; Holdens and guest beers kept
well, real cider, bargain home-made food
(reduced choice after 3pm, kitchen closed
Sun), helpful friendly staff, traditional
front bar, other rooms including neat
dining conservatory, interesting railway
memorabilia, open fires; TV; children and
dogs welcome, maybe summer barbecues in
yard, open all day and busy with Wolves fans
on match days. *(Dave Braisted, Alan C Curran)*

WOOTTON WAWEN SP1563
Bulls Head (01564) 795803
Stratford Road, just off A3400; B95 6BD
Attractive black and white dining pub with
good choice of enjoyable traditional food
from baguettes up, Marstons, Ringwood and
a guest, friendly helpful staff, Elizabethan
beams and timbers, stone and quarry-tiled
floors, log fires; children welcome, dogs in
bar, outside tables front and back, handy
for one of England's finest churches and
Stratford Canal walks, open all day (till
8pm Sun). *(Gerry and Pam Pollard)*

Wiltshire

ALDBOURNE   SU2675 Map 2
Blue Boar 🍺 £
(01672) 540237 – www.theblueboarpub.co.uk
The Green (off B4192 in centre); SN8 2EN

Busy local with simple pubby furnishings in bar, cottagey restaurant and seats outside

Cheerful staff and plenty of locals create a relaxed, chatty atmosphere in the heavily beamed bar. It has built-in wooden window seats, tall farmhouse and other red-cushioned pubby chairs on flagstones or bare boards, a woodburning stove in an inglenook fireplace with a stuffed boar's head and large clock above it, and horsebrasses on the bressumer beam; a noticeboard has news of beer festivals and live music events. Wadworths IPA, 6X and a guest beer on handpump, eight wines by the glass, 17 malt whiskies and a farm cider. The back restaurant is beamed and cottagey with standing timbers, dark wooden chairs and tables on floorboards and rugs, and plates on a dresser. Picnic-sets at the front make the most of the charming location by the pretty village green and the window boxes are lovely and colourful in summer.

🍴 Fairly priced, traditional food includes lunchtime sandwiches and baguettes, deep-fried breaded whitebait with tartare sauce, smoked mackerel pâté, home-cooked ham and free-range eggs, pumpkin and parmesan ravioli with green pesto, lambs liver and bacon with mash, butterflied chicken breast with white wine and tarragon sauce, salmon fillet with lemon and parsley butter, sirloin steak with red wine sauce and chips, and puddings such as Baileys and dark chocolate cheesecake and lemon tart. *Benchmark main dish: steak and kidney pie £9.50. Two-course evening meal £16.50.*

Wadworths ~ Tenants Michael and Joanne Hehir ~ Real ale ~ Open 11.30-3, 5.30-11.30; 11.30am-midnight Fri, Sat; 12-11 Sun ~ Bar food 12-2 (2.30 Fri, Sat), 6.30-9; 12-4 Sun ~ Restaurant ~ Children welcome ~ Dogs allowed in bar ~ Wi-fi ~ Live music regularly (phone to check) *Recommended by Roy and Gill Payne, Julian Thorpe, Andrew Vincent, Simon Day*

BRADFORD-ON-AVON   ST8261 Map 2
Castle 🍺
(01225) 865657 – www.flatcappers.co.uk
Mount Pleasant, by junction with A363, N edge of town; extremely limited pub parking but spaces in nearby streets; BA15 1SJ

Substantial stone inn with local ales, popular food, plenty of character and fine views; bedrooms

The seats at the front of this handsome stone building offer sweeping town views, while in the back garden you look across lovely countryside. Inside, the unspoilt bar has a lot of individual character: a wide range of seats (church chairs, leather armchairs, cushioned wall seating, brass-studded leather dining chairs) around chunky pine tables on dark flagstones, church candles, fringed lamps and a good log fire; daily papers, background music and board games. A bare-boards snug on the right is similar in style. Cheerful staff serve a beer named for the pub (from Three Castles), Arbor Oz Bomb, Blindmans Buff, Dorset Yachtsman, Hop Back Minstrel and Three Castles Barbury Castle on handpump and several wines by the glass; they hold a beer and music festival twice a year. The boldly decorated bedrooms are comfortable and have spacious bathrooms. Back wheelchair access.

Food is good and includes breakfast (8.30am-midday), sharing boards, burgers with toppings, coleslaw, sauce and chips, sausages of the week, smoked haddock and cockle chowder, mushroom duxelles, chestnut and mozzarella wellington with buttered kale and sultanas and soy jus, chicken suprême with smoked paprika sauce, calves liver and smoked bacon with lyonnaise sauce, and puddings such as crumble of the day and chocolate and hazelnut brownie with chocolate sauce. *Benchmark main dish: cider-battered fish and chips £11.95. Two-course evening meal £16.50.*

Free house ~ Licensee Tori Hill ~ Real ale ~ Open 8.30am-11pm ~ Bar food 8.30am-10pm (9.30pm Sun) ~ Children welcome but must be seated from 7.30pm ~ Dogs welcome ~ Wi fi Bedrooms: /£100 *Recommended by Dr and Mrs A K Clarke, Max Simons, Jeff Davies, Rupert and Sandy Newton, Taff Thomas*

BRADFORD-ON-AVON
Timbrells Yard ♀ ◖ ⇌

ST8260 Map 2

(01225) 869492 – www.timbrellsyard.com
St Margarets Street; BA15 1DE

Town-centre pub next to the river, with interesting décor, a thoughtful choice of drinks and food, and cheerful staff; bedrooms

Beside the River Avon in the centre of town, this Grade II listed 18th-c building has been given a clever makeover by blending original features with quirky, contemporary décor and furnishings. The bar has stripped floorboards, walls of exposed stone, planking and grey paintwork, there are dining chairs, upholstered and modern ones, scatter-cushioned wall seats, cubed or leather-topped stools, wooden tables of every size and shape, mirrors, hanging lamps, a group of sofas and armchairs and both a woodburning stove and an open fire; it's all very entertaining, with a wide mix of customers and a bustling, chatty atmosphere. From the tiled counter, friendly, efficient staff serve Bristol Beer Factory Nova, Kettlesmith Faultline, Otter Bitter and Twisted Rider on handpump, 22 wines by the glass, local cider and perry and cocktails. The light and airy restaurant is similarly furnished, and the sunny front terrace has seats and tables. Stylish, up-to-date bedrooms (some have mezzanines) are deeply comfortable and well equipped.

As well as breakfasts (8.30-11am; 8-10.30am Sunday) and all-day cakes and coffee, the rewarding food includes ciabattas, smoked lamb scrumpets with rémoulade, radish and chicory, fresh crab on toast with grilled fennel, lemon and capers, chargrilled chicken and bacon caesar salad, parsnip and polenta gnocchi with mushroom ragoût and olive and truffle oil pesto, grilled fresh fish of the day with chips, chimichurri beef burger with paprika mayonnaise and chips, pork belly stuffed with nettles with beetroot, greens and apple sauce, and puddings such as buttermilk pannacotta with honey-roasted rhubarb and pumpkin seed praline and rocky road sundae with toffee sauce and vanilla-ice-cream. *Benchmark main dish: spiced haddock fishcake with a poached egg £14.50. Two-course evening meal £22.00.*

Free house ~ Licensee Henry Gray ~ Real ale ~ Open 7.30am-11pm; 8am-10.30pm Sun ~
Bar food 12-3, 6-9.45 (9 Sun) ~ Restaurant ~ Children welcome ~ Dogs allowed in bar and
bedrooms ~ Bedrooms: /£100 *Recommended by Chris and Sophie Baxter, Alexander and Trish
Gendall, Ben and Jenny Settle*

 CHICKSGROVE   ST9729   Map 2

Compasses ★ 🎖 ♀ 🛏

(01722) 714318 – www.thecompassesinn.com

*From A30 5.5 miles W of B3089 junction, take lane on N side signposted 'Sutton
Mandeville, Sutton Row', then first left fork (small signs point the way to the pub in
Lower Chicksgrove; look out for the car park); can also be reached off B3089 W of
Dinton, passing the glorious spire of Teffont Evias church; SP3 6NB*

**Excellent all-rounder with enjoyable food, a friendly welcome,
four real ales and seats in the quiet garden; attractive bedrooms**

This 14th-c thatched inn is extremely popular with both locals and
visitors. You'll get a genuine welcome and the unchanging bar has plenty
of real character: old bottles and jugs hanging from beams above the roughly
timbered counter, farm tools and traps on the part-stripped stone walls,
high-backed wooden settles forming snug booths around tables on the mostly
flagstoned floor, and a log fire. Bristol Beer Factory Nova, Butcombe Bitter and
Three Daggers Daggers Edge on handpump, a dozen wines by the glass, eight
malt whiskies and farm cider. The quiet garden behind has seating on terraces
and in a flagstoned courtyard. The comfortable bedrooms make this a lovely
place to stay; they also have a self-catering cottage. Fine surrounding walks.

🎖 The highly thought-of food includes lunchtime sandwiches, duck liver parfait
with red onion jam, seared scallops with pork belly, pea purée and apple sauce,
roasted vegetable, spinach and ricotta tart with sun-dried tomato sauce, merguez
sausages with onion gravy and mash, lancashire hotpot, beef curry, mussel and clam
bouillabaisse, tandoori chicken with onion bhaji, and puddings such as apple and
rhubarb crumble with strawberry crunch ice-cream and sticky toffee pudding with
honeycomb ice-cream. *Benchmark main dish: slow-roast pork belly with dauphinoise
potatoes £13.50. Two-course evening meal £18.00.*

Free house ~ Licensee Ben Maschler ~ Real ale ~ Open 11-11 (10.30 Sun); 11-3,
6-11 weekdays in winter ~ Bar food 12-2.30, 6.30-9; 12-3 Sun ~ Children welcome ~
Dogs welcome ~ Wi-fi ~ Bedrooms: £75/£95 *Recommended by Michael Doswell, S Holder,
Edward Mirzoeff, Robin and Anne Triggs, Mary and Douglas McDowell*

 COMPTON BASSETT   SU0372   Map 2

White Horse 🎖 🛏

(01249) 813118 – www.whitehorse-comptonbassett.co.uk

At N end of village; SN11 8RG

**Bustling pub with four ales, good wines by the glass, interesting food
and seats in big garden; pretty bedrooms**

You can make the most of the lovely countryside surrounding this 18th-c
inn by staying in the attractive and well equipped bedrooms, which are in
a separate building overlooking the grounds; good breakfasts. The friendly,
bustling bar has cushioned window and wall seats and settles, chunky
wood and leather dining chairs around assorted tables on parquet flooring,
a woodburning stove, and bar stools against the counter where they keep
Box Steam Golden Bolt and Piston Broke and Wadworths 6X on handpump,
15 wines by the glass, 13 malt whiskies, a good range of spirits and farm
cider. The dining room has dark red walls and carpet at one end and bare

floorboards and pale paintwork at the other; throughout there are beams and joists and miscellaneous antique tables and chairs. There's another woodburning stove, and background music and board games. The large, neatly kept garden has picnic-sets and other seats, while the paddock is home to pigs and geese.

First class food using local, seasonal produce includes sandwiches, chicken liver parfait with sherry jelly and date chutney, gilt-head bream with braised gem, girolle mushrooms and vanilla beurre blanc, chicken breast with smoked mash, pak choi and niçoise sauce, malaysian-style noodles with tofu, mandarin, bean sprouts, mushrooms and sugar snap peas, wreckfish with sticky black rice, king oyster mushrooms, plantain and red onion, chilli, ginger and maple dressing, rabbit lasagne, and puddings such as buttermilk and rosemary pannacotta with blackcurrant sorbet and meringue and dark chocolate and salted caramel fondant with salted caramel ice-cream. *Benchmark main dish: local pork belly with artichoke purée, asparagus and jus £19.00. Two-course evening meal £23.00.*

Free house ~ Licensee Kristian Goodwin ~ Real ale ~ Open 12-11; 12-6 Sun; closed Mon ~ Bar food 12-2.30, 6-9; 12-4 Sun; no food Tues lunchtime ~ Restaurant ~ Children welcome ~ Dogs allowed in bar ~ Wi-fi ~ Bedrooms: £75/£85 *Recommended by Sally and Lance Oldham, Andy and Louise Ramwell, Nicola and Nigel Matthews, Karl and Frieda Bujeya*

CORSHAM
Methuen Arms 🌟 ♀ 🛏

ST8670 Map 2

(01249) 717060 – www.themethuenarms.com
High Street; SN13 0HB

Charming hotel with character bars, friendly staff, imaginative food, good wines and ales, and seats outside; comfortable bedrooms

There's always a pleasing mix of drinkers and diners in this handsome Georgian inn and the atmosphere is civilised yet informal. The proper little front bar has a log fire, a big old clock under a sizeable mirror, an assortment of antique dining chairs and tables, rugs on elm floorboards and evening candlelight. Drinks include Butcombe Bitter, Otter Bright and a changing guest beer on handpump, 12 wines by the glass, ten malt whiskies and quite a few gins; background music. Across the green-painted bar counter is a second small bar, with similar furnishings, bare boards and rugs and a couple of armchairs. The dining room has settles (carved and plain), high-backed dining chairs with wooden arms around old sewing-machine tables, an open fire with tea-lights, black and white photographs of large local houses on sage-green paintwork and swagged curtains. Another room leads off here, and there's also a restaurant at the back. The garden to the side of the building has seats and tables.

As well as breakfasts for non-residents (7.30-10.30am), the excellent food from a thoughtful menu includes lunchtime sandwiches, crab tortellini with bisque, lamb short rib with peas, morels, radicchio and mint vinaigrette, roasted cauliflower curry with sultanas, coconut and apple, braised chilli sausages with cheesy polenta mash and tomato ragoût, chicken with vegetable stew and hazelnut and lemon granola, duck breast pie with confit leg, creamed leeks and duck fat chips, osso bucco with garlic marrowbone butter, and puddings such as baked egg custard with rhubarb and dark chocolate cheesecake with dulce de leche and honeycomb. *Benchmark main dish: burger with coleslaw, pickle, relish and fries £13.00. Two-course evening meal £21.00.*

Butcombe ~ Tenants Drew and Andrew Reilly-Sanderson ~ Real ale ~ Open 11-11 (midnight Sat) ~ Bar food 12-3, 6-9 ~ Restaurant ~ Children welcome ~ Dogs allowed in bar and bedrooms ~ Wi-fi ~ Bedrooms: £120/£140 *Recommended by Dr and Mrs A K Clarke, Michael Doswell, Mike Gleave, Jacqui and Alan Swan*

CRICKLADE
THE GOOD PUB GUIDE

Red Lion 🍺 🛏️

SU1093 Map 4

(01793) 750776 – www.theredlioncricklade.co.uk

Off A419 Swindon–Cirencester; High Street; SN6 6DD

16th-c inn with well liked food in two dining rooms, ten real ales, friendly, relaxed atmosphere and big garden; bedrooms

Our readers enjoy the community atmosphere and traditional décor here – as well as, of course, the fine choice of real ales. From their on-site Hop Kettle microbrewery, there might be Hop Kettle C.O.B, Dawn Til Dusk, Heather Beehiving Badly and North Wall and up to ten quickly changing guests. They also keep 60 bottled beers, five farm ciders, ten wines by the glass, 18 malt whiskies and 15 gins (gin hour is 5.30-6.30pm). The bar has stools by the nice old counter, wheelbacks and other chairs around dark wooden tables on red patterned carpet, an open fire and all sorts of bric-a-brac on the stone walls including stuffed fish, animal heads and old street signs. You can eat here or in the slightly more formal dining room, furnished with pale wooden farmhouse chairs and tables, beige carpeting and a woodburning stove in a brick fireplace. There are plenty of picnic-sets in the big back garden. Bedrooms are comfortable and breakfasts good. You can walk along the nearby Thames Path or around the historic, pretty town.

🍴 The rewarding food includes lunchtime sandwiches (not Sunday), chicken and ham hock terrine with pickled vegetables, mussels in ale with stilton and bacon, honey and mustard ham with free-range eggs, twice-baked gruyère soufflé with leek and mustard sauce, corn-fed chicken breast with braised leg, bacon and brie pomme purée and roast garlic and thyme sauce, sea bass with langoustine bisque, crab won ton, saffron potatoes, fennel and samphire, and puddings such as steamed treacle sponge with orange and Cointreau ice-cream and chocolate and raspberry mousse with malted milk ice-cream and praline. *Benchmark main dish: burger with toppings, cucumber and pepper relish and triple-cooked chips £12.95. Two-course evening meal £21.00.*

Free house ~ Licensee Tom Gee ~ Real ale ~ Open 12-11; 12-midnight Fri, Sat; 12-10.30 Sun ~ Bar food 12-2.30, 6.30-9; 12-2.30, 6.30-9.30 Fri, Sat; 12-3, 6.30-9 Sun ~ Restaurant ~ Children welcome ~ Dogs welcome ~ Wi-fi ~ Bedrooms: /$85 *Recommended by Phil and Jane Villiers, Alison and Tony Livesley, Gerry and Pam Pollard, Catherine and Daniel King*

CRUDWELL
THE GOOD PUB GUIDE

Potting Shed 🏅 ♍ 🍷 🍺

ST9592 Map 4

(01666) 577833 – www.thepottingshedpub.com

A429 N of Malmesbury; The Street; SN16 9EW

Friendly dining pub with low-beamed rooms, an interesting range of drinks and food, and seats in the big garden

Rambling around the bar in this civilised pub, the low-beamed rooms have bare stone walls, open fires and woodburning stoves (one in a big worn stone fireplace), mixed plain tables and chairs on pale flagstones, armchairs and a sofa in one corner and daily papers. Four steps lead up into a high-raftered area with wood flooring, and there's another separate, smaller room that's ideal for a lunch or dinner party. Also, lots of country prints and more modern pictures, fresh flowers, candles and some quirky, rustic decorations such as a garden-fork door handle, garden-spade beer pumps and so forth. Butcombe Gold and Rare Breed and a couple of guests such as Bath Gem and Prescott Hill Climb on handpump, as well as carefully chosen wines and champagne by the glass, home-made seasonal cocktails and local fruit liqueurs; background music and board games. There are teak seats around cask tables among the weeping willows, as well as a boules piste. Good access for those in need of extra assistance. Sister business the Rectory Hotel is a stone's throw away.

 Using some home-grown produce, the appetising food includes smoke-cured hogget with mint and rhubarb, fish stew with hake, mussels and rouille, wild garlic risotto with a crispy egg and mint pesto, hake with braised bacon, swiss chard and creamed polenta, pigeon with cauliflower gratin, black pudding and sprouting broccoli, calves liver and smoked bacon with mash, greens and bone marrow jus, rib-eye steak with peppercorn or béarnaise sauce and triple-cooked chips, and puddings such as lime parfait with strawberries and almond crumble and raspberry crème brûlée with lavender shortbread. *Benchmark main dish: wagyu burger with toppings, home-made ketchup and triple-cooked chips £14.00. Two-course evening meal £20.00.*

Enterprise ~ Lease Alex Payne ~ Real ale ~ Open 11-11 ~ Bar food 12-2.30, 6.30-9.30; 12-4.30, 6.30-8.30 Sun ~ Restaurant ~ Children welcome ~ Dogs welcome ~ Wi-fi
Recommended by Geoffrey Sutton, Alistair Forsyth, Michael Sargent, Mrs Zara Elliott, Beverley and Andy Butcher, Holly and Tim Waite

EAST CHISENBURY
Red Lion ⭐ ♀ 🛏

SU1352   Map 2

(01980) 671124 – www.redlionfreehouse.com
At S end of village; SN9 6AQ

● ●
Wiltshire Dining Pub of the Year

Country inn in peaceful village run by hard-working chef-owners, contemporary décor, an informal atmosphere and excellent food; fine bedrooms

Those who love good food come from far and wide to sample the wonderful dishes cooked by Mr and Mrs Manning (who are both top chefs) in this thatched inn. They also keep a fine range of drinks, and locals congregate at high chairs by the counter for a pint and a chat: Box Steam Tunnel Vision, Flack Manor Flacks Double Drop and Otter Ale on handpump, 30 wines by the glass, home-made cordial and quite a range of gins and malt whiskies. One long room is split into different areas by brick and green-planked uprights. A big woodburner sits in a brick inglenook fireplace at one end; at the other is a comfortable black leather sofa and armchairs, and in between are high-backed and farmhouse wooden dining chairs around various tables on bare boards or stone tiles, with pretty flowers and church candles dotted about. There's an additional dining area too and an upstairs private dining room; background music. Outside, the terrace and grassed area above it have picnic-sets and tables and chairs. This is a special place to stay and the very well equipped, boutique-style bedrooms are in a separate building with private decks just a few metres from the River Avon; breakfasts are delicious and the bloody marys and bucks fizz are complimentary. They make their own dog treats and can organise a packed lunch for walkers.

 They raise their own pigs, keep chickens and grow some produce for the delicious food: rabbit and foie gras terrine wrapped in air-dried ham with vegetable salad and toasted sourdough, warm crab tart with dressed fennel, citrus tabbouleh with asparagus, pink grapefruit, toasted seeds and labneh (strained yoghurt), herb-roasted guinea fowl breast with potato millefeuille, girolles, broad beans and jus, halibut with asparagus, braised gem, grelot onions, shiitake mushrooms and lobster velouté, roast rib of beef with béarnaise sauce (for two), and puddings such as carrot cake with cream cheese crémeux, poached raisins, candied walnuts and caramel carrot sorbet and strawberries with almonds, white balsamic jelly and basil ice cream. *Benchmark main dish: hake with olive oil mash, provençale tomatoes and gremolata £18.00. Two-course evening meal £30.00.*

Free house ~ Licensees Britt and Guy Manning ~ Real ale ~ Open 9am-11pm; 9am-5pm Sun; closed Sun evening, Mon, Tues ~ Bar food 12-2.30, 6-9; 12-3 ~ Children welcome ~ Dogs allowed in bar and bedrooms ~ Wi-fi ~ Bedrooms: /£195 *Recommended by Penny and David Shepherd, Simon and Alex Knight, Rosie and Marcus Heatherley, Dan and Nicki Barton, Barbara and Phil Bowie*

EAST KNOYLE   ST8731 Map 2
Fox & Hounds ♀
(01747) 830573 ~ www.foxandhounds-eastknoyle.co.uk
Village signposted off A350 S of A303; The Green (named on some road atlases), a mile NW at OS Sheet 183 map reference 872313; or follow signpost off B3089, about 0.5 miles E of A303 junction near Little Chef; SP3 6BN

Pretty thatched village pub with splendid views, welcoming service, good beers and popular, enjoyable food

On a clear day you can enjoy remarkable views into Somerset and Dorset from the picnic-sets facing the green in front of this partly thatched old place. The nearby woods are good for a stroll and the Wiltshire Cycleway passes through the village. Three linked areas – on different levels around the central horseshoe-shaped servery – have big log fires, plentiful oak woodwork and flagstones, comfortably padded dining chairs around big scrubbed tables, and a couple of leather sofas; the furnishings are all very individual and uncluttered. There's also a small light-painted conservatory restaurant. Butcombe Rare Breed, Hop Back Summer Lightning, Palmers Copper Ale and Tolchards Devon Coast on handpump, a dozen wines by the glass and Thatcher's farm cider; background music, board games and skittle alley.

Rewarding food includes whitebait with garlic mayonnaise, deep-fried rosemary and garlic-crusted brie wedges with cranberry sauce, falafel and spinach burger with halloumi, coleslaw and onion rings, pizzas, beef casserole, duck breast with rösti potato and port sauce, slow-cooked pork belly with creamy cider and apple sauce, beer-battered fresh fish of the day and chips, bacon-wrapped chicken with pesto and cream, and puddings such as lemon posset with shortbread and sticky toffee pudding. *Benchmark main dish: prawn and crab risotto £14.00. Two-course evening meal £22.00.*

Free house ~ Licensee Murray Seator ~ Real ale ~ Open 11.30-3, 5-11 ~ Bar food 12-2.15, 6-9 ~ Children welcome ~ Dogs welcome ~ Wi-fi *Recommended by Douglas Power, Valerie Sayer, John and Abigail Prescott, Glen and Patricia Fuller, Camilla and Jose Ferrera, Sally and Colin Allen*

EDINGTON   ST9353 Map 2
Three Daggers ◖
(01380) 830940 ~ www.threedaggers.co.uk
Westbury Road (B3098); BA13 4PG

Rejuvenated village pub with open fires, beams and candlelight, helpful staff, enjoyable food and own-brew beers; bedrooms

There's an easy-going atmosphere here and the heavily beamed and open-plan layout is most appealing: leather sofas and armchairs at one end in front of a woodburning stove, kitchen and chapel chairs and built-in planked wall seats with scatter cushions, leather-topped stools against the counter, and a cosy nook with just one table. A two-way fireplace opens into the candlelit restaurant, which has similar tables and chairs on a dark slate floor, and lots of photos of local people and views. The thoughtful choice of drinks includes their own Three Daggers hand-pumped Daggers beers – Ale, Black, Blonde and Edge (brewed in the farm-shop building) – 14 wines by the glass, ten malt whiskies and a couple of farm ciders. Stairs lead up to another dining room with beams in a high roof and some unusual large wooden chandeliers; background music, darts and board games. The airy conservatory has tea-lights or church candles on scrubbed kitchen tables and wooden dining chairs. Just beyond this are picnic-sets on grass plus a fenced-off, well equipped children's play area. The three bedrooms are pretty and they've just opened luxury rooms with a spa available. Do visit their farm shop opposite.

 Starting with breakfast, the highly rated food includes mackerel pâté with pickles, pigeon breast with celeriac, roasted beetroot and pistachios, tomato and goats cheese tagliatelle, chicken caesar salad, a pie of the day, guinea fowl with wild mushrooms and artichokes, salmon fillet with fennel and herb dressing, duck breast with fondant potato and blackberries, locally bred steak with beef dripping chips, and puddings such as banana parfait with white chocolate sorbet, peanuts, macaroons and glazed banana and sticky toffee pudding with toffee sauce; they also offer a two-course lunch menu. *Benchmark main dish: lamb rump with dauphinoise potatoes and salsa verde £17.95. Two-course evening meal £22.00.*

Free house ~ Licensee Robin Brown ~ Real ale ~ Open 10am-11pm (10.30pm Sun) ~ Bar food 12-2.30, 6-9; 12-4, 6-8 Sun ~ Restaurant ~ Children welcome ~ Dogs allowed in bar ~ Wi-fi ~ Bedrooms: £85/£95 *Recommended by Hilary and Neil Christopher, Rob Anderson, Beth Aldridge, Thomas Green, Charlotte and William Mason*

FONTHILL GIFFORD
Beckford Arms 🍴⭐ ♀ 🛏

ST9231   Map 2

(01747) 870385 – www.beckfordarms.com
Hindon Lane; from Fonthill Bishop, bear left after tea rooms through Estate gate; from Hindon follow High Street signed for Tisbury; SP3 6PX

Handsome 18th-c inn with character bar and restaurant, unfailingly good food, thoughtful choice of drinks and an easy-going atmosphere; comfortable bedrooms

On the edge of the lovely rolling parkland of the Fonthill Estate is this elegant Georgian coaching inn with a civilised but informal and friendly atmosphere. There's a genuine welcome for both locals and visitors and the main bar has various old wooden dining chairs and tables on parquet flooring, a huge fireplace and bar stools beside the counter where they keep an interesting range of drinks. This includes Butcombe Bitter, Keystone Phoenix (named for them) and Timothy Taylors Landlord on handpump, 15 wines by the glass, 20 malt whiskies, farm cider, winter mulled wine and cider, and cocktails such as a bellini using locally produced peach liqueur and a bloody mary using home-grown horseradish. The cosy sitting room is stylish with comfortable sofas facing one another across a low table with newspapers, an appealing built-in window seat among other chairs and tables, and an open fire in a stone fireplace with candles in brass candlesticks and fresh flowers on the mantelpiece. There's also a separate restaurant and private dining room. Much of the artwork on the walls is by local artists. They host film nights on occasional Sundays and will provide water and bones for dogs (the pub dog is called Elsa). The mature rambling garden is equipped with seats on a brick terrace, hammocks under trees, games for children, a dog bath and boules. Bedrooms are individually decorated and breakfasts are good and generous.

Seasonal local produce (some is home-grown) is the mainstay of the excellent food: clam chowder with samphire, chicken, hazelnut and smoked bacon terrine with onion chutney and pickle gel, garlic-fried fregola with confit leeks, artichoke purée and smoked almonds, burger with toppings, beetroot chilli coleslaw and chips, whole gurnard with chimichurri, braised fennel, pickled radish and brown caper butter, slow-braised lamb shoulder with puy lentils, artichokes, celeriac purée and roasting juices, and puddings such as steamed chocolate and cola cake with bourbon sauce and clotted cream ice-cream and fennel marshmallow with lemon custard and lemon sorbet. *Benchmark main dish: beer-battered fish and chips £14.50. Two-course evening meal £25.00.*

Free house ~ Licensees Dan Brod and Charlie Luxton ~ Real ale ~ Open 8am-11pm (10.30pm Sun) ~ Bar food 12-3, 6-9.30 (9 Sun) ~ Children welcome ~ Dogs welcome ~ Wi-fi ~ Bedrooms: /£95 *Recommended by Bob and Margaret Holder, Richard and Penny Gibbs, S G N Bennett, Edward Mirzoeff, Rosie and Marcus Heatherley, Lee and Jill Stafford, Frances and Hamish Porter*

GREAT BEDWYN
SU2764   Map 2

Three Tuns 🌟 ♀

(01672) 870280 – www.threetunsbedwyn.co.uk

Village signposted off A338 S of Hungerford, or off A4 W of Hungerford via Little Bedwyn; High Street; SN8 3NU

Friendly village pub with highly rated food and local ales; seats outside

How things have changed since this was the village bakery. It's been carefully refurbished and the chef-owner and his wife work hard to keep standards consistently high. The beamed front bar is traditional and simply furnished with pubby stools and chairs on bare floorboards, and has an open fire, artwork by local artists on the walls and plenty of original features. They keep quickly changing ales include Bath Gem, Butcombe Bitter and Otter Bitter on handpump, 14 wines by the glass, several malt whiskies, gins and vodkas and Sheppy's farm cider. French doors in the back dining room lead into the garden where there are tables and chairs and an outdoor grill. The Kennet & Avon Canal runs through the village and the pub is on the edge of Savernake Forest, which has lovely walks and cycle routes.

 Making everything in-house and using the best local produce, the chef-landlord produces lovely food: crispy fried chicken with kimchi, roll mops with beetroot rémoulade and gremolata, orecchiette pasta with black trompette mushrooms, bocconcini mozzarella and truffle ragoût, house-smoked barbecue pulled lamb with coleslaw, pickled cucumber and chips, confit duck leg with cauliflower and sticky red cabbage, sea bass with chorizo-braised butter beans, spinach and aioli, and puddings such as dark chocolate mousse with Hob Nob crumbs, popcorn and salted caramel sauce and pear, apple and cranberry nut crumble with vanilla custard. *Benchmark main dish: bavette steak with café de paris butter and chips £18.00. Two-course evening meal £23.00.*

Free house ~ Licensees James and Ashley Wilsey ~ Real ale ~ Open 10am-midnight; 12-6 Sun; closed Sun evening, Mon, first week Jan ~ Bar food 12.30-2.30, 6-9.30; 12.30-9.30 Fri, Sat; 12-3 Sun ~ Restaurant ~ Children welcome ~ Dogs welcome ~ Wi-fi *Recommended by Caroline Prescott, Alan and Alice Morgan, Edward and William Johnston, Alfie Bayliss, Buster and Helena Hastings, Belinda Stamp*

The star-on-a-plate award, 🌟, distinguishes pubs where the food is of exceptional quality. The knife-and-fork symbol just means the pub serves food.

GRITTLETON

ST8680 Map 2

Neeld Arms 🍺 🛏

(01249) 782470 – www.neeldarms.co.uk

*From M4 junction 17, follow A429 to Cirencester and immediately left, signed
Stanton St Quinton and Grittleton; SN14 6AP*

**Bustling village pub with popular food and drink and friendly staff;
bedrooms**

An attractive Cotswold-stone building on a village lane, this is a very
nice, civilised yet unstuffy pub with a relaxed, chatty atmosphere and
welcoming licensees. The open-plan rooms have Cotswold-stone walls,
contemporary colours on wood panelling and a pleasant mix of seating
ranging from bar stools and traditional settles to window seats and pale
wooden dining chairs around an assortment of tables – each set with fresh
flowers. The little brick fireplace houses a woodburning stove and there's
an inglenook fireplace on the right. Flying Monk Habit, Ramsbury Gold,
Stonehenge Pigswill and Wadworths 6X on handpump and decent wines,
served from the blue-painted panelled and oak-topped bar counter. The
back dining area has another inglenook with a big woodburning stove and
white-painted chairs and settles around solid tables; even back here, you
still feel thoroughly part of the action. Bedrooms are attractive, neatly kept
and comfortable. There's an outdoor terrace with a pergola and a few tables
behind a low roadside wall at the front.

 Enjoyable food includes freshly made lunchtime ciabattas, moules marinière, local
wild boar salami and parma ham, local sausages and mash, goats cheese, tomato
and basil pesto tart, whole sea bass with butter and parsley sauce, lambs kidneys with
dijon mustard, pork medallions with apple and calvados, local sirloin steak with all the
trimmings, and puddings such as lemon tart with mango and passion-fruit sorbet and
chocolate st emilion on rum-soaked macaroons. *Benchmark main dish: pie of the day
£10.95. Two-course evening meal £19.00.*

Free house ~ Licensees Charlie and Boo West ~ Real ale ~ Open 12-3, 5.30-11.30;
12-midnight Sun ~ Bar food 12-2, 6.30-9.30; 12-2.30, 7-9 Sun ~ Restaurant ~ Children
welcome ~ Dogs welcome ~ Wi-fi ~ Bedrooms: £60/£80 *Recommended by Ruth Ridge,
Simon and Mandy King, Tom and Lorna Harding, Claire and Emma Braithwaite,
Charlotte and William Mason*

HOLT

ST8561 Map 2

Toll Gate 🛏

(01225) 782326 – www.tollgateinn.co.uk

Ham Green; B3107 W of Melksham; BA14 6PX

**16th-c stone pub with cheerful staff, woodburning stoves in bars,
real ales and popular food; pretty bedrooms**

Once they've discovered this well run and friendly former weavers' shed,
our readers return on a regular basis. The relaxed bar has real character,
with seats by a woodburner, a mix of tables and chairs on pale floorboards
and plenty of paintings by local artists for sale. Box Steam Half Sovereign
and Tunnel Vision (the brewery is in the village), Butcombe Bitter and Rare
Breed, Sharps Doom Bar and Tollgate Gold (named for them from Box Steam)
on handpump, 16 wines by the glass, interesting gins and three farm ciders;
background music and board games. The dining room leads off the bar with
high-backed leather and other cushioned chairs, a second woodburner, fresh
flowers and cream window blinds. Up a few steps, the high-raftered restaurant
is similarly furnished with white deer heads on a dark blue wall and church

windows (this used to be a workers' chapel). The sun-shaded and paved back terrace has seats and tables, and there's a boules pitch. Bedrooms, some of which are in their old farm shop, have open fires; there's also a holiday cottage for rent. Wheelchair access to bar (but not to loos).

🍴 Food is good and includes lunchtime ciabattas (till 6pm Saturday), blue cheese mousse with caramelised walnuts, pickled apple and fennel and asparagus salad, smoked trout fishcake with samphire and sweet chilli jam, home sugar-roasted ham and eggs, wild mushroom and ricotta tortellini with pine nuts and lemon butter sauce, braised lamb rump and shoulder with pea and leek fricassée, rabbit and black pudding wellington with carrot purée and spinach and tarragon gravy, and puddings such as mango and coconut parfait with rum-infused pineapple and coconut marshmallow and dark chocolate tart with kirsch-infused cherries and cherry sorbet. *Benchmark main dish: duo of pork with roasted fillet and crispy belly £16.80. Two-course evening meal £20.00.*

Free house ~ Licensees Laura Boulton and Mark Hodges ~ Real ale ~ Open 9.30am-11pm (midnight Sat); 10-3 Sun; closed Sun evening ~ Bar food 12-2, 6.30-9; 12-9 Sat; 12-2.30 Sun ~ Restaurant ~ Children welcome ~ Wi-fi ~ Bedrooms: £60/£70 *Recommended by Chris and Angela Buckell, Michael Doswell, Sophie Ellison, Guy Henderson, Dr and Mrs A K Clarke, Martin and Sue Neville*

HORNINGSHAM
Bath Arms 🛏

ST8041   Map 2

(01985) 844308 – www.batharms.co.uk
By tradesmen's entrance to Longleat House; BA12 7LY

Character country pub with plenty of space, rustic furnishings, interesting food and real ales; bedrooms

On the Longleat Estate and opposite a sloping village green, this is a handsome old stone-built inn with a proper country atmosphere and several linked bar and dining areas. A simple end room has an open fire, paintings and photos of the village and cushioned pews, wall seats and dining chairs around big tables on wide floorboards. You go through a smaller dining room into the character main bar, where there's another open fire with a large mirror above it, rustic tables and chairs and a long cushioned settle on rugs and bare boards, candles in big wooden candlesticks and paintings of fancy-plumaged birds. Butcombe Bitter and Wessex Golden Apostle and Longleat Pride on handpump, Weston's cider and a good choice of wines and other drinks. The restaurant is similarly furnished, with chandeliers and a big painting of a sultan. A pleasant back garden has a two-level terrace with circular picnic-sets and there are more at the front and on gravel under pollarded trees. Bedrooms are attractively furnished and comfortable. Wheelchair access to bars is via a side door.

🍴 Using the best local, seasonal produce, the good quality food includes sandwiches, scallops with black pudding and pea purée, ham and leek terrine with piccalilli, beetroot and ricotta ravioli with sesame seed butter, burger with toppings and chips, pie of the day, blackened cod with chorizo and bean ragout, confit duck leg with fondant potato and red cabbage, daube of venison with horseradish mash, and puddings such as jam roly-poly with custard and raspberry crème brûlée. *Benchmark main dish: twice-cooked chicken breast with potato cake and spinach £14.50. Two-course evening meal £18.00.*

Free house ~ Licensee Des Jones ~ Real ale ~ Open 11am-1am ~ Bar food 12-3, 6-9.30; 12-9 Sun ~ Restaurant ~ Children welcome ~ Dogs allowed in bar and bedrooms ~ Wi-fi ~ Bedrooms: £95/£105 *Recommended by Belinda Stamp, John Harris, Chris and Angela Buckell, Elise and Charles Mackinlay, Jennifer and Nicholas Thompson*

LOWER CHUTE

SU3153 Map 2

Hatchet 🍽 🛏

(01264) 730229 – www.thehatchetinn.com

The Chutes well signposted via Appleshaw off A342, 2.5 miles W of Andover; SP11 9DX

Neatly kept 13th-c thatched inn with a friendly welcome for all, real ales and enjoyable food; comfortable bedrooms

The snug bedrooms here make this a fine place to stay (dogs are welcome in one room) and breakfasts are hearty. It's a tucked-away country cottage and the beamed bar has a peaceful local feel, a splendid 16th-c fireback in a huge fireplace (and a roaring winter log fire) and various comfortable seats around oak tables; there's also an extensive restaurant. You'll get a warm welcome from the convivial landlord and, despite the rural setting, plenty of customers find their way here. Timothy Taylors Landlord and a couple of guests such as Greene King Old Golden Hen and Triple fff Moondance on handpump, eight wines by the glass, 20 malt whiskies and several farm ciders; board games. There are seats out on a terrace and the side grass and a safe play area for children.

 Tasty food includes baguettes, creamy garlic mushrooms, tempura prawns with sweet chilli sauce, spinach and red pepper lasagne, lambs liver and bacon, chicken breast with leek, bacon and stilton sauce, beef bourguignon, fish pie, pork medallions with grain mustard sauce and sauté potatoes, and puddings. *Benchmark main dish: steak in ale pie £10.95. Two-course evening meal £17.00.*

Free house ~ Licensee Jeremy McKay ~ Real ale ~ Open 11.30-3, 6-11 (all day Fri); 12-4, 7-10.30 Sun ~ Bar food 12-2.15, 6.30-9.45; 12-3, 7-9 Sun ~ Restaurant ~ Children welcome ~ Dogs allowed in bar and one bedroom ~ Wi-fi ~ Bedrooms: £70/£80 *Recommended by S Holder, Pip White, Alison and Graeme Spicer, Serena and Adam Furber*

MARSTON MEYSEY

SU1297 Map 4

Old Spotted Cow 🍽⭐ ♉

(01285) 810264 – www.theoldspottedcow.co.uk

Off A419 Swindon–Cirencester; SN6 6LQ

An easy-going atmosphere in cottagey bar rooms, friendly young staff, lots to look at, well kept ales and enjoyable food; bedrooms

'A delightful pub' and 'what charming, friendly staff' are just two comments from our readers on this well run small pub. You'll see many cows of all sorts around the bars, and some of them actually are spotted: paintings, drawings, postcards, all manner and colour of china objects and embroidery and toy ones too. The main bar has high-backed cushioned dining chairs around chunky pine tables on wooden floorboards or parquet, a few rugs here and there, an open fire at each end of the room (with comfortable sofas in front of one), fresh flowers and brass candlesticks with candles, and beer mats and bank notes pinned to beams. Butcombe Gold, Otter Bitter and Sharps Doom Bar on handpump, 12 wines by the glass, summer farm cider and quite a few gins and malt whiskies. Two cottagey dining rooms lead off here with similar tables and chairs, a couple of long pews and a big bookshelf. There are seats and picnic-sets on the front grass and a children's play area beyond a big willow tree. A classic car show is held here on the late May Bank Holiday with live music and local beers.

⭐ Popular, interesting food cooked by the landlady includes sandwiches, tapas (patatas bravas, chilli king prawns, quail eggs with paprika salt), macaroni cheese with white truffle crumb, bubble and squeak with bacon, mustard cream sauce and poached free-range egg, cajun chicken wrap with salsa, smoked cheese, peppers and avocado and chipotle mayonnaise, moroccan-style lamb and sour cherry meatballs with tomato sauce and chickpea, pistachio and apricot pilaf, calves liver strips with pancetta and baby onions and red wine gravy, sirloin steak with an interesting choice of toppings, and puddings such as banana and walnut bread and butter pudding with ice-cream and baked cappuccino cheesecake with chocolate ice-cream. *Benchmark main dish: spicy fish stew with coconut rice £14.00. Two-course evening meal £18.50.*

Free house ~ Licensee Anna Langley-Poole ~ Real ale ~ Open 11-11; 11-6.30 Sun ~ Bar food 12-2, 7-9; 12-3 Sun ~ Restaurant ~ Children welcome but must be over 8 in bar ~ Dogs allowed in bar ~ Wi-fi ~ Bedrooms: /£95 *Recommended by Edward Mirzoeff, Ben and Diane Bowie, Keith Perry, Adam Jones, Andrea and Philip Crispin*

NEWTON TONY
Malet Arms 🎯 ◖

SU2140   Map 2

(01980) 629279 – www.maletarms.com
Village signposted off A338 Swindon–Salisbury; SP4 0HF

Smashing village pub with no pretensions, a good choice of local beers and highly regarded food

For many people, this is the real deal – a proper country local (perhaps a little worn about the edges for those who like their pubs neat and tidy) – but just perfect for our readers who love genuinely friendly places with plenty of unspoilt character. The low-beamed interconnecting rooms have a mix of tables of different sizes with high-winged wall settles, carved pews, chapel and carver chairs, and lots of pictures of local scenes and from imperial days. The main front windows are said to be made from the stern of a ship, and there's a log and coal fire in a huge fireplace. The snug is noteworthy for its fantastic collection of photographs and prints celebrating the local aviation history of Boscombe Down, alongside archive photographs of Stonehenge festivals of the 1970s and '80s. At the back is a homely, red-painted dining room. Four real ales on handpump come from breweries such as Butcombe, Fullers, Hop Back, Itchen Valley, Palmers, Plain, Ramsbury, Stonehenge and Triple fff and they also keep 40 malt whiskies, ten wines by the glass and farm cider; board games. There are seats on the small front terrace with more on grass and in the back garden. The road leading to the pub goes through a ford, and it may be best to use an alternative route in winter when the water can be quite deep. There's an all-weather cricket pitch on the village green.

Using seasonal game from local shoots (some bagged by the landlord), lamb raised in the surrounding fields and free-range local pork, the country cooking includes venison liver pâté with spicy home-made plum chutney, roasted red pepper stuffed with baba ganoush, millionaire's fish pie (scallops, prawns, pollack and smoked salmon), venison, mushroom and Guinness pie, lamb shoulder with mash and minted pea purée, and puddings (some are gluten-free) such as a changing cheesecake and chocolate brownies. *Benchmark main dish: home-cooked salt beef burger with sauerkraut, swiss cheese and mustard mayonnaise £10.50. Two-course evening meal £19.00.*

Free house ~ Licensees Noel and Annie Cardew ~ Real ale ~ Open 11-3, 6-11; 12-4 Sun; closed Sun evening ~ Bar food 12-2.30, 6.30-9.30; 12-2.30 Sun ~ Restaurant ~ Children allowed only in restaurant or snug ~ Dogs allowed in bar *Recommended by Roger and Donna Huggins, Steve Whalley, Edward Mirzoeff, Randy Alden, Mrs Zara Elliott, M J Daly*

The ◖ symbol shows pubs that keep their beer unusually well,
have a particularly good range or brew their own.

 **RAMSBURY**
Bell 🌟 ⌂

SU2771 Map 2

(01672) 520230 – www.thebellramsbury.com

Off B4192 NW of Hungerford, or A4 W; SN8 2PE

Lovely old coaching inn with a civilised feel, character bar and dining rooms, and a thoughtful choice of both drinks and food; spotless bedrooms

Our readers very much enjoy their visits to this handsome and civilised 300-year-old inn – especially for the friendly welcome and first class food. Throughout, the original features and contemporary paintwork and furnishings blend well together. The two rooms of the bar have tartan-cushioned wall seats and pale wooden dining chairs around assorted tables, country and wildlife paintings, interesting stained-glass windows and a woodburning stove. Neat, efficient staff serve Ramsbury Bitter and Gold and a guest such as Downton Quadhop on handpump, a dozen wines by the glass and 20 malt whiskies. A cosy room between the bar and restaurant has much-prized armchairs and sofas before an open fire, a table of magazines and papers, a couple of portraits, stuffed birds and a squirrel, books on shelves and patterned wallpaper. Smart and relaxed, the restaurant is similarly furnished to the bar with white-clothed tables on bare boards or rugs, oil paintings and winter-scene photographs on beige walls; fresh flowers decorate each table. A nice surprise is the charming back café with white-painted farmhouse, tub and wicker chairs on floorboards, where they offer toasties, buns, cakes and so forth – it's very popular for morning coffee and afternoon tea. The garden has picnic-sets on a lower terrace and raised lawn, with more on a little terrace towards the front. Well equipped, restful bedrooms are named after game birds or fish.

 Using seasonal, local and some home-grown produce, the creative food includes smoked salmon with ewes milk yoghurt and beetroot, rare-breed pressed pig head with pickles and mustard dressing, spinach and home-made ricotta cannelloni of leek, spelt, romanesco sauce, pine nuts and black olive oil, beer-battered haddock with triple-cooked chips, hay-flamed hogget with lamb-fat potatoes, barbecued cabbage and rosemary sauce, ox tongue and cheek with braised red cabbage, mushrooms and red wine sauce, brill with crushed potatoes, salsify, horns of plenty (mushrooms), apple and sorrel sauce, and puddings such as dark chocolate cylinder with beetroot ice and ginger and date and ale sticky pudding with stout sauce and vanilla ice-cream. *Benchmark main dish: cornish mussels with a cider, cream and seaweed sauce and fries £15.00. Two-course evening meal £21.00.*

Free house ~ Licensee Alistair Ewing ~ Real ale ~ Open 12-11 (10 Sun) ~ Bar food 12-2.30, 6-9; 12-3, 6-8 Sun ~ Restaurant ~ Children welcome ~ Dogs allowed in bar ~ Wi-fi ~ Bedrooms: /£130 *Recommended by Hilary and Neil Christopher, James Allsopp, David Phillips, V Brogden, Richard Tilbrook, Sally Harrison, Michael and Sarah Lockley, Sam Cole, Darrell Barton*

ROWDE
George & Dragon 🌟 ⌂

ST9762 Map 2

(01380) 723053 – www.thegeorgeanddragonrowde.co.uk

A342 Devizes–Chippenham; SN10 2PN

Gently upmarket inn with good food, west country ales and a relaxed atmosphere; bedrooms

As the food has received much praise from our readers, we've given this former coaching inn a Food Award this year. The two low-ceilinged rooms have plenty of character, beams, large open fireplaces, wooden dining chairs (some straightforward and others rather elegant) and wall seats with scatter cushions around candlelit tables, antique rugs and walls hung with old pictures and portraits; the atmosphere is pleasantly chatty. From the rustic bar counter, friendly staff serve Butcombe Bitter, Listers American Pale Ale and a guest from a brewery such as Castle Combe on handpump and several wines by the glass. There are tables and chairs in the pretty garden. Bedrooms are individually furnished and well equipped, and you can walk from here along the nearby Kennet & Avon Canal.

Fresh fish from Cornwall (dishes are listed on blackboards) is the highlight: crispy salt cod fritters with garlic aioli, hake with prawn and whiskey chowder and cod fillet with heritage tomato-stuffed peppers and olive sauce, but they also offer twice-baked soufflé with parmesan cream, asparagus, garden pea and parmesan risotto with pesto oil, salmon with teriyaki, ginger and soy sauce, slow-roasted belly pork with borlotti beans and salsa verde, and puddings such as chocolate and espresso roulade with jersey pouring cream and lemon posset with grapefruit mint salad. *Benchmark main dish: roast monkfish wrapped in parma ham with wild mushroom and grain mustard sauce £19.00. Two-course evening meal £25.00.*

Free house ~ Licensee Christopher Day ~ Real ale ~ Open 12-3 (4 Sat), 6-11; 12-4 Sun; closed Sun evening ~ Bar food 12-3 (4 weekends), 6-10 ~ Restaurant ~ Children welcome ~ Dogs allowed in bar and bedrooms ~ Bedrooms: £75/£95 *Recommended by Pauline and Mark Evans, Rosie and John Moore, Sophia and Hamish Greenfield, Ian Herdman, Amanda Shipley, Susie and Spencer Gray*

SHERSTON
Rattlebone ♀

ST8585 Map 2

(01666) 840871 – www.therattlebone.co.uk
Church Street; B4040 Malmesbury–Chipping Sodbury; SN16 0LR

17th-c village pub with rambling rooms, real ales and good bar food using local and free-range produce; friendly staff

They manage to strike an enjoyable balance between the pub and restaurant sides here – all helped along nicely by the easy-going atmosphere and chatty customers. The rambling rooms are softly lit and in the public bar and long back dining room you'll find beams, standing timbers and flagstones, pews, settles and country kitchen chairs around an assortment of tables, and armchairs and sofas by roaring fires. Butcombe Bitter, Flying Monk Elmers and St Austell Tribute on handpump, 20 wines by the glass from a thoughtful list, local cider and home-made lemonade; background music, darts, board games, TV and games machine. Outside is a skittle alley and three boules pitches, often in use by one of the many pub teams; a boules festival is held in July, as well as mangold hurling (similar to boules, but using cattle-feed turnips) and other events. The two pretty gardens include an extended terrace where they hold barbecues and spit roasts. Wheelchair access.

Enjoyable food includes lunchtime ciabattas and hot open sandwiches on rosemary focaccia, spicy potted octopus with chilli, garlic oil and sherry vinegar, ballotine of free-range chicken leg with pistachio, spinach and sage, sharing platters, roasted vegetable orzo pasta with crispy almonds, dried apricots and feta cheese, chicken kiev with confit garlic, garlic butter and fries, a pie of the day, goan fish curry with chilli bread, slow-braised acorn-fed ibérico pork belly with roasted red peppers, chorizo, pancetta and creamy mash, and puddings such as white and dark chocolate mousse with fresh minted shortbread and coconut pannacotta with rhubarb compote; Monday is gourmet burger night. *Benchmark main dish: local venison ragoût with red wine and thyme £11.50. Two-course evening meal £21.00.*

Youngs ~ Tenant Jason Read ~ Real ale ~ Open 12-3, 5-11; 12-midnight Fri, Sat; 12-11 Sun ~ Bar food 12-2.30, 6-9.30; 12-8.30 Sun (pizzas only 5-8.30) ~ Restaurant ~ Children welcome ~ Dogs allowed in bar ~ Wi-fi ~ Live music last weekend of month *Recommended by Hilary and Neil Christopher, Chris and Angela Buckell, Freddie and Sarah Banks, Amy Ledbetter*

 SOUTH WRAXALL   ST8364   Map 2

Longs Arms

(01225) 864450 – www.thelongsarms.com
Upper S Wraxall, off B3109 N of Bradford-on-Avon; BA15 2SB

Friendly licensees for well run and handsome old stone inn with plenty of character, real ales and first class food

A favourite with many and run by a generous, warm-hearted owner-chef, this convivial inn comes in for much praise. The bar has windsor and other pubby chairs around wooden tables on flagstones, a fireplace with a woodburning stove and high chairs by the counter where they keep Wadworths Horizon and 6X and a changing guest on handpump, ten wines and prosecco by the glass, ten gins and farm cider. Another room has cushioned and other dining chairs, a nice old settle and a wall banquette around a mix of tables on carpeting, fresh flowers and lots of prints and paintings; background music, board games and a skittle alley. There are tables and chairs in the pretty walled back garden, which also has raised beds and a greenhouse for salad leaves and herbs.

Excellent food cooked by the landlord includes sandwiches, home-cured smoked salmon with sweet pickled cucumber and seaweed, omelette arnold bennett, twice-baked cheese soufflé with walnuts and tomatoes, free-range sausages with mash and onion gravy, chicken breast with smoked bacon, hen-of-the-woods mushrooms and wild garlic, kid loin and kidney with elderberry jelly, pistachios and fondant potato, short rib of aberdeen angus beef with blue murder (a scottish blue cheese), walnuts and beetroot sauce, and puddings such as salted caramel fondant with pistachio and nougatine and Valrhona chocolate tart with raspberry. *Benchmark main dish: local free-range pork belly with truffle mash, black pudding, apple sauce and crackling £18.00. Two-course evening meal £22.00.*

Wadworths ~ Tenants Rob and Liz Allcock ~ Real ale ~ Open 12-3.30, 6-11.30; 12-5 Sun; closed Sun evening, Mon, Tues ~ Bar food 12-2.30, 6-9.30; 12-3 Sun ~ Children welcome ~ Dogs welcome ~ Wi-fi *Recommended by Michael Doswell, Alistair Holdoway, Taff Thomas, Sarah Le Fevre, Gerry and Pam Pollard, Robin and Anne Triggs, Dr and Mrs A K Clarke, Monica and Steph Evans*

 SWALLOWCLIFFE   ST9627   Map 2

Royal Oak ♀ ⇦

(01747) 870211 – www.royaloakswallowcliffe.com
Signed just off A30 Wilton–Shaftesbury; Common Lane; SP3 5PA

Thoughtfully restored inn on a quiet village lane with attractive, clean décor in bar and dining rooms, a good choice of drinks and food and seats in garden; bedrooms

After a long closure, this pretty part-thatched building has been transformed by a group of villagers into a welcoming, gently civilised and stylishly furnished inn. There are contemporary and locally made pale oak chairs, benches and tables on flagstones, light paintwork and a log fire in an inglenook fireplace in the bar. A row of stools line the planked counter where helpful staff serve a beer named for the pub (from Butcombe), Hop Back Admiral and a changing guest on handpump, 14 wines by the glass, ten gins, local cider and perry and a good choice of teas and coffee; board games. The new conservatory dining room, beautifully beamed and timbered, is similarly furnished to the bar, with logs piled tightly into fireplaces and wall-to-wall windows. Doors open from here on to the terrace and garden, where there are rustic tables surrounded by chairs and benches. The six bedrooms are spotlessly clean, deeply comfortable and up to date; breakfasts are first class. Plenty of surrounding walks and places to visit.

Local, seasonal ingredients are at the heart of the food: sandwiches, cured local rainbow trout with pickled vegetables and jerusalem artichoke, local charcuterie with roquefort, olives and sourdough, burger with toppings, bourbon jam and skinny chips, globe artichoke and asparagus tagliatelle with lemon butter, parmesan and coriander, sous-vide lamb rump with basil and goats cheese risotto with rosemary and verjus, seared cod with dauphinoise potatoes, mussel chowder and sea vegetables, and puddings such as warm orange polenta sponge with orange curd and nut parfait and dark chocolate délice with hazelnut crémeux and praline brittle. *Benchmark main dish: pork belly with pomme purée £16.95. Two-course evening meal £25.00.*

Free house ~ Licensee Steve Radford ~ Real ale ~ Open 11-11 ~ Bar food 12-2.30, 6-9 ~ Restaurant ~ Dogs allowed in bar and bedrooms ~ Wi-fi ~ Occasional live music first Mon of month ~ Bedrooms: /£100 *Recommended by Sally and Lance Oldham, Michael and Sarah Lockley, Rupert and Sandy Newton*

SWINDON
Weighbridge Brewhouse ♀ ◀

SU1384 Map 2

(01793) 881500 – www.weighbridgebrewhouse.co.uk
Penzance Drive; SN5 7JL

Stunning building with stylish modern décor, own microbrewery ales, a huge wine list, a big range of popular food and helpful staff

There is indeed a brewhouse in this fantastic building (you can peek through a glass viewing panel to see all the equipment) and they serve six of their own Weighbridge ales at any one time. These might include Best, Brinkworth Village, Craft Lager, GWR 175 Special Mild, Pooleys Golden and Swindon Pale Ale; also, 20 wines by the glass, 30 malt whiskies and a cocktail menu. The bar area has comfortable brown leather chesterfields and wood and leather armchairs around a few tables on dark flagstones, much-used blue bar chairs against the long dimpled and polished steel counter and a sizeable carved wooden eagle on a stand. The stylishly modern, open-plan dining room is the only place you can eat and you need to book in advance; this has a steel-tensioned high-raftered roof (the big central skylight adds even more light), attractive high-backed striped chairs and long wall banquettes, bare brick walls, candles in red glass jars on windowsills and a glass cabinet at the end displaying about 1,000 bottled beers from around the world. Metal stairs lead up to an area overlooking the dining room with big sofas and chairs beside a glass piano; another room on the same level is used for cosier dining occasions. There are seats on an outside terrace.

Highly regarded and very popular food includes lunchtime dishes such as mushroom stroganoff, salad of smoked mackerel, smoked salmon and prawns in marie rose sauce, and bubble and squeak (crushed new potatoes, onion, savoy cabbage, crispy bacon and free-range eggs) as well as crispy half duck with redcurrant jelly, cherry wine and cream sauce, lamb rump in rosemary, red wine and wild mushroom sauce with diced black pudding, thai-style crocodile with coconut milk and rice, tuna with chilli, ginger, spring onions, tomatoes, spinach and brandy butter, and puddings such as limoncello and mint sorbet and Baileys and white chocolate brûlée. *Benchmark main dish: pork tenderloin in creamy mushroom, bacon, onion and red wine sauce with crispy cheese dumplings £23.00. Two-course evening meal £28.00.*

Free house ~ Licensees Anthony and Allyson Windle ~ Real ale ~ Open 12-10.30; 12-11 Sat; 12-8 Sun ~ Restaurant ~ Children welcome before 8pm ~ Dogs allowed in bar ~ Live music Thurs-Sat evenings *Recommended by Gus Swan, Charlie May, Sarah Roberts, Edward Edmonton, Caroline and Steve Archer, Max and Steph Warren*

TOLLARD ROYAL
King John 🍽️◑ 🛏️

ST9317   Map 2

(01725) 516207 – www.kingjohninn.co.uk
B3081 Shaftesbury–Sixpenny Handley; SP5 5PS

Pleasing contemporary furnishings in carefully opened-up pub, courteous, helpful service, good drinks and excellent food; pretty bedrooms

The inventive food here is what most customers come to enjoy, but regulars do drop in for a pint and a chat and the atmosphere is gently civilised and friendly. The open-plan L-shaped bar has a log fire, nice little touches such as a rosemary plant and tiny metal buckets of salt and pepper on scrubbed kitchen tables, dog-motif cushions, a screen made up of the sides of wine boxes, and candles in big glass jars. An attractive mix of seats takes in spindlebacks, captain's and chapel chairs (some built into the bay windows) plus the odd cushioned settle, and there are big terracotta floor tiles, lantern-style wall lights, hound, hunting and other photographs, and prints of early 19th-c scientists. A beer named for the pub (from Marstons), Sharps Doom Bar and Waylands Sixpenny 6d Gold on handpump and wines from a good list. A second log fire has fender seats on each side and leather chesterfields in front, and there's also a stuffed heron and grouse and daily papers. Outside at the front are seats and tables beneath parasols, with more up steps in the raised garden where there's also an outdoor kitchen pavilion. Bedrooms are comfortable and pretty.

🍽️ Impressive food includes venison meatballs with pasta, thai-style green mussels, burger with toppings, coleslaw and fries, beer-battered fish and chips, best end of lamb with fondant potato and ratatouille, hake fillet with brown shrimps, a poached egg and caper butter, braised pig cheeks with vegetable broth, duck breast with crushed new potatoes and wild mushrooms, venison ragoût with pasta, rib of beef on the bone with béarnaise sauce (for two), and puddings such as apple doughnuts with toffee sauce and salted chocolate fondant with chocolate ice-cream. *Benchmark main dish: twice-baked cheese soufflé with fries £14.50. Two-course evening meal £27.00.*

Free house ~ Licensee John Lacombe ~ Real ale ~ Open 11-11 ~ Bar food 12-2.30, 7-9.30; 12-3, 7-9 Sun ~ Restaurant ~ Children welcome ~ Dogs allowed in bar and bedrooms ~ Wi-fi ~ Bedrooms: /£89 *Recommended by Emma Scofield, Mike Kavaney, Lyn and Freddie Roberts, Colin Humphreys, Robert and Diana Myers, Sam Cole*

'Children welcome' means the pub says it lets children inside without any special restriction. If it allows them in, but to restricted areas such as an eating area or family room, we specify this. Places with separate restaurants often let children use them, and hotels usually let children into public areas such as lounges. Some pubs impose an evening time limit – let us know if you find one earlier than 9pm.

Also Worth a Visit in Wiltshire

Besides the fully inspected pubs, you might like to try these pubs that have been recommended to us and described by readers. Do tell us what you think of them: feedback@goodguides.com

---

BADBURY   SU1980

★**Plough** (01793) 740342

A346 (Marlborough Road) just S of M4 junction 15; SN4 0EP Busy country pub with wide choice of good fairly priced food, well kept Arkells beers and decent wines, friendly efficient service, large rambling bar with log fire, light airy dining room; background music; children and dogs welcome, far-reaching views from tree-shaded garden, open all day, food all day weekends, useful M4 stop. *(Jacqui and Alan Swan)*

BARFORD ST MARTIN   SU0531

★**Barford Inn** (01722) 742242

B3089 W of Salisbury (Grovely Road), just off A30; SP3 4AB Welcoming 16th-c coaching inn; dark panelled front bar with big log fire, other interlinking rooms, old utensils and farming tools on walls and ceiling, beamed bare-brick restaurant, wide choice of popular reasonably priced food (not Sun evening) including good value deals, prompt friendly service, well kept Badger ales and decent wines by the glass; children welcome, dogs in bar, disabled access (not to bar) and loos, terrace tables, more in back garden, four comfortable annexe bedrooms, good walks, open all day. *(Edward Mirzoeff)*

BECKHAMPTON   SU0868

Waggon & Horses (01672) 539418

A4 Marlborough–Calne; SN8 1QJ Handsome stone and thatch former coaching inn; decent choice of enjoyable fairly priced food (not Sun evening) including gluten-free menu in open-plan beamed bar or separate dining area, well kept Wadworths ales, friendly service; background music; children and dogs welcome, pleasant raised garden with play area, handy for Avebury (NT), open all day. *(Sam Cole)*

BERWICK ST JAMES   SU0739

★**Boot** (01722) 790243

High Street (B3083); SP3 4TN Welcoming 18th-c flint and stone pub not far from Stonehenge; good locally sourced food (not Sun evening, Mon) from daily changing blackboard menu cooked by landlord-chef, friendly efficient staff, well kept Wadworths ales and a guest, huge log fire in inglenook at one end, sporting prints over brick fireplace the other, small back dining room with collection of celebrity boots; children

and dogs welcome, sheltered side lawn, open 6-8pm Mon. *(Lee and Jill Stafford)*

BERWICK ST JOHN   ST9422

★**Talbot** (01747) 828222

Village signed from A30 E of Shaftesbury; SP7 0HA Unspoilt 17th-c pub in attractive village, simple furnishings and big inglenook in heavily beamed bar, Ringwood Best, Wadworths 6X and a guest, several wines by the glass, good choice of popular home-made food including decent vegetarian options, friendly service, restaurant; darts, free wi-fi; children and dogs (pub has its own) welcome, seats outside, good local walks, closed Sun evening, Mon. *(Tom and Lorna Harding)*

BIDDESTONE   ST8673

★**Biddestone Arms** (01249) 714377

Off A420 W of Chippenham; The Green; SN14 7DG Spacious whitewashed stone pub mostly set out for dining; very popular food from standards up including signature home-made pies, some good vegetarian options and gluten-free menu, Sun carvery, friendly efficient service despite being busy, well kept Sharps, Wadworths and guests, nice open fire; children and dogs (in front bar) welcome, pretty back garden, picturesque old village. *(Dr and Mrs A K Clarke)*

BIDDESTONE   ST8673

White Horse (01249) 713305

The Green; SN14 7DG Prettily placed 16th-c three-room local near the village duck pond; a couple of real ales and enjoyable fairly pubby food (not Sun evening) including a few specials and menu for smaller appetites, friendly staff; children and dogs welcome, tables out at front and in back garden with clematis-covered pergola and play area, open all day Sun, closed Mon. *(Michael Doswell, Dr and Mrs A K Clarke)*

BISHOPSTONE   SU2483

Royal Oak (01793) 790481

Cues Lane; near Swindon; at first exit roundabout from A419 N of M4 junction 15, follow sign for Wanborough then Bishopstone, at small sign on telegraph pole turn left; SN6 8PP Informal dining pub run by local farmers using seasonal produce including properly hung home-reared steaks for their good daily changing menu; mainly scrubbed-wood furnishings on bare boards or parquet, animal pictures

---

We say if we know a pub allows dogs.

for sale, log fire on left and little maze of dark pews, Arkells beers, organic wines, and good choice of whiskies and gins, additional recently refurbished upstairs dining area (on same level as garden) with own bar and good disabled access/loos; children and dogs welcome, picnic-sets on grass and among trees, smarter modern tables on front deck, 12 bedrooms in separate newly converted building, pretty village below Ridgeway and White Horse, open all day weekends, Sun till 8pm (6pm winter). *(Richard Maccabee)*

BOX　　　　　　　　　　　　　　　ST8168
Northey Arms　(01225) 742333
A4, Bath side; SN13 8AE 19th-c stone-built dining pub with good interesting food from snacks up including children's menu, well kept Wadworths ales and plenty of wines by the glass (happy hour 4-6.30pm Fri), friendly young staff, fresh contemporary décor with chunky modern tables and high-backed rattan chairs, afternoon teas (not Sun); background music; seats in garden behind, ten well appointed bedrooms, open (and food) all day from 8am for breakfast. *(Gavin Markwick, Dr and Mrs A K Clarke)*

BOX　　　　　　　　　　　　　　　ST8369
★Quarrymans Arms　(01225) 743569
Pub signed from A4 at Box Hill in both directions; SN13 8HN Enjoyable unpretentious pub with friendly staff and informal relaxed atmosphere, plenty of mining-related photographs and memorabilia (once a local for Bath-stone miners – you can hire a key to visit the extensive mines or take a guided tour), well kept Butcombe, Moles, Wadworths and guests, 60 malt whiskies and several wines by the glass, decent choice of fairly priced food (all day Sun) including daily specials; children and dogs welcome, picnic-sets on terrace with sweeping views, popular with walkers and potholers, four bedrooms, open all day. *(Taff Thomas, Dr and Mrs A K Clarke)*

BRADFORD-ON-AVON　　　　　ST8260
Barge　(01225) 863403
Frome Road; BA15 2EA Large modernised stone inn set down from canal, well kept ales such as Brakspears, Fullers, Marstons and Ringwood, nice wines by the glass and enjoyable pub food including children's choices, good friendly staff and atmosphere, open-plan interior with stripped stone, flagstones and solid furniture, woodburners; wheelchair access, garden with smokers' pavilion, steps up to canalside picnic-sets, moorings, five bedrooms. *(Dr and Mrs A K Clarke, Taff Thomas)*

BRADFORD-ON-AVON　　　　　ST8261
Bunch of Grapes　(01225) 938088
Silver Street; BA15 1JY Attractively renovated bar-restaurant with good french-influenced cooking including set menu

choices, local ales such as Butcombe along with craft beers (sampling trays), plenty of well chosen french wines, nice coffee and cakes too, friendly efficient service, upstairs dining room; children welcome, open all day Fri-Sun, closed lunchtime Mon-Weds. *(Mo Moncreiff-Jury, Dan Rodeck)*

BRADFORD-ON-AVON　　　　　ST8161
Dog & Fox　(01225) 862137
Ashley Road; BA15 1RT Welcoming unpretentious two-room pub on country outskirts, beams and painted half-panelling, well kept Bath Gem, Courage Best and Sharps Doom Bar, four draught ciders, enjoyable affordably priced traditional food, right-hand part with little serving hatch and comfy seating by woodburner, carpeted dining area behind, small bare-boards bar to the left with darts; children and dogs welcome, picnic-sets and play area in lawned garden, open all day Fri-Sun. *(Taff Thomas)*

BRADFORD-ON-AVON　　　　　ST8261
★George　(01225) 865650
Woolley Street; BA15 1AQ Neatly updated 18th-c stone dining pub, very good food with some imaginative touches including evening set menu (Mon, Tues), also weekend breakfast (from 9.30am) and afternoon teas (Fri-Sun), efficient friendly service, a house beer from Butcombe and a couple of guests, good choice of wines and whiskies, two smallish rooms either side of entrance (one with open kitchen), mix of tables and chairs on wood floors, pictures for sale, cosy back lounge bar with sofas and wing chairs by log fire; children and dogs welcome, split-level back garden, two new self-catering apartments, parking can be difficult, open all day Fri, Sat, till 6pm Sun. *(Taff Thomas, Alistair Holdoway, Mr and Mrs P R Thomas, Michael Doswell)*

BROAD HINTON　　　　　　　　SU1176
Barbury　(01793) 731510
On A4361 Swindon–Devizes, E of village; SN4 9PF Roadside sister pub to the Vine Tree in Norton; long bar with woodburner at each end, a few wicker armchairs and tables on bare boards, hunting and shooting prints, Regency-style striped modern armchairs around counter serving well kept/priced ales such as Butcombe, 30 wines by the glass, steps up to carpeted dining room, good food from shortish interesting menu (not Sun evening, Mon); background music, daily newspapers, free wi-fi; children and dogs welcome, seats and tables on partly covered back terrace, closed Mon lunchtime, otherwise open all day. *(Paul A Moore)*

BROKENBOROUGH　　　　　　　ST9189
★Horse Guards　(01666) 822302
Signed from Malmesbury on Tetbury road; SN16 0HZ Well run 18th-c village dining pub with fresh modern décor, beams

and some bare stone walls in cosy bar, large two-way woodburner, lower plainer back part mainly for eating, good home-made food using local ingredients including seasonal game, well kept Uley and a guest, interesting wines from shortish list, welcoming owners and friendly staff; children and dogs allowed, two comfortable bedrooms, closed Mon lunchtime. *(Michael Doswell, Guy Vowles, Theocsbrian)*

BROMHAM ST9665
Greyhound (01380) 850241
Off A342; High Street; SN15 2HA
Popular old beamed dining pub refurbished under welcoming new owners; bar with light modern décor, snug area to the right, dining part to the left, wood and blue tartan-carpeted floors, woodburner, back restaurant with walk-across well, old local photographs and OS map wallpaper, good reasonably priced food (not Sun evening, Mon) from landlord-chef including weekday lunch deal, efficient friendly service, well kept Wadworths ales and wide choice of wines, upstairs skittle alley/overflow restaurant; background music, live acoustic session first Mon of month; children welcome, dogs in bar, picnic-sets in big enclosed garden with play equipment, ample parking in square opposite, closed Mon lunchtime, otherwise open all day (till 7pm Sun), hours may extend in summer (best to check website). *(Barry Collett, Michael Doswell)*

BULKINGTON ST9458
Well (01380) 828287
High Street; SN10 1SJ Popular dining pub with modernised open-plan interior, good food from sandwiches and traditional favourites up, efficient friendly service, four real ales including Sharps and Timothy Taylors, well priced wines; background music, free wi-fi; children and dogs (in bar) welcome, wheelchair access, closed Mon except first of month when there's a themed food night. *(Taff Thomas)*

BURCOMBE SU0631
★Ship (01722) 744879
Burcombe Lane; brown sign to pub off A30 W of Salisbury, then turn right; SP2 0EJ Busy welcoming pub with most here for the good fairly traditional food from sandwiches to popular dry-aged steaks; section by entrance with log fire, beams and leather-cushioned wall and window seats on slate tiles, step up to spreading area of pale wood dining chairs around bleached tables, three changing ales, Symonds cider, nice wines by the glass and good range of gins/whiskies, friendly helpful staff; quiz last Thurs of month, free wi-fi; well supervised children welcome, dogs and muddy boots in bar, picnic-sets and pond in pretty back garden sloping down to willows by mill stream, three new bedrooms, open (and food) all day Fri-Sun. *(Ashley O'Connor)*

CASTLE COMBE ST8477
Castle Inn (01249) 783030
Off A420; SN14 7HN Handsome old inn under new ownership; beamed bar with big stone fireplace, padded bar stools and fine old settle, some vintage french posters, ales such as Castle Combe and St Austell from oak servery, 18 wines by the glass including champagne, well liked traditional food served by friendly attentive staff, two snug lounges, formal dining rooms and big upstairs conservatory opening on to charming little terrace; children and dogs (in bar) welcome, tables out at front looking down idyllic main street of this remarkably preserved Cotswold village, fascinating medieval church clock, 12 bedrooms, car park shared with next-door hotel, open all day from 9.30am (food from midday). *(Tony Scott)*

CHILMARK ST9732
Black Dog (01722) 716344
B3089 Salisbury–Hindon; SP3 5AH Cosy 15th-c beamed village pub with several linked areas; cushioned window seats, inglenook woodburner, a suit of armour in one part, black and white film star pictures in another, decent home-made food from lunchtime sandwiches and pizzas up, Wadworths ales; free wi-fi; children and dogs welcome, disabled access, good-sized garden fenced from road, closed Sun evening, also Tues Oct-Mar. *(Sam Cole)*

CHIPPENHAM ST9173
Old Road Tavern (01249) 247080
Old Road, by N side of station; SN15 1JA Old-fashioned 19th-c town pub, very friendly, with public bar and two-part lounge, half a dozen well kept ales including Bath, Otter and Wye Valley Butty Bach, straightforward lunchtime food Thurs-Sat; frequent live music and comedy nights in side barn; pool; nice secluded back garden, open all day. *(Dr and Mrs A K Clarke)*

CHOLDERTON SU2242
Crown (01980) 629247
A338 Tidworth–Salisbury roundabout, just off A303; SP4 0DW Thatched low-beamed cottage with nicely informal eating areas in L-shaped bar, a couple of well kept ales and good home-made food cooked by landlord-chef including regular themed evenings, woodburner, restaurant; quiz first Weds of month, open mike nights, Sept beer festival; children and dogs welcome, picnic-sets out at front and in garden with play area, open (and food) all day Sun. *(Dennis and Doreen Haward)*

COLERNE ST8171
Six Bells (01225) 742413
High Street; SN14 8DD 17th-c stone pub with good well presented food from chef-landlord including generous Sun roasts, efficient friendly service, well kept

Butcombe Gold and Sharps Doom Bar, single room with regimental badges and horsebrasses on black beams, bare boards and carpeted floor, assorted pictures, boar's head and flag-draped mirror on green walls, woodburner in stone fireplace; background and some live music, skittle alley; children and dogs welcome, open all day weekends (no food Sun evening), closed weekday lunchtimes. *(Michael Doswell)*

COLLINGBOURNE DUCIS SU2453
Tipple Inn (01264) 850050
High Street; SN8 3EQ Comfortable 18th-c village pub well cared for by present friendly landlord, three changing ales and enjoyable fairly standard home-cooked food (not Sun evening, Tues, Weds) from good baguettes up, woodburners in bar and smallish restaurant with light wood furniture and some vibrant artwork; quiz and live music nights, sports TV, pool, darts and free wi-fi; children, walkers and dogs welcome, small roadside terrace with pretty hanging baskets, grassy garden behind beyond car park, one bedroom, open all day weekends, closed Tues. *(Michael Doswell)*

CORTON ST9340
★Dove (01985) 850109
Off A36 at Upton Lovell, SE of Warminster; BA12 0SZ Modernised brick pub on edge of small Wylye Valley village not far from the A303; popular well prepared food from sandwiches and pub favourites to more enterprising dishes including generous fish boards, well kept ales such as Otter and Wadworths, Thatcher's cider and nice wines by the glass from good list, chatty helpful staff, opened-up rooms with flagstones and light oak boards, pale green dados and lots of animal pictures/figurines, flowers on good quality dining tables, woodburner in bar, sunny conservatory; children and dogs welcome, wheelchair access/loos, picnic-sets outside, five comfortable bedrooms in courtyard annexe, self-catering cottage, open all day and can get very busy. *(Chris and Angela Buckell)*

CROCKERTON ST8642
★Bath Arms (01985) 212262
Off A350 Warminster–Blandford; BA12 8AJ Welcoming old dining pub (some refurbishment), beamed bar with plush banquettes and matching chairs, well spaced tables on parquet, woodburner, two Wessex ales and a weekend guest, real cider and several wines by the glass, good food from interesting changing menu (booking advised) including frequent themed nights, helpful friendly staff, two restaurant areas and a garden room; background music, free wi-fi; children and dogs (in bar) welcome, plenty

of picnic-sets in well divided garden, gets crowded during school holidays (Longleat close by), good local walks, two bedrooms, open all day (till 9pm Sun). *(John Hazel)*

DEVIZES SU0061
Bear (01380) 722444
Market Place; SN10 1HS Ancient coaching inn with big carpeted main bar, log fires, winged wall settles and upholstered bucket chairs, steps up to room named after portrait painter Thomas Lawrence with oak panelling and large open fireplace, well kept Wadworths, a couple of decent ciders and extensive choice of wines by the glass, good food from sandwiches and light dishes up (they may ask for a credit card if you run a tab), Bear Grills bistro, cellar bar with live music and comedy nights; children welcome, dogs in front bar, wheelchair access throughout, mediterranean-style courtyard, 25 bedrooms, open all day. *(JPC)*

DEVIZES SU0061
Black Swan (01380) 698070
Market Place; SN10 1JQ Traditional 17th-c coaching inn with plenty of atmosphere; quirky bare-boards interior filled with antiques and interesting bits and pieces (lots for sale), candles and open fire, Wadworths ales and a guest, sensibly priced food (not Sun evening) from short varied menu, friendly service, function room for live music (Fri, Sat), quiz Sun; children and dogs welcome (there's a resident lurcher), nice courtyard garden, 12 bedrooms and shepherd's hut, open all day. *(Paul Humphreys)*

DEVIZES SU0061
British Lion (01380) 720665
A361 Swindon roundabout; SN10 1LQ Chatty little drinkers' pub with four well kept quickly changing ales and a proper cider, bare-boards bar with brewery mirrors and gas fire, back part with pool and darts, garden behind, open all day. *(Ben and Jenny Steele)*

DONHEAD ST ANDREW ST9124
★Forester (01747) 828038
Village signposted off A30 E of Shaftesbury, just E of Ludwell; Lower Street; SP7 9EE Attractive 14th-c thatched restaurant-pub in charming village; relaxed atmosphere in nice bar, stripped tables on wood floors, log fire in inglenook, alcove with sofa and magazines, Butcombe Bitter and a guest, good selection of wines by the glass including champagne, well presented popular food from bar tapas up with much emphasis on fresh fish/seafood, good service, comfortable restaurant with well spaced country kitchen tables, second cosier

---

If we know a pub has an outdoor play area for children, we mention it.

dining room; children and dogs welcome, seats on good-sized terrace with country views, can walk up White Sheet Hill and past the old and 'new' Wardour castles, closed Sun evening, Mon. *(Darrell Barton)*

DOWNTON   SU1721
Wooden Spoon (01725) 511899
High Street (A338 S of Salisbury); SP5 3PG Popular 18th-c red-brick pub, good reasonably priced food from blackboard menus cooked by landlady, well kept Ringwood and a guest, friendly efficient service, two bars, open fire, extensive banknote collection; children and dogs welcome, nice garden behind, closes 9pm Sun. *(Sam Cole)*

EBBESBOURNE WAKE   ST9924
★Horseshoe (01722) 780474
On A354 S of Salisbury, right at signpost at Coombe Bissett; village about 8 miles further; SP5 5JF Unspoilt country pub in pretty village with plenty of regular customers, welcoming long-serving landlord and friendly staff, well kept Bowman, Otter, Palmers and guests tapped from the cask, farm cider, generous helpings of good traditional food (not Mon), neatly kept and comfortable character bar, collection of farm tools and bric-a-brac on beams, conservatory extension and small restaurant; children (away from bar) and dogs welcome, seats in pretty little garden with views over Ebble Valley, play area, chickens and goat in paddock, good nearby walks, one bedroom, closed Sun evening, Mon lunchtime. *(Michael Hill, Marianne and Peter Stevens, David and Judy Robison)*

ENFORD   SU14351
Swan (01980) 670338
Long Street, off A345; SN9 6DD Attractive and welcoming thatched village pub much improved under current licensees; opened-up beamed interior with log fire in large fireplace, five well kept changing ales and good locally sourced home-made food from lunchtime sandwiches and snacks up; darts and board games, various charity events including Tues quiz, beer/music festival Aug Bank Holiday; children, walkers and dogs welcome (pub dogs are Digger and Pickle), seats out on small front terrace and in big landscaped garden behind, gallows-style inn sign spanning the road, open (and some food) all day Fri-Sun, closed Mon lunchtime. *(Peter Meister, Mrs Zara Elliott)*

FARLEIGH WICK   ST8063
Fox & Hounds (01225) 863122
A363 NW of Bradford-on-Avon; BA15 2PU Rambling low-beamed 16th-c roadside pub with wide range of enjoyable food including good value lunchtime set deal (Tues-Sat), can eat in three distinct areas (largest is the L-shaped bar), well kept Bath Gem and six wines by the glass,

friendly efficient service, oak and flagstone floors, log fire; children and dogs (in one part) welcome, attractive well maintained garden, closed Mon. *(Michael Doswell)*

FORD   ST8474
White Hart (01249) 782213
Off A420 Chippenham–Bristol; SN14 8RP Handsome 16th-c Marstons-managed country inn; beamed bars with bare boards or quarry tiles, lots of prints on bold paintwork, dining and tub chairs, cushioned wall seats, leather-padded benches and button-back sofas, log fire and woodburner, three real ales including Bath Gem and a beer badged for the pub, 20 wines by the glass and good range of other drinks, popular food from sandwiches/baguettes to signature steaks cooked in charcoal oven, friendly efficient staff; free wi-fi; children and dogs (in bar) welcome, front courtyard and terrace, trout stream by small stone bridge, comfortable modern bedrooms, open (and food) all day. *(Dennis and Doreen Haward, Steve Blatchford, Dr and Mrs A K Clarke)*

FOXHAM   ST9777
Foxham Inn (01249) 740665
NE of Chippenham; SN15 4NQ Small tucked-away country dining pub with simple traditional décor, enterprising food strong on local produce along with more straightforward bar meals, well kept ales such as Butcombe and Sharps, nice choice of wines by the glass and good coffee, woodburner, more contemporary conservatory-style restaurant with kitchen view, own bread, chutneys, jams etc for sale; children and dogs welcome, disabled access and facilities, terrace with pergola, extensive views from front, two comfortable bedrooms, closed Mon. *(Mr and Mrs P R Thomas, Michael Doswell)*

GASTARD   ST8868
Harp & Crown (01249) 715697
Velley Hill; SN13 9PU Spacious village pub divided into several distinct dining areas including flagstoned conservatory, grey colour scheme with traditional and modern furniture, popular sensibly priced home-made food from shortish menu (not Sun evening, Mon), weekday lunch deal, well kept Moles and guests, friendly staff; children welcome, picnic-sets in well maintained back garden, open all day weekends, closed Mon lunchtime. *(Michael Doswell)*

GREAT DURNFORD   SU1337
Black Horse (01722) 782270
Follow Woodfords sign from A345 High Post traffic lights; SP4 6AY Traditional red-brick country pub under welcoming licensees and popular with locals and visitors alike; four cosy unpretentious rooms with lots of quirky bits and pieces, large inglenook woodburner in one, well kept ales including Ringwood Razorback,

real cider, generous helpings of good straightforward home-made food; darts and table skittles; children and dogs welcome, big informal garden with play area, closed Sun evening, Mon. *(Tony and Rachel Schendel)*

HAMPTWORTH SU2419

Cuckoo (01794) 390302
Hamptworth Road; SP5 2DU Welcoming 17th-c thatched New Forest pub owned by the Hamptworth Estate; peaceful and unspoilt, with friendly mix of customers from farmers to families in four compact rooms around tiny servery, up to nine real ales such as Hop Back and Palmers tapped from the cask, real ciders/perry, simple food including sandwiches, ploughman's, pasties and pies, basic wooden furniture (some tables made using Estate trees), open fire and woodburner; shove-ha'penny, shut the box and other traditional games, live music Thurs; children (till 9pm) and dogs welcome, big garden with view of golf course, two pétanque pitches, open all day Fri-Sun. *(Charlotte and William Mason)*

HANNINGTON SU1703

Jolly Tar (01793) 762245
Off B4019 W of Highworth; Queens Road; SN6 7RP Old painted stone pub in pretty village, relaxing beamed bar with big log fire, steps up to flagstoned and stripped-stone dining area, good reasonably priced home-made food including popular Sun lunch (should book, no food Sun evening), well kept Arkells ales, friendly helpful service; free wi-fi; children and dogs (in bar) welcome, picnic-sets on front terrace and in big garden with play area, four comfortable bedrooms, good breakfast, closed Mon lunchtime. *(Simon Day)*

HEDDINGTON ST9966

Ivy (01380) 859652
Off A3102 S of Calne; SN11 0PL Picturesque thatched 15th-c village local; good inglenook log fire in L-shaped bar, heavy low beams, timbered walls, assorted furnishings on parquet floor, cask-tapped Wadworths ales, good wine choice and well cooked/priced pubby food including Sun carvery, back dining room; children and dogs welcome, disabled access, picnic-sets in small side garden, open all day Sat, till 8pm Sun, closed Mon and lunchtime Tues. *(Mrs Zara Elliott)*

HINDON ST9132

Lamb (01747) 820573
B3089 Wilton–Mere; SP3 6DP Attractive refurbished old hotel; long roomy log-fire bar, two flagstoned lower sections with very long polished table, high-backed pews and settles, steps up to a third, bigger area, well kept Youngs, Wells Bombardier and a guest, several wines by the glass and around 25 malt whiskies, cocktails and cuban cigars, enjoyable bar and restaurant food (service charge added), friendly helpful staff; can get very busy; children and dogs welcome, tables on roadside terrace and in garden across road with boules, 19 bedrooms, good breakfast, open all day from 7.30am for breakfast. *(Roger and Donna Huggins)*

KILMINGTON ST7835

Red Lion (01985) 844263
B3092 Mere–Frome, 2.5 miles S of Maiden Bradley; 3 miles from A303 Mere turn-off; BA12 6RP NT-owned country pub under welcoming management; low-beamed flagstoned bar with cushioned wall and window seats, curved high-backed settle, woodburners in big fireplaces at either end, well kept ales such as Butcombe and Wessex, traditional ciders and enjoyable straightforward home-made food including lunchtime sandwiches, newer big-windowed back dining area; children and dogs (in bar) welcome, picnic-sets in attractive big garden with fine views, White Sheet Hill (hang-gliding) and Stourhead gardens (NT) nearby, open all day till 6pm Sun, 8pm Mon and Tues, 9pm other days, evening food Weds-Sat. *(Edward Mirzoeff)*

KINGTON ST MICHAEL ST9077

Jolly Huntsman (01249) 750305
Handy for M4 junction 17; SN14 6JB Roomy 18th-c stone-built pub, Moles, Wadworths and a couple of guests, proper cider and well liked home-made food from pub standards to unusual things like alpaca, friendly service, carpeted interior with some scrubbed tables, comfortable sofas and good log fire; children and dogs (in bar) welcome, nine bedrooms in separate block. *(Darrell Barton)*

LACOCK ST9268

Bell (01249) 730308
E of village; SN15 2PJ Extended cottagey pub with warm welcome; local ales including a house brew from Bath Ales (beer festivals), traditional ciders, interesting wines by the glass and good selection of malt whiskies and gins, enjoyable generously served food from lunchtime platters through pub favourites and grills up, friendly efficient young staff, linked rooms off bar including more formal restaurant and bright conservatory; children and dogs (in bar) welcome, disabled access from car park, sheltered well tended garden with smokers' shelter (the Coughing Shed) and play area, open (and food) all day weekends. *(Tony and Wendy Hobden, Chris and Angela Buckell, Dr and Mrs A K Clarke)*

LACOCK ST9168

George (01249) 730263
West Street; village signed off A350 S of Chippenham; SN15 2LH Rambling inn at centre of busy NT tourist village; low-beamed bar with upright timbers creating cosy corners, armchairs and windsor chairs around close-set tables,

seats in stone-mullioned windows, some flagstones, dog treadwheel in outer breast of central fireplace, lots of old pictures and bric-a-brac, souvenirs from filming *Cranford* and *Harry Potter* in the village, Wadworths beers and Weston's cider, bar food from snacks up; background music; children and dogs welcome, tricky wheelchair access, picnic-sets on grass and in attractive courtyard with pillory and well, open all day in summer. *(Sam Cole)*

LACOCK ST9168
Red Lion (01249) 730456
High Street; SN15 2LQ Popular NT-owned Georgian inn, sizeable opened-up interior with log fire in big stone fireplace, bare boards and flagstones, roughly carved screens here and there and some cosy alcoves, well kept Wadworths ales, Thatcher's and Weston's ciders, enjoyable food from sandwiches and sharing plates up; background music, free wi-fi; children and dogs welcome, wheelchair access to main bar area only, picnic-sets out on gravel, four modern bedrooms, open (and food) all day. *(Frances and Hamish Porter)*

LACOCK ST9367
Rising Sun (01249) 730363
Bewley Common, Bowden Hill – out towards Sandy Lane, up hill past abbey; OS Sheet 173 map reference 935679; SN15 2PP Old stone pub with three knocked-together simply furnished rooms, beams and log fires, Moles ales, real cider and enjoyable fairly traditional food (not Sun evening) from snacks and sharing boards up, friendly attentive service; background music (live every other Weds), free wi-fi; well behaved children welcome, dogs in bar, no wheelchair access, wonderful views across Avon Valley from conservatory and two-level terrace, closed Mon evening, otherwise open all day (till 9pm Sun), winter hours may vary. *(Dr and Mrs A K Clarke)*

LITTLE SOMERFORD ST9784
Somerford Arms (01666) 826535
Signed off B4042 Malmesbury–Brinkworth; SN15 5JP Popular modernised village pub with opened-up interior, easy chairs in front of two-way woodburner, green-painted half-panelling and stone flooring, chunky candles on assorted tables, wall of clocks in one part, enjoyable home-made food from pub standards up, three well kept changing ales and lots of wines by the glass, friendly helpful service; children, dogs (pub boxer is Nutmeg) and muddy boots welcome, open all day Fri-Sun, from 4pm Mon and Tues, no food Sun evening. *(Michael Doswell)*

LONGBRIDGE DEVERILL ST8640
George (01985) 840396
A350/B3095; BA12 7DG Popular updated and extended roadside inn owned by Upham, their beers kept well and

generous helpings of enjoyable freshly made food, Sun carvery, amiable if not always speedy service, conservatory; children welcome, big riverside garden with play area, 12 bedrooms, handy for Longleat, open all day (breakfast for non-residents from 8am Mon-Sat). *(Edward Mirzoeff)*

LUCKINGTON ST8384
Old Royal Ship (01666) 840222
Off B4040 SW of Malmesbury; SN14 6PA Friendly pub by village green, opened up inside with one long bar divided into three areas, ales such as Sharps and Wadworths from central servery, also traditional cider and several wines by the glass, good range of food including vegetarian choices, decent coffee, neat tables, spindleback chairs and small cushioned settles on dark boards, some stripped masonry and small open fire, skittle alley; background music; children welcome, plenty of seats in garden (beyond car park) with boules and play area, Badminton House close by, open all day weekends. *(Sally and Lance Oldham)*

MANTON SU1768
★Outside Chance (01672) 512352
Village (and pub) signposted off A4 just W of Marlborough; High Street; SN8 4HW Popular country pub with three small linked rooms, hops on beams, flagstones or bare boards, plain pub furnishings such as chapel chairs and a long-cushioned pew, one room has more cosseted feel with comfortable banquette, décor celebrates unlikely horse-racing winners such as Mr Spooner's Only Dreams (a 100-1 shot at Leicester in 2007), log fire in big main fireplace, wide choice of enjoyable food, Wadworths ales and eight wines by the glass; background music, board games; children and dogs welcome, suntrap side terrace with contemporary tables, more rustic furniture under ash trees in good-sized garden, private access to local playing fields and play area, open all day. *(Simon Rodway, Lenny and Ruth Walters, Val and Malcolm Travers, Neil Allen)*

MARDEN SU0857
★Millstream (01380) 848490
Village signposted off A342 SE of Devizes; SN10 3RH Rather smart red-brick dining pub in leafy setting at top end of this attractive village; highly regarded food cooked by landlady-chef including fish/seafood specials and great value Sun lunch (best to book), well kept Wadworths ales, friendly efficient young staff, appealing layout of linked cosy areas, beams and log fires, red-cushioned dark pews and small padded dining chairs around sturdy oak and other good tables, comfy sofas in one part; free wi-fi; children and dogs welcome (resident pointers are Sophie and Francesca), disabled access/loos, neat terrace by entrance and big lawned garden down to tree-lined

stream, 12th-c church worth a visit, closed Sun and Mon evenings. *(Michael Doswell)*

MARKET LAVINGTON   SU0154
Green Dragon (01380) 813235
High Street; SN10 4AG Rambling early 17th-c red-brick pub, well kept Wadworths ales and two guests, good value wines and enjoyable reasonably priced food from sandwiches and baked potatoes up, friendly welcoming staff; collection of vintage wireless sets, darts, free wi-fi; children and dogs welcome, wheelchair access, large back garden with shelter, six pleasant bedrooms (four in converted outbuildings), hearty breakfast, open all day. *(Revd R P Tickle, Mrs Zara Elliott)*

MARLBOROUGH   SU1869
★ Lamb (01672) 512668
The Parade; SN8 1NE Bustling town local with good mix of customers, cheerful atmosphere in main bar, hop bines, wall banquettes and wheelback chairs around wooden tables on parquet flooring, Cecil Aldin prints on red walls, candles in bottles and a two-way woodburning stove, generous helpings of traditional home-made food (not Fri-Sun evenings), Wadworths ales tapped from the cask, ten wines by the glass and 15 malt whiskies; juke box, games machine, darts and TV; tables in pleasant back courtyard, pretty summer window boxes, cottagey bedrooms and hearty breakfast, open all day. *(Peter Brix, Mark Morgan, Thomas Green, Celia and Rupert Lemming)*

NETHERHAMPTON   SU1129
★ Victoria & Albert (01722) 743174
Just off A3094 W of Salisbury; SP2 8PU Cosy black-beamed bar in simple thatched cottage, old-fashioned cushioned wall settles on ancient floor tiles, log fire, three well kept changing ales, proper cider and decent wines, welcoming helpful staff, popular home-made food from sandwiches up (gluten-free diets catered for), sensible prices and local supplies, restaurant; children and dogs welcome, hatch service for sizeable terrace and garden behind, handy for Wilton House and Nadder Valley walks. *(David and Laura Young)*

NORTON   ST8884
Vine Tree (01666) 837654
4 miles from M4 junction 17; A429 towards Malmesbury, then left at Hullavington, Sherston signpost, then follow Norton signposts; in village turn right at Foxley signpost, which takes you into Honey Lane; SN16 0JP Civilised dining pub (sister to the Barbury in Broad Hinton); three neat small rooms, beams, old settles and unvarnished wooden tables on flagstones, sporting prints and church candles, large fireplace in central bar, woodburner in restaurant, ales such

as St Austell and Butcombe, 40 wines by the glass, 35 gins and several malt whiskies, well liked food from sharing boards up; children and dogs welcome, hitching rail for horses, picnic-sets and play area in two-acre garden, suntrap terrace, closed Sun evening. *(Simon Day)*

OGBOURNE ST ANDREW   SU1871
Silks on the Downs (01672) 841229
A345 N of Marlborough; SN8 1RZ Popular civilised restauranty pub with horse-racing theme, good variety of enjoyable food (best to book), Ramsbury Gold and a guest, proper cider and decent wines by the glass, good friendly service, stylish décor with mix of dining tables on polished wood floors, some good prints and photographs as well as framed racing silks; well behaved children allowed, no dogs inside, small decked area and garden, closed Sun evening. *(Michael Sargent)*

PEWSEY   SU1561
Waterfront (01672) 564020
Pewsey Wharf (A345 just N); SN9 5NU Bar-bistro in converted wharf building next to canal, ample helpings of good reasonably priced food including daily specials, three well kept changing ales tapped from the cask in upstairs bar with views (can eat here too), good quality wines, efficient friendly staff; children and dogs (not downstairs) welcome, waterside picnic-sets, nice walks, parking fee to the Kennet & Avon Canal Trust, open all day Fri-Sun. *(Dave Snowden, Ian Herdman)*

PITTON   SU2131
★ Silver Plough (01722) 712266
Village signed from A30 E of Salisbury (follow brown signs); SP5 1DU New owners should have taken over as you read this – reports please; has been lots to look at in front bar with hundreds of antique boot warmers and stretchers, pewter and china tankards, copper kettles and toby jugs hanging from black beams, cushioned antique settles around rustic pine tables, counter made from carved Elizabethan overmantel serving Badger ales and good range of wines by the glass, food has been good, simpler back bar, a couple of woodburners; skittle alley; quiet south-facing lawn with picnic-sets and other tables under parasols, more seats on heated terrace, bedrooms, good nearby walks including Clarendon Way. *(Edward Mirzoeff, Helen and Brian Edgeley, Rod and Diana Pearce, Ian Duncan, Charlie May)*

POULSHOT   ST9760
★ Raven (01380) 828271
Off A361; SN10 1RW Attractive half-timbered pub opposite village green, two cosy neatly kept black-beamed rooms with comfortable banquettes and other pubby furniture, open fire, Wadworths IPA and 6X

plus a changing guest tapped from the cask, 13 wines by the glass, good popular food cooked by landlord, friendly efficient service; background music in dining room only, free wi-fi; children welcome, dogs in bar (their jack russell is called Faith and the doberman Harvey), picnic-sets under parasols in walled back garden, nearby walks, closed Sun evening Oct–Easter, Mon end Oct–early May. *(Peter and Penny Bull, Susan Eccleston, Mr and Mrs P R Thomas, Taff Thomas, Muriel and Spencer Harrop)*

REDLYNCH SU2021
Kings Head (01725) 510420
Off A338 via B3080; The Row; SP5 2JT Early 18th-c pub on edge of New Forest; three or four well kept ales such as Hop Back and Ringwood, decent house wines and coffee, good value home-made food from pub favourites up, beamed and flagstoned main bar with woodburner in large brick fireplace, small conservatory; free wi-fi; children, dogs and muddy boots welcome, picnic-sets out in front and in side garden, nice Pepperbox Hill (NT) walks nearby, closed Mon lunchtime. *(Chris and Sophie Baxter)*

SALISBURY SU1430
Avon Brewery (01722) 416184
Castle Street; SP1 3SP Long narrow city bar under new management; frosted and engraved bow window, dark mahogany and two open fires, friendly staff and regulars, well kept Ringwood ales and a Marstons-related guest, enjoyable pubby food; regular live music; sheltered courtyard garden overlooking river, open all day. *(Lee and Jill Stafford)*

SALISBURY SU1429
Haunch of Venison (01722) 411313
Minster Street, opposite Market Cross; SP1 1TB Ancient jettied pub with tiny downstairs rooms dating from 1320, massive beams, stout oak benches built into timbered walls, log fires, tiny snug with unique pewter counter and rare set of antique taps for gravity-fed spirits, four well kept ales, generous pubby lunchtime food, more restauranty evening choice, friendly staff; halfway upstairs is panelled room with splendid fireplace and (behind glass) the mummified hand of an 18th-c card sharp still clutching cards; open all day. *(Ann and Colin Hunt, Mike Kavaney)*

SALISBURY SU1429
New Inn (01722) 326662
New Street; SP1 2PH Much extended old building with massive beams and timbers, good choice of home-made food from pub staples up, well kept Badger ales and decent house wines, flagstones, bare boards and carpet, quiet cosy alcoves, inglenook log fire; children welcome, pretty walled garden with striking view of nearby cathedral spire, three bedrooms, open all day. *(Mike Kavaney)*

SALISBURY SU1329
Old Mill (01722) 327517
Town Path, West Harnham; SP2 8EU Charming old pub-hotel in tranquil setting (parts date to the 15th c), beamed and flagstoned bar with prized window tables, well kept local ales and decent choice of food from snacks and sharing boards up, attractive restaurant showing mill race; children welcome, small floodlit garden by duck-filled millpond, delightful stroll across water meadows from cathedral (classic view of it from bridge beyond garden), 11 bedrooms, open all day. *(M G Hart)*

SALISBURY SU1430
Wyndham Arms (01722) 331026
Estcourt Road; SP1 3AS Corner red-brick local with unpretentious modern décor, popular and friendly, with full Hop Back range (brewery was originally based here) and a guest, bottled beers and country wines, no food, small front and side rooms, longer main bar; darts and board games; children and dogs welcome, open all day Thurs–Sun, from 4.30pm other days. *(Tony and Rachel Schendel)*

SEEND ST9361
Barge (01380) 828230
Seend Cleeve; signed off A361 Devizes–Trowbridge; SN12 6QB Busy waterside pub with plenty of seats in garden making most of boating activity on Kennet & Avon Canal (moorings), rambling interior with log fires, some unusual seating in bar including painted milk churns, Wadworths ales and extensive range of wines by the glass, decent choice of well cooked/priced food, efficient service; background music, free wi-fi; children and dogs welcome, summer barbecues, open all day. *(Tracey and Stephen Groves, Dr and Mrs A K Clarke)*

SEEND ST9562
Three Magpies (01380) 828389
Sells Green – A365 towards Melksham; SN12 6RN Traditional partly 18th-c roadside pub with well kept Wadworths ales and decent choice of wines by the glass, enjoyable fairly pubby food at reasonable prices from baguettes up, good friendly service, two warm fires; free wi-fi; children and dogs (in bar) welcome, big garden with play area, campsite next door, Kennet & Avon Canal close by, open all day. *(Susie and Spencer Gray)*

SEMINGTON ST9259
Lamb (01380) 870263
The Strand; A361 Devizes–Trowbridge; BA14 6LL Modernised dining pub with various eating areas including bar with wood-strip floor and log fire, enjoyable food (not Sun evening) from pub favourites to specials including good value set menu (Mon, Tues), a couple of Box Steam ales,

friendly staff; background music; children and dogs welcome, pleasant garden with views to the Bowood Estate, play area, two self-catering cottages. *(Sam Cole)*

SHALBOURNE   SU3162
Plough (01672) 870295
Off A338; SN8 3QF Low-beamed traditional pub by small village green, good variety of enjoyable fairly priced food cooked by landlord including vegetarian choices, Butcombe and Wadworths, friendly helpful landlady and staff, open fire in neat bar, separate carpeted restaurant with central woodburner; free wi-fi; children and dogs welcome, disabled access, play area in small garden, closed Mon. *(Tom and Lorna Harding)*

STEEPLE ASHTON   ST9056
Longs Arms (01380) 870245
High Street; BA14 6EU Attractively presented 17th-c stone coaching inn with friendly local atmosphere, Sharps and Wadworths ales kept well, plenty of wines by the glass and very good locally sourced food from lunchtime sandwiches/ciabattas and home-made pizzas up, bar with lots of pictures and old photos, adjacent dining area, woodburner; quiz and live music nights, free wi-fi; children and dogs welcome, big garden with play area and boules, adjoining self-catering cottage, delightful village, open all day weekends if busy. *(Richard Tilbrook)*

STIBB GREEN   SU2262
Three Horseshoes (01672) 810324
Just N of Burbage; SN8 3AE Popular and welcoming thatched village pub, enjoyable affordably priced food including blackboard specials, well kept Wadworths ales, inglenook log fire in comfortable beamed front bar, railway memorabilia, small dining room; dogs welcome, seats in nice garden, closed Mon lunchtime. *(Darrell Barton)*

SUTTON VENY   ST8941
Woolpack (01985) 840834
High Street; BA12 7AW Small well run 1920s village local, good food including some inventive dishes cooked by landlord-chef from reassuringly short blackboard menu (best to book), home-made chutneys, pickles etc for sale, a couple of real ales and sensibly priced wines by the glass, prompt friendly service, modernised interior with compact side dining area screened from bare-boards bar, woodburner; background music; closed Sun evening, Mon lunchtime. *(Mrs Zara Elliott, Edward Mirzoeff)*

TISBURY   ST9429
Boot (01747) 870363
High Street; SP3 6PS Ancient unpretentious village local under welcoming long-serving licensees, three well kept changing ales tapped from the cask, cider/perry, range of pizzas and reasonably priced pubby food, open fire;

dogs welcome, tables in good-sized back garden, closed Sun evening and lunchtimes Mon, Tues. *(Sally and Lance Oldham)*

UPAVON   SU1355
Ship (01980) 630313
High Street; SN9 6EA Large thatched pub with good choice of enjoyable home-made food including wood-fired pizzas (Thurs-Sat evenings), Weds steak night, well kept changing ales such as Butcombe and Wadworth, a couple of traditional ciders and decent range of wines and whiskies, some interesting nautical memorabilia; occasional live music; dogs welcome, picnic-sets in front and on small side terrace, parking can be tricky, open all day. *(Simon Day)*

UPTON LOVELL   ST9441
Prince Leopold (01985) 850460
Up Street, village signed from A36; BA12 0JP Prettily tucked-away Victorian country pub with simply furnished bar, ales such as Butcombe and Plain from hand-crafted elm counter, also 16 wines by the glass and interesting spirits, cosy snug leading off with open fire, book lined wall and comfortable sofas, two other linked rooms have bare boards, scrubbed tables and watercolours on pale walls, well liked food from sandwiches and pub favourites up, friendly service, airy back restaurant overlooking River Wylye (as do some outdoor balcony tables); children and dogs welcome, garden with own bar and waterside tables, comfortable cottagey bedrooms, open all day Sat, till 9.30pm (5pm winter) Sun. *(S G N Bennett, Hugh Roberts, Edward Mirzoeff, Pete and Sarah)*

UPTON SCUDAMORE   ST8647
★ Angel (01985) 213225
Off A350 N of Warminster; BA12 0AG 16th-c inn well placed for Longleat; bare-boards bar with farmhouse tables and chairs and leather sofa, Butcombe Bitter and Sharps Doom Bar, good wines by the glass, well liked food from lunchtime ciabattas up, friendly service, a couple of steps up to informal dining room with some sizeable paintings, more steps to restaurant with elegant chairs around polished tables on tartan carpet; children and dogs (in bar) welcome, terraced back garden with modern tables and chairs under parasols, well equipped comfortable bedrooms, closed Sun evening, Mon. *(Neil Allen, John Harris, Roger and Donna Huggins, Dave Sutton, James and Becky Plath, Francis and Mandy Robertson)*

URCHFONT   SU0357
Lamb (01380) 848848
The Green; SN10 4QU Welcoming part-thatched village local, well kept Wadworths ales and enjoyable good value pubby food from baguettes up, homely feel with several rooms around bar; skittle alley, darts; children and dogs welcome, picnic-sets

on back lawn, pétanque, smokers' shelter, open all day Sun (food till 6pm), closed Mon lunchtime. *(Paul Humphreys)*

WARMINSTER ST8745
Organ (01985) 211777
High Street; BA12 9AQ Former 18th-c inn (reopened 2006 after 93 years as a shop), front bar, snug and traditional games room, welcoming owners and chatty regulars, three regional beers including one named for them, real ciders/perries, good cheap lunchtime cheeseboard, skittle alley, local art in upstairs gallery; regular live music and games events; no under-21s, dogs welcome, open all day Sat, from 4pm other days. *(Susie and Spencer Gray)*

WARMINSTER ST8744
Snooty Fox (01985) 846505
Fore Street/Brook Street; BA12 8DN Modernised restauranty pub on the outskirts, neat clean and comfortable, with good varied choice of popular food cooked by owner-chef from lunchtime ciabattas and pub favourites up, ales such as Bath and Wadworths from brick-faced counter, good friendly service; free wi-fi; seats out on terrace and small lawn, open all day Sun (till 4pm in winter), closed Mon. *(Marianne and Peter Stevens)*

WARMINSTER ST8745
★Weymouth Arms (01985) 216995
Emwell Street; BA12 8JA Charming backstreet pub with snug panelled entrance bar, log fire in fine stone fireplace, ancient books on mantelpiece, leather tub chairs around walnut and satinwood table, more seats against the walls, daily newspapers, Butcombe, Wadworths 6X and half a dozen wines by the glass, second heavily panelled room with wide floorboards and smaller fireplace, candles in brass sticks, split-level dining room stretching back to open kitchen serving good food from snacks and pub favourites up, friendly helpful service; children and dogs (in bar) welcome, seats in flower-filled back courtyard, six well equipped comfortable bedrooms, closed Mon lunchtime. *(Andrew McDonald, Edward Mirzoeff)*

WEST OVERTON SU1368
Bell (01672) 861099
A4 Marlborough–Calne; SN8 1QD Early 19th-c coaching inn with good imaginative cooking from owner-chef using fresh local ingredients, lunchtime sandwiches and some pubby choices too, bar with woodburner, spacious restaurant beyond, well kept Moles and other local beers, attentive friendly uniformed staff;

background music; disabled access, nice secluded back garden with terrace and own bar, country views, good walks nearby, closed Sun evening, Mon. *(Sam Cole)*

WESTWOOD ST8159
★New Inn (01225) 863123
Off B3109 S of Bradford-on-Avon; BA15 2AE Traditional 18th-c country pub with linked rooms; beams and stripped stonework, scrubbed tables on slate floor, lots of pictures, log fires, highly rated good value food cooked by chef-owner from pub staples to more imaginative choices, Bath Gem and a couple of Wadworths ales kept well, good service and cheerful buzzy atmosphere; children and dogs welcome, paved back garden with sturdy furniture and gazebo, pretty village – Westwood Manor (NT) in road opposite, good surrounding walks, closed Sun evening. *(Alistair Holdoway, Taff Thomas, Robert Henderson)*

WHITLEY ST8866
Pear Tree (01225) 704966
Off B3353 S of Corsham; SN12 8QX Attractive stone dining pub (former 17th-c farmhouse), revamped beamed interior with lots of contemporary/rustic charm in front bar, restaurant and airy garden room, good food from varied if not particularly cheap menu, three real ales including Bath Gem, interesting wine list (plenty by the glass) and good range of other drinks, friendly attentive service; events such as comedy nights and flower workshops; children welcome, terrace and pretty garden, eight well equipped bedrooms (four in converted barn), open all day from 7.30am (8.30am Sun). *(Taff Thomas, Alistair Holdoway, Brian Wheeldon)*

WILTON SU2661
★Swan (01672) 870274
The village S of Great Bedwyn; SN8 3SS Popular light and airy 1930s pub, good well presented seasonal food (not Sun evening) including daily specials, two Ramsbury ales and up to three local cask-tapped guests, real ciders and good value wines from extensive list, friendly efficient staff, stripped pine tables, high-backed settles and pews on bare boards, woodburner; children and dogs welcome, disabled access, front garden with picnic-sets, picturesque village with windmill, open all day weekends. *(Mrs Zara Elliott)*

WINGFIELD ST8256
Poplars (01225) 752426
B3109 S of Bradford-on-Avon (Shop Lane); BA14 9LN Appealing country pub with warm friendly atmosphere, beams and log fires, enjoyable sensibly priced food from pub staples to interesting specials,

---

Virtually all pubs in this book sell wine by the glass. We mention wines if they are a cut above the average.

Wadworths ales (including seasonal) and Weston's cider, airy family dining extension; quiz first Sun of month; nice garden and own cricket pitch. *(Darrell Barton)*

WINSLEY ST7960

★ **Seven Stars** (01225) 722204
Off B3108 bypass W of Bradford-on-Avon; BA15 2LQ Handsome bustling inn with low-beamed linked areas, pastel paintwork and stripped-stone walls, farmhouse chairs around candlelit tables on flagstones or coir, woodburner, very good freshly made food from well constructed menu, prompt friendly service, changing west country ales, Thatcher's and Weston's ciders, nice wines by the glass; background music; children and dogs (in bar) welcome, disabled access using ramp, tables under parasols on terrace and neat grassy surrounds, bowling green opposite, closed Sun evening. *(B and F A Hannam, Alistair Holdoway, Taff Thomas, Michael Doswell)*

WINTERBOURNE BASSETT SU1075

White Horse (01793) 731257
Off A4361 S of Swindon; SN4 9QB Welcoming roadside dining pub with gently old-fashioned feel; part-carpeted bar with plenty of wood, plush-topped stools and cushioned dining chairs, Wadworths ales and several wines by the glass, enjoyable home-made food including daily specials (seasonal game) and bargain lunchtime deal (Mon-Fri),

dining rooms with country kitchen furniture on wood floors, old prints and paintings, woodburner in little brick fireplace, flagstoned conservatory; background music, bar billiards, TV, free wi-fi; children and dogs (in bar) welcome, tables on good-sized lawn, closed Sun evening, Mon and Tues lunchtime. *(Frances and Hamish Porter)*

WOOTTON RIVERS SU1963

Royal Oak (01672) 810322
Off A346, A345 or B3087; SN8 4NQ Cosy 16th-c thatched pub, ales such as Ramsbury and Wadworths 6X, plenty of wines by the glass and enjoyable food from lunchtime sandwiches up, Tues pie night, comfortable L-shaped dining lounge with woodburner, timbered bar and small games area; free wi-fi; children and dogs welcome, tables out in yard, pleasant village near Kennet & Avon Canal, good local walks, bedrooms in adjoining building, open (and food) all day Sun. *(David and Judy Robison, Dave Braisted)*

ZEALS ST7831

Bell & Crown (01747) 840404
A303; BA12 6NJ Nicely laid-out beamed dining pub with good fairly priced food cooked by chef-landlord, ales such as Butcombe, Palmers and Otter, a dozen wines by the glass including champagne, flagstoned bar with big log fire, parquet-floored restaurant; closed Sun evening, Mon. *(Ben and Jenny Settle)*

Worcestershire

BAUGHTON
SO8742 Map 4

Jockey 🏵 🍷

(01684) 592153 – www.thejockeyinn.co.uk

4 miles from M50 junction 1; A38 northwards, then right on to A4104
Upton–Pershore; WR8 9DQ

Smart bar and dining rooms in elegantly redesigned pub with a fine choice of drinks, rewarding food, courteous staff and seats outside

The open-plan, contemporary interior in this extended and stylishly refurbished pub has distinct drinking and dining areas that work well. The smart dining rooms have high-backed upholstered chairs, long button-back wall seats, a mix of pale-topped tables and bare floorboards with décor that takes in an unusual woven wicker wall, deer antler chandeliers, oil portraits, a large black and white painting of a jockey on a racehorse, horse-racing photographs, bookshelves, stubby candles in glass lanterns, old jockey saddles and up-to-date paintwork. Stools on flagstones line the counter in the beamed bar, where friendly, attentive staff serve Butcombe Rare Breed, Sharps Doom Bar and Wye Valley Butty Bach and HPA on handpump, and 32 wines by the glass (including champagne and sweet wines) from the large glass walk-in wine cellar on display behind the bar; also, cocktails and 30 gins. Background music. Big leather armchairs, sofas and pouffes are grouped together and there's an open fire and a neat ceiling-high stack of logs beside a two-way woodburning stove. Outside, the attractive paved courtyard has glass-topped gables, dark wicker chairs and large heated parasols surrounded by bamboo and wild herbs in planters.

From a seasonal menu, with everything made in-house, the food includes sandwiches, braised pork bonbons with apple, onion and sage and crackling, salmon and cod fishcakes with a free-range poached egg and caper and dill hollandaise, sharing and meze boards, stone-baked pizzas, spicy mushroom and spinach strudel with roasted tomato and sesame chutney and raita, duck breast and confit leg with braised red cabbage and morello cherry and red wine reduction, sea bass with spiced mixed bean cassoulet, poussin with spring onion and chive pomme purée and three mustard and chestnut mushroom sauce, and puddings such as caramel pannacotta with sticky ginger cake and caramel sauce and chocolate torte with mascarpone and morello cherry griottines; they also offer a two- and three-course lunch menu. *Benchmark main dish: steak burger with toppings, coleslaw and skinny fries £13.95. Two-course evening meal £20.00.*

Free house ~ Licensee Rebekah Seddon-Wickens ~ Real ale ~ Open 11.30am-11pm (11.30pm Sat); 12-6 Sun; closed Mon except bank holidays ~ Bar food 12-9 (9.30 Fri, Sat); 12-4 Sun ~ Children welcome ~ Wi-fi *Recommended by Mrs Zara Elliott, Charles Welch, Colin Humphreys, Chris and Angela Buckell, Bernard Stradling*

BRANSFORD
Bear & Ragged Staff ♀

SO8052 Map 4

(01886) 833399 – www.bearatbransford.co.uk

Off A4103 SW of Worcester; Station Road; WR6 5JH

Well run dining pub with pleasant places to sit both inside and out and popular food and drink

This is a friendly, gently civilised dining pub that also contains a relaxing bar: Hobsons Twisted Spire and Sharps Doom Bar on handpump, ten wines by the glass, several malt whiskies and quite a few brandies and liqueurs. The restaurant is more formal with upholstered dining chairs, proper tablecloths and linen napkins. These interconnecting rooms give fine views of attractive rolling country (as do the pretty garden and terrace). In winter, there's a warming open fire; background music and darts. Good disabled access and facilities.

Making everything in-house and using local produce (and home-grown vegetables, fruit and salads), the enjoyable food includes sandwiches, baked whole camembert with red onion marmalade, ham hock terrine with pea purée, wild mushroom and cheese fritters with panko-breaded deep-fried cauliflower cheese and ratatouille, gammon and free-range eggs, burger with toppings and triple-cooked chips, chicken breast and southern-fried confit leg with chilli and peppercorn sauce, a curry of the day, plaice, prawn, spinach and samphire linguine with caper and dill butter, and puddings such as egg custard tart with apple and dill compote and caramel sauce and raspberry and lemongrass crème brûlée with raspberry sorbet; they also offer a two- and three-course set lunch (not Sunday). *Benchmark main dish: pulled braised leg of lamb with spinach and mint purée, redcurrant jus and dauphinoise potatoes £16.95. Two-course evening meal £20.50.*

Free house ~ Licensee Lynda Williams ~ Real ale ~ Open 12-2.30, 6-10; 12-11 Fri; 12-2.30, 6-11 Sat; 12-3 Sun; closed Sun evening ~ Bar food 12-2, 6-9; 12-2.30 Sun ~ Restaurant ~ Children welcome ~ Dogs allowed in bar ~ Wi-fi *Recommended by Jamie and Lizzie McEwan, Charles Welch, Gary and Marie Miller*

BRETFORTON
Fleece ★  £

SP0943 Map 4

(01386) 831173 – www.thefleeceinn.co.uk

B4035 E of Evesham: turn S off this road into village; pub is in central square by church; there's a sizeable car park at one side of the church; WR11 7JE

Marvellously unspoilt medieval pub owned by the National Trust; bedrooms

Although bequeathed to the National Trust in 1977, for 500 years before that this lovely former farm was owned by the same family and many of the furnishings here are original heirlooms. The fine country rooms include a great oak dresser holding a priceless 48-piece set of Stuart pewter, two grandfather clocks, ancient kitchen chairs, curved high-backed settles, a rocking chair and a rack of heavy pointed iron shafts, probably for spit roasting in one of the huge inglenook fireplaces; two other log fires. As well as massive beams and exposed timbers, there are worn and crazed flagstones (scored with marks to keep out demons) and plenty of oddities such as a great cheese press and set of cheese moulds and a rare dough-proving table; a leaflet details the more bizarre items. Uley Pigs Ear and Wye Valley Bitter with guests such as Oakham Citra, Wychwood Hobgoblin and Woods Shropshire Lad on handpump, nine wines by the glass, a similar number of malt whiskies and four farm ciders; board games. They hold an asparagus auction at the end of May, as part of the Vale of Evesham Asparagus Festival, and also host the village fête on August Bank Holiday Monday. The calendar of events also includes morris dancing and the village silver band plays here regularly. The lawn, with fruit trees around a beautifully restored thatched and timbered barn, is a lovely place to sit, and there are more picnic-sets and a stone pump-trough in the front courtyard. If you're visiting to enjoy the famous historic interior, it's a good idea to go midweek as it can get very busy at weekends.

Bar food includes plenty of asparagus in season, sandwiches, ham hock terrine, whitebait with tartare dip, nut roast with tomato and rosemary gravy, calves liver on shallot mash with red wine sauce, local faggots with gravy, mustard-baked ham and eggs, poached smoked haddock with leek mornay, pork belly with celeriac purée and port sauce, steaks with a choice of sauce, and puddings such as lemon meringue cheesecake and crumble of the day with custard. *Benchmark main dish: pie of the day £11.95. Two-course evening meal £17.00.*

Free house ~ Licensee Nigel Smith ~ Real ale ~ Open 10.30am-11pm (midnight Sat) ~ Bar food 12-2.30, 6.30-9; 12-8.30 Sun ~ Children welcome ~ Dogs welcome ~ Wi-fi ~ Bedrooms: /£97.50 *Recommended by Revd Michael Vockins, John Saville, Beth Aldridge, John and Abigail Prescott*

BROADWAY
Crown & Trumpet 🍺 £

SP0937 Map 4

(01386) 853202 – www.crownandtrumpet.co.uk
Church Street; WR12 7AE

Honest local with good real ale and decent food; bedrooms

Our readers enjoy their visits to this old-fashioned and unpretentious pub and all are welcomed by the charming landlord and his helpful staff. The bustling beamed and timbered bar has a cheerful, easy-going feel, antique high-backed dark settles, large solid tables and a blazing log fire. You'll find a beer named for the pub (from Stanway) plus Prescott Chequered Flag, Stroud Tom Long and Timothy Taylors Landlord on handpump, alongside nine wines by the glass, ten malt whiskies, Black Rat perry and cider, Orchard Pig chilli and ginger or marmalade ciders, mulled wine and a good range of soft drinks. There's an assortment of pub games, including darts, cribbage, shut the box, dominoes, bar skittles and ring the bull, as well as a games machine, TV and background music. The hardwood tables and chairs outside, set among flowers on a slightly raised front terrace, are popular with walkers.

Incredibly good value, popular food includes lunchtime baguettes, deep-fried brie with cranberry sauce, devilled whitebait with mayonnaise dip, scrambled eggs with salmon and chives, duck and apricot sausages with plum gravy, omelettes, meat or vegetarian lasagne, faggots with mushy peas and chips, steak and kidney pie, chilli con carne, and puddings such as apple and cinnamon crumble and spotted dick and custard. *Benchmark main dish: beef and worcestershire sauce pie £8.45. Two-course evening meal £12.00.*

Laurel (Enterprise) ~ Lease Andrew Scott ~ Real ale ~ Open 11-11 (midnight Sat); 11-11 Sun ~ Bar food 12-2.30, 5.45-9.30; 12-9.30 Fri-Sun ~ Children welcome ~ Dogs allowed in bar ~ Wi-fi ~ Live jazz/blues Thurs evening, acoustic pop Fri evening, 1960s-'80s music Sat evening ~ Bedrooms: /£78 *Recommended by Phil and Jane Villiers, M G Hart, Theocsbrian, Guy Vowles, Naomi and Andrew Randall, Stuart and Natalie Granville*

> If we know a featured-entry pub does sandwiches, we always say so – if they're not mentioned, you'll have to assume you can't get one.

CHILDSWICKHAM　　　　　　　　　SP0738　Map 4

Childswickham Inn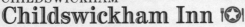

(01386) 852461 – www.childswickhaminn.co.uk

Off A44 NW of Broadway; WR12 7HP

Bustling dining pub with highly regarded food, good drinks choice, attentive staff and seats in neat garden

In a peaceful village, this is a bustling country pub surrounded by many lovely walks. The chatty bar is full of friendly regulars (often with their dogs too) and there are leather sofas and armchairs and Greene King Abbot, Sharps Atlantic and Wells Bombardier Burning Gold on handpump, ten wines by the glass (Friday evening special deals on champagne and prosecco), malt whiskies and farm cider; background music. There are two dining areas, one with high-backed dark leather chairs on terracotta tiles, the other with country kitchen chairs on bare floorboards. Both have contemporary artwork on part-timbered walls painted cream or pale violet; an open fire and a woodburning stove. The neat garden has rush-seated chairs and tables on decking and also separate areas under parasols. Disabled facilities.

 Creative food includes paninis and wraps, king prawns and scallops in creamy cajun sauce, ham hock and black pudding scotch egg with maple parsnip and butternut squash purée and green peppercorn and brandy sauce, quorn mince scotch pie with neeps and tatties, creamed garlic kale and balsamic jus, sea bream fillet with tempura king prawns, curried coriander and crab potato cake, pak choi and thai green curry sauce, chicken suprême wrapped in serrano ham, with goats cheese and tomato-crushed sweet potato and wild mushroom and pancetta sauce, and puddings such as black cherry and apple cobbler with toffee ice-cream and sticky date pudding with butterscotch sauce; Thursday is steak night and the third Friday of the month is fish night. *Benchmark main dish: pie of the day £12.50. Two-course evening meal £20.50.*

Punch ~ Tenant Carol Marshall ~ Real ale ~ Open 11.30-11; 12-11 Sun ~ Bar food 12-2, 6-9; 12-6 Sun ~ Restaurant closed Sun evening and Mon lunch ~ Children welcome ~ Dogs allowed in bar ~ Wi-fi *Recommended by P and J Shapley, Ian Duncan, Richard Kennell, Guy Vowles*

 CLENT　　　　　　　　　　　　　SO9279　Map 4

Fountain 🌟 ♀

(01562) 883286 – www.thefountainatclent.co.uk

Adams Hill/Odnall Lane; off A491 at Holy Cross/Clent exit roundabout, via Violet Lane, then right at T junction; DY9 9PU

Restauranty pub often packed to overflowing, with imaginative dishes and good choice of drinks

After a good walk in the surrounding Clent Hills, make your way to this spotlessly kept, friendly pub for a reliably good lunch. The long carpeted dining bar (consisting of three knocked-together areas) is fairly traditional, with teak chairs and pedestal tables and some comfortably cushioned brocaded wall seats. There are nicely framed local photographs on the rag-rolled pinkish walls above a dark panelled dado, pretty wall lights and candles on the tables (flowers in summer). The changing real ales on handpump include Brakspears Oxford Gold, Marstons EPA and Ringwood Boondoggle and most of their wines are available by the glass; also farm cider, speciality teas and good coffees. Background music and skittle alley. There are tables outside on a decked area.

A wide choice of highly popular food includes open and grilled sandwiches, tiger prawns with garlic butter, chicken liver pâté with onion marmalade, porcini and raddichio risotto, hake fillet with crab, white wine, chilli and tomato sauce, corn-fed chicken with shallot tarte tatin with red wine and bacon sauce, herb-crusted rack of lamb with redcurrant sauce, steaks with a choice of seven sauces, and puddings such as lime cheesecake and black forest gateau; they also offer a two- and three-course menu (lunch Mon-Sat, 6 and 6.30pm sittings Mon-Thurs). *Benchmark main dish: lamb pot roast £16.95. Two-course evening meal £25.00.*

Marstons ~ Lease Richard and Jacque Macey ~ Real ale ~ Open 11-11; 12-6 Sun; closed Sun evening ~ Bar food 12-2, 6-9 (9.30 Fri, Sat); 12-6 Sun ~ Children welcome ~ Wi-fi
Recommended by Anne Taylor, Lionel Smith, Carol and Barry Craddock, Sarah and David Gibbs

CUTNALL GREEN
SO8868 Map 4

Chequers 🏅 ♀

(01299) 851292 – www.chequerscutnallgreen.co.uk
Kidderminster Road; WR9 0PJ

Bustling roadside pub with plenty of drinking and dining space in interesting rooms, and rewarding food

A clever mix of ancient and modern, this interesting pub was built on the site of an old coaching inn. There are red-painted walls between beams and timbering, broad floorboards and weathered quarry tiles, and warm winter fires. Also, leather sofas and tub chairs, high-backed purple and red or ladderback dining chairs around all sorts of tables, plenty of mirrors giving the impression of even more space, brass plates and mugs, candles and fresh flowers. Ringwood Boondoggle, Sharps Doom Bar and Wye Valley HPA on handpump and 14 wines by the glass. One elegant but cosy room, known as the Players Lounge, has photographs of the landlord Mr Narbett, who is a former chef for the England football team. The pretty garden has three 'beach huts' available to hire, as well as chairs with barrel tables and sofas, heaters and parasols.

 As well as offering weekend breakfasts (9-11am), the interesting food includes sandwiches, box-baked camembert studded with garlic and rosemary, sticky barbecue ribs with onion, chilli, avocado and sour cream in a soft taco, stone-baked pizzas, portobello mushroom welsh rarebit with beetroot, spinach and parmentier potatoes, beer-battered cod and chips, calves liver and bacon with champ mash, a pie of the day, slow-cooked lamb shoulder with mushrooms, bacon and dauphinoise potatoes, and puddings such as banoffi pie cheesecake with caramel sauce and banana fudge ice-cream and boozy chocolate and raspberry mousse with honeycomb crunch. *Benchmark main dish: chicken escalope saltimbocca £14.95. Two-course evening meal £19.00.*

Free house ~ Licensees Roger and Jo Narbett ~ Real ale ~ Open 12-11 (10.30 Sun) ~ Bar food 12-9; 12-8.30 Sun ~ Restaurant ~ Children welcome ~ Dogs allowed in bar ~ Wi-fi
Recommended by Lynda and Trevor Smith, Susan and John Douglas, Camilla and Jose Ferrera, Liz and Mike Newton

HOLY CROSS
SO9278 Map 4

Bell & Cross

(01562) 730319 – www.bellandcrossclent.co.uk
2 miles from M5 junction 3: A491 towards Stourbridge, then follow Clent signpost off on left; DY9 9QL

Pretty garden, an attractive old interior and up-to-date food

In good weather, the lovely garden here with its spacious lawn and terrace is just the place to head for. New owners have made some changes to the food and décor, but locals still enjoy Enville Ale, Timothy Taylors Landlord, and Wye Valley HPA on handpump and good wines by the glass in the bar. The four attractively decorated dining rooms (with a choice of carpet, bare boards, lino or nice old quarry tiles) have a variety of moods, from snug and chatty to bright and airy, and most have coal fires; background music. The pub is handy for the M5.

Quite a choice of food includes duck and orange terrine with fig chutney, chilli-crusted squid with tabbouleh, a pie of the day, burger with toppings and skinny fries, squash, chestnut mushroom and cauliflower lasagne with pecorino, calves liver with smoked bacon and thyme jus, hake fillet with shrimps, leek and chervil risotto and vermouth cream sauce, north indian chicken curry, chargilled steaks with confit garlic and shallot butter and fries, and puddings. *Benchmark main dish: slow-cooked lamb shoulder with chorizo dauphinoise potatoes and red wine jus £16.95. Two-course evening meal £22.00.*

Enterprise ~ Lease Sam Hami ~ Real ale ~ Open 12-3, 6-11; 12-9 Sun ~ Bar food 12-2, 6-9; 12-7 Sun ~ Restaurant ~ Children welcome ~ Dogs allowed in bar ~ Wi-fi *Recommended by Dr D J and Mrs S C Walker, Susan and John Douglas*

KNIGHTWICK SO7355 Map 4
Talbot 🍴 ♀ 🍺 🛏

(01886) 821235 – www.the-talbot.co.uk
Knightsford Bridge; B4197 just off A44 Worcester–Bromyard; WR6 5PH

Worcestershire Dining Pub of the Year

Interesting old coaching inn with good own-brewed beers and riverside garden; bedrooms

This former coaching inn's own Teme Valley microbrewery uses locally grown hops to produce Talbot Blonde, That, This, T'Other and a seasonal ale on handpump, and they hold regular beer festivals; they also serve a dozen wines by the glass and 16 malt whiskies. The heavily beamed and extended lounge bar is traditionally furnished with a variety of seats from small carved or leatherette armchairs to winged settles by the windows, and there's both a warm log fire and a vast stove in a big central stone hearth. The bar opens into a light and airy garden room. The back public bar has pool on a raised side area, a TV, darts, a juke box and cribbage; in contrast, the dining room is a sedate place for a quiet meal. In warm weather, it's lovely to use the tables on the lawn beside the River Teme (it's across the lane from the inn, but they serve out here too) or you can sit in front of the building on old-fashioned seats. A farmers' market takes place here on the second Sunday of the month.

The enjoyable food uses some home-grown produce and they make their own preserves, bread, raised pies and black pudding: smoked pigeon and sauté pigeon breasts with crispy bacon and tarragon vinaigrette, home-cured salmon gravadlax with horseradish crème fraîche, sausage and egg with chips, wild mushroom timbale with roast vegetable couscous and poached free-range duck egg, game cassoulet (locally shot rabbit, muntjac and pigeon), slow-roast pork belly with griddled black pudding and apple fritters, cod fillet with cheese, herb and breadcrumb topping and tomato sauce, and puddings such as chocolate truffle cake and treacle hollygog (pastry rolled with golden syrup and baked in milk). *Benchmark main dish: chicken and leek pie £14.00. Two-course evening meal £20.00.*

Own brew ~ Licensee Annie Clift ~ Real ale ~ Open 8am-11pm ~ Bar food 8am-9pm ~ Restaurant ~ Children welcome ~ Dogs welcome ~ Wi-fi ~ Bedrooms: £65/£110
Recommended by Alan and Angela Scouller, Dr and Mrs Paul Cartwright, Ben and Diane Bowie, Nicola and Stuart Parsons, Lenny and Ruth Walters

MALVERN
SO7845   Map 4

Nags Head 🍺

(01684) 574373 – www.nagsheadmalvern.co.uk

Bottom end of Bank Street, steep turn down off A449; WR14 2JG

A delightfully eclectic layout and décor, remarkable choice of ales, tasty lunchtime bar food and warmly welcoming atmosphere

'One of my favourite all-time pubs,' says one reader with enthusiasm – and so many agree. This is a particularly well run, cheerful place and always packed with customers keen to enjoy the marvellous range of ales and the easy-going atmosphere. A series of snug, individually decorated rooms, separated by a couple of steps and with two open fires, have leather armchairs, pews sometimes arranged as booths and a mix of tables (including sturdy ones stained different colours). There are bare boards here, flagstones there, carpet elsewhere, plenty of interesting pictures and homely touches such as house plants, shelves of well thumbed books and daily papers; board games. If you struggle to choose from the 15 or so beers on handpump, you'll be offered a taster by the professional, friendly staff: Banks's Bitter, Bathams Best Bitter, Ringwood Fortyniner, St Georges Charger, Dragons Blood and Friar Tuck, and Woods Shropshire Lad with around eight changing guests. Also, two farm ciders, 30 malt whiskies, a dozen gins, ten bottled craft ales/lagers and ten wines by the glass including pudding ones. The front terrace and garden have picnic-sets, benches and rustic tables as well as parasols and heaters.

🍴 Tasty lunchtime food includes sandwiches, home-cooked ham and eggs, beef in ale pie, butternut squash and sage gnocchi with creamy white wine sauce and fried smoked haddock macaroni cheese cakes with tomato chilli purée, with evening meals (served in the barn extension dining room only) such as tempura courgette chips with beetroot hummus and roasted pepper salsa, sausage casserole with sweet potato mash, crispy duck with hoisin, orange and pineapple sauce and pak choi, escalope of lamb with leek fool, sea bass fillet with crab bonbons and confit cerry tomato, and puddings. *Benchmark main dish: beer-battered fresh cod and chips £13.20. Two-course evening meal £19.50.*

Free house ~ Licensee Alex Whistance ~ Real ale ~ Open 11am-11.15pm; 11am-11.30pm Fri, Sat; 12-11 Sun ~ Bar food 12-2.30, 6.30-8.30; 12-2.30, 7-8.30 Sun ~ Restaurant ~ Children welcome ~ Dogs welcome ~ Wi-fi *Recommended by Guy Vowles, Mark Hamill, Barry Collett, Katherine Matthews, Patti and James Davidson, Lee and Jill Stafford*

NEWLAND
SO7948   Map 4

Swan 🍺

(01886) 832224 – www.theswaninnmalvern.co.uk

Worcester Road (set well back from A449 just NW of Malvern); WR13 5AY

Popular, interesting pub with eight real ales and seats in the big garden

With up to eight real ales on handpump, it's not surprising that this creeper-clad pub is always so busy. The dimly lit dark-beamed bar is quite traditional, with a forest canopy of hops, whisky-water jugs, beakers and tankards. Several of the comfortable and clearly individually chosen seats are worth a close look for their carving, and the wall tapestries are interesting. From the carved counter friendly staff serve Purity Mad Goose and Ringwood Fortyniner plus guest ales such as Otter Amber, Purity Pure Gold, St Georges Dragons Blood, Dreamweaver and Friar Tuck and Woods Shropshire Lad on handpump, as well as several wines, malt whiskies and four farm ciders. On the right is a broadly similar red-carpeted dining room and beyond it, in complete contrast, an ultra-modern glass garden room; board games. The garden is as individual as the pub, with a cluster of huge casks topped with flowers, even a piano doing flower-tub duty, and a set of stocks on the pretty front terrace.

Enjoyable food includes lunchtime sandwiches, ham hock terrine with piccalilli, potted goats cheese with red onion marmalade, cheddar and spinach quiche in walnut pastry, venison casserole with spring onion mash, cod on kedgeree with coriander cream, guinea fowl with leek and potato rarebit with red wine jus, chicken curry with mint yoghurt and rice, pork schnitzel with chips, and puddings. *Benchmark main dish: beef in ale pie £12.50. Two-course evening meal £17.00.*

Free house ~ Licensee Duncan Ironmonger ~ Real ale ~ Open 12-11 ~ Bar food 12-2.30, 6.30-9 ~ Restaurant ~ Children allowed ~ Dogs welcome ~ Wi-fi *Recommended by Mike and Mary Carter, Jack Trussler, Chris Stevenson, Alister and Margery Bacon, Chantelle and Tony Redman*

TENBURY WELLS

Talbot 🍴🌟 ♀ 🛏

SO6468 Map 4

(01584) 781941 – www.talbotinnnewnhambridge.co.uk
Newnham Bridge; A456; WR15 8JF

Carefully refurbished coaching inn with character bar and dining rooms and highly rated food; bedrooms

To make the most of the lovely Teme Valley countryside and surrounding towns, stay for a few days in the thoughtfully decorated and well equipped bedrooms here; breakfasts are regarded too. There's a friendly, gently civilised atmosphere, nice old red and black and original quarry tiles, bare floorboards, open fires, hops and candlelight – and the bar and dining rooms are quite different in style. There's an assortment of dark pubby, high-backed painted wooden and comfortably upholstered dining chairs around a mix of tables, leather tub chairs and sofas, bookshelves, old photographs of the local area, table lights and standard lamps, and some elegant antiques. It gets pretty busy at the weekend, when you'll need to book a table in advance. Hobsons Twisted Spire and Wye Valley Bitter on handpump, local cider and good wines by the glass.

Imaginative food includes sandwiches, dorset snail fricassée, scallops, celeriac and cumin oil, roasted tomato and fennel risotto, chicken breast with parsnip, pear and cider fondant potato, monkfish with curried cauliflower, mango, kale and parmentier potatoes, duck breast with turnip, kale and rhubarb, lobster with béarnaise sauce and french fries, and puddings such as caramel pineapple with banana and passion-fruit sorbet and vanilla pannacotta with black pepper meringues. *Benchmark main dish: sirloin steak with green peppercorn and parsley butter and chips £18.00. Two-course evening meal £24.00.*

Free house ~ Licensee Barnaby Williams ~ Real ale ~ Open 7am-11; 9am-midnight Sat; 9am-10pm Sun; closed first two weeks Jan ~ Bar food 12-2.30, 6-9.30; 12-7.30 Sun ~ Children welcome ~ Dogs allowed in bar and bedrooms ~ Wi-fi ~ Bedrooms: £80/£90 *Recommended by Ian Malone, Jacob Vaughan, Lance and Sarah Milligan, Kerry and Guy Trooper, Graham Smart*

A star symbol after the name of a pub shows exceptional character and appeal. It doesn't mean extra comfort. And it's nothing to do with exceptional food quality, for which there's a separate star-on-a-plate symbol. Even quite a basic pub can win a star, if it's individual enough.

WELLAND
SO8039 Map 4

Inn at Welland ⭐ ♟

(01684) 592317 – www.theinnatwelland.co.uk

Drake Street; A4104 W of Upton upon Severn; WR13 6LN

**Stylish contemporary country dining bar with good food
and wines and nice tables outside**

The good-sized neat garden here, offering tranquil views of the Malvern
Hills, has tables with comfortable teak or wicker chairs on a biggish
sheltered deck or on individual separate terraces set into lawn. Inside, there's
a lively buzz of conversation and a gently civilised atmosphere, cool grey
paintwork, a few carefully chosen modern prints and attractive seat fabrics,
with beige flagstones in the central area, wood flooring to the sides and
a woodburning stove at one end. Ledbury Bitter, Otter Bitter and Wye Valley
Butty Bach on handpump, 25 wines by the glass including an unusually wide
range of pudding wines, mocktails, cocktails and quite a few gins – all served
by neatly dressed, efficient staff; background music. The pub is handy for the
Three Counties Showground.

Making everything in-house and championing local produce, the tempting food
includes rillettes of local smoked salmon with chive crème fraîche and pickled
cucumber, croquette of slow-braised oxtail with thyme and red wine jus and vegetable
escabeche, english charcuterie plate with vegetable crudités, omelette arnold bennett,
fresh potato gnocchi with wild mushrooms and truffled parmesan cream, beer-braised
free-range chicken with potato purée and charred baby gem and fennel, calves liver
with glazed baby shallots and red wine jus, pork schnitzel with caper butter and sauté
potatoes, and puddings such as rhubarb and custard trifle and tonka bean pannacotta
with amaretto ice-cream and caramelised orange salad. *Benchmark main dish: pork
tenderloin with honey and sesame, carrot and ginger jus and cabbage parcel £15.90.
Two-course evening meal £27.00.*

Free house ~ Licensees David and Gillian Pinchbeck ~ Real ale ~ Open 12-3.30, 5.30-11;
12-3.30 Sun; closed Sun evening, Mon ~ Bar food 12-2.30, 5.30-9.30; 12-2.30 Sun ~
Restaurant ~ Children welcome ~ Wi-fi *Recommended by Louise and Anton Parsons,
Bernard Stradling, Andy and Louise Ramwell, Val and Malcolm Travers*

Also Worth a Visit in Worcestershire

Besides the fully inspected pubs, you might like to try these pubs that
have been recommended to us and described by readers. Do tell us what
you think of them: feedback@goodguides.com

ABBERLEY   SO7567
Manor Arms (01299) 890300
Netherton Lane; WR6 6BN Modernised
country inn tucked away in quiet village
backwater opposite fine Norman church;
changing ales and decent selection of wines,
good food from pub favourites up including
daily specials, afternoon tea, friendly service;
sports TV; children and dogs welcome, two-
level deck with lovely valley views, good walks
(on Worcestershire Way), six bedrooms, open
(and food) all day. *(Susan and Tim Boyle)*

ALVECHURCH   SP0172
Weighbridge (0121) 445 5111
Scarfield Wharf; B48 7SQ Little red-brick

pub (former weighbridge office) by Worcester
& Birmingham Canal marina, bar and a
couple of small rooms, half a dozen well
kept ales including Kinver Bargee Bitter
and Weatheroak Tillermans Tipple (beer
festivals), simple low-priced food (not Tues,
Weds); tables outside. *(Beth Aldridge)*

ASHTON UNDER HILL   SO9038
Star (01386) 881325
Elmley Road; WR11 7SN Smallish pub
perched above road in quiet village at
foot of Bredon Hill; linked beamed rooms
around bar, one with flagstones and log
fire, steps up to pitch-roofed dining room
with woodburner, well liked food (not Sun
or Mon evenings) from good freshly baked

baguettes to specials, meal deals Mon-Fri lunchtime and Tues evening, real ales such as Black Sheep and Greene King IPA, friendly welcoming staff; background music, TV and games machine; children and dogs welcome, picnic-sets in pleasant garden, good walks (Wyche Way passes nearby), open all day. *(Guy Vowles, Peter Young)*

BELBROUGHTON   SO9277
Olde Horse Shoe (01562) 731663
High Street; DY9 9ST Popular old beamed corner pub with smallish stone-floored bar and separate restaurant, usually three real ales including St Austell and Wye Valley, good range of well liked freshly made food (not Sun evening, Mon), afternoon teas, friendly service, open fires, may be paintings for sale; occasional live music including tribute acts; children and dogs welcome, big back garden, closed Mon till 4pm, otherwise open all day. *(Clifford Blakemore)*

BELBROUGHTON   SO9177
Queens (01562) 730276
Queens Hill (B4188 E of Kidderminster); DY9 0DU Old red-brick pub by Belne Brook, several linked areas including beamed slate-floor bar, very good modern food alongside pub standards, three well kept beers such as Ringwood and a nice selection of wines, friendly staff coping well at busy times; disabled facilities, small roadside terrace, pleasant village and handy for M5 (junction 4), open all day, till 6pm Sun. *(Graham and Elizabeth Hargreaves)*

BERROW   SO7835
Duke of York (01684) 833449
Junction A438/B4208; WR13 6JQ Bustling old country pub with two linked rooms, beams, nooks and crannies and log fire, welcoming friendly staff, good food from baguettes up including specials, well kept Banks's, Wye Valley and a guest; restaurant; big garden behind, handy for Malvern Hills. *(Jake)*

BEWDLEY   SO7775
Hop Pole (01299) 401295
Hop Pole Lane; DY12 2QH Modernised 19th-c pub with good choice of well liked food (booking advised) from pub favourites up including evening set menu, three well kept Marstons-related ales and several wines by the glass, country-chic décor, cast-iron range in dining area; live music Fri and other events such as cookery demonstrations, free wi-fi; children and dogs (in bar) welcome, seats on raised front terrace, vegetable garden to the side, back play area, open all day. *(Frances and Hamish Porter)*

BEWDLEY   SO7875
Mug House (01299) 402543
Severn Side North; DY12 2EE 18th-c bay-windowed pub in charming spot by River Severn, good food from traditional choices up including set menus, can eat in bar or more upmarket evening restaurant with lobster tank, six well kept ales such as Bewdley, Purity, Timothy Taylors and Wye Valley (May beer festival), log fire; children (daytime only) and dogs welcome, disabled access, glass-covered terrace behind, seven river-view bedrooms, open all day, no food Sun. *(Gary and Marie Miller)*

BIRLINGHAM   SO9343
Swan (01386) 750485
Church Street; off A4104 S of Pershore, via B4080 Eckington Road, turn off at sign to Birlingham with integral 'The Swan Inn' brown sign (not the 'Birlingham (village only)' road), then left; WR10 3AQ Pretty family-run thatched and timbered cottage, updated beamed quarry-tiled bar with woodburner in big stone fireplace, well kept ales such as Hook Norton and Purity, real cider, good food from reasonably priced varied menu including fresh fish specials, friendly efficient service, dining conservatory; nice back garden, handy for River Avon walks, open all day Sun till 7pm, closed Mon except bank holidays. *(Dr and Mrs H J Field, Peter Young)*

BISHAMPTON   SO9445
Dolphin (01386) 462343
Main Street; WR10 2LX Comfortably updated village pub with good reasonably priced food (not Mon) cooked by landlord-chef including daily specials and some weekday lunchtime bargains, Tues curry and Weds steak night, Fullers London Pride, Wye Valley HPA and a guest such as local Pershore, well chosen wines by the glass, efficient friendly staff; children and dogs welcome, seats on paved terrace and small raised deck, open all day Sun till 9pm, closed Mon lunchtime. *(Dave Braisted)*

BOURNHEATH   SO9474
Gate (01527) 878169
Handy for M5 junction 4 via A491 and B4091; Dodford Road; B61 9JR Comfortable tiled-floor country dining pub with popular American/Mexican-influenced menu, real ales and craft beers such as Brakspears, Purity and Shipyard, plenty of wines by the glass and cocktails, friendly service, conservatory; children welcome, sheltered garden, open all day Fri-Sun. *(Dave Braisted)*

BREDON   SO9236
★ Fox & Hounds (01684) 772377
4.5 miles from M5 junction 9; A438 to Northway, left at B4079, in Bredon follow sign to church; GL20 7LA Cottagey 16th-c thatched pub with open-plan carpeted bar, low beams, stone pillars and stripped timbers, central woodburner, traditional furnishings including upholstered settles, a variety of wheelback, tub and kitchen chairs around handsome mahogany and

cast-iron-framed tables, elegant wall lamps, smaller side bar, Butcombe, Charles Wells Bombardier, Wadworths 6X and Wye Valley HPA, nice wines by the glass and wide choice of enjoyable food including specials, fast friendly service; background music, quiz Sun evening (no food then); children welcome, dogs in bar, outside picnic-sets (some under cover) and pretty hanging baskets, closed Mon. *(R J Herd)*

BROADWAS-ON-TEME   SO7555
Royal Oak   (01886) 821353
A44; WR6 5NE Red-brick roadside pub with various areas including unusual lofty-raftered medieval-style dining hall, popular good value daily carvery and other enjoyable food, weekday set menus, well kept Marstons-related ales and decent wines by the glass, friendly helpful service; free wi-fi; children welcome, no dogs inside, disabled access, garden with play area, open (and food) all day. *(Jake)*

BROADWAY   SP0937
Swan   (01386) 852278
The Green (B4362); WR12 7AA Sizeable Mitchells & Butlers dining pub with imaginative décor in several linked areas, popular sensibly priced food including good value fixed-price menu (till 6pm Mon-Sat), three well kept changing ales, plenty of wines by the glass and good range of cocktails, polite friendly young staff; children welcome, tables under parasols on small front terrace looking over road to village green, open all day. *(Richard Kennell)*

CALLOW END   SO8349
Blue Bell   (01905) 830261
Upton Road; WR2 4TY Popular Marstons local with two bars and dining area, their well kept ales and wide variety of enjoyable food including lots of specials (some good vegetarian choices), friendly welcoming staff, open fire; quiz last Thurs of the month; children allowed, dogs in garden only, open all day weekends. *(Susan and Tim Boyle)*

CALLOW HILL   SP0164
Brook Inn   (01527) 543209
Elcocks Brook, off B4504; B97 5UD Modernised country dining pub with well liked fairly priced food from lunchtime sandwiches and baps up, Marstons-related ales, friendly staff; tables out at front and in pleasant back beer garden, open all day. *(Dave Braisted)*

CALLOW HILL   SO7473
Royal Forester   (01299) 266286
Near Wyre Forest visitor centre; DY14 9XW Dining pub dating in part from the 15th c, good food including regular themed evenings, friendly helpful service, well kept ales such as Hobsons and Otter, Robinson's cider, relaxed lounge bar and restaurant; regular live music,

Sun quiz; children and dogs welcome, seats outside, seven contemporary bedrooms, open all day. *(Beth Aldridge)*

CAUNSALL   SO8480
Anchor   (01562) 850254
Caunsall Road, off A449; DY11 5YL Traditional unchanging two-room pub (in same family since 1927), welcoming atmosphere and can get very busy, five well kept ales such as Hobsons, Three Tuns and Wye Valley, traditional ciders and good value generously filled cobs, friendly efficient service; dogs welcome, large outside seating area behind, near Staffordshire & Worcestershire Canal. *(Brian and Anna Marsden)*

CHADDESLEY CORBETT   SO8973
Swan   (01562) 777302
Off A448 Bromsgrove–Kidderminster; DY10 4SD Popular old local, lively and friendly, with well kept Bathams and enjoyable good value pubby food from sandwiches and pizzas up, various rooms including large lofty lounge; Thurs jazz, TV, games machine; children and dogs welcome, picnic-sets in big lawned garden with play area and country views, handy for Harvington Hall, open all day. *(Dave Braisted)*

CLAINES   SO8558
Mug House   (01905) 456649
Claines Lane, off A449 3 miles W of M5 junction 3; WR3 7RN Fine views from this ancient country tavern in unique churchyard setting by fields below the Malvern Hills; several small rooms around central bar, low doorways and heavy oak beams, well kept Banks's and other Marstons-related ales, simple lunchtime pub food; no credit cards, outside lavatories; children (away from servery) and dogs welcome, open all day weekends. *(Beth Aldridge)*

CROPTHORNE   SO9944
Bell   (01386) 861860
Main Road (B4084); WR10 3NE Isolated rather stark-looking roadside pub with contrasting brightly modernised interior, L-shaped bar with painted beams, bare boards and colourful carpet, well divided seating areas (one down a couple of steps), log fire, small back conservatory, emphasis on dining with popular freshly made food from good ploughman's up, children's choices, Sharps Doom Bar and a guest, welcoming efficient service; background music; open all day Sat, till 8pm Sun, closed Mon (and Tues in winter). *(Richard Kennell)*

CROWLE   SO9256
Chequers   (01905) 381772
Crowle Green, not far from M5 junction 6; WR7 4AA Busy refurbished beamed dining pub (sister to the Forest at Feckenham); good food (some quite pricey) from sandwiches and one or two pubby

choices up, well kept ales such as Purity and Wye Valley, lots of wines by the glass and good range of other drinks, friendly attentive staff; children and dogs (in bar) welcome, open all day. *(Dave Braisted)*

DEFFORD   SO9042

★**Monkey House** (01386) 750234

A4104, after passing Oak pub on right, it's the last of a small group of cottages; WR8 9BW Tiny black and white thatched cider house, a wonderful time warp and in the same family for over 150 years; ciders and a perry tapped from barrels into pottery mugs and served by landlady from a hatch, no other drinks or food (can bring your own); children welcome, no dogs (resident rottweilers), garden with caravans, sheds and Mandy the horse, small spartan outbuilding with a couple of plain tables, settle and fireplace, open Fri and Sun lunchtimes, Weds and Sat evenings. *(Jake)*

DEFFORD   SO9042

Oak (01386) 750327

Woodmancote (A4104), WR8 9DW Modernised 17th-c beamed country pub with two front bars and back restaurant, well kept ales such as Holdens and Wye Valley, Thatcher's cider, good fairly priced food (all day Sat, till 7pm Sun) including weekday OAP deal, friendly staff; occasional live music; children and dogs welcome, vine-covered front pergola, garden with orchard and chickens, open all day. *(Alister and Margery Bacon)*

DODFORD   SO9372

Dodford Inn (01527) 835825

Whinfield Road; B61 9BG Mid 19th-c red-brick country pub tucked away in six-acre grounds, fresh modern refurbishment, up to four well kept ales including Purity and Wye Valley, good home-made food (all day Sat, not Sun evening) from sandwiches and pizzas up, friendly staff; children welcome, no dogs inside, nice views over wooded valley from terrace tables, good walks, open till 7pm Sun. *(Dave Braisted)*

DROITWICH   SO8963

Gardeners Arms (01905) 772936

Vines Lane; WR9 8LU Individual place on the edge of town; cosy traditional bar to the right, bistro-style restaurant to the left with red gingham tablecloths and lots of pictures (mostly for sale), four Marstons-related ales, well priced food from varied menu including range of good local sausages; regular live music and quiz nights, also themed food evenings, whisky tastings and a cigar club; children and dogs welcome, outside seating areas on different levels below railway embankment with quirky mix of furniture, play area, camping, close to Droitwich Canal, open all day. *(Pete Carr)*

DROITWICH   SO9063

Hop Pole (01905) 770155

Friar Street; WR9 8ED Heavy-beamed local with panelled rooms on different levels, well kept Malvern Hills, Wye Valley and a guest, bargain home-made lunchtime food including doorstep sandwiches; dominoes, darts and pool, occasional live music; children welcome, partly canopied back garden, open all day. *(Pete Carr)*

DUNLEY   SO7969

Dog (01299) 822833

A451 S of Stourport; DY13 0UE Attractive creeper-clad roadside dining pub, good choice of well priced enjoyable food from bar meals up including lunchtime OAP deal, well kept Wye Valley and guests, friendly staff; free wi-fi; children and dogs welcome, garden with play area and bowling green, three bedrooms, open all day. *(Lynda and Trevor Smith)*

ELDERSFIELD   SO8131

★**Butchers Arms** (01452) 840381

Village signposted from B4211; Lime Street (coming from A417, go past the Eldersfield turn and take the next one), OS Sheet 150 map reference 815314; also signposted from B4208 N of Staunton; GL19 4NX Pretty 16th-c cottage with deliberately simple unspoilt little locals' bar, ales such as St Austell, Wickwar and Wye Valley tapped from the cask, a proper cider and short but well chosen wine list, just a dozen seats in candlelit dining room and booking essential for owner-chef's highly regarded imaginative food (not cheap); no under-10s, garden picnic-sets and nice surroundings, open and food lunchtime Fri-Sun, evening Tues-Sat, closes for two weeks Dec-Jan and the latter part of Aug; for sale as we went to press so may be changes. *(Susan and Tim Boyle)*

EVESHAM   SP0344

Old Red Horse (01386) 442784

Vine Street; WR11 4RE Attractive black and white former coaching inn, two bars with beams, bare boards and open fires, three real ales, enjoyable reasonably priced pub food including weekday set menu and steak nights (Tues, Weds), good cheerful service; TV, darts and machines; children and dogs welcome, nice covered inner courtyard with small pond, five bedrooms, open all day, no evening food weekends. *(Gary and Marie Miller)*

FECKENHAM   SP0061

Forest (01527) 894422

B4090 Droitwich–Alcester; B96 6JE Contemporary décor and good interesting food at this village dining pub (sister to Chequers at Crowle) from lunchtime sandwiches and sharing boards up, well kept Hook Norton and Timothy Taylors, efficient friendly service, oak-floored bar with light-wood stools at high tables and some other more comfortable seating, panels of bookshelf wallpaper dotted about, woodburner, adjoining restaurant with upholstered booth seats, conservatory; children welcome, disabled access/facilities, rattan furniture on block-paved terrace with big outdoor fireplace, more tables on raised lawn, open all day. *(Mike and Mary Carter)*

FLADBURY   SO9946
Chequers (01386) 861854
Chequers Lane; WR10 2PZ Modernised old pub in peaceful village; long beamed bar with log fire in old-fashioned range, ales such as Sharps Doom Bar and Wye Valley, Aspall's and Weston's ciders, enjoyable sensibly priced home-made food including Mon grill night, timbered back restaurant with conservatory; background music, free wi-fi; children welcome, steps up to walled terrace, play area on lawn with country views, eight bedrooms in extension, open all day Fri-Sun, closed Mon lunchtime. *(Beth Aldridge)*

FLYFORD FLAVELL   SO9754
Boot (01386) 462658
Off A422 Worcester–Alcester; Radford Road; WR7 4BS Popular range of home-made food including two-course lunch deal, cook your own steak on a hot stone and blackboard specials, Fullers London Pride and Sharps Doom Bar, good friendly service, log fires in ancient heavily beamed and timbered core, modern conservatory; background music, games room with pool and TV; children and dogs (in bar) welcome, tables on split-level terrace and small lawned area, popular with walkers, five bedrooms, open all day. *(Mike and Mary Carter)*

GRIMLEY   SO8359
Camp House (01905) 640288
A443 5 miles N from Worcester, right to Grimley, right at village T junction; WR2 6LX Simple unspoilt old pub in same family since 1939, appealing Severn-side setting (prone to flooding) with own landing stage, generous home-made food at bargain prices, well kept Bathams and guests, Thatcher's and Robinson's ciders, friendly relaxed atmosphere; no credit cards; children and well behaved dogs welcome, attractive lawns (maybe wandering peacocks), small campsite, open all day. *(Pete Carr)*

HADLEY   SO8662
Bowling Green (01905) 620294
Hadley Heath; off A4133 Droitwich–Ombersley; WR9 0AR Popular and welcoming 16th-c inn with beams and big log fire, well kept Wadworths ales and decent wines by the glass, good food (all day

Sun) from sandwiches and deli boards up, comfortable back lounge and restaurant; children welcome, tables out overlooking own bowling green (UK's oldest), 12 comfortable bedrooms, nice walks (footpath starts from car park), open all day. *(Andy Dolan)*

HALLOW   SO8258
Crown (01905) 640408
Main Road; WR2 6LB Large low-beamed 17th-c pub with modern/rustic décor, good food from sandwiches up including lunchtime set menu, ales such as St Austell and Wye Valley; children welcome, no dogs inside, tables under parasols on terrace and lawn, big tipi with fire pit, open (and food) all day. *(Jake)*

HANBURY   SO9662
Vernon (01527) 821236
Droitwich Road (B4090); B60 4DB 18th-c former coaching inn, contemporary interior and much emphasis on food, but serves up to four real ales in beamed bar with woodburner, nice food from sandwiches and light choices through pub favourites to more enterprising dishes, OAP lunch menu too, good friendly service; children and dogs welcome, modern terrace seating, five boutique-style bedrooms, open all day. *(Dave Braisted)*

HANLEY CASTLE   SO8342
★ **Three Kings** (01684) 592686
Church End, off B4211 N of Upton upon Severn; WR8 0BL Timeless, hospitable and by no means smart – in same family for over 100 years and a favourite with those who put unspoilt character and individuality first; cheerful, homely tiled-floor tap room separated from entrance corridor by monumental built-in settle, equally vast inglenook fireplace, room on left with darts and board games, separate entrance to timbered lounge with second inglenook and neatly blacked kitchen range, leatherette armchairs, spindleback chairs and antique winged settle, well kept Butcombe, Hobsons and three guests from smaller brewers, Weston's cider and around 75 malt whiskies, simple snacks; live music; children and dogs welcome, old-fashioned wood and iron seats on front terrace looking across to great cedar shading tiny green, on Wyche Way long-distance path. *(Guy Vowles, Barry Collett)*

HANLEY SWAN   SO8142
★ **Swan** (01684) 311870
B4209 Malvern–Upton; WR8 0EA Contemporary/rustic décor and furnishings blending well with old low beams (some painted), bare boards and log fire, extended back part set for their good well presented

---

'Children welcome' means the pub says it lets children inside without any special restriction; some may impose an evening time limit earlier than 9pm – please tell us if you find this.

food (all day Sat, not Sun evening) from sandwiches/baguettes and pub favourites to more restaurانty dishes (booking advised), friendly helpful staff, St Austell Tribute, Sharps Doom Bar and Wye Valley HPA, seven wines by the glass, oak-framed conservatory; children and dogs welcome, disabled access/loos, seats out on paved terrace and grass, nice spot facing green and big duck pond, five comfortable good value bedrooms, open all day, weekend breakfast from 8am. *(Martin and Alison Stainsby, Dave Braisted, Richard Kennell)*

HIMBLETON   SO9458
Galton Arms (01905) 391672
Harrow Lane; WR9 7LQ Friendly old black and white bay-windowed country pub, good food including daily specials in split-level beamed bar or restaurant, well kept ales such as Banks's, Bathams and Wye Valley, woodburner; sports TV; children and dogs welcome, picnic-sets in small part-paved garden, local walks, open all day Sun, closed Mon lunchtime. *(Andy and Louise Ramwell)*

INKBERROW   SP0157
Old Bull (01386) 792428
Off A422 on the green – note that this is quite different from the nearby Bulls Head; WR7 4DZ Photogenic black and white Tudor pub with lots of *Archers* memorabilia (it's the model for the Ambridge Bull); tasty pub food and well kept ales such as Wye Valley, friendly service, log fire in huge inglenook, bulging walls, flagstones, oak beams and trusses, brasswork and other bits and pieces; children and dogs welcome, plenty of tables outside, open all day. *(Andy G)*

KEMERTON   SO9437
Crown (01386) 725020
Back road Bredon–Beckford; GL20 7HP Small 18th-c pub in pretty village; hospitable landlord and cheerful staff, good freshly made food (not Sun evening) from sandwiches up including sharing dishes and daily specials, ales such as Wye Valley, local cider, flagstoned bar with log fire, restaurant; dogs welcome (may get a treat), roadside tables and peaceful courtyard garden behind, good walks over Bredon Hill, four pleasant bedrooms, closed Mon lunchtime, otherwise open all day. *(Gerald Warner)*

KIDDERMINSTER   SO8376
King & Castle (01562) 747505
Severn Valley Railway station, Comberton Hill; DY10 1QX Neatly recreated Edwardian refreshment room in Severn Valley Railway terminus – steam trains outside and railway memorabilia and photographs inside; eight real ales including Bathams, Bewdley and Hobsons, three traditional ciders, cobs at the bar or reasonably priced straightforward food in

adjacent dining room; children welcome, little railway museum close by, open all day and busy bank holidays/railway gala days, open (and food) all day. *(Dave Braisted)*

LONGDON   SO8434
Hunters Inn (01684) 833388
B4211 S, towards Tewkesbury; GL20 6AR Beamed and timbered country pub with flagstone floors, stripped brickwork and log fires, enjoyable locally sourced food including Sun carvery, real ales such as Donnington and Otter, local ciders and decent wines by the glass, friendly service, raftered dining area with linen-clothed tables, good views; some live music, darts; children welcome, extensive well tended garden, campsite, closed Mon. *(Jamie and Lizzie McEwan)*

MALVERN   SO7746
Foley Arms (01684) 573397
Worcester Road; WR14 4QS Substantial Georgian hotel (former coaching inn) owned by Wetherspoons, friendly staff and usual good value; free wi-fi; children welcome, splendid views from sunny terrace and back bedrooms, open all day from 7am. *(Jake)*

MALVERN   SO7746
Red Lion (01684) 564787
St Anns Road; WR14 4RG Enjoyable food (all day Sat) from substantial sandwiches and baguettes up, also very good adjacent thai restaurant, well kept Marstons-related ales such as Ringwood, cheerful prompt service, airy modern décor with stripped pine, bare boards, flagstones and pastel colours; background and live music including frequent jazz nights, darts; attractive partly covered front terrace, well placed for walks, open (and food) all day Sat, closed Sun-Thurs lunchtimes. *(Pete Carr)*

MALVERN   SO7643
Wyche (01684) 575396
Wyche Road; WR14 4EQ Comfortable busy pub near top of Malvern Hills, splendid views and popular with walkers, Wye Valley and guests, decent range of affordable pubby food from sandwiches up, good service; pool and games machine in one bar; children and dogs welcome, four bedrooms plus self-catering apartments, open all day. *(Guy Vowles)*

OMBERSLEY   SO8463
Cross Keys (01905) 620588
Just off A449; Main Road (A4133, Kidderminster end); WR9 0DS Under new management and some refurbishment; carpeted bar with fire, archways opening into several separate areas, beams, banquettes and brassware, Timothy Taylors Landlord and Wye Valley HPA, well liked food from baguettes to daily specials, friendly helpful service, dining conservatory; background music; children and dogs welcome, terrace seating, open all day Sun (food till 7pm), closed Mon. *(Frances and Hamish Porter)*

OMBERSLEY   SO8463
Crown & Sandys   (01905) 620252
A4133; WR9 0EW Big open-plan inn (part
of the small Scoff & Quaff group); good
range of enjoyable food from sandwiches,
sharing plates and pubby dishes up, set menu
choices Mon-Thurs, ales such as Wye Valley
and plenty of wines by the glass, friendly
efficient staff, spotlessly clean interior
mixing modern décor with 17th-c beams
and inglenook, some interesting old local
pictures and photographs; background music;
children welcome, terrace with fountain,
more tables in sizeable garden, six bedrooms,
open (and food) all day. *(Robert W Buckle)*

OMBERSLEY   SO8463
Kings Arms   (01905) 620142
Main Road (A4133); WR9 0EW Imposing
beamed and timbered Tudor pub; low-
ceilinged brick-floored bar with built-in
panelled wall seat and woodburner in large
fireplace, three dining areas, steps down
to one, another with Charles II coat of
arms decorating the ceiling, good food and
service (popular with older diners), well
kept Marstons-related ales; background
music; children and dogs welcome, seats on
tree-sheltered courtyard, colourful hanging
baskets and tubs, open all day, food all day
weekends. *(Lynda and Trevor Smith)*

PENSAX   SO7368
★ Bell   (01299) 896677
*B4202 Abberley–Clows Top, Snead
Common part of village; WR6 6AE*
Mock-Tudor roadside pub with good local
atmosphere, half a dozen ever changing
ales such as Exmoor and Hobsons (festival
last weekend of June), also cider and perry,
well liked good value pubby food (not Sun
evening) from sandwiches up, L-shaped main
bar with traditional décor, cushioned pews
and pubby tables on bare boards, vintage
beer ads and wartime front pages, two open
fires and woodburner, dining room with
french windows opening on to deck; children
and dogs (in bar) welcome, country-view
garden, closed Mon lunchtime. *(Dave
Braisted, Lynda and Trevor Smith)*

PEOPLETON   SO9350
Crown   (01905) 840222
*Village and pub signed off A44 at
Allens Hill; WR10 2EE* Cosy and
welcoming village pub with friendly mix
of drinkers and diners; beamed bar with
big inglenook, well laid-out eating area,
good food (must book) from sandwiches
and pub favourites up including set menu
and regular themed evening deals, well
kept ales such as Fullers, Sharps and Wye
Valley, nice wines by the glass, efficient

pleasant service; children (till 9pm) and
dogs (in bar) welcome, flower-filled back
garden, open all day. *(Revd Michael Vockins)*

SEVERN STOKE   SO8544
Rose & Crown   (01905) 371249
A38 S of Worcester; WR8 9JQ Attractive
16th-c black and white pub, low beams,
good fire and various knick-knacks in
character bar, some cushioned wall seats
and high-backed settles among more
modern pub furniture, well kept Marstons-
related ales and decent choice of enjoyable
sensibly priced food, good friendly service,
carpeted back restaurant; fortnightly quiz
Weds, monthly folk night; dogs welcome,
wheelchair access with help, picnic-sets
in big garden with play area, Malvern Hills
views and good walks, open (and food) all
day. *(Dave Braisted, Chris and Angela Buckell)*

SHATTERFORD   SO7981
Bellmans Cross   (01299) 861322
Bridgnorth Road (A442); DY12 1RN
Welcoming 19th-c mock-Tudor dining pub
with good well presented food cooked by
french chef-landlord including lunchtime
set menu and weekday themed evenings,
restaurant with kitchen view, Enville and
a couple of guests from neat timber-effect
bar, good choice of wines, teas and coffees;
children welcome, picnic-sets outside, handy
for Severn Woods walks, open (and food) all
day weekends. *(Dennis and Doreen Haward)*

STOKE POUND   SO9667
Queens Head   (01527) 557007
*Sugarbrook Lane, by Bridge 48,
Worcester & Birmingham Canal;
B60 3AU* Smartly modernised by the
small Lovely Pubs group; fairly large bar
with comfortable seating area, dedicated
dining part beyond, good choice of food
including sharing plates, wood-fired pizzas
and charcoal spit-roasts, early evening
discount (Mon-Fri) and two-for-one pizzas
(Mon-Thurs), well kept ales such as Purity,
Sharps and Wye Valley, large selection of
wines from glass-fronted store, helpful
pleasant staff; Thurs live music; children
welcome, waterside garden with tipi,
moorings, good walk up the 30 locks of
Tardebigge Steps, quite handy for Avoncroft
Museum, open (and food) all day. *(Pete Carr)*

STOKE WORKS   SO9365
Bowling Green   (01527) 861291
*A mile from M5 junction 5, via
Stoke Lane; handy for Worcester &
Birmingham Canal; B60 4BH*
Friendly comfortable pub with enjoyable
straightforward food at bargain prices
(particularly good faggots), well kept
Banks's ales and a Marstons guest, wall

There are report forms at the back of the book.

chart showing cost of a pint over the years; children welcome, big garden with play area and well tended bowling green, camping, open all day, no food Sun. *(Dave Braisted)*

TENBURY WELLS   SO5968
Pembroke House   (01584) 810301
Cross Street; WR15 8EQ Striking timbered building, oldest in town, with pubby beamed bar and two dining rooms, good popular food (not Sun evening, Mon, best to book) including themed nights, friendly efficient staff, Hobsons Best and a guest such as Ludlow, woodburner, games area with pool, darts and TV; background and some live music; children welcome, no dogs inside, smokers' shelter and pleasant garden, open all day Fri-Sun, closed Mon lunchtime. *(Alister and Margery Bacon)*

UPHAMPTON   SO8464
Fruiterers Arms   (01905) 620305
Off A449 N of Ombersley; WR9 0JW Homely and friendly country local (looks like a private house, and has been in the same family since the mid 19th c), good value Cannon Royall ales brewed at the back of the pub and a couple of guests, farm cider and perry, simple rustic Jacobean panelled bar and lounge with comfortable armchairs, beams and log fire, lots of photographs and memorabilia, snacky food such as rolls and pork pies; children till 9pm, dogs welcome in one area, back terrace and some seats out in front, open all day. *(Susan and Tim Boyle)*

WEST MALVERN   SO7645
Brewers Arms   (01684) 575408
The Dingle, signed off B4232; WR14 4BQ Attractive little two-bar beamed country local down steep path, well kept Malvern Hills, Wye Valley and up to five guests at busy times, good value pubby food, airy dining room; free wi-fi; children, walkers and dogs welcome, glorious view from small garden, open all day. *(Pete Carr)*

WILDMOOR   SO9675
Wildmoor Oak   (0121) 453 2696
A mile from M5 junction 4 – first left off A491 towards Stourbridge; Top Road; B61 0RB Busy country local with good choice of enjoyable food (all day Fri-Sun) including caribbean dishes cooked by landlord, changing real ales, ciders and perries, friendly atmosphere; music nights second Fri and last Thurs of the month, free wi-fi; small sloping terrace and garden, closed Mon lunchtime, otherwise open all day (winter hours may differ). *(Dave Braisted)*

WILLERSEY   SP1039
New Inn   (01386) 853226
Main Street; WR12 7PJ Friendly old stone-built local in lovely village, generous good value pub food (not Sun evening) from sandwiches up, well kept Donnington ales, flagstoned bar with raised quarry-tiled end section, some black beams, games room with pool and darts, separate skittle alley; background music, TV; rattan-style tables and chairs outside, good local walks, open all day. *(Andy and Louise Ramwell)*

WITHYBED GREEN   SP0172
Crown   (0121) 445 2300
Near Bridge 61, Worcester & Birmingham Canal; B48 7PN Tucked-away pub in row of former canal workers' cottages overlooking fields, Greene King Abbot and a couple of guests such as Marstons and Wye Valley, simple low-priced food (not Sun), series of lived-in small rooms with two open fires; background and some live music, Thurs quiz; children and dogs welcome, picnic-sets out in front and on terrace, open all day. *(Dave Braisted)*

WORCESTER   SO8554
Cardinals Hat   (01905) 724006
Friar Street; just off A44 near cathedral; WR1 2NA Dating from the 14th c with three small character rooms (one with fine oak panelling), half a dozen changing ales, real ciders and plenty of bottled beers, friendly well informed staff, good bar snacks and cheese/meat platters; free wi-fi; children welcome, pleasant little brick-paved terrace behind, four good bedrooms (continental breakfast), closed Mon lunchtime, otherwise open all day. *(Dave Braisted)*

WORCESTER   SO8455
Dragon   (01905) 25845
The Tything (A38); WR1 1JT Refurbished alehouse under friendly newish landlady, carpeted L-shaped bar with woodburner, six well kept Church End ales and a couple of guests, traditional cider and seven wines by the glass, snacky food such as pork pies and sausage rolls, more room (and loos) upstairs; no children inside, dogs welcome, partly covered back terrace, open all day Fri-Sun, from 4pm other days. *(Beth Aldridge)*

WORCESTER   SO8454
Farriers Arms   (01905) 27569
Fish Street; WR1 2HN Welcoming and relaxed old timbered pub off the High Street, compact interior with bar and dining areas wrapping around central bar, enjoyable inexpensive food, well kept ales such as Wells Bombardier and St Austell Tribute, decent house wines, good cheerful service; pool, darts, TV and machines; children welcome away from bar, beer garden, handy for cathedral, open all day and gets busy lunchtimes. *(Dave Braisted)*

WORCESTER   SO8554
King Charles II   (01905) 726100
New Street; WR1 2DP Small jettied Tudor building, heavy beams, fine panelling and woodburners in carved fireplaces, settles and pews on bare boards, eight well kept ales from Craddocks and associated Bridgnorth

and Two Thirsty Brewers, traditional ciders, enjoyable range of Pieminister pies served with peas and different types of mash (limited range of other food), friendly helpful staff, upstairs area with bench seating, old tapestry and some leather easy chairs; ask about the skeleton under the floor; open all day (food all day weekends). *(Dave Braisted, Tony and Wendy Hobden, Stephen Funnell)*

WORCESTER   SO8455

★**Marwood** (01905) 330460
The Tything (A38); some nearby parking; WR1 1JL Easy to miss this old building; quirky and civilised with a long narrow series of small linked areas, dark flagstones and broad floorboards, stripped or cast-iron-framed tables, the odd chandelier and art deco poster, open fires, upstairs room looking across to law courts, four well kept changing ales, enjoyable food from open sandwiches and tapas up, Mon steak night; background music; children (not in bar after 7.30pm) and dogs welcome, sunny flagstoned courtyard, open all day. *(Beth Aldridge)*

WORCESTER   SO8555

Plough (01905) 21381
Fish Street; WR1 2HN Traditional corner pub with two simple rooms off entrance lobby, six well kept interesting ales including Hobsons and Malvern Hills, farm cider/perry and good whisky choice, straightforward food available Fri, Sat lunchtimes plus rolls all day weekends and Sun roast; outside lavatories; small back terrace with cathedral view, open all day. *(Beth Aldridge)*

Post Office address codings confusingly give the impression that some pubs are in Worcestershire, when they're really in Gloucestershire, Herefordshire, Shropshire or Warwickshire (which is where we list them).

Yorkshire

 BECK HOLE
Birch Hall
NZ8202 Map 10

(01947) 896245 – www.beckhole.info/bhi.htm

Off A169 SW of Whitby, from top of Sleights Moor; YO22 5LE

Extraordinary place in lovely valley with friendly landlady, real ales and simple snacks

'What a treasure this is,' says one reader enthusiastically. It's a resolutely unchanging and tiny pub-cum-village shop in stunning surroundings by a bridge over a river and close to Thomason Foss waterfall; many customers are walkers with their dogs. The two simple rooms have built-in cushioned wall seats, wooden tables (one embedded with 136 pennies), flagstones or composition flooring, unusual items such as a tube of toothpaste priced 1/-3d, and a model train running around a head-height shelf. Black Sheep, North Yorkshire Beckwatter and a guest such as Half Moon Imbibe on handpump and several malt whiskies and wines by the glass. The shop sells postcards, sweets and ice-creams. There are benches outside in a streamside garden and one of the wonderful nearby walks is along a disused railway. They have a self-catering cottage for hire.

🍴 Bar snacks only, such as local pork pie, butties, scones and their famous beer cake.

Free house ~ Licensee Glenys Crampton ~ Real ale ~ No credit cards ~ Open 11-11; 11-3, 7.30-11 Weds-Sun in winter; closed Mon evening in winter, all day Tues Nov-Apr ~ Bar food available during opening hours ~ Children in small family room ~ Dogs welcome
Recommended by Elizabeth and Peter May, Sally and Colin Allen, Alexander and Trish Gendall, Thomas Green

 BLAKEY RIDGE
Lion 🍺 🛏
SE6799 Map 10

(01751) 417320 – www.lionblakey.co.uk

From A171 Guisborough–Whitby follow 'Castleton, Hutton-le-Hole' signposts; from A170 Kirkby Moorside–Pickering follow 'Keldholm, Hutton-le-Hole, Castleton' signposts; OS Sheet 100 map reference 679996; YO62 7LQ

Extended pub in fine scenery and open all day; popular food; bedrooms

Given its isolated position, it's always a surprise to find this 16th-c inn packed with customers. The low-beamed rambling bars have open fires, a few big high-backed rustic settles around cast-iron-framed tables, lots of small dining chairs, a nice leather sofa and stone walls hung with old engravings and photographs of the pub under snow (it can easily get cut off in winter – 40 days is the record so far). The fine choice of beers on handpump might include Black Sheep Best, Copper Dragon Golden Pippin, Great Yorkshire Yorkshire Golden, Theakstons Best, Old Peculier and XB and Thwaites Wainwright, they have 13 wines by the glass and several malt whiskies; background music and games machine. If you wish to stay here, you'll need to book well in advance as the inn is situated at the highest point of the North York Moors National Park (1,325-ft above sea level) with breathtaking valley views; breakfasts are first class.

Generous helpings of popular food includes sandwiches, deep-fried brie with cranberry sauce, prawn cocktail, mushroom stroganoff, home-cooked ham and egg, beef curry, duck breast in orange sauce, lamb chops in minted gravy, salmon in creamy white wine and prawn sauce, fillet steak with mushrooms and onion rings, and puddings such as hot chocolate fudge cake and banana split. *Benchmark main dish: steak and mushroom pie £11.95. Two-course evening meal £17.50.*

Free house ~ Licensees Barry, Diana, Paul and David Crossland ~ Real ale ~ Open 10am-11pm (midnight Sat) ~ Bar food 12-10 ~ Restaurant ~ Children welcome ~ Dogs allowed in bar ~ Wi-fi ~ Bedrooms: £42.50/£86 *Recommended by Ian Herdman, Dr J Barrie Jones, WAH, Martin and Joanne Sharp, Mike and Sarah Abbot*

BOROUGHBRIDGE
SE3966 Map 7
Black Bull £
(01423) 322413 – www.blackbullboroughbridge.co.uk
St James Square; B6265, just off A1(M); YO51 9AR

Bustling town pub with real ales, several wines by the glass and traditional bar food; bedrooms

If you're fed up with the A1, just drop in here for a break. It dates back to the 13th c and has been welcoming customers – travelling between England and Scotland – for hundreds of years. It's an attractive place with lots of separate drinking and eating areas where cheerful regulars drop in for a pint and a chat. The main bar area has a big stone fireplace and comfortable seats and is served through an old-fashioned hatch; there's also a cosy snug with traditional wall settles, and a tap room, lounge bar and restaurant. John Smiths Cask, Timothy Taylors Boltmaker and Wells Bombardier on handpump, six wines by the glass and 21 malt whiskies; dominoes and board games. The borzoi dog is called Spot and the two cats are Kia and Mershka. The hanging baskets are lovely.

Our Value Award is for the bar snacks menu: pork sausages with mash and onion gravy, thai-style beef strips with egg noodles and stir-fried vegetables in hot and sour sauce, gammon and egg, and spicy chicken goujons with chips, but they also offer chicken liver pâté with cumberland sauce, crispy duck salad with hoisin and plum sauce, pork tenderloin with pink peppercorn and calvados sauce, chicken wrapped in parma ham with wild mushrooms in port and garlic sauce, 10oz sirloin steak with trimmings and chips, and puddings such as jam sponge and custard and dark chocolate truffle torte. *Benchmark main dish: beer-battered haddock and chips £8.75. Two-course evening meal £15.00.*

Free house ~ Licensee Anthony Burgess ~ Real ale ~ Open 11-11 (midnight Fri, Sat); 11.30-11 Sun ~ Bar food 12-2, 6-9 (9.30 Fri, Sat); 12-2.30, 6-9 Sun ~ Restaurant ~ Children welcome ~ Dogs welcome ~ Wi-fi ~ Bedrooms: £50/£75 *Recommended by Denis and Margaret Kilner, Andrew and Michele Revell, Melanie and David Lawson, Michael Butler, Angela and Steve Heard*

BRADFIELD
SK2290 Map 7

Strines Inn £ 🛏

(0114) 285 1247 – www.thestrinesinn.webs.com

From A57 heading E of junction with A6013 (Ladybower Reservoir) take first left turn (signposted with Bradfield) then bear left; with a map can also be reached more circuitously from Strines signpost on A616 at head of Underbank Reservoir, W of Stocksbridge; S6 6JE

On the edge of the Peak District National Park, this bustling inn is popular with quite a mix of customers; bedrooms

In an area known as Little Switzerland, this isolated moorland inn was originally built as a manor house in 1275, although most of the building dates from the 16th c. The main bar has black beams liberally decked with copper kettles and so forth, a coal fire in a rather grand stone fireplace, quite a menagerie of stuffed animals, and homely red plush-cushioned traditional wooden wall benches and small chairs; background music. Two other rooms, to the right and left, are similarly furnished. Acorn Yorkshire Pride, Jennings Cocker Hoop and Marstons Pedigree on handpump, nine wines by the glass and eight malt whiskies. There are plenty of picnic-sets outside, as well as swings, a play area and peacocks and geese. The bedrooms have four-poster beds and a dining table (they serve breakfast in your room) and our readers enjoy staying here; the front room overlooks the Strines Reservoir and the surrounding scenery is superb.

 Hearty food includes hot and cold sandwiches, chicken liver and redcurrant pâté, smoked mackerel salad, broccoli, mushroom and stilton pasta bake, giant yorkshire pudding filled with cheese, parsley sauce or sausages, burgers with chips, cajun chicken, gammon with egg or pineapple, mammoth mixed grill, and puddings such as treacle sponge with custard and chocolate fudge cake with cream. *Benchmark main dish: steak in ale pie £9.99. Two-course evening meal £15.00.*

Free house ~ Licensee Bruce Howarth ~ Real ale ~ Open 10.30am-11pm ~ Bar food 12-9; 12-2.30, 5.30-8.30 weekdays in winter ~ Children welcome ~ Dogs welcome ~ Bedrooms: £70/£90 *Recommended by Dave Sutton, Edward and William Johnston, Julie Braeburn, Susan and Tim Boyle, Diana and Bertie Farr*

BROUGHTON
SD9450 Map 7

Bull 🌟 ♀

(01756) 792065 – www.thebullatbroughton.com

A59; BD23 3AE

Handsome, carefully refurbished inn making good use of pale oak and contemporary paintwork, fine choice of drinks and enjoyable bar food

Even when really busy – which this handsome stone inn deservedly usually is – staff remain warmly friendly and helpful. The various carefully furnished rooms have lots of pale oak, handsome flagstones, open log fires, exposed stone walls, built-in wall seats and a mix of dining chairs around polished tables and contemporary paintwork hung with photographs of local suppliers. Bowland Hen Harrier, Dark Horse Hetton Pale Ale, Moorhouses Premier Bitter and Thwaites 1709 on handpump, 15 malt whiskies, 11 wines by the glass and eight gins; background music and TV. In warm weather you can sit at the solid chairs and tables on the attractive terrace in front of the building. There's a lot to do and see nearby, including walking through Broughton Hall Estate's 3,000 acres of beautiful countryside and parkland.

First class food includes sandwiches (until 6pm; not Sunday), black pudding with a toasted muffin, fried onions, poached free-range egg and brown sauce, ham hock croquette with piccalilli and crackling salad, purple sprouting broccoli and jersey royal bake with cheese topping, steak in ale pie, tandoori chicken skewers with spicy potato and spinach, onion fritter and coriander yoghurt, fell-bred lamb burger with toppings, mint slaw and chips, seafood platter, lancashire hotpot, 30-day-aged rib-eye steak with dripping chips with a choice of sauces, and puddings such as warm sticky banana cake with toffee sauce and build your own sundae. *Benchmark main dish: beer-battered fish and chips £10.50. Two-course evening meal £17.50.*

Ribble Valley Inns ~ Manager Paul Morris ~ Real ale ~ Open 12-11 (10.30 Sun) ~ Bar food 12-9 (9.30 Fri, Sat); 12-8 Sun ~ Children welcome ~ Dogs allowed in bar ~ Wi-fi
Recommended by Steve Whalley, John and Sylvia Harrop, David Norris, Michael Butler, Chloe and Michael Swettenham, Pat and Tony Martin

COLTON
SE5444 Map 7
Old Sun 🏅 ⚲ ◖

(01904) 744261 – www.yeoldsuninn.co.uk
Off A64 York–Tadcaster; LS24 8EP

Whitewashed inn in pretty village with five real ales, highly thought-of food, and seats and an outside bar in the garden

Although many customers come to this neat 18th-c place for the attractively presented and very good food, this is a proper pub with loyal regulars and hard-working, hands-on licensees. The simply furnished bar has stools and small tables on bare boards, built-in window seats and high chairs against the bar where they serve Black Sheep and guests such as Pennine Amber Necker, Stancill Barnsley Bitter, Timothy Taylors Landlord and Yorkshire Heart Hearty Bitter on handpump and 13 wines by the glass. In the corner of the bar is a little shop selling locally produced chutney, oils, chocolates and so forth. Dining areas fan out from here with solid wooden and tartan-upholstered chairs and cushioned wall seats around polished tables on carpet, terracotta and stripped wooden floors, there's some exposed old brickwork and both open fires and a woodburning stove; background music. Outside, they have a log cabin-style garden bar with a wood-fired pizza oven, plus seats on a sunny front terrace and in the rambling garden with country views. Bedrooms are planned.

Cooked by the landlord, the interesting food includes lunchtime sandwiches and wraps, spiced lamb skewers on onion-seed flatbread with tzatziki dressing, creamy wild and button mushrooms in garlic and herb butter on toasted focaccia with goats cheese, spinach and broccoli frittata with sweet potatoes, pie of the day, tandoori-spiced snapper fillet with bombay potatoes, carrot bhaji and coriander yoghurt, chorizo-stuffed chicken breast with black pepper cauliflower and roasted onion cream, 10oz rib-eye steak with a choice of sauce and chips, and puddings such as crème brûlée of the day and chocolate, espresso and kumquat torte; they also offer afternoon teas. *Benchmark main dish: beer-battered fish and chips £9.95. Two-course evening meal £20.00.*

Free house ~ Licensees Ashley and Kelly McCarthy ~ Real ale ~ Open 12-3, 6-11; 6-11 Tues; 12-11 Fri, Sat; 12-10.30 Sun; closed Mon, lunchtime Tues ~ Bar food 12-2, 6-9; 12-9 Fri; 12-9.30 Sat; 12-8 Sun ~ Restaurant ~ Children in eating area of bar ~ Dogs welcome ~ Wi-fi
Recommended by John and Eleanor Holdsworth, Chloe and Michael Swettenham, Amy and Luke Buchanan

---

Children – if the details at the end of a featured entry don't mention them, you should assume that the pub does not allow them inside.

CONSTABLE BURTON

Wyvill Arms 🌟 ♀ 🍴 🛏

SE1690   Map 10

(01677) 450581 – www.thewyvillarms.co.uk

A684 E of Leyburn; DL8 5LH

Well run, friendly dining pub with interesting food, a dozen wines by the glass, real ales and efficient helpful service; bedrooms

As a stylish former farmhouse with lovely dales views, this is just right for lunch after visiting Constable Burton Hall opposite. The small bar area has a finely worked plaster ceiling with the Wyvill family's coat of arms, a mix of seating and an elaborate stone fireplace with a warm winter fire. The second bar has a lower ceiling with fans, leather seating, old oak tables, various alcoves and a model train on a railway track running around the room; a reception area includes a huge leather sofa that can seat up to eight people, another carved stone fireplace and an old leaded stained-glass church window partition. Both rooms are hung with pictures of local scenes. Theakstons Best, Wensleydale Coverdale Gamekeeper and a guest beer on handpump, plus nine wines by the glass and nine malt whiskies; chess, backgammon and dominoes. There are several large wooden benches under sizeable white parasols for outdoor dining and picnic-sets by a well. Bedrooms are comfortable (they've just opened three new ones) and breakfasts are generous.

 Good quality food includes lunchtime swandwiches, ham hock, chicken and cheese terrine with pear and apple chutney, pigeon breast with wild mushrooms and madeira sauce, spicy egyptian-style aubergine, courgette and red pepper stew topped with mozzarella, steak and onion pie, pork fillet, belly, cheek and black pudding with grain mustard mash and cider sauce, salmon on steamed leeks with a coarse-grain mustard sauce, duck confit on cabbage and bacon with black cherry sauce, rare-breed steaks with a choice of sauces, and puddings such as three-way brûlée (vanilla, blueberry and strawberry) and pecan pie. *Benchmark main dish: venison on haggis with fondant potato and blueberry and redcurrant sauce £17.95. Two-course evening meal £20.00.*

Free house ~ Licensee Nigel Stevens ~ Real ale ~ Open 11-3, 5.30 (6 Sun)-11; closed Mon ~ Bar food 12-2.15, 5.30-9 ~ Restaurant ~ Children welcome until 8.30 ~ Dogs allowed in bar ~ Wi-fi ~ Bedrooms: £65/£90 *Recommended by Hilary and Neil Christopher, Michael Doswell, Millie and Peter Downing, Barbara Brown, Christine and Tony Garrett, Frances and Hamish Porter*

CRAYKE

Durham Ox 🌟 ♀ 🛏

SE5670   Map 7

(01347) 821506 – www.thedurhamox.com

Off B1363 at Brandsby, towards Easingwold; West Way; YO61 4TE

Friendly, well run inn, with interesting décor in old-fashioned rooms, fine drinks and smashing food; comfortable bedrooms

In warm weather you can make the most of the seats in the courtyard garden, the bottom of which offers views on three sides over the Vale of York; on the fourth is a charming view to the medieval church on the hill – supposedly the very hill up which the Grand Old Duke of York marched his men. This is a civilised inn that appeals to both locals and visitors, who enjoy the pubby bar, excellent food and comfortable bedrooms. The old-fashioned lounge bar has venerable tables, antique seats and settles on flagstones, pictures and photographs on dark red walls, interesting satirical carvings in the panelling (Victorian copies of medieval pew ends), polished copper and brass and an enormous inglenook fireplace. In the bottom bar is a framed illustrated account of local history (some of it gruesome) dating to the 12th c, and a large framed print of the famous Durham Ox, which weighed 171 stone. The Burns Bar has a woodburning stove, exposed brickwork and large french windows that open on to a balcony. Black Sheep Best, Isaac Poad No.84 India Pale Ale, Timothy Taylors Boltmaker and York Guzzler on handpump, 20 wines by the glass, a dozen malt whiskies and interesting spirits; background music and board games. Bedrooms, in the main building or in renovated farm cottages (dogs allowed here), are well equipped, spacious and comfortable, and breakfasts are very good. The nearby A19 leads straight to a park & ride for York city centre. This is part of the Provenance Inns & Hotels group.

Highly rated food from a seasonal menu includes lunchtime sandwiches (not Sunday), chicken and wild mushroom terrine with celeriac rémoulade, salt and pepper squid with saffron aioli, cauliflower and almond gratin with parmesan and pine nut crust, chicken breast with rösti potato, wild mushrooms, confit shallot and chicken jus, barbecue sticky pork ribs with onion rings, coleslaw and skinny fries, singapore-style chilli soft shell crab with ginger, coriander and garlic, crispy pork belly with bacon jam, balsamic-glazed carrots and black pudding hash brown, lobster thermidor, and puddings such as crème brûlée of the day and crêpes suzette; they also offer a two- and three-course set lunch plus seven dishes at £7 (5.30-6.30pm except Saturday). *Benchmark main dish: seafood platter £24.00. Two-course evening meal £22.00.*

Free house ~ Licensee Michael Ibbotson ~ Real ale ~ Open 12-11.30 (10.30 Sun) ~ Bar food 12-2.30, 5.30-9.30; 12-3, 5.30-8.30 Sun ~ Restaurant ~ Children welcome ~ Dogs allowed in bar and bedrooms ~ Wi-fi ~ Bedrooms: £100/£120 *Recommended by Dr Peter Crawshaw, Naomi and Andrew Randall, Alister and Margery Bacon, Jamie and Lizzie McEwan*

EAST WITTON
Blue Lion 🏅 ♟ 🛏

SE1486 Map 10

(01969) 624273 – www.thebluelion.co.uk
A6108 Leyburn–Ripon; DL8 4SN

Civilised dining pub with a proper bar, real ales, highly enjoyable food and courteous service; comfortable bedrooms

Once found, our readers tend to return to this lovely 18th-c coaching inn on a regular basis – usually staying for a few days in the comfortable bedrooms with their pretty country furnishings; some are in the main house, others are in converted stables across the courtyard (these are dog-friendly). You'll find the welcome just as warm if you're only dropping in for a pint by the fire after a damp walk. The big squarish bar is civilised but informal with soft lighting, high-backed antique settles and old windsor chairs on turkish rugs and flagstones, ham hooks in the high ceiling decorated with dried wheat, teazles and so forth, a delft shelf filled with bric-a-brac, plus several prints, sporting caricatures and other pictures; daily papers. Black Sheep Best and Golden Sheep and Theakstons Best on handpump, an impressive wine list including a dozen (plus champagne) by the glass and 21 malt whiskies. The candlelit, high-ceilinged and elegant dining room has another open fire. Picnic-sets on the gravel outside look beyond the stone houses on the far side of the village green to Witton Fell, and there's also a large attractive garden at the back.

From a seasonal menu, the imaginative food includes sandwiches, seared king scallops with lemon risotto and crispy leeks, pigeon with toasted hazelnut, crispy bacon and sultana salad, potato and thyme rösti with mushroom, garlic and leek fricassée, braised blade of beef with roasted vegetables and baby onion, thyme and red wine sauce, salmon fillet with tomato compote and potato rösti, slow-roast honey-glazed duckling with apple gravy, venison haunch with celeriac purée and redcurrant sauce, and puddings such as iced liquorice terrine with roast fig and milk chocolate and amaretto tart with coffee cream and caramel sauce; there's also a two- and three-course set lunch (not Sunday). *Benchmark main dish: poached smoked haddock with mushroom and leek cream, a poached egg and gruyère £18.95. Two-course evening meal £24.00.*

Free house ~ Licensee Paul Klein ~ Real ale ~ Open 11-11 ~ Bar food 12-2, 7-9.15; 12-9.15 Sun ~ Restaurant ~ Children welcome ~ Dogs allowed in bar and bedrooms ~ Wi-fi ~ Bedrooms: /£94 *Recommended by Comus and Sarah Elliott, Simon Cleasby, Clive and Fran Dutson, Neil and Angela Huxter, Richard Kennell, Tim and Sue Halstead*

 ELSLACK SD9249 Map 7

Tempest Arms

(01282) 842450 – www.tempestarms.co.uk
Just off A56 Earby–Skipton; BD23 3AY

Busy inn with three log fires in stylish rooms, six real ales, good wines and well regarded food; bedrooms

Surrounded by lovely walks in beautiful scenery, this stylish 18th-c stone inn has a good mix of customers and plenty of character in the bar and surrounding dining areas. There are cushioned armchairs, built-in wall seats with comfortable cushions, stools, plenty of tables and three log fires – one greets you at the entrance and divides the bar and restaurant. Also, quite a bit of exposed stonework, amusing prints on cream walls, half a dozen real ales such as Dark Horse Hetton Pale Ale, Greene King Old Speckled Hen, Theakstons Best and Thwaites Wainwright on handpump, 12 wines by the glass, 30 malt whiskies and 20 gins; background music and board games. The tables outside are largely screened from the road by a raised bank. The bedrooms are comfortable and well equipped and make a perfect base for exploring the area.

 High quality, popular food includes sandwiches, box-baked camembert with garlic and basil topping, beer-soaked button mushrooms with creamy stilton sauce, sharing boards, vegetable curry with pineapple chutney, lasagne, chicken caesar salad, beef bourguignon, sea bream fillet with bacon and pea fricassée and salsa verde, slow-braised lamb with roasted root vegetables and mint and redcurrant gravy, fish and prawn pie with cheese topping, and puddings such as sherry trifle and sticky toffee pudding with toffee sauce. *Benchmark main dish: steak and mushroom in ale pudding £12.95. Two-course evening meal £21.00.*

Individual Inns ~ Managers Martin and Veronica Clarkson ~ Real ale ~ Open 11-11 (10.30 Sun) ~ Bar food 12-2.30, 6-9; 12-7.30 Sun ~ Restaurant ~ Children welcome ~ Dogs allowed in bar and bedrooms ~ Wi-fi ~ Bedrooms: £80/£105 *Recommended by John and Eleanor Holdsworth, John and Sylvia Harrop, David Fowler, Robert and Diana Ringstone*

FELIXKIRK SE4684 Map 10

Carpenters Arms ⭐ ♀

(01845) 537369 – www.thecarpentersarmsfelixkirk.com
Village signed off A170 E of Thirsk; YO7 2DP

Stylishly refurbished village pub with spacious rooms, real ales and highly regarded food; lodge-style bedrooms

True to its name, this friendly, moors-edge pub was once a carpenter's workshop. The opened-up bars are spacious and relaxed with dark beams and joists, candlelight and fresh flowers, stools against the panelled counter where they keep Black Sheep Best, Timothy Taylors Boltmaker, York Guzzler and a guest such as Black Sheep BAA BAA on handpump, around 24 wines by the glass, 18 malt whiskies, quite a few gins and farm cider, and a mix of chairs and tables on big flagstones or carpet. There's also a snug seating area with tartan armchairs in front of a double-sided woodburning stove. The red-walled dining room has a mix of antique and country kitchen chairs around scrubbed tables, and the walls throughout are hung with traditional prints, local pictures and maps; background music. There are seats and tables on a raised decked terrace overlooking the landscaped garden and picnic-sets at the front. The ultra-modern, well equipped bedrooms come with a drying wardrobe for wet days and a log-effect gas fire – they make a good base for both short walks and long-distance hikes (the Cleveland Way is in the locality); dogs are welcome. This is part of Provenance Inns & Hotels.

The appetising, seasonal food includes lunchtime sandwiches, sweet marinated mackerel escabeche with pickled vegetables, ham hock and parsley terrine with piccalilli, wild mushroom ravioli with girolles, sage and parmesan butter, beer-battered fish and chips, chicken breast with piperade and basil mash, seafood linguine with tomato and chilli, rare-breed 28-day-aged rib-eye steak with a choice of sauce, venison haunch steak with white bean cassoulet, and puddings such as grappa pannacotta with cherry compote and pine nut praline and pear frangipane tart with gingerbread ice-cream; they also offer a two- and three-course set lunch (not Sunday); steak night is Wednesday. *Benchmark main dish: roast halibut fillet with clams, saffron and potato and fennel broth £17.95. Two-course evening meal £23.00.*

Free house ~ Licensee Michael Ibbotson ~ Real ale ~ Open 8am–11pm ~ Bar food 12-2.30, 5.30-9.30; 12-3, 5.30-8.30 Sun ~ Restaurant ~ Children welcome ~ Dogs allowed in bar and bedrooms ~ Wi-fi ~ Bedrooms: £110/£120 *Recommended by Jim and Sue James, Mike Benton, Dave Webster, Michael Doswell, Comus and Sarah Elliott*

GRANTLEY

Grantley Arms ★☆ ♀

SE2369 Map 7

(01765) 620227 – www.grantleyarms.com
Village signposted off B6265 W of Ripon; HG4 3PJ

Relaxed and interesting dining pub with good food

The affable, hands-on licensees here make all their customers, both locals and visitors, genuinely welcome. The front bar has an easy-going local atmosphere, beams, a huge fireplace built of massive stone blocks and housing a woodburning stove, traditional furnishings such as comfortable dining chairs and polished tables set with evening tea-lights and some of the landlady's own paintings of ponies and dogs. The back dining room has crisp linen tablecloths, decorative plates and more paintings, mainly landscapes. Theakstons Best and a guest from a brewery such as Isaac Poad on handpump, nine wines by the glass, eight malt whiskies, a local farm cider and attentive friendly service. Teak tables and chairs on the flagstoned front terrace have a pleasant outlook, and Fountains Abbey and Studley Royal Water Garden (National Trust) is nearby.

Quite a choice of reliably good food (they make everything in-house) includes lunchtime open sandwiches, chicken liver parfait with plum chutney, prawns in lemon mayonnaise with avocado purée and lime and cucumber sorbet, mushroom stroganoff, a pie of the week, lager-battered haddock and chips, pork sausage meat wrapped in bacon and black pudding with cumberland and green peppercorn sauce, fresh fish dish of the day, confit rare-breed pork belly with apple purée, crackling and red wine sauce, and puddings such as a trio of chocolate terrine and pear and ginger sponge with custard; breakfast and coffee are served from 9am

Tuesday-Saturday and they offer a two- and three-course set lunch (not Monday or Sunday). *Benchmark main dish: fish pie £13.95. Two-course evening meal £20.50.*

Free house ~ Licensees Valerie Sails and Eric Broadwith ~ Real ale ~ Open 12-3, 5.30-10.30; 12-3, 5.30-11 Fri, Sat; 12-10.30 Sun; closed Mon except bank holidays ~ Bar food 12-2, 5.30-9 (9.30 Sat); 12-3.30, 5.30-8 Sun ~ Restaurant ~ Well behaved children welcome ~ Wi-fi
Recommended by Rona Mackinlay, Rosie and John Moore, Sophia and Hamish Greenfield, Kate Moran, John Stephenson, Trish and Karl Soloman

 GRINTON   SE0498   Map 10
Bridge Inn ▟ ⇌
(01748) 884224 – www.bridgeinn-grinton.co.uk
B6270 W of Richmond; DL11 6HH

Bustling pub with traditional, comfortable bars, log fires, real ales, malt whiskies and tasty bar food; neat bedrooms

This friendly old pub is in a pretty village opposite a lovely church known as the Cathedral of the Dales. There's a relaxing, comfortable atmosphere, bow-window seats and a pair of stripped traditional settles among more usual pub seats (all well cushioned), a good log fire and Jennings Cumberland, Marstons 61 Deep, Ringwood Boondoggle and Thwaites Wainwright on handpump; also, eight wines by the glass, 20 malt whiskies, ten gins and farm cider. On the right, a few steps lead down into a room with darts and ring the bull. On the left, past leather armchairs and a sofa next to a second log fire (and a glass chess set), is a large two-part dining room with décor in cream and shades of brown, and a modicum of fishing memorabilia. The bedrooms are neat, simple and comfortable, and breakfasts good. There are picnic-sets outside and fine surrounding walks.

 Decent food includes lunchtime baguettes, deep-fried breaded brie with cranberry sauce, crayfish cocktail in spicy marie rose sauce, a risotto of the day, beer-battered cod and chips, rare-breed burger with toppings, onion rings and chips, duck breast with garlic mash and star anise jus, gammon with egg or pineapple, 28-day-aged beef with trimmings, and puddings such as lemon and lime cheesecake with fruit compote and ginger sponge with toffee sauce and vanilla ice-cream. *Benchmark main dish: steak in ale pie £11.50. Two-course evening meal £17.00.*

Jennings (Marstons) ~ Lease Andrew Atkin ~ Real ale ~ Open 12-11 ~ Bar food 12-2.30, 6-9 ~ Restaurant ~ Children welcome ~ Dogs allowed in bar and bedrooms ~ Wi-fi ~ Live music Thurs evening ~ Bedrooms: £51/£82 *Recommended by Sabina and Gerald Grimshaw, Margaret McDonald, Liz and Mike Newton*

HALIFAX   SE1027   Map 7
Shibden Mill ◉ ♟ ▟ ⇌
(01422) 365840 – www.shibdenmillinn.com
Off A58 into Kell Lane at Stump Cross Inn, near A6036 junction; keep on, pub signposted from Kell Lane on left; HX3 7UL

Yorkshire Dining Pub of the Year

300-year-old interesting pub with a cosy rambling bar, four real ales and inventive, top class bar food; luxury bedrooms

To make the most of the lovely surrounding countryside, our readers regularly stay in the stylish and well equipped bedrooms here. The rambling bar is full of nooks and crannies and the bustling atmosphere is helped along by a good mix of locals and visitors. Some cosy side areas have banquettes heaped with cushions and rugs, well spaced attractive old tables and chairs, and candles in elegant iron holders giving a feeling of real intimacy; also, old hunting prints, country landscapes and a couple of big log fires. A beer named for them (from Moorhouses) plus Black Sheep, Little Valley Withens IPA and Stod Fold Gold on handpump, 27 wines by the glass from a wide list, 22 malt whiskies and 20 gins. There's also an upstairs restaurant; background music. Outside on the pleasant heated terrace are plenty of seats and tables, and the building is prettily floodlit at night.

Excellent food includes sandwiches, sea bream with squid ink pasta, brown crab ketchup and lemon purée, chicken liver parfait with chicken skin butter and tomato relish, burger with toppings, pickle and skinny fries, sweet potato and quinoa fritters with cauliflower purée and chargrilled and baked courgettes, duck breast and leg meat crispy pie with cherries, rhubarb and confit potatoes, curry-spiced monkfish with vermouth sauce, steamed and pickled mussels, sea herbs and shellfish oil, roe deer with potted rabbit, home-made salted butter, red cabbage and honey, and puddings such as lemon tart with raspberry sorbet and chocolate fondant, cocoa sorbet, white chocolate tuiles and dark chocolate sauce; they also offer a two- and three-course set lunch/early-bird menu (5.30-7pm, not weekends). *Benchmark main dish: trio of local lamb (rump, breast, cutlet) with aubergine fondant, tomatoes and black olives £19.00. Two-course evening meal £25.00.*

Free house ~ Licensee Glen Pearson ~ Real ale ~ Open 12-11 (10.30 Sun) ~ Bar food 12-2, 5.30-9; 12-2.30, 5.30-9.30 Fri, Sat; 12-7.30 Sun ~ Restaurant ~ Children welcome ~ Dogs allowed in bar ~ Wi-fi ~ Bedrooms: £105/£130 *Recommended by Laura Reid, Gordon and Margaret Ormondroyd, John and Eleanor Holdsworth, Pat and Tony Martin, Mr and Mrs P R Thomas, Celia and Geoff Clay*

HELPERBY

SE4370 Map 7

Oak Tree 🏅 ♀ 🛏

(01423) 789189 – www.theoaktreehelperby.com

Raskelf Road; YO61 2PH

Attractive pub with real ales in friendly bar, fine food in cosy dining rooms and seats on terrace; comfortable bedrooms

This is a handsome stone inn that's much enjoyed by both drinkers and diners. The informal bar has church chairs and elegant wooden dining chairs around a mix of wooden tables on old quarry tiles, flagstones and oak floorboards, prints and paintings on bold red walls, and open fires; background music. Stools line the counter where they keep Black Sheep Best, Timothy Taylors Boltmaker and a guest or two such as York Guzzler and Timothy Taylors Ram Tam on handpump, 24 wines by the glass, good collections of malt whiskies and gin, and farm cider. The main dining room has a large woodburner in a huge brick fireplace, a big central flower arrangement, high-backed burgundy and graceful wooden chairs around nice old tables on oak flooring, ornate mirrors and some striking artwork on exposed brick walls. French windows lead out to the terrace where there are plenty of seats and tables for summer dining. Upstairs, a private dining room has a two-way woodburner, a sitting room and doors to a terrace. The bedrooms are comfortable and well equipped. This belongs to the Provenance Inns & Hotels group.

As well as weekend breakfasts (8-11.30am), the highly thought-of food majors on first class steaks and grills – as well as serving lunchtime sandwiches, ham hock terrine with piccalilli, prawn cocktail, wild mushroom ravioli with girolles, sage and parmesan butter, beer-battered fish and chips, beef and onion pie, half roast chicken with piri-piri sauce, cajun salmon with sweet potato fries, corn and sour cream, and puddings such as mixed berry cheesecake and chocolate fudge cake; they also offer a two- and three-course set lunch (not Sunday). *Benchmark main dish: baby rack barbecue ribs £15.95. Two-course evening meal £21.00.*

Free house ~ Licensee Michael Ibbotson ~ Real ale ~ Open 12-2.30, 5.30-11; 12-3, 5.30-10.30 Sun ~ Bar food 12-2.30, 5.30-9.30 (8.30 Sun) ~ Restaurant ~ Children welcome ~ Dogs allowed in bar and bedrooms ~ Wi-fi ~ Bedrooms: £90/£100 *Recommended by George and Alison Bishop, Dr and Mrs R G J Telfer, Louise and Simon Peters, Dan and Belinda Smallbone*

ILKLEY
SE1347 Map 7
Wheatley Arms ♀ 🍴 🛏
(01943) 816496 – www.wheatleyarms.co.uk
Wheatley Lane, Ben Rhydding; LS29 8PP

Smart stone inn with a cosy bar, restful dining rooms, professional service and good food and drink; comfortable bedrooms

Always deservedly busy with plenty of contented customers, this is a substantial inn close to wonderful walks. The interconnected dining rooms have all manner of nice antique and upholstered chairs and stools and prettily cushioned wooden or rush-seated settles around assorted tables, rugs on bare boards, some bold wallpaper, various prints and two log fires; our readers like the smart garden room. One half of the locals' bar has tub armchairs and other comfortable seats, the other has tartan-cushioned wall seats and mate's chairs, with classic wooden stools against the counter where they keep Ilkley Mary Jane, Thwaites Original, Wharfedale Blonde and a quickly changing guest on handpump. Also, 23 wines by the glass (including prosecco and champagne), a dozen malt whiskies and a farm cider; background music and TV. There are seats and tables on the terrace. Bedrooms are individually decorated, well equipped and comfortable (some have a private roof terrace) and breakfasts are good.

As well as breakfasts (8-11am Monday-Saturday; 8-10.30 Sunday), the reliably good food includes sandwiches (until 5.30pm), smoked salmon and crab ballotine with soused cucumber salad, lemon crème fraîche and dill oil, ham hock terrine with pea pannacotta, chicken caesar salad, beetroot and chive risotto with parmesan, sharing boards, fish pie with herb crumb topping, lamb burger with toppings, harissa yoghurt, onion rings and chips, thyme and garlic roasted chicken ballotine, beetroot dauphinoise, shallot purée and mustard and chervil cream, and puddings such as iced passion-fruit parfait with raspberry and mango coulis and sticky toffee pudding with toffee sauce. *Benchmark main dish: lamb shoulder, cauliflower and cumin purée, coriander croquette and date dressing £16.95. Two-course evening meal £22.00.*

Individual Inns ~ Licensee Steve Benson ~ Real ale ~ Open 11-11 (midnight Sat); 11-10.30 Sun ~ Bar food 12-2, 5.30-9; 12-7 Sun ~ Restaurant ~ Children welcome ~ Dogs allowed in bar ~ Wi-fi ~ Live jazz first Sun lunchtime of month ~ Bedrooms: £80/£90 *Recommended by Michael Butler, Caroline Sullivan, Gordon and Margaret Ormondroyd, Dan and Nicki Barton, Colin Humphreys*

KIRKBY FLEETHAM
SE2894 Map 10
Black Horse ♀ 🍴 🛏
(01609) 749010 – www.blackhorseinnkirkbyfleetham.com
Village signposted off A1 S of Catterick; Lumley Lane; DL7 0SH

Attractively reworked country inn with well liked food, good drinks choice and cheerful atmosphere; comfortable bedrooms

This is a charming village inn with plenty of stylish character. The long softly lit beamed bar on the right has flagstones, cushioned wall seats, some little settles and high-backed dining chairs by the log fire at one end, Black Sheep Best, Timothy Taylors Landlord and York Guzzler on handpump and 11 wines by the glass. The cosy snug has darts. A dining room towards the back is light and open, with big bow windows on either side and a casual contemporary look thanks to loose-covered dining chairs or pastel garden settles with scatter cushions around tables painted pale green; background pop music. The neat sheltered back lawn and flagstoned side terrace have teak seats and tables and there are picnic-sets at the front; quoits. Bedrooms are attractive and comfortable with plenty of antique charm; breakfasts are good.

Enjoyable food includes confit chicken, leek and wild mushroom terrine with apricot-dressed leaves, twice-baked goats cheese soufflé with pear, walnut and watercress, mushroom, sage and hazlenut tagliatelle with parmesan, a pie of the day, chicken shawarma with flatbread, garlic aioli, mint yoghurt and skinny fries, moroccan-spiced lamb shank with couscous, apricot and ras el hanout spices, beer-battered fish and chips, pork three-ways (belly, fillet, black pudding) with bubble and squeak, apple and cider jus, and puddings such as chocolate mousse with cherry textures and pineapple frangipane tart with coconut sorbet and mango gel; fish and chip night is Friday (takeaway too) and steak night is Tuesday. *Benchmark main dish: medley of fresh fish of the day with chips £20.00. Two-course evening meal £24.00.*

Free house ~ Licensee Simon Wade ~ Real ale ~ Open 12-11.30 ~ Bar food 12-2.30, 5-9; 12-8 Sun ~ Restaurant ~ Children welcome ~ Dogs allowed in bar and bedrooms ~ Wi-fi ~ Bedrooms: /£120 *Recommended by Chantelle and Tony Redman, Karl and Frieda Bujeya, Andrea and Philip Crispin*

LEDSHAM
SE4529 Map 7

Chequers 🌟 ♀

(01977) 683135 – www.thechequersinn.com

1.5 miles from A1(M) junction 42: follow Leeds signs, then Ledsham signposted; Claypit Lane; LS25 5LP

Friendly pub with hands-on landlord, log fires in several beamed rooms, real ales and interesting food; pretty back terrace

This neatly kept and very well run pub is in an attractive village and handy for the A1, so it's not surprising that you need to book in advance to be sure of a table here. The several small, individually decorated rooms have plenty of character, with low beams, log fires, lots of cosy alcoves, toby jugs and all sorts of knick-knacks on the walls and ceilings (cricket fans will be interested to see a large photo in one room of four yorkshire heroes). From the little old-fashioned, panelled-in central servery they offer Brown Cow Sessions Pale Ale, Leeds Best, Theakstons Best, Timothy Taylors Landlord and a guest beer on handpump and eight wines by the glass. The lovely sheltered two-level terrace at the back has lots of tables among roses, and the hanging baskets and flowers are very pretty. RSPB Fairburn Ings reserve is not far and the ancient village church is worth a visit.

High quality food includes baguettes, chicken liver pâté with spiced chutney, king prawns in creamy garlic sauce, puy lentil and sweet potato pie in garlic and tomato sauce, corn beef hash layered with onions and potatoes, venison steak with apple and cranberry jus and braised red cabbage, calves liver on mash with shallot and red wine sauce, duck breast with stir-fried vegetables and soy, pancetta-wrapped monkfish on pea purée, and puddings such as cheesecake of the day and chocolate sponge pudding with hot chocolate sauce. *Benchmark main dish: steak in ale pie £13.45. Two-course evening meal £21.00.*

Free house ~ Licensee Chris Wraith ~ Real ale ~ Open 11-11; 12-6 Sun; closed Sun evening ~ Bar food 12-9; 12-5 Sun ~ Restaurant ~ Children allowed until 8.30pm ~ Dogs allowed in bar ~ Wi-fi *Recommended by Stephen Woad, Denis and Margaret Kilner, Noel and Judy Garner, John and Eleanor Holdsworth, Gerald Warner*

LEVISHAM
Horseshoe 🏆 🛏

SE8390　Map 10

(01751) 460240 – www.horseshoelevisham.co.uk
Off A169 N of Pickering; YO18 7NL

Friendly village pub with super food, neat rooms, real ales and seats on the village green; bedrooms

We get enthusiastic praise on all aspects of this particularly well run pub from our readers. The bustling bars have beams, blue banquettes, wheelback and captain's chairs around a variety of tables on polished wooden floors, vibrant landscapes by a local artist on the walls and a log fire in the stone fireplace; an adjoining snug has a woodburning stove, comfortable leather sofas and old photographs of the pub and the lovely village. Served by the courteous staff are Black Sheep and guests such as Cropton Yorkshire Moors and Timothy Taylors Golden Best on handpump, 14 wines by the glass and 15 malt whiskies. There are seats on the attractive green, with more in the back garden. The clean, comfortable bedrooms make a good base for exploring the North York Moors National Park; breakfasts are hearty. The historic church is worth a visit. This is sister pub to the Fox & Rabbit in Lockton.

 Super food cooked by one of the landlords includes sandwiches, crab and smoked salmon terrine, black pudding wrapped in bacon with sauté potatoes and apple sauce, butternut squash, leek and pine nut risotto with parmesan, steak in ale pie, gammon with egg or pineapple, lamb shank with rosemary mash and mint gravy, pork stroganoff with rice, chicken wrapped in bacon on creamed leeks, sea bass with peppers, onions and spinach, and puddings such as lime cheesecake and chocolate truffle torte. *Benchmark main dish: rare-breed pork belly with thyme mash and cider and apple gravy £13.95. Two-course evening meal £20.50.*

Free house ~ Licensees Toby and Charles Wood ~ Real ale ~ Open 11-11 (10.30 Sun) ~ Bar food 12-2, 6-8.30 ~ Children welcome ~ Dogs allowed in bar ~ Wi-fi ~ Bedrooms: £45/£85 *Recommended by Ian Herdman, Ian and Rose Lock, John Robinson, Dr and Mrs F McGinn, John Coatsworth, Stuart and Natalie Granville, Alex Macdonald, Dr K Nesbitt*

LEYBURN
Sandpiper 🏆 ♟ 🛏

SE1190　Map 10

(01969) 622206 – www.sandpiperinn.co.uk
Just off Market Place; DL8 5AT

Appealing food and cosy bar for drinkers in 17th-c inn, real ales and impressive choice of whisky; bedrooms

There's a fair balance in this pretty little stone cottage between those dropping in for a drink and a chat and diners keen to enjoy the highly regarded and interesting food. The cosy bar has a couple of black beams in the low ceiling, a log fire and wooden or cushioned built-in wall seats around a few tables. The back snug, up three steps, features lovely dales photographs – get here early if you want a seat. There are photographs and a woodburning stove in a stone fireplace by the linenfold panelled bar counter; to the left is the attractive restaurant, with dark wooden tables and chairs on bare boards and fresh flowers. Black Sheep Best and a couple of guests such as Wensleydale Semer Water and Yorkshire Dales Nappa Scar on handpump, 100 malt whiskies, good wines by the glass and a growing number of gins; background music and dominoes. In good weather, you can enjoy a drink on the front terrace among the pretty hanging baskets and flowering climbers. Bedrooms are well equipped and comfortable.

 Cooked by the chef-patron, the enjoyable food includes sandwiches, caramelised pork belly with seared scallops and butternut squash purée, game scotch egg with beer kethcup, twice-cooked cheese soufflé with roasted beetroot, rib burger with toppings and fries, sea bass on leek and smoked salmon risotto, local venison with chorizo and caramelised shallots, 36-day-aged rib-eye steak with peppercorn sauce, and puddings such as chocolate marquise with frozen salted caramel custard, blow-torched marshmallow and popcorn and cinnamon and nutmeg rice pudding with mango compote. *Benchmark main dish: crispy duck leg with mushrooms, smoked bacon and roasted onions £16.95. Two-course evening meal £22.00.*

Free house ~ Licensees Jonathan and Janine Harrison ~ Real ale ~ Open 11.30-3, 6-10.30 (11 Sat); 11.30-3, 6-10 Sun; closed Mon, some winter Tues, two weeks early Jan ~ Bar food 12-2.30, 6.30-8.30 (9 Sat); 12-2.30, 6-8 Sun ~ Restaurant ~ Children welcome ~ Dogs allowed in bar and bedrooms ~ Wi-fi ~ Bedrooms: £90/£100 *Recommended by Mary Hunstings, Lynda and Trevor Smith, Clive and Fran Dutson, Caroline and Steve Archer, Dan and Belinda Smallbone*

LINTON IN CRAVEN
SD9962 Map 7
Fountaine ◀

(01756) 752210 – www.fountaineinnatlinton.co.uk
Off B6265 Skipton–Grassington; BD23 5HJ

Neatly kept pub with attractive furnishings, open fires, five real ales and popular food; bedrooms

'What a big shame this pub is so far from our home,' says one reader – and many others agree. It's the civilised and friendly sort of place that customers visit regularly, particularly after enjoying one of the fine nearby walks. The bars have beams and white-painted joists in low ceilings, log fires (one in a beautifully carved heavy wooden fireplace), attractive built-in cushioned wall benches and stools around a mix of copper-topped tables, little wall lamps and quite a few prints on the pale walls. John Smiths, Tetleys Cask, Thwaites Original and guests such as Dark Horse Hetton Pale Ale and Thwaites Wainwright on handpump, 17 wines by the glass and a dozen malt whiskies served by efficient staff; background music, darts and board games. The terrace, looking across the road to the duck pond, has teak benches and tables under green parasols, and the hanging baskets are most attractive. The well equipped bedrooms are in a converted barn behind the pub.

Good country cooking includes dishes such as sandwiches, chicken, chorizo and black pudding salad, crispy duck pancakes, sharing platters, mushroom, cranberry and brie wellington with creamy herb sauce, cumberland sausage with bacon, cabbage and gravy, roasted half duck with spring onion, ginger and honey sauce, beer-battered fish and chips, slow-braised lamb shank with redcurrant and mint sauce, fish stew in tomato sauce, slow-cooked beef in ale with mash and yorkshire pudding, and puddings such as lemon posset with home-made shortbread and banoffi pie. *Benchmark main dish: steak pie £11.95. Two-course evening meal £20.00.*

Individual Inns ~ Manager Christopher Gregson ~ Real ale ~ Open 11-11; 12-10.30 Sun ~ Bar food 12-9 ~ Restaurant ~ Children welcome ~ Dogs allowed in bar ~ Wi-fi ~ Bedrooms: £75/£99 *Recommended by Gordon and Margaret Ormondroyd, Lynda and Trevor Smith, B and M Kendall, Peter Smith and Judith Brown, Michael Breeze, Dr and Mrs F McGinn*

LOCKTON   SE8488   Map 10

Fox & Rabbit

(01751) 460213 – www.foxandrabbit.co.uk

A169 N of Pickering; YO18 7NQ

**Neatly kept pub with fine views, a friendly atmosphere,
real ales and highly regarded food**

The two brothers running this bustling pub work hard to make sure
standards remain as high as ever. The interconnected rooms have
beams, panelling and some exposed stonework, wall settles and banquettes,
dark pubby chairs and tables on tartan carpet, a log fire and an inviting
atmosphere; fresh flowers, brasses, china plates, prints and old local
photographs too. The locals' bar is busy and cheerful and there are
panoramic views from the comfortable restaurant – it's worth arriving early
to bag a window seat. Black Sheep, Cropton Yorkshire Moors and Timothy
Taylors Golden Best on handpump, seven wines by the glass, 12 malt
whiskies and home-made elderflower cordial; background music, games
machine, pool, juke box and board games. Outside are seats under parasols
and some picnic sets. The inn is in the North York Moors National Park, so
there are plenty of surrounding walks. They have a caravan site. This is sister
pub to the Horseshoe in Levisham.

Pleasing seasonal food includes lunchtime sandwiches, crab and smoked salmon
terrine, deep-fried brie with sweet chilli sauce, wild mushroom and spinach
cannelloni, a curry of the day, venison burger with toppings, onion rings, coleslaw and
chips, slow-cooked rare-breed pork belly with dauphinoise potatoes, apple sauce and
cider jus, lamb shank with yorkshire pudding, beef stroganoff, sea bass fillet with garlic
king prawns, samphire, mixed peppers and tomatoes, and puddings such as lemon tart
and sticky toffee pudding with toffee sauce. *Benchmark main dish: steak in ale pie
£11.95. Two-course evening meal £20.50.*

Free house – Licensees Toby and Charles Wood ~ Real ale ~ Open 11-11 ~ Bar food 12-2,
5-8.30; light snacks 2-4pm ~ Restaurant ~ Children welcome ~ Dogs allowed in bar ~ Wi-fi
*Recommended by Ian Herdman, Ian and Rose Lock, Michael Butler, Joe and Belinda Smart,
Mark Hamill*

LOW CATTON   SE7053   Map 7

Gold Cup

(01759) 371354 – www.goldcuplowcatton.com

*Village signposted with High Catton off A166 in Stamford Bridge or A1079
at Kexby Bridge; YO41 1EA*

**Friendly, pleasant pub with attractive bars, real ales, decent
dependable food, seats in garden and ponies in paddock**

You can be sure of a warm welcome from the long-serving licensees in
this bustling village pub. The neatly kept bar has a cheerful atmosphere,
plenty of smart tables and chairs on stripped wooden floors, quite a few
pictures, an open fire at one end opposite a gas-effect stove and coach lights
on the rustic-looking walls. The spacious restaurant, with solid wooden pews
and tables (said to be made from a single oak tree), has pleasant views of the
surrounding fields. John Smiths Cask and Theakstons Best on handpump;
background music and pool. There's a grassed area in the garden for children
and the back paddock houses three ponies, Cinderella, Dobbin and Polly. The
pub has fishing rights on the adjacent River Derwent.

Good food includes lunchtime sandwiches (not Sunday), beer-battered mushrooms with garlic mayonnaise, smoked salmon, prawn and crayfish in marie rose sauce, thai red vegetarian curry, roast beef and yorkshire pudding, slow-cooked lamb rump in red wine gravy, salmon fillet with spinach and mushroom sauce, marinated chicken with tomato and basil sauce topped with stilton, steak in ale pie, whitby scampi and chips, and puddings; they also offer a two- and three-course candlelit weekday supper menu. *Benchmark main dish: crispy pork belly and black pudding with redcurrant gravy £14.95. Two-course evening meal £20.50.*

Free house ~ Licensees Pat and Ray Hales ~ Real ale ~ Open 12-2.30, 6-11; 12-11 Sat; 12-10.30 Sun; closed Mon lunchtime ~ Bar food 12-2, 6-8.30; 12-8.30 Sat; 12-8 Sun ~ Restaurant ~ Children welcome ~ Dogs allowed in bar ~ Wi-fi *Recommended by Dave Braisted, Gordon and Margaret Ormondroyd, John Saville, Mark and Sîan Edwards*

MALHAM
SD9062   Map 7

Lister Arms ♀ ◖ ⇌

(01729) 830330 – www.listerarms.co.uk
Off A65 NW of Skipton; BD23 4DB

Friendly inn in fine countryside with cosy bars and dining room, enjoyable food and seats outside; comfortable bedrooms

This is a handsome, creeper-covered inn with views over the Yorkshire Dales National Park. One bar has a medley of cushioned dining chairs and leather or upholstered armchairs around antique wooden tables on slate flooring, with a big deer's head above the inglenook fireplace. A second bar has a small brick fireplace with logs piled to each side, rustic slab tables, cushioned wheelback chairs and comfortable wall seats. Thwaites Original Bitter, Lancaster Bomber, Nutty Black and Wainwright and guests such as Dark Horse Hetton Pale Ale and Settle Signal Main Line on handpump, 20 wines by the glass and Weston's farm cider. A woodburning stove stands in the fireplace of the airy dining room which has swagged curtains and smartly upholstered high-backed and pale wooden farmhouse chairs around rustic tables on bare floorboards. The flagstoned and gravelled courtyard has seats and benches around tables under parasols – some overlook the small green at the front. The bedrooms (in the pub, next-door cottage and barn conversion) are attractive, warm and comfortable with views over the village green, and breakfasts are good and hearty.

Rewarding food in generous helpings includes sandwiches, chicken liver and wild mushroom pâté, box-baked camembert with tomato jam, platters, home-cooked honey-glazed ham and free-range eggs, local pork sausages with mash and onion gravy, burgers with toppings, tomato relish and fries, sunblush tomatoes, tomato pesto and spring onion pasta, moules marinière with chips, cajun chicken with coleslaw and fries, roast salmon with pea and green bean risotto, and puddings such as chocolate and hazelnut brownie with hot chocolate sauce and chocolate ice-cream and caramelised lemon tart with citrus crème fraîche. *Benchmark main dish: pie of the day £13.50. Two-course evening meal £20.00.*

Thwaites ~ Manager Darren Dunn ~ Real ale ~ Open 8am-11pm ~ Bar food 12-9.30 (10 Fri, Sat in summer) ~ Restaurant ~ Children welcome ~ Dogs allowed in bar and bedrooms ~ Wi-fi ~ Bedrooms: £97/£103 *Recommended by John and Sylvia Harrop, Tim and Sue Halstead, Steve Whalley, Gary and Marie Miller*

MARTON-CUM-GRAFTON

SE4263 Map 7

Punch Bowl 🏮❉ ⚲

(01423) 322519 – www.thepunchbowlmartoncumgrafton.com

Signed off A1 3 miles N of A59; YO51 9QY

Refurbished old inn in lovely village, with character bar and dining rooms, real ales, interesting food and seats on terrace

There are plenty of original features in this handsome and particularly well run old inn. The main bar is beamed and timbered with a built-in window seat at one end, lots of red leather-topped stools, and cushioned settles and church chairs around pubby tables on flagstones or bare floorboards. Black Sheep Best, Timothy Taylors Boltmaker and guests such as Great Yorkshire Yorkshire Lager and Rudgate Jorvik Blonde on handpump, 24 wines by the glass and a good number of malt whiskies and gins. Open doorways lead to five separate dining areas, each with an open fire, heavy beams and an attractive mix of cushioned wall seats and wooden or high-backed red-leather dining chairs around antique tables on oak floors; the red walls are covered with photographs of vintage car races and racing drivers, sporting-themed cartoons and old photographs of the pub and village. Up a spiral staircase is a coffee loft and a private dining room. There are seats and tables in the back courtyard where they hold summer barbecues. This is part of Provenance Inns & Hotels.

 Interesting food from a seasonal menu includes lunchtime sandwiches, king scallops with black pudding, peas and pancetta, ham hock terrine with piccalilli, caramelised onion and blue cheese tart with charred broccoli and walnut salad, burger with toppings, onion rings and fries, seafood linguine with chilli and tomato sauce, chicken breast with celeriac gratin and mustard and tarragon cream, fillet of beef chateaubriand (for two) with chunky chips and a choice of sauces, and puddings such as baked alaska and grappa pannacotta with cherry compote and pine nut praline; they also offer an early-bird menu (5.30-6.45, not Saturday). *Benchmark main dish: braised beef with creamy mash and shallot and mushroom jus £15.95. Two-course evening meal £21.00.*

Free house ~ Licensee Michael Ibbotson ~ Real ale ~ Open 12-3, 5-11; 12-11 Sat; 12-10.30 Sun ~ Bar food 12-2.30, 5.30-9.30; 12-8 Sun ~ Children welcome ~ Dogs allowed in bar ~ Wi-fi *Recommended by Gordon and Margaret Ormondroyd, Ian Duncan, Paul Scofield, Daphne and Robert Staples, Sue Parry Davies, Alison and Tony Livesley, Jacob Matt*

MASHAM

SE2281 Map 10

Black Sheep Brewery ◀

(01765) 680100 – www.blacksheepbrewery.co.uk

Brewery signed off Leyburn Road (A6108); HG4 4EN

Lively place with friendly staff, unusual décor in big warehouse room, well kept beers and popular food

There's a bar in the huge upper warehouse room here where they keep their own-brewed Black Sheep Ale, Best, Golden Sheep and Riggwelter plus a couple of other changing Black Sheep beers such as BAA BAA and Shearer on handpump, several wines by the glass and a fair choice of soft drinks. Most of the good-sized tables have cheery gingham tablecloths and brightly cushioned green café chairs, and there are some modern pubbier tables near the bar. The space is partly divided by free-standing partitions and there's a good deal of bare woodwork, with cream-painted rough stonework and green-painted steel girders and pillars; background music and friendly service. The tours of the sizeable brewery are popular and a glass wall lets you see into the brewing exhibition centre; there's also a shop selling beers and beer-related items from pub games and T-shirts to pottery and fudge. Picnic-sets out on the grass.

🍴 Good pubby food choices include sandwiches, chestnut mushrooms filled with blue cheese pâté with cumberland sauce, scallops in garlic and herb butter with white wine and gruyère sauce, grazing and sharing plates, tomato and cauliflower macaroni cheese, rack of baby back barbecue ribs with coleslaw and skinny fries, local pork sausages in ale and onion gravy with mash, cajun chicken with tomato salsa and burgers with toppings – both with fries, lamb shank in ale with sage mash, flat-iron steak with onion rings and a choice of sauces, and puddings such as sticky toffee pudding with stout and toffee sauce and cinnamon doughnuts with hot chocolate sauce. *Benchmark main dish: steak in ale pie £12.50. Two-course evening meal £18.00.*

Free house ~ Licensee Paul Casterton ~ Real ale ~ Open 10am-5pm Sun-Weds, 10am-11pm Thurs, Fri, Sat ~ Bar food 12-2.30 Sun-Weds; 12-2.30, 6-8.30 Thurs-Sat; 12-3 Sun ~ Children welcome ~ Wi-fi *Recommended by Janet and Peter Race, Jeremy Snow, Nigel Havers, Tony and Wendy Hobden, Barbara and Phil Bowie, Stuart and Natalie Granville*

 MOULTON   NZ2303   Map 10
Black Bull 🏅 ♎

(01325) 377556 – www.theblackbullmoulton.com
Just E of A1, a mile E of Scotch Corner; DL10 6QJ

Character pub with a traditional bar, a large open restaurant, high quality food and courteous efficient service; bedrooms

They stress that they're a pub with good food rather than a restaurant with a bar, and they certainly serve a fine range of drinks, including Black Sheep Best, Timothy Taylors Boltmaker and a guest such as Theakstons Black Bull Bitter on handpump, 24 wines by the glass and over 20 malt whiskies. There's a convivial atmosphere, some original panelling and leather wall seating topped with scatter cushions, plus a dining area with cushioned wooden chairs around a mix of tables on pale flagstones, a couple of leather armchairs in front of a woodburner in a brick fireplace, and horse tack, stone bottles, wooden pails and copper items on windowsills. The dining extension has high windows, a wooden floor, attractive brown-orange high-backed dining chairs or cushioned settles and a rather nice wire bull; background music. Doors from here lead out to a neat terrace with modern seats and tables among pots of rosemary or tall bay trees. They hope to open bedrooms in the near future. This is part of Provenance Inns & Hotels.

🌟 Accomplished food includes sandwiches, crispy duck salad with noodles and orange and sesame dressing, prawn cocktail, pea and mint risotto topped with cheese, braised pig cheeks with ham hock bonbon, baby fennel, apple compote and mustard mash, stone bass with celeriac, samphire, mushrooms and red wine, chicken breast with thyme fondants, girolle mushrooms and madeira jus, 10oz 30-day-aged sirloin steak with chips and a choice of sauce, and puddings such as banana arctic roll with passion fruit, popcorn and chocolate and lemon and coconut posset; they also offer a two- and three-course set lunch. *Benchmark main dish: gourmet fish pie £16.50. Two-course evening meal £23.00.*

Free house ~ Licensee Michael Ibbotson ~ Real ale ~ Open 12-3, 5-11; 12-11 Fri-Sun ~ Bar food 12-2.30, 5.30-9.30; 12-3, 5.30-8.30 Sun ~ Restaurant ~ Children welcome ~ Dogs allowed in bar ~ Wi-fi *Recommended by Christopher Mannings, Tony Selinger, Richard and Tessa Ibbot, Professor James Burke, Julia and Fiona Barnes*

It's very helpful if you let us know up-to-date food prices when you report on pubs.

NUN MONKTON

SE5057   Map 7

Alice Hawthorn 🏠⭐ ♀

(01423) 330303 – www.thealicehawthorn.com

Off A59 York–Harrogate; The Green; YO26 8EW

Carefully and attractively renovated pub with appealing décor, imaginative food and picturesque setting

This is a lovely village and the pub (formerly called the Bluebell Inn) is by the broad green where cattle graze and England's tallest maypole stands. There's a cosy bar (dogs and boots are welcome here), with comfortable seats and an open fire, Black Sheep BAA BAA, Timothy Taylors Landlord, Yorkshire Heart Hearty Bitter (brewed in the village) and a guest beer on handpump and good wines by the glass served by friendly, helpful staff. The elegant dining rooms are divided by a two-way open fire and have button-back wall seating and beige plush and upholstered chairs around all manner of tables, plus candles in lanterns; a snug (the oldest part of the building) leads off here with big piles of logs to each side of another log fire. They grow their own fruit and vegetables in raised beds in the sunny garden which has plenty of seats and tables.

 Imaginative food using local, seasonal produce includes queen scallops with garlic butter, cheddar and gruyère, fresh tuna spring rolls with wasabi and asian slaw, chilli and lime rice wine dressing, salt-baked sweet potato, chorizo, miso hash, labneh, poached egg, cashew and anise brittle, beer-battered fish and triple-cooked chips, crisp confit duck leg with fried duck egg and maple glaze, venison haunch with crisp potato, mulled spice beetroot, chervil root and roast plum and red wine reduction, and puddings such as lemon tart with raspberry coulis and chocolate brownie sundae with salted caramel sauce. *Benchmark main dish: confit duck on a waffle with duck egg and jus £15.00. Two-course evening meal £21.00.*

Free house ~ Licensee Katherine Doughty ~ Real ale ~ Open 12-11; 12-8 Sun; closed Mon, Tues ~ Bar food 12-2.30, 5.30-9; 12-5 Sun ~ Restaurant ~ Children welcome ~ Dogs allowed in bar ~ Wi-fi *Recommended by John and Eleanor Holdsworth, Sarah and David Gibbs, Ben and Jenny Settle*

RIPPONDEN

SE0419   Map 7

Old Bridge ♀ 🍺

(01422) 822595   www.theoldbridgeinn.co.uk

From A58, best approach is Elland Road (opposite the Golden Lion), park opposite the church in pub's car park and walk back over ancient hump-back bridge; HX6 4DF

Pleasant old pub run by a long-serving family with relaxed communicating rooms and well-liked food

If you have trouble finding this family-run 14th-c pub (there's no traditional pub sign outside), just head for the church which is next door. The three communicating rooms, each on a slightly different level, have oak settles built into window recesses in the thick stone walls, antique oak tables, rush-seated chairs and comfortably cushioned free-standing settles, a few well chosen pictures and prints on the panelled or painted walls and a big woodburning stove. Timothy Taylors Best, Golden Best, Landlord and Ram Tam, a couple of guests such as Abbeydale Deception and Goose Eye Chinook Blonde on handpump, quite a few foreign bottled beers, 15 wines by the glass, 30 malt whiskies and farm cider; quick, efficient service. Seats in the garden overlook the little River Ryburn. Do note the beautiful medieval packhorse bridge.

The ever-popular weekday lunchtime cold meat and salad buffet has been running since 1963 (they also offer soup and sandwiches at lunch). Evening and weekend choices include bacon and black pudding salad with poached egg and mustard and honey dressing, king scallops on carrot and cumin purée with bacon crumb, a pie and a risotto of the day, sea bass with king prawns and charred asparagus with lemon and herb butter sauce, chicken wrapped in bacon with garlic roast potatoes and creamy wholegrain mustard sauce, lamb rump with rosemary mash and red wine and redcurrant jus, beer-battered haddock and dripping chips, and puddings such as ginger sponge with ginger sauce and crumble of the day. *Benchmark main dish: smoked haddock and spinach pancakes £11.25. Two-course evening meal £21.00.*

Free house ~ Licensees Tim and Lindsay Eaton Walker ~ Real ale ~ Open 12-3, 5-11; 12-11 Sat; 12-10.30 Sun ~ Bar food 12-2, 5-9 (9.30 Fri, Sat); 12-4 Sun ~ Children allowed until 8pm but must be seated away from bar ~ Wi-fi *Recommended by Steve Whalley, Jill and Dick Archer, Maria and Henry Lazenby, Graeme and Sally Mendham*

ROECLIFFE
Crown 🏅 ♀ 🍺 🛏

SE3765   Map 7

(01423) 322300 – www.crowninnroecliffe.com

Off A168 just W of Boroughbridge; handy for A1(M) junction 48; YO51 9LY

Attractively placed pub with a civilised bar, first class enterprising food and a fine choice of drinks; charming bedrooms

This is a lovely inn run by the warmly friendly Mainey family, and our readers continue to send us enthusiastic reports on the caring service, excellent food and comfortable bedrooms. The bar has a contemporary colour scheme of dark reds and off-whites with pleasant prints carefully grouped and lit; one area has chunky pine tables on flagstones, while another, with a log fire, has dark tables on plaid carpet. Black Sheep BAA BAA and Best, Saltaire Blonde and Timothy Taylors Landlord on handpump, 20 wines by the glass, eight malt whiskies and eight gins. For meals, you can choose between a small candlelit olive-green bistro with nice tables, a longcase clock and a couple of paintings, and a more formal restaurant; background music. The garden has rattan sofas and tables set out on decking. This is a most enjoyable place to stay in cosy, country-style bedrooms. The village green is opposite.

Using small local producers, the delicious, weekly changing food includes sandwiches, fresh crab cakes with guacamole and tomato and coriander salsa, twice-baked cheese and cranberry soufflé with sunblush tomato chutney, tomato and tarragon risotto with goats cheese, bacon chop with duck egg, charred pineapple salsa and skinny fries, lamb cutlet, lamb shoulder tagine and crispy lamb tongue with roasted root vegetables and mint gel, pork fillet in parma ham with slow-cooked pork belly bonbons, calvados sauce, apple and vanilla, sea bass fillet with king prawns, fresh basil linguine and basil and vermouth sauce, and puddings such as belgian chocolate and orange fondant with salted butter caramel sauce and Cointreau and rhubarb jelly with rhubarb sherbert and honey pannacotta. *Benchmark main dish: steak in ale pie £13.95. Two-course evening meal £24.00.*

Free house ~ Licensee Karl Mainey ~ Real ale ~ Open 12-11; 12-10 Sun ~ Bar food 12-2.15, 6-9.30; 12-7 Sun ~ Restaurant ~ Children welcome ~ Dogs allowed in bar and bedrooms ~ Wi-fi ~ Bedrooms: £80/£100 *Recommended by Comus and Sarah Elliott, Janet and Peter Race, Peter and Anne Hollindale, Richard Cole, Simon Cleasby, Dr and Mrs F McGinn, R L Borthwick, Dr K Nesbitt*

Bedroom prices include full english breakfast, VAT and any inclusive service charge that we know of.

SANCTON

SE9039 Map 7

Star ⭐◫ ♀ 🍺

(01430) 827269 – www.thestaratsancton.co.uk

King Street (A1034 S of Market Weighton); YO43 4QP

Bustling bar with up to four real ales, more formal dining rooms with accomplished food, and a friendly, easy-going atmosphere

The hard-working licensees continue to run their extended 800-year-old pub with enthusiasm and care – and it shows. There's a bar with a woodburning stove, traditional red plush stools around a mix of tables, and a cheerful atmosphere. Ales from breweries such as Black Sheep, Great Newsome, Great Yorkshire and Wold Top are served on handpump from the brick counter and they keep 19 wines by the glass including prosecco and champagne, 20 gins and over 20 malt whiskies. The more formal (though still relaxed) dining rooms have comfortable high-backed dark leather dining chairs around wooden tables on carpeting, and prints on red- or cream-painted walls; background music. There are picnic-sets outside at the back. As this is at the foot of the Yorkshire Wolds Railway, many walkers and cyclists use it as a base for both a pint and a chat and a good meal.

 Using the best local, seasonal produce, the inventive modern food includes pressed duck terrine with rhubarb and juniper tartare, watercress and clementine, sticky pig cheek with home-made black pudding, burnt apple purée and clapshot (carrot and swede mash) with maple and cider reduction, smoked potato gnocchi with roasted beetroot, cheese, broad beans, toasted seeds and rapeseed dressing, cumberland sausage with roasted root vegetable mash, braised onions and ale gravy, wild sea bass with samphire, brown shrimps, warm potato salad and dill, crispy duck breast with carrot terrine, caraway and swede fondants and spiced duck jus, and puddings such as treacle and liquorice tart with black treacle sauce and malted chocolate fondant with peanut butter ice-cream and white chocolate fudge. *Benchmark main dish: steak in ale pie £14.95. Two-course evening meal £28.00.*

Free house ~ Licensees Ben and Lindsey Cox ~ Real ale ~ Open 12-3.30, 6-11.30; 12-10 Sun; closed Mon, first week Jan ~ Bar food 12-2, 6-9.30; 12-3, 6-8 Sun ~ Restaurant ~ Children welcome *Recommended by Gordon and Margaret Ormondroyd, Pat and Graham Williamson, Richard Cole, Alison and Graeme Spicer, Monica and Steph Evans*

SANDHUTTON

SE3882 Map 10

Kings Arms 🍺

(01845) 587887 – www.thekingsarmssandhutton.co.uk

A167, a mile N of A61 Thirsk–Ripon; YO7 4RW

Cheerful pub with friendly service, interesting food and beer and comfortable furnishings; bedrooms

The same friendly father and son team continue to run this charming inn and it remains the hub of the village. There's a traditional pubby atmosphere and the bar has an unusual circular woodburner in one corner, a high central table with four equally high stools, modern ladder-back wooden dining chairs around light pine tables, a couple of cushioned wicker armchairs, some attractive modern bar stools and photographs of the pub in years gone by. Black Sheep, Isaac Poad 1863 Best Bitter, Rudgate Jorvik Blonde and Village Brewer White Boar Bitter on handpump, 11 wines by the glass and efficient, friendly service. The two connecting dining rooms have similar furnishings to the bar (plus some high-backed brown leather dining chairs), arty flower photographs on cream walls and a small woodburning stove; background music, darts, board games and TV. There's a small beer garden and they have secure bike storage with air and puncture repair kits and a heated towel rail for drying wet kit. The pub does get pretty packed on race days at Thirsk Racecourse.

 Tasty food includes lunchtime sandwiches, spicy lamb kofta with minted sour cream, smoked salmon and prawn cocktail, slow-roasted vegetable lasagne, burger with toppings and chips, harissa chicken with sag aloo potatoes, raita and lime pickle, chilli con carne, fish pie, a plate of game (partridge, pigeon breast, pheasant goujons and venison sausage) with creamy mash, sea bass with chilli and polenta chips, parsnip purée and beetroot syrup, and puddings such as peanut butter crème brûlée and Toblerone cheesecake. *Benchmark main dish: salmon, cod and prawn fishcake with sweet chilli sauce £10.95. Two-course evening meal £17.00.*

Free house ~ Licensees Raymond and Alexander Boynton ~ Real ale ~ Open 12-11; 12-10 Sun ~ Bar food 12-2.30, 6-9; 12-5 Sun ~ Restaurant ~ Children welcome ~ Dogs allowed in bar ~ Wi-fi ~ Bedrooms: £45/£70 *Recommended by Michael Butler, Jeremy Snaithe, Helena and Trevor Fraser, Maggie and Matthew Lyons, Gail and Frank Hackett*

SHEFFIELD
SK4086 Map 7
Kelham Island Tavern 🍷 £
(0114) 272 2482 – www.kelhamtavern.co.uk
Kelham Island; S3 8RY

Busy little local with fantastic real ales, basic but decent lunchtime food, a friendly welcome and pretty back garden

Our readers love this busy backstreet local and the 13 interesting ales on handpump are well kept by knowledgeable, organised and friendly staff. There's always a mild and a stout or porter on offer and their regulars include Abbeydale Deception, Acorn Barnsley Bitter, Bradfield Farmers Blonde and Pictish Brewers Gold, with guests such as Blue Bee Ginger Beer, Hop Studio XS, North Riding Mosaic Pale Ale, Ramsgate Gadds Faithful Dogbolter Porter, Tiny Rebel Fubar – to name just a few; also, a changing craft beer, a german wheat beer, a belgian fruit beer, an interesting range of bottled ales, two farm ciders and around 40 malt whiskies. Furnishings are pubby and simple and there's always a wide array of cheerful customers; dominoes and board games. The unusual flower-filled back courtyard garden has plenty of seats and tables, and the front window boxes regularly win awards.

 Tasty and very good value pubby food – served weekday lunchtimes only – includes sandwiches, locally made pork pies and lunchtime hot dishes such as casseroles, mushroom and red pepper stroganoff, burgers with chips and various curries. *Benchmark main dish: steak in ale pie £5.60.*

Free house ~ Licensee Trevor Wraith ~ Real ale ~ Open 12-midnight ~ Bar food 12-3 (not Sun) ~ Children allowed in back room ~ Dogs welcome ~ Live folk Sun evenings *Recommended by Neil Allen, Sandra Morgan, William Slade, Rosie and John Moore, Sophia and Hamish Greenfield*

THORNTON WATLASS
SE2385 Map 10
Buck 🍷 🛏
(01677) 422461 – www.buckwatlass.co.uk
Village signposted off B6268 Bedale–Masham; HG4 4AH

Honest village pub with up to five real ales, a traditional bar and dining room, well-liked food and popular Sunday jazz; bedrooms

This is a friendly country pub and part of a row of low stone cottages; the village green is opposite. The pleasantly traditional bar on the right has upholstered wall settles on carpet, a fine mahogany bar counter, local artwork on the walls and a brick fireplace; background music, TV and board games. The Long Room (overlooking the cricket green) has photos from Thornton Watlass cricket teams of the past, and is the venue for the Sunday afternoon jazz sessions. Black Sheep, Theakstons Best, Walls Gun Dog Bitter and Wensleydale Coverdale Gamekeeper on handpump, eight wines by the glass and a dozen interesting malt whiskies. The sheltered garden has picnic-sets with more at the front. Bedrooms are simply furnished and comfortable.

Home-cooked food includes hot and cold sandwiches and rolls, deep-fried whitebait with tartare sauce, black pudding and apple stack with mustard sauce, broccoli and pesto pasta, steak and kidney pudding, haddock and chorizo fishcakes, chicken breast stuffed with pesto and mozzarella and wrapped in parma ham, lambs liver and bacon with mash and onion gravy, rib-eye steak with a choice of sauces, and puddings such as baked alaska and cheesecake of the day. *Benchmark main dish: steak in ale pie £10.95. Two-course evening meal £16.00.*

Free house ~ Licensees Victoria and Tony Jowett ~ Real ale ~ Open 12-11 (10.30 Sun) ~ Bar food 12-2, 6-9; 12-3, 6-8.30 Sun ~ Restaurant ~ Children welcome ~ Dogs allowed in bar and bedrooms ~ Wi-fi ~ Live trad jazz Sun lunchtime monthly (best to phone) ~ Bedrooms: £60/£90 *Recommended by Richard Kennell, Peter and Caroline Waites, Martine and Fabio Lockley*

WELBURN
SE7168 Map 7

Crown & Cushion ♀ ◀

(01653) 618777 – www.thecrownandcushionwelburn.com
Off A64; YO60 7DZ

Plenty of dining and drinking space in well run inn with real ales and particularly good food – and seats outside

The contemporary tables and chairs on the outdoor terrace and picnic-sets below, with long-reaching views across to the Howardian Hills, are popular in warm weather. This is a handsome, carefully refurbished inn and the little tap room has rustic tables and chairs on wide floorboards, high stools around an equally high central table, beams and timbering, with Black Sheep, Rudgate Jorvik Blonde and Timothy Taylors Boltmaker on handpump, a good choice of malt whiskies and gins, 24 wines by the glass and farm cider. The other attractively refurbished, interconnecting rooms are for dining and on different levels: smart high-backed chairs mix with wooden ones and an assortment of cushioned settles and wall seats around various tables on flagstones or red and black floor tiles. There are open fires and a woodburning stove, old prints of the pub and local scenes on painted or exposed stone walls and lots of horsebrasses, copper pans and kettles and old stone bottles; background music. The pub is handy for Castle Howard. This is part of Provenance Inns & Hotels.

Pleasing food includes sandwiches, confit duck terrine with glazed oranges and spiced orange syrup, queen scallops with garlic and parsley butter and a cheddar and gruyère crust, pearl barley and root vegetable risotto with butter-roasted salsify, crisp kale and poached duck egg, beer-battered fish and chips, chicken breast with sauté gnocchi, courgette ribbons and wild mushroom and madeira sauce, guinea fowl breast with crispy thigh croquette, smoked bacon, leeks and creamy lentils, chargrilled lamb chop with redcurrant mint glaze, and puddings such as toffee and banana parfait with walnut bread and caramel sauce and glazed lemon tart with lemon sorbet and raspberry coulis; they also offer an early-bird menu (5.30-6.45pm Sunday to Friday). *Benchmark main dish: barbecue sticky pork ribs £15.95. Two-course evening meal £21.00.*

Free house ~ Licensee Michael Ibbotson ~ Real ale ~ Open 12-3.30, 5.30-11; 12-11 Sat; 12-10.30 Sun ~ Bar food 12-2.30, 5.30-9.30; 12-8.30 Sun ~ Restaurant ~ Children welcome ~ Dogs allowed in bar ~ Wi-fi *Recommended by Pat and Graham Williamson, Mike Benton, Simon Sharpe, Jane and Philip Saunders*

WIDDOP

SD9531 Map 7

Pack Horse ◀ £

(01422) 842803 – www.packhorseinn.pub

The Ridge; from A646 on W side of Hebden Bridge, turn off at Heptonstall signpost (as it's a sharp turn, coming out of Hebden Bridge the road signs direct you around a turning circle), then follow Slack and Widdop signposts; can also be reached from Nelson and Colne, on high, pretty road; OS Sheet 103 map reference 952317; HX7 7AT

Friendly pub up on the moors and liked by walkers for generous, tasty honest food, four real ales and lots of malt whiskies

Pennine Way walkers use this isolated moorland pub with its friendly atmosphere as a cosy haven. The bar has welcoming winter fires, window seats cut into the partly panelled stripped-stone walls (from where you can take in the beautiful views), sturdy furnishings and horsey mementoes. Black Sheep and Thwaites Wainwright plus guests such as Black Sheep BAA BAA and Cottage Bombshell on handpump, over 100 single malt whiskies plus some irish ones, and a dozen wines by the glass. The friendly golden retrievers are called Padge and Purdey. There are seats outside in the cobblestoned beer garden and pretty summer hanging baskets. They have a smart self-catering apartment for rent.

🍴 Well regarded food includes sandwiches, baked camembert with plum chutney, queen scallops grilled with garlic and cheese, mushroom stroganoff, sausages with mash and sizzled onions, steak and kidney or fish pie, cottage hotpot, chicken breast with mushroom and brandy sauce, gammon and eggs, pheasant breasts with stuffing and bacon, and puddings. *Benchmark main dish: rack of lamb with a changing jus £13.95. Two-course evening meal £17.00.*

Free house ~ Licensee Andrew Hollinrake ~ Real ale ~ Open 12-3, 6.30-11; 12-10 Sun; closed Mon except bank holidays; closed weekday lunchtimes in winter ~ Bar food 12-2, 5.30-9; 12-7 Sun ~ Children welcome ~ Dogs welcome *Recommended by Alan and Alice Morgan, Simon and Alex Knight, Diane Abbott, WAH, Professor James Burke*

YORK

SE5951 Map 7

Judges Lodging ♀ ⇐

(01904) 639312 – www.judgeslodgingyork.co.uk

Lendal; YO1 8AQ

Lovely Georgian townhouse with a modern interior, character cellar bar, several dining rooms, well liked food and outside seating; stylish bedrooms

Right in the centre of this lovely city stands this Grade I listed Georgian house with an interestingly refurbished, contemporary interior. The proper bar is in the cellar (and open for drinks and food all day) with fine vaulted ceilings, upholstered dining chairs and sofas on big flagstones, Thwaites Original and Wainwright and Treboom Yorkshire Sparkle on handpump and good wines by the glass; this leads through a dining room to a bright and airy garden room, both of which have green-painted farmhouse chairs around blonde wooden tables on pale floorboards. On the first floor is what they call the Medicine Cabinet – a reception room for both the dining rooms and hotel – with quirky men's trouser leg stools by the bar counter, a couple of grey button-back leather armchairs on either side of the fireplace and plaster judges' heads on Farrow & Ball paintwork. Leading off here, the two restaurants have leather chesterfields and more upholstered chairs around a mix of tables on bare boards, painted panelling, tall window shutters, chandeliers, gilt-edged mirrors and some unusual wire sculptures

– it's all very smart and civilised. There are modern seats and tables at the front of the building between lavender pots, white metal furniture beside the garden room and traditional wooden chairs, tables and picnic-sets in the back courtyard. Bedrooms are modern, well equipped and comfortable (one at the very top has York Minster views).

🍴 Rewarding food includes sandwiches, salt and pepper squid with sweet chilli and teriyaki dip, prosciutto, chicken and sweet pepper terrine with grape and walnut salad and golden raisin purée, vegetable moussaka, asian moules frites, superfood salad with pomegranate and honey dressing, burgers with toppings, chutney and skinny fries, corn-fed chicken with mushrooms, pancetta, potato purée and tarragon butter sauce, sea bass and scallops with herb pasta, pea purée, crispy capers and langoustine oil, and puddings such as dark chocolate tiffin with macerated red berries and clotted cream and caramelised rice pudding with exotic fruit salad. *Benchmark main dish: beef in ale pie £12.50. Two-course evening meal £18.00.*

Thwaites ~ Lease Rachel Guy ~ Real ale ~ Open 10am-11pm; 10am-10.30pm Sun ~ Bar food 12-10 ~ Restaurant ~ Children welcome ~ Wi-fi ~ Bedrooms: £109/£115 *Recommended by Lionel Smith, Beth Aldridge, Rona Mackinlay, Phil and Jane Villiers, Julian Thorpe, Alice Wright*

YORK
Maltings 🍺 £

SE5951   Map 7

(01904) 655387 – www.maltings.co.uk
Tanners Moat/Wellington Row, below Lendal Bridge; YO1 6HU

Bustling, friendly city pub with cheerful landlord, interesting real ales and other drinks plus good value standard food

There's a fine range of interesting drinks in this cheerful, busy pub – all served by the hard-working, convivial landlord. The permanent beers on handpump are Black Sheep Best, Treboom Yorkshire Sparkle and York Guzzler with guests such as Adnams Cashmere IPA, Flash House Original Porter, JW Lees Dirty Dozen, North Riding A Slap Up North IPA and Totally Brewed Passion Fruit In the Face. They also keep six continental beers on tap, four craft beers, lots of bottled beers, six farm ciders, 15 country wines and 25 whiskies from all over the world. The atmosphere is bustling and friendly and the tricksy décor is strong on salvaged, somewhat quirky junk: old doors for the bar front and much of the ceiling, a marvellous collection of railway signs and amusing notices, an old chocolate dispensing machine, cigarette and tobacco advertisements alongside cough and chest remedies, what looks like a suburban front door for the entrance to the ladies', partly stripped orange brick walls and even a lavatory pan in one corner; games machine. The day's papers are framed in the gents'. The pub is very handy for the National Railway Museum and the station; nearby parking is difficult. Please note that dogs are allowed only after food service has finished.

🍴 Exceptional value food includes sandwiches and toasties, baked potatoes with lots of fillings, ham and egg, sausage and chips, beef in ale pie, mushroom and spinach lasagne, chilli tacos, and burgers. *Benchmark main dish: chilli chips £4.95.*

Free house ~ Licensee Shaun Collinge ~ Real ale ~ No credit cards ~ Open 11am-11.30pm; 12-10.30 Sun ~ Bar food 12-2 weekdays; 12-4 weekends ~ Children allowed only during meal times ~ Wi-fi ~ Live music Mon and Tues evenings *Recommended by Dr J Barrie Jones, Roger and Donna Huggins, David Thorpe, Rob Anderson, Professor James Burke*

Anyone claiming to arrange, or prevent, inclusion of a pub in the *Guide* is a fraud. Pubs are included only if recommended by readers and if our own anonymous inspection confirms that they are suitable.

Also Worth a Visit in Yorkshire

Besides the fully inspected pubs, you might like to try these pubs that have been recommended to us and described by readers. Do tell us what you think of them: feedback@goodguides.com

AINDERBY STEEPLE   SE3392
Wellington Heifer (01609) 775718
A684, 3 miles from A1; opposite church; DL7 9PU Nicely refurbished late 18th-c pub with four connecting rooms, flagstone floors and log fires, comfortable scatter-cushion bench seating and sturdy tables, good range of beers and wines from carved counter, enjoyable food including good value lunchtime/early-evening set menu, restaurant at end of corridor; children welcome, two well appointed bedrooms, open and food all day Sun. *(Jill and Dick Archer)*

AINTHORPE   NZ7007
Fox & Hounds (01287) 660218
Brook Lane; YO21 2LD Traditional beamed moorland inn dating from the 16th c, tranquil setting with sheep grazing freely and wonderful views; nice open fire in unusual stone fireplace, comfortable seating, well kept Theakstons and good choice of wines by the glass, generous fairly priced food including daily specials, friendly staff, restaurant, games room; free wi-fi; dogs welcome (great walks from the door), seven bedrooms and attached self-catering cottage, open all day. *(Jimmy)*

AISLABY   SE8508
Forge (01947) 811522
Main Road, off A171 W of Whitby; YO21 1SW Refurbished mellow-stone village pub with opened-up interior, light wood floor, upholstered wall benches and woodburner in brick fireplace, well kept ales such as Black Sheep from small central servery, good home-made food at sensible prices including popular Sun roasts served till 7pm, friendly accommodating staff; Tues quiz; children and dogs welcome, six bedrooms. *(John Robinson)*

ALDBOROUGH   SE4166
Ship (01423) 322749
Off B6265 just S of Boroughbridge, close to A1; YO51 9ER Attractive 14th-c beamed village dining pub adjacent to medieval church; good food from sandwiches and pub standards up including early-bird deal, cheerful helpful service, well kept Black Sheep and Theakstons, extensive affordably priced wine list, some old-fashioned seats around cast-iron-framed tables, lots of copper and brass, inglenook fire, candlelit back restaurant; children and dogs welcome, a few picnic-sets outside, handy for Roman remains and museum, open all day weekends (food till 6pm Sun), closed Mon lunchtime. *(Stuart Lymath)*

APPLETON-LE-MOORS   SE7388
★**Moors** (01751) 417435
N of A170, just under 1.5 miles E of Kirkby Moorside; YO62 6TF Traditional 17th-c stone-built village pub; beamed bar with built-in high-backed settle next to old kitchen fireplace, plenty of other seating, three changing regional ales and wide range of malt whiskies and gins, good sensibly priced food from sandwiches/ciabattas and pub favourites up including daily specials, dining room with leather chairs at polished tables, friendly helpful staff; background music; children and dogs welcome, tables in lovely walled garden with quiet country views, walks to Rosedale Abbey or Hartoft End, eight good bedrooms, open all day. *(Luke Bruce)*

APPLETON-LE-STREET   SE7373
Cresswell Arms (01653) 693647
B1257/Appleton Lane; YO17 6PG Modernised stone-built country inn dating from the 1800s, pleasant carpeted bar with log fire, good-sized bare-boards restaurant with pine furniture and fittings, well kept Wold Top and a guest, enjoyable pubby food from sandwiches up; children welcome, ten bedrooms, open all day weekends, may close weekday lunchtimes (best to check). *(Ben and Jenny Settle)*

APPLETREEWICK   SE0560
★**Craven Arms** (01756) 720270
Off B6160 Burnsall–Bolton Abbey; BD23 6DA Character creeper-clad 16th-c beamed pub; cushioned settles and rugs on flagstones, open fires (one in old range), gas lighting and lots of interesting pictures and bric-a-brac, up to eight well kept ales including cask-tapped Theakstons Old Peculier and a house beer from Dark Horse, real cider and several wines by the glass, enjoyable home-made food (not Mon or Tues lunchtimes) from hot or cold sandwiches up, friendly helpful service, small dining room and splendid thatched and raftered cruck barn with gallery; free wi-fi; children, dogs and muddy boots welcome (plenty of surrounding walks), wheelchair access, nice country views from front picnic-sets, more seats in back garden, shepherd-hut accommodation, open all day. *(Stuart Doughty)*

ARNCLIFFE   SD9371
★**Falcon** (01756) 770205
Off B6160 N of Grassington; BD23 5QE Basic no-frills country tavern in lovely setting on village green, coal fire in small

bar with elderly furnishings, well kept Timothy Taylors Boltmaker and a guest either from handpump or tapped from cask to stoneware jugs in central hatch-style servery, inexpensive simple lunchtime food (non-residents must book for evening meals), friendly service, attractive watercolours, sepia photographs and humorous sporting prints, back sun-room overlooking pleasant garden; quiz first Fri of month; children (till 9pm) and dogs welcome, four miles of trout fishing, nice walks, six bedrooms (two with own bathroom), open all day. (*Neil and Angela Huxter, Peter Smith and Judith Brown*)

ASENBY   SE3975
★ **Crab & Lobster** (01845) 577286
Dishforth Road; village signed off A168 – handy for A1; YO7 3QL Main emphasis on civilised hotel and restaurant side, but has rambling L-shaped bar serving a yorkshire ale; interesting jumble of seats from antique high-backed settles through sofas and wing armchairs to rather theatrical corner seats, mix of tables too and a jungle of bric-a-brac, cosy main restaurant and dining pavilion with big tropical plants, nautical bits and pieces and Edwardian sofas, very good if not cheap food, efficient service; background music; well behaved children allowed, seats on mediterranean-style terrace, opulent bedrooms in nearby Crab Manor with seven acres of gardens and 180-metre golf hole, open all day till midnight. (*Pat and Graham Williamson, Helena and Trevor Fraser*)

ASKRIGG   SD9491
Crown (01969) 650387
Main Street; DL8 3HQ Open-plan local in James Herriot village, three areas off main bar, open fires (one in old-fashioned range), enjoyable simple pub food at reasonable prices including deals, ales such as Black Sheep, Theakstons and a guest, friendly buzzy atmosphere; children, walkers and dogs welcome, tables outside, open all day. (*Jackie Robinson*)

ASKRIGG   SD9491
Kings Arms (01969) 650113
Signed from A684 Leyburn–Sedbergh in Bainbridge; DL8 3HQ Popular 18th-c coaching inn (the Drovers in TV's *All Creatures Great and Small*) under same ownership as the Charles Bathurst at Langthwaite and the Punch Bowl at Low Row; high-ceilinged flagstoned main bar with good log fire, traditional furnishings and décor, a couple of well kept house beers from nearby Yorkshire Dales plus Black Sheep, Theakstons and a guest, 13 wines by the glass, enjoyable reasonably priced food including some evening offers, friendly efficient service, more modern restaurant with inglenook, games room in former barrel-vaulted beer cellar; background music, TV; children and dogs (in bar) welcome, side courtyard, bedrooms run separately as part of

Holiday Property Bond complex behind, open all day. (*John and Enid Morris, Ian Wilson*)

AUSTWICK   SD7668
★ **Game Cock** (01524) 251226
Just off A65 Settle–Kirkby Lonsdale; LA2 8BB Quaint civilised place in pretty spot below Three Peaks; friendly old-fashioned beamed back bar with bare-boards and good log fire, well kept Thwaites and a guest, winter mulled wine and nice coffee, cheerful efficient staff, plenty of emphasis on french chef-owner's good fairly priced food, two refurbished restaurant areas and small conservatory-style extension; children, walkers, cyclists and dogs welcome, garden with play equipment, four bedrooms, closed Mon, otherwise open all day (till 1am if busy). (*Colin Hammond, Steve Lumb*)

AYSGARTH   SE0188
Aysgarth Falls (01969) 663775
A684; DL8 3SR Creeper-clad moorland hotel with good food and welcoming accommodating service, ales such as Black Sheep, Theakstons and Wensleydale in log-fire bar where dogs on leads welcome, comfortable eating areas, some interesting ancient masonry at the back recalling its days as a pilgrims' inn; great scenery near broad waterfalls, 13 bedrooms, camping (adults only). (*Mary Hunstings*)

AYSGARTH   SE0088
★ **George & Dragon** (01969) 663358
Just off A684; DL8 3AD Welcoming 17th-c posting inn with emphasis on good locally sourced food from sandwiches up, two big dining areas and small beamed and panelled bar with log fire, well kept ales including Black Sheep, Theakstons and a house beer from Yorkshire Dales, good choice of wines by the glass, friendly helpful staff; may be background music, free wi-fi; children and dogs (in bar) welcome, nice paved garden, lovely scenery and walks, handy for Aysgarth Falls, seven bedrooms, open all day. (*Liz and Mike Newton*)

BAILDON   SE1538
Junction (01274) 582009
Baildon Road; BD17 6AB Friendly wedge-shaped local with three traditional linked rooms, seven well kept ales including own Junction brews (July festival), generous helpings of good value home-made food weekday lunchtimes, games part with pool; live music Sun evening, Thurs quiz, sports TV; children welcome, open all day. (*Andy Barker*)

BARDSEY   SE3642
Bingley Arms (01937) 572462
Church Lane; LS17 9DR Ancient pub with spacious lounge divided into separate areas, substantial beams and huge fireplace, well kept ales such as Black Sheep, Sharps and Timothy Taylors,

and good range of home-cooked food, afternoon teas, friendly staff, smaller public bar, upstairs raftered restaurant; children welcome, attractive terraced garden, lovely Saxon church nearby, open all day. *(Nigel and Sue Foster, Michael Butler)*

BARKISLAND   SE0419
★**Fleece** (01422) 820687
B6113 towards Ripponden; HX4 0DJ
Large well renovated and extended 18th-c beamed moorland dining pub, very good popular food including weekday set menu and Thurs grill night, efficient friendly uniformed staff, Timothy Taylors Landlord and a couple of other well kept ales such as Ilkley and Stod Fold; background music; children welcome, front disabled access, lovely Pennine views from first-floor terrace and garden, summer barbecues, five bedrooms, handy for M62, open all day from 8am for breakfast, food till 7pm Sun. *(Gordon and Margaret Ormondroyd)*

BARMBY-ON-THE-MARSH   SE6828
Kings Head (01757) 630705
High Street; DN14 7HT Renovated and extended early 19th-c beamed village pub, good locally sourced food including yorkshire tapas and Sun lunchtime carvery, four well kept local ales, bar, lounge, restaurant and deli (home-baked bread to order); children welcome, disabled access/facilities, open all day weekends, closed Mon and lunchtime Tues. *(Jimmy)*

BARNSLEY   SE3400
Cock (01226) 744227
Pilley Hill, Birdwell; S70 5UD
Welcoming village local set down from the road, enjoyable reasonably priced home-made food and several well kept ales including Tetleys, cheerful helpful staff, main bar with beams, stone floor and open fire, lounge and back dining room; children and dogs welcome, open all day (from 4pm Mon). *(David H Bennett)*

BARNSLEY   SE3203
Strafford Arms (01226) 287488
Near Northern College, about 2.5 miles NW of M1 junction 36; S75 3EW Pretty stone-built village pub (Fine & Country Inns) with opened-up contemporary interior, decent choice of food from lunchtime sandwiches and platters to Josper grills, local ales such as Timothy Taylors and Bradfield, good range of wines and cocktails, friendly service, log fires including one in big Yorkshire range; Tues quiz, free wi-fi; children, dogs and muddy boots welcome, garden with play area, on Trans Pennine Trail and by entrance to Wentworth Castle, open (and food) all day. *(Gordon and Margaret Ormondroyd)*

BEDALE   SE2688
Old Black Swan (01677) 422973
Market Place; DL8 1ED Popular old pub with attractive bay-windowed frontage, well kept ales including Theakstons and generous helpings of good value food, friendly efficient staff, log fire; darts, pool, sports TV; children and dogs welcome, disabled facilities, small covered back terrace, Tues market, open all day. *(Mick Allen)*

BEVERLEY   TA0339
★**White Horse** (01482) 861973
Hengate, off North Bar; HU17 8BN
Timeless place known locally as Nellie's; carefully preserved Victorian interior with basic little rooms huddled around central bar, brown leatherette seats (high-backed settles in one little snug) and plain chairs/benches on bare boards, antique cartoons and sentimental engravings, gas lighting including chandelier, coal fires, bargain Sam Smiths beers and guests, straightforward food, friendly staff, more space upstairs; charity quiz Tues, games room; children till 7pm, no dogs inside, courtyard picnic-sets, open all day. *(Steve and Alex Cardis)*

BEVERLEY   TA0239
Woolpack (01482) 867095
Westwood Road, W of centre; HU17 8EN
Small proper pub at end of 19th-c row of terrace cottages, generous helpings of good traditional food at reasonable prices including Tues pie-and-pint night and popular Sun roasts, seven well kept Marstons-related beers, helpful prompt service, open fires and simple furnishings, brasses, knick-knacks and prints, cosy snug; Thurs quiz; contemporary seats and tables in beer garden, open all day weekends, closed Mon lunchtime (kitchen closed all day then). *(John Saville)*

BILTON   SE4750
Chequers (01423) 359637
Pub signed just off B1224; YO26 7NN
Quietly placed cream-washed village inn; well kept Black Sheep, Timothy Taylors and a summer guest, nice selection of wines by the glass and generous helpings of good freshly made often interesting food from sandwiches up, linked areas with comfortable seating including leather armchairs and banquettes, woodburner, some open shelving separating part-panelled dining room; picnic-sets in small garden with extensive country views, three bedrooms, open all day (food all day weekends). *(John and Eleanor Holdsworth)*

BINGLEY   SE1039
Brown Cow (01274) 564345
B6429 just W of junction with A650; BD16 2QX Open-plan pub in nice riverside spot (renovations after flood damage),

Timothy Taylors range and good choice of generously served enjoyable food, friendly staff; live music Sat; children and dogs welcome, tables out on sheltered terrace, open all day. *(John and Eleanor Holdsworth)*

BINGLEY SE1242

Dick Hudsons (01274) 552121

Otley Road, High Eldwick; BD16 3BA Well run Vintage Inn family dining pub named after a former landlord, their usual reasonably priced food including set menu choices, ales such as Black Sheep, Marstons and Timothy Taylors, lots of wines by the glass, efficient friendly staff; tables outside with great views over Baildon Moor, open all day. *(John and Eleanor Holdsworth)*

BIRSTWITH SE2459

★Station Hotel (01423) 770254

Off B6165 W of Ripley; HG3 3AG Welcoming immaculately kept stone-built dales pub; bar, log-fire restaurant and garden room, good home-made food from extensive menu including lunchtime/early-evening set deal, four local ales and 14 wines by the glass, friendly efficient staff; Mon quiz and monthly open mike night; tables in landscaped garden with heated smokers' shelter, picturesque valley, five bedrooms, open (and food) all day. *(John and Eleanor Holdsworth)*

BISHOPTHORPE SE5947

Woodman (01904) 706507

Village signed just off A64 York S bypass; Main Street; YO23 2RB Welcoming open-plan pub with good range of enjoyable food cooked by landlord-chef including OAP weekday deal, four regional ales and decent choice of wines by the glass, friendly efficient service, woodburner; background music; children and dogs welcome, seats out in front and in large back garden with play equipment, handy for York Racecourse, closed Mon and Tues, otherwise open all day, food all day weekends. *(Gordon and Margaret Ormondroyd, Rob Jones)*

BOLTON ABBEY SE0754

Devonshire Arms (01756) 710441

B6160; BD23 6AJ Comfortable and elegant 18th-c hotel in wonderful position on edge of Bolton Abbey Estate; good if pricey food from light meals up in bright modern brasserie-bar, contemporary paintings (some for sale) on roughcast walls, colourful armchairs around cast-iron-framed tables on pale wood floor, four well kept Copper Dragon ales and good wines by the glass, afternoon teas, more formal restaurant; tables in spacious courtyard with extensive views, Estate and Strid river-valley walks, bedrooms in old and new wings, open all day. *(WAH)*

BRADFIELD SK2692

Old Horns (0114) 285 1207

High Bradfield; S6 6LG Welcoming old stone pub in hill village with stunning views;

good hearty food including themed evenings, bargain weekday lunchtime deal and Sun carvery, can eat in part-flagstoned bar or carpeted pitch-roofed dining room, half a dozen predominantly Thwaites beers, friendly helpful staff; background music, Tues quiz, TV; children welcome, raised terrace taking in the view, picnic-sets and play area in garden, next to interesting 14th-c church, good walks, open (and food) all day. *(Kerry and Guy Trooper)*

BRADFORD SE1533

Fighting Cock (01274) 726907

Preston Street (off B6145); BD7 1JE Busy bare-boards traditional alehouse by industrial estate, a dozen well kept changing ales, foreign draught/bottled beers and real ciders, friendly staff and lively atmosphere, all-day sandwiches plus good simple lunchtime hot dishes (not Sun), coal fires; beer festivals; dogs welcome, open all day. *(Joe Oswald)*

BRADFORD SE1533

New Beehive (01274) 721784

Westgate; BD1 3AA Robustly old-fashioned five-room Edwardian inn, plenty of period features including gas lighting, big mirrors, interesting paintings and coal fires, changing ales (mostly from smaller brewers) along with continental bottled beers, welcoming staff and friendly atmosphere (busy on BCFC match days), weekend live music in cellar bar; pool and bar billiards; children welcome, back courtyard, 17 simple bedrooms, open all day from around 2pm (6pm Sun), till late Fri, Sat. *(Joe Oswald)*

BRADFORD SE1633

Sparrow Bier Café (01274) 270772

North Parade; BD1 3HZ Bare-boards bar with great selection of bottled beers, draught continentals, craft beers and local real ales, friendly knowledgeable staff, food including range of pies, meat and cheese platters and pizzas from nearby italian restaurant, more tables in cellar bar; background music; open all day. *(Joe Oswald)*

BRADFORD SE1938

Stansfield Arms (0113) 250 2659

Apperley Lane, Apperley Bridge; off A658 NE; BD10 0NP Popular ivy-clad pub dating from the 16th c, good food including daily specials and early-evening deal, well kept Timothy Taylors Landlord and a couple of local guests, friendly helpful service, beams, stripped stone and dark panelling, open fires, restaurant; children and dogs (in bar) welcome, tables out on front decking, pleasant setting, open all day till midnight (1am Fri, Sat) and can get very busy. *(John and Eleanor Holdsworth)*

BRAMHAM SE4242

Swan (01937) 843570

Just off A1 2 miles N of A64; LS23 6QA Unspoilt and unchanging little local up steep hill from village square – also known as the 'Top Pub'; friendly atmosphere and good mix of customers, well kept ales such as Black Sheep, Hambleton and Leeds, no food, two coal fires; open all day Sat, from 4pm weekdays. *(Shirley Blenkinsopp)*

BRANTINGHAM   SE9329

Triton (01482) 667261

Ellerker Road; HU15 1QE Spacious comfortably refurbished and extended old stone pub, good choice of enjoyable home-made food in bar and restaurant, three local ales, good friendly service; children, walkers and dogs welcome, tables out at front and in sheltered back garden, open all day weekends (food all day Sat, till 6pm Sun), closed Mon. *(John Robinson)*

BREARTON   SE3260

★ Malt Shovel (01423) 862929

Village signposted off A61 N of Harrogate; HG3 3BX Welcoming 15th-c dining pub; heavily beamed rooms with two open fires and woodburner, attractive mix of tables and chairs on wood or slate floors, some partitioning separating good eating areas, good food including set lunch menu, helpful friendly staff, well kept Black Sheep, Timothy Taylors Landlord and a guest from linenfold oak counter, plenty of wines by the glass, airy conservatory; children welcome, tables under parasols in garden and pretty summer hanging baskets, circular walks from the pub, closed Sun evening, Mon. *(Mick Allen)*

BRIDGE HEWICK   SE3370

Black-a-moor (01765) 603511

Boroughbridge Road (B6265 E of Ripon); HG4 5AA Roomy family-run dining pub with good choice of popular home-cooked food including set menu till 6pm, well kept local beers and decent wines, friendly young staff, sofas and woodburner in bar area; free wi-fi; children welcome, dogs in snug, five comfortable bedrooms, open (and food) all day, kitchen closes 7pm Sun. *(Sarah and David Gibbs)*

BRIGHOUSE   SE1320

Four Sons (01484) 308904

Clough Lane, A6107 towards Fixby; HD6 3QL Light modern refurbishment (formerly the Clough House) under new owners, popular reasonably priced food cooked to order including OAP lunch, ales such as Oakham, Ossett and Timothy Taylors, friendly helpful staff, woodburner; some live music, back games room with pool; children welcome, attractive beer garden, open all day, no food Sun evening. *(Gordon and Margaret Ormondroyd)*

BURN   SE5928

★ Wheatsheaf (01757) 270614

Main Road (A19 Selby–Doncaster); YO8 8LJ Busy but welcoming 19th-c roadside pub; comfortable seats in partly divided open-plan bar with masses to look at – air force wartime memorabilia, gleaming copper kettles, polished buffalo horns, cases of model vans and lorries, decorative mugs above one bow-window seat, a drying rack over the log fire, well kept Copper Dragon, Timothy Taylors and four guests, 20 malt whiskies, straightforward good value food (not Mon or Tues evenings), roast only on Sun; games machine, TV and may be unobtrusive background music; children and dogs welcome, picnic-sets on terrace in small back garden, open all day. *(Hilary Forrest)*

BURNISTON   TA0193

Three Jolly Sailors (01723) 871259

A171 N of Scarborough; High Street; YO13 0HJ Comfortable and welcoming village pub with wide range of enjoyable reasonably priced food from sandwiches up, OAP and children's menus, ales such as Timothy Taylors Landlord, main bar, restaurant and conservatory, open fires; dogs welcome, tables under parasols in small side garden, handy for Cleveland Way and coastal walks, open (and food) all day. *(D W Stokes)*

BURTON LEONARD   SE3263

★ Hare & Hounds (01765) 677355

Off A61 Ripon–Harrogate, handy for A1(M) junction 48; HG3 3SG Civilised and welcoming 19th-c village dining pub; good popular food (till 6pm Sun) from lunchtime sandwiches up using fresh local ingredients, set menu choices, well kept ales such as Black Sheep and Theakstons, nice wines by the glass and decent coffee, efficient friendly service, cosy carpeted bar with woodburner, large dining area beyond; children in eating areas, pretty little back garden. *(Dan and Belinda Smallbone)*

CARLTON   SE0684

Foresters Arms (01969) 640272

Off A684 W of Leyburn; DL8 4BB Old stone pub owned by local co-operative; log fire bar with dark low beams and flagstones, four well kept yorkshire-brewed ales and good range of popular affordably priced food (not Sun evening, Mon, Tues lunchtime), carpeted restaurant; events including fortnightly quiz and monthly live music; dogs welcome, disabled access/loos, a few picnic-sets out at front, pretty village in heart of Yorkshire Dales National Park, lovely views, three bedrooms, open all day weekends, closed Mon lunchtime (and Tues lunchtime in winter). *(John and Enid Morris)*

CARLTON HUSTHWAITE   SE4976

Carlton Inn (01845) 501265

Butt Lane; YO7 2BW Cosy modernised beamed dining pub; good fairly priced food cooked by landlady including daily specials and lunchtime/early-evening set menu, friendly helpful service, John Smiths and Theakstons, local cider, mix of country furniture including some old settles, open fire; children welcome, dogs in back bar area, garden picnic-sets, open all day Sun, closed Mon. *(Dr and Mrs R G J Telfer)*

CARPERBY SE0089
Wheatsheaf (01969) 663216
A mile NW of Aysgarth; DL8 4DF
Friendly early 19th-c inn set in quiet dales village and popular with walkers; cosy traditional bar with warming fire, three or four well kept ales such as Black Sheep and Jennings, enjoyable good value home-cooked food, lounge and dining room; children and dogs welcome, 13 comfortable bedrooms (James Herriot spent his honeymoon here in 1941), good breakfast, lovely walks including to Aysgarth Falls, open all day. *(Randy Alden)*

CARTHORPE SE3083
★Fox & Hounds (01845) 567433
Village signed from A1 N of Ripon, via B6285; DL8 2LG Neatly kept pub run by same family since 1983 and emphasis on very good well presented food, attractive high-raftered restaurant with lots of farm and smithy tools, Black Sheep and Worthington in L-shaped bar with two log fires, plush seating, plates on stripped beams and evocative Victorian photographs of Whitby, some theatrical memorabilia in corridors, good friendly service; background classical music; children welcome, handy for A1, closed Mon and maybe first week Jan. *(Trish and Karl Soloman)*

CATTAL SE4455
Victoria (01423) 330249
Station Road; YO26 8EB Bustling Victorian themed dining pub with extensive choice of good attractively presented food, charming attentive service, well kept ales including one from local Rudgate named for the landlord, good value wines; children welcome, picnic-sets in gravelled back garden, open (and food) all day Sun, from 4pm Tues-Sat, shut Mon, handy for the station. *(Jackie Robinson)*

CAWOOD SE5737
Ferry (01757) 268515
King Street (B1222 NW of Selby), by Ouse swing bridge; YO8 3TL Interesting 16th-c inn with several comfortable areas, low beams and stripped brickwork, woodburner in massive inglenook, five well kept ales and enjoyable food including deals; Tues bingo, Aug charity music festival, sports TV; children and dogs welcome, nice flagstone terrace and lawn down to river, bedrooms, open all day Thurs-Sun (till 1am Fri, Sat), otherwise from 4pm, no food Sun evening-Weds. *(Dave Braisted)*

CHAPEL-LE-DALE SD7477
★Old Hill Inn (01524) 241256
B5655 Ingleton–Hawes, 3 miles N of Ingleton; LA6 3AR Welcoming former farmhouse with fantastic views to Ingleborough and Whernside; clean rustic interior, beams, log fires and bare-stone recesses, straightforward furniture on stripped-wood floors, nice pictures and some interesting local artefacts, Black Sheep, Dent and a guest, good wholesome food including lovely puddings (look out for the landlord's sugar sculptures), separate dining room and sun lounge, relaxed chatty atmosphere; children welcome, dogs in bar, wonderful remote surrounding walks, two bedrooms and space for five caravans, open all day Sat, closed Mon. *(Lynda and Trevor Smith)*

CLIFTON SE1622
★Black Horse (01484) 713862
Westgate/Coalpit Lane; signed off Brighouse Road from M62 junction 25; HD6 4HJ Friendly 17th-c inn-restaurant with good interesting food in front dining rooms including a few pubby dishes and set menu (Fri, Sat), can be pricey, efficient uniformed staff, open fire in back bar with beam-and-plank ceiling, well kept Timothy Taylors Landlord and a house beer brewed by Brass Monkey, good range of wines; nice courtyard, 22 comfortable bedrooms, pleasant village, open all day Fri-Sun, from 4pm other days. *(Michael Butler)*

CLOUGHTON SE9798
Falcon (01723) 870717
Pub signed just off A171 out towards Whitby; YO13 0DY Newish licensees for this big 19th-c country inn set in five-acre grounds, well divided opened-up interior including log-fire lounge and dining conservatory, enjoyable pubby food from sandwiches to daily specials, steak night Thurs, beers such as Theakstons and good choice of wines, distant sea view from end windows; background music; children welcome, picnic-sets in neat walled garden, good walks (leave muddy boots by the door), eight bedrooms and 11 glamping pods, may close Mon and Tues in winter. *(Alan McQuilan)*

CLOUGHTON NEWLANDS TA0195
Bryherstones (01723) 870744
Newlands Road, off A171 in Cloughton; YO13 0AR Popular traditional stone pub with several interconnecting rooms including dining room up on right and flagstoned stable-theme bar on left, very well liked food using local produce, Timothy Taylors and a few guests, good friendly service, games room (pool and darts); children and dogs welcome, picnic-sets and play area in sheltered back garden, closed lunchtimes Mon-Weds. *(Mick Allen)*

COLEY SE1226
Brown Horse (01422) 202112
Lane Ends, Denholme Gate Road (A644 Brighouse–Keighley, a mile N of Hipperholme); HX3 7SD Popular roadside pub (some recent renovations) with

enjoyable reasonably priced home-made food (not Sun evening), well kept Brakspears, Saltaire, Timothy Taylors Landlord and a guest, cheerful attentive staff, open fires, small back conservatory overlooking beer garden; children welcome, no dogs inside, open all day. *(John and Eleanor Holdsworth, Gordon and Margaret Ormondroyd)*

CONEYTHORPE   SE3958
★ Tiger (01423) 863632
2.3 miles from A1(M) junction 47; A59 towards York, then village signposted (and brown sign to Tiger Inn); bear left at brown sign in Flaxby; HG5 0RY Spreading red-carpeted bar with hundreds of pewter tankards hanging from ochre-painted joists, padded wall seats, pews and settles around sturdy scrubbed tables, olde-worlde prints, china figurines in one arched alcove, open fire, more formal back dining area, tasty sensibly priced food from lunchtime sandwiches through pub favourites, also set deals, well kept Black Sheep, Copper Dragon and Timothy Taylors Landlord, good range of wines, friendly helpful staff; background music; picnic-sets on front gravel terrace and on small green opposite, open all day. *(Margaret and Peter Staples, John and Eleanor Holdsworth)*

COXWOLD   SE5377
Fauconberg Arms (01347) 868214
Off A170 Thirsk–Helmsley, via Kilburn or Wass; easily found off A19 too; YO61 4AD 17th-c village pub with heavily beamed flagstoned bar, log fires in both linked areas (one in unusual arched fireplace in a broad low inglenook), some attractive oak chairs made by local craftsmen alongside more usual pub furnishings, old local photographs and copper implements, Theakstons and a couple of guests, proper cider and good range of malt whiskies, well liked traditional home-cooked food, friendly service, elegant, gently upmarket dining room; live music some weekends, pool, free wi-fi; children welcome, dogs in bar, views from terrace over fields to Byland Abbey (EH), picnic-sets on front cobbles, eight comfortable bedrooms, open all day weekends; still for sale last we heard, so things may change. *(John Harris, Gus Swan, Richard Kennell)*

CRAY   SD9479
★ White Lion (01756) 760262
B6160 N of Kettlewell; BD23 5JB Refurbished beamed drovers' inn set in lovely countryside high up on Buckden Pike; flagstoned bar with button-back leather chesterfields and armchairs in front of woodburner, cushioned window seat and shelves of books, simple little back room (good for wet dogs), ales such as Black Sheep, Hop Studio and Wharfedale, eight wines by the glass and good food from short but varied menu including lunchtime

sandwiches, more flagstones in attractive dining room with antique-style chairs around chunky tables, some exposed stonework and old farming equipment; background music, free wi-fi; children welcome, comfortable bedrooms in pub and converted barn, picnic-sets above quiet steep lane or can sit on flat limestone slabs in shallow stream opposite, open all day. *(Kate Moran, Luke Morgan, Peter and Emma Kelly, Susan and Callum Slade)*

CROPTON   SE7588
New Inn (01751) 417330
Village signposted off A170 W of Pickering; YO18 8HH Modernised village pub with own Great Yorkshire beers and guests (can tour brewery Tues-Sat lunchtime for £7.50 – includes a pint); public bar with plush seating, panelling and small fire, downstairs conservatory (doubles as visitor centre at busy times) and elegant restaurant with local artwork, fairly straightforward food from sandwiches up; background music, TV, games machine, darts and pool; well behaved children and dogs (in bar) welcome, garden and brewery shop, bedrooms, open all day. *(Alister and Margery Bacon)*

DACRE BANKS   SE1961
★ Royal Oak (01423) 780200
B6451 S of Pateley Bridge; HG3 4EN Popular 18th-c stone pub with lovely Nidderdale views from the back, good traditional food (not Sun or Mon evenings) along with daily specials and events such as summer seafood festival, attentive friendly staff, half a dozen well kept changing ales and good choice of wines and gins, beams and panelling, log-fire dining room, games room with darts, dominoes and pool; background music, TV, free wi-fi; children welcome in eating areas, no dogs, seats on front terrace and in back garden, three bedrooms, big breakfast, open all day. *(Michael Butler)*

DANBY   NZ7008
Duke of Wellington (01287) 660351
West Lane; YO21 2LY 18th-c creeper-clad inn overlooking village green, usually four yorkshire ales such as Copper Dragon and Daleside, enjoyable home-made food from shortish menu; children and dogs welcome, clean tidy bedrooms. *(Mick Allen)*

DARLEY   SE1961
Wellington Inn (01423) 780362
B6451; Darley Head; HG3 2QQ Extended roadside stone inn with fine Nidderdale views; beams and big open fire in bar, modern restaurant with light wood floor and small conservatory, enjoyable freshly made food (all day weekends in summer) from sandwiches up, well kept Black Sheep, Copper Dragon, Timothy Taylors and Tetleys, helpful friendly staff; children and dogs (in bar) welcome, seats on large grassed area, 12 bedrooms, good breakfast, open all day. *(Jill and Dick Archer)*

DEWSBURY   SE2622

Huntsman (01924) 275700

Walker Cottages, Chidswell Lane, Shaw Cross – pub signed; WF12 7SW Cosy low-beamed converted cottages alongside urban-fringe farm, original features including an old range in the snug, agricultural bric-a-brac, brassware, plates and bottles on delft shelving, blazing woodburner, small front extension, four changing local beers such as Bosuns, Partners and Timothy Taylors, well priced traditional home-made food (Thurs-Sat, till 4pm Sun), friendly staff and nice relaxed atmosphere; children welcome, no dogs inside, open all day Fri-Sun, closed Mon and lunchtimes Tues, Weds. *(Michael Butler)*

DEWSBURY   SE2421

★West Riding Licensed Refreshment Rooms (01924) 459193

Station (Platform 2), Wellington Road; WF13 1HF Convivial three-room early Victorian station bar, eight well kept changing ales, foreign bottled beers and farm ciders, good value food such as all-day breakfast, burgers and pizzas, friendly staff, lots of railway memorabilia and pictures, coal fire; juke box and live music; children till 6pm in two end rooms, disabled access, on Transpennine Rail Ale Trail, open all day. *(Jimmy)*

DONCASTER   SE5702

Corner Pin (01302) 340670

St Sepulchre Gate West, Cleveland Street; DN1 3AH Traditional corner pub with plush beamed lounge and cheery public bar, five well kept ales, good value traditional home-made food (not Mon-Thurs) including popular Sun lunch; juke box, TV, Sun quiz; children welcome, seats on back decking, open all day. *(Gary and Marie Miller)*

DOWNHOLME   SE1197

★Bolton Arms (01748) 823716

Village signposted just off A6108 Leyburn–Richmond; DL11 6AE Stone-built pub with wonderful Swaledale views from garden and dining conservatory; simply furnished carpeted bar down a few steps with two smallish linked areas, plush wall banquettes, collection of gleaming brass and few small country pictures, log fire in neat fireplace, ales such as Timothy Taylors and Wensleydale, ten wines by the glass and eight malt whiskies, good food from lunchtime baguettes up; background music, free wi-fi; children welcome, two bedrooms sharing bathroom, closed Tues lunchtime. *(Mungo Shipley, Patricia Hawkins, Caroline Sullivan)*

EASINGWOLD   SE5270

★George (01347) 821698

Market Place; YO61 3AD Neat market town hotel (former 18th-c coaching inn) with slightly old-fashioned feel and popular with older customers, quiet corners even when

busy, well kept Black Sheep, Timothy Taylors and a guest, good sensibly priced food in bar and restaurant including daily specials, helpful cheerful service; soft background music, free wi-fi; children welcome, no dogs, disabled access, pleasant bedrooms and good breakfast, open all day. *(Charlotte and William Mason)*

EAST MARTON   SD9050

Cross Keys (01282) 844326

A59 Gisburn–Skipton; BD23 3LP Spacious refurbished 17th-c pub behind small green looking down on Leeds & Liverpool Canal; black beams, bare boards and patterned carpet, woodburner in big stone fireplace, good generous food from hot and cold sandwiches, sharing plates and pub favourites up, well kept Copper Dragon and Greyhawk ales, friendly service, further dining area down steps; background music; children, walkers and dogs welcome, picnic-sets on front deck, near Pennine Way, open (and food) all day weekends in winter, may open all day in summer. *(John and Eleanor Holdsworth)*

EAST MORTON   SE0941

Busfeild Arms (01274) 563169

Main Road; BD20 5SP Attractive 19th-c stone-built village pub (originally a school); traditionally furnished beamed and flagstoned bar with woodburner, Saltaire, Timothy Taylors, Tetleys and a guest, good range of enjoyable well priced food including gluten-free menu, weekday early-bird deal (5.30-6.30pm), efficient cheerful service, restaurant; Thurs quiz, live music Sat, sports TV; children welcome, picnic-sets on front terrace, three bedrooms, open all day, food till 6pm Sun. *(Gordon and Margaret Ormondroyd)*

EAST WITTON   SE1487

★Cover Bridge Inn (01969) 623250

A6108 out towards Middleham; DL8 4SQ Cosy and welcoming 16th-c flagstoned country local, good choice of well kept yorkshire-brewed ales and enjoyable generously served pub food at sensible prices, small restaurant, roaring fires; children and dogs welcome, riverside garden with play area, three bedrooms, open all day. *(Ben and Jenny Settle)*

EBBERSTON   SE8983

Grapes (01723) 859273

High Street (A170); YO13 9PA Modernised roadside pub, plenty of emphasis on their good well presented food from short if not particularly cheap menu, nice wines and a couple of real ales such as Greene King; children and dogs welcome, open all day weekends. *(Sara Fulton, Roger Baker)*

EGTON   NZ8006

★Wheatsheaf (01947) 895271

Village centre; YO21 1TZ 19th-c village pub of real character, interesting pictures and collectables in small bare-boards bar with fire in old range, very good generously served food including daily specials, friendly service, Black Sheep, Timothy Taylors Landlord and a summer guest, several wines by the glass, restaurant; four bedrooms in adjacent cottage, closed Mon, no food Sun evening. *(John Robinson)*

EGTON BRIDGE   NZ8005
Horseshoe (01947) 895245
Village signed off A171 W of Whitby; YO21 1XE Attractively placed 18th-c stone inn; open fire, high-backed built-in winged settles, wall seats and spindleback chairs, various odds and ends including a big stuffed trout (caught nearby in 1913), Theakstons Best and a couple of guests, popular food using their own eggs and vegetables and locally sourced meat; background music, free wi-fi; children welcome, dogs in side bar during mealtimes, seats on quiet terrace in nice mature garden by small River Esk, good walks (on Coast to Coast path), six bedrooms, open all day weekends (food till 7pm Sun). *(Kerry and Guy Trooper)*

EGTON BRIDGE   NZ8005
★ ## Postgate (01947) 895241
Village signed off A171 W of Whitby; YO21 1UX Moorland village pub next to railway station; good imaginative food at fair prices including fresh local fish (lots of blackboard menus), friendly staff, well kept Black Sheep and a guest, traditional quarry-tiled bar with beams, panelled dado and coal fire in antique range, elegant restaurant; children and dogs welcome, walled front garden with picnic-sets either side of brick path, three comfortable bedrooms. *(Maria and Bertie Farr)*

ELLAND   SE1021
Barge & Barrel (01422) 254604
Quite handy for M62 junction 24; Park Road (A6025, via A629 and B6114); HX5 9HP Large roadside pub by Calder & Hebble Navigation, own-brew beers and plenty of guests, pubby food including Fri steak night, lounge bar, snug with open fire and games room; Thurs quiz and occasional live music, free wi-fi; children (until 8pm) and dogs welcome, waterside seats and moorings, limited parking, open all day. *(Barbara and Phil Bowie)*

EMBSAY   SE0053
Elm Tree (01756) 790717
Elm Tree Square; BD23 6RB Popular open-plan beamed village pub, hearty helpings of good value food including blackboard specials, four well kept ales such as Tetleys and Thwaites, cheerful young staff; comfortable bedrooms, handy for Embsay & Bolton Abbey Steam Railway. *(Jimmy)*

FACEBY   NZ4903
Sutton Arms (01642) 700382
Mill Lane/Bank Lane; TS9 7BW Welcoming village dining pub at foot of Cleveland Hills, clean, comfortable and cosy,

with low beamed central bar flanked by eating areas, highly regarded freshly made food (best to book) from pub favourites to more restauranty choices including excellent steaks, well kept ales such as Thwaites Wainwright and good selection of wines, friendly attentive service; tables on tiered front deck, three simply furnished but well appointed bedrooms, good hearty breakfast, closed Sun evening, Mon, Tues and lunchtimes apart from Sun. *(Michael Doswell)*

FEARBY   SE1980
Black Swan (01765) 689477
Keld Bank; HG4 4NF Recently refurbished after fire, beamed bar with dining area to the right, woodburner in pale stone fireplace, Black Sheep, Theakstons and a couple of regional summer guests, several wines by the glass and good food from varied menu including daily specials (seafood and game festivals), friendly helpful service, lovely valley views from back restaurant (more rustic in style); children welcome till 7pm, dogs in bar, 14 modern bedrooms (12 in annexe), camping, open all day summer (from 3pm weekdays, all day weekends in winter). *(Charlotte and William Mason)*

FERRENSBY   SE3660
★ ## General Tarleton (01423) 340284
A655 N of Knaresborough; HG5 0PZ Carefully renovated 18th-c coaching inn, more restaurant-with-rooms than pub, but there's an informal bar with sofas and woodburner serving well kept Black Sheep, Timothy Taylors Landlord and a dozen wines by the glass; other open-plan rooms with low beams, exposed stonework and brick pillars creating alcoves, dark leather high-backed dining chairs around wooden tables, first class modern cooking from owner-chef along with more traditional food and children's menu, pleasant well trained staff; seats in covered courtyard and tree-lined garden, pretty rural views, 13 stylish bedrooms, good breakfast. *(Janet and Peter Race, Peter and Anne Hollindale)*

FILEY   TA1180
Bonhommes (01723) 515325
The Crescent; YO14 9JH Friendly old-fasianed bustling bar with up to five well kept ales and four ciders, good value food (not Sun evening) including home-made pizzas; regular live music, bingo (Thurs), karaoke (Fri), quiz (Thurs and Sat); children and dogs welcome, open all day till midnight. *(Joe Oswald)*

FINGHALL   SE1889
★ ## Queens Head (01677) 450259
Off A684 E of Leyburn; DL8 5ND Welcoming comfortable dining pub, log fires either end of low-beamed carpeted bar with stone archway, settles making stalls around big tables, four real ales such as Theakstons and Wensleydale, good food from

deli boards and traditional favourites up including lunchtime/early-evening set menus, efficient service, extended dining room with Wensleydale view; children welcome, no dogs inside, disabled access/facilities, back garden with decking sharing same view, three bedrooms, may stay open all day on busy weekends. *(Clive and Fran Dutson)*

FIXBY   SE1119
Nags Head (01727) 871100
New Hey Road, by M62 junction 24 south side, past Hilton; HD2 2EA Spacious ivy-clad chain dining pub, busy pubby bar with four well kept ales, wide choice of enjoyable fairly priced food, friendly efficient service, linked areas with wood and slate floors, restaurant on two levels; garden tables, bedrooms in next-door Premier Inn, open all day from 7am.
(Gordon and Margaret Ormondroyd)

GARGRAVE   SD9253
Masons Arms (01756) 749510
Church Street/Marton Road (off A65 NW of Skipton); BD23 3NL Traditional beamed pub with welcoming local atmosphere; open interior divided into bar, lounge and restaurant, log fire, ample helpings of enjoyable home-made food at very fair prices, well kept ales such as Black Sheep, Copper Dragon, Tetleys and Timothy Taylors from ornate counter, friendly efficient staff; live acoustic music first Fri of month in winter, darts; children and dogs welcome, tables out behind overlooking own bowling green, charming village on Pennine Way and not far from Leeds & Liverpool Canal, six barn conversion bedrooms, open (and food) all day. *(Jill and Dick Archer)*

GIGGLESWICK   SD8164
★**Black Horse** (01729) 822506
Church Street – take care with the car park; BD24 0BE Hospitable licensees at this 17th-c village pub prettily set by church; cosy bar with gleaming copper and brass, bric-a-brac and coal-effect fire, good value generously served food, well kept Timothy Taylors, Tetleys and guests, quick friendly service, intimate dining room; piano (often played), monthly quiz; children welcome till 9pm, no dogs (the resident doberman is Trevor), heated back terrace, smokers' shelter, three reasonably priced comfortable bedrooms, good breakfast, open all day weekends. *(Shirley Blenkinsopp)*

GIGGLESWICK   SD8164
Harts Head (01729) 822086
Belle Hill; BD24 0BA 18th-c village inn refurbished under new management (same owners as the Plough at Lupton – see Cumbria Main Entries); bar/lounge and restaurant, half a dozen well kept ales including Black Sheep, good food from varied fairly priced menu, friendly helpful staff; children and dogs (in bar) welcome,

picnic-sets on sloping lawn, seven bedrooms, open (and food) all day. *(Shirley Blenkinsopp)*

GILLAMOOR   SE6890
★**Royal Oak** (01751) 431414
Off A170 in Kirkbymoorside; YO62 7HX 18th-c stone-built dining pub with good food at sensible prices including vegetarian options and daily specials (evening menu has greater more varied choice), friendly staff, ales such as Black Sheep and Copper Dragon, reasonably priced wines, roomy bar with heavy dark beams, log fires in two tall stone fireplaces (one with old kitchen range), overspill dining room where dogs allowed; children welcome, eight comfortable modern bedrooms, good breakfast, attractive village handy for Barnsdale Moor walks. *(Ian and Rose Lock)*

GILLING EAST   SE6176
★**Fairfax Arms** (01439) 788212
Main Street (B1363, off A170 via Oswaldkirk); YO62 4JH Smartly presented pub in pleasant village; beamed bar with woodburner, Black Sheep, Tetleys and a couple of local guests from handsome oak counter, interesting wines by the glass, two-part carpeted dining room with big hunting prints, nicely old-fashioned floral curtains and some padded oak settles, good modern food along with sandwiches and pub favourites, neat attentive staff, newly added orangery and outside seating area by floodlit roadside stream; well placed for Howardian Hills and North York Moors, comfortable up-to-date bedrooms, good breakfast, open all day, food till 7pm Sun. *(John Coatsworth)*

GILLING WEST   NZ1805
White Swan (01748) 825122
High Street (B6274 just N of Richmond); DL10 5JG Welcoming 17th-c family-run village inn with open-plan bar and dining room, log fires, well kept ales including a house beer brewed by Mithril, enjoyable home-made food from yorkshire tapas, through burgers and fresh fish to steaks, Sat brunch, friendly accommodating staff; live music; children and dogs welcome, tables in courtyard, four bedrooms, open all day (from 4pm Tues). *(Comus and Sarah Elliott)*

GOATHLAND   NZ8200
Mallyan Spout Hotel (01947) 896486 *Opposite church; YO22 5AN* Old creeper-clad stone hotel with three spacious lounges and traditional bar, roaring fires and fine views, popular fairly priced bar food including Sun lunchtime carvery, three real ales, good wines and malt whiskies, friendly helpful staff, smart restaurant (separate evening menu); well behaved children welcome in eating areas, dogs in bar, handy for namesake waterfall, comfortable bedrooms and good buffet breakfast, open all day. *(Jimmy)*

GOODMANHAM   SE8943
Goodmanham Arms (01430) 873849
Main Street; YO43 3JA Unpretentious
little red-brick country pub (not to
everyone's taste) with three traditional
linked areas, beam-and-plank ceilings,
some red and black floor tiles, mix of new
and old furniture and plenty of interesting
odds and ends, even a Harley-Davidson,
seven real ales – three from on-site All
Hallows microbrewery, unfussy food from
italian owner (no starters), maybe a winter
casserole cooked over the open fire, evening
meals served 5-7pm Mon (steak and pies)
and Fri only; folk night first Thurs of month,
jazz/blues third Thurs, quiz every other Weds;
children and dogs welcome, good walks
(on Wolds Way), open all day. *(Mick Allen)*

GRANGE MOOR   SE2215
Kaye Arms (01924) 840228
Wakefield Road (A642); WF4 4BG
Smartly updated spotless dining pub
divided into three distinct areas, popular
good value food including meal deal for
two (not Sat evening, Sun), well kept ales
such as Black Sheep and plenty of wines
by the glass, efficient friendly service;
children welcome, handy for National Coal
Mining Museum, open (and food) all day
weekends. *(Gordon and Margaret Ormondroyd)*

GRASSINGTON   SE0064
Foresters Arms (01756) 752349
Main Street; BD23 5AA Comfortable
opened-up coaching inn with friendly
bustling atmosphere, six well kept regional
ales such as Black Sheep and Tetleys, decent
reasonably priced hearty food including
pizzas, log fires; popular Mon quiz, sports
TV, darts and pool; children and dogs
welcome, a few tables out at front, seven
affordable bedrooms, good breakfast, open
all day. *(Dan and Belinda Smallbone)*

GREAT AYTON   NZ5610
Royal Oak (01642) 200283
*Off A173 – follow village signs; High
Green; TS9 6BW* Popular 18th-c village inn
with good promptly served food including
set menu (till 6.30pm), well kept Caledonian
Deuchars IPA and Theakstons, convivial
bar with log fire, beam-and-plank ceiling
and bulgy old partly panelled stone walls,
traditional furnishings including antique
settles, pleasant views of elegant green
from bay windows, two linked dining rooms,
back one appealingly old-fashioned and
catering for tour groups; children welcome,
dogs in bar, four comfortable bedrooms,
handy for Cleveland Way, open (and food)
all day. *(Tony and Wendy Hobden)*

GREAT BROUGHTON   NZ5405
Bay Horse (01642) 712319
High Street; TS9 7HA Big creeper-
clad dining pub in attractive village,
wide choice of food including blackboard
specials and good value set lunch,
friendly attentive service, real ales such
as Camerons and Jennings, restaurant;
children welcome (under-5s till 8pm),
seats outside, open (and food) all day
weekends. *(Trish and Karl Soloman)*

GREAT HABTON   SE7576
★Grapes (01653) 669166
*Corner of Habton Lane and Kirby
Misperton Lane; YO17 6TU* Popular
and genuinely welcoming beamed dining
pub in small village, homely and cosy, with
good cooking including fresh local fish
and game, Marstons-related ales, open
fire, small public bar with darts and TV;
background music; a few roadside picnic-
sets, nice walks, open all day Sun, closed
Mon, weekday lunchtimes. *(Mick Allen)*

GUISELEY   SE1941
Coopers (01943) 878835
Otley Road; LS20 8AH Market Town
Tavern conversion of former Co-op store,
open-plan bare-boards bar with good range
of well priced food from ciabattas and snacks
up, eight real ales including Okells, Roosters
and Timothy Taylors, also craft kegs, bottled
beers and decent range of wines, good
friendly service, upstairs function/dining
room; sports TV, free wi-fi; dogs welcome,
open (and food) all day. *(Jackie Robinson)*

GUNNERSIDE   SD9598
Kings Head (01748) 886261
B6270, road down Swaledale; DL11 6LD
Small two-room pub (former 17th-c
blacksmith's) in pretty riverside dales
village, Black Sheep ales, decent wines
and enjoyable reasonably priced pubby
food from baguettes up, woodburner in big
stone fireplace, flagstones and carpet, old
village photographs; children, walkers and
dogs welcome, picnic sets out at front near
bridge, open all day. *(Roy and Gill Payne)*

HALIFAX   SE0925
Mill (01422) 647494
Dean Clough; HX3 5AX Newly opened
bar in former carpet mill, good choice of
craft beers, wines and cocktails, enjoyable
food from italian leaning menu including
good pizzas, friendly efficient service;
background music; handy for Northern
Broadsides theatre, open all day till 10pm
(midnight Fri, Sat). *(Jimmy)*

HALIFAX   SE0924
Three Pigeons (01422) 347001
*Sun Fold, South Parade; off Church
Street; HX1 2LX* Carefully restored,
four-room 1930s pub (Grade II listed), art
deco fittings, ceiling painting in octagonal
main area, original flooring, panelling
and tiled fireplaces, range of Ossett beers
along with guests such as Fernandes and
Rat, good Robinson's pies, friendly chatty

staff; tables outside, handy for Eureka! museum and Shay Stadium (pub very busy on match days), open all day Fri-Sun, otherwise from 4pm. *(Pat and Tony Martin)*

HAROME
SE6482

★**Star** (01439) 770397

High Street; village signed S of A170, E of Helmsley; YO62 5JE Pretty 14th-c thatched pub-restaurant; bar with bowed beam-and-plank ceiling, plenty of bric-a-brac and interesting furniture including 'Mouseman' Thompson pieces, log fire and well polished tiled kitchen range, three changing ales and plenty of wines by the glass, smart restaurant for chef-owner's highly regarded inventive cooking (not cheap), also snacks in cocktail bar and a coffee loft in the eaves, well trained helpful staff; background music; children welcome, seats on sheltered front terrace, more in garden, nine bedrooms (some quirky touches) in building across the road, very good breakfast, open all day Sun, closed Mon lunchtime. *(John and Penny Wildon, Mr and Mrs Richard Osborne)*

HARPHAM
TA0961

St Quintin Arms (01262) 490329

Main Street; YO25 4QY Comfortable old village pub with enjoyable reasonably priced home-made food including plenty of specials, well kept Tetleys and Wold Top, good friendly service, bar and small dining room; sports TV, daily papers; children welcome, sheltered garden with pond, on National Cycle Route 1, three bedrooms, open all day Weds-Sat, closed lunchtimes Mon and Tues. *(Kerry and Guy Trooper)*

HARROGATE
SE3155

Coach & Horses (01423) 561802

West Park; HG1 1BJ Friendly bustling pub with up to eight good yorkshire-brewed ales, 80 malt whiskies and over 30 gins, enjoyable good value lunchtime food (not Sat) plus some themed evenings, comfortable interior arranged around central bar with booths and other cosy areas; regular Fri charity raffle, Sun quiz; no children or dogs, open all day. *(Chris Sale)*

HARROGATE
SE2955

★**Hales** (01423) 725570

Crescent Road; HG1 2RS Classic Victorian décor in 18th-c gas-lit local close to the Pump Rooms; leather seats in alcoves, stuffed birds, comfortable saloon and tiny snug, half a dozen ales including Daleside, simple good value lunchtime food, friendly helpful staff; can get lively weekend evenings, open all day. *(Mick Allen)*

HARROGATE
SE2955

Old Bell (01423) 507930

Royal Parade; HG1 2SZ Recently refurbished Market Town Tavern with seven real ales, eight craft beers and good selection of wines and gins, friendly helpful

staff, fairly traditional food from ciabattas up, mix of furniture including iron-framed tables and leather tub chairs on wood floors, Anaglypta dado, servery made from an old mahogany dresser, some vintage sweet shop ads, further seating upstairs; children (if eating) and dogs welcome, open all day, food all day Fri, Sat, till 7pm Sun. *(Steve Whalley)*

HARROGATE
SE3155

Winter Gardens (01423) 877010

Royal Baths, Crescent Road; HG1 2RR Interesting Wetherspoons conversion of former ballroom in landmark building, plenty of well kept ales and their usual good value food, many original features, comfortable sofas in lofty hall, upper gallery; TVs, free wi-fi; children welcome, seats on attractive terrace, open all day and can be very busy late evening. *(Chris Sale)*

HARTSHEAD
SE1822

★**Gray Ox** (01274) 872845

3.5 miles from M62 junction 25; A644 towards Dewsbury, left on to A62, next left on to B6119, first left into Fall Lane, left into Hartshead Lane – pub on right; WF15 8AL Rather smart stone-built moorland dining pub; main bar with beams, flagstones and roaring log fire, bentwood chairs and leather stools around stripped-pine tables, Jennings, Thwaites and a guest, 15 wines by the glass and range of cocktails, comfortable carpeted dining areas off with high-backed chairs around polished tables, very popular inventive food including lunchtime/early-evening set menu, good cheerful service; background music; children welcome, fine views over Calder Valley to the distant outskirts of Huddersfield from outside tables, open all day weekends, food till 7pm Sun. *(Michael Butler, John and Eleanor Holdsworth, Gordon and Margaret Ormondroyd)*

HAWES
SD8789

Crown (01969) 667212

Market Place; DL8 3RD Welcoming traditional market town local divided into four areas, open fires/woodburners and some interesting old photographs, well kept ales including a couple from Theakstons, hearty helpings of good value pub food including deals, friendly helpful staff; free wi-fi; children, walkers and dogs welcome, seats out on cobbled front forecourt and in back split-level beer garden with lovely Wensleydale views, three bedrooms, open all day. *(Joe Oswald)*

HAWES
SD8789

White Hart (01969) 667214

Main Street; DL8 3QL Welcoming 16th-c coaching inn on cobbled street, emphasis on good fairly priced food, but also four well kept regional ales, friendly quick service, bar with fire in antique range, daily papers, restaurant; children and dogs welcome, five bedrooms, open (and food) all day. *(WAH)*

HAWNBY   SE5489
Inn at Hawnby (01439) 798202
*Aka Hawnby Hotel; off B1257 NW of
Helmsley; YO62 5QS* Welcoming stone-
built inn set in pretty moorland village, good
food from traditional choices up, ales such as
Black Sheep and Great Newsome, ten wines
by the glass, helpful friendly service; children
welcome, dogs in bar (but must ask first),
lovely views from restaurant and garden
tables, good walking country, nine quiet
bedrooms (three in converted stables over
road), open all day Fri-Sun. *(Dave Braisted)*

HEADINGLEY   SE2736
Arcadia (0113) 274 5599
Arndale Centre; LS6 2UE Glass-fronted
Market Town Tavern in former bank, eight
changing regional ales, a couple of craft
kegs and over 100 bottled beers, good
range of wines too, friendly knowledgeable
staff, snacky food including very good local
cheese, stairs to mezzanine; no children;
open all day. *(Peter Smith and Judith Brown)*

HEATH   SE3520
Kings Arms (01924) 377527
*Village signposted from A655 Wakefield–
Normanton – or, more directly, turn
off to the left opposite Horse & Groom;
WF1 5SL* Popular old-fashioned gas-lit
pub of genuine character; fire in black
range (long row of smoothing irons on the
mantelpiece), plain elm stools, built-in
oak settles and dark panelling, well kept
Ossett and several guests, standard food
(all day Fri and Sat, till 7pm Sun), more
comfortable extension preserving original
style, two other small flagstoned rooms and
a conservatory; summer folk events, Tues
quiz, free wi-fi; children and dogs (in bar)
welcome, benches out at front facing village
green (surrounded by fine 19th-c stone
merchants' houses), picnic-sets on side lawn
and in nice walled garden, usually open all
day (may shut early if quiet). *(Michael Butler)*

HEBDEN   SE0263
Clarendon (01756) 752446
B6265; BD23 5DE Well cared-for
modernised inn surrounded by wonderful
moorland walking country; bar, snug and
restaurant, open fire, ales such as Black
Sheep, Thwaites and Timothy Taylors, good
range of enjoyable food (till 7pm Sun) from
pubby choices up including blackboard
specials, cheerful relaxed atmosphere;
Sun quiz, Oct beer/food festival; children
welcome, farm shop, five bedrooms, open
all day weekends. *(John and Eleanor
Holdsworth, Hunter and Christine Wright)*

HEBDEN BRIDGE   SD9922
Hinchcliffe Arms (01422) 883256
Off B6138; HX7 5TA Tucked-away
stone-built pub in great walking country
on the Calderdale Way and near Stoodley

Pike; refurbished under present owners
with open-plan bar to the left and
restaurant on the right, three Lees ales
and a guest, enjoyable fairly traditional
home-made food from sandwiches up,
friendly service; children, dogs (in bar)
and walkers welcome, a few seats out
at front, picturesque setting close to
stream and Victorian church, open (and
food) all day weekends, Sun till 9pm
(6pm), closed Mon. *(Gordon and Margaret
Ormondroyd, John and Eleanor Holdsworth)*

HEBDEN BRIDGE   SD9927
Old Gate (01422) 843993
Oldgate; HX7 8JP Busy bar-restaurant
with wide choice of popular food served
from 10am breakfast on, eight well kept
ales, plenty of bottled beers and good
range of wines by the glass including
champagne, helpful friendly service,
upstairs room for comedy club (second
Sun of month) and assorted other
events; children welcome, tables outside,
open (and food) all day. *(WAH)*

HEBDEN BRIDGE   SD9827
Stubbings Wharf (01422) 844107
About a mile W; HX7 6LU Friendly
pub in good spot by Rochdale Canal,
popular good value food from sandwiches
and light meals up, half a dozen well kept
regional ales, proper ciders, comfortable
carpeted interior with local pictures;
children and dogs welcome, adjacent
moorings and boat trips, open (and food)
all day. *(Gordon and Margaret Ormondroyd)*

HELMSLEY   SE6183
Feathers (01439) 770275
Market Place; YO62 5BH Substantial
old stone inn overlooking the market
square, enjoyable food (all day Sat)
from sandwiches to popular Sun carvery,
well kept Black Sheep, Tetleys and
a local guest, good friendly service,
several rooms with comfortable seats,
oak and walnut tables (some by Robert
'Mouseman' Thompson – as is the bar
counter), flagstones or tartan carpet, heavy
medieval beams and huge inglenook log
fire; children and dogs (in bar) welcome,
terrace tables with heaters, 22 bedrooms,
open all day. *(Tony and Wendy Hobden)*

HELWITH BRIDGE   SD8169
Helwith Bridge Inn (01729) 860220
Off B6479 N of Stainforth; BD24 0EH
Friendly unpretentious village local
popular with walkers, up to eight well
kept ales in flagstoned bar, enjoyable
reasonably priced pub food including
Thurs steak night, dining room with light
wood furniture on bare boards; free wi-fi;
children and dogs welcome, camping and
basic bunkhouse, by River Ribble and
Settle–Carlisle railway, open all day, food
all day weekends. *(Jill and Dick Archer)*

HEPWORTH SE1606
Butchers Arms (01484) 687147
*Village signposted off A616 SE of
Holmfirth; Towngate; HD9 1TE* Old
country dining pub with french-influenced
cooking including themed evenings, three
well kept Yorkshire ales, decent wines
by the glass and cocktails, flagstones by
counter, bare boards elsewhere, log fire,
low beams (handsomely carved in room on
right); regular live music and quiz nights;
children, walkers and dogs welcome,
terrace seating, closed Mon, otherwise
open (and food) all day. *(James Knight)*

HETTON SD9658
★**Angel** (01756) 730263
*Off B6265 Skipton–Grassington;
BD23 6LT* Creeper-clad former drover's
inn with plenty of emphasis on their good
imaginative food; most informal part is the
beamed and timbered bar-brasserie with
copper kettles, bed warmers, horsebrasses
and so forth on red-painted walls, working
Victorian range in big stone fireplace,
ales such as Black Sheep, Dark Horse and
Hetton, an award-winning wine list with
20 by the glass and a large choice of malt
whiskies, also two smart restaurant rooms
with high-backed and plush tub chairs
around white-clothed tables; children
welcome, front terrace with tables under
awnings, individually styled bedrooms in
converted barn or more modern Sycamore
Bank opposite, good breakfast, open all day.
*(W K Wood, Peter Smith and Judith Brown,
Nick Higgins, Hunter and Christine Wright)*

HIGH HOYLAND SE2710
Cherry Tree (01226) 382541
*Bank End Lane; 3 miles W of M1
junction 38; S75 4BE* Split-level
whitewashed village pub, well kept
Acorn Barnsley Bitter, Black Sheep and
a couple of guests, good range of enjoyable
generously served food (not Sun evening),
competitive prices and friendly young staff,
beams and open fire, dining areas each
end of bar and separate small restaurant;
background music; children and dogs
welcome, front roadside picnic-sets with
lovely views over Cannon Hall Country
Park, open all day. *(Michael Butler)*

HOLMFIRTH SD1408
Nook (01484) 681568
Victoria Square/South Lane; HD9 2DN
Friendly tucked-away 18th-c stone local
run by same family for two generations,
own-brew beers and guests, low-priced
home-made pubby food including good
burgers, no-frills bar areas with flagstones

and quarry tiles, big open fire; juke box,
pool; heated streamside terrace, bedrooms,
open (and food) all day. *(Angie Mayer)*

HOPPERTON SE4256
Masons (01423) 330442
Hopperton Street; HG5 8NX Village
dining pub with good food from standards
up, a couple of real ales and decent range
of gins, friendly helpful staff, snug pubby
bar, extended restaurant with high-backed
leather chairs at mix of table on tiled floor,
open fires; background music, free wi-fi;
children and dogs (in bar) welcome, closed
Mon and Tues, no food Sun evening. *(John
and Eleanor Holdsworth, Graham Gill)*

HORBURY SE2918
Boons (01924) 277267
Queen Street; WF4 6LP Comfortably
unpretentious flagstoned local, chatty
and relaxed, with Clarks, John Smiths,
Timothy Taylors Landlord and up to
four quickly changing guests, pleasant
young staff, no food or children, rugby
league memorabilia, warm fire, back tap
room with pool and TV; courtyard tables,
open all day Fri-Sun. *(Michael Butler)*

HORBURY SE2918
Cricketers (01924) 267032
Cluntergate; WF4 5AG Welcoming
refurbished Edwardian pub; Bosuns,
Timothy Taylors and six local guests, also
craft beers such as BrewDog, real cider and
good selection of spirits, reasonably priced
cheeseboards and meze platters; regular
beer festivals and tap takeovers; open all day
Fri-Sun, from 4pm other days. *(Mick Allen)*

HORSFORTH SE2438
Town Street Tavern (0113) 281 9996
Town Street; LS18 4RJ Market Town
Tavern with eight well kept ales and lots
of draught/bottled continental beers, good
food in small bar or upstairs restaurant,
friendly helpful service; children and dogs
(downstairs) welcome, small terrace, open all
day, food all day Sat, till 6pm Sun. *(Jimmy)*

HUBBERHOLME SD9278
★**George** (01756) 760223
Dubbs Lane; BD23 5JE Ancient little
dales inn, beautifully placed and run by
friendly licensees; heavy beams, flagstones
and stripped stone, enjoyable fairly priced
home-made food (booking advised evenings)
from lunchtime sandwiches (not Sun)
up, Black Sheep and three guests, open
fire, perpetual candle on bar; outside
lavatories; children allowed in dining
area, well-behaved dogs in bar (pub jack
russell is George), terrace seating, River

We include some hotels with a good bar that offers facilities comparable
to those of a pub.

Wharfe fishing rights, six comfortable clean bedrooms (three in annexe), good breakfast, open all day Sat, till 5pm Sun, closed Mon lunchtime, Tues. *(Steve Lumb)*

HUDDERSFIELD   SE1416
Grove (01484) 430113
Spring Grove Street; HD1 4BP Friendly two-bar pub with huge selection of bottled beers (some gluten-free), 19 well kept/priced ales including Oakham, Timothy Taylors and Thornbridge, 120 malt whiskies and 60 vodkas, also real cider, knowledgeable staff, no food but choice of snacks from dried crickets to biltong; live music Tues and Thurs evenings, art gallery; children and dogs welcome, back terrace, open 12-11 Fri-Sun, from 2pm other days. *(Shirley Blenkinsopp)*

HUDDERSFIELD   SE1416
Kings Head (01484) 511058
Station, St Georges Square; HD1 1JF Friendly well run pub in renovated Victorian station building; spacious high-ceilinged main bar with original tiled floor, ten well kept beers and good sandwiches/cobs, other rooms off; regular live music, Jimi Hendrix pub sign; dogs welcome, disabled access via platform 1, open all day. *(Shirley Blenkinsopp)*

HUDDERSFIELD   SE1416
Rat & Ratchet (01484) 542400
Chapel Hill; HD1 3EB Popular split-level pub with own-brew beers and several guests including Ossett, good range of ciders/perries too, pork pies and sausage rolls, friendly staff; open all day Fri-Sun, from 3pm other days. *(James Knight)*

HUDDERSFIELD   SE1417
Slubbers Arms (01484) 429032
Halifax Old Road; HD1 6HW Friendly V-shaped traditional three-room pub, good range of beers including Timothy Taylors from horseshoe bar, pie-and-peas menu, black and white photographs and old wartime posters, warm fire, games room; well behaved dogs welcome, terrace for smokers, open from 4pm Mon-Thurs, 3pm Fri, Sat, 2pm Sun. *(Shirley Blenkinsopp)*

HUDDERSFIELD   SE1417
Sportsman (01484) 421929
St Johns Road; HD1 5AY Same owners as the West Riding Licensed Refreshment Rooms at Dewsbury; restored 1930s interior with lounge and two cosy side rooms, eight real ales and four craft beers, friendly knowledgeable staff, pie menu served Fri-Sun; live music Sat; dogs welcome, handy for station, open all day. *(Shirley Blenkinsopp)*

HUDDERSFIELD   SE1415
Star (01484) 545443
Albert Street, Lockwood; HD1 3PJ Unpretentious friendly local with excellent range of competitively priced ales kept well by enthusiastic landlady, continental beers

and real cider too, beer festivals in back marquee, open fire; open all day weekends, closed Mon and lunchtimes Tues-Fri. *(JMB)*

HUDSWELL   NZ1400
George & Dragon (01748) 518373
Hudswell Lane; DL11 6BL Popular community-owned village pub run by welcoming landlord, enjoyable good value home-made food from short menu (not Sun evening) plus a few daily specials, five well kept ales such as Copper Dragon, Rudgate and Wensleydale, various craft beers too, friendly atmosphere; small shop and library, free wi-fi; children and dogs welcome, panoramic Swaledale views from back terrace, open all day weekends. *(Alister and Margery Bacon)*

HULL   TA1028
★**Olde White Harte** (01482) 326363
Passage off Silver Street; HU1 1JG Dating from the 16th c with Civil War history, carved heavy beams, attractive stained glass, oak panelling and two big inglenooks with frieze of delft tiles, well kept Caledonian, Theakstons and guests from copper-topped counter, 80 or so malt whiskies; old skull (found here in the 19th c) displayed in Perspex case; children welcome, dogs in bar, heated courtyard, open all day. *(Jimmy)*

HUNMANBY   TA1077
Piebald (01723) 447577
Sands Lane; E of level crossing; YO14 0LT Comfortably renovated pub with well stocked bar and separate dining room, popular generously served food featuring more than 50 different pies, up to five real ales including a house beer from Greene King, friendly helpful staff; children welcome, picnic-sets on side terrace and lawn bordering railway line, camping, open (and food) all day. *(Stephen Woad)*

HUTTON-LE-HOLE   SE7089
Crown (01751) 417343
The Green; YO62 6UA Overlooking pretty village green with wandering sheep in classic coach-trip country; enjoyable home-made pubby food (not Sun evening), Black Sheep, Tetleys and a guest, decent wines by the glass, cheerful efficient service, opened-up bar with varnished woodwork, dining area; quiz first Sun of month; children and clean dogs welcome, small site available for caravans behind, Ryedale Folk Museum next door and handy for Farndale walks, open all day. *(Joe Oswald)*

ILKLEY   SE1147
Bar t'at (01943) 608888
Cunliffe Road; LS29 9DZ Extended Market Town Tavern with eight well kept mainly local ales and good wine and bottled beer choice, enjoyable well priced pubby food from sandwiches and snacks up, steak night first Fri of the month, candlelit cellar

dining area, friendly service; upstairs loos; dogs welcome, back terrace with heated canopy, open all day (food all day Fri, Sat and till 6pm Sun). *(Kerry and Guy Trooper)*

KEIGHLEY SE0641
Boltmakers Arms (01535) 661936
East Parade; BD21 5HX Small open-plan split-level character local, friendly and bustling, with full Timothy Taylors range and a guest kept well, traditional cider and several malt whiskies, lots to look at including brewing pictures and celebrity photos, coal fire; Tues quiz, Weds live music, sports TV; small beer garden, short walk from Keighley & Worth Valley Railway, open all day. *(Trish and Karl Soloman)*

KELD NY8900
Keld Lodge (01748) 886259
Butthouse Rigg (B6270); DL11 6LL Remote former youth hostel now serving as village inn, three well kept Black Sheep ales and tasty sensibly priced food, good service, various rooms including conservatory-style restaurant with superb Swaledale views; children and dogs welcome, popular with Coast to Coast walkers, 11 bedrooms, open all day. *(Gary and Marie Miller)*

KETTLESING SE2257
★**Queens Head** (01423) 770263
Village signposted off A59 W of Harrogate; HG3 2LB Popular stone pub with very good well priced traditional food, L-shaped carpeted main bar with lots of close-set cushioned dining chairs and tables, open fires, little heraldic shields on the walls along with 19th-c song sheet covers and lithographs of Queen Victoria, delft shelf of blue and white china, smaller bar on left with built-in red banquettes and cricketing prints, life-size portrait of Elizabeth I in lobby, well kept Black Sheep, Roosters and Theakstons, efficient friendly service; background music, free wi-fi; children welcome, seats in neatly kept suntrap back garden, benches in front by lane, eight bedrooms, open all day Sun. *(John and Eleanor Holdsworth)*

KETTLEWELL SD9672
Blue Bell (01756) 760230
Middle Lane; BD23 5QX Roomy knocked-through former coaching inn under welcoming new management, Theakstons, Wharfedale and plenty of guests kept well, enjoyable generously served food, friendly helpful staff, low beams and simple furnishings, old country photographs, woodburner; Sun quiz, TV, free wi-fi; children, walkers and dogs welcome, shaded picnic-sets on cobbles facing bridge over the River Wharfe, seven annexe bedrooms, open (and food) all day. *(Dan and Belinda Smallbone)*

KETTLEWELL SD9772
★**Kings Head** (01756) 761600
The Green; BD23 5RD Welcoming old pub tucked away near church, flagstoned main bar with log fire in big arched inglenook, three local ales and well chosen wines, good affordably priced food (all day Sun till 7pm) cooked by chef-landlord from pub favourites to imaginative restaurant dishes, efficient friendly service; children welcome, no dogs inside, six bedrooms named after kings, attractive village and good surrounding walks, closed Mon (Oct-end Mar), otherwise open all day. *(Lewis Canning)*

KETTLEWELL SD9672
Racehorses (01756) 760233
B6160 N of Skipton; BD23 5QZ Comfortable and friendly two-bar inn next to River Wharfe (across from the Blue Bell); tasty sensibly priced home-made food and three well kept Timothy Taylors ales, log fires, separate dining areas; children and dogs (in some parts) welcome, front and back terrace seating, pretty village well placed for Whartedale walks, parking can be difficult, 13 good bedrooms, open all day. *(Jeremy King)*

KILBURN SE5179
Forresters Arms (01347) 868386
Between A170 and A19 SW of Thirsk; YO61 4AH Welcoming beamed inn next to the Robert Thompson furniture workshops (early examples of his work in both bars); roaring fires, well kept local ales and good choice of home-made food, restaurant; background music; children welcome, dogs in some areas, suntrap seats out in front, smokers' shelter behind, ten bedrooms, open all day from 8am. *(Mick Allen)*

KIRBY HILL NZ1406
Shoulder of Mutton (01748) 822772
Off A66 NW of Scotch Corner, via Ravensworth; DL11 7JH Traditional 18th-c ivy-clad village inn, four local beers and well liked food from pub favourites up, front bar areas linking to long back restaurant, log fires; children and dogs welcome, fine Holmedale views from picnic-sets behind and bedrooms (you do hear the tuneful church bell), open all day Sun, from 5pm weekdays. *(Michael Doswell)*

KIRKBYMOORSIDE SE6986
George & Dragon (01751) 433334
Market Place; YO62 6AA Friendly 17th-c family-run coaching inn; front bar with beams and panelling, tub seats around wooden tables on carpet or stripped wood, log fire, well kept changing ales and several malt whiskies, wide choice of enjoyable generously served bar food, good

service, also a snug, bistro and more formal restaurant; background music; children welcome, seats and heaters on front and back terraces, 20 bedrooms, Weds market day, open all day. *(Barbara and Phil Bowie)*

KNARESBOROUGH   SE3457
Mitre (01423) 868948
Station Road; HG5 9AA Red-brick 1920s Market Town Tavern by the station, clean fresh décor and friendly staff, up to eight real ales including Black Sheep, Roosters and Okells, interesting continental beers, enjoyable sensibly priced food (all day Fri-Sun) in bar and dining room; children and dogs welcome, terrace tables under parasols, four bedrooms, open all day. *(B and M Kendall)*

KNAYTON   SE4388
Dog & Gun (01845) 537368
Moor Road, off A19; YO7 4AZ Attractive well cared-for family-run pub, cosy and comfortable, with roaring fire at one end, tables laid for their popular traditional home-made food (till 6pm Sun, not Tues, best to book) including blackboard specials, Black Sheep and Copper Dragon, good friendly service; late summer charity music festival; children and dogs welcome, heated outside seating area, open all day weekends, closed Mon and lunchtimes Tues-Fri. *(Tony and Wendy Hobden)*

LANGTHWAITE   NY0002
★Charles Bathurst (01748) 884567
Arkengarthdale, a mile N towards Tan Hill; DL11 6EN Welcoming busy 18th-c country inn (sister to the Kings Arms at Askrigg and Punch Bowl at Low Row); strong emphasis on dining and bedrooms, but pubby feel in long bar, scrubbed pine tables and country chairs on stripped floors, snug alcoves, open fire, Black Sheep, Caledonian Deuchars IPA and a local guest, several wines by the glass and good choice of popular interesting food, cheerful helpful staff, dining room with Robert 'Mousey' Thompson furniture and views of Scar House, several other eating areas; background music, TV, pool and darts; children welcome, dogs in bar, lovely walks from the door and views over village and Arkengarthdale, 19 smart bedrooms (best not above dining room), open all day; worth checking there are no corporate events/weddings before you visit. *(Jackie Robinson)*

LANGTHWAITE   NZ0002
★Red Lion (01748) 884218
Just off Arkengarthdale Road, Reeth–Brough; DL11 6RE Proper pub dating from 17th c in charming dales village with ancient bridge; long-serving character landlady and homely old-fashioned atmosphere, lunchtime sandwiches, pasties and sausage rolls, a couple of well kept Black Sheep ales, Thatcher's cider, country wines, tea

and coffee, well behaved children allowed lunchtime in low-ceilinged side snug, newspapers and postcards; the ladies' is a genuine bathroom; no dogs inside, a few picnic-sets out at front, good walks including circular ones from the pub – maps and guides for sale. *(Sarah and David Gibbs)*

LASTINGHAM   SE7290
★Blacksmiths Arms (01751) 417247
Off A170 W of Pickering; YO62 6TL 17th-c pub opposite beautiful Saxon church in charming village; log fire in open range, tankards hanging from beams, traditional furnishings, well kept Theakstons and other regional ales, several wines by the glass and good sensibly priced home-made food (not Sun evening), prompt service, two dining rooms; background music, darts and board games; children, walkers and dogs welcome, seats out at front and in back beer garden, three bedrooms, open all day. *(Dr Peter Crawshaw, Peter and Anne Hollindale, Richard Stanfield)*

LEALHOLM   NZ7607
★Board (01947) 897279
Off A171 W of Whitby; YO21 2AJ In wonderful moorland village spot by wide pool of River Esk; homely bare-boards bar on right with squashy old sofa and armchairs by big black stove, local landscape photographs on stripped-stone or maroon walls, china cabinet and piano, left-hand bar with another fire, traditional pub furniture, darts and a stuffed otter, carpeted dining room, three well kept changing ales, five ciders and dozens of whiskies, good seasonal food using meat from own farm and other local produce, friendly helpful landlady; children, dogs and muddy boots welcome, secluded waterside garden with decking, bedrooms (good breakfast) and self-catering cottage, open all day. *(Liz and Mike Newton)*

LEAVENING   SE7863
Jolly Farmers (01653) 658276
Main Street; YO17 9SA Bustling village local, friendly and welcoming, with four regional ales and popular good value traditional food (not Mon, Tues), front bar with eating area behind, separate dining room; some live music; children and dogs welcome, open all day weekends, closed weekday lunchtimes. *(James Knight)*

LEEDS   SE2932
Cross Keys (0113) 243 3711
Water Lane, Holbeck; LS11 5WD Welcoming early 19th-c pub; flagstones and bare boards, stripped brick, original tiling and timbers, old prints and photographs, a collection of clocks in one part, three or four interesting yorkshire-brewed ales plus imported bottled beers, shortish choice of good well prepared food (not Sun evening), winding stairs up to function/dining room; newspapers and board games,

free wi-fi; children and dogs welcome, tables under big parasols in sheltered back courtyard, open all day. (*Mick Allen*)

LEEDS SE3131
Garden Gate (0113) 345 1234
Whitfield Place, Hunslet; LS10 2QB Impressive Edwardian pub (Grade II* listed) owned by Leeds Brewery; their well kept ales from rare curved ceramic counter, a wealth of other fine period features in rooms off central drinking corridor including intricate glass and woodwork, art nouveau tiling, moulded ceilings and mosaic floors; dogs welcome, tables out in front, open all day. (*Mick Allen*)

LEEDS SE2932
★**Grove** (0113) 243 9254
Back Row, Holbeck; LS11 5PL Unspoilt and lived-in 1930s-feel local overshadowed by towering office blocks, tables and stools in main bar with marble floor, panelling and original fireplace, large back room and snug off drinking corridor, eight well kept regional ales including Daleside and Theakstons, Weston's cider, lunchtime food (not Sat), friendly staff; regular live music including folk club; open all day. (*Joe Oswald*)

LEEDS SE3033
Kirkstall Bridge (0113) 278 4044
Bridge Road, Headingley–Kirkstall; LS5 3BW Welcoming traditionally renovated pub by bridge over River Aire; main bare-boards bar with lots of breweriana and other rescued items from closed pubs, well kept Kirkstall beers and several guests, generous helpings of popular reasonably priced food from deli boards and pizzas up, downstairs flagstoned bar (dogs welcome here) leading out to riverside garden; Weds quiz, some live music, free wi-fi; handy for Kirkstall Abbey, open (and food) all day, kitchen closes 5pm Sun. (*Andrew Bosi*)

LEEDS SE2932
Midnight Bell (0113) 244 5044
Water Lane, Holbeck; LS11 5QN Leeds Brewery pub on two floors in Holbeck Urban Village, their ales and guests kept well, enjoyable home-made food, friendly staff, light contemporary décor mixing with original beams and stripped brickwork; children welcome, dogs in courtyard beer garden only, open (and food) all day. (*Joe Oswald*)

LEEDS SE3037
Mustard Pot (0113) 269 5699
Strainbeck Lane, Chapel Allerton; LS7 3QY Relaxed easy-going dining pub, enjoyable food (all day Sun) from lunchtime sandwiches to daily specials, Marstons-related ales plus monthly guests, decent wines by the glass, mix of furniture from farmhouse tables and chairs to comfortable banquettes and leather chesterfields, half-panelling and open fire; background music;

children welcome, pleasant front garden with heaters, open all day. (*Jill and Dick Archer*)

LEEDS SE3033
Scarbrough (0113) 243 4590
Bishopgate Street, opposite station; LS1 5DY Nicholsons pub with ornate tiled façade, eight well kept changing ales served by friendly knowledgeable staff, enjoyable food including speciality pies and breakfasts; sports TV; open all day and busy lunchtime and early evening. (*Andrew Bosi, Mick Allen*)

LEEDS SE3033
Victoria (0113) 245 1386
Great George Street; LS1 3DL Opulent early Victorian pub with grand cut and etched mirrors, impressive globe lamps extending from majestic bar, carved beams and leather-seat booths with working snob screens, smaller rooms off, eight real ales and standard Nicholsons menu (including afternoon tea) in separate room with serving hatch, friendly efficient service; open all day. (*Mick Allen*)

LEEDS SE3033
★**Whitelocks** (0113) 245 3950
Turks Head Yard, off Briggate; LS1 6HB Classic Victorian pub, perhaps a little worn around the edges but full of character; long narrow bar with fine tiled counter, grand mirrors, mahogany and glass screens, heavy copper-topped tables and red leather seating, coal fire, well kept Theakstons ales and enjoyable food; children welcome, tables in narrow courtyard (open and food) all day, can be crowded at lunchtime. (*Jimmy*)

LINTHWAITE SE1014
★**Sair** (01484) 842370
Lane Top, Hoyle Ing, off A62; HD7 5SG Old-fashioned four-room pub brewing its own good value Linfit beers; pews and chairs on rough flagstones or wood floors, log-burning ranges, dominoes, cribbage and shove-ha'penny, piano and vintage rock juke box; no food or credit cards; children (till 8pm) and dogs welcome, plenty of tables out in front with fine Colne Valley views, restored Huddersfield Narrow Canal nearby, open all day weekends, from 5pm weekdays. (*Ben and Jenny Settle*)

LINTON SE3846
★**Windmill** (01937) 582209
Off A661 W of Wetherby; LS22 4HT Smart 16th-c inn on different levels, beams and stripped stone, antique settles around copper-topped tables, three log fires; tasty up-to-date food plus more traditional dishes (pie night Weds, steak night Thurs), ales such as Theakstons Best and several wines by the glass, restaurant and airy conservatory; background music; children and dogs (in bar) welcome, sunny back terrace and sheltered garden with pear tree (raised from seed brought back from

the Napoleonic Wars), two bedrooms in annexe, open all day Fri–Sun, food all day Sat, till 6pm Sun. *(Jackie Robinson)*

LITTON   SD9074
Queens Arms (01756) 770096
Off B6160 N of Grassington; BD23 5QJ
Beautifully placed 17th-c dales pub; main bar with stone floor and beam-and-plank ceiling, old photographs on rough stone walls, coal fire, plainer carpeted dining room with woodburner, ales such as Greene King, Thwaites and Wharfedale, enjoyable freshly made food, friendly staff; children and dogs welcome, plenty of seats in two-tier garden, country views and good surrounding walks, six bedrooms, open all day Fri–Sun, closed Mon except bank holidays. *(Liz and Mike Newton)*

LOFTHOUSE   SE1073
Crown (01423) 755206
Pub signed from main road; Nidderdale; HG3 5RZ Prettily placed dales inn, friendly and relaxed, with hearty simple food from sandwiches up, well kept Black Sheep and Theakstons, small public bar, comfortable dining extension where children allowed, open fire; no credit cards, outside gents'; dogs welcome, nice garden and good walks from the door, bedrooms. *(B and M Kendall)*

LOW BRADFIELD   SK2691
Plough (0114) 285 1280
Village signposted off B6077 and B6076 NW of Sheffield; New Road; S6 6HW
Comfortably modernised old pub ideally placed for some of South Yorkshire's finest scenery; L-shaped bar with stone walls, button-back banquettes and captain's chairs, log fire in big arched fireplace, well kept Bradfield, Thwaites and a guest, good value food from sandwiches and baked potatoes to grills, also bargain two-for-one deals and Sun carvery; background music, Weds quiz, sports TV and free wi-fi; children and dogs welcome, seats on back verandah, terrace and lawn, Damflask and Agden Reservoirs close by, open (and food) all day. *(Michael Butler)*

LOW ROW   SD9898
★Punch Bowl (01748) 886233
B6270 Reeth–Muker; DL11 6PF 17th-c country inn under same ownership as the Charles Bathurst at Langthwaite and Kings Arms at Askrigg; long bare-boards bar with peaceful view over Swaledale, stripped kitchen tables and a variety of seats including armchairs and sofa by woodburner, good food (menu on huge mirror with some interesting choices), nice wines by the glass, well kept Black Sheep ales and a guest, cheerful

efficient staff, separate dining room similar in style; wide views from terrace set above road, comfortable bedrooms, good breakfast, open all day. *(Roy and Gill Payne, WAH)*

LOWER DUNSFORTH   SE4465
Dunsforth (01423) 320700
Mary Lane; YO26 9SA Painted-brick dining pub in centre of peaceful village, highly regarded attractively presented food from chef-patron including lunchtime/early-evening set deal and tasting menus, well kept Theakstons Best and Timothy Taylors Landlord, nice wines by the glass from well chosen list, friendly attentive service, cosy bar with scatter-cushion pews, small dining area just inside main entrance, much bigger one behind with polished wood flooring, some exposed brickwork and hunting print wallpaper, open fire; picnic-sets on front terrace among tubs and hanging baskets, outside bar, barbecue and pizza oven, open all weekends, closed Mon, Tues. *(Michael Doswell)*

LUND   SE9748
★Wellington (01377) 217294
Off B1248 SW of Driffield; YO25 9TE Smart busy pub with cosy Farmers' Bar, beams, well polished wooden banquettes and square tables, quirky fireplace, plainer side room with flagstones and wine-theme décor, Yorkstone walkway to further room with village's Britain in Bloom awards, well kept ales including Timothy Taylors and Theakstons, good wine list and 25 malt whiskies, highly rated well presented food (not Sun evening and not cheap) in restaurant and bistro dining area, friendly efficient staff; background music, TV; children welcome, disabled access, benches in pretty back courtyard, open all day Sun, closed Mon lunchtime. *(Pat and Stewart Gordon, Huw Jones, Colin and Angela Boocock)*

MALTON   SE7972
Spotted Cow
Cattle Market; YO17 7JN Unspoilt early 18th-c pub overlooking cattle and sheep market (popular with local farmers on market days), small traditional rooms including tap room on left with tiled floor, wooden furniture and vintage brewery mirror, well kept Marstons, Tetleys and a guest; pool in back bar; dogs welcome, open from 4pm Mon, Weds, Thurs, otherwise open all day. *(Mike and Eleanor Anderson)*

MANFIELD   NZ2213
Crown (01325) 374243
Vicars Lane; DL2 2RF Unpretentious two-bar village local, friendly and welcoming,

---

If you report on a pub that's not a featured entry, please tell us any lunchtimes or evenings when it doesn't serve bar food.

with eight interesting ales including Village Brewer, enjoyable home-made food, open fires, games room with pool and darts; occasional live music; children and dogs welcome, beer garden, good walks nearby, open all day weekends, closed lunchtimes Mon, Tues. *(Ben and Jenny Settle)*

MARSDEN   SE0411
Riverhead Brewery Tap
(01484) 841270 *Peel Street, next to Co-op; just off A62 Huddersfield–Oldham; HD7 6BR* Owned by Ossett with up to ten well kept ales including Riverhead range (microbrewery visible from bare-boards bar), bustling friendly atmosphere, airy upstairs beamed restaurant with stripped tables (moors view from some) and open kitchen, good choice of enjoyable food (all day weekends, not Mon or Tues); background and some live music, Tues quiz; dogs welcome, wheelchair access, some riverside tables, open all day. *(Mick Allen)*

MASHAM   SE2281
White Bear (01765) 689319
Wellgarth, Crosshills; signed off A6108 opposite turn into town; HG4 4EN Comfortably updated beamed inn, small public bar with full Theakstons range kept well and several wines by the glass, welcoming coal fire in larger lounge, decent choice of food, from sandwiches/baguettes up, afternoon teas, friendly efficient staff, restaurant extension; background music; children and dogs (in bar) welcome, terrace tables, 14 bedrooms, open all day. *(Shirley Blenkinsopp)*

MAUNBY   SE3586
Buck (01845) 587777
Off A167 S of Northallerton; YO7 4HD Brick-built dining pub in quiet out-of-the-way village by River Swale; ales such as Theakstons and York, eight wines by the glass and good food (not Sun evening) from lunchtime sandwiches and traditional choices up (shortish menu), friendly helpful service, carpeted beamed bar with comfy leather sofa and captain's chest in front of inviting fire, more contemporary restaurant and conservatory with one huge table; children welcome, dogs in bar, open all day weekends, closed Mon. *(Kerry and Guy Trooper)*

MENSTON   SE1744
Fox (01943) 873024
Bradford Road (A65/A6038); LS29 6EB Contemporary Mitchells & Butlers dining pub in former coaching inn on busy junction, enjoyable fairly priced food served by efficient friendly staff, Black Sheep, Timothy Taylors Landlord and a guest, Aspall's cider, big fireplace, flagstones and polished boards in one part; background music, free wi-fi; two terraces looking beyond

car park to cricket field, open (and food) all day. *(John and Eleanor Holdsworth)*

MIDDLEHAM   SE1288
Richard III (01969) 623240
Market Place; DL8 4NP Traditional 17th-c beamed inn with friendly landlady and locals, cosy front bar, Black Sheep, John Smiths and Theakstons, good range of generous food cooked by landlord, back bar and restaurant, lots of racehorse pictures; sports TV; tables out by square, six bedrooms, open all day, food all day Fri-Sun. *(Barbara and Phil Bowie)*

MIDDLEHAM   SE1287
★**White Swan** (01969) 622093
Market Place; DL8 4PE Extended coaching inn opposite cobbled market square; beamed and flagstoned entrance bar with log fire, well kept Theakstons ales, nice wines by the glass and several malt whiskies, good choice of enjoyable food (all day Sun) in modern brasserie with large fireplace or back dining room, cream teas, friendly efficient staff; background music; children welcome, 17 comfortable bedrooms, hearty breakfast. *(Barbara and Phil Bowie)*

MIDDLESMOOR   SE0974
Crown (01423) 755204
Top of Nidderdale Road from Pateley Bridge; HG3 5ST Remote unpretentious family-run inn with beautiful view over stone-built hamlet high in upper Nidderdale, warmly welcoming character landlord and good local atmosphere, well kept Black Sheep and guests, several whiskies and simple wholesome food, blazing fires in cosy spotless rooms, old photographs and bric-a-brac, homely dining room; children and dogs welcome, small garden, seven good value bedrooms, camping and self-catering cottage, open all day weekends. *(Joe Oswald)*

MIDDLETON TYAS   NZ2205
Shoulder of Mutton (01325) 377271
Just E of A1 Scotch Corner roundabout; DL10 6QX Welcoming old pub with three softly lit low-ceilinged rooms on different levels, good freshly made food from snacks up, three well kept changing ales, friendly service; children welcome, a useful A1/A66 stop, open all day Sun, closed Mon lunchtime. *(Tony Selinger)*

MILLINGTON   SE8351
Gait (01759) 302045
Main Street; YO42 1TX Friendly 16th-c beamed local, five well kept regional ales (July beer festival) and enjoyable straightforward home-made food, nice mix of old and newer furnishings, large map of Yorkshire on the ceiling, big inglenook log fire; live music or quiz Weds; children and dogs welcome, garden picnic-sets, appealing village in good wolds walking country, closed Mon and lunchtimes Tues-Thurs. *(James Knight)*

MIRFIELD   SE2019
Flower Pot (01924) 496939
Calder Road; WF14 8NN Comfortably
refurbished three-room Ossett pub with
their well kept beers and four local guests,
short but enjoyable lunchtime menu
including good sandwiches and locally
made pies, real fires; children and dogs
welcome, flowering tubs in nice riverside
garden, open all day. *(Pat and Tony Martin)*

MOORSHOLM   NZ6912
Jolly Sailor (01287) 660270
A171 nearly a mile E; TS12 3LN
Remotely placed dining pub with good
variety of enjoyable food, well kept
Black Sheep and a guest, friendly staff,
long beamed and stripped-stone bar,
restaurant; children and dogs welcome,
tables looking out to the surrounding
moors, open all day. *(WAH)*

MUKER   SD9097
★**Farmers Arms** (01748) 886297
B6270 W of Reeth; DL11 6QG Small
down-to-earth pub in beautiful valley
village popular with walkers and other
visitors (can get very busy); warmly
welcoming, with four well kept local ales
such as Yorkshire Dales and good choice
of wines by the glass, teas and coffees,
enjoyable good value home-made food
(delivered by dumb waiter from upstairs
kitchen), good service, clean interior with
warm fire, simple modern pine furniture,
flagstones and panelling; soft background
music, darts and dominoes; children, dogs
and muddy boots welcome, hill views from
terrace tables, self-catering apartment,
open all day; still up for sale last we heard,
but business as usual – news please.
(Roy and Gill Payne, Clive and Fran Dutson)

NEWTON-ON-OUSE   SE5160
★**Dawnay Arms** (01347) 848345
Off A19 N of York; YO30 2BR 18th-c pub
with two bars and airy river-view dining room,
low beams, stripped masonry, open fire and
inglenook woodburner, chunky pine tables
and old pews on bare boards and flagstones,
fishing memorabilia, highly regarded original
food (till 6pm Sun), also good lunchtime
sandwiches (home-baked bread), fixed-price
menu (not Sat evening or Sun), interesting
vegetarian menu and children's choices, ales
such as Tetleys and Timothy Taylors, good
range of wines by the glass, friendly efficient
service; terrace tables, lawn running down
to Ouse moorings, handy for Beningbrough
Hall (NT), open till 6pm Sun, closed Mon
except bank holidays. *(Mick Allen)*

NORTH DALTON   SE9352
Star (01377) 217688
B1246 Pocklington–Driffield; YO25 9UX
Picturesque 18th-c red-brick inn next to
village pond, good range of changing ales

and well cooked classic pub food (not Tues),
open fire in pubby bar, restaurant; some live
music including open mike nights; children
and dogs welcome, open all day weekends,
from 2pm Fri, 5pm other days. *(Dan and
Belinda Smallbone)*

NORTH RIGTON   SE2749
Square & Compass (01423) 733031
Hall Green Lane/Rigton Hill; LS17 0DJ
Substantial stone building with smart
modern interior, beamed bar serving Leeds,
Theakstons and Washburn, good range of
bottled beers and plenty of wines by the
glass, food from sandwiches, sharing boards
and pizzas up, friendly efficient service
by aproned staff, restaurant; children and
dogs (in bar) welcome, tables on tiered
terrace, peaceful village, open (and food)
all day. *(Gordon and Margaret Ormondroyd)*

NORWOOD GREEN   SE1326
Old White Beare (01274) 676645
*Signed off A641 in Wyke, or off A58
Halifax–Leeds just W of Wyke; Village
Street; HX3 8QG* Nicely renovated and
extended 16th-c pub named after ship
whose timbers it incorporates; well kept
Copper Dragon, Timothy Taylors and
a guest, decent choice of enjoyable food
(not Sun evening) including weekday
fixed-price menu, good friendly service,
bar with steps up to dining area, small
character snug and imposing galleried barn
restaurant; children and dogs welcome,
a few tables in front and in back garden,
Calderdale Way and Brontë Way pass the
door, open all day. *(Michael Butler)*

NUNNINGTON   SE6679
Royal Oak (01439) 748271
*Church Street; at back of village, which
is signposted from A170 and B1257;
YO62 5US* Welcoming neatly updated
old stone pub; bar with high beams and
some farming memorabilia on bare-stone
wall, nice mix of furniture, dining area
linked by double-sided woodburner, good
food (not Sun evening) with some tuscan
influences, Theakstons, York and a guest
such as Timothy Taylors, nice wines and
italian coffee; bar billiards; children and
dogs welcome, terrace seating, handy
for Nunnington Hall (NT), open all day
weekends, closed Mon, Tues. *(Angie Mayer)*

OLDFIELD   SE0138
Grouse (01535) 643073
*Harehills; 2 miles towards Colne;
BD22 0RX* Comfortable old pub in
undisturbed moorland hamlet, enjoyable
food from light lunches to good steaks
and daily specials, well kept Timothy
Taylors ales, friendly attentive service;
children and dogs (in snug) welcome,
picnic-sets on terrace with lovely Pennine
views, open (and food) all day.
(Gordon and Margaret Ormondroyd)

OSMOTHERLEY SE4597

★**Golden Lion** (01609) 883526

The Green, West End; off A19 N of Thirsk; DL6 3AA Attractive and welcoming old stone pub, roomy beamed bar on left with old pews and a few decorations, ales such as Timothy Taylors and around 50 malt whiskies, similarly unpretentious eating area on right plus weekend dining room, popular pubby food, good service; background music; children and dogs (in bar) welcome, benches out at front overlooking village green, more seats in covered courtyard, 40-mile Lyke Wake Walk starts here and Coast to Coast path nearby, seven comfortable bedrooms, open all day weekends, closed Mon and Tues lunchtimes. *(WAH)*

OSMOTHERLEY SE4597

Three Tuns (01609) 883301

South End, off A19 N of Thirsk; DL6 3BN Small stylish pub-restaurant with décor inspired by Charles Rennie Mackintosh; very good freshly made food in bistro setting with pale oak furniture and panelling, friendly efficient service, flagstoned bar with built-in cushioned wall benches, stripped-pine tables and pale stone fireplace, well kept ales such as Timothy Taylors, good friendly service; children welcome, dogs in bar, seats out at front and in charming terrace garden, good nearby walks, comfortable bedrooms. *(M and GR)*

OSSETT SE2719

★**Brewers Pride** (01924) 273865

Low Mill Road/Healey Lane (long cul-de-sac by railway sidings, off B6128); WF5 8ND Friendly local with own Horbury ales (brewed at back of pub) along with Rudgate Ruby Mild and seven guests, cosy front rooms and flagstoned bar, brewery memorabilia, open fires, good well priced food (not Sun evening) including weekday set lunch and Tues evening tapas, modern back dining extension (Millers Restaurant); live music Sat, quiz and pie night Mon; well behaved children and dogs welcome, big back garden, near Calder & Hebble Navigation, open all day. *(Michael Butler)*

OSSETT SE2820

Old Vic (01924) 273516

Manor Road, just off Horbury Road; WF5 0AU Friendly four-room roadside pub; well kept Ossett ales and guests including Fullers London Pride, competitively priced home-cooked food (not Sun evening, Mon), traditional décor with old local photographs, shelves of bottles and antique range; pool room, darts; children and dogs welcome, open all day Fri-Sun, from 4pm other days. *(Michael Butler)*

OSSETT SE2719

Tap (01924) 272215

The Green; WF5 8JS Cosy tap for the Ossett Brewery; simple traditional décor with flagstones, bare boards and woodburner, mix of seating including upholstered banquettes and padded stools, photos of other Ossett pubs, their well kept ales and guests plus competitively priced wines by the glass, friendly relaxed atmosphere; dogs on the lead welcome, small car park (other nearby parking can be difficult), open all day Thurs-Sun, from 3pm other days. *(Michael Butler)*

OTLEY SE2045

Chevin (01943) 876109

West Chevin Road, off A660; LS29 6BE Popular 18th-c roadside pub largely rebuilt after fire, good home-made food including seasonal game, weekday early-bird deal (5-7pm) and other offers, Timothy Taylors Landlord and a guest, helpful friendly young staff; children and dogs welcome, garden with splendid Wharfedale views, handy for Leeds airport and right on the flight path, open (and food) all day. *(John and Eleanor Holdsworth)*

OTLEY SE2045

Old Cock (01943) 464424

Crossgate; LS21 1AA Traditional two-room drinkers' pub with nine mainly local ales and a couple of ciders, also foreign imports and range of gluten-free bottled beers, beer festivals, no cooked food but good pork pies and sandwiches, more room upstairs; no under-18s, dogs welcome, open all day. *(Trish and Karl Soloman)*

OTLEY SE2047

★**Roebuck** (01943) 463063

Roebuck Terrace; LS21 2EY Smartly modernised 18th-c beamed pub, good food from sandwiches and sharing plates up including range of hearty pies, Black Sheep and five changing local beers, plenty of wines by the glass, friendly helpful service, log fire and woodburner, raftered restaurant with mix of old furniture including pews on wood floor; children and dogs (in bar) welcome, wheelchair access, tables out on terrace and small lawn, open all day (closed Mon in winter), food all day Sun until 7pm. *(John and Eleanor Holdsworth)*

OXENHOPE SE0335

Bay Horse (01535) 642921

Upper Town; BD22 9LN Bustling community pub with friendly enthusiastic licensees, good value food cooked to order and half a dozen well kept local ales; free wi-fi; children, walkers and dogs welcome, seats outside. *(Brian and Anna Marsden)*

It's very helpful if you let us know up-to-date food prices when you report on pubs.

OXENHOPE   SE0434
★**Dog & Gun**   (01535) 643159
Off B6141 towards Denholme; BD22 9SN
Spacious beautifully placed 17th-c moorland
pub, smartly extended and comfortable, with
wide choice of good generously served free
from sandwiches to daily specials, cheerful,
welcoming staff, full Timothy Taylors range
kept well and good selection of malt whiskies,
beamery, copper, brasses, plates and jugs, big
log fire each end, padded settles and stools,
glass-covered well in one dining area, super
views; five bedrooms in adjoining hotel,
open all day weekends (food all day Sun).
(Gordon and Margaret Ormondroyd)

PICKERING   SE7983
Black Swan   (01751) 472288
Birdgate; YO18 7AL Refurbished old
coaching inn with half a dozen local
ales such as Brass Castle (tasting trays
available), several ciders and good choice
of wines by the glass, enjoyable home-made
food including Thurs steak nights and pie/
curry evenings alternate Tues, friendly
staff, cosy bar with log fire, bay-windowed
lounge (another fire) and restaurant;
background and maybe live music, free
wi-fi; children and dogs welcome, bedrooms
(some in converted stables). *(Joe Oswald)*

PICKERING   SE7984
White Swan   (01751) 472288
Market Place, just off A170; YO18 7AA
Civilised and welcoming 16th-c coaching
inn run by the same family for 35 years;
cosy, properly pubby bar, sofas and a few
tables, panelling and log fire, Black Sheep,
Timothy Taylors Landlord and a dozen
wines by the glass, second bare-boards
room with big bow window and handsome
art nouveau iron fireplace, good food
(everything made in-house, even ketchup),
flagstoned restaurant and next-door deli,
efficient friendly staff, residents' lounge
in converted beamed barn; children and
dogs (in bar) welcome, bedrooms, open
all day from 7.30am. *(Jimmy, Joe Oswald)*

PICKHILL   SE3483
★**Nags Head**   (01845) 567391
*A1 junction 50 (northbound) or
junction 51 (southbound), village
signed off A6055, Street Lane;
YO7 4JG* Welcoming dining inn under
long-serving owners, many tables set for
eating, but bustling tap room on left (lots
of ties, jugs, coach horns and ale-yards)
serves Black Sheep, Rudgate, Theakstons
and a guest along with 30 malt whiskies,
vintage Armagnacs and ten wines by
the glass, smarter lounge bar with
deep green plush banquettes, pictures
for sale and open fire, library-themed
restaurant, good food from wide-ranging
menu (all day Sun); background music,
TV, free wi-fi; well behaved children

till 7.30pm (after that in dining room),
dogs in bar, front verandah, boules/
quoits pitch and nine-hole putting green,
seven comfortable bedrooms, buffet-style
breakfast, open all day. *(Michael Butler)*

POOL   SE2445
★**White Hart**   (0113) 203 7862
*Just off A658 S of Harrogate, A659
E of Otley; LS21 1LH* Popular light and
airy Mitchells & Butlers dining pub (bigger
inside than it looks), good food from sharing
plates and pizzas to more restauranty dishes,
fixed-price menu too, efficient friendly
young staff, 25 wines by the glass including
champagne, cocktails and three well kept
ales, stylishly simple bistro eating areas,
armchairs and sofas on bar's flagstones
and bare boards, welcoming log fires and
relaxing atmosphere; background music;
children and dogs welcome, plenty of tables
outside, open (and food) all day. *(John
and Sylvia Harrop, Gordon and Margaret
Ormondroyd, Michael Butler, Derek Stafford)*

PUDSEY   SE2037
Thornhill Arms   (0113) 256 5492
Town Gate; LS28 5NF Fully updated
17th-c pub with wide range of enjoyable
food from meze sharing plates, mexican
choices, burgers and hot dogs up, real ales
such as Theakstons and plenty of wines by
the glass, friendly efficient staff; free wi-fi;
children welcome, seats outside, open (and
food) all day. *(John and Eleanor Holdsworth)*

REDMIRE   SE0491
Bolton Arms   (01969) 624336
Hargill Lane; DL8 4EA Welcoming village
dining pub (former 17th-c farmhouse)
with enjoyable fairly traditional food
at reasonable prices, well kept Black
Sheep, Theakstons, Wensleydale and a
guest, efficient friendly service even at
busy times, woodburner in comfortable
carpeted bar, attractive dining room; free
wi-fi; children and dogs (in bar) welcome,
disabled facilities, picnic-sets in small
part-paved garden, good walks and handy
for Wensleydale Railway and Bolton Castle,
five bedrooms (two with views from shared
balcony, others in converted outbuilding),
open all day. *(Clive and Fran Dutson)*

REETH   SE0499
Buck   (01748) 884210
*Arkengarthdale Road/Silver Street;
DL11 6SW* Friendly 18th-c coaching inn
adjacent to village green, ales such as Black
Sheep, Ossett and Wensleydale, enjoyable
fairly pubby food, part-carpeted beamed
bar with open fire, steps up to dining area;
some live music, July beer festival, free
wi-fi; children welcome, dogs in bar (theirs
is Marley), a few tables out in front, hidden
walled garden with play equipment, good
walking country, ten comfortable bedrooms,
open all day. *(Liz and Mike Newton)*

RIPLEY   SE2860
Boars Head (01423) 771888
Off A61 Harrogate–Ripon; HG3 3AY
Informal and relaxed old hotel belonging to
the Ripley Castle Estate; long bar-bistro with
nice mix of dining chairs and tables, walls
hung with golf clubs, cricket bats, some jolly
cricketing/hunting drawings, a boar's head
and interesting religious carving, ales such
as Black Sheep, Daleside and Theakstons, 20
wines by the glass and several malt whiskies,
good food including Estate produce, separate
restaurant; children welcome, dogs in bar
and bedrooms, pleasant little garden, open
all day. *(Charlotte and William Mason)*

RIPON   SE3171
★ One-Eyed Rat (01765) 607704
Allhallowgate; HG4 1LQ Small friendly
pub with seven well kept changing ales,
draught continentals and traditional cider,
long narrow bare-boards bar with roaring
fire, back carpeted area with piano and TV
projector for sports; no food; some live music
and a couple of beer festivals; dogs welcome,
outside seating area, open all day Fri-Sun,
from 5pm other days. *(Gary and Marie Miller)*

RIPON   SE3171
Royal Oak (01765) 602284
Kirkgate; HG4 1PB Centrally placed
18th-c coaching inn on pedestrianised
street; smart modern décor, Timothy Taylors
ales and guests kept well, good choice of
wines, split-level dining area serving good
food from pub staples to more enterprising
restauranty dishes, two-course deal 5-6.30pm
(not Sat), friendly service; background
music; children and dogs (in bar) welcome,
seats in courtyard with retractable awning,
eight bedrooms, open (and food) all day.
(Richard Tingle, Janet and Peter Race)

RISHWORTH   SE0316
Booth Wood (01422) 825600
Oldham Road (A672); HX6 4QU
Welcoming beamed and flagstoned country
dining pub, good range of enjoyable well
priced food from sandwiches to blackboard
specials, lunchtime/early-evening bargains,
local Oates beers and guests, friendly staff,
some leather sofas and wing-back chairs,
two blazing woodburners; regular live music
including folk nights; children welcome, open
(and food) all day weekends. *(Stuart Paulley)*

ROBIN HOOD'S BAY   NZ9504
Bay Hotel (01947) 880278
The Dock, Bay Town; YO22 4SJ Old
village inn perched on edge of the bay with
fine sea views from cosy picture-window
upstairs bar (Wainwright bar downstairs
open too if busy), ales including Caledonian
Deuchars IPA and Theakstons, reasonably
priced home-made food in bar and separate
dining area from sandwiches to blackboard
specials, log fires; background music, TV;
children and dogs welcome, popular with
walkers (at end of the 191-mile Coast
to Coast path), lots of tables outside,
bedrooms, steep road down and no parking
at bottom, open all day. *(Dr J Barrie Jones)*

ROBIN HOOD'S BAY   NZ9505
★ Laurel (01947) 880400
*Bay Bank; village signed off A171 S of
Whitby; YO22 4SE* Charming little pub
at bottom of row of fishermen's cottages
in especially pretty and unspoilt fishing
village; beamed main bar with open fire,
old local photographs, Victorian prints and
brasses, Adnams and Theakstons ales, no
food or credit cards; background music,
darts and board games; children in snug
bar only, dogs welcome, open all day in
summer, best to check winter hours; may
be changes as long-serving landlord has
recently retired. *(Diane Abbott, Elizabeth
and Peter May, Simon and Alex Knight)*

ROBIN HOOD'S BAY   NZ9505
Victoria (01947) 880205
Station Road; YO22 4RL Clifftop Victorian
hotel with great bay views, good choice of
local beers from curved counter in traditional
carpeted bar, enjoyable fresh food here, in
restaurant or large family room, also a coffee
shop/tea room; dogs welcome, useful car
park, play area and picnic-sets in big garden
overlooking sea and village, comfortable
bedrooms, good breakfast. *(Chris Allen)*

SANDAL   SE3418
Star (01924) 229674
Standbridge Lane; WF2 7DY Friendly
19th-c local under newish ownership,
relaxed and comfortable, with well kept
ales including own good microbrews (not
always available), simple well priced
lunchtime food (evening sharing plates);
Tues quiz and some live music; children
and dogs welcome, garden with decked
area, open all day. *(Michael Butler)*

SANDSEND   NZ8612
Hart (01947) 893304
East Row; YO21 3SU Shoreside pub with
good choice of generously served traditional
food including fish/seafood (best to book),
well kept ales such as Black Sheep and
Greene King, prompt friendly service, log fire
in beamed and flagstoned bar, upstairs dining
room; free wi-fi; children and dogs welcome,
picnic-sets on small side terrace, open all day
(till 6pm Sun). *(Michael Butler, Stephen Woad)*

SAWDON   TA9484
Anvil (01723) 859896
Main Street; YO13 9DY Attractive
high-raftered former smithy under new
owners – reports please; ales from yorkshire
brewers and good range of wines, pleasant
attentive service, feature smith's hearth
with anvil and old tools, scrubbed pine
tables on wood floor, logburner, lower-

ceilinged second bar leading to small dining room; children and dogs (in bar) welcome, terrace seating, self-catering cottage, closed Mon, Tues. *(Ben and Jenny Settle)*

SAWLEY SE2467

★**Sawley Arms** (01765) 620642
Village signposted off B6265 W of Ripon; HG4 3EQ Village dining pub with friendly busy atmosphere, well liked modern food from sandwiches and light meals up, Theakstons Best and Timothy Taylors Landlord, a dozen wines by the glass, welcoming helpful staff, comfortable interior with log fire and conservatory; children welcome, seats on terrace and in attractive garden, close to Fountains Abbey (NT), open (and food) all day. *(John and Eleanor Holdsworth, Janet and Peter Race)*

SCARBOROUGH TA0588

Golden Ball (01723) 353899
Sandside, opposite harbour; YO11 1PG Tall mock-Tudor seafront pub with good harbour and bay views from highly prized window seats (busy in summer), panelled bar with good mix of visitors and locals, some nautical memorabilia and open fire, well kept low-priced Sam Smiths; family lounge upstairs, tables out in yard, open all day. *(Angie Mayer)*

SCARBOROUGH TA0387

Valley (01723) 372593
Valley Road; YO11 2LX Family-run Victorian pub with basement bar, up to six well kept changing ales, eight ciders/perries and excellent choice of bottled belgian beers, friendly staff, no food, more seats upstairs and pool room; bedrooms, open all day. *(Angie Mayer)*

SCORTON NZ2500

Farmers Arms (01748) 812533
Northside; DL10 6DW Comfortably modernised little pub in terrace of old cottages overlooking green, well kept Sharps Doom Bar, Thwaites Wainwright and a guest such as Black Sheep, decent wines and good freshly made food including popular Sun lunch, friendly accommodating staff, bar with open fire, darts and dominoes, restaurant; background music, fortnightly quiz and bingo nights; children and dogs welcome, open all day weekends, closed Mon lunchtime. *(Pat and Stewart Gordon, Ian and Rose Lock, Tony and Wendy Hobden)*

SCOTTON SE3259

Guy Fawkes Arms (01423) 862598
Main Street; HG5 9HU Hospitable neatly refurbished village pub run by two local families, very popular food (must book; not Mon) including plenty of fish and good value set lunch, well kept Black Sheep, Copper Dragon and three local guests, charming staff; Mon quiz; children and dogs (not at food times) welcome, open from

4pm Mon, otherwise open all day (food till 7pm Sun). *(Maria and Bertie Farr)*

SETTLE SD8163

Lion (01729) 823459
B6480 (main road through town), off A65 bypass; BD24 0HB Market town inn with grand staircase sweeping down into baronial-style high-beamed bar, lovely log fire, second bar with bare boards and dark half-panelling, lots of old local photographs and another fire, enjoyable good value food including deli boards and specials, well kept Thwaites and occasional guests, decent wines by the glass, helpful welcoming staff, restaurant; Tues jazz, silent TV and games machine; children and dogs welcome, courtyard tables, 14 bedrooms, open (and food) all day. *(Chris Allen)*

SHAROW SE3371

Half Moon (01765) 278524
Sharow Lane; HG4 5BP Nice little village pub with well kept Black Sheep ales and tasty home-made food from sandwiches up, early-bird deal Tues-Thurs (5.30-7pm), Victorian pictures and ornate gilded mirror on grey-green walls, lots of pine furniture, sofa and easy chairs one end, cosy dining room the other with open fire, small gift shop; quiz nights; children welcome, dogs in bar area, open all day Sun till 7.45pm, closed Mon and lunchtime Tues. *(Jackie Robinson)*

SHEFFIELD SK3487

Bath (0114) 249 5151
Victoria Street, off Glossop Road; S3 7QL Victorian corner pub with well restored 1930s interior, two rooms and a drinking corridor, well kept Thornbridge and guests, simple snacky food including weekend hot pork sandwiches, friendly staff; live music Weds with some emphasis on jazz/blues, Thurs quiz; closed Sun and bank holiday Mon, otherwise open all day. *(Jimmy)*

SHEFFIELD SK3687

Fat Cat (0114) 249 4801
Alma Street; S3 8SA Cheerfully busy little Victorian pub with a dozen interesting beers on handpump including next-door Kelham Island, also draught/bottled continentals and traditional cider, friendly knowledgeable staff, straightforward bargain food (not Sun evening) catering for vegetarians/vegans; Mon quiz; seats in back courtyard, open all day. *(Chris Sale)*

SHEFFIELD SK3687

Gardeners Rest (0114) 272 4978
Neepsend Lane; S3 8AT Community-oriented pub recently bought by local consortium; bar, snug and back conservatory, old brewery memorabilia and local artwork, several interesting changing beers including Sheffield, no food (plans to build a kitchen); live music, film nights and other regular events, traditional games

including bar billiards; children and dogs welcome, tables out in quirky garden overlooking River Don, open all day Fri-Sun, from 3pm other days. *(James Knight)*

SHEFFIELD SK3588
Harlequin (0114) 275 8195
Nursery Street; S3 8GG Welcoming open-plan corner pub owned by nearby Exit 33, their well kept ales and great selection of changing guests, also bottled imports and real ciders/perries, straightforward cheap lunchtime food including Sun roasts; weekend live music plus jazz second Thurs of month, Weds quiz, beer festivals; children till 7pm and dogs welcome, outside seating, open all day. *(Jimmy)*

SHEFFIELD SK3290
★ **New Barrack** (0114) 232 4225
Penistone Road, Hillsborough; S6 2GA Friendly and lively with nine real ales including Castle Rock and lots of bottled belgian beers, traditional good value bar food, comfortable front lounge with log fire and upholstered seats on old pine floors, tap room with another fire, function room (own bar); live music and comedy nights, pool, darts, sports TV; children till 9pm and dogs welcome, attractive little walled garden, difficult parking nearby, closed lunchtimes Mon-Weds, otherwise open all day. *(Chris Sale)*

SHEFFIELD SK3186
Ranmoor (0114) 230 1325
Fulwood Road (across from church); S10 3GD Comfortable and welcoming open-plan 19th-c local, four well kept ales including Abbeydale and Bradfield, enjoyable food, etched bay windows, big mirrors and period fireplaces; two outside seating areas, open all day. *(James Knight)*

SHEFFIELD SK3185
Rising Sun (0114) 230 3855
Fulwood Road; S10 3QA Extended community pub with a dozen ales (several from Abbeydale) and good selection of craft beers, tasty fairly priced food, friendly service; background music, quiz Weds and Sun; children welcome, a few tables out in front, more on back terrace, open all day. *(Ewan and Sue Hewitt)*

SHEFFIELD SK3586
Sheffield Tap (0114) 273 7558
Station, platform 1B; S1 2BP Busy station bar in restored Edwardian refreshment room, popular for its extensive range of international beers on draught and in bottles, also own Tapped ales from visible microbrewery and plenty of guests including Thornbridge, knowledgeable helpful staff, snacky food, spacious tiled interior with vaulted ceiling; open all day. *(Chris Sale)*

SHEFFIELD SK3687
★ **Wellington** (0114) 249 2295
Henry Street; by Shalesmoor tram stop; S3 7EQ Unpretentious and relaxed corner pub with up to ten changing beers including own bargain Little Ale Cart brews, also bottled imports and real cider, coal fire in lounge, photographs of old Sheffield, daily papers and pub games, friendly staff; tables out behind, open all day Fri-Sun, from 3pm Mon-Thurs. *(Jimmy)*

SHEFFIELD SK3584
White Lion (0114) 255 1500
London Road; S2 4HT Terrace-row pub dating from the late 18th c with various small lounges and snugs off central corridor, ten well kept changing ales (marked on blackboard) and good selection of whiskies, friendly relaxed atmosphere; regular live music in back room, Weds quiz; open all day from 4pm (midday Sat, 2pm Sun). *(James Knight)*

SHELLEY SE2112
★ **Three Acres** (01484) 602606
Roydhouse (not signed); from B6116 towards Skelmanthorpe, turn left in Shelley (signposted Flockton, Elmley, Elmley Moor), go up lane for 2 miles towards radio mast; HD8 8LR Civilised former coaching inn with emphasis on hotel and dining side; roomy lounge with leather chesterfields, old prints and so forth, tankards hanging from main beam, well kept Copper Dragon, 40 malt whiskies and up to 17 wines by the glass from serious (not cheap) list, several formal dining rooms, wide choice of good if expensive food from lunchtime sandwiches up, competent friendly service; conferences, weddings and events; children welcome, fine moorland setting and lovely views, smart well equipped bedrooms. *(W K Wood)*

SHEPLEY SE1809
Farmers Boy (01484) 605355
Marsh Lane, W of village – off A629 at Black Bull (leads on past pub to A635); HD8 8AP Smart stone-built dining pub; small traditional beamed bar on right serving Black Sheep, Bradfield and Copper Dragon, bare-boards area on left with coal fire and sturdy country tables, carpeted part rambling back through plenty of neat linen-set dining tables, barn restaurant with own terrace, popular often imaginative food from lunchtime sandwiches up, not cheap but they do offer a lunchtime/

early-evening set menu, friendly service; unobtrusive background music; children welcome, disabled access (via restaurant entrance) and loos, picnic-sets out in front, open all day. *(Sarah and David Gibbs)*

SHERIFF HUTTON SE6566
Highwayman (01347) 878328
The Square; YO60 6QZ Friendly comfortably refurbished family-run pub, good value home-made food from sandwiches and baguettes up including generous Sun lunch, a house beer from Pennine (Stand & Deliver), Theakstons and a guest, beamed interior with bar, restaurant and games room (pool and darts); Thurs quiz, TV; children and dogs welcome, picnic-sets in big garden, attractive village with castle ruins and 12th-c church, open all day weekends, closed Mon lunchtime, no food Sun evening, Mon. *(Pat and Tony Martin)*

SHIPLEY SE1437
Fannys Ale House (01274) 591419
Saltaire Road; BD18 3JN Bare-boards alehouse on two floors, cosy and friendly, with eight well kept ales including Timothy Taylors, also bottled beers and traditional ciders, gas lighting, brewery memorabilia, log fire and woodburner, back extension; dogs welcome, closed Mon lunchtime, otherwise open all day and can get crowded weekend evenings. *(Jill and Dick Archer)*

SHIPLEY SE1337
Hop (01274) 582111
Bingley Road; BD18 4DH Cavernous glass-fronted tramshed conversion, high pitched ceilings with some rather grand chandeliers, raised seating areas and stairs up to gallery, well kept Ossett range and guests from central curved counter, good choice of enjoyable food including sandwiches, sharing boards and wood-fired pizzas, early-bird weekday set menu (5-7pm), friendly helpful service; live music Sat, quiz Tues; no under-18s after 8pm, picnic-sets out at front among the old tram tracks, on edge of Saltaire World Heritage Site, open all day (food all day Fri, Sat and till 7pm Sun). *(Steve Whalley)*

SICKLINGHALL SE3648
Scotts Arms (01937) 582100
Main Street; LS22 4BD Hospitable and popular 17th-c pub with enjoyable generously served food (all day weekends) including blackboard specials, rambling interior with interesting nooks and crannies, low beams, old timbers and log fires (one in lovely fireplace), four well kept ales including Timothy Taylors Landlord and Theakstons Old Peculier, good wine range, friendly efficient staff; free wi-fi; children welcome, disabled access/loos, big garden with teak furniture on paved terrace, open all day. *(Gordon and Margaret Ormondroyd)*

SINNINGTON SE7485
★**Fox & Hounds** (01751) 431577
Off A170 W of Pickering; YO62 6SQ Popular 18th-c coaching house in pretty village, carpeted beamed bar with two-way woodburner, comfortable seating, various pictures and old artefacts, well kept Black Sheep and a guest such as Thwaites, several wines by the glass and some interesting whiskies, appealing attractively presented food including a light lunch/early-evening menu, friendly helpful service, lounge and smart restaurant; background music, free wi-fi; children and dogs welcome, picnic-sets out at front and in garden, ten good comfortable bedrooms. *(Pat and Stewart Gordon, Michael Butler, Michael Doswell)*

SKIPTON SD9851
★**Narrow Boat** (01756) 797922
Victoria Street; pub signed down alley off Coach Street; BD23 1JE Lively pub down cobbled alley, eight well kept ales, fruit and wheat beers, traditional cider/perry, dining chairs, pews and stools around wooden tables on bare boards, various breweriana, upstairs galleried area with interesting canal mural, fair-priced pubby food (all day Sat, not Sun evening); live music Mon; children allowed if eating, dogs welcome, picnic-sets under front colonnade, Leeds & Liverpool Canal nearby, open all day. *(Steve Whalley)*

SKIPTON SD9851
Woolly Sheep (01756) 700966
Sheep Street; BD23 1HY Bustling narrow pub just off the High Street, full Timothy Taylors range kept well, several wines by the glass and good range of gins, whiskies and cocktails, friendly service, two beamed bars off flagstoned passage, exposed brickwork, coal fire in stone fireplace, split-level dining area at the back, good choice of enjoyable reasonably priced food; children welcome, wheelchair access with help, rattan furniture in covered back terrace, 12 bedrooms, good breakfast, open (and food) all day. *(Comus and Sarah Elliott, Steve Whalley, Michael Butler)*

SLEDMERE SE9364
★**Triton** (01377) 236078
B1252/B1253 junction, NW of Great Driffield; YO25 3XQ Handsome old inn by Sledmere House; open-plan bar with old-fashioned atmosphere, dark wooden furniture on red patterned carpet, 15 clocks ranging from grandfather to cuckoo, lots of willow pattern plates, paintings and pictures, open fire, Greene King, Timothy Taylors, Tetleys and Wold Top, 50 gins, generous helpings of well liked freshly cooked food (only take bookings in separate restaurant), friendly helpful staff; children welcome till 8pm, wheelchair access to bar and restaurant, five good bedrooms, generous breakfast, open (and food) all day Sun till 9pm. *(Joe Oswald)*

SLINGSBY   SE6975
Grapes (01653) 628076
*Off B1257 Malton–Hovingham; Railway
Street; YO62 4AL* Stone-built 18th-c
village pub, good sensibly priced food (not
Sun evening) from traditional menu, well
kept Black Sheep, Copper Dragon, Timothy
Taylors and Theakstons, cheerful staff, bare
boards, flagstones and painted beams, nice
mix of old furniture and some interesting
bits and pieces including a tusky boar's head
above one of the woodburners, games area
with bar billiards; tables out behind, open
all day Fri-Sun, closed Mon. *(Angie Mayer)*

SNAITH   SE6422
Brewers Arms (01405) 862404
Pontefract Road; DN14 9JS Georgian
inn tied to local Old Mill Brewery, their
distinctive range from brick and timber-
fronted servery, decent home-made food
including fresh fish/seafood (June crab
festival), friendly helpful staff, open-
plan carpeted interior, old well complete
with skeleton; children welcome in
eating areas, attractive, good quality
bedrooms, open all day but may close
early if quiet; refurbishment planned as
we went to press. *(Liz and Mike Newton)*

SNAPE   SE2684
★Castle Arms (01677) 470270
Off B6268 Masham–Bedale; DL8 2TB
Welcoming homely pub in pretty village,
flagstoned bar with straightforward pubby
furniture, horsebrasses on beams and
open fire, Marstons-related ales, enjoyable
food from good sandwiches up, dining
room (also flagstoned) with dark tables
and chairs and another fire; children and
dogs welcome, picnic-sets out at front
and in courtyard, fine walks in Yorkshire
Dales and on North York Moors, nine
good bedrooms. *(Maria and Bertie Farr)*

SOUTH DALTON   SE9645
★Pipe & Glass (01430) 810246
*West End; brown sign to pub off B1248
NW of Beverley; HU17 7PN* Attractive
tucked-away village pub with main emphasis
on landlord-chef's excellent food; beamed
and bow-windowed bar, copper pans hanging
above woodburner in sizeable fireplace,
cushioned window seats and high-backed
wooden dining chairs around mix of tables,
Black Sheep, a house beer (Two Chefs)
from Great Yorkshire and a couple of
guests, 15 wines by the glass and some 40
malt whiskies, friendly staff, contemporary
area beyond with leather chesterfields
and another woodburner leading to airy
restaurant overlooking parkland; background
music, free wi-fi; children welcome, tables

on lawn and front terrace, ancient yew tree,
stylish bedrooms including three luxury
suites, charming village with 62-metre church
spire, closed Mon, otherwise open (and food)
all day, kitchen closes 4pm Sun. *(Michael
Doswell, Chris Stevenson, Penny and David
Shepherd, Tim and Sarah Smythe-Brown)*

SOUTH KILVINGTON   SE4284
Old Oak Tree (01845) 523276
Stockton Road (A61); YO7 2NL Spacious
low-ceilinged pub with three linked rooms
and long back conservatory, large choice
of good honest food from sandwiches up
including lunchtime/early-evening two-course
deal, three well kept beers, friendly staff;
children welcome, tables on sloping lawn,
five bedrooms. *(Charlotte and William Mason)*

SOWERBY BRIDGE   SE0623
Hogs Head (01422) 836585
Stanley Street; HX6 2AH Brewpub in
former 18th-c maltings, one large bare-
boards room with heavy beams and big
woodburner, brewery visible behind glass,
their good beers and several mainly local
guests, no food, open from 3pm weekdays,
midday weekends. *(Pat and Tony Martin)*

SOWERBY BRIDGE   SE0523
Hollins Mill (01422) 647410
Hollins Mill Lane, off A58; HX6 2QG
Large airy bare-boards pub in converted
joinery workshop by Rochdale Canal,
seating from pews to comfortable sofas, up
to eight well kept ales including Phoenix
and Timothy Taylors, craft beers, a couple
of ciders and decent range of gins, good
value home-made food from baguettes up,
efficient young staff; music nights in big
upstairs room; children and dogs welcome,
disabled facilities, backyard (covered in poor
weather), open all day, food all day weekends
till early evening. *(Pat and Tony Martin)*

STAMFORD BRIDGE   SE7055
Three Cups (01759) 377381
A166 W of town; YO41 1AX Family
dining pub (Vintage Inn) with popular
food including meal deals, plenty of wines
by the glass and three well kept beers,
friendly helpful staff, pleasant rustic
décor with two blazing fires, glass-topped
well in bar; disabled access, play area
behind, river walks nearby, open (and
food) all day. *(Ben and Jenny Settle)*

STANBURY   SE0037
Old Silent (01535) 647437
Hob Lane; BD22 0HW Welcoming
moorland dining inn, enjoyable fairly
priced home-made food (all day weekends),
Timothy Taylors Landlord, Theakstons
Old Peculier and guests, attentive helpful

If you know a pub is ever open all day, please tell us.

service, character linked rooms with beams, flagstones, mullioned windows and open fires, restaurant and conservatory; free wi-fi; children and dogs welcome, open all day. *(John and Eleanor Holdsworth)*

STAVELEY SE3662

Royal Oak (01423) 340267

Signed off A6055 Knaresborough–Boroughbridge; HG5 9LD Popular pub in village conservation area; beams, panelling and open fires, broad bay windows overlooking small front garden, well kept Black Sheep, Timothy Taylors and two local guests, several wines by the glass, enjoyable fairly priced food in bar and restaurant cooked by landlord-chef; children welcome, open all day, kitchen closed Mon, Tues. *(Alister and Margery Bacon)*

STILLINGTON SE5867

Bay Tree (01347) 811394

Main Street; leave York on outer ring road (A1237) to Scarborough, first exit on left signposted B1363 to Helmsley; YO61 1JU Cottagey pub-restaurant in pretty village's main street; modern bar areas with comfortable cushioned wall seats and kitchen chairs around mix of tables, central gas-effect coal fire, real ales such as Black Sheep, several wines by the glass and extensive range of gins, good interesting food from chef-owner along with some pub favourites and lunchtime sandwiches, steps up to cosy dining area, larger conservatory-style back restaurant; background music; children and dogs (in bar) welcome, seats in garden and a couple of picnic-sets at front, closed Mon and Tues. *(Shirley Blenkinsopp)*

STOKESLEY NZ5208

White Swan (01642) 710263

West End; TS9 5BL Good Captain Cook ales brewed at this attractive 18th-c flower-decked local, L-shaped bar with three relaxing seating areas, log fire, assorted memorabilia and nice bar counter with carved panels, speciality pies; Weds quiz, regular live music and beer festivals; no children, dogs welcome, open all day. *(Jackie Robinson)*

SUTTON UPON DERWENT SE7047

★ St Vincent Arms (01904) 608349

Main Street (B1228 SE of York); YO41 4BN Busy pub with seven well kept ales including Fullers, lots of wines by the glass and popular food from lunchtime sandwiches up, parlour-style front bar with panelling, traditional high-backed settles, windsor chairs, cushioned bow-window seat and gas-effect coal fire, another lounge and separate dining room; children and dogs (in bar) welcome, garden tables, handy for Yorkshire Air Museum. *(Michael Doswell, Margaret and Peter Staples)*

SUTTON-UNDER-WHITESTONECLIFFE SE4983

Whitestonecliffe Inn (01845) 597271

A170 E of Thirsk; YO7 2PR Well located 18th-c beamed roadside pub, enjoyable fairly priced food from traditional menu along with blackboard specials, three well kept ales including Black Sheep, friendly staff, log fire and some exposed stonework in bar, separate restaurant, games room with pool and darts; quiz last Fri of month; children and dogs welcome, six self-catering cottages, open all day weekends, closed Weds lunchtime. *(Comus and Sarah Elliott, Tony and Wendy Hobden)*

TAN HILL NY8906

★ Tan Hill Inn (01833) 628246

Arkengarthdale Road, Reeth–Brough, at junction Keld/West Stonesdale Road; DL11 6ED Basic old pub (Britain's highest) in wonderful bleak setting on Pennine Way, often snowbound; full of bric-a-brac and interesting photographs, simple sturdy furniture on flagstones and an ever-burning log fire with prized stone side seats, five well kept ales including one badged for them from Dent, good cheap pubby food, family room; live weekend music; dogs welcome, seven bedrooms, bunk rooms and camping, wandering ducks and chickens, Swaledale sheep show here last Thurs in May, open (and some food) all day, can get very crowded. *(Ian and Rose Lock)*

THIRSK SE4282

Golden Fleece (01845) 523108

Market Place; YO7 1LL Major recent refurbishment for this old brick coaching inn; good food from snacks and sharing plates up including pub staples and stone-baked pizzas, friendly helpful service, ales such as Black Sheep and Copper Dragon, craft beers and over 20 wines by the glass, good range of gins too, clean contemporary décor in bar and separate dining rooms, view across marketplace from bay windows; children and dogs (in some areas) welcome, part-covered back courtyard, 26 bedrooms, open (and food) all day. *(Jeremy King)*

THIXENDALE SE8461

Cross Keys (01377) 288272

Off A166 3 miles N of Fridaythorpe; YO17 9TG Unspoilt country pub in deep valley below the rolling wolds and popular with walkers; cosy and relaxed L-shaped bar with fitted wall seats, well kept Tetleys and a couple of guests, generous uncomplicated blackboard food; no children or dogs inside, views from big back garden, handy for Wharram Percy earthworks, comfortable bedrooms in converted stables, good breakfast, closed Mon-Thurs lunchtimes (unless pre-booked by walking group). *(Lee and Jill Stafford)*

THOLTHORPE   SE4766
New Inn   (01347) 838329
Flawith Road; YO61 1SL Updated
beamed village-green pub with log-fire
bar and candlelit restaurant, good food
(allergies catered for) from sandwiches
and wood-fired pizzas up including popular
Sun lunch, Fri evening fish and chips deal,
John Smiths and a local guest, friendly
helpful staff; small shop; children welcome,
closed Mon and lunchtime Tues.
(Patti and James Davidson)

THORNTON   SE0832
White Horse   (01274) 834268
Well Heads; BD13 3SJ Deceptively large
country pub popular for its wide choice of
good food including early-bird menu, five
well kept Timothy Taylors ales, pleasant
helpful staff, four separate areas, two with
log fires, bustling atmosphere; children
welcome, upstairs lavatories (disabled
ones on ground level), also disabled
parking, open all day, food all day weekends
(till 7.45pm Sun). *(Gordon and Margaret
Ormondroyd, John and Eleanor Holdsworth)*

THORNTON DALE   SE8383
New Inn   (01751) 474226
The Square; YO18 7LF Friendly early
18th-c beamed coaching inn – packed
weekend evenings; well kept ales and
good traditional food cooked by landlord
including deals; children and dogs (in bar)
welcome, courtyard tables, six bedrooms
and self-catering cottage, pretty village
on edge of Dalby Forest, open all day in
summer. *(Sara Fulton, Roger Baker)*

THORNTON-LE-CLAY   SE6865
White Swan   (01653) 618286
*Off A64 SW of Malton, via Foston;
Low Street; YO60 7TG* Refurbished
19th-c family-run village pub; a house beer
from Helmsley with guests such as Black
Sheep and York, nice wines by the glass
and enjoyable well priced home-made
food including daily specials, early-bird
discount 5-6.30pm (not Sun), friendly
helpful young staff, some local chutneys,
preserves etc for sale; live music and
quiz nights; children welcome, large
garden, attractive countryside nearby and
Castle Howard, open all day Sun, closed
Mon, Tues. *(Kerry and Guy Trooper)*

THORP ARCH   SE4346
Pax   (01937) 843183
The Village; LS23 7AR Welcoming
19th-c village pub with enjoyable home-
made food at sensible prices (notable
steak and ale pie), ales such as Abbeydale,
Moorhouses and Roosters, friendly helpful
service, two bar areas, open fire, back
dining area; children and dogs welcome,
useful A1 stop, open all day weekends, no
food Sun evening. *(Liz and Mike Newton)*

THRESHFIELD   SD9863
Old Hall Inn   (01756) 752441
*B6160/B6265 just outside Grassington;
BD23 5HB* Old creeper-clad village inn set
back from the road, enjoyable food served
by attentive friendly staff, good choice of
beers and wines, flagstoned bar with dining
rooms either side, open fires (one in fine
blacked kitchen range), high beam-and-
plank ceiling, cushioned wall pews; neat
garden and pretty hanging baskets, seven
comfortable bedrooms, self-catering
cottage, open (and food) all day. *(Jimmy)*

THRINTOFT   SE3293
New Inn   (01609) 771961
*Thrintoft Moor Lane, off Bramper Lane;
DL7 0PN* Friendly 18th-c village local with
good variety of generously served home-
made food including popular Sun lunch,
well kept Black Sheep and a guest such
as nearby Walls County Town, restaurant,
open fire and woodburner; quiz first Thurs
of month, free wi-fi; children welcome, no
dogs inside, disabled access, front garden
with two quoits pitches, closed Mon, no
food Tues lunchtime. *(Steve Thornley)*

TIMBLE   SE1852
★ Timble Inn   (01943) 880530
*Off Otley–Blubberhouses moors road;
LS21 2NN* Smartly restored 18th-c dining
inn tucked away in quiet farmland hamlet,
good food from pub favourites up including
well aged Nidderdale beef (booking advised),
ales such as Copper Dragon, Ilkley and
Theakstons; children welcome, no dogs
at food times, good walks from the door,
seven well appointed bedrooms, closed Sun
evening to Weds lunchtime. *(Chris Allen)*

TONG   SE2230
Greyhound   (0113) 285 2427
Tong Lane; BD4 0RR Traditional low-
beamed and flagstoned local by village
cricket field, distinctive areas including
cosy dining room, generous helpings of
enjoyable good value food, ales such as Black
Sheep, Leeds, Timothy Taylors and Tetleys,
several wines by the glass, good friendly
service; tables outside, open all day (food
till 5.45pm Sun). *(Barbara and Phil Bowie)*

TOPCLIFFE   SE4076
Angel   (01845) 578000
*Off A1, take A168 to Thirsk, after 3
miles follow signs for Topcliffe; Long
Street; YO7 3RW* Part of the West Park
Inns group; softly lit bare-boards bar with
log fire, real ales and good choice of wines
by the glass, enjoyable food in carpeted
grill restaurant, weekday early-bird deal
(till 6.30pm), cheerful helpful service;
background music, comedy night (usually
first Tues of month); children welcome,
nice garden, 16 bedrooms, open all day
(food all day Sun till 8pm). *(Joe Oswald)*

TOWTON SE4839
Rockingham Arms (01937) 530948
A162 Tadcaster–Ferrybridge; LS24 9PB
Comfortable roadside village pub with
enjoyable home-made food from lunchtime
sandwiches up, efficient friendly service, ales
such as Black Sheep and Theakstons, back
conservatory; children and dogs welcome,
garden tables, handy for Towton Battlefield,
closed Sun evening, Mon, otherwise open
all day. *(John and Eleanor Holdsworth)*

ULLESKELF SE5140
Ulleskelf Arms (01937) 835515
Church Fenton Lane; LS24 9DS Village
pub refurbished under friendly new
management, four well kept ales including
Timothy Taylors Boltmaker, good value
home-made food (till 6pm Sun evening, not
Tues) including Mon pie night, open-plan
interior with mix of old and new furniture
on laminate flooring; background music;
children, walkers and dogs welcome, beer
garden behind, open all day Sun, closed
lunchtimes Mon and Tues. *(Nick Wilkinson)*

WAKEFIELD SE3417
Castle (01924) 256981
Barnsley Road, Sandal; WF2 6AS
Popular roadside dining pub with good
affordably priced food including set menu
till 6pm, well kept Black Sheep and
a couple of guests, friendly staff and
pleasant relaxed atmosphere; unobtrusive
background music; children welcome, dogs
in bar, rattan-style furniture on paved back
terrace overlooking bowling green, open
all day. *(John and Eleanor Holdsworth)*

WAKEFIELD SE3320
Fernandes Brewery Tap (01924)
386348 *Avison Yard, Kirkgate; WF1 1UA*
Owned by Ossett but still brewing Fernandes
ales in the cellar, interesting guest beers,
bottled imports and traditional ciders,
ground-floor bar with flagstones, bare brick
and panelling, original raftered top-floor
bar has some unusual breweriana; monthly
folk and open mike nights, quiz Weds;
dogs welcome, open all day Fri-Sun (when
some lunchtime food available), from
4pm other days. *(Kerry and Guy Trooper)*

WAKEFIELD SE3220
Harrys Bar (01924) 373773
Westgate; WF1 1EL Cheery little one-room
local with good selection of real ales and
bottled beers, stripped-brick walls, open fire;
live music Mon and Weds, free wi-fi; small
back garden, open all day Sun from 5pm
Mon-Fri, 4pm Sat. *(Kerry and Guy Trooper)*

WALKINGTON SE9937
Dog & Duck (01482) 423026
B1230, East End; HU17 8RX Popular
comfortably modernised pub with well liked
generously served food including blackboard

specials, four well kept Marstons-related
beers, friendly helpful service; sports TV;
children welcome, garden and terrace with
pizza oven and barbecue, charming village,
open (and food) all day. *(Jack Robinson)*

WALTON SE4447
Fox & Hounds (01937) 842192
*Hall Park Road, off back road Wetherby–
Tadcaster; LS23 7DQ* Popular dining
pub with good reasonably priced food from
sandwiches to specials (should book Sun
lunch), evening set menu Tues-Sat, well kept
ales such as John Smiths, friendly thriving
atmosphere; children welcome, handy A1
stop, closed Mon. *(Gary and Marie Miller)*

WALTON SE3517
New Inn (01924) 255447
Shay Lane; WF2 6LA Open-plan village
pub with friendly staff and buoyant
atmosphere, well kept Ossett and guests,
several wines by the glass and good helpings
of tasty well priced food cooked by landlord,
split-level back dining extension; quiz
nights Sun and Mon; children welcome,
dogs in bar, garden play area, open
(and food) all day. *(Michael Butler)*

WARLEY TOWN SE0524
Maypole (01422) 835861
*Signed off A646 just W of Halifax;
HX2 7RZ* Friendly open-plan village dining
pub, enjoyable good value food from fairly
traditional menu including lunchtime/early-
evening set deal Tues-Fri, well kept ales such
as Black Sheep, pleasant young staff, two-way
woodburner; children welcome, open all day
Fri-Sun, closed Mon lunchtime. *(Angie Mayer)*

WASS SE5579
Stapylton Arms (01347) 868280
*Back road W of Ampleforth; or follow
brown sign for Byland Abbey off
A170 Thirsk–Helmsley; YO61 4BE*
Two refurbished bustling bars with log fires,
a beer or two from Helmsley or Theakstons,
restaurant in 18th-c granary serving good
popular food including specials, friendly staff;
children welcome, no dogs, pretty village
and surrounding countryside, near ruins
of Byland Abbey (EH), three comfortable
well equipped bedrooms. *(James Knight)*

WATH SE3277
George (01765) 641324
Main Street; village N of Ripon; HG4 5EN
Friendly refurbished village pub with good
range of enjoyable traditional food (till
7pm Sun) using local ingredients, ales such
as Black Sheep, Rudgate and Theakstons,
decent choice of wines; five comfortable
bedrooms, open all day weekends, closed
lunchtimes Mon-Weds. *(Michael Butler)*

WATH-IN-NIDDERDALE SE1467
★**Sportsmans Arms** (01423) 711306
Nidderdale road off B6265 in Pateley

Bridge; village and pub signposted over hump-back bridge, on right after a couple of miles; HG3 5PP Civilised, beautifully located restaurant with rooms run by long-serving owner; although most emphasis on the excellent food and bedrooms, it does have a proper welcoming bar with open fire, well kept Black Sheep and Timothy Taylors, Thatcher's cider, lots of wines by the glass (extensive list) and 40 malt whiskies, also a highly rated ploughman's and other bar food, helpful hospitable staff, elegant dining room; background music; children welcome, dogs in bar, benches and tables outside, pretty garden with croquet, own fishing on River Nidd. *(Stephen Woad, Lynda and Trevor Smith, Hunter and Christine Wright)*

WENSLEY   SE0989

Three Horseshoes (01969) 622327

A684; DL8 4HJ Old whitewashed stone pub with neat beamed and flagstoned bar, five well kept ales including Black Sheep, Theakstons and Wensleydale, enjoyable straightforward food at reasonable prices from sandwiches up, pizzas only Mon evening, friendly helpful service, woodburner and open fire; children and dogs welcome, lovely views from paved terrace, popular with walkers, open all day. *(Clive and Fran Dutson)*

WENTWORTH   SK3898

Rockingham Arms (01226) 742075

3 miles from M1 junction 36; B6090, signed off A6135; Main Street; S62 7TL Welcoming 19th-c ivy-clad inn (John Barras group) in pretty village, comfortable traditional furnishings, stripped stone and open fires, bar with two snug rooms off, more formal dining room, several ales including Theakstons and good choice of wines by the glass, enjoyable well priced traditional food served by energetic young staff; background music, TV; dogs allowed in one part, attractive garden with bowling green, 11 bedrooms, open (and food) all day. *(Peter Hacker)*

WEST TANFIELD   SE2678

Bruce Arms (01677) 470325

Main Street (A6108 N of Ripon); HG4 5JJ Smart dining pub (18th-c coaching inn) under same ownership as the nearby Bull; good restaurant-style food served by friendly attentive staff, well kept Theakstons and good range of wines, gins and malt whiskies; terrace tables, three comfortable bedrooms, good breakfast, closed Sun evening to Weds lunchtime. *(Peter and Eleanor Kenyon, Michael Butler)*

WEST TANFIELD   SE2678

Bull (01677) 470678

Church Street (A6108 N of Ripon); HG4 5JQ Busy pub in picturesque riverside setting; flagstoned bar and slightly raised dining area, popular fairly standard food

---

(all day Sat, till 7pm Sun), well kept Black Sheep and Theakstons, pleasant service; background and live music once or twice a month (Sun), free wi-fi; children (away from bar) and dogs welcome, tables on terraces in attractive garden sloping steeply to River Ure and its old bridge, five bedrooms, open all day. *(Michael Butler)*

WEST WITTON   SE0588

★**Wensleydale Heifer** (01969) 622322

A684 W of Leyburn; DL8 4LS Stylish restaurant-with-rooms rather than pub, but can pop in for a drink; excellent food with emphasis on fish/seafood and grills (not cheap and best to book), also early-bird menu (6-6.30pm), sandwiches and snacks, good wines, cosy dining bar with Black Sheep and a house beer brewed by Yorkshire, much bigger and more formal restaurant, attentive helpful service; children welcome, dogs in some areas, 13 good bedrooms (back ones quietest), generous breakfast, open all day. *(John and Penny Wildon, John and Enid Morris, Ian Wilson)*

WESTOW   SE7565

Blacksmiths Arms (01653) 619606

Off A64 York–Malton; Main Street; YO60 7NE Updated 18th-c family-run pub with attractive beamed bar, woodburner in brick inglenook and original bread oven, beers such as Copper Dragon, Tetleys and Thwaites, enjoyable home-made, locally sourced food from sandwiches and pub favourites up (steaks a speciality), restaurant; picnic-sets on side terrace, open all day. *(Sarah and David Gibbs)*

WETHERBY   SE4048

Swan & Talbot (01937) 582040

Handy for A1; North Street; LS22 6NN Comfortable traditional town pub (former posting inn) with large bar area and restaurant, four well kept ales and several wines by the glass, food from sandwiches and sharing plates up, busy friendly staff; background music, TV; children welcome, courtyard tables, open all day from 9am for breakfast. *(Chris Allen)*

WHITBY   NZ9011

Black Horse (01947) 602906

Church Street; YO22 4BH Small traditional two-room pub, much older than its Victorian frontage, and previously a funeral parlour and brothel; friendly and down to earth with five changing ales, continental beers and a proper cider, range of yorkshire tapas, tins of snuff for sale; dogs welcome, four cosy bedrooms, open all day. *(Shirley Blenkinsopp)*

WHITBY   NZ9011

Board (01947) 602884

Church Street; YO22 4DE Busy pub in good spot opposite fish quay, faux-beamed bar with nice old range in one part, banquettes and other pubby furniture on patterned carpet, modern dining room downstairs with fine harbour view from big windows, well kept Caledonian Deuchars IPA and Theakstons, good value traditional food, friendly staff; background music, live bands Thurs and Fri, Weds quiz, TV and games machine; bedrooms. *(James Knight)*

WHITBY NZ9011
★Duke of York (01947) 600324
Church Street, Harbour East Side; YO22 4DE Busy pub in fine harbourside position, good views and handy for the famous 199 steps leading up to abbey; comfortable beamed lounge bar with fishing memorabilia, five well kept ales such as Black Sheep and Caledonian, decent wines and several malt whiskies, enjoyable straightforward bar food at reasonable prices, attentive service; background music, TV, games machine, free wi-fi; children welcome, bedrooms overlooking water, no nearby parking, open (and food) all day. *(Shirley Blenkinsopp)*

WHITBY NZ8911
Station Inn (01947) 603937
New Quay Road; YO21 1DH Friendly three-room drinkers' pub across from the station and harbour, good mix of customers, eight well kept ales including a house beer brewed by Whitby, Weston's cider and good wines by the glass, traditional games; background and regular live music, quiz Thurs; dogs welcome, three new bedrooms, open all day. *(Mick Allen)*

WHITBY NZ9011
White Horse & Griffin (01947)
604857 *Church Street; YO22 4BH* Historic 17th-c coaching inn; tall narrow front bar with bare boards and a couple of large chandeliers, ales such as Black Sheep and Timothy Taylors, good wines and over 30 gins, steps down to low-beamed bistro-style dining area with flagstones and log fire, good interesting food, friendly staff; ten bedrooms, close to the 199 steps, open all day. *(Randy Alden)*

WIGHILL SE4746
White Swan (01937) 832217
Main Street; LS24 8BQ Fairly modern family-run village pub with two cosy front rooms and larger side extension, well kept Black Sheep Bitter, a house beer from Moorhouses and a guest, enjoyable interesting food, friendly staff; children welcome, no dogs inside, wheelchair access with help (steps down to lavatories), picnic-sets on side lawn, open (and food) all day. *(Michael Butler)*

WITHERNWICK TA1940
Falcon (01964) 527925
Main Street; HU11 4TA Welcoming 18th-c beamed corner pub, popular good

value food from fairly pubby menu, well kept Timothy Taylors Landlord, Tetleys and a guest; children welcome, a few seats outside, closed Mon and lunchtimes apart from Sun. *(Douglas Power, Kate Moran)*

WOMBLETON SE6683
Plough (01751) 431356
Main Street; YO62 7RW Welcoming 15th-c village local with good home-made food including blackboard specials, ales such as Black Sheep, John Smiths, Tetleys and Theakstons, bar eating area and restaurant; tables outside, open all day Fri-Sun, closed Mon lunchtime. *(Michael Doswell)*

WORTLEY SK3099
Wortley Arms (0114) 288 8749
A629 N of Sheffield; S35 7DB 18th-c stone-built coaching inn with several comfortably furnished rooms, beams, panelling and large inglenook, wide choice of food (all day Sat) and five well kept ales including Timothy Taylors and Wentworth; occasional live music; children and dogs (in bar) welcome, nice village about ten minutes from M1, open all day (till 8pm Sun). *(Stuart Paulley)*

YORK SE6051
Black Swan (01904) 679131
Peaseholme Green (inner ring road); YO1 7PR Striking black and white Tudor building; compact panelled front bar, crooked-floored central hall with fine period staircase and black-beamed back bar with vast inglenook, good choice of real ales, decent wines and generous helpings of reasonably priced pubby food from sandwiches up; background music, Thurs folk club; children welcome, useful car park behind, bedrooms, open all day, no food weekend evenings. *(Jamie and Lizzie McEwan)*

YORK SE6051
★Blue Bell (01904) 654904
Fossgate; YO1 9TF Delightfully old-fashioned little Edwardian pub, very friendly and chatty, with well kept Bradfield, Rudgate, Timothy Taylors Landlord and three guests (a dark mild always available), good value lunchtime sandwiches (not Sun), tiny tiled-floor front bar with roaring fire, panelled ceiling and stained glass, corridor to small back room with hatch service, lamps and candles, pub games; soft background music; no children, dogs welcome, open all day (but maybe just for locals on busy nights due to its size). *(Roger and Donna Huggins)*

YORK SE5951
★Brigantes (01904) 675355
Micklegate; YO1 6JX Bar-bistro (Market Town Tavern) with shop-style frontage, wooden tables and chairs on bare boards, blue-painted half-panelling and screens forming booths, ten well kept mainly local

ales (York Brewery is in street behind), good range of bottled beers, decent wines and coffee, good food from fairly priced varied menu, cheerful service, upstairs function room; children and dogs welcome, open (and food) all day. *(Pat and Tony Martin)*

YORK   SE6051
Golden Ball (01904) 652211
Cromwell Road/Victor Street; YO1 6DU Friendly well preserved four-room Edwardian corner pub owned by local co-operative, up to seven well kept ales, no food apart from bar snacks, bar billiards, cards and dominoes; Sun folk night and other live music, quiz Tues, TV; lovely small walled garden, open all day weekends, closed weekday lunchtimes. *(Naomi and Andrew Randall)*

YORK   SE6051
Golden Fleece (01904) 625171
Pavement; YO1 9UP Popular little city-centre pub with four well kept ales including Copper Dragon and Timothy Taylors, long corridor from bar to comfortable back dining room (sloping floors – it dates from 1503), interesting décor with quite a library, lots of pictures and ghost stories; background music and occasional folk evenings; children allowed if eating, no dogs, four bedrooms, open all day. *(Michael Butler)*

YORK   SE6052
Guy Fawkes (01904) 466674
High Petergate; YO1 7HP Splendid spot next to the Minster; dark panelled interior with small bar to the left, half a dozen real ales including Timothy Taylors and York, enjoyable sensibly priced food (not Sun evening) from shortish menu plus blackboard specials, good helpful service, dining rooms lit by gas wall-lights and candles, open fires; courtyard tables, 13 bedrooms, open all day. *(Phil and Jane Villiers)*

YORK   SE6051
Harkers (01904) 672795
St Helens Square; YO1 8QN Nicholsons pub in handsome late Georgian building (basement features part of a Roman gateway), spacious split-level bar with high ceilings and columns, a couple of smaller rooms off, half a dozen ales including Rudgate, John Smiths and York from long counter, their usual good value food; open all day. *(Naomi and Andrew Randall)*

YORK   SE6052
House of Trembling Madness (01904) 640009
Stonegate; YO1 8AS Unusual place above own off-licence; impressive high-raftered medieval room with collection of stuffed animal heads from moles to lions, eclectic mix of furniture including cask seats and pews on bare boards, lovely old brick fireplace, real ales and craft beers from

pulpit servery, also huge selection of bottled beers (all available to buy downstairs), good knowledgeable staff, hearty reasonably priced food all day including various platters; two self-catering apartments in ancient courtyard behind, open all day till midnight. *(Roger and Donna Huggins)*

YORK   SE6052
Lamb & Lion (01904) 612078
High Petergate; YO1 7EH Appealing Georgian inn next to Bootham Bar; five well kept local ales and nice choice of wines by the glass, good food from sandwiches and pub favourites to more restauranty choices, friendly helpful staff, bare-boards bar and series of compact rooms off narrow corridors; steep steps up to attractive paved garden below city wall and looking up to the Minster, 12 bedrooms, open all day, food all day Sun. *(Marianne and Peter Stevens, Phil and Jane Villiers)*

YORK   SE6052
Old White Swan (01904) 540911
Goodramgate; YO1 7LF Spacious Nicholsons pub with Victorian, Georgian and Tudor-themed bars, wide choice of fair value food, eight well kept ales and good whisky choice, central glass-covered courtyard (dogs allowed here); background and monthly live music, big-screen sports TV, games machines; children allowed till 9pm if eating, open all day. *(Louise and Simon Peters)*

YORK   SE6051
Phoenix (01904) 656401
George Street; YO1 9PT Friendly little pub next to city walls, proper front public bar and comfortable back horseshoe-shaped lounge, five well kept ales from yorkshire brewers, decent wines and simple food; live jazz two or three times a week, bar billiards; beer garden, handy for Barbican, open all day. *(Sally and Colin Allen)*

YORK   SE6051
Pivni (01904) 635464
Patrick Pool; YO1 8BB Old black and white pub close to the Shambles, extensive range of foreign draught and bottled beers (some unusual choices), also good selection of local ales, friendly knowledgeable staff, small narrow bar, more seats upstairs, snacky food and good coffee; dogs welcome, open all day. *(Naomi and Andrew Randall)*

YORK   SE6051
Punch Bowl (01904) 655147
Stonegate; YO1 8AN Bustling 17th-c black and white-fronted pub with small panelled rooms off corridor, good choice of well kept ales, decent wines and sensibly priced Nicholsons menu, efficient friendly service, dining room at back with fireplace; background music; a couple of tables out by pavement, open (and food) all day. *(Sally and Colin Allen)*

YORK　　　　　　　　　　SE6052

Snickleway　(01904) 656138

Goodramgate; YO1 7LS Interesting
little open-plan pub behind big shop-front
window, lots of antiques, copper and
brass, cosy fires, five well kept ales, some
lunchtime food (not Sun) including good
sandwiches, cheery landlord and prompt
friendly service, stories of various ghosts
including Mrs Tulliver and her cat; closed
Sun, otherwise open all day. *(Mick Allen)*

YORK　　　　　　　　　　SE6052

Star Inn the City　(01904) 619208

Museum Street; YO1 7DR Restauranty
place (sister to the Star at Harome) in
wonderful central riverside setting – a
former 19th-c pumping station with modern
glass extension; very good but not cheap
food (they also do a weekday set menu till
early evening), beers including a house
ale (Two Chefs) from Great Yorkshire
and Pilsner Urquell dispensed from two
large copper tanks, good range of wines
by the glass and cocktails, afternoon teas,
friendly service; open all day from 9.30am
for breakfast. *(Jamie and Lizzie McEwan)*

YORK　　　　　　　　　　SE6051

Swan　(01904) 634968

*Bishopgate Street, Clementhorpe;
YO23 1JH* Unspoilt 1930s pub (Grade
II listed) with two small rooms either
side of lobby bar, several changing ales
and ciders, friendly knowledgeable staff;
pleasant little walled garden, near city
walls, open all day weekends, from 4pm
weekdays. *(Stuart and Natalie Granville)*

YORK　　　　　　　　　　SE6052

★ Three Legged Mare　(01904) 638246

High Petergate; YO1 7EN Bustling
light and airy modern café-bar with York
Brewery's full range and guests kept
well (12 handpumps), plenty of belgian
beers too, quick friendly young staff,
interesting sandwiches and some basic

lunchtime hot food, back conservatory;
no children, disabled facilities (other
lavatories down spiral stairs), back
garden with replica gallows after which
pub is named, open all day till midnight
(11pm Sun). *(Jamie and Lizzie McEwan)*

YORK　　　　　　　　　　SE6051

Warmgate Ale House　(01904)

629222 *Walmgate; YO1 9TX* 17th-c
city-centre pub on three levels; ground-
floor bar with half a dozen yorkshire
ales and good range of wines, snacks
including sausage rolls and local cheeses,
upstairs bistro with wide choice of
enjoyable food including set menu choices
and weekend brunch (from 9.30am),
further loft dining area, friendly service;
children welcome, closed Mon, Tues
lunchtime otherwise open (and food)
all day. *(Stuart and Natalie Granville)*

YORK　　　　　　　　　　SE5951

Whippet　(01904) 500660

*Opposite Park Inn Hotel, North Street;
YO1 6JD* Steak and alehouse in street set
back from the river, good popular food
including signature dry-aged steaks, small
bar area with four well kept ales from
yorkshire brewers, lots of wines by the glass,
interesting cocktails and excellent range of
gins, friendly well informed staff; no children,
open all day. *(Pat and Graham Williamson,
Pat Martin)*

YORK　　　　　　　　　　SE5951

York Tap　(01904) 659009

Station, Station Road; YO24 1AB
Restored Edwardian bar at York train
station; high ceiling with feature stained-
glass cupolas, columns and iron fretwork,
bentwood chairs and stools on terrazzo floor,
button-back banquettes, period fireplaces,
great selection of real ales from circular
counter with brass footrail, also bottled
beers listed on blackboard, good pork pies
(three types); seats out by platform, open all
day from 10am. *(Roger and Donna Huggins)*

London

CENTRAL LONDON
Admiral Codrington ♀

Map 13

(020) 7581 0005 – www.theadmiralcodrington.co.uk

Mossop Street; ⊖ South Kensington; SW3 2LY

Long-standing Chelsea landmark with easy-going bar and pretty restaurant, popular food and seats outside

Customers drop in and out of this busy, tucked-away pub all day and the atmosphere is gently civilised and friendly. A central dark-panelled bar has high red chairs beside the counter with more around equally high tables on either side of the log-effect gas fire, button-back wall banquettes with cream and red patterned seats, little stools and plain wooden chairs around a medley of tables on black-painted floorboards, patterned wallpaper above a dado and a shelf with daily papers. There are ornate flower arrangements, a big portrait above the fire, several naval prints and quiet background music. The friendly, helpful staff serve London Beer Factory Chelsea Blonde, Marstons 61 Deep and Wychwood Hobgoblin on handpump and good wines by the glass. The light and airy restaurant area is a total contrast: high-backed pretty wall seats and plush dining chairs around light tables, an open kitchen, fish prints on pale blue paintwork, a second fireplace and an impressive skylight. The back garden has chunky benches and tables under a summer awning.

🍴 Enjoyable food includes sandwiches (until 5pm), beef carpaccio, pickles and horseradish cream, orkney king scallops, pancetta and peas, cumberland sausages with mash and caramelised onions, goats cheese, potato and onion pasty with baby beetroots and hollandaise, cheese burger with house-cured bacon, gherkins and chips, sea trout with samphire and shrimp brown butter, steak of the day with béarnaise sauce and triple-cooked chips, and puddings such as chocolate torte with kirsch cherries, chocolate soil and cherry sorbet and sticky toffee pudding with orange butterscotch and stem ginger ice-cream. *Benchmark main dish: somerset chicken with girolle mushrooms and cabbage £16.50. Two-course evening meal £22.00.*

Free house ~ Licensee Adam Byallas ~ Real ale ~ Open 11.30-11 (midnight Weds, Thurs); 11.30-1am Fri, Sat; 12-10 Sun ~ Bar food 12-3, 6-10 (11 Fri); 12-4, 6-11 Sat; 12-9 Sun ~ Restaurant ~ Children welcome ~ Dogs allowed in bar ~ Wi-fi *Recommended by Margaret McDonald, Tom Stone, Alister and Margery Bacon, Ian Duncan*

Real ale may be served from handpumps, electric pumps (not just the on-off switches used for keg beer) or – common in Scotland – tall taps called founts (pronounced 'fonts') where a separate pump pushes the beer up under air pressure.

CENTRAL LONDON
Alfred Tennyson 🏠⭐ ♀

Map 13

(020) 7730 6074 – www.thealfredtennyson.co.uk

Motcomb Street; ⊖ *Knightsbridge; SW1X 8LA*

Bustling and civilised with good drinks choice, rewarding food and friendly, helpful service

In a quiet residential area, this civilised pub draws in plenty of customers who enjoy the interesting food and drinks. Apart from one table surrounded by stools beside the bar counter, there are high-backed upholstered dining chairs around wooden tables on parquet flooring, comfortable leather wall seats and eclectic décor that encompasses 19th-c postcards to nobility, envelopes displayed address-side out, Edward Lear illustrations and World War II prints – plus antique books on windowsills. Friendly, helpful staff serve Cubitt 1788 (named for the pub from Canopy) on handpump, cocktails and 23 wines by the glass. The upstairs restaurant has leather chairs and wooden tables on more parquet and a huge mirror above an open fire. Above that is a room for private hire, while up again is a cosy loft used for monthly events such as cheese tastings. Outside on the front pavement are tables and chairs beneath a striped awning.

 As well as weekend breakfasts (9-11.30am), the enjoyable food includes smoked duck breast with goats curd, beetroot relish and spiced hazelnuts, a charcuterie board with rhubarb chutney (to share), dry-aged beef burger with tomato relish, dill pickles and horseradish mayonnaise, loin and leg of rabbit with heritage carrots and pickled morel mushrooms, beetroots and manouri cheese with pistachio granola and lemon and honey dressing, chicken breast with girolle mushrooms, baby onions, peas and tarragon velouté, cod fillet with wild nettle gnocchi, sea herbs and lemon pickle, and puddings such as white chocolate cheesecake with roasted peaches and peach sorbet and apple pie with salted caramel and vanilla ice-cream. *Benchmark main dish: beer-battered fish and chips £15.00. Two-course evening meal £23.00.*

Cubitt House ~ Lease Adam Quigley ~ Real ale ~ Open 12-11; 9am-11pm Sat, Sun ~ Bar food 12-10 ~ Children welcome ~ Dogs allowed in bar ~ Wi-fi *Recommended by Neil Tipler, Michael Butler, Sam Cole, Stuart and Natalie Granville*

CENTRAL LONDON
Black Friar ◀

Map 13

(020) 7236 5474 – www.nicholsonspubs.co.uk

Queen Victoria Street; ⊖ *Mansion House, Temple* ⊖ ⇌ *Blackfriars; EC4V 4EG*

Remarkable art nouveau décor, a fine choice of ales, friendly atmosphere and popular all-day food

After a stunning restoration, this architectural gem of a pub has reopened. It includes some of the best Edwardian bronze and marble art nouveau work to be found anywhere. The inner back room has big bas-relief friezes of jolly monks set into richly coloured florentine marble walls, an opulent marble-pillared inglenook fireplace, a low vaulted mosaic ceiling, gleaming mirrors, seats built into rich golden marble recesses and tongue-in-cheek verbal embellishments such as Silence is Golden and Finery is Foolish. The other large room has a fireplace and plenty of seats and tables. They keep a fantastic range of around ten real ales including their core three – Fullers London Pride, Nicholsons Pale Ale (named for the pub from St Austell) and Sharps Doom Bar – on handpump with guests from breweries such as Adnams, Belhaven, Dark Star, Harbour, Hop Back, Hop Stuff, Ilkley, Purity, Roosters, Titanic and so forth, and several wines by the glass. Staff are helpful, efficient and friendly, despite the crowds; background music. In warmer weather, people spill out on to the wide forecourt, near the approach to Blackfriars Bridge.

 As well as their sausage and chop menu (ten different sausages and four types of chop) the well thought-of food includes sandwiches (until 5pm), potted crab with toast, ham hock and pistachio rillettes with golden beetroot piccalilli, smoked salmon fishcakes, ale-glazed chicken with lemon aioli, coleslaw and triple-cooked chips, steak or vegetarian burger with toppings and triple-cooked chips, mixed grill, and puddings such as belgian chocolate brownie and lemon tart. *Benchmark main dish: beer-battered fish and chips £13.00. Two-course evening meal £19.00.*

Nicholsons ~ Manager John McKeone ~ Real ale ~ Open 10am-11pm; 9am-11pm Sat; 12-10.30 Sun ~ Bar food 10-10; 9am-10pm Sat; 12-9.30 Sun ~ Children welcome ~ Dogs allowed in bar ~ Wi-fi *Recommended by Tony Scott, Giles and Annie Francis, Darrell Barton, Diana and Bertie Farr*

CENTRAL LONDON   Map 12

Cross Keys ♀

(020) 7351 0686 – www.thecrosskeyschelsea.co.uk
Lawrence Street; ✪ *Sloane Square (some distance away); SW3 5NB*

Popular pub with a friendly bar, airy back restaurant, real ales and modern bar food

A civilised and friendly Chelsea landmark, this place is always busy with a chatty crowd of mixed customers. The central counter has bars areas to each side with simple furnishings: distressed panelled walls, some exposed brickwork, a couple of open fires, framed tobacco postcards and display cases of butterflies, mirrors, tankards on a rack, industrial-style ceiling lights, and a mix of cushioned wooden dining chairs, wheelbacks and plush stools around scrubbed tables on bare boards. At the back, the airy conservatory-style dining room has button-back wall seating and similar chairs and tables. On handpumps beside a stuffed rabbit holding a gun, friendly staff serve Long Arm Lucky Penny, Otter Ale, Truman Swift, seasonal cocktails and good wines by the glass; background music and TV.

 From an up-to-date menu, enjoyable food includes seared tuna with avocado purée, pickled shimeji mushrooms and soy dressing, beef fillet carpaccio with beetroot, watercress and manchego, shallot tarte tatin with mushroom purée, wilted greens and kale pesto, cumberland sausage and mash with wholegrain mustard jus, roast cod with brown shrimps, broccoli salad, roasted almond and chicken jus, braised lamb shoulder hotpot with crushed carrot and swede and pickled red cabbage, pork fillet and black pudding wellington with mustard mash, and puddings such as crème brûlée and hot chocolate fondant with blackcurrant sorbet. *Benchmark main dish: veal schnitzel £20.00. Two-course evening meal £27.00.*

Free house ~ Licensee George Wales ~ Open 12-midnight; 12-11 Sun ~ Bar food 12-3, 6-10; 11-4, 6-10 Sat; 12-9 Sun ~ Restaurant ~ Children welcome ~ Dogs welcome *Recommended by Dan and Belinda Smallbone, Sandra and Miles Spencer, James and Sylvia Hewitt*

CENTRAL LONDON   Map 13

Grazing Goat ⚏ ♀ ⇖

(020) 7724 7243 – www.thegrazinggoat.co.uk
New Quebec Street; ✪ *Marble Arch; W1H 7RQ*

A good mixed crowd of customers, restful décor, a thoughtful choice of drinks and good interesting food; bedrooms

If you want to escape the hustle and bustle of Oxford Street and Marble Arch, head for this stylish pub. The bar has a big gilt-edged mirror above an open fire and plenty of spreading dining space with white cushioned and beige dining chairs around pale tables on bare boards, sage green or pale oak-panelled walls, hanging lamps and lanterns and some goat memorabilia dotted about. Efficient, friendly staff serve Cubitt 1788 (named for the pub from Canopy), 23 wines by the glass and Weston's cider. The upstairs restaurant is more formal. Glass doors open on to the street where there are a few wooden-slatted chairs and tables. The bedrooms are modern and well equipped, with good bathrooms.

As well as breakfast (8-11.15am), the imaginative food includes crab with samphire and cucumber and orange dressing, house-cured charcuterie board with marinated olives, feta, piccalilli and smoked tomato relish (to share), artichoke fritter with charred broccoli, courgettes and toasted almond granola, chicken and ham hock pie, beer-battered fish and chips, pork loin with trotter, potato and bacon fritter, onions and rhubarb, a fresh fish dish of the day, rose veal chop with a choice of sauce, and puddings such as apple pie with salted caramel and vanilla ice-cream and strawberry and vanilla cheesecake with frozen yoghurt. *Benchmark main dish: dry-aged beef burger with coppa, fennel remoulade and caramelised onions £16.00. Two-course evening meal £22.00.*

Cubitt House ~ Lease Adam Quigley ~ Real ale ~ Open 7.30am-11pm (10.30pm Sun) ~ Bar food 12-10 (9.30 Sun) ~ Restaurant ~ Children welcome ~ Dogs allowed in bar ~ Wi-fi ~ Bedrooms: £210/£250 *Recommended by Tim and Sarah Smythe-Brown, Charles Todd, Laura Reid, Dr and Mrs A K Clarke, Heather and Richard Jones*

CENTRAL LONDON   Map 13

Harp 🍺

(020) 7836 0291 – www.harpcoventgarden.com
47 Chandos Place; ⊖ ⇄ *Charing Cross* ⊖ *Leicester Square; WC2N 4HS*

Ten real ales and lots of ciders and perries in bustling narrow pub

A favourite with many, this is a little gem. It pretty much consists of one long narrow, very traditional bar, with lots of high bar stools along the wall counter and around elbow tables, big mirrors on the red walls, some lovely stained glass and loads of interesting, quirkily executed celebrity portraits. If you're lucky, you may be able to snare one of the prized seats by the front windows. A little room upstairs is much quieter, with comfortable furniture and a window overlooking the road below. The ten real ales on handpump are particularly well kept and quickly changing, though they always have Harveys Best, Dark Star American Pale Ale and Hophead and Fullers London Pride with guests sourced from all over the country – as well as up to nine farm ciders, three perries and quite a few malt whiskies. At any time of day, the pub is always packed; at peak times, customers are happy to spill out on to the pavement or the back alley. The hanging baskets are a wonderful sight in summer.

Food – served lunchtime only – consists of sandwiches, sausage rolls and pork pies. *Benchmark main dish: sausages in a bap £4.00.*

Free house ~ Licensee Paul Bancroft ~ Real ale ~ Open 10.30am-11.30pm; 10.30am-midnight Fri, Sat; 12-10.30 Sun ~ Bar food 12-2 ~ Wi-fi *Recommended by Edward and William Johnston, William Slade, Dr and Mrs A K Clarke, Miles Green*

The 🍺 symbol shows pubs that keep their beer unusually well, have
a particularly good range or brew their own.

CENTRAL LONDON   Map 13

Lamb & Flag 🍺 £

(020) 7497 9504 – www.lambandflagcoventgarden.co.uk

Rose Street, off Garrick Street; ⊖ *Covent Garden, Leicester Square; WC2E 9EB*

Historic yet unpretentious, full of character and atmosphere, and with six real ales and pubby food

Unspoilt and, in places, rather basic, this old tavern has plenty of character. The more spartan front room leads into a cosy, atmospheric, low-ceilinged back bar with high-backed black settles and an open fire. Fullers ESB, London Pride, Olivers Island and Seafarers plus three guest beers on handpump, as well as 12 wines by the glass and 25 malt whiskies. The upstairs Dryden Room is often less crowded and has more seats (though fewer beers). There's a lively and well documented history: Dryden was nearly beaten to death by hired thugs outside, and Dickens made fun of the Middle Temple lawyers who frequented it when he was working in nearby Catherine Street.

 Tasty food, served upstairs, includes sandwiches, duck liver pâté with caramelised onion jam, nachos with salsa, soured cream, guacamole and jalapenos, pasta with tomato, ginger, spinach and parmesan with rosemary and chilli breadcrumbs, pie of the day, burger with toppings and a secret sauce, thyme and rosemary chicken with courgettes, broad beans, peas, mozzarella and lemon dressing, 35-day-aged rib-eye steak with chips, and puddings such as chocolate brownie with salted caramel ice-cream and sticky toffee pudding. *Benchmark main dish: beer-battered fish and chips £14.00. Two-course evening meal £20.00.*

Fullers ~ Manager Tim Adams ~ Real ale ~ Open 11-11; 12-10.30 Sun ~ Bar food 12-9 ~ Restaurant ~ Children in upstairs dining room only ~ Dogs allowed in bar ~ Wi-fi
Recommended by Philip J Alderton, Max Simons, Peter Brix

CENTRAL LONDON   Map 13

Old Bank of England ♀ 🍺

(020) 7430 2255 – www.oldbankofengland.co.uk

Fleet Street; ⊖ *Chancery Lane, Temple* ⊖ ⇌ *Blackfriars; EC4A 2LT*

Dramatically converted former bank building, with gleaming chandeliers in impressive soaring bar, well kept Fullers beers and tasty food

The interior here is quite astounding. It was once a subsidiary branch of the Bank of England and is a Grade I listed Italianate building – the splendid spacious bar has three gleaming chandeliers hanging from an exquisitely plastered ceiling that's high above an unusually tall island bar counter crowned with a clock. The end wall has huge paintings and murals that look like 18th-c depictions of Justice, but, in fact, feature members of the Fuller, Smith and Turner families, who set up the brewery that owns the pub. There are well polished dark wooden furnishings, luxurious curtains swagging massive windows, plenty of framed prints and, despite the grandeur, some surprisingly cosy corners, with screens between tables creating an unexpectedly intimate feel. The quieter galleried section upstairs offers a bird's-eye view of the action; some smaller rooms (used mainly for functions) open off. Fullers ESB, London Pride, Olivers Island, Seafarers and a seasonal guest beer on handpump alongside a good choice of malt whiskies and a dozen wines by the glass. At lunchtime, the background music is generally classical or easy listening; it's louder and livelier in the evenings. There's also a garden with seats (one of the few pubs in the area to have one).

Pies have a long if rather dubious pedigree in this area: it was in the vaults and tunnels below the Old Bank and the surrounding buildings that Sweeney Todd butchered the clients destined to provide the fillings at his mistress Mrs Lovett's nearby pie shop. The popular food here does indeed include pies, and also sandwiches, black pudding scotch eggs, prawns in marie rose sauce, ham and eggs with pineapple salsa, beer-battered fish and chips, poached salmon with lemon and herb dressing, lamb steak with chargrilled vegetable, pine nut and spelt salad, and puddings such as chocolate brownie with vanilla ice-cream and banoffi cheesecake with salted caramel sauce. *Benchmark main dish: pie of the day £13.00. Two-course evening meal £18.00.*

Fullers ~ Manager Sarah Corcoran ~ Real ale ~ Open 11-11; 12-8 Sat; closed Sun ~ Bar food 12-9 Mon-Fri; 12-4 Sat ~ Children welcome until 6pm ~ Wi-fi *Recommended by Barry Collett, Mrs Maureen Pye, Tony Scott, Dr and Mrs A K Clarke, Nik and Gloria Clarke*

CENTRAL LONDON Map 13
Olde Mitre 🍺 £

(020) 7405 4751 – www.yeoldemitreholburn.co.uk

Ely Place; the easiest way to find it is from the narrow passageway beside 8 Hatton Garden; ⊖ Chancery Lane ⊖ ⇄ Farringdon; EC1N 6SJ

Hard to find but well worth it – an unspoilt old pub with lovely atmosphere, unusual guest beers and bargain toasted sandwiches

---

Although the current building dates from 1782, there's actually been a tavern here since 1546 – it's hard to believe you're so close to Holborn and the edge of the City. The cosy small rooms have lots of dark panelling as well as antique settles and (particularly in the popular back room where there are more seats) old local pictures and so forth. It gets good-naturedly packed with the City suited-and-booted between 12.30pm and 2.15pm, filling up again in the early evening, but in the early afternoons and by around 8pm is a good deal more tranquil. An upstairs room, mainly used for functions, may double as an overflow area at peak periods. They serve Fullers London Pride, Olivers Island and Seafarers with guests from breweries such as Electric Bear and Pheasantry on handpump, and they hold three beer festivals a year; eight farm ciders and several wines by the glass. No music, TV or machines – the only games here are cribbage and dominoes. There's some space for outside drinking by the pot plants and jasmine in the narrow yard between the pub and St Etheldreda's church (which is worth a look). Note the pub doesn't open on weekends or bank holidays. The best way to get there is from Hatton Garden, walking up the right-hand side away from Chancery Lane; an easily missed sign on a lamp-post points the way down a narrow alley. No children.

 Served all day, bar snacks are limited to scotch eggs, pork pies, sausage rolls and really good value toasties. *Benchmark main dish: sausage roll £3.00.*

Fullers ~ Manager Judith Norman ~ Real ale ~ Open 11-11; closed weekends and bank holidays ~ Bar food 11-9.30 ~ Wi-fi *Recommended by Daniel England, Tony Scott, Margaret McDonald, Adam Jones*

CENTRAL LONDON Map 13
Orange 🏠 ♀ 🛏

(020) 7881 9844 – www.theorange.co.uk

Pimlico Road; ⊖ Sloane Square; SW1W 8NE

Carefully restored pub with simply decorated rooms, thoughtful choice of drinks and good modern cooking; bedrooms

This restored Georgian inn is a comfortable place to stay in well equipped bedrooms – and the breakfasts are first class. The two floors of the pub have huge sash windows on all sides making the interconnected rooms light and airy; throughout, the décor is shabby-chic and simple and the atmosphere easy-going and chatty. The high-ceilinged downstairs bar has wooden dining chairs around pale tables on bare boards, an open fire at one end and a big carved counter where friendly staff keep Cubitt 1788 (named for the pub from Canopy), 23 wines by the glass, Weston's cider and a lengthy cocktail list. The dining room to the right, usually packed with cheerful customers, is decorated with prints, glass bottles and soda siphons, large house plants and a few rustic knick-knacks. Upstairs, the linked restaurant rooms are similarly furnished with old french travel posters and circus prints on cream walls, more open fireplaces, big glass ceiling lights and chandeliers and quiet background music.

Good modern food includes chilli salt squid with smoked chilli and lime, duck leg croquette with asparagus and a poached duck egg with béarnaise sauce, nettle gnocchi with courgette flower, pickled peppers and charred lemon, wood-fired pizzas, chalk-stream trout with salt cod fritters and horseradish cream, venison with hasselback potatoes, pancetta, onions and cherries, duck breast with grilled cabbage, hazelnuts, wild thyme and honey, and puddings such as orange and olive oil almond cake with marsala custard and milk chocolate crémeux with dark chocolate crumbs and pistachios. *Benchmark main dish: spicy sausage, burrata, tomato and rocket pizza £16.50. Two-course evening meal £22.00.*

Cubitt House ~ Lease Adam Quigley ~ Real ale ~ Open 8am-11.30pm (midnight Fri, Sat); 8am-10.30pm Sun ~ Bar food 12-10; 12-10.30 Fri, Sat; 12-9.30 Sun ~ Restaurant ~ Children welcome ~ Dogs allowed in bar ~ Wi-fi ~ Bedrooms: £205/£240 *Recommended by Rosie and John Moore, Penny and David Shepherd, Elizabeth and Peter May, Ian Herdman, Michael Butler*

CENTRAL LONDON   Map 13

Punchbowl ♀

(020) 7493 6841 – www.punchbowllondon.com

Farm Street; ⊖ *Green Park; W1J 5RP*

Bustling, rather civilised pub with good wines and ales, enjoyable food and helpful service

Our readers enjoy this tucked-away Mayfair pub very much. Perhaps the nicest part is at the back where several panelled booths have suede bench seating, animal scatter cushions, some etched glasswork and church candles on tables. Elegant spoked chairs are grouped around dark tables on worn floorboards, a couple of long elbow shelves are lined with high chairs and one fireplace has a coal fire while the other is piled with logs. At the front it's simpler, with cushioned bench seating and pubby tables and chairs on floor tiles. All sorts of artwork from cartoons to oil paintings line the walls and the ceiling has interesting old hand-drawn street maps; background music. Caledonian Deuchars IPA, a beer named for the pub (also from Caledonian), and a guest from Theakstons on handpump, good wines by the glass and professional, friendly service. The smart dining room upstairs has plush furnishings, large artworks and a huge gilt mirror above an open fire; there are private dining facilities too.

Rewarding food includes lunchtime sandwiches and wraps, crab on toast with brown crab mayonnaise, duck and chicken terrine with spicy apricot chutney, crispy courgette flowers with goats cheese curd, shaved courgette, asparagus and pomegranate, beer-battered fresh fish of the day and chips, stuffed rabbit saddle saltimbocca with swiss ruby chard, sea trout with lemon butter, samphire, razor clams and sauce vierge, lamb rump with baked beetroot and rosemary jus, and puddings such as apple and sultana crumble with cinnamon ice-cream and Nutella doughnuts with mulled berries and hot chocolate sauce; they also offer a two- and three-course weekday set menu. *Benchmark main dish: burger with toppings and chips £14.00. Two-course evening meal £22.00.*

Free house ~ Licensee Ben Newton ~ Real ale ~ Open 12-11 (10.30 Sun) ~ Bar food 12-3.30, 5.30-10; 12-10 Sat; 12-9 Sun ~ Restaurant ~ Children welcome if seated and dining ~ Dogs allowed in bar ~ Wi-fi *Recommended by Laura Reid, Jeff Davies, Maggie and Stevan Hollis, Samuel and Melissa Turnbull*

CENTRAL LONDON
Map 13

Seven Stars ◖

(020) 7242 8521 – www.thesevenstars1602.co.uk
Carey Street; ⊖ *Temple, Holborn, Chancery Lane, Holborn; WC2A 2JB*

Quirky pub with cheerful staff, an interesting mix of customers and a good choice of drinks and food

A favourite haunt of lawyers, Church of England music directors and choir singers, this character pub faces the back of the law courts. Numerous caricatures of barristers and judges line the red-painted walls of the two main rooms and there are posters of legal-themed british films, big ceiling fans and checked tablecloths that add a quirky, almost continental touch. A third area, in what was formerly a legal wig shop next door, still retains its original frontage, with a neat display of wigs in the window. It's worth arriving early as they don't take bookings and tables get snapped up quickly. Adnams Broadside, Dark Star Hophead, Sharps Cornish Coaster and a couple of guests from breweries such as Sambrooks and Whitstable on handpump and six wines by the glass (they import wine from France); they do a particularly good dry martini. On busy evenings, customers overflow on to the quiet road in front; things generally quieten down after 8pm and there can be a nice, sleepy atmosphere some afternoons. The Elizabethan stairs up to the loos are rather steep, but there's a good strong handrail. The pub cat, who wears a ruff, is called Peabody. No children.

Cooked according to the landlady's fancy, the good, interesting food includes chicken liver pâté, black bean and sweetcorn soup, rabbit and chicken pie, merguez sausages with pilaf rice, spiced lamb filo parcels and linguine with prawns and squid or cream and parmesan. *Benchmark main dish: soused herring and potato salad £11.50. Two-course evening meal £15.50.*

Free house ~ Licensee Roxy Beaujolais ~ Real ale ~ Open 11-11; 12-11 Sat; 12-10 Sun ~ Bar food 12-9.30; 1-9 weekends ~ Wi-fi *Recommended by Dr J Barrie Jones*

CENTRAL LONDON
Map 13

Star ◖

(020) 7235 3019 – www.star-tavern-belgravia.co.uk
Belgrave Mews West, behind the German Embassy, off Belgrave Square; ⊖ *Hyde Park Corner, Knightsbridge; SW1X 8HT*

Bustling local with restful bar, upstairs dining room, Fullers ales, well liked bar food and colourful hanging baskets

Outside peak times, there's a peaceful, local feel to this tucked-away pub in its cobbled mews. The small bar is pleasant, with sash windows, a wooden floor, stools by the counter, an open winter fire and Fullers ESB, London Pride and Olivers Island plus a couple of guest beers on handpump, nine wines by the glass and a few malt whiskies. An arch leads to the main seating area with well polished tables and chairs and good lighting; there's also an upstairs dining room. In summer, the front of the building is covered with an astonishing array of hanging baskets and flowering tubs. It's said that this is where the Great Train Robbery was planned.

🍴 Food is good and includes lunchtime sandwiches, potted duck with spiced pear chutney, smoked salmon with caper butter and horseradish, pea and broad bean risotto with parmesan, bacon chop with free-range eggs, lamb rump with rosemary polenta, burnt aubergine purée and mint and anchovy dressing, grilled sardines with crushed potatoes and lemon and lime salsa, chicken with pineapple, bacon crisp and garlic mayonnaise, and puddings such as pear and almond tart and chocolate brownie with orange chocolate chip ice-cream. *Benchmark main dish: beer-battered fish and chips £14.00. Two-course evening meal £20.00.*

Fullers ~ Manager Marta Lemieszewska ~ Real ale ~ Open 11-11; 10.30am-11pm Sat; 12-10.30 Sun ~ Bar food 12-3, 5-9 weekdays; 10.30-10 Sat; 12-4, 5-9 Sun ~ Restaurant ~ Children welcome ~ Dogs welcome ~ Wi-fi *Recommended by Helen McLagan, Philip J Alderton, Phoebe Peacock, Caroline Prescott*

CENTRAL LONDON
Thomas Cubitt 🏵 ♀

Map 13

(020) 7730 6060 ~ www.thethomascubitt.co.uk
Elizabeth Street; ⊖ *Sloane Square* ⊖ ⇄ *Victoria; SW1W 9PA*

Belgravia pub with a civilised and friendly atmosphere and enjoyable food and drink

We get a lot of praise from our readers for this bustling, well run pub in well heeled Elizabeth Street. The bar has miscellaneous Edwardian-style dining chairs around wooden tables on stripped parquet flooring, and architectural prints and antlers on panelled or painted walls; open fires and lovely flower arrangements. Attentive staff serve Canopy Journeyman and Cubitt 1788 (named for the pub from Canopy), 23 wines by the glass, Weston's cider and cocktails. The more formal dining room upstairs has smart upholstered wooden chairs around white-clothed tables, candles in wall holders, a few prints, house plants and window blinds; background music. In warm weather, the floor-to-ceiling glass doors are pulled back to the street where there are cordoned-off tables and chairs on the pavement.

🏵 Enterprising food includes crab with heritage tomatoes, green strawberries and basil, rabbit scotch egg with coronation dressing, octopus carpaccio with avocado and samphire and squid ink dressing, nettle dumplings with minted peas, grilled baby gem and black garlic, dry-aged beef burger with toppings, smoked garlic mayonnaise and gherkins, chicken with baby artichokes and chervil sauce, plaice fillets with fennel confit, pistachios and pickled cherries, and puddings such as warm cinnamon and apple doughnuts with Guinness caramel and bread and butter pudding with rum and bananas. *Benchmark main dish: beer-battered fish and chips £15.00. Two-course evening meal £22.00.*

Cubitt House ~ Lease Adam Quigley ~ Real ale ~ Open 12-11 (10.30 Sun) ~ Bar food 12-3, 6-10; 12-9.30 Sun ~ Restaurant ~ Children welcome ~ Dogs allowed in bar ~ Wi-fi *Recommended by Tim and Sarah Smythe-Brown, Peter and Emma Kelly, John Robinson, Barbara and Phil Bowie*

Cribbage is a card game using a block of wood with holes for matchsticks or special pins to score with; regulars in cribbage pubs are usually happy to teach strangers how to play.

NORTH LONDON
Hare

Map 5

(020) 8954 4949 – www.hareoldredding.com

Brookshill/Old Redding; ⇌ Hatch End (some distance away); HA3 6SD

Carefully modernised old pub with plenty of drinking and dining space, friendly staff and enjoyable food

In decent weather, the garden behind this early 19th-c pub really comes into its own – there are seats and tables under a gazebo, deck chairs on the lawn and piles of blankets for cooler temperatures; some picnic-sets out in front too. The interior is attractively contemporary with interconnected bar and dining rooms. The bar has tartan cushions on a long leather wall seat, upholstered and leather dining chairs around a medley of tables and a long counter lined with bar stools. Sharps Doom Bar and Timothy Taylors Landlord on handpump and several wines by the glass. The stylish brasserie has a woodburning stove, a long beige button-back leather wall seat, leather-seated chairs around simple tables, rugs on bare boards and candles in lanterns, and there's also a similarly furnished dining area with more rugs on black slates. A little room with burgundy-painted wall planking is just right for a small group. Throughout, there are church candles on substantial holders, dried lavender in rustic jugs and modern artwork.

 Interesting food includes cheese soufflé with cheddar sauce, trout gravadlax with dill mustard sauce and lemon crème fraîche, ravioli duo (goats cheese with rosemary and pea and mint), a pie of the week, chicken and green pawpaw salad, coriander, mint, cashews and thai-style dressing, beef bourguignon, bouillabaisse, 30-day dry-aged steaks with a choice of sauce, and puddings such as chocolate délice with chocolate mousse, pannacotta cream with kirsch and hazelnuts and gooseberry compote with almond, ginger and cinnamon crumble with vanilla ice-cream. *Benchmark main dish: duck leg confit with black cherry sauce and dauphinoise potatoes £16.55. Two-course evening meal £22.00.*

White Brasserie Company ~ Manager James Scott ~ Real ale ~ Open 11-11 (10 Sun) ~ Bar food 12-10; 12-10.30 Fri, Sat; 12-9 Sun ~ Restaurant ~ Children welcome ~ Dogs allowed in bar ~ Wi-fi *Recommended by Geoff and Ann Marston, Andrew and Michele Revell, Charles Todd, Patricia and Gordon Tucker*

NORTH LONDON
Holly Bush ♀ ◖

Map 12

(020) 7435 2892 – www.hollybushhampstead.co.uk

Holly Mount; ⊖ Hampstead; NW3 6SG

Unique village local, with good food and drinks, and lovely unspoilt feel

A timeless old favourite, this was originally a stable block and is tucked away among some of Hampstead's most villagey streets. The old-fashioned front bar has a dark sagging ceiling, brown and cream panelled walls (decorated with old advertisements and a few hanging plates), open fires, bare boards and secretive bays formed by partly glazed partitions. The slightly more intimate back room, named after the painter George Romney, has an embossed red ceiling, panelled and etched glass alcoves, and ochre-painted brick walls covered with small prints; lots of board and card games. Fullers ESB, London Pride and Olivers Island plus a guest on handpump, as well as 15 malt whiskies and 14 wines by the glass from a good wine list. The upstairs dining room has table service at the weekend, as does the rest of the pub on Sundays. There are benches on the pavement outside.

🍴 Food is popular and includes grilled sardines with pine nut pesto dressing, confit rabbit terrine with parsley and cornichon salad, quinoa with chargrilled sprouting broccoli, green olives, almonds and dates in tahini dressing, corn-fed chicken with wild mushroom gnocchi and spinach, lamb rump with burnt aubergine purée, rosemary polenta and mint and anchovy dressing, seared trout with spicy couscous, pickled cucumber and mint yoghurt, cold smoked duck breast with pomegranate and orange wild rice salad and port dressing, and puddings such as caramel fondant with berries and cherry and almond clafoutis; they also offer a two- and three-course set lunch. *Benchmark main dish: pie of the day £16.50. Two-course evening meal £22.00.*

Fullers ~ Manager Ben Ralph ~ Real ale ~ Open 12-11 (10.30 Sun) ~ Bar food 12-10; 12-8 Sun ~ Restaurant ~ Children welcome ~ Dogs welcome ~ Wi-fi *Recommended by Isobel Mackinlay, John and Mary Warner, John Wooll, Mark Morgan, Philip Chesington*

 NORTH LONDON   Map 13

Princess of Wales

(020) 7722 0354 ~ www.lovetheprincess.com

Fitzroy Road/Chalcot Road; ⊖ *Chalk Farm via Regents Park Road and footbridge; NW1 8LL*

Friendly place with three different seating areas, enjoyable food, wide choice of drinks and funky garden

Spread over three floors, this bustling pub usefully offers some kind of food all day at weekends. The main bar, at ground level, is open-plan and light with big windows looking out to the street, wooden tables and chairs on bare boards and plenty of high chairs against the counter: Sambrooks Wandle and a beer named for the pub (also from Sambrooks) plus a changing guest ale on handpump, 16 wines by the glass, 11 malt whiskies and good cocktails. Upstairs, the smarter dining room has beige- and white-painted chairs, leather sofas and stools around wooden tables on more bare boards, big gilt-edged mirrors and chandeliers; two TVs. The refurbished Garden Room downstairs has a bar, three connected areas and access to the suntrap garden with its Bansky-style mural, framed wall mirrors and picnic-sets (some painted pink and purple) under parasols.

🍴 Interesting food includes lunchtime sandwiches (not weekends), crispy salt and chilli squid with aioli, buttermilk chicken in polenta and parmesan crumb with burnt lemon mayonnaise, chicken caesar salad, pizzas, linguine with white wine and chive sauce, spatchcock poussin with tomato, red pepper and herb couscous, pie of the day, roasted salmon with gnocchi, broad bean and cucumber fricassée and beetroot pesto, and puddings such as banoffi pie and bakewell tart. *Benchmark main dish: burger with toppings, onion rings and skinny fries £12.95. Two-course evening meal £20.50.*

Free house ~ Licensee Lawrence Santi ~ Real ale ~ Open 11am-midnight; 10am-midnight Sat; 10am-11.30pm Sun ~ Bar food 12-3, 6-10; 12-10.30 weekends ~ Restaurant ~ Children welcome until 6.30pm ~ Dogs allowed in bar ~ Wi-fi ~ Live jazz Sun lunchtime, live music Friday 6.30pm *Recommended by Laura Reid, Alf and Sally Garner, Glen and Patricia Fuller, Jamie Green*

 SOUTH LONDON   Map 12

Earl Spencer 🍷 🍴

(020) 8870 9244 ~ www.theearlspencer.co.uk

Merton Road; ⊖ *Southfields; SW18 5JL*

Good, interesting food and local ales in busy but friendly pub

Well run and with a cheerful chatty atmosphere, this sizeable Edwardian pub is much enjoyed by our readers. There are cushioned wooden, farmhouse and leather dining tables around all sorts of tables on bare boards, standard lamps, modern art on the walls and an open fire. The back bar has long tables, pews and benches, and stools line the U-shaped counter where efficient, friendly staff serve By the Horns The Mayor of Garratt, Sambrooks Wandle and Wimbledon Common Pale Ale on handpump. Also, 20 wines by the glass, 50 british gins, 12 british vodkas and 20 malt whiskies; they also sell 23 kinds of cigar. There are picnic-sets out on the front terrace.

 Highly regarded food includes vietnamese beef and white cabbage salad with chilli, mint and peanuts, home-smoked prawns with aioli, lemon and gazpacho, wild mushroom and spinach risotto with truffle oil, fishcakes with a poached egg and hollandaise, chilli con carne, sun-dried tomato and mozzarella-stuffed chicken breast with couscous, white wine and garlic butter, and puddings such as dark chocolate, Cointreau and orange pannacotta and sticky ginger pudding with toffee sauce. *Benchmark main dish: bavette steak with a changing butter £18.50. Two-course evening meal £23.00.*

Enterprise ~ Lease Michael Mann ~ Real ale ~ Open 4-11pm Mon-Thurs; 11am-midnight Fri, Sat; 12-10.30 Sun ~ Bar food 7-10pm Mon-Thurs; 12.30-3.30, 7-10 Fri, Sat; 12.30-4, 7-9.30 Sun ~ Children welcome ~ Dogs allowed in bar ~ Wi-fi *Recommended by Belinda May, James Landor, Rona Mackinlay, Chantelle and Tony Redman*

SOUTH LONDON

Map 12

Guildford Arms 🍴⭐ 🍷

(020) 8691 6293 – www.theguildfordarms.co.uk

Guildford Grove/Devonshire Drive; ⊖ ⇌ Greenwich, ⊖ Deptford Bridge; SE10 8JY

London Dining Pub of the Year

Stylish bar and restaurant on two floors, imaginative food, thoughtful choice of drinks, helpful staff and friendly feel; lovely garden

A bow-fronted, Georgian dining pub in a residential area, this civilised place is designed more for an excellent meal than a casual drink – though they do have a small bar where they keep real ales on handpump and good wines by the glass. The ground-floor bar is open-plan and modern with minimalist décor, contemporary chairs and tables on bare boards and high chairs by the counter with more by window shelves. Brockley Golden Ale and Phipps NBC India Pale Ale on handpump, a cocktail list and 17 wines by the glass from a good list; background music. Upstairs, the restaurant is stylish with abstract art and photos of food producers on pale grey walls and dark chairs and tables on carpet. The back garden is lovely with picnic-sets, seats and tables under cover, big parasols, trees and lighting.

Beautifully presented and first class, the food includes crispy lamb shoulder with aubergine, spiced tomato jam, dukkah and yoghurt, poached salmon with pickled celery, cucumber and honey and mustard dressing, herb polenta with caponata, olives, asparagus and tomato sauce, burger with crispy onions, bloody mary ketchup and chips, hake with samphire, green beans and tomato butter, pork chop with beetroot, spinach and roast garlic dressing, rib-eye steak with truffle mayonnaise and triple-cooked chips, and puddings such as berry and elderflower eton mess and chocolate délice with caramelised hazelnuts, salted caramel and crème fraîche. *Benchmark main dish: cod with a chorizo crust, clams, mussels and cider broth £16.00. Two-course evening meal £22.00.*

Free house ~ Licensee Guy Awford ~ Real ale ~ Open 12-11 (midnight Sat); closed Mon ~ Bar food 12-3, 6-10; all day Fri, Sat; 12-4, 5-10 Sun ~ Restaurant ~ Children welcome ~ Dogs allowed in bar ~ Wi-fi *Recommended by Louise and Simon Peters, Charlie and Mark Todd, Ben and Jenny Settle*

SOUTH LONDON
Rose & Crown ♀ ◖

Map 12

(01689) 869029 – www.the-roseandcrown.co.uk

Farnborough Way (A21); ⇌ Chelsfield (some distance away); BR6 6BT

Sizeable pub on the edge of London with large back garden, character bars, a wide choice of food and drink and cheerful service

The big garden behind this renovated pub is quite a surprise – it has colourful beach huts and cabanas, chairs and tables on a terrace, picnic-sets on grass and a sizeable children's play area. Inside, the open-plan, interconnected rooms (there are alcoves and smaller, cosier areas too) are interestingly furnished. There's every shape and size of Edwardian-style dining chair, leather tub seats, upholstered stools and coloured button-back banquettes grouped around polished tables on rugs, bare boards or black and white tiles, and the walls are hung with frame-to-frame prints and pictures; also, house plants, church candles, lots of mirrors, hundreds of books on shelves and three log fires (one is a woodburner). Friendly, efficient young staff serve a beer named for the pub (from Youngs), Courage Directors, Westerham Single Hop Flyer and Youngs Bitter and Hummingbird on handpump, and 16 wines by the glass.

Good, popular food includes sandwiches (until 6pm), deep-fried whitebait with aioli, thai chicken salad, sweet potato and courgette crumble with halloumi and beetroot pesto, pork and leek sausages with onion and thyme gravy, cajun-spiced chicken burger with guacamole and skinny fries, cod fillet with lemon-zested potatoes, streaky bacon, leeks and samphire, guinea fowl breast with mushroom duxelles, carrot purée and fondant potato, 28-day-hung sirloin steak with a choice of sauces, and puddings such as bakewell tart with lemon curd ice-cream and chocolate brownie with chocolate sauce. *Benchmark main dish: beer-battered fish and chips £10.95. Two-course evening meal £20.00.*

Whiting & Hammond ~ Manager Lee Scott ~ Real ale ~ Open 11-11; 9am-11pm Sat; 9am-10.30pm Sun ~ Bar food 12-9.30 (9 Sun) ~ Restaurant ~ Children welcome ~ Dogs allowed in bar ~ Wi-fi *Recommended by Christian Mole, Lionel Smith, Daphne and Robert Staples, B and M Kendall, Philip Chesington*

SOUTH LONDON
Royal Oak ◖

Map 13

(020) 7357 7173 – www.harveys.org.uk/pubs/the-royal-oak-london/

Tabard Street/Nebraska Street; ⊖ Borough ⊖ ⇌ London Bridge; SE1 4JU

Old-fashioned corner house with particularly well kept beers and honest food

This bustling pub has the look and feel of a traditional London alehouse – you'd never imagine it had been painstakingly transformed by Sussex brewery Harveys from a standard Victorian boozer. The place is always packed with customers of varying ages, all keen to enjoy the full range of Harveys ales plus a guest from Fullers on handpump and Thatcher's cider. The two little L-shaped rooms (the front bar is larger and brighter, the back room cosier with dimmer lighting) meander around the central wooden servery, which has a fine old clock in the middle. The rooms are done out with patterned rugs on wooden floors, plates running along a delft shelf, black and white scenes or period sheet music displayed on red-painted walls, and an assortment of wooden tables and chairs. There's disabled access at the Nebraska Street entrance.

🍴 Tasty food includes sandwiches, deep-fried whitebait, duck liver pâté, seasonal fresh crab salad, bubble and squeak with black pudding, bacon and duck egg, rabbit in mustard sauce, game pie, goats cheese and beetroot salad, and puddings such as lemon tart and sherry trifle. *Benchmark main dish: steak and kidney pudding £11.75. Two-course evening meal £16.50.*

Harveys ~ Tenants John Porteous, Frank Taylor ~ Real ale ~ Open 11-11; 12-9 Sun ~ Bar food 12-2.45, 5-9.15; 12-8 Sun ~ Children welcome until 9pm ~ Dogs welcome *Recommended by Tony Scott, Tom Stone, Patricia Hawkins, Giles and Annie Francis, Dr and Mrs A K Clarke, Patricia and Gordon Tucker*

 WEST LONDON Map 12

Bell

(020) 8941 9799 – www.thebellinnhampton.co.uk
Thames Street, Hampton; ⇌ *Hampton; TW12 2EA*

Bustling pub by the Thames with seats outside, real ales, a good choice of food and friendly service

In warm weather, head for the garden of this friendly riverside pub – there you'll find plenty of contemporary chairs and tables plus booth seating, heaters, lighting and barbecues. Inside, a wide mix of customers create a good bustling atmosphere in the interconnected rooms: wooden dining and tub chairs around copper-topped or chunky wooden tables, comfortably upholstered wall seats with scatter cushions, mirrors, old photographs and lots of church candles. From the long panelled bar counter, helpful staff serve Caledonian Deuchars IPA and guests such as Adnams Jack Brand Mosaic Pale Ale, Sambrooks Wandle and Sharps Doom Bar on handpump, 20 wines by the glass and speciality teas and coffees.

🍴 Quite a choice of pleasing food includes braised pig cheeks with apple and ginger purée and crispy bacon, chorizo scotch egg with spicy mayonnaise, sharing platters, goats cheese pasta with creamy basil sauce, pie of the day, piri-piri spatchcock chicken with sweet potato chips and coleslaw, lamb rump with minted pea purée and red wine and rosemary jus, plaice fillets with shrimp and lemon butter sauce and sauté potatoes, and puddings such as a seasonal crumble with custard and dark chocolate brownie with vanilla bean ice-cream. *Benchmark main dish: burger with toppings, coleslaw and chips £11.95. Two-course evening meal £20.00.*

Authentic Inns ~ Lease Simon Bailey ~ Real ale ~ Open 11-11; 11-midnight Fri, Sat ~ Bar food 12-3, 6-10; 12-10 Sat; 12-9 Sun ~ Restaurant ~ Children welcome ~ Dogs allowed in bar ~ Wi-fi ~ Live music Sat evening, quiz Sun evening *Recommended by Maddie Purvis, Hilary and Neil Christopher, Carol and Barry Craddock, Martin and Sue Neville*

 WEST LONDON Map 12

Brown Cow ♀

(020) 7384 9559 – www.thebrowncowpub.co.uk
Fulham Road; ⊖ *Parsons Green; SW6 5SA*

Busy pub with food and drinks served all day by cheerful staff

As this efficiently run dining pub is open (and serves food) all day, there are always plenty of customers popping in and out. The open-plan bar is furnished and decorated in a minimalist style with wooden and cushioned dining chairs and leather-topped stools around rustic tables on bare boards, button-back wall banquettes, prints on pale painted walls, a few suitcases on racks, house plants and industrial-style ceiling lamps. From a small bar counter lined with stools, friendly staff serve Otter Bitter, Sharps Doom Bar and a guest such as Twickenham Spring Ale on handpump, good wines by the glass and a growing collection of gins; background music and TV. Outside there are one or two tables on a side road.

🍴 As well as offering weekend brunches, the enjoyable food includes smoked beef carpaccio with celeriac rémoulade, asparagus and mint risotto with truffle and parmesan, barbecue jacob's ladder with macaroni cheese and red cabbage slaw, grilled mackerel with sauce vierge, confit chicken leg with french fries, shepherd's pie, 8oz bavette steak with triple-cooked chips, garlic green beans and bordelaise sauce, brill with celeriac purée, baby new potatoes and shrimp butter, and puddings such as rhubarb and pear crumble and peanut butter parfait with cherry compote. *Benchmark main dish: burger with toppings and chips £14.00. Two-course evening meal £23.00.*

Free house ~ Licensee Kyle Turner ~ Real ale ~ Open 12-midnight; 10.30-midnight Sat; 10.30-11 Sun ~ Bar food 12-3, 6-10; 12-10 Sat; 12-9 Sun ~ Restaurant ~ Children welcome ~ Dogs welcome ~ Wi-fi *Recommended by Gail and Arthur Roberts, Sally and Colin Allen, Julia and Fiona Barnes*

WEST LONDON   Map 12
Dove 🍷 📷

(020) 8748 9474 – www.dovehammersmith.co.uk
Upper Mall; ⊖ *Ravenscourt Park; W6 9TA*

Character pub with a lovely riverside terrace, cosily traditional front bar and an interesting history

As ever, our readers love this old-fashioned riverside place and it certainly gets packed at peak times – particularly the front snug which is in the *Guinness World Records* for having the smallest bar room – a mere 1.3 metres by 2.4 metres. The main bar is cosy, traditional and unchanging, with black panelling and red leatherette cushioned built-in wall settles and stools around assorted tables. It leads to a bigger, similarly furnished back room that's more geared to eating, which in turn leads to a conservatory. Fullers ESB, London Pride, Olivers Island, a changing seasonal ale plus a guest or two on handpump and 19 wines by the glass including champagne and sparkling wine. Head down steps at the back to reach the verandah with its highly prized tables looking over a low river wall to the Thames Reach just above Hammersmith Bridge; a tiny exclusive area, reached up a spiral staircase, is a prime spot for watching rowers on the water. The pub has played host to many writers, actors and artists over the years (there's a fascinating framed list on a wall); it's said to be where 'Rule Britannia' was composed and was a favourite with Turner, who painted the view of the Thames from the delightful back terrace, and with Graham Greene. The street itself is associated with the foundation of the arts and crafts movement – William Morris's old residence Kelmscott House (open certain afternoons) is nearby.

🍴 Good, well regarded food includes confit rabbit terrine with parma ham, parsley and cornichon salad, smoked mackerel pâté with crème fraîche, orzo pasta salad with mozzarella and pine nut pesto, crab and prawn linguine with white wine and parsley sauce, corn-fed chicken breast with spinach and chorizo butter, pork medallions wrapped in pancetta with peppercorn sauce, lamb rump with rosemary polenta, burnt aubergine purée and mint and anchovy dressing, and puddings such as passion-fruit crème brûlée and pistachio tiramisu with pistachio brittle. *Benchmark main dish: beer-battered fish and chips £14.00. Two-course evening meal £20.50.*

Fullers ~ Manager Sonia Labatut ~ Real ale ~ Open 11-11; 12-10.30 Sun ~ Bar food 12-10; 12-9 Sun ~ Children welcome ~ Dogs welcome ~ Wi-fi *Recommended by Chantelle and Tony Redman, Belinda and Neil Garth, Gary and Marie Miller*

WEST LONDON
Mute Swan ♀ ◗
Map 12

(020) 8941 5959 – www.brunningandprice.co.uk/muteswan
Palace Gate, Hampton Court Road; ⇌ *Hampton Court; KT8 9BN*

Handsome pub close to the Thames with sunny seats outside, relaxed bar, upstairs dining room and imaginative food and drinks choice

Always busy and friendly, this well run pub is just yards from the River Thames (though there's no view). The light and airy bar has four big leather armchairs grouped around a low table in the centre, while the rest of the room has brown leather wall seats, high-backed Edwardian-style cushioned dining chairs around dark tables and rugs on bare boards. The walls are covered in interesting photographs, maps, prints and posters and there are sizeable house plants, glass and stone bottles on the windowsills and a woodburning stove; the atmosphere is informal and relaxed. Brunning & Price Phoenix Original, Hogs Back TEA and a couple of guests on handpump, a carefully chosen wine list with 30 by the glass, 42 gins, 75 malt whiskies and farm cider; staff are efficient and helpful. A metal spiral staircase – presided over by an elegant metal chandelier – leads up to the dining area where there are brass-studded caramel leather chairs around well spaced tables on bare boards or carpeting, and numerous photos and prints. The tables and chairs on the front terrace get snapped up quickly and the pub is opposite the gates to Hampton Court Palace. There are a few parking spaces available in front, but you'll probably have to park somewhere else.

 Rewarding up-to-date food includes sandwiches (until 5pm), chicken liver pâté with rhubarb and apple chutney, scallops with celeriac purée, black pudding and apple sauce, sweet potato gnocchi with pesto and tomato and fennel sauce, smoked haddock fishcake with poached egg and tomato concasse, steak burger with toppings, coleslaw and chips, pork and leek sausages with mash and gravy, lamb shoulder with dauphinoise potatoes and red wine and rosemary gravy, cod loin with clam chowder and sweetcorn fritters, and puddings such as dark chocolate and hazelnut praline tart with salted caramel ice-cream and crème brûlée. *Benchmark main dish: chicken and ham hock pie £14.95. Two-course evening meal £21.00.*

Brunning & Price ~ Manager Sal Morgan ~ Real ale ~ Open 11-11 (midnight Sat); 11-10.30 Sun ~ Bar food 12-10 (9 Sun) ~ Restaurant ~ Children welcome in upstairs restaurant only ~ Dogs allowed in bar ~ Wi-fi *Recommended by Atle Helgedagsrud, Belinda May, Alf Wright, Miranda and Jeff Davidson*

WEST LONDON
Old Orchard ♀ ◗
Map 3

(01895) 822631 – www.brunningandprice.co.uk/oldorchard
Off Park Lane, Harefield; ⇌ *Denham (some distance away), UB9 6HJ*

Wonderful views from the front garden, a good choice of drinks and interesting brasserie-style food

Tables on the front terrace and in the garden have a stunning view down to the narrowboats on the canal way below and across to the lakes that are part of the conservation area known as the Colne Valley Regional Park – it's a haven for wildlife. Inside, the open-plan rooms have an attractive mix of cushioned dining chairs around all sizes and shapes of dark wooden tables, lots of prints, maps and pictures covering the walls, books on shelves, old glass bottles on windowsills and rugs on wood or parquet flooring. One room is hung with a large rug and some tapestry. There are daily papers to read, three cosy coal fires, big pot plants and fresh flowers. Half a dozen real ales on handpump served by friendly, efficient staff include Phoenix Brunning & Price Original and six guests from breweries such as Leighton Buzzard, London Fields, Mighty Oak, Oakham, Red Squirrel and Tring; also, 24 wines by the glass, 140 malt whiskies and farm cider.

🍴 Interesting food includes sandwiches (until 6pm), dill and vodka-cured trout with bloody mary sauce, smoked duck breast with basil blinis, chive crème fraîche and raspberry vinaigrette, mussels in cider and fennel, with parsley cream sauce, butternut squash and pea risotto with goats cheese and pumpkin seed pesto, hake with hazelnut and bacon crumb, white onion and fennel purée and tempura baby fennel, barbecue jerk chicken breast with lime and mango yoghurt and lentil, coriander, pepper and spring onion salad, pork belly with sage new potatoes, pineapple purée, samphire and crackling, and puddings such as crème brûlée and lemon tart with raspberry ripple ice-cream. *Benchmark main dish: burger with toppings, coleslaw and chips £12.95. Two-course evening meal £21.00.*

Brunning & Price ~ Manager Kate Lomax ~ Real ale ~ Open 11.30-11; 12-10.30 Sun ~ Bar food 12-10 (9.30 Sun) ~ Children welcome ~ Dogs welcome ~ Wi-fi *Recommended by Simon Rodway, Nigel and Sue Foster, Trevor and Michele Street, Buster and Helena Hastings*

WEST LONDON   Map 12
Sands End ♀

(020) 7731 7823 – www.thesandsend.co.uk
Stephendale Road; ⇄ Imperial Wharf; SW6 2PR

Simply furnished, bustling pub in a quiet street with interesting food and a thoughtful range of drinks; seats outside

Busy and friendly with lots of young locals and visitors, this Fulham dining pub has an informal but gently civilised atmosphere. The open-plan bar features a mix of wooden dining chairs, the odd settle and cushioned wall seat and scrubbed pine, painted or polished wooden tables on bare boards; the dining area is quieter and more spacious. There's an open fire, large house plants, a few wall prints, a TV and background music. From the solid, central counter efficient staff serve Otter Bitter, Sambrooks Wandle, Trumans Swift and Twickenham Naked Ladies on handpump and good wines by the glass. Upstairs is a private dining room. At the front of the pub are seats and tables on the quiet residential street.

🍴 Good food includes seared scallops with peas, broad beans, shallots, mint and madeira jus, foie gras and chicken liver parfait, pea and pecorino risotto with mascarpone, preserved lemon and pine nuts, crab fettucine with crab bisque and slow-roast tomatoes, slow-roast pork belly with pig head croquettes, burnt apple, hispi cabbage and hazelnuts, black bream with herb gnocchi, tarragon and artichokes, and puddings such as passion-fruit cheesecake with coconut ice-cream and chocolate tart with lime butterscotch, crémeux and burnt caramel ice-cream. *Benchmark main dish: turbot with roast leeks, cauliflower purée and brown shrimp butter £19.50. Two-course evening meal £28.00.*

Free house ~ Licensee James Hardesty ~ Real ale ~ Open 12-midnight (11 Sun) ~ Bar food 12-3, 6-10; 12-4, 6-10 Sat; 12-9 Sun ~ Restaurant ~ Children allowed but no high chairs ~ Dogs welcome *Recommended by John and Claire Masters, Patricia and Anton Larkham, Lucy and Giles Gibbon*

WEST LONDON
Windsor Castle ◀

Map 12

(020) 7243 8797 – www.thewindsorcastlekensington.co.uk

Campden Hill Road; ⊖ *Notting Hill Gate; W8 7AR*

Genuinely unspoilt, with lots of atmosphere in tiny, dark rooms and lovely summer garden

To enjoy the old-fashioned charm here, try to visit at lunchtime when it's quieter. Unchanging and full of character, the pub has a wealth of dark oak furnishings, sturdy high-backed built-in elm benches, time-smoked ceilings, soft lighting and a coal-effect fire. Three of the tiny unspoilt rooms have their own entrance from the street, but it's much more fun trying to navigate through the minuscule doors between them inside. The panelled and wood-floored dining room at the back overlooks the garden. St Austell Skipper and Proper Job, Sharps Doom Bar, Timothy Taylors Landlord, West Berkshire Good Old Boy, Woodfordes Wherry and up to four guest beers on handpump, decent house wines, farm ciders, malt whiskies and jugs of Pimms. The garden, on several levels, has tables and chairs on flagstones and feels secluded thanks to the high ivy-covered walls; there are heaters for when evenings are cooler.

Good, popular food includes seared scallops with roasted cauliflower and curried bean purée, chicken and sauternes parfait with toasted sourdough, sharing boards, butternut squash risotto with pecorino, salmon and crab fishcakes with asian slaw and hollandaise, sausage and spring onion mash with crispy onions and red wine jus, guinea fowl stuffed with spinach and cheese with broccoli, cod with cauliflower purée, cauliflower fritters, sun-dried tomato and sunflower seed and herb dressing, and puddings such as chocolate brownie with hazelnut ice-cream and lemon tart with raspberries. *Benchmark main dish: beer-battered fish and chips £14.25. Two-course evening meal £21.00.*

Mitchells & Butlers ~ Manager Carl Clayton ~ Real ale ~ Open 12-11 (10.30 Sun) ~ Bar food 12-10 (9 Sun) ~ Restaurant ~ Children allowed in dining area ~ Dogs welcome ~ Wi-fi
Recommended by Hilary and Neil Christopher, Harvey Brown, Tony Scott, Neil Allen

---

Also Worth a Visit in London

Besides the fully inspected pubs, you might like to try these pubs that have been recommended to us and described by readers. Do tell us what you think of them: feedback@goodguides.com

CENTRAL LONDON

EC1
Bishops Finger (020) 7248 2341
West Smithfield; EC1A 9JR Welcoming little pub close to Smithfield Market, Shepherd Neame ales including seasonals, good range of sausages and other food in bar or upstairs room; children welcome, seats out in front, closed weekends and bank holidays, otherwise open all day and can get crowded, no food Fri evening. *(Diana and Bertie Farr)*

Butchers Hook & Cleaver
(020) 7600 9181 *West Smithfield; EC1A 9DY* Fullers conversion of bank and adjoining butcher's shop, their full range kept well and enjoyable pubby food including various pies, helpful efficient service, spiral stairs to mezzanine; background music, free wi-fi; closed weekends, otherwise open (and food) all day, gets busy with after-work drinkers. *(Sam Cole)*

Craft Beer Company
(020) 7404 7049 *Leather Lane; EC1N 7TR* Corner drinkers' pub with excellent selection of real ales and craft beers plus an extensive bottled range, good choice of wines and spirits too, high stools and tables on bare boards, big chandelier hanging from mirrored ceiling, food limited to snacks, more room upstairs; open all day and can get very busy. *(Sam Cole)*

Dovetail (020) 7490 7321
Jerusalem Passage; EC1V 4JP Fairly
small and can get very busy with drinkers
spilling into alleyway, specialises in
draught/bottled belgian beers and serves
popular food including some belgian and
vegetarian/vegan dishes, efficient staff
coping well at peak times; open all day
(from 2pm Sun). *(Louise and Simon Peters)*

Fox & Anchor (020) 7250 1300
Charterhouse Street; EC1M 6AA
Beautifully restored late Victorian pub/
boutique hotel by Smithfield Market (note
the art nouveau façade); long slender
bar with unusual pewter-topped counter,
lots of mahogany, green leather and
etched glass, small back snugs, Youngs
ales and guests, enjoyable food from
brunch onwards, friendly efficient staff;
six individual well appointed bedrooms,
good breakfast, open all day from 7am
(8.30am Sat, 11am Sun). *(Tony Scott)*

★**Hand & Shears** (020) 7600 0257
Middle Street; EC1A 7JA Traditional
unspoilt Smithfield corner pub, three
rooms and small snug arranged around
central servery, bare boards, panelling
and a couple of gas fires, interesting
prints and old photographs, up to six
changing ales, friendly service; open
all day (bustling lunchtime and early
evening), closed weekends. *(John Poulter)*

★**Jerusalem Tavern** (020) 7490 4281
Britton Street; EC1M 5UQ Atmospheric
re-creation of a dark 18th-c tavern (1720
merchant's house with shopfront added
1810); tiny dimly lit bar with simple wood
furnishings on bare boards, some remarkable
old wall tiles, coal fires and candlelight,
stairs to a precarious-feeling (though
perfectly secure) balcony, plainer back
room, St Peters beers tapped from the cask
and in bottles, short choice of lunchtime
food including good sandwiches, friendly
attentive young staff; no children but dogs
welcome, seats out on pavement (plastic
glasses if you drink out here), open all day
weekdays, closed weekends, bank holidays
and 24 Dec-2 Jan; can get very crowded at
peak times. *(Roger and Donna Huggins)*

Ninth Ward (020) 7833 2949
Farringdon Road; EC1R 3BN American-
themed bar/grill (has sister restaurant
in New York) with unusual New Orleans-
inspired interior (quite dark), tasty food
such as burgers and fried chicken, good
range of craft and bottled beers, cocktails,
friendly staff; background music; closed
Sat lunchtime and all day Sun, otherwise
open all day till late. *(Sam Cole)*

Old Fountain (020) 7253 2970
Baldwin Street; EC1V 9NU Popular
traditional old pub in same family since

1964; long bar serving two rooms, excellent
range of real ales and craft beers chalked
up on blackboard, friendly knowledgeable
staff, enjoyable good value food (not Sat
lunchtime) from open kitchen, main
carpeted part with wooden tables and chairs,
padded stools and fish tank; function room
for live music, darts; nice roof terrace;
open all day. *(Tony Scott, Tony Taylor)*

Old Red Cow (020) 7726 2595
Long Lane; EC1A 9EJ Cheerful little
pub close to the Barbican and within
sight of Smithfield Market, fine changing
selection of cask, craft and bottled beers,
tasters offered by friendly knowledgeable
staff, nine wines by the glass, well liked if
not particularly cheap food from sharing
boards and home-made pies to good Sun
roasts, modernised interior with larger
room upstairs; open all day and popular
with after-work drinkers. *(Tony Scott)*

EC2

★**Dirty Dicks** (020) 7283 5888
Bishopsgate; EC2M 4NR Refurbished
but keeping olde tavern feel, bare boards,
chunky low beams and timbers, exposed
brickwork and some interesting old prints,
Youngs ales and guests such as Meantime
and Sambrooks, lots of wines by the glass
and good variety of fairly priced food,
upstairs dining room, cellar cocktail bar with
barrel-vaulted ceiling; background music;
open all day (till 3am Thurs-Sat), handy
for Liverpool Street station. *(Tony Scott)*

George (020) 7618 7300
*Great Eastern Hotel, Liverpool Street;
EC2M 7QN* Part of hotel but good pubby
atmosphere in spacious oak-panelled room
with latticed windows and fine Victorian
coffered ceiling, some high tables and
stools on wood floor, mural behind bar
of Bishopsgate in 1620, decent food from
pub favourites up including a 'crackling'
menu to accompany their range of craft
beers; sports TV; children welcome,
handy for Liverpool Street station, open
all day, till 7pm Sun. *(Philip Chesington)*

Hamilton Hall (020) 7247 3579
*Bishopsgate; also entrance from
Liverpool Street station; EC2M 7PY*
Showpiece Wetherspoons with
flamboyant Victorian baroque décor
mixing with contemporary bar counter
and modern tables and chairs, good-
sized comfortable mezzanine, lots of
real ales including interesting guests,
decent wines and coffee, their usual
food and competitive pricing, friendly
staff coping well at busy times; silenced
machines, free wi-fi, screens showing
train times; good disabled access,
café-style furniture out in front, open
all day from 7am, can get very crowded
after work. *(Diana and Bertie Farr)*

Lord Aberconway (020) 7929 1743

Old Broad Street; EC2M 1QT Victorian
feel with high moulded ceiling, dark
panelling, some red leather bench seating
and drinking booths, six well kept ales
and reasonably priced Nicholsons menu
from sandwiches up, dining gallery;
silent fruit machine; handy for Liverpool
Street station, gets busy with after-work
drinkers, open till 10pm Sat, 6pm Sun,
otherwise open all day. *(Susan Eccleston)*

EC3

★ **Counting House** (020) 7283 7123

Cornhill; EC3V 3PD Spacious bank
conversion retaining original Victorian
character, impressive glass dome and grand
ceiling, chandeliers, rich polished mahogany,
mosaics, island bar topped with four-sided
clock, gallery seating, Fullers ale choice kept
well and enjoyable food including range of
pies, efficient friendly service; wheelchair
access, closed weekends, otherwise open
(and food) all day. *(Ross Balaam)*

East India Arms (020) 7265 5121

Fenchurch Street; EC3M 4BR Standing-
room 19th-c corner pub popular with City
workers, small single room with wood
floor, half-panelling, old local photographs
and brewery mirrors, well kept Shepherd
Neame ales served by efficient staff; tables
outside, closed weekends and may shut
by 9pm weekdays. *(Philip Chesington)*

Hoop & Grapes (020) 7481 4583

Aldgate High Street; EC3N 1AL Originally
17th-c (dismantled and rebuilt 1983) and
much bigger inside than it looks; long
partitioned bare-boards bar with beams,
timbers, exposed brickwork and panelling,
mix of seating including some button-back
wall benches, seven real ales and standard
Nicholsons menu (popular lunchtime),
friendly efficient service; muted sports TV;
a few seats in front, closed Sun, otherwise
open (and food) all day. *(Tony Scott, Aiden)*

Jamaica Wine House

(020) 7929 6972 *St Michaels Alley,
Cornhill; EC3V 9DS* Red-stone 19th-c
pub (site of London's first coffee house) in
warren of small alleys; known to locals as
the Jampot; traditional Victorian décor with
ornate coffered ceiling, oak panelling,
booths and bare boards, Shepherd
Neame ales and wide choice of wines,
friendly helpful service and bustling
atmosphere (quietens after 8pm),
food in bar or downstairs dining room;
closed weekends. *(Tony Scott)*

Lamb (020) 7626 2454

Leadenhall Market; EC3V 1LR Well
run stand-up bar with friendly staff coping
admirably with hordes of after-work
drinkers, Youngs ales and good choice of
wines, dark panelling, engraved glass and
plenty of ledges and shelves, spiral stairs
up to small carpeted gallery overlooking
market's central crossing, corner servery
for lunchtime food from sandwiches up,
separate stairs to nice bright dining room
(not cheap), also basement bar with shiny
wall tiles and own entrance; tables out under
splendid Victorian market roof – crowds
here in warmer months, open (and food)
all day, closed weekends. *(Darrell Barton)*

Ship (020) 7929 3903

Talbot Court, off Eastcheap; EC3V 0BP
Interesting Nicholsons pub tucked down
alleyway; busy bare-boards bar with soft
lighting and ornate décor, candles in
galleried dining area, friendly efficient
staff, several well kept ales including their
house beer from St Austell, well liked
good value food; closed Sun, otherwise
open all day, till 6pm Sat. *(Tony Scott)*

Ship (020) 7702 4422

Hart Street; EC3R 7NB Tiny one-room
19th-c City pub with ornate flower-decked
façade; Caledonian ales and two well kept
guests, some food including sandwiches,
burgers and weekday deals, friendly
staff, limited seating and can get packed,
upstairs dining room; spiral stairs down to
lavatories; closed weekends. *(Sam Cole)*

Simpsons Tavern (020) 7626 9985

Just off Cornhill; EC3V 9DR Pleasingly
old-fashioned place founded in 1757; small
narrow panelled bar serving five real
ales including Adnams, Bass and Fullers,
traditional chophouse with upright stall
seating (expect to share a table) and
similar upstairs restaurant, straightforward
good value food from sandwiches and
snacks up, further bar downstairs; open
weekday lunchtimes and from 8am
Tues-Fri for breakfast. *(Susan Eccleston)*

Swan (020) 7929 6550

*Ship Tavern Passage, off Gracechurch
Street; EC3V 1LY* Traditional Fullers
pub with bustling narrow flagstoned
bar, their well kept ales and lunchtime
sandwiches/burgers, friendly efficient
service, neatly kept Victorian panelled
décor, low lighting, larger more ordinary
carpeted bar upstairs; silent TV; covered
alley used by smokers, open all day Mon-Fri,
shuts at weekends. *(Darrell Barton)*

EC4

Cockpit (020) 7248 7315

*St Andrews Hill/Ireland Place, off Queen
Victoria Street; EC4V 5BY* Plenty of
atmosphere in this little corner pub near
St Paul's Cathedral; as name suggests, a
former cockfighting venue with surviving
spectators' gallery; good selection of
ales such as Adnams, St Austell and
Shepherd Neame, lunchtime food; open
all day. *(Alister and Margery Bacon)*

Old Bell (020) 7583 0216
Fleet Street, near Ludgate Circus;
EC4Y 1DH Dimly lit 17th-c tavern backing
on to St Bride's Church; stained-glass bow
window, heavy black beams, bare boards
and flagstones, half a dozen or more well
kept changing beers from island servery
(can try before you buy, tasting trays
available), usual Nicholsons food, friendly
helpful young staff and cheery atmosphere,
various seating nooks, brass-topped tables,
coal fire; background music; covered and
heated outside area, open all day (may close
early weekend evenings). *(Tony Scott)*

★ **Olde Cheshire Cheese**
(020) 7353 6170 *Wine Office Court, off*
145 Fleet Street; EC4A 2BU Best to visit
this 17th-c former chophouse outside peak
times as it can be packed (early evening
especially); soaked in history with warren
of old-fashioned unpretentious rooms,
high beams, bare boards, old built-in black
benches, Victorian paintings on dark brown
walls, big open fires, tiny snug and steep
stone steps down to unexpected series
of cosy areas and secluded alcoves, Sam
Smiths beers, all-day pubby food; Coco the
profane parrot – also look out for Polly (now
stuffed) who entertained distinguished
guests for over 40 years; children allowed
in eating area lunchtime only, closed Sun
evening. *(Giles and Annie Francis, Tony Scott)*

Olde Watling (020) 7248 8935
Watling Street; EC4M 9BR Heavy-beamed
and timbered post-blitz replica of pub built
by Wren in 1668; interesting choice of well
kept beers, standard Nicholsons menu, good
service, quieter back bar and upstairs dining
room; open all day. *(Philip Chesington)*

SW1

Albert (020) 7222 5577
Victoria Street; SW1H 0NP Airy open-
plan bar with gleaming mahogany, cut
and etched glass, ornate ceiling and solid
comfortable furnishings, enjoyable pubby
food from sandwiches up, well kept Fullers,
Greene King and guests, 24 wines by the
glass, efficient cheerful service, handsome
staircase lined with portraits of prime
ministers leading up to carvery/dining room;
background music, some live music, games
machine, sports TV, lavatories down steep
stairs; children welcome if eating, open (and
food) all day. *(Patricia and Gordon Tucker)*

Antelope (020) 7824 8512
Eaton Terrace; SW1W 8EZ Pretty little
flower-decked local in Belgravia, traditional
interior with snug seating areas, bare boards
and panelling, mix of old and new furniture
including leather bucket chairs, interesting
prints, gas-effect coal fire in tiled Victorian
fireplace, etched windows, well kept Fullers
ales from central servery and decent house
wines, upstairs dining room (children

allowed) serving decent pubby food including
popular Sun roasts; TVs, free wi-fi, daily
papers; dogs welcome, open all day and can
get crowded in the evening. *(Michael Butler)*

Buckingham Arms (020) 7222 3386
Petty France; SW1H 9EU Welcoming
and relaxed bow-windowed early 19th-c
local, Youngs ales and a guest from long
curved bar, good range of wines by the
glass and well liked pubby food from back
open kitchen, elegant mirrors and dark
woodwork, stained-glass screens, stools
at modern high tables, some armchairs
and upholstered banquettes, unusual side
corridor with elbow ledge for drinkers;
background music, TV; dogs welcome,
handy for Buckingham Palace, Westminster
Abbey and St James's Park, open all day,
till 6pm weekends. *(Dr and Mrs A K Clarke)*

Cask & Glass (020) 7834 7630
Palace Street; SW1E 5HN Snug
one-room traditional pub with good range
of Shepherd Neame ales, friendly staff and
atmosphere, good value lunchtime toasties,
old prints and shiny black panelling; quiet
corner TV, free wi-fi; hanging baskets and
a few tables outside, handy for Queen's
Gallery, open all day, till 8pm Sat, closed
Sun. *(Patricia and Gordon Tucker)*

Cask Pub & Kitchen
(020) 7630 7225 *Charlwood Street/*
Tachbrook Street; SW1V 2EE Modern,
spacious and simply furnished, excellent
choice of draught beers with over 500 more
in bottles, decent range of wines too, friendly
knowledgeable staff, good burgers and other
enjoyable food including Sun roasts, chatty
atmosphere – can get packed and noisy in the
evening; Sun live music, regular beer-related
events such as Meet the Brewer; downstairs
gents'; some outside seating, open all day, food
all day weekends. *(Richard Tilbrook, Tony Scott)*

Clarence (020) 7930 4808
Whitehall; SW1A 2HP Popular beamed
corner pub (Geronimo Inn), Youngs and
guests, decent wines by the glass and good
food from snacks up, friendly chatty staff,
quirky cheerful décor with well spaced
tables and varied seating including tub
chairs and banquettes, upstairs dining
area; pavement tables, open (and food) all
day. *(Dr and Mrs A K Clarke, Jon Isherwood)*

★ **Fox & Hounds** (020) 7730 6367
Passmore Street/Graham Terrace;
SW1W 8HR Small flower-decked Youngs
pub in backstreets below Sloane Square,
their well kept ales and interesting
guests, warm red décor with lots of old
pictures, prints and photographs, wall
benches and leather chesterfields, back
room with skylight, coal-effect gas fire;
open all day and can get crowded early
evening. *(Richard and Penny Gibbs)*

★**Grenadier** (020) 7235 3074
Wilton Row; the turning off Wilton Crescent looks prohibitive, but the barrier and watchman are there to keep out cars; SW1X 7NR Steps up to cosy old mews pub with lots of character and military history, but not much space (packed 5-7pm); simple unfussy panelled bar, stools and wooden benches on bare boards, changing ales such as Fullers, Timothy Taylors, Woodfordes and Youngs from rare pewter-topped counter, famous bloody marys, well liked pubby food, intimate back restaurant; children over 8 and dogs allowed, hanging baskets, sentry box and single table outside, open (and food) all day. *(Caroline Prescott)*

Grosvenor (020) 7821 8786
Grosvenor Road; SW1V 3LA Traditional pub across from river (no views), chatty and relaxed, with three well kept ales including Sharps and nice selection of wines, enjoyable reasonably priced pub food including good fish and chips and popular Sun roasts, friendly staff; some tables out by road, secluded beer garden behind, open (and food) all day. *(Jamie Davies)*

Jugged Hare (020) 7828 1543
Vauxhall Bridge Road/Rochester Row; SW1V 1DX Popular Fullers pub in former colonnaded bank; iron pillars, dark woodwork and large chandelier, old photographs of London, smaller back panelled dining room, stairs up to gallery, four well kept ales and reasonably priced food including range of pies, good friendly service; background music, TVs, silent fruit machine; open all day. *(Dr and Mrs A K Clarke)*

★**Lord Moon of the Mall**
(020) 7839 7701 *Whitehall; SW1A 2DY* Popular Wetherspoons bank conversion; elegant main room with big arched windows looking over Whitehall, old prints and a large portrait of Tim Martin (the chain's founder); through an arch the style is more recognisably Wetherspoons with neatly tiled areas and bookshelves opposite long servery, ten real ales and their good value food (from breakfasts up); children (if eating) and dogs welcome, open all day from 8am (till midnight Fri, Sat). *(Stephen Shepherd, B and M Kendall, Dr and Mrs A K Clarke, Dave Braisted)*

Morpeth Arms (020) 7834 6442
Millbank; SW1P 4RW Victorian pub facing the Thames, roomy and comfortable, with view over to MI6 headquarters from upstairs Spy Room, etched and cut glass, lots of mirrors, paintings, prints and old photographs (some of british spies), well kept Youngs ales and guests, decent choice of wines and fair value standard food, welcoming efficient staff, built on site of Millbank Prison and cells remain below; background music; seats outside (a lot of traffic), handy for Tate Britain and Thames Path walkers, open (and food) all day. *(Nigel and Sue Foster)*

Nags Head (020) 7235 1135
Kinnerton Street; SW1X 8ED Unspoilt and unchanging little mews pub with no-nonsense plain-talking landlord, low-ceilinged panelled front room with unusual sunken counter, log-effect gas fire in old range, narrow passage down to even smaller bar, well kept Adnams from 19th-c handpumps, uncomplicated food, theatrical mementoes and other interesting memorabilia including what-the-butler-saw machine and one-armed bandit; no mobiles, individual background music; well behaved children and dogs allowed, a few seats outside, open (and food) all day. *(Helen McLagan, Richard and Penny Gibbs)*

Red Lion (020) 7930 5826
Parliament Street; SW1A 2NH Victorian pub by Houses of Parliament, used by Foreign Office staff and MPs, divided bare-boards bar with showy chandeliers suspended from fine moulded ceiling, parliamentary cartoons and prints, Fullers/Gales beers and decent wines from long counter, good range of food, efficient staff, also clubby cellar bar and upstairs panelled dining room; free wi-fi; children welcome, outside bench seating, open all day (till 9pm Sun). *(Martin Day, Dr and Mrs A K Clarke)*

Red Lion (020) 7930 4141
Crown Passage, behind St James's Street; SW1Y 6PP Cheerful traditional little pub tucked down narrow passage near St James's Palace; dark panelling and leaded lights, upholstered settles and stools on patterned carpet, lots of prints, decorative plates and horsebrasses, well kept Adnams, St Austell and decent range of malt whiskies, friendly service, lunchtime sandwiches (no hot food), narrow overflow room upstairs; sports TV; colourful hanging baskets, closed Sun, otherwise open all day. *(Tony Scott)*

★**Red Lion** (020) 7321 0782
Duke of York Street; SW1Y 6JP Pretty little flower-decked Victorian pub, remarkably preserved and packed with customers often spilling out on to the pavement; series of small rooms with profusion of polished mahogany, gleaming mirrors, cut/etched windows and chandeliers, striking ornamental plaster ceiling, Fullers/Gales beers and traditional lunchtime food; no children; dogs welcome, closed Sun and bank holidays, otherwise open all day. *(Patricia and Gordon Tucker)*

We say if we know a pub allows dogs.

Speaker (020) 7222 1749
Great Peter Street; SW1P 2HA Bustling
chatty atmosphere in unpretentious smallish
corner pub (can get packed at peak times),
well kept Timothy Taylors and guests,
bottled beers and lots of whiskies, short
choice of enjoyable simple food, friendly
staff, panelling, political cartoons and
prints, notes here and there on etiquette;
no mobiles, background music or children;
open (and food) all day weekdays, closed
weekends. *(Dr and Mrs A K Clarke)*

★**St Stephens Tavern** (020) 7925 2286
Parliament Street; SW1A 2JR Victorian
pub opposite Houses of Parliament and
Big Ben (so quite touristy); lofty ceilings
with brass chandeliers, tall windows with
etched glass and swagged curtains, gleaming
mahogany, charming upper gallery bar (may
be reserved for functions), four well kept
Badger ales from handsome counter with
pedestal lamps, fairly priced traditional
food including burgers and pies, friendly
efficient staff, division bell for MPs and
lots of parliamentary memorabilia; open
(and food) all day. *(Dr and Mrs A K Clarke)*

Tom Cribb (020) 7839 3801
Panton Street; SW1Y 4EA Small
Shepherd Neame corner pub named after
19th-c boxer, tiled exterior and traditional
bare-boards bar, four real ales, short choice
of pubby food till 6pm (5pm Sun), friendly
service; sports TV; no children, open all
day (till 9.30 Sun). *(Eddie Edwards)*

White Swan (020) 7821 8568
Vauxhall Bridge Road; SW1V 2SA Roomy
corner pub handy for Tate Britain, lots of
dark dining tables on three levels in long
room, well cooked reasonably priced pubby
food, six or more ales including Adnams,
Fullers, St Austell and Youngs, decent wines
by the glass, uniformed staff; background
music; open all day and can get very busy at
peak times. *(John Wooll, Dr and Mrs A K Clarke)*

Windsor Castle (020) 7834 7260
Francis Street; SW1P 1DN Traditionally
restored 19th-c pub directly behind
Westminster Cathedral (was the Cardinal);
new etched glass and rebuilt screened
snugs matching the original architect's
drawings, fine Victorian moulded ceiling,
open fires, well kept/priced Sam Smiths
beers and enjoyable good value food (not
Sun) such as fish and chips and steak and
kidney pudding, friendly staff, parquet-
floored back dining lounge with half-
panelled and papered walls, another bar
upstairs (not always open); no children,
open all day. *(Susan and John Douglas)*

SW3

Coopers Arms (020) 7376 3120
Flood Street; SW3 5TB Useful bolthole
for King's Road shoppers (so can get busy);
comfortable bar with good mix of tables
and chairs on stripped boards, large moose
head on one wall, Youngs ales and guests,
good selection of other drinks including
over 20 wines by the glass, decent food
from fairly pubby menu; Tues quiz; well
behaved children till 7pm, dogs allowed
in bar, courtyard garden, open (and food)
all day. *(Richard and Penny Gibbs)*

Hour Glass (020) 7581 2497
Brompton Road; SW3 2DY Under same
ownership as nearby Brompton Food Market
deli; compact wood-floored bar with open
brick fireplace, red leather banquette
at each end, stools along drinking shelf
overlooking street, Fullers London Pride
and a couple of guests, proper cider, highly
regarded interesting food from bar snacks
up (all day Sat, till 6pm Sun), panelled
upstairs dining room with open kitchen,
friendly helpful service; children and dogs
(in bar) welcome, handy for V&A and other
nearby museums, open all day. *(Sam Cole)*

Surprise (020) 7351 6954
Christchurch Terrace; SW3 4AJ Late
Victorian Chelsea pub (Geronimo Inn)
popular with well heeled locals; Sharps,
Youngs and a house beer (HMS Surprise)
from light wood servery, champagne and
plenty of other wines by the glass, interesting
food (all day weekends) including british
tapas-style canapé boards, friendly service,
soft grey décor and comfortable furnishings
with floral sofas and armchairs on sturdy
floorboards, stained-glass partitioning, a
model ship or two, upstairs dining room,
daily papers; open all day. *(Darrell Barton)*

W1

★**Argyll Arms** (020) 7734 6117
Argyll Street; W1F 7TP Popular and
individual Nicholsons pub with three
interesting little front cubicle rooms
(essentially unchanged since 1860s),
wooden partitions and impressive frosted
and engraved glass, mirrored corridor to
spacious back room, around eight real
ales from well stocked bar and decent
reasonably priced food, upstairs dining
room overlooking pedestrianised street;
background music, fruit machine; children
welcome till 8pm, pavement tables, handy
for the Palladium, open (and food) all day.
(Tony Scott, John Beeken)

Audley (020) 7499 1843
Mount Street; W1K 2RX Classic late
Victorian Mayfair pub; opulent red plush,
mahogany panelling and engraved glass,
clock in extravagantly carved bracket and
chandeliers hanging from ornately corniced
ceiling, long polished bar serving Greene
King ales and guests, good choice of pub
food (reasonably priced for the area),
upstairs panelled dining room, cellar wine
bar; quiet background music, TV, pool, free

wi-fi; children till 6pm, pavement tables, open (and food) all day. *(Tony Scott)*

Clachan (020) 7494 0834

Kingly Street; W1B 5QH Nicholsons corner pub behind Liberty (and once owned by them), ornate plaster ceiling supported by fluted pillars, comfortable screened leather banquettes, smaller drinking alcove up three or four steps, fine selection of real ales from handsome mahogany counter, affordably priced food served all day, dining room upstairs; open all day and can get very busy. *(Giles and Annie Francis)*

Crown & Two Chairmen

(020) 7437 8192 *Bateman Street/Dean Street; W1D 3SB* Large main room with smaller area off to the right, different height tables on bare boards, four real ales such as Sharps and Windsor & Eton along with craft beers, interesting up-to-date food from bar snacks up including weekday breakfasts (from 10am) and Sun roasts, upstairs dining room, good mix of customers (gets busy with after-work drinkers); free wi-fi; open (and food) all day. *(Jamie Davies)*

★ Dog & Duck (020) 7494 0697

Bateman Street/Frith Street; W1D 3AJ Bags of character in this tiny Soho pub – best enjoyed in the afternoon when not so packed; unusual old tiles and mosaics (the dog with tongue hanging out in hot pursuit of a duck is notable), heavy old advertising mirrors and open fire, Fullers London Pride and guests from unusual little counter and quite a few wines by the glass, enjoyable well priced food (including pre-theatre menu) in cosy upstairs dining room where children welcome; background music; dogs allowed in bar, open (and food) all day with drinkers often spilling on to the pavement. *(Richard and Penny Gibbs)*

Flying Horse (020) 7636 8324

Oxford Street, near junction with Tottenham Court Road; W1D 1AN Ornate late Victorian pub with long narrow bar, old tiling, mirrors, mahogany fittings and so forth, also three notable murals behind glass of voluptuous nymphs, dark floorboards and leather banquettes, half a dozen real ales, over 20 gins and enjoyable all-day food from Nicholsons menu, friendly service, bar and dining room downstairs; background music, free wi-fi; children welcome until 9pm, can get very busy at lunchtime. *(Sandra Hollies)*

French House (020) 7437 2477

Dean Street; W1D 5BG Small character Soho pub with impressive range of wines, bottled beers and other unusual drinks, some draught beers but no real ales or pint glasses, lively chatty atmosphere (mainly standing room), theatre memorabilia, shortish choice of modern food (Mon-Fri till 3.30pm) in bar or upstairs restaurant, efficient staff;

no music or mobile phones; can get very busy evenings with customers spilling on to the street, open all day. *(Sam Cole)*

★ Grapes (020) 7493 4216

Shepherd Market; W1J 7QQ Genuinely old-fashioned pub with dimly lit bar, plenty of well worn plush red furnishings, stuffed birds and fish in display cases, some old guns, wood floors, panelling, coal fire and snug back alcove, six ales including Fullers, Sharps and a house beer from Brains, good choice of authentic all-day thai food (some english dishes too), lots of customers (especially lunchtime and early evening) congregating out on the square; children till 6pm weekdays (anytime weekends), open all day. *(Maggie and Stevan Hollis)*

★ Guinea (020) 7409 1728

Bruton Place; W1J 6NL Lovely hanging baskets and chatty customers outside this tiny 17th-c Mayfair mews pub, standing room only at peak times, a few cushioned wooden seats and tables on tartan carpet, side elbow shelf and snug back area, old-fashioned prints, planked ceiling, Youngs and a couple of guests from striking counter, good range of wines and whiskies, famous steak and kidney pie, grills and some sandwiches, smart Guinea Grill restaurant, highish prices; no children; open all day (till 8pm Sun), no food Sat lunchtime or Sun evening. *(Dr and Mrs A K Clarke)*

Prince Regent (020) 7486 7395

Marylebone High Street; W1U 5JN Victorian corner pub in Marylebone village, flamboyant (if slightly worn) bare-boards interior with richly coloured furnishings, large gilt mirrors and opulent chandeliers, four changing ales, good range of wines and decent sensibly priced home-made food, friendly staff, upstairs 'Opium Room'; quiz Mon, free wi-fi; open all day from 8am (11am weekends) for breakfast. *(Dr and Mrs A K Clarke)*

Running Horse (020) 7493 1275

Davies Street/Davies Mews; W1K 5JE Stylish 18th-c pub with open-plan bare-boards bar, appealing collection of dining chairs and cushioned settles around mix of tables, tartan armchairs in front of green-tiled fireplace, ales such as Rebellion, lots of wines by the glass and good imaginative food from bar snacks up, friendly service, horse-racing prints on plain or navy-painted panelling, projector showing live televised racing, upstairs cocktail bar with button-back club chairs, brass chandeliers and more horsey prints on racing colours wallpaper; background music, free wi-fi; children and dogs welcome, contemporary wicker seats and tables out on the pavement, open all day (till 8pm Sun) from 9.30am for breakfast. *(Richard and Penny Gibbs)*

Shakespeares Head

(020) 7734 2911 *Great Marlborough Street; W1F 7HZ* Taylor Walker corner pub dating from the early 18th c (though largely rebuilt in the 1920s), dark beams, panelling and soft lighting, well kept ales including Fullers and Sharps, pubby food from sandwiches and baked potatoes up, upstairs dining room overlooking Carnaby Street; sports TV, free wi-fi; open (and food) all day. *(M J Winterton)*

Three Tuns (020) 7408 0330

Portman Mews S; W1H 6HP Large bare-boards front bar and sizeable lounge/dining area with beams and nooks and crannies, Fullers, Timothy Taylors and guests, enjoyable reasonably priced pubby food, good friendly staff and vibrant atmosphere; regular music quiz; open (and food) all day. *(Philip Chesington)*

W2   TQ2680

Leinster Arms (020) 7402 4670

Leinster Terrace; W2 3EU Small traditional flower-decked pub in Bayswater close to Hyde Park, friendly and busy, with Fullers London Pride, three guest ales and well liked pubby food at sensible prices; sports TV, free wi-fi; children and dogs welcome, a few pavement tables, open (and food) all day. *(Dr and Mrs A K Clarke)*

Mad Bishop & Bear

(020) 7402 2441 *Paddington station; W2 1HB* Fuller's pub up escalator from concourse, their beers kept well and good choice of wines, reasonably priced standard food quickly served including breakfast from 8am (10am Sun), airy interior with ornate plasterwork and mirrored columns, high tables and chairs on light wood or tiled floors, raised carpeted dining area with some booth seating; background music, games machines and TVs (including train times); tables out at front, open all day till 11pm (10.30pm Sun). *(Roger and Donna Huggins, Ian Herdman, Dr and Mrs A K Clarke)*

★Victoria (020) 7724 1191

Strathearn Place; W2 2NH Well run bare-boards pub with lots of Victorian pictures and memorabilia, cast-iron fireplaces, gilded mirrors and mahogany panelling, brass mock-gas lamps above attractive horseshoe bar serving Fullers ales and guests from smaller breweries, several wines by the glass and reasonably priced popular food, friendly service and chatty relaxed atmosphere; upstairs has small library/snug and replica of Gaiety Theatre bar (mostly for private functions now); quiet background music, TV; pavement tables, pretty hanging baskets, open all day. *(Dr and Mrs A K Clarke, Michael Domeney)*

WC1

Bountiful Cow (020) 7404 0200

Eagle Street; WC1R 4AP Popular for its excellent burgers and steaks; informal bar with booth seating and raised area by the windows, chrome stools against counter serving ales such as Adnams and ten wines by the glass, smallish upper room with wicker dining chairs around oak tables, larger downstairs dining room; background music, free wi-fi; children welcome, closed Sun, otherwise open all day. *(Louise and Simon Peters)*

★Cittie of Yorke (020) 7242 7670

High Holborn; WC1V 6BN Splendid back bar rather like a baronial hall with extraordinarily extended counter, 1,000-gallon wine vats resting above gantry, bulbous lights hanging from soaring raftered roof, intimate ornately carved booths and triangular fireplace with grates on all three sides, smaller comfortable panelled room with lots of little prints of York, cheap Sam Smiths beers and reasonably priced bar food, lots of students, lawyers and City types but plenty of space to absorb the crowds; children welcome, closed Sun, otherwise open all day. *(Tony Scott)*

Harrison (020) 7278 3966

Harrison Street; WC1H 8JF Tucked-away 1930s red-brick corner pub, modernised bar with simple mix of tables and chairs on bare boards, sofas by woodburner, enjoyable generously served food from snacks up (plenty for vegetarians), good friendly service; regular live music (mainly folk), comedy nights and cinema in basement; pavement picnic-sets, four bedrooms, closed Sat lunchtime, otherwise open all day. *(Jon Tickner)*

★Lamb (020) 7405 0713

Lambs Conduit Street; WC1N 3LZ Authentic 19th-c Bloomsbury pub with green-tiled frontage, bank of cut-glass swivelling snob screens around U-shaped counter, sepia photographs of 1890s actresses on ochre-panelled walls, traditional cast-iron-framed tables and button-back wall benches on stripped boards, snug little back room, Youngs ales and guests kept well, good choice of wines and malt whiskies, decent food from sandwiches, sharing boards and pub favourites up, function room upstairs; Sun quiz; children welcome till 5pm, seats in small paved courtyard behind, Foundling Museum nearby, open all day (till midnight Thurs-Sat) and can get very busy. *(Helen McLagan, Tracey and Stephen Groves)*

Museum Tavern (020) 7242 8987

Museum Street/Great Russell Street;
WC1B 3BA Traditional high-ceilinged
ornate Victorian pub facing British
Museum, busy lunchtime and early
evening, half a dozen well kept ales and
several wines by the glass, standard Taylor
Walker menu, friendly helpful staff; one
or two tables out under gas lamps, open
all day. *(Robert and Diana Ringstone)*

Norfolk Arms (020) 7388 3937

Leigh Street; WC1H 9EP Atmospheric
tile-fronted pub with ornate ceiling and other
high Victorian features, very good tapas,
a couple of well kept changing ales and nice
wines, close-set tables in bustling U-shaped
bar, prompt, friendly efficient service;
open all day. *(Tracey and Stephen Groves)*

★Princess Louise (020) 7405 8816

High Holborn; WC1V 7EP Splendid
Victorian gin palace with extravagant décor –
even the gents' has its own preservation
order; gloriously opulent main bar with wood
and glass partitions, fine etched and gilt
mirrors, brightly coloured and fruit-shaped
tiles, slender Portland stone columns soaring
towards the lofty and deeply moulded plaster
ceiling, open fire, cheap Sam Smiths from
long counter, competitively priced pubby
food (not Fri-Sun) in quieter upstairs room;
no children, open all day and gets crowded
early weekday evenings. *(Barry Collett)*

Queens Head (020) 7713 5772

Acton Street; WC1X 9NB Small Victorian
terraced pub attracting good mix of
customers; wide ever-changing range of UK
and European draught beers (plenty more
in bottles), real ciders and extensive whisky
choice, friendly knowledgeable staff, food
such as pork pies and meat/cheese boards,
traditional interior with several large
mirrors, wood floors and skylit back part,
piano; live jazz last Thurs of month; open
all day. *(Shaun Flook, Heather Campbell)*

Queens Larder (020) 7837 5627

Queen Square; WC1N 3AR Small
character pub on corner of traffic-free square
and cobbled Cosmo Place, also known as
Queen Charlotte (it's where she stored food
for her mad husband George III, who was
being cared for nearby); circular cast-iron
tables, wall benches and stools around
attractive U-shaped bar, theatre posters
on dark panelled walls, Greene King ales,
decent pubby food, upstairs function room;
background jazz; dogs welcome, picnic-sets
and heater outside. *(Adam Jones)*

Skinners Arms (020) 7837 5621

Judd Street; WC1H 9NT Richly decorated,
with glorious woodwork, marble pillars,
high ceilings and ornate windows, lots of
London prints on busy wallpaper, interesting
layout including comfortable back seating

area, coal fire, Greene King and guests from
attractive long bar, enjoyable home-made
food; unobtrusive background music and
muted TV; pavement picnic-sets, handy
for British Library, closed Sun, otherwise
open all day. *(Tracey and Stephen Groves)*

WC2   TQ2980

Admiralty (020) 7930 0066

Trafalgar Square; WC2N 5DS Handsome
naval-theme pub by Trafalgar Square;
button-back leather seating in booths by
big windows, high stools and elbow tables,
grand chandeliers and lots of interesting
prints, flagstaff with white ensigns and
union jacks, eight Fullers/Gales beers
from traditional counter, grand steps up to
mezzanine with leather-seated dining chairs
at wooden tables, also atmospheric vaulted
cellar bar with painted brick or planked
walls, arched seating alcoves, nautical
pictures and knick-knacks, standard pub
food including speciality pies, efficient
staff; children welcome, a few pavement
tables, open all day from 8am (10am
weekends) for breakfast. *(David Jackman)*

Bear & Staff (020) 7930 5261

Bear Street; WC2H 7AX Traditional
Nicholsons corner pub with six well kept
changing ales and standard pubby food
from sandwiches and sharing plates
up, friendly staff, upstairs dining room
named after Charlie Chaplin who was
a customer; open all day. *(Darrell Barton)*

Cheshire Cheese (020) 7836 2347

Little Essex Street/Milford Lane;
WC2R 3LD Small cosy 1920s corner pub,
leaded bow windows, beams and panelling,
cushioned oak settles and assorted seats
on patterned carpet, bric-a-brac hanging
from beams, well kept St Austell Tribute,
Sharps Doom Bar and guests, good value
wines and pubby food, friendly staff,
downstairs games room with bar billiards,
darts and table skittles, upstairs dining/
function room; background music, sports
TVs; closed weekends, otherwise open all day,
food till 3pm. *(Alister and Margery Bacon)*

Coal Hole (020) 7379 9883

Strand; WC2R 0DW Well preserved
Edwardian pub adjacent to the Savoy;
original leaded windows, classical wall
reliefs, mock-baronial high ceiling and
raised back gallery, nine changing ales
from central servery, standard Nicholsons
menu, wine bar downstairs; sports TV;
open all day and can get very busy. *(Simon
Collett-Jones, Tony Scott, Dr and Mrs A K Clarke)*

Cross Keys (020) 7836 5185

Endell Street/Betterton Street; WC2H 9EB
Flower-decked Covent Garden pub with
fascinating interior, masses of photographs,
pictures and posters including Beatles
memorabilia, all kinds of brassware and

bric-a-brac from stuffed fish to musical instruments, well kept Brodies ales and a couple of guests (usually smaller London brewers), decent wines by the glass, good lunchtime sandwiches and a few bargain hot dishes including Sun roast; fruit machine, gents' downstairs; sheltered outside cobbled area with flower tubs, open all day. *(Robert and Diana Ringstone)*

Edgar Wallace (020) 7353 3120

Essex Street; WC2R 3JE Simple spacious open-plan pub dating from the 18th c, eight well kept ales including a house beer brewed by Nethergate, enjoyable good value traditional food from sandwiches up, friendly efficient service, half-panelled walls and red ceilings covered in beer mats, interesting Edgar Wallace memorabilia and lots of old beer and cigarette adverts, upstairs dining room; a few high tables in side alleyway, closed weekends, otherwise open all day. *(Maggie and Stevan Hollis)*

George (020) 7353 9638

Strand; WC2R 1AP Timbered pub near the law courts with long narrow bare-boards bar, nine real ales and a dozen wines by the glass, lunchtime food from sandwiches up, also upstairs bar/restaurant with fixed-price weekday menu; open all day. *(Tony Scott, Dr and Mrs A K Clarke)*

Knights Templar (020) 7831 2660

Chancery Lane; WC2A 1DT Good well managed Wetherspoons in big-windowed former bank, marble pillars, handsome fittings and plasterwork, bustling atmosphere on two levels, ever-changing range of well kept/priced ales, good wine choice and enjoyable bargain food, friendly efficient staff; free wi-fi; open all day Mon-Fri, till 6.30pm Sat, closed Sun. *(Ian Herdman, Dr and Mrs A K Clarke)*

Mr Foggs Tavern (020) 7581 3992

St Martins Lane; WC2N 4EA Themed around Jules Verne's Phileas Fogg, small Victorian-style bar with appropriate pictures and stuffed animals on panelled walls, masses of bric-a-brac hanging from ceiling including model boats, bird cages, brass instruments, even an old pram, craft beers and over a dozen wines by the glass from metal-topped servery, friendly staff in period dress, enjoyable food including bar snacks, sharing plates and range of pies, atmospheric upstairs re-creation of 19th-c salon/gin parlour, swagged curtains, chinese wallpaper and chaises longues, extensive selection of gins plus cocktails; open all day, upstairs from 4pm (1pm Sat). *(Alf and Sally Garner)*

Nell Gwynne (020) 7240 5579

Bull Inn Court, off Strand; WC2R 0NP Narrow dimly lit old pub tucked down alleyway, character bare-boards interior with lots of pictures (some of Nell Gwynne)

on papered walls, a few tables but mainly standing room and drinkers spill outside at busy times, ales such as Adnams, Fullers and St Austell, some interesting bottled beers including Camden Town and extensive range of spirits; good juke box, TV, darts; open all day. *(Brian Glozier)*

Porterhouse (020) 7379 7917

Maiden Lane; WC2E 7NA London outpost of Dublin's Porterhouse brewery, their interesting beers along with guests and lots of bottled imports, good choice of wines by the glass, pubby food; three-level labyrinth of stairs (lifts for disabled), galleries, gleaming copper ducting and piping, a large sonorous open-work clock suspended from the ceiling, neatly cased bottled beer displays; background and live music, sports TV (also in gents'); tables on front terrace, open all day and can get packed evenings. *(Miles Green)*

Salisbury (020) 7836 5863

St Martins Lane; WC2N 4AP Gleaming Victorian pub in the heart of the West End, a wealth of cut-glass and mahogany, wonderfully ornate bronze light fittings and etched mirrors, some interesting photographs including Dylan Thomas enjoying a drink here in 1941, up to six well kept ales, usual Taylor Walker menu from sharing platters up, cheerful staff; steep stairs down to lavatories; children allowed till 5pm, fine details on building exterior, seats in pedestrianised side alley, open (and food) all day. *(Miles Green)*

Ship (020) 7405 1992

Gate Street; WC2A 3HP Tucked-away bare-boards pub with roomy minimally furnished bar, some booth seating, chesterfields by open fire, quite dark with leaded lights, panelling and plaster-relief ceiling, six changing ales and enjoyable bar food, upstairs restaurant with good separate menu, friendly service; background music; open (and food) all day. *(Michael Zeitlyn, David Hartshorne)*

★ Ship & Shovell (020) 7839 1311

Craven Passage, off Craven Street; WC2N 5PH Unusually split between two facing buildings; well kept Badger ales and a guest, decent reasonably priced food including wide range of baguettes, other bar snacks and pubby choices, good friendly service; one side brightly lit with dark wood, etched mirrors and interesting mainly naval pictures, plenty of tables, some stall seating and open fire; other side (across 'Underneath the Arches' alley) has a cosily partitioned bar; open all day, closed Sun. *(Tony Scott, Ian Phillips)*

Temple Brew House (020) 7936 2536

Essex Street; WC2R 3JF Popular refurbished basement bar; fine range of beers including some from on-site microbrewery, lots of wines by the glass and well liked food from sandwiches, small plates and burgers up (own smokehouse), friendly service from enthusiastic knowledgeable young staff; open (and food) all day. *(Dr and Mrs A K Clarke)*

Wellington (020) 7836 2789
Strand/Wellington Street; WC2R 0HS
Long narrow traditional corner pub next to the Lyceum; eight real ales including Trumans and Sharps, a couple of craft beers and several wines by the glass, usual Nicholsons menu, friendly staff, quieter upstairs bar/restaurant; sports TV; tables outside, open all day. *(Tony Scott, Dr and Mrs A K Clarke)*

EAST LONDON

E1
Captain Kidd (020) 7480 5759
Wapping High Street; E1W 2NE
Converted Wapping warehouse worth knowing for its great Thames views from jutting bay windows and waterside terrace; hefty timbers and flagstones providing plenty of old-world atmosphere, cheap Sam Smiths beers and pubby food, bare-boards restaurant upstairs; children and dogs welcome, open all day. *(Susan and John Douglas)*

★ Prospect of Whitby (020) 3603 4041
Wapping Wall; E1W 3SH Claims to be oldest pub on the Thames, dating from 1520 (although largely rebuilt after much later fire), was known as the Devil's Tavern and has a colourful history (Pepys and Dickens used it regularly and Turner came for weeks at a time to study the river views) – tourists love it; L-shaped bare-boards bar with plenty of beams, flagstones and panelling, five changing ales served from fine pewter counter, good choice of wines by the glass, bar food and more formal restaurant upstairs, cheerful helpful staff; children welcome (only if eating after 5.30pm), unbeatable views towards Docklands from tables on waterfront courtyard, open all day. *(Alastair and Sheree Hepburn, B and M Kendall)*

Town of Ramsgate (020) 7481 8000
Wapping High Street; E1W 2PN
Interesting olde-London Thames-side setting, restricted but evocative river view from small back floodlit terrace with mock gallows (hanging dock was nearby), long narrow dimly lit chatty bar with squared oak panelling, Fullers and Youngs ales, good choice of traditional food (all day Sun) including daily specials and deals, friendly helpful service; background music, Mon quiz; children and dogs welcome, open all day. *(Sally and David Champion)*

Water Poet (020) 7426 0495
Folgate Street; E1 6BX Large rambling Spitalfields pub with enjoyable food in bar and dining room including popular

Sun roasts, good selection of real ales and craft beers, decent wines, friendly staff, comfortable leather sofas and armchairs on wood floor, basement bar/function room (comedy club), separate games room with two pool tables; sports TV, regular quiz nights; children allowed till 7pm, enclosed outside area (dogs welcome here) with 'barn' room and barbecue, open all day. *(Sophie and John Moor)*

Williams (020) 7247 5163
Artillery Lane; E1 7LS Busy pub with wide range of real ales including Greene King and several from smaller London brewers, proper ciders too, decent choice of well liked food, comfortable seating areas including some leather sofas, pictures of old London breweries on the walls; weekend live music; closed Sun otherwise open (and food) all day. *(Martin and Sue Neville)*

E2
Carpenters Arms (020) 7739 6342
Cheshire Street; E2 6EG Welcoming neatly looked-after little corner pub just off Brick Lane and once owned by the Kray twins, well kept ales such as Timothy Taylors Landlord, enjoyable blackboard food; beer garden at back, closed Mon-Weds till 4pm, otherwise open all day. *(Sally and David Champion)*

Sun (020) 7739 4097
Bethnal Green Road; E2 0AN Updated 19th-c bar with good choice of local beers and other drinks including cocktails, friendly helpful service, padded stools around copper-topped counter with lanterns above, bare boards, exposed brickwork and some leather banquettes, bar snacks and sharing boards; open all day. *(Susan Eccleston)*

E3
Crown (020) 8880 7261
Grove Road/Old Ford Road; E3 5SN
Geronimo Inn with relaxed welcoming bar, chunky tables on polished boards, big bay window with comfortable scatter cushion seating area, books etc on open shelves, well kept Youngs and guests, good choice of wines by the glass, three individually decorated upstairs dining areas overlooking Victoria Park, imaginative food (all day Sun); background music; children and dogs welcome, open all day. *(Sam Cole)*

Palm Tree (020) 8980 2918
Haverfield Road; E3 5BH Lone survivor of blitzed East End terrace tucked away in Mile End Park by Regent's Canal; two Edwardian bars around oval servery, old-fashioned and unchanging under long-serving licensees, a couple of well kept ales, lunchtime sandwiches, good local atmosphere with popular weekend jazz; no credit cards; open all day (till late Sat). *(Sam Cole)*

E7

Forest Tavern (020) 8503 0868

Forest Lane across from Forest Gate station; E7 9BB Part of the Antic group, relaxed and unsmart, with six real ales, craft beers and enjoyable food from pub favourites to more unusual choices, friendly staff; live music, DJ nights and monthly vinyl market, games including table football; children and dogs welcome, seats out on decking, open all day weekends, from 4pm other days and till 1am Fri and Sat. *(Michael Maher)*

E11

Red Lion (020) 8988 2929

High Road Leytonstone; E11 3AA Large 19th-c corner pub (Antic group) with plenty of quirky character, high-ceilinged open-plan interior with lots of pictures, mirrors, books and general bric-a-brac, ten changing ales, craft kegs and real ciders, enjoyable interesting food along with some pub staples, bar billiards and table football; weekend DJs and live music, Mon quiz, Tues cinema, monthly comedy night; children and dogs welcome, picnic-sets out at front and in good-sized back garden, open all day. *(Miles Green)*

E13

Black Lion (020) 8472 2351

High Road, Plaistow; E13 0AD Beamed 18th-c coaching inn surviving among 20th-c development, up to six real ales including Courage, Mighty Oak and Sharps, enjoyable well priced pubby food (good fish and chips), friendly staff; sports TVs; picnic-sets on terrace and grass, open all day, no food weekends except on West Ham match days. *(David Jackman)*

E14

George (020) 3637 5993

Glengall Grove; E14 3ND Refurbished 1930s corner pub (Hippo Inns) on the Isle of Dogs, two bars, snug and conservatory, traditional food from snacks up including pie, mash and liquor menu, four mainstream ales and over two dozen wines by the glass; background and some live music, sports TV, darts; children welcome, nice back garden with vine clad arbour, open all day. *(Steve Manning)*

★Grapes (020) 7987 4396

Narrow Street; E14 8BP Relatively unchanged since Charles Dickens used it as a model for his Six Jolly Fellowship Porters in *Our Mutual Friend*; a proper traditional tavern with friendly atmosphere and good mix of customers, partly panelled bar with prints of actors, old local maps and the pub itself, elaborately etched windows, plates along a shelf, larger back area leading to small deck looking over river towards Canary Wharf; Adnams, Black Sheep, Timothy Taylors and two guests, good value tasty bar food, upstairs restaurant with fine

views; no children, dogs welcome on the lead, open all day, food all day Sat, kitchen closed Sun evening. *(B and M Kendall)*

★Gun (020) 7515 5222

Coldharbour; E14 9NS Dining pub with great views from riverside terrace of the O2 arena; smart front restaurant and two character bars – busy flagstoned drinkers' one with antique guns and log fire, cosy red-painted next-door room with leather sofas and armchairs, stuffed boar's heads and modern prints, Fullers ales, several wines by the glass and good modern food (also cheaper bar menu), efficient service from friendly staff; background music; children welcome till 8pm, open all day. *(Miles Green)*

Narrow (020) 7592 7950

Narrow Street; E14 8DJ Stylish dining pub (part of Gordon Ramsay's chain) worth knowing for its great Thames views from window seats and covered terrace; simple but smart bar with white walls and blue woodwork, mosaic-tiled fireplaces and colourful striped armchairs, beers such as Fullers London Pride, good wines, food from bar snacks to pricier restaurant meals, dining room also white with matching furnishings, local maps, prints and a suspended boat; background music (live Weds); open all day. *(Sophie and John Moor)*

E17

Queens Arms (020) 8520 9184

Orford Road; E17 9NJ Refurbished 19th-c corner pub in Walthamstow village, spacious and comfortable, with well kept ales such as Timothy Taylors Landlord and numerous wines by the glass, good food from interesting changing menu, friendly service and good buoyant atmosphere; background music; children very welcome, seats outside, open all day. *(Michael Butler)*

NORTH LONDON

N1

Camden Head (020) 7359 0851

Camden Walk; N1 8DY Comfortably preserved Victorian pub in pedestrianised street, lots of fine etched glass and mahogany panelling, unusual clock suspended from ceiling, button-back leather wall seats and a few small booths, half a dozen well kept changing ales including Greene King from oval servery, fairly priced pubby food (order at the bar); free nightly comedy club upstairs; children welcome till 7pm, no dogs, chunky picnic-sets on front terrace, open (and food) all day. *(Adam Jones)*

Charles Lamb (020) 7837 5040

Elia Street; N1 8DE Small friendly backstreet corner pub with four well kept ales such as Dark Star and Windsor & Eton, interesting bottled beers and decent choice of wines by the glass including own-label, good blackboard food (brunch Sat from 11am), no bookings, big windows, polished boards and simple traditional furniture; background jazz; pavement tables, closed Mon and Tues lunchtimes, otherwise open all day. *(Martin and Sue Neville)*

Craft Beer Company

(020) 7278 4560 *White Lion Street; N1 9PP* Flower-decked Islington pub with extensive choice of interesting draught and bottled beers, good range of wines and spirits too, cosy and softly lit with dark green walls, wood-strip or red carpeted floors, a couple of ornate Victorian pillars, leather armchairs under a portrait of Churchill, high tables in main bar, low ones in adjacent areas, good mix of customers, burger menu; occasional live acoustic music; small side garden, open all day Fri-Sun, from 4pm other days. *(Margaret McDonald)*

Duke of Cambridge (020) 7359 3066

St Peters Street; N1 8JT Well established as London's first organic pub; simply decorated busy main room with chunky wooden tables, pews and benches on bare boards, corridor past open kitchen to more formal dining room and conservatory, ales from small breweries, also organic draught lagers, ciders, spirits and wines, interesting bar food using seasonal produce (not cheap and they add a service charge), teas and coffees; children welcome, dogs in bar, open all day. *(Max Simons)*

Earl of Essex (020) 7424 5828

Danbury Street; N1 8LE One-room pub brewing its own Earl ales, great choice of other beers too on draught (listed on boards) and in bottles, friendly staff will offer tasters, varied menu from small plates up including suggested beer pairings; back walled garden, open (and food) all day. *(Max Simons)*

Hemingford Arms (020) 7607 3303

Hemingford Road; N1 1DF 19th-c ivy-clad pub filled with bric-a-brac, good choice of real ales from central servery, thai evening food plus Sunday roasts, open fire, upstairs bar/function room; live music including Mon bluegrass, quiz second Weds of month, sports TV, machines; picnic-sets outside, open all day. *(Peter Brix)*

Islington Townhouse

(020) 3637 6424 *Liverpool Road; N1 0RW* Corner pub recently refurbished by Hippo Inns; stylish modern décor over three floors, good selection of beers and other drinks including cocktails and over 20 wines by the glass, enjoyable sensibly priced food from open sandwiches and assorted small plates up, Sat brunch, friendly engaging staff; background music, Tues quiz; children welcome, open (and food) all day. *(Sally and David Champion)*

Lighterman (020) 3846 3400

Granary Square, Regent's Canal; N1C 4BH Ultra-modern bar-cum-restaurant on three floors in redeveloped plaza behind King's Cross station, views over Granary Square fountains and Regent's Canal; light airy feel with floor-to-ceiling windows, wood-strip floors and minimalist décor, Crate Golden Ale, Hiver Honey IPA and a guest, 20 wines by the glass and seasonal cocktails, popular food from breakfast on including wood-fired grills, efficient friendly young staff; background music; waterside terrace and wrap-around first-floor deck making most of the view, open (and food) all day from 8am (9am weekends). *(Brian Glozier, Maggie and Stevan Hollis, Adam and Natalie Davis, Robert and Diana Ringstone)*

Marquess Tavern (020) 7359 4615

Canonbury Street/Marquess Road; N1 2TB Imposing revamped Victorian pub; bare boards and a mix of furniture including sofas around big horseshoe servery, a couple of fireplaces and lots of prints (some recalling George Orwell who used to drink here), Youngs beers, good selection of wines, gins and cocktails, traditional and more adventurous food in bar or back skylit dining room with classical wall columns, large mirrors and modern lights dangling from high ceiling; background music, TV; children and dogs welcome, a few seats out behind front railings, open (and food) all day. *(Sally)*

★Parcel Yard (020) 7713 7258

King's Cross station, N end of new concourse, up stairs (or lift); N1C 4AH Impressive restoration of listed Victorian parcel sorting office; lots of interesting bare-boards rooms off corridors around airy central atrium, pleasing old-fashioned feel with exposed pipework and ducting adding to the effect, back bar serving full range of well kept Fullers beers plus guests from long modern counter, plenty of wines by the glass, similar upstairs area with old and new furniture including comfortable sofas, railway memorabilia and some nice touches like Victorian-envelope wallpaper, good bistro-pub food from bar snacks up, breakfast till 11.45am, attentive friendly service; power points to recharge phones/laptops, screens for train times, platform views; seats out at front, open all day from 8am (9am Sun). *(Roger and Donna Huggins, Tony Scott, Susan and John Douglas)*

Wenlock Arms (020) 7608 3406

Wenlock Road; N1 7TA Friendly corner local with excellent choice of real ales, craft beers and ciders from central servery, plenty of foreign bottled beers too, simple food, alcove seating, coal fires; darts, free wi-fi; children (until 8pm) and dogs welcome, open all day. *(Max Simons)*

N6

★**Flask** (020) 8348 7346

Highgate West Hill; N6 6BU Traditional
Georgian pub with intriguing up-and-down
layout; unusual sash-windowed bar hatch,
panelling and bare boards in snug lower
area, log fires, Fullers beers and a guest,
good variety of food from sandwiches
and snacks up, barrel-vaulted flagstoned
dining area; children and dogs welcome,
picnic-sets out in front courtyard, handy
for strolls around Highgate village or
Hampstead Heath, open all day, food all
day Sun till 7pm. *(Jim and Sue James)*

Red Lion & Sun (020) 8340 1780

North Road (B519); N6 4BE 1920s
Highgate Village dining pub with good
variety of well liked food (can be pricey)
from oysters to pub favourites, they also
do takeaway fish and chips, four real
ales including Morland Original, lots
of wines by the glass (good list) and
extensive range of whiskies, cheerful
helpful service; well behaved children
and dogs welcome, tables on leafy front
terrace and in smaller back courtyard,
open (and food) all day. *(Victoria Brooks)*

N16

Railway Tavern (020) 3092 3344

*St Jude Street/King Henrys Walk;
N16 8JT* 19th-c bow-fronted single-bar
pub, half a dozen well kept ales along
with craft kegs and bottled beers, good
authentic thai food (just roasts on Sun),
reasonable prices and friendly relaxed
atmosphere, some railway memorabilia;
Tues quiz and acoustic live music; children
and dogs welcome, open all day weekends,
from 4pm other days. *(Andrew Bosi)*

NW1

Bree Louise (020) 7681 4930

Cobourg Street/Euston Street; NW1 2HH
No-frills corner pub with wide selection of
well kept ales on handpump and gravity,
good choice of ciders too and some
decent reasonably priced wines, food
emphasising pies (Mon-Thurs bargains),
basic décor and well worn furnishings;
can get very busy early evening; pavement
tables, handy for Euston station, open
all day. *(Dr J Barrie Jones, Liz and Brian
Barnard, Phil and Jane Villiers, Tony Scott)*

★**Chapel** (020) 7402 9220

Chapel Street; NW1 5DP Corner dining
pub attracting equal share of drinkers (busy
and noisy in the evening); spacious rooms
dominated by open kitchen, smart but
simple furnishings, sofas at lounge end by
big fireplace, a couple of real ales such as
Greene King and Black Sheep, good choice
of wines by the glass, several coffees and
teas, decent food from weekly changing
menu, brisk friendly service; children

and dogs welcome, picnic-sets in sizeable
back garden, more seats on decking under
heated parasols, covered smokers' area,
open all day. *(Trevor and Michele Street)*

Constitution (020) 7380 0767

St Pancras Way; NW1 0QT Traditional
standalone 19th-c pub close to Camden
Lock and a quieter alternative to the busy
market area; three local beers and good
selection of wines by the glass, pubby
lunchtime food Mon-Fri, friendly staff
and pleasant atmosphere; pool, darts and
juke box, cellar bar for live music (every
Weds); barbecues in lovely sunny garden
overlooking canal, open all day. *(Adam Jones)*

★**Doric Arch** (020) 7388 2221

Eversholt Street; NW1 2DN Virtually
part of Euston station (up stairs from the
bus terminus) and a welcome retreat from
the busy concourse; well kept Fullers ales,
guest beers and enjoyable well priced
pubby food from snacks and sharing plates
to specials, friendly efficient service,
compact bare-boards bar with railway
memorabilia and pretty Victorian fireplace,
some button-back bench seating and a
cosy boothed alcove, steps up to carpeted
back dining area; background music,
TVs (including train times); open (and
food) all day. *(Dr and Mrs A K Clarke)*

Euston Tap (020) 3137 8837

Euston Road; NW1 2EF Two small
19th-c neoclassical lodges in front of
Euston station, good selection of around
16 quickly changing real ales, along
with craft kegs and huge bottled range,
friendly knowledgeable staff, limited
seating but more space and lavatories
up spiral stairs; outside tables, open all
day from noon. *(Dr and Mrs A K Clarke)*

Metropolitan (020) 7486 3489

*Baker Street tube station, Marylebone
Road; NW1 5LA* Flight of steps up to
spacious Wetherspoons in impressively
ornate pillared hall (designed by
Metropolitan Railway architect Charles
W Clarke), some recent refurbishment
with lots of tables on one side, very long
bar the other, ten or more real ales, good
coffee and their usual inexpensive food;
free wi-fi; family area, open all day from
8am (10am Sun). *(Tony and Wendy Hobden)*

Queens Head & Artichoke

(020) 7916 6206 *Albany Street;
NW1 4EA* Corner pub-restaurant near
Regent's Park with good fairly priced modern
food including lots of smaller tapas-style
plates, five well kept ales and good choice of
wines from Edwardian counter, bare boards
and panelling, large leaded windows, quieter
upstairs dining room; may be background
music; pavement picnic-sets under
awnings, open all day. *(Alistair Holdoway)*

Somerstown Coffee House
(020) 7691 9136 *Chalton Street (tucked away between Euston and St Pancras stations); NW1 1HS* Despite its name (there was a coffee house here in the 18th c) this is a busy pub with a fine range of well kept ales including Wells and Youngs and enjoyable food from british tapas up, friendly service, spacious interior with main bar on the ground floor, basement cocktail bar (from 5pm) and upstairs private dining rooms; background music; children and dogs welcome, tables out at front and back, open all day from 8am (10am weekends) for breakfast. *(David Hunt)*

Tapping the Admiral
(020) 7267 6118 *Castle Road; NW1 8SU* Friendly local with fine range of well kept ales mainly from London brewers, fairly priced home-made food including range of pies; quiz Weds, live music Thurs, free wi-fi; children welcome till 7pm, heated beer garden, open all day. *(Maggie and Stevan Hollis)*

NW3
★**Flask** (020) 7435 4580
Flask Walk; NW3 1HE Bustling local with two traditional front bars divided by unique Victorian screen, smart banquettes, panelling and lots of little prints, attractive fireplace, Youngs and a guest, plenty of wines by the glass and maybe winter mulled wine, popular all-day food, good friendly service, dining conservatory; background music, TV; children (till 8pm) and dogs welcome, seats and tables in alley, open (and food) all day. *(Buster and Helena Hastings)*

Spaniards Inn (020) 8731 8406
Spaniards Lane; NW3 7JJ Busy 16th-c pub next to Hampstead Heath with charming garden – flagstoned walk among roses, side arbour with climbing plants and plenty of seats on crazy-paved terrace (arrive early weekends as popular with dog walkers and families); attractive and characterful low-ceilinged rooms with oak panelling, antique winged settles, snug alcoves and open fires, up to five real ales, continental draught beers and several wines by glass, decent fairly pubby food including range of burgers, upstairs dining room; July beer festival, free wi-fi; car park fills fast and nearby parking difficult, open (and food) all day. *(Martin and Sue Neville)*

NW5   TQ2886
★**Bull & Last** (020) 7267 3641
Highgate Road; NW5 1QS Traditional décor with a stylish twist in this Victorian corner dining pub; single room with big windows, colonial-style fans in planked ceiling, bulls' heads and other stuffed animals, stone fireplace at one end along with collection of tankards and big faded map of London, much emphasis on their good

imaginative food (not cheap), takeaways including picnic hampers for Hampstead Heath, well kept changing ales and a house craft beer, good selection of wines, whiskies and gins, friendly staff, upstairs restaurant; children (away from bar) and dogs welcome, hanging baskets and picnic-sets by street, open all day. *(Michael Butler)*

Junction Tavern (020) 7485 9400
Fortess Road; NW5 1AG Black-painted Victorian corner pub with good interesting food from front dining area's open kitchen, well kept ales including Sambrooks and plenty of wines by the glass in ornate panelled bar, friendly helpful staff, conservatory; background music; no children after 7pm, picnic-sets under big parasols in paved back garden, open all day weekends, closed Mon-Thurs till 5pm. *(Peter Brix)*

Southampton Arms 07958 780073
Highgate Road; NW5 1LE Simply furnished drinkers' pub with one long room, wall seats and stools around tables on bare boards, up to ten changing beers and eight ciders, bar snacks, no credit cards; live piano some evenings, Mon quiz; garden at back and handy for Hampstead Heath, open all day. *(Tony Scott)*

SOUTH LONDON

SE1
Anchor (020) 7407 1577
Bankside; SE1 9EF In great Thames-side spot with river views from upper floors and roof terrace, beams, stripped brickwork and old-world corners, well kept ales including Greene King and good choice of wines by the glass, popular fish and chip bar and other sensibly priced food, breakfast/tea room, can get very busy; background music, machines; provision for children, disabled access, more tables under big parasols on raised riverside terrace, bedrooms in Premier Inn behind, open (and food) all day. *(B and M Kendall)*

Dean Swift (020) 7357 0748
Gainsford Street; SE1 2NE Comfortably updated corner pub tucked away behind Tower Bridge, five cask ales, lots of craft beers and several wines by the glass, friendly well informed staff, rewarding choice of food from bar snacks to Sun roasts, upstairs restaurant; sports TV; open (and food) all day, Sat brunch from 11am. *(B and M Kendall)*

Fire Station (020) 7620 2226
Waterloo Road; SE1 8SB Unusual fire station conversion, busy and noisy, with two big refurbished knocked-through rooms, burger and pizza menu, craft beers such as Beavertown, Meantime and Revisionist, 11 wines by the glass and cocktails, friendly staff; background music; children welcome, a few tables out in front, handy

for Old Vic theatre and Waterloo station, open (and food) all day from 7am (9am weekends) for breakfast. *(Adam Jones)*

★**Founders Arms** (020) 7928 1899
Hopton Street; SE1 9JH Modern glass-walled building in superb location – outstanding terrace views along Thames and handy for South Bank attractions; plenty of customers (City types, tourists, theatre- and gallery-goers) spilling on to pavement and river walls, Youngs Bitter and a guest, lots of wines by the glass, extensive choice of well priced bar food all day (weekend breakfasts from 9am), tea and coffee from separate servery, cheerful service; background music; children welcome (till 9pm) away from bar, open till midnight Fri, Sat. *(B and M Kendall)*

Garrison (020) 7089 9355
Bermondsey Street; SE1 3XB Interesting and very busy tile-fronted dining pub with idiosyncratic mix of styling, popular modern food including breakfast from 8am (9am weekends), a real ale or two but perhaps more emphasis on wine than beer, buzzy atmosphere; cinema/function room downstairs; open all day. *(Jamie Davies)*

★**George** (020) 7407 2056
Off 77 Borough High Street; SE1 1NH Tucked-away 16th-c coaching inn mentioned in *Little Dorrit*, owned by the National Trust and beautifully preserved; lots of tables in bustling cobbled courtyard with views of the tiered exterior galleries, series of no-frills ground-floor rooms with black beams, square-latticed windows and some panelling, plain oak or elm tables on bare boards, old-fashioned built-in settles, dimpled glass lanterns and a 1797 Act of Parliament clock, impressive central staircase up to a series of dining rooms and balcony, well kept Greene King ales and a beer badged for the pub, traditional food from sandwiches up; children welcome away from bar, open (and food) all day. *(Simon Collett-Jones, Brian Glozier, B and M Kendall)*

★**Kings Arms** (020) 7207 0784
Roupell Street; SE1 8TB Proper corner local tucked away amid terrace houses, bustling and friendly, with curved servery dividing traditional bar and lounge, bare boards, open fire and various bits and pieces including local road signs on the walls, nine well kept changing beers, good wine and malt whisky choice, welcoming helpful staff, enjoyable reasonably priced food from thai dishes to Sun roasts, big back extension with conservatory/courtyard dining area; background music; open all day. *(Simon Collett-Jones, B and M Kendall)*

★**Market Porter** (020) 7407 2495
Stoney Street; SE1 9AA Properly pubby no-frills place opening at 6am weekdays for workers at neighbouring Borough Market, up to ten unusual real ales (over 60 guests a week) often from far-flung brewers and in top condition, particularly helpful friendly service, bare boards and open fire, beams with barrels balanced on them, simple furnishings, food in bar and upstairs lunchtime restaurant with view over market; background music; children allowed weekends till 7pm, dogs welcome, gets very busy with drinkers spilling on to the street, open all day. *(Tony Scott, Jamie Davies)*

Rake (020) 7407 0557
Winchester Walk; SE1 9AG Tiny discreetly modern Borough Market bar with amazing bottled beer range in wall-wide cooler, also half a dozen continental lagers on tap and three real ales, good friendly service; fair-sized covered and heated outside area. *(Peter Brix)*

Ring (020) 7620 0811
Blackfriars Road/The Cut, opposite Southwark tube station; SE1 8HA Popular chatty local recalling the historic boxing ring that used to be opposite, single bare-boards bar with lots of boxing photographs and memorabilia, simple seating including some upholstered wall benches, Sharps Doom Bar and interesting guests, straightforward food such as burgers and hot dogs, friendly helpful service; background music, TV for major sports; picnic-sets out at front, open all day. *(Simon Collett-Jones)*

Sheaf (020) 7407 9934
Southwark Street; SE1 1TY In cellars beneath the Hop Exchange; brick vaulted ceilings and iron pillars, button back benches, sofas and some high tables, lots of framed black and white photographs of former regulars, ten real ales and decent pubby food; sports TVs; open all day. *(Trevor and Michele Street)*

Wheatsheaf (020) 7940 3880
Stoney Street; opposite Borough Market main entrance under new railway bridge; SE1 9AA Cheerful Youngs pub with comfortably refurbished interior, three of their well kept beers and a guest, food from side campervan kitchen; live music; heated back garden, open (and food) all day from 9am (10am Sun). *(Sophie and John Moor)*

White Hart (020) 7928 9190
Cornwall Road/Whittlesey Street; SE1 8TJ Backstreet corner pub near Waterloo station; friendly community bustle, comfortable sofas, stripped boards and so forth, real ales, craft kegs and lots of bottled beers, good range of ciders, wines and artisan spirits too, sensibly priced up-to-date blackboard food along with pub standards, Sunday bloody marys and newspapers, fresh flowers on tables; background music, free wi-fi; disabled facilities, open all day, food till early evening. *(Simon Collett-Jones, B and M Kendall)*

SE5

★ Crooked Well (020) 7252 7798

Grove Lane; SE5 8SY Popular early 19th-c restaurant pub in heart of Camberwell; button-back sofas, wall seats and variety of wooden dining chairs and tables on bare boards, very good imaginative food including express lunch menu, nice wines and cocktails (happy hour 5-7pm), craft beers and a couple of real ales, welcoming helpful staff, private dining/function rooms upstairs; children welcome, pavement picnic-sets, closed Mon lunchtime, otherwise open all day. *(Peter Brix)*

SE8

Dog & Bell (020) 8692 5664

Prince Street; SE8 3JD Friendly old-fashioned local tucked away on Thames Path; wood benches around bright cheerfully decorated L-shaped bar, open fire, up to half a dozen well kept ales including Fullers, bottled belgian beers, prompt friendly service, reasonably priced pub food from good sandwiches up, dining room; TV, bar billiards; tables in yard, open all day. *(Laura Read)*

SE9

Park Tavern (020) 8850 3216

Passey Place; SE9 5DA Traditional Victorian corner pub off Eltham High Street, eight well kept changing ales and 14 wines by the glass, log fire, friendly easy-going atmosphere; background music; pleasant little garden behind, open all day. *(Margaret McDonald)*

SE10

Cutty Sark (020) 8858 3146

Ballast Quay, off Lassell Street; SE10 9PD Great Thames views from this early 19th-c Greenwich tavern; genuinely unspoilt old-fashioned bar, dark flagstones, simple furnishings including barrel seats, open fires, narrow openings to tiny side snugs, upstairs room (reached by winding staircase) with ship-deck feel and prized seat in big bow window, Youngs ales and a couple of guests, organic wines, malt whiskies and wide choice of enjoyable bar food; background music; children and dogs welcome, busy riverside terrace across narrow cobbled lane, open (and food) all day. *(Sanjeev)*

★ Greenwich Union (020) 8692 6258

Royal Hill; SE10 8RT Feels more like a bar than a pub with full Meantime craft range, over 150 bottled beers, unusual spirits and interesting choice of teas and coffees, enjoyable food from lunchtime sandwiches and pub favourites up, friendly brisk service; long narrow stone-flagged room with simple front area, wooden furniture, stove and daily papers, comfortable part with sofas and cushioned pews, booth seating in end conservatory; free wi-fi; well behaved children and dogs welcome, paved terrace with teak furniture, old-fashioned lamp posts and end fence painted as a poppy field, open (and food) all day. *(Peter Brix)*

Pilot (020) 8858 5910

River Way, Blackwall Lane; SE10 0BE Early 19th-c pub surviving amid O2 development; opened-up interior on three levels with roof terrace overlooking park, well kept Fullers/Gales beers, good choice of food (all day Fri, Sat, till 6pm Sun) from pubby choices and charcoal grills to daily specials; background music, newspapers and free wi-fi; dogs welcome, picnic-sets in front, more seating in enclosed back garden with paving, lawn and covered area, ten well equipped boutique bedrooms, open all day. *(Taff Thomas)*

Prince of Greenwich (020) 8692 6089

Royal Hill; SE10 8RT Victorian pub under warmly welcoming Sicilian owners, good italian food from freshly made pizzas up, Fullers London Pride, Sharps Doom Bar and nice wines by the glass, quirky décor and unusual furnishings, lots of black and white jazz photos/posters (regular live jazz); italian film night Thurs; children and well behaved dogs welcome, closed Mon, open from 4pm Tues-Fri, 12.30pm weekends. *(Sandra Hollis, Sanjeev)*

Sail Loft (020) 8222 9310

Victoria Parade, Greenwich; SE10 9FR Airy modern Thames-side pub on two floors, excellent views over to Canary Wharf from floor-to-ceiling windows, Fullers/Gales beers and plenty of wines by the glass, short but varied choice of food from open kitchen; background music, free wi-fi; children and dogs welcome, terrace with covered seating booths taking in the view, open all day. *(Alister and Margery Bacon)*

SE11

Prince of Wales (020) 7735 9916

Cleaver Square; SE11 4EA Comfortably traditional little Edwardian pub in smart quiet Georgian square near the Oval, well kept Shepherd Neame ales and simple pub food from sandwiches up, warm friendly atmosphere; pavement seats, boules available to play in the square, open all day. *(Tracey and Stephen Groves)*

SE12 TQ3974

Lord Northbrook (020) 8318 1127

Burnt Ash Road; SE12 8PU Opened-up bare-boards Victorian corner pub, contemporary paintwork and lots of pictures, good mix of seating including a couple of chesterfields by Victorian fireplace, well kept Fullers/Gales beers, decent food from shortish menu, friendly staff, conservatory; children and dogs welcome, paved split-level back garden; open (and food) all day. *(Sanjeev)*

SE15 TQ3575

Ivy House (020) 7277 8233

Stuart Road; SE15 3BE Co-operative
owned pub with eight real ales and good
range of craft beers and ciders, well priced
food (not lunchtimes Mon, Tues) including
burgers and hot dogs, old-fashioned
panelled interior, stage in back room for
live music, comedy and theatre nights;
children (till 8pm) and dogs welcome, rack
for cyclists, open all day. *(Laura Reed)*

Old Nuns Head (020) 7639 4007

Nunhead Green; SE15 3QQ Popular
open-plan 1930s brick and timber pub
on edge of small green, half a dozen
interesting changing beers and enjoyable
food provided by pop-up kitchens including
burgers, greek grills and indian street food,
roasts only on Sun, cheerful efficient staff;
music, quiz and comedy nights; children
welcome, back garden and a few seats
out in front, handy for fascinating gothic
Nunhead Cemetery, open all day (till 1am
Fri, Sat), food from 6pm weekdays, midday
weekends. *(Patricia and Gordon Tucker)*

SE16

★Mayflower (020) 7237 4088

Rotherhithe Street; SE16 4NF Unchanging
cosy old riverside pub in unusual street
with lovely early 18th-c church; generous
bar food including more upmarket daily
specials, well kept Greene King and guests,
good value wines and decent coffee,
friendly young staff, black beams, panelling,
high-backed settle and coal fires, nautical
bric-a-brac, great Thames views from upstairs
candlelit evening restaurant; background
music, Tues quiz; children welcome, fun
jetty/terrace over water (barbecues), handy
for Brunel Museum, open (and food) all day.
(Jeremy King, Tony Scott)

SE22

Clockhouse (020) 8693 2001

Peckham Rye/Barry Road; SE22 9QA
Light and airy restyled Victorian pub, well
kept Youngs and guests, decent wines and
cocktail list, fairly priced food served by
friendly helpful staff, cheerfully decorated
front bar with dining area behind, upstairs
bar/function room; background music,
Tues quiz; children (till 7pm) and dogs
welcome, tables on front terrace looking
across to Peckham Rye, open (and food)
all day. *(Chantelle and Tony Redman)*

SE24

Florence (020) 7326 4987

Dulwich Road; SE24 0NG Tile-fronted
Victorian pub in Herne Hill with opened-up
contemporary bar, own-brew beers plus
guests, real cider and several wines by the
glass from central counter, good varied
choice of enjoyable food including brunch;
children (till 7pm) and dogs welcome, a few

tables out in front under awning, more on
back terrace, open (and food) all day (till
1am Fri, Sat). *(Samuel and Melissa Turnbull)*

SW4

Windmill (020) 8673 4578

*Clapham Common South Side;
SW4 9DE* Big bustling pub by the common,
contemporary front bar, quite a few original
Victorian features, pillared dining room
leading through to conservatory-style
eating area, popular varied choice of
food all day (breakfast from 7am), Wells
Bombardier, Youngs Bitter and decent
wines by the glass; background music,
live Sat (4-9pm), Sun quiz; children
welcome, tables under umbrellas along
front, more seats in side garden, good
bedrooms, open all day. *(Sanjeev)*

SW11

Eagle Ale House (020) 7228 2328

Chatham Road; SW11 6HG Unpretentious
backstreet local, seven well kept changing
ales including southern brewers like
Harveys, Surrey Hills and Westerham,
welcoming efficient service, L-shaped
carpeted bar with simple pubby furniture,
shelves of books either side of Victorian
fireplace; some live music, big-screen
sports TV; children and dogs welcome, back
terrace with heated marquee, small front
terrace too, open all day weekends, from
4pm Mon-Thurs, 3pm Fri. *(Sam Cole)*

Fox & Hounds (020) 7924 5483

Latchmere Road; SW11 2JU Victorian
pub with good italian-influenced food
(all day Sun, not Mon-Thurs lunchtimes),
St Austell and two local ales, several wines
by glass, spacious straightforward bar
with big windows overlooking street, bare
boards, mismatched tables and chairs,
photographs on walls, fresh flowers,
view of kitchen behind; background
music, TV, daily newspapers; children
and dogs welcome, terrace picnic-
sets, open all day Fri-Sun, closed Mon
lunchtime. *(Peter Brix, Laura Reed)*

Latchmere (020) 7223 3549

Battersea Park Road; SW11 3BW
Popular Battersea corner pub with award-
winning theatre upstairs; open-plan bare-
boards interior, Edwardian-style dining
chairs, two-sided banquettes and red
leather wall seats around wooden tables,
sofas either side of log fire, big mirrors,
model yachts, animal print and posters,
stools by counter serving St Austell, Sharps
and Timothy Taylors, 19 wines by the glass
and cocktails, enjoyable food including
pre-theatre set menu; children (till 7pm)
and dogs welcome, heated terrace with
booths down one side and plenty of other
seating, open all day, food all day Sun.
*(Donald Allsopp, Caroline Sullivan, Sophie
Ellison, Julian Thorpe)*

Westbridge (020) 7228 6482

Battersea Bridge Road; SW11 3AG Draft House pub with interesting ever-changing choice of real ales, craft beers and ciders served by friendly knowledgeable staff, tasting trays available, good reasonably priced food from open kitchen, can eat in bar or restaurant; background music (often blues/jazz), sports TV; small garden, open (and food) all day. *(Richard and Penny Gibbs)*

Woodman (020) 7228 2968

Battersea High Street; SW11 3HX Village feel in busy pub (especially in summer); enjoyable food from sandwiches up, Badger ales and several wines by the glass, good friendly service; children and dogs welcome, back garden with heaters and wood-fired pizza oven, open (and food) all day. *(Richard and Penny Gibbs)*

SW12
Avalon (020) 8675 8613

Balham Hill; SW12 9EB Part of south London's Three Cheers group; popular food including weekend brunch, well kept changing ales and good choice of wines by the glass, plenty of room in split-level bar and back dining area, big murals, stuffed animals and coal fires; sports TV; children welcome, front terrace and good large garden behind, open all day (till 1am Fri, Sat). *(Sam Cole)*

★Nightingale (020) 8673 1637

Nightingale Lane; SW12 8NX Early Victorian local, cosy and civilised, with small front bar opening into larger back area and attractive family conservatory, well kept Youngs and guests, decent wines and enjoyable sensibly priced bar food, friendly service, open fire; dogs welcome, nice secluded back beer garden with summer barbecues, open all day. *(David Seward)*

SW13
Red Lion (020) 8748 2984

Castelnau; SW13 9RU Roomy and relaxed 19th-c Fullers pub, their well kept ales and good choice of wines from stainless-steel counter, friendly staff, decent fairly priced food from varied menu (order at bar); back dining part has most character with impressive Victorian woodwork, big arched windows and high ceiling with stained-glass skylight, comfortable fireside sofas; TV; children and dogs welcome, disabled access/loo, big back garden with heated terrace and lawn (occasional outdoor theatre), open all day, food all day weekends. *(Simon and Mandy King, Susan and John Douglas, Edward Mirzoeff)*

White Hart (020) 8876 5177

The Terrace; SW13 0NR Open-plan Barnes dining pub with fine river views, well kept Wells and Youngs ales along with craft beers such as Camden Town and Meantime from island servery, good selection of wines by the glass, popular food in bar or upstairs restaurant with open kitchen and balcony; seats outside, open (and food) all day. *(Sanjeev)*

SW15
Bricklayers Arms (020) 8789 0222

Down cul-de-sac off Lower Richmond Road near Putney Bridge; SW15 1DD Welcoming tucked-away little 19th-c local with up to ten well kept changing ales, also proper cider/perry and good selection of english wines, efficient friendly staff, long L-shaped room with pitched-roof section, pine tables on bare boards, lots of pictures on painted panelling, log fire; background music, sports TV; paved side terrace, open all day Fri-Sun, from 4pm other days. *(M J Winterton)*

Half Moon (020) 8780 9383

Lower Richmond Road; SW15 1EU Good long-standing music venue, Youngs and a couple of guests from elegant curved counter, food from burgers and hot dogs to more elaborate choices and a brunch menu; free lunchtime jazz, nightly gigs in back music room; open all day (till 1am Fri, Sat). *(Chantelle and Tony Redman)*

Jolly Gardeners (020) 8789 2539

Lacy Road; SW15 1NT Slightly quirky bare-boards pub in residential Putney; gardening theme with trowels and watering cans on walls, potted flowers and botanical prints, bucket lampshades, a reclining gnome and row of colourful heated sheds in the back garden; four changing ales and several other draught beers, good selection of wines, enjoyable varied choice of food from sandwiches and sharing boards up; Tues quiz, sports TV, newspapers and free wi-fi; front fairy-lit terrace, open (and food) all day. *(Peter Brix)*

★Telegraph (020) 8788 2011

Telegraph Road; SW15 3TU Big pub on Putney Heath named after 19th-c admiralty telegraph station that was sited nearby; two attractively modernised rooms with leather armchairs and sofas, rugs on wood floors, eight real ales including a beer badged for them, enjoyable bistro-style food, upstairs function/overspill rooms; background and live music, sports TV, newspapers and board games; children and dogs welcome, great rural-feeling garden, open all day. *(Susan and John Douglas, Sanjeev)*

SW16
Earl Ferrers (020) 8835 8333

Ellora Road; SW16 6JF Opened-up Streatham corner pub with Sambrooks and several other well kept ales (tasters offered), interesting food along with pub standards including popular Sat brunch and Sun roasts, good friendly service, mixed tables and chairs, sofas, old photographs; music nights Mon and Thurs, pool and darts;

children welcome, some tables outside with tractor-seat stools, open all day weekends, from 5pm weekdays. *(Barbara and Phil Bowie)*

Railway (020) 8769 9448
Greyhound Lane; SW16 5SD Busy Streatham corner local with two big rooms (back one for families), rotating ales from London brewers such as Meantime, Redemption, Sambrooks and Trumans, enjoyable freshly made food, friendly staff, events including Tues quiz and monthly farmers' market; walled back garden, open all day (till 1am Fri, Sat). *(Barbara and Phil Bowie)*

SW18

Alma (020) 8870 2537
York Road, opposite Wandsworth Town station; SW18 1TF Corner Victorian pub-hotel with well kept Wells and Youngs ales and good choice of wines from island bar, sofas and informal mix of tables and chairs on wood floor, mosaic plaques and painted mirrors, wide range of good food from bar snacks up, back restaurant, friendly helpful staff; 23 bedrooms, open (and food) all day from 7am (8am weekends). *(Laura Reed)*

Cats Back (020) 8617 3448
Point Pleasant; SW18 1NN Traditionally refurbished 19th-c Harveys corner pub, four of their ales along with bottled beers, enjoyable food from sandwiches to Sun roasts, friendly staff; upstairs live music and film nights; partially covered beer garden with heaters, open all day. *(Jamie Davies)*

Jolly Gardeners (020) 8870 8417
Garrett Lane; SW18 4EA Bustling Victorian corner pub with L-shaped front bar, black leather dining chairs around straightforward tables on pale floorboards, stools at high tables and at counter serving ales such as Belleville and Sambrooks plus a dozen wines by the glass, good modern food (not Sun evening), dining area with open fire, friendly chatty staff and easy-going atmosphere, simply furnished conservatory opening on to courtyard garden with heaters, summer barbecues; children and dogs (in bar) welcome, open all day, till 8pm Sun; some restructuring planned, so may be changes. *(Millie and Peter Downing, Edward Nile, L Wright)*

Ship (020) 8870 9667
Jews Row; SW18 1TB Popular riverside pub by Wandsworth Bridge; light and airy conservatory-style décor, mix of furnishings on bare boards, church candles on tables, more basic public bar, well kept Youngs ales, Sambrooks and a guest, freshly cooked interesting bistro food (not particularly cheap) in extended restaurant with own garden; children and dogs welcome, good-sized terrace with barbecue and outside bar, open all day. *(Adam Jones)*

SW19

Alexandra (020) 8947 7691
Wimbledon Hill Road; SW19 7NE Busy 19th-c Youngs pub, their well kept beers and guests from central servery, good wine choice, enjoyable food from sandwiches and sharing boards to good Sun roasts, friendly attentive service, linked rooms with comfortable fairly traditional décor, more contemporary upstairs bar with burger menu; sports TVs; tables out in mews and on attractive popular roof terrace, open (and food) all day. *(Martin and Sue Neville)*

Crooked Billet (020) 8946 4942
Wimbledon Common; SW19 4RQ Busy 18th-c pub popular for its position by Wimbledon Common (almost next door to the Hand in Hand); Youngs ales and guests, good choice of wines and well liked up-to-date food in open-plan bar or dining room, mix of wooden dining chairs, high-backed settles and scrubbed pine tables on oak boards, some interesting old prints, winter fire; Mon quiz board games, children (away from bar) and dogs welcome, plastic glasses for outside, open (and food) all day. *(Martin and Sue Neville)*

Fox & Grapes (020) 8619 1300
Camp Road; SW19 4UN Popular 18th-c dining pub by Wimbledon Common; modern bistro feel but keeping some original features in the two linked areas (step between), enjoyable food from short but varied menu (not particularly cheap and they add a service charge), view into kitchen from high-ceilinged upper room with its unusual chandeliers, well chosen wines by the glass, Sambrooks Wandle and a guest from central servery, pleasant relaxed atmosphere; children and dogs welcome, three bedrooms, open all day, food all day Sun. *(Robert and Diana Ringstone)*

Hand in Hand (020) 8946 5720
Crooked Billet; SW19 4RQ Friendly Youngs local on edge of Wimbledon Common, their ales and guests kept well, enjoyable home-made pubby food, several areas off central bar with leather armchairs, sofas and built in wall seats, bookshelves, photos and prints on papered walls, stubby candles and a log fire; front courtyard, benches out by common, open all day. *(Max Simons)*

Sultan (020) 8544 9323
Norman Road; SW19 1BN Popular red-brick 1950s drinkers' pub owned by Hop Back and hidden in a tangle of suburban roads; their well kept ales plus a guest, some snacky food, friendly staff and locals, big scrubbed tables, darts in public bar; nice walled beer garden with summer barbecues, open all day. *(Darrell Barton)*

WEST LONDON

SW6

★**Atlas** (020) 7385 9129
Seagrave Road; SW6 1RX Busy ivy-clad pub with long simple bar, plenty of panelling and dark wall benches, mix of old tables and chairs on bare boards, brick fireplaces, good italian-influenced food (all day Sun), four well kept ales, plenty of wines by the glass and decent coffee, friendly service; background music, summer quiz Tues; children (till 7pm) and dogs welcome, attractively planted side terrace, open all day weekends, closed Mon lunchtime. *(Alister and Margery Bacon)*

Eight Bells (020) 7736 6307
Fulham High Street/Ranelagh Gardens; SW6 3JS Friendly traditional local tucked away near Putney Bridge, Fullers London Pride, Sharps Doom Bar and a guest, good value standard pub menu; sports TV; dogs welcome, seats outside under awning, close to Bishop's Park, open all day and busy with away supporters on Fulham match days. *(Susan and John Douglas)*

Harwood Arms (020) 7386 1847
Walham Grove; SW6 1QP Popular bare-boards Fulham restaurant-pub (Michelin-starred) with top notch food including set menu choices (not cheap), a couple of well kept changing ales and extensive wine list, opened-up informal bare-boards interior with all tables set for dining, stools at bar for drinkers; credit card required for booking with penalty for late or no show; closed Mon lunchtime, otherwise open all day. *(Susan and John Douglas)*

Malt House (020) 7084 6888
Vanston Place; SW6 1AY Large updated Fulham pub dating from the 18th c; U-shaped bar with high ceilings and big windows, green leather button-back wall seats and dark wooden dining chairs around mix of tables, groups of sofas and armchairs on wood or tiled floors, pictures on panelled walls, Brakspears, Marstons and a guest, nice wines by the glass and 11 malt whiskies, good varied choice of well liked food, helpful staff; children and dogs welcome, small paved back garden with candy-striped benches, pretty hanging baskets, fairy lights and candle-lit lanterns, comfortable airy bedrooms, open (and food) all day including breakfasts for non-residents. *(Susan Eccleston, Sally and David Champion, Geoff and Ann Marston)*

White Horse (020) 7736 2115
Parsons Green; SW6 4UL Busy pub with modernised U-shaped bar, huge windows with slatted blinds, leather chesterfields and wooden tables on bare boards, winter fires (one in elegant marble fireplace), upstairs dining room (own bar), enjoyable food from short but varied menu, Harveys Best, Oakham JHB and several guests, eight craft kegs, Trappist beers and around 135 other foreign bottled beers, 20 wines by the glass too; three annual beer festivals; children and dogs welcome, plenty of tables on front terrace overlooking Parsons Green, open (and food) all day from 9.30am for breakfast. *(Edward May, Jim and Sue James, Jeff Davies)*

SW7

★**Anglesea Arms** (020) 7373 7960
Selwood Terrace; SW7 3QG Very busy 19th-c pub, well run and friendly, with mix of cast-iron tables on wood-strip floor, central elbow tables, panelling and heavy portraits, large brass chandeliers hanging from dark ceilings, big windows and swagged curtains, several booths at one end with partly glazed screens, Greene King Abbott, IPA and four guests, around 20 malt whiskies and 15 wines by the glass, interesting bar food, steps down to dining room; children welcome, dogs in bar, heated front terrace, open all day. *(Max Simons)*

Queens Arms (020) 7823 9293
Queens Gate Mews; SW7 5QL Popular Victorian corner pub with open-plan bare-boards bar, generous helpings of enjoyable good value home-made food, decent wines by the glass and good selection of beers including Fullers and Sharps, friendly helpful service; TV; children welcome, disabled facilities, handy for Royal Albert Hall, open all day. *(Caroline Prescott)*

SW10

Chelsea Ram (020) 7351 4008
Burnaby Street; SW10 0PL Corner Geronimo Inn tucked away in residential streets; modern interior with broad mix of furniture on bare boards or stripy carpet, shelves of books and lots of pictures, tiled Victorian fireplace, Youngs ales and guests, good food including daily specials and popular Sun roasts, friendly service; some pavement seating, open (and food) all day. *(Adam Jones)*

W4

★**Bell & Crown** (020) 8994 4164
Strand on the Green; W4 3PF Fullers local with great Thames views from back bar and conservatory, interesting food and good friendly staff, panelling and log fire, lots of atmosphere and can get very busy weekends; dogs welcome, terrace and towpath area, good walks, open (and food) all day. *(Martin and Sue Neville)*

Bulls Head (020) 8994 1204
Strand on the Green; W4 3PQ Cleanly updated old Thames-side pub (said to have served as Cromwell's HQ during the Civil War), seats by windows overlooking the water in beamed rooms, steps up and down, Greene King IPA and London Glory along with four guests, several wines by

the glass and decent pubby food served by friendly staff; background music; children and dogs (in bar) welcome, seats out by river, pretty hanging baskets, open (and food) all day. *(Susan and John Douglas)*

City Barge (020) 8994 2148

Strand on the Green; W4 3PH Attractively furnished old riverside pub; light modern split-level interior keeping a few original features such as Victorian panelling and open fires, good choice of ales/craft beers and wines by the glass (prosecco on tap), interesting food from open kitchen including good fish choice; background music; children and dogs welcome, waterside picnic-sets facing Oliver's Island, deck chairs on grass and more formal terrace, open all day. *(Miles Green)*

★ Duke of Sussex (020) 8742 8801

South Parade; W4 5LF Big bonus for this attractively restored Victorian local is the excellent back garden with tables under parasols, nicely laid out plants and carefully positioned lighting and heaters; classy simply furnished bar with huge windows overlooking Acton Green, chapel and farmhouse chairs around scrubbed pine and dark wood tables, original etched glass, large horseshoe counter serving four real ales including a house beer from Greene King, 30 wines by the glass and 15 malt whiskies, good imaginative modern food, parquet-floored dining room with booth seating and a splendid skylight framed by colourfully painted cherubs; children and dogs (in bar) welcome, open (and food) all day. *(Ben and Diane Bowie, Sophia and Hamish Greenfield, Philip J Alderton)*

Roebuck (020) 8995 4392

Chiswick High Road; W4 1PU Popular relaxed Victorian dining pub with bare boards and high ceilings, front bar and roomy back dining area opening on to delightful paved garden, enjoyable well presented food (all day weekends) from open kitchen, daily changing menu, four real ales and good choice of wines by the glass; dogs welcome, open all day. *(Simon Rodway)*

Swan (020) 8994 8262

Evershed Walk, Acton Lane; W4 5HH Cosy 19th-c local with good mix of customers and convivial atmosphere, well liked interesting food along with more pubby choices, friendly staff, a dozen or so wines by the glass, St Austell, Sambrook and Twickenham, two bars with wood floors and panelling, leather chesterfields by open fire; dogs very welcome, children till 7.30pm, picnic-sets on good spacious terrace, open (and food) all day weekends, from 5pm other days. *(Trevor and Michele Street)*

Tabard (020) 8994 3492

Bath Road; W4 1LW Roomy Chiswick pub built in 1880, pleasant chatty atmosphere,

up to ten changing ales, decent choice of wines and all-day pubby food, friendly efficient staff, arts and crafts interior with lots of nooks and corners, period mirrors and high frieze of William de Morgan tiles; fringe theatre upstairs, free wi-fi; well behaved children and dogs welcome, disabled access, terrace tables by busy road, open all day. *(Jim and Sue James)*

W6

Anglesea Arms (020) 8749 1291

Wingate Road; W6 0UR Bustling Victorian corner pub with four changing ales and good range of wines by the glass, bare-boards panelled bar with open fire, generally well liked food from short but interesting menu (not Mon-Thurs lunchtimes), close-set tables in sky lit bare-brick dining room; children and dogs welcome, tables out by quiet street, open all day Fri-Sun, closed Mon lunchtime. *(Darrell Barton)*

Blue Anchor (020) 8748 5774

Lower Mall; W6 9DJ Right on the Thames a short walk from Hammersmith Bridge; two traditional linked areas with oak floors and panelling, mirrors one end with oars above, a house beer brewed by Nelsons and three well kept guests, enjoyable food from light meals up (all day weekends), pleasant river-view dining room upstairs with balcony; TV; disabled facilities, waterside pavement tables, open all day. *(Sam Cole)*

Hampshire Hog (020) 8748 3391

King Street; W6 9JT Spacious Hammersmith pub with light airy interior, plenty of emphasis on food from interesting if not extensive menu, good choice of wines including 50cl carafes, cocktails, prices can be high; background music; nice big garden with some seats under cover, closed Sun evening, otherwise open (and food) all day from 10am for breakfast/brunch. *(Simon Rodway)*

Latymers (020) 8748 3446

Hammersmith Road; W6 7JP Big popular bar with mirrored ceiling in 1980s corner building, well kept Fullers ales and good reasonably priced thai food, friendly staff, spacious back restaurant; free wi-fi; children and dogs welcome, pavement seating, open all day. *(Susan and John Douglas)*

Pear Tree (020) 7381 1787

Margravine Road; W6 8HJ Arts and crafts building (plenty of original features) tucked away behind Charing Cross Hospital; cleanly kept cosily lived-in interior with heavy curtains, drapes on doors and cushions on well worn seating, soft lighting and candlelight, fresh flowers and crisp white evening tablecloths, open fires, good modern pub food from bar snacks up, well kept mainstream ales and good range of wines by the glass, efficient service; background music; dogs welcome, seats in small garden, open (and food) all day Fri-Sun, closed Mon-Thurs lunchtimes. *(Susan and John Douglas)*

Queens Head (020) 7603 3174
Brook Green; W6 7BL Spacious refurbished Fullers pub dating from the early 19th c, cosy linked areas with beams and open fire, good menu from lunchtime sandwiches and bar snacks up, four well kept ales, craft beers and nice wines by the glass; Mon quiz; children and dogs welcome, big garden behind, open (and food) all day. *(Diana and Bertie Farr)*

W7

Fox (020) 8567 4021
Green Lane; W7 2PJ Friendly open-plan 19th-c local in quiet cul-de-sac near Grand Union Canal, several real ales including Fullers, Sharps and Timothy Taylors, craft beers and decent wines by the glass, popular well priced food, panelling and stained glass, farm tools hanging from ceiling; quiz Thurs; children and dogs welcome, Tea Barn in garden serving cakes, teas and coffees, food/crafts market last Sat of month, towpath walks, open all day. *(Susan Eccleston)*

W8

Britannia (020) 7937 6905
Allen Street, off Kensington High Street; W8 6UX Smartly presented Youngs pub with spacious front bar, pastel green walls contrasting dark panelling, patterned rugs on bare boards, banquettes, leather tub chairs and sofas, steps down to back area with wall-sized photo-print of the demolished Britannia Brewery, dining conservatory beyond, good freshly prepared food including pub staples, spiral staircase up to overflow/function room; background music, Tues quiz, sports TV; children welcome, wheelchair access (side passage to back part), open (and food) all day. *(Simon and Mandy King)*

★**Churchill Arms** (020) 7727 4242
Kensington Church Street; W8 7LN Character long-serving irish landlord at this bustling welcoming old pub, eclectic interior dense with bric-a-brac, countless lamps, miners' lights, horse tack, bedpans and brasses hanging from ceiling, prints of american presidents and lots of Churchill memorabilia, a couple of interesting carved figures and statuettes behind central counter, well kept Fullers ales, 18 wines by the glass and good value thai food, spacious rather smart plant-filled dining conservatory; free wi-fi; children and dogs welcome, some chrome tables and chairs outside, stunning display of window boxes and hanging baskets, open (and food) all day. *(Tony Scott)*

Scarsdale (020) 7937 1811
Edwardes Square; W8 6HE Popular easy-going Georgian pub in leafy square, scrubbed pine tables, simple cushioned dining chairs,

pews and built-in wall seats on bare boards, oil paintings in fancy gilt frames and old local photographs, heavily swagged curtains, coal-effect gas fires, Adnams, Fullers and a guest, 16 wines by the glass and a dozen malt whiskies, well liked food; free wi-fi; children (in dining area) and dogs welcome, seats and tables under parasols on attractive front terrace, open (and food) all day. *(Tony Scott)*

W9

Prince Alfred (020) 7286 3287
Formosa Street; W9 1EE Well preserved ornate Victorian corner pub with wonderful etched-glass frontage, five separate bar areas (lots of mahogany) arranged around central servery, snob screens and duck-through doors, Youngs ales, guest beers and good choice of wines by the glass, enjoyable food including some imaginative choices in airy modern dining room with large centre skylight, cellar function rooms; background music; open (and food) all day. *(Giles and Annie Francis)*

Warwick Castle (020) 7266 0921
Warwick Place; W9 2PX Popular character pub in narrow street near Little Venice; open-fronted with a few pavement tables, comfortable Victorian-feel rooms, real ales including Greene King IPA, wide choice of food from sandwiches and pub standards up (all day Fri-Sun); quiz night Weds; dogs welcome, open all day. *(Susan Eccleston)*

W10

Eagle (020) 3757 8051
Ladbroke Grove/Telford Road; W10 5LP Stylishly refurbished Victorian corner pub (Hippo Inns) arranged over two floors, numerous beers including Trumans Raw lager dispensed from copper tanks above island servery, good selection of other drinks and highly rated food from snacks up including some bavarian influences, Sat brunch from 10am, friendly knowledgeable aproned staff; Tues quiz, Fri live music; children and dogs welcome, pavement tables under awning, open (and food) all day. *(Miles Green)*

W12

Oak (020) 8741 7700
Goldhawk Road; W12 8EU Large refurbished Victorian pub serving interesting mediterranean-influenced food including speciality wood-fired pizzas, good range of beers and wine, friendly staff; open all day weekends, from 6pm other days. *(Simon Rodway)*

W13

Duke of Kent (020) 8991 7820
Scotch Common; W13 8DL Large Ealing pub built in 1929 (Grade II listed) with warren of interesting linked areas, mix of old and new furniture on wood floors, panelling and coal fires, several Fullers ales and guests, good food from pub standards

up, friendly staff; live music Sun evening, free wi-fi; children and dogs welcome, steps down to big garden with partly covered terrace, picnic-sets and play area, open (and food) all day. *(Susan and John Douglas)*

W14 TQ2477

⋆**Colton Arms** (020) 3757 8050
Greyhound Road; W14 9SD Cosy pub next to the Queen's Club tennis courts revamped by new owners (Hippo Inns); small front Dot's Bar (named after former long-serving landlady) with handsomely carved high-backed oak bench, bare boards, painted panelling and log fire, real ales such as Fullers and over 20 wines by the glass from copper-topped servery, extended skylit back dining area serving good variety of enjoyable food from snacks up, friendly young staff, some quirky touches including colourful stuffed birds in cages, other taxidermy and eclectic range of artwork; background music; little back terrace, open (and food) all day. *(Robert and Diana Ringstone)*

Crown & Sceptre (020) 7603 2007
Holland Road; W14 8BA Civilised Victorian corner pub with light airy interior; sofas, antique-style dining chairs and leather cube stools around wooden tables, rugs on bare boards, gas fire, Caledonian Golden XPA, Courage Directors and a guest, plenty of wines by the glass and extensive range of whiskies and gins, enjoyable food including pub favourites and range of burgers, friendly service, cosy cellar bar with banquettes, candles in bottles and big prints on rough wood walls; background music, TV, board games; children and dogs (in bar) welcome, pavement tables, comfortable bedrooms, handy for Olympia exhibition centre and Design Museum, open all day from 7.30am. *(Edward May, Neil)*

⋆**Havelock Tavern** (020) 7603 5374
Masbro Road; W14 0LS Busy 19th-c corner dining pub with blue-tiled frontage, light airy L-shaped bar with plain unfussy décor, second smaller room behind, Sambrooks Wandle, Sharps Doom Bar and guests, wide choice of interesting wines by the glass, good imaginative food from short changing menu, friendly efficient service; free wi-fi; children and dogs welcome, picnic-sets on small paved terrace, open all day. *(Michael Robinson)*

OUTER LONDON

BARNET EN5 TQ2496

Black Horse (020) 8449 2230
Wood Street/Union Street; EN5 4HY Attractively updated 19th-c pub with eight real ales including own Barnet beers from back microbrewery, good range of food (all day weekends); children and dogs (in bar) welcome, terrace seating, open all day. *(Trevor and Michele Street)*

Gate (020) 8449 7292
Barnet Road (A411, near Hendon Wood Lane); EN5 3LA Modernised country pub feel with comfortably opened-up areas, beams and log fires, good choice of enjoyable brasserie-style food from lunchtime sandwiches/ciabattas up, well kept Greene King, Sharps and a guest, friendly staff and atmosphere; children welcome, open (and food) all day. *(Sanjeev)*

BECKENHAM BR3 TQ3769

George (020) 8663 3468
High Street; BR3 1AG Busy weatherboarded pub with half a dozen real ales and enjoyable food from sandwiches to grills, efficient staff; regular quiz nights; children welcome, side garden with terrace, open all day. *(Sparky)*

Jolly Woodman (020) 8663 1031
Chancery Lane; BR3 6NR Welcoming old-fashioned local in conservation area, cosy L-shaped bar with woodburner, five or so well kept ales such as Harveys Best and Timothy Taylors Landlord, good choice of whiskies, reasonably priced home-made food (weekday lunchtimes only) including sandwiches; children in back bar only; dogs welcome, pavement tables and sunny flower-filled courtyard, open all day (from 4pm Mon). *(Laura Reed, Sparky)*

BEXLEY DA5 TQ4973

Kings Head (01322) 553137
Bexley High Street; DA5 1AA Dating from 14th c, linked rooms with low beams and brasses, traditional furniture, open fires, well kept Greene King ales and tasty pub food including all-day breakfast, friendly staff; jazz Mon evening; open all day. *(Ben and Jenny Settle)*

BEXLEYHEATH DA6 TQ4875

Robin Hood & Little John
(020) 8303 1128 *Lion Road; DA6 8PF* Small 19th-c family-run local in residential area, welcoming and spotless, with eight well kept ales such as Adnams, Bexley, Fullers and Harveys, popular bargain pubby lunchtime food (not Sun); seats out at front and in back garden. *(Nik and Gloria Clarke)*

BROMLEY BR1 TQ4069

Red Lion (020) 8460 2691
North Road; BR1 3LG Chatty backstreet local in conservation area, traditional dimly lit interior with wood floor, tiling, green velvet drapes and shelves of books, well kept Greene King, Harveys and guests, lunchtime food, good friendly service; tables out in front, open all day. *(Jamie Davies)*

BROMLEY BR2 TQ4265

Two Doves (020) 8462 1627
Oakley Road (A233); BR2 8HD Popular Victorian local, comfortable and

unpretentious, with cheerful staff and regulars, well kept Wells, Youngs and a guest, snacky lunchtime food such as rolls and baked potatoes, modern back conservatory and lovely garden; open all day Fri-Sun. *(Julian and Fiona Barnes)*

CHELSFIELD BR6   TQ4864
Five Bells   (01689) 821044
Church Road; just off A224 Orpington bypass; BR6 7RE Chatty 17th-c white weatherboarded village local, two separate bars and dining area, inglenook fireplace, well kept Courage, Harveys and a couple of guests, reasonably priced food from lunchtime sandwiches up, evening meals Thurs-Sat only, Sun breakfast 9-11am; live music including jazz and open mike nights, Tues quiz, sports TV; children welcome, picnic-sets among flowers out in front, open all day. *(Mary Joyce)*

CHISLEHURST BR7   TQ4469
Crown   (020) 8467 7326
School Road; BR7 5PQ Imposing Victorian pub overlooking common, simple attractive interior with flagstoned bar and several dining areas, well kept Shepherd Neame ales and good quality food from sandwiches and traditional choices up, friendly helpful service; events including open mike night first Tues of month; children welcome, terrace tables, pétanque, seven bedrooms, open all day. *(David Jackman, B and M Kendall)*

EASTCOTE HA5   TQ1089
Case is Altered   (020) 8866 0476
High Road/Southill Lane; HA5 2EW Attractive recently refurbished 17th-c pub in quiet setting adjacent to cricket ground; main bar, flagstoned snug and barn seating/dining area, Rebellion, Oakham, West Berkshire and a couple of guests, draught and bottled craft beers, lots of wines by the glass (can be pricey) and good range of other drinks, enjoyable food from sandwiches and snacks to charcoal grills from open kitchen, friendly staff; background music, weekly quiz, free wi-fi; children and dogs welcome, nice front garden with outside bar (very popular in fine weather), handy for Eastcote House Gardens, open (and food) all day. *(Maureen Eaton)*

GREENFORD UB6   TQ1382
Black Horse   (020) 8578 1384
Oldfield Lane; UB6 OAS Spacious canalside pub on two levels, well kept Fullers ales, a dozen wines by the glass and decent choice of enjoyable reasonably priced food from sandwiches and snacks up, efficient friendly service; weekend live music, sports TV, darts and machines; children and dogs welcome, balcony

tables overlooking Grand Union Canal and big garden fenced from towpath, open all day, food all day Fri-Sun. *(Tony Hobden)*

HAMPTON TW12   TQ1469
Jolly Coopers   (020) 8979 3384
High Street; TW12 2SJ Friendly end of terrace Georgian local with four or five well kept ales and good choice of wines, well liked freshly cooked food in back restaurant extension including good evening tapas and Sun lunch till 5pm; pretty terrace with climbing plants and summer barbecues, open all day. *(Trevor and Michele Street)*

HAMPTON COURT KT8   TQ1668
★ Kings Arms   (020) 8977 1729
Hampton Court Road, by Lion Gate; KT8 9DD Civilised and well run pub by Hampton Court itself (so can get busy with tourists), comfortable furnishings including sofas in back area, open fires, lots of oak panelling, beams and some stained glass, well kept Badger beers and good choice of wines by the glass, friendly service, enjoyable food from sandwiches up, restaurant too; background music, free wi-fi; children and dogs welcome, picnic-sets on roadside front terrace, limited parking, 12 bedrooms, open all day, food all day weekends. *(Peter Brix)*

HARROW HA1   TQ1587
Castle   (020) 8422 3155
West Street; HA1 3EF Edwardian Fullers pub in picturesque part (steps up from street), their ales and guests kept well, decent food from lunchtime sandwiches up including Thurs burger night and weekend brunch, several rooms around central servery, open fires, rugs on bare boards and lots of panelling, collection of clocks in cheery front bar, more sedate back lounge; children welcome, nice garden behind with rattan furniture, open (and food) all day. *(Aiden Nunn)*

ISLEWORTH TW7   TQ1675
London Apprentice   (020) 8560 1915
Church Street; TW7 6BG Large Thames-side Taylor Walker pub, reasonably priced food from sandwiches up – may be a wait, well kept ales and good wine choice, log fire, pleasant service, upstairs river-view restaurant; weekly music quiz; children welcome, attractive riverside terrace with tables under parasols, open all day. *(Georgie)*

KINGSTON KT2   TQ1869
Boaters   (020) 8541 4672
Canbury Gardens (park in Lower Ham Road if you can); KT2 5AU Family-friendly pub by the Thames in small park, good selection of beers such as Bedlam, BrewDog, Hogs Back, Sambrooks and Trumans, decent wines and varied choice of

---

Half pints: by law, a pub should not charge more for half a pint than half the price of a full pint, unless it shows that half-pint price on its price list.

enjoyable food from changing menu (service charge added), comfortable banquettes in split-level wood-floored bar; Sun evening jazz, quiz nights; riverside terrace and balcony, parking nearby can be difficult, open (and food) all day. *(Sam Cole)*

Canbury Arms (020) 8255 9129
Canbury Park Road; KT2 6LQ Popular open-plan Victorian corner pub with simple contemporary décor, bare boards, big windows and high ceilings, open fire, relaxed friendly atmosphere, well regarded up-to-date food along with pub favourites and good Sun roasts, pleasant young staff, five well kept ales including Harveys, Park (brewed nearby) and Timothy Taylors Landlord, nice choice of wines, side conservatory; regular events such as quiz and music nights, wine tasting and camera club; children and dogs welcome, picnic-sets out behind metal fence, open all day (till 8pm Sun). *(David and Sally Frost, Garry Galvin)*

Queens Head (020) 8546 9162
Richmond Road/Windoor Road; KT2 5ILA Large recently refurbished red-brick Fullers pub; modern interior arranged around traditional wooden servery (rescued from another London pub), four real ales and good variety of enjoyable all-day food from snacks up, helpful young staff; background music, free wi-fi; children welcome, part-covered front deck, paved back terrace with wooden planters and cabins, play area, ten bedrooms, open all day from 9am. *(David and Sally Frost)*

ORPINGTON BR6   TQ4963
★**Bo-Peep** (01959) 534457
Hewitts Road, Chelsfield; 1.7 miles from M25 junction 4; BR6 7QL Useful M25 country-feel dining pub, old low beams and enormous inglenook in carpeted bar, two cosy candlelit dining rooms, airy side room overlooking lane and fields, well kept Sharps Doom Bar, a changing beer from Westerham and a guest, cheerful efficient staff, good helpings of enjoyable food (all day Sat, not Sun evening) from traditional choices up and weekend afternoon tea; background music; children welcome, dogs in bar, picnic-sets on big brick terrace, open all day. *(David Jackman)*

RICHMOND UPON THAMES TW9   TQ1874
Mitre (020) 8940 1336
Just off the Upper Richmond Road; TW9 1UY Refurbished Victorian local with ten changing ales and four draught ciders/perries (tasters offered), some simple food such as toasties and ploughman's, friendly staff and pub dog (others welcome), bare boards, leaded windows and woodburner; music nights; seats on small front terrace, open all day weekends, from 3pm other days. *(Buster and Helena Hastings)*

Princes Head (020) 8940 1572
The Green; TW9 1LX Spacious open-plan pub overlooking cricket green, clean and well run, with low-ceilinged panelled areas off island servery, well kept Fullers ales, popular sensibly priced pub food from sandwiches up, friendly young staff and chatty locals, coal-effect fire; background music, TV and daily papers; children allowed in certain areas, circular picnic-sets outside, handy for Richmond Theatre, open (and food) all day. *(Peter Brix)*

Watermans Arms (020) 8940 2893
Water Lane; TW9 1TJ Friendly old-fashioned Youngs local with their well kept ales and a couple of guests from Twickenham, enjoyable thai food plus some standard english dishes, traditional layout with open fire, upstairs restaurant; handy for the river. *(Brian and Anna Marsden, Tony and Wendy Hobden)*

★**White Cross** (020) 8940 6844
Water Lane; TW9 1TH Lovely garden with terrific Thames views, seats on paved area, outside bar and boats to Kingston and Hampton Court; two chatty main rooms with local prints and photographs, three log fires (one unusually below a window), well kept Youngs and guests from old-fashioned island servery, a dozen wines by the glass and enjoyable fairly pubby food from 10am brunch on, also bright and airy upstairs room (children welcome here till 6pm) with pretty cast-iron balcony for splendid river view; background music, TV; dogs allowed, tides can reach the pub entrance (wellies provided), open (and food) all day. *(Michael Massey)*

White Swan (020) 8940 0959
Old Palace Lane; TW9 1PG Small 18th-c cottagey pub, civilised and relaxed, with rustic dark-beamed open-plan bar, well kept Otter, St Austell, Sharps and Timothy Taylors, enjoyable food, coal-effect fires, back dining conservatory and upstairs restaurant; soft background music; children (till 6.30pm) and dogs welcome, some seats on narrow paved area at front, more in pretty walled back terrace below railway, open all day. *(Sally and David Champion)*

RICHMOND UPON THAMES TW10   TQ1874
White Horse (020) 8940 2418
Worple Way, off Sheen Road; TW10 6DF Large open-plan Fullers pub, their ales and good choice of wines from long aluminium counter, airy interior with pastel shades, exposed brickwork and mix of old and new furniture on bare boards including some easy chairs, enjoyable food from traditional favourites up, friendly helpful service; free wi-fi; children welcome (playground next door), two-level back terrace, open (and food) all day. *(Margaret McDonald)*

ROMFORD RM1   TQ5188
Golden Lion   (01708) 740081
High Street; RM1 1HR Busy former
coaching inn (one of the town's oldest
buildings) with spacious beamed
interior, four or five well kept ales, food
including sharing platters, burgers
and chicken buckets, friendly staff
and good mix of customers; weekend
live music, sports TV, free wi-fi; open
(and food) all day. *(Sandra Hollis)*

ROMFORD RM2   TQ5188
Ship   (01708) 741571
Main Road; RM2 5EL Friendly
18th-c black and white pub, low beams,
panelling and woodburner in fine brick
fireplace, Adnams, Courage, Sharps,
Timothy Taylors and guests, enjoyable
good value food (not weekend evenings)
from sandwiches and sharing boards up;
live weekend music; children and dogs
welcome, picnic-sets in back garden under
parasols, open all day. *(Robert Lester)*

SURBITON KT6   TQ1767
Antelope   (020) 8399 5565
Maple Road; KT6 4AW Double-fronted
Victorian pub with civilised properly pubby
atmosphere, excellent range of real ales
and craft kegs including own Big Smoke
unfined beers from on-site microbrewery,
several ciders too, friendly knowledgeable
staff, split-level bare-boards interior with
mix of comfortable seating including some
button-back banquettes, grey-painted
and tiled walls, lots of pump clips, open
fire, tasty food including range of burgers;
background music from vinyl collection,
board games; dogs welcome, paved back
terrace, open all day. *(Rob Unsworth)*

TEDDINGTON TW11   TQ1671
Kings Head   (020) 3166 2900
High Street; TW11 8HG Comfortably
updated bare-boards front bar with easy
chairs and button-back wall benches,
modern artwork and photographs on vibrant
coloured walls, woodburners, Fullers London
Pride, Meantime London Pale Ale and

Sharps Doom Bar, lots of wines by the glass
including champagne, well separated back
dining part with similar décor and open
kitchen, enjoyable interesting food including
good value set menu till 6.30pm (not Sun),
courteous helpful service; background
music; children and dogs welcome, seats
out at front and on enclosed back terrace,
open (and food) all day. *(Robert W Buckle)*

TWICKENHAM TW1
★ Crown   (020) 8892 5896
Richmond Road, St Margarets; TW1 2NH
Popular Georgian pub with emphasis on
good food from sandwiches and sharing
plates to restaurant choices, several large
dining areas including splendid Victorian
back hall, also well kept ales, nice wines
by the glass and good coffee, friendly
efficient staff, open fire; newspapers and
free wi-fi; children welcome, picnic-sets in
sunny courtyard garden, open (and food)
all day. *(Taff Thomas, David and Sally Frost)*

White Swan   (020) 8892 2166
Riverside; TW1 3DN Refurbished
17th-c Thames-side pub up steep anti-
flood steps; bare-boards L-shaped bar with
cosy log fire, river views from prized bay
window with leather banquettes, Fullers,
Sharps and guests such as Twickenham,
enjoyable fairly priced food (all day Sat, Sun
till 6pm), friendly local atmosphere, board
games; live acoustic music and quiz nights;
children and dogs welcome, tranquil setting
opposite Eel Pie Island with well used
balcony and waterside terrace (liable to
flooding) across quiet lane, open all day.
(Taff Thomas)

TWICKENHAM TW2   TQ1572
Sussex Arms   (020) 8894 7468
Staines Road; TW2 5BG Traditional
bare-boards pub with 18 handpumps plus
ciders and perries from long counter,
plenty in bottles too, simple food including
good home-made pies, pizzas and burgers,
friendly staff, walls and ceilings covered
in beer mats and pump clips, open fire;
some live acoustic music; large back garden
with boules, open all day. *(Adam Jones)*

SCOTLAND

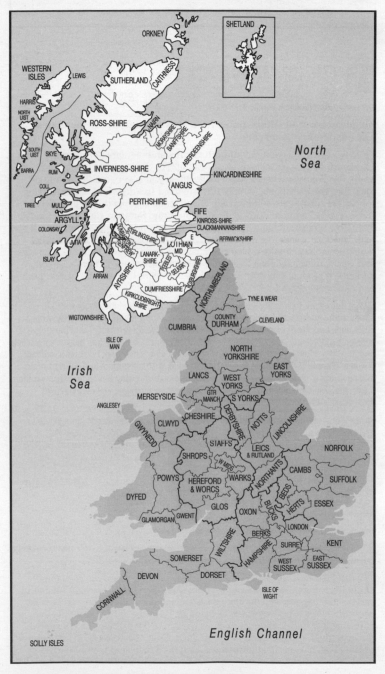

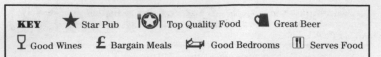

KEY ★ Star Pub 🍴 Top Quality Food 🍺 Great Beer
 ♀ Good Wines £ Bargain Meals 🛏 Good Bedrooms ▥ Serves Food

ANCRUM
NT6224 Map 10

Cross Keys 🍴 ♀

(01835) 830242 – www.ancrumcrosskeys.com

Off A68 Jedburgh–Edinburgh; TD8 6XH

Simply decorated village pub with a high reputation for local ales and particularly good food

There's always a good mix of both visitors and regulars here and the cheerful atmosphere is most appealing. The 200-year-old pub is perched above Ale Water and beside the village green and is very much the hub of local life. The easy-going, simply furnished bar has dogs and regulars vying for the fire, wall seats, minimal décor and stools against the counter where they serve Born in the Borders Foxy Blonde and Summer Cloud and Ilkley Holy Cow on handpump, a good choice of wines and a healthy number of malt whiskies; a side bar is for both drinking and eating. The blue-walled dining room has chunky tables and chairs on bare boards, an open kitchen and, again, minimal décor. Service is helpful and friendly. There's a back garden with picnic-sets and a gate that leads down to the water. A few tables and chairs are set out in front of the stone building.

 Innovative food using local and foraged ingredients includes haggis scotch egg with pancetta and creamy Drambuie sauce, tempura king prawns with sweet chilli, lime and soy dip, pumpkin tortellini with garlic and herb butter and parmesan, smoked haddock and seafood chowder with cheddar crumble, chicken burger with black pudding, blue cheese dressing, coleslaw and chips, slow-roast pork belly with cabbage, bacon and apple and rosemary sauce, rib-eye steak with mushroom and sherry cream, and puddings such as espresso and chocolate crème brûlée and lemon tart with vanilla ice-cream. *Benchmark main dish: tempura-battered haddock and chips £12.00. Two-course evening meal £19.00.*

Free house ~ Licensee John Henderson ~ Real ale ~ Open 5pm-midnight (1am Fri, Sat); 12-11 Sun; closed weekday lunchtimes ~ Bar food 5.30-9 Weds-Sun; 12-2, 5.30-9 Sat; 12-2, 5.30-8 Sun ~ Restaurant ~ Children welcome ~ Dogs allowed in bar ~ Wi-fi *Recommended by Isobel Mackinlay, Alan and Alice Morgan, Elizabeth and Peter May, Molly and Stewart Lindsay*

APPLECROSS
NG7144 Map 11

Applecross Inn ★ 🛏

(01520) 744262 – www.applecross.uk.com

Off A896 S of Shieldaig; IV54 8LR

Isolated pub on famously scenic route on west coast, with particularly friendly welcome, real ales and good seafood; bedrooms

Judith Fish welcomes customers from all over the world into her remote but lively pub – as one of our readers said, 'the conversation in the bar in various languages is fascinating'; it's a special place. The exhilarating west coast drive to get here over the Bealach na Bà (Pass of the Cattle), is one of the highest in Britain and not to be tried in bad weather. The alternative route, along the single-track lane winding around the coast from just south of Shieldaig, has equally glorious sea loch (and then sea) views nearly all the way. Once reached, the no-nonsense, welcoming bar has a woodburning stove, exposed stone walls, upholstered pine furnishings and a stone floor; An Teallach Crofters Pale Ale and Isle of Skye Red on handpump, more than 50 malt whiskies and a good, varied wine list; board games. The tables in the shoreside garden enjoy magnificent views and there's now an outdoor eating area for summer use. If you wish to stay here, you'll have to book months ahead. Some disabled facilities.

The first class fresh local fish and seafood includes squat lobsters, oysters, fresh haddock, langoustines, a seafood platter, king scallops and dressed crab with smoked salmon – but they also offer local haggis flambéed in Drambuie topped with cream, gammon and egg, thai green chicken curry, venison burger with chips, duck breast in soy and honey marinade, sirloin steak with peppercorn sauce, and puddings such as a seasonal crumble and sticky toffee pudding. *Benchmark main dish: fresh local langoustines £22.00. Two-course evening meal £25.00.*

Free house ~ Licensee Judith Fish ~ Real ale ~ Open 11am-11.30pm (midnight Sat); 12.30-11.30 Sun ~ Bar food 12-9 ~ Children welcome till 8.30pm ~ Dogs welcome ~ Wi-fi ~ Live music first Sun of month 3-6pm ~ Bedrooms: £90/£140 *Recommended by Barry Collett, Roy and Gill Payne, Neil and Angela Huxter, Mandy and Gary Redstone*

DALKEITH
NR3264 Map 11

Sun 🏠🍽️ 🍷 🛏️

(0131) 663 2456 – www.thesuninnedinburgh.co.uk
A7 S; EH22 4TR

Family-run inn with charming bar and restaurant, open fires, leafy garden, local ale and delicious food; comfortable, airy bedrooms

This is the perfect retreat from a day in the city – Edinburgh is a mere 20 minutes away – but surrounded by five acres of wooded grounds and close to the River Esk, you'd never believe it. The bars have been carefully renovated with walls stripped back to the original stone (or with hunting-theme wallpaper), bare floorboards and refurbished fireplaces. There are cushioned built-in settles, all sorts of wooden dining chairs around an appealing collection of tables, gilt-edged mirrors and high stools against the counter where friendly staff serve Inveralmond Lia Fail and Stewart Pentland IPA on handpump and good wines by the glass; background music. Seats on the covered courtyard overlook the garden where they hold popular summer barbecues. Bedrooms are thoughtfully equipped and comfortable and breakfasts highly rated.

As well as breakfasts (8.30-10.30am), the excellent food is cooked by the landlord and his son: korean-style lamb chop with watermelon, feta and toasted peanut salad, lobster tempura with pineapple and mango salsa, soft shell crab tacos and lobster mayonnaise, chestnut mushroom and cheese pasta, roasted pork sausages with mustard seed mash, gravy and crispy onion rings, duck breast and leg croquettes with bacon and pea fricassée, lamb rump with potato rösti, goats curd and wild garlic pesto, hake with rarebit topping, pea and bacon cream and sauté potatoes, and puddings such as triple chocolate brownie with chocolate sauce and apple crumble tart. *Benchmark main dish: pork fillet, belly and cheek with red wine jus and apple purée £18.00. Two-course evening meal £22.00.*

Free house ~ Licensee Bernadette McCarron ~ Real ale ~ Open 12-11 (midnight Sat) ~ Bar food 12-2, 6-9; 12-7 Sun ~ Children welcome ~ Wi-fi ~ Live monthly tribute evenings ~ Bedrooms: £75/£95 *Recommended by Laura Reid, Jeff Davies, Lance and Sarah Milligan, Molly and Stewart Lindsay*

EDINBURGH   NT2574   Map 11

Bow Bar ◀

(0131) 226 7667

West Bow; EH1 2HH

Cosy, enjoyably unpretentious pub with an excellent choice of well kept beers

This is a cheerfully traditional alehouse and a haven of old-fashioned drinking with a splendid range of real ales served by knowledgeable staff. The rectangular bar has an impressive carved mahogany gantry and from the tall 1920s founts on the bar counter, eight well kept real ales are dispensed: regulars such as Fallen Odyssey, Tempest Cascadian Blonde and Stewart 80/- and five quickly changing guests from breweries such as Cloudwater, Cromarty, Swannay and Wild Beer; regular beer festivals. Also on offer are some 370 malts, including five 'malts of the moment', a good choice of rums, 60 international bottled beers and 20 gins. The walls are decorated with a fine collection of enamel advertising signs and handsome antique brewery mirrors, and there are sturdy leatherette wall seats and café-style bar seats around heavy narrow tables on the wooden floor. No children allowed.

Lunchtime-only food is limited to pies.

Free house ~ Licensee Mike Smith ~ Real ale ~ Open 12-midnight; 12.30-11.30 Sun ~ Bar food 12-3; 12.30-3 Sun ~ Dogs welcome ~ Wi-fi *Recommended by Roger and Donna Huggins, Sarah and David Gibbs, Nicola and Holly Lyons, Jane Rigby*

EDINBURGH   NT2574   Map 11

Guildford Arms ◀ £

(0131) 556 4312 – www.guildfordarms.com

West Register Street; EH2 2AA

Busy and friendly with spectacular Victorian décor, a marvellous range of real ales and good food

The splendid Victorian décor is the chief glory here. Opulently excessive, this features ornate painted plasterwork on lofty ceilings, dark mahogany fittings, heavy swagged velvet curtains and a busy patterned carpet. Tables and stools are lined up along towering arched windows opposite the bar, where knowledgeable, efficient staff might offer a taste of the ten, quickly changing ales before you choose what you want; beers come from breweries such as Belhaven, Fallen, Fyne Ales, Oakham, Orkney, Mordue, Speyside Craft, Stewart, Swannay and Wells. Also, ten wines by the glass, 50 malt whiskies and a dozen rums and a dozen gins; TV and background music. The snug upstairs gallery restaurant, with contrasting modern décor, gives a fine dress-circle view of the main bar.

Tasty food includes sandwiches, fish chowder, crab and mackerel pâté, vegetable wellington, minted lamb cutlets, haggis-stuffed chicken breast, rib-eye steak with chips and a choice of sauce, and puddings such as bread and butter and sticky toffee puddings. *Benchmark main dish: steak in ale pie £10.25. Two-course evening meal £16.00.*

Stewart ~ Lease Steve Jackson ~ Real ale ~ Open 11-11; 11am-midnight Thurs-Sat ~ Bar food 12-2.30 (3 Sun), 5.30-9.30; 12-10 Sat; snacks throughout afternoon except Fri, Sat ~ Restaurant 12 (12.30 Sun)-2.30, 6-9.30 (10 Fri, Sat) ~ Children welcome in upstairs gallery if dining and over 5 ~ Dogs allowed in bar ~ Wi-fi ~ Live music during Edinburgh Festival *Recommended by Roger and Donna Huggins, Barry Collett, Charles Fraser, Rob Anderson*

EDINBURGH
Kays Bar ❦ £

NT2574   Map 11

(0131) 225 1858 – www.kaysbar.co.uk

Jamaica Street West; off India Street; EH3 6HF

Cosy, enjoyably chatty backstreet pub with good value lunchtime food and an excellent choice of well kept beers

They keep a marvellous choice of drinks in this busy little backstreet pub that includes seven real ales on handpump such as Caledonian Deuchars IPA and Theakstons Best, plus guests such as Campbells Gunner, Hop Studio Blonde, Stewart Telos, Thwaites Wainwright, Tryst Double Chocolate Porter and Timothy Taylors Landlord; they also stock more than 50 malt whiskies aged from eight to 50 years old, 15 gins and half a dozen wines by the glass. There's an eclectic mix of customers and an enjoyable local feel, with long, curving, well worn, red plush wall banquettes and stools around cast-iron tables on red carpet, and red pillars supporting a red ceiling. Décor is simple with big casks and vats arranged along the walls, old wine and spirits merchants' notices and gas-type lamps. A quiet panelled back room (a bit like a library) leads off, with a narrow, plank-panelled pitched ceiling and a collection of books ranging from dictionaries to ancient steam-train books for boys; a lovely coal fire in winter, and board games. In days past, the pub was owned by John Kay, a whisky and wine merchant; wine barrels were hoisted up to the first floor and dispensed through pipes attached to nipples that are still visible around the ceiling light rose. Dogs may be allowed outside food service times.

 Lunchtime food is very good value and includes stovies, pâté with toast, chicken or beef curries, steak pie, chilli con carne, prawn salad, and puddings such as chocolate fudge cake. *Benchmark main dish: mince and tatties £4.50.*

Free house ~ Licensee Fraser Gillespie ~ Real ale ~ Open 11am-midnight; 11am-1am Fri, Sat; 12.30-11 Sun ~ Bar food 12-2.30; not Sun ~ Wi-fi *Recommended by Rona Mackinlay, Roger and Donna Huggins, Molly and Stewart Lindsay*

EDINBURGH
Scran & Scallie ⭐ ♀

NT2374   Map 11

(0131) 332 6281 – www.scranandscallie.com

Comely Bank Road; EH4 1DT

First class food from top chefs in two dining rooms, scottish real ales in proper bar, scandinavian-style furnishings and courteous, knowledgeable staff

Of course, most customers are here to enjoy the exceptional food (well, with two of Scotland's high-ranking chefs involved – Tom Kitchin and Dominic Jack – that's not surprising) but there is a proper bar too, and scottish ales such as Campervan Blonde Voyage, Harviestoun Summer Legend and Stewart Pentland IPA on handpump; also an impressive whisky choice and inventive house cocktails. Throughout, furnishings are simple and contemporary with tweed and tartan fabrics, the odd fur throw and pale floorboards. The bar has stools against the counter, a high corner table with equally high chairs, just a few tables and wooden dining chairs down each side of the room and blue paintwork. The sizeable dining area (with a smaller room leading off) has a cream-coloured woodburning stove, mismatched wooden dining chairs around a medley of tables, bare and painted brick walls (hung with old Scottish recipes and menus), contemporary wallpaper and the odd brick pillar here and there. Staff are interested and helpful.

From a seasonal menu using the best local suppliers, the seriously good modern food includes roe deer terrine with rhubarb, their own take on cullen skink, roast bone marrow, oxtail and mushrooms, grain salad and hot smoked salmon, spelt and lentil burger, smoked haddock and pearl barley kedgeree, home-made beef sausage and mash, game pie, breaded chicken escalope and a fried egg, fish pie, and puddings such as dark chocolate fondant with orange sauce and buttermilk ice-cream, and rhubarb crumble tart with vanilla ice-cream; they also offer a three-course set weekday lunch and weekend breakfasts (8.30-11am). *Benchmark main dish: steak pie £16.50. Two-course evening meal £26.00.*

Free house ~ Licensees Tom Kitchin and Dominic Jack ~ Real ale ~ Bar food 12-3, 5-10 (reduced menu 3-5); 8.30am-10pm weekends ~ Restaurant ~ Children welcome ~ Dogs welcome ~ Wi-fi *Recommended by Samuel and Melissa Turnbull, Belinda and Neil Garth, Penny Barr, Charlotte and William Mason*

GLASGOW NS5965 Map 11
Babbity Bowster ♀
(0141) 552 5055 – www.babbitybowster.com
Blackfriars Street; G1 1PE

A lively mix of traditional and modern with a continental feel too; bedrooms

This 18th-c former tobacco merchant's house remains very much a Glasgow institution with a thoroughly convivial atmosphere and a good mix of locals and visitors. The simply decorated, light-filled interior has fine tall windows, plush stools and cushioned ladder-back chairs around a mix of dark tables on bare boards, some wall bench seating, open fires and attractive plant prints on light paintwork. The bar opens on to a pleasant terrace with picnic-sets under parasols and there's another back terrace too. High chairs line the counter where they keep Caledonian Deuchars IPA and a couple of guests such as Fyne Ales Jarl and Kelburn Jaguar on air-pressure tall fount, and a remarkably sound collection of wines and malt whiskies; good tea and coffee too. On Saturday evenings, the pub has live traditional scottish music, while at other times you may find games of boules in progress outside. Note the bedroom price is for the room only.

A short choice of enjoyable food includes sandwiches, goats cheese filo parcel with onion jam, mussels in creamy saffron sauce, vegetarian risotto, corn-fed chicken paupiette with mushroom mousse and a creamy brandy sauce, braised ox cheeks with port wine and mushroom sauce, duck breast with orange and star anise, herb-crusted lamb rack with dijon mustard and white wine jus, saddle of deer in oatmeal and black pepper with whisky sauce, and puddings such as seasonal fruit tart and clootie dumpling with toffee sauce. *Benchmark main dish: cullen skink £6.25. Two-course evening meal £19.00.*

Free house ~ Licensee Fraser Laurie ~ Real ale ~ Open 11am-midnight; 12.30-midnight Sun ~ Bar food 12-10 ~ Restaurant ~ Children welcome if eating ~ Wi-fi ~ Live traditional music Weds afternoon, Sat early evening ~ Bedrooms: £55/£70 *Recommended by Mungo Shipley, Dave Braisted, Rona Mackinlay, Barry Collett, Barry and Daphne Gregson*

GLASGOW NS5765 Map 11
Bon Accord ⬤ £
(0141) 248 4427 – www.bonaccordweb.co.uk
North Street; G3 7DA

Remarkable choice of drinks, a good welcome and bargain food

You can find an extraordinary range of drinks in this cheerful tavern, from an amazing 400 malt whiskies alongside Caledonian Deuchars IPA and nine daily changing guests sourced from breweries around Britain served from swan-necked handpumps. Also, continental bottled beers, a farm cider and, in a remarkable display behind the counter, 50 gins and lots of vodkas and rums. Staff are knowledgeable, so do ask for help if you need it. The several linked traditional bars are warmly understated with cream or terracotta walls, a mix of chairs and tables, a leather sofa and plenty of bar stools on polished bare boards or carpeting; TV, background music and board games. There are circular picnic-sets on a small terrace, and modern tables and chairs out in front.

Incredibly good value food includes baguettes, peppered mushrooms with garlic bread, giant yorkshire pudding filled with sausages and onion gravy, chilli con carne, all-day breakfast, battered fresh haddock and chips, cajun chicken or burger both with french fries, gammon and egg, and puddings such as clootie dumpling or apple pie with custard. *Benchmark main dish: steak pie £6.95. Two-course evening meal £9.50.*

Free house ~ Licensee Paul McDonagh ~ Real ale ~ Open 11am-midnight; 12.30-midnight Sun ~ Bar food 11-8; 12.30-8 Sun ~ Children welcome until 8pm ~ Wi-fi ~ Live band Sat evening, quiz Weds evening *Recommended by Neil Allen, Helena and Trevor Fraser, Dave Sutton, Edward and William Johnston, Sophia and Hamish Greenfield*

ISLE OF WHITHORN
Steam Packet ♥ ⇤

NX4736 Map 9

(01988) 500334 – www.thesteampacketinn.biz
Harbour Row; DG8 8LL

Waterside views from friendly, family-run inn with up to eight real ales and tasty food; bedrooms

They brew their own ales here at the Five Kingdoms Brewery and also keep Belhaven IPA, Fyne Ales Highlander, Greene King Old Speckled Hen and guests from other breweries such as Kelburn and Orkney on handpump – plus 12 gins, 23 malt whiskies, nine wines by the glass and a couple of farm ciders. The friendly, family-run inn is in a pretty fishing village on the tip of the south-west peninsula and sits right on the quayside; big picture windows overlook the bustle of yachts and inshore fishing boats – a view that's shared by some of the bedrooms. The comfortable low-ceilinged bar is split into two: on the right, plush button-back banquettes and boat pictures, and on the left, stools around cast-iron-framed tables on big stone tiles, and a woodburning stove in the bare stone wall; TV, dominoes and pool. There's a lower beamed dining room with high-backed leather dining chairs around square tables on wooden flooring plus another woodburner, a small eating area off the lounge bar and an airy conservatory leading into the garden. You can walk from here up to the isolated remains of St Ninian's kirk, on a headland behind the village.

Food is popular and includes chicken liver pâté, cullen skink, battered fresh fish and chips, vegetable curry, burger with toppings, onion rings and chips, seafood platter, sirloin steak with a choice of sauces, and puddings such as Drambuie crème brûlée and apple and blueberry crumble. *Benchmark main dish: battered fish and chips £10.95. Two-course evening meal £17.00.*

Free house ~ Licensee Alastair Scoular ~ Real ale ~ Open 8am-midnight ~ Bar food 12-2, 6.30-9 ~ Restaurant ~ Children welcome except in public bar ~ Dogs allowed in bar and bedrooms ~ Wi-fi ~ Folk music third Sun of month ~ Bedrooms: £30/£60 *Recommended by David and Betty Gittins, Jack Trussler, Mike Benton, Paddy and Sian O'Leary*

MEIKLEOUR
Meikleour Arms 🛏

NO1539 Map 11

(01250) 883206 – www.meikleourarms.co.uk

A984 W of Coupar Angus; PH2 6EB

Traditional and welcoming 19th-c inn with a thoughtful choice of drinks and interesting food; bedrooms

This enjoyable country inn is part of the Meikleour Estate and there's a lot to see and do nearby – including one of the best salmon beats in Scotland. This year, a lot of work has been done: there's a big new kitchen, a new dining room opened in a converted barn, six bedrooms added to the pretty existing ones and a comfortable new sitting room. The main lounge bar is basically two rooms (one carpeted, the other with a stone floor) with comfortable seating, some angling equipment and fishing/shooting pictures, exposed stone walls and open wood fires. There's a beer named for the pub (from Inveralmond), Belhaven Best, Orkney Dark Island and Strathbraan Due South on handpump, 50 malt whiskies and 12 wines by the glass, served by attentive, friendly staff; background music. Seats in the garden and on a small colonnaded verandah, with more on a sloping lawn, have distant highland views. Do visit the spectacular beech hedge just 300 metres away which was planted over 250 years ago – it's the tallest in the world, at 30 metres high.

🍴 Pleasing food using Estate produce and some from their walled garden includes local smoked trout pâté in choux buns with sweet cured cucumber, black pudding scotch egg with tomato chutney, butternut squash, goats cheese and spinach lasagne, shrimp, scallop and calamari salad with lemon vinaigrette, chicken pernod pie, burger with toppings, chilli jam and chips, pork belly with parsnip purée and blueberry compote, rolled lemon sole with white wine and parsley sauce, stuffed tenderloin of pork with creamed spinach and caramelised baby turnips, and puddings such as rhubarb and custard tart and white chocolate and raspberry cheesecake. *Benchmark main dish: crumbed haddock with chips and broad bean purée £12.95. Two-course evening meal £18.50.*

Free house ~ Licensees Sam and Claire Mercer Nairne ~ Real ale ~ Open 11am-midnight ~ Bar food 12-9 ~ Restaurant ~ Children welcome ~ Dogs welcome ~ Wi-fi ~ Bedrooms: £90/£110 *Recommended by Pat and Stewart Gordon, Patricia and Gordon Tucker, Jamie and Lizzie McEwan*

MELROSE
Burts Hotel 🍴 🛏

NT5433 Map 9

(01896) 822285 – www.burtshotel.co.uk

B6374, Market Square; TD6 9PL

●●●

Scotland Dining Pub of the Year

Comfortable town-centre hotel with imaginative food and a fine array of malt whiskies; bedrooms

Right at the heart of an attractive border town, this smart, family-run hotel is just a few steps away from the abbey ruins and makes a lovely base for exploring the area. The bedrooms, though quite small, are immaculate and comfortably decorated and the breakfasts highly regarded. Neat public areas are maintained with attention to detail. The welcoming red-carpeted bar has a warming fire, tidy pub tables between cushioned wall seats and windsor armchairs, scottish prints on pale green walls and a long dark wood counter serving Born in the Borders Foxy Blonde, Broughton Hopopotamus IPA and

Tempest Cascadian Blonde on handpump, 12 wines by the glass from a good wine list, a farm cider and around 80 malt whiskies. The elegant restaurant with its swagged curtains, dark blue wallpaper and tables laid with white linen offers a smarter dining experience; background music. In summer you can sit out in the well tended garden.

 Outstanding food using premium local ingredients includes haggis croquette with root vegetable purée, parsley and whisky sauce, home-smoked local venison with peppered pear, beetroot and port reduction and sweet potato, chicken caesar salad, butternut squash, red onion and feta tart with herb salad, burger with toppings, pickle relish and chips, sea bream with potato and spinach salad, pancetta and herb butter sauce, steak pudding with horseradish mash, parsnip purée, smoked bacon and mushroom jus, and puddings such as chocolate délice with chocolate fondant and white chocolate ice-cream and passion-fruit mousse with caramelised pineapple, pina colada and mango sorbet. *Benchmark main dish: harissa-roasted lamb rump with spiced vegetable purée, rösti potato and cumin jus £18.25. Two-course evening meal £24.00.*

Free house ~ Licensees Graham and Nick Henderson ~ Real ale ~ Open 11-2.30, 5-11; 12-2.30, 6-11 Sun; closed 6-12 Feb 2018 ~ Bar food 12-2, 6-9 ~ Restaurant ~ Children welcome ~ Dogs allowed in bar and bedrooms ~ Wi-fi ~ Bedrooms: £75/£140 *Recommended by John Poulter, Martin Day, Nick Higgins, Barbara and Phil Bowie, Dan and Belinda Smallbone*

PLOCKTON
Plockton Hotel ★ 🏵️ 🛏️
NG8033 Map 11

(01599) 544274 – www.plocktonhotel.co.uk
Village signposted from A87 near Kyle of Lochalsh; IV52 8TN

Neat little hotel with wonderful views, very good food with emphasis on local seafood and real ales; bedrooms

At the centre of a National Trust village, this family-run hotel is right by Loch Carron with seats in the front garden that look out past the village's trademark palm trees to a shore lined with colourful flowering shrubs and across the sheltered anchorage to rugged mountains. Inside, the welcoming, comfortably furnished lounge bar has window seats with views of the harbour boats, as well as antique dark red leather seating around neat Regency-style tables on a tartan carpet, and three model ships set into the woodwork and partly panelled stone walls. The separate public bar has pool, board games, TV, a games machine, a juke box and background music. Cromarty Happy Chappy, Fyne Ales Jarl and a guest beer on handpump, 20 malt whiskies, several wines by the glass and scottish gins. Half the comfortable bedrooms have extraordinary water views, while the others, some with balconies, look over the hillside garden; breakfasts are good. There's a hotel nearby called the Plockton, so don't get the two confused.

 Food is highly thought-of and includes lunchtime sandwiches and paninis, king prawn tails in garlic butter, country pâté laced with whisky, a vegetarian dish of the day, haggis, neeps and tatties, venison casserole with red wine, juniper berries and redcurrant jelly, pork medallions with brandied apricots and cream, chicken stuffed with smoked ham and cheese in a sun-dried tomato, garlic and basil sauce, seafood platter, chargrilled aberdeen angus steaks with a choice of sauces, and puddings. *Benchmark main dish: local langoustines £19.00. Two-course evening meal £20.50.*

Free house ~ Licensee Alan Pearson ~ Real ale ~ Open 11-midnight; 12-11 Sun; closed first two weeks Jan ~ Bar food 12-2.15, 6-9 ~ Restaurant ~ Children welcome ~ Wi-fi ~ Live music Weds evening Apr-Oct ~ Bedrooms: £70/£140 *Recommended by Laura Reid, Dr A McCormick, Philip Chesington, Amy and Luke Buchanan, Sophia and Hamish Greenfield*

RATHO
NT1470   Map 11

Bridge 🏮 ⚲ ◧

(0131) 333 1320 – www.bridgeinn.com

Baird Road; EH28 8RA

**Canalside inn with cosy bar and airy restaurant, a thoughtful choice
of drinks and enjoyable food; attractive bedrooms**

Right by the Union Canal, this is a charming inn and seats on the terrace overlook the water. The cosy bar has an open fire with leather armchairs to either side and a larger area with a two-way fireplace and upholstered tub and cushioned wooden chairs on pale boards around a mix of tables; a contemporary and elegant dining room leads off. A beer named for the pub (from Stewart), Alchemy Starlaw and Orkney Red MacGregor on handpump, 36 wines by the glass and 50 malt whiskies. The main restaurant is light and airy with up-to-date pale oak settles, antique-style chairs and big windows overlooking the canal. The individually decorated and well equipped bedrooms also have fine views and breakfasts are lovely. A unique part of the friendly licensees' business is their summer restaurant barge, which travels from the inn down the canal to the Almondell Aqueduct over the River Almond; there's a full kitchen team on board and you can have lunch, afternoon tea or supper.

 Using produce grown in their walled garden and own-bred pork, the interesting food includes lunchtime sandwiches, pigeon breast with jerusalem artichoke, burnt onion and crispy lamb haggis, scallops with pea velouté, pea shoots and crispy smoked pork crumb, sharing plates, oyster mushroom, butternut squash and green bean curry with roast aubergine caviar, burger with toppings, onion rings and skinny fries, roe deer (seared loin and crispy haunch) with textures of squash, chard, truffled mushrooms, blackberry gel and jus, hake with confit potato, mussels, turnip purée, wasabi crème fraîche and parsley dressing, and puddings such as yoghurt pannacotta with rhubarb confit, orange, toasted oat and ginger cookie and raspberry crumb and sticky toffee date pudding with tomato caramel and ice-cream. *Benchmark main dish: pie of the day £14.40. Two-course evening meal £20.50.*

Free house ~ Licensees Graham and Rachel Bucknall ~ Real ale ~ Open 9am-11pm; 9am-midnight Fri, Sat; 9am-11pm Sun ~ Bar food 12-3, 5-9; 12-4, 5-9 Sat; 12-4, 5-8 Sun ~ Restaurant ~ Children welcome but not in bar after 8pm ~ Dogs allowed in bar ~ Wi-fi ~ Live music monthly (phone for details) ~ Bedrooms: £75/£90 *Recommended by Pat and Stewart Gordon, Mr and Mrs P R Thomas, Victoria and James Sargeant, Angela and Steve Heard*

SHIELDAIG
NG8153   Map 11

Tigh an Eilean Hotel 🛏

(01520) 755251 – www.tighaneilean.co.uk

Village signposted just off A896 Lochcarron–Gairloch; IV54 8XN

**Wonderfully set hotel with separate contemporary bar,
real ales and enjoyable food; tranquil bedrooms**

If you're lucky you might see otters, sea eagles, seals or even the rare pine marten around here as this is a stunningly set inn looking over the forested Shieldaig Island to Loch Torridon and then out to the sea beyond. Separate from the hotel, the bright, attractive bar is on two storeys with an open staircase; dining is on the first floor and a decked balcony has a magnificent loch and village view. The place is gently contemporary and nicely relaxed with timbered floors, timber-boarded walls, shiny bolts through exposed timber roof beams and an open kitchen. A couple of changing ales from An Teallach on handpump and up to a dozen wines by the glass; background music, TV, darts, pool and board games. Tables outside in a sheltered little courtyard are well placed to enjoy the gorgeous position. To preserve the peace and quiet, the comfortable bedrooms have no TVs and no telephones, though each has its own sitting area; good, ample breakfasts.

As well as shellfish delivered fresh from the jetty, the reliably good food includes moules marinière, hand-dived scallops with garlic or chilli butter, aubergine parmigiana, pizzas from a wood-fired oven, battered fresh haddock and chips, haggis, neeps and tatties, fresh crab cakes with lemon mayonnaise, a plate of langoustines, slow-roasted rack of pork ribs with barbecue sauce, aged rib-eye steak frites, and puddings such as crème brûlée and sticky toffee and date pudding with vanilla ice-cream. *Benchmark main dish: seafood stew £18.50. Two-course evening meal £21.00.*

Free house ~ Licensee Cathryn Field ~ Real ale ~ Open 11-11 (midnight Sat); closed Mon and Tues Jan ~ Bar food 12-9; 12-2.30, 6.30-9 in winter ~ Restaurant ~ Children welcome ~ Dogs allowed in bar and bedrooms ~ Wi-fi ~ Traditional live folk music Fri or Sat in summer ~ Bedrooms: £70/£140 *Recommended by Rona Mackinlay, Brian and Sally Wakeham, William Slade, William and Ann Reid, Robert and Diana Ringstone*

SLIGACHAN
Sligachan Hotel 🍺 🛏️

NG4930 Map 11

(01478) 650204 ~ www.sligachan.co.uk
A87 Broadford–Portree, junction with A863; IV47 8SW

Spectacularly set mountain hotel with walkers' bar and plusher side, all-day food and impressive range of whiskies

The huge, modern, pine-clad main bar in this stunningly set hotel falls somewhere between a basic climbers' bar and the plusher, more sedate hotel side. It's spaciously open to the ceiling rafters and has geometrically laid-out dark tables and chairs on neat carpets; pool, TV and board games. As well as their own Cuillin Black Face, Eagle and Pinnacle, they keep a guest on handpump plus an incredible display of over 400 malt whiskies at one end of the counter. It can get quite lively in here some nights, but there's a more sedate lounge bar with leather bucket armchairs on plush carpets and a coal fire; background highland and islands music. The separate restaurant is in the hotel itself. The interesting little museum, well worth a visit, charts the history of the hotel and its famous climbers, with photographs and climbing and angling records. There are tables out in the garden and a big play area for children, which can be seen from the bar. The bedrooms are comfortable, bright and modern, and they also offer self-catering and have a campsite with caravan hook-ups. Dogs are allowed only in the main bar and not in the hotel's cocktail bar – but may stay in some bedrooms. Some of the most testing walks in Britain are right on the doorstep.

Some sort of food is on offer all day: cullen skink, smoked duck with blueberries, blue cheese and spiced pecans, asparagus, prosciutto, a soft boiled egg and local cheddar, venison burger with pickles and fries, smoked halloumi with warm chickpea and spinach salad with basil pesto, pork belly with black pudding, apple and crispy oyster, loin, shoulder and flank of lamb with peas, baby gems and Talisker jus, and puddings such as chocolate fondant and sticky toffee pudding. *Benchmark main dish: beer-battered fresh fish and chips £11.95. Two-course evening meal £19.00.*

Own brew ~ Licensee Sandy Coghill ~ Real ale ~ Open 11am-1am; closed 7 Jan-1 Mar 2018 ~ Bar food 11-9 ~ Restaurant ~ Children welcome ~ Dogs allowed in bar and bedrooms ~ Wi-fi ~ Live music every Sat and midweek May-Sept ~ Bedrooms: £70/£140 *Recommended by Caroline Prescott, Anne and Ben Smith, Charles Welch, Angus Light, Matthew and Elisabeth Reeves*

STEIN

NG2656 Map 11

Stein Inn

(01470) 592362 – www.steininn.co.uk

End of B886 N of Dunvegan in Waternish, off A850 Dunvegan–Portree; OS Sheet 23
map reference 263564; IV55 8GA

Inn of character on the island's Waternish peninsula with good,
simple food and lots of whiskies; a rewarding place to stay

A lovely setting on Skye's northern corner for this welcoming 18th-c inn with marvellous views across Loch Bay. The unpretentious original public bar makes a particularly inviting retreat from the elements, with sturdy country furnishings, flagstones, beam-and-plank ceiling, partly panelled stripped-stone walls and a warming double-sided stove between the two rooms. Caledonian Deuchars IPA and a couple of local guests such as Cairngorm Gold and Isle of Skye Red on handpump, ten wines by the glass, 130 malt whiskies and 18 gins. Good service from smartly uniformed staff. Pool, darts, board games, dominoes and cribbage in the games area, and maybe background music. There's a lively indoor play area for children and showers for yachtsmen. Benches outside look over the water – as do all the bedrooms; it's worth pre-ordering the smoked kippers as part of the tasty breakfasts. Dogs are welcome but not during evening food service.

Using highland meat and local fish the tempting food includes hand-dived scallops in white wine and cream, black pudding with whisky and mustard dressing, butternut squash stuffed with feta cheese, spinach and pine nuts, steak in ale pie, fresh fish dish of the day, venison casserole, langoustines with fries, sirloin steak with whisky cream or pepper sauce, and puddings such as seasonal fruit crumble and sticky toffee pudding. *Benchmark main dish: beer-battered haddock and chips £9.50. Two-course evening meal £15.00.*

Free house ~ Licensees Angus and Teresa McGhie ~ Real ale ~ Open 11am-midnight; 11-11 Sun; 12-11 (midnight Sat) in winter ~ Bar food 12-4, 6-9.30; 12.30-4, 6-9 Sun ~ Children welcome ~ Dogs allowed in bar and bedrooms ~ Wi-fi ~ Bedrooms: £50/£80 *Recommended by Alison and Michael Harper, Rob Anderson, Daniel King, Angus Light, Molly and Stewart Lindsay, Stuart and Natalie Granville*

SWINTON

NT8347 Map 10

Wheatsheaf 🏅 ♀ 🏠

(01890) 860257 – www.wheatsheaf-swinton.co.uk

A6112 N of Coldstream; TD11 3JJ

Civilised place with small bar for drinkers, comfortable lounges, top
quality food and drinks and professional service; appealing bedrooms

To make the best of the surrounding rolling countryside, why not stay in the well equipped and comfortable bedrooms here – breakfasts are good and hearty. And although there's also quite an emphasis on the enjoyable food, the attentive, friendly staff welcome customers into the little bar and informal lounges too. Here they keep Belhaven IPA on handpump alongside 50 malt whiskies and 18 wines by the glass. There are comfortable plush armchairs, several nice old oak settles with cushions, a little open fire, sporting prints and china plates on the bottle-green walls in the bar and small agricultural prints and a fishing theme décor on the painted or bare-stone walls in the lounges. The dining room and front conservatory with its vaulted pine ceiling have carpet on the floor and high-backed slate-grey chairs around pale wood tables set with fresh flowers, while the more formal restaurant has black leather high-backed dining chairs around clothed tables; background music. This is a pretty village just a few miles from the River Tweed.

There are traditional dishes such as linguine with king prawns, chilli and tomatoes or chicken with garlic, tomatoes, parmesan and cream, steak burger with toppings, barbecue sauce and chips, and mixed grill plus more creative choices like smoked ham terrine with apricot and pickled vegetables, home-made gnocchi with tomatoes, smoked paprika, mascarpone and olives, corn-fed chicken breast with haggis and whisky, duck breast with udon noodles and lemongrass and coriander broth, and puddings such as vanilla cream profiteroles with chocolate sauce and strawberry cheesecake. *Benchmark main dish: fresh fish dish of the day £17.25. Two-course evening meal £22.00.*

Free house ~ Licensee Michael Lawrence ~ Real ale ~ Open 11-11 (midnight Sat); 11-11 Sun ~ Bar food 12-2, 6-9 ~ Restaurant ~ Children welcome ~ Dogs allowed in bar and bedrooms ~ Wi-fi ~ Bedrooms: £93/£124 *Recommended by Belinda May, Nick Sharpe, Michael Doswell, Rosie and Marcus Heatherley, Kerry and Guy Trooper*

THORNHILL
Lion & Unicorn

NS6699 Map 11

(01786) 850204 – www.lion-unicorn.co.uk
Main Street (A873); FK8 3PJ

Busy, interesting pub with emphasis on its home-made food; friendly staff and bedrooms

There are three log fires in this family-owned and neatly kept inn – one is in an original fireplace with a high brazier almost big enough to drive a car into. Parts of the place date from 1635 and the pubby character back bar has some exposed stone walls, wooden flooring and stools lined along the counter where they keep An Teallach Ale and Caledonian Deuchars IPA on handpump and several wines by the glass; log fires. This opens to a games room with a pool table, juke box, fruit machine, darts, TV and board games. The more restauranty-feeling beamed and carpeted front room is traditionally furnished and set for dining; background music. Outside there are benches in a gravelled garden and a lawn with a play area.

Well regarded food includes sandwiches, haggis fritters with whisky, honey and grain mustard dip, local moules marinière, leek, mushroom and parsnip crumble, beer-battered fresh haddock and chips, steak burger with toppings, chicken, leek and mushroom pie, rib-eye of beef with yorkshire pudding and red wine sauce, and puddings such as assorted ice-creams and sticky toffee pudding. *Benchmark main dish: chicken topped with haggis, wrapped in bacon with a whisky cream sauce £12.95. Two-course evening meal £20.00.*

Free house ~ Licensee Fiona Stevenson ~ Real ale ~ Open 12-midnight (1am Fri, Sat) ~ Bar food 12-9 ~ Restaurant ~ Children welcome ~ Dogs allowed in bar ~ Wi-fi ~ Bedrooms: £65/£80 *Recommended by John Evans, Frances Parsons, Charles and Maddie Bishop, Patricia Healey*

Please tell us if the décor, atmosphere, food or drink at a pub is different from our description. We rely on readers' reports to keep us up to date: feedback@goodguides.com, or (no stamp needed) The Good Pub Guide, FREEPOST RTXY–ZCBC–BBAZ, Stream Lane, Sedlescombe, Battle TN33 0PB.

Also Worth a Visit in Scotland

Besides the fully inspected pubs, you might like to try these pubs that have been recommended to us and described by readers. Do tell us what you think of them: feedback@goodguides.com

ABERDEENSHIRE

ABERDEEN
NJ9305
Grill (01224) 573530
Union Street; AB11 6BA Don't be put off by the exterior of this 19th-c granite building – the remodelled 1920s interior is well worth a look; long wood-floored bar with fine moulded ceiling, mahogany panelling and original button-back leather wall benches, ornate servery with glazed cabinets housing some of the 550 whiskies (a few from the 1930s, and 60 from outside Scotland), five well kept ales including Caledonian 80/- and Harviestoun Bitter & Twisted, basic snacks; no children or dogs; open all day. *(Belinda and Neil Garth)*

ABERDEEN
NJ9406
★ **Prince of Wales** (01224) 640597
St Nicholas Lane; AB10 1HF Individual and convivial old tavern with eight changing ales from very long counter, bargain hearty food, painted floorboards, flagstones or carpet, pews and screened booths, original tiled spittoon running length of bar; live acoustic music Sun evening, quiz Mon, games machines; children over 5 welcome if eating, open all day from 10am (11am Sun).
(Stuart and Natalie Granville)

ABOYNE
NO5298
★ **Boat** (01339) 886137
Charlestown Road (B968, just off A93); AB34 5EL Friendly and busy country inn with fine views across River Dee; bareboards bar with contemporary paintwork, scatter cushions on built-in wall seats, antlers, animal hides and scottish pictures, model train chugging its way around just below ceiling height, woodburner in stone fireplace, three well kept ales, decent wines and some 30 malt whiskies, particularly good food from 7am breakfast on, more elaborate seasonal evening menu, additional dining area; background music, games in public bar end; children and dogs welcome, six comfortable well equipped bedrooms, open all day. *(Dr A McCormick, S G N Bennett)*

ALFORD
NJ5617
Forbes Arms (01975) 562108
A944; by the bridge; AB33 8QJ Small riverside hotel with two bars, restaurant and conservatory, fair-priced pubby food including high teas, a changing scottish ale; TV projector for sports; seats in garden sloping down to River Don (fishing permits available), nine comfortable bedrooms, open all day. *(Philip Chesington)*

BALMEDIE
NJ9619
Cock & Bull (01358) 743249
A90 N of Balmedie; AB23 8XY Pleasant atmosphere and interesting décor in this country dining pub, good locally sourced food from sandwiches up, a well kept ale such as Burnside, afternoon teas, obliging service, beamed log-fire lounge, restaurant and conservatory; children and dogs (in bar) welcome, four bedrooms in converted cottage, open (and food) all day. *(Philip Chesington)*

OLDMELDRUM
NJ8127
Redgarth (01651) 872353
Kirk Brae, off A957; AB51 0DJ Good-sized comfortable lounge with traditional décor, two or three well kept ales and interesting range of malt whiskies (village distillery), popular reasonably priced food, friendly attentive service, restaurant; children welcome, lovely views to Bennachie, bedrooms (get booked quickly); open all day Sun. *(Belinda and Neil Garth)*

PENNAN
NJ8465
Pennan Inn (01346) 561201
Just off B9031 Banff-Fraserburgh; AB43 6JB Whitewashed building in long row of old fishermen's cottages, wonderful spot right by the sea – scenes from the film *Local Hero* (1983) shot here; small bar with simple furniture and exposed stone walls, modern décor in separate restaurant, enjoyable sensibly priced food from shortish menu including some thai dishes, at least one real ale; five bedrooms, at foot of steep winding road and parking along front limited, closed Mon, Tues, and throughout Jan and Feb. *(Philip Chesington)*

ANGUS

BROUGHTY FERRY
NO4630
★ **Fishermans Tavern** (01382) 775941
Fort Street; turning off shore road; DD5 2AD Once a row of fishermen's cottages, this friendly pub is just steps from the beach; up to eight well kept changing ales (May beer festival) and good range of malt whiskies, comfortable lounge with coal fire, small snug and back dining area with another fire, popular fair-priced pubby food from sandwiches up; sports TV; children and dogs welcome, disabled facilities, tables on front pavement, more in secluded little walled garden, 12 bedrooms, open (and food) all day, till 1am Thurs-Sat. *(Stuart Douglas)*

CLOVA N03273
Glen Clova Hotel (01575) 550350
B955 NW of Wheen; DD8 4QS Tucked-
away 19th-c hotel's unpretentious climbers'
bar; flagstones, bench seats and stone
fireplace with woodburner, bric-a-brac
and old photographs, a couple of well kept
changing beers, 18 malts and plenty of
wines by the glass, good food (same menu
as their restaurant) using home-reared beef
and lamb and venison from surrounding
hills, friendly staff; children and dogs
welcome, ten bedrooms, eight garden lodges
and bunkhouse, glorious walks nearby,
open all day. *(Pat and Stewart Gordon)*

ARGYLL

ARDFERN NM8004
Galley of Lorne (01852) 500284
*B8002; village and inn signposted off
A816 Lochgilphead–Oban; PA31 8QN*
17th-c drovers' inn on edge of Loch
Craignish, cosy beamed and flagstoned bar
with warming log fire, some black panelling
and unfussy assortment of furniture
including settles, up to four real ales and
50 whiskies, good choice of food from
lunchtime sandwiches up, lounge bar with
woodburner and spacious picture-window
restaurant; background music, small pool
room, darts, games machine, sports TV; good
sea and loch views from sheltered terrace
and deck, seven bedrooms in extension,
open all day summer. *(David Todd)*

BRIDGE OF ORCHY NN2939
★**Bridge of Orchy Hotel**
(01838) 400208 *A82 Tyndrum–
Glencoe; PA36 4AB* Spectacular spot
on West Highland Way, very welcoming
with good fairly priced food in bar, lounge
and smarter restaurant, decent choice
of well kept ales, house wines and malt
whiskies, interesting mountain photographs,
open fires; dogs welcome; ten good
bedrooms, more in airy riverside annexe,
open (and food) all day. *(Lexie Booth)*

CAIRNDOW NN1811
★**Cairndow Stagecoach Inn** (01499)
600286 *Village and pub signed off A83;
PA26 8BN* 17th-c coaching inn in wonderful
position on edge of Loch Fyne, good sensibly
priced food including local venison and fresh
fish, ales from nearby Fyne and 37 malt
whiskies (including a whisky of the month),
friendly accommodating staff; children
and dogs welcome, lovely peaceful lochside
garden, 13 comfortable bedrooms, six more
in modern annexe with balconies overlooking

the water, good breakfast, open (and food)
all day. *(Roy and Lindsey Fentiman, Pat and
Stewart Gordon, David J Austin, Dr A McCormick)*

CONNEL NM9034
Oyster (01631) 710666
A85, W of Connel Bridge; PA37 1PJ
18th-c inn opposite former ferry slipway,
lovely view across the water (especially
at sunset), decent-sized bar (the Glue
Pot) with friendly highland atmosphere,
log fire in stone fireplace, Caledonian
Deuchars IPA, good range of wines, gins
and malts, enjoyable all-day food from
pubby choices to local seafood including
two-course menu till 5pm, friendly attentive
service; sports TV; modern hotel part
with 11 bedrooms and separate evening
restaurant (closed winter). *(Lexie Booth)*

GLENCOE NN1058
★**Clachaig** (01855) 811252
*Old Glencoe Road, behind NTS Visitor
Centre; PH49 4HX* 18th-c climbers' and
walkers' inn surrounded by the scenic
grandeur of Glencoe; Boots Bar with 14
scottish ales, some 300 malts and interesting
range of artisan gins, vodkas and rums
from across Scotland, slate-floored snug
with whisky barrel-panelled walls and open
fire, lounge (children allowed here) has
mix of tables and booths, photos signed by
famous climbers and local artwork, hearty
food; background music, live bands Sat,
pool, free wi-fi; dogs welcome, comfortable
bedrooms in adjoining hotel plus self-
catering, open (and food) all day. *(CDM)*

INVERARAY NN0908
★**George** (01499) 302111
Main Street East; PA32 8TT Georgian
hotel (packed in high season) at hub of
this appealing small town; pubby bar with
exposed joists, bare stone walls, old tiles
and big flagstones, antique settles, carved
wooden benches and cushioned stone
slabs along the walls, four log/peat fires,
a couple of real ales and 100 malt whiskies,
good food in bar and smarter restaurant,
conservatory; live entertainment Fri, Sat;
children and dogs welcome, well laid-out
terraces with plenty of seats, 17 bedrooms,
Inveraray Castle and walks close by, open
(and food) all day till 1am. *(Lexie Booth)*

KILCHRENAN NN0323
Kilchrenan Inn (01866) 833232
B845; PA35 1HD Newly refurbished 18th-c
country inn with stylish modern décor,
friendly staff and nice relaxed atmosphere,
good food from sensibly short menu (not
Sun evening), well kept local ales such
as Fyne, scottish gins and several malts;

dogs welcome, picnic-sets out at front, lovely drive along Loch Awe to the pub and beyond to Ardanaiseig gardens, three good bedrooms, open all day. *(Stuart Douglas)*

OBAN   NM8530

Cuan Mor (01631) 565078

George Street; PA34 5SD Contemporary quayside bar-restaurant with lots of kitchen-style chairs and tables on bare boards, snug bar with open fire, more than 100 malts and their own-brewed ales, wide choice of competitively priced food all day from sizeable menu (Sunday brunch 10.30-12.30am), friendly service; children welcome, some seats outside. *(CDM)*

OBAN   NM8529

Lorne (01631) 570020

Stevenson Street; PA34 5NA Victorian décor including tiles and island bar with ornate brasswork, well kept Oban Bay, reasonably priced food such as pies and burgers, good service; weekend live music and DJs, Weds quiz; children and dogs welcome, sheltered beer garden with contemporary chairs and tables, open all day till late. *(CDM)*

OTTER FERRY   NR9384

Oystercatcher (01700) 821229

B8000, by the water; PA21 2DH Refurbished pub-restaurant in old building in outstanding spot overlooking Loch Fyne, good food using local fish and shellfish, well kept ales including Fyne from pine-clad bar, decent wine list, friendly staff; dogs welcome in bar; lots of tables out on spit, free moorings, open all day (closed Weds). *(Lexie Booth)*

PORT APPIN   NM9045

Pierhouse (01631) 730302

In Appin, turn right at the Port Appin/ Lismore Ferry sign; PA38 4DE Beautiful location overlooking Loch Linnhe to Lismore and beyond, smallish bar with attractive terrace, good range of wines and beers, 100 malt whiskies and 37 gins (many scottish), excellent seafood (plus other bar food), picture-window restaurant taking in the fine view, helpful friendly staff; children welcome, 12 comfortable bedrooms, moorings for visiting yachts, open all day. *(Pat and Stewart Gordon)*

TARBERT   NR8365

West Loch Hotel (01880) 820283

A83, a mile S; PA29 6YF Friendly 18th-c inn overlooking sea loch, comfortably updated with exposed stone walls, pale-wood tables and dark high-backed dining chairs, relaxing lounges with fine views or warming open fire, enjoyable food using local produce, Belhaven and good selection

of whiskies and gins, helpful cheerful service; children and dogs welcome, eight bedrooms (some with loch view), handy for ferry terminal. *(Philip Chesington)*

TAYVALLICH   NR7487

Tayvallich Inn (01546) 870282

B8025; PA31 8PL Small single-storey bar-restaurant by Loch Sween specialising in good local seafood; pale pine furnishings on quarry tiles, local nautical charts, good range of whiskies and usually a couple of beers from Loch Ness, friendly atmosphere; background music (live first Fri of month); children and dogs welcome, a few rustic picnic-sets on front deck with lovely views over yacht anchorage, open all day. *(Lexie Booth)*

AYRSHIRE

DUNURE   NS2515

Dunure (01292) 500549

Just off A719 SW of Ayr; KA7 4LN Busy place attractively set by ruined harbourside castle; updated bar, lounge and restaurant, varied food including fresh fish/seafood, good service, nice wines but no real ales; courtyard tables, bedrooms and two cottages, not far from Culzean Castle (NTS). *(Dan and Belinda Smallbone)*

SORN   NS5526

Sorn Inn (01290) 551305

Village signed from Mauchline (A76); Main Street; KA5 6HU Restaurany pub in tiny conservation village, highly regarded imaginative food from brasserie dishes up in two restaurant areas, also smallish bar serving an Orkney ale, friendly staff; children and dogs (not in restaurant) welcome, four comfortable well appointed bedrooms, good breakfast, open (and food) all day weekends, closed Mon. *(David and Betty Gittins)*

SYMINGTON   NS3831

Wheatsheaf (01563) 830307

Just off A77 Ayr–Kilmarnock; Main Street; KA1 5QB Single-storey former 17th-c posting inn, charming and cosy, with first class food (must book weekends) including lunchtime/early-evening set menu, efficient friendly service, log fire; children welcome, tables outside, quiet pretty village, open (and food) all day. *(Dan and Belinda Smallbone)*

BERWICKSHIRE

ALLANTON   NT8654

★ Allanton Inn (01890) 818260

B6347 S of Chirnside; TD11 3JZ Well run 18th-c stone-built village inn with attractive open-plan interior, very good fairly priced

---

If we know a pub has an outdoor play area for children, we mention it.

food with emphasis on fresh fish/seafood from daily changing menu, a couple of well kept ales such as Born in the Borders, good wine list and speciality gins, friendly efficient service, cosy bare-boards bar with scatter cushions on bench seats, immaculate dining areas, log fire; background music; children welcome, no dogs inside, picnic-sets in sheltered garden behind, nice views, seven bedrooms, open all day. *(Ruaraidh)*

AUCHENCROW   NT8560
Craw (01890) 761253
B6438 NE of Duns; pub signed off A1; TD14 5LS Delightful little 18th-c village pub in row of cream-washed slate-roofed cottages, friendly and welcoming, with enjoyable well presented food, changing ales from smaller brewers (early Nov beer festival), good wine list, beams decorated with hundreds of pump clips, pictures on panelled walls, woodburner, more formal back restaurant; children welcome, tables on decking behind and out on village green, three bedrooms and self-catering, open all day Fri-Sun. *(Victoria and James Sargeant)*

LAUDER   NT5347
Black Bull (01578) 722208
Market Place; TD2 6SR Comfortable white-painted 18th-c inn festooned with cheerful window boxes and hanging baskets, cosy rustic-feel bar with country scenes on panelled walls, quieter room off and restaurant, well kept Campbells Gunner and Stewart Edinburgh Gold, enjoyable sensibly priced food using local seasonal produce, friendly service; background music, sports TV, free wi-fi; children and dogs (in bar) welcome, eight bedrooms, open (and food) all day. *(Victoria and James Sergeant)*

BORDERS

AYTON   NT9261
Hemelvaart Bier Café 07968 359917
High Street; TD14 5QL Welcoming village bar (former Black Bull) with plenty of community spirit; two real ales, six craft kegs and extensive range of bottled beers, interesting collection of gins too, friendly knowledgeable staff, enjoyable good value food including range of burgers and locally made pies, Thurs curry night, also good coffee and home-made cakes; regular live music, comedy evenings and other events; children and dogs welcome, closed Tues and Weds, otherwise open (and food) all day, till midnight Fri, Sat. *(Ruaraidh)*

CAITHNESS

MEY   ND2872
Castle Arms (01847) 851244
A836; KW14 8XH Whitewashed 19th-c coaching inn under newish ownership; well liked food in evening restaurant (may be shut winter – telephone to check) including good locally smoked produce, friendly helpful service, lounge bar with plenty of malt whiskies and bottled beers (no cask ales), views of Dunnet Head and across Pentland Firth to the Orkneys; nine comfortable bedrooms (five in converted stable block, one with disabled facilities), well placed for north coast of Caithness, Gills Bay ferry and Castle of Mey, open from 6pm to non-residents. *(CDM)*

DUMFRIESSHIRE

BARGRENNAN   NX3576
House O' Hill (01671) 840243
Off A714, road opposite church; DG8 6RN Small pub on edge of Galloway Forest (mountain biking), good popular food from fair-priced varied menu including daily specials, a couple of real ales and decent wine list, afternoon teas, friendly helpful staff; children and dogs (in bar) welcome, two comfortable bedrooms and self-catering cottage, open all day. *(Charles Fraser)*

BEATTOCK   NT0702
Old Stables (01683) 300134
Smith Way; 0.25 mile from M74 junction 15; DG10 9QX Turreted 19th-c pub at edge of the village, Belhaven beers and bargain home-cooked food, friendly staff, bar and second railway-themed room with memorabilia from the old Beattock line (famous for its steep gradients); live music, pool, darts, big-screen TVs and fruit machine; children and dogs welcome, covered outside seating area, three bedrooms and parking for campervans, open all day. *(Charles and Maddie Bishop)*

DUMFRIES   NX9776
★ Cavens Arms (01387) 252896
Buccleuch Street; DG1 2AH Good generously served home-made food (all day weekends, not Mon) from pubby standards up, seven well kept interesting ales, traditional ciders and fine choice of malts, friendly attentive service, civilised front part with lots of wood, drinkers' area at back with bar stools, banquettes and traditional cast-iron tables, more recently added lounge/restaurant areas; discreet TV; no children or dogs allowed, disabled facilities, small terrace at back, open all day and can get very busy. *(Dr J Barrie Jones)*

DUMFRIES   NX9775
Globe (01387) 252335
High Street; DG1 2JA Proper town pub with strong Burns connections, especially in the dark-panelled 17th-century snug and little museum-like room beyond; main part is more modern in feel; ales such as Caledonian and Sulwath, plenty of whiskies and good value pubby food, friendly service; live music

Mon, children welcome in eating areas, terrace seating, open all day. (*Charles Fraser*)

DUNBARTONSHIRE

ARROCHAR   NN2903
Village Inn (01301) 702279
A814, just off A83 W of Loch Lomond; G83 7AX Friendly lochside inn with well kept ales such as Caledonian and Fyne and several dozen malts, wide choice of popular food in simple dining area including breakfasts (till midday) and weekday two-course menu, heavy beams, bare boards, panelling and roaring fire, steps down to unpretentious bar; background music, sports TV; children welcome in eating areas till 8pm, no dogs, tables out on deck and lawn with lovely loch and hill views, neat comfortable bedrooms (more spacious ones in former barn), good breakfast, open (and food) all day. (*Stuart and Natalie Granville*)

LUSS   NS3498
Inn on Loch Lomond (01436) 860678 *A82, about 3 miles N; G83 8PD* Large open-plan inn across the road from Loch Lomond with tables out overlooking it, decent choice of enjoyable food all day including local fish in bar and restaurant, well kept beers, some 30 wines by the glass and good range of whiskies, friendly helpful staff; children welcome, private jetty with boat trips, bedrooms including eight in water's edge lodge – great views. (*Dr A McCormick*)

EAST LOTHIAN

ABERLADY   NT4679
Old Aberlady (01875) 870503
Main Street; EH32 0NF In pretty coastal village with lots to do nearby; varied choice of enjoyable food including breakfast from 8am, Caledonian Deuchars IPA and a guest, good wine and whisky selection, friendly staff; children and dogs welcome, six bedrooms, open (and food) all day. (*Charles and Maddie Bishop*)

GULLANE   NT4882
★**Old Clubhouse** (01620) 842008
East Links Road; EH31 2AF Single-storey building in nice position overlooking Gullane Links; cosy bar and more formal dining room, seating from wooden dining chairs and banquettes to big squashy leather armchairs and sofas, Victorian pictures and cartoons, stuffed birds, sheet music covers, golfing and other memorabilia, open fires, good choice of home-made food including own ice-cream, Caledonian Deuchars IPA, Timothy Taylors Landlord and a couple of guests, nice house wines, friendly helpful service; under-10s till 8pm, dogs welcome in bar, plenty of seats out at front, open (and food) all day. (*Paul Baxter*)

HADDINGTON   NT5173
Victoria (01620) 823332
Court Street; EH41 3JD Popular bar-restaurant with good imaginative local food cooked by chef-landlord, Belhaven ales and short but decent wine list, prompt friendly service, mix of cushioned dining chairs and wall banquettes on wooden flooring or carpets, woodburning stove; five bedrooms, open all day. (*Charles and Maddie Bishop*)

FIFE

CULROSS   NS9885
Red Lion (01383) 880225
Low Causeway; KY12 8HN Convivial old pub in pretty NTS village, wide choice of fair value food, a beer from Inveralmond and several wines by the glass, beams and amazing painted ceilings; seats outside, open (and food) all day. (*Belinda and Neil Garth*)

CUPAR   NO3714
Boudingait (01334) 654681
Bonnygate; KY15 4BU Bustling bar with captain's and cushion-seated chairs around dark tables on wood flooring, open fire, high chairs against counter serving a couple of changing ales, good choice of well liked traditional food at reasonable prices, afternoon teas, friendly attentive staff; quiz Weds, live folk third Thurs of month; children welcome, open (and some food) all day. (*Caroline Prescott*)

ELIE   NO4999
Ship (01333) 330246
The Toft, off A917 (High Street) towards harbour; KY9 1DT Attractively updated and in great position for enjoying a drink overlooking the sandy bay; bar and two restaurants (one upstairs), good seasonal food, friendly service; children and dogs welcome, seats on terrace (own bar) looking out to stone granary and pier, maybe beach cricket, six boutique-style bedrooms, open all day. (*Pat and Stewart Gordon*)

INVERNESS-SHIRE

ARDGOUR   NN0163
Inn at Ardgour (01855) 841225
From A82 follow signs for Strontian A861 and take Corran Ferry across loch to the inn; note that ferry does not sail over Christmas period; PH33 7AA Traditional fairly remote roadside inn by Corran Ferry slipway with fine Loch Linnhe views; enjoyable food and decent beer and whisky choice, friendly accommodating staff, restaurant; children and well behaved dogs welcome, a few tables outside, clean bedrooms (dogs allowed in some), open all day in season (from 4pm winter). (*Dr A McCormick*)

AVIEMORE   NH8612
Cairngorm (01479) 810233
Grampian Road (A9); PH22 1PE Large
flagstoned bar in traditional turreted hotel,
lively and friendly, with good value food from
wide-ranging menu using local produce,
Cairngorm ales and good choice of other
drinks, prompt helpful service, tartan-walled
and carpeted restaurant; daily live music
(not Tues when there's a quiz), sports TV;
children welcome, comfortable smart
bedrooms (some with stunning views), open
(and food) all day. *(Sarah and David Gibbs)*

CARRBRIDGE   NH9022
Cairn (01479) 841212
Main Road; PH23 3AS Welcoming
traditionally furnished hotel bar, pubby food
using local produce, three well kept ales
including Cairngorm, old local pictures,
warm coal fire, separate more formal
dining room; pool and sports TV; children
and dogs welcome, seats and tables out in
front, seven comfortable bedrooms, open
all day. *(Johnston and Maureen Anderson)*

DORES   NH5934
★Dores (01463) 751203
B852 SW of Inverness; IV2 6TR
Traditional country pub with exposed stone
walls and low ceilings in delightful spot on
the shore of Loch Ness; small attractive
bar on right with two or three well kept
changing scottish ales and several whiskies,
two-part dining area to the left serving good
food from breakfasts and pub favourites up,
friendly staff; children and dogs welcome,
sheltered front garden, lots of picnic-sets out
behind taking in the spectacular view, open
(and food) all day. *(Sarah and David Gibbs)*

FORT WILLIAM   NN1274
Ben Nevis Inn (01397) 701227
N off A82: Achintee; PH33 6TE Roomy
converted stone barn in stunning spot
by path up to Ben Nevis, good mainly
straightforward food (lots of walkers so
best to book), ales such as Cairngorm
and Isle of Skye, prompt cheery service,
bare-boards dining area with steps up to
bar; live music (Tues in summer, maybe
first and third Thurs in winter); children
welcome, no dogs, seats out at front and
back, bunkhouse below, open all day Apr-Oct,
otherwise closed Mon-Weds. *(CDM)*

GLEN SHIEL   NH0711
Cluanie Inn (01320) 340238
*A87 Invergarry–Kyle of Lochalsh, on
Loch Cluanie; IV63 7YW* Welcoming
inn in lovely isolated setting by Loch
Cluanie with stunning views; friendly table
service for drinks including well kept
Isle of Skye and excellent malt whisky
range, enjoyable food (good local game
and salmon) in three knocked-together
rooms and restaurant, warm log fire, chatty

parrots in lobby; children allowed, dogs
too (owners have several of their own),
big comfortable pine-furnished modern
bedrooms, self-catering club house, good
breakfast (non-residents welcome), open
all day. *(Molly and Stewart Lindsay)*

GLENFINNAN   NM9080
Glenfinnan House (01397) 722235
*Take A830 off A32 to Glenfinnan, turn
left after Glenfinnan Monument Visitors
Centre; PH37 4LT* Beautifully placed
18th-c hotel by Loch Shiel, traditional bar
with well kept ales and over 50 whiskies,
good food including fish/seafood and local
venison, restaurant; lawns down to the
water, comfortable bedrooms, may close
during the winter. *(Belinda and Neil Garth)*

GLENUIG   NM6576
Glenuig Inn (01687) 470219
*A861 SW of Lochailort, off A830 Fort
William–Mallaig; PH38 4NG* Friendly
bar set on picturesque bay, enjoyable
locally sourced food including some
from next-door smokery, well kept
Cairngorm ales and a scottish cider
on tap, lots of bottled beers and good
range of whiskies, dining room with
woodburner; dogs welcome, bedrooms in
adjoining block, also bunkhouse popular
with walkers and divers, moorings for
visiting yachts, open (and food) all day.
(Charlotte and William Mason)

INVERIE   NG7500
★Old Forge (01687) 462267
Park in Mallaig for ferry; PH41 4PL
Utterly remote waterside stone pub
with stunning views across Loch Nevis;
comfortable mix of old furnishings, lots of
charts and sailing prints, open fire, good
reasonably priced bar food including fresh
local seafood (excellent langoustines)
and venison burgers, a well kept house ale
(Remoteness IPA) and other draught beers,
lots of whiskies and good wine choice,
restaurant extension; live music and ceilidhs
(instruments provided); children and dogs
welcome, six bedrooms (get booked early),
closed Weds, otherwise open all day from
3pm, evening food only in winter; the snag
is getting here – boat (jetty moorings and
new pier), Mallaig foot-ferry six times a day
(four in winter) or 15-mile walk through
Knoydart from nearest road. *(David Todd)*

INVERMORISTON   NH4216
Glenmoriston Arms (01320) 351206
A82/A887; IV63 7YA Small civilised
hotel dating in part from 1740 when it was
a drovers' inn; bare-boards bar with open
fire and big old stag's head, a well kept
beer such as Orkney and over 100 malt
whiskies, good food here from lunchtime
sandwiches up or in neatly laid-out evening
restaurant with antique rifles, friendly
staff; children welcome, handy for Loch

Ness, ten bedrooms (three in converted outbuilding), open all day, from 4pm Nov-Mar. *(Charlotte and William Mason)*

INVERNESS NH6645

Black Isle (01463) 229920

Church Street; IV1 1EN Buzzy new corner bar owned by Black Isle brewery, more than 20 draught beers (listed on screens) plus extensive bottled range from slabby wood counter, long rustic tables, benches and mix of wooden chairs on bare boards, full-length windows at front, some colourful murals and high ceiling with exposed ducting, enjoyable food including cheese/charcuterie boards and good wood-fired pizzas, friendly knowledgeable staff; barrel tables and seats made from pallets on part-covered terrace, 14 bedrooms. *(the Dutchman)*

INVERNESS NH6645

Number 27 (01463) 241999

Castle Street; IV2 3DU Busy pub opposite the castle, friendly and welcoming, with plenty of draught and bottled beers and good choice of well liked/priced food including Mon steak night, restaurant at back; children welcome, open (and food) all day. *(Philip Chesington)*

INVERNESS NH6645

Phoenix Ale House (01463) 240300

Academy Street; IV1 1LX Much-liked 1890s bare-boards bar with fine oval servery, up to ten real ales and enjoyable reasonably priced food, neatly furnished adjoining dining room; sports TV; open (and food) all day. *(Philip Chesington)*

MALLAIG NM6796

Steam (01687) 462002

Davies Brae; PH41 4PU Popular Victorian inn run by mother and daughter team, good choice of food including freshly landed fish/seafood (takeaway menu too), speedy service, bar with open fire, split-level bare-boards restaurant with high-backed dark leather chairs around pale tables; live music; children and dogs welcome (resident great dane), tables in back beer garden, five simple but comfortable bedrooms (no breakfast), open all day. *(Angus Light)*

ONICH NN0263

Four Seasons (01855) 821393

Off A82, signed for Inchree, N of village; PH33 6SE Wooden building – part of Inchree holiday complex; bare-boards bar with cushioned wall benches, up to three scottish ales and decent choice of whiskies, central log fire in dining area serving reasonably priced evening food from varied menu, local maps and guidebooks for sale, daily weather forecast and free wi-fi; children (till 8.30pm) and dogs welcome, hostel, lodge and chalet accommodation, handy for Corran Ferry, open from 2.30pm, best to check winter hours. *(Stuart and Natalie Granville)*

WHITEBRIDGE NH4815

Whitebridge (01456) 486226

B862 SW of village; IV2 6UN Old-style hunting, shooting and fishing hotel set in the foothills of the Monadhliath Mountains, popular and cheerful, with good traditional food, well kept ales such as Cairngorm, Cromarty and Loch Ness and some 50 malts, two bars with woodburners, summer restaurant; well behaved dogs welcome, 12 bedrooms, open all day in summer, all day weekends winter. *(John Poulter)*

KINCARDINESHIRE

FETTERCAIRN NO6573

Ramsay Arms (01561) 340334

Burnside Road; AB30 1XX Hotel with tasty traditional food in tartan-carpeted bar and smart oak-panelled restaurant, friendly service, well kept ales and a dozen malts including the local Fettercairn; children welcome, picnic-sets in garden, attractive village (liked by Queen Victoria who stayed at the hotel), 12 comfortable bedrooms, good breakfast. *(Samuel and Melissa Turnbull)*

STONEHAVEN NO8595

Lairhillock (01569) 730001

Netherley; 6 miles N of Stonehaven, 6 miles S of Aberdeen, take the Durris turn-off from the A90; AB39 3QS Extended 200-year-old family-run inn; beamed bar with dark woodwork, panelled wall benches and attractive mix of old seats, lots of brass and copper, nice open fire, Timothy Taylors Landlord and a guest, several wines by the glass, good malt whiskies, generally well liked food from lunchtime baguettes up, spacious lounge with unusual central fire, panoramic views from back conservatory; children and dogs (in bar) welcome, open all day. *(Gus Swan, Neil Allen)*

STONEHAVEN NO8785

Marine Hotel (01569) 762155

Shore Head; AB39 2JY Popular harbourside pub with six well kept ales, 165 bottled belgian beers and plenty of whiskies, good food especially local fish/seafood, efficient service, large stripped-stone bar with log fire in cosy side room, upstairs sea-view restaurant; live acoustic music last Thurs of month; children welcome, pavement tables, bedrooms, open all day (till 1am Fri, Sat). *(Samuel and Melissa Turnbull)*

STONEHAVEN NO8785

Ship (01569) 762617

Shore Head; AB39 2JY Whitewashed 18th-c waterside inn with bustling local atmosphere, good selection of changing beers and over 100 whiskies, well liked food in bar or modern restaurant, friendly staff; sports TV; children and dogs (in bar) welcome, disabled access/loos, tables out overlooking pretty harbour, 11 bedrooms, open all day, food all day weekends. *(Dr A McCormick)*

KIRKCUDBRIGHTSHIRE

CASTLE DOUGLAS NX7662
Sulwath Brewery (01556) 504525
King Street; DG7 1DT Convivial bar attached to this small brewery, six Sulwath ales in top condition and their bottled beers, Weston's cider, limited food (hot pies), stools and barrel tables, off-sales and souvenirs, brewery tours Mon and Fri at 1pm (unless by prior arrangement); dogs welcome, disabled access, open 10am-6pm Mon-Sat. *(Giles and Annie Francis)*

DALRY NX6281
Clachan (01644) 430241
A713 Castle Douglas–Ayr; DG7 3UW Cheerful traditional inn with plenty of character, beams, dark woodwork and open fires, some large stuffed fish in display cases and other interesting bits and pieces, two well kept changing ales and good selection of other drinks from carved counter, popular good value food from lunchtime sandwiches and pub favourites up, friendly efficient service, woodburner in pitched-ceiling timbered restaurant; TV, fruit machine; children and dogs welcome, on Southern Upland Way, bedrooms, open all day. *(Phil Papworth)*

GATEHOUSE OF FLEET NX6056
Masonic Arms (01557) 814335
Ann Street; off B727; DG7 2HU Spacious dining pub with comfortable two-room pubby bar, traditional seating, pictures on timbered walls, plates on delft shelf, stuffed fish above brick fireplace, a couple of real ales and good choice of malts, enjoyable food in bar and contemporary restaurant, attractive terracotta-tiled conservatory with cane furniture; background music (live Thurs), quiz Fri, free wi-fi; children and dogs (in bar) welcome, picnic-sets under parasols in neatly kept sheltered garden, more seats in front, open all day. *(Stuart Douglas)*

GATEHOUSE OF FLEET NX5956
Ship (01557) 814217
Fleet Street; DG7 2JT Late Victorian village inn on the banks of the River Fleet, popular food, Belhaven beers, over 100 malt whiskies and several local artisan gins, neatly kept interior with woodburner, restaurant (only for residents in evening), pleasant service; waterside garden, comfortable bedrooms and good breakfast; Dorothy Sayers wrote *Five Red Herrings* while staying here in the 1930s. *(Jamie and Lizzie McEwan)*

HAUGH OF URR NX8066
Laurie Arms (01556) 660246
B794 N of Dalbeattie; Main Street; DG7 3YA Welcoming 19th-c village pub with good local atmosphere, traditional furnishings in carpeted log-fire bar with steps up to similar area, restaurant, tasty reasonably priced home-made food including good steaks, well kept changing ales and decent wines by the glass, friendly service, games room with darts and pool; quiz first Fri of month; children welcome, dogs in bar, tables out at front and on sheltered terrace behind, open (and food) all day weekends. *(Jamie and Lizzie McEwan)*

KIPPFORD NX8355
Anchor (01556) 620205
Off A710 S of Dalbeattie; DG5 4LN Popular waterfront inn overlooking yachting estuary and peaceful hills, nautical theme décor and slightly old-fashioned feel, open fire in small traditional back bar with local photographs, more tables in area off, bright roomy dining room, good choice of generously served pubby food including local fish, two or three ales such as Harviestoun and Sulwath, lots of malts; background music, TV; children and dogs welcome, tables out at front, good walks and bird-watching, on Seven Stanes cycle route, seven bedrooms, open all day in summer. *(David and Betty Gittins)*

KIRKCUDBRIGHT NX6850
Selkirk Arms (01557) 330402
High Street; DG6 4JG Comfortable well run 18th-c hotel in pleasant spot by mouth of the Dee, simple locals' front bar (own street entrance), partitioned high-ceilinged and tartan-carpeted lounge with upholstered armchairs, wall banquettes and paintings for sale, ales including a house beer from local Sulwath, enjoyable food in bistro and evening restaurant from pub standards up, efficient service; background music, TV; children (not in bar) and dogs welcome, smart wooden furniture under blue parasols in neat garden with 15th-c font, 17 comfortable bedrooms, open all day. *(Jamie and Lizzie McEwan)*

LANARKSHIRE

BALMAHA NS4290
Oak Tree (01360) 870357
B837; G63 0JQ Family-run slate-clad inn on Loch Lomond's quiet side; beams, timbers and panelling, pubby bar with lots of old photographs, farm tools, stuffed animals and collection of grandfather clocks, log fire, good choice of enjoyable food from sandwiches and snacks up, own-brew ales along with

---

We mention bottled beers and spirits only if there is something unusual about them – imported belgian real ales, say, or dozens of malt whiskies; so do please let us know about them in your reports.

other scottish beers and over 50 whiskies, restaurant, coffee shop and ice-cream parlour, village shop; children welcome, plenty of tables out around ancient oak tree, popular with West Highland Way walkers, seven attractive bedrooms, two bunkhouses and four cottages. *(Mandy and Gary Redstone)*

BIGGAR
NT0437
Crown (01899) 220116
High Street (A702); ML12 6DL Friendly old pub with enjoyable food all day including vegetarian choices and good value Sun carvery, two well kept changing ales (annual beer festival – see website), open fire in beamed front bar, panelled lounge with old local pictures, restaurant; live music every other Fri; children welcome, open (and food) all day. *(CDM)*

FINTRY
NS6186
Fintry (01360) 860224
Main Street; G63 0XA Refurbished village pub with beers from on-site microbrewery and enjoyable food, friendly relaxed atmosphere; live traditional music Weds evening, Sun afternoon and first Sat of the month, quiz last Mon; children welcome, dogs in pool room or suntrap back garden, open all day. *(Martin Turner)*

GLASGOW
NS5767
Belle (0141) 339 2299
Great Western Road; G12 8HX Busy pub with wide mix of customers; leather-topped stools, modern and traditional chairs around all sorts of tables on polished wood floor, stags' heads and unusual mirrors on painted or exposed stone walls, open fire, american craft beers and european lagers; dogs welcome, tables and chairs on pavement and in tiny leafy back garden, open all day. *(Charles Fraser)*

GLASGOW
NS5965
Counting House (0141) 225 0160
St Vincent Place/George Square; G1 2DH Wetherspoons in converted 19th-c bank, imposing interior rising into lofty richly decorated coffered ceiling culminating in great central dome, big windows, decorative glasswork, statues and wall-safes, smaller rooms (former managers' offices) around perimeter, one like a well stocked library, a few themed with pictures and prints of historical characters, fine choice of beers from far and wide and lots of malt whiskies, usual good value food all day; children welcome if eating, open 8am-midnight. *(Charles Fraser, Ruaraidh)*

GLASGOW
NS5865
Drum & Monkey (0141) 221 6636
St Vincent Street; G2 5TF Busy Nicholsons bank conversion, lots of carved mahogany, granite pillars and ornate ceiling, island bar serving beers such as Caledonian, over 20 gins and decent range of wines,

good value food, pleasant staff, quieter back area; open all day. *(Charles Fraser)*

GLASGOW
NS5865
Pot Still (0141) 333 0980
Hope Street; G2 2TH Comfortable and welcoming little pub with over 700 malt whiskies (good value whisky of the month), traditional bare-boards interior with raised back part, button-back leather bench seats, dark panelling, etched and stained glass, columns up to ornately corniced ceiling, four changing ales and interesting bottled beers from nice old-fashioned servery, friendly knowledgeable staff; silent fruit machine; open all day and can get packed. *(Ken Tay)*

GLASGOW
NS5965
★**Sloans** (0141) 221 8886
Argyle Arcade; G2 8BG Restored Grade A listed building over three floors, many original features including fine mahogany staircase, etched glass, ornate woodwork and moulded ceilings, ales such as Caledonian and Kelburn, enjoyable modern food in ground-floor bar-bistro and upstairs restaurant, friendly staff; lots of events from life drawing to live music and quiz nights in impressive barrel-vaulted parquet-floored ballroom; children welcome, tables in courtyard, weekend market, open all day (till late Fri, Sat). *(Charles Fraser)*

GLASGOW
NS5865
State (0141) 332 2159
Holland Street; G2 4NG High-ceilinged bar with marble pillars, lots of carved wood including handsome oak island servery, half a dozen or so well kept changing ales, bargain basic lunchtime food up (not weekends), some areas set for dining, good atmosphere and friendly staff, armchairs among other comfortable seats, coal-effect fire in big wooden fireplace, old prints and theatrical posters; background music (live weekends and comedy nights), silent sports TVs, games machine; open all day. *(Ken Tay)*

GLASGOW
NS5666
Tennents (0141) 339 7203
Byres Road; G12 8TN Big busy high-ceilinged Victorian corner pub near the university, ornate plasterwork, panelling and paintings, traditional tables and chairs, stools and wall seating, a dozen well kept ales and keenly priced wines, wide range of good value food from sandwiches and wraps up including breakfasts till midday; basement bar for weekend DJs, sports TVs; open all day. *(Ruaraidh)*

GLASGOW
NS5666
Three Judges (0141) 337 3055
Dumbarton Road, opposite Byres Road; G11 6PR Traditional corner bar with eight quickly changing ales from small breweries far and wide (they get through several hundred a year), friendly staff offer

tasters; live jazz Sun afternoons, TV; dogs welcome, open all day. *(Charles Fraser)*

GLASGOW NS5466
St Louis (0141) 339 1742
Dumbarton Road, by the roundabout; G11 6RD Relaxed bar-café with simple stylish décor, Williams beers and enjoyable reasonably priced food including range of burgers, friendly staff; weekend live music, free wi-fi; dogs welcome, open (and food) all day. *(Michael Butler)*

MIDLOTHIAN

CRAMOND NT1877
Cramond Inn (0131) 336 2035
Cramond Glebe Road (off A90 W of Edinburgh); EH4 6NU New canadian licensees for this charming 17th-c inn near the quayside; softly lit smallish traditional beamed rooms, open fires, old local photographs on dark brown walls, large carved settle, popular well priced pubby food, Sam Smiths keg beers, friendly service (can be slow at busy times); children and dogs welcome, picturesque village at mouth of River Almond, delightful views from tables out on grass, open (and food) all day. *(Lexie Booth)*

EDINBURGH NT2574
★**Abbotsford** (0131) 225 5276
Rose Street; E end, beside South St David Street; EH2 2PR Busy city pub with unchanging feel; hefty Victorian island bar (ornately carved from dark spanish mahogany and highly polished) serving ales such as Atlas, Caledonian, Fyne, Harviestoun, Orkney and Stewart, also selection of bottled american beers and around 70 malt whiskies, traditional food (all day Fri, Sat), long wooden tables and leatherette benches, high panelled walls and handsome green and gold moulded ceiling, smarter upstairs restaurant where children allowed; open all day. *(Charles and Maddie Bishop)*

EDINBURGH NT2574
★**Café Royal** (0131) 556 1884
West Register Street; EH2 2AA Wonderful Victorian baroque interior – floors and stairway laid with marble, chandeliers hanging from magnificent plasterwork ceilings, superb series of Doulton tilework portraits of historical innovators (Watt, Faraday, Stephenson, Caxton, Benjamin Franklin and Robert Peel), substantial island bar serving well kept Greene King IPA, Belhaven 80/-, Stewart Edinburgh Gold and four guests, several wines by the glass and 40 malts, very well liked food with emphasis on fresh seafood, good friendly

service, the restaurant's stained glass is also worth a look (children welcome here); background music; open all day (till 1am Fri, Sat), can get very busy. *(Pat and Stewart Gordon, Comus and Sarah Elliott, Anthony, Roger and Donna Huggins, Barry Collett)*

EDINBURGH NT2573
Deacon Brodies (0131) 225 6531
Lawnmarket; EH1 2NT Commemorating the notorious highwayman town councillor who was eventually hanged on the scaffold he'd designed; very busy city bar with wonderfully ornate high ceiling, well kept ales and decent selection of whiskies from long counter, good choice of reasonably priced food in upstairs dining lounge where children allowed; background music, TV; pavement seating. *(Tony Scott)*

EDINBURGH NT2573
Doric (0131) 225 1084
Market Street; EH1 1DE Welcoming 17th-c pub-restaurant with plenty of atmosphere, simple furnishings in small bar with wood floor and lots of pictures, four cask ales and good range of bottled beers, 50 single malts, friendly young staff, interesting modern food (must book) in upstairs wine bar (children welcome) and bistro; handy for Waverley station, open all day. *(Lexie Booth)*

EDINBURGH NT2573
Ensign Ewart (0131) 225 7440
Lawnmarket, Royal Mile; last pub on right before castle; EH1 2PE Charming dimly lit old-world pub handy for castle (so gets busy), beams peppered with brasses, huge painting of Ewart at Waterloo capturing french banner, assorted furniture including elbow tables, well kept Caledonian ales and lots of whiskies, straightforward bar food; background and regular live music (not Tues, Thurs), games machine, keypad entry to lavatories; open all day. *(CDM)*

EDINBURGH NT2573
★**Halfway House** (0131) 225 7101
Fleshmarket Close (steps between Cockburn Street and Market Street, opposite Waverley station); EH1 1BX Tiny one-room character pub off steep steps, part carpeted, part tiled, with a few small tables and high-backed settles, lots of prints (some golf and railway themes), four well kept scottish ales and good range of malt whiskies, short choice of decent low-priced food, friendly staff; dogs welcome, open (and food) all day. *(Alf Wright)*

EDINBURGH NT2473
Hanging Bat (0131) 229 0759
Lothian Road; EH3 9AB Modern bar on three levels with own microbrewery, six real

---

We accept no free drinks or meals and inspections are anonymous.

ales, 14 craft kegs and 120 bottled beers, food such as ribs and hot dogs; children till 8pm, open (and food) all day. *(CDM, Ruaraidh)*

EDINBURGH NT2573
Inn on the Mile (0131) 556 9940
High Street; EH1 1LL Centrally placed pub-restaurant-boutique hotel in former bank; long high-ceilinged bar with booth seating, good selection of beers including Mile Ale badged for them, plenty of wines, whiskies and cocktails, well priced food from panini to hearty helpings of pubby food, good friendly service; nightly live music, projector for sports TV, free wi-fi; children welcome, a few seats outside, nine bedrooms, open all day (till 1am Fri, Sat when can be lively). *(Charles Fraser)*

EDINBURGH NT2573
Jolly Judge (0131) 225 2669
James Court, by 495 Lawnmarket; EH1 2PB Small comfortable basement of 16th-c tenement with interesting fruit- and flower-painted wooden ceiling, welcoming relaxed atmosphere, two changing ales and good range of malts, lunchtime bar meals, log fire; no children, open all day. *(Tony Scott)*

EDINBURGH NT1968
Kinleith Mill (0131) 453 3214
Lanark Road (A70); EH14 5EN Refurbished pub (former Kinleith Arms) with contemporary bar, well kept ales and popular food including early-bird menu; sports TV, darts; suntrap back garden; open all day. *(Charles Fraser)*

EDINBURGH NT2473
Oxford (0131) 539 7119
Young Street; EH2 4JB Friendly no-frills backstreet local with links to Ian Rankin and other scottish writers and artists; tiny bustling bar with a couple of built-in wall settles, steps up to quieter back room, four well kept regional beers and good range of whiskies, no food or children; TV; dogs welcome, open all day. *(Comus and Sarah Elliott)*

EDINBURGH NT2573
Sandy Bells (0131) 225 1156
Forrest Road; EH1 2QH Small unpretentious place popular for its nightly folk music, eight scottish ales and wide choice of whiskies, simple food, good mix of customers and friendly atmosphere; open all day. *(Lexie Booth)*

EDINBURGH NT2872
Sheep Heid (0131) 661 7974
The Causeway, Duddingston; EH15 3QA Comfortably updated former coaching house in lovely spot near King Arthur's Seat, long history and some famous guests

such as Mary, Queen of Scots, fine rounded servery in main room, well kept beers and good, enterprising food including children's menu, friendly young staff, attractive dining rooms, skittle alley; courtyard tables, open (and food) all day. *(CDM)*

EDINBURGH NT2574
Standing Order (0131) 225 4460
George Street; EH2 2LR Grand Wetherspoons bank conversion in three elegant Georgian houses, enormous main room with elaborate colourful ceiling, lots of tables and smaller side booths, other rooms including two with floor-to-ceiling bookshelves, comfortable clubby seats, various portraits and an Adam fireplace, wide range of real ales from long counter, usual bar food, gets very busy (particularly Sat night) but staff cope well; weekend live music, sports TV, free wi-fi; children welcome, disabled facilities, open 8am-1am. *(Roger and Donna Huggins)*

EDINBURGH NT2574
★**Starbank** (0131) 552 4141
Laverockbank Road, off Starbank Road, just off A901 Granton–Leith; EH5 3BZ Cheerful pub in a fine spot with terrific views over the Firth of Forth, long airy bare-boards bar with leather bench and tub seats, up to eight well kept ales and good choice of malt whiskies, interesting food (and set menus) in conservatory restaurant; background and regular live music nights, quiz every second Weds, sports TV, fruit machine; children welcome till 9pm if eating, dogs on leads, sheltered back terrace, parking on adjacent hilly street, open all day. *(CDM, Lexie Booth)*

EDINBURGH NT2574
Stockbridge Tap (0131) 343 3000
Raeburn Place, Stockbridge; EH4 1HN Welcoming corner pub with traditional L-shaped interior, seven interesting beers and good reasonably priced food (not Mon or Tues); no children, dogs welcome, open all day (till 1am Fri, Sat). *(Anthony)*

MORAYSHIRE

FINDHORN NJ0464
Crown & Anchor (01309) 690243
Off A96; IV36 3YF Nice village setting adjacent to small sheltered harbour, enjoyable food including good fresh fish/seafood specials, a couple of real ales and plenty of whiskies, woodburner in cosy bar; sports TV; children welcome (under-14s in conservatory and restaurant till 8pm), outside seating and smokers' shelter 'the Smokooterie', seven bedrooms, sand dune walks and good boating in Findhorn Bay, open all day. *(John Evans)*

We say if we know a pub has background music.

NAIRNSHIRE

CAWDOR   NH8449
Cawdor Tavern (01667) 404777
Pub signed from B9090; IV12 5XP
Popular dining pub in lovely conservation
village near the castle, well kept Orkney
ales, nine wines by the glass (comprehensive
list) and good range of malt whiskies,
enjoyable freshly cooked food from traditional
choices up, friendly staff, oak-panelled
lounge with log fire, pool in public bar,
restaurant; children welcome, seats on
front terrace, open (and food) all day in
summer. *(the Dutchman, John Evans)*

PEEBLESSHIRE

INNERLEITHEN   NT3336
★**Traquair Arms** (01896) 830229
*B709, just off A72 Peebles–Galashiels;
follow signs for Traquair House;
EH44 6PD* Old stone inn at heart of this
pretty borders village; one of the few places
serving Traquair ale (produced in original
oak vessels in 18th-c brewhouse at nearby
Traquair House), also Tempest Cascadian
and Timothy Taylors Landlord, over 40 malt
whiskies, enjoyable traditional food with some
spanish influences (all day Fri-Sun), main
bar with warm open fire, another in relaxed
bistro-style restaurant, good mix of customers;
background music; children welcome, dogs in
bar, seats out at front and in attractive back
garden, 14 bedrooms and six self-catering
cottages, open all day. *(Belinda and Neil Garth)*

PERTHSHIRE

BANKFOOT   NO0635
Bankfoot (01738) 787243
Main Street; PH1 4AB Traditional
coaching inn dating from 1760, two bars
and restaurant, well kept local ales and
enjoyable food cooked by landlady, friendly
helpful staff, open fires; live folk night Weds;
dogs welcome, six comfortable bedrooms,
open all day weekends, closed lunchtimes
Mon, Tues (food for residents only on
those days). *(Jamie and Lizzie McEwan)*

BLAIR ATHOLL   NN8765
★**Atholl Arms** (01796) 481205
B8079; PH18 5SG Sizeable stone hotel with
nice old-fashioned scottish feel; two cosy bar
rooms (one beamed and tartan-carpeted),
open fires, armchairs, sofas and traditional
tables, chairs and benches, four local Moulin
ales, grand dining room with suit of armour
and stag's head, good well priced food
using local salmon and meat, quick friendly
service; 31 good value bedrooms, self-catering
cottage, lovely setting near the castle, open
(and food) all day. *(Sarah and David Gibbs)*

BRIG O' TURK   NN5306
★**Byre** (01877) 376292
*A821 Callander–Trossachs, just outside
village; FK17 8HT* Newly refurbished and
beautifully placed byre conversion with slate-
floored log-fire bar and roomier high-raftered
restaurant, good popular food (best to book)
including local game and fish, a couple
of changing scottish ales and nice wines,
friendly helpful staff; children welcome,
outside tables and boules piste, lovely walks,
may close Mon, Tues during winter (and all
Jan), otherwise open all day. *(Paul Baxter)*

CALLANDER   NN6208
Old Rectory (01877) 339215
Leny Road (A84); FK17 8AL Friendly
19th-c stone inn away from the town
centre, cosy little bar with fine range of
whiskies, well liked reasonably priced food
in small adjoining restaurant including
good Sun roasts, pleasant helpful staff;
live folk music Weds and some weekends,
quiz second Tues of month, free wi-fi; dogs
welcome, four bedrooms, handy for Trossachs
National Park, open all day. *(John Evans)*

DUNBLANE   NN7801
Tappit Hen (01786) 825226
Kirk Street; FK15 0AL Small drinkers' pub
across close from cathedral, five changing
ales and good range of malt whiskies, friendly
busy atmosphere; sports TV; open all day
(till 1am Fri, Sat). *(Les and Sandra Brown)*

DUNKELD   NO0243
Atholl Arms (01350) 727219
Atholl Street (A923); PH8 0AQ Sizeable
Victorian hotel with smallish bar and
lounge, open fires, good choice of well
kept ales such as Inveralmond, decent
all-day food from varied menu including
cullen skink and beef stovies, pleasant
service; 17 bedrooms (some with views
of River Tay). *(Sarah and David Gibbs)*

DUNNING   NO0114
Kirkstyle (01764) 684248
*B9141, off A9 S of Perth; Kirkstyle
Square; PH2 0RR* Unpretentious 18th-c
streamside pub under new owners who are
gradually renovating the building; log fire
in snug bar, up to three real ales including
one named for the pub and good choice
of whiskies, enjoyable reasonably priced
home-made food, attentive friendly service,
split-level stripped-stone back restaurant;
background music; children and dogs
welcome, open all day weekends. *(CDM)*

KENMORE   NN7745
Kenmore Hotel (01887) 830205
A827 W of Aberfeldy; PH15 2NU Small
hotel dating from the 16th c in pretty Loch
Tay village; comfortable traditional front
lounge with warm log fire (there's a poem
pencilled by Burns himself on the chimney

breast), dozens of malts helpfully arranged alphabetically, friendly attentive staff, modern restaurant with balcony; back bar and terrace overlooking River Tay with enjoyable food from lunchtime soup and sandwiches to grills, Inveralmond Ossian and decent wines by the glass; pool and winter darts, juke box, TV, fruit machine; children and dogs welcome, 40 bedrooms plus lodges, open all day. *(Sarah and David Gibbs)*

KILMAHOG   NN6008
★**Lade** (01877) 330152
A84 just NW of Callander, by A821 junction; FK17 8HD Lively family-run place with strong scottish theme – traditional weekend music, shop with over 190 bottled beers from regional microbreweries plus their own WayLade ales; plenty of character in several cosy beamed areas with panelling and stripped stone, highland prints and works by local artists, 40 malt whiskies, good home-made food from bar snacks up (booking advised), big-windowed restaurant, friendly staff; background music; children and dogs (in bar) welcome, disabled access, terrace and pleasant garden with fish ponds, open all day (till 1am Fri, Sat, but may close early in winter if quiet). *(Mollie and Stewart Lindsay)*

KIRKTON OF GLENISLA   NO2160
Glenisla Hotel (01575) 582223
B951 N of Kirriemuir and Alyth; PH11 8PH Attractively refurbished 17th-c coaching inn with good local atmosphere in traditional split-level bar, beams, flagstones and warm log fire, two well kept scottish ales and eight wines by the glass, popular home-made food using local produce from bar snacks up, good friendly service; children and dogs welcome, garden with play area, bedrooms, good walks from the door (on Cateran Trail), open all day in season. *(CDM)*

PERTH   NO1223
Greyfriars (01738) 633036
South Street; PH2 8PG Small comfortable local in old part of town, a couple of well kept changing ales and good whisky/gin range, enjoyable lunchtime food (not Sun) in bar or little upstairs dining room, friendly welcoming staff; live music Thurs (open mike) and Sat; open all day. *(Tony Scott)*

PITLOCHRY   NN9163
★**Killiecrankie Hotel** (01796) 473220
Killiecrankie, off A9 N; PH16 5LG Comfortable splendidly placed country hotel with attractive panelled bar and airy conservatory, well kept ales, over 40 malt whiskies and well chosen wines, good imaginative food in bar or more formal evening restaurant, friendly efficient service; children in eating areas, dogs welcome, extensive peaceful grounds with dramatic views, ten bedrooms. *(Caroline Prescott)*

PITLOCHRY   NN9459
★**Moulin** (01796) 472196
Kirkmichael Road, Moulin; A924 NE of Pitlochry centre; PH16 5EH Attractive much-extended inn brewing its own good beers in stables across the street, decent wines by the glass too and around 45 malt whiskies, cheerfully busy down-to-earth bar in oldest part with traditional character, smaller bare-boards room and bigger carpeted area with cushioned booths divided by stained-glass country scenes, popular quickly served food, separate restaurant; bar billiards and 1960s one-arm bandit; children and dogs (in bar) welcome, picnic-sets on gravel looking across to village kirk, good nearby walks, 15 comfortable bedrooms and two self-catering cottages, open all day. *(Barry Collett, Johnston and Maureen Anderson)*

PITLOCHRY   NN9358
Old Mill (01796) 474020
Mill Lane; PH16 5BH Welcoming family-run inn (former 19th-c watermill) with enjoyable food from sandwiches and sharing plates up, four real ales including Strathbraan and good wine and whisky choice, quick friendly service; live music Fri, Sat, free wi-fi; courtyard tables by Moulin Burn, comfortable well equipped bedrooms, open all day. *(Dr A McCormick)*

WEEM   NN8449
★**Ailean Chraggan** (01887) 820346
B846; PH15 2LD There's plenty to do and see close to this little hotel (now under new management); chatty bar with good mix of customers, local Strathbraan ales and around 100 malt whiskies, popular food including Sun carvery, efficient good-humoured service, adjoining neatly old-fashioned dining room and a comfortable carpeted modern lounge; quiz nights; children and dogs (in bar) welcome, covered terrace and garden behind, views stretching beyond the Tay to Ben Lawers (the highest peak in this part of Scotland), four spacious bedrooms, open all day Thurs-Sun, from 5pm other days. *(Neil and Angela Huxter, John Evans)*

ROSS-SHIRE

BADACHRO   NG7873
★**Badachro Inn** (01445) 741255
2.5 miles S of Gairloch village turn off A832 on to B8056, then after another 3.25 miles turn right in Badachro to the quay and inn; IV21 2AA Superbly positioned by Loch Gairloch with terrific views from decking down to water's edge, popular (especially summer) with mix of sailing visitors (free moorings) and chatty locals; welcoming bar with interesting photographs, An Teallach, Caledonian and a guest ale, about 50 malt whiskies and eight

wines by the glass, quieter eating area with big log fire, dining conservatory overlooking bay, fair-priced food including locally smoked fish and seafood; background music; children and dogs welcome, one bedroom, open all day. *(Barbara and Phil Bowie)*

GLENELG   NG8119
Glenelg Inn (01599) 522273
Unmarked road from Shiel Bridge (A87) towards Skye; IV40 8JR Unpretentious mountain cabin-like bar in small hotel reached by dramatic drive with spectacular views of Loch Duich to Skye; beams, wood-clad walls and big fireplace, a couple of well kept ales and good fresh local food including seafood from daily changing menu, friendly welcoming staff, dining room; regular live music; children and dogs welcome, lovely garden, views from some bedrooms, summer ferry to Skye, open all day. *(David Todd)*

PLOCKTON   NG8033
★**Plockton Inn** (01599) 544222
Innes Street; unconnected to Plockton Hotel (see Main Entries); IV52 8TW Close to the harbour in this lovely village, congenial bustling atmosphere even in winter, good fairly priced food with emphasis on local fish/seafood (some from own back smokery), friendly efficient service, well kept changing beers and good range of malts, lively public bar with traditional music Thurs (also Tues in summer); children welcome, seats out on decking, 14 bedrooms (seven in annexe over road), good breakfast, open all day. *(Barry Collett)*

SHIEL BRIDGE   NG9319
Kintail Lodge (01599) 511275
A87, N of Shiel Bridge; IV40 8HL Large bar adjoining hotel nestled down by Loch Duich, convivial bustle in season, Isle of Skye Red and plenty of malt whiskies, good food from same kitchen as restaurant/conservatory with magnificent view to Skye, friendly efficient service; 12 comfortable bedrooms, bunkhouse and moorings for visiting yachts, good breakfast, dogs welcome, open all day from Easter, best to check out of season hours. *(Charles Fraser)*

ULLAPOOL   NH1293
★**Ceilidh Place** (01854) 612103
West Argyle Street; IV26 2TY Pretty white house and more arty café-bar than pub with gallery, bookshop and coffee shop; conservatory-style main area with mix of dining chairs around dark wood tables, cosy bar and other rooms filled with armchairs, sofas and scatter-cushioned wall seats, rugs on floors, woodburner, a beer from An Teallach, lots of wines by the glass and 75 malt whiskies, tasty food (something available all day); regular jazz, folk and classical music; children welcome but must leave bar by 7pm, tables on front terrace looking over houses to distant hills beyond natural harbour, comfortable bedrooms, open all day, closed Jan. *(CDM)*

ULLAPOOL   NH1294
Morefield Motel (01854) 612161
A835 N edge of town; IV26 2TQ Modern family-run place, clean and bright, with cheerful L-shaped lounge bar, reliably good food including local fish and seafood, well kept changing ales, decent wines and over 50 malt whiskies, large conservatory; background music, pool and darts; children welcome, terrace tables, bike lock-up, bedrooms, open all day. *(Johnston and Maureen Anderson)*

ROXBURGHSHIRE

KELSO   NT7234
★**Cobbles** (01573) 223548
Bowmont Street; TD5 7JH Small comfortably refurbished 19th-c dining pub just off the main square, friendly and well run with good range of food from pub standards to more enterprising dishes, local Tempest beers and decent range of wines and malts, open fire and pubby furnishings in bar, elegantly furnished restaurant with overspill room upstairs; folk music Fri evening; children welcome, disabled facilities, open all day (till late Fri, Sat).
(David Longhurst, Rona Mackinlay)

KIRK YETHOLM   NT8328
★**Border** (01573) 420237
Village signposted off B6352/B6401 crossroads, SE of Kelso, The Green; TD5 8PQ Comfortable family-run inn facing village green, nice traditional bar with beams, flagstones and log fire, snug side rooms, two or three ales including Hadrian Border, decent wines and numerous whiskies, good home-made food from snacks and pub favourites up, charming friendly service, spacious dining room with fishing theme, lounge with another fire and neat conservatory; background music; children and dogs (in bar) welcome, sheltered back terrace, five well appointed bedrooms, good breakfast, at end of Pennine Way and start of Scottish National Trail, open all day. *(Sara Fulton, Roger Baker)*

MELROSE   NT5434
Kings Arms (01896) 800335
High Street; TD6 9PB Popular late 18th-c inn, bare-boards bar with pews and other wooden furniture, rugby memorabilia and sports TV, cosy log fire, comfortable dining room, ales such as Caledonian, Harviestoun, Inveralmond and Stewart, good choice of malt whiskies and wide range of enjoyable food including vegetarian dishes and Tues steak night, cheerful helpful young staff; children and dogs welcome, bedrooms, open all day. *(Johnston and Maureen Anderson)*

ST BOSWELLS   NT5930
Buccleuch Arms (01835) 822243
A68 just S of Newtown St Boswells;
TD6 0EW Civilised 19th-c sandstone hotel
opposite village green; bar, comfortable
lounge and bistro, good popular food from
bar snacks up, prompt friendly service, two
or three real ales such as Belhaven, open
fires; children and dogs welcome, tables
in attractive garden behind, 19 bedrooms,
open (and food) all day. *(Martin Day)*

SELKIRKSHIRE

MOUNTBENGER   NT3324
Gordon Arms (01750) 82261
A708/B709; TD7 5LE Nice old pub – an
oasis in these empty moorlands; a couple
of real ales and enjoyable reasonably
priced pubby food cooked by landlord,
good regular traditional music (there's
a recording studio on site); children and
dogs welcome, comfortable bedrooms,
good walking country, open (and food)
all day in summer, has shut Mon-Weds in
winter – best to check website. *(Ruaraidh)*

STIRLINGSHIRE

KIPPEN   NS6594
★Cross Keys (01786) 870293
Main Street; village signposted off
A811 W of Stirling; FK8 3DN Cosy
and gently civilised 18th-c inn; log fires
in two bars, exposed stonework, bare
boards or carpeting, built-in wall seating,
wooden dining chairs and stools against
counter serving a couple of Fallen ales
(one brewed for the pub), a guest beer,
20 malt whiskies and a dozen wines by
the glass, very good food including lighter
lunch menu, friendly staff; background
music, live folk first and third Sun of
month, free wi-fi; children (till 9pm) and
dogs welcome, tables in garden looking
across to the Ochil Hills, play area, three
comfortable bedrooms, generous breakfast,
open (and food) all day weekends. *(Roy*
and Gill Payne, Iain Waterson, John Evans)

STRATHCLYDE

CAIRNDOW   NN1810
Stagecoach (01499) 600286
Just off and signed from A83; PA26 8BN
Old inn run by same family for 46 years in
lovely setting overlooking Loch Fyne; good
local fish and seasonal produce in bar and
restaurant, Fyne ales and plenty of whiskies,
efficient friendly service; live music and quiz
nights; children welcome, garden picnic-sets,
19 bedrooms (some in separate building with
balconies taking in the view), open (and
food) all day. *(Mandy and Gary Redstone)*

SUTHERLAND

KYLESKU   NC2333
★Kylesku Hotel (01971) 502231
A894, S side of former ferry crossing;
IV27 4HW Remote but surprisingly busy
hotel on shores of Loch Glendhu; pleasant
tartan-carpeted bar facing glorious mountain
and loch view, with seals and red-throated
divers often in sight (tables outside too);
wonderfully fresh seafood along with other
good locally sourced food (booking advisable),
friendly accommodating staff, well kept
ales such as An Teallach, nice wines by the
glass and numerous malt whiskies, more
expensive restaurant extension overlooking
loch; children welcome, eight comfortable
bedrooms, good boat trips from hotel slipway,
closed winter. *(Neil and Angela Huxter)*

LAIRG   NC5224
★Crask Inn (01549) 411241
A836 13 miles N towards Altnaharra;
IV27 4AB Remote homely inn on single-
track road through peaceful moorland, recent
change of management but things remain
much the same; comfortably basic bar with
large stove, interesting books and harmonium,
a couple of Black Isle ales with more in
bottles, good simple food cooked by landlord
including own lamb, friendly helpful service,
pleasant separate dining room; church service
third Thurs of month (the pub is church-
owned); children and dogs welcome, four
bedrooms, camping (no facilities), closed till
1pm Tues, otherwise open all day. *(CDM)*

LOCHINVER   NC0922
★Caberfeidh (01571) 844321
Culag Road (A837); IV27 4JY Delightful
lochside position and lovely views; cosy
bar, conservatory and more formal evening
restaurant, two woodburners, good popular
food (best to book) from shortish changing
menu with emphasis on local seafood (one
or two large plates and a selection of smaller
tapas-style dishes), a couple of well kept
ales such as An Teallach, good choice of
wines, whiskies and gins, friendly helpful
staff; children and dogs (in bar) allowed,
small garden with nice view of the loch,
open all day in summer apart from Mon
lunchtime, closed Mon-Weds in winter,
and all Jan. *(Neil and Angela Huxter)*

WEST LOTHIAN

BO'NESS   NS9981
Corbie (01506) 825307
A904 Corbiehall; EH51 0AS Neatly
furnished pub with up to six well kept local
ales including own Kinneil brewed behind,
70 malt whiskies (tasting evenings) and
quite a choice of enjoyable food at fair
prices, friendly staff; children welcome,

garden with play area, open (and food) all day. *(Samuel and Melissa Turnbull)*

LINLITHGOW   NS0077

★**Four Marys** (01506) 842171
High Street; 2 miles from M9 junction 3 (and little further from junction 4) – town signposted; EH49 7ED Named after Mary, Queen of Scots' four ladies-in-waiting and filled with mementoes of the ill-fated queen including pictures and written records, pieces of bed curtain and clothing, even a facsimile of her death-mask; L-shaped room with traditional and more modern seating on wood-block floor, mainly stripped-stone walls (some remarkable masonry in the inner area), elaborate Victorian dresser serving as part of the bar, seven well kept ales (taster glasses available, May, Oct festivals), good range of malt whiskies and gins, enjoyable reasonably priced food, friendly staff, tartan carpeted dining area where children allowed (till 8pm); background and live music; enclosed terrace, open all day. *(Paul Baxter)*

WIGTOWNSHIRE

BLADNOCH   NX4254

Bladnoch Inn (01988) 402200
Corner of A714 and B7005; DG8 9AB Roadside pub across from Bladnoch distillery (tours) in nice riverside setting, cheerful neat bar with eating area, separate restaurant, tasty pubby food from sandwiches up including set menus and Sun carvery, a couple of changing real ales, friendly obliging service; background music; children and dogs welcome, four good value bedrooms, open all day. *(Barbara and Phil Bowie)*

PORTPATRICK   NW9954

Crown (01776) 810261
North Crescent; DG9 8SX Popular seafront hotel in delightful harbourside village, enjoyable reasonably priced food including notable seafood and local game, friendly prompt service, several dozen malts and decent wines by the glass, warm fire in rambling traditional bar with cosy corners, sewing-machine tables, old photographs and posters, attractively decorated early 20th-c dining room opening through conservatory into sheltered back garden; background music, TV; children and dogs welcome, tables out in front, open (and food) all day. *(Robert and Diana Ringstone)*

STRANRAER   NX0660

Grapes (01776) 703386
Bridge Street; DG9 7HY Popular and welcoming 19th-c local, simple and old-fashioned, with a couple of well kept ales and over 60 malts, regular traditional music in bar or upstairs room; dogs welcome, courtyard seating, open all day. *(Robert and Diana Ringstone)*

Scottish Islands

ARRAN

CATACOL   NR9049

Catacol Bay (01770) 830231
A841; KA27 8HN Unpretentious hotel rather than pub run by same family for 38 years, wonderful setting just yards from the sea looking across to Kintyre; simple bar with log fire, Timothy Taylors Landlord and a guest, all-day food (Sun buffet until 4pm) and hearty breakfasts; pool, TV; tables outside and children's play area, six simple bedrooms with washbasins (ones at front have the view), own mooring, open all day in summer, closed Mon, Tues winter. *(Charles Fraser)*

BARRA

CASTLEBAY   NL6698

Castlebay Hotel (01871) 810223
By aeroplane from Glasgow or ferry from Oban; HS9 5XD Comfortable cheerful bar next to the hotel, popular food from sandwiches up, keg and bottled beers, also two-level lounge/restaurant with great harbour view, pleasant young staff; regular live music; decent bedrooms. *(Charlie)*

BUTE

ROTHESAY   NS0864

Black Bull (01700) 502366
W Princes Street; PA20 9AF Traditional comfortably furnished pub under new management; enjoyable reasonably priced bar food and three well kept ales, good friendly service; weekend live music, TV; children welcome till 8pm, no dogs, opposite pier with its wonderfully restored Victorian gents', open all day, no food Mon, or evenings apart from Fri and Sat. *(Dan and Belinda Smallbone)*

COLONSAY

SCALASAIG   NR3893

★**Colonsay** (01951) 200316
W on B8086; PA61 7YP Extended stylish 18th-c hotel, a haven for ramblers and birders; chatty bar is hub of the island and full of locals and visitors, comfortable sofas and armchairs on painted boards, pastel walls hung with interesting old islander pictures, log fires, Colonsay IPA, several wines by the glass and interesting selection of whiskies, relaxed informal restaurant overlooking the harbour, good food using home-grown produce (own oyster farm) including pre-ferry two-course offer, friendly efficient service; children and

dogs (in bar) welcome, nice views from garden, ten comfortable pretty bedrooms, closed Nov-Feb except Christmas and New Year, otherwise open all day (till 1am Sat). *(Mary Kirkwood, Neil Allen)*

CUMBRAE

MILLPORT   NS1554
Frasers (01475) 530518
Cardiff Street; KA28 0AS Small cheerful pub set just back from the harbour; bar with old paddle-steamer pictures and woodburner, back vaulted dining room, a couple of changing beers and enjoyable very reasonably priced pubby food, friendly staff; children welcome till 8pm, no dogs, tables in yard behind, open all day. *(Charlotte and William Mason)*

HARRIS

TARBERT   NB1500
★ **Harris Hotel** (01859) 502154
Scott Road; HS3 3DL Large hotel in same family for over a century; small welcoming panelled bar with hebridean-brewed ales and fine selection of malt whiskies including some rarities, interesting food using local game and seafood from lunchtime baguettes and afternoon teas up, friendly accommodating staff, smart (but relaxed) airy restaurant; 23 comfortable sea-view bedrooms (some up narrow stairs). *(Mr and Mrs P R Thomas)*

ISLAY

BOWMORE   NR3159
★ **Harbour Inn** (01496) 810330
The Square; PA43 7JR Refurbished inn with lovely harbour/loch views from dining room and conservatory, good fish/seafood and other local sourced food, nice wines and plenty of Islay malts including some rarities, traditional bar with unusual barrel counter, friendly helpful staff; children welcome, seven bedrooms with views. *(Charlie)*

PORT ASKAIG   NR4369
Port Askaig (01496) 840245
A846, by port; PA46 7RD Family-run inn on shores of the Sound of Islay overlooking ferry pier; snug, tartan-carpeted bar with good range of malt whiskies, local bottled ales and popular food, neat sea-view restaurant and traditional residents' lounge; dogs welcome in bar, plenty of picnic-sets on waterside grass, eight neat bedrooms

and self-catering apartment, open (and food) all day. *(Jamie and Lizzie McEwan)*

PORT CHARLOTTE   NR2558
★ **Port Charlotte Hotel**
(01496) 850360 *Main Street; PA48 7TU* Most beautiful of Islay's Georgian villages and in lovely position with sweeping views over Loch Indaal; exceptional collection of some 150 Islay malts including rarities, two changing local ales and decent wines by the glass, good food using local meat, game and seafood, civilised bare-boards pubby bar with padded wall seats, open fire and modern artwork, second comfortable back bar, neatly kept restaurant and roomy conservatory (overlooking beach); traditional live music Weds and Sun in high season; children welcome, garden tables, near sandy beach, ten attractive bedrooms (nine with sea view), open all day till 1am. *(Jamie and Lizzie McEwan)*

PORTNAHAVEN   NN1652
An Tighe Seinnse (01496) 860224
Queen Street; PA47 7SJ Friendly little end-of-terrace harbourside pub tucked away in this remote attractive fishing village, cosy bar with room off, open fire, fair-priced tasty food including local seafood, Belhaven keg beer and bottled Islay ales, good choice of malts; sports TV and occasional live music; can get crowded, open all day. *(Jamie and Lizzie McEwan)*

JURA

CRAIGHOUSE   NR5266
Jura Hotel (01496) 820243
A846, opposite distillery; PA60 7XU Family-run and in superb setting with views over the Small Isles to the mainland; bar, two lounges and restaurant, good food using local fish, seafood and game (breakfasts for non-residents if capacity allows); garden down to water's edge, 17 bedrooms (most with sea view), camping. *(Simon Rigby)*

MULL

DERVAIG   NM4251
★ **Bellachroy** (01688) 400314
B8073; PA75 6QW Island's oldest inn dating from 1608; pub and restaurant food including local seafood, afternoon teas, ales such as Isle of Mull and good choice of whiskies and wines, traditional bar with darts, attractive dining area, comfortable residents' lounge with games and TV; children and dogs welcome, covered outside

---

A star symbol before the name of a pub shows exceptional character and appeal. It doesn't mean extra comfort. Even quite a basic pub can win a star, if it's individual enough.

area plus plenty of picnic-sets, nice spot in sleepy lochside village, six comfortable bedrooms, open all year. *(Philip Chesington)*

TOBERMORY   NM5055
Mishnish   (01688) 302500
Main Street – the yellow building; PA75 6NU Popular and lively place right on the bay, dimly lit two-room bar with cask tables, old photographs and nautical/fishing bric-a-brac, woodburner, little snugs, well kept Belhaven and Isle of Mull, enjoyable bar food, can also eat in next-door Mishdish or italian restaurant upstairs; background and live music, pool; beer garden behind, 14 attractive bedrooms (some with sea view), good breakfast, open all day till late. *(Dave Braisted)*

ORKNEY

DOUNBY   HY3001
Merkister   (01856) 771366
Russland Road, by Harray Loch; KW17 2LF Fishing hotel in great location on the loch shore, bar dominated by prize catches, good food here and in evening restaurant including hand-dived scallops and local aberdeen angus steaks, local bottled beers, good friendly service; 16 bedrooms, open all day. *(Sarah and David Gibbs)*

ST MARY'S   HY4700
Commodore   (01856) 781788
A961; KW17 2RU Modern single-storey building with stunning views over Scapa Flow, bar with well kept Orkney beers, pool and darts, good food using local produce in contemporary restaurant (Fri, Sat 6-8.45pm only); open all day. *(Sarah and David Gibbs)*

WESTRAY   HY4348
Pierowall Hotel   (01857) 677472
Centre of Pierowall village, B9066; KW17 2BZ Comfortable pub-hotel near ferry, enjoyable food from sandwiches and snacks to good freshly landed fish, bottled Orkney beers and plenty of malts, lounge bar with warming stove, public bar and separate restaurant; six bedrooms with bay or hill views; tables out on front grass, for sale, so may be changes. *(Sarah and David Gibbs)*

SKYE

ARDVASAR   NG6303
Ardvasar Hotel   (01471) 844223
A851 at S of island, near Armadale pier; IV45 8RS Wonderful sea and mountain views from this comfortable peacefully placed white-stone inn, charming owner (will pick you up from the ferry) and friendly efficient staff, good home-made food using local fish and meat, over 30 malt whiskies, real ales including Caledonian and Isle of Skye, two bars and games room; background

music, TV; children welcome in eating areas, tables outside, lovely walks, ten bedrooms (front ones overlook the sound), open all day. *(Patricia and Gordon Tucker)*

CARBOST   NG3731
★ Old Inn   (01478) 640205
B8009; IV47 8SR Unpretentious waterside pub with stunning views and well positioned for walkers and climbers; simply furnished chatty bar with exposed stone walls, bare-board or tiled floors, open fire, Cuillin ales and a guest, traditional cider and quite a few malt whiskies, tasty fair priced food using local fish and highland meat (breakfasts 7.45-9.30am); background music (live Weds, Thurs, Fri), darts and pool; children and dogs welcome, picnic-sets on terrace by the water, bedrooms and bunkhouse also enjoying the views, Talisker distillery nearby, closed afternoons in winter, otherwise open (and food) all day. *(Patricia and Gordon Tucker)*

EDINBAINE   NG3451
Edinbaine   (01470) 582414
Just off A850, signed for Meadhan a Bhaile; IV51 9PW Friendly former farmhouse with simply furnished modernised bar, light wood flooring and woodburner in stone fireplace, well kept Isle of Skye beers, airy carpeted dining room serving good attractively presented food including local fish/seafood, friendly staff; live traditional music (Sun); children and dogs welcome, open all day (but best to check winter hours). *(Patricia and Gordon Tucker)*

ISLE ORNSAY   NG7012
★ Eilean Iarmain   (01471) 833332
Off A851 Broadford–Armadale; IV43 8QR Smartly old-fashioned 19th-c hotel in beautiful location looking over the Sound of Sleat; cosy traditional bar with panelling and open fire, well kept Isle of Skye and good choice of vatted (blended) malt whiskies including their own Gaelic Whisky Collection, good food here or in charming sea-view restaurant, friendly efficient service; traditional background and live music; children welcome, outside tables with spectacular views, 16 comfortable bedrooms, open all day. *(Charlotte and William Mason)*

SOUTH UIST

LOCH CARNAN   NF8144
Orasay Inn   (01870) 610298
Signed off A865 S of Creagorry; HS8 5PD Wonderful remote spot overlooking the sea (lovely sunsets), good local fish/seafood and beef from own herd in comfortable modern lounge or conservatory-style restaurant, friendly service, pleasant simply furnished public bar; seats outside on raised decked area, compact comfortable bedrooms (two with terraces), open all day at least in summer. *(Charles Fraser)*

WALES

ORKNEY

SHETLAND

WESTERN
ISLES

LEWIS

SUTHERLAND

CATHNESS

HARRIS

NORTH
UIST

ROSS-SHIRE

NAIRN

MORAYSHIRE

BANFFSHIRE

ABERDEENSHIRE

*North
Sea*

SOUTH
UIST

SKYE

BARRA

RUM

INVERNESS-SHIRE

KINCARDINESHIRE

COLL

ANGUS

TIREE

MULL

PERTHSHIRE

FIFE

ARGYLL

KINROSS-SHIRE

COLONSAY

CLACKMANNANSHIRE

STIRLINGSHIRE

DUNBARTON

W

BERWICKSHIRE

II IRA

JURA

RENFREW

E

LOTHIAN

MID

ISLAY

LANARK-
SHIRE

PEEBLES

AYRSHIRE

SELKIRK

ROXBURGHSHIRE

ARRAN

DUMFRIESSHIRE

NORTHUMBERLAND

KIRKCUDBRIGHT-
SHIRE

TYNE & WEAR

WIGTOWNSHIRE

CUMBRIA

COUNTY
DURHAM

CLEVELAND

*Irish
Sea*

ISLE OF
MAN

NORTH
YORKSHIRE

ANGLESEY

LANCS

WEST
YORKS

EAST
YORKS

MERSEYSIDE

GTR
MANCH.

S YORKS

GWYNEDD

CLWYD

CHESHIRE

DERBYSHIRE

NOTTS

LINCOLNSHIRE

STAFFS

SHROPS

LEICS
& RUTLAND

NORFOLK

W MIDS

POWYS

HEREFORD
& WORCS

WARKS

NORTHANTS

CAMBS

SUFFOLK

DYFED

BEDS

GLOS

OXON

BUCKS

HERTS

ESSEX

GLAMORGAN

GWENT

LONDON

BERKS

WILTSHIRE

HAMPSHIRE

SURREY

KENT

SOMERSET

WEST
SUSSEX

EAST
SUSSEX

DORSET

DEVON

ISLE OF
WIGHT

CORNWALL

SCILLY ISLES

English Channel

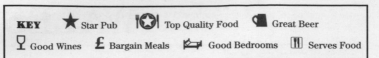

KEY ★ Star Pub 🌟 Top Quality Food 🍺 Great Beer
🍷 Good Wines £ Bargain Meals 🛏 Good Bedrooms 🍴 Serves Food

ABERAERON
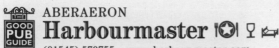
Harbourmaster 🌟 🍷 🛏

SN4562 Map 6

(01545) 570755 – www.harbour-master.com

Quay Parade; SA46 0BA

Charming small hotel with a lively bar, simply furnished dining room, local ales and first class food; bedrooms

With a prime location on the yacht-filled harbour lined by colourwashed buildings, this handsome small hotel is extremely well run and deservedly popular. The buzzing bar has all sorts of chairs around tables on bare boards, brown leather wall banquettes, some bright blue armchairs and stools lining the bar where friendly staff keep a beer named for the inn (from Purple Moose), Grey Trees Afghan Pale Ale, Heavy Industry 77 and Mantle Moho on handpump, 21 good wines by the glass, 11 malt whiskies and farm cider. The dining room has blue leather chairs, sea-blue walls and seaside-inspired art. Bedrooms are comfortable and breakfasts are particularly good. You can sit outside on a bench and take in the view. Disabled access.

 Using the best local, seasonal produce and starting with breakfasts (8-11.45am), the imaginative food includes crispy cockles with chilli vinegar, twice-cooked cheese soufflé with pineapple salsa, pea and mint risotto with hazelnut granola, burger with toppings and skinny fries, sea bream fillets with orange, fennel, beetroot and spinach, lamb neck fillet with a dukkah crust, kale, feta, lemon, yoghurt, harissa and crispy chickpeas, short rib of beef with chilli kale, chimichurri and chips, chicken suprême with chicken faggot, popcorn, carrot and passion-fruit purée, and puddings such as white chocolate mousse with hazelnut purée, cherries and chocolate crumb and treacle tart with lemon caramel and crème fraîche sorbet. *Benchmark main dish: crab linguine £14.00. Two-course evening meal £20.00.*

Free house ~ Licensees Glyn and Menna Heulyn ~ Real ale ~ Open 8am-11.30pm ~ Bar food 12-2.30, 6-9 ~ Restaurant ~ Children over 5 if staying ~ Wi-fi ~ Bedrooms: £75/£120
Recommended by Mr and Mrs P R Thomas, R T and J C Moggridge, Anna and Mark Evans, Paul Baxter

ABERTHIN
Hare & Hounds 🌟 🍷

ST0075 Map 6

(01446) 774892 – www.hareandhoundsaberthin.com

NE of Cowbridge; CF71 7HB

Excellent food in easy-going country pub, interesting drinks, helpful courteous service and seats in garden

Of course, the fine food cooked by the chef-landlord in this homely country pub is the main draw, but this is a proper pub where locals gather for a pint and a chat just as they've done for 300 years. The simply furnished rooms have a relaxed, informal atmosphere, whitewashed walls, mate's chairs and wheelbacks around wooden tables on bare boards, posies of flowers dotted around, a dresser stocked with home-made preserves, a woodburning stove in an inglenook fireplace, bookshelves with cookbooks and an open kitchen. Rhymney Golden Ale, Vale of Glamorgan South Island, Wye Valley HPA and a guest ale on handpump, local cider, home-made seasonal drinks such as damson gin, and 24 wines plus sparkling ones by the glass from a thoughtful list; darts. The hanging baskets at the front of the building are pretty and there are benches and picnic-sets in the garden. They hope to have opened bedrooms by the time this *Guide* is published.

Using local, seasonal and some home-grown produce and making everything from sourdough bread to home-cultured butter, fresh pasta and charcuterie in their kitchen, the first class food includes crispy pig cheeks with chicory, mustard and pickled apple, braised cuttlefish with smoked eel, fennel and radish, cheese and potato gnocchi with red onion, squash, kale and blue cheese, breast and leg of duck with bacon, wild mushrooms and dauphinoise potatoes, red mullet with leeks, cockles and mussels, roast hanger steak with béarnaise sauce and chips, calves liver and bacon with onion, parsley and confit potatoes, and puddings such as champagne rhubarb soufflé and buttermilk pudding with honeycomb and bramley apple; they also offer a two- and three-course lunch. *Benchmark main dish: local lamb with mint sauce £17.00. Two-course evening meal £23.00.*

Free house ~ Licensees Tom Watts-Jones, Alex Howells ~ Real ale ~ Open 12-midnight; 3-11.30 Mon, Tues; 12-11 Sun; closed Mon, lunchtime Tues ~ Bar food 12-2.30, 6-9; 12-3 Sun ~ Restaurant ~ Children welcome but must leave bar by 7.30pm ~ Dogs allowed in bar ~ Wi-fi *Recommended by Susan and Callum Slade, Alister and Margery Bacon, Naomi and Andrew Randall*

BEAUMARIS
Bull 🏮 ♀ 🛏

SH6076   Map 6

(01248) 810329 – www.bullsheadinn.co.uk
Castle Street; LL58 8AP

Interesting historic inn with plenty of interest, a rambling bar, stylish brasserie and restaurant; well equipped bedrooms

The heart of this 15th-c inn – close to the castle – is the charming rambling and beamed bar with its fine log fire and interesting reminders of the town's past such as a rare 17th-c brass water clock, a bloodthirsty crew of cutlasses and even an oak ducking stool tucked in the snug alcove. Seats range from comfortable low-seated settles and leather-cushioned window seats, there are lots of copper and china jugs and courteous staff serve Bass, Hancocks HB and guests such as Itchen Valley Leprechauns Gold, RCH Pitchfork and St Peters Honey Porter on handpump, as well as 26 gins with interesting tonics; board games. In contrast, the busy brasserie behind is lively and stylishly modern with around 14 wines by the glass, while the exceptionally good upstairs restaurant is an elegantly smart choice for a more formal meal and has a wine list running to 120 bottles. The entrance to the pretty courtyard is closed by a huge simple-hinged door that's an astonishing 3.3 metres wide and 4 metres high. Bedrooms are named after characters in Dickens' novels (Dickens himself popped in for a drink in 1859) and are very well equipped; some are traditional, others more contemporary in style. They also have bedrooms in the Townhouse, an adjacent property with disabled access.

Beautifully presented and first class, the food includes lunchtime sandwiches, arbroath smokies (smoked haddock, cream, tomato and parmesan), a charcuterie board, chargrilled vegetables and halloumi stack with skinny fries, burger with toppings, crispy onion rings and chips, king prawn and pesto pasta, malaysian coconut chicken with coriander noodles, salmon wellington with tomato and rocket, crisp pork belly with bubble and squeak and black pudding bonbon, sea bass with chive mash, creamed leeks and prawn tempura, and puddings such as vanilla and blueberry pannacotta with berry compote and bakewell tart with vanilla bean custard. *Benchmark main dish: slow-cooked lamb shoulder with onion mash, rosemary and redcurrant jus £16.00. Two-course evening meal £22.00.*

Free house ~ Licensees Kate and David Robertson ~ Real ale ~ Open 11-11 (10.30 Sun) ~ Bar food 12-2, 7-9; food is served in the bar lunchtime only ~ Restaurant ~ Children welcome in bar annexe ~ Dogs allowed in bar ~ Wi-fi ~ Bedrooms: £85/£110 *Recommended by Andrew Vincent, Tim King, Donald Allsopp, Elizabeth and Andrew Harvey, Holly and Tim Waite*

BODFARI
Dinorben Arms ♀ ◖

SJ0970 Map 6

(01745) 775090 – www.brunningandprice.co.uk/dinorbenarms
Off A541, near church; LL16 4DA

Renovated village pub with interesting furnishings in open-plan bars, fine choice of drinks and rewarding food; seats with far-reaching country views

A traditional pub in the shadow of the village church, this was completely renovated and reopened by Brunning & Price early in 2017. It's basically one big open-plan bar with cosier areas – the oldest of which is heavily beamed and has antique settles, stone bottles on a delft shelf and a woodburning stove. There's a glassed-over well in one corner, a curved central counter, leather armchairs grouped around one open fire (there are others), all manner of wooden dining chairs around tables on rugs or bare boards, elegant metal chandeliers, hundreds of prints on pale painted or exposed stone walls, large house plants and sizeable gilt-edged mirrors. Brunning & Price Phoenix Original plus Caledonian Deuchars IPA, Facers North Star Porter, Timothy Taylors Boltmaker and three quickly changing guests on handpump, lots of wines by the glass and a good choice of spirits. A new high tower has been added to the back of the building, where there's also a spacious partly covered terrace with good quality seats and tables and fine views over rolling countryside; picnic-sets on grass too.

Modern, brasserie-style food includes sandwiches, prawn cocktail, five-spice duck leg with hoisin sauce, spring onions and pancakes, sharing boards, crispy lamb salad with fennel, pea falafel and pomegranate and yoghurt mint dip, butternut squash, spinach and blue cheese pie, sausages with mash and onion gravy, steak and kidney pudding, malaysian fish stew with coconut rice, braised shoulder of lamb with dauphinoise potatoes and rosemary gravy, and puddings such as crème brûlée and triple chocolate brownie with chocolate sauce. *Benchmark main dish: chicken in a basket £12.95. Two-course evening meal £21.00.*

Brunning & Price ~ Licensee John Unsworth ~ Real ale ~ Open 11-11; 12-10.30 Sun ~ Bar food 12-10 (9.30 Sun) ~ Restaurant ~ Children welcome ~ Dogs allowed in bar ~ Wi-fi
Recommended by Richard and Tessa Ibbot, Maggie and Stevan Hollis, Chloe and Michael Swettenham

COLWYN BAY
Pen-y-Bryn ♀ ◖

SH8478 Map 6

(01492) 533360 – www.brunningandprice.co.uk/penybryn
B5113 Llanwrst Road, on southern outskirts; when you see the pub, turn off into Wentworth Avenue for the car park; LL29 6DD

Spacious, open-plan, one-storey building overlooking the bay with brasserie-style all-day food, good range of drinks and obliging staff

The views alone are reason enough to seek out this very well run place, which is much more special than its bungalow exterior suggests. Extending around the three long sides of the bar counter, you'll find welcoming coal fires, oriental rugs on pale stripped boards, a mix of seating and well spaced tables, shelves of books, a profusion of pictures, big pot plants, careful lighting and dark green old-fashioned school radiators. A fine choice of drinks served by knowledgeable young staff includes Phoenix Brunning & Price Original plus Castle Rock Harvest Pale, Conwy Beachcomber Blonde, Cross Bay Halo and Purple Moose Snowdonia Ale on handpump, well chosen good value wines including 19 by the glass and 65 malt whiskies; board games and background music. The big windows at the back look over seats and tables on the terraces and in the sizeable garden and then out to the sea and the Great Orme. In summer, the award-winning flowering tubs and hanging baskets are lovely.

From an extensive menu, the well presented food includes sandwiches, tempura king prawns with pineapple, mint and chilli salsa, pigeon breast with wild mushroom sausage and beetroot fondant, pumpkin, spinach, red pepper and lentil pie, pork and leek sausages with mash and onion gravy, smoked haddock with bacon, leek mash, a poached egg and white wine sauce, malaysian chicken curry with coconut rice, pork tenderloin with prosciutto, black pudding, braised pig cheeks, apple purée and cider gravy, and puddings such as cherry and white chocolate bakewell with cherry crumble ice-cream and crème brûlée. *Benchmark main dish: braised shoulder of lamb with dauphinoise potatoes and gravy £16.95. Two-course evening meal £21.00.*

Brunning & Price ~ Manager Andrew Grant ~ Real ale ~ Open 11-11; 12-10.30 Sun ~ Bar food 12 0.30 (9 Sun) ~ Children welcome ~ Dogs allowed in bar ~ Wi-fi *Recommended by Tony Smaithe, Pauline and Mark Evans, Mike and Wena Stevenson, Fiona and Jack Henderson*

CRICKHOWELL
Bear ★ ♀ ⇌

SO2118 Map 6

(01873) 810408 – www.bearhotel.co.uk
Brecon Road; A40; NP8 1BW

Convivial and interesting inn, a splendid, old-fashioned bar area warmed by a log fire and rewarding food; comfortable bedrooms

Thankfully, the same long-serving and warmly welcoming family continue to run this lovely old inn and our readers enjoy their visits as much as ever. Customers of all ages mix happily together in the heavily beamed, bustling bar with little plush-seated bentwood armchairs and handsome old cushioned settles, fresh flowers on tables, and a window seat that looks down on the market square. Next to the great roaring log fire are a big sofa and leather easy chairs on oak parquet flooring with rugs and antiques including lots of pewter mugs and brassware, a longcase clock and interesting prints. Brains Rev James, Greene King Old Speckled Hen, Sharps Doom Bar and a guest from a brewery such as Horny Goat on handpump, alongside 32 malt whiskies, local ciders, vintage and late-bottled ports and unusual wines (with ten by the glass); disabled lavatories. This is a particularly appealing place to stay with quite a choice of bedrooms; the older ones in the main building have antiques, others are in a country style – and the luxury ones have hot tubs and four-poster beds. Breakfasts are excellent. Reception rooms are comfortably furnished, and there are seats in the small garden.

Notably good food using top quality local produce includes lunchtime sandwiches, warm squid salad with lemon, coriander and chilli, duck liver pâté with onion marmalade, wild mushroom ravioli with concasse tomato and parmesan, jamaican-style beef ribs with sweet potato fries, gammon and egg, steak and mushroom in ale pie, chicken with wild mushroom, marsala and peppercorn sauce with sauté potatoes, sea bass fillet with roasted mediterranean vegetables and chorizo, and puddings such as pecan pie with coffee ice-cream and chocolate and fruit roulade with Oreo

ice-cream. *Benchmark main dish: local lamb shank with spring onion mash,
seasonal vegetables and braising juices £15.95. Two-course evening meal £20.00.*

Free house ~ Licensee Judy Hindmarsh ~ Real ale ~ Open 10am-11pm; 11am-10.30pm Sun
~ Bar food 11-10; 12-9.30 Sun ~ Restaurant ~ Children welcome ~ Dogs allowed in bar
and bedrooms ~ Wi-fi ~ Bedrooms: £96/£115 *Recommended by Mike and Mary Carter,
B and M Kendall, Lorna and Jack Mulgrave, Miranda and Jeff Davidson*

DALE

SM8105   Map 6

Griffin

(01646) 636227 – www.griffininndale.co.uk

B4327, by sea on one-way system; SA62 3RB

**Friendly waterside pub with fresh fish and shellfish, local ales
and two attractive upstairs rooms**

Our readers enjoy this friendly old pub very much, with plenty of praise
for the fresh fish and shellfish dishes. You can also be sure of a genuine
welcome from the helpful licensees. The two imaginatively decorated rooms
have an easy-going atmosphere, open fires, wood panelling and traditional
red quarry tiles. Brains Rev James, Cwrw Iâl Hâf Gwyn and Harbwr Tenby
North Star on handpump, six wines by the glass, local cider and malt
whiskies – including a welsh one; background music and board games. The
pub is right by the water with a pontoon and a seawall, and picnic-sets on the
front terrace make the most of the delightful views of the estuary. There are
fine coastal walks to either side.

The pub co-owns a local fishing boat and the menu offers prawns, lobsters, crab,
razor clams, scallops, whole sea bream, hake, cod and haddock. Also, a changing
pâté with sun-dried tomato chutney, goats cheese on toasted brioche with red onion
marmalade, vegetable lasagne, beef in ale or chicken and leek pies, steak burger with
onion rings and chips, gammon with free-range eggs, local rump steak with beer-
battered rings and peppercorn sauce, and puddings. *Benchmark main dish: john dory
with chilli jam, king prawns and slow-roasted potatoes £27.50. Two-course evening
meal £22.00.*

Free house ~ Licensees Sian Mathias and Simon Vickers ~ Real ale ~ Open 12-11; check
website for times in winter ~ Bar food 12-2.30, 6-8.30 ~ Restaurant ~ Children welcome ~
Wi-fi *Recommended by Harvey Brown, S and L McPhee, Simon Sharpe, Ted and Mary Bates*

EAST ABERTHAW

ST0366   Map 6

Blue Anchor £

(01446) 750329 – www.blueanchoraberthaw.com

Village signed off B4265; CF62 3DD

**Thatched character pub with cosy range of low-beamed little rooms,
making a memorable spot for a drink**

This ancient place dates back to 1380 and is one of the oldest pubs in
Wales. A warren of low-beamed and atmospheric little rooms lead off the
central server with tiny doorways, open fires (including one in an inglenook
with antique oak seats built into the stripped stonework) and other seats and
tables worked into a series of small, chatty alcoves. The more open front bar
still has an ancient lime-ash floor and keeps Brains Bitter, Theakstons Old
Peculier, Wadworths 6X, Wye Valley HPA and a guest beer on handpump, as
well as farm cider and eight wines by the glass. Outside, rustic seats shelter
peacefully among tubs and troughs of flowers, with stone tables on a newer
terrace. The pub can get very full in the evenings and on summer weekends.
A path from here leads to the shingle flats of the estuary.

🍴 Popular food includes baguettes, breaded salmon and prawn fishcakes with tomato and mango salsa, mussels in garlic, shallots, white wine and cream, butternut squash, chickpea and spinach strudel with spiced curry sauce, pork and leek sausages on wholegrain mustard mash with red wine gravy, thai green chicken curry, sea trout with braised fennel, crab arancini and white wine and creamy crayfish sauce, slow-braised pork belly with parsnip mash, pork faggot and onion gravy, steak and chips, beef stroganoff, and puddings such as sticky toffee pudding with toffee sauce and a changing cheesecake. *Benchmark main dish: pie of the day £11.95. Two-course evening meal £19.50.*

Free house ~ Licensee Jeremy Coleman ~ Real ale ~ Open 11-11; 12-10.30 Sun ~ Bar food 12-2, 6-9; 12-3 Sun ~ Restaurant ~ Children welcome ~ Dogs allowed in bar ~ Wi-fi
Recommended by Alfie Bayliss, Harvey Brown, Melvyn Jones, Ian Duncan, Sandra and Miles Spencer, Monty Green

FELINFACH   SO0933   Map 6
Griffin 🍽⭐ 🍷 🍺 🛏

(01874) 620111 – www.eatdrinksleep.ltd.uk
A470 NE of Brecon; LD3 0UB

Wales Dining Pub of the Year

Highly thought-of dining pub with excellent food, a fine range of drinks and upbeat rustic décor; inviting bedrooms

As ever, our readers very much enjoy their visits to this civilised but easy-going and genuinely friendly inn. The back bar is quite pubby in an up-to-date way, with four leather sofas around a low table on pitted quarry tiles by a high slate hearth with a log fire. Behind them are mixed stripped seats around scrubbed kitchen tables on bare boards, and a bright blue and ochre colour scheme with some modern prints; background music, board games and plenty of books. Efficient staff serve interesting drinks, many from smaller independent suppliers, including well chosen wines (18 by the glass and carafe, and they have a wine shop), welsh spirits, cocktails, local bottled cider, locally sourced apple juice, non-alcoholic cocktails made with produce from their garden, unusual continental and local bottled beers and a range of sherries. Montys Pale Ale and Wye Valley Butty Bach on handpump. The two smallish front dining rooms that link to the back bar are attractive. On the left: mixed dining chairs around mainly stripped tables on flagstones and white-painted rough stone walls, with a cream-coloured Aga in a big stripped-stone embrasure. On the right: similar furniture on bare boards, big modern prints on terracotta walls and smart dark curtains. Dogs may sit with their owners at certain tables while dining. There are seats and tables outside. The comfortable, tastefully decorated bedrooms make an excellent base for exploring the area and the hearty breakfasts are nicely informal – you make your own toast and help yourself to home-made marmalade and jam. Good wheelchair access.

⭐ Exceptional food using home-grown and other local produce includes smoked pork rillettes with crispy pork and celeriac rémoulade, rabbit loin with curried leg, pickled cauliflower and sultanas, gnocchi with roasted squash, chard, goats curd and pine nuts, ray wing with confit potato, savoy cabbage, pancetta and almonds, duck breast with chicory, duck fat mash, oranges and star anise, lamb breast with sweetbreads, white bean mash and salsa verde, cod with creamed leeks, crab, cauliflower and capers, and puddings such as dark chocolate mousse with pecans and caramel and coconut and cardamom rice pudding with lime and mango. *Benchmark main dish: rump of beef with girolles, onions and black truffle £21.00. Two-course evening meal £25.00.*

Free house ~ Licensees Charles and Edmund Inkin and Julie Bell ~ Real ale ~ Open 11-11 ~ Bar food 12-2.30, 6-9 (9.30 Fri, Sat) ~ Restaurant ~ Children welcome ~ Dogs allowed in bar and bedrooms ~ Wi-fi ~ Bedrooms: £110/£135 *Recommended by Guy Vowles, Brian and Sally Wakeham, Bernard Stradling, Barry Collett, Roger Mallard, Megan and William Revell, Ian Herdman*

GRESFORD   SJ3453 Map 6
Pant-yr-Ochain ♀ ⬤

(01978) 853525 – www.brunningandprice.co.uk/pantyrochain

Off A483 on N edge of Wrexham: at roundabout take A5156 (A534) towards Nantwich, then first left towards the Flash; LL12 8TY

Particularly well run dining pub with good food all day, a very wide range of drinks and lovely lakeside garden

Feeling more like a country house than a traditional pub, this 16th-c place is reached down a long drive and surrounded by attractive grounds with a small lake; tables and chairs on the front terrace and picnic-sets on the lawn enjoy the view. The light and airy rooms inside are stylishly decorated with a wide range of interesting prints and bric-a-brac, and a good mix of individually chosen country furnishings, including comfortable seats for relaxing as well as more upright ones for eating. One area is set out as a library, with floor-to-ceiling bookshelves, there's a log fire in an inglenook fireplace, and a popular dining conservatory overlooking the pretty garden; board games. An impressive line-up of drinks served by well trained staff includes Phoenix Brunning & Price Original and guests such as Big Hand Havok, Castle Rock Harvest Pale, Hawkshead Iti, Purple Moose Snowdonia Ale and Stonehouse Off the Rails on handpump, a farm cider, 20 wines by the glass, around 80 malt whiskies, 50 gins and 30 rums. Good disabled access.

Very good modern food includes sandwiches, rabbit, pheasant and prune faggot with carrot purée and cider gravy, potted prawn and crayfish with spiced butter, butternut squash, red pepper and sage quiche, coq au vin, steak in ale pie, sea bass fillets with glazed pineapple, chilli, coriander and sesame salad, duck breast with poached pear, dauphinoise potatoes and blackberry jus, rump steak salad with roasted onions, blue cheese, walnuts and red wine dressing, and puddings such as meringue with berry compote and lemon curd cream and apple and blackberry crumble with custard. *Benchmark main dish: steak burger with toppings, coleslaw and chips £12.95. Two-course evening meal £20.00.*

Brunning & Price ~ Licensee James Meakin ~ Real ale ~ Open 11-11; 12-10.30 Sun ~ Bar food 12-9.30 (9 Sun) ~ Children welcome ~ Dogs allowed in bar ~ Wi-fi *Recommended by Miles Green, Sandra Morgan, Mike and Wena Stevenson, Rosie Fielder, Trish and Karl Soloman, Douglas Power*

HAWARDEN   SJ3266 Map 6
Glynne Arms ⋈ ♀

(01244) 569988 – www.theglynnearms.co.uk

Glynne Way; CH5 3NS

Golden-stone Georgian pub with simply furnished bars, imaginative food, four real ales and charming staff

This handsome early 19th-c stone coaching inn (part of the Hawarden Estate) has been nicely renovated and is much enjoyed by the village. The character rooms are interconnected with built-in blue or brown leather wall seats, dark pubby and other simple chairs around a mix of tables on bare boards or parquet, a few bright rugs, pale walls hung with mirrors and framed posters and bills, and three open fires. A few quirky touches include bobbins on a delft shelf, jelly moulds, antlers and crossed axes and log-end wallpaper. From the stripped and attractively panelled bar counter (lined by stools), friendly staff serve Facers This Spendid Ale, Weetwood Cheshire Cat and a couple of guest ales on handpump and eight wines by the glass; background music, board games and TV. The back courtyard has some picnic-sets for good weather.

Using Estate produce, the interesting food includes sandwiches, scallops with burnt onion, black pudding beignet, parmesan crisp and truffle oil, chicken caesar croquettes with chicken thigh, anchovies, parmesan and little gem, miso-glazed aubergine steak with quinoa tabbouleh, pomegranate, pistachios and coriander pesto, sausages with wholegrain mash, kibbled onions and gravy, panko katsu chicken breast with peanuts, coconut cream and stir-fry vegetables, lamb neck fillet with olive tapenade, black garlic potato, rainbow chard and red pepper jus, and puddings such as dark chocolate délice with mango, coconut sorbet and pistachio popcorn and rhubarb trifle and custard. *Benchmark main dish: burger with toppings, onion rings and chips £16.95. Two-course evening meal £21.00.*

Free house ~ Licensee Alan Downes ~ Real ale ~ Open 11-11 (midnight Sat) ~ Bar food 12-9 ~ Restaurant ~ Children welcome ~ Dogs allowed in bar ~ Wi-fi
Recommended by Joe and Belinda Smart, Julian Richardson, Heather and Richard Jones

LITTLE HAVEN
Swan ♀ ◖

SM8512 Map 6

(01437) 781880 – www.theswanlittlehaven.co.uk
Point Road; SA62 3UL

Charming village pub with sea views from both inside and an outdoor terrace, and enjoyable food and ales

Quaint and unchanging, this little pub is nestled in one of the prettiest coastal villages in west Wales. Seats in the bay window or on the heated terrace (where there are rattan-style chairs and tables) give good views across a broad and sandy hill-sheltered cove to the sea, and it's right on the Pembrokeshire Coast Path. The traditional oak-floored bar has a mix of furniture including cask tables, a couple of leather armchairs by an open fire at one end, and a woodburning stove at the other, while the snug has a large table suitable for around ten diners. From the heavily panelled counter, helpful staff serve Brains Rev James and Sharps Doom Bar on handpump alongside two quickly changing guests, and ten wines by the glass from an extensive list. There's a blue-painted dining room and a more contemporary upstairs restaurant.

Enjoyable food includes panko chicken with sweet chilli and spring onion sauce, local crab with pickled radish and beetroot and apple coleslaw, roasted butternut squash with cranberries, sage and toasted nuts, ale-battered fresh fish and chips, confit pork belly with black pudding bonbons and apple, lamb cannon with leeks, beetroot and red wine jus, and puddings such as pistachio pannacotta with pistachio cake and black cherries and macerated strawberries in champagne jelly with elderflower sorbet. *Benchmark main dish: fresh fish dish of the day £17.95. Two-course evening meal £22.00.*

Free house ~ Licensees Matt and Helen John ~ Real ale ~ No credit cards ~ Open 12-midnight; 12pm-1am Fri, Sat ~ Bar food 12-2.30, 6-8.30 ~ Restaurant ~ Children welcome ~ Dogs allowed in bar ~ Wi-fi *Recommended by Nik and Gloria Clarke, Alison and Graeme Spicer, William and Sophia Renton*

LLANBERIS
Pen-y-Gwryd 🏠

SH6655 Map 6

(01286) 870211 – www.pyg.co.uk

Nant Gwynant; at junction of A498 and A4086, ie across mountains from Llanberis – OS Sheet 115 map reference 660558; LL55 4NT

Atmospheric and unchanged mountaineers' haunt in the wilds of Snowdonia, run by the same family since 1947; bedrooms

Apart from its magnificent setting, one of the main draws of this cheerful and simple inn is the wonderful atmosphere – it's long been a favourite among the mountaineer fraternity. It's packed with items left by past climbers and you can still make out the fading signatures scrawled on the ceiling by the 1953 Everest team, who used this as a training base; on display is the very rope that connected Hillary and Tenzing on top of the mountain. One snug little room in the homely slate-floored log cabin bar has built-in wall benches and sturdy country chairs. From here you can look out to precipitous Moel Siabod beyond the lake opposite. A smaller room has a worthy collection of illustrious boots from famous climbs, while a cosy panelled smoke room has more fascinating climbing mementoes and equipment; darts, pool, board games, bar billiards and table tennis. Purple Moose Glaslyn and Madogs are on handpump and they have several malts. Staying in the comfortable but basic bedrooms can be quite an experience, and there's an excellent traditional breakfast (served 8.30-9am, though they may serve earlier). The inn has its own chapel (built for the millennium and dedicated by the Archbishop of Wales), sauna and outdoor natural pool, and the garden overlooks a lake.

The short choice of simple, good-value lunchtime food includes rolls, ploughman's, pies, salads and quiche of the day as well as daily specials such as roast beef. The hearty three- or five-course set meal in the evening restaurant is signalled by a gong at 7.30pm (if you're late, you'll miss it): maybe chicken liver pâté or smoked salmon followed by loin of pork with leeks, cannellini beans and cream, beef in ale pie or salmon fillet with hollandaise and puddings such as banoffi pie or chocolate bread and butter pudding. *Benchmark main dish: roast leg of local lamb £9.50. Two-course evening meal £25.00.*

Free house ~ Licensee Nicholas Pullee ~ Real ale ~ Open 11-11; closed weekdays Nov; closed Jan, Feb ~ Bar food 12-2; evening meal 7.30pm ~ Restaurant ~ Children welcome ~ Dogs allowed in bar and bedrooms ~ Wi-fi ~ Bedrooms: $45/$90 *Recommended by Isobel Mackinlay, Alison and Michael Harper, Peter and Emma Kelly, Helena and Trevor Fraser, Anna and Mark Evans*

LLANDUDNO JUNCTION
Queens Head ⭐ ♀

SH8180 Map 6

(01492) 546570 – www.queensheadglanwydden.co.uk

Glanwydden; heading towards Llandudno on B5115 from Colwyn Bay, turn left into Llanrhos Road at roundabout as you enter the Penrhyn Bay speed limit; Glanwydden is signed as the first left turn; LL31 9JP

Consistently good food served all day at comfortably modern dining pub

To be sure of a table you must book here in advance – as those in the know always do. Modest from the outside it may be, but the food inside is excellent and customers travel miles for it. The spacious modern lounge bar (partly divided by a white wall of broad arches) has beams, beige plush wall banquettes, rush-seated or cushioned wooden and high-backed black leather dining chairs around neat black tables on tartan carpeting, an open woodburning stove and fresh flowers. The little public bar keeps Adnams Best and Salopian Shropshire Gold or Wild Horse Palomino Pale Ale on handpump, 12 decent wines by the glass, several malt whiskies and good coffee; background music. There's a pleasing mix of seats and tables under parasols outside. Northern Snowdonia is within easy reach, and a pretty stone cottage (which sleeps two) across the road is for rent.

 Extremely good seasonal food includes lunchtime open ciabatta sandwiches, crispy lamb and feta salad with olives and mint and yoghurt dressing, smoked salmon and trout mousse, portobello mushroom burger with toppings and chips, scallops with pea purée and chorizo, braised pork belly on wholegrain mustard mash with home-made black pudding, apple purée, crackling and cider jus, flaked smoked haddock in cream with tomato and parmesan, marinated chicken breast with moroccan-style couscous, coriander, crème fraîche and sweet chilli, and puddings such as chocolate, nut and raisin fudge pie and brioche bread and butter pudding. *Benchmark main dish: fresh local plaice £14.95. Two-course evening meal £21.00.*

Free house ~ Licensees Robert and Sally Cureton ~ Real ale ~ Open 11.30-11 ~ Bar food 12-9 ~ Restaurant ~ Children welcome ~ Wi-fi *Recommended by Mike and Mary Carter, Graham Smart, Barry and Daphne Gregson, John and Abigail Prescott*

LLANELIAN-YN-RHOS
White Lion
SH8676 Map 6

(01492) 515807 ~ www.whitelioninn.co.uk

Signed off A5830 (shown as B5383 on some maps) and B5381, S of Colwyn Bay; LL29 8YA

Bustling local with bar and spacious dining areas, tasty food, real ales and helpful staff

Though the present building is only a few centuries old, there's been some sort of place here for 1,200 years. There are two distinct parts inside, linked by a broad flight of steps, and each has its own cheery personality. Up at the top is a very spacious and neat dining area, while at the other end is a traditional old bar with antique high-backed settles fitting snugly around a big fireplace, and flagstones by the counter. Jennings Golden Host, Great Orme Celtica and Marstons Saddle Tank on handpump, 15 wines by the glass, farm cider, several gins including welsh ones and ten malt whiskies are served by helpful staff. Off to the left is another dining room with jugs hanging from beams and teapots above the windows; background music. There are tables in an attractive courtyard (also used for parking) next to the church.

Hearty food includes lunchtime sandwiches and baguettes, pâté of the week, moules marinière, beetroot, goats cheese and walnut salad with honey and wholegrain mustard dressing, pie of the day, barbecue ribs with coleslaw and chips, beer-battered hake and chips, chicken topped with bacon, cheese and mushrooms in cider, rosemary and sage sauce, fish, shellfish and sweet potato curry, sirloin steak with a choice of sauce and chips, and puddings; they may also offer a two-course weekday lunchtime menu. *Benchmark main dish: traditional roast beef £10.95. Two-course evening meal £16.70.*

Free house ~ Licensee Simon Cole ~ Real ale ~ Open 11.30-3.30, 6-11; 11.30-3.30, 5-11 Sat; 12-10 Sun; closed Mon except school and bank holidays ~ Bar food 12-2, 6-9; 12-2, 5-9 Fri, Sat; 12-8.30 Sun ~ Restaurant ~ Children welcome ~ Wi-fi ~ Live jazz Tues evening, live music Weds evening, sing-along first Sun, welsh singing third Sat of month *Recommended by George Sanderson, Darrell Barton, Patricia and Gordon Tucker, Louise and Anton Parsons*

LLANGOLLEN
SJ2142 Map 6

Corn Mill ♀ ☖

(01978) 869555 – www.brunningandprice.co.uk/cornmill

Dee Lane, very narrow lane off Castle Street (A539) just S of bridge; nearby parking can be tricky, may be best to use public car park on Parade Street/East Street and walk; LL20 8PN

Fascinating riverside building with fine views, personable young staff, super food all day and good beers

In addition to inventive food, this cleverly restored watermill has a fine range of drinks served by helpful young staff: Phoenix Brunning & Price Original and Facers DHB on handpump with guests such as Brimstage Elderflower Wheat, Facers North Star Porter and Salopian Oracle, farm cider, around 50 sensibly priced malt whiskies and a decent wine choice with around a dozen by the glass. The interior is interestingly fitted out with pale pine flooring on stout beams, a striking open stairway with gleaming timber and tensioned steel rails, and mainly stripped stone walls. Quite a lot of the old machinery is still in place, including the huge waterwheel (often turning) and there are good-sized dining tables, big rugs, thoughtfully chosen pictures (many to do with water) and several pot plants. One of the two serving bars, away from the water, has a much more local feel with regulars sitting on bar stools, pews on dark slate flagstones and daily papers. There are seats on a raised deck at the front that overlook the rushing mill race and rapids below; you can also watch steam trains arriving and leaving the station on the opposite riverbank.

 High standards of interesting food includes sandwiches, crispy ham hock and mustard terrine with pea and broad bean purée, a charcuterie plate to share, crab linguine with ginger, coriander and chilli, cauliflower with aubergine and chickpea dhal, red onion bhaji and mint yoghurt, chicken with smoked pancetta and leek mash and wild mushroom and button onion sauce, duck breast and duck croquette with orange purée, slow-roast belly pork with white bean casserole, lemon and butternut squash purée and crisp chorizo, and puddings such as chocolate torte with cherry compote and crème brûlée. *Benchmark main dish: beer-battered cod and chips £13.45. Two-course evening meal £20.00.*

Brunning & Price ~ Manager Andrew Barker ~ Real ale ~ Open 11-11 (10.30 Sun) ~ Bar food 12-9.30 (9 Sun) ~ Restaurant ~ Children welcome ~ Dogs allowed in bar ~ Wi-fi
Recommended by Helen McLagan, Mike and Wena Stevenson, Andrew and Ruth Simmonds, Mark Hamill

LLANMADOC
SS4493 Map 6

Britannia

(01792) 386624 – www.britanniainngower.co.uk
The Gower, near Whiteford Burrows (NT); SA3 1DB

Fine views from seats behind this popular pub with more in the big garden, well liked food and ales and friendly staff

The picnic-sets on the raised decked area at the back of this bustling dining pub have marvellous views over the Loughor estuary and do get snapped up quickly; there are also tables out in front and in the big garden. They have a rabbit hutch and an aviary with budgies, cockatiels, quails and a parrot. The refurbished beamed bar has a woodburning stove and plenty of space to enjoy a pint of Sharps Atlantic and Doom Bar and Wye Valley HPA on handpump and several wines by the glass; background music, darts, TV and board games. The beamed restaurant has attractive modern wooden tables and chairs on a striped carpet, paintings on exposed stone walls and another woodburning stove. Good surrounding walks.

🍴 High quality food includes lunchtime baguettes, local mussels in white wine, garlic, chilli and confit tomato broth, saddle of rabbit with prosciutto, carrot and cumin purée, wild mushrooms and beetroot, thai vegetable curry, slow-cooked barbecue spare ribs with chips, salt marsh lamb, shoulder, loin and chop with dauphinoise potatoes, pearl barley, salsa verde and lamb gravy, ballotine of chicken with crispy chicken wing and mixed bean tagine, parma ham-wrapped monkfish with spiced pearl barley and curried parsnip purée, Tia Maria and espresso crème brûlée and chamomile pannacotta with strawberry compote; they also offer a two- and three-course set lunch. *Benchmark main dish: steak in ale pie £10.95. Two-course evening meal £19.00.*

Enterprise ~ Tenants Martin and Lindsey Davies ~ Real ale ~ Open 12-11 ~ Bar food 12-3, 6-9 ~ Restaurant ~ Children welcome ~ Dogs allowed in bar ~ Wi-fi
Recommended by Hugh Roberts, Trevor and Michele Street, Rosie and John Moore

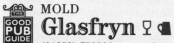

MOLD
Glasfryn 🍷 🍺

SJ2465 Map 6

(01352) 750500 – www.brunningandprice.co.uk/glasfryn
N of the centre on Raikes Lane (parallel to the A5119), just past the well signposted Theatr Clwyd; CH7 6LR

Busy open-plan bistro-style pub with inventive all-day food, nice décor and wide choice of drinks

Although unassuming from the outside, there's a wide mix of customers and a lively, cheerful atmosphere here. The open-plan interior is cleverly laid out to create plenty of nice quiet corners with a mix of informal, attractive country furnishings, turkey-style rugs on bare boards, deep red ceilings (some high), shelves of books, house plants, a warming fire and plenty of close-hung homely pictures; background music. Phoenix Brunning & Price Original plus guests such as Hobsons Best Bitter, Purple Moose Snowdonia Ale, Timothy Taylors Boltmaker, Titanic Plum Porter and Weetwood Cheshire Cat on handpump, 22 wines by the glass, 30 gins, 25 rums, 60 malt whiskies and farm cider. On warm days, the wooden tables on the large front terrace are a restful place to sit, providing sweeping views of the Clwydian Hills. Theatre Clwyd is just over the road.

🍴 Good, attractively presented food includes sandwiches, rabbit and wild mushroom sausage with garlic and herb risotto and beetroot and thyme dressing, monkfish scampi with bloody mary ketchup, butternut squash, borlotti bean and aubergine lasagne, moroccan-spiced chicken thighs with lemon couscous and apricot, date and pomegranate salad, steak burger with toppings, coleslaw and chips, duck breast with polenta chips and orange jus, teriyaki sea bass with crispy wasabi balls, pickled ginger and soy and sesame dressing, and puddings such as millionaire cheescake with salted caramel sauce and cherry meringue pie with pistachio nut ice-cream. *Benchmark main dish: chicken with haggis potato cake, neeps and tatties £13.95. Two-course evening meal £20.00.*

Brunning & Price ~ Manager Graham Arathoon ~ Real ale ~ Open 11.30-11; 12-10.30 Sun ~ Bar food 12-9.30 (9 Sun) ~ Children welcome ~ Dogs allowed in bar ~ Wi-fi
Recommended by Stuart Paulley, Mike and Wena Stevenson, Molly and Stewart Lindsay, Chantelle and Tony Redman

---

Bedroom prices are for high summer. Even then you may get reductions for more than one night, or (outside tourist areas) weekends. Winter special rates are common, and many inns reduce bedroom prices if you have a full evening meal.

MONKNASH
SS9170 Map 6
Plough & Harrow 🍺 £
(01656) 890209

Signposted 'Marcross, Broughton' off B4265 St Brides Major–Llantwit Major –
turn left at end of Water Street; OS Sheet 170 map reference 920706; CF71 7QQ

**Old building full of history and character, with a huge log fire
and a good choice of real ales**

Dating back almost nine centuries, this was originally part of a monastic grange. The unspoilt main bar with its massively thick stone walls used to be the scriptures room and mortuary with ancient ham hooks in the heavily beamed ceiling, an intriguing arched doorway at the back, broad flagstones and a comfortably informal mix of furnishings that includes three fine stripped-pine settles. There's a log fire in a huge fireplace with a side bread oven large enough to feed a village. Real ales on handpump or tapped from the cask might include Bass, Cwrw Iâl Hâf Gwyn, Grey Trees Mosaic Pale Ale, Sharps Atlantic, Wye Valley HPA and a guest from Mumbles or Tomos Watkin; they usually hold beer festivals in August. Also, a good range of local farm cider and quite a few gins and malt whiskies; background music in the left-hand room. The front garden has some picnic-sets. A path from the pub leads through the wooded valley of Cwm Nash to the coast, revealing a spectacular stretch of cliffs around Nash Point.

Tasty food includes garlic mushrooms, burgers with toppings and chips, a changing vegetarian risotto, fresh fish of the day, cajun chicken with sauté potatoes, lamb shank in red wine jus, and puddings such as apple crumble and sticky toffee pudding. *Benchmark main dish: steak in ale pie £9.50. Two-course evening meal £18.00.*

Free house ~ Licensee Paula Jones ~ Real ale ~ Open 12-11 (10.30 Sun) ~ Bar food 12-2.30, 6-9; 12-5, 6-9 Sat; 12-5 Sun ~ Restaurant ~ Children welcome ~ Dogs allowed in bar ~ Live music Sat evening *Recommended by Alan and Alice Morgan, Audrey and Paul Summers, Sandra King*

NEWPORT
SN0539 Map 6
Golden Lion
(01239) 820321 – www.goldenlionpembrokeshire.co.uk
East Street (A487); SA42 0SY

**Attractive, friendly local, with tasty food and pleasant staff;
well appointed bedrooms**

Enthusiastic reports once again from our readers who thoroughly enjoy their visits to this cheerful local. The genuinely pubby bar has Sharps Doom Bar and a couple of guest ales from the nearby Bluestone Brewery on handpump, several malt whiskies, wines by the glass and Gwynt y Ddraig cider; background music, TV, pool, juke box, darts and games machine. There's also a cosy series of beamed rooms with distinctive old settles and the dining room has elegant blond oak furniture, whitewashed walls and potted plants; service is efficient and friendly. You can sit outside at the front and in a side garden. This coastal village makes a fine base for exploring northern Pembrokeshire and the bedrooms are comfortable and fair value; good disabled access and facilities.

Popular, enjoyable food includes lunchtime sandwiches and platters, creamy garlic mushrooms, sizzling chilli and garlic prawns, roasted mediterranean vegetable lasagne, pie of the day, thai green chicken curry, burger with toppings, mustard mayonnaise and fries, a fresh fish dish of the day, gammon with leek, mustard and melted cheese topping, lamb chops with rosemary and mint sauce, rib-eye steak with peppercorn and brandy sauce, and puddings such as dark chocolate and peanut butter brownie and crumble of the day with custard. *Benchmark main dish: beer-battered fresh cod and chips £12.95. Two-course evening meal £18.00.*

Free house ~ Licensee Daron Paish ~ Real ale ~ Open 12pm-2am ~ Bar food 12-2.30, 6.30-9 ~ Restaurant ~ Children welcome ~ Dogs allowed in bar and bedrooms ~ Wi-fi ~ Live music Sat Sept-March ~ Bedrooms: £80/£100 *Recommended by R T and J C Moggridge, Mark Hamill, Colin and Daniel Gibbs, Peter Brix*

OLD RADNOR
Harp 🏵 ⇐   SO2459 Map 6

(01544) 350655 – www.harpinnradnor.co.uk

Village signposted off A44 Kington–New Radnor in Walton; LD8 2RH

Charming inn in beautiful spot, with cottagey bar, tasty food and well kept ales; comfortable bedrooms

'A real find' is how one of our readers describes this delightful old place in its glorious hilltop position at the end of a lane in a tiny village. You'll get a warm welcome from the hands-on licensees and the public bar has a great deal of character plus high-backed settles, an antique reader's chair and other venerable chairs around a log fire; board games, cribbage, darts and quoits. The snug slate-floored bar contains a handsome curved antique settle, a log fire in a fine inglenook and lots of local books, maps and guides for residents; a quieter dining area off to the right extends into another dining room with a woodburning stove. Ludlow Gold and Three Tuns XXX on handpump, as well as five wines and prosecco by the glass, local cider and local gins, vodka and whiskies. Tables outside make the most of the view overlooking the heights of Radnor Forest. The spic and span bedrooms are highly sought after (no door keys) and share the same lovely views; good breakfasts too. The impressive village church is worth a look for its early organ case (Britain's oldest), fine rood screen and ancient font.

 Rewarding food using local produce includes sandwiches, scallops with black pudding, pea purée and pork crackling, game ballotine with celeriac purée, wild mushroom, leek and chestnut pearl barley risotto with a poached egg, home-cooked ham and eggs, beer-battered fish and chips, pot-roasted pheasant with chorizo, butter bean and carrot broth, hake with bubble and squeak cake, beetroot and brown shrimp beurre blanc, barnsley lamb chop with salsa verde, and puddings such as vanilla crème brûlée and chocolate brownie with pistachio ice-cream. *Benchmark main dish: rump steak and chips £15.00. Two-course evening meal £22.00.*

Free house ~ Licensees Chris and Angela Ireland ~ Real ale ~ Open 6-11 Weds, Thurs; 12-3, 6-11 Fri, Sat; 12-3, 6-10.30 Sun; closed Mon except bank holidays, Tues ~ Bar food 12-2 Fri-Sun; 6-9 Weds-Sat ~ Children welcome ~ Dogs allowed in bar and bedrooms ~ Wi-fi ~ Bedrooms: £75/£105 *Recommended by Anne and Ben Smith, Alison and Michael Harper, P and J Shapley, Professor James Burke, Peter and Emma Kelly*

OVERTON BRIDGE
Cross Foxes ♀   SJ3542 Map 6

(01978) 780380 – www.brunningandprice.co.uk/crossfoxes

A539 W of Overton, near Erbistock; LL13 0DR

Terrific river views, contemporary food and an extensive range of drinks in bustling, well run pub

The River Dee sweeps past this substantial 18th-c coaching inn and big windows in the airy dining conservatory look over the water – as do seats and tables on the raised terrace and picnic-sets on grass; there's also a swing, a slide and a tractor. The ancient low-beamed bar has a red tiled floor, dark timbers, a warm fire in the big inglenook and built-in old pews, and several dining areas have turkey rugs, big pot plants and frame-to-frame wall pictures; board games and newspapers. A fine range of drinks includes 40 malt whiskies, 30 Armagnacs, 45 gins and lots of wines by the glass – plus Phoenix Brunning & Price Original, Brakspears Bitter, Jennings Cumberland, Ludlow Gold and Marstons EPA on handpump and a farm cider. Service is friendly and efficient.

Attractively presented modern food includes sandwiches, chicken, ham and leek terrine with fruit chutney, wild boar scotch egg with pickled vegetables, satay chicken with chinese leaves, mango, spring onion and cashews, sweet potato, cauliflower and chickpea tagine with lemon and coriander couscous, steamed game pudding, spicy vietnamese king prawn and rice noodle salad with peanuts, lime and chilli dressing, sea bass fillets with lemon and basil gnocchi and warm gazpacho sauce, and puddings such as dark chocolate marquise with boozy cherries and pistachio ice-cream and custard tart with poached rhubarb. *Benchmark main dish: braised lamb shoulder with dauphinoise potatoes and rosemary gravy £17.25. Two-course evening meal £22.00.*

Brunning & Price ~ Manager Ian Pritchard-Jones ~ Real ale ~ Open 11-11; 12-10.30 Sun ~ Bar food 12-9.30 (9 Sun) ~ Children welcome ~ Dogs allowed in bar ~ Wi-fi *Recommended by David Longhurst, Julie Swift, Christopher Mannings, Samuel and Melissa Turnbull, Nicholas and Lucy Sage*

PANTYGELLI
Crown 🏵 ♀ 🍺
SO3017 Map 6

(01873) 853314 – www.thecrownatpantygelli.com
Old Hereford Road N of Abergavenny; off A40 by war memorial via Pen Y Pound, passing leisure centre; Pantygelli also signposted from A465; NP7 7HR

Country pub in fine scenery, attractive inside and out, with good food and drinks

After a walk up the nearby Sugar Loaf, head to this warmly friendly and very well run pub afterwards for refreshment. The dark flagstoned bar, with sturdy timber props and beams, has a log fire in a stone fireplace, a piano at the back with darts opposite, Bass, Rhymney Best, Wye Valley HPA and a guest such as Baa Best on handpump from the slate-roofed counter, Gwatkin's farm cider, seven good wines by the glass, local organic apple juice and good coffees. On the left are four smallish, linked, carpeted dining rooms, the front pair separated by a massive stone chimneybreast; thoughtfully chosen individual furnishings and lots of attractive prints by local artists make it all thoroughly civilised. Also, background music, darts and board games. On the flower-filled front terrace, wrought-iron and wicker chairs look up from the lush valley to the hills and there's also a smaller back terrace surrounded by lavender.

Reliably good food includes king prawn, herring and locally smoked salmon salad, chicken caesar salad, goats cheese, tomato and onion tart, home-cooked ham platter with mango chutney and chips, venison sausages with mash and red onion gravy, chicken with crushed chestnuts and potatoes, sauté wild mushrooms and butternut squash purée, rosemary-roasted monkfish on burgundy wine risotto, a spicy dish of the day, pheasant suprême in marsala wine sauce with grilled artichokes, fresh figs and fondant potato, 10oz rib-eye steak with chips and red wine jus, and puddings such as orange crème brûlée and Baileys and white chocolate cheesecake. *Benchmark main dish: steak in ale pie £11.00. Two-course evening meal £20.50.*

Free house ~ Licensees Steve and Cherrie Chadwick ~ Real ale ~ Open 12-2.30 (3 Sat), 6-11; 12-3, 6-10.30 Sun; closed Mon lunchtime ~ Bar food 12-2, 7-9; not Sun evening or Mon ~ Restaurant ~ Children welcome ~ Dogs allowed in bar ~ Wi-fi *Recommended by Christopher Mannings, Julian Richardson, Tim King, R T and J C Moggridge, Liz and Martin Eldon*

PENNAL
SH6900 Map 6
Riverside ⭐ 🍺
(01654) 791285 – www.riversidehotel-pennal.co.uk
A493; opposite church; SY20 9DW

Carefully refurbished pub with tasty food and local beers, and efficient young staff; bedrooms

Most people come to this bustling pub to enjoy the wide choice of good quality food, but there's quite a range of thoughtful drinks too. The neatly furnished rooms have green and white walls, slate tiles on the floor, a woodburning stove, modern light wood dining furniture and some funky fabrics. High-backed stools are lined up along the stone-fronted counter where they serve Hancocks HB, Purple Moose Glaslyn, Sharps Atlantic, Salopian Golden Thread and Tiny Rebel Cwtch on handpump, 30 malt whiskies, 30 gins, 12 wines by the glass and farm cider. There are seats and tables in the garden. As the pub is just inside the southern boundary of Snowdonia National Park, there are plenty of fine surrounding walks. They also run a Georgian guesthouse in the pretty village.

 Pleasing food includes baguettes, salmon and smoked haddock fishcake with lemon mayonnaise, welsh rarebit with bacon and a poached egg, sharing platters, vegetarian nut roast with sauté potatoes and gravy, steak burger with toppings and skinny fries, chicken kiev with sweet potato fries, spicy mediterranean fish stew, loin of venison with creamed leeks and red wine sauce, herb-crusted cod with samphire, king prawns and salsa verde, and puddings such as chocolate and brandy truffle cake with salted caramel ice-cream and apple and blackberry crumble with custard. *Benchmark main dish: lamb steak with dauphinoise potatoes and red wine jus £18.50. Two-course evening meal £21.00.*

Free house ~ Licensees Glyn and Corina Davies ~ Real ale ~ Open 12-3, 6-11.30; 12-midnight Sat; 12-11.30 Sun; closed Mon; three weeks Jan ~ Bar food 12-2 (2.30 Sun), 6-9 ~ Restaurant ~ Children welcome ~ Dogs allowed in bar ~ Wi-fi ~ Bedrooms: £55/£75 *Recommended by Mike and Mary Carter, John Evans, Alf Wright, Mike and Wena Stevenson*

PENTYRCH
ST1081 Map 6
Kings Arms �
(029) 2089 0202 – www.kingsarmspentyrch.co.uk
Church Road; CF15 9QF

Village pub very much part of the community with a perky bar, civilised lounge and top class food

Both locals and visitors are drawn to this 16th-c longhouse for the highly regarded food, but this is no straightforward dining place. It's very much a proper pub with plenty of regulars popping in for a drink and a chat, and the cosy bar has a cheerful atmosphere, an open log fire in a sizeable brick fireplace and a mix of seats on flagstones. There's Brains Bitter, Rev James and SA and a guest such as Lacons Encore on handpump, 14 wines by the glass and up to ten malt whiskies, all served by helpful, friendly staff. There's also a comfortable lounge and a cosy restaurant. Plenty of seats on a terrace and picnic-sets are set out under parasols in the garden.

Cooked by the landlady, the well thought-of food includes pork loin ribs marinated in chilli and chocolate with a hickory barbecue glaze, ham hock terrine with carrot chutney, sharing boards, halloumi and vegetable pasta, pork, spring onion and cheddar sausages with carrot and parsnip mash, caramelised onions and red wine gravy, burger with toppings and cajun fries, beer-battered fish fingers with skinny fries, chilli and lime salmon with courgettes, aubergines and green beans in chilli dressing, duck breast with spiced plum sauce, and puddings. *Benchmark main dish: rib-eye steak with chips £17.50. Two-course evening meal £19.00.*

Free house ~ Licensee Owen Robbins ~ Real ale ~ Open 12-11 (midnight Sat); 12-8 Sun ~ Bar food 12-3, 5-9; 12-5 Sun ~ Restaurant ~ Children welcome ~ Dogs allowed in bar ~ Wi-fi *Recommended by Sally and David Champion, Sabina and Gerald Grimshaw, Margo and Derek Stapley*

PONTYPRIDD   ST0790   Map 6

Bunch of Grapes 🍽️ ♀ 🍺

(01443) 402934 – www.bunchofgrapes.org.uk
Off A4054; Ynysangharad Road; CF37 4DA

Bustling pub with a fine choice of drinks in friendly, relaxed bar, first class inventive food and a warm welcome for all

As well as brewing their own beer and baking fresh bread daily, this particularly well run 18th-c pub is known for its delicious inventive food. Knowledgeable, friendly and efficient staff also serve a fantastic range of drinks. This might include their own Otley O2 Croeso and three Otley guests plus other quickly changing guests such as Amber Chocolate Orange Stout, Oakham Citra, Redemption Hopspur and Salopian Lemon Dream on handpump. They hold around six beer and music festivals each year, and also keep continental and american ales on draught or in bottles, a couple of local ciders or perrys, nine wines by the glass and a growing gin collection. The cosy bar has an informal, relaxed atmosphere, comfortable leather sofas, wooden chairs and tables, a roaring log fire, newspapers to read and background music and board games. There's also a restaurant with elegant high-backed wooden dining chairs around a mix of tables and black and white local photo-prints taken by the landlord (an ex-professional photographer). A deli offers home-baked bread and chutneys, home-cooked ham, local eggs and quite a choice of welsh cheeses and so forth, and they hold regular themed cookery evenings. There are seats outside on decking.

Using the best local, seasonal produce, the excellent food includes bar choices plus more elaborate restaurant meals: chicken terrine with pickle salad, cured sea trout with beetroot, burgers with toppings and chips, pea, spinach, almond and rocket pesto risotto, pork loin with cumin gnocchi, spiced apple and pak choi, veal with pickled mustard potato terrine and cauliflower, halibut with sorrel and lettuce, slow-cooked barbecue beef short rib with green slaw and fries, and puddings such as lemon tart with raspberry sorbet and lemon balm and banana, peanuts and yuzu (japanese citrus fruit). *Benchmark main dish: ox cheek with wild garlic £15.50. Two-course evening meal £24.00.*

Free house ~ Licensee Nick Otley ~ Real ale ~ Open 11am-11.30pm; 12-11 Sun ~ Bar food 12-8.30; 12-6.30 Fri, Sat; 12-4 Sun ~ Restaurant ~ Children welcome ~ Dogs allowed in bar ~ Wi-fi *Recommended by Christopher Mannings, Edward Edmonton, Barry and Daphne Gregson, Elizabeth and Peter May, Kerry and Guy Trooper*

PUMSAINT
SN6540 Map 6

Dolaucothi Arms 🛏

(01558) 650237 – www.thedolaucothiarms.co.uk

A482 Lampeter–Llandovery; SA19 8UW

**Friendly owners for enjoyable inn with simply furnished bar
and dining room, local beers and riverside garden; bedrooms**

Our readers very much enjoy this genuinely welcoming inn that's part of the Dolaucothi Estate and owned by the National Trust. The chatty bar has a chesterfield and button-back armchair on red and black tiles to one side of the woodburning stove, stone bottles on the mantelpiece, some tables and chairs near the counter and Evan Evans Cwrw and Grey Trees Mosaic Pale Ale on handpump, eight wines by the glass and farm cider; darts, background music and board games. The terracotta-painted dining room has another woodburning stove, heavy welsh dressers and all sorts of nice old dining chairs and tables on big flagstones; walls are hung with local art, maps and old photos of the pub, the village and the Estate. Picnic-sets in a neat garden overlook the Cothi River where the pub has four miles of fishing rights. This is a warm and cosy place to stay, with simply furnished bedrooms complete with a decanter of port and fresh biscuits.

 Tempting food includes their popular home-made pies plus sandwiches using home-baked bread, black pudding fritters with curried mayonnaise, smoked mackerel pâté with pickled rhubarb, mushroom suet pudding with carrots, burger with toppings, coleslaw and chips, lamb shanks in stout and honey with champ, crab cakes with tartare sauce, rib-eye steak with garlic and herb field mushroom and beer-battered onion rings, and puddings such as plum and apple crumble and chocolate and cherry brownie with salted caramel ice-cream. *Benchmark main dish: pie of the day £11.00. Two-course evening meal £16.00.*

Free house ~ Licensee David Joy ~ Real ale ~ Open 12-11; 4-11 Tues (Tues-Thurs in winter); 12-9 Sun; closed Mon; closed two weeks Jan except Fri, Sat evenings ~ Bar food 12 3, 6 8.30; 6-8.30 Tues; 12-2.30 Sun (and Sun evening in July, Aug) ~ Restaurant ~ Children welcome ~ Dogs allowed in bar ~ Wi-fi ~ Bedrooms: £60/£80
Recommended by David Longhurst, Peter Barrett, James Allsopp, Christine and Tony Garrett

RAGLAN
SO3609 Map 6

Clytha Arms ⭐ ♀ 🍺 🛏

(01873) 840206 – www.clytha-arms.com

Clytha, off Abergavenny road – former A40, now declassified; 3 miles W of Raglan; NP7 9BW

**Fine setting in spacious grounds, a relaxing spot for enjoying good
food and impressive range of drinks; comfortable bedrooms**

Just a short stroll from the riverside path by the Usk, this civilised old country inn stands in its own extensive well cared-for grounds on the edge of Clytha Park; long heated verandahs and diamond-paned windows take in the view. It appeals to a wide array of customers which creates a chatty, easy-going atmosphere, and the bar and lounge are comfortable, light and airy, with a good mix of nice old furniture, pine settles, window seats with big cushions, scrubbed wooden floors and a couple of open log fires; the contemporary restaurant is linen-set. A notable array of drinks includes Bass, Uley Pigs Ear, Untapped Raglan Mild and Sundown (from a little brewery just down the road) and Wye Valley Bitter on handpump, an extensive wine list with eight by the glass, 20 malt whiskies, three farm ciders, their own perry and various continental beers; they hold a cider and beer festival over the late May Bank

Holiday weekend. Darts, bar skittles, boules, board games and large-screen TV for rugby matches. The bedrooms are comfortable and the welsh breakfasts good. Dogs are welcome – the pub has its own labrador and collie.

 Interesting, reliably good food includes tapas (piri-piri chicken skewers, pork belly and black pudding with apple, three local cheeses with local honey and so forth) plus snails with goats cheese and herb butter, black pasta with bacon, leeks and cockles, leek and laverbread rissoles with beetroot chutney, pie of the day, lemongrass chicken curry, wild boar sausage and german sausage with potato pancakes, rabbit in cider with bacon and herb dumplings, ham with bubble and squeak and parsley sauce, fresh fish dish of the day, and puddings such as treacle pudding with custard and chocolate and local whisky cup. *Benchmark main dish: smoked haddock with local cheese sauce £15.50. Two-course evening meal £24.00.*

Free house ~ Licensees Andrew and Beverley Canning ~ Real ale ~ Open 12-3, 6-11; 12-11 Fri, Sat; 12-10.30 Sun; closed Mon lunchtime ~ Bar food 12.30-2.15, 7-9.30; 12.30-2.30 Sun ~ Restaurant ~ Children welcome ~ Dogs allowed in bar and bedrooms ~ Wi-fi ~ Bedrooms: £70/£90 *Recommended by Andrew Stone, Heather and Richard Jones, Simon and Miranda Davies, Roy and Gill Payne, Terry Davis*

SKENFRITH
SO4520 Map 6

Bell 🌟 ♀ 🛏
(01600) 750235 – www.skenfrith.co.uk
Just off B4521, NE of Abergavenny and N of Monmouth; NP7 8UH

Elegant but relaxed inn much praised for classy food and thoughtful choice of drinks; excellent bedrooms

After enjoying one of the fine circular walks created by this former 17th-c coaching inn and visiting the impressive ruins of nearby Skenfrith Castle (National Trust), why not stay overnight in the individually decorated bedrooms (named after brown trout fishing flies); dogs are welcome in some rooms. The two bars have flagstoned floors and one welcomes dogs and walkers. The main bar has a big inglenook fireplace with comfortable sofas, a couple of pews and lots of tables and chairs. From the bleached oak counter they serve Bespoke Saved by the Bell, Wickwar BOB and Wye Valley Butty Bach on handpump, bottled local cider and perry, 15 wines by the glass from an impressive list, local sparkling wine, early-landed cognacs and a good range of spirits; background music. There's a sitting room for resident guests with more sofas and tables and plenty of books, magazines and board games. The terrace has good solid tables under parasols, with steps leading up to a sloping lawn and an orchard area (ideal for families and they'll make a picnic and provide a rug for you to sit on); the kitchen garden is immaculate. Good disabled access.

 High quality food using home-grown and local produce includes sandwiches, blue cheese brûlée with poached pear and walnut brittle, marinated crab tian with pickled cucumber, fennel and wasabi mayonnaise, sharing boards, wild mushroom, spinach and crème fraîche risotto, pork sausages with pomme purée and onion gravy, rack of pork, ham hock croquette, sautéed cabbage and mustard and rosemary cream, wild sea bass with samphire and prawn and caper butter, and puddings such as plum jam and frangipane tart with vanilla ice-cream and white chocolate and raspberry cheesecake with strawberry ice-cream; steak night is Tuesday. *Benchmark main dish: local steaks £21.00. Two-course evening meal £25.00.*

Free house ~ Licensee Richard Ireton ~ Real ale ~ Open 11-11 (10.30 Sun); closed one week Nov, one week Jan ~ Bar food 12-2.30, 6.30-8.30; all day weekends ~ Restaurant ~ Well behaved children welcome ~ Dogs allowed in bar and bedrooms ~ Wi-fi ~ Bedrooms: £90/£150 *Recommended by Peter Harrison, Robin and Anne Triggs, Gerry and Pam Pollard, Jennifer and Nicholas Thompson*

ST GEORGE   SH9775 Map 6

Kinmel Arms 🌟 🛏

(01745) 832207 – www.thekinmelarms.co.uk

Off A547 or B5381 SE of Abergele; LL22 9BP

**Stylish food in bustling inn, a wide choice of drinks,
courteous staff and lovely position; bedrooms**

Some kind of good, interesting food is available all day here and our
readers are full of high praise for all the meals they've enjoyed. It's
a 17th-c sandstone inn with mullioned windows and handsome carriage
lamps at the front, plus plenty of picnic-sets. There's a bar with sofas on
either side of a woodburning stove, an attractive mix of nice old wooden
chairs and tables on the wooden floor and seats against the counter where
they keep Facers DHB, Heavy Industry Diawl Bach and Thwaites Original
on handpump, 21 wines by the glass, 55 malt whiskies and farm cider;
service is helpful and friendly. The restaurant, with rattan chairs around
marble-topped tables, has big house plants, contemporary art painted by
Tim Watson (one of the owners) and evening candles and twinkling lights;
background music. A tea room with silver teapots and pretty bone-china
cups and saucers also sells hampers, chutneys, port and cheese boxes and
so forth. The surrounding countryside is stunning and there are good walks
from the front door. The bedrooms consist of comfortable contemporary
suites, each with their own decked area.

 Using carefully sourced local produce, the creative food includes lunchtime
croque monsieur or madame, mushroom brûlée with truffle butter, king
scallops with squash and squid ink, caramelised aubergine with lentils, carrots and
lemongrass and chervil velouté, pie of the day, local mussels in curry sauce, loin of
veal with white asparagus and wild mushrooms, guinea fowl with pickled cabbage and
french-style beans, and puddings such as apple and blackberry crumble with damson
ice-cream and chocolate tart with salted caramel and morello cherries; they also
offer a two- and three-course menu (6-7pm Tuesday-Thursday). *Benchmark main
dish: lamb rump with soubise (creamy onion sauce) £24.00. Two-course evening
meal £25.00.*

Free house ~ Licensees Lynn Cunnah-Watson and Tim Watson ~ Real ale ~ Open 11-11
(11.30 Sat); closed Sun ~ Bar food 12-2, 5.45-9.30; coffee and cake from 11am, afternoon
tea 2-4.30pm ~ Restaurant ~ Children welcome ~ Dogs allowed in bar ~ Wi-fi ~ Bedrooms:
£115/£135 *Recommended by Pip White, Alison and Michael Harper, Geoff and Ann Marston,
Brian and Sally Wakeham, Julie and Andrew Blanchett, John and Delia Franks*

STACKPOLE   SR9896 Map 6

Stackpole Inn 🌟 🛏

(01646) 672324 – www.stackpoleinn.co.uk

Village signed off B4319 S of Pembroke; SA71 5DF

**Busy pub, a good base for the area, with enjoyable food
and friendly service; comfortable bedrooms**

Walkers, climbers and bird-watchers crowd into this popular pub,
particularly at lunchtime when they offer a walkers' lunch menu; two
stunning beaches are also close by. There's an area around the bar with pine
tables and chairs, but most of the pub, L-shaped on four different levels,
is given over to diners, with neat light oak furnishings, ash beams and low
ceilings to match; background music and board games. They serve Brains
Rev James, Felinfoel Double Dragon and IPA and a changing guest ale on
handpump, 14 wines by the glass, 15 malt whiskies and two farm ciders.

Attractive gardens feature colourful flower beds and mature trees and there are plenty of picnic-sets on grass at the front. The comfortable bedrooms are spotless and the breakfasts enjoyable.

Fresh fish is the speciality here and dishes come with a choice of sauce and double-cooked chips; other options include lunchtime rolls, smoked bacon, pork and cranberry terrine with caper and mustard dressing, home-cured gravadlax with celeriac rémoulade, roasted onion and mushroom tagliatelle in creamy madeira sauce, local sausages with cider gravy, salmon fillet with chorizo, tomato and cannellini bean cassoulet, lamb rump with lyonnaise potatoes, celeriac purée and lamb jus, rib of beef (for two) with garlic and herb butter, rarebit-topped mushrooms and red wine jus, and puddings such as coconut pannacotta with marinated pineapple and belgian chocolate and orange brownie with honeycomb ice-cream. *Benchmark main dish: fresh fish dish of the day £15.00. Two-course evening meal £20.00.*

Free house ~ Licensees Gary and Becky Evans ~ Real ale ~ Open 12-3, 6-11; 12-11 Sat; closed Sun evening in winter ~ Bar food 12-2.15, 6.30-9 ~ Restaurant ~ Children welcome ~ Dogs allowed in bar ~ Wi-fi ~ Bedrooms: £60/£90 *Recommended by Hugh Roberts, S and L McPhee, Mike Benton, Jamie Green, Alexander and Trish Gendall*

TINTERN
Anchor
SO5300 Map 6

(01291) 689582 – www.theanchortintern.co.uk
Off A466 at brown sign for Tintern Abbey; NP16 6TE

Wonderful setting for ancient inn next to Tintern Abbey ruins and river, historic features, plenty of space and good ales and food

There are wonderful views from picnic-sets on the terrace and in the front garden and also from the Garden Room, of Tintern Abbey's magnificent ruins (floodlit at night) right next door to this medieval building. The bar was originally a cider mill attached to the abbey's orchard and the horse-drawn cider press is the central feature; also, little plush stools around circular tables, heavy beams, flagstones, Otter Bitter, Wye Valley Butty Bach and a quickly changing guest on handpump and local ciders served by friendly staff. The restaurant was once the ferryman's cottage and boat house and is connected to the abbey's north wall: bare stone walls, high-backed leather dining chairs around all sorts of tables and more flagstones. There's also an airy café (open 9am-5pm) with colourfully painted chairs and a 100-year-old olive tree. The River Wye is just behind and there are plenty of surrounding walks.

Well liked food includes lunchtime sandwiches, ham hock terrine with pickled vegetables, chicken and bacon caesar salad, tomato, red pepper, spinach and cheese tart, sausages of the week with a giant yorkshire pudding and cider gravy, steak in ale pie, chicken curry, burgers with toppings, coleslaw and fries, confit duck leg with puy lentils, braised red cabbage and balsamic jus, hake fillet with chorizo and mussel and tomato sauce, and puddings such as Baileys pannacotta with salted caramel sauce and apple crumble with custard. *Benchmark main dish: beer-battered haddock and chips £12.00. Two-course evening meal £18.00.*

Free house ~ Real ale ~ Open 12-midnight; 12-8.30 Sun ~ Bar food 12-2, 6-9.30; 12-6 Sun ~ Restaurant ~ Children welcome ~ Dogs allowed in bar ~ Wi-fi *Recommended by Ian and Rose Lock, Simon and Miranda Davies, Charles Todd, Julie Braeburn, Anna and Mark Evans*

Post Office address codings confusingly give the impression that some pubs are in Gwent or Powys, Wales, when they're really in Gloucestershire or Shropshire (which is where we list them).

USK

Nags Head ♀

(01291) 672820 – www.nagsheadusk.co.uk

SO3700 Map 6

The Square; NP15 1BH

Spotlessly kept and traditional in style with a hearty welcome and good food and drinks

The Key family who run this handsome old coaching inn have been at the helm for more than 50 years and you'll always be personally welcomed by one of them. The traditional main bar is cheerily chatty and cosy, with lots of well polished tables and chairs packed under its beams (some of these have farming tools, lanterns or horsebrasses and harness attached), as well as leatherette wall benches, and various sets of sporting prints and local pictures – look out for the original deeds to the pub. Tucked away at the front is an intimate little corner with some african masks, while on the other side of the room a passageway leads to a dining area; background music. They offer nine wines by the glass, along with Brains Rev James and Sharps Atlantic and Doom Bar on handpump. There are seats outside at the front under the fantastic hanging baskets. The church is well worth a look. The pub has no parking and nearby street parking can be limited.

Tasty food using local meat and seasonal game includes sandwiches, snails in garlic butter, grilled sardines, vegetable pancakes topped with melting cheese, faggots with mushy peas and onion gravy, rabbit or steak pie, beer-battered cod and chips, seasonal pheasant in port wine sauce, crispy half duck in orange and Cointreau sauce, gammon with eggs or pineapple, guinea fowl with wine and fig sauce, and puddings such as treacle and walnut tart and sticky toffee pudding. *Benchmark main dish: rabbit pie £10.50. Two-course evening meal £16.00.*

Free house ~ Licensee Key family ~ Real ale ~ Open 10-3, 5-11 ~ Bar food 11.30-2, 5.30-9 ~ Restaurant ~ Children welcome ~ Dogs welcome ~ Wi-fi *Recommended by Peter Barrett, Caroline Sullivan, M G Hart, Diana and Bertie Farr, Louise and Simon Peters*

Also Worth a Visit in Wales

Besides the fully inspected pubs, you might like to try these pubs that have been recommended to us and described by readers. Do tell us what you think of them: feedback@goodguides.com

ANGLESEY

ABERFFRAW SH3568
Crown (01407) 840222
Bodorgan Square; LL63 5BX Village-square pub with two well kept ales, good selection of gins and enjoyable home-made food including daily specials, quick friendly service; sports TV; well behaved children and dogs welcome, suntrap beer garden with sturdy furniture and views towards the dunes, open all day, food all day Sat, till 6pm Sun. *(Sandra and Miles Spencer)*

GAERWEN SH4972
Gaerwen Arms (01248) 421906
Chapel Street; LL60 6DW Dining pub with bare-boards bar, farmhouse chairs, stools and wall seats around wooden tables, tartan-carpeted dining area with upholstered or leather armchairs and open fire, good well presented food at sensible prices, local Coppertown beers, efficient friendly service; children welcome, seats outside with views over to Snowdonia, play area, useful stop before Holyhead for the Irish ferries, open (and food) all day weekends. *(Sandra and Miles Spencer)*

MENAI BRIDGE SH5773
Gazelle (01248) 713364
Glyngarth; A545, halfway towards Beaumaris; LL59 5PD Hotel and restaurant rather than pub in outstanding waterside position looking across to Snowdonia, main bar with smaller rooms off, up to three Robinsons ales kept well and seven wines by the glass, decent bar food; children and dogs (in bar) welcome,

steep garden behind (and walk down from car park), 30 bedrooms including suites, slipway and mooring for visiting boats, open all day weekends. *(Alan McQuilan)*

MENAI BRIDGE   SH5572
Liverpool Arms (01248) 712453
St Georges Road/Water Street; LL59 5EY
Refurbished pub close to the quay and not far from the famous suspension bridge; ales such as Bass, Facers and Greene King, enjoyable home-made food (all day Fri-Sun) including daily specials and Mon steak night, quick friendly service; quiz Weds and Sun; children welcome, part-covered terrace, open all day (till 1am Fri, Sat). *(Dave Braisted)*

MOELFRE   SH5186
Kinmel Arms (01248) 410231
Moelfre Bay; LL72 8LL Popular sea-view pub with nautical-theme interior, four Robinsons ales and generous helpings of enjoyable traditional food from sandwiches and baked potatoes up, friendly service; dogs welcome, picnic-sets on paved front terrace, open all day. *(Brian and Anna Marsden)*

PENTRAETH   SH5278
Panton Arms (01248) 450959
The Square; LL75 8AZ Welcoming roadside pub with spacious cleanly presented interior, enjoyable good value food and three well kept ales such as Black Sheep, Purple Moose and Thornbridge; free wi-fi; children and dogs (in bar) welcome, good-sized back garden with play area, open all day in summer, food all day weekends. *(Brian and Anna Marsden)*

RED WHARF BAY   SH5281
Ship (01248) 852568
Village signed off A5025 N of Pentraeth; LL75 8RJ Whitewashed 18th-c pub right on Anglesey's east coast – fantastic views of miles of tidal sands; big old-fashioned rooms either side of bar counter, nautical bric-a-brac, long varnished wall pews, cast-iron-framed tables and open fires, three well kept ales including Adnams, 48 malt whiskies and decent choice of wines, enjoyable food (if you run a tab they lock your card in a numbered box); background music; children welcome in room on left, dogs in bar, limited disabled access, numerous outside tables, open all day. *(Paul Humphreys)*

RHOSCOLYN   SH2675
★**White Eagle** (01407) 860267
Off B4545 S of Holyhead; LL65 2NJ
Remote place rebuilt almost from scratch on site of an old pub; airy modern feel in neatly kept rooms, relaxed atmosphere and nice winter fire, Conwy, Weetwood and three guests from smart oak counter, several wines by the glass, extensive choice of good locally sourced interesting food (all day weekends and school holidays, best to book), friendly helpful service,

restaurant; children welcome, dogs in bar (biscuits for them), terrific sea views from decking and picnic-sets in good-sized garden, lane down to beach, open all day. *(Sandra and Miles Spencer)*

RHOSNEIGR   SH3272
Oystercatcher (01407) 812829
A4080; LL64 5JP Modern glass-fronted Huf Haus set in dunes close to the sea – same owners as the White Eagle at Rhoscolyn but not really a pub (created as a restaurant/chefs' academy); great views from upstairs restaurant and bar with good range of enjoyable food, well kept ales and decent choice of wines by the glass, ground-floor coffee/wine bar serving lighter meals till 6pm; children welcome, upper terrace with rattan sofas and colourful beach huts, full wheelchair access, open all day. *(Alister and Margery Bacon)*

CLWYD

CAERWYS   SJ1373
Piccadilly (01352) 720284
North Street; CH7 5AW Pleasantly modernised pub-restaurant; high-ceilinged bare-boards bar with raised central woodburner, dining room across corridor with white-painted beams and tartan carpet, spacious slate-floor restaurant behind has banquettes and light wood furniture, stairs up to further eating area, enjoyable modern food, three real ales and good friendly service; background music, daily papers; children welcome, partly covered side terrace, open (and food) all day, till 7.30pm Sun. *(Nicholas and Lucy Sage)*

CARROG   SJ1143
Grouse (01490) 430272
B5436, signed off A5 Llangollen–Corwen; LL21 9AT Small unpretentious pub with superb views over River Dee and beyond from bay window and balcony, Lees ales, decent food from sandwiches up including gluten-free choices, reasonable prices, friendly helpful staff, local pictures, pool in games room; background music; children welcome, wheelchair access (side door a bit tight), tables in pretty walled garden, covered terrace, narrow turn into car park, handy for Llangollen steam railway; open (and food) all day. *(Fiona and Jack Henderson)*

COLWYN BAY   SH8479
Picture House (01492) 535286
Princes Drive; LL29 8LA Interesting Wetherspoons conversion of 1914 cinema, good range of well kept beers, decent wines and their usual competitively priced food, seating areas on different levels, efficient service; open all day from 8am. *(Paul Humphreys)*

COLWYN BAY SH8579
Toad (01492) 532726
Promenade; LL28 4BU Seafront pub overlooking the prom and beach, enjoyable varied choice of food including fixed-price menu, good wine list and real ales such as Jennings, friendly efficient service; children welcome, seats out at front, open all day Sun. *(Paul Humphreys)*

GRAIG FECHAN SJ1454
Three Pigeons (01824) 703178
Signed off B5429 S of Ruthin; LL15 2EU Extended largely 18th-c pub with enjoyable inexpensive food (all day Sun, not Tues) from sandwiches up, friendly licensees, good range of quickly changing real ales and plenty of wines by the glass, various nooks and corners, interesting mix of furniture and some old signs on the walls, great country views from restaurant; children allowed if eating, big garden with terrace and same views, good walks, two self-catering apartments, closed Mon and lunchtime Tues. *(Mike and Wena Stevenson)*

LLANARMON DYFFRYN
CEIRIOG SJ1532
★ Hand (01691) 600666
B4500 from Chirk; LL20 7LD Peaceful former farmhouse at heart of Upper Ceiriog valley set against backdrop of the Berwyn Mountains; low-beamed bar with inglenook log fire, sturdy tables and a mix of seating including settles, wheelbacks and mate's chairs on carpet, old prints on the walls, ales such as Big Hand and Weetwood, seven wines by the glass and 17 malt whiskies, good popular food, woodburner in largely stripped-stone restaurant, quiet lounge and games room with darts and pool; children welcome (not in bar after 8pm), dogs in some areas, picnic-sets on crazy-paved front terrace, more tables in garden, not far from Pistyll Rhaeadr (Wales's highest waterfall), well equipped spacious bedrooms, good breakfast, open all day. *(Dennis and Doreen Haward, Julie Braeburn)*

LLANARMON DYFFRYN
CEIRIOG SJ1532
★ West Arms (01691) 600665
End of B4500 W of Chirk; LL20 7LD Former drovers' inn with fine surrounding walks; small back public bar plus smarter beamed and timbered lounge with antique settles, sofas and even an elaborately carved confessional, old-fashioned entrance hall with more sofas, several log fires, attractive slightly more formal restaurant, wide range of good food, Brains Rev James, Sharps Doom Bar and Wye Valley HPA, friendly staff; background music, darts and board games, free wi-fi; children and dogs (in bar) welcome, pretty lawn running down to River Ceiriog (fishing for residents), character bedrooms in main building,

more contemporary ones at the back, open all day. *(Isobel Mackinlay, Belinda May, Dave Sutton, Sally and David Champion)*

LLANFERRES SJ1860
Druid (01352) 810225
A494 Mold–Ruthin; CH7 5SN Extended 17th-c whitewashed inn set in fine walking country – Alyn Valley towards Loggerheads Country Park, or up Offa's Dyke Path to Moel Famau; views from broad bay window in civilised plush lounge and from bigger beamed back bar with two handsome antique oak settles, pleasant mix of more modern furnishings and quarry-tiled area by log fire. Marstons-related ales, 30 malt whiskies, reasonably priced traditional food plus specials, games room with darts and pool; background music, TV; children welcome, dogs in bar and bedrooms, open all day Fri-Sun. *(Nicholas and Lucy Sage)*

LLANGOLLEN SJ2142
Chainbridge (01978) 860215
2 miles W; LL20 8BS Refurbished 19th-c hotel in great position overlooking River Dee rapids, chain bridge and renovated steam railway, bar, lounge, restaurant and good outside spaces, enjoyable food from sandwiches and pubby choices up, helpful friendly service; children and dogs welcome, 32 bedrooms (some with river-view balconies), good walks, open all day. *(Mike and Wena Stevenson)*

MINERA SJ2651
Tyn-y-Capel (01978) 269347
Church Road; LL11 3DA Community-owned pub with good locally sourced food and four real ales including one badged for them; regular live music, Sun quiz; children and dogs (in bar) welcome, lovely hill views from terrace, park opposite with play area, open all day. *(Nicholas and Lucy Sage)*

RUABON SJ3043
Bridge End (01978) 810881
Bridge Street; LL14 6DA Proper old-fashioned pub serving own McGivern ales (brewed here) alongside several guests and ciders, friendly staff and cheerful local atmosphere, snacky food such as sandwiches and pies, black beams, open fires; Tues quiz, regular summer live music; children and dogs welcome, garden, open all day weekends, from 5pm weekdays (4pm Fri). *(Alister and Margery Bacon)*

DYFED

ABERAERON SN4562
Cadwgan (01545) 570149
Market Street; SA46 0AU Small brightly painted late 18th-c pub opposite the harbour, fairly basic with friendly regulars, well kept Hancocks HB and a couple of guests, some nautical memorabilia and interesting

old photographs, open fire, no food; sports TV; children and dogs welcome, pavement seats and little garden behind, closed Sun evening, Mon lunchtime, otherwise open all day. *(Elizabeth and Andrew Harvey)*

ABERAERON
SN4562

Castle (01545) 570205

Market Street; SA46 0AU Red-painted early 19th-c corner building with popular boldly decorated café-bar and elegant wood-floored restaurant upstairs, friendly efficient service, quite a choice of food and sensibly priced wine list, Evan Evans or Sharps Doom Bar, welsh whisky; background music, sports TV; eight comfortable bedrooms and self-catering apartment, open all day. *(Louise and Simon Peters)*

ABERCYCH
SN2539

★ **Nags Head** (01239) 841200

Off B4332 Cenarth–Boncath; SA37 0HJ Friendly tucked-away riverside pub with dimly lit beamed and flagstoned bar, stripped wood tables and woodburner in big fireplace, hundreds of beer bottles, clocks showing time around the world, photographs of locals on brick and stone walls, a coracle hanging from the ceiling in one part, even a large stuffed rat, Mantle Cwrw Teifi and two guests, pubby food and specials in two sizeable dining areas; background music, piano; children and dogs welcome, benches (some under cover) in garden overlooking river (fishing rights), play area with wooden castle, barbecues, three bedrooms, open all day Fri-Sun, closed Mon lunchtime (no food Mon in winter). *(Anna and Mark Evans)*

ABERGORLECH
SN5833

★ **Black Lion** (01558) 685271

B4310; SA32 7SN Friendly old pub in fine rural position; traditional stripped-stone beamed bar, oak furniture and black settles on flagstones, old jugs and other bits and pieces on shelves, local paintings, woodburner, Rhymney and a guest beer, proper ciders and varied choice of fair-priced home-cooked food including good daily specials, dining extension with another woodburner; background music, free wi-fi; children and dogs welcome, lovely views of Cothi Valley from riverside garden, two self-catering cottages, good nearby mountain biking, open all day weekends, closed Mon, Tues-Weds lunchtimes. *(Mike and Anita Beach)*

ABERYSTWYTH
SN6777

Halfway Inn (01970) 880631

Pisgah – A4120 right out towards Devils Bridge; SY23 4NE Panoramic views from this friendly roadside country pub, log fire, beams, stripped stone and flagstones, scrubbed tables and settles, well kept Sharps Doom Bar and enjoyable good value home-cooked food; background music, pool; children and dogs (in bar) welcome, picnic-sets outside, two comfortable bedrooms, free overnight camping if you buy a meal, may close Mon-Weds in winter. *(Anna and Mark Evans)*

ANGLE
SM8603

Hibernia (01646) 641517

B4320; SA71 5AT Welcoming village pub with good home-made food at reasonable prices, Sharps Doom Bar and a guest, traditional bar with coal fire, more modern dining room; some live music, sports TV, pool; children and dogs welcome, one bedroom plus a caravan to rent, open all day in high summer. *(Alec and Susan Hamilton)*

ANGLE
SM8703

★ **Old Point House** (01646) 641205

Signed off B4320 in village, along long rough waterside track; SA71 5AS Quaint simple place in idyllic spot overlooking sheltered anchorage; new owners have opened up the bar, wooden tables and chairs on stone floor, log fire, a couple of real ales, farm cider and several wines by the glass, enjoyable pubby food in carpeted lounge; outside lavatories; children and dogs welcome, picnic-sets on grass with charming views across the water, lovely surrounding walks (on Pembrokeshire Coast Path), open (and food) all day in summer, check website for winter hours; note that the road from Angle is unmade and gets cut off by spring tides about four times a year for a couple of hours. *(Jamie Green)*

BORTH
SN6089

Victoria (01970) 871417

High Street; SY24 5HZ Stone-built pub backing on to the beach and popular with locals and tourists; five well kept ales including Sharps Doom Bar and Wye Valley, good variety of enjoyable reasonably priced food from children's meals to well cooked fish, friendly accommodating staff even when busy, more space upstairs and sea-view balcony; live music, sports TV; dogs welcome, tables on back deck with steps down to the shingle, open all day. *(Dave Snowden)*

BOSHERSTON
SR9694

St Govans Country Inn (01646) 661311 *Off B4319 S of Pembroke; SA71 5DN* Busy pub with big modernised open-plan bar, cheery and simple, with several changing ales and well priced pubby food, good climbing photographs and murals of local beauty spots, log fire in large stone fireplace; background music,

---

We include some hotels with a good bar that offers facilities comparable to those of a pub.

TV, games machine and pool (winter only); children and dogs welcome, picnic-sets on small front terrace, four good value bedrooms (residents' parking), handy for water-lily lakes, beach and cliff walks, open all day in season (all day weekends at other times). *(Elizabeth and Andrew Harvey)*

BRECHFA   SN5230
Forest Arms (01267) 202288
Opposite church (B4310); SA32 7RA
Renovated stone-built village inn with well kept ales and enjoyable reasonably priced food, friendly helpful staff, two beamed bars, one with big inglenook and angling theme (pub can arrange fishing on River Cothi), the other in two sections, note Bob the stuffed raven, also dining/function room with pitched ceiling and another log fire; children and dogs welcome, picnic-sets in back garden, good walks and mountain bike trails, three comfortable bedrooms and self-catering holiday cottage, closed Mon and lunchtimes Thurs-Sat. *(Nicholas and Lucy Sage)*

BROAD HAVEN   SM8614
★Druidstone Hotel (01437) 781221
N on coast road, bear left for about 1.5 miles then follow sign left to Druidstone Haven; SA62 3NE Cheerfully informal country house hotel in grand spot above the sea, individual, relaxed and with terrific views; inventive cooking using fresh often organic ingredients (best to book) including good value themed 'feast evenings', helpful efficient service, cellar bar with local ale tapped from the cask, country wines and other drinks, ceilidhs and folk events, friendly pub dogs (others welcome); attractive high-walled garden, all sorts of sporting activities from boules to sand-yachting, spacious homely bedrooms and self-catering cottages, closed Jan, Nov, restaurant closed Sun evening. *(Joe and Belinda Smart)*

BURTON   SM9805
Jolly Sailor (01646) 600378
Just off Trinity Terrace; SA73 1NX
Popular unpretentious pub with great views of River Cleddau, toll bridge and Milford Haven beyond from lounge and conservatory restaurant, generous helpings of enjoyable home-made food at reasonable prices, well kept Brains Rev James and a couple of local guests; children welcome, dogs in bar, waterside garden with play area, can moor a small boat at jetty. *(Alec and Susan Hamilton)*

CAIO   SN6739
Brunant Arms (01558) 650483
Off A482 Llanwrda–Lampeter; SA19 8RD
Unpretentious village pub, comfortable and friendly with helpful staff, beams, old settles, china on delft shelving and nice log fire, a couple of ales such as Evan Evans, enjoyable regularly changing home-made food from baguettes up, stripped-stone public bar with games including pool; some live

music, sports TV; children and dogs welcome, small Perspex-roofed verandah and lower terrace, two bedrooms, handy for Dolaucothi Gold Mines (NT), closed Sun evening to Tues evening. *(Joe and Belinda Smart)*

CAREW   SN0403
★Carew Inn (01646) 651267
A4075 off A477; SA70 8SL Stone-built pub with appealing cottagey atmosphere, unpretentious small panelled public bar, nice old bentwood stools and mix of tables and chairs on bare boards, small dining area, lounge bar with low tables, warm open fires, two changing beers and enjoyable generously served food (Tues curry, Thurs steak night), two upstairs dining rooms with leather chairs at black tables; background music, dominoes, darts; children and dogs (in bar) welcome, enclosed back garden with play equipment, view of imposing Carew Castle ruins and remarkable 9th-c celtic cross, open all day. *(Nicholas and Lucy Sage)*

CILYCWM   SN7540
Neuadd Fawr Arms (01550) 721644
By church entrance; SA20 0ST Nicely placed 18th-c drovers' inn above River Gwenlais among lanes to Llyn Brianne; eclectic mix of old furniture on huge slate flagstones, woodburners, good seasonal food with interesting specials in bar or smaller dining room, one or two changing local ales, friendly helpful service and chatty locals; children and dogs welcome, open all day weekends, closed Mon-Thurs lunchtimes. *(Nicholas and Lucy Sage)*

COSHESTON   SN0003
Brewery Inn (01646) 686678
Signed E from village crossroads; SA72 4UD Welcoming 17th-c village pub with attractively furnished bar, flagstones and exposed stone walls, enjoyable food including good grill choices, a locally brewed house beer and guest, ten gins, helpful friendly service; quiz Weds, live music last Sat of month; children and dogs welcome, closed Sun evening, Mon. *(Joe and Belinda Smart)*

CRESSWELL QUAY   SN0506
★Cresselly Arms (01646) 651210
Village signed from A4075; SA68 0TE
Simple unchanging alehouse overlooking tidal creek; plenty of local customers in two welcoming old-fashioned linked rooms, built-in wall benches, kitchen chairs and plain tables on red and black tiles, open fire in one room, Aga in the other with lots of pictorial china hanging from high beam-and-plank ceiling, third more conventionally furnished red-carpeted room, a house beer from Caffle along with Hancocks, Sharps and a rotating guest such as Evan Evans; no children or dogs, seats outside making most of view, you can arrive by boat if tide is right, open all day in summer. *(Ted and Mary Bates)*

CWM GWAUN   SN0333
★ Dyffryn Arms (01348) 881305
*Cwm Gwaun and Pontfaen signed off
B4313 E of Fishguard; SA65 9SE* Classic
rural time warp known locally as Bessie's
after the much-loved veteran landlady (her
farming family have run it since 1840 and
she's been in charge for well over a third of
that time); basic 1920s front parlour with
plain deal furniture and draughts boards
inlaid into tables, red and black quarry tiles,
woodburner, well kept Bass served by jug
through sliding hatch, low prices, World War
I prints and posters, a young portrait of the
Queen and large collection of banknotes,
darts; may be duck eggs for sale; lovely
outside view and walks in nearby Preseli
Hills, open more or less all day (may close
if no customers). *(Giles and Annie Francis)*

DINAS   SN0139
Old Sailors (01348) 811491
*Pwllgwaelod; from A487 in Dinas
Cross follow Bryn-henllan signpost;
SA42 0SE* Shack-like building in superb
position, snugged down into the sand by
isolated cove below Dinas Head with its
bracing walks; good local fish/seafood (often
crab and lobster), also snacks, coffee and
summer cream teas, well kept Felinfoel
Double Dragon and decent wine, maritime
bric-a-brac; children welcome, no dogs
inside, picnic-sets on grass overlooking
beach with views across to Fishguard,
closed Mon. *(Liz and Martin Eldon)*

FISHGUARD   SM9537
★ Fishguard Arms (01348) 872763
Main Street (A487); SA65 9HJ Tiny
unspoilt bay-windowed terrace pub with
friendly community atmosphere and
character landlord, front bar with unusually
high counter serving well kept/priced Bass
direct from the cask, rugby photographs
and open fire, back snug with woodburner,
traditional games and sports TV, no food;
smokers' area out behind, open all day,
closed Weds evening. *(Giles and Annie Francis)*

FISHGUARD   SM9537
Royal Oak (01348) 218632
Market Square, Upper Town; SA65 9HA
Recently refurbished under new
management; stripped beams, exposed stone
and slate flagstones, big picture-window
dining extension, plaque commemorating
defeat of bizarre french raid in 1797 (peace
treaty was signed in the pub), Brains,
Glamorgan and Sharps, farm cider, good
choice of well liked fairly priced food,
friendly prompt service; folk night Tues;
children and dogs welcome, pleasant
terrace with view down to Lower Town bay,
open all day. *(Nicholas and Lucy Sage)*

FISHGUARD   SM9637
Ship (01348) 874033
Newport Road, Lower Town; SA65 9ND
New welcoming licensees for this softly lit
18th-c pub near the old harbour, beams and
coal fire, lots of boat pictures, model ships
and photos of actors such as Richard Burton
and Peter O'Toole who drank here while
filming locally, well kept Bass, Felinfoel
and Hancocks, no food; Sat live music;
children and dogs welcome, open all day
weekends, closed Mon, Tues and lunchtimes
Weds-Fri. *(Giles and Annie Francis)*

HERMON   SN2031
Lamb (01239) 831864
Taylors Row; SA36 0DS Friendly
family-run pub dating from the 17th c,
homely and comfortable, with generously
served food cooked by landlady; well
behaved dogs welcome, three good value
refurbished bedrooms, caravan pitches.
(Anna and Mark Evans)

JAMESTON   SS0699
Tudor Lodge (01834) 871212
A4139, E of Jameston; SA70 7SS
Friendly family-run inn close to the coast;
two character bars with open fire and
woodburner, Sharps Doom Bar and several
wines by the glass, airy carpeted dining
room with pale beams and high-backed
chairs around sturdy tables, second dining
room with modern artwork, decent choice
of well liked food including early-bird deal
Mon-Fri; children welcome, play area and
plenty of picnic-sets outside, five stylish
comfortable bedrooms, good breakfast,
open (and food) all day weekends,
from 4pm weekdays. *(M G Hart)*

LITTLE HAVEN   SM8512
Castle Inn (01437) 781445
Grove Place; SA62 3UF Welcoming pub
well placed by green looking over sandy
bay (lovely sunsets), popular generously
served food including pizzas and good
local fish, Marstons-related ales, decent
choice of wines by the glass, tea and
cafetière coffee, bare-boards bar and
carpeted dining area with big oak tables,
beams, some stripped stone, castle prints;
children and dogs welcome, picnic-sets
out in front, New Year's Day charity swim,
open all day. *(Roy and Gill Payne)*

LITTLE HAVEN   SM8512
St Brides Inn (01437) 781266
St Brides Road, SA62 3UN Just
20 metres from Pembrokeshire Coast
Path; neat stripped-stone bar and
linked carpeted dining area, traditional
furnishings, log fire, interesting well in
back corner grotto thought to be partly

Pubs close to motorway junctions are listed at the back of the book.

Roman, Banks's, Marstons and a guest, enjoyable bar food including fresh fish and other local produce; background music and TV; children welcome, no dogs inside, seats in sheltered suntrap terrace garden across road, two bedrooms, open all day summer. *(John and Enid Morris)*

LLANDDAROG   SN5016

★**Butchers Arms** (01267) 275330

On back road by church; SA32 8NS New owners for this ancient black-beamed local but few changes; three intimate eating areas off small central bar, popular food, Felinfoel ales tapped from the cask and nice wines by the glass, conventional pub furniture, gleaming brassware and open woodburner in biggish fireplace; background music; children welcome, tables outside and pretty window boxes, bedroom in converted stables, closed Sun, Mon. *(Joe and Belinda Smart)*

LLANDDAROG   SN5016

White Hart (01267) 275395

Aka Yr Hydd Gwyn; off A48 E of Carmarthen, via D4310, SA32 8NT Ancient thatched pub brewing beers using water from 90-metre borehole, also own ciders; comfortable lived-in beamed rooms with lots of engaging bric-a-brac and antiques including a suit of armour, 17th-c carved settles by huge log fire, interestingly furnished high-raftered dining room, generous if not cheap food (surcharge if paying by credit card), home-made jams, chutneys and honey for sale; background music; children welcome, no dogs inside, disabled access (ramps provided), picnic-sets on front terrace and in back garden with play area, closed Weds. *(Nicholas and Lucy Sage)*

LLANDEILO   SN6226

Angel (01558) 822765

Rhosmaen Street; SA19 6EN Town-centre local painted a distinctive pale blue, comfortably furnished front bar with ales such as Evan Evans from central servery, step up to popular back restaurant serving very good food at reasonable prices including daily specials, friendly helpful staff; children welcome, walled beer garden behind, closed Sun. *(Simon and Mandy King)*

LLANDOVERY   SN7634

Castle (01550) 720343

Kings Road; SA20 0AP Popular and welcoming hotel next to castle ruins, good attractively presented food from sandwiches and deli boards to charcoal grills and fresh fish specials, afternoon teas, courteous efficient service, well kept Gower and a couple of guests; children and dogs welcome, picnic-sets out in front under parasols, comfortable bedrooms, open (and food) all day from 8am for breakfast. *(Ted and Mary Bates)*

LLANDOVERY   SN7634

Kings Head (01550) 720393

Market Square; SA20 0AB Early 18th-c beamed coaching inn, pattern-carpeted bar with exposed stonework and large woodburner, three well kept ales including Evan Evans, enjoyable food from snacks and bar meals up including Fri steak night, friendly service; children and dogs welcome, nine bedrooms, open all day. *(Professor James Burke)*

LLANFIHANGEL-Y-CREUDDYN   SN6676

★**Y Ffarmers** (01974) 261275

Village signed off A4120 W of Pisgah; SY23 4LA New owners for a pub that's been a hub of the community; carefully and simply refurbished rooms, mate's chairs and cushioned armed wheelbacks around dark tables, stripped oak boards, woodburner in little fireplace, highly regarded food from pub favourites to more restauranty dishes (children eat for free 5-6.30pm in school holidays), two changing ales such as Montys and Wye Valley, a craft beer, real cider and interesting selection of gins including eight from welsh distillers, good friendly service; dogs welcome (not in restaurant), back terrace with steps up to lawn, 13th-c village church opposite, new self-catering apartment, open all day weekends (no food Sun evening), closed Mon and lunchtime Tues. *(B and M Kendall, Dr Simon Innes)*

LLANGRANNOG   SN3154

Pentre Arms (01239) 654345

On the front; SA44 6SP Friendly old seafront pub beautifully placed in this pretty coastal village, magnificent sunset and sea views from picture window, well kept Gales, St Austell and a guest, standard food including good steaks and often fresh fish, separate restaurant, pool room with games machines and TV; regular live music; children and dogs (in bar) welcome, seven bedrooms (some directly overlooking the small bay), staff will advise on dolphin-watching, handy for coast path, open all day. *(Martyn Davies)*

LLANGRANNOG   SN3154

Ship (01239) 654510

Near the front, by car park entrance; SA44 6SL Just back from the bay with tables out by beachside car park; good generous food including local fish/ seafood (booking advised weekends), friendly accommodating staff, well kept ales such as Mantle and good selection of gins, refurbished bare-boards bar with burnt-orange walls and big woodburner, further spacious upstairs eating area, local artwork for sale, games room with pool; weekend live music; children and dogs welcome, car parking charge refunded against food, open all day and can get very busy in summer. *(Martyn Davies)*

MATHRY SM8831
Farmers Arms (01348) 831284
*Brynamlwg, off A487 Fishguard–
St Davids; SA62 5HB* Popular pub with
traditional beamed bar, well kept Felinfoel
Double Dragon and guests, several gins
and ample helpings of enjoyable good
value pubby food, friendly staff and locals,
large vine-covered dining conservatory;
background music, TV, games machine,
pool; children welcome, dogs in bar, nearby
campsite, open all day. *(Rock Dweller)*

NEWCHAPEL SN2239
Ffynnone Arms (01239) 841800
B4332; SA37 0EH Welcoming 18th-c
beamed pub with enjoyable traditional
food including popular Sun carvery,
special diets catered for and some
produce home-grown, a couple of changing
ales, local cider and afternoon teas in
season, two woodburners; darts, pool
and table skittles; disabled facilities,
picnic-sets in small garden, open all day
weekends (from 2pm Sat), closed weekday
lunchtimes, food served Wed evening to
Sun lunchtime. *(Professor James Burke)*

NEWPORT SN0539
Castle (01239) 820742
Bridge Street; SA42 0TB Welcoming
old pub with split bar – one part panelled
with open fire, the other with pool, darts,
juke box and projector for major sports;
enjoyable home-made food including
Sun carvery, ales from Mantle and Wye
Valley, pleasant service, restaurant; some
live music; children and dogs welcome,
three bedrooms, handy for Parrog estuary
walk (especially for bird-watchers),
open all day. *(Nicholas and Lucy Sage)*

PEMBROKE DOCK SM9603
Shipwright (01646) 682090
Front Street; SA72 6JX Little blue-
painted end-of-terrace pub on waterfront
overlooking estuary, enjoyable home-made
food and a couple of well kept ales, friendly
efficient staff, bare-boards interior with
nautical and other memorabilia, some booth
seating; children welcome, five minutes from
Ireland ferry terminal. *(Hywel Thomas)*

PENRHIWLLAN SN3641
Daffodil (01559) 370343
*A475 Newcastle Emlyn–Lampeter;
SA44 5NG* Contemporary open-plan
dining pub with comfortable welcoming
bar, sofas and leather tub chairs on pale
limestone floor, woodburner, Greene
King Abbot, Hancocks HB and maybe a
guest from granite-panelled counter, two
lower-ceilinged end rooms with big oriental
rugs, steps down to a couple of airy dining
rooms, one with picture windows by open
kitchen, particularly good food including
daily specials and two-course lunch menu;

background music; children and dogs (in
bar) welcome, nicely furnished decked area
outside with valley views. *(Kristin Warry)*

PONTRHYDFENDIGAID SN7366
Black Lion (01974) 831624
*Off B4343 Tregaron–Devils Bridge;
SY25 6BE* Relaxed country inn run well
by friendly landlord; smallish main bar
with dark beams and exposed stonework,
old country furniture on bare boards,
woodburner and big pot-irons in vast
fireplace, copper, brass and so forth on
mantelpiece, historical photographs,
Felinfoel Double Dragon and a local guest,
seven wines by the glass and enjoyable
good value home-cooked food, quarry-
tiled back restaurant, small games room
with pool and darts; background music;
children and dogs (away from diners)
welcome, back courtyard and tree-
shaded garden, seven bedrooms (five in
converted stables), good walking/cycling
country and not far from Strata Florida
Abbey, open all day. *(Hywel Thomas)*

RHANDIRMWYN SN7843
Royal Oak (01550) 760201
7 miles N of Llandovery; SA20 0NY
Friendly 17th-c stone-built inn set in remote
peaceful walking country, comfortable
traditional bar with log fire, four well kept
local ales, ciders and perries, good variety of
popular sensibly priced food sourced locally,
big dining area, pool room; children and dogs
welcome, hill views from garden and cottagey
bedrooms, handy for Brecon Beacons, closed
Sun evening, Mon. *(Ted and Mary Bates)*

ROSEBUSH SN0729
★ Tafarn Sinc (01437) 532214
*B4329 Haverfordwest–Cardigan;
SA66 7QU* Former Victorian hotel on
long-defunct railway that served the nearby
slate quarries; extraordinary maroon-
painted corrugated structure, the halt
itself has been re-created with life-size
dummy passengers on the platform and the
sizeable garden is enlivened by sounds of
steam trains broadcast from a replica signal
box; interior reminiscent of a local history
museum with sawdust floors, hams, washing
and plenty more hanging from the ceiling,
bar has plank panelling, informal mix of old
chairs and pews and a woodburner, Cwrw
Tafarn Sinc (brewed locally for them) and
Sharps Doom Bar, simple food, buoyant
atmosphere with welsh spoken; background
music, darts, games machine, board games
and TV; children welcome, closed Mon
(except Aug and bank holidays), otherwise
open all day. *(John and Enid Morris)*

ST DAVIDS SM7525
Farmers Arms (01437) 721666
Goat Street; SA62 6RF Bustling old-
fashioned low-ceilinged pub by cathedral
gate, cheerful and unpretentiously pubby,

mainly drinking on the left and eating on the right, central servery with three well kept ales including Felinfoel Double Dragon, decent food (summer only) from sandwiches to specials, friendly staff and atmosphere; TV for rugby, pool, free wi-fi; children and dogs welcome, cathedral view from large tables on big back suntrap terrace, open all day in summer, closed weekday lunchtimes winter. *(Hywel Thomas)*

ST DOGMAELS   SN1646
Ferry (01239) 615172

B4546; SA43 3LF Old stone building with spectacular views of Teifi estuary and hills from attractively furnished picture-window dining extension, good popular freshly made food, character bar with pine tables, interesting old photographs and chalk board with humorous quotes, Brains and summer guests, several wines by the glass, pleasant attentive staff; background music; children and dogs welcome, plenty of room outside on linked decked areas, open all day. *(Frank Price)*

TRESAITH   SN2751
Ship (01239) 811816

Off A487 E of Cardigan; bear right in village and keep on down – pub car park fills quickly; SA43 2JL Excellent position beside broad sandy surfing beach (maybe dolphins), seats under canopy on heated deck and picnic-sets on two-level terrace; front dining area with same view, room behind with winter log fire plus two further back rooms (one with stove), Brains Rev James and SA, food can be good; children and dogs welcome, four sea-view bedrooms and lovely coastal walks from this steep little village, open all day. *(Louise and Simon Peters)*

GLAMORGAN

BISHOPSTON   SS5789
Joiners Arms (01792) 232658

Bishopston Road, just off B4436 SW of Swansea; SA3 3EJ Thriving 19th-c stone local with own good value Swansea ales along with well kept guests, ample helpings of enjoyable freshly made pub food (not Sun evening, Mon), friendly staff, unpretentious quarry-tiled bar with massive solid-fuel stove, comfortable lounge; TV for rugby; children and dogs welcome, open all day (from 3pm Mon and Tues). *(M G Hart)*

BISHOPSTON   SS5889
Plough & Harrow (01792) 234459

Off B4436 Bishopston–Swansea; SA3 3DJ Cleanly modernised and renovated old pub with L-shaped bar and restaurant, good imaginative food from chef-owner including good value two-course lunch deal and antipasti/pizza menu Sun evening, ales such as Brains, Fullers and St Austell, a dozen wines by the glass, helpful courteous

service; quiz Mon evening; open all day Sun, closed Mon lunchtime. *(Mrs Julie Thomas)*

CARDIFF
Cambrian Tap (029) 2064 4952

St Mary Street/Caroline Street; CF10 1AD Revamped city-centre corner pub popular for its good range of Brains cask and keg beers plus guests, several more in bottles, friendly knowledgeable staff, nice home-made pies; Tues comedy night, Weds quiz; open all day. *(Taff Thomas)*

CARDIFF   ST1876
City Arms (029) 2064 1913

Quay Street; CF10 1EA City-centre alehouse with four Brains beers and ten regularly changing guests (some cask-tapped), tasting trays available, also plenty of draught/bottled continentals and real cider, friendly knowledgeable staff, no food; some live music, darts, free wi-fi; open all day (till 2am Fri, Sat), very busy on rugby match days. *(Maggie and Stevan Hollis)*

CARDIFF   ST1776
Crickcters (029) 2034 5102

Cathedral Road; CF11 9LL Victorian townhouse in quiet residential area backing on to Glamorgan CC, well kept Evan Evans ales and enjoyable freshly made food (all day Fri, Sat, until 5pm Sun); children welcome, sunny back garden, open all day. *(Patricia and Gordon Tucker)*

CARDIFF   ST1876
Zero Degrees (029) 2022 9494

Westgate Street; CF10 1DD Lively contemporary placc on two levels visibly brewing its own interesting beers, good selection of other drinks too, enjoyable food including pizzas from wood-fired oven, risotto and pasta dishes, friendly staff; background music, sports TVs, free wi-fi; open all day. *(Nik and Gloria Clarke)*

COWBRIDGE   SS9974
★**Bear** (01446) 774814

High Street, with car park behind off North Street; signed off A48; CF71 7AF Busy Georgian coaching inn in smart village, well kept Brains, Hancocks and guests, decent house wines, enjoyable food from good sandwiches and wraps up, lunchtime weekday set menu, friendly helpful service, three attractively furnished bars with flagstones, bare boards or carpet, some stripped stone and panelling, big hot open fires, barrel-vaulted cellar restaurant; children and dogs (in one bar) welcome, courtyard tables, comfortable quiet bedrooms, disabled parking, open all day. *(TD)*

GWAELOD-Y-GARTH   ST1183
Gwaelod y Garth Inn (029) 2081 0408

Main Road; CF15 9HH Meaning 'foot of the mountain', this stone-built village pub has wonderful valley views and is popular with walkers on the Taff Ely Ridgeway Path; highly thought-of well presented food (all day Fri and Sat, not Sun evening), friendly efficient service, own-brew beer along with Wye Valley and guests from pine-clad bar, log fires, upstairs restaurant (disabled access from back car park); some live music Fri and Sat; table skittles, pool, juke box; children and dogs welcome, three bedrooms, open all day. *(Professor James Burke)*

KENFIG   SS8081

★ **Prince of Wales** (01656) 740356
2.2 miles from M4 junction 37; A4229 towards Porthcawl, then right when dual carriageway narrows on bend, signed 'Maudlam, Kenfig'; CF33 4PR Ancient local with plenty of individuality by historic sand dunes, well kept ales tapped from the cask, decent wines and good choice of malts, generously served straightforward food at fair prices, friendly staff, chatty panelled room off main bar, log fires, stripped stone and lots of wreck pictures, restaurant with upstairs overspill room; TV for special rugby events; children allowed till 9pm, dogs in bar, handy for nature reserve (June orchids), open all day, no food Sun evening, Mon. *(Robin and Anna Triggs)*

LISVANE   ST1883

Ty Mawr Arms (01222) 754456
From B4562 on E edge turn N into Church Road, bear left into Llwyn y Pia Road, keep on along Graig Road; CF14 0UF Large welcoming country pub with good choice of popular food, well kept Brains and guests, decent wines by the glass, teas and coffees, friendly service, great views over Cardiff from spacious bay-windowed dining area off traditional log-fire bar; children welcome, disabled access with help to main bar area, attractive big garden with pond, open all day. *(Sandra and Miles Spencer)*

LLANBLETHIAN   SS9873

Cross (01446) 772995
Church Road; CF71 7JF Welcoming former staging inn, enjoyable freshly made food from pubby choices up in bar or airy split-level restaurant, reasonable prices and various deals, well kept Wye Valley and guests, good choice of wines, woodburner and open fire; children welcome, dogs in bar, tables out on decking, open all day. *(Elizabeth and Andrew Harvey)*

LLANCARFAN   ST0570

Fox & Hounds (01446) 781287
Signed off A4226; can also be reached from A48 from Bonvilston or B4265 via Llancadle; CF62 3AD Newish owners and some redecoration for this comfortably modernised village pub, snug bar, good interesting food, local ales and nice choice of wines; tables on covered terrace (dogs

allowed here), charming streamside setting by interesting church, eight comfortable bedrooms, good breakfast, open all day (from 3pm Mon, Tues). *(Louise and Simon Peters)*

LLANGENNITH   SS4291

Kings Head (01792) 386212
Clos St Cenydd, opposite church; SA3 1HX Extended 17th-c stone-built inn with wide choice of popular food (best to book) including good curries and pizzas, own Gower beers (brewed at sister pub, the Greyhound at Oldwalls), over 100 malt whiskies, friendly staff; pool and juke box in lively public bar – back bar quieter with dining areas; children and dogs welcome, large terrace with village views, good walks, not far from great surfing beach and large campsite, bedrooms in separate buildings to the side and rear, open (and food) all day, breakfast for non-residents (8.30-10.30am). *(John and Enid Morris)*

LLANRHIDIAN   SS4992

Welcome to Town (01792) 390015
Mill Lane, opposite the green; SA3 1EH Refurbished old dining pub with well liked food from sandwiches, pizzas and pub favourites to more restauranty dishes, various good value weekly deals, Glamorgan and Gower ales and good choice of wines by the glass, afternoon teas, upstairs restaurant, friendly efficient service; live music and quiz nights; well behaved children and dogs (in bar) welcome, tables out on front terrace, open (and food) all day. *(Molly and Stewart Lindsay)*

MUMBLES   SS6287

Pilot 07897 895511
Mumbles Road; SA3 4EL Friendly 19th-c seafront local with half a dozen well kept ales including some from own back microbrewery, slate-floored bar with woodburning stove, boat suspended from planked ceiling, no food; daily newspapers, TV, free wi-fi; dogs welcome, open all day. *(Chris Marsh)*

OLDWALLS   SS4891

Greyhound (01792) 391027
W of Llanrhidian; SA3 1HA 19th-c sister pub to the Kings Head at Llangennith; spacious beamed and dark-panelled carpeted lounge bar, well kept ales including own Gower brews, decent wine and coffee, wide choice of popular food from sandwiches, baguettes and wraps up, friendly staff, hot coal fires, back dining room and upstairs overspill/function room; children and dogs welcome, picnic-sets in big garden with terrace, play area and good views, open all day. *(Christopher Mannings)*

PENARTH   ST1771

Pilot (029) 2071 0615
Queens Road; CF64 1DJ End-of-terrace pub set high in residential area overlooking Cardiff Bay; good often interesting food

from changing menu, four well kept ales, friendly welcoming staff; regular live music, cocktail evenings and summer beer/cider festival; children and dogs allowed, tables out in narrow front area, open all day. *(Maggie and Stevan Hollis)*

PENDERYN   SN9408
Red Lion (01685) 811914
Off A4059 at Lamb, then up Church Road (narrow hill from T junction); CF44 9JR Friendly old stone-built pub (former drovers' inn) set high in good walking country opposite church; dark beams, flagstones and blazing log fires, antique settles and interesting bits and pieces including some military memorabilia, good range of real ales and ciders tapped from the cask, also whiskies and other spirits from the local Penderyn distillery, highly regarded imaginative food (best to book); children and dogs (in bar) welcome, great views from big garden, open all day weekends (no food Sun evening), closed Mon. *(David Evans)*

PONTNEDDFECHAN   SN8907
Angel (01639) 722013
Just off A465; Pontneathvaughan Road; SA11 5NR Comfortably opened-up 16th-c pub, well kept ales and wide choice of enjoyable fairly priced pub food, masses of jugs on beams, ancient houseware and old kitchen range, separate flagstoned bar; children welcome, terrace tables, good walks including the waterfalls, open all day in summer. *(Anna and Mark Evans)*

REYNOLDSTON   SS4889
★**King Arthur** (01792) 390775
Higher Green, off A4118; SA3 1AD Cheerful pub-hotel with timbered main bar, country-style restaurant and summer family dining area (games room with pool in winter), good fairly priced food from sandwiches and pub favourites up, afternoon teas, Felinfoel and guests kept well, log fires and country house bric-a-brac, buoyant local atmosphere in the evening; background music; tables out on green, play area, 18 bedrooms and self-catering cottage, open (and bar food) all day. *(M G Hart, Christian Mole)*

ST HILARY   ST0173
Bush (01446) 776888
Off A48 E of Cowbridge; CF71 7DP Cosily restored 16th-c thatched and beamed pub; flagstoned main bar with inglenook, bare-boards lounge and snug, nice mix of old furniture, Bass, Greene King, Hancocks and a guest, Weston's cider and good wines by the glass, enjoyable food including home-made pies and wellingtons, gluten-free choices too, friendly service, restaurant; children and dogs (in bar) welcome, some picnic benches out at front, garden behind, open all day Fri-Sun. *(Ted and Mary Bates)*

SWANSEA   SS6492
Brunswick (01792) 465676
Duke Street; SA1 4HS Large rambling local with traditional pubby furnishings, lots of knick-knacks, artwork and prints for sale, good value popular weekday food till 7.30pm (also Sun lunch), half a dozen well kept ales, friendly helpful service, regular live music, quiz night Mon; no dogs, open all day. *(H Powell)*

TAFFS WELL   ST1283
Fagins (029) 2081 1800
Cardiff Road, Glan-y-Llyn; CF15 7QD Terrace-row pub with interesting range of cask-tapped ales, friendly olde-worlde atmosphere, benches, pine tables and other pubby furniture on flagstones, faux black beams, woodburner, good value straightforward food (not Sun evening, Mon) from lunchtime baguettes up, restaurant; live music, sports TV; children and dogs welcome, open all day, closed Mon. *(Robin and Anna Triggs)*

THREE CROSSES   SS5604
Poundffald Inn (01792) 931061
Tirmynydd Road, NW end; SA4 3PB New licensees and refurbishment for this 17th-c beamed and timbered pub, farmhouse, mate's and attractively upholstered chairs around wooden tables on patterned carpet, woodburner, changing real ales and enjoyable pubby food including deals, sports TV in separate bar; dogs welcome, picnic-sets under parasols on side terrace, open (and food) all day, apart from Sun when kitchen closes at 6pm. *(PJT)*

GWENT

ABERGAVENNY   SO2914
Angel (01873) 857121
Cross Street, by town hall; NP7 5EN Comfortable late Georgian coaching inn; good local atmosphere in two-level bar, rugs on flagstones, big sofas, armchairs and settles, some lovely bevelled glass behind counter serving Evan Evans, Hereford, Rhymney and Wye Valley, proper cider and good choice of wines and malt whiskies, well liked food, friendly helpful staff, attractive lounge (popular afternoon tea) and smart dining room; free wi-fi; children and dogs (in bar) welcome, pretty candlelit courtyard, 35 bedrooms (some in other buildings), open all day. *(Nik and Gloria Clarke)*

ABERGAVENNY   SO3111
★**Hardwick** (01873) 854220
Hardwick; B4598 SE, off A40 at A465/ A4042 exit – coming from E on A40, go right round the exit system, as B4598 is final road out; NP7 9AA Restaurant-with-rooms and you'll need to book for owner-chef's highly regarded imaginative

food; drinkers welcome in simple bar with spindleback chairs around pub tables, stripped brickwork by fireplace and small corner counter serving Rhymney and Wye Valley, local perry and a dozen wines by the glass, two dining rooms, one with beams, bare boards and huge fireplace, the other in lighter carpeted extension, friendly service; background music; no under-8s in restaurant after 8pm, teak tables and chairs under umbrellas by car park, neat garden, bedrooms, open all day (till 10pm Sun). *(Mike and Mary Carter)*

CAERLEON   ST3490
Bell (01633) 420613
Bulmore Road; off M4 junction 24 via B4237 and B4236; NP18 1QQ Old stone coaching inn under newish management; good variety of enjoyable food including vegetarian choices and daily specials (some dishes served on boards or slates), three well kept changing ales and ten welsh ciders/perries, friendly helpful staff, linked beamed areas, big open fireplace; children and dogs (menu for them) welcome, pretty back terrace, open all day Fri and Sat, closed Mon and Tues lunchtime (all day Tues in winter). *(M G Hart)*

CHEPSTOW   ST5394
Three Tuns (01291) 645797
Bridge Street; NP16 5EY Early 17th-c and a pub for much of that time; bare-boards interior with painted farmhouse pine furniture, a couple of mismatched sofas by woodburner, dresser with china plates, five local ales and ciders from nice wooden counter at unusual angle, very reasonably priced home-made lunchtime only bar food including speciality pies, friendly staff; background and regular live music; dogs welcome, wheelchair access, four bedrooms (one suitable for disabled customers), open all day. *(Maggie and Stevan Hollis)*

GROSMONT   SO4024
Angel (01981) 240646
Corner of B4347 and Poorscript Lane; NP7 8EP Small welcoming 17th-c local, rustic interior with simple wooden furniture, Wye Valley Butty Bach, a couple of guests and local cider (regular summer beer/cider festivals), reasonably priced traditional food (not Sun, Weds or Thurs evenings), pool room with darts; TV for rugby, no lavatories – public ones close by; dogs welcome, seats out by ancient market cross on attractive steep street in sight of castle, back garden with boules, good local walks, open all day Sat, closed Sun evening and weekday lunchtimes. *(Charles Thomas)*

LLANDENNY   SO4103
★**Raglan Arms** (01291) 690800
Centre of village; NP15 1DL Well run dining pub with interesting freshly cooked food, Wye Valley Butty Bach

and good selection of wines, friendly welcoming young staff, big pine tables and a couple of leather sofas in linked dining rooms leading to conservatory, log fire in flagstoned bar's handsome stone fireplace, relaxed informal atmosphere; children welcome, garden tables, closed Sun evening, Mon. *(Fiona and Jack Henderson)*

LLANGATTOCK LINGOED   SO3620
Hunters Moon (01873) 821499
Off B4521 just E of Llanvetherine; NP7 8RR Attractive tucked-away pub dating from the 13th c, beams, dark stripped stone and flagstones, woodburner, friendly licensees and locals, welsh ales tapped from the cask and enjoyable straightforward food, separate dining room; children welcome, tables out on deck and in charming dell with waterfall, glorious country on Offa's Dyke Path, four comfortable bedrooms, open (and food) all day. *(Anna and Mark Evans)*

LLANGYBI   ST3797
White Hart (01633) 450258
On main road; NP15 1NP Friendly village dining pub in delightful 12th-c monastery building (part of Jane Seymour's dowry); pubby bar with roaring log fire, steps up to pleasant light restaurant, decent pubby food, well kept mainly welsh ales and good choice of wines by the glass; children welcome, two nice bedrooms, closed Sun evening and Mon, otherwise open all day. *(Alister and Margery Bacon)*

LLANISHEN   SO4703
Carpenters Arms (01600) 860812
B4293 north of Chepstow; NP16 6QH Old cottagey pub with good food cooked by landlady including blackboard specials, Bass and a local guest kept well, friendly welcoming staff, comfortable bar/lounge, coal fire, back games room with pool; flagstoned terrace and little side lawn up steps, self-catering cottage, closed Mon and lunchtimes Tues and Weds, no food Sun evening. *(Bob and Margaret Holder)*

LLANOVER   SO2907
★**Goose & Cuckoo** (01873) 880277
Upper Llanover signed up track off A4042 S of Abergavenny; after 0.5 miles take first left; NP7 9ER Remote pub looking over picturesque valley just inside Brecon Beacons National Park; essentially one little rustically furnished room with woodburner in arched stone fireplace, small picture-window extension making most of the view, four well kept ales, over 45 whiskies and generous helpings of simple tasty home-cooked food; live music, board games, cribbage and darts; children and dogs welcome, picnic-sets out on gravel below, bedrooms and self-catering, closed Mon, open all day Fri-Sun. *(Elizabeth and Andrew Harvey)*

LLANTHONY SO2827
★**Priory Hotel** (01873) 890487
Aka Abbey Hotel, Llanthony Priory; off A465, back road Llanvihangel Crucorney–Hay; NP7 7NN Magical setting for plain bar in dimly lit vaulted crypt of graceful ruined Norman abbey, lovely in summer with lawns around and the peaceful border hills beyond; well kept Felinfoel Double Dragon and a couple of summer guests, enjoyable good value food (more restaurauty in the evening), friendly efficient staff; no mobile phone signal; children welcome but not in hotel part (seven non-ensuite bedrooms in restored abbey walls), no dogs, open all day weekends Apr-Oct (all day July, Aug), closed in winter apart from Fri evening, Sat and lunchtime Sun. *(Ian Herdman)*

LLANTRISANT FAWR ST3997
Greyhound (01291) 672505
Off A449 near Usk; NP15 1LE Prettily set 18th-c country inn with relaxed homely feel in three linked beamed rooms (steps between two), nice mix of furnishings and rustic decorations, enjoyable home cooking at sensible prices, efficient service, two or more well kept ales, decent wines by the glass, log fires, pleasant panelled dining room; muddy boots/dogs welcome in one bar, disabled access, attractive garden with big fountain, hill views, comfortable bedrooms in converted stable block (dogs allowed in one room), closed Sun evening. *(Charles Thomas)*

LLANVIHANGEL CRUCORNEY SO3220
Skirrid (01873) 890258
Signed off A465; NP7 8DH One of Britain's oldest pubs, dating partly from 1110 and a former courthouse – plenty of atmosphere and ghostly tales; ancient studded door to high-ceilinged main bar, exposed stone, flagstones and panelling, huge log fire, well kept ales and pubby food, separate dining room; children and dogs welcome, tables on terrace and small sloping back lawn, bedrooms, closed Sun evening, Mon lunchtime. *(R T and J C Moggridge)*

MAGOR ST4287
Wheatsheaf (01633) 880608
A mile from M4 junction 23; Newport Road off B4245; NP26 3HN Welcoming white-painted pub with some exposed stone walls and lots of black beams, pubby furniture on wood, flagstone or quarry-tiled floors, woodburner in big fireplace, ales such as Rhymney, Sharps and Seren, decent wines and 20 gins, well priced food from bar snacks to full meals, good service, carpeted restaurant, pool and darts in tap room; children welcome, wheelchair access (ramp for restaurant), open all day. *(Chris and Angela Buckell)*

MAMHILAD SO3004
Horseshoe (01873) 880542
Old Abergavenny Road; NP4 8QZ Old beamed country pub with slate-floor bar, traditional pubby furniture and a couple of unusual posts acting as elbow tables, original Hancocks pub sign, ornate woodburner in stone fireplace, tasty fairly priced food from lunchtime baguettes up, Great Orme and Wye Valley ales, Blaengawney cider; children welcome, dogs away from dining area, lovely views particularly from tables by car park over road, open all day Fri-Sun. *(Aled)*

PANDY SO3322
Old Pandy (01873) 890208
A465 Abergavenny–Hereford; NP7 8DR Welcoming 17th-c beamed roadside pub on edge of the Black Mountains and popular with walkers; good reasonably priced food from fairly traditional menu, well kept ales including Brains and Wye Valley, friendly service; pool, darts; children and dogs welcome, adjacent walkers' bunkhouse, open (and food) all day. *(Phil and Jane Hodson)*

PENALLT SO5209
★**Inn at Penallt** (01600) 772765
Village signed off B4293; at crossroads in village turn left; NP25 4SE 17th-c stone inn with good imaginative food using local produce including set lunch, well priced wine list, welsh ales and cider, courteous efficient service, roaring woodburner in airy slate-floored bar, restaurant and small back conservatory (fine Forest of Dean views); children and dogs welcome, big garden with terrace and play area, four bedrooms, closed Mon-Thurs, open all day Fri-Sun. *(Aled)*

RAGLAN SO4107
Beaufort Arms (01291) 690412
High Street; NP15 2DY Pub-hotel (former 16th-c coaching inn) with two character beamed bars, one with big stone fireplace and comfortable seats on slate floor, well kept local ales, carefully sourced food (some home-grown produce) including good seafood and set lunch/early-evening menu, light airy brasserie, friendly attentive service; background music; children welcome, terrace tables, 17 bedrooms, open all day from 7am. *(Patricia and Gordon Tucker)*

'Children welcome' means the pub says it lets children inside without any special restriction. If it allows them in, but to restricted areas such as an eating area or family room, we specify this. Some pubs may impose an evening time limit. We do not mention limits after 9pm as we assume children are home by then.

REDBROOK SO5309

★**Boat** (01600) 712615

Car park signed on A466 Chepstow–
Monmouth, then 30-metre footbridge
over Wye; or very narrow steep car
access from Penallt in Wales; NP25 4AJ
Beautifully set riverside pub with well kept
Wye Valley and guests tapped from the
cask, lots of ciders, perries and country
wines, enjoyable fair value food (not Sun
evening) from baguettes and baked potatoes
up, helpful staff, unchanging interior
with stripped-stone walls, flagstones and
woodburner; live bands Thurs evening;
children and dogs welcome, home-built rustic
seats in informal tiered suntrap garden with
stream spilling down into duck pond, open
all day in summer, in winter closed Tues, and
from 9pm Sun, Mon. *(Louise and Simon Peters)*

TALYCOED SO4115

Warwicks (01600) 780227

B4233 Monmouth–Abergavenny; though
its postal address is Llantilio Crossenny,
the inn is actually in Talycoed, a mile
or two E; NP7 8TL Pretty wisteria-clad
17th-c beamed pub under enthusiastic
welcoming management; softly lit snug
bar with friendly locals, good log fire in
stone fireplace, settles and mix of other
old furniture, horsebrasses and assorted
memorabilia, well kept Otter Bitter, good
quality food (cooked by landlady) including
daily specials, cosy little dining room; quiz
last Weds of month; children welcome, dogs
in bar, seats on front terrace and in neat
garden, lovely countryside and surrounding
walks, open all day weekends, closed Mon,
Tues and lunchtime Weds. *(Derek Stafford)*

TRELLECK SO5005

Lion (01600) 860322

B4293 6 miles S of Monmouth; NP25 4PA
Open-plan bar with one or two low black
beams, nice mix of old furniture and two
log fires, ales such as Butcombe, Felinfoel
and Wye Valley, wide range of fair-priced
food, takeaway pizzas, traditional games
including shove-ha'penny, ring the bull and
table skittles; background music; children
and dogs welcome, picnic-sets on grass, side
courtyard overlooking church, self-catering
cottage, open (and food) all day, kitchen
closes 6pm Sun. *(Maggie and Stevan Hollis)*

TRELLECK GRANGE SO5001

Fountain (01291) 689303

Minor road Tintern–Llanishen, SE
of village; NP16 6QW Traditional
17th-c country pub under friendly family
management, enjoyable local food from
pub favourites to game specials, three well
kept welsh ales, farm cider/perry, roomy
low-beamed flagstoned bar with log fire; dogs
welcome, small walled garden, peaceful spot
on small winding road, comfortable bedrooms
(no children), camping, open all day
weekends, closed Mon and lunchtimes Tues-
Fri, shuts 9pm Tues. *(Robin and Anna Triggs)*

USK SO3700

Kings Head (01291) 672963

Old Market Street; NP15 1AL Popular
16th-c family-run inn, chatty and relaxed,
with generously served traditional food and
well kept beers, friendly efficient staff, huge
log fire in superb fireplace; sports TV; nine
bedrooms, open all day. *(Charles Thomas)*

GWYNEDD

ABERDARON SH1726

Ty Newydd Hotel (01758) 760207

B4413, by the sea; LL53 8BE Hotel right
by sea with lovely views, good choice of
enjoyable food including Sun carvery, welsh
real ales; panoramic terrace within feet
of the waves, 11 bedrooms. *(Steve Parry)*

ABERDOVEY SN6196

★**Penhelig Arms** (01654) 767215

Opposite Penhelig station; LL35 0LT
Fine harbourside location for this popular
18th-c hotel; traditional bar with warm fire
in central stone fireplace, some panelling,
Brains ales and a guest, good choice
of wines and malt whiskies, enjoyable
food including home-made pizzas and
afternoon tea; children welcome, dogs
allowed in bar and comfortable bedrooms
(some have balconies overlooking estuary,
ones nearest road can be noisy), open
(and food) all day. *(Simon Sharpe)*

BETWS-Y-COED SH7955

★**Ty Gwyn** (01690) 710383

A5 just S of bridge to village; LL24 0SG
Family-run restaurant-with-rooms rather
than pub (you must eat or stay overnight to
be served drinks), but pubby feel in character
beamed lounge bar with ancient cooking
range, easy chairs, antiques, old prints and
bric-a-brac, highly regarded interesting
food using local produce including own fruit
and vegetables, beers such as Brains and
Great Orme, friendly professional service;
background music; children welcome, 14
comfortable bedrooms and holiday cottage,
closed Christmas and ten days in Jan. *(Aled)*

BLAENAU FFESTINIOG SH7041

Pengwern Arms (01766) 762200

Church Square, Ffestiniog; LL41 4PB
Co-operative-owned pub on village square
with well kept/priced ales in panelled bar,
dining area serving good value food evenings

If we know a pub has an outdoor play area for children, we mention it.

(not Sun) and weekend lunchtimes, friendly local atmosphere; games room, live music; dogs welcome, fine views from back garden, eight bedrooms, open all day weekends, from 6pm Mon-Thurs, 5pm Fri. *(Graham Smart)*

CAERNARFON SH4762
★ **Black Boy** (01286) 673604
Northgate Street; LL55 1RW Busy traditional 16th-c inn with cosy beamed lounge bar, sumptuously furnished and packed with tables, additional dining room across corridor and dimly lit atmospheric public bar, well kept ales, several wines by the glass and good generous food from sandwiches up (try the traditional 'lobsgows' stew), lunchtime set deal, good friendly service and lots of welsh chat; background music, TV, free wi-fi; disabled access (ramps) and loos, a few pavement tables, 16 bedrooms (ten in separate townhouse), open (and food) all day. *(Ian Herdman, Peter and Anne Hollindale)*

CAPEL CURIG SH7257
★ **Bryn Tyrch** (01690) 720223
A5 E; LL24 0EL Family-owned roadside inn perfectly placed for mountains of Snowdonia; bistro-bar with open fire (enjoyed by walkers) and amazing picture-windows views, Conwy Welsh Pride and a guest, quite a few malt whiskies, comprehensive choice of good well presented food including packed lunches and hampers, second bar with big menu boards, leather sofas and mix of tables on bare boards; children and dogs welcome, steep little side garden, more seats on terrace and across road by stream, 11 bedrooms including two bunk rooms, open all day in summer. *(Stuart Doughty)*

CAPEL CURIG SH7357
Tyn y Coed (01690) 720331
A5 SE of village; LL24 0EE Bustling community inn across from River Llugwy; enjoyable home-made food using local produce, well kept Purple Moose and three guests, pleasant quick service, log fires, pool room with juke box; nice side terrace, good surrounding walks, comfortable bedrooms, cycle storage and drying room, closed weekday lunchtimes out of season, otherwise open all day. *(Graham Smart)*

CONWY SH7777
Albion (01492) 582484
Uppergate Street; LL32 8RF Interesting sensitively restored 1920s pub under collective ownership of four welsh brewers – Conwy, Great Orme, Nant and Purple Moose, their beers and guests kept well (tasting trays available), friendly staff, some snacky food including pies, three linked rooms with plenty of well preserved features including stained glass and huge baronial fireplace, back part with serving hatch is quieter; open all day. *(Simon Collett-Jones, Dr and Mrs A K Clarke, Stuart Doughty)*

DOLGELLAU SH7318
Royal Ship (01341) 4222209
Queens Square; LL40 1AR Small civilised central hotel (19th-c coaching inn) with good well priced food from sandwiches and sharing boards up, well kept Robinsons ales and decent choice of wines by the glass, friendly service; children welcome, comfortable bedrooms, open (and food) all day. *(John Wooll)*

LLANDUDNO SH7882
Cottage Loaf (01492) 870762
Market Street; LL30 2SR Popular former bakery with three linked rooms, dark beams and timbers, rugs on pale flagstones or bare boards, good mix of tables, benches, cushioned settles and dining chairs, woodburners, decent brasserie-style food from sandwiches up, well kept Conwy, Courage, Brains and a couple of guests (often from local microbreweries), friendly service, big garden room extension; teak furniture on front and back terraces, children welcome, open (and food) all day. *(Simon Collett-Jones, David H Bennett)*

LLANDUDNO SH7882
Queen Victoria (01492) 860952
Church Walks; LL30 2HD Traditional Victorian pub away from the high-street bustle, five well kept Marstons-related beers and good choice of affordable pubby food in bar or upstairs restaurant (steaks cooked on a hot stone here), congenial atmosphere and good service; background music, free wi-fi; children and dogs welcome, a few seats out in front, not far from the Great Orme Tramway, open (and food) all day. *(Simon Collett-Jones)*

LLANFAETHLU SH3286
Black Lion (01407) 730718
A5025; LL65 4NL Renovated 18th-c inn with simple elegant décor, cosy bar with wooden tables and chairs on black slates, woodburner, oak-topped counter serving Marstons Pedigree, Purple Moose and a summer guest, seven wines by the glass, welsh whisky and gin, high-raftered dining room with another woodburner, enjoyable food using Anglesey produce including meat from own farm; children and dogs (in bar) welcome, terrace with lovely views to Snowdonia, two spacious bedrooms, open all day weekends (no Sun evening food), closed Mon, Tues and lunchtime Weds, check website for opening hours outside school holidays. *(Rob Anderson, Alison and Michael Harper, Pip White)*

LLANFROTHEN SH6141
Brondanw Arms (01766) 770555
Aka Y Ring; A4085 just N of B4410; LL48 6AQ Welsh-speaking village pub at end of short whitewashed terrace, main bar with slate floor and woodburner in large fireplace, pews and window benches, old

farm tools on the ceiling, snug with panelled booths and potbelly stove, long spacious dining room behind with contrasting red walls, good home-cooked food, Robinsons ales, friendly helpful staff; free wi-fi; children welcome, wheelchair access (two long shallow steps at front), Snowdonia National Park views from garden with play area, camping and good walks, handy for Plas Brondanw Gardens, open all day. *(Aled)*

LLANUWCHLLYN — SH8730
Eagles (01678) 540278

Aka Eryrod; A494/B4403; LL23 7UB Family-run and welcoming with good reasonably priced food (not Mon lunchtime) using own farm produce, ales such as Purple Moose, limited wine choice in small bottles, opened-up slate-floor bar with log fire, beams and stripped stone, back picture-window view of mountains with Lake Bala in the distance; small general stores open from 7am; sports TV; children welcome, metal tables and chairs on flower-filled back terrace, touring caravan and campsite, open all day summer (afternoon break Mon). *(Mike and Wena Stevenson)*

MAENTWROG — SH6640
Grapes (01766) 590365

A496; village signed from A470; LL41 4HN Handsome 17th-c inn, three bars and good-sized conservatory with views of steam trains on Ffestiniog Railway, enjoyable reasonably priced pubby food, ales such as Hancocks, Llŷn and Purple Moose, friendly helpful staff; children welcome, seats on pleasant terrace, six simply furnished clean bedrooms, open all day. *(Aiden)*

PENMAENPOOL — SH6918
George III (01341) 422525

Just off A493, near Dolgellau; LL40 1YD Attractive inn dating from 1650, lovely views over Mawddach estuary from partly panelled upstairs bar opening into cosy inglenook lounge, more basic beamed and flagstoned downstairs bar, three well kept ales and decent food including Sun carvery, restaurant; children and dogs welcome, sheltered terrace, 11 bedrooms (some in converted station – line now a walkway), open all day. *(John Evans)*

PORTH DINLLAEN — SH2741
★ **Ty Coch** (01758) 720498

Beach car park signed from Morfa Nefyn, then 15-minute walk; LL53 6DB Former 19th-c vicarage in idyllic location right on the beach with wonderful views, far from roads and only reached on foot; bar crammed with nautical paraphernalia, pewter, old miners' and railway lamps and other memorabilia, simple furnishings, coal fire, up to three real ales and a craft beer (served in plastic as worried about glass on beach), short lunchtime bar menu; children and dogs welcome, open all

day in season and school holidays (till 5pm Sun), 12-4pm weekends only during winter. *(Alister and Margery Bacon)*

PORTHMADOG — SH5639
Australia (01766) 515957

High Street; LL49 9LR Attractively refurbished tap for Purple Moose, their well kept ales and guests, decent wines by the glass and tasty pub food, chunky contemporary wooden furniture, beer barrel tables and banquettes on bare boards; occasional quiz and live music nights; children welcome, seats outside, open all day. *(Aled)*

PWLLHELI — SH3735
Whitehall (01758) 614091

Gaol Street; LL53 5RG Family-run pub-bistro in centre of this market town, local ales such as Llŷn and good choice of wines, popular freshly made food using local produce from shortish menu, early-bird weekday deal before 6.30pm, Fri steak night, friendly staff, spiral staircase to upstairs dining room; TV in bar; children welcome, open all day (till late Fri, Sat). *(Hefina Pritchard)*

RHYD DDU — SH5652
Cwellyn Arms (01766) 890321

A4085 N of Beddgelert; LL54 6TL Simple 18th-c village pub (same owners for over 30 years) not far below Welsh Highland Railway top terminus, up to nine real ales and good choice of popular seasonal food from home-baked rolls to blackboard specials, friendly helpful staff, two cosy bars and restaurant, log fires and woodburning stove; children, walkers and dogs welcome, spectacular Snowdon views from garden tables, babbling stream just over wall, campsite, bedrooms and bunkhouses, open all day. *(Charles Thomas)*

TREFRIW — SH7863
Old Ship (01492) 640013

B5106; LL27 0JH Well run old pub with nice staff and cheerful local atmosphere, good home-made food from daily changing blackboard menu, Marstons-related beers and local guests in top condition, good selection of wines/malt whiskies, log fire and inglenook woodburner; garden with picnic-sets by stream, children welcome, open all day (and food served all day) weekends, closed Mon except bank holidays. *(Martin Cawley, Mike and Wena Stevenson)*

TREMADOG — SH5640
Union (01766) 512748

Market Square; LL49 9RB Traditional early 19th-c stone-built pub in terrace overlooking square, cosy and comfortable, with quiet panelled lounge and carpeted public bar with exposed stone walls and woodburner, well kept ales such as Great Orme and Purple Moose, enjoyable pubby food from lunchtime sandwiches up, friendly staff, back restaurant; darts and TV; children and dogs welcome, paved terrace behind. *(Tony and Wendy Hobden)*

TUDWEILIOG   SH2336
Lion (01758) 659724
Nefyn Road (B4417), Llŷn Peninsula; LL53 8ND Cheerful village inn with enjoyable sensibly priced food from baguettes to blackboard specials, traditional furnishings in lounge bar and two dining rooms (one for families, other with woodburner), quick friendly service, real ales such as Purple Moose (up to three in summer), dozens of malt whiskies and decent wines; pool and board games in public bar; pleasant front garden, four bedrooms, open all day in season. *(Alison Griffiths)*

Y FELINHELI   SH5267
Garddfôn Inn (01248) 670359
Beach Road, off A487 SW of Bangor; LL56 4RQ Welcoming whitewashed pub facing the Menai Straits; quaint nautical-theme bar, Robinsons ales and decent choice of enjoyable fairly priced food using local suppliers, large back dining room, good friendly service; children welcome, great views from tables over the road on grass, five bedrooms, open all day. *(Hilary Forrest)*

POWYS

ABEREDW   SO0847
Seven Stars (01982) 560494
Just off B4567 SE of Builth Wells; LD2 3UW Cosy local with good generously served pub food and well kept ales such as Sharps Doom Bar and Wye Valley Butty Bach, prompt friendly service, low beams and stripped stone, log fire, restaurant; some live music; children and dogs welcome, open all day. *(Miranda and Jeff Davidson)*

BEGUILDY   SO1979
Radnorshire Arms (01547) 510634
B4355 Knighton–Newtown; LD7 1YE 17th-c black and white beamed country pub with enjoyable good value food, Ludlow, Stonehouse and a beer badged for them, friendly helpful service, inglenook woodburner; pool; no dogs inside, beer garden, closed Mon. *(Heather and Richard Jones)*

BLEDDFA   SO2068
Hundred House (01547) 550441
A488 Knighton–Penybont; LD7 1PA 16th-c pub (former courthouse) opposite village green; bar with pitched ceiling,

oak flooring and two-sided woodburner, three changing local ales and interesting choice of pies, slate-floored dining room; children welcome, tables in side garden with play area, lovely countryside, open all day weekends, closed Mon and Tues. *(Liz and Martin Eldon)*

CILMERY   SO0051
Prince Llewelyn (01982) 552694
A483; LD2 3NU Friendly new owners for this country pub, plush dining chairs and button-back banquettes in dining room, woodburner in carpeted bar, a couple of real ales and enjoyable food using local produce; children and dogs welcome, lovely surrounding walks, open all day. *(Sandra and Miles Spencer)*

CRICKHOWELL   SO2118
Dragon (01873) 810362
High Street; NP8 1BE Welcoming old family-owned inn, more hotel-restaurant than pub, but with neat small bar serving Rhymney, stone and wood floors, sofas and armchairs by open fire, enjoyable traditional food including welsh choices in tidy dining room, good friendly service; 15 bedrooms; open (and food) all day. *(Liz and Martin Eldon)*

CRICKHOWELL   SO1919
★ **Nantyffin Cider Mill** (01873) 810775
A40/A479 NW; NP8 1SG Former 16th-c drovers' inn facing River Usk in lovely Black Mountains countryside – charming views from tables on lawn; bar with solid furniture on tiles or carpet, woodburner in broad fireplace, Felinfoel Double Dragon, proper ciders and several wines by the glass, open-plan main area with beams, standing timbers and open fire in grey stonework wall, striking high-raftered restaurant with old cider press, good home-made food from sandwiches to grills; background music; children and dogs (in bar) welcome, bedrooms, handy for Tretower Court and Castle, closed Mon and Tues, otherwise open all day. *(Roger Mallard)*

DERWENLAS   SN7299
★ **Black Lion** (01654) 703913
A487 just S of Machynlleth; SY20 8TN Cosy 16th-c country pub with extensive range of good well priced food including children's menu and daily specials, friendly staff coping well at busy times, Wye Valley Butty Bach and a guest, decent wines, heavy black beams and timbering, thick walls, carpet over big slate flagstones, good log fire; background music; garden behind with play area and steps up into woods, limited parking, bedrooms, closed Mon. *(John Evans)*

DINAS MAWDDWY   SH8514
Red Lion (01650) 531247
*Dyfi Road; off A470 (N of A458
junction); SY20 9JA* Two small traditional
front bars and more modern back extension,
changing ales and decent food including
popular pies and Sunday carvery, friendly
efficient service, open fire, beams and lots
of brassware; children welcome, six simple
bedrooms (four ensuite), pub named in
welsh (Llew Coch). *(Liz and Martin Eldon)*

FELINFACH   SO0933
Plough & Harrow (01874) 622709
*Village and pub signed from A470,
4 miles N of Brecon; LD3 0UB* Small
village pub under welcoming long-serving
licensees, simple bar, comfortable lounge
area with woodburner and dining room, well
kept Sharps Doom Bar and a guest, good
reasonably priced home-made food (evenings
only); three bedrooms. *(Barry Collett)*

GLADESTRY   SO2355
Royal Oak (01544) 370669
B4594; HR5 3NR Friendly old-fashioned
village pub on Offa's Dyke Path, simple
stripped-stone slate-floored walkers' bar,
beams hung with tankards and lanterns,
carpeted lounge, open fires, Golden
Valley and Wye Valley ales, uncomplicated
home-made food from sandwiches up;
no credit cards; children welcome, dogs
in bar, sheltered sunny back garden,
four bedrooms, camping, closed Sun
evening, Mon, Tues and lunchtimes
Weds-Fri. *(Louise and Simon Peters)*

GLANGRWYNEY   SO2416
Bell (01873) 811115
A40 Crickhowell–Abergavenny; NP8 1EH
Updated old beamed village pub under
new management, Brains ales and good
well presented food, friendly attentive staff;
children and dogs (in bar) welcome, garden
picnic-sets, good surrounding walks, four
bedrooms, open (and food) all day Fri, Sat.
(Aled Powell)

GLASBURY   SO1839
Harp (01497) 847373
*B4350 towards Hay, just N of A438;
HR3 5NR* Welcoming homely old place
with good value pubby food (not Mon)
cooked by landlady including proper
pies, curries and takeaway pizzas, log-fire
lounge with eating areas, black beamed
bar, well kept local ales, picture windows
over wooded garden sloping to River
Wye; some live folk music, regular quiz

evenings, darts; river views from picnic-
sets on terrace and back bedrooms, good
breakfast. *(Fiona and Jack Henderson)*

HAY-ON-WYE   SO2242
★Blue Boar (01497) 820884
Castle Street/Oxford Road; HR3 5DF
Medieval bar in character pub, cosy
corners, dark panelling, pews and country
chairs, open fire in Edwardian fireplace,
four well kept ales including Brains Rev
James and Timothy Taylors Landlord,
organic bottled cider and several wines by
the glass, decent food in quite different
long café/dining room, bright light décor,
local artwork for sale and another open
fire, friendly service; background music;
children and dogs welcome, tables in
tree-shaded garden, open all day from 9am
for breakfast. *(Nicholas and Lucy Sage)*

HAY-ON-WYE   SO2242
★Three Tuns (01497) 821855
Broad Street; HR3 5DB Sizeable old pub
with low beams, exposed stone walls and
woodburners in hefty fireplaces (one with a
beautiful old curved settle beside it), upstairs
summer restaurant, well kept ales and good
wine choice, popular freshly prepared food
from ciabattas, pizzas and pubby choices
to pricier upscale dishes, prompt helpful
service (they may ask for a credit card
if you run a tab); children welcome till
7pm, no dogs, disabled access/facilities,
seats under big parasols in sheltered
courtyard. *(Samuel and Melissa Turnbull)*

HUNDRED HOUSE   SO1154
Hundred House Inn (01982) 570231
A481 NE of Builth Wells; LD1 5RY
Traditional two-room roadside country
pub under welcoming licensees, well
liked food including Tues curry, Weds and
Thurs steak night and Fri evening fish
and chips, one or more well kept ales,
woodburner in public bar; pool and sports
TV; children welcome, garden picnic-sets,
four cosy bedrooms and camping, open all
day weekends. *(Anna and Mark Evans)*

KNIGHTON   SO2872
Horse & Jockey (01547) 520062
Wylcwm Place; LD7 1AE Popular old
family-run pub with several cosy areas,
one with woodburning stove, enjoyable
good value food cooked by owner from
traditional choices and pizzas up in bar
and adjoining restaurant, cheerful service,
well kept beers; tables in pleasant medieval
courtyard, six bedrooms, handy for Offa's
Dyke Path, open all day Sun. *(Hywel Thomas)*

A star symbol before the name of a pub shows exceptional character and appeal.
It doesn't mean extra comfort. Even quite a basic pub can win a star,
if it's individual enough.

LIBANUS SN9926
Tai'r Bull (01874) 622600
A470 SW of Brecon; LD3 8EL Welcoming
old roadside village pub with well kept
ales such as Greene King and Wye Valley,
decent food from good sandwiches up,
woodburner in large stone fireplace,
light and airy restaurant; great views of
Pen-y-Fan from small front terrace, five
bedrooms. *(Brian and Jacky Wilson)*

LLANBEDR SO2320
Red Lion (01873) 810754
Off A40 at Crickhowell; NP8 1SR Quaint
old local in pretty village set in dell, charming
landlady, heavy beams, antique settles in
lounge and snug, log fires, well kept Rhymney,
Wye Valley and a guest ale, front dining
area with fair value home-made food; good
walking country (porch for muddy boots),
open all day weekends, closed Mon and
weekday lunchtimes. *(Nik and Gloria Clarke)*

LLANFIHANGEL-
NANT-MELAN SO1958
Red Lion (01544) 350220
A44 10 miles W of Kington; LD8 2TN
Stripped-stone and beamed 16th-c roadside
dining pub; roomy main bar with flagstones
and woodburner, carpeted restaurant, front
sun porch, good reasonably priced home-made
food from shortish interesting menu, Brains
and changing guests, friendly service, back
bar with another woodburner; pool and
darts; children and dogs welcome, country
views from pleasant garden, five bedrooms
(three in annexe), handy for Radnor Forest
walks and near impressive waterfall, open
all day Sun till 7pm. *(Anna and Mark Evans)*

LLANGEDWYN SJ1924
Green Inn (01691) 828234
B4396 E of village; SY10 9JW Old country
dining pub with various snug alcoves,
nooks and crannies, good mix of furnishings
including oak settles and leather sofas,
woodburner, Sharps Doom Bar, Stonehouse
and a guest, enjoyable well priced pubby
food, OAP lunch deal Thurs, friendly
helpful staff; children and dogs welcome,
attractive garden over road running
down towards River Tanat, closed Mon
and maybe winter Tues, otherwise open
all day. *(Alister and Margery Bacon)*

LLANGURIG SN9079
Blue Bell (01686) 440254
A44 opposite church; SY18 6SG Friendly
old-fashioned village inn with comfortable
flagstoned bar, well kept Brains Rev James
and Wye Valley Butty Bach, Thatcher's cider,
ample helpings of good value pubby food,
small dining room, games room with darts,
dominoes and pool; background music;
children welcome, no dogs, eight simple
inexpensive bedrooms, open all day.
(Patricia and Gordon Tucker)

LLANGYNIDR SO1519
Coach & Horses (01874) 730245
*Cwm Crawnon Road (B4558 W of
Crickhowell); NP8 1LS* Popular flower-
decked country dining pub, three well
kept ales and enjoyable generously served
food from chef-owner, beams, stripped
stone and big log fire, restaurant; children
and dogs (in some areas) welcome,
picnic-sets and play area across fairly
busy road in fenced sloping garden by
lock of Monmouthshire & Brecon Canal,
bedrooms, open all day (shuts 3-5pm
in winter). *(Giles and Annie Francis)*

LLANIDLOES SN9584
Crown & Anchor (01686) 412398
Long Bridge Street; SY18 6EF Friendly
unspoilt town-centre pub known locally
as Ruby's after landlady who has run it
for over 50 years (been in her family for
a lot longer), well kept Brains Rev James
and Wye Valley Bitter, chatty locals' bar,
lounge, snug and two other rooms, one
with pool and games machine separated
by central hallway; open all day. *(KD)*

LLANWRTYD WELLS SN8746
Neuadd Arms (01591) 610236
The Square; LD5 4RB Sizeable 19th-c
hotel (friendly and by no means upmarket)
brewing its own good value Heart of Wales
beers in back stable block (ten on at once),
enjoyable straightforward home-made food,
log fires in lounge and small tiled public
bar still with old service bells, restaurant,
games room; well behaved dogs welcome in
bars, a few tables out at front, 20 bedrooms
(front ones can be noisy), engaging very
small town in good walking area, novel
events such as bogsnorkelling and man
v horse, open all day. *(Nik and Gloria Clarke)*

MALLWYD SH8612
Brigands (01650) 511999
*A470 by roundabout in village; SY20
9HJ* Sizeable 15th-c beamed coaching
inn with gently civilised atmosphere,
enjoyable food using local produce,
popular afternoon teas, Cader ales and
a summer guest, friendly efficient staff;
children and dogs welcome, extensive
lawns with lovely views, can arrange
fishing on River Dovey, nine bedrooms,
open (and some food) all day. *(KD)*

PAINSCASTLE SO1646
★ Roast Ox (01497) 851398
*Off A470 Brecon–Builth Wells, or from
A438 at Clyro; LD2 3JL* Well restored
pub with beams, flagstones and stripped
stone, appropriate simple furnishings and
some rustic bric-a-brac, huge antlers above
open fire, ales tapped from the cask and
good range of ciders and malt whiskies,
popular freshly made food including good
fish and chips, friendly quick service;

children and dogs welcome, picnic-sets outside, attractive hill country, ten comfortable neat bedrooms. *(Tony Hough)*

PENCELLI   SO0925
Royal Oak (01874) 665396
B4558 SE of Brecon; LD3 7LX New licensees for this country pub; two small unpretentious bars, low beams and log fires, assorted furniture on flagstones, well kept Brains Rev James and a couple of guests, quite a choice of home-made food (12-6 Sun roasts), simple modern dining room; children and dogs welcome, terraces backing on to Monmouthshire & Brecon Canal (nearby moorings), lovely canalside walks and handy for Taff Trail, open all day in summer, may close Jan. *(Giles and Annie Francis, Frank Price)*

PENYCAE   SN8313
Ancient Briton (01639) 730273
Brecon Road (A4067); SA9 1YY Friendly opened-up roadside pub, log fire in bar, seven or more well kept ales from far and wide, local cider and enjoyable reasonably priced home-made food; children and dogs welcome, seats outside and play area, four bedrooms, campsite (good facilities including disabled loo and shower), handy for Dan-yr-Ogof caves, Henrhyd Waterfall and Craig-y-Nos Country Park, open all day. *(Fiona and Jack Henderson)*

RHAYADER   SN9668
★**Triangle** (01597) 810537
Cwmdauddwr; B4518 by bridge over River Wye, SW of centre; LD6 5AR Interesting little 16th-c pub with buoyant local atmosphere, shortish choice of good value home-made pubby food (best to book evenings), well kept Brains Rev James, Hancocks HB and reasonably priced wines, friendly staff, dining area with nice view over park to River Wye; darts; self-catering cottage opposite, three tables on small front terrace, parking can be difficult, closed Mon lunchtime. *(Anna and Mark Evans)*

A little further afield

CHANNEL ISLANDS

GUERNSEY

FOREST
Deerhound (01481) 238585
Le Bourg; GY8 0AN Spacious roadside dining pub with modern interior, food including summer seafood menu can be good, Liberation ales, friendly helpful service; free wi-fi; children welcome, sunny sheltered terrace with parasols, handy for the airport, open all day. *(Adam Jones)*

KING'S MILLS
★**Fleur du Jardin** (01481) 257996
Kings Mills Road; GY5 7JT Lovely 15th-c country hotel in pretty walled garden with solar-heated swimming pool; low-beamed bar with log fire, Liberation and guests, local cider and plenty of wines by the glass, very good attractively presented food, afternoon teas, friendly helpful service, restaurant; background music; children and small dogs welcome, plenty of tables on back terrace, 15 stylish, contemporary bedrooms, open all day. *(Adam Jones, Dan and Nicki Barton)*

ST MARTIN
Les Douvres (01481) 238731
La Fosse; GY4 6ER Sister hotel to the Fleur du Jardin at King's Mills; popular beamed bar with country pub feel, three changing ales and plenty of wines by the glass, decent range of enjoyable fairly priced food including burgers and pizzas, friendly helpful staff; live music Fri; garden with swimming pool, 19 bedrooms, good breakfast, open all day. *(Charlie Walker)*

ST PETER PORT
Ship & Crown (01481) 728994
Opposite Crown Pier, Esplanade; GY1 2NB Bustling old town pub with bay windows overlooking harbour; interesting photographs (especially of World War II occupation, also boats and local shipwrecks), decent all-day bar food from sandwiches up, ales such as Butcombe and Fullers London Pride, welcoming prompt service even when busy, more modern-feel Crow's Nest brasserie upstairs with good views; sports TVs in bar; open all day from 10am till late. *(Richard)*

VALE
Houmet (01481) 242214
Grande Havre; GY6 8JR Modern building overlooking Grande Havre Bay; front restaurant/bar with conservatory, good choice of reasonably priced popular food (best to book) including fresh fish and seafood, friendly service, a couple of real ales and several wines by the glass, back public bar with pool, darts and big-screen sports TV (dogs allowed here); regular quiz nights; children welcome, tables out on sheltered deck, open all day (not Sun evening). *(Adam Jones)*

JERSEY

GRÈVE DE LECQ
★**Moulin de Lecq** (01534) 482818
Mont de la Grève de Lecq; JE3 2DT Cheerful family-friendly mill conversion dating from the 12th c with massive waterwheel dominating the softly lit beamed bar, good varied choice of enjoyable food, four changing ales and a couple of real ciders, friendly service and chatty regulars, restaurant extension, upstairs games room with pool and TV; dogs welcome in bar, terrace picnic-sets and adventure playground, peaceful streamside spot with good walks, open all day in summer. *(Susan and John Douglas)*

ST AUBIN
Boat House (01534) 747141
North Quay; JE3 8BS Modern steel and timber-clad harbourside building with great views (window tables for diners), bar serving well kept local ales and several wines by

the glass, good food ranging from tapas to Josper grills, airy upstairs restaurant (evenings, weekends, closed Tues and Weds); balcony and decked terrace overlooking harbour, open all day. *(Mary Joyce)*

ST AUBIN
★ Old Court House Inn (01534)
746433 *Harbour Boulevard; JE3 8AB* Attractively updated and prettily positioned harbourside inn; bustling bar with low beams and open fire, other rambling areas including bistro, popular generously served food from sandwiches and pubby choices to good fresh fish/seafood, well kept Liberation ales and 15 wines by the glass, handsome upstairs restaurant with lovely views across the bay to St Helier, efficient service; children welcome, front deck overlooking harbour, more seats in courtyard behind, ten comfortable well equipped bedrooms, open all day (food all day in summer). *(Susan and John Douglas)*

ST AUBIN
Tenby (01534) 741224
Harbour Boulevard, towards St Helier; JE3 8AB Randalls pub overlooking the harbour; large bar and several other rooms, decent choice of food (all day Sun) from sandwiches and wraps to good seafood, a couple of real ales such as Skinners, helpful service; children welcome, disabled access/loos, seats out on small front deck under awning, more on paved side terrace, open all day. *(Paul Humphreys)*

ST BRELADE
Old Smugglers (01534) 741510
Ouaisne Bay; OS map reference 595476; JE3 8AW Unpretentious pub just above Ouaisne beach; up to four well kept ales, proper cider and enjoyable traditional food, friendly service, black beams, built-in settles and log fires, restaurant; occasional live music, sports TV, darts, cribbage and dominoes; children and dogs welcome, sun porch with coast views, open all day in summer. *(Andrew Wall)*

ST HELIER
Cock & Bottle (01534) 722184
Royal Square; JE2 4WA Big lively outside eating area in Royal Square with lovely large hanging baskets, rattan tables and chairs under parasols, heaters and blankets for cooler evenings; pleasantly old-fashioned and pubby inside with upholstered settles and small stools in front of large fireplace, wide choice of good food from sandwiches and wraps through pub favourites and bistro choices to summer seafood menu, well kept Liberation ales; open all day, no food Fri-Sun evenings. *(Susan and John Douglas)*

ST HELIER
Halkett (01534) 732769
Halkett Place; JE2 4WG Modern pub-cum-bar close to tree-lined square, mix of traditional and contemporary décor and furnishings, Liberation ales, 17 wines by the glass and wide choice of food from pubby and brasserie dishes to summer seafood menu; very busy with visitors and locals; Fri and Sat DJs playing 1980s music; open all day, no food Sun evening. *(Andrew Wall)*

ST HELIER
★ Lamplighter (01534) 723119
Mulcaster Street; JE2 3NJ Small friendly pub with up to eight well kept ales, real ciders and more than 150 malt whiskies from pewter-topped counter, low-priced pubby food including good crab sandwiches and popular steak nights (Tues and Thurs), traditional décor with lots of pump clips on heavy timbers and some old gas light fittings; sports TV, can get very busy; wheelchair access (no disabled loos), interesting patriotic façade (the only union flag visible during Nazi occupation), open all day, no evening food Fri-Sun. *(Adam Jones, Neil Allen)*

ST HELIER
Post Horn (01534) 872853
Hue Street; JE2 3RE Popular centrally placed pub with modernised interior, four well kept ales including Liberation and eight wines by the glass, fair value pubby food (not Fri or Sat evenings, Sun), open fire; darts, cribbage, sports TV; tables out in front, open all day. *(Adam Jones)*

ISLE OF MAN

BALDRINE   SC4180
Liverpool Arms (01624) 674787
Main Road; IM4 6AE Former coaching inn with wide choice of reasonably priced pubby food (all day Fri-Sun), Okells Bitter and a summer guest, friendly welcoming staff, open fires; sports TV, pool and darts; picnic-sets outside, children and dogs (in bar) allowed, open all day. *(Chris Webster)*

DOUGLAS   SC3875
Rovers Return
Church Street; IM1 3LX Lively old-fashioned pub tucked down alleyway attracting good mix of customers; several rambling bars, mainly Bushy ales but some mainland guests, generous straightforward lunchtime food, friendly staff, back room filled with Blackburn Rovers memorabilia (landlord is a fan); rock juke box, TV, pool and darts; no children, tables outside, open all day. *(Dave Braisted)*

All *Guide* inspections are anonymous. Anyone claiming to be a *Good Pub Guide* inspector is a fraud. Please let us know.

LAXEY
SC4382

Shore (01624) 861509

Old Laxey Hill; IM4 7DA Friendly nautically themed village pub brewing its own Old Laxey Bosun Bitter, good value wines by the glass and enjoyable pubby lunchtime food (regular curry and steak nights); children welcome till 9pm, picnic-sets out by lovely stream, nice walk to Laxey waterwheel, open all day. *(Liz and Mike Newton)*

PEEL
SC2484

Creek (01624) 842216

Station Place/North Quay; IM5 1AT In lovely setting on the ancient quayside opposite the House of Manannan heritage centre and very busy at peak times; wide choice of highly thought-of food including fish, crab and lobster fresh from the boats, good local kippers too, ten well kept changing ales (always some from Okells), nautical-themed lounge bar with etched mirrors and mainly old woodwork; TVs and weekend live music in public bar; children welcome, tables outside overlooking harbour, open (and food) all day from 10am. *(Chris Webster)*

PORT ERIN
SC1969

Falcon's Nest (01624) 834077

Station Road; IM9 6AF Friendly family-run hotel overlooking the bay, enjoyable food including local fish/seafood and Sun carvery, up to five well kept ales and some 60 malt whiskies, two bars, one with open fire, conservatory and restaurant; sports TV; children welcome, 39 bedrooms, many with sea view, also eight self-catering apartments, handy for steam rail terminus, open all day. *(Max Simons, Charlie May)*

Pubs that serve food all day

We list here all the pubs (in the Main Entries) that have told us they plan to serve food all day, even if it's only one day of the week. The individual entries for the pubs themselves show the actual details.

Bedfordshire
Ireland, Black Horse
Oakley, Bedford Arms

Berkshire
Kintbury, Dundas Arms
Pangbourne, Elephant
Peasemore, Fox
Sonning, Bull
White Waltham, Beehive

Buckinghamshire
Coleshill, Harte & Magpies
Forty Green, Royal Standard of England
Stoke Mandeville, Bell

Cambridgeshire
Cambridge, Punter
Peterborough, Brewery Tap
Stilton, Bell

Cheshire
Aldford, Grosvenor Arms
Allostock, Three Greyhounds Inn
Astbury, Egerton Arms
Aston, Bhurtpore
Bostock Green, Hayhurst Arms
Bunbury, Dysart Arms
Burleydam, Combermere Arms
Burwardsley, Pheasant
Chester, Architect
Chester, Mill
Chester, Old Harkers Arms
Cholmondeley, Cholmondeley Arms
Cotebrook, Fox & Barrel
Delamere, Fishpool
Haughton Moss, Nags Head
Macclesfield, Sutton Hall
Mobberley, Bulls Head
Mobberley, Church Inn
Mobberley, Roebuck
Mottram St Andrew, Bulls Head
Nether Alderley, Wizard
Thelwall, Little Manor
Warmingham, Bears Paw

Cornwall
Morwenstow, Bush
Mylor Bridge, Pandora
Polgooth, Polgooth Inn

Porthtowan, Blue
Wainhouse Corner, Old Wainhouse

Cumbria
Cartmel Fell, Masons Arms
Crosthwaite, Punch Bowl
Elterwater, Britannia
Ings, Watermill
Levens, Strickland Arms
Lupton, Plough
Ravenstonedale, Black Swan
Threlkeld, Horse & Farrier

Derbyshire
Chelmorton, Church Inn
Fenny Bentley, Coach & Horses
Hathersage, Plough
Hayfield, Royal
Ladybower Reservoir, Yorkshire
  Bridge

Devon
Cockwood, Anchor
Iddesleigh, Duke of York
Postbridge, Warren House
Sidbury, Hare & Hounds
Topsham, Globe

Dorset
Weymouth, Red Lion
Worth Matravers, Square &
  Compass

Essex
Feering, Sun
Fyfield, Queens Head
Little Walden, Crown
South Hanningfield, Old Windmill

Gloucestershire
Didmarton, Kings Arms
Guiting Power, Hollow Bottom

Nailsworth, Weighbridge
Sheepscombe, Butchers Arms

Hampshire
Bransgore, Three Tuns
Cadnam, White Hart
Littleton, Running Horse
Portsmouth, Old Customs House

Hertfordshire
Ashwell, Three Tuns
Barnet, Duke of York
Berkhamsted, Highwayman
St Albans, Prae Wood Arms

Isle of Wight
Fishbourne, Fishbourne Inn
Hulverstone, Sun
Niton, Buddle
Seaview, Boathouse
Shorwell, Crown

Kent
Chiddingstone Causeway, Little
  Brown Jug
Langton Green, Hare
Penshurst, Bottle House
Sevenoaks, White Hart
Shipbourne, Chaser
Stalisfield Green, Plough

Lancashire
Bashall Eaves, Red Pump
Bispham Green, Eagle & Child
Formby, Sparrowhawk
Great Mitton, Aspinall Arms
Great Mitton, Three Fishes
Manchester, Wharf
Nether Burrow, Highwayman
Pleasington, Clog & Billycock
Preston, Haighton Manor
Uppermill, Church Inn

Leicestershire
Lyddington, Marquess of Exeter
Swithland, Griffin

Lincolnshire
Kirkby la Thorpe, Queens Head
Stamford, George of Stamford

Norfolk
King's Lynn, Bank House
Larling, Angel
Morston, Anchor
Salthouse, Dun Cow
Thorpe Market, Gunton Arms
Woodbastwick, Fur & Feather

Northamptonshire
Ashby St Ledgers, Olde Coach House
Oundle, Ship

Northumbria
Blanchland, Lord Crewe Arms
Carterway Heads, Manor House Inn
Corbridge, Angel
Newton, Duke of Wellington

Oxfordshire
Kingham, Plough
Oxford, Bear
Oxford, Punter
Sparsholt, Star
Wolvercote, Jacobs Inn
Woodstock, Woodstock Arms

Shropshire
Chetwynd Aston, Fox
Shipley, Inn at Shipley
Shrewsbury, Armoury

Somerset
Dunster, Luttrell Arms
Hinton St George, Lord Poulett Arms
Stanton Wick, Carpenters Arms
Wedmore, Swan

Staffordshire
Brewood, Oakley
Longdon Green, Red Lion
Salt, Holly Bush
Wrinehill, Hand & Trumpet

Suffolk
Chelmondiston, Butt & Oyster
Snape, Plough & Sail
Stoke-by-Nayland, Crown
Waldringfield, Maybush

Surrey
Buckland, Pheasant
Chiddingfold, Swan
Chobham, White Hart
Elstead, Mill at Elstead
Englefield Green, Bailiwick
Milford, Refectory
Norwood Hill, Fox Revived

Sussex
Alfriston, George
Charlton, Fox Goes Free
Eridge Green, Nevill Crest & Gun
Friday Street, Farm at Friday Street
Horsham, Black Jug
Ringmer, Cock

Warwickshire
Birmingham, Old Joint Stock
Birmingham, Physician
Hunningham, Red Lion
Long Compton, Red Lion

Shipston-on-Stour, Black Horse
Warmington, Falcon
Welford-on-Avon, Bell

Wiltshire
Bradford-on-Avon, Castle

Yorkshire
Beck Hole, Birch Hall
Blakey Ridge, Lion
Bradfield, Strines Inn
Broughton, Bull
Elslack, Tempest Arms
Grinton, Bridge Inn
Halifax, Shibden Mill
Ledsham, Chequers
Linton in Craven, Fountaine
Welburn, Crown & Cushion
Widdop, Pack Horse
York, Judges Lodging

London
Central London, Black Friar
Central London, Old Bank of
    England
Central London, Olde Mitre
Central London, Seven Stars
Central London, Thomas Cubitt

Hampton Court, Mute Swan
North London, Hare
North London, Holly Bush
West London, Dove
West London, Old Orchard
West London, Windsor Castle

Scotland
Applecross, Applecross Inn
Edinburgh, Guildford Arms
Edinburgh, Scran & Scallie
Glasgow, Babbity Bowster
Glasgow, Bon Accord
Shieldaig, Tigh an Eilean Hotel
Sligachan, Sligachan Hotel
Thornhill, Lion & Unicorn

Wales
Colwyn Bay, Pen-y-Bryn
Gresford, Pant-yr-Ochain
Hawarden, Glynne Arms
Llandudno Junction, Queens Head
Llanelian-yn-Rhos, White Lion
Llangollen, Corn Mill
Mold, Glasfryn
Overton Bridge, Cross Foxes
Pontypridd, Bunch of Grapes

Pubs near motorway junctions

The number at the start of each line is the number of the junction. Detailed directions are given in the Main Entry for each pub. In this section, to help you find the pubs quickly before you're past the junction, we give the name of the chapter where you'll find the text.

M1

9: Redbourn, Cricketers (Hertfordshire) 3.2 miles

13: Woburn, Birch (Bedfordshire) 3.5 miles

18: Ashby St Ledgers, Olde Coach House (Northamptonshire) 4 miles

M3

1: Sunbury, Flower Pot (Surrey) 1.6 miles

3: West End, The Inn West End (Surrey) 2.4 miles; Chobham, White Hart (Surrey) 4 miles

5: North Warnborough, Mill House (Hampshire) 1 mile; Hook, Hogget (Hampshire) 1.1 miles

M4

9: Bray, Crown (Berkshire) 1.75 miles

13: Curridge, Bunk (Berkshire) 3 miles; Chieveley, Crab & Boar (Berkshire) 3.5 miles; Peasemore, Fox (Berkshire) 4 miles

14: Shefford Woodlands, Pheasant (Berkshire) 0.3 miles

M5

4: Holy Cross, Bell & Cross (Worcestershire) 4 miles

10: Coombe Hill, Gloucester Old Spot (Gloucestershire) 1 mile

13: Eastington, Old Badger (Gloucestershire) 1 mile

19: Clapton-in-Gordano, Black Horse (Somerset) 4 miles

30: Topsham, Globe (Devon) 2 miles; Woodbury Salterton, Diggers Rest (Devon) 3.5 miles

M6

16: Barthomley, White Lion (Cheshire) 1 mile

17: Sandbach, Old Hall (Cheshire) 1.2 miles

18: Allostock, Three Greyhounds Inn (Cheshire) 4.7 miles

19: Mobberley, Bulls Head (Cheshire) 4 miles

33: Bay Horse, Bay Horse (Lancashire) 1.2 miles

36: Lupton, Plough (Cumbria) 2 miles; Levens, Strickland Arms (Cumbria) 4 miles

40: Yanwath, Gate Inn (Cumbria) 2.25 miles; Tirril, Queens Head (Cumbria) 3.5 miles

M11

9: Hinxton, Red Lion (Cambridgeshire) 2 miles

10: Duxford, John Barleycorn (Cambridgeshire) 1.8 miles; Whittlesford, Tickell Arms (Cambridgeshire) 2.4 miles

M25

5: Chipstead, George & Dragon (Kent) 1.25 miles

8: Walton on the Hill, Blue Ball (Surrey) miles

18: Flaunden, Bricklayers Arms (Hertfordshire) 4 miles

21A: Potters Crouch, Holly Bush (Hertfordshire) 2.3 miles

M27

1: Cadnam, White Hart (Hampshire) 0.5 miles; Fritham, Royal Oak (Hampshire) 4 miles

M40

2: Hedgerley, White Horse (Buckinghamshire) 2.4 miles; Forty Green, Royal Standard of England (Buckinghamshire) 3.5 miles

12: Gaydon, Malt Shovel (Warwickshire) 0.9 miles

M42

5: Barston, Malt Shovel (Warwickshire) 3 miles

6: Hampton-in-Arden, White Lion (Warwickshire) 1.25 miles

M50

1: Baughton, Jockey (Worcestershire) 4 miles

3: Kilcot, Kilcot Inn (Gloucestershire) 2.3 miles

M60

13: Worsley, Worsley Old Hall (Lancashire) 1 mile

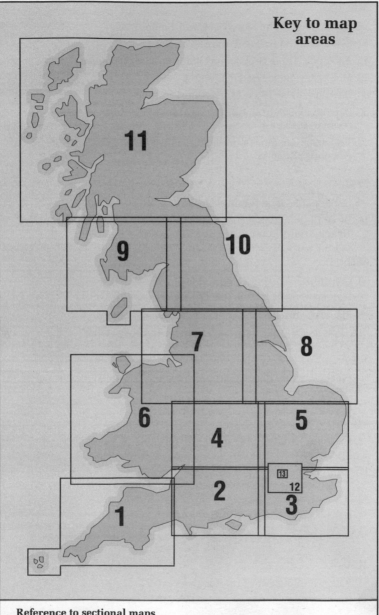

Key to map areas

11

9   **10**

7   **8**

6   **4**   **5**

2   13
          12

1   **3**

Reference to sectional maps

— Motorway

— Major road

----- County boundary

● Main Entry

◉ Main Entry with accommodation

■ Place name to assist navigation

MAPS

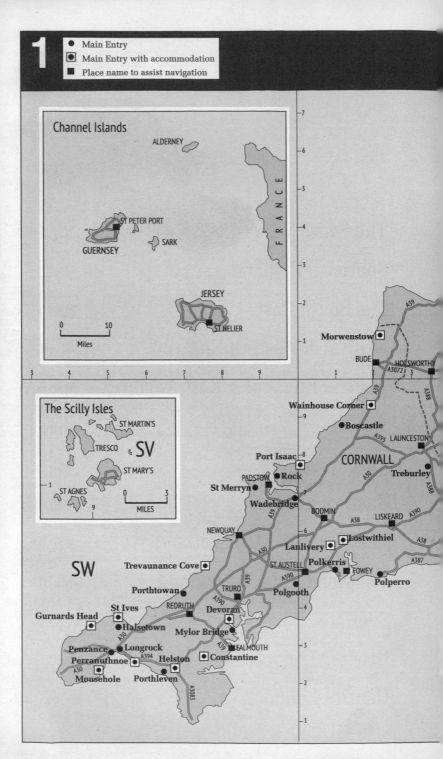

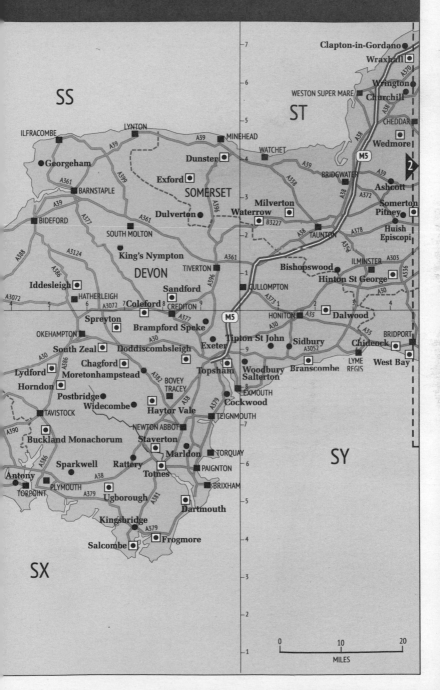

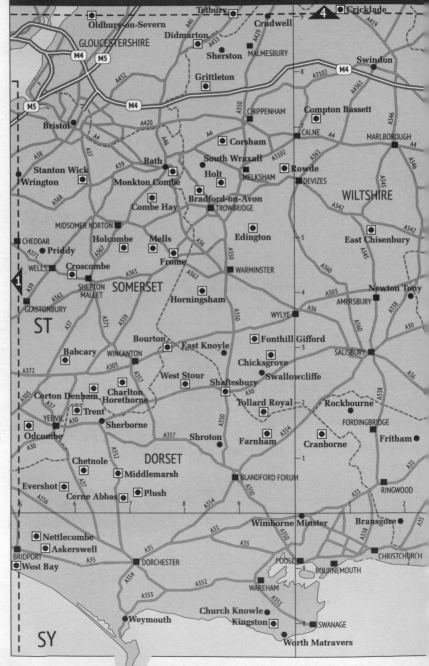

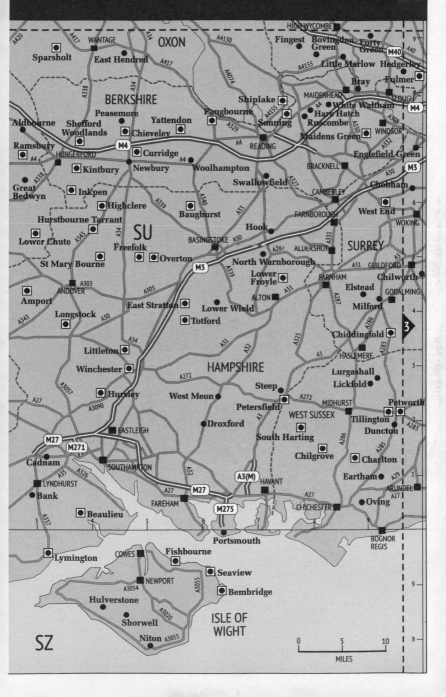

2

SZ

3

BUCKS

M1 M11 5

M25 A127

● Harefield (see West London section)

GREATER LONDON

Horndon-on-the-Hill

A13

● Hedgerley
M40
● Fulmer UXBRIDGE

BERKS
M25 M4

A128

TILBURY ■

■ GRAVESEND

■ Englefield Green ■ STAINES

DARTFORD A2

ROCHESTER

A30
M3 ◉ Sunbury

Meopham ●

M2

● Chobham Esher ●

M25 M20 A227 M20

A3

M6
● Ripley Walton on the Hill ● Chipstead ●

Chipstead ● M26

MAIDSTONE

WOKING
◉ Mickleham

M25 WESTERHAM Ivy Hatch ■

Sevenoaks ● Shipbourne ●

TQ

A246 A24 ● Buckland

A25 A227 A26

GUILDFORD
DORKING REIGATE

Chiddingstone ● TONBRIDGE ■

● Chilworth SURREY

A217 A23 A22

Penshurst ● Bidborough ● Matfield ●

● Norwood Hill

Goudhurst ●

● Shamley Green M23 A264

Langton Green ●

A262

A281 A24 CRAWLEY ◉ Copthorne EAST GRINSTEAD

Tunbridge Wells ●

2 A264 West Hoathly ◉ Withyham ● Eridge Green ● Mark Cross ●

● Horsham Horsted Keynes ◉

A21

● Lower Beeding ◉ Warninglid Danehill ◉ A275 A26 CROWBOROUGH

Ticehurst ●

A272 HAYWARDS HEATH Fletching ◉

A265 Salehurst ●

◉ Petworth ◉ Dial Post BURGESS HILL A272 ● Uckfield

Robertsbridge ●

A283 A23 A273

A26 A267

EAST SUSSEX

WEST SUSSEX Ditchling ◉ A275 ● Ringmer

A271

A29 A27 LEWES HAILSHAM ■

BEXHILL

ARUNDEL A27 A26 Firle ● A259

A259 WORTHING BRIGHTON A259 NEWHAVEN Alfriston ◉ ● Friday Street

EASTBOURNE

◉ East Dean

TV

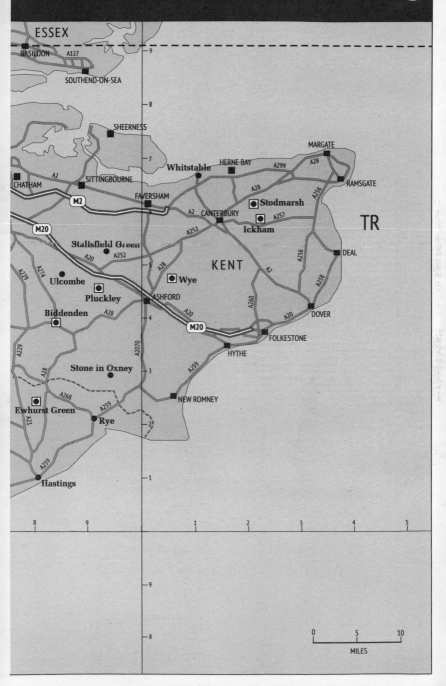

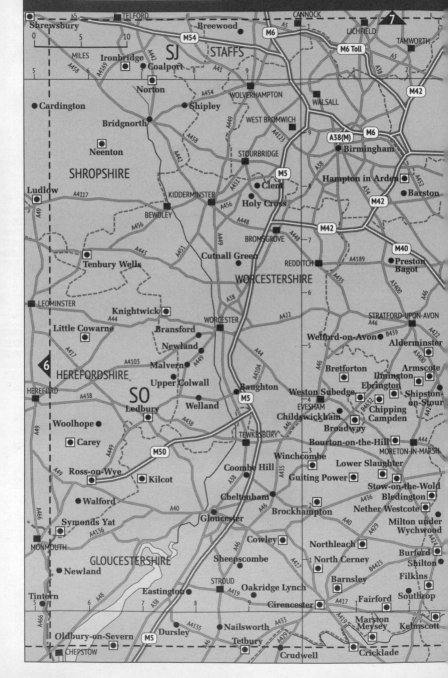

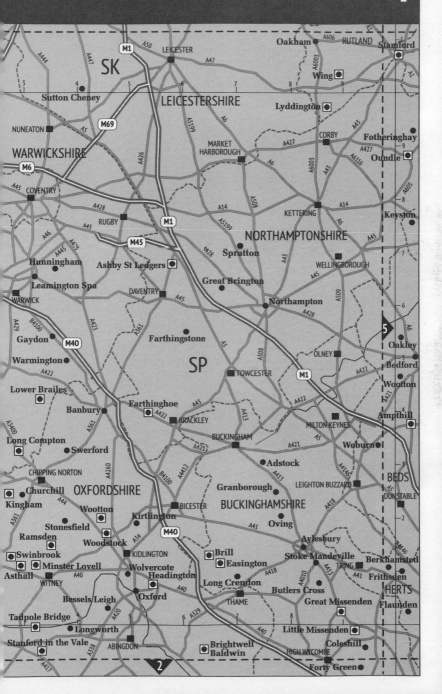

M1 · A50 · LEICESTER · A47 · Oakham · A606 · RUTLAND · Stamford
A444 · A447 · SK · LEICESTERSHIRE · A6003 · Wing · A1
3 · 4 · Sutton Cheney · 5 · 6 · 7 · Lyddington · 8 · 9
NUNEATON · M69 · A5 · A5199 · A6 · A427 · CORBY · A43 · Fotheringhay
WARWICKSHIRE · A426 · MARKET HARBOROUGH · A6003 · A43 · A6116 · Oundle · 9
M6 · A6 · A508 · A14 · Keyston
A45 · COVENTRY · A428 · A14 · KETTERING · A14 · 8
RUGBY · M1 · A5199 · NORTHAMPTONSHIRE · A45
M45 · A428 · Spratton · A43 · WELLINGBOROUGH · 7
Hunningham · A445 · A45 · Ashby St Ledgers · Great Brington · A45 · A509
Leamington Spa · DAVENTRY · A45 · Northampton · 6
WARWICK · A361 · A428 · A509
A429 · B4100 · Farthingstone · A5 · A508 · Olney · 5
Gaydon · M40 · Oakley
Warmington · TOWCESTER · M1 · Bedford
A422 · SP · Wootton
Lower Brailes · Farthinghoe · A43 · A422 · Ampthill
Banbury · A422 · BRACKLEY · A413 · MILTON KEYNES · 4
Long Compton · A361 · BUCKINGHAM · A5 · Woburn · 3
Swerford · A421 · A4146 · BEDS
CHIPPING NORTON · B4100 · B4412 · Adstock · A413 · LEIGHTON BUZZARD · DUNSTABLE
Churchill · OXFORDSHIRE · Granborough · BUCKINGHAMSHIRE · A418 · 2
Kingham · A44 · Wootton · BICESTER · Oving · A41
A361 · Kirtlington · A41 · Aylesbury
Stonesfield · A34 · M40 · Stoke Mandeville · Berkhamsted
Ramsden · Woodstock · Brill · TRING · Frithsden
Swinbrook · Minster Lovell · KIDLINGTON · Easington · A418 · A4010 · A413 · A41 · HERTS
Asthall · WITNEY · Wolvercote · Headington · A40 · Long Crendon · Butlers Cross · Flaunden
Bessels Leigh · A40 · Oxford · THAME · Great Missenden
Tadpole Bridge · A420 · Longworth · A329 · Little Missenden · Coleshill
Stanford in the Vale · A338 · ABINGDON · Brightwell Baldwin · HIGH WYCOMBE · Forty Green
A417 · 2

5

- Main Entry
- Main Entry with accommodation
- Place name to assist navigation

LINCS

A1175

A154 • Shouldham

WISBECH

8

A10

A1122

• Stamford

A15

A1

Ufford

A16

A47

DOWNHAM MARKET

A1122

Oxborough

A47

TF

A134

A15

Thorney

A605

A1122

A10

A134

Peterborough

Elton

A605

A141

• Brandon Creek

Fotheringhay

A427

A505

Stilton

CAMBRIDGESHIRE

A10

A134

Oundle

A1(M)

CHATTERIS

A142

A1101

A11

NORTHANTS

Sutton Gault

A141

ELY

MILDENHALL

A45

A14

A1123

A142

• Keyston

Huntingdon

Hemingford Abbots

A10

• Reach

NEWMARKET

4

B645

• Hemingford Grey

• Fen Drayton

A1

A14

Horningsea

A14

Madingley

A14

6

A428

Cambridge

• Great Wilbraham

A1198

A11

TL

A603

A10

A1307

• Oakley

A6

A1307

A1309

Balsham

• Bedford

A1145

BEDFORDSHIRE

A505

Whittlesford

A1307

A1092

• Wootton

Ireland

A1

ROYSTON

Duxford

Hinxton

A1017

Ampthill

A507

Ashwell

A505

• Little Walden

• Flitton

A6

A505

Chrishall

• Saffron Walden

A600

A507

A10

Cottered

M11

ESSEX

M1

HITCHIN

HERTFORDSHIRE

A505

STEVENAGE

A120

BRAINTREE

DUNSTABLE

Preston

A1(M)

A602

BISHOP'S STORTFORD

A120

Littley Green

LUTON

Watton-at-Stone

A119

Hatfield Broad Oak

A131

HARPENDEN

HERTFORD

• Fuller Street

A1081

A414

A1060

Berkhamsted

Redbourn

Hertford Heath

• Fyfield

A17

Frithsden

St Albans

HATFIELD

HARLOW

CHELMSFORD

A41

HEMEL HEMPSTEAD

Epping Green

A10

A414

Flaunden

Potters Crouch

A1000

Margaretting Tye

A12

A404

Sarratt

M1

A183

Barnet

TQ

M25

EPPING

• Stock

M25

A1000

ENFIELD

South Hanningfield •

A409

Harrow (see North London section)

BRENTWOOD

3

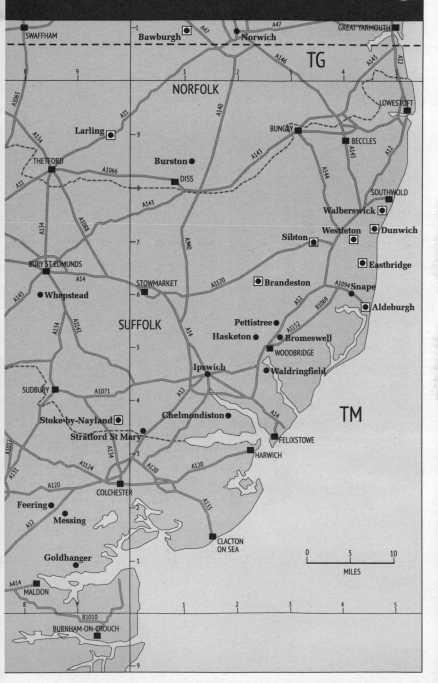

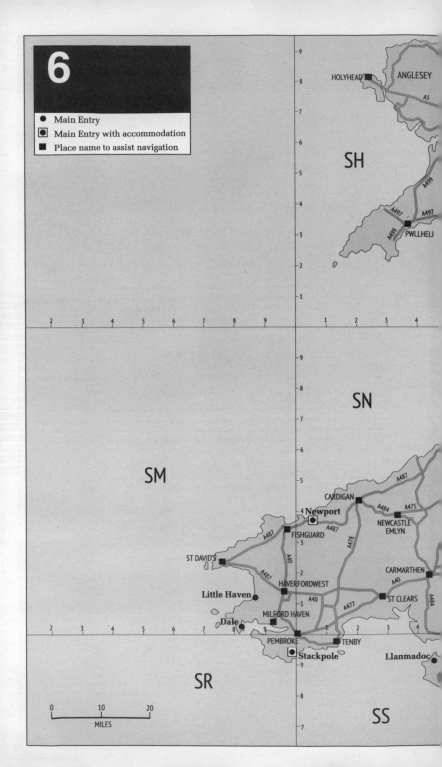

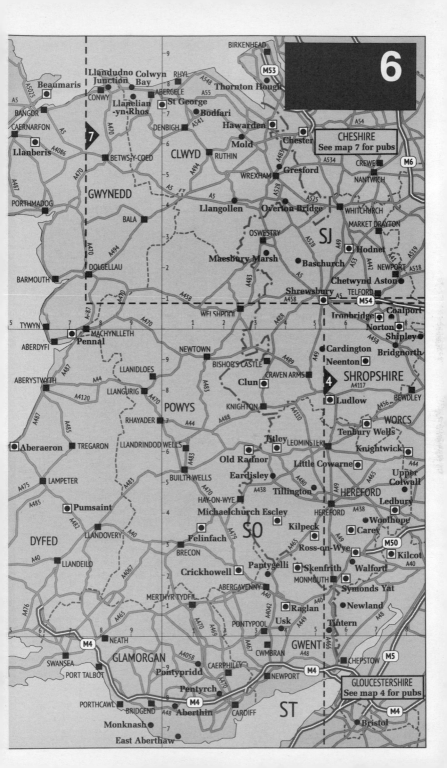

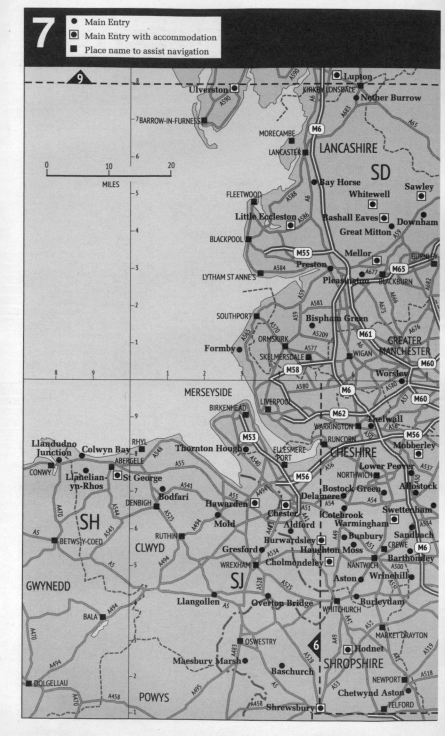

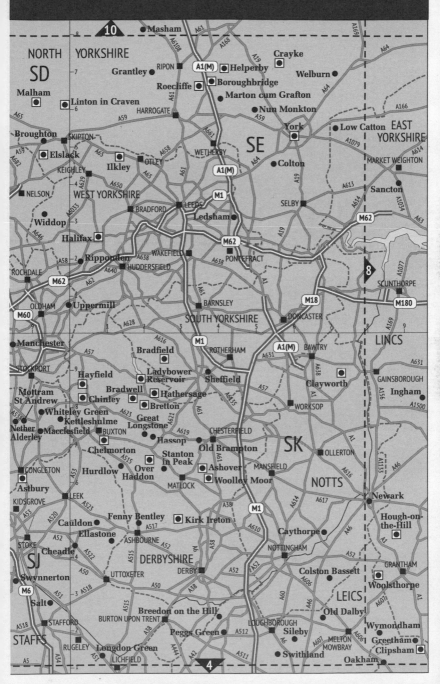

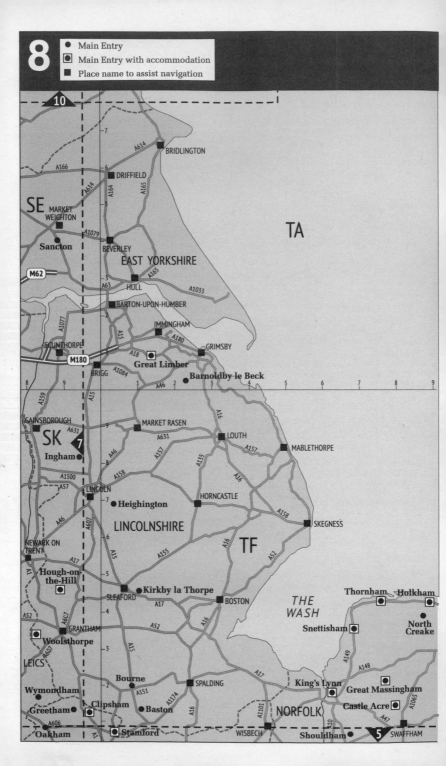

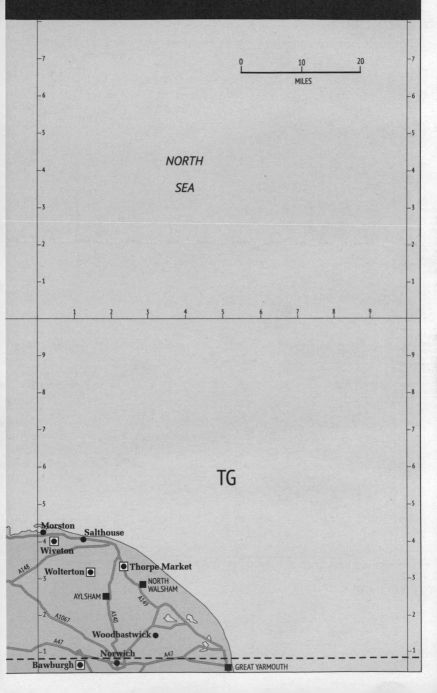

NORTH

SEA

TG

Morston
Salthouse
Wiveton
A148
Wolterton
Thorpe Market
NORTH
WALSHAM
AYLSHAM
A149
A140
A1067
Woodbastwick
A47
A47
Norwich
Bawburgh
GREAT YARMOUTH

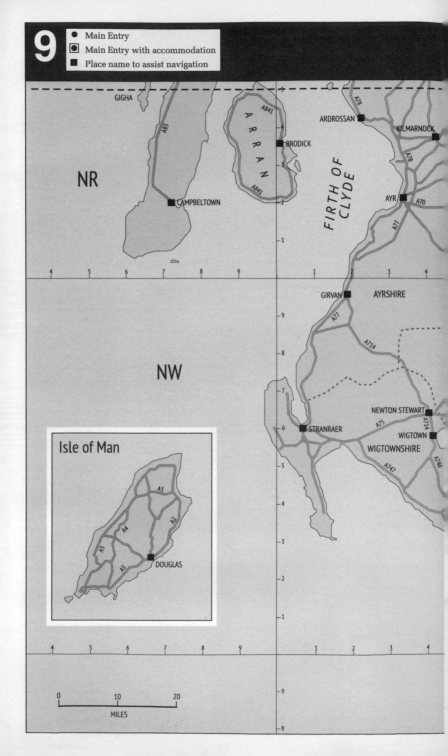

- Main Entry
- Main Entry with accommodation
- Place name to assist navigation

GIGHA

ARRAN

A841

BRODICK

ARDROSSAN

KILMARNOCK

A78

A78

NR

FIRTH OF CLYDE

A841

CAMPBELTOWN

AYR

A70

A77

GIRVAN

AYRSHIRE

A77

A714

NW

NEWTON STEWART

A714

A75

WIGTOWN

STRANRAER

A726

WIGTOWNSHIRE

A747

Isle of Man

A3

A2

A4

A3

A5

DOUGLAS

MILES

0   10   20

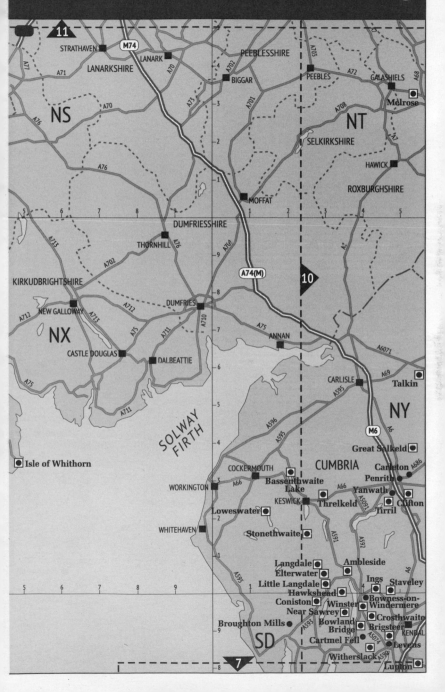

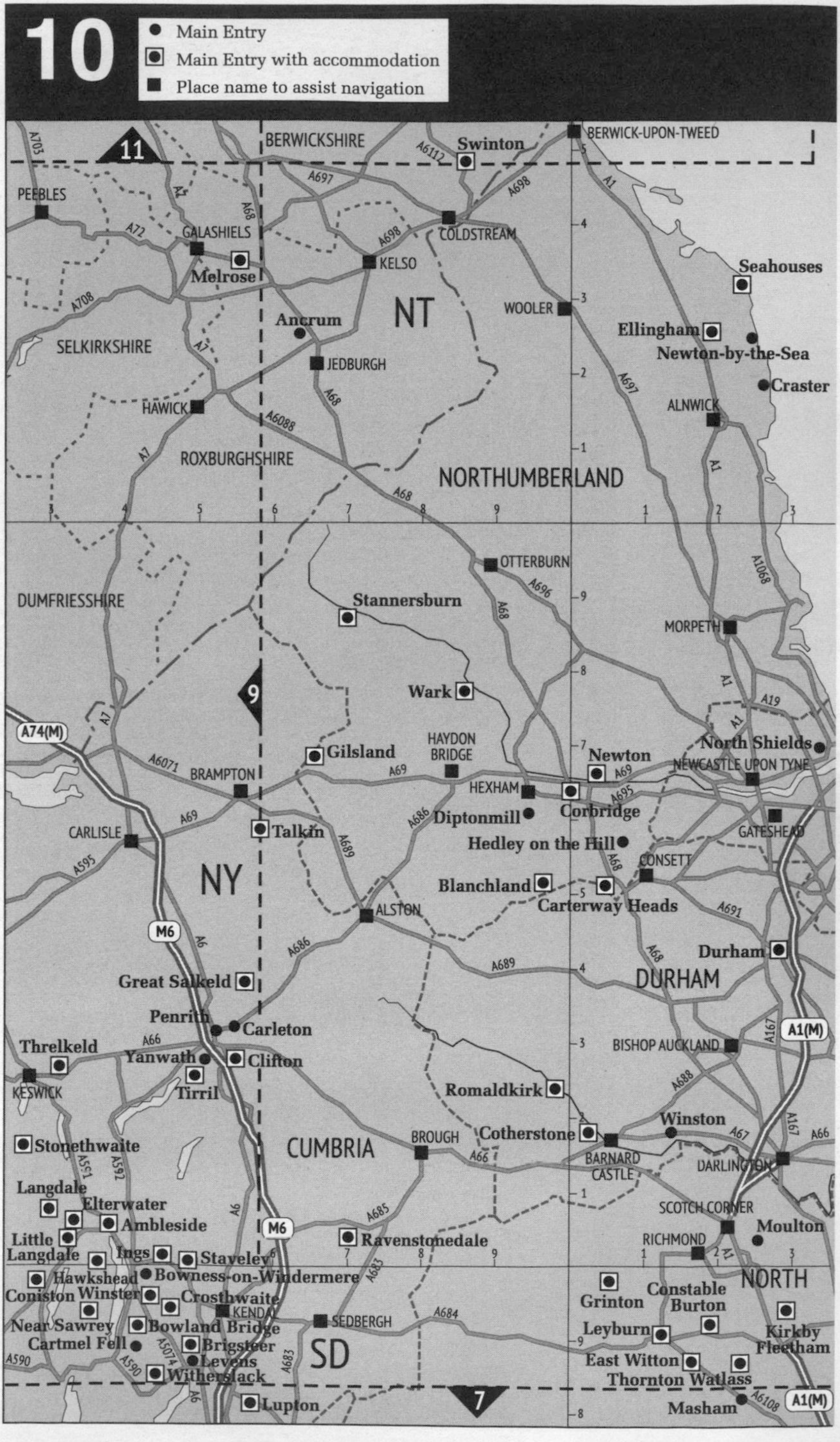
10
Main Entry
Main Entry with accommodation
Place name to assist navigation
11
BERWICKSHIRE
Swinton
BERWICK-UPON-TWEED
PEEBLES
GALASHIELS
Melrose
COLDSTREAM
KELSO
Seahouses
NT
WOOLER
Ancrum
Ellingham
Newton-by-the-Sea
SELKIRKSHIRE
JEDBURGH
Craster
HAWICK
ALNWICK
ROXBURGHSHIRE
NORTHUMBERLAND
OTTERBURN
DUMFRIESSHIRE
Stannersburn
MORPETH
Wark
9
A74(M)
Gilsland
HAYDON BRIDGE
Newton
North Shields
NEWCASTLE UPON TYNE
BRAMPTON
HEXHAM
Corbridge
Diptonmill
GATESHEAD
CARLISLE
Talkin
Hedley on the Hill
CONSETT
NY
Blanchland
Carterway Heads
ALSTON
M6
Durham
Great Salkeld
DURHAM
Penrith
Carleton
A1(M)
Threlkeld
Yanwath
Clifton
BISHOP AUCKLAND
KESWICK
Tirril
Romaldkirk
Winston
Stonethwaite
CUMBRIA
BROUGH
Cotherstone
BARNARD CASTLE
DARLINGTON
Langdale
Elterwater
Ambleside
SCOTCH CORNER
Moulton
Little Langdale
Ings
Staveley
Ravenstonedale
RICHMOND
Hawkshead
Bowness-on-Windermere
NORTH
Coniston
Winster
Crosthwaite
Grinton
Constable Burton
KENDAL
Near Sawrey
Bowland Bridge
SEDBERGH
Leyburn
Kirkby Fleetham
Cartmel Fell
Brigsteer
Levens
SD
East Witton
Witherslack
Thornton Watlass
Lupton
7
Masham
A1(M)

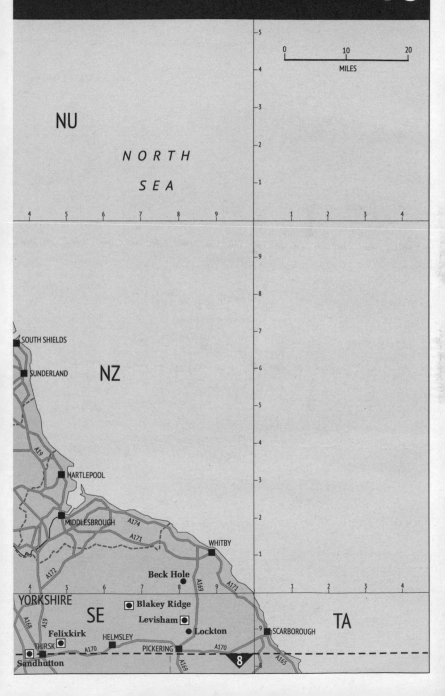

NU

N O R T H

S E A

0   10   20
MILES

NZ

■ SOUTH SHIELDS

■ SUNDERLAND

A19

■ HARTLEPOOL

■ MIDDLESBROUGH A174

A171

■ WHITBY

A172

Beck Hole ●

A169 A171

YORKSHIRE

◉ Blakey Ridge

SE   Levisham ◉

Felixkirk   ● Lockton

A168 A19 HELMSLEY   ■ SCARBOROUGH   TA

◉ THIRSK A170 PICKERING ■ A170

Sandhutton   A169 **8** A165

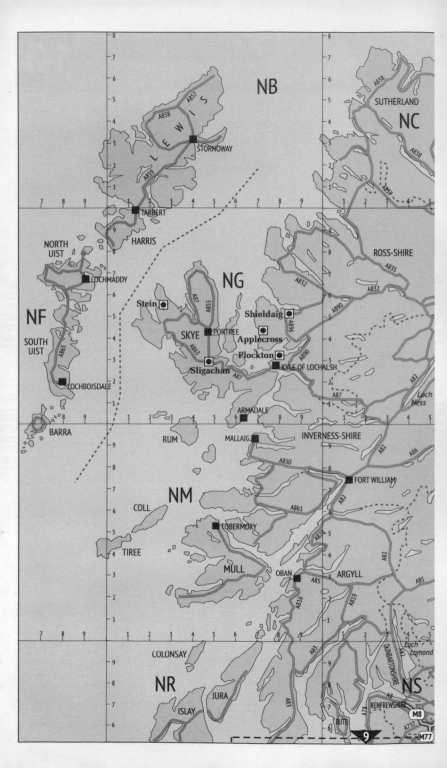

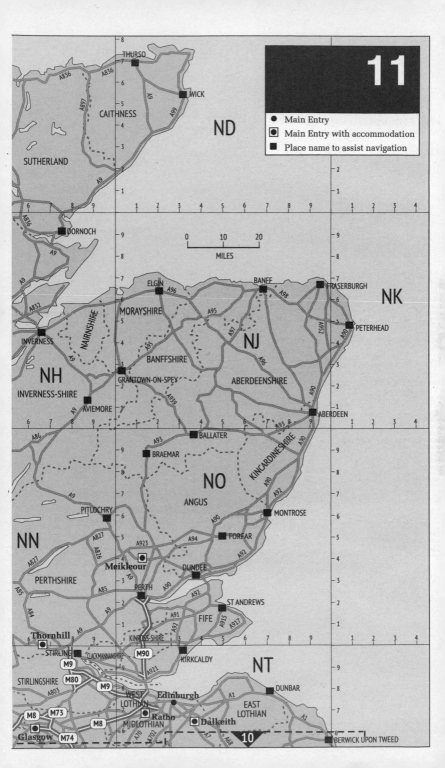

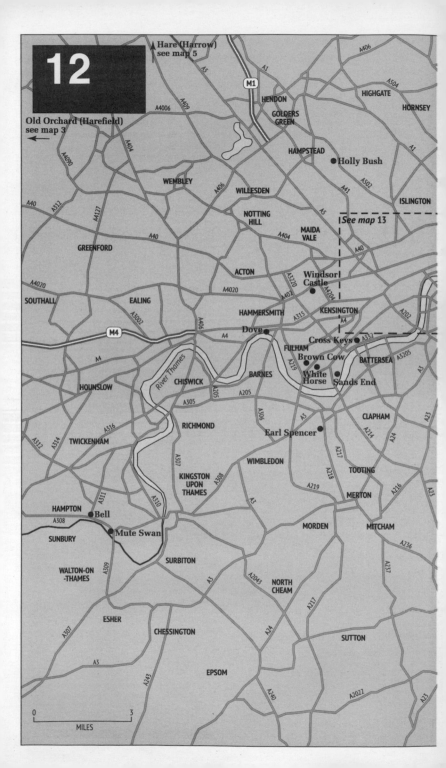

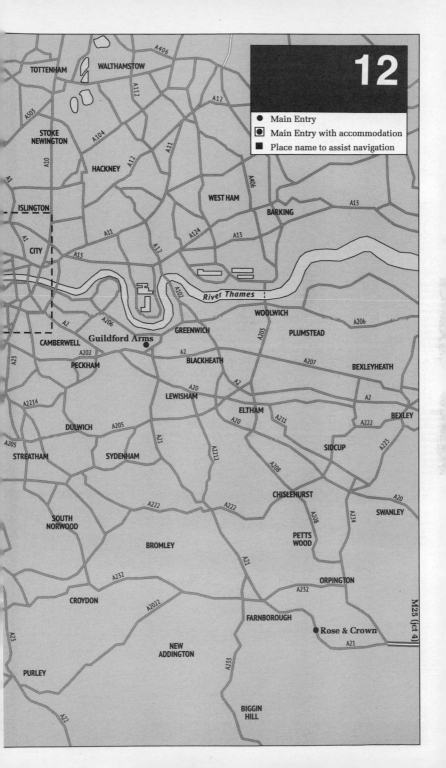

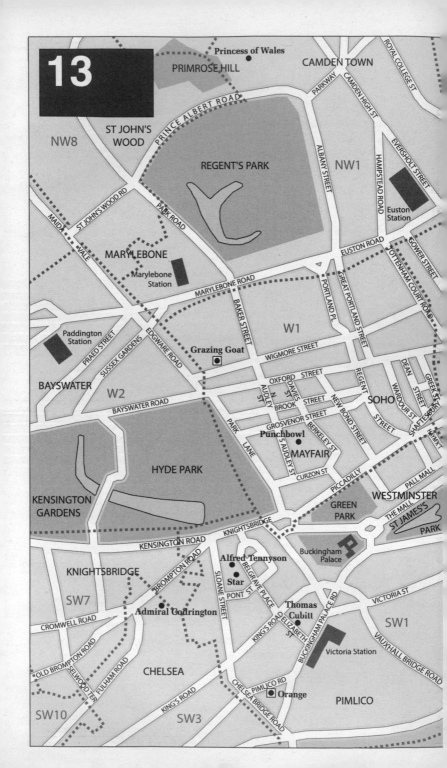

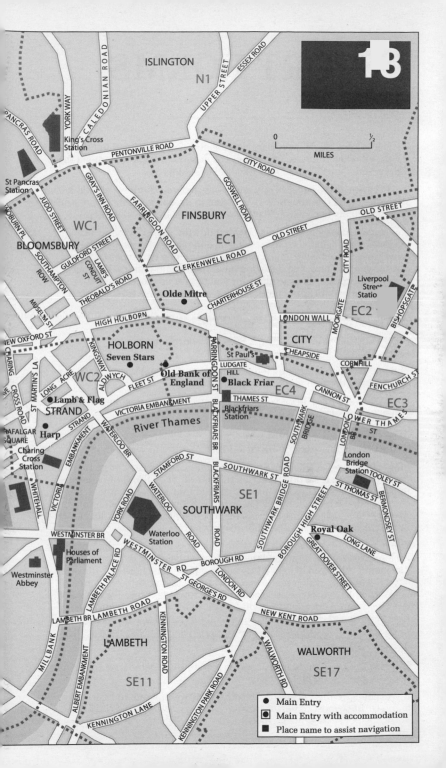

REPORT FORMS

We would very much appreciate hearing about your visits to pubs in this *Guide*, whether you have found them as described and recommend them for continued inclusion or noticed a fall in standards.

We'd also be glad to hear of any new pubs that you think we should know about. Readers' reports are very valuable to us, and sometimes pubs are dropped simply because we have had no up-to-date news on them.

You can use the tear-out forms on the following pages, email us at feedback@goodguides.co.uk or send us comments via our website (www.thegoodpubguide.co.uk) or app. We include two types of form: one for you to simply list pubs you have visited and confirm that our review is accurate, and the other for you to give us more detailed information on individual pubs. If you would like more forms, please write to us at:

The Good Pub Guide

FREEPOST RTXY–ZCBC–BBAZ, Stream Lane, Sedlescombe, Battle TN33 0PB

Though we try to answer all letters, please understand if there's a delay (particularly in summer, our busiest period).

We'll assume we can print your name or initials as a recommender unless you tell us otherwise.

MAIN ENTRY OR 'ALSO WORTH A VISIT'?

Please try to gauge whether a pub should be a Main Entry or go in the Also Worth a Visit section (and tick the relevant box). Main Entries need to have qualities that would make it worth other readers' while to travel some distance to them. If a pub is an entirely new recommendation, the Also Worth a Visit section may be the best place for it to start its career in the *Guide* – to encourage other readers to report on it.

The more detail you can put into your description of a pub, the better. Any information on how good the landlord or landlady is, what it looks like inside, what you like about the atmosphere and character, the quality and type of food, which real ales are available and whether they're well kept, whether bedrooms are available, and how big/attractive the garden is. Other helpful information includes prices for food and bedrooms, food service and opening hours, and if children or dogs are welcome.

If the food or accommodation is outstanding, tick the FOOD AWARD or the STAY AWARD box.

If you're in a position to gauge a pub's suitability or otherwise for people with disabilities, do please tell us about that.

If you can, give the full address or directions for any pub not currently in the *Guide* – most of all, please give us its postcode. If we can't find a pub's postcode, we don't include it in the *Guide*.

I have been to the following pubs in *The Good Pub Guide 2018* **in the last few months, found them as described, and confirm that they deserve continued inclusion:**

continued overleaf

PLEASE GIVE YOUR NAME AND ADDRESS ON THE BACK OF THIS FORM

Pubs visited continued..........

Your own name and address *(block capitals please)*

....

....

....

Postcode...

Please return to

The Good Pub Guide
FREEPOST RTXY–ZCBC–BBAZ,
Stream Lane,
Sedlescombe, Battle
TN33 0PB

IF YOU PREFER, YOU CAN SEND
US REPORTS BY EMAIL:

feedback@goodguides.com

I have been to the following pubs in *The Good Pub Guide 2018* in the last few months, found them as described, and confirm that they deserve continued inclusion:

continued overleaf

PLEASE GIVE YOUR NAME AND ADDRESS ON THE BACK OF THIS FORM

Pubs visited continued..........

Your own name and address *(block capitals please)*

....

....

....

Postcode...

Please return to

The Good Pub Guide
FREEPOST RTXY–ZCBC–BBAZ,
Stream Lane,
Sedlescombe, Battle
TN33 0PB

IF YOU PREFER, YOU CAN SEND
US REPORTS BY EMAIL:

feedback@goodguides.com

I have been to the following pubs in *The Good Pub Guide 2018* in the last few months, found them as described, and confirm that they deserve continued inclusion:

continued overleaf

PLEASE GIVE YOUR NAME AND ADDRESS ON THE BACK OF THIS FORM

Pubs visited continued..........

By returning this form, you consent to the collection, recording and use of the information you submit by The Random House Group Ltd. Any personal details which you provide from which we can identify you are held and processed in accordance with the Data Protection Act 1998 and will not be passed on to any third parties. The Random House Group Ltd may wish to send you further information on its associated products.

Please tick box if you do not wish to receive any such information. ☐

Your own name and address *(block capitals please)*

....

....

....

Postcode...

In returning this form I confirm my agreement that the information I provide may be used by The Random House Group Ltd, its assignees and/or licensees in any media or medium whatsoever.

Please return to

The Good Pub Guide
FREEPOST RTXY–ZCBC–BBAZ,
Stream Lane,
Sedlescombe, Battle
TN33 0PB

IF YOU PREFER, YOU CAN SEND
US REPORTS BY EMAIL:

feedback@goodguides.com

I have been to the following pubs in *The Good Pub Guide 2018* in the last few months, found them as described, and confirm that they deserve continued inclusion:

continued overleaf

PLEASE GIVE YOUR NAME AND ADDRESS ON THE BACK OF THIS FORM

Pubs visited continued..........

Your own name and address *(block capitals please)*

....

....

....

Postcode..

Please return to

The Good Pub Guide
FREEPOST RTXY–ZCBC–BBAZ,
Stream Lane,
Sedlescombe, Battle
TN33 0PB

IF YOU PREFER, YOU CAN SEND
US REPORTS BY EMAIL:

feedback@goodguides.com

I have been to the following pubs in *The Good Pub Guide 2018* in the last few months, found them as described, and confirm that they deserve continued inclusion:

continued overleaf

PLEASE GIVE YOUR NAME AND ADDRESS ON THE BACK OF THIS FORM

Pubs visited continued..........

Your own name and address *(block capitals please)*

....

....

....

Postcode...

Please return to

The Good Pub Guide
FREEPOST RTXY–ZCBC–BBAZ,
Stream Lane,
Sedlescombe, Battle
TN33 0PB

IF YOU PREFER, YOU CAN SEND
US REPORTS BY EMAIL:

feedback@goodguides.com

**I have been to the following pubs in *The Good Pub Guide 2018*
in the last few months, found them as described, and confirm
that they deserve continued inclusion:**

continued overleaf

PLEASE GIVE YOUR NAME AND ADDRESS ON THE BACK OF THIS FORM

Pubs visited continued..........

Your own name and address *(block capitals please)*

....

....

....

Postcode..

Please return to

The Good Pub Guide
FREEPOST RTXY–ZCBC–BBAZ,
Stream Lane,
Sedlescombe, Battle
TN33 0PB

IF YOU PREFER, YOU CAN SEND
US REPORTS BY EMAIL:

feedback@goodguides.com

Report on (pub's name)

....

Pub's address

....

☐ YES MAIN ENTRY ☐ YES WORTH A VISIT ☐ NO don't include

Please tick one of these boxes to show your verdict, and give reasons, descriptive comments, prices and the date of your visit

☐ Deserves **FOOD Award** ☐ Deserves **STAY Award** 2018:1

PLEASE GIVE YOUR NAME AND ADDRESS ON THE BACK OF THIS FORM

✂ ....

Report on (pub's name)

....

Pub's address

....

☐ YES MAIN ENTRY ☐ YES WORTH A VISIT ☐ NO don't include

Please tick one of these boxes to show your verdict, and give reasons, descriptive comments, prices and the date of your visit

☐ Deserves **FOOD Award** ☐ Deserves **STAY Award** 2018:2

PLEASE GIVE YOUR NAME AND ADDRESS ON THE BACK OF THIS FORM

Your own name and address *(block capitals please)*

In returning this form I confirm my agreement that the information I provide may be used by The Random House Group Ltd, its assignees and/or licensees in any media or medium whatsoever.

DO NOT USE THIS SIDE OF THE PAGE FOR WRITING ABOUT PUBS

By returning this form, you consent to the collection, recording and use of the information you submit by The Random House Group Ltd. Any personal details which you provide from which we can identify you are held and processed in accordance with the Data Protection Act 1998 and will not be passed on to any third parties. The Random House Group Ltd may wish to send you further information on its associated products. Please tick box if you do not wish to receive any such information.

☐

✂ ....

Your own name and address *(block capitals please)*

In returning this form I confirm my agreement that the information I provide may be used by The Random House Group Ltd, its assignees and/or licensees in any media or medium whatsoever.

DO NOT USE THIS SIDE OF THE PAGE FOR WRITING ABOUT PUBS

By returning this form, you consent to the collection, recording and use of the information you submit by The Random House Group Ltd. Any personal details which you provide from which we can identify you are held and processed in accordance with the Data Protection Act 1998 and will not be passed on to any third parties. The Random House Group Ltd may wish to send you further information on its associated products. Please tick box if you do not wish to receive any such information.

☐

Report on (pub's name)

....

Pub's address

....

☐ YES MAIN ENTRY ☐ YES WORTH A VISIT ☐ NO don't include

Please tick one of these boxes to show your verdict, and give reasons, descriptive comments, prices and the date of your visit

☐ Deserves **FOOD Award** ☐ Deserves **STAY Award** 2018: 3

PLEASE GIVE YOUR NAME AND ADDRESS ON THE BACK OF THIS FORM

✂ ....

Report on (pub's name)

....

Pub's address

....

☐ YES MAIN ENTRY ☐ YES WORTH A VISIT ☐ NO don't include

Please tick one of these boxes to show your verdict, and give reasons, descriptive comments, prices and the date of your visit

☐ Deserves **FOOD Award** ☐ Deserves **STAY Award** 2018: 4

PLEASE GIVE YOUR NAME AND ADDRESS ON THE BACK OF THIS FORM

Your own name and address *(block capitals please)*

In returning this form I confirm my agreement that the information I provide may be used by The Random House Group Ltd, its assignees and/or licensees in any media or medium whatsoever.

DO NOT USE THIS SIDE OF THE PAGE FOR WRITING ABOUT PUBS

By returning this form, you consent to the collection, recording and use of the information you submit by The Random House Group Ltd. Any personal details which you provide from which we can identify you are held and processed in accordance with the Data Protection Act 1998 and will not be passed on to any third parties. The Random House Group Ltd may wish to send you further information on its associated products. Please tick box if you do not wish to receive any such information.

✂ ....

Your own name and address *(block capitals please)*

In returning this form I confirm my agreement that the information I provide may be used by The Random House Group Ltd, its assignees and/or licensees in any media or medium whatsoever.

DO NOT USE THIS SIDE OF THE PAGE FOR WRITING ABOUT PUBS

By returning this form, you consent to the collection, recording and use of the information you submit by The Random House Group Ltd. Any personal details which you provide from which we can identify you are held and processed in accordance with the Data Protection Act 1998 and will not be passed on to any third parties. The Random House Group Ltd may wish to send you further information on its associated products. Please tick box if you do not wish to receive any such information.